# Travel Disc

This coupon entitles
when you book your trip through the

## RESERVATION SERVICE

### Hotels ♦ Airlines ♦ Car Rentals ♦ Cruises
### All Your Travel Needs

Here's what you get: *

♦ A discount of $50 USD on a booking of $1,000** or more for two or more people!

♦ A discount of $25 USD on a booking of $500** or more for one person!

♦ Free membership for three years, and 1,000 free miles on enrollment in the unique Travel Network Miles-to-Go® frequent-traveler program. Earn one mile for every dollar spent through the program. Redeem miles for free hotel stays starting at 5,000 miles. Earn free roundtrip airline tickets starting at 25,000 miles.

♦ Personal help in planning your own, customized trip.

♦ Fast, confirmed reservations at any property recommended in this guide, subject to availability.***

♦ Special discounts on bookings in the U.S. and around the world.

♦ Low-cost visa and passport service.

♦ Reduced-rate cruise packages and special car rental programs worldwide.

> Visit our website at http://www.travelnetwork.com/Frommer or call us globally at 201-567-8500, ext. 55. In the U.S., call toll-free at 1-888-940-5000, or fax 201-567-1838. In Canada, call at 1-905-707-7222, or fax 905-707-8108. In Asia, call 60-3-7191044, or fax 60-3-7185415.

* To qualify for these travel discounts, at least a portion of your trip must include destinations covered in this guide. No more than one coupon discount may be used in any 12-month period, for destinations covered in this guide. Cannot be combined with any other discount or promotion.

**These are U.S. dollars spent on commissionable bookings.

*** A $10 USD fee, plus fax and/or phone charges, will be added to the cost of bookings at each hotel not linked to the reservation service. Customers must approve these fees in advance. If only hotels of this kind are booked, the traveler(s) must also purchase roundtrip air tickets from Travel Network for the trip.

Valid until December 31, 1999. Terms and conditions of the Miles-to-Go® program are available on request by calling 201-567-8500, ext 55.

USA234

"Amazingly easy to use. Very portable, very complete."

*—Booklist*

♦

"The only mainstream guide to list specific prices. The Walter Cronkite of guidebooks—with all that implies."

*—Travel & Leisure*

♦

"Complete, concise, and filled with useful information."

*—New York Daily News*

♦

"Hotel information is close to encyclopedic."

*—Des Moines Sunday Register*

# Frommer's

5th Edition

# USA

## Edited and Compiled by
## Bill Goodwin

Macmillan • USA

Born and raised in North Carolina, **Bill Goodwin** was an award-winning newspaper reporter before becoming a legal counsel and speechwriter for two U.S. senators, Sam Nunn of Georgia and the late Sam J. Ervin, Jr., of North Carolina. Now a full-time travel writer based in northern Virginia, Goodwin is the author of *Frommer's South Pacific* and *Frommer's Virginia* and co-author of *Frommer's Florida*. He was regional editor for the first edition of *Frommer's America on Wheels Mid-Atlantic*.

## MACMILLAN TRAVEL

A Simon & Schuster Macmillan Company
1633 Broadway
New York, NY 10019

Find us online at **www.frommers.com**

Copyright © 1998 by Simon & Schuster, Inc.
Maps copyright © by Simon & Schuster, Inc.

ISBN 0-02-861846-7
ISSN 1094-0227

Design by Michele Laseau
Digital Cartography by John Decamillis, Roberta Stockwell, and Ortelius Design

### SPECIAL SALES

Bulk purchases (10+ copies) of Frommer's and selected Macmillan travel guides are available to corporations, organizations, mail-order catalogs, institutions, and charities at special discounts, and can be customized to suit individual needs. For more information write to: Special Sales, Macmillan General Reference, 1633 Broadway, New York, NY 10019.

Manufactured in the United States of America

# Contents

## 8  The Northwest   791

## 9  Alaska   876

## 10  Hawaii   916

## Appendix 961

## Index 969

# List of Maps

# Acknowledgments

Thanks to the authors of Frommer guides who helped to prepare their work for this book: Stephanie Avnet, Jane Aukshunas, Wayne Curtis, Victoria Pesce Elliott, Adam Feibelman, Jeanette Foster, Jay Golan, Elizabeth Hansen, Edie Jarolim, Don and Barbara Laine, Erika Lenkert, Mary Meehan, Marie Morris, Matthew Poole, Karl Samson, and Charles Wohlforth.

Special thanks to Carol Gallant and Don and Barbara Laine for their editorial assistance.

And thanks to all the in-house editors, freelance editors, and researchers who helped to put the book together: Ron Boudreau, Janet P. Cave, Sophia Dembling, Cheryl Farr, Tammy Hale, Walker Morgan, Kelly Regan, Robin M. Krueger, Suzanne Jannetta, Rob Robertson, John Rosenthal, and Jeremy Woan.

## AN INVITATION TO THE READER

In researching this book, we discovered many wonderful places—hotels, restaurants, shops, and more. We're sure you'll find others. Please tell us about them, so we can share the information with your fellow travelers in upcoming editions. If you were disappointed with a recommendation, we'd love to know that, too. Please write to:

*Frommer's U.S.A.,* 5th Edition
Macmillan Travel
1633 Broadway
New York, NY 10019

## AN ADDITIONAL NOTE

Please be advised that travel information is subject to change at any time—and this is especially true of prices. We therefore suggest that you write or call ahead for confirmation when making your travel plans. The authors, editors, and publisher cannot be held responsible for the experiences of readers while traveling. Your safety is important to us, however, so we encourage you to stay alert and be aware of your surroundings. Keep a close eye on cameras, purses, and wallets, all favorite targets of thieves and pickpockets.

## FIND FROMMER'S ONLINE

Arthur Frommer's Outspoken Encyclopedia of Travel (www.frommers.com) offers more than 6,000 pages of up-to-the-minute travel information—including the latest bargains and candid, personal articles updated daily by Arthur Frommer himself. No other Web site offers such comprehensive and timely coverage of the world of travel.

## WHAT THE SYMBOLS MEAN

### ✪ Frommer's Favorites

Our favorite places and experiences—outstanding for quality, value, or both.

The following abbreviations are used for credit cards:

| AE | American Express | EU | Eurocard |
|------|------------------|------|-------------------|
| CB | Carte Blanche | JCB | Japan Credit Bank |
| DC | Diners Club | MC | MasterCard |
| DISC | Discover | V | Visa |
| ER | enRoute | | |

# See the USA

*By Bill Goodwin*

The United States has one defining quality, its variety. Indeed, this vast area of some 3.6 million square miles—it's 2,500 miles (4,000km) from New York to Los Angeles, and that again to Hawaii—has something for everyone.

Our terrain varies from the flat coastal plains of the Southeast to the soaring alpine mountains of the West, from the humid swamps of Florida's Everglades to the bone-dry desert of California's Death Valley. In January you can bask on a beach in Florida, California, or Hawaii—or go skiing in Colorado or snowmobiling in Alaska. In July you can hear the Boston Symphony Orchestra perform outdoors in New England's Berkshire hills—or listen to country music's greats down in air-conditioned Nashville, Branson, or Myrtle Beach. You can dine on haute cuisine in New York or Los Angeles—or get down-and-dirty at a lobster shack in Maine or a barbecue joint in the Carolinas. You can whitewater raft through the bowels of the Grand Canyon—or cavort with Mickey Mouse at Disney World or Disneyland.

Although we are a nation of more than 260 million souls—a quarter of them in the Boston–New York–Philadelphia–Washington, D.C., corridor—we still have plenty of wide-open spaces. Fortunately some of the best is preserved in national parks, monuments, forests, and wildlife refuges. From Acadia in Maine down to the Everglades in Florida, from the Grand Canyon in Arizona up to the magnficient mountains of Yellowstone, Yosemite, and Glacier, our parks give us ample opportunity to commune with nature and enjoy some of its grandest spectacles.

You'll experience great variety even if you don't get beyond our world-class cities. The great melting pot of New York is a major player on the international scene. The world's political power broker, tree-shrouded Washington, D.C., is the most European of all our cities. Sitting by its gorgeous bay, San Francisco ranks as our most beautiful. New Orleans gives us its funky French Quarter, Cajun cuisine, and nonstop partying. Sprawling Los Angeles sets our style, giving us trends and movie stars. Built by beef, grain, and railroads, Chicago is perhaps our most quintessentially American city.

Other unique metropoli beckon beyond the Hudson and Potomac rivers, out on the Great Plains, and even in the desert. Up in New England, Boston has its universities and history. Down south, Miami loves its Cuban sandwiches and art deco South Beach, Atlanta sends Coca-Cola and CNN news around the world, and Spanish moss–draped Charleston and Savannah preserve the Old South. Over in Tennessee, Memphis has its blues, barbecue, and Elvis shrine, while Nashville sports the Grand Ole Opry. Down in the Texas Hill Country, San Antonio strolls by its charming Riverwalk, and Austin creates unique music. Out in the southwestern desert, Phoenix plays golf on irrigated greens, while neon-lit Las Vegas lives for the ever-illusive jackpot. And up in the Northwest, soggy but lovely Seattle started our craze for coffee.

Although television, suburbs, strip malls, and chain restaurants are having a homogenizing effect on our citizenry, the USA is not a monolithic place. As you travel around, you will find that each region speaks with its own accent, enjoys its own favorite foods, and has its own political and social attitudes. And even within the regions, you'll discover a great variety of race, religion, ethnic origin, and general outlook on life. Indeed, foreign travelers often go away with the impression that we are not one nation but an amalgam of 50 little countries.

Whatever you want to see, do, or eat, you are likely to find it within the vast and very diverse confines of the United States of America.

## 1 50 Great American Experiences

With a platter so full, it's difficult to pick the best of the USA, but here are 50 experiences that capture the spirit and beauty of the land from coast to coast, from the Great Lakes to the Gulf of Mexico, and on to Hawaii and Alaska. They appear here not in order of importance but as you will come to them in the following chapters.

- **Autumn Leaves.** New Yorkers and Bostonians may love their cities, but come late September you'll find them driving the backroads of Vermont and New Hampshire when the changing leaves paint the hills the colors of fire. See the driving tours in chapter 2. The changing leaves move south in October, with more spectacular viewing along Virginia's Skyline Drive. See chapter 3.
- **Miss Liberty.** Standing tall in New York harbor for more than a century, Miss Liberty welcomes visitors and immigrants to our shores. And you won't soon forget the view of Manhattan's famous skyline from the ferry. See chapter 2.
- **Stars on Broadway.** Not even London's West End has better theater than New York's Broadway. Professional, whacky, or both, Broadway is a metaphor for the city itself. See chapter 2.
- **Where Masterpieces Rule.** Masterpieces are the rule rather than the exception at New York's Metropolitan Museum of Art, perhaps our finest repository, where the whole world's cultures are on display. See chapter 2.
- **The Midnight Ride of Paul Revere.** The American Revolution began when the midnight ride of Paul Revere roused the patriots to fire the "shot heard 'round the world" at Lexington in 1775. More battles followed at Concord and Bunker Hill. You can follow Revere's route through what is now suburban Boston. See the driving tour in chapter 2.
- **Classic Home Runs.** Our national pastime doesn't get any better than when played at a classic baseball yard like Boston's Fenway Park with its hallowed "Green Monster" left-field fence. Yankee Stadium in New York is of more recent vintage, but it's just as storied. See chapter 2. New parks built like old ones reincarnate the hallowed spirit in Atlanta, Baltimore, Cleveland, and Arlington, Texas.
- **July Fourth with the Boston Pops.** It's not often you hear the *1812 Overture* with real cannons, church bells, and fireworks, but big crowds with picnic suppers do on Independence Day in Boston. See chapter 2.
- **Summer on Cape Cod.** The political Kennedys and nearly everyone else flees to Cape Cod to escape summer's heat. There's a little of everything out here, from Cape Cod National Seashore to small-town Americana in Chatham to Provincetown's funky, artsy party scene with a crowd of gay travelers. See chapter 2.

# Major Interstate Highways

- **Down and Dirty in Maine.** Succulent Maine lobsters are one of our national delicacies, and they don't get any better, fresher, or cheaper than right off the boat at a down-and-dirty lobster pound on the Maine coast. See chapter 2.
- **Halls of Fame.** In 1839, Abner Doubleday drew the first diamond and wrote the first rules for a game called baseball. The sport's history is immortalized in the National Baseball Hall of Fame where it all began in Cooperstown, New York. See chapter 2. The pro football hall of fame is in Canton, Ohio (☎ 330/456-8207); basketball, in Springfield, Massachusetts (☎ 413/781-6500); bowling, in St. Louis, Missouri (☎ 314/231-6340); golf, in Far Hills, New Jersey (☎ 908/234-2300); swimming, in Ft. Lauderdale, Florida (☎ 305/462-6536); and tennis, in Newport, Rhode Island (☎ 401/849-3990).
- **Honeymooning at the Falls.** Not everyone is as enraptured as Jérôme Bonaparte, but Niagara Falls has been the honeymoon capital of the world since Napoléon's brother brought his bride here in 1803. Everyone else comes to look at the misty falls. See chapter 2.
- **Mr. Smithson's Universe.** Our most diverse collection of museums, the Smithsonian Institution in Washington has everything from dinosaur bones to spaceships. See chapter 3.
- **Not a Dry Eye.** Washington is full of memorials to our national heroes, but none is as emotionally wrenching as the names of the 58,000 Americans who died during the Vietnam conflict etched into the polished black granite wall of the Vietnam Veterans Memorial. See chapter 3.
- **Scandals, Gangsters & Graves.** It's not surprising that a nation seemingly obsessed with seemy tabloid television would love escorted tours of scandalous sites in Washington (see chapter 3), gangster gore in Chicago (see chapter 5), and a ride in a converted hearse to movie star graves in Los Angeles (see chapter 7).
- **A Capital Fourth.** Boston may have its Pops on the Esplanade, but it doesn't top Washington's Fourth of July celebration, when half a million mob the mall for concerts, monstrous fireworks over the Washington Monument, and the Smithsonian Festival of American Folklife. See chapter 3.
- **Roof of the East.** The most scenic route in the east, the Skyline Drive snakes along the crest of the Blue Ridge Mountains through Shenandoah National Park, offering vistas down over Virginia's horse country on one side, the Shenandoah Valley on the other. The Blue Ridge Parkway continues south to Asheville, North Carolina. See the driving tour in chapter 3.
- **Fine Old Homes.** Virginia has carefully preserved George Washington's Mount Vernon, Thomas Jefferson's Monticello, and many other homes of our Founding Fathers. In fact, the entire town of Williamsburg looks exactly as it did in colonial times. See chapter 3.
- **Liberty Bell.** Few places will let you feel the spirit of American freedom as in Philadelphia, where the Liberty Bell proclaimed our independence and the Founding Fathers ran the Revolutionary War and crafted our enduring Constitution. See chapter 3.
- **Horses and Buggies.** The USA might be a modern car culture, but you'll see as many horse-drawn carriages in Pennsylvania's Amish Country, where simpler ways survive. See chapter 3.
- **Blood and Guts at Gettysburg.** The Civil War raged throughout the Southeast, but the turning point came in 1863 on a ridge outside the village of Gettysburg in south-central Pennsylvania. Today a touching battlefield memorial reminds us of the price our forebears paid to preserve the Union. See chapter 3.

- **Straights, Gays, and Cigars.** Miami Beach's art deco South Beach is one of our hippest neighborhoods, chock-full of clubs and cafes filled with gay and straight vacationers, working models, photographers, musicians, and writers, many puffing on illicit Cuban stogies and all enjoying the exciting and sophisticated atmosphere. See chapter 4.

- **Mickey and Friends.** If you let your kids pick where you'll go on vacation, chances are they'll vote for Walt Disney World in Orlando (see chapter 4) or Disneyland near Los Angeles (see chapter 7). These are the USA's most popular family attractions, after all.

- **Midnight in the Garden.** Made famous by John Berendt's best-selling novel *Midnight in the Garden of Good and Evil,* Savannah's beautifully restored historic area has all the Deep South images that are disappearing elsewhere. See chapter 4.

- **On Top of Old Smoky.** Shrouded in blue mist—not all of it natural—the Great Smoky Mountains National Park has some of the East's highest peaks and a multitude of plants, trees, mammals, birds, and fish. See chapter 4.

- **Honkey Tonks and the Grand Ole Opry.** Out of the Mississippi Delta and the Appalachian foothills have sprung the USA's great contributions to the music scene: blues, jazz, and country-and-western. They're played everywhere now (Chicago is famous for its blues clubs), but you can still hear the best in New Orleans's French Quarter, Memphis's Beale Street, and Nashville's Grand Ole Opry, with country offshoots in Branson and Myrtle Beach. See chapter 4.

- **Nawlins All Night.** Infused with a *joie de vivre* from its French heritage, New Orleans—or *Nawlins* to the locals—seems to party around the clock, even when it's not Mardi Gras. Sober up with a breakfast of beignets at Café du Monde. See chapter 4.

- **Sunsets in Margaritaville.** No trip to the Florida Keys is complete without joining everyone on funky Key West's Mallory Docks for the most famous sunsets in the eastern USA. See chapter 4.

- **Barbecue and Crayfish.** Maine might love its lobsters, but in the Southeast and across the Great Plains, they claim barbecue and spicy Cajun cuisine to be the national dishes. Every town has its favorite barbecue joint and Cajun kitchen. See chapter 4.

- **A Better Chicago.** Home of Frank Lloyd Wright's "Prairie School" and Ludwig Mies van der Rohe's Bauhaus modernism, Chicago is at the forefront of American architecture. Terrific bus, boat, and walking tours explore the city's best. See chapter 5.

- **Art on the Plains.** Standing with New York's Met among our major museums, the Art Institute of Chicago houses a notable Impressionist collection including Grant Wood's *American Gothic,* Seurat's pointilist masterpiece *A Sunday on La Grande Jatte,* and Marc Chagall's wonderful stained-glass windows. See chapter 5.

- **500 Miles in Indy.** At the end of May, nearly 400,000 spectators throng to a 2.5-mile oval course to watch the world's cutting-edge autos run the Indianapolis 500. Indy's racing hall of fame is in the oval. See chapter 5.

- **Old Man River.** Much legend surrounds the mighty Mississippi River and its tributaries, the major central USA thoroughfares before railroads and highways. You can relive those old days on modern versions of paddlewheel steamers cruising out of New Orleans, Cincinnati, and other river cities. See chapters 4 and 5.

- **Old Stonefaces.** Visible 60 miles away, Mount Rushmore stands as a silent memorial to George Washington, Thomas Jefferson, Abraham Lincoln, and Theodore Roosevelt, whose stoney images stare across the South Dakota plains from the

Black Hills. See chapter 5. Not to be fogotten, Stone Mountain near Atlanta sports a huge carving of Confederate heroes (see chapter 4).

- **Horses, Hogs, and Quilts.** Cows, horses, hogs, quilts, preserves, cakes, big-name musical acts (preferably country-and-western), and a Midway with dizzying carnival rides—you'll find them all at state fairs throughout the country every autumn. Indianapolis (see chapter 5) and Dallas (see chapter 6) have two of the biggest. Contact each state's visitor information offices for dates and details.

- **The World's Largest Ditch.** Awesome is the only word to describe standing on the edge of the mile-deep Grand Canyon, one of the world's great natural spectacles. It's so huge that it looks painted rather than real. To see how real it is, ride a mule or hike to the bottom—or raft through it. See chapter 6.

- **Cowboys . . .** The very symbol of the American West, cowboys still ride the range, tending herds and rounding up cattle. You can see them in action at rodeos, especially at Denver's National Western Stock Show, Rodeo, and Horse Show in January and during Frontier Days in Cheyenne, Wyoming, in July. See "The USA's Top Festivals & Events," below.

- **. . . and Indians.** One of the great tragedies of American history is the treatment of the American Indians by the white newcomers, who hearded the native tribes into reservations. The largest—and by far the most beautiful—of these are the Hopi and Navajo reservations in the northeastern Arizona desert. Here and in the strikingly beautiful Canyon de Chelly National Monument, you can see the ancient cliff dwellings of the Anasazi, who lived here long before the Hopi and Navajo. See chapter 6.

- **Master Sculptor.** Nature has sculpted an otherworldly landscape on the Utah–Arizona line known as Monument Valley—officially Monument Valley Navajo Tribal Park. Don't be surprised if you've seen these monoliths and spires before—they have appeared in numerous movies. See chapter 6.

- **City Slickers.** You do more than watch cowboys doing their thing at guest ranches in Arizona and Wyoming: A la Billy Crystal in the *City Slickers* movies, you can do it yourself. See chapters 6 and 8.

- **Old Roads.** You can see wonderful scenery from the interstate highways crisscrossing the USA, but to experience the real America, get off onto the old roads such as U.S. 66 through the Southwest or U.S. 11 down the Shenandoah Valley. You'll see up close the small towns that the superhighways miss.

- **Last Stand in Texas.** To find the real heart of Texas, visit the Alamo in downtown San Antonio, where Davy Crockett, Jim Bowie, and 186 others died while fighting for the state's freedom from Mexico. See chapter 6.

- **Fruit of the Vine.** Vineyards have sprung up from sea to shining sea, but the best places to sample the vintages are still the Napa and Sonoma valleys in California's Wine Country. See chapter 7.

- **Big Views at Big Sur.** The USA has some great vistas, but nowhere else do mountains and sea combine to thrill the eye as along California's Big Sur coast. See the driving tour in chapter 7.

- **Atop El Capitan.** You don't have to be a rock climber to enjoy the stunning views from atop the sheer face of El Capitan in Yosemite, one of our most magnificent national parks. See chapter 7.

- **Glitz Capital.** The neon-lit desert oasis of Las Vegas is America at its most excessive—from the world's largest hotel to its most glamorous floor shows—and a copy of the Eiffel Tower is on the drawing boards. See chapter 7.

- **Dry and Hot.** Visitors have long linked the Creator with California's Death Valley—not as a heavenly spot, but as hell on earth. Today the Western Hemisphere's lowest, driest, and hottest place is a national park with air-conditioned hotel rooms, well-maintained campgrounds, and a saloon serving cold brews. See chapter 7.

- **Whales and Rocky Headlands.** It rains more along the Oregon coast than down on California's Big Sur coast, but this stretch of shoreline is just as dramatic, with heavily forested mountains forming windswept headlands falling into the sea, hundreds of offshore monoliths and tiny islands sheltering seabirds, sea lions, and seals, and gray whales passing close ashore twice a year. See the driving tour in chapter 8.
- **Old Faithful and Grizzly Bears.** Although it's best known for a thermal geyser named Old Faithful, Yellowstone National Park is a diverse wilderness of pristine forests, blue-ribbon trout streams, great herds of bison, and a multitude of wildlife including fearsome grizzly bears. See chapter 8.
- **Fire and Brimstone.** Wiffs of sulfur, eye-stinging plumes of smoke, red-hot burning lava, and miles of scorched black earth. Doesn't sound like the Hawaii of tropical dreams, but this is what you'll find in Hawaii Volcanoes National Park on the Big Island, where Kilauea has been erupting since 1983. See chapter 9.
- **Big and Wild.** The only way into Denali National Park and its Mount McKinley, at 20,320 feet the tallest mountain in North America, is by bus, which means that grizzly bears and Alaska's other wild things are still doing what they would be doing even if you weren't there. See chapter 10.

## 2  The Wild, the Weird & the Wacky: Offbeat America

Anyone in love with the bizarre could spend several delightful years exploring the USA. We have everything here from shrines to soft drinks and fast-food restaurants to museums dedicated to flushing toilets and vacuum cleaners. Here's a selection from the land of the free, home of the bizarre.

If you want to know of many more, pick up a copy of *The New Roadside America* by Doug Kirby, Ken Smith, and Mike Wilkins (Simon & Schuster, 1992), or *The Cockroach Hall of Fame and 101 Other Off-the-Wall Museums* by Sandra Gurvis (Citadel Press, 1994).

- **Hollerin', Jumping Frogs, and Men's Legs.** Among our wacky festivals, entrants see just how loud they can yell during the National Hollerin' Contest in Spivey's Corner, North Carolina, every June. Mark Twain thought California's Calaveras County Jumping Frog Jubilee in May was so funny he wrote a story about it. And in January men vie to see who has the best legs at the Goodland Mullet Festival in Marco Island, Florida, an annual that also features the Buzzard Lope dance. See "The USA's Top Festivals & Events," below.
- **Toil and Trouble.** Some people say that despite purging itself in the 17th century, Salem, Massachusetts, is still home to many practicing witches who take their craft very seriously. You may not knowingly meet one, but you can visit the **Salem Witch Museum** and buy witchcraft accessories from several local shops. See chapter 2.
- **Brushes and Flushes.** While you're touring around Boston, you can drive over to Worcester to the **American Sanitary Plumbing Museum** (☎ 508/754-9453), the only place in the world that exhibits, well, sanitary plumbing.
- **Tails and Scales.** Drive north of Clearwater, Florida, for an hour on U.S. 19 and you'll come to **Weeki Wachee Spring** (☎ 800/678-9335 or 352/596-2062), where "mermaids" have been putting on acrobatic swimming shows since 1947. It's a sight to see them doing their dances in waters that come from one of America's most prolific freshwater springs.

- **Pins and Needles.** The Big Easy has always been a little different from the rest of the USA, and the dark, musty **New Orleans Historic Voodoo Museum** proves it. See chapter 4.

- **Pop Bottles.** Lest we forget Atlanta's first great contribution to the world (before CNN news), **The World of Coca-Cola** reminds us with "Coke" memorabilia ranging from endorsements by Clark Gable to campy commercials sung by the Supremes. See chapter 4.

- **Heirs and Assigns.** The King of Rock-and-Roll may be gone, but Elvis's **Graceland** mansion in Memphis draws more visitors than any other place in town. His heirs and assigns have turned it into a mini–theme park, with plenty of opportunities to spend money. See chapter 4.

- **Oil Money.** It would be just another Texas ranch had **Southfork** not been the setting for the hit TV series *Dallas.* Today Southfork is a tourist attraction, with a tram tour, visits to J. R. Ewing's mansion, and a *Dallas* museum. See chapter 6.

- **Pork Paddle.** That's no mermaid at **Aquarena Springs Resort** (☎ 800/ 999-9767 or 512/396-8900), near San Marcos in the Texas Hill Country. It's Ralph the Swimming Pig, who performs at a submarine theater. See chapter 6.

- **Big Mac, Fries, and a Coke.** The first McDonald's opened in San Bernadino, California, in 1948, but the actual fast-food chain we know today began on April 15, 1955, in Des Plaines, Illinois. Today that golden-arched structure is **McDonald's Museum Store #1,** complete with vintage 1950s cars parked out front (☎ 708/297-5022).

- **Suction Sweepers.** In the mid-1800s, women had to rock back and forth atop the machine to make a vacuum cleaner work. Then along came electricity and the Hoover Suction Sweeper Company. Cleaning has been getting easier ever since, as you will discover at the **Hoover Historical Center** in North Canton, Ohio (☎ 216/499-0287).

- **Art of the Bark.** You'll learn everything you ever wanted to know about man's best friend at the **Dog Museum** in St. Louis. Owners display their pedigreed pets on Sunday. See chapter 5.

- **Bigger Dreams.** One machine promised to enlarge a woman's breasts, while another claimed it would do the same for a man's prowess. If they worked, they wouldn't be in the **Museum of Questionable Medical Devices** in Minneapolis (☎ 612/545-1113), which exhibits more than 250 quack machines.

- **Car Druids.** Could there be a better shrine in a nation obsessed with automobiles than a replica of England's Stonehenge built of junked cars? It's called **Carhenge,** and it's in Alliance, a small town in western Nebraska. If you miss the signs, call the local chamber of commerce at ☎ 308/762-1520.

- **The Great Bubble.** For 2 years beginning in September 1991, four men and four women locked inside **Biosphere 2,** an airtight, 3-acre greenhouse in the desert 35 miles north of Tucson near the town of Oracle, Arizona, conducted experiments on how the earth manages to support all the planet's life forms. Today this giant science project is a major tourist attraction. See chapter 6.

- **Unidentified Objects.** The desert town of Roswell in southeastern New Mexico is the Unidentified Flying Object capital of the world. This was, after all, the site of an alleged UFO crash (and subsequent military cover-up) in 1947. You can learn more at two museums—the **International UFO Museum and Research Center** (☎ 505/625-9495) and the **UFO Enigma Museum** (☎ 505/ 347-2275)—devoted to the "incident." Each July the town hosts a UFO Festival. You can also visit the alleged crash site and videotape your own UFO sighting at the **Midway Sightings Location Site** (☎ 505/347-4228). Your tape will even be sent off for "analysis."

- **Stoney Mirage.** In the mid-1960s the British government decided to sell the **London Bridge,** which was sinking into the Thames River. An American developer bought it and shipped it stone-by-stone to Lake Havasu City in western Arizona. At first the 900-foot-long bridge connected only desert to more desert. Although a channel eventually was dredged under it, the London Bridge sits like a mirage in this dusty desert resort. See chapter 7.
- **Stars Down Under.** Old movie stars don't just fade away; they end up in Los Angeles's wacky **Forest Lawn Memorial Park,** America's most famous cemetery. The living use it, too: Ronald Reagan married Jane Wyman here. See chapter 7.
- **Barbie My Love.** More than half a billion Barbie dolls have been sold, and you'll find an example of all but a few models at the **Barbie Doll Hall of Fame** in Palo Alto, California, south of San Francisco (☎ 415/326-5841).
- **Stuffed and Mounted.** Passing through Victorville, California, it's tough to miss a log fort visible from I-15, with the words **"Roy Rogers and Dale Evans Museum"** emblazoned Las Vegas–style on its side (☎ 619/243-4547). Fans of cowboy lore know this as the final resting place of Roy's faithful horse Trigger, whom he had stuffed and mounted.
- **Tassles and G-strings.** Halfway between Hollywood and Las Vegas, Helendale, California, is as good a place as any for **Exotic World: The Burlesque Hall of Fame** (☎ 619/243-5261), dedicated to the rich lore of burlesque dancing. You can see memorabilia of Sally Rand, Lily St. Cyr, Blaze Starr, Tempest Storm, and other strippers here.
- **Mr. Flamboyant.** Few American entertainers have been as outrageously flamboyant as the late Walter Valentino Liberace, so it's fitting that his dazzling costumes and glittering stage jewelry be preserved in Las Vegas. Also in the **Liberace Museum** are his spectacular cars, antique and custom-made pianos, and 3,000 miniature pianos his fans gave him. See chapter 7.

## 3  Planning Your Trip

With such a large country to visit, doing a little homework before you leave home can save a lot of time, trouble, and money later. Following are some advance-planning details that can help you enjoy a smooth, successful trip.

### VISITOR INFORMATION

The American federal government has abolished the U.S. Travel and Tourism Administration, so there is no central visitor information office for the entire country. Your best bet is to contact the state or local visitor information offices mentioned in this book, or one of the state tourism offices listed in the appendix. If you live in another country, check with the U.S. Information Agency (USIA) office at an American embassy or consulate in your home country.

### WHEN TO GO

**CLIMATE**  There is no one climate in the USA. When it's shivering cold in New England, the upper central states, and Alaska, it's sunny and warm in Florida, California, and Hawaii. When it's raining cats and dogs along the Northwest coast, it's dry as a bone in the Southwest desert. It can be a pleasant 75°F on the beaches of southern California in summer, yet 120°F just a few miles inland. And even in tropical Hawaii, it can be simultaneously warm down by the sea and snowing atop Mauna Loa on the Big Island.

Nor is there a nationwide high or low season. In summer, room rates are highest on the Northeast and Mid-Atlantic beaches but lowest on the sands of hot-and-humid Florida. Winter snows virtually close the great Rocky Mountain national parks, but they bring crowds to the nearby ski slopes. It all depends on when a region has the best weather for its special attractions and activities.

The Northeast and Mid-Atlantic states have their summer beach season June to Labor Day and their great fall foliage in September and October. Summer can be brutally hot and humid in the Southeast, but spring and fall last longer there, and winter is mild, with snow the exception rather than the rule. Southern Florida's best season is January to April, although cold snaps can turn it nippy for a few days. The central states see brutal winters and scorching summers. The Southwest varies from hot-and-humid summers and mild winters along the east Texas coast to 110°F-but-dry summers and pleasant-and-dry winters in Arizona. The mountains of Colorado, Utah, and the Northwest have dry, moderately hot summers and cold, snowy winters. The California coast is fine all year except early spring, when it rains, while the Northwest coast is wet all the time except July.

The long and short of it: Late spring and early fall are the best times to visit most of the country.

**NATIONAL HOLIDAYS**    Banks, government offices, post offices, and many stores, restaurants, and museums are closed on legal national holidays: January 1 (New Year's Day), the third Monday in January (Martin Luther King, Jr. Day), the third Monday in February (Presidents' Day, Washington's Birthday), the last Monday in May (Memorial Day), July 4 (Independence Day), the first Monday in September (Labor Day), the second Monday in October (Columbus Day), November 11 (Veterans' Day/Armistice Day), the last Thursday in November (Thanksgiving), and December 25 (Christmas). Also, the Tuesday following the first Monday in November is Election Day, which is a federal government holiday in presidential-election years (1996 was the most recent, 2000 is the next).

See "Festivals & Events," below, for more dates around which to plan your trip.

## HEALTH, INSURANCE & SAFETY

**HEALTH**    The U.S. doesn't present any unusual health hazards to domestic or foreign visitors. Tap water is safe to drink throughout the country. You aren't likely to catch any dangerous diseases, but AIDS (acquired immunodeficiency syndrome) is very present here, so exercise the same safe-sex practices as you would at home.

If you have a serious condition or allergy, consider wearing a Medic Alert identification bracelet; contact the **Medic Alert Foundation,** P.O. Box 1009, Turlock, CA 95381-1009 (☎ 800/432-5378). If you have dental problems, a nationwide referral service known as **1-800-DENTIST** (☎ 800/336-8478) will give you the name of a nearby dentist or clinic.

When heading into the great outdoors, keep in mind that injuries often occur when people fail to follow instructions. Believe the experts who tell you to stay on the established ski trails, hike only in designated areas, follow the marine charts if piloting your own boat, carry rain gear, and wear a life jacket when rafting. Mountain weather can be fickle at any time of the year. And watch out for summer thunderstorms that can send bolts of lightening your way and leave you drenched.

**INSURANCE**    Foreign travelers should be aware that unlike Canada and Europe, there is no national health system in the United States, and the cost of medical care is extremely high. For this reason, many travelers buy insurance policies providing health and accident coverage as well as trip-cancellation or -interruption and lost-luggage protection. The coverage you should consider depends on how you're getting here and how much protection is already contained in your existing policies. Some credit- and charge-card companies will insure you against travel accidents if you buy plane, train, or bus tickets with their cards.

Some American firms offering travel insurance are: **Travel Assistance International (TAI)** (☎ 800/821-2828 or 202/347-2025), **Travel Guard International** (☎ 800/782-5151 or 715/345-0505), **Access America** (☎ 800/284-8300 or 804/285-3300), or **Mutual of Omaha** (☎ 800/228-9792). The **Divers Alert Network (DAN)** (☎ 800/446-2671 or 919/684-2948) insures scuba divers.

**SAFETY**   While tourist areas are generally safe, and violent crime has been decreasing in many parts of the country, U.S. urban areas tend to be less safe than those in Europe or Japan. It is wise to ask your hotel front desk staff or the city's or area's tourist office if you're in doubt about which neighborhoods are safe.

Recently more and more crime has involved vehicles, so safety while driving is particularly important. Question your rental agency about personal safety, or ask for a brochure of traveler safety tips when you pick up your car. Obtain written directions, or a map with the route clearly marked, from the agency showing how to get to your destination.

If you have a minor accident, or an accident on the highway, never get out of your car. Stay in your car with the doors locked until you assess the situation or the police arrive. If you see someone on a street or highway who indicates a need for help, don't stop—drive on to the nearest well-lighted area and telephone the police by dialing ☎ 911. Park in well-lighted areas, and never leave any packages or valuables in sight in your car.

## RESOURCES FOR TRAVELERS WITH SPECIAL NEEDS

**FOR TRAVELERS WITH DISABILITIES**   Some nationwide resources include **Mobility International USA** (☎ 503/343-1284), which offers its members travel-accessibility information and has many interesting travel programs for the disabled; the **Travel Information Service** (☎ 215/456-9600); and the **Society for the Advancement of Travel for the Handicapped** (☎ 212/447-7284). In addition, **Twin Peaks Press**, P.O. Box 129, Vancouver, WA 98666 (☎ 360/694-2462), specializes in travel-related books for people with disabilities.

Companies offering tours for those with physical or mental disabilities include **Accessible Journeys** (☎ 800/TINGLES or 610/521-0339), **Flying Wheels Travel** (☎ 800/535-6790 or 507/451-5005), **The Guided Tour, Inc.** (☎ 215/782-1370), and **Wilderness Inquiry** (☎ 800/728-0719 or 612/379-3858).

In addition, both **Amtrak** (☎ 800/USA-RAIL) and **Greyhound** (☎ 800/752-4841) offer special fares and services for the disabled. Call at least a week in advance of your trip for details.

**FOR SENIORS**   Senior citizen discounts are widespread, so mention the fact that you're a senior when you first make your travel arrangements. For example, **Amtrak** (☎ 800/USA-RAIL) and many airlines offer discounted senior fares. And don't forget that hotels and motels also have discounts for seniors. For example, in 1996 the Econo Lodge chain instituted a 30% break for anyone 50 or older.

Members of the **American Association of Retired Persons (AARP)**, 601 E St. NW, Washington, DC 22049 (☎ 800/424-3410 or 202/434-2277), get discounts not only on hotels but on airfares and car rentals, too.

Other helpful organizations include the nonprofit **National Council of Senior Citizens**, 1331 F St. NW, Washington, DC 20004 (☎ 202/347-8800), part of whose magazine is devoted to travel tips. **Mature Outlook**, 6001 N. Clark St., Chicago, IL 60660 (☎ 800/336-6330), offers discounts at ITC-member hotels and savings on selected auto rentals and restaurants. **Golden Companions,** P.O. Box 5249, Reno, NV 89513 (☎ 702/324-2227), helps travelers 45-plus find compatible companions through a personal voicebox mail service. Contact them for more information. **Elderhostel,** 75 Federal St., Boston, MA 02110-1941 (☎ 617/426-7788), sponsors learning vacations on college campuses. Participants must be 55 or older; however, if two people go as a couple, only one has to be of the required age.

Companies specializing in senior travel include **Grand Circle Travel,** 347 Congress St., Suite 3A, Boston, MA 02210 (☎ 800/221-2610 or 617/350-7500); and **SAGA International Holidays,** 222 Berkeley St., Boston, MA 02115 (☎ 800/343-0273).

The National Park Service issues a **"Golden Age Passport"** to any citizen or person who lives in the United States and is 62 or older, providing free admittance to all national parks. Obtain this lifetime admission permit for $10 at any Park Service property; proof of age is necessary.

**FOR FAMILIES**  Many hotels and resorts have children's programs, and baby-sitting services are often available. Hotels and restaurants in destinations like Florida that especially attract families are always willing and eager to cater to people traveling with children.

**FOR STUDENTS**  You'll need your valid high school or college identification for discounted admission to museums and other attractions. An international hosteling card entitles you to members' rates in hostels; to join, contact **Hosteling International–American Youth Hostels,** 733 15th St. NW, Washington, DC 20005 (☎ 202/783-6161), or **Hosteling International–Canada,** 205 Catherine St., Suite 400, Ottawa, Ontario K2P 1C3 (☎ 613/237-7884). Remember that by law, alcoholic beverages cannot be sold to anyone under 21, so if you intend to imbibe, you'll need your driver's license or passport to prove your date of birth.

**FOR GAY & LESBIAN TRAVELERS**  While many American cities are friendly to gays and lesbians—San Francisco, New York City, Key West, Miami's South Beach, and Washington, D.C., leap to mind—there are places where intolerance still reigns. *Out and About,* 8 W. 19th St., Suite 401, New York, NY 10011 (☎ 800/929-2268), profiles the best gay or gay-friendly hotels, gyms, clubs, and other places in destinations throughout the world. *Our World,* 1104 N. Nova Rd., Suite 251, Daytona Beach, FL 32117 (☎ 904/441-5367), is a magazine devoted to options and bargains for gay and lesbian travel worldwide.

The **International Gay Travel Association (IGTA),** P.O. Box 4974, Key West, FL 33041 (☎ 800/448-8550, or 305/292-0217 for voice mail), links travelers up with the appropriate gay-friendly service organization or tour specialist. Contact IGTA for a list of its member agencies, who will be tied into IGTA's information resources.

## GETTING TO THE USA

Many international carriers and several U.S. airlines offer service to the USA. The major gateway cities are Boston, New York, Washington, D.C. (and nearby Baltimore), Atlanta, Orlando, Miami, Houston, Dallas, Chicago, Los Angeles, San Francisco, Seattle, Anchorage, and Honolulu. You can also fly direct—though there are less frequent flights—to many other cities. Call the airlines' local offices or contact your travel agent.

If you're coming from the United Kingdom or Europe, **Virgin Atlantic Airways** (☎ 800/662-8621 in the USA, or 01/293-74-77-47 in the U.K.) has cut-rate fares on its flights from London and Manchester to New York, Washington, D.C., Miami, and Orlando. **Laker Airways** (☎ 888/525-3724 in the USA, or 011-44-129-377-2020 in the U.K.) is flying again from Manchester and London's Gatwick Airport to New York, Boston, Los Angeles, Miami, Orlando, and San Francisco. If you're coming from

Canada, ask your travel agent about cheap seasonal charters to Florida and other USA destinations offered by **Canada 3000** (☎ **416/674-0257**).

Regardless of the airline, you should always ask about **APEX (Advance Purchase Excursion) fares,** which represent substantial savings over regular fares. Most require tickets to be bought up to 3 weeks prior to departure.

No matter at which airport you land, getting through Immigration Control may take as long as 2 hours on some days, especially summer weekends, so make very generous allowances for delays when planning connections between international and domestic flights. In contrast, travelers arriving by car or by rail from Canada will find border-crossing formalities streamlined to the vanishing point. And air travelers from Canada, Bermuda, and some places in the Caribbean can sometimes go through Customs and Immigration at the point of departure, which is much quicker and less painful.

Travel agents offer hundreds of **package tour** options to the USA. Quite often a package tour will result in savings not just on airfares but on hotels and other activities as well. Packages always cover airfare, transfers, and accommodations, and sometimes meals and certain activities are thrown in. The specifics vary, so consult your travel agent to find out the best deals at the time you want to travel.

## GETTING AROUND THE USA

**BY AIR**   Flying is the quickest and most comfortable way to get around this large country. If you're from overseas, ask your travel agent or local airline office about a **Visit USA** discount ticket sold by some large American airlines (for example, American, Delta, Northwest, TWA, and United) to travelers on their transatlantic or transpacific flights. It allows travel between many USA destinations at minimum rates. The ticket must be purchased before you leave your home point of departure. The conditions attached to these discount tickets can be changed without warning.

Ask the airlines for their *lowest* fares, and ask if it's cheaper to book in advance, fly in midweek, or stay over a Saturday night. Don't stop at the 7-day advance purchase; ask how much the 14- and 30-day plans cost. Decide when you want to go before you call, since many of the best deals are nonrefundable.

So-called no-frills airlines—low fares but no meals or other amenities—have been increasing in recent years. **Southwest Airlines** (☎ 800/435-9792), the oldest, biggest, and best, has flights to and from many U.S. cities. Their success caused Delta to launch **Delta Express** (☎ 800/325-5205), which at presstime was flying from several East Coast cities. An arm of the popular cruise line, **Carnival Air** (☎ 800/824-7386) flies from New York and Washington, D.C., to Fort Lauderdale, Florida. Others worth calling are **Air South** (☎ 800/247-7688), **Airtran** (☎ 800/247-8726), **America Trans Air** (☎ 800/225-2995), **Kiwi** (☎ 800/538-5494), **Midway** (☎ 800/44-MIDWAY), **Midwest Express** (☎ 800/452-2022), **SunJet** (☎ 800/478-6538), **Pan American** (☎ 800/359-7262), **Spirit** (☎ 800/772-7117), **Sun Country** (☎ 800/752-1218), **Sun Jet** (☎ 800/478-6538), **Tower Air** (☎ 800/348-6937), **Vanguard** (☎ 800/826-4827), and **Western Pacific** (☎ 800/930-3030).

You might also get a low fare by calling a "consolidator" such as **TFI Tours International** (☎ **800/745-8000** or 212/736-1140), which serves as a clearinghouse for unused seats, or a "rebator" such as **Travel Avenue** (☎ **800/333-3335** or 312/876-1116) or **The Smart Traveller** (☎ **800/448-3338** in the USA, or 305/448-3338), which rebates part of its commission to you. A travel agent can tell you more about consolidators and can shop among them to find their best deals. Look in your local newspaper's Sunday travel section for rebators' usually tiny advertisements.

Another possibility is to use a travel club such as **Moment's Notice** (☎ **718/234-6295**) and **Sears Discount Travel Club** (☎ **800/433-9383,** or 800/255-1487 to join), which supplies unsold tickets at discounted prices. You pay an annual membership fee to get the club's hotline number. Of course, you're limited to what's available, so you have to be flexible.

**BY CAR**    If you're not in a hurry, traveling by car is the best way to see the USA. It gives you the freedom to make—and alter—your itinerary to suit your own needs and interests. You can visit some of the off-the-beaten path locations, places that cannot be reached easily—or at all—by public transportation.

If you're a member, your local branch of the **American Automobile Association (AAA)** will provide a free trip-routing plan. AAA's nationwide **emergency road service** phone number is ☎ 800/AAA-HELP. (For more information about AAA, see "Automobile Organizations" in "Fast Facts: For the Foreign Traveler," below.)

The international **rental-car agencies** have offices at most airports and in many cities. Most of them pad their profits by selling Loss-Damage Waiver (LDW) insurance. You may already be covered by your insurance carrier and credit- or charge-card companies, so check with them before succumbing to the hard-sell. Also, the rental companies will offer to refill your gas tank at "competitive" prices when you return, but fuel usually is less expensive in town.

Most also require a minimum age, ranging from 19 to 25, and some also set maximum ages. Others deny cars to anyone with a bad driving record. Ask about rental requirements and restrictions when you book to avoid problems later. You must have a valid credit card to rent a vehicle.

Many packages are available that include airfare, accommodations, and a rental car with unlimited mileage. Compare these prices with the cost of booking airline tickets and renting a car separately to see if these offers are good deals.

Foreign visitors please note: In the USA we drive on the **right side of the road** as in Europe, not on the left side as in the United Kingdom, Australia, and New Zealand.

**BY TRAIN**    Long-distance trains in the United States are operated by **Amtrak** (☎ 800/USA-RAIL), the national rail passenger corporation. Be aware, however, that with a few notable exceptions (for instance, the Northeast Corridor line between Boston and Washington, D.C.), intercity service is not up to European standards. Delays are common, routes are limited and often infrequently served, and fares are seldom significantly lower than discount airfares. Thus cross-country train travel should be approached with caution.

If you intend to stop off along the way, you can save money with Amtrak's **All Aboard America** fares, which are based on three regions of the country. In 1997, for example, you could stop three times in the eastern states for $318 in summer, $198 during the off-season.

International visitors can buy a **USA Railpass,** good for 15 or 30 days of unlimited travel on Amtrak. The pass is available through many foreign travel agents, and with a foreign passport, you can also buy them at some Amtrak offices in the United States, including Boston, Chicago, Los Angeles, Miami, New York, San Francisco, and Washington, D.C. The prices are based on a zone system: eastern, central, and western United States. In 1997, a 15-day pass good in the eastern third of the country ranged from $190 to $230, depending on the time of travel, while 30-day passes ranged from $215 to $290. The highest prices are in summer and on holidays. Reservations are generally required and should be made for each part of your trip as early as possible.

**BY BUS**    Although it's the least expensive way to get around the country, long-distance bus service here can be both slow and uncomfortable, so it's not for everyone. The only national bus company is **Greyhound** (☎ 800/231-2222 in the USA), which offers a **New Ameripass** for unlimited travel anywhere on its system. In 1997, prices for a 7-day pass started at $179; 15 days, at $289; 30 days, at $399; and 60 days, at

$599. Senior citizen discounts ranged from $20 to $60. There are also local **Trailways** bus options.

## TIPS ON ACCOMMODATIONS

The USA has a vast array of accommodations, from rock-bottom roadside motels to some of the world's finest resorts. Whether you spend a pittance or a bundle depends on your budget and your tastes. In the words of that well-worn phrase, you can enjoy "champagne on a beer budget"—if you plan carefully and possess a little knowledge of how the hotel industry works.

If business is slow, many hotels will accept less than their published "rack" rates, which are their highest regular rates (rack rates are quoted in this book). Most rack rates include commissions of 20% or more for travel agents, which many will knock off rather than have a room go empty. You might save, therefore, if you make your own reservations and bargain a little.

Most hotels also give discounts to corporate travelers, government employees, senior citizens, automobile club members, active duty military personnel, and others. They usually don't advertise these discounted rates or even volunteer them at the front desk, but you can ask politely if there's a special rate that applies to you.

Downtown hotels catering to business travelers during the week usually have big discounts on Friday, Saturday, and Sunday nights. If you're staying in a city over a weekend, always ask about a weekend rate or package deal. Weekend rates don't apply in resort areas, so you should ask there about weekday or weeklong vacation packages.

Parking fees can run up the cost at downtown hotels, especially for long-term stays. And many hotels jack up the price of long-distance phone calls made from your room. Accordingly, always inquire about the costs of parking, and use a pay phone if the hotel tacks a hefty surcharge on calls.

## FAST FACTS: For Foreign Travelers

**Automobile Organizations**   The **American Automobile Association (AAA)** is the major auto club in the U.S. If you belong to an auto club in your home country, inquire about AAA reciprocity before you leave. You may be able to join AAA even if you're not a member of a reciprocal club; to inquire, call AAA (☎ **800/ 222-4357**). AAA's nationwide emergency road service telephone number is **800/ AAA-HELP.**

**Automobile Rentals**   See "Getting Around the USA," above.

**Business Hours**   Opening hours for stores, offices, banks, and other establishments vary from place to place. In general, offices are open weekdays 9am–5pm, while stores in malls usually operate Mon–Sat 10am–9pm, Sun noon–5pm. Banks normally are open weekdays 9am–3pm, and some have Saturday morning hours.

**Currency and Currency Exchange**   The U.S. monetary system has a decimal base: one American **dollar** ($1) = 100 **cents** (100¢). Notes come in $1 ("a buck"), $5, $10, $20, $50, and $100 denominations (the last two are not welcome when paying for small purchases and are not accepted in taxis or at subway ticket booths). There are also $2 bills, but you rarely see one. There are six denominations of coins: 1¢ (one cent, known here as a "penny"), 5¢ (five cents or a "nickel"), 10¢ (ten cents or a "dime"), 25¢ (twenty-five cents or a "quarter"), 50¢ (fifty cents or a "half dollar"), and the rare $1 piece.

Changing foreign currency in the United States is a hassle, so leave your own currency at home—few banks will be able to change it into U.S. dollars. An exception is **Thomas Cook Foreign Exchange,** which changes foreign currency and sells

commission-free foreign and U.S. traveler's checks, drafts, and wire transfers. Call
☎ 800/287-7362 for branch locations and hours.

**Traveler's checks** denominated in U.S. dollars are readily accepted at most hotels,
motels, restaurants, and large stores (but personal checks are not). Do not bring
traveler's checks denominated in other currencies.

**Credit and charge cards** are the most widely used form of payment in the United
States: Visa (Barclaycard in Britain), MasterCard (EuroCard in Europe, Access in
Britain, Chargex in Canada), American Express, Diners Club, Discover, and Carte
Blanche. You must have a credit or charge card to rent a car. **Automatic Teller
Machines (ATMs)** are ubiquitous, and will allow you to draw U.S. currency against
your bank and credit cards. Check with your bank before leaving home, to be sure
your Personal Identification Number (PIN) number will work in U.S. ATMs.

**Customs Requirements**   Every adult visitor may bring in free of duty: 1 liter of
wine or hard liquor; 200 cigarettes or 100 cigars (but no cigars made in Cuba) or
3 pounds of smoking tobacco; and $100 worth of gifts. You must spend at least
72 hours in the United States and have not claimed the excemptions within the
preceding 6 months. It is altogether forbidden to bring into the country foodstuffs
(particularly cheese, fruit, and cooked meats) or plants (vegetables, seeds, tropical
plants, and so on). Foreign tourists may bring in or take out up to $10,000 in U.S.
or foreign currency with no formalities; larger sums must be declared to Customs
upon entering or leaving.

Penalties are severe for smuggling illegal narcotics into the United States, so if you
need medications containing narcotics or other controlled substances, or medication
administered by syringe, carry a valid signed prescription from your physician.

See "Entry Requirements," below, for documents you will need to enter the U.S.

**Electricity**   Like Canada, the United States uses 110–120 volts AC, 60 cycles,
compared to 220–250 volts AC, 50 cycles in most of Europe, Australia, and New
Zealand. If your small appliances use 220–250 volts, you'll need a 110-volt transformer and an adapter with two flat, vertical plugs to operate them here. Down-
ward converters that change 220–250 volts to 110–120 volts are difficult to find in
the U.S., so bring one with you.

**Entry Requirements**   Immigration laws have been a hot political issue in the USA
in recent years, so it's wise to check at any U.S. embassy or consulate for current
information and requirements. You can also plug into the U.S. State Department's
Internet site at **http://www.state.gov**.

Canadians may enter the U.S. without passports or visas; you need only proof of
residence.

The U.S. State Department has a **Visa Waiver Program** allowing citizens of
certain countries to enter the United States without a visa for stays of up to 90
days. At press time these included Andorra, Argentina, Australia, Austria, Belgium,
Brunei, Denmark, Finland, France, Germany, Iceland, Ireland, Italy, Japan,
Liechtenstein, Luxembourg, Monaco, the Netherlands, New Zealand, Norway, San
Marino, Spain, Sweden, Switzerland, and the United Kingdom. If you're from one
of these countries, you will need only a valid passport and a round-trip air or cruise
ticket in your possession upon arrival. Once here, you may then visit Mexico,
Canada, Bermuda, and/or the Caribbean islands and return to the United States
without further formality. Information is available from any U.S. embassy or
consulate.

If you are from a country not listed above, you must have (1) a valid passport
with an expiration date at least 6 months later than the scheduled end of your visit;
and (2) a tourist visa that may be obtained without charge from the nearest U.S.

consulate. To obtain a visa, submit a completed application form with a 1$^1$/$_2$-inch square photo and demonstrate binding ties to your residence abroad. Contact the nearest U.S. embassy or consulate for directions if you are applying by mail. Your travel agent or airline office may also be able to provide you with the visa application forms and instructions. The U.S. embassy or consulate where you apply will determine whether you receive a multiple- or single-entry visa and any restrictions regarding the length of your stay.

No **inoculations** are needed to enter the United States unless you are coming from, or have stopped over in, areas known to be suffering from epidemics, particularly cholera or yellow fever.

Foreign **driver's licenses** are recognized in most states, but you may want to get an international driver's license written in English.

See "Customs Requirements," above, for what you can bring into the U.S. without paying duty.

**Embassies and Consulates**   All embassies are located in the national capital, Washington, D.C. Some consulates are located in major U.S. cities, and most nations have a mission to the United Nations in New York City.

The embassy of **Australia** is at 1601 Massachusetts Ave. NW, Washington, DC 20036 (☎ 202/797-3000). There are consulates in New York, Honolulu, Houston, Los Angeles, and San Francisco.

The embassy of **Canada** is at 501 Pennsylvania Ave. NW, Washington, DC 20001 (☎ 202/682-1740). Canadian consulates are in Atlanta, Buffalo (N.Y.), Chicago, Cleveland, Dallas, Detroit, Los Angeles, Miami, Minneapolis, New York, and Seattle.

The embassy of the **Republic of Ireland** is at 2234 Massachusetts Ave. NW, Washington, DC 20008 (☎ 202/462-3939). Irish consulates are in Boston, Chicago, New York, and San Francisco.

The embassy of **New Zealand** is at 37 Observatory Circle NW, Washington, DC 20008 (☎ 202/328-4800). New Zealand consulates are in Los Angeles, Salt Lake City, San Francisco, and Seattle.

The embassy of the **United Kingdom** is at 3100 Massachusetts Ave. NW, Washington, DC 20008 (☎ 202/462-1340). In Florida, there's a full-service British consulate in Miami at Suite 2110, Brickell Bay Office Tower, 1001 S. Bayshore Dr. (☎ 305/374-1522), and a vice consulate for emergency situations in Orlando at the Sun Trust Center, Suite 2110, 200 S. Orange Ave. (☎ 407/426-7855). British consulates are in Atlanta, Boston, Chicago, Cleveland, Dallas, Houston, Los Angeles, Miami, New York, and Orlando.

**Emergencies**   Call ☎ **911** to report a fire, call the police, or get an ambulance anywhere in the United States. This is a toll-free call (no coins are required at public telephones). If 911 is not available in the area where you are traveling, dial "O" for operator assistance.

If you encounter problems, check the local telephone directory to find an office of the **Traveler's Aid Society,** a nationwide, nonprofit, social-service organization geared to helping travelers in difficult straits.

**Gasoline (Petrol)**   Petrol is known as gasoline (or simply "gas") in the United States, and it's bought at gas stations or service stations. Gasoline costs about half as much here as it does in Europe (about $1.25 per gallon at press time). One U.S. gallon equals 3.8 liters or .85 Imperial gallons.

**Health**   See "Health, Insurance & Safety" under "Planning Your Trip," above.

**Holidays**   See "When to Go" under "Planning Your Trip," above.

**Insurance**   See "Health, Insurance & Safety" under "Planning Your Trip," above.

**Legal Aid**    Foreign visitors will probably never become involved with the American legal system. If you are "pulled over" for a minor infraction (exceeding the speed limit, for example), never attempt to pay the fine directly to a police officer; this could be construed as attempted bribery, a much more serious crime. Pay fines by mail, or directly into the hands of the clerk of the court. If accused of a more serious offense, say and do nothing before consulting a lawyer, since here the burden is on the state to prove a person's guilt, and everyone has the right to remain silent, whether suspected of a crime or actually arrested. Once arrested, a person can make one telephone call to a party of his or her choice. Call your embassy or consulate.

**Liquor Laws**    You must be at least 21 years old to purchase alcoholic beverages anywhere in the U.S., and photo identification will be required if there is any question about your age. Each state has its own laws about who can sell beer, wine, and liquor by the bottle; your hotel staff will direct you to the appropriate vendor.

**Mail**    If you aren't sure what your address will be in the United States, mail can be sent, in your name, **c/o General Delivery** at the main post office of the city or region where you expect to be. You must pick it up in person and must produce proof of identity (driver's license, passport, etc.).

Generally to be found at intersections, mailboxes are blue with a red-and-white stripe and carry the inscription U.S. MAIL. If your mail is addressed to a U.S. destination, don't forget to add the five-digit postal code, or ZIP Code, after the two-letter abbreviation of the state.

Our postal service has been raising prices lately. At press time domestic postage rates were expected to rise from 20¢ to 22¢ for a postcard and from 32¢ to 34¢ for a letter. Airmail postcards to Canada cost 30¢ at press time, while letters cost 46¢. Airmail letters to other countries are 60¢ for the first half ounce. These rates are also expected to increase.

**Money**    See "Currency and Currency Exchange," above.

**Newspapers/Magazines**    Every American city has its own daily newspaper. *USA Today* and the *Wall Street Journal* are distributed nationally. In many areas you can also buy the *New York Times.* Newsstands are loaded with a plethora of magazines aimed at every special interest. The major weekly news magazines are *Time, Newsweek,* and *U.S. News & World Report.*

**Safety**    See "Safety" under "Planning Your Trip," above.

**Shopping**    Many foreign visitors find the United States to be a shopping bargain basement. The U.S. federal government charges very low duties on imports compared to the rest of the world, so you can get some excellent deals here on imported electronic goods, cameras, and clothing. Of course, it all depends on the value of your home currency versus the dollar, and how much duty you'll have to pay on your purchases when you get home. You'll pay a "sales tax," which varies from state to state and is added to the price of items you buy, but the USA has no Value-Added Tax (VAT).

The national "discount" chain stores consistently offer some of our best shopping deals. For televisions, VCRs, radios, camcorders, computers, and other electronic goods, go to **Circuit City** and **Best Buy.** Best Buy also has a wide selection of music. **CompUSA** and **Micro Center** specialize in computer hardware, accessories, and software, while **Egghead Software** has competitive prices on software. **Service Merchandise** is one of our best chains for cameras, and it also has electronics, jewelry, and many other items.

Most computers and other electronic equipment sold here use only 110- to 120-volt, 60-cycle electricity. You will need a transformer to use them at home if your power is 220–240 volts, 50 cycles. Be sure to ask the salesperson if an item has a universal power adapter.

Our major department store chains are **Sears, Macy's, Saks Fifth Avenue, Lord & Taylor,** and **JC Penney.** You'll also find **Burdines, Jordan Marsh,** and **Dillard's** in many locales. You get real deals in department stores only during sales, when selected merchandise is marked down 25% or more. The **Marshall's** and **TJ Maxx** chains carry name-brand clothing at department-store sale prices, but their stock tends to vary greatly.

Another source are **outlet malls** in which manufacturers operate their own shops, selling directly to the consumer. Sometimes you can get very good buys at the outlets, especially when sales are going on. Most lingerie and china outlets have good prices when compared to department stores, but that's not necessarily the case with designer clothing. In addition, some manufacturers produce items of lesser quality so they can charge less at their outlets, so inspect all merchandise carefully. The main advantage to outlet malls is that if you are looking for a specific brand—Levi's jeans, for example—the company's outlet will have it.

You'll find national chain stores, department stores, and outlet malls throughout the USA. Look in the White Pages of the local telephone directory for their addresses and phone numbers.

**Smoking**   The USA has more restrictions on smoking than any other country. Federal and state laws prohibit tobacco products from being sold to anyone under 18 years old, and tobacco vendors are required by federal law to request a photo identification of any customer under the age of 27. Other rules vary from state to state and city to city, but smoking is absolutely prohibited on all airplanes, trains, and buses, and in most public and private buildings. Nonsmoking hotel rooms and seating sections in most restaurants and bars now far outnumber those in which you can light up. If you smoke, ask for a smoking room when you make your hotel reservations.

**Taxes**   There is no Value-Added Tax (VAT) or other indirect tax at the national level. Every state, county, and city has the right to levy its own local tax on all purchases, including hotel and restaurant checks, airline tickets, and so on. These are known as "sales taxes" and are added to your bill.

**Telephone, Telegraph, Telex & Fax**   The telephone system in the United States is run by private corporations, so rates, especially for long-distance service and operator-assisted calls, can vary widely. Generally, hotel surcharges on long-distance and local calls are astronomical, so you're usually better off using a **public pay telephone,** which you'll find clearly marked in most public buildings and private establishments as well as on the street. Convenience grocery stores and gas stations always have them. Many convenience groceries and packaging services sell prepaid calling cards in denominations up to $50; these can be the least expensive way to call home. Many public phones at airports now accept American Express, MasterCard, and Visa credit cards. Local calls made from public pay phones usually cost 25¢.

Most **long-distance and international calls** can be dialed directly from any phone. For calls within the United States and to Canada, dial 1 followed by the area code and the seven-digit number. For other international calls, dial 011 followed by the country code, city code, and the telephone number of the person you are calling.

Calls to area codes 800 and 888 are **toll free.** However, calls to numbers in area codes 700 and 900 (chat lines, bulletin boards, "dating" services, etc.) can be very expensive—usually a charge of 95¢ to $3 or more per minute, and they sometimes have minimum charges that can run as high as $15 or more.

For **reversed-charge or collect calls,** and for **person-to-person calls,** dial 0 (zero, *not* the letter O) followed by the area code and number you want; an operator will then come on the line, and you should specify that you are calling collect, or person-to-person, or both. If your operator-assisted call is international, ask for the overseas operator.

For local **directory assistance** ("information"), dial ☎ 411; for **long-distance information,** dial 1, then the appropriate area code and 555-1212.

**Telegraph and telex services** are provided primarily by Western Union, which has hundreds of offices across the country (☎ 800/325-6000 for the nearest location). You can also telegraph money, or have it telegraphed to you, very quickly over the Western Union system, but this service can cost as much as 15% to 25% of the amount sent.

Most hotels have **fax** machines available for guest use (be sure to ask about the charge to use it), and many hotel rooms are even wired for guests' fax machines. A less expensive way to send and receive faxes may be at stores such as **Mail Boxes Etc.,** a national chain of packing service shops (look in the Yellow Pages directory under "Packing Services").

There are two kinds of telephone directories in the United States. The so-called **White Pages** list private and business subscribers in alphabetical order. The inside front cover lists emergency numbers for police, fire, ambulance, the Coast Guard, poison-control center, crime-victims hotline, and so on. The first few pages will tell you how to make long-distance and international calls, complete with country codes and area codes. Government numbers usually are on pages printed on blue paper. Printed on yellow paper, the so-called **Yellow Pages** list all local services, businesses, industries, churches, and synagogues by type of activity, with an index at the front or back. The Yellow Pages also include city plans or detailed area maps, often showing postal ZIP Codes and public transportation routes.

**Time** The continental United States is divided into four time zones: eastern standard time (EST), central standard time (CST), mountain standard time (MST), and Pacific standard time (PST). Alaska and Hawaii have their own zones. For example, noon in New York City (EST) is 11am in Chicago (CST), 10am in Denver (MST), 9am in Los Angeles (PST), 8am in Anchorage (AST), and 7am in Honolulu (HST).

Daylight saving time is in effect from 1am on the first Sunday in April through 1am the last Sunday in October.

**Tipping** Tipping is so ingrained in the American way of life that the annual income tax of tip-earning service personnel is based on how much they should have received in light of their employers' gross revenues. Accordingly, they may have to pay tax on a tip you didn't actually give them.

Here are some rules of thumb: Bartenders, 10–15% of the check; bellhops, at least 50¢ per bag, or $2–$3 for a lot of luggage; cab drivers, 15% of the fare; chambermaids, $1 per day; checkroom attendants, $1 per garment; hairdressers and barbers, 15–20% of the bill; waiters and waitresses, 15–20% of the check; valet parking attendants, $1 per vehicle; restroom attendants, 25¢. We do not tip theater ushers, gas station attendants, or the staff at cafeterias and fast-food restaurants.

**Toilets** You won't find public toilets (euphemistically referred to here as "restrooms") on the streets in most U.S. cities, but they can be found in hotel lobbies, bars, restaurants, museums, department stores, railway and bus stations, or service stations. Note, however, that restaurants and bars in resorts, large cities, or heavily visited areas may reserve their restrooms for the use of their patrons.

# FESTIVALS & EVENTS

January

- **Tournament of Roses,** Pasadena, California. A spectacular parade with lavish floats, music, and extraordinary equestrian entries precedes the annual Rose Bowl college football game. Jan. 1. ☎ 818/449-4100.
- **Mummer's Parade,** Philadelphia. Some 30,000 spangled strutters march down Broad Street with feathers and banjos in a celebration that must have had pagan origins. Jan. 1. ☎ 215/336-3050.
- **Elvis Presley's Birthday Tribute,** Memphis. International gathering of The King's fans to celebrate his birthday at Graceland, his home. Around Jan. 8. ☎ 901/332-3322.
- **National Western Stock Show, Rodeo, and Horse Show,** Denver. The world's largest livestock show and indoor rodeo, beginning with a parade through downtown. Second and third weeks of Jan. ☎ 303/295-1660.
- **Martin Luther King Jr.'s Birthday,** Washington, D.C. The great civil rights leader's "I Have a Dream" speech is read on the steps of the Lincoln Memorial. Third Monday in Jan. ☎ 202/789-7000.
- **Martin Luther King Week,** Atlanta. More than 300,000 attend speeches by Mrs. Coretta Scott King and other notables, concerts by the likes of Stevie Wonder, plays, films, seminars, parade. Second week in Jan. ☎ 404/624-5600.
- **Art Deco Weekend,** South Beach, Miami. Bands, food stands, antique vendors, tours, and other festivities celebrate the whimsical architecture that has made South Beach one of America's most unique neighborhoods. Usually third weekend in Jan. ☎ 305/672-2014.
- **Goodland Mullet Festival,** Marco Island, Florida. Stan Gober's Idle Hour Seafood Restaurant is mobbed during a riotous country music party featuring the Buzzard Lope dance and the Best Men's Legs Contest. Sunday before Super Bowl. ☎ 941/394-3041.

February

- **Mardi Gras,** New Orleans. Almost synonymous with the Big Easy is the world famous partying that ends 2-week Carnival. Tickets to the balls and most events are either unavailable or hard to come by, but street action and parades are free. Tuesday before Ash Wednesday (46 days before Easter). ☎ 504/566-5055.
- **Edison Pageant of Light,** Fort Myers, Florida. The spectacular Parade of Lights tops off arts-and-crafts shows, pageants, and a 5km race. First 2 weeks in Feb. ☎ 800/237-6444 or 941/334-2550.
- **Gasparilla Pirate Festival,** Tampa, Florida. Hundreds of boats and rowdy "pirates" invade the city, showering crowds with beads and coins. Early Feb. ☎ 813/272-1939.
- **Chinese New Year Festival and Parade,** San Francisco. Golden Dragon parade with lion dancing, bands, street fair, flower sale, festive food during America's largest Chinese celebration. On Chinese New Year. ☎ 415/982-3000.
- **Miami Film Festival,** Miami. A 10-day festival provides an important screening opportunity for Latin American cinema and American independents. Small, well priced, easily accessible. Mid-Feb. ☎ 305/377-FILM.
- **George Washington's Birthday,** Alexandria, Virginia. Colonial costume dinner and ball, Revolutionary War encampment, parade in historic Old Town. Presidents' Day weekend. ☎ 703/838-5005 or 703/838-4200.
- **Coconut Grove Art Festival,** Coconut Grove, Miami. More than 300 artists are selected from thousands of entries to show their works at Florida's largest art

festival. Almost every medium represented, including the culinary arts. Presidents' Day weekend. ☎ **305/447-0401.**

- **Westminster Kennel Club Dog Show,** New York City. Some 30,000 dog fanciers from all over the world congregate at Madison Square Garden for the "World Series of Dogdom." Mid-Feb. ☎ **212/465-6000.**
- **Newport Seafood & Wine Festival,** Newport, Oregon. One of America's largest wine festivals features vinters from California, Oregon, Washington, plus seafood specialties from the West's best chefs. Third weekend in Feb. ☎ **800/ 262-7844** or 541/265-8801.
- **Winter Fiesta,** Santa Fe, New Mexico. Midwinter break appeals to skiers and non-skiers alike. Snow sculpture, snowshoe races, Great Santa Fe Chili Cookoff, more. Last weekend in Feb. ☎ **505/982-4429.**
- **Philadelphia Flower and Garden Show,** Philadelphia. Largest in the country, with acres of gardens and rustic settings. Late Feb. ☎ **215/625-8250.**

March

- **Sanibel Shell Fair,** Sanibel and Captiva islands, Florida. A show of shells from around the world and the sale of unusual shell art. Begins first Thursday in Mar. ☎ **941/472-2155.**
- **Calle Ocho Festival,** Miami. One of the world's biggest block parties held along 23 blocks of Little Havana's SW 8th Street. Early to mid-Mar. ☎ **305/644-8888.**
- **Cherry Blossom Festival,** Washington, D.C. Blossoming of the famous Japanese cherry trees around the Tidal Basin brings a week of festivities in the capital. Late Mar. or early Apr. ☎ **202/789-7038** or 202/547-1500.
- **South by Southwest (SXSW) Music & Media Conference,** Austin. The Austin Music Awards kick off this huge conference, with hundreds of concerts at dozens of venues. Aspiring music industry types sign up months in advance. Mid-Mar. ☎ **512/467-7979.**
- **St. Patrick's Day/Evacuation Day,** Boston. Five-mile parade salutes the city's Irish heritage and the day British troops left Boston in 1776. Music, dancing, food, and plenty of Irish spirit. Mar. 17. ☎ **800/888-5515.**
- **Patriots Day,** Lexington and Concord, Massachusetts. Reenactment of the battles that began the American Revolution at Lexington Green and Concord North Bridge, with real musket fire but no bullets. Third Monday in Apr. ☎ **508/ 369-6944** or 617/862-1450.
- **Return of the Swallows,** San Juan Capistrano, California. Parade, dances, and special programs welcome home the swallows to this coastal town. Mid-Mar. ☎ **916/583-7652.**
- **Spring Break,** Miami Beach, Key West, Fort Lauderdale, and other Florida beaches. College students from all over the U.S. and Canada arrive for endless partying, wet T-shirt and bikini contests, free concerts, volleyball tournaments, and more. See it on MTV. Three weeks in Mar. Call the local visitor information offices.
- **Tennessee Williams/New Orleans Literary Festival,** New Orleans. The Big Easy honors the illustrious writer with his plays, readings, symposiums, panel discussions, and walking tours of his French Quarter haunts. Late Mar. or early Apr. ☎ **504/286-6680.**

April

- **White House Easter Egg Roll,** Washington, D.C. Kids 3–6 crowd the White House lawn in search of 1,000 Easter eggs. Famous names or acts entertain. Easter Monday ☎ **202/208-1631.**

- **World's Largest Easter Egg Hunt,** Bradenton, Florida. The city tries to break into the *Guinness Book of World Records* by burying 200,000 eggs in the sand of Coquina Beach. Easter week. ☎ 941/746-7117.
- **Easter Parade,** New York City. The city's gentry used to saunter down Fifth Avenue in their finest and most outrageous Easter hats. Today it's more likely to be simply outrageous (as in flamboyance and exhibitionism). Easter morning.
- **San Francisco International Film Festival,** San Francisco. One of America's oldest film festivals features more than 100 films and videos from 30-plus countries. Inexpensive tickets and accessible screenings. Two weeks in early Apr. ☎ 415/931-FILM.
- **New Orleans Jazz and Heritage Festival,** New Orleans. One of America's top music fests features top musicians plus mimes, artists, craftspeople, and chefs. Mid-Apr. ☎ 504/522-4786.
- **Boston Marathon,** Boston. International stars and local amateurs run in the world's oldest and most famous foot race. Third Monday in Apr. ☎ 617/236-1652.
- **Merrie Monarch Hula Festival,** Hilo, Big Island, Hawaii. The islands' biggest hula festival with 3 nights of modern and ancient dance competition in honor of King David Kalakaua, the "merrie monarch" who revived the dance. Usually week after Easter. ☎ 808/935-9168.
- **World Series of Poker,** Las Vegas. It costs $10,000 to enter but nothing to watch high-stakes gamblers and show-biz types compete for six-figure purses at Binion's Horseshoe Casino. Three weeks in Apr. ☎ 702/382-1600.
- **Fiesta San Antonio,** San Antonio. What started as a modest marking of Texas's independence more than a century ago is now a huge celebration, with an elaborately costumed royal court presiding over 10 days of reverly. Starts third week in Apr. ☎ 210/227-5191.
- **Historic Garden Week in Virginia.** A statewide celebration with tours of 200 Virginia landmarks, including plantations and other sites open only during this week. Last week in April. Contact Garden Club of Virginia (☎ 804/644-7776).

## May

- **Taos Spring Arts Celebration,** Taos, New Mexico. Contemporary visual, performing, and literary arts are highlighted. May 1–15. ☎ 800/732-TAOS or 505/758-3873.
- **Memphis in May International Festival,** Memphis. A nation is honored, but the blues festival, barbecue cooking championship, and symphony concerts get most of the attention. All of May. ☎ 901/527-BLUE.
- **Cinco de Mayo,** Miami, Los Angeles, San Diego, Tucson, Phoenix, San Antonio, other cities. Merriment in honor of the Mexican victory over the French in a famous 1862 battle. May 5. Check with local visitor information offices.
- **Shenandoah Apple Blossom Festival,** Winchester, Virginia. Acres of orchards in bloom, plus 5 days of bands, parades, beauty pageants, carnivals, arts and crafts. Usually first weekend in May. ☎ 540/662-3863.
- **Preakness Celebration,** Baltimore. Weeklong hoopla culminates in the Preakness Stakes, middle jewel in horse racing's Triple Crown. Mid-May. ☎ 800/638-3811 or 410/542-9400.
- **Calaveras County Fair and Jumping Frog Jubilee,** Angels Camp, California. The frog race inspired by Mark Twain's story "The Celebrated Jumping Frog of Calaveras County." Also children's parade, livestock competition, rodeo, carnival, fireworks. Third weekend in May. ☎ 209/736-2561.

- **Wright Plus Tour,** Oak Park, Illinois. Annual tour of Frank Lloyd Wright's home and studio in Chicago suburb. Second or third week in May. ☎ 708/848-1976.
- **Carnival,** San Francisco. Weeklong festivities culminate with a parade on Mission Street with more than a half-million spectators. Memorial Day weekend. ☎ 415/826-1401.
- **Spoleto Festival USA,** Charleston, South Carolina. The famous American counterpart to the equally celebrated one in Spoleto, Italy, showcases world-renowned performers in drama, dance, music, and art. Late May–early June. ☎ 803/722-2764.

June
- **Portland Rose Festival,** Portland, Oregon. Dating to 1888, festivities include the rose show, floral parade, beauty contest, music, boat races, and air show. First 3 weeks of June. ☎ 503/227-2681.
- **Shakespeare in the Park,** New York City. The Delacorte Theater in Central Park hosts first-rate free performances under the stars. Be prepared to wait hours for two tickets. June–Aug. ☎ 212/598-7100.
- **International Country Music Fan Fair,** Nashville. Country artists and their fans greet each other in a weeklong music celebration. Concerts, shows, barbecue, autographs. Early June. ☎ 615/889-7503.
- **Coconut Grove Goombay Festival,** Miami. Bahamian bacchanalia with dancing in the streets of Coconut Grove during one of the country's largest black-heritage festivals, celebrating Miami's Caribbean connection. Early June. ☎ 305/372-9966.
- **Chicago Blues Festival,** Chicago. A much-awaited and heavily attended event with dozens of acts, at Petrillo Music Shell in Grant Park. Usually second weekend in June. The **Gospel Festival** follows on the next weekend at the same venue. For information about both, call ☎ 312/744-3315.
- **National Hollerin' Contest,** Spivey's Corner, North Carolina. A true slice of Americana celebrataes hollerin' as a traditional form of communication. Mid-June. ☎ 910/567-2156.
- **Smithsonian Festival of American Folklife,** Washington, D.C. Uniquely American music, crafts, foods, games, and culture are celebrated on the Mall. Late June to July 4. ☎ 202/357-2700.

July
- **Independence Week,** Boston. Concerts, exhibits, and special events culminate in the famous Boston Pops Fourth of July concert in Hatch Memorial Shell on the Esplanade. After real cannons during Tchaikovsky's *1812 Overture,* mammoth fireworks go off over the Charles River. Week of July 4. ☎ 800/888-5515 or 617/536-4100.
- **Welcome America!,** Philadelphia. The whole town celebrates the independence proclaimed here in 1776. Special July 4 ceremonies in Independence Square see reading of Declaration of Independence, presentation of the prestigious Freedom Medal, and parade. Week before July 4. ☎ 215/636-1666.
- **Independence Day on the Mall,** Washington, D.C. Parades, bands, ceremonies, big-name entertainment, National Symphony Orchestra concert, and massive fireworks over the Washington Monument draw some 500,000 to the Mall. July 4. ☎ 202/789-7000.
- **Fourth of July in the Rose Bowl,** Pasadena, California. Southern California's most spectacular fireworks follows an evening of live entertainment in the huge stadium. July 4. ☎ 818/577-3100.

- **Grandfather Mountain Highland Games and Gathering of the Scottish Clans,** Linville, North Carolina. Complete with Scottish dance, music, and athletic competitions. Early July. ☎ 704/733-1333.
- **World Championship Over-the-Line Tournament,** San Diego. Beach softball event features 1,000 three-person teams. Gets pretty risque, so don't bring children. Second and third weekends in July. ☎ 619/688-0817.
- **Seafair,** Seattle. Parades, boat races, the navy's Blue Angels, ethnic festivals, sporting events, open house on U.S. Navy ships. Third weekend in July to first weekend in Aug. ☎ 206/728-0123.
- **Hemingway Days Festival,** Key West, Florida. Locals and visitors pay homage to the tortured novelist by putting on Ernest Hemingway look-alike contests, attracting participants from all over the U.S. and sometimes other countries. Writers' workshops and conferences for the more serious-minded. Third week in July. ☎ 305/294-4440.
- **Tanglewood,** near Lenox, Massachusetts. The summer season of the Boston Symphony Orchestra brings concerts and solo recitals to the Berkshire hills. July–Aug. Call ☎ 617/266-1492 or 413/637-1666.
- **Frontier Days,** Cheyenne, Wyoming. One of the country's most popular rodeos, the "Daddy of 'em All" entertains standing-room-only crowds. Last full week of July. ☎ 800/227-6336.

## August

- **Maine Lobster Festival,** Rockland, Maine. Some 60,000 hungry souls threaten to make the Maine lobster an endangered species in just one long weekend. Parade, Great Lobster Crate Race, too. First weekend in Aug. ☎ 207/596-0376.
- **Old Time Fiddlers' Convention,** Galax, Virginia. Dating to 1935, one of the world's largest and oldest gatherings of fiddlers. Street festival, too. Early Aug. ☎ 540/236-8681.
- **Newport Folk Festival & JVC Jazz Festival,** Newport, Rhode Island. Thousands gather at Fort Adams State Park to hear the best. Alternate weekends July–Aug. ☎ 401/847-3700 for information, 401/331-2211 for tickets.
- **Annual Tennessee Walking Horse National Celebration,** Shelbyville, Tennessee (40 miles southeast of Nashville). The World Grand Championship of the much-loved Tennessee walking horse, plus trade fairs and dog shows. Late Aug. ☎ 615/684-5915.

## September

- **Chicago Jazz Festival,** Chicago. The music is Chicago style and plenty steamy in Petrillo Music Shell in Grant Park. Labor Day weekend. ☎ 312/744-3370.
- **Bumbershoot,** Seattle. Named for British term for umbrella, Seattle's second most popular event has lots of music, arts and crafts, other events. Labor Day weekend. ☎ 206/682-4386.
- **U.S. Open Tennis Championship,** New York City. Top pros vie for one of four grand-slam events, at Flushing Meadow Park, Queens. Around Labor Day. ☎ 718/271-5100.
- **La Fiesta de Santa Fe,** Santa Fe, New Mexico. America's oldest (1720) community celebration sees an exuberant combination of spirit, history, and general merrymaking. "Old Man Gloom" effigy is burned to revitalize community. First Friday after Labor Day. ☎ 505/988-7575.
- **La Jolla Rough-Water Swim,** La Jolla, California. Country's largest rough-water swimming competition began in 1916. Features 1-mile race for all levels (shorter for juniors). First Sunday after Labor Day. ☎ 619/456-2100.

- **Aloha Festivals,** statewide in Hawaii. Parades and other events celebrate Hawaiian culture and friendliness. Mid-Sept. ☎ **808/545-1771** or 808/885-8086.
- **Monterey Jazz Festival,** Monterey, California. Top names in traditional and modern jazz at one of the world's oldest such festivals. Mid-Sept. ☎ **408/373-3366.**
- **Festivals Acadiens,** Lafayette, Louisiana. Food, music, crafts, fairs, and trade shows pay tribute to Louisiana's unique Cajun culture and heritage. ☎ **800/346-1958** or 318/232-3808 in the U.S., 800/543-5340 in Canada.

October

- **Fantasy Fest,** Key West, Florida. Inane, world-famous Halloween festival is Florida's version of Mardi Gras. Crazy costumes, wild parades, and colorful revelers doing things mom said not to do. Last week of Oct. ☎ **305/296-1817.**

November

- **Macy's Thanksgiving Day Parade,** New York City. Huge hot-air balloons of Rocky and Bullwinkle, Snoopy, Underdog, the Pink Panther, Betty Boop, and more. Check Upper West Side streets the night before for surreal sight of balloons being inflated. Thanksgiving Day.

December

- **National Finals Rodeo,** Las Vegas. Nearly 170,000 people attend this superbowl of rodeos featuring top 15 male stars competing in roping, bulldogging, bull riding, bronco riding, and more. First 2 weeks in Dec. ☎ **702/895-3900.**
- **San Diego Harbor Parade of Lights,** San Diego. Lighted boats cruise the city's beautiful harbor as prelude to Christmas. Early Dec. ☎ **619/236-1212.**
- **King Orange Jamboree Parade,** Miami. The world's largest nighttime parade is followed by a long night of festivities leading up to the Orange Bowl football game. Usually Dec. 31. ☎ **305/539-3063.**

## 4   A Special-Interest Vacation Planner

Whatever your tastes, the USA has something to offer. Here's a rundown of some companies offering escorted adventures and tours, a preview of your favorite activities mentioned in this book, and where you can get more information.

**ADVENTURE-TRAVEL COMPANIES**   Scores of "soft" and "hard" adventure-travel companies have sprung up in recent years. Most travel agents have their catalogs listing upcoming trips. **All Adventure Travel** (☎ 800/537-4025; fax 303/440-4160) represents a number of adventure-travel choices and will book your trip. Another good source of up-to-date information is the monthly "Active Traveler" section in *Outside* magazine (☎ 800/678-1131 or 303/604-1464), available on newsstands throughout the USA. It's slightly dated now, but *The Ultimate Adventure Sourcebook* (Turner Publishing, 1992), contains a thorough rundown of activities both here and overseas.

   **Mountain Travel • Sobek** (☎ 800/227-2384 or 510/527-8100; fax 510/525-7710) is perhaps the granddaddy of adventure-travel companies, guiding its own trips and acting as an agent for other outfitters. It began with river rafting, which is still its strong suit. **Backroads Active Vacations!** (☎ 800/462-2848 or 510/527-1555; fax 510/527-1444) started out running bicycle tours but now has walking, hiking, cross-country skiing, trail running, and other trips. **Backcountry** (☎ 800/575-1540 or 406/586-4288; fax 406/586-4288) is another firm that started with bikes but now has hiking, skiing, and other packages. The venerable **Sierra Club** (☎ 415/977-5588; fax 415/977-5795) offers a number of trips each year. **Alyson Adventures** (☎ 800/825-9766) specializes in gay and lesbian adventure travel.

These and other operators plan their adventures at least a year ahead of time, so ask them or your travel agent for their schedules and catalogs as far in advance as possible.

**BEACHES**   Miami and Florida's west coast, southern California, and all of Hawaii have our best beaches (see chapters 4, 7, and 10, respectively), but the entire Atlantic is lined with sand where you can sun and swim during summer. You can even find a little undeveloped solitude at the Cape Cod National Seashore in Massachusetts (see chapter 2) and at Cape Hatteras National Seashore on North Carolina's Outer Banks (see chapter 3). The water's nippy even in summer, but you'll find beaches almost hidden in the nooks and crannies along the Oregon coast (see chapter 8).

**BICYCLING**   Except for the interstate highways, you can bike on most roads in the USA. In fact, it's a great way to see the country up close and personal. Among the best places for two-wheel touring are the Maine coast, Cape Cod, and the hills of New England (see chapter 2); Virginia's rolling Shenandoah Valley, the combined Skyline Drive and Blue Ridge Parkway in Virginia and North Carolina, and Maryland's flat eastern shore (see chapter 3); the dramatic California coast (see chapter 7); and the Oregon coast and San Juan Islands near Seattle (see chapters 7 and 8). Biking is an excellent way to see some of our national parks, especially Shenandoah (chapter 3), Yosemite (chapter 7), and Yellowstone, Grand Tetons, and Glacier (chapter 8).

Off the roads, an ongoing nationwide program is converting some 50,000 miles of abandoned railroad beds into biking-and-walking paths. For a list, contact the **Rails to Trails Conservancy,** 1325 Massachusetts Ave. NW, Washington, DC 20005 (☎ 202/797-5400).

Several companies and organizations offer escorted bike excursions, including **Backroads** and **Backcountry** (see "Adventure-Travel Companies," above). **American Youth Hostels** (☎ 202/783-6161) has trips for its members. **CROSSROADS Bike Tours** (☎ 800/971-2453) has nationwide excursions, including California-to-Massachusetts and Maine-to-Florida. **Vermont Bicycle Touring** (☎ 802/453-4811) has inn-to-inn tours through New England and occasionally in Virginia and the Carolinas. In the Northwest, **Bicycle Adventures** (☎ 800/443-6060 or 360/786-0989; fax 360/786-9661) has trips in the San Juan Islands, the Oregon Cascades, the Columbia River gorge, the Oregon coast, and Olympic Peninsula. **Volcano View Mountain Bike Tours** (☎ 360/274-4341) will lead you though the Mt. St. Helens blast zone.

See "Mountain Biking," below, for more ideas.

**BIRD-WATCHING**   There's great bird watching almost everywhere in the USA, especially those species which migrate from the Arctic to warmer climes in spring, back in autumn. For example, the entire East Coast is on the Atlantic Flyway for migrating waterbirds and waterfowl. You can see them all the way from the Maine coast, particularly Monhegan and Machias islands, to the Wellfleet Wildlife Sanctuary on Cape Cod (see chapter 2), and on south to Maryland's eastern shore (chapter 3), where Chincoteague National Wildlife Refuge on the Maryland–Virginia line is the best bet (☎ 757/336-6122).

Shorebirds also migrate along the Pacific side of the country, with good viewing anywhere along the Washington and Oregon coasts but especially in Malheur National Wildlife Refuge in southeastern Oregon (see chapter 8).

Once endangered, the bald eagle is now widespread across the country. You could spot our national symbol as far south as the Florida Everglades in winter (chapter 4). Dozens make their winter home at Lake Cachuma near Santa Barbara in California (chapter 7). In January they flock to the Skagit River north of Seattle to feast on salmon, and you can even spot them while riding a Washington State ferry through the San Juan Islands (chapter 8). In September, look for them along Alaska's southeastern coast, especially in the Chilkat River Valley. Alaska has many other birds not found in the lower 48 states (chapter 9).

In the Arizona desert, Ramsey Canyon Preserve is internationally known as home to 14 species of hummingbird, more than anywhere else in the USA. San Pedro Riparian National Conservation Area is another good spot, with more than 300 species. See chapter 6.

For tropical species, head to Florida, especially to Everglades National Park. The J. N. "Ding" Darling National Wildlife Refuge on Sanibel Island is another good spot, as is Corkscrew Swamp Sanctuary near Naples, home to countless wood storks. You can see rare white pelicans on wintertime cruises from Captiva Island. See chapter 4. Hawaii's tropical birds are found nowhere else on earth, including the rare o'o, whose yellow feathers Hawaiians once plucked to make royal capes. Large colonies of seabirds nest at Kilauea National Wildlife Preserve and along the Na Pali coast on Kauai, and Molokai's Kamakou Preserve is home to the Molokai thrust and Molokai creeper, found nowhere else. See chapter 10.

For information about escorted bird-watching trips, contact **Field Guide** (☎ 512/327-4953; fax 512/327-9231), **Victor Emanual Nature Tours** (☎ 800/328-VENT or 512/328-5221; fax 512/328-2919), or **Wings** (☎ 602/749-1967; fax 602/749-3175). Also, the **National Audubon Ecology Camp** (☎ 203/869-2017) runs superb bird-watching programs for both aspiring and experienced naturalists, including a study camp on 333-acre Hog Island off the Maine coast. The world-famous Laboratory of Ornithology of **Cornell University,** at Ithaca, New York, has weeklong observation workshops in the Finger Lakes region (☎ 607/255-6260).

**CANOEING & KAYAKING**  The USA offers a wide variety of rivers, streams, lakes, and sounds for canoeing and kayaking enthusiasts. In fact, most cities with rivers running through them now have a contingent of activists.

Out in the hinterlands, some of the best paddling is along Maine's coast (see chapter 2) or through its 92-mile Allagash Wilderness Waterway, a series of remote rivers, lakes, and ponds. Call **North Woods Ways** (☎ 207/997-3723), offering canoe trips on several northern Maine rivers. It's hot and humid in Florida's Everglades National Park during summer (see chapter 4), but winter offers great opportunities along a maze of well-marked trails. You can rent canoes at the main park center at Flamingo, or go with **North American Canoe Tours** (☎ 941/695-4666 Nov–Apr or 860/739-0791 May–Oct), based in Everglades City on the park's western side during winter. The peaceful lakes of Minnesota's Boundary Waters Canoe Area north of Minneapolis (see chapter 6) are another good choice. Contact **Nor'Wester Outfitters** (☎ 800/992-4FUN) or **Top of the Trail Outfitters** (☎ 800/869-0883). Puget Sound's San Juan Islands near Seattle (see chapter 8) also are enchanting when seen by canoe or kayak. **San Juan Kayak Expeditions** (☎ 360/378-4436) and **Shearwater Adventures** (☎ 360/376-4699) both have multiday trips to the islands, and biologists and naturalists lead educational expeditions sponsored by the nonprofit **Sea Quest Expedition/Zoetic Research** (☎ 360-378-5767). For a truly unique kayaking experience, you can paddle among the humpback whales taking their winter break in Hawaii. Contact **South Pacific Kayaks** (☎ 800/776-2326 or 808/661-8400).

For general information, contact the **American Canoe Association,** 7432 Alban Station Blvd., Suite B226, Springfield, VA 22150 (☎ 703/451-0141), the nation's largest organization, for lists of trips and local clubs.

See "River Rafting," below, for information about the best places for whitewater canoeing and kayaking.

**CIVIL WAR BATTLEFIELDS**  The Civil War started in 1861 at Fort Sumter in Charleston, South Carolina (see chapter 4). Battles raged all over the South during the next 4 years. General Ulysses S. Grant took Vicksburg, Mississippi, after a long siege, and General William Tecumseh Sherman burned Atlanta, but the most famous fighting took place within 100 miles of Washington, D.C. This area has more national battlefield parks than any other part of the country.

It won't be in chronological order, but you can tour them by starting at the battles of Fredericksburg, Chancellorsville, and The Wilderness in and near Fredericksburg, Virginia. Proceed north to the two Battles of Manassas (or Bull Run) southwest of Washington, then north across the Potomac River to the Battle of Antietam at Sharpsburg, Maryland. From there, go northwest through Harpers Ferry to the Battle of Gettysburg in south central Pennsylvania, turning point of the war. You'll also pass several battlefields on the driving tour of the Shenandoah Valley. See chapter 3.

**Civil War Tours** (☎ 800/295-4428 or 301/745-4400) has escorted 3-day tours of Manassas, Gettysburg, and Antietam.

**FALL FOLIAGE**   Fall in New England is one of the great natural spectacles of the USA, with the rolling hills blanketed with brilliant reds and stunning oranges. The colors start reaching their peak in mid-September at the higher altitudes in the Green and White Mountains of Vermont and New Hampshire, then working lower into the Berkshires of Massachusetts (see chapter 2). The colors move progressively south down the East Coast into October, when bumper-to-bumper traffic jams Virginia's Skyline Drive through Shenandoah National Park (see chapter 3). The precise dates of prime color vary from year to year depending on temperature and amount of rain, but the local newspapers and TV stations keep close track of when the best viewing will occur.

**Tauck Tours** (☎ 800/468-2825 or 203/226-6911), **Maupintour** (☎ 800/255-4266 or 913/843-1211), and several other escorted tour operators have foliage tours; see your travel agent.

**FISHING**   From surf casting off Cape Cod or Cape Hatteras to flicking a fly in Maine or Montana, the USA has every type of fishing yet invented, and some record-setting catches to brag about.

Fly-fishing camps are as prolific as the fish in the Maine woods. **Grant's Kennebago Camps** in Oquossoc (☎ 800/633-4815 or 207/864-3608) has 18 of them built on Kennebago Lake in 1905. **Tim Pond Wilderness Camps** in Eustis (☎ 207/243-2947) has been in business since the 1860s and is billed as "the oldest continuously operating sporting camp in America." If you want to learn or develop your skills, the famous outdoor clothing merchant offers **L. L. Bean Fly-Fishing School,** in Freeport, Maine (☎ 800/341-4341, ext. 6666). Over in Vermont, **Orvis** in Manchester (☎ 800/235-9763) runs one of the top fly-fishing schools in the country.

The nation's other great fly-fishing area is in the Montana and Wyoming mountains near Yellowstone National Park, made famous by recent movies such as *A River Runs Through It.* The top river out here is Montana's Madison, with headquarters starting in the park, but cutthroat trout make the Snake River over in Wyoming almost as good—and the resort of Jackson Hole offers luxury relief within casting distance (see chapter 8). Good outfitters out here are **Montana Troutfitters Orvis Shop** in Boseman, Montana (☎ 406/587-4707); **High Country Flies** (☎ 307/733-7210) and **Jack Dennis Outdoor Shop** (☎ 307/733-3270), both in Jackson, Wyoming; and **Bud Lilly's Trout Shop** (☎ 406/646-9570) and Madison River Outfitters (☎ 406/646-9644), both in West Yellowstone, Wyoming.

Most ports along the nation's seaboards have deep-sea charter-fishing fleets and less expensive party boats (all you have to do is show up for the latter). The best tropical strikes are in the Florida Keys (see chapter 4) and off the Kona coast of the Big Island in Hawaii (see chapter 10). Florida's southwest coast is noted for fighting snook and tarpon (see the driving tour in chapter 4). Alaska is famous for summertime salmon and halibut fishing, with the biggest in the Kenai River and on Kodiak Island, which has the state's best roadside salmon fishing (see chapter 9).

**FLOWERS & GARDENS**   Flower lovers will have many opportunities to stop and smell the roses, so to speak, especially in Portland, Oregon, which calls itself the City of Roses (see chapter 8). Many other cities have gardens of note, including Atlanta, Denver, New Orleans, New York, Seattle, and Tucson (see their sections in the following chapters). Longwood Gardens in the Brandywine Valley is noted for its greenhouses as well as its grounds (see chapter 3). The Biltmore Estate in Asheville, North Carolina, has a walled English garden on its 25 acres (see chapter 4). And **Magnolia Plantation** near Charleston, South Carolina, is famed for its azaleas, camellias, and 60-acre cypress swamp (☎ 803/571-1266). And if you like gardens from the Elizabethan era, head for Colonial Williamsburg, Virginia (see chapter 3).

If you're passing their way, don't miss **Bellingrath Gardens and Home** in Theodore, near Mobile, Alabama (☎ 800/247-8420); **Huntington Botanical Gardens** in San Marino, California (☎ 818/405-2100); **Cypress Gardens** in Cypress Gardens, Florida (☎ 813/324-2111); **Callaway Gardens** in Pine Mountain, Georgia (☎ 404/663-2281); the **Morton Arboretum** in Lisle, Illinois, near Chicago (☎ 312/968-0074); and **Brookgreen Gardens** in Murrels Inlet, near Myrtle Beach, South Carolina (☎ 803/237-4218).

A few travel companies have escorted tours of gardens, others include them on their general sightseeing excursions, and still others organize trips for local botanical gardens or gardening and horticultural groups (check with those in your hometown for upcoming trips). Check with **Expo Garden Tours** (☎ 800/448-2685 or 212/677-6704), **Learned Journeys** (☎ 800/682-6191 or 805/682-6191), **Maupintour** (☎ 800/255-4266 or 913/843-1211), or **Tours à la Carte** (☎ 610/687-4185).

**GOLF & TENNIS**   You can play golf and tennis almost anywhere in the USA, although the best is across the southern tier of states where the outdoor seasons are longest. In the Southeast, top golfing destinations are the North Carolina Sandhills, Hilton Head Island, South Carolina, and almost anywhere in Florida, with the highest concentration of courses on the southwest coast around Naples (see chapter 4). In the Southwest, the twin desert cities of Phoenix and Scottsdale have some of the country's most luxurious golf resorts (see chapter 6). The same can be said of Palm Springs and the Monterey coast in California (see chapter 7). And Hawaii has some of our most famous courses (see chapter 10).

Most of the nation's top golf resorts also have excellent tennis facilities. For the top 50 tennis resorts, see *Tennis* magazine's rankings each November. The **Colony Beach & Tennis Resort** on Longboat Key, Florida (☎ 800/4-COLONY or 941/383-6464), and **Sea Pines Plantation** on Hilton Head, South Carolina (☎ 800/SEA-PINES or 803/785-3333), seem to swap the number-one position every year or two.

**HISTORY**   The USA is a young country by European standards, but Americans are proud of their history and are quick to preserve the sites where momentous events took place. In New England, for example, you can easily visit Boston and its suburbs, where the Revolutionary War began (see chapter 2). In the Mid-Atlantic, you can see where our independence was proclaimed in Philadelphia or see what colonial life was like at the remarkably restored town of Williamsburg (see chapter 3).

You can visit more than one historic location and be escorted by knowledgeable guides or even historians on a variety of tours. The **National Trust for Historic Preservation** (☎ 202/673-4000) has guided trips ranging from Virginia's historic homes to Route 66 through the Southwest. Commercial tour operators often combine Washington, D.C., Williamsburg, and the Pennsylvania Dutch Country, as **Tauck Tours** did recently (☎ 800/468-2825). But history trips can be more offbeat, such as an excursion by **HistoryAmerica Tours** (☎ 800/628-8542), which examined the Sioux Wars on the Northern Plains, including a visit to the Little Big Horn, where Crazy Horse wiped out Custer. See your travel agent for upcoming tours.

**LITERARY SITES** Aficionados of the written word can see where some of our great writers put pen to paper, especially in the Berkshires of Massachusetts, where Nathaniel Hawthorne, Herman Melville, Edith Wharton, and others came for mild summers and seclusion (see chapter 2). Homes of writers are preserved all over the country, such as Edgar Allen Poe's and H. L. Mencken's in Baltimore (see chapter 3) and O. Henry's in Austin (see chapter 6). Your travel agent should know of escorted literary tours.

**MOUNTAIN BIKING** If mountain bikes are your thing, you'll find plenty of dirt roads and backcountry pathways to explore. Many national parks and forests have a good selection of trails—Acadia National Park's carriage roads, for example, are unique in this country (see chapter 2). You also can take guided tours through 60 miles of connected trails in the Sebago Lake area, near the New Hampshire border, with **Back Country Excursions** (☎ 207/625-8189), which operates a mountain-biking playground called the "Palace" in Limerick, Maine.

Out in bike-happy Colorado, ski areas often open their lifts to bikers in the summer, with **Winter Park** considered the state's mountain-bike capital (☎ 800/903-PARK or 970/726-4118). The state's single best route, the 30-mile **Tipperary Creek Trail,** ends at Winter Park. **Crested Butte** is another good choice, with trails for beginners to highly skilled. Contact **Gunnison National Forest** (☎ 970/641-0471).

In **Deschutes National Forest,** outside the town of Bend in central Oregon, dry ponderosa pine forests are laced with trails past lakes, waterfalls, and great views of the surrounding mountains. Contact the **Bend/Fort Rock Ranger Station** (☎ 541/388-5664). You can go on guided rides in this area with **High Cascade Descent Guide Service** (☎ 541/389-0562) or **Pacific Crest Peddlers** (☎ 541/593-8369). Another popular fat-tire area is the Bryce, Zion, and Canyonlands regions of southern Utah. Contact **Rim Tours** (☎ 800/626-7335) or **Kaibab Mountain Bike Tours** (☎ 800/451-1133), based in the town of Moab.

The companies mentioned under "Bicycling," above, also have mountain expeditions throughout the country and abroad.

**NATURE & ECOLOGY** A better way to see more of our national parks than just driving through them—and to learn a great deal about nature while you're at it—is with a program sponsored by one of the associations dedicated to preserving and improving these treasures. To find out what's being offered, contact the **Yosemite Association** (☎ 209/379-2646), **Yellowstone Institute** (☎ 307/344-2294), **Rocky Mountain Nature Association** (☎ 303/586-1265), or **Glacier Institute** (☎ 406/756-3911). See chapters 7 and 8 for general information about the parks.

Not just for bird-watchers, the **National Audubon Society** (☎ 203/869-2017) has its Ecology Camp on Hog Island off the Maine coast and another in the Grand Tetons of Wyoming, and it sponsors ecology excursions to such places as California's Death Valley. The **Sierra Club** maintains base camps in the Rockies (☎ 415/776-2211) and sponsors a wide variety of nature- and conservation-oriented trips (☎ 415/977-5630; fax 415/977-5795). And the **National Wildlife Federation** has four annual "conservation summits" dedicated to preserving the great outdoors, including one on Hawaii's Big Island (☎ 800/245-5484 or 703/790-4265).

**RIVER RAFTING** Our most famous place to run the rapids is the Grand Canyon, whose steep walls tower above as you race down the Colorado River (see chapter 6). It's also the most popular, with bumper-to-bumper rafts in summer. You may have less company on the Colorado upstream in Utah, which also has good rafting on the Green River. Call the **Utah Travel Council** (☎ 800/220-1160 or 801/538-1030) and ask for a copy of *Raft Utah*. The Snake River south of Yellowstone National Park near Jackson Hole, Wyoming, also is a best if somewhat popular bet (see chapter 8). The Snake River flows on down into Idaho, where its wild Hells Canyon, plus the Salmon and Middle Fork rivers, offer exciting rides. Contact **Hughes River Expeditions** (☎ 800/262-1882). Up in Alaska, you can see plenty of birds and the occasional moose on the Kenai River. Contact **Kenai Peninsula Rafting and Wilderness** (☎ 800/334-8730 or 907/783-2928).

The New River cuts a dramatic 2,000-foot-deep gorge through the Appalachian Mountains near the town of Beckley, West Virginia, making it the most scenic route in the east. Among the outfitters here are **Ace Whitewater** (☎ 800/787-3982 or 304/469-2651) and **Appalachian Wildwaters** (☎ 800/624-8060), or call the **Southern West Virginia Convention & Visitors Bureau** for general information (☎ 800/VISIT-WV or 304/252-2244).

**SCENIC DRIVES**    The driving tours in this book follow a few of the USA's many exceptionally beautiful roads. The tour of New Hampshire's Green Mountains follows a loop, but the dramatic Kancamagus Highway (N.H. 112) cuts through them between Lincoln and Conway. Nearby is the privately owned Mount Washington Auto Road, to the top of one of the tallest peaks in the east. The loop road in Maine's Acadia National Park is another beauty (see chapter 2). In the Mid-Atlantic, you can't beat Virginia's Skyline Drive (see chapter 3), and the Blue Ridge Parkway, which continues south to North Carolina's Great Smoky Mountains near Asheville (see chapter 4).

Out west, driving doesn't get any more dramatic than along the California and Oregon coasts (see the tours in chapters 7 and 8). In the Arizona desert, the drive from Phoenix through Prescott and Sedona includes huge red rocks and the cool oasis of Oak Creek Canyon, but the desert's most spectacular scenery is in Monument Valley on the Arizona–Utah border in the Navajo and Hopi country and the nearby Canyonlands (see chapter 6).

In Colorado, the driving tour of the Western Slope follows the Million Dollar Highway (U.S. 550) across 11,008-foot Red Mountain Pass, an unforgettable drive (see chapter 6). In Montana, the driving tour of Glacier Country puts you on Going-to-the-Sun Road through Glacier National Park, one of our great summertime drives. Over the border in Wyoming, the Beartooth Scenic Byway (U.S. 212) from the northern part of Yellowstone National Park east to Red Lodge climbs over 10,947-foot Beartooth Pass, from where you can see mile upon mile of Wyoming and Montana mountains (see chapter 8).

Up in Alaska, one of the world's great drives begins in Anchorage and leads roughly 50 miles south on the Seward Highway to Portage Glacier; chipped from the rocky Chugach Mountains, the Turnagain Arm provides a platform to see an untouched landscape full of wildlife (see chapter 9).

Out in Hawaii, the drive from Honolulu to Oahu's Windward coast on Hi. 61 provides an unparalleled view down from the near-vertical Pali cliff, while the narrow, winding Hana Road on Maui will reward your driving skills with wonderful seascapes (see chapter 10).

**SKIING**    New England may have started downhill skiing in the USA, but for the best, head for the deep powder out west. Colorado is endowed with more than two dozen ski resorts, including world-renown Aspen, Vail, Breckenridge, and Wolf Creek; Utah is home to Alta, Beaver Mountain, Snowbasin, Park City, and Deer Valley; and Santa Fe and Taos in New Mexico have well-known slopes (see chapter 6). In California's Sierras, Lake Tahoe is home to Alpine Meadows, Heavenly Resort, the famous Squaw Valley USA, and others (see chapter 7). And there's Jackson Hole near Yellowstone and the Grand Tetons national parks (see chapter 8).

New England does have good cross-country skiing, especially at the **Trapp Family Lodge Cross-Country Ski Center** (☎ **800/826-7000** or 802/253-8511) in Stowe, Vermont, and the entire village of Jackson, New Hampshire, which is laced with a network of ski trails maintained by the **Jackson Ski Touring Foundation** (☎ **603/ 383-9355**). Out west, many of the downhill resorts mentioned above have cross-country trails, but the best is in Yosemite, Yellowstone, and Glacier national parks (see chapters 7 and 8). And the rims of the Grand Canyon and Bryce Canyon national parks present some unusual venues (see chapter 6).

**WHALE & WILDLIFE WATCHING**    The best whale-watching on the East Coast leaves from Provincetown on Cape Cod, where some boats sight humpbacks, finbacks, and others 99% of the time April to November (see chapter 2). On the West Coast, you can see Pacific gray whales during their spring and fall migrations from Point Reyes National Seashore north of San Francisco (see chapter 7), Depot Bay and other points on the Oregon coast, and the San Juan Islands near Seattle, which have orcas, too (see chapter 8). The ports of Petersburg and Sitka in southeastern Alaska and Kenai Fjords National Park and nearby Seward are great spots to watch the humpbacks feeding in summer, plus a profusion of seals, otters, and other marine mammals (see chapter 9). For many humpbacks, the fall migration takes them south to sunny Hawaii, where they frolic in the warm waters from December to May. They are best seen here from Maui's west coast (see chapter 10).

For wildlife watching, you can see moose in Baxter State Park in Maine (see chapter 2), maybe a bear in the Great Smoky Mountains, or alligators and other critters in Florida's Everglades (see chapter 3), but the best is in our national parks out west and in Alaska. Without question, Yellowstone offers some of the top opportunities, with an abundance of elk and bison walking up to your car, while Glacier has these plus mountain elk and an occasional grizzly bear (see chapter 8). Your best chance of seeing a bear, grizzly or otherwise, is in Alaska's Denali and Katmai national parks, particularly at the Brooks Camp Lodge in Katmai, where they walk right by on their way to a salmon spawning area (see chapter 9).

# The Northeast

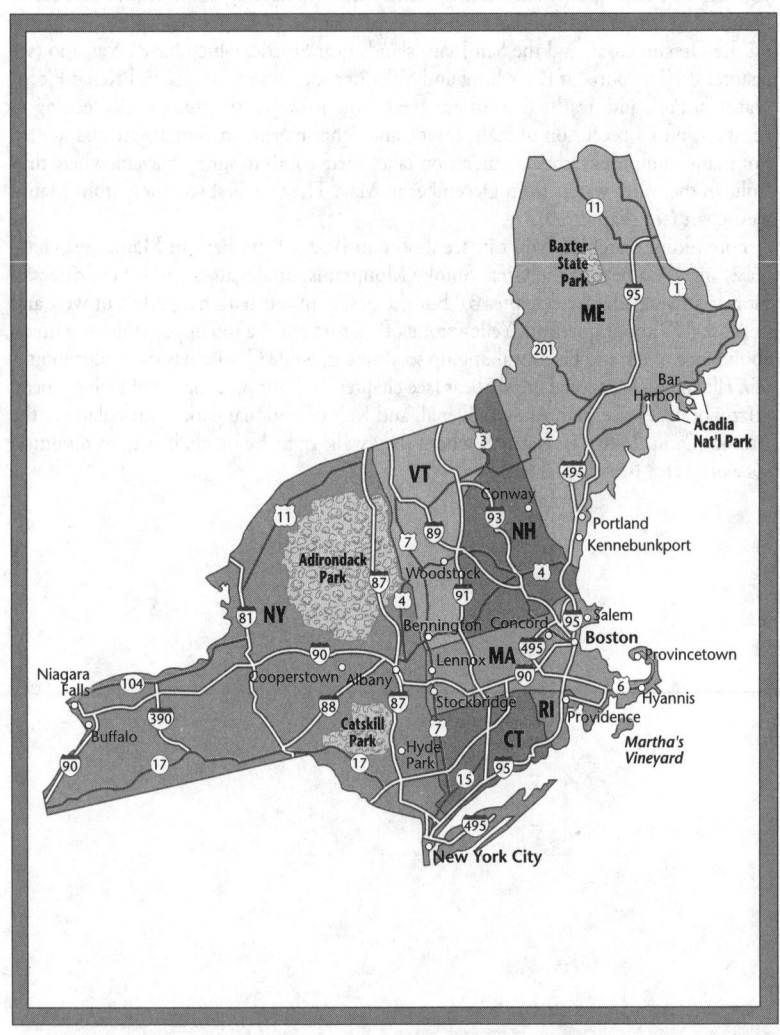

The Northeastern United States presents a face of enormous contrast to the visitor, from the dynamism of America's greatest city to the wooded hills, historic mansions, and peaceful meadows of the Hudson Valley; from historic, urban Boston to the rural villages of northern New England.

Much that is American was forged in the Northeast, and much that is intrinsic to the American spirit was born in New England—the independence, enterprise, hard work, ingenuity, and respect for education that characterized the early settlers. History is everywhere in New England. As you travel around these states, you'll find it not only in the monuments—Plymouth Rock, Bunker Hill, and the many Revolutionary War sites—but in the graceful villages and rolling hills of Vermont; the coastal towns of Maine, Rhode Island, and Connecticut where clipper ships once docked; in the rugged mountains of New Hampshire; and in Massachusetts's historic towns. New Englanders love their region because of its history, and they cherish their traditions.

Once the most highly industrialized part of the country and an economic leader, New England in the 20th century found itself losing out as other parts of the country developed; its whaling industry came to an end, and its factories began moving south where wages were lower. In recent times, however, this trend has started to reverse, as high-tech industries and service businesses expand in New England. Upper New York State suffered a similar experience, but has not yet, for the most part, found a way to turn things around.

Paradoxically, New England's fading prosperity helped save it from the trash-the-old-and-replace-with-the-new that afflicted so much of the country in the decades that followed World War II. Consequently, much that we admire today was preserved and has been restored to give the visitor pleasure. New England's cuisine is often joked about, but this also is the land of maple syrup, lobsters, clambakes, wild blueberries, and the famous Vermont cheddar cheese.

And what about the great international city of New York? New York just won't sit still long enough for anyone to capture its definitive portrait. It constantly reinvents itself right before your eyes. Today Broadway theater is booming, crime is down, and you'll either be enthralled and excited by the glitter, the variety, and the tempo or disturbed by the noise, the dirt, and the juxtaposition of grinding poverty and incredible wealth. New York attracts the gifted, the creative, and the ambitious from all over the world. The cumulative effect of the city—its energy, its beauty, its sense of unlimited opportunity—is an inescapable feeling that this is where it's all happening.

## DRIVING TOUR
## Historic Massachusetts

**Start:** Boston
**Finish:** Concord
**Distance:** 23 miles
**Time:** 1 day
**Highlights:** The cradle of American liberty and American *belles lettres,* Harvard University, Revolutionary battle sites, historic homes, and literary hangouts

This journey basically retraces the route Paul Revere took that fateful night of April 18, 1775, to warn the colonial rebels that the Redcoats were about to make their move. The tour begins with the cultural sights of Cambridge and then takes you to the rural beauty, resonant with history, of Concord and Lexington. The best time to take the drive is in the fall, when resplendent foliage enhances New England with burnished beauty. Travel midweek, if possible, to enjoy more elbow room at these top tourist spots.

The tour makes an easy excursion from Boston, but if you want to stay in Cambridge, the **Charles Hotel** (☎ **800/882-1818** or 617/864-1200) is steps from Harvard Square, overlooking the Charles River. It has a full-scale spa and contains one of Boston's most accomplished restaurants, Rialto. Around the corner is Harvard's **American Repertory Theatre.** Just off I-95, Boston's peripheral artery, the **Sheraton Tara Lexington Inn** (☎ **800/THE TARA** or 617/862-8700), with peaceful, secluded grounds and an outdoor pool, is ideally suited for exploring the area.

Before you begin the tour, take a walking tour of the historic landmarks of Boston's North End, or visit them by tourist trolley: the circa 1677 **Paul Revere's House,** 19 North Square (see "Historic Houses" in section 2); **Old North Church,** 193 Salem St. (Boston's oldest, built in 1727), where lanterns were hung to signal the British offensive; and on Mill Street, **Copp's Hill Burying Ground,** a 1659 graveyard (originally known as "Corpse Hill") whose headstones remain riddled by British bullets. Lack of parking makes exploring this area by car difficult.

Departing from the Faneuil Hall area in Boston, head out the Charlestown Bridge for a quick glimpse of the USS *Constitution,* invincible "Old Ironsides" built in 1797, and the **Bunker Hill Monument,** site of a pivotal 1775 Revolutionary victory. Returning back over the bridge, take a right on Causeway Street (past the Fleet Center sports arena) and continue along Staniford Street until you reach Cambridge Street, where another right will lead you across the Longfellow Bridge. Popularly known as the "Salt and Pepper" bridge for its shakerlike turrets, it affords a fantastic view of the Boston skyline. Make a cloverleaf right turn at the end of the bridge, circle under it, and emerge westbound on Route 3 (Cambridge Parkway, becoming Memorial Drive). On your right, you'll pass the **Massachusetts Institute of Technology,** distinguished by its capitol-like dome.

Your destination, about a mile upriver, is Cambridge. Look for the 1909 **Weld Boathouse,** where the university's sculls are stored, as a signal to turn right on JFK Street. **Harvard Square** is 3 blocks ahead. Stop at:

1. **Harvard University.** Stop by the **Harvard University Information Office** in Holyoke Center (☎ **617/495-1573**). They can load you up with literature, including a map outlining a self-guided walking tour; student volunteers also offer free hour-long tours. A highlight of the campus is the **Fogg Art Museum** (☎ **617/495-5573**), packed with treasures ranging from Fra Angelico to Pollock, and its two satellite museums, the **Sackler** and **Busch–Reisinger.** Harvard's outstanding **Museums of Natural History** (☎ **617/495-3045**) cover archeology, comparative zoology, mineralogy, and botany; the latter collection includes the

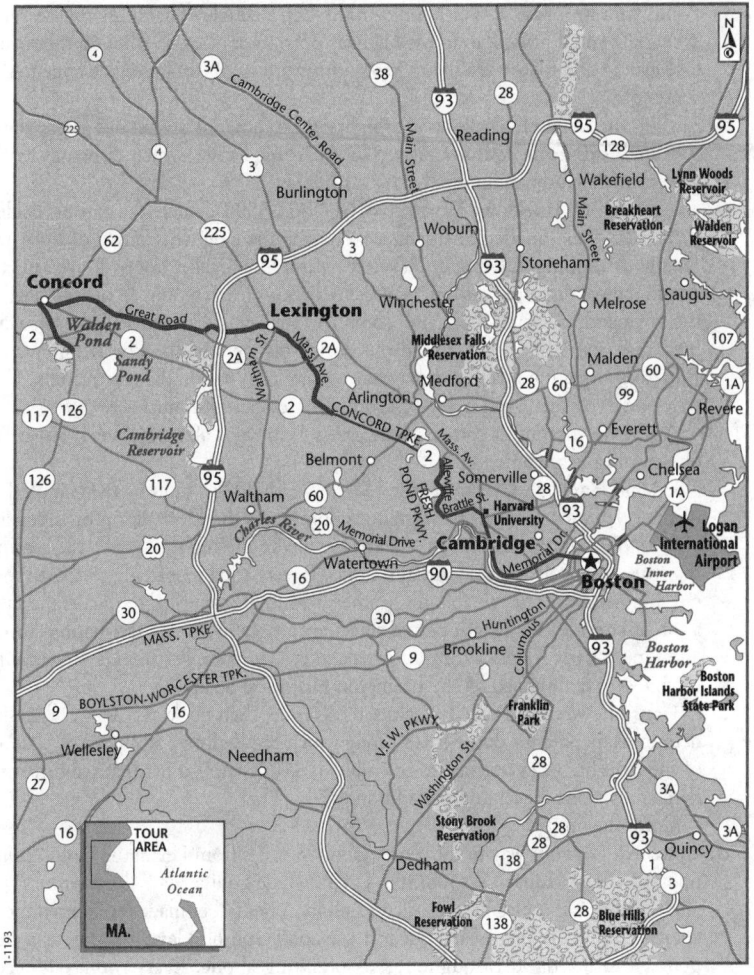

famed "glass flowers," representing over 840 species. Walk back through Harvard Yard and look for such campus landmarks as **Memorial Hall,** a 1878 Ruskinian Gothic church commemorating the university's Civil War dead; the 1963 **Carpenter Center for the Visual Arts,** the only Le Corbusier structure in North America; and **Widener Library.**

**☕ TAKE A BREAK**   Decorated with panels illustrating an amusing fauxbiography of "John Harvard, brewmaster" (the college's benefactor was actually the son of a brewer), **John Harvard's Brew House** (☎ 617/868-3585) doubles as a microbrewery and a surprisingly accomplished yet affordably priced restaurant.

Returning to your car, take the most scenic means of egress from the square:
2. **Brattle Street,** once known as "Tory Row." Many of the houses here date back to pre-Revolutionary days. On the right you'll pass the **Henry Wadsworth Longfellow House** (see "Historic Houses" in section 2) and the 1688 **Hooper–Lee–Nichols House,** Cambridge's oldest. Brattle Street will bring you to Fresh

Pond Parkway (Mass. 2 West); forge on through a couple of daunting rotaries, and eventually you'll make it onto the highway portion of Mass. 2. About 6 miles out, take exit 54 and follow Waltham Street northward to Massachusetts Avenue to the center of:

**3. Lexington.** Within 2 blocks on your right, at the corner of the famous green, you'll spot the **Lexington Visitor Center** (☎ 617/862-1450), which dispenses useful tourist information. A hundred yards farther is:

**4.** The circa 1709 **Buckman Tavern** (☎ 617/862-5598), where the patriots cooled their heels—and quaffed fortifying ale—during the long, tense night of April 18. Finally concluding that despite Revere's alarum, the royalist troops *weren't* in fact coming, most dispersed during the predawn hours, leaving only 77 men to defend the town and its munitions against some 700 Redcoats. No one really knows who fired that first "shot heard 'round the world" (as memorialized by Ralph Waldo Emerson); legend holds that it may have come from within the tavern itself. This well-preserved site (open mid-April through October) is a must-see.

At the northernmost corner of the green, bear right along Hancock Street for one-third mile to come to:

**5.** The 1638 **Hancock-Clarke House** (☎ 617/861-0928), built by the grandfather of the celebrated rebel whose signature dominates the Declaration of Independence. John Hancock and Sam Adams slept here the night of April 18. Fearing that they might be targeted as figureheads, Revere tried repeatedly to roust them out, but naturally, the two founding fathers-to-be felt compelled to discuss the situation at considerable length before agreeing to decamp. Some fascinating stories and superb Early American antiques make this a worthwhile stop. Like the tavern, the house is maintained by the Lexington Historical Society.

Continue westward on Massachusetts Avenue, then on Mass. 2A west, taking detours as marked for Battle Road, along which the Redcoats advanced. A portion of the road has been restored to resemble its 1775 state—a hardpacked dirt road flanked by stone fences and period houses.

Continue on to:

**6. Concord.** On your way to the center (about 8 miles from Lexington, you'll come upon **Orchard House** (☎ 508/369-4118), where Louisa May Alcott wrote *Little Women.* The radical leanings of Alcott's philosopher father made for an even more colorful home life that is described in the book, and his clever touches as a carpenter can be found throughout this rambling abode. Every room—indeed, every artifact, such as Louisa's "mood pillow"—has its stories. During the time described in *Little Women,* the Alcotts actually lived next door, at **The Wayside,** which was to acquire further literary luster when it was bought by Nathaniel Hawthorne: He added a three-story tower to achieve the quiet he craved. The property is now part of the **Minute Man National Historical Park** (☎ 508/369-6993), and Park Service rangers offer guided tours mid-April through October. Here you can pick up a weekly "broadside" describing other nearby MMNHP properties and special events.

About a quarter-mile west, take a sharp left on the Cambridge Turnpike (Mass. 2) to learn more about local authors and philosophers at:

**7.** The **Concord Museum** (☎ 508/369-9609), a spiffy facility with extraordinary holdings covering both the Revolutionary era and the 19th-century Transcendentalist movement. Entire rooms have been re-created here, such as Emerson's study (his house stands across the road) and Henry David Thoreau's Walden Pond cabin (long gone); the artifacts are authentic. Returning to Mass. 2A, proceed about 1 mile farther west to the center of town. Turn right on Bedford Road to visit:

8. **"Author's Ridge"** at the Sleepy Hollow Cemetery where Emerson, Thoreau, Hawthorne, and the Alcotts are convened in death as they were in life. Avid fans keep the dialogue alive with appreciative tributes. Return to the town square.

☕ **TAKE A BREAK**   At the extensively remodeled 1716 **Colonial Inn** (☎ **800/370-9200** or 508/369-9200), you can take tea, complete with fresh-baked crumpets and scones. Thoreau lived here before heading for the woods. Although the century-old hotel is a bit of a decorative hodgepodge, with Victoriana taking the upper hand, the colonnaded front porch is still a good place to catch the pulse of the town.

Head north on Monument Street toward the battle site:

9. **The Old Manse** (☎ **508/369-3909**)—so named by Hawthorne, who spent a rapturous midlife honeymoon here—overlooks the battleground at **North Bridge.** From his handsome gambrel-roofed house, then only five years old, Ralph Waldo Emerson's grandfather, Rev. William Emerson, observed the melee that his sermons had helped to stir up. By this time, the numbers favored the upstarts: Thanks to Revere's timely warnings, some 500 rebels had convened on the western bank of the sleepy Concord River, prepared to hold the line against a royalist contingent numbering only about 100. The "embattled farmers" (Emerson again) might have stood their ground right there had the king's troops not moved to dismantle the bridge. The rebels advanced, the Redcoats opened fire, and the war began in earnest.

Stroll across the bridge—a replica, but nonetheless evocative—for a glimpse of the stirring *Minute Man* statue forged by Daniel Chester French, who studied under May Alcott, Louisa's sister, early in his career. Then take in the inspirational simplicity of the Manse, where Emerson wrote his first book *(Nature)* and the newly wed Hawthornes left poetic mementos in the form of windowpane "graffiti" carved with Sophia's diamond ring. It's easy to imagine them here, "in the gold light," enjoying the freedom that their ancestors had suffered to ensure.

Head out Walden Street south on Mass. 126 for a look at:

10. **Walden Pond.** At the **Walden Pond State Reservation** (☎ **508/369-3254**) a pile of stones marks the spot where Henry David Thoreau had his cabin and lived from 1845 to 1847. Call for a schedule of interpretive programs. From Mass. 126 you can rejoin Mass. 2 for the trip back to Cambridge.

## DRIVING TOUR
## Vermont's Southern Green Mountains

**Start and Finish:** Bennington
**Distance:** 220 miles
**Time:** 1 or 2 days
**Highlights:** Farms, idyllic villages, marble quarries, covered bridges, Revolutionary War sites, stops on the Underground Railroad, finely preserved colonial and Federal architecture, and nature trails

Beginning on Vt. 7A, which runs northward, roughly parallel to the New York border, this tour passes through some of Vermont's loveliest and richest valleys before crossing over the spine of the Green Mountains and its surrounding Green Mountain National Forest.

Although some of the roads on the tour are back-road byways, all are numbered routes, well marked by signs. The roads are paved, and in good repair, but some are hilly and winding, so drivers will need to judge their speeds accordingly. Road signs usually indicate sharp curves or intersections ahead, as well as areas where wildlife frequently cross the road. Since the roads form the main streets of towns without sidewalks, motorists will need to be alert for pedestrians and cyclists.

NY 67, U.S. 7, and Vt. 9 all bring the traveler easily to the first stop:

1. **Bennington,** in the southwest corner of the state. Just a mile from its center is the settlement of **Old Bennington,** where stately homes and a fine white clapboard church surround a hilltop green. Just down the hill, in the old churchyard, is the grave of the poet Robert Frost with its well-known epitaph referring to his "lover's quarrel with the world."

Just beyond, past a row of historic buildings that includes the **Catamount Tavern,** where Ethan Allen and his Green Mountain Boys frequently gathered, is the **Bennington Battle Monument.** Although the actual battle was fought just over the line in New York, its purpose was the control of Bennington. You can ascend to the top of the obelisk for a fine view of the surrounding valley.

Places to stay in Bennington are the **Kirkside Motor Lodge,** 250 W. Main St. (☎ 802/447-7596), a friendly mom-and-pop motel right in the center of town; and the **Paradise Motor Inn,** 141 W. Main St. (☎ 802/442-8351), tucked away from traffic and street noise in its own compound.

Between Old Bennington and the "new" town is the **Bennington Museum,** best known for its collection of early glassware and pottery, and for the Grandma Moses Schoolhouse, where her paintings are displayed.

At **Bennington Potters,** on County Street, you may recognize the style of the pottery from having seen it in decorator shops. Here you can buy it at factory store prices. From the pottery, 1 block takes you to Vt. 7A; go north (right) to:

2. **Shaftsbury,** a small town full of historic homes, with a designated historic district. The **Shaftsbury Historical Museum** is located in an 1846 church. Not far beyond, still on 7A, is **Shaftsbury State Park,** with a fine beach, picnic area, and a nature trail around the pond. Pick up a booklet at the park office explaining the features of this trail. VT 7A continues north and into the center of:

3. **Arlington,** best known as the home of Norman Rockwell. The town provided the inspiration and the models for many of Rockwell's best-known magazine covers. At the Arlington Gallery at the **Norman Rockwell Exhibition,** you can meet people pictured in his work; many of them still work here as guides. Rockwell lived here until 1953, and the small-town America he portrayed was pure Arlington. Avid readers will want to stop at the tent in front of the library to browse for secondhand books and magazines.

Just north of the library, a side trip on Vt. 313 leads along the **Batten Kill River.** Flowing through one of the loveliest of Vermont's many valleys, the Batten Kill is lined with farms and spanned by a covered bridge. Batten Kill Canoe, a short distance north on Vt. 7A, rents canoes to those who want to see the valley from water level; a van will return you and canoe to the starting point. From Arlington, continue north on Vt. 7A, where you will soon see the long bulk of Mt. Equinox on your left. This mountain reaches almost to the main street of:

4. **Manchester Village,** which faces the elegant facade of **The Equinox.** The inn's original building, now a restaurant, was a meeting place for the rebellious Green Mountain Boys before and during the Revolution, and the inn, a grand summer resort, hosted Mary Todd Lincoln and her sons. It was during his stay here that Robert Todd Lincoln first fell in love with Manchester—later he built his own summer estate, **Hildene.** The stately home, with its gardens overlooking the valley far below, are well worth a stop, and in the house you'll see President

# Driving Tour: Southern Green Mountains

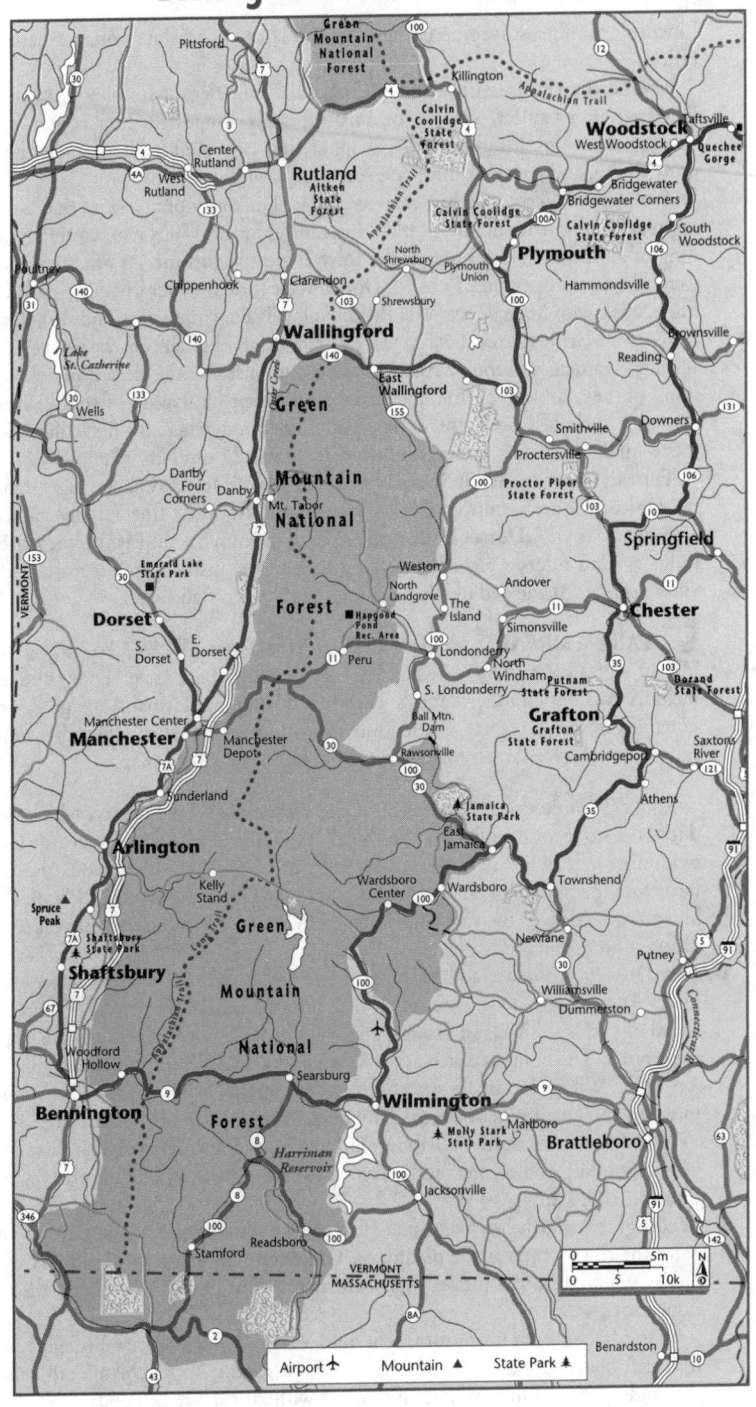

Lincoln's familiar stovepipe hat and the Bible on which he swore his oath of office.

Beyond the village, with its marble sidewalks and elegant summer "cottages," is Manchester Center, known for an impossibly congested intersection with VT 30, where a multitude of outlet shops are in newly built malls. Turn left here, onto Vt. 30, and continue until you reach the town line of:

5. **Dorset,** site of Vermont's first marble quarry. Discovery of a vein of fine building marble on the mountain overlooking Dorset in the 1700s marked the beginning of an industry that brought the town fame and fortune. At one time there were 28 quarries operating. Look for Dorset West Road on your left, a little past the intersection with Manchester West Road. Follow it along the valley, and slow down to glimpse **Marble House,** built in two different colors of locally quarried stone, with Italianate gardens and fountains. Not far beyond, just past the elegant marble columns of the Marble West Inn, look for a **monument** (in marble, of course) at the corner of Nichols Road. It marks the sight of the tavern where the first convention met to draft Vermont's constitution when it separated from New Hampshire.

Turn right onto Church Street into the village of Dorset. On the right stands the **United Church,** built entirely of marble and featuring fine Tiffany stained-glass windows. The **Dorset Historical Society** museum has displays on the marble industry, and offers a recorded walking tour of the historic architecture of the village center. At the end of The Green is Vt. 30; turn right here.

☕ **TAKE A BREAK** The **Inn at West View Farm** (☎ 802/867-5715), on VT 30, dates back to 1870, when it was a working dairy farm. Today the inn includes two restaurants, Clancy's Tavern and the more formal Auberge Room. Fillet of venison in cognac, braised rosemary quail with polenta, and other innovative entrees have earned them a dot on Vermont's culinary map.

About 2½ miles south on VT 30 is the **Norcross–West Quarry,** which produced the stone for the pillars of the New York Public Library. Now a favorite local swimming hole, it is easy to spot on the left side of the road. About a quarter-mile farther on the right, look for a sign pointing to the Dorset Elementary School. Follow the direction of the sign onto Morse Hill Road (to the left) until you reach U.S. 7, and turn left into:

6. **East Dorset,** birthplace and boyhood home of Bill Wilson, who founded Alcoholics Anonymous. Turn right off U.S. 7 into the center of the village. Directly ahead of you is the **Wilson House,** and Bill's boyhood home is just to the left of the church. The home is much as it was when the family lived there; just walk in. Ask at the Wilson House for directions to the cemetery where "Bill W" is buried, to see the poignant tokens left there by thousands grateful for his guidance.

U.S. 7 continues north past **Emerald Lake State Park,** set around a clear lake, with swimming and picnicking facilities as well as nature and hiking trails. Continue on U.S. 7 to:

7. **Wallingford,** which has many fine 19th-century buildings. On the right as you enter the town center is the distinctive **Old Stone Shop** where pitchforks were made. Wallingford is a pleasant place to stretch your legs and browse in the antique shops.

From the center of town, turn right onto Vt. 140, which climbs through a narrow cleft between moss-covered ledges and crosses the Appalachian Trail before the land opens out into rolling hills dotted with farms. Vt. 140 ends at Vt. 103; travel south (right) until you reach VT 100. Go north (left) past a series of small lakes to the village of Plymouth Union, and turn right onto Vt. 100A to:

8. **Plymouth,** birthplace and boyhood home of President Calvin Coolidge. On your left, not far from the intersection, is the **Calvin Coolidge Birthplace** in the Plymouth Notch Historic District. Ten historic buildings are open, including homes, barns, a church, a store, and a working cheese factory.

   In Bridgewater Corners, Vt. 100A ends at U.S. 4, where you go east (right) along the pleasant river valley and into:

9. **Woodstock,** one of Vermont's best-known towns. It's easy to see why. Set around a quiet green, Woodstock is the picture of prosperous mid-19th-century New England. Fine buildings, many dating from the Federal period, are almost perfectly preserved. Stop at the **Dana House,** built in 1807 and now a museum, and at **F. H. Gillingham & Sons,** both on Elm Street. The latter recalls an old-fashioned country store, but has been updated; many of the gourmet foods are locally produced. Continue along Elm Street to **Billings Farm and Museum,** a working demonstration of rural life and farming in the 1890s.

   ☕ **TAKE A BREAK**   Woodstock's upscale business district offers several eateries, including **Bentley's** (☎ 802/457-3232) on the corner facing the common. Best known for its lunches and brunches, Bentley's serves up its famous coffee cake fresh from the oven (on Sunday to the accompaniment of live jazz).

   For staying overnight, the modern **Woodstock Inn and Resort** (☎ 802/457-1100), with full recreational facilities, is right in the center of town. Historic **Kedron Valley Inn** (☎ 802/457-1473), once a waystation in the Underground Railroad, is only a few minutes away in South Woodstock. The latter is as well known for its outstanding dining room. The **Shire Motel** on Pleasant Street (☎ 802/457-2211) is a budget-level option.

   From Woodstock a 5-mile detour east on U.S. 4 will take you to **Quechee Gorge.** This cleft, more than 150 feet deep, was cut by the Ottauquechee River, which appears as a tiny ribbon from the highway bridge spanning the gorge. An easy walking path leads to the bottom for a different view of the towering cliffs and river. Between Woodstock and the gorge, you will pass the **Taftsville Covered Bridge,** built in 1836.

   Back in Woodstock, take Vt. 106 through South Woodstock, a route through peaceful farm country with meadows framed by mountain views until it reaches an intersection with Vt. 10 near North Springfield. Go west (right) here, until you reach Vt. 103; turn left and head southward into:

10. **Chester,** perhaps Vermont's most quintessentially Victorian town. The main street is lined with well-preserved homes spanning the century between 1820 and 1920. Stop by the small museum and art gallery in the imposing brick Academy building. There, or in the visitors' kiosk nearby, you can pick up a map and brochure for a short walking tour that points out the many fine examples of architecture in the town; 156 of them are listed on the National Register.

    ☕ **TAKE A BREAK**   Nothing could be more fitting in this Victorian town than a genteel teatime. The **Rose Arbor Tea Room** (☎ 802/875-4767), in an elegant home just off the main square on School Street, serves scones fresh from the oven, along with delicious cakes and other treats. They also serve lunches.

    A short drive north, on Vt. 103, is Chester's remarkable **Stone Village,** known for its active role in the Underground Railroad. On the way, you will pass the **Victorian Depot,** built in 1872 and now terminus of the Green Mountain Flyer.

The 2-hour scenic train ride crosses another dramatic rock gorge and passes several miles of covered bridges.

Back in Chester, take Vt. 35 south, along a quiet, wooded byway to:

11. **Grafton,** a village so perfectly frozen in the early 19th century that many regard it as a museum town. The entire village is owned by a foundation created to preserve it from 20th-century change. **The Old Tavern,** a distinguished inn with a double-tiered front porch, forms the village nucleus. Close by are several small craft shops and the **Windham Foundation Museum** with displays on early farming. Farther along Vt. 35 is a working cheese factory, where you can see the famous Vermont cheddar in the making.

Continue on Vt. 35, still a quiet road lined with fields, stone walls, and mossy boulders, to Townsend, where it meets Vt. 30. Go west (right), passing Vermont's longest covered bridge, until Vt. 100 intersects in East Jamaica. Go left onto Vt. 100; travel through several villages and past Mt. Snow Ski Area until you reach Vt. 9 in the busy town of **Wilmington,** where you may want to stop and browse in its many small shops.

From Wilmington, follow Vt. 9 west, passing the northern shore of Harriman Reservoir. The road winds alongside a river, then climbs over the Green Mountains, passing through a **National Forest Wilderness Area** and **Woodford State Park,** with its shaded picnic grove. From the top of this mountain ridge, Vt. 9 drops down a long hill and brings you back to your starting point in Bennington.

# DRIVING TOUR
## New Hampshire's White Mountains

**Start and Finish:** Plymouth
**Distance:** 200 miles
**Time:** 1 or 2 days
**Highlights:** Views of the White Mountains, waterfalls, the Old Man of the Mountains, the flume, classic New England villages, a majestic old pine forest, and Squam Lake, the "Golden Pond" of movie fame. Most attractions on this tour are free

Mountain scenery, mixed with forests, farms, and small towns, fill this tour, which includes the two main notches of the White Mountains, Crawford on the east and Franconia on the west. These notches, great glacial scours that formed passes low enough for the early settlers to build roads through, once provided the only link between the vast areas of northern New Hampshire and the supply centers and cities on the coast. Today the area is full of reminders of its Golden Age as a summer resort haven. Some of its grand turn-of-the-century resort hotels are still welcoming guests. The route is lined with natural wonders: waterfalls dropping over granite ledges, crystal lakes, New England's tallest mountains, deep forests, and geological phenomena caused by glaciers and the eroding powers of water. New Hampshire's trademark, the Old Man of the Mountains, looks down upon the route. Expect spectacular views, covered bridges, quiet country lanes, and, just maybe, a moose.

The portion of the trip on N.H. 16 from Chocorua to Conway can be very busy during summer weekends, but this itinerary misses the most congested section, from Conway to North Conway, by taking an easy-to-find unnumbered road directly to the town of Bartlett. Several of the roads you will follow are byways that tourists seldom find. A few are winding and hilly, but well maintained and well marked with signs alerting drivers to sudden curves or intersections. The biggest problem the driver will have is remembering to watch the road when there are so many fine views to enjoy.

# Driving Tour: The White Mountains

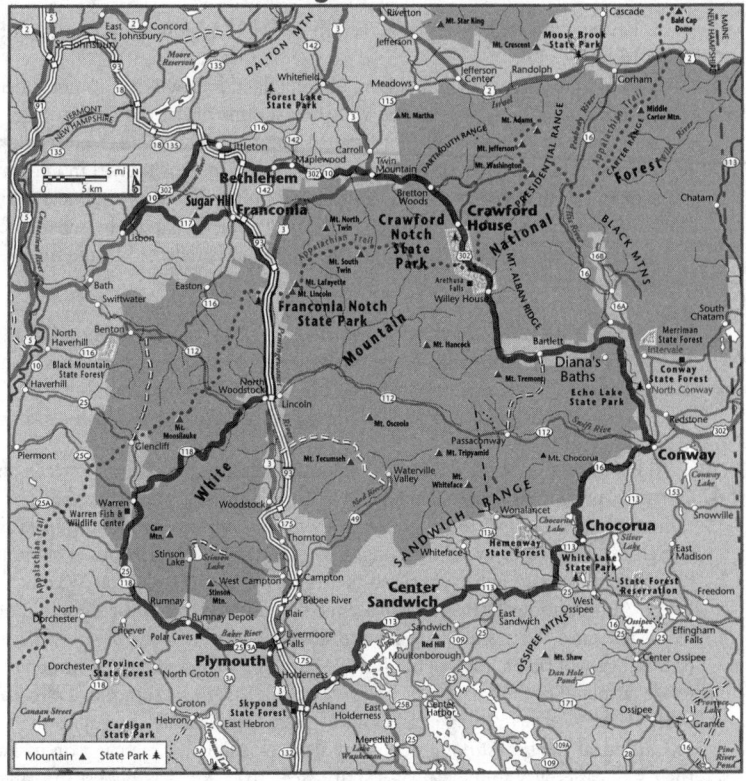

I-93 connects Boston and the New Hampshire's major cities along the Merrimack Valley to the White Mountains. Exits 25 and 26 lead into:

1. **Plymouth,** where the tour begins. Follow U.S. 3 south to Ashland and on to Holderness, on the shores of **Squam Lake.** This largely undeveloped lake was the setting for the film, *On Golden Pond,* and is habitat for loons, which can find quiet nesting sites in the many coves of its irregular shore line. The **Sailing Center,** on U.S. 3, rents both canoes and sailboats for those who want to explore the lake. In Holderness, turn right onto N.H. 113, where you will come almost immediately to the **Science Center of New Hampshire.** A nature education facility for adults and children, the center has marked trails in six different environments, including a boardwalk over a marsh.

The road snakes along the curving shore of Squam Lake and through woodlands until it reaches:

2. **Center Sandwich,** a classic New England village of white clapboard churches and homes. Most of these date from the early 1800s, when the village was a thriving farming center. Now it is a quiet, tree-shaded town with craft and antique shops and a good **Historical Society Museum** filled with tools, household furnishings, and other 19th-century artifacts. Continue on N.H. 113 past rambling stone walls that enclose farm pastures until you reach N.H. 113A in North Sandwich. Take this to Wonalancet; ahead are fine views of Whiteface Mountain. After Wonalancet, with its tiny church, you will come to **Big Pines Natural Area,** with a nature trail leading beneath its grove of unusually tall pines.

In Tamworth, shortly beyond, rejoin N.H. 113, which in 2 miles joins N.H. 16 in:

**3. Chocorua,** a small settlement beside an old mill dam. Follow N.H. 16 north (left), to the top of a long hill, where you will soon see one of the most photographed sights in the state—here Mount Chocorua's pointed summit and tree-clad slopes drop to the shores of Chocorua Lake, and the entire scene is framed in tall white birch trees. No one with a camera can resist stopping. The view is almost as fine from the foot of the hill, where the shore of the lake is shaded by magnificent red pines, and the entire silhouette of the mountain is reflected in the mirror of the lake.

☕ **TAKE A BREAK**   In summer weather, the **Dam Ice Cream Shop** (☎ 603/323-8745), has custom-made ice cream and sundaes, and also sandwiches. When cooler weather arrives in September, you can stop at the same place, but it will be called **Teahouse by the Dam** and will be transformed into an English tea shop.

NH 16, which can be quite busy on summer and fall weekends, leads directly into:

**4. Conway,** passing the southern terminus of the **Conway Scenic Railroad.** The train runs to the resort town of North Conway. You may want to bypass this stretch of N.H. 16 to avoid the congested traffic past the many outlet shopping malls: Continue through Conway to the traffic lights and go left on Washington Street. Almost immediately you will see the first of **two covered bridges,** but bear to the left onto West Side Road instead of passing through the bridge. The second bridge will be on your right after the turn. This road takes you through the fertile farmland of the Saco River Valley. You will pass the entrance to **Echo Lake State Park,** with swimming beaches and a picnic area, before coming to the foot of **Cathedral Ledge.** Although you may see rock climbers practicing on its face, there's an easier way to the top via a short, steep road, for views across the valley.

Shortly after Cathedral Ledge, look for a short, straight gravel lane to the left between two horse pastures; the road ends abruptly at the edge of the woods only a few yards away. Follow the easy, level trail at the end of the road for about a half-mile to reach **Diana's Baths,** a long series of waterfalls deep in the forest. Back on the road, continue past the foot of another set of cliffs, and along the banks of the Saco to join U.S. 302, where you turn left. After passing through the town of Bartlett, the road enters the reservation of:

**5. Crawford Notch,** one of the most scenic areas in the White Mountains. If the day is clear, you will see Mount Washington and other peaks of the Presidential Range ahead as you drive along the banks of the Saco River. Almost at the top of the long climb through the notch, **Silver Cascade** drops over a series of steep ledges right beside the road. A nearby pullout area offers a fine panorama southward back down the notch. At the head of the notch is a Victorian railway station, now a checkpoint for hikers and climbers.

Along the next few miles of road, you will see low muddy areas where moose often come at dawn and dusk. Look across the valley to your right for glimpses of the rooftop and towers of the **Mount Washington Hotel** (☎ 800/258-0330 or 603/278-1000), which will soon come into full view, with a backdrop of the entire Presidential Range. This landmark was the scene of the Bretton Woods Monetary Conference at the close of World War II, and its rooms still bear the brass plaques noting the royalty and heads of state who stayed in them.

About 3 miles past the resort, a short drive to the right takes you to **Lower Falls,** a series of cascades over low ledges. Continue on U.S. 302 until you reach:

**6. Bethlehem,** one of the earliest White Mountain resort towns. At one time Bethlehem had dozens of fine hotels, including the grand Maplewood, whose casino and golf course will be on the right. Notice the many different architectural styles along Main Street—Bethlehem is thought to have more examples of different styles than any other town its size in New England.

On your left, at the far end of town, look for **The Rocks,** a 19th-century estate farm, with restored gardens and marked walking trails. The barns and outbuildings were built from stone cleared from the rocky fields.

☕ **TAKE A BREAK**   As you enter Littleton, **Bishop's Homemade Ice Cream Shoppe** (☎ 603/444-6039) will be on your right. Flavors range from the standard ones to fruit sherbets and Bishop's popular brandy Alexander ice cream. Sundaes are their specialty. They're open daily from mid-April to mid-October.

Continue on U.S. 302 through Littleton, and west toward Lisbon, until you reach N.H. 117. Turn left, climbing steadily to:

**7. Sugar Hill,** whose maple-lined main street stretches along a scenic hillside. Be sure to stop at **Harman's Store** for aged cheddar and maple syrup, and at the **Historical Museum,** to see their collection of photographs and mementos from the Golden Age of the resort hotels, when Sugar Hill was one of the most fashionable resort towns in New England.

☕ **TAKE A BREAK**   It's the views that made Sugar Hill famous, and the best place to enjoy them is from the dining room of the **Sunset Hill House** (☎ 800/SUN-HILL or 603/823-5522). The food is equal to the view, and influences from a variety of cuisines are blended with a deft hand. The main building of this grand hotel is gone, but a second one, built in 1882, has been restored and is an elegant inn.

Continuing on N.H. 117, the views unfold as you drop down into the valley and the town of:

**8. Franconia,** once the home of Robert Frost. N.H. 117 ends here, and you should go right on N.H. 18. Shortly after the turn, the last remaining **iron furnace** in the state is on the right. The giant stone tower stands across the river, where iron ore from Sugar Hill was smelted until 1850. The centrally located Franconia–Sugar Hill area is a good base for lodgings, with a wide choice available. **Sunset Hill House** is recommended above, and the **Franconia Inn** on Easton Road (☎ 603/823-5542) has great views and an elegant restaurant. For a less-expensive option, try the **Gale River Motel** (☎ 603/823-5655) on N.H. 18.

Just south of the village of Franconia, N.H. 18 meets U.S. 3, close to:

**9. Franconia Notch,** which has so many attractions that you could spend an entire day enjoying them. The **Aerial Tramway** carries visitors to the top of Cannon Mountain for views that reach all the way to Canada. At its base is the **New England Ski Museum,** which contains early ski equipment, Olympic memorabilia, and other historic displays. From the same parking lot you can take the short trail to Echo Lake, where you will see the state's trademark, the **Old Man of the Mountains,** above. This stone profile is actually composed of three separate ledges, but from below they blend into one craggy face. Telescopes are mounted near the lake for closer views.

Farther down the notch, on the right, is **The Basin,** a pool carved into the rocks by the constant swirling action of flowing water as it drops over a short falls. If you follow the trail into the woods behind it, you will come to a long series of cascades over ledges.

**The Flume** is a giant cleft in the earth through which a small stream flows. The walk through the flume (on a boardwalk) and to the scenic Liberty Pool is well graded and fairly level. This is one of the very few of New Hampshire's scenic attractions for which you must pay an admission fee. As you leave the notch, look up to your right to see the **Indian Head,** another cliff profile, this one with a feather headdress of pointed fir trees.

Leave U.S. 3 in the town of North Woodstock, going west on N.H. 118, and follow the signs to Warren. Here N.H. 118 joins N.H. 25 briefly. When they split again in West Rumney, go left on N.H. 25. On your right will be **Polar Caves,** a glacial rock formation of caves, tunnels, and crevices; in places, ice remains year-round. N.H. 25 continues on to Plymouth, completing the tour.

## 1 New York City

Seductively uncontrollable and willful, New York City insists on displaying many contrary moods at once. Its past, present, and future tug at one another right before your eyes; its sometimes unruly facades veil charms that will intoxicate you—once you get beyond the surface, delving deeper than the glass, steel, and concrete skin to try to touch the city's soul.

Despite its charms, this city can be as tough as a New Yorker. Either you'll be enthralled by the dazzle, the tempo, and the sense of discovery, or you'll be stunned by the noise, the blatant juxtaposition of inhuman poverty and unimaginable wealth, the smog, and the callousness of the natives. Take heart, because New Yorkers have the old love–hate relationship with their town. They talk endlessly about escaping for the weekend, commiserate about subways that arrive late, bemoan the recent spate of cab drivers who don't seem to know Lincoln Center from Grant's Tomb, and on and on. Yet still they stay.

New York's magnetism pulls in the intelligent, the creative, the determined, the overbearing, and the overblown from all over the world. Just about any language and any dialect is spoken in this great melting pot, from Brooklynese to Mandarin. And this is the nerve of the world's finance and trade; the international hub of advertising, publishing, and fashion; and the creative core for theater, ballet, and music.

It's the cumulative effect of all that—the energy, the beauty, the watery setting, the options, and the opportunities—that keeps New Yorkers here. The unrestrained, inescapable feeling that they're somewhere where things are happening. And those characteristics are exactly what make New York impossible to resist for millions.

### ARRIVING & DEPARTING

**BY PLANE** Three major airports serve the New York metropolitan area: **John F. Kennedy International Airport (JFK)** and **La Guardia Airport** are both in Queens, and **Newark International Airport,** across the Hudson River in New Jersey. Almost every major domestic carrier serves the New York area, including America West, American, Continental, Delta, Northwest, TWA, US Airways, and United. So do some of the less-expensive, no-frills airlines, including Air South, Carnival, Midway, Midwest Express, and Tower Air.

For transportation information for all three airports, call **Air-Ride** at ☎ **800/ 247-7433;** it gives recorded information on bus and shuttle companies and private car services registered with the New York and New Jersey Port Authority. On the arrivals level at each airport the Port Authority also has information counters where you can make reservations. Most transportation companies have courtesy phones near the baggage-claim area.

Taxis wait curbside at all three airports. Fares into New York City are metered and cost approximately $30–$35 from JKF, $25–$35 from La Guardia, and $30 from Newark, plus tolls. Take only metered cabs and be wary of drivers demanding huge sums; pay *exactly* what the meter says. The rides usually take about 45 minutes from JFK, 30 minutes from La Guardia or Newark.

**BY TRAIN & BUS**  Amtrak (☎ **800/USA-RAIL**) runs frequent service to New York City's Pennsylvania Station (Seventh Avenue between 31st and 33rd streets), where you can easily transfer to your hotel by taxi, subway, or bus.

Greyhound/Trailways (☎ **800/231-2222**) buses arrive at the Port Authority Terminal (Eighth Avenue between 40th and 42nd streets), where you can easily transfer to your hotel by taxi, subway, or bus.

**BY CAR**  From the New Jersey Turnpike (I-95) and points west, there are three Hudson River crossings into the city: the Holland Tunnel (Lower Manhattan), the Lincoln Tunnel (Midtown), and the George Washington Bridge (Upper Manhattan). The toll at each is $4 for cars heading into the city; there's no outbound toll.

From upstate New York, take the New York State Thruway (I-87), which crosses the Hudson on the Tappan Zee Bridge ($2.50 toll) and becomes the Major Deegan Expressway (I-87) through The Bronx. For the east side, continue to the Triborough Bridge ($3.50 toll) and then down the FDR Drive. For the west side, take the Cross Bronx Expressway (I-95) to the Henry Hudson Parkway or the Taconic State Parkway to the Saw Mill River Parkway to the Henry Hudson Parkway ($1.50 toll) on the west side.

From New England, the New England Thruway (I-95) connects with the Bruckner Expressway (I-278), which leads to the Triborough Bridge and the FDR on the east side. For the west side, take the Bruckner to the Cross Bronx Expressway (I-95) to the Henry Hudson Parkway south.

Once you arrive in Manhattan, park your car in a garage (expect to pay at least $20–$30 per day) and leave it there. Do not use it for traveling within the city.

## ESSENTIALS

**VISITOR INFORMATION**  The best source for general travel information on New York City is the **New York Convention and Visitor Bureau,** 2 Columbus Circle, New York, NY 10019. (Note, however, that the bureau plans to move sometime soon, so check on the address.) Before you arrive, call the 24-hour hotline at ☎ **800/ NYC-VISIT** from anywhere in the United States and Canada (from outside North America or once you're in New York City, dial ☎ **212/397-8222**).

**RESOURCES FOR TRAVELERS WITH SPECIAL NEEDS**  For a copy of *Access for All,* a guide on accessibility to many of the city's cultural institutions, send a $5 check to **Hospital Audiences, Inc.,** 220 W. 42nd St., 13th floor, New York, NY 10036 (☎ **212/575-7676;** TDD: 212/575-7673). For a packet on accessible hotels, restaurants, transportation, museums, and sites, send a $5 check to the **Society for the Advancement of Travel for the Handicapped (SATH),** 347 Fifth Ave., Suite 610, New York, NY 10016 (☎ **212/447-7284;** fax 212/725-8253).

Gray Line Air Shuttle (☎ **800/451-0455** or 212/315-3006) operates minibuses with lifts from JKF and La Guardia airports to Midtown hotels by reservation only. Public buses are supposed to be equipped with wheelchair lifts, and disabled passengers ride for half price (75¢). The subway isn't yet fully wheelchair accessible, but a free brochure, **Accessible Transfer Points,** is available by contacting MTA Customer Assistance, 370 J St., Room 702, Brooklyn, NY 11201 (☎ **718/330-3322;** TTY: 718/ 596-8273).

# New York: Midtown

1-1196

52

E 67th St
E 66th St
E 65th St
E 64th St
E 63rd St
E 62nd St
E 61st St
E 60th St
E 59th St
E 58th St
E 57th St
E 56th St
E 55th St
E 54th St
E 53rd St
E 52nd St
E 51st St
E 50th St
E 49th St
E 48th St
E 47th St
E 46th St
E 45th St
E 44th St
E 43rd St
E 42nd St
E 41st St
E 40th St
E 39th St
E 38th St
E 37th St
E 36th St
E 35th St
E 34th St
E 33rd St
E 32nd St
E 31st St
E 30th St
E 29th St
E 28th St
E 27th St
E 26th St
E 25th St
E 24th St
E 23rd St
E 22nd St
E 21st St
E 20th St
E 19th St
E 18th St
E 17th St
E 16th St
E 15th St
E 14th St
E 13th St

0    440 y
     400 m

N

Central Park S
The Pond
East Drive

York Av
Roosevelt Island Tram
Queensboro Bridge

Queens

From Lower Level
To Upper Level

Sutton Pl
Sutton Pl South
Beekman Place
Mitchell Place

MIDTOWN EAST
Rockefeller Center

Sixth Av
Fifth Av
Madison Av
Park Av
Vanderbilt Av
Depew Pl
Lexington Av
Third Av
Second Av
First Av
FDR Drive

Grand Central Terminal

Bryant Park
New York Public Library

MURRAY HILL

United Nations

Queens-Midtown Tunnel

Tunnel Exit
Tunnel Entrance

East River

Empire State Bldg.

Broadway

Park Av. S.

Madison Square Park

FLATIRON DISTRICT

Gramercy Park

GRAMERCY PARK

Union Sq W
Union Square
Union Sq E
Irving Pl
Periman Pl

Asser Levy Pl
Av. C

Peter Cooper Village

Stuyvesant Town

Subway stop M

53

Other helpful organizations are **The Lighthouse, Inc.,** 111 E. 59th St., New York, NY 10017 (☎ **800/334-5497** or 212/821-9200), which stages special concerts and art exhibitions for people with impaired vision and sells braille subway maps; the **New York Society for the Deaf,** 817 Broadway, 7th floor, New York, NY 10003 (☎ and TDD: **212/777-3900**); and the **American Foundation for the Blind,** 11 Penn Plaza, Suite 300, New York, NY 10001 (☎ **800/232-5463** or 212/502-7600).

Seniors 65 and older pay half fare (75¢) on New York subway and buses, and many museums and sites (and some theaters and performance halls) offer them discounted entrance and tickets.

Gay and lesbian culture is as much a part of the city's identity as yellow cabs, high rises, obnoxious but amusing characters, and fabulous theater. You'll find musical events and outrageous festivals like **Wigstock.** The **Lesbian and Gay Community Services Center,** 208 W. 13th St., between Seventh and Eighth avenues (☎ **212/620-7310**), is open daily 9am–11pm; a meeting facility for lesbian, gay, and bisexual organizations, it issues a calendar of events and has the city's largest lending library for gay and lesbian literature. The **Gay Men's Health Crisis (GMHC),** 129 W. 20th St. (AIDS hotline: **212/807-6655**), sponsors health programs. Pick up *Homo Xtra (HX),* a weekly magazine in bars, clubs, and stores throughout town.

**EMERGENCIES & SAFETY**　Dial ☎ **911** for **fire, police,** and **ambulance** in an emergency. There is crime in New York, but millions of people spend their lives here without being robbed and assaulted even once. In fact, New York is safer than most big American cities. Still, visitors can make particularly easy and usually obvious targets for con men and pickpockets, so trust your instincts. A general rule is to avoid deserted or poorly lighted areas, and stay out of city parks at night. If you plan to sightsee in Harlem, its best to take a tour.

## GETTING AROUND

Don't even think about getting around by car. For New Yorkers, walking is the major means of self-propulsion, and they stride across wide but crowded pavements with speedy skill, dexterously dodging taxis, buses, bike messengers, in-line skaters, unscooped doggie poop, and other pedestrians. Don't take your cue from them until you feel really comfortable with the city: Wait for walk signals and pay attention to such things as cars and buses that don't yield the right of way and to bikers who blithely fly along the sidewalks.

**BY SUBWAY**　It screeches, and it may look scary, but the subway—or train, as it's called here—is as much a part of the city as the Empire State Building, and it's by far the fastest way to get around. In general, the subways are safe, especially in Manhattan. The subway fare is $1.50 (half price for seniors and the disabled), and children under 3 feet 8 inches tall ride free. Fares can be paid with tokens or MetroCards—magnetic strip "credit" cards that debit the fare when swiped through the turnstile, for sale at token booths located in the stations. Maps are available at most token booths and tourist information centers.

The system basically recapitulates the lay of the land aboveground, with most lines in Manhattan running north and south under the avenues, with a few lines going east and west under streets. Subway stations are at main intersections and often marked with green lights on posts. Watch for entrances marked uptown (northbound) or downtown (southbound), these signs mean you can't cross over to the other side at this station. There are express lines that skip many stops, and locals that stop at every station. For travel directions and information, call the **New York City Transit's Travel Information Center** at ☎ **718/330-1234** (daily 6am–9pm).

# New York: Downtown

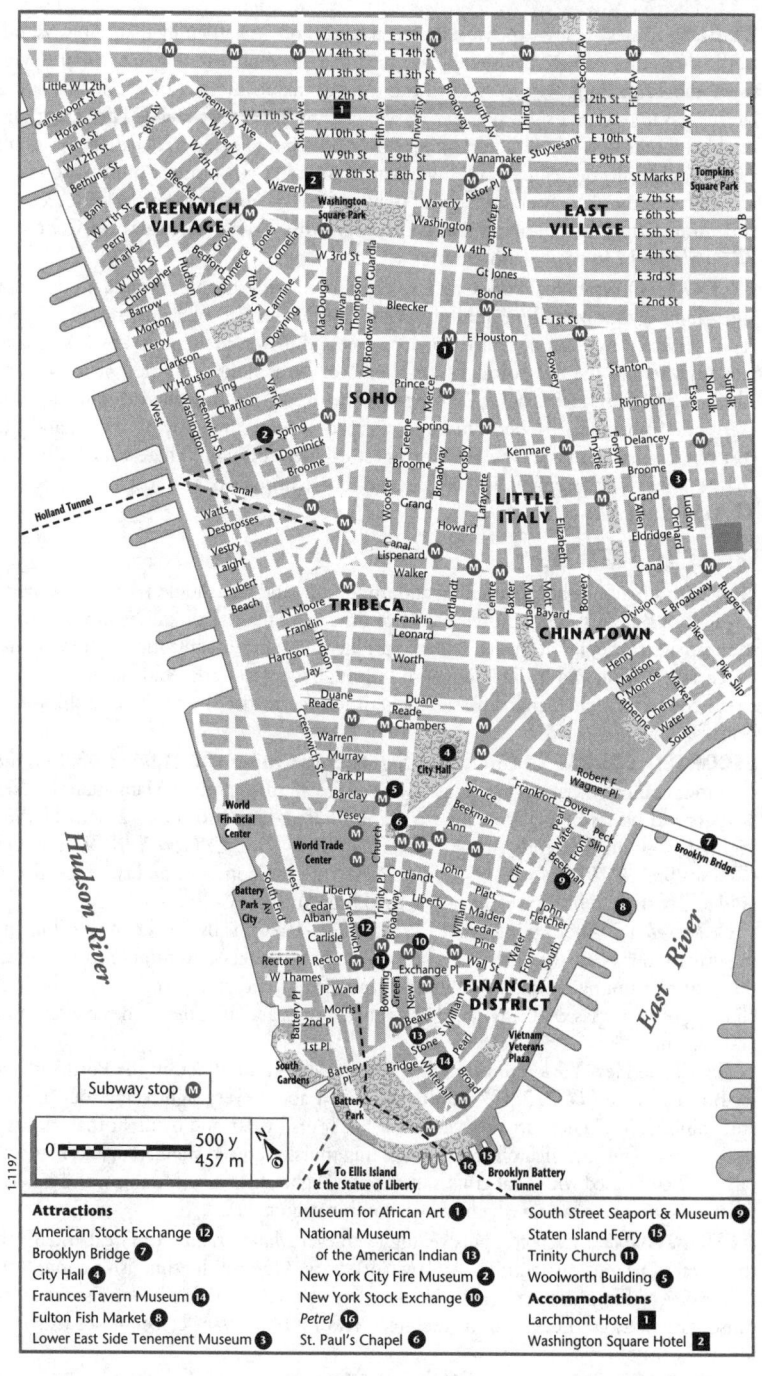

**Attractions**
American Stock Exchange 12
Brooklyn Bridge 7
City Hall 4
Fraunces Tavern Museum 14
Fulton Fish Market 8
Lower East Side Tenement Museum 3

Museum for African Art 1
National Museum
of the American Indian 13
New York City Fire Museum 2
New York Stock Exchange 10
Petrel 16
St. Paul's Chapel 6

South Street Seaport & Museum 9
Staten Island Ferry 15
Trinity Church 11
Woolworth Building 5
**Accommodations**
Larchmont Hotel 1
Washington Square Hotel 2

55

**BY BUS**  Buses are less expensive than taxis and more user-friendly than subways, but traffic slows them down. Each major avenue has a bus route running uptown or downtown and connecting with crosstown bus lines at major intersections. The bus fare is $1.50, payable with a subway token, a MetroCard, or exact change. The senior and disabled fare is 75¢ and children under 3 feet 8 inches tall ride free. Fare boxes don't accept dollar bills or pennies. Bus maps can be found at most tourist information centers and in some subway stations, but rarely on buses themselves. For travel directions and information, call the **New York City Transit's Travel Information Center** at ☎ **718/330-1234** (daily 6am–9pm).

**BY TAXI**  Official New York City taxis are yellow, with the rates printed on the door and a light with a medallion number on the roof. Never accept a ride from any other "taxi" service. Taxis can be hailed on any street and drivers are required by law to take you anywhere in the five boroughs, to Nassau or Westchester counties, or to Newark Airport. The base fare is $2 ($2.50 8pm–6am) upon entering the cab plus 30¢ for every one-fifth mile, 20¢ per minute in stopped or very slow-moving traffic, and the cost of all tolls. Don't let the few dishonest cabbies con you: There's no additional charge for extra passengers or for luggage. For complaints and lost property, call ☎ **212/221-TAXI**.

## WHAT TO SEE & DO

New York's major sights are exciting and important, and you should try to see as many as you can. But also allow yourself plenty of time to let the city sink in by osmosis: time to rummage through Greenwich Village antique stores, explore historic neighborhoods, watch lovers stroll and in-line skaters roll through Central Park, enjoy an impromptu street concert, or sip a martini at a cocktail lounge in the sky as the city shimmers below.

**ESCORTED TOURS**  ✪ **Circle Line Sightseeing Cruises** (☎ **212/563-3200**) is the only tour company that circumnavigates the entire 35 miles around Manhattan. It takes 3 hours and passes by many major attractions. Circle Line also runs a 2-hour Harbor Lights Cruise on weekends Apr–Oct and daily May–Oct. ✪ **New York Waterways** (☎ **800/533-3779**) also has a 90-minute New York Harbor cruise and two exceptional guided day trips to historic sights along the Hudson River Valley.

✪ *Petrel,* a 70-foot sailing yacht (☎ **212/825-1976**), is by far the most exhilarating way to tour New York Harbor. There are no loud speakers, no rumbling of engines, no children running on deck—only the sound of the wind and waves and the civilized clinking of wine glasses. Daily sails last about 2 hours and are offered in the afternoon and evening.

**Gray Line New York Tours,** Eighth Avenue and 42nd Street, in the Port Authority Bus Terminal (☎ **212/397-2600**), offers just about every sightseeing tour option and combination. There are double-decker bus tours by day and by night that run uptown, downtown, and all around town; walking tours of Lower Manhattan and Harlem; bus tours combined with boat cruises, helicopter flights, museum entrances, and guided visits of sights. You can save by buying a combination ticket.

**ATTRACTIONS**  Even compulsive, high-achiever Manhattanites can't experience all the attractions and distractions in New York City. One full lifetime isn't enough to fathom everything Gotham has to offer—whether you're a refined connoisseur of its museums, an awed observer of its architecture, or a bon-vivant consumer of its street life.

✪ **American Museum of Natural History.** *Central Park West (at 77th St.).* ☎ *212/769-5100. Suggested admission $8 adults, $6 seniors, $4.50 children. Sun–Thurs 10am–5:45pm, Fri–Sat 10am–8:45pm. Subway: B, C to 81st St.; 1, 9 to 79th St.*

Occupying a 4-block area, the American Museum of Natural History houses the world's greatest natural science collection in a group of buildings made in a mishmash of architectural styles. The diversity is astounding: some 36 million specimens ranging from microscopic organisms to the world's largest cut gem, the Brazilian Princess Topaz (21,005 carats). The museum's fourth-floor dinosaur displays are the most popular exhibitions. Other favorites include the animal habitat dioramas and the children's discovery room with hands-on exhibitions and experiments. The best of the best can be seen on daily highlight tours departing from the second-floor Hall of African Mammals. The museum also has a four-story-screen **IMAX Theater** (☎ 212/769-5034).

✪ **Bronx Zoo/Wildlife Conservation Park.** *Fordham Rd. and Bronx River Pkwy., the Bronx.* ☎ *718/367-1010. Admission Nov–Mar, $3 adults, $1.50 seniors and children under 12; Apr–Oct, $6.75 adults, $3 seniors and children under 12; free Wed year-round. Nov–Mar, daily 10am–4:30pm; Apr–Oct, Mon–Fri 10am–5pm, Sat–Sun 10am–5:30pm. Subway: No. 2 train to Pelham Pkwy., then walk 2 blocks west.* Founded in 1899, the Bronx Zoo is the largest metropolitan animal park in the United States, with more than 4,000 nonhumans living in 265 acres. Most of the old-fashioned cages have been replaced by natural settings. The **Wild Asia Complex** is a zoo-within-a-zoo over which the Bengali Express Monorail (open seasonally) goes high above free-roaming tigers, elephants, rhinoceroses, and other Asian animals. The **Children's Zoo** (open Apr–Oct) allows kids to see animals in their natural habitat as well as by imitation. A special **Butterfly Zone** in an amusing caterpillar-like tube is aflutter Apr–Sept with 1,000 colorful specimens.

✪ **Brooklyn Bridge.** *Sidewalk entrance on Park Row. Subway: 4, 5, 6 to Brooklyn Bridge/City Hall.* This great span of gothic-inspired stone pylons and intricate steel-cable webs has moved poets like Walt Whitman and Hart Crane to sing its body impressive. You can view it from afar and then, on the wood-plank pedestrian walkway elevated above the traffic, take a relatively peaceful walk. It provides a great vantage point from which to contemplate the New York skyline and the East River and a grand entryway for a tour of Brooklyn Heights. You'll be surprised at the number of walkers and bikers who regularly cross the bridge, but it's best to promenade with a friend.

✪ **Central Park.** *59th to 110th sts. from Fifth Ave. to Central Park West.* ☎ *212/794-6564 (Dairy Visitor and Information Center) or 212/360-3444 (recorded events). Subway to main southern entrances: N, R to Fifth Ave.; A, B, C, D, 1, 9 to Columbus Circle/59th St.* New Yorkers come to Central Park's lakes, streams, meadows, and forests to escape the frazzles of the city. Stop first at the **Information Center** in the **Dairy,** midpark at about 65th Street, for more information on sights and events and an exhibition on park history and design. The **urban park rangers** (☎ 212/427-4040) offer free walking tours. Near the Dairy is the **carousel** with 58 hand-carved horses, the **zoo** (see below), and the **Wollman Rink** for roller or ice skating (☎ 212/396-1010). The **Mall,** a long formal walkway lined with elm-shaded benches and sculptures of writers, leads to the focal point of Central Park, the grandly sculpted **Bethesda Fountain** (along the 72nd Street Transverse), which borders a large lake where dogs fetch sticks and rowboaters romantically glide by. You can rent a rowboat or take a gondola ride at **Loeb Boathouse** (☎ 212/517-2233), at the eastern end of the lake. **Sheep Meadow** on the southwestern side of the park is a designated quiet zone. Another peaceful respite is **Strawberry Fields,** at 72nd Street on the park's west side, a memorial to Beatle John Lennon, who was murdered nearby at the Dakota apartment building (72nd Street and Central Park West). **Bow Bridge,** a graceful cast-iron span designed by Calvert Vaux, crosses over the lake and leads to the **Ramble,** a bucolic, dense 38-acre woodland with a lacework of spiraling paths, rocky outcroppings, and a stream (the best spot for bird-watching). In midpark north of the Ramble, **Belvedere Castle** is home to the Henry

# New York: Uptown

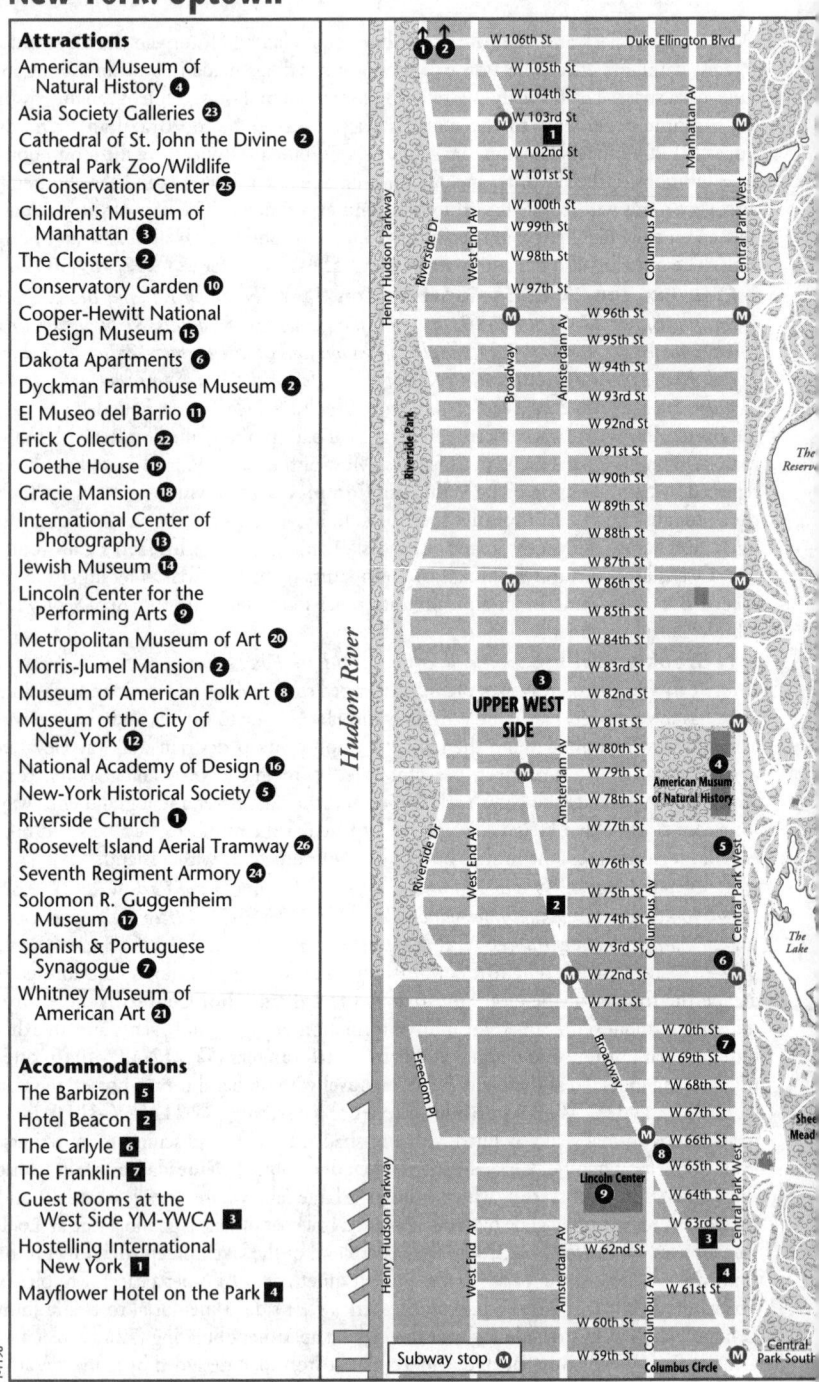

## Attractions

American Museum of Natural History ❹

Asia Society Galleries ㉓

Cathedral of St. John the Divine ❷

Central Park Zoo/Wildlife Conservation Center ㉕

Children's Museum of Manhattan ❸

The Cloisters ❷

Conservatory Garden ❿

Cooper-Hewitt National Design Museum ⓯

Dakota Apartments ❻

Dyckman Farmhouse Museum ❷

El Museo del Barrio ⓫

Frick Collection ㉒

Goethe House ⓳

Gracie Mansion ⓲

International Center of Photography ⓭

Jewish Museum ⓮

Lincoln Center for the Performing Arts ❾

Metropolitan Museum of Art ⓴

Morris-Jumel Mansion ❷

Museum of American Folk Art ❽

Museum of the City of New York ⓬

National Academy of Design ⓰

New-York Historical Society ❺

Riverside Church ❶

Roosevelt Island Aerial Tramway ㉖

Seventh Regiment Armory ㉔

Solomon R. Guggenheim Museum ⓱

Spanish & Portuguese Synagogue ❼

Whitney Museum of American Art ㉑

## Accommodations

The Barbizon ❺

Hotel Beacon ❷

The Carlyle ❻

The Franklin ❼

Guest Rooms at the West Side YM-YWCA ❸

Hostelling International New York ❶

Mayflower Hotel on the Park ❹

1-1198

58

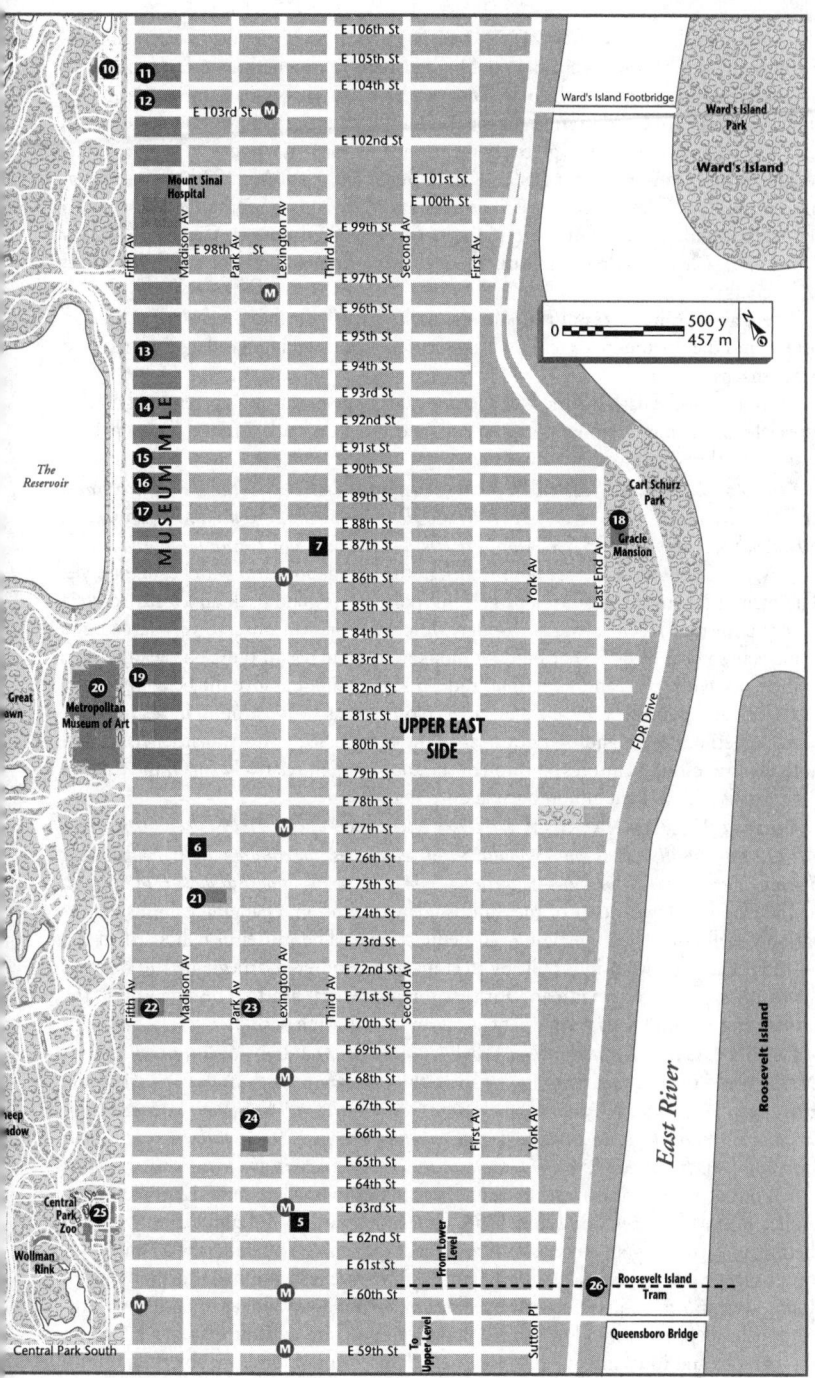

E 106th St
E 105th St
E 104th St
E 103rd St
E 102nd St
E 101st St
E 100th St
E 99th St
E 98th St
E 97th St
E 96th St
E 95th St
E 94th St
E 93rd St
E 92nd St
E 91st St
E 90th St
E 89th St
E 88th St
E 87th St
E 86th St
E 85th St
E 84th St
E 83rd St
E 82nd St
E 81st St
E 80th St
E 79th St
E 78th St
E 77th St
E 76th St
E 75th St
E 74th St
E 73rd St
E 72nd St
E 71st St
E 70th St
E 69th St
E 68th St
E 67th St
E 66th St
E 65th St
E 64th St
E 63rd St
E 62nd St
E 61st St
E 60th St
E 59th St

Ward's Island Footbridge
Ward's Island Park
Ward's Island

Mount Sinai Hospital

MUSEUM MILE

The Reservoir

Carl Schurz Park
Gracie Mansion

Great Lawn

Metropolitan Museum of Art

UPPER EAST SIDE

East River

Roosevelt Island

FDR Drive

Fifth Av
Madison Av
Park Av
Lexington Av
Third Av
Second Av
First Av
York Av
East End Av

Central Park Zoo
Wollman Rink
Central Park South

Sheep Meadow

Front Lower Level
To Upper Level
Sutton Pl

Roosevelt Island Tram
Queensboro Bridge

0 ____ 500 y
     457 m

Luce Nature Observatory (☎ 212/772-0210), worth a visit if you're with children. From the Castle set on Vista Rock, the highest point in the park, you can look down on the **Great Lawn** and **Delacorte Theater,** home to Shakespeare in the Park. The small **Shakespeare Garden** south of the theater is a bit scruffy, but it does have plants, herbs, trees, and other bits of greenery mentioned by the playwright.

The formal **Conservatory Garden** (105th Street and Fifth Avenue) presents a magnificent display of flowers and trees. The **Harlem Meer** and its boathouse were recently renovated, and the boathouse now berths the **Dana Discovery Center** (☎ 212/860-1370), where children can learn about the environment and borrow fishing poles at no charge.

There are two main **restaurants** in the park, Tavern on the Green (see "Dining," below) and the Boathouse Cafe. You'll also find food carts selling hot dogs, pretzels, and other snacks.

Even though the park has the lowest crime rate of any of the city's precincts, be wary, especially in the more remote northern end, and avoid the park unless there's a performance or other event after the sun sets.

**Central Park Zoo/Wildlife Conservation Center.** *Near the park entrance at Fifth Ave. and E. 64th St.* ☎ *212/861-6030. Admission $2.50 adults, $1.25 seniors, 50¢ children 3–12, under 3 free. Mon–Fri 10am–5pm, Sat–Sun 10:30am–5:30pm. Subway: N, R to Fifth Ave.* Lithe sea lions frolic in the central pool area with beguiling style. The incomprehensibly gigantic but graceful polar bears glide back and forth across a watery pool that has glass walls through which visitors can observe very large paws doing very smooth strokes. The outdoor monkeys seem to regard those on the other side of the fence with great, and sometimes rude, disdain. Children love the penguin house. In the hot and humid Tropical Zone, large colorful birds swoop around in relative freedom, sometimes even landing right next to the nonplussed visitors. Gardeners should note the interesting plantings all through the zoo. Though relatively small, the Central Park Zoo is still, as Paul Simon once said it, "a gas."

**Cooper-Hewitt National Design Museum.** *2 E. 91st St. (at Fifth Ave.).* ☎ *212/860-6868. Admission $3 adults, $1.50 seniors, free for children under 12; free Tues 5–9pm. Tues 10am–9pm, Wed–Sat 10am–5pm, Sun noon–5pm. Subway: 6 to 86th St.* At the Cooper-Hewitt, part of the Smithsonian Institution, changing exhibits are invariably well conceived, engaging, and educational. The museum is housed in the 64-room Carnegie Mansion, built by steel magnate Andrew Carnegie in 1901. It was the first home in the city with an Otis elevator and central heating. Be sure to visit the garden ringed with Central Park benches from various time periods.

**✪ Ellis Island.** *Located in New York Harbor.* ☎ *212/363-7620 (general info) or 212/269-5755 (ticket and ferry info). Ferry ticket and admission to Statue of Liberty and Ellis Island, $7 adults, $5 seniors, $3 children 3–17. Daily 9:30am–5pm; extended hours in summer. Subway to ticket booth: 4, 5 to Bowling Green; 1, 9 to South Ferry (the platform onto which you exit here is shorter than the train, so ride in the first five cars).* More than 4 out of 10 Americans trace their ancestry to this spot where some 12 million newcomers arrived between 1892 and 1954. The Immigration Museum skillfully relates their story by putting an emphasis on personal experience. You enter the Main Building's baggage room, just as the immigrants did, then climb the stairs to the Registry Room, with its dramatic vaulted tiled ceiling, where millions waited anxiously for medical and legal processing. The Through America's Gate exhibit displays haunting photographs and touching oral histories. In Treasures from Home are objects and photographs donated by descendants of immigrants. Outside, the American Immigrant Wall of Honor commemorates more than 500,000 individuals and families, including some of America's most famous. You won't leave here unmoved.

**○ Empire State Building.** *Fifth Ave. (at 34th St.).* ☎ *212/736-3100. Observatory admission $4.50 adults, $2.25 seniors and children under 12. Daily 9:30am–midnight (tickets sold until 11:30pm). Subway: B, D, F, N, Q, R to 34th St.* Built in 1931, this gleaming structure is the Manhattan skyscraper par excellence with its graceful proportions, fabulous setbacks, and distinctive pinnacle. At an impressive 102 floors, its still among the world's tallest buildings. There are two **observation decks** where you can gaze awestruck down on Manhattan. The 86th-floor observatory, at 1,050 feet, has a glass-enclosed area, but you should head outside into the bracing wind on the terrace (take a pocketful of quarters for the high-power binoculars). The 102nd-floor observatory, at 1,250 feet, is entirely glass enclosed.

**Frick Collection.** *1 E. 70th St. (at Fifth Ave.).* ☎ *212/288-0700. Admission $5 adults, $3 seniors, children under 10 not admitted. Tues–Sat 10am–6pm, Sun 1–6pm. Subway: 6 to 68th St./Hunter College.* Henry Clay Frick, an associate of Andrew Carnegie, built this 18th-century French-style mansion (1914), one of the most beautiful remaining on Fifth Avenue. Most appealing about the Frick is its intimate size and setting. The interior still resembles a private home, albeit one with masterpieces by major European painters. A highlight of the collection is the Fragonard Room, graced with the sensual rococo series *The Progress of Love.* The portrait of Montesquiou by Whistler is stunning. Sculpture, furniture, Chinese vases, and French enamels complement the paintings and round out the collection.

**Intrepid Sea-Air-Space Museum.** *Pier 86 (W. 46th St. at Twelfth Ave.).* ☎ *212/245-0072. Admission $10 adults, $7.50 seniors, $5 children 6–11, first child under 6 free, each additional $1. May–Sept, Mon–Sat 10am–5pm (last admission 4pm), Sun 10am–6pm (last admission 5pm); Oct–Apr, Wed–Sun 10am–5pm (last admission 4pm). Subway: A, C, E to 42nd St. Bus: M42 crosstown.* If you've wondered how jet planes thunder onto ship decks without plunging off the other end, the answer is here at the USS *Intrepid,* a decommissioned aircraft carrier. The world's largest naval museum is dedicated to the history of the U.S. Navy, space and undersea exploration, and aviation. On board are more than 40 aircraft, displays of memorabilia, and lots of skinny halls and winding staircases to wander through. There are also daily guided tours of the destroyer *Edison,* the submarine *Growler,* and lightship *Nantucket,* part of the museum complex. The annual Fleet Week celebration in May brings an invasion of active ships and thousands of service personnel here.

**Jewish Museum.** *1109 Fifth Ave. (at 92nd St.).* ☎ *212/423-3230. Admission $7 adults, $5 seniors, free for children under 12; Tues 5–8pm pay what you wish. Sun, Mon, Wed, Thurs 11am–5:45pm, Tues 11am–8pm. Subway: 6 to 96th St.* A gothic-style mansion gives the Jewish Museum a world-class space to showcase its remarkable collection of Jewish art, history, and culture. The excellent permanent installation "Culture and Continuity: The Jewish Journey" occupies two floors and traces the development of 4,000 years of Jewish experience. There's a great collection of TV programs (Jewish comedy contributed mightily to television's Golden Age in the 1950s).

**○ Metropolitan Museum of Art.** *Fifth Ave. (at 82nd St.).* ☎ *212/535-7710. Suggested admission $8 adults, $4 seniors, free for children under 12; includes admission to the Cloisters. Tues–Thurs and Sun 9:30am–5:15pm, Fri–Sat 9:30am–8:45pm. No strollers allowed Sun. Subway: 4, 5, 6 to 86th St.* The "Met" attracts more visitors than any other site in the city. Its magnificent collections include art from every place and time—nearly the whole world's cultures are on display. And masterpieces from each of them are the rule. Its Egyption collections are justly famous. One good way to get an overview is to take advantage of the little-known **Highlights Tour** (☎ 212/570-3930). For reconstructed medieval architecture and medieval art, head to the **Cloisters,** a branch of the Met in Uptown Manhattan.

**✪ Museum of Modern Art.** *11 W. 53rd St. (Fifth and Sixth aves.).* ☎ *212/ 708-9480. Admission $8.50 adults, $5.50 seniors, free for children under 16; Thurs and Fri 5:30–8:30pm pay as you wish. Sun–Tues 11am–6pm, Thurs–Fri noon–8:30pm. Subway: E, F to Fifth Ave./43rd St.* The Museum of Modern Art (MoMA, or "the Modern" as it's known to New Yorkers) boasts the world's greatest collection of 20th-century art, including everything from van Gogh *(The Starry Night)* and early Picasso *(Les Demoiselles d'Avignon)* to contemporary design. Crowd-pleasing galleries are dedicated to Matisse *(Dance* and *Goldfish)* and Monet *(Water Lilies).* The Sculpture Garden is a rare oasis of sunlight, trees, fountains, and art in Midtown. A self-guided tour stops at the collection's highlights, chosen by the different departments' curators; it's a quick and nearly complete way for first-time visitors to appreciate the museum.

**Museum of Television and Radio.** *25 W. 52nd St. (Fifth and Sixth aves.).* ☎ *212/621-6800. Admission $6 adults, $4 seniors, $3 children 12 and under. Tues–Sun noon–6pm (until 8pm Thurs). Subway: 1, 9 to 50th St.; N, R to 49th St.* Founded in 1975 by William S. Paley, former chairman of CBS, this limestone tower is a repository for more than 75,000 TV and radio programs and commercials spanning more than 7 decades. You can see virtually every famous TV moment—the Beatles' first appearance on *The Ed Sullivan Show,* Neil Armstrong alighting on the moon, the falling of the Berlin Wall (five sections of which can be found, graffiti intact, in front of 520 E. 53rd St.), and much more.

**New York Stock Exchange.** *20 Broad St. (at Wall St.).* ☎ *212/656-5165. Free admission. Mon–Fri 9:15am–4:30pm. Subway: 2, 3, 4, 5 to Wall St.* The world's largest stock exchange is housed in a classic-style building completed in 1903. The highlight of the self-guided visit is the observation gallery overlooking the deceptively orderly and calm trading floor where fortunes are fashioned or destroyed with the flash of a hand signal. Try to be there for the ceremonial opening or closing bell. Free tickets are distributed starting at 9am; lines are long, but things move pretty quickly. You can skip the video and most of the other exhibits along the way to the observation gallery, now lined in glass to prevent shenanigans like the Yippies' tossing down of dollar bills back in the 1970s.

**Rockefeller Center.** *In the area bounded by 48th and 51st sts. from Fifth Ave. to Sixth Ave.* ☎ *212/632-3975. Subway: B, D, F, Q to 47th–50th sts./Rockefeller Center.* An art deco masterpiece of architecture and sculpture, Rockefeller Center's foyers, facades, and gardens showcase works by more than 40 artists. There are also famous murals like *American Progress* and *Time,* by José Marie Sert, in the black marble lobby of the **GE Building,** 30 Rockefeller Plaza, a towering 70-story showpiece with the Rainbow Room ensconced on high. Most dazzling is the interior of the 6,200-seat **Radio City Music Hall,** 1260 Sixth Ave. at 50th Street. You can take the illuminating 1-hour backstage tour of Radio City Music Hall (☎ **212/632-4041**), including an encounter with a Rockette. A walking tour brochure highlighting the center's art and architecture is available at the main information desk in the GE Building. **NBC Studio tours** (☎ **212/664-4000**) leave from the GE Building lobby (no children under 6).

**Solomon R. Guggenheim Museum.** *1071 Fifth Ave. (at 88th St.).* ☎ *212/ 423-3500. Admission $8 adults, $5 seniors, free for children under 12. Sun–Wed 10am–6pm, Fri–Sat 10am–8pm. Subway: 4, 5, 6 to 86th St.* It has been called a bun, a snail, a concrete tornado, and even a gigantic wedding cake tilted to one side. Whatever, Frank Lloyd Wright's only New York building, completed in 1959, is perhaps best summed up as assertively undeniable. It's a brilliant work of architecture, so consistently brilliant it competes with the art for your attention. Inside, a spiraling rotunda circles over a slowly inclined ramp that leads you down and around from the sixth floor past changing exhibitions. Permanent exhibitions of 20th-century art are on display in a new annex called the Tower Galleries.

**South Street Seaport and Museum.** *Water St. to the East River between John St. and Peck Slip.* ☎ *212/669-9400 (general info) or 212/748-8600 (museum). Museum admission $6 adults, $5 seniors, $3 children. Museum, Apr–Sept, daily 10am–6pm, Thurs 10am–8pm; Oct–Mar, Wed–Mon 10am–5pm. Subway: 2, 3, 4, 5 to Fulton St.* You can explore most of this complex on your own, but you'll need a ticket for the museum, whose galleries recount the district's history and whose holdings include the ships berthed at the pier. Start at the South Street Seaport **Visitor Center** at 12 Fulton St. to pick up a free map and guide. On the north side of the street you'll note a row of early 19th-century buildings called **Schermerhorn Row.** These once served as counting houses for the cargo unloaded on the docks at the foot of Fulton. Head next to the third level of Pier 17 overlooking the East River, where you can see south to the Statue of Liberty and north to the Brooklyn Bridge. Across the river is Brooklyn Heights and at the west end of the pier is the famous Fulton Fish Market. The stores here are mostly what you'll find anywhere else, with the great exception of the **Strand bookstore** (art tomes are an especially good buy).

**✪ Staten Island Ferry.** *Departs from the Staten Island Ferry Terminal at the southern tip of Manhattan.* ☎ *212/806-6940. Free. Hours vary seasonally, but it runs 24 hours daily every 20–30 min (less frequently late at night). Subway: 1, 9, N, R to South Ferry.* As this magical ride begins, the ferry loudly churns the waters and tosses out from its old wood-piling–lined slip into New York Harbor. The spectacular city skyline rises and then recedes behind you. As the ferry passes the Statue of Liberty, you're rewarded with the same view that immigrants early in this century had. This is a wonderful alternative to sightseeing cruises and is particularly lovely at night.

**✪ Statue of Liberty.** *On Liberty Island in New York Harbor.* ☎ *212/363-7620 (general info) or 212/269-5755 (ticket and ferry info). Ferry ticket and admission to Statue of Liberty and Ellis Island, $7 adults, $5 seniors, $3 children 3–17. Daily 9:30am–5pm; extended hours in summer. Subway: 4, 5 to Bowling Green; 1, 9 to South Ferry (the platform onto which you exit here is shorter than the train, so ride in the first five cars).* On October 28, 1886, more than a million people watched as the French tricolor veil concealing Lady Liberty's face was pulled away. This gift to the United States from France was meant to commemorate the two countries' friendship dating back to the American Revolution. The statue soon became an enduring symbol of much more, for no other monument so embodies the notion of political freedom and economic potential as does Lady Liberty. Get on the first ferry of the day; otherwise expect a 3-hour wait in line. Ferries depart every 30 to 45 minutes from 9:15am to 4:30pm. Tickets are for sale inside Castle Clinton, in Battery Park, and include transportation and entrance to both the Statue of Liberty and Ellis Island.

**United Nations.** *At First Ave. and 46th St.* ☎ *212/963-7713. Guided tours $7.50 adults, $5.50 seniors and students, $3.50 children (under 5 not permitted). Daily tours every 30 min. 9:15am–4:45pm, except weekends Jan–Feb. Subway: 4, 5, 6, 7, S to 42nd St./Grand Central.* U.N. headquarters occupies 18 acres of international territory—neither New York City nor the United States has jurisdiction here—along the East River from 42nd to 48th streets. The complex, completed in 1952, was designed by an international team of architects. Guided 1-hour tours take you to the General Assembly Hall and the Security Council Chamber and introduce you to the history and activities of the United Nations. Along the tour are donated objects and artwork, including artifacts that survived the atomic bombs at Hiroshima and Nagasaki, stained-glass windows by Chagall, a replica of the first *Sputnik,* and a Norman Rockwell mosaic.

**Whitney Museum of American Art.** *945 Madison Ave. (at 75th St.).* ☎ *212/ 570-3676. Admission $8 adults, $6 seniors, free for children under 12; free Thurs 6–8pm. Wed and Fri–Sun 11am–6pm, Thurs 1–8pm. Subway: 6 to 77th St.* You'll find arguably the finest collection of 20th-century American art in the world here, thanks to the efforts of Gertrude Vanderbilt Whitney, herself a sculptor, who assembled a sizable personal collection and founded the museum in 1930. Her museum is an imposing presence on Madison Avenue—an inverted three-tiered pyramid of concrete and gray granite with seven seemingly random windows, designed by Marcel Breuer (1966), a member of the Bauhaus group. In contrast to the sober exterior, the sprightly figures of Alexander Calder's *Circus* greet you in the entrance. In addition to the permanent collection, there are usually several temporary shows. The Whitney's most important exhibit, the Biennial, is an invitational show of work produced in America during the preceding two years.

**World Trade Center.** *Bounded by Church, Vesey, Liberty, and West sts.* ☎ *212/ 435-4170. Subway: C, E to World Trade Center; 1, 9, N, R to Cortlandt St.* The World Trade Center, created by the Port Authority of New York and New Jersey and opened in 1970, is an immense complex of seven buildings on 16 acres that comprise offices, restaurants, a Marriott hotel, an underground shopping mall, and an outdoor plaza with fountains, sculpture, and summer concerts and performances. Most famous are the tall Twin Towers, each 1,350 feet high at 110 floors, with the world's highest open-air observation deck on the 107th floor of Two World Trade Center (☎ **212/232-2340;** open daily 9:30am–9:30pm, until 11:30pm in summer; $10 adults, $5 children). For a more pampered sky-high viewing experience, make dinner reservations well in advance at **Windows on the World** (see "Dining," below) or stop for a cocktail at the restaurant's Greatest Bar on Earth, both on the 107th floor of One World Trade Center.

**SPORTS** When it comes to professional sports, New York has its fair share of teams and events. Baseball's **New York Yankees** play at famous Yankee Stadium, 161st Street and River Avenue, in the Bronx (☎ **718/293-6000** for the box office or 718/307-1212 for TicketMaster), while the **New York Mets** play at Shea Stadium, 126th Street and Roosevelt Avenue, in Flushing, Queens (☎ **718/507-8499**). Pro basketball's **New York Knicks** play at Madison Square Garden, Seventh Avenue between 31st and 33rd streets (☎ **212/465-JUMP,** or 212/307-7171 for TicketMaster). Hockey's **New York Rangers** also play at Madison Square Garden (☎ **212/308-NYRS** or 212/307-7171 for TicketMaster). Tickets are almost impossible to get for either team. Madison Square Garden (☎ **212/465-6741**) is also a venue for professional boxing.

The **New York Giants** and **New York Jets** both play in Giants Stadium, in the Meadowlands Sports Complex, East Rutherford, New Jersey (☎ **201/935-3900** for the box office or 212/307-7171 for TicketMaster).

You can watch thoroughbreds race at **Belmont Park Racetrack,** Hempstead Turnpike, Elmont, Long Island (☎ **718/641-4700**) and at **Aqueduct Racetrack,** Rockaway Boulevard and 110th Street, Ozone Park, Queens (☎ **718/641-4700**). The famous Belmont Stakes, the third jewel in the Triple Crown, takes place in early June. There's harness racing year-round at **Yonkers Raceway,** Central Avenue, Yonkers (☎ **718/ 562-9500**).

From late August to early September, the hottest ticket in town is to the **U.S. Open Tennis Championships** at the National Tennis Center in Flushing Meadows–Corona Park (☎ **718/760-6200,** or 212/239-6250 for Tele-charge). Tickets go on sale in May. The **Women's Tennis Association Tour Championships** at Madison Square Garden (☎ **212/ 465-6741**) in mid-November attracts the top 16 singles players and 8 doubles teams.

**SHOPPING** One of the beauties of New York shopping is that there are stores everywhere, and every part of the city has a distinct personality. Many chains have shops in each of the various neighborhoods; other stores are only in certain parts of town and have helped define the lifestyle and flavor of their neighborhoods, such as SoHo.

The heart of Manhattan retail is on **Fifth Avenue** at 57th Street, but the avenue changes personality many times as it runs from Uptown to Downtown. Midtown from 59th to 23rd streets is a designer and big-name shopping scene (several new stores have been opening up in the East 50s). Downtown, starting at the famous Flatiron Building on the corner of Fifth Avenue and 23rd Street, is hip and funky. Also note that **Rockefeller Center** has a promenade lined with stores. **57th Street** from Fifth Avenue east to Lexington Avenue has a dense selection of designer boutiques, galleries, antique shops, and discounters. The first block west of Fifth houses many designer shops and unusual specialty stores.

A few years ago **Madison Avenue** was defined as the home of the hotsy-totsy European designers like Ungaro, Givenchy, and Rykiel. Now Madison is alive with affordable choices along with the exorbitant. Upper Madison avenue is like a museum of art galleries and antique shops.

**Greenwich Village** has several personalities and shopping areas. There are serious antiques shops on Bleecker Street and serious coffee and chocolates on Christopher Street. East of Broadway, the **East Village** is the "in" spot for teenagers and tourists alike. Note that this is a night person's playground: Stores don't open until noon or 1pm and stay open until 8pm or later. Street fashions are translated into trends on East 9th from First Avenue to Avenue A. Seventh Street is home to antique shops and new designers and an assortment of eclectic stores. **St. Mark's Place,** 1 block over from East 9th Street, is the place for bootleg tapes and CDs of live concerts.

The most European of New York's neighborhoods, **SoHo** is almost like a small village overlaid with a grid of streets offering cutting-edge art galleries and boutiques. Most don't open until 11am but do stay open until later at night. Mostly, this is the land of the independent dream, where original is the name of the game and the scene is to be seen.

The **Lower East Side** was popular in the days before discounters opened on Sunday everywhere else. Still, if you want some good pickles or pumpernickel, it's a nice place to eat, munch, and discover a part of New York that's really disappearing.

**Chelsea** is the hot new neighborhood for gays and lesbians, so look for trendy new shops along Seventh and especially Eighth avenues. In recent years, galleries have been moving to Chelsea to escape the higher rents along Madison Avenue.

On the **Upper West Side** there's shopping on Columbus Avenue, Amsterdam Avenue, and Broadway from the sixties to the eighties. Small shops line both sides of Columbus and the Sunday flea market in the schoolyard on 78th Street gives you a good look at the neighborhood's lifestyle.

**South Street Seaport** (see "Attractions," above) and nearby **Pier 71** have plenty of branch stores of your favorite chains. The **Financial District** is home of the bulls, the bears, and **Century 21** and **Sym's,** major discounters where you can find name-brand clothing for a fraction of regular retail. There are also excellent business- and formal-wear standbys all over the neighborhood.

New York has lots of famous **department stores.** One of those you've-just-gotta-see-it-before-you-die stores is **Barneys,** 660 Madison Ave., at 61st Street (☎ 212/826-8900)—eight floors of menswear and eight floors of cutting-edge women's wear and accessories. **Bergdorf Goodman,** 754 Fifth Ave., at 57th Street (☎ 212/753-7300), competes with Barneys around the corner for the high-end market. **Bergdorf Goodman Man,** 745 Fifth Ave., at 58th Street (☎ 212/753-7300), is very expensive, but the women's side of the street is more accessible; there's a terrific gift and tabletop floor. The small scale of the shop makes it feel intimate.

You'll find everything at the original **Bloomingdale's,** 1000 Third Ave., at 59th Street (☎ 212/355-5900); **Macy's** at Herald Square, West 34th Street and Broadway (☎ **212/695-4400**); **Lord & Taylor,** 424 Fifth Avenue, at 39th Street (☎ 212/391-3344); and **Saks Fifth Avenue,** 611 Fifth Ave., at 50th Street (☎ **212/ 753-4000**).

## ACCOMMODATIONS

There's one important rule for booking rooms in New York, no matter what the price category: *Always ask for the lowest-priced package available.* Ask what packages are offered; reservation clerks won't volunteer such information—you have to pull it out of them. After you've reserved with the hotel, call a reservation service to see if they have a price better than the one you just negotiated. They can also be helpful if you can't get a room in your favorite hotel, since they often hold reservations themselves. Try **Accommodations Express** (☎ 800/950-4685), **Express Hotel Reservations** (☎ 800/356-1123), or **Hotel Reservations Network** (☎ 800/96-HOTEL).

**Ameritania.** *1701 Broadway (at 54th St.), New York, NY 10019.* ☎ *800/922-0330 or 212/247-5000. Fax 212/247-3316. 183 rms, 14 suites. $165–$205 double; $215–$350 suite. Children 16 and under stay free in parents' room. AE, JCB, MC, V. Parking $20.* Fans of *The Late Show with David Letterman* know Ameritania gift-shop clerks Mujibur and Sirajul, who were discovered by Letterman's prying cameras. With marble baths, guest rooms are comfortable, junior suites ideal for families. There's a small exercise room. Characters, the hotel's restaurant, has a hilarious wait staff who impersonate famous movie stars.

**Barbizon.** *140 E. 63rd St. (at Lexington Ave.), New York, NY 10021.* ☎ *800/ 223-1020 or 212/838-5700. Fax 212/888-4271. 287 rms, 13 suites. $190–$225 double; $375–$800 suite. Children under 12 stay free in parents' room. AE, DC, MC, V. Parking $29.* This neo-Gothic building is the hotel of choice for New Yorkers putting up weekend guests and visiting parents and in-laws. It has recently undergone a $40 million renovation that transformed it into a more upscale, pricier place. There's a new breakfast room and lobby bar/lounge. It has no restaurant, but the neighborhood has lots of good options.

✪ **Carlyle.** *35 E. 76th St. (at Madison Ave.), New York, NY 10021.* ☎ *800/ 227-5737 or 212/744-1600. Fax 212/717-4682. 130 rms, 50 suites. $355–$525 double; $550–$2,400 suite. AE, CB, DC, MC, V. Valet parking $35.* Movie stars and heads of state check into the Carlyle, whose English manor–style decor is luxurious without being excessive. The formal Carlyle Restaurant serves a famous Sunday brunch. Cafe Carlyle supper club is here (see "New York After Dark," below), and charming Bemelmans Bar also offers live entertainment. The Gallery serves afternoon tea. Extras include a concierge, 24-hour room service, business/secretarial services, newspaper delivery, fitness center with sauna and massage.

**Chelsea Savoy Hotel.** *204 W. 23rd St. (at Seventh Ave.), New York, NY 10011.* ☎ *212/929-9353. Fax 212/741-6309. 90 rms. A/C TV TEL. $99–$155 double. Children under 13 free in parents' room. AE, MC, V. Parking $20.* The new Chelsea Savoy is a much-needed addition to Chelsea, a neighborhood suddenly blooming with art galleries and weekend flea markets. While most of the city's new hotels were carved out of existing buildings, the six-story Chelsea Savoy was built from the ground up. The furnishings and decor are simple: There's a large, brightly lit sitting room off the small lobby; the rooms are painted off-white, with plain wood furniture; the boxlike baths are tiled floor to ceiling. To keep the rates low, services and amenities are kept to a minimum. The rooms in back are quieter, but some overlooking Seventh Avenue have Empire State Building views, if you crane your neck.

**Doubletree Guest Suites.** *1568 Broadway (47th St. and Seventh Ave.), New York, NY 10036.* ☎ *800/222-TREE or 212/719-1600. Fax 212/921-5112. 460 suites. $225–$245 suite; $350–$450 conference suite. Extra person $20. Children under 12 stay free in parents' room. AE, DC, DISC, JCB, MC, V. Parking $32.* You get a suite here for less than the cost of a room in most nearby Times Square hotels, and this is a family-friendly hotel with childproof suites and a Kids Club designed by Philadelphia's Please Touch Museum. There are a restaurant and piano bar, concierge, 24-hour room service, free newspaper, and fitness center.

**Drake Swissôtel.** *440 Park Ave. (at 56th St.), New York, NY 10022.* ☎ *800/DRAKENY or 212/421-0900. Fax 212/688-8053. 380 rms, 107 suites. $235–$385 double; $325–$550 one-bedroom suite; $750 two-bedroom suite. Extra person $30. Children 14 and under stay free in parents' room. AE, CB, DC, DISC, EU, JCB, MC, V. Valet parking $24.* The efficient Drake originally was an apartment house, so each room is large. The Kidsôtel program provides children with a welcome backpack, special menu, TV movies, bedtime stories by phone, and milk and cookies at tuck-in time. Guests enjoy the restaurant, 24-hour room service, complimentary limousine service to Wall Street weekday mornings, business center, and fitness center.

✪ **Four Seasons Hotel New York.** *57 E. 57th St. (Park and Madison aves.), New York, NY 10022.* ☎ *800/332-3442 in the U.S., 800/268-6282 in Canada, or 212/758-5700. Fax 212/758-5711. 309 rms, 61 suites. $525–$715 double; $875–$4,500 one-bedroom suite; $2,225–$2,600 two-bedroom suite. Room with terrace $50 extra. AE, DC, DISC, EU, JCB, MC, V. Valet parking $30.* Designed by I. M. Pei, this limestone-clad tower is known for its spectacular interior design and exceptional service. The luxuriously equipped guest rooms are among New York's largest. Fifty-Seven, Fifty-Seven is a popular power-breakfast spot. On the premises guests will find a lobby lounge, concierge, 24-hour room service, 1-hour pressing and valet service, complimentary shoe shine, business center, spa, and fully equipped fitness center.

**Franklin.** *164 E. 87th St. (Lexington and Third aves.), New York, NY 10128.* ☎ *800/600-8787 or 212/369-1000. Fax 212/369-8000. 53 rms. $169–$189 double. Rates include continental breakfast. AE, MC, V. Free parking.* You can stay on the Upper East Side in style without paying outrageous prices here. The small rooms have style—illuminated canopied beds, custom cherrywood-and-steel furniture, cedar closets, and modern baths. Black-and-white photos of the 87th Street area add an extra touch of class. Good service only adds to the hotel's appeal.

**Guest Rooms at the West Side YMCA.** *5 W. 63rd St. (Broadway and Central Park West), New York, NY 10023.* ☎ *800/348-YMCA or 212/787-4400. Fax 212/875-1334. 525 rms, 25 with bath. $65 double without bath; $90 double with bath. MC, V. Parking $10–$20 nearby.* This building next to Lincoln Center and Central Park is a National Historic Landmark, but a multi-million-dollar renovation has made it attractive. Showers and bathrooms are down the hall, but the small rooms do have air-conditioning, TVs, and maid and even room service. Overnight guests can use the athletic facilities. Book early.

**Herald Square Hotel.** *19 W. 31st St. (Fifth Ave. and Broadway), New York, NY 10001.* ☎ *800/727-1888 or 212/279-4017. Fax 212/643-9208. 120 rms, most with bath. $75–$105 standard double; $95–$125 large double. AE, DISC, JCB, MC, V. Parking $18.* Near the Empire State Building, the former home of *Life* magazine is now this clean, comfortable hotel. Welcoming guests is Phillip Martiny's sculpted cherub known as *Winged Life* over the entrance, and *Life* covers adorn the lobby, halls, and rooms. The accommodations are small but have air-conditioning and color TVs.

**Hostelling International New York.** *891 Amsterdam Ave. (at 103rd St.), New York, NY 10025.* ☎ *800/909-4776 or 212/932-2300. Fax 212/932-2574. 624 beds,*

*4 rms with bath. $22–$24 AYH members; $3 additional for nonmembers. Stays limited to 7 days. JCB, MC, V.* Cheap here doesn't mean so-bad-you-could-die, but you do need a sense of adventure. Housed in a 100-year-old renovated neoclassical landmark, the hostel has a coffee bar, a cafeteria, and a large, friendly garden out back where guests mingle. Many restaurants and clubs are nearby, but all tourist attractions are a sometimes long subway ride away.

○ **Hotel Metro.** *45 W. 35th St. (Fifth and Sixth aves.), New York, NY 10001.* ☎ *800/356-3870 or 212/947-2500. Fax 212/279-1310. 155 rms, 20 suites. $150–$200 double; $200–$275 suite. Rates include continental breakfast. AE, DC, MC, V. Parking $18.* Foreign travelers have known for years that this art deco jewel near Herald Square is New York's best budget hotel. The stylish rooms are larger than the price, with phone, data port, voice mail, TVs with movie channels, and marble baths with hair dryers. The rooftop terrace view of the Empire State Building is spectacular.

**Larchmont Hotel.** *27 W. 11th St. (Fifth and Sixth aves.), New York, NY 10011.* ☎ *212/989-9333. Fax 212/989-9496. 55 rms, none with bath. $90–$95 double. Rates include continental breakfast. AE, DC, DISC, MC, V. Parking $20 nearby.* On a landmark brownst1 block in a quiet residential part of the Village, this is one of New York's most affordable and delightful small hotels. You share a bath, but the guest rooms are tastefully done with rattan furniture and writing desks, wash basins, TVs, and ceiling fans. Every floor has a small kitchen. Book well in advance.

**Mansfield.** *12 W. 44th St. (Fifth and Sixth aves.), New York, NY 10019.* ☎ *800/255-5167 or 212/944-6050. Fax 212/764-4477. 103 rms, 26 suites. $225 double; $245 suite; $270–$650 penthouse. Rates include continental breakfast. AE, DC, MC, V. Free parking.* This formerly lackluster property is now a reasonably priced, stylish home away from home. Rooms in this 1904 residence for well-to-do bachelors are tastefully decorated. For the price, the free extras are unequaled: continental breakfast, cappuccino in the lobby, after-theater dessert buffet Monday to Saturday accompanied by live harp music, and best of all, free parking.

**Plaza Hotel.** *768 Fifth Ave. (58th and 59th sts.), New York, NY 10019.* ☎ *800/759-3000 or 212/759-3000. Fax 212/759-3167. 805 rms, 96 suites. $235–$475 double; $500–$15,000 suite. Weekend packages available. AE, DC, DISC, JCB, MC, V. Valet parking $35.* This 1907 French Renaissance–style palace rightfully deserves its National Historic Landmark status and boasts the most idyllic location of any hotel in the city. Some guest rooms are small and lack views, but the amenities throughout are first class. The gardenlike Palm Court is a favorite for tea or Sunday brunch. The Oak Room and Edwardian Room serve in a men's-club setting. The Oyster Bar (not the better one at Grand Central) is a casual fish house/pub. Guests have at their disposal a concierge, 24-hour room service, business services, laundry/valet, free *New York Times,* theater desk, exercise room, and use of a nearby health club.

**Shoreham.** *33 W. 55th St. (Fifth and Sixth aves.), New York, NY 10019.* ☎ *800/553-3347 or 212/247-6700. Fax 212/765-9741. 47 rms, 37 suites. $245 double; $295 suite. Rates include continental breakfast. AE, DC, MC, V. Parking $14.* This boutique hotel is sleekly modern without compromising comfort. The guest rooms have perforated steel headboards through which tiny beams of light shine, sofas and chairs covered in velveteen, refrigerators stocked with complimentary Perrier, cedar-lined closets, and CD players and VCRs. Young children get rubber bath toys. An evening dessert buffet, coffee bar, and health club passes are available.

**Vanderbilt YMCA.** *224 E. 47th St. (Second and Third aves.), New York, NY 10017.* ☎ *212/756-9600. Fax 212/755-7579. 415 rms without bath, 6 suites. $66–$81 double; $81–$91 triple; $101–$121 quad; $121 suite. MC, V. Parking $20 nearby.* This coed Y boasts a friendly, youthful atmosphere and a good Midtown location within walking distance of many key sights. The *tiny* rooms are spartan, but they have TVs, dressers, and desks. The more expensive rooms have sinks; the suites have private baths. You get towels and soap, and there are two pools and athletic facilities. Book early.

✪ **Waldorf-Astoria and Waldorf Towers.** *301 Park Ave. (49th and 50th sts.), New York, NY 10022.* ☎ *800/WALDORF or 212/355-3000. Fax 212/421-8103. 1,180 rms, 200 suites. Waldorf-Astoria: $287–$324 double; $400 minisuite; $450–$800 one-bedroom suite; $675–$875 two-bedroom suite. Waldorf Towers: $425–$450 double; $475–$6,500 suite. AE, DC, DISC, EU, MC, V. Valet parking $34.* The legend lives on thanks to Hilton Hotels' spending $200 million to renovate this quintessential New York hotel. The more expensive Waldorf Towers occupies floors 28 to 42 and has a separate entrance and excellent butler service. Many Tower units have dining rooms, full kitchens, and maid's quarters. The Waldorf Salad was invented in Peacock Alley, the elegant French dining room. Bull & Bear, Oscar's, Ingaiku, and Sir Harry's Bar are other choices. The hotel has a concierge, 24-hour room service, theater and tour desks, business center, fitness center, and beauty salon.

**Washington Square Hotel.** *103 Waverly Place (Fifth and Sixth aves.), New York, NY 10011.* ☎ *800/222-0418 or 212/777-9515. Fax 212/979-8373. 180 rms. $115–$120 double; $122–$140 twin; $144–$160 quad. Rates include continental breakfast. AE, MC, JCB, V. Parking $19 nearby.* Overlooking Washington Square Park in the heart of Greenwich Village, this European-style hotel is family owned and managed. The rooms are plain, compact, and quiet—it's well worth paying a few extra dollars for a larger, recently renovated deluxe room, especially one facing south higher up. Minimum services keep the prices down, but the staff is helpful and accommodating.

## DINING

Nearly every New Yorker has a favorite Chinatown haunt, is convinced of the superiority of a certain Italian hideaway, knows the best place for the ubiquitous pizza by the slice, and claims to control the superlative list of hip sidewalk cafes, cozy gardens, and late-night eateries. Here is the roster of merit.

**Arizona 206.** *206 E. 60th St. (Second and Third aves.).* ☎ *212/838-0440. Reservations recommended. Main courses $18–$29. AE, DC, DISC, MC, V. Mon–Sat noon–3pm; Mon–Thurs 5:30–11pm, Fri–Sat 5:30–11:30pm, Sun 5:30–10pm. Subway: 4, 5, 6 to 59th St.; N, R to Lexington Ave. SOUTHWESTERN.* Here you'll find a sassy Southwestern menu served up in an animated dining room that evokes an adobe. Eclectic entrees such as seared trout with black mole and hash browns rank this hot restaurant among New York's best. **Arizona 206 Cafe** at the same address has comparable great food at gentler prices.

**Bombay Dining.** *320 E. 6th St. (First and Second aves.).* ☎ *212/260-8229. Main courses $5–$11. AE, MC, V. Daily noon–midnight. Subway: F to Second Ave. INDIAN.* Among the dozens of Indian restaurants on this block, Bombay Dining stands out thanks to well-prepared dishes that can't be beat for the price. Main courses include meats, seafood, and vegetables that are well seasoned with mild or hot exotic spices. Bring your own beer or wine and linger to enjoy the live sitar music.

**Bryant Park Grill.** *25 W. 40th St. (in Bryant Park, 42nd St. between Fifth and Sixth aves.).* ☎ *212/840-6500. Reservations recommended. Main courses $10–$20. AE, DC, MC, V. Mon–Sat 11:30am–11:30pm, Sun 11:30am–10:30pm. Subway: B, D, F, Q to 42nd St. CONTEMPORARY AMERICAN.* This solarium-like space is sophisticated and casual, with 1,000 seats inside and on a large terrace. Main courses range from morel mushroom pasta to marinated pork loin. The **Terrace,** on the Grill's roof, serves a cold seafood menu. The less expensive **Cafe** has small tables beneath a canopy of trees for outdoor dining.

**Café Asean.** *117 W. 10th St. (Sixth and Greenwich aves.).* ☎ *212/633-0348. Main courses $7–$13. No credit cards. Sun–Thurs noon–10:30pm, Fri–Sat noon–11:30pm. Subway: A, C, E, L to 14th St. SOUTHEAST ASIAN.* If you're looking for old-fashioned enchantment and inventive Vietnamese, Thai, and Malaysian cooking, this Village spot fits the bill. Dine in a tiny but charmingly simple rustic dining room or a lovely small garden. The curried squid and the shrimp are worth trying. The prices here are a real bargain.

✪ **Daniel.** *20 E. 76th St. (in the Hotel Surrey, Fifth and Madison aves.).* ☎ *212/288-0033. Reservations required 1 month in advance. Jacket/tie required. Main courses $30–$38; fixed-price dinners $69, $85, and $110. AE, DC, MC, V. Tues–Fri noon–2:15pm; Mon–Thurs 5:45–11pm, Fri–Sat 5:45–11:30pm. Closed 1 week in late Aug. Subway: 6 to 77th St. FRENCH.* The *New York Times* awarded chef/owner Daniel Boulud's place four stars, and Patricia Wells named it one of the *world's* top 10 restaurants. You'll forgive the unbridled praise when you experience Daniel's cuisine. The decor is unassuming beige against which the flower arrangements explode with color and the Bernardaud and Limoges china gleams. Be aware that in late 1998 Boulud plans to move his restaurant to the space once occupied by Le Cirque, 620 Park Ave.

**Florent.** *69 Gansevoort St. (Greenwich and Washington sts.).* ☎ *212/989-5779. Reservations recommended. Main courses $8–$18; fixed-price dinner $16.50 (before 7:30pm) or $18.50 (7:30pm–midnight). No credit cards. Mon–Fri 9am–5am, Sat–Sun 24 hours. Subway: A, C, E, L to 14th St. FRENCH BISTRO/DINER.* If you get a 3am craving for homemade rillettes, boudin noir, or steak frites and can't decide whether you'd like to eat with club kids, partying celebrities, cross-dressed revelers, truckers from Jersey, or the odd stockbroker, get down to this nearly 24-hour diner *avec* bistro where you can have it all.

✪ **Gotham Bar & Grill.** *12 E. 12th St. (Fifth Ave. and University Place).* ☎ *212/620-4020. Reservations recommended. Main courses $24–$29. AE, CB, DC, DISC, MC, V. Mon–Fri noon–2:30pm; Sun–Thurs 5:30–10:30pm, Fri–Sat 5:30–11pm. Subway: L, N, R, 4, 5, 6 to 14th St./Union Square. CONTEMPORARY AMERICAN.* This is one of New York's best restaurants and one of the best American-food restaurants anywhere. Much of what we take for "New American" came from chef Alfred Portale's kitchen, and he was the prime architect of "high-rise food"—towers of chicken thighs and other usually low-rise dishes. Dessert chef Won Yee Tom's pear napoleon could conquer any continent.

**Jackson Hole.** *232 E. 64th St. (Second and Third aves.).* ☎ *212/371-7187. Main courses and sandwiches $4.25–$11. AE. Daily 10:30am–1am. Subway: 6 to 68th St. AMERICAN.* This small, satisfying fast-food chain is a couple of giant steps above McDonald's and can placate even the largest appetite. Two trademarked combinations are the Eastsider, a bacon cheeseburger topped with ham, mushrooms, tomatoes, and fried onions, and the Eastsider Bronco, grilled chicken topped with the same. This location has garden dining.

**Jing Fong.** *20 Elizabeth St. (Bayard and Canal sts.).* ☎ *212/964-5256. Reservations recommended. Main courses $9–$20. AE, MC, V. Daily 9am–11pm; dim sum 9am–2pm. Subway: N, R, 6 to Canal St. CHINESE.* This immense, industrial-like hall is justly famous for great dim sum. If you're seated with Chinese at countless round tables, follow their lead in ordering from the dim sum cart. The dumplings are particularly memorable. You also can order fresh seafood at a counter in the center of all the hubbub.

**John's Pizzeria.** *278 Bleecker St. (Sixth and Seventh aves.).* ☎ *212/243-1680. Reservations accepted for six or more. Main courses $6–$16. No credit cards. Mon–Thurs 11:30am–12.30am, Fri–Sat 11:30am–1am, Sun noon–12:30am. Subway: A, B, C, D, E, F, Q to W. 4th St./Washington Square. PIZZA.* Thin-crusted, properly sauced, and fresh, John's pizza has long been one of New York's best. You order a whole pie, not by the slice, so come with friends or family. This place is *popular*, and there's often a wait. Other John's are near Lincoln Center, 48 W. 65th St. (☎ 212/721-7001), and on the Upper East Side, 408 E. 64th St. (☎ **212/935-2895**).

**✪ La Côte Basque.** *60 W. 55th St. (Fifth and Sixth aves.).* ☎ *212/688-6525. Reservations required well in advance. Jacket/tie required. Fixed-price lunch $33; fixed-price dinner $59. AE, DC, MC, V. Mon–Sat noon–2:30pm; Mon–Thurs 5:30–10:30pm, Fri– Sat 5:30–11:30pm, Sun 5:30–10pm. Closed Sun in summer. Subway: E, F to Fifth Ave./53rd St. CLASSIC FRENCH.* For many years, serious New York diners went to La Côte Basque to bask in its sublime food, crisp service, wonderful murals depicting scenes from St-Jean-de-Luz in the Basque area of France—and, most important, to be seen. Now in a new home, with the wonderful murals intact, La Côte Basque serves food as glorious as ever.

**✪ Le Bernardin.** *155 W. 51st St. (Sixth and Seventh aves.).* ☎ *212/489-1515. Reservations required 1 month in advance. Jacket required/tie optional. Fixed-price lunches $32 and $42; fixed-price dinner $68. AE, DC, DISC, JCB, MC, V. Mon–Fri noon– 2:30pm; Mon–Thurs 5:30–10:30pm, Fri–Sat 5:30–11pm. Subway: 1, 9 to 50th St.; N, R to 49th St. FRENCH/SEAFOOD.* Le Bernardin's seafood is probably the best in New York, if not the world. And the fixed-price lunch is a bargain, given the masterful work in the kitchen. The tuna tartare always exhilarates, its Asian seasoning adding a welcome exotic touch. Among lightly cooked dishes that shine are herbed crabmeat in saffron ravioli and a shellfish-tarragon reduction.

**✪ Le Madri.** *168 W. 18th St. (at Seventh Ave.).* ☎ *212/727-8022. Reservations recommended. Main courses $18–$34. AE, DC, MC, V. Mon–Fri noon–2:45pm and 5:30–midnight, Sat–Sun 5–10:30pm. Subway: 1, 9 to 18th St. ITALIAN.* In a former stable redone to resemble a lovely country home in Tuscany, Le Madri strives to provide the best Italian home cooking (the restaurant's name means "mothers"). The menu changes seasonally but the thin-crust pizzas, prepared in wood-burning ovens, and the pastas (like saffron cavatelli with broccoli rape and sausage) are always excellent.

**Lucky Cheng's.** *24 First Ave. (1st and 2nd sts.).* ☎ *212/473-0516. Reservations recommended. Main courses $10–$18. AE, DC, DISC, MC, V. Sun–Thurs 6pm–midnight, Fri–Sat 6pm–2am; brunch Sun noon–4pm. Subway: F to Second Ave. ASIAN FUSION.* With waiters dressed like waitresses, this fun place has a mixed crowd—suits and jeans, yuppies and gays. Bemused out-of-towners spice the brew. The wit and sheer exaggerated abnormality make it impossible to dislike. The food is Asian fusion, with dishes from across the continent. The chicken satay was good and the calamari crisp.

**✪ Mesa Grill.** *102 Fifth Ave. (15th and 16th sts.).* ☎ *212/807-7400. Reservations recommended. Main courses $18–$27. AE, DC, DISC, MC, V. Mon–Fri noon–2:30pm; Sun–Thurs 5:30–10:30pm, Fri–Sat 5:30–11pm; brunch Sat–Sun 11:30am–3pm. Subway: L, N, R, 4, 5, 6 to 14th St./Union Square. SOUTHWESTERN.* Chef/owner Bobby Flay's room with Corinthian columns and "giddyup"-style banquettes feels as if it's on the cutting edge while paradoxically having become a classic. Flay has made a new tradition out of his sometimes thrillingly inventive dishes. The tuna is perfectly cooked, with bracing spices; the pasta specials are innovative and quirky. For delicious and bold food in a more casual setting where the prices are lower, try Flay's new **Mesa City,** 1059 Third Ave. at 63rd Street (☎ **212/207-1919**).

**New Pasteur.** *85 Baxter St. (Bayard and Canal sts.).* ☎ *212/608-3656. Reservations recommended, especially on weekends. Main courses $4–$9. No credit cards. Daily 11am–10pm. Subway: N, R, 6 to Canal St. VIETNAMESE.* In the middle of an unofficial Little Saigon section of Chinatown, the unassuming New Pasteur has some of New York's best Vietnamese food. One of the many outstanding main courses is barbecued fish, which comes whole, tender, and mouth-meltingly delicious. Be prepared for worth-the-wait lines on weekends.

✪ **Nobu.** *105 Hudson St. (at Franklin St.).* ☎ *212/219-0500. Reservations required (accepted 10am–5pm) far in advance. Main courses $20–$30. AE, DC, MC, V. Mon–Fri 11:45am–2:15pm; Mon–Sat 5:45–10:15pm. Subway: 1, 9 to Franklin St. NEW JAPANESE.* This is one of New York's most exciting places, deserving winner of the prestigious James Beard Award for Best New Restaurant of 1995. You'd never think so much could be done to humble raw fish. Traditional Japanese crosses extravagantly with Latin American and nouvelle Californian influences, adding up to flavors you've never encountered.

**Osteria del Circo.** *120 W. 55th St. (Sixth and Seventh aves.).* ☎ *212/265-3636. Reservations recommended. Main courses $16–$27. AE, MC, V. Mon–Thurs 11:30am–2:30pm and 5:30–11pm, Fri–Sat 11:30am–2:30pm and 5:30–11:30pm, Sun 5:30–11pm. Subway: N, R to 57th St. ITALIAN.* In a bright, airy space, this winningly upbeat place is run by the three sons and wife of the legendary Sirio Maccioni, of Le Cirque fame. As befits such a family of restaurateurs, the first review in the *New York Times* awarded Circo a well-deserved two stars.

**Oyster Bar.** *In Grand Central Terminal, lower level (Vanderbilt and Lexington aves.).* ☎ *212/490-6650. Reservations recommended. Main courses $8.95–$28.95. AE, DC, DISC, MC, V. Mon–Fri 11:30am–9:30pm. Subway: 4, 5, 6, 7, S to 42nd St./Grand Central. SEAFOOD.* This New York institution located right in Grand Central Terminal offers a completely new menu every day, since only the freshest fish gets served. The oysters are irresistible. The prices can be steep, so sit at the counter for a filling lunch of smoked rainbow trout appetizer (around $7).

**Patria.** *250 Park Ave. S. (at 20th St.).* ☎ *212/777-6211. Reservations necessary. Main courses $19–$29. AE, DC, MC, V. Mon–Thurs noon–2:30pm and 6–11pm, Fri noon–2:30pm and 5:30pm–midnight, Sat 5:30–midnight, Sun 5–10:30pm. Subway: 6, R to 23rd St. CONTEMPORARY SOUTH AMERICAN.* Maybe it's the potent rum concoctions or the dizzying effect of the trilevel dining room, but Patria's patriots are wildly devoted. Its menu takes a bite from Ecuador, a taste from Colombia, a dash of Dominican, and a pinch of Peru to create a "New Latin" cuisine.

✪ **Rosa Mexicano.** *1063 First Ave. (at 58th St.).* ☎ *212/753-7407. Reservations recommended. Main courses $16–$28. AE, CB, DC, MC, V. Daily 5pm–midnight. Subway: 4, 5, 6, to 59th St.; N, R to Lexington Ave. MEXICAN.* Nachos, burritos, and quesadillas are what most people think are Mexican food, but here you get *real* Mexican foods like rajas, mole poblano, pozole, and ceviche, served up in a pink dining room with polished touches like the hammered-copper service plates and ornate wooden chairs. Grilled meats and seafood also are fine bets.

**Sylvia's Restaurant.** *328 Lenox Ave. (126th and 127th sts.).* ☎ *212/996-0660. Reservations accepted for 10 or more. Main courses $7–$16. AE. Mon–Sat 7:30am–10:30pm, Sun 12:30–7pm. Subway: 2, 3 to 125th St. SOUL FOOD.* The "Queen of Soul Food" since 1962, Sylvia's should also bill itself as Queen of the Bargain. Fried chicken, baked ham, and smothered pork chops will soon put you in mind of swinging slowly on a large wooden porch under the elms as you sip sweetened iced tea.

**Tavern on the Green.** *In Central Park (at W. 67th St.).* ☎ *212/873-3200. Reservations recommended, necessary on holidays. Main courses $13–$30; pretheater fixed-price dinner $23–$25. AE, DC, MC, V. Mon–Fri 11:30am–3:30pm; Sun–Fri 5–11pm, Sat 5pm–1am; brunch Sat–Sun 10am–3:30pm. Subway: 1, 9 to 66th St./Lincoln Center. CONTEMPORARY AMERICAN/CONTINENTAL.* Tiny twinkling lights glimmer on nearby trees and the views of the park are wonderful from Warner LeRoy's Central Park fantasy palace. Ask to be seated in the Crystal Room, where a festive spirit prevails, especially at Christmas. In warm weather, a magical little garden has a "cookout" menu.

Good-value pretheater dinners and fixed-price lunches are available Monday through Friday.

**Tribeca Grill.** *375 Greenwich St. (at Franklin St.).* ☎ *212/941-3900. Reservations recommended. Main courses $16–$26. AE, DC, MC, V. Mon–Thurs 11:30am–2:45pm and 5:30–11pm, Fri 11:30am–2:45pm and 5:30–11:30pm, Sat 5:30–11:30pm, Sun 5:30–9:30pm; brunch Sun 11:30am–2:45pm. Subway: 1, 9 to Franklin St. CONTEMPORARY AMERICAN.* Whether it's co-owner Robert DeNiro, or Bruce Springsteen, or a business powerhouse, Tribeca Grill has them. The restaurant is part of the Tribeca Film Center, where many premieres are held, but takes its integrity seriously. An old mahogany bar and exposed brick walls lend a feeling of historic charm. The food is American with an international touch, especially Japanese.

**✪ Union Square Cafe.** *21 E. 16th St. (Fifth Ave. and Union Square West).* ☎ *212/243-4020. Reservations required. Main courses $18–$28. AE, DC, MC, V. Mon–Sat noon–2:30pm; Sun–Thurs 6–10:30pm, Fri–Sat 6–11:30pm; soup and oysters at bar between lunch and dinner. Subway: L, N, R, 4, 5, 6 to 14th St./Union Square. CONTEMPORARY AMERICAN.* This simple yet sophisticated restaurant has been turning out acclaimed food for 10 years. Limousines of advertising executives, photographers, and publishers line the block, and you'll need dinner reservations weeks in advance. Main courses include crisp roasted lemon-pepper duck, with quinoa-basmati pilaf and spicy pear-apple chutney. Be sure to get some hot garlic potato chips.

**Viceroy.** *160 Eighth Ave. (at 18th St.).* ☎ *212/633-8484. Reservations accepted until 7:30pm. Main courses $8–$19. AE, CB, DC, DISC, MC, V. Mon–Fri 11:30am–3pm; Mon–Wed 5:30pm–midnight, Thurs–Sat 5:30pm–1am; brunch Sat–Sun 11:30am–4pm. Subway: 1, 9 to 18th St. CONTEMPORARY AMERICAN.* It's in Chelsea, so this attractive place is gay-*mobbed.* Rightly popular here are the barbecue quail salad, the seared peppered tuna with stir-fry Asian vegetables, and a very nicely done roast chicken with rosemary, haricots verts, sweet corn, and garlic whipped potatoes. The crowds especially line up for the $12 brunch, so come early.

**✪ Vong.** *200 E. 54th St. (at Third Ave.).* ☎ *212/486-9592. Reservations recommended. Jacket/tie requested. Main courses $19–$32. AE, MC, V. Mon–Fri noon–2:30pm and 6–11pm, Sat 5:30–11pm, Sun 5:30–10pm. Subway: 6 to 51st St.; E, F to Lexington/ Third aves. and 53rd St. FRENCH THAI.* Chef/owner Jean-Georges Vongerichten's vibrant imagination is expressed in both cooking and decor here. Teak wall treatments, liberal use of gold leaf, and a pagoda set a Southeast Asian scene, while a small patio is perfect in warm weather. The cuisine is an exotic fusion of French technique and Thai spices that woos a fashionable crowd.

**✪ Windows on the World.** *One World Trade Center, 107th Floor (on West St., between Liberty and Vesey sts.).* ☎ *212/524-7000. Reservations recommended well in advance. Jacket required. Main courses $23–$35; buffet lunch (Sun 11:30am–3pm) $37.50. AE, CB, DC, JCB, MC, V. Mon–Fri noon–2pm (limited lunch reservations); Mon–Thurs 5–10:30pm, Fri–Sat 5–11:30pm, Sun 5–10pm. Subway: E to World Trade Center; 1, 9, R to Cortlandt St. CONTEMPORARY AMERICAN.* Windows, which had for years reigned over the city from its high perch but disappointed serious diners, has reemerged from a long renovation with a "great dishes of the world" menu in capable kitchen hands. In addition to Windows, the main dining room, there's the **Greatest Bar on Earth** for drinks, à la carte dining, and dancing; the **Skybox,** a smoking lounge where cigars are definitely permitted; and **Cellar in the Sky,** a restaurant that serves five-course fixed-price dinners, with specially chosen wines.

**✪ Zarela.** *953 Second Ave. (50th and 51st sts.).* ☎ *212/644-6740. Reservations recommended. Main courses $13–$17. AE, DC. Mon–Fri noon–3pm; Mon–Thurs 5–11pm,*

*Fri–Sat 5–11:30pm, Sun 5–10pm. Subway: 6 to 51st St.; E, F to Lexington/Third aves. and 53rd St. MEXICAN.* A friendly assortment of connoisseurs come here for Zarela Martinez's unsurpassed authentic Mexican food and Manhattan's best margaritas. The fajitas, grilled marinated skirt steak in flour tortillas, melt in your mouth. Here you'll understand that Mexican food is so much more than you ever thought. The desserts are great, too.

**THEME RESTAURANTS**    It began when the **Hard Rock Cafe** opened in the early 1980s at 221 W. 57th St., between Broadway and Seventh Avenue (☎ 212/459-9320). Actors Arnold Schwarzenegger, Bruce Willis, Sylvester Stallone, and producer/director John Hughes joined forces to back **Planet Hollywood,** 140 W. 57th St., between Sixth and Seventh avenues (☎ 212/333-7827), and an avalanche of copycats soon made West 57th Street the site of the most "theme" restaurants in Manhattan. ✪ **Jekyll & Hyde Club,** 1409 Sixth Ave., between 57th and 58th streets (☎ 212/541-9505), is entered through a small dark room with a sinking ceiling and a fetching corpse. Kids love the laboratory, mausoleum, and observatory dining rooms, all with bizarre artifacts. **Harley-Davidson Cafe,** 1370 Sixth Ave., at 56th Street (☎ 212/245-6000), roars back through 90 years of Hog history. **Motown Cafe,** 104 W. 57th St., between Sixth and Seventh avenues (☎ 212/489-0097), has a proto-Motown group sliding, harmonizing, and wailing its choreographed way through lunch. **Brooklyn Diner USA,** 212 W. 57th St., Broadway and Seventh Avenue (☎ 212/581-8900), looks like an old-fashioned diner on the outside, but inside there are linen tablecloths and fresh-cut flowers, and the food isn't traditional diner fare either: lump crab cakes and Valrhona chocolate fudge sundaes, for example.

Nearby, **Fashion Cafe,** 51 Rockefeller Plaza, at 51st Street (☎ 212/765-3131), is to Coco Chanel what Planet Hollywood is to Fred Astaire. Supermodels Claudia Schiffer, Elle Macpherson, Naomi Campbell, and Christy Turlington joined up with entrepreneur Tommaso Buti to put it together. And the **Official All Star Café,** 1540 Broadway, at 45th Street (☎ 212/840-8326), is creation of jocks Andre Agassi, Wayne Gretzky, Ken Griffey Jr., Joe Montana, Shaquille O'Neal, Monica Seles, and restaurateur Robert Earl. Appropriately, the food is straight from the ballpark—hot dogs and hamburgers, St. Louis ribs, Philly cheese steak sandwiches, and the like.

## NEW YORK AFTER DARK

New York has some of the world's best opera, dance, and classical musicians, plus a wide range of high and low arts, bars, clubs, stand-up comedy, and just about everything else. Broadway and other theater performances are themselves enough to fill a year's vacation.

For the best local listings consult the *New York Times,* especially on Friday and Sunday; the *Village Voice; New York* magazine; and *New York Press.* The **New York Convention and Visitor Bureau** (☎ 800/NYC-VISIT) is a gold mine of information about the after-dark scene. **NYC/On Stage** (☎ 800/STAGE-NY or 212/768-1818 in New York State) is a recorded service giving schedules of theater and performance, dance and music, the off-price TKTS booths (see below), and family entertainment. Once you've listened to descriptions, you can be transferred to a ticket seller like **Tele-charge** (☎ 212/239-6200) or **TicketMaster** (☎ 212/307-4100).

If you arrive without tickets, call the box offices first. You can make rounds of Broadway theaters about 6pm, when unclaimed "house seats" are made available to the public at face value. The **TKTS booth,** 47th Street and Broadway, sells discounted day-of-performance tickets for both Broadway and off-Broadway shows (open daily 3–8pm for evening performances, 10am–2pm for Wed and Sat matinees, noon–6:30pm Sun for all performances; cash and traveler's checks only, with small surcharge). The TKTS outlet on the mezzanine of Two World Trade Center usually has shorter lines and you wait indoors. **Broadway Cares/Equity Fights AIDS** (☎ 212/840-0770) doubles face value but donates half to people with AIDs. Some hotel concierges hold tickets or can provide them for a fee.

**THE PERFORMING ARTS**   Not even London has better theater than New York. Professional, wacky, or both, New York theater is a metaphor for the city itself—always on, often uplifting and engaging, occasionally disenchanting or exasperating. Note that the terms *Broadway, Off Broadway,* and *Off Off Broadway* don't necessarily refer to location—many are in Times Square on 44th and 45th streets, or along the blocks of Sixth to Eighth avenues, north to about 53rd Street. There's even a Broadway theater outside Times Square, the Vivian Beaumont, in Lincoln Center at Broadway and 65th Street.

As it is for the theater, New York is one of the world's capitals for opera, classical music, and dance. Most organizations limit their major offerings to "seasons" between about September and May, though summer is full of festivals and free outdoor performances. The ☻ **Metropolitan Opera** in Lincoln Center, at the **Metropolitan Opera House,** Broadway and 64th Street (☎ 212/362-6000), produces a classic repertory and full schedule of grand sopranos and tenors. The **New York City Opera** (☎ 212/ 870-5570) in Lincoln Center at the **New York State Theater,** is another superb company with a more innovative repertory.

The ☻ **New York Philharmonic** (☎ 212/875-5030), plays everything from Bach to the avant garde, often with classical international stars as soloists, at **Avery Fisher Hall** in Lincoln Center. There's a summer season in July. Chamber music, recitals, and smaller concerts take place at **Alice Tully Hall,** just across 65th Street from Lincoln Center (☎ 212/875-5050). The renowned **Juilliard School,** 60 Lincoln Center Plaza, Broadway and 65th Street (☎ 212/769-7406), sponsors about 550 performances of high quality—and at the lowest prices (it's one of New York's greatest cultural bargains). **Bargemusic,** at the Fulton Ferry Landing just south of the Brooklyn Bridge in Brooklyn (☎ 718/624-2083), is a 40-year-old barge transformed into an internationally reputed recital room.

New York is a mecca for dance. The **New York City Ballet,** at the New York State Theater in Lincoln Center  (☎ 212/870-5570), is one of the world's best and renders with happy regularity the works of two of America's most important choreographers, George Balanchine and Jerome Robbins. The **American Ballet Theatre** and other major companies visit the Metropolitan Opera House May–July, when the opera season is over (☎ 212/362-6000). The Moorish palace–style **City Center,** 131 W. 55th St. (☎ 212/581-7907), hosts regular performances by such companies as Merce Cunningham, Martha Graham, Paul Taylor, and Alvin Ailey. The City Center is also home to the Manhattan Theatre Club and the Encore! series of great American musicals in concert.  The **Joyce Theater,** 175 Eighth Ave. at 19th Street (☎ 212/ 242-0800), a rehabbed neighborhood movie house, has everything from Native American ceremonial dance to the Bill T. Jones/Arnie Zane Dance Company.

**MAJOR CONCERT HALLS & LANDMARK VENUES**   In addition to its major music and dance tenants, **Lincoln Center for the Performing Arts** (☎ 212/ 875-5400) is a focal point of creative and social energy. There's jitterbugging in summer, big bands in the central Fountain Plaza, and jazz orchestras conducted by Wynton Marsalis. (call Tele-charge, ☎ 212/239-6200); The Broadway Theater Vivian Beaumont and the Off Broadway Mitzi E. Newhouse (call Tele-charge, ☎ 212/239-6200), and the Walter Reade Theater, home of the highly respected New York Film Festival (☎ 212/875-5600), are also here.

Perhaps the world's most famous performance space, ☻ **Carnegie Hall,** 57th Street and Seventh Avenue (☎ 212/247-7800), offers everything from grand classics to Liza Minnelli overdoing it live.

The ○ **Brooklyn Academy of Music,** 30 Lafayette Ave., Brooklyn (☎ 718/636-4100), is the site of some of New York's most important contemporary performances— dance, performance art, outdoor jazz concerts, experimental theater, and visiting opera companies. Especially important is the Next Wave Festival with new works by re- nowned and more experimental American and international artists, held October to December.

The stunningly beautiful, 6,200-seat art deco ○ **Radio City Music Hall,** 1260 Sixth Ave. at 50th Street (☎ 212/247-4777), continues to be a choice venue, where the the- ater alone adds a dash of panache to any performance. It features the Rockettes, the Christmas and Easter pageants, and various visiting chart-toppers, mostly in the pop- music category.

When the Knicks and Rangers aren't playing, **Madison Square Garden,** Seventh Avenue from 31st to 33rd streets (☎ 212/465-MSG1), fills its 20,000 seats with rock concerts (you may have to squint to see Tina Turner). In the same complex and with the same phone number, **The Theater at Madison Square Garden** is a 5,600-seat amphitheater-style auditorium that hosts major pop stars as well as shows like *The Wizard of Oz.*

Up in Harlem, the **Apollo Theater,** 253 W. 125th St. between Adam Clayton Powell Jr. and Frederick Douglass blvds. (☎ 212/749-5838), became famous in the 1930s when it featured Count Basie, Duke Ellington, Ella Fitzgerald, and Billie Holiday. Today it's internationally renowned for its African-American acts of all musical genres.

**JAZZ & ROCK**   The ○ **Knitting Factory,** 74 Leonard St. between Broadway and Church Street (☎ 212/219-3055), has firmly established itself as Downtown's premier cutting-edge arts venue for alternative rock, experimental jazz, videos, and more on its main stage and the AlterKnit Theater. The Tap Bar serves microbrewed beers, shows films, and hosts the Late Night Players Hang.

Wear black to ○ **CBGB & OMFUG,** 315 Bowery at Bleecker Street (☎ 212/ 982-4052), with its roots in the prehistory of the New York punk–and–art-school rock movement. It launched such stars as the Ramones, Blondie, and Talking Heads and is as close as New York gets to a rock-and-roll hall of fame.

For jazz, the ○ **Blue Note, Jazz Club & Restaurant,** 131 W. 3rd St. at Sixth Av- enue (☎ 212/475-8592), attracts the biggest names to its intimate setting. With door charges that can rise to $60 and a drink minimum (usually about $5), it can get expen- sive, but you'll hear the greatest of the great. Dinner is served (about $30–$35 per person).

**CABARETS**   No other city has anything to match the range of choices, quality of per- formers, or simple chic of New York's best cabarets. All those who know cabaret need to know is that Bobby Short plays at the ○ **Cafe Carlyle,** in the Carlyle Hotel, 781 Madison Ave. at 76th Street (☎ 212/744-1600). He's the quintessential suave, witty, and intelligent interpreter of the greats like Porter and the Gershwins. Eartha Kitt also does her purring here. Closed in summer.

It used to be a gay bar, but the **Duplex Cabaret,** 61 Christopher St. at Sheridan Square (☎ 212/255-5438), draws a decidedly mixed clientele. The upstairs cabaret runs the gamut from drag revues to stand-up comedy. Classic Manhattan chic reigns at ○ **Rainbow & Stars,** 30 Rockefeller Plaza, 30th floor, 49th and 50th streets (☎ 212/632-5000 for reservations or 212/632-5100 for information), where the dramatic art deco decor and views over the city enhance superb vocalists from Tony Bennett to Rosemary Clooney. There's dancing on a revolving floor. Jackets and ties are required.

**DANCE CLUBS**   The cartographers of cool are continuously remapping their noctur- nal dance world. The terribly hip **Mother,** 432 W. 14th St., at Washington Street

(☎ 212/366-5680), hosts various events throughout the week, such as Jackie 60 (☎ 212/677-6060) on Tuesday, wherein the mood of Warhol and the Velvet Underground is resurrected by the art-graduate crowd mixed with professional nightlifers, cross-dressers, and other denizens of the dark. This is what still gives New York a cool-camp edge. There are occasional performances, poetry readings, and the like.

**Nell's,** 246 W. 14th St. (☎ 212/675-1567), is civilized and attracts everyone from gays to Wall Streeters. The glamorous **Roxy,** 515 W. 18th St., at Tenth Avenue (☎ 212/645-5156), could be the single best place to see the Manhattan night mix: fashion models, wide-eyed suburban kids, straight folk (on Friday), and gays (Saturday after 1am), lights, sound, and action. There's even in-line skating to music on Tuesday (predominantly gay) and Wednesday (mixed). And a $12-million renovation of what used to be the Village Gate has established **Life,** 158 Bleecker St. at Thompson Street (☎212/420–1999), as the dance club hotspot—for the moment. The formula changes every night.

**THE BAR SCENE**   Elegant or rough, unassuming or frenetic, the New York bar scene encompasses something for everyone, whether you like to wear a tuxedo, a Marie Antoinette–style wig, basic black with pearls, or jeans and a Gap T-shirt. Many bars in the city stay open until 4am or later, but by law they must close for at least 2 hours during any 24-hour period.

There's no sign at the superbly appointed **Merc Bar,** 151 Mercer St. (☎ 212/966-2727), but just look for the steady stream of beautiful people flowing in. This is SoHo at its most fabulous. **McSorley's Old Ale House,** 15 E. 7th St., between Second and Third avenues (☎ 212/473-9148), claims to be New York's longest-established watering hole, supposedly founded in 1854. It's a must-see for a glimpse of old New York. The clandestine **Chumley's,** 86 Bedford St., between Grove and Barrow streets (☎ 212/675-4449), feels as if you're sneaking into a slightly disreputable place. The door is unmarked, with a grill on the small window; another entrance is at 70 Barrow St., where you go in through a back courtyard. **B. Smith's,** 771 Eighth Ave., at 47th Street (☎ 212/247-2222), a stylish Theater District hangout, is for the well dressed and well heeled, especially a suave African-American crowd. The **King Cole Room,** in the St. Regis Hotel, 2 E. 55th St., at Fifth Avenue (☎ 212/339-6721), is great for a sophisticated tête-à-tête. The real oak in the **Oak Bar,** in the Plaza Hotel, 768 Fifth Ave. at 59th Street (☎ 212/546-5320), sets a warm and elegant tone everywhere. Sumptuous red chairs and old-time waiters dressed as properly as the clientele paint the right mood for a power after-work drink.

**THE LESBIAN & GAY SCENE**   Everything you could want—and many things you fear—is in Manhattan. To get a thorough, up-to-date take on what's happening in gay and lesbian nightlife, pick up a free copy of *Homo Xtra (HX);* another choice is *Next* magazine, also free. Always remember that asking other people in one bar can lead you to discover another that fits your taste—or tastelessness.

As its name implies, **The Clit Club,** at Mother, 432 W. 14th St. at Washington Street (☎ 212/366-5680), becomes the site of a very hip women's scene on Friday, when the likes of Madonna have been spotted. **Meow Mix,** 269 E. Houston St. (☎ 212/254-1434), is now a fixture on the women's scene. **Stonewall,** 53 Christopher St., east of Seventh Avenue South (☎ 212/463-0950), draws a mixed male crowd—old and young. At **g,** 223 W. 19th St. between Seventh and Eight avenues (☎ 212/919-1085), you'll find big crowds of big muscles, making it a popular place for meeting dream dates. If your idea of masculine beauty is buffed bodies and beefed go-go boys, **Champs,** 17 W. 19th St. (☎ 212/633-1717), is your place. Very popular, very cruisy. Preppy gays mixed with gym bunnies watch the go-go guys get wet onstage at **Splash,** 50 W. 17th St. (☎ 212/691-0073). The crowd includes lots of visitors as well as locals. **The Web,** 40 E. 58th St., between Madison and Park avenues (☎ 212/308-1546), formerly known as Club 58, is a cellar full of noise, with many different events throughout the week for a heavily Asian crowd (and the Western men who love them). Go late or it's Dullsville.

## 2　Boston & Cambridge

In a glorious waterfront setting that has attracted travelers for hundreds of years, Boston offers cosmopolitan sophistication on a comfortable scale. From the narrow, crowded streets near the harbor to the spacious boulevards along the Charles River, a sense of history permeates the city. Eighteenth-century landmarks sit alongside space-age office towers, and the thousands of students who make the area feel like the world's biggest college town rush to lectures in red-brick buildings.

The Boston area (including adjacent Cambridge) balances romantic celebration of the past and pursuit of the future. Skyscrapers bear plaques describing the deeds and misdeeds of centuries past. The city's museums showcase the treasures of antiquity and cutting-edge technology. And the waterfront has been reclaimed from squalor and disrepair and restored to a condition that outshines its former glory.

It's not perfect, of course. Even a brief visit will confirm that the city's drivers have earned their terrible reputation, and the local accents are as ear-splitting as any in Brooklyn or Chicago. Wander into the wrong part of town and you may be ordered to "pahk yuh cah" (park your car) somewhere else—pronto. And college town or not, there isn't much of a late-night scene outside of convenience stores and photocopy shops.

### ARRIVING & DEPARTING

**BY PLANE**　Most major domestic and international carriers fly into Boston's **Logan International Airport** (☎ 617/561-1919), in East Boston, 3 miles across the harbor from downtown. The **subway** (known as the "T" by locals) is cheap (85¢) and fast (10 minutes to Government Center). Free shuttle buses run from each terminal to the airport subway station 5:30am–1am.

Some hotels have their own **limos;** ask about them when you make your reservations. A **cab** from the airport to downtown costs $16–$22. The ride into town takes anywhere from 10 to 45 minutes, depending on the time of day. If you must travel during rush hour or on Sunday afternoon, allow extra time, or take the subway.

The **Airport Water Shuttle** cruises to Rowes Wharf on Atlantic Avenue, a 7-minute cruise (perfect for the Boston Harbor Hotel, Marriott Long Wharf, or cab service). Courtesy buses from all terminals connect with the heated boats, which sail every 15 minutes 6am–8pm weekdays, every half hour on Friday until 11pm, Saturday 10am–11pm, Sunday 10am–8pm. The one-way fare is $8 for adults, $4 for senior citizens, free for children under 12.

If you're headed for the suburbs, the Massachusetts Port Authority coordinates **bus service** (☎ 800/23-LOGAN) from the airport to suburban hubs in Braintree, Framingham, and Woburn. You can also try the **Share-A-Cab booths** at each terminal and save up to half the fare. **Limousine** and bus service north, south, and west of the city is available, usually by prearrangement. Call **Carey Limousine Boston** (☎ 800/743-2282 or 617/623-8700) or **Stagecoach Executive Sedan Services, Inc.** (☎ 800/922-9500 or 617/723-9393).

**BY TRAIN & BUS**　Boston has three rail centers: **South Station** on Atlantic Avenue, **Back Bay Station** at 145 Dartmouth St., and **North Station** on Causeway Street. Amtrak (☎ 800/USA-RAIL or 617/482-3660) serves South Station and Back Bay Station. The T's red line stops at South Station, while the orange line connects Back Bay Station with the rest of the city. The **MBTA** (☎ 617/222-3200) operates trains to

Ipswich, Rockport, and Fitchburg from North Station, and commuter lines to points south of Boston from South Station.

The **South Station Transportation Center** (a fancy name for the bus terminal) is at 700 Atlantic Ave., right next to the train station. It's the city's hub for **Greyhound** (☎ **800/231-2222** or 617/526-1810), **Peter Pan Trailways** (☎ **800/343-9999**), and other bus companies.

## ESSENTIALS

**VISITOR INFORMATION**  The **Greater Boston Convention and Visitor Bureau,** P.O. Box 990468, Prudential Tower, Suite 400, Boston, MA 02199 (☎ **800/888-5515** outside MA or 617/536-4100; fax 617/424-7664), offers a free travel planner, a comprehensive guidebook, and a *Kids Love Boston* guidebook. It operates **Boston by Phone** (☎ **800/SEE-BOSTON**), providing information on attractions, dining, performing arts and nightlife, shopping, and travel services.

You can also contact the **Massachusetts Office of Travel and Tourism,** 100 Cambridge St., 13th floor, Boston, MA 02202 (☎ **800/447-6277** or 617/727-3201; fax 617/727-6525; e-mail: vacationinfo@state.ma.us); they'll send you a free "Getaway Guide" magazine that includes information about attractions and lodgings, a map, and a seasonal calendar. For information about Cambridge, contact **Cambridge Discovery, Inc.,** P.O. Box 1987, Cambridge, MA 02238 (☎ **617/497-1630**). Information about Boston is also available on the Internet. The Convention and Visitor Bureau's site at **http://www.dvm.com/users/dvm/boston** offers listings of visitor services that can be reached through toll-free numbers.

Once you're in town, three convenient visitor centers are open daily: the **Boston National Historic Park Visitor Center,** 15 State St. (☎ **617/242-5642**), which is staffed by National Park Service rangers; and the **Boston Common Information Center,** 146 Tremont St., and **Prudential Information Center,** Center Court, Prudential Center main level, 800 Boylston St., both run by the Greater Boston Convention and Visitor Bureau (☎ **617/536-4100**). In Cambridge, **Cambridge Discovery,** P.O. Box 1987, Cambridge, MA 02238 (☎ **617/497-1630**), operates an information kiosk in the heart of Harvard Square.

**RESOURCES FOR TRAVELERS WITH SPECIAL NEEDS**  Boston offers many discounts to **seniors** with identification. Seniors can ride the MBTA subways for 20¢ and local buses for 15¢. You must purchase an MBTA senior citizen card, available at the Downtown Crossing "T" station (☎ **617/222-5438**) weekdays 8:30am–4:15pm.

An excellent source of information for the disabled is the **Information Center for Individuals with Disabilities,** 29 Stanhope St., 4th floor, P.O. Box 256, Boston, MA 02117 (☎ **800/462-5015** in MA or 617/450-9888; TDD: 617/424-6855). Although Boston has made progress, some wheelchair-dependent travelers have recently reported difficulty negotiating curbs and buses. All MBTA buses should have lifts or kneelers (call ☎ **800/LIFT-BUS** for more information). The green line subway is not wheelchair accessible, but most stations on other lines are. In addition, there is now an **Airport Handicap Van** (☎ **617/561-1769**).

The **Gay and Lesbian Helpline** (☎ **617/267-9001**) offers information Mon–Fri 4–11pm, Sat 6–8:30pm, and Sun 6–10pm. You can also contact the **Boston Alliance of Gay and Lesbian Youth,** or BAGLY (☎ **800/422-2459**). *In Publications,* 258 Shawmut Ave., Boston, MA 02118 (☎ **617/426-8246**), and *Bay Windows,* 1523 Washington St., Boston, MA 02118 (☎ **617/266-6670**), publish weekly newspapers that concentrate on upcoming gay-related events, news, and features.

**EMERGENCIES**  Call ☎ **911** for fire, ambulance, or the Boston, Brookline, or Cambridge police. For the state police, call ☎ **617/523-1212. Massachusetts**

# Boston

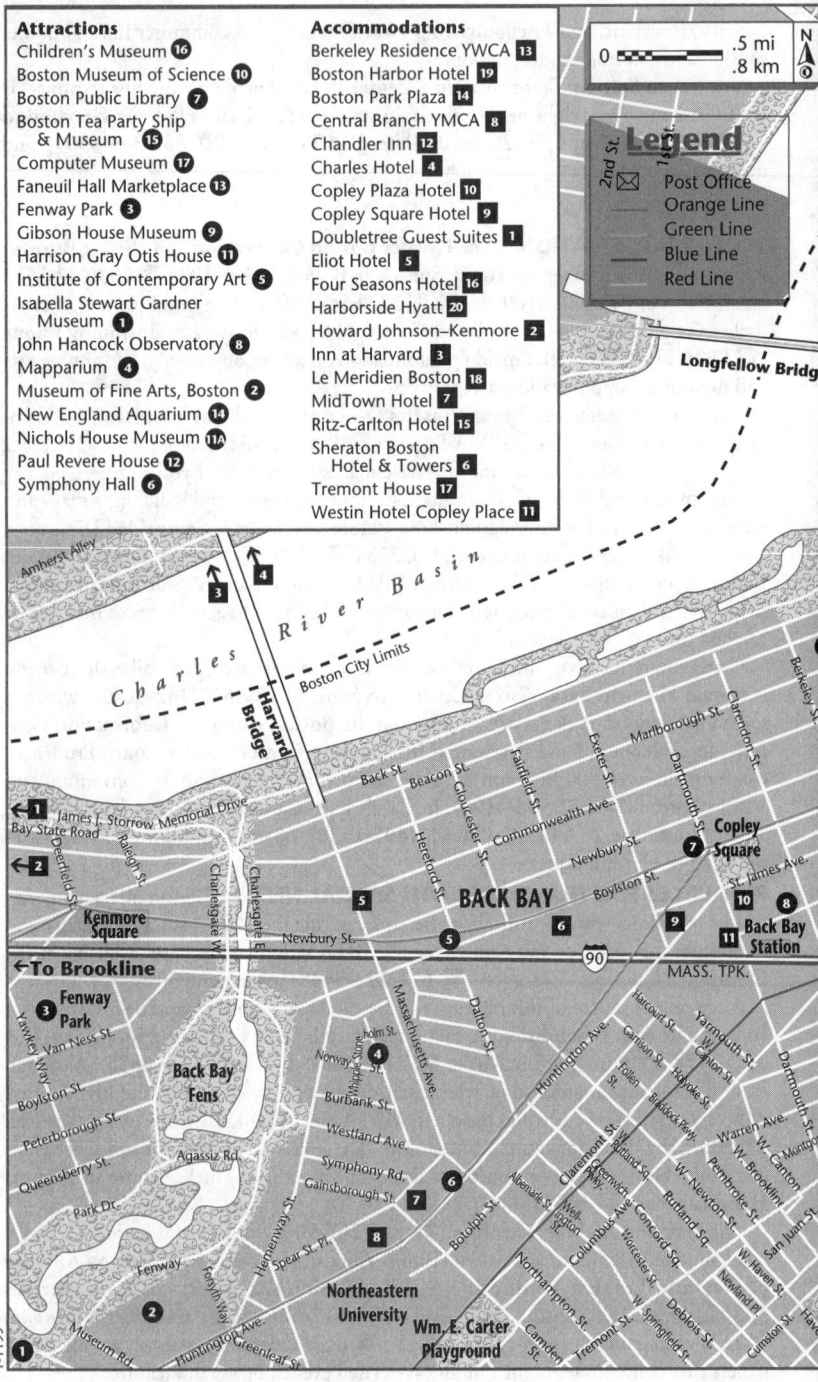

## Attractions

Children's Museum **16**
Boston Museum of Science **10**
Boston Public Library **7**
Boston Tea Party Ship & Museum **15**
Computer Museum **17**
Faneuil Hall Marketplace **13**
Fenway Park **3**
Gibson House Museum **9**
Harrison Gray Otis House **11**
Institute of Contemporary Art **5**
Isabella Stewart Gardner Museum **1**
John Hancock Observatory **8**
Mapparium **4**
Museum of Fine Arts, Boston **2**
New England Aquarium **14**
Nichols House Museum **11A**
Paul Revere House **12**
Symphony Hall **6**

## Accommodations

Berkeley Residence YWCA **13**
Boston Harbor Hotel **19**
Boston Park Plaza **14**
Central Branch YMCA **8**
Chandler Inn **12**
Charles Hotel **4**
Copley Plaza Hotel **10**
Copley Square Hotel **9**
Doubletree Guest Suites **1**
Eliot Hotel **5**
Four Seasons Hotel **16**
Harborside Hyatt **20**
Howard Johnson–Kenmore **2**
Inn at Harvard **3**
Le Meridien Boston **18**
MidTown Hotel **7**
Ritz-Carlton Hotel **15**
Sheraton Boston Hotel & Towers **6**
Tremont House **17**
Westin Hotel Copley Place **11**

## Legend

✉ Post Office
Orange Line
Green Line
Blue Line
Red Line

0 .5 mi
.8 km

N

Longfellow Bridge

*Charles River Basin*

Boston City Limits

Amherst Alley

Harvard Bridge

James J. Storrow Memorial Drive
Bay State Road

Back St.
Beacon St.
Marlborough St.
Commonwealth Ave.
Newbury St.
Boylston St.
St. James Ave.

Deerfield St.
Raleigh St.
Charlesgate E.
Charlesgate W.
Hereford St.
Gloucester St.
Fairfield St.
Exeter St.
Dartmouth St.
Clarendon St.
Berkeley St.

Kenmore Square

**BACK BAY**

Copley Square

Back Bay Station

Newbury St.

←To Brookline

Fenway Park
Yawkey Way
Van Ness St.
Boylston St.
Peterborough St.
Queensberry St.
Park Dr.

Back Bay Fens

Agassiz Rd.

Westland Ave.
Burbank St.
Norway St.
Whipple St.
Stoneholm St.
Symphony Rd.
Gainsborough St.

Massachusetts Ave.
Dalton St.

Huntington Ave.
Harcourt St.
Garrison St.
Follen St.
Braddock Pwy.

MASS. TPK.
90

Fenway
Forsyth Way
Hemenway St.
Spear St. Pl.

**Northeastern University**
**Wm. E. Carter Playground**

Museum Rd.
Huntington Ave.
Greenleaf St.

Claremont St.
Greenwich St.
Concord Sq.
Columbus Ave.
Worcester Sq.
Northampton St.
Albemarle St.
Melnea Station
Botolph St.

Warren Ave.
W. Canton St.
Pembroke St.
W. Brookline St.
W. Newton St.
Rutland Sq.
W. Canton St. Montgomery
Newland Pl.
W. Springfield St.
W. Dedham St.
Tremont St.
Camden St.
Cunston St.

Yarmouth St.
Holyoke St.
St. San Juan St.
W. Haven St.

Columbus Ave.
Concord St.
Rutland St.
Worcester St.
Deblois St.
Springfield St.

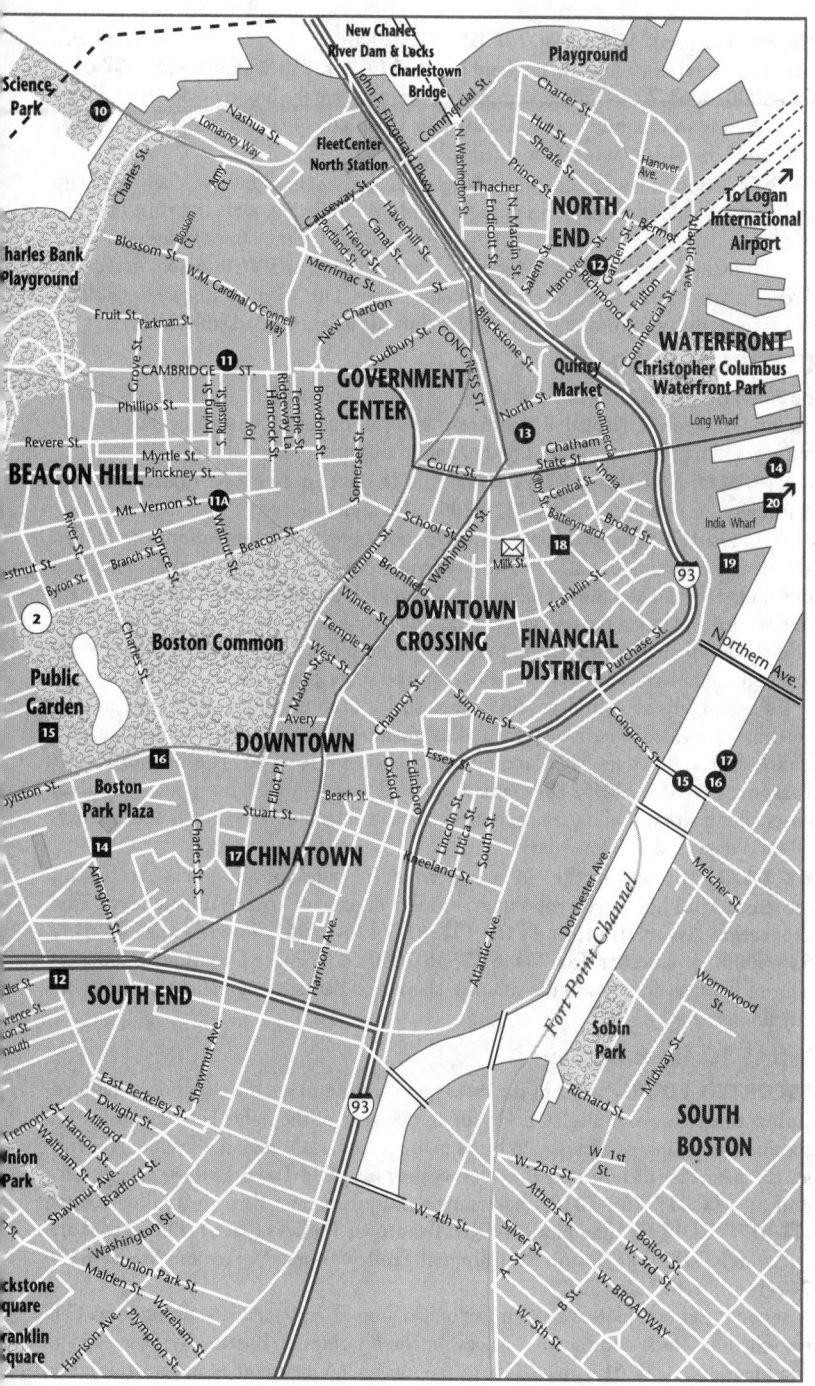

**General Hospital,** 55 Fruit St. (☎ **617/726-2000,** or 617/726-4100 for children's emergency services), and **New England Medical Center,** 750 Washington St. (☎ **617/636-5000,** or 617/636-5566 for emergency services), are the hospitals closest to downtown Boston. In Cambridge go to **Cambridge Hospital,** 1493 Cambridge St. (☎ **617/498-1000,** or 617/498-1429 for emergency services).

**SAFETY**   Boston is a safe city for walking, though the general caveats of any large city still apply. Stay out of the parks at night unless you're in a crowd, and trust your instincts—a dark, deserted street is probably deserted for a reason. Specific areas to avoid at night include Boylston Street between Tremont Street and Washington Street, and Tremont Street from Stuart Street to Boylston Street. The "Combat Zone," or red-light district, has shrunk almost out of existence, but the neighborhood still isn't great.

## GETTING AROUND

Boston bills itself as "America's Walking City," and walking is by far the easiest way to get around. Legend has it that the streets were laid out along cow paths, but the layout owes more to 17th-century London and to Boston's original shoreline.

**BY PUBLIC TRANSPORTATION**   The **Massachusetts Bay Transportation Authority,** or MBTA (☎ 617/222-3200), also known as the "T" (its logo is the letter T in a circle), runs the subways, trolleys, and buses in Boston and many suburbs, as well as the commuter rail. The **subways** and green line trolleys will take you around Boston faster than any other mode of transportation except walking. The subways are color coded and called the red, green, blue, and orange lines (commuter rail to the suburbs shows up on system maps in purple). The local fare is 85¢, and tokens are available at all stations. Service begins about 5am and shuts down around 12:30am.

Buses and "trackless trolleys" (indistinguishable from buses except for their electric antennae) provide service crosstown and to and around the suburbs. The local bus fare is 60¢; express buses are $1.50 and up. Exact change is required. The **Boston Visitor Passport** (☎ 617/222-5218) grants unlimited travel on all subway lines and local buses, plus discounts on museums, restaurants, and entertainment. It costs $5 for 1 day, $9 for 3 days, and $18 for 7 days.

**BY TAXI**   All taxis in the city are metered. They're not always easy to flag on the street. Most hotels have cab stands, or call a dispatcher: try the **Independent Taxi Operators Association,** or ITOA (☎ 617/426-8700), **Town Taxi** (☎ 617/536-5000), or **Checker Taxi** (☎ 617/536-7000). The Police Department publishes a list of flat rates for trips to the suburbs; charging a flat rate is not allowed within the city limits.

## WHAT TO SEE & DO

**ESCORTED TOURS**   One of the most popular ways to see the city is on a narrated **trolley tour.** Use your all-day ticket for an overview of the sights before focusing on specific attractions, or as a way to hit as many places as possible in a few hours. Trolley companies are identified by the colors of their cars. **Old Town Trolley,** 329 W. Second St. (☎ 617/269-7010), has orange-and-green cars; **Boston Trolley Tours** (☎ 617/TROLLEY) uses blue cars; **Red Beantown Trolleys** (☎ 617/236-2148) are red; and the **Discover Boston Multilingual Trolley Tours,** 73 Tremont St. (☎ 617/742-1440), vehicle is white.

If you prefer to explore with your feet on the ground, try a guided **walking tour.** Call for schedules, fees, and meeting places for the offerings of·**Boston By Foot,** 77 N. Washington St. (☎ 617/367-2345, or 617/367-3766 for recorded information); the **Society for the Preservation of New England Antiquities,** 141 Cambridge St. (☎ 617/227-3956); the **Historic Neighborhoods Foundation,** 99 Bedford St. (☎ 617/426-1885); and the **Boston Park Rangers** (☎ 617/635-7383).

Perhaps the best way to see Boston is with **Boston Duck Tours** (☎ 617/ 723-DUCK) aboard a "duck," a reconditioned World War II amphibious landing craft, which departs from behind the Prudential Center at 101 Huntington Ave. The 80-minute narrated tour hits the key attractions, but the real high point comes when the duck lumbers down a ramp and splashes into the Charles River for a spin around the basin.

**SIGHTSEEING CRUISES**   Call ahead for descriptions, schedules, and fares for the narrated harbor tours given by **Boston Harbor Cruises,** Long Wharf (☎ 617/ 227-4321); **Bay State Cruise Company, Inc.,** Long Wharf (☎ 617/723-7800); and **Massachusetts Bay Lines,** Rowes Wharf (☎ 617/542-8000). For almost a full day at sea, Bay State Cruises' *MV Provincetown II* sails from Commonwealth Pier daily from mid-June to Labor Day, and on weekends May to September. The all-day trip includes a few hours in Provincetown at the tip of Cape Cod.

**WHALE-WATCHING**   The magnificent sight of migrating whales is a favorite of locals and visitors alike. Excursions to Stellwagen Bank, about 27 miles east of Boston, last 4 to 6$^1$/$_2$ hours. Bundle up—whales migrate from April to October, but it gets chilly on the open sea. For information and reservations, call the **New England Aquarium,** Central Wharf (☎ 617/973-5281); **Boston Harbor Whale Watch,** Rowes Wharf (☎ 617/345-9866); or **A. C. Cruise Line,** 290 Northern Ave. (☎ 800/422-8419 or 617/261-6633).

**ATTRACTIONS**   Boston's top people-magnet is the **Quincy Market and Faneuil Hall Marketplace** complex (see below), which attracts 14 million visitors a year. The **Freedom Trail** is second, with about 5 million visitors a year, a number the city is trying to increase with renovations and improvements of the attractions along the trail. The trail links 16 historical sights with a 3-mile line of red paint or brick on or in the sidewalk. First painted in 1958, the trail begins at Boston Common (established as the country's first public park in 1634) and ends in Charlestown at the Bunker Hill Monument. National Park Service rangers lead free tours of the trail from the **Boston National Historic Park Visitor Center,** 15 State St. (☎ 617/242-5642), across the street from the Old State House and the State Street "T" station. If you prefer to set your own pace, pick up a pamphlet and start at **Boston Common Information Center,** 146 Tremont St.

✪ **Boston Museum of Science.** *Science Park.* ☎ *617/723-2500. Admission to the exhibit halls, the Mugar Omni Theater, the Hayden Planetarium, or the laser theater, $8 adults, $6 seniors and children 3–14, free for children under 3. Tickets to two or three parts of the complex available at discounted prices. Daily 9am–5pm, Fri until 9pm. Closed Thanksgiving and Christmas.* More than 450 exhibits feature demonstrations, experiments, and interactive displays that introduce facts and concepts so effortlessly that everyone learns something. The separate-admission theaters are worth planning for. Buy all your tickets at once—it's cheaper and you won't get sold out. The **Mugar Omni Theater** bombards you with images on a four-story domed screen and sounds from a 84-speaker system. The **Charles Hayden Planetarium** takes you deep into space with daily star shows and shows on special topics that change several times a year. On weekends, rock-and-roll laser shows take over—Pink Floyd fans, this is the place for you.

**Boston Public Library.** *666 Boylston St., at Copley Square.* ☎ *617/536-5400. Admission free. Mon–Thurs 9am–9pm, Fri–Sat 9am–5pm. Sun (Oct–May only) 1–5pm. Closed legal holidays.* The central branch of the city's library system is an architectural as well as intellectual monument. The original 1895 building, a registered National Historic Landmark designed by Charles F. McKim, is an Italian Renaissance–style masterpiece that fairly drips with art. The front doors are by Daniel Chester French; the murals are by John Singer Sargent and Pierre Puvis de Chavannes, among others. The addition was designed by Philip Johnson and opened in 1972. Visitors are welcome to wander throughout both buildings, but you must have a library card to check out materials.

**Boston Tea Party Ship and Museum.** *Congress Street Bridge.* ☎ *617/ 338-1773. Admission $7 adults, $5 students, $3 children 6–12, free for children under 6. Ship and museum, Mar 1–Nov 30, daily 9am–dusk (about 6pm in summer, 5pm in winter). Closed Dec 1–Feb 28 and Thanksgiving.* On December 16, 1773, a public meeting of independent-minded Bostonians led to the symbolic act of resistance that's commemorated here. The brig *Beaver II,* a full-size replica of one of the three merchant ships emptied by colonists poorly disguised as Indians on the night of the raid, is alongside a museum with exhibits on the "tea party." You can even dump your own bale of tea into Boston Harbor (it will be retrieved by the museum staff).

**Computer Museum.** *300 Congress St. (Museum Wharf).* ☎ *617/426-2800, or 617/423-6758 for the "Talking Computer." Web site: http://www.tcm.org. Admission $7 adults, $5 students and senior citizens, free for children under 5. Fall, winter, and spring, Tues–Sun 10am–5pm; summer, daily 10am–6pm.* As computer technology develops, the world's premier computer museum changes and grows with it. The exhibits tell the story of computers from their origins in the 1940s to the latest in PCs and virtual reality. The signature exhibit is the Walk-Through Computer 2000™, a networked multimedia machine 50 times larger than the real thing. When the computer's the size of a two-story house, the mouse is the size of a car, the CD-ROM drive is 8 feet long, and the monitor is 12 feet high. The exhibit is so cutting-edge that it even has a 7-foot-square Pentium processor.

✪ **Faneuil Hall Marketplace.** *Bounded by North, Congress, and State sts. and I-93.* ☎ *617/338-2323. Marketplace, Mon–Sat 10am–9pm, Sun noon–6pm; Colonnade food court opens earlier; some restaurants open early for Sun brunch and remain open until 2am daily.* The original "festival market," Faneuil Hall Marketplace opened in 1976, and the complex of shops, food stands, restaurants, bars, and public spaces has been widely imitated around the country. The marketplace includes five buildings—the central three-building complex is listed on the National Register of Historic Places—set on brick and stone plazas that teem with crowds shopping, eating, performing, and just people-watching. Quincy Market itself (you'll hear the whole complex called by that name as well) is a three-level Greek Revival–style building reopened after renovations on August 26, 1976, 150 years after Mayor Josiah Quincy opened the original market.

✪ **Isabella Stewart Gardner Museum.** *280 The Fenway.* ☎ *617/566-1401. Admission $7 adults, $5 seniors and college students with valid ID, $3 youths ages 12–17, free for children under 12. Tues–Sun 11am–5pm.* Isabella Stewart Gardner (1840–1924) designed her home in the style of a 15th-century Venetian palace and filled it with European, American, and Asian painting and sculpture. You'll see works by Titian, Botticelli, Raphael, Rembrandt, Matisse, and Mrs. Gardner's friends James McNeill Whistler and John Singer Sargent. The building, which was opened to the public after Mrs. Gardner's death, features furniture and architectural details imported from European churches and palaces. The pièce de résistance is a magnificent interior skylit courtyard filled year-round with fresh flowers, stained-glass windows, and exquisite antique furnishings. A special exhibition gallery features changing exhibitions.

✪ **John F. Kennedy Presidential Library and Museum.** *Columbia Point, Dorchester.* ☎ *617/929-4523. Admission $6 adults, $4 seniors and students with ID, $2 children age 6–16, free for children under 6. Daily 9am–5pm (last film begins at 3:50pm).* The Kennedy era springs to life at this dramatic library, museum, and educational research complex. Your visit begins with a 17-minute film narrated by the former president himself. Then you're turned loose to spend as much or as little time as you like on exhibits like souvenirs from the 1960 campaign, film from the Kennedy–Nixon debates, replicas of the Oval Office, and a darkened chamber where news reports of Kennedy's assassination and funeral play in a continuous loop. The final room, entitled "Legacy," houses archival documents and interactive computers that explain the programs JFK initiated and how they affect the world today.

**Mapparium.** *World Headquarters of the First Church of Christ, Scientist, 250 Massachusetts Ave. (at Huntington Ave.). ☎ 617/450-3790. Admission free. Mon–Sat 10am–4pm. Closed major holidays.* For a real insider's view of the world, step inside the world! This unique hollow globe 30 feet across is a work of both art and history. The 608 stained-glass panels are connected by a bronze framework and surrounded by electric lights, and because sound bounces off the nonporous surfaces, the acoustics are as unusual as the aesthetics. As you cross the glass bridge just south of the equator, you'll see the political divisions of the world from 1932 to 1935, when the globe was constructed.

**✪ Museum of Fine Arts, Boston.** *465 Huntington Ave. ☎ 617/267-9300. Web site: http://www.mfa.org. Admission $10 adults, $8 students and senior citizens, free for children under 18. Admission is reduced by $2 if only the West Wing is open and is free for all Wed 4–9:45pm. Entire museum, Tues, Thurs, Fri, and summer and holiday Mondays, 10am–4:45pm; Wed 10am–9:45pm; Sat–Sun 10am–5:45pm. West Wing only, Thurs–Fri 5–9:45pm. Closed Mon mid-Sept–late May and major holidays.* Not content with the reputation as the second-best museum in the country (after New York's Metropolitan Museum of Art), the MFA works nonstop to make its collections more accessible and interesting. Your visit is guided by the best sort of curatorial attitude, the kind that makes even those who go only out of obligation leave with a sense of discovery and wonder. The MFA is especially noted for its Asian and Old Kingdom Egyptian collections, its Buddhist temple, and medieval sculpture and tapestries, but you may find its American and European Impressionist paintings and sculpture more familiar.

**New England Aquarium.** *Central Wharf. ☎ 617/973-5200. Admission $9 adults, $5 children 3–11, $8 senior citizens; free for children under 3. July 1–Labor Day, Mon–Tues and Fri 9am–6pm, Wed–Thurs 9am–8pm, Sat–Sun and holidays 9am–7pm. Early Sept–June, Mon–Wed and Fri 9am–5pm, Thurs 9am–8pm, Sat–Sun and holidays 9am–6pm.* The aquarium is an entertaining complex, home to more than 7,000 fish and aquatic mammals. You might be tempted to settle in near the outdoor seal display, especially at feeding time. Indoors, you can commune with the penguin colony, then climb the four-story spiral ramp that encircles the Giant Ocean Tank. It contains 187,000 gallons of salt water, a replica of a Caribbean coral reef, and a conglomeration of sea creatures who coexist amazingly well. That's partly because scuba divers feed the sharks five times a day. Leave time for the floating marine mammal pavilion, where sea lions perform every 90 minutes.

**USS Constitution.** *In Charlestown Navy Yard, Constitution Rd. ☎ 617/242-5670. Admission free. Daily 9:30am–3:50pm.* "Old Ironsides," one of the U.S. Navy's six original frigates and the oldest warship afloat, never lost a battle. She was constructed from 1794 to 1797 at a cost of $302,718. She earned her nickname during an engagement on August 19, 1812, with the French warship HMS *Guerriere,* whose shots bounced off her oak hull as if it were iron. Retired from combat in 1815, she was rescued from destruction by an 1830 preservation movement. She was completely overhauled in 1995–96 in preparation for her 1997 bicentennial. Free tours are given by active-duty sailors in 1812 dress uniforms. Just inland from the vessel is the **USS** *Constitution* **Museum** (☎ 617/426-1812). It has several participatory exhibits that allow visitors to hoist a flag, fire a cannon, and learn more about the ship.

**GREAT VIEWS** The **John Hancock Observatory,** 200 Clarendon St. (☎ 617/ 572-6429), would be a good introduction to Boston even if it didn't have a sensational

60th-floor view. The exhibits include a multimedia show that chronicles the events leading to the Revolutionary War and demonstrates how Boston's landmass has changed. The **Prudential Center Skywalk,** on the 50th floor of the Prudential Tower, 800 Boylston St. (☎ 617/236-3318), offers the only 360° view of Boston and beyond. On a clear day, you can see the mountaintops of southern New Hampshire to the north and the beaches of Cape Cod to the south.

**SWAN BOATS**　　Located in the spectacular **Public Garden,** the swan boats (☎ 617/522-1966 or 617/451-8558) are a quintessential Boston experience. For many people, the official return of spring coincides with the return of the pedal-powered vessels to the lagoon in mid-April.

**HISTORIC HOUSES**　　The oldest and most historic home in Boston is the **Paul Revere House,** 19 North Sq. (☎ 617/523-2338). The self-guided tour brings to life the legendary revolutionary who warned that the British were coming. Revere had 16 children with two wives, supported them with his thriving silversmith's trade, and then put the whole operation in jeopardy with his role in the Revolution. The Federal-style **Harrison Gray Otis House,** 141 Cambridge St. (☎ 617/227-3956), was designed in 1796 for an up-and-coming young lawyer who later became mayor of Boston. The **Nichols House Museum,** 55 Mount Vernon St. (☎ 617/227-6993), is an 1804 Beacon Hill home with beautiful antique furnishings collected by several generations of the Nichols family. In the Back Bay, the **Gibson House Museum,** 137 Beacon St. (☎ 617/267-6338), is an 1859 brownstone that embodies the word *Victorian.* You'll see petrified-wood hat racks, a sequined pink-velvet pagoda for the cat, and a Victrola. In Cambridge, the ravishing yellow mansion at 105 Brattle St. is the **Longfellow National Historic Site** (☎ 617/876-4491), where the books and furniture have remained intact since the poet died there in 1882. During the siege of Boston in 1775–76, the house served as the headquarters of Gen. George Washington.

**HARVARD UNIVERSITY**　　The country's oldest and most famous university lends its name to any number of things, including the neighborhood that represents the crossroads of Cambridge. Harvard Square is a hodgepodge of students, instructors, commuters, street performers, and sightseers. Restaurants and stores line the streets that spread out from the center of the square and the streets that intersect them. The colorful area is well worth a visit. Free student-led tours of the university leave from the Holyoke Center Information Office, 1350 Massachusetts Ave. (☎ 617/495-1573), twice a day during the school year (only once on Saturday) and four times a day in summer (twice on Sunday). Also see the driving tour "Historic Massachusetts," at the beginning of the chapter.

**BEST BETS FOR KIDS**　　The ✪ **Children's Museum,** 300 Congress St. (Museum Wharf) (☎ 617/426-8855), is one of the best in the country. No matter their age, everyone behaves like a little kid at this delightful museum. Touching is not only encouraged, it's required if you're going to enjoy the exhibits. Some favorites: "Under the Dock," an environmental exhibit that teaches youngsters about the Boston waterfront and allows them to dress up in a crab suit; the "Kids' Bridge," where interactive videos allow a virtual visit to Boston's ethnic neighborhoods to learn about cultural differences; and the "Dress-Up Shop," a souped-up version of playing in Grandma's closet. Admission is $7 adults, $6 children aged 2–15 and seniors, $2 aged 1–2, free for children under 1, Fri 5–9pm, $1 for all. It's open Sept–June, Tues–Sun 10am–5pm, Fri until 9pm; June–Aug, daily 10am–5pm, Fri until 9pm.

　　See the listings above for the hands-on exhibits at the **New England Aquarium,** the **Computer Museum,** and the **Boston Tea Party Ship and Museum;** shows by the street performers at **Faneuil Hall Marketplace;** and the **John F. Kennedy Presidential Library and Museum.** Young children will delight in the 75-minute *Make Way for Ducklings* tour offered by the **Historic Neighborhoods Foundation** (☎ 617/426-1885), which follows the path of the Mallard family described in Robert McCloskey's famous book, and ends at the **Public Garden.** For a lengthier walk, **Boston By Foot** (☎ 617/367-2345,** or 617/367-3766 for recorded information) offers a 1-hour **Boston By Little Feet** city tour geared for children 6–12 years old and their parents.

**SPORTS**   Few experiences in sports match watching the **Boston Red Sox** play at **Fenway Park** (☎ **617/267-8661** for information, 617/267-1700 for tickets). The quirkiness of the oldest park in the major leagues (built in 1912) and the fact that the team last won the World Series in 1918 only add to the mystique. The **FleetCenter,** 150 Causeway St. (☎ **617/624-1000**), recently replaced aging Boston Garden as the home of the NBA's **Celtics** and the NHL's **Bruins.**

The city's most famous sporting event is the **Boston Marathon,** which starts at noon on Patriots' Day (the third Monday in April) in Hopkinton, Massachusetts, and ends in Copley Square in Boston. Another riotous outdoor event is the **Head of the Charles Regatta,** conducted in late October. The country's largest crew event attracts rowers by the hundreds and preppies by the thousands to the banks of the Charles.

**SHOPPING**   Good money-spending destinations include the Back Bay, home to the celebrated art galleries of Newbury Street, the Shops at Prudential Center, and upscale Copley Place. Another notable stop is Faneuil Hall Marketplace, the busiest attraction in Boston, not only because of its smorgasbord of food outlets, but also because of its shops, boutiques, and pushcarts filled with everything from rubber stamps to costume jewelry (see "Attractions," above). Charles Street, at the foot of Beacon Hill, is a short but commercially dense (and picturesque) street noted for its antique and gift shops.

**Downtown Crossing** is a traffic-free pedestrian mall best known as the home of **Filene's Basement,** 426 Washington St. (☎ **617/542-2011**). "The Basement" has spoiled New England shoppers with retail discounts since 1908. After 2 weeks on the selling floor, merchandise is automatically marked down 25%. Prices continue to fall for the next 3 weeks. If 75% discounts don't result in a sale, the merchandise is donated to charity.

**Harvard Square** in Cambridge, with its bookstores, boutiques, and T-shirt shops, is about 15 minutes from Boston on the red line. An aggressive neighborhood association has kept the area from being swallowed up by chain stores, though the Bohemian days of "the Square" are long gone.

## ACCOMMODATIONS

The lodging market in Boston and Cambridge (included here) is thriving, with many centrally located hotels operating at or near capacity during the busy periods around graduation (May–June), summer vacation (June–Aug), and foliage season (Sept–Oct). To avoid paying through the nose, be willing to scout around and perhaps stay a little out of town. Rates downtown tend to be lower on the weekends. And if you don't mind cold and snow, great deals are available all over town from December to March, particularly for weekend packages. Boston charges a 9.7% tax on all hotel rooms.

If you prefer a bed-and-breakfast, the two largest agencies in the area are **Bed and Breakfast Associates Bay Colony Ltd.,** P.O. Box 57-166, Babson Park Branch, Boston, MA 02157 (☎ **800/347-5088** or 617/449-5302; fax 617/449-5958), and **Bed and Breakfast Agency of Boston,** 47 Commercial Wharf, Boston, MA 02110 (☎ **800/CITY-BNB** or 617/720-3540; fax 617/523-5761; from the United Kingdom, call 0800/89-5128).

**Berkeley Residence YWCA.** *40 Berkeley St., Boston, MA 02116.* ☎ *617/482-8850. Fax 617/482-9692. 200 rms (none with bath). $35 single; $50 double; $60 triple. Long-term stay (4-week minimum) $130 per week, including breakfast and dinner daily. JCB, MC, V. Parking $14 in public lot 1 block away.* This pleasant, conveniently located residence hotel for women offers a dining room, patio garden, pianos, library, and laundry facilities. The rooms are basic, containing little more than a bed, but are clean and comfortable. Passes are available to the pool and exercise room at the nearby YWCA fitness center.

✪ **Boston Harbor Hotel.** *70 Rowes Wharf (entrance on Atlantic Ave.), Boston, MA 02110.* ☎ *800/752-7077 or 617/439-7000. Fax 617/330-9450. 230 rms, 26 suites. $235–$385 double; from $350 suite. Weekend packages available. AE, DC, DISC, MC, V. Self-parking $21 weekdays; valet parking $23 daily.* This is the prettiest hotel in town. You'll forget about the Central Artery construction raging out front the minute you glimpse the water. The hotel is within walking distance of downtown and the waterfront, and prides itself on top-notch service. Each luxurious bedroom/living room combination has a view of the harbor or the skyline. The hotel has two restaurants, a bar, lounge, concierge, health club and spa with 60-foot lap pool, beauty salon, and state-of-the-art business center with professional staff.

**Boston Park Plaza Hotel and Towers.** *64 Arlington St. (at Park Plaza), Boston, MA 02116.* ☎ *800/225-2008 or 617/426-2000. Fax 617/426-1708. 960 rms, 10 suites. Main hotel, $175–$265 double. Towers, $195–$245 double; $375–$2,000 suite. Senior discounts and special packages available. AE, DC, MC, V. Valet parking $18.* The crystal chandeliers and red-carpeted corridors remain from the roaring '20s, when this was the Statler Hilton, but the rest of the hotel is thoroughly modern. The decor and size of rooms vary greatly, but the location can't be beat. It's within walking distance to Boston Common, the Public Garden, and the Theater District. On the premises you will find a travel agency, pharmacy, four restaurants (including the famous Legal Seafood), concierge, health club, kids' video/game room, hairdresser, and beauty salon.

**Central Branch YMCA.** *316 Huntington Ave., Boston, MA 02115.* ☎ *617/536-7800. 67–150 rms, depending on season (none with bath). $39 single; $56 double. AE, DISC, MC, V. Rates include breakfast.* The Central Branch Y is about 10 minutes from downtown, near Symphony Hall and the Museum of Fine Arts. The gloomy lobby is slated for renovations that should bring it up to the level of the modern (but not air-conditioned) guest rooms. Rates include the use of the pool, indoor track, and fitness center, and there's a cafeteria.

**Chandler Inn.** *26 Chandler St. (at Berkeley St.), Boston, MA 02116.* ☎ *800/842-3450 or 617/482-3450. Fax 617/542-3428. 56 rms. Nov–Apr $79 double; May–Oct $99 double. AE, CB, DC, DISC, MC, V. Parking available in nearby garages.* Technically in the South End, the Chandler Inn is so convenient to the Back Bay and such a good deal that you won't mind the less-toney address. The guest rooms were recently redecorated, and, more importantly, air-conditioned. They're still nothing fancy, but meet basic needs. And the staff is friendly and helpful.

✪ **Charles Hotel.** *1 Bennett St., Cambridge, MA 02138.* ☎ *800/882-1818 outside MA, or 617/864-1200. Fax 617/864-5715. 252 rms, 45 suites. $239–$259 double; $325–$1,500 suite. Weekend packages available. AE, CB, DC, DISC, JCB, MC, V. Parking $18.* The Charles has been *the* place to stay in Cambridge since it opened in 1985. Much of its fame derives from its excellent restaurants, jazz bar, and spa. The service is equally exalted. In the guest rooms, the style is contemporary country, with big, fluffy down quilts on the beds. Extras include two restaurants (Henrietta's Table offers the best Sunday brunch in the area), a jazz bar, concierge, laundry, indoor pool, and health club. Special spa weekends are offered.

**Copley Plaza Hotel.** *138 St. James Ave., Boston, MA 02116.* ☎ *800/527-4727 or 617/267-5300. Fax 617/247-6681. 373 rms, 61 suites. $275–$374 double; $395–$1,400 suite. AE, CB, DC, JCB, MC, V. Valet parking $22.* With next-door neighbors like Trinity Church and the Boston Public Library to keep up with, the Renaissance revival Copley Plaza Hotel has been synonymous with elegance since it opened in 1912. The hotel has entertained royalty, celebrities, and every U.S. president since Taft. Guest rooms are equally opulent, furnished with reproduction Edwardian antiques. Two restaurants, three bars, concierge, dry cleaning and laundry service, fitness center, complimentary use of the nearby Le Pli Spa (with pool and sauna), and a beauty salon are conveniences.

**Copley Square Hotel.** *47 Huntington Ave., Boston, MA 02116.* ☎ *800/225-7062 or 617/536-9000. Fax 617/236-0351. 143 rms, 12 suites. $155–$185 double; $260 suite. AE, DISC, JCB, MC, V. Parking available in adjacent lot for $16.* This seven-story hotel sits literally in the shadow of the megahotels around Copley Place, but its attractively decorated rooms and excellent service allow it to hold its own. Each room has a unique layout and comfortable furnishings. An exceptionally good value in a good location. Three restaurants, including Café Budapest, one of Boston's finest eateries, are in the hotel.

**Doubletree Guest Suites.** *400 Soldiers Field Rd., Boston, MA 02134.* ☎ *800/ 222-TREE or 617/783-0090. Fax 617/783-0897. 310 rms. $169–$229 double. Extra person $20. Children 18 and under stay free in parents' room. Weekend packages from $109 per night. AE, CB, DC, DISC, JCB, MC, V. Parking $14 Sun–Thurs, $7 Fri–Sat.* This all-suite hotel is a great deal. Most bedrooms have king-size beds; living rooms feature sofa beds, a dining table, and a refrigerator, making this an excellent choice for families. Overlooking the Charles River near a turnpike exit, the hotel isn't in an actual neighborhood, but complimentary van service to downtown is available. Extras include a restaurant, lounge, jazz club, newspaper delivery, indoor pool, exercise room, spa, and laundry room.

✪ **Eliot Hotel.** *370 Commonwealth Ave. (at Massachusetts Ave.), Boston, MA 02215.* ☎ *800/44-ELIOT or 617/267-1607. Fax 617/536-9114. 16 rms, 78 suites. $195–$225 double; $225–$265 suite for two. AE, DC, MC, V. Valet parking $18.* This exquisite hotel combines the flavor of Yankee Boston with European-style service. Built in 1925 as a retirement residence for Harvard alumni, the hotel underwent a complete renovation from 1990 to 1994. The spacious suites are furnished with antique furnishings. The hotel is convenient to Boston University and MIT (across the river). Guests have access to a concierge, valet parking, and health club.

✪ **Four Seasons Hotel.** *200 Boylston St., Boston, MA 02116.* ☎ *800/332-3442 or 617/338-4400. Fax 617/423-0154. 288 rms, 80 suites. $320–$495 double; from $650 one-bedroom suite; from $1,100 two-bedroom suite. Weekend packages available. AE, CB, DC, DISC, JCB, MC, V. Valet parking $22.* No other hotel in Boston offers everything you expect from a luxury hotel quite so seamlessly and pleasingly as the Four Seasons. Each room is elegantly appointed and has a striking view (many overlooking the Public Garden). Two restaurants include Aujourd'hui, a fine French restaurant (see "Dining," below). The hotel has a concierge, complimentary limousine service to downtown, indoor pool, extensive health club, and business center. Small pets are welcome.

**Harborside Hyatt Conference Center and Hotel.** *101 Harborside Dr., Boston, MA 02129.* ☎ *800/233-1284 or 617/568-1234. Fax 617/568-6080. 270 rms. $220 double. AE, CB, DC, DISC, JCB, MC, V. Parking $7.* This striking waterfront hotel, which opened in 1993, has unobstructed views of the harbor and city skyline. Inside, fiber-optic stars change color in the skydome ceiling in the reception area. The first-class guest rooms have all the amenities you'd expect from a deluxe hotel, plus extras like irons and ironing boards. Guests enjoy the restaurant with spectacular views, 24-hour airport shuttle service, health club with indoor lap pool, and business center.

**Harvard Square Hotel.** *110 Mount Auburn St., Cambridge, MA 02138.* ☎ *800/ 458-5886 or 617/864-5200. Fax 617/864-2409. 73 rms. $125–$160 single or double.*

*Corporate, AAA, and AARP rates available. AE, DC, DISC, JCB, MC, V. Parking $15.* Smack in the middle of Harvard Square, this hotel is a favorite with visiting parents and budget-conscious business travelers. In early 1996 the former Harvard Manor House was renamed and completely refurbished. Some rooms overlook Harvard Square and the atmosphere everywhere is comfortable and unpretentious. Complimentary newspapers and laundry service are available. Guests may dine at the Inn at Harvard, which is managed by the same company, or at the Harvard Faculty Club.

**Inn at Harvard.** *1201 Massachusetts Ave., Cambridge, MA 02138.* ☎ *800/ 458-5886 or 617/491-2222. Fax 617/491-6520. 109 rms, 4 suites. $165–$249 double; $450 presidential suite. Senior, AAA, and AARP discounts available. AE, CB, DC, MC, V. Parking $18.* Located a stone's throw from Harvard Yard, the Inn at Harvard's red-brick architecture would fit nicely on campus. Step inside, though, and there's no mistaking it for anything other than a first-class business hotel. Guest rooms have cherry furniture and an original painting from the nearby Fogg Art Museum. Extras include a restaurant (guests can also lunch at the nearby Faculty Club), business center, and complimentary newspaper delivery.

**✪ Le Meridien Boston.** *250 Franklin St. (at Post Office Sq.), Boston, MA 02110.* ☎ *800/543-4300 or 617/451-1900. Fax 617/423-2844. 326 rms, 22 suites. $285–$335 double; $450–$800 suite. Weekend rates from $145. AE, CB, DC, MC, V. Parking $24.* Located in the old Federal Reserve Bank—the original marble staircase remains—this hotel is an architectural marvel. The location, in the heart of the Financial District, is perfect for business travelers or those vacationing near the waterfront. And the multi-lingual staff provides superb service. The already plush guest rooms were renovated in 1995. The hotel has an award-winning restaurant, bar, outdoor cafe, concierge, indoor pool, well-equipped health club, and full-service business center with library and full-time staff.

**MidTown Hotel.** *220 Huntington Ave., Boston, MA 02115.* ☎ *800/343-1177 or 617/262-1000. Fax 617/262-8739. 159 rms. $109–$149 double. AARP and government employee discounts. AE, DC, DISC, MC, V. Free parking.* Even without free parking, this hotel would be a good deal. It's on a busy street within easy walking distance of Symphony Hall, the Museum of Fine Arts, and other Back Bay attractions. The good-sized rooms are bright and attractively outfitted with contemporary furnishings; some have connecting bedrooms for families. Facilities include a heated outdoor pool and restaurant.

**Ritz-Carlton.** *15 Arlington St., Boston, MA 02117.* ☎ *800/241-3333 or 617/ 536-5700. Fax 617/536-1335. 237 rms, 48 suites. $270–$370 double; $500–$2,000 one-bedroom suite; $720–$2,100 two-bedroom suite. Weekend packages available. AE, CB, DC, DISC, JCB, MC, V. Valet parking $20.* Overlooking the Public Garden, the Ritz-Carlton has a tradition of gracious service that has made it famous since it opened in 1927. The service and attention to detail are legendary, with the highest staff-to-guest ratio in the city. The guest rooms have French provincial furnishings accented with imported floral fabrics and crystal chandeliers. The hotel offers two restaurants, a bar, rooftop night-club, concierge, complimentary newspaper delivery, well-equipped fitness center with massage room, use of pool at nearby Le Pli Health Spa, and beauty salon.

**Sheraton Boston Hotel and Towers.** *39 Dalton St., Boston, MA 02199.* ☎ *800/325-3535 or 617/236-2000. Fax 617/236-1702. 1,208 rms, 85 suites. $210– $255 double; suites from $255. 25% discount for students, faculty, and retired persons. Weekend packages available. AE, CB, DC, DISC, JCB, MC, V. Parking $16.* You won't have any trouble finding this gigantic hotel, but you might get lost inside. The lavish convention facilities make it a business traveler's favorite. It's connected to the Hynes Convention Center, the new Shops at Prudential Center, and Copley Place. Standard rooms are large, with traditional mahogany and cherry-wood furnishings. The complex contains two restaurants, a sports bar with dance floor, concierge, heated indoor/outdoor pool with retractable dome, and well-equipped health club.

**Tremont House.** *275 Tremont St., Boston, MA 02116.* ☎ *800/331-9998 or 617/426-1400. Fax 617/482-6730. 281 rms, 34 suites. $139–$199 double; $170–$270 suite. Weekend packages and AAA discount available. AE, CB, DC, DISC, MC, V. Parking $15 in nearby garage or lot.* Tremont House is as close to Boston's theaters as a balcony seat, and convenient to downtown and the Back Bay. A complete renovation restored the style that prevailed when the hotel was built in 1924. The hotel is geared to budget-minded travelers, but it has many services found in luxury hotels such as a restaurant, two nightclubs, secretarial services, and valet laundry.

**Westin Hotel.** *10 Huntington Ave., Boston, MA 02116.* ☎ *800/228-3000 or 617/262-9600. Fax 617/424-7483. 800 rms, 46 suites. $179–$250 double; $285–$1,500 suite. Weekend packages available. AE, CB, DC, DISC, JCB, MC, V. Valet parking $21.* High above Copley Place, the Westin is popular with conventioneers and shoppers. Determined consumers don't even have to step outside—the hotel is linked by sky bridges to Copley Place and the Prudential Center. The spacious guest rooms are comfortably furnished, but you'll hardly notice once you see the stunning views of downtown Boston. The hotel offers three restaurants, two bars, a concierge, indoor pool, well-equipped health club, business center with computer rentals and secretarial services.

**OTHER ACCOMMODATIONS**  The Howard Johnson chain has three hotels here worth considering. The **Howard Johnson Hotel Cambridge,** 777 Memorial Dr. in Cambridge (☎ **617/492-7777**), is near the major college campuses and just a 10-minute drive from downtown Boston. Rooms on the higher floors have a panoramic view of the Boston skyline. In Boston, the **Howard Johnson Hotel—Kenmore,** 575 Commonwealth Ave. (☎ **617/267-3100**), is surrounded by the Boston University campus, with the subway to downtown out front and Kenmore Square and Fenway Park nearby. The **Howard Johnson Lodge Fenway,** 1271 Boylston St. (☎ **617/267-8300**), is also convenient to the Back Bay colleges, the Museum of Fine Arts, and the Isabella Stewart Gardner Museum. When the Red Sox are playing, guests contend with crowded sidewalks and raucous baseball fans who flood the area. The hotel has a restaurant, outdoor pool, and lounge. The toll-free reservation number for all three is ☎ **800/654-2000.**

## DINING

You don't have to love seafood to enjoy eating in the Boston area, but it helps. Across the culinary and economic spectrum, fish and shellfish crop up on menus all over the place. Carnivores and vegetarians will also find plenty of options to keep them happy and full. If you prefer to eat and run, remember that the food offerings at Faneuil Hall Marketplace are almost as numerous as the bricks (see "Attractions," above).

**Algiers Coffeehouse.** *40 Brattle St., Cambridge.* ☎ *617/492-1557. Main courses $2–$8. AE, MC, V. Mon–Thurs 8am–midnight, Fri–Sat 8am–1am. MIDDLE EASTERN.* Long known as a dark, smoke-filled literary hangout, the new Algiers (which resulted from a fire in the 1980s) is upstairs in Brattle Hall, and still a favorite with Cambridge intellectuals, would-be intellectuals, and tired Harvard Square shoppers. The food is terrific and the Algiers mint coffee is one-of-a-kind.

**✪ Ambrosia on Huntington.** *116 Brattle Ave.* ☎ *617/247-2400. Reservations recommended at dinner. Main courses $5–$12 at lunch, $16–$29 at dinner. AE, DISC, MC, V. Mon–Fri 11:30am–2:30pm; Mon–Thurs 5:30–10pm, Fri–Sat 5–11pm, Sun 5–9pm. FRENCH/ASIAN.* Felicitously named proprietors Tony and

Dorene Ambrose (he's the chef) have turned the vacant ground floor of an office building into a dazzling room. Every dish here is a feast for the eyes as well as the mouth with rich, unusual flavors. Try the Peruvian purple potato spring roll in crispy paper.

✪ **Aujourd'hui.** *In the Four Seasons Hotel, 200 Boylston St.* ☎ *617/451-1392. Reservations strongly recommended. Main courses $17–$20 at lunch, $35–$45 at dinner; Sun buffet brunch $39. AE, CB, DC, MC, V. Daily 6:30–10:30am; Mon–Fri 11:30am–2:30pm, Sun 11:30am–2:30pm (brunch); Mon–Sat 5:30–10:30pm, Sun 6–10:30pm. INTERNATIONAL.* On the second floor of the city's premier luxury hotel, the most beautiful restaurant in town has floor-to-ceiling windows overlooking the Public Garden, and the service may even outstrip the setting. A favorite among all the delicious entrees: juniper-roasted venison chop with a sweet potato, and turnip cake and cider-glazed chard.

✪ **Bartley's Burger Cottage.** *1246 Massachusetts Ave., Cambridge.* ☎ *617/354-6559. Most items under $8. No credit cards. Mon–Sat 11am–10pm. AMERICAN.* Harvard students and regular folks alike make this a perennial favorite for great burgers and the best onion rings anywhere. Burgers bear the names of celebrities; the names change, but the ingredients stay the same. You can still get a real raspberry lime rickey here—raspberry syrup, lime juice, lime wedges, and club soda.

**Biba Food Hall.** *272 Boylston St.* ☎ *617/426-7878. Reservations recommended. Main courses $17–$34 at dinner; bar menu $4–$9. CB, DC, DISC, MC, V. Mon–Fri 11:30am–2pm, Sun 11:30am–2:30pm; Sun–Thurs 5:30–9:30pm, Fri–Sat 5:30–10:30pm. Bar menu offered until 2am. ECLECTIC.* Legendary chef Lydia Shire's regularly changing menu is well past the cutting edge, divided into categories that include "offal" (organ meats) and "legumina" (vegetables), as well as her signature lobster pizza and steak au poivre. The restaurant, in the posh Heritage on the Garden complex across from the Public Garden, attracts a chic crowd.

**Café Jaffa.** *48 Gloucester St.* ☎ *617/536-0230. Reservations not accepted. Main courses $3–$9. AE, MC, V. Mon–Thurs 11am–10:30pm, Fri–Sat 11am–11pm, Sun 1–10pm. MIDDLE EASTERN.* Café Jaffa looks more like a snazzy pizza place than the wonderful Middle Eastern restaurant it is. Young people flock here, drawn by the low prices, excellent quality, and large portions of food, which includes burgers and steak tips as well as traditional Middle Eastern offerings like falafel and babaghanoush.

**Daily Catch.** *261 Northern Ave.* ☎ *617/338-3093. Reservations not accepted. Main courses $10–$17. AE. Sun–Thurs noon–10:30pm, Fri–Sat noon–11pm. SOUTHERN ITALIAN/SEAFOOD.* Go with friends to this Fish Pier institution, because you're going to emanate garlic for at least a day. It's no secret that this unassuming storefront has some of the best seafood in town, so you'll have to wait forever for a table and put up with an often-overwhelmed wait staff. There are two other branches of this minichain: in the North End, at 323 Hanover St. (☎ 617/523-8567), and in Brookline, at 441A Harvard St. (☎ 617/734-5696).

**Durgin-Park.** *340 Faneuil Hall Marketplace.* ☎ *617/227-2038. Reservations not accepted. Main courses $5–$17, specials $16–$25. AE, MC, V. Daily 11:30am–2:30pm; Mon–Sat 2:30–10pm, Sun 2:30–9pm. NEW ENGLAND.* Some 2,000 people a day line up at this Boston institution so they can partake of huge portions of fresh delicious food (Boston baked beans are a specialty), enjoy a rowdy atmosphere where CEOs share tables with students, and be served by the famously cranky waitresses.

**Elephant Walk.** *900 Beacon St.* ☎ *617/247-1500. Reservations recommended at dinner Sun–Thurs, not accepted Fri–Sat. Main courses $6–$19 at lunch, $10–$19 at dinner. AE, DISC, MC, V. Mon–Sat 11:30am–2:30pm; Mon–Thurs 5–10pm, Fri 5–11pm, Sat 4:30–11pm, Sun 4:30–10pm. FRENCH/CAMBODIAN.* France meets Cambodia at the Boston–Brookline border near Kenmore Square. This madly popular spot has a two-part menu (French on one side, Cambodian on the other), but the boundary seems quite porous. Many of the Cambodian dishes have part-French names, and most of the French dishes have an Asian persuasion.

**Grill 23 & Bar.** *161 Berkeley St.* ☎ *617/542-2255. Reservations recommended. Main courses $19–$30. AE, CB, DC, DISC, MC, V. Mon–Thurs 5:30–10:30pm, Fri–Sat 5:30–11pm, Sun 5:30–10pm. AMERICAN.* Grill 23 is a steak house on par with any in New York or Chicago, but it's also much more. Slabs of beef are the stars here, but less aggressively carnivorous entrees attract equal attention. Lamb chops are so tender that your knife glides through them. Desserts show similarly little restraint.

**Hamersley's Bistro.** 553 Tremont St. ☎ *617/423-2700. Reservations recommended. Main courses $19–$27. AE, DISC, MC, V. Mon–Fri 6–10pm, Sat 5:30–10pm, Sun 5:30–9:30pm. ECLECTIC.* The husband-and-wife team of Gordon and Fiona Hamersley put the South End on Boston's culinary map. You'll have to quiz your server about the delicious-looking appetizer of potato galette, smoked salmon, crème fraîche, and three caviars that just went to another table. The menu changes seasonally.

**✪ The Helmand.** *143 First St., Cambridge.* ☎ *617/492-4646. Reservations recommended. Main courses $9–$15. AE, MC, V. Sun–Thurs 5–10pm, Fri–Sat 5–11pm. AFGHAN.* Even in cosmopolitan Cambridge, Afghan food is novel, and if competitors are aiming at The Helmand, they're contemplating a daunting task. The elegant setting belies the reasonable prices at this spacious spot near the CambridgeSide Galleria mall. The food is distinctly Middle Eastern with Indian and Pakistani influences. Many vegetarian dishes are offered.

**House of Blues.** *96 Winthrop St., Cambridge.* ☎ *617/491-2583. Reservations not accepted. Main courses $5–$15. AE, MC, V. Sun–Wed 11:30am–1am, Thurs–Sat 11:30am–2am. CAJUN/PIZZA/INTERNATIONAL.* This is the original House of Blues, in a blue clapboard house near Harvard Square. Everything is blue here, including the live blues every night at 10 and on Saturday afternoon. The menu is essentially bar food, with enough variety to keep the legions of tourists who flock here contented. Try the buffalo legs (like the wings, only bigger), or pizzas topped with feta cheese and garlic.

**✪ Icarus.** *3 Appleton St.* ☎ *617/426-1790. Reservations recommended. Main courses $20–$30; "Square Meal" $38. AE, CB, DC, MC, V. Sun 11am–3pm (brunch); Sun–Thurs 6–10pm, Fri 6–11pm, Sat 5:30–11pm. ECLECTIC.* This subterranean restaurant, which is both spacious and cozy, provides a memorable dining experience from start to finish. Chef Chris Douglass's menu uses choice local seafood, poultry, meats, and produce in a combination that seems almost more like alchemy than cooking. Witness: cod encased in a shredded potato cake. Desserts are unbelievable.

**Jimbo's Fish Shanty.** *245 Northern Ave.* ☎ *617/542-5600. Main courses $6–$14. AE, DC, MC, V. Mon–Thurs 11:30am–9:30pm, Fri–Sat 11:30am–10pm, Sun noon–8pm. SEAFOOD.* Bring your sense of humor to this jam-packed restaurant, where model trains run on tracks suspended from the low ceiling, and the waitresses call you "honey." Under the same management as Jimmy's Harborside across the street, Jimbo's serves good, fresh seafood, skewers threaded with fish or beef, and pasta dishes.

**✪ Legal Sea Foods.** *800 Boylston St., in the Prudential Center.* ☎ *617/266-6800. Reservations recommended at lunch. Main courses $6–$13 at lunch, $14–$24 at dinner. AE, CB, DC, DISC, MC, V. Mon–Thurs 11am–10pm, Fri–Sat 11am–11pm, Sun noon–10pm. SEAFOOD.* Legal's has had a reputation for the freshest seafood in town ever since it opened in 1968. The menu includes regular selections like scrod, salmon, shrimp, calamari, and lobster, plus whatever looked good at the market that morning. The clam chowder is a winner, and the seafood casserole is sinfully good. There are also branches at the Boston Park Plaza Hotel and Towers, 35 Columbus Ave. (☎ 617/426-4444); Copley Place, 100 Huntington Ave. (☎ 617/266-7775); Kendall Square, 5 Cambridge Center (☎ 617/864-3400); and eight other locations.

❂ **L'Espalier.** *30 Gloucester St.* ☎ *617/262-3023. Reservations required. Fixed-price dinner (four courses) $62; vegetable dégustation menu (six courses) $68; dégustation menu (seven courses) $78. AE, DISC, MC, V. Mon–Sat 6–10pm. NEW ENGLAND/FRENCH.* Dining here is like eating at the home of a dear friend who happens to have 12 chefs in the kitchen. Service is beyond excellent, as if the waiter just read your mind. The food—try chimney-roasted Maine lobster with lemongrass and star anise broth—may exceed the trappings.

**Locke-Ober.** *3 and 4 Winter Place.* ☎ *617/542-1340. Reservations required. Main courses $8–$25 at lunch, $17–$40 at dinner. AE, DC, MC, V. Mon–Fri 11:30am–3pm; Fri 3–10pm, Sat 5:30–10:30pm, Sun 5:30–10pm. Closed Sun in summer. AMERICAN.* "Locke-Ober's" is *the* traditional Boston restaurant, a favorite since 1875, where some Bostonians eat lunch at the same table every day. Oysters Rockefeller and the famous lobster Savannah seem perfectly in place at this clubby, wood-paneled dining room, but don't be surprised to see tofu and "lower-fat specials" on the menu.

❂ **Maison Robert.** *45 School St.* ☎ *617/227-3370. Reservations recommended. Main courses $9–$22 at lunch, $17–$30 at dinner. Le Café has a fixed-price menu ($18 or $25) as well as à la carte selections. AE, CB, DC, MC, V. Mon–Fri 11:45am–2:30pm; Mon–Sat 5:30–10pm. INNOVATIVE FRENCH.* This is one of the finest French restaurants anywhere. Majestic crystal chandeliers and tall windows overlook the peaceful Old Granary Burying Ground from the site of the former Boston City Hall. The food is every bit the equal of the setting. The splendid rack of lamb comes with an equally delicious potato cake.

❂ **Mamma Maria.** *3 North Sq.* ☎ *617/523-0077. Reservations recommended. Main courses $10–$15 at lunch, $18–$28 at dinner. AE, DC, DISC, MC, V. Tues–Sat 11:30am–2pm; daily 5:30–10pm. NORTHERN ITALIAN.* You'll find innovative cuisine in this traditional town house overlooking North Square and the Paul Revere House. The bread, pasta, and desserts are homemade, the service is exceptional, and the cool, whitewashed rooms are among the most popular in town for getting engaged. Try goat cheese ravioli with arugula, walnuts, and oven-cured tomatoes.

❂ **Olives.** *10 City Sq., Charlestown.* ☎ *617/242-1999. Reservations accepted only for parties of six or more. Main courses $16–$30. AE, DC, MC, V. Tues–Fri 5:30–10pm, Sat 5–10:30pm. ECLECTIC.* Expect to wait at least an hour for a table at this small, informal bistro, and then suffer uneven service, small tables, and a loud atmosphere. Why? Because the food is worth the aggravation. Braised lamb shank with a sherry-and-olive sauce is so tender it falls off the bone.

**Original Sports Saloon.** *In the Copley Square Hotel, 47 Huntington Ave.* ☎ *617/536-9000. Main courses $7–$18. AE, DC, DISC, MC, V. Daily 11:30am–1:30am. Full menu served until 10pm, appetizers until closing. AMERICAN/BARBECUE.* This tiny saloon serves award-winning barbecue in a pleasant, if loud, room with 11 large-screen TVs. The specialty is barbecued baby-back ribs, which take more than 30 hours to prepare. The ribs are slow-cooked, using an authentic Memphis smoker, over a secret blend of hickory, ash, cherry, and apple woods.

**Piccola Venezia.** *263 Hanover St.* ☎ *617/523-3888. Reservations not accepted. Main courses $10–$17. AE, DISC, MC, V. Daily 11:30am–10pm. ITALIAN.* There's seldom a slow night at this glass-fronted restaurant with the exposed-brick dining room filled with happy patrons. Portions are large and the food tends to be heavy on red sauce, but more sophisticated specials are available. Traditional specialties like spaghetti and meatballs or chicken parmigiana reign.

❂ **Providence.** *1223 Beacon St., Brookline.* ☎ *617/232-0300. Reservations recommended. Main courses $12–$25. AE, DC, MC, V. Tues–Thurs 5:30–10pm; Fri–Sat 5:30–11pm, Sun 5–9:30pm. ECLECTIC.* Providence's columns and intricate moldings suggest a formal dining room, but the warm tones of the paint lend a casual air. The helpful staff can help you navigate the list of specials, which is almost as long as the menu. The food is the definition of eclectic: veal pastrami comes with sweet-potato dumplings

✪ **Rialto.** *One Bennett St., in the Charles Hotel, Cambridge.* ☎ *617/661-5050. Reservations recommended. Main courses $19–$29. AE, DC, MC, V. Sun–Thurs 5:30–10pm, Fri–Sat 5:30–11pm. MEDITERRANEAN.* Rialto may very well be the best restaurant in the Boston area. It attracts a chic crowd, but it's not a "scene." The staff is solicitous without being smothering, and the food speaks for itself. Main courses are so good that you might as well just close your eyes and point.

**Top of the Hub.** *800 Boylston St., Prudential Center.* ☎ *617/536-1775. Reservations recommended. Jacket advised for men. Main courses $7–$16 at lunch, $16–$29 at dinner. Menu dégustation $65 per person (two-person minimum). Sun brunch $29 adults, $14 children. AE, DC, DISC, MC, V. Mon–Fri 11:30am–2pm, Sat noon–3pm, Sun 11am–2:30pm (brunch); Sun–Thurs 5:30–10pm, Fri–Sat 5:30–11pm. CONTEMPORARY AMERICAN.* For many years, the answer to the question "How's the food at Top of the Hub?" was, "The view is spectacular." The cuisine has been dramatically improved, courtesy of a 1995 menu overhaul, so it nearly measures up to the 52nd-story panorama outside. Ask for a window table.

**Ye Olde Union Oyster House.** *41 Union St. (between North and Hanover sts.).* ☎ *617/227-2750. Reservations recommended. Main courses $7–$14 at lunch, $9–$19 at dinner; lobster $22–$35. AE, CB, DC, DISC, MC, V. Sun–Thurs 11am–9:30pm, Fri–Sat 11am–10pm. Lunch served until 5pm Sun–Thurs, until 6pm Fri–Sat. NEW ENGLAND/SEAFOOD.* America's oldest restaurant opened in 1826, and the booths and oyster bar haven't moved since. Daniel Webster ate here, as did John F. Kennedy, whose favorite booth is marked with a plaque. The food is tasty, traditional New England fare: Try the sampler, a mixed appetizer of oysters, clams, and scampi.

**Zuma's Tex-Mex Café.** *7 N. Market St., Faneuil Hall Marketplace.* ☎ *617/367-9114. Main courses $5–$14. AE, CB, DC, DISC, MC, V. Mon–Thurs 11:30am–11pm, Fri–Sat 11:30am–midnight, Sun noon–10pm. TEX-MEX.* Because of its great location, Zuma's could probably get away with serving so-so food and still draw enormous crowds. Happily, its Southwestern cuisine is excellent, with guacamole and salsa cruda made from scratch, and tortilla chips cut and fried throughout the day right in the dining room. Portions are large, especially considering the low prices.

## BOSTON AFTER DARK

For up-to-date entertainment listings, consult the "Calendar" section of the Thursday *Boston Globe,* the "Scene" section of the Friday *Boston Herald,* and the Sunday arts sections of both papers. The weekly *Boston Phoenix* (published on Thursday) has especially good club listings, and the twice-monthly *Improper Bostonian* has extensive live music listings. For discount tickets, visit the **BosTix** (☎ 617/723-5181) booths at Faneuil Hall Marketplace and in Copley Square, where same-day tickets to musical and theatrical performances (subject to availability) are on sale for half price. Credit cards are not accepted.

**THE PERFORMING ARTS** The city's best-known concert venue is **Symphony Hall,** 301 Massachusetts Ave., at Huntington Avenue (☎ 617/266-1492, 617/CONCERT for program information, or 617/266-1200 for Symphony Charge). Symphony Hall is home to the legendary ✪ **Boston Symphony Orchestra.** The **Boston Pops** also plays there, and the **Hatch Shell** amphitheater on the Esplanade (☎ 617/727-1300, ext. 555) is the scene of the Pops' Fourth of July concert (which always ends with Tchaikovsky's *1812 Overture* with real cannons). Almost every other night in the summer, free music and dance performances and films take over the Hatch Shell stage to the delight of the crowds on the lawn. Smaller professional venues include the Berklee College of Music's **Berklee Performance Center,** 136 Massachusetts Ave. (☎ 617/266-7455 for concert line or 617/266-1400, ext. 261), where programs run to jazz and popular music, and the **Boston Center for the Arts,** 539 Tremont St. (☎ 617/426-7700 for events line, or 617/426-0320 for box office), for contemporary theater, music, and dance.

The multipurpose **Wang Center for the Performing Arts,** 270 Tremont St. (☎ 617/482-9393 or 617/931-2000), in the Theater District, is home to the **Boston Ballet** (☎ 617/695-6950) and numerous touring dramatic, dance, and music companies. In the same neighborhood, you'll find shows headed to or on hiatus from Broadway at the **Colonial Theatre,** 106 Boylston St. (☎ 617/426-9366); the **Shubert Theatre,** 265 Tremont St. (☎ 617/426-4520); and the **Wilbur Theater,** 246 Tremont St. (☎ 617/423-7440).

The excellent local theater scene boasts the **Huntington Theatre Company,** which performs at the Boston University Theatre, 264 Huntington Ave. (☎ 617/266-0800), and the **American Repertory Theatre (ART),** which makes its home at Harvard University's Loeb Drama Center, 64 Brattle St., Cambridge (☎ 617/547-8300).

**THE CLUB & BAR SCENE**   Clubs and bars are thickly concentrated along Lansdowne Street, near Kenmore Square, and along Boylston Place, off Boylston Street near the Common and the Theater District. The drinking age is 21, and only a valid driver's license or passport will do as proof of age.

The **Bull & Finch Pub,** 84 Beacon St. (☎ 617/227-9605), looks like "Cheers" from the outside, but not the inside. It really is a neighborhood bar, but today it's far better known for attracting legions of out-of-towners, who find good pub grub, drinks, and plenty of souvenirs. Whenever the door swings open at the **Cantab Lounge,** 738 Massachusetts Ave., Cambridge (☎ 617/354-2685), the deafening music comes spilling out. The source on weekends most likely is Little Joe Cook and the Thrillers, headliners since the early '80s, whose catchy tunes you'll dance to all night and hum all the next day. The 33rd-floor view from the **Custom House Lounge,** in the Bay Tower, 60 State St., Faneuil Hall Marketplace (☎ 617/723-1666), and the 52nd-floor view from **Top of the Hub,** Prudential Center (☎ 617/536-1775), are both amazing, and each also boasts live music and dancing.

The following hotel bars are also worth a separate listing: **The Bar at the Ritz,** Ritz–Carlton Hotel, 15 Arlington St. (☎ 617/536-5700), with its magnificent view of the Public Garden; and the **Bristol Lounge,** Four Seasons Hotel, 200 Boylston St. (☎ 617/351-2000), a perfect after-theater choice.

Popular brew pubs include **Beer Works,** 61 Brookline Ave. (☎ 617/536-2337), across the street from Fenway Park (and always crowded, even when the Red Sox are away); **Brew Moon Restaurant & Microbrewery,** 115 Stuart St. (☎ 617/523-6467), where the food is as good as the beer; **Commonwealth Brewing Company,** 138 Portland St. (☎ 617/523-8383), the city's first brew pub, dating back to 1986; and **John Harvard's Brew House,** 33 Dunster St., Cambridge (☎ 617/868-3585), a clublike, subterranean Harvard Square hangout.

Members of the Boston-based band Aerosmith co-own **Mama Kin** and the adjacent **Mama Kin Music Hall,** 41 Lansdowne St. (☎ 617/536-2100). You probably won't see Steven Tyler, but you will see up-and-comers early in the week, and more established artists toward the weekend. **Middle East,** 472–480 Massachusetts Ave., Central Square, Cambridge (☎ 617/864-EAST), is a restaurant that offers progressive and alternative rock, as well as tasty Middle Eastern fare, and has become a very popular hangout among a younger crowd. For more than 20 years, the **Rathskeller (The Rat),** 528 Commonwealth Ave. (☎ 617/536-2750, or 617/536-6508 for the concert line), has been in the heart of Kenmore Square dispensing rock and riding out the fickle whims of musical fashion. There's nothing glamorous here—just live music Tuesday to Sunday night.

**Johnny D's,** 17 Holland St., Davis Square, Somerville (☎ 617/776-2004 or 617/776-9667 for the concert line), attracts local and national acts alike, with music ranging from zydeco to rock, rockabilly to jazz, blues to ska. Folk predominates at **Kendall Cafe,** 233 Cardinal Medeiros Way, Cambridge (☎ 617/661-0093), but you might also hear up-and-coming rock, country, or blues artists in the tiny back room. The **Western Front,** 343 Western Ave., Cambridge (☎ 617/492-7772), attracts an integrated crowd to hear world-beat music, blues, and especially reggae. **Club Passim,** 47 Palmer St., Cambridge (☎ 617/492-7679), has launched more careers than the mass production of acoustic guitars—Joan Baez, Suzanne Vega, and Michelle Shocked started out here. **The Nameless Coffee House,** 3 Church St., Cambridge (☎ 617/864-1630), represents a foot in the door for a wide range of musicians. The young crowd comes for the promising talent, the storytelling, and the free refreshments (coffee, cider, tea, cocoa, and cookies).

The original **House of Blues,** 96 Winthrop St., Cambridge (☎ 617/491-BLUE), packs 'em in for evening and weekend matinee shows, attracting big names and hordes of fans. **Regattabar,** in the Charles Hotel, 1 Bennett St., Cambridge (☎ 617/661-5000 or 617/876-7777), features a selection of local and international artists considered the best in the area. Cassandra Wilson, Branford Marsalis, Tito Puente, and the Count Basie Orchestra have appeared within the past 2 years. During an evening at **Ryles Jazz Club,** 212 Hampshire St., Inman Square, Cambridge (☎ 617/876-9330), you can shuttle back and forth between the two levels or settle on one floor for the evening. **Scullers Jazz Club,** in the Doubletree Guest Suites Hotel, 400 Soldiers Field Rd. (☎ 617/783-0811), books top jazz singers and instrumentalists in a comfortable, newly expanded room.

Boston's only women-only club, **Coco's Lazy Lounge & Dance Club,** 965 Massachusetts Ave. (☎ 617/427-7807), boasts three dance spaces filled with patrons of all descriptions and often features lesbian performers. **Club Cafe,** 209 Columbus Ave. (☎ 617/536-0966), a trendy South End spot, draws men and women for conversation (the noise level is reasonable), dining, live music in the front room, and video entertainment in the back room, called Moonshine. **Luxor,** 69 Church St., Park Square (☎ 617/423-6969), is a gay video bar, drawing a diverse crowd to see the latest music clips and compilations of snippets from movies and old TV shows concocted by the veejays. Also note that Sunday night is gay night at many nightclubs.

The nightclub scene isn't as snooty as in New York, but at most clubs, T-shirts and jeans are forbidden. **Avalon,** 15 Lansdowne St. (☎ 617/262-2424), is a cavernous dance club with a full concert stage, large dance floors, and a spectacular light show. A hotel ballroom–turned–dance club, **The Roxy,** 279 Tremont St., is in the Tremont House (☎ 617/338-7699). The cover is $8–$10 and the club boasts excellent deejays and live music, a huge dance floor, concert stage, and balcony (perfect for checking out the action down below). **Zanzibar,** 1 Boylston Place (☎ 617/351-2560), is an atrium with a balcony and 25-foot-tall palm trees, where enthusiastic dancers gyrate to contemporary hits. The upscale clientele take breaks from dancing in the billiard room.

## A DAY TRIP TO SALEM

Settled in 1626 (4 years before Boston), Salem later became known around the world as a center of merchant shipping and the China trade, but it's internationally famous today for a 7-month episode in 1692. The witchcraft trial hysteria led to 20 deaths, 3 centuries of notoriety, countless lessons on the evils of prejudice, and dozens of bad puns ("Stop by for a spell" is a favorite slogan). Unable to live down its association with witches, Salem has embraced it. The high school sports teams are called the Witches, and the logo of the *Salem Evening News* is a silhouette of a witch. Should you find yourself in town at the end of October, you won't be able to miss **Haunted Happenings,** the city's 2-week Halloween celebration.

An excellent place to start your visit is the **National Park Service Visitor Center,** 2 New Liberty St. (☎ 508/741-3648), where exhibits highlight early settlement, maritime history, and the leather and textiles industries. At the Essex Street side of the visitor center, you can board the **Salem Trolley** (☎ 508/744-5469) for a 1-hour narrated tour. Or you can walk the **Heritage Trail,** a 1.7-mile route that begins at the visitor center. It's marked by a red line painted on the sidewalk and connects many of the major attractions.

Many 18th-century houses still stand in Salem, some with original furnishings. Ship captains lived near the water at the east end of downtown, while their employers, the shipping company owners, built their homes away from the water (and the accompanying aromas). Many of them lived on **Chestnut Street,** which is preserved as a registered National Historic Landmark.

With the decline of the shipping trade in the early 19th century, Salem's wharves fell into disrepair, a state the National Park Service began to remedy in 1938 when it took over a small piece of the waterfront. Derby Wharf is now a finger of parkland extending into the harbor, part of the 9 acres, dotted with explanatory markers, that make up the **Salem Maritime National Historic Site,** 174 Derby St. (☎ 508/745-1470).

Built by Capt. John Turner in 1668, the **House of the Seven Gables,** 54 Turner St. (☎ 508/744-0991), was later occupied by a cousin of Nathaniel Hawthorne's, and his 1851 novel was inspired by stories and legends of the house and its inhabitants. If you haven't read the book, don't let that keep you away—begin your visit with the audiovisual program, which tells the story.

The 1992 merger of the Peabody Museum and the Essex Institute into the **Peabody Essex Museum,** East India Square (☎ 800/745-4054 or 508/745-9500), combined fascinating collections that illustrate Salem's adventures abroad and its development at home. The treasures have all been arranged in well-planned displays that help you understand the significance of each artifact.

A re-creation of life in Salem just 4 years after European settlement, **Salem 1630: Pioneer Village,** Forest River Park, off West Avenue (☎ 508/745-0525 or 508/744-0991), is a Puritan village staffed by costumed interpreters who lead tours, demonstrate crafts, and tend to farm animals. The village inherited a large collection of authentic and reproduction props used in the 1996 movie *The Crucible.*

So what about the witches? Find out all about them at **Salem Witch Museum,** 19½ Washington Square (☎ 508/744-1692), a huge room lined with displays that are lighted in sequence. The 30-minute narration tells the story of the witchcraft trials and the accompanying hysteria. Several local shops specialize in witchcraft accessories. **The Broom Closet,** 3–5 Central St. (☎ 508/741-3669), and **Crow's Haven Corner,** 125 Essex St. (☎ 508/745-8763), sell everything from crystals to clothing and cast a modern-day light on age-old customs—just bear in mind that Salem is home to many practicing witches who take their craft very seriously.

**Essentials:** Salem is 17 miles northeast of Boston. Take Route 1A north, or take I-93 or Route 1 to Route 128, then Route 114 into downtown Salem. Once there, follow the signs, which are color coordinated—brown for the visitor center, blue for parking, and green for museums and historic sites. From Boston, the **MBTA** (☎ 617/222-3200) runs bus route 450 from the Haymarket "T" station and commuter trains from North Station. The bus takes about an hour, the train 30 minutes.

# 3  The Berkshires

They're more than hills but less than mountains, so the Taconic and Hoosac ranges that define this region at the western end of Massachusetts go by the collective name of "The Berkshires." The hamlets, villages, and two small cities that have long drawn energy and sustenance from the region's kindly Housatonic River and its gentle tributaries are as representative an evocation of greater New England as can be found.

Mohawks and Mohegans lived and hunted here, and while missionaries established settlements at Stockbridge and elsewhere in an attempt to Christianize the native tribes, the Indians eventually moved on west. Farmers, drawn to the narrow but fertile flood-plains of the Housatonic, were supplanted in the 19th century by manufacturers, who erected the brick mills that drew their power from the rushing river.

At the same time, Nathaniel Hawthorne, Herman Melville, Edith Wharton, and other writers and artists came here for the mild summers and seclusion these hills and lakes offered. By the last decades of the 19th century and the arrival of the rails, wealthy New Yorkers and Bostonians had discovered the region and begun to erect extravagant summer "cottages" on tailored wooded acres. With their support, theater, dance, and concerts had established themselves as sturdily regular summer fixtures by the 1930s. Tanglewood, Jacob's Pillow, and the Berkshire and Williamstown Theatre Festivals are events that draw tens of thousands of visitors every July and August.

## ARRIVING & DEPARTING

The Massachusetts Turnpike (I-90) runs east–west from Boston to the Berkshires, with an exit near Lee and Stockbridge. From New York City, the scenic Taconic State Park-way connects with I-90 not far from Pittsfield. **Amtrak's** daily *Lake Shore Limited* between Boston and Chicago stops in Pittsfield (☎ **800/USA-RAIL**).

## ESSENTIALS

**VISITOR INFORMATION**   Pittsfield's **Berkshire Visitor Bureau,** Berkshire Common (off South Street, near the entrance to the Hilton), Pittsfield, MA 01201 (☎ **800/237-5747** or 413/443-9186), provides brochures and answers questions for the region. In addition, local chambers of commerce and other civic groups maintain info booths at central locations in Great Barrington, Lee, Lenox, Stockbridge, and Williamstown. Internet surfers go to **www.berkshires.org**.

## SHEFFIELD

The first settlement of any size that you'll encounter after crossing the Connecticut bor-der north on U.S. 7 (if you're approaching from the south), Sheffield occupies a flood-plain beside the Housatonic River, with the Berkshires rising to the west. Agriculture has been the principal occupation of its residents, and it still is, to a large degree. Ev-eryone else sells antiques, or so it might seem while you continue along U.S. 7 (aka Main Street or Sheffield Plain). The wide road and generously spaced, well-maintained houses cultivate an impression of prosperous tranquility.

### WHAT TO SEE & DO

**ATTRACTIONS**   The **Colonel Ashley House,** Cooper Hill Road (☎ **413/229-8600**), is in Ashley Falls. Built in 1735, this small modified saltbox is believed to be the old-est house in Berkshire County. It was built by a Colonel Ashley, a person of consider-able repute in colonial western Massachusetts, a pioneer in the area, an officer in one of the French and Indian Wars, and later a lawyer and judge. Furnishings and farm tools appropriate to the period inform the interior. To find it, drive south on U.S. 7, watching for U.S. 7A on the left toward Ashley Falls. After a short distance on 7A, bear right on Rannappo Road. At the Y intersection, turn right on Copper Hill Road and drive for about 200 yards. Visiting times are sharply restricted. Open Sat, Sun, and holiday Mon 1–5pm in June, Sept, and Oct; Wed–Sun July–Labor Day.

A 278-acre nature reservation, **Bartholomew's Cobble,** U.S. 7A (☎ **413/229-8600**), lies beside an ox-bow bend in the Housatonic. It's latticed with 6 miles of trails suitable for gentle hiking in summer and for cross-country skiing in winter. They cross

# The Berkshires

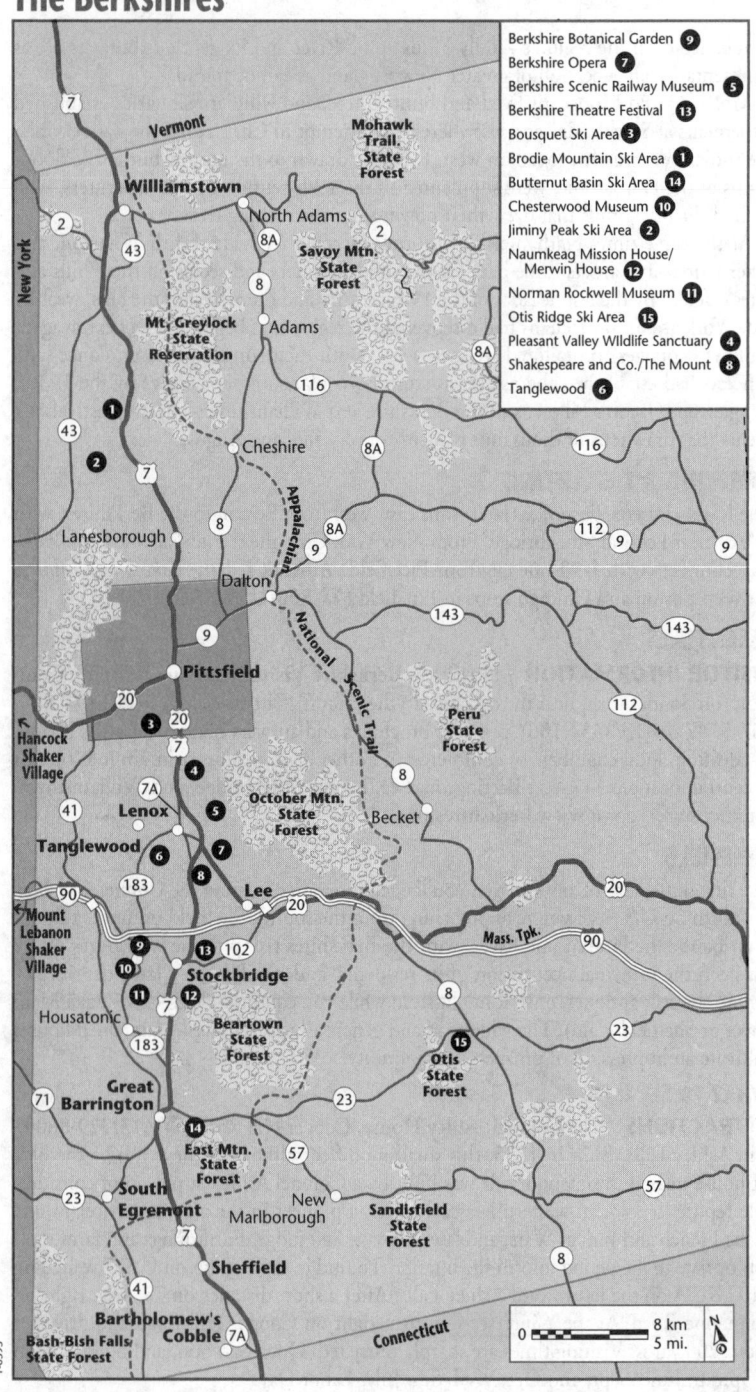

Berkshire Botanical Garden **9**
Berkshire Opera **7**
Berkshire Scenic Railway Museum **5**
Berkshire Theatre Festival **13**
Bousquet Ski Area **3**
Brodie Mountain Ski Area **1**
Butternut Basin Ski Area **14**
Chesterwood Museum **10**
Jiminy Peak Ski Area **2**
Naumkeag Mission House/
Merwin House **12**
Norman Rockwell Museum **11**
Otis Ridge Ski Area **15**
Pleasant Valley Wildlife Sanctuary **4**
Shakespeare and Co./The Mount **8**
Tanglewood **6**

1-0595

pastures and penetrate forests and provide a fine vista of the river and its valley from the area's high point, Hurlburt's Hill. Picnicking is permitted. A sign near the entrance claims there are 700 varieties of plants, 125 types of trees, and 450 kinds of wildflowers. Birders should take their binoculars, for many species are attracted to the flora and the feeders set up near the the administrative cabin. The requested donations are $3 adults, $1 children 6–12. To get there, follow the directions for the Colonel Ashley House (above), except at the end of Rannappo Road, bear left on Weatogue Road and follow it to the reservation entrance.

**SHOPPING**   Sheffield can lay claim to the title of antiques capital of the Berkshires. While you're driving north on U.S. 7, the jumbled display of birdhouses on the right will drag your eye to the Antiques Center of Sheffield, 33 S. Main St. (‰ 413/229-3400). The garrulous owner claims it has been an antique store since 1860. His stock isn't afflicted by excessive tidiness, but it's diverse, including railroad lanterns, military mementos, and wildly varied Americana. Across the street is Darr Antiques, Main Street, P.O. Box 130 (☎ 413/229-7773), a well-ordered shop in pristine contrast to its neighbor—one of the owners is an interior designer. Darr specializes in formal 18th- and 19th-century English and American furniture, with some Chinese accessories. Open year-round, it closes Tues–Wed in winter.

Farther north along U.S. 7, on the right, **Dovetail Antiques,** 440 Sheffield Plain (☎ 413/229-2628), specializes in American clocks, especially those made in Connecticut in the 19th century. Some have gears, cogs, and other internal parts made of wood. Continuing along Route 7, on the left at the edge of town you'll come to **Susan Silver** (☎ 413/229-8169). On display are meticulously restored 18th- and 19th-century English library furniture and French accessories of comparable age.

### ACCOMMODATIONS

No decorator had a hand in assembling the stolid, comfortable furnishings of the **Ivanhoe Country House,** 254 S. Undermountain Rd. (Rte. 41), Sheffield, MA 01257 (☎ 413/229-2143). The rooms have double beds or twins and a refrigerator. Three have fireplaces. The only TV is in the common Chestnut Room. A double costs $65–$85 in winter, $85–$110 in summer; breakfast is included, and credit cards are not accepted. No children under 15 are allowed on weekends July–Aug. Dogs are accepted ($10 a day) but must be leashed at all times and cannot be left alone in the rooms.

## SOUTH EGREMONT

As the larger, busier half of the town of Egremont, this enjoyably diverting village borders Mass. 23, the most-used gateway to the southern Berkshires from Mass. 23 and the Taconic Parkway in New York State. It was once a stop on the stagecoach route between Hartford and Albany and retains many structures from that era, including mills that utilized the stream that still rushes by. Those circumstances make it a magnet for antique dealers, restaurateurs of varying levels of ambition, and refugee urban professionals who have made the precarious leap into innkeeping and retailing.

### OUTDOOR ACTIVITIES

In warmer months, scenic **Bash Bish Falls State Park,** Mass. 23 (☎ 413/528-0330), makes a rewarding day outing for hiking, birding, and fishing. (No camping or picnicking.) Getting there from South Egremont isn't too complicated. Drive west on Mass. 23 from the town center, turning south on Route 41, and immediately right on Mt. Washington Road. Keep alert for signs directing the way to Mt. Washington State Forest and Bash Bish Falls. After 8 miles, a sign indicates a right turn toward the falls. Look for it opposite a board-and-batten church with an unusual steeple. The road begins to follow the course of a mountain stream, going downhill. In about 3 miles, on the left, is a large parking place next to a craggy promontory and a sign prohibiting alcohol, camping, and fires and pointing to a trail down to the falls, which should be negotiated only by reasonably fit adults. First, mount the promontory for a splendid view across the Hudson Valley to the pale blue ridgeline of the Catskills, between two rounded peaks off to the west. You'll hear the falls, but won't see them yet, down to the left. If the trail seems too steep, continue down the road to another parking area, on the left. From here, a gentler trail a little over a mile long leads into the falls. The falls themselves are quite impressive, crashing down from over 50 feet into a deep pool. The park is open from dawn to dusk. Admission is free.

At the western edge of the township, touching the New York border, is the **Catamount Ski Area,** Mass. 23 (☎ 413/528-1262). About 2 hours from Manhattan, it's popular with New Yorkers, who must drive twice as long to get to Vermont's higher peaks. It has 24 trails, including the daunting Catapult, the steepest run in the Berkshires (for experts only), and four double chairlifts. There's also night skiing on 13 trails.

## ACCOMMODATIONS

City escapees have opened some interesting inns in renovated houses in Egremont/South Egremont area.

**Egremont Inn.** *Old Sheffield Rd. (P.O. Box 418), South Egremont, MA 01258.* ☎ *413/528-2111. Fax 413/528-3284. 18 rms. July–Aug, $90–$165 double; lower rest of year. Rates include breakfast. AE, DISC, MC, V.* The Egremont has been a tavern/inn since 1780. The present owners have been here for a little over 2 years, and their renovations have included the merging of smaller rooms to create five suites. The Egremont is a restaurant as well (dinner Wed–Sun all year, Sun brunch July to mid-Oct), serving "Country American" food.

**Weathervane Inn.** *Mass. 23, South Egremont, MA 01258.* ☎ *800/528-9580 or 413/528-9580. Fax 413/528-1713. 12 rms. Sun–Thurs, $95–$135 double including breakfast and afternoon tea; Fri–Sat, $175–$205 double including breakfast, and tea. MAP (breakfast and lunch included in rate) and 2-night minimum required weekends; no dinner Mar–Apr.* "Screw the Golden Years" reads a sampler pillow in the sitting room, a reflection of the owners' nose-thumbing views. An affectionate cat is more welcoming, as are the rooms, many with four-posters. The building's core was a 1735 farmhouse, and the Greek Revival appearance dates to an 1835 renovation. No smoking indoors.

## DINING

Some imaginative dining options are in the area—they offer traditional dishes with a twist.

**John Andrew's.** *Mass. 23.* ☎ *413/528-3469. Reservations recommended Sat–Sun. Main courses $13–$22. MC, V. June–Aug, Mon–Sat 5:30–10pm, Sun 11am–3pm. Sept–May, Thurs–Tues 5:30–10pm. ECLECTIC AMERICAN.* A fertile imagination is at work here, one that conjures up dishes like wilted beet greens with artichoke hearts and sundried tomato vinaigrette as well as seared sea scallops with couscous and sweet-pea mint coulis. A choice of breads arrive with the generous martinis. Espresso and brandies are available, and desserts feature homemade ice cream.

**Mom's Cafe.** *Main St.* ☎ *413/528-2414. Main courses $4.95–$12.95. MC, V. Daily 6:30am–9:30pm. ECLECTIC.* "Mom" is Rich Altman, and his menu runs from omelets and pancakes to pizzas with toppings as diverse as avocado and pineapple. A couple of years ago, he added Spanish tapas in the evening. In good weather, elect to eat on the deck. The restaurant also serves beer and wine.

## GREAT BARRINGTON

Even with a population well under 8,000, this pleasant commercial and retail center is the largest town in the southernmost part of the county. Rapids in the Housatonic provided power for a number of mills in centuries past, most of which are now gone, and in 1886 it was one of the first communities in the world to have electricity on its streets and in its homes. More recently, it was spared by the killer tornado of Memorial Day 1995 that hopped over Great Barrington only to touch down again a few miles east around Monterey, tearing off hundreds of trees halfway up their trunks. That devastation will be seen along Mass. 23 for decades to come.

Great Barrington has no sights or monuments of significant interest, leaving you ample time to browse its many antique galleries and specialty shops. Convenient as a home base for excursions to such nearby attractions as Monument Mountain, Bash Bish Falls, Butternut Basin, Tanglewood concerts, and the museums and historic houses of Stockbridge, it has a number of unremarkable but adequate motels along U.S. 7 north of the town center that tend to fill up slower on weekends than the better-known inns in the area. It's something of a dining center, too, compared to other Berkshire towns.

The **Southern Berkshire Chamber of Commerce** maintains an information booth at 362 Main St. (☎ **413/528-1510**), near the town hall, open Mon–Fri 9:30am–4:30pm, Sat 9:30am–3:30pm.

## WHAT TO SEE & DO

**Butternut Basin,** Mass. 23 (☎ **413/528-2000**), 2 miles east of town, is known for its family ski programs. A children's center provides day care for kids 2$^1$/$_2$–6 daily from December 23 to the end of the season, and the SKIwee program offers full and half-day programs for children 4–12 that include lunch, ski instruction, and a lift ticket. Six double and quad chairlifts provide access to 22 trails, the longest of which is a 1$^1$/$_2$-mile run. There are also 5 miles of cross-country trails.

A little over 4 miles north of town, west of U.S. 7, is **Monument Mountain,** with two hiking trails to the summit. The easier one is called the Indian Monument Trail, about an hour's hike to the top; the more difficult Hickey Trail isn't much longer but takes the steep way up and should probably be avoided by novice hikers. The summit, called Squaw Peak for an Indian maiden who allegedly leapt to her death from the spot, offers splendid views. Nathaniel Hawthorne and Herman Melville, members of the remarkable mid–19th-century literary set that summered in the Berkshires, first met here on a hiking trip.

Camping and hiking equipment, as well as free advice on area trails, are available at **Appalachian Mountain Gear,** 777 S. Main St. (☎ **413/528-8811**). The owner guides free hikes on Sunday.

Shoppers will want to take a turn off of Main Street onto Railroad Street, the town's best shopping strip. Start on the corner, at **T. P. Saddle Blanket & Trading Co.,** 304 Main St. (☎ **413/528-6500**), an unlikely but fascinating emporium that looks like it was lifted whole from the Colorado Rockies. Packed to the walls with western gear—boots, hats, plates, Indian jewelry, pitchers, jars of salsas, rugs, blankets—it's open every day. Down the left side of Railroad Street is **Bleu Lavande,** U.S. 7 (☎ **413/528-1618**), whose French Canadian owner parades her good taste with a stock of Gallic tableware, bed linens, country furniture, and nightwear. Open daily.

## ACCOMMODATIONS

The Great Barrington area has a number of good overnight options. Many inns have plans that include breakfast and lunch or dinner (MAP).

**Old Inn on the Green & Gedney Farm.** *Route 57, New Marlborough, MA 01230.* ☎ ***800/286-3139** or 413/229-3131. 8 rms, 5 suites. $120–$285 double. Rates include breakfast. MC, V. Take Mass. 23 east from Great Barrington, picking up Route 57 after 3.4 miles. After 5.7 miles, you'll see the the Old Inn on the left. Continue another quarter mile to the barns on the left. Registration is in the gray barn.* This establishment is a

1760 tavern/general store/post office on the village green and two barns down the road. The restaurant is in the Old Inn (dinner Nov–June, Thurs–Sun; July–Oct, Wed–Mon). While the baths in the inn have been redone, the most desirable rooms are in the barns, combining contemporary furnishings with oriental rugs.

**Windflower Inn.** *684 S. Egremomt Rd. (P.O. Box 25), Great Barrington, MA 01230.* ☎ *800/992-1993 or 413/528-2720. Fax 413/528-5147. 13 rms. $100–$160 double with breakfast and afternoon tea; $170–$220 double, MAP. AE.* Built in the mid-19th century in Federal style, the Windflower has attained its high quality under the current owners, who bought it in 1980. All rooms have black-and-white TVs, six have fireplaces, and four have canopied beds. Dinner is served Thursday to Sunday in summer. Smoking in the living room only. Children are welcome; pets aren't.

### DINING

A brewery, a bistro, and ecclectic international cuisine are among the less traditional restaurants in the area.

**Barrington Brewery.** *U.S. 7 (in the Jennifer House complex, north of town).* ☎ *413/528-8282. Main courses $8.95–$14.95. AE, MC, V. Daily 11:30am–10 or 11pm (depending on business). ECLECTIC AMERICAN.* This converted barn retains its rough siding and beams. The excellent beers and ales are made on the premises. Grub is of the bratwurst, burger, and nacho variety, but you'll find good pot pies and grilled strip steaks too. The restaurant bakes its own breads and desserts. In summer, a tented dining area is erected outside.

**Boiler Room Cafe.** *405 Stockbridge Rd. (U.S. 7).* ☎ *413/528-4280. Main courses $9–$21. MC, V. Tues–Sat 5–10pm. ECLECTIC/INTERNATIONAL.* The menu describes the fare as "cuisine locale," but it's replete with raclette, soy-marinated tuna with sesame noodles, and braised lamb shanks with avocado salsa. A recent special was a Mediterranean platter, with sausage of lamb, pork, and fennel; white beans; shrimp; asparagus; goat cheese; olives; smoked mussels; and grilled bread.

**Castle Street Cafe.** *10 Castle St. (near the Town Hall).* ☎ *413/528-5244. Main courses $9–$21. AE, DISC, MC, V. Wed–Mon 5–9pm (until 10pm Fri–Sat). NEW AMERICAN.* This storefront bistro has ruled the Great Barrington roost for some time, with fare like grilled veal chop with roast garlic sauce and "homemade" mashed potatoes or roast duck with black-currant sauce. Pastas are so big that half portions are available. There's a short bar to have a drink while checking out the menu.

## STOCKBRIDGE

Stockbridge's ready accessibility to Boston and New York, each about 2$^1$/$_2$ hours away by road and reachable by rail, transformed the original frontier settlement into a Gilded Age summer retreat for the superrich and the merely wealthy. The town has long been popular among artists and writers as well, including Norman Rockwell, who lived here for 25 years and who rendered the Main Street of his adopted town in a famous painting. Along and near Main Street are a number of historic homes and other attractions, enough to fill the hours of a long weekend, even without the Tanglewood concert season in nearby Lenox.

The chamber of commerce maintains a self-service seasonal information booth opposite the row of stores Rockwell depicted. It's open 24 hours a day May through October, with stocks of pamphlets and notices about area attractions and lodgings.

### WHAT TO SEE & DO

**ATTRACTIONS** The **Berkshire Botanical Garden,** Mass. 102 and 183 (☎ 413/298-3926), comprises 15 acres of flower beds, shrubs, ponds, and raised vegetable and herb gardens. The first weekend in October is devoted to a harvest festival, which features jugs of cider, displays of pumpkins, and hayrides. Admission is $5 adults, $4 seniors, free for children under 12. Open May–Oct, daily 10am–5pm. Drive west from downtown Stockbridge on Main Street, picking up Church Street (Route 102) northwest and driving about 2 miles.

Sculptor Daniel Chester French used **Chesterwood,** 4 Williamsville Rd. (☎ 413/298-3579), as his summer home and studio for over 30 years. His famous sculpture of the *Minute Man* at the Old North Bridge in Concord, completed in 1875 at the age of 25, launched his successful career. Subsequent commissions included a bust of Ralph Waldo Emerson at Harvard, the statue of *Alma Mater* at Columbia University, and one of the most moving monuments in America, the Abraham Lincoln Memorial in Washington, D.C. His house and studio here were designed by his friend and collaborator on the Lincoln Memorial, Henry Bacon. A visit can easily be combined with one to the Rockwell Museum, under a mile away. Admission is $7 adults, $3.50 children 13–18, $1.50 children 6–12. Open May–Oct, daily 10am–5pm. Drive west on Main Street and south on Route 183 about 1 mile to the Chesterwood sign.

Rev. John Sergeant had the most benevolent, if paternalistic, of intentions: He sought to build a house among the Stockbridge Indians of the Housatonic tribe, hoping to convert them to civilized (English) ways through proximity to his godly self and his small band of settlers. The **Mission House,** Main and Sergeant streets (Route 102) (☎ 413/298-3239), built in 1739, was the site of this Christianizing process, and it was moved here, understandably weathered, in 1928. A few of the furnishings were owned by Sergeant. Visits are by guided tour and include a stroll around the herb garden. Admission is $5 adults, $2.50 children. Open daily Memorial Day–Columbus Day 10am–5pm.

Celebrated architect Stanford White of New York designed the 26-room **Naumkeag,** Prospect Hill (☎ 413/298-3239), for Joseph Hodge Choate and his family in 1886. Choate was a lawyer and served as U.S. ambassador to the Court of St. James. His many-gabled and chimneyed house is largely of the New England shingle style, surrounded by impressive gardens. Admission is by guided tour only, but worth it for the glimpses of the rich interior, fully furnished and decorated in the manner of the period, including many paintings and an extensive collection of Chinese export porcelain. Admission is $7 adults, $2.50 children. Open daily Memorial Day–Columbus Day 10am–5pm. From the Cat and Dog Fountain in the intersection next to the Red Lion Inn, drive north on Prospect Hill Road about 2 miles.

The striking ✪ **Norman Rockwell Museum,** Route 183 (☎ 413/298-4100), was erected at a cost of $4.4 million in 1993 to house the works of Stockbridge's favorite son. The beloved illustrator used both his neighbors and the town where he lived for the last third of his life to tell stories about an America rapidly fading from memory. Most of Rockwell's paintings adorned covers of the weekly *Saturday Evening Post,* warm and often humorous depictions of homecomings, first proms, visits to the doctor, and the marriage license bureau. He displayed serious concerns, too, notably with his series on the "Four Freedoms" and his poignant portrait of a little African-American girl in a white dress being escorted by U.S. marshals into a previously segregated school. Selections of his illustrations are rotated into view from the large permanent collection, the pity being that none of his ingenious April Fool's covers are included. A couple of galleries show the works of other illustrators of the past hundred years, including Howard Pyle, Charles Dana Gibson, and N. C. Wyeth. The lovely 36-acre grounds contain Rockwell's last studio, moved here to a point overlooking a bend in the Housatonic. Picnic tables are provided. Admission is $9 adults, $2 children 6–18, $20 family. Open year-round, daily 10am–5pm. Take Main Street (Route 102) west to the junction with Route 183, with its traffic signal. Turn left (south). In about a half-mile, the entrance to the museum is on the left.

## ACCOMMODATIONS & DINING

Stockbridge is the place to experience a stay at a historic inn. A dining option outside of the inn dining rooms is **Michael's,** Elm Street (off Main Street, (☎ **413/298-3530**), a tavern with a sports flavor that serves pretty good Italian/American food. Main courses cost $8.95–$16.95, and the dining room stays open all day.

**Inn at Stockbridge.** *30 East St. (U.S. 7; Box 618), Stockbridge, MA 01262.* ☎ *413/298-3337. Fax 413/298-3406. 12 rms. June–Oct, $100–$260 double; Nov–May, $98–$190 double. Rates include breakfast. AE, MC, V.* The owners of this 1906 neoclassical building serve breakfast by candlelight and afternoon spreads of cheese and wine. They intend to add four rooms, but the best of the existing accommodations is the Terrace Room, with a deck, a private entrance, a Jacuzzi, and the only bedroom TV. No smoking and no pets, and children must be 12 or over.

**Red Lion.** *Main St., Stockbridge, MA 01262.* ☎ *413/298-5545. Fax 413/298-5130. 111 rms. Late Apr–late Oct, $94–$159 double; rest of year, $87–$123. AE, CB, DC, DISC, MC, V.* This famous and eternally busy inn had its origins as a stagecoach tavern in 1773. Most rooms have TVs. You can take sustenance in the moderately formal dining room, the Widow Bingham Tavern, the basement Lion's Den, or, in good weather, the courtyard out back. Make reservations *far* in advance.

**Taggart House.** *Main St., Stockbridge, MA 01262.* ☎ *413/298-4303. Fax 413/ 298-4303. 4 rms. July–Oct, $275–$355; rest of year, $175–$275. Rates include breakfast. Two- and 3-day minimum stays apply summer and fall weekends. AE, CB, DC, DISC, MC, V.* The decor and furnishings of this 1850 Victorian/colonial mansion are breathtaking. The dining room's inlaid mahogany table is over a century old and the site of elaborate candlelight breakfasts. There's a paneled library and even a ballroom. Upstairs are beds with fur throws or East Indian silk coverlets or velvet canopies and chests painted with turtleshell and bois effects.

## LEE

While Stockbridge and Lenox were developing into luxurious recreational centers for the satraps of Boston and New York, Lee was a thriving paper-mill town. That inevitably meant it was shunned by the wealthy summer people and thus essentially remained a town of workers and merchants. It has a somewhat raffish, though not unappealing, aspect, its center clustered with shops and offices, and few of the stately homes and broad lawns that characterize the neighboring communities. The town's contribution to the Berkshire cultural calendar is the Jacob's Pillow Dance Festival, which first thrived on a fabled alliance between founder Ted Shawn and Martha Graham.

The Lee Chamber of Commerce operates an **information center** during summer and early fall on Railroad Street (Route 20) (☎ **413/243-0852**). They can assist in obtaining lodging in the area, often in modest guesthouses and B&Bs that are rarely as grand as those in Lenox but nearly always significantly cheaper. That's something to remember when every other place near Tanglewood seems to be booked or quoting $200 a night or more.

## WHAT TO SEE & DO

There's no immediate obligatory historic homes or museums, so visitors in search of attractions routinely make the short excursion to the hamlet of Tyringham. To get there, take U.S. 20 south to Route 102, near the no. 2 interchange of the Massachusetts Turnpike. Following the signs through the complicated intersection, pick up Tyringham Road and drive south about 4 miles.

You'll know when you get where you're going. It's on the left, an odd fairy-tale structure often called the "Gingerbread House." At the front wall are jagged limestone outcroppings, in back are conical turrets topping towers, and the shingled roof rolls like waves on the ocean. Erected at the turn of the century as a studio for sculptor Henry

Hudson Kitson, it now houses the **Tyringham Art Galleries** (☎ 413/243-0654), showcasing the works of competent, if not breathtaking, Berkshire artists. Open Memorial Day–Columbus Day, daily 10am–5pm. Admission is $1 adults, free for children.

**Jacob's Pillow**   On George Carter Road in Becket, Jacob's Pillow (☎ 413/243-0745) is to dance what Tanglewood is to classical music, each showcasing talent of equal stature. Known as a regular summer venue for the late dancer and choreographer Martha Graham, the theater has long welcomed troupes of international reputation such as the Mark Morris Dance Group, the Paul Taylor Company, and Feld Ballet/NY, as well as repertory companies whose work is based on jazz, flamenco, and Indian and Asian music. The season is late June to late August, and tickets go on sale May 1. The more prominent companies are seen in the main Ted Shawn Theatre; other troupes are assigned to the less expensive Studio/Theatre.

## ACCOMMODATIONS

**October Mountain State Forest** offers 50 campsites (with showers) and over 16,000 acres for hiking and walking, canoeing and other nonmotorized boating, cross-country skiing, and snowmobiling. To get there, drive northwest on U.S. 20 into town, turn right on Center Street, and follow the signs.

**Applegate.** *279 W. Park St., Lee, MA 01238.* ☎ *800/691-9012 or 413/243-4451. 6 rms. $85–$225 double. MC, V. From Stockbridge, drive north on U.S. 7. In about a half-mile, take a right on Stockbridge Rd. The inn is 2 miles ahead, on the right.* In this 1920s Georgian colonial, the most desirable lodging has a huge canopied bed, Queen Anne reproductions, a walk-around steam shower, and a fireplace. Other rooms are similar, albeit smaller. Breakfast is by candlelight, and the innkeepers set out wine and cheese in the afternoon. No children 12 and under and no pets.

## LENOX & TANGLEWOOD

With its many stately homes and fabulous mansions, Lenox is a repository of extravagant domestic architecture, surpassed only by such fabled resorts of the wealthy as Newport and Palm Beach. Many of these beautiful buildings have been converted into inns and hotels. In a town with a permanent population of barely 5,000, the reason for so many hostelries—over two dozen post signs and others take in guests through B&B networks—is Tanglewood, a series of concerts presented by the Boston Symphony Orchestra every summer on a nearby estate. While the weekend performances of the BSO are the big draw, there are also solo recitals, chamber concerts, and appearances by the privileged young musicians who study at the prestigious Tanglewood Music Center.

The **Lenox Chamber of Commerce** operates an information center in the Lenox Academy Building, 75 Main St. (☎ 413/637-3646). It has public restrooms, and attendants can assist in obtaining lodgings.

### WHAT TO SEE & DO

**ATTRACTIONS**   Housed in a deactivated and restored train station, the **Berkshire Scenic Railway Museum,** Housatonic Street and Willow Creek Road (☎ 413/637-2210), has displays of model railroads, a gift shop, and a real caboose. Fifteen-minute train rides are also offered. This is one of the few attractions in Lenox likely to appeal to children. Guided tours are June–Oct Sat–Sun and holidays.

Edith Wharton, who won a Pulitzer for *The Age of Innocence,* was singularly equipped to write this subtle and deftly detailed examination of the upper classes of the Gilded Age. She was born into that stratum of society in 1862 and traveled in those circles that made the Berkshires a regular stop on their restless movements among New York, Florida, Newport, and the Continent. She had her own "cottage," now the **Edith Wharton Restoration,** Plunkett Street, at the intersection of U.S. 7, 7A, and 20 (☎ 413/637-1899), built on this 130-acre lakeside property in 1902, where she lived for 10 years before leaving for France, never to return. She took an active hand in the overall design and execution of its details, as would be expected of the author of an up-scale 1897 how-to guide called *The Decoration of Houses.* Grand by today's standards, it wasn't especially large for that time in Lenox history. Called "The Mount," it's often used by the actors of the Shakespeare & Co. troupe in stage productions. Restoration is ongoing, but tours continue as scheduled. Guided tours are Memorial Day–Oct, Sat–Sun 9am–2pm. Admission is $6 adults, $4.50 children 13–18, free for children under 13.

The estate of **Tanglewood,** West Street, Stockbridge, MA 01262 (☎ 413/637-1940, box office for concerts, June–Aug), over 500 gorgeous acres of manicured lawns, gardens, and groves of ancient trees, much of it overlooking Stockbridge Bowl Lake, was put together starting in 1849 by William Aspinwall Tappan. At the outset, the only structure was a modest something referred to as the Little Red Shanty. In 1851, it was rented to Nathaniel Hawthorne and his wife, Sophia. The author of *The Scarlet Letter* and *The House of the Seven Gables* stayed there long enough to write a children's book, *Tanglewood Tales,* and meet Herman Melville, who lived nearby in Dalton and became a close friend. The existing Hawthorne Cottage is a replica, now serving as practice studios. It isn't open to the public. On the grounds is the original Tappan mansion, with fine views, and the 1938 Koussevitsky Music Shed, an open-ended auditorium seating 5,000 where the Boston Symphony performs every summer. Two smaller structures of more recent vintage provide space for recitals, lectures, and chamber concerts. Admission to the grounds is free, except for concerts (prices vary). Drive 1 1/2 miles southwest on Mass. 183.

The **Pleasant Valley Wildlife Sanctuary,** West Mountain Road (☎ 413/637-0320), has a small museum and 7 miles of hiking and snowshoeing trails crossing its 1,000 acres. Beaver lodges and dams can be glimpsed from a distance, and waterfowl and other birds are found in abundance, rewarding targets for those who come equipped with binoculars. Open Tues–Sun, dawn–sunset. Admission is $3 adults, $1 children 6–12. To get there, drive north 3 miles on Routes 7 and 20 and turn left on West Mountain Road.

**THE PERFORMING ARTS**　Lenox is filled with music every July and August, and the undisputed headliners are Seiji Ozawa and the Boston Symphony Orchestra, of which he is music director. Concerts, under the baton of Ozawa and other famous guest conductors and often featuring top soloists like Jessye Norman and Itzak Perlman, are given at the famous **Tanglewood** estate, usually beginning the last weekend in June and ending the weekend before Labor Day. While the BSO is Tanglewood's 800-pound cultural gorilla, the program features a menagerie of other performers and musical idioms. These run the gamut from popular artists (past performers have included James Taylor and Peter, Paul, and Mary) and jazz vocalists and combos (including Dave Brubeck, Betty Carter, and Joe Williams), to chamber music to performances by Tanglewood's own music students and faculty. Large visiting ensembles like the Kirov Orchestra and Chorus are also featured.

Large concerts take place in The Shed, an open-ended auditorium that seats 5,000, and also plays to an outdor audience pickniking or lounging on the huge surrounding lawn. Smaller groups and individual soloists appear in Ozawa Hall and the separate theater. For information on programs, call ☎ 617/266-1492 (Boston) or 413/637-5165 (Lenox). For weekly updates on the performance schedule, call ☎ 413/637-1666. To order tickets by mail before June, write the **Tanglewood Ticket Office** at Symphony Hall, Boston, MA 02115. After the first week in June, write the Tanglewood Ticket Office, Lenox, MA 01240. Tickets can be charged by phone through Symphonycharge (☎ 800/274-0808 outside Boston, or 617/266-1200 in Boston).

As all-consuming as the events at Tanglewood are, there's even more. **Shakespeare & Company** uses buildings and outdoor amphitheaters on the grounds of The Mount to stage its late May–late August season of plays by the Bard as well as new American playwrights. Performances by dance troupes, student actors, and even puppets flesh out the schedule. There are two outdoor amphitheaters, Mainstage and Oxford Court, and two indoor stages, Stables and Wharton. Staggered performances take place Tues–Sun noon–8:30pm. Call the box office at ☎ **413/637-3353.** Lunch and dinner picnic baskets can be purchased on site.

The **National Music Center,** 70 Kemble St. (☎ **413/637-1800** for information, 413/637-4718 for tickets), is home to the **Berkshire Performing Arts Theatre,** which presents a June–September season of music—jazz, pop, folk, and blues—in its 1,200-seat hall. And, on selected Saturdays from Oct to May, chamber music recitals are presented at the Lenox Town Hall by **Armstrong Chamber Concerts,** P.O. Box 367, Washington Depot, CT 06794 (☎ **860/868-0522**).

## ACCOMMODATIONS

While it may seem that every other house in town puts up guests, most can only accommodate small numbers. The Tanglewood concert season is a powerful draw, so prices are highest in summer and reservations must be made far in advance. This also applies to the brief fall foliage season, usually around Columbus Day. Zoning restrictions prohibit some B&Bs from hanging signs out front. To find one, contact **Berkshire B&B Homes,** Main Street, Box 211, Williamsburg, MA 01096 (☎ **413/268-7244;** fax 413/268-7243). Inns vary greatly in facilities and ambience, so choose carefully.

When all the area's inns are fully booked, or if you want to be assured the full quota of 20th-century comforts and gadgets, U.S. 7 and 20 north and south of town harbor a number of conventional motels. Among the possibilities are the **Mayflower Motor Inn** (☎ **413/443-4468**), **Susse Chalet** (☎ **413/637-3560**), and the **Lenox Motel** (☎ **413/499-0324**).

**Amadeus House.** *15 Cliffwood St. (near the corner of Main St.), Lenox, MA 01240.* ☎ *800/205-4770 or 413/637-4770. 8 rms, 6 with bath. July–Labor Day, $60–$175 double; mid-May–June and Sept–Oct, $60–$160 double; Nov–mid-May, $60–$135 double. Rates include breakfast. AE, DISC, MC, V.* The owners are classical music lovers and they've named the rooms Bach and Brahms and the like. Beethoven is a two-bedroom suite with a sitting area and kitchen. Only one room has air-conditioning; most of the rest have ceiling fans. Breakfast incorporates a hot entree and afternoon tea is served. No smoking, children 10 or under, or pets.

**Cranwell Resort & Golf Club.** *55 Lee Rd., Lenox, MA 01240.* ☎ *800/272-6935 or 413/637-1364. Fax 413/637-4364. 65 rms. Jan–May, $99–$239 double; June–Labor Day, $199–$389 double; Sept–Dec, $99–$329. Rates include breakfast. 3-night minimum stay July–Aug. AE, DC, DISC, MC, V. From Lenox Center, go north to U.S. 20 east. The resort is on the left.* The most expensive rooms are in a century-old mansion at the center of this 380-acre resort; the rest are in smaller buildings. Some of the latter have wet bars or kitchenettes. There's an 18-hole golf course, and the gentle slopes serve as cross-country ski trails. Three dining rooms range from formal to pubby.

**Gables Inn.** *103 Walker St., Lenox, MA 01240.* ☎ *413/637-3416. 15 rms, 3 suites. $150–$210 double. Rates include breakfast. DISC, MC, V.* Edith Wharton made this Queen Anne mansion her home while The Mount was being built. That may be enough to satisfy her fans, but there's much more here that will appeal, including the canopied four-poster bed and fireplace in Edith's bedroom. No rooms have phones, but have TVs, VCRs, and refrigerators. Children under 12 aren't made welcome.

**Wheatleigh.** *W. Hawthorne Rd., Lenox, MA 01240.* ☎ *413/637-0610. Fax 413/ 637-4507. 17 rms. $175–$565 double. AE, DC, MC, V.* At this 1893 replica of a 16th-century Italian palazzo, the new French manager is striving to give requisite value for the rates. He has added TVs, an exercise room is being added, and a pool and tennis court are available. The dining room admirably rounds out the experience—the year-round fixed-price menu is $58–$90; reservations recommended on weekends.

**Whistler's Inn.** *5 Greenwood St., Lenox, MA 01240.* ☎ *413/637-0975. 14 rms, 3 suites. $90–$250 double and suites. Rates include breakfast. AE, DISC, MC, V.* The inn-keepers are travelers and bring things back from every trip, filling their Tudor mansion with cut glass, assorted Victoriana, and lavish furniture. The result is rooms that aren't so much decorated as gathered; 10 are air-conditioned. Breakfast is enormous, and a bottle of sherry or port is kept in the library. Concerts are often held in summer.

## DINING

In addition to the choices below, many of the inns have dining rooms or bars open to the public, which will give you a chance to see some of the town's beautiful buildings from the inside.

**Church Street Cafe.** *65 Church St.* ☎ *413/637-2745. Reservations recommended on weekends. Main courses $14.95–$17.95. MC, V. Daily 11:30am–2pm and 5:30–10pm (closed Mon in winter). ECLECTIC AMERICAN.* The town's most popular eatery got that way by delivering fanciful combinations like the lunchtime "cafe sandwich," lay-ered grilled eggplant, roasted red peppers, goat cheese, watercress, red onion, and to-mato on wholegrain bread. Another example is the dinner plate of potato cake, roast ratatouille, sautéed greens, and grilled bread drizzled with oil.

**Lenox 218.** *28 Main St. (U.S. 7A).* ☎ *413/637-4218. Main courses $12.95–$21.95. AE, CB, DC, DISC, MC, V. Mon–Sat 11:30am–2:30pm and 5–9:30pm. ITALIAN/ AMERICAN.* Largely black and white, with hanging ivy, the decor at this restaurant falls short of the sophistication it evidently seeks. So does the food, mainly simple fare like veal piccata, chicken cacciatore, and meat loaf with peas, carrots, and mashed potatoes. It's cooked and assembled well enough, and the service is at least pleasant.

## PITTSFIELD

Berkshire County's largest city (population 48,000) and a commerical and industrial center, Pittsfield presents little of the charm that marks such popular destinations as Stockbridge and Lenox. Still, it's a convenient base for day excursions to other Berk-shire attractions, and you can visit the house where Herman Melville wrote *Moby Dick* and an eccentric little museum with a theater showing art films much of the year.

The **Berkshire Visitors Bureau** (☎ 800/237-5747 or 413/443-9186) is in the same block of buildings as the Hilton, on Berkshire Common.

## WHAT TO SEE & DO

**ATTRACTIONS**    Herman Melville, just one prominent member of the Berkshires' literary and artistic community, bought **Arrowhead,** 780 Holmes Rd. (☎ 413/ 442-1793), in 1850 and lived here until 1863. It was here that he wrote his master-piece, *Moby Dick,* and a number of lesser works. He conversed regularly with best friend Nathaniel Hawthorne in the upstairs study and at a table beside the large fireplace in the kitchen. In truth, however, the house is only likely to be interesting to literature stu-dents and avid readers. Visits are by guided tour only. Admission is $5 adults, $4.50 seniors, $3.50 children 6–16. Open late May–Labor Day, daily 10am–5pm; Labor Day–end of Oct, Fri–Mon 10am–5pm; rest of year, by appointment only. Drive east from Park Square on East Street, turn right on Elm Street, and right again on Holmes Road.

The **Berkshire Museum,** 39 South St., 1 block south of Park Square (☎ 413/ 443-7171), began in 1903 as the Museum of Natural History and Art, the words chiseled in stone above the entrance. The holdings bounce from Babylonian cuneiform tablets to stuffed birds to mineral displays to tanks of live fish in the aquarium. An auditorium seating 300 serves as the Little Cinema, which has a season of art and foreign films during warmer months. Apart from the aquarium, the greatest interest may be generated by the art and archeological artifacts assembled on the second floor. A sculpture gallery has full-size casts of important 16th-century Italian sculptures and a 19th-century *Diana* by American Augustus Saint-Gaudens. While those looking for "name" artists will generally be disappointed, there are a number of canvases and sculptures by contemporary artists that deserve attention, and here and there are minor Alexander Calders, a Reginald Marsh, and a couple of landscapes by Alfred Bierstedt. Among cases of 2nd-century Mediterranean glassware and Roman funerary busts are pieces of pre-Christian Egyptian jewelry and pottery and a delicate necklace from Thebes dating to at least 1500 B.C. Kids will love the mummy and the tropical and native fish and amphibians. Admission is $3 adults, $2 seniors and students, $1 children 12–18. Open Tues–Sat 10am–5pm (open Mon July–Aug), Sun 1–5pm.

**OUTDOOR ACTIVITIES**   **Plaine's Bike Golf Ski Golf,** 55 W. Housatonic St. (☎ 413/499-0294), rents bikes by the day and week and carries equipment for all the sports its name suggests. It's on U.S. 20, west of the city center, at the corner of Center Street. **Onota Boat Livery,** 463 Peck Rd. (☎ 413/442-1724), rents canoes and motorboats for use on Onota Lake, conveniently located at the western edge of the city. Nonmember golfers are welcome on the 18-hole course at **Pontoosuc Lake Country Club,** Kirkwood Drive (☎ 413/445-4217), for reasonable greens fees.

South of the city center, off U.S. 7, is the **Bousquet Ski Area,** Dan Fox Drive (☎ 413/442-2436). It has 21 trails, the longest over 1 mile and with a vertical drop of 750 feet, with two double chairlifts and two rope tows. Night skiing is Monday to Saturday; equipment can be rented for moderate rates.

About 9 miles in the other direction, off U.S. 7 in the town of New Ashford, is the **Bodie Mountain Ski Area** (☎ 413/443-4752), with a vertical drop of 1,250 feet and a long run of $2^1/_2$ miles. Midweek ski school packages are attractive, and in summer they offer raquetball, tennis, and campsites.

Alternatively, turn west a mile short of Bodie on Brodie Mountain Road and continue about 3 miles to **Jiminy Peak,** Hancock, MA 01237 (☎ 413/738-5500, or 413/ 738-7325 for 24-hour ski reports). This expanding resort aspires to four-season activity, so skiing on 28 trails (18 open at night) with 7 lifts is supplemented the rest of the year with horseback riding, trapshooting, fishing in a stocked pond, six tennis courts, mountain biking, pools, and golf at the nearby Waubeeka Springs course.

## ACCOMMODATIONS

A prime recreational preserve is **Pittsfield State Forest,** Cascade Street (☎ 413/442-8992), a little over 3 miles west of the center of town on West Street. Its 10,000 acres have 31 campsites, boat ramps, streams for canoeing and fishing, and trails for hiking, horseback riding, and cross-country skiing. Open daily 8am–8pm. Admission is $2 per car.

   ✪ **Country Inn at Jiminy Peak.** *Brodie Mountain Rd. (near Route 43), Hancock, MA 01237.* ☎ *800/882-8859 or 413/738-5500. Fax 413/738-5513. 105 suites. $95–$195 suite. Rates include breakfast. AE, CB, DC, DISC, MC, V.* All units are one-bedroom suites with kitchens and pullout sofas. A buffet breakfast is served late June–mid-Oct and mid-Dec–Apr. There are two pools and abundant recreational facilities. However, most guests could probably live without the reminders that they "could be part of the Jiminy Peak family" by buying a condo.

   **Hilton Inn Berkshire.** *West St., Pittsfield, MA 01201.* ☎ *800/445-8667 or 413/ 499-2000. Fax 413/442-0449. 175 rms. $79–$189 double. AE, CB, DC, DISC, MC, V.* At 14 stories, the tallest building in town, the Hilton isn't hard to find (look for signs to Berkshire Common, west of South Street). With all the rooms, chances are better for copping a bed for Tanglewood weekends, and unlike at most area inns, children are welcome. Seven floors are no-smoking.

## DINING

While most inns have dining rooms, you may want a change of pace.

**Giovanni's.** *U.S. 7 north (north of the center).* ☎ *413/443-2441. Main courses $7–$18. AE, DC, DISC, MC, V. Mon–Sat noon–3pm, Fri–Sat 4:30–10pm, Sun 10am–2pm; Mon–Thurs 5–10pm. ITALIAN/AMERICAN.* The menu hearkens back to an era when iceberg lettuce was salad king. But Giovanni's does have its high points. The portions are gargantuan. And though you've seen veal amandine and baked stuffed shrimp before, they taste good. A specialty is chicken ricco with shrimp, broccoli, mushrooms, onions, and bell peppers on linguine.

## ON THE SHAKER TRAIL: A DRIVING TOUR

The former Ann Lee, Mother Ann arrived in near-Revolutionary New York State in 1774 with eight disciples. She was previously imprisoned for her excess of religious zeal, having proclaimed a vision that anointed her the leader of the United Society of Believers in Christ's Second Coming. That austere Protestant sect was popularly known as "the Shakers" for their spastic movements when in the throes of religious ecstacy.

Mother Lee established their first communal settlement in Watervliet, near Albany, New York. By the time of her death in 1784 she had made many converts, who then fanned out across the country to form colonies from Maine to Indiana. Two of the most important communities straddled the Massachusetts–New York border, within miles of each other near Pittsfield and New Lebanon, New York. Farther west, a Shaker Museum has been established at Old Chatham.

Shaker society produced highly disciplined farmers and craftspeople, whose products were much in demand in the outside world. They sold seeds, invented early agricultural machinery and hand tools, and erected large buildings of several stories and exquisite simplicity. Their spare, clean-lined furniture and accessories anticipated the so-called "Danish Modern" style by a century, and in recent years have drawn astonishingly high prices at auction.

Start your tour in Pittsfield and heading west on U.S. 20. In about 5 miles, on the left, is the Hancock Shaker Village, Routes 20 and 41, Pittsfield, MA 01202 (☎ 800/817-1137 or 413/443-0188). Of the 20 restored buildings that make up the village, the signature structure is clearly the 1826 round stone barn. The Shaker preoccupation with primacy of functionalism and purity of line and material is no more clear than here. The precise joinery of the roof beams and support pillars is a joy to examine. A brick dwelling contained the communal dining room, kitchens, and upstairs sleeping quarters. Sexes were separated here (a prime Shaker tenet being celibacy). Other buildings of note are the Meeting House, where religious services were held, and the laundry and machine shop. While present-day artisans and docents labor in herb and vegetable gardens and in shops demonstrating Shaker crafts and techniques, they're not in costume and don't pretend to be Shaker inhabitants. They dispense such nuggets as explanations of the Shaker discipline that required members to dress the right side first, to button from right to left, and to step with the right foot first. The museum shop is excellent, and a cafe serves lunches from Memorial Day through October. On Saturday night from July through October, the village presents tours and Shaker four-course dinners by candlelight; reservations are essential (☎ 413/443-0188).

Admission to the village is $12.50 adults, $5 children 6–17, $25 families. Open Apr–Memorial Day and late Oct–late Nov (guided tours only), daily 10am–3pm;

Memorial Day–third week in Oct, daily 9:30am–5pm. Also open first weekend in Dec, Christmas weekend, and third week in Feb (call for times and events).

Continue to the far end of the village, taking the rutted gravel road down to the red barn on the left. From Hancock, turn left (west) on U.S. 20. In about 5 miles, on the left, is the private **Darrow School,** which has taken over most of the buildings that were once part of one of the Shaker movement's most important communities. They're easy to spot after a visit to the Hancock Village, with their sober, simple dimensions and utter lack of ornamental detailing. Some of the buildings have been set aside as the **Mount Lebanon Shaker Village,** on U.S. 20 in New Lebanon, New York (☎ **518/794-9500**). This was the first self-contained Shaker community in America, established in 1787. In the red barn is a gift shop and a small museum of tools, furniture, farm implements, and related items. Guided tours are available (on a sporadic basis) of buildings not in use by the school, the most interesting of which are the meetinghouse and a stone dairy barn. Past fund-raising auctions held on the school grounds helped send prices for antique Shaker furniture and artifacts into the stratosphere, especially after enthusiasts Oprah Winfrey and Bill Cosby showed up.

Admission to the village is $6 adults, $3 children 7–18. Open Memorial Day–Labor Day weekends (and some Mon holidays) 10–4pm.

Leaving the Mount Lebanon Village, turn left (west) on U.S. 20. After Brainard (about 8 miles), watch for the turn south on Mass. 66. Continue to the hamlet of Old Chatham, where you'll pick up County Road 13. This is tricky, so watch closely for the sign next to the general store pointing to the **Shaker Museum and Library,** 88 Shaker Museum Rd. in Old Chatham, New York (☎ **518/794-9100**). Obviously better funded and pampered than the Mount Lebanon Village, this concentration of barns and outbuildings contains a substantial collection of about 8,000 Shaker tools, pieces of furniture, machinery, and smaller items, such as the famous oval boxes that held everything from seeds to sewing materials. The collection fills 24 galleries, most of which offer illuminating essays, reproductions of Shaker writings, and helpful descriptive labels. Many of the galleries are arranged as period rooms, including living quarters, kitchen areas, weaving shops, a classroom, and a blacksmith's shop. Periodic special events are mounted, which have included, in the recent past, antique fairs, apple harvest breakfasts, herb and plant sales, concerts, and kite-flying demonstrations.

Admission to the village is $6 adults, $5 seniors, $3 children 8–17. Open late Apr–early Nov, Wed–Mon 10am–5pm.

### ACCOMMODATIONS & DINING

The **Old Chatham Sheepherding Company Inn,** 99 Shaker Museum Rd., Old Chatham, NY 12136 (☎ **518/794-9774**; fax 518/794-9779) rents eight sumptuous rooms in the main house and in cottages, three with fireplaces. The owners of this Georgian manor have 2,000 sheep. Their interest is in developing sheep's milk products—cheeses, ice cream, yogurt—and you can watch them in the milking parlor. The chef makes maximum use of the farm's own products. Rates are $150-$325 for a double, including breakfast. There's no smoking. Children under 12 are not accepted.

## WILLIAMSTOWN

Entering the town on U.S. 7 or intersecting Mass. 2, you'll see a central green shaded by tall trees. In the middle is a weathered building that looks authentic but turns out to be a replica of a 1753 dwelling. It was made with period tools in celebration of the town's bicentennial. The town and its prestigious liberal arts Williams College were named for Col. Ephraim Williams, who was killed in 1755 in one of the French and Indian Wars. He bequeathed the land for creation of a school and a town. His college grew, spreading east from the central common along both sides of Main Street

(Mass. 2). Since it has been around for over 200 years, every new building was erected in one of the styles popular at the time of construction. That makes Main Street a virtual museum of institutional architecture, with representatives of the Georgian, Federalist, Gothic Revival, Romanesque, and Victorian modes and a few that are yet to be labeled. They stand at dignified distances from each other, so what might have been a tumultuous visual hodgepodge is a stately lesson in historical design.

A free weekly newspaper, *The Advocate,* produces a useful *Guide to the Northern Berkshires* that mainly covers Williamstown. For a copy, send a check for $3.50 to *The Advocate,* P.O. Box 95, 38 Spring St., Williamstown, MA 01267. An unattended **information booth** at the corner of North Street (U.S. 7) and Main Street (Route 2) has an abundance of pamphlets and brochures free for the taking.

## WHAT TO SEE & DO

**ATTRACTIONS**   The **Sterling and Francine Clark Art Institute** is at 225 South St. (☎ 413/458-9545). The eponymous Mr. Clark was an art lover. He was also an heir to the Singer fortune, which allowed him to pursue his avocation and bestow this remarkable repository on his community. Clark's donation funded the modern wing to the original white marble neoclassical building and covered all acquisitions, upkeep, and recent renovations; in addition, he specified in his bequest that no admission be charged. It's a remarkable gift, for this is not the collection of an undisciplined, self-absorbed millionaire. Within these walls are canvases by Renoir, Degas, Gauguin, Toulouse-Lautrec, Pissaro, and their predecessor Corot. While they're the stars, there are also 15th- and 16th-century Dutch portraitists, English and European genre and landscape painters, and Americans Sargent and Homer, as well as fine porcelain, silverware, and antique furnishings. This qualifies as one of the great cultural resources of the Berkshires and the state. Admission is free. Open Tues–Sun (and some Mon holidays) 10am–5pm.

The second, lesser leg of Williamstown's two prominent art repositories, the **Williams College Museum of Art,** Main Street (☎ 413/597-2429), exists in large part due to the college's collection of almost 400 paintings by the American modernists Maurice and Charles Prendergast. Some of their works are always rotated into view, and while they're of moderate interest, you're more likely to be drawn to such names as Juan Gris, Fernand Leger, Giorgio de Chirico, James Whistler, and Pablo Picasso. These are salted with more contemporary pieces by Andy Warhol and Edward Hopper and supplemented by frequently changed temporary exhibitions. The striking three-story entrance atrium was designed by architect Charles Moore. Admission is free. Open Tues–Sat (and some Mon holidays) 10am–5pm, Sun 1–5pm.

**OUTDOOR ACTIVITIES**   The **Waubeeka Golf Links,** Routes 7 and 43, South Williamstown, MA 01267 (☎ 413/458-5869), is open to the public, with highest weekend greens fees of only $22. The clubhouse can seat 150 people in three dining rooms.

**Mt. Greylock State Reservation** contains the highest peak (3,487 feet) in Massachusetts and a section of the Appalachian Trail. A road allows cars to be driven almost to the summit, where the War Memorial Tower is located—even the sedentary visitor can enjoy 360° vistas of the Taconic and Hoosac ranges, far into Vermont and New York. More active people will find hiking trails radiating from the parking lot near **Bascom Lodge,** P.O. Box 1800, Lanesborough, MA 01237 (☎ 413/743-1591), a grandly rustic creation of the Civilian Conservation Corps in the New Deal 1930s. Simple dorm beds and four private rooms are available by the night from mid-May to late October. Dinners are available by reservation. Look for Greylock Road off U.S. 7 in New Ashford.

**SHOPPING**   In South Williamstown, the white frame building on the right (going north on U.S. 7) looks like a recycled general store, and it is. Once a basic small-town emporium, **The Store at Five Corners,** Routes 7 and 43 (☎ 413/458-3176), now stocks more upscale merchandise like stylish takeouts and picnics comprised of pâtés, baguettes, French cheeses, wines, deli meats, and salads. Meals can also be eaten on the premises. Open daily 7am–8pm.

**Saddleback Antiques,** 1395 Cold Spring Rd. (☎ 413/458-5852), features country, wicker, and Victorian furniture and a variety of collectibles, while **Collectors Warehouse,** 105 North St. (☎ 413/458-9686), has a bit of everything—jewelry, books, dolls, furniture, glassware. Both are on U.S. 7, the first to the south of the town center, the second slightly to the north.

### ACCOMMODATIONS

This is a college town, so remember that in addition to the usual peak periods of July, August, and the October foliage season, lodgings fill up during graduation (late May–early June) and on football weekends.

**Field Farm Guesthouse.** *554 Sloan Rd., Williamstown, MA 01262.* ☎ *413/458-3135. 5 rms. $100 double. MC, V. Follow U.S. 7 to its intersection with Route 43. Turn west, then make an immediate right turn on Sloan Rd. Continue 1 mile to the Field Farm entrance, on the right.* In 1948, this pristine example of postwar modern architecture rose on a 294-acre estate. Most rooms look over meadows and on up to the summit of Mt. Greylock. All are free of clutter and decorated in muted colors. Breakfast is a hearty meal of waffles and five-cheese omelets. No smoking or pets, but well-behaved children are welcome.

**Williams Inn.** *1090 Main St. (Routes 7 and 2), Williamstown, MA 01267.* ☎ *800/828-0133 or 413/458-9371. Fax 413/458-2767. 100 rms. $100–$150 double. Children under 14 stay free in parents' room. AE, CB, DC, DISC, MC, V.* This is a standard motel but with most conveniences. Even the smallest rooms are ample, and there's an indoor pool and a Jacuzzi and saunas. Pets are permitted on the first floor. The dining room serves expectables like veal scallopini and chicken amandine; the tavern menu offers burgers and such.

### WILLIAMSTOWN AFTER DARK

Williamstown's premier attraction each summer is the **Williamstown Theatre Festival,** held at the Adams Memorial Theatre, Main Street, P.O. Box 517, MA 01267 (☎ 413/597-3400). Staging classic and new plays during its performance season (late June–Aug), the festival attracts many top actors and directors. There are two venues: The Main Stage showcases works by major playwrights, while the Other Stage features more experimental works.

## 4  Cape Cod

Massachusetts' great curling arm of sand known as Cape Cod encompasses hundreds of miles of beaches, more freshwater ponds than there are days in the year, more than a dozen lovely, richly historic New England villages, scores of classic clam shacks and soft–ice-cream stands—and just about everyone's idea of the perfect summer vacation. More than 17 million visitors flock from around the world to enjoy summertime's nonstop carnival.

If anything, "The Cape" is perhaps a bit too popular at full swing: Cognoscenti are beginning to discover the subtler appeal of the off-season, when prices plummet along with the population and travelers have the prospect of taking long, solitary strolls on a windswept beach, with only the gulls as company. Hyannis and Provincetown, however, are populous enough to weather the winter in style, and it's in this downtime that you're most likely to experience the "real" Cape—an elusive entity amid the summer madness.

# Cape Cod

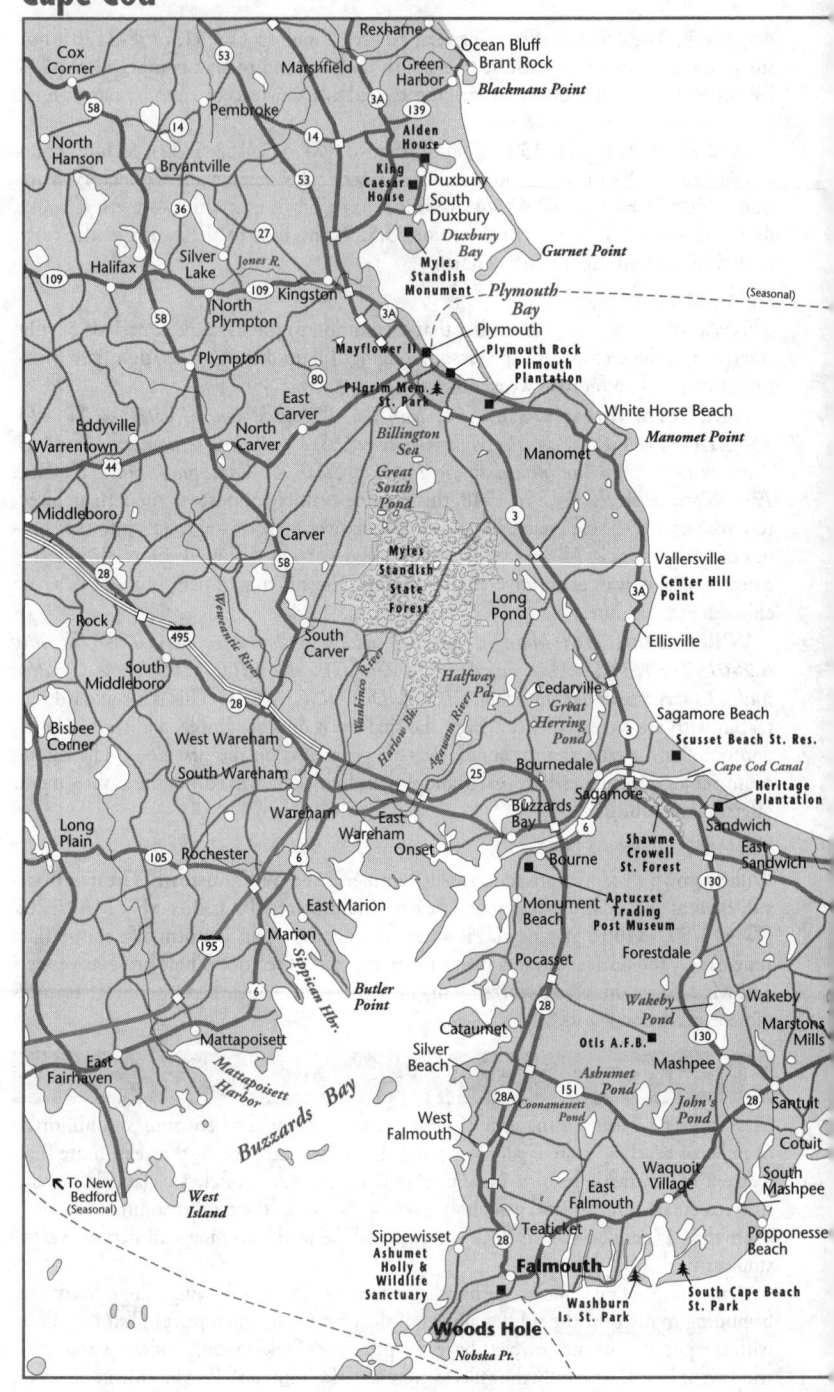

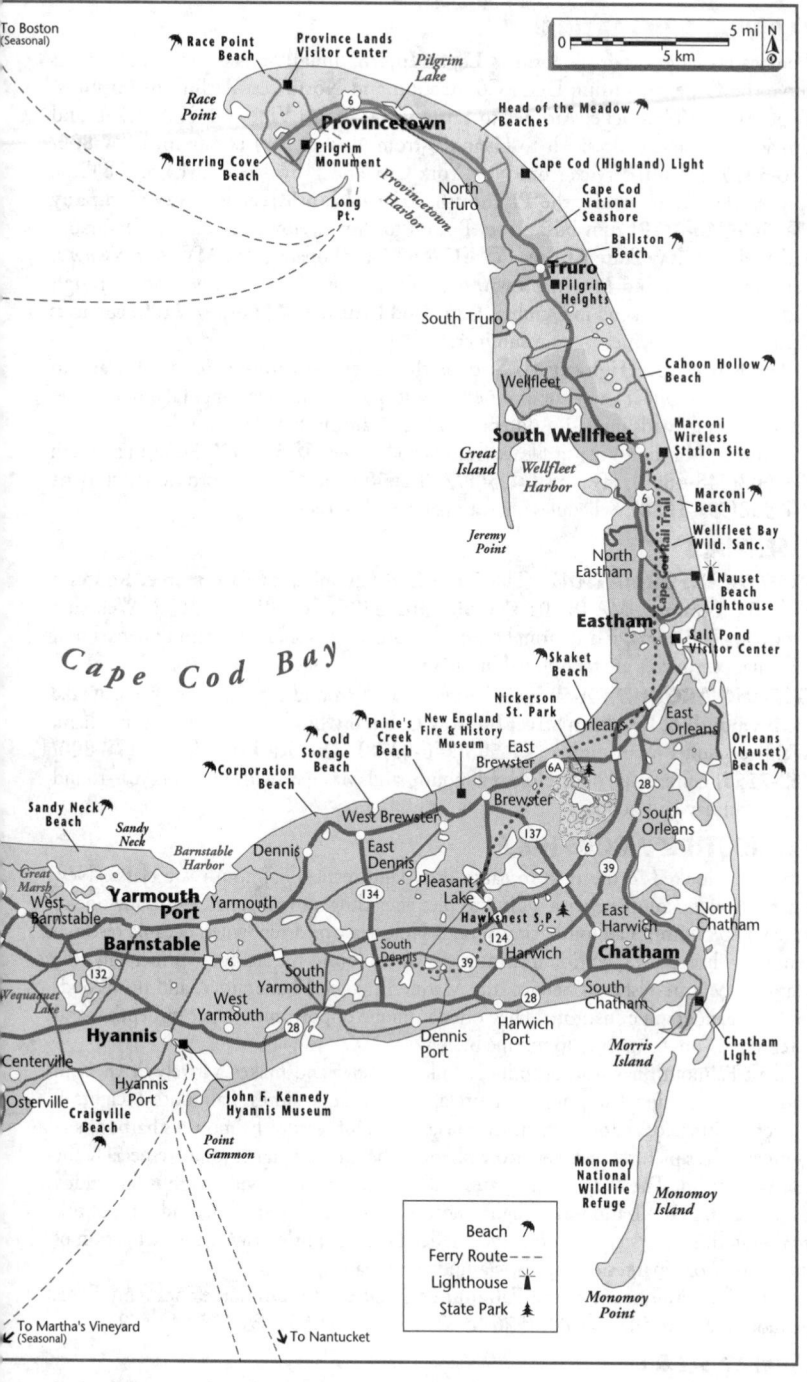

## ARRIVING & DEPARTING

The nearest large airport is Boston's **Logan International.** Several commuter airlines serve the Cape, including Delta Connection and Northwest Airlink to Hyannis; Cape Air and Nantucket Airlines to Hyannis, Martha's Vineyard, Nantucket, and Provicetown; and Colgan Air to Hyannis (from Newark, N.J.). **Bonanza** (☎ 800/556-3815) has bus service from New York City and Providence (R.I.) to the Cape towns. Despite its name, the **Plymouth & Brockton Street Railway Company** (☎ 508/746-0378) runs buses from Boston to Provincetown via Orleans, Eastham, and Wellfleet. **Bay State Cruises** (☎ 617/457-1428) operates the MV *Provicetown II* between Boston and Provincetown, daily during summer and weekends through Columbus Day weekend in October. **Cape Cod Cruises** (☎ 508/747-2400) connects Plymouth and Provincetown in summer.

The **Mid-Cape Highway (U.S. 6)** is the fastest road route along the Cape to Provincetown, but it's not the prettiest way to go. If you have time, take one of the smaller, scenic roads instead. Addresses on U.S. 6 are given as "Route 6."

Ferries to Martha's Vineyard leave from Woods Hole (☎ 508/477-8600); Falmouth (☎ 508/548-4800); Hyannis (☎ 508/778-2600); and New Bedford, Massachusetts (☎ 508/997-1688). Schedules are seasonal, so call ahead.

## ESSENTIALS

**VISITOR INFORMATION**   The **Cape Cod Chamber of Commerce,** Routes 6 and 132, Hyannis, MA 02601 (☎ 508/362-3225; fax 508/362-3698; Web site: www.capecod.com), is a clearinghouse of information about vacationing here. Local information sources are mentioned in the specific town sections below.

**GETTING AROUND**   A car is the best way to get around the Cape, but you can take the **Plymouth & Brockton Street Railway Company** bus between Orleans, Eastham, Wellfleet, and Provincetown (☎ 508/746-0378). The **Sea Line shuttle** (☎ 800/352-7155) connects Woods Hole, Falmouth, and Mashpee with Hyannis year-round except Sunday and holidays.

## FALMOUTH & WOODS HOLE

Often overlooked in the rush to catch the island ferries, Falmouth is a classic New England town, complete with white steeples encircling a town green. Officially one of nine villages within Falmouth, tiny Woods Hole is a world-renowned oceanic research center, with various scientific institutes crowded around the harbor—principally, the National Marine Fisheries Service, the Marine Biological Laboratory, and the Woods Hole Oceanographic Institute. They offer a unique opportunity to get in-depth—and often hands-on—exposure to marine biology.

West Falmouth has held onto its bucolic character and makes a lovely drive, with perhaps an occasional stop for the more alluring antique stores. Falmouth Heights, a cluster of shingled Victorian summer houses on a bluff east of Falmouth's harbor, is as popular as it is picturesque; its narrow ribbon of beach is a magnet for all, especially the younger crowd. The Waquoit Bay area, a few miles east of town, has thus far eluded the overcommercialization that blights most of Mass. 28. Several thousand acres of this vital estuarine ecosystem are now under federal custody, primarily at the instigation of the region's original residents, the Mashpee Wampanoags.

For information, contact the **Falmouth Chamber of Commerce,** Academy Lane, Falmouth, MA 02541 (☎ 800/526-8532 or 508/548-8500; fax 508/540-4724).

### WHAT TO SEE & DO

**ATTRACTIONS**   A visit to the cutting-edge think tank, the **Marine Biological Laboratory,** Water Street (at MBL Street, in the center of town), Woods Hole (☎ 508/289-7623), housed in an 1836 candle factory, requires a little forethought—the MBL prefers that reservations be made a week in advance—but will definitely reward the curious. The MBL's area of inquiry isn't limited to the aquatic but encompasses the "biological process common to all life forms." Admission is free. Tours June–Aug, Mon–Fri at 1, 2, and 3pm. Closed to the public Sept–May.

A great family excursion, the 1¹/₂-hour harbor cruises offered by **OceanQuest,** Water Street (in the center of town), Woods Hole (☎ **800/376-2326** or 508/457-0508), actually accomplish real marine research, with passengers serving as bona-fide data collectors, since you get to examine the specimens hauled up by the dredger. The fee is $14 adults, $10 children 3–12. Cruises mid-June to early Sept, daily at 10am, noon, 2, and 4pm.

Western-facing (great for sunsets) and relatively placid, **Old Silver Beach,** off Mass. 28A in West Falmouth, is a popular pick and often crowded (parking $10 a day). **Nobska Beach,** by the Nobska Lighthouse in Woods Hole, is accessible by bike, via the Shining Sea Bicycle Path, and boasts a magnificent view. **Surf Drive Beach,** off Shore Street in Falmouth, is about a mile from downtown and appealing to families; it's a serviceable choice with limited pay parking.

The **Shining Sea Bicycle Path** (☎ **508/548-8500**) is a 3.6-mile beauty skirting the Sound from Falmouth to Woods Hole, by way of the scenic Nobska Lighthouse; it also connects with a 23-mile scenic-road loop through pretty Sippewissett. You can park at the trailhead on Locust Street in Falmouth, or any nonmetered spot in town (parking in Woods Hole is scarce). The closest shop is **Corner Cycle** at Palmer Avenue and North Main Street (☎ **508/540-4195**). For a broad selection, visit **Holiday Cycles** at 465 Grand Ave. in Falmouth Heights (☎ **508/540-3549**).

Both boards and boats can be rented at **Cape Water Sports,** 145 Falmouth Heights Rd., E. Falmouth (☎ **508/548-7700**), or **Cape Cod Windsurfing Academy & Watersports Rentals** (☎ **508/495-0008**), at the Surfside Holiday Motel on Maravista Beach in East Falmouth; the latter also offers classes by appointment.

## ACCOMMODATIONS

The area around the historic Village Green (given over to military exercises in the pre-Revolutionary days) is a veritable hotbed of B&Bs.

**Coonamessett Inn.** *Jones Rd. and Gifford St. (about a half-mile north of Main St.), Falmouth, MA 02540.* ☎ *508/438-2300. 24 suites, 1 cottage. Summer, $95–$120 double. AE, CB, DISC, MC, V.* The Coonamessett has been the social center of town since the century's teens. On 7 lushly landscaped acres, it has the feel of a country club where all comers are welcome. Some of the rooms, decorated in reproduction antiques, can be a bit somber, so try to get one with good light. The dining room is formal and surprisingly good.

**Mostly Hall.** *27 W. Main St. (west of the Village Green), Falmouth, MA 02540.* ☎ *800/682-0565 or 508/548-3786. Fax 508/457-1572. 6 rms. Summer (including full breakfast), $95–$110 double. MC, V. Closed Jan to mid-Feb.* This plantation-style house exudes Southern graciousness. Longtime innkeepers Caroline and Jim Lloyd have mastered the art, providing memorable breakfasts, loaner bikes, and plenty of valuable advice for making the most of your stay. The stately rooms each boast a canopied four-poster. The gardens are lovely, and the gazebo makes a pleasant retreat.

## DINING

**Peking Palace.** *452 Main St. (in the center of town), Falmouth.* ☎ *508/540-8204. Fax 508/540-8382. Main courses $8–$12. AE, DC, MC, V. Jun–Aug, daily 11:30am–2am; Sept–May, Sun–Thurs 11:30am–midnight, Fri–Sat 11:30am–1:30am. CHINESE.* The best Chinese restaurant on the Cape, this smallish restaurant has been infused with TLC at every turn. There are 300-plus items on the menu, spanning Cantonese, Mandarin, and Szechuan cuisines, as well as Polynesian. Be sure to solicit your server's opinion: That's how I encountered some heavenly spicy chilled squid.

**The Regatta at Falmouth-by-the-Sea.** *217 Clinton Ave. (off Scranton Ave., about 1 mile south of Main St.), Falmouth.* ☎ *508/548-5400. Reservations recommended. Main courses $20–$27. AE, MC, V. May–Sept, daily 4:30–10pm. Closed Oct–Apr. INTERNATIONAL.* This restaurant has it all: a harbor view, polished yet innovative cuisine, and superb service. Certain menu offerings are inviolable; these include a celestial lobster-and-corn chowder and lamb *en chemise*—stuffed with chevre, spinach, and pine nuts, baked in puff pastry, and cloaked in a cabernet sauvignon sauce. For dessert, order the "trilogy."

## BARNSTABLE & HYANNIS

As the commercial center and transportation hub of the Cape, hyperdeveloped Hyannis grossly overshadows the actual seat of government in the bucolic village of Barnstable. The two locales couldn't be more dissimilar. As peaceful as Hyannis is hectic, the bay area along historic U.S. 6A unfolds in a blur of greenery and well-kept colonial houses. No wonder many visitors experience "post-Camelot letdown" the first time they venture southward to Hyannis. The downtown area, sapped by the strip development that proliferated at the edges of town after the Cape Cod Mall was built in 1970, is making a valiant comeback, with attractive banners and a pretty public park flanking the wharf where frequent ferries depart for the islands. If you were to confine your visit to this one town, however, you'd get a very warped view of the Cape. Along Routes 132 and 28, you could be visiting Anywhere, USA: They're lined by the standard chain stores, restaurants, and hotels, and enmired by maddening traffic.

Hyannis has more beds and better "rack rates" than anywhere else on the Cape, but there's little rationale for staying right in town or along the highways. Even full resort facilities can't begin to compensate for the lack of local color. The best strategy is to stay somewhere peaceful near the edge of town, in one of the moneyed villages—Centerville, Osterville, Marstons Mills, and Cotuit—to the west, or in the bayside villages of Barnstable due north, and just go into the "city" to sample the restaurants and nightlife.

For information, contact the **Hyannis Area Chamber of Commerce,** 1471 Rte. 132, Hyannis, MA 02601 (☎ **800/449-6647** or 508/362-5230).

### WHAT TO SEE & DO

**BEACHES & WHALE WATCHING**　Barnstable's primary bay beach is **Sandy Neck,** accessed through East Sandwich. Most of the sound beaches are fairly protected and not big in terms of surf. Beach parking costs $8 a day, usually payable at the lot; for a weeklong parking sticker ($35), visit the **Recreation Department** at 141 Basset Lane, behind the Kennedy Memorial Skating Rink (☎ **508/790-6345**).

**Craigville Beach,** off Craigville Beach Road in Centerville, was once a magnet for Methodist "camp" meetings (conference centers still line the shore). This broad expanse of sand boasts lifeguards and restrooms. A magnet for the bronzed and buffed, it's known as "Muscle Beach." **Kalmus Beach,** off Gosnold Street in Hyannisport, is an 800-foot spit of sand stretching toward the mouth of the harbor; it makes an ideal launching site for windsurfing. The surf is tame, the slope shallow—the conditions are ideal for little kids and lifeguards, a snack bar, and restrooms facilitate family outings.

The **Goose Hummock Shop,** 2 Route 132 (☎ **508/778-0877**), rents the usual craft; **Eastern Mountain Sports,** 1513 Iyanough Rd. (☎ **508/362-8690**), offers rental kayaks—tents and sleeping bags, too—and sponsors occasional overnights to Washburn Island in Waquoit Bay, as well as free clinics.

If you can't get to Provincetown to watch the whales in their preferred feeding grounds, then hop aboard at **Hyannis Whale Watch Cruises,** Barnstable Harbor (about a half-mile north of U.S. 6A on Mill Way), Barnstable (☎ **800/287-0374** or 508/362-6088; fax 508/362-9739), for a 4-hour voyage on a 100-foot high-speed cruiser. Naturalists provide the narration, and should you fail to spot a whale, your next trek is free. Closed Nov–Mar.

**SHOPPING**   Of the hundreds of antiques shops scattered through the region, perhaps a dozen qualify as destinations for well-schooled collectors. **Harden Studios,** 3264 U.S. 6A (in the center of town), Barnstable (☎ **508/362-7711**), is one. Owner Charles M. Harden, ASID, used to supply only to the trade dealers in the Boston Design Center. An architect by training, he renovated this deaconage, built around 1720, to display his finds. Some items, such as the primitive portraits and mourning embroidery, are all but extinct outside of museums. **Country Store,** 877 Main St. in the center of Osterville (☎ **508/428-2097**), is the essence of an old-fashioned general store.

## ACCOMMODATIONS

If you should miss the last ferry, or you want to stay near Hyannis's nightlife, try one of the nearby inns below.

   **Inn at Fernbrook.** *481 Main St. (about a half-mile south of Mass. 28), Centerville, MA 02632.* ☎ *508/775-4334. Fax 508/778-4455. 5 suites, 1 cottage. Summer (including full breakfast and afternoon tea), $135–$290 suite; $135 cottage. AE, DISC, MC, V.* Owners Brian Gallo and Sal DiFlorio have restored this 1881 showplace to not-too-fussy Victorian splendor, while retaining subsequent architectural quirks. The Spellman Room has an elaborate canopied bed. The two-bedroom Olmsted Suite, occupying the entire third floor, boasts a fireplaced living room and stairs leading to a balcony and sundeck.

   **Sea Breeze Inn.** *397 Sea St. (about 1 mile south of the West End Rotary), Hyannis, MA 02601.* ☎ *508/771-7213. 14 rms. Summer (including continental breakfast), $70–$130 double. AE, DISC, MC, V.* This shingled house has been decked out with the totems of small-town America: a picket fence, exuberant plantings, and a rocker for two couples. All this attention to the exterior is mirrored in the cheerful interior. Also on the grounds are three cottages that rent by the week, including one with a honeymooners' Jacuzzi.

## DINING

They really *are* the world's best: **Cape Cod Potato Chips,** on Breed's Hill Road at Independence Way, off Mass. 132 in Hyannis (☎ **508/775-7253**). (Free factory tours are offered Mon–Fri 9am–5pm.)

   **Alberto's Ristorante.** *360 Main St., Hyannis.* ☎ *508/778-1770. Reservations recommended. Main courses $13–$25. AE, CB, DC, DISC, MC, V. Daily 11am–11pm. ITALIAN.* Owner-chef Felisberto Barreiro's sole Florentine consists of sole topped with lobster, spinach, and Fontina and then a beurre blanc. Hand-cut pasta is a specialty, including seafood ravioli in saffron cream sauce. Locals who appreciate a bargain know to come between 4 and 6pm, when a full dinner, with soup, salad, and dessert, costs $11.

   **East Bay Lodge.** *199 East Bay Rd. (a half-mile southeast of Main St.), Osterville.* ☎ *508/428-5200. Fax 508/428-5432. Reservations recommended; jacket requested. Main courses $14–$19. AE, CB, DC, DISC, MC, V. Late May to mid-Oct, Tues–Fri 6–9pm, Sat 5:30–9pm, Sun 11am–2pm and 5:30–9pm; off-season, dinner only. AMERICAN.* This century-old restaurant is *the* place to eat in Osterville. The Sunday brunch segues into an evening shellfish buffet, and piano accompaniment adds panache to weekend suppers. The menu looks a little stodgy, but it's jazzed up by garlicky red pepper coulis with sautéed jumbo shrimp and ratatouille with grilled swordfish.

## THE YARMOUTHS

This cross-section represents the Cape at its best—and worst. Yarmouthport, on the bay, is an enchanting town, clustered with interesting shops and architectural pearls, whereas the sound-side "villages" of West to South Yarmouth are an object lesson in unbridled development run amuck. This section of Mass. 28 is a nightmarish gauntlet of tacky accommodations and "attractions." Yet even here you'll find a few spots worthy of the name. You've got the north shore for culture and refinement, the south shore for kitsch. Take your pick, or ricochet schizophrenically, enjoying the best of both worlds.

Yarmouth boasts 11 saltwater and 2 pond beaches open to the public. The body-per-square-yard ratio can be pretty intense along the sound, but so's the social scene, so no one seems to mind. **Bass River Beach,** off South Shore Drive in Bass River, is at the mouth of the largest tidal river on the eastern seaboard; this sound beach offers the usual, plus a bonus—a wheelchair-accessible fishing pier. **Grays Beach,** off Centre Street in Yarmouth, offers tame waters excellent for children; it adjoins the Callery–Darling Conservation Area. **Seagull Beach,** off South Sea Avenue in West Yarmouth, features rolling dunes, a boardwalk, and all the facilities to attract a young crowd. Bring bug spray, though.

Contact the **Yarmouth Area Chamber of Commerce,** 657 Route 28, West Yarmouth, MA 02673 (☎ **508/778-1008**).

## ACCOMMODATIONS

If you're impressed by the antiques in the local inns below, check out the shops on U.S. 6A in Yarmouth and Yarmouthport.

**Captain Farris House.** *308 Old Main St. (about a quarter-mile west of the Bass River Bridge), S. Yarmouth, MA 02664.* ☎ *800/350-9477 or 508/760-2818. Fax 508/398-1262. 10 rms and suites. $85–$175 double; $175–$225 suite. Rates include full breakfast. AE, MC, V.* Lavished with fine antiques and striking contemporary touches, this 1845 manse has been carved into lovely spaces designed for relaxing. Some suites are apartment-size, with fireplaced sitting rooms and whirlpool-tubbed bathrooms bigger than the average bedroom. Innkeeper Scott Toney whips up gourmet breakfasts replete with home-baked sweet breads.

**Wedgewood Inn.** *83 Mass. 6A (in the center of town), Yarmouthport, MA 02675.* ☎ *508/362-5157. 9 rms. Summer, $115–$160 double. Rates include full breakfast. AE, DISC, MC, V.* This 1812 Federal home sits atop its lawn with pride. Gerrie Graham provides a warm welcome, complete with tea delivered to your room: one of the four front rooms (all with fireplaces, some with porches), the two romantic hideaways under the eaves, or the three spacious rooms, with fireplaces and decks, in the barn.

## DINING

Don't miss **Hallet's** old-fashioned frappes and floats, on U.S. 6A in the center of Yarmouthport (☎ **508/362-3362**): Unsuspecting passersby invariably do a double-take when they happen on this 1889 drugstore; Mary Hallet Clark, granddaughter of the founder, is the one dishing out from the original marble soda fountain.

**Fiesta Grande.** *737 Mass. 28 (midway between W. Yarmouth and Bass River), S. Yarmouth.* ☎ *508/760-2924. Main courses $5–$11. AE, DC, DISC, MC, V. June–Aug noon–10pm; call for off-season hours. MEXICAN.* Most of the Mexican food you'll encounter on the Cape is a well-intentioned approximation, but this is the real thing, whipped up by a chef from Mazatlán. Locally inspired specialties include shrimp fajitas and crabmeat enchiladas. The menu is so enticingly priced, it's tempting to try a bit of everything.

**Lobster Boat.** *681 Mass. 28 (midway between W. Yarmouth and Bass River), W. Yarmouth.* ☎ *508/775-0486. Main courses $10–18. AE, MC, V. May–Oct, daily 4–10pm. SEAFOOD.* Just about every town seems to have one of these barnlike restaurants serving the usual array of seafood in the usual manner, from deep-fried to boiled or broiled. True to its sound-side setting, this place advertises itself with a facade featuring the hull of a ship grafted onto a shingled shack.

## CHATHAM

Chatham was one of the first spots to attract early explorers. Samuel de Champlain stopped by in 1606 but got into a tussle with the prior occupants over some copper cooking pots and had to leave in a hurry. The first colonist to stick around was William Nickerson, from Yarmouth, who befriended a local sachem (tribal leader) and built a house beside his wigwam in 1656. One prospered; the other—for obvious reasons—didn't.

Chatham, along with Provincetown, is the only area on the Cape to support a commercial fishing fleet—against increasing odds. Overfishing has resulted in closely monitored limits, to give the stock time to bounce back. Boats must now go out as far as 100 miles to catch their fill. Despite the difficulties, it's a way of life few locals would willingly relinquish.

With its tree-shaded Main Street lined with specialty stores, Chatham offers a nonpareil opportunity to shop and stroll. The **Chatham Chamber of Commerce** is at 533 Main St., Chatham, MA 02633 (☎ **800/715-5567** or 508/945-5199).

### BEACHES & BIRD-WATCHING

Chatham has an unusual array of beach styles, from the peaceful shores of the Nantucket Sound to the treacherous, shifting shoals along the Atlantic. **Cockle Cove Beach, Ridgevale Beach,** and **Hardings Beach** are lined up along the sound, each at the end of its namesake road south of Mass. 28; these family-pleasing beaches offer gentle surf suitable for all ages, as well as full facilities. Extending all the way south from Orleans, the 5-mile **North Beach** is accessible from Chatham only by boat; for a fee, you can hop a water taxi from the Chatham Fish Pier on Shore Road (☎ 508/430-2346). Inquire about other possible dropoff points if you'd like to beach around.

Chatham's natural bonanza lies southward: the uninhabited **Monomoy Island,** 2,750 acres of brush-covered sand favored by some 285 species of migrating birds as the perfect pit stop along the Atlantic Flyway. Hundreds of gray and harbor seals carpet the coastline from late November to May. If you go out during that time, you won't have any trouble seeing them. Shuttle service to South Island is available aboard the *Rip Ryder* out of the Stage Harbor Marina (☎ 508/945-5450), but you'll get a lot more out of the trip—and probably leave this unspoiled landscape in better shape—if you let a naturalist lead the way. Both the **Wellfleet Bay Wildlife Sanctuary** operated by the Audubon Society (☎ 508/349-2615) and Brewster's **Cape Cod Museum of Natural History** (☎ 508/896-3867) offer guided trips.

### ACCOMMODATIONS

**Captain's House Inn.** *369–377 Old Harbor Rd. (about a half-mile north of the rotary), Chatham, MA 02633.* ☎ *800/315-0728 or 508/945-0127. Fax 508/945-0866. 14 rms, 2 suites. Summer, $135–$325 double. Rates include full breakfast and afternoon tea. AE, MC, V.* This lovely 1839 Greek Revival house, along with a cottage and carriage house, is set on 2 acres. The rooms, named for Capt. Hiram Harding's ships, are richly furnished. The window-walled breakfast room is also the site of a traditional tea, presided over by the innkeeper, Englishman Jan McMasters.

**Chatham Bars Inn.** *Shore Rd. (off Seaview St., about a half-mile northwest of town center), Chatham, MA 02633.* ☎ *800/527-4884 or 508/945-0096. Fax 508/945-5491. 132 rms, 20 suites. Summer, $190–$375 double; $405–$675 one-bedroom suite; $580–$1,000 two-bedroom suite. MAP and off-season packages available. AE, DC, MC, V.* This brick building—surrounded by 26 shingled cottages on 20 acres—has regained its glory days. The best spot to take in the grandeur (as well as the sweeping views) is the veranda.

The **Main Dining Room,** presided over by Al Hynes, is highly recommended. Two other restaurants are the North Beach Tavern & Grille, and the Beach House Grill. There are many recreational facilities.

## DINING

**Christian's.** *443 Main St. (in the center of town).* ☎ *508/945-3362. Reservations recommended. Main courses $10–$20. AE, CB, DC, DISC, MC, V. Apr–Dec, 11:30am–3pm and 5–10pm; call for off-season hours. NEW AMERICAN.* Owned by innovative Christian Schultz, this restaurant has a split personality: The summer-only downstairs dining rooms enjoy a French country decor, whereas Upstairs at Christian's (open year-round) is British clubby. The same cinematic-motif menu applies to both: Famous movie titles are accorded to specialties like escargots in marsala sauce—aka *Casablanca.*

# EASTHAM: GATEWAY TO THE CAPE COD NATIONAL SEASHORE

One thing you won't see in Eastham is tanned socialites clutching thousand-dollar Nantucket baskets as they peruse the latest shipment of distressed continental antiques. Despite its optimal location (the distance from bay to ocean is as little as 1 mile in spots), Eastham is one of the least pretentious locales on the Cape—and yet highly popular, as the gateway to the magnificent Cape Cod National Seashore.

The downside—or up, depending on how you look at it—is that there aren't a whole lot of shops or attractions, or at least few worth checking out. Most visitors won't bother. You can tell as soon as you pull into town: This is a place meant for kicking back—for letting the sun, surf, and sand dictate your day.

Contact the **Eastham Chamber of Commerce,** U.S. 6 at Fort Hill Road, Eastham, MA 02642 (☎ **508/255-3444**).

## BEACHES & NATURE TRAILS

Since you're undoubtedly going to spend a fair amount of time on the beach, you might as well find out how it came to be, what other creatures you'll be sharing it with, and how not to harm them or it. Occupying more than half the landmass north of Orleans and covering the 30-mile oceanfront, the 44,000-acre **Cape Cod National Seashore** was set aside as a sanctuary in 1961. Get your tax money's worth at the excellent educational exhibits and continuous film loops offered at the **Salt Pond Visitor Center,** on Salt Pond Road, east of U.S. 6 (☎ **508/255-3421**). Particularly fascinating is a video about the accidental 1990 discovery of an 11,000-year-old campsite amid the storm-ravaged dunes of Coast Guard Beach—which was about 5 miles inland when these early settlers spent their summers here. After absorbing some of the local history, be sure to take time to venture out—on your own or with a ranger guide—on some of the surrounding trails.

With plenty of free parking, the visitor center makes a convenient access point for the **Cape Cod Rail Trail** (☎ **508/896-3491**). Northward, it's about 5 wildflower-lined miles to Wellfleet, where the trail currently ends. A 1.6-mile spur trail, winding through locust and apple groves, links the visitor center with glorious Coast Guard Beach: It's for bikes only (no blades). Rentals are available at the **Little Capistrano Bike Shop** (☎ **508/255-6515**), on Salt Pond Road just west of U.S. 6, or **Idle Times,** 4550 U.S. 6 in the center of North Eastham (☎ **800/924-8281** on the Cape, or 508/255-8281), which also carries in-line skates.

Shorter nature trails here include the 1¹⁄₂-mile **Fort Hill Trail** off Fort Hill Road (turn off U.S. 6, about 1 mile south of town center), which passes "Indian Rock" and scenic vantage points overlooking the channel-carved marsh—keep an eye out for egrets and great blue herons. The Fort Hill Trail hooks up with the half-mile **Red Cedar**

**Swamp Trail,** offering boardwalk views of an ecology otherwise inaccessible. Check with the Salt Pond Visitor Center for maps of other trails.

From here on up, the Atlantic beaches are best reserved for strong swimmers: Waves are *big* and the undertow can be treacherous. The flat, nearly placid bay beaches, on the other hand, are just right for families. When the tide recedes (twice daily), it leaves a mile-wide playground of rippled sand full of fascinating creatures, including horseshoe and hermit crabs. **Coast Guard** and **Nauset Light,** off Ocean View Drive, are connected to outlying parking lots by a free shuttle; these pristine National Seashore beaches have lifeguards and restrooms. **First Encounter, Thumpertown, Campground,** and **Sunken Meadow** are town-operated bay beaches.

The best way to experience Nauset Marsh is by kayak or canoe. Rentals are available in neighboring towns: The closest source would be the **Goose Hummock Outdoor Center,** 15 U.S. 6A in Orleans (☎ 508/255-0455). **Jack's Boat Rentals** (☎ 508/349-9808) has a seasonal outlet on Wellfleet's Gull Pond, which connects to Higgins Pond by way of a narrow channel lined with red maples and choked with yellow water lilies. Jack's also offers guided paddle tours of Eastham's Herring River. Inquire about trips sponsored by the **Cape Cod Museum of Natural History** (☎ 800/479-3867 or 508/896-3867) and the **Wellfleet Bay Wildlife Sanctuary** (☎ 508/349-2615).

## WELLFLEET

Wedged between tame Eastham and Truro, Wellfleet—with the well-tended look of a classic New England town—is the golden mean, the perfect destination for artists, writers, off-duty psychiatrists, and other contemplative types. Distinguished literati such as Edna St. Vincent Millay and Edmund Wilson put this rural village on the map in the 1920s, in the wake of Provincetown's Bohemian heyday. In her brief and tumultuous tenure as Wilson's wife, Mary McCarthy pilloried the pretensions of the summer population in *A Charmed Life* but had to concede that the region boasts a certain natural beauty: "steel-blue fresh-water ponds and pine forests and mushrooms and white bluffs dropping to a strangely pebbled beach."

To this day, Wellfleet remains remarkably unspoiled. Once you depart from U.S. 6, commercialism is kept to a minimum, though the town boasts plenty of appealing shops—including a score of distinguished galleries—and a couple of excellent New American restaurants. It's hard to imagine any other community on the Cape supporting so sophisticated an undertaking as the Wellfleet Harbor Actors Theatre or hosting such a wholesome event as public square dancing on the adjacent Town Pier. And where else could you find, next door to an outstanding nature preserve (the Wellfleet Bay Wildlife Sanctuary), a thriving drive-in movie theater? And it has what is arguably the best dance club on Cape Cod—**The Beachcomber** (☎ 508/349-6055), just south of Old Cahoon Hollow Beach—so close that beachgoers on summer weekends can count on a free concert: reggae or the homegrown "Incredible Casuals."

There's just one drawback: Unlike Provincetown, which has something to offer virtually year-round, Wellfleet pretty much rolls up its sidewalks come Columbus Day.

Contact the **Wellfleet Chamber of Commerce,** off U.S. 6, Wellfleet, MA 02663 (☎ 508/349-2510).

### BEACHES & WILDLIFE

Though the profiles are far from hard and fast, Wellfleet's fabulous ocean beaches tend to sort themselves demographically: **LeCount Hollow** is popular with families, **Newcomb Hollow** with high schoolers, **White Crest** with the college crowd (including surfers and off-hours hang gliders), and **Cahoon** with 30-somethings. Only the latter two beaches permit parking by nonresidents. To enjoy the other two, as well as **Burton Baker Beach** on the harbor and **Duck Harbor** on the bay, plus three freshwater ponds, you'll have to walk or bike in, or see if you qualify for a sticker ($25 per week). Bring proof of residency to the seasonal Beach Sticker Booth on the Town Pier, or call the **Wellfleet Recreation Department** (☎ 508/349-0818).

The **Cape Cod National Seashore** maintains two spectacular self-guided trails: The 1¹/₄-mile **Atlantic White Cedar Swamp Trail,** off the parking area for the Marconi Wireless Station, is a warmup for magnificent **Great Island,** jutting 4 miles into the bay (off the western end of Chequessett Neck Road) to cup Wellfleet Harbor. The "island" is uninhabited and a true refuge for those strong enough to go the distance. Just be sure to cover up, wear sturdy shoes, bring water, and venture to Jeremy Point—the very tip—*only* if you're sure the tide is going out.

A spiffy new eco-friendly visitor center serves as both introduction and gateway to **Wellfleet Bay Wildlife Sanctuary,** a 1,000-acre refuge. You'll see plenty of wildlife— especially red-winged blackbirds and osprey—as you follow 5 miles of looping trails through pine forests, saltmarsh, and moors. Naturalists guide walks throughout the day and sometimes into the night. Also inquire about special workshops for children and about canoeing, snorkeling, birding, and off-season seal-watching excursions. The visitor center is off West Road, about 1 mile north of Eastham border, in South Wellfleet (☎ 508/349-2615).

## ACCOMMODATIONS

Slightly north of the Town pier, **Holden Inn,** 140 Commercial St., Wellfleet, MA 02663 (☎ 508/349-3450), has been run by the same family since 1924. This three-building complex—centered on an 1840 captain's house fronted by a welcoming porch and picket fence—projects the leisurely ease of a bygone era. Furnishings tend to be well worn but homey, and the hospitality is genuinely gracious. About half the rooms have shared baths. Summer rates are $58–$68 double; the one suite (for four) is $110. No credit cards are accepted, and it's closed mid-Oct to mid-Apr.

## DINING

**Aesop's Tables,** 316 Main St. (☎ 508/349-6450) has it all: a handsome, relaxed setting and delectable New American cuisine turned out by Peter Rennert. Brian Dunne is owner/host. The scallops and oysters come from the bay, and you must try "Clementine's Citrus Tart," a rich pâté sable with a mousse of fruit and white chocolate. Main courses are $16–$23. It's open for lunch Wed–Sun noon–3pm, and for dinner daily 5:30–9:30pm; closed mid-Oct to mid-May.

Kate Painter presents "simple food in a funky place" at **Painter's,** 50 Main St. (☎ 508/349-3003). Though the setting is low-key, her culinary skills are topnotch. Main courses are $12–$20, and it's open daily May–Oct.

## TRURO

Truro is one of those blink-and-you'll-miss-it towns. With only 1,600 year-round residents (fewer than it boasted in 1840, when Pamet Harbor was a whaling and ship-building port), the town amounts to little more than a scattering of stores and public buildings and lots of low-profile houses hidden in the woods and dunes. As in Wellfleet, writers, artists, and vacationing therapists are drawn to the quiet and calm. Edward Hopper lived in contented isolation in a South Truro cottage for nearly 4 decades.

If you find yourself craving cultural stimulation or other kinds of excitement, however, Provincetown is only a 10-minute drive. The natives manage to entertain themselves pretty well with get-togethers at the Truro Center for the Arts or, more simply, among themselves. However much money may be circulating in this rusticated community (a *lot*), inconspicuous consumption is the rule of the day. The culmination of the social season, tellingly enough, is the late-September "dump dance" at Truro's recycling center.

The **North Truro Shuttle System** (☎ 508/487-6870) connects the town with Provincetown in season, for only $2 one way. For information, contact the **Truro Chamber of Commerce,** U.S. 6A at Head of the Meadow Road, Truro, MA 02666 (☎ 508/487-1288).

## BEACHES & NATURE TRAILS

Here you can visit such natural wonders as **Ballston Beach,** where all you'll see is silky sand and grass-etched dunes. **Head of the Meadow,** off Head of the Meadow Road, is among the more remote Cape Cod National Seashore beaches; this spot (with restrooms) is known for its excellent surf. **Corn Hill Beach,** off Corn Hill Road, offers lifeguard supervision and restrooms; this bay beach—near the hill where the Pilgrims found the seed corn that ensured their survival—is open to nonresidents for a parking fee of $5 a day.

The **Cape Cod National Seashore**—comprising 70% of Truro's land—offers three self-guided nature trails. The half-mile **Cranberry Bog Trail** leads from the Little America youth hostel parking lot past a number of previously cultivated bogs reverting to their natural state. The **Pilgrim Spring Trail** and **Small Swamp Trail** (each a 3/4-mile loop) head out from the CCNS parking lot just east of Pilgrim Lake. Pilgrim Spring is where the parched colonists sipped their first fresh water in months—with "much delight," according to a contemporary account. Small Swamp is named for Thomas Small, a rather overoptimistic 19th-century farmer who tried to cultivate fruit trees in a soil more suited to salt hay. Both paths overlook Salt Meadow, a freshwater marsh favored by hawks and osprey.

## ACCOMMODATIONS

An alternative to staying in crowded Provincetown are the two places below.

**Outer Reach Motel.** *535 Route 6 (midway between N. Truro center and Provincetown border), N. Truro, MA 02652.* ☎ *800/942-5388 or 508/487-9090. Fax 508/942-5388. 59 rms. Summer, $79–$114 double. MC, V. Closed mid-Oct to mid-May.* This sprawling motel offers glorious vistas of Provincetown, where you have privileges at the Provincetown Inn. Here you'll find an outdoor pool and tennis court; the ocean is a sylvan mile east. The rooms are standard-issue, but there's a terrific independent restaurant, Adrian's (see "Dining," below).

**South Hollow Vineyards Bed and Breakfast Inn.** *11 Shore Rd. (U.S. 6A, off Route 6, a half-mile south of town center), N. Truro, MA 02652.* ☎ *508/487-6200. Fax 508/487-4248. 4 rms, 1 suite. Summer, $89–$99 double; $129 suite. Rates include continental breakfast. MC, V.* This beautiful 1836 B&B is set amid 5 vine-covered acres. Each room—including the Vintage Suite, with its double Jacuzzi—comes with a four-poster. For those not into wine, the draw is likely to be the bucolic setting (this is one of the last working farms on the Outer Cape) 6 miles from Provincetown.

## DINING

Seeing as this deli/bakery/grocery is basically *it* in terms of downtown Truro, and seasonal to boot, it's a good thing **Jams,** 14 Truro Center Rd., off U.S. 6 (☎ 508/349-1616), is so delightful. It's full of tantalizing aromas: fresh creative pizzas, rotisseried fowl, cookies straight from the oven. The pastry and deli selections deserve their own four-star restaurant but are all the more savory as part of a picnic. Closed early Sept–late May.

**Adrian's.** *535 U.S. 6 (midway between N. Truro center and Provincetown border), N. Truro.* ☎ *508/487-4360. Fax 508/487-6510. Reservations recommended. Main courses $7–$17. AE, MC, V. Mid-June to early Sept, Mon–Fri 8am–noon and 5:30–10pm; Sat–Sun 8am–1pm and 5:30–10pm; call for off-season hours. Closed mid-Oct to mid-May. NORTHERN ITALIAN.* Adrian Salcedo Cyr's stylish restaurant is greatly prized—

not just for its wood-fired *pizzette* and other creative fare, but for its superb breakfasts. Try for a table on the deck overlooking Provincetown Harbor and sample eye-openers like orange-cinnamon French toast. Come back for the sunset and the Tuscan bread-and-tomato soup or fabulous pastas.

**Terra Luna.** *104 Shore Rd. (in the center of town), N. Truro.* ☎ *508/487-1019. Main courses $8–$16. AE, MC, V. Late May to mid-Oct, daily 7am–1pm and 5:30–10pm. Closed mid-Oct to late May. FUSION.* People come from miles around to sample the outstanding breakfasts here: fresh muffins and scones and entrees like breakfast burritos and raisin French toast stuffed with cream cheese and walnuts. At dinner, try the well-priced Pacific Rim and/or neo-Italian fare.

## PROVINCETOWN

You made it! Explorer Bartholomew Gosnold must have felt much the same thrill in 1602 when he and his crew happened on a "great stoare of codfysshes" here (it wasn't quite the gold they were seeking, but valuable enough to warrant changing the peninsula's name). The Pilgrims were ecstatic when they dragged into the harbor 18 years later: Never mind that they'd landed several hundred miles off course—it was a miracle they'd made it round the treacherous Outer Cape at all. And Charles Hawthorne, the painter who "discovered" this fishing town in the late 1890s and introduced it to the Greenwich Village intelligentsia, was besotted by this "jumble of color in the intense sunlight accentuated by the brilliant blue of the harbor."

He'd probably be aghast at the commercial circus his enthusiasm has wrought—though proud, perhaps, to find the Provincetown Art Association and Museum, which he helped found in 1914, still going strong. Though it's bound to experience the occasional off year or dull stretch, the town is extraordinarily dedicated to creative expression, and right now it's on a roll. Some would ascribe the inspiration to the quality of the light or the solitude afforded by long lonely winters. Still, the general atmosphere of open-mindedness certainly plays a pivotal role in allowing a very varied assortment of individuals to pull together in pushing the boundaries of the avant-garde.

That same warm embrace of lifestyles accounts in part for Provincetown's ascendancy as a gay and lesbian resort. During peak season, Provincetown's streets are a celebration of any individual's freedom to be as "out" as imagination allows.

Contact the **Provincetown Chamber of Commerce,** 307 Commercial St., Provincetown, MA 02657 (☎ **508/487-3424;** fax 508/487-8966); or the gay-oriented **Provincetown Business Guild,** 115 Bradford St., Provincetown, MA 02657 (☎ **800/ 637-8696** or 508/487-2313).

### WHAT TO SEE & DO
**THE CAPE COD NATIONAL SEASHORE**   With nine-tenths of its territory (basically all but the "downtown" area) protected by the **Cape Cod National Seashore,** Provincetown has miles of beaches. The 3-mile bay beach that lines the harbor, though certainly swimmable, isn't all that inviting compared to the magnificent ocean beaches overseen by the CCNS. The two official access areas (see below) tend to be crowded; however, you can always find a less densely populated stretch if you're willing to hike. *Note:* Local beachgoers have been mobilizing for "clothing-optional" beaches for years, but the rangers routinely issue tickets, so stand forewarned.

**Herring Cove** and **Race Point** are national seashore beaches known for their spectacular sunsets: Observers often applaud. Race Point, on the ocean side, is rougher, and you might actually spot whales en route to Stellwagen Bank. Accessible by shuttle, calmer Herring Cove is a haven for same-sex couples, who tend to sort themselves by gender. Parking costs $5 a day, $15 a season.

North of town, nestled amid the Cape Cod National Seashore preserve, is one of the more spectacular bike paths in New England, the 7-mile **Province Lands Trail.** With its free parking, the **Province Lands Visitor Center** (☎ 508/487-1256) is a good place to start: You can survey the landscape from the observation tower to try to get your bearings before setting off amid the dizzying maze. With any luck, you'll find a spur path leading to one of the beaches—Race Point or Herring Cove—lining the shore. Bike rentals are offered seasonally by **Nelson's Bike Shop,** 43 Race Point Rd. (☎ 508/487-0034). It's also an easy jaunt from town, where you'll find plenty of good bike shops.

**ART & ANTIQUES**  The **Provincetown Art Association and Museum,** 460 Commercial St., in the East End (☎ 508/487-1750), is an extraordinary cache of 20th-century Americana. Founded in 1914, the museum was the site of innumerable "space wars" as classicists and modernists vied for square footage; an uneasy truce was struck in 1927 when each camp was accorded its own show. In today's more ecumenical atmosphere it's not unusual to see a tame still life hanging alongside a statement of Generation X angst. Open late May–early Sept, daily noon–5pm and 7–9pm; call for off-season hours.

Of the several dozen art galleries in town, only a handful are reliably worthwhile. For in-depth coverage of the local arts scene, look to *Provincetown Arts,* a glossy annual sold at the Provincetown Art Association and Museum shop. In season, most of the galleries and even some of the shops take a suppertime siesta so as to reopen later and greet visitors as late as 10 or 11pm. Shows usually open Friday evening, prompting a "stroll" tradition spanning the many receptions.

The second-story **Clifford–Williams Antiques,** 225 Commercial St. (☎ 508/487-4174), is packed to the gills with substantial English furniture. You'd have to go to Boston—or abroad—to view estate jewelry as fine as that at **Small Pleasures,** 359 Commercial St. (☎ 508/487-3712). Virginia McKenna's hand-selected stock ranges from romantic Victorian settings to sleek silver for the 1920s-era male. **Remembrances of Things Past,** 376 Commercial St. (☎ 508/487-9443), is a fun kitsch-fest; and **West End Antiques,** 146 Commercial St. (☎ 508/487-6723), is more of a nostalgia-fest.

## ACCOMMODATIONS

Though Provincetown is full of places to stay, it's crowded in the summer, so make your reservations here as early as possible.

**Boatslip Beach Club.** *161 Commercial St. (in the West End), Provincetown, MA 02657.* ☎ *800/451-7547 or 508/487-1669. Fax 508/487-6021. 45 rms. Summer, $120–$160 double. MC, V. Closed Nov–early Apr.* As the site of "tea dances," this waterside motel is Party Central—mostly for gays, but also for anyone who wants to hang around. Some snazzy specimens can be found around the pool or the sundeck. Just as you can expect to be scoped out, you can count on making interesting friends.

**Brass Key Guesthouse.** *9 Court St. (in the center of town), Provincetown, MA 02657.* ☎ *800/842-9858 or 508/487-9005. Fax 508/487-9020. 10 rms, 2 cottages. Summer, $155–$220 double; $190 cottage. Rates include continental breakfast. AE, DISC, MC, V.* Michael MacIntyre and Bob Anderson operate an ideal inn. The service is attentive and the amenities topnotch. They're a powerful social force in town, sponsoring winemaker dinners and importing cultural events. Most guests repair to the whirlpool after a night of dancing. There's a rooftop deck for nude sunbathing.

**Inn at Cook Street.** *7 Cook St. (at Bradford St., in the East End), Provincetown, MA 02657.* ☎ *888/COOK-655 or 508/487-3894. 3 rms, 2 suites, 1 cottage. Summer, $85 double; $110–$120 suite; $100 cottage. Rates include continental breakfast. MC, V.*

This 1836 Greek Revival beauty exudes tasteful warmth. The handsomely appointed rooms are oriented to the hidden garden, with private and shared decks, and the tiny rose-trellised cottage, with sleeping loft, is an integral part of its charm. The enthusiasm of Paul Church and Dana Mitton is evident in every welcoming touch.

**Land's End Inn.** *22 Commercial St. (in the West End), Provincetown, MA 02657.* ☎ *800/276-7088 or 508/487-0706. 17 rms (1 with bath), 2 apts, 1 suite. Summer, $110–$285 double; $140–$150 apt; $285 suite. Rates include continental breakfast. MC, V.* Atop Gull Hill, this 1907 bungalow is stuffed with outlandish antiques. Some rooms would suit a 19th-century sheik, others your everyday hedonist. The octagonal loft suite, poised to take in views in every direction, is a spectacular setting for romance. Though the inn is predominantly gay, all cosmopolitan visitors will feel welcome.

**Watermark Inn.** *603 Commercial St. (in the East End), Provincetown, MA 02657.* ☎ *800/734-0165 or 508/487-0165. Fax 508/487-2383. 10 suites. Summer, $130–$275 double. AE, MC, V.* Innkeeper/architect Kevin Shea carved this beachfront manor into 10 dazzling suites: The prize ones, on the top floor, have peaked picture windows and sweeping views from their own 80-foot deck. Even the lack of breakfast is a plus: You have an excuse to stockpile goodies from **Martin's Market,** 467 Commercial St. (☎ **508/487-4858**).

## DINING

There's no shortage of restaurants here, with some of the best food on the Cape.

**Cafe Heaven.** *199 Commercial St. (in the center of town).* ☎ *508/487-9639. Reservations not accepted. Most items under $10. No credit cards. Late May–early Sept daily 8am–3pm and 6:30–10pm; call for off-season hours. Closed Nov–Apr. AMERICAN.* Prized for its leisurely country breakfasts, this modernist storefront also turns out substantive sandwiches, burgers, and pastas. The salads are lightly doused with dilled sour cream and tossed with tomatoes and grapes.

**Dancing Lobster Cafe/Trattoria.** *9 Ryder St. Extension (on Fisherman's Wharf, off Commercial St.).* ☎ *508/487-0900. No reservations. Main courses $10–$14. No credit cards. May–Oct, daily 5:30–11pm. Closed Nov–Apr. MEDITERRANEAN.* It's worth lining up 90 minutes or more for one of native son Nils "Pepe" Berg's 20 hotly contested tables. Try the grilled-squid *bruschetta,* saffrony Venetian *zuppa di pesce,* or asparagus ravioli or steamed mussels with basil aïoli. And don't miss the *rustica* tiramisù.

✪ **Cafe Edwige.** *333 Commercial St.* ☎ *508/487-2008. Reservations recommended. Main courses $15–$18. AE, DC, MC, V. July–Aug daily 8am–1pm and 6–11pm; call for off-season hours. Closed late Oct–Mar. NEW AMERICAN/FUSION.* You could easily miss this little second-story place where the masterful cuisine of Chef Steve Frappolli, a veteran of New York's New American cuisine landmark, An American Place, holds sway. He's in his element here, dishing up the likes of planked codfish with ginger carrot broth and wildberry shortcake. It's a great place to start the day with superlative breakfasts in a healthful mode, featuring everything from tofu frittatas to broiled flounder with stir-fried vegetables. At night, the cathedral-ceilinged space with its subdued lighting takes on a romantic aura.

**Martin House.** *157 Commercial St.* ☎ *508/487-1327. Fax 508/487-4514. Reservations recommended. Main courses $14–$26. AE, CB, DC, DISC, MC, V. July–Oct, Mon–Sat 6–11pm, Sun 3:30–11pm; call for off-season hours. Closed early Dec. FUSION.* Co-owner Gary Martin is the conceptualizer behind the regional menu, and chef Alex Mazzocca the gifted creator. Both favor regional delicacies, like the *mizuma* (a Japanese bitter herb) that jazzes up a gingered dipping sauce for the Asian steamed buns. By far the most esoteric item around is the farm-raised organic ostrich fillet.

**Mews Restaurant & Cafe Mews.** *429 Commercial St.* ☎ *508/487-1500. Reservations recommended. Main courses $15–$22. AE, CB, DC, DISC, MC, V. Mid-June* *to mid-Sept, daily 11am–3pm, 5:30–10:30pm. Closed late Dec (except New Year's Eve) to mid-Feb. NEW AMERICAN.* The formal dining room is right on the beach. Standouts include the marsala-marinated portobellos and mixed seafood carpaccio. Among the showier entrees is "captured scallops": prime Wellfleet specimens enclosed with a shrimp-and-crab mousse in a crisp wonton pouch and served atop filet mignon. The Cafe has a lighter menu.

## PROVINCETOWN AFTER DARK

There's so much going on in season on any given night, you might want to simplify your search by calling or stopping in at the **Provincetown Reservations System** office at 293 Commercial St. in the center of town (☎ 508/487-6400).

Open year-round, the **Atlantic House,** 6 Masonic Place, off Commercial Street, two blocks west of Town Hall (☎ 508/487-3821), the nation's premiere gay bar, also welcomes straights of both sexes, except in the leather-oriented Macho Bar upstairs. Late in the evening, there's usually plenty going on in the Big Room dance bar. Check out the Tennessee Williams memorabilia, including a portrait *au naturel;* there's more across the street, in a new restaurant called Grand Central. Cover for the Big Room is $5.

Come late afternoon, if you wonder where all the beachgoers went, it's a safe guess that they're at the gay-lesbian tea dance held daily in season 3:30–6:30pm on the pool deck of the **Boatslip Beach Club,** 161 Commercial St. (☎ 508/487-2660). Later in the evening, after a posttea dance at Pied Piper (below), they'll probably be back for some disco or two-stepping. Cover varies. In season, a "parade" of gay revelers descends in early evening from the Boatslip to the **Pied Piper,** 293A Commercial St. (☎ 508/ 487-1527), for its After Tea T-Dance. The late-night wave consists of a fair number of women, or fairly convincing semblance thereof (Monday and Wednesday nights feature the "female illusionists" of the Drag Factory). For a glimpse of stars-in-the-making, check out "Putting on the Hits," a sampling of local talent held Tuesday at 10pm. Cover varies; call for schedule. Closed November to mid-April.

Provincetown's oldest hotel was overhauled in 1995, yielding **Vixen,** Pilgrim House, 336 Commercial St. (☎ 508/487-6424), a chic new women's bar. On the roster are jazz, blues, and comedy acts—including the unabashedly butch (even in a prom dress) and hilarious Lea Delaria, who resembles a punk Bud Costello. Cover varies; call for schedule.

# 5 Martha's Vineyard

For a place with such a chichi reputation, this good-sized island (New England's largest, at 100 square miles) can seem surprisingly dowdy at first glance. It presents its showiest side in the trim port of Edgartown, where impressive captains' mansions, uniformly white with black trim, bespeak the riches that prior generations wrested from the sea. Inland, you might forget you're on an island at all: The rolling meadows and dense forests are more reminiscent of landscapes back on the mainland.

Most visitors cling to the shore, usually making a circuit of Vineyard Haven; Oak Bluffs; buttoned-down Edgartown, still the seat of money and power; and Gay Head, where the remarkable multicolored clay cliffs remain under the stewardship of their original caretakers, the Wampanoag Indians. Visitors with a bit more time and latitude will also want to take in the rough-hewn fishing port of Menemsha and wander the rural back roads of Chilmark, where a loose-knit federation of artists, writers, actors, and musicians—some rather well known—seek and sometimes even find inspiration.

## ESSENTIALS

**VISITOR INFORMATION** Contact the **Martha's Vineyard Chamber of Commerce** at Beach Road, Vineyard Haven, MA 02568 (☎ 508/693-0085;

fax 508/693-7589). Their office is 2 blocks up from the ferry terminal in Vineyard Haven. There are also **information booths** at the ferry terminal in Vineyard Haven, across from the Flying Horses Carousel in Oak Bluffs, and on Church Street in Edgartown.

**GETTING AROUND**   Leave your car at home if you're going to stick to the down-island towns, since traffic and parking on the island can be brutal in summer. The national car-rental chains and local agencies are at the airport and in Vineyard Haven and Oak Bluffs; many of them also rent jeeps, mopeds, and bikes. It's also easy to take the **Martha's Vineyard Transit Authority** shuttle buses (☎ 508/627-7448) from town to town. Edgartown operates its own **trolleys** in season, which circle throughout town or out to South Beach. They stop at the free parking lots just north of the town center. Most taxi outfits operate cars as well as vans for larger groups and travelers with bikes. Call **Adam Cab** (☎ 800/281-4462 or 508/693-3332) or **All Island Taxi** (☎ 800/693-TAXI or 508/693-2929).

## OUTDOORS ON THE VINEYARD

Most of the Vineyard's magnificent shoreline is privately owned or restricted to residents or renters with beach stickers, available at the town halls. **Oak Bluffs Town Beach,** Seaview Avenue, is a sandy strip extending from both sides of the ferry wharf, which makes it a convenient place to linger while waiting for the next boat. The **Joseph A. Sylvia State Beach,** midway between Oak Bluffs and Edgartown, stretches a mile and is flanked by a paved bike path; this placid beach has views of Cape Cod and Nantucket Sound and is prized for its gentle and warm waves. If you can't get up-island, head to **South Beach (Katama Beach),** about 4 miles south of Edgartown on Katama Road; it's a 3-mile barrier strand that boasts heavy wave action, sweeping dunes, and relatively ample parking.

A triangle of paved bike paths, roughly 8 miles to a side, links the down-island towns of Oak Bluffs, Edgartown, and West Tisbury (flanked by water on both sides, the Sound portion along Beach Road is especially enjoyable). From Edgartown, you can also follow the bike path to South Beach. For a more woodsy ride, there are paved paths in the **Manuel E. Correllus State Forest** (☎ 508/693-2540), a vast spread of scrub oak and pine smack dab in the middle of the island. The up-island roads leading to Chilmark, Menemsha, and Gay Head are a cyclist's paradise, with sprawling pastureland, old farmhouses, and brilliant sea views. Keep in mind that the terrain is often hilly and the roads are narrow and a little rough around the edges. Try **South Road** from the town of West Tisbury to Chilmark Center (about 5 miles), or **Middle Road,** another lovely ride that will also get you from West Tisbury to Chilmark (it's usually less trafficked too.)

**Wind's Up** at 95 Beach Rd. in Vineyard Haven (☎ 508/693-4252) rents canoes, kayaks, and various sailing craft, including Windsurfers, and offers instruction on-site, on a placid pond; they also rent out surfboards and boogie boards. For **scuba** equipment, visit **Vineyard Scuba** on South Circuit Avenue in Oak Bluffs (☎ 508/693-0288).

## STROLLING AROUND EDGARTOWN

Depending on how long you linger at each stop, you can walk about Edgartown in 2 to 3 hours. Start at the **Edgartown Visitors Center** on Church Street. Around the corner, the **Dr. Daniel Fisher House,** 99 Main St. (☎ 508/627-8017), is a prime example of Edgartown's trademark Greek Revival opulence. Built in 1840, this prosperous-and-proud mansion boasts such classical elements as colonnaded porticos, as well as a delicate roof-walk. The only way to view the interior is with a guided **Edgartown Historic Walking Tour** originating next door at the **Vincent House Museum,** off Main Street between Planting Field Way and Church Street (☎ 508/627-8619),

# Martha's Vineyard

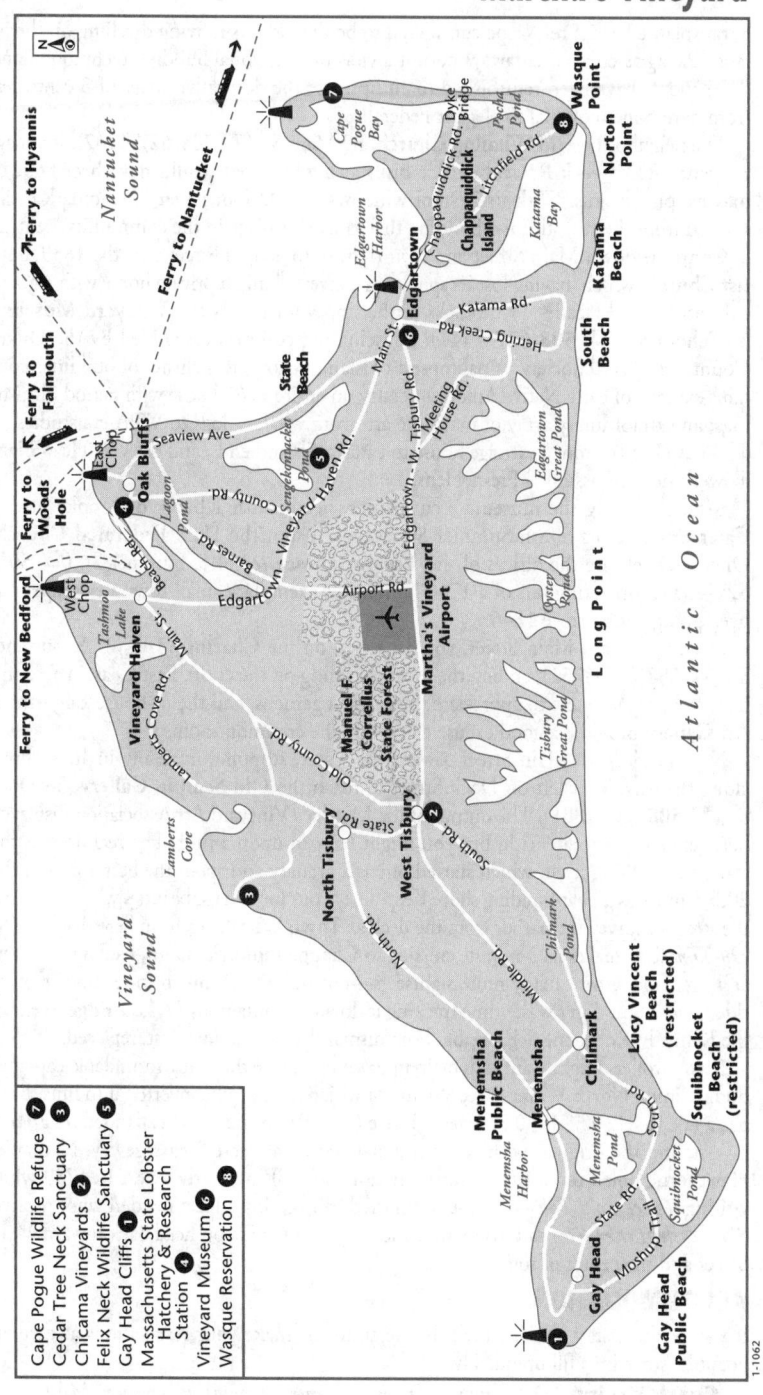

a transplanted 1672 full Cape considered to be the oldest surviving dwelling on the island. Plexiglas-covered cutaways permit a view of traditional building techniques, and three rooms have been refurbished to encapsulate the decorative styles of 3 centuries, from bare-bones colonial to elegant Federal.

The neighboring **Old Whaling Church,** 89 Main St. (☎ 508/627-4442), is a magnificent 1843 Greek Revival edifice built as a whaleboat would have been, out of massive pine beams. With its 27-foot windows and 92-foot tower (a landmark easily spotted from the sea), this is a building that knows its place in the community: central.

Continue down Main Street and turn right onto School Street past the 1839 **Baptist Church,** which, having lost its spire, was converted into a private home with a grand column-fronted facade. Two blocks farther, on your left, is the **Vineyard Museum,** 59 School St. (☎ 508/627-4441), a fascinating complex assembled by the Dukes County Historical Society. A palimpsest of island history, this cluster of buildings contains exhibits of early Native American crafts; an entire 1765 house with period furnishings; an extraordinary array of maritime art, from whalers' logs to WPA-era studies by Thomas Hart Benton; a carriage house to catch odds and ends; and the Gay Head Light Tower's decommissioned Fresnel lens.

After exploring the museum's curiosities, head south 1 block on Cooke Street. Catercorner across South Summer Street, you'll spot the 1828 **Federated Church.** One block left are the offices of the *Vineyard Gazette,* 34 S. Summer St. (☎ 508/627-4311); operating out of a 1760 house, this exemplary small-town newspaper has been going strong since 1846.

Heading toward Main Street, you'll happen on the **Charlotte Inn,** 27 S. Summer St. (☎ 508/627-4751), among the most charming on the entire East Coast. You don't have to be a guest here to appreciate the English gardens, and the in-house **Edgartown Art Gallery** provides a good excuse to explore the common rooms.

Now head down Main Street toward the water, stopping in at any inviting shops along the way. Veer left on Dock Street to reach the **Old Sculpin Gallery,** 58 Dock St. (☎ 508/627-4881). The output of the Martha's Vineyard Art Association displayed here tends to be amateurish, but you might happen upon a find. The real draw is the stark old building itself, which started out as a granary and spent the better part of the 20th century as a boat-building shop. Keep an eye out for vintage beauties when you cross the street to survey the harbor from the deck at **Town Wharf.** It's from here that the tiny *On-Time* ferry makes its 3-minute crossing to **Chappaquiddick Island,** hauling three cars at a time and a great many more sightseers—not that there's much to see on the other side. Just so you don't waste time tracking it down, the infamous **Dyke Bridge,** scene of the Kennedy/Kopechne debacle, has been dismantled and, at long last, replaced.

Mere strollers might want to remain in town to admire the many formidable captains' homes lining **North Water Street,** many of which have been converted into inns. Each has a tale to tell. The 1750 **Daggett House** (no. 59), for instance, expanded on a 1660 tavern, and the original beehive oven is flanked by a "secret" passageway. Nathaniel Hawthorne holed up at the **Edgartown Inn** (no. 56) for nearly a year in 1789 while writing *Twice Told Tales*—and, it is rumored, romancing a local maiden who inspired *The Scarlet Letter.* You can make up stories of your own as you head back toward Main Street and the center of town.

## ACCOMMODATIONS

If you want to stay in Edgartown in the summer, make your reservations as early as possible, since inns fill up quickly.

**Charlotte Inn.** *27 S. Summer St. (in the center of town), Edgartown, MA 02539.* ☎ *508/627-4751. Fax 508/627-4652. 22 rms, 3 suites. Summer (including continental* *breakfast and afternoon tea), $260–$450 double; $495–$575 suite. AE, MC, V. Open year-round.* Gery and Paul Conover have been fine-tuning this cluster of 18th- and 19th-century houses since 1971. Each house has a distinctive look, though the predominant mode is English country house. The Carriage House contains some of the more desirable quarters. L'Etoile is one of Edgartown's finest restaurants (see below).

**Kelley House.** *23 Kelley St. (in the center of town), Edgartown, MA 02539.* ☎ *800/ 225-6005 or 508/627-4394. Fax 508/627-4394. 51 rms, 8 suites. Summer (including continental breakfast and afternoon tea), $215 double; $215–$525 suite. AE, CB, DC, MC, V. Closed Nov–Apr.* The rooms, many with harbor views, are large and airy, with handsome pine furnishings and low-key country accents. If fresh decor and luxurious amenities (like a heated outdoor pool) are important to you, this place might win out over a more intimate B&B. Overnight laundry and baby-sitting can be arranged.

**Oak House.** *Seaview Ave. (on the Sound), Oak Bluffs, MA 02557.* ☎ *508/ 693-4187. Fax 508/696-7385. 8 rms, 2 suites. Summer, $140–$180 double; $250 suite. Rates include continental breakfast and afternoon tea. AE, DISC, MC, V. Closed mid-Oct to mid-May.* This 1872 Queen Anne beauty is owned by Betsi Convery-Luce. The rooms in back are quieter, but the front ones have Nantucket Sound views. Throughout, the furnishings are opulent Victorian. Anyone intent on destressing is sure to benefit from this immersion course on the era that invented the leisure class.

**Point Way Inn.** *104 Main St. (at Pease's Point Way, in the center of town), Edgartown, MA 02539.* ☎ *800/942-9569 or 508/627-8633. Fax 508/627-8579. 15 rms. Summer, $110–$260 double. Rates include continental breakfast and afternoon tea. AE, MC, V. Open year-round.* This homey inn is owned by Ben and Linda Smith. Days begin with the scent of Linda's delectable breakfast breads wafting from the kitchen; you'll also get an afternoon boost of lemonade and cookies in the gazebo. The living room is especially welcoming in the pre- and postdinner hours. The rooms aren't too fancy, but rather effortlessly romantic.

## DINING

Outside Oak Bluffs and Edgartown, all of Martha's Vineyard is "dry," including Vineyard Haven, so bring your own alcoholic beverages; some restaurants charge a fee for uncorking.

**L'Etoile.** *Charlotte Inn, 27 S. Summer St. (off Main St.).* ☎ *508/627-5187. Reservations required. Jacket recommended. Fixed-price dinner $62 and up. AE, MC, V. May–early Sept, daily 6:30–9:45pm; call for off-season hours. Closed late Dec–Apr. FRENCH.* Chef Michael Brisson is determined to dazzle with an ever-evolving menu. Sevruga may appear as a garnish for chilled leek soup. An étouffée of lobster with champagne sauce might come with fish-roe ravioli or warm Mission figs might offset seared pheasant breast in Armagnac-sage sauce.

**Oyster Bar.** *162 Circuit Ave. (in the center of town).* ☎ *508/693-3300. Fax 508/ 693-6439. Reservations recommended. Main courses $28–$44. MC, V. July–Aug, daily 6pm–12:30am; call for off-season hours. Closed Oct–Apr. NEW AMERICAN.* Chef/owner Raymond Schilcher's creativity is considerable, yet the subliminal message is that the "O-Bar" output is meant not so much to be studied as savored. He'll whip up some white truffle polenta or concoct seafood couscous featuring wood-roasted monkfish and homemade lobster sausage. Desserts range from tiramisù to hot chocolate mousse.

**Savoir Fare.** *14 Church St. (Old Post Office Square, off Main St. in the center of town).* ☎ *508/627-9864. Reservations recommended. Main courses $18–$28. AE, MC, V. Late May to mid-Oct, Mon–Sat 11:30am–2:30pm; daily 6–10pm; call for off-season hours. Closed Nov to mid-Apr. NEW AMERICAN.* Scott Caskey opened this stylish space as a gourmet deli/catering concern, then switched to haute restaurateuring. Some of the prettiest seating is outside, under the graceful pergola, where champagne and shellfish are always on ice. The mostly Mediterranean fare is substantial and lyrical, and Scott has a winning way with unusual desserts.

**Zapotec.** *10 Kennebec Ave. (in the center of town).* ☎ *508/693-6800. No reservations. Main courses $10–$17. AE, MC, V. Mid-May to mid-Oct, daily 11:30am–2pm and 5–10pm. Closed mid-Oct to mid-May. MEXICAN.* The chile-pepper lights outside this clapboard cottage are a beacon leading to tasty food, from Mussels Oaxaca (with chipotles, cilantro, lime, and cream) to Crab Cakes Tulum (with codfish, grilled peppers, and dual salsas), plus chicken and beef burritos. You can accompany the good *mole* with Mexico's unbeatable beers or well-priced wines.

## 6 Acadia National Park & the Maine Coast

Summer on the Maine Coast brings ospreys diving for fish off wooded points; gleaming cumulus clouds building over the steely blue, rounded peaks of the western mountains; and the haunting whoop of loons echoing off the dense forest walls bordering the lakes. A placid stay in the right spot can rejuvenate even the most jangled nerves.

The trick comes in finding that right spot. Those who arrive without a clear plan may find themselves cursing their travel decision. Maine's Route 1 along the coast has its moments, but for the most part it's rather charmless, lined with places catering to bus tours. Acadia National Park can be congested, Mount Katahdin's summit can get crowded, and some of the more popular lakes become obstacle courses of jet skis.

But Maine's size works to the traveler's advantage. There are 3,500 miles of coastline and some 3,000 coastal islands. In addition, inland are millions of acres of undeveloped woodland. In fact, more than half the state exists as the "unorganized territories" with few inhabitants. With all this space and a little planning, you'll be able to find your piece of Maine.

### ARRIVING & DEPARTING

The best way to reach the Maine Coast is by car. While major airlines serve the **Portland International Jetport,** and commuter carriers including **Colgan Air** (☎ **800/ 272-5488** or 207/667-7171) go to small airports at Rockport and Bar Harbor, you'll save on airfares and have a wider choice of flight times by flying into Boston's **Logan International Airport,** then renting a car and driving to Portland, a 2-hour trip. Coming from the south, take I-95 (the Maine Turnpike), which parallels the southern coast until it veers inland just north of Portland at Brunswick. From here the rest of the coast is accessible via Route 1.

**Concord Trailways** (☎ **800/639-3317**) operates a coastal bus route with several stops from Brunswick to Searsport, including Bath, Rockland, Camden, Rockport, and Belfast; Concord also serves Portland. **Vermont Transit Lines** (☎ **800/451-3292** or 800/642-3133), affiliated with Greyhound, runs buses to/from Portland, Brunswick, Lewiston, and Augusta.

Wrangling over track upgrades and other issues has severely delayed resumption of rail service from Boston to Portland. Contact **Amtrak** (☎ **800/872-7245**) for more information.

### BAR HARBOR & ACADIA NATIONAL PARK

When Yankees talk about a "downeaster," they mean someone from Maine, but when somebody from Maine says that, they mean someone from the region of Bar Harbor—or "Bah Hah-bah," as it's pronounced up here. The French influence was paramount in these parts for a long time, which explains another local pronunciation: "Mount Dez-*zert*" instead of Mount Desert.

# Acadia National Park

When steamships opened up America in the 1800s, they also opened up Bar Harbor, a little town on the rocky Mount Desert Island. The big attractions are the town itself, cruise boats that leave here for Nova Scotia, and Acadia National Park. The only national park in New England, Acadia takes up about half of Mount Desert Island and much of the surrounding islet.

**VISITOR INFORMATION**   As you enter Mt. Desert Island on Route 3 you'll come to the **Thompson Island Information Center** (☎ 207/288-3411), open May to mid-October. It's a good stop for lodging and restaurant information. The National Park Service's **Hulls Cove Visitor Center** (☎ 207/288-5262), on Route 3 about 7¹/₂ miles beyond Thompson Island, is the best place for information about the park (open mid-April to October). In winter, information is available at the park's **headquarters,** on Route 233 between Bar Harbor and Somes Sound (☎ 207/288-3338).

**TOURING THE PARK**   The **Park Loop Road** is Acadia's premier attraction. This 20-mile road runs along the island's eastern shore, then loops inland along Jordan Pond and Eagle Lake. The road runs alternately high along the shoulders of brawny coastal mountains, then dips down along the boulder-strewn coastlines. The dark granite is broken by the spires of spruce and fir, and the earthy tones contrast sharply with the frothy white surf and the azure sea. The two-lane road is one-way along the coastal stretches; the right-hand lane serves as a parking area, so it's easy to make frequent stops to admire the vistas.

Ideally, you should take at least two trips on the loop road: the first for the sheer ex-hilaration and to get a feel for the lay of the land, the second to stop more frequently, leaving your car to explore the trails and coastline.

Attractions along the coastal loop include scenic **Sand Beach,** which is the only sand beach on the island and offers good swimming during infrequent hot spells and brutally cold swimming the rest of the time; **Thunder Hole** is a shallow oceanside cav-ern into which the surf surges, compresses, and bursts out with explosive force and a concussive sound (kids seem to be endlessly mesmerized); and **Cadillac Mountain,** at 1,530 feet the highest point on the island and the place in the United States first touched by the sun during certain times of year. The mountaintop is accessible by car, but the lot at the summit is often overflowing. You're better off hiking to the top or scaling a more remote peak.

On the tip of the eastern lobe of Mt. Desert Island is the staid, prosperous commu-nity of **Northeast Harbor,** long one of the retreats among the Eastern Seaboard's up-per crust. One of the best, least publicized places for enjoying views of the harbor is from the understatedly spectacular **Asticou Terraces** (☎ **207/276-5130**). Finding the park-ing lot can be tricky: Head a half-mile south on Route 3 from the junction with Route 198 and look for the gravel lot on the water side of the road with a sign reading ASTICOU TERRACES. Park here, cross the road on foot, and set off up a magnificent path made of local rock that scales the sheer hillside with expanding views of the harbor and town. This pathway, with its precise stonework and the occasional bench and gazebo, is one of the Northeast's hidden marvels. Created by Boston landscape architect Joseph Curtis, who summered here for many years prior to his death in 1928, the pathway seems to blend in almost preternaturally with its spruce-and-fir surroundings, as if it were created by an act of God rather than of human. Curtis donated the property to the public for quiet enjoyment.

Continue on the trail at the top of the hillside and you'll soon arrive at Curtis's cabin (open to the public daily in summer), behind which lies the formal **Thuya Gardens,** which are as manicured as the terraces are natural. These wonderfully maintained gar-dens, designed by Charles K. Savage, attract flower enthusiasts, students of landscape architecture, and local folks looking for a quiet place to rest. It's well worth the trip. A donation of $2 is requested of visitors to the garden; the terraces are free.

**HIKING**   Acadia National Park has 120 miles of hiking trails. The park is studded with low "mountains" affording superb views over the island and ocean. The trails weren't simply hacked out of the hillside; they were crafted by experienced stonemasons and others with high aesthetic intent. The routes aren't the most direct, but they're often the most scenic, taking advantage of fractures in the rocks, picturesque ledges, and sud-den vistas. The Hulls Cove Visitor Center (above) offers a one-page chart of area hikes; combined with the park map, this is all you'll need since the trails are well maintained and well marked. It's not hard to cobble together loop hikes to make your trips more varied. Coordinate your hiking with the weather; if it's damp or foggy, you'll stay drier and warmer strolling the carriage roads. If it's clear and dry, head for the highest peaks with the best views.

Among the most extraordinary trails is the **Dorr Ladder Trail,** which departs from Route 3 near The Tarn just south of the Sieur de Monts entrance to the Loop Road. This trail begins with a Homeric series of stone steps ascending along the base of a vast slab of granite, then passes through crevasses (not for the wide of girth) and up ladders affixed to the unyielding granite. The views are superb.

An easy lowland hike is around **Jordan Pond,** with the northward leg along the pond's east shore on a hiking trail, and the return via carriage road. It's mostly level, with the total loop measuring 3.3 miles. At the north end of Jordan Pond, consider detouring up the prominent, oddly symmetrical mounds called **The Bubbles.** The ascents shouldn't take much more than 20 minutes each; look for signs off the Jordan Pond Shore Trail.

**MOUNTAIN BIKING**　The 57 miles of carriage roads built by John D. Rockefeller Jr. are among the park's most extraordinary hidden treasures. While built for horse and carriage, these grass-and-gravel roads with their fine stonework bridges are ideal for cruising by mountain bike. Park your car near Jordan Pond and plumb the tree-shrouded roads lacing the area. Afterward, stop for tea and popovers at the Jordan Pond House (see "Dining," below), an island tradition for over a century.

The grassy lanes and gravel roads were maintained by Rockefeller until his death in 1960. Today the roads are superbly restored and maintained. Where the carriage roads cross private land (generally between Seal Harbor and Northeast Harbor), they're closed to mountains bikes. Please respect these restrictions. A map of the carriage roads is available at the park's visitor center. More detailed guidebooks are sold at area bookstores.

You can find mountain bike rentals along Cottage Street in Bar Harbor. Some bike shops include locks and helmets as basic equipment; ask what's included before you rent. Try **Bar Harbor Bicycle Shop** (☎ 207/288-3886) at 141 Cottage St.; **Acadia Outfitters** (☎ 207/288-8118) at 106 Cottage St.; or **Acadia Bike & Canoe** (☎ 207/288-9605) at 48 Cottage St.

For a unique adventure, consider watching the sunrise from atop Cadillac Mountain followed by a zippy bike descent back to Bar Harbor. For $29 per person, **Acadia Downhill,** part of Acadia Bike and Canoe, 48 Cottage St. (☎ 207/288-9605), will haul you and a rental bike to the top of the island's highest peak via van, serve you coffee and a light breakfast while you watch the sun edge over the horizon, then lead you on a brisk coasting and pedaling trip 6 miles back down the mountain and into Bar Harbor. This is an *early*-morning adventure: Tours meet at about 3:30am in June (about 5am by August) and last about 3 hours. Trips are offered Monday to Friday and reservations are recommended.

**SEA KAYAKING**　Experienced sea kayakers flock to Acadia to test their paddling skills along the surf at the base of rocky cliffs, venture out to the offshore islands, and probe the still waters of Somes Sound. Novice sea kayakers can take guided tours, which are offered by several outfitters. Tours vary in quality. The following outfitters offer half- and full-day tours: **Acadia Outfitters** (☎ 207/288-8118) at 106 Cottage St., **Coastal Kayaking Tours** (☎ 207/288-9605) at 48 Cottage St., and **National Park Sea Kayak Tours** (☎ 207/288-0342) at 137 Cottage St.

**WHALE-WATCHING**　Bar Harbor makes a terrific base for **whale-watching.** Several tour operators offer excursions in search of humpbacks, finbacks, and others. The largest of the fleet is the *Friendship* (☎ 800/942-5374 or 207/288-2386), operating out of the Regency Holiday Inn on Eden Street, about a mile north of Bar Harbor. The tours are on a twin-hulled excursion boat that can hold 200 passengers in two heated cabins. **Sea Bird Watcher Company** (☎ 800/247-3794 or 207/288-2025) runs whale tours on a 72-foot boat from the Golden Anchor Pier in Bar Harbor; it also offers birdwatching trips to offshore islands to view puffins and terns. **Frenchman Bay Boat Cruises** (☎ 800/508-1499 or 207/288-3322) takes passengers in search of whales aboard the 105-foot *Whale Watcher* and offers a handy pickup service at many hotels and inns.

**BAR HARBOR AFTER DARK**　One of Bar Harbor's special attractions is the **Criterion Theater** (☎ 207/288-3441), a movie house built in 1932 in a classic art deco style. The 900-seat theater, on Cottage Street, shows first-run movies in summer and is worth the price of admission for the beautiful interiors.

## ACCOMMODATIONS

In peak season, it's best to make reservations as far in advance as possible.

**Acadia Hotel.** *20 Mt. Desert St., Bar Harbor, ME 04609.* ☎ *207/288-5721. 10 rms. Peak season, $59–$115 double; off-season, $45–$85 double. Rates include continental breakfast. AE, DISC, MC, V.* The Acadia overlooks the Village Green and is easily accessible to all in-town activities. This handsome home from the late 19th century has a wraparound porch (where you can breakfast in summer) and attractive guest rooms. The rooms vary in size and amenities; ask for the specifics when you book.

**Balance Rock Inn.** *21 Albert Meadow, Bar Harbor, ME 04609.* ☎ *800/ 753-0494 or 207/288-2610. 21 rms. Peak season, $195–$395 double; off-season, $150– $265 double. Rates include full breakfast. Open early May–late Oct. AE, DISC, MC, V. Albert Meadow is off Main Street at Butterfield's grocery store.* This 1903 mansion is an elaborate affair of gray shingles with cream, maroon, and forest-green trim. A favored spot is the front patio with its small bar. And then there's the view: You look across a wonderful pool and down a lawn framed by hardwoods to Frenchman Bay. The rooms are wonderful, many with whirlpools or fireplaces.

**Claremont.** *P.O. Box 137, Southwest Harbor, ME 04679.* ☎ *800/244-5036 or 207/244-5036. Fax 207/244-3512. 30 rms, 2 with tub only; 12 cottages. July–Labor Day, $130–$150 double, including breakfast; $172–$192 double, including breakfast and dinner; off-season, $110–$130 double, including breakfast. Open early June to mid-Oct.* The Claremont offers classic New England grace. Most of the rooms are bright and airy. Rooms overlooking the water are more expensive—and worth it. There's also a series of cottages, available for a 3-day minimum. Meals are mainly reprises of American classics like grilled salmon, steamed lobster, and ribeye steak.

**Inn at Southwest.** *Main St. (P.O. Box 593), Southwest Harbor, ME 04679.* ☎ *207/244-3835. 9 rms, 3 with shower only, 2 with hall bath. Summer and early fall, $105–$124 double; off-season, $60–$90 double. Rates include full breakfast. Open Apr– Oct. MC, V.* Owner Jill Lewis has done a fine job with this mansard-roofed Victorian. The rooms are named after Maine lighthouses and contain contemporary and antique furniture. Among the most pleasant is Blue Hill Bay, with its large bath, oak bed and bureau, and glimpses of the harbor. Breakfasts feature specialties like poached pears in wine sauce and eggs Florentine.

**Ledgelawn Inn.** *66 Mt. Desert St., Bar Harbor, ME 04609.* ☎ *800/274-5334 or 207/288-4596. Fax 207/288-9968. 33 rms, 9 with shower only. July–Aug, $145–$195 double; discounts in off-season. Rates include full breakfast. Open May–late Oct. AE, DISC, MC, V.* This cream-and-maroon 1904 "cottage" sits on a village lot amid towering oaks and maples and has a midcentury elegance. The common area around the fireplace has a plush feel; the breakfast room is more formal. The guest rooms vary in size and mood but all are comfortably if not stylishly furnished.

**Lindenwood Inn.** *118 Clark Point Rd. (P.O. Box 1328), Southwest Harbor, ME 04679.* ☎ *207/244-5335. 23 rms, some with shower only. July–Aug, $85–$195 double; Sept to mid-Oct, $75–$185 double; mid-Oct to June $65–$175 double. Rates include full breakfast. AE, MC, V.* A handsome 1902 Queen Anne at the harbor's edge, this no-smoking inn offers uncluttered modern rooms. The suites have great harbor views. If you're on a tighter budget, ask for a room in the annex, a minute's walk down the block. The dining room is one of the best (if most expensive) on the island.

**Primrose Inn.** *73 Mount Desert St., Bar Harbor, ME 04609.* ☎ *800/543-7842 or 207/288-4031. 10 rms plus 5 efficiencies, 1 with shower only. Peak season, $90–$145 double; shoulder season, $85–$140 double; $650–$850 suite per week. Daily rates include breakfast. Open May–late Oct. AE, DISC, MC, V.* This handsome Victorian is comfortable and elegant, though it has an informal air, which encourages guests to mingle in the common room. Many of the rooms feature whirlpools or fireplaces. The suites are spacious and the efficiencies make sense for families (for rent by the week only).

**St. Saviour's Parish Hall Youth Hostel.** *27 Kennebec St. (P.O. Box 32), Bar Harbor, ME 04609.* ☎ *800/444-6111 or 207/288-5587. 20 beds, none with bath. $15 single ($12 American Youth Hostel members). No credit cards.* Behind St. Saviour's church, this AYH-sanctioned hostel in a handsome building offers inexpensive dorms for men or women. This is a good bet if low cost is a high priority and privacy a low one. Reservations are accepted by phone only, or you can stop by to see if beds are available. The office is open daily 7–9am and 5–8:30pm.

## DINING

Whether your taste runs to lobster, brewpubs, or afternoon tea, you'll find something you'll like in the Bar Harbor area.

**Burning Tree.** *Route 3, Otter Creek.* ☎ *207/288-9331. Reservations recommended. Main courses $14–$20. Wed–Mon 5–9pm (daily in Aug). Closed Columbus Day to mid-June. SEAFOOD/ORGANIC.* Between Bar Harbor and Northeast Harbor, this restaurant serves the area's freshest food, prepared with imagination and skill. A typical appetizer is smoked salmon with corn-and-caper relish. Entrees might include crab-and-lobster au gratin or grilled swordfish with watercress-lime sauce. A standout dessert is the ginger-orange cheesecake.

**George's.** *7 Stephens Lane, Bar Harbor.* ☎ *207/288-4505. Reservations recommended. Main courses $20; appetizer, main course, and dessert packages $29. AE, DISC, MC, V. Daily 5:30–10pm; shorter hours after Labor Day. Closed Nov–early May. MEDITERRANEAN-INSPIRED AMERICAN.* Behind Main Street's First National Bank, George's offers fine dining in informal surroundings. The service is upbeat, and the meals are wonderfully prepared. Main courses include salad, vegetable, and potato or rice. You can't go wrong with steamed lobster or roast chicken, but do try more adventurous fare like tangerine scallops, game, or lamb.

**Jordan Pond House.** *Park Loop Rd., Acadia National Park (near Seal Harbor).* ☎ *207/276-3316. Reservations recommended for lunch and dinner. Lunch $6–$12; dinner $8–$14. AE, DISC, MC, V. Late May–late Oct, daily 11:30am–8pm (until 9pm July–Aug). AMERICAN.* This modern bilevel dining room boasts a great location. If the weather is right, ask for a seat on the lawn. Afternoon tea is a tradition, with everyone feasting on tasty popovers and strawberry jam served with tea or lemonade. The reasonably priced dinners include classics like prime rib, steamed lobster, and baked haddock.

**Lompoc Cafe and Brewpub.** *32 Rodick St., Bar Harbor.* ☎ *207/288-9392. Reservations not accepted. Sandwiches $4–$6; dinner $10–$14. DISC, MC, V. May–Nov, daily 11:30am–1am. Closed Dec–Apr. AMERICAN/ECLECTIC.* The cafe has three sections—the original bar in the pine-floored dining room, a small garden just outside, and a barnlike structure at the garden's edge. The on-site brewery produces five unique beers, including a blueberry ale. The menu has some surprises, with main courses like Indonesian chicken, Mediterranean scallops, and Vermont pork tenderloin.

**Porcupine Grill.** *123 Cottage St., Bar Harbor.* ☎ *207/288-3884. Reservations recommended. Main courses $17–$22. AE, DC, MC, V. Summer and fall daily, 5:30–9:30pm; off-season, Fri–Sun only. NEW AMERICAN.* At the Porcupine Grill you can sit upstairs or down amid a smattering of antiques. You might begin with salmon cakes accompanied by ginger, chili, and coconut sauce, then try filet mignon with portobello mushrooms and wild-boar bacon. The Porcupine stew is a mélange of lobster, scallops, fish, and mussels in tomato-caper broth.

**Redfield's.** *Main St., Northeast Harbor.* ☎ *207/276-5283. Reservations strongly recommended in summer. Main courses $18–$21. AE, MC, V. June–Oct, Mon–Sat 6–9pm; Nov–May, Fri–Sat only. CONTEMPORARY.* Here you can enjoy a drink at the marble bar, then peruse the menu. Appetizer choices may be smoked mussels with a sauce of corn, tomato, and serrano chile or eggplant and roasted red peppers baked with cheddar on a corn tortilla. Entrees include salmon fillet with ginger-tamari sauce and venison tenderloin with dried cranberries and blueberries.

**Restaurant XYZ.** *Shore Rd., Manset.* ☎ *207/244-5221. Reservations recommended weekends. Main courses $11–$15. MC, V. Summer, daily 5:30–9:30pm; off-season, limited hours (usually weekends only). MEXICAN.* Drawing on the traditions of central Mexico and the Yucatán, the fare is spicy and tangy. Expect a savory mole and a chipotle salsa that sings. Among the notable main courses are tatemado (pork loin baked with guajillo and ancho chiles) and Yucatecan-style pork rubbed with achiote paste and marinated with citrus. The flan is a great dessert.

# YORK

John Hancock is famed for his oversized signature on the Declaration of Independence. What's not so well known about him is his failure as a businessman. Hancock was the proprietor of Hancock Wharf, a failed enterprise that's only one of the intriguing sites open in **York Village,** a fine destination for those curious about early American history.

First settled in 1624, York Village has several early homes open mid-June to September. The **Old York Historical Society** (☎ **207/363-4974**) operates a community museum comprised of seven buildings spanning three centuries in this quiet riverside town. One ticket ($6 adults, $2.50 children 6–16) provides admission to all buildings, or you can buy admission to individual buildings ($2). The museum is open Tues–Sat 10am–5pm and Sun 1–5pm.

Tickets are available across from the handsome old burying ground at **Jefferds Tavern,** where changing exhibits document facets of early life. Next door is the **School House,** furnished as it might have been in the last century. A 10-minute walk away on lightly traveled Lindsay Road is **Hancock Wharf,** next door to the George Marshall Store. Also nearby is the **Elizabeth Perkins House** with its well-preserved Colonial Revival interiors. The newest acquisition is an old bank building that houses the society's library and offices. The library is open to historical society members only.

The two don't-miss buildings in the society's collection are the intriguing 1719 **Old Gaol,** with now-musty dungeons for criminals and debtors. The jail is the oldest surviving public building in the United States. Just down the knoll from the jail is the **Emerson–Wilcox House,** built in the mid-1700s. Added on to periodically over the years, it's a virtual catalog of architectural styles and early decorative arts. Docents make the building come alive during a tour.

## ACCOMMODATIONS

For basic accommodations, try York Beach, which has a proliferation of motels and guest cottages facing Long Sands Beach. If the following places are booked, try these: **Anchorage Motor Inn** (☎ 207/363-5112), **Sea Latch Motor Inn** (☎ 800/441-2993 or 207/363-4400), or **Sunrise Motel** (☎ 800/242-0752 or 207/363-4542).

**Dockside Guest Quarters.** *Harris Island (P.O. Box 205), York, ME 03909.* ☎ *207/363-2868. Fax 207/363-1977. 21 rms, 2 with shared bath. Mid-June to early Sept, $70–$155 double. Rates up to 30% lower off-season. MC, V. Closed weekdays Nov–May. Drive south on Route 103 from Route 1A; after bridge, turn left and follow signs.* David and Harriet Lusty opened this retreat in 1954 and recent additions haven't taken away the friendly flavor. On an island connected to the mainland by a small bridge, the

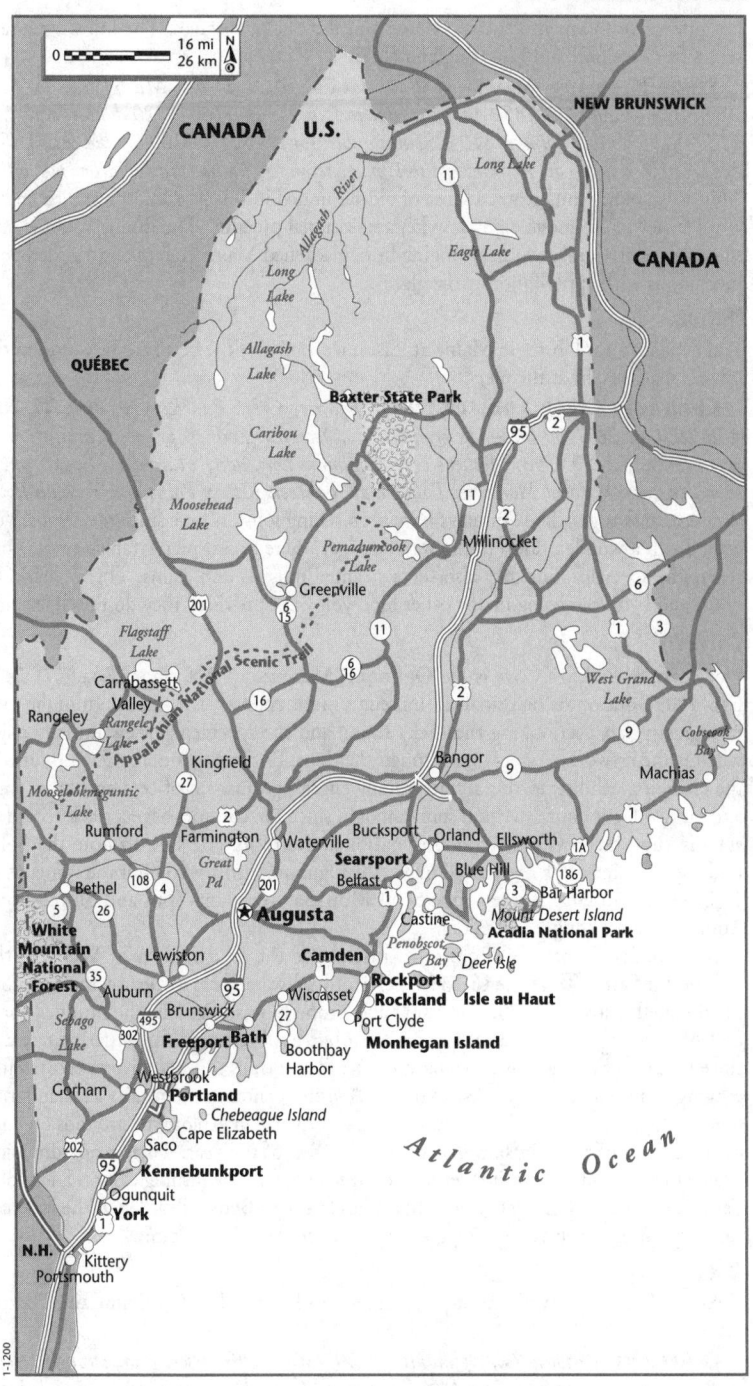

# The Maine Coast

CANADA   U.S.

NEW BRUNSWICK

Long Lake

(11)

Eagle Lake

CANADA

QUÉBEC

Allagash River

Long Lake

Allagash Lake

1

Baxter State Park

95   2

Caribou Lake

Moosehead Lake

(11)   2

Pemadumcook Lake   Millinocket

Greenville   6

201   16
13

Flagstaff Lake   (11)

6
16

Carrabassett Valley   Appalachian National Scenic Trail   16

Rangeley   Rangeley Lake

2

West Grand Lake

Cobscook Bay

Kingfield   27   9   Machias

Mooselookmeguntic Lake

Rumford   2   Bangor   9   1

Farmington   Waterville   Bucksport   Orland   Ellsworth

Bethel   108   4   Great Pd   201   Searsport   Blue Hill   1A

5   26   Belfast   3   186

White Mountain National Forest   ★ Augusta   Castine   Bar Harbor

Lewiston   1   Camden   Penobscot Bay   Deer Isle   Mount Desert Island

35   Rockport   Acadia National Park

Auburn   95   Wiscasset   Rockland   Isle au Haut

Brunswick   27   Port Clyde

495   Bath   Monhegan Island

Freeport   Boothbay Harbor

302   Westbrook

Gorham   Portland   Chebeague Island

Sebago Lake   Cape Elizabeth   Atlantic Ocean

202   Saco

95   Kennebunkport

Ogunquit

1   York

N.H.   Kittery
Portsmouth

inn offers five rooms in the main house and the rest in cottages. The inn's restaurant serves fresh seafood and New England classics.

**Stage Neck Inn.** *Stage Neck (P.O. Box 70), York Harbor, ME 03911.* ☎ *800/ 222-3238 or 207/363-3850. 60 rms. June to Labor Day, $160–$220 double; early fall, $130–$195 double; winter, $105–$140 double; spring, $110–$160 double. AE, DISC, MC, V. Head north on 1A from Route 1; make second right after York Harbor post office.* This no-smoking inn creates a sense of old-fashioned intimacy. Almost every room has a water view, and guests enjoy low-key recreational pursuits. The dining room is outstanding, offering main courses ranging from blackened Maine crab cakes to grilled pork medallions with apple-Dijon-garlic glaze.

### DINING

You'll want to eat lobster in Maine at least once. Some of the best is to be found in the lobster shacks right at the piers.

**Chauncey Creek Lobster Pier.** *Chauncey Creek Rd., Kittery Point.* ☎ *207/ 439-1030 or 207/439-9024. Reservations not accepted. Lobsters priced to market; other main courses $2–$9. Open Mother's Day–Columbus Day, daily 11am–8pm (until 7pm in shoulder season); closed Mon after Labor Day. Between Kittery Point and York on Route 103; watch for signs.* The Spinneys have been selling lobsters here since the 1950s. You walk down a wooden ramp to the water's edge, where bright picnic tables await. Lobster is the specialty, but they also serve steamed mussels and clams. There's a BYOB policy, and you can bring in any other food you want provided they don't sell it here.

## OGUNQUIT

Not far from Perkin's Cove is the **Ogunquit Museum of Art,** Shore Road (☎ 207/ 646-4909), one of the best small art museums in the country. It's set back from the road in a grassy glen overlooking the rocky shore, and the spectacular view initially overwhelms the artwork as you walk through the door. But stick around a few minutes—the changing exhibits in this architecturally engaging museum of cement block, slate, and glass will get your attention soon enough, since the curators have a track record of staging superb shows and attracting national attention. (Be sure to note the bold, underappreciated work of Henry Strater, the Ogunquit artist who built the museum in 1953.) The museum is open July–Sept, Mon–Sat 10:30am–5pm and Sun 2–5pm. Admission is $3 adults, $2 seniors.

A short drive north of Ogunquit, just above the beach town of Wells, is the **Laudholm Farm** (☎ 207/646-1555), a historic saltwater farm owned by the nonprofit Laudholm Trust since 1986. The 1,600-acre property was originally the summer home of 19th-century railroad baron George Lord but has been used for estuarine research since taken over by the trust. The farm has 7 miles of trails through diverse ecosystems, ranging from salt marsh to forest to dunes. A visitor center in the regal Victorian farmhouse will get you oriented. Tours are available, or you can explore the grounds on your own. Parking costs $5 in summer; it's free the rest of the year. There's no admission charge to the grounds or visitor center. You reach the farm by turning east on Laudholm Farm Road at the blinking light just north of Harding's Books. Bear left at the fork and turn right into the entrance. The grounds are open daily 8am–5pm.

### DINING

Two of Maine's finest dining experiences are to be found in Ogunquit and Perkins Cove.

✪ **Arrows.** *Berwick Rd., Ogunquit.* ☎ *207/361-1100. Reservations strongly recommended. Main courses $26–$30. MC, V. May and Columbus Day–Thanksgiving, Fri–Sat 6–9pm; June and Sept–Columbus Day, Wed–Sun 6–9pm; July–Aug, Tues–Sun 6–9pm.*

*Closed Thanksgiving to Apr. Turn uphill at the Key Bank in the village; the restaurant is 1.9 miles on your right. REGIONAL/NEW AMERICAN.* Owner/chefs Marc Gaier and Clark Frasier have put Ogunquit on the culinary map. The atmosphere is that of a European inn, and the food is concocted with some exotic twists. Main courses may include grilled yellowfin tuna or smoked duck breast with jasmine rice fritters. The wine list is superb.

✪ **Hurricane.** *Oarweed Dr., Perkins Cove, Ogunquit.* ☎ *207/646-6348. Reservations recommended. Lunch items $7–$13; main dinner courses $14–$25. AE, DC, DISC, MC, V. Mon–Sat 11:30am–4pm, Sun 11:30am–4:30pm; Mon–Thurs 5:30–9:30pm, Fri–Sat 5:30–10:30pm. NEW AMERICAN.* The dining room is divided into small halves, but soaring windows overlooking the Gulf of Maine make the rooms feel much larger. The cuisine offers appetizers like deviled Maine lobster cakes with salsa. Main courses include lobster cannelloni with mascarpone and baked salmon and brie baklava with key-lime béarnaise. Try the best martinis in town.

## KENNEBUNKPORT

A short drive north of Kennebunkport on Log Cabin Road is one of the quirkiest and most engaging museums in the state: the **Seashore Trolley Museum** (☎ 207/967-2800). A place with an excess of character and an intriguing history, this is well worth a visit. This scrap-yard-masquerading-as-a-museum ("world's oldest and largest museum of its type") was founded in 1939 to preserve a disappearing way of life, and today the collection contains more than 200 trolleys from around the world, including Glasgow, Moscow, San Francisco, and Rome. Naturally, there's also a streetcar named Desire from New Orleans. About 40 of the cars still operate, and the admission ($7 adults, $4 children 6–16, $5 seniors) includes unlimited rides on a 2-mile track. The other cars, some of which still contain turn-of-the-century advertising, are on display outdoors and in vast storage sheds. The museum is open daily from May to mid-October, but weekends only from mid-October to mid-November. Head north from Kennebunkport on North Street; look for signs.

### ACCOMMODATIONS & DINING

**Captain Lord.** *Pleasant St. and Green St. (P.O. Box 800), Kennebunkport, ME 04046.* ☎ *207/967-3141. Fax 207/967-3172. 20 rms. A/C TEL. $155–$349 double; $60 off during midweek in Jan–Apr. Two-night minimum on weekends. Rates include breakfast. DISC, MC, V.* The no-smoking Captain Lord is one of the most architecturally distinguished inns anywhere, in a superb location. Off the front hall is a comfortable common area with piped-in classical music and a fireplace. The rooms are furnished with splendid antiques. The only complaint I've heard is that it's too perfect, too friendly. Go figure.

✪ **The Colony.** *Ocean Ave. (about a mile from Dock Square; P.O. Box 511), Kennebunkport, ME 04046.* ☎ *800/552-2363 or 207/967-3331. Fax 207/967-8738. E-mail: colony@cybertours.com. 135 rms. $199–$299 double. Rates include breakfast and dinner. Closed mid-Oct to mid-May. AE, MC, V.* The Georgian Revival main inn has 105 cheery rooms, furnished with summer cottage antiques. Rooms in two of the three outbuildings carry over the rustic elegance; the exception is the East House, with charmless rooms. Dinners begin with a relish tray but progress to more contemporary fare like rainbow tortellini with lobster marinara sauce.

✪ **White Barn Inn.** *Beach St. (a quarter-mile east of junction of Routes 9 and 35; P.O. Box 560), Kennebunkport, ME 04046.* ☎ *207/967-2321. Fax 207/967-1100. 24 rms. $140–$205 double; up to $375 suite. Rates include breakfast. AE, MC, V.* Upon checking in, you're offered sherry or brandy while valets gather your luggage and park your car. The no-smoking inn has a European atmosphere, with an emphasis on service. Nice touches include robes, fresh flowers, bottled water, and turndown service. The inn serves some of the best fare in Maine in the adjoining barn.

# PORTLAND

Cities in Maine have never have had a reputation for chic or avant-garde ambience, but Portland may be changing that. The Civic Center draws sports events, conventions, and big-name entertainers, and the Old Port Exchange—its revitalized waterfront—is now even more attractive than in its Victorian heyday when railroads, a huge sailing fleet, and trade in lumber and fish made Portland a thriving commercial center. It's still Maine's largest city, its transportation hub, and its business center.

## WHAT TO SEE & DO

**ATTRACTIONS**    Any visit to Portland should start with a stroll around the historic **Old Port.** Bounded by Commercial, Congress, Union, and Pearl streets, this area near the waterfront contains some of the best commercial architecture in town, many fine restaurants and boutiques, and bars thicker than north woods black flies in June. The narrow streets and intricate brick facades reflect the mid-Victorian era; most of the area was built following a devastating fire in 1866. Leafy, quaint **Exchange Street** is the heart of the Old Port, with other attractive streets running off and around it.

A 10-minute drive from downtown Portland is the ✪ **Portland Head Light & Museum,** Fort Williams Park, 1000 Shore Rd., Cape Elizabeth (☎ **207/799-2661**), a picturesque 1794 lighthouse. The light marks the entrance to Portland Harbor and was occupied continuously from its construction until 1989, when it was automated and the graceful keeper's house (1891) converted to a town-owned museum on the history of navigation. The lighthouse is still active and thus closed to the public, but you can wander the park grounds, sit on the rocky headlands, and watch the sailboats and ships come and go. The park has a pebble beach, grassy lawns with ocean vistas, and picnic areas for barbecues. Admission to the museum is $2 adults, $1 children 6–18. The grounds are open daily year-round sunrise to sunset (until 8:30pm in summer); the museum is open June–Oct, daily 10am–4pm (weekends only spring and late fall). From Portland, follow State Street across the Fore River to the T intersection at Broadway and turn left. At the second light turn right on Cottage Road, which soon becomes Shore Road; follow this about 2 miles until you arrive at the park, on your left.

The bold, modern **Portland Museum of Art,** 7 Congress Square, at the corner of Congress and High streets (☎ **207/775-6148**), was designed by I. M. Pei Associates in 1983 and includes selections from its own fine collections and a parade of touring exhibits. It's particularly strong in American artists who had a connection to Maine, including Winslow Homer, Andrew Wyeth, and Edward Hopper, and has fine displays of early American furniture and crafts. The museum shares the Joan Whitney Payson Collection with Colby College (the college gets it one semester every other year). It also features works by Renoir, Degas, and Picasso. The museum is open Tues–Wed and Sat 10am–5pm, Thurs–Fri 10am–9pm, and Sun noon–5pm (July–Columbus Day, also Mon 10am–5pm). Admission is $6 adults, $5 students and seniors, $1 children 6–12; free Fri 5–9pm.

One of the most elaborate Victorian brownstones in existence, **Victoria Mansion,** also known as the Morse–Libby House, 109 Danforth St. (☎ **207/772-4841**), is a remarkable display of high Victorian style. Built between 1859 and 1863 for a Maine businessman who had made a fortune in the New Orleans hotel trade, the slightly foreboding home is a prime example of the Italiante style then in vogue. Inside, it appears that not a square inch of wall space was left unmolested by craftsmen or artists (11 artists were hired to paint the murals). The decor is ponderous and somber, but it offers an engaging look at a bygone era. The home is open May–Oct, Tues–Sat 10am–4pm and Sun 1–5pm; closed the rest of the year, except for special Christmas tours. Admission is $5 adults, $2 children under 18. From the Old Port, head west on Fore Street to Danforth Street, near Stonecoast Brewing; bear right and proceed three blocks to the mansion.

**ISLAND TOURS**   Six of the Casco Bay islands have year-round populations and are served by ferries from Portland. (Most of these are part of the city of Portland; the exception is Long Island, which broke away a few years ago.) The **Casco Bay Lines,** Commercial and Franklin streets (☎ 207/774-7871), offer an inexpensive way to view the bustling harbor and get a taste of Maine's islands. Trips range from a 20-minute excursion to Peaks Island (the closest thing to an island suburb with 1,200 year-round residents), to the 5$^{1}$/2-hour cruise to Bailey Island and back. All the islands are well suited to walking; Peaks has a rocky back shore that's easily accessible via the paved perimeter road (bring a picnic lunch). Cliff Island is the most remote and has a sedate turn-of-the-century feel. Fares vary depending on the run, but are generally $4.50–$13.75 round-trip. There are frequent departures from 6am to midnight.

**Eagle Island Tours,** Long Wharf (Commercial St.) (☎ 207/774-6498), offers one 4-hour excursion daily from Portland to Eagle Island, including a 1$^{1}$/2-hour stopover on the island. Eagle Island was the summer home of famed Arctic explorer and Portland native Robert E. Peary, who claimed in 1909 to be the first person to reach the North Pole. (His accomplishments have been the subject of exhaustive debates among Arctic scholars.) In 1904 Peary built this simple home on a 17-acre island at the edge of Casco Bay; in 1912 he added two low stone towers. After his death in 1920 his family kept up the home, then donated it to the state, which has since managed it as a state park. The home is open to the public, maintained much the way it was when Peary lived here. Island footpaths through the forest allow exploration to the open, seagull-clotted cliffs at the southern tip. The trip costs $15 adults, $9 children under 9 (plus state park fee of $1.50 adults, 50¢ children).

**SHOPPING**   Aficionados of antiques and junk stores love Portland. You'll find good browsing on Congress Street. Check out the stretches between State and High streets in the arts district and from India Street to Washington Avenue on Munjoy Hill. There are about a dozen shops of varying quality in these areas. For new items, the Old Port, with its dozens of boutiques and storefronts, is well worth browsing.

More serious antique hounds will want to take in an **auction** or two. Almost any day of the week you'll be able to find an auction within an hour's drive of Portland, often in the town of Gray, which has an exit off the Maine Turnpike. The best source of information is the *Maine Sunday Telegram.* Look under the classifieds for listings of auctions scheduled for the following week.

## ACCOMMODATIONS

The **Holiday Inn by the Bay,** 88 Spring St. (☎ 207/775-2311), offers great views of the harbor from about half the rooms. The **Radisson Eastland,** 157 High St. (☎ 207/775-5411), features two restaurants, a rooftop lounge, and a spacious lobby imbued with an old-world elegance.

Budget travelers can find accommodations by the Maine Mall in South Portland and off the Maine Turnpike near Westbrook, charmless areas, but only 10 minutes away from downtown. Try **Days Inn** (☎ 207/772-3450) or **Coastline Inn** (☎ 207/772-3838) near the mall; or the **Super 8 Motel** (☎ 207/854-1881) or **Susse Chalet** (☎ 207/774-6101) off turnpike exit 8 near the Westbrook town line.

✪ **Pomegranate Inn.** *49 Neal St., Portland, ME 04102.* ☎ *800/356-0408 or 207/772-1006. 8 rms. $95–$165 double. Rates include full breakfast. AE, DISC, MC, V.*

*From the Old Port, take Middle St. (which turns into Spring) to Neal St. in the West End (about 1 mile); turn right and proceed to the inn. On-street parking.* In this handsome Italianate home, the interiors are decorated with whimsy and elegance. If you can, peek in some of the unoccupied rooms—they're all different, with painted floors and faux-marble woodwork. The best is in the carriage house, with its own terrace and fireplace. Breakfasts are creative and tasty. No smoking.

**Portland Regency Hotel.** *20 Milk St., Portland, ME 04101.* ☎ *800/727-3436 or 207/774-4200. Fax 207/775-2150. 95 rms. Summer, $159–$229 double; off-season, $89–$175 double. AE, CB, DC, DISC, MC, V.* In a historic brick armory, the hotel offers modern guest rooms furnished with all the amenities. It has a well-regarded dining room, a tavern, and a well-equipped fitness room. Note that the walls are a bit thin, and on weekends the street noise can penetrate even the dense exterior walls.

## DINING

Portland has an exceptionally vibrant dining scene, with dozens of restaurants offering up a smorgasbord of cuisines at a wide range of prices. Restaurants seem to line every Old Port street and are tucked down every alley around town. For a city of this size, the selection is dazzling.

**Café Uffa!** *190 State St, Portland.* ☎ *207/775-3380. Reservations not accepted. Main courses $8–$13. MC, V. Wed–Sat 5:30–10pm; Sun 9am–2pm. MULTIETHNIC.* It consistently manages to impress Portland's picky eaters with its creative international fare. The specialty is fish grilled to perfect tenderness, but there's plenty else to choose from. With mismatched chairs, flea-market decor, and high ceilings, Uffa attracts a young crowd. Sunday brunches are superb, but be prepared to wait.

**Silly's.** *40 Washington Ave., Portland.* ☎ *207/772-0360. No reservations. Lunch and dinner $2–$6; pizza $7–$17. No credit cards. Mon–Sat 10am–10pm. ECLECTIC/ TAKEOUT.* The interior is informal, with 1950s-era funky accessories. The menu is creative and the selections tasty. A lot of the meals are served in hubcap-sized pita bread (the shish kebab roll-up is great). Don't overlook the french fries or the huge milkshakes and malts. There's free delivery for orders over $6.

✪ **Street & Co.** *33 Wharf St., Portland.* ☎ *207/775-0887. Reservations strongly recommended. Main courses $12–$18. AE, MC, V. Sun–Thurs 5:30–9:30pm, Fri–Sat 5:30–10pm. SEAFOOD/CONTEMPORARY.* This is one of the state's best seafood restaurants. Try the lobster diavolo—a spicy mélange of lobster, mussels, and clams in a delectable red sauce. If you're partial to calamari, be sure to order it here—they know how to cook it so it's perfectly tender.

**West Side Restaurant.** *58 Pine St., Portland.* ☎ *207/773-8223. Reservations recommended. Main courses $12–$19. MC, V. Tues–Thurs 11:30am–2pm and 5–9pm, Fri 11:30am–2pm and 5–10pm, Sat 9am–1pm and 5–10pm, Sun 9am–2pm and 5–9pm. NEW AMERICAN.* This intimate bistro is hugely popular. The menu often features a good selection of game dishes: Maine venison medaillons with a wild mushroom, tarragon, and red-wine sauce; or tangy cassoulet with duck, lamb sausage, and pork. Other choices are delicate preparations of quail, veal, and salmon. Weekend breakfasts and weekday lunches are first-rate.

## PORTLAND AFTER DARK

Portland has a small but lively theater community. Many companies take the summer off, but call or check the local papers for special performances.

In an intimate theater incongruously on the commercial strip of outer Forest Avenue, the **Mad Horse Theatre Company,** 955 Forest Ave. (☎ 207/797-3338), offers up a good mix of dramas and comedies ably performed by an ensemble of local actors. At press time, the theater was scouting for a new home downtown; call for more information.

The 90-seat black-box **Oak Street Theatre,** 92 Oak St. (☎ 207/799-1421), in the downtown arts district is used by several theater groups and visiting performers through-out the year. Shows range from classical to avant garde. Call for the current lineup.

The most professional of Portland's theater groups, the **Portland Stage Company,** Portland Performing Arts Center, 25A Forest Ave. (☎ 207/774-0465), offers slick pro-ductions starring local and imported equity actors in a handsome second-story theater. The season runs October–May. Call to ask about special summer shows.

The bar scene here is lively in the evenings, especially on summer weekends when young men and women prowl the dozens of bars and spill over onto the streets. Among the bars favored by locals are **Three-Dollar Dewey's** at the corner of Commercial and Union streets, **Gritty McDuff's Brew Pub** on Fore Street near the foot of Exchange Street, and **Brian Ború,** slightly out of the Old Port on Center Street.

Portland's oldest gay club is **The Underground,** 3 Spring St., near the Old Port (☎ 207/773-3315). Half of the place is a tidy, friendly bar and hangout; the other half is a disco with pulsing lights and loud music. Other places to visit are **Blackstones,** 6 Pine St. (☎ 207/775-2885), which has a low-key neighborhood bar feel to it, and **Sisters,** 45 Danforth (☎ 207/774-1505), which draws many of the city's lesbians.

Portland's newest nightclub, the **Stone Coast,** 14 York St. (☎ 207/773-2337), houses a restaurant (with a Cajun menu) and brew pub in a renovated 19th-century cannery at the edge of the Old Port. Performers who take the stage upstairs range from local acoustic rock groups to touring acts like New Riders of the Purple Sage. This is the most upscale of Portland's live-music venues.

### A Side Trip from Portland

Ma. 26 from Portland to Norway is a speedy road through hilly farmland, past new housing developments. At one point the road pinches through a cluster of stately his-toric buildings standing proudly beneath towering elms. That's the **Sabbathday Lake Shaker Community** (☎ 207/926-4597), the last active Shaker community in the na-tion. The dozen or so Shakers living here still embrace the old Shaker beliefs and main-tain a communal, pastoral way of life. The bulk of the community's income comes from the sale of herbs, which have been grown here since 1799.

This community is open to the public daily in summer except on Sunday (when visi-tors are invited to attend Sunday services). Docents offer tours of the grounds and several of the buildings, including the graceful 1794 meetinghouse. Exhibits in the buildings showcase the famed furniture lovingly crafted by the Shakers and include antiques made by Shakers at other U.S. communes. You'll learn a lot about the Shaker ideology with its emphasis on simplicity, industry, and celibacy. After your tour, browse the gift shop for Shaker herbs and teas. Tours last either 1 hour ($5 adults, $2 children 6–12) or 1 3/4 hours ($6.50 adults). It's open Memorial Day–Columbus Day, Mon–Sat 10am–4:30pm.

The Shaker village is about 45 minutes from Portland. Head north on Me. 26 (Wash-ington Avenue in Portland). The village is 8 miles from exit 11 (Gray) of the Maine Turnpike.

## FREEPORT

Freeport is almost synonymous with the monster retailer **L. L. Bean,** Main and Bow streets (☎ 800/341-4341), which traces its roots to the day Leon Leonwood Bean de-cided that what the world really needed was a good weatherproof hunting shoe. He married a watertight gumshoe bottom with a laced leather upper. Hunters liked it. The store grew. An empire was born.

Today L. L. Bean sells millions of dollars worth of clothing and outdoor goods through its catalogs and continues to draw hundreds of thousands through its doors. This multilevel store is the size of a regional mall, but tastefully done with its own indoor trout pond and lots of natural wood. L. L. Bean is open 365 days a year, 24 hours a day (note the lack of locks or latches on the front doors), and it's popular even in the dead of night, especially around summer and holidays.

In addition to the main store, L. L. Bean stocks an outlet shop with a relatively small but rapidly changing inventory at discount prices. It's located in a back lot between Main Street and Depot Street—ask at the front desk of the main store for walking directions.

In addition, Freeport has more than 100 retail shops between exit 19 off I-95 at the far lower end of Main Street and Mallett Road, which connects to exit 20. Shops have recently begun to spread south of exit 19 toward Yarmouth. If you can't stand missing a single one, get off at exit 17 and head north on Route 1. Most major manufacturers have outlets here.

### ACCOMMODATIONS

Two blocks north of L. L. Bean is the **Harraseeket Inn,** 162 Main St., Freeport, ME 05032 (☎ **800/342-6423** or 207/865-9377). A late-19th-century home is the soul of the hotel, but most of the rooms are in an addition that dwarfs the old house. Rooms are large and tasteful, with quarter-canopy beds; about half have fireplaces, and a number have whirlpools. Summer and fall, doubles cost $145–$235 double; spring and early summer, $130–$235; and in winter prices are $105–$215 for a double; rates include breakfast buffet, and there's a 10% discount midweek. Take exit 20 off I-95 to Main St.

### DINING

For a quick and simple meal, you might head down Mechanic Street to the **Corsican Restaurant,** 9 Mechanic St. (☎ 207/865-9421), for a 10-inch pizza, calzone, or king-sized sandwich. Nearby is tiny **Chowder Express and Sandwich Shop,** 2 Mechanic St. (☎ 207/865-3404), where you can pick up a New England chowder, sandwich, bagel, or muffin. A favorite spot among locals for quick, reasonably priced lunch close to L. L. Bean is the **Falcon Restaurant,** 8 Bow St. (☎ 207/865-4031). A popular lobster pound is at a boatyard on the Harraseeket River, the **Harraseeket Lunch & Lobster,** Main St., South Freeport (☎ 207/865-4888). Lobsters are market price (typically $6–$9), and it's open for lunch and dinner May to mid-Oct. From I-95 take exit 17 and head north on Route 1; turn right at the huge Indian statue; continue to stop sign in South Freeport; turn right to waterfront. From Freeport take South St. (off Bow St.) to Main St. in South Freeport; turn left to water.

### A SIDE TRIP TO BATH

You don't have to be a ship aficionado to enjoy the **Maine Maritime Museum and Shipyard,** 243 Washington St. in Bath (☎ 207/443-1316), on U.S. 1 off I-95. This up-to-date museum on the shores of the Kennebec River (just south of Bath Iron Works) features displays and exhibits related to the boat-building art. It's sited at the former shipyard of Percy and Small, which built some 42 schooners in the late 19th and early 20th centuries. Indeed, the largest wooden ship ever built in America—the 329-foot *Wyoming*—was constructed on this lot in 1909. The centerpiece is the striking brick Maritime History Building, where you'll find changing exhibits of maritime art and artifacts. The 10-acre property houses plenty of other displays, including an intriguing exhibit on lobstering and a complete shipbuilding shop, called the Apprenticeshop. Kids enjoy the play area (look for pirates from the crow's nest of the play boat). Be sure to wander down to the docks on the river to see what's tied up or to ask about cruises on the river (extra charge). The museum is open daily 9:30am–5pm. Admission is $7.75 adults, $5 children 6–17, $22 family.

## MONHEGAN ISLAND

Brawny and remote, Monhegan is Maine's premier island destination. Visited by Europeans as early as 1497 (some insist earlier Norsemen carved primitive runes on nearby Mañana Island), the island was settled by fishermen attracted to the sea's bounty in the offshore waters. Starting in the 1870s and continuing to the present day, noted artists discovered the island and came to stay for a spell. These included Rockwell Kent (the artist most closely associated with the island), George Bellows, Edward Hopper, and Robert Henri. The artists gathered in the kitchen of the lighthouse to chat and drink coffee; it's said that the wife of the lighthouse keeper accumulated a tremendously valuable collection of paintings. Today, Jamie Wyeth, scion of the Wyeth clan, claims the island as his part-time home.

It's not hard to figure why artists have long been attracted to the place: There's a mystical quality to it, from the thin light to the startling contrasts of the dark cliffs and the foamy white surf. If you have the time, I'd strongly recommend an overnight on the island. Day trips are popular and affordable, but the island's true character doesn't start to emerge until the last day the boat sails away and its quiet, rustic appeal starts to percolate back to the surface.

Access to Monhegan Island is via boat from either New Harbor, Boothbay Harbor, or Port Clyde. The 1-hour 10-minute trip on the *Laura B.* from Port Clyde is the favored route among longtime island visitors. The trip is very picturesque as it passes the Marshall Point Lighthouse and a series of spruce-clad islands before setting out across the open sea. The *Laura B.* is a doughty work boat (cargo including propane tanks and boxes of food is loaded on first; passengers fill in the available niches on the deck and in the small cabin). You can't bring your car, so pack light and wear sturdy shoes. Reservations are advised: **Monhegan Boat Line,** P.O. Box 238, Port Clyde, ME 04855 (☎ 207/372-8848). Parking is available near the dock for a slight extra charge.

**ACCOMMODATIONS**  The **Trailing Yew,** Monhegan Island, ME 04852 (☎ 207/596-0440), is a friendly, informal place, popular with hikers and bird-watchers. Rooms are eclectic and simply furnished; only one has a private bath. Of the four guest buildings, one has electricity in the guestrooms (all bathrooms have electricity), others are lighted with kerosene lamps. A double costs $108; rates include breakfast, dinner, taxes, and tips. It's open mid-May–mid-October.

## ROCKLAND

Noted sculptor Louise Nevelson grew up in Rockland, and in 1935 cranky philanthropist Lucy Farnsworth bequeathed a fortune large enough to establish Rockland's **Farnsworth Museum,** 352 Main St. (☎ 207/596-6457). The Farnsworth has a compact but superb collection of paintings and sculptures by renowned American artists with some connection to Maine. This includes not only Louise Nevelson and three generations of Wyeths (N.C., Andrew, and Jamie), but Rockwell Kent, Childe Hassam, and Maurice Prendergast. The display space is modern and well designed, and the shows are professionally prepared. The Farnsworth owns two other buildings: The **Farnsworth Homestead,** behind the museum, offers a glimpse into the life of prosperous coastal Victorians. And a 25-minute drive away in the village of Cushing is the **Olson House,** immortalized in the background of Andrew Wyeth's famous *Christina's World.* Ask at the museum for directions and information. The museum is open in the summer, Mon–Sat 10am–5pm and Sun noon–5pm; closed Mon from Columbus Day–Memorial Day). Admission is $5 adults, $4 seniors, $3 children 8–18.

The **Owls Head Transportation Museum,** Route 73, Owls Head (☎ 207/594-4418), is 3 miles south of Rockland. Founded in 1974, the museum has an extraordinary collection of cars, motorcycles, bicycles, and planes, nicely displayed in a hangarlike building at the edge of the Knox County Airport. Look for the beautiful early Harley–Davidson and the sleek Rolls Royce Phantom from 1929. The museum is also a popular destination for hobbyists and tinkerers, who drive and fly their classic vehicles here for frequent weekend rallies in summer. Call ahead to ask about special events. The museum is open Apr–Oct, daily 10am–5pm; Nov–Mar, Mon–Fri 10am–4pm and Sat–Sun 10am–3pm. Admission is $6 adults, $5 seniors, $4 children 5–12, $16 families.

## WINDJAMMER CRUISES

Maine is the capital of windjammer cruising in the United States, and two of the most active Maine harbors are Rockland and Camden. Windjammer vacations combine adventure with limited creature comforts—sort of like lodging at a backcountry cabin on the water. You typically bunk in small two-person cabins, which usually offer cold running water and a porthole to let in fresh air, but not much else. Cruises last from 3 days to a week. It's a superb way to explore Maine's coast. The price runs around $100 per day per person, with modest discounts early and late in the season.

At least a dozen windjammers offer cruises in the Penobscot Bay region during summer (many migrate south to the Caribbean in the winter). The ships vary widely in size and vintage, and guest accommodations range from cramped and rustic to reasonably spacious and well appointed. Ideally, you'll have a chance to look at a couple of ships to find one that suits you before signing up. If that's not practical, call ahead to the **Maine Windjammer Association** (☎ 800/807-9463) and request a packet of brochures. For a last-minute cruise, stop by the Chamber of Commerce office at the Rockland waterfront and ask if any berths are available.

While all the commercial windjammers are Coast Guard–inspected, each has its own charm. Among the notable are the 44-passenger *Victory Chimes* (☎ 800/745-5651 or 207/594-0755), the largest schooner at 132 feet. The smallest in the fleet is the seven-passenger *Summertime* (☎ 800/562-8290), a 53-foot schooner based in Rockland. And the 31-passenger *Angelique* (☎ 800/282-9989 or 207/236-8873), based in Camden, may be the most handsome ship in the fleet, featuring two below-deck hot-water showers.

### ACCOMMODATIONS

The **Capt. Lindsey House Inn,** 5 Lindsey St., Rockland, ME 04841 (☎ 800/523-2145 or 207/596-7950; fax 207/236-0585; e-mail: kebarnes@midcoast.com.) has nine rooms, seven have shower only, decorated in a contemporary country style. Doubles in peak season cost $95–$160 and include continental breakfast and afternoon tea. From Columbus Day–Memorial Day the cost goes down to $65–$110. All rooms have handmade bedspreads, hair dryers, down comforters, and bathrobes. The Waterworks is the hotel's restaurant.

## CAMDEN

Camden is quintessential coastal Maine, set around a picturesque harbor that no Hollywood movie could improve upon. The best way to enjoy the town is to reconnoiter on foot and browse among the boutiques and galleries. Don't miss the town park behind the library, designed by the firm of the famous landscape architect Frederick Law Olmstead.

### OUTDOOR ACTIVITIES

**Camden Hills State Park** (☎ 207/236-3109) is about a mile north of Camden's village center on Route 1. This 6,500-acre park features an oceanside picnic area, camping at 112 sites, a winding toll road up 800-foot Mt. Battie with spectacular views from the summit, and a variety of well-marked hiking trails.

One easy hike I'd recommend strongly is an ascent to the ledges of **Mt. Megunticook,** preferably early in the morning before the crowds have amassed and when the mist still lingers in the valleys. Leave from near the campground and follow the well-maintained trail to these open ledges, which requires only about 30 to 45 minutes' exertion. Spectacular, improbable views of the harbor await, as well as glimpses inland to the gentle valleys. Depending on your stamina and desires, you can continue on the park's trail network to Mt. Battie or into the less-trammeled woodlands on the east side of the Camden Hills.

**Maine Sports Outfitters** (☎ **800/722-0826** or 207/236-8797) offers sea-kayaking tours of Camden's scenic harbor. The standard tour lasts 4 hours and takes paddlers out to Curtis Island at the outer edge of the harbor. This is an easy, delightful way to get a taste of the area's maritime culture. Longer trips are also available. The outfitter's main shop, on Route 1 in Rockport, is worth a stop for outdoor enthusiasts gearing up for local adventures or heading on to Acadia.

For windjammer cruises departing from Camden, see "Rockland," above.

## ACCOMMODATIONS

Camden vies with Kennebunkport and Manchester, Vermont, for the title of bed-and-breakfast capital of New England. They're everywhere. Route 1 north of the village center—locally called High Street—is a virtual B&B alley, with many handsome homes converted to lodging. Others are tucked off on side streets.

Despite the preponderance of B&Bs, the total number of rooms is fairly limited and lodging during peak season is tight. It's best to reserve far in advance. You might also try **Camden Accommodations and Reservations** (☎ 800/236-1920), which offers assistance with everything from booking rooms at resorts to finding cottages for seasonal rental.

On Route 1 north of town, there's the **Lighthouse Motel** (☎ 207/236-2758) and the **Mount Battie Motel** (☎ 800/224-3870). A bit closer to the village center are the **Cedar Crest Motel,** 115 Elm St. (tel **207/236-4839**), and the **Towne Motel,** 68 Elm St. (☎ **207/236-3377**). And smack in town, across the footbridge, is the modern **Camden Riverhouse Hotel,** 11 Tannery Lane (☎ **800/755-7483** or 207/236-0500).

✪ **Maine Stay.** *22 High St., Camden, ME 04843.* ☎ *207/236-9636. 8 rms, 6 with bath, 4 with shower only. $75–$125 double; discounts during off-season. Rates include breakfast. AE, MC, V.* The no-smoking Maine Stay is a classic slate-roofed New England homestead. The rooms have ceiling fans and are furnished with antiques and special decorative touches. My favorite: the downstairs Carriage House Room, boasting a stone patio. The hosts—Peter Smith, his wife, Donny, and her twin sister, Diana Robson—are marvelous.

**Whitehall Inn.** *52 High St., Camden, ME 04843.* ☎ *207/236-3391. 50 rms, including 10 rms across the street in 2 cottages, 5 rms with shared bath. July–late Oct, $135–$165 double, including breakfast and dinner ($100–$135 with breakfast only). Discounts in late May–June. Open late May–late Oct. AE, MC, V.* This three-story inn has a striking integrity with its columns, gables, and long roofline. The antique furnishings—including the handsome Seth Thomas clock—are well cared for. The guest rooms are simple but appealing. The dining room boasts reliable fare like veal with vermouth, sage, and prosciutto or baked shrimp-stuffed haddock.

## DINING

**Frogwater Cafe.** *31 Elm St., Camden.* ☎ *207/236-8998. Main courses $8–$15. MC, V. Tues–Sun 5–9:30pm (slightly later on weekends). BISTRO.* The Frogwater is cozy and comfortable—there's a shower stall in one corner, but it's for storage, not hygiene. The meals are well above average and range from downhome (twice-cooked spaghetti cake, double hamburgers) to borderline elegant (oven-roasted lamb chops). The wild-mushroom ravioli is delectable.

**Peter Ott's.** *16 Bayview St., Camden.* ☎ *207/236-4032. Reservations not accepted. Main courses $13.95–$22.95 (most $14–$16). MC, V. Daily 5:30–9:30pm during season; closed for a couple of months in winter. AMERICAN.* While Ott's poses as a steak house with its wooden tables and chairs and meat dishes (like charbroiled Black Angus with mushrooms and onions), it's grown beyond that. It offers some of the best seafood in town, including a pan-blackened seafood sampler and grilled salmon with lemon-caper sauce. The lemon-almond crumb tart is great.

## SEARSPORT & ISLE AU HAUT

In tiny downtown Searsport, the **Penobscot Marine Museum,** Church Street at Route 1 (☎ 207/548-2529), is one of the best small museums in New England. Housed in eight historic buildings atop a gentle rise, the museum does a deft job in educating you about the local shipbuilding industry, the essential role of international trade to daily life in the 19th century, and the hazards of life at sea. The exhibits are uniformly well organized, and wandering from building to building induces a keen sense of wonderment at the vast enterprise that was Maine's maritime trade.

Among the more intriguing exhibits are a wide selection of dramatic marine paintings (including one stunning rendition of whaling in the Arctic), black-and-white photographs of many of the 286 weathered sea captains who once called Searsport home, photographs of a 1902 voyage to Argentina, and an early home decorated in the style of sea captain, complete with lacquered furniture and accessories hauled back from trade missions to the Orient. It's well worth the price if you're the least interested in Maine's rich culture of the sea. The museum is open Memorial Day to mid-Oct, Mon–Sat 10am–5pm and Sun noon–5pm. Admission is $5 adults, $3.50 seniors, $1.50 children 7–15.

Rocky and remote Isle au Haut offers the most unique hiking and camping experience in northern New England. This 6- by 3-mile island, 6 miles south of Stonington, was originally named Ille Haut (High Island) in 1604 by French explorer Samuel de Champlain. The name and its pronunciation evolved—today, it's generally pronounced "aisle-a-ho"—but the island itself has remained steadfastly unchanged over the centuries.

About half of the island is owned by the National Park Service and maintained as an outpost of Acadia National Park (see the beginning of this chapter). A 60-passenger "mailboat" makes a stop in the morning and late afternoon at Duck Harbor, allowing for a solid day of hiking while still returning to Stonington by nightfall. At Duck Harbor the NPS also maintains a cluster of five Adirondack-style lean-tos, which are available for overnight camping. Reservations are essential. Contact **Acadia National Park,** Bar Harbor, ME 04609, or call ☎ **207/288-3338.**

A network of superb hiking trails radiates from Duck Harbor. Be sure to ascend the island's highest point, 543-foot **Duck Harbor Mountain,** for exceptional views of the Camden Hills to the west and Mount Desert Island to the east. Nor should you miss the Cliff or Western Head trails, which track along high, rocky bluffs and coastal outcroppings capped with damp, tangled fog forests of spruce. The trails periodically descend down to cobblestone coves, which issue forth with a deep rumble with every incoming wave. A hand pump near Duck Harbor provides drinking water, but be sure to bring food and refreshments for hiking.

The other half of the island is privately owned, some by fishermen who can trace their island ancestry back 3 centuries and some by summer rusticators, whose forebears discovered the bucolic splendor of Isle au Haut in the 1880s. The summer population of the island is about 300, with about 50 diehards remaining year-round. The mail boat also stops at the small harborside village, which has a few old homes, a handsome church, and a tiny schoolhouse, post office, and store. Day-trippers will be better served ferrying straight to Duck Harbor.

The **mail boat** (☎ 207/367-5193) to Isle au Haut leaves from Stonington. In summer, the *Miss Lizzie* departs from the dock at the end of Seabreeze Avenue (1 block east of the former Atlantic Avenue location) to the village of Isle au Haut daily at 7 and

11am; the *Mink* departs for Duck Harbor daily at 10am. The round-trip boat fare is $20 for adults to either the village or Duck Harbor. Children under 12 are half price. Reservations aren't accepted, but surprisingly few passengers are turned away, even in midsummer. Parking is sometimes a problem, so plan to show up half an hour before departure.

## 6  More Northeast Highlights

### THE HISTORIC HUDSON VALLEY

The Hudson Valley begins just north of New York City and stretches 140 miles to the state capital of Albany. The natural beauty of the river and the landscape with its palisades, wooded hillsides, pine forests, and mountain lakes and streams inspired an art movement known as the Hudson River School. The area is dotted with Revolutionary battle sites, great mansions, and picturesque Victorian towns. U.S. 9 travels through the valley up the east bank of the Hudson, and U.S. 9W goes up the river's west bank.

Here's a sample of the towns where you may want to stop or at least drive through. **Cold Spring** is a charming little town, with streets lined with antiques shops. **Rhinebeck** has notable Victorian architecture, and a famous inn, the Beekman Arms. **Saugerties** also boasts many antiques shops on its restored downtown street. **Woodstock** is a center for craftspeople, old hippies, and a combination of fine crafts shops and the usual gift shops. **New Paltz** was originally a Huguenot settlement. Its street of ancient Flemish-style stone houses is one of the oldest in the country; tours can be arranged through the Huguenot Historical Society (☎ **914/255-1660** or 914/255-1889). **Kingston** was once an important New York State town; its restored downtown and Rondout Landing area (at the end of Broadway) suggests a bit of the town's former glory as a river shipping center.

In Tarrytown near Irvington, off U.S. 9, is **Sunnyside,** (☎ **914/631-8200**), the meticulously restored retreat of Washington Irving, author of *Rip van Winkle* and *The Legend of Sleepy Hollow.* The house holds his library and many of his furnishings and personal belongings. Visitors may stroll in the grounds, laid out by Irving himself. He is buried nearby in Sleepy Hollow Cemetery.

✪ **Boscobel,** on N.Y. 9D, near Garrison (☎ **914/265-3638**), was begun in 1804 and is an outstanding example of a Federal-style house. Its exterior is elegantly festooned with carved swags connecting the columns of the pediment, and the interior furniture was made by the 19th-century cabinetmaker Duncan Phyfe. The grounds have a spectacular view over the Hudson.

The **Roosevelt–Vanderbilt National Historic Site,** operated by the National Park Service, is in Hyde Park. The ✪ **Franklin D. Roosevelt Home** (☎ **914/229-7770**) was the family home of the Roosevelts. Besides a museum, the house contains FDR's library and the original furnishings, including personal belongings that movingly evoke FDR's life. Eleanor Roosevelt's own private retreat, **Val-Kill,** built for her by FDR, is set on 172 wooded acres. Nearby is the large, ornate, and imposing 54-room **Vanderbilt Mansion** (☎ **914/229-7770**), looking out on the shores of the Hudson.

One of the most interesting estates in the area is the **Mills Mansion,** Mills-Norrie State Park, on U.S. 9 in Staatsburg (☎ **914/889-4100**). This beaux arts mansion has a different ambience from most along the Hudson, with its elevated ceilings, French furniture, and Flemish tapestries. The estate has river views and hiking trails. Another interesting house is **Clermont,** Route 9G (☎ **518/537-4240),** at Clermont State Historic Site near Germantown, the home of Robert R. Livingston, one of the drafters of the Declaration of Independence. There are a formal garden, hiking trails, and an exhibition on Livingston.

✪ **Olana,** N.Y. 9G (☎ 518/828-0135), should not be missed. The home of landscape painter Frederic Edwin Church, a leader of the Hudson River School, is a Moorish-style castle, complete with tiles, Persian carpets, and decorative arts; some of Church's paintings are on display, and the vistas of the Hudson from the house and grounds will recall his landscape paintings. Tours are limited; it's wise to reserve in advance.

On the bluffs overlooking the Hudson on the west side of the river is the granite army citadel of **West Point,** the oldest and most distinguished U.S. military academy. Enter by Thayer Gate and stop at the Visitor Center (☎ 914/446-4724) for a map of the grounds. Next door is the West Point Museum, containing an important military collection. You can stay overnight at the academy by reserving at the Hotel Thayer (☎ 800/247-5047).

The largest outdoor recreation area in the valley is **Bear Mountain State Park,** just off U.S. 9W, which offers year-round activities, including hiking, swimming, fishing, and cross-country skiing. The **Mohonk Preserve,** west of New Paltz (from U.S. 9W take N.Y. 299 to N.Y. 4455), offers hiking, rock climbing, cross-country skiing, and other outdoor activities; you can also stay at the stately Victorian Mohonk Mountain House (☎ 914/255-4500). Cruises of the Hudson are offered by the *Rip Van Winkle* at the Rondout Waterfront in Kingston (☎ 914/255-6515).

Along U.S. 9W are a number of wineries that can be toured: **Adair Vineyards,** 75 Allhusen Rd., New Paltz (☎ 914/255-1377); **Baldwin Vineyards,** 1786 Hardenburgh Rd., Pine Bush (☎ 914/744-2226); **Benmarl Winery,** Highland Avenue (off 9W), Marlboro (☎ 914/236-4265); **Brimstone Hill Vineyards,** 61 Brimstone Hill Rd., Pine Bush (☎ 914/744-2231); **Walker Valley Vineyards,** N.Y. 52 and Oregon Trail Road, Walker Valley (☎ 914/744-3449); **West Park Wine Cellars,** U.S. 9W, West Park (☎ 914/384-6709).

**Essentials:** The Hudson Valley is best seen by car. Leaving from the west side of Manhattan, follow the Henry Hudson Parkway (State Road 9A or the West Side Highway) north for about 12 miles to exit 23, and take U.S. 9 (Broadway) north.

## COOPERSTOWN

Baseball fans come to this charming small town to tour the ✪ **National Baseball Hall of Fame and Museum,** Main Street (☎ 607/547-7200), where they can see exhibits on every possible aspect of the national game. The museum has a collection of more than 1,000 artifacts, including bats used by famous players, and other memorabilia from all the baseball greats—Babe Ruth's locker, Ty Cobb's spikes, Hank Aaron's bat, and a score of others.

In earlier days, Cooperstown was the home of James Fenimore Cooper, author of *The Last of the Mohicans,* who used the town as a setting for his Leatherstocking tales. A museum, the **Fenimore House,** houses a collection of folk art. Across the street is the **Farmers' Museum and Village Crossroads,** a re-created 19th-century village with original buildings.

Places to stay in Cooperstown are **Best Western Inn at the Commons,** N.Y. 28, Commons Drive (☎ 800/528-1234 or 607/547-9439); and the **Cooper Inn,** Lake Street at Chestnut (☎ 800/348-6222; fax 607/547-1271).

**Essentials:** From New York City, take the New York State Thruway and connect with N.Y. 28 at Kingston. For information, contact the **Cooperstown Chamber of Commerce,** 31 Chestnut St. (☎ 607/547-9983).

## NIAGARA FALLS

This is the grandest—and certainly the most famous—spectacle in New York State. The American Falls cascades 190 feet to the rocks below, and the Horseshoe Falls on the

Canadian side, with its broad crescent, plummets 185 feet, creating rainbows and sending clouds of mist into the air. At night, colored lights play across the spectacle. Cross to the Canadian side to view the Horseshoe Falls.

The American Falls are best seen in the morning from Prospect Point. Goat Island offers a striking view of Horseshoe Falls, while visitors can view the American and Bridal Veil falls from Luna Island, reached from Goat Island by footbridge. Some ways to experience close views of the falls are from the **Cave of the Winds** (☎ 716/278-1730) at the foot of the American Falls; the **Journey Behind the Falls** (☎ 905/358-3268); the **Great Gorge Adventure** (☎ 905/374-1221); and by taking a boat ride to the base of the falls on the *Maid of the Mist* (☎ 716/284-8897).

Niagara Falls has always been popular with honeymooners, and there are places to stay for all tastes. The **Red Coach Inn,** 2 Buffalo Ave. ☎ **716/282-1459**), overlooking the Upper Rapids, has an old-English ambience, with antiques and woodburning fireplaces and an award-winning restaurant. **Comfort Inn the Pointe,** 1 Prospect Pointe (☎ **800/228-5150** or 716/284-6835; fax 716/284-5177), is just off Main Street near the falls. **Horseshoe Falls Motor Inn,** 5481 Dunn St. (☎ **905/358-9353**), is 2 blocks from the falls on the Canadian side.

**Essentials:** Access from the west is by the New York State Thruway, I-90. For information, contact **Niagara County Tourism,** 139 Niagara St., Lockport, NY 14094 (☎ **800/338-7890**), or stop by **Niagara Falls Convention and Visitors Bureau,** 310 4th St. (☎ **716/285-2400**).

# The Mid-Atlantic

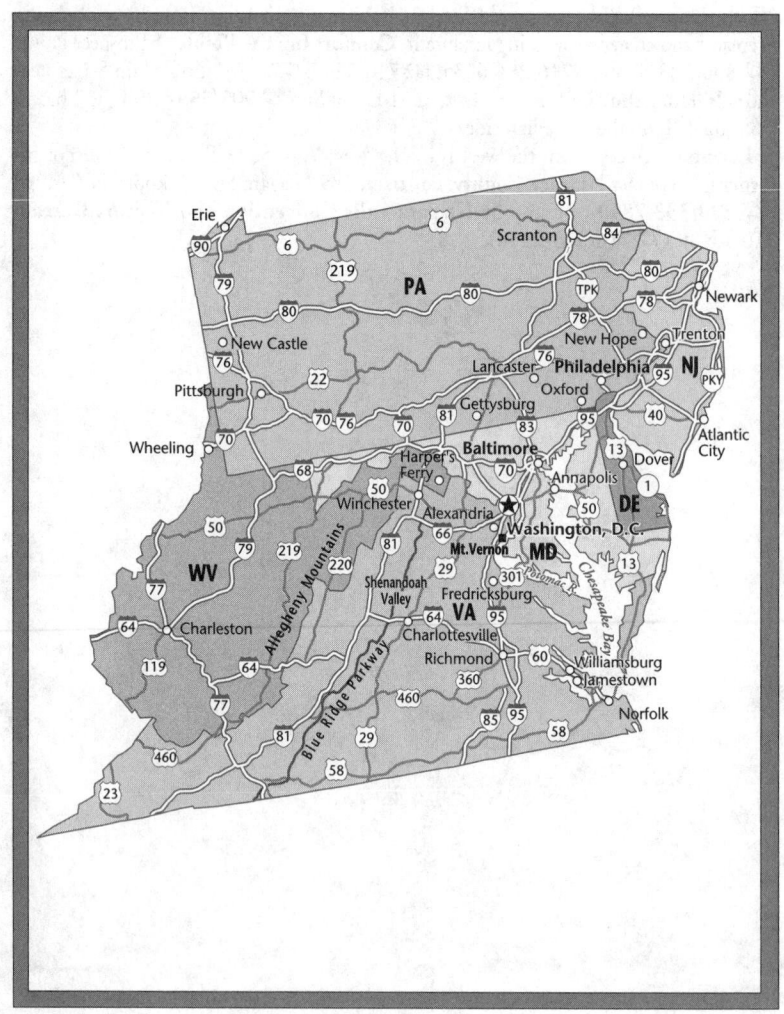

**P**art of the thrill of visiting the Mid-Atlantic states is following in the footsteps of George Washington, Thomas Jefferson, Abraham Lincoln, Robert E. Lee, and many others who cut wide paths through American history.

In Philadelphia, you can see where the Founding Fathers proclaimed the Declaration of Independence and crafted the U.S. Constitution. In Washington, D.C., you can view those monumental documents in one of the great temples of the federal government. In Baltimore, you can dine on Chesapeake Bay crabs near where Francis Scott Key wrote the words to "The Star Spangled Banner." Williamsburg, Jamestown, and Yorktown recapture America's earliest beginnings, and the battlefields at Fredericksburg and Gettysburg vividly recall the Civil War.

Just as the perfectly straight Mason–Dixon line separated Pennsylvania from Maryland, free state from slave state, this region still divides North and South. Although it's changing rapidly, Virginia remains very much Southern, a land with its own accent, smoked country ham, and red-eye gravy. Pennsylvania is very much Northern, just as when it fostered abolitionist spirit and harbored runaway slaves. As it did then, Maryland stands on the border, a mixture of Yankee and Rebel tradition. Despite their differences, however, they all share a deep and abiding sense of history.

Today Philadelphia, Baltimore, and Washington are part of the great East Coast megalopolis running south from Boston, but you can easily escape to the broad bays, wide rivers, rolling piedmont, gentle mountains, and quaint small towns that make this region lovely and charming. You can drive out to Charlottesville, hometown of "Mr. Jefferson," and through a dramatic gap in the Blue Ridge Mountains to beautiful Harpers Ferry, where John Brown's fanatical raid presaged the Civil War. Up in the mountains, the Shenandoah National Park is bisected by the Skyline Drive, one of America's most scenic routes overlooking the lovely Shenandoah Valley.

In Pennsylvania and bordering Delaware, you can visit the great mansions-turned-museums in the Brandywine Valley, then follow horse-drawn carts through southern Pennsylvania's fascinatingly quaint Amish Country. In Maryland, you can visit Annapolis, one of America's oldest towns, then cross the soaring Chesapeake Bay Bridge to relatively unchanged 18th-century hamlets on the eastern shore.

Indeed, you'll find much to see and do as you make your own tracks through the Mid-Atlantic.

# DRIVING TOUR
## The Shenandoah Valley

**Start:** Winchester
**Finish:** Natural Bridge
**Distance:** 175 miles
**Time:** 2–4 days
**Highlights:** Rolling hills dotted with farms and apple orchards; magnificent underground caverns and the 215-foot-high Natural Bridge; Civil War battlefields and museums; graves of Robert E. Lee and Stonewall Jackson; birthplace of Woodrow Wilson

Following the route of I-81 (one of America's most scenic interstate highways) and U.S. 11 (the historic Valley Pike), this tour takes you the length of Virginia's lovely Shenandoah Valley, whose Shawnee name means "Daughter of the Stars." The two highways go up and down over hill and dale through some of the Mid-Atlantic's most beautiful countryside. As a backdrop, the gentle folds of the Blue Ridge Mountains rise to the east of the valley; to the west begin the rugged Allegheny Mountains. At the end of the tour, U.S. 11 actually crosses the awesome Natural Bridge, where George Washington carved his initials. In addition to this wonder, you'll visit several underground caverns, and you can detour into the primordial woodlands of Shenandoah National Park and the George Washington National Forest. As the "Breadbasket of the Confederacy," the valley was fought over throughout the Civil War, and several battlefields and museums will remind you of that bloody conflict.

Atop the Blue Ridge Mountains to the east run two of America's premier scenic roads: the Skyline Drive and the Blue Ridge Parkway. A multitude of sharp curves and a strictly enforced 35-mph speed limit translate into slow-going traffic, but the mountain vistas make a detour on either road worth the extra time.

I-81, U.S. 11, U.S. 50, U.S. 340, U.S. 522, and Va. 7 all give easy access to the first stop:

1. **Winchester,** the valley's oldest town and its unofficial "Apple Capital," settled in 1732 by Quakers and Germans. George Washington commanded Virginia's militia during the French and Indian wars, and you'll want to visit the small stone building that was **Washington's Office,** at West Cork and South Braddock streets (☎ 540/662-4412). During the Civil War, when Winchester changed hands 70 times, **Gen. Thomas J. "Stonewall" Jackson's Headquarters** were 5 blocks north of Washington's at 415 N. Braddock St. (☎ 540/667-3242).

   Begin your tour of these and other historic attractions by taking exit 313 off I-81 and following signs to the **Winchester–Frederick County Visitor Center,** 1360 S. Pleasant Valley Rd. (☎ 540/662-4135). It's on the grounds of **Abram's Delight,** Winchester's oldest home, built of native limestone in 1754 on an attractive site by a lake; or you can go straight to the **Old Town Welcome Center,** North Cameron and Boscawen streets (☎ 540/722-6367), in the heart of the historic district. Both centers have walking-tour brochures and are open daily 9am–5pm. One walking tour visits youthful haunts of country music legend Patsy Cline, a Winchester native whose grave is south of town on Va. 644 just west of U.S. 522.

   From Winchester, both I-81 and U.S. 11 go 12 miles "up" the valley (that is, south) to:

2. **Middletown,** a small roadside village noted for its antique shops; the **Wayside Theater,** Main Street (☎ 540/869-1776), which presents excellent theatrical productions from the end of May to mid-October; and **Belle Grove Plantation** (☎ 540/869-2028), a late 18th-century gray-stone manor house 2 miles south of

# Driving Tour: The Shenandoah Valley

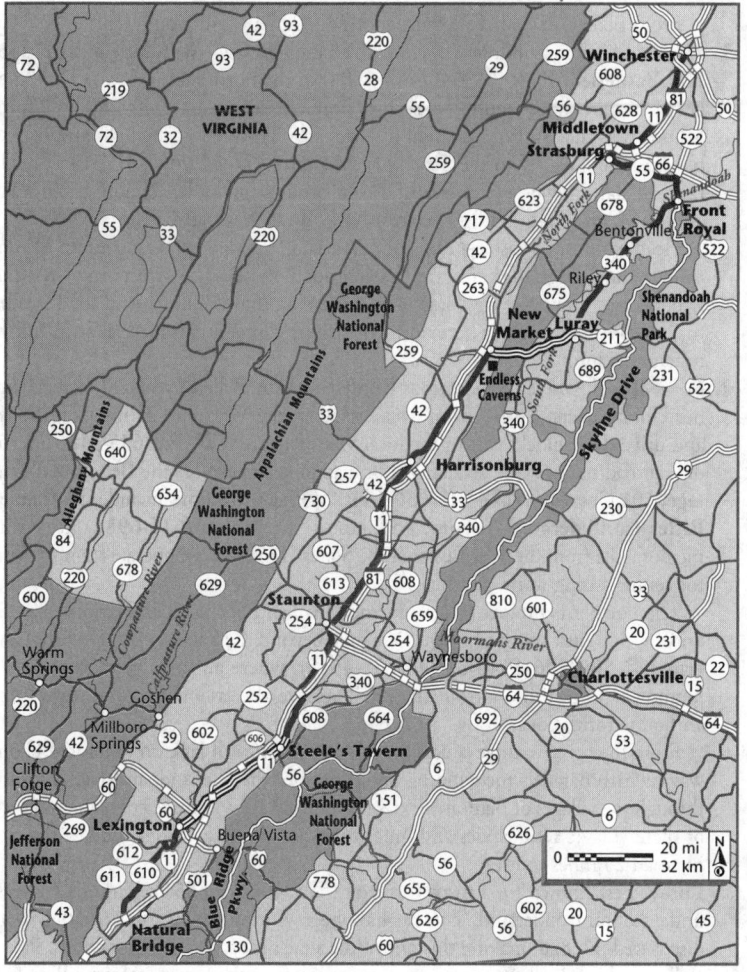

town off U.S. 11. Now a National Trust museum, Belle Grove was built between 1794 and 1979 by Maj. Isaac Hite, who relied on his brother-in-law, Thomas Jefferson, for architectural advice. The building has Palladian-style front windows and columns, and the interior is furnished with period antiques.

During the Civil War, Union Gen. Philip Sheridan's troops were camped on the open fields around the house when Confederate forces under Gen. Jubal Early staged a surprise attack. The Rebels initially won the Battle of Cedar Creek, but Sheridan rallied his troops and turned defeat into victory. There's a small battle-field visitor center on the road to the plantation.

☕ **TAKE A BREAK**   You can sample more colonial charm at the **Wayside Inn** (☎ 540/869-1797), on U.S. 11 in the heart of Middletown. Travelers have been taking meals and renting rooms at this establishment since 1797. Today, the beautifully restored dining room serves fine traditional Virginian cuisine, some from recipes handed down since Jeffersonian times. Lunch entrees cost $6–$11; dinner main courses cost $13–$25.

From Belle Grove, drive 3 miles south on U.S. 11 until you reach:

3. **Strasburg,** where children will enjoy the hands-on Civil War museum at **Hupps Hill Battlefield Park** (☎ 540/465-5884) at the north end of town. The number of antique shops around Strasburg's stoplight demonstrate why this little town is known as the "Antique Capital of Virginia." Turn left at the light and drive a block east on Va. 55 to the **Strasburg Museum** (☎ 540/465-3175) in the old railroad station, where Stonewall Jackson brought his stolen Union locomotives after the Great Train Raid on Martinsburg, West Virginia.

Head east from Strasburg on Va. 55. Ahead of you looms **Massanutten Mountain,** a long ridge that cuts the Shenandoah Valley into two parts. I-81 and U.S. 11 run down the west side. You'll drive around the north end for 11 miles to U.S. 340. Turn right here and drive south along a commercial strip full of restaurants into:

4. **Front Royal,** where the notorious Confederate spy Belle Boyd pried secrets from her Union lovers. Turn left on Main Street at the Warrren County Courthouse and drive three blocks east to the local **visitor center** (☎ 540/635-3185) in the old railroad station. Get a walking-tour map here and explore the **Belle Boyd Cottage,** 101 Chester St. (☎ 540/636-1446). Other attractions include the **Warren Rifles Confederate Museum,** 95 Chester St. (☎ 540/636-6982), featuring memorabilia from the War Between the States. Trolley tours operate from the visitor center during warm weather.

The northern entrance to the Skyline Drive and Shenandoah National Park is on U.S. 340, just south of town. One mile beyond the entrance are **Skyline Caverns** (☎ 800/296-4545 or 540/635-4545), where an underground waterfall plummets 37 feet into a trout stream. The cave also is noted for rare, flowerlike anthodite formations.

From the caverns, drive south on U.S. 340 (Stonewall Jackson Memorial Highway), which parallels the winding South Fork of the Shenandoah River and runs through the villages of Bentonville, Compton, and Riley. Private companies in each of these villages rent canoes and inner tubes for river excursions. Follow the scenic road 24 miles south to:

5. **Luray,** best known for **Luray Caverns** (☎ 540/743-6551), Virginia's largest underground wonderland. Tourists have been visiting the caverns since they were discovered in 1878, making this one of the state's most popular attractions. Paved walkways lead down to such cavernous wonders as the Great Stalactite Pipe Organ, which can actually play music. Outside the cavern stands a carillon and the Can and Carriage Caravan, a fine collection of antique automobiles and carriages.

The caverns are 2 miles west of Luray on the U.S. 211 Bypass, upon which you'll continue up and over Massanutten Mountain for 15 miles. This is the most scenic part of the tour, so stop at the overlooks for views back across the valley. At the top of **New Market Pass** sits the **visitor center** (☎ 540/740-8310) of George Washington National Forest. From here, proceed down the mountain's west side to:

6. **New Market,** where the entire student body of Virginia Military Institute (VMI) marched up from Lexington to help defeat a larger Union force on May 15, 1864. Turn right just west of I-81 and drive to the end of the service road to the **New Market Battlefield Historical Park** (☎ 540/740-3101). Maintained by VMI, the battlefield and its Hall of Valor Civil War Museum are dedicated to the Civil War students and all other young men who have served their country. (On the way to the park, you'll pass a cavalry museum and the **New Market Battlefield Military Museum;** neither is part of the VMI operation.) The **Shenandoah Valley**

**Travel Association** has a tourist information office (☎ 540/740-3132) opposite the Battlefield Park turnoff; it has a free reservations phone, in case you decide to stay overnight at one of the chain motels in the area.

🍴 **TAKE A BREAK**  New Market has the usual collection of fast-food restaurants at its I-81 interchange, but for good home cooking, visit the **Southern Kitchen** (☎ 540/740-3514), on U.S. 11 less than a half mile south of the stoplight. Loaded with small-town ambience, it has been serving lightly breaded fried chicken and other local fare since 1955. Main courses cost $6–$12.

For another look underground, proceed 3 miles south of New Market on U.S. 11 to **Endless Caverns** (☎ 800/544-CAVE or 540/740-3993). As far as anyone knows, this cave really is endless; you'll see stalactites, stalagmites, giant columns, and limestone pendants. From here, keep driving 18 miles south on either I-81 or U.S. 11 to **Harrisonburg,** an agricultural center, home of James Madison University, and a good stopping place for a meal or an overnight stay (there are ample chain motels at the I-81 exits). If you choose not to rest here, push on south another 25 miles to:

7. **Staunton,** pronounced "STAN-ton" by the locals, where President Woodrow Wilson was born in 1856 in the Presbyterian Manse. His minister-father soon moved to a church in Georgia, but Staunton still claims the World War I leader as its own. **Woodrow Wilson's Birthplace,** Coalter and Frederick streets (☎ 540/885-0897), a handsome Greek Revival building, is now a national shrine and the local welcome center. A next-door museum has exhibits on Wilson's life.

Across the street is **Mary Baldwin College,** a noted "finishing" school for girls. Tour maps for Staunton's Victorian downtown are available at Wilson's Birthplace and at the **Staunton/Augusta County Travel Information Office** (☎ 540/332-3972), near exit 222 off I-81 (follow U.S. 250 west and the tourist information signs).

Also worth a visit is the nearby **Museum of American Frontier Culture,** also off U.S. 250 west of exit 222 (☎ 540/332-7850). This living museum contains working 19th-century farms, one local and one each from England, northern Ireland, and Germany. Staff members in period costumes plant fields and tend livestock.

Staunton offers a good place for an overnight rest. The town has good chain motels near exit 222 off I-81 (near the tourist information office and the Museum of American Frontier Culture). Two properties in town have their own special ambience: the **Belle Grae Inn,** 515 W. Frederick St. (☎ 540/886-5151), with rooms in a well-restored Victorian house; and the European-style **Frederick House,** 28 N. New St. (☎ 800/334-5575 or 540/885-4220).

From Staunton, continue south on I-81 or U.S. 11 for 16 miles to Steele's Tavern. Turn left there on Va. 606 and drive a mile east to:

8. **McCormick's Farm Historic Wayside** (☎ 540/377-2255), where Cyrus McCormick revolutionized farming by building the first effective grain reaper in 1831. The farm's log blacksmith shop and grist mill are now a museum where you can see one of Cyrus's first machines.

Return to U.S. 11 or I-81 and head south 16 miles to:

9. **Lexington,** among the most historic and photogenic towns in the country, with a lovingly restored downtown, Washington and Lee (W&L) University, and the Virginia Military Institute (VMI). You'll have much to see in this resting place of generals Stonewall Jackson, Robert E. Lee, and George C. Marshall— and Jackson's and Lee's horses. Begin at the **Lexington Visitor Center,**

106 E. Washington St. (☎ 540/463-3777), which provides an excellent brochure with walking and driving tour maps. Be sure to visit the **Stonewall Jackson House,** 8 E. Washington St. (☎ 540/463-2552), where the Confederate hero lived while teaching philosophy at VMI. The home features many of his possessions and has photographs and a slide show about Jackson's residency here. The **Virginia Military Institute Museum** in Jackson Memorial Hall, VMI campus (☎ 540/464-7232), facing VMI's fabled Parade Ground, contains Jackson's stuffed horse and the bullet-pierced raincoat he was wearing the night his own men accidentally shot him at Chancellorville. The VMI campus also is home to the **George C. Marshall Museum and Library** (☎ 540/463-7103), named in honor of the 1906 alumnus who became the army's chief of staff during World War II and who, as Secretary of State, won the Nobel Peace Prize for creating the Marshall Plan.

From the end of the Civil War until his death in 1870, Gen. Robert E. Lee served as president of Washington and Lee University, which adjoins VMI (the brick sidewalks belong to VMI; the concrete ones to Washington and Lee). Lee designed the president's house on campus and supervised the building of the Victorian–Gothic **Lee Chapel** (☎ 540/463-8768), his burial place and shrine. The chapel, which today is used for concerts and other events, contains both Edward Valentine's white marble statue of Lee and Charles Wilson Peale's portrait of George Washington. Lee's office in the lower level of the building has been preserved as a museum, and his famous horse Traveller is buried in a plot outside.

From Lexington, a gorgeous 60-mile side trip follows the Virginia byway (Va. 39) northwest from Lexington through the **Goshen Pass,** where the Maury River cuts an 1,800-foot-deep gorge through the Allegheny Mountains. Return via Va. 42 and I-64, certainly one of the most beautiful interstate highways anywhere.

From Lexington, drive 12 miles south on U.S. 11, where the highway actually crosses:

**10.** **Natural Bridge** (☎ 800/533-1410 or 540/291-2121), a 215-foot-tall limestone arch over Cedar Creek. Some people consider this 90-foot-long structure to be one of the world's greatest natural wonders. George Washington surveyed the property in the mid-1700s and carved his initials on the arch, and Thomas Jefferson bought it in 1774. Even though the bridge is a major commercial tourist attraction today, it is still fascinating to walk along the creek under the soaring bridge and see Washington's initials.

Also here are the **Natural Bridge Zoo** and the **Natural Bridge Wax Museum,** which has more than 100 life-size figures of leading characters in the area's history and folklore. And you can make a final foray underground into **Natural Bridge Caverns.** The Natural Bridge area has a restaurant and lodging facilities on the premises.

From Natural Bridge, both I-81 and U.S. 11 go 39 miles south to Roanoke, the largest city in western Virginia and the gateway to the state's ruggedly beautiful Southwest Highlands. Or you can backtrack to Lexington and take I-64 east to Charlottesville and Richmond.

## DRIVING TOUR
## The Brandywine Valley

**Start:** Longwood Gardens (near Kennett Square)
**Finish:** Historic Yellow Springs (near Chester Springs)

**Distance:** Approximately 85 miles
**Time:** 1–2 days
**Highlights:** Historic homes; battlefield; wineries; magnificent gardens; noted art museum; unique mushroom museum; sculptural furniture studio; 18th- and 19th-century villages

This tour runs through the rolling hills of the lovely Brandywine Valley of southeastern Pennsylvania and northern Delaware, where immigrant families from all over Europe began settling some 300 years ago. They built cabins, taverns, and houses of logs, stone, and brick; some of them still stand and can be visited. The architecture reflects familiar English and German styles such as medieval leaded-glass windows, raised hearths, and herb gardens. During the American Revolution, the Continental Army suffered a crushing defeat at Brandywine Battlefield. In more modern times, the Du Ponts, one of America's premier industrial families, built palatial mansions surrounded by magnificent gardens in the valley. Thanks to them, we can visit Longwood Gardens and the Winterthur and Hagley museums, some of the nation's finest.

Howard Pyle, a painter and illustrator of adventure tales, established an art school here in the late 19th century. Some of his students, including N. C. Wyeth, Frank Schoonover, and Harvey Dunn, eventually became known as the Brandywine School of painters. The prolific Wyeths still live and paint here. The Brandywine River Museum is a tribute to them and to other area artists.

The **Brandywine Valley Tourist Office Center** (☎ 610/388-2900), at the entrance to Longwood Gardens, is a good place to stop for detailed information, including current hours for the valley's many attractions.

Begin your tour on U.S. 1 just east of Kennet Square and the junction of Pa. 52 at:

1. **Longwood Gardens,** on land sold by William Penn to the Peirce family in 1700 (☎ 610/388-1000). Joshua and Samuel Peirce began collecting specimens for a private arboretum in 1789. Pierre S. Du Pont bought the property in 1906 and continued to develop the horticultural garden. Today, 4 acres of massive bronze and glass conservatories guarantee splashes of color throughout the year. Outdoors, a topiary garden of closely pruned trees surrounds a 37-foot sundial, and a Fountain Garden spews up illuminated jets of water. There's also an open-air theater with performances during the summer.

Nearby on U.S. 1, the **Mushroom Museum at Phillips Place** (☎ 610/388-6082) is a good place to learn about the history, lore, and development of mushrooms, from the ordinary to the exotic.

☕ **TAKE A BREAK**   The **Terrace Restaurant at Longwood Gardens** (☎ 610/388-6771) offers a full-service dining room with a seasonal regional menu; crab cakes and mushroom dishes are among the specialties. Afternoon tea is also available. Entrees are $12–$20.

From Longwood Gardens, backtrack to Kennet Square and head south on Pa. 52 into Delaware until you reach the valley's star attraction, the:

2. **Winterthur Museum,** the world's premier collection of American antiques and decorative arts (☎ 800/448-3883 or 302/888-4600). Named after a town in Switzerland, this nine-story mansion and country estate once comprised the country home of the late Henry Francis Du Pont, a collector of furniture. His trove, including Chippendale furniture, silver tankards by Paul Revere, and a dinner service made for George Washington, is displayed in more than 175 period rooms. Start your tour at The Galleries, a two-story pavilion in which the Henry S. McNeil Gallery offers an exhibition of tools and workshops used in furniture

making. Adding to the splendid aura of the house, the 980-acre grounds are meticulously landscaped with native and exotic plants.

From Winterthur, continue south on Del. 52 until you come to the:

3. **Delaware Museum of Natural History,** which houses more than 100 exhibits of birds, shells, and mammals from far and near, including displays of the Great Barrier Reef, an African water hole, and various Delaware fauna (☎ **302/658-9111**). For young visitors, there's a hands-on Discovery Room, as well as a continuous showing of nature films.

From the museum, continue south on Del. 52, turn east on Del. 141, and proceed to the:

4. **Hagley Museum,** on the spot where French émigré Eleuthère Irénée Du Pont de Nemours established a black-powder mill in 1802, the first of the large Du Pont chemical factories (☎ **302/658-2400**). Today, this 240-acre outdoor museum re-creates the original 19th-century mill village through a series of restored buildings and gardens. The highlight is the first (1803) Du Pont home in America, a Georgian-style residence furnished to reflect five generations of the Du Ponts.

Next to the Hagley, the **Delaware Toy & Miniature Museum** (☎ **302/427-TOYS**) has an outstanding collection of toys and miniature dollhouses.

Now backtrack west to Del. 100 and head north into Pennsylvania to:

5. **Chadds Ford,** site of an old Native American trail that forded the Brandywine Creek, and named after John Chad, a Quaker immigrant who purchased the land from William Penn. Near the center of the village, the **Brandywine River Museum** (☎ **610/388-2700**) is housed in the 1864 Hoffman's Gristmill and features the work of three generations of the Wyeth family: N. C., his son Andrew, and his grandson Jamie. The Andrew Wyeth Gallery houses the world's largest collection of his work. There's also a section of trompe l'oeil work. Across the street, the **Christian C. Sanderson Museum** (☎ **610/388-6545**) has all the sketches and paintings the Wyeths gave to their friend Chris Sanderson over the years. A little farther along Pa. 100, the **John Chad House** (☎ **610/388-7376** or 610/388-1132) was built of bluestone by the village's founder about 1725. John Chad's widow Elizabeth could have witnessed the Brandywine Battle from her attic window. Today, living-history interpreters bake colonial breads in her beehive oven and make traditional crafts in her parlor. Across the road, the **Chadds Ford Historical Society** (☎ **610/388-7376**) is housed in an attractive barn-style building that contains displays and information on Chadds Ford.

On U.S. 1, you can watch grapes being crushed and have a taste of the produce at the **Chaddsford Winery** (☎ **610/388-6221**). From the winery, you can walk along a path to the 1714 **Barns–Brinton House** (☎ **610/388-7376**), of handsome Flemish-bond brickwork with patterned gables. It served as a tavern and inn from 1722 until 1731, and the old cage bar has been restored. Guides in colonial dress discuss tavern life.

You can overnight in the Chadds Ford area at some lovely inns. **Sweetwater Farm** (☎ **610/459-4711**), 50 Sweetwater Rd., offers seven guest rooms in an elegant 18th-century fieldstone mansion (five guest cottages are also available). The late Princess Grace of Monaco was aunt to one of the owners, Grace LeVine, and family pictures are on display. **Fairville Inn** (☎ **610/388-5900**), located south of town on Pa. 52 between U.S. 1 and the Delaware Museums, offers 15 guest rooms in an 1820s house. **Chadds Ford Inn,** at the junction of Pa. 100 and U.S. 1 (☎ **610/388-7361**), offers lunch, dinner, and Sunday brunch in a 1736 building. Brandywine decor gives atmosphere to the dining rooms. Dinner entrees are $15–$25. **Pace One Restaurant and Country Inn,** on the Concord–Thornton

# Driving Tour: The Brandywine Valley

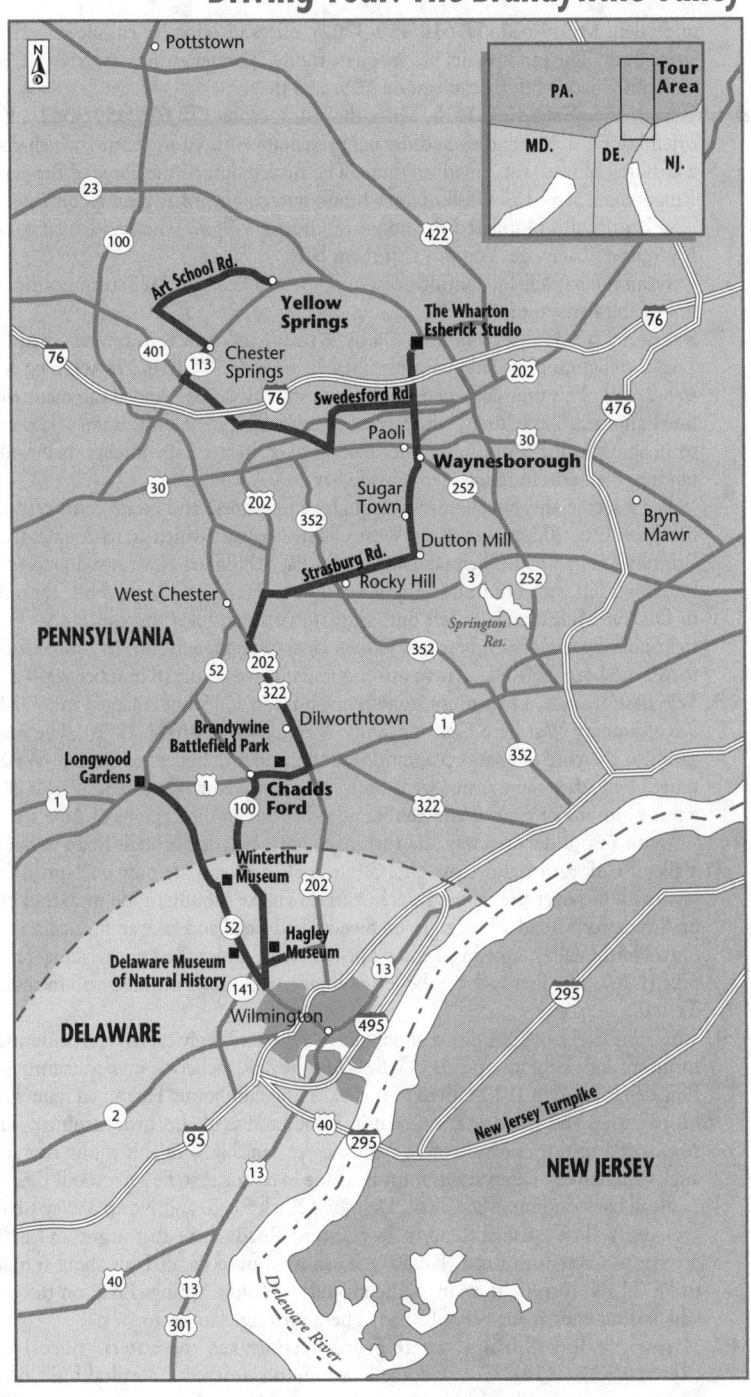

and Glens Mills Road (☎ 610/459-3702), offers imaginative cuisine in a 1740s stone barn. The inn upstairs has six guest rooms. Dinner entrees are $18–$27.

From Chadds Ford, head east on U.S. 1 to the:

6. **Brandywine Battlefield Park,** where the visitor center (☎ 610/459-3342) offers orientation exhibits and an audiovisual presentation about the battle, which dealt a crushing blow to the American cause. The British burned the home of Benjamin Ring, which served as Washington's headquarters, but it has been reconstructed. The British also plundered the house of Gideon Gilpin, who had lent it to the Marquis de Lafayette. You can visit them both.

From the battlefield, continue east on U.S. 1 to U.S. 202/322, turn north, and follow the signs to the:

7. **Brinton 1704 House,** built in 1704 by William and Ann Brinton, who had fled English religious persecution against Quakers in 1684 (☎ 610/399-0913 or 302/478-2853). This unusually fine stone house still displays 27 leaded casement windows and bedroom closets, which were often lacking in colonial homes. It is easy to imagine Ann Brinton filling her baking oven in the large kitchen below and tending the herbs in the garden outside her door.

For a scenic and bucolic drive through rolling horse and estate country, head north on U.S. 202, and take the West Chester Bypass, which starts 3 miles from Brinton Bridge Road. Then take the exit for Pa. 3E (signed Newtown Square) and look for a left turn onto Strasburg Road. Cross Pa. 352 at Rocky Hill, continue to Dutton Mill, then turn left onto Sugartown Road for a short distance. Turn right onto Spring, which becomes Jaffrey, cross Warren, and turn left onto Grubb to Waynesborough Road. There turn right and drive 1 mile to number 2049 and:

8. **Waynesborough,** a two-room stone home built in 1715 but enlarged in 1792 by Revolutionary War hero Gen. Anthony Wayne (☎ 610/647-1779). The mansion was the core of a large plantation on more than 1,000 acres of land. Wayne retired here after the war but went back into service when President Washington named him major general and commander-in-chief of the Legions of America.

Come out of the driveway and turn right onto Waynesborough Road to South Valley Road, turn right, cross U.S. 30 in Paoli, and you are now on North Valley Road. Go over the railroad tracks and down the mountainside to a dead end on Swedesford Road. Head right on Swedesford Road and take an immediate left onto North Valley, crossing Yellow Springs Road under the Pennsylvania Turnpike (I-76). The first fork on the left will take you one-tenth mile on Horseshoe Trail to:

9. **Wharton Escherick Studio,** a visual marvel with strikingly carved and sculptured furniture and decorative pieces (☎ 610/644-5822). Escherick studied painting in Philadelphia and in 1913 moved to this old stone farmhouse. He carved frames for his paintings and woodcuts, sculpted in wood, and made his own furniture. The shapes and textures provide more than the eye can follow in this studio of many angles and curves. Reservations must be made in advance, so be sure to call ahead.

Head back on Horseshoe Trail, Diamond Rock Road, and North Valley Road, crossing Yellow Springs Road to Swedesford Road; there turn right and drive 5 miles to Conestoga Road (Pa. 401). Turn right onto Pa. 401 for about 6 miles to Pa. 113N, turn right again, and continue to Yellow Springs Road on the left, which dead ends at Art School Road. There turn right to get to:

10. **Historic Yellow Springs,** where people have "taken the waters" since 1722 (☎ 610/827-7414). Gen. George Washington ordered a hospital built here, which was used for the sick and injured from the Valley Forge encampment. The three springs were a health spa until 1860. Iron Spring, now under a gazebo, is

named for the yellow, iron-rich water that patients drank and bathed in. Jenny Lind may have used the sulfur spring and also slept in the stone farmhouse on the grounds.

To return to Chadds Ford the fast way, take Pa. 100 to U.S. 202 back to U.S. 1, a 20-mile drive.

# 1 Washington, D.C.

As capital of the world's sole remaining superpower, Washington, D.C., offers its own special brand of excitement. While the city's full-time residents are dealing with a serious urban crisis, this isn't the face that visitors typically see. Here, you can can linger in the halls and chambers where great leaders have engaged in the democratic process; listen to Senate debates; hear the Supreme Court in session; visit the National Archives, where the Declaration of Independence, the Constitution, the Bill of Rights, and other cherished U.S. documents are enshrined; find inspiration in magnificent monuments to the greatest American presidents and check out the palatial digs of the current chief executive; wander the vast museums of the Smithsonian Institution; learn how the FBI works to thwart crime; and see dollar bills being churned out at the Bureau of Engraving and Printing. In short, visitors can experience firsthand just how the government of the United States works.

All this is set in a showplace of gleaming marble monuments, wide boulevards lined with architecturally impressive buildings, and grassy malls and verdant parks. No one who's visited in April is likely to forget the sight of the city's Japanese cherry blossoms bursting into bloom along the Tidal Basin, resembling a pink snowstorm. There's the pleasure of exploring the city's neighborhoods, from the town houses and cafes of Georgetown to the ethnic restaurants and funky boutiques of Adams–Morgan. And you can get to most of this on Washington's clean, efficient subway system.

There's more to see than just the capital in this region, for across the Potomac River sits Arlington National Cemetery, where an eternal flame burns above the grave of President John F. Kennedy. The George Washington Memorial Parkway runs along the river through the charming old town of Alexandria, where our first president went to church, and then to Mount Vernon, his impressive plantation home overlooking the river.

## ARRIVING & DEPARTING

**BY PLANE**  Washington is served by three major airports. **Washington National Airport** is just across the Potomac in Virginia and a 15-minute drive from downtown. **Washington Dulles International Airport** also is in Virginia, about 45 minutes west of downtown. **Baltimore–Washington International (BWI) Airport** is northeast of the city near Baltimore, about 45 minutes from downtown. National Airport is a domestic-only facility served by American, America West, Continental, Delta, Northwest, TWA, United, and US Airways. Delta and US Airways both have shuttle service between National and New York's La Guardia Airport. Delta, United, and Valujet fly to Washington Dulles, as do Air Canada, Air France, All Nippon Airways, British Airways, KLM, Lufthansa, Saudi Arabian Airlines, Swissair, and Virgin Atlantic. British Airways, El Al, and Icelandair fly into BWI.

Covered walkways connect National Airport's modern new terminal to its own **Metro** station, on the blue and yellow lines (see "Getting Around," below). **SuperShuttle** (☎ **800/258-3826**) has frequent van service between National, Dulles, and BWI airports (check in at ground transportation desks in the baggage claim areas) and the **Airport Terminal Building,** downtown at 1517 K St. NW. Fares to/from National are $8 one way, $14 round-trip; to/from Dulles $16 one way, $26 round-trip; to/from

BWI, $21 one way, $31 round-trip. Childeren 6 and under ride free. A free loop shuttle connects 8 downtown hotels to the Airport Terminal Building. Although their trains run much less frequently than SuperShuttle's vans, both **Amtrak** (☎ **800/USA-RAIL**) and **MARC**, Maryland's commuter rail system (☎ **800/325-RAIL**), link BWI Airport to Washington's Union Station.

   **Taxi** fares come to about $10 from National Airport to downtown, $40 to $45 from Dulles or BWI. The traffic directors at the airport taxi stands will give you the official fares. **SuperShuttle** (☎ **800/258-3826**) has door-to-door shuttle van service from National Airport, and may begin operating to and from Dulles in 1998.

**BY CAR**   From New York or other points north, take I-95 south to U.S. 50 west, which becomes New York Avenue in D.C. From the south, exit off I-95 onto I-395 to downtown. From the west, I-66 is restricted inside the Capitol Beltway (I-495) to three-occupant vehicles eastbound during morning rush hour, westbound during the evening. If you're caught going east on I-66 during the morning rush, exit on I-495 north, then take the George Washington Memorial Parkway south to the I-66 east or I-395 north exits. From the northwest on I-270, take I-495 south (toward northern Virginia) to the George Washington Memorial Parkway south to I-66 or I-395 east. The Convention and Visitors Association (☎ **202/789-7000**) can help you find the way; have a map in front of you when you call. WTOP Radio (1500 AM) has frequent traffic reports round the clock, or you can call **SmarTraveler** (☎ **202/863-1313**) for free up-to-the-minute conditions Mon–Fri 5:30am–7pm.

**BY TRAIN & BUS**   Amtrak trains (☎ **800/USA-RAIL**) arrive at historic **Union Station,** 50 Massachusetts Ave. NE, a turn-of-the-century beaux-arts masterpiece that was magnificently restored in the late 1980s to house shops, restaurants, and movie theaters. It's conveniently located near the Capitol, has a Metro subway station, and there are always lots of taxis waiting.

   The **Greyhound/Trailways** station is at 1005 1st St. NE at L Street (☎ **800/231-2222**). The closest Metro station is Union Station, four blocks away. The neighborhood isn't safe after dark, so take a taxi.

## ESSENTIALS

**VISITOR INFORMATION**   Contact the **Washington, D.C., Convention and Visitors Association,** 1212 New York Ave. NW, Washington, DC 20005 (☎ **202/789-7000**), for a free copy of the *Washington, D.C., Visitors Guide* detailing hotels, restaurants, sights, shops, and more. Also write or call the **D.C. Committee to Promote Washington,** P.O. Box 27489, Washington, DC 20038-7489 (☎ **800/422-8644** or 202/724-4091), for a free copy of *Discover Washington, D.C.,* which lists low weekend rates at dozens of Washington hotels. In town, the walk-in **Washington Visitor Information Center** is in the Willard Collection of Shops, next to the Willard Inter-Continental Hotel at Pennsylvania Avenue and 14th Street NW (☎ **202/789-7038**). It's open Mon–Sat 9am–5pm.

**RESOURCES FOR TRAVELERS WITH SPECIAL NEEDS**   Washington is one of the most accessible cities in the world for the disabled, with virtually every public building in town having special entrances and other facilities. The **Information, Protection, and Advocacy Center for People with Disabilities** (☎ **202/966-8081**) publishes a series of pamphlets called *Access Washington: A Guide to Metropolitan Washington for the Physically Disabled,* which cover everything from hotels to restaurants to sightseeing attractions. There's a nominal fee for mailing, but it's well worth it.

   The **D.C. Office on Aging,** 441 4th St. NW (☎ **202/724-5626**), publishes a free directory, *Golden Washingtonian Club Gold Mine,* listing numerous establishments offering discounts to seniors.

The complete information source for the gay and lesbian community is the *Washington Blade* (☎ 202/797-7000), a comprehensive weekly newspaper distributed free at about 700 locations in the District. Every issue provides an extensive events calendar and a list of hundreds of resources.

**EMERGENCIES & SAFETY**   Call ☎ 911 to reach the police, fire, or ambulance. George Washington University Hospital has an emergency room downtown at Washington Circle, Pennsylvania Avenue at 23rd Street NW. Washington has a high crime rate, but the major tourist areas are heavily patroled by local and federal police. None of the restaurants listed here will take you into dangerous or sparsely populated areas at night. The Metro in Washington is quite safe. On the other hand, there are unsafe neighborhoods within walking distance of the major tourist attractions, so don't wander away from the beaten path, and be especially cautious at night.

## GETTING AROUND

Washington is one of the easiest U.S. cities in which to get around. The area's clean, efficient, and safe Metro subway system is one of its pride and joys. There's also a complex bus system with routes covering all major D.C. arteries, and it's easy to hail a taxi anywhere at any time. Finally, Washington is pretty compact, with most of the key attractions on or near the Mall, so often the best way to get from one place to another is on foot.

**BY SUBWAY & BUS**   Known here as "Metro," the **Metrorail subway** services almost every sightseeing attraction and extends to suburban Maryland and Virginia. Stations are indicated by discreet brown columns bearing the station's name and topped by the letter *M*. Station managers can provide a free "Metro System Pocket Guide" containing a system map, explaining how it works and listing the closest Metro stops to points of interest. Computerized fare cards are used to enter and exit the system. Charts posted near the fare-card machines explain the fares, which start at $1.10 and go up according to distance and time of day. Metrorail operates Mon–Fri 5:30am–midnight and on weekends and most holidays 8am–midnight.

The **Metrobus** system is considerably more complex. For routing information, call ☎ 202/637-7000; a transit information agent can tell you the most efficient route from where you are to where you want to go (using bus and/or subway) almost instantly. The starting fare is $1.10, and exact change is required.

**BY TAXI**   Taxis are plentiful in the District of Columbia, with fares based on a zone system rather than meters. The base fare in Zone 1 (extending from the U.S. Capitol through most of downtown) starts at $3.50 for one person, but there's a $1.25 charge for each additional passenger and surcharges for trips 4–6:30pm weekdays, for large pieces of luggage, and for arranging a pickup by telephone. Fares in the Maryland and Virginia suburbs are metered, with each local jurisdiction setting its own fares.

**BY TOURMOBILE & TROLLEY**   You can see most Washington landmarks in comfort aboard **Tourmobiles** (☎ 202/544-5100), open-air blue-and-white sightseeing trams that make 15 stops along the Mall Arlington National Cemetery. Tickets are sold for a tour of Washington and Arlington Cemetery or for the cemetery alone; you may get off and reboard. Fares are $12 adult, $6 children 3–11. Tourmobile coaches also run to Mount Vernon, departing from the Arlington National Cemetery Visitor Center and the Washington Monument Apr–Oct at 10am and 2pm. Fares are $20 adults, $10 children 3–11.

**Old Town Trolley Tours of Washington** (☎ 202/832-9800) stops at or near the same sightseeing attractions visited by Tourmobile, but they also go to Georgetown, Embassy Row, the National Zoo, and Washington National Cathedral. For a fixed price, you can get on and off as often as you like. You can board without a ticket and

# Washington, D.C.

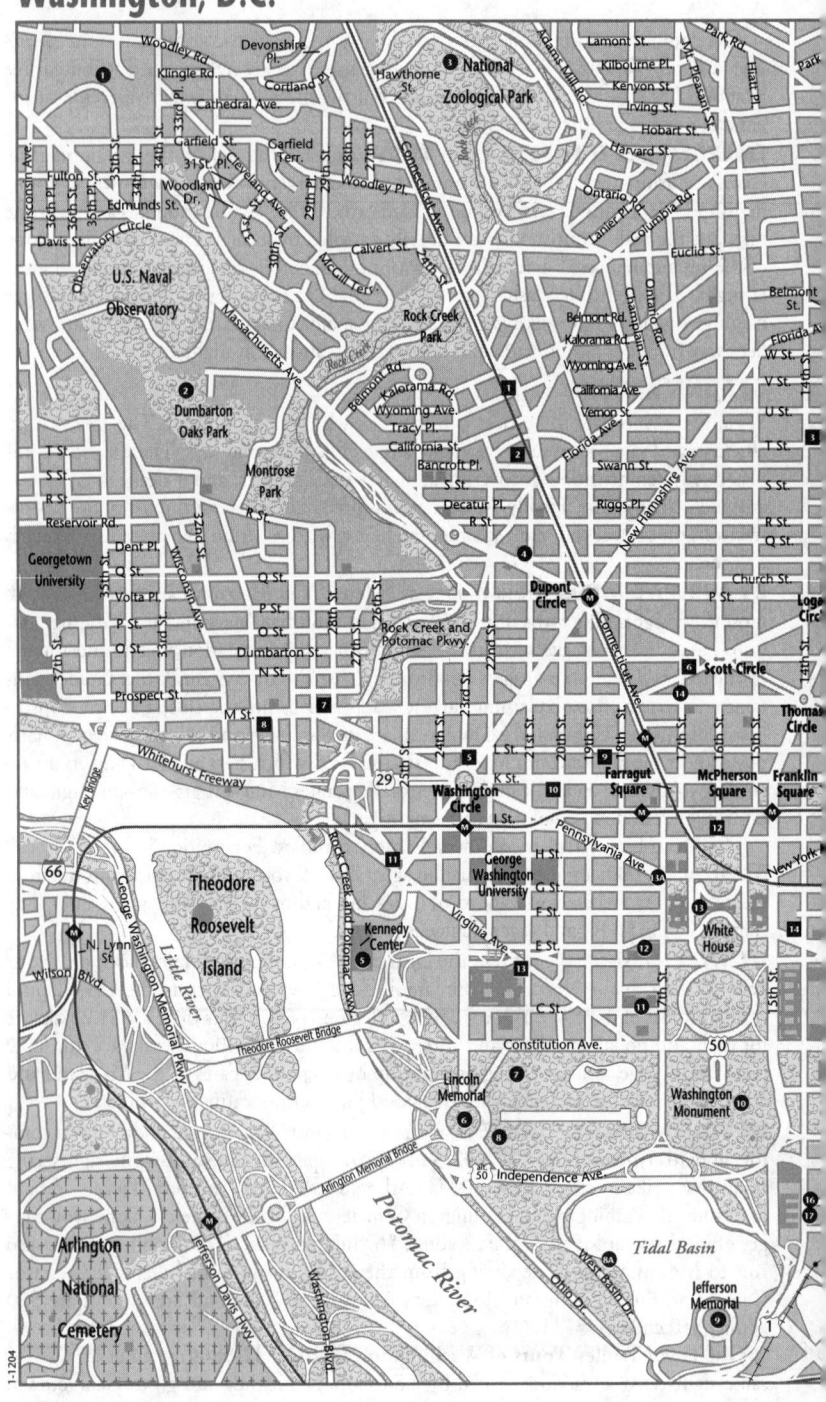

## Attractions

Arthur M. Sackler Gallery ⑲
Arts & Industries Building ㉑
Bureau of Engraving
  and Printing ⑰
Capitol ㊱
Constitution Hall ⑪
Corcoran Gallery ⑫
Dumbarton Oaks ②
Enid A. Haupt Garden ⑱A
FDR Memorial ⑥A
Federal Bureau
  of Investigation ㉗
Folger Shakespeare Library ㉞
Ford's Theatre ㉘
Freer Gallery of Art ⑱
Hirshhorn Museum ㉓
Jefferson Memorial ⑨
Kennedy Center ⑤
Korean War Veterans
  Memorial ⑧
Library of Congress ㉟
Lincoln Memorial ⑥
Nat'l Air and Space Museum ㉔
National Archives ㉖
National Gallery of Art ㉕
Nat'l Geographic Society's
  Explorers Hall ⑭

National Museum
  of African Art ⑳
Nat'l Museum
  of American Art ㉚
Nat'l Museum
  of American History ⑮
Nat'l Museum
  of Natural History ㉒
Nat'l Musuem
  of Women in the Arts ⑭A
National Portrait Gallery ㉙
National Postal Museum ㉛
National Zoological Park ③
Phillips Collection ❶
Renwick Gallery ⑬A
Supreme Court ㉝
Union Station ㉜
U.S. Botanic Garden ㊲
U.S. Holocaust Memorial
  Museum ⑯
U.S. Navy Memorial ㉕A
Vietnam Veterans
  Memorial ⑦
Washington
  National Cathedral ❶
Washington Monument ⑩
White House ⑬

## Accommodations

Capitol Hill Suites ⑳
Channel Inn ⑲
Days Inn Downtown ⑯
Four Seasons ❼
Hay-Adams ⑫
Hostelling International ⑰
Hotel Lombardy ⑩
Howard Johnson's
  Premier Hotel ⑪
J. W. Marriott ⑱
The Latham ❽
Lincoln Suites Downtown ❾
Morrison Clark Inn ⑮
Normandy Inn ❶
One Washington Circle
  Hotel ❺
Quality Hotel Downtown ❻
Reeds' B&B ❹
State Plaza Hotel ⑬
Washington Courtyard
  by Marriott ❷
Willard Inter-Continental ⑭
Windsor Inn ❸

purchase it en route. The trolleys operate daily year-round, on seasonal schedules. Fares are $20 adults, $11 children 5–20.

## WHAT TO SEE & DO

Don't expect to see all the capital's sights in one weekend. The Smithsonian Institution alone consists of more than a dozen museums plus the National Zoo. Fortunately most of the key attractions are on or near the **Mall,** the great open stretch that runs from the U.S. Capitol to the Lincoln Memorial, with the **Ellipse** branching off to the White House.

**AVOIDING THE CROWDS**   Ask your senator or representative for tickets to a **VIP tour** of the Capitol, the White House, the FBI, the Bureau of Engraving and Printing, and the Kennedy Center so you won't have to stand in line. Write as far in advance as possible—6 months ahead is not too early—specifying the exact dates you will visit and the number of tickets you need. Address requests to representatives at the U.S. House of Representatives, Washington, DC 20515; and to senators at the U.S. Senate, Washington, DC 20510. You might try calling your senator or congressperson's local office; some will even issue passes by phone.

**SPECIAL EVENTS**   Washington's best-known annual event is the **Cherry Blossom Festival** when the famous Japanese cherry trees around the Tidal Basin bloom in late March or early April. The biggest crowd-pleaser is the **Independence Day Celebration,** when upward of 500,000 persons gather on the Mall on July 4 for concerts, fireworks, and the **Smithsonian Festival of American Folklife,** a major exhibition of traditional American music, crafts, foods, games, concerts, and exhibits. Mall celebrations also are held on Memorial Day and Labor Day weekends. A good chance to see the president is when he lights the national Christmas tree during the **Christmas Pageant of Peace/ National Tree Lighting,** on the Ellipse in early December. The lighting inaugurates the 3-week Pageant of Peace, a tremendous holiday celebration with seasonal music, caroling, a nativity scene, 50 state trees, and a burning yule log.

**ESCORTED TOURS**   The **Gray Line** (☎ 202/289-1995) offers a variety of tours to all the sights, including Arlington National Cemetery, Mount Vernon, and Alexandria. There are also trips as far afield as Williamsburg, Harper's Ferry, Gettysburg, and Charlottesville. A local company, **All About Town, Inc.,** 519 6th St. NW (☎ 202/ 393-3696), offers a similar range of tours. The hilarious **Scandal Tours** (☎ 301/ 587-4291), a creation of the brilliantly talented D.C. political-comedy group Gross National Product, visits Washington's sleaziest sites Saturday Apr–Labor Day. Reservations are required. ABC News anchor Peter Jennings called it "a worm's-eye view of Washington."

   And don't forget that the Tourmobile and Old Town Trolley of Washington provide narration during their junkets around town (see "Getting Around," above).

**BOAT TOURS**   Washington's beauty can also be appreciated from the Potomac River. **Spirit of Washington Cruises,** Pier 4 at 6th and Water streets SW (☎ 202/ 554-7447), offers a variety of lunch, dinner, and moonlight dance cruises daily Mar–Dec, including a half-day excursion to Mount Vernon. **DC Ducks** (☎ 202/966-3825) features unique land and water tours of Washington aboard a DUKW, an amphibious army vehicle from World War II that accommodates 30 passengers. Ninety-minute guided tours Apr–Nov aboard the open-air canopied craft include a land portion taking in major sights and a 30-minute Potomac cruise. Buy tickets and board just outside the main entrance to Union Station.

**THE THREE BRANCHES OF GOVERNMENT**   Three of the most visited sights in Washington are the buildings housing the executive, legislative, and judicial branches of the U.S. government: the White House, the Capitol, and the Supreme

Court. All stunning edifices, they offer considerable insight into the workings of our republic.

**✪ The Capitol.** *At the east end of the Mall, entrance on E. Capitol St. and 1st St. NW.* ☎ *202/225-6827. Admission free. Daily 9am–4:30pm (tours 9am–3:45pm). Rotunda open 9am–8pm Memorial Day–Labor Day most years (hours decided each year). Closed New Year's Day, Thanksgiving, and Christmas. Parking at Union Station. Metro: Capitol South.* The U.S. Congress has met here since 1800. The hub of the building is the **Rotunda,** under the soaring 180-foot-high Capitol dome. The adjoining **National Statuary Hall** originally was the House chamber. The Senate used to meet in the **Old Supreme Court Chamber,** now beautifully restored. Senators and representatives hand out free tickets to the House and Senate galleries at their offices across Constitution and Independence avenues.

**✪ The Supreme Court.** *1st St. NE (between E. Capitol St. and Maryland Ave.).* ☎ *202/479-3000. Admission free. Mon–Fri 9am–4:30pm. Closed weekends and all federal holidays. Metro: Capitol South.* The Supreme Court hears and decides its cases in this stately Corinthian marble temple Mon–Wed 10am–3pm, with a lunch-hour recess noon–1pm, from the first Monday in October through late April. Arrive at least an hour early—even earlier for a highly publicized case—to line up for the 150 seats allotted to the general public. If the Court is not in session, you can attend a free lecture in the courtroom about the Court Mon–Fri 9:30am–3:30pm every hour on the half hour.

**✪ The White House.** *1600 Pennsylvania Ave. NW (visitor entrance gate on E. Executive Ave.).* ☎ *202/456-7041 or 202/755-7798. Admission free. Tues–Sat 10am–noon. Closed some days for official functions; check before leaving your hotel by calling the 24-hour number. Metro: McPherson Square.* The official residence and office of American presidents since the 1790s, the White House is the central theater of American government. Its interior is a repository of art and furnishings. You won't see the president's Oval Office, but tours of the public areas include the gold-and-white East Room, scene of great and gala receptions and other dazzling events; the Green Room, used as a sitting room; the oval Blue Room, where presidents and first ladies officially receive guests; the Red Room, used as a reception room and for afternoon teas; and the gold-accented State Dining Room, a superb setting for state dinners and luncheons. You must have tickets from mid-Mar–Labor Day weekend. Get them free at the **The White House Visitor Center,** Pennsylvania Avenue between 14th and 15th streets NW (☎ **202/ 208-1631;** 202/456-7041 for recorded information), which provides extensive interpretive data about the White House and other Washington attractions. Other times, line up at the southeast gate at E Street and Executive Avenue.

**THE MEMORIALS & MONUMENTS**   A highlight of any visit to the Mall are the grand memorials to presidents, famous figures, and veterans of the nation's wars. The first to be built, to George Washington, was begun in 1848. More keep being added, with construction to begin soon on one to World War II veterans.

**Arlington National Cemetery.** *Arlington, Va. (across Memorial Bridge from Lincoln Memorial).* ☎ *703/692-0931. Admission free. Tourmobile $4 adults, $2 children 3–11. Apr–Sept, daily 8am–7pm; Oct–Mar, daily 8am–5pm. Parking $2 per hour. Metro: Arlington Cemetery.* Since the Civil War these 612 wooded acres on a ridge overlooking the Potomac River and Washington have been a cherished shrine to members of the U.S. armed forces. At its center, **Arlington House** (☎ **703/557-0613**) was the home of Robert E. Lee, who left here in 1861 to take command of the Confederate army (to spite him, the Union army buried its dead in his front yard). The **Grave of President John F. Kennedy** is marked by an eternal flame. Jacqueline Kennedy Onassis is buried next to her first husband, and nearby stands a simple white cross at the grave of his brother, Robert F. Kennedy. America's most distinguished honor guard watches over the **Tomb of the Unknowns,** dedicated to all Americans who gave their lives in war. Plan to see the changing of the guard daily every hour on the hour Oct–Mar, every half hour the rest of the year. The **U.S. Marine Corps War Memorial,** with its famous statue of the 1945 flag raising on Iwo Jima, is on the northern periphery of the cemetery, just off Va. 110.

**Franklin Delano Roosevelt Memorial.** *In West Potomac Park about midway between the Lincoln and Jefferson memorials (on the west shore of the Tidal Basin).* ☎ *202/ 426-6841. Admission free. Park staff on duty 8am–midnight daily. Transportation: Tourmobile.* This latest D.C. presidential memorial was near completion at press time. Set amid waterfalls and quiet pools, "outdoor rooms" are devoted to one of Roosevelt's four terms in office (1933 to 1945). Ten bronze sculptures honor Franklin and wife Eleanor Roosevelt and memorialize the institution of the presidency, the struggles of the Great Depression, and America's rise to world leadership.

✪ **Jefferson Memorial.** *South of the Washington Monument on Ohio Dr. (on the south shore of the Tidal Basin).* ☎ *202/426-6822. Admission free. Park staff on duty 8am– midnight daily. Parking free for 1 hour. Transportation: Tourmobile.* The domed interior of this beautiful columned rotunda in the style of the Pantheon in Rome contains a 19-foot bronze statue of Thomas Jefferson, our third president, who also served as ambassador to France, secretary of state, and vice president—and still found time to pen the Declaration of Independence, found the University of Virginia, and to pursue wide-ranging interests including architecture, astronomy, anthropology, music, and farming. Rangers give 35-minute programs throughout the day June–Sept; on request the rest of the year.

**Korean War Veterans Memorial.** *Just across from the Lincoln Memorial (east of French Dr., between 21st and 23rd sts. NW).* ☎ *202/634-1568. Admission free. Rangers on duty 8am–midnight daily. Metro: Foggy Bottom.* This privately funded memorial, focusing on an American flag, honors those who served in Korea, a 3-year conflict (1950–1953) that produced almost as many casualties as Vietnam. It consists of a circular "Pool of Remembrance" in a grove of trees and a triangular "Field of Service"— the latter highlighted by statues of 19 infantrymen. A 164-foot-long black granite wall depicts the array of combat and combat support troops that served in Korea.

✪ **Lincoln Memorial.** *Directly west of the Mall in Potomac Park (at 23rd St. NW, between Constitution and Independence aves.).* ☎ *202/426-6895. Admission free. Park staff on duty 8am–midnight daily. Metro: Foggy Bottom.* This beautiful neoclassical templelike structure, similar in architectural design to the Parthenon in Greece, is a moving testament to the great Civil War president. Visitors are silently awed in the presence of Daniel Chester French's 19-foot-high seated statue of Lincoln in deep contemplation, and few aren't touched when reading his enormously powerful Gettysburg Address engraved on the interior walls. Especially at night, the view from the steps across the Reflecting Pool to the Washington Monument and the Capitol beyond is one of the city's most beautiful. Ranger programs are presented throughout the day June–Sept, by request the rest of the year.

✪ **United States Holocaust Memorial Museum.** *100 Raoul Wallenberg Place (formerly 15th St. SW; near Independence Ave., just off the Mall).* ☎ *202/488-0400. Admission free. Daily 10am–5:30pm. Closed Yom Kippur and Christmas. Metro: Smithsonian.* Telling the full story of Nazi genocide during the World War II era, this extraordinarily powerful museum reminds us of what can happen when civilization goes awry. An outer wall is reminiscent of an extermination camp's exterior brickwork, and towers evoke the guard towers of Auschwitz. A reconstructed Auschwitz barracks, the yellow stars that Jews were forced to wear, instruments of genocide, and a gas-chamber door are among the thousands of artifacts on display. If you bring children under 12 to this museum, prepare them beforehand for what they'll see. Tickets specifying a visit time are required; reserve them via **PROTIX** (☎ 800/955-5566 or 703/218-6500). There's a small service charge. You can also get them at the museum box office (14th Street entrance); lines form early for the 10am daily opening. If you can't obtain tickets, there are some portions of the museum you can see without them.

**United States Navy Memorial.** *701 Pennsylvania Ave., at 7th St. NW.* ☎ *800/831-8892 or 202/737-2300. Admission free. Mon–Sat 9:30am–5pm, Sun noon–5pm. Closed New Year's Day, Thanksgiving, and Christmas. Metro: Archives/Navy Memorial.* A statue of *The Lone Sailor* watches over a 100-foot-diameter circular plaza bearing a granite world map flanked by fountains and waterfalls salted with waters from the seven seas. The adjoining building houses a naval heritage center, including an exciting, wide-screen Surroundsound film called *At Sea,* which plays every hour on the hour 10am–4pm; admission is $3.75 adults, $3 seniors and students 18 and under. Guided tours are available from the front desk, subject to staff availability.

**✪ Vietnam Veterans Memorial.** *Just across from the Lincoln Memorial (east of Henry Bacon Dr. between 21st and 22nd sts. NW).* ☎ *202/634-1568. Admission free. Rangers on duty 8am–midnight daily. Ranger-led programs throughout the day June–Labor Day. Metro: Foggy Bottom.* It's emotionally wrenching to watch visitors grimly studying the directories at either end of this 492-foot-long, sunken black granite wall inscribed with the names of the 58,000 American men and women who gave their lives, or remain missing, in the longest war in our nation's history. Nearby statues honor both the men and women who served in Vietnam.

**✪ Washington Monument.** *15th St. and Constitution Ave. NW, directly south of the White House.* ☎ *202/426-6839. Admission free. Easter Sunday–Labor Day, daily 8am–midnight; rest of the year, daily 9am–5pm. Last elevators depart 15 minutes before closing. Closed July 4 (after noon) and Christmas. Metro: Smithsonian.* The 555-foot stark marble obelisk that shimmers in the sun and glows under floodlights at night is the city's most visible landmark. Like the Eiffel Tower in Paris or London's Big Ben, it's a symbol of the city. Climbing the 897 steps is verboten, but a large elevator whisks visitors to the top in just 70 seconds. The 360° views from atop are spectacular. Rangers give 30-minute talks throughout the day June–Sept. During tourist season, arrive before 8am to avoid long lines. **"Down the Steps" tours** are given, subject to staff availability, weekends at 10am and 2pm (more often in summer). There's free 2-hour parking at the 16th Street Oval.

**THE SMITHSONIAN MUSEUMS**   Once referred to as "the nation's attic," the Smithsonian Institution's 140 million objects now pertain to the entire world. Although its trademark is the famous brick "Castle" building on the Mall, the sprawling institution now comprises nine immense buildings located between the Washington Monument and the Capitol. Other facilities are within walking distance of the Mall, and farther out are the National Zoological Park (the zoo) and the Anacostia Museum. (The National Gallery of Art is not a Smithsonian museum but is well worth a visit; see "More Top Attractions," below.)

Begin your visit at the original Castle, now serving as the **Smithsonian Information Center,** on the Mall at 1000 Jefferson Dr. SW (☎ 202/357-2700). Daily Smithsonian events are displayed on monitors, and the multilingual staff can answer questions and help you plan a Smithsonian itinerary. The crypt of James Smithson, the Scotsman whose fortune founded the institution, is on the premises. The Smithsonian Metro station is next door. Open daily 9am–5:30pm except Christmas.

**Anacostia Museum.** *1901 Fort Place SE (off Martin Luther King Ave.).* ☎ *202/287-3382 or 202/357-2700. Admission free. Daily 10am–5pm. Closed Christmas. Metro:*

*Anacostia; then take a W1 or W2 bus directly to the museum.* This unique Smithsonian establishment was created in 1967 as a neighborhood museum serving African-Americans in the Anacostia community. It's now a national resource devoted to the identification, documentation, protection, and interpretation of the African-American experience, focusing on Washington, D.C., and the Upper South.

✪ **Arthur M. Sackler Gallery.** *1050 Independence Ave. SW.* ☎ *202/357-2700. Admission free. Daily 10am–5:30pm. Closed Christmas. Metro: Smithsonian.* A museum of Asian art, the Sackler presents traveling exhibitions from major overseas cultural institutions. The extensive permanent collection includes Chinese bronzes from the Shang (1700–1028 B.C.) through the Han (206 B.C.–A.D. 220) dynasties. The Sackler is linked to the adjoining National Museum of African Art. Be sure to browse the vast gallery shop.

**Arts and Industries Building.** *900 Jefferson Dr. SW (on the south side of the Mall).* ☎ *202/357-2700. Admission free. Daily 10am–5:30pm. Closed Christmas. Metro: Smithsonian.* Completed in 1881 as the first national museum, this red-brick-and-sandstone structure houses exhibits from the 1876 U.S. International Exposition in Philadelphia, when steam and gas engines, printing presses, corn mills, refrigerator compresses, and technological advances evoked oohs and aahs. Singers, dancers, puppeteers, and mimes perform in the **Discovery Theater** (Oct–July, Tues–Sat; call ☎ **202/357-1500** for show times and ticket information). Weather permitting, there's a 19th-century carousel in operation across the street.

**Freer Gallery of Art.** *On the south side of the Mall (at Jefferson Dr. and 12th St. SW).* ☎ *202/357-2700. Admission free. Daily 10am–5:30pm. Closed Christmas. Metro: Smithsonian.* A gift to the nation of 9,000 works from Charles Lang Freer, a collector of Asian art and American art from the 19th and early 20th centuries, the Freer Gallery has added objects of the highest quality to the Asian collection. Among the American works are more than 1,200 pieces by Whistler, including the famous *Peacock Dining Room,* permanently installed here. The museum's **Meyer Auditorium** is the setting for free chamber music concerts, dance performances, Asian feature films, and other programs.

✪ **Hirshhorn Museum and Sculpture Garden.** *On the south side of the Mall (at Independence Ave. and 7th St. SW).* ☎ *202/357-2700. Admission free. Daily 10am–5:30pm; Sculpture Garden 7:30am–dusk. Closed Christmas. Metro: L'Enfant Plaza.* This museum of modern and contemporary art is named after Latvian-born Joseph H. Hirshhorn, who donated his collection of more than 11,500 drawings, paintings, and other works. Sculpture is displayed in a verdant plaza courtyard. A rotating show of about 600 pieces is on view at all times. The collection features just about every well-known 20th-century artist and provides a comprehensive overview of major trends in Western art from the late 19th century to the present.

✪ **National Air and Space Museum.** *On the south side of the Mall (between 4th and 7th sts. SW), with entrances on Jefferson Dr. and Independence Ave.* ☎ *202/357-2700; 202/357-1686 for IMAX ticket information. Admission free. Daily 10am–5:30pm (some years the museum has extended hours during summer). Closed Christmas. Metro: L'Enfant Plaza.* A hit with kids of all ages, the National Air and Space Museum chronicles the story of man's mastery of flight, from Kitty Hawk to outer space, including the Wright Brothers' first plane, Charles Lindbergh's *Spirit of St. Louis,* and the Apollo moon ships. Arrive before 10am to make a rush for the film-ticket line, for the IMAX films shown here are not to be missed.

**National Museum of African Art.** *950 Independence Ave. SW.* ☎ *202/357-2700 or 202/357-4600. Admission free. Daily 10am–5:30pm. Closed Christmas. Metro: Smithsonian.* Sharing a subterranean space with the Arthur M. Sackler Gallery (see above), this is the only national art museum in the United States devoted to research in, and the collection and exhibition of, African art. Its permanent collection of more than 7,000 objects highlights the traditional arts of the vast sub-Saharan region.

**National Museum of American Art.** *8th and G sts. NW.* ☎ *202/357-2700. Admission free. Daily 10am–5:30pm. Closed Christmas. Metro: Gallery Place.* NMAA owns more than 37,500 works representing two centuries of our national art history. About 1,000 of these works are on display at any given time, along with special exhibitions highlighting various aspects of American art. The collection, along with the National Portrait Gallery (see below), is housed in the palatial quarters of the 19th-century Greek Revival Old Patent Office Building (4,000 revelers celebrated Lincoln's second inaugural here in 1865). *Note:* The museum will be closed for 2 years for renovations beginning early in 2000.

✪ **National Museum of American History.** *On the north side of the Mall (between 12th and 14th sts. NW), with entrances on Constitution Ave. and Madison Dr.* ☎ *202/357-2700. Admission free. Daily 10am–5:30pm. Summer hours, sometimes extended, are determined annually. Closed Christmas. Metro: Smithsonian or Federal Triangle.* Dealing with "everyday life in the American past," the massive contents here run the gamut from a Revolutionary War general's tent to Archie Bunker's chair. If you enter from the Mall, you'll find yourself facing the original Star-Spangled Banner that inspired Francis Scott Key to write the U.S. national anthem in 1814.

✪ **National Museum of Natural History.** *On the north side of the Mall (between 9th and 12th sts. NW), with entrances on Madison Dr. and Constitution Ave.* ☎ *202/357-2700. Admission free. Daily 10am–5:30pm, with extended hours in summer some years. Closed Christmas. Metro: Smithsonian or Federal Triangle.* Another hit with kids, this fascinating museum contains more than 120 million artifacts and specimens—everything from one of the largest African elephants ever bagged by a hunter to the legendary Hope Diamond, the Star of Bombay sapphire that belonged to Mary Pickford, and Marie Antoinette's diamond earrings. Dinosaurs loom large, including a life-size model of the pterosaur, which had a 40-foot wingspan. A **Discovery Room,** filled with creative hands-on exhibits for children, is on the first floor; it's open Mon–Fri noon–2:30pm, Sat–Sun 10:30am–3:30pm.

**National Portrait Gallery.** *8th and F sts. NW.* ☎ *202/357-2700. Admission free. Daily 10am–5:30pm. Closed Christmas. Metro: Gallery Place.* "Heroes and villains, thinkers and doers, conservatives and radicals" are represented here in paintings, sculpture, photography, and other forms of portraiture. Notable is Gilbert Stuart's famed "Lansdowne" portrait of George Washington. The Civil War is documented in portraiture, including one of the last photographs ever taken of Abraham Lincoln. Take a look at the magnificent Great Hall on the third floor; originally designed as a showcase for patent models, it was a Civil War hospital where Walt Whitman came to "soothe and relieve wounded troops." *Note:* The gallery will be closed for 2 years for renovations beginning early in 2000.

**National Postal Museum.** *2 Massachusetts Ave. NE (at 1st St., opposite Union Station).* ☎ *202/357-2700. Admission free. Daily 10am–5:30pm. Closed Christmas. Metro: Union Station.* Occupying the palatial beaux-arts quarters of the City Post Office Building designed by brilliant architect Daniel Burnham, this surprisingly fun museum documents America's postal history back to 1673, about 170 years before the advent of stamps, envelopes, and mailboxes. Dozens of intriguing interactive exhibits include a video game that challenges visitors to get 20 bags of mail from Philadelphia to New Orleans in the 1850s via train, boat, or stagecoach (17,000 problems can arise en route!). The museum houses a vast research library for philatelic researchers and scholars, a stamp store, and a museum shop.

✪ **National Zoological Park.** *Adjacent to Rock Creek Park, main entrance in the 3000 block of Connecticut Ave. NW.* ☎ *202/673-4800 or 202/673-4717. Admission free. Apr 15–Oct 15, daily (weather permitting): grounds, 8am–8pm; animal buildings, 9am–4:30pm. Oct 16–Apr 14, daily: grounds, 6am–8pm; animal buildings, 10am–6pm. Closed Christmas. Metro: Cleveland Park or Woodley Park–Zoo.* Established in 1889, the National Zoo is home to several thousand animals of some 500 species, many of them rare and/or endangered. Star resident is Hsing-Hsing, a giant panda donated by the People's Republic of China. He's best observed at feeding times, 11am and 3pm, and he's generally livelier at the morning feeding. Pick up a map and find out about feeding times at the Education Building, just inside the Connecticut Avenue entry.

**Renwick Gallery of the National Museum of American Art.** *Pennsylvania Ave. and 17th St. NW.* ☎ *202/357-2700. Admission free. Daily 10am–5:30pm. Closed Christmas. Metro: Farragut West or Farragut North.* A showcase for American creativity in crafts, the Renwick is housed in a historic mid-1800s landmark building of the French Second Empire style. The rich and diverse display includes both changing crafts exhibitions and contemporary works from the museum's permanent collection. There's a comprehensive schedule of crafts demonstrations, lectures, and films. The museum shop is great for books on crafts, design, and decorative arts, as well as craft items, many of them for children.

**MORE TOP ATTRACTIONS** Many of Washington's most popular attractions aren't memorials or part of the Smithsonian. While many visitors are waiting in line at the White House, others are off to see how criminals are caught by the Federal Bureau of Investigation and how money is printed by the Bureau of Engraving and Printing.

✪ **Bureau of Engraving and Printing.** *14th and C sts. SW.* ☎ *202/874-3188 or 202/874-2330. Admission free. Apr 1–Sept 30, Mon–Fri 9am–1:50pm; June 1–Aug 31, Mon–Fri additional evening tours 4–7:30pm; Oct 1–Mar 31, Mon–Fri 9am–2pm. Closed Dec. 25–Jan. 1 and federal holidays. Metro: Smithsonian (Independence Ave. exit).* As many as 5,000 people line up each day to get a peek at $103 *billion* of moolah being printed each year around the clock. Get a VIP ticket from your senator or congressperson, or arrive early, especially during the peak tourist season. Apr–Sept you must obtain a ticket that specifies a tour time. No ticket is needed the rest of the year; just line up. Allow time to explore the **Visitor Center** (open 8:30am–3:30pm, plus 4–8:30pm in summer). You can buy unique gifts ranging from bags of shredded money to copies of documents such as the Gettysburg Address.

**Corcoran Gallery of Art.** *17th St. NW (between E St. and New York Ave.).* ☎ *202/639-1700. Admission free. Wed and Fri–Mon 10am–5pm, Thurs 10am–9pm. Closed New Year's Day and Christmas. Metro: Farragut West or Farragut North.* Washington's first art museum and one of the nation's first, the Corcoran occupies a beaux-arts building just west of the White House. Shown in rotating exhibits, the collection comprehensively spans American art from 18th-century portraiture to 20th-century moderns like Nevelson, Warhol, and Rothko. There's also an eclectic grouping of Dutch and Flemish masters, European painters, French impressionists, Barbizon landscapes, Delft porcelains, and a Louis XVI salon doré transported in toto from Paris. Free 30-minute tours are given at 12:30pm (and on Thursday also at 7:30pm).

**Federal Bureau of Investigation.** *J. Edgar Hoover FBI Building, E St. NW (between 9th and 10th sts.).* ☎ *202/324-3447. Admission free. Mon–Fri 8:45am–4:15pm. Closed New Year's Day, Christmas, and other federal holidays. Metro: Metro Center or Federal Triangle.* You can learn why crime doesn't pay by touring the FBI headquarters. You'll see some of the weapons used by big-time gangsters like Al Capone, John Dillinger, Bonnie and Clyde, and "Pretty Boy" Floyd; an exhibit on counterintelligence operations; and photos of the 10 most wanted fugitives. The attraction is especially popular with kids. To beat the crowds, arrive for the 1-hour tour before 8:45am or write to a senator or congressperson for a VIP tour.

✪ **Ford's Theatre and Lincoln Museum.** *511 10th St. NW (between E and F sts.).* ☎ *202/426-6924. Admission free. Daily 9am–5pm. Closed Christmas. Metro: Metro Center.* President Lincoln was assassinated by John Wilkes Booth here on April 14, 1865, while eveyone was laughing at a funny line from Tom Taylor's celebrated comedy, *Our American Cousin.* Booth escaped by jumping to the stage, mounting his horse in the back alley, and galloping off. The theater was remodeled and restored in the 1960s to its appearance on the night of the tragedy. The **Lincoln Museum** in the basement has exhibits on Lincoln's life and times, including Booth's Derringer pistol. Doctors carried Lincoln across the street to the house of William Petersen, where the president died the next morning. Today, **The House Where Lincoln Died,** 516 10th St. NW (☎ 202/426-6924), is open daily 9am–5pm except Thanksgiving and Christmas. It looks much as it did on that fateful night. Admission is free.

**Library of Congress.** *1st St. SE (between Independence Ave. and E. Capitol St.).* ☎ *202/707-5458. Admission free. Madison Building, Mon–Fri 8:30am–9:30pm, Sat 8:30am–6pm. Jefferson Building, Mon–Sat 10am–5:30pm. Call ahead for tour information. Closed most major holidays. Metro: Capitol South.* Starting with Thomas Jefferson's personal collection of 6,487 books, the nation's library has grown to be the world's largest, with a mind-boggling 2 billion items. As impressive is its original home—the ornate Italian Renaissance–style **Thomas Jefferson Building,** erected between 1888 and 1897, and its exquisite marble Great Hall and the Main Reading Room, the latter under a 160-foot dome. Intended to hold at least 150 years of collecting, the building was filled up in 13 years. It is now supplemented by the **James Madison Memorial Building** and the **John Adams Building.**

✪ **National Archives.** *Constitution Ave. NW (between 7th and 9th sts.).* ☎ *202/ 501-5000. Admission free. Exhibition Hall, Apr–Labor Day, daily 10am–9pm; day after Labor Day–Mar, daily 10am–5:30pm. Call for research hours. Closed Christmas. Metro: Archives.* Here you can examine our most cherished treasures in appropriately awe-inspiring surroundings. The Declaration of Independence, the Constitution of the United States, and its Bill of Rights are lowered 20 feet into a 50-ton vault under the Rotunda of the Exhibition Hall for safekeeping every night. Nearby are changing exhibits of documents relating to American history, such as the Louisiana Purchase Treaty signed by Napoléon. The neoclassical building is an impressive example of the beaux-arts style. Free docent tours weekdays at 10:15am and 1:15pm by appointment only; call ☎ 202/501-5205 for details.

✪ **National Gallery of Art.** *On the north side of the Mall (between 3rd and 7th sts. NW), with entrances at 6th St., Constitution Ave., Madison Dr., 4th and 7th sts.* ☎ *202/737-4215. Admission free. Mon–Sat 10am–5pm, Sun 11am–6pm. Closed New Year's Day and Christmas. Metro: Archives or Judiciary Square.* Housing one of the world's foremost collections of Western painting, sculpture, and graphic arts from the Middle Ages through the 20th century, the National Gallery has a dual personality. You'll find the masters in the original **West Building,** a neoclassic marble masterpiece with a domed rotunda over a colonnaded fountain. The ultramodern **East Building,** composed of two adjoining triangles with glass walls and lofty tetrahedron skylights, appropriately houses an important collection of 20th-century art, including a massive aluminum Calder mobile under a seven-story skylight.

✪ **Phillips Collection.** *1600 21st St. NW (at Q St.).* ☎ *202/387-0961. Admission Sat–Sun, $6.50 adults, $3.25 seniors and students, free for children under 18; contribution suggested. Tues–Wed and Fri–Sat 10am–5pm, Thurs 10am–8:30pm. Closed New Year's Day, July 4, Thanksgiving, and Christmas. Metro: Dupont Circle (Q St. exit).*

Conceived as "a museum of modern art and its sources," this intimate establishment houses—in an elegant 1890s Georgian Revival mansion plus an added wing—the exquisite collection of Duncan and Marjorie Phillips, avid collectors and proselytizers of modernism. The original building was once the Phillipses' elegant abode, and it still has the warmth of a home. Among the highlights are some splendid small Vuillards, five van Goghs, Renoir's *Luncheon of the Boating Party,* seven Cézannes, and six works by Georgia O'Keeffe. Free tours are given on Wednesday and Saturday at 2pm.

**GREAT VIEWS**   The extraordinary view over the city is well worth a trip up the **Washington Monument.** The nighttime view from the **Lincoln Memorial** across the Reflecting Pool to the Washington Monument and the Capitol dome shouldn't be missed. You'll get that same angle plus a wonderful panorama over the river and city from **Arlington House,** in Arlington National Cemetery. Other lookouts in town are from the **Bell Tower of the Old Post Office,** Pennsylvania Avenue at 11th Street NW, and from the tower of **Washington National Cathedral,** Wisconsin and Massachusetts avenues NW.

**BEST BETS FOR KIDS**   Among the biggest kid-pleasers in this great family destination is the **National Air and Space Museum,** with its spectacular IMAX films, planetarium shows, missiles, rockets, and a walk-through orbital workshop. The **National Museum of Natural History** has a Discovery Room just for youngsters, an insect zoo, shrunken heads, and dinosaurs. The **National Museum of American History** has its Foucault Pendulum perpetually swinging back and forth, locomotives, Archie Bunker's chair, and an old-fashioned ice-cream parlor. The **Federal Bureau of Investigation** displays gangster memorabilia, crime-solving methods, espionage devices, and a sharpshooting demonstration. Kids enjoy seeing the immense piles of money at the **Bureau of Engraving and Printing** just as much as you do.

Children always love a zoo, and the **National Zoological Park** is an especially nice one, starring Hsing-Hsing the panda. Most also get a kick out of **Ford's Theatre and Lincoln Museum** and **The House Where Lincoln Died,** with Booth's gun and diary, the clothes Lincoln was wearing the night he was assassinated, and other such grisly artifacts. It's easy to get them up to the top of the **Washington Monument,** and hard to get them down. If only they could use the steps, they'd be in heaven! The **Arts and Industries Building** has performances just for children in its Discovery Theater. Call the **Kennedy Center** and **National Theatre** to find out about children's shows (see "Washington After Dark," below). And getting around on the **Metro** is fun in itself; let the kids purchase the tickets and insert their own fare cards.

**SPORTS**   Football's **Washington Redskins (☎ 202/546-2222)** play in the new Jack Cooke Stadium in Landover, Md.,but tickets have been sold out since 1966. For a price, you can get them from agencies listed under "Tickets" in the *Washington Post* classified section or from scalpers outside the gate on game day. Formerly the Bullets, basketball's **Washington Wizzards (☎ 800/551-SEAT** or 301/NBA-DUNK) and hockey's **Washington Capitals (☎ 800/551-SEAT** or 301/336-CAPS) also are moving in 1998, to the new MCI Center, 7th and H sts. NW, in downtown Washington (☎ 202/624-9732).

**SHOPPING**   The city's most delightful shopping area is historic Georgetown, with its hundreds of boutiques, antique shops, and **The Shops at Georgetown Park** (M Street at Wisconsin Avenue NW), a neo-Victorian shopping center that provides excellent browsing. Most stores front Wisconsin Avenue and M Street NW, making for a great shopping stroll. The eclectic **Adams–Morgan** neighborhood is another good area, with numerous boutiques at Columbia Road and 18th Street NW selling a wide array of imported art, clothing, handcrafts, and spices.

The only department store left downtown is **Hecht's** (12th and G streets NW; Metro Center Metro), a fun store with moderate- to higher-priced merchandise. The city's only real mall is **Mazza Gallerie** (Wisconsin and Western avenues NW; Friendship Heights Metro), a *très chic* answer to Rodeo Drive. Here you'll find Neiman-Marcus and a multi-level Ann Taylor, plus such other upscale outlets as Stephene Kelian. Lord & Taylor is next door, and Saks Fifth Avenue is 2 blocks north.

A sightseeing attraction in its own right, **The Pavilion at the Old Post Office** (Pennsylvania Avenue at 11th Street NW; Federal Triangle Metro) is in one of the capital's oldest buildings; today you'll find upscale boutiques and a food court behind the old stamp windows. Also a historic attraction, the beautiful beaux-arts **Union Station** (40 Massachusetts Ave.; Union Station Metro) now has shops, restaurants, and movie theaters. You might see a famous correspondent or two at **The Shops at National Place** (14th and F streets NW; Metro Center Metro), which occupy the lower level of the National Press Building.

Just across the Potomac River in Arlington, the **Fashion Center at Pentagon Center** (South Hayes Street at Army–Navy Drive; Pentagon City Metro) is anchored by Nordstrom and Macy's. A Price Club and Best Buy electronics outlet are across the street.

Believe it or not, one of the most popular tourist attractions in northern Virginia is **Potomac Mills,** a collection of 240-plus outlet and discount stores 25 miles south of Washington via I-395 and I-95 (☎ **800/VA-MILLS** or 703/643-1770). Nearly every outlet merchant is represented here, plus Nordstrom, Saks Fifth Avenue, and JC Penney leftover stores. Call ☎ **703/551-1050** for bus transportation from Arlington.

**Museum Shops**   Plan to work in a little shopping while sightseeing, for many of the major attractions mentioned above have shops specializing in their particular fields. For example, the shops in the **National Gallery of Art** and the **Arthur M. Sackler Gallery** sell a wide variety of posters, art reproductions, Christmas cards, and art books; likewise at the **Corcoran Gallery of Art,** whose shop has a terrific selection of art reproductions, books, jewelry, and art nouveau glassware. There are several shops at the **Smithsonian Institution** museums, including the National Museum of American Art (the Smithsonian's bookstore is here), the National Museum of Natural History, and the National Air and Space Museum. Stamp collectors will like the shop in the National Postal Museum, and if crafts are your game, check out the offerings at the Renwick Gallery of the National Museum of American Art.

In addition to sheets of uncut currency, the **Bureau of Engraving and Printing** sells engravings, including portraits of presidents and Supreme Court justices, scenes of Washington landmarks, and government seals, plus prints of Lincoln's Gettysburg Address. The **Lincoln Memorial** also has a bookshop, where you can pick up historical tomes.

In addition, the **Indian Crafts Shop** at the Department of the Interior, 18th and C streets NW, carries very high-quality handcrafts produced by American Indians. There's another outlet in Georgetown Park Mall (M Street at Wisconsin Avenue NW).

**Specialty Stores & Boutiques**   The city's favorite bookstore is **Kramerbooks & Afterwords** (1517 Connecticut Ave. NW at Dupont Circle), a San Francisco–style shop where you can buy a book and read it over lunch or dinner (see "Dining," below). A large branch of **Borders Books & Music** (L Street at 18th Street NW) also is a cultural center of sorts, with book signings, poetry readings, Saturday morning storytelling for kids, and more. It's also a good source for out-of-town newspapers. **Yes! Bookshop** (1035 31st St. NW in Georgetown) has a wealth of literature on personal growth, health, and transformation. **Lambda Rising** (1625 Connecticut Ave. NW between Q and R streets) is the city's main gay and lesbian bookstore. The **Government Printing Office Bookstore** (710 N. Capitol St. at H Street NW) sells close to 16,000 government publications covering every conceivable subject. There's another GPO outlet at 1510 H St. NW.

Antiquers can browse the premises at **Georgetown Antiques Center** (2918 M St. NW), which houses the **Cherub Antiques Gallery** and **Michael Getz Antiques.** Nearby, **Ashburner Beargie Antiques** and **The Proud American** share premises on the second floor of 1529 Wisconsin Ave. NW.

Washington society women must change their wardrobes frequently, for the city's consignment shops are filled with great second-hand buys. In Georgetown, try **Christ Child Opportunity Shop** (1427 Wisconsin Ave. NW), whose proceeds go to children's charities, and **Secondhand Rose** (1516 Wisconsin Ave. NW), specializing in designer merchandise. West of Georgetown, **Once Is Not Enough** (4830 MacArthur Blvd. NW near Reservoir Road) carries top-quality women's clothing.

**Appalachian Spring** (1415 Wisconsin Ave. NW) brings quality country crafts to citified Georgetown, all made by hand in the United States. There's another branch in Union Station.

**Markets**   Old-fashioned shopping still lives at the **Eastern Market** (7th Street at Independence Avenue SE; Eastern Market Metro), in the gentrified Capitol Hill neighborhood. Here you can buy fresh fruits and vegetables, enjoy one of the best breakfasts in town, and browse small boutiques across the street. For the freshest seafood, everyone heads to the barges moored at **Southwest Waterfront Fish Market,** on the Potomac River at Maine Avenue between 11th and 12th streets SW.

## ACCOMMODATIONS

The District's 63,600 hotel and motel rooms cover every price category, so you shouldn't have trouble finding affordable accommodations. If the establishments listed below don't have space available, **Capitol Reservations,** 1730 Rhode Island Ave. NW, Suite 506, Washington, D.C. 20036 (☎ **800/VISIT-DC** or 202/452-1270; fax 202/452-0537), will find you a hotel that meets your requirements and is within your price range. Their service is free, and they screen all hotels for cleanliness and other desirability factors, and they're all in safe neighborhoods.

Be sure to inquire about discounted weekend rates and packages. The **D.C. Committee to Promote Washington,** P.O. Box 27489, Washington, D.C. 20038-7489 (☎ **800/422-8644** or 202/724-4091), publishes "Discover Washington, D.C.," listing weekend rates at more than 90 hotels in all price ranges.

**Capitol Hill Suites.** *200 C St. SE, Washington, D.C. 20003.* ☎ *800/424-9165 or 202/543-6000. Fax 202/547-2608. 152 suites. Weekdays $159–$199 double. Weekends $99–$119 double. Extra person $20. Children under 18 stay free in parents' room. AE, CB, DC, DISC, MC, V. Valet parking $12. Metro: Capitol South.* This well-run allsuite property is on a residential street close to the Library of Congress, the Capitol, and Mall attractions. Residential decor features 18th-century mahogany reproduction furnishings. There's no on-premises restaurant, but there are plenty of inexpensive eateries on Pennsylvania Avenue SE just a block away. There are coin-op washers/dryers, and guests enjoy free use of the nearby Washington Sports Club.

**Channel Inn.** *650 Water St. SW (at 7th St. and Maine Ave.), Washington, D.C. 20024.* ☎ *800/368-5668 or 202/554-2400. Fax 202/863-1164. 100 rms. Weekdays $110–$125 double. Weekends $80–$90 double. Extra person $10. Children under 12 stay free in parents' room. Call toll-free number for best rates. AE, CB, DC, DISC, JCB, MC, V. Free parking. Metro: Waterfront.* The city's only waterfront hotel offers wonderful views of the boat-filled Washington Channel. Beautifully decorated rooms sport balconies, mahogany furnishings, and plush armchairs. Some have high cathedral ceilings. A restaurant with marina views offers moderately priced fare, and a sunny coffee shop serves cafeteria-style breakfasts. Guests use a nearby fitness club. Golf course and indoor/outdoor tennis are within walking distance.

**Days Inn Downtown.** *1201 K St. NW, Washington, D.C. 20005.* ☎ *800/562-3350, 800/325-2525, or 202/842-1020. Fax 202/289-0336. 220 rms. Weekdays $89–$109 double. Weekends $58–$89 double. Extra person $10. Children under 18 stay free in parents' room. AE, CB, DC, DISC, MC, V. Parking $11. Metro: McPherson Square.* Close to the Convention Center, the city's best inexpensive hotel has newly renovated, cheerful rooms equipped with hair dryers and coffeemakers; some also offer kitchenettes and/or cafes. A pleasant restaurant specializes in reasonably priced steak, seafood, and pasta dishes. An adjoining lounge has sports TVs. Facilities and services include a small rooftop pool, video-game arcade, room service, and a small fitness center. Call the toll-free number for "Super Saver" rates (about $59).

✪ **Four Seasons.** *2800 Pennsylvania Ave. NW, Washington, D.C. 20007.* ☎ *800/332-2442 or 202/342-0444. Fax 202/944-2076. 166 rms, 30 suites. Weekdays $325–$370 double. Weekends $245–$265 double. $725–$2,350 suites. Extra person $30. Children under 18 stay free in parents' room. AE, CB, DC, ER, JCB, MC, V. Parking $20. Metro: Foggy Bottom, then M St. buses.* The most glamorous of Washington's haute hotels has hosted everyone from Billy Joel to King Hussein of Jordan. A lobby with thousands of live plants and palm trees gives way to exceptional accommodations, many overlooking Rock Creek Park or the C&O Canal. Amenities include large desks, plump cushioned armchairs with hassocks, VCRs, CD players, and three phones. Dining includes the elegant Seasons and the delightful Garden Terrace overlooking the canal. The warmly intimate Desirée is a private on-premises nightclub. Guests can enjoy a beauty salon, gift shop, jogging trail, children's programs, and the best fitness club in town.

✪ **Hay-Adams.** *16th and H sts. NW, Washington, D.C. 20006.* ☎ *800/424-5054 or 202/638-6600. Fax 202/638-3803. 117 rms, 19 suites. Weekdays $250–$425 double. Weekends $143–$210 double. $625–$1,975 suites; $550 junior suite. Extra person $30. Children under 12 stay free in parents' room. AE, CB, DC, JCB, MC, V. Parking $19. Metro: Farragut West or McPherson Square.* The rich and famous have stayed at the elegant Hay-Adams since it was built in 1927. Its architecture evokes an Italian Renaissance palazzo with Doric, Ionic, and Corinthian orders and intricate ceiling motifs. Rooms are individually furnished with antiques and appointments far superior to those usually found in today's hotels. Overlooking the White House, the sunny Lafayette Restaurant is an elegant venue with French Empire crystal candelabra chandeliers. Guests have access to a local health club.

**Hostelling International—Washington, D.C.** *1009 11th St. NW (at K St.), Washington, D.C. 20001.* ☎ *202/737-2333. 250 beds. $18 for AYH members, $21 for nonmembers. MC, V. Metro: Metro Center.* This spiffy youth hostel in a fully renovated eight-story brick building offers air-conditioned dorm rooms (4 to 14 beds, segregated by sex) and clean baths down the hall. A limited number of rooms for families and couples are available Oct–Mar (reserve early). Sleeping bags are not allowed, but linens and pillows are provided (bring your own soap and towel). Guests can use a huge kitchen, dining room, comfortable lounge, coin-op washers/dryers, storage lockers, indoor parking for bicycles, and comprehensive information desk.

**Hotel Lombardy.** *2019 I St. NW, Washington, D.C. 20006.* ☎ *800/424-5486 or 202/828-2600. Fax 202/872-0503. 85 rms, 41 suites. Weekdays $130–$140 double; $165–$185 suite for two. Weekends (and sometimes off-season weekdays) $69–$89 double; $119–$140 suite for two. Extra person $20. Children under 16 stay free in parents' room. AE, CB, DC, MC, V. Parking $15. Metro: Farragut West or Foggy Bottom.* From its rich wood-paneled lobby with carved Tudor ceilings to its appealing restaurant and rooms, the Lombardy offers a lot of luxury for the price and location, about five blocks west of the White House. Rooms are charmingly residential, most with fully equipped kitchens, dining nooks, ceiling fans, and fine cherrywood furnishings. The Café Lombardy with open-air seating in fine weather serves delicious northern Italian fare. Coin-op washers/dryers are available.

**Howard Johnson's Premier Hotel.** *2601 Virginia Ave. NW (at New Hampshire Ave.), Washington, DC 20037.* ☎ *800/965-6869 or 202/965-2700. Fax 202/337-5417. 192 rms. $89–$139 double; concierge floor $20 additional. Extra person $10. Children under 18 stay free in parents' room. AE, DC, DISC, JCB, MC, V. Parking $9. Metro: Foggy Bottom.* Just two blocks from the Kennedy Center, this recently renovated property offers a concierge, a business center, a large L-shaped rooftop pool, a workout room, a Ping-Pong room, video games, coin-op washers and dryers, sightseeing bus tours, and a gift shop. An upscale contemporary diner provides room service; a bar/lounge adjoins. (History buffs note: President Nixon's burglars kept a lookout here while they broke into the Watergate office building across the street in 1972.)

**J. W. Marriott.** *1331 Pennsylvania Ave. NW (at E St.), Washington, D.C. 20004.* ☎ *800/228-9290 or 202/393-2000. Fax 202/626-6991. 721 rms, 51 suites. Weekdays $199–$209 double; $219–$229 concierge level double. Weekends $119–$159 double with full breakfast. Extra person free. AE, DC, DISC, ER, JCB, MC, V. Parking $16. Metro: Metro Center.* The Marriott chain's flagship property is adjacent to the National and Warner theaters, near the Mall, and two blocks from the White House. It's stunning, combining futuristic architecture with warm color schemes and lush plantings to create an exciting but very livable environment. The elegant Celadon dining room provides an Eastern ambience for American/continental fare. In fine weather, alfresco seating is available at the National Café and at SRO, a friendly pub. The skylit Garden Terrace has piano entertainment and jazz bands nightly. The Shops at National Place (see "Shopping," above) are connected to the hotel.

**The Latham.** *3000 M St. NW, Washington, D.C. 20007.* ☎ *800/368-5922 or 202/726-5000. Fax 202/342-1800. 121 rms, 22 suites. Weekdays $175–$195 double. Weekends $165–$185 double; $195–$325 suite. Extra person $20. Children under 12 stay free in parents' room. AE, CB, DC, DISC, JCB, MC, V. Valet parking $14. Metro: Foggy Bottom, then M St. buses.* The Latham is at the very hub of Georgetown's trendy nightlife/restaurant/shopping scene, but since its accommodations are set back from the street, none of the noise of nighttime revelers will reach your room. Charming earth-toned rooms are decorated in French-country motif, with multipaned windows that open, pine furnishings, and gilt-framed works of art adorning striped wallpaper. Tenth-floor rooms offer gorgeous river views. The Citronelle serves gourmet fare. Guests can enjoy a small outdoor pool and sundeck and an adjacent health club.

**Lincoln Suites Downtown.** *1823 L St. NW, Washington, D.C. 20036.* ☎ *800/424-2970 or 202/223-4320. Fax 202/223-8546. 99 suites. Weekdays $129–$149 suite for one person, $15 for each additional person. Weekends $69–$99 suite for two people, $15 for each additional person. Children under 16 stay free in parents' suite. AE, CB, DC, DISC, JCB, MC, V. Parking $10 (at nearby garage). Metro: Farragut North or Farragut West.* This recently renovated downtown hotel five blocks from the White House offers large, comfortable suites—some with full kitchens, others with refrigerators, wet bars, coffeemakers, and microwaves. They're delightfully decorated in forest green/sienna color schemes, with traditional mahogany furnishings and attractive striped wallpaper. There are two restaurants on the premises, and guests can use a nearby Bally's health club.

**Normandy Inn.** *2118 Wyoming Ave. NW (at Connecticut Ave.), Washington, D.C. 20008.* ☎ *800/424-3729 or 202/483-1350. Fax 202/387-8241. 75 rms. Weekdays $113* *double. Weekends $79 double. Extra person $10. Children under 12 stay free in parents'* *room. AE, CB, DC, MC, V. Parking $10. Metro: Dupont Circle.* This gracious small hotel blends in perfectly with neighboring embassies. Pristinely charming rooms have tapestry upholstered mahogany furnishings in 18th-century styles. Amenities include refrigerators and coffeemakers. Continental breakfast is available. Guests can use a swimming pool 1 block away.

**One Washington Circle Hotel.** *One Washington Circle NW, Washington, D.C.* *20037.* ☎ *800/424-9671 or 202/872-1680. Fax 202/887-4989. 151 suites. A/C TV* *TEL. Weekdays $115–$195. Weekends $59–$149. Extra person $15. Rates of $135 or* *higher include continental breakfast weekdays and cocktails/hor d'oeuvres Mon–Thurs.* *Children under 18 free. AE, CB, DC, MC, V. Underground valet parking $8–$15. No-* *smoking rooms available. Metro: Foggy Bottom.* This was the city's first all-suite hotel. Five types of suites range in size from 390 to 710 square feet. Suites have sofabeds and dining areas, kitchens, and walk-out balconies, some overlooking the circle and George Washington's statue. Across the circle is George Washington University Hospital's busy emergency room entrance—the hotel is well-insulated, but guests may want to ask for a suite on the L Street side. President Nixon liked to stay here on his visits to Washington (in suite 615). The clientele is mostly corporate, but families like the outdoor pool, kitchen facilities, and the prime location near Georgetown and the Metro. The West End Cafe features contemporary American cuisine in a garden room/greenhouse setting; Tuesday through Saturday nights, a pianist plays jazz. Services and facilities include concierge; room service; dry cleaning, laundry service and coin-operated washer/dryer; outdoor pool; complimentary passes to nearby healthclub with indoor pool, racquetball court, and exercise room. A conference center is on the premises.

**Quality Hotel Downtown.** *1315 16th St. NW (between Rhode Island Ave. and* *O St.), Washington, D.C. 20036.* ☎ *800/368-5689 or 202/232-8000. Fax 202/* *667-9827. 125 rms, 10 suites. Weekdays $89–$129 double; $99–$140 one-bedroom suite.* *Weekends $79–$99 double. Extra person $15. Children under 18 stay free in parents' room.* *AE, CB, DC, DISC, ER, JCB, MC, V. Parking $8.50. Metro: Dupont Circle.* This very central and pleasantly plush-looking hotel offers a lot of bang for your buck, for each large double here is like a suite, with a fully equipped kitchen and in most dining areas, sofas, and dressing rooms. A few rooms feature Murphy beds. Two dining rooms and a lounge are on premises. Guests can use the nearby YMCA health center and a swimming pool, coin-op washers/dryers, and a business center.

**✪ State Plaza Hotel.** *2117 E. St. NW, Washington, D.C. 20037.* ☎ *800/424-2859* *or 202/861-8200. Fax 202/659-8601. 221 suites. Weekdays $125–$150 efficiency suite* *for one or two people; $175–$225 large one-bedroom suite (with dining room) for up to four* *people. Weekends (also, subject to availability, off-season weeknights) $69–$109. Rates in-* *clude continental breakfast. Extra person $20. Children under 18 stay free in parents' room.* *AE, DC, ER, MC, V. Parking $12. Metro: Foggy Bottom.* You'll be charmed by the State Plaza from the moment you enter its antique-furnished lobby. This all-suite hotel is deservedly popular with performers (including many ballet troupes) from the nearby Kennedy Center. The spacious, lovely accommodations have Federal-style mahogany beds and Queen Anne chests, plus fully equipped kitchens. The pristinely pretty Garden Café has an awning-covered patio for alfresco dining. Coin-op washers/dryers and a fitness center are on the premises.

**Washington Courtyard by Marriott.** *1900 Connecticut Ave. NW (at Leroy* *Place), Washington, D.C. 20009.* ☎ *800/842-4211 or 202/332-9300. Fax 202/* *328-7039. 147 rms. Weekdays $120–$170 double. Weekends $69–$120 double. Extra* *person $15. Children under 18 stay free in parents' room. AE, CB, DC, DISC, MC, V.*

*Parking $10. Metro: Dupont Circle.* This Courtyard has the well-heeled look of a much more expensive hostelry with the amenities to match. Very nice residentially furnished guest rooms are equipped with coffeemakers and phones with modem jacks. Accommodations on higher floors offer panoramic views, and some rooms have stocked minibars. Claret's rather elegant restaurant serves moderately priced American fare at breakfast and dinner. A clubby bar adjoins. There is an outdoor pool, and guests can use the Washington Sports Club just across the street for a fee.

✪ **Willard Inter-Continental.** *1401 Pennsylvania Ave. NW, Washington, D.C. 20004.* ☎ *800/327-0200 or 202/628-9100. Fax 202/637-7326. 304 rms, 37 suites. Weekdays $295–$380 double. Weekends $199 double. $800–$2,000 suite. Extra person $30. Children under 12 stay free in parents' room. AE, DC, DISC, JCB, MC, V. Parking $15.75. Metro: Metro Center.* Worth a stop just to see, this French Second Empire beaux-arts palace is the crown jewel of all Washington hotels. Lincoln spent the eve of his inaugural here, and it was at the Willard that Julia Ward Howe penned the words to the "Battle Hymn of the Republic." It was saved as a national landmark in 1974 and beautifully restored in the 1980s. The main lobby today is again an awesome entranceway, with massive marble columns ascending to a lofty ceiling decorated with 48 state seals. Rooms are suitably sumptuous, furnished in Edwardian and Federal-period reproductions and adorned with beautiful gilt-framed French prints. Dining choices here include the stunning Willard Room, which epitomizes the term *power lunch.* A business center and complete fitness center are on the premises.

**BED & BREAKFASTS**   In addition to the bed-and-breakfasts mentioned below, more than 100 in the metro area are represented by **Bed and Breakfast League/Sweet Dreams and Toast,** P.O. Box 9490, Washington, D.C. 20016 (☎ 202/363-7767), and by **Bed & Breakfast Accommodations Ltd.,** P.O. Box 12011, Washington, D.C. 20005 (☎ 202/328-3510; fax 202/332-3885). Many are in historic districts.

✪ **Morrison Clark Inn.** *Massachusetts Ave. NW (at 11th St.), Washington, D.C. 20001.* ☎ *800/332-7898 or 202/898-1200. Fax 202/289-8576. 40 rms (all with bath), 14 suites. Weekdays $155–$185 double. Weekends $85 double. Rates include continental breakfast. Extra person $20. Children under 12 stay free in parents' room. AE, CB, DC, DISC, MC, V. Parking $15. Metro: Metro Center.* On the National Register of Historic Places, this magnificent inn occupies twin 1865 Victorian brick town houses, with a newer wing in converted stables across an interior courtyard. Exquisite, high-ceilinged guest rooms are individually decorated, some with antique wicker pieces, others with floral swag friezes and/or decorative fireplaces. Some rooms have private porches or bay windows; many have plant-filled balconies overlooking a fountained courtyard garden. Room service is available from the inn's highly acclaimed restaurant (see "Dining," below). There is a fitness center.

**Reeds' Bed & Breakfast.** *P.O. Box 12011, Washington, D.C. 20005.* ☎ *202/238-3510. 5 rms (with shared bath), 1 apt (with bath). $60–$85 double with breakfast. Apt (no breakfast) $75–$85 for two. Extra person $15. Children 18 and under $10; crib $5 extra. AE, DC, MC, V. Parking $5. Metro: McPherson Square or Dupont Circle (about six blocks from either).* Charles and Jackie Reed's restored Victorian mansion is a gorgeous Victorian/art nouveau showplace masterpiece adorned with period/reproduction furnishings and art, plus a landscaped garden with fountains. Reached by a grand carved-oak staircase, rooms are charmingly decorated in period styles. A one-bedroom apartment in another building easily accommodates five people but has no maid service. This facility offers free local calls and washers and dryers. The Reeds don't take walk-ins, so you must write or call to reserve.

**Windsor Inn.** *1842 16th St. NW (at T St.), Washington, D.C. 20009.* ☎ *800/423-9111 or 202/667-0300. Fax 202/667-4503. 44 rms (all with bath), 2 suites. Weekdays*

*$79–$125 double; $125–$150 suite accommodating up to five people. Weekends $59 double. Rates include continental breakfast. Extra person $10. Children under 14 stay free in parents' room. AE, CB, DC, MC, V. Metro: Dupont Circle.* Built as a boardinghouse in the 1920s, this neat brick structure and the adjacent building were converted in the late 1980s. Rooms are neat as a pin and handsomely furnished. You may get a sofa and/ or decorative fireplace. Suites are worthy of a first-class hotel—but much cheaper. There are ice machines and a refrigerator for guest use. A very friendly multilingual staff is a big plus. *Note:* There is no elevator, and parking is on the street.

## DINING

Once a culinary boondocks, Washington is now on a par with major American cities and European capitals. Here you will find dozens of first-rate restaurants, whose chefs are not only up-to-date on the latest culinary trends but in the vanguard. And in a city filled with foreign embassies and a large immigrant population, numerous eateries offer everything from Spanish tapas to Ethiopian zilzil wat. Here, too, you can join the rich and powerful over gravlax and champagne, or perhaps rub elbows with a justice at the Supreme Court cafeteria or with your senator in a Capitol restaurant. It all adds up to an excitingly diverse dining scene.

M Street and Wisconsin Avenue NW in Georgetown, and 18th Street at Columbia Road NW in Adams–Morgan are packed with excellent ethnic restaurants, many inexpensive. Over in Virginia, the Clarendon station on Metro's orange line comes up in the middle of Arlington's "Little Saigon," another area of cheap but very good places to eat.

**Aditi.** *3299 M St. NW.* ☎ *202/625-6825. Reservations recommended. Main courses $5–$7.50 at lunch, $7–$14 at dinner. AE, DC, DISC, MC, V. Mon–Sat 11:30am–2:30pm, Sun noon–2:30pm; Sun–Thurs 5:30–10pm, Fri–Sat 5:30–10:30pm. INDIAN.* This pristinely charming Georgetown restaurant provides a serene setting in which to enjoy first-rate Indian cookery. You enter a small, red-carpeted, cream-walled front room, where the tables are set with white linen, fresh flowers, and candles. Soft Indian music sets the tone. Excellent is the chicken pasanda (in a mild yogurt-cream sauce seasoned with onion, cumin, fresh cilantro, and almond paste).

**Clyde's.** *3236 M St. NW.* ☎ *202/333-9180. Reservations recommended. Main courses mostly $7–$11 at lunch/brunch, $10–$17 at dinner (most under $12); burgers and sandwiches under $7 all day. AE, DC, DISC, MC, V. Mon–Thurs 11:30am–2am, Fri 11:30am–3am, Sat 9am–3am, Sun 9am–2am; brunch Sat–Sun 9am–4pm. AMERICAN.* Clyde's has been a favorite watering hole for an eclectic mix of Washingtonians since 1963. A warren of pubby bars and cozy dining areas offers burgers, delicious Maryland crab-cake sandwiches, award-winning chili, and salads—plus daily specials such as fresh-made fettuccine tossed with Cajun andouille sausage, tomatoes, and herbs.

✪ **Coco Loco.** *810 7th St. NW (between H and I sts.).* ☎ *202/289-2626. Reservations recommended. Tapas mostly $3.95–$7.95; churrascaria with antipasti bar $15.95 lunch, $24.95 dinner; antipasti bar only $9.95 lunch, $15.95 dinner. AE, DC, MC, V. Mon–Fri 11:30am–2:30pm; Sun–Wed 5:30–10pm, Thurs–Sat 5:30–11pm. Valet parking $4 evenings. Metro: Gallery Place. CONTEMPORARY MEXICAN (TAPAS)/BRAZILIAN CHURRASCARIA.* Crackling with excitement, this large and festive downtown restaurant focuses on a daily changing buffet table where antipasti items are temptingly arranged on palm fronds and banana leaves. The tapas are diverse and subtly flavored. The wine list here is small but well chosen; the service warm and competent.

**Kramerbooks & Afterwords, A Café.** *1517 Connecticut Ave. NW (between Q St. and Dupont Circle).* ☎ *202/387-1462. Reservations not accepted. Main courses mostly $8.75–$12.25. AE, DISC, MC, V. Mon–Thurs 7:30am–1am, around the clock Fri*

*7:30am–Mon 1am. Metro: Dupont Circle. AMERICAN.* This schmoozy bookstore-cum-cafe is the kind of congenial place you go for cappuccino after the movie or to linger over a good book and a cognac (you can buy both here). Fare at lunch or dinner includes salads, sandwiches, and hot entrees like cheese-filled tortellini tossed with pancetta and field mushrooms in creamy basil Parmesan sauce. There's cozy seating indoors and out.

✪ **Le Lion d'Or.** *1150 Connecticut Ave. NW (at M St.).* ☎ *202/296-7972. Reservations required. Main courses $20–$32. AE, CB, DC, MC, V. Mon–Sat 6–10pm. Metro: Farragut North. FRENCH.* Owner/chef Jean Pierre Goyenvalle's Le Lion d'Or is one of Washington's most highly esteemed bastions of classic French cuisine at its best, beautifully presented and graciously served. You'll quickly forget you're underground because of the delightful French country setting with seating in dark-brown tufted-leather banquettes under tented silk canopies.

**Mixtec.** *1792 Columbia Rd.* ☎ *202/332-1011. Reservations not accepted. Main courses $4.75–$10, full breakfasts $6.25–$8.75. MC, V. Mon–Tues 7am–11:30pm, Fri–Sat 7am–1am, Sun 7am–11pm. Metro: Woodley Park–Zoo. MEXICAN REGIONAL.* This open kitchen in Adams–Morgan serves up authentic regional cuisines of Mexico in a cheerful setting, with colorful *faroles* (paper lanterns) hanging overhead. A few individual dishes in the $2.50–$4.50 range make a hearty meal of diverse culinary thrills. Come here, too, for hearty Mexican breakfasts.

✪ **Morrison Clark Inn.** *Massachusetts Ave. NW (at 11th St.).* ☎ *202/898-1200. Reservations recommended. Main courses $10.50–$14 at lunch, $16.25–$21.50 at dinner; three-course Sun brunch (including unlimited champagne) $19.50. AE, CB, DC, MC, V. Mon–Fri 11:30am–2:30pm, Sun 11:30am–2pm; nightly 6–9pm. Metro: Metro Center. AMERICAN REGIONAL.* This elegant dining room is one of the District's most fashionable restaurants. Chef Richard Mahan's seasonally changing menus are inspired, offering the likes of sautéed red snapper in a citrusy pan sauce served with marinated black olives, tomato marmalade, and crispy-creamy pommes Lyonnaises. A reasonably priced wine list offers premium vintages by the glass.

✪ **Nora.** *2132 Florida Ave. NW (at R St.).* ☎ *202/462-5143. Reservations recommended. Main courses $20–$25. MC, V. Mon–Thurs 6–10pm, Fri–Sat 6–10:30pm. Metro: Dupont Circle. ORGANIC/MULTIETHNIC.* Owner-chef Nora Pouillon's healthful organic cookery is a favorite of the Clintons, Gores, Kennedys, and the ever fit Jane Fonda when she's in town. The skylit main dining room is in a converted stable, and there's an intimate brick-walled patio with a large shade tree. The chemical-free, organically grown, free-range fare is extremely healthful, with vivid and earthy flavors of natural foods.

**Old Ebbitt Grill.** *675 15th St. NW (between F and G sts.).* ☎ *202/347-4801. Reservations recommended. Main courses $4.50–$7 at breakfast, $6–$10 at brunch, $7–$11 at lunch, $10–$15 at dinner; burgers and sandwiches $6.25–$11. AE, DC, DISC, MC, V. Mon–Fri 7:30am–midnight, Sat 8am–midnight, Sun 9:30am–midnight. Bar, Sun–Thurs until 2am, Fri–Sat until 3am. Metro: McPherson Square or Metro Center. Complimentary valet parking Mon–Sat from 6pm, Sun from noon. AMERICAN.* Although recently moved around the corner from its original 1856 location two blocks from the White House, this is the city's oldest saloon. The plush new facility is loosely based on the original, but beveled mirrors, gas lighting, etched-glass panels, and such Old Ebbitt heirlooms as animal trophies bagged by Teddy Roosevelt make this a stunning setting for meals, cocktails, or a romantic rendezvous. Menus change daily but always feature sandwiches, burgers, and Maryland crab cakes.

**Patisserie Café Didier.** *3206 Grace St. NW (off Wisconsin Ave. just below M St.).* ☎ *202/342-9083. Main courses $8–$9; breakfast pastries, muffins, croissants, and desserts $1.10–$5. DC, DISC, MC, V. Tues–Sat 8am–7pm, Sun 8am–5pm. CONTINENTAL/ PATISSERIE.* Former pastry chef at New York's haute-cuisine bastions Le Cirque and La Côte Basque, Dieter Schorner has created Washington's most delightful place for continental breakfasts, light lunches, and afternoon teas. After decadently eating cake for breakfast, come back at lunch for homemade soups, fresh-baked breads, quiches, soufflés, sandwiches, salads, small European-style pizzas, cold platters, and hot items such as crab cakes and lamb couscous.

✪ **Petitto's.** *2653 Connecticut Ave. NW (between Calvert St. and Woodley Rd.).* ☎ *202/667-5350. Reservations recommended. Main courses $11–$17.75. AE, CB, DC, DISC, MC, V. Mon–Sat 6–10:30pm, Sun 6–9:30pm. Dolce Finale, Mon–Thurs 5pm– 12:30am, Fri–Sat 5pm–1:30am. Metro: Woodley Park–Zoo. NORTHERN ITALIAN.* In a row of interesting restaurants near the zoo, the superb Petitto's serves the cuisine of Rome and Abruzzi in a converted turn-of-the-century town house with working fire-places. Operatic arias (sometimes live) enhance the atmosphere. Dolce Finale, in the cozily candlelit wine cellar, features cappuccinos, wines, grappas, liqueurs, fruits, cheeses, and sumptuous desserts.

**Peyote Café.** *2319 18th St. NW (between Belmont and Kalorama rds.).* ☎ *202/ 462-8330. Reservations recommended. Sandwiches, salads, burgers $3.50–$7.95; main courses $5.95–$14.95 at dinner, mostly $3.95–$7.95 at brunch. AE, CB, DC, MC, V. Mon–Fri 5–11pm, Sat–Sun 11:30am–midnight. Bar, Sun–Thurs until 2am, Fri–Sat until 3am. Metro: Woodley Park–Zoo. SOUTHWESTERN/TEX-MEX.* Although it occupies an Adams–Morgan town house, the Peyote Café evokes a Southwestern roadside eat-ery. It's a casual place, but there's nothing casual about the kitchen, with the chili, mixed grill, tacos al carbón, and other offerings at Lone Star State quality. You can dine at the bar or sit on high chairs at round tables.

✪ **Pizzeria Paradiso.** *2029 P St. NW.* ☎ *202/223-1245. Reservations not accepted. Pizzas $6.50–$16, sandwiches and salads $4–$6. DC, MC, V. Mon–Thurs 11am–11pm, Fri–Sat 11am–midnight, Sun noon–10pm. Metro: Dupont Circle. ITALIAN REGIONAL PIZZA AND PANINI.* Housed on the second floor of a Dupont Circle town house, Pizzeria Paradiso is pristinely charming. An exhibition kitchen basks in the rosy glow of an oak-burning pizza oven. Also on the menu: panini (sandwiches), great salads, and desserts. There are only about 16 tables, so come either early or late to avoid waiting.

**Prime Rib.** *2020 K St. NW.* ☎ *202/466-8811. Reservations recommended. Main courses $10–$16.50 at lunch, $18–$28 at dinner. AE, CB, DC, MC, V. Mon–Fri 11:30am–3pm; Mon–Thurs 5–11pm, Fri–Sat 5–11:30pm. Free valet parking after 6pm. Metro: Farragut West. STEAKS/CHOPS/SEAFOOD.* A perennial favorite of well-heeled lobbyists and politicos, the glamorous Prime Rib is one of the best celebrity-watching spots in town. They come here to gorge on thick, perfectly prepared steak and roast beef, plus about a dozen seafood entrees. Bar drinks here are made with fresh-squeezed juices and Evian water.

**Red Sage.** *605 14th St. NW.* ☎ *202/638-4444. Reservations recommended. Main courses $11–$16 at lunch, $16–$31.95 at dinner; Cafe/Chili Bar items are almost all under $10. AE, CB, DC, MC, V. Restaurant, Mon–Fri 11:30am–2:15pm and 5:30–10:30pm, Sat 5:30–10:30pm, Sun 5–10pm. Cafe/Chili Bar, Mon–Sat 11:30am–11:30pm, Sun 4:30–11:30pm. Metro: Metro Center. SOUTHWESTERN/CONTEMPORARY AMERICAN.* One of the brightest stars in Washington's culinary galaxy, Red Sage is the creation of renowned chef Mark Miller, who brings brilliant inspiration to

Southwestern-nuanced American cuisine. His warren of downstairs dining rooms is an elegantly whimsical Wild West fantasy. The Chili Bar and Cafe offer inexpensive light fare ranging from barbecued brisket quesadillas to a sandwich of grilled chicken, smoked prosciutto, sun-dried tomato spread, mozzarella, and Monterey Jack on roast garlic/herb focaccia.

**Reeve's Restaurant and Bakery.** *1306 G St. NW.* ☎ *202/628-6350. Main courses $5.50–$8; sandwiches $3.50–$6; buffet breakfast $5.25 Mon–Fri, $6.25 Sat and holidays. MC, V. Mon–Sat 7am–6pm. Metro: Metro Center. AMERICAN.* Reeve's has been a downtown institution since 1886 (J. Edgar Hoover used to send a G-man for chicken sandwiches). You can't beat the all-you-can-eat breakfast buffet or hot lunch entrees running the gamut from crab cakes to fried chicken with mashed potatoes and gravy. And leave room for one of Reeve's fabulous pies. No alcoholic beverages here.

**Sholl's Cafeteria.** *In the Esplanade Mall, 1990 K St. NW.* ☎ *202/296-3065. Main courses $1.65–$5.25. No credit cards. Mon–Sat 7am–8pm, Sun 8:30am–6pm. Metro: Farragut West. AMERICAN.* Pennsylvania Dutchman Evan A. Sholl opened this homey, simple establishment in 1928, offering fresh, wholesome, inexpensive fare, prayers, and patriotism. His nephew still does. Everything served here is prepared on the premises using fresh produce. Add a vegetable or a scoop of mashed potatoes for another 75¢ to 85¢, a piece of homemade peach or pumpkin pie for $1.05.

**Sequoia.** *3000 K St. NW (at the Washington Harbour).* ☎ *202/944-4200. Reservations recommended (not accepted for outdoor seating). Main courses $10.95–$20.95, salads and sandwiches $7.95–$14.95. AE, DISC, MC, V. Sun–Thurs 11:30am–midnight, Fri–Sat 11:30am–1am. Paid parking available at the Harbour, discounted to restaurant patrons at dinner on weekends. AMERICAN REGIONAL.* Although the Potomac River vista outshines the food, this Georgetown waterfront eatery is one of Washington's most popular restaurants (the Clintons bring Chelsea here). The extensive menu runs the gamut from burgers and fries to a warm grilled Thai chicken salad served over rice noodles. It's casual; wear jeans. Singles pack the outdoor bar on Friday evening.

**The Tombs.** *1226 36th St. NW (at Prospect St.).* ☎ *202/337-6668. Reservations not accepted. Burgers, sandwiches, salads $3.95–$7.95; main courses $6.95–$10.95. AE, DISC, MC, V. Mon–Thurs 11:30am–2am, Fri 11:30am–3am, Sat 11am–3am, Sun 9:30am–2am; brunch Sun 10am–3pm. Note: The kitchen closes a few hours before the bar. AMERICAN.* Low beer prices and lunch and dinner specials attract the college crowd to this classic watering hole in a converted 19th-century Federal-style house near Georgetown University. The menu offers a wide selection of burgers and sandwiches served with steak fries, chili, and salads, along with a few more serious entrees. Arrive at off-peak hours to avoid waiting.

**Trio.** *1537 17th St. NW (at Q St.).* ☎ *202/232-6305. Reservations not accepted. Main courses $5.75–$9.50 at lunch and dinner; burgers and sandwiches $1.75–$5.75; full breakfasts $2.75–$5.95. AE, MC, V. Daily 7:30am–midnight. Metro: Dupont Circle (Q St. exit). AMERICAN.* A relic from the 1950s, Trio's roomy red leather booths (with coat hooks) usually are filled with Dupont Circle residents taking advantage of low-priced specials such as fried oysters and crab cakes, grilled pork chops with applesauce, and turkey with cornbread dressing and cranberry sauce. There's a full bar, and an old-fashioned soda fountain turns out hot-fudge sundaes and milkshakes.

✪ **Vidalia.** *1990 M St. NW.* ☎ *202/659-1990. Reservations recommended. Main courses $12.50–$16.85 at lunch, $16–$20 at dinner. AE, DC, MC, V. Mon–Fri 11:30am–2:30pm; Mon–Thurs 5:30–10pm, Fri–Sat 5:30–10:30pm. Complimentary valet parking at dinner. Metro: Dupont Circle. PROVINCIAL AMERICAN.* Near Dupont Circle, the charmingly country-cozy Vidalia offers "high-flauting" Southern cuisine by Chef Jeff Buben. His menus change frequently. A mouthwatering recent offering: sautéed shrimp on a mound of creamed grits and caramelized onions in a chopped tomato and fresh thyme sauce. There are hearty sandwiches at lunch, and tapas are served in the adjoining Onion Bar.

**Zed's.** *3318 M St. NW.* ☎ *202/333-4710. Reservations accepted for large parties only. Main courses $5.95–$10.75 at lunch, mostly $6.95–$12.95 at dinner. AE, MC, V. Sun– Thurs 11am–11pm, Fri–Sat 11am–1am. ETHIOPIAN.* Although the city has a number of Ethiopian restaurants, the best of this spicy cuisine is at Zed's, a charming little Georgetown place. You eat here *sans* utensils—a sourdough crepelike bread called injera is used to scoop up food. Tops here are the chicken dishes such as Doro watt (stewed in a tangy hot red-chili-pepper sauce).

**DINING AT SIGHTSEEING ATTRACTIONS**   Given the hectic pace of seeing Washington, you'll sometimes want to save time by having lunch at or near the major attractions.

On Capitol Hill, you might run into your senator or representative in the **Refectory,** on the first floor of the Senate side of the Capitol (☎ 202/224-4870), or in the **House of Representatives Restaurant,** first floor of the House side (☎ 202/225-6300). Mostly senate staffers use the inexpensive **Dirksen Senate Office Building South Buffet,** 1st and C Streets NE (☎ 202/224-4249). Across the street, the **Supreme Court Cafeteria** (☎ 202/479-3246) and the cafeteria and Montpelier Dining Room in the James Madison Building of the **Library of Congress** (☎ 202/707-8300) also offer reasonably priced lunchtime fare.

Down on the Mall, you can grab a bite at the National Air and Space Museum's **Flight Line** (☎ 202/371-8778) and **The Wright Place** (☎ 202/371-8778), both open for lunch daily. The National Gallery of Art (☎ 202/347-9401) has four outlets including the **Garden Café** under a skylight and the **Terrace Café** overlooking the Mall.

You can also slip off to the food courts and restaurants in the **Pavilion at the Old Post Office, Union Station,** and **The Shops at National Place** (see "Shopping," above).

## WASHINGTON AFTER DARK

Washington has a lot to keep you busy after seeing the sights, all of it chronicled in the Friday "Weekend" section of the *Washington Post.* Equally comprehensive is the *City Paper,* a free weekly available in newpaper boxes outside Metro stations and at many restaurants, clubs, and bars. The monthly *Washingtonian* magazine is another good source.

**TICKETplace,** located in the Old Post Office Pavilion, Pennsylvania Avenue at 11th Street NW (☎ 202/TICKETS), sells half-price (cash only) day-of-performance tickets to most major theaters and concert halls (on Saturday for Sunday and Monday shows). The facility also serves as a **Ticketmaster** outlet (☎ 800/551-SEAT or 202/ 432-SEAT), which also has an office at **Hecht's Department Store,** 12th and G streets NW. A similar ticket outlet is **PROTIX** (☎ 800/955-5566 or 703/218-6500). Several private agencies are listed under "Tickets" in the *Washington Post* classified ads.

**THE PERFORMING ARTS**   The hub of the city's cultural and entertainment scene is the ✪ **John F. Kennedy Center for the Performing Arts,** at the southern end of New Hampshire Avenue NW and Rock Creek Parkway (☎ 800/444-1324 or 202/ 467-4600). The center's Eisenhower Theater, Opera House, Concert Hall, Terrace Theater, and Theater Lab host a wide variety of performances, from pre-Broadway plays to pop stars to the National Symphony Orchestra. Half-price tickets are available for full-time students, senior citizens, enlisted personnel, and the disabled (☎ 202/416-8340 for details). The Kennedy Center also is home to the **American Film Institute** (☎ **202/ 828-4000** for information, or 202/785-4600 for tickets), a marvelous facility featuring classic films, works of independent filmmakers, foreign films, themed festivals, and the like.

The nation's third oldest theater, the luxurious, Federal-style **National Theatre,** 1321 Pennsylvania Ave. NW (☎ 800/447-7400 or 202/628-6161), has been operating since 1835 and is the closest thing Washington has to a Broadway-style playhouse, offering star-studded hits. Headliners often are booked at **Constitution Hall,** 18th and D streets NW (☎ 202/638-2661 or 202/628-4780), a beautiful 3,746-seat Federal-style auditorium at the DAR's national headquarters. Opened in 1924 and recently restored to its original plush magnificence, the **Warner Theatre,** 1299 Pennsylvania Ave. at 13th Street NW (☎ 202/783-4000), offers year-round entertainment.

Buffs of the Bard shouldn't miss the **Shakespeare Theatre,** 450 7th St. NW, between D and E streets (☎ 202/393-2700), where an internationally renowned classical ensemble company performs three Shakespearean productions and one other classical work Sept–June. The company used to perform at **The Folger,** 201 E. Capitol St. SE (☎ 202/544-7077), which still provides a medieval and Renaissance music ensemble and a full October-to-June season of theatrical programs relating to Shakespeare and other literary greats.

Although it was closed for more than a century after Lincoln's assassination, the restored **Ford's Theatre,** 511 10th St., between E and F streets NW (☎ 202/347-4833 for listings; 800/955-5566 or 703/218-6500 for tickets), now hosts a variety of plays and the annual Festival at Ford's, a celebrity-studded bash.

**Arena Stage,** 6th Street and Maine Avenue SW (☎ 202/488-3300), is a nationally recognized reportory company founded by the brilliant Zelda Fichandler and now in its fifth decade. Eight annual productions are presented on two stages—the **Fichandler** (a theater-in-the-round), and the smaller, fan-shaped **Kreeger.** In addition, the Arena houses the **Old Vat,** a space used for new play readings and the special productions.

The country's only national park devoted to the performing arts, **Wolf Trap Farm Park for the Performing Arts,** 1551 Trap Rd., Vienna, Va. (☎ 703/255-1868 or PROTIX 703/218-6500 to charge tickets), offers a star-studded Summer Festival Season from late May to mid-Sept. in its open-air pavilion. Year-round, jazz, pop, country, folk, bluegrass, and chamber musicians perform in the pre-Revolutionary, 350-seat **German Barn** at 1635 Trap Rd. (☎ 703/938-2404), also the summer home of the Wolf Trap Opera Company. Wolf Trap is 30 minutes by car from downtown via I-66, and there's a summertime shuttle from the West Falls Church Metro station.

Rock stars often play at the 55,000-seat **Robert F. Kennedy Memorial Stadium,** 2400 E. Capitol St. SE (☎ 202/547-9077 or 202/546-3337), and at the 19,000-seat **U.S. Air Arena,** in Landover, Md. (☎ 301/350-3400).

**THE CLUB & MUSIC SCENE** Georgetown is the best place to hear live music in a nightclub setting. Funky and cavelike, **The Bayou,** 3135 K St. NW under the Whitehurst Fairway near Wisconsin Avenue (☎ 202/333-2897), features a mixed bag of progressive, reggae, and alternative sounds, with occasional big names coming home for old time's sake. **Blues Alley,** 1073 Wisconsin Ave. NW in an alley below M Street (☎ 202/337-4141), has been Washington's top jazz club since 1965, featuring such artists as Nancy Wilson, Wynton Marsalis, and Maynard Ferguson. There are usually two shows nightly at 8 and 10pm. Reservations are essential (call after noon).

For dancing, **Coco Loco,** 810 7th St. NW, between H and I streets downtown (☎ 202/289-2626), is among D.C.'s hottest spots. A sexy 11pm Friday and Saturday floor show features Brazilian exhibition dancers who shed their feathers and sequins down to a bare minimum. Usually packed on weekends, **Deja Vu,** 2119 M St. NW (☎ 202/452-1966), has a dance floor, eight bars, and two restaurants. The **Spy Club,** 805 15th St. NW, between H and I streets in Zel Alley (☎ 202/289-1779), has a dance floor punctuated by "Gothic" columns, and there are cozy nooks including a billiards room. In a vast converted warehouse, **9:30 Club,** 815 V St. NW (☎ 202/393-0930), is a major live-music venue, hosting frequent record company parties and featuring a wide range of top performers.

Up in Adams–Morgan, **Kilimanjaro,** 1724 California St. NW, between 18th Street and Florida Avenue (☎ **202/328-3838** or 202/328-3839), is the hub of Washington's Caribbean music scene. This lively, international neighborhood is home to a variety of bars that frequently have Latin, Caribbean, African, and other live music. Just wander along the 2400 block of 18th Street NW to the likes of **Latin Quarter** (☎ **202/ 234-0774**), with deejays and live Latin bands; **Meskerem** (☎ **202/799-7673**), with Ethiopian musicians on weekends; **Bukom Café** (☎ **202/265-4600**), with very good African bands; **Kala Kala** (☎ **202/232-5433**), with a deejay playing tunes from Africa, the French Caribbean, and Trinidad; and the upscale **Cities** (☎ **202/328-7194**), with Latin and contemporary deejay music.

Nationally known comedians play the major venues here, but you can also laugh at both local and national comics at **The Improv,** 1140 Connecticut Ave. NW, between L and M streets (☎ **202/296-7008**), featuring top performers on the national comedy-club circuit as well as comic plays and one-person shows. Political satirist Mark Russell got his start at the **Marquee Cabaret,** in the OMNI Shoreham Hotel, 2500 Calvert St. NW at Connecticut Avenue (☎ **202/234-0700**), which today features an extremely funny musical comedy revue called *Mrs. Foggybottom & Friends* Thurs–Sat.

**BARS & LOUNGES**   The town's premier sports bar is **Champions,** 1206 Wisconsin Ave. NW just north of M Street in Georgetown (☎ **202/965-4005**). Lots of rugby players and other athletes also hang out at the **Bottom Line,** 1716 I St. NW downtown (☎ **202/298-8488**), where there's dancing to deejay music Tues–Sat and frequent zany promotions. See "Dining," above, for details about three of the more popular upscale watering holes: **Clyde's,** 3236 M St. NW (☎ **202/333-9180**), and **Sequoia,** 3000 K St. NW at Washington Harbour (☎ **202/944-4200**), both in Georgetown, and **Old Ebbitt Grill,** 675 15th St. NW, between F and G streets downtown (☎ **202/ 347-4801**).

Dupont Circle is Washington's gay and lesbian hub, with at least 10 gay bars within easy walking of each other. The **Circle Bar and Tavern,** 1629 Connecticut Ave. NW (☎ **202/462-5775**), is the largest, attracting a racially mixed gay and lesbian crowd, mostly 25–35. The more intimate **J.R.'s,** 1517 17th St. NW, between Q and Church streets (☎ **202/328-0090**), is all-male. Down south of the Capitol, there's good dancing at **Tracks,** 1111 1st St. SE (☎ **202/488-3320**), in a converted auto dealership.

## DAY TRIPS FROM WASHINGTON

**MOUNT VERNON**   No visit to the region is complete without a trip to ✪ **Mount Vernon,** George Washington's stunning southern plantation that dates back to a 1674 land grant to his great-grandfather. The restoration by the Mount Vernon Ladies' Association is an unmarred beauty; many of the furnishings are original pieces acquired by Washington, and the rooms have been repainted in the original colors favored by George and Martha.

Some 500 of the original 8,000 acres overlooking the Potomac are still intact. The house itself is interesting as an outstanding prototype of colonial architecture, as an example of the aristocratic lifestyle in the 18th century, and of course, as the home of our first president. There are a number of family portraits, and the rooms are appointed as if actually in day-to-day use. After leaving the house, you can tour the kitchen, slave quarters, storeroom, smokehouse, overseer's quarters, coach house, stables, and a 4-acre exhibit area called "George Washington, Pioneer Farmer."

A museum on the property exhibits Washington memorabilia, and details of the restoration are explained in the museum's annex; there's also a gift shop on the premises. You'll

want to walk around the grounds, see the wharf, the slave burial ground, the greenhouse a
nd gardens, and the tomb containing George and Martha Washington's sarcophagi.

There's no formal tour of the plantation, but attendants stationed throughout the
house and grounds provide brief orientations and answer questions. Avoid weekends and
holidays if possible during the heavy tourist months. A snack bar at the entrance serves
light fare, and you can also dine at the **Mount Vernon Inn,** near the entrance (☎ 703/
780-0011).

**Essentials:** Mount Vernon is 16 miles south of Washington via the George Washington Memorial Parkway (Va. 400). Tourmobile buses (☎ 203/554-5100) depart
Washington daily Apr–Oct (see "Getting Around," above). You can also get there on
the Spirit of Washington Cruises, which travel down the Potomac Mar–Dec from Pier
4, at 6th and Water streets SW (☎ 202/554-8000 for departure times). The house and
grounds are open daily Apr–Aug 8am–5pm; Mar, Sept, and Oct 9am–5pm; and Nov–
Feb 9am–4pm. Admission is $8 for adults, $7.50 for senior citizens, $4 for children
6 to 11, under 6 free. For more information, call ☎ 703/780-2000.

**OLD TOWN ALEXANDRIA**   Founded by a group of Scottish tobacco merchants,
the seaport town of Alexandria came into being in 1749. Today the original 60 acres
of lots in the hometown of George Washington and Robert E. Lee are the heart of **Old
Town,** a multi-million-dollar urban-renewal historic district. Though the present can
be seen in the abundance of quaint shops, boutiques, art galleries, and restaurants capi-
talizing on the volume of tourism, it's still easy to imagine yourself in colonial times.

Your first stop should be the **Alexandria Convention & Visitor Bureau** at Ramsay
House, 221 King St., at Fairfax Street (☎ 703/838-4200, or 703/838-5005 for a 24-
hour events recording), which is open daily from 9am to 5pm except January 1, Thanksgiving, and Christmas. Here you can obtain a self-guided walking tour map, brochures
about the area, a guide to antique stores, and a free 1-day parking permit. *Note:* Many
Alexandria attractions are closed on Monday.

The top attractions here include **Gadsby's Tavern,** 134 N. Royal St. at Cameron St.
(☎ 703/838-4242 museum, 703/548-1288 restaurant), consisting of two buildings
dating from circa 1770 and 1792, respectively. George Washington, Thomas Jefferson,
James Madison, and Lafayette all dined here, and today you can sample the authentic
colonial fare served in their time. The **Boyhood Home of Robert E. Lee,** 607 Oronoco
St. between St. Asaph and Washington streets (☎ 703/548-8454), provides a glimpse
into the gracious lifestyle of Alexandria's gentry. The **Lee-Fendall House,** 614 Oronoco
St. at Washington Street (☎ 703/548-1789), is another veritable Lee family museum
of furniture, heirlooms, and documents. The **Carlyle House,** 121 N. Fairfax St. at
Cameron Street (☎ 703/549-2997), is regarded as one of Virginia's most architecturally impressive 18th-century houses. **Christ Church,** 118 N. Washington St. at
Cameron Street (☎ 703/549-1450), would be an important national landmark even
if its two most distinguished members had not been Washington and Lee. It has been
in continuous use since 1773. The **Stabler-Leadbeater Apothecary Museum,**
105–107 S. Fairfax St. near King Street (☎ 703/836-3713), looks much as it did in
colonial times, its shelves lined with the most valuable collection of antique medicinal
bottles in the country.

Most attractions charge admission, but you can pick up a money-saving **block ticket**
for admission to Gadsby's Tavern, Lee's Boyhood Home, the Carlyle House, Stabler–
Leadbeater Apothecary Shop, and the Lee–Fendall House. It's available at those sites
and at the visitor bureau.

Plan to browse through Old Town's hundreds of charming boutiques, antique stores,
and gift shops selling everything from souvenir T-shirts to 18th-century reproductions.
Most are clustered on King and Cameron streets and their connecting cross streets.

**Essentials:** Old Town Alexandria is 5 miles south of Washington via the George Washington Memorial Parkway (Va. 400), which becomes King Street, Alexandria's main thoroughfare. Take the Metro yellow line to the King Street station, but be sure to get a transfer to a blue-and-gold DASH bus (AT2 or AT5 eastbound).

## 2   Shenandoah National Park & the Skyline Drive

Native Americans called the 200-mile-long valley in northwestern Virginia "Shenandoah," meaning Daughter of the Stars. Overlooking the valley from the spine of the Blue Ridge Mountains, the Shenandoah National Park provides spectacular landscapes and a plethora of hiking and riding trails. Running the length of the park along the Blue Ridge crest, the 105-mile-long Skyline Drive—one of America's great scenic roads—connects directly with the Blue Ridge Parkway, which continues south into North Carolina.

Although long and skinny, the park encompasses some 300 square miles of mountains, forests, waterfalls, and rock formations. It has more than 60 mountain peaks higher than 2,000 feet, with two exceeding 4,000 feet. More than two-fifths of the park is considered wilderness, with more than 100 species of trees and animals like deer, bear, bobcat, turkey, deer, and smaller animals.

The Skyline Drive provides the only road access to the park's visitor facilities and to more than 500 miles of glorious hiking and horse trails, including the Maine-to-Georgia Appalachian Trail.

In addition to the park, you won't want to miss the many picturesque small towns down in the valley. Many of them are steeped in American history dating to the early 1700s. George Washington surveyed the valley and carved his initials on Natural Bridge near Lexington. Winchester has preserved the office he occupied during the French and Indian Wars. During the Civil War, Stonewall Jackson left his home and work at Lexington's Virginia Military Institute to become one of the leading figures of the Confederacy. Major valley engagements included the legendary battle at New Market, when the entire VMI Corps of Cadets fought heroically. After the war, Robert E. Lee settled in Lexington as president of what is now Washington and Lee University, and both he and Jackson are buried there. And President Woodrow Wilson was born just before the war in Staunton. See the driving tour in this chapter for details.

### ESSENTIALS

**ARRIVING & DEPARTING**   Washington Dulles International Airport is the nearest large facility, 50 miles east of Front Royal via I-66. Amtrak has service directly to Staunton, but both the park and the valley are best seen by car, since local public transportation is almost nonexistent. Valley roads are open year-round, but wintertime snow and ice can close the Skyline Drive—and hence, Shenandoah National Park.

The park and Skyline Drive have four **entrances** that are open 24 hours a day. Most used is the northernmost **Front Royal** entry on U.S. 340 near the junction of I-81 and I-66, about 1 mile south of Front Royal and 90 miles west of Washington, D.C. Other entrances are at **Thornton Gap,** 33 miles south of Front Royal on U.S. 211; at **Swift Run Gap,** 68 miles south of Front Royal on U.S. 33; and at **Rockfish Gap,** 105 miles south of Front Royal at I-64 and U.S. 250. The Skyline Drive is marked with mile posts, starting at zero and increasing as you go south.

**VISITOR INFORMATION**   For free information, call or write **Shenandoah National Park,** Route 4, Box 348, Luray, VA 22835 (☎ 540/999-3500). The best source from which to purchase information is the **Shenandoah Natural History Association,** at that same address (☎ 540/999-3582). We highly recommend the association's

# Shenandoah National Park

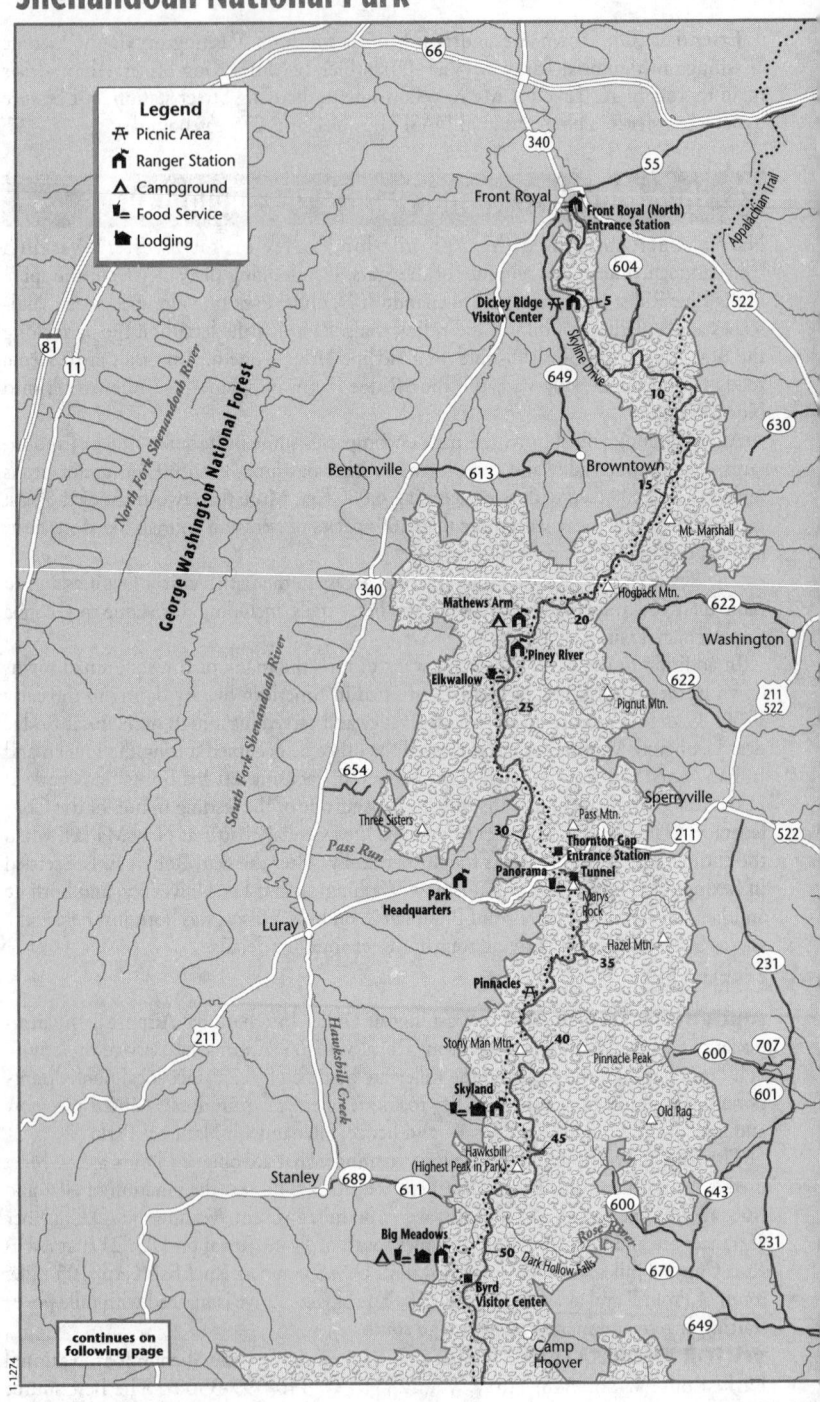

## Legend
🏕 Picnic Area
🏠 Ranger Station
△ Campground
🍴 Food Service
🏨 Lodging

66

340

55

Front Royal

Front Royal (North)
Entrance Station

Appalachian Trail

604

522

Dickey Ridge
Visitor Center

5

81

11

649

Skyline Drive

10

630

Bentonville

613

Browntown

15

George Washington National Forest

North Fork Shenandoah River

Mt. Marshall

340

Mathews Arm

Hogback Mtn.

622

20

Piney River

Washington

Elkwallow

Pignut Mtn.

622

211
522

25

South Fork Shenandoah River

654

Three Sisters

Pass Mtn.

Sperryville

30

Thornton Gap
Entrance Station

211

522

Pass Run

Panorama

Tunnel

Marys
Rock

Park
Headquarters

Hazel Mtn.

231

Luray

35

Pinnacles

707

Stony Man Mtn.

40

Pinnacle Peak

600

601

211

Skyland

Old Rag

Hawksbill Creek

45

Hawksbill
(Highest Peak in Park)

Stanley

689

611

600

643

231

Big Meadows

50

Dark Hollow Falls

Rose River

670

Byrd
Visitor Center

649

Camp
Hoover

continues on
following page

1-1274

198

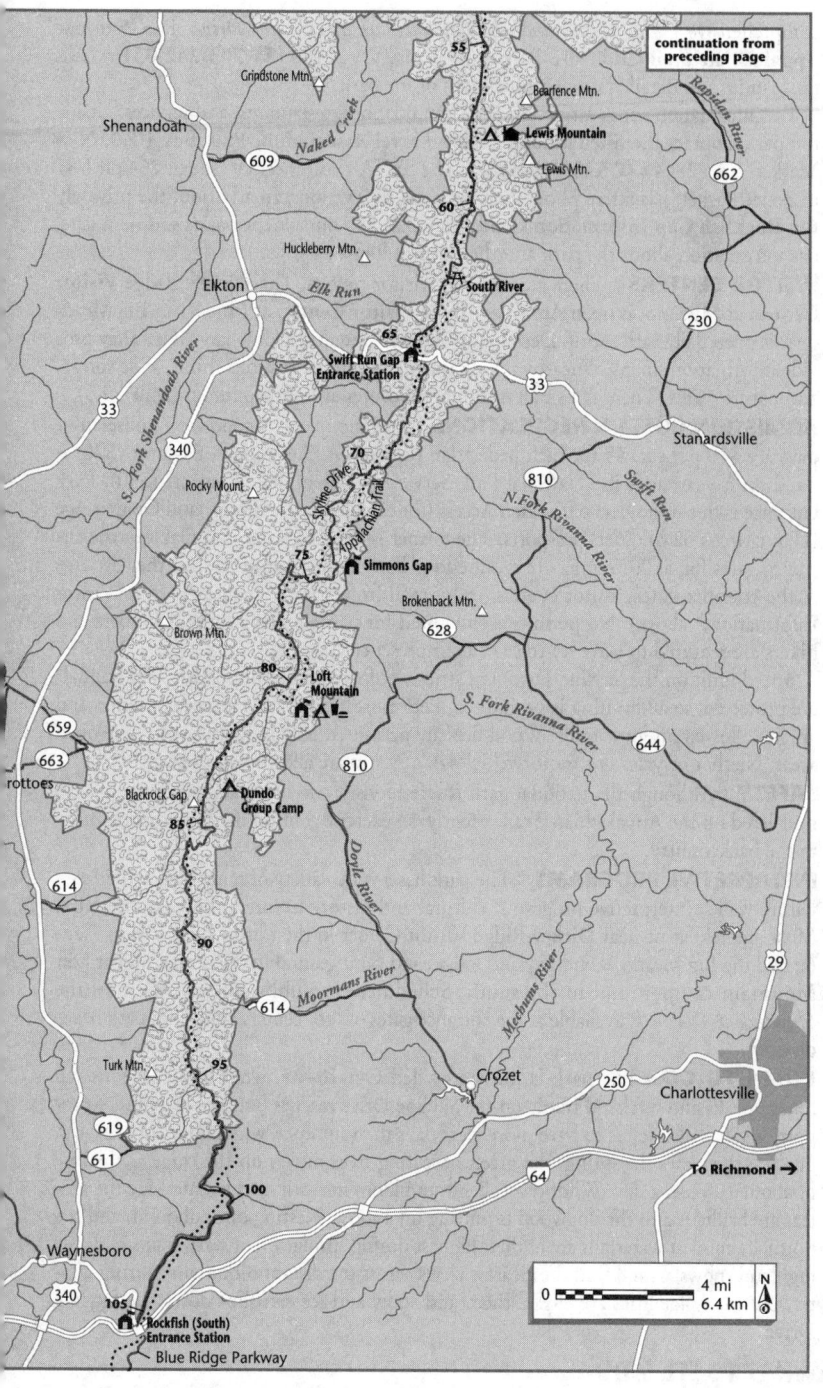

**continuation from preceding page**

Grindstone Mtn.

Bearfence Mtn.

Lewis Mountain

Shenandoah

609

Naked Creek

Lewis Mtn.

662

Rapidan River

60

Huckleberry Mtn.

Elk Run

South River

Elkton

65

Swift Run Gap
Entrance Station

33

230

Stanardsville

33

340

Rocky Mount.

70

Skyline Drive

Appalachian Trail

810

N.Fork Rivanna River

Swift Run

75

Simmons Gap

Brokenback Mtn.

628

Brown Mtn.

80

Loft
Mountain

S. Fork Rivanna River

644

659

663

rottoes

810

Blackrock Gap

Dundo
Group Camp

85

Doyle River

614

90

Mechums River

29

614

Moormans River

Turk Mtn.

95

Crozet

250

Charlottesville

619

611

64

To Richmond →

100

Waynesboro

340

105

Rockfish (South)
Entrance Station

Blue Ridge Parkway

0    4 mi
     6.4 km

N

199

comprehensive *Guide to Shenandoah National Park and Skyline Drive.* The **Potomac Appalachian Trail Club,** 118 Park St., Vienna, VA 22180 (☎ **703/242-0315**), sells trail guides and detailed topographic maps of the park.

For information about attractions, accommodations, restaurants, and services outside the park, contact the **Shenandoah Valley Travel Association,** P.O. Box 1040, New Market, VA 22844 (☎ **540/740-3132**). The SVTA's visitor center, at exit 264 off I-81 in New Market, has a free phone line for hotel reservations. In addition, the privately run **Rockfish Gap Information Center,** on U.S. 211 outside the park's southern gate, has information about the park and the surrounding area.

**VISITOR CENTERS**   There are two park visitor centers. The **Dickey Ridge Visitor Center,** at Mile 4.6, is open Apr–Nov. **Byrd Visitor Center,** at Mile 51 in Big Meadows, is open daily early April–Dec and on an intermittent schedule Jan–Mar. They provide information, maps of nearby hiking trails, interpretive exhibits, films, slide shows, and nature walks. There is a small information center at Loft Mountain (Mile 79.5).

**ADMISSION COSTS & REGULATIONS**   Entrance permits good for 7 consecutive days are $10 per car, $5 for each pedestrian or biker. A Shenandoah Passport ($20) is good for 1 year, as is the National Park Service's Golden Eagle Passport ($50). Park entrance is free to holders of Golden Access (for disabled U.S. citizens) and Golden Age (U.S. citizens 62 or older) passports. The former is free; the latter is available at the entrance gates for $10. Permits are required for backcountry camping, but they are free at the entrance gates, visitor centers, or by mail from park headquarters (see "Visitor Information," above). No permits are required for backcountry hiking. Campers and hikers are required to leave no trace of their presence.

Speed limit on the Skyline Drive is a strictly enforced 35 m.p.h. Plants and animals are protected, so all hunting is prohibited. Pets must be kept on a leash at all times and are not allowed on some trails. Wood fires are permitted only in fireplaces in developed areas. Neither bicycles nor motor vehicles of any sort are allowed on the trails.

**SAFETY**   Although the national park is safe to visit, two backpacking campers were murdered on the Appalachian Trail recently, so exercise caution if you're overnighting in the backcountry.

**INTERPRETIVE PROGRAMS**   The park has a wide variety of ranger-led activities—nature walks, interpretive programs, cultural and history lectures, and campfire talks. Most are held at or near Dickey Ridge Visitor Center in the north; Byrd Visitor Center and the Big Meadows and Skyland lodges and campground in the center; and at Loft Mountain campground in the south. Schedules are published seasonally in the *Shenandoah Overlook,* available at the entrance gates, visitor centers, and from park headquarters.

**WHEN TO GO**   The park is most crowded Oct 10–25, when the gorgeous fall foliage peaks and weekend traffic on the Skyline Drive reaches bumper-to-bumper proportions. Fall also tends to have more clear days than summer, when lingering haze can obscure the views. In spring, the green of leafing trees moves up the ridge at the rate of about 100 feet a day. Wildflowers begin to bloom in April, and by late May the azaleas are brilliant and the dogwood is putting on a show. Nesting birds abound, and the normally modest waterfalls are at their highest during spring, when warm rains melt the highland snows. You'll find the clearest views across the distant mountains during winter, but many facilities are closed then, and snow and ice can shut down the Skyline Drive.

## WHAT TO SEE & DO

Unless you're caught in heavy traffic on fall foliage weekends, you can drive the entire length of the Skyline Drive in about 3 hours without stopping. But why rush? Give yourself at least a day for this drive, so lovely are the views from its 75 designated scenic overlooks. Stop for lunch at a wayside snack bar, a lodge, or one of seven picnic grounds. Get out of your car and take at least a short hike down one of the hollows to a waterfall.

If you have only 1 day, head directly to the Central District between Thornton Gap and Swift Run Gap, the most developed but also the most interesting part of the park. It has the highest mountains, best views, nearly half of the park's 500 miles of hiking trails, and the park's only stables and overnight accommodations. Most visitors make Big Meadows or Skyland lodges their base of operations for stays of more than a day, but if you plan to do this, *place your lodge reservations early* (see "Accommodations," below).

**HIKING**   The number-1 outdoor activity here is hiking. The park's 112 hiking trails total more than 500 miles, varying in length from short walks to a 95-mile segment of the **Appalachian Trail** running the entire length of the park. Access to the trails is marked along the Skyline Drive. There are parking lots at the major trailheads, but these quickly fill on weekends. We strongly recommend that you obtain maps and trail descriptions before setting out—even before leaving home if possible (see "Visitor Information," above). Free maps of each trail are available at the visitor centers, which also sell the topographic maps.

At the minimum, take one of the short hikes on nature trails at Dickey Ridge Visitor Center, Byrd Visitor Center/Big Meadows, and Lewis Mountain. For an easy excursion, a 1-mile trial at Mile 50.7 near the Byrd Visitor Center goes to **Dark Hollow Falls,** the closest cascade to the Skyline Drive. There's also an excellent 1.6-mile nature hike at Stoney Man (Mile 41.7).

Among the more popular trails are **White Oak Canyon,** beginning at Mile 42.6 just south of Skyland. This steep gorge has been described as the park's "scenic gem." The 5-mile trail goes through an area of wild beauty, passing no less than six waterfalls and cascades. The upper reaches to the first falls are relatively easy, but farther down the track can be rough and rocky.

**FISHING**   The park's streams are short, with limited fishing. Only native brook trout may be taken, and some streams are "catch-and-release," meaning you must release your catch back into the water. Only artificial lures are allowed, and you must get a Virginia fishing license (available at the entry gates, visitor centers, wayside facilities, and camp stores inside the park, or at sporting goods stores outside). The park publishes a free recreational fishing brochure and an annual list of streams open for fishing; both are available from park headquarters or at the visitor centers.

**HORSEBACK RIDING**   Horses are allowed only on trails marked with yellow, and even then only via guided expeditions with **Skyland Stables** (☎ 540/999-2210), on the Skyland Lodge grounds (Mile 41.8). Rides cost $10 per hour. Pony rides for children are $5 per 30 minutes. Children must be 58 inches tall to ride the horses. The stables operate Apr–Nov, depending on the spring and fall weather.

**CAMPING**   The park has three campgrounds with tent and trailer sites: **Big Meadows** (Mile 51.2), **Lewis Mountain** (Mile 57.5), and **Loft Mountain** (Mile 79.5). The Lewis Mountain and Loft Mountain campgrounds are on a first-come, first-served basis at $14 per site per night. They are open mid-May to late October. Big Meadows is open early April through October, and reservations can be made up to 6 months in advance by writing or calling DESTINET, P.O. Box 85705, San Diego, CA 92138 (☎ 800/365-CAMP). If you phone in your reservation, use SHEN as the four-letter designator when asked. Big Meadows charges $16 per night.

## ACCOMMODATIONS

The park concessionaire is **Aramark Virginia Sky-Line Co.,** P.O. Box 727, Luray, VA 22835 (☎ 800/999-4714 or 540/743-5108), which operates all lodging, food, and other services for park visitors. Reservations, especially for the peak fall season, should be made with Aramark as much as a year in advance. Aramark also rents **housekeeping cottages** at Lewis Mountain. The **Shenandoah Valley Travel Association,** P.O. Box 1040, New Market, VA 22844 (☎ **540/740-3132**), provides information about accommodations and private campgrounds outside the park. There is no shortage of chain motels along I-81 in Winchester, New Market, Harrisonburg, Staunton, and Lexington.

**Big Meadows Lodge.** *Mile 51.2.* ☎ *800/999-4714 or 540/999-2221. 92 rms. $65–$105 main lodge; $79–$102 motel; $112–$122 suite; $67–$76 cabin rms. Extra person $5. Highest rates in Oct. Weekday packages available off-season. MC, V. Closed Dec–Mar.* Accommodations at Big Meadows comprise rooms in the main lodge and in rustic cabins, and multiunit lodges with modern suites, many of them with spectacular westward views over the valley. The dining room features traditional regional dishes like fried chicken, mountain trout, and country ham. During the season live entertainment keeps the Taproom busy. You won't have phones, TVs, or air-conditioners in your units.

**Cabins at Brookside.** *U.S. 211 East, Luray, VA 22835.* ☎ *800/299-2655 or 540/743-5698. 8 cabins. $70–$180 double. AE, DC, DISC, MC, V.* The closest privately owned accommodation to the park, this 1940s roadside service station/motel has been remodeled into a collection of cozy, log-look cabins with comfortable Williamsburg-style furnishings throughout. Although they lie along busy U.S. 211 near the park headquarters, the rear of the cabins open to decks or sunrooms overlooking a bubbling brook, and road noise dies down after dark. Three units have hot tubs, four have fireplaces, and one has a kitchen (the others, refrigerators). The rustic Brookside Restaurant on the premises serves inexpensive home cooking.

**Skyland Lodge.** *Mile 41.8.* ☎ *800/999-4714 or 540/999-2211. 151 rms, 20 cabins, 6 suites. Doubles $83–$102 in lodge, $48–$104 in cabins, $112–$160 in suites. Extra person $5. Highest rates in Oct. Weekday packages available off-season. AE, DC, DISC, MC, V. Closed Nov–Apr.* Atop the highest point on the drive, Skyland offers rustic wood-paneled cabins as well as modern motel-type accommodations with wonderful views. Some of the buildings are dark-brown clapboard, others fieldstone, and all nestle among the trees. The central building has a lobby with a huge stone fireplace, TV (also in some, but not all, rooms), and comfortable seating areas. Complete breakfast, lunch, and dinner menus are offered at reasonable prices. Dinner entrees include vegetarian lasagna, steak, roast turkey, and pan-fried rainbow trout. There's a fully stocked taproom.

## DINING

In addition to the lodges, there are daytime restaurants and snack bars at Elkwallow Wayside (Mile 24.1), Panorama–Thornton Gap (Mile 31.5), and Loft Mountain (Mile 79.5). Picnic areas with tables, fireplaces, water fountains, and restrooms are at Dickey Ridge (Mile 4.6), Elkwallow (Mile 24.1), Pinnacles (Mile 36.7), Big Meadows (Mile 51), Lewis Mountain (Mile 57.5), South River (Mile 62.8), and Loft Mountain (Mile 79.5).

## 3 Williamsburg & Colonial Virginia

The United States can trace its roots to the narrow peninsula between the James and York rivers in southeastern Virginia. In 1607 the English established their first permanent North American colony at Jamestown. Colonial legislators meeting in Williamsburg some 150 years later sewed the seeds of rebellion by railing against "taxation without representation." And in 1781 those leaders' dreams of independence became reality with George Washington's convincing victory over Lord Cornwallis at Yorktown.

Today you can virtually relive that early history in the beautifully restored 18th-century town of Colonial Williamsburg, see the remaining traces of the Jamestown colony, and walk Washington's ramparts at Yorktown. And along the James River you can tour the magnificent tobacco plantations that created Virginia's first great wealth.

Indeed, Colonial Williamsburg is unique even in history-revering Virginia. Here women wear long dresses and ruffled caps, men don powdered wigs, colonial fare is served in restaurants, blacksmiths' and harnessmakers' shops line cobblestone streets, and the local militia drills on Market Square. He may be a modern actor, but your casual conversation with "Thomas Jefferson" about the rights of man will seem almost real.

The area today is one of America's family vacation meccas, and not only for the great history lesson it teaches us and our children. Busch Gardens Williamsburg brims with entertainment and thrilling rides, while Water Country USA beckons with wet and wild rides and attractions. And there's world-class shopping in authentic colonial shops and numerous modern factory outlet stores. With so much to see and do—for all ages—you'll find this "Historic Triangle" a wonderful place to explore.

## ARRIVING & DEPARTING

**ARRIVING**   Newport News/Williamsburg Airport (☎ 757/877-0221) is 14 miles east of Williamsburg, but most flights to the area come into **Norfolk International Airport** (☎ 757/857-3351) or **Richmond International Airport** (☎ 757/226-3052), both of which are about 45 miles from town via I-64.

Amtrak trains (☎ 800/872-7245) and **Greyhound/Trailways** buses (☎ 800/231-2222) stop at a single station at Boundary and Lafayette streets, within walking distance of the historic area.

## ESSENTIALS

**VISITOR INFORMATION**   The **Colonial Williamsburg Visitor Center,** P.O. Box 1776, Williamsburg, VA 23187 (☎ 800/HISTORY or 757/220-7645), offers maps and guidebooks, tours, and information on lodgings, dining, and evening activities. Most important, the center is where you park and buy your **tickets** for the dozens of attractions that make up Colonial Williamsburg (see "What to See & Do," below). The center is off U.S. 60 Bypass, just east of Va. 132 (take exit 238 off I-64). Bright-green signs point the way from all access roads to Williamsburg. It's open 365 days a year, Memorial Day to Labor Day 9am–8pm, the rest of the year 9am–5pm.

In addition, visitor information and one of the best maps of the area is available from the **Williamsburg Area Convention & Visitor Bureau,** 201 Penniman Rd., Williamsburg, VA 23187 (☎ 800/368-6511 or 757/253-0192).

## GETTING AROUND

Cars are not allowed in the Historic Area daily 8am–10pm. Colonial Williamsburg ticket holders can use shuttle buses from the visitor center to and around the Historic Area daily 8:45am–10pm. There's also a footpath from the visitor center to the Historic Area. You can ride bicycles in the Historic Area; Williamburg Lodge and Williamsburg Woodlands (see "Accommodations," below) rent them Apr–Oct for $5 an hour, $18.50 per day. Horse-drawn carriage rides depart from several Historic Area attractions; they last 15 minutes and cost $7 for ticket holders, $12 for everyone else.

## WHAT TO SEE & DO

Williamsburg was founded in 1699, when the beleaguered Virginia Colony abandoned the mosquito-infested swamp at Jamestown for a planned colonial city 8 miles inland. Royal Gov. Francis Nicholson laid out the new capital with grid streets, public greens, and a half acre of land for every house on 99-foot-wide Duke of Gloucester Street, the main drag. People grew vegetables and raised livestock on their lots. Most houses were whitewashed wood frame, and kitchens were in separate structures to keep the houses from burning down.

Williamsburg played a major role as the colony's seat of royal government and later as a hotbed of revolution. Many of the seminal events leading up to the Declaration of Independence occurred here. During the Revolution, Williamsburg served as the wartime capital for 4 years. Washington planned the siege of Yorktown in George Wythe's house.

After the state government moved to Richmond in 1780, Williamsburg remained a quaintly charming Virginia town for another century and a half, unique only in that it changed so little. As late as 1926, the colonial town plan was virtually intact, including numerous original 18th-century buildings. Then with money from John D. Rockefeller Jr., restoration of Williamsburg began. Today the **Historic Area** covers 173 acres of the original 220-acre town and encompasses 88 preserved and restored houses, shops, taverns, public buildings, and outbuildings that survived to the 20th century. More than 500 additional buildings and smaller structures have been rebuilt on their original sites after extensive archeological, architectural, and historical research.

Shops, crafts, and trade exhibits throughout the Historic Area demonstrate numerous 18th-century crafts that were a facet of everyday life in the preindustrial era. Interesting in a morbid way is the apothecary shop, where sore feet were treated with leeches between the toes, a headache with leeches across the forehead, and a sore throat with leeches on the neck.

**TICKETS**    You can stroll the Historic Area streets for free, but you'll need a ticket to enter most attractions and to use the shuttle bus. They are available at the visitor center and at **ticket booths** on Duke of Gloucester Street at the Palace Green and at the Merchants Square shops, on Henry Street at Duke of Gloucester Street.

A **Basic Admission Ticket** admits you to all attractions except the museums and Carter's Grove plantation for 1 day. It costs $25 for adults, $15 for children 6–12. A much better buy is a **Basic Plus Ticket,** admitting you to all the attractions and museums except Basset Hall for 2 consecutive days. It costs $29 for adults, $17 for children 6–12. If you have longer to stay, a **Patriot's Pass** lets you into all attractions and museums for 1 year and includes special-interest guided tours and exhibits. It costs $33 for adults, $19 for children.

A **Museums Ticket** combines the Wallace Gallery, the Folk Art Center, and Bassett Hall. These cost $10 for adults, $6.50 for children for 1 day; $17 for adults and $10 for children for 1 year. You can also buy tickets just to the Governor's Palace ($17 per person) and Carter's Grove ($15 adults, $9 children). **Evening Program Tickets** cost $10 per person, $5 for Patriot's Pass holders. Children under 6 are admitted free to all attractions.

American Express, Diners' Club, Discover, MasterCard, and Visa credit cards are accepted at all Colonial Williamsburg ticket outlets, attractions, hotels, and taverns.

**HOURS**    Historic Area attractions normally are open Apr–Oct daily 9am–6pm, Nov–Mar daily 9:30am–4:30pm. Precise hours—and closing days for some attractions—are given in the *Colonial Williamsburg Visitor's Companion,* a tabloid newspaper pubished weekly and available free at the visitor center and ticket offices. The taverns are open evenings, and you can stroll the streets anytime.

**HISTORIC AREA ATTRACTIONS**    Duke of Gloucester Street still is the principal east–west artery of the Historic Area. The Capitol building sits at its eastern end, the Wren building of the College of William and Mary at the western end. Except for Carter's Grove, Historic Area sights are on or a block off Duke of Gloucester Street and can be visited on foot.

# Williamsburg

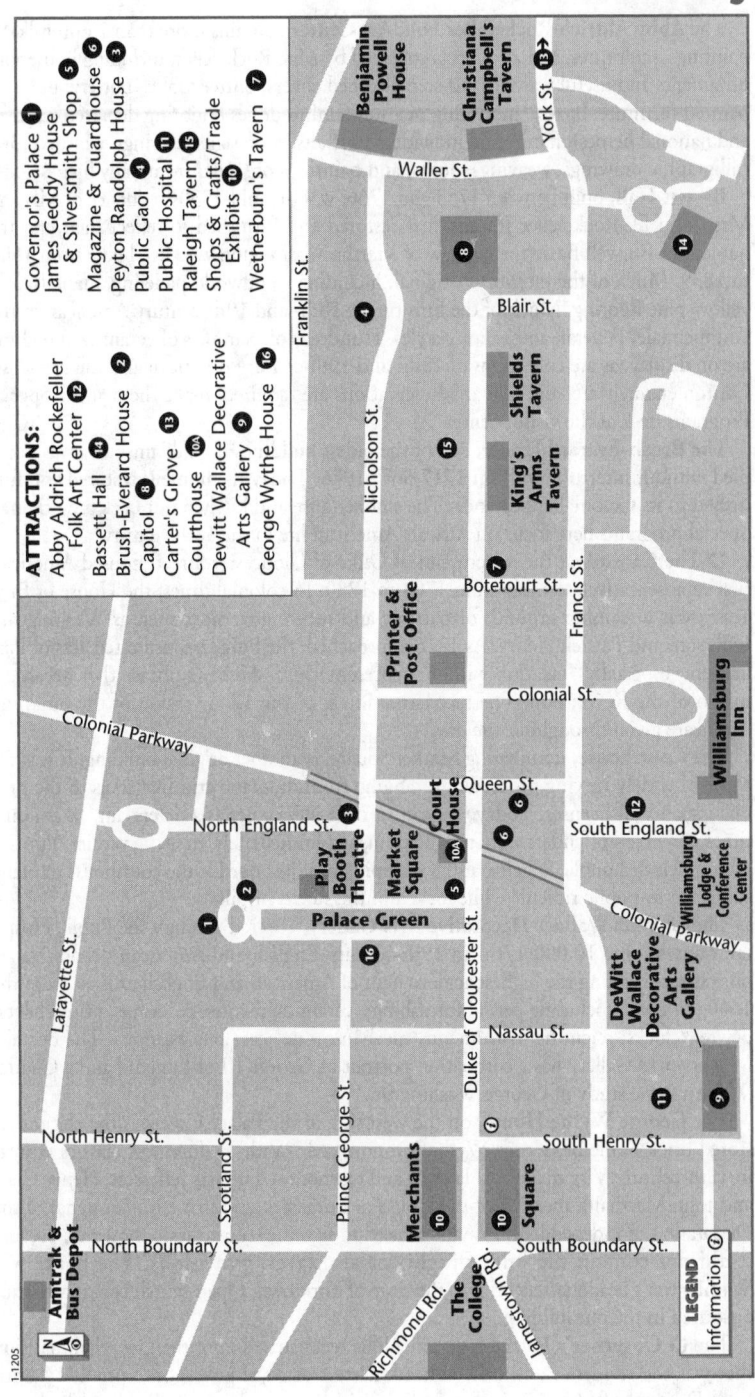

ATTRACTIONS:

Abby Aldrich Rockefeller Folk Art Center 12
Bassett Hall 14
Brush-Everard House 2
Capitol 8
Carter's Grove 13
Courthouse 10A
Dewitt Wallace Decorative Arts Gallery 9
George Wythe House 16

Governor's Palace 1
James Geddy House & Silversmith Shop 5
Magazine & Guardhouse 6
Peyton Randolph House 3
Public Gaol 4
Public Hospital 11
Raleigh Tavern 15
Shops & Crafts/Trade Exhibits 10
Wetherburn's Tavern 7

LEGEND
Information i

1-1205

The **Abby Aldrich Rockefeller Folk Art Center** contains more than 2,600 folk-art paintings, sculptures, and art objects collected by Mrs. Rockefeller, including household ornaments and useful wares (hand-stenciled bed covers, butter molds, pottery, utensils, painted furniture, boxes), mourning pictures (embroideries honoring departed relatives and national heroes), family and individual portraits, shop signs, carvings, whittled toys, calligraphic drawings, weavings, quilts, and paintings of scenes from daily life.

**Bassett Hall,** built between 1753 and 1766, was the mid-1930s residence of Mr. and Mrs. John D. Rockefeller Jr., and it is restored and furnished to reflect their era. It's named for Burwell Bassett, a nephew of Martha Washington who lived here from 1800 to 1839. Much of the interior is original, including woodwork, paneling, mantels, and yellow-pine flooring. Much of the furniture is 18th- and 19th-century American in the Chippendale, Federal, and Empire styles. Hundreds of examples of ceramics and china are on display, as are collections of 18th- and 19th-century American and English glass, Canton enamelware, and folk art. Reservations are required; make them at the Special Programs desk at the visitor center.

The **Brush-Everard House,** one of the oldest buildings in Williamsburg, was occupied without interruption from 1717 until 1946. Today the home is restored and furnished to its Colonial appearance. The smokehouse and kitchen out back are original. Special programs here focus on African-American life in the 18th century.

✪ **The Capitol,** at the eastern end of Duke of Gloucester Street, housed America's first representative assembly from 1704 to 1780. In colonial times, the House of Burgesses was a training ground for patriots and future governors such as Washington, Jefferson, and Patrick Henry. As 1776 approached, the burgesses protested acts of Parliament, especially "taxation without representation," Henry's phrase that became a motto of the Revolution. The reconstruction is of the 1704 version of the building. Tours are given throughout the day.

The **Courthouse,** dominating Market Square, is another original building. It was the scene of widely varying proceedings, ranging from dramatic criminal trials to the prosaic issuance of licenses. Today you can sit on a jury or act as a defendant. In colonial times convicted offenders were usually punished immediately after the verdict. Punishments included public flogging at the whipping post just outside the courthouse or being subjected to public ridicule while locked in the stocks or pillory.

The **DeWitt Wallace Decorative Arts Gallery,** entered through the Public Hospital, houses some 10,000 17th- to 19th-century English and American decorative art objects representing the highest achievement of American and English artisans from the 1640s to 1800, including period furnishings, ceramics, textiles, paintings, prints, silver, pewter, clocks, scientific instruments, mechanical devices, and weapons. The upstairs Masterworks Gallery has a coronation portrait of George III of England and a Charles Willson Peale study of George Washington.

The **George Wythe House,** on the west side of the Palace Green, is the elegant restored brick home of George Wythe (pronounced "With")—foremost classics scholar in 18th-century Virginia, noted lawyer, and teacher (of Thomas Jefferson, Henry Clay, and John Marshall), member of the House of Burgesses, and first Virginia signer of the Declaration of Independence. Wythe refused to sign the Constitution, however, because it did not contain the Bill of Rights or antislavery provisions. The house was Washington's headquarters prior to the siege of Yorktown. Open-hearth cooking is demonstrated in the outbuilding.

The ✪ **Governor's Palace** is a meticulous reconstruction of the Georgian mansion that was the residence and official headquarters of royal governors from 1714 until Lord Dunmore fled in 1775, thus ending British rule in Virginia. By then, the king's representative was little more than a functionary of great prestige and little power.

Given continuously throughout the day, tours wind up in the 10 acres of formal gardens.

The **James Geddy House & Silversmith Shop,** built in 1762, is an original building. Unlike the fancier abodes you'll visit, the Geddy House has no wallpaper or oil paintings; a mirror and spinet from England, however, indicate relative affluence. Craftsmen cast silver, pewter, bronze, and brass items at a forge on the premises.

The **Magazine & Guardhouse,** a sturdy octagonal brick building, was constructed in 1715 to house ammunition and arms for the defense of the British colony and has survived intact to the present day. The high wall and guardhouse were built during the French and Indian War to protect the magazine's 60,000 pounds of gunpowder. Today the building is stocked with 18th-century equipment: British-made flintlock muskets, cannons and cannonballs, barrels of powder, bayonets, and drums, the latter for communication purposes.

The **Peyton Randolph House** was home to one of the most prominent—and wealthy—families in colonial Virginia. Sir John Randolph was the only colonial-born Virginian ever to be knighted. His son, Peyton, was unanimously elected president of 1774's First Continental Congress in Philadelphia. Thomas Jefferson purchased the Randolph family books at auction; they eventually became the nucleus of the Library of Congress in Washington, D.C. Actually two connected homes, the house dates to 1715. Robertson's Windmill out back is a type of post mill popular in the early 18th century.

The **Public Gaol** didn't coddle criminals in the 18th century, for punishments included not only public ridicule (stocks and pillories) but also whipping, branding, mutilation, and hanging—not only for murder and treason but for burglary, forgery, and horse stealing. Beds were rudimentary piles of straw; leg irons, shackles, and chains were used frequently. During the Revolution, redcoats, spies, traitors, and deserters were locked up here. The building is restored to its 1720s appearance.

The **Public Hospital** opened in 1773 as America's first lunatic asylum. On a self-guided tour, you'll see a 1773 cell with a filthy straw-filled mattress on the floor, ragged blanket, and manacles. The so-called Moral Management Period (1820–65) saw patients treated with kindness, especially during the administration of John Minson Galt II (1841–62), who created the carpentry and shoemaking shops, a games room, and sewing, spinning, and weaving rooms.

The **Raleigh Tavern** is the most famous of Williamsburg's historic watering holes. After the Governor's Palace, it was the social and political hub of the town, especially during crowded Publick Times when the legislature was in session. Washington, Jefferson, and others met here in 1774 to discuss revolution, and Patrick Henry's troops treated their commander to a farewell dinner at the Raleigh in 1776. The original tavern was destroyed by fire in 1859; the present structure was reconstructed on the original site in 1932.

**Wetherburn's Tavern,** though less important than the Raleigh, also was mobbed during Publick Times and frequently served as a center of sedition and a rendezvous of Revolutionary patriots. The yellow-pine floors are original, so you can actually walk in Washington's footsteps. Twenty-five-minute tours are given throughout the day.

**CARTER'S GROVE**   Although it's 8 miles east of the Historic Area on U.S. 60, ✪ **Carter's Grove** is administered by the Colonial Williamsburg Foundation. This magnificent James River plantation has been continuously occupied since 1755. It's also the site of the "lost" village of Wolstenholme Towne, destroyed by American Indians in 1622. Robert "King" Carter, Virginia's wealthiest planter, purchased the property for his daughter, Elizabeth. Her son, Carter Burwell, built the beautiful Georgian mansion between 1751 and 1754. Legend says that southern belles Mary Cary and Rebecca Burwell rejected marriage proposals here from George Washington and Thomas

Jefferson, respectively. The **Winthrop Rockefeller Archaeology Museum,** nestled into a hillside southeast of the Carter's Grove mansion, identifies and interprets the Martin's Hundred clues and artifacts discovered on the site of the partially reconstructed Wolstenholme Towne.

**THEME PARKS**   When the kids have seen enough history, you can keep them occupied at the two nearby amusement parks that help make Williamsburg a major family destination.

   ✪ **Busch Gardens Williamsburg.** *One Busch Gardens Blvd.* ☎ *757/253-3350. Admission $31 adults, $24 children 3–6 for unlimited rides, shows, and attractions (children 2 and under free). Parking $5. Open late Mar–early Oct. Hours vary considerably, so call ahead. From Williamsburg, go 3 miles east on U.S. 60.* This 360-acre family entertainment park is historically themed, with attractions in nine authentically detailed 17th-century European hamlets. Rides include the world's tallest and fastest inverted roller coaster, but most rides and attractions are geared to younger visitors. Admission includes unlimited rides and top-quality musical entertainment, bird shows, ice-skating revues, and more.

   **Water Country USA.** *Va. 199.* ☎ *757/253-3350. Admission (including parking) $23 adults, $16 children 3–6, free for children 2 and under. Open mid-May–mid-Sept. Hours vary greatly, so call ahead. Take Va. 199 to I-64 and follow the signs.* A wet and sometimes wild break from the summer heat, this water-oriented amusement park features exciting water slides, rides, and entertainment set to a 1950s and '60s surf theme. The Big Daddy Falls takes the entire family on a colossal river rafting adventure, or you can twist and turn on giant inner tubes through flumes, tunnels, water "explosions," and down a waterfall to "splashdown."

**BEST BETS FOR KIDS**   In addition to the excitement at Busch Gardens Williamsburg and Water Country USA, families can enjoy many hands-on activities in the Historic Area. At the **Powell House,** on Waller Street near Christiana Campbell's Tavern, families can participate in keeping a garden and managing a kitchen; here kids can dress up in 18th-century style. Another fun activity is at the **Governor's Palace,** where the dancing master gives lessons. During the summer kids can "enlist" in the militia and practice marching and drilling (we still have a snapshot of us holding a flintlock back in the 1950s). Inquire at the visitor center for special themed tours in areas of your children's specific interest. You don't have to be a guest of the Williamsburg Inn (see "Accommodations," below) to take your kids to **Felicity's Tea,** a children's version of high English tea, daily from 3:30 to 5pm in the inn's Regency Lounge.

**SHOPPING**   Give yourself plenty of browsing time along **Duke of Gloucester Street** in the Historic Area, where present-day craftspeople ply the trades of our 18th-century forefathers, offering hand-wrought silver jewelry at the Sign of the Golden Ball, hats at the Mary Dickenson shop, pomanders to ward off the plague at McKenzie's Apothecary, hand-woven linens at Prentis Store, books bound in leather and hand-printed newspapers at the post office, gingerbread cakes at the Raleigh Tavern Bake Shop, and everything from foodstuffs to fishhooks at Greenhow and Tarpley's, a general store. The **Craft House** in Merchants Square and near the Abby Aldrich Rockefeller Folk Art Center features exquisite works by master craftspeople and authentic reproductions of colonial furnishings.

   The modern "shoppes" in **Merchants Square,** at the west end of Duke of Gloucester Street, offer a wide range of merchandise: antiquarian books and prints, 18th-century–style floral arrangements, candy, toys, handcrafted pewter and silver items, needlework supplies, and oriental rugs. You can also find a camera shop, upscale clothing stores, and a drugstore offering aspirin in lieu of leeches. Merchants Square has free 2-hour parking for its customers.

The biggest merchandising draws are in Lightfoot, 5 to 7 miles west of town on Richmond Road (U.S. 60). Leading the list is the **Williamsburg Pottery Factory** (☎ 757/564-3326), a 200-acre shopping complex with more than 31 tin buildings offering plenty of quality and plenty of kitsch from all over the world: Christmas decorations, garden furnishings, lamps, art prints, dried and silk flowers, luggage, linens, baskets, hardware, glassware, cookware, candles, wine, toys, crafts, clothing, food, jewelry, plants—and yes, even pottery. It even has its own **Pottery Factory Outlets,** with discount offerings of 20 major manufacturers.

In fact, Lightfoot is a major destination for outlet shoppers, with every manufacturer represented at **Berkeley Commons Outlet Center** and **Williamsburg Outlet Mall,** both on U.S. 60.

Two unusual shops are in Norge, on U.S. 60 west of Lightfoot. The **Williamsburg Doll Factory** (☎ 757/564-9703) has limited-edition porcelain collector's dolls. You can observe the doll-making process and even buy parts to make your own. Other items sold here are stuffed animals, clowns, and books on dolls. At the **Williamsburg Soap & Candle Company,** another quarter-mile west on U.S. 60 (☎ 757/564-3354), you can buy an incredible variety of candles and watch them being made. There are interesting shops and an inexpensive country-style restaurant on the premises.

## ACCOMMODATIONS

Williamsburg has nearly 10,000 hotel rooms, but you're well advised to reserve in advance, especially during the summer months and on holiday weekends. The **Williamsburg Hotel/Motel Association** (☎ 800/446-9244 or 757/220-3330) will make reservations in any price range. It's a free service.

**COLONIAL WILLIAMSBURG HOTELS** The Colonial Williamsburg Foundation operates the following establishments within or adjacent to the Historic Area. For reservations, write P.O. Box 1776, Williamsburg, VA 23187, or call the visitor center reservations service (☎ 800/HISTORY). Ask about special packages, which represent the best deals here. Room rates depend not only on the season but on special events such as conventions. They can vary greatly from day to day, which is another reason to book early.

All guests at these properties are invited to a special 2-hour guided walking tour of the Historic Area.

**Governor's Inn.** *Va. 132 (Henry St.) (P.O. Box 1776), Williamsburg, VA 23187.* ☎ *800/HISTORY or 757/229-1000. 200 rms. $50–$90. AE, DC, DISC, MC, V. Free parking. Closed Jan–Feb.* The foundation recently took over this contemporary motel and completely renovated and redecorated it. Furnishings are clean and bright. A new wing was added as well as an outdoor swimming pool. It's near the visitor center on Va. 132, an extension of North Henry Street.

✪ **Williamsburg Inn.** *136 Francis St. (P.O. Box 1776), Williamsburg, VA 23187.* ☎ *800/HISTORY or 757/229-1000. Fax 757/220-7096. 102 rms. $235–$300 double main building; $125–$400 in taverns, houses, and Providence Hall. AE, DC, DISC, MC, V.* With three top courses, this rambling white-brick Regency-style inn is a distinguished golf resort as well as luxurious hotel. Exquisite rooms have Regency reproductions, fresh flowers, and French-milled soap. Another 84 units are in charming colonial houses and taverns; they are less expensive and can accommodate 2 to 12. Rooms in the adjacent, modern Providence Hall are furnished in a blend of 18th-century and oriental styles. The inn's lounge offers cocktails, light suppers, entertainment, and hosts Felicity's Tea for children. The dining room features fine classic American cuisine. Rates include complimentary tea and baby-sitting. Facilities include croquet, a fitness center, lawn bowling, two outdoor pools, eight tennis courts, and a nature trail.

**Williamsburg Lodge.** *S. England St. (P.O. Box 1776), Williamsburg, VA 23187.* ☎ *800/HISTORY or 757/229-1000. Fax 757/220-7685. 315 rms. $105–$250 double. Extra person $12. Children under 18 stay free in parents' room. AE, DC, DISC, MC, V.* The Lodge offers a pleasantly rustic, lodgelike interior and all the sports facilities of the nearby Williamsburg Inn. Contemporary accommodations are warm and homey, with folk art and handcrafted furniture. Some have fireplaces. The dining room overlooks a garden with a fountain. Guests can enjoy a golf course, pool, fitness center with indoor lap pool, and aerobic classes.

**Williamsburg Woodlands.** *Va. 132 off U.S. 60 Bypass (P.O. Box 1776), Williamsburg, VA 23187.* ☎ *800/HISTORY or 757/229-1000. Fax 757/220-7941. 315 rms. $70–$115 double. Extra person $8. Children under 18 stay free in parents' room. AE, DC, DISC, MC, V.* Adjacent to the visitor center, the Woodlands offers a lot for your money, with cheerful rooms, a restaurant, and a grill room with cafeteria-style breakfast and lunch. You will also find a jogging path, golf putting green, miniature golf course, shuffleboard, playground, horseshoes, volleyball, badminton, swimming pool and sundeck, and toddler's pool.

**OTHER ACCOMMODATIONS**   Most national motel chains are represented here, most on Richmond Road and Chelsea Bypass (both U.S. 60), a short drive west of the Historic Area. The local **Motel 6,** 3030 Richmond Rd. (☎ **800/466-8356** or 757/ 565-3433), is one of the largest and best members of this budget chain, but you should reserve far in advance. Rates are $32–$42 single; $6 each additional adult.

**Carolynn Court.** *1446 Richmond Rd., Williamsburg, VA 23185.* ☎ *800/666-5880 or 757/229-6666. Fax 757/220-9917. 65 rms. $32–$52 double. Extra person $7. AE, CB, DC, DISC, MC, V.* This older, family-owned motel offers comfort at budget prices within 10 minutes of the Historic Area. Plain but comfortable rooms are clean and inviting, with wood-paneled walls. All rooms face the courtyard and outdoor pool.

**Courtyard by Marriott.** *470 McLaws Circle, Williamsburg, VA 23185.* ☎ *800/ 321-2211 or 757/221-0700. Fax 757/221-0741. 142 rms, 9 suites. $49–$119 double; $89–$169 suite. Children under 18 stay free in parents' room. AE, CB, DC, DISC, MC, V. From Williamsburg, follow U.S. 60 east about 2 miles to the right on McLaws Circle.* This member of the fine chain designed by business travelers (and very comfortable for the rest of us) surrounds a courtyard with a pool. Rooms feature large desks, separate seating areas, irons and boards, and piping-hot faucets for instant coffee or tea. There is a breakfast buffet in the lobby. Facilities include an exercise room with Jacuzzi.

**Kingsmill Resort.** *1010 Kingsmill Rd., Williamsburg, VA 23185.* ☎ *800/832-5665 or 757/253-1703. Fax 757/253-3993. 352 units. $115–$165 double; $135–$550 suite. Packages available. Rates include shuttle to Colonial Williamsburg, Busch Gardens Williamsburg, Water Country USA. AE, DC, DISC, MC, V. From I-64, take Va. 199 (exit 243) west to U.S. 60; go east to right turn at sign for Kingsmill on the James.* On the James River, this gray-clapboard resort sports the world-famous River Golf Course. Accommodations range from rooms to three-bedroom condo units. Most suites have complete kitchens and living rooms with fireplaces. Four dining rooms overlook the river. There are three golf courses, 15 tennis courts, indoor and outdoor pools, racquetball courts, a children's program, exercise room, saunas, Jacuzzi, billiards, a marina, gift shop, and pro shop.

**Liberty Rose.** *1022 Jamestown Rd., Williamsburg, VA 23185.* ☎ *800/545-1825 or 757/253-1260. 4 rms. $110–$180 double. Rates include full breakfast. AE, MC, V.* Williamsburg's most romantic B&B, this 70-year-old two-story white-clapboard residence enjoys a premier location on a wooded hilltop just 1 mile from the Historic Area. You'll find Victorian, French, and English country furnishings, and 18th-century antiques and reproductions. Luxurious guest rooms are distinctively decorated and have TVs and phones. A full breakfast is served on the morning porch.

**Williamsburg Hospitality House.** *415 Richmond Rd., Williamsburg, VA 23185.* ☎ *800/932-9192 or 757/229-4020. Fax 757/220-1560. 297 rms, 9 suites. $79–$150 double; $350 one-bedroom suite; $430 two-bedroom suite. AE, CB, DC, DISC, MC, V.* Just 2 blocks from Colonial Williamsburg opposite William and Mary College, this four-story brick hotel is built around a central courtyard with flowering trees and plants and umbrella tables. Guest rooms and public areas are appointed with a gracious blend of 18th-century reproductions. Two restaurants, an outdoor pool, and a gift shop are on the premises.

**Williamsburg Manor Bed & Breakfast.** *600 Richmond Rd., Williamsburg, VA 23185.* ☎ *800/422-8011 or 757/220-8011. Fax 757/220-0245. 5 rms. $95 double. Rates include full breakfast. MC, V.* Right in the heart of Williamsburg, two blocks from the Historic Area, this gracious 1928 Georgian Revival brick residence offers traditional comfort. Accommodations vary in size and furnishings, but expect four-poster beds, oriental rugs, and wing chairs. Set with Villeroy & Boche china, breakfast might include eggs in puff pastry with Surry bacon.

## DINING

Williamsburg abounds in restaurants catering to tourists. Most national chain fast-food and family restaurants have outlets on Richmond Road (U.S. 60) on the west side of town.

**COLONIAL WILLIAMSBURG FOUNDATION TAVERNS** A dining highlight here, the Historic Area's reconstructed 18th-century "ordinaries," or taverns, aim at authenticity in fare, ambience, and costuming of the staff. All offer colonial fare such as peanut soup, salad with chutney dressing, Brunswick stew, sautéed backfin crabmeat and ham topped with butter and laced with sherry, Sally Lunn bread, and deep-dish Shenandoah apple pie. All have alfresco dining in good weather on brick patios under grape arbors. Low-priced children's menus are available.

If dinner reservations are required at your choice, make them first thing in the morning—if not up to 60 days in advance from spring to early fall—by calling ☎ **800/ TAVERNS** or 757/229-2141. Their seasonal menus are posted by a reservations phone at the ticket office on Henry Street at Duke of Gloucester Street. None of the taverns take reservations for lunch. Their business hours can vary slightly, especially in January and February when they can be closed for annual upkeep.

**Christiana Campbell's Tavern.** *Waller St.* ☎ *757/229-2141. Reservations required at dinner. Main courses $17.50–$24. AE, DC, DISC, MC, V. Mon–Sat 5–9:15pm. COLONIAL.* George Washington recorded in his diary that he dined at Christiana Campbell's Tavern 10 times over a 22-month period. In its heyday, the tavern was famous for seafood, and today that is once again the specialty. Flutists and balladeers entertain diners.

**Josiah Chowning's Tavern.** *Duke of Gloucester St.* ☎ *757/229-2141. Reservations not accepted. Main courses $15–$20. AE, DC, DISC, MC, V. Daily 11:30am–9pm; Gambols Pub, daily 9pm–midnight. COLONIAL.* Josiah Chowning opened this establishment in 1765, and it serves the same English pub fare today as then. It's very charming, with low beamed ceilings, raw pine floors, fireplaces, and sturdy country-made furnishings. Gambols Pub has magicians and 18th-century games.

**Kings Arms Tavern.** *Duke of Gloucester St.* ☎ *757/229-2141. Reservations required. Main courses $17.50–$25.50. AE, DC, DISC, MC, V. Daily 11:30am–2:30pm; dinner, with three nightly seatings, 5–9:30pm. COLONIAL.* The Kings Arms Tavern, on the site of a 1772 establishment, is actually a re-creation of the tavern and an adjoining home. The 11 dining rooms (eight with fireplaces) are the most elegant of all the taverns, painted and furnished following authentic early-Virginia style. Balladeers wander the rooms during dinner and entertain.

**Shields Tavern.** *Duke of Gloucester St.* ☎ *757/229-2141. Reservations essential. Main courses $16.50–$23.50. AE, DC, DISC, MC, V. Daily 8:30–10am, 11:30am–3:30pm, and 5:30–9:30pm. COLONIAL.* The largest of the Historic Area's taverns, this one is named for James Shields, who ran a much-frequented hostelry on this site in the mid-1700s. A specially designed rotisserie unit in the kitchen allows the chefs to approximate 18th-century roasting techniques. Shields is the only tavern open for breakfast. Strolling balladeers entertain at night.

**OTHER HISTORIC AREA RESTAURANTS** Merchants Square, on the west end of the Historic Area, has a number of privately owned restaurants, one of them offering gourmet fare. All of them have outdoor seating in pleasant weather. There are benches throughout the Historic Area and scenic picnic areas off the Colonial Parkway. **The Cheese Shop,** on Prince George Street in Merchants Square (☎ **757/220-0298**), sells take-out sandwiches and other fixings.

**Berret's.** *199 S. Boundary St.* ☎ *757/253-1847. Reservations recommended for dinner. Main courses $14.50–$19. AE, MC, V. Jan–Feb, Tues–Sun 11:30am–5pm and 5:30–10pm; Mar–Dec, daily 11:30am–5pm and 5:30–10pm. SEAFOOD.* A great place to relax over a libation, congenial and casual Berret's has a popular outdoor raw bar where people at picnic tables crack open steamed Chesapeake Bay crabs. The adjoining restaurant is bright and airy, with seating at nautical-blue leather booths and light-wood tables covered with matching blue cloth. For an entree, try soft-shell crabs served with peanut-bourbon butter.

**A Good Place to Eat.** *410 Duke of Gloucester St., Merchants Square.* ☎ *757/229-4370. Breakfast $2.75–$4.50; lunch/dinner $2.50–$6.50. MC, V. Jan to mid-Mar, daily 8am–6pm; mid-Mar to Aug, daily 8am–10pm; Sept–Oct, daily 8am–8pm; Nov–Dec, daily 8am–7pm. AMERICAN.* This is an especially good place for family meals featuring high quality for a fast-food operation—burger meat is prepared from the best cuts of chuck and round, breads and cakes are fresh baked, and even the ice cream is homemade.

✪ **Old Chickahominy House.** *1211 Jamestown Rd., at Va. 199.* ☎ *757/229-4689. Reservations not accepted. Breakfast $3.50–$6.50; lunch $4–$7.50. MC, V. Daily 8:30–10:15am and 11:30am–2:15pm. REGIONAL AMERICAN.* One of the best places in the state to enjoy a traditional Virginia breakfast or lunch, this reconstructed 18th-century house has mantels from old Gloucester homes and wainscoting from Carter's Grove. The entire effect is extremely cozy and charming. Miss Melinda's lunch special is a cup of delightfully spicy Brunswick stew, hot Virginia ham biscuits, fruit salad, and dessert (luscious lemon chess pie made with buttermilk is a don't-miss). The rest of the house is an antique/gift shop. Also check out the Shirley Pewter Shop next door.

✪ **Trellis Cafe, Restaurant & Grill.** *Duke of Gloucester St., Merchants Square.* ☎ *757/229-8610. Reservations suggested at dinner. Main courses $6–$15 at lunch, $14–$23 at dinner; fixed-price dinner $22. AE, MC, V. Mon–Sat 11:30am–9:30pm, Sun 11:30am–3pm and 5–9:30pm. AMERICAN.* A grapevine-covered trellis leads into this fine establishment, to which co-owner–executive chef Marcel Desaulniers has brought national recognition with his outstanding regional dishes. The author of three best-selling cookbooks, including *Death by Chocolate,* he changes the menu every season to take advantage of fresh produce, imaginatively preparing the best in foods from different regions of the United States.

## DAY TRIPS FROM WILLIAMSBURG

No visit to Williamsburg is complete without seeing nearby Jamestown and Yorktown. Both are linked to Williamsburg by the Colonial Parkway, a scenic excursion in itself as it skirts the banks of the James and York rivers. The picnic areas overlooking the York are particularly appealing. To the west of Williamsburg, the John Tyler Highway (Va. 5) is known as the Plantation Route, since it is lined with historic 18th-century manor houses built with tobacco profits.

**JAMESTOWN**   Today two important sites commemorate the first permanent English colony in the New World, established in 1607 at Jamestown, 8 miles southwest of Williamsburg. Here you can examine Capt. John Smith's legendary rescue from execution by the Native American princess Pocahontas; the arrival of the first slaves from Africa; and a vivid picture of life in 17th-century Virginia. Archeologists recently uncovered the remains of what appears to be the original fort. They already had excavated more than 100 building frames, evidence of manufacturing ventures (pottery, wine making, brick making, and glass blowing), early wells, and old roads, as well as scores of artifacts of everyday life—tools, utensils, ceramic dishes, armor, keys, and the like.

**Jamestown Island,** now part of Colonial National Historical Park (which also includes Yorktown Battlefield), was the actual site of the first colony. Begin at the visitor center, where you can rent a recorded walking tour of the town site and a driving tour of the island ($2 each). Be sure to inquire about special programs and tours for kids. Footpaths lead you through the actual site of "James Cittie," where rubbly brick foundations of the 17th-century buildings are enhanced by artists' renderings, text, and audio stations. Most complete are the remains of the tower of one of the first brick churches in Virginia (1639). There are demonstrations of 17th-century pottery making from spring through fall at the Dale House Pottery, near the church.

Beginning at the visitor center parking lot, a fascinating 5-mile loop drive winds through 1,500 wilderness acres of woodland and marsh that have been allowed to return to their natural state in order to approximate the landscape as 17th-century settlers found it.

Admission to the island is $5 per person, which includes entrance to Yorktown Battlefield. The gate is open daily 8:30am–4:30pm except Christmas. The visitor center stays open until 5pm, and you can remain on the grounds until dusk.

**Jamestown Settlement** is an indoor-outdoor museum, operated by the Commonwealth of Virginia on the mainland near Jamestown Island. Three large permanent museum galleries feature artifacts, documents, decorative objects, dioramas, and graphics relating to the Jamestown period. The Powhatan Indian Village represents the culture and technology of a highly organized chiefdom of 32 tribes that inhabited coastal Virginia in the early 17th century. Historical interpreters tend gardens, tan animal hides, and make bone and stone tools and pottery. Triangular James Fort is a re-creation of the wooden stockade built by the Jamestown colonists in 1607. Inside are primitive wattle-and-daub structures with thatched roofs like Jamestown's earliest buildings. Interpreters are engaged in activities typical of early 17th-century life. You can board reproductions of the *Susan Constant, Godspeed,* and *Discovery,* the three ships that brought the 104 colonists to Virginia.

Jamestown Settlement is open daily 9am–5pm except New Year's Day and Christmas. Admission is $9.75 for adults and $4.75 for children 6 to 12 (under 6 free). If you're also planning to visit the Yorktown Victory Center (see below), purchase a money-saving combination ticket to both museums for $13.25 for adults and $6.50 for children. A fast-food restaurant is on the premises, and parking is free.

**Essentials:** Jamestown is 8 miles south of Williamsburg via Jamestown Road (Va. 31) or the Colonial Parkway. For information about Jamestown Island, contact the National

Park Service, P.O. Box 210, Yorktown, VA 23690 (☎ **757/229-1733**). For Jamestown Settlement information, write P.O. Box 1607, Williamsburg, VA 23187 (☎ **757/ 253-4838**). Other than the cafe at Jamestown Settlement, there are few restaurants, so you may want to take advantage of the picnic areas at the National Park Service site.

**YORKTOWN** "I have the Honor to inform Congress, that a Reduction of the British Army under the Command of Lord Cornwallis, is most happily effected," George Washington wrote to the Continental Congress on October 19, 1781. Though it would be 2 years before a peace treaty was signed and sporadic fighting would continue, Washington's stunning victory at Yorktown for all intents and purposes won the Revolution.

✪ **Yorktown Battlefield National Park** preserves the battleground. The visitor center shows a 16-minute documentary called *Siege at Yorktown,* and its museum displays Washington's actual military headquarters tent, objects recovered from the York River, exhibits about Cornwallis's surrender and the events leading up to it, and dioramas detailing the siege. Spring and fall weekends, and daily in summer, national park rangers give free tours of the British inner defense line. The center is open daily 8:30am–5:30pm in summer, 8:30am–5pm spring and fall, 9am–5pm winter except Christmas. Admission is $5 per person, which includes entrance to Jamestown Island.

The visitor center is the starting point for two self-guided tours, a 7-mile Battlefield route and a 10.2-mile Encampment route. You'll be given a map indicating both routes and detailing major sites, but for the most interesting experience, rent a cassette player and tape at the visitor center ($2). Narrated by "British and American colonels," whose polite hostilities to each other are most amusing, the taped commentary further elucidates the battlefield sites. You won't stay in your car the whole time; it's frequently necessary to park, get out, and walk to redoubts and earthworks. A lot of the drive is very scenic, winding through woods and fields abundant with birdlife; the Encampment route is especially beautiful. If you rent the cassette, listen to the introduction in the parking lot; it will tell you when to depart.

Be sure to stop at the Grand French Battery, from which French soldiers fired on British and German mercenary troops; the Moore House, where the two sides negotiated the surrender (open Mon–Fri 1–4:30pm and Sat–Sun 10am–4:30pm in summer; Sat–Sun 1–4:30pm spring and fall); and Surrender Field, where the British laid down their arms.

✪ **Yorktown Victory Center,** on old route Va. 238 overlooking part of the battlefield, offers an excellent orientation to Yorktown attractions, including an evocative 18-minute dramatic film set in an encampment during the battle. There's also a living-history program and museum exhibits. Admission is $6.75 for adults, $3.25 for children 6 to 12 (under 6 free); or you can purchase a combination ticket for this and Jamestown Settlement for $13.25 for adults, $6.50 for children 6 to 12 (under 6 free). Open 9am–5pm daily except New Year's Day and Christmas.

**Old Yorktown** itself is worth exploring. Self-guided or ranger-led walking tours of the village are available at the Battlefield Visitor Center. Key sites include the 98-foot-tall Victory Monument, erected by Congress to commemorate the battle; Cornwallis Cave, where the British commander allegedly lived during the final days of the siege; the Dudley Digges House, a restored 18th-century white weatherboard house that is now a private residence closed to the public; the **Nelson House,** damaged but not destoryed during the battle (open daily 1am–4:30pm in summer; Mon–Fri 1–4:30pm in spring and fall); the Sessions House, built in 1692 and the oldest home in Yorktown; the Customhouse, which dates to 1721; Grace Episcopal Church, which has been an active house of worship since 1697; and the **Swan Tavern,** a reconstruction of Yorktown's leading hostelry that predated Williamsburg's Raleigh Tavern (it's now an antique shop).

**Essentials:** Yorktown is 14 miles from Williamsburg at the eastern end of the Colonial Parkway. For more information about Yorktown Victory Center, contact P.O. Box 1607, Williamsburg, VA 23187 (☎ 757/253-4838). For information about the battlefield, contact **Yorktown Battlefield Visitor Center,** P.O. Box 210, Yorktown, VA 23690 (☎ 757/898-3400).

**JAMES RIVER PLANTATIONS**   While Williamsburg was the political capital of Virginia during the 18th century, its economic livelihood depended on the great tobacco plantations like Carter's Grove. Several more of the mansions still stand along the banks of the James River, some occupied to this day by the same families that have produced generals, governors, and two U.S. presidents. They provide an authentic feel for 18th-century plantation life.

They all are on Va. 5, which covers a distance of 55 miles between Williamsburg and Richmond and makes an excellent scenic driving tour between the two cities. Allow a full day to visit all the plantations and to take a break for lunch. We list them here east to west as you come to them from Williamsburg. If you're driving from Richmond, start at Shirley and work backward.

The owners of Sherwood Forest, Evelynton, Berkeley, and Shirley offer a **block ticket** to all of their homes for $25.50 for adults (it's less expensive to buy children's tickets to each home), available at any of their four plantations. Otherwise, admission at each runs $7–$8.50 adults, $3.50–$4.50 students. Unless otherwise noted, the plantations are open daily 9am–5pm except Christmas.

**Sherwood Forest,** 20 miles west of Williamsburg (☎ 757/829-5377), was owned by President William Henry Harrison in the 1790s and was the home of President John Tyler after he retired from the White House in 1845. Tyler extended the one-room-deep home built in 1730 to its present length of 301 feet, making it the longest wood-frame house in America. All furnishings are family heirlooms or similar period pieces.

**Evelynton,** 25 miles west of Williamsburg (☎ 800/473-5075 or 757/829-5075), was named for William Byrd's daughter Evelyn (pronounced "EVE-lyn"), who is said to have died of a broken heart because her father refused to let her marry her chosen suitor. Legend says her ghost still roams the premises. The original house was destroyed in 1862 during the fierce but short-lived Battle of Evelynton Heights. The present structure, a magnificent example of Colonial Revival style, was built in 1935.

**Berkeley,** 30 miles west of Williamsburg (☎ 757/829-6018), is where 38 English settlers sent by the Berkeley Company put ashore on December 4, 1619, after a 3-month voyage. They fell on their knees in a prayer of thanksgiving. If you're here on the first Sunday of November, you can participate in the annual commemoration of that first official Thanksgiving in the New World. The aristocratic Harrison family bought Berkeley in 1691. Benjamin Harrison V was a signer of the Declaration of Independence and thrice governor of Virginia. The next generation produced William Henry Harrison, the frontier fighter whose nickname "Old Tippecanoe" helped him get elected as our 9th president. His grandson, another Benjamin Harrison, took the presidential oath 47 years later. During the Civil War, Union Gen. Dan Butterfield composed "Taps" here.

**Take a Break:** Berkeley is a good place to stop for lunch, for moderately priced sandwiches, soups, and salads are served in its old carriage house, now appropriately named the **Coach House Tavern** (☎ 757/829-6003). Open daily 11am–3pm.

**Westover** shares Berkeley's lane off Va. 5 (☎ 757/829-2882). This beautiful 1730s Georgian manor house directly on the banks of the James is open to the public only for 5 days during Garden Week (last week in April), but visitors are invited to walk around the grounds and gardens year-round, daily 9am–6pm. Admission is $2.

**Shirley,** 35 miles west of Williamsburg (☎ 757/829-5121), was founded in 1613, with the present mansion dating to 1723. Because of its continuous ownership, many original furnishings, portraits, and memorabilia remain, making this one of the most interesting plantations open to public view. The carved-walnut staircase, rising three stories with no visible means of support, is the only one of its kind in America. A group of superb brick outbuildings form a unique Queen Anne forecourt.

**Essentials:** The plantations are on John Tyler Memorial Highway (Va. 5) between Williamsburg and Richmond. For information in advance, contact the individual plantations or the **Williamsburg Area Convention & Visitor Bureau,** 201 Penniman Rd., Williamsburg, VA 23187 (☎ 800/368-6511 or 757/253-0192).

## 4  Baltimore

Baltimore today has its share of industrial eyesores and some crime-ridden neighborhoods, but the famous Harborplace has revitalized the downtown waterfront area known as the Inner Harbor, as has the excellent National Aquarium and exciting Camden Yards, the modern but very traditional home of baseball's Baltimore Orioles. And work has begun on an adjoining football stadium for the Baltimore Ravens, the former Cleveland Browns who replaced the city's beloved Colts in 1996. Indeed, the Inner Harbor serves as an interesting focal point for this old but revitalized city.

Away from the Inner Harbor and downtown's anonymous glass skyscrapers, there's still an authentic, Old World charm in Baltimore's ethnic neighborhoods such as Little Italy, Little Lithuania, Greektown, Highlandtown (once heavily Polish), and the old Jewish area named Corned Beef Row because of its numerous delicatessens. Once the original seaport, Fells Point is now the city's funkiest area, a denizen of restaurants and clubs.

There are old-style markets here where you can watch a dozen oysters being shucked before you down them on the half shell. More than likely they were harvested from the Chesapeake Bay, the great estuary that has helped make Baltimore a key seaport since the American Revolution and an important manufacturing center since the Industrial Revolution. During the War of 1812, the rockets' red glare over Baltimore Harbor inspired Francis Scott Key to write the words to "The Star-Spangled Banner." The famous Baltimore clipper ships were built here, and the city was the starting point for the first American railroad and the site of the country's first railroad passenger and freight station. The first telegraph communication was sent to Baltimore in 1844, and the nation's oldest cathedral is also here.

### ARRIVING & DEPARTING

**BY PLANE**  The no-frills Southwest Airlines, which has a major hub here, and most other major domestic airlines fly to **Baltimore–Washington International Airport (BWI),** 10 miles south of downtown off the Baltimore–Washington Parkway (Md. 295), which will take you north into the heart of downtown via Russell Street in 15 minutes if you're driving or taking a taxi ($17 fare). It takes slightly longer to the downtown hotels via **SuperShuttle** (☎ 800/BLUE-VAN or 410/859-0800) vans, running daily every 30 minutes 5:45am–11:15pm. The fare is $10 per person one way or $15 round-trip. Baltimore's light rail system (see "Getting Around," below) should open a station in BWI's international terminal in 1998, thus providing a link directly to downtown.

**BY TRAIN & BUS**  Northeast corridor **Amtrak** trains stop at Baltimore's beaux-arts–style Pennsylvania Station, 1500 N. Charles St., at Falls Road (☎ 800/USA-RAIL or 410/291-4260). Both Amtrak and **MARC,** the state's commuter rail system, provide

# Baltimore

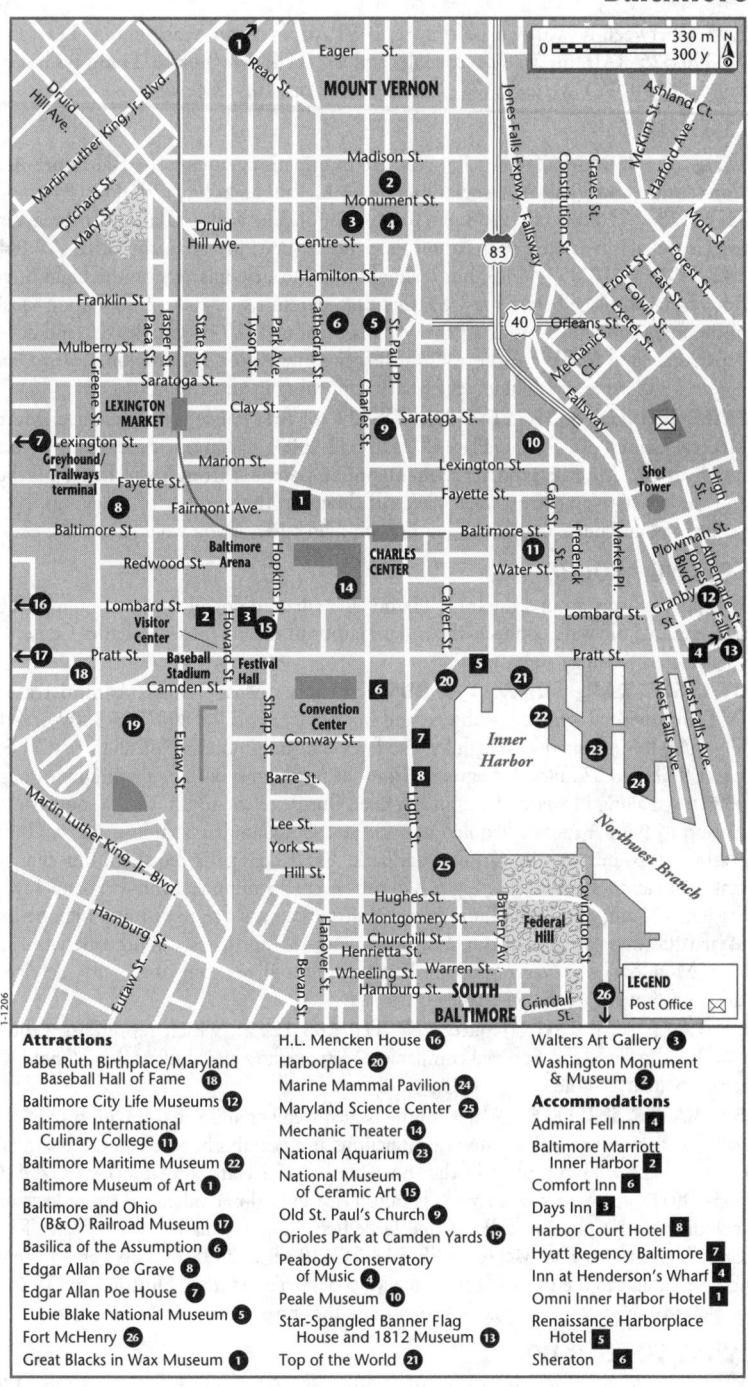

0    330 m
0    300 y

**LEGEND**
Post Office ✉

## Attractions

Babe Ruth Birthplace/Maryland Baseball Hall of Fame 18

Baltimore City Life Museums 12

Baltimore International Culinary College 11

Baltimore Maritime Museum 22

Baltimore Museum of Art 1

Baltimore and Ohio (B&O) Railroad Museum 17

Basilica of the Assumption 6

Edgar Allan Poe Grave 8

Edgar Allan Poe House 7

Eubie Blake National Museum 5

Fort McHenry 26

Great Blacks in Wax Museum 1

H.L. Mencken House 16

Harborplace 20

Marine Mammal Pavilion 24

Maryland Science Center 25

Mechanic Theater 14

National Aquarium 23

National Museum of Ceramic Art 15

Old St. Paul's Church 9

Orioles Park at Camden Yards 19

Peabody Conservatory of Music 4

Peale Museum 10

Star-Spangled Banner Flag House and 1812 Museum 13

Top of the World 21

Walters Art Gallery 3

Washington Monument & Museum 2

## Accommodations

Admiral Fell Inn 4

Baltimore Marriott Inner Harbor 2

Comfort Inn 6

Days Inn 3

Harbor Court Hotel 8

Hyatt Regency Baltimore 7

Inn at Henderson's Wharf 4

Omni Inner Harbor Hotel 1

Renaissance Harborplace Hotel 5

Sheraton 6

service between downtown Baltimore, BWI Airport, and Washington, D.C. Call
☎ 800/325-RAIL for MARC schedules and fares. The **Greyhound/Trailways** bus station is at 210 W. Fayette St. (☎ **800/231-2222** or 410/744-9311).

## ESSENTIALS

**VISITOR INFORMATION**   For advance information, contact the **Baltimore Area
Convention and Visitors Association (BACVA),** 100 Light St., 12th floor, Baltimore,
MD 21202 (☎ **800/343-3468** or 410/659-7300). The walk-in **Baltimore Area Visitor Center** has been at Constellation Pier, 301 E. Pratt St., at Harborplace (☎ **800/
282-6632** or 410/837-4636), but it should move to new quarters on the Light Street
side of Harborplace before the USS *Constitution* returns in 2000. Information kiosks
in the main lobby of Amtrak's Pennsylvania Station, 1525 N. Charles St., and at the
departures level of BWI Airport also dispense some visitor information. *Guest Quick
Guide,* a magazine-style guide, tells what's happening in and around the city.

**EMERGENCIES & SAFETY**   Dial ☎ **911** for fire, police, or ambulance. **Mercy
Medical Center,** 301 St. Paul Place (☎ **410/332-9000**), has an emergency room 6 blocks
north of the Inner Harbor. Frequent police patrols through the Inner Harbor and
the other main tourist areas have cut down on the number of muggings, pick-
pocketings, and purse snatchings, but use common sense, as you would anywhere else.

## GETTING AROUND

You can easily get around the Inner Harbor and adjacent downtown areas on foot. The
safe, elevated Skywalk connects the Inner Harbor to the downtown Charles Center (at
Charles and Saratoga streets).

**BY LIGHT RAIL, SUBWAY & BUS**   The city's **Mass Transit Administration
(MTA)** provides Light Rail, subway, and bus service. Call ☎ **800/543-9809** or 410/
539-5000 for information, schedules, and fares. The minimum fare on all three is $1.50.
**Light Rail** runs 27 miles aboveground from the northern suburb of Timonium through
downtown along Howard Street and to Glen Burnie to the south, with a southern extension to BWI Airport scheduled to open in 1998. Camden Station is the key Inner
Harbor stop, next to the Orioles' ballpark. Exact change is required, but change-
making machines are on site. Light Rail runs every 15 minutes Mon–Fri 6am–11pm;
Sat 8am–11pm; and Sun 11am–7pm. Of little practical use to visitors, the one-line
**Metro** subway system connects downtown with the northwest suburbs. Service runs
from Mon–Sat, with varying hours. **Buses** connect all sections of the city. Service is
daily, but hours vary. Exact change is necessary.

**BY TAXI**   Call **Taxi Dispatch** (☎ **410/685-1212**), which represents Yellow,
Checker, Jimmy's, and Sun taxi companies. Metered fares are $1.40 at flag fall plus 10¢
for every quarter-mile.

**BY WATER SHUTTLE**   Water shuttle is a convenient and very pleasant way to hop
between Baltimore's major waterside attractions and neighborhoods. You can board any
of them behind Harborplace in the Inner Harbor. **Ed Kane's Water Taxi** (☎ **410/
563-3901**) runs year-round between Harbor Place and a dozen other waterfront locations
including Harborplace, Fells Point, and Little Italy. Stops are marked with "Water Taxi"
signs. The narrated **Fort McHenry Shuttle** (☎ **410/685-4288**) connects Fort McHenry
and Fells Point to the Inner Harbor daily May–Sept. The **Harbor Shuttle Co.** (☎ **410/
675-2900**) operates to 10 major points along the Inner Harbor daily Apr–Sept.

## WHAT TO SEE & DO

You can save on admissions to many Baltimore attractions and tours at **City Life
Tickets,** between the pavilions at Harborplace, corner of Light and Pratt streets
(☎ **410/396-8342**). Open daily 10am–4pm.

**ESCORTED TOURS**   One of the best ways to tour Baltimore is via the fully narrated ✪ **Baltimore Trolley** (☎ 410/752-2015), a bus built to resemble the city's original cabled vehicles. Starting at Harborplace, it stops at all major hotels and attractions daily 10am–4pm, with a slightly reduced schedule Oct–Apr. You can get on at any point along the route and reboard as many times as you wish.

Baltimore City Life Museums (☎ 410/396-3279) sponsor occasional walking and bus tours, focusing on different historical, social, and cultural aspects of the city. The topics change monthly, so check in advance. Reservations are required. **Baltimore Heritage Walking Tours** (☎ 410/625-2585) also offers 2-hour guided walking tours of the city's unique neighborhoods and historic areas. Tours and itineraries change monthly, so phone ahead. Reservations are required.

**CRUISES & BOAT TOURS**   Several boats docked at Harborplace offer sightseeing cruises of the harbor, the Patapsco River, and the Chesapeake Bay. Schedules and prices change with the season, so call ahead for information and reservations. The ✪ *Bay Lady/ Lady Baltimore* (☎ 800/695-BOAT or 410/727-5552) are two 450-passenger, three-deck luxury cruise ships. The sleek, 149-passenger *Clipper City* (☎ 410/539-6277) is a replica of an 1854 vessel and one of the largest tall ships licensed in the United States to carry passengers. *Harbor Belle* (☎ 800/777-0850 or 410/752-7545) replicates a turn-of-the-century paddlewheel riverboat.

**ATTRACTIONS**   Although much of Baltimore's business activity takes place along Charles Street, the focus of the city for visitors is the ✪ **Inner Harbor,** home of the Baltimore Convention Center and Festival Hall Exhibit Center, the Baltimore Area Visitor Center, the National Aquarium and other museums, the Pier 6 Concert Pavilion, historic and working ships, a host of major hotels, dozens of restaurants and shops, Orioles Park at Camden Yards, and soon the new football stadium.

**Harborplace** is the centerpiece of it all, occupying two full blocks right on the waterfront along Light and Pratt streets. Built in 1981, this complex is to Baltimore what Station Square is to Pittsburgh, Faneuil Hall to Boston, South Street Seaport to New York, or Ghirardelli Square to San Francisco—a historic setting transformed into a contemporary complex of restaurants, food markets, curiosity shops, and trendy boutiques. Its two pavilions are named after the streets they occupy: Light Street and Pratt Street. Most cruise boats and water taxis dock at Pier 1, in front of the two pavilions, and a fleet of paddleboats wait to be rented. Shops are open Mon–Sat 10am–10pm, Sun noon–6pm, with later hours for restaurants and entertainment.

Heading east along the north shore of the Inner Harbor, you'll come first to **Little Italy,** whose narrow streets seem to be lined with Italian restaurants, and then **Fell's Point,** whose restored Thames and Fleet streets and the board boulevard known as South Broadway are the center of lively dining, shopping, and nightlife. Going due north from the Inner Harbor, Charles Street leads uphill to **Mount Vernon,** where a restaurant row occupies the 2 blocks south of the Walters Art Gallery.

**Babe Ruth Birthplace and Museum/Maryland Baseball Hall of Fame.** *216 Emory St.* ☎ *410/727-1539. Admission $5 adults, $3 seniors, $2 children 5–16. Daily 10am–4pm (until 7pm on Orioles home game days).* Located 2 blocks west of Oriole Park at Camden Yards, this restored house and adjoining museum contain personal mementos of George Herman ("Babe") Ruth, who was born here on February 6, 1895. You can reach out and touch the Babe's own hats, bats, and gloves, or watch an audiovisual presentation about him, the World Series, the Orioles, and more.

**Baltimore and Ohio (B&O) Railroad Museum.** *901 W. Pratt St.* ☎ *410/752-2490. Admission $6.50 adults, $5.50 seniors, $4 children 3–12, free for children under 3; train rides $2 per person. Museum, daily 10am–5pm; train rides, Sat–Sun at 11:30am, 12:30, 2:30, and 3:30pm. Closed Thanksgiving and Christmas.* This fascinating museum commemorates the city's trailblazing role in American railroading, with old steam loco-motives, the 1830 Mount Clare Station (the nation's first), and the 1844 roundhouse with the original B&O tracks and turntable. Peter Cooper built and tested his famous Tom Thumb on this site, and Samuel Morse strung his first telegraph wires through this depot. On weekends a steam train will also chug you along on a 150-year round-trip through the history of American train travel.

**Baltimore City Life Museums.** *35 S. Front St.* ☎ *410/396-3523. Admission (covers all Museum Row sites) $6 adults, $4 children 4–18. Wed–Fri 10am–4pm, Sat–Sun 10am–5pm.* This is a collection of museums and historic sites, four of which are clus-tered together on "Museum Row," northeast of the Inner Harbor at Brewers' Park, site of a 1783 brewery. **Carroll Mansion,** home of Charles Carroll, last surviving signer of the Declaration of Independence, illustrates the lifestyle of a wealthy 19th-century Bal-timore family. The **Center for Urban Archaeology** shows archaeologists uncovering ceramics and glassware from 18th- and 19th-century homes. The **1840 House** features living history dramas about the lifestyle and social issues of mid-19th-century Baltimore. The **Shot Tower,** several blocks north at 801 E. Fayette St., is a 215-foot-tall brick local landmark built in 1828 for the production of lead ammunition (a sound-and-light show tells how it was done).

**✪ Baltimore International College (BIC).** *206 Water St.* ☎ *410/752-4710, 410/752-8813 for tickets. Admission $20 per person per course. Classes Tues–Thurs 6–8pm.* Founded in 1972, BIC's School of Culinary Arts is now a prestigious training center for chefs-to-be. You, too, can learn the art of gourmet cooking by attending minicourses such as "Tourtes and Gâteaux and Centerpieces." Call for a schedule; advance registra-tion is required.

**Baltimore Maritime Museum.** *Pier 4, Pratt St.* ☎ *410/396-3453. Admission $5 adults, $4 seniors, $2.50 children 5–12, free for children under 5. Apr–Oct, daily 10am–6pm. Winter, Fri–Sun 11am–5pm.* This outdoor complex is the home of the U.S. Coast Guard cutter *Taney,* the last ship still afloat that fought in Pearl Harbor; the subma-rine USS *Torsk,* which sank the last enemy ship in World War II; and the lightship *Chesapeake,* a floating lighthouse built in 1930.

**Baltimore Museum of Art.** *N. Charles St. and 31st St.* ☎ *410/396-7100. Admission Fri–Wed $5.50 adults, $3.50 seniors and students, $1.50 children 7–18; Thurs free. Wed–Fri 10am–4pm, weekends 11am–6pm.* Located on the northern edge of the city near Johns Hopkins University and about 4 miles from the Inner Harbor, this is the largest museum in Maryland, with exhibits of art from all periods, most notably an Impressionist collection and two outdoor sculpture gardens. Present is the largest ensem-ble of paintings by Andy Warhol outside of the Andy Warhol Museum in Pittsburgh.

**✪ Basilica of the Assumption.** *Cathedral and Mulberry sts.* ☎ *410/727-3564. Admission free, but donations welcome. Daily 7:30am–4pm. Tours by appointment.* Dat-ing from 1806, this was the first metropolitan Catholic cathedral in the United States. A fine example of neoclassical architecture, it was designed by Benjamin Henry Latrobe, who designed the nation's capitol. Highlights include a grand organ dating from 1821, a high altar from 1822, stained-glass windows installed between 1943 and 1947, and paintings that were gifts from European kings.

**Eubie Blake National Museum & Cultural Center.** *34 Market Place* ☎ *410/625-3113. Admission free, but donations welcome. Mon–Fri 8:30am–4:30pm.* Within walking distance of Haborplace, this museum showcases photos, sheet music, manuscripts, letters, and newspaper clippings reflecting on the 100-year-long life of Baltimore-born ragtime and vaudeville great James Hubert ("Eubie") Blake. *Note:* At press time there were plans to relocate this museum to its original site, at 409 N. Charles St. Call in advance to check.

○ **Fort McHenry National Monument and Historic Shrine.** *E. Fort Ave.* ☎ *410/962-4290. Admission $2; visitors under 17 and seniors 62 and over admitted free. Day after Labor Day to mid-June, daily 8am–5pm; mid-June to Labor Day, daily 8am– 8pm. Closed New Year's Day and Christmas.* The sight of our flag flying over this star-shaped fort during the 1814 Battle of Baltimore inspired Francis Scott Key to write the words to "The Star-Spangled Banner." The American forces repulsed the British, and the fort never again came under attack. It remained an active military base until it became a national park in 1925. There are historical and military exhibits, a 15-minute film shown every half hour, and explanatory maps. Guided activities are regularly scheduled during summer.

○ **Great Blacks in Wax Museum.** *1601–03 E. North Ave.* ☎ *410/563-3404. Admission $5.50 adults, $5 seniors and college students, $3.50 children 12–17, $3 children 2–11. Tues–Sat 9am–5pm, Sun noon–5pm. Open Mon during Feb for Black History Month.* In the city's northeast corner, this is the nation's first and only wax museum dedicated to famous black heroes and historical legends, from ancient Africa to slavery and the Civil War to the civil rights era.

○ **National Aquarium.** *501 E. Pratt St.* ☎ *410/576-3800. Admission $11.95 adults, $10.50 seniors, $7.50 children 3–11, free for children under 3. Sat–Thurs 10am– 5pm, Fri 10am–8pm.* Stretching over Piers 3 and 4, this spectacular five-level glass-and-steel structure is the centerpiece of the Inner Harbor. It contains more than 5,000 specimens of mammals, fish, rare birds, reptiles, and amphibians. All the creatures are on view in settings that re-create their natural habitats, including a South American rain forest; a 335,000-gallon Atlantic coral reef; a 225,000-gallon Open Ocean Exhibit; and the Marine Mammal Pavilion, in which visitors literally can go dolphin-watching indoors.

**Old St. Paul's Church.** *Charles and Saratoga sts.* ☎ *410/685-3404. Admission free, but donations welcome. Mon–Fri 11am–1pm, Sun 8:30am–12:30pm.* Opened in 1856, this is the sixth church of a parish dating from 1692. Designed by Richard Upjohn in the basilica style, it is noted for its Tiffany windows and inlaid mosaic work including marble reliefs of Moses and Christ dating from 1812. Don't miss a chance to hear the church bells ring or to hear the choir of men and boys, one of the most notable in North America, which sings every Sunday from September to May at 10:30am.

**Oriole Park at Camden Yards.** *333 W. Camden St.* ☎ *410/685-9800. Tours $5 adults, $4 seniors and children under 13. Tours Mon–Fri at 1pm, Sat at 11am and 2pm, Sun at 12:30pm and 2pm.* Although it looks like it was built in the 1890s, the Orioles' 1990s ballpark has all the latest amenities and short, slugger-friendly fences. Behind-the-scenes tours are available on a first-come, first-served basis at the box office except when the "Os" are playing an afternoon home game.

**Peale Museum.** *225 Holliday St.* ☎ *410/396-3523. Admission $2 adults, $1.50 children 4–18. Sat 10am–5pm, Sun noon–4pm.* Built in 1814 by American portrait painter Rembrandt Peale, this is reputed to be the oldest museum building in the United States. It served as Baltimore's first city hall. Today it houses a fine collection of historical photographs, prints, and paintings of Baltimore and the Peale family. The garden is enhanced by 19th- and 20th-century relief carvings and sculptures.

**Star-Spangled Banner Flag House and 1812 Museum.** *844 E. Pratt St.* ☎ *410/837-1793. Admission $4 adults, $3 seniors, $1 students 13–18, 50¢ children 6–12. Tues–Sun 10am–3:20pm. Closed major holidays.* A national historic landmark, this Federal-style house (1793) was once the home of Mary Pickersgill, the seamstress who made the 30-by-42-foot red, white, and blue Fort McHenry flag that inspired Francis Scott Key to write the poem that was to become our national anthem. Adjacent is a museum of 1812 military artifacts commemorating the defense of Baltimore. Outside, an unusual garden features a map of the continental United States made of stones native to each state.

✪ **Walters Art Gallery.** *600 N. Charles St.* ☎ *410/547-9000. Admission $4 adults, $3 seniors, free for children 18 and under, free Sat 11am–noon. Tues–Sun 11am–5pm (until 8pm Thurs).* Designed in an Italianate palazzo style, this museum houses more than 30,000 works of art spanning some 5,000 years, including Asian, Egyptian, Greek, Roman, Byzantine, medieval, Renaissance, baroque, romantic, Impressionist, and art nouveau works. In addition, there are exhibits of historic jewelry, medieval armor, and illuminated manuscripts.

**LITERARY ATTRACTIONS**   The tiny **Edgar Allan Poe House,** 203 N. Amity St. (☎ 410/396-7932), was home to the horror-story writer from 1832 to 1835. He wrote many of his great works while living here, and courted his cousin, whom he later married. Admission $3 adults, $1 children under 12. Open Wed–Sat noon–3:45pm.

Author, journalist, and literary critic Henry Louis Mencken, the "Sage of Baltimore," lived for 70 years in the **H. L. Mencken House,** 1524 Hollins St. (☎ 410/396-3523), a 19th-century row house in historic Union Square on the city's west side. Now one of the City Life Museums, it has been restored to include many of Mencken's original furnishings and belongings. Admission $2 adults, $1.50 children 18 and under. Open Sat noon–4pm.

**GREAT VIEWS**   The 178-foot-tall **Washington Monument and Museum,** Mount Vernon Place (☎ 420/396-0929), stands as the country's first major architectural memorial to George Washington. Begun in 1815, it was designed by Robert Mills, who also designed the Washington Monument in Washington, D.C. Those who are physically fit can climb the 228 steps to the top of the tower and see why this spot is often called the best view in Baltimore. Donation $1 per person. Open Wed–Sun 10am–4pm.

The most awesome view is from **Top of the World,** the sky-high observatory on the 27th floor of the World Trade Center, 401 E. Pratt St. opposite Harborplace (☎ 410/837-4515), the world's tallest pentagonal building. Exhibits, hands-on displays, and multimedia presentations tell about Baltimore. Admission $2 adults, $1 children 5 to 15 and seniors over 60. Open Mon–Sat 10am–5pm, Sun 11am–5pm.

**Federal Hill Park,** at Warren and Battery avenues, provides a spendid view back over the Inner Harbor and downtown. Just walk south around the Inner Harbor and climb the hill.

**BEST BETS FOR KIDS**   Kids can learn how machines work and how various industries helped Baltimore to develop into the city it is today at the **Baltimore Museum of Industry,** 1415 Key Hwy. (☎ 410/727-4808), housed in an 1865 oyster cannery. It illustrates the city's industrial history through a series of 19th-century workshop settings—from a machine shop and a print shop to a clothing factory and cannery works. The **Baltimore Zoo,** Greenspring Avenue, Druid Hill Park (☎ 410/396-7102), is the third-oldest zoo in the United States, an agreeable habitat to more than 1,200 animals, birds, and reptiles from seven continents. For young visitors, there's also an 8-acre interactive children's zoo. On the edge of the Inner Harbor, the **Maryland Science Center,** 601 Light St. (☎ 410/685-5225), features hundreds of hands-on activities, live demonstrations, and interactive displays ranging from a simulated space station control center to experiments revealing the properties of sight, sound, magnetism, light, and mechanics. There are film presentations in the five-story IMAX movie theater and scientific shows in the Davis Planetarium.

**SPORTS**   Taking in a **Baltimore Orioles** game at Camden Yards is an experience not to be missed. A few tickets are sold on game day, but it's best to purchase in advance (☎ 410/685-9800). The NFL's **Baltimore Ravens** (☎ 410/547-5696) will play their home games at Memorial Stadium, on 33rd Street at Ellersbie Avenue, until the new complex is completed at Camden Yards. **Pimlico Race Course,** Park Heights and Belvedere avenues (☎ 410/542-9400), is Maryland's oldest track and the site of the annual Preakness Stakes, second leg of Thoroughbred racing's Triple Crown, in May. The full racing season extends from mid-March to the end of May and early August to early October.

**SHOPPING**   For visitors, Baltimore's prime shopping scene is centered around the Inner Harbor. **Harborplace,** Pratt and Light streets (☎ 410/332-4191), features more than 135 shops, markets, craft vendors, restaurants, and cafes. You'll find everything from bonbons and books to scrimshaw and silks. To add to the ambience, from April through September free concerts are staged in the amphitheater in front of the pavilions. Across the street is the **Gallery at Harborplace,** Pratt and Light streets (☎ 410/332-4191), a four-story brass and mahogany atrium-style shopping mall of more than 70 shops.

Certain parts of the city are known for specific types of shopping. Broadway and its side streets in **Fells Point** are rich in antique, art, souvenir, and craft shops. **Antique Row,** along the 700 and 800 blocks of North Howard Street (at West Read Street), offers more than 75 independently owned antiques shops; it's eight blocks north of the Inner Harbor.

**Markets**   Established in 1782, ✪ **Lexington Market,** 400 W. Lexington St. (☎ 410/685-6169), claims to be the oldest continuously operating market in the United States. It houses more than 140 merchants, selling prepared ethnic foods (for eat-in or take-away), fresh seafood, produce, meats, baked goods, sweets, and more. It's a real slice of Baltimore, well worth a visit for the aromas, flavors, sounds, and sights, as well as good shopping. Open Mon–Sat 8:30am–6pm.

Sitting in the median strip dividing South Broadway between Fleet and Lancaster streets in the heart of Fells Point, the 200-year-old **Broadway Market** (☎ 410/396-9780) offers the smells and tastes of Baltimore's original seaport. Local vendors sell fresh produce, flowers, crafts, and an assortment of ethnic and raw bar foods, ideal for snacking, a quick lunch, or a picnic. Open daily 8am–6pm.

## ACCOMMODATIONS

The most convenient place to stay for sightseeing or an Orioles game is the Inner Harbor and adjacent downtown, but you'll be competing with conventioneers and business travelers for rooms here during the week, when doubles for under $100 are scarce. You can also opt for one of two inns in Fells Point, requiring transportation to the Inner Harbor but leaving a stroll home after dinner and entertainment. Rates are highest for harbor-view rooms and during April–October.

Less expensive chain motels are concentrated in two suburban areas. North of the city off I-83, **Hunt Valley** has Courtyard by Marriott, Holiday Inn, and Hampton Inn. From here, you can take the Light Rail line from Timonium to downtown. Another bevy of motels is on **Security Boulevard,** west of town at exit 17 off I-695. Here you'll find Best Western, Comfort Inn, Days Inn, Holiday Inn, Motel 6, and Ramada Inn. In addition, the southern suburb of Linthicum, near **BWI Airport,** has a Courtyard by Marriott, a regular Marriott, and a Hampton Inn, Holiday Inn, and Motel 6.

✪ **Admiral Fell Inn.** *888 S. Broadway (at Thames St.), Baltimore, MD 21231.* ☎ *800/292-4667 or 410/522-7377. Fax 410/522-0707. 80 rms. $125–$225 double. AE, MC, V. Free parking. Complimentary van to downtown.* Orignally a boardinghouse for sailors and later a YMCA, this charming, seven-building Fells Point inn now includes an antique-filled lobby and parlor, a restaurant, an English-style pub, and Savannah's, a basement restaurant serving "American fare with a Southern accent." Individually decorated guest rooms have modern bathrooms. Many have canopied four-poster beds and Jacuzzis. They range from small standard models to a two-room suite.

**Baltimore Marriott Inner Harbor.** *110 S. Eutaw St. (at N. Lombard St.), Baltimore, MD 21201.* ☎ *800/228-9290 or 410/962-0202. Fax 410/962-8585. 525 rms, 12 suites. $209–$229 double; $237–$305 suite. AE, DC, MC, V. Parking $10.* This dramatic 10-story, crescent-shaped hotel is a great base for Orioles fans—across the street from Camden Yards and four blocks from Harborplace. Facilities include a restaurant, cocktail dance bar, game room, indoor swimming pool, and fitness center with sauna and whirlpool.

**Days Inn Inner Harbor.** *100 Hopkins Place (between Lombard and Pratt sts.), Baltimore, MD 21202.* ☎ *800/325-2525 or 410/576-1000. Fax 410/576-9437. 251 rms. $69–$149 double. AE, DC, MC, V. Parking $8.* This modern nine-story hotel is one of the Inner Harbor area's best bargains. It is conveniently situated between the arena and Convention Center. Guest rooms offer standard chain motel furnishings. The hotel has an outdoor heated pool, patio courtyard, and full-service restaurant.

✪ **Harbor Court Hotel.** *550 Light St., Baltimore, MD 21202.* ☎ *800/824-0076 or 410/234-0550. Fax 410/659-5925. 203 rms, 25 suites. $270–$280 double; $300–$650 suite. AE, DC, MC, V. Self-parking $10; valet parking $15.* More than half the spacious rooms overlook the Inner Harbor at this posh, intimate property. A distinctive brick facade fronts Old World charm: marble floors, crystal chandeliers, paneled walls, masterful artworks, and fine reproduction furniture. You'll find a formal gourmet dining room, informal cafe, cozy lounge with piano music nightly, health club, swimming pool, whirlpool, saunas, racquetball, squash, tennis, and croquet.

**Holiday Inn Inner Harbor.** *301 W. Lombard St., Baltimore, MD 21201.* ☎ *800/ HOLIDAY or 410/685-3500. Fax 410/727-6169. 374 rms. $115–$159 double. AE, DC, DISC, MC, V. Parking $8.* This old-timer between the Baltimore Arena and the Convention Center offers good value and location. An updated executive tower with 175 rooms is geared to business travelers. Guest rooms have desks and reclining chairs, brass fixtures, watercolor art, and wide windows with views of the skyline. Guests can take advantage of a restaurant, lounge, and health center with indoor swimming pool.

✪ **Hyatt Regency Baltimore.** *300 Light St., Baltimore, MD 21202.* ☎ *800/ 233-1234 or 410/528-1234. Fax 410/685-3362. 490 rms. $139–$239 double. AE, DC, MC, V. Self-parking $10; valet parking $15.* A bank of rounded glass elevators whisks guests from the customary Hyatt atrium to spacious bedrooms with views of the city or the Inner Harbor across Light Street. The Hyatt has a dining room, informal bistro, spacious lobby-level bar, outdoor pool, tennis courts, jogging track, health club, gift shop, and business center.

**Inn at Henderson's Wharf.** *1000 Fell St., Baltimore, MD 21231.* ☎ *800/ 522-2088 or 410/522-7777. Fax 410/522-7087. 38 rms. $99–$130 double. Rates include continental breakfast. AE, DC, MC, V. Free parking.* Located on the waterfront at Fells Point, this inn occupies the ground floor of a former B&O railroad warehouse dating from the 1800s and restored in 1991. The guest rooms, which face the water or the central courtyard with English-style gardens, are decorated with period reproduction furniture, paneled or brick walls, floral quilted fabrics, nautical art, and brass fixtures.

**Omni Inner Harbor Hotel.** *101 W. Fayette St., Baltimore, MD 21201.* ☎ *800/ THE-OMNI or 410/752-1100. Fax 410/752-6832. 702 rms. $99–$190 double. AE, DC, MC, V. Self-parking $9; valet parking $14.* In the heart of downtown, these two beige skyscrapers comprise the largest hotel in Maryland, popular with conventions and groups. Most bedrooms are L-shaped, with mirrored closets, traditional dark-wood furnishings, and designer fabrics. The Grill Room restaurant, cafe, bar, outdoor swimming pool, fitness center, and gift shop are on the premises.

**Renaissance Harborplace Hotel.** *202 E. Pratt St., Baltimore, MD 21202.* ☎ *800/468-3571 or 410/547-1200. Fax 410/539-5780. 622 rms. $215–$265 double; weekend packages available. AE, DC, MC, V. Self-parking $10; valet parking $14.* Harbor views are a draw at this large hotel, part of the Gallery at Harborplace, a glass-enclosed atrium of 75 shops and restaurants. Extras include an all-day restaurant/lounge, lobby bar, indoor pool, health club, sauna, and whirlpool.

**Sheraton Inner Harbor.** *300 S. Charles St., Baltimore, MD 21201.* ☎ *800/325-3535 or 410/962-8300. Fax 410/962-8211. 339 rms. $162–$200 double. AE, DC, MC, V. Parking $10.* More expensive rooms have water views at this hotel near Harborplace, the Convention Center, Camden Yards, and the Skywalk. The decor is accented with American art, with emphasis on works by Maryland artists. The bright, modern rooms offer light wood furnishings and mirrored closets. The hotel contains a restaurant, lobby-level piano bar, baseball-themed bar, indoor swimming pool, health club, and sauna.

## DINING

"Crabtown" along the waterfront has always been well known for its excellent seafood restaurants, and the development of the Inner Harbor has provided an ideal setting for even more places emphasizing the bounty from the bay. The stretch of Charles Street just south of the Walters Art Gallery is known locally as "Restaurant Row." And you'll find something to pique your appetite in Little Italy and Fells Point. For quality quick meals, don't forget the Lexington and Broadway markets (see "Markets," above) and the food court in Harborplace's Light Street Pavilion.

**Adrian's Book Café.** *714 S. Broadway (Fells Point).* ☎ *410/732-1048. All items $4–$7. AE, DISC, MC, V. Sun–Thurs 11am–11:30pm, Fri–Sat 11am–midnight. AMERICAN.* Situated in the heart of Fells Point, this ground-floor bookstore and upstairs cafe provides a bit of tranquility amid the bustle of Broadway. It's named after New York artist Adrian Rappin, whose paintings line the walls. The menu is simple: pastas, pizzas, salads, sandwiches, quiches, chilis, and desserts, but all are made fresh daily on the premises.

**Bertha's.** *734 S. Broadway, at Lancaster St. (Fells Point).* ☎ *410/327-5795. Reservations accepted only for parties of six or more. Main courses $8–$20; lunch $5–$12. MC, V. Sun–Thurs 11:30am–11pm, Fri–Sat 11:30am–midnight. INTERNATIONAL/ SEAFOOD.* Don't miss this yesteryear Fells Point landmark known for its mussels and music. A dozen different preparations of mussels headline the menu throughout the day. Other specialties include Bertha's shrimp, broiled in tomato, lemon, and garlic sauce with scallions. Scottish-style afternoon tea is served Mon–Sat 3–5pm (reservations required).

**Burke's Café.** *36 Light St., at Lombard St. (Inner Harbor).* ☎ *410/752-4189. Reservations recommended for dinner. Main courses $8–$22; lunch $3.50–$10. AE, MC, V. Daily 7am–2am. INTERNATIONAL.* Located a block north of Harborplace, this dark, tavern-style restaurant with ceiling fans, aged barrels, pewter tankards, and a long, dark-wood bar has been a downtown fixture for more than half a century. The crab cakes are a perennial standout, and deep-fried onion rings are a house specialty.

**Chiapparelli's.** *237 S. High St., at Fawn St. (Little Italy).* ☎ *410/837-0309. Reservations required. Main courses $10–$22; lunch $6–$15. AE, DC, DISC, MC, V. Mon–Thurs 11am–10pm, Fri–Sat 11am–midnight, Sun 3–10pm. ITALIAN.* In the heart of Little Italy, Chiapparelli's is a longtime favorite for southern Italian dishes. Special plaudits go to Mom Chiapparelli's raviolis stuffed with spinach and ricotta, but veal is the star of the menu, cooked at least half a dozen different ways.

**Louie's Bookstore Cafe.** *518 N. Charles St. (between Centre and Hamilton sts., Mount Vernon).* ☎ *410/962-1224. Reservations not accepted. Main courses $8–$14; lunch $4–$8. MC, V. Mon 11:30am–midnight, Tues–Thurs 11:30am–12:30am, Fri 10am–1:30am, Sat 11:30am–1:30am, Sun 10:30am–midnight. INTERNATIONAL.* Artists and musicians staff this eclectic bookstore cafe on "Restaurant Row." Dinner entrees include a crab-cake platter, vegetable stir-fry, crab and shrimp casserole, steaks, and "Chestertown Chicken" (white meat marinated in a curry, garlic, and lemon sauce). There is live solo or duo classical music every night and during Sunday brunch.

✪ **Obrycki's.** *1727 E. Pratt St. (between S. Broadway and S. Register sts., Fells Point).* ☎ *410/732-6399. Reservations accepted only for lunch or for dinner parties of 10 or more. Main courses $14–$25; lunch/light fare $6–$10. AE, DC, MC, V. Mon–Sat noon–11pm, Sun noon–9:30pm. Closed Dec–Mar. SEAFOOD.* Stained-glass windows, brick archways, and wainscoting along the walls render charming atmosphere to this quintessential crab house—where you can crack them open steamed in their shells and feast on the tender, succulent meat to your heart's content. The service is extremely attentive.

**Paolo's.** *In Light St. Pavilion, Harborplace, 301 Light St. (Inner Harbor).* ☎ *410/539-7060. Reservations not accepted. Main courses $8–$17; lunch $5–$9. AE, DC, MC, V. Daily 11am–midnight, Sat–Sun brunch 10:30am–4pm. ITALIAN/AMERICAN.* In the Light Street Pavilion, this informal, wide-windowed restaurant offers indoor and outdoor seating overlooking the harbor. From their open kitchen, chefs prepare pizzas, pastas, and entrees such as veal with saffron risotto. The same menu is served all day.

**Phillips Harborplace.** *In Light St. Pavilion, Harborplace, 301 Light St. (Inner Harbor).* ☎ *410/685-6600. Reservations not accepted. Main courses $12–$25; lunch $5–$9. AE, DISC, MC, V. Sun–Thurs 11am–11pm, Fri–Sat 11am–midnight. SEAFOOD.* Okay, this branch of a very successful chain begun in Ocean City, Maryland, in 1956 is crowded and touristy, but it's a fun restaurant with a lively sing-along piano bar and entertainment at night. Dinner is a feast of fresh local seafood, highlighted by crab in many forms. Also in the Light Street Pavilion, **Phillips Seafood Buffet** offers quick and less expensive fare.

**Purple Orchid.** *419 N. Charles St., at Franklin St. (Mount Vernon).* ☎ *410/837-0080. Reservations recommended for dinner. Main courses $18–$28; lunch $9–$14. AE, MC, V. Tues–Fri 11:30am–2:30pm and 5–10:30pm, Sat 5–11pm, Sun 4–9:30pm. FRENCH/ASIAN.* Classic French dishes with creative Asian accents prevail in this converted row house with a fireplace, crisp linens, brass chandeliers, and, of course, orchids on each table. House favorites include spicy tuna with fresh mango in a warm sesame sauce.

**Sabatino's.** *901 Fawn St., at High St. (Little Italy).* ☎ *410/727-9414. Reservations advised. Main courses $10–$24.50; lunch $5–$12. AE, DC, DISC, MC, V. Daily noon–3am. ITALIAN.* Both northern and southern Italian cuisine are featured at this Little Italy restaurant with a plain stucco facade and a colorful interior. This is a particularly good late-night dining spot since it's open every day until 3am. Dinner entrees include two dozen pastas such as spaghetti with broccoli and anchovy sauce.

**Washington Café.** *In Mount Vernon Hotel, 24 W. Franklin St. (Mount Vernon).* ☎ *410/727-2000. Reservations recommended for dinner. Main courses $6–$9.50. AE, DC, DISC, MC, V. Daily 7am–9pm. INTERNATIONAL.* Staff and students of the Baltimore International College (see "Attractions," above) show off the latest in culinary treats at low prices here. The decor is an eclectic reflection of Old Baltimore, including a ceiling painted with blue sky and clouds. There is an appealing and healthful menu for children aged 12 and under.

✪ **Women's Industrial Exchange Tea Room.** *333 N. Charles St.* ☎ *410/ 685-4388. Main courses $4–$7. MC, V. Mon–Fri 7am–2pm; lunch counter 10:30am–2pm; bakery 8am–3:30pm. Closed major holidays. AMERICAN.* Carrying on a 19th-century Baltimore tradition, this restaurant is in the back room of the craft shop/bakery. The 1815 building has fine Flemish bond work, wrought-iron railings, marble steps, historic wall murals, a black-and-white tile floor, ceiling fans, fireplace, and motherly and grandmotherly waitresses (Miss Marguerite made her acting debut at age 92 in the movie *Sleepless in Seattle,* part of which was filmed here). The menu is simple— homemade soups, salads, sandwiches, omelets, meat or fish platters, and luscious desserts (charlotte russe is a specialty). There is also a lunch counter in the building's basement (entrance from Pleasant Street).

## BALTIMORE AFTER DARK

The most complete source for entertainment information and schedules is the weekly *City Paper,* available in yellow newspaper boxes at most Inner Harbor street corners. Also check the arts and entertainment pages of the *Baltimore Sun* for daily listings and ticket information. **City Life Tickets** (☎ 410/396-8342), on Light Street between Harbor- place and the Maryland Science Center on the Inner Harbor, sells tickets to theaters, concerts, sports events, museums, attractions, tours, and cruises. It's open daily 10am– 4pm or later. You can also call **TicketMaster** (☎ 410/481-SEAT).

**THE PERFORMING ARTS**    The city's prime theatrical showplace is the ultramod- ern **Morris Mechanic Theatre,** Hopkins Plaza, Baltimore and Charles streets (☎ 410/ 625-1400), which stages contemporary plays with original casts en route to or from Broadway. Smaller venues include **Arena Players,** 801 McCulloch St. (☎ 410/ 728-6500), a prominent black theater company, and the intimate **Center Stage,** 700 N. Calvert St. (☎ 410/332-0033), recognized as Maryland's resident professional theater and the state theater of Maryland.

The Baltimore music scene is led by the ✪ **Joseph Meyerhoff Symphony Hall,** 1212 Cathedral St. (☎ 410/783-8000), home of the Baltimore Symphony Orchestra and Baltimore Symphony Chorus. A replica of Germany's Leipzig music hall, the **Lyric Opera House,** 1404 W. Mt. Royal Ave. (☎ 410/685-0692), is home to the Baltimore Opera Company, which performs the world's great operas from October to May. A division of Johns Hopkins University, the ✪ **Peabody Conservatory of Music,** 1 E. Mt. Vernon Place (☎ 410/659-8124), is America's oldest school of music, dating from 1866. More than 60 school-year events feature the Peabody Symphony Orchestra and student performers. Concerts take place in the Miriam A. Friedberg Concert Hall.

**Pier Six Concert Pavilion,** Pier 6 off Pratt Street, Inner Harbor (☎ 410/837-4636), a 4,300-seat concert pavilion that is an open-air, six-point aluminum tent, presents the top names of the music industry in live concerts from May through September. The city's all-purpose venue is the 16,000-seat **Baltimore Arena,** 201 W. Baltimore St. (☎ 410/347-2000), with an ever-changing program including sports events, concerts, plays, circuses, and ice shows.

**THE CLUB & BAR SCENE**    The city's hot area is **Fells Point,** where numerous res- taurants and pubs offer live entertainment, especially on weekends. Stroll along South Broadway and its side streets to see what's happening at places like **Adrian's Bookstore Café** and **Bertha's** (see "Dining," above); the **Full Moon Saloon,** 1710 Aliceanna St., (☎ 410/276-6388), Baltimore's top blues spot; and **Fletcher's,** 710 S. Bond St. (☎ 410/880-8124), whose upstairs has live music.

Popular pubs in the Inner Harbor and adjacent downtown include **Baja Beach Club** at the Brokerage, 55 Market Place at East Lombard Street (☎ 410/727-0468), with progressive deejay dance music Wed–Sun; **Buddies Pub & Jazz Club,** 313 N. Charles

St. (☎ 410/332-4200), known for live jazz sessions Wed–Sat; **The Club at Spike and Charlie's,** 25 Cathedral St., opposite Myeroff Symphony Hall (☎ 410/752-8144), with jazz sessions weekends; **Louie's Bookstore,** 518 N. Charles St. (☎ 410/962-1224), presenting live classical music every night; and **Mick O'Shea's,** 328 N. Charles St. (☎ 410/539-7504), for live Irish tunes. Also downtown, the **Comedy Factory,** above Burke's Restaurant, 36 Light St. at Lombard Street (☎ 410/752-4189), presents live comedy acts Thurs–Sat.

## 5 Philadelphia & the Amish Country

It was in Philadelphia that the United States declared its independence on July 4, 1776, that the Continental Congress managed the Revolutionary War, and that the Founding Fathers wrote our Constitution in 1781. Today the Liberty Bell that proclaimed our freedom from Great Britain, Independence Hall in which it all took place, and dozens of other historic treasures are preserved here in the largest colonial district in the country.

But you'll find a lot more than history and old buildings in Philadelphia today. Its smart Center City core has some of America's best dining values and several of its finest restaurants. It's a stroller's paradise of restored Georgian and Federal structures integrated with sleek shops and contemporary row-house courts, all creating a working urban environment. It's a city filled with art, crafts, and music for every taste, with boulevards made for street fairs and parades all year long. From row-house boutiques to the Second Continental Congress's favorite tavern, from an Ivy League campus to street artists and musicians, from gleaming skyscrapers and a state-of-the-art convention center to Italian marketplaces and more than 7,800 acres of parkland, Philadelphia is a tourist destination of unexpected quality and pleasure.

The colonial view of Philadelphians as reflective, sophisticated, and tolerant has long been succeeded by the stereotype of brash, good-hearted ethnics made famous by the "Rocky" movies. Of course, both characterizations have their points. There's a tremendous diversity of 1.6 million people spread over 129 square miles—there's a lot of distance between the boxes at the Academy of Music, the dining room of Zanzibar Blue, and the bleachers of Veterans Stadium.

Situated some 60 miles inland in the Delaware Valley, Philadelphia is the country's busiest freshwater port. It's a natural stopping place between New York and Washington, D.C., with easy access by rail and road. And the Revolutionary War sites of Valley Forge and Brandywine, the great Du Pont family mansions, and Pennsylvania Dutch country all lie within 90 minutes.

### ARRIVING & DEPARTING

**BY PLANE** All flights into and from Philadelphia use **Philadelphia International Airport** (☎ 215/937-6800), a just-improved and expanded facility at the southwest corner of the city via I-95. It's about 25 minutes from the heart of downtown by car, and slightly longer with the high-speed rail link with direct service daily every 30 minutes 5:30am–11:25pm; fare is $5 for adults, $1.50 for children weekdays and $1 weekends, and family fare is $15. For up-to-the-minute information on airline arrival and departure times and gate assignments, call ☎ 800/PHL-GATE.

**BY TRAIN & BUS** Philadelphia is a major **Amtrak** stop on the Boston–Washington, D.C., northeast corridor (☎ 800/USA-RAIL). The handsomely restored terminal is Penn (30th Street) Station, about 15 blocks from City Hall. **SEPTA** commuter trains also connect 30th Street Station and several Center City stations to Trenton, N.J., with a New Jersey Transit connection to New York for under half the Amtrak price (☎ 800/582-5946 or 215/569-3752).

**Greyhound Lines** buses stop at the city bus terminal on 11th Street between Filbert and Arch streets opposite the Convention Center (☎ **800/231-2222**). **New Jersey Transit** (☎ **215/569-3752**) also operates buses between Philadelphia and Camden, Atlantic City, and other nearby destinations.

## ESSENTIALS

**VISITOR INFORMATION**   The **Philadelphia Visitor Center,** 16th Street and John F. Kennedy Boulevard, Philadelphia, PA 19102 (☎ **800/537-7676** or 215/636-1666), offers a wealth of publications, from seasonal calendars of events to maps; knowledgeable volunteers staff their phones. If you obtain nothing else, request the "Official Visitors Guide," an annual compendium. They also have an increasing number of package tours combining events like special museum exhibitions, concerts, or sporting events with discount hotel prices, free city transit passes, and Amtrak discounts. Once you're in town, note that many bus tours, historic trolley rides, tours of City Hall, and walking tours start from here.

The **Visitor Center of Independence National Historical Park** (☎ **215/597-8974**), at 3rd and Walnut streets, specializes in historic materials, but does have general city information along with spotless restrooms and cool benches. Penn Station (see above) and the **Pennsylvania Convention Center,** between 11th and 13th streets (☎ **215/418-4728**), also maintain information booths.

**RESOURCES FOR TRAVELERS WITH SPECIAL NEEDS**   Seniors should bring some form of photo ID to take advantage of special discounts at city attractions, especially during weekdays. Some hotels, too, will shift their rates, particularly on weekends. The Convention and Visitor Bureau (see above) publishes "Seniors on the Go," which lists dozens of specific benefits around town from flat taxi fares to museum admissions. They'll also give you a "Ben's Pass for Senior Citizens," good for a calendar year. You can pick up a Golden Age Passport at Independence National Historical Park if you are 62 or over. Discounted local transportation is available through the SEPTA DayPass or the PHLASH vans (see "Getting Around," below).

Favorite tourist areas are accessible to the disabled. Some streets in Society Hill and bordering Independence National Historical Park have uneven brick sidewalks or cobblestones, but all curbs are well cut at intersections. The same is true for Chestnut Street, the Benjamin Franklin Parkway, and the University of Pennsylvania campus. Virtually all theaters and stadiums accommodate wheelchairs. The Academy of Music provides free infrared headsets for concerts; the Annenberg Center rents them for $2.

For basic information, contact the **Mayor's Commission on People with Disabilities,** Room 143, City Hall, Philadelphia, PA 19107 (☎ **215/686-2798**). SEPTA publishes a special "Transit Guide for the Disabled"; you can request it from **SEPTA Special Services,** 130 S. 9th St., Philadelphia, PA 19107 (☎ **215/580-7365**). All SEPTA bus routes are lift-equipped; Market East subway station is wheelchair accessible, but other stops are not. The Free Library of Philadelphia runs a **Library for the Blind and Physically Handicapped,** very conveniently located at 919 Walnut St. (☎ **215/925-3213**); it's open Mon–Fri 9am–5pm.

Center City is used to, and tolerant of, homosexual populations, and the rectangle bordered by 9th and 18th streets and by Walnut and South streets is filled with gay social services, restaurants, bookstores, and clubs. **Giovanni's Room,** 345 S. 12th St., Philadelphia, PA 19107 (☎ **215/923-2960**), is a national resource for publications produced by and for gays and lesbians, as well as for feminist and progressive literature. The **Gay Switchboard** (open daily 7–10pm) is at ☎ **215/546-7100;** the **Lesbian Hotline** is at ☎ **215/222-5110.** For meetings, classes, gallery exhibitions, and social

# Philadelphia

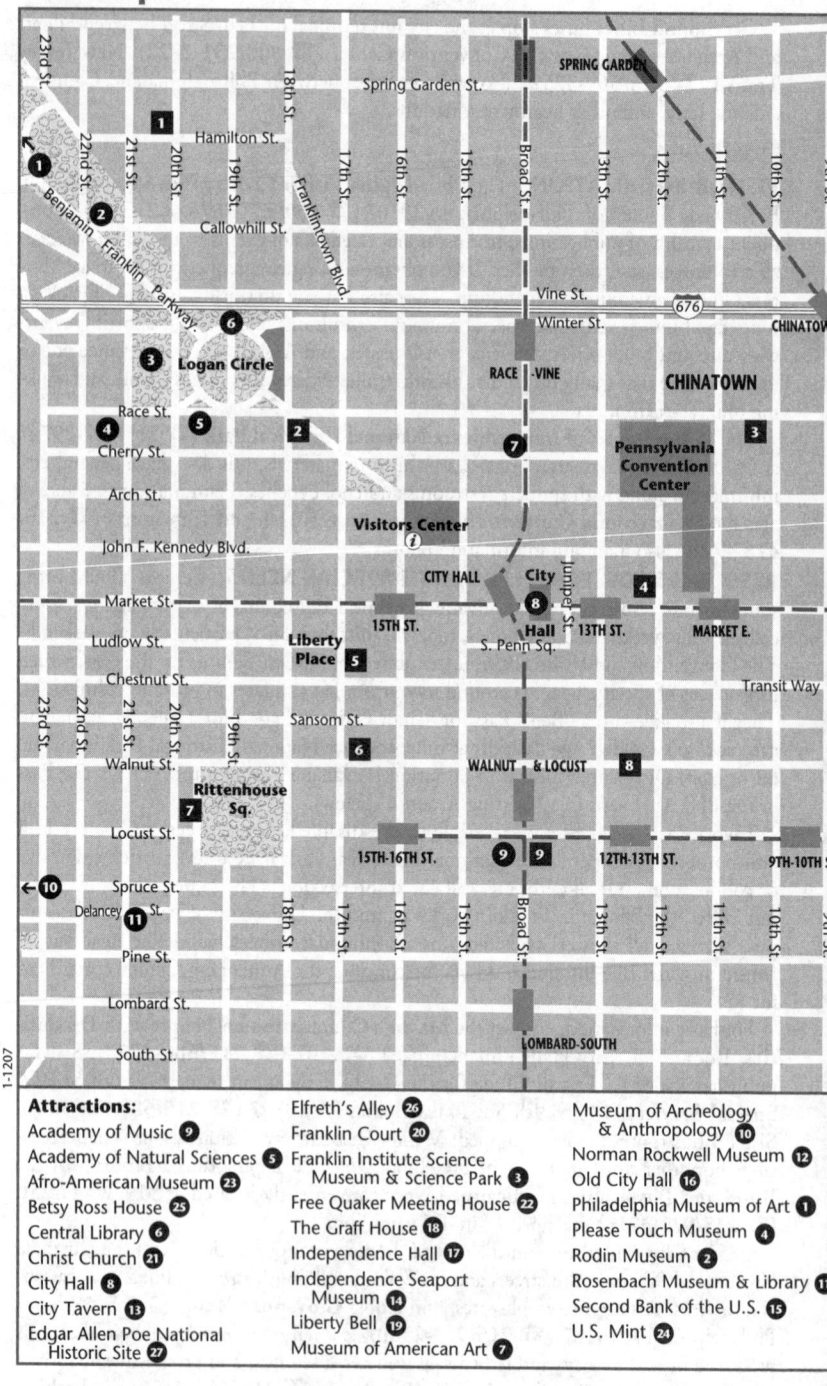

**Attractions:**

Academy of Music ⑨
Academy of Natural Sciences ⑤
Afro-American Museum ㉓
Betsy Ross House ㉕
Central Library ⑥
Christ Church ㉑
City Hall ⑧
City Tavern ⑬
Edgar Allen Poe National Historic Site ㉗

Elfreth's Alley ㉖
Franklin Court ⑳
Franklin Institute Science Museum & Science Park ③
Free Quaker Meeting House ㉒
The Graff House ⑱
Independence Hall ⑰
Independence Seaport Museum ⑭
Liberty Bell ⑲
Museum of American Art ⑦

Museum of Archeology & Anthropology ⑩
Norman Rockwell Museum ⑫
Old City Hall ⑯
Philadelphia Museum of Art ①
Please Touch Museum ④
Rodin Museum ②
Rosenbach Museum & Library ⑪
Second Bank of the U.S. ⑮
U.S. Mint ㉔

1-1207

events, consult **Penguin Place,** 201 S. Camac St. (☎ **215/723-2220**). *Philadelphia Gay News* is widely available at newsstands.

**EMERGENCIES & SAFETY**  Dial ☎ **911** for fire, police, or ambulance. Major Center City hospitals include **Graduate Hospital,** 1800 Lombard St. (☎ **215/893-2000**); **Hahnemann,** Broad and Vine streets (☎ **215/762-7000**); **University of Pennsylvania Hospital,** 3400 Spruce St. (☎ **215/662-4000**); **Pennsylvania Hospital,** 8th and Spruce streets (☎ **215/829-3000**); and **Thomas Jefferson,** 11th and Walnut streets (☎ **215/955-6000**).

Like most large American cities, Philadelphia has its share of crime. Center City core has a vigilant combination of police staffing and specially identified "Community Ambassadors," so incidents here are rare. If you are planning to explore unusual neighborhoods, the college campuses in West Philadelphia, or at unusual hours, use common sense, and walk only in well-lighted, well-populated streets. If your car looks attractive or stuffed with merchandise, please spring for an indoor garage.

## GETTING AROUND

William Penn's grid for Center City has been walkable for 350 years, and you should organize your time into tours of neighborhoods of chief interest, using the city's varied connections between them.

**BY LIGHT RAIL, SUBWAY & BUS**  SEPTA (Southeastern Pennsylvania Transportation Authority; ☎ **215/580-7800**) operates a complicated and extensive network of trolleys, buses, commuter trains, and subways. Certain buses and trolleys run 24 hours a day. Fares for any SEPTA route are $1.60, with 40¢ more for a transfer. Exact change or tokens are required. Seniors ride free and the disabled pay half fare during off-peak hours. Anyone can purchase a 5-pack for $5.75 or a 10-pack for $11.50. A $5 DayPass is good for all buses, subways, and one ride on the airport loop; a $16 weekly TransPass is good from Monday to the next Sunday.

**Rapid Transit** cars speed under Broad Street and Market Street, intersecting under City Hall. The Broad Street line connects directly to major league sporting events to the south. The Market Street line stops at seven popular destinations and stretches to the west and northeast. Both run all night, but exercise caution at night.

The **PATCO** commuter rail line (☎ **215/922-4600**) begins at Walnut and Locust streets around Broad Street, connects with rapid transit at 8th and Market streets, and crosses the Ben Franklin Bridge to Camden and its New Jersey State Aquarium, via the Aqualink Shuttle.

Purple **PHLASH** vans (☎ **215/474-5274**) link Independence Park sites, the Delaware River waterfront, the Convention Center, Rittenhouse Square shopping, and the cultural institutions at Logan Circle. The total loop takes 50 minutes and makes 30 stops. A one-time pass is $1.50, but take the all-day unlimited-ride pass for $3. Hours are every 10 minutes 10am–12:30am in summer, 10am–6:30pm mid-September to mid-May.

Route 76, the **Ben FrankLine,** is also a subsidized tourism deal at 50¢; it connects Society Hill at 3rd and Chestnut streets to the Parkway all the way to the Museum of Art and the Zoo. It operates 9am–6:11pm every 10 minutes weekdays, every 20 minutes weekends.

**BY TRAIN**  The "Main Line," or the posh suburbs north and west of Philadelphia, is served by one of the great commuter-rail networks in America. From **Suburban Station** at 16th Street and JFK Boulevard or **Reading Terminal** at 12th and Market streets, you can reach Chestnut Hill, an enclave of fine shops; the great Barnes Foundation art collection in Merion; the colleges of Bryn Mawr, Haverford, Swarthmore, and

Villanova; and Devon's great horse and country fair. One-way fares for all destinations are under $6, and you can buy tickets at station counters or vending machines.

**BY TAXI**   The three largest taxi fleets are **Olde City Taxi** (☎ **215/247-7678**), **United Cab** (☎ **215/238-9500**), and **Quaker City** (☎ **215/728-8000**). Fares are $1.80 for the first one-seventh mile and 30¢ for each additional one-seventh mile or minute of immobility.

## WHAT TO SEE & DO

**ESCORTED TOURS**   To get the feel of Philadelphia as it was, try a narrated horse-drawn carriage ride. Operated daily by the **76 Carriage Co.** (☎ **215/923-8516**), tours begin at 5th and Chestnut streets in front of Independence Hall from 10am to 5pm, with later hours in summer. Reservations are not necessary.

Replicas of 1930s open-air trolleys operate as 39-seat buses run by **American Trolley Bus** (☎ **215/333-0320**) and **Old Town Trolley** (☎ **215/928-8687**), with guides who point out all the high spots. Pickup spots include Liberty Bell Pavilion, Independence Park Visitor Center, and the Franklin Institute.

Many specific-interest tours such as African-American Philadelphia, architectural walks, Jewish sites in Society Hill, and the Italian Market exist. Check the **Visitor Center** (☎ **215/636-3300**) for information.

From May through October, **Centipede Tours, Inc.** (☎ **215/735-3123**) has evening tours of the historic area led by costumed guides. They leave from Welcome Park at 2nd and Walnut streets at 6:30pm. Tours of Old City (Fri) and Society Hill (Sat) take 90 minutes. Call for reservations.

**CRUISES & BOAT TOURS**   Two choices are available at Penn's Landing. The *Spirit of Philadelphia* (☎ **215/923-1419**) at the Great Plaza combines lunch, brunch, or dinner with a cruise on a 600-person passenger ship, fully climate controlled, with two enclosed decks and two open-air decks. Trips require reservations.

The *Liberty Belle II* (☎ **215/629-1131**) boards from Lombard Street Circle, near the Chart House restaurant at the southern end of Penn's Landing, and can accommodate up to 475 passengers on three decks.

The *Riverbus* (☎ **609/365-1400**) provides a 10-minute crossing from a landing just outside the Independence Seaport Museum and the New Jersey State Aquarium. It has a large interior, and the views of the Philadelphia skyline are great. Departures from Penn's Landing are on the hour; from Camden, on the half hour. Hours are 9am–5pm daily.

**ATTRACTIONS**   The city's top attraction is ✪ **Independence National Historical Park,** centering around Chestnut Street between 5th and 6th streets. The Declaration of Independence was written and announced here in 1776, the U.S. Constitution was written in 1787, and Philadelphia was the nation's capital for 10 years while awaiting the construction of the new capital at Washington, D.C. The National Historical Park comprises 40 buildings on 45 acres of Center City real estate, with **Independence Hall** and the **Liberty Bell** in its glass pavilion as the most prominent. **Graff (Declaration) House, City Tavern, Pemberton House,** and **Library Hall** all were reconstructed on the original sites; **Liberty Bell Pavilion, Franklin Court,** and the **Visitor Center** are contemporary structures.

A park ranger must lead you through Independence Hall, and you must reserve a place for the free and frequent guided tours of the Bishop White House and the Todd House. Avoid waits by arriving early to sign up. This can be done at the **Visitor Center,** 3rd and Chestnut streets (☎ **215/597-8974**). Hours for all park sites are 9am–5pm, but grounds are never closed.

**Academy of Natural Sciences.** *19th St. and Benjamin Franklin Pkwy.* ☎ *215/ 299-1000. Admission $6.75 adults, $6 seniors, $5.75 children 3–12, free for children under 3. Mon–Fri 10am–4:30pm, Sat–Sun and holidays 10am–5pm. Bus: PHLASH, 32, 33, 76.* If you're looking for dinosaurs, the academy is the best place to find them. Kids love the big diorama halls, with cases of several species mounted and posed in authentic settings, and a $2.5-million permanent display, "Discovering Dinosaurs," which features more than a dozen specimens, including a huge *Tyrannosaurus rex* with jaws agape. The rest of the space covers flora and fauna from around the world, with frequent live demonstrations with rocks, birds, plants, and animals.

✪ **Barnes Foundation.** *300 N. Latches Lane, Merion Station, PA 19066.* ☎ *610/ 667-0290. Admission $5. Thurs 12:30–3pm, Fri–Sun 9:30am–5pm. Hours may expand in the future. SEPTA: Take Paoli local train to Merion; walk up Merion Ave. and turn left onto Latches Lane. Bus: 44 to Old Lancaster Rd. and Latches Lane. Auto: I-76 (Schuylkill Expressway) north to City Line Ave., then south on City Line 1$^1/_2$ miles to Old Lancaster Rd. Turn right onto Old Lancaster, continue 4 blocks, and turn left onto Latches Lane.* If you're interested in art, the Barnes Foundation will stun you with its magnificence. Eccentric Albert Barnes crammed his French provincial mansion with over 1,000 masterpieces—180 Renoirs, 69 Cézannes, innumerable Impressionists and post-Impressionists, and a generous sampling of European art from the Italian primitives onward. The stars of the collection have recently been cleaned, and admission policies may become more user-friendly.

**Betsy Ross House.** *239 Arch St.* ☎ *215/627-5343. Admission free, but suggested contribution of $1 adult, 25¢ child. Tues–Sun 10am–5pm. Bus: PHLASH, 5, 17, 33, 48.* One colonial home everybody knows about is this one near Christ Church, restored in 1937 and distinguished by the Stars and Stripes outside. Elizabeth (Betsy) Ross was a Quaker needlewoman, newly widowed in 1776; nobody knows if she did the original American flag of 13 stars set in a field of 13 red and white stripes, but she was commissioned to sew new ships' flags for the Revolutionary War fleet. The house takes only a minute or two to walk through, and it's a great picture of "normal" colonial life, from low ceilings to the cellar kitchen (standard placement for this room), tiny bedrooms, and model working areas for upholstering, making musket balls, and the like.

**Christ Church.** *2nd St., one-half block north of Market St.* ☎ *215/922-1695. Admission free, although donations are welcome. Mon–Sat 9am–5pm, Sun 1–5pm. Sun services at 9 and 11am. Closed Mon–Tues Jan–Feb and major holidays. Bus: PHLASH, 5, 17, 33, 48.* The most beautiful colonial building (1724–54) north of Market Street, its spire gleams white from anywhere in the neighborhood. The interior spans one large arch, with galleries above the sides as demanded by the Anglican church. Behind the altar, the massive Palladian window was the wonder of worshipers and probably the model for the one in Independence Hall. Seating is by pew—Washington's is marked with a plaque—and it's impossible to avoid the history in its stones, memorials, plaques, and grassy park with benches.

✪ **Elfreth's Alley.** *2nd St. between Arch and Race sts.* ☎ *215/574-0560. Admission: Street is public; Mantua Maker's House $1 adults, 50¢ children, $2.50 families. Tues– Sat 10am–4pm, Sun noon–4pm. Bus: PHLASH, 5, 48, 76.* The modern Benjamin Franklin Bridge shadows Elfreth's Alley, the oldest continuously inhabited street in America. Most of colonial Philadelphia looked much like this: cobblestone lanes between the major thoroughfares; small two-story homes; and pent eaves over doors and windows, a local trademark. Note the busybody mirrors that let residents see who was at their door (or someone else's) from the second-story bedroom. Jews, blacks, Welsh, and Germans made it a miniature melting pot. Number 126, the 1755 **Mantua**

**Maker's House** (cape maker), now serves as a museum and is the only house open to the public.

**Franklin Court.** *Chestnut St. between 3rd and 4th sts., with another entrance at 316–318 Market St. Admission free. Daily 9am–5pm, including the post office and postal museum. Bus: PHLASH, 76.* Franklin Court is an imaginative, informative, and downright fun museum, built under and around the site of Ben Franklin's local mansion and run by the National Park Service. The exhibits reflect Franklin's almost limitless interests as scientist, inventor, statesman, printer, and politician, and minitheaters reenact critical scenes from his career in London, Paris, and at Independence Hall. You reach Franklin Court through arched passages from either Market or Chestnut streets, and the Market entrance adjoins Franklin's reconstructed and fully operating post office.

**Franklin Institute Science Museum.** *Logan Circle, 20th St. and Benjamin Franklin Pkwy.* ☎ *215/448-1200 or 215/564-3375 for a taped message. Admission $8.50 adults, $7.50 children; additional charges for certain exhibits. Science Center, daily 9:30am–5pm; Futures Center, Mon–Wed 9:30am–5pm, Thurs–Sat 9:30am–9pm, Sun 9:30am–6pm. Bus: PHLASH, 33, 76.* The science museum is a thoroughly imaginative trip that shows us the influence of the world of science on our lives. The complex actually has four parts: a memorial to Ben Franklin; exhibitions such as a gigantic walk-through heart, ship models, and antique airplanes; a new Futures Center addition with eight permanent, interactive exhibits on space, earth, computers, chemistry, and health; and a new summer science park outside. The texts throughout are witty and disarming. There are good dining choices in the museum.

✪ **Independence Seaport Museum.** *Penn's Landing at 211 S. Columbus Blvd.* ☎ *215/925-5439. Admission $5 adults, $4 seniors, 2.50 children. Combined admission to the museum and Historic Ship Zone (USS* Olympia *and USS* Becuna; *see below) $7.50 adults, $6 seniors, $3.50 children. Daily 10am–5pm except major holidays.* This 1995 star of the Penn's Landing waterfront is a user-friendly maritime museum, beautifully laid out and blending a first-class collection with interactive techniques for a trip through time that engages all ages. One of the museum's most attractive features is the **Workshop on the Water,** where you can watch classes and amateurs undertake traditional wooden boat building and restoration throughout the year.

**Liberty Bell.** *Chestnut St. between 5th and 6th sts. Admission free. Summer, daily 9am–8pm; rest of year, daily 9am–5pm. Bus: PHLASH, 76.* The Liberty Bell, America's symbol of independence, "proclaims liberty throughout the land." It was commissioned in 1751 and recast 2 years later, cracking beyond use in 1846. Since 1976, the Liberty Bell has had its own glass Liberty Bell Pavilion across the street from its original location, once the site of the Executive Mansion. You can no longer touch the bell, but you can photograph it. You can even see it through the glass walls at night.

**Museum of American Art of the Pennsylvania Academy of Fine Arts.** *118 N. Broad St. at Cherry St.* ☎ *215/972-7600. Admission $5.95 adults, $4.95 seniors and students with ID, $3.95 children 5–12. Mon–Sat 10am–5pm; Sun 11am–5pm. Tours free with admission. Leave from the Grand Stairhall Sat–Sun at 12:30 and 2pm. Bus: C, 48.* Located two blocks north of City Hall, the Museum of American Art of PAFA continues the work of the first art school in the country in a beautifully restored beaux-arts Frank Furness building. Following a renovation in late 1994, the academy unveiled a major reinstallation of 300 works out of their 6,000 canvases, including 18th- and 19th-century masters such as Allston, the Peale family, and Gilbert Stuart. The ground floor houses an excellent bookstore and cafe.

✪ **Penn's Landing.** *Delaware River waterfront between Market and South sts.* ☎ *215/ 629-3200. Open-air esplanade never restricted; several sites have separate admissions and* *hours. Bus: PHLASH, 17, 21, 33, and 76 go directly to Penn's Landing; 42 is an easy walk from 2nd St. On Foot: Pedestrian walkways across Front St., on Market, Chestnut, Walnut, Spruce, or South sts.; Front St. connects directly at Spruce St. Auto: From I-95 use the Columbus Blvd./Washington St. exit and turn left onto Columbus Blvd. From I-76 take I-676 across Center City to I-95 south. Ample parking available onsite.* Philadelphia started out as a major freshwater port of the Delaware River valley, and tourism is increasingly nudging it back to the water after 50 years of neglect. A complete waterfront park is now at Penn's Landing on Columbus Boulevard between Market and Lombard streets, and includes the Independence Seaport Museum (see above) and an assembly of historic ships, performance and park areas, a skating rink, restaurants, cruise facilities, and a marina. There are pedestrian bridges over I-95, between the city and the riverfront, and there's an ongoing project to install wider sidewalks, lighting, and kiosks along Columbus Boulevard, with sites and transport connecting them all. Penn's Landing has a pleasantly spacious feeling, and in time will be equivalent to Baltimore's Inner Harbor.

○ **Philadelphia Museum of Art.** *26th St. and Ben Franklin Pkwy. ☎ 215/763-8100 or 215/684-7500 for 24-hour information. Admission $7 adults; $4 students, seniors, and children 5–18; free for children under 5; free Sun 10am–1pm. Tues–Sun 10am–5pm; Wed evening hours until 8:45pm with music, talks, movies, and socializing. Bus: 7, 32, 38, 43, 76; this last is door-to-door, but runs only until 6pm.* Even on a hazy day you can see America's third-largest art museum from City Hall—resplendent, huge, a temple on a hill. Aided by magnificent donations, energetic management, and a recent blockbuster on Cézanne, it's undoubtedly one of the "hottest" groupings of art objects in America, strong in American arts and crafts and in most aspects of classical European art. Upstairs is a chronological sweep in 83 galleries of European arts from medieval times through about 1850. The 19th-century gallery has many works by Philadelphia's Thomas Eakins, which evoke the spirit of the city in watercolors and oils. Late hours on Wednesday, with films, music, and drinks have quickly become a city social favorite.

**University of Pennsylvania Museum of Archaeology and Anthropology.** *33rd and Spruce sts. ☎ 215/898-4000. Admission $5 donation adults, $2.50 students and seniors; free for children under 6. Tues–Sat 10am–4:30pm, Sun 1–5pm. Closed holidays and Sun Memorial Day–Labor Day. Bus: 21, 30 (from 30th St. Station), 40, 42, 90.* This Ivy League university got into the work of excavations and fieldwork on the ground floor, and the romanesque brick structure houses some real gems of Benin bronzes, ancient cuneiform texts, Mesopotamian masterpieces, Pre-Colombian gold, and other artifacts of every continent. The basement Egyptian galleries, including colossal architectural remains from Memphis and "The Egyptian Mummy: Secrets and Science," are family favorites. Probably the most famous excavation display is a spectacular Sumerian trove of jewelry and household objects from the royal tombs of the ancient city of Ur. The Ancient Greek Gallery in the classical-world collection has 400 superb objects.

**U.S. Mint.** *5th and Arch sts. ☎ 215/597-7350. Admission free. May–June, Mon–Sat 9am–4:30pm; July–Aug, daily 9am–4:30pm; Sept–April, Mon–Fri 9am–4:30pm. Closed New Year's Day, Christmas. Bus: 5, 48, 76.* This U.S. Mint was the first authorized by the federal government in Washington's first term. About 1,500,000 coins are turned out every hour. A self-guided walk takes you through the processes of melting raw metal, rolling sheets to coin thinness, punching out blank coins, and pressing on the designs. A counting machine automatically sews lots of 5,000 into bags, headed for Federal Reserve Banks.

**LITERARY ATTRACTIONS**   The **Rosenbach Museum and Library,** 2010 Delancey Place, between Spruce and Pine streets (**☎ 215/732-1600**) now houses their collection of 30,000 books and 270,000 documents in a charming town house. The Rosenbach specializes in illuminated manuscripts, parchment, rough drafts, and first editions. An admission fee ($3.50 adults, $2.50 students and seniors) allows you a 75-minute guided tour. Holdings include the original manuscript of Joyce's *Ulysses* and first editions of Melville, in Melville's own bookcase. The **Central Library** of the **Free Library of Philadelphia,** Logan Circle at 19th and Vine streets (☎ **215/686-5322**), has some rare collections along with interesting exhibitions on local history and travel.

**GREAT VIEWS** **City Hall,** Broad and Market streets (☎ **215/569-3187**), offers free admission to what was until recently the highest, and remains the most central, spot in town. When construction of City Hall began in 1871, it was planned to be the tallest structure in the world. It's long since lost that claim, but there's still general love for the crowning 37-foot statue of William Penn by A. M. Calder and the tower view. Take any corner elevator to the seventh floor and follow the red tape to two escalators and a waiting area for the tower elevator. The elevator to the Penn statue's recently renovated shoestrings, at 480 feet, can hold only eight people, and the outdoor cupola cannot hold many more. The view from the top encompasses not only the city but also the upper and lower Delaware Valley and port, western New Jersey, and suburban Philadelphia.

**BEST BETS FOR KIDS** In Center City, top honors go to the **Please Touch Museum,** 210 N. 21st St. (☎ **215/963-0667**), especially for kids 7 or younger. Its creative, thoughtful areas involve the whole family in how a TV studio works, the journey food makes to our tables, and play in motion, mixing gymnastics and science. The **Free Library of Philadelphia Children's Department** across Logan Circle, at Vine and 19th streets, is a joy, with a separate entrance, 100,000 books, and microcomputers in a playground-like space, and weekend hours. The **Philadelphia Zoological Garden** in Fairmount Park, 34th Street and Girard Avenue (☎ **215/243-1100**), was the nation's first and remains strong, with white lions as a major new attraction and 1,500 other animals. **Rittenhouse Square** at 18th and Walnut streets has a small playground and space to eat and relax in the heart of the city. Near Independence Hall, try **Delancey Park,** at Delancey between 3rd and 4th streets (with lots of fountains and animal sculptures to climb on), or **Starr Garden,** at 6th and Lombard streets.

The **Great Plaza** at Penn's Landing has free children's theater performances by American Family Theater on Friday at 7pm in July and August. The **Philadelphia Museum of Art** has Sunday-morning and early-afternoon programs for children at minimal or no charge.

**SPORTS** Philadelphia boasts two adjoining stadiums on South Broad Street. **Veterans Stadium** (☎ **215/686-1776**), a graceful bowl with undulating ramps, can seat 58,000 for the Phillies in baseball and 68,000 for the Eagles in football. The **CoreStates Center** (☎ **215/336-3600**) hosts the Philadelphia Flyers pro hockey and Philadelphia 76ers basketball teams. For ticket information, call the **Phillies** (☎ **215/463-1000**), the **Eagles** (☎ **215/463-5500**), the **76ers** (☎ **215/339-7676**), or the **Flyers** (☎ **215/465-5500**). Philadelphia is also a hotbed of college rowing along the Schuylkill River; track and field; college basketball; and annual marathons, tennis tournaments, and pro cycling.

**SHOPPING** The best places to look for high fashion and international wares are the specialty shops around **Liberty Place** and the nearby **Rittenhouse Square. The Shops at Liberty Place,** 1625 Chestnut St., between 16th and 17th streets (☎ **215/851-9055**), are the real thing, with 70 stores and stalls in a handsome 60-story tower that provide enjoyable, comfortable shopping for quality merchandise, complete with a great food court and public atrium. The once-funky area on **South Street** has turned into big business. Because restaurants and nightlife now line South Street from Front to 8th streets, many of the 180 stores here are open well into the evening and offer goods ranging from the gentrified to the somewhat grotesque.

There are two enormous malls to the north of the city: **King of Prussia,** a 450-store behemoth second only to Minnesota's Mall of America, and **Franklin Mills,** an outlet mall that draws four times the traffic of the Liberty Bell.

Certain parts of the city are known for specific types of shopping. **Pine Street** from 9th to 12th streets is "Antique Row"; **Sansom Street** from 7th to 9th streets is "Jeweler's Row." **Old City,** just north of the historic park, and **Manayunk,** a northwestern corner of the city, specialize in hip contemporary crafts.

**Markets**    Philadelphia has always been a market town, and covered markets with stalls continue to be a local feature, adapted to the modern indoor mall. **Reading Terminal Market,** 12th and Arch streets (☎ **215/922-2317**), is a century-old national landmark with a combination of restaurants and greengrocers, snack shops, bakeries, butchers, fish markets, Amish specialties, and gourmet grocer/charcuteries. Scrapple, mangoes, clam chowder, pretzels—you name it, if it's fresh and unpackaged, it's there. You can still see the Amish in the big city on their market days of Wednesday and Saturday, and you can buy sticky buns at **Beiler's Pies,** soft pretzels made before your eyes at **Fisher's,** and individual egg custards (75¢) and chicken pot pie at **The Dutch Eating Place.**

While touring South Street or South Philadelphia, be sure to visit the **Italian Market,** centering around 9th Street between Christian and Federal streets, between dawn and dusk for the freshest produce, pasta, seafood, and other culinary delights. Fast-talking vendors, opera-singing butchers, and try-it-before-you-buy-it cheese merchants hawk their wares.

## ACCOMMODATIONS

Given growing numbers of conventions, increased occupancy is driving rates up, so expect to pay at least $110 for moderate doubles. Most hotels offer weekend packages and discounts for specific ages and groups. Older hotels in the Rittenhouse Square area often have larger, more individualized spaces. Between City Hall and the Philadelphia Museum of Art you'll find sleek 1980s hotels, with a lesser surge of smaller hotels in or near historic Society Hill. Outside Center City, West Philadelphia and the airport are only a bus or train ride away and rates are a bit cheaper.

**Abigail Adams Bed & Breakfast.** *1208 Walnut St., Philadelphia, PA 19107.* ☎ *800/887-1776 or 215/546-7336. Fax 215/546-7573. 32 rooms. $90 single or double; $120 suite. Rates include continental breakfast. AE, DC, DISC, MC, V.* This late 19th-century shell was restored in 1992, and the nearby Convention Center and hospitals send some 30 people a night who save at least $50 from the Marriott's prices. There are seven floors of comfortable, bigger-than-average rooms with solid-core doors, private baths, cable TV, phones, and a restaurant.

**Best Western Independence Park Inn.** *235 Chestnut St., Philadelphia, PA 19106.* ☎ *800/528-1234 or 215/922-4443. Fax 215/922-4487. 36 rms. $99–$135 for one to three people. Rates include breakfast and afternoon tea. Children under 12 stay free in parents' room. AE, DC, DISC, MC, V. Parking $9.* The top choice here for bed-and-breakfast–style accommodations, this 1856 former dry-goods store with eight floors is only two blocks from Independence Hall. Interiors have armoires, lathed bedposts, and lots of illumination and mirrors. All the windows are triple casement and double glazed. There isn't a restaurant, but continental breakfast and tea in a glass-enclosed garden courtyard are served.

**Clarion Suites Convention Center.** *1010 Race St., Philadelphia, PA 19107.* ☎ *800/272-6232 or 215/922-1730. Fax 215/922-6258. 92 suites. $120 single; $130 double. Rates include continental breakfast. AE, DC, MC, V. Parking $8.* Rooms are spacious at this 1880s renovated handsome dark-red-brick building with lots of terra-cotta tiling and wide arches. It retains 13-foot ceilings, solid floors, and wood cross beams. Other bonuses include a new breakfast room/bar, small fitness center, very clean and well-stocked Chinese market directly across the street, and a location two blocks from Reading Terminal Market.

**Comfort Inn at Penn's Landing.** *100 N. Columbus Blvd. (formerly Delaware Ave.), Philadelphia, PA 19106.* ☎ *800/228-5150 or 215/627-7900. Fax 215/238-0809. 185 rms. $119 double. Rates include continental breakfast. Children under 18 stay free in parents' room. AE, DC, MC, V.* This is Old City's only hotel, nestled into a corner between I-95 and the Delaware River, built to airport-area noise specifications, with insulated windows and other features to lessen the din of traffic. The eastern views of the river on upper floors are stupendous. Guests can use a shuttle van to Center City, coin laundry, and fitness room. There is no restaurant.

**Doubletree Hotel Philadelphia.** *Broad St. at Locust St., Philadelphia, PA 19107.* ☎ *800/222-8733 or 215/893-1600. Fax 215/893-1663. 427 rms. $199 single or double; $185–$200 deluxe. Weekday and weekend specials available. AE, DC, MC, V. Self-parking $13; valet parking $17.* The hotel is fairly bland looking except for the four-story atrium, but has handsome rooms and a prime tourist location for shopping and nightlife, with the Academy of Music across the street. Recently renovated guest rooms each have two views of town because of the sawtooth design. Ten rooms are designed for the disabled. Conveniences include a restaurant, health club, two racquetball courts, a small jogging track, and turndown service with chocolate-chip cookies.

**Embassy Suites Center City.** *1776 Benjamin Franklin Pkwy. at Logan Square, Philadelphia, PA 19103.* ☎ *800/362-2779 or 215/561-1776. Fax 215/963-0122. 288 suites. $169 single; $184 double, with full complimentary breakfast. Weekend packages from $116. AE, DC, MC, V. Parking $15.50 weekdays, $10 weekends.* The big cylinder of marble and glass, designed as luxury apartments, looks dated, but actually works well within their "room plus kitchenette plus living room area" format. Grace Kelly's family had the last penthouse here. Guests can enjoy a full breakfast at TGI Friday's (the connected restaurant), fitness room, nightly managers' reception, balcony terraces, and Please Touch Too room with games and PCs for the kids.

**✪ KormanSuites Hotel and Conference Center.** *2001 Hamilton St. (just off the Parkway), Philadelphia, PA 19130.* ☎ *888/4-KORMAN or 215/569-7300. Fax 215/569-0584. 182 rms. $169 efficiency; $189 two-bedroom plus kitchen; $229 one-bedroom suite with connecting den. Rates include continental breakfast. Discounts for stays of 2 weeks or more. Children stay free in parents' room. AE, DC, MC, V. Parking free.* The amenities and location make this an excellent value; the weekend packages are outstanding. KormanSuites is really a grand hotel, but it's in separate pieces. A 28-story tower is connected by a marble-and-mahogany lobby and a glass-enclosed corridor to a restaurant and lush Japanese sculpture garden and pool. The standard "living" areas have full dining table for four, TV, full couch, and three double closets. Each bedroom has a queen-size bed and extra TV, and the adjoining bath has a stacked washer/dryer. On the premises are a restaurant, complimentary shuttle van running hourly through Center City to Independence Park, concierge, outdoor pool, Jacuzzi, two tennis and platform tennis courts, high-tech spa and fitness center, full-service hair salon, and ATM.

**The Latham.** *135 S. 17th St. at Walnut St., Philadelphia, PA 19103.* ☎ *800/ 528-4261 or 215/563-7474. Fax 215/563-4034. 140 rms, 3 suites. $165 standard single; $185 double; $195–$215 superior with king-size bed. Basic weekend package $99–$109 double per night including breakfast and parking. One or two children stay free in parents' room. AE, DC, MC, V. Valet parking $14.* The Latham brings to mind a small, superbly run Swiss hostelry, with its charm, congeniality, and small attentions. Weekdays see mostly a business clientele, with no convention groups. The hotel has a restaurant, concierge, turndown service with Godiva chocolate mints, and free access to a nearby fitness club with indoor pool.

**Omni Hotel at Independence Park.** *4th and Chestnut sts., Philadelphia, PA 19106.* ☎ *800/843-6664 or 215/925-0000. Fax 215/925-1263. 141 rms, 9 suites. $179–$229 double. Weekend rates available from $119 double per night. Children stay free in parents' room. AE, CB, DC, DISC, MC, V. Self-parking $13.50; valet parking $19.50.* This medium-sized, polished hotel opened in 1990 and is located in the middle of Independence National Historical Park. All rooms have Independence Park views, and horse-drawn carriages clip-clop past. Rooms are cheery, and have plants, state-of-the-art room keys, voice mail, VCR, two telephones, and windows that open. Extras include a noted restaurant, afternoon tea in lobby lounge, 24-hour room service, concierge, complimentary van to Center City stops (weekdays 7am–7pm), indoor lap pool, whirlpool and health club, and a Ritz 5 movie theater tucked into the back corner.

**Penn Tower Hotel.** *Civic Center Blvd. at 34th St., Philadelphia, PA 19104.* ☎ *800/356-7366 or 215/387-8333. Fax 215/386-8306. 175 rms, 7 suites. $144 double. Packages start at $99 per couple per night. AE, DC, MC, V. Parking $9.* Penn Tower, a 1980s rough concrete former Hilton in West Philadelphia, is steps from the University of Pennsylvania and its medical center, 30th Street Station, and Drexel University. The hotel has a restaurant, complimentary van service to airport and Independence Park/historic district, and complimentary guest passes to Penn's nearby Hutchinson Health Complex.

**Philadelphia Marriott.** *12th and Market sts., Philadelphia, PA 19107.* ☎ *800/228-9290 or 215/972-6700. Fax 215/972-6704. 1,200 rms. $190–$210 double. Weekend specials from $138. AE, DC, MC, V. Valet parking $20.* The Marriott chain hotel is the biggest in Pennsylvania, linked by an elevated covered walkway to the Reading Terminal Shed of the Convention Center. It's grand, tasteful without luxury, and convenient to everything; service is superb. Rooms feature dark woods, a TV armoire, club chair and ottoman, round table plus a separate desk. Facilities include restaurants, corporate and some luxury services, complimentary health club with indoor lap pool, whirlpool, aerobics/fitness room, locker rooms, and wet and dry saunas. There is a direct internal connection to SEPTA subways and airport train.

**✪ Rittenhouse Hotel.** *210 W. Rittenhouse Square. Philadelphia, PA 19103.* ☎ *800/635-1042 or 215/546-9000. Fax 215/732-3364. 98 rms. From $230 single; from $285 double. Weekend rates from $160. Packages including health club, dinners, etc. usually available. AE, DC, MC, V. Parking $21.* Among Philadelphia's luxury hotels, the Rittenhouse has the fewest and largest rooms, the most satisfying views, and the most homegrown Philadelphia feel. Built in 1989, it's a jagged concrete-and-glass high rise off the western edge of Philadelphia's most distinguished public square, with two restaurants, tearoom, 24-hour room service, concierge, turndown service, twice-daily room cleaning, and a health facility available.

**✪ Ritz-Carlton Philadelphia.** *17th and Chestnut sts. at Liberty Place, Philadelphia, PA 19103.* ☎ *800/241-3333 or 215/563-1600. Fax 215/564-9559. 290 rms, 17 suites. $205–$265 double. Weekend rates from $169. Packages available. AE, DC, MC, V. Self-parking $17.50; valet parking $22.* Opened in 1990, this luxury hotel with over-the-top service is connected to Liberty Place, a major urban mall below, but is 18th century in feel, and romantic. The guest rooms feature bedside walnut tables, desks, and beds; modern baths are outfitted with black-and-white marble and silverplate fixtures. Three noted restaurants, 24-hour room service and concierge, turndown service, complimentary morning newspapers, transport to and from airport, small exercise and sauna facility make the hotel a great place to stay.

**Sheraton Society Hill.** *1 Dock St., Philadelphia, PA 19106.* ☎ *800/325-3535 or 215/238-6000. Fax 215/922-2709. 365 rms, 17 suites. $210–$220 double. Weekend packages $159–$179 double per night. Children under 17 stay free in parents' room. AE, DC, MC, V. Parking $12.50.* The 1986 hotel fits in the tree-lined cobblestoned streets of the historic district, with Flemish Bond brickwork and only four stories. Rooms are small and low, but furnishings are top-quality Drexel Heritage mahogany and dark marble baths. Conveniences include a restaurant, lounge, 24-hour room service, free shuttle van to Center City, indoor pool (open daily from 6am to 10pm), whirlpool, and small health club.

**OTHER ACCOMMODATIONS**   A **Bed & Breakfast Connection/Bed & Breakfast of Philadelphia,** Box 21, Devon, PA 19333 (☎ **800/448-3169** or 610/687-3565; fax 610/995-9524), represents more than 100 personally inspected accommodations in Philadelphia, Valley Forge, the Brandywine Valley, and Lancaster, Montgomery, and Bucks counties. Philadelphia accommodations include a contemporary loft with a great Delaware River view, a mid-18th-century inn, and a town house tucked in an alley seconds from Rittenhouse Square. Rates range from $45 to $225 double. Phone reservations accepted Mon–Fri 9am–7pm, Sat 9am–5pm.

The best hotels near the airport are **Doubletree Guest Suites,** 4101 Island Ave., Philadelphia, PA 19153 (☎ **800/424-2900** or 215/365-6600; fax 215/492-9858), with suites surrounding a dramatic atrium; and the new-in-1995 **Philadelphia Airport Marriott Hotel,** Arrivals Road, Philadelphia, PA 19153 (☎ **800/228-9290** or 215/492-9009; fax 215/492-6799), with 419 new rooms and the only hotel linked by skywalk to the airport.

## DINING

Philadelphia has many traditional early colonial favorites, and traditional ethnic restaurants. In 1994, *Condé Nast Traveler*'s readers rated seven Philadelphia restaurants among America's top 50, including Le Bec-Fin as number one. Today literally dozens of young entrepreneurs are producing excellent gourmet fare in Center City and in Manayunk, a hot enclave along the Schuylkill River in the northeast. Most kitchens stop serving at 10pm in summer, 9pm other seasons.

**Chart House.** *555 S. Columbus Blvd. (formerly Delaware Ave.) at Penn's Landing.* ☎ *215/625-8383. Reservations recommended. Main courses $16–$36. Sun fixed-price brunch $20. AE, DC, MC, V. Mon–Thurs 4–11pm, Fri 5pm–midnight, Sat 4pm–midnight, Sun 4–10pm; Sun brunch 10:30am–2pm. STEAKHOUSE/SEAFOOD.* The busiest restaurant in all Philadelphia has to be the Chart House, right on the Delaware River. Expect a spirited crowd and frequent birthday celebrations, but they have a track record for reasonably priced dinners, with soup, fresh molasses or sourdough bread, and an unlimited salad bar included. All seats have spectacular views, and the service will make you wish you had had camp counselors that enthusiastic. Children's menu available.

**Circa.** *1518 Walnut St.* ☎ *215/545-6800. Reservations recommended. Main courses $9–$18; lunch $6–$13. AE, MC, V. Tues–Fri 11:30am–2:30pm, Mon–Thurs 4:30–10pm, Fri–Sat 4:30–11pm, Sun 4:30–9:30pm. Dancing Fri–Sat 10:30pm–2:20am, Labor Day to Memorial Day. AMERICAN/MEDITERRANEAN.* This 1994 labor of love is one of Philadelphia's hottest spots. With great food on a great restaurant block, it combines dinner with a sophisticated dance club. It's magnificent and yet engaging and comfortable, and it's cheaper than you think it's going to be. Cuisine is Mediterranean with a twist up and westward—strong, flavorful food like duck ravioli, goat cheese, and sun-dried cherries or roast salmon osso buco. Friday and Saturday nights after 10:30, the ground floor and mezzanine become a club with a jammed dance floor.

✪ **City Tavern.** *138 S. 2nd St., near Walnut St.* ☎ *215/413-1443. Reservations recommended. Main courses $16–$26, lunch $8–$15. AE, CB, DC, MC, V. Mon–Fri 11:30am–10pm, Fri–Sat 11:30am–11pm, Sun 11:30am–9pm. AMERICAN.* You can relive the 1780s in this reconstruction of the same tavern that members of the Constitutional Convention used as a coffee shop, ballroom, and club. The U.S. government now owns the building, and the concessionaire is terrific, with dishes like local brook trout, stews over noodles, and meat pies. The "shrubs" or punches pack a wallop, inside or in the garden areas adjoining the park.

**DiNardo's Famous Crabs.** *312 Race St.* ☎ *215/925-5115. Reservations required for six or more. Appetizers $3.75–$8; crabs $2.50 each; other main courses $12–$22; lunch $5–$9. AE, CB, DC, MC, V. Mon–Thurs 11am–11pm, Fri–Sat 11am–midnight, Sun 4–9pm. SEAFOOD.* This is the best moderately priced spot in the area around the Betsy Ross House and Elfreth's Alley. DiNardo's has two unique factors—the site, which dates from the Revolutionary War, and the prices, which are very reasonable thanks to huge volume. Experienced hands dredge Gulf of Mexico crabs with the house seasoning of 24 spices and pack heavy-gauge steel hampers with them; other seafood choices abound.

**Dock Street Brewing Company.** *2 Logan Sq. (corner of 18th and Cherry sts.).* ☎ *215/496-0413. Reservations required for six or more. Main courses $7–$15; lunch $5–$11. Fresh-brewed tap beer $2.50–$3.50 per glass. AE, CB, DC, DISC, MC, V. Mon–Thurs 11am–midnight, Fri–Sat 11am–2am, Sun noon–11pm. INTERNATIONAL.* This brew pub is just right for the 1990s: relaxed and tasty fare, with a definite hook in the spotless on-premises microbrewery. Six or more fresh Dock Street beers, ales, stouts, and porters are on tap. Lunch brings soups, several fresh salads, and pub-style sandwiches; dinner main courses include maple-chipotle barbecued salmon, hand-carved roast beef, and traditional English fish-and-chips with malt vinegar.

✪ **The Garden.** *1617 Spruce St., near Rittenhouse Square.* ☎ *215/546-4455. Reservations recommended. Main courses $15–$25; lunch $10–$22. AE, CB, DC, MC, V. Mon–Fri 11:30am–1:45pm (appetizers 2:30–5:30pm); Mon–Sat 5:30–10pm. Closed Sat–Sun July–Aug. CONTINENTAL.* This former music academy captures the city's sense of style of taste without ornateness, with antique tables and bars and 19th-century prints of fruit and animals. The three softly lit dining areas and bedecked back garden present high-quality, comfortable dishes like breaded Dover sole, calves' liver with fried potato and shallots, and chateaubriand with Roquefort sauce. The chocolate sampler plate is frighteningly good.

**Golden Pond.** *1006 Race St.* ☎ *215/923-0303. Reservations recommended. Main courses $8–$16; lunch special $6. MC, V. Mon–Fri 11:30am–10pm, Sat–Sun noon–11pm. CHINESE.* This very stylish Hong Kong–style place costs a bit more than others in the neighborhood, but the impeccable service and the obviously fresh preparation are worth it. This Chinese cuisine features some potato dishes, chicken, duck, and seafood, but no pork or beef. It's one of the few places that serves brown rice.

✪ **Jack's Firehouse.** *2130 Fairmount Ave.* ☎ *215/232-9000. Reservations recommended. Main courses $17–$23; fixed-price menus $45 and $52. Bar service available; sandwiches from $7. AE, DC, MC, V. Mon–Sat 11:30am–10:30pm; Sun brunch 11am–3pm. Bar open nightly until 2am. CONTEMPORARY AMERICAN.* This is one of the most provocative restaurants in town. Chef Jack McDavid, after raves for Reading Terminal's Down Home Diner, took a turn-of-the-century firehouse and incorporated dramatic American ingredients and flavors in a warm, homey space. The game—bear, bison, and beaver tail to name a few—is outstanding. Seafood and organic vegetables round out the choices. The desserts could be a smooth peanut-butter-and-chocolate cake or sweet pecan pie.

**Jake & Oliver's House of Brews.** *22 S. 3rd St.* ☎ *215/627-4825. Reservations recommended for dinner. Main courses $10–$16; pizzas $8–$9. AE, DC, MC, V. Mon–Fri 11:30am–11:30pm, Sat–Sun 11:30am–12:30am. Bar and dancing daily until 2am. AMERICAN/CONTINENTAL.* This 1837 Greek Revival church has been transformed into a relaxed and improbably good combination of restaurant, bar, and nightclub, steps from Franklin Court. The first-floor restaurant has a new oak floor and a back bar like a Georgian altar, featuring the products of 40 microbreweries from throughout the country along with gourmet pizzas in a brick oven and simple, quickly braised or baked fish and poultry. If you come for dinner, you can stay for the dancing until 2am Thurs–Sat upstairs ($5–$10 cover charge).

**✪ Le Bec-Fin.** *1523 Walnut St.* ☎ *215/567-1000. Reservations required a week ahead for weeknights, months ahead for Fri–Sat. Fixed-price lunch $32; fixed-price dinner $94. AE, DC, MC, V. Lunch seatings Mon–Fri 11:30am and 1:30pm; dinner seatings Mon–Thurs 6 and 9pm, Fri–Sat 6 and 9:30pm. Bar Lyonnais downstairs serves food and drink until midnight. FRENCH.* There's no doubt that Le Bec-Fin is the best in Philadelphia and certainly one of the top 10 in the country. Patron Georges Perrier hails from Lyon, France's gastronomic capital, and commands the respect of restaurateurs on two continents. The opulence of the fixed-price meal will stagger you, as it waltzes through hors d'oeuvres, a fish course, a main course, a salad, cheese, a dessert, and coffee with petits fours. And those dessert carts—unforgettable! Decor is elegant and comfortable, with deep red silk covering acoustic panels.

**Marabella's.** *1420 Locust St.* ☎ *215/545-1845. Reservations not accepted for dinner. Main courses $9–$16; lunch $4–$7. AE, DC, MC, V. Mon–Thurs 11:30am–11pm, Fri–Sat 11:30am–midnight, Sun 3–11pm. INTERNATIONAL.* This trendy trattoria offers pastas, pizza, sandwiches, and grilled seafood, all with contemporary flair and reasonable prices (almost every item under $14). This and another branch on Benjamin Franklin Parkway at 17th Street (☎ *215/981-5555*) are convenient for families and posttheater dining. There are contemporary dishes such as tortellini with goat cheese, sun-dried tomatoes, and olives, and the old standards—spaghetti and meatballs, pizza, and lasagna with meat sauce—are also very well done.

**✪ Ralph's.** *760 S. 9th St.* ☎ *215/627-6011. Reservations recommended. Main courses $9–$16. No credit cards. Lunch and dinner Sun–Thurs noon–9:45pm, Fri–Sat noon–10:45pm. ITALIAN.* South Philly—literally square miles of basic row houses in straight lines between Bainbridge Street and the sports stadiums—is the best place on earth for one particular cuisine: the adaptation of the dishes of south and central Italy to American ingredients and meal sizes. This two-story restaurant a few blocks above the Italian Market is the epitome of the "red gravy" style: unpretentious, comfortable, reasonable, owned by the same family for decades. The baked lasagna and spaghetti with sausage have fans all over the city, but the whole menu is huge. Service is friendly and attentive.

**Sansom Street Oyster House.** *1516 Sansom St.* ☎ *215/567-7683. Reservations not accepted. Main courses $11–$20; lunch $5–$11. Four-course fixed-price dinner $18. AE, DC, MC, V. Mon–Sat 11am–10pm. SEAFOOD.* Chef David Mink knows oysters from every angle—where they come from, how their flavors differ, and how to prepare them. The ambience is traditional seafood parlor, with a tiled floor (instead of sawdust) and plywood paneling. The blackboards listing the daily specials perch beside an endless collection of antique oyster plates and nautical lithographs. In 1989, Mink added the Samuel Adams Brew House upstairs, with two ales and porter on tap.

**✪ Striped Bass.** *1500 Walnut St.* ☎ *215/732-4444. Reservations essential. Main courses $15–28; lunch $13.50–$20. AE, DC, MC, V. Mon–Fri 11:30am–2:30pm,*

*Mon–Sun 5–11pm; brunch Sat–Sun 11am–2:30pm. SEAFOOD.* This spectacular ambience, with a 16-foot steel sculpture of a leaping bass poised over the exposed kitchen and rows of plateaued banquettes, houses what's called the hottest seafood restaurant in the country. The kitchen delivers creative, simple preparations of seafood, with the emphasis on fresh herbs and clean flavors. This is the type of restaurant where you can feel comfortable asking the wait staff for advice.

✪ **Susanna Foo.** *1512 Walnut St.* ☎ *215/545-2666. Reservations recommended for dinner. Main courses $15–$24; lunch $9–$16. AE, MC, V. Mon–Fri 11:30am– 2:30pm; Mon–Thurs 5–10pm, Fri–Sat 5–11pm. CHINESE.* Susanna Foo has been touted in *Gourmet* and *Esquire* magazines and just about everywhere else as providing one of the best blends of Asian and Western cuisines in this country. Appetizers feature such delicacies as curried chicken ravioli with grilled eggplant, slightly crispy but not oily. Noodle dishes, salads, and main courses similarly combine East and West.

✪ **White Dog Café.** *3420 Sansom St.* ☎ *215/386-9224. Reservations recommended. Main courses $14–$19; lunch $8–$16. AE, DC, MC, V. Mon–Fri 11:30am–2:30pm; Mon– Thurs 5:30–10pm, Fri–Sat 5:30–11pm, Sun 5–10pm; brunch Sat–Sun 11am–2:30pm. AMERICAN.* The White Dog attracts everyone, from Penn students to the mayor. Sophisticated kitchen equipment and electronics in two funky row houses are concealed behind an eclectic mélange of checkered tablecloths, antique furniture and lights, and white dogs, dogs, and dogs. The three-counter bar specializes in all-American beers, and the staff offers frequently changing menus as well as "theme" dinners based on the season or a particular American region. They buy produce locally, which eliminates the middleman and results in dishes that "underprice" the market by $3–$5.

**LOCAL FAVORITES** Philadelphia is famous for its cheesesteak hoagie sandwiches (known as submarines, grinders, and torpedoes elsewhere). Preparing them involves ribbons of thinly sliced steak cooked quickly (with onions if you like) and slapped on a roll on top of overlapping slices of provolone or a thick smear of Cheez Wiz. You can find the best at **Jim's Steaks,** 400 South St. (☎ **215/928-1911**), or at **Lee's Hoagies,** in Center City at 44 S. 17th St. (☎ **215/564-1264**), or all over South Philly. For pretzels, try the Amish stalls at **Reading Terminal,** the new **Pretzel Museum** at 312 Market St., or pushcart vendors.

**FOOD COURTS** The **Food Court at Liberty Place,** between Chestnut and Market streets and 16th and 17th streets, has Reading Terminal alumni like Bain's Deli, Bassett's Original Turkey, and Original Philly Steaks joined by Mandarin Express, Montesini Pizza and Pasta Gourmet, Sbarro, and Chick-fil-A. The prepared sandwiches at **New World Coffee** are outstanding. It's spotless, large, and reasonable, with full lunches from $3.50, and you'll find it easy to keep your eyes on the kids as they wander. Open Mon–Sat 9:30am–7pm, Sun noon–6pm.

## PHILADELPHIA AFTER DARK

On the piers along the Delaware River, Old City north of Society Hill, and the northwest quadrant of Center City have joined South Broad Street and Rittenhouse Square as lively areas for cafe- or barhopping and live entertainment. A project to make South Broad Street into "Avenue of the Arts" is picking up steam, with the new ARTS BANK, Clef Club, and Wilma Theater performance spaces, the revitalized Merriam Theater, and an impending new home for the Philadelphia Orchestra and alternate use for the Academy of Music.

The best sources for what's current are the "Weekend" supplement of Friday's *Philadelphia Inquirer* and the free tabloids *City Paper* and *Philadelphia Weekly,* copies of which are distributed throughout Center City. Most cultural attractions have individual box offices open until curtain time. **Upstages** (☎ **215/893-1145**), the city's premier nonprofit box-office service, sells tickets at the Visitor Center, 16th Street and John F. Kennedy Boulevard (☎ **215/567-0670**); the ARTS BANK, 601 S. Broad St.; Plays and Players Theater, 1714 Delancey St.; and at the top of the escalators at Liberty Place, 1625 Chestnut St. The Liberty Place location also offers half-price tickets on the day of the show. There's a small service charge.

**THE PERFORMING ARTS**   Philadelphia's crown jewel in music is the smooth, powerful ✪ **Philadelphia Orchestra,** which performs at the Academy of Music, Broad and Walnut streets (☎ **215/893-1900**), and moves to Mann Music Center in Fairmount Park for 6 weeks of free summer concerts. The Academy of Music also presents visiting classical and pop artists and local opera. **Curtis Institute of Music,** 1726 Locust St. (☎ **215/893-5252**), is a world-famous conservatory and provides mostly free, excellent concerts, operas, and recitals several times weekly in its small hall. The **Philadelphia Chamber Music Society** (☎ **215/569-8587**) brings 35 renowned international soloists, chamber players, and jazz artists annually to the Pennsylvania Convention Center's 600-seat hall, with exceptionally low ticket prices.

✪ **Wilma Theater,** Broad and Spruce streets (☎ **215/963-0249**), is the premier modern theater in town, with a brand-new building, NEA grants, and premieres from the pens of Athol Fugard, Tom Stoppard, and Tina Howe. The **Annenberg Center** on the campus of the University of Pennsylvania, 3680 Walnut St. (☎ **215/898-6791**), has two stages for campus productions as well as for **Philadelphia Drama Guild, Philadephia Festival Theatre for New Plays,** and the like. Casts to or from Broadway are at **Merriam Theater,** Broad and Locust streets (☎ **215/732-5446**), or **The Forrest,** 11th and Walnut streets (☎ **215/923-1515**).

In dance, the **Pennsylvania Ballet** (☎ **215/551-7014**) is tops, with frequent performances at the Academy of Music, Annenberg Center, and the Merriam Theater.

Two firms now control the presentation of large rock concerts in town. The long-established local is **Electric Factory Concerts** (☎ **215/569-9416** or 215/568-3222), which usually books major talent like the Eagles into the CoreStates Spectrum (box office ☎ **215/336-3600**), the city's major indoor arena in South Philly. They also present out of their own **The Electric Factory,** 421 N. 7th St., a plain industrial rehab, for smaller shows like Mary Chapin Carpenter. Recently, Houston-based **Pace Concerts** has begun muscling in national acts such as Diana Ross and Barry Manilow through their exclusive contract with the spanking new **Blockbuster–Sony Music Entertainment Centre at the Waterfront** across the river in Camden, N.J. Locally, try the box office (☎ **609/365-1300**), or purchase tickets in advance through **Tele-Charge** (☎ **800/833-0800**).

**THE CLUB & BAR SCENE**   With huge spaces of fantasyland and night lights shimmering off the water, the piers and warehouses of Columbus Boulevard along the Delaware River have become the hottest social scene in town, both north and south of the Ben Franklin Bridge. In the interests of reducing drunk driving, the club owners run free **water taxis** with surrey tops 9pm–2am along the piers on weekend nights; other nights, charges are minimal. While names are changing rapidly, try **Maui, Egypt, KatManDu,** and **Rock Lobster** for dancing, **Dave & Buster's** for games and sports, and **Moshulu** for dining and conversation.

A number of new clubs and bars have opened in Old City just to the west: **The Bank,** 600 Spring Garden St. (☎ **215/351-9404**), with a large dance floor, and **Silk City Lounge,** 5th and Spring Garden streets (☎ **215/592-8838**), a postmodern hip dive, are two of the best. South Street has always been a late-night hangout; try the **Love Lounge** of the **Knave of Hearts,** 232 South St. (☎ **215/922-3956**), and **Xero,** 613 S. 4th St. (☎ **215/629-0565**). For straight bar ambience, **Cutters,** 2005 Market St.

(☎ 215/851-6262), is a yuppie capital with massive choices, and **Society Hill Hotel,** 3rd and Chestnut streets (☎ 215/925-1919), is always convivial in the historic dis trict.

Philadelphia is a great American hothouse for jazz and blues. Tops are **Warmdaddy's,** Front and Market streets (☎ 215/627-2500), for Southern sounds and acts like Koko Taylor, and **Zanzibar Blue,** 305 S. 11th St. (☎ 215/829-0300), for elegant jazz combos.

## DAY TRIPS FROM PHILADELPHIA

Within 75 minutes, it's an easy jaunt (except on summer weekends) from Center City to some of this country's richest, most historical, and picturesque destinations. These include the historic estates and antique stores and country inns of Bucks County; the Du Pont fiefdoms and American art of Brandywine Valley; and the lush, quiet farmlands of Amish Country and Lancaster County.

**BUCKS COUNTY** New Hope is a former colonial town turned artists' colony; it's somewhat commercial and parking is cramped, but it is a regional center for antiques, specialty stores, restaurants, galleries, and country inns. **Bucks County Playhouse,** 70 S. Main St. (☎ 215/862-2041), is the center of town entertainment, with summer theater featuring Broadway hits and musical revivals in a former gristmill. **Lambertville,** just across the Delaware River in New Jersey, has more scenic routes along the river and, many say, better restaurants. You can find cycles, river rafts and tubes, steam railways, and mule barges along this stretch of the Delaware and a 19th-century adjoining canal winding lazily along green fields and woods. Four miles south on Route 32 is **Washington Crossing State Park,** where George Washington crossed in a small boat on Christmas Eve of 1776 to attack the British; interpreters in period dress enliven the experience. This area also has some of the most elegant country inns on the East Coast, including **Whitehall Inn,** 1370 Pineville Rd., New Hope, PA 18938 (☎ 215/598-7945), and **Evermay,** River Road, Erwinna, PA 18920 (☎ 215/294-9100).

**Doylestown,** the county seat, is pleasant in itself, but notable for three collections all endowed by Henry Mercer (1856–1930), a collector, local archeologist, and master of pottery. **Fonthill** (☎ 215/348-9461) was his home, a castle made of reinforced concrete of his own design; the **Mercer Museum** (☎ 215/345-0210) is a fantastic group of thousands of early American tools, vehicles, cooking pieces, looms, and even weather vanes; and the **Moravian Pottery and Tile Works** (☎ 215/345-6722) is still an impressive working factory.

**Sesame Place,** 100 Sesame Rd., Langhorne, PA 19047 (☎ 215/752-7070), is the nation's only theme park based on the award-winning show, and is good for a totally involving and fun day of rides, parades, and activities for preteens and their parents.

**Essentials:** The best automobile route into Bucks County from Center City is I-95 north. Pa. 32 intersects I-95 in Yardley and runs along the Delaware past Washington Crossing State Park to New Hope, which connects to Doylestown by U.S. 202. From New York, take the New Jersey Turnpike to I-78 west; follow to exit 29 and pick up Route 287 south to Route 202, which crosses the Delaware River at Lambertville straight into New Hope. For more information, contact the **Bucks County Tourist Commission,** 152 Swamp Rd., Doylestown, PA 18901 (☎ 800/836-2825 or 215/345-4552).

**THE AMISH COUNTRY** Fifty miles west of Philadelphia is a quietly beautiful region of rolling hills, winding creeks, neatly cultivated farms, covered bridges, and towns with picturesque names like Paradise and Bird-in-Hand. The real attraction here is the Amish people themselves, who steadfastly retain a life of agrarian simplicity, centered around religious worship and family cohesiveness. The preservation of their world evokes feelings of curiosity, nostalgia, amazement, and respect.

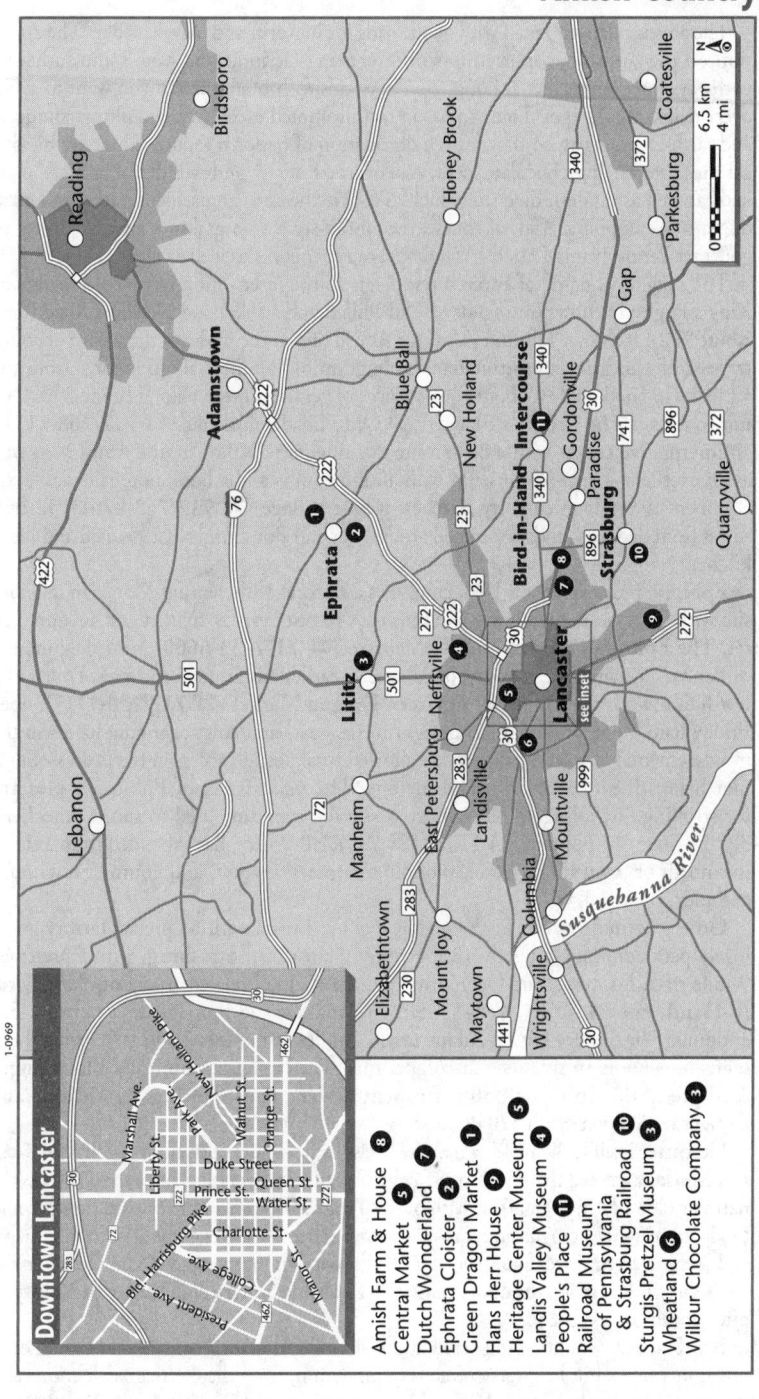

# Amish Country

**Downtown Lancaster**

Amish Farm & House 8
Central Market 5
Dutch Wonderland 7
Ephrata Cloister 2
Green Dragon Market 1
Hans Herr House 9
Heritage Center Museum 5
Landis Valley Museum 4
People's Place 11
Railroad Museum
of Pennsylvania
& Strasburg Railroad 10
Sturgis Pretzel Museum 3
Wheatland 6
Wilbur Chocolate Company 3

1-0969

The area is relatively small with good roads for motorist and bicyclist alike. The attention on the Amish has spurred lots of interesting facsimile and even some authentic pathways into Amish life, although you have to sift through them if you want to avoid overt religious messages. Tourism has in fact promoted excellence in quilting, antiques, and farm-based crafts, so the area is a destination of national repute. There are historical sites, pretzel and chocolate factories, covered bridges, and wonderful farmers' markets, as well as modern diversions such as movie theaters, amusement parks, and great outlet-mall shopping. And, of course, the family-style, smorgasbord, all-you-can-eat or gourmet Pennsylvania Dutch restaurants are experiences as well as meals.

The suggestive name of **Intercourse** refers to the intersection of two old roads, the King's Highway (now Route 340 or Old Philadelphia Pike) and Newport Road (now Route 772). It's now "Ground Zero" for Amish life, in the midst of the wedge of country east of Lancaster; unfortunately the buildup of commercial attractions, from the schlocky to good quality, about equals places of genuine interest along Route 340. One not to miss is **The People's Place,** 3513 Old Philadelphia Pike (☎ 717/768-7171), an interpretive center with a 30-minute documentary "Who Are the Amish?" as well as an excellent hands-on museum with antique quilts and a bookshop/gallery. Of the commercial developments, try **Kitchen Kettle Village** (☎ 717/768-8261), 32 craft stores from decoys to fudge, grouped around Pat and Bob Burnley's 1954 jam and relish kitchen.

**Ephrata,** near exit 21 off I-76, combines a historic 18th-century Moravian religious site with some pleasant country and the area's largest farmers' market and auction center. **The Ephrata Cloister,** 632 W. Main St. (☎ 717/733-6600), near the junction of Penna. 272 and 322, was one of America's earliest communal societies. Four miles north of town is the wonderful ✪ **Green Dragon Market** (☎ 717/738-1117), open Friday 6am–7pm. It's an amazing sight to see goats and cows changing hands in the most elemental way, and children are allowed total petting access in the process. Summer brings fresh corn, fruit, and melons. The main street of Ephrata is pleasant for strolling, including an old rail car where the train line used to run. **Doneckers,** 322 N. State St., Ephrata, PA 17522 (☎ 717/738-9502), has expanded from a single inn north of town into a hotel, shopping, farmers' market, and gourmet restaurant complex, open daily.

Other charming towns in the region include **Lititz,** with its pretzel factory and a lovely park adjoining a purely 18th-century main street; **Strasburg,** with a preserved 9-mile track for iron steam locomotive and assorted rail-related attractions; and **Bird-in-Hand,** known for its Wed–Sat farmers' market and homemade ice cream. For antiquing, the Sunday fairs in **Adamstown,** 2 miles east of exit 21 off I-76, bring thousands of vendors to six or seven competitors. The largest are **Stoudt's Black Angus Antique Mall,** with over 350 permanent dealers, and **Renninger's Antique and Collectors Market,** with 370 dealers.

**Lancaster** itself is slightly down at the heels. In town, the one visitor highlight is **Central Market,** erected in 1889 just off Penn Square but operating since the 1730s as the nation's oldest farmers' market, with over 80 stalls. You can savor regional produce and foods, from sweet bologna and scrapple, breads, cheeses, and egg noodles, to shoofly pie and "schnitzel" or dried apple. Open Tues–Fri 6am–4:30pm and Sat 6am–2pm. To the city's east on Route 30, the outlet centers of **Rockvale Square** and **Tanger at Millwood** offer dozens of top brands.

Ben Franklin would be staggered at the size of a modern Pennsylvania Dutch meal or smorgasbord, but he'd recognize everything on it, from the German-style meats and pot pies with boiled vegetables to the sweet desserts. **Groff's Farm Restaurant,** 650 Pinkerton Rd., Mount Joy, PA (☎ 717/653-2048), is the top regional restaurant, where Pennsylvania Dutch cuisine's emphasis on fresh ingredients and rib-sticking heartiness receives an injection of the 20th century's lighter touch. Among the smorgasbords and family-style restaurants open Mon–Sat, try **Good 'N' Plenty Restaurant,** Route 896 between Routes 30 and 340, Smoketown (☎ **717/394-7111**); **Miller's Smorgasbord/Country Fare Restaurant,** Route 30 at Ronks Road, 5 miles east of Lancaster (☎ **800/669-3568** or 717/687-6621), which has served the official Pennsylvania Dutch smorgasbord to millions since 1929; or **Plain & Fancy Farm & Dining Room,** Route 340, 7 miles east of Lancaster in Bird-in-Hand (☎ **717/768-8281**). Also, don't neglect road signs or newspaper notices for church or firehouse pancake breakfasts, corn roasts, or barbecue or game suppers. You can also catch annual festivals, such as the rhubarb fair in Intercourse and the Dutch Food and Folk Fair in Bird-in-Hand in June.

**Essentials:** Lancaster County is 57 miles or a 90-minute drive west of Philadelphia, directly on Route 30. From the Northeast, the easiest route is to take I-95 south from New York City onto the New Jersey Turnpike, then take exit 6 onto the Pennsylvania Turnpike (I-76), turning south to Lancaster City via exit 20 or 21. Travel time is $2\frac{1}{4}$ hours, and tolls amount to $6. From the south, follow I-83 north for 90 minutes from Baltimore, then head east on Route 30 from York into the county. If you're in Brandywine County or Longwood Gardens, you're only minutes from Amish farms in Gap, via routes 41 and 741. Amtrak takes 70 minutes from 30th Street Station in Philadelphia to the great old Lancaster station.

The **Pennsylvania Dutch Convention & Visitors Bureau,** 501 Greenfield Rd., Lancaster, PA 17601 (☎ **800/PA DUTCH** or 717/299-8901, ext. 2405), provides an excellent detailed map and visitors' guide to the region, along with answers to specific questions and interests. Onsite (Route 30 Bypass east of Lancaster), the bureau has direct telephone links to many local hotels and a multi-image overview slide show. Many towns such as Intercourse, Strasburg, and Lancaster have local information centers, and the **Exit 21 Tourist Information Center** on Route 272 just south of I-76 is open 10am–2pm daily. It's next to **Zinn's Diner** (☎ **717/336-2210**), which looks suspect with its statue of "Big Amos," batting cages, and miniature golf, but the menu, portions, and clientele are very typically Pennsylvania Dutch (open daily 6am–11pm).

## 6 More Mid-Atlantic Highlights

### ANNAPOLIS

As you stroll up from Annapolis's waterfront today, you can't help thinking that not much has changed since this picturesque town's radiating streets were laid out in 1694 at the confluence of the Severn River and the Chesapeake Bay. Indeed, Maryland's capital is a vista of 18th-century mansions, churches, and public buildings. The original layout is still in place—narrow brick streets fanning out from two circular thoroughfares, State Circle and Church Circle.

A prosperous seaport because of the tobacco trade, Annapolis had its golden years as the commercial, political, and social center of Maryland from 1750 to 1790. The first library in the colonies, as well as the first theater, is believed to have been founded in Annapolis during those years, as was St. John's College, one of the first public schools in America.

Today this charming seaport city, with a population of about 35,000, is the home of the ✪ **U.S. Naval Academy,** whose Armel–Leftwich Visitor Center, Gate 1, King George and Randall streets (☎ **410/263-6933**), has guided walking tours of the campus daily.

Another key attraction is the **Maryland State House,** State Circle (☎ 410/269-3400). In the middle of town, it was built between 1772 and 1779, making it the oldest U.S. state capitol in continuous use. The building served as the U.S. capitol from November 16, 1783, to August 13, 1784. The *Treaty of Paris* ending the American Revolution was ratified here, and George Washington turned in his commission as commander of the Continental Army in the Old Senate Chamber. Free guided tours leave at 11am and 3pm from the visitor center on the first floor.

The best way to tour the town is on foot, especially with a **"Historic Annapolis Walk with Walter Cronkite,"** a self-guided audiocassette tour narrated by the famous TV news broadcaster and avid yachtie (Annapolis is the Chesapeake's largest yachting and boating center). Covering 19 historic and architectural sites, Cronkite's 45-minute commentary can be completed at a leisurely pace. It's only available at the **Maritime Museum,** 77 Main St. (☎ 410/268-5576). The museum is open daily 10am–4pm. Cassette rentals cost $7.

To see the town and Naval Academy from the water, **Chesapeake Marine Tours,** Slip 20, City Dock (☎ 410/268-7600), has a variety of cruises in the harbor and out on the bay from Memorial Day to October.

**Essentials:** Annapolis is 28 miles south of Baltimore via I-97, or 35 miles east of Washington, D.C., via U.S. 50. Either is a drive of about 45 minutes. From U.S. 50, take Rowe Boulevard south into the historic district. For more information, contact the **Annapolis and Anne Arundel Conference and Visitors Bureau,** 26 West St., Annapolis, MD 21401 (☎ 410/280-0445 or 410/268-TOUR).

## MARYLAND'S EASTERN SHORE

Relatively isolated for 3 centuries until the Chesapeake Bay Bridge opened in 1954, Maryland's eastern shore has a personality of its own. Much of James Michener's novel *Chesapeake* was inspired by the independent lifestyle of the "watermen" who earn a hard living from the bay. Thanks to them, this part of the world is known for its succulent crabs, oysters, and other seafood. Top-class restaurants and down-home "crab houses" line the shore.

This part of Maryland is also one of the chief resting areas for migrating wildfowl along the Atlantic flyway and is famed for its bird-watching and duck and goose hunting.

**Easton,** once known as the colonial capital of Maryland's eastern shore, is today a quiet little community of 8,500 souls. Closely tied to the nearby Miles and Tred Avon rivers, Easton and its neighbors were an ideal locale for shipbuilding in the 18th century. Centered around the Talbot County Courthouse, Easton has more than 40 beautifully restored and preserved public buildings, churches, and private homes, all dating back to the 18th and 19th centuries. Easton is 60 miles southeast of Baltimore on U.S. 50.

✪ **St. Michaels** on the Miles River is one of the oldest settlements along the Chesapeake, and today is an aesthetic delight—no billboards or fast-food chains, just quiet tree-lined streets, rows of boutiques housed in graceful old restored buildings, and a marina so clean that it seems to sparkle. At least 20,000 boats a year pull into this idyllic harbor just 11 miles west of Easton via Md. 33. Yachties and wheeled visitors alike visit the **Chesapeake Bay Maritime Museum** on the waterfront (☎ 410/745-2916), whose large collection of Chesapeake watercraft includes fine examples of the skipjack and log-bottom bugeye, two sailing craft unique to the area. Centerpiece here is an 1879 "screwpile" lighthouse like those that once guided mariners up and down the bay. Next door, the **Crab Claw,** one of the bay's most famous crab houses (☎ 410/745-2900), serves up the crustaceons in every form imaginable at prices ranging from $8 to $19. Neither reservations nor credit cards are accepted at this fun eatery.

St. Michaels also is home to one of America's most luxurious country inns, ✪ **The Inn at Perry Cabin** (☎ **800/722-2200** or 410/745-2000). Sir Bernard Ashley has extensively decorated this 19th-century colonial Revival manor house on the Miles River with the fabrics and furnishings of his late wife, the designer Laura Ashley. Rooms and suites range from $175 to $525, including full breakfast, afternoon tea, and considerable pampering.

✪ **Oxford** on the Tred Avon River also is one of Maryland's oldest towns. Here lived Robert Morris Jr., who befriended George Washington and then used his own savings to help finance the American Revolution. Oxford seems hardly touched by time, with a pervasive quiet charm and views of the water at every turn. Plan to dine or stay at the **Robert Morris Inn,** 314 N. Morris St., Oxford, MD 21645 (☎ **410/226-5111**), built by ships' carpenters with wooden-pegged paneling and hand-hewn beams, all of which remain today. Double rooms range from $70 to $220.

All this is worth the 10-mile drive from St. Michaels via the **Oxford-Bellevue Ferry** (☎ **410/745-9023**), America's oldest operating private ferry. Fares for a car and two persons are $4.50 one way, $7 round-trip; extra car passenger, 50¢; bicycles, $1.50; walk-on passengers, $1.

**Outdoor activities** abound on the eastern shore. Most roads are flat and have wide shoulders, making biking a favorite sport. Rental boats are available at several marinas in St. Michaels and Oxford, and the fishing is excellent.

**Essentials:** The nearest airport is **Baltimore–Washington International,** near Baltimore. U.S. 50/301 is the main route across the Chesapeake Bay Bridge to the eastern shore. Easton is 60 miles southeast of Baltimore via I-97 south and U.S. 50/301 east across the Bay Bridge ($2.50 toll east bound, free west bound). From Easton, take Md. 33 west to St. Michaels or Md. 333 west to Oxford. Follow the signs off Md. 33 to the Oxford–Bellevue Ferry. For complete information about Easton, St. Michaels, and Oxford, contact the **Talbot County Chamber of Commerce,** Tred Avon Square (P.O. Box 1366), Easton, MD 21601 (☎ **888/BAY-STAY** or 410/822-4606).

## HISTORIC NEW CASTLE

New Castle was Delaware's original capital and a major colonial seaport on the Delaware River. It remains much the way it was in the 17th and 18th centuries. Original houses and public buildings have been restored and preserved; the sidewalks are made of brick and the streets of cobblestones.

Small and compact, New Castle is ideal for walking. In less than an hour, you can stroll past old homes and churches and such historic sights as Packet Alley, a well-worn pathway named after the many packet boats that used to travel to New Castle in the 18th and 19th centuries.

At the center of it all, the ✪ **Old Courthouse** (☎ **302/323-4453**) was built of brick in 1732 and served as Delaware's colonial capitol and meeting place of the state assembly until 1777. The building's cupola is the center of a 12-mile circle that marks the northern boundary between Delaware and Pennsylvania. As in many English colonial towns, it sits at the end of the town green. Walking tours start here.

Facing the Green, **The Dutch House** (☎ **302/322-9168**) is one of the oldest brick houses in Delaware, almost unchanged since its construction around 1700. Although it burned in 1980, the 1703 **Immanuel Episcopal Church** (☎ **302/328-2413**) has been carefully restored. Gravestones in the adjoining graveyard date from 1707.

Nearby at 4th and Delaware streets, the **Amstel House** (☎ **302/322-2794**) dates from the 1730s and is a fine example of 18th-century Georgian architecture. It's furnished with antiques and decorative arts of the period. The unique hexagonal **Old Library Museum,** on 3rd Street (☎ **302/328-2923**), was erected in 1892 and is now used for exhibits by the New Castle Historical Society. Built between 1791 and 1804 near the banks of the Delaware, the 22-room ✪ **Read House and Garden,** on The Strand (☎ **302/322-8411**), is a fine example of Federal architecture with elaborately carved woodwork, relief plasterwork, gilded fanlights, and silver door hardware. The surrounding 1¹/₂-acre formal garden was installed in 1847.

There is good shopping in New Castle, especially for antiques and collectibles. Try the **Antique Co-Op of Historic New Castle,** 116 Delaware St. (☎ **302/328-6362**).

You can stay in the heart of the historic district opposite the courthouse at the **Terry House** (☎ **302/322-2505**), a bed-and-breakfast in a three-story brick Federal town house dating from 1860. The spacious guest rooms look out over either the Delaware River or the courthouse.

**Essentials:** New Castle is 7 miles south of Wilmington via Del. 9. You can obtain brochures and information from the **New Castle Visitor Bureau,** P.O. Box 465, New Castle, DE 19720 (☎ **800/758-1550** or 302/322-8411).

## GETTYSBURG

Pennsylvania emancipated all its slaves in 1781, and when the Civil War broke out 80 years later, it was strongly antislavery and became an arsenal for President Abraham Lincoln's Union army. Pennsylvania saw only two battles in that conflict, but one of them played a monumental role in determining the war's outcome.

In June 1863, the 75,000-man Confederate army of northern Virginia under Gen. Robert E. Lee invaded south-central Pennsylvania, hoping to cut the Union's supply lines and win a major victory and thus convince Lincoln to end the war. In early July, Lee ran into Gen. George Meade's 88,000-man Union army at the little town of Gettysburg, where four highways converged near the Maryland border. During the next 3 days, a total of more than 7,000 men died and another 33,000 were wounded in the bloodiest battle ever fought on American soil. Lee retreated after Gen. George E. Pickett's ill-fated charge up Cemetery Ridge, but the Union army was too exhausted to pursue. Although he escaped to Virginia and fought on for almost 2 more years, Gettysburg was the beginning of Lee's road to surrender at Appomattox.

Lincoln traveled to Gettysburg 4 months after the battle to dedicate the cemetery that held 3,706 casualties, a third of them unknown. "Four score and seven years ago," Lincoln began his brief address—the most famous speech by any American president.

The battle and Lincoln's address are commemorated at **Gettysburg National Military Park Battlefield,** the country's premier battlefield shrine with 1,000 monuments and cannons along 23 scenic miles. The visitor center (☎ **717/334-1124**) on Pa. 134 explains the battle, and the nearby Cyclorama holds Paul Philippoteaux's round painting of Pickett's charge. Tour guides are available at the center for a fee, or you can rent self-drive audiotapes from local vendors.

You can also sign up at the visitor center for a bus tour of the **Eisenhower National Historic Site,** the farm next to the battlefield where President Dwight D. Eisenhower and wife Mamie spent presidential weekends and later retired. Such global luminaries as Nikita Khruschev, Konrad Adenauer, and Charles de Gaulle visited them here.

The battle is often reenacted, especially during **Gettysburg Civil War Heritage Days,** July 1–7.

**Essentials:** Gettysburg is on U.S. 15 about 30 miles southwest of Harrisburg, Pa., the nearest airport. For information about accommodations, restaurants, shopping, and other local attractions, contact the **Gettysburg Travel Council,** 35 Carlisle St., Getysburg, PA 17325 (☎ **717/334-6274**).

## HARPERS FERRY

Thomas Jefferson wrote of Harpers Ferry in 1783, "the view is worth a voyage across the Atlantic." The **Harpers Ferry National Historical Park** now preserves much of that breathtaking view where the Potomac and Shenandoah rivers merge in West Virginia's Eastern Panhandle and cut a gap through the Blue Ridge Mountains. The quaint town is worth a visit from anyone interested in discovering a wealth of American history.

Harpers Ferry is best remembered for John Brown's Raid, which presaged the Civil War. After his friend, abolitionist editor Elijah Lovejoy, was murdered by a mob in 1837, Brown dedicated his life to the destruction of slavery. Seeking weapons, he captured the federal arsenal at Harpers Ferry on October 16, 1859. The next day, 90 U.S. Marines under the command of then-Col. Robert E. Lee surrounded the arsenal, and Col. J. E. B. Stuart twice delivered surrender demands to Brown. When he refused, a party of 12 marines smashed the door and captured Brown and the surviving raiders. Brown was tried for treason and hanged in nearby Charles Town, W. Va., on December 2. Less than 2 years later, Lee and Stuart joined the Confederate army and fought to preserve slavery.

You can hop a free shuttle bus from the **Visitor Center** and parking lot to the Historic Area, a half mile away, where the **John Brown Museum** vividly recounts the story with photographs, documents, and a slide show. Many original stone buildings are open, including a restored dry-goods store, a blacksmith shop, and an armorer's house. In addition, the area is a terrific place for **hiking,** since several scenic walking tracks, including the **Overlook Cliff Trail,** lead to a dramatic clifftop view over the town and the two rivers.

Sitting atop another ridge with a stunning view over the Potomac River, the historic **Hilltop House Hotel,** Ridge Street (P.O. Box 930), Harpers Ferry, WV 25425 (☎ **800/338-8319** or 304/535-2135; fax 304/535-6322), has 65 rooms and a dining room serving excellent Southern fare.

**Essentials:** The nearest airport is Washington–Dulles International. The visitor center is on U.S. 340 about 1 mile west of the Shenandoah River. For information, contact the **Harpers Ferry National Historical Park,** P.O. Box 65, Harpers Ferry, WV 25425 (☎ **304/535-6298**). Admission is $5 per car, $3 per pedestrian, bicyclist, person age 17–61, and bus passenger. Open daily 8am–5pm except Christmas.

## CHARLOTTESVILLE

It was in Charlottesville that Thomas Jefferson built his famous mountaintop home, Monticello; selected the site for and helped plan James Monroe's Ash Lawn–Highland; designed his "academical village," the University of Virginia; and died at Monticello exactly 50 years after the Declaration of Independence he wrote was proclaimed on July 4, 1776.

Along with neighbor James Madison, Jefferson and Monroe were instrumental in developing the emerging nation. In addition to writing the Declaration of Independence, Jefferson advocated freedom of religion, public education, and the abolition of slavery. Madison was instrumental in developing the Constitution and its Bill of Rights. One of the two American presidents actually to fight in the Revolution, Monroe nearly doubled the new nation's size by negotiating the Louisiana Purchase, and he kept colonial powers out of the Americas by declaring the Monroe Doctrine.

Established in 1762 as the county seat for Albemarle, Charlottesville still has its Court Square complete with courthouse—albeit without the whipping post, pillory, and stocks that kept fractious colonials in line. The courthouse doubled as marketplace in those early days and served as a church with rotating services for different denominations (Jefferson called it the "Common Temple"). Elections were held in Court Square followed by raucous political celebrations. The taverns across the street were well patronized.

Though today's Charlottesville is a cosmopolitan center, it is still sufficiently unchanged and pastoral for visitors to imagine themselves back in colonial times. "Mr. Jefferson's" university and home are major attractions open to the public.

**Essentials:** US Airways, Delta, and United fly to **Charlottesville–Albemarle Airport.** Amtrak (☎ 800/872-7245) and **Greyhound/Trailways** (☎ 800/231-2222) have service to points north and south. For information, contact the **Charlottesville/Albemarle Information Center,** P.O. Box 161, Charlottesville, VA 22902 (☎ 804/977-1783), in the Thomas Jefferson Visitor Center on Va. 20, at exit 121 off I-64. Tours of Monticello begin here.

## FREDERICKSBURG

Though George Washington always called Alexandria his hometown, he spent his formative years in the Fredericksburg area at Ferry Farm (where he supposedly never told a lie about chopping down the cherry tree). His mother later lived in a house he bought her on Charles Street, and she is buried on the former Kenmore estate, home of his sister, Betty Washington Lewis.

The town was a hotbed of revolutionary zeal in the 1770s. Troops drilled on the courthouse green on Princess Anne Street, and it was in Fredericksburg that Thomas Jefferson, George Mason, and other Founding Fathers met in 1777 to draft what later became the Virginia Statute of Religious Freedoms, the basis for the First Amendment guaranteeing separation of church and state. President James Monroe began his law career in Fredericksburg in 1786.

Fredericksburg's strategic location on the Rappahannock River equidistant from Washington and Richmond made it a fierce battlefield during the Civil War. Clara Barton nursed wounded Federal soldiers in the still-extant Presbyterian church. Cannonballs embedded in the walls of some prominent buildings and the graves of 17,000 Civil War soldiers in the town's cemeteries are grim reminders of that tragic era.

The **Fredericksburg Battlefield Visitor Center,** 1013 Lafayette Blvd. (U.S. 1 Business) at Sunken Road (☎ 540/373-6122), is the starting point for a 75-mile self-guided tour covering the battles of Fredericksburg, Chancellorsville, The Wilderness, and Chancellorsville Courthouse.

**Essentials:** The nearest airports are in Washington, 50 miles to the north via I-95. Amtrak (☎ 800/872-7245) has several trains daily from Washington and Richmond. **Virginia Railway Express** (☎ 800/743-3843 or 703/497-7777) provides weekday commuter trains to and from Washington. **Greyhound/Trailways** has bus service (☎ 800/231-2222). Stop first at the **Fredericksburg Visitor Center,** 706 Caroline St., Fredericksburg, VA 22401 (☎ 800/678-4748 or 540/373-1776).

# The Southeast

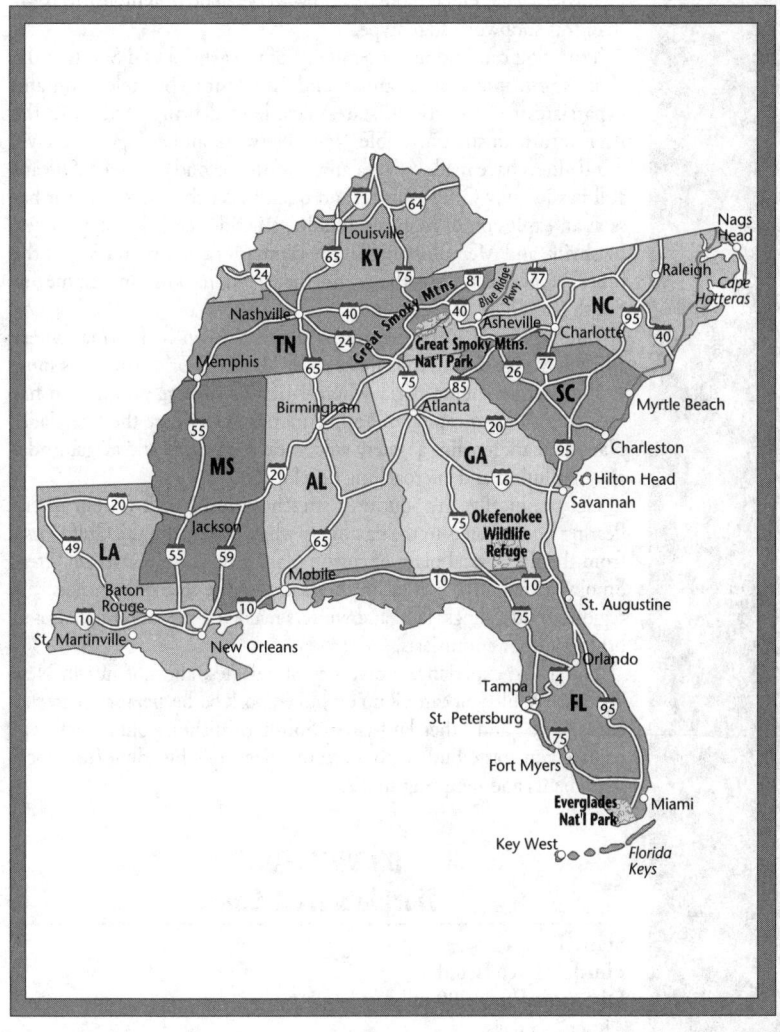

In the popular mind, the Southeastern states are often seen as the Old South, a land of magnolias and Spanish moss, of plantation manses and the Lost Cause of the Civil War, of Scarlett O'Hara and Rhett Butler fleeing through Atlanta's burning streets. But the states of the Old Confederacy are much more modern—and a good deal more diverse—than this shopworn stereotype.

True, you can find many remnants of the genteel Old South in the charming seaports of Savannah and Charleston, but television and expatriates from northern states have helped bring Dixie into the American mainstream. Cable News Network and an agressive civic mindedness have made Atlanta an up-to-the-second city. New Orleans still has its firey Cajun cuisine and quaint French Quarter, but it has seen an explosion of high-rise buildings beside the Mississippi River. Nashville and Memphis are still the capitals of country music and the blues, respectively, but they send their stars packing in summer to South Carolina's Myrtle Beach.

The region's diversity reaches its peak down in Florida, where Mickey Mouse and friends make Walt Disney World America's most visited family theme park, where Miami's diverse population has created a de facto capital of Latin America, and where the Everglades National Park remains a watery wilderness of sawgrass and alligators despite pollution and encroaching development.

Geographically, the Southeast stretches from North Carolina's endearing Outer Banks to the dazzlingly white beaches on the Gulf Coast, from the flat coastal plain of cotton plantations to the mystical Great Smoky Mountains, highest in the east. Despite steamy summers, the region's mild springs, falls, and winters make it a mecca for golfers and other outdoor enthusiasts.

You'll also experience a diversity of cuisines, and not just in New Orleans. While you can fill up on pulled pork barbecue, turnip greens, cheese grits, and other lard-laden Southern dishes, young chefs will titillate your taste buds with a creative new style blending fresh local ingredients and tempting spices.

## DRIVING TOUR
## Florida's West Coast

**Start:** Tampa
**Finish:** Marco Island
**Distance:** About 200 miles
**Time:** 2–3 days
**Highlights:** White sand beaches, Florida's cultural center, quaint beach towns, beautiful islands, shopping, and glamorous resorts

This tour runs down the heart of Florida's west coast from the Tampa Bay area south to Marco Island. Along the way you'll visit Thomas Edison's winter home in historic Fort Myers, lovely Sanibel and Captiva islands, and ritzy but relaxed Naples. Culture fans will especially enjoy Sarasota, with its performing arts and the Ringling Museum Complex. You'll stop at pleasant beach villages and lively resorts with plenty of opportunities for shopping, water sports, and fine dining. The trip allows you to be comfortable in sandals and shorts, but you can also dress up, if you wish, for a night on the town.

From top to bottom, the west coast is a resort area. Except during the high season in January to April, you should have no problem finding accommodations in all price ranges, or places to eat the bounty of seafood harvested from the Gulf of Mexico.

The tour begins in on the northern shore of Tampa Bay in the city of:

1. **Tampa,** perhaps best known as the home of **Busch Gardens Tampa Bay** (☎ 813/987-5171), one of Florida's major theme parks that also is one of the world's largest zoos, and of the **Florida Aquarium** (☎ 813/273-4000), where you and the kids can learn all about the state's sea life. You will also want to explore historic **Ybor City,** the old Cuban enclave along 7th Avenue that was once the cigar capital of the world; it's now a restored and very lively dining, shopping, and nightlife center. At Ybor City's hub is one of Florida's most famous restaurants, **The Columbia,** 2117 7th Ave. (☎ 813/248-4961), which dishes up authentic Spanish fare and flamenco dancing.

   For information about Tampa, contact the **Tampa/Hillsborough Convention and Visitor Association,** 400 N. Tampa St., Tampa, FL 33602-4706 (☎ 800/44-TAMPA or 813/223-2752).

   From Tampa's city center, go west 20 miles on Fla. 60 across the Courtney Campbell Causeway, through the mainland town of Clearwater, and across another causeway to:

2. **Clearwater Beach,** on the northernmost of a 20-mile-long chain of barrier islands fringing the Pinellas peninsula. Just off the causeway, the **Clearwater Marine Aquarium** (☎ 813/447-0980) is dedicated to the rescue and rehabilitation of marine mammals and sea turtles. At the end of the causeway, you'll come to a fine public beach with a children's playground. Across the street, the **Clearwater Beach Marina** has every imaginable waterborne activity, from boating to windsurfing. Across the high-rise bridge to the south is **Sand Key Park,** one of Florida's finest municipal beach parks.

   Head south on Fla. 699, the only highway along the barrier islands. You will pass through the residential communities of Belleair Beach, Indian Rocks Beach, and Indian Shores to Redington Shores, where you can stop for a look at the **Suncoast Seabird Sanctuary** (☎ 813/391-6211), the nation's largest wild-bird hospital. From there continue south to Madeira Beach and **John's Pass Village,** a restored fishing settlement now filled with shops, restaurants, and marinas. The village sits on John's Pass, across which Fla. 699 will take you over Treasure Island to:

3. **St. Pete Beach,** the most developed of the Pinellas County resorts. Among its many hotels is the **Don CeSar Beach Resort,** 3400 Gulf Blvd. (☎ 813/360-1881), a big pink national landmark hotel built in 1928 combining Moorish and Mediterranean architecture. You'll enjoy looking at its elegant interior, with classic high windows and archways, crystal chandeliers, marble floors, and artworks on display. A less expensive but still charming place to stay is **Island's End Resort,** 1 Pass-a-Grille Way (☎ 813/360-5023), a collection of beachside cottages at the south end of the island and away from the maddening crowd.

For information, contact the **St. Petersburg/Clearwater Area Convention and Visitor Bureau,** 14450 46th St. N., Clearwater, FL 34622 (☎ **800/345-6710** or 813/464-7200). The toll-free number connects to a free hotel reservation service.

From the Don CeSar, head due east on the Pinellas Byway (Fla. 682), a toll road that connects to I-275. At the interstate, you can detour 7 miles north via I-375 to downtown **St. Petersburg** and its famous pier and museums, including one devoted to the works of Salvador Dalí. But the tour heads south on I-275 across the soaring **Sunshine Skyway** over the mouth of Tampa Bay. At the junction of U.S. 19, head south across the Manatee River and into the pleasant town of Bradenton. Turn right there on Manatee Boulevard (Fla. 64) and drive due west to:

**4. Anna Maria Island,** whose narrow streets are a favorite of cyclists and walkers who come to the town of Anna Maria to explore its old buildings and quaint boutiques and craft shops. The town shares the island with two other communities, Holmes Beach and Bradenton Beach. The latter has a mile-long public beach fringed by casuarina pines. The **Chamber of Commerce,** south of Manatee Avenue on East Bay Drive (☎ **941/778-1541**), has a tourist information center. For more information in advance, contact the **Greater Bradenton Area Convention and Visitor Bureau,** P.O. Box 1000, Bradenton, FL 34206 (☎ **941/729-9177**). The walk-in **Manatee County Welcome Center** is northeast of Bradenton, on U.S. 301, just east of exit 43 off I-75.

☕ **TAKE A BREAK**    Overlooking the Gulf of Mexico from the north end of Anna Maria Island, **The Sandbar,** 100 Spring Ave. (☎ **941/778-0444**), has a menu of seafood combo plates, steaks, pastas, and chicken to be consumed at umbrella tables on a gulfside patio. Another local favorite, **Rotten Ralph's,** 902 S. Bay Blvd., Anna Maria Island (☎ **941/778-3953**), offers crab cakes, deep-fried oysters, and other fish platters.

From Bradenton Beach, follow Gulf of Mexico Drive (Fla. 789) south onto:

**5. Longboat Key,** one of Florida's wealthiest areas, with expensive private homes and condominiums in gated communities between the Gulf of Mexico and Sarasota Bay. A number of hotels along the gulf shore provide fine accommodations in a variety of settings. Although this is not an area for economy lodging, Longboat has a number of resorts, starting with the **Holiday Inn Longboat Key,** 4949 Gulf of Mexico Dr. (☎ **941/383-3771**), and followed by **Longboat Key Hilton Beach Resort,** 4711 Gulf of Mexico Dr. (☎ **941/383-2451**), the **Colony Beach & Tennis Resort,** 1620 Gulf of Mexico Dr. (☎ **941/383-6464**), and the **Resort of Longboat Key Club,** 301 Gulf of Mexico Dr. (☎ **941/383-8821**).

On City Island, at the south end of Longboat, you can pull into the **Mote Marine Aquarium** (☎ **800/691-MOTE** or 941/388-4441) and watch sharks and other sea life. Nearby, **Pelican Man's Bird Sanctuary** (☎ **941/388-4444**) treats more than 5,000 injured birds and other wildlife each year.

From Longboat, keep heading south across a bridge to:

**6. St. Armands Key,** a delightful enclave with a traffic rotary, known as St. Armands Circle, lined with flower beds and filled with trendy shops, boutiques, sidewalk cafes, and restaurants. Plan to spend a couple of hours here looking at shops and relaxing at a sidewalk cafe as you people-watch.

☕ **TAKE A BREAK**    Most of St. Armands Circle's restaurants are moderate and up, but you can get inexpensive diner-style fare at **The Buttery,** 470 John Ringling Blvd. (☎ **941/388-1523**). For fun as well as good seafood, climb the stairs to the Key West–style **Hemingway's,** on Boulevard of the Presidents

# Driving Tour: Florida's West Coast

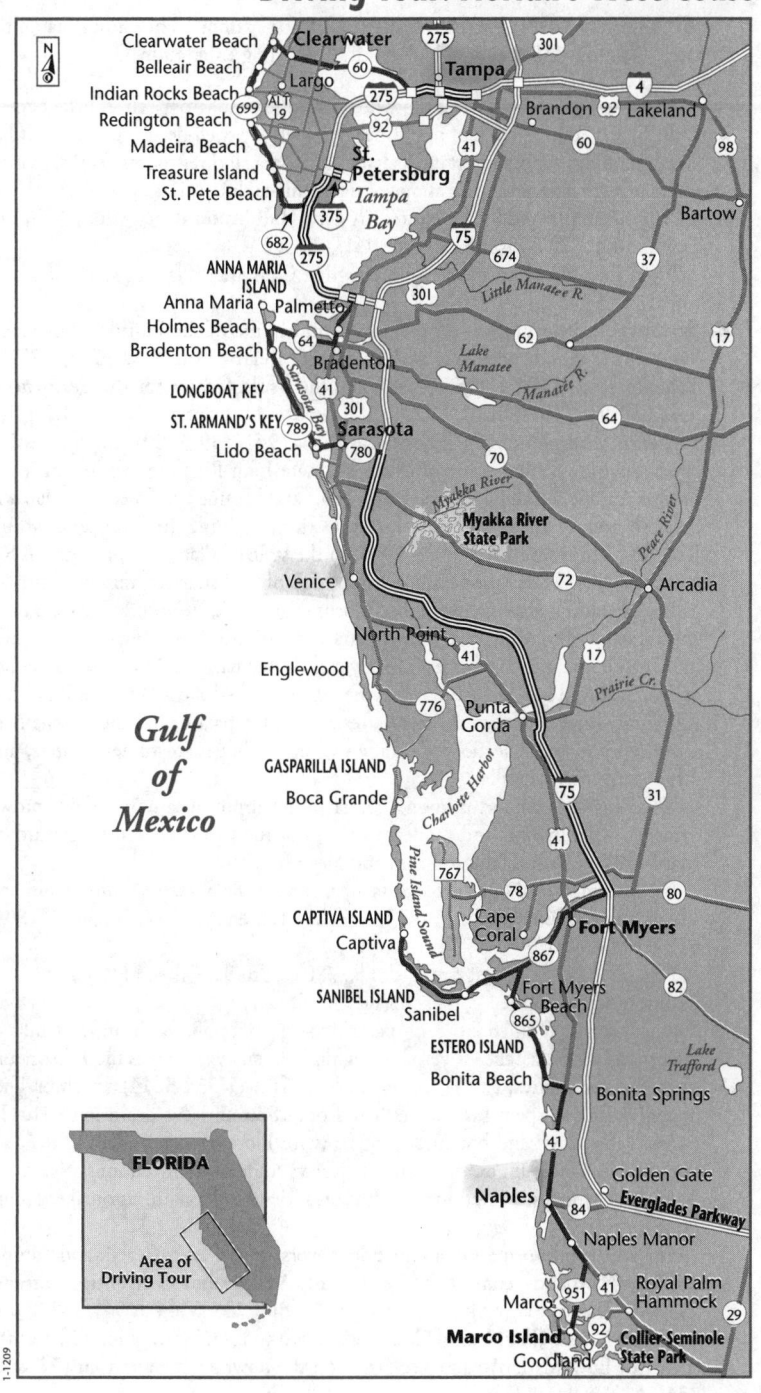

(☎ 941/388-3948). There's a branch of Tampa's famous **The Columbia** on the circle (☎ 941/338-3987), which has lively evening entertainment.

From St. Armands Circle, follow the signs due west across a short bridge to:

**7. Lido Beach,** a fine stretch of public beach on a lively, well-developed island. It has ample parking, concession stands, changing rooms, and restrooms. You can bring lunch in a cooler here and sit at one of the picnic tables. Among several hotels here are a Holiday Inn and the beachside, art deco **Half Moon Beach Club,** 2050 Ben Franklin Dr. (☎ 800/358-3245 or 941/388-3694).

From Lido Beach, take the John Ringling Causeway (Fla. 789) east to downtown:

**8. Sarasota,** the cultural center of Florida and home of the Florida West Coast Symphony, which performs at **Van Wezel Performing Arts Hall,** 777 N. Tamiami Trail (☎ 941/953-3366); and the **Asolo Center for the Performing Arts** (☎ 941/351-8000). During the day, you'll want to visit the **Ringling Museum Complex,** 5401 Bayshore Rd. (☎ 941/359-5700), the impressive, larger-than-life former estate of circus magnate John Ringling, who spent much time in Europe searching for fine works of art and became enamored of Italian and Spanish architecture. To house his collection, he built the **John and Mable Ringling Museum of Art** in the 1920s in the style of a fabulous pink Italian Renaissance villa. Today the building is Florida's official state art museum, with 22 galleries featuring exquisite works by Rubens, Van Dyck, Velázquez, Hals, Poussin, and others. It also displays decorative arts and antiques as well as traveling exhibits. Outside the museum are elaborate gardens, one with a 17-foot bronze replica of Michelangelo's *David.* Also here is the 30-room **Ca'd'Zan** (House of John), the Ringling winter residence modeled after a Venetian palace, and the **Circus Museum,** with a vast collection of parade wagons, calliopes, costumes, posters, and other circus memorabilia.

The Ringling complex is in on U.S. 41 in the airport area north of downtown Sarasota, where you'll find modern versions of the Comfort Inn, Courtyard by Marriott, Days Inn, Hampton Inn, and Sleep Inn.

For information about the Sarasota area, contact the **Sarasota Convention and Vistor Bureau,** 655 N. Tamiami Trail (U.S. 41), Sarasota, FL 34236 (☎ 800/522-9799 or 941/957-1877).

From U.S. 41 in downtown, take Fla. 780 east to I-75, then head south for 75 minutes to exit 25, then go west on Fla. 80 into:

**9. Fort Myers,** a dignified city with palm tree–covered boulevards on the banks of the broad Caloosahatchee River. The highlight of any visit here is the **Edison and Ford Winter Estates,** 2350 McGregor Blvd. (☎ 941/334-3614). Inventor Thomas Alva Edison spent his winters here from 1886 until his death in 1931. His retreat, laboratory, and botanical gardens (with Florida's largest banyan tree) are open daily. A museum on the grounds displays some of his inventions. Next door is the rather modest winter home of Edison's friend, billionaire automaker Henry Ford.

For advance information about Fort Myers, Fort Myers Beach, and Sanibel and Captiva islands, contact the **Lee County Visitor and Convention Bureau,** 2180 W. First St., Fort Myers, FL 33901 (☎ 800/237-6444 or 941/338-3500). The **Fort Myers Chamber of Commerce** has a walk-in information office at the corner of Edwards Drive and Lee Street on the downtown waterfront (☎ 800/336-3622 or 941/332-3624).

☕ **TAKE A BREAK**   Before or after touring the Edison and Ford homes, have a scenic alfresco lunch at the riverside **Shooters Waterfront Café USA,** at the Holiday Inn Sunspree, 2220 W. First St. (☎ 941/334-2727), dishing up reliable grouper sandwiches and other typically modern pub fare. Shooters is Fort Myers's most popular watering hole and often gets noisy and crowded after sunset, but the daytime view is unmatched hereabouts.

Make your way back to McGregor Bouelvard (Fla. 867) and head south and west for about 17 miles, following the signs across a causeway ($3 round-trip toll) to:

10. **Sanibel and Captiva islands,** where the main drag, Periwinkle Way, runs under a canopy of whispery pines, gnarled oaks, and twisted banyans so thick they almost obscure the signs for chic shops and restaurants. This wooded ambience is the work of local voters, who have saved their trees, limited the size and appearance of signs, and prohibited any building taller than the tallest palm. And they won't let noisy motorized beach toys within 300 yards of their world-famous shelling beaches.

Indeed, shelling is so good here that visitors and local residents alike can be seen hunched over in the "Sanibel stoop" in search of some 200 species found on its shores. From February to April or after any storm are the best times to look. Before hitting the beach, visit the **Baily–Mathews Shell Museum,** on Sanibel–Captiva Road (☎ 941/395-2233), the only museum in the U.S. devoted solely to shells.

Furthermore, the 5,000-acre ✪ **J. N. (Ding) Darling National Wildlife Refuge** (☎ 941/472-1100) occupies more than a third of Sanibel. If you protect yourself from the mosquitoes and sand flies, the refuge is a great place for hiking, kayaking, and canoeing—all the while bird- and wildlife-watching.

All this makes Sanibel and Captiva an extraordinarily appealing but relatively expensive destination. The only two chain hotels on the islands are the **Best Western Sanibel Island Beach Resort** and the **Holiday Inn Beach Resort,** and neither is inexpensive. You also can call **South Seas Resorts** (☎ 800/554-5454), a company that manages several hotels on the islands. The best of the few inexpensive choices here is the **Palm View Motel,** 706 Donax St., Sanibel Island, FL 33957 (☎ 941/472-6733), a block from the beach.

For visitor information, contact the **Sanibel–Captiva Islands Chamber of Commerce,** 1159 Causeway Rd., Sanibel Island, FL 33957 (☎ 941/472-1080; fax 941/472-1070). The chamber is on the right as you drive onto Sanibel. It has phones for making hotel reservations.

☕ **TAKE A BREAK**   Once you've driven to the far north end of Captiva, stop for refreshments at the **Mucky Duck,** a lively pub directly on the beach at the west end of Andy Rosse Lane (☎ 941/472-3434). The beach here is Captiva's center of water-sports activities. Back on Sanibel, the fun-filled, inexpensive **Hungry Heron,** in Palm Ridge Place at the corner of Palm Ridge Road and Periwinkle Way (☎ 941/395-2300), features cartoons and a magician to entertain the kids.

From Sanibel, go back across the causeway and keep going straight on Summerlin Road (Fla. 869) to San Carlos Boulevard (Fla. 865). Turn right there and drive 3 miles south across the tall bridge over Mantanzas Pass onto Estero Island and:

11. **Fort Myers Beach,** a casual, laid-back community, with quaint cottages, garden apartments, high-rise hotels, and a busy beach area known locally as Times Square.

Fishing, windsurfing, waterskiing, sailing, and jet skiing are popular here, and nature lovers can take guided boat tours to see dolphins and manatees out in **Estero Bay,** an official Florida marine sanctuary. The beach has plenty of pretty shells to collect, and bird-watchers can spot many species, especially at **Carl E. Johnson–Lover's Key State Recreation Area** (☎ 941/463-4259), 2 miles south of Fort Myers Beach, where you must walk or take a tractor-pulled tram to a magnificent stretch of undeveloped white sand beach on Lover's Key.

Of several chain hotels here, the popular, family-oriented **Best Western Pink Shell Beach Resort** (☎ 800/554-5454 or 941/463-6161) is quietly situated near Estero Island's north end; it has hotel rooms, suites, apartments, and old-fashioned cottages. Another good choice is the **Sandpiper Gulf Resort,** 5550 Estero Blvd., Fort Myers Beach, FL 33931 (☎ 941/463-5721), where you can stay on the beach for as little as $65 a night off season.

For more information, contact the **Fort Myers Beach Chamber of Commerce,** 17200 San Carlos Blvd., Fort Myers Beach, FL 33931 (☎ 800/782-9283 or 941/454-7500). The chamber is on the right just south of Summerlin Road.

From Fort Myers Beach, continue 19 miles south on Estero Boulevard (Fla. 865) to U.S. 41, then turn south 8 miles until you reach:

**12. Naples,** easily southwest Florida's most sophisticated city. Many of the boutiques and galleries along **Fifth Avenue South** and **Third Street South** would upstage those in Palm Beach or Beverly Hills, and the municipal tennis courts in Cambier Park could easily belong to a deluxe resort. Naples began in 1886, when wealthy Midwesterners built **Millionaires' Row** along Gulf Shore Boulevard. Known today as **Olde Naples** and carefully protected by its modern residents, the original settlement still retains the air of that Victorian era more than a century ago. Just as it did then, **Naples Pier** still reaches into the Gulf of Mexico, offering fabulous sunsets and views of the millionaires' mansions. In addition to Olde Naples's very own beach, a 3,000-foot boardwalk wanders through a mangrove swamp to the lovely sands at **Clam Pass County Park,** where you can share beach equipment, kayaks, and canoes with guests at the luxury Registry Resort. And north of town at Vanderbilt Beach, **Delnor–Wiggins State Recreation Area** has been rated as having one of America's top 20 beaches.

You can also experience southwest Florida's abundant natural life at **Big Cypress National Preserve,** accessible by I-75 and U.S. 41 (☎ 914/695-4111), a 2,000-square-mile sanctuary for alligators, deer, and numerous birds; the **Conservancy Nature Center,** Goodlette Road on 14th Avenue N. (☎ 941/262-0304), with a science museum, nature trails, butterfly atrium, and aviary; and **Corkscrew Swamp Sanctuary,** Sanctuary Road (☎ 941/657-3771), an 11,000-acre wilderness, maintained by the National Audubon Society, that features alligators as well as migratory and wading birds.

It isn't surprising that Naples is home to some of Florida's finest lodgings, including the **Ritz-Carlton Naples,** 280 Vanderbilt Beach Rd. (☎ 800/241-3333 or 941/598-3300). The **Naples Beach Hotel & Golf Club,** 851 Gulf Shore Blvd. N. (☎ 800/237-7600 or 941/261-2222), is less expensive and is infused with more Old Florida charm. And you can find some surprisingly affordable places to stay, including the **Tides Inn of Naples,** 1801 Gulf Shore Blvd. N. (☎ 800/438-8763 or 941/262-6196), which is right on the gulf.

The **Naples Area Chamber of Commerce** maintains a visitor center at 895 5th Ave. S., Naples, FL 34102 (☎ 941/262-6141; fax 941/262-8374).

From Naples, drive 8 miles south on U.S. 41 to Isle of Capri Road (Fla. 951), turn right and go south 7 miles, and go over the bridge to:

**13. Marco Island,** largest of the Ten Thousand Islands marking this coastline all the way into the Everglades National Park. A trader named William Collier settled here in 1871 and built the **Old Marco Inn** to house fishermen. The building still stands (it's a fine restaurant), but most of what you see here today is the creation of a massive real estate development begun in 1965. As a result, Marco Island offers much to do—but none of the charm found on Sanibel and Captiva. A long crescent beach stretches along the western shore; most of it is lined with condos and Marriott, Hilton, and Radisson resorts, but you get away from the congestion at **Tigertail Public Beach,** on the north end, where a sandbar offshore creates a shallow lagoon perfect for learning to windsurf.

For more information, contact the **Marco Island Area Chamber of Commerce,** 1102 N. Collier Blvd., Marco Island, FL 34145 (☎ **800/788-6272** or 941/394-7549).

☕ **TAKE A BREAK**    **Stan's Idle Hour Seafood Restaurant** (☎ **941/394-3041**) is located in Goodland, a 10-minute drive east from Marco Island's center, just off to the right before the bridge on Fla. 92. An Ernest Hemingway look-alike, Stan Gober owns this rustic seafood eatery on the dock, where locals like to gather for good food and drinks. Hundreds if not thousands show up on Sunday afternoon for live country music, and Stan hosts the Goodland Mullet Festival, one of Florida's biggest bashes, in January on the Sunday before the Super Bowl.

## DRIVING TOUR
## North Carolina's Outer Banks

**Start:** Kitty Hawk/Kill Devil Hills
**Finish:** Beaufort
**Distance:** Approximately 115 miles
**Time:** 1–2 days
**Highlights:** Sea, sand, and surf; the Wright Brothers National Memorial; national seashores; outdoor drama; 16th-century sailing vessel; English gardens; lighthouses; ghost town; historic homes and cemeteries

This tour runs along the Outer Banks, an enchanting chain of skinny barrier islands stretching for 120 miles down North Carolina's northern coastline. They are best known for their endless beaches, many of them preserved in their magnificent natural state by the Cape Hatteras National Seashore, but this also is where the first English colonists in the New World mysteriously disappeared in 1587, where the infamous Blackbeard and other 18th-century pirates supposedly buried their loot, where the "Graveyard of the Atlantic" claimed innumerable ships, and where the Wright Brothers flew the world's first airplane in 1903.

We will follow N.C. 12, the only highway on the banks. There are plenty of places to pull off the road, so you can easily find your own deserted stretch of beach. In planning your drive, factor in waiting time for the ferries, which depart every half hour in the summer and every hour in the winter and are loaded on a first-come, first-served basis. Some businesses are closed during the winter months, and the bridges to the islands can be jammed during summer weekends, so plan accordingly.

The northern beaches from Kitty Hawk to Nags Head have ample accommodations, but book ahead during the busy summer season. For details, contact the **Dare County Tourist Bureau,** P.O. Box 399, Manteo, NC 27945 (☎ **800/446-6262** or 919/473-2138), or drop in at the **Aycock Brown Welcome Center** on N.C. 12 in Kitty

Hawk. For Ocracoke Island, call or write the **Ocracoke Civic and Business Associa-tion,** P.O. Box 456, Ocracoke, NC 27960 (☎ **919/928-6711**).

To reach the Outer Banks, take U.S. 158 or U.S. 64/264 from the mainland to the north end of the islands and your first stop:

1. **Kitty Hawk/Kill Devil Hills,** where Orville and Wilbur Wright set humanity soaring with the first powered aircraft flight in 1903. Even though it lasted only 12 seconds and covered only 120 feet, it launched aviation as we know it today. The site of their historic flight is marked by the **Wright Brothers National Me-morial** (☎ **919/441-7430**), a granite monument resembling the tail of an airplane and sitting high on a grass-covered sand dune. The site includes a reconstructed hangar and a museum containing a wind tunnel used by the Wrights, their 1902 gliders, and a replica of their 1903 Wright Flyer.

It's 4 miles south on N.C. 12 to:

2. **Nags Head,** where according to legend, local pirates lured unsuspecting ships into the dangerous surf by tying lanterns around horses' necks and walking them back and forth, thus making it falsely appear that other ships were safely at anchor. Whether it's true or not, residents claim this is how Nags Head got its name. To-day this long community is a popular vacation spot with a multitude of hotels, motels, condominiums, rental cottages, restaurants, and shopping centers. You can watch present-day flight enthusiasts launch their hang gliders from the tops of the 140-foot sand dunes of **Jockey's Ridge State Park** (☎ **919/441-7132**).

At the south end of Nags Head, make a brief 7-mile detour west on U.S. 64/264 to:

3. **Roanoke Island,** site of the mysterious Lost Colony. Sponsored by Sir Walter Raleigh, a total of 112 Englishmen, women, and children arrived in 1585 and erected a log fort. The leader of the band, John White, went back to England for supplies, but when he returned the following spring, all the settlers had disappeared without a trace. **Fort Raleigh National Historic Site** (☎ **919/473-5772**), on the island's north end 4 miles from the town of **Manteo** (follow the signs), marks the site with a reconstructed fort and the **Elizabethan Gardens,** a re-creation of a 16th-century formal pleasure garden (open mid-Mar to Nov; ☎ **919/473-3234**). *The Lost Colony,* an outdoor drama performed during the summer at the Water-side Amphitheater next door to Fort Raleigh, tells of the colonists' lives, hardships, and baffling disappearance (☎ **919/473-3414**).

At Manteo's waterfront, the *Elizabeth II,* a 69-foot, square-rigged ship mod-eled on the 16th-century sailing vessel that brought the colonists to these shores, serves as the visitor center for the *Elizabeth II* **State Historic Site** (☎ **919/ 473-1144**). Also here, the **North Carolina Aquarium** displays marine life (☎ **919/473-3493**).

**TAKE A BREAK** Although you'd expect a 16th-century Elizabethan mo-tif, the **Elizabethan Inn,** U.S. 64 (☎ **919/473-2101**), actually specializes in Ital-ian and seafood entrees. Luncheon choices cost $4–$6, dinner entrees $10–$15.

Retrace U.S. 64/264 back onto the Outer Banks and turn south on N.C. 12 for 12 miles. When you cross the high-rise bridge over Oregon Inlet to Hatteras Island, you will enter:

4. **Cape Hatteras National Seashore,** created in 1953 as the nation's first national seashore to preserve the beaches in their natural state. This gorgeous stretch of beach and dunes runs 70 miles south through Ocracoke Island. Along with swim-ming, sunning, and shelling, the beaches are famous for surf fishing. Deep-sea

# Driving Tour: The Outer Banks

charters are available from marinas in the towns, as are charters for inland/intracoastal fishing in the bays and estuaries. On the left, you'll pass **Coquina Beach,** with picnic shelters, bathhouses, and the 1921 wreck of the *Laura Barnes.*

Keep going south to the village of:

5. **Rodanthe,** where you can watch the many varieties of waterfowl that live at least part of the year on the 5,000 marshy acres of the **Pea Island National Wildlife Refuge.** Parts of the **Chicamacomico U.S. Lifesaving Service Station,** established in 1875, are open in the summer. Its museum tells the story of the 24 stations that once lined the coast; living history reenactments are held in the summer.

Follow N.C. 12 south to:

6. **Hatteras,** near the south end of the island, where the 208-foot-tall, candy-striped **Cape Hatteras Lighthouse** (☎ **919/995-4474**) was built in 1870 and is still the tallest of America's lighthouses—the 269 steps to the top are quite a climb. When it was constructed, the tower stood 1,500 feet inland from the sea, but by 1935 waves lapping around the base forced the Coast Guard to abandon it. The light

was restored to the tower in 1950, but the structure may eventually be moved inland. Memorabilia relating to the history of the lighthouse is the focus of the **Museum of the Sea,** in the restored keeper's cottage.

The iron balcony at the top of the lighthouse provides a stunning panorama of the island, the ocean, and the inland sounds between here and the mainland. You can't see them, but offshore lie the remains of the *Monitor,* the famous ironclad Union ship that sank in 1862 after its battle in Hampton Roads with the Confederate *Merrimac.* The *Monitor* went down in the turbulent seas caused by the cold Labrador Current converging with the warm Gulf Stream over **Diamond Shoals,** just off the southern tip of Cape Hatteras.

**Canadian Hole,** on the sound side of Hatteras Island opposite the lighthouse, has evolved into the windsurfing capital of the Outer Banks. Strong, consistent winds make the area ideal for both the neophyte and the master windsurfer. Almost any day you drop by, you'll see surfers gathered to hone their skills.

From Hatteras, take the free auto ferry to:

7. **Ocracoke Island,** once a sanctuary for pirates like the infamous Blackbeard, who was captured in nearby waters and, according to local legend, buried part of his booty somewhere in this vicinity. On the way to **Ocracoke Village,** watch for the ponies descended from beasts brought here by Spanish and English sailors. In the village, which is built around a little round harbor, the **British Cemetery** is the last resting place of four British sailors killed when a German U-boat sunk the HMS *Bedfordshire* 40 miles offshore during World War II. A British flag flies over the plot of ground, deeded to Britain forever. Built in 1823, **Ocracoke Lighthouse** is the oldest operating lighthouse in North Carolina.

Accommodations are available in Ocracoke at the **Island Inn** (☎ 919/928-4351), a turn-of-the-century hotel with a front porch filled with rocking chairs; the **Anchorage Inn** (☎ 919/928-1581), with breathtaking views of the harbor; the **Boyette House** (☎ 919/928-4261), a motel resembling a quiet country inn; and the **Harborside Motel** (☎ 919/928-3111), a simple seaside motel.

☕ **TAKE A BREAK**  Best known for its oyster omelets, crab cakes, and hush puppies, the dining room at the **Island Inn** (☎ 919/928-7821) is filled with Outer Banks character. For lunch, ask for a soft-shell crab sandwich; dinner often includes crab cakes, other seafood, beef, chicken, and pasta. Entrees are $5–$12; reservations are advised for dinner.

From Ocracoke, take the toll ferry to Cedar Island, a 2-hour ride, then follow N.C. 12 south to U.S. 70 east. Depending on which of the three national seashore islands you want to visit, passenger ferry service is available from Harkers Island to Shackleford Banks or the southern tip of South Core Banks; Davis to the midpoint of South Core Banks; and Atlantic to the southern end of North Core Banks—all components of the:

8. **Cape Lookout National Seashore,** a protected 55-mile span of three unconnected barrier islands of deserted beaches and superb fishing. The seashore has few roads; if you have a four-wheel-drive vehicle, motoring on the beach is the best method of transportation. You can camp anywhere, but there are no facilities.

It's a 40-minute drive from the ferry landing to Portsmouth Village, a modern-day ghost town. Established in 1753, this was at one time North Carolina's busiest seaport, but the last family deserted the island in 1971. Of the 21 remaining structures, two are open to the public: the **church** and the **Dixon/Salter House,** which is used as a visitor center. On display are a town genealogy, old photos, and other memorabilia. Portsmouth is also accessible by ferry from Ocracoke and then a short walk from the dock.

At the southern end of South Core Banks is the **Cape Lookout Lighthouse.** Constructed in 1859, it is still operational. The old keeper's house serves as a visitor center (staffed Mar–Nov). Continue around the point to see massive, partially submerged gun mounts that served as submarine defenses during World War II.

Return on the ferry and continue south on U.S. 70 for 25 miles to the picturesque waterfront town of:

9. **Beaufort,** a popular stop on the Intracoastal Waterway. Settled in 1710, Beaufort was once North Carolina's third-largest port. Pirates attacked it in 1747. Several structures from the 1700s and 1800s are part of an extensive preservation and restoration project in the historic district. You can visit the **Old Burying Grounds** (built in 1731), the **Joseph Bell House** (1767), the **Carteret County Courthouse** (1796), the **J. Pigott House** (1830), and the **Apothecary Shop and Doctor's Office** (1859). Learn more about the role the sea has played in North Carolina's history at the **North Carolina Maritime Museum,** on Front Street, where exhibits include boats, boat models, and natural history displays. At the **Harvey W. Smith Watercraft Center,** Front Street, visitors can watch boats being constructed or restored.

From Beaufort, you can go to New Bern via U.S. 70, or continue south along North Carolina's coast via U.S. 17 to Wilmington.

# DRIVING TOUR
## Louisiana's Cajun Country

**Start:** Houma
**Finish:** Lafayette
**Distance:** 150 miles
**Time:** 2 days
**Highlights:** Bayous, riverbanks, and swamps; fishing villages; an aviation museum; historic towns; Cajun dance halls, theme parks, and museums

This tour explores the colorful, fascinating Cajun culture that thrives in the bayous and along the riverbanks of "Acadiana," the official designation for the 22 southwestern Louisiana parishes collectively known as "Cajun Country." Cajun music and food became a nationwide fad in the 1980s.

Deeply religious and hardworking, Cajuns are also warm and friendly, and welcome strangers to "pass a good time" on the bayous. Many inhabitants of this unique region are descendants of the French colonists expelled by the British in the mid–18th century from *l'Acadie*—the old French name for Nova Scotia and the other Canadian maritime provinces ("Cajun" is a corruption of "Acadian"). The majority of residents speak a 17th-century form of French, learned from ancestors who had long been isolated from Mother France. Yet language poses no barriers to the excitement that pulses throughout the region. Almost everyone speaks English and most can speak or understand standard French as well. Here, the fiddles and accordions of Cajun bands raise the rafters in dance halls for *fais-do-dos* (dances), and restaurants serve piles of étouffées, jambalaya, red beans and rice, and bread pudding. Food and fun are plentiful in the place where the motto is "Laissez les bon temps rouler"—let the good times roll. And roll they do.

The gateway to Cajun Country lies 57 miles south of New Orleans on U.S. 90 in:

1. **Houma,** the seat of Terrebonne Parish and a major shrimping and boating area. Several swamp tours take off from here. One of the state's prettiest drives is the circular loop along La. 56 and La. 57, which dips all the way down from Houma to the Gulf of Mexico and passes through the fishing villages of Dulac and Chauvin en route to Cocodrie on the gulf. At Cocodrie ("crocodile" in French), Coco Marina, abutting the gulf, is loaded with fishing guides and charter services. The **Houma-Terrebonne Parish Tourist Commission** at 1702 S. St. Charles St. (☎ 504/868-2732), has maps, brochures, and free advice about the region.

From Houma, continue 16 miles northwest on U.S. 90 to:

2. **Gibson,** home to **Wildlife Gardens** (at the intersection of La. 311 and U.S. 90; ☎ 504/575-3676 for information). Here you can take guided tours of a 20-acre preserved swamp, luxuriant with subtropical flowers, trees, and plants. Visitors can lure the resident alligators in for a closer look by tossing dog food over the fence; big buckets are passed out by park personnel. There is also an authentic trapper's cabin for overnight stays.

From Gibson, continue west on U.S. 90 for 13 miles to:

3. **Morgan City,** which sits on the Atchafalaya River, close to the Gulf of Mexico. Morgan City became a boomtown in November 1947, when oil was struck offshore and ushered in the "black gold rush." The original 1917 film *Tarzan of the Apes* was filmed in and around Morgan City; a video of the film is shown at the **Morgan City Tourist Commission,** 725 Myrtle St. (☎ 504/384-3343). Adjacent to the office is the 22-foot-high flood wall of the Atchafalaya River, which is accessible and provides a good view of the river.

Cross the Atchafalaya River bridge west of Morgan City to Patterson. Just before the Calumet Bridge, turn right on Zenor Road and drive less than a mile to the **Wedell-Williams Memorial Aviation Museum,** 394 Airport Circle (☎ 504/395-7067). In the early 1930s, James Wedell, a nationally known pioneer aviation ace, teamed with Harry Williams, mayor of Patterson, to form a commercial airmail service and build speed planes. This museum pays tribute to the two flyers and contains memorabilia pertaining to their careers.

Go a mile west of Patterson to Calumet before veering right on Route 182, which closely follows the winding Bayou Teche, Louisiana's largest bayou. Drive 19 miles to:

4. **Franklin.** This beautiful little town, an official Main Street USA town, boasts more than 400 historic houses and buildings. In fact, the entire town is listed on the National Register of Historic Places. The pretty main street with its oak trees and antique street lanterns is lined with Greek Revival mansions. Franklin is not a Cajun town; it was settled by Northerners, who sided with the Union during the Civil War. Stop at the **City of Franklin Tourist Commission,** 300 Iberia St. (☎ 800/962-6889 or 318/828-6323), to pick up walking and driving tour maps of the historic area. Among the mansions open to the public for tours are **Arlington Plantation** and the **Grevemberg House.**

☕ **TAKE A BREAK** The **Yellow Bowl Restaurant** (☎ 318/276-5512), located 7 miles west of Franklin and 3 miles east of Jeanerette on La. 182, is famous in these parts for its crawfish étouffée and other Cajun specialties (priced at $8–$10).

From Franklin, continue northwest on La. 182 for 23 miles to:

5. **New Iberia,** the "Queen City of the Teche." This small town offers several worthwhile attractions. Stop in the **Iberia Tourist Center,** 2704 La. 14 (☎ 318/365-1540), for information about the town and the region. Note that

in downtown New Iberia, La. 182 splits into two one-way streets: Main Street (westbound) and St. Peter Street (eastbound). The town's most famous site is stately **Shadows-on-the-Teche,** 317 E. Main St. (☎ 318/369-6446). Shaded by giant moss-draped oak trees on the banks of Bayou Teche, this lovely historic home was built by sugar planter David Weeks in 1834. The bricks used in its construction were made of clay taken from the banks of the bayou. Period antiques are among the house's beautiful furnishings. Nearby, tours are conducted of the **Conrad Rice Mill,** one of the nation's oldest rice mills (it produces Wild Pecan Rice). New Iberia is also home to **Trappey's Fine Foods,** 900 Main St. (☎ 318/365-8281), which manufactures spices and condiments.

☕ **TAKE A BREAK  Café Lagniappe Too,** 204 E. Main St. (☎ 318/365-9419), a block from the Shadows, is a cozy little restaurant decorated with paintings and handmade dolls created by chefs/owners Al and Elaine Landry. Lunchtime fare is mostly soups, salads, and sandwiches, but the changing dinner menu might feature grilled quail, crab-and-corn bisque, steaks, or pan-fried catfish. Entrees cost $8 to $10.

In New Iberia, a picturesque place to stay is the **Inn at le Rosier,** 314 E. Main St. (☎ 318/367-5305), a small white cottage directly across the street from the Shadows. The inn offers four tiny, moderately priced, antique-filled rooms with private baths, plus a restaurant serving breakfast, lunch, and dinner. There is also a **Best Western,** 2714 La. 14 (☎ 318/364-3030), and the **Holiday Inn New Iberia/Avery Island,** 2915 La. 14 (☎ 318/367-7877).

New Iberia is the jumping-off point for trips to Avery Island and Live Oak Gardens. On La. 329, 7 miles southwest of New Iberia is:

6. **Avery Island.** This is not an island in the usual sense, but rather a salt dome covered with luxuriant subtropical vegetation, rising gently out of the surrounding marshlands. The 2,500-acre island is the property of descendants of Edmund McIlhenny, who invented **Tabasco sauce** here in the 1880s. The hot sauce, once a condiment on every Deep South table and now world famous, is still manufactured on Avery Island, and free tours of the factory are conducted every day except Sunday. Avery Island is also home to **Jungle Gardens,** with its bird sanctuary and profusion of exotic year-round blooms.

Six miles southwest of New Iberia on La. 14 is:

7. **Live Oak Gardens.** Also called Jefferson Island, like Avery Island it is a salt dome covered with splendid gardens. In the late 19th century, actor Joseph Jefferson, famous for the role of Rip Van Winkle, built his country estate here. Parts of the landscaped gardens were destroyed in 1980 when an oil company drilling in nearby Lake Peigneur pierced the salt dome. However, Jefferson's Moorish-Gothic mansion was not damaged, and today the house and 20 acres of stunning theme gardens are open for tours.

From New Iberia, La. 31 heads north along Bayou Teche for 10 miles to:

8. **St. Martinville.** In the center of the town is the **Arcadian Memorial,** which commemorates the exiled Arcadians. The Acadians were romanticized and immortalized in Longfellow's poem *Evangeline,* which was based on a real-life love affair between Emmeline Labiche and Louis Areceneux. According to the legend, the couple was separated after *Le Grand Derangement,* when the British forced the Acadians out of Nova Scotia. They were reunited in St. Martinville, but by that time Louis was betrothed to another. The town is dotted with icons of the legend. The **Evangeline Oak** is said to be the site where Emmeline/Evangeline came ashore and met Louis. Local musicians and storytellers often congregate under the oak to entertain locals and visitors. On the town square, behind the St. Martin de Tours Church, a bronze statue of Evangeline looks out over the small cemetery.

Two miles north of downtown on La. 31 is the **Longfellow-Evangeline State Commemorative Area,** a luxuriant 160-acre park with a number of sites for interpretation of Acadian culture.

Bed-and-breakfast accommodations and a full-service restaurant are offered at **Place d'Evangeline/Old Castillo Hotel,** 220 Evangeline Blvd. (☎ **318/394-4010**), a historic building next to the Evangeline Oak on Bayou Teche. The five moderately priced rooms feature high ceilings and period antiques; all have private baths. The restaurant specializes in seafood, including crawfish, catfish, and alligator boulettes. Entrees are $8 to $10.

On La. 31, 11 miles north of the park, is:

9. **Breaux Bridge,** a sleepy little hamlet that rouses itself each May for one of the state's major festivals. Breaux Bridge is the "Crawfish Capital of the World," and its annual crustacean festival draws upward of 200,000 people. The town is also home to **La Poussiere,** one of the oldest and best Cajun dance halls. Cajun bands play every Saturday night for lively two-stepping, jigs, and Cajun waltzes.

☕ **TAKE A BREAK** Mulate's, 325 Mills Ave. (☎ **318/332-4648**) in Breaux Bridge, is known nationally as a down-home Cajun restaurant and dance hall. A simple roadhouse, it serves up prodigious portions of seafood—broiled, fried, baked, and étoufféed—while Cajun bands jam daily during lunch and dinner. Meals cost around $12.

Traveling 8 miles west of Breaux Bridge via La. 94 will lead you to the last stop on the tour:

10. **Lafayette,** the unofficial capital of Cajun Country. This laid-back city of about 150,000 brings Cajun culture to life through theme parks such as **Vermilionville** and **Acadian Village,** and the **Lafayette Museum,** downtown, and the **Acadian Cultural Center,** operated by the Jean Lafayette National Historic Park Service. Nowhere, however, is Cajun culture livelier and more evident than in the city's several dance halls. **Grant Street** and **Antler's** are both longtime rustic bastions of live music and dancing. Zydeco is featured at **El Sido** and **Hamilton's** dance halls, and you can enjoy both food and live music at **Randol's** and **Prejean's.** Lafayette's two biggest festivals are the Festival International de Louisiana in April and the Festival Arcadiens in September, both of which feature plenty of food and live music. If you want to take a break from the Cajun deluge, the **Natural History Museum,** with its planetarium, has many exhibits and activities, and is a popular place for family outings.

Overnight lodgings in Lafayette range from chain motels to quaint bed-and-breakfasts. The **Best Western Hotel Acadiana,** 1801 W. Pinhook Rd. (☎ **800/826-8386** out of state, or 318/233-8120), is a sleek, modern, moderately priced hotel with a restaurant and lounge. More expensive are bed-and-breakfast accommodations at **A la Bonne Viellee,** off La. 339 west of Lafayette (☎ **318/937-5495**). Two bedrooms and a kitchen are in a charming Arcadian cottage with a fireplace and TVs upstairs and down.

# 1 Miami & Miami Beach

The Spanish first colonized Florida's southeastern coast in the 16th century, and since then the Miami area has attracted sun-seekers, retirees, immigrants, entrepreneurs, and drifters—all lured by its predictable year-round warmth and its location, on a lush peninsula surrounded by deep waters, facing emphatically toward the Caribbean and the rest of the Americas.

But the city has not been without its share of troubles. A spate of tourist murders in the early '90s contributed to Miami's status as the nation's murder capital; a steady wave of immigration had the world believing that Cuban rafts floated onto the beaches every afternoon. And in 1997, after news of corruption scandals and a huge fiscal deficit hit the papers, citizens even introduced a referendum to abolish the city of Miami.

Despite lingering fears of crime and news of financial crisis, visitors continue to set upon the city's shores. Miami is a sprawling metropolis made up of countless neighborhoods—from the whimsical art deco landmarks of cutting-edge South Beach to the circa-'50s megaresorts of Miami Beach proper; from the boho enclaves-turned-hip nightspots of Coconut Grove to the Mediterranean-style hotels and restaurants that line the fountained plazas in Coral Gables; and from Key Biscayne's tony mansions and golf courses to Little Havana's "Calle Ocho," where cigar-chomping gents play dominoes to a pulsating salsa backbeat.

## ARRIVING & DEPARTING

**BY PLANE** Most domestic and many international carriers serve **Miami International Airport (MIA),** about 6 miles west of downtown and about 12 miles from the beaches. A **taxi** should take no more than 30 minutes to Coral Gables or the beaches. Fares are about $14 to Coral Gables, $22–$26 to Miami Beach, including South Beach. **SuperShuttle** vans cost $12–$24 per person for door-to-door service to any part of Dade County (☎ **800/BLUE-VAN** or 305/871-2000). Virtually every major car-rental company has a desk at the airport. Though notoriously inefficient, **public buses** leave the airport for downtown only once every 30–40 minutes from the arrivals level. They cost $1.25 for adults and 60¢ for seniors. For detailed route information or a map, call ☎ 305/638-6700 weekdays 6am–10pm, weekends 9am–5pm. Flat fares of $22–$46 apply to taxis.

**BY TRAIN & BUS** Amtrak's East Coast line terminates in Miami; the terminal is at 8303 NW 37th Ave., off of 79th St. (☎ 800/USA-RAIL). **Greyhound/Trailways** (☎ 800/231-2222) buses pull into a number of stations, including 700 Biscayne Blvd. downtown and 1650 NE 6th Ave. in North Miami Beach.

## ESSENTIALS

**VISITOR INFORMATION** The **Greater Miami Convention and Visitor Bureau,** 701 Brickell Ave., Suite 2700, Miami, FL 33131 (☎ 800/283-2707 or 305/539-3063), provides an informative free magazine, *Greater Miami and the Beaches Visitor's Guide,* and will put you in touch with Greater Miami's various chambers of commerce for maps and details on particular regions.

**RESOURCES FOR TRAVELERS WITH SPECIAL NEEDS** The Greater Miami Convention and Visitor Bureau (see above) has up-to-date information on hotels that offer special accommodations and services for travelers with disabilities. The **Deaf Services Bureau** (☎ 305/668-DEAF) and the **Division of Blind Services** (☎ 305/377-5339) will answer any questions you have about traveling in and around Miami.

With a large population of retirees, Miami is well versed in catering to seniors. Ask for discounts everywhere—hotels, movies, museums, restaurants, and attractions. Numerous restaurants offer early-bird specials, and most places will honor AARP membership.

Miami, particularly South Beach, has a large gay community, supported by a wide range of services. The **Gay and Lesbian Community Hotline** (☎ 305/759-3661) is an interactive, informative recording that can be accessed by a touch-tone phone. The **Lambda Passages/Gay Community Bookstore,** 7545 Biscayne Blvd. (☎ 305/754-6900), has literature, newspapers, videos, music, cards, and more. *TWN* is a gay publication distributed free in Miami in lavender boxes.

**EMERGENCIES & SAFETY** Call ☎ 911 for fire, police, or ambulance. Among area hospitals is the **Health South Doctors' Hospital,** 5000 University Dr., Coral Gables (☎ 305/666-2111). When driving around Miami, always have a good map and know where you're going. Don't walk alone at night, and be extra wary when walking or driving through Little Haiti and areas in and around downtown. If you arrive late in the evening, consider going to your hotel by taxi, then renting a car the next day.

## GETTING AROUND

Unless you're going to spend your entire vacation at a self-contained resort or in pedestrian-friendly South Beach, a car is a necessity here, although parking—especially in South Beach, Miami Beach, and Coconut Grove—is a hassle. A reliable map is essential. The City of Miami is divided into quadrants—NE, NW, SE, and SW—by the intersection of Flagler Street and North Miami Avenue. These two roads meet in the city center. Street and avenue numbers increase from this intersection. Addresses are usually descriptive; 12301 Biscayne Blvd. is located at 123rd Street. It's also helpful to remember that avenues generally run north–south, while streets go east–west.

**BY RAIL & BUS** Notoriously inefficient, Greater Miami's mass transit system is operated by the **Metro-Dade Transit Agency** (☎ 305/638-6700 for route information). Free schedules, maps, and a "First-Time Rider's Kit" are available at Government Center Station, 111 NW 1st St. (1 block from Flagler Street), in downtown Miami, or by mail from the address above.

**Metrorail,** the city's modern high-speed commuter train, is a 21-mile elevated line that connects Miami's northern and southern suburbs to downtown, but it simply doesn't go most places that tourists go. If you're staying in Coral Gables or Coconut Grove, you can park your car at a nearby station and ride the rail downtown. Metrorail operates daily 6am–midnight, every $7^1/_2$ minutes during rush hours, and every 15 minutes at other times. The fare is $1.25.

The Disneyesque **Metromover,** a $4^1/_2$-mile elevated line, circles the city center in two big loops, and connects with Metrorail at Government Center and Brickell Station. The single-train car winds through some of the city's most important business and retail locations, including the Omni International Mall and the Brickell Financial District, and is one of Miami's best sightseeing bargains at 25¢ a ride. Service runs daily 6am–midnight about every 5 minutes. Transfers to Metrorail are $1.

Miami's suburban layout is not conducive to getting around by bus, although **Metrobus** provides service with widely varying frequency. Standard fare is $1.25, though some express routes cost $2.75. Disabled passengers, students, and those over 65 pay only 60¢. Exact change is required.

**BY TAXI**   If you'll be traveling only short distances, an occasional taxi is a good alternative to renting a car. Fares start at $1.10 for the first one-seventh of a mile, and increase at the rate of $1.75 for each additional mile. Major cab companies include **Metro** (☎ 305/888-8888) and **Yellow** (☎ 305/444-4444). On Miami Beach, the reigning cab company is **Central** (☎ 305/532-5555).

## WHAT TO SEE & DO

**ESCORTED TOURS**   There's no better way to see *all* of Miami than with **Fun Flight Miami, Inc.** (☎ 305/769-9353), offering air tours in an open, ultra-light plane. Flights leave from Rickenbacker Causeway at the marina in Key Biscayne, Tues–Sun 8am–6pm, weather permitting.

**Miami Nice Excursion, Inc.** (☎ 305/949-9180) tours will take you to the Everglades, Fort Lauderdale, the Seaquarium, or even The Bahamas. Included in most Miami trips is a comprehensive city tour. Tours run daily 7am–10pm; call ahead for directions to various pickup areas.

The **Miami Design Preservation League** (☎ 305/672-2014) sponsors $1^1/_2$-hour walking tours of the Art Deco District on Thursday at 6:30pm and Saturday at 10:30am from the Art Deco Welcome Center, 1001 Ocean Dr.; call for updated schedules. If you'd rather see the district on two wheels, reserve a spot on the **Art Deco Cycling Tour** (☎ 305/674-0150). Tours depart on the first and last Sunday of the month at 10:30am from the Miami Beach Bicycle Center, 601 5th St. (where you can also rent a bike).

On the first Friday of the month, from 7 to 10pm, vans shuttle art lovers to the more than 20 Coral Gables galleries that participate in **"Gables Night."** Tours are free, and participants sip wine as they view the art. For more information, call Richard Arregui (☎ 305/447-3973), or stop by any of the area galleries.

**CRUISES & BOAT TOURS**   Cruise along Biscayne Bay and check out the waterfront mansions on the *Lady Lucille* (☎ 305/534-7000), an air-conditioned 150-passenger boat, complete with snacks and two full bars. The 3-hour cruise leaves across from the Fontainebleau Hotel daily at 11am, 1:30 and 4pm.

The *Sea Kruz* (☎ 800/688-PLAY or 305/538-8300) takes you 3 miles off the coast into international waters for lunch or dinner cruises that offer gambling, music, and dancing. (Free chips or coupons are usually offered for the asking.) Departures are from the South Beach pier at 1280 5th St.; call for schedules.

More adventure than tour, a 2-hour cruise on the *Heritage Miami II* **Topsail Schooner** (☎ 305/442-9697) passes Villa Vizcaya, Coconut Grove, and Key Biscayne,

# Miami

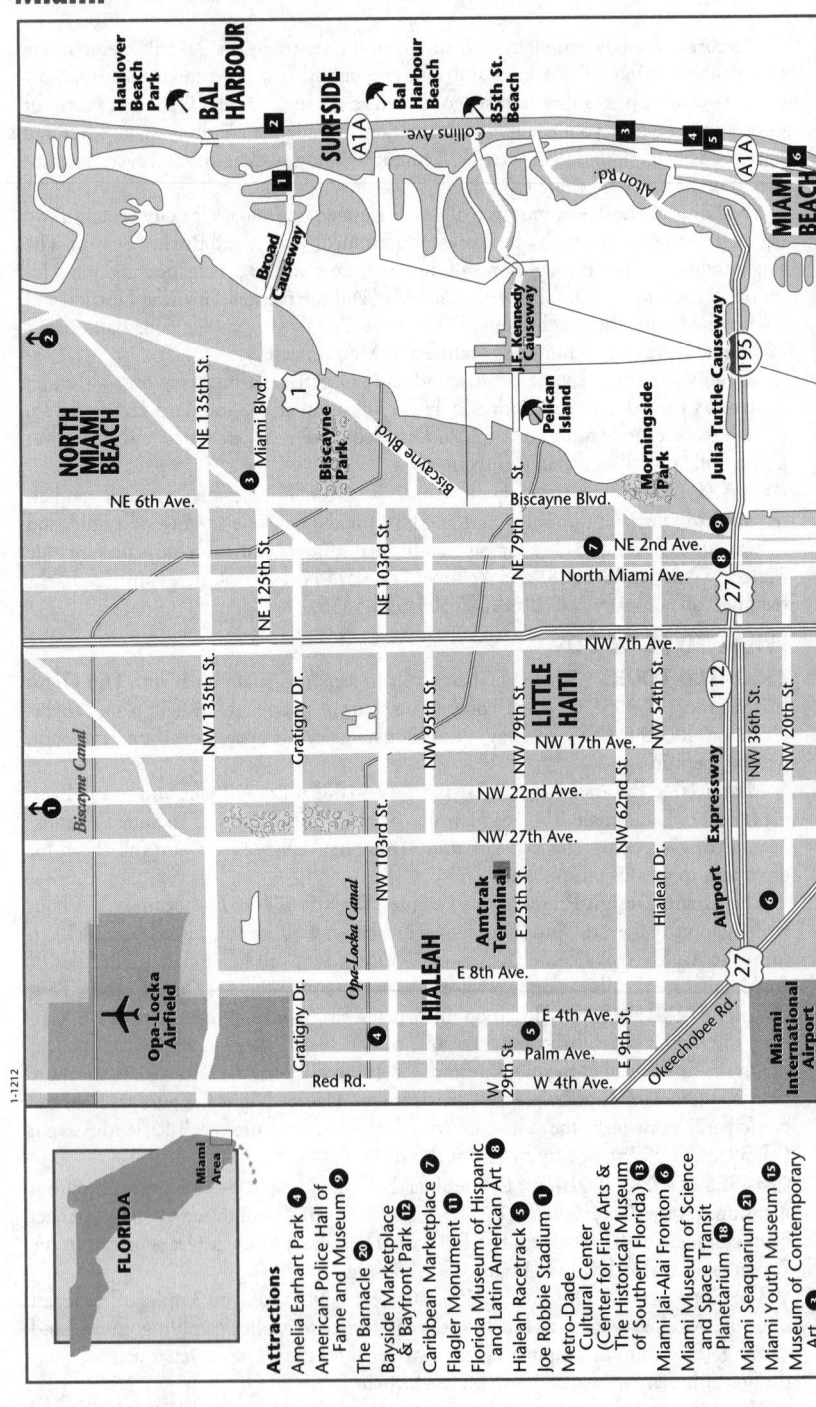

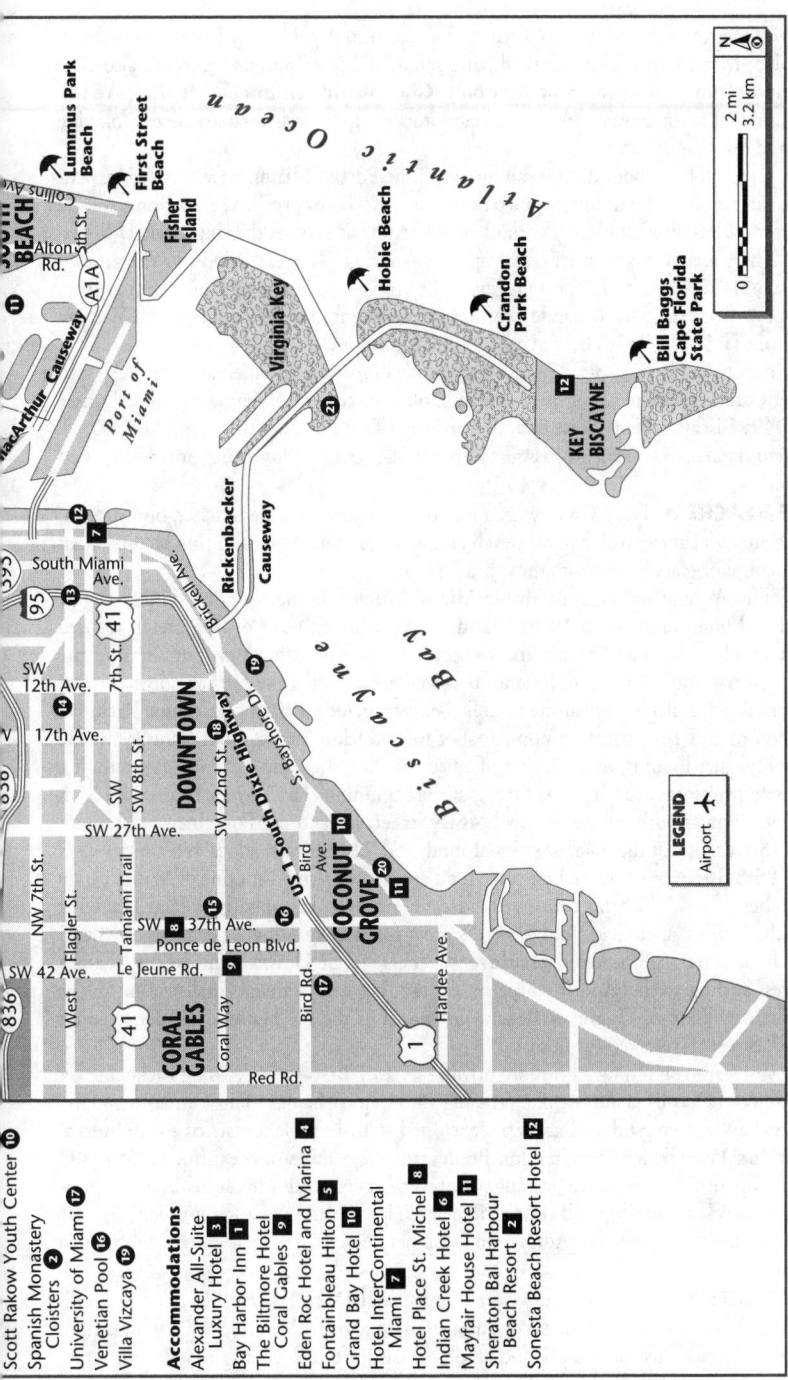

Scott Rakow Youth Center ⓪

Spanish Monastery
Cloisters ②

University of Miami ⑯

Venetian Pool ⑲

Villa Vizcaya ⑲

**Accommodations**

Alexander All-Suite
Luxury Hotel ③

Bay Harbor Inn ①

The Biltmore Hotel
Coral Gables ⑨

Eden Roc Hotel and Marina ⑤

Fontainbleau Hilton ⑤

Grand Bay Hotel ⑩

Hotel InterContinental
Miami ⑦

Hotel Place St. Michel ⑧

Indian Creek Hotel ⑥

Mayfair House Hotel ⑪

Sheraton Bal Harbour
Beach Resort ②

Sonesta Beach Resort Hotel ⑫

providing great views of the city skyline. The tall ship departs daily from Bayside Marketplace Marina, 401 Biscayne Blvd., at 1:30, 4, and 6pm, and on weekends also at 9, 10, and 11pm. Cruises run Sept–May only. **Gondola Adventures** (☎ 305/573-1818), also moored at the Bayside Marina, takes visitors on an honest-to-goodness gondola ride around Bayside.

Most Caribbean-bound ships sailing out of the Port of Miami are relatively inexpensive, can be booked without advance notice, and make for excellent excursions. All the shorter cruises offer gambling, with casinos opening as soon as the ship clears U.S. waters. There are dozens of other cruise options—from a 1-day excursion to a trip around the world. Pick up the *Passport to Adventure,* an up-to-date list of cruises sailing from the port, from the **Metro–Dade Seaport Department,** 1015 North America Way, in Miami (☎ 305/371-7678), open Mon–Fri 8am–5pm.

Most of the big lines offer 3- and 4-day excursions to The Bahamas, Key West, and other Caribbean islands. For more information, contact The **Bahamas Tourist Office,** at 19495 Biscayne Blvd., Suite 809, in Aventura (☎ 800/422-4262 or 305/932-0051). Passengers must travel with a passport or proof of citizenship for reentry into the United States.

**THE BEACHES** Dade County has more than 35 miles of wide beaches, but in short, there are two alternatives: Miami Beach and Key Biscayne. You can bring picnics—but no alcohol or glass bottles—to most beaches.

Collins Avenue and Ocean Drive in **Miami Beach** front nearly a dozen miles of gray sand and blue waters from 1st to 192nd streets. Though most of this stretch is lined with a wall of hotels and condos, beach access is plentiful. Bring lots of quarters for the metered parking. In general, beaches become less crowded the farther north you go. Miami Beach's lifeguard-protected public beaches include ultrachic **Lummus Park,** between 6th and 14th streets, a popular spot for modeling photo shoots (check out the funky lifeguard stands, in the shapes of a bed, a rocket ship, and a Shinto-style temple). For safe swimming, also try **21st Street,** at the beginning of a $1^1/_2$-mile boardwalk; **35th Street,** popular with an older crowd; **46th Street,** next to the Fontainebleau Hilton; **64th Street,** one of the quietest strips around; and **72nd Street,** a local old-timers' spot. The **85th Street** beach is the best place for a crowd-free swim—it's one of Miami's only stretches of sand with no condos or hotels looming over sunbathers. **Bal Harbour Beach,** Collins Avenue at 96th Street, is great for shell-hunting. Just north of Miami Beach, at about 108th Street, **Haulover Beach/Harbor House** seems to get Miami's biggest surfing swells. And if you're set on tanning *au naturel,* a small section in the southern portion of **Haulover Beach,** just north of the Bal Harbour border at about 106th Street, is reserved for nudists.

If you want something a bit more private, try **Key Biscayne.** Crossing Rickenbacker Causeway ($1 toll) is almost like crossing into The Bahamas. The 5 miles of public beach have softer sand and are less developed than hotel-laden strips to the north. **Crandon Park Beach,** on Crandon Boulevard, has 3 miles of oceanfront beach, 493 acres of park, 75 grills, three parking lots, several soccer and softball fields, and a public 18-hole championship golf course. The beach is wide and the water is usually so clear ~~~~ ~~ to the bottom. Admission is $2 per vehicle; it's open daily from 8am to

**AT**~~~~ ~~~~ ~~~~est sight is the ✪ **Art Deco District.** Located in South Beach, it's a comm~~~~ up of outrageous, fanciful 1920s and 1930s architecture, roughly bounded by the ~~~~ntic Ocean on the east, Alton Road on the west, 6th Street to the south, and Dade Boulevard (along the Collins Canal) to the north. Most of the district's best buildings are concentrated along Ocean Drive, Collins Avenue, and Washington Avenue.

# Miami: South Beach

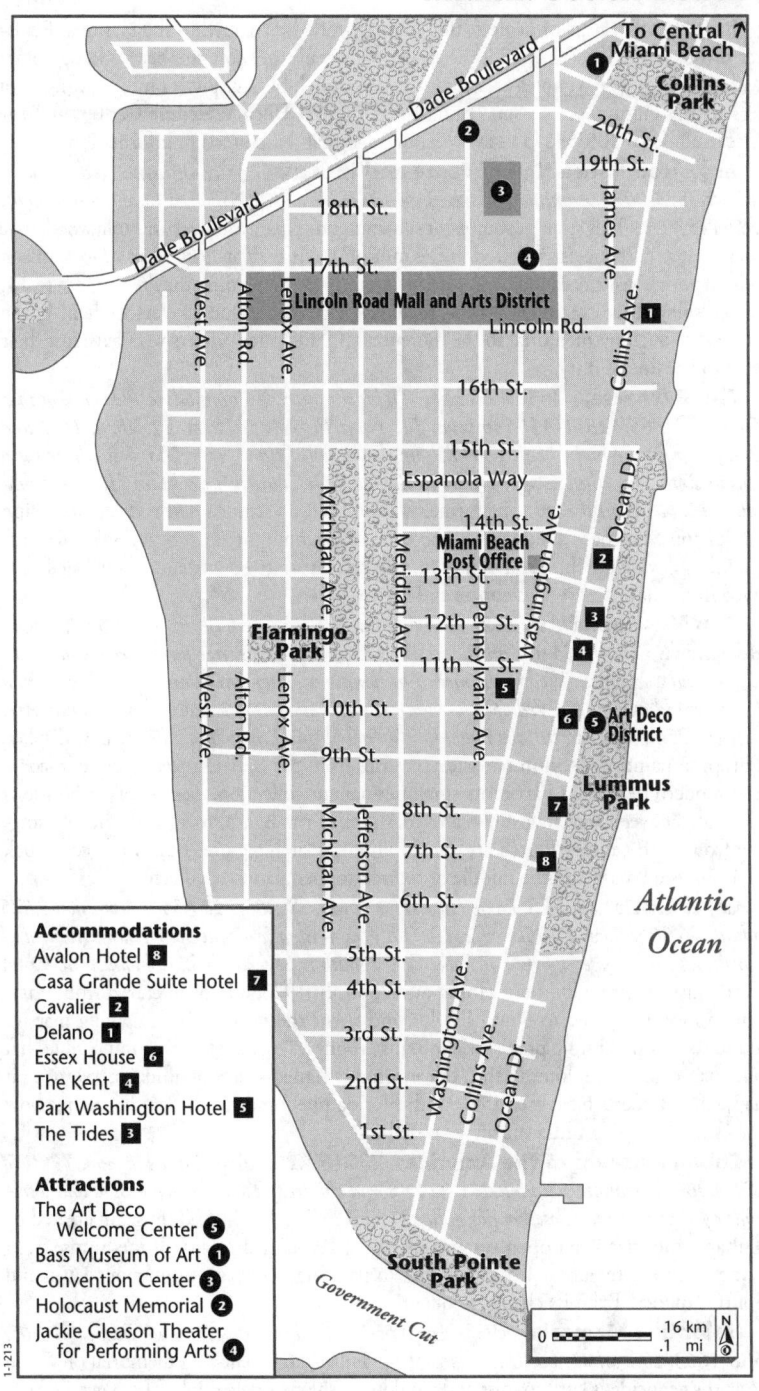

To Central Miami Beach

Collins Park

Dade Boulevard

20th St.
19th St.
18th St.
17th St.

James Ave.
Collins Ave.

**Lincoln Road Mall and Arts District**
Lincoln Rd.

16th St.
15th St.
Espanola Way
14th St.

West Ave.
Alton Rd.
Lenox Ave.
Michigan Ave.
Meridian Ave.
Washington Ave.
Ocean Dr.

**Miami Beach Post Office**
13th St.
12th St.
11th St.

**Flamingo Park**

Pennsylvania Ave.

10th St.
9th St.
8th St.
7th St.
6th St.

Jefferson Ave.
Michigan Ave.

**Art Deco District**

**Lummus Park**

*Atlantic Ocean*

5th St.
4th St.
3rd St.
2nd St.
1st St.

Washington Ave.
Collins Ave.
Ocean Dr.

**South Pointe Park**

*Government Cut*

0    .16 km
     .1  mi

N

## Accommodations
Avalon Hotel **8**
Casa Grande Suite Hotel **7**
Cavalier **2**
Delano **1**
Essex House **6**
The Kent **4**
Park Washington Hotel **5**
The Tides **3**

## Attractions
The Art Deco Welcome Center **5**
Bass Museum of Art **1**
Convention Center **3**
Holocaust Memorial **2**
Jackie Gleason Theater for Performing Arts **4**

1-1213

In 1979, after years of neglect, this 1 square mile was named to the National Register of Historic Places. Long-lost architectural details and soft sherbet building colors were unveiled. Today, hotels, restaurants, and nightclubs have put it on the cutting edge of Miami's cultural scene. Start your visit at the **Art Deco Welcome Center,** at 1001 Ocean Dr. (☎ 305/531-3484), which has maps and architecture information.

**American Police Hall of Fame and Museum.** *3801 Biscayne Blvd., Miami.* ☎ *305/573-0070. Admission $6 adults, $4 seniors over 61, $3 children 11 and under. Daily 10am–5:30pm.* This strange, somewhat silly museum is part tribute, part Hollywood-style drama. Just past the car featured in the motion picture *Blade Runner* is a mock prison cell, in which visitors can take pictures of themselves pretending they're doing 5 to 10. Also displayed are execution devices, including a guillotine and an electric chair. In the entry is a touching memorial to the more than 3,000 police officers who have lost their lives in the line of duty.

**The Barnacle.** *3485 Main Hwy. (1 block south of Commodore Plaza), Coconut Grove.* ☎ *305/448-9445. Admission $1. Tours Fri–Sat at 10am, 11:30am, 1pm, and 2:30pm from the main house porch. From downtown Miami, take U.S. 1 south; make a left on 27th Ave., then a right on South Bayshore Dr. Turn left on Main Hwy.; the museum is 2 blocks on the left.* The former home of naval architect and early settler Ralph Middleton Munroe is a museum in the heart of Coconut Grove. The house's quiet surroundings, wide porches, and period furnishings illustrate how Miami's privileged class lived in the days before skyscrapers and luxury hotels.

**Bass Museum of Art.** *2121 Park Ave. (at 21st St.), South Beach.* ☎ *305/673-7530. Admission $5 adults, $3 students with ID and senior citizens, free for children 6 and under; second and fourth Wed of the month by donation. Tues–Sat 10am–5pm, Sun 1–5pm (every second and fourth Wed open 1–9pm). Closed holidays. One block west of Collins Ave. between 21st and 22nd sts.; the museum is directly behind the public library.* Bass displays European paintings, sculptures, and tapestries from the Renaissance, baroque, rococo, and modern periods as part of its small permanent collection. Temporary exhibitions alternate between traveling shows and rotations of the Bass's stock, with themes ranging from 17th-century Dutch art to contemporary architecture. Built from coral rock in 1930, the Bass sits in the middle of six tree-topped, landscaped acres.

**Coral Castle.** *28655 S. Dixie Hwy., Homestead.* ☎ *305/248-6344. Admission $7.75 adults, $6.50 seniors, $5 children 7–12. Daily 9am–6pm (closes at 3pm Thanksgiving and Christmas Eve). Closed Christmas. Take U.S. 1 south to SW 286th St. in Homestead.* Coral Castle just might be Florida's zaniest attraction. In 1923, a Latvian crazed from unrequited love emigrated to South Florida and spent the next 25 years carving massive amounts of stone into a prehistoric-looking, roofless "castle." It seems impossible that one man could have done all this, but neighbors signed scores of affidavits swearing it happened. Experts have used this South Florida phenomenon to help figure out how the Great Pyramids and Stonehenge were built.

**Cuban Museum of the Americas.** *1300 SW 12th Ave., Little Havana.* ☎ *305/858-8006. Donations $3 adults, $1 students and children. Tues–Fri noon–6pm and weekends by appointment. Closed major holidays.* This politically charged museum created by Cuban exiles has been open on and off since 1974. It displays all mediums, from ceramics to photography, from sculpture to painting, by artists throughout Latin and South America. Exhibits change frequently.

**Holocaust Memorial.** *1933 Meridian Ave. (at Dade Blvd.), South Beach.* ☎ *305/538-1663. Free admission. Daily 9am–9pm.* This heart-wrenching memorial of World War II's genocide is hard to miss and would be a shame to overlook. The powerful centerpiece is a bronze statue by Kenneth Treister that depicts millions of people crawling into an open hand to freedom. You can walk through an open hallway lined with photographs and the names of concentration camps and their victims. From the street, you'll see the outstretched arm, but do stop and tour the sculpture at ground level. What's hidden behind the beautiful stone facade is extremely moving.

✪ **Miami Art Museum at the Metro–Dade Cultural Center.** *101 W. Flagler St., Miami.* ☎ *305/375-1700. Metro–Dade Cultural Center,* ☎ *305/375-3000. Admission $5 adults, $2.50 senior citizens and students with ID, free for children 11 and under, free for everyone Thurs 5–9pm. Tues–Wed and Fri 10am–5pm; Thurs 10am–9pm; Sat–Sun noon–5pm. Closed major holidays. From I-95 south, exit at Orange Bowl–NW 8th St. and continue south to NW 2nd St.; turn left at NW 2nd St. and go 1¹/₂ blocks to NW 2nd Ave., turn right, and park at the Metro–Dade Garage. Bring the parking ticket to the lobby for validation.* The recently renamed Miami Art Museum (it was the Center for the Fine Arts until 1996) features modern and contemporary works by such artists as Eric Fischl, Max Beckman, Jim Dine, and Stuart Davis. Rotating exhibitions often focus on Latin American or Caribbean artists. The Metro–Dade Cultural Center, where the museum is located, also houses the main branch of the **Metro–Dade Public Library** and the **Historical Museum of Southern Florida,** which highlights the fascinating history of Florida, and in particular the state's southern region.

**Miami Metrozoo.** *SW 152nd St. and SW 124th Ave., south of Coral Gables.* ☎ *305/ 251-0403. Admission $8 adults, $4 children 3–12. Daily 9:30am–5:30pm (ticket booth closes at 4pm). From U.S. 1, take the SW 152nd St. exit west three blocks to the Metrozoo entrance.* Rarely does a zoo warrant mention as a city's top attraction, but this huge 290-acre complex is completely cageless—animals are kept at bay by cleverly designed moats. Star attractions include two rare white Bengal tigers, a Komodo dragon, rare koala bears, and a monorail "safari." Especially appealing for both adults and children is PAWS, a unique petting zoo. You can even ride an elephant.

**Miami Museum of Science and Space Transit Planetarium.** *3280 S. Miami Ave., Coconut Grove.* ☎ *305/854-4247 for general information, 305/854-2222 for planetarium show times. Museum of Science, $6 adults, $4 seniors and children 3–12, free for children 2 and under; planetarium, $5 adults, $2.50 children and seniors; combination ticket, $9 adults, $5.50 children and seniors. Museum of Science, daily 10am–6pm; call for planetarium show times. Closed major holidays. Metrorail: Vizcaya station. Auto: Take I-95 south to exit 1 and follow the signs.* The Museum of Science features more than 140 hands-on exhibits that explore the mysteries of the universe. Live demonstrations and collections of rare natural history specimens make a visit here fun and informative. The adjacent Space Transit Planetarium projects astronomy and laser shows and has interactive demonstrations of upcoming computer technology and cyberspace features.

**Miami Seaquarium.** *4400 Rickenbacker Causeway (south side), Key Biscayne.* ☎ *305/ 361-5705. Admission $18.95 adults, $13.95 seniors over 55, $16.95 children 3–9. Daily 9:30am–6pm (ticket booth closes at 4:30pm).* Allot 4 hours to tour the 35-acre oceanarium, if you want to see all four daily shows starring trained dolphins, killer whales, and frolicking sea lions. You can even volunteer for one of their wet fishy kisses! If you're a fan of the old TV show *Flipper,* come see one of the original dolphins who played the title role.

**Monkey Jungle.** *14805 SW 216th St., Greater Miami South.* ☎ *305/235-1611. Admission $11.50 adults, $9.50 seniors and active-duty military, $6 children 4–12. Daily 9:30am–5pm (tickets sold until 4pm).* See rare Brazilian golden lion tamarins. Watch the "skin-diving" Asian macaques. It's primate paradise! No cages restrain the antics of the monkeys as they swing, chatter, and play their way into your heart. Screened-in trails wind through acres of "jungle," and daily shows feature the talents of the park's most progressive pupils. But you've got to love primates to get over the heavy smell of the jungle.

✪ **Museum of Contemporary Art (MOCA).** *In the Joan Lehman Building, 770 NE 125th St., North Miami.* ☎ *305/893-6211. Admission $4 adults, $2 seniors and students with ID, free for children 11 and under. Tues–Sat 10am–5pm, Sun noon–5pm. Closed major holidays.* MOCA recently acquired a new 23,000-square-foot space in which to display its impressive collection of internationally acclaimed art. You can see works by Jasper Johns, Roy Lichtenstein, Larry Rivers, Duane Michaels, and Claes Oldenberg. Guided tours are offered in English, Spanish, French, Creole, Portuguese, German, and Italian. A new screening facility allows for film presentations that will complement the exhibitions. Although the new facility is somewhat out of the way, the quality of the art makes it worth the trip.

**Parrot Jungle and Gardens.** *11000 SW 57th Ave., Greater Miami South.* ☎ *305/666-7834. Admission $12.95 adults, $8.95 children 3–10, $11.95 seniors. Daily 9:30am–6pm.* Not just parrots, but hundreds of brilliantly colored macaws, peacocks, cockatoos, and flamingos occupy this over-50-year-old park. Continuous shows in the Parrot Bowl Theater star roller-skating cockatoos, card-playing macaws, and more stunt-happy parrots than you ever thought possible. Alligators, tortoises, and iguanas are also on exhibit. Other attractions include a show focusing on indigenous Florida animals, an area called "Primate Experience," a children's playground, and a petting zoo. *Note:* Parrot Jungle is planning to move to its own island midway between downtown Miami and the beaches; the move is scheduled to be completed by 1999.

✪ **Spanish Monastery Cloisters.** *16711 W. Dixie Hwy. (at NE 167th St.), North Miami Beach.* ☎ *305/945-1461. Admission $4.50 adults, $2.50 seniors, $1 children 11 and under. Mon–Sat 10am–4pm, Sun noon–4pm. From downtown, take U.S. 1 north and turn left onto 163rd St.; take the first right onto West Dixie Hwy. and the Cloisters are 3 blocks ahead on the right.* Did you know that the oldest building in the Western Hemisphere dates from A.D. 1141 and is located in Miami? Well, not originally, but . . . The Spanish Monastery Cloisters were first erected in Segovia, Spain. Centuries later, newspaper magnate William Randolph Hearst purchased and brought the Cloisters to America in pieces. The carefully numbered stones were quarantined for years until they were finally reassembled on the present site in 1954. You'll want to spend about an hour touring the cold, ancient structure, the beautiful grounds, and gift shop.

**Venetian Pool.** *2701 DeSoto Blvd. (at Toledo St.), Coral Gables.* ☎ *305/460-5356. Admission $5 adults, $4 teens, $2 children 3–12 and under (children under 3 not allowed in the water). June–Aug, Mon–Fri 11am–7:30pm, Sat–Sun 10am–4:30pm; Apr–May and Sept–Oct, Tues–Fri 11am–5:30pm, Sat–Sun 10am–4:30pm; Nov–Mar, Tues–Fri 10am–4:30pm, Sat–Sun 10am–4:30pm.* Miami's most unusual swimming pool, dating from 1924, is hidden behind pastel stucco walls. Underground artesian wells feed the free-form lagoon, which is shaded by three-story Spanish porticos and features both fountains and waterfalls. Visitors are free to swim and sunbathe here year-round, just as Esther Williams and Johnny Weissmuller did decades ago.

✪ **Villa Vizcaya.** *3251 S. Miami Ave. (just south of Rickenbacker Causeway), North Coconut Grove.* ☎ *305/250-9133. Admission $10 adults, $5 children 6–12, free for children 5 and under. Villa, daily 9:30am–5pm (ticket booth closes at 4:30pm); gardens, daily 9:30am–5:30pm. Closed Christmas. Take I-95 south to exit 1 and follow the signs to Vizcaya.* Sometimes called the "Hearst Castle of the East," this magnificent villa was built in 1916 as a winter retreat for James Deering, cofounder and former vice president of International Harvester. The industrialist was fascinated by 16th-century art and architecture, and his ornate mansion—which took 1,000 artisans 5 years to build—became a celebration of these designs. Most of the original furnishings and paintings are still intact. Outside, lush formal gardens front an enormous swath of Biscayne Bay.

**The Wolfsonian.** *1001 Washington Ave., South Beach.* ☎ *305/531-1001. Admission $6 adults; $4 senior citizens, students, and children 11 and under; $7 tour-group members. Tues–Thurs and Sat 10am–6pm, Fri 10am–9pm, Sun noon–5pm.* Mickey Wolfson, Jr., an eccentric collector of late 19th- and 20th-century art and other paraphernalia, was spending so much money storing his booty that he decided to buy the warehouse and retrofit it to display his glass, ceramics, sculptures, paintings, photographs, and other items. In 1997, he gifted the collection to a local university; the future of the exhibitions remains in question. Call for details.

**PARKS & GARDENS**    The **Fairchild Tropical Gardens,** 10901 Old Cutler Rd. (☎ 305/667-1651), features a veritable rain forest of both rare and exotic plants on 83 acres. Palmettos, vine pergola, palm glades, and other unique species create a scenic, lush environment. It's well worth taking the free hourly tram to learn what you always wanted to know about the various flowers and trees on a 30-minute narrated tour.

The **Preston B. Bird and Mary Heinlein Fruit and Spice Park,** 24801 SW 187th Ave., Homestead (☎ 305/247-5727), harbors rare fruit trees that cannot survive elsewhere in the country. Ask for a guide to learn about this 30-acre living plant museum where the most exotic varieties of fruits and spices, including ackee, mango, ugly fruits, carambola, and breadfruit, grow on strange-looking trees with unpronounceable names. The best part? You're free to take anything that falls to the ground. You'll find samples of interesting fruits and jellies made from the park's bounty in the gift store, which also carries exotic cookbooks.

**BEST BETS FOR KIDS**    This interactive **Miami Youth Museum,** 3301 Coral Way, Coral Gables (☎ 305/446-4FUN), is more like a theater than a museum, since it's a place where kids can role-play in the "grown-up world." A great selection of hands-on exhibits includes a mini-grocery store complete with cashier and stockboy assignments, and an office for "Dr. Smiles" the dentist, or the "Hot off the Press" exhibit, where kids publish their own newspaper. Tours are offered in English and Spanish. The **Scott Rakow Youth Center,** 2700 Sheridan Ave. (☎ 305/673-7767), is a hidden treasure on Miami Beach. This two-story facility boasts an ice-skating rink, bowling alleys, a basketball court, gymnasium equipment, and full-time supervision for kids. Call for a complete schedule of organized events. **Amelia Earhart Park,** 401 E. 65th St., Hialeah (☎ 305/685-8389), is the best park in Miami for kids—they'll love the petting zoo with cows, sheep, and goats, the pony rides, and the private island with hidden tunnels.

**WATER SPORTS**    You can rent sailboats and catamarans through the beachfront concessions desk of several top resorts. Private boat-rental outfits include **Beach Boat Rentals,** 2400 Collins Ave., Miami Beach (☎ 305/534-4307); **Club Nautico of Coconut Grove,** 2560 S. Bayshore Dr., Coconut Grove (☎ 305/858-6258); and **Sailboats of Key Biscayne Rentals and Sailing School,** 4000 Crandon Blvd., Key Biscayne (☎ 305/361-0328 days, 305/279-7424 evenings).

For jet skis and Wave Runners, try **Tony's Jet Ski Rentals,** 3601 Rickenbacker Causeway, Key Biscayne (☎ 305/361-8280). **Urban Trails Kayak Company** rents kayaks from 10800 Collins Ave., Miami Beach (☎ 305/947-1302), and will provide maps of scenic routes as well as guided tours.

Several scuba-diving shops around the city offer organized weekend outings, either to the reefs or to one of over a dozen old shipwrecks around Miami's shores. Check "Divers" in the Yellow Pages for rental equipment and for a full list of undersea tour operators. **Divers Paradise of Key Biscayne,** 4000 Crandon Blvd. (☎ 305/361-3483), takes daily expeditions as well as 3-day certification courses.

Many hotels rent **Windsurfers** to their guests. Otherwise, head for Key Biscayne; **Sailboards Miami,** on Rickenbacker Causeway (☎ 305/361-SAIL), operates out of big yellow trucks on Hobie Beach.

**MORE OUTDOOR ACTIVITIES**   Most of the big beach hotels rent bicycles, as does **Miami Beach Bicycle Center,** 601 5th St., South Beach (☎ 305/674-0150); **Intra Mark,** 350 Ocean Dr., Key Biscayne (☎ 305/365-9762 or 305/578-3013); and **Key Cycling,** 61 Harbor Dr., Key Biscayne (☎ 305/361-0061). Bikers can enjoy more than 130 miles of paved paths throughout Miami. Coral Gables, Coconut Grove, and Key Biscayne offer some of the best scenery.

**Bridge fishing** is popular in Miami; you'll see people with poles over most every waterway. Some of the best **surf casting** in the city is at Haulover Beach Park (Collins Avenue at 105th Street), where there's a bait-and-tackle shop right on the pier. South Pointe Park, at the southern tip of Miami Beach, is another popular fishing spot. For **deep-sea fishing,** try **Kelley Fishing Fleet** (☎ 305/945-3801) and the charter boat *Helen C* (☎ 305/947-4081), both at the Haulover Marina, 10800 Collins Ave. (at 108th Street), Miami Beach. For those deep-sea enthusiasts willing to get their hands dirty and pay a lot, head for the Key Biscayne Marina. Competition among the boats is fierce; some will even take you out to the Upper Keys if fish aren't biting in Miami.

There are more than 50 private and public golf courses in the Greater Miami area. Contact the **Greater Miami Convention and Visitor Bureau** (☎ 800/283-2707 or 305/539-3063) for a complete list of courses and costs. Some of the area's best and most expensive are at the big resorts, many of which allow nonguests to play—the Doral Blue Course at the Doral Resort and Spa in West Miami, and the Biltmore in Coral Gables are just two (see "Accommodations," below). ✪ **Crandon Park Golf Course,** formerly known as The Links, 6700 Crandon Blvd., Key Biscayne (☎ 305/361-9129), is the number-one-ranked municipal course in the state. The **Golf Club of Miami,** 6801 Miami Gardens Dr. (☎ 305/829-8456), has three 18-hole courses of varying degrees of difficulty.

**Miami's flat** terrain makes in-line skating easy. Popular rental firms include **Extreme Skate & Sport,** 7876 SW 40th St., Coral Gables (☎ 305/261-6699), and **Skate 2000,** 1200 Ocean Dr., South Beach (☎ 305/538-8282), which also offers free lessons by a certified instructor on South Beach's boardwalk every Sunday at 10am.

Hundreds of tennis courts in South Florida are open to the public for a minimal fee. For information and directions to the one nearest where you're staying, call one of these government offices: the **City of Miami Beach Recreation, Culture, and Parks Department** (☎ 305/673-7730); the **City of Miami Parks and Recreation Department** (☎ 305/575-5240); or the **Metro–Dade Park and Recreation Department** (☎ 305/533-2000). The three hard courts and seven clay courts at the **Key Biscayne Tennis Association** (The Links, 6702 Crandon Blvd., ☎ 305/361-5263) get crowded on weekends since they're some of Miami's most beautiful courts.

The clear, warm waters of Biscayne National Park, 35 miles south of Miami, are packed with colorful tropical fish that swim in the offshore reefs. **Biscayne National Underwater Park Inc.** (☎ 305/230-1100) operates daily snorkel trips that last about 4 hours and cost $27.95 per person. They run two-tank dives for certified scuba divers and instruction for beginners, and they have scheduled glass-bottom-boat trips.

**SPORTS**   Pro Player Stadium (☎ 305/626-7426) is home to baseball's **Florida Marlins** and pro football's **Miami Dolphins.** You'll find the NBA's **Miami Heat** (☎ 305/577-HEAT), as well as hockey's recent Stanley Cup finalist **Florida Panthers** (☎ 954/768-1900), at **Miami Arena**—though the Panthers plan a move to Broward Arena in 1998. **Gulfstream Park** (☎ 305/931-7223), in Hallandale, and **Hialeah Park** (☎ 305/885-8000), in Hialeah, are the local horse-racing venues. Jai alai, sort of a Spanish-style indoor lacrosse, is played at the **Miami Jai Alai Fronton** (☎ 305/633-6400).

**SHOPPING**   This shopping capital of Latin America (yes, people fly in just to spend money) has strip malls, boutiques, and enclosed malls in every conceivable nook and cranny of the city. Among the city's choice shopping areas: the boutique-lined sidewalks along **Main Highway** and **Grand Avenue** in Coconut Grove; the old-fashioned ladies' shops along **Miracle Mile** in Coral Gables; **Lincoln Road,** a luxurious pedestrian mall in South Beach; and the wheeler-dealers around **Flagler Street** and **Miami Avenue** downtown (watch for rip-offs!).

The **Aventura Mall** is an enclosed mall with more than 200 generic shops and Macy's. The **Bal Harbour Shops** have high-end names like Chanel, Hermès, Versace, and Tiffany & Co. The **Bayside Marketplace** consists of 16 beautiful acres along Biscayne Bay. Kendall's **Dadeland Mall** is the granddaddy of Miami's suburban mall scene, anchored by five department stores. **The Falls** is an outdoor shopping center set amid tropical waterfalls, with Miami's only Bloomingdales. Coconut Grove's newly renovated **Streets of Mayfair** is a small open-air complex, just across the street from Cocowalk.

For a few unusual souvenirs, **Miami Twice** (☎ 305/666-0127), in Coral Gables, is the place to hunt for deco memorabilia. It's illegal to bring Cuban cigars into this country, but you'll find excellent hand-rolled cigars at **Ba-balú** (☎ 305/538-0679) and **South Beach News and Tobacco** (☎ 305/673-3002), both in South Beach; **La Gloria Cubana** (☎ 305/858-4162), in Little Havana; and Mike's Cigars (☎ 305/866-2277), in Bay Harbor Island.

Citrus-fruit stores that will ship home are a dying breed—try **Todd's Fruit Shippers** (☎ 305/448-5215); they take phone orders. **Casino Records, Inc.** (☎ 305/856-6888), in Little Havana, has the largest selection of Latin music in Miami.

If you can't leave town without some seafood, Miami's most famous restaurant, **Joe's Stone Crab** (☎ 800/780-CRAB or 305/673-0365), makes overnight air shipments of stone crabs to anywhere in the country. **East Coast Fisheries,** 330 W. Flagler St. (☎ 305/577-3000), has shipped millions of pounds of seafood worldwide from its own fishing fleet. They'll wrap and send 5- or 10-pound packages of stone crab claws, Florida lobsters, and other delicacies via overnight mail.

## ACCOMMODATIONS

South Florida's tourist season begins in mid-November and lasts until Easter. During the off-season, hotel rates are typically 30% to 50% lower than their winter highs. Rates quoted don't include state and city taxes, which, in some parts of Miami, are as high as 12.5%. Some hotels, especially those in South Beach, also tack on an additional service charge.

✪ **Alexander All-Suite Luxury Hotel.** *5225 Collins Ave., Miami Beach, FL 33140.* ☎ *800/327-6121 or 305/865-6500. Fax 305/864-8525. 150 suites. Winter, $310–$420 suite; off-season, $225–$325 suite. Additional person $35 extra. Children 17 and under stay free in parents' room. AE, CB, DC, DISC, MC, V. Valet parking $8.50.* Each of these elegant one- and two-bedroom mini-apartments has a living room, kitchen, two baths, and a balcony. Two oceanfront pools are surrounded by lush vegetation, and one is fed by a waterfall. You'll pay for the luxury, service, and attention, but it's worth it. **Dominique's** restaurant offers excellent French cuisine.

**Avalon Hotel.** *700 Ocean Dr., South Beach, FL 33139.* ☎ *800/933-3306 or 305/538-0133. Fax 305/534-0258. 106 rms. Winter, $120–$180 double; off-season, $65–$145 double. Rates include continental breakfast, full breakfast off-season. Additional person $10 extra. Children 11 and under stay free in parents' room. 10% discount for stays of 7 days or more. AE, CB, DC, DISC, MC, V. Valet parking $14.* Classic deco digs on the beach. Rooms are decorated in traditional 1930s style. The casual lobby restaurant is best for lunch, especially on the breezy patio. The cozy bar is a romantic place to linger. If the Avalon is full, get a room across the street in its sister, the Majestic.

○ **Bay Harbor Inn.** *9660 E. Bay Harbor Dr., Bay Harbor Island, FL 33154.* ☎ *305/868-4141. Fax 305/868-4141, ext. 602. 48 rms. Winter (including continental breakfast), $120 double; off-season, $80 double; additional person $25 extra. Children 12 and under stay free in parents' room. AE, CB, DC, MC, V. Free parking.* This quaint little inn looks straight out of Vermont, but it's moments from the beach, fine restaurants, and great city shopping. The rooms have oak-framed mirrors, canopied beds, and Victorian chairs. Some are slightly larger and boast another half bath at no extra cost. Students from a nearby culinary institute run the restaurant and bar.

○ **Biltmore Hotel Coral Gables.** *1200 Anastasia Ave., Coral Gables, FL 33134.* ☎ *800/727-1926 or 305/445-1926, or Westin at 800/228-3000. Fax 305/442-9496. 240 rms, 30 suites. Winter, $259 double; $379 suite; off-season, $189 double; $309 suite. Additional person $20 extra. Children 17 and under stay free in parents' room. Special packages available. AE, CB, DC, DISC, MC, V. Valet parking $9.* Recently designated a National Historical Landmark, the Biltmore is a Spanish Mediterranean–style estate (with a majestic 300-foot tower modeled after the Giralda, in Seville) situated on a challenging, beautiful 18-hole course. Rooms are furnished with tasteful period reproductions. It's 5 minutes from the airport and about 20 minutes from Miami Beach.

**Brigham Gardens.** *1411 Collins Ave., South Beach, FL 33139.* ☎ *305/531-1331. Fax 305/538-9898. 19 rms and suites. Winter, $75–$125 double; off-season, $50–$95 double. Additional person $5 extra. Pets stay for $6 a night and children stay free in parents' room. 10% discount on all stays of 1 week or longer. AE, MC, V.* Enter through a lush, tropical garden amid chirping macaws and parrots. The quaint Mediterranean hotel buildings are pleasant but need some sprucing. Many rooms have kitchens; you can make coffee and do laundry here. This happy spot is run by a mother and daughter who work hard at pampering guests.

○ **Casa Grande Suite Hotel.** *834 Ocean Dr., South Beach, FL 33139.* ☎ *800/ OUTPOST or 305/672-7003. Fax 305/673-3669. 33 suites. Winter, $230–$1,125 suite; off-season, $150–$700 suite. Additional person $15 extra. Children 11 and under stay free in parents' room. AE, CB, DC, DISC, MC, V. Valet parking $14.* Perhaps the most desirable hotel on South Beach, right on "Deco Drive." Suites have kitchenettes, reed rugs, mahogany beds, batik prints, and antiques from the world over, especially Indonesia. There's no pool, but you can see the ocean, stock your own fridge, and veg out with a stereo and VCR.

**Cavalier.** *1320 Ocean Dr., South Beach, FL 33139.* ☎ *800/OUTPOST or 305/ 534-2135. Fax 305/531-5543. 46 rms. Winter, $145–$350; off-season, $95–$240. Additional person $15 extra. Children 11 and under stay free in parents' room. AE, DC, DISC, MC, V. Self-parking $6; valet parking $14.* A hip, well-priced hotel with an unbeatable oceanfront location, adjacent to shops and restaurants. Funky prints cover tequila-sunrise–colored walls. The young staff offers good advice about local clubs, restaurants, and shopping. Most rooms are quiet, considering the Ocean Drive address.

**Clay Hotel & Youth Hostel.** *438 Washington Ave., South Beach, FL 33139.* ☎ *305/534-2988. Fax 305/673-0346. 350 beds. $30–$35 single; $35–39 double; $12–$13 per person in a dorm bed. Sheets $2 extra. Weekly rates available. JCB, MC, V.* A member of the International Youth Hostel Federation, the Clay occupies a beautiful 1920s-style Spanish Mediterranean building on Española Way. It's open to all ages; and the usual smattering of Europeans, Australians, and other budget travelers makes this the clearinghouse of "insider" travel information.

**The Delano.** *1685 Collins Ave., South Beach, FL 33139.* ☎ *800/555-5001 or 305/ 672-2000. Fax 305/532-0099. 208 rms. Winter, $295–$2,000; off-season, $200–$1,500. Additional person $35 extra. Children 17 and under stay free in parents' room. AE, DC, DISC, MC, V. Valet parking $16.* There's no sign, so look for the distinctive neon blue archway. This whimsical, renowned hotel has fur-covered beds in the all-white rooms. Poolside cabanas are spacious but noisy. The location is ideal—just north of the Deco District, near Lincoln Road Mall, and on the ocean. Its Blue Door is one of *the* places to be seen.

**Eden Roc Hotel and Marina.** *4525 Collins Ave., Miami Beach, FL 33140.* ☎ *800/327-8337 or 305/531-0000. Fax 305/531-6955. 306 rms, 45 suites. Winter, $195–$359 double, $650–$1,500 suite; off-season, $125–$275 double, $450-$1,000 suite. Additional person $15 extra. Children 16 and under stay free in parents' room. All-inclusive resort and spa packages available. AE, CB, DC, DISC, MC, V. Valet parking $8.50.* One of the big, gaudy hotels that gives Miami Beach its flamboyance. Still, the amenities make up for the ostentation. The huge, modern spa has excellent facilities. The pool deck overlooking the ocean is a popular hangout. Rooms, uniformly outfitted in purple and aqua with retouched 1930s furnishings, are spacious.

**Essex House.** *1001 Collins Ave., South Beach, FL 33139.* ☎ *800/55-ESSEX or 305/534-2700. Fax 305/532-3827. 50 rms. Winter, $125–$300; off-season, $75–$175. Rates include breakfast. 10% service charge extra. Minimum stay 2 nights on weekends, 3 nights on holidays. Additional person $10 extra. Nearby parking available for $4 weekdays, $6 weekends and holidays. AE, DC, MC, V.* This TraveLodge is one of South Beach's gems, a textbook example of Streamline Moderne—porthole windows, etched glass-work, and ziggurat arches. The solid-oak furnishings have been carefully restored. Some-what of a chainlike atmosphere, but the staff is quite pleasant. Families are scarce at the Essex; according to hotel staff, children are "inappropriate" here.

**Fontainebleau Hilton.** *4441 Collins Ave., Miami Beach, FL 33140.* ☎ *800/ HILTONS or 305/538-2000. Fax 305/674-4607. 1,146 rms, 60 suites. Winter, $275–$395 double; off-season, $235–$350 double; year-round, $475–$830 suite. Additional person $25 extra. Children under 18 stay free in parents' room. Weekend and other pack-ages available. AE, CB, DC, DISC, MC, V. Overnight valet parking $10.* The Fontainebleau just might be the quintessential Miami hotel, garish excess and all (the James Bond thriller *Goldfinger* was filmed here). But it's huge and easy to get lost. The lobby is crowded, the staff overworked, and lines long. If nothing else, don't miss the incredible lagoon-style pool and waterfall.

✪ **Grand Bay Hotel.** *2669 S. Bayshore Dr., Coconut Grove, FL 33133.* ☎ *800/ 327-2788 or 305/858-9600. Fax 305/858-1532. E-mail: grandbay@run.net. 131 rms, 47 suites. MINIBAR. Winter, $255–$295 double; off-season, $205–$255 double; year-round, $350–$1,200 suite. Additional person $20 extra. Packages available. AE, CB, DC, MC, V. Valet parking $13.* A stunning pyramid-shaped hotel, the elegant Grand Bay is a masterpiece inside and out. Rooms are luxurious, with high-quality linens, overstuffed love seats, and writing desks. Original art and fresh flowers are generously displayed. High-profile guests come here to be pampered and to be seen.

**Hotel Inter-Continental Miami.** *100 Chopin Plaza, Miami, FL 33131.* ☎ *800/ 327-3005 or 305/577-1000. Fax 305/577-0384. 612 rms, 34 suites. Winter, $209–$289 double; off-season, $189–$249 double; year-round $329–$450 suite. Additional person $20 extra. Weekend and other packages available. AE, CB, DC, MC, V. Valet parking $12.* The Inter-Continental is downtown's swankiest hotel. Boasting more marble than a mau-soleum, it's frequently warmed by colorful, homey palm trees and wicker furniture. Brilliant downtown and bay views add luster to already-posh rooms that are outfitted with every convenience known to hoteldom; some suites have kitchenettes.

✪ **Hotel Place St. Michel.** *162 Alcazar Ave., Coral Gables, FL 33134.* ☎ *800/ 848-4683 or 305/444-1666. Fax 305/529-0074. 27 rms. Winter (including continental breakfast), $165–$200; off-season, $95–$160. Additional person $10 extra. Children 11 and under stay free in parents' room. Senior discounts available. AE, DC, MC, V.*

*Parking $7.* One of the city's most romantic options, the accommodations are straight out of Old World Europe—dark wood-paneled walls, cozy beds, beautiful antiques, and a quiet elegance that seems out of place in trendy Miami. One-of-a-kind furnishings make each room special. Guests receive fresh fruit baskets upon arrival.

✪ **Indian Creek Hotel.** *2727 Indian Creek Dr., Miami Beach, FL 33140.* ☎ *800/ 207-2727 or 305/531-2727. 61 rms. Winter, $120–$200 double; off-season, $90–$150 double. Additional person $10 extra. Group packages available. 18% gratuity added to room service, 15% added to restaurant check. AE, CB, DC, DISC, MC, V. Limited parking available on street.* This hotel is slightly removed from hectic South Beach, yet close enough to walk to most activities there. Every detail of the 1936 building has been restored; modest rooms have deco furnishings and tropical prints. A landscaped pool area is a great place to lounge. A cozy pan-Caribbean restaurant/bar serves innovative fare.

**The Kent.** *1131 Collins Ave., South Beach, FL 33139.* ☎ *800/OUTPOST or 305/ 531-6771. Fax 305/531-0720. 54 rms. Winter (including continental breakfast), $95– $175 double; off-season, $65–$125 double. Additional person $15 extra. Children 11 and under stay free in parents' room. AE, DC, DISC, MC, V. Self-parking $6; valet parking $14.* For the price, this is an excellent value right in South Beach's active center. The mostly Caribbean staff caters to a large fashion-industry clientele (photo shoots are often coordinated in the lobby and conference room). Thanks to a vacant lot in the backyard (for now), some rooms in the rear offer nice views of the ocean. The decor is modest but tasteful.

✪ **Mayfair House Hotel.** *3000 Florida Ave., Coconut Grove, FL 33133.* ☎ *800/ 433-4555 or 305/441-0000. Fax 305/441-1647. 182 suites. Winter, $235–$450 suite; off-season, $205–$450 suite. Packages available. AE, DC, DISC, MC, V. Self-parking $6; valet parking $15.* Situated inside Coconut Grove's posh Mayfair Shops complex, this all-suite hotel is as centrally located as you can get. Each guest unit has been individually designed. Some suites are downright opulent. Most of the more expensive accommodations include a private, outdoor, Japanese-style hot tub.

**Park Washington Hotel.** *1020 Washington Ave., South Beach, FL 33139.* ☎ *305/532-1930. Fax 305/672-6706. 36 rms. Winter, $69–$129; off-season, $49–$99. Rates include breakfast. Additional person $10 extra. Children stay free in parents' room. AE, MC, V.* Located 2 blocks from the ocean, this hotel offers quality accommodations at incredible prices. Most rooms have original deco furnishings and well-kept interiors; some have kitchenettes. A decent-sized outdoor heated pool has a sundeck, and bikes are for rent. The management also runs the adjacent Taft House and Kenmore hotels; all three attract a large gay clientele.

✪ **Sheraton Bal Harbour Beach Resort.** *9701 Collins Ave., Bal Harbour, FL 33154.* ☎ *800/999-9898 or 305/865-7511. Fax 305/864-2601. 644 rms. Winter, $220–$650; off-season, $130–$650. Additional person $25 extra. Children 17 and under stay free in parents' room. Weekend and other packages and senior discounts available. Lowest rates reflect bookings made at least 14 days in advance and rooms without ocean views. AE, CB, DC, DISC, JCB, MC, V. Valet parking $12.* This hotel has the best location in Bal Harbour, on the ocean and just across from the swanky Bal Harbour Shops. (Bill and Hillary Clinton have stayed here.) Large, well-decorated rooms include convenient extras like coffeemakers and hair dryers. Popular with the convention crowd, but the main sections remain relatively uncongested.

✪ **Sonesta Beach Resort Hotel Key Biscayne.** *350 Ocean Dr., Key Biscayne, FL 33149.* ☎ *800/SONESTA or 305/361-2021. Fax 305/361-3096. 303 rms. Winter, $195–$1,350; off-season, $150–$1,350. Up to two children 11 and under stay free in parents' room. 15% gratuity added to food and beverage bills. Special packages available. AE, CD, DC, DISC, EURO, JCB, MC, V. Valet parking $9.25.* This is one of South

Florida's most luxurious resorts. If you like sports, everything from tennis to jet skiing awaits. If you leave the lush grounds, Bill Baggs State Park and the best beaches are right at hand. Still, you're only 15 minutes from Miami Beach and even closer to Coconut Grove.

**The Tides.** *1220 Ocean Dr., South Beach, FL 33139.* ☎ *800/OUTPOST or 305/ 604-5000. Fax 305/672-6288. 45 suites. MINIBAR . Winter, $275–$2,000 suite; off-season, $150–$1,100 suite. Rates include continental breakfast. Additional person $20 extra. AE, DC, DISC, MC, V. Valet parking $15.* Due for completion by the end of 1997, this 12-story Art Deco building is the tallest on Ocean Drive. Amenities will include terrace exercise facilities, a freshwater pool on the rear mezzanine, and two alfresco restaurants featuring Mediterranean cuisine and fresh seafood.

**Turnberry Isle Resort and Club.** *19999 W. Country Club Dr., Aventura, FL 33180.* ☎ *800/327-7028 or 305/932-6200. Fax 305/933-6550. 340 rms and suites. Winter, $295–$495; off-season, $150–$300. AE, DC, DISC, MC, V. Free self-parking; valet parking $8.* This gorgeous 300-acre compound has two renovated Trent Jones golf courses available only to members and guests. Stay in the resort (not the yacht club) section—you'll be closer to the spa and the renowned Veranda restaurant. Rooms are tiled to match the Mediterranean architecture. Nearby North Miami Beach has excellent dining and shopping.

**OTHER ACCOMMODATIONS**　　If you have trouble getting a room, look along Miami Beach's Collins Avenue. There are dozens of hotels and motels on this strip—in all price categories—so unless you arrive on a holiday weekend in midwinter, there's bound to be a vacancy. **Central Reservations** (☎ **800/950-0232** or 305/274-6832) works with many of Miami's hotels and can often secure discounts of up to 40% for otherwise unyielding hotels; the **South Florida Hotel Network** lists more than 300 hotels throughout Palm Beach to Miami and the Keys (☎ **800/538-3616** or 305/ 538-3616).

Among the area's chain hotels, the **Howard Johnson Tudor Hotel,** 1111 Collins Ave. (☎ **800/446-4656** or 305/534-2934), is 1 block from the beach; rates start at $195 a night in season. **Days Inn,** 100 21st St., off Collins Avenue (☎ **800/325-2525** or 305/538-6631), and **Holiday Inn,** 2201 Collins Ave. (☎ **800/327-5476** or 305/ 534-1511), are at the north edge of South Beach's historic district and within walking distance to the social scene.

## DINING

Miami's cuisine encompasses the varied tastes of the Caribbean (especially Cuba), as well as an old-time rural Florida influence. The chefs who pioneered what's been dubbed "New World Cuisine" have fused the many influences into an ever-changing style. Think of mango-infused oils dotted on tuna tartar with jicama slaw served in a cracked coconut—not for the xenophobic or the meat-and-potatoes crowd.

**At's a Nice.** *2779 Bird Ave. (off SW 27th Ave.).* ☎ *305/441-9119. Pizza $6–$16; entrees $9–$16. AE, MC, V. Tues–Sun 4–11pm. ITALIAN.* This Italian eatery has won immediate fans for its superb pizza and good pastas. The Coconut Grove setting is as casual as you can get, with a wood deck and plastic patio furniture.

**Bayside Seafood Restaurant and Hidden Cove Bar.** *3501 Rickenbacker Causeway.* ☎ *305/361-0808. Reservations accepted for parties of 16 or more. Raw clams or oysters $7 per dozen; salads and sandwiches $4.50–$6; platters $7–$13. AE, MC, V. Sun–Thurs noon–9 or 10pm, Fri–Sat noon–11pm. SEAFOOD.* Locals call it "the Hut," a ramshackle joint that serves sandwiches and fresh fish on paper plates. Happy hour is a deal—open bar and snacks for $25 per person. On weekends a band plays reggae and calypso. Ask for bug spray, or bring your own; mosquitoes can be pesky.

**Cafe Prima Pasta.** *414 71st St. (half a block east of the Byron–Carlyle movie theater).* ☎ *305/867-0106. Main courses $12–$14; pastas $7–$9. No credit cards. Mon–Fri noon–3pm; Mon–Thurs 5:45–11pm, Fri–Sat 5:45pm–midnight, Sun 4–11pm. ITALIAN.* Another tiny pasta joint serving phenomenal homemade noodles in good old Italian sauces. The restaurant feels a bit cramped, but it's not a problem squeezing in with this laid-back crowd. The stuffed agnolotti—with pesto, spinach, and ricotta, or tomato—is incredibly delicate and flavorful.

✪ **Caffé Abracci.** *318 Aragon Ave. (between Le Jeune Rd. and the Miracle Mile).* ☎ *305/441-0700. Reservations recommended for dinner. Main courses $16–$24; pasta $14–$20. AE, CB, DC, MC, V. Mon–Fri 11:30am–3pm and 6–11pm, Sat 6pm–midnight, Sun 6–11pm. NORTHERN ITALIAN.* You'll be greeted with a hug by the owner/maitre d' Nino. Appetizers are remarkable; the excellent risottos are served in half portions to save room for the indescribable fish dishes. Perfect service in a wood-and-marble setting—the only drawback is the loud dining room.

**Caribbean Delite.** *236 NE 1st Ave. (across the street from Miami Dade Community College).* ☎ *305/381-9254. Full meals $5.50–$9. AE, MC, V. Daily 8:30am–7pm. Closed sometimes on Sun. JAMAICAN.* Look hard for this tiny storefront diner; the aroma of succulent jerk chicken and pork beckons regulars from all over. Try Jamaican specialties like the curried goat or oxtail stew. The kitchen can be stingy with the spectacular sauces, so ask for an extra helping on the side.

✪ **Chef Allen's.** *19088 NE 29th Ave. (on the mainland at 190th St., near the Dade County line), North Miami Beach.* ☎ *305/935-2900. Reservations accepted. Main courses $20–$27. AE, MC, V. Sun–Thurs 6–10:30pm, Fri–Sat 6–11pm. MIAMI REGIONAL.* One of South Florida's finest dining experiences. Owner/chef Allen Susser has built a classy, relaxed deco restaurant with a hot-pink neon swirl on the ceiling. The homemade breadsticks are sublime, but don't miss the lobster and crab cake appetizer served with strawberry-ginger chutney, or the entree of crisp roast duck with cranberry sauce.

✪ **Fishbone Grille.** *650 S. Miami Ave. (at SW 7th Ave., next to Tobacco Rd.).* ☎ *305/530-1915. Reservations recommended Fri–Sat. Main courses $7–$16. AE, DC, MC, V. Mon–Thurs 11:30am–10pm, Fri 11:30am–11pm, Sat 5:30–11pm. SEAFOOD.* This casual spot is by far Miami's most reasonably priced seafood restaurant, though there's not much atmosphere except for a lively fish tank. Try the excellent ceviche; the kicky spice doesn't overwhelm the super-fresh flavor. The stews, crab cakes, and all the starters are superb.

**Forge Restaurant.** *432 Arthur Godfrey Rd. (at 41st St.).* ☎ *305/538-8533. Reservations required. Main courses $18–$35. AE, DC, MC, V. Sun–Thurs 4pm–midnight, Fri–Sat 5pm–3am. AMERICAN.* English oak paneling and Tiffany glass suggest the high prices and haute cuisine found here. The menu has a northern Italian bias, but fish, poultry, and beef dishes also rate, many prepared on an oak grill. Ask the knowledgeable, affable head wine steward, Gino Santangelo, for a tour of the impressive cellar.

**Hy-Vong.** *3458 SW 8th St. (between 34th and 35th aves.).* ☎ *305/446-3674. Reservations not accepted. Main courses $8–$12. No credit cards. Tues–Sun 6–11pm. Closed 2 weeks in Aug. VIETNAMESE.* Expect to wait hours for a table, but don't complain. Just enjoy the wait with a traditional Vietnamese beer and lots of company. Service is painfully slow in this tiny storefront, but the food is elegant, simple, and superspicy. Entrees include pastry-enclosed chicken with watercress/cream-cheese sauce.

**Joe's Stone Crab Restaurant.** *227 Biscayne St. (at the corner of Washington Ave.).* ☎ *305/673-0365. Reservations not accepted. No shorts allowed. Market price varies but averages $37 for jumbo crab claws, $27 for large claws. AE, CB, DC, MC, V. Sun–Mon 5–10pm; Tues–Thurs 11:30am–2pm and 5–10pm (until 11pm on nights of Miami Heat* *home games), Fri–Sat 11:30am–2pm and 5–11pm. SEAFOOD.* Open since 1913, this restaurant is famous in Florida and beyond, as evidenced by the long lines waiting to get in. The claws are pricier here than at other restaurants, but you're paying for history. To avoid the wait and the attitude, try Monty's, just a few doors down (see below).

**Kaleidoscope.** *3112 Commodore Plaza (one block from Main Hwy.).* ☎ *305/ 446-5010. Reservations recommended. Pastas $12–$15; main courses $14–$20. AE, CB, DC, DISC, MC, V. Mon 6–11pm; Tues–Sun 11:30am–3pm; Tues–Sat 6pm–midnight; Sun 5:30–10pm. NEW AMERICAN.* A low-key spot just off Coconut Grove's main drag on a second-floor terrace, which assures a good view. The pastas, topped with sauces like seafood and fresh basil or pesto with grilled yellowfin tuna, are especially tasty. A good choice for pretheater dinner—it's near the Coconut Grove Playhouse.

**La Sandwicherie.** *229 14th St. (east of Washington Ave., behind the Amoco Station).* ☎ *305/532-8934. Sandwiches and salads $4.50–$7. No credit cards. Sun–Mon 10am– 5am. Delivery Sun–Mon 10am–6pm. FRENCH SNACK BAR.* A green-and-white awning hides this fabulous sandwich counter. Choose from pâté, saussion, prosciutto, salami, turkey, or any of the perfect meats or cheeses on display. If the few stools are taken, stand and watch the tattoo artist through the glass wall next door.

**Mark's Place.** *2286 NE 123rd St. (just east of Biscayne Blvd.), North Miami.* ☎ *305/ 893-6888. Reservations recommended. Main courses $24–$30. AE, MC, V. Mon–Thurs 6–10:30pm; Fri–Sun 6–11pm. MIAMI REGIONAL.* A smart, modern bistro that shines with off-white walls, an aquamarine ceiling, and contemporary glass sculptures. Owner/ chef Mark Militello's food is inspired and unusual; appetizers include oak-grilled mozzarella and prosciutto, and curry-breaded fried oysters. The best entrees are Florida conch stew and flank steak in sesame marinade.

**Monty's Bayshore Restaurant.** *2560 S. Bayshore Dr.* ☎ *305/858-1431. Reservations recommended upstairs Sat–Sun. Sandwiches $6–$8; platters $7–$12; main courses $19–$35. AE, CB, DC, MC, V. Daily 11:30am–midnight. Call for hours of each of the three restaurants; some are open later. SEAFOOD.* This place has a lounge, a raw bar, and an elegant restaurant serving everything from steak and seafood to munchies. There's live music at the dockside bar. In season (Oct–Apr), splurge on the all-you can-eat stone crab claws, which cost less than a small plateful at Joe's.

**Mrs. Mendoza's Tacos al Carbon.** *1040 Alton Rd.* ☎ *305/535-0808. Main courses $3–$5; side dishes 80¢–$3. No credit cards. Mon–Thurs 11am–10pm, Fri–Sat 11am–11pm, Sun noon–10pm. FAST FOOD/MEXICAN.* Popular with locals, this hard-to-spot storefront is the only fresh California-style Mexican joint in town; the steak and chicken are grilled as you wait and then stuffed into homemade flour or corn wrappings.

✪ **Norma's.** *646 Lincoln Rd.* ☎ *305/532-2809. Reservations recommended. Main courses $12–$24. AE, DC, DISC, MC, V. Tues–Thurs noon–11pm, Fri–Sat noon– midnight, Sun noon–10:30pm. JAMAICAN/NEW WORLD CARIBBEAN.* This tiny jewel on Lincoln Road sparkles with an eclectic mix of classical and Caribbean cooking. The multilingual staff is polite, if sometimes flustered. The extensive list of daily specials is always good, but arrive early—they sell out quickly.

✪ **South Pointe Seafood House and Brewing Company.** *1 Washington Ave. No phone. Fax 305/673-1708. Reservations recommended. Main courses $15–$34. AE, CB, DC, DISC, MC, V. Mon–Thurs 11:30am–3pm and 5–11pm, Fri–Sat 11:30am– 3pm and 5pm–midnight, Sun 11am–3pm (brunch) and 5–10:30pm. SEAFOOD.* Besides its spectacular view and selection of home-brewed beers, this casual joint at the southernmost tip of South Beach serves up exquisitely prepared food as well. Enjoy their seafood chowder while you watch the cruise and cargo ships slowly ease their way in and out of port.

**Sundays on the Bay.** *5420 Crandon Blvd.* ☎ *305/361-6777. Reservations accepted; recommended for Sun brunch. Main courses $15–$24; Sun brunch $18.95. AE, CB, DC, MC, V. Mon–Sat 11:30am–11:30pm, Sun 10:30am–11:30pm. AMERICAN.* Popular with boaters who dock at the marina, Sundays is known more for its tropical bar than its food, which is fine, but not as spectacular as the view. The menu features grouper, tuna, snapper, and good shellfish in season.

**Versailles.** *3555 SW 8th St.* ☎ *305/444-0240. Main courses $5–$8. DC, MC, V. Mon–Thurs 8am–1:30am, Fri–Sat 8am–3:30am, Sun 9am–1:30am. CUBAN.* For a taste of real Cuban cooking in a kitschy diner, come to where Miami's Cuban power brokers meet daily over Sunday breakfast or a simple *café con leche.* Specialties include *ropa vieja* (a tasty stew of shredded meat) and fried whole fish with black beans and rice.

**Wolfie Cohen's Rascal House.** *17190 Collins Ave., Sunny Isles.* ☎ *305/947-4581. Omelets and sandwiches $4–$6; other dishes $5–$14. AE, MC, V. Daily 7am–12:45am. JEWISH/DELICATESSEN.* This Miami Beach institution packs them in for all the favorite Jewish goodies—corned beef, schmaltz herring, brisket, kreplach, and chicken soup. Expect a wait, and don't forget to take leftovers (and the free rolls) home in a doggy bag.

**World Resources.** *719 Lincoln Rd.* ☎ *305/534-9095. Main courses $6–$8; sushi hand rolls $3–$4. AE, DC, MC, V. Daily noon–midnight. JAPANESE/THAI.* This excellent cafe/sushi bar/Indonesian furniture and bric-a-brac store is great for people-watching. Local hippie types and Eurotourists frequent this cheap hangout, where they eat good food from paper plates while listening to live World music outside.

✪ **Yuca.** *501 Lincoln Rd. (corner of Drexel Ave.).* ☎ *305/532-9822. Reservations required. Main courses $18–$29. AE, CB, DC, MC, V. Daily 11:30am–5pm and 6pm–midnight. NOUVELLE CUBAN.* It's pronounced yoo-ka—an acronym for Young Upscale Cuban-Americans, and that's the clientele here. Try any of the fresh fish and meat dishes, including an excellent veal chop with lobster potatoes. The menu is badly translated, so ask for a waiter who speaks English if you don't *habla español.*

**OTHER DINING**   A number of chains that originated here are worth trying for a quick and inexpensive bite. Try **Pollo Tropical,** a Cuban fast-food chain serving delicious moist chicken, rice and beans, and garlic-drenched yucca (a potato-like root vegetable). Locations include 18710 S. Dixie Hwy. (at 186th Street), South Miami (☎ 305/225-7858); 1454 Alton Rd., Miami Beach (☎ 305/672-8888); and 11806 Biscayne Blvd., North Miami (☎ 305/895-0274).

## MIAMI AFTER DARK

On any given night in Miami, you'll find opera and dance as well as grinding rock and seductive salsa. Restaurants and bars are open late; many clubs, especially on South Beach, stay open past dawn. For up-to-date entertainment listings, check the *Miami Herald's* "Weekend" section, which runs on Friday, or Miami's free alternative weekly, *New Times,* which comes out each Wednesday.

Tickets for most performances can be purchased by phone through **Ticketmaster** (☎ 305/358-5885), whose phone lines are open 24 hours daily. One well-known ticket broker is **Ultimate Travel & Entertainment** (☎ 305/444-8499).

**THE PERFORMING ARTS**   Miami has an active theater community, thanks in large part to the patronage of New York transplants. South Beach standouts are the **Jackie Gleason Theater of the Performing Arts,** 1700 Washington Ave. (☎ 305/673-7300), and the **Colony Theater,** 1040 Lincoln Rd. (☎ 305/674-1026). Home base for the **Actors' Playhouse** is the newly restored Miracle Mile Theater in Coral Gables (☎ 305/444-9293), a grand 1948 art deco movie palace. The **Area Stage Company** (☎ 305/673-8002) has won respect from local and national audiences for their dramatic work in contemporary theater. The **Coconut Grove Playhouse,** 3500 Main Hwy., Coconut Grove (☎ 305/442-4000), was also a former movie house, built in 1927 in an ornate Spanish rococo style. The Biltmore Hotel houses the **Florida Shakespeare Theatre,** Anastasia Ave., Coral Gables (☎ 305/446-1116); they stage at least one Shakespeare play, one classic, and one contemporary piece a year.

One of the most important and longest-running concert series is produced by the **Concert Association of Florida (CAF),** 555 17th St., South Beach (☎ 305/532-3491), which schedules world-renowned dance companies and seasoned virtuosi. **Florida Grand Opera,** 1200 Coral Way, Coral Gables (☎ 800/741-1010 or 305/854-1643), has had featured singers from America's and Europe's top houses. The **New World Symphony,** Lincoln Road, South Beach (☎ 305/673-3331), is a stepping stone for gifted young musicians seeking professional careers. The **Florida Philharmonic Orchestra,** 169 E. Flagler St. (☎ 800/226-1812 or 305/930-1812), is South Florida's premier symphony orchestra, under the direction of James Judd. An excellent inexpensive alternative to the high-priced classical venues is the **Miami Chamber Symphony,** 5690 N. Kendall Dr., Kendall (☎ 305/858-3500).

Several local dance companies train and perform in the Greater Miami area. ۞ **Miami City Ballet,** Lincoln Road Mall at 9th Street, South Beach (☎ 305/532-4880), has emerged as a top troupe under artistic director Edward Villela, with a repertoire of more than 75 works, many by George Balanchine. Look also for such special performances as **Ballet Flamenco La Rosa** (☎ 305/672-0552), a local flamenco and Afro-Caribbean dance troupe.

**THE CLUB & MUSIC SCENE**   In South Beach, there are lots of clubs and bars on Washington Avenue between 5th and 14th streets. Another good place to hang out after dark is Cocowalk, in Coconut Grove. The three-story complex has bars, restaurants, and clubs.

South Florida's jazz scene is very much alive with traditional and contemporary performers. Call the **Blues Hotline** (☎ 305/666-MOJO) for the most up-to-date bookings. **MoJazz Cafe,** 928 71st St., Miami Beach (☎ 305/867-0950 or 305/865-2636), has Latin jazz every Thursday and Brazilian jazz every Sunday. ۞ **Tobacco Road,** 626 S. Miami Ave. (☎ 305/374-1198), has offered blues, zydeco, brass, jazz, and more since 1912; it's a Miami institution. There's live *free* music 7 seven nights a week at **Van Dyke Cafe,** 846 Lincoln Rd., South Beach (☎ 305/534-3600).

A new trend in Miami's club scene is the popularity of **"one-off" nights**—events organized by a promoter and held in established venues on irregular schedules. Local advertising and listings in the free weekly *New Times* are the best way to find out about them.

In South Beach, **Bash,** 655 Washington Ave. (☎ 305/538-2274), has "theme days" and is always reliably hot—which accounts for the stoic bouncers. **Liquid,** 1439 Washington Ave. (☎ 305/532-9154), smacks of the 80s New York club scene, a cavernous space with up-to-the-minute dance music and two beautiful bars. **Chili Pepper's,** 621 Washington Ave. (☎ 305/531-9661), never has a cover; you'll hear alternative and dance music from Wednesday through Sunday. **Sticky Fingers,** 3399 Virginia St. (in the Mayfair Mall), Coconut Grove (☎ 305/461-3313), a relatively new addition to the after-dark scene, has mellow jazz or blues weekdays; Fridays have a mix of rock, rave, retro, and Latin music; on Sunday there's good-old-fashioned disco. Cover is $5–$8.

For a taste of Miami's Latino culture, try **Cafe Nostalgia,** 2212 SW 8th St. (Calle Ocho), Little Havana (☎ 305/541-2631), which celebrates Old Cuba with films and hot Afro-Cuban jazz. **Mango's,** 900 Ocean Dr., South Beach (☎ 305/673-4422), sports a funky, loud Brazilian beat—samba till you drop! Every Tuesday and Thursday night, **Casa Panza,** 1620 SW 8th St. (Calle Ocho), Little Havana (☎ 305/643-5343), becomes the House of Flamenco, with shows at 8 and 11pm.

**821,** 821 Lincoln Rd., South Beach (☎ **305/531-1188**), is a neighborhood gay bar/nightclub with a live deejay every night. **Twist,** 1057 Washington Ave. (☎ **305/53-TWIST**), is one of South Beach's first and still most popular cruise bars; it attracts mostly gay male customers but welcomes anyone.

**BARS & LOUNGES**     South Beach is the hub of most of the area's nightlife. In Coconut Grove, bars and clubs are clustered in **Cocowalk** and the adjacent **Streets of Mayfair,** right on Main Highway.

There are dozens of late-night bars in South Beach clustered along Washington Avenue between 6th and 8th streets. If you want to rack a few, head to **Brandt's Break. Ready Bar,** 560 Washington Ave. (☎ **305/534-8847**), features events from drag shows to barbecues. The upstairs deck at **Wet Willies,** 760 Ocean Dr. (☎ **305/532-5650**), is a prime spot to take in the South Beach scene; beware of the potent frozen concoctions they serve. Stop in to **China Grill,** 404 Washington Ave. (☎ **305/534-2211**), for an overpriced drink—it's another fine people-watching spot. **The Clevelander,** 1021 Ocean Dr. (☎ **305/531-3485**), is an old South Beach standby, where crowds gather around the large outdoor pool until 5am.

Step back in time at **The Forge,** 432 41st St., Miami Beach (☎ **305/538-8533**), an ultra-elegant restaurant/bar where Wednesday is the night to hang with singles in Armani and Versace. **Dan Marino's American Sports Bar & Grill,** 3015 Grand Ave., Coconut Grove (☎ **305/567-0013**), in Cocowalk, is packed with young sports fans day and night.

# 2   Everglades National Park

Described poetically as the "river of grass" by conservationist Marjory Stoneman Douglas in her 1947 book *The Everglades: River of Grass,* the Everglades actually is a shallow, 40-mile-wide, slow-moving river. Rarely more than knee-deep, the water is the lifeblood of this wilderness. Subtle shifts in water level dictate the life cycle of plants and animals.

Everglades National Park comprises 1.5 million acres, less than 20% of the Everglades wilderness. In the 1800s, the only inhabited piece of this wilderness was a quiet fishing village called Flamingo, today the main center for visitor activities and a jumping-off point for backcountry camping and exploration. On the way, you'll find Indian villages, alligator farms, and boat rides. An excellent tram tour goes deep into the park along a trail that's also terrific for biking.

## ESSENTIALS

**ARRIVING & DEPARTING**     Miami International Airport is the nearest large facility. From there, you'll need a car to reach the park and travel around it.

Most visitors approach by the **main entrance** in Homestead, on the park's east side 10 miles southeast of Florida City. Signs there will point you southwest onto Fla. 9336, the road into the park. The main entrance's Park Ranger Station is open 24 hours. The **Shark Valley entrance,** on the park's north side, is on U.S. 41 about 35 miles west of downtown Miami. Shark Valley is known for its 15-mile trail loop that's used for an excellent interpretive tram tour, bicycling, and walking. This entrance is open daily 8:30am–5:30pm, with some seasonal variation. Call ahead.

Popular primarily with day visitors, picnickers, and campers, the **Chekika entrance** is halfway between the main and Shark Valley entrances in the northeast section of the park. There are picnic facilities and a 20-site campground.

If you're on Florida's west coast, there is a visitor center and boat tours at **Everglades City,** off U.S. 41 about 35 miles southeast of Naples and 75 miles west of Miami. This side of the park features a maze of islands and swamps that can only be reached by boat.

# Everglades National Park

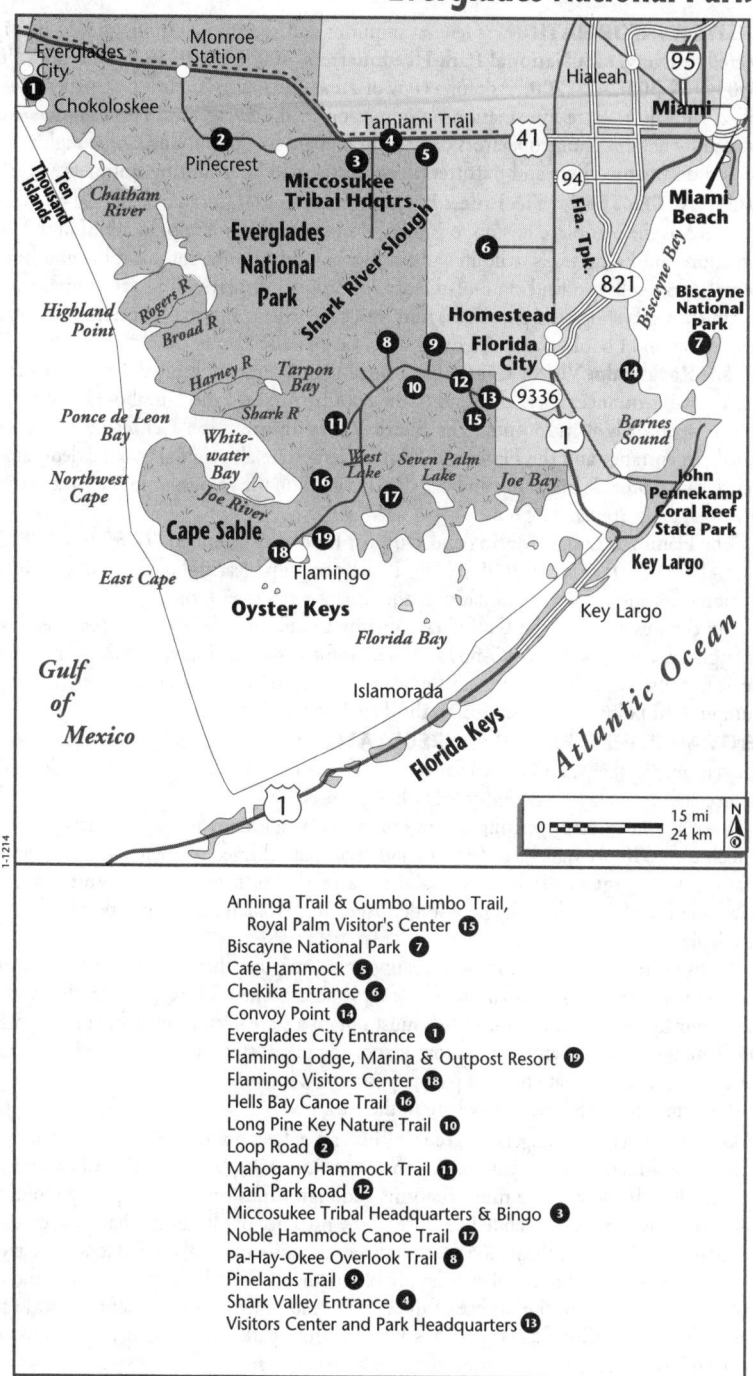

Anhinga Trail & Gumbo Limbo Trail,
Royal Palm Visitor's Center **15**
Biscayne National Park **7**
Cafe Hammock **5**
Chekika Entrance **6**
Convoy Point **14**
Everglades City Entrance **1**
Flamingo Lodge, Marina & Outpost Resort **19**
Flamingo Visitors Center **18**
Hells Bay Canoe Trail **16**
Long Pine Key Nature Trail **10**
Loop Road **2**
Mahogany Hammock Trail **11**
Main Park Road **12**
Miccosukee Tribal Headquarters & Bingo **3**
Noble Hammock Canoe Trail **17**
Pa-Hay-Okee Overlook Trail **8**
Pinelands Trail **9**
Shark Valley Entrance **4**
Visitors Center and Park Headquarters **13**

**VISITOR INFORMATION**   General inquiries and specific questions should be directed to **Everglades National Park Headquarters,** 40001 Fla. 9336, Homestead, FL 33034 (☎ **305/242-7700**). Ask for a copy of *Parks and Preserves,* a free newspaper that's filled with up-to-date information on goings-on in the Everglades. Headquarters are staffed by helpful phone operators daily from 8:30am to 4:30pm during the high winter season (many offices and outfitters keep abbreviated hours during summer).

**VISITOR CENTERS**   The **Ernest F. Coe Visitor Center,** located at the park's main entrance, is the best place to stop to gather information for your trip. In addition to free brochures outlining trails, wildlife, and activities, and information on tours and boat rentals, you will also find state-of-the-art educational displays, films, and interactive exhibits. A gift shop sells postcards, film, insect repellent, unusual gift items, and the best selection of books about the Everglades. Open daily 8am to 5pm.

The **Royal Palm Visitor Center** has a small nature museum located 3 miles past the park's main entrance. It's at the head of the popular Anhinga and Gumbo–Limbo trails and is open daily 8am to 4pm. The **Shark Valley Information Center** at the park's northern entrance and the **Flamingo Visitor Center** are also staffed by knowledgeable rangers who provide brochures and personal insight into the goings-on in the park. They are open daily 8:30am to 5pm.

The **Flamingo Lodge, Marina and Outpost Resort,** in Flamingo (☎ **800/600-3813** or 941/695-3101; fax 941/695-3921), is the one-stop clearinghouse—and the only option—for in-park accommodations, equipment rentals, and tours.

On the western side, the **Gulf Coast Visitor Center,** on Fla. 29 at the south end of Everglades City (☎ **941/695-3311**), offers information and advice during the high season daily from 8:30am to 4:30pm, and intermittently in the summer. It's the jumping-off point for boat cruises to the Ten Thousand Islands area.

**ENTRANCE FEES, PERMITS & REGULATIONS**   Permits and passes can be purchased only at the Main Park entrance, the Chekika entrance, or the Shark Valley entrance stations. There is no entry fee at Everglades City.

Even if you are only visiting for an afternoon, you'll need to buy a 7-day permit, which costs $10 per vehicle. Pedestrians and cyclists are charged $5 each and $4 at Shark Valley. An **Everglades Park Pass,** valid for a year's worth of unlimited entrances, is available for $20. Golden Eagle, Golden Age, and Golden Access passports are also available.

Permits are required for campers wishing to overnight either in the backcountry or in primitive campsites, and you must file an itinerary when camping overnight in the backcountry. Those who want to fish must obtain a state license, available in the park at Flamingo Lodge or any tackle shop or sporting goods store nearby (charter captains carry vessel licenses that cover all paying passengers, but ask to be sure).

Firearms are not allowed anywhere in the park.

**SAFETY**   There are dangers inherent in this vast wilderness area. Always let someone know your itinerary before you set out on an extended hike. When on the water, watch for weather changes; severe thunderstorms and high winds often develop very rapidly. Swimming is not recommended because of the presence of alligators, sharks, and barracudas. Watch out for the region's four indigenous poisonous snakes: diamondback and pygmy rattlesnakes, coral snakes (identifiable by their colorful rings), and water moccasins (which swim on the surface of the water). And bring insect repellent to ward off mosquitoes and biting flies. First aid is available from park rangers. The nearest hospital is in Homestead, 10 miles from the park's main entrance.

**INTERPRETIVE PROGRAMS**   More than 50 free ranger programs are offered each month during high season. Since times, programs, and locations vary from month to month, check a schedule, available at any of the visitor centers (see above). If you can, stay for the 7pm program, available during high season at the **Long Pine Key Amphitheater.** This talk by one of the park's rangers, along with the accompanying slide show, gives a detailed overview of the park's history, natural resources, wildlife, and threats to its survival. **Glade Glimpses,** walking tours during which rangers point out flora and fauna and discuss issues affecting the Everglades' survival, are scheduled daily at 10:15am, noon, and 3:30pm. The **Anhinga Ambles,** a similar program that takes place on the Anhinga Trail, starts at 10:30am, 1:30pm, and 4pm.

Offered occasionally, the **Slough Slog** journey takes you wading into the park and through the muck, stopping at an alligator hole, which is a particularly interesting and vital ecological community unto itself. Lace-up shoes and long pants (preferably ones you don't care about) are required on this walking trip.

**WHEN TO GO**    There are two distinct seasons in the Everglades: high season and mosquito season. High season is also dry season and lasts approximately from late November to May. This is the best time to visit, as low water levels attract the largest variety of wading birds and their predators. As the dry season wanes, wildlife follows the receding water, and by the end of May, the only living things you are sure to spot will cause you to itch. Many establishments and operators in the area either close or curtail offerings in the summer, so always call ahead to check schedules.

## EXPLORING THE EVERGLADES

Shark Valley provides a fine introduction to the wonder of the Everglades, but don't expect to spend more than a few hours there. If you want to see a greater array of plant and animal life, make sure to venture into the park through the main entrance, pick up a trail map, and dedicate at least a day to exploring from here.

Stop first along the Anhinga and Gumbo–Limbo trails, which start right next to one another, 3 miles from the park's main entrance. These trails provide a thorough introduction to Everglades flora and fauna, and are highly recommended to first-time visitors. There's more water and wildlife here than in most parts of the Everglades, especially during dry season. Alligators, turtles, river otters, herons, egrets, and other animals abound, making this one of the best trails for seeing wildlife. Arrive early to spot the widest selection of exotic birds; like the Anhinga Trail's namesake, a large, black fishing bird that is used to humans, many of these birds build their nests in plain view. Others travel deeper into the park during daylight hours. Take your time—at least an hour is recommended. If you treat the trails and modern boardwalk as pathways to get through quickly, rather than as destinations to experience and savor slowly, you'll miss out on the still beauty and hidden treasures that await.

Those who love to mountain bike, and who prefer solitude, might check out the infrequently traveled **Old Ingraham Highway.** This dirt road delves deeper into the Glades and isn't used by most visitors. Since this pathway is sometimes closed, check at the visitor center when you arrive.

Also, it's worth climbing the **observation tower** at the end of the quarter-mile-long Pa-hay-okee Trail. The panoramic view of undulating grass and seemingly endless vistas gives the impression of a semiaquatic Serengeti. Flocks of tropical and semitropical birds traverse the landscape, alligators and fish stir the surface of the water, small grottos of trees thrust up from the sea of grass marking higher ground, and the vastness of the hidden world you've entered seems unparalleled.

If you want to get closer to nature, a few hours in a canoe along any of the trails allow paddlers the chance to sense the park's fluid motion and to become a part of the ecosphere. Visitors who choose this option end up feeling more like explorers than merely observers.

**BIKING**  The relatively flat 38-mile paved **Main Park Road** is excellent for bicycling, as are many park trails, including **Long Pine Key.** Cyclers should expect to spend 2 to 3 hours along the path. If the park isn't flooded from excess rain (which it has been for several months in recent years), **Shark Valley** is South Florida's most scenic bicycle trail. You can ride this paved 17-mile loop with other bikers and a menagerie of wildlife as company. You can rent bikes at the **Flamingo Lodge, Marina and Outpost Resort** (see "Accommodations," below) and from **Shark Valley Tram Tours,** at the park's Shark Valley entrance (☎ **305/221-8455**).

**BIRDING**  More than 350 species of birds make their homes here—tropical birds from the Caribbean, temperate species from North America, even exotics blown in from more distant regions. **Eco and Mrazek ponds,** located near Flamingo, are two of the best places for birding, especially in early morning or late afternoon in the dry winter months. Pick up a free birding checklist from a visitor center (see "Essentials," above), and ask a park ranger what's been spotted in recent days.

**BOATING & CANOEING**  Environmentalists are taking stock of the damage motorboats inflict on the delicate ecosystem, so if you choose to motor, remember that most of the areas near land are "no-wake" zones, and for the protection of nesting birds, landing is prohibited on most of the little mangrove islands. There's a long list of restrictions and restricted areas, so get a copy of the park's boating rules from National Park Headquarters before setting out (see "Essentials," above).

Everglades National Park's longest "trails" are designed for boat and canoe travel and many are marked as clearly as walking trails. The **Noble Hammock Trail,** a 2-mile loop, takes 1 to 2 hours, and is recommended for beginning canoers. The **Hell's Bay Trail,** a 3- to 6-mile course for hardier paddlers, takes 2 to 6 hours, depending on how far you choose to go. Park rangers can recommend other trails that best suit your abilities, time limitations, and interests.

**Flamingo Lodge, Marina and Outpost Resort,** located in Flamingo, rents canoes and skiffs with 15-horsepower engines (☎ **941/695-3101,** ext. 304). Skiffs, kayaks, and tandem kayaks are also available. The concessionaire will shuttle your party to the trailhead of your choice and pick you up afterward.

**FISHING**  Open water comprises about one-third of Everglades National Park. Freshwater fishing is popular in brackish Nine-Mile Pond (25 miles from the main entrance) and other spots along the Main Park Road, but because of the high mercury levels found in the Everglades, freshwater fishers shouldn't eat their catch. Before casting, check in at a visitor center, as many of the park's lakes are preserved for observation only. Fishing licenses are required. See "Essentials," above.

Saltwater anglers will find that snapper and sea trout are plentiful. Charter boats and guides are available at **Flamingo Lodge, Marina and Outpost Resort** (see "Accommodations," below). Phone for information and reservations.

**AIRBOAT TOURS**  Shallow-draft, fan-powered airboats are not permitted in the park, since these noisy craft tend to inflict severe damage on the animals and plants. Nevertheless, many operators offer rides outside the boundaries. At **Miccosukee Indian Village,** just west of the Shark Valley entrance on U.S. 41 (☎ **305/223-8380**), Native American guides will take you through the reserve's rushes at high speed and stop along the way to point out alligators, native plants, and exotic birds. Prices are just $7. The **Everglades Alligator Farm,** 4 miles west of Palm Drive (Fla. 9336), offers half-hour guided airboat tours daily from 9am to 6pm (☎ **305/247-2628**). Also, you'll find several airboat operators in and near Everglades City.

**MOTORBOAT TOURS**  Both Florida Bay and backcountry tours are offered at the **Flamingo Lodge, Marina and Outpost Resort** (see "Accommodations," below). Both are available in 1¹/₂- and 2-hour versions that cost an average of $16 adults, $8 children;

free for children under 6. There are also charter-fishing and sightseeing boats that can be booked through the main reservation number (☎ 941/695-3101). Florida Bay tours cruise nearby estuaries and sandbars, while six-passenger backcountry boats visit smaller sloughs. Tours depart throughout the day, and reservations are recommended.

Over in Everglades City, **Everglades National Park Boat Tours,** at the Gulf Coast Visitor Center (☎ 800/445-7724 in Florida, or 941/695-2591), depart daily, every half hour from 9am to 5pm (less frequently off-season). The cruises last about 90 minutes and cost $11 for adults, $5.50 for children 6–12. Reservations are not accepted.

Also in Everglades City, naturalists Frank and Georgia Garrett of ✪ **Majestic Everglades Excursions** (☎ 941/695-2777) take up to six passengers on 4-hour excursions through the islands on their covered-deck boat and explain the bird, marine, animal, and plant life. The trips cost $65 for adults, $35 for children 11 and under. Reservations are required.

**TRAM TOURS**   At the park's Shark Valley entrance, open-air tram buses take visitors on 2-hour naturalist-led tours that delve $7^{1}/_{2}$ miles into the wilderness. At the trail's midsection, passengers can disembark and climb a 65-foot observation tower that offers good views of the Glades. The tour offers visitors considerable views that include plenty of wildlife and endless acres of sawgrass. Tours run November to April only, daily 9am to 4pm, and are sometimes stalled by flooding or particularly heavy mosquito infestation. Reservations are recommended December to March. The cost is $8 for adults, $4 for children 12 and under, and $7 for seniors. For further information, contact **Shark Valley Tram Tours** (☎ 305/221-8455).

**CAMPING**   Campgrounds are available in **Flamingo** and **Long Pine Key,** where there are more than 300 campsites designed for tents and RVs. There are no electrical hookups and showers are cold water. Private ground fires are not permitted, but supervised campfire programs are conducted during winter months. Reservations may be made in advance through **Destinet** (☎ 800/365-CAMP). Campsites are $14 per night with a 14-day consecutive stay limit, 30 days a year maximum.

Camping is also available in the backcountry year-round on a first-come first-served basis and is only accessible by boat, foot, or bicycle. Campers must register in person or by telephone no more than 24 hours prior to the start of their trip. Free permits must be obtained at ranger stations in either Flamingo or Everglades City. Campers can use only designated campsites, which are plentiful and well marked on visitor maps.

Many backcountry sites are chickees—covered wooden platforms on stilts. They're only accessible by canoe. Ground sites are located along interior bays and rivers, and beach camping is also popular. In summer especially, mosquito repellent is necessary gear.

## ACCOMMODATIONS

**Flamingo Lodge, Marina and Outpost Resort.** *1 Flamingo Lodge Hwy., Flamingo, FL 33034.* ☎ *800/600-3813 or 941/695-3101. Fax 941/695-3921. 102 rms, 24 cottages, 1 suite. High season, $75–$89 double, $99–$125 cottage, $110–$130 suite; summer and fall, $65 double, from $79 cottage, from $85 suite. AE, DC, DISC, MC, V.* The only lodging actually located within the boundaries of Everglades National Park, this woodsy sprawling complex offers rooms overlooking the Florida Bay in either a two-story simple motel or in the lodge. Situated right in the center of the action (with boat, canoe, and kayak rentals), it can sometimes feel like summer camp. The larger, more private and romantic cottages are an especially good choice if you plan to stay more than a night or two since they come with small kitchens, equipped with dishes and flatware, but no televisions. Facilities include a very good restaurant (see "Dining," below), bar, freshwater swimming pool, gift shop, and coin-op laundry.

**HOUSEBOAT RENTALS**    Motorized houseboats make it possible to explore some of the park's more remote regions without having to worry about being back by nightfall. You can choose from two different types of houseboats: a 40-foot pontoon boat sleeping six to eight in a single large room for $254 per night, and a newer, sleeker Gibson fiberglass boat sleeping six for $280 per night (both with a 2-night minimum).

Boating experience is helpful, but not mandatory, as the boats only cruise up to 6 miles per hour and are surprisingly easy to use. Reservations should be made far in advance; call **Flamingo Lodge, Marina and Outpost Resort** (☎ 800/600-3813 or 941/695-3101).

**NEARBY ACCOMMODATIONS**    Located about 10 miles from the park's main entrance, along U.S. 1, 35 miles south of Miami, the somewhat rural towns of Homestead and Florida City offer several chain hotels, including a Days Inn in Homestead and a Hampton Inn right off the turnpike in Florida City. The best option is the **Best Western Gateway to the Keys,** 1 Strano Blvd. (U.S. 1), Florida City, FL 33034 (☎ 800/528-1234 or 305/246-5100), with rates in high season starting at $85. Its suites and some larger rooms offer convenient extras like a microwave, coffeemaker, extra sink, and small fridge. There's also a swimming pool, Jacuzzi, and self-service Laundromat.

On the park's western side, the **Rod & Gun Lodge,** Riverside Drive and Broadway (P.O. Box 190), Everglades City, FL 33929 (☎ 941/695-2101), was originally built as a private residence in the 1830s but was turned into a cozy hunting lodge in the 1920s. President Herbert Hoover vacationed here after his 1928 election victory, and President Harry S. Truman flew in to sign Everglades National Park into existence in 1947. Rooms cost $85 double in winter, $65 double off-season. No credit cards.

## DINING

The only dining option in the park is a very civilized **Flamingo Restaurant** (☎ 941/695-3101), in the Flamingo Lodge (see "Accommodations," above). Besides the spectacular view of Florida Bay and numerous keys from the large, airy dining room, you'll also find fresh fish grilled, blackened, or deep-fried. The large menu has something for everyone, including basic and very tasty sandwiches, pastas, burgers, and salads. You may need reservations for dinner, especially in season. Prices are surprisingly moderate, with full meals starting at about $11 and going no higher than $20.

**NEARBY DINING**    You won't find fancy nouvelle cuisine in this suburbanized farm country, but there are plenty of fast-food chains along U.S. 1 and a few old favorites worth checking out.

Housed in a squat, one-story, windowless stone building that looks something like a medieval fort, the **Capri Restaurant,** 935 N. Krome Ave., Florida City (☎ 305/247-1542), has been serving hearty Italian-American fare since 1958. Great pastas and salads complement a full menu of meat and fish dishes. Portions are big. They serve lunch and dinner Mon–Sat until 11pm.

Another landmark is **Potlikker's,** 591 Washington Ave. (at the corner of NE 6th Street) in Homestead (☎ 305/248-0835), featuring fried fish and shrimp baskets, along with barbecued chicken and ribs, roast pork, grilled fish, and lots of local veggies. It's good, unadulterated Southern feed at popular prices. Main courses range from $6 to $13. The kitchen is open daily 7am–9pm.

The **Miccosukee Restaurant** (☎ 305/223-8380), just west of the Shark Valley entrance on the Tamiami Trail (U.S. 41), serves authentic pumpkin bread, fry bread, fish, and not-so-authentic Native American interpretations of tacos and fried chicken. This interesting spot is worth a stop for lunch or dinner, served daily from 8am until 3pm. Meals cost from $5 to $14.

In Everglades City, you can get your fill of fresh seafood at the **Oyster House,** on Fla. 29 opposite the national park visitor center (☎ **941/695-2073**), where a narrow, screened front porch here is a fine place to sip a drink while watching the sunset over the Everglades. Main courses cost $12–$17; sandwiches $4.50–$9.50. Open daily 11am–9pm. The down-home **Oar House Restaurant,** 305 Collier Ave. (Fla. 29) in Everglades City (☎ **941/695-3535**), offers "cooters, legs, and tails" (turtles, frogs' legs, and alligator tails) as specialties. Main courses go for $8–$16, sandwiches and seafood baskets $2–$8. Open daily 6am–9pm.

## 3  Walt Disney World & Orlando

Orlando was a sleepy Southern town ringed with sparkling lakes, pine forests, and citrus groves until Walt Disney turned 43 square miles of swampland into the Magical Kingdom known as Walt Disney World (WDW). He sparked an unprecedented building boom, as hotels, restaurants, and scores of additional attractions arose to take advantage of the tourist traffic he had generated. The world's most famous mouse changed central Florida forever. Thanks to Disney and what followed, Orlando today is one of the world's most popular family destinations.

Though the citrus industry still exists here, orange groves have largely given way to neighborhoods, hotels and resorts, and shopping malls. Competition has increased in recent years with Universal Studios Florida becoming a real force, with its own park and an entertainment district, the E-Zone. The expansion will continue in 1999 with Universal's Islands of Adventure, a second major theme park, and the Portofino Bay Resort, a 750-room Loews hotel, plus three more hotels by 2005. After years of cowering to the mouse, Universal and other non-Disney attractions are now banning together to offer special packages and discounts.

Of course, Disney is going about its ever expanding business, going out to sea with its own cruise line and creating another theme park, Animal Kingdom.

### ARRIVING & DEPARTING

**BY PLANE**   User-friendly **Orlando International Airport,** 25 miles from Walt Disney World, is served by American, American Trans Air, British Airways, Continental, Delta, Delta Express, Kiwi, Midway, Northwest, SunJet, Transbrasil, TWA, United, US Airways, and Virginia Atlantic. All major car-rental companies are at the airport. **Mears Transportation Group** (☎ **407/423-5566**) shuttle vans depart every 15 to 25 minutes around the clock to all Disney resorts and official hotels, as well as many other hostelries. Round-trip for adults is $21 between the airport and downtown Orlando or International Drive, $25 for Walt Disney World/Lake Buena Vista or Kissimmee/ U.S. 192. Children 4 to 11 are charged about $15; children 3 and under ride free.

**BY TRAIN & BUS**   Amtrak trains (☎ **800/USA-RAIL**) arrive at 1400 Sligh Blvd. in downtown Orlando (about 23 miles from Disney) and 111 Dakin Ave. in Kissimmee (about 15 miles from Disney). Amtrak's overnight **Auto Train** will bring you and your car from Lorton, Virginia, to Sanford, Florida, about 23 miles northeast of Orlando (reserve early). **Greyhound/Trailways** buses (☎ **800/231-2222**) also serve the two cities.

**PACKAGE TOURS**   Frankly, the number and diversity of money-saving package tours to Orlando is staggering. To choose the one that's right for you, first obtain the *Walt Disney World Vacations* guide (☎ **407/934-7639**), which lists the company's own packages. Also contact **Universal City Travel Company** (☎ **800/224-3838**), whose packages highlight Universal City. Then go to a sizable travel agency and pick up brochures from **American Express Vacations** (☎ **800/241-1700**), **Delta's Dream**

Vacations (☎ 800/872-7786), **American Airlines' Fly Away Vacations** (☎ 800/321-2121), **US Airways Vacations** (☎ 800/455-0123), and **Continental Vacations** (☎ 800/634-5555). Many hotels and other airlines also offer package deals; ask when you make your reservations.

## ESSENTIALS

**VISITOR INFORMATION**   The **Orlando/Orange County Convention and Visitor Bureau,** 8723 International Dr., Suite 101 (in the Mercado Shopping Village), Orlando, FL 32819 (☎ **407/363-5871**), will send you maps, brochures (including the informative *Official Visitors Guide,* the *Official Attractions Guide,* the *Official Accommodations Guide,* and the *African-American Visitors Guide*), and the Magicard (good for discounts of 10–50% on accommodations, car rentals, etc). The staff can also make dining reservations and hotel referrals.

The **Kissimmee–St. Cloud Convention and Visitor Bureau,** 1925 E. Irlo Bronson Memorial Hwy. (P.O. Box 422007), Kissimmee, FL 34742-2007 (☎ **800/327-9159** or 407/847-5000), will also send maps, brochures, discount coupon books, and the *Kissimmee–St. Cloud Vacation Guide* that details the area's accommodations and attractions.

For general information about WDW and a copy of the informative *Walt Disney World Vacations* guide, write or call the **Walt Disney World Co.,** P.O. Box 10000, Lake Buena Vista, FL 32830-1000 (☎ **407/934-7639**). If driving, stop at **Disney/AAA Travel Center** in Ocala, Florida, near the intersection of I-75 (exit 68) and Fla. 200, about 90 miles north of Orlando (☎ **904/854-0770**). Here you can purchase tickets, get help planning your park itinerary, and make hotel reservations. It's open daily 9am–6pm (until 7pm June–Aug). And at the Orlando International Airport, stroll over to **Greetings from Walt Disney World Resort,** a shop and information center on the third floor in the main lobby behind the Northwest Airlines counter, where you can buy WDW multiday park tickets or annual passes and make dinner-show and hotel reservations at Disney properties.

**RESOURCES FOR TRAVELERS WITH SPECIAL NEEDS**   Walt Disney World offers the *Guidebook for Guests with Disabilities;* write Guest Letters, P.O. Box 10040, Lake Buena Vista, FL 32830-0040 (☎ **407/824-4321**). At **Universal Studios** go to Guest Services just inside the main entrance for a *Disabled Guest Guidebook,* a Telecommunications Device for the Deaf (TDD), an audiocassette for visually impaired guests, or sign language guides and scripts for the hearing impaired (advanced notice required; call ☎ **407/363-8000**). **Sea World** has a guide for guests with disabilities, a braille guide, and a brief synopsis of shows for the hearing impaired (☎ **407/351-2600**).

When staying at Disney you can get a shuttle bus from your hotel that will also accommodate wheelchairs. In addition, all public buses in Orlando have a hydraulic lift and restraining belts for wheelchairs. **Wheelers Inc.** (☎ **407/826-0616**) and **Vantage Mini Vans** (☎ **407/521-8002**) both rent wheelchair vans.

**EMERGENCIES**   Dial ☎ **911** to contact the police or fire department or to call an ambulance. All major theme parks have first-aid centers. A local 24-hour service called **HouseMed** (☎ **407/396-1195**) has doctors who make "house calls" to local hotels.

## GETTING AROUND

You can get to and around Disney and other major attractions without a car, but it's handy to have one. All major car-rental companies have desks at the airport.

**BY BUS**   **Disney shuttle buses** serve all Disney resorts and official hotels and other properties offering unlimited complimentary transportation via bus, monorail, ferry, and/or water taxi to all three parks from 2 hours prior to opening until 2 hours after closing. Most area hotels and motels offer transportation to Disney and other attractions, but it can be pricey. **Mears Transportation Group** (☎ 407/423-5566) operates buses to all major attractions.

**BY TAXI**    Taxis line up in front of major hotels, or call **Yellow Cab** (☎ 407/699-9999). They charge $2.75 for the first mile, $1.50 per mile thereafter.

## WHAT TO SEE & DO

**ESCORTED TOURS**    The Disney parks offer a number of walking tours and learning programs (☎ 407/939-8687). The **Hidden Treasures of World Showcase** focuses on the architecture and entertainment offerings of Epcot's international pavilions. **Gardens of the World,** a 3-hour tour of the extraordinary landscaping at Epcot, is led by a Disney horticulturist. The 4-hour **Keys to the Kingdom** provides an orientation to the Magic Kingdom and a glimpse into the high-tech operational systems behind the magic. There are also learning programs (☎ 407/363-6000) on subjects ranging from animation to international cultures.

At **Sea World** visitors can take 90-minute behind-the-scenes **tours** of the park's breeding, research, and training facilities and/or attend a 45-minute presentation about Sea World's animal behavior and training techniques.

**ATTRACTIONS**    Mickey Mouse has evolved in Orlando into a vast entertainment empire offering everything from miniature golf and thrill rides to nightclubs and high-end eateries. Within the Disney world alone there are five major attractions: **Magic Kingdom, Epcot, MGM Studios, Pleasure Island,** and **Animal Kingdom.** Add to that an array of smaller attractions such as **Typhoon Lagoon** and **Blizzard Beach** and you have an entertainment extravaganza. You can eat, sleep, play, shop, even get married without ever stepping foot off of Disney property.

Of course, there are lots of other things to see and do in "O-town." Other major theme parks include **Universal Studios Florida** and **Sea World.** Toss into the mix attractions such as the popular **Wet 'n' Wild,** an elaborate water park, and even a few nontourist highlights like the **Orlando Science Center,** and you will have plenty of options. And there are increasing opportunities for adults, including three entertainment complexes—Disney's **Pleasure Island,** Universal's **City Walk,** and downtown Orlando's **Church Street Station.**

### THE MAJOR THEME PARKS

**Animal Kingdom.** *In the heart of Disney property about 25 miles outside of Orlando. Although not available at press time, hours and prices should be comparable with those at Magic Kingdom (see below).* Slated to open in 1998, Disney's fifth park combines animals, elaborate landscapes, and rides to create yet another reason not to venture outside of the Disney world. Animal Kingdom is divided into three "regions": one dedicated to the wildlife in Africa today; one to mythical creatures such as unicorns and dragons; and the third focusing on extinction. The park covers more than 500 acres, more than double the size of the Magic Kingdom. At the heart of it all is a 14-story "Tree of Life," a free-form representation of animals hand-crafted by Disney artists, nearly as tall as the silver golf-ball dome, also known as Spaceship Earth, that has come to symbolize Epcot.

**Disney–MGM Studios.** *Located in the heart of Disney property, about 25 miles outside of Orlando.* ☎ *407/934-7639. One-day admission $40.81 adults, $32.86 children, plus tax. Hours generally daily 9am–7pm, with extended hours—sometimes as late as midnight—during major holidays and summer. Parking $5.* Shows and rides with movie and TV themes are here, and behind-the-scenes "reel-life" and costumed character actors add atmosphere. This is also a working movie and TV studio, where shows such as *Star Search* are in production even as you tour the 110 acres. **Twilight Zone Tower**

# Walt Disney World

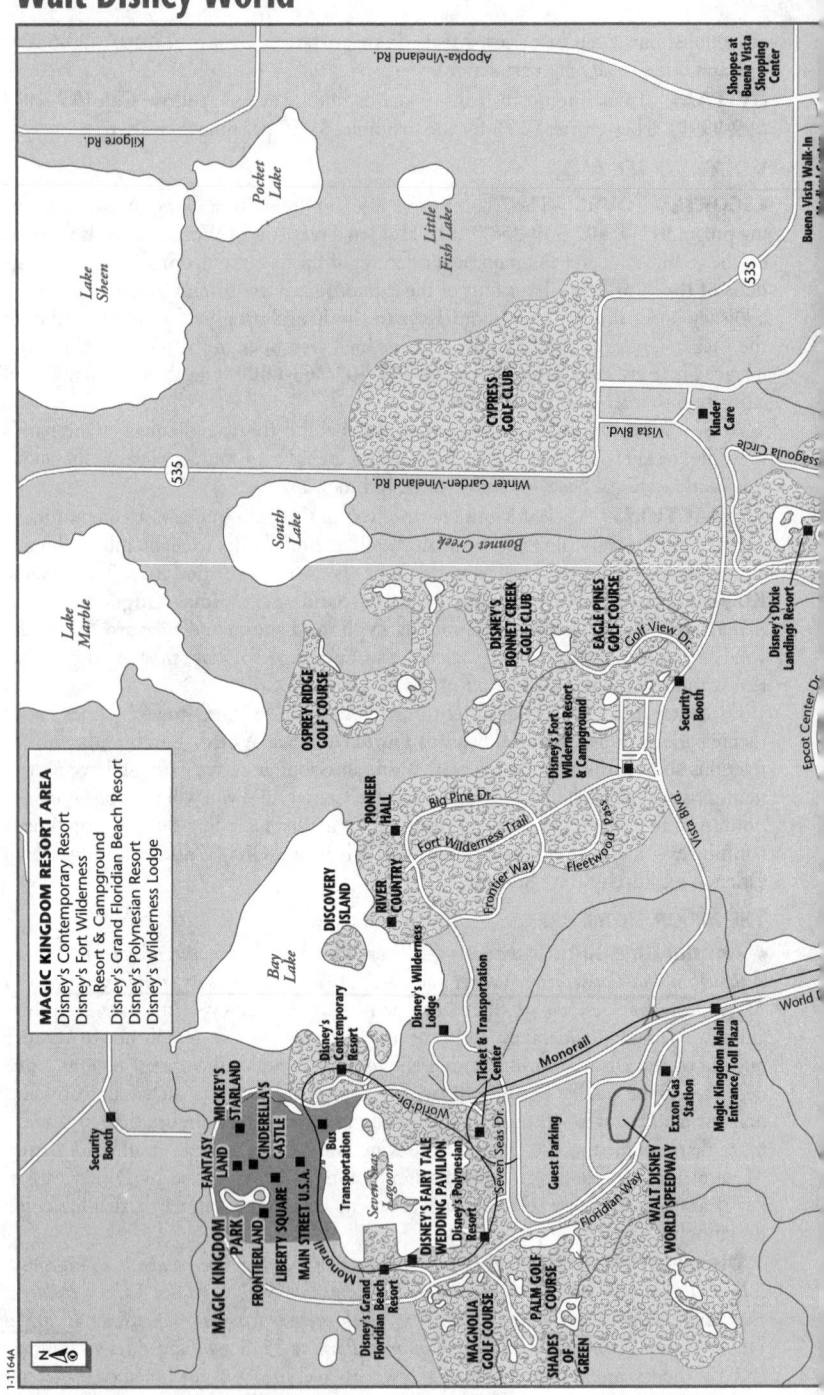

**MAGIC KINGDOM RESORT AREA**
Disney's Contemporary Resort
Disney's Fort Wilderness
Resort & Campground
Disney's Grand Floridian Beach Resort
Disney's Polynesian Resort
Disney's Wilderness Lodge

Lake Sheen

Pocket Lake

Kilgore Rd.

Apopka-Vineland Rd.

Shoppes at Buena Vista Shopping Center

Buena Vista Walk-In

535

Little Fish Lake

Lake Marble

South Lake

Winter Garden-Vineland Rd.

535

Bonnet Creek

CYPRESS GOLF CLUB

Vista Blvd.

Kinder Care

Issaqoula Circle

OSPREY RIDGE GOLF COURSE

DISNEY'S BONNET CREEK GOLF CLUB

EAGLE PINES GOLF COURSE

Golf View Dr.

Security Booth

Disney's Dixie Landing Resort

Epcot Center Dr

PIONEER HALL

Big Pine Dr.

Fort Wilderness Trail

Disney's Fort Wilderness Resort & Campground

Frontier Way

Fleetwood Pass

Vista Blvd.

Bay Lake

DISCOVERY ISLAND

RIVER COUNTRY

Disney's Wilderness Lodge

Ticket & Transportation Center

World Dr.

Monorail

World Dr.

MICKEY'S STARLAND

Disney's Contemporary Resort

FANTASY LAND

CINDERELLA'S CASTLE

Bus Transportation

Seven Seas Lagoon

Seven Seas Dr.

Guest Parking

Exxon Gas Station

Magic Kingdom Main Entrance/Toll Plaza

Security Booth

MAGIC KINGDOM PARK

FRONTIERLAND

LIBERTY SQUARE

MAIN STREET U.S.A.

Monorail

DISNEY'S FAIRY TALE WEDDING PAVILION

Disney's Polynesian Resort

Disney's Grand Floridian Beach Resort

Floridian Way

WALT DISNEY WORLD SPEEDWAY

MAGNOLIA GOLF COURSE

PALM GOLF COURSE

SHADES OF GREEN

1-1164A

302

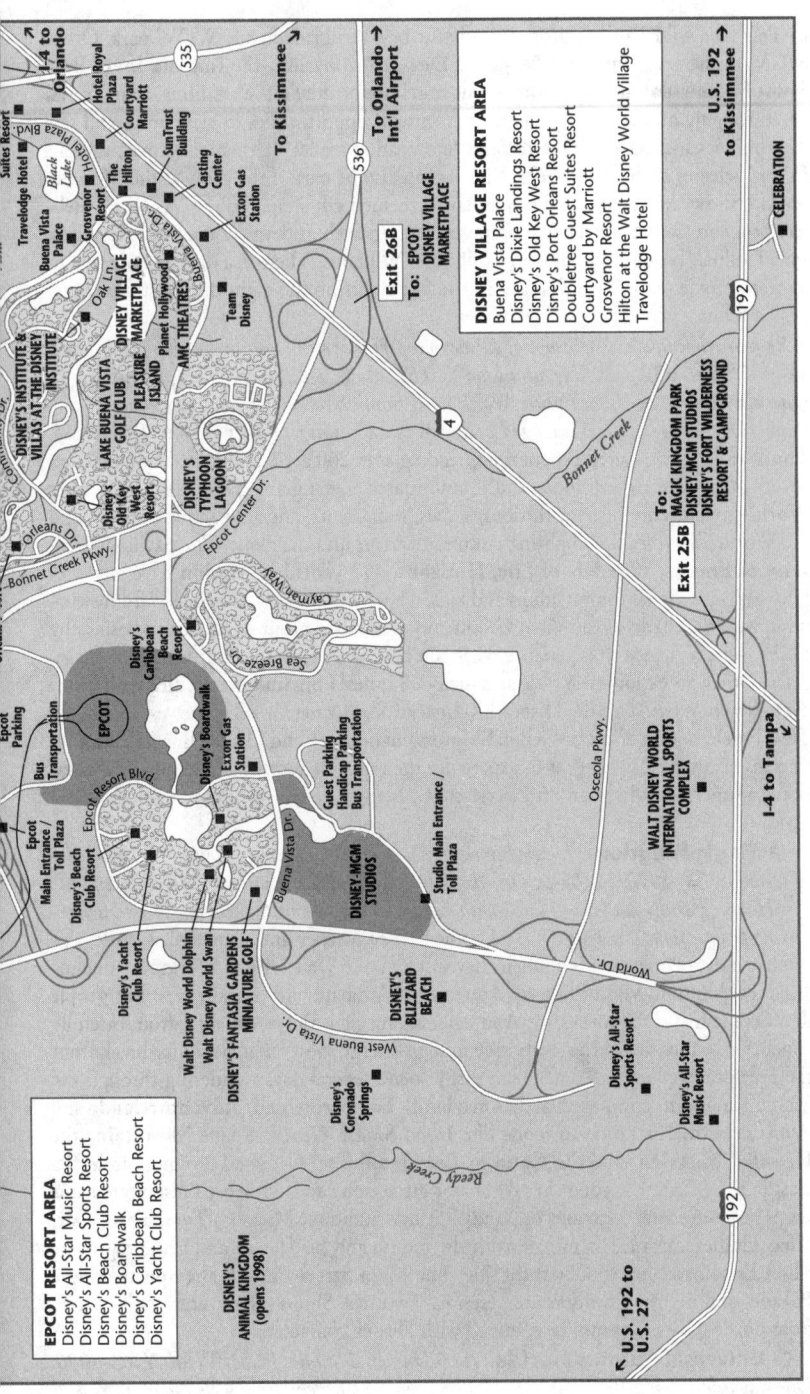

**EPCOT RESORT AREA**
Disney's All-Star Music Resort
Disney's All-Star Sports Resort
Disney's Beach Club Resort
Disney's Boardwalk
Disney's Caribbean Beach Resort
Disney's Yacht Club Resort

**DISNEY VILLAGE RESORT AREA**
Buena Vista Palace
Disney's Dixie Landings Resort
Disney's Old Key West Resort
Disney's Port Orleans Resort
Doubletree Guest Suites Resort
Courtyard by Marriott
Grosvenor Resort
Hilton at the Walt Disney World Village
Travelodge Hotel

**Exit 26B**
To: EPCOT
DISNEY VILLAGE
MARKETPLACE

**Exit 25B**
To:
MAGIC KINGDOM PARK
DISNEY-MGM STUDIOS
DISNEY'S FORT WILDERNESS
RESORT & CAMPGROUND

I-4 to Orlando
To Orlando →
To Orlando →
Int'l Airport
To Kissimmee
U.S. 192 →
to Kissimmee
I-4 to Tampa
← U.S. 192 to
U.S. 27

CELEBRATION

WALT DISNEY WORLD
INTERNATIONAL SPORTS
COMPLEX

Disney's All-Star
Sports Resort

Disney's All-Star
Music Resort

DISNEY'S
BLIZZARD
BEACH

DISNEY'S FANTASIA GARDENS
MINIATURE GOLF

Disney's
Coronado
Springs

DISNEY'S
ANIMAL KINGDOM
(opens 1998)

Walt Disney World Dolphin
Walt Disney World Swan

Disney's Yacht
Club Resort

Disney's Beach
Club Resort

Epcot
Main Entrance /
Toll Plaza

EPCOT
Parking

EPCOT

Bus
Transportation

Disney's
Caribbean
Beach
Resort

Disney's Boardwalk

Exxon Gas
Station

Guest Parking
Handicap Parking
Bus Transportation

Studio Main Entrance /
Toll Plaza

DISNEY-MGM
STUDIOS

Disney's
Old Key
West
Resort

DISNEY'S
TYPHOON
LAGOON

DISNEY INSTITUTE &
VILLAS AT THE DISNEY
INSTITUTE

LAKE BUENA VISTA
GOLF CLUB

DISNEY VILLAGE
MARKETPLACE

PLEASURE
ISLAND

AMC THEATRES

Planet Hollywood

Team
Disney

Buena Vista
Palace

Grosvenor
Resort

The
Hilton

SunTrust
Building

Casting
Center

Exxon Gas
Station

Suites Resort
Travelodge Hotel
Hotel Royal
Plaza
Courtyard
Marriott

535
536
4
192

Bonnet Creek

Bonnet Creek Pkwy

Osceola Pkwy

World Dr.

West Buena Vista Dr.

Buena Vista Dr.

Epcot Center Dr.

Resort Blvd

Cayman Way

Sea Breeze Dr.

Reedy Creek

Black
Lake

Orleans Dr.

**of Terror,** a wild 13-floor drop, is easily the best thrill ride in any WDW park. Other MGM must-sees include the **Magic of Disney Animation,** the **Indiana Jones Epic Stunt Spectacular** and, with the recent re-release of the Star Wars films, **Star Tours,** based roughly on the trilogy. There are plenty of opportunities to view props and sets from movies such as *101 Dalmatians.* Shows and parades are themed to match recent Disney releases such as *Hercules.* Visitors can also be part of the show at the **Monster Sound Show.** Most rides and shows have a themed gift shop and the **Visiting Celebrity** program features frequent appearances by stars such as Betty White, Burt Reynolds, Joan Collins, Leonard Nimoy, and Billy Dee Williams. There is a daily parade tied to a recent movie release and **Sorcery in the Sky** lights up the night during summer and peak seasons.

**Epcot.** *Located in the heart of Disney property, about 25 miles outside of Orlando.* ☎ *407/934-7639. One-day admission $40.81 adults, $32.86 children, plus tax. Hours generally daily 9am–9pm; Future World daily 9am–9pm; World Showcase daily 11am–9pm. Hours are sometimes extended as late as midnight during peak seasons. Parking $5.* This is really a two-tiered experience spreading over 260 acres dominated by a massive, silvery geosphere (which looks to the uninitiated like a giant golf ball). The **Future World** pavilions are filled with rides, shows, restaurants, and interactive exhibits, and the World Showcase, highlighting cultures from around the globe. The pavilions **Universe of Energy, Wonders of Life, Horizons,** and **World of Motion** have plenty of nifty gadgets that are fun for adults and kids. The **virtual reality offerings**—from swimming with the sharks at the Vivid Group pod to a walking tour of St. Peter's Basilica by ENEL—are a chance to experience what you have been reading about in science magazines. Other, more low-tech pleasures include **Honey I Shrunk the Audience,** a funny 3-D attraction based on the Disney hit *Honey I Shrunk the Kids.* The newest attraction, **Test Track,** a joint effort of General Motors engineering and Disney Imagineering™, puts guests in the driver's seat to experience the rigors of automobile testing. Illuminations, a water, laser-light and fireworks show, is a way to end your day at Epcot with a bang.

**✪ Magic Kingdom.** *Located in the heart of Disney property, about 25 miles outside of Orlando.* ☎ *407/934-7639. One-day admission $40.81 adults, $32.86 children, plus tax. Hours generally daily 9am–7pm, with extended hours—sometimes as late as midnight—during peak seasons. Parking $5.* The home base of Mickey and Cinderella's castle, this is what most people envision when they think about Walt Disney World, the uncluttered, cobblestone **Main Street** of America that probably never really was. But people don't come to WDW for reality. And, after all, magic is the watchword, from carefully concocted stories to go with every ride to high-energy shows that are a nice break from the ever-present long lines. You can easily spend several days wandering through the Magic Kingdom, composed of **Fantasyland, Tomorrowland, Adventureland,** and **Frontierland.** It's home to icons like **It's a Small World, Space Mountain,** the **Haunted Mansion,** and the **Country Bear Jamboree.** Centered around Cinderella Castle, the Magic Kingdom has 45 major attractions and numerous restaurants and shops in seven themed sections or "lands." A new addition, **Mickey's Toon Town Fair,** offers kiddies a chance to mingle with the mouse and his friends and get autographs. **Alien Encounter** is a spooky thrill ride. The **Main Street Parade,** the **SpectroMagic Parade,** and nightly fireworks are perennial favorites. Shops offer everything possible, from boxer shorts to earmuffs, stamped with Disney characters.

**✪ Universal Studios Florida.** *1000 Universal Studios Plaza.* ☎ *407/363-8000. One-day admission $40.81 for ages 10 and over, $32 for children 3–9; 2-day ticket $55 for ages 10 and over, $44 for children 3–9; annual pass $69 for ages 10 and over, $59 for children 3–9; free for children 2 and under. Parking $5 per vehicle, $6 for RVs and* *trailers. The park is open 365 days a year from 9am; closing hours vary seasonally.* This is a working motion-picture and television production studio, although most of the production goes on inside on the Nickelodeon sound stages. But remember cable's *The Swamp Thing* or the short-lived *SeaQuest?* Yes, they were filmed here. You will amble amid reel history displayed in the form of some 40 actual sets along "Hollywood Boulevard" and "Rodeo Drive." On hand to greet visitors are Hanna-Barbera characters (Yogi Bear, Scooby Doo, Fred Flintstone, and others) and a talented group of actors representing Universal stars from Harpo Marx to the Blues Brothers. Some attractions, such as **A Day in the Park with Barney** and **E.T. Adventure,** are targeted at wee ones. But the park specialty is really harum-scarum thrill rides like **Terminator 2: 3-D Battle Across Time, Jaws,** and **Back to the Future.** These are fast-moving, high-tech adventures. Shows, like the **Wild, Wild, Wild West Show** and **Beetlejuice Graveyard Revue,** are a little more freewheeling than Disney, with not quite so many dimpled chorus members and lots more humor. Kids love seeing **Nickelodeon** and several of the network's wacky, messy game shows are filmed at the park. Visitors can be part of the audience and, sometimes, part of the show. More than 25 **shops** in the park sell everything from Lucy collectibles to Bates Motel towels, and **restaurants** run the gamut from Mel's Drive-In (of *American Graffiti* fame), to the Hard Rock Cafe, to Schwab's.

**OTHER DISNEY ATTRACTIONS**   **Typhoon Lagoon is** off Lake Buena Vista Drive halfway between Disney Village and Disney–MGM Studios. **Blizzard Beach** is Disney's newest and zaniest water park—a 66-acre "ski resort" in the midst of a tropical lagoon. **River Country** is one of the many recreational facilities at Fort Wilderness Resort campground, a mini–water park themed after Tom Sawyer's swimming hole. **Discovery Island,** a lushly tropical 11½-acre zoological sanctuary—just a short boat ride away from the Magic Kingdom entrance—provides a tranquil counterpoint to Walt Disney World dazzle. **Fantasia Gardens** is an 18-hole miniature golf course based on the characters of the classic Disney animated film *Fantasia.* Hippos dance, broomsticks leap, and magic abounds, but it's still up to you to sink that hole in one.

**DISNEY TICKET OPTIONS**   Disney offers several ticket options, all providing unlimited use of the WDW transportation system. Most people get the best value from 4- and 5-day passes. The prices quoted below do *not* include sales tax, and they are, of course, subject to change. Increases, which come sporadically, are usually not increments of more than $1.50 per 1-day ticket. If you're staying at any Walt Disney World resort or "official" hotel, you're also eligible for a money-saving **Be Our Guest Pass** priced according to length of stay. It also offers special perks. Adult prices are paid by anyone over 10 years of age, while kids under 3 get in free.

The **4-Day Value Pass** provides admission for 1 day at the Magic Kingdom, 1 day at Epcot, 1 day at Disney–MGM Studios, and 1 day at your choice of any of those three parks; you can use it on any 4 days following purchase, but you cannot visit more than one park on any given day. Adults pay $136.74; children, $109.18.

The **4-Day Park-Hopper Pass** provides unlimited admission to the three major parks on any 4 days; in other words, you can hop from park to park on any given day. Adults pay $152.64; children, $121.90.

The **5-Day World-Hopper Pass** provides unlimited admission to the Magic Kingdom, Epcot, and Disney–MGM Studios on any 5 days; you can visit any combination of parks on any given day. It also includes admission to Typhoon Lagoon, River Country, Blizzard Beach, Discovery Island, and Pleasure Island for a period of 7 days beginning the first date stamped. Adults pay $207.76; children, $166.42.

## OTHER ATTRACTIONS

   **Gatorland.** *14501 S. Orange Blossom Trail (U.S. 441, between Osceola Pkwy. and Hunter's Creek Blvd.).* ☎ *407/855-5496. Admission $13.95 adults, $8.95 children*

*10–12, $6.50 children 3–9, free for children 2 and under. Daily 8am–6pm. Free parking.*
Gatorworld features thousands of alligators and crocodiles on a 70-acre spread. Breeding pens, nurseries, and rearing ponds are situated throughout the park, which also displays monkeys, snakes, birds, a Galápagos tortoise, and many other animals. A 2,000-foot boardwalk winds through a cypress swamp and a 10-acre breeding marsh with an observation tower, or you can take the free Gatorland Express Train around the park. Educational shows are scheduled throughout the day. An open-air restaurant, shop, and picnic facilities are on the premises.

**Harry P. Leu Gardens.** *1920 N. Forest Ave. (between Nebraska St. and Corrine Dr.).*
☎ *407/246-2620. Admission $3 adults, $1 children 6–16, free for children 5 and under. Gardens, daily 9am–5pm. Leu House tours, Sun–Mon 1–3:30pm, Tues–Sat 10am–3:30pm. Closed Christmas. Take I-4 east to exit 43 (Princeton St.), follow Princeton St. east, make a right on Mills Ave., turn left on Virginia Dr., and look for the gardens on your left.*
At this delightful 50-acre botanical garden on the shores of Lake Rowena, meandering paths lead through forests of giant camphors, moss-draped oaks, palms, cycads, and camellias. Exquisite formal rose gardens display 75 varieties. Free 20-minute tours of the Leu House, built in 1888, and a veritable decorative arts museum, take place on the half-hour.

**Orlando Museum of Art.** *2416 N. Mills Ave. (off U.S. 17/92), in Loch Haven Park.* ☎ *407/896-4231. Admission $4 adults, $2 children 4–11, free for children 3 and under. Museum, Tues–Sat 9am–5pm, Sun noon–5pm. Art Encounter, Tues–Fri and Sun noon–5pm, Sat 10am–5pm. Closed New Year's Day, Memorial Day, July 4, Labor Day, Thanksgiving, and Christmas. Free parking. Take I-4 east to exit 43 (Princeton St.) and follow the signs to Loch Haven Park.* Also undergoing a multi-million-dollar expansion, the museum displays its permanent collection of 19th- and 20th-century American art, pre-Colombian art, and African art on a rotating basis. "Art Encounter" is an interactive hands-on area for children. At this writing, an expansion is under way, which will allow for major exhibitions.

✪ **Orlando Science Center.** *777 E. Princeton St. (between Orange and Mills aves.), in Loch Haven Park.* ☎ *407/896-7151. Admission $6.50 adults, $5.50 children 3–11, free for children 2 and under. Mon–Thurs and Sat 9am–5pm, Fri 9am–9pm, Sun noon–5pm. Closed Thanksgiving and Christmas. Take I-4 east to exit 43 (Princeton St.). It is the building with the large, shiny silver dome.* A $44-million expansion completed in 1997 made the Orlando Science Center the largest center of its kind in the southeastern United States. The exhibits are state of the art and geared toward encouraging kids to touch, and have fun while learning. The CineDome projects images onto an eight-story domed screen with a powerful audio system.

**Ripley's Believe It or Not! Museum.** *8201 International Dr. (1¹/₂ blocks south of Sand Lake Rd.).* ☎ *407/345-0501. Admission $9.95 adults, $6.95 children 4–12, free for children 3 and under. Daily 10am–midnight.* It's always fun to peruse a Ripley collection of oddities, curiosities, and fascinating artifacts from faraway places. Among the hundreds of items and mannequins on display here are a 1,069-pound man, a five-legged cow, a mosaic of the *Mona Lisa* created from 1,426 pieces of toast, torture devices from the Spanish Inquisition, a Tibetan flute made from human bones, and Ubangi women with wooden plates in their lips. A mini–baby boom among workers in 1995 was attributed to a fertility idol and attracted other women hoping for similar luck.

✪ **Sea World.** *7007 Sea World Dr.* ☎ *407/351-3600. One-day ticket $37.95 for ages 10 and over, $31.80 for children 3–9; 2-day ticket $42.95 for ages 10 and over, $36.80 for children 3–9; free for children 2 and under. Parking $5 per vehicle, $7 for RVs and trailers. Daily 9am–7pm, later during summer and holidays.* This popular 200-plus-acre marine-life park explores the mysteries of the deep in a format that combines entertainment with environmental awareness. (No drinking straws here, because if swallowed, they can injure the animals.) Its beautifully landscaped grounds, centering on a 17-acre lagoon, include flamingo and pelican ponds and a lush tropical rain forest. **Shamu,** a killer whale, is the star of the park along with his expanding family, including several baby whales. The pace is much more laid-back than either Universal or Disney, and is a good way to end a long week of trudging through the other parks. There are lots of wild animal shows and chances to stroke, feed, and generally marvel at a variety of sea life. **Wild Artic,** a simulation ride/polar bear exhibit, is among the newest and most amibitious attractions. Other highlights include **Manatees: The Last Generation, Key West Dolphin Fest,** and **Pacific Point Preserve,** home to dozens of sea lions willing to literally sing for their supper. **Baywatch Nights** is a watery stunt-driving exhibition based on the television series. There are dozens of shops and eateries.

    **Splendid China.** *Formosa Gardens Blvd., off W. Irlo Bronson Memorial Hwy. (U.S. 192; between Entry Point Blvd./Sherbeth Rd. and Black Lake Rd.).* ☎ *407/396-7111. Admission $23.55 adults, $13.90 children 5–12, free for children 4 and under. Daily from 9:30am; closing hours vary seasonally (call ahead). Free parking.* This 76-acre outdoor attraction features more than 60 miniaturized replicas of China's wonders. Park highlights include a half-mile-long copy of the 4,200-mile Great Wall; the Forbidden City's 9,999-room Imperial Palace; Tibet's sacred Potala Palace; the Stone Forest of Yunan; and the Mongolian mausoleum of Genghis Khan. Live shows (acrobats, martial-arts demonstrations, puppetry, and more) take place throughout the day; check your entertainment schedule. There's a recorded commentary at each attraction.

    **Wet 'n' Wild.** *6200 International Dr. (at Republic Dr.).* ☎ *800/992-WILD or 407/351-WILD. Admission $23.95 adults, $18.95 children 3–9, free for children 2 and under. Open daily; hours vary seasonally (call before you go). Free parking. Take I-4 east to exit 30A and follow the signs.* When temperatures soar, head for this 25-acre water park and cool off jumping waves, careening down steep flumes, and running rapids. Among the highlights: **Fuji Flyer** (a six-story toboggan ride along 450 feet of banked curves); **The Surge** (one of the longest, fastest tube rides in the Southeast); **Bomb Bay** (a speedy vertical flight straight down to a target pool); **Black Hole** (step into a spaceship and board a two-person raft for a 30-second, 500-foot, twisting, turning reentry through total darkness propelled by a 1,000-gallon-a-minute blast of water!). There are additional flumes, a vast wave pool, a large and innovative children's water playground, a sunbathing area, and a picnic area.

**BEST BETS FOR KIDS**   Of course, **Magic Kingdom,** but if you have younger children, be sure to go to **Mickey's Toon Town Fair.** Older kids will be more interested in thrill rides such as **Space Mountain.** The interactive pavilions at Epcot are the place for kids, not the World Showcase. There are **character meals** galore offered through Disney, and kids, especially those under 10, love the opportunity to spend a little time with their favorite animated characters. Older children will get a kick out of one of the many Orlando dinner shows, especially **Medieval Times** and **King Henry's Feast.** At **Universal** you can't go wrong with **A Day in the Park with Barney** for younger kids and almost any of the thrill rides for teens. **Sea World** is a hit for animal lovers of all ages, and children especially love being able to pet a dolphin or feel the velvetlike skin of a stingray. The **Orlando Science Center** is a nice change of pace, not to mention educational, with lots of hands-on exhibits for kids of all ages. Gatorland, while a bit cheesy, is always a hoot. Of the many water parks, **Wet 'n' Wild** is the most popular, especially with older children and teens.

**SPORTS**   Pro basketball's **Orlando Magic** play at the **Orlando Arena,** 600 W. Amelia St., between I-4 and Parramore Avenue (☎ **407/849-2020** for information, 407/839-3900 to charge tickets). Orlando is also home to several other professional teams, including the **Predators,** an area football team, and the **Solar Bears,** an ice hockey team. **Spring training** for the **Houston Astros** runs mid-February to March, with exhibition games at the **Osceola County Stadium** in Kissimmee (☎ **407/933-2520**). The **Florida Citrus Bowl,** in downtown Orlando (☎ **407/896-2442** for information, 407/839-3900 to charge tickets), seats 70,000 people for major sporting events including the annual CompUSA Florida Citrus Bowl game, college football games, and NFL preseason games. The **Bay Hill Invitational Golf Tournament** is held mid-March at Arnold Palmer's Bay Hill Club, 9000 Bay Hill Blvd. (☎ **407/876-2888** for details). Another stop on the PGA tour is the **Walt Disney World Oldsmobile Golf Classic** (☎ **407/824-4321**) in October.

**SHOPPING**   **Belz Factory Outlet World,** 5401 W. Oak Ridge Rd., at the north end of International Drive (☎ **407/354-0126** or 407/352-9600), has 180 stores in two huge, enclosed malls and four shopping annexes. **The Mercado,** 8445 International Dr., just south of Sand Lake Road (☎ **407/345-9337**) is a Mediterranean-style shopping center with brick and cobblestone streets, terra-cotta–roofed buildings, and more than 60 specialty shops. Aside from a 500-room Sheraton Hotel plopped in its center, the **Florida Mall,** 8001 S. Orange Blossom Trail, at Sand Lake Road (☎ **407/851-6255**), is a typical, massive American shopping mall with more than 200 shops, restaurants, and services.

## ACCOMMODATIONS

As one of the world's hottest tourist destinations, accommodations of all kinds are available in Orlando. Consider the cost of parking or shuttle buses to and from Disney and other theme parks in determining your hotel choice. It can add up to quite a bit. Remember, too, to factor in the 11% tax.

   **Courtyard by Marriott.** *1805 Hotel Plaza Blvd. (between Lake Buena Vista Dr. and Apopka–Vineland Rd./Fla. 535), Lake Buena Vista, FL 32830.* ☎ *800/223-9930 or 407/828-8888. Fax 407/827-4623. 321 rms, 2 suites. $89–$149 double, depending on view and season. AE, CB, DC, DISC, JCB, MC, V. Free parking.* Recently renovated rooms here—most with balconies—have in-room safes, coffeemakers, pay-movie options, and Nintendo; refrigerators are available. Guests appreciate the restaurant, guest-services desk, two pools, whirlpool, playground, boat rental (at nearby Disney Village Marina), exercise room, coin-op laundry, arcade.

   **Days Inn.** *4104 and 4125 W. Irlo Bronson Memorial Hwy. (U.S. 192, at Hoagland Blvd. N.), Kissimmee, FL 34741.* ☎ *800/647-0010, 800/DAYS-INN, or 407/846-4714. Fax 407/932-2699. 194 rms, 32 efficiencies. $29–$59 room for up to four, depending on season; $37–$63 efficiency; $55–$75 Jacuzzi room (for one or two people). Rates include continental breakfast. Rates may be higher during major events. AE, CB, DC, DISC, MC, V. Free parking.* Good value for your hotel dollar, two Days Inns—on either side of U.S. 192—share facilities, including two pools, coin-op washers/dryers, and an arcade. Several restaurants (which deliver), a large shopping mall with a 12-theater movie house, and a supermarket are within walking distance.

   **Disney's All-Star Music Resort.** *1801 W. Buena Vista Dr. (at World Dr. and Osceola Pkwy.; P.O. Box 10000), Lake Buena Vista, FL 32830-1000.* ☎ *407/W-DISNEY or 407/939-6000. Fax 407/354-1866. 1,920 rms. $69–$79 double. Additional person $8 extra. Children 17 and under stay free in parents' room. AE, MC, V. Free parking.* Rooms here are small but the price is right. Ten musically themed buildings include country, jazz, rock, calypso, and Broadway show tunes. Rooms have musically themed bedspreads, paintings, and wallpaper borders. Extras include pizza-only room service, food court, bar, two pools, playground, coin-op laundry, and arcade.

**Disney's All-Star Sports Resort.** *1701 W. Buena Vista Dr. (at World Dr. and Osceola Pkwy.; P.O. Box 10000), Lake Buena Vista, FL 32830-1000.* ☎ *407/ W-DISNEY or 407/939-5000. Fax 407/354-1866. 1,920 rms. $79–$89 double. Additional person $8 extra. Children 17 and under stay free in parents' room. AE, MC, V. Free parking.* Buildings designed around football, baseball, basketball, tennis, and surfing highlight this sports-style resort. Immense public-area "icons" here include four-story football helmets. Cheerful rooms feature sports-motif bedspreads and paintings, and on the premises you'll find a food court, bar, two pools, playground, coin-op laundry, shop, and arcade.

✪ **Disney's Beach Club Resort.** *1800 Epcot Resorts Blvd. (off Buena Vista Dr.; P.O. Box 10000), Lake Buena Vista, FL 32830-0100.* ☎ *407/W-DISNEY or 407/ 934-8000. Fax 407/354-1866. 584 rms, 17 suites. $225–$295 double. Additional person $15 extra. Children under 17 stay free in parents' room. AE, MC, V. Free valet and self-parking.* Manicured gardens, ceiling fans, and furniture of bleached wood re-create a luxurious Victorian Cape Cod resort. The elegant Ariel's serves dinner. Cape May Café hosts character breakfasts and New England clambakes. The hotel offers complimentary boat transport to MGM, a sand beach, extensive sporting facilities, a health club, a coin-op laundry, a salon, shops, an arcade, a children's center, and Stormalong Bay (a vast pool/water park).

✪ **Disney's BoardWalk.** *2101 N. Epcot Resorts Blvd. (off Buena Vista Dr.; P.O. Box 10000), Lake Buena Vista, FL 32830-1000.* ☎ *407/W-DISNEY or 407/939-5100, 407/ 939-6200 for villas. Fax 407/354-1866. 358 rms, 20 suites, 532 villas. $225–$305 double; $380–$450 concierge-level double; $540–$1,525 suite. Villas, $210–$250 studio; $285– $310 one-bedroom; $385–$405 two-bedroom; $780 grand villa. Rates depend on view and season. Additional person $15 extra. Children under 17 stay free in parents' room. AE, MC, V. Free valet and self-parking.* This Disney property resembles a 1920s seaside resort with quaint B&B style. Villas offer kitchens and washer/dryers. Restaurants, a sports bar, and street performers line the boardwalk. There is boat transport to Epcot and MGM. Facilities include several lounges, a pool bar, three pools, extensive sporting facilities, a health club, a business center, two arcades, a community hall, and a children's center.

**Disney's Caribbean Beach Resort.** *900 Cayman Way (off Buena Vista Dr.; P.O. Box 10000), Lake Buena Vista, FL 32830-1000.* ☎ *407/W-DISNEY or 407/934- 3400. Fax 407/354-1866. 2,112 rms. $95–$129 double. Additional person $12 extra. Children 16 and under stay free in parents' room. AE, MC, V. Free parking.* This island-style hotel is good family value. Rooms with oak furnishings and floral-print spreads also offer coffeemakers, ceiling fans, and verandas. You'll also find a restaurant, food court, pizza-only room service, shuttle around the grounds, seven pools, pool bar, arcade, shops, boat rentals, bicycle rental, coin-op laundry, and playgrounds.

**Disney's Fort Wilderness Resort and Campground.** *3520 N. Fort Wilderness Trail (P.O. Box 10000), Lake Buena Vista, FL 32830-1000.* ☎ *407/W-DISNEY or 407/824-2900. Fax 407/354-1866. 784 campsites, 408 wilderness homes. $35–$54 campsite (depending on season, location, number of people, size, and extent of hookup); $180–$215 wilderness home. AE, MC, V. Free self-parking.* This woodsy 780-acre resort has both campsites and one-bedroom cabins. Nightly campfire programs carry out the theme. Hoop-Dee-Doo Musical Revue takes place in Pioneer Hall, one of two restaurants here. The resort offers boat transport, laundry rooms, two pools, a beach, fishing, volleyball, ballfields, shuffleboard, bike rentals, boat rentals, a nature trail, jogging, two tennis courts, two golf courses, shops, a kennel, and two arcades.

**Disney's Grand Floridian Beach Resort.** *4401 Floridian Way (P.O. Box 10000), Lake Buena Vista, FL 32830-1000.* ☎ *407/W-DISNEY or 407/824-3000. Fax 407/ 354-1866. 899 rms, 34 suites. $290–$365 double, depending on view and season; $450– $490 concierge-floor double; $580–$1,810 suite. Additional person $15 extra. Children 17 and under stay free in parents' room. AE, MC, V. Free valet and self-parking.* This luxurious, romantic choice has sunny rooms with floral-chintz spreads and private balconies overlooking formal gardens. Victoria & Albert's, Orlando's finest restaurant (see "Dining," below), is one of three choices here. The resort has monorail, boat, and trolley transport, a masseuse, pool, tennis, boat rentals, waterskiing, croquet, volleyball, jogging, fishing, beach, salon, coin-op laundry, shops, car-rental desk, spa, arcade, and children's activity center.

**Disney's Polynesian Resort.** *1600 Seven Seas Dr. (P.O. Box 10000), Lake Buena Vista, FL 32830-1000.* ☎ *407/W-DISNEY or 407/824-2000. Fax 407/354-1866. 841 rms, 12 suites. $260–$315 double, depending on view and season; $335–$395 concierge-floor double; $385–$1,100 suite. Additional person $15 extra. Children 17 and under stay free in parents' room. AE, MC, V. Free valet and self-parking.* A beach overlooking a lagoon and an immense pool with waterfalls and slide highlight this South Seas–style resort. Large, beautiful rooms have canopied beds and rattan furnishings. Luau Cove hosts Mickey's Tropical Luau, a Polynesian dinner show. Facilities include several other restaurants and bars, an ice-cream parlor, monorail, boat transport, kiddie pool, boat rental, waterskiing, volleyball, playground, jogging, fishing, coin-op laundry, shops, arcade, and children's activity center.

✪ **Disney's Wilderness Lodge.** *901 W. Timberline Dr. (on the southwest shore of Bay Lake just east of the Magic Kingdom; P.O. Box 10000), Lake Buena Vista, FL 32830-1000.* ☎ *407/W-DISNEY or 407/824-3200. Fax 407/354-1866. 697 rms, 25 junior suites, 6 suites. $159–$215 double, depending on view and season; $270–$290 junior suite; $580–$625 suite. Additional person $15 extra. Children 17 and under stay free in parents' room. AE, MC, V. Free valet and self-parking.* This hotel replicates a turn-of-the century national park lodge complete with cascading waterfall, a large, spewing geyser, and creek running through the lobby. Rooms are in Mission style with paintings of the Northwest. The resort offers two restaurants, bars, snack bars, transport to theme parks, a large pool, boat and bicycle rentals, a jogging and bike trail, arcade, shop, and children's activity center.

✪ **Disney's Yacht Club Resort.** *1700 Epcot Resorts Blvd. (off Buena Vista Dr.; P.O. Box 10000), Lake Buena Vista, FL 32830-1000.* ☎ *407/W-DISNEY or 407/ 934-7000. Fax 407/354-1866. 630 rms, 12 suites. $225–$305 double, depending on view and season; $370–$405 concierge-level double. AE, MC, V. Additional person $15 extra. Children 17 and under stay free in parents' room. Free valet and self-parking.* With marina atmosphere, nautically themed rooms here come in snappy blue and white with French doors opening onto balconies. The concierge level will appeal to business travelers. There are two restaurants, two bars, boat transport to MGM and Epcot, and a tram. The Yacht Club is identical to those of Disney's Beach Club Resort (see above).

**Holiday Inn Sunspree Resort Lake Buena Vista.** *13351 Fla. 535 (between Fla. 536 and I-4), Lake Buena Vista, FL 32821.* ☎ *800/FON-MAXX or 407/239-4500. Fax 407/239-7713. 507 rms. $89–$129 room for up to four people, depending on season. AE, CB, DC, DISC, JCB, MC, V. Free parking.* This Holiday Inn caters to children in a big way with special kid suites designed as igloos or Noah's Ark. There is transportation to area attractions, and facilities include a pool, kiddie pool, playground, fitness center, coin-op laundry, shops, arcade, children's activity center, and restaurant.

✪ **Hyatt Regency Grand Cypress.** *1 Grand Cypress Blvd. (off Fla. 535), Orlando, FL 32836.* ☎ *800/233-1234 or 407/239-1234; 800/835-7377 or 407/239-4700 for villas. Fax 407/239-3800; 407/239-7219 for villas. 676 rms, 74 suites, 146 villas.*

*$185–$310 room for up to five; $305–$410 Regency Club double; $190–$1,400 one- to four-bedroom villa. Range reflects room size, view, and season. AE, CB, DC, DISC, JCB, MC, V. Free self-parking; valet parking $9.* The villas are especially lavish at this deluxe property. There are six restaurants, a pool bar, snack bars, a shuttle to WDW, airport shuttle, salon, health club, shops, a helicopter pad, arcade, children's activity center, and playground. Sports include golf and tennis instruction, nature walk, jogging, and racquetball, volleyball, and shuffleboard courts.

✪ **Marriott's Orlando World Center.** *8701 World Center Dr. (on Fla. 536 between I-4 and Fla. 535), Orlando, FL 32821.* ☎ *800/621-0638 or 407/239-4200. Fax 407/238-8777. 1,504 rms, 85 suites. $159–$209 room for up to five people (range reflects season); $169–$219 pool-view room (14-day advance-purchase rates $129–$169, subject to availability); $265–$2,400 suite. AE, CB, DC, DISC, JCB, MC, V. Free self-parking; valet parking $8.* This sprawling 230-acre luxury resort has spacious rooms in pastel. There are four restaurants, several bars, snack bars, four pools, a kiddie pool, salon, health club, coin-op laundry, shops, an arcade, and children's activity center. Sports include golf and tennis pro shops and instruction, miniature golf, and volleyball.

✪ **Peabody Orlando.** *9801 International Dr. (between the Beeline Expressway and Sand Lake Rd.), Orlando, FL 32819.* ☎ *800/PEABODY or 407/352-4000. Fax 407/351-0073. 834 rms, 57 suites. $240–$300 room for up to three people; $300 Peabody Club room; $450–$1,350 suite. Children 17 and under stay free in parents' room; seniors 50 and over pay $89. Inquire about packages and holiday/summer discounts. AE, CB, DC, DISC, JCB, MC, V. Free self-parking; valet parking $7.* This deluxe 27-story resort is one of Florida's finest, with plush rooms complete with laser-disc movie setups. Extras include three restaurants, two bars, afternoon tea, transport to WDW parks, pool, kiddie pool, tennis courts, jogging, salon, health club, shops, arcade, and golf privileges.

✪ **Residence Inn by Marriott.** *8800 Meadow Creek Dr. (just off Fla. 535 between Fla. 536 and I-4), Orlando, FL 32821.* ☎ *800/331-3131 or 407/239-7700. Fax 407/239-7605. 688 suites. $159–$199 one-bedroom suite for up to four; $199–$219 two-bedroom suite for up to six. Range reflects season. Rates include full breakfast. AE, CB, DC, DISC, JCB, MC, V. Free parking.* Good for long-term stays, these tastefully decorated accommodations have fully equipped eat-in kitchens, private balconies or patios, and large living rooms. Guests enjoy two restaurants, food-shopping service, airport shuttle, three pools, sports court, tennis, playground, coin-op laundry, shops, and two arcades.

**OTHER ACCOMMODATIONS**     There are scores of other inexpensive but perfectly serviceable motels within a few miles of the WDW parks. All have swimming pools and all sell tickets to attractions and arrange transportation to them for a fee.

Kids love the **Viking Motel,** 4539 W. Irlo Bronson Memorial Hwy. (U.S. 192), between FL 535 and Hoagland Blvd. N. (☎ 407/396-8860), a family-owned property housed in a fantasy castle, with towers topped by little Viking ships. With its large, on-premises water park (Watermania), playground, poolside picnic tables, barbecue grills, and cheerful on-site Shoney's restaurant, **Larson's Lodge Main Gate,** 6075 W. Irlo Bronson Memorial Hwy. (U.S. 192), just east of I-4 (☎ 800/327-9074 or 407/396-6100), is a good choice for families. Families also will appreciate picnic tables and a children's play area on the lawn at the **Avista Inn,** 5245 W. Irlo Bronson Memorial Hwy. (U.S. 192), between Poinciana and Polynesian Isle blvds. (☎ 800/423-3864 or 407/396-7700).

Among national chains, there's the **Comfort Inn Maingate,** the **Econo Lodge Maingate East,** and the **Ramada Inn.**

## DINING

Since most visitors spend the majority of their time in the Disney area, we focus below on the best choices throughout that vast enchanted empire. In addition, all the theme parks offer both fast-food and sit-down restaurants. Some are quite good, especially the restaurants at the various "countries" in the Epcot World Showcase.

There are many other options in the Orlando area. Just about every restaurant offers a low-priced children's menu. If you're looking for a quiet meal away from children, head for restaurants on International Drive, which are farther from the Disney parks, or patronize the more expensive places.

**Ariel's.** *At Disney's Beach Club Resort, 1800 Epcot Resorts Blvd.* ☎ *407/WDW-DINE for priority seating. Main courses $17.95–$24. AE, MC, V. Daily 6–10pm. SEAFOOD.* Named for the *Little Mermaid* character, the focal point of this exquisite restaurant is a 2,000-gallon coral-reef tank filled with tropical fish, under a vaulted ceiling decorated with whimsical fish mobiles and glass bubbles. Try the paella or the Maine lobster sautéed with shiitake mushrooms and served atop a nest of tricolor pasta with lemon-butter sauce. Ariel's has an extensive wine list.

✪ **Bahama Breeze.** *8849 International Dr., Orlando.* ☎ *407/248-2499. Reservations not accepted. Main courses $6.95–$14.95; sandwiches and salads $5.95–$6.95. AE, MC, V. Sun–Thurs 4pm–1am, Fri–Sat 4pm–2am.* Traditional Caribbean foods are transformed into unusual treats like "fish in a bag"—strips of mahimahi in a parchment pillow. Traditionalists can stick with the first-rate paella. Sample from a drink menu of over 50 beers and pseudo-exotic drinks like Very Berry Daiquiris while watching the chefs in the open kitchen.

✪ **Cafe Tu Tu Tango.** *8625 International Dr. (just west of the Mercado).* ☎ *407/ 248-2222. Reservations accepted. Tapas (tasting portions) $3–$7.95. AE, DISC, MC, V. Sun–Thur 11:30am–11pm, Fri–Sat 11:30am–1am. INTERNATIONAL TAPAS.* Tu Tu's puts on a show—belly dancers wriggle by as sword swallowers perform cutting-edge acts—but food like Cajun eggrolls or tuna sashimi is the real attraction here. Two selections—meant to be shared—will sate most appetites. International wines can be ordered by the glass or bottle.

**California Grill.** *At Disney's Contemporary Resort, 4600 N. World Dr.* ☎ *407/ 824-1576 or 407/WDW-DINE for reservations. Main courses $14.75–$27.50. AE, MC, V. Daily 5:30–10pm. CALIFORNIA.* High above the Magic Kingdom, this restaurant offers scenic views, plus an exhibition kitchen with a wood-burning oven. A sushi sampler or goat cheese ravioli makes a good beginning. Choice entrees include braised lamb shank or grilled pork tenderloin with a crispy fried sage garnish. For dessert, try the butterscotch crème brûlée. The restaurant has a good selection of California wines.

✪ **Cape May Café.** *At Disney's Beach Club Resort, 1800 Epcot Resorts Blvd.* ☎ *407/ WDW-DINE for priority seating. Buffet $18.95 adults, $9.50 children 7–11, $4.50 children 3–6, free for children 2 and under. Lobster is additional. AE, MC, V. Daily 5:30– 9:30pm. CLAMBAKE BUFFET.* A nightly New England clambake serves up chowder, steamed clams and mussels, corn on the cob, chicken, lobster, and redskin potatoes from a crackling rockweed steamer pit. All this plus dozens of salads, hot dishes (barbecued pork ribs, smoked sausage, pastas), and an array of oven-fresh breads and desserts. There's a full bar.

✪ **Dux.** *In the Peabody Orlando, 9801 International Dr.* ☎ *407/345-4550. Reservations recommended. Main courses $19–$45.95. AE, CB, DC, DISC, JCB, MC, OPT, V. Mon–Thur 6–10pm, Fri–Sat 6–11pm. INTERNATIONAL.* Named for the hotel's signature ducks that parade ceremoniously into the lobby each morning, this is one of central Florida's most acclaimed restaurants. The internationally nuanced menu changes seasonally but can feature entrees such as grilled Florida black grouper marinated in West Indian spices with a plantain-yam mash and tropical chutney. Dux has an extensive, award-winning wine list.

**Fireworks Factory.** *1630 Lake Buena Vista Dr., Pleasure Island.* ☎ *407/934-8989. Reservations recommended. Main courses mostly $13.95–$25. AE, MC, V. Daily 11:30am– 11:30pm (dinner served from 4pm, light fare and drinks served until 2am). AMERICAN REGIONAL.* Order the appetizer sampler of chicken wings, shrimp quesadillas, and baby-back ribs. Entrees range from Cajun shrimp pasta to oak-roasted salmon served with tomato/corn relish. Indulge in a giant Toll House cookie topped with ice cream and hot fudge or one of 46 varieties of beer, ale, and stout. A good, casual choice for family dining in a faux-warehouse.

✪ **Hemingway's.** *In the Hyatt Regency Grand Cypress, 1 Grand Cypress Blvd. (off Fla. 535).* ☎ *407/239-1234. Reservations recommended. Main courses $7.50–$19.75 at lunch, $20–$28 at dinner. AE, CB, DC, DISC, JCB, MC, V. Tues–Sat 11:30am–2:30pm; daily 6–10:30pm. Free validated valet and self-parking. SEAFOOD.* Fronted by a waterfall that cascades into stone-bedded streams, Hemingway's evokes Key West by honoring its most famous denizen "Papa." Start with an appetizer of deep-fried baby squid and grilled eggplant in garlicky herb-seasoned tomato coulis. Follow up with an entree of beer-battered coconut shrimp served with roasted potatoes and an orange marmalade horseradish. For dessert, what else but key-lime pie.

**Ming Court.** *9188 International Dr. (between Sand Lake Rd. and the Beeline Express-way).* ☎ *407/351-9988. Reservations recommended. Dim sum items mostly $1.95–$2.50; main courses $12.50–$19.95. AE, CB, DC, DISC, JCB, MC, V. Daily 11am–2:30pm and 4:30pm–midnight. Free parking. CHINESE REGIONAL.* The specialty here is sophisticated Chinese fare amid a candlelit interior decorated in soft earth tones, overlooking lotus ponds filled with koi. The menu offers specialties from diverse regions of China. Pair Mandarin pot stickers with Szechuan charcoal-grilled filet mignon. The wine list is extensive.

**Planet Hollywood.** *1506 E. Buena Vista Dr., Pleasure Island.* ☎ *407/827-7827. Reservations not accepted. Main courses $7.50–$18.95 (most under $13). AE, DC, MC, V. Daily 11am–2am. AMERICAN.* This branch of the trendy chain features a fiber-optic ceiling that creates a planetarium effect. There are displays of more than 300 items from Peter O'Toole's *Lawrence of Arabia* costume to the *Speed* bus. Nosh on appetizers—hickory-smoked buffalo wings, pot stickers, or nachos—burgers, salads, pizzas, pastas, and platters of grilled steak, ribs, or pork chops. Save room for dessert.

✪ **RainForest Cafe.** *In the Disney Village Marketplace, 1800 E. Buena Vista Dr., Buena Vista.* ☎ *407/827-8500. Reservations not accepted. Main courses $5.50–$17.95. AE, DISC, MC, V. Sun–Thurs 10:30am–11pm, Fri–Sat 10:30am–midnight. CALIFOR-NIA.* It's a jungle in here, complete with erupting volcano. Comfort food like mashed potatoes and veggie delights such as Rasta Pasta with a pesto cream sauce come in huge, tasty portions. Top it off with coconut bread pudding with dried apricots. *Warning:* The wait can be hours, so prepare to shop in the Disney Village Marketplace.

✪ **Victoria & Albert's.** *In Disney's Grand Floridian Beach Resort, 4401 Floridian Way.* ☎ *407/WDW-DINE. Reservations required. Jackets required for men. Fixed-price dinner $80 per person; $25 additional for the Royal Wine Pairing. AE, MC, V. Daily seat-ings at 6–6:45pm and 9–9:45pm. AMERICAN REGIONAL.* This is the world's (well, Walt Disney's world) most elite restaurant. A maid and butler provide gracious service while a harpist softly plays. The seven-course dinner changes nightly and includes delicacies such as vermouth-poached jumbo sea scallops served in a crisp rice-noodle basket, sautéed Peking duck breast with wild rice and crabapple chutney, and a hazelnut and Frangelico soufflé. There is, of course, an extensive wine list.

**DINING WITH DISNEY CHARACTERS** Especially for the 10-and-under set, it's a thrill to dine in a restaurant where costumed Disney characters show up to greet the customers, sign autographs, pose in family photos, and interact with little kids. Make reservations as far in advance as possible for these very popular meals. There are about a dozen options that feature everything from Mickey and his pals to to the characters from *The Hunchback of Notre Dame*. For information on all character meals, call ☎ 407/WDW-DINE.

## WALT DISNEY WORLD & ORLANDO AFTER DARK

Although known for family fun and theme parks, Orlando has plenty to do after dark. The huge multiclub entertainment complexes such as **Church Street Station, Pleasure Island,** and **E-Zone** (see below) offer access to all clubs for one admission price. There are dozens of independent bars and clubs in downtown Orlando and along International Drive, not to mention a unique array of dinner shows featuring everything from gladiators to knights on horseback.

Check the "Calendar" section of Friday's *Orlando Sentinel* for details on what's happening. Tickets to many performances are handled by **Ticketmaster** (☎ 407/839-3900).

**PERFORMING ARTS**    The area's major cultural venue is the **Bob Carr Performing Arts Centre,** 401 W. Livingston St., between I-4 and Parramore Avenue (☎ 407/849-2020 for information, 407/839-3900 to charge tickets). This 2,500-seat facility is home to the **Orlando Opera Company** and the **Southern Ballet Theater,** both of which have Oct–May seasons. The **Orlando Broadway Series** (Sept–May) features original-cast Broadway shows such as *Damn Yankees* and *Cats.*

**THE CLUB & BAR SCENE**    There are dozens of clubs and restaurants along Orange Avenue, the main street in downtown. A free public transportation system call **Lymmo** runs in a designated lane that connects many of these clubs once you get into downtown. Big hair, leather, and heavy-metal music are the standards at **Jani Lane's Sunset Strip,** 25 S. Orange Ave., corner of Orange Avenue and Pine Street (☎ 407/649-4803), a large, loud downtown favorite. A magnet for Generation X types who dig Tony Bennett on the jukebox, **Kit Kat Club,** 23 Wall Street Plaza, off of Orange Avenue (☎ 407/422-6990), is a swinging, plush joint with red velvet couches, pool tables, and a cigarette girl. **Eight Seconds,** 100 W. Livingston Ave. (☎ 407/839-4800), is a honky-tonk, complete with "Buckin' Bull Nights"—and it's a real mechanical bull, à la *Urban Cowboy.* Local and national acts both perform at **Sapphire Supper Club,** 54 N. Orange Ave. (☎ 407/246-1419), a laid-back club with vintage brick walls and an extensive martini menu. Muscled bouncers and servers in G-strings populate **Zuma Beach,** 46 N. Orange Ave. (☎ 407/648-8363), which one local newspaper dubbed the "Best Pickup Place"—if you can hear over the pumping dance music.

**ENTERTAINMENT COMPLEXES**    Universal's answer to Disney's Pleasure Island is a high-energy 12-acre entertainment complex called **City Walk.** It is home to the world's largest Hard Rock Cafe—the grande dame of all theme restaurants—but also the NASCAR Cafe, the Motown Cafe, and Marvel Mania, a theme send-up to villains and superheroes. There are also several upscale restaurants and a 16-screen Cineplex Odeon movie theater.

**Pleasure Island,** adjacent to Disney Village Marketplace (☎ 407/934-7781), is a rollicking, 6-acre complex of nightclubs, restaurants, shops, and movie theaters. Due to double in size in the near future, the park is designed to evoke an abandoned waterfront industrial district with clubs in "converted" ramshackle lofts, factories, and warehouses, but the streets are festive with brightly colored lights and balloons. There are nightly fireworks.

**Church Street Station,** 129 W. Church St., off I-4 between Garland and Orange avenues in downtown Orlando (☎ 407/422-2434), occupies a cobblestone city block lined with turn-of-the-century buildings (real ones). It, too, is a shopping/dining/

nightclub complex offering a diverse evening of entertainment for a single admission price. There are 20 live shows nightly plus an array of street performers. Major blowout celebrations are held for special events such as St. Patrick's Day and the Super Bowl.

**DINNER SHOWS**   The rustic log-beamed Pioneer Hall at Disney's Fort Wilderness Resort and Campground (☎ 407/WDW-DINE) is the setting for the **Hoop-Dee-Doo Musical Revue,** a 2-hour foot-stompin', hand-clappin', down-home musical revue. The delightful 2-hour **Polynesian Luau Dinner Show** at Disney's Polynesian Resort (☎ 407/WDW-DINE) is a big favorite with kids, who are all invited on the stage. It features a colorfully costumed cast of entertainers from the South Pacific performing on a flower-bedecked stage. The **Arabian Nights,** 6225 W. Irlo Bronson Memorial Hwy. (U.S. 192), just east of I-4 at exit 25A, Kissimmee (☎ 800/553-6116 or 407/ 239-9223), has everything from prancing Royal Lippizan Stallions to chariot races. The 2-hour show claims to have more characters, costumes, and lights than any on Broadway. The 90-minute, action-packed **Gladiator Arena,** 5515 W. Irlo Bronson Memorial Hwy. (U.S. 192), between I-4 and Fla. 535, Kissimmee (☎ 800/BATTLE-4 or 407/390-0000), features qualified contenders battling in areas such as assault, breakthrough and conquer, joust, powerball, the wall, and whiplash. A long-time favorite for Orlando visitors, **Medieval Times,** 4510 W. Irlo Bronson Memorial Hwy. (U.S. 192), 11 miles east of the main Disney entrance in Kissimmee (☎ 800/229-8300 or 407/ 239-0214), features jousting contests, armored clashes, and 80 Andalusian stallions performing with military precision.

# 4  Atlanta

If only General Sherman could rise from the grave to witness the phenomenal growth of Atlanta, the city he burned to the ground during the Civil War. Ever bustling and not always growing attractively, Atlanta was a world-class city even before it hosted the 1996 Summer Olympics. Thanks in no small part to home-grown Coca-Cola and the Cable News Network, it's now one of the centers of the universe. The city's airport is so busy that Southerners wisecrack that to get to heaven, they'll have to change planes in Atlanta.

The Olympics brought Atlanta more attention than anything since *Gone With the Wind* premiered here in 1939, but in spite of local boosterism, the *Atlanta Journal–Constitution* admits that the city still lacks "the culture and sophistication found in genuine international cities." Yet Atlanta can be a lot of fun. You can enjoy its glittering skyscraper hotels, its bevy of new restaurants that now place it among the top dining meccas of the South, and the many late-night diversions that prove Atlanta is hardly an old folks' home (the median age is only 28, at last count). More than ever before, there are concerts and cabarets, art galleries and avant-garde "happenings"—and the influx of restaurants featuring international cuisine has made it harder and harder to find fried chicken, country ham, hot biscuits, and grits. Locals like to boast that Atlanta has arrived—and they'll be happy to take you by the hand and prove it.

## ARRIVING & DEPARTING

**BY PLANE**   **Hartsfield International Airport** is the home of **Delta Airlines** (☎ 800/ 221-1212) and is served by more than a dozen other carriers, including American, British Airways, Continental, Japan Airlines, Lufthansa, Northwest/KLM, Swissair, TWA, United, and US Airways. All major car-rental agencies are present at the airport.

The **Atlanta Airport shuttle** (☎ 800/842-2770 or 404/524-3400) connects the airport with major downtown hotels. The fare is $8. MARTA's **rapid-rail trains** run from 4:35am to 1:42am, with a downtown fare of $1.25. **Taxi** fare to downtown is $15 for one passenger, $8 each for two, $6 each for three. Be sure the taxi driver knows how to get to where you want to go before you leave the airport.

**BY TRAIN & BUS**  Amtrak trains arrive at the Brookwood Railway Station, 1688 Peachtree St. (☎ **800/USA-RAIL**). This is a very central location, within easy reach of most downtown or midtown hotels. The **Greyhound/Trailways** bus station is at 232 Forsyth St. (☎ **800/231-2222**).

## ESSENTIALS

**VISITOR INFORMATION**  The **Atlanta Convention and Visitor Bureau (ACVB),** 233 Peachtree St. NE, Suite 2000, Atlanta, GA 30303 (☎ **800/ATLANTA,** or 404/ 521-6600 for an informational recording), supplies a wealth of information on sightseeing, accommodations, dining, cultural happenings, and special interests. Its *International Visitors Guide* is available in five lanaguages. The ACVB has walk-in visitor information centers at Hartsfield Atlanta International Airport (near the car-rental booths); in the Lenox Square Shopping Center (Buckhead), at 3393 Peachtree Rd.; and in Underground Atlanta, 65 Upper Alabama St. The ACVB also has a booth in the huge **Welcome South Visitor Center,** at the corner of Spring Street and International Boulevard (☎ **404/224-2000**), which provides information about the entire Southeast.

**RESOURCES FOR TRAVELERS WITH SPECIAL NEEDS**  The **Georgia Department of Industry, Trade and Tourism** publishes a guide, *Georgia on My Mind,* that lists attractions and accommodations with access for the disabled. To receive a copy, contact Tour Georgia, P.O Box 1776, Atlanta, GA 30301 (☎ **800/VISIT-GA**, ext. 1903). For transportation, disabled individuals can call **Rent-A-Van of Atlanta** (☎ **404/422-9025**) or **Wheelchair Getaways, Inc.** (☎ **404/467-9851**). MARTA provides transportation services for the disabled (☎ **404/848-5389**).

You can access Atlanta's large gay community via the free *Etcetera Magazine* (☎ **404/ 525-3821**) and *Creative Loafing,* both available in front of MARTA stops and in many shops, bars, and restaurants. Another free gay publication is *Southern Voice* (☎ **404/ 876-1819**). The month of June has many gay-oriented events, including the annual Gay Pride Parade. For details, call ☎ **770/662-4533.**

**EMERGENCIES**  Call ☎ **911** in case of emergencies. There are 24-hour emergency rooms at the Georgia Baptist Medical Center, 300 Boulevard NE (☎ **404/265-4000**), and Grady Memorial Hospital, 80 Butler St. (☎ **404/616-4307**). For physician referrals, contact the Medical Association of Atlanta (☎ **404/752-1564**).

**SAFETY**  Atlanta is one of the most dangerous cities in America. More than 80% of its crimes are property crimes, including many thefts from parked cars. Purse snatching is also commonplace, as are muggings, especially after dark in the downtown and midtown areas. Proceed with caution, just as you would in any other urban area.

## GETTING AROUND

**BY SUBWAY & BUS**  The **Metropolitan Atlanta Rapid Transit Authority (MARTA)** provides Atlanta with its rapid-rail and bus transportation system. With 36 stations, **MARTA rapid rail** extends south to the airport, and east–west and north–south lines intersect at the Five Points Station in downtown. Extentions are under way, including a north line to parallel Ga. 400. It operates daily from 5am to 1am, and the regular fare is $1.50, payable in exact change. There are token vending machines at all stations, and transfers are free.

MARTA also operates some 150 **bus** routes, which connect with all rapid-rail stations. You must have exact change for the $1.50 fare, and transfers are free.

For route and schedule information about rapid rail or buses, call ☎ **404/848-4711** Mon–Fri 6am–10pm, Sat–Sun and holidays 8am–4pm.

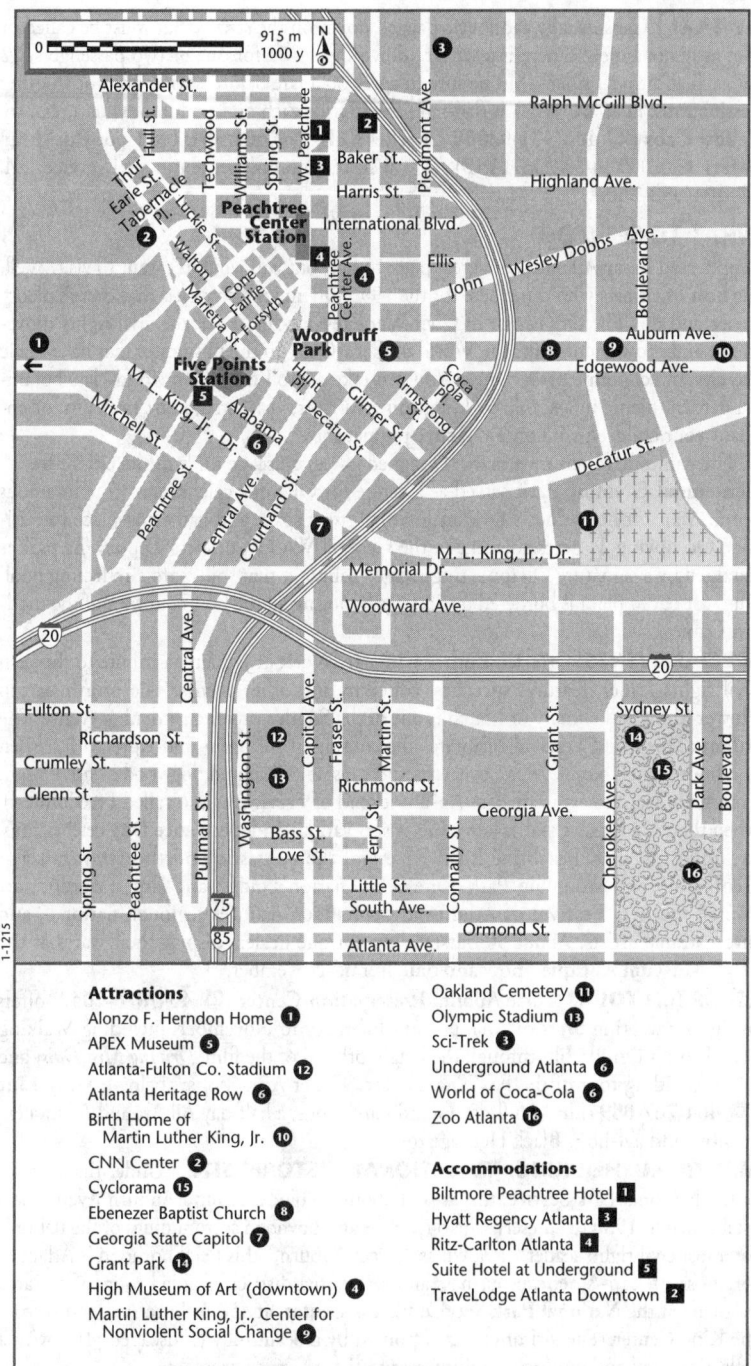

# Downtown Atlanta

**Attractions**

Alonzo F. Herndon Home ➊

APEX Museum ➎

Atlanta-Fulton Co. Stadium ⑫

Atlanta Heritage Row ➏

Birth Home of
Martin Luther King, Jr. ⑩

CNN Center ➋

Cyclorama ⑮

Ebenezer Baptist Church ➑

Georgia State Capitol ➐

Grant Park ⑭

High Museum of Art (downtown) ➍

Martin Luther King, Jr., Center for
Nonviolent Social Change ➒

Oakland Cemetery ⑪

Olympic Stadium ⑬

Sci-Trek ➌

Underground Atlanta ➏

World of Coca-Cola ➏

Zoo Atlanta ⑯

**Accommodations**

Biltmore Peachtree Hotel **1**

Hyatt Regency Atlanta **3**

Ritz-Carlton Atlanta **4**

Suite Hotel at Underground **5**

TraveLodge Atlanta Downtown **2**

**BY TAXI**　Cabs usually cannot be flagged down on the streets, but must be called or met at major hotels. There is a set fare downtown—$4 for one or two passengers, $2 for each additional rider—but be sure to agree on a fare before setting off. For all other destinations, fares are $1.50 at flag-fall plus 20¢ for each one-sixth mile. For a taxi, try **Yellow Cabs** (☎ 404/521-0200), **Checker Cabs** (☎ 404/351-1111), or **Buckhead Safety Cab** (☎ 404/233-1152). If you have a complaint about taxi service, call ☎ 404/658-7600.

## WHAT TO SEE & DO

People used to say Atlanta was a great place to live, but you wouldn't want to visit. Well, the host of visitors who came here for the 1996 Olympics discovered that there's plenty to see and do. The city is rich in Civil War sites, landmarks of the civil rights movement, and monuments (like the World of Coca-Cola) to the businesses that have made the city an economic powerhouse. You can take a stroll through a world-class botanical garden, picnic in a scenic park, raft down a river, visit a major art museum, or enchant your children with an interactive puppet show.

The games left their own mark. Designed as "a landscape quilt in the city of trees," **Centennial Olympic Park** served as a venue for Olympic celebrations (the infamous bomb went off here) and is now an inviting green space and gathering place for visitors. Occupying 21 acres adjacent to the Georgia World Congress Center, the park is heralded by a signature Olympic ring-shaped fountain that spills into a reflecting pool. The vast paved plaza is bordered by 23 flags honoring all the host countries of the modern Games.

**SPECIAL EVENTS**　**Martin Luther King, Jr. Week** in January, a tribute to the slain civil rights leader, features speeches, concerts, and other events. The **Southeastern Flower Show** in February or March is one of the South's premier gardening events. The **Atlanta Dogwood Festival** celebrates the coming of spring in mid-April with garden and house tours, bicycle tours, concerts, and tons of azaleas and dogwood in full bloom. You might want to avoid the late-April weekend of **Freaknik** (also called Freedomfest), when there are massive traffic jams. July 4 sees various **Independence Day** celebrations, including the 10K Peachtree Road Race and the Fantastic Fourth extravaganza at Georgia's Stone Mountain Park. One of the nation's oldest and largest outdoor art events, the **Arts Festival of Atlanta** in September, features regional, national, and international artists. About 50 outstanding antique dealers display their wares at the **High Museum Antique Show and Sale** in mid-November.

**ESCORTED TOURS**　The **Atlanta Preservation Center** (☎ 404/876-2040) offers intriguing walking tours of Atlanta from February to November, including Walking Miss Daisy's Druid Hills through the neighborhood of the film *Driving Miss Daisy* and an outstanding tour of the Fox Theatre (see "Other Attractions," below). **Gray Line** (☎ 404/767-0594) has a full-day Grand Circle tour, a half-day All Around Atlanta excursion, and a 4-hour Black Heritage tour.

**MARTIN LUTHER KING, JR. NATIONAL HISTORIC SITE**　Under the auspices of the National Park Service, this area of about 10 blocks around Auburn Avenue was established in 1980 to "preserve the birthplace and boyhood surroundings of the nation's foremost civil rights leader." Known as "Sweet Auburn," this neighborhood is Atlanta's foremost African-American business and residential district. Guided tours of the area originate at the **National Park Service Visitor Center,** at 450 Auburn Ave. across from the King Center. The visitor center is fronted by a beautifully landscaped plaza with a reflecting pool and outdoor amphitheater for Park Service programs.

　　**Birth Home of Martin Luther King, Jr.** *501 Auburn Ave. (at Hogue St.).* ☎ *404/ 331-3920. Admission free. (obtain tickets at 449 Auburn Ave.). Daily 10am–5pm. Closed*

# Central Atlanta

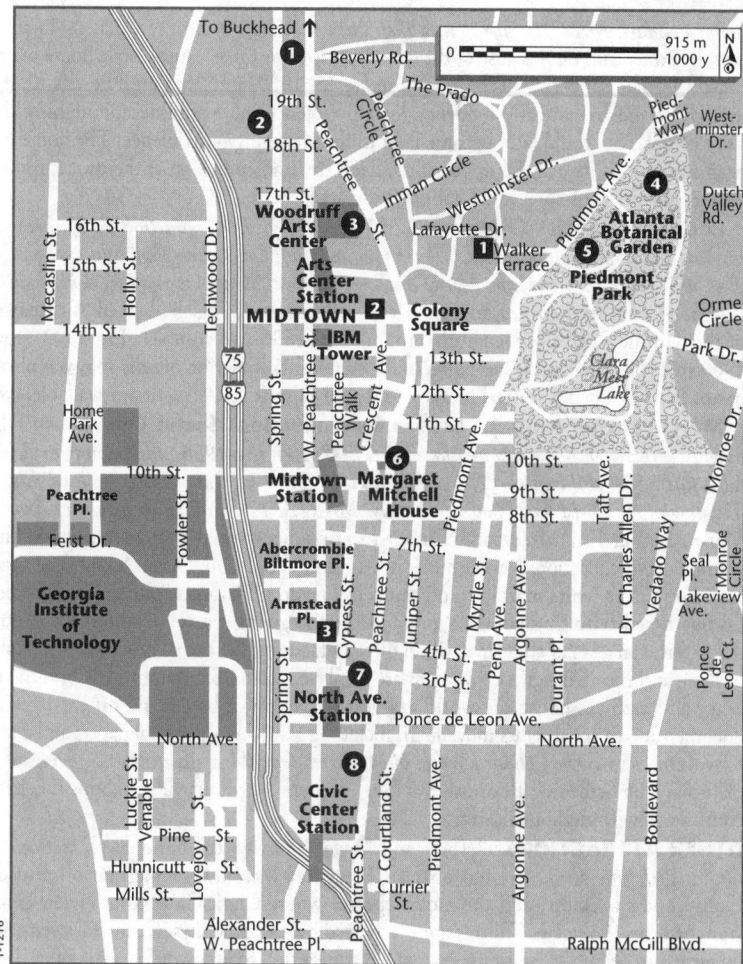

To Buckhead ↑
Beverly Rd.
The Prado
19th St.
18th St.
Piedmont Way
Westminster Dr.
17th St.
Woodruff Arts Center
Inman Circle
Lafayette Dr.
Atlanta Botanical Garden
Dutch Valley Rd.
Walker Terrace
Arts Center Station
Piedmont Park
Orme Circle
Park Dr.
MIDTOWN
Colony Square
IBM Tower
13th St.
Clara Meer Lake
12th St.
11th St.
Midtown Station
10th St.
9th St.
Margaret Mitchell House
8th St.
Peachtree Pl.
Ferst Dr.
Abercrombie Biltmore Pl.
7th St.
Georgia Institute of Technology
Armstead Pl.
Cypress St.
4th St.
3rd St.
North Ave. Station
Fox Theatre
North Ave.
Ponce de Leon Ave.
North Ave.
Civic Center Station
Pine St.
Hunnicutt St.
Mills St.
Currier St.
Alexander St.
W. Peachtree Pl.
Ralph McGill Blvd.

Home Park Ave.
Mecaslin St.
16th St.
15th St.
Holly St.
14th St.
Techwood Dr.
75
85
Spring St.
W. Peachtree St.
Peachtree Walk
Crescent Ave.
Piedmont Ave.
Peachtree St.
Juniper St.
Myrtle St.
Penn Ave.
Argonne Ave.
Durant Pl.
Dr. Charles Allen Dr.
Vedado Way
Taft Ave.
Seal Pl.
Lakeview Ave.
Ponce de Leon Ct.
Monroe Circle
Monroe Dr.
Westminster Dr.
Boulevard
Courtland St.
Piedmont Ave.
Argonne Ave.
Luckie St.
Venable St.
Lovejoy St.
Fowler St.
Spring St.

0    915 m / 1000 y
N

## Attractions
Atlanta Botanical Garden ⑤
Atlanta College of Art Gallery ③
Atlanta Museum ⑧
Center for Puppetry Arts ②
Fox Theatre ⑦
High Museum of Art ③
Margaret Mitchell House ⑥
Piedmont Park ④
Rhodes Memorial Hall ①

## Accommodations
Ansley Inn 1
Biltmore Suites II 3
Grand Hotel Atlanta 2

1-1216

319

*major holidays. MARTA: Five Points, then bus no. 3.* If you can get a ticket—in summer they often run out because of the crowds—visit this Queen Anne–style house where Martin Luther King, Jr., was born on January 15, 1929, and lived until he was 12. Although he showed an early tendency toward violence (he would decapitate his older sister's dolls), he would later become famous for preaching nonviolence. The home has been restored to its original appearance. Even the linoleum is an authentic reproduction. A great deal of King memorabilia is displayed here.

**Ebenezer Baptist Church.** *407–413 Auburn Ave.* ☎ *404/688-7263. Free admission, but donations welcomed. Mon–Fri 9am–4pm; Sat 11am–2pm; Sun only for services, at 7:45am and 10:45am. MARTA: King Memorial Station; then a long 8-block walk. Bus: no. 3 from stops on Peachtree St.* Dr. Martin Luther King, Jr., served as co-pastor of this Gothic Revival–style church, founded in 1886 and completed in 1922, from 1960 to 1968. Martin Luther King, Sr., a civil rights leader before his son, was also a pastor here. A taped historical message and a 10-minute guided tour are available.

**Martin Luther King, Jr. Center for Nonviolent Social Change.** *449 Auburn Ave. (between Boulevard and Jackson sts.).* ☎ *404/524-1956. Admission free. Videos, $1 adults, 50¢ children 6–12, free for children under 6. Daily 9am–5:30pm. Closed Thanksgiving, Christmas, New Year's Day. MARTA: Five Points, then take bus no. 3.* Martin Luther King, Jr.'s commitment to nonviolent social change lives on at this memorial and educational center under the direction of his son, Dexter Scott King. Outside, Dr. King's white marble crypt stands in Freedom Plaza, surrounded by a beautiful five-tiered reflecting pool, a symbol of the life-giving nature of water. An eternal flame burns in a small circular pavilion directly fronting the crypt. Inside, memorabilia of King and the civil rights movement are displayed in the Exhibition Hall, and the library and archives house the world's largest collection of books and other materials documenting the civil rights movement, including Dr. King's personal papers and a rare 87-volume set of *The Collected Works of Mahatma Gandhi*, a gift from the government of India. The Screening Room shows four excellent half-hour videos about Dr. King continuously throughout the day.

**OTHER ATTRACTIONS**   "Tara" and "Twelve Oaks," the fictional plantations in *Gone With the Wind*, existed only in Margaret Mitchell's imagination and on Hollywood's backlots, and the movie theater where Clark Gable and Vivien Leigh launched the 1939 classic film is gone, replaced by a marble skyscraper. But even with no great antebellum plantations, Atlanta has a great deal to keep you busy for a few days.

**Alonzo F. Herndon Home.** *587 University Place (between Vine and Walnut sts.).* ☎ *404/581-9813. Free admission, but donations welcomed. Tues–Sat 10am–4pm (tours on the hour). Closed major holidays. MARTA: Vine City.* Although born into slavery in 1858, Alonzo F. Herndon founded the Atlanta Life Insurance Company, the nation's largest black-owned insurer, and by 1895 was one of the richest black men in America. He built this lavish mansion in the Beaux Arts Neoclassical style, complete with a colonnaded entrance, and furnished it with the antiques and art he amassed. The building stands at the Vine Street edge of the Morris Brown University campus.

**Atlanta Heritage Row: The Museum at Underground.** *55 Upper Alabama St. (at Underground Atlanta).* ☎ *404/584-7879. Admission $3 adults, $2 children 5–18 and seniors 65 and older, free for children 4 and under. Tues–Sat 10am–5pm, Sun 1–5pm. MARTA: Five Points.* Part of the Underground Atlanta complex (see below), this museum celebrates Atlanta's colorful past, ranging from the siege by General Sherman through the "I Have a Dream" years of Martin Luther King, Jr., right up to the successful bid for the 1996 Summer Olympics.

**Atlanta History Center.** *130 W. Paces Ferry Rd. (at Slaton Dr.).* ☎ *404/814-4000. Admission $7 adults, $5 seniors and students 18 or older, $4 children 6–17, free for* *children 5 and under. Swan House and Tullie Smith Farm, each $1 extra. Mon–Sat 10am–5:30pm, Sun noon–5:30pm. MARTA: Lenox, then bus no. 23 to Peachtree St. and W. Paces Ferry Rd., then a 3-block walk.* From cotton fields back home to the coming of the railway, from the Civil War to the civil rights movement, Atlanta's history is vividly displayed in this vast museum. There's even a collection of memorabilia from *Gone With the Wind* author Margaret Mitchell. On the grounds, the Swan House and Gardens is considered to be the finest residential design of architect Philip Trammell Schutze (it's on the National Register of Historic Places), and the Tullie Smith Farm shows how Georgia farmers lived before the Civil War.

**Carter Presidential Center.** *One Copenhill, 453 Freedom Pkwy.* ☎ *404/331-3942. Admission $4 adults, $3 seniors, free for children under 16. Mon–Sat 9am–4:45pm, Sun noon–4:45pm.* Opened in 1986, this center is the site from which former U.S. President Jimmy Carter undertakes his work to advance peace and human rights. On the grounds is the **Jimmy Carter Library and Museum,** housing millions of documents, photos, gifts, and memorabilia of Carter's years in the White House, including a full-scale reproduction of the Oval Office. Exhibits follow Carter's career from his boyhood in Plains, Georgia, through his presidency. *Presidents,* a 30-minute film, looks at the crises and triumphs that marked his administration. Displays of gifts he and Mrs. Carter received range from silver, ivory, and crystal from heads of state to paintings and peanut carvings from around the world. The center is 2 miles east of the center of downtown Atlanta, with the skyline as a dramatic backdrop.

✪ **CNN Center.** *One CNN Center (at Marietta St. and Techwood Dr.).* ☎ *800/410-4CNN or 404/827-2300 for reservations and tickets. Admission $7 adults, $5 senior citizens 65 and over, $4.50 children 11 and under; $24.50 VIP tour. Tours every 35 minutes daily 9am–6pm. Studio and stores, daily 9:30am–7pm. Closed major holidays. MARTA: Omni.* In the heart of downtown, this is the global headquarters of Ted Turner's broadcasting empire, housing CNN, Headline News, and CNN International Studios. In addition to guided tours, you can reserve seating in the studio audience of *TalkBack Live,* CNN's weekday talk show; create your own tape by reading the news at an actual CNN anchor desk; and have your photo taken on the pitcher's mound with electronically created likenesses of your favorite Atlanta Braves players (Turner owns the team), or relaxing with Scarlett O'Hara and Rhett Butler in a scene from *Gone With the Wind* or with more than 40 other backgrounds from MGM movies (Turner owns the old MGM films, too). The Atrium features a food court and more than 40 retail stores, including one selling Braves paraphernalia. *Note:* Tickets are available on a first-come, first-served basis on the day of the tours. Arrive early for the tour you wish to take, since only 35 tickets are sold per tour, and they often sell out. Your best bet is to reserve in advance via American Express, MasterCard, or VISA.

✪ **Cyclorama.** *800 Cherokee Ave., in Grant Park.* ☎ *404/624-1071. Admission $5 adults, $4 seniors, $3 children 6–12, free for children under 6. Daily June–Labor Day 9:20am–5:30pm, the day after Labor Day–May 31 9:20am–4:30pm. Shows begin every half hour on the half hour starting at 9:30am. Closed Thanksgiving, Christmas, New Year's Day, and Martin Luther King, Jr. Day. MARTA: Five Points, then bus no. 97 (Georgia Ave.).* For a breathtaking view of the Battle of Atlanta, go by the neoclassical building that houses this 42-foot-high, 356-foot-circumference, 1880s painting with a three-dimensional foreground and special lighting, music, and sound effects. When you see this monumental work, you'll know why Sherman said, "War is hell." One of only three cycloramas in the United States, this one is an artistic and historical treasure that many visitors to Atlanta miss, erroneously thinking it is "strictly for kids." There are 15 shows daily.

**Fernbank Museum of Natural History.** *767 Clifton Rd. (off Ponce de León Ave.).* ☎ *404/378-0127. Admission $9.50 adults ($14.50 inclusive of an IMAX Theater* *ticket), $8 students and seniors ($12 inclusive of an IMAX Theater ticket), $7 children 3–12 ($10 inclusive of an IMAX Theater ticket), free for children 2 and under. IMAX Theater admission alone, $7 adults, $6 students and seniors, $5 children 3–12, free for children under 3. Mon–Sat 10am–5pm, Sun noon–5pm. The IMAX Theater is open until 9pm on Friday. Closed Thanksgiving and Christmas. MARTA: North Ave., then bus no. 2 to Clifton Way.* The largest museum of natural sciences in the Southeast, this $43-million complex abuts 65 acres of virgin forest. The permanent exhibition, "A Walk Through Time in Georgia," takes you through more than a dozen galleries exploring Georgia's scenic wonders. Adventures here include stepping inside a life-size kaleidoscope, and an IMAX Theater shows films on a six-story screen.

**Fernbank Science Center.** *156 Heaton Park Dr. NE (at Artwood Rd., off Ponce de León Ave.).* ☎ *404/378-4311. Admission free. Planetarium shows, $2 adults, $1 students, free for senior citizens. Note: Children under 5 not admitted to the planetarium. Mon 8:30am–5pm, Tues–Fri 8:30am–10pm, Sat 10am–5pm, Sun 1–5pm. Planetarium shows Tues–Fri at 8pm and Wed and Fri–Sun at 3pm. Observatory, Thurs–Fri 8pm (or whenever it gets dark) to 10:30pm, weather permitting. Forest trails, Sun–Fri 2–5pm, Sat 10am– 5pm. Greenhouse, Sun 1–5pm. Closed all school holidays.* Next to the 65-acre Fernbank Forest, this is a planetarium, observatory, and museum all rolled into one. It's a branch of the Fernbank Museum of Natural History (see above). A 1 1/2-mile forest trail showcases some of the state's most popular trees such as magnolias and dogwoods. Inside, you can see the original *Apollo 6* space capsule and an astronaut's spacesuit, as well as a replica of the Okefenokee Swamp in South Georgia. The greenhouse, 2 1/2 miles from the center, is open only on Sunday.

✪ **Fox Theatre.** *660 Peachtree St. NE.* ☎ *404/881-2100. Tours, $5 adults, $4 seniors, $3 students. The Atlanta Preservation Center conducts walking tours of the Fox Theatre and its surrounding area Mon and Thurs at 10am and Sat at 10 and 11:30am. Call to verify tour times before you go. MARTA: North Ave.* With its minarets and onion domes, this block-long Moorish–Egyptian extravaganza began life as a Shriners' temple back in 1916. Movie mogul William Fox turned it into a cinema in 1929 with a skyscape ceiling that could be transformed to sunrise, sunset, or starry night skies as the occasion demanded, and hung a striped bedouin canopy over the balcony. Unfortunately, the Great Depression forced it into bankruptcy. It reopened in the 1940s but closed its doors again in the 1970s. A civic effort saved the Fox from demolition and restored it to its former glory.

**Georgia State Capitol.** *Capitol Square.* ☎ *404/656-2844. Admission free. Mon– Fri 7:30am–5pm, Sat 10am–4pm, Sun noon–4pm. Tours given weekdays only at 10 and 11am and 1 and 2pm, but self-guided tours are possible at any time the capitol is open. Closed major holidays, including state holidays. Parking lot behind the capitol building on Capitol Ave. is closed to the public during legislative sessions; other lots are on Martin Luther King, Jr. Dr. at Central Ave. and on Courtland St. between Martin Luther King, Jr. Dr. and Central Ave. MARTA: Georgia State.* Built in 1884, the capitol building is distinguished by its gold-topped dome rising 237 feet above Atlanta. Besides a Hall of Fame (with busts of famous Georgians), and a Hall of Flags (U.S., state, and Confederate), it houses the **Georgia State Museum of Science and Industry,** which has collections of Georgia minerals and Indian artifacts, dioramas of famous places, and fish and wildlife exhibits. Legislators meet here in late January through February.

✪ **High Museum of Art.** *In the Woodruff Arts Center, 1280 Peachtree St. NE.* ☎ *404/733-4200, or 404/733-HIGH for 24-hour information. Admission $5 adults, $4 senior citizens and college students, $3 children 6–17. High Museum of Art members and children under 6 free. Daily 10am–5pm. MARTA: Arts Center.* Although not one of the world's great museums, this little gem is the finest in Georgia, showcasing first-rate traveling exhibitions along with its permanent collection of some 10,000 pieces, including works by John Singer Sargent, Mattie Lou O'Kelley, and Howard Finster. There's also an extensive collection of sub-Saharan African art and the Virginia Carroll Crawford Collection of American Decorative Arts, covering changing tastes from 1825 to 1917.

✪ **Michael C. Carlos Museum of Emory University.** *Kilgo St. (near the junction of Oxford and N. Decatur rds. on the Main Quadrangle of the Emory campus).* ☎ *404/727-4282. $3 donation suggested. Mon–Thurs 10am–5pm, Fri 10am–9pm, Sat 10am–5pm, Sun noon–5pm. Closed New Year's Day, Thanksgiving, and Christmas.* There's nothing in Georgia to equal this collection of Mediterranean, African tribal, and pre-Colombian art. Only a tenth of its collections are on display, but you can count on something interesting even if it's only a small piece of the Carlos pie. The 1916 Beaux Arts building is listed on the National Register of Historic Places. *Note:* Parking can be difficult on the Emory campus. Paid visitor parking is available in the Boisfeuillet Jones Center lot; free parking is allowed anywhere on campus except in 24-hour restricted areas or reserved spaces.

✪ **Oakland Cemetery.** *248 Oakland Ave. SE (main entrance at Oakland Ave. and Martin Luther King, Jr. Dr.).* ☎ *404/688-2107. Admission free. Daily sunrise–7pm (until 6pm in winter). Visitor Center, Mon–Fri 9am–5pm. Purchase an informative self-guided walking tour map brochure at the Visitor Center for $1.25. Parking inside the cemetery, near the Visitor Center. MARTA: King Memorial. Gone With the Wind* author Margaret Mitchell and golfing great Bobby Jones are buried in this 88-acre outdoor museum of funerary architecture. Founded 10 years before the Civil War, it also is the resting place of nearly 50,000 soldiers, both Confederate and Union. The visitor center distributes a self-guided walking-tour map and brochure for $1.25.

✪ **Underground Atlanta.** *Bounded by Peachtree, Wall and Washington sts., and Martin Luther King, Jr. Dr.* ☎ *404/523-2311. Admission free. Mon–Sat 10am–9:30pm, Sun noon–6pm. Most restaurants and clubs stay open until midnight (or later) nightly. MARTA: Five Points Station (a pedestrian tunnel goes directly to the underground).* Right in town, Underground Atlanta is the city's birthplace, where the Zero Milepost of the Western and Atlantic Railroad was planted in 1837. In post–Civil War days, railroad viaducts were built over its rococo buildings, which then lay deserted for the better part of a century. A group of Atlanta businesspeople restored the crumbling area in the 1960s into an authentic, completely charming picture of Atlanta in the 1800s. It includes more than 200 establishments, including shops, restaurants, and nightspots. There is a charge for parking in the garages off Martin Luther King, Jr. Dr., but it's reduced if you get your ticket validated at a store or restaurant.

**World of Coca-Cola.** *55 Martin Luther King, Jr. Dr. SW (at Central Ave., adjacent to Underground Atlanta).* ☎ *404/676-5151. Admission $4.50 adults, $3.50 seniors 55 and over, $2.75 children 6–12, free for children under 6. Mon–Sat 10am–8:30pm, Sun noon–5pm. Closed New Year's Day, the second Sun in Jan, Easter, Thanksgiving, Christmas Eve, and Christmas Day. MARTA: Five Points.* Its recipe still a secret, Atlanta-born Coca-Cola has been consumed by people all over the world. "Coke" memorabilia ranges from endorsements from fabled stars of yesterday, including those by actors Clark Gable and Claudette Colbert, to campy commercials sung by the Supremes. The pavilion boasts the most innovative outdoor neon sign ever created for a company, an 11-ton extravaganza hanging 18 feet above the entrance. There's a parking garage on Central Avenue off Martin Luther King, Jr. Drive.

**PARKS & GARDENS**    Sprawling across 30 acres of Piedmont Park, the ✪ **Atlanta Botanical Garden,** at Piedmont Avenue and the Prado (☎ **404/876-5859**), has been a hit with Atlantans ever since it opened in 1977. It's their most tranquil urban retreat, embracing a 15-acre hardwood forest. A highlight is the glass-walled Dorothy Chapman Fuqua Conservatory. Admission is $6 for adults, $5 for seniors, $3 for students, and free for children 4 and under. It's open Tues–Sun 9am–7pm (until 6pm off-season).

**BEST BETS FOR KIDS**   Be sure to take the kids for a day at the Fernbank Museum of Natural History and the Fernbank Science Center (see "Other Attractions," above). Also on the science front, ✪ **SciTrek (Science and Technology Museum of Atlanta),** 395 Piedmont Ave. between Ralph McGill Boulevard and Pine Street (☎ **404/ 522-5500**), houses more than 150 interactive exhibits, including KIDSPACE, geared to the 2- to 7-year-old set.

**Zoo Atlanta,** 800 Cherokee Ave. in Grant Park (☎ **404/624-5600**), is an exciting and creatively run facility, with animals housed in large open enclosures simulating their natural habitats. There are frequent animal demonstrations, African storytelling, and educational programs. The **Yellow River Wildlife Game Ranch,** 4525 Hwy. 78 in Lilburn (☎ **770/972-6643**), offers a chance to view, pet, feed, and generally mingle with some 600 animals (always including quite a few babies) living in open enclosures or right out in the open.

**Wren's Nest,** 1050 Ralph David Abernathy Blvd., 2 blocks from Ashby Street (☎ **404/753-7735**), is the former home of Joel Chandler Harris, who chronicled the wily deeds of Br'er Rabbit and Br'er Fox. Call ahead to find out when storyteller-in-residence Akbar Imhotep is at work; it's a real treat. Even if you don't have kids in tow, consider visiting the **Center for Puppetry Arts,** 1404 Spring St. NW, at 18th Street (☎ **404/873-3089;** box office 404/873-3391), which is dedicated to expanding public awareness of puppetry as a fine art (Kermit the Frog cut the ribbon when it opened in 1978). Some of the riveting, elaborately staged puppet shows are family oriented; others, with nighttime showings, are geared to adults.

If a theme park appeals, **Six Flags Over Georgia,** 7561 Six Flags Rd. SW, in Austell at the Six Flags exit off I-20W (☎ **770/948-9290**), is one of Georgia's major family attractions, with eight themed areas reflecting the historical heritage of the region. The Spanish section contains Bugs Bunny World, which is especially geared to young children. Thrill rides include several wet ones. There's another 40 acres of wet-and-wild fun at **White Water,** 240 N. Cobb Pkwy. NE in Marietta at exit 113 off I-75 (☎ **770/ 424-9283**). Next door is **American Adventures** (☎ **770/424-9283**), an indoor/outdoor family amusement park featuring 15 children's rides including a classic carousel.

**SHOPPING**   There's nothing in the American Southeast to equal Atlanta as a shopping bazaar, primarily because the area has one seemingly endless suburban mall after another. For high fashion—and high prices too—Atlantans head for **Buckhead,** 8 miles north of downtown. There are at least 200 specialty stores in the Greater Buckhead area, and **Lenox Square Mall** has branches of Neiman Marcus and the like. Virtually across the street is the exclusive **Phipps Plaza,** with upscale branches of such stores as Tiffany & Co., Saks Fifth Avenue, and Lord & Taylor. Also in Buckhead, **Oxford Books,** in Peachtree Battle Shopping Center, 2345 Peachtree Rd. NE (☎ **404/364-2700**), is the largest independently owned bookstore in the Southeast.

But if you'd like something a little more imaginative, head for **Virginia–Highland,** which has been referred to as "New York's SoHo a decade ago." Around the junction of Highland Avenue at Virginia Avenue and Ponce de León Avenue; it offers five different art galleries, at least 30 restaurants, a scattering of artsy cafes, and endless rows of stores devoted to clothing, flea-market junk, antiques, jewelry, and everything from high to low camp.

For **antiques,** one of the densest concentrations of stores in Greater Atlanta lies near the T-junction of Peachtree Road and Broad Street, in the northeastern suburb of Chamblee, 17 miles from central Atlanta.

In Tanger, 77 miles northeast of Atlanta at exit 53 off I-85, **Tanger Factory Outlet** (☎ 706/335-4537) is a destination for dozens of tour buses bringing hordes of shoppers to browse its 100-plus factory stores.

**Markets**   The ✪ **Atlanta State Farmer's Market,** 16 Forest Pkwy. in Forest Park (☎ 404/366-6910), is the largest food outlet in the Southeast, covering 146 acres. About half the vendors insist on selling only to wholesalers, but the other half sell to the public, purveying meats, poultry, plants, flowers, fruits, vegetables, and a staggering variety of home-canned jams, pickles, and relishes. Most vendors don't accept credit or charge cards. Open 24 hours daily.

Out in Decatur, east of the city, the ✪ **Dekalb Farmer's Market,** 3000 E. Ponce de León Ave. (☎ 404/377-6400), isn't strictly a farmer's market, but it is one of the largest, best-stocked, and most atmospheric grocery stores in Atlanta, rustically outfitted like your fantasy version of a country fair.

## ACCOMMODATIONS

Downtown hotels primarily cater to business and convention travelers, but they are close to many key attractions. Midtown hotels tend to be low-key, attracting families and other visitors. Joggers and outdoor enthusiasts will appreciate Midtown's Piedmont Park, and the Woodruff Arts Center is here. Buckhead is the optimum hotel location, combining the quiet residential appeal of Midtown accommodations with the luxury of downtown hotels. Many of Atlanta's best restaurants are close by.

Chain hotels are numerous here. In the city center you'll find the Clarion Downtown, Comfort Inn, and Days Inn Downtown. Midtown has the Comfort Inn Buckhead, Days Inn Peachtree, and Marriott's Fairfield Inn Midtown. And in Buckhead there's the Holiday Inn at Lenox. Econo Lodge and Motel 6 both have inexpensive units on I-20, a 10-minute drive east of downtown.

Most hotels and motels are busiest weekdays but offer attractive weekend deals. You'll pay a 13% hotel and motel tax.

✪ **Ansley Inn.** *253 15th St. NE (at Lafayette Dr., between Piedmont Ave. and Peachtree St., Midtown), Atlanta, GA 30309.* ☎ *800/446-5416 or 404/872-9000. Fax 404/892-2318. 33 rms, 1 cottage. $115–$450 double; $200 two-bedroom cottage (sleeps six). Additional person $10 extra. Rates include continental breakfast. AE, DC, DISC, ER, MC, V. MARTA: Arts Center.* Atlanta's most romantic hotel occupies a 1907 yellow-brick Tudor mansion amid magnolias and oaks in Ansley Park, one of the city's most beautiful and chic residential areas. Antiques and art add to a refined, hospitable ambience. Elegant rooms have wet bars and whirlpool tubs; some have lofty cathedral ceilings and working fireplaces. The hotel provides a concierge, complimentary newspaper, and health club privileges ($10 a day). An outdoor pool/sundeck is in the works.

**Biltmore Peachtree Hotel.** *330 Peachtree St. NE (between Baker St. and Ralph McGill Blvd., Downtown), Atlanta, GA 30308.* ☎ *800/241-4288 or 404/577-1980. Fax 404/688-3706. 94 rms. $59–$250 double (high end reflects major special events). Rates include continental breakfast. Children 16 and under stay free in parents' room. AE, CB, DC, DISC, MC, V. Self-parking $6.50. MARTA: Peachtree Center or Civic Center.* This pleasant hotel offers a lot for the price. Rooms are large and equipped with a desk, two armchairs or a sofa, and a compact kitchen. Complimentary continental breakfast is served in a comfortably furnished room off the lobby or outdoors at patio tables. Free *USA Today* in lobby.

**Biltmore Suites.** *30 5th St. NE (at W. Peachtree St., Midtown), Atlanta, GA 30308.* ☎ *800/822-0824 or 404/874-0824. Fax 404/458-5384. 60 suites. $75–$110 studios and one-bedroom suites; $99–$165 two-bedroom suites. Rates include continental breakfast. AE, DISC, MC, V. Self-parking $5. MARTA: North Ave.* In its heyday, this

1924-vintage, white-columned building hosted *GWTW* stars Vivien Leigh and Olivia de Havilland. Refurbished in 1986, its lovely suites sport fully equipped kitchens, glossy oak floors, brass bathroom fixtures, French doors, and more. Extras include a complimentary shuttle to/from airport and anywhere within a 5-mile radius of the hotel, health club privileges, and coin-op laundry.

**Cheshire Motor Inn.** *1865 Cheshire Bridge Rd. NE (between Wellborne Dr. NE and Manchester St. NE, Midtown), Atlanta, GA 30324.* ☎ *800/827-9628 or 404/ 872-9628. 58 rms. $52–$55 double (may be higher during special events). Extra person $6. Children under 12 stay free in parents' room. AE, DC, DISC, MC, V. MARTA: Take bus no. 27 from Lindbergh Station, which is about 1 mile away.* The Lacy family has been providing homelike hospitality at this attractive motel for decades. Though not fancy, their rooms are spacious and nicely kept. The famous Colonnade restaurant is here (see "Dining," below). The restaurant and motel are quite respectable despite several sleazy bars nearby. Free newspapers and coffee are in the lobby.

**Grand Hotel Atlanta.** *75 14th St. (between Peachtree and West Peachtree sts., Midtown), Atlanta, GA 30309.* ☎ *800/952-0702 or 404/881-9898. Fax 404/888-8669. 228 rms, 18 suites. Sun–Thurs, $170–$275 double; Fri–Sat, $118–$138 double; $410– $1,500 suite. Additional person $20 extra. Children under 18 stay free in parents' room. Inquire about packages. AE, CB, DC, DISC, ER, JCB, MC, V. Self-parking $11.50; valet parking $15. MARTA: Arts Center.* Atlanta's trendiest hotel sports Old World elegance. Earth-toned accommodations come with luxuries like gilt-framed artworks lit by gallery lights. The notable Florencia Restaurant is here, as is the Café Opera, the Segovia Bar, and Overtures lounge, the latter overlooking a lavish grand staircase. Service is as exceptional as the setting. Facilities include a complete health club, large indoor pool, outdoor sundeck, whirlpool, steam room, sauna, full-service hair/beauty salon, extensive business services, and gift shop.

**Hyatt Regency Atlanta.** *265 Peachtree St. NE (between Baker and Harris sts., Downtown), Atlanta, GA 30303.* ☎ *800/233-1234 or 404/577-1234. Fax 404/ 588-4137. 1,279 rms, 58 suites. $250–$300 double; $405–$690 suite. Children under 18 stay free in parents' room. Packages and promotional rates often available. AE, CB, DC, DISC, ER, JCB, MC, V. Valet parking $15. MARTA: Peachtree Center.* Designed in 1967 by famed Atlanta architect John Portman, this hotel was the prototype for hotel design throughout America. It features a 23-story atrium lobby filled with lush greenery thriving under a lofty skylight. Rooms feature plush modern furnishings (expense account junkies like those in the International Tower with panoramic views of Atlanta). The blue dome capping the Polaris revolving rooftop restaurant is a landmark on the city's skyline. Facilities include full health club, indoor pool with hot tub, business center, and fitness room. A covered walkway connects to the Peachtree Center shopping mall.

**JW Marriott at Lenox.** *3300 Lenox Rd. NE (a few blocks east of Peachtree Rd. at E. Paces Ferry Rd., Buckhead), Atlanta, GA 30326.* ☎ *800/228-9290 or 404/262-3344. Fax 404/262-8603. 361 rms, 10 suites. Mon–Thurs, $155–$230 for up to four people; Fri–Sun, $124–$230 per room. AE, CB, DC, DISC, ER, MC, V. Self-parking $7; valet parking $12. MARTA: Lenox.* This striking, luxurious Marriott enjoys one of the best locations in town. Rooms are charmingly furnished with Chippendale-style mahogany pieces and gilt-framed watercolors of Buckhead mansions. Picture windows offer great views of Buckhead or the downtown skyline. There's a restaurant and two lounges. Guests enjoy the large Roman bathlike indoor pool, health club, full business center, and pastry shop.

**Lenox Inn.** *3387 Lenox Rd. NE (between Peachtree and E. Paces Ferry rds.), Atlanta, GA 30326.* ☎ *800/241-0200 or 404/261-5500. Fax 404/261-6140. 174 rms, 6 suites. $79–$125 double. Additional person $15 extra. Children under 18 stay free in parents'* *room. AE, CB, DC, MC, V. Free parking. MARTA: Lenox.* A great bargain, this cost-conscious annex of the Terrace Garden Inn (see below) sits opposite Lennox Square Mall in the heart of Buckhead. Simple yet comfortable bedrooms have Early American themes. Not all of the two- and three-story buildings here have elevators. There are two outdoor swimming pools. Local phone calls are free.

**Marriott Residence Inn Buckhead.** *2960 Piedmont Rd. NE (just south of Pharr Rd., Buckhead), Atlanta, GA 30305.* ☎ *800/331-3131 or 404/239-0677. Fax 404/262-9638. 136 suites. $135 studio suite (for up to three); $169 penthouse suite (for up to six). Rates include breakfast. Weekly rates available. AE, DC, DISC, MC, V. MARTA: Take the no. 5 bus from Lindbergh Station to corner of Pharr Rd. and Piedmont Rd., about a half block away.* This home-away-from-home is marvelous for families. Accommodations include kitchens and comfortable living-room areas. About half the suites have working fireplaces. Five attractively landscaped acres backed by woods surround the property. The hotel has an outdoor pool and adjoining whirlpool, coin-op washers/dryers, outdoor barbecue grills, sports courts, and complimentary use of a nearby health club.

**Ritz-Carlton Buckhead.** *3434 Peachtree Rd. NE (at Lenox Rd., Buckhead), Atlanta, GA 30326.* ☎ *800/241-3333 or 404/237-2700. Fax 404/239-0078. 524 rms, 29 suites. Mon–Thurs, $170–$260 double; Fri–Sun, $155–$260 double. Club Floor, $260–$495 double. Children under 12 stay free in parents' room. Packages available. AE, DC, DISC, JCB, MC, V. Self-parking $8; valet parking $12. MARTA: Buckhead or Lenox.* Ritz fans will find the familiar Persian carpets, cut-crystal chandeliers, afternoon tea, and snap-to service here, plus a location opposite two upscale malls and near Buckhead's fine restaurants and nightspots. Large bay windows augment the rooms' exquisite decor. The Dining Room is one of Atlanta's finest, the mahogany-walled Lobby Lounge has a glowing fireplace, the Café offers a lavish Sunday brunch and weekend dancing, and Expresso's has indoor and outdoor seating. Facilities include a full business center, swimming and fitness center, steam and sauna rooms, Jacuzzi, and gift shop.

The **Ritz-Carlton Atlanta,** 181 Peachtree St. NE, Atlanta, GA 30303 (☎ **800/241-3333** or 404/659-0400; fax 404/688-0400), is equally elegant and more convenient for doing business or seeing the sights downtown. Rates are the same as the Ritz-Carlton Buckhead.

✪ **Suite Hotel Underground Atlanta.** *54 Peachtree St. SW (Downtown), Atlanta, GA 30303.* ☎ *800/477-5549 or 404/223-5555. Fax 404/223-0467. 156 suites. Mon–Thurs, $165–$250 suite; Fri–Sat, $89–$250 suite. (Higher rate applies for suite with Jacuzzi.) Children up to 16 stay free in parents' suite. Packages available. AE, DC, DISC, JCB, MC, V. Valet parking $12. MARTA: Five Points.* On the top level of Underground Atlanta, this all-suites hotel is elegant and understated. Each luxuriously appointed suite has a small living room, a separate bedroom and marble bath (some with Jacuzzis), wet bar, refrigerator, two TVs, and three phones. Many have views of the downtown skyline. A dining room serves Southern fare. The hotel has limited room service, a complimentary shuttle within a 5-block radius of the hotel, a business center, and health club privileges ($10).

**Summerfield Suites Hotel Buckhead.** *505 Pharr Rd. (about a block off Piedmont Rd., Buckhead), Atlanta, GA 30305.* ☎ *800/833-4353 or 404/262-7880. Fax 404/262-3734. 88 suites. $109–$159 one-bedroom suite (for up to three); $129–$189 two-bedroom suite (for up to five). (The higher rates apply during special events.) Weekend rates and summer packages available. AE, DISC, JCB, MC, V. Free parking. MARTA: Take the no. 5 bus from Lindbergh Station to corner of Pharr Rd. and Piedmont Rd., about a block away.* This is a great Buckhead location at less than usual Buckhead prices. Several fine restaurants, nightspots, and a park with tennis courts are nearby. Accommodations include a spacious one- or two-bedroom suite with a fully equipped kitchen. Extras include a complimentary shuttle within a 3-mile radius of the hotel and to MARTA rail, a medium-size outdoor pool, Jacuzzi, exercise room, convenience store/gift shop, and coin-op laundry.

**Terrace Garden Inn.** *3405 Lenox Rd. NE (between Peachtree and E. Paces Ferry rds., Buckhead), Atlanta, GA 30326.* ☎ *800/241-8260 or 404/261-9250. Fax 404/ 848-7391. 360 rms, 6 suites. Mon–Thurs, $135–$190 double; Fri–Sun, $95–$150 double. Children under 18 stay free in parents' room. AE, DC, DISC, MC, V. Self-parking $5 in covered garage. MARTA: Lenox.* This stylish hotel offers abundant services and facilities plus a great location opposite Lenox Square Mall. Rooms are furnished with French country and 18th-century–reproduction mahogany pieces (some have four-poster or brass beds). The two-level, garden-themed Café is one of Atlanta's prettiest hotel dining rooms. Facilities include an extensive health club with indoor pool, outdoor pool with waterfalls, car and airline desks, and gift shop.

**TraveLodge Atlanta Downtown.** *311 Courtland St. NE (between Baker St. and Ralph McGill Blvd., Downtown), Atlanta, GA 30303.* ☎ *800/578-7878 or 404/ 659-4545. Fax 404/659-5934. 71 rms. $64–$114 double. Rates include continental breakfast. Additional person $8 extra. Children under 18 stay free in parents' room. AE, CB, DC, DISC, ER, MC, V. Free self-parking. MARTA: Peachtree Center.* Family operated since 1964, this small TraveLodge has clean and fresh rooms with new furniture, carpet, drapes, and bedspreads. Each is equipped with a safe and a coffeemaker. Numerous restaurants are within walking distance. Free daily newspapers are another plus. The hotel has a heated outdoor pool and offers use of a nearby health club ($10 a day).

**OTHER ACCOMMODATIONS**   Atlanta B&Bs range from modest, middle-class houses to some of the city's finest residences. Among the best is the cozy, somewhat eccentric **Beverly Hills Inn,** 65 Sheridan Dr. NE, Atlanta, GA 30305 (☎ **800/ 331-8520** or 404/233-8520; fax 404/233-8520), an English-style establishment on a choice parcel near Buckhead's shops and restaurants. The **Buckhead Bed & Breakfast Inn,** 70 Lenox Pointe NE, Atlanta, GA 30324 (☎ **404/261-8284;** fax 404/237-9224), is a new, elegant property and one of the best bargains available in this pricey neighborhood.

**Gaslight Inn,** 1001 St. Charles Ave., Atlanta, GA 30306 (☎ **404/875-1001;** fax 404/876-1001), is a charming Craftsman-style 1913 house in convenient and charming Virginia–Highland. In Midtown, **Woodruff Bed & Breakfast Inn,** 223 Ponce de León Ave. NE, Atlanta, GA 30308 (☎ **800/473-9449** or 404/875-9449; fax 404/ 875-2882), occupies a three-story white-brick Victorian house built in 1906 but used in the 1950s as a house of ill repute (present owners display light boards used to keep track of the rooms in use). Also in Midtown, the **Shellmont Bed and Breakfast Lodge,** 821 Piedmont Ave. NE, Atlanta, GA 30308 (☎ **404/872-9290;** fax 404/872-5379), looks from the outside like a Wedgwood fairy-tale house embellished with ribbons, bows, garlands, and shells. Built in 1891, it's on the National Register of Historic Places.

For more options, contact **Bed & Breakfast Atlanta,** 1801 Piedmont Ave., Suite 208, Atlanta, GA 30324 (☎ **800/96-PEACH** or 404/875-0525; fax 404/875-9672). There's no booking fee, and American Express, MasterCard, and Visa are accepted.

## DINING

Not too many years ago, most of what was offered in Atlanta's restaurants was standard, fairly uninventive American fare or down-home Southern cooking. The Colonnade and Thelma's Kitchen still turn out some of the best Southern cooking you'll ever put in your mouth, but the current rage in many kitchens is to take heirloom recipes and give them a contemporary twist. So pork chops might be stuffed with eggplant and andouille sausage, collard greens sautéed and seasoned with balsamic vinegar, and the comfy, familiar grits spiked with Stilton.

**Atlanta Fish Market.** *265 Pharr Rd. (between Peachtree Rd. and N. Fulton Dr.), Buckhead.* ☎ *404/262-3165. Reservations recommended. Main courses $12.50–$27.50 (most under $16); lunch sandwiches $8–$10. AE, CB, DC, DISC, ER, MC, V. Mon–Fri 11:30am–2:30pm; Mon–Thurs 5:30–11pm, Fri–Sat 5:30pm–midnight, Sun 5–10pm. The Geechee Crab Lounge and Porch are open daily 2:30–5:30pm for light fare and desserts. Complimentary valet parking. MARTA: Buckhead. SEAFOOD.* Even Madonna and Gov. Zell Miller agree that the pecan-crusted catfish and the Carolina mountain trout here are the best in Atlanta. Locals are won over by the grilled halibut over creamy grits and garnished with shards of apple-smoked bacon. The jazzy, 475-seat dining room is like a Southern train station in 1902.

**Bacchanalia.** *3125 Piedmont Rd., Buckhead.* ☎ *404/365-3125. Reservations essential. Four-course fixed-price menu $35; $55 with accompanying wines. AE, DC, MC, V. Tues–Thurs 6–9:30pm, Fri–Sat 6–10pm. Closed Christmas Eve–New Year's Eve and 2 weeks in Aug. Free parking in adjacent lot. NEW AMERICAN.* The most inventive cooking in Atlanta draws discriminating diners to this 1920s house and its quartet of intimate dining rooms with brick fireplaces. The portions are small in size but big on flavor. Some recipes have been criticized as "pretentiously experimental," but try the charred Georgia quail served over a mound of creamy collard greens.

**Bone's.** *3130 Piedmont Rd. NE (half a block below Peachtree Rd.), Buckhead.* ☎ *404/ 237-2663. Reservations required. Main courses $9–$35 at lunch, lunch specials $10–$20; main courses $20–$35 at dinner. AE, CB, DC, DISC, MC, V. Mon–Fri 11:30am–2:30pm; daily 6–11pm. Closed most major holidays. Complimentary valet parking. MARTA: Buckhead. STEAK/SEAFOOD.* Atlanta's best and most famous steak house, Bone's is a top power-lunch venue for the expense-account crowd, who are provided with notepads and phones at the midday meal. As many deals as steaks are cut here (yes, that's Ted Turner). Bone's flies in Maine lobster and serves fresh Gulf Coast crabmeat and shrimp.

**Brasserie Le Coze.** *In Lennox Square Mall, 3393 Peachtree Rd. NE, Buckhead.* ☎ *404/266-1440. Reservations recommended. Main courses at lunch $9–$16, sandwiches $7–$9; main courses at dinner $17–$22. AE, DC, MC, V. Main dining room, Mon–Thurs 11:30am–2:30pm and 5:30–10pm; Fri 11:30am–3pm and 5:30–11pm; Sat 11:30am–3:30pm and 5:30–11pm. Bar and cafe, Mon–Thurs 11:30am–10pm, Fri–Sat 11:30am–11pm. Complimentary valet parking. MARTA: Lenox. TRADITIONAL FRENCH.* The fish is whisked from the fire and served perfectly at this Paris bistro. Believe it or not, some foodies come here for the perfectly done roast chicken with its crisp skin and the best mashed potatoes in Atlanta—creamy and laced with butter and chives.

**۞ Buckhead Diner.** *3073 Piedmont Rd. (at E. Paces Ferry Rd.), Buckhead.* ☎ *404/ 262-3336. Reservations not accepted. Snacks, sandwiches, and salads $4.50–$10; main courses $8–$13 at lunch, $9–$18 at dinner. AE, CB, DC, DISC, MC, V. Mon–Sat 11am–midnight, Sun (including brunch) 10:30am–10pm. Complimentary valet parking. MARTA: Buckhead. AMERICAN.* You'll know that this is no ordinary diner when a valet rushes to park your car and you find yourself waiting in line with the likes of Elton John or Princess Caroline of Monaco. Try the crisp spicy barbecued oysters served over creamy succotash with a Cajun rémoulade on the side.

**Ciboulette.** *1529 Piedmont Ave. NE (at Monroe Dr.), Midtown.* ☎ *404/874-7600. Reservations recommended. Main courses $15.95–$23.95. AE, CB, DC, MC, V.*

*Mon–Thurs 6–10pm, Fri–Sat 5:30–11pm. Free parking in lot out front. MODERN FRENCH.* The stylish Ciboulette offers some of the city's most inventive French cuisine in a posh and comfortable setting to which an open kitchen adds energy. The house specialties are fish and game, and there are always several well-chosen appetizer and entree specials on the changing menu.

**City Grill.** *50 Hurt Plaza (at Edgewood Ave.), Downtown.* ☎ *404/524-2489. Reservations recommended. Main courses, salads, and sandwiches $7.50–$15 at lunch; main courses $17–$26 at dinner. AE, CB, DC, MC, V. Mon–Fri 11:30am–2:30pm; Mon–Sat 5:30–10pm. Complimentary valet parking at dinner. MARTA: Peachtree Center or Five Points. CONTEMPORARY SOUTHERN.* One of Atlanta's most opulent restaurants and a focus for power lunches, City Grill is entered via a gold-leaf-adorned rotunda of the lavishly refurbished Hurt Building. It's a fitting backdrop for the dazzling, Southern-inspired creations of chef Roger Kaplan, such as blue crab cakes on corn chowder and country grits spoonbread.

**Colonnade.** *1879 Cheshire Bridge Rd. NE (between Wellborne Dr. and Manchester St.), Buckhead.* ☎ *404/874-5642. Reservations not accepted. Main courses $6–$9 at lunch, $8–$14 at dinner. No credit cards. Mon–Sat 11am–2:30pm; Mon–Thurs 5–9pm, Fri–Sat 5–10pm; Sun 11am–9pm. MARTA: Lindbergh, then bus no. 27. SOUTHERN.* An Atlanta favorite since 1927, this friendly joint offers great value with its down-home cookery and gargantuan portions. Inexpensive steaks, chops, seafood, and the inevitable Southern fried chicken come with vegetables boiled all day long. One regular comes here every day to order sugar-cured ham with red-eye gravy.

**Mary Mac's Tea Room.** *224 Ponce de León Ave. NE (at Myrtle St.), Midtown.* ☎ *404/876-1800. Reservations not accepted. Dinner $8–$13. No credit cards. Mon–Sat 11am–9pm, Sun 8am–5pm. MARTA: North Ave. SOUTHERN.* You might see Georgia's governor at this landmark where the fried chicken and country ham are really good. So are the fresh but overcooked vegetables and the fresh-from-the-oven breads. Best bet: sautéed North Carolina rainbow trout. For dessert, don't dare order anything but the fresh Georgia peach cobbler.

**Mick's.** *In Underground Atlanta, corner of Pryor and Alabama sts., Downtown.* ☎ *404/ 525-2825. Reservations not accepted. Main courses $7–$13; burgers, salads, and sandwiches $4–$8. AE, CB, DC, MC, V. Mon–Thurs 11am–11pm, Fri–Sat 11am–1am, Sun noon–10:30pm. MARTA: Five Points. AMERICAN.* One of the best of a dozen or so Underground eateries, Mick's is a Victorian-themed two-story restaurant with a gaslit, wrought-iron enclosed porch for viewing the indoor "street" action. It's best known for solid casual fare from snacks to full meals. Nachos here are as good as they get. Other Mick's are at 557 Peachtree St. (☎ 404/875-6425), 229 Peachtree St. (☎ 404/688-6425), the Lenox Square Mall (☎ 404/262-6425), and 2110 Peachtree Rd. (☎ 404/351-6425).

**Pano's & Paul's.** *In West Paces Ferry Shopping Center, 1232 W. Paces Ferry Rd. (at Northside Pkwy.), Buckhead.* ☎ *404/261-3662. Reservations essential. Main courses $15.95–$32. AE, CB, DC, DISC, MC, V. Mon–Sat 6–11pm. Free parking. AMERICAN/ CONTINENTAL.* Pano Karatassos and Paul Albrecht have provided big-city sophistication at their posh, almost bordello-like eatery since 1979. Their impeccable service, refined cuisine, and extensive wine list drown out complaints that their place is snobby and overpriced. The broiled dry-aged sirloin steak or the roast double beef filet is about the best you'll get in Atlanta.

✪ **Riviera.** *519 E. Paces Ferry Rd. NE (one block west of Piedmont Rd.), Buckhead.* ☎ *404/262-7112. Reservations essential. Main courses $19–$24. AE, DC, MC, V. Mon–Thurs 6–10pm, Fri–Sat 5:30–11pm. MARTA: Buckhead. FRENCH.* Opened in 1995, this is the most elegant French restaurant in Atlanta, with top-notch cuisine that has taken the city's *grande bourgeoisie* by storm. It's the domain of master chef Jean Banchet, who learned his art from Paul Bocuse and knows how to make classic cuisine intriguing and unforgettable. Set in an old house, it's casual and unassuming.

**Thelma's Kitchen.** *764 Marietta St. NW (just north of Means St.), Downtown.* ☎ *404/688-5855. Everything under $7. No credit cards. Mon–Fri 7:30am–4:30pm. Free parking out front and on neighboring streets. Or take the no. 1 Howell Mill bus from downtown. TRADITIONAL SOUTHERN.* Sitting opposite the Georgia Tech campus, Thelma's serves up good Southern-style home cooking dirt cheap. The general ambience is that of a grade-school cafeteria, but the fried chicken is like it ought to be. There's also excellent country fried steak, barbecued ribs, fried fish, and Brunswick stew, as well as daily specials.

**OTHER DINING** Some 16,000 people a day munch hot dogs, hamburgers, french fries, and 300 gallons of chili at **The Varsity,** 61 North Ave. at Spring St. (☎ **404/ 881-1706**), the world's largest drive-in, which opened in 1928. Service is fast both carside and inside, and the prices definitely are low. Yes, the orange freezes are just like the ones you had after the senior prom.

## ATLANTA AFTER DARK

Atlanta sizzles after dark, with numerous music clubs featuring jazz, rock, country, and blues. It also offers a comprehensive cultural scene, including symphony, ballet, opera, and theater productions. And major artists headline regularly at Atlanta's many large-scale performance facilities.

To find out what's on during your stay, consult the *Atlanta Journal–Constitution.* Its "Preview" section, published every Friday, covers the entire scene. The newpaper's Saturday "Leisure" section offers mini–movie reviews and extensive listings of events for the weekend and the week ahead. Or pick up copies of *Where, Key: This Week in Atlanta, After Hours,* and *Creative Loafing,* free publications you'll see in stores, restaurants, and other places around town. Another source is the **ARTS Hotline** (☎ **404/ 853-3278**), a 24-hour recording that provides up-to-the-minute listings of concerts, plays, films, and other cultural events.

Tickets to many performances are handled by **Ticketmaster** (☎ **404/249-6400,** or 404/817-8700 to charge tickets). Half-price tickets to some events are available the day of the performance at the Ticketmaster location in Blockbuster Music and Video, 2099 Peachtree Rd. NE (☎ **404/605-7131**). These tickets are not available by phone, they must be paid for with cash, and a surcharge is applied. Call ☎ **404/614-1212** to check on availability.

**THE PERFORMING ARTS** The ✪ **Atlanta Symphony Orchestra,** performing in the Woodruff Arts Center, 1280 Peachtree St. NE, at 15th Street (☎ **404/733-4900,** or 404/733-5000 for the box office), under Music Director Yoel Levi, is one of America's acclaimed orchestras. It's complemented by the 200-voice ✪ **Atlanta Symphony Orchestra Chorus,** formerly the Robert Shaw Chorale. The principal season runs Sept–May, while in summer its Classic Chastain Summer Concerts are held in the 7,000-acre **Chastain Park Amphitheater,** 449 Stella Dr. at Powers Ferry Road (☎ **404/231-5888**). The venue also hosts other concerts and big-name performers during summer (picnics are *de rigeur*).

The **Atlanta Opera** presents a trio of fully staged productions each summer at the historic **Fox Theatre,** 660 Peachtree St. NE, at Ponce de León Avenue (☎ **404/733-4900** or 404/355-3311), plus various productions at other venues. The season runs late May to Labor Day. The **Atlanta Ballet** also performs at the Fox Theatre (☎ **404/881-2000** or 404/892-3303).

**Seven Stages,** 1105 Euclid Ave. (☎ 404/523-7647), in the Little Five Points district, is Atlanta's leading producer of new and contemporary plays and hosts touring international companies. The **Alliance Theatre Company,** at the Woodruff Arts Center, 1280 Peachtree St. NE (☎ 404/733-4710), is the largest resident professional theater troupe in the Deep South. It produces about 10 plays a year.

Other major venues include the **Atlanta Civic Center,** 395 Piedmont Ave. NE, between Ralph McGill Boulevard and Pine Street (☎ 404/523-6275), with a mixed bag of headliners, touring Broadway shows, traveling symphonies and opera companies, fashion shows, and body-builder contests. The **Coca-Cola Lakewood Amphitheatre,** 202 Lakewood Way (☎ 404/627-9704), at the Lakewood exit of I-75/85, 3¹/₂ miles south of downtown, is a vast facility used for major shows and music festivals.

**THE CLUB & MUSIC SCENE** Nightlife tunes up all over Atlanta. Buckhead is like a huge fraternity party, especially on weekends when streets are mobbed with revelers. Numerous nightspots make this an ideal base for club-hopping. Virginia–Highland draws older adults. Little Five Points gets an eclectic mix of wildly, weirdly dressed folks and neighborhood regulars. Downtown has Underground Atlanta and out-of-town visitors and convention goers. Nightclubs come and go, so it's always a good idea to call ahead. Most clubs are open until 2, 3, or even 4am.

At the center of the Buckhead action, **Tongue & Groove,** 3055 Peachtree Rd. between East Paces Ferry Road and Buckhead Avenue (☎ 404/261-2325), attracts an older group than many establishments here. You might see some of the Atlanta Braves hanging out at the T&G. Thursday is basically a members-only/private party night, but if you look snazzy you might get in. Also in Buckhead, **Otto's,** 265 E. Paces Ferry Rd. NE, a block off Peachtree Road (☎ 404/233-1133), attracts a sophisticated, well-dressed late-20s-to-40s single crowd looking for dancing and easy listening music.

Actually afloat in murky waters, **Dante's Down the Hatch,** 3380 Peachtree Rd., opposite Lenox Square Mall (☎ 404/266-1600), provides a nautical setting for a jazz-oriented supper club. **Yin Yang Café,** 64 Third St. NE, between Spring Street and I-75/85 at Georgia Tech (☎ 404/607-0682), is a comfortable, casual, and hip jazz venue. The crowd of all ages is most definitely not mainstream. Wednesday is coffee-house night, and there's live music the rest of the week.

For serious dancing, **Johnny's Hideaway,** 3771 Roswell Rd., 2 blocks north of Piedmont Rd. (☎ 404/233-8026), is one of Atlanta's hottest spots, with music primarily big-band era to '50s and '60s oldies. So is the crowd. Occasional live oldies concerts feature groups like the Four Freshmen.

Housed in a century-old stone-walled Romanesque former excelsior factory, **Masquerade,** 695 North Ave. NE, just east of Boulevard Street (☎ 404/577-8178), is divided into three main areas. Downstairs, **Purgatory** offers music videos, pool tables, pinball, video games, and a photo machine, while **Hell** is adorned with hanging chains (Wedneday is S&M fetish night). Ascend the stairs to **Heaven,** its walls painted blue with fluffy clouds, where live local and national acts perform. In addition, there's a 4,000-seat outdoor **Music Park** behind the club for performances from April to October by Porno for Pyro, The Connells, 311, and the like (tickets available via Ticketmaster, ☎ 404/249-6400). An alfresco bar with a tree-shaded wooden deck enclosed by a picket fence is away from the action.

You comedy-lovers can get your laughs at **Punchline Comedy Club,** 280 Hildebrand Dr. NE, off Roswell Road (☎ 404/252-5233), about a 40-minute drive from downtown in the Balconies Shopping Center in Sandy Springs. It's best to reserve by phone using a major credit card.

In **Underground Atlanta,** many nightclubs offering various entertainment formats are grouped conveniently in **Kenny's Alley.** Here you'll find the original **Dante's Down** the Hatch (☎ 404/577-1800), where well-known artists sometimes jam with the house band; and **Fat Tuesday** (☎ 404/523-7404), a New Orleans concept club with a bar similar to a Mardi Gras float.

**THE BAR SCENE**   The Virginia–Highland neighborhood has some of Atlanta's friendliest bars. In fact, the town's journalists, politicos, cops, students, and writers hang out at ✪ **Manuel's Tavern,** 602 N. Highland Ave. NE at North Avenue (☎ 404/ 525-3447). Former President Jimmy Carter often drops by with the Secret Service in tow. Nearby, there's a friendly and mellow ambience at **Atkins Park,** 794 N. Highland Ave. NE at St. Charles Place, 1 block north of Ponce de León Avenue (☎ 404/ 876-7249). It began as a deli in 1922 and holds the oldest existing tavern license in the city. **Dark Horse Tavern,** 816 N. Highland Ave. NE, 2 blocks north of Ponce de León Ave. (☎ 404/873-3607), attracts a regular mix of young professionals during the week and college students on the weekend. There's a small downstairs bar with nightly live entertainment, usually rock bands. The kitchen is open until well after midnight.

Up in Buckhead, ✪ **fado'** at 3035 Peachtree Rd. NE, at the corner of Buckhead Ave. (☎ 404/841-0066), is the place for a good pint or two of Guinness (fado' is Gaelic for "long ago"). This charming pub is as authentic as you get outside of Ireland. In the same block, **John Harvard's Brew House,** 3041 Peachtree Rd. NE at Buckhead Avenue (☎ 404/816-2739), brews and serves its own beer on the premises. It's right in the middle of Buckhead nightclub territory and is packed Thursday to Saturday.

Elvis fans head for the **Star Community Bar,** 437 Moreland Ave. NE, between Euclid and Mansfield aves. (☎ 404/681-9081), a funky and cavernous club featuring the "GraceVault"—a small shrine filled with The King's posters, an all-Elvis jukebox, Elvis clocks, and other memorabilia.

Popular sports bars include the local branches of **Champions,** in the Marriott Marquis, 265 Peachtree Center Ave. between Baker and Harris streets (☎ 404/586-6017), and **Damon's Clubhouse,** 76 Wall St., aboveground at Underground Atlanta near the Esplanade Fountains (☎ 404/659-7427).

**The Armory,** 836 Juniper St. NE (☎ 404/881-9280), is the largest gay dance club in town, with what some fans claim is Atlanta's finest sound system. **Bulldog & Co.,** 893 Peachtree St. NE (☎ 404/872-3025), is a gay-lifestyle staple for men aged 30 and over who, while maybe not addicted to the leather life, don't necessarily flinch at it, either. **Revolution,** 293 Pharr Rd. (☎ 404/816-5455), is Atlanta's premier women's bar, a cavernous establishment in otherwise conservative Buckhead that on popular nights crams in as many as 1,000 drinkers and dancers (80% of them female). **The Otherside,** 1924 Piedmont Rd. just north of Cheshire Bridge Road (☎ 404/875-5238), defies description, with a radical eclecticism of clients—married couples, single gay men, lesbians, and gender-benders in between.

## DAY TRIPS FROM ATLANTA

**STONE MOUNTAIN**   Standing 16 miles northeast of downtown, Stone Mountain is the world's largest monolithic gray granite outcropping, but it's mostly famous because on one side it is a carved massive monument to the Confederacy. It's Georgia's number-one tourist mecca and the third most visited paid attraction in the United States.

Over half a century in the making, the neoclassic carving—90 feet high and 190 feet wide—is the world's largest piece of sculpture. Originally conceived by Gutzon Borglum, who later carved South Dakota's Mount Rushmore, it depicts Confederate leaders Jefferson Davis, Robert E. Lee, and Stonewall Jackson galloping on horseback throughout eternity. The best view is from below, but you can ascend a walking trail up its moss-covered slopes (especially lovely in spring when they're blanketed in wildflowers) or take the narrated tram ride to the top.

Today the mountain is part of **Georgia's Stone Mountain Park,** a major recreation area. A highlight here is **Lasershow,** a spectacular display of laser lights and fireworks with animation and music that operates from April to September. Other major park attractions include a railroad around the base of Stone Mountain, paddlewheel riverboat cruises on Stone Mountain Lake, the Antique Auto and Music Museum, a 19-building Antebellum Plantation, and Confederate Hall, an information center that houses a large narrated exhibit of the Civil War in Georgia. There's also a top-rated 36-hole course designed by Robert Trent Jones and John LaFoy, miniature golf, eight night-lit Laykold tennis courts, a sizable stretch of sandy lakefront beach with wonderful water slides, 20 acres of wildlife trails with natural animal habitats and a petting zoo, carillon concerts, rowboats, canoes, sailboats, paddleboats, bicycle rental, fishing, hiking, picnicking, and more.

**Essentials:** Stone Mountain is 16 miles east of downtown on U.S. 78. Take a MARTA train to Indian Trail Station where you can transfer to a bus to Memorial Hall in the park. Call ☎ **404/498-5600** for park schedules and ticket prices. You can stay inside the park at **Stone Mountain Park Inn,** Jefferson Davis Road (U.S. 78 east; P.O. Box 775), Stone Mountain Park, Stone Mountain, GA 30086 (☎ **800/227-0007** or 404/469-3311), but don't expect a view of the monolith.

**KENNESAW** The **Kennesaw Mountain Battlefield National Park** (☎ **404/427-4686**) honors the sites of two major Civil War engagements: the Battle of Kolb Farmhouse on June 22, 1864, and the Battle of Kennesaw Mountain on June 27, 1864. Both served as only temporary setbacks for the infamous march of Union Army general, William Sherman, who eventually bypassed the site's Confederate strongholds to capture Atlanta. Today the site is marked as a bloody setback for Union troops—Sherman lost 2,000 members of his 16,000-man army—and an icon of Confederate pride.

The only Civil War structure in the park, the Kolb family homestead, is closed to visitors, but historians often hike along 15 miles of walking trails that meander adjacent to 11 miles of once-bloody trench lines and bunkers. Energetic visitors climb the signposted trail leading to the top of **Big Kennesaw Mountain** (1,808 feet above sea level), where a view extends over Marietta and faraway Atlanta.

The **Kennesaw Civil War Museum,** 2829 Cherokee St. (☎ **404/427-2117**), houses *The General,* a steam-driven boat highjacked by Union spies in 1862. Admission is $3 for adults, $2.50 for seniors, $1.50 for children 7–15, and free for children 6 and under. It's open Mar–Nov, daily 9:30am–5:30pm; Dec–Feb, Mon–Sat 10am–4pm, Sun noon–4pm.

**Essentials:** The national battlefield park is located 2 miles north of Marietta, off Cobb Parkway (U.S. 41). From Atlanta, take I-75 north to exit 116 (Barrett Parkway) and follow the signs to the park. The visitor center is open daily 8:30am–5pm (until 6pm on midsummer weekends). The park itself is open daily 8am–8:30pm. During weekends throughout the year, there's a free shuttle between the visitor center and the top of Kennesaw Mountain. Admission is free.

# 5 Savannah

Savannah is familiar to moviegoers who saw Tom Hanks in *Forrest Gump,* to viewers of the steamy TV series named for the city, and to readers of John Berendt's best-selling novel *Midnight in the Garden of Good and Evil,* soon to be a major motion picture directed by Clint Eastwood, all of them set in this genteel Georgia seaport. If you're not among them, you should guess that Savannah is special. Its free spirit, passion, and even its decadence resemble Key West or New Orleans more than the down-home, Bible-thumping interior of Georgia. Why, they even have water fountains for dogs in Savannah.

The big draw for visitors is the city's picture-perfect restored and maintained historic area. Here you'll find all the images of the Deep South: oak trees dripping with

Spanish moss, stately antebellum mansions, mint juleps on the veranda, peaceful marshes, horse-drawn carriages, ships sailing up the river (though no longer laden with cotton), and even General Sherman—no one's favorite military hero here. More than 800 of Old Savannah's 1,100 historic buildings have been restored, using original paint colors—pinks and reds and blues and greens. This "living museum" is now the largest urban National Historic Landmark District in the country—some 2½ square miles, including twenty 1-acre squares that still survive from Gen. James Oglethorpe's 1733 dream of a gracious city.

## ARRIVING & DEPARTING

**BY PLANE**    **Savannah International Airport,** 11 miles west of downtown just off I-16, is served by American, Delta, United, and US Airways. **Limousine service** to downtown locations (☎ 912/966-5364) has a one-way fare of $15. The 15-minute taxi ride costs $15 for one person, $3 for each additional passenger.

**BY TRAIN & BUS**    The **Amtrak** train station is at 2611 Seaboard Coastline Dr. (☎ 800/USA-RAIL), some 4 miles southwest of downtown; cab fare into the city is around $4. The **Greyhound/Trailways** bus station is at the corner of Oglethorpe Avenue and Fahm Street (☎ 800/231-2222).

## ESSENTIALS

**VISITOR INFORMATION**    For advance information and hotel reservations, contact the **Savannah Area Convention and Visitor Bureau,** 222 W. Oglethorpe Ave., Savannah, GA 31401 (☎ 800/444-2427 or 912/944-0456). The bureau's walk-in **Savannah Visitor Center** is at 301 Martin Luther King, Jr. Blvd.; it's open Mon–Fri 8:30am–5pm, Sat–Sun 9am–5pm. For information on current happenings, call ☎ 912/233-ARTS.

**EMERGENCIES & SAFETY**    Dial ☎ 911 for police, ambulance, or fire emergencies. There are 24-hour emergency-room services at **Candler General Hospital,** 5353 Reynolds St. (☎ 912/692-6000). Although it's reasonably safe to explore the historic districts during the day, the situation changes at night. Although the bars and restaurants along the riverfront report very little crime, muggings and drug dealing are common in the poorer neighborhoods.

## GETTING AROUND

The historic district is best seen on foot, and a real point of your visit should be to take leisurely strolls with frequent stops in the many squares.

You'll need exact change for the $1.20 **bus** fare, plus 5¢ for a transfer, to ride the **Chatham Area Transit (CAT)** buses (☎ 912/233-5767 for routes and schedules).

For 24-hour **taxi** service, call **Adam Cab Co.** (☎ 912/927-7466). The base fare is 60¢ plus $1.20 for each mile.

## WHAT TO SEE & DO

**ESCORTED TOURS**    You'll have a wide choice of organized tours of Savannah and the nearby Low Country. Most of the town tours depart from the walk-in Savannah Visitor Center at 301 Martin Luther King, Jr. Blvd., where you'll find their representatives.

A delightful way to see the historic area is on an authentic horse-drawn carriage ride with **Carriage Tours of Savannah** (☎ 912/236-6756). For a regular or a haunted history tour via trolley, contact **Old Town Trolley Tours** (☎ 912/233-0083). **Gray Line Savannah Tours** (☎ 912/236-9604) has joined forces with **Historic Savannah Foundation Tours** (☎ 912/234-TOUR) to feature narrated bus tours of museums, squares, parks, and homes. The **Negro Heritage Trail Tour,** 502 E. Harris St. (☎ 912/234-8000), offers organized tours from the African-American perspective.

From a literary angle, **Tours by BJ, Inc.** (☎ 912/233-2335) walks the sights of *Midnight in the Garden of Good and Evil* every Sunday. **Ghost Talk Ghost Walk** takes you through colonial Savannah on a journey based on Margaret Debolt's book, *Savannah Spectres and Other Strange Tales.* Call Jack Richards at New Forest Studios, 127 E. Congress St. (☎ 912/233-3896).

**Savannah Riverboat Cruises** (☎ 800/786-6404 or 912/232-6404) are offered aboard the *Savannah River Queen.* **Low Country River Excursions** (☎ 912/898-9225) takes passengers on pontoon boats *Natures Way* and *Dolphin's Dream* for an encounter with friendly bottle-nose dolphins.

**ATTRACTIONS**     Savannah's **Historic District** is bordered by the Savannah River and Forsyth Park at Gaston Street, and Montgomery and Price streets. Laid out in a grid system in 1733 by General Oglethorpe, Georgia's founder, it contains more than 2,350 architecturally significant historic buildings. **Riverfront** is the most popular tourist district. The old warehouses of River Street, along the Savannah River, that once held King Cotton are now restaurants, art galleries, shops, and bars. The **City Market,** at Jefferson and West Julian streets two blocks from River Street, once was the city's social and business mecca. Its old warehouses are also filled with restaurants and shops. Live music often fills the nighttime air around the market, including some of Savannah's best jazz.

To the south, the **Victorian District** holds some of the finest examples of post–Civil War architecture in the Deep South. It's bounded by Martin Luther King, Jr. Boulevard and East Broad, Gwinnett, and Anderson streets. The **Savannah History Museum,** 303 Martin Luther King, Jr., Blvd., behind the visitor center at Liberty Street (☎ 912/238-1779), provides a good introduction to the city. *The Siege of Savannah* is replayed, and there's an exhibition hall displaying memorabilia from every era of the city's history. Admission $3 adults, $2.50 senior citizens and students. Open daily 8:30am–5pm.

**Andrew Low House.** *329 Abercorn St.* ☎ *912/233-6854. Admission $6 adults, $3 children 6–12, free for children 5 and under. Mon–Wed and Fri–Sat 10:30am–4pm, Sun noon–4pm. Closed major holidays.* This classic, 1848 house facing Lafayette Square is of stucco over brick with elaborate ironwork, shuttered piazzas, carved woodwork, and crystal chandeliers. Juliette Gordon Low lived here when she founded the Girl Scouts. She died on the premises in 1927. William Makepeace Thackeray visited here twice (the desk at which he worked is in one bedroom), and Robert E. Lee was entertained at a gala reception in the double parlors in 1870.

**Davenport House Museum.** *324 E. State St.* ☎ *912/236-8097. Admission $5 adults, $3 children 6–18, free for children 5 and under. Daily 10am–4pm. Closed major holidays.* Constructed between 1815 and 1820 by master builder Isaiah Davenport, this is one of the truly great Federal-style houses in the United States, with delicate ironwork and a handsome elliptical stairway. Seven determined women saved it from demolition in 1954, thus starting the movement that has preserved the entire Historic District.

**Green-Meldrim Home.** *14 W. Macon St.* ☎ *912/233-3845. Admission $4 adults, $2 children and students. Tues and Thurs–Sat 10am–4pm.* This impressive house was built on Madison Square for cotton merchant Charleston Green, but its moment in history came when it served as Gen. William Tecumseh Sherman's final headquarters during his "March to the Sea" in 1864. While here, Sherman offered the house to President Lincoln as a Christmas gift. It's now the Parish House for St. John's Episcopal Church.

**Hamilton-Turner House and Ghost House.** *330 Abercorn St.* ☎ *912/233-4800. Admission $5. Tours daily 10am–4:30pm.* The only Victorian house in town that's open to the public, this Second Empire masterpiece is said to be haunted. Featured in the novel *Midnight in the Garden of Good and Evil,* it once was a setting

# Savannah

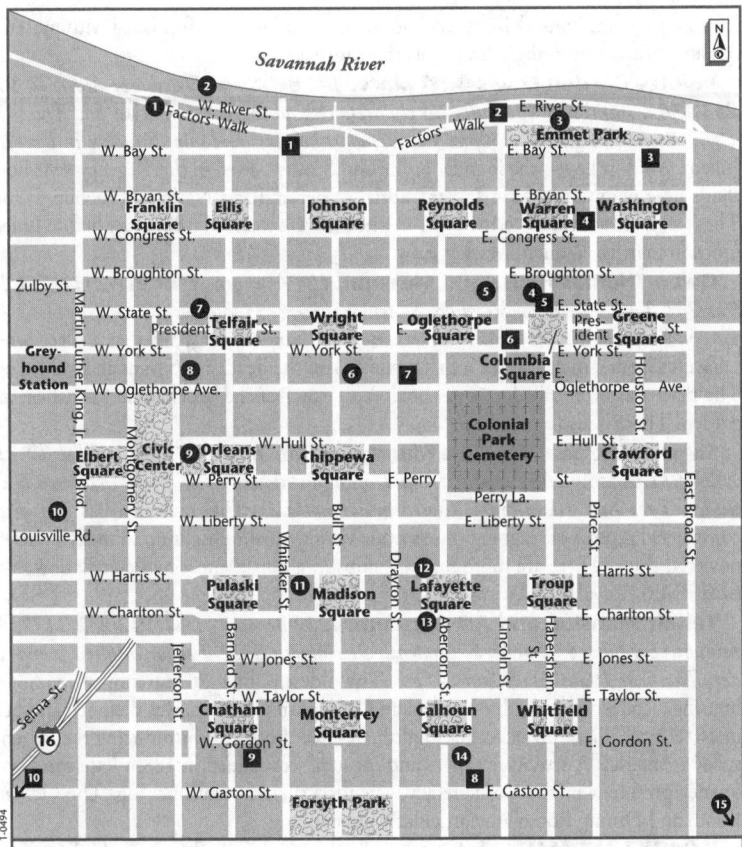

## Attractions

Andrew Low House **13**
Chamber of Commerce **8**
Davenport House Museum **4**
Factors' Walk **1**
Green-Meldrim Home **11**
Hamilton-Turner House **12**
J. G. Low's Birthplace **6**
Massie Heritage
  Interpretation Center **14**
Municipal Auditorium **9**
Owen-Thomas House & Museum **5**
River Street Train Museum **2**
Savannah History Museum **10**
Savannah Science Museum **15**
Ships of the Sea Maritime Museum **3**
Telfair Mansion & Art Museum **7**
Visitors Center **10**

## Accommodations

Ballastone Inn **7**
Bed and Breakfast Inn **9**
Courtyard by Marriott **10**
Gastonian **8**
Hyatt Regency Savannah **1**
Kehoe House **5**
The Mulberry (Holiday Inn) **3**
River Street Inn **2**
St. Julian Street B&B **4**
17 Hundred 90 **6**

for countless cotillions, debuts, receptions, and weddings. It's furnished with museum-quality antiques from the 17th and 18th centuries.

**Juliette Gordon Low's Birthplace.** *142 Bull St. (at Oglethorpe Ave.).* ☎ *912/233-4501. Admission $5 adults, $4 children 18 and under. Mon–Tues and Thurs–Sat 10am–4pm, Sun 12:30–4:30pm. Closed major holidays and some Sundays in Dec–Jan.* Juliette Gordon Low—the founder of the Girl Scouts—lived in this Regency-style house that's now maintained both as a memorial to her and as a National Program Center. The Victorian additions to the 1818–21 house were made in 1886, just before Juliette Gordon married William Mackay Low.

**Owen-Thomas House and Museum.** *124 Abercorn St.* ☎ *912/233-9743. Fax 912/233-0102. Admission $6 adults, $4 senior citizens, $3 students, $2 children 6–12, free for children 5 and under. Tues–Sat 10am–5pm, Sun 2–5pm.* Famed as a place where Lafayette spent a night in 1825, this house evokes the heyday of Savannah's golden age. The place has been called a "jewel box." You can visit the bedchambers, kitchen, and garden. There is also a gift shop.

**Ships of the Sea Maritime Museum.** *41 Martin Luther King, Jr. Blvd.* ☎ *912/232-1511. Admission $5 adults, $4 students and children 7–12, free for children 6 and under. Tues–Sun 10am–5pm. Closed major holidays.* This museum has intricately constructed models of seagoing vessels from Viking warships right up to today's nuclear-powered ships. There are more than 75 ships in a bottle, most by Peter Barlow, a retired British Royal Naval commander.

**Telfair Mansion and Art Museum.** *1212 Bernard St.* ☎ *912/232-1177. Admission $5 adults, $3 seniors, $2 students, $1 children 6–12, free for children 5 and under. Tues–Sat 10am–5pm, Sun 2–5pm.* The oldest public art museum in the South, housing a collection of both American and European paintings, was designed and built in 1818 by William Jay, a young English architect noted for introducing the Regency style in America. A sculpture gallery and rotunda were added in 1883; Jefferson Davis, former president of the Confederacy, attended their formal opening. The Octagon Room and Dining Room are particularly outstanding.

**LITERARY LANDMARKS** As for "the book" (the local reference to *Midnight in the Garden of Good and Evil*), you might want to check out the **Mercer House** at 429 Bull St., the splendid Italianate mansion where the songwriter Johnny Mercer grew up and which Jacqueline Onassis once tried to purchase for $2 million. This was the home of Jim Williams, the rich, gay Savannah antiques dealer, who was acquitted four times for shooting the male hustler Danny Hansford. The incident was the inspiration of John Berendt's best-seller.

The American poet, critic, writer, and Pulitzer Prize winner Conrad Aiken (1889–1973) was born in Savannah and lived at both 228 and 230 E. Oglethorpe Ave. In *Midnight in the Garden,* Mary Hardy and its author sipped martinis at Aiken's bench-shaped tombstone in **Bonaventure Cemetery.**

Flannery O'Connor (1924–64), author of such novels as the 1952 *Wise Blood* and the 1960 *The Violent Bear It Away,* and short stories such as the collection *A Good Man Is Hard to Find* (1955), was raised at the **Flannery O'Connor Childhood Home,** 207 E. Charlton St. (☎ 912/233-6014). It's open Sept–May, Sat–Sun 1–4pm; June–Aug, Sat 1–4pm. Admission is free.

**BLACK HISTORY SITES** Savannah boasts the first African Baptist church in North America, the **First African Baptist Church** at 23 Montgomery St. (☎ 912/233-6597). It was established by George Leile, a slave whose master allowed him to preach to other slaves. After being granted his freedom in 1777, Leile raised some $1,500 to purchase the present church from a white congregation, making it the first brick building in

Georgia to be owned by African-Americans. Slaves built the pews on either side of the organ. Morning worship is at 11:30am daily.

The **Ralph Mark Gilbert Civil Rights Museum,** 460 Martin Luther King, Jr. Blvd. (☎ 912/231-8900), close to the Savannah Visitor Center, is dedicated to the life and service of African-Americans and their contributions to the civil rights movement in Savannah.

**BEST BETS FOR KIDS**   To everyone who was given a set of model trains, **River Street Train Museum,** 315 W. River St. (☎ 912/233-6175), evokes keen memories. Toy train displays from the 1930s are featured, including both die-cast and plastic-coated models, and there's a gift shop.

Geared to school-aged children, **Massie Heritage Interpretation Center,** 207 E. Gordon St. (☎ 912/651-7022), features exhibits about Savannah, including the city's Greek, Roman, and Gothic architecture. There's a period costume room and a classroom where kids can experience what school was like in the 19th century.

A mile east of downtown Savannah, the **Savannah Science Museum,** 4405 Paulsen St. (☎ 912/355-6705), features hands-on exhibits in natural history, astronomy, and science. Reptiles and amphibians of Georgia are also featured, and planetarium shows realistically re-create night skies Saturday at 1pm and Sunday at 2:30pm.

**NEARBY FORTS**   About $2^1/2$ miles east of the center of Savannah via the Islands Expressway, **Old Fort Jackson,** 1 Fort Jackson Rd. (☎ 912/232-3945), is the oldest standing fort in Georgia, with a 9-foot-deep tidal moat around its brick walls. The original brick fort was begun in 1808 to replace an earthen battery constructed during the Revolutionary War. It saw its greatest use as headquarters for the Confederate river defenses during the Civil War. The fort is open Tues–Sat 9am–5pm, Sun noon–5pm. Admission is $2.50 for adults, $2 for seniors and children 6–18, free for chidren under 6.

**Fort McAllister,** Richmond Hill, 10 miles southwest on U.S. 17 (☎ 912/727-2339), was a Confederate earthwork fortification on the banks of the Great Ogeechee River. It withstood nearly 2 years of bombardments before it finally fell on December 13, 1864, in a bayonet charge that ended General Sherman's infamous "March to the Sea." It's open Tues–Sat 9am–5pm and Sun 2–5pm. Admission is $2 for adults and $1 for children.

**Fort Pulaski,** a national monument, stands 15 miles east of Savannah off U.S. 80 on Cockspur and McQueen islands at the very mouth of the Savannah River. Its $7^1/2$-foot-thick walls took 18 years to build, yet it was captured in just 30 hours by Union forces using rifled cannons. This new Union weapon marked the end of the era of masonry fortifications. You can still find shells from 1862 embedded in the walls. It's open daily (except Christmas) from 8:30am to 5:15pm. Admission is $2 for adults, free to those 16 and under, with a $4 maximum per car.

**SHOPPING**   River Street is a shopper's delight, with some 9 blocks (including Riverfront Plaza) of interesting stores, offering everything from crafts to clothing to souvenirs. The **City Market,** between Ellis and Franklin squares on West St. Julian Street, has art galleries, boutiques, and sidewalk cafes. Bookstores, boutiques, and antique shops are located between Wright Square and Forsyth Park. **Oglethorpe Mall,** at 7804 Abercorn St., has more than 100 specialty shops and four major department stores, while **Savannah Mall,** 14045 Abercorn St. (☎ 912/927-7467), is Savannah's newest, offering two floors of shopping. **Savannah Festival Factory Stores,** Abercorn Street at I-95 (☎ 912/925-3089), has some 30 manufacturer-owned stores. **Keller's Flea Market,** 5901 Ogeechee Rd. (☎ 912/927-4848), has more than 400 booths (try Janie Arkwright's Kitchen and Snack Bar, serving barbecue, popped pork pellets, corn dogs, and burgers).

## ACCOMMODATIONS

The undisputed stars here are the small inns in the historic district, most in restored old homes that have been renovated. A very expensive inn might also have some smaller and more moderately priced units, so it pays to ask. Advance reservations are necessary in most cases, since many of the best properties are quite small.

The least expensive lodgings remain the chain hotels and motels on the periphery of the historic area, although most of these are pretty generic.

✪ **Ballastone Inn.** *14 Oglethorpe Ave., Savannah, GA 31401.* ☎ *800/822-4553* or *912/236-1484. Fax 912/236-4626. 18 rms, 3 suites. $135–$255 double; $255 suite. Rates include continental breakfast. AE, MC, V. Free parking.* This dignified 1838 building sits next to the Juliette Gordon Low house (see "Attractions," above). It's rich with hardwoods, elaborate draperies, antique furniture, and art objects that would thrill any decorator, but no closets (they were taxed as extra rooms in the old days). The suites are in a clapboard town house a 5-minute walk away.

**Bed and Breakfast Inn.** *117 W. Gordon St. (at Chatham Square), Savannah, GA 31401.* ☎ *912/238-0518. Fax 912/233-2537. 14 rms, 7 with bath. $50 double without bath; $80 double with bath. Rates include full breakfast. AE, DISC, MC, V.* Set adjacent to Chatham Square, in the oldest part of historic Savannah, this is a dignified stone-fronted, four-story town house originally built in 1853. Guests climb a gracefully curved front stoop to reach the cool, high-ceilinged interior, outfitted with a combination of antique and reproduction furniture. Some accommodations contain refrigerators. There is no smoking.

**Courtyard by Marriott.** *6703 Abercorn St., Savannah, GA 31405.* ☎ *800/ 321-2211* or *912/354-7878. Fax 912/352-1432. 144 rms, 12 suites. $92 double, from $102 suite. Children 15 and under stay free in parents' room. Senior discounts available. AE, DC, DISC, MC, V. From I-16, take exit 34A to I-516 east and turn right on Abercorn St.* Bordering the historic district, this Courtyard is friendly to both families and business travelers, offering bedrooms with separate seating areas, oversized desks, and private patios or balconies, plus a coin laundry, free cribs, pool, whirlpool, and exercise equipment. The restaurant serves à la carte and buffet breakfasts.

**Fairfield Inn by Marriott.** *2 Lee Blvd. (at Abercorn Rd.), Savannah, GA 31405.* ☎ *800/228-2800* or *912/353-7100. Fax 912/353-7100. 135 rms. $54 double. Children 17 and under stay free in parents' room. AE, DC, DISC, MC, V. From I-16, take exit 34A to I-516 east, then turn right on Abercorn St. and go right again onto Lee Blvd.* Not quite as good as the Courtyard by Marriott, this reliable budget hotel offers standard but comfortably appointed bedrooms with a large, well-lit desk. The big attraction here is an outdoor pool. Health-club privileges are available nearby, as are several good, moderately priced restaurants.

✪ **The Gastonian.** *220 E. Gaston St., Savannah, GA 31401.* ☎ *800/322-6603* or *912/232-2869. Fax 912/232-0710. 13 rms, 3 suites. $125–$200 double; $250–$285 suite. Rates include full breakfast and afternoon tea. AE, MC, V. No children under 12.* This plush B&B incorporates a pair of Italianate Regency buildings, both built in 1868 and restored in 1984. A skillfully crafted serpentine bridge across a verdant semitropical garden connects the two buildings. Today everything here is a testimonial to Victorian charm. Afternoon tea is served in a formal, English-inspired drawing room.

**Hyatt Regency Savannah.** *2 W. Bay St., Savannah, GA 31401.* ☎ *800/233-1234* or *912/238-1234. Fax 912/944-3678. 346 rms, 28 suites. $135–$155 double; $165–$185 suite. AE, DC, DISC, MC, V. Parking $10.* Boxy and bulky, Savannah's biggest hotel contrasts sharply to the restored warehouses that flank it beside the river. Many of the modern bedrooms have balconies overlooking a typical Hyatt atrium. There's a stylish bar and two restaurants with river views. Facilities include a health club, indoor swimming pool, and small fitness room.

✪ **Kehoe House.** *123 Habersham St., Savannah, GA 31401.* ☎ *800/820-1020 or 912/232-1020. Fax 912/231-0208. 13 rms, 2 suites. $105–$250 double; $250 suite. Rates include full breakfast. AE, DC, DISC, MC, V.* Tom Hanks stayed at this spectacularly beautiful and opulent B&B when he filmed *Forrest Gump.* He surely appreciated the almost forbiddingly valuable collection of fabrics and furniture. You will tread softly among decor that is considered a model of historic authenticity. Afternoon tea is part of the ritual. Don't bring children.

**The Mulberry (Holiday Inn).** *601 E. Bay St., Savannah, GA 31401.* ☎ *800/ 465-4329 or 912/238-1200. Fax 912/236-2184. 96 rms, 21 suites. $125–$175 double; $165–$195 suite. Children under 18 stay free in parents' room. AE, DC, DISC, MC, V. Parking $5.* Built in 1868 as a stable and cotton warehouse, this suprisingly elegant hotel has a lobby like that of a grand hotel in London and a brick-covered patio evoking New Orleans. Although small, bedrooms have a formal, English country–house look with a Southern accent. The hotel has a bar, two restaurants, and access to a nearby health club.

✪ **River Street Inn.** *115 E. River St., Savannah, GA 31401.* ☎ *800/253-4229 or 912/234-6400. Fax 912/234-1478. 44 rms. $89–$149 double. Rates include breakfast. Children 17 and under stay free in parents' room. AE, DC, MC, V. Free parking.* Built in 1818 of ballast stone, this old warehouse is now a lynchpin of the River District. Its warren of brick-lined storerooms now are some of the most comfortable and well-managed bedrooms in town. The location is a plus, near tons of bars, restaurants, and nightclubs. Breakfast is served in Huey's Restaurant.

**St. Julian Street B&B.** *501 E. St. Julian St., Savannah, GA 31401.* ☎ *and fax 912/ 236-9939. 3 rms, 1 with bath. $75–$85 double without bath; $100 double with bath. Rates include breakfast. AE, DISC, MC, V.* In a small residential pocket near the commercial heart of town, this B&B is a refreshingly simple alternative to Savannah's grandiose historic inns. It's homey and modern-day, with a loquacious charm provided by hosts Bill and Judy Strong. Bedrooms contain a combination of modern and antique furniture but no phones.

**17 Hundred 90.** *307 E. President St., Savannah, GA 31401.* ☎ *800/487-1790 or 912/236-7122. Fax 912/236-7123. 14 rms. $109–$169 double. AE, MC, V.* This severely dignified brick and clapboard-sided house is the oldest inn in Savannah, permeated with conversation and laughter from the basement-level bar and restaurant. Accessible via cramped hallways, the bedrooms are small yet charming, and outfitted with the colonial trappings. About a dozen contain fireplaces and small refrigerators. There's a resident ghost.

## DINING

You'll find plenty of dining options along the riverfront and in the historic area, plus a few choices nearby.

**Boar's Head.** *1 N. Lincoln St. (at River St.).* ☎ *912/232-3196. Reservations recommended. Main courses $8–$30. AE, MC, V. Mon–Thurs 5–10pm, Fri–Sun 11:30am– 10pm. CONTINENTAL/AMERICAN.* Original stone walls and wooden ceiling beams create a faux-medieval pub effect in this cotton warehouse-cum-restaurant, one of the most popular on the waterfront since the 1960s. The river view is better than the usual array of seafood, beef, chicken, veal, lamb, and the inevitable pasta dishes. A continuous exhibition of paintings is for sale.

**Clary's Café.** *404 Abercorn St. (at Jones St.).* ☎ *912/233-0402. Main courses $6.95–$10.95. AE, DC, DISC, MC, V. Mon–Thurs 6am–4pm and 5–10pm, Fri–Sat*

*8am–4pm and 5–11pm, Sun 8am–3pm and 5–10pm. AMERICAN.* Author John Berendt featured Clary's in *Midnight in the Garden of Good and Evil,* and you might see him ordering a lunch of fresh salads, sandwiches, stir-fries, homemade chicken soup, or flame-broiled burgers, or perhaps a dinner of chicken pot pie, stuffed pork loin, or planked fish (fillet of fresh red snapper).

✪ **Elizabeth on 37th.** *105 E. 37th St.* ☎ *912/236-5547. Reservations required. Main courses $22.50–$29.50. AE, DC, DISC, MC, V. Mon–Sat 6–9:30pm. MODERN SOUTHERN.* Built in 1900, this palatial neoclassical-style villa is ringed with semitropical landscaping and cascades of Spanish moss. Award-winning chef Elizabeth Terry's menu may include roast quail with mustard-and-pepper sauce and an apricot-pecan chutney, herb-seasoned rack of lamb, or broiled salmon with a mustard-garlic glaze. Her desserts are Savannah's best.

✪ **45 South at the Pirates' House.** *20 E. Broad St.* ☎ *912/233-1881. Reservations required. Jackets "advised" for men. Main courses $18.50–$27.50. AE, CB, DC, MC, V. Mon–Thurs 6–9pm, Fri–Sat 6–9:30pm; closed Sun. INTERNATIONAL.* This deluxe restaurant featuring "gourmet Southern" cuisine is elegant and ritzy, small and stylish. The ever-changing menu is likely to feature smoked North Carolina trout, rack of lamb flavored with crushed sesame seeds, grilled venison with a gratin of sweet potatoes, or sliced breast of pheasant with foie gras. The service is impeccable.

✪ **Huey's.** *In the River Street Inn, 115 E. River St.* ☎ *912/234-7385. Reservations not accepted. Main courses $8.95–$15.95. AE, DISC, MC, V. Mon–Thurs 7am–10pm, Fri 7am–11pm, Sat 8am–11pm, Sun 8am–10pm. CAJUN/CREOLE.* Fine food distinguishes Huey's from the other restaurants in restored waterfront warehouses. Under Louisiana-born chef Mike Jones, the kitchen manages to please visitors from New Orleans with the likes of jambalaya with andouille sausage, crayfish étouffée, and crab and shrimp au gratin. A jazz brunch is featured weekends 8am–3pm. The place is often packed.

**Mrs. Wilkes' Boarding House.** *107 W. Jones St. (west of Bull St.).* ☎ *912/232-5997. Reservations not accepted. Breakfast $5; lunch $10. No credit cards. Mon–Fri 8–9am and 11am–3pm. SOUTHERN.* Mrs. Selma Wilkes has been serving family-style meals to locals and travelers since the 1940s. Her food is pure home-cooked Southern: fried or barbecued chicken, red rice and sausage, black-eyed peas, corn on the cob, squash and yams, fried okra, cornbread, and collard greens. There's no sign; look for the long line.

✪ **Olde Pink House Restaurant.** *23 Abercorn St.* ☎ *912/232-4286. Reservations recommended. Main courses $17.95–$18.95. AE, MC, V. Daily 6–10:30pm. SEAFOOD/AMERICAN.* One of Sherman's generals headquartered in this 1771 house, glowing pink from stucco over antique bricks. Today its interior is severe and dignified, with stiff-backed chairs and bare wooden floors (the basement piano bar is more relaxed). The cuisine is richly Low Country, such as black grouper stuffed with blue crab and drenched in Vidalia onion sauce.

**Pirates' House.** *E. Broad and Bay sts.* ☎ *912/233-5757. Reservations recommended. Main courses $15.95–$18.95; Sun brunch $14.95. AE, DC, MC, V. Mon–Sat 11:30am–2:30pm and 5:30–9:15pm, Sun 11am–3pm and 5:30–9:15pm. SEAFOOD/LOW COUNTRY.* Robert Louis Stevenson used the labyrinth of rooms in this 1754 Bay Street Inn, once a rendezvous for pirates and sailors, as a setting in *Treasure Island.* Bring the kids: They may love the place more than you do, unless they're future Julia Childs or James Beards in the making.

**River House.** *125 W. River St.* ☎ *912/234-1900. Reservations recommended. Main courses $9–$22. AE, MC, V. Mon–Thurs 11am–10pm, Fri–Sat 11am–11pm, Sun* *noon–10pm. SEAFOOD.* This converted riverfront cotton warehouse excels in fresh seafood, making it one of the best dining choices along the river. The menu depends on the catch of the day, ranging from deviled crab to charcoal-broiled swordfish. Sam Harris, the pastry chef, makes Georgia pecan pie a house specialty.

**606 East Café (Cow Patio).** *319 W. Congress St.* ☎ *912/233-7927. Salads, burgers, sandwiches $3.50–$6.95; platters $4.50–$14.95. AE, MC, V. Mon–Wed 11am–10pm, Thurs–Sat 11am–11pm, Sun noon–10pm. AMERICAN.* This eclectic, offbeat, irreverent, and good-natured restaurant is the whimsical creation of owner and muralist Sandi Baumer, a self-described "hater of plain white walls." Cyndi Lauper look-alikes in short, crinoline skirts serve vegetarian lasagna, burgers, pasta primavera, shrimp tempura, and an "amazing" meat-loaf sandwich. Live music is usually featured on a side terrace.

## SAVANNAH AFTER DARK

**River Street,** along the Savannah River, is the major entertainment venue. Many night owls stroll the waterfront until they hear the sound of music they like—then follow their ears inside.

In summer, concerts of jazz, big band, and Dixieland music fill downtown **Johnson Square** with lots of foot-tapping sounds that thrill both locals and visitors. Some of Savannah's finest musicians perform regularly on this historic site.

**THE PERFORMING ARTS** The **Savannah Symphony Orchestra** has city-sponsored outdoor concerts in addition to its regular ticketed events in the Savannah Civic Center's **Johnny Mercer Theater** at Orleans Square (☎ 800/537-7894 or 912/236-9536), which is also home to ballet, musicals, and Broadway shows. The **Savannah Theater,** Chippewa Square (☎ 912/233-7764), presents contemporary plays. September is the venue for the 5-day **Savannah Jazz Festival** (☎ 912/232-2222), with nationally known musicians appearing around the city.

**THE CLUB, MUSIC & BAR SCENE** The most popular music venue in Savannah, ✪ **Hannah's East,** at the Pirates' House, 20 E. Broad St. (☎ 912/233-2225), is the showcase for jazz great Ben Tucker and also for Emma Kelly—"The Lady of 6,000 Songs"—who was one of the foremost characters in John Berendt's *Midnight in the Garden of Good and Evil.*

Try your hand at singing during Tuesday's open mike at **The Crossroads,** 219 W. St. Julian St. (☎ 912/234-5438), which features live entertainment from 10pm to 2am, showcasing the blues. Nostalgia is the catchphrase at **Hip Huggers,** 9 W. Bay St. (☎ 912/233-6999), a disco offering dance music from the 1970s and 1980s. On Thursday night a complimentary buffet is served.

✪ **Planters Tavern,** in the Olde Pink House, 23 Abercorn St. (☎ 912/232-4286), is probably the most beloved tavern in Savannah, graced with a sprawling and convivial bar and a pair of fireplaces that cast a welcome glow over a decor of antique bricks and carefully polished and darkened hardwoods. You can order food from the Olde Pink House Restaurant (see "Dining," above). Foremost among the divas who perform is the endearingly elegant Gail Thurmond, one of Savannah's most legendary songstresses.

**The Zoo,** 121 W. Congress St. (☎ 912/236-6266), actually is three clubs in one, offering the Top 40s, alternative bands, and acid rock. The 25-screen video wall is one of the largest in the Southeast.

Local affection for the plain, unpretentious **Crystal Beer Parlor,** 301 W. Jones St., west of Bull Street (☎ 912/232-5763), has dimmed not a whit since it opened its doors in the Depression days of 1933 and sold huge sandwiches for a dime. Owner Conrad Thomson still serves up fried oysters and shrimp-salad sandwiches, crab stew, and chili. The seafood gumbo is one of the best in the southern Atlantic region. Parking is available in the lot off Jones Street. A new, second location is at 6710 Waters Ave. (☎ 912/691-1069).

✪ **Club One,** 1 Jefferson St. (☎ **912/232-0200**), defines itself as the premier gay bar in a town that prides itself on a level of decadence that falls somewhere between New Orleans and Key West. Clients include a coterie of lesbians and gay men from the coastal islands, visiting urbanites from Atlanta, New York, and Los Angeles. There's also likely to be a healthy helping of voyeurs who've read *Midnight in the Garden of Good and Evil.* Although not as aggressively noisy, **The Rail,** 405 W. Congress St. (☎ **912/238-1311**), is a convivial watering hole that attracts Savannah's writers, artists, and eccentrics.

**DINNER CRUISES** The *Savannah River Queen* (☎ 912/232-6404) offers a 2-hour cruise with a prime rib or fish dinner and live entertainment. Reservations are necessary. Departures are Saturday at 7pm.

## DAY TRIPS FROM SAVANNAH

**SAVANNAH NATIONAL WILDLIFE REFUGE** A 10-minute drive across the river from downtown Savannah delivers you to the Savannah National Wildlife Refuge (☎ 912/652-4415), which was once the site of rice plantations in the 1800s, and is today a wide expanse of woodland and marsh, ideal for a scenic drive, a canoe ride, a hike, a picnic, and most definitely a look at a variety of animals including alligators.

**Essentials:** From Savannah, take U.S. 17A across the Talmadge Bridge about 8 miles to the intersection of U.S. 17 and 17A. The refuge entrance is named Laurel Hill Wildlife Drive.

**TYBEE ISLAND** For more than 150 years, Tybee Island has lured those who wanted to go swimming, sailing, fishing, and picnicking. Pronounced " *Tie*-bee," a Euchee Indian word for "salt," the island offers 5 miles of unspoiled sandy beaches. On the northern tip is Fort Screven, a coastal artillery station that evolved into a training camp for troops in both world wars. The **Tybee Museum,** housed in what was a battery of **Fort Screven,** displays a collection of photographs, memorabilia, art, and dioramas depicting the island's history. Across the street is the **Tybee Lighthouse** (☎ 912/786-5801), built in 1742 and the third-oldest lighthouse in America. From its panoramic deck you get a sense of "the length and breadth of the marshes," as related in the Sidney Lanier poem "The Marshes of Glynn." There are picnic tables here, and access to the beach is easy.

Tybee Island is a favorite destination for families, the major activity centering around the **Tybee Amusement Park,** 16th Street (☎ **912/786-8806**). Children's rides are available, as are a small roller coaster, a merry-go-round, and a Ferris wheel, among other attractions. The **Tybee Island Marine Science Center,** in the 14th Street parking lot (☎ 912/786-5917), has aquariums with species indigenous to the coast of southern Georgia. On display are the usual cast of marine mammals, sharks, and other creatures.

**Essentials:** Tybee Island is 14 miles east of Savannah via U.S. 80. The **Tybee Island Visitor Center** (☎ 800/868-BEACH or 912/786-4043) provides complete information. If you're interested in daily or weekly rentals of a condo or beach house, contact **Tybee Beach Rentals,** P.O. Box 1440, Tybee Island, GA 31328 (☎ **800/755-8562** or 912/944-0444).

---

# 6 Charleston

In the closing pages of *Gone With the Wind*, Rhett Butler tells Scarlett O'Hara that he's going back home to Charleston, where a little grace and charm are still left. What was true in 1865 is still true, for this South Carolina seaport evokes the Old South more than any other city. In fact, Rhett would feel right at home here today.

Charleston was a center of gentility and culture for a century before the Civil War, which started here with the attack on Fort Sumter in 1861. Wealthy rice and indigo planters pleasured themselves with imported luxuries and built stately town houses to which they regularly repaired in the summer, to escape backcountry mosquitoes and malaria. These Southern aristocrats supported the first theater in the United States, held glittering socials, and invented the Planter's punch cocktail.

Today their stately antebellum homes still stand, and courtly manners and gracious hospitality remain facts of everyday life. With cobblestone streets and horse-drawn carriages, Charleston is a place of visual and sensory pleasures. Tea, jasmine, and wisteria fragrances fill the air, and the aroma of she-crab soup wafts from sidewalk cafes. Your simplest encounter with Charleston natives will seem invested with a social air, as though they mean to please a valued guest. Yet some detect a certain snobbishness in Charleston, and—truth be told—you'd have to stay a few hundred years before you'd be considered an insider here.

## ARRIVING & DEPARTING

**BY PLANE**   **Charleston International Airport** in North Charleston on I-26, about 12 miles west of the city, is served by American, Continental, Delta, United, and USAirways. Taxi fare into the city runs about $24. **Airport limousines** (☎ 803/767-7111) cost $9 per person. All major car-rental facilities are available at the airport.

**BY TRAIN & BUS**   Charleston is on **Amtrak's** New York–to–Miami route (☎ 800/USA-RAIL). **Greyhound/Trailways** (☎ 800/231-2222) has bus service to Charleston.

## ESSENTIALS

**VISITOR INFORMATION**   The helpful staff at the **Visitor Reception and Transportation Center (VRTC),** 375 Meeting St. (P.O. Box 975), Charleston, SC 29402 (☎ 803/853-8000), at John Street, will provide brochures and tour information, and will assist you in finding accommodations and planning your stay. A free map called *The Map Guide—Charleston* is especially useful. Numerous tours depart hourly from the VRTC, and restroom facilities and parking are available. Allow time to view the 24-minute multi-image presentation "Forever Charleston." The center is open Apr–Oct, Mon–Fri 8:30am–5:30pm, Sat–Sun 8am–5pm; Nov–Mar, daily 8:30am–5:30pm.

**RESOURCES FOR TRAVELERS WITH SPECIAL NEEDS**   The State of South Carolina provides numerous agencies to assist those with disabilities. For specific information, call the **South Carolina Handicapped Services Information System** (☎ 803/777-5732). Two other agencies that may prove helpful are the **South Carolina Protection and Advocacy System for the Handicapped** (☎ 803/782-0639) and the **Commission for the Blind** (☎ 803/734-7520).

Gay hotlines in Charleston fall under the 24-hour **crisis prevention network** (☎ 803/744-4357). For general information, you can contact the **Low Country Gay and Lesbian Alliance** (☎ 803/720-8088).

**EMERGENCIES & SAFETY**   In an emergency, dial ☎ **911.** Charleston Memorial Hospital, 326 Calhoun St. (☎ 803/577-0600), has a 24-hour emergency room and a physician referral service. You can generally walk about Charleston at night without fear of violence. Of course, the later the evening progresses, the more likely it is that you will become the victim of a mugging. The local trolley system, DASH, closes down at 10:30pm. After that, it's better to call a taxi than to walk through dark streets.

## GETTING AROUND

**BY BUS & TROLLEY**   The **Downtown Area Shuttle (DASH)** is the quickest way to get around the main downtown area daily. The fare is 75¢, and you'll need exact change. A pass good for the whole day costs $2. For hours and routes, call ☎ 803/724-7420. **City buses** run from 5:35am to 10pm (until 1am to North Charleston). Fares are 75¢, but senior citizens and the disabled pay 25¢ from 9:30am to 3:30pm. Exact change is required. For route and schedule information, call ☎ 803/722-2226.

**BY TAXI**   Leading taxi companies are **Yellow Cab** (☎ 803/577-6565) and **Safety Cab** (☎ 803/722-4066); each company has its own fare structure, but fares seldom exceed $3 or $4 in the city. You must call for a taxi—there are no pickups on the street.

**BY CAR**   If you're staying in the city proper, park your car and save it for day trips to outlying areas. You'll find parking facilities scattered about the city, with some of the most convenient at Hutson Street and Calhoun Street near Marion Square; on King Street between Queen and Broad; and on George Street between King and Meeting.

## WHAT TO SEE & DO

In 1861, according to one Charlestonian, "South Carolina seceded from the Union, Charleston seceded from South Carolina, and south of Broad Street seceded from Charleston." The city preserves its early years in its Historic District, at its southernmost point, the conjunction of the Cooper and Ashley rivers. The White Point Gardens, right in the "elbow" of the two rivers, provide a sort of gateway into this area, where virtually every home is of historic or architectural interest. Between Broad Street and Murray Boulevard (which runs along the south waterfront), you'll find such sightseeing highlights as St. Michael's Episcopal Church, the Calhoun Mansion, the Edmonston–Alston House, the Old Exchange/Provost Dungeon, the Heyward–Washington House, Catfish Row, and the Nathaniel Russell House. See "Day Trips from Charleston," below, for information about nearby plantations that you can visit.

**SPECIAL EVENTS**   Many of Charleston's historic homes are open during the **Festival of Houses and Gardens** from mid-March to mid-April. One of the nation's top events, the ✪ **Spoleto Festival USA** in May and early June is the American counterpart to the one in Spoleto, Italy. World-renowned performers in drama, dance, music, and art perform in various venues throughout the city. Call ☎ 803/722-2764 for information.

**ESCORTED TOURS**   You can stroll down cobblestone streets with **Jack Thomson** (☎ 803/722-7033) and listen to his accounts and anecdotes of Charleston during its years of siege by Union troops. The 2-hour **Charleston Tea Party Walking Tour** (☎ 803/577-5896) gives an offbeat view of the city. **Charleston Carriage Co.** (☎ 803/577-0042) offers narrated horse-drawn tours through the historic district, while **Palmetto Carriage Tours** (☎ 803/723-8145) uses mule teams instead of horses.

**ATTRACTIONS**   The only way to get to ✪ **Fort Sumter,** target of the opening shots of the Civil War, is by boat with Fort Sumter Tours (☎ 803/722-1691), departing daily from the City Marina and from the Patriots Point Maritime Museum. The company also has an interesting Charleston Harbor Tour, departing daily from Patriots Point.

  **Calhoun Mansion.** *16 Meeting St. (between South Battery and Atlantic sts.).* ☎ *803/722-8205. Admission $10 adults, $5 children 6–14, free for children 5 and under. Wed–Sun 10am–4pm. Closed holidays and January.* This 1876 Victorian showplace is complete with period furnishings (including a few original pieces), porcelain and etched-glass gas chandeliers, ornate plastering, and woodwork of cherry, oak, and walnut. The ballroom's 45-foot-high ceiling has a skylight.

# Charleston

## Attractions

Aiken-Rhett Mansion **2**
Calhoun Mansion **11**
Charleston Museum **3**
The Citadel **1**
Dock Street Theatre **6**
Edmonston-Alston House **10**
Gibbes Museum of Art **5**
Heyward-Washington House **8**
Joseph Manigault House **3**
Nathaniel Russell House **9**
Old Exchange & Provost Dungeon **7**
Thomas Elfe Workshop **4**
White Point Gardens **12**

## Accommodations

Anchorage Inn **11**
Ansonborough Inn **6**
Barksdale House Inn **4**
Best Western King Charles Inn **5**
Cannonboro Inn **1**
Charleston Columns Guesthouse **2**
Charleston Place Hotel **8**
Hawthorn Suites Hotel **7**
John Rutledge House Inn **12**
Maison DuPré **3**
Mills House Hotel **10**
Planters Inn **9**
Two Meeting Street Inn **13**

✪ **Charles Towne Landing.** *1500 Old Towne Rd. (S.C. 171, between U.S. 17 and I-126).* ☎ *803/852-4200. Admission $5 adults, $2.50 seniors and children 6–14, free for children 5 and under and for the disabled. Daily 9am–5pm.* This 663-acre park with huge old oaks and freshwater lagoons is located on the site of the first 1670 settlement. There's a re-creation of a small village; a colonial-era crop garden growing rice, indigo, and cotton; a full-scale replica of the 17th-century trading ship *Adventure;* and an Animal Forest with the same species that lived here in 1670. You can take a tram tour or rent a bike.

✪ **Charleston Museum.** *360 Meeting St.* ☎ *803/722-2996. Admission $6 adults, $3 children 3–12, free for children 2 and under; combination ticket to the Joseph Manigault House and Heyward–Washington House, $15. Mon–Sat 9am–5pm, Sun 1–5pm.* Founded in 1773, this is the first and oldest museum in America. The collections preserve and interpret the social and natural history of Charleston and the South Carolina coastal region. The full-scale replica of the famed Confederate submarine *Hunley* is one of the most photographed subjects in the city. The museum also exhibits the largest Charleston silver collection, early crafts, historic relics, and the state's only children's "Discover Me" room with hands-on exhibits for children.

**The Citadel.** *Moultrie St. and Elmwood Ave. (between Hampton Park and Ashley River).* ☎ *803/953-5006. Fax 803/953-6767. Free admission. Daily 8am–6pm; museum Sun–Fri 2–5pm, Sat noon–5pm. Closed religious and school holidays. Free visitor parking.* Famous for its controversy over women cadets, this military college was built in 1842 as an arsenal and refuge for whites in case of a slave uprising. The buildings are of Moorish design, featuring crenellated battlements and sentry towers. The public is invited to a precision drill on the quadrangle Friday at 3:45pm when school is in session. For a history of The Citadel, stop at The Citadel Memorial Archives Museum (☎ 803/953-6846).

✪ **Edmondston-Alston House.** *21 East Battery St.* ☎ *803/722-7171. Admission $7. Guided tours Tues–Sat 10am–4:30pm, Sun–Mon 1:30–4:30pm.* Charles Edmondston, a merchant and wharf owner, built this late Federal-style house in 1825 on High Battery, an elegant section of Charleston. He sold it to Charles Alston, a Low Country rice planter, who modified the style more to Greek Revival (popular at the time). The Alston family opens the first two floors to visitors, who can view their heirloom furnishings, silver, and painting collection.

**Fort Moultrie.** *Middle St., on Sullivan's Island.* ☎ *803/883-3123. Free admission. Daily 9am–5pm. Take U.S. 17/701 east and follow the signs (it's about a 10-mile drive).* This fort was only half completed when Col. William Moultrie's troops repelled a British fleet in 1776, thus winning one of the first decisive American victories of the Revolution. The fort was subsequently enlarged into a five-sided structure with earth and timber walls 17 feet high. Osceola, the fabled leader of the Seminoles in Florida, was incarcerated and died here. Edgar Allen Poe served as a soldier here in the 1830s and set his famous short story *The Gold Bug* on Sullivan's Island.

**Gibbes Museum of Art.** *135 Meeting St.* ☎ *803/722-2706. Admission $5 adults, $4 seniors and students 6–17, free for children 5 and under. Tues–Sat 10am–5pm, Sun–Mon 1–5pm. Closed holidays.* Established in 1905, the Gibbes Museum contains an intriguing collection of prints and drawings from the 18th century to the present. On display are landscapes, genre scenes, panoramic views of Charleston harbor, and portraits of South Carolinians, including one of John C. Calhoun by Rembrandt Peale. The museum's collection of some 400 miniature portraits is one of the more comprehensive in the country. The Wallace Exhibit includes ten rooms, eight replicated from historic American buildings and two from classic French styles.

○ **Heyward-Washington House.** *87 Church St. (between Tradd and Elliott sts.).*
☎ *803/722-0354. Admission $6 adults, $3 children 3–12, free for children 2 and under; combination ticket to the Charleston Museum and Joseph Manigault House, $15. Open for tours Mon–Sat 10am–4:30pm, Sun 1–5pm.* In the Cabbage Row, this 1772 house was built by Daniel Heyward, the so-called rice king, and was the setting for Dubose Heyward's *Porgy.* George Washington bedded down here in 1791. It was also the home of Thomas Heyward, Jr., a signer of the Declaration of Independence. Many of the fine period pieces in the house were the work of Thomas Elfe, one of America's most famous cabinetmakers. The restored kitchen from the 1700s is the only historic one in the city open to the public.

**Joseph Manigault House.** *350 Meeting St. (at John St.).* ☎ *803/722-2996. Admission $6 adults, $3 children 3–12, free for children 2 and under; combination ticket to the Heyward–Washington House and Charleston Museum, $15. Mon–Sat 10am–5pm, Sun 1–5pm.* This 1803 Adams-style residence, a National Historic Landmark, features a curving central staircase and an outstanding collection of Charleston, American, English, and French period furnishings. It's diagonally across from the visitor center.

○ **Nathaniel Russell House.** *51 Meeting St.* ☎ *803/722-3405. Admission $6. Guided tours Mon–Sat 10am–4:30pm, Sun and holidays 2–4:30pm.* One of America's finest examples of Federal architecture, this 1808 house is celebrated for its "free-flying" staircase, spiraling unsupported for three floors. The staircase's elliptical shape is repeated throughout the house. The interiors are ornate with period furnishings, especially the elegant music room with its golden harp and neoclassical-style sofa.

**Old Exchange and Provost Dungeon.** *122 E. Bay St.* ☎ *803/727-2165. Admission $6 adults, $5.50 seniors, $3.50 children 7–12, free for children 6 and under; $5 group rate. Daily 9am–5pm. Closed major holidays.* This is considered one of the three most important colonial buildings in the United States because of its role as a prison during the American Revolution. In 1873 the building became City Hall. You'll also find a large collection of antique chairs (each of the Daughters of the American Revolution brought a chair here from home in 1921).

**BEST BETS FOR KIDS** Kids and navy vets will love visiting **Patriots Point,** the world's largest naval and maritime museum, 2 miles east of the Cooper River Bridge. Here you can board the aircraft carrier **USS *Yorktown*** and wander through its bridge wheelhouse, flight and hangar decks, chapel, sick bay, and several other areas, and view the film *The Fighting Lady,* depicting life aboard the carrier. You can also tour the *Savannah,* the world's first nuclear-powered merchant ship; the World War II destroyer *Laffey;* the World War II submarine *Clamagore;* and the cutter *Ingham.* Patriots Point is open Apr–Oct, daily 9am–6pm; Nov–Mar, daily 9am–5pm. Admission is $9 for adults, $8 for seniors over 62 and military personnel in uniform, $4 for children 6–11, and free for children 5 and under. Adjoining is the fine 18-hole public **Patriots Point Golf Course.** For further information, call ☎ **803/884-2727.**

Another kid pleaser, **Best Friend,** adjacent to the visitor center on Ann Street (☎ 803/973-7269), combines a museum and an antique train featuring a full-size replica of the 1830 locomotive that was the first steam engine in the United States to establish regularly scheduled passenger service. The present train was constructed from the original plans in 1928 and donated to Charleston in 1993. It's open Mon–Sat 9am–5pm, Sun 1–5pm; admission is free.

**SHOPPING** **King Street** is lined with many special shops and boutiques. The **Shops at Charleston Place,** 130 Market St., is an upscale complex of top designer clothing shops (Gucci, Jaeger, Ralph Lauren), and the lively **State Street Market,** just down from the City Market, is another cluster of shops and restaurants. The **African-American Art**

**Gallery,** 43 John St. (☎ 803/722-8224), is the largest African-American art gallery in the South. On permanent display are the works of prominent artists, including Dr. Leo Twiggs and historical artist Joe Pinckney.

## ACCOMMODATIONS

Charleston ranks among the top cities of America for hotels and inns of charm and character. Bed-and-breakfast accommodations range from historic homes to carriage houses to simple cottages, and they're found in virtually every section of the city. For full details and reservations, contact **Historic Charleston Bed and Breakfast,** 60 Broad St., Charleston, SC 29401 (☎ 800/743-3583 or 803/722-6606).

The hotels and motels are priced in direct ratio to their proximity to the 789-acre historic district; the least expensive are west of the Ashley River. Rates skyrocket during the Festival of Houses and the Spoleto Festival, when advance reservations are essential (see "Special Events," above). From mid-November to mid-February, you can get a Courtesy Discount Card that gives reductions of 10% to 50% off the cost of certain hotels, restaurants, tours, and even purchases. Contact the **Charleston Trident Convention and Visitor Bureau,** P.O. Box 975, Charleston, SC 29402 (☎ 803/853-8000).

Most chains are represented in the area, including the **Hampton Inn,** 345 Meeting St. (☎ 800/426-7866 or 803/723-4000), across from the visitor center.

✪ **Anchorage Inn.** *26 Vendue Range, Charleston, SC 29401.* ☎ *800/421-2952 or 803/723-8300. Fax 803/723-9543. 17 rms, 2 suites. Sun–Thurs $89–$139 double, Fri–Sat $109–$179 double; $240 suite. Rates include continental breakfast and afternoon tea. AE, MC, V.* Few ornaments mark this bulky structure, built in the 1840s as a cotton warehouse but radically renovated and upgraded in 1991. A mock-Tudor interior boasts lots of dark paneling, canopied beds with matching tapestries, leaded casement windows, and in some places, half timbering. The most expensive rooms overlook the street, but most have views of the sky-lit lobby.

**Ansonborough Inn.** *21 Hassell St., Charleston, SC 29401.* ☎ *800/522-2073 or 803/723-1655. Fax 803/577-6888. 37 suites. Sun–Thurs, $79–$149 suite; Fri–Sat $109–$179 suite. Rates include continental breakfast. Children 12 and under stay free in parents' room. AE, DISC, MC, V. Free parking.* Most visitors really like the unusual configuration of rooms in this massive building near the waterfront. Rooms have ceilings of 14 to 16 feet and are outfitted with copies of 18th-century furniture and accessories. Many have sleeping lofts (good for families). Only the motel-style baths are disappointing. The rooftop terrace has a hot tub and panoramic views.

**Barksdale House Inn.** *27 George St., Charleston, SC 29401.* ☎ *803/577-4800. Fax 803/853-0482. 14 rms. $80–$180 double. Rates include continental breakfast. MC, V. Free parking. No children under 7.* Built in 1778 as an inn and later massively altered and enlarged, this neat, tidy, and well-proportioned Italianate building near the City Market now evokes the late 19th century. The bedrooms often contain four-poster beds and working fireplaces, and about half a dozen have whirlpool tubs. Evening sherry and tea are served on the back porch.

**Best Western King Charles Inn.** *237 Meeting St. (between Wentworth and Society sts.), Charleston, SC 29401.* ☎ *800/528-1234 or 803/723-7451. Fax 803/723-2041. 91 rms. $69–$159 double. Children 17 and under stay free in parents' room. AE, DC, DISC, MC, V. Free parking.* One block from the historic market area, this three-story hotel is one of Charleston's best family values. The rooms are better than you might expect from a motel, and are likely to be discounted off-season. Some have balconies, but views are limited. A colonial-inspired restaurant serves breakfast. There's a small pool.

**Cannonboro Inn.** *184 Ashley Ave., Charleston, SC 29403.* ☎ *803/723-8572.* Fax *803/723-8007. 6 rms, 1 suite. $69–$135 double; $135–$165 suite. Rates include full breakfast. AE, DISC, MC, V. Free parking. No children under 10.* Originally a rice planter's home built in 1856, this buff- and beige-colored house isn't as carefully coordinated or as relentlessly upscale as many of its competitors. There's the sense of folksy informality throughout. Accommodations lack phones, and baths are dated and cramped, but rooms do have canopy beds and formal, old-fashioned furniture.

✪ **Charleston Place Hotel.** *130 Market St., Charleston, SC 29401.* ☎ *800/843-6664 or 803/722-4900. Fax 803/724-7215. 403 rms, 47 suites. $295 double; $375–$2,000 suite. Seasonal packages available. AE, DC, MC, V. Parking $9.* Charleston's premier hostelry, this brick landmark rises eight stories in the historic district. Acres of Italian marble grace the place, leading to plush bedrooms with decor inspired by colonial Carolina. Louis's Charleston Grill is a deluxe restaurant, while a cafe provides a more casual option. The hotel has a whirlpool, men's steam bath, aerobics studio, and sundeck.

**Hawthorn Suites Hotel.** *181 Church St., Charleston, SC 29401.* ☎ *800/527-1133 or 803/577-2644. Fax 803/577-2697. 181 suites. $89–$189 one-bedroom suite; $194–$299 two-bedroom suite. Rates include buffet breakfast. AE, DC, DISC, MC, V. Parking $10.* This somber, five-story 1991 building adjacent to the historic City Market offers all suites, each outfitted with some type of cooking equipment. They tend to receive heavy use, thanks to their appeal to families, tour groups, and business travelers. Breakfast is the only meal served. There's parking in the underground garage. Facilities include a bar/lounge, fitness center, pool, and coin laundry.

✪ **John Rutledge House Inn.** *116 Broad St., Charleston SC 29401.* ☎ *800/476-9741 or 803/723-7999. Fax 803/720-2615. 15 rms, 4 suites. $165–$245 double; $270–$325 suite. Rates include continental breakfast. AE, DC, DISC, MC, V. Free parking.* Many meetings that culminated in the United States becoming a nation were conducted in this fine 1763 house, impeccably restored to its Federalist grandeur and now Charleston's most prestigious inn. Tea and afternoon sherry are served in a spacious upstairs sitting room, where historic mementos and marble fireplaces help to enhance the building's distinguished aura.

**Maison DuPré.** *317 E. Bay St., Charleston, SC 29401.* ☎ *800/844-4667 or 803/723-8691. 12 rms, 3 suites. $89–$145 double; $145–$200 suite. Rates include continental breakfast and afternoon tea. DISC, MC, V.* More than any other B&B in Charleston, this one evokes the aura of a French country inn. Its central core dates from 1803, but now three adjacent houses and two carriage houses are unified by a brick-paved courtyard with fountains. You'll find bold 18th-century colors and good-quality reproductions of antique sleigh beds, armoires, and four-posters.

**Mills House Hotel.** *115 Meeting St. (between Queen and Broad sts.), Charleston, SC 29401.* ☎ *800/874-9600 or 803/577-2400. Fax 803/722-2112. 200 rms, 14 suites. $135–$190 double; $195–$225 suite. Children 18 and under stay free in parents' room. AE, CB, DC, DISC, MC, V. Parking $15 nearby.* This slightly faded but charming landmark contains many of the architectural adornments of the original Mills House, built in 1853 but later demolished. Rooms are traditionally furnished with antique reproductions and, most often, half-tester beds. The hotel's Barbados Room is one of the finest hotel eateries in town. There's a small indoor pool.

**Planters Inn.** *Market and Meeting sts., Charleston, SC 29401.* ☎ *800/845-7082 or 803/722-2345. Fax 803/577-2125. 56 rms, 6 suites. $105–$195 double; $175–$250 suite. Rates include continental breakfast. AE, MC, V. Parking $5.* A massive renovation has transformed this distinguished inn next to the City Market into a cozy but tasteful and opulent enclave of colonial charm. Spacious bedrooms have hardwood floors, marble baths, and unique 18th-century decor. Afternoon tea is served in the lobby, and meals are offered by the fine Planter's Café.

✪ **Two Meeting Street Inn.** *2 Meeting St., Charleston, SC 29401.* ☎ *803/723-7322. 9 rms. $150–$235 double. Rates include continental breakfast and afternoon tea. No credit cards. No children under 12.* Near the Battery, this house was built in 1892 with proportions as lavish and gracious as the Gilded Age could provide. You'll see stained-glass windows, mementos, and paintings that were part of the original decorations or collected by the present owners. Most bedrooms contain four-poster beds and ceiling fans. Some open to a network of balconies.

## DINING

Foodies from all over the Carolinas and Georgia flock to Charleston for some of the finest dining in the tri-state area. You get not only the most refined cookery of the Low Country but an array of French and international specialties as well. For a culinary experience unique to Charleston, try the **Market Street Food Court,** between South Market and Church streets.

✪ **Anson.** *12 Anson St.* ☎ *803/577-0551. Reservations recommended. Main courses $14–$23. AE, DC, DISC, MC, V. Sun–Thurs 5:30–11pm, Fri–Sat 5:30pm–midnight. LOW COUNTRY/MODERN AMERICAN.* This century-old, brick-sided ice warehouse now has New Orleans–style iron balconies, Corinthian pilasters salvaged from colonial houses, and enough Victorian rococo to make diners feel pampered. Charleston's finest cuisine is inspired by Low Country traditions but isn't down-home cookery, as you'll see by sampling the crispy flounder.

**A. W. Shucks.** *70 State St.* ☎ *803/723-1151. Reservations not necessary. Main courses $9–$15. AE, DC, DISC, MC, V. Sun–Thurs 11:30am–10pm, Fri–Sat 11am–11pm. SEAFOOD.* Absolutely no one cares how you dress at this hearty oyster bar in a rough-hewn warehouse a short walk from the Public Market. The menu highlights oysters and clams on the half shell, seafood chowders, and oysters prepared in at least a half a dozen different ways. A wide selection of international beers is sold.

**Bay Trading Company.** *161 E. Bay St.* ☎ *803/722-0722. Reservations recommended. Main courses $9.95–$19.95. AE, MC, V. Mon–Thurs and Sun 5:30–10pm, Fri–Sat 5:30–11pm. Closed Sun in winter. AMERICAN.* This 1880s warehouse now is a three-story dining emporium. Upstairs enjoys a view over the singles-bar action in the atrium below, while the downstairs atmosphere is considerably more intense. Menu items include fresh seafood such as a casserole of "drunken fishes" laced with bourbon. Come here not for haute cuisine but for the large portions, conviviality, and reasonable prices.

**Carolina's.** *10 Exchange St.* ☎ *803/724-3800. Reservations recommended. Main courses $9.85–$23. AE, DC, DISC, MC, V. Mon–Thurs 5–11pm, Fri–Sat 5pm–midnight, Sun 5–10pm. AMERICAN.* This antique warehouse is one of the few noteworthy local bistros—a stylish, minimalist enclave of hip whose black, pink, and white decor is more Californian than Carolinian. Old-time dishes are prepared with uptown flair—Carolina quail with goat cheese, salmon with coriander sauce, and the best crab cakes in town.

**82 Queen.** *82 Queen St.* ☎ *803/723-7591. Reservations recommended for dinner. Main courses $9.95–$21.95. AE, MC, V. Daily 11:30am–2:30pm and 6–10pm. LOW COUNTRY.* These three 18th- and 19th-century houses are clustered around an ancient magnolia tree, with outdoor tables arranged in its shade. Menu items filled with flavor and flair include an award-winning version of she-crab soup laced with sherry. Or try fried Carolina alligator with black-bean sauce, fresh tomato salsa, and sour cream.

**Hyman's Seafood Company Restaurant.** *215 Meeting St.* ☎ *803/723-6000. Seafood dinners and platters $5.95–$26. DISC, MC, V. Daily 11am–11pm. SEAFOOD.* Hyman's sprawls over most of a city block in Charleston's commercial heart. Inside are at least six dining rooms and a take-away deli loaded with salmon, lox, and smoked herring—all displayed in the style of the great kosher delis of New York City. Another section offers a delectably messy choice of fish, shellfish, lobsters, and oysters.

✪ **Louis' Charleston Grill.** *In the Charleston Place Hotel, 224 King St.* ☎ *803/ 577-4522. Reservations recommended. Main courses $14.75–$21. AE, DC, MC, V. Mon– Thurs 6–11pm, Fri–Sat 6pm–midnight, Sun 6–10am (brunch) and 6–11pm. LOW COUNTRY/MODERN AMERICAN.* South Carolinian Louis Osteen's mahogany-sheathed dining room is one of the city's most luxurious and artful dining venues. Un-like the posh decor, the food recognizes local traditions. Fresh twists to classic dishes are the rule of the day. Seasonal menus might include McClellanville lump crabmeat with lobster cakes and mustard sauce.

**Magnolias.** *185 E. Bay St.* ☎ *803/577-7771. Reservations recommended. Main courses $7–$25. AE, DC, MC, V. Sun–Thurs 11:30am–11pm, Fri–Sat 11:30am– midnight. SOUTHERN.* Occupying the completely rebuilt Customs House, Magnolias seems like a sprawling network of interconnected New York City loft apartments. Everybody's favorite lunch here is a rather dull open-face veal meat-loaf sandwich, but the soups and salads tend to be excellent. Down South dinners include chicken and dumplings with shiitake mushrooms.

✪ **Planters Café.** *In the Planters Inn, 112 N. Market St. (at Meeting St.).* ☎ *803/ 723-0700. Reservations recommended. Main courses $14.50–$27. AE, MC, V. Mon– Thurs 5:30–10pm, Fri–Sat 5:30–11pm, Sun 5:30–9pm. INTERNATIONAL.* Stylish, upscale, and amusing, this postmodern establishment is one of the historic district's most likable and best-managed restaurants, a fit rival to the nearby Anson. It seems like an upscale, artsy European bistro. The food is imaginative, such as lightly spiced tuna steak with a curried salsa. There are also low-cholesterol, low-calorie dishes.

✪ **Restaurant Million.** *2 Unity Alley.* ☎ *803/577-3141. Reservations required. Main courses $23–$27; fixed-price dinner $55. AE, CB, DC, MC, V. Tues–Sat 6:30– 10pm. Closed the first 2 weeks of Jan. FRENCH.* Built as a tavern in 1788, this is as French and as upscale as anything you're likely to find in all of South Carolina, a well-coifed gem evocative of 18th-century Williamsburg. Opened by French-born celeb chef Philippe Million, and now under the eye of classically trained Chef Josè de Anacleto, the best of French cuisine is combined with a touch of American fare. The menu in-cludes sophisticated preparations such as turbot layered with escargot, served with steamed spinach and sauce of garden vegetables, and domestic rack of lamb with fen-nel mousse. Million is tucked away down a narrow brick alley in an elegant long room on the second floor of an 18th-century building where Edward McCrady opened a tav-ern in 1788. In 1791 during his visit to Charleston, George Washington enjoyed an exclusive dinner here.

**S.N.O.B. (Slightly North of Broad).** *192 E. Bay St.* ☎ *803/723-3424. Res-ervations accepted only for parties of six or more. Main courses $9–$19. AE, CB, DC, DISC, MC, V. Mon–Fri 11:30am–3pm and 5:30–11pm, Sat–Sun 5:30–11pm. SOUTHERN.* There's an exposed kitchen, a high ceiling crisscrossed with ventilation ducts, and vague references to the Old South in this snazzily rehabbed warehouse. Flounder stuffed with deviled crab, grilled dolphin glazed with pesto on a bed of tomatoes, and grilled ten-derloin of beef with green-peppercorn sauce are examples of this place's well-prepared but not particularly Southern menu. Main courses can be ordered in medium or large sizes.

**OTHER DINING**    If you just want to hang out and people-watch in the evening, head for **Café Rainbow,** 282 King St. (☎ 803/965-5000), where the granola set is always playing chess on a large board in the front window, while others sit on sacks of coffee beans and watch. Have a muffin or cookies, with coffee, hot cocoa, or iced mochaccino. Open daily until 11pm.

Step back to the 1950s at **Mickey's Diner,** 137 Market St. (☎ 803/723-7121), where even at 3am you can order the kind of food that Elvis used to fill up on while listening to himself on the jukebox. Open daily 24 hours.

Visitors who like New York's SoHo will feel at home at **Kaminsky's Most Excellent Café,** 78 N. Market St. (☎ 803/853-8270). The handsome bar offers a wide selection of wines and is ideal for people-watching. The desserts are sinful, especially the Italian cream cake or mountain chocolate cake.

## CHARLESTON AFTER DARK

Charleston isn't New York or Washington, but you will find plenty to keep you entertained. A local distributor of tickets is **S.C.A.T.** (☎ 803/577-4500 for tickets and information about performances).

**THE PERFORMING ARTS**    Charleston's major cultural venue is the **Dock Street Theater,** 135 Church St. (☎ 803/965-4032), which hosts performances ranging from Shakespeare to *My Fair Lady*. It's most active at the annual Spoleto Festival USA in May and June. The **Robert Ivey Ballet,** 1910 Savannah Hwy. (☎ 803/556-1343), offers both classical and contemporary dance as well as children's ballet programs. The **Charleston Ballet Theatre,** 477 King St. (☎ 803/723-7334), is one of South Carolina's professional ballet companies. The season runs late October to early spring. The **Charleston Symphony Orchestra,** 14 George St. (☎ 803/723-7528), performs throughout the state, but its main venues are the Gaillard Auditorium and Charleston Southern University. The season runs from September to May.

**Low Country Legends Music Hall,** 30 Cumberland St. (☎ 803/722-1829), offers entertainment in Old Charleston style, ranging from ghost stories to contemporary folk rock to African spirituals.

**THE CLUB & MUSIC SCENE**    A dinner club and jazz club, **Chef & Clef,** 102 N. Market St. (☎ 803/722-0732), is *the* place to go in the City Market area in the heart of Charleston. **Henry's,** 54 N. Market St. (☎ 803/723-4363), is one of the city's best places for jazz on Friday and Saturday; otherwise, you get taped Top 40 music for listening and dancing. Live Irish entertainment is presented Wednesday to Sunday at **Tommy Condon's Irish Pub,** 160 Church St. (☎ 803/577-3818), in a restored warehouse in the City Market area. It's also a family restaurant filled with memorabilia of Old Ireland. Every evening there's a band playing in the patio of the **Market Street Mill,** 99 S. Market St. (☎ 803/722-6100).

**THE BAR SCENE**    Local yuppies come to mingle at **Acme Bar & Grill,** 413 Coleman Blvd., Mt. Pleasant (☎ 803/884-1949). **Charleston Sports Pub & Grill,** 4 Linguard Alley (☎ 803/577-8887), is situated in the center of activity at South Market Street. Visiting celebrities have been spotted at the elegant **First Shot Bar,** in the Mills House Hotel, 115 Meeting St. (☎ 803/577-2400). Local people-watching is good at **Arizona's Inside,** 14 Chapter St. (☎ 803/577-5090), whose large bar is packed for Friday happy hour. **Vickery's Bar & Grill,** 15 Beaufain (☎ 803/577-5300), is one of the most popular gathering places with the younger crowd, especially students.

Catering with equal ease to gay men and women, **The Arcade,** 5 Liberty St. (☎ 803/722-5656), in the heart of historic Charleston, is the largest and most high-energy dance bar in Charleston. **Déjà Vu II,** 445 Savannah Hwy., West Ashley (☎ 803/556-5588), is the newest, and some say, coziest and warmest, of the lesbian bars in the Southeast.

**Dudley's,** 346 King St. (☎ 803/723-2784), is a gay version of "Cheers" because of its wood paneling, bricks, and amused and bemused sense of blasé permissiveness.

## DAY TRIPS FROM CHARLESTON

**KIAWAH ISLAND**   The most pristine beach within an easy drive of Charleston is on Kiawah Island, a private residential resort community 21 miles south of downtown. The best front here is at the **Beachwalker County Park,** on the southern end of the island. Go before noon on Saturday or Sunday to get a parking space. Canoe rentals are available for use on the Kiawah River, and the park offers a boardwalk, restrooms, showers, and a changing area. Kiawah also boasts many challenging golf courses and **Kiawah Island Resort** (☎ 800/654-2924 or 803/768-2122; fax 803/768-9386), which offers a wide range of accommodations and dining options. To get here, take U.S. 17 west to S.C. 171 south (Folly Beach Road), turn right onto S.C. 700 (Maybank Highway), and turn left onto C.R. 20 to Kiawah Island.

**THE ISLE OF PALMS**   A residential beach community 10 miles north of Charleston, this island with its salt marshes and wildlife is a self-contained resort, with shops, dining, an array of accommodations, plus two championship golf courses. Seven miles of wide, white sandy beach is the island's main attraction, and sailing and windsurfing are popular. Offering villas and condos, **Wild Dunes Resort** (☎ 800/845-8880 or 803/886-6000; fax 803/886-2916) has two widely acclaimed golf courses and an array of other outdoor activities. Take I-26 and I-526, which goes directly to the island.

**EDISTO ISLAND**   Offering a kind of melancholy beauty, isolated Edisto lies some 45 miles south of Charleston. By the late 18th century, Sea Island cotton made the islanders wealthy, and some plantations from that era still stand. Edisto Island today attracts families from Charleston and the Low Country intent on enjoying the white sandy beaches. Water sports include shrimping, surf casting, deep-sea fishing, and sailing. **Edisto Beach State Park,** on State Cabin Road, sprawls across 1,255 acres, opening onto 2 miles of beach. It has a well-signposted nature trail, 103 campsites, and five cabins. To get here from Charleston, take U.S. 17 south for 21 miles, then head east along Hwy. 174.

**✪ CYPRESS GARDENS**   Giant cypress trees draped with Spanish moss provide an unforgettable setting for flat-bottom boat rides through this 163-acre swamp garden, on U.S. 52 in Moncks Corner, 24 miles north of Charleston (☎ 803/553-0515). Footpaths wind through a profusion of azaleas, camellias, daffodils, and other colorful blooms. You will share the swamp with alligators, pileated woodpeckers, wood ducks, otters, barred owls, and other abundant species. Admission Mar–Apr (including boat rides), $9 adults, $7 seniors, $3 children 6–16, free for children 5 and under; off-season, $8 adults, $6 seniors, $2 children 6–16, free for children 5 and under. Open daily 9am–5pm.

**NEARBY PLANTATIONS**   In the old days, Charleston owed its livelihood to the great Low Country plantations that produced rice, indigo, and cotton. Today several of these great manses are open to the public. They charge admissions ranging from $7 to $14 for adults, $3 to $7 for children.

  **✪ Middleton Place,** on Ashley River Road (☎ 803/556-6020), was the home of Henry Middleton, president of the First Continental Congress, whose son Arthur signed the Declaration of Independence. It includes America's oldest landscaped gardens and collections of fine silver, furniture, rare first editions by Catesby and Audubon, and portraits by Benjamin West and Thomas Sully. Enjoy a plantation lunch in the very fine Middleton Place Restaurant, a replica of an original rice mill.

  Ten generations of the Drayton family have lived at **✪ Magnolia Plantation,** on S.C. 61 (☎ 803/571-1266), since the 1670s. The existing simple, pre-Revolutionary house was barged down from Summerville. The flowery gardens of camellias and azaleas are among America's most beautiful. Also on the grounds, the **Audubon Swamp Garden** is a 60-acre cypress swamp offering a close look at egrets, alligators, wood ducks, otters, turtles, herons, and other wildlife.

Built in 1738, **Drayton Hall,** on Old Ashley River Road (S.C. 61) (☎ 803/766-0188), is one of the oldest surviving plantations. Its hand-carved woodwork and plasterwork represent New World craftsmanship at its finest. There are no modern amenities such as electricity, plumbing, and central heating here.

The unique **Boone Hall Plantation,** on Long Point Road (U.S. 17/701), Mount Pleasant (☎ 803/884-4371), is approached by a famous avenue of huge, moss-draped oaks planted in 1743. You can tour the elegantly furnished first floor. Outbuildings include the circular smokehouse and slave cabins constructed of bricks made on the plantation.

## 7 Great Smoky Mountains National Park

Straddling the North Carolina–Tennessee border, the Great Smoky Mountains National Park contains some of the oldest peaks in the world, ranging in elevation from 840 to 6,642 feet. More than 9 million visitors a year come to these 520,000 acres of forests, streams, rivers, waterfalls, and hiking trails, which will take you through valleys to peaks with panoramic overlooks.

The United Nations has designated the park as an International Biosphere Reserve because of its multitude of plants, trees, mammals, birds, and fish. More than 100 species of trees thrive here, and the park's abundant wildflowers offer a kaleidoscope of colors in spring and early summer. In mid-June you'll find rhododendron, mountain laurel, and azaleas displayed in all their beauty. The park is home to more than 200 species of birds, more than 70 types of fish, and 30 varieties of amphibians. It's known especially for its black bear, averaging 200 to 300 pounds. Other mammals you may see are white-tailed deer, groundhogs, raccoons, skunks, and bobcats.

As you ascend the peaks, you'll travel through the "smoke"—actually blue mist—which gives these mountains their name. Once the mist was wholly the result of mother nature, but now almost 70% of it comes from pollution sent this way by factories and cities. Unfortunately, this pollution has reduced visibility by 30% over the past several decades.

Yet, as you traverse the park, the mists still surround you with an aura of mystery that has been present here since the Great Smokies were part of the mountain empire of the Cherokee Indians. They lived in harmony with nature in small communities along the streams, but advancing colonists pushed their settlements into the hills. It's estimated that 95% of the Cherokee died of diseases brought by the foreigners. Many others were "removed" to Oklahoma along the "Trail of Tears" in the 1830s, but about 1,000 of them hid in the mountains. Today their descendants live on the Cherokee Indian Reservation, on the park's southern boundary. Here you can visit the Oconaluftee Indian Village and see the summertime outdoor drama *Unto These Hills,* which powerfully tells the Cherokee story.

### ESSENTIALS

**ARRIVING & DEPARTING**   The nearest airports are in Asheville, North Carolina, 50 miles east of the park's southern entrance, and at Knoxville, Tennessee, 40 miles west of the northern entrance. There is no public transportation to, from, or within the park, so rent a vehicle at the airports.

Both the northern and southern **entrances** are on Newfound Gap Road (U.S. 441), a 33-mile road that winds north–south through the center of the park. The southern

# Great Smoky Mountains National Park

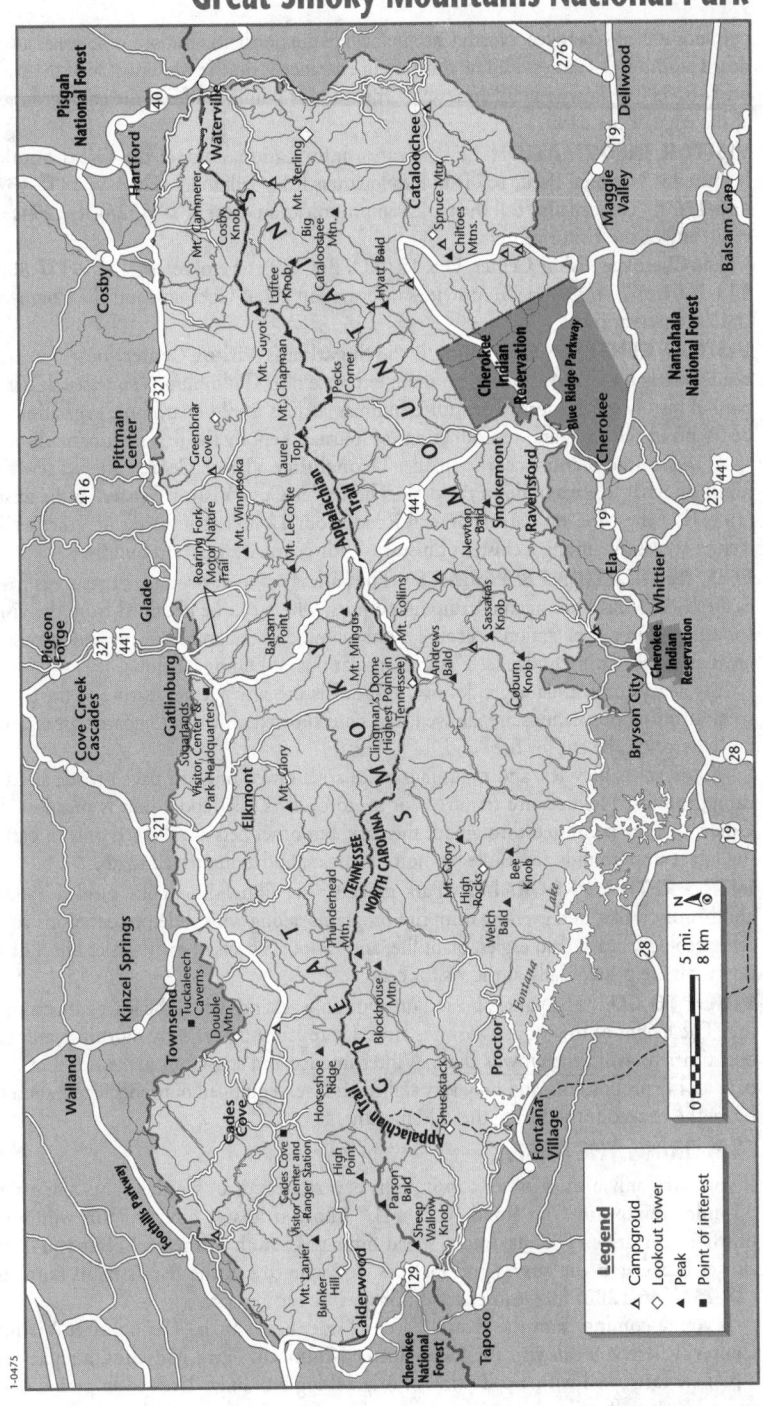

Pisgah National Forest

Hartford

Cosby

Pittman Center

Pigeon Forge

Gatlinburg

Glade

Cove Creek Cascades

Kinzel Springs

Townsend

Walland

Cades Cove

Calderwood

Tapoco

Cherokee National Forest

Waterville

Mt. Cammerer

Cosby Knob

Mt. Sterling

Big Cataloochee Mtn.

Cataloochee

Spruce Mtn.

Chiltoes Mtns.

Maggie Valley

Dellwood

Balsam Gap

Nantahala National Forest

Cherokee Indian Reservation

Blue Ridge Parkway

Cherokee

Whittier

Cherokee Indian Reservation

Bryson City

Fontana Lake

Fontana Village

Proctor

Shuckstack

Parson Bald

Sheep Wallow Knob

Mt. Lanier

Bunker Hill

High Point

Cades Cove Visitor Center and Ranger Station

Horseshoe Ridge

Blockhouse Mtn.

Thunderhead Mtn.

Double Mtn.

Tuckaleech Caverns

Mt. Glory

Elkmont

Sugarlands Visitor Center & Park Headquarters

Balsam Point

Mt. Mingus

Clingman's Dome (Highest Point in Tennessee)

Mt. Collins

Andrews Bald

Sassafras Knob

Coburn Knob

Newton Bald

Smokemont

Ravensford

Ela

Mt. Glory

High Rock

Bee Knob

Welch Bald

Roaring Fork Motor Nature Trail

Mt. LeConte

Mt. Winnesoka

Greenbriar Cove

Laurel Top

Appalachian Trail

Pecks Corner

Mt. Chapman

Mt. Guyot

Luftee Knob

Hyatt Bald

TENNESSEE

NORTH CAROLINA

GREAT SMOKY MOUNTAINS

19

40

321

416

321

441

441

321

129

28

28

19

19

23 441

276

Foothill parkway

## Legend

△ Campground

◇ Lookout tower

▲ Peak

■ Point of interest

N

5 mi.

8 km

0

357

1-0475

entrance is near Cherokee, North Carolina, while the northern entrance is 33 miles away near Gatlinburg, Tennessee. The third main entrance is on the western side of the park off U.S. 321 at Townsend, Tennessee. Other access points are from the campgrounds at the edge of the park.

**VISITOR INFORMATION**   For advance information, contact the **Great Smoky Mountains National Park,** 107 Park Headquarters Rd., Gatlinburg, TN 37738 (☎ 432/436-1200). You can also call the park's communication center (☎ 432/436-1294) to reach any of the visitor centers.

The **Cherokee Visitor Center,** U.S. 19 (P.O. Box 460), Cherokee, NC 28719 (☎ 800/438-1601 or 704/497-9195), provides information about Cherokee and the Cherokee Indian Reservation.

**VISITOR CENTERS**   The largest is the **Sugarlands Visitor Center,** near the park headquarters on U.S. 441 at the northern entrance near Gatlinburg, Tennessee. It has a natural history exhibit featuring stuffed animals such as a wild boar, some vegetation to be found in the park, and reproductions of journals kept by the first park naturalists.

At the southern entrance, the smaller **Oconaluftee Visitor Center** offers a few exhibits on what to see and do in the park. The **Cades Cove Visitor Center,** at the western end of the park, on Parson Branch Road about 12 miles southwest of Townsend, Tennessee, is set among a cluster of historic 19th-century farms and buildings.

**FEES, REGULATIONS & PERMITS**   The park is open year-round. Entrance is free, as are backcountry hiking and camping permits, which can be obtained from the visitor centers and ranger stations. Alcohol is only allowed in designated picnic and campsite areas and at LeConte Lodge (see "Accommodations & Dining," below).

It is illegal to pick, damage, destroy, and/or disturb any natural feature of the park, so no hunting or weapons are allowed. Fires are allowed only in designated areas, and no live tree can be cut for firewood.

Motorcycles, bicycles, and mountain bikes are allowed only on paved roads and in campgrounds. Helmets are required for motorcyclists. Skateboarding is prohibited. Guide dogs are permitted throughout the park, but other pets are allowed only in parking lots, campgrounds accessible by motor vehicles, and along paved roads.

**INTREPRETIVE PROGRAMS**   Park rangers offer films, short talks, guided nature and history walks, and evening campfire programs, along with slide presentations covering geology, bears, bald eagles, plant life, and various aspects of early settler life. These programs are posted daily at the visitor centers.

**WHEN TO GO**   The park is busiest on autumn weekends when the leaves are changing. The height of the tourist season is late May to late August; early mornings are the best times to avoid the crowds then. Wintertime ice and snow can make travel in the park an iffy proposition, and only very skilled and well-equipped outdoorspeople should brave the backcountry during the cold months.

## EXPLORING THE PARK

If you have only a short time to visit, your best strategy is to see the sights along the 33-mile **Newfound Gap Road** (U.S. 441). Allow at least 1 hour for this winding, north–south drive. The maximum speed limit is 45 mph in the park, but you'll go slower because of the curves and inclines. It's wise to call the park's main number (☎ 432/436-1200) for weather conditions before setting out.

If you're coming from the North Carolina side, begin at the **Oconaluftee Visitor Center,** where you can visit the **Oconaluftee Mountain Farm Museum,** a replica of a pioneer farmstead with a collection of original log buildings. Dressed in period costumes, park staff make this a living-history farm from April to October. About a half mile north, the Mingus Mill was constructed in 1886 by Dr. John Jacob Mingus, son of this area's first permanent white settler. This water-powered mill still grinds wheat and corn for flour and cornmeal from mid-April to October.

As you travel north, you'll come to a turnoff for **Clingmans Dome,** the highest peak in the park, soaring 6,642 feet. The turnoff leads 7 miles southwest to a parking lot, where you can walk a steep half-mile to a platform with one of the park's best views. The platform usually is closed from December to April.

Next comes **Newfound Gap,** the center of the park at 5,048 feet. A path that Cherokees traveled was located 2 miles west of the present-day gap. Later it was widened and renamed Indian Gap Road. If the sky is clear, you can see for miles around; on other days you find yourself literally in the clouds.

The next point of interest is **Chimney Tops,** twin peaks rising close to 2,000 feet. The Cherokee named these peaks Duniskwalguni, meaning Forked Antlers, whereas the settlers called them chimney tops because of the 30-foot-deep fluelike cavity located in one of them. If you'd like a closer look, you can hike a 4-mile trail round-trip.

Near the north side of the park is the **Sugarlands Visitor Center,** where you can stroll through the nature exhibit, view a slide show, or browse through the gift shop.

**HIKING**    With more than 800 miles of trails, the park offers all fitness levels a chance to experience the great outdoors firsthand. Even couch potatoes can walk about a dozen self-guided **nature trails,** which are staked and keyed to pamphlets available at the visitor centers and stands at the trailheads. All easy, they range in length from a third of a mile to 6 miles through peaceful surroundings.

A number of trails begin from U.S. 441. From Alum Cave parking area, you can hike to **Alum Cave Bluffs** (5 miles round-trip), where rose-purple rhododendron bloom in mid-June. The stronger hiker may climb **Chimney Tops** (4 miles and 3 hours round-trip), a high, rocky perch. The **Cove Hardwoods Trail** is an easy one, passing through an area where settlers once cultivated the land, then plunging through a virgin forest. A flat and easy paved trail leads to **Laurel Falls** (1$^1$/$_4$ miles), making it the most popular waterfall trail. Beginning near Deep Creek Campground, another easy walk goes to **Indian Creek Falls Trail** (1 mile).

A 68-mile stretch of the Maine-to-Georgia **Appalachian Trail** follows the Smokies' ridgeline almost the entire length of the park. Access points are at Newfound Gap, Clingmans Dome, the end of Tenn. 32 just north of the Big Creek Campground, and the Fontana Dam. The most popular section is from Newfound Gap to **Charlies Bunion,** a strenuous 4-mile trek to a 1,000-foot-high cliff.

**BIKING**    Though much of the park's terrain is too steep, the 11-mile loop through Cades Cove is ideal for cycling. The Cades Cove Campground Store rents bikes.

**BIRD-WATCHING**    More than 200 species have been recorded in the park. Spring migration and summer nesting season are generally the best times. Watch hardwood forests and rhododendron thickets for nesting species.

**FISHING**    The park contains more than 700 miles of streams suitable for fishing, including **Abrams Creek, Big Creek, Fontana Lake,** and **Little River.** The optimum seasons are spring and fall. Fishers must have a valid North Carolina or Tennessee state fishing license, but trout stamps are not required. The limit is five fish, but you can't take brook trout.

**HORSEBACK RIDING**    The park offers some of the region's most panoramic scenery for equestrians, but you'll have to stay on trails marked for horses. Anthony Creek, Big Creek, Cataloochee, Round Bottom, and Towstring horse camps offer easy access to designated horse trails. Reservations can be made 30 days in advance with the park's backcountry office (☎ 432/436-1231). If you have your own horse, ask for an information packet on trails, campsites, and regulations.

Concessionaires rent horses from April to October. They are **Cades Cove** (☎ 432/448-6286); **McCarter's Riding Stables,** Newfound Gap Road, near park headquarters (☎ 432/436-5354); **Smokemont Campground** (☎ 704/497-2373); and **Smoky Mountains Riding Stables,** U.S. 321 (☎ 432/436-5634). A guide must accompany all rental treks.

**WHITEWATER RAFTING**  Starting at the Waterville Power Plant, a 5-mile stretch of the Pigeon River has 10 rapids and offers some of the most challenging whitewater rafting in the South. Contact **Rafting in the Smokies** (☎ 800/770-7238).

**CAMPING**  The park contains 10 campgrounds with picnic tables, fire grills, cold running water, and flush toilets, but they don't have showers or water and electrical hookups. The three major campgrounds are **Cades Cove,** featuring a camp store, bike rentals, a disposal station, wood for sale, naturalist programs held in the small amphitheater, and 161 sites; **Elkmont,** offering a disposal station, firewood for sale, vending machines, a telephone, and 220 sites; and **Smokemont,** boasting a disposal station, firewood for sale, and 140 sites. Fees at each are $12 a night, $15 a night if you make reservations. **Reservations** (☎ 800/365-CAMP) can be made up to 5 months in advance, and you definitely should make them at least a month in advance from July to October.

**Backcountry campers** must have free permits and are only allowed to use designated campsites and shelters. There's a rationing program at 13 of the 80 campsites and at all 18 of the shelters, so it's best to plan your route before visiting the park to determine if you'll use any of these designated areas, what permits you will need, and whether you should make reservations. Contact the park's backcountry office (☎ 432/436-1297). For nonrationed sites, you can register yourself at any ranger station or visitor center when you arrive.

## ACCOMMODATIONS & DINING

The only accommodation inside the park is **LeConte Lodge,** P.O. Box 350, Gatlinburg, TN 37738 (☎ 432/429-5704 for reservations), atop Mt. LeConte. You'll have to hike 4 miles to this rustic facility with no electricity, phone, or indoor plumbing. Per person costs, including meals, range from $66.50 to $107.50 a night, depending on how many people occupy a unit. No credit cards. Reservations should be made in October for the next year. The lodge is open March to mid-November.

Most national chains have motels in Cherokee on the North Carolina side of the park and in Gatlinburg on the Tennessee side. You can also find accommodations in North Carolina at Bryson City, Dillsboro, Fontana Dam, and Maggie Valley, and in Tennessee at Pigeon Forge.

Both Cherokee and Gatlinburg have some nifty, inexpensive retro motels that are straight out of a family trip in the 1940s and 1950s. For example, **Newfound Lodge,** 34 U.S. 441 North, Cherokee, NC 28719 (☎ 704/497-2746), is divided into two sections, one on the mountainside, the other across the street with balconied rooms overlooking the Oconaluftee River. The rooms are spacious, although bathrooms are rather small. The grounds include a swimming pool, restaurant, and picnic areas. **Riverside Motel,** U.S. 441 south at Old Route 441 (P.O. Box 58), Cherokee, NC 28719 (☎ 704/497-9311), is a stone structure that fits in well with the environment and also overlooks the river. The grounds hold a swimming pool and a sheltered picnic area with grills.

There are no restaurants in the park, so pack a lunch to eat at the many picnic sites. As for nearby dining, most restaurants here serve your basic chicken, steak, seafood, and freshwater fish from local waters, with many a chef's idea of a good dinner being a frozen hamburger slapped on the grill. Your best bets are joints serving good country cooking or the standard national chains, which abound around Cherokee and Gatlinburg.

# 8 Nashville

Nashville may be the capital of Tennessee, but it's much better known as Music City USA, the country music capital of the world. This is where the country music "thang" happens, where the deals are cut, where the stars are made, and where the Grand Ole Opry broadcasts. Country music's increased popularity has brought a newfound importance to the city, and a rejuvenation to its neigborhoods, from the historic but once nearly abandoned District that now bustles with clubs and restaurants, to the upscale West End, adjacent to Vanderbilt University, offering nice shops and good restaurants. There's also Music Valley, home of the Grand Ole Opry, and Music Row, the center of the country music recording industry.

Downtown has also become the site of the new 20,000-seat Nashville Arena (it will soon be home to professional football's Houston Oilers), and a Bicentennial Mall complex has been built north of the State Capitol. Adjacent to the mall is the new Farmer's Market building, with vendors, restaurants, and specialty shops.

## ARRIVING & DEPARTING

**BY PLANE**   **Nashville International Airport** is some 8 miles east of downtown Nashville and just south of I-40. By car it takes about 15 minutes to reach downtown. The **Gray Line Airport Express** (☎ 615/275-1180) operates two shuttle routes between the airport and downtown and West End hotels every 15–20 minutes daily 6am–11pm. Fares are $9 one way and $15 round-trip. **Metropolitan Transit Authority buses** (☎ 615/862-5950) between the airport and downtown charge $1.35 each way for the 40-minute ride, with exact change required. Buses from the airport leave at the ground-level curbside, and heading to the airport they depart from Shelter C at Deaderick Street and Fourth Avenue. A taxi from the airport into downtown costs about $17.

**BY BUS**   Greyhound (☎ 800/231-2222) offers service to Nashville from around the country. The Greyhound bus station is on the south side of downtown Nashville at 200 Eighth Ave. S. There is no Amtrak service to Nashville.

## ESSENTIALS

**VISITOR INFORMATION**   The **Nashville Convention and Visitor Bureau,** 161 Fourth Ave. N. (☎ 615/259-4700), is convenient if you're downtown. A **Nashville Visitor Center** is located at the Nashville Arena and connected by tunnel to the Nashville Convention Center. The **Nashville International Airport Welcome Center** is on the baggage-claim level.

**RESOURCES FOR TRAVELERS WITH SPECIAL NEEDS**   The public transit systems in Nashville have either handicapped-accessible regular vehicles or offer special transportation services for the disabled. Call **Access Ride** (☎ 615/880-3970). Call the **Disability Information Office,** 25 Middleton St. (☎ 615/862-6492) for the *Nashville City Vacation Guide,* which lists restaurants, hotels, and other barrier-free places.

**EMERGENCIES & SAFETY**   Phone ☎ 911 for fire, police, emergency, or ambulance. **Vanderbilt University Medical Center,** 1211 22nd Ave. S., in the downtown/Vanderbilt area (☎ 615/322-3391), offers emergency medical treatment. Nashville has its share of crime. Be alert for pickpockets in crowds. At night, try to park your car in a garage, not on the street. Stick to the busier streets when walking downtown at night. The lower Broadway area, though popular with visitors, also attracts a rather unruly crowd to its many bars.

## GETTING AROUND

Downtown Nashville is the only area where you're likely to do much walking around. Here you can visit numerous attractions, shop, eat, and go to a club without ever getting in your car.

# Nashville

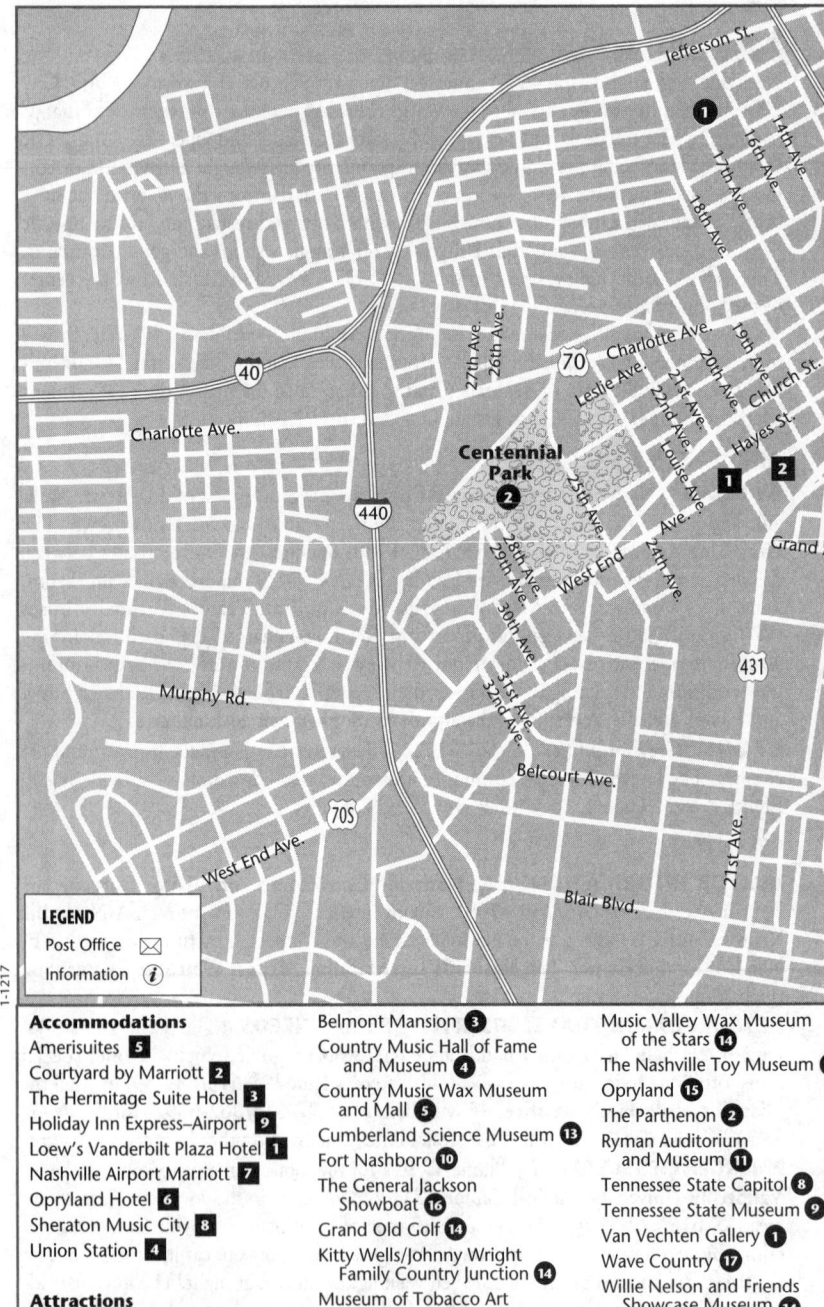

**LEGEND**
Post Office ✉
Information ⓘ

**Accommodations**
Amerisuites **5**
Courtyard by Marriott **2**
The Hermitage Suite Hotel **3**
Holiday Inn Express–Airport **9**
Loew's Vanderbilt Plaza Hotel **1**
Nashville Airport Marriott **7**
Opryland Hotel **6**
Sheraton Music City **8**
Union Station **4**

**Attractions**
Barbara Mandrell Country **6**
Belle Carol Riverboat Co. **12**

Belmont Mansion **3**
Country Music Hall of Fame
and Museum **4**
Country Music Wax Museum
and Mall **5**
Cumberland Science Museum **13**
Fort Nashboro **10**
The General Jackson
Showboat **16**
Grand Old Golf **14**
Kitty Wells/Johnny Wright
Family Country Junction **14**
Museum of Tobacco Art
and Industry **7**
Music Valley Car Museum **14**

Music Valley Wax Museum
of the Stars **14**
The Nashville Toy Museum
Opryland **15**
The Parthenon **2**
Ryman Auditorium
and Museum **11**
Tennessee State Capitol **8**
Tennessee State Museum **9**
Van Vechten Gallery **1**
Wave Country **17**
Willie Nelson and Friends
Showcase Museum **14**

362

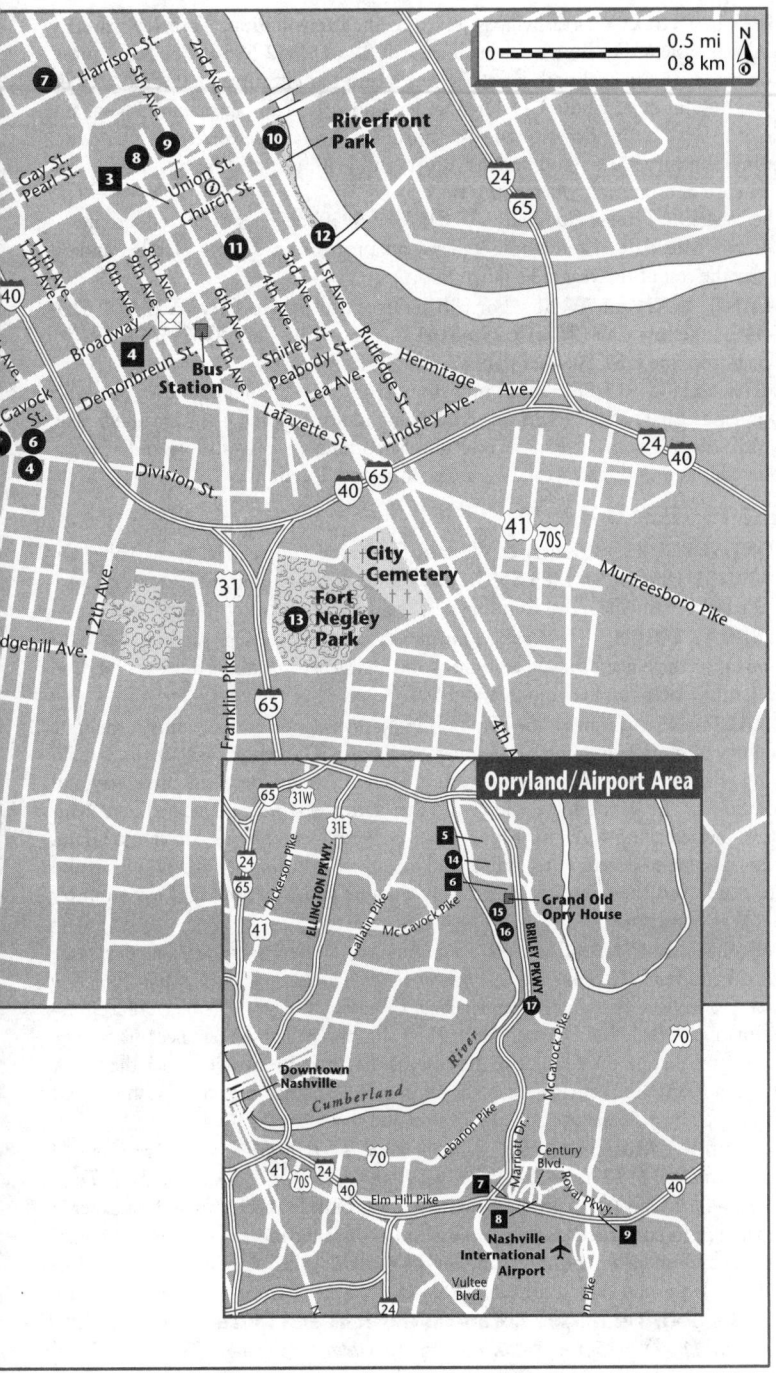

N
0   0.5 mi
    0.8 km

**7** Harrison St.

5th Ave.
2nd Ave.

**Riverfront Park**

**10**

24
65

Gay St.
Pearl St.

**3**  **8**  **9**

Union St.
Church St.

11th Ave.
12th Ave.

8th Ave.
9th Ave.
10th Ave.

**11**

**12**

3rd Ave.
4th Ave.
1st Ave.

40

Broadway

6th Ave.
7th Ave.

**4**

Demonbreun St.
**Bus Station**

Shirley St.
Peabody St.
Lea Ave.
Rutledge St.

Hermitage

Ave.

Gavock St.

**6**
**4**

Lafayette St.
Lindsley Ave.

Division St.

40  65

**City Cemetery**

41  70S

Murfreesboro Pike

12th Ave.

31

**Fort Negley Park**

**13**

dgehill Ave.

Franklin Pike

65

4th A

**Opryland/Airport Area**

65  31W

31E

24
65

Dickerson Pike

ELLINGTON PKWY

**5**

**14**

**6**

**15**

**16**

**Grand Old Opry House**

41

Gallatin Pike

McGavock Pike

BRILEY PKWY

**17**

70

**Downtown Nashville**

River

Cumberland

McGavock Pike

Lebanon Pike

Marriott Dr.

Century Blvd.

Royal Pkwy.

41  70S  24
40

70

**7**

Elm Hill Pike

**8**

**9**

40

**Nashville International Airport**

Vultee Blvd.

24

**BY BUS & TROLLEY**   Nashville is served by the **Metropolitan Transit Authority (MTA)** bus system. For routes or schedules, call ☎ **615/862-5950.** The MTA information center and ticket booth is on Deaderick Street at Fifth Avenue. Adult fares are $1.35 ($1.65 for express buses); children under 4 ride free. You can ride for 30¢ on any MTA bus within the downtown area bordered by James Robertson Parkway, Demonbreun Street, the Cumberland River, and I-40; just ask the bus driver for a **RUSH card** and return it when you leave.

The **Nashville Trolley Company** (☎ 615/862-5950) operates three trolley routes—downtown, Music Row, and Music Valley—on a regular basis April–October and on Saturday the rest of the year. The fare is 95¢.

**BY LAND & RIVER TAXI**   For cab service, call **Music City Taxi** (☎ 615/262-0451), **Yellow Cab** (☎ 615/256-0101), or **Nashville Cab** (☎ 615/242-7070). The flag-drop rate is $1.50; after that it's $1.50 per mile.

A **river taxi** (☎ 615/889-6611) runs from Riverfront Park in downtown Nashville to Opryland year-round. Tickets cost $11.95 for adults; children 4–11 are $8.95. The river taxi leaves Riverfront Park at odd-numbered hours; it leaves Opryland at even-numbered hours, and tickets can be purchased at both locations.

## WHAT TO SEE & DO

**ESCORTED TOURS**   **Country & Western/Gray Line Tours,** 2416 Music Valley Dr. (☎ 800/251-1864 or 615/883-5555), offers tours ranging from historic and country music–related Nashville sights to riding past the homes of country-music stars.

**RIVERBOAT TOURS**   The *General Jackson* showboat, 2812 Opryland Dr. (☎ 615/889-6611), is the biggest showboat in the world and departs from the dock at Opryland USA. Cruise prices run between $18 and $41.

**ATTRACTIONS**   Although the emphasis in Nashville is on country music, the state capital city also offers museums and other attractions. The center of Nashville's main evening entertainment area, the District, is Second Avenue between Broadway and Union Street. The Wild Horse Saloon and the Hard Rock Cafe are located here. Music Row, located along 16th and 17th avenues between Demonbreun Street and Grand Avenue, is home to dozens of recording studios and record-company offices. This is also where you'll find the Country Music Hall of Fame and Museum, and the Country Music Wax Museum.

**Belle Meade Plantation.** *5025 Harding Rd.* ☎ *615/356-0501. Admission $7 adults, $6.50 seniors, $2 children 6–12, free for children under 6. Mon–Sat 9am–5pm, Sun 1–5pm. Closed New Year's Day, Thanksgiving, Christmas.* Called the "Queen of Tennessee Plantations," Belle Meade was built in 1853 after this plantation had become famous as a stud farm that produced some of the best race horses in the South. Today the Greek Revival mansion is the centerpiece of the affluent Belle Meade region of Nashville and is surrounded by 30 acres of manicured lawns and shade trees.

✪ **Belmont Mansion.** *1900 Belmont Blvd.* ☎ *615/460-5459. Admission $6 adults, $2 children 6–12. June–Aug, Mon–Sat 10am–4pm, Sun 2–5pm; Sept–May, Tues–Sat 10am–4pm.* This terra-cotta Italianate villa was built in the 1850s and no expense was spared in its construction. Belmont's grand salon is the most elegant and elaborate room ever built in an antebellum home. In the gardens is the largest collection of 19th-century garden ornaments in the United States.

**Cheekwood, Tennessee Botanical Gardens and Museum of Art.** *1200 Forrest Park Dr.* ☎ *615/356-8000. Admission $6 adults, $5 seniors, $3 children 7–17. Mon–Sat 9am–5pm, Sun 11am–5pm. Open later hours in summer. Closed first Sat in June, Thanksgiving, Dec 24–25, and Dec 31–Jan 1.* Once a private estate, today the museum and gardens are situated in a 55-acre park. The museum itself is housed in the original

Georgian-style Cheek family mansion and the grounds also offer a variety of pleasures, from a greenhouse of orchids to a Japanese garden. You'll also find a gift shop and restaurant.

**✪ Country Music Hall of Fame and Museum.** *4 Music Square E.* ☎ *615/255-5333. Admission $9.95 adults, $4.95 children 6–11. Memorial Day–Labor Day, daily 8am–6pm; Labor Day–Memorial Day, daily 9am–5pm.* The museum is pretty loose with its definition of country music, so you'll find displays on bluegrass, cowboy music, country swing, rockabilly, Cajun, honky tonk, and contemporary country. You'll even see Elvis's "gold" Cadillac. Your ticket also admits you to the Studio B recording studio, 2 blocks away.

**Fort Nashboro.** *170 First Ave. N. No phone. Admission free. Daily 9am–5pm.* Though it's much smaller than the original, this reconstruction of Nashville's first settlement includes several buildings that reproduce 18th-century life in this frontier outpost. The fort is located on the edge of Riverfront Park.

**The Hermitage.** *Old Hickory Blvd., Hermitage.* ☎ *615/889-2941. Admission $8 adults, $7 seniors, $4 children 6–12, free for children under 6. Daily 9am–5pm. Closed Thanksgiving, Christmas, and third week of Jan. Take I-40 east to exit 221, then north 4 miles.* Lawyer, congressman, U.S. president Andrew Jackson built The Hermitage in 1821 in the Federal style. It acquired its current classic Greek Revival facade when it was remodeled in 1836. In addition to the main house, you can also visit Jackson's tomb, an original log cabin, and nearby Old Hermitage Church and Tulip Grove mansion.

**Opryland.** *2802 Opryland Dr.* ☎ *615/889-6611. Admission $32 adults, $22 children 4–11; add a second day for $13 (includes all rides and all shows except "Nashville On Stage" concerts, which are $16–$23 extra). Three-day Opryland USA Passport, about $120 (includes 2 days' park admission, General Jackson showboat cruise, "Grand Ole Opry" or "Prime Time Country" performance, Nashville city tour, and "Nashville On Stage" concert). Ask about discount programs in effect during your visit. Open early Apr–early May, Sat–Sun; early May–mid-May, Fri–Sun; late May–Labor Day, daily. Opening and closing times vary depending on season and day of week; call for exact hours. Special "Christmas in the Park" hours: mid-Nov–Dec, daily 4–10pm.* Opryland's country music theme park is where Disneyland meets the "Grand Ole Opry," with everything from roller coasters to musical shows. There are special shows and rides for the littlest kids, and lots of restaurants and snack bars. Enjoy daily concerts in the Chevrolet/GEO Celebrity Theater with country singer greats, then go out the park's front gates to visit the three country music museums—the Grand Ole Opry Museum, the Roy Acuff Museum, and the Minnie Pearl Museum—and the Grand Ole Opry House itself, home of the famous live broadcasts of country music shows.

**The Parthenon.** *Centennial Park, West End Ave.* ☎ *615/862-8431. Admission $2.50 adults, $1.25 seniors and children 4–17. Tues–Sat 9am–4:30pm; Sun 12:30–4:30pm in summer.* Centennial Park, as its name implies, was built for the Tennessee Centennial Exposition of 1897, and this full-size replica of the Parthenon in Athens was the exposition's centerpiece. It was reconstructed in 1931 to duplicate the original floor plan of the Parthenon in Greece and houses a 42-foot statue of Athena Parthenos, the largest piece of indoor sculpture in the country. In the basement galleries there is an excellent collection of 19th- and 20th-century American art.

**Ryman Auditorium and Museum.** *116 Fifth Ave. N.* ☎ *615/254-1445. Admission $5.50 adults, $2.25 children 11 and under. Daily 8:30am–4pm.* Known as the "Mother Church of Country Music," the Ryman Auditorium is the single most historic site in the world of country music. Its 1892 stage once saw the likes of Sarah Bernhardt, Caruso, and Will Rogers, and the "Grand Ole Opry" broadcast from here from 1943 until 1974. The Ryman underwent renovation in 1994, unfortunately robbing it of much of its historic character, but it is once again home to country music as well as other performances.

**Tennessee State Museum.** *Fifth Ave. between Union and Deaderick sts.* ☎ *615/ 741-2692. Admission free. Tues–Sat 10am–5pm, Sun 1–5pm. Closed Easter, Thanksgiving, Dec 25, Jan 1.* To gain an understanding of Tennessee history, stop by this modern museum in the basement of the Tennessee Performing Arts Center. It houses everything from Indian artifacts and Davy Crockett's rifle to displays on famous Tennesseans and replicas of old buildings. One block west on Union Street is the museum's Military Branch.

**ARCHITECTURAL HIGHLIGHTS**  The **Opryland Hotel Conservatory, Cascades, and Delta,** 2800 Opryland Dr. (☎ **615/889-1000**), offers two vast atrium greenhouses, with everything from waterfalls to pathways. In the evenings there is a light show and a harp player. Open 24 hours a day with free admission. Completed in 1859, the Greek Revival **Tennessee State Capitol,** Charlotte Avenue between Sixth and Seventh avenues (☎ **615/741-2692**), sits atop a hill on the north side of downtown Nashville, with ornate detail, frescoes, and several rooms of 19th-century furnishings. President and Mrs. James K. Polk are buried on the capitol's east lawn. Open Tues–Sat 10am–5pm, Sun 1–5pm; closed state holidays. Admission is free.

**ESPECIALLY FOR KIDS**  The **Nashville Zoo,** 1710 Ridge Rd. Circle, Joelton (☎ **615/370-3333**), is located on 150 acres of rolling hills near Nashville and has more than 600 residents. At the **Cumberland Science Museum,** 800 Ft. Negley Blvd. (☎ **615/862-5160**), learning about the environment, technology, and health can be fun for the whole family through the interactive displays in this modern, hands-on museum. There is also a planetarium.

**SPORTS**  Pro football's Houston Oilers are scheduled to move here in 1999. Meanwhile, you can enjoy some four-legged "pros" at several horse shows. The most important one of the year is the **Annual Tennessee Walking Horse National Celebration** (☎ **615/684-5915**), which takes place in late August and early September in Shelbyville, 40 miles southeast of Nashville. The annual running of the **Iroquois Steeplechase** (☎ **615/322-7284**), the oldest steeplechase in the country, takes place the second Saturday in May at Percy Warner Park. The **Sara Lee Classic LPGA Golf Tournament** (☎ **615/847-5017**) is held each year in early May at the Hermitage Golf Course on Old Hickory Boulevard.

**SHOPPING**  Most of the city's best shopping is found in the large shopping malls scattered around the newer suburbs, but there are also interesting and exclusive shops in the West End area. In downtown Nashville there are gift and souvenir shops, antique stores, and musical instrument and record stores that cater to country musicians and fans. Second Avenue North, in the historic district area downtown, is becoming a souvenir and gallery district, with some antique stores.

## ACCOMMODATIONS

Because Nashville caters to country music fans, there is an abundance of inexpensive and moderately priced hotels close to Opryland, plus downtown's luxury and historic hotels.

**AmeriSuites-Nashville/Across from Opryland.** *220 Rudy's Circle, Nashville, TN 37214.* ☎ *800/833-1516 or 615/872-0422. Fax 615/872-9283. 125 rms. $99– $140 double. All rates include continental breakfast. AE, DC, DISC, MC, V.* This midrise hotel, just off Music Valley Drive, has guest rooms larger than most, but they are not full suites. Extras include large televisions, VCRs and video rental, microwaves, refrigerators, and a small outdoor pool.

**Courtyard by Marriott.** *1901 West End Ave., Nashville, TN 37203.* ☎ *800/ 321-2211 or 615/327-9900. Fax 615/327-8127. 136 rms. $90–$105 double. AE, CB, DC, DISC, MC, V.* This new high-rise hotel on West End Avenue, close to Music Row, fills the moderate price and service gap between the Vanderbilt Plaza and less expensive motels in Nashville. Guest rooms are none too large, but those with king beds are set up with the business traveler in mind. Facilities include a restaurant, whirlpool, and exercise room.

○ **Hermitage Suite Hotel.** *231 Sixth Ave. N., Nashville, TN 37219.* ☎ *800/ 251-1908 or 615/244-3121. Fax 615/254-6909. 120 suites. $150–$170 suite. AE, CB, DC, DISC, MC, V. Parking $8.* This downtown historic 1910 hotel recently underwent a $4 million renovation that produced an elegant lobby and comfortable, newly furnished guest rooms, all of which are suites of varying sizes with nice touches like porcelain decorations. North-side rooms have good views of the capitol. The hotel has a restaurant, two lounges, and a lobby bar.

**Holiday Inn Express–Airport.** *1111 Airport Center Dr., Nashville, TN 37214.* ☎ *800/HOLIDAY or 615/883-1366. Fax 615/889-6867. 206 rms. $79–$99 double. All rates include continental breakfast. AE, CB, DC, DISC, JCB, MC, V.* This great value hotel, with mountain lodge decor, offers fairly spacious rooms with country pine furniture and extra-large bathrooms. Some have balconies overlooking the courtyard gardens. Guests have use of the outdoor pool and a fitness center 5 miles away.

○ **Loew's Vanderbilt Plaza Hotel.** *2100 West End Ave., Nashville, TN 37203.* ☎ *800/23-LOEWS or 615/320-1700. Fax 615/320-5019. 338 rms, 12 suites. $189– $209 double; $200–$600 suite. AE, CB, DC, DISC, MC, V. Self-parking $6.50; valet parking $8.50.* This luxurious high-rise hotel across from Vanderbilt University offers guest rooms with contemporary European styling, all with antique reproduction furnishings. The spacious concierge-level rooms include breakfast, fax machine, and lounge. All rooms have hair dryers, irons/ironing boards, and coffeemakers. Facilities include a restaurant, lounge with live music, exercise room, and hair salon.

○ **Nashville Airport Marriott.** *600 Marriott Dr., Nashville, TN 37214-5010.* ☎ *800/228-9290 or 615/889-9300. Fax 615/889-9315. 399 rms, 6 suites. $148–$162 double; $330–$456 suite. AE, CB, DC, DISC, ER, JCB, MC, V.* This resortlike hotel, on 17 mostly wooded acres (though near the highway), has guest rooms featuring elegant furnishings and business traveler conveniences (modem hookups, concierge level). Families may prefer poolside rooms. Extras include a restaurant, lounge, indoor/outdoor pool, health club, tennis courts, basektball and volleyball court, complimentary airport shuttle, weekday complimentary newspaper, and coffee.

○ **Opryland Hotel.** *2800 Opryland Dr., Nashville, TN 37214-1297.* ☎ *615/ 883-2211 or 615/889-1000. Fax 615/871-5828. 2,882 rms, 120 suites. $209–$249 double; $500–$900 suite. AE, CB, DC, DISC, MC, V. Self-parking $5; valet parking $10.* The hotel offers spectacular lobbies (waterfalls, antebellum mansion) and average rooms, with colonial American decor, some overlooking atriums. Guests have access to five restaurants, a cafe, five lounges (one revolving, one with entertainment), three outdoor pools, a fitness center, saunas, hot tubs, tennis courts, a pro shop, specialty shops, a beauty salon, Opryland tickets, a travel agency, and a car-rental desk.

**Regal Maxwell House.** *2025 MetroCenter Blvd., Nashville, TN 37228-1505.* ☎ *800/457-4460 or 615/259-4343. Fax 615/313-1327. 289 rms, 12 suites. $88–$108 double; $165–$300 suite. AE, CB, DC, DISC, ER, JCB, MC, V.* Convenient to both downtown and Opryland, this high-rise hotel, off I-265, offers commanding views of Nashville from its upper floors, glass elevators, and restaurant. Guest rooms are large-windowed with traditional furnishings, including wingback chairs. Facilities include a restaurant (dinner only), lounge with pool tables, outdoor pool, tennis courts, whirlpool, and steam and exercise rooms.

✪ **Sheraton Music City.** *777 McGavock Pike, Nashville, TN 37214.* ☎ *800/325-3535 or 615/885-2200. Fax 615/871-0926. 412 rms, 64 suites. $119–$149 double; $136–$159 suite. AE, CB, DC, DISC, ER, JCB, MC, V. Valet and self-parking $6.* Set on 23 acres in a business park near the airport, this hotel offers a commanding vista. Georgian styling lends elegance, and well-designed guest rooms have three phones, large desks, and comfy chairs. The hotel has a restaurant, lounge, complimentary airport shuttle, outdoor and indoor pools, and access to tennis courts and health club.

✪ **Union Station.** *1001 Broadway, Nashville, TN 37203.* ☎ *800/331-2123 or 615/726-1001. Fax 615/248-3554. 124 rms, 13 suites. $105–$145 double; $205 suite. AE, CB, DC, DISC, MC, V. Valet parking $8.* Housed in the former 1900 Union Station, this is Nashville's most elegant hotel, with no two rooms alike. Some overlook railroad tracks, but others offer high ceilings and large windows. Furnishings are showing some wear. Extras include two restaurants, a bistro, complimentary downtown shuttle, and sundries shop.

## DINING

You can find plain southern food right along with everything from French to Vietnamese dining here, but as long as you're below the Mason–Dixon line, you should try a bit of country cookin'. Barbecued and fried catfish are two staples, or old-fashioned "meat-and-three (vegetables)." But to find out what Southern cooking is capable of, try the New Southern or New American cuisine, made with traditional and not-so-traditional Southern ingredients.

✪ **Blackstone Restaurant & Brewery.** *1918 West End Ave.* ☎ *615/327-9969. Reservations not necessary. Sandwiches, pizza, and main dishes $6–$15. AE, DC, MC, V. Mon–Thurs 11am–11pm, Fri–Sat 11am–midnight, Sun noon–10pm. BURGERS/NEW AMERICAN.* Brewing tanks in the front window add to the pub atmosphere, but there is also a sparely elegant dining area and a cozy library alcove with couches and game tables. Lighter fare is available, or heaftier offerings, like meaty pork loin with apple chutney, garlic, and juniper berries.

✪ **The Bound'ry.** *911 20th Ave. S.* ☎ *615/321-3043. Reservations accepted for large parties. Tapas $4–$8; main courses $13–$22. AE, DC, DISC, MC, V. Tues–Thurs 5–10:30pm, Fri–Sat 5–11pm, Sun 5:30–10pm. NEW AMERICAN/NEW SOUTHERN.* You'll find everyone from families to businessmen at this fun yet sophisticated bastion of the trendy near Vanderbilt University. Wild-colored murals and jazz add to the energy, and the food is upbeat. Try the yin yang soup, melding white bean with cheddar soup and Cuban black bean soup.

**Houston's.** *3000 West End Ave.* ☎ *615/269-3481. Reservations not accepted; phone ahead for wait list. Main courses $9–$16. AE, MC, V. Sun–Thurs 11am–10pm, Fri–Sat 11am–11pm. STEAKS.* West End Avenue has a number of good restaurants, moderately priced and appealing to students from nearby Vanderbilt University. Houston's is one of the more popular, and it is often packed. The salads and burgers here are consistently voted the best in town. Vegetarian dishes are available.

**Loveless Café.** *8400 Tenn. 100.* ☎ *615/646-9700. Breakfast $4–$9; dinner entrees $9–$15. AE, MC, V. Mon–Fri 8am–2pm and 5–9pm, Sat–Sun 8am–9pm. TRADITIONAL SOUTHERN.* Country cooking in a country place, that's the Loveless. This old roadhouse is a Nashville institution. People rave about the cooking because the food, like country ham with red-eye gravy and homemade biscuits, is just like granny used to make.

○ **Sunset Grill.** *2001 Belcourt Ave.* ☎ *615/386-FOOD. Reservations recommended. Main courses $6–$24. AE, CB, DC, DISC, MC, V. Mon–Fri 11am–1:30am, Sat 5pm– 1:30am, Sun 5–11pm. NEW AMERICAN/NEW SOUTHERN.* Located in the West End neighborhood of Hillsboro Village, this trendy spot is many Nashvillians' favorite restaurant. The decor is minimalist and monochromatic with original paintings to liven it up. The menu highlights contemporary flavor combinations and healthy preparations. Try the hickory-smoked bucksnort trout.

**Sylvan Park Restaurant, Green Hills.** *2201 Bandywood Ave.* ☎ *615/292-6449. Reservations not accepted. Main courses $5–$6. MC, V. Mon–Sat 11am–7:45pm. AMERICAN.* Serving Nashville old-fashioned Southern cooking for more than 50 years, this is a down-home friendly spot with oilcloth tablecloths and tiled floor. It is Mom's "meat-and-three" cooking. Try the homemade pie. Other Sylvan Park locations include 4502 Murphy Rd. (☎ **615/292-9275**), 221 Sixth Ave. N. (☎ **615/255-1562**), and 5207 Nolensville Rd. (☎ **615/781-3077**).

**Uncle Bud's Catfish.** *714 Stewart's Ferry Pike (near the airport).* ☎ *615/ 872-7700. Reservations not accepted. Main courses $6–$15. DISC, MC, V. Mon–Thurs 4–9pm, Fri 4–10pm, Sat 11am–10pm, Sun 11am–9pm. SOUTHERN.* Located near the airport, Uncle Bud's is both rough-hewn and country kitchen, with a thousand ball caps suspended from the ceiling. (Bring one to trade.) The raison d'être is succulent fried catfish with crunchy hush puppies. They'll keep the food comin', and cater to kids, so bring the family.

○ **Whitt's Barbecue.** *5310 Harding Rd.* ☎ *615/356-3435. Plates $5–$7; barbecue $6–$7 per pound. No credit cards. Mon–Sat 10:30am–8pm. BARBECUE.* Walk in, drive up, or get it delivered, there's no in-restaurant seating, but Whitt's was voted "Best Barbecue" by *Nashville Scene* readers. The pork barbecue sandwiches, topped with a zesty dryish coleslaw, are a favorite. Other Whitt's are at 2535 Lebanon Rd. (☎ **615/ 883-6907**) and 3621 Nolensville Rd. (☎ **615/831-0309**).

○ **Wild Boar.** *2014 Broadway.* ☎ *615/329-1313. Reservations highly recommended. Lunch main courses $8–$13; three-course lunch tasting menu with wines $36; dinner main courses $20–$30; six-course dinner tasting menu with wines $140. AE, CB, DC, DISC, MC, V. Mon–Fri 11:30am–2pm; Mon–Thurs 6–10pm, Fri–Sat 6–10:30pm. NEW AMERICAN/NEW SOUTHERN.* Dining in this palatial four-star restaurant may be pricey, but the food is superb, and the wine cellar is among the country's best. Seared duck foie gras over caramelized apples with cracked pistachios and warm balsamic vinegar will reveal the chef's skill. There's live piano music Friday and Saturday evenings.

## NASHVILLE AFTER DARK

The *Nashville Scene* is the city's arts-and-entertainment weekly. On Thursday, the *Nashville Banner* newspaper publishes its "Weekender" section. Every Sunday, *The Tennessean,* Nashville's morning daily, publishes "USA Weekend," a similar guide to the weekend's entertainment scene.

The downtown area known as the District is the heart of the Nashville entertainment scene. Here you'll find the Wildhorse Saloon, the Hard Rock Cafe, Tootsie's Orchid Lounge, and several clubs and pubs. Also, within a few blocks of the District, you'll find the Tennessee Performing Arts Center and several other clubs.

Tickets to major concerts and sporting events can be purchased through **Ticketmaster** (☎ **615/255-9600**).

**COUNTRY MUSIC**   The **Grand Ole Opry,** 2804 Opryland Dr. (☎ **615/889-6611**), is the country's longest continuously running radio show and airs every weekend. Before moving to its theater at the Opryland theme park, the Opry played at **Ryman**

**Auditorium,** 116 Fifth Ave. N. (☎ 615/889-6611), which today hosts performances with a country music slant, like bluegrass night, or the Sunday night gospel show. **TNN: The Nashville Network,** 2806 Opryland Dr., is a cable-television network dedicated to country music that reaches more than 64 million homes. Call ☎ 615/883-7000 or 615/889-6611 for reservations to its most popular show, "Prime Time Country." Call ☎ 615/251-1000 or 615/885-1593 for information about Wildhorse Saloon tapings. Other live shows do not require a reservation.

The ✪ **Bluebird Café,** 4104 Hillsboro Rd. (☎ 615/383-1461), is Nashville's premier venue for both up-and-coming songwriters and those who have hit the big time. There are two shows a night and reservations are recommended. **Tootsie's Orchid Lounge,** 422 Broadway (☎ 615/726-0463), is a country bar that has been a Nashville tradition for many years. There's free live country music here, from mid-morning to early morning, and celebrities still make the scene. The ✪ **Wildhorse Saloon,** 120 Second Ave. N. (☎ 615/251-1000), is a massive dance hall attracting everyone from country music stars to line-dancing senior citizens. It's the scene to make in town, with live music most nights and frequent videotapings by TNN. The **Ace of Clubs,** 114 Second Ave. S. (☎ 615/254-ACES), is big, loud, and packed, with live rock with local performers and lesser-known national acts several nights a week. The **Music City Mix Factory,** 300 Second Ave. S. (☎ 615/251-8899), bills itself as the "South's ultimate progressive entertainment complex," and vies for the biggest club; with live and recorded rock music and nightly themes and drink specials, it attracts the single college crowd.

**THE PERFORMING ARTS**   The **Tennessee Performing Arts Center (TPAC),** 505 Deaderick St. (☎ 615/741-7975 for information, or 800/333-4849, 615/737-4849, or 615/741-7777 for tickets), is Nashville's premier performing arts venue and houses three theaters—the Andrew Johnson, the Andrew Jackson, and the James K. Polk (named for Tennessee's three U.S. presidents). Performance companies that appear here include the following: the **Nashville Ballet** (☎ 615/244-7233); the **Nashville Symphony** (☎ 615/255-5600), which offers a children's series; and the **Nashville Opera** (☎ 615/292-5710). The **Tennessee Repertory Theatre** (☎ 615/244-4878) is Tennessee's largest professional theater company and stages five productions each season, from September to May.

**ELEGANT BARS**   The lively **Sunset Grill,** 2000A Belcourt Ave. (☎ 615/386-3663), offers great drinks and beautiful people. The piano bar at the **Wild Boar,** 2014 Broadway (☎ 615/329-1313), is located in Nashville's most exclusive restaurant, so enjoy the atmosphere and dress accordingly.

## DAY TRIPS FROM NASHVILLE

More Civil War battles were fought in Tennessee than in any other state except Virginia, and the bloodiest of these was the Battle of Stones River. In the two decades that followed the war, Tennessee recovered and developed two of the state's most famous commodities—Tennessee sippin' whisky and Tennessee walking horses. For a view of it all, head south on I-24.

Located 30 miles south of Nashville near the town of Murfreesboro, the **Stones River National Battlefield** (☎ 615/893-9501) preserves over 351 acres where 23,000 soldiers died. It includes a national cemetery and the oldest Civil War memorial in the U.S.

Take exit 105 off I-24 to the **George Dickel Distillery,** on Cascade Road in Tullahoma (☎ 615/857-3124), which offers a tour of the distillery, some history, and a stop at Miss Annie's General Store. What it doesn't offer is a sip of Dickel's finest; it's in a dry county. The most famous and oldest of American distilleries, the **Jack Daniel's Distillery** is located on Tenn. 55 off I-24 at Lynchburg (☎ 615/759-6180). Founded in 1866 by "Mr. Jack," the distillery whisky's distinctive taste comes from

Cave Spring water and sugar maple. You'll learn more on the tour (totally wheelchair accessible). You can also purchase a special bottle of the good stuff while visiting, though nowhere else in the dry county. ✪ **Miss Mary Bobo's Boarding House,** on Main Street in Lynchburg (☎ 615/759-7394), offers Southern dining in an antebellum-style mansion. It's so popular that it requires reservations weeks in advance (months for Saturday lunch). There's a set menu of $11 adults, $5 for children under 10, and no credit cards accepted. Lunch seatings are Mon–Sat at 11am and 1pm.

In the rolling hills of middle Tennessee, the world's premier breed of show horse is bred. At the **Tennessee Walking Horse Museum** at Shelbyville, 40 miles southeast of Nashville (☎ 615/684-0314), you'll find displays and hands-on exhibits on this high-stepping horse's history. Visitors other than horse enthusiasts will find much to enjoy. Go north on Tenn. 55 from Lynchburg and then north on Tenn. 82; or Tenn. 82 from I-24.

# 9 Memphis

A trip to Memphis is a pilgrimage for those yearning to see Elvis Presley's mansion, Graceland (the second most visited house in the country after the White House), or for music fans drawn to the birthplace of the most important musical styles of the 20th century—blues, soul, and rock 'n' roll. Memphis is barbecue and Beale Street, the Mighty Mississippi and urban sprawl, Federal Express and John Grisham's novel-turned-movie *The Firm.*

Located at the far western end of Tennessee, Memphis sits on a bluff overlooking the Mississippi River. It looks across the river to Arkansas, and a few miles to the south lies Mississippi. With a metropolitan area of 1 million, it is a sprawling city, with highrises sprouting in suburban neighborhoods. The wealthy live, do businesss, and shop in East Memphis, but in recent years Midtown, with its old homes and tree-lined streets, has been rediscovered and blossoms with hip restaurants, boutiques, and nightlife.

But it is the renovation of Beale Street that has succeeded in bringing businesses and people back downtown. Beale Street was home to W. C. Handy, B. B. King, Muddy Waters, and others who merged the gospel singing and cotton-field work songs of the Mississippi delta into a music called the blues. Memphis remains a city of music, and of Elvis memories.

## ARRIVING & DEPARTING

**BY PLANE**  **Memphis International Airport** (☎ 901/922-8000) is about 11 miles south of downtown and some 9 miles from East Memphis. It's about 20 minutes via I-240 to downtown, about 15 minutes to East Memphis—more during rush hour. The **Memphis Area Transit Authority (MATA)** (☎ 901/274-MATA) operates buses between the airport and downtown Memphis from Monday to Saturday; the fare is $1.20. There are usually plenty of taxis around, but if not, call **Yellow Cab** (☎ 901/577-7777) or **City Wide Cab Company** (☎ 901/324-4202). The fare to downtown is about $18; to East Memphis, about $17.

**BY TRAIN & BUS**  Memphis is on **Amtrak's** north–south line between Chicago and New Orleans (☎ 800/872-7245). The train station is at 545 S. Main St. near Calhoun Street. It is a questionable neighborhood, especially after dark, so take a cab to your destination. The **Greyhound** bus station (☎ 800/231-2222 or 901/523-9253) is at 203 Union Ave. within the heart of downtown and 2 blocks from the Peabody Hotel.

## ESSENTIALS

**VISITOR INFORMATION**  Contact the **Visitor Information Center,** 340 Beale St., Memphis, TN 38103 (☎ 901/543-5333). At the airport, information boards provide

# Memphis

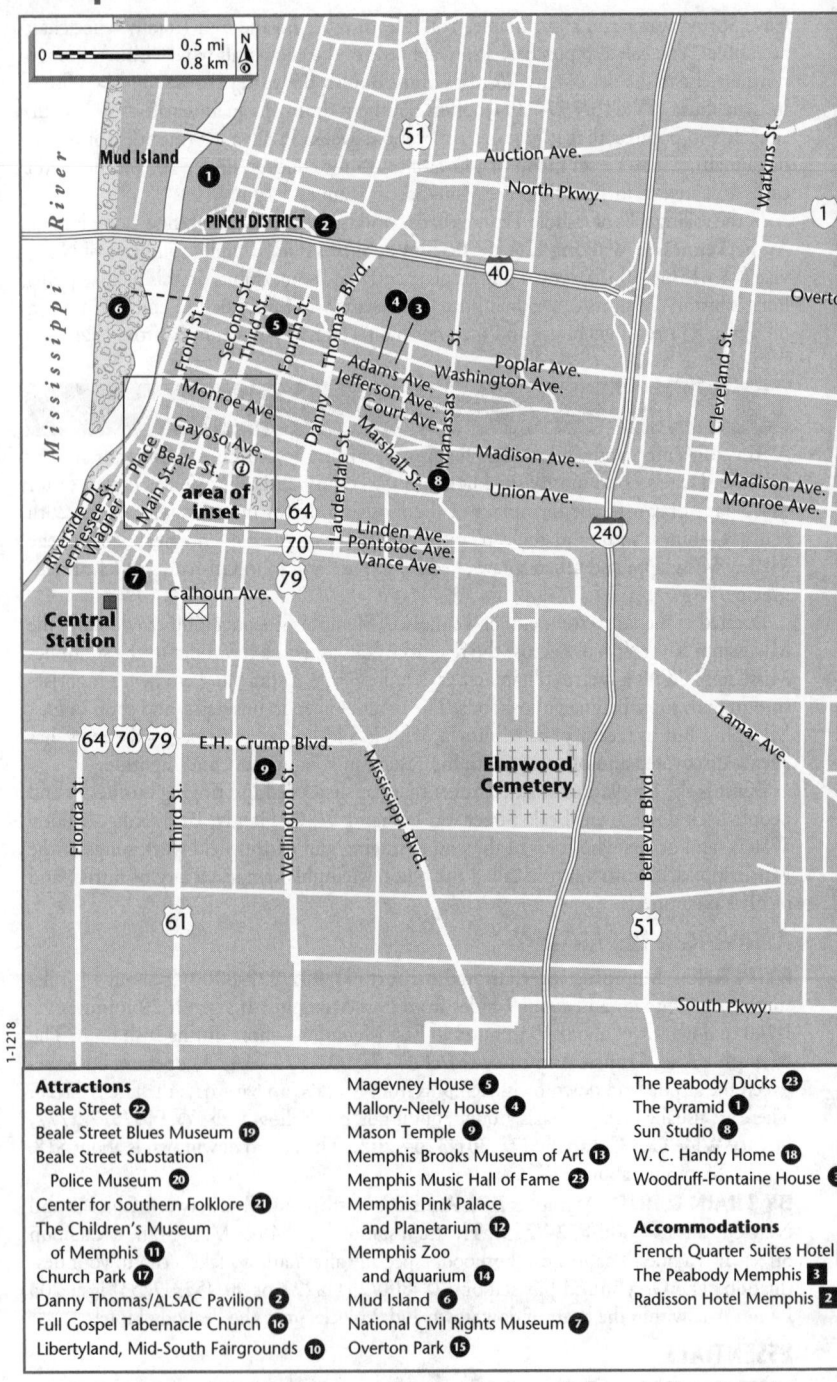

**Attractions**
Beale Street 22
Beale Street Blues Museum 19
Beale Street Substation
  Police Museum 20
Center for Southern Folklore 21
The Children's Museum
  of Memphis 11
Church Park 17
Danny Thomas/ALSAC Pavilion 2
Full Gospel Tabernacle Church 16
Libertyland, Mid-South Fairgrounds 10

Magevney House 5
Mallory-Neely House 4
Mason Temple 9
Memphis Brooks Museum of Art 13
Memphis Music Hall of Fame 23
Memphis Pink Palace
  and Planetarium 12
Memphis Zoo
  and Aquarium 14
Mud Island 6
National Civil Rights Museum 7
Overton Park 15

The Peabody Ducks 23
The Pyramid 1
Sun Studio 8
W. C. Handy Home 18
Woodruff-Fontaine House 3

**Accommodations**
French Quarter Suites Hotel
The Peabody Memphis 3
Radisson Hotel Memphis 2

1-1218

372

helpful telephone numbers, including those for hotels. A **state welcome center** at 119 N. Riverside Dr. on the banks of the Mississippi River is open 24 hours a day.

**EMERGENCIES & SAFETY**   For police, fire, or medical emergencies, phone ☎ **911.** The **Baptist Memorial Hospital Medical Center** has emergency rooms at 899 Madison Ave. (☎ **901/227-2727**) and at 6019 Walnut Grove Rd. in East Memphis (☎ **901/226-5000**). Memphis is a large urban city, and all the normal precautions that apply in other cities hold true here. Be especially alert to pickpockets in crowds. At night, try to park your car in a garage, not on the street. If you walk around town at night, stick to the busier streets. Outside of the area of Beale Street or the Peabody Hotel, downtown Memphis can be quite deserted at night.

## GETTING AROUND

Downtown Memphis is compact and walkable, but the rest of the city is spread out and can be confusing and difficult to get around. Traffic congestion on main east–west avenues is bad throughout the day, so you're usually better off taking the interstate around the outskirts of the city when crossing town. A car is nearly a necessity for travel between downtown and East Memphis, yet traffic congestion can make this a 45-minute trip.

**BY BUS & STREETCAR**   The **Memphis Area Transit Authority (MATA)** (☎ **901/274-MATA**) operates citywide bus service with stops indicated by green-and-white signs. The standard fare is $1.10 and exact change is required.

The **Main Street Trolley** operates renovated 1920s trolley cars that run along a north–south route down the Main Street Mall from the Pyramid to the National Civil Rights Museum. The fare is 50¢ each way, with a lunch-hour special rate of 25¢ 11am–1:30pm. An all-day pass is $2. Exact change is required and passengers may board at any of the 20 stations along Main Street. Trolleys are wheelchair accessible.

**BY TAXI**   Call **Yellow Cab** (☎ **901/577-7777**) or **City Wide Cab Company** (☎ **901/324-4202**). The flag-drop rate is $1.50, then $1.40 per mile. Each additional passenger pays 50¢.

## WHAT TO SEE & DO

**ESCORTED TOURS**   **Blues City Tours of Memphis,** 164 Union Ave. (☎ **901/522-9229**), offers a half-day city tour that takes you past the city's most important attractions. There are also Graceland tours, Beale Street night-on-the-town tours, and a casino tour to Mississippi. Lined up in front of the Peabody Hotel most evenings are horse-drawn carriages operated by **Carriage Tours of Memphis** (☎ **901/527-7542**) for downtown tours. **Stardust Tours/Gray Line of Memphis,** 3677 Elvis Presley Blvd. (☎ **901/346-8687**), offers a "Blues, Booze & Barbeque Tour" that includes Beale Street clubs, drinks, and barbecue dinner.

**RIVER TOURS**   The **Memphis Queen Line** (☎ **901/527-5694**) operates four paddlewheelers on the Mississippi River that all leave from a dock at the foot of Monroe Avenue, downtown. In summer, there are 1¹/₂-hour sightseeing cruises, sunset dinner cruises, and party cruises. The dinner cruises include live Dixieland and big-band music.

**ATTRACTIONS**   Though much of downtown Memphis is deserted after dark, **Beale Street** continues to draw music fans and tourists as a major attraction. It was here that W. C. Handy penned and performed "The Memphis Blues," the first published blues song, and here that the most famous musicians in the blues world got their start. Nightclubs line Beale Street between Second and Fourth streets, and it's also home to theaters and museums. Historic markers relate the area's colorful past.

✪ **Dixon Gallery and Gardens.** *4339 Park Ave.* ☎ *901/761-5250. Admission $5 adults, $4 seniors, $3 students, $1 children under 12; half price on Mon to gardens.*

*Tues–Sat 10am–5pm, Sun 1–5pm.* The South's finest collection of French and American Impressionist and post-Impressionist artworks is the highlight of this exquisite little museum amid 17 acres of formal and informal gardens. Twice a year the Memphis Symphony Orchestra performs here. Across the street is the Memphis Botanic Garden.

✪ **Graceland.** *3675 Elvis Presley Blvd.* ☎ *800/238-2000 or 901/332-3322. Graceland Mansion Tour, $10 adults, $9 seniors, $5 children 7–12. Platinum Tour (includes admittance to all Graceland attractions), $18.50 adults, $16.65 seniors, $11 children 7–12. Tour reservations can be made 24 hours in advance and are recommended. Memorial Day–Labor Day, daily 8am–6pm; Labor Day–Memorial Day, daily 9am–5pm (Nov–Feb, the mansion tour does not operate Tues). Closed New Year's Day, Thanksgiving, Christmas.* Graceland today is far more than the former home of "The King" of rock 'n' roll; it is Memphis's biggest attraction and resembles a small theme park or shopping mall in scope and design. There are Elvis Presley's two personal jets, the Elvis Presley Automobile Museum, the Sincerely Elvis collection of personal belongings, the *Walk a Mile in My Shoes* video, and, of course, Graceland itself. On most mornings, early risers can take a free walk up to Elvis's grave during a 90-minute period that ends 30 minutes before the mansion opens.

✪ **Memphis Music Hall of Fame.** *97 S. Second St.* ☎ *901/525-4007. Admission $7.50 adults, $2.50 children 5–12. Apr 1–Nov 1, Mon–Fri 10am–6pm, Sat 10am–8pm, Sun noon–6pm; Nov 2–Mar 31, Mon–Sat 10am–5pm, Sun noon–5pm.* Among the displays here are instruments used by some of the most famous Memphis musicians, with a focus on Elvis. However, Memphis's music from World War II to the present is chronicled, including videos of famous performers.

**Memphis Pink Palace Museum and Planetarium.** *3050 Central Ave.* ☎ *901/320-6320 or 901/763-IMAX for IMAX schedule. Museum, $5.50 adults, $5 seniors, $4 children 3–12, free for children under 3 and for everyone Thurs 5–8pm. Planetarium, $3.50 adults, $3 seniors, $2.50 children 3–12 (children under 2 not admitted). IMAX, $5.50 adults, $5 seniors, $4 children 3–12. Combination tickets available. Memorial Day–Labor Day, Mon–Wed 9am–5pm, Thurs–Sat and holidays 9am–9pm, Sun noon–5pm. Labor Day–Memorial Day, Mon–Wed 9am–4pm, Thurs 9am–8pm, Fri–Sat and holidays 9am–9pm, Sun noon–5pm.* This ostentatious pink-marble mansion was built shortly after World War I by grocery-store magnate Clarence Saunders, who revolutionized grocery shopping with the first Piggly Wiggly self-service market in 1916. Among the walk-through exhibits is a reproduction of the original Piggly Wiggly, and, with Memphis a major medical center, an extensive medical history exhibit. The planetarium presents a variety of shows, and there is also an IMAX movie theater.

**Mud Island.** *Mud Island Rd.* ☎ *800/507-6507 or 901/576-7241. Grounds and Mississippi River Museum, $8 adults, $6 seniors and children 4–11. Grounds only, $4 adults, $3 seniors and children 4–11. Parking $3. Apr–Memorial Day and Labor Day–Oct, Tues–Sun 10am–4pm; Memorial Day–Labor Day, daily 10am–7pm. Beach and pool: Memorial Day–Labor Day, daily noon–7pm. To reach Mud Island, take the monorail from Front St. at Adams Ave.* This island is home to a 52-acre park that includes several attractions. River Walk is a 5-block-long scale model of 900 miles of the Mississippi River, including the Gulf of Mexico, which is a huge public swimming pool with a view of the Memphis skyline. The Mississippi River Museum, the most entertaining museum in Memphis, offers more than 10,000 years of river history in engrossing life-size reconstructions. The *Memphis Belle,* perhaps the most famous B-17 bomber of World War II, is here, and the first Sunday of each month there are guided tours of its interior. Summer evenings, the Mud Island Amphitheater hosts top-name performers.

✪ **National Civil Rights Museum.** *450 Mulberry St.* ☎ *901/521-9699. Admission $5 adults, $4 seniors and students, $3 children 6–12, free for children under 6. June–Sept, Mon and Wed–Sat 10am–6pm, Sun noon–5pm; Oct–May, Mon and Wed–Sat 10am–5pm.* Civil rights leader Dr. Martin Luther King, Jr. always stayed at the Lorraine Motel when in Memphis, and it was here on a hotel balcony that he was assassinated on April 4, 1968. Saved from demolition, the Lorraine Motel was remodeled and today serves as the nation's memorial to the civil rights movement, with evocative displays and walk-through tableaux.

**The Pyramid.** *1 Auction Ave.* ☎ *901/526-5177. Guided tours, $3.75 adults, $2.75 seniors and children 4–11. Tours, mid-Apr–Labor Day, Mon–Sat 10am–4pm, Sun noon–4pm. Labor Day–mid-Apr, limited days and hours.* Named for the ancient capital of Egypt, Memphis has always evoked its namesake in various buildings and public artworks. The 32-story stainless-steel Pyramid is Memphis's answer to the sports dome, with a base the size of six football fields. Self-guided tours of the public areas and guided tours of the backstage areas are held year-round.

✪ **Sun Studio.** *706 Union Ave.* ☎ *901/521-0664. Admission $7.50 adults, free for children under 12 with parents. Daily 9am–7pm.* In the early 1950s, owner and recording engineer Sam Phillips recorded local artists here, like Elvis and Jerry Lee Lewis, who were creating a sound that would become rock 'n' roll. Greats like B. B. King and Johnny Cash also started here. Sun Studio has remained an active recording studio, used by such artists as U2 and Bonnie Raitt.

**PARKS & GARDENS**    Located in Midtown and bounded by Poplar Avenue, East Parkway, North Parkway, and McLean Boulevard, Overton Park, one of Memphis's largest parks, includes not only the Memphis Zoo and Aquarium but the Memphis Brooks Museum of Art, the Memphis College of Art, the Overton Park Municipal Golf Course, tennis courts, hiking and biking trails, and an open-air theater. The surrounding residential neighborhoods are some of the wealthiest in the city. Farther east, Audubon Park, bounded by Park Avenue, Perkins Road, Southern Avenue, and Goodlet Street, contains the W. C. Paul Arboretum, the Memphis Botanic Garden, Theatre Memphis, and the Audubon Park Municipal Golf Course.

**BEST BETS FOR KIDS**    The **Memphis Pink Palace Museum and Planetarium** (see "Attractions," above) offers an array of sights and fun, including a real mastodon skeleton and an animated hand-carved miniature circus. The **Peabody Ducks** are famous as the waddling little quackers who spend each day in the lobby of the posh Peabody Hotel, 149 Union Ave. (☎ **901/529-4000**). **Mud Island** (see "Attractions," above) offers a huge swimming pool. The ✪ **Memphis Zoo and Aquarium,** Overton Park, 2000 Galloway Ave. (☎ **901/276-WILD**), offers not only wild animals but also farm animals, a discovery center, and children's rides. The **Lichterman Nature Center,** 1680 Lynnfield Rd. (☎ **901/767-7322**), is a 65-acre nature preserve that serves as both an environmental education center and a wildlife sanctuary.

**SPORTS**    The **Memphis Chicks Baseball Club** (☎ **901/272-1687**), a farm team of the Kansas City Royals, plays at Tim McCarver Stadium on the Mid-South Fairgrounds at the corner of East Parkway and Central Avenue. Tickets are available through Ticketmaster (☎ **901/527-5700**). The **Liberty Bowl Football Classic** (☎ **901/795-7700**) is the biggest football event of the year in Memphis, pitting two of the top college teams in a December postseason game at the Liberty Bowl Memorial Stadium, also on the Mid-South Fairgrounds. The **Federal Express St. Jude Golf Classic** (☎ **901/748-0534**), a PGA charity tournament, is held each year in June or July at the Tournament Players Club at Southwind. Horse shows are popular and the biggest of the year is the **Germantown Charity Horse Show** held each June at the Germantown Horse Show Arena, just off Poplar Pike at Melanie Smith Lane in Germantown. The

**Kroger St. Jude International Indoor Tennis Championships** (☎ 901/765-4400), which are a part of the Association of Tournament Players Tour, is held each year in February at the Racquet Club of Memphis.

**SHOPPING** The dozens of shopping malls and plazas in East Memphis are where the majority of people head for quality merchandise. However, in recent years some interesting and trendy shops have appeared in the Midtown area, particularly around Overton Square and the Cooper–Young area. The main antique districts are at the intersection of Central Avenue and East Parkway, on Cooper Street between Overton Square and Young Street in Midtown, and along Summer Avenue in East Memphis. A favorite store is **A. Schwab Dry Goods Store,** 163 Beale St. (☎ 901/523-9782), as much a Memphis attraction as a place to shop.

## ACCOMMODATIONS

There are only a few downtown Memphis hotels, and although a few, including the elegant Peabody Hotel, are among the best in the city, most are below the standards (and rates) of downtown hotels in other cities. Most of the better hotels, whether expensive or not, are in East Memphis, which is more than 20 miles from downtown Memphis. Luckily, East Memphis is also where you'll find most of the better restaurants. If you're on a family trip or on business, you may prefer East Memphis. If you're here to sample the Beale Street nightlife, then consider staying downtown. The Midtown area is another option, and is convenient to Beale Street, many midtown museums, and the East Memphis restaurants.

**✪ Adam's Mark Hotel.** *939 Ridge Lake Blvd., Memphis, TN 38120.* ☎ *800/ 444-ADAM or 901/684-6664. Fax 901/762-7411. 379 rms, 13 suites. $114–$165 double; $350–$600 suite. Special discounts available. AE, CB, DC, DISC, MC, V. North of Poplar Ave. on the west side of I-240 (turn left at the bottom of the hill and go under the bridge).* With its glass tower rising out of a pond, this is Memphis's most dramatic hotel. Most guest rooms are wedge-shaped, making them attractively different, and bathrooms offer dressing areas. The restaurant features singing waiters, and the lounge offers live music some nights. Extras include complimentary airport shuttle, secretarial services, and an outdoor pool.

**✪ French Quarter Suites Hotel.** *2144 Madison Ave., Memphis, TN 38104.* ☎ *800/843-0353 or 901/728-4000. Fax 901/278-1262. 104 suites. $110–$145 double. All rates include continental breakfast. AE, CB, DC, DISC, MC, V.* Located in Overton Square, one of Memphis's entertainment districts, this hotel draws on New Orleans for architectural theme and room decor. Double whirlpool tubs and private balconies in some rooms make it popular with honeymooners. The bar features live music some nights. The hotel has a cafe and outdoor pool, and offers an evening social hour and complimentary newspaper.

**Holiday Inn Memphis East.** *5795 Poplar Ave., Memphis, TN 38119.* ☎ *800/ HOLIDAY or 901/682-7881. Fax 901/682-7881. 243 rms, 3 suites. $89–$139 double; $129–$149 suite. AE, CB, DC, DISC, ER, JCB, MC, V.* At the interchange of I-240 and Poplar Avenue, convenient to both east-side businesses and the interstate, this high-rise hotel, though geared to corporate travelers, appeals to vacationers with its sunny indoor pool area. Lackluster rooms do offer upper-floor views, and corner king rooms are spacious. All offer amenities such as coffeemakers. Conveniences include a restaurant, lounge, and complimentary airport shuttle.

**Homewood Suites.** *5811 Poplar Ave., Memphis, TN 38119.* ☎ *800/CALL-HOME or 901/763-0500. Fax 901/763-0132. 140 suites. $109–$159 suite. Rates include continental breakfast. AE, CB, DC, DISC, MC, V.* Offering some of Memphis's most attractive and spacious accommodations, Homewood features rooms around a landscaped courtyard with a swimming pool and basketball court, and early-American rooms with fireplaces. Nearby restaurants offer room service. Extras include a complimentary airport and shopping shuttle, morning newspaper, outdoor pool, hot tub, convenience store, and executive center.

**Memphis Marriott.** *2625 Thousand Oaks Blvd., Memphis, TN 38118.* ☎ *800/ 627-3587 or 901/362-6200. Fax 901/360-8836. 320 rms, 4 suites. $54–$154 double; $300 suite. AE, CB, DC, DISC, MC, V.* Located just south of I-240 at the Perkins Road exit, this modern high-rise hotel is about midway between the airport and the East Memphis exit, and near the Mall of Memphis. The rooms are small, some with a view, but king rooms offer desks and a sofa. The hotel has a piano bar, dining room, dance lounge, complimentary airport shuttle, indoor and outdoor pools, hot tub, and sauna.

✪ **Peabody Memphis.** *149 Union Ave., Memphis, TN 38103.* ☎ *800/ PEABODY or 901/529-4000. 468 rms, 15 suites. $160–$315 double; $595 suite. AE, CB, DC, DISC, ER, MC, V. Parking $10.* The elegant Peabody, one of the finest hotels in the South, features its famous ducks playing in a lobby fountain. Guest rooms offer French styling and king-size beds. A bar, deli/pastry shop, and two restaurants are here, including the noted Chez Philippe (see "Dining," below). Full athletic facility and shopping arcade.

**Radisson Hotel Memphis.** *185 Union Ave., Memphis, TN 38103.* ☎ *800/ 333-3333 or 901/528-1800. Fax 901/525-8509. 280 rms, 7 suites. $109–$115 double; $145–$240 suite. AE, CB, DC, DISC, MC, V. Parking $4.* The Radisson, in a restored building with a good location, is popular with tour groups. Regular rooms are large with modern furnishings, and for a bit more money there are king resort rooms and spacious corner rooms offering three walls of windows. Facilities include restaurant, ice-cream parlor, bar, outdoor pool, hot tub, and sauna.

✪ **Ridgeway Inn.** *5679 Poplar Ave. (at I-240), Memphis, TN 38119.* ☎ *800/ 822-3360 or 901/766-4000. Fax 901/763-1857. 155 rms, 4 suites. $94–$96 double; $195–$295 suite. AE, CB, DC, DISC, ER, MC, V.* Located just west of I-240 at the Poplar Avenue exit in East Memphis, and operated by the company that runs the Peabody, this popular hotel offers comparable accommodations in a modern building. It's a favorite of business travelers, and the early-American guest rooms cater to them with king rooms offering desks and couches. There are concierge-level rooms, a restaurant, bar, and outdoor pool.

**Wilson World Hotel.** *2715 Cherry Rd., Memphis, TN 38118.* ☎ *800/WILSONS or 901/366-0000. Fax 901/366-6361. 178 rms, 72 suites. $81 double; $86 suite. AE, CB, DC, DISC, MC, V.* Though the facade looks plain, the glitzy atrium lobby offers a sunken lounge with a stage above the bar and behind that a swimming pool and hot tubs. All rooms offer wet bars and refrigerators, with suites only slightly larger. Facilities include restaurant, snack bar, airport shuttle, and barber/beauty salon.

**Wilson World Hotel–Graceland.** *3677 Elvis Presley Blvd., Memphis, TN 38116.* ☎ *800/WILSONS or 901/332-1000. Fax 901/332-2107. 134 rms, 60 suites. $51 double; $54–$65 suite. AE, CB, DC, DISC, MC, V.* This hotel has a gate right into the Graceland parking lot, and the decor would fit right in at Elvis's home. The rooms, with refrigerators and microwaves, may have seen too many Elvis fans, but they're clean and comfortable. Room TVs offer 24-hour Elvis videos.

## DINING

Memphis claims the title of pork barbecue capital of the world. There is also old-fashioned American food—here known as "meat-and-three," referring to the three vegetables you get with whatever meat you order. Some excellent restaurants offer contemporary creations with Southern and international influences.

**Aubergine.** *5007 Black Rd.* ☎ *901/767-7840. Reservations recommended. Main courses $18–$22. AE, CB, MC, V. Tues–Fri 11:30am–2:30pm; Tues–Sat 6–9:30pm, Fri–Sat 6–10pm. CONTEMPORARY FRENCH.* In this intimate restaurant in the parking lot of an older shopping plaza, you'll find businesspeople and gentrified Memphians enjoying French cuisine with a twist, set amid colorful faux-painted walls and flower arrangements. This is a good place for both fish and wild game in season. Try the scallops roasted in a potato crust.

**Automatic Slim's Tonga Club.** *83 S. Second St.* ☎ *901/525-7948. Reservations recommended. Main courses $15–$22. AE, MC, V. Mon–Fri 11am–2:30pm; Mon–Thurs 4–10pm, Fri–Sat 4–11pm. NEW AMERICAN.* Named for a blues song and local teen hangout, this downtown restaurant's decor was created by artists from New York and Memphis, including zebra-print banquettes. The food here is also creative, including Caribbean voodoo stew with mussels, shrimp, whitefish, and crab legs with rice. Vegetarian main courses are available. If you like Automatic Slim's, check out their new restaurant called **Cielo** (☎ **901/524-1886**), in a renovated Victorian mansion in the Victorian Village historic district at 726 Adams Ave.

**✪ Chez Philippe.** *In the Peabody Memphis Hotel, 149 Union Ave.* ☎ *901/529-4188. Reservations recommended. Main courses $20–$30. AE, MC, V. Mon–Sat 6–10pm. FRENCH/SOUTHERN.* This palatial restaurant, with marble columns and chandeliers, features dining on three levels. It offers a mix of contemporary French and down-home New Southern dishes, with some Asian influences offered by Chef José Gutierrez, who changes the menu constantly. Main courses might include a roasted monkfish with crispy country ham.

**✪ Corky's Bar-B-Q.** *5259 Poplar Ave.* ☎ *901/685-9744. Reservations not accepted. Dinners $6–$7. AE, CB, DC, DISC, MC, V. Sun–Thurs 10:45am–10pm, Fri–Sat 10:45am–10:30pm. BARBECUE.* With rock 'n' roll piped indoors and out, big crowds, and the aromatic barbecue smells, this is a jolly place with the largest barbecue pit in the state. Corky's has a drive-up window and an 800 number (800/926-7597) for ribs shipped "anywhere." Try Memphis-style pulled pork shoulder.

**The Cupboard.** *1495 Union Ave.* ☎ *901/276-8015. Reservations not accepted. Meat and two vegetables $5.50. No credit cards. Mon–Fri 11am–8pm, Sat–Sun 11am–3pm. SOUTHERN.* This place is usually packed with Memphians having a filling home-cooked meal of Southern-style vegetables and meat. Vegetables range from turnip greens to fried green tomatoes. Try the pecan pie for dessert.

**La Tourelle Restaurant/Tower Café.** *2146 Monroe Ave.* ☎ *901/726-5771. Reservations recommended. Main courses $20–$27; tasting menu $50; bistro menu $20. MC, V. Daily 6–9:30pm; Sun brunch 11:30am–2pm. FRENCH.* The exterior of this turn-of-the century house in the Overton Square neighborhood belies the elegance inside. An entree might be rack of lamb marinated in molasses and garlic. The Tower Café menu, served in The Tower, offers three courses for $20. Sunday brunch is elegant.

**Maxwell's.** *948 S. Cooper St. (at Young Ave.).* ☎ *901/725-1009. Reservations accepted for eight or more. Main courses $10–$17. AE, DC, MC, V. Mon–Fri 11am–2am, Sat–Sun 5pm–2am. MEDITERRANEAN/NEW AMERICAN.* The Cooper-Young intersection is one of the hippest corners in Memphis, and this neighborhood restaurant is part of the reason why. The clientele tends to be urban sophisticates with artistic inclinations, which is reflected in the restaurant's decor of dark walls with a cosmic theme. A main dish offering is braised lamb shank with burgundy sauce.

**✪ Puck's.** *22 S. Cooper St.* ☎ *901/722-8744. Reservations recommended. Main courses $16–$20. MC, V. Wed–Sun 5–10pm. NEW AMERICAN.* This small, unassuming restaurant in Overton Square has captured the heart of savvy diners with its artful presentation of imaginative food combinations. The emphasis is on fresh local products. A favorite here is grilled rack of lamb with roasted garlic and plum sauce.

**Raji.** *712 W. Brookhaven Circle.* ☎ *901/685-8723. Reservations required. Fixed-price dinner $35 for three courses; weekend dinners with wine $50–$70. AE, MC, V. Tues–Sat 6–10pm, last seating at 9:30pm. FRENCH/INDIAN.* On a side street in a little house, chef Raji Jallepalli has for several years served up amazing combinations of continental and Indian cuisines. In the simple, elegant dining rooms, a meal might be Atlantic salmon with dill-turmeric emulsion and mango-ginger sauce. Some weekends Raji presents multicourse dinners with wine.

✪ **Rendezvous.** *52 S. Second St.* ☎ *901/523-2746. Main plates $7–$13. AE, CB, DC, MC, V. Tues–Thurs 4:30–11:30pm; Fri–Sat noon–midnight. BARBECUE.* This Memphis institution for great barbecue is down General Washburn Alley, across from the Peabody Hotel. Downtown since 1948, the Rendezvous offers a museum-like display in a cozy cellar. Ask for the red beans and rice, not on the menu but served free every night until they run out.

**Sun Studio Café.** *710 Union Ave.* ☎ *901/521-0664. Main courses $4–$6. AE, DISC, MC, V. Sept–May, daily 10am–6pm; June–Aug, daily 9am–7pm. DINER.* Located next to Sun Studio, this historic cafe has long been a place for recording engineers and musicians to grab a bite to eat. Old photos and memorabilia abound and the jukebox is reputed to be the best in Memphis. Try the famous Dixie fried-banana pie with ice cream.

## MEMPHIS AFTER DARK

For information on the entertainment scene, pick up a copy of the *Memphis Flyer,* the arts and entertainment weekly, which comes out on Thursday, or try the Friday edition of the *Commercial Appeal,* Memphis's morning daily newspaper. For tickets to sporting events and performances at the Pyramid, Mud Island Amphitheater, and the Mid-South Coliseum, contact **Ticketmaster** (☎ **901/525-1515**).

**BLUES & BEALE STREET**    Beale Street is the center of Memphis's nightclub scene. However, Beale Street is primarily a tourist scene. For genuine blues, head out to more out-of-the-way spots, for Earnestine and Hazel's, and Newby's are now the true home of Memphis blues.

Yes, the "king of the blues" does occasionally play at the **B. B. King's Blues Club,** 143 Beale St. (☎ **901/524-5464**), but any night you can catch blazing blues with some of the best bands, and sometimes famous musicians who drop by to jam. ✪ **Rum Boogie Cafe and Mr. Handy's Blues Hall,** 182 Beale St. (☎ **901/528-0150**), offers live music nightly, with the house band playing everything from blues to country, and occasional performances by touring blues bands. Once a dive, today ✪ **Earnestine and Hazel's,** 531 S. Main St. at the corner of Calhoun Street (☎ **901/523-9754**), is one of Memphis's hottest nightspots. Though there's Friday evening happy-hour jazz and R&B on Sunday afternoons, things don't really get cookin' here until after midnight on Friday and Saturday. The music is a mix of blues, R&B, and rock, and the clientele is equally mixed.

Located near the University of Memphis, the cavernous **Newby's,** 539 S. Highland St. (☎ **901/452-8408**), is a popular college hangout with two stages—one large, one small. On Tuesday night, the small stage plays host to the Memphis Musicians Jam, featuring up-and-coming local talent. It's live rock most other nights.

At the **New Daisy Theatre,** 330 Beale St. (☎ **901/525-8979** or 901/525-8981), you'll find regional and national rock bands. The New Daisy showcases musicians with past hits who no longer draw the crowds.

**THE PERFORMING ARTS**   Memphis's main performance hall, the **Orpheum Theatre,** 203 S. Main Ave., was built in 1928 as a vaudeville hall, and its opera house elegance makes it the most spectacular performance venue in the city. It is home to **Opera Memphis** (☎ 901/678-2706), which annually stages four operas plus a concert, and the **Ballet Memphis** (☎ 901/763-0139). The **Memphis Symphony Orchestra** (☎ 901/324-3627) performs most concerts at the Christ United Methodist Church, at the corner of Poplar Avenue and Laurelwood, across from the Chickasaw Oaks Plaza.

**CLUBS & BARS**   **Hernando's Hideaway,** 3210 Old Hernando Rd. (☎ 901/398-7496), on the south side near Graceland, is a legendary honky tonk where country music and rock greats have been known to drop by just to listen to the live music or play a few songs. **Automatic Slim's Tonga Club,** 83 S. Second St. (☎ 901/525-7948), with hip decor and a great menu, offers live music on weekends and attracts the arty and upscale 30- and 40-something crowd. Anchoring the trendiest corner in Memphis, ✪ **Maxwell's,** 948 S. Cooper St. (☎ 901/725-1009), is one of the city's hottest restaurants and a lively bar for the young and fashionable to gather. The **Peabody Lobby Bar,** Peabody Hotel, 149 Union Ave. (☎ 901/529-4000), is the most elegant place for drinks, but arrive after the departure of the 5pm crowds for the march of the Peabody ducks.

## DAY TRIPS FROM MEMPHIS

**ALEX HALEY'S HOME**   This attraction is enjoyable for any fans of Haley's Pulitzer Prize book *Roots,* or those interested in African-American history. The **Alex Haley House and Museum** (☎ 901/738-2240) is located in the small town of Henning, about 45 miles north of downtown Memphis on U.S. 51. Nearby is the family burial site, where Haley and many of his ancestors, including Chicken George (the television series' most endearing character), are buried.

**MISSISSIPPI CASINOS**   In recent years the days of showboats and games of chance have returned to the Mississippi River in states bordering Tennessee. You still won't find any blackjack tables in God-fearing Tennessee, but you don't have to drive far for some Las Vegas–style action. In fact, you don't have to drive at all, since **Kirby Tours** (☎ 800/748-1659) will pick you up at your Memphis hotel and take you to the new casinos across the state line in and near Tunica, Mississippi, for between $20 and $25. If you drive, take either Tenn. 61 or I-55 south. Exit either Miss. 304 or Miss. 4 off the interstate. Head west to the river, watching for signs. The casinos closest to Tunica are about 35 miles.

The closest casinos to Memphis are 12 miles south of the state line off U.S. 61. Here you'll find **Circus Circus Casino** (☎ 601/357-1111), **Horseshoe Casino and Hotel** (☎ 800/303-7463), and Sheraton Casino (☎ 800/391-3777). Continuing south on U.S. 61 and then west on Miss. 304, you'll come to a half dozen more casinos.

## 10  New Orleans

New Orleans is not like any other place in the United States. Its French and Spanish origins, mixed with Caribbean and Acadian influences, have produced a distinctive and different culture. Inscrutable, renegade, and occasionally lawless, it's a town of inside jokes and clever ruses, and in its earliest days it was a haven for schemers, tricksters, and charming criminals. The rule here is *laissez les bon temps rouler*—let the good times roll.

In spite its crowds of visitors, its past at times seems palpably, almost spookily alive. As you walk the narrow streets of the French Quarter or ride the historic streetcar that still goes up St. Charles Avenue or wander in the Old South ambience of the Garden District, the city's past will be present all around you.

# New Orleans

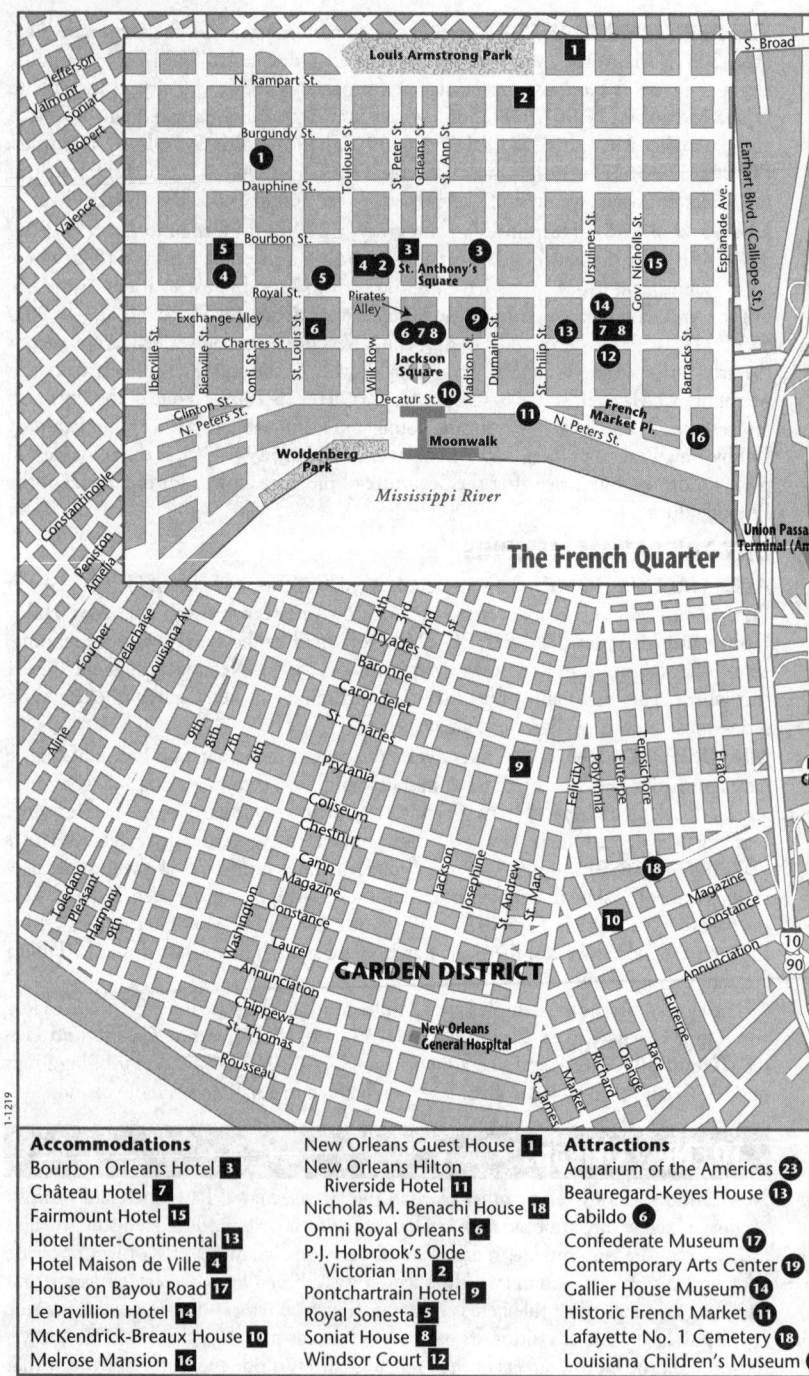

**Accommodations**

Bourbon Orleans Hotel **3**
Château Hotel **7**
Fairmount Hotel **15**
Hotel Inter-Continental **13**
Hotel Maison de Ville **4**
House on Bayou Road **17**
Le Pavillion Hotel **14**
McKendrick-Breaux House **10**
Melrose Mansion **16**

New Orleans Guest House **1**
New Orleans Hilton
  Riverside Hotel **11**
Nicholas M. Benachi House **18**
Omni Royal Orleans **6**
P.J. Holbrook's Olde
  Victorian Inn **2**
Pontchartrain Hotel **9**
Royal Sonesta **5**
Soniat House **8**
Windsor Court **12**

**Attractions**

Aquarium of the Americas **23**
Beauregard-Keyes House **13**
Cabildo **6**
Confederate Museum **17**
Contemporary Arts Center **19**
Gallier House Museum **14**
Historic French Market **11**
Lafayette No. 1 Cemetery **18**
Louisiana Children's Museum **2**

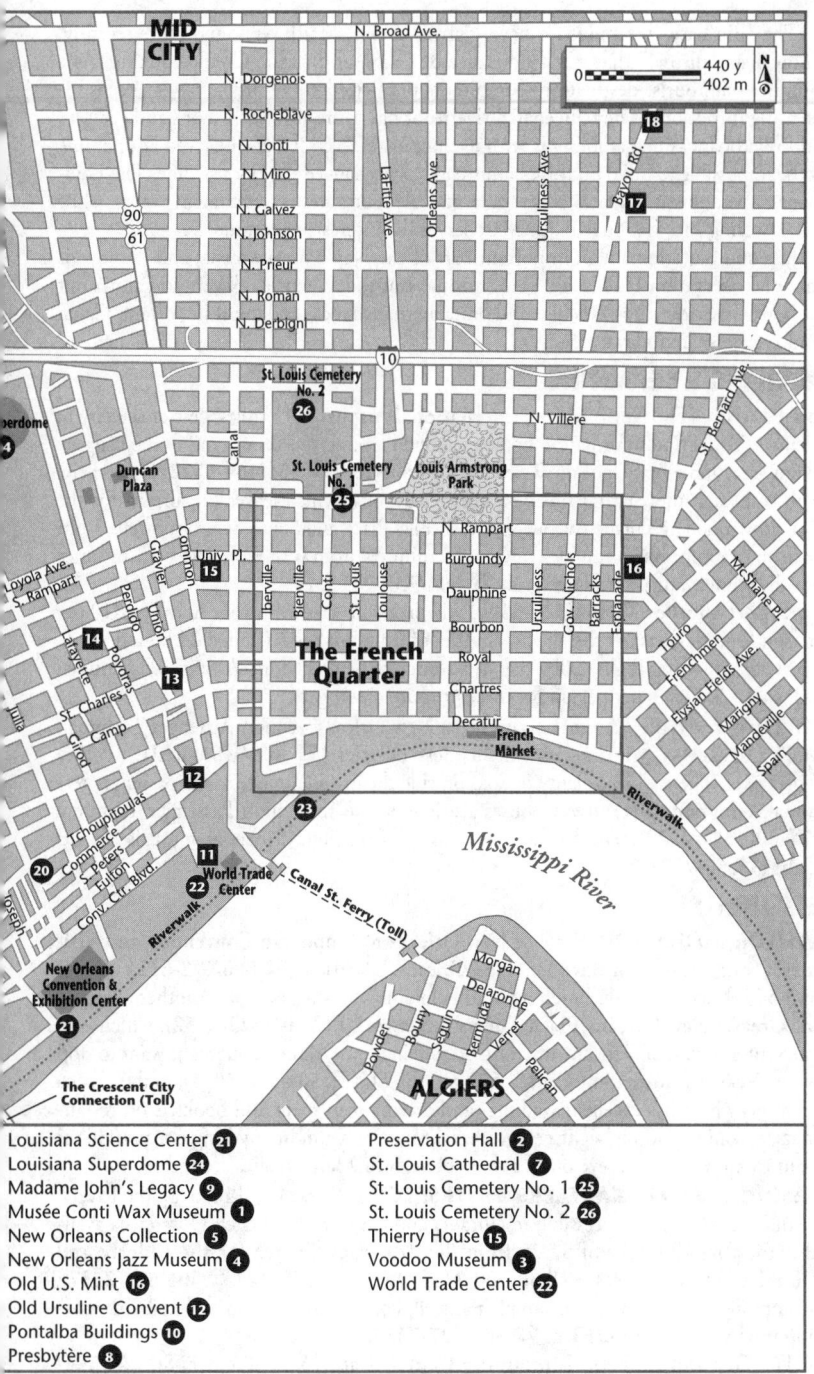

MID CITY

N. Broad Ave.

N. Dorgenois
N. Rocheblave
N. Tonti
N. Miro
N. Galvez
N. Johnson
N. Prieur
N. Roman
N. Derbigni

LaFitte Ave.
Orleans Ave.
Ursuliness Ave.
Bayou Rd.

0    440 y / 402 m

90 / 61

18
17

10

St. Louis Cemetery No. 2
26

N. Villere

Superdome
24

Duncan Plaza

Canal
Common
Univ. Pl.

St. Louis Cemetery No. 1
25

Louis Armstrong Park

N. Rampart
Burgundy
Dauphine
Bourbon
Royal
Chartres
Decatur

Ursuliness
Gov. Nichols
Barracks
Esplanade

16

McShane Pl.

Gravier
Loyola Ave.
S. Rampart
Perdido
Union

Iberville
Bienville
Conti
St. Louis
Toulouse

The French Quarter

Touro
Frenchmen

Elysian Fields Ave.

St. Bernard Ave.

Lafayette
Poydras

13

14

Julia
St. Charles
Girod
Camp

French Market

Mangny
Mandeville
Spain

12

23

Mississippi River

Tchoupitoulas
Commerce
S. Peters
Fulton
Conv. Ctr. Blvd.

11
World Trade Center
22

Canal St. Ferry (Toll)

Riverwalk

Riverwalk

20

New Orleans Convention & Exhibition Center

21

Morgan
Delaronde
Bermuda

Powder
Bouny
Seguin
Verret
Pelican

The Crescent City Connection (Toll)

ALGIERS

Louisiana Science Center **21**
Louisiana Superdome **24**
Madame John's Legacy **9**
Musée Conti Wax Museum **1**
New Orleans Collection **5**
New Orleans Jazz Museum **4**
Old U.S. Mint **16**
Old Ursuline Convent **12**
Pontalba Buildings **10**
Presbytère **8**

Preservation Hall **2**
St. Louis Cathedral **7**
St. Louis Cemetery No. 1 **25**
St. Louis Cemetery No. 2 **26**
Thierry House **15**
Voodoo Museum **3**
World Trade Center **22**

The "Big Easy" is famous for having given us jazz, Mardi Gras, and more recently, "Louisiana cuisine," that trendy mixture of Cajun and classic Creole cooking. As a number-one tourist destination—despite its publicized crime problems—it keeps increasing its options. The rejuvenated riverfront has come alive with shops and eateries, and riverboat casino gambling is with us once again. Skyscrapers, believed at one time to be impossible to build on this swampy site, have changed the city's skyline. The Louisiana Superdome is the focal point for large-scale sports and entertainment events, while the towering International Trade Mart serves the interests of commerce.

Jazz and blues remain an important part of the New Orleans scene, and the joyous jazz of Preservation Hall is still going strong. But today, music of every sort flows out of Bourbon Street clubs. R&B, world beat, alternative rock, and, most important, Cajun and zydeco share today's scene.

## ARRIVING & DEPARTING

**BY PLANE**  The **New Orleans International Airport** is 15 miles west of the city in Kenner. You'll find information booths scattered around the airport and in the baggage claim area, and a branch of the **Travelers Aid Society** (☎ 504/464-3522) is also here. You can reach the Central Business District by **bus,** which leaves the airport for the downtown side of Tulane Avenue, between Elks Place and South Saratoga Street, from 6am to 6:30pm; buses run every 12 to 15 minutes from 6 to 9am, every 23 minutes at other times. For information, call ☎ 504/737-9611.

**Airport Shuttle** (☎ 504/522-3500) will take you directly to your hotel for $10 per person (one way); ask at the airport shuttle information desks (staffed 24 hours). *Note:* For your departing flight, call a day in advance to be picked up. A **taxi** to downtown will cost $21, or $8 per person for three or more passengers.

**BY TRAIN & BUS**  **Amtrak** trains reach New Orleans's Union Passenger Terminal, 1001 Loyola Ave., in the Central Business District (☎ 800/USA-RAIL or 504/524-7571). There will be plenty of taxis outside the main entrance of the passenger terminal. **Greyhound–Trailways** buses also come into the Union Passenger Terminal (☎ 800/231-2222). There should be taxis out front, but if there aren't, call **United Cabs** (☎ 504/522-9771).

## ESSENTIALS

**VISITOR INFORMATION**  The **New Orleans Metropolitan Convention and Visitor Bureau,** 1520 Sugar Bowl Dr., New Orleans, LA 70112 (☎ 800/672-6124 or 504/566-5055), will mail you brochures and help you with information. Another source is the **Greater New Orleans Black Tourism Network** (☎ 504/523-5652), which provides information on African-American culture in New Orleans. You might want to stop by the **Visitor Information Center,** 529 St. Ann St. (☎ 504/566-5031), in the French Quarter, which has excellent walking- and driving-tour maps and booklets on restaurants, accommodations, sightseeing, special tours, and almost anything else you might want to know. Keep an eye out for the mobile **Info à la Cart** sites around town.

**RESOURCES FOR TRAVELERS WITH SPECIAL NEEDS**  "Rollin' by the River," a guide to wheelchair-accessible restaurants and clubs in the French Quarter, is available for a handling fee of $2.25 from the **Advocacy Center for the Elderly and Disabled,** 210 O'Keefe Ave., Suite 700, New Orleans, LA 70112 (☎ 504/522-2337). Seniors are welcome to use this number as well. For information about specialized transportation systems, call **LIFT** at ☎ 504/827-7433.

The **Gay and Lesbian Community Center** is at 816 N. Rampart St. (☎ 504/522-1103). The **NO/AIDS** task force has a 24-hour hotline (☎ 504/945-4000). *Ambush Mag 2000,* 828A Bourbon St., New Orleans, LA 70116 (☎ 504/522-8049), is the Gulf South weekly entertainment/news publication for the gay and lesbian community. *Impact Gulf South Gay News* is another area publication.

**EMERGENCIES & SAFETY**   For fire, ambulance, and police, dial ☎ **911.** If no doctor is available in your hotel or guesthouse, call or go to the emergency room at **Ochsner Medical Institutions,** 880 Commerce Rd. W. (☎ **504/842-3460**).

New Orleans has a high street-crime rate. Don't walk alone at night. Don't go into the cemeteries alone at any time. Ask around locally before you go anywhere—people will tell you if you should take a cab.

## GETTING AROUND

If you drive, drive defensively—there are a lot of reckless drivers around. Traffic officers are fairly tolerant of moving violations but are murder on illegal parking. French Quarter sightseeing is best done on foot—streets there are one way, and on weekdays during daylight hours, most of Royal and Bourbon streets are closed to traffic.

**BY BUS & STREETCAR**   For complete bus information, call the **Regional Transit Authority (RTA)** (☎ **504/248-3900**) or pick up an excellent city map at the **Visitor Information Center,** 529 St. Ann St., in the French Quarter. Fares are $1 (you must have exact change, and transfers are an extra 10¢); express buses are $1.25. A **VisiTour** pass entitles you to an unlimited number of rides on all streetcar and bus lines, and costs $4 for 1 day and $8 for 3 days. Ask your hotel to point you to the nearest vendor or call the RTA.

The **Riverfront streetcars** are vintage trolleys that run for 1.9 miles along the riverfront from the Old Mint, across Canal Street, to Riverview. The fare is $1.25; there are stops along the way and ramp access for the disabled. Don't miss the 1 1/2-hour ride down St. Charles Avenue on the old **streetcar line** (a national historic landmark). Streetcars run 24 hours a day at frequent intervals, and the fare is $1 each way (you must have exact change). Board at Canal and Carondelet streets (directly across Canal from Bourbon Street). Lafayette Square is at the 500 block of St. Charles, and across from it is Gallier Hall, built in the 1840s, the seat of the city's government for 100 years. The Garden District begins at Jackson Avenue, and you may want to get off to explore. Loyola and Tulane universities are at the 6000 block, across from Audubon Park.

**BY TAXI**   Taxis are plentiful and respond quickly to telephone calls. They can be hailed on the street in the French Quarter and some parts of the Central Business District. Rates are $1.70 when you enter the taxi and $1 per mile thereafter. During special events (like Mardi Gras and Jazz Fest) the rate is $3 per person (or the meter rate if it's greater) no matter where you go. The city's most reliable company is **United Cabs** (☎ **504/524-9606**).

## WHAT TO SEE & DO

**SPECIAL EVENTS**   The **USF&G Sugar Bowl Classic** pits two of the country's top-ranking college football teams on New Year's Day. February brings **Mardi Gras,** the famous culmination of the 2-month-long Carnival season. March sees the **Black Heritage Festival** and the **Tennessee Williams New Orleans Literary Festival,** a 4-day series of events. In late March or early April, the **Spring Fiesta** begins its events. In April, the **French Quarter Festival** celebrates New Orleans's history with a parade down Bourbon Street, visits to historic homes, and other events. The **New Orleans Jazz and Heritage Festival** is usually held the last weekend in April and the first weekend in May.

**ESCORTED TOURS**   The nonprofit volunteer group **Friends of the Cabildo** (☎ **504/523-3939**) offers a guided 2-hour walking tour of the French Quarter that leaves from in front of the Museum Store, 523 St. Ann St., on Tuesday through Sunday at 10am and 1:30pm and Monday at 1:30pm, except holidays. A donation of $10 for adults or $8 for seniors and those ages 13–20 is requested. No reservations are necessary—just show up. National Park Service rangers offer excellent free walking tours on a variety of themes; contact them at the Jean Lafitte National Park and Preserve's **Folklife and Visitor Center,** 419 Decatur St. (☎ 504/589-2636). Only the Faubourg Promenade Tour through the Garden District requires booking ahead.

**Tours by Isabelle** (☎ 504/391-3544) takes small groups on a 3-hour minibus tour that covers the French Quarter, the cemeteries, and other points of interest in the city. Departure times are 9am and 1:30pm, and the fee is $30; book as far in advance as possible. The afternoon Combo Tour adds Longue Vue Gardens to the itinerary.

✪ **Magic Walking Tours** (☎ 504/593-9693), at 1015 Iberville St., offers guided walking tours daily of St. Louis Cemetery No. 1, the French Quarter, and the Garden District, as well as the Voodoo, Haunted House, and the Vampire Tour. Call ahead for tour schedules. Tours cost between $9 and $13 for adults and all children tour free.

**"Roots" of New Orleans, A Heritage City Tour,** 1215 Prytania St., no. 238 (☎ 504/522-7414), offers two black heritage tours daily, from Thursday to Saturday (at press time there were plans to offer the tours 6 days a week, so call ahead to see if the schedule has changed).

Fans of Anne Rice can take one of **Anne Rice's New Orleans Tours** (☎ 888/ SEE-RICE or 504/592-0560), sponsored by the author who introduced vampires to New Orleans. **Haunted History Tours,** 2814 Robert St. (☎ 504/897-2030), are entertaining outings featuring more authentic New Orleans legends, complete with theatrical guides.

**Gray Line** (☎ 800/535-7786 or 504/587-0861) has bus and trolley tours of the entire city. The trolley tour costs $18 for a 1-day pass and $25 for a 2-day pass with unlimited boarding and departing privileges.

**BOAT TOURS** The steamboat *Natchez,* 1340 World Trade Center of New Orleans (☎ 800/233-BOAT or 504/586-8777), a three-deck sternwheeler, offers two 2-hour daytime or evening cruises daily. There is a jazz dinner cruise every evening. Call for the schedules and the prices.

The sternwheeler *John James Audubon* (☎ 800/233-BOAT or 504/586-8777) offers four trips daily with stopovers at the zoo, the aquarium, and other attractions. Call for prices, sailing schedules, and reservations.

**PLANTATION TOURS** A 7-hour River Road tour is offered by **Gray Line** (☎ 504/ 587-0861). Nottoway and Oak Alley plantations are visited for an all-inclusive $50 charge. Tours at 9am on Tuesday, Thursday, and Sunday pick you up at your hotel. **Tours by Isabelle** (☎ 504/391-3544) takes a small group to Oak Alley, Madewood, and Nottoway plantations, including lunch at Madewood. This outfit also offers a Cajun Bayou Tour and a more extensive plantation tour.

**THE FRENCH QUARTER** Residents here may rue the fact and struggle against it, but the French Quarter is essentially one huge, living tourist attraction. At times its narrow old streets, seemingly ancient French- and Spanish-style buildings, and eccentric characters evoke an Old European town center. Other times, the place feels more like Disneyland. In either case, the Quarter packs a lot of history, architecture, entertainment, and commerce into approximately 80 small square blocks. The city was laid out in 1718 by a French royal engineer named Adrien de Pauger, and today it is a great anomaly in contemporary America. Only a few other American cities can claim an original town center, complete with original structures, that has maintained the vitality of its finest days. Activity in the French Quarter emanates outward from the lush green park below Andrew Jackson's equestrian statue: Jackson Square. Decatur, Chartres, Bourbon, and Royal—these streets are witness to a year-long carnival. The Quarter is a little frayed at some of its edges. Farthest from Jackson Square are the quiet residential areas. In the heart of the Quarter, the first floors of most buildings contain some form of commercial venture—palatial antique shops, museum-like retail stores, bizarre specialty shops, bars, and dining rooms.

The most impressive spots in the Quarter are all but hidden from the visitor: the courtyards. You can occasionally glimpse through the iron gates of an old carriageway. These can be an artful combination of red brick, flagstone, tropical greenery, and flowers—often with some kind of fountain or pool thrown in for good measure.

The Vieux Carré Commission is ever vigilant to balance contemporary economic interests in the Quarter with concerns over historic preservation. Not only has the commission encouraged restoration, but it has also joined in the battle to hold back certain modern would-be intruders. There's not a traffic light within the whole of the French Quarter—they're relegated to fringe streets—and streetlights are of the old gaslight style. In 1996, large city buses were banned from the neighborhood.

**Cabildo.** *701 Chartres St.* ☎ *504/568-6968. Admission $4 adults, $3 students, seniors, and children over 12. Tues–Sun 9am–5pm.* The Louisiana Purchase Transfer was signed on this site. Reopened in 1994 following an extensive restoration, this national historic landmark now houses a comprehensive exhibit that traces Louisiana's past from exploration through the Civil War and Reconstruction from a multicultural perspective.

**Gallier House Museum.** *1132 Royal St.* ☎ *504/523-6722. Admission $4 adults, $3 seniors and students, $2.25 children 5–11. Mon–Sat 10am–4:30pm, Sun noon–4pm.* Built by architect James Gallier, Jr. as his residence in 1857, the house has been carefully restored. The adjoining building houses historical exhibits. There is a cafe and plenty of free parking.

**Historic French Market.** *Decatur St., just down from Jackson Square. Farmer's Market open daily 24 hours.* Legend has it that the French Market began as a Native American bartering place. The European-style market has been here for well over 150 years, and today it has a farmer's market, a flea market, all sorts of shops, and nonpareil people-watching.

✪ **Historic New Orleans Collection–Museum/Research Center.** *533 Royal St.* ☎ *504/523-4662. Admission free. Tours, $2, given Tues–Sat at 10 and 11am and 2 and 3pm. Tues–Sat 10am–4:45pm. Closed major holidays and Mardi Gras. Wheelchair accommodation is available.* The research collection is housed in a complex of historic buildings, the oldest constructed in the late 18th century. The Williams Gallery presents changing exhibitions that focus on Louisiana's history and culture. Guided tours are available of both the founders' residence, one of the "hidden" houses of the Vieux Carré, and the Louisiana History Galleries.

✪ **New Orleans Historic Voodoo Museum.** *724 Dumaine St.* ☎ *504/522-5223. Admission $5 adults, $4 students and seniors. French Quarter tour, $18 per person. Cemetery tour, $10 per person. Daily 10am–dusk.* Its dark, musty interior seems exactly the right setting to view artifacts of the occult and learn about that curious mixture of African and Catholic ritual brought to New Orleans in the 1700s from Santo Domingo. The museum offers walking tours and can arrange visits to voodoo rituals.

**Old Ursuline Convent.** *1114 Chartres St.* ☎ *504/529-3040. Admission $4 adults, $2 students, seniors, and children over 8. Tours, Tues–Fri at 10 and 11am and 1, 2, and 3pm; Sat–Sun at 11:15am and 1 and 2pm.* The convent is the oldest building of record in the Mississippi Valley and the only surviving French colonial building. In the complex is the beautiful restored 1845 Chapel of the Archbishops. The Ursuline nuns were teachers and nurses, and established the first schools for Catholic girls, African-Americans, and Native Americans, and set up the first orphanage in New Orleans. It now houses Catholic archives from 1718.

**Old U.S. Mint.** *400 Esplanade Ave.* ☎ *504/568-6968. Admission $4 adults, $3 seniors, students, and children over 12. Tues–Sun 9am–5pm.* The mint houses exhibits on New Orleans jazz and Carnival celebrations, and a collection of Mardi Gras costumes. Louis Armstrong's first trumpet is here.

**Presbytère.** *751 Chartres St.* ☎ *504/568-6968. Admission $4 adults, $3 students, seniors, and children over 12. Tues–Sun 9am–5pm.* The Presbytère exhibits the paintings of Louisianan artists as well as displays on local history and culture.

**St. Louis Cathedral.** *615 Père Antoine's Alley.* ☎ *504/525-9585. Free tours Mon–Sat 9am–5pm.* The oldest cathedral in the United States (1794) dominates Jackson Square. This is the third building to stand on this spot. It is of Spanish design, brick covered with stucco, with a tower at each end and a higher central tower. Inside, look for the six stained-glass windows depicting the life of its patron saint, Louis IX. St. Louis is also seen in a spectacular painting on the wall above the main altar, proclaiming the Seventh Crusade from the steps of Notre Dame.

Running from Royal Street alongside the cathedral is **Pirates Alley,** where William Faulkner once lived and wrote his first novel.

**St. Louis Cemetery No. 1.** *400 block of Basin St.* and **St. Louis Cemetery No. 2.** *Claiborne Ave.* No. 1 was established in the 1740s. Because of the soggy ground, in these "Cities of the Dead" people were buried in aboveground tombs that look a little like tiny windowless houses, arranged along narrow paths, many of which have "street" names. Along the outer walls of the cemeteries, you'll see rows of wall vaults, or "ovens," which hold the remains of the city's poor. The same tomb is used over and over—after two years the old remains are moved to a lower level, and a new body entombed in the vacated space. The grave of voodoo queen Marie Laveau, just inside the Basin Street entrance of No. 1, is marked with red crosses. And if you see one of the "ovens" in No. 2 marked with red crosses, that's the place where her daughter, voodoo queen Marie Laveau II, may or may not be resting. *Warning:* Only go into the cemeteries on a guided tour.

**HISTORIC BUILDINGS**   A number of historic residences are open to the public. The **Beauregard–Keyes House,** 1113 Chartres St. (☎ 504/523-7257) is a "raised cottage," with Doric columns and handsome twin staircases, built in 1826. It was once the home of Frances Parkinson Keyes, who wrote many novels about this region. It's open Mon–Sat 10am–3pm. Tours are given on the hour. The historic **Pontalba Apartments,** 523 St. Ann St. (☎ 504/568-6968), are in the Lower Pontalba Buildings, in a restored 1850 house. They're authentically furnished from parlor to kitchen to servants' quarters, and are open Tues–Sun 10am–5pm. The **Spring Fiesta Historic House,** 826 St. Ann St. (☎ 504/945-0322), is owned by the New Orleans Spring Fiesta Association and furnished in Victorian style. Call ☎ 504/581-1367 on Friday for an appointment. **Madame John's Legacy,** 632 Dumaine St. (part of the Louisiana State Museum complex), was erected in 1726, and is a fine example of a French "raised cottage." The aboveground basement is a brick-between-posts construction, and the hipped, dormered roof extends over the veranda. With its classic portico, the **Thierry House,** 721 Governor Nicholls St., started an architectural trend that spread Greek Revival style throughout the state. It was designed in 1814 by architect Benjamin Henry Latrobe when he was just 19 years old.

Two bars with historic connections are the **Old Absinthe House,** 240 Bourbon St., and **Lafitte's Blacksmith Shop,** at St. Philip and Bourbon streets. The Old Absinthe House was where Andrew Jackson and the Lafitte brothers planned the defense of New Orleans against the British in 1815. Lafitte's was used as a front by Jean Lafitte and his brother during their pirate days.

**UPTOWN & THE GARDEN DISTRICT** "American" New Orleans came into being because of Creole snobbery—they closed ranks against the Americans who flooded into the city after the 1803 Louisiana Purchase. The newcomers simply bought land upriver from Canal Street, and very soon they dominated the business scene and began to construct the mansions of the Garden District as their homes. It wasn't until 1852 that the various sections of the city came together to become New Orleans.

**Jackson Barracks.** *6400 St. Claude Ave.* ☎ *504/271-6262, ext. 242, or 504/ 278-6242. Admission free. Mon–Fri 7:30am–3:30pm.* On an extension of Rampart Street downriver from the French Quarter, this series of fine old brick buildings with white columns was built in 1834–35 for troops stationed at the river forts. They now serve as headquarters for the Louisiana National Guard. A military museum is in the old powder magazine. Call to confirm that the barracks and museum are open.

**Confederate Museum.** *929 Camp St.* ☎ *504/523-4522. Admission $4 adults, $2 children under 12. Mon–Sat 10am–4pm.* Not far from the French Quarter, the Confederate Museum was established in 1899. There are battle flags, weapons, and the personal effects of Confederate president Jefferson Davis and General Beauregard, and many portraits of Confederate military and civilian personalities.

✪ **Contemporary Arts Center.** *900 Camp St.* ☎ *504/523-1216. Admission $3 adults, $2 students and seniors, free to members and to everyone on Thurs. Performance prices range from $3 to $15. Mon–Sat 10am–5pm, Sun 11am–5pm.* The Contemporary Arts Center is a main anchor of New Orleans's young arts district (once the city's old Warehouse District), now home to a handful of leading local galleries. Over the past two decades, the center has been a consistent exhibitor of influential and groundbreaking artwork of regional, national, and international artists. The building, an old warehouse, was redesigned and renovated in 1990 to much applause and design awards. The CAC staggers its shows, so there should always be something hanging on the walls worth seeing.

✪ **New Orleans Museum of Art.** *Lelong Ave., in City Park.* ☎ *504/488-2631. Admission $6 adults, $3 seniors and children, free to everyone on Thurs. Tues–Sun 10am– 5pm.* NOMA completed a $23-million expansion project in 1994. The front portion of the museum is the original imposing neoclassical building; the rear is a striking contrast of curves and the contemporary. The museum houses European painting, pre-Colombian and Native American ethnographic art, and one of the largest glass collections in the United States. Note the first-floor Delgado Great Hall with its branched staircase.

**Pitot House.** *1440 Moss St.* ☎ *504/482-0312. Admission $3 adults, $2 seniors, $1 children under 12. Wed–Sat 10am–3pm.* A typical West Indies–style plantation home dating from 1799, it has been restored and furnished with Louisianan and American antiques. It has wide galleries on the sides and large columns supporting the second floor.

✪ **Superdome.** *1500 block of Poydras St.* ☎ *504/587-3810. Tours, $6 adults, $5 seniors, $4 children 5–10. Guided tours daily on the hour 10am–4pm (except during events).* Tall as a 27-story building, with a seating capacity of 76,000, the windowless structure with a computerized climate-control system is one of the largest buildings in the world in diameter (680 feet). Movable partitions and seats give it flexibility and allow it to be configured for any kind of event. In addition to sports, conventions, and trade shows, large theatrical and musical productions happen here.

**PARKS & GARDENS** Along the Mississippi riverfront in the French Quarter, **Woldenberg River Park** is an oasis of greenery in the heart of the city, the setting for the Audubon Institute's million-gallon aquarium. ✪ **Audubon Park,** 6500 Magazine St. (☎ **504/861-2538**), is across the street from Loyola and Tulane universities. It reaches from the end of St. Charles Avenue all the way to the Mississippi River. Some of the park's ancient live oaks, whose spreading branches turn walkways into covered alleys, go back to the days when this area was a plantation. There's an 18-hole golf course, picnic facilities, tennis courts, a jogging track, and the zoo (see below).

✪ **City Park,** 1 Dreyfous Ave. (☎ **504/483-9358**), is the home of the famous dueling oaks. The extensive, beautifully landscaped grounds hold a botanical garden and conservatory, four golf courses, a restaurant, lagoons for boating and fishing, tennis courts, horses for hire, and the New Orleans Museum of Art.

Just off Metarie Road you'll find **Longue Vue House and Gardens,** 7 Bamboo Rd. (☎ **504/488-5488**), which is listed on the National Register of Historic Places. The mansion is designed in the classical tradition, to foster a close rapport between indoor and outdoor vistas. Highlights in the grounds are the Canal Garden, Walled Garden, Wild Garden (which features native iris), and Spanish Court. It's open Mon–Sat 10am–4:30pm, Sun 1–5pm.

**VIEWS, ZOOS & THE AQUARIUM**   For a panorama of the city and harbor and a stunning ride, take the outside elevator to Viewpoint, the observation deck on the 31st floor of the **World Trade Center of New Orleans,** 2 Canal St. (☎ **504/581-4888**).

✪ **Aquarium of the Americas.** ☎ *504/861-2537. Aquarium admission, $10.50 adults, $8 seniors 65 and up, $5 children 2–12. IMAX admission, $7.50 adults, $6.50 seniors 65 and up, $5 children 2–12. Combination tickets, $15 adults, $12 seniors 65 and up, $9 children 2–12. Aquarium, Sun–Thurs 9:30am–6pm, Fri–Sat 9:30am–7pm. IMAX, Sun–Thurs 10am–6pm, Fri–Sat 10am–8pm.* The aquarium has five major exhibit areas and dozens of smaller displays. Highlights of the million-gallon aquarium are the exhibits of North and South American fish in their natural environments, the Caribbean reef exhibit where you can take a walk through an underwater tunnel, a re-creation of the Gulf of Mexico environment, and the tropical rain forest with piranha and tropical birds. "Fatal Beauties," a new display of deadly and poisonous creatures, opened in 1997.

✪ **Audubon Zoo.** *6500 Magazine St.* ☎ *504/861-5101. Admission $8 adults, $4 seniors 65 and older and children 2–12. Daily 9:30am–5:30pm (the zoo remains open until 6pm on Sat and Sun in summer). Closed holidays.* The Audubon Zoo is one of the top five in the country, where some 1,800 animals (including rare and endangered species) live in natural habitats. The new Butterflies in Flight exhibit houses over 1,000 butterflies as well as a pupae hatchery ($2 extra).

**BEST BETS FOR KIDS**   **Accents on Arrangements,** 938 Lafayette St., No. 410 (☎ 504/524-1227), offers tours specially designed to interest children. Kids love the **Riverfront streetcar,** and of course they enjoy visiting the **Superdome,** the **zoo,** and the **aquarium** (see above). A museum especially for kids is the ✪ **Louisiana Children's Museum,** 420 Julia St. (☎ 504/523-1357), full of dynamic "hands-on" exhibits; open Tues–Sat 9:30am–5pm, Sun noon–5pm; admission $5. **Children's Storyland,** in City Park (☎ 504/483-9381), is a playground where kids can slide down Jack and Jill's hill, climb Little Miss Muffet's spiderweb, or have an imaginary sword fight on Captain Hook's pirate ship. Hours vary; call for information. The **Musée Conti Wax Museum,** 917 Conti St. (☎ 504/525-2605), with its life-size historical figures, appeals to children. Kids will also like the puppet shows about New Orleans history and the collection of puppets at **Pontalba Historical Puppetorium,** 514 St. Peter St. (☎ **504/522-0344** or 504/944-8144).

**OUTDOOR ACTIVITIES & SPECTATOR SPORTS**   One of the most spine-tingling activities in the New Orleans area is a canoe ride through a bayou. Locals will tell you that alligators are really shy and harmless, but when you see a big one up close, that will seem anything but the case. Near Jean Lafitte National Park, just outside the city, you can rent a canoe for this adventure for $25 at **Earl's Bar & Canoe Rentals** (☎ 504/ 689-3271), open daily. Earl will drop you and your canoe off at the Jean Lafitte Park bayou.

Audubon Park and City Park are both good spots for golfers, tennis players, joggers, and bicyclists. **Olympic Bike Rentals,** 1618 Prytania St. (☎ 504/523-1314 or 504/ 522-6797), is a full-service bike-rental establishment.

New Orleans's NFL team, the **Saints,** plays in the Superdome every year, from August to December. Tickets for games are fairly easy to come by; call **Ticketmaster** (☎ 504/522-5555 or 504/733-0255 for information) to find out availability. Every year, two college football teams participate in the **Sugar Bowl,** played in the Superdome. Last-minute tickets are virtually impossible to get, so make plans in advance. If horse racing is your thing, head to the **Fair Grounds Race Course,** 1751 Gentilly Blvd. (☎ 504/944-5515). The race track here is one of the oldest in the country and has been a setting for such figures as Pat Garrett, Jesse James's brother, Frank, and generals Ulysses S. Grant and George Custer.

**SHOPPING**  Antiques are special here, from furniture, porcelains, and estate jewelry to dolls, culinary items, and collectibles. The emphasis New Orleans's past placed on fine home furnishings has left a residue of both high-quality European pieces and furniture crafted right in the city. Antiquing tours are offered by Macon Riddle's **Let's Go Antiquing!** (☎ 504/899-3027). The **Royal Street Guild** (☎ 504/949-2222), an association of antique dealers, has put together brochures that are available at most hotels. Antiques shops and art galleries line **Royal Street** and are also found on **Chartres Street** and **Bienville Street.**

The **Warehouse District** has many art and crafts galleries; pick up a brochure, "Arts in the Warehouse District." Along **Julia Street,** from Camp Street over toward the river, you'll find art galleries showing contemporary works. **Magazine Street** is a major uptown thoroughfare of some 6 miles of shopping, including many important antique shops and more art galleries.

**Canal Place,** 365 Canal St., an upscale three-tiered mall with a landscaped atrium, is a sophisticated setting for such stores as Jaeger, Bally of Switzerland, Saks Fifth Avenue, and Laura Ashley. **The Esplanade,** 1401 West Esplanade, houses more than 150 shops such as Macy's, Yvonne LaFleur, and The Limited; there is also a large food court. In addition to the Farmer's Market, the **French Market** (see above) has candy and praline shops, and cookware, craft, toy, and candle shops. Just across from Jackson Square at 600–620 Decatur St., the old **Jackson Brewery** building has been transformed into a jumble of shops, cafes, delicatessens, restaurants, and entertainment. The **New Orleans Centre,** 1400 Poydras, is New Orleans's newest shopping center, with many upscale specialty stores. **Riverwalk,** 1 Poydras St., is a covered mall that runs along the river with about 140 specialty shops including Eddie Bauer, Sharper Image, and Banana Republic.

## ACCOMMODATIONS

The city has a large and diverse selection of hotels, guesthouses, and B&Bs where you'll probably be treated like a friend; grand old hotels and young boutique inns; and towering institutions mostly for business travelers. Many of the best accommodations in New Orleans are concentrated in and around the French Quarter and the Central Business District. In addition to the selections below, the people at **Bed and Breakfast Reservation Service,** 1021 Moss St. (P.O. Box 52257), New Orleans, LA 70152 (☎ 800/ 729-4640 or 504/488-4640), are experts at matching guests and hosts.

**Bourbon Orleans Hotel.** *717 Orleans St., New Orleans, LA 70116.* ☎ *504/ 523-2222. Fax 504/525-8166. 216 rms, 50 suites. MINIBAR. $115–$185 petit queen or twin; $135–$205 deluxe king or double; $170–$245 junior suite; $225–$375* *town-house suite; $250–$450 town house with balcony. Extra person $20. AE, CB, DC, DISC, MC, V. Valet parking $12.* The hotel's pale salmon and moss green exterior takes up an entire block in the Quarter. The Orleans Ballroom, the oldest part of the hotel, was constructed in 1815 as a venue for the city's masquerade, carnival, and quadroon balls. The hotel occupies three buildings and has recently undergone a $6-million renovation. Public spaces are lavishly decorated with chandeliers, oriental rugs, and marble flooring, and guest rooms have recently been completely redecorated. There are standard-size rooms, as well as bilevel suites that have a living room with a pullout queen sofa. Bathrooms are outfitted with Italian marble, telephones, and hair dryers, and you can order room service through your TV. Café Lafayette is the hotel's restaurant.

**Château Hotel.** *1001 Chartres St., New Orleans, LA 70116.* ☎ **504/524-9636.** *Fax 504/525-2989. 45 rms. $89–$109 double. Rates include continental breakfast. 10% senior discount. AE, CB, DC, MC, V. Free parking.* This is one of the best buys in town. A bit removed from the well-traveled sections of the French Quarter, it is still a short walk from all attractions. Each room is distinctively decorated. Some have king-size four-poster beds, while others feature painted iron beds, and all have armchairs and/or couches. There are even a few bed/living-room combinations. Its outdoor swimming pool is surrounded by a flagstone-paved courtyard dotted with chaise longues.

✪ **Fairmont Hotel.** *At University Place, 123 Baronne St., New Orleans, LA 70140.* ☎ *800/527-4727 or 504/529-7111. Fax 504/529-4775. 615 rms, 85 suites. $229–$289 double. Additional person $25 extra. AE, DC, DISC, MC, V. Self-parking $10; valet parking $14.* New Orleanians still think of it as the Roosevelt—perhaps you remember those old radio broadcasts "from the Blue Room of the Hotel Roosevelt in downtown New Orleans." The blue-and-gold decor and French period furnishings have changed very little over the years, and on Sunday, there's a sumptuous brunch. The hotel upholds its predecessor's tradition of elegance. Guest rooms were overhauled in 1996; they are spacious, with high ceilings and many extras; beds are luxuriously outfitted with all-cotton sheets, down pillows, and comforters. For the business traveler, the Fairmont offers in-room computer hookups and fax machines in the suites. For fine dining, there's the romantic **Sazerac Restaurant.** Extras include a rooftop health club, pool, tennis courts, business center, and currency exchange.

✪ **Hotel Inter-Continental.** *444 St. Charles Ave., New Orleans, LA 70130.* ☎ *800/327-0200 or 504/525-5566. Fax 504/523-7310. 482 rms, 20 suites. $220–$280 double; $400–$1,750 suite. AE, CB, DC, DISC, MC, V. Valet parking $14.* The red-granite hotel rises from the heart of the Central Business District, within walking distance of the French Quarter and the Mississippi River attractions. Its luxurious rooms and suites blend classic and contemporary styling and feature separate dressing areas, built-in hair dryers, and telephone extensions and TVs in the bathrooms. It is surely a traveling businessperson's dream. The Governor's Floor (the 14th) is reminiscent of Louisiana's romantic past, and has a VIP lounge, which entitles guests to a complimentary continental breakfast and evening cocktails. The **Veranda Restaurant** is highly recommended. Facilities include a health club and pool, and business center.

**Hotel Maison de Ville.** *727 Toulouse St., New Orleans, LA 70130.* ☎ *800/634-1600 or 504/561-5858. Fax 504/528-9939. 23 rms. MINIBAR. $165–$185 double; $275–$295 suite; $375–$525 two-bedroom cottage. AE, DC, MC, V. Valet parking $15.* Dating from before 1742, today's Maison sits on its original site. It has been restored to old-time elegance with marble fireplaces, fine French antiques, and gilt-framed mirrors. Guest rooms surround a brick courtyard, where Tennessee Williams reworked *A Streetcar Named Desire,* sitting at one of the wrought-iron tables; his usual room was today's room 9. Another famous tenant was John James Audubon, who lived for a time in one of the Audubon Cottages; today they are furnished with antiques and reflect a warm country elegance. **Le Bistro,** the hotel's restaurant, is intimate and inviting.

○ **House on Bayou Road.** *2275 Bayou Rd. (just off Esplanade Ave.), New Orleans, LA 70119.* ☎ *800/882-2968 or 504/949-7711. 4 rms, 2 cottages. $150–$230 double. Rates include breakfast. AE, MC, V. Free parking.* Owner Cynthia Reeves has lovingly restored this intimate late-1700s Creole plantation home surrounded by beautifully manicured grounds. Rooms are light and airy. A large cottage has three rooms that can be rented separately or by a family, while the small Creole cottage is a great romantic getaway spot. A pool is available for guest use.

**Le Pavillon Hotel.** *833 Poydras St., New Orleans, LA 70140.* ☎ *800/535-9095 or 504/581-3111. Fax 504/522-5543. 219 rms, 7 suites. From $109 double; from $495 suite. AE, CB, DC, DISC, MC, V. Valet parking $14.* Le Pavillon was the first hotel in New Orleans to have elevators. Opened in 1907 in the Business District, it is a member of Historic Hotels of America. The building is a long, slendor rectangle with a prominent columned motor entrance on Poydras Street and a grand, high-ceilinged lobby. Paintings from the hotel's fine-arts collection hang in the halls. Standard guest rooms all have similar furnishings but differ in size. The Pavillon has some fine suites for reasonable rates—if you like art deco, you're sure to love the two-bedroom art deco suite. The Antiques Suite contains a collection of furnishings that include pieces by Mallard, C. Lee (who, as a slave, studied under Mallard), Mitchell Rammelsberg, Belter, Badouine, and Marcotte; beds have feather mattresses and elaborate canopies. Facilities include a heated rooftop pool, fitness center, and whirlpool spa.

**McKendrick–Breaux House.** *1474 Magazine St., New Orleans, LA 70130.* ☎ *888/570-1700 in the U.S. or Canada, or 504/586-1700. Fax 504/522-7138. 5 rms. $90–$135 double. Rates include breakfast. AE, MC, V. Limited free off-street parking is available.* You'd be hard-pressed to find more gracious hosts than Lisa and Eddie Breaux. The young couple saved the two houses on this property from ultimate destruction. The original house was built in 1865 by Scottish immigrant Daniel McKendrick, but was virtually unrecognizable by the time the Breauxes got their hands on it in 1992. They gutted the structure and started from scratch (original medallions, some woodwork, and some flooring remain). Rooms are located both in the main house and in the building directly across the quiet courtyard; all are extremely spacious and furnished with antiques and family collectibles. Bathrooms are large, and in the main house they have beautiful claw-foot tubs, while those in the building opposite have modern fixtures. Fresh flowers greet you on arrival, and Lisa and Eddie will help plan day and evening activities.

○ **Melrose Mansion.** *937 Esplanade Ave., New Orleans, LA 70116.* ☎ *504/ 944-2255. Fax 504/945-1794. 8 rms. MINIBAR. $250–$275 double; $350–$450 suite. Rates include airport limousine service, full breakfast, and cocktail hour. AE, DISC, MC, V. Free parking on the street.* Rosemary and Melvin Jones have restored this three-story 1884 Victorian mansion to combine the utmost in luxury with the warm hospitality of a private home. The Donecio Suite, for example, includes a Rice four-poster bed, a marble bathroom complete with Jacuzzi and separate dressing room, and a wide balcony where breakfast can be served. (Lady Bird Johnson was its first tenant and gave it a rave review.) The Sol Owens Suite houses a fitness and health area. The best feature of this place may well be its staff—including Rosemary, Melvin, and the mansion's butler. Book as far in advance as possible.

**New Orleans Guest House.** *1118 Ursulines St., New Orleans, LA 70116.* ☎ *504/566-1177. 14 rms. $79–$89 queen or twin; $89–$99 king or two full beds. Rates include continental breakfast. Extra person $25. AE, MC, V. Free parking.* The exterior of the New Orleans Guest House is painted hot pink—a clue to its gay-friendly character. Off the beaten path, it's located just outside the French Quarter, across North Rampart Street on the border of a less than desirable neighborhood. Ray Cronk and Alvin Payne have been running this renovated Creole cottage, dating from 1848, for more than 10 years now. There are rooms in the main house and somewhat smaller rooms in what used to be the old slave quarters, all decorated with period furniture. They all open onto the lush New Orleans–style courtyard, which is a veritable tropical garden. There is a new covered breakfast room with an outdoor patio.

**New Orleans Hilton Riverside Hotel.** *2 Poydras St., New Orleans, LA 70140.* ☎ *800/445-8667 or 504/561-0500. Fax 504/568-1721. 1,602 rms. $275–$295 double; $580–$1,870 suite. Special packages available. AE, CB, DC, DISC, JCB, MC, V. Parking $12 for 24 hours.* No sterile, impersonal hotel, the Hilton sits right at the riverfront, adjacent to the World Trade Center and the New Orleans Convention Center. Guest rooms are spacious, and most have views of the river or the city. The Tower rooms and suites and the low-rise complex opening to the river are the epitome of luxury. The hotel offers health club privileges with outdoor and indoor tennis courts, squash and racquetball courts, a rooftop jogging track, aerobics classes, and a golf studio.

**Nicolas M. Benachi House.** *2257 Bayou Rd., New Orleans, LA 70119.* ☎ *800/308-7040 or 504/525-7040. Fax 504/525-9760. 4 rms. $95–$130 double. AE, DISC, MC, V. Free parking.* This house was originally constructed in 1858 on what was then an estate on the outskirts of town for Mr. Benachi, a cotton broker and the Greek consul. Jim Derbes, a lawyer and university instructor, is the fourth owner of the house. Under his care it was restored to its current condition (he received a 1985 Honor Award for restoration). The guest rooms are named for the Benachi children—Belasario's room holds a lovely Victorian double bed and writing desk; Marie's room features a balcony and shares a bath with Irene's room (a good choice for families); a favorite is Pandia's room, on the first floor, with a Rococo Revival dresser and American mahogany double bed. TVs are available on request, and smoking is allowed outdoors only.

✪ **Omni Royal Orleans.** *621 St. Louis St., New Orleans, LA 70140.* ☎ *800/ THE-OMNI in the U.S. and Canada, or 504/529-5333. Fax 504/529-7089. 346 rms, 16 suites. $185–$245 double; $320–$605 suite. Children 17 and under stay free in parents' room. AE, CB, DC, DISC, MC, V. Valet parking $14 with in/out privileges.* The Omni Royal Orleans opened its doors in 1960 on the site of the 1836 St. Louis Exchange Hotel, which was a center of New Orleans social life until the final years of the Civil War. The present hotel is a worthy successor, with an elegant marble lobby and guest rooms that come equipped with umbrellas, irons, and ironing boards as well as the usual amenities. The classic Rib Room is a favorite dining spot. The rooftop poolside La Riviera bar and restaurant has unobstructed views of the French Quarter. Facilities include a health club, heated pool, and business center.

**P. J. Holbrook's Olde Victorian Inn.** *914 N. Rampart St., New Orleans, LA 70116.* ☎ *800/725-2446 or 504/522-2446. 6 rms. A/C. $120–$170 double. Rates include full breakfast. Senior citizen discount. Weekly rates available. AE, MC, V. Parking on street only.* Walking into P.J.'s is like walking through time into an old Victorian home. Most rooms have fireplaces, and each room has its own bathroom, though the private baths of a couple of units are across the hall. P.J. herself is a most gracious host who will look after your every need and cook up a breakfast that could probably keep you going for an entire week. The house is nonsmoking. P.J.'s dog, Olivia, guards the house. Be sure to sit and chat with P.J .and her staff—they've got some great New Orleans stories to tell.

**Pontchartrain Hotel.** *2031 St. Charles Ave., New Orleans, LA 70140.* ☎ *800/ 777-6193 or 504/524-0581. Fax 504/529-1165. 102 rms. $95–$380 based on single* *occupancy. Additional person $25 extra. Seasonal packages and special promotional rates available. AE, CB, DC, DISC, MC, V. Parking $10.* In the Garden District on the St. Charles streetcar line and easily accessible from the French Quarter, this elegant landmark hotel was erected in 1927, and many original furnishings and antiques are still found in the guest rooms. Novelist Anne Rice set part of her *The Witching Hour* here. The gourmet cuisine of the **Caribbean Room** is internationally known.

**Royal Sonesta.** *300 Bourbon St., New Orleans, LA 70140.* ☎ *800/766-3782 or 504/586-0300. 500 rms. $160–$280 double; $325–$1,100 suite. Package and seasonal rates may be available. AE, CB, DC, DISC, MC, V. Parking $14.* In an ideal location, this hotel is adorned with lacy New Orleans balconies, and rooms are furnished with period reproductions. Rooms overlooking inner patios are preferable to those facing noisy Bourbon Street. The hotel has a pool, exercise room, and business center.

✪ **Soniat House.** *1133 Chartres St., New Orleans, LA 70116.* ☎ *800/544-8808 or 504/522-0570. Fax 504/522-7208. 31 rms. $145–$235 standard room; $235–$500 suite; $575 two-bedroom suite. AE, MC, V. Valet parking $14.* Life seems a little more precious in the courtyard of the Soniat House—the air is a little lighter, the colors a little softer. It is a special place and, not surprisingly, it has received international acclaim in recent years. Built in 1829 by wealthy plantation owner Joseph Soniat Dufossat, the building itself is an interesting combination of Creole style and Greek Revival detail. Rodney and Frances Smith have created the perfect blend of guesthouse and hotel. Most rooms have balconies and face the courtyard; they differ in size and decor, but all are furnished with antiques and feature polished hardwood floors covered with antique oriental rugs. Some rooms have held paintings on loan from the New Orleans Museum of Art.

✪ **Windsor Court.** *Gravier St., New Orleans, LA 70130.* ☎ *800/262-2662 or 504/523-6000. Fax 504/596-4513. 319 rms and suites. $250–$360 standard guest room; $325–$460 junior suite; $410–$650 full suite; $600–$1,000 two-bedroom suite. Children under 12 stay free in parents' room. AE, CB, DC, DISC, MC, V. Valet parking $17.* In recent years, the centrally located Windsor Court has enjoyed the reputation of being New Orleans's premier luxury hotel. The pink-granite facade is somewhat unassuming, unlike the interior—Italian marble and antique furnishings distinguish public spaces, and two corridors downstairs are mini-galleries displaying works of art. Standard rooms are spacious, and each suite features large bay windows or private balconies overlooking the river or city, a private foyer, large living room, bedroom entered through French doors, marble bath, separate his-and-her dressing rooms, and a "petite kitchen." Afternoon tea accompanied by live chamber music is served in the lobby lounge. The **Grill Room,** featuring chef Jeff Tunks's New American cuisine, is highly recommended. Facilities include a health club with a resort-size pool, sauna, and steam room. Numerous conveniences and luxurious conference areas are available for business travelers.

**OTHER ACCOMMODATIONS**   The **YMCA International Hotel** at 920 St. Charles Ave., New Orleans, LA 70130 (☎ **504/558-9622;** fax 504/523-7174), charges $29 for a single room, $35 for a double, $41 for a triple, and $46 for a quad. A room key deposit of $5 is required and refundable at checkout. Rooms are air-conditioned and have TVs. Within walking distance of the French Quarter, there is a fitness facility (free for hotel guests), an indoor pool, and a restaurant. The **Marquette House New Orleans International Hostel,** 2253 Carondelet St., New Orleans, LA 70130 (☎ **504/ 523-3014;** fax 504/529-5933), in a century-old home, offers a community kitchen, dining area, reading rooms, garden patio, and laundry facilities to guests. Dormitory beds are $14.95 a night, and private rooms with private baths are $39.95. Parking is on the street.

Downtown New Orleans is only a 15-minute drive from the airport (located in nearby Kenner). The **New Orleans Airport Hilton,** 901 Airline Hwy., Kenner, LA 70062 (☎ **800/445-8667** or 504/469-5000), features a lighted tennis court, fitness center, putting green, restaurant, and business center. The **Holiday Inn New Orleans–Airport,** 2929 Williams Blvd., Kenner, LA 70062 (☎ **800/465-4329** or 504/467-5611), is a less expensive alternative. It also has a restaurant, exercise room, pool, and sauna. Both hotels offer airport transfer.

## DINING

From the simplest of po-boy sandwiches to the fanciest prosciutto-wrapped filet, cooking is perhaps the city's most important art. The local cuisine has its traditional chefs of haute Creole cooking, and its "folk" and "roots" elements in Cajun and rural Creole cooking, with dishes like gumbo, jambalaya, and red beans and rice. And now the contemporary free-form and multicultural approach is firmly in vogue: Today's hot New Orleans chefs are toying with Asian Creole, Californian Creole, and endless mystifying combinations of American and European dishes.

In addition to the restaurants listed below, there are the legendary places, serving classic New Orleans French and Creole cuisine, and usually expensive, formal, and requiring reservations. Who hasn't heard of **Antoine's,** 713 St. Louis St. (☎ **504/581-4422**), in the same family for more than 150 years, or dreamed of at least one meal in this fabled restaurant? For the first time, English translation has recently been added to the menu. Historic **Arnaud's,** 813 Bienville St. (☎ **504/523-5433**), in a building from the 1700s, came back from the doldrums in a 1970s restoration, and the kitchen is now presided over by Chef Kevin Davis. **Brennan's,** 417 Royal St. (☎ **504/525-9711**), is one of the best known, if not the oldest, with fine food, good service, and exceptional atmosphere. The sumptuous "Breakfast at Brennan's" has, of course, gained international fame. The **Court of Two Sisters,** 613 Royal St. (☎ **504/522-7261**), is one of the most atmospheric, with its huge courtyard filled with flowers, fountains, and low-hanging willows, but the cuisine and service doesn't always measure up.

And there's **K-Paul's Louisiana Kitchen** (☎ **504/524-7394**), where all the hoopla about Cajun cooking began, offering some of the best—and hottest—Cajun food around.

**Acme Oyster House.** *724 Iberville St.* ☎ *504/522-5973. Reservations not accepted. Oysters $3.50–$6; New Orleans specialties $5.25–$5.75; seafood $7.75–$9.75; po-boys $4–$5. AE, DC, DISC, JCB, MC, V. Mon–Sat 11am–10pm, Sun noon–7pm. SEAFOOD.* This place is always loud, often crowded, but if you're an oyster lover, there's nothing quite like standing at the oyster bar eating a dozen or so freshly shucked oysters on the half shell. (You can have them at a table, but somehow they taste better at the bar.) If you can't quite stomach them raw, try the oyster po-boy off the sandwich menu, with beer, of course, as the perfect accompaniment. Acme offers fresh baked bread pudding and cheesecake on the dessert menu.

✪ **Bacco.** *310 Chartres St.* ☎ *504/522-2426. Reservations recommended. Main courses $19.50–$25. AE, DC, MC, V. Mon–Fri 7–10am, Sat–Sun 8:30–10am; Mon–Sat 11:30am–2:30pm; Sun brunch 10:30am–2:30pm; daily 6–10pm. ITALIAN/CREOLE.* Owned and operated by brother and sister Ralph and Cindy Brennan, this is a newcomer to the New Orleans scene. The menu changes with the season. Bacco jumbo shrimp is roasted in a wood-burning oven and served in a garlic pepper oil. The hickory grilled pork chop is wrapped with apple-smoked bacon and served with a wild mushroom–sage sauce and sweet potato mash. For dessert try the frozen cappuccino or the praline cinnamon ice-cream sandwich.

✪ **Bayona.** *430 Dauphine St.* ☎ *504/525-4455. Reservations required at dinner; recommended at lunch. Main courses $9–$21. AE, CB, DC, DISC, MC, V.*

*Mon–Fri 11:30am–1:30pm; Mon–Thurs 6–9:30pm, Fri–Sat 6–10:30pm. Closed Sun.*
INTERNATIONAL. Innovative Chef Susan Spicer opened her own restaurant in a century-old Creole cottage, and those who have sampled her innovative dishes agree— Spicer never misses. Begin your meal with Spicer's signature garlic soup, and go on to a main dish such as grilled duck breast with a pepper-jelly glaze, or Parmesan-crusted rabbit with a lemon-sage sauce. The wine list is excellent. The menu changes seasonally.

✪ **Bella Luna.** *914 N. Peters.* ☎ *504/529-1583. Reservations recommended. Main courses $15–$24.75. AE, DC, DISC, MC, V. Mon–Sat 6–10:30pm, Sun 6–9:30pm.* ECLECTIC/ITALIAN. Noted for its expansive, romantic view of the Mississippi River, Bella Luna has an interior that feels like an Italian villa. Chef Horst Pfeifer, originally from Germany, draws upon almost every imaginable cuisine. He is adventurous and creative, even by New Orleans standards. Main courses might include herb-crusted roasted loin of lamb or house-cured pork chop in a New Orleans–style pecan crust with horseradish mashed potatoes and an Abita beer sauce. Pastas are a specialty here. The dessert menu changes frequently, but if the chocolate bellini napoleon is on the menu, give it a try. If you want a culinary adventure on a romantic moonlit evening, you can't do better than Bella Luna. It's worth noting that Chef Pfeifer grows the herbs and spices he uses on a small plot on the grounds of the historic Ursuline Convent in the Quarter.

✪ **Brigtsen's.** *723 Dante St.* ☎ *504/861-7610. Reservations required a week or two in advance. Main courses $14–$28. AE, DC, MC, V. Tues–Sat 5:30–10pm. CAJUN/ CREOLE.* Brigtsen's is set in a quiet corner of the Riverbend area. The trappings here— from the new interior wall paintings to the handwritten menus—are appealing yet modest for a fine dining establishment. Frank Brigtsen, a former chef at K-Paul's, writes a new menu every day himself. To fully appreciate the Frank Brigtsen phenomenon, you have to see him tucked into the restaurant's very small kitchen casually preparing six entrees at once. If the setting is understated, the quality of Brigtsen's food speaks for itself. Popular dishes in the past have included a roast duck with "dirty" rice and honey-pecan gravy, and broiled gulf fish with a crabmeat Parmesan crust and lemon mousse-line. If you're looking for a bargain, Brigtsen's three-course "Early Evening" dinner special (for $14.95, offered Tues–Thurs 5:30–6:30pm) is as good as you'll find.

✪ **Cafe Sbisa.** *1011 Decatur St.* ☎ *504/522-5565. Reservations recommended. Main courses $11–$23. AE, CB, DC, DISC, MC, V. Sun–Thurs 5:30–10:30pm, Fri–Sat 5:30–11pm; Sun brunch 11am–3pm. CREOLE.* Cafe Sbisa first opened in 1899—the building is old, but the interior is classy and cosmopolitan. There are two floors of dining rooms (tables on the upper floor near the interior balcony are the best), and there is a small courtyard. Today the Napoli family has transformed the menu so dramatically that it's nipping at the heels of Emeril's (see below) in terms of creativity. The turtle soup is superb, as is the charcoal-grilled shrimp with a red Thai curry and barbecue relish. Desserts are equally creative, especially the white chocolate bread pudding. This is also a good choice for a Sunday jazz brunch.

**Christian's.** *3835 Iberville St.* ☎ *504/482-4924. Reservations recommended. Main courses $13.25–$23.95. AE, CB, DC, MC, V. Tues–Fri 11:30am–2pm and 5:30–10pm; Sat 5:30–10pm. FRENCH/CREOLE.* Ever had a three-course meal in a church? This lovely restaurant serves seafood with the most delicate of French sauces. Try the shrimp en brochette (grilled shrimp with slices of onion and bell pepper in a lemon butter sauce over angel-hair pasta), and for dessert, baked Alaska or profiteroles aux chocolate. The exterior of the little church building is unaltered; inside it's been beautifully restored.

✪ **Commander's Palace.** *1403 Washington Ave.* ☎ *504/899-8221. Reservations required, sometimes days in advance. Main courses $22–$30; full brunch $20–$32; full* *dinner $29–$32. AE, CB, DC, DISC, MC, V. Mon–Fri 11:30am–2pm; daily 6–10pm; brunch Sat 11:30am–12:30pm and Sun 10:30am–1pm. Jackets required. HAUTE CREOLE.* In an unusual, rather grand blue-and-white Victorian building at the corner of Washington Avenue and Coliseum Street, Commander's Palace has played an important role in New Orleans's culinary history, employing such chefs as Emeril Lagasse, Paul Prudhomme, and Frank Brigtsen. The patio, fountains, and soft colors are a perfect backdrop for mouthwatering Creole specialties. If this is your first visit, start your meal with the Soups 1–1–1, a half serving of turtle soup au sherry, Creole gumbo du jour, and the soup of the day. The corn-fried oysters with shoestring potatoes and a horseradish cream sauce are also excellent. Outstanding entrees include Mississippi quail with a rock shrimp stuffing and a port-wine sauce; and an oven-roasted, molasses glazed duck, served with red cabbage slaw and caramelized potatoes. There is an excellent wine list, and the menu offers suggestions with each entree. Perhaps the best way to experience Commander's is during one of its famous jazz brunches (Saturday or Sunday).

✪ **Emeril's.** *800 Tchoupitoulas St.* ☎ *504/528-9393. Reservations required at dinner. Main courses $14–$32. AE, CB, DC, DISC, MC, V. Mon–Fri 11:30am–2pm; Mon–Thurs 6–10pm, Fri–Sat 6–10:30pm. CREOLE/NEW AMERICAN.* Emeril Lagasse is another young, daring, but traditionally schooled chef. He gained national recognition with his own show, *The Essence of Emeril,* on the cable TV Food Network. His zealous approach to his work is quite contagious—the fever has been caught by his entire staff, who are among the best in New Orleans. Lagasse makes everything from scratch, including sausage and even the ketchup. Try the grilled homemade andouille sausage with his famous homemade Worcestershire sauce, or the pameed Mississippi quail, served with roasted garlic, smashed root vegetables, crispy bacon, stewed barbecued quail legs, and a drizzle of sweet barbecue sauce. The wine list recently won awards from *Wine Spectator* magazine.

✪ **Gabrielle.** *3201 Esplanade Ave.* ☎ *504/948-6233. Reservations recommended. Main courses $14.50–$24. AE, CB, DC, DISC, MC, V. Tues–Sat 5:30–10pm. Lunch 11:30am–2pm, Fri only, Oct–May. INTERNATIONAL.* In an unpretentious setting, Chef Sonnier (who studied under Paul Prudhomme and Frank Brigtsen) specializes in delectable homemade sausages. The pan-fried trout with shrimp and roasted pecan butter blends its flavors perfectly. Desserts are less sophisticated than they might be for a restaurant that rivals some of the best in the city.

**Galatoire's.** *209 Bourbon St.* ☎ *504/525-2021. Reservations not accepted. Main courses $12–$24. AE, MC, V. Tues–Sat 11:30am–9pm, Sun noon–9pm. Closed holidays. FRENCH.* Family run since 1905, and in one of the loveliest dining rooms in town, Galatoire's traditions remain intact and unchanging. Sunday afternoon dinner here is still a ritual for many local family groups. Seafood is a specialty. Try trout amandine or marguéry or the perfectly broiled pompano meunière. There is also a good selection of meat dishes. To avoid waiting in line, go before noon or before 6pm. Jackets are required after 5pm and on Sunday.

**Lola's.** *3312 Esplanade Ave.* ☎ *504/488-6946. Reservations not accepted. Main courses $7.75–$14. No credit cards accepted; no out-of-town checks accepted. Daily 6–10pm. SPANISH/INTERNATIONAL.* How can a restaurant survive that does not accept reservations or credit cards, does not serve wine, and hardly advertises itself? Word of mouth is that Lola's is a special place. About a half mile from City Park in a small storefront, there are a handfull of tables. Your best bet is to arrive 15 to 30 minutes before opening time and wait in line. Once you're inside, service is attentive and food comes quickly. Spanish dishes are specialties here, especially the meat, seafood, and vegetarian paellas (made with arborio rice) and fideuas (with angel-hair pasta). These come in sizzling, mountainous portions. There are plenty of other entrees, too, and excellent appetizers.

✪ **Louis XVI.** *730 Bienville St.* ☎ *504/581-7000. Reservations recommended. Main courses $16.50–$30. AE, CB, DISC, MC, V. Mon–Fri 7–11am, Sat–Sun 7am–noon; daily 6–10pm. FRENCH.* Set in the small, stylish St. Louis Hotel, Louis XVI is one of New Orleans's finest restaurants. The elegant 1920s Parisian-style dining rooms look onto a lush courtyard complete with a sparkling fountain. The menu, like the decor, is decidedly French, although in recent years it has been lightened slightly with the addition of dishes like fillet de poisson grille au beurre de mangue (grilled fish of the day with a composed butter of mango, orange, and cilantro). However, you'll still find traditional cream sauces over shrimp and scallops and filet mignon with béarnaise sauce here. Enticing desserts are chocolate hazelnut cake and charlotte au chocolate et la banane (chocolate and banana mousse surrounded by lady fingers with Chantilly cream in an English rum sauce).

**Louisiana Pizza Kitchen.** *2800 Esplanade Ave.* ☎ *504/488-2800. Reservations not required. Pizzas $5.95–$7.95; pastas $4.50–$10.95. AE, CB, DC, DISC, MC, V. Sun–Thurs 5–10pm, Fri–Sat 5–11pm. ITALIAN.* It's favored locally for its creative pies as well as for the atmosphere. About 20 blocks from the French Quarter (take a taxi in the evening) on a quiet section of Esplanade, its dining room allows patrons a lovely view. While pastas have a place on the menu, it's the individually sized pizzas, baked in a wood-fired oven and offered with a wide variety of toppings, that diners come for. Other locations are at 95 French Market Place (☎ **504/522-9500**) and 615 S. Carrollton Ave. (☎ **504/866-5900**).

**Mother's.** *401 Poydras St.* ☎ *504/523-9656. Reservations not accepted. Menu items $1.75–$16.50. No credit cards. Mon–Sat 5am–10pm, Sun 7am–10pm. SANDWICHES/ CREOLE.* Be sure to allow time to stand in line for the best po-boy sandwiches in New Orleans. Made on crisp French bread so fresh that it's just cooled down from the oven, the po-boys here are real creations. It's always crowded, but the line moves quickly. It's within walking distance of the Louisiana Superdome.

✪ **Palace Café.** *605 Canal St.* ☎ *504/523-1661. Reservations recommended. Main courses $8.75–$25. AE, DC, MC, V. Mon–Sat 11:30am–2:30pm; Sun brunch 10:30am– 2:30pm; daily 5:30–10pm. CONTEMPORARY CREOLE.* This grand cafe is operated by Ti Martin, daughter of Ella Brennan. The restaurant was recently renovated and redecorated, and an acoustic engineer worked wonders—despite the large tile-floored dining room, noise is now hardly noticeable. Chef Robert Bruce moved to the Palace in 1995 after a tutelage under Emeril Lagasse, and within a year, was winning awards as the city's favored chef. The crabmeat batons (ginger-wrapped Louisiana crabmeat with wasabi cream and soy dipping sauce) are a good appetizer choice and a highlight of Bruce's cooking style. He is a high-energy cook and seems to use the daily specials as an outlet for his creativity; if in doubt, go with a special. For dessert, try the white chocolate bread pudding. The staff is attentive and friendly. Brunch on Sunday brings live blues entertainment by Betty Shirley.

✪ **Pelican Club.** *312 Exchange Alley.* ☎ *504/523-1504. Reservations recommended. Main courses $17.50–$22.50. Fixed-price "early dinner" $19.50. AE, DC, DISC, MC, V. Daily 5:30–closing; early dinner nightly 5:30–6pm.* Located in a 19th-century Creole town house are three distinctive dining rooms decorated with art on consignment from area galleries. The overall cosmopolitan feeling here, combined with the talents of chefs Richard Hughes and Chin Ling, has drawn locals, visitors, and big-name stars alike over the past 3 years. Signature dishes include veal and shrimp pot stickers with garlic-chili and ginger-soy sauces to start; clay pot seafood with shrimp, scallops, fish, mussels, clams, and vegetables in a broth flavored with chili, garlic, lime, and cilantro as a main course; and vanilla brandy crème brûlée for dessert. The Pelican Club has earned *Wine Spectator*'s "Award of Excellence" for the past 5 years.

**Praline Connection.** *542 Frenchmen St.* ☎ *504/943-3934. Reservations not accepted. Main courses $4–$13.95. AE, DC, DISC, MC, V. Sun–Thurs 11am–10:30pm, Fri–Sat 11am–midnight. CREOLE/SOUL FOOD.* This is a locally famous institution on Frenchmen Street, which is just behind Esplanade Avenue. The interior is bright and airy, with stainless-steel ceiling fans and a black-and-white tiled floor. The noise level can be quite daunting, but food is wonderful, plentiful, and very reasonably priced Southern soul cooking at its best. Praline Connection II, at 901 South Peters St. (☎ *504/523-3973*), offers the same menu and a larger dining room.

**Sapphire.** *228 Camp St.* ☎ *504/571-7500. Reservations recommended. Main courses $15–$31. AE, CB, DC, DISC, MC, V. Daily 6:30–10:30am and 11:30am–2pm; Sun–Thurs 6:30–10:30pm, Fri–Sat 6:30–11pm. NEW AMERICAN.* Before opening Sapphire, chef Kevin Graham made his reputation at the Windsor Court's Grill Room and with his ultra-hip Graham's restaurant. Sapphire is his showcase; it is without peer or precedent in New Orleans. The decor is by designer Mario Villa, whose individualistic and eclectic aesthetics are exploded upon the interior of the restaurant. The cuisine is in a category of its own. A smoked salmon appetizer may combine slivers of salmon with a beet garnish, crunchy Parmesan sticks, and a splash of creamy sauce, but there is harmony in these tastes. The same is true of the trout wrapped in thin slices of prosciutto with spinach risotto. Each dish is carefully and artfully presented with a great sense of proportion.

**Uglesich's Restaurant and Bar.** *1238 Barrone St.* ☎ *504/523-8571. Reservations not required. Lunch $6–$11. No credit cards. Mon–Fri 9:30am–4pm. SANDWICHES.* Though it's old and more than a little rundown in appearance, it is well loved locally for its freshly prepared sandwiches of fried food. If you feel like being part of the neighborhood scene, you won't regret the trip here.

**PASTRY & ICE CREAM**   Since 1905, New Orleans has depended on **Angelo Brocato's Ice Cream and Confectionery,** 214 N. Carrollton Ave. (☎ **504/486-0078**), to cater fabulous ice cream and pastries for parties. The **Café du Monde,** in the French Market at 813 Decatur (☎ **504/581-2914**), is an indispensable part of the New Orleans scene. Here's where you go after a night on the town, or any other time, for cafe au lait and beignets, those square, deep-fried confections that arrive hot, crisp, and covered with confectioner's sugar. It's open daily, 24 hours. **La Madeleine,** 547 St. Ann St. at Chartres (☎ **504/568-9950**), a delightful place for breakfast or afternoon coffee or a light lunch, turns out marvelous pastries, croissants, and brioches. It's open daily 7am–9pm. **La Marquise,** 625 Chartres St. (☎ **504/524-0420**), serves French pastries on a small but delightful patio under the guiding hand of master baker Maurice Delechelle. It's open daily 7am–5:30pm.

## NEW ORLEANS AFTER DARK

From the moment Buddy Bolden blew the first notes of jazz from his cornet a century ago, New Orleans has been a music city. Jazz greats such as Louis Armstrong, Jelly Roll Morton, and later Harry Connick, Jr. and the Marsalises honed their skills in French Quarter clubs. In the past several decades, however, Cajun, zydeco, R&B, world beat, and New Orleans funk (a combination of Afro-Caribbean and R&B) have come to share the music marquee with jazz and blues.

New Orleans nightlife happens around the clock. There are no legal closing hours, no restrictions on when or where liquor can be sold, and the ambience encourages partying. *Warning:* Don't go wandering about deserted streets alone, especially late at night; and take a cab to and from nightspots outside the French Quarter.

For up-to-date information on what's happening around town, look for current editions of *Gambit, Offbeat,* and *Where,* all of which are free and are distributed in most hotels. You can also check out *Offbeat* magazine on the Internet before your trip (http://www.nola.com). Other sources include the *Times–Picayune's* daily entertainment calendar as well as Friday's *Lagniappe* section of the newspaper. Additionally, **WWOZ** (90.7 FM) broadcasts the local music schedule several times throughout the day.

**JAZZ & BLUES**    Dear to the hearts of all jazz devotees is **Preservation Hall,** 726 St. Peter St. (☎ 504/523-8939), a unique institution where jazz is found in a very pure form, uncluttered by such refinements as air-conditioning, drinks, or even (unless you arrive very early—a good 45 minutes before the doors open at 8pm) a place to sit. The shabby old building offers only hot, foot-tapping, body-swaying music, played by a solid core of old-time greats who never left New Orleans.

**Carrollton Station,** 8140 Willow St. (☎ 504/865-9190), offers everything from acoustic blues to fusion jazz. **Cosima's Bar,** 1201 Burgundy St. (☎ 504/586-0444), is a great place for traditional jazz, especially jazz piano. On the edge of the French Quarter, **Donna's,** 800 N. Rampart St. (☎ 504/596-6914), showcases talented local brass bands; you may find a member of the Marsalis family scheduled here. **Dragon's Den,** 435 Esplanade Ave. (☎504/949-1750), is an intimate and casual place to hear good modern jazz. **Funky Butt,** 714 N. Rampart St. (☎ 504/558-0872), is another new venue for modern jazz artists. **House of Blues,** 225 Decatur St. (☎ 504/529-2583), is one of the largest and most advanced music performance venues. There's a gospel brunch every Sunday at 11am and 2pm (reservations recommended). **Maxwell's Toulouse Cabaret,** 615 Toulouse St. (☎ 504/523-4207), is a piano bar where Harry Connick (father of the singer) and the Dukes of Dixieland perform.

**John Wehner's Famous Door,** 339 Bourbon St. (☎ 504/522-7626), is the oldest music club on Bourbon Street. There's jazz in the afternoon and dancing in the evening. The **New Showcase Lounge,** 1915 N. Broad St. (☎ 504/945-5612), is one of the newest clubs in town, and the showcase is modern jazz with an occasional blues singer. The **Palm Court Café,** 1204 Decatur St. (☎ 504/525-0200), is one of the Quarter's most stylish jazz haunts; top-notch jazz groups are featured. **Pampy's,** 2005 N. Broad St. (☎ 504/949-7970), a tiny club frequented mainly by locals, has live jazz. **Pete Fountain's,** in the New Orleans Hilton, 2 Poydras St. (☎ 504/523-4374 or 504/561-0500), is a re-creation of Pete's former Bourbon Street club in a plush setting. Pete is featured in one show a night, Tues–Sat at 10pm. You'll need reservations.

The 9,000-square-foot **Praline Connection Gospel and Blues Hall,** 901 S. Peters St. (☎ 504/523-3973), offers live entertainment. Every Sunday brings a great gospel brunch (reservations recommended). **Snug Harbor,** 626 Frenchmen St. (☎ 504/949-0696), has contemporary jazz nightly at 9 and 11pm; this is the place to find Ellis Marsalis, grandfather of the dynasty.

**CAJUN & ZYDECO**    The **Maple Leaf Bar,** 8316 Oak St. (☎ 504/866-9359), uptown in the Carrollton area, may be the best place outside the bayous to hear some of the leading local and national lights of Cajun and zydeco music. Some nights it's rhythm and blues or R&B, so call for a schedule. In the Warehouse District, you'll find good Cajun music at **Michaul's on St. Charles,** 840 St. Charles Ave. (☎ 504/522-5517). **Mulate's,** 201 Julia St. (☎ 504/522-1492), a Cajun restaurant, has a stage for live Cajun music, and dancing takes place nightly. **Patout's Cajun Cabin,** 501 Bourbon St. (☎ 504/529-4256), features music from the country side of Cajun in a lighthearted, raucous atmosphere.

**OTHER LIVE MUSIC**   **Café Brasil,** 2100 Chartres St. (☎ 504/947-9386), features Latin and Caribbean music, R&B, or jazz almost every night to a fashionable if casual and cool crowd. **Checkpoint Charlie's,** 501 Esplanade Ave. (☎ 504/949-7012), has been a reliable venue for rock and R&B for many years. **Dream Palace,** 534 Frenchmen St. (☎ 504/945-2040), is one of the newer clubs in Faubourg Marigny, providing a venue for Latin music, rock, R&B, and blues to a 20s crowd. **Howlin' Wolf,** 828 Peters St. (☎ 504/523-2551), is New Orleans's stop on the underground/indie rock railroad. **Jimmy Buffetts' Margaritaville Cafe & Storyville Tavern,** 1104 Decatur St. (☎ 504/592-2565, concert line 592-2552), has a loyal following for its nightly live entertainment.

Lion's Den, 2655 Gravier St. (☎ 504/821-3745), features Irma Thomas, one of the great live R&B/soul acts; call to see if she's performing. **Mid-City Lanes Rock and Bowl,** 4133 S. Carrollton Ave. (☎ 504/482-3133), is a spot for some good ol' rock 'n' roll. It's a rock club and a bowling alley—you literally rock *and* bowl. **Tipitina's,** 501 Napoleon Ave. (☎ 504/895-8477, concert line 504/897-3943), has jazz, rhythm and blues, and almost every other form of music, depending on the artist playing.

**THE PERFORMING ARTS**   The **Louisiana Philharmonic Orchestra** (☎ 504/523-6530) has a standard repertory and gives a subscription series during the fall-to-spring season; its home is the ornate **Orpheum Theater,** 129 University Place. The **New Orleans Opera Association** (☎ 504/529-2278) mounts four productions a year. The **New Orleans Ballet Association** (☎ 504/522-0996) performs in the New Orleans Theater of the Performing Arts Center.

New Orleans's **Municipal Auditorium,** 1201 St. Peter St. (☎ 504/565-7470, or 504/565-7490 for ticket information), is used for just about every kind of entertainment—most of the Mardi Gras balls are held here. The **Mahalia Jackson Theatre of the Performing Arts,** 801 N. Rampart St. (☎ 504/565-7470), is the venue for the Opera Association's performances as well as touring musicals, circuses, prizefights, ice shows, and the summer pops symphony concerts.

New Orleans has only one Equity theater, the **Southern Repertory Company,** Canal Place Shopping Center, third level (☎ 504/861-8163). In the Warehouse District, the **Contemporary Arts Center,** 900 Camp St. (☎ 504/523-1216), is best known for its changing art exhibitions, but it also features experimental works by local playwrights as well as dance recitals and concerts. Call for the current schedule. **Le Petit Théâtre du Vieux Carré,** 616 St. Peter St. (☎ 504/522-2081), is right in the heart of the French Quarter, one of the oldest nonprofessional theater troupes in the country. The **Saenger Theatre,** 143 N. Rampart St. (☎ 504/525-1052), has been restored to its former opulence and hosts Broadway productions. **Theatre Marigny,** 616 Frenchmen St. (☎ 504/944-2653), is known for avant-garde works.

**COFFEEHOUSES**   Several of the city's coffeehouses offer live entertainment. **Kaldi's Coffee House and Museum,** 941 Decatur St. (☎ 504/586-8989), has live jazz and gospel music on the weekends. In the Warehouse District the place to go is **True Brew Cafe and Theater,** at 200 Julia St. (☎ 504/524-8441), where live music alternates with one-act plays weekly. Uptown **Neutral Ground Coffee House,** 5110 Daneel St. (☎ 504/891-3381), features high-comfort-level armchairs and all sorts of performers.

**THE BAR & DISCO SCENE**   A French Quarter watering hole with lots of atmosphere is **The Abbey,** 1123 Decatur St. (no phone). Locals love to play darts at the **Apple Barrel,** 609 Frenchmen St. (☎ 504/949-9399). **Apres,** 709 St. Charles St. (☎ 504/566-7000), is a new bar riding the current trends of martinis and cigars. **City Lights,** 310 Howard Ave. (☎ 504/568-1700), is a dance club popular with the 30-something well-heeled crowd. **Hyttops Sports Bar,** in the Hyatt Hotel, 500 Poydras

Plaza (☎ **504/561-1234**), has TVs tuned, via satellite, to sporting events around the country. **Lafitte's Blacksmith Shop,** 941 Bourbon St. (☎ **504/523-0066**), dates from 1772, and legend has it that the privateer brothers Pierre and Jean Lafitte used the smithy as a "blind" for their lucrative trade in contraband. **Madigan's,** 800 S. Carrollton Ave. (☎ **504/866-9455**), in the Uptown section, is a home to blues musician John Mooney on Sunday. Atmosphere is a big draw at the landmark **Napoleon House Bar and Cafe,** 500 Chartres St. (☎ **504/524-9752**). The haunted courtyard is the draw at **O'Flaherty's Irish Channel Pub,** 514 Toulouse St. (☎ **504/ 529-1317** or 504/529-4570); there's Irish dancing on Saturday night. Touristy **Pat O'Brien's,** 718 St. Peter St. (☎ **504/525-4823**), is famous for its gigantic, rum-based Mighty Hurricane drink, served in 29-ounce hurricane lamp-style glasses. The **"R" Bar,** 1431 Royal St. (☎ **504/948-7499**), is the quintessential neighborhood bar. **Voodoo Grove,** 216 Bourbon St. (☎ **504/523-2020**), is the best bet for an alternative music dance club.

For something more upscale, stop by the **Esplanade Lounge,** in the Royal Orleans, 621 St. Louis St. (☎ **504/529-5333**), for a nightcap to the strains of top-notch piano music. The **Polo Lounge,** in the elegant Windsor Court Hotel, 300 Gravier St. (☎ **504/523-6000**), is the place to go if you're feeling particularly stylish. The **Sazerac Bar,** in the Fairmont Hotel, University Place (☎ **504/529-4733**), is a favorite with the city's young professionals. **Top of the Mart,** World Trade Center of New Orleans, 2 Canal St. (☎ **504/522-9795**), has a breathtaking view, especially after dark. **Vino Vino,** 1119 Decatur St. (☎ **504/529-4553**), as its name suggests, is a wine bar.

**SKIN SHOWS & CABARET**  Bourbon Street's legendary skin shows are offered at a number of establishments along the 300 and 400 blocks, and club owners frequently open their doors to lure in the paying public with music and a view of the strippers inside. A more traditional cabaret is at **Chris Owens Club,** 735 St. Louis St., corner of Bourbon Street (☎ **504/523-6400**), where talented Chris Owens puts on a sexy show backed by jazz, pop, country and western, and blues. Trumpeteer Al Hirt performs several times a week at 8pm; call for reservations. **Maiden Voyage,** 225 Bourbon St. (☎ **504/524-0010**), is the city's most upscale spot; upstairs is a "boardroom suite," but you'll have to do your own research for that.

**THE GAY & LESBIAN SCENE**  Check *Ambush Mag 2000* (http://www.gaybars.com/ states/louisian.htm), a great source for gay community activities.

**Bourbon Pub–Parade Disco,** 801 Bourbon St. (☎ **504/529-2107**), attracts a young male crowd with a high-tech dance floor and a Sunday-night T dance. **Café Lafitte in Exile,** 901 Bourbon St. (☎ **504/522-8397**), is the oldest and most famous of men's gay bars. **Charlene's,** 940 Elysian Fields (☎ **504/945-9328**), is a longstanding social spot for the lesbian community. It's a little out of the way if you're staying in the Quarter, but there's dancing and live entertainment; take a cab. **LeRoundup,** 819 St. Louis St. (☎ **504/561-8340**), attracts a diverse crowd of friendly locals, from transsexuals to men in khakis and Levis. **The Mint,** 504 Esplande Ave. (☎ **504/525-2000**), has live entertainment all the time. **Oz,** 800 Bourbon St. (☎ **504/593-9491**), is one of the newest dance clubs, the place to see and be seen. High-tech lighting and sound makes **Rubyfruit Jungle,** 640 Frenchmen St. (☎ **504/947-4000**), one of the city's hottest gay and lesbian clubs. **Rawhide,** 740 Burgundy St. (☎ **504/586-0644**), is a leather-and-Levi's scene. **Wolfendale's,** 834 N. Rampart St. (☎ **504/523-7764**), has a lovely courtyard, a raised dance floor, and a pool table, and is popular with the city's · gay African-American population.

**CASINOS**  The **Flamingo Casino New Orleans** (☎ **800/587-LUCK** or 504/587-5777) is an authentic re-creation of a 19th-century riverboat casino, docked at Riverwalk Marketplace, next to the New Orleans Hilton Riverside Hotel on Poydras Street.

Cruises last 90 minutes and take place every 3 hours. The **Treasure Chest Casino** is docked on Lake Ponchartrain in Kenner (☎ **504/443-8000** for information).

**CRUISES**   The *Creole Queen* (☎ **800/445-4109** or 504/524-0814), a paddlewheeler, offers dinner and jazz cruises with dancing nightly. Departures are at 8pm, boarding at 7pm from the Canal Street Wharf. **Steamboat** *Natchez* (☎ **800/233-BOAT** or 504/ 586-8777) boards at Toulouse Street Wharf at 6pm for a buffet and jazz and Dixieland cruise 7–9pm.

## 11  More Southeast Highlights

### THE FLORIDA KEYS

Juan Ponce de León, the 16th-century Spanish explorer who was searching for the Fountain of Youth, found the Florida Keys instead. He couldn't have missed, for this magical chain of 400 tropical islands arches from Miami halfway to Cuba. The best known are the 34 islands connected to the mainland by the Overseas Highway (U.S. 1); crossing 42 bridges and 34 islands, it's one of the greatest road trips anywhere. Away from the highway, most "backcountry" keys are wildlife refuges protected by either the federal government or the Nature Conservancy, a private environmental organization.

Surrounding the Keys is the world's third-largest barrier-reef system, a variety of living corals that supports a complex and delicate ecosystem of plants and animals. According to readers of *Scuba Diving* magazine, the Keys are the best place to dive in America, topping even California and Hawaii. Here you can also go snorkeling, biking, birdwatching, hiking, fishing, kayaking, and canoeing.

Although the northern or Upper Keys from Key Largo through Islamaroda to Marathon are commercial and overdeveloped, that's not the case farther south in the Lower Keys, thanks to environmental activism and governmental protection. Here in places like **Great White Heron National Wildlife Refuge** you'll find a rich variety of indigenous plants and animals, including many endangered species. Eagles, egrets, and Key deer are some of the most visible, as are gumbo-limbo trees, mangroves, royal poincianas, banyans, and aloe.

Literally at the end of the road, famous **Key West** operates on "island time"—you'd think there was an ordinance against wearing watches in this land of perennial vacation. It has long attracted luminaries, among them Ernest Hemingway, John James Audubon, and Tennessee Williams, and was once one of the wealthiest towns in America. Today the majority of the island's residents are drifters who headed south until they could drift no farther. They brought with them a very tolerant live-and-let-live attitude and a burning devotion to personal independence and individual freedom. This liberal philosophy has made Key West especially welcoming to gays, but it has fostered unchecked growth. Only recently has concern about the environment been building among Key West's residents. AIDS has claimed the lives of many of the island's most creative characters, and increasing tourism and gentrification have sapped the once-funky fishing village of much of its charm. T-shirt shops are edging out smart boutiques and old gin joints, and strollers are less likely to be longtime locals than cruise-ship passengers on a few hours' leave.

But Key West is still entertaining to visit, for hedonism still outpaces consumerism here. It's a great place to pocket your watch and take a long stroll down **Duval Street,** the island's famously fun thoroughfare. Although Duval was tamed long ago by gourmet ice-cream parlors and tacky T-shirt shops, pubbing through the many open-air bars remains one of the world's best crawls. Be sure to end up at **Mallory Docks** for the town's famous sunsets.

To see the "real" Key West, you'll need to get off Duval Street and wander (or bicycle) around the byways of the island's compact Old Town. Lined with "conch"

# The Florida Keys

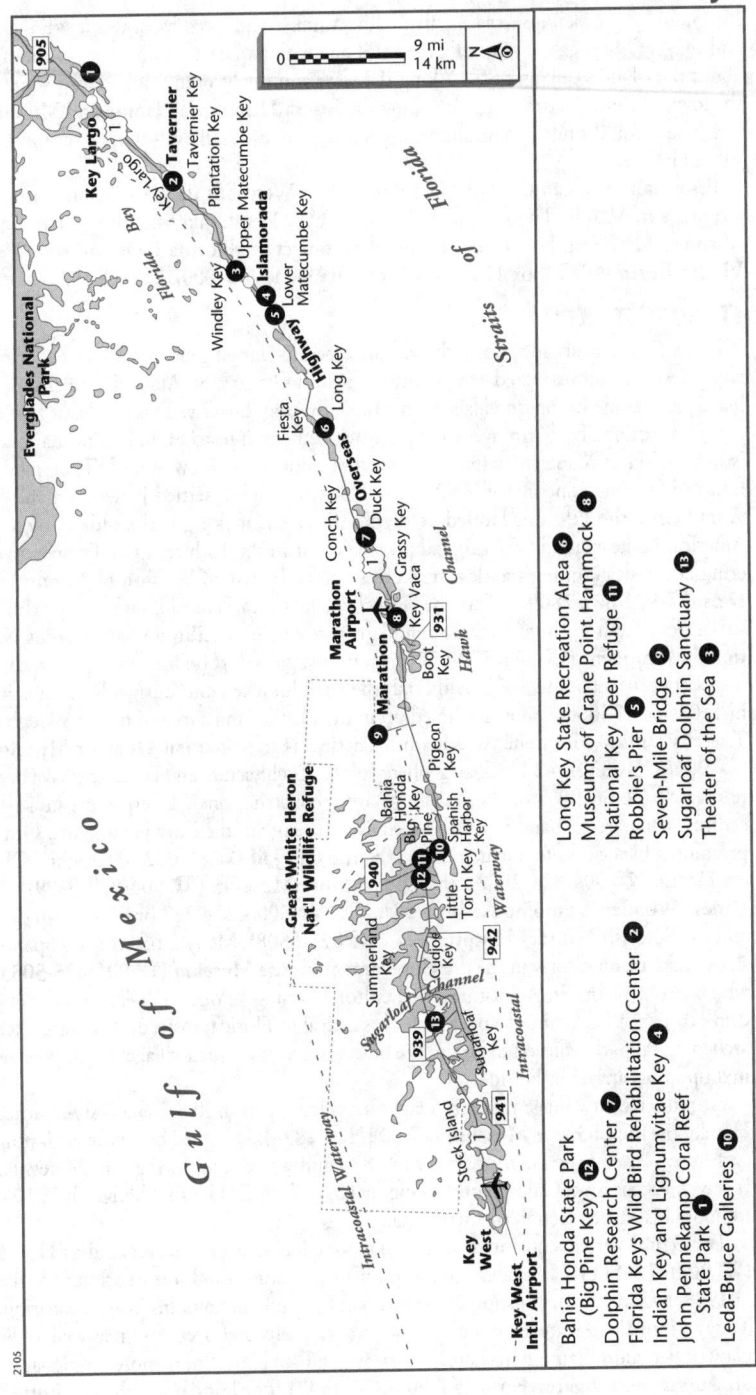

Bahia Honda State Park (Big Pine Key) 12

Dolphin Research Center 7

Florida Keys Wild Bird Rehabilitation Center 2

Indian Key and Lignumvitae Key 4

John Pennekamp Coral Reef State Park 1

Leda-Bruce Galleries 10

Long Key State Recreation Area 6

Museums of Crane Point Hammock 8

National Key Deer Refuge 11

Robbie's Pier 5

Seven-Mile Bridge 9

Sugarloaf Dolphin Sanctuary 13

Theater of the Sea 3

(pronounced "conk") houses that are architecturally influenced by both New England and the Caribbean, these smaller streets still retain a unique charm that speaks volumes about the island's quixotic past. Along the way, you might even want to visit some of the town's historical attractions, including the **Ernest Hemingway Home and Museum** (elsewhere you'll find the famous author's image used to sell everything from beer to suntan lotion).

**Essentials:** You can fly into Marathon or Key West, but the nearest international airport is in Miami. The Overseas Highway (U.S. 1) will take you all the way from Miami to Key West. For visitor information, contact the **Florida Keys and Key West Visitor Bureau,** P.O. Box 1147, Key West, FL 33041 (☎ 800/FLA-KEYS).

## ST. AUGUSTINE

With its 17th-century fort, horse-drawn carriages clip-clopping along narrow streets, old city gates, and reconstructed 18th-century Spanish Quarter, St. Augustine seems more like a picturesque European village than a modern American city. This northeast Florida city is exceptionally charming. It has palm-fringed ocean beaches, but its primary lure is historic. Here Western civilization first took root in the New World. The Spanish founded St. Augustine in 1565, 42 years before the English settled Jamestown and 55 years before the Pilgrims landed at Plymouth Rock, making it the oldest town in America. Its heart is still the original plaza laid out in the 16th century. Today a towering 208-foot gleaming stainless-steel cross marks the **site of Mission of Nombre de Dios** (☎ 904/824-2809), where the Gospel was first preached. Although many existing structures date from much later, a highlight here is the **Castillo de San Marcos National Monument** (☎ 904/829-6506), an impregnable fort built by the Spanish colonists between 1669 and 1695. Although the British sacked and burned St. Augustine in 1702 and 1740, the populace holed up in the Castillo and survived both onslaughts. The city's most comprehensive historic section is the **Spanish Quarter Museum** (☎ 904/825-6830), a 2-block area where colonial architecture and landscape have been re-created (about 90% of the buildings are reconstructions). Interpreters in 18th-century attire are on hand to help you envision the life of the early inhabitants. Other prominent historical sites include the **Authentic Old Jail** (☎ 904/829-3800), the **Oldest House** (☎ 904/824-2872), the **Oldest Store Museum** (☎ 904/829-9729), the **Oldest Wooden Schoolhouse in the U.S.A.** (☎ 800/428-0222 or 904/824-0192), and the **Spanish Military Hospital** (☎ 904/825-6808). Many artifacts from Spanish shipwrecks are on display in the the **Government House Museum** (☎ 904/825-5033), which also explains St. Augustine's rich cultural heritage. Ponce de Léon didn't really drink from the Fountain of Youth upon his arrival in Florida; instead, this is a 25-acre archeological park believed to be the site of the American Indian village of Seloy he visited upon his arrival in Florida.

Of more recent vintage is Henry Flagler's opulent Spanish Renaissance–style Alcazar Hotel, now the **Lightner Museum** (☎ 904/824-2874). Designed by Thomas Hastings and John Carrère, the hotel was built in 1889 and was closed during the Depression. It stayed vacant until Chicago publishing magnate Otto C. Lightner bought it in 1948 to house his vast collection of Victoriana.

To become better acquainted with local marine life, visit the **Marineland of Florida** (☎ 904/471-1111), an underwater motion-picture studio and tourist attraction that, in 1938, became the first institution to successfully maintain dolphins in an oceanarium. Today Marineland features dolphin shows in a vast saltwater oceanarium as well as displays of penguins, flamingos, sharks, alligators, and sea lions. Enjoy more reptiles at the **St. Augustine Alligator Farm** (☎ 904/824-3337). For less damp subjects, **Potter's Wax Museum** (☎ 904/829-9056) features more than 150 wax figures. You can even take in a dose of weirdness at St. Augustine's edition of **Ripley's Believe It or Not! Museum** (☎ **904/824-1606**).

**Essentials**: St. Augustine is about equidistant (an hour's drive) from airports in Jacksonville and Daytona Beach. Start your visit at the **St. Augustine Visitor Information Center,** 10 Castillo Dr., at San Marco Avenue (☎ **904/825-1000**), where you can buy tickets for sightseeing trolleys, trains, and horse-drawn carriage tours. Before you go, write or call the **St. Johns County Visitors and Convention Bureau,** 88 Riberia St., Suite 250, St. Augustine, FL 32084 (☎ **904/829-1711**).

## HILTON HEAD

The largest sea island between New Jersey and Florida, and one of America's great resort meccas, Hilton Head is surrounded by the Low Country, where all the romance, beauty, and graciousness of the Old South survive. Its coastline is among the most scenic in the Southeast. Broad, white sandy beaches are backed by rolling dunes held in place by swaying sea oats. Palms mingle with live oaks, dogwoods, and pines, and it seems that everything is draped in Spanish moss. Warmed by the Gulf Stream, the climate makes all this beauty the ideal setting for golf, tennis, fishing, bicycling, kayaking, horseback riding, and a plethora of other outdoor pursuits. It's a far more sophisticated and upscale destination than Myrtle Beach and the Grand Strand (see below). Its country club–like resorts preserve something of the leisurely Southern lifestyle that's always held sway here.

Although the island is only 12 miles long and 5 miles wide, it feels spacious, thanks to judicious planning from the start of its development in 1952. And that's a blessing, since about half a million resort guests visit annually (the permanent population is about 25,000). The broad beaches on its ocean side, sea marshes on the sound, and natural wooded areas of live and water oak, pine, bay, and palmetto trees in between have all been carefully preserved amid the commercial explosion. This lovely setting attracts artists, writers, musicians, theater groups, and craftspeople. The only city (of sorts) is **Harbour Town,** a Mediterranean-style cluster of shops and restaurants.

With 22 challenging golf courses, and an additional 9 within a 30-minute drive, this is heaven for professional and novice golfers. Some of golf's most celebrated architects, including George and Tom Fazio, Robert Trent Jones, Pete Dye, and Jack Nicklaus, have designed championship courses on the island with wide, scenic fairways and rolling greens.

No other American destination can boast of a greater concentration of tennis facilities, with more than 300 courts ideal for players of all skill levels. A wide variety of tennis clinics and lessons will let you learn or hone your game.

The oldest and most comprehensive hotel reservation service on the island, **Hilton Head Central Reservation Service** (☎ **800/845-7018**) can book you into any hotel room or villa on the island, and there's no fee. To rent private homes, villas, and condos, contact **Island Rentals and Real Estate,** P.O. Box 5915, Hilton Head Island, SC 29938 (☎ **800/845-6134** or 803/785-3813).

**Essentials:** The nearest airports are at Savannah, 52 miles to the south, and at Charleston, 65 miles to the north. The **Hilton Head Visitor and Convention Bureau** (Chamber of Commerce), 1 Chamber Dr., Hilton Head Island, SC 29938 (☎ **803/785-3673**), offers free maps of the area and will assist you in finding places of interest and outdoor activities. The **Island Visitor Information Center** (☎ **803/757-4472**) is on U.S. 278 at S.C. 46 just before you cross over from the mainland. It offers a free "Where to Go" booklet, including a visitor map and guide.

# Myrtle Beach & the Grand Strand

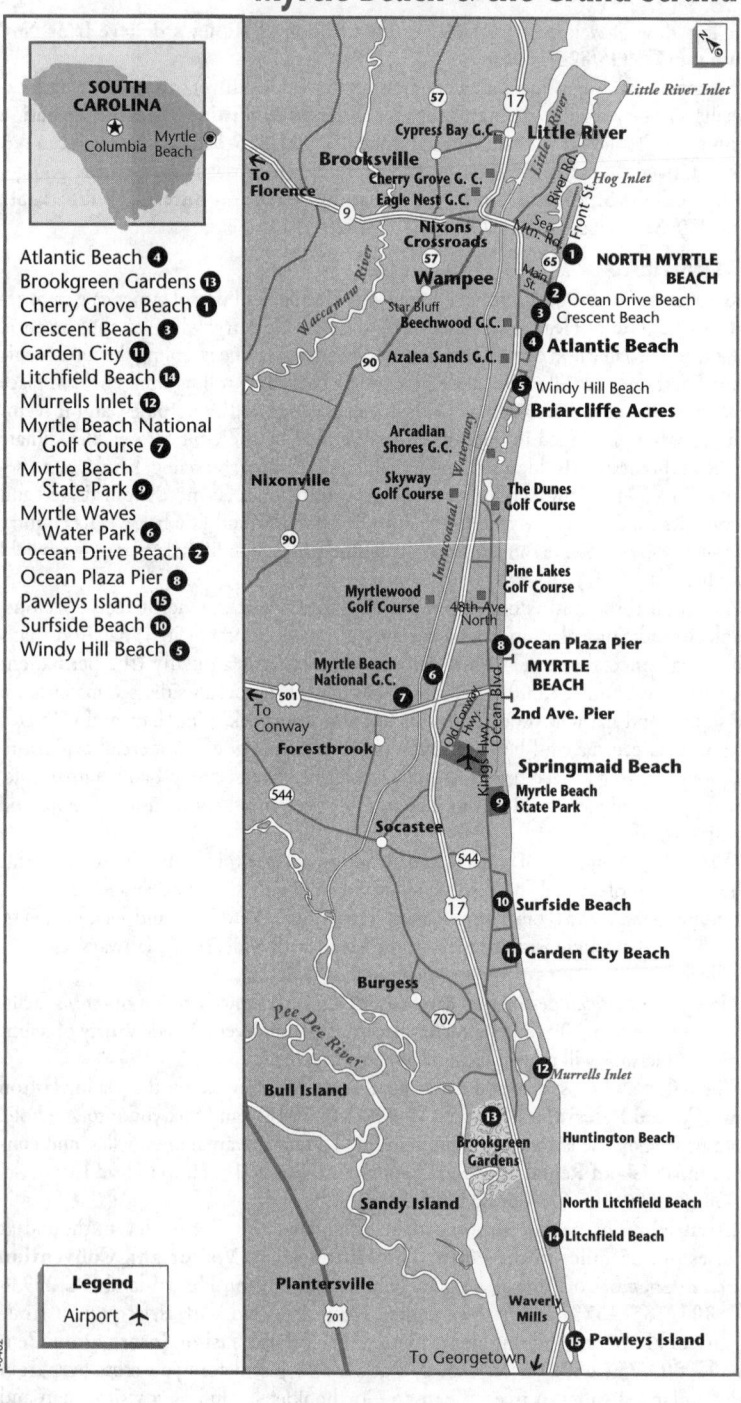

Atlantic Beach ④
Brookgreen Gardens ⑬
Cherry Grove Beach ①
Crescent Beach ③
Garden City ⑪
Litchfield Beach ⑭
Murrells Inlet ⑫
Myrtle Beach National
  Golf Course ⑦
Myrtle Beach
  State Park ⑨
Myrtle Waves
  Water Park ⑥
Ocean Drive Beach ②
Ocean Plaza Pier ⑧
Pawleys Island ⑮
Surfside Beach ⑩
Windy Hill Beach ⑤

SOUTH
CAROLINA

Columbia ★    Myrtle ◉
              Beach

To
Florence ←

Little River Inlet

Cypress Bay G.C.    Little River

Brooksville
Cherry Grove G. C.
Eagle Nest G.C.

Nixons
Crossroads

Wampee

Star Bluff
Beechwood G.C.

Azalea Sands G.C.

Hog Inlet

❶ Cherry Grove Beach

NORTH MYRTLE
BEACH

❷ Ocean Drive Beach
❸ Crescent Beach

❹ Atlantic Beach

❺ Windy Hill Beach

Briarcliffe Acres

Nixonville

Arcadian
Shores G.C.

Skyway
Golf Course

The Dunes
Golf Course

Pine Lakes
Golf Course

Myrtlewood
Golf Course

48th Ave.
North

❽ Ocean Plaza Pier

MYRTLE
BEACH

2nd Ave. Pier

Myrtle Beach
National G.C.

❻
❼

← 501
To
Conway

Forestbrook

Springmaid Beach
Myrtle Beach
❾ State Park

Socastee

❿ Surfside Beach

⓫ Garden City Beach

Burgess

Pee Dee River

Bull Island

⓬ Murrells Inlet

Brookgreen
Gardens    Huntington Beach

⓭

Sandy Island    North Litchfield Beach

⓮ Litchfield Beach

Plantersville

Waverly
Mills    ⓯ Pawleys Island

To Georgetown ↓

Legend

Airport ✈

1-0482

## MYRTLE BEACH & THE GRAND STRAND

Once a ghost town after Labor Day, South Carolina's Grand Strand—a 60-mile-long coastal playground northeast of Charleston—has grown into a year-round destination. Coupled with shopping, golf, tennis, and outdoor activities, this area's seemingly endless beach attracts more than half a million people on a hot summer day. Even in the winter months, visitors flock to theaters combining several styles of music with comedy, circus acts, ice skating, and more. In the world of country music, the Grand Strand is quickly becoming a Nashville or Branson by the beach.

The flood of visitors has brought dramatic changes to the area, and some longtime promoters fear that the Grand Strand's family-friendly atmosphere may be threatened. Thong bathing suits have been banned, and so far topless nightclubs have been exiled to an industrial park. But big-time theme parks are on the way as the coast increasingly becomes a junior-size version of Disneyland and Las Vegas (albeit without the gambling casinos). But for now, families still make up the most important part of the trade.

Some 98 miles northeast of Charleston, **Myrtle Beach** is at the center of the Grand Strand and its largest beach resort. Named for the area's abundant myrtle trees, it has more facilities, entertainment, and restaurants than its neighbors—Little River, Cherry Grove, Crescent Beach, Ocean Drive, Atlantic Beach, Surfside Beach, Garden City, Murrells Inlet, Litchfield Beach, and Pawleys Island.

The big attraction here is the beach and all that goes with it: sunbathing, swimming, boating, sailing, fishing, windsurfing, scuba diving, and other water sports.

The Grand Strand also is a major golf mecca, with more than 87 courses in a variety of shapes, sizes, and degrees of difficulty. You can play all year, although spring and autumn are the busiest seasons. Most hotels and motels provide guest membership privileges entitling you to reduced greens fees, and a plethora of golf packages include room and board as well as fees. For information, call **Golf Holiday** (☎ **800/845-4653** or 803/448-5942). And there are over 200 public and private tennis courts here.

The Strand's entertainment venues offer something for every taste. The country music supergroup Alabama plays at least 10 times a year at their **Alabama Theatre** (☎ **800/ 342-2262** or 803/272-1111). Kenny Rogers, Bill Cosby, and the Righteous Brothers have appeared at the **Palace at Myrtle Beach** (☎ **800/905-4228** or 803/448-0588). Dolly Parton's hokie **Dixie Stampede** (☎ **800/433-4401** or 803/497-9700) features a rodeo and a dinner theater in which patrons chow down on Southern food with their fingers. The **Carolina Opry** (☎ **800/843-6779** or 803/238-8888) stages elaborate country, bluegrass, western swing, big band, and other shows. The hottest pickers and comedians play at The **Dixie Jubilee** (☎ **800/843-6779** or 803/238-8888). And **Legends in Concert** (☎ **800/843-6779** or 803/238-8888) aren't the real legends, only impersonators making like Elvis, Michael Jackson, the Beatles, and others.

Needless to say, the Grand Stand has a multutide of places to stay, and at very reasonable rates when compared to other destinations. Most chains have establishments here, including Radisson's **Kingston Plantation** (☎ **800/333-3333** or 803/449-0006), the most desirable choice.

**Essentials:** Air South, Continental, Delta, Myrtle Jet Express, and US Airways fly to the **Myrtle Beach Jetport. Greyhound/Trailways** has bus service to Myrtle Beach (☎ **800/231-2222**). For information, contact the **Myrtle Beach Area Chamber of Commerce** at 1200 N. Oak St. (P.O. Box 2115), Myrtle Beach, SC 29578 (☎ **800/ 356-3016** or 803/626-7444).

## THE NORTH CAROLINA SANDHILLS

The porous, sandy soil of North Carolina's Sandhills region, 50 miles west of I-95 at Fayetteville, provides the ideal drainage that's crucial to the area's standing as the "Golf

Capital of the World," for no matter what the rainfall, no puddles accumulate on its rolling courses. The likes of Ben Hogan, Bobby Jones, Sam Snead, Arnold Palmer, Gary Player, and Jack Nicklaus have been drawn to the area's 35 courses, some among the highest rated in the world. And with mean temperatures ranging between 44°F and 78°F, the game is played here year-round.

**Pinehurst** has a New England village air, with a town green and shaded residential streets. Year-round greenery is provided by pines, with color by camellias, azaleas, wisteria, peach trees, dogwoods, and summer-blooming yard flowers. For years, golfing on the superb courses of the **Pinehurst Country Club** was by invitation only. Although the golf world's top players consider Pinehurst their own turf, today you don't have to wait for an invitation, or be a millionaire, to play. Prices are certainly high enough at Pinehurst, but they're not exorbitant in comparison with other luxury resorts around the country. And there's a profusion of other hotels and motels in almost any price range. And expert or duffer, guests can always play the Pinehurst courses. If there's a hotel or motel in the area that doesn't arrange play for its guests, we couldn't find it. Most can also set you up for tennis, cycling, horseback riding, skeet shooting, archery, or boat rentals on one of the many lakes around.

In September 1974 President Gerald Ford presided at the opening of the **World Golf Hall of Fame,** overlooking the famous Pinehurst Number Two Course, one of the top 10 in the country.

Over the years, Pinehurst and the nearby village of **Southern Pines** have become renowned meccas for artists, craftspeople, and potters. Scattered around the vicinity in rustic, pine-sheltered workshops, many of the potters welcome visitors, and most are quite happy to have you watch them at their work. **Midland Crafters,** between Pinehurst and Southern Pines on Midland Road (N.C. 2), is a virtual gallery of American crafts, ranging from beanbags to paintings to furniture to candles to pottery to glassware to almost any handcraft you can conjure up.

What Park Avenue is to New York or Michigan Avenue is to Chicago, Midland Road is to the Pinehurst and Southern Pines area. It has somewhat the feel of the 17-mile drive on the Monterey peninsula in California. More than a third of the area's courses are accessible via this road, with its stately 6-mile row of pine trees in the median.

**Essentials:** Raleigh/Durham is the nearest commercial airport. Amtrak (☎ 800/USA-RAIL) has one northbound and one southbound train daily through Southern Pines. For visitor information, contact the **Pinehurst Area Convention and Visitor Bureau,** P.O. Box 2270, Southern Pines, NC 28388 (☎ 800/346-5362 or 910/692-3330).

## ASHEVILLE

Asheville is the largest and most important city in North Carolina's gorgeous High Country, its pleasant climate and mountainous scenery long drawing rich and famous residents. For cities of its size, Asheville is one of America's most desirable places to live. It's the closest North Carolina city to Great Smoky Mountains National Park (see section 7 of this chapter).

F. Scott Fitzgerald and wife Zelda were among Asheville's most famous part-time residents (Fitzgerald arrived in the summer of 1935 to recuperate from tuberculosis, while Zelda was incarcerated at Highland Hospital, a private sanatorium, for treatment of nervous breakdowns).

But Asheville is most famous as novelist Thomas Wolfe's hometown. His mother's boardinghouse was thinly disguised as "Dixieland" in Wolfe's autobiographical novel, *Look Homeward, Angel,* which caused such a stir it was blacklisted here as late as 1949. Although Wolfe claimed "You can't go home again," he eventually did—upon his premature death in 1938, when thousands assembled outside the boardinghouse to bid him farewell. His mother's establishment, the **Old Kentucky Home,** 48 Spruce St. (☎ **704/253-8304**), is maintained as a literary shrine.

Both Wolfe and William Sydney Porter (better known as the short story–writer O. Henry) are buried in **Riverside Cemetery** (entrance on Birch Street off Pearson Drive).

As interesting as these literary attractions may be, they're dwarfed by the ✪ **Biltmore Estate,** 2 miles north of I-40 on U.S. 25 (☎ **800/543-2961** or 704/274-6333). This 250-room French Renaissance château was built by multi-millionaire George W. Vanderbilt between 1890 and 1895 of Indiana limestone transported by a special railway spur he installed to the site. The great house remains the largest private residence in the United States, a National Historic Landmark still owned by the Vanderbilt family. There isn't an ordinary spot in the place, not even the kitchen. Vanderbilt gathered furnishings and art treasures from all over the world for this palace (Napoleón's chess set and table from St. Helena are here). The formal gardens are among the most lavish you'll ever see, with more than 200 varieties of azaleas and thousands of other plants and shrubs. In addition to the gardens, there are three restaurants and endless gift shops, plus tours of the **Biltmore Estate Winery.**

You'll find other interesting attractions near Asheville, including the scenic **Blue Ridge Parkway.** At milepost 382 on the parkway, some 5 miles east of downtown, the **Folk Art Center** (☎ **704/298-7928**) houses and sells the finest traditional and contemporary handcrafts of the region (the **Allanstand Craft Shop** is one of the oldest craft shops in the country, established in 1895). Stately **Mount Mitchell,** highest point east of the Mississippi River, is some 33 miles northeast via the parkway, then 5 miles north on N.C. 128. The surrounding state park has a museum, a tower, an observation lodge, camping, and picnicking.

**Chimney Rock Park,** 25 miles to the southeast via U.S. 64/74A, is a granite monolith rising 315 feet; you can reach the views from on top by stairway, trail, or elevator. *The Last of the Mohicans* was filmed here. About 30 miles southeast of Asheville on I-26 is the little town of **Flat Rock,** home of the late Carl Sandburg, the two-time Pulitzer Prize–winning writer, poet, and historian. His beloved home, **Connemara,** on Little River Road just west of I-25 (☎ **704/693-4178**), is open daily for tours. At the North Carolina State Theater's **Flat Rock Playhouse** (☎ **704/693-0731**), which opened in 1952, the popular Vagabond Players present *The World of Carl Sandburg* and *The Rootabaga Stories* annually.

In addition to many chain hotels, Asheville is blessed with several fine bed-and-breakfasts and the famous **Grove Park Inn** (☎ **800/438-5800** or 704/252-2711), built in 1913 on the side of Sunset Mountain overlooking the city and the Blue Ridge Mountains. On the National Register of Historic Places, it's a favorite year-round destination, with panoramic views, Old World charm, massive fireplaces, and a long tradition of hospitality—plus an 18-hole golf course, tennis courts, and numerous other modern sports facilities.

**Essentials:** American Eagle, Delta, United Express, and US Airways serve **Asheville Airport.** I-40 connects Asheville to points east and west, I-26 to points south. For information, contact the **Asheville Convention and Visitor Bureau,** 151 Haywood St. (P.O. Box 1011), Asheville, NC 28802 (☎ **800/257-1300** or 704/258-6109).

# The Central States

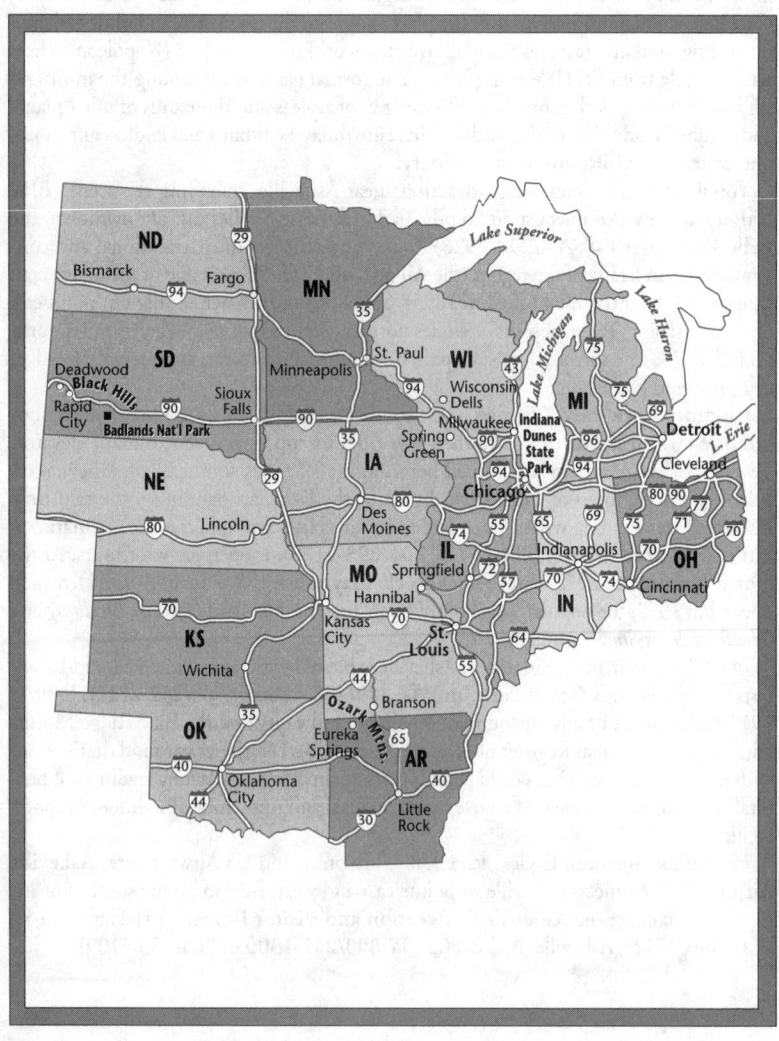

The north-central states, especially the Midwestern states, are America's heartland, where the ideal of small-town America and the values that go with it are epitomized. The area evokes images of neat farmlands, tree-lined small town streets, and hard-working, industrialized cities. When a sociological study of a typical American community was proposed, it was Muncie, Indiana that became America's "Middletown."

This chapter concentrates on an area loosely composed of the states that originally made up the Northwest Territory: Illinois, Indiana, Michigan, Minnesota, Ohio, and Wisconsin, together with Missouri and South Dakota. America's richest farmland is found here as well as some of America's most important big cities, including the great metropolis of Chicago. In recent years, news from the area has emphasized the ongoing economic problems that have plagued many of the cities—plant closings, unemployment, and deterioration of the infrastructure. However, today the cities are busy refurbishing their downtowns, building convention centers and restoring historic areas, and enhancing their parks, museums, and zoos. You'll find that every major city has important art museums and supports a world-class symphony orchestra, and some of America's most vital and innovative theater groups are found in Chicago and Minneapolis.

The ideal small town still exists, and as you travel through the area you'll discover that people really do seem more open, friendly, and down-to-earth—even the cities have a sense of community. Sports are a way of life here, from rooting for your baseball or basketball team—national or local—to hiking, skiing, or biking in gently rolling landscape or rugged terrain. Many acres of forest and lakeshore have been set aside for preserves, from the stark beauty of the South Dakota Badlands to the wetlands and forests of the Indiana Dunes. And history is everywhere, reflecting the Midwest's immigrant heritage, its Native American legacy, the pioneers of every nationality who first came to settle this land, and its famous people, from Abraham Lincoln to Mark Twain to Garrison Keillor and David Letterman.

## DRIVING TOUR
## The Land of Lincoln

**Start:** Vandalia Statehouse, Vandalia
**Finish:** Lincoln Tomb, Springfield
**Distance:** Approximately 250 miles
**Time:** 2 days
**Highlights:** The restored village where Abraham Lincoln lived and worked, the only home he ever owned, and his final resting place

Illinois was settled from south to north. The state's first capital was Kaskaskia, on the banks of the Mississippi River. Cairo, at the southernmost tip, was a thriving, bustling river port and, in 1830, businessmen from the north were denied a loan at the State Bank because "Chicago was too far from Shawneetown to ever amount to anything." But, the people moved forward and northward, often migrating west and north from Indiana, as the Thomas and Sarah Lincoln family did. The state's founding fathers moved the capital in 1820 about 90 miles northeast to Vandalia, where it remained until 1839. Largely due to the efforts of a young legislator named Abraham Lincoln, the capital again moved north to the center of the state in Springfield. While Chicago has grown larger than the early pioneers could have imagined, the capital and resulting Lincoln history remain in central Illinois.

The topography of the tour route, while vastly prairie, varies. The southern quarter offers winding, hilly roads lined with wildflowers and prairie grass near fields of sunflowers and sorghum. The central section stretches for miles in every direction with open road, fields of corn and beans, and horizons that deliver spectacular evening sunsets. Keep in mind that the seemingly spare Illinois prairie landscape hides the rich black earth that yields much of the nation's food source.

This tour assumes a south to north route toward Chicago with numerous stopping points, not all connected with the 16th president, but interesting nonetheless. Lincoln's life is, however, the focal point, while not entirely chronological or complete. Should you wish to follow his life in the order he lived it, you can contact the **Springfield Convention and Visitor Bureau** (☎ **217/789-2360**) or the **Central Illinois Tourism Council** (☎ **217/525-7980**) for a copy of the history of Lincoln's life.

Near the end of the tour, the city of Springfield contains the majority of historic sites connected to Abraham Lincoln. Plan to stay there overnight and start fresh for a second full day of touring.

From St. Louis, Missouri, take I-70 east to the center of Vandalia, Illinois, and the:

1. **Vandalia Statehouse,** 315 W. Gallatin (☎ **618/283-1161**), the oldest statehouse still standing in Illinois. The legislature met in this gracious, Federal-style building in 1836–39, and as a state legislator, Lincoln delivered his first speech against the injustice of slavery in this building. Located on the town square, the site is now surrounded by 4 blocks of storefront boasting five antique shops. A delightful urban garden with piped-in music offers a quiet summertime place to reflect on the history of Lincoln Land. A historical marker and an unusual statue, Madonna of the Prairie, featuring a pioneer mother and two children, pay tribute to the strength of women settlers and the western terminus of the famous Cumberland Trail.

Take U.S. 40 east out of Vandalia for an interesting, rather hilly (for Illinois), two–lane drive through small rural towns and open fields to Effingham. At this point, get on I-70 east for approximately 27 miles to exit 119 toward Charleston. Follow the signs to Lincoln Log Cabin for approximately 17 miles on State Road 130 north. Stop at the Lost Creek Orchard roadside stand for seasonal fruits and vegetables. Watch carefully for the sign to Lincoln Log Cabin approximately 6 miles down Ill. 130 and turn left on the road between a farmhouse and a grain bin. Note the abandoned one-room schoolhouse on the left about a mile down. The entrance is well marked to:

2. **Lincoln Log Cabin** (☎ **217/345-6489**), which preserves the last home of Abraham Lincoln's father and stepmother, Thomas and Sarah Bush Lincoln. Abraham said good-bye to his family before they left their first Illinois homestead near Decatur and moved to the farm called Goosenest Prairie. He went to seek his

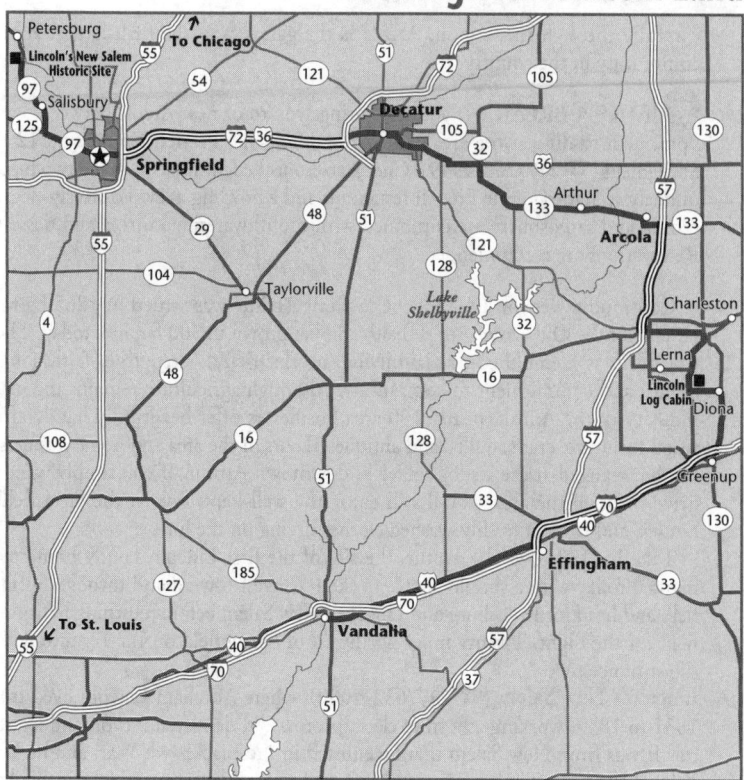

fortune on the flatboats between New Salem and New Orleans. His family intended to return to Indiana when they stopped to visit relatives and decided to stay. By 1845, there were as many as 18 people—many of them Sarah's extended family—living in the small two-room cabin. Abraham's visits were seldom. He did not come home for his father's funeral but visited the grave site in Shiloh Cemetery (1 mile from the cabin) in 1861 on his way to Washington as president-elect. Today the site staff adopt the persona of a family member or neighbor and speak as though they lived in 1845. The site includes the log cabin, large log barn, smokehouse, root cellar, and a garden and orchard filled with 19th-century crop varieties. Nearby is the **Sargent Farm;** in marked contrast to the Lincoln farm, it shows a wealthier lifestyle of the same period.

The next Lincoln-related historic site is not for another 125 miles, so sit back and enjoy the landscape through Amish country. When leaving the Lincoln Log Cabin site, turn right and head for Ill. 16. This country road will lead you through a portion of the town of Charleston for approximately 8 miles. Take the I-57 exit north toward Champaign. At exit 203 head west for the Amish community of:

3. **Arcola,** known as the broom corn capital of the world (three companies make them here). Shops all over town also sell Raggedy Ann and Andy dolls, in tribute to the town's native son, Johnny Gruelle, the doll's creator. If you stop here, you'll likely begin to notice the townsfolk's dress (women in white gauzelike bonnets, plain dresses in dark colors, and white socks and black tennis shoes; men in dark suits or bib overalls) and the horse and buggies on the side of the road. Drive

carefully through this region. Arcola is the gateway to the fifth-largest Amish community in the country.

☕ **TAKE A BREAK**   If your trip brings you to or near Arcola between 5 and 9pm, plan to dine at the area's finest restaurant, the **French Embassy,** 112 W. Springfield (☎ 217/268-4949). Chef Jean-Louis Ledent has combined two highly unlikely scenarios, a fine French restaurant and a bowling alley. Positively elegant dining and atmosphere are combined with mouthwatering entrees and desserts. Reservations are recommended.

Continuing west on Ill. 133, the town of **Arthur** was settled in 1865 by four families of the Old Order Amish Faith and has grown to 300 families today. Their way of life is exemplified by plain living (no electricity), strength of faith, family bonds, and commitment to community. Although agriculture remains the main industry of the Amish, nearly 100 area businesses offer beautifully handcrafted wood furniture, crafts, quilts, and antiques. Tours of the area and home businesses can be arranged at the visitor center in downtown Arthur. If you simply want to drive through the area, you'll still enjoy the well-kept look of the farm fields, houses, and rows of freshly-washed clothes drying on the line.

Take Ill. 133 toward Decatur, the site of the first Lincoln family homestead marked today with a simple plaque. Take I-72 west toward and through Springfield and head for Petersburg and Lincoln's New Salem before returning to Springfield for the night. Twenty miles northwest of Springfield on Ill. 97, turn left at the entrance to:

4. **Lincoln's New Salem** (☎ 217/632-4000), where Abraham Lincoln lived from 1831 to 1837, working as a store clerk, postmaster, deputy surveyor, and legislator. It was from New Salem that he enlisted in the Blackhawk War, and he later studied law here. Timber houses, shops, and stores reconstructed by the Civilian Conservation Corps in the 1930s replicate the 1830s village. Costumed interpreters go about their daily chores of gardening, spinning wool, or tending the animals. Don't miss the wonderful gift shop at the end of the village. During the summer, on the nearby Sangamon River, where Lincoln once piloted a flatboat, the **Talisman Riverboat** offers leisurely trips to tourists for a small admission.

One last stop on your way back to Springfield: the primitive folk art shop and home of George Colin in Salisbury on Route 97. You can't miss it! Bright, colorfully painted Lincolns, alligators, watermelon benches and tables, and cows grace the front lawn of this special place on the main road through town. If you meet Winnie Colin, George's wife, you'll probably get a great deal on a special memento. Colin's art is on display (and for sale) in his Chicago showroom, but the best place to see it is in its natural surroundings.

Head back east on Ill. 97 to:

5. **Springfield,** "the city Lincoln loved" and the present state capital. When he left for Washington—to return only to be buried after his assassination in 1865—he said, "No one, not in my situation, can appreciate my feelings of sadness at this parting." It is a place to savor the taste of Lincoln history slowly and fully.

If you planned on spending the night in Springfield, you might want to try the **Mansion View Inn and Suites** (☎ 800/252-1083 or 217/544-7411). Located across the street from the Governor's Mansion and near the historic district, it's a good bet for couples or families. The **Holiday Inn East** (☎ 217/529-7171) is about 10 minutes from downtown and offers a large Holidome area for active families with children. Both offer moderately priced rooms.

☕ **TAKE A BREAK** **Gumbo Ya Yas,** 700 E. Adams St. (☎ 217/789-1530), offers the best view of the city from the 30th floor of the downtown Springfield Hilton Hotel, plus a fun family atmosphere and cuisine with a Cajun flair. Prices are reasonable and a children's menu is available. Bronzed or blackened fish entrees are superb. The Cajun Caesar salad is the house specialty.

Start your second day of touring early at the:

6. **Lincoln-Herndon Law Offices,** at the corner of 6th and Adams (☎ 217/785-7289), the only surviving structure in which Lincoln maintained working law offices. Lincoln and partners Stephen Logan (1843–44) and William Herndon (1844–65) practiced law in offices located above Seth Tinsley's store and local post office and across the street from the new capitol.

From the law offices walk out the front door and across the square to the:

7. **Old State Capitol** (☎ 217/785-7961), where Lincoln delivered his famous "House Divided" speech in the turbulent days leading up to the Civil War. Today you are taken on guided tours of the building where Lincoln tried more than 200 cases in the Supreme Court, borrowed books from the State Library, served as legislator, and spent time with the other lawyers and politicians of the day. An original copy of the Gettysburg Address is on display.

From here, walk 2 blocks south on 6th Street and east 1 block to 7th Street, where you will find the **Lincoln Home Visitor Center.** It is a good idea to stop here early in the day to get your free tickets to tour the:

8. **Lincoln Home,** 8th and Jackson streets (☎ 217/492-4150), the only National Historic Site in Illinois and a memorial to the Abraham Lincoln family, who resided in this Quaker brown house for 17 years. It has been meticulously restored to its 1860s style. Tours led by National Park Service rangers will give you a real sense of Lincoln's family life. You'll see the parlor where Lincoln learned that he had been nominated as the Whig Party's candidate for president, as well as the Lincolns' bedrooms. The home is located in the midst of a restored 4-block historic neighborhood managed by the National Park Service.

If you're visiting in April to August, walk 2 blocks north and 1 block east to the:

9. **Lincoln Depot,** 10th and Monroe (☎ 217/544-8695), where Lincoln left as president-elect for Washington, D.C., in 1861. Today you can walk through the building's restored waiting rooms (one for ladies, one for the luggage and tobacco-spitting men) and view a slide show that re-creates Lincoln's 12-day journey to his inauguration.

☕ **TAKE A BREAK** **Maldaners Restaurant,** 222 S. 6th St. (☎ 217/522-4313), has been around since the 19th century. Lunchtime favorites on the seasonally changing menu include the turkey curry sandwich, fresh spinach salad, or chicken teriyaki salad. Lunch entrees cost $3–$7.

After lunch you can visit two non-Lincoln attractions. Keep heading south to the next stop, the:

10. **State Capitol,** 2nd Street and Capitol Avenue (☎ 217/782-2099), which hosted its first legislative session in 1877. Today it's the center of Illinois government, and you can watch politics in action from balcony-level seating when the legislature is in session.

Head 2 blocks south to the corner of 4th Street and Lawrence to the:

11. **Dana-Thomas House,** 301 E. Lawrence (☎ 217/782-6776), was designed by Frank Lloyd Wright and is one of the finest and most complete of his Prairie-style

residences. Built in 1902 for Springfield socialite and activist, Susan Lawrence Dana, it was his largest commission for many years. Tours are offered Wednesday to Sunday. A small admission is charged.

The final stop on your tour of Lincoln Land was also Lincoln's final stop. You will find yourself deeply moved by the:

**12. Lincoln Tomb,** Oak Ridge Cemetery (☎ 217/782-2717), the final resting place for Abraham, wife Mary Todd Lincoln, and children Tad, Eddie, and Willie. Abraham was buried here at the request of Mrs. Lincoln after his assassination in 1865. The monument was designed by sculptor Larken Mead and completed in 1874. Be sure to rub the nose of the large Lincoln bust at the tomb's entrance—it's said to bring good luck! The statues surrounding the obelisk at the top of the tomb depict the four military branches of the time and were made from melted-down Civil War cannons. Also on site is the original receiving vault in which Lincoln's body was placed while the monument was built.

## DRIVING TOUR
## The Mississippi River Valley

**Start:** Hannibal
**Finish:** Ste. Genevieve
**Distance:** Approximately 188 miles
**Time:** 3–4 days
**Highlights:** The mighty Mississippi River, historic river towns including Mark Twain's Hannibal, antique and craft shops, and restored homes open to the public

The Mississippi River, the most widely known and widely used river in the United States, is a constant and powerful backdrop to this tour, which begins fittingly enough in Hannibal, the boyhood hometown of Mark Twain, immortalized in *The Adventures of Tom Sawyer* and *Adventures of Huckleberry Finn.* Following the winding contours of the fertile river valley, you'll then head south and stop off in the picture-perfect historic town of St. Charles. You'll pass through St. Louis (see section 5) to Ste. Genevieve, the first white settlement on the west bank of the Mississippi and boasting more 18th-century Creole buildings than any other city in North America.

U.S. 36, U.S. 61, and Mo. 79 all provide easy access to:

**1. Hannibal,** located about 120 miles north of St. Louis on the banks of the Mississippi. If Mark Twain had not grown up here, Hannibal would undoubtedly be just another sleepy river town, but as it is, about a quarter of a million visitors come annually to pay tribute to one of America's greatest authors and humorists. Hannibal capitalizes on its favorite son by conjuring up storybook attractions and naming everything from motels to restaurants after Twain, who no doubt would have something sarcastically witty to say about that. And yet, Hannibal is not nearly the tourist trap it could be—it's simply not sophisticated enough for that. It remains remarkably and refreshingly small-town, friendly, charming, and unassuming, and probably not much different from the days when a young Samuel Clemens restlessly roamed its streets. It's a great family destination.

After stopping off at the **Hannibal Visitor Bureau,** 505 N. Broadway (☎ 573/221-2477), it's just a minute's walk to the town's foremost attraction, the **Mark Twain Boyhood Home and Museum,** 208 Hill St., where a narrated slide show presents a short biography of Samuel Clemens, who moved to Hannibal with his family when he was 4 years old. Next door is the small white clapboard

# Driving Tour: The Mississippi River Valley

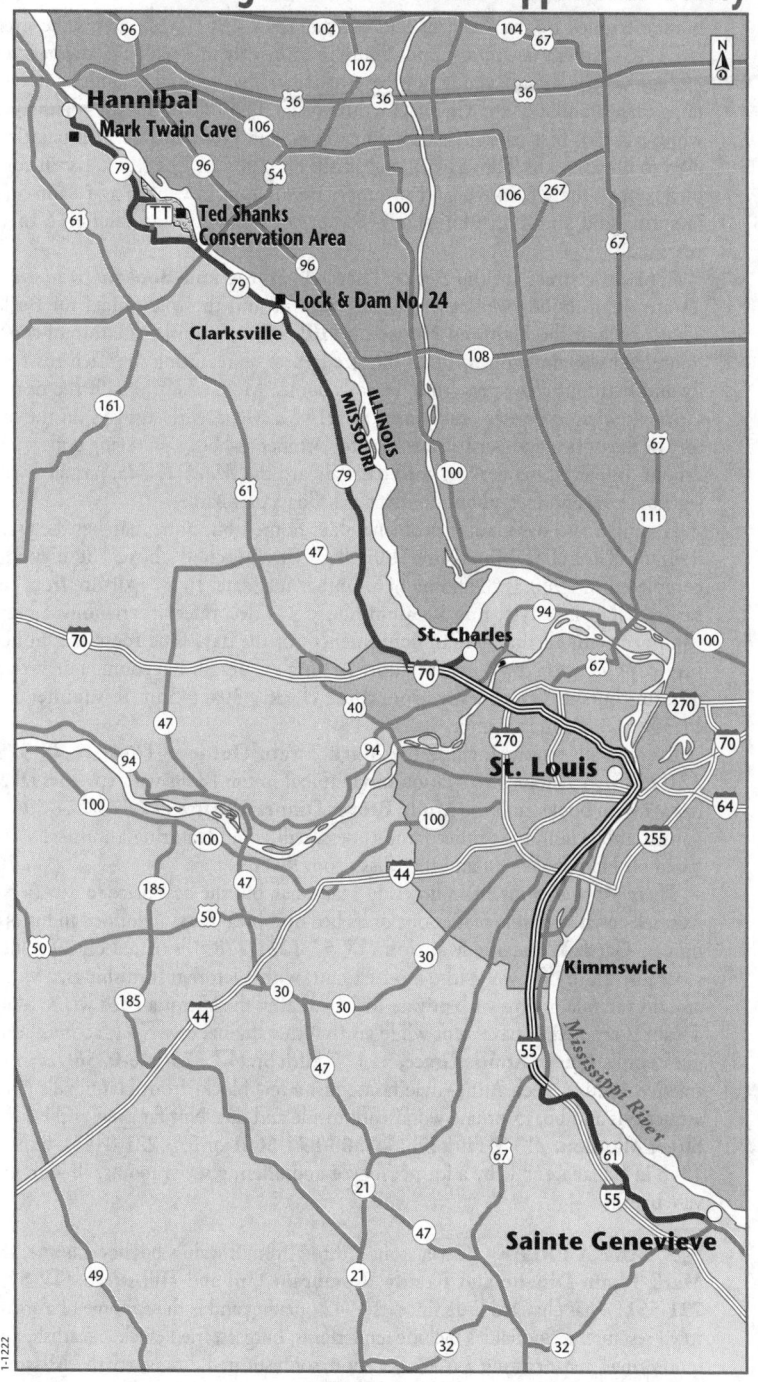

home occupied by the Clemens family from 1844–1853, while across the street is Twain's father's law office. Both figure prominently in Twain's *The Adventures of Tom Sawyer,* about a young boy patterned after Twain himself. A museum contains memorabilia of the Clemens family (including one of Twain's trademark white jackets), first editions of Twain's works, and Norman Rockwell paintings used to illustrate the Tom Sawyer and Huck Finn novels. The Mark Twain complex is open daily 8am–6pm in summer, 10am–4pm in winter, and 8am–5pm in spring and autumn. Admission is $4 for adults and $2 for children 6 to 12 years old.

Across the street are the **Becky Thatcher House and Bookshop,** home of Twain's childhood sweetheart Laura Hawkins and the role model for Becky Thatcher, and the **Haunted House on Hill Street,** a quirky mixture of spook house and wax museum, with 27 life-size figures representing the Clemens family and fictitious characters from Twain's books. More educational is the nearby **Optical Science Center and Museum,** 214 N. Main, with displays on the history of the optical industry. From May to October, 1-hour sightseeing cruises and 2-hour dinner cruises are launched daily aboard the *Mark Twain,* narrated with legends, lore, and facts about the river as it floats past barges.

Hannibal also has a number of fine older homes, but none matches the grandeur of **Rockcliff Mansion,** 1000 Bird St., perched above the city and completed in 1900 as the home of a lumber magnate. In a departure from the earlier Victorian style, this 30-room house was decorated in art nouveau and equipped with all the modern conveniences of the day. One room is a miniature copy of the New York Waldorf Astoria's Turkish ballroom. Forty-five-minute tours are given daily around the clock 9:30am–5pm in summer and 11:30am–3:30pm in winter.

Evening diversions include the **Mark Twain Outdoor Theatre** (☎ 573/221-2945), a 2-hour presentation of Hannibal in the 1840s with episodes taken from Twain books, and the **Molly Brown Dinner Theatre** (☎ 573/221-8940), named after Hannibal's other famous personality and featuring a musical revue based on Hannibal's past and the Mississippi River.

There are numerous chain hotels in Hannibal, but the best place to experience its small-town atmosphere is at one of its bed-and-breakfasts, all located in historic homes. **Garth Woodside Mansion** (☎ 573/221-2789), situated on 39 rolling acres just south of town, is the most elegant, with Victorian furnishings, a wrap-around veranda, rooms with private bath, and even the Victorian bed where Mark Twain is reputed to have slept while visiting the original owners. It accepts adult guests only. **Queen Anne's Grace,** 313 N. Fifth St. (☎ 573/248-0756), is an attractive 1880s Queen Anne–style home just a few blocks from Hannibal's main attractions and boasts ornate woodwork inside and out. Not far away is the **Fifth Street Mansion,** 213 S. Fifth St. (☎ 800/874-5661 or 573/221-0445), built in 1858 in Italianate style by a former mayor and offering seven rooms, all with private bath.

**☕ TAKE A BREAK** Just a stone's throw from Twain's boyhood home, the **Mark Twain Dinette and Family Restaurant,** 3rd and Hill streets (☎ 573/221-5511), has changed little since its 1942 opening and is the epitome of a small-town restaurant. Specialties include tenderloins, burgers, fried chicken, catfish, and onion rings, most costing $4–$7. For more sophisticated dining, try the **Missouri Territory Steakhouse,** 600 Broadway (☎ 573/248-1440), occupying a former federal court house, an impressive limestone building dating from 1888 but somewhat gaudily decorated inside. Steaks range from $10 to $18. It's open for dinner Tues–Sat 4–9pm; lunch on Sun.

Depart Hannibal by heading south on Mo. 79 (Third Street). After 1¹/₂ miles, to your right will be the:

2. **Mark Twain Cave,** discovered in 1819. Sam Clemens played here as a young boy, later using it in *Tom Sawyer* and *Huckleberry Finn* as the cave containing buried treasure, where Tom and Becky were lost, and where Injun Joe met his demise. One-hour guided tours depart every 15 minutes and cover less than a mile along smooth walkways. Across the highway is **Sawyer's Creek,** a family amusement center with miniature golf, bumper boats, a carousel, a shooting gallery, games arcade, and shops, including a year-round Christmas store. Its **Riverview Cafe** offers great views of the Mississippi, especially from its covered outdoor deck.

Continue south on Mo. 79, dubbed the "Great River Road," as it hugs the curves of the Mississippi and railroad tracks and winds past limestone bluffs and riots of wildflowers in summer and glorious changing leaves in autumn. If you're a bird-watcher, turn left after about 16 miles onto Country Road TT, which will bring you to the:

3. **Ted Shanks Conservation Area,** with 6,600 acres of bottom wetlands, marsh, and lakes bordering 6 miles of the Mississippi. Although hunting, camping, fishing, and hiking are allowed, bird-watching is the main activity, especially during spring and fall migrations. A room at the visitor center is stocked with binoculars; if you're lucky you might see bald eagles, warblers, American bitterns, king rails, and various waterfowl.

After another 23 miles south on Mo. 79, passing through the tiny town of Louisiana with its 2-block Victorian downtown along the way, you'll come to:

4. **Clarksville,** with a thriving population of 480. To your left as you enter town is the **Clarksville Visitor Center** (☎ **573/242-3132**), with displays on river traffic and river habitat. Across the street is the **Skylift,** which will take you to a bluff 670 feet above the river for an unparalleled view of the surrounding countryside—on clear days you can see 800 square miles. Beside the hilltop observation tower are empty frontierlike wooden buildings, constructed in a wave of entrepreneurial optimism and now dusty and cobwebbed from neglect, giving the whole bluff an eerie, ghost-town-like atmosphere. In January, it's a premier spot for eagle-watching.

The other key attraction here is the Mississippi's **lock and dam no. 24,** managed by the U.S. Army Corps of Engineers, which can be toured if enough personnel are on duty. You can straddle two states at once in the middle of the river.

From Clarksville, the river valley flattens into farmland and open pastures, with old farmhouses, silos, barns, churches, and cemeteries dotting the landscape. After approximately 45 miles, you'll reach I-70, where you should head east about 9 miles to exit 229, where Fifth Street North will take you to the historic heart of:

5. **St. Charles,** established in 1769 as a fur-trading post on the banks of the Missouri River. In 1804, Lewis and Clark spent 5 days here preparing for their historic explorations of the Louisiana Territory. When Missouri became the 24th state in 1821, St. Charles served as the temporary capital while the city of Jefferson was being built in the center of the state's wilderness. The **First State Capitol of Missouri,** 200–216 S. Main St., a Federal-style brick building, looks pretty much as it did back then, with a general store, carpenter shop, and private residence on the ground floor and Senate and House chambers on the second. It's open for tours.

More of St. Charles's history is presented in the **Lewis & Clark Center,** 701 Riverside Dr., which describes the famous expedition with dioramas and displays.

One of the best things to do in St. Charles is to stroll several blocks along South Main Street, a brick road lined with quaint two-story brick and stone buildings, most dating from about 1799 to 1860 and constructed in French colonial and Federal styles and now housing craft shops and restaurants. If you like antiques, be sure to drive to **Frenchtown,** the original French settlement, with about 20 antique shops spread along the 800–1700 blocks of North Second Street. There's also a riverboat casino moored close to the historic district.

🌀 **TAKE A BREAK**　**Lewis and Clark's,** 217 S. Main St. (☎ 573/947-3334), is a family restaurant across the street from the First Capitol. Upstairs an atrium skylight bathes the dining area in a white glow, while the third-floor balcony overlooks Main Street. Hamburgers, sandwiches, steaks, chicken, pasta, soups, salads, and Mexican fare are featured on the extensive menu, with entrees priced $5–$17. For casual dining, snacks, or drinks, there's no better place than **Winery of the Little Hills,** 501 S. Main St. (☎ 573/946-9339), which specializes in Missouri wines, sausages, and cheeses and offers outdoor patio seating in fine weather.

Back on I-70 heading east, you'll soon find yourself in **St. Louis** (see section 5 for details). After your visit to the big city, head south on I-55 for approximately 25 miles to exit 186 and County Road K. Take it to the riverside hamlet of:

6. **Kimmswick,** founded and settled by Germans in the mid-1800s. A dreamy, low-key, and increasingly popular destination for St. Louis day-trippers, it consists of just a few streets dotted with homes and individually standing buildings, many dating from the 1880s through the turn of the century and now housing antique and craft shops.

Return to I-55 and continue south another 12 miles or so to exit 170, where you can then take the more scenic and much pleasanter two-lane Mo. 61 south another 25 miles to:

7. **Ste. Genevieve,** where Market Street will take you into the heart of its historic district. Ste. Genevieve was the first settlement on the west bank of the Mississippi, founded in the 1730s and predating even St. Louis. It boasts more 18th-century French Creole–style buildings than any other city in North America, with more than 30 dating back 200 years to French colonial times. Your first stop should be the **Great River Road Interpretive Center,** at the corner of Market and South Main streets, offering information about Ste. Genevieve and displays relating to the town's history.

You can tour several of the old buildings. The oldest is the **Bolduc House,** 125 S. Main, built in 1770 and one of the finest examples of French Creole architecture in the entire nation. The **Maison Guibourd–Valle,** 4th and Merchant streets, built about 1784, is known for its attic with Norman truss and hand-hewn oak beams. It's the most elaborately furnished house open to the public, with French antiques. The **Felix Valle House,** Merchant and 2nd streets, was built in 1818 in the Federal style—a marked departure from the wooden log structures built during the French colonial period. It has been restored as much as possible to its original state and is furnished with American Empire furniture dating from 1830–1840.

Of the several bed-and-breakfasts in Ste. Genevieve, a particular standout is the **Southern Hotel,** 146 South Third St. (☎ 573/883-3493), first built as a home in 1790 and becoming a hotel in 1805. A rambling brick structure, it features eight rooms filled with country Victorian antiques and private baths, 12 fireplaces, a beautiful garden, nightly happy hours, and wonderful French breakfasts. Adult guests only.

# 1 Chicago

Today's Chicago is more glittery than gritty, more Paris than prairie, a cultured, sophisticated, and cosmopolitan city. But if it is no longer, in Carl Sandburg's words, "Hog Butcher for the World . . . City of the Big Shoulders," and has long left behind its gangsterism image, Chicago yet remains the quintessential American city.

The visitor's first impression may be the city's brilliant, varied skyline. When the Great Fire of 1871 reduced the city to ashes, waiting in the wings was a group of outstandingly talented architects whose work coincided with the development of new materials and engineering innovations, a combination that created the Chicago we see today. The city owes its parks, its lakefront development, and its general livability to the early urban planning of Louis Sullivan, Dankmar Adler, and, particularly, Daniel Burnham. Later they were to be joined by Frank Lloyd Wright's "Prairie School" and Ludwig Mies van der Rohe's Bauhaus modernism.

Chicago first came into existence because its strategic location at a key point on an inland water route made it the great engine of America's westward expansion. It has always been a city of diversity, fitting for a place that began as a trading post founded in 1781 by a French/black/Native American trader named Jean Baptiste DuSable. While some of Chicago's old ethnic areas have disappeared, new ones have grown up. And unlike many other American cities, middle-class Chicagoans have not fled to the suburbs; the city has remained vital and attractive to young professionals and to the artistic community.

## ARRIVING & DEPARTING

**BY PLANE** **O'Hare International Airport** is northwest of the city proper, about a 25- to 30-minute drive from downtown; a cab will cost $25 or more. From the airport, the west–northwest subway (Blue Line) will take you to the Loop. On the southwest side of the city is Chicago's other major airport, **Midway,** smaller than O'Hare, and servicing fewer airlines. An El train will take you to the Loop.

**Continental Air Transport** (☎ 312/454-7800) services most first-class hotels in Chicago; check with your bell captain. The cost is $13.75 one way ($25.50 round-trip) to O'Hare, and $9.75 one way ($19 round-trip) to Midway. For limo service from either O'Hare or Midway, call **Carey of Chicago** (☎ 312/663-1220), or **Chicago Limousine Services** (☎ 312/726-1035). Cost, with tip and tax, comes to about $75.

**BY TRAIN & BUS** Chicago remains the hub of the national passenger rail system. Amtrak trains pull into **Union Station** at Adams and Canal streets (☎ 800/USA-RAIL or 312/558-1075 in Chicago). The station is west across the river from the Loop. Bus nos. 1, 60, 151, and 156 all stop at the station. The nearest subway stop is at Congress and Clinton, a fair walk away.

The **Greyhound** bus station is at 630 W. Harrison (☎ 800/231-2222), not far from Union Station. Bus no. 61 passes in front of the terminal building, and the nearest El stop is at Clinton and Congress.

## ESSENTIALS

**VISITOR INFORMATION** The **Chicago Office of Tourism,** Chicago Cultural Center, 78 E. Washington St., Chicago, IL 60602 (☎ 312/744-2400; online at www.ci.chi.il.us/tourism; TDD: 312/744-2947), will mail you a packet of material,

# Chicago

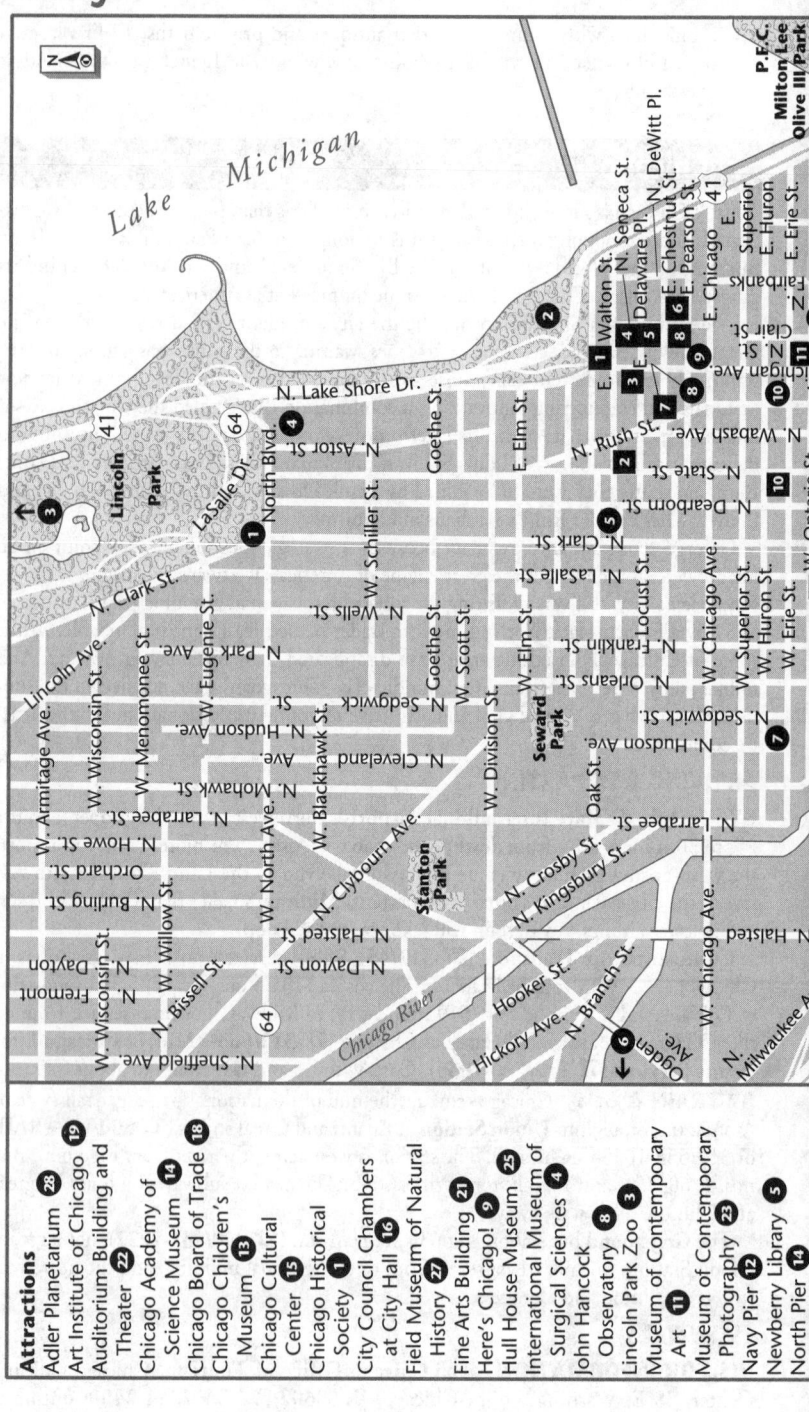

**Attractions**

Adler Planetarium 28
Art Institute of Chicago 19
Auditorium Building and Theater 22
Chicago Academy of Science Museum 14
Chicago Board of Trade 18
Chicago Children's Museum 13
Chicago Cultural Center 15
Chicago Historical Society 1
City Council Chambers at City Hall 16
Field Museum of Natural History 27
Fine Arts Building 21
Here's Chicago! 9
Hull House Museum 25
International Museum of Surgical Sciences 4
John Hancock Observatory 8
Lincoln Park Zoo 3
Museum of Contemporary Art 11
Museum of Contemporary Photography 23
Navy Pier 12
Newberry Library 5
North Pier 14

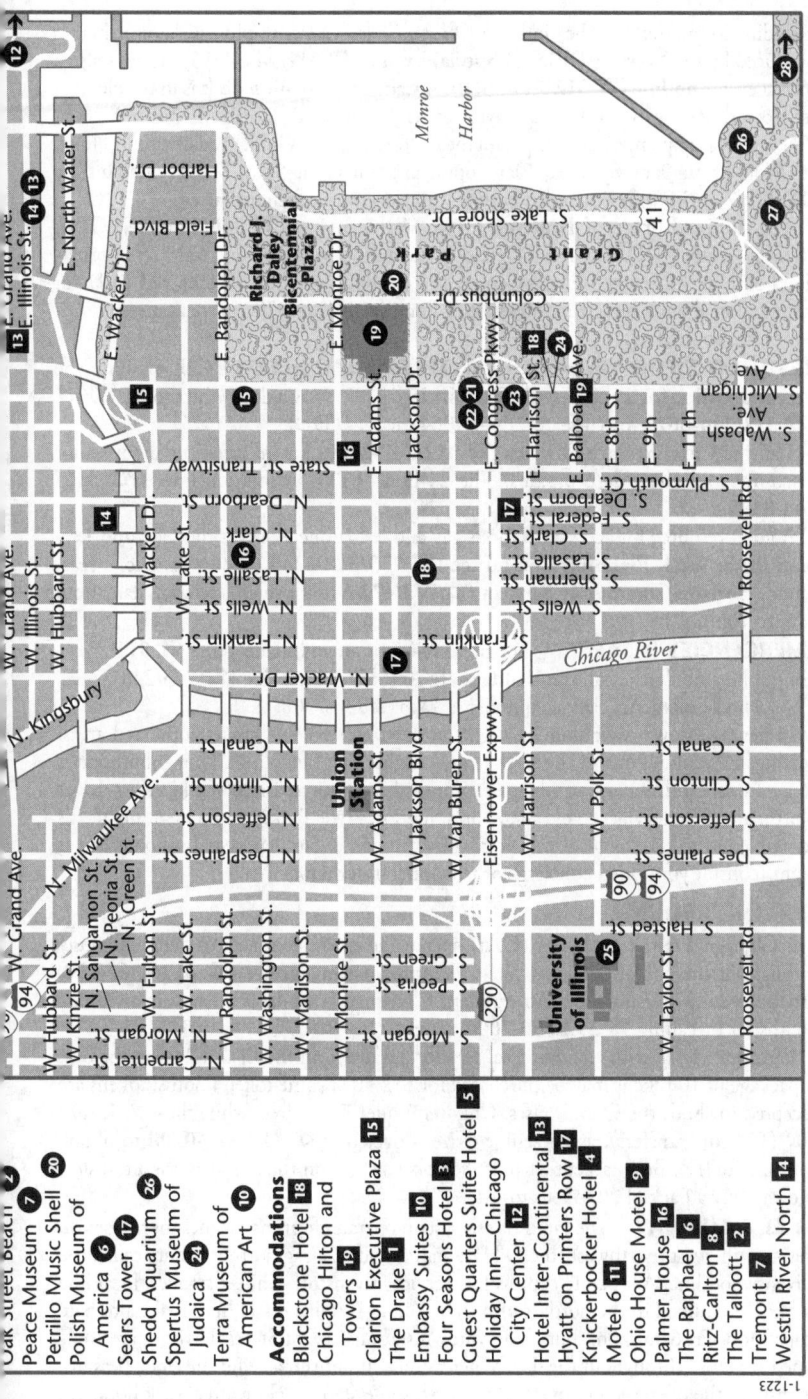

including its quarterly publication, the *Chicago Illinois Calendar,* plus the latest materials produced by the **Mayor's Office of Special Events** (☎ 312/744-3315). There's also a special events **hotline** (☎ 312/744-3370). A **visitor information desk** is in the old Water Tower, Michigan and Chicago avenues, at the corner of North Michigan Avenue. You can pick up pamphlets, a map, and the "Loop Sculpture Guide" walking tour. Hours are Mon–Fri 9:30am–6pm, Sat 10am–6pm, and Sun 11am–5pm. The **Events Hotline** (☎ 312/744-3370) is a recorded hotline listing events throughout the city.

The **Illinois Bureau of Tourism,** 310 S. Michigan Ave. (☎ **800/2CONNECT** or 800/487-2446; TDD 800/406-6418), operates a drop-in center, and staffs an information booth in the State of Illinois Center, 100 W. Randolph St. (☎ **800/223-0121** for information about Chicago and the state of Illinois; 800/822-0292 to speak directly with a vacation counselor).

**RESOURCES FOR TRAVELERS WITH SPECIAL NEEDS** Call or write the **Mayor's Office for People with Disabilities,** 2102 W. Ogden, Chicago, IL 60611 (☎ 312/744-6673 for voice; 312/744-4964 for TT/TDD).

Call the **Chicago Park District** (☎ 312/747-2200) for information about senior discounts and citywide programs. The 24-hour **TTY** information line is ☎ 312/744-8599.

A good resource for access to various gay and lesbian networks is the **Gay and Lesbian Pride Week Planning Committee** (☎ 773/348-8243), which functions year-round. **Horizon Community Services** (☎ 773/472-6469) provides referrals daily from 7am to 10pm.

**EMERGENCIES & SAFETY** For fire, police, or an ambulance, dial ☎ **911.** For a nonpublic ambulance, call the **Vandenberg Ambulance Service** (☎ 773/248-2712). The Dental Emergency Service number is ☎ 312/836-7300.

In general, don't walk alone at night on deserted streets; stick to populated areas. Michigan Avenue is one of the safer areas at night. The Lincoln Park neighborhood is generally safe (but stay out of the park proper after dark), as are the Gold Coast, River North, and Wrigleyville. Avoid the Loop's interior, Hyde Park, and Pilsen at night. It's advisable not to take long subway or El rides through unfamiliar neighborhoods late at night (consult your hotel concierge or personnel if in doubt).

## GETTING AROUND

The **Chicago Transit Authority (CTA)** operates an extensive system of trains and buses throughout the city of Chicago. The CTA **information service** (☎ 312/836-7000) functions daily 4:45am–1am. An excellent CTA map is available at subway or El fare booths, or by calling ☎ 312/836-7000.

Fares are $1.50, with an additional 30¢ for a transfer on the El and 25¢ on the bus. A package of 10 tokens may be purchased for $12.50 at some token booths; tokens are accepted for both the El and buses. Children under 7 ride free, while those 7–11 pay 90¢ (15¢ for transfers), as do senior citizens over 65 (☎ 312/814-0700 to obtain appropriate ID). Buses accept $1 bills. Seniors pay 75¢ on the bus (10¢ for a transfer) and can buy a pack of 20 tokens for $12.

**BY EL & SUBWAY** The rapid transit system operates four major lines, north–south, west–south, west–northwest (the O'Hare train), and a zigzag northern route called the Ravenswood line. A separate express line services Evanston, while a smaller, local line in Skokie is linked to the north–south train. A and B trains on all lines make alternate stops Mon–Fri 6am–7pm, but all downtown stations except State/Harrison, are combined AB stops throughout the day. Whereas most trains run around the clock (less frequently in the off-peak and overnight hours), some stations close after work hours (as early as 8:30pm) and remain closed weekends and holidays. Please note that you may not use your transfer on the line where you first obtained it.

**BY BUS**   Particulary handy for visitors are two buses: the No. 151 Sheridan passes through Lincoln Park onto North Lake Shore Drive and then along Michigan Avenue as far south as Adams Street, where it turns west into the Loop; the No. 156 LaSalle goes through Lincoln Park and then down the Loop's main street. PACE buses service the suburban zones.

**BY TRAIN**   The **Metra** commuter railroad (☎ 312/322-6777 Mon–Fri 8am–5pm; 312/836-7000 other times), which services the surrounding suburban zones, has terminals at several downtown locations, including Union Station at Adams and Canal, LaSalle Street Station at LaSalle and Van Buren, Northwestern Station at Madison and Canal, and Randolph Street Station at Randolph and Michigan.

**BY TAXI**   Chicago cabs charge $1.50 at flag fall, plus $1.20 for each mile and 50¢ for each additional rider aged 12–65. Taxis are easy to hail in the Loop, on the Magnificent Mile and the Gold Coast, in River North, and in Lincoln Park, but if you go much beyond these key areas, you may need to call. Cab companies are **American** (☎ 773/248-7600), **Flash** (☎ 773/561-1444), and **Yellow/Checker** (☎ 312/ TAXI-CAB or 312/829-4222).

**BY BOAT**   A shuttle boat operates daily April–October between a dock adjacent to the Michigan Avenue bridge and Northwestern Station, a commuter train station across the river from the Loop. The ride takes about 10 minutes and costs $1.25 each way. The service operates 7:45–8:45am from the station, and 4:45–5:27pm from the bridge.

## WHAT TO SEE & DO

**SPECIAL EVENTS**   **Wright Plus Tour,** the second or third week in May, is an annual event in Oak Park when privately owned Frank Lloyd Wright houses are open to visitors (☎ 708/848-1976 for information). The second weekend in June the **Chicago Blues Festival** usually takes place in the Petrillo Music Shell, Jackson and Columbus drives in Grant Park. The **Gospel Festival** follows on the next weekend at the same venue. For information about both these popular events, call ☎ 312/744-3315. The free outdoor **Grant Park Concerts** (☎ 312/294-2920) in the Petrillo Music Shell begin the last week in June. Scores of Chicago's restaurants cart their fare to food stands set up throughout Grant Park for 8 days of **Taste of Chicago** street feasting in late June and the first week of July. The **Air & Water Show,** an aquatic and aerial spectacular, takes place at North Avenue Beach toward the end of August; call the hotline ☎ 312/ 744-3370 for details. The **Jazz Festival** is Chicago style, and happens over Labor Day weekend; call ☎ 312/744-3370 for information. The **Chicago International Film Festival** (☎ 312/425-9400) is held the third week of October at various theaters.

**ESCORTED TOURS**   **American Sightseeing** (☎ 312/427-3100) offers a selection of 2- to 5-hour bus tours covering daytime sights and nightlife. "Double Decker Bus Rides," narrated 1-hour tours of the Loop, downtown, and the lakefront, are offered by **Chicago Motor Coach** (☎ 312/666-1000). Board the buses at the Sears Tower, the Water Tower, or Mercury Boat, and buy your ticket from the driver. You can get off at any number of attractions along the way and reboard throughout the day. **Untouchable Tours,** or so-called Gangster Tours (☎ 773/881-1195), has bus tours of old hoodlum hangouts from the Prohibition era.

The **Friends of the Chicago River** (☎ 312/939-0490) offers docent-guided walks along eight sections of the river, scheduled on many weekends from May to October. The **Chicago Architecture Foundation** (☎ 312/922-3432) has guided programs by foot, bike, and bus to more than 50 different architectural sites and environments in and around Chicago, including a Frank Lloyd Wright bus tour.

**BOAT TOURS**   The Chicago Architecture Foundation also organizes **river trips** that leave from the south side of the Chicago River, at Michigan Avenue and Lower Wacker

Drive, and cruise along both the north and south branches, accompanied by a lecturer who points out both landmark and notable contemporary buildings.

Sightseeing cruises on Lake Michigan give you a look at that incredible skyline from an offshore vantage point. **Mercury Chicago Skyline Cruiseline,** Michigan Avenue and Wacker Drive (☎ 312/332-1353), also offers frequent water tours, usually combining the river and the lake. The **Wendella Streamliner** (☎ 312/337-1446), also located under the Michigan Avenue Bridge at Michigan Avenue and Wacker Drive, offers 1- and 2-hour cruises of the lake. Scheduling depends on the season and the weather, so call ahead for the current hours. **Shoreline Marine Sightseeing** (☎ 312/222-9328) schedules 1-hour lake cruises. **Chicago from the Lake Ltd.,** 455 E. Illinois (☎ 312/527-2002), home ports in the Ogden Slip adjacent to North Pier at the end of East Illinois Street. The company runs both architectural river tours and lake and river historical tours from May through September.

The **Spirit of Chicago** (☎ 312/836-7899) has evening dinner cruises that depart daily from Navy Pier, offering dancing to a live band and a floor show 7–10pm, brunch and luncheon trips, and moonlight cocktail cruises Friday and Saturday.

**MUSEUMS & MONUMENTS**    With the help of a very comprehensive map and pamphlet, "The Loop Sculpture Guide," you can guide yourself through Grant Park and much of the Loop to view some 65 examples of Chicago's monumental public art, from pieces by Picasso, Chagall, Miró, Calder, and Moore to more traditional monuments by 19th-century sculptors Augustus Saint-Gaudens and Lorado Taft. Pick up the guide free at one of the visitor information centers.

✪ **Art Institute of Chicago.** *Michigan Ave. (at Adams St.).* ☎ *312/443-3600. Admission $7 adults; $3.50 children, students, and seniors; free on Tues. Mon and Wed–Fri 10:30am–4:30pm, Tues 10:30am–8pm, Sat 10am–5pm, Sun and holidays noon–5pm. Closed Thanksgiving and Christmas. Bus: 3, 4, 60, 145, 147, 151. Subway/El: Take the Lake/Dan Ryan, Evanston, or Ravenswood line to Adams, or the Howard line to Monroe or Jackson.* This major museum houses an extensive painting collection, from medieval times to all the modernists. Especially notable is the Impressionist collection. Famous works here are Grant Wood's *American Gothic* and Seurat's pointilist masterpiece *A Sunday on La Grande Jatte;* and don't miss Marc Chagall's wonderful stained-glass windows. Other attractions are the exhibits of photography, furnishings, ceramics, and Asian art, and the original Trading Room of the old Chicago Stock Exchange.

**Chicago Historical Society.** *1601 N. Clark St. (at North Ave.).* ☎ *312/642-4600. Admission $3 adults, $2 seniors and students, $1 children 6–17; free on Mon. Mon–Sat 9:30am–4:30pm, Sun noon–5pm. Bus: 11, 22, 36, 72, 151, 156.* At the southwestern tip of Lincoln Park, this interesting exhibition covers both Chicago and U.S. history. Some highlights are "We the People," with many rare documents relating to social and mercantile history on display, and an emotionally charged exhibit on the Civil War, "A House Divided," that draws on the society's antebellum Lincoln and Civil War holdings.

**DuSable Museum of African-American History.** *740 E. 56th Place.* ☎ *773/947-0600. Admission $3 adults, $1 children 6–13, $2 students and seniors; free on Thurs. Mon–Sat 10am–4pm, Sun noon–4pm, Thurs 10am–6pm. Bus: 4. Subway/El: Take the Howard line to Jackson Park.* The museum is a repository of the history, art, and artifacts pertaining to the African-American experience and culture from the late 1930s to today, with rather sketchy exhibits tracing the earlier African-American experience in the United States. The museum, located in Hyde Park on the eastern edge of Washington Park, also has a gift shop, research library, and extensive program of community-related events.

○ **Field Museum of Natural History.** *Roosevelt Rd. and Lake Shore Dr.* ☎ *312/ 922-9410. Admission $5 adults; $3 children 3–17, students with ID, and seniors; free for children 2 and under, members, teachers, and armed forces personnel in uniform. Maximum family charge $16; free on Wed. Daily 9am–5pm. Closed Thanksgiving, Christmas, and New Year's Day. Bus: 146.* The museum's home is a tour de force of classicism in marble, designed by Daniel Burnham after the Erechtheum in Athens. Spread over the museum's acres of floor space are both interactive exhibits and traditional diorama and taxidermy presentations. A notable permanent exhibit is "Inside Ancient Egypt," where a *mastaba,* the tomb of Pharaoh Unis-ankh from the 5th century B.C., forms the core of a spellbinding exhibit that realistically depicts scenes from Egyptian everyday life as well as funeral and religious rites. Other interactive exhibits include "Traveling the Pacific" and a Pawnee earth lodge for storytelling on Native American life and lore.

**Museum of Contemporary Art.** *220 E. Chicago Ave.* ☎ *312/280-2660 for a recorded announcement. Admission $6.50 adults; $4 children 12–16, students, and seniors; free for children under 12; free on the first Tues of every month. Tues and Thurs–Fri 11am–6pm, Wed 11am–9pm, Sat–Sun 10am–6pm. Bus: 151. Subway/El: Take the Howard line to Chicago Ave.* Housed in a new building, designed by Berlin's Josef Paul Kleihues, the MCA opened in July 1996. The MCA emphasizes experimentation, and while exhibits change frequently, there is a permanent collection of more than 3,300 pieces, highlighting the work of Chicago artists.

○ **Museum of Science and Industry.** *57th St. and Lake Shore Dr.* ☎ *773/ 684-1414. TDD: 773/684-DEAF. Admission to museum only, $6 adults, $5 seniors, $2.50 children 5–12, free for children under 5; free on Thurs. Museum and Omnimax Theater, $11 adults, $9 seniors, $5 children, children under 5 free on an adult's lap. Omnimax Theater only, Thurs and evening shows $6 adults, $5 seniors, $4 children, free for children under 5 if on adult's lap. Summer, daily 9:30am–5:30pm; fall–spring, Mon–Fri 9:30am–4pm, Sat–Sun and holidays 9:30am–5:30pm. Bus: 151 or 156.* This world-famous museum is the granddaddy of all interactive museums. A headline attraction is the Henry Crown Space Center, where the story of space exploration is documented. A favorite is the descent into a full-scale replica of a southern Illinois coal mine. From historic railroad trains to submarines to space capsules, from special effects to the mysteries of the human immune system, you will find the object of your curiosity somewhere in this amazing place. The Omnimax Theater offers Friday and Saturday evening showings at 7 and 8pm.

**OTHER TOP ATTRACTIONS**   Chicago is full of museums, exhibits, and attractions.

**Adler Planetarium.** *1300 S. Lake Shore Dr.* ☎ *312/322-0304, or 312/922-STAR for a recorded message. Admission $3 adults, $2 children 4–17; $2 additional fee for sky shows. Free on Tues. Mon–Thurs 9am–5pm, Fri 9am–9pm, Sat–Sun 9am–6pm. Sky shows at numerous times throughout the day; call 922-STAR for current times. Bus: 146.* The zodiacal 12-sided planetarium sits on a promontory at the end of ornamental Solidarity Drive, just up the road from the aquarium. Multimedia sky shows re-create the nighttime skies and current topics in space exploration. A closed-circuit monitor connected to the planetarium's Doane Observatory telescope allows visitors to view dramatic close-ups of the moon, the planets, and distant galaxies (Friday after the 8pm sky show). To find out what to look for in this month's sky, call the Nightwatch 24-Hour Hot Line (☎ 312/922-STAR), or check in on the Internet at http://astro.vchicago.edv/adler.

○ **Chicago Board of Trade.** *141 W. Jackson.* ☎ *312/435-3590. Admission free. Visitor center, Mon–Fri 9am–1:15pm. For groups of 10 or more, call for reservations. Bus: 1, 7, 60, 126, 151, 156. Subway/El: Take the Ravenswood or Evanston line to Quincy or Van Buren.* Live, improvisational acting in the city isn't necessarily at the theater. The

Trading Pit at the Chicago Board of Trade can provide the best entertainment in town. Watched over by a statue of Ceres, goddess of grain, the traders' frantic dealings in commodities, financial futures, and options peak in a shouting frenzy at the closing hour, after which individual gamblers in pinstripes will count up their chips and learn if they've come out winners or losers for the day.

**Here's Chicago! & the Water Tower Pumping Station.** *163 E. Pearson (corner of N. Michigan Ave.). No phone. Show tickets, $5.75 adults; $4.50 seniors, students, the handicapped, and children under 12; $12 family. Daily 9:30am–6pm. Shows every 30 minutes until 4pm Mon–Thurs, until 5pm Sat–Sun. Bus: 125, 145, 146, 147, 151. Subway/El: Take the Howard line to Chicago Ave.* The limestone Pumping Station and the Water Tower across the street were the only two buildings in the path of the Great Fire that withstood the blaze. The 45-minute *Here's Chicago!* show begins with a brief tour of the Pumping Station's machinery, and goes on to exhibits and computerized slides about Chicago's history, ending with a film entitled *City of Dreams,* which takes you on a simulated helicopter ride over the city.

✪ **Lincoln Park Zoo.** *2200 N. Cannon Dr. ☎ 312/742-2000. Admission free. Daily 9am–5pm. Zoo buildings, 9am–5pm. Bus: 151, 156.* The zoo is humanely and imaginatively designed, with animals occupying separate habitats appropriate to their species. The best time to visit the zoo, of course, is in good weather, for that is when the park itself is at its most animated. The zoo has a gorilla breeding program, and a population of more than 1,200 animals, birds, and reptiles, large and small. There is an adjoining children's zoo (see below, "Best Bets for Kids").

✪ **Navy Pier.** *600 E. Grand Ave. ☎ 312/595-PIER. Bus: 29, 56, 65.* This is a place for Chicagoans to come to relax and to be entertained. Developers have resurrected the old Chicago ballroom, installed a winter garden, a concert stage, a space that holds an ice rink in winter and a merry-go-round in summer, and a giant 15-story Ferris wheel. The 50 acres of pier and lakefront property is home to many shops and restaurants, and hosts the huge annual art show. The pier is also home to the **Chicago Children's Museum** (☎ 312/527-1000; see "Best Bets for Kids," below).

✪ **Shedd Aquarium.** *1200 S. Lake Shore Dr. ☎ 312/939-2438. Admission to both Aquarium and Oceanarium, $8 adults, $6 children 3–11 and seniors, free for children under 3. Admission to Oceanarium on Thurs, $6 adults, $5 children 3–11 and seniors. Admission to original Aquarium galleries only, $4 adults, $3 children 3–11 and seniors; free to everyone on Thurs. Aquarium tickets available on a limited, first-come, first-served basis, so it's recommended you purchase tickets in advance at any Ticketmaster outlet. Daily 9am–6pm; last entry into Oceanarium 5:15pm. Bus: 146.* The aquarium's most popular entertainment is the twice-daily (at 11am and 2pm; additional show at 3pm on Saturday and Sunday) feeding of the sharks and other creatures from the hands of divers who swim among them in a 90,000-gallon tank, the world's largest indoor aquarium. The Oceanarium, a marine mammal pavilion, re-creates a Pacific Northwest coastal environment—as you follow a winding nature trail, you encounter whales, dolphins, sea otters, and harbor seals. In the large pool surrounded by an amphitheater, the whales and dolphins are put through their paces of leaps and dives by a crew of friendly trainers at scheduled times.

**GREAT VIEWS**   The **John Hancock Observatory,** on the 94th floor of the John Hancock Center, 875 N. Michigan (☎ 312/751-3681), delivers a panorama of the city and nearby Lake Michigan. On a clear day you can see four states—Illinois, Michigan, Indiana, and Wisconsin—a radius of 80 miles. The view is spectacular at night. The observatory reopened in May, 1997 after a renovation that added new attractions, including a virtual reality tour of the city's high points. Enter on Delaware; admission is $7 for adults, $5 students and seniors, free for children under 5 and military personnel, and it's open daily from 9am until midnight. Take the Howard line to Chicago Avenue or buses 125, 145, 146, 147, or 151.

The view from the world's second tallest skyscraper, the **Sears Tower,** 233 S. Wacker Dr. (☎ **312/875-9696**), is everything you'd expect it to be, a momentary suspension between earth and sky. From the Skydeck 100 floors up, the city spreads out, both intimate and colossal. Enter on Jackson. Admission is $6.75 for adults, $4.75 seniors, $4 children 5–17, free for children under 4, $18.50 family (two adults and up to three children). The Skydeck is open daily from March to September from 9am to 11pm; from October to February, daily 9am to 10pm. Take the Ravenswood or Evanston line to Quincy or buses 7, 126, 151, or 156.

**CHICAGO'S PARKS**   **Grant Park** is a patchwork of giant lawns pieced together by major roadways. The immense Buckingham Fountain is the baroque centerpiece, spurting columns of water up to 100 feet in the air, illuminated after dark by a whirl of colored lights. Outdoor concerts are staged at the Petrillo Music Shell (see "Special Events," above). At the north end of the park is a covered outdoor sports plaza with 12 lighted tennis courts, a rink for ice skating (winter) or roller skating (summer), a cross-country ski trail, and a field house. Notable sculptures in the park are the Native American on horseback (at Congress and Michigan) and Saint-Gaudens Lincoln statue (Congress between Michigan and Columbus Drive). Buses 3, 4, 6, 60, 146, or 151 go to the park.

**Lincoln Park** is the city's largest. Straight and narrow, the park begins at North Avenue and follows the shoreline of Lake Michigan northward as far as Ardmore Avenue. Many attractions are here, including beaches, a golf course, tennis courts, and the **Lincoln Park Conservatory** (☎ **312/294-4770**), the closest thing Chicago has to a botanical garden within the city limits. Buses 22, 145, 146, 147, 151, or 156 go to the park.

**A FRANK LLOYD WRIGHT TOUR**   Oak Park has 30 homes and buildings designed and constructed by Wright between 1899 and 1913; they constitute the core output of his Prairie School period. To get to Oak Park, take the Lake Street/Dan Ryan El to the Harlem/Marion stop, roughly a 25-minute ride from downtown. Exit the station onto Harlem Avenue, then backtrack along North Boulevard one block until reaching Forest Avenue; turn left (north) and walk another block to Lake Street. On this corner you will find the **Visitor Center,** 158 Forest Ave. (☎ **708/848-1976**), open daily from 10am to 5pm. Stop here for orientation, maps, guidebooks, and tour tickets. By car, take the Eisenhower Expressway (I-290) to the exit north of Harlem Avenue (Ill. 43), and follow the brown-and-white signs to the parking lot at Forest Avenue and Lake Street. Most of the homes are privately owned, and only their exteriors can be viewed, but once a year many are open to the public during the Wright Plus Tour (see "Special Events," above).

The **Chicago Architecture Foundation** (☎ **312/922-3432** for reservations and tickets) offers tours of Oak Park and of Frank Lloyd Wright houses in Hyde Park and other locations. There is a guided walking tour of the Oak Park area as well as a bus tour, leaving from downtown.

You can also take an extensive walking tour, guided or with cassette, from the **Ginko Tree Book Shop,** 951 Chicago Ave., weekdays at 11am, 1pm, and 3pm, and continuously on weekends from 11am to 4pm.

✪ **Frank Lloyd Wright Home & Studio.** *951 Chicago Ave., Oak Park.* ☎ *708/848-1976. General admission $8; $6 for children under 18 and seniors. Guided tours, Mon–Fri 11am and 1 and 3pm, Sat–Sun every 15 minutes 11am–4pm. Additional hours in summer. Handicapped access is limited; please call in advance.* The home began as a simple shingled cottage in 1889, but became a work in progress as Wright, up to

1911, remodeled it to suit his family's changing needs. Wright's showcase and laboratory, the house is not an architect's masterpiece, but the master's home, and every room reflects the workings of a remarkable mind.

✪ **Unity Temple.** *875 Lake St. Admission $3 adults, $2 for students and seniors on Mon–Fri; $5 adults, $3 for students and seniors on weekends.* Using poured concrete with metal reinforcements, Wright created a building that contains the entire architectural alphabet of the Prairie School. Wright used color sparingly, achieving the pale, natural effects by adding pigment to the plaster. His exciting use of wood for trim and other decorative touches reflects his sensitivity to grain and tone.

**BEST BETS FOR KIDS**   The **Museum of Science and Industry** has high-tech, push-button, and interactive exhibits for children. Kids are particularly awed by the large-screen Omnimax Theater. The **Field Museum of Natural History** has a "place for wonder" with many curiosities that children can touch. Most kids also go nuts over the dinosaurs and the mummies. The **Adler Planetarium** offers special "sky shows" for children on Saturday morning. Children love the Belugas at the **Shedd Aquarium** and the divers that hand-feed the sharks. The **Chicago Children's Museum,** on Navy Pier (☎ 312/527-1000), has areas for preschoolers as well as older children, and allows kids a maximum of hands-on fun with imaginative permanent installations and special programs. It's open Tuesday to Friday from 12:30 to 4:30pm, and weekends it opens at 10am. The **Chicago Cultural Center,** 78 E. Washington St. (☎ 312/744-6630 for a listing of current events), offers films for children every Saturday, and a special program of activities in summer. The **Art Institute of Chicago** has designated five galleries as a "junior museum" where children can engage in art projects of their own. The **DuSable Museum of African-American History** has a summer program offering cultural and educational activities for children. Every kid should get to go to a **Cubs baseball game** at Wrigley Field. In the Lincoln Park Zoo, the **Pritzker Children's Zoo and Nursery** (☎ 312/742-2000) gives kids the opportunity to touch many animals, and at the Farm-in-the-Zoo, kids will discover a working reproduction of a midwestern farm, complete with a barnyard full of livestock.

**BEACHES**   Chicago is unusual among cities in that even downtown, public beaches line Lake Michigan. A few of the most popular are **Oak Street Beach,** at the northern tip of the Magnificent Mile; the **North Avenue Beach,** about six blocks farther north; and the **Belmont Avenue strip,** where gays congregate.

**SPORTS**   A **Chicago Cubs** game in Wrigley Field, 1060 W. Addison St. (☎ 773/404-2827), is a must for baseball fans. With its ivy-covered outfield walls, its hand-operated scoreboard, and its view of the shimmering lake from the upper deck, it's one of baseball's perfect places. Take the B train on the north–south line to the Addison stop or the no. 22 bus, which runs up Clark Street. The **Chicago White Sox** play at Comiskey Park, 333 W. 35th St. (☎ 312/674-1000), in the South Side neighborhood of Bridgeport; to get there by subway/El, take the Lake/Dan Ryan line to Sox/35th Street. Game times and schedules are available by writing to the Chicago Office of Tourism, 78 E. Washington, Chicago, IL 60602.

Michael Jordan and the NBA's **Chicago Bulls** play at the **United Center,** 1901 W. Madison St. (☎ 312/455-4500). Tickets are tough to come by. Try your concierge or a ticket broker, such as Gold Coast Tickets (☎ 312/644-6446) or Center Stage (☎ 773/233-8686). Pro football's **Chicago Bears** play at **Soldier Field,** 425 E. McFetridge Dr. (☎ 312/663-5408).

**SHOPPING**   Chicago just happens to be one of the best cities in the world to shop. The quality of the stores is top-notch, and, since so many of the best are concentrated on North Michigan Avenue, the convenience is unmatched.

The **Magnificent Mile** refers to the roughly mile-long stretch of North Michigan Avenue between the Chicago River and Oak Street. A combination of department stores and specialty shops and three vertical malls make for a density of first-rate shopping unmatched anywhere. Marshall Field's, Crate & Barrel, F. A. O. Schwarz, Borders, Hammacher Schlemmer, NIKETOWN (a great tourist attraction, a shrine to Michael Jordan), the fascinating Sony Gallery of Consumer Electronics, Neiman Marcus, and others too numerous to name are all here. **Oak Street** at the north end of the Mile is lined with chic designer boutiques. As a general rule, **shop hours** are Mon–Sat 10am–8pm and Sun noon–6pm.

**State Street** was once the center of Chicago retailing. Worth exploring are Marshall Field's restored flagship store with its Tiffany skylight and the Louis Sullivan–designed Carson Pirie Scott building. The revival of shopping in **the Loop** has drawn a mixture of moderately priced stores, open in daytime hours only and closed Sunday.

**River North** is Chicago's primary art gallery district, and along Wells Street from Kinzie Street to Chicago Avenue are many interesting shops. **North Pier,** 435 E. Illinois St. (☎ **312/836-4300**) houses nearly four dozen specialty shops and boutiques as well as nightspots and restaurants. Antique shops are concentrated west of Sheffield Avenue on **Belmont,** or along **Halsted Street.**

## ACCOMMODATIONS

Make your reservations well in advance to ensure the best rate available. If you're interested in an option other than a hotel, **Bed & Breakfast/Chicago,** P.O. Box 14088, Chicago, IL 60614, offers a range of accommodations from rooms in private homes to guesthouses or inns.

**Blackstone Hotel.** *636 S. Michigan Ave., Chicago, IL 60605.* ☎ *800/622-6330 or 312/427-4300. Fax 312/427-4300. Telex 721507. 280 rms. $109–$129 double weekdays; $69–$89 double weekends. Rates include continental breakfast. AE, DC, DISC, JCB, MC, V. Valet parking $16.* When a suitable location was needed for the banquet scene in the movie *The Untouchables,* the period style of the Blackstone Hotel with its imposing lobby and grand staircase was the clear choice. Guest rooms are large and comfortable, with views over the harbor lighthouse or Grant Park. Some rooms are relatively inexpensive. There is a game-and-billiards room, and a health club available to guests at $10 a day.

**Chicago Hilton and Towers.** *730 S. Michigan Ave., Chicago, IL 60605.* ☎ *800/HILTONS or 312/922-4400. Fax 312/922-5240. 1,543 rms. $175–$250 double. Special weekend rates:$149 for a Tower room. AE, CB, DC, DISC, JCB, MC. V. Self-parking $19; valet parking $21.* Mammoth it may be, but it's easily the loveliest place to stay in the southern part of downtown, and is five blocks from the Art Institute and a 10-minute walk from the Shedd Aquarium, Field Museum, and Adler Planetarium. Most standard rooms are large and have two bathrooms. Four restaurants provide culinary options, and there is a complete fitness center.

**Clarion Executive Plaza.** *71 E. Wacker Dr., Chicago, IL 60601.* ☎ *800/621-4005. Fax 312/346-1721. 417 rms. $179–$279 double. Weekend rates $119–$179. AE, CB, DC, DISC, MC, V. Parking $19.75 with in/out privileges.* This hotel is very modern, with a great river location. The rooms are spacious, furnished in tasteful, contemporary style, and have either a city or a river view. Club-floor rooms are priced slightly higher. There's a concierge, restaurant, fitness center, and business center.

**✪ The Drake.** *140 E. Walton Place (at Michigan Ave.), Chicago, IL 60611.* ☎ *800/55-DRAKE or 312/787-2200. Fax 312/787-1431. 535 rms and suites. TV. $225–$265 double; $320 executive floor; $595–$795 suite. AE, CB, DC, DISC, ER, JCB, MC, V. Valet parking $23.75 with in/out privileges.* The historic Drake's landmark building fronts East Lake Shore Drive, looking out over a quiet park to the beach and Lake Michigan. From the lobby on, you sense that the Drake is a special place, an eminently civilized hotel. Bedrooms are generous in size, with sitting areas, writing desks, and bathrooms with marble floors. Tea in the opulent Palm Court is a special treat.

**Embassy Suites.** *600 N. State St., Chicago, IL 60610.* ☎ *312/943-3800. Fax 312/ 943-7629. 358 suites. $189–$249 king suite; $219–$279 double suite. AE, DC, DISC, JCB, MC, V. Valet parking $22 with in/out privileges.* Although it bills itself as a business hotel, it is a very family-friendly hotel. Suites have two rooms, a living room with a sleeper sofa and a bedroom with one king-size or two double beds, and a minikitchen outfitted with a refrigerator, microwave, coffeemaker, and minibar. The suites surround a central atrium filled with greenery. Facilities include a pool, sauna, whirlpool, and workout room. The hotel has a good restaurant, Papagus Greek Taverna.

✪ **Four Seasons Hotel.** *120 E. Delaware Place, Chicago, IL 60611.* ☎ *800/ 332-3442 or 312/280-8800. Fax 312/280-7585. 343 rms. $340–$380 double; $360– $995 suite. Weekend rates from $285. AE, CB, DC, DISC, MC, V. Self-parking $15; valet parking $22.* Above the city's most upscale vertical mall is Chicago's tallest hotel, with spectacular views. Guest rooms have English furnishings, custom-woven carpets and tapestries, marble bathrooms with luxurious amenities, and windows that open to let in fresh air. The Seasons Restaurant serves elegant American and continental fare. The hotel has an excellent health spa with a 50-foot pool, a sundeck, and an outdoor jogging track.

**Guest Quarters Suite Hotel.** *198 E. Delaware Place, Chicago, IL 60611.* ☎ *800/424-2900 or 312/664-1100. Fax 312/664-9881. 345 suites. TV. $139–$250 suite. Weekend and summer promotional rates start at $119. Children under 18 stay free in parents' room. AE, CB, DC, DISC, MC, V. Valet parking $23.75 per day with in/out privileges.* Each full-service suite features a separate living room and bedroom, deluxe bath, refrigerator, two telephones, and two TVs. Rooms aren't huge, but are spotless, and there are those little extras that can make a difference, such as complimentary coffee and newspaper every morning. There is a rooftop health club with a pool. Most nights, the hotel also has live entertainment featuring jazz and contemporary music.

**Holiday Inn–Chicago City Center.** *300 E. Ohio St., Chicago, IL 60611.* ☎ *800/HOLIDAY or 312/787-6100. Fax 312/787-6238. 500 rms. $118–$240 double. AE, CB, DC, DISC, MC, V. Parking $17.50.* North of the Chicago River and east of the Magnificent Mile is the recently renovated Holiday Inn. Right next door is the McClurg Court Sports Complex, where guests may enjoy the facilities free of charge. With its own fifth-floor outdoor pool and sundeck, and the hotel's proximity to such attractions as the North Pier mall and the Navy Pier, the Holiday Inn is a good choice for summer visitors.

**Hotel Inter-Continental.** *505 N. Michigan Ave., Chicago, IL 60611.* ☎ *800/ 327-0200 or 312/944-4100. Fax 312/944-1320. 844 rms. $245–$309 double. AE, CB, DC, DISC, MC, V. Valet parking $24.50 with in/out privileges.* In a landmark building at the foot of the Magnificent Mile, the hotel also occupies a more modern structure where the feeling is both elegant and intimate, with spacious rooms in attractive, muted tones. The bathrooms have sleek pedestal sinks and separate tubs and glass-enclosed showers. Each room also comes equipped with a refrigerator, three dual-line phones, and a large desk, and other amenities. Facilities include two restaurants, the Salon, which serves tea by day and cocktails by night with musical entertainment, a complete fitness center, and a junior Olympic-size indoor pool. The pool is complimentary for guests, but there is a charge for use of the fitness center.

**Hyatt on Printer's Row.** *500 S. Dearborn St., Chicago, IL 60605.* ☎ *800/ 233-1234 or 312/986-1234. Fax 312/939-2468. 161 rms. $225 double; $99 double* *weekends. AE, CB, DC, DISC, ER, JCB, MC, V. Valet parking $16.50 weekends, $20 weekdays; self-parking $13, all with in/out privileges.* The Hyatt's national historic landmark building and discreet and tasteful lobby remind you of a fine European establishment. It's an easy walk from the financial district and the Art Institute and other attractions. Prairie, one of the city's best restaurants, is here, rooms come with all amenities, and there's a fitness room as well as access to a nearby health club, the City Club.

**Knickerbocker Hotel.** *163 E. Walton St., Chicago, IL 60611.* ☎ **800/621-8140** *or 312/751-8100. Fax 312/751-0370. 254 rms. $135–$250 double. AE, DC, DISC, MC, V. Parking $22 with in/out privileges.* At one time part of Hugh Hefner's *Playboy* empire, the Knickerbocker, after a $10.5-million renovation, is seeking a new image as a serious business hotel. The hotel has a good location, a block from the 900 N. Michigan shops and right across the street from the Drake, and guest rooms have a fresh look. A bonus for couples or families: About one-third of the rooms have two bathrooms.

**Motel 6 Chicago Downtown.** *162 E. Ontario St., Chicago, IL 60611.* ☎ **312/787-3580.** *Fax 312/787-1299. 191 rms. $89–$99 double; 10% AARP discount. AE, DC, DISC, MC, V. Parking $14 with no in/out privileges.* Just east of North Michigan Avenue, Motel 6 is practically spitting distance from Crate & Barrel and the Tribune Tower. Formerly the Richmont Hotel, its rooms are on the small side, but they're comfortable, and the location can't be beat. The lobby is clean and bright.

**Ohio House Motel.** *600 N. La Salle St., Chicago, IL 60610.* ☎ **312/943-6000.** *Fax 312/943-6063. 50 rms. $75 king-size bed; $97 four-person occupancy. AE, DC, DISC, MC, V. Free parking.* This motel is a real bargain, located in one of the hottest entertainment and restaurant districts. It's clean and well maintained. Breakfast at the Ohio House Coffee Shop, served all day, is on the grand scale: two eggs, two strips of bacon, two sausages, and two pancakes for $2.95.

**Palmer House.** *17 E. Monroe St., Chicago, IL 60690.* ☎ **800/HILTONS** *or 312/716-7500. Fax 312/263-2556. 1,639 rms. $200–$325 double; $650–$900 suite. Weekend rates available. AE, DC, DISC, MC, V. Parking $9.75 weekdays, $8.75 weekends; self-parking across the street.* The grand building you see was constructed in 1925. Escalators lead up to the second-floor lobby, an absolutely cavernous room, gilded in a way that modern architects can only dream about. Guest rooms are large and bright, but not deluxe. The Empire Room still attracts a fashionable luncheon crowd.

**The Raphael.** *201 E. Delaware Place, Chicago, IL 60611.* ☎ **800/821-5343** *or 312/943-5000. Fax 312/943-9483. 172 rms and suites. $150–$185 double weekdays; $110–$140 double weekends. AE, CB, DC, DISC, MC, V. Parking $21 with in/out privileges.* A small hotel with an intimate feel, The Raphael stands among residential buildings a couple of blocks east of Michigan Avenue. The lobby, with its peculiar wood chandelier and Gothic ambience, is about as old world as Chicago gets. Guest rooms are spacious, if a little dark. Suites here cost less than rooms in comparable hotels. Off the lobby are a small continental restaurant and the chummy Raphael bar. The hotel offers $10 discount passes to a nearby health club.

✪ **Ritz-Carlton.** *160 E. Pearson St., Chicago, IL 60611.* ☎ **800/621-6906** *or 312/266-1000. Fax 312/266-1194. 431 rms, 82 suites. $240–$380 double; $435–$3,500 suite. Weekend rates $205–$295. Valet parking $25.50 with in/out privileges; $23 self-parking with no in/out privileges.* Book as far ahead as possible—the hotel is often full. The location adjacent to Water Tower Place is excellent. Standard rooms have king-size beds, armoires, desks—traditional without being heavy—and generously sized marble bathrooms. Lake views cost more, but are spectacular. The Greenhouse restaurant has a glass roof, and the Dining Room serves continental cuisine. An elegant high tea is served from 3:30 to 5pm in the 12th-floor lobby. A health and exercise facility can be used for a small charge.

**Talbott Hotel.** *20 E. Delaware Place, Chicago, IL 60611.* ☎ *800/621-8506 or 312/943-0161. Fax 312/944-7241. 98 rms, 50 suites. Rates include continental breakfast. $185 double; $255–$395 suite. Weekend packages available. AE, DC, MC, V. Parking $11 across the street in a lot.* The Talbott is a European-style gem. Rooms are spacious; all contain either kitchenettes or full kitchens. The lobby, with its leather sofas and fireplace, the cozy bar, and the complimentary evening coffee and brownies create an intimate, collegial atmosphere.

✪ **Tremont.** *100 E. Chestnut St., Chicago, IL 60611.* ☎ *800/621-8133 outside Illinois, or 312/751-1900. Fax 312/280-1304. 118 rms and suites. $190–$255 double; $350–$950 suite. Weekend rates start at $159. AE, DC, DISC, MC, V. Parking $23 per day with no in/out privileges.* If you're looking for an intimate European-style hotel, the Tremont will appeal to you. Recent renovations opted for a cheerful yellow and green color scheme that nicely complements the bright sunshine that fills many rooms. Every room comes with a VCR and a CD player. Access is offered to a nearby health club. Off the lobby is a somewhat overpriced restaurant.

✪ **Westin River North.** *320 N. Dearborn St., Chicago, IL 60610.* ☎ *800/WESTIN-1 or 312/744-1900. Fax 312/527-2664. 422 rms. $285–$355 double; $500–$2,500 suite. Packages available. Valet parking $23 with in/out privileges.* Formerly a Nikko hotel, the place has kept its Japanese sensibility. A small Japanese garden separates the Nikko from its Riverfront Park, a 300-foot-long landscaped strip between Dearborn and Clark streets. The lobby has a sleek design, with black marble, and minimalist fountain. The well-organized guest rooms are being gradually renovated, with new furniture and accessories. Every Sunday from 9:30am–2pm, the hotel hosts a jazz brunch in its Les Célébrités restaurant. Facilities include a fitness center.

**Other Accommodations**    Near O'Hare airport, the **Hotel Sofitel,** 5550 N. River Rd., Rosemont, IL 60018 (☎ **800/233-5959** or 847/678-4488; fax 847/678-4422) is linked to the O'Hare Exposition Center by a heated tunnel. The lobby recalls the monumental, and the hotel has two restaurants and a health club with a swimming pool. Directly adjacent to O'Hare is the **Westin Hotel O'Hare.** 6100 N. River Rd., Rosemont, IL 60018 (☎ **800/228-3000** or 847/698-6000; fax 847/698-4591), where, in decorous, sleek surroundings, guests are offered aerobics classes, racquetball courts, Nautilus equipment, and a swimming pool. Guest rooms are spacious, with oversized desks, two telephones, and TVs in the bathroom. The Westin's Bakery Café has a strong local following.

## DINING

With the advent of such restaurants as Charlie Trotter's and Everest, Chicago's culinary reputation has expanded considerably. The newest trend is midwestern cuisine, putting a new twist on old favorites and emphasizing regionally produced fruits, vegetables, meat, and game.

✪ **Ambria.** *2300 Lincoln Park West.* ☎ *773/472-0076. Reservations required. Main courses $19.50–$29.95; fixed-price meals $42–$55. AE, DC, DISC, MC, V. Mon–Thurs 6–9:30pm; Fri–Sat 6–10:30pm. FRENCH.* Near the Lincoln Park Conservatory in the impressive former Belden Stratford Hotel, Ambria, one of Chicago's finest restaurants, is clublike and eminently civilized. On the frequently changing menu you'll find dishes such as the flaky napoleon of lobster, bacalhao, and crispy potato, and roasted medaillons of New Zealand venison with wild rice pancakes, caramelized rhubarb, and root vegetables, accompanied by a blackberry sauce. On the wine list are many of those wonderful private cellar selections for which the Napa Valley is justly famous.

**Ann Sather's.** *929 W. Belmont.* ☎ *773/348-2378. Reservations accepted for parties of six or more. Main courses $6.95–$11.95. AE, MC, V. Sun–Thurs 7am–10pm;*

*Fri–Sat 7am–11pm. SWEDISH/AMERICAN.* This is a real Chicago institution. All meals include appetizer, main course, vegetable, potato, and dessert. It's the sticky cinammon rolls, though, that make addicts out of diners. On Monday night there are live performances upstairs in a cabaret setting. There is another branch at 5207 N. Clark (☎ 773/271-6677).

✪ **Arun's.** *4156 N. Kedzie (Irving Park).* ☎ **773/539-1909.** *Reservations recommended. Main courses $13.95–$24.95. AE, CB, DC, DISC, MC, V. Tues–Sat 5–10pm; Sun 5–9pm. THAI.* It's been called the best Thai restaurant in the city—possibly the country. Chef/owner Arun Sampanthavivat prepares a refined traditional cuisine that's authentic and flavorful. House specialties include khao kriab (steamed rice dumplings filled with crabmeat, shrimp, chicken, peanuts, and garlic) and golden baskets (flower-shaped bite-size pastries filled with shrimp, chicken, sweet corn, and shiitake mushrooms).

**Avanzare.** *161 E. Huron.* ☎ **312/337-8056.** *Reservations required. Main courses $12–$26 at lunch, $10.75–$27.75 at dinner. AE, DC, DISC, MC, V. Mon–Thurs 11:30am–2pm and 5:30–10pm; Fri 11:30am–2pm and 5–11pm; Sat 5–11pm; Sun 5–9:30pm. NORTHERN ITALIAN.* Avanzare is one of those hangar-size continental-style cafes with wraparound windows and moderate prices. Some dishes, such as the tortellini di pollo affumicato (smoked chicken-filled pasta with a sauce of provolone and spinach) and the spiedini di manzo con aglio (a skewer of sirloin tips rubbed with garlic), are of gourmet quality; other dishes are merely "good."

**The Berghoff.** *17 W. Adams.* ☎ **312/427-3170.** *Reservations recommended. Main courses $5.50–$9.95 at lunch, $8.75–$17.95 at dinner. AE, MC, V. Mon–Thurs 11am–9pm; Fri–Sat 11am–9:30pm. GERMAN/AMERICAN.* The immense 700-seat restaurant is a Chicago landmark, housed in a landmark building with a cast-iron facade. The Berghoff holds Chicago liquor license no. 1, issued at the close of Prohibition. While the menu rotates seasonally, the German standard-bearers like Wiener schnitzel or sauerbraten are always available, plus lighter fare in the form of salads, broiled fish, and vegetarian dishes.

**Bice.** *158 E. Ontario St.* ☎ **312/664-1474.** *Reservations required. Main courses $11–$24. AE, DC, MC, V. Mon–Fri 11:30am–10pm, Sat 11:30am–11:30pm, Sun 5pm–10pm. NORTHERN ITALIAN.* Direct from Milano, Bice occupies a lovely two-story building just minutes from North Michigan Avenue. The northern Italian menu, which changes daily, offers such dishes as insalata d'aragosta (lobster salad with arugula, Belgian endive, and hearts of palm), carpaccio of tuna or swordfish, and veal scallopini sautéed with roasted peppers, oregano, and basil. Desserts are all made on the premises, including the ice cream.

**Bistro 110.** *110 E. Pearson St.* ☎ **312/266-3110.** *Reservations accepted. Main courses $9.95–$21.95. AE, CB, DC, DISC, MC, V. Mon–Thurs and Sun 11:30am–10pm, Fri–Sat 11:30am–11pm. CONTINENTAL.* Neighborhood cronies tend to congregate in the sidewalk cafe or the large back room, drawn by the reasonably priced daily specials. A sample dinner might begin with half a dozen raw oysters, followed by steak au poivre or a fillet of salmon served with a whole squadron of veggies. For dessert try the crème brûlée or a creamy white-chocolate mousse with fresh raspberry sauce.

✪ **Blackhawk Lodge.** *41 E. Superior St.* ☎ **312/280-4080.** *Reservations recommended. Main courses $10.95–$21.95. Lunch prices slightly lower. AE, CB, DC, DISC, MC, V. Mon–Thurs and Sun 11:30am–3pm and 5–10pm; Fri–Sat 11:30am–3pm and 5–11pm. REGIONAL AMERICAN.* New Executive Chef Scott Birch prepares comfort food with a twist. Grilled pork chops with sautéed apples, shoestring potatoes with mustard sauce, and pan-fried Idaho brook trout with pecan rice and lime butter are served up in a rustic setting of early-American furniture and pine-knot paneling.

**Café Ba-Ba-Reeba!** *2024 N. Halsted.* ☎ *773/935-5000. Limited reservations accepted. Tapas $1.95–$7.50; main courses $8.95–$14.95. AE, DC, MC, V. Mon 5:30–10:30pm; Tues–Thurs 11:30am–2:30pm and 5:30–10:30pm; Fri–Sat 11:30am–midnight; Sun noon–10pm. SPANISH/TAPAS.* Ba-Ba-Reeba! is a valiant attempt to popularize the merits of the Iberian snack tradition. The bright acrylic and oil paintings, mostly pop portraiture, are delightful, and the plato de la casa of traditional meats and cheeses is very satisfactory. It's frequented by a young Lincoln Park crowd.

✪ **Carson's.** *612 N. Wells.* ☎ *312/280-9200. Reservations not accepted. Main courses $8.95–$25.95. Carry-out prices slightly lower. AE, CB, DC, DISC, MC, V. Mon–Thurs and Sun 11am–11pm; Fri–Sat 11am–12:30am. Closed Thanksgiving. AMERICAN/BARBECUE.* A true Chicago institution, Carson's calls itself "The Place for Ribs," and boy, is it ever. The barbecue sauce is sweet and tangy, and the ribs are meaty. Carson's also barbecues chicken and pork chops. For dinner, there's often a wait, and popularity has led to something of a factory mentality among management, which evidently feels the need to herd 'em in and out.

✪ **Charlie Trotter's.** *816 W. Armitage.* ☎ *773/248-6228. Reservations required (far in advance). Fixed-price dinners $70 and $90. AE, CB, DC, MC, V. Tues–Sat from 5:30pm. NOUVELLE.* He has been called the greatest American-born chef of his generation. The grand menu dégustation, which changes daily, is the perfect introduction to the innovative creations of the owner/chef. His cuisine clearly has roots in the French style, but Charlie Trotter feels no constraints. Much of the produce used is grown organically, and most of the meat is pasture raised. The real show is best seen from the table for four in the kitchen (reservations needed very far in advance). A vegetarian dégustation menu ($55) is also available.

✪ **Coco Pazzo.** *300 W. Hubbard.* ☎ *312/836-0900. Reservations accepted. Main courses $10–$11.50 at lunch, $12.50–$26 at dinner. AE, DC, MC, V. Daily 11:30am–2:30pm; Mon–Thurs 5:30–10pm, Fri–Sat 5:30–11:30pm, Sun 5–10pm. REGIONAL ITALIAN.* From Milan to Chicago by way of New York, Coco Pazzo wins high marks for its northern Italian food, which is traditionally simple, allowing the ingredients to shine through. The menu undergoes periodic changes, but there is always a tempting risotto del giorno. Desserts might include a tart filled with fresh raspberries and topped with champagne-spiked zabaglione. The atmosphere is open, light, and airy, though service can be slow.

**Eli's the Place for Steak.** *215 E. Chicago Ave.* ☎ *312/642-1393. Reservations recommended. Main courses $17.95–$29.95. AE, DC, DISC, MC, V. Mon–Fri 11am–2:30pm and 4–10:30pm; Sat–Sun 4–10:30pm. STEAKS/CHOPS.* A friendly formality, a commitment to quality, and generous servings is Eli's formula in a nutshell. The restaurant's signature appetizer is the shrimp de jonghe, baked to succulent perfection with garlic and bread crumbs. The 20-ounce T-bone is perfect—full-flavored, juicy. Liver connoisseurs will appreciate calf's liver Eli, a truly delicate and palate-pleasing selection. Be sure to save some room for a slice of Eli's famous cheesecake—50 varieties are available.

✪ **Everest.** *440 S. La Salle St.* ☎ *312/663-8920. Reservations required. Main courses $26.50–$32.50; fixed-price meal from $79; three-course pretheater dinner $39, including complimentary parking. AE, DC, DISC, MC, V. Tues–Thurs 5:30–8:30pm, Fri–Sat 5:30–10pm. ALSATIAN.* Dining room windows overlook the shimmering nightscape of downtown Chicago 40 stories above the Stock Exchange. Chef (and owner) Jean Joho, a baker in his youth in Strasbourg, France, has created a menu with a rare delicacy of touch and imagination. The elaborate menu dégustation, from the appetizer to the pièce de résistance—possibly Texas-bred saddle of venison with wild huckleberries and gray shallots—is always an extraordinary and memorable culinary event.

✪ **Frontera Grill & Topolobampo.** *445 N. Clark St.* ☎ *312/661-1434. Reservations accepted at Frontera Grill only for parties of five or more; accepted at Topolobampo. Main courses $8.95–$21. AE, DC, DISC, MC, V. Tues–Thurs 11:30am–2pm and 5:30–10pm; Fri 11:30am–2pm and 5–11pm; Sat 10:30am–2:30pm and 5–11pm. MEXICAN/MESOAMERICAN.* Owners Rick and Deann Groen Bayless offer authentic Mexican cooking in the Grill. Topolobampo is a more formal and expensive establishment under the same roof with an intimate atmosphere and its own menu of subtle and interesting dishes. The chef offers a "tasting dinner" of five courses for $39.

**Gino's East.** *160 E. Superior.* ☎ *312/943-1124. Reservations not required. Pizza $6.95–$17.40. AE, CB, DC, DISC, MC, V. Mon–Thurs 11am–11pm, Fri–Sat 11am–midnight, Sun noon–10pm. PIZZA.* Gino's East is perhaps the only Chicago restaurant where patrons wait outside nightly for pizza. Gino's looks like a condemned building, but the prerenovation look is a studied part of the "ambience." The pizza is elaborate and tasty, "a banquet served on a lush, amber bed of dough," or so one critic described it. Next to the restaurant is Gino's carry-out, with its own phone number (☎ 312/988-4200).

**Lou Malnati's Pizzeria.** *439 N. Wells.* ☎ *312/828-9800. Pizza $15–$20. AE, DISC, MC, V. Mon–Thurs 11am–11pm, Fri–Sat 11am–midnight, Sun noon–10pm. PIZZA.* In River North, Lou Malnati bakes both Chicago-style thick-crusted deep-dish pizza and thin-crusted pizza. He even has a low-fat cheese option.

**Michael Jordan's.** *500 N. La Salle St.* ☎ *312/644-DUNK. Reservations not accepted. Main courses $6–$12.50 at lunch, $12–$22 at dinner. AE, CB, DC, DISC, MC, V. Sun–Thurs 11:30am–10pm, Fri–Sat 11:30am–midnight. AMERICAN.* Despite the restaurant's mass popularity (you might have to wait for some time to be seated), the owners have kept Michael Jordan's affordable to families, especially at lunchtime, when there is a very economical children's menu. The food is surprisingly good, and appeals both to adults and young people.

**Nick's Fishmarket.** *First National Bank Plaza at Monroe and North Dearborn.* ☎ *312/621-0200. Reservations recommended. Main courses $14–$55; fixed-price lunch $21. AE, CB, DC, DISC, JCB, MC, V. Mon–Fri 11:30am–3pm and 5:30–10:30pm; Sat 5:30pm–midnight. SEAFOOD.* Taking the elevator down below street level to Nick's feels a little like plunging underwater in a submarine. Nick offers everything from California abalone, Maine lobster, and Dover sole to Atlantic swordfish, catfish, and salmon. With a piano player tickling the ivories Tuesday through Saturday evenings, it's a lovely choice for an old-fashioned evening of good food and music.

**Pizzeria Due.** *618 N. Wabash (at the corner of Ontario).* ☎ *312/943-2400. Pizza $4.99–$20. AE, CB, DC, DISC, MC, V. Mon–Thurs 11am–1am; Fri–Sat 11:30am–2am; Sun 11:30am–1pm. PIZZA.* In a lovely gray Victorian town house this restaurant serves gourmet Chicago-style deep-dish pizza. A popular feature is the express lunch, a choice of soup and a personal-size pizza for $4.95.

✪ **Prairie.** *In the Hyatt on Printer's Row, 500 S. Dearborn.* ☎ *312/663-1143. Reservations required. Main courses $15–$30. Half portions of many dishes available for lunch. AE, CB, DC, MC, V. Mon–Fri 6:30am–10pm, Sat 7am–10pm, Sun 7am–9pm. MIDWESTERN.* With an interior inspired by Frank Lloyd Wright, the restaurant uses only ingredients from the 14 midwestern states. Don't expect, however, anything homespun or plain. The tomato soup is multitoned, in swirls of yellow, red, and green, with sour cream and sturgeon caviar floating in the center. The must-sample is the buffalo steak, served in its natural juices, or the duck, cooked in a delicious dried cherry port-wine sauce. For dessert, have a hot-fudge sundae with real bittersweet chocolate.

**RoseAngelis.** *1314 W. Wrightwood Ave. (Lakewood).* ☎ *773/296-0081. Reservations accepted for parties of eight or more. Main courses $7.95–$9.95. DISC, MC, V.*

*Tues–Thurs 5–10pm, Fri–Sat 5–11pm, Sun 4:30–9pm. ITALIAN.* Two former lawyers traded in their law books for pots and pans to open RoseAngelis about 5 years ago. Ensconced in an old house in a residential section of Lincoln Park, the restaurant charms with its series of small dining rooms and garden patio and then delights with its exceptional and affordable Italian food. Try the outstanding, garlicky chicken Vesuvio or the substantial lasagna.

**Thai Borrahn.** *16 E. Huron St.* ☎ *312/440-6003. Reservations accepted only for large groups. Main courses $6.25–$16.50. AE, MC, V. Mon–Thurs 11am–10pm, Fri 11am–11pm, Sat 4–11pm, Sun 4–10pm. THAI.* It's moved 2 blocks from its old location, but has the same terrific, authentic Thai fare. Start with the classic tom yum soup, a spicy broth with lemongrass, straw mushrooms, crushed chili peppers, cilantro, lime, and huge tender prawns. The classic pad thai has a wonderful combination of flavors and textures.

**✪ Trattoria No. 10.** *10 N. Dearborn.* ☎ *312/984-1718. Reservations recommended. Main courses $10.95–$21.95. AE, CB, DC, DISC, MC, V. Mon–Fri 11:30am–2pm and 5:30–9pm; Sat 5:30–10pm. ITALIAN.* The decor with its ceramic floor tiles is straight out of Tuscany, and the food contemporary Italian. Ravioli is the house specialty. Start with *gamberi aromatici,* grilled shrimp with thyme and vegetable reduction, and follow with ravioli al tre funghi with crimini caps and wild mushroom ricotta in a porcini cream sauce. Another interesting pasta dish is farfalle con anatra with duck confit, asparagus, caramelized onions, and pine nuts.

**✪ Yoshi's Cafe.** *3257 Halsted St.* ☎ *773/248-6160. Reservations required. Main courses $17–$25. AE, MC, V. Tues–Thurs 5:30–10pm, Fri–Sat 5:30–10:30pm, Sun 5–9:30pm. NOUVELLE FRENCH.* Despite having won raves from *Condé Nast Traveler* and *Zagat's,* Yoshi's is a surprisingly low-key though elegant and intimate spot. Preparations are intriguing, with very light sauces and combinations chosen to enhance the flavors and textures of the ingredients. The menu, which frequently changes, lists predominantly seafood choices, and reflects a strong Japanese influence. Chef Yoshi Katsumura himself often comes out from the kitchen to visit each table and make sure everyone is happy. Highly recommended.

## CHICAGO AFTER DARK

Hearing the world-class Chicago Symphony Orchestra, attending a performance of the critically acclaimed Lyric Opera of Chicago, and seeing the Tony Award–winning Steppenwolf and Goodman companies are a few of the best—but by no means the only—ways to spend your evenings in the city. Chicago has a thriving music scene, with clubs devoted to everything from jazz and blues to alternative rock, country, and Latin beats. Clubs are found on Rush Street, Old Town, Lincoln Park, and New Town. And if you're just looking to hang out, you won't have to go far in any neighborhood to find a tavern filled with locals.

For up-to-date entertainment listings, check the local newspapers and magazines, particularly the "Weekend" and "What's Happening" sections of the two dailies, the *Chicago Tribune* and the *Chicago Sun–Times;* the *Reader* and *New City,* both free weekly tabloids; and the monthly *Chicago* magazine. **Hot Tix Hotline** (☎ 312/977-1755) offers a recorded message listing all performances for the evening on which you call, and on Friday the message lists the weekend theater schedule for the entire city. For current information on classical music and opera, call the **Chicago Musical Alliance** (☎ 312/987-1123).

To order tickets for many plays and events, call **Ticketmaster Arts Line** (☎ 312/902-1500), a centralized phone-reservation system that allows you to charge full-price tickets for productions at more than 50 Chicago theaters with a major credit card. For hard-to-get tickets, try the **Ticket Exchange** (☎ **800/666-0779** or 312/902-1888). For half-price tickets on the day of the show, drop by the **Hot Tix Ticket Center,** located in the Loop at 24 S. State St., or call ☎ **312/831-2822** to order by phone, ☎ 312/977-1755 for information. Hot Tix also offers advance-purchase tickets at full price. It's open Mon noon–6pm, Tues–Fri 10am–6pm, and Sat 10am–5pm.

**THE PERFORMING ARTS**    Chicago's symphony and opera and dance are world-class, and the city is known for its vibrant and innovative off-Loop theaters.

The ✪ **Chicago Symphony** is among the 10 or so best orchestras in the world. It performs at historic Orchestra Hall, 220 S. Michigan Ave. (☎ **312/294-3000;** fax 312/435-9032), under the direction of Daniel Barenboim and laureate director Sir Georg Solti. Summertime visitors have an opportunity to hear a CSO performance at the delightful **Ravinia Festival** (☎ **773/RAVINIA**) in suburban Highland Park, led by well-known guest conductors. Other classical music groups are the **Civic Orchestra of Chicago,** training orchestra of the Chicago Symphony; the **Chicago Chamber Musicians** (☎ **312/558-1404**), which presents chamber music concerts by groups from around the world; the **Vermeer Quartet** (for information, write to 410 S. Michigan Ave., Suite 911, Chicago, IL 60605); and the **Chicago Chamber Orchestra** (☎ **312/922-5570**). A series of free outdoor concerts is given in the summer by the **Grant Park Symphony and Chorus** at the James C. Petrillo Music Shell (☎ **312/294-2420** for information).

The ✪ **Lyric Opera of Chicago** is a major American opera company that attracts top-notch singers from all over the world. It performs at the art deco Civic Opera House, Madison Street and Wacker Drive (☎ **312/332-2244**).

Chicago has two major dance companies. The ✪ **Joffrey Ballet** (☎ **312/739-0120**), directed by Gerald Arpino, recently relocated from New York, presented its second Chicago season in spring 1997. The contemporary **Hubbard Street Dance Chicago** (☎ **312/663-0853**), under the artistic direction of Lou Conte, has long been a Chicago institution. Other companies include **Ballet Chicago,** 222 S. Riverside Plaza (☎ 312/251-8838), led by artistic director Daniel Duell; and a new and entertaining group, **River North Dance Company,** 1016 N. Dearborn Pkwy. (☎ 312/944-2888). For complete information call the **Chicago Dance Coalition** (☎ **312/419-8383**).

Chicago is particularly rich in theater offerings, from splashy Broadway musicals to avant garde productions in basement-level spaces. The **Goodman Theatre,** 200 S. Columbus Dr. (☎ **312/443-3800**), is the dean of Chicago theaters. Under artistic director Robert Falls, the Goodman produces both original productions and familiar standards. The brilliant repertory company, ✪ **Steppenwolf Theater,** 1650 N. Halsted (☎ **312/335-1650**), has garnered many awards, including five Tonys. Other interesting off-Loop theaters are the **Bailiwick Arts Center,** 1229 W. Belmont (☎ **773/883-1090**), a young and exciting regional theater; **Blue Rider,** 1822 S. Halsted (☎ **312/733-4668**), one of Chicago's most controversial experimental theaters; and the small **Briar Street Theater,** 3133 N. Halsted (☎ **773/348-4000**), which has premiered the work of Chicago native David Mamet. The **Annoyance Theatre,** 3747 N. Clark St. (☎ **773/929-6200**), has its own definition of the word irreverent; **Lookingglass Theatre Company** (☎ **773/477-9257** for information) is a young company with a style all its own; and the well-regarded **Shakespeare Repertory Company** (☎ **312/642-2273** for information) produces three of the Bard's plays every year.

For more mainstream entertainment downtown, the **Arie Crown Theater,** at 23rd Street and Lake Shore Drive (☎ **312/791-6000**), is a showcase for Broadway-style traveling musicals. The **Chicago Theater,** 175 N. State St. (☎ **312/443-1130**), an ornate restored landmark movie-house theater, hosts visiting dance companies, touring concerts, and Broadway shows.

**MAJOR VENUES** The **Auditorium Theater,** 50 E. Congress Pkwy. (☎ 312/902-1500 for box office information, 312/431-2354 for tour information), was designed and built in 1889 by Louis Sullivan and Dankmar Adler. The building now belongs to Roosevelt University, but the landmark restored theater hosts a season of dance and musical performances and plays. The art deco ✪ **Civic Opera House** (see above) was built in 1929, and is the enduring monument of its founder, Samuel Insull, whose speculative empire crumbled during the 1929 crash, dragging down thousands of small investors in its wake. ✪ **Orchestra Hall** (see above) and neighboring buildings are now undergoing renovation; a new Symphony Center opened in the fall of 1997.

**COMEDY CLUBS** The mid-1970s *Saturday Night Live* brought Chicago-style comedy to national attention. **Second City,** 1616 N. Wells (☎ 312/337-3992), remains the top comedy club in Chicago. Just down the street is **Zanies Comedy Club,** 1548 N. Wells (☎ 312/337-4027). **All Jokes Aside,** 1000 S. Wabash Ave. (☎ 312/922-0577), spotlights African-American and Latino comic artists.

**JAZZ** Born in the Storyville section of New Orleans, jazz moved upriver to Chicago some 75 years ago, and is still going strong. **Andy's,** 11 E. Hubbard (☎ 312/642-6805), appeals to both hard-core and neophyte jazz enthusiasts with the likes of Dr. Bop and the Headliners' Rock and Roll Revival. **The Backroom,** 1007 N. Rush St. (☎ 312/751-2433), one of the original Rush Street clubs, still packs them in. **Gold Star Sardine Bar,** 680 N. Lake Shore Dr. (☎ 312/664-4215), has live jazz Monday through Saturday. **Green Dolphin Street,** 2200 N. Ashland Ave. (☎ 773/395-0066), the newest jazz club in town, attracts a well-heeled cigar/martini crowd. **Green Mill,** 4802 N. Broadway (☎ 773/878-5552), still has its speakeasy atmosphere and flavor from the days when Al Capone was a regular and the headliners included Sophie Tucker. **Jazz Bulls,** 1916 N. Lincoln Park West (☎ 773/337-3000), one of the liveliest spots, offers new-age jazz among other entertainment. **Jazz Showcase,** 59 W. Grant St. at Clark (☎ 312/670-2473), Joe Segal's old club, now run by his son Wayne, is a must (reservations recommended), **Pops for Champagne,** 2934 N. Sheffield (☎ 773/472-1000), is a very civilized, elegant way to enjoy jazz. The electic offerings at **The Vu,** 2624 N. Lincoln (☎ 773/871-0205), encompass everything from jazz jams, to country music, to big-band sounds.

**BLUES** With a few notable exceptions, Chicago's best and most popular blues showcases are located in entertainment districts of the Near North Side. **Blue Chicago,** 937 N. State St. near Oak Street; (☎ 312/642-6261), features women vocalists. **B.L.U.E.S.,** 2519 N. Halsted (☎ 773/528-1012)—the name says it all. **B.L.U.E.S. Etcetera,** 1124 W. Belmont, at the corner of Clifton (☎ 773/525-8989), attracts the big names. Run by the gifted guitarist, **Buddy Guy's Legends,** 754 S. Wabash Ave. (☎ 312/427-0333), is one of the most comfortable and popular clubs in town. **Kingston Mines,** 2548 N. Halsted (☎ 773/477-4646), is where musicians congregate after their own gigs to jam together and to socialize. **Lilly's,** 2513 N. Lincoln (☎ 773/525-2422), still enshrines the old-time blues every Thursday night. **New Checkerboard Lounge,** 423 E. 43rd St. (☎ 773/624-3240), located in a marginal neighborhood, is the real thing, close to its Mississippi roots. **Rosa's Lounge,** 3420 W. Armitage at Kimball (☎ 773/342-0452), is strictly a neighborhood hangout, but it has live blues every night.

**ROCK, FOLK & ETHNIC MUSIC** Lately Chicagoans—or at least some Chicagoans—have taken pride in the city's burgeoning alternative rock scene, which has produced such names as Liz Phair, Smashing Pumpkins, Urge Overkill, and Veruca Salt. **Abbey Pub,** 3420 W. Grace St. (☎ 773/478-4408), is a gathering place for rock, and folk acts local and international. **Double Door,** 1572 N. Milwaukee

Ave. (☎ 773/489-3160), is a relatively new club that brings buzz bands and unknowns to its stage. **The Metro,** 3730 N. Clark (☎ 773/549-0203), has live alternative/rock music most nights. **Park West,** 322 W. Armitage Ave. (☎ 773/929-5959), is a fine place for folk, jazz, and alternative rock. The major rock concert tours, on the o ther hand, generally play such huge places as the **Rosemont Horizon,** near O'Hare Airport, and tickets sell way in advance, generally through **Ticketmaster** (☎ 312/ 902-1500).

**DANCE CLUBS/DISCOS**   Dancing takes place these days in clubs and bars that either specialize in one brand of music or that offer an ever-changing mix of rhythms and beats. The polka is alive and kicking in the **Baby Doll Polka Club,** 6102 S. Central (☎ 773/582-9706). **Bossa Nova,** 1960 N. Clybourn Ave. (☎ 773/248-4800), is a thoroughly modern version of the old-fashioned supper club, featuring world beat music. **Ka-Boom!,** 747 N. Green (☎ 312/243-8600), is huge and offers high-energy dance music in the main room, alternative rock in the rock room, and disco or '80s beats in the cabaret. For new wave, it's **Neo,** 2350 N. Clark (☎ 773/528-2622). The hallmark of the **950 Club,** 950 W. Wrightwood (☎ 773/929-8955), is alternative music à la Patti Smith. Underground house and funk music at **Shelter,** 564 W. Fulton (☎ 312/ 648-5500), attracts a young dance crowd. The **Wild Hare and Singing Armadillo Frog Sanctuary,** 3530 N. Clark St. (☎ 773/327-4273), number one on Chicago's reggae charts, is well out of the tourist area, but the crowd is safely mainstream.

**THE GAY & LESBIAN SCENE**   Pick up a copy of the **Pink Pages,** a free community telephone book that lists bars and clubs catering to gays and lesbians. If you'd like to order a copy in advance of your trip, send $5 to D.A.C. Marketing, 3023 N. Clark St., No. 779, Chicago, IL 60657. Another good resource is **Nightlines,** a weekly publication with an emphasis on entertainment.

Shades of the Weimar period are the intended vibes at **Berlin,** 954 W. Belmont (☎ 773/348-4975), which describes the crowd as "pansexual," a blend of straights and gays. **The Closet,** 3325 N. Broadway (☎ 773/477-8533), is mostly gay, but also has a sports crowd. **Cocktail,** 3357 N. Halsted St. (☎ 773/477-1420), is a neighborhood spot on the Halsted strip. **Manhole,** 3458 N. Halsted (☎ 773/975-9244), attracts a youthful late-night clientele with recorded dance music. **Sidetrack,** 3349 N. Halsted (☎ 773/477-9189), is a video bar where the American musical is the sound of choice. **Paris Dance,** 1122 W. Montrose Ave. (☎) 773/369-0602), is an attractive lesbian disco. **Roscoe's Tavern and Cafe,** 3356 N. Halsted St. (☎ 773/281-3355), and Sidetrack are across the street from each other, two of the city's biggest bars.

**THE BAR SCENE**   For the atmosphere of a neighborhood tavern or a sports bar, it's best to venture beyond downtown. Some of the many neighborhood bars that dot Chicago are **Burwood Tap,** 724 W. Wrightwood (☎ 773/525-2593), dominated by postcollege singles and young marrieds; **Old Town Ale House,** 219 W. North (☎ 312/ 944-7020), a legendary hangout since the late '50s; **Sheffield's,** 3258 N. Sheffield (☎ 773/281-4989), a gathering spot for the theater crowd; and **Sterch's,** 2236 N. Lincoln (☎ 773/281-2653). Sports bars and yuppie hangouts are **Corner Pocket,** 2610 N. Halsted St. (☎ 773/281-0050), started by a few Ivy League types who'd rather shoot pool than crunch numbers; **Gamekeepers,** 345 W. Armitage St. (☎ 773/549-0400), Lincoln Park's most popular sports bar; **Glascott's Groggery,** 2158 N. Halsted St. (☎ 773/281-1205), at the top of any self-respecting Lincoln Park yuppie's list of meeting places; **River Shannon,** 425 W. Armitage (☎ 312/944-5087), part singles hangout and part sports bar.

The **John Barleycorn Memorial Pub,** 658 W. Belden (☎ 773/348-8899), offers classical music and a continuous slide show of art masterpieces, and **Otis,**

2150 N. Halsted (☎ **773/348-1900**), is more than just a bar, offering live music from Southern rock to reggae and blues 3 nights a week.

Around Rush Street are what a bygone era called singles bars—attracting primarily a college-aged contingent that give a frat party feel to the street. An "institution" on Rush that still caters to construction-worker types in the daytime and businesspeople at night is **Jay's,** 930 N. Rush (☎ **312/664-4333**).

Division Street is still the place where pitchmen stand on the sidewalk trying to attract customers. The bars lining Division Street include the **House of Beer,** 16 W. Division (☎ 312/642-2344); **Butch McGuire's,** 20 W. Division (☎ 312/337-9080); the **Lodge,** 21 W. Division (☎ 312/642-4406); and **Mother's,** 26 W. Division (☎ 312/642-7251).

## 2 Indianapolis

Indianapolis, the capital city of Indiana, is also a spectator sport–oriented city. The Indianapolis 500 attracts hundreds of thousands of visitors to the city in the month of May. The city also bills itself as the "Amateur Sports Capital of the World," and boasts world-class sports facilities. Indy natives rally behind the city's pro franchises—the NBA's Indiana Pacers and the NFL's Indianapolis Colts—but they also follow with fervor their local high school teams, especially the basketball teams, thus giving rise to the term "Hoosier Hysteria."

In its passion for sports, however, the city does not neglect the arts and is home to world-class art museums. Indianapolis also has neighborhoods worth exploring: the Lockerbie Square district downtown with renovated Victorian homes on cobblestone streets; Broad Ripple Village, a canalside neighborhood with boutiques, restaurants, and nightlife; and the historic village of Zionsville, 20 minutes north of Indianapolis, with Victorian homes, antique shops, and brick-paved streets.

### ARRIVING & DEPARTING

**BY PLANE** Flights arrive at **Indianapolis International Airport.** There is no public transportation into town; taxis cost about $17 to downtown, but can go as high as $35 elsewhere.

**BY TRAIN & BUS** Amtrak trains come into **Indianapolis Union Station,** 350 S. Illinois St. (☎ **317/263-0550**). The **Greyhound Bus Terminal** is at 350 S. Illinois St. (☎ **317/267-3074**).

### ESSENTIALS

**VISITOR INFORMATION** The **Indianpolis Convention & Visitor Bureau** is at One RCA Dome, No. 100, Indianapolis, IN 46225 (☎ **317/639-4282**). The **Indiana Tourism Hotline** is ☎ **800/824-INDY.**

**EMERGENCIES & SAFETY** In an emergency, call ☎ **911.** As in all unfamiliar cities, be alert and avoid deserted places. Downtown Indianapolis empties out at night; be careful walking alone to your car in large outdoor parking lots.

### GETTING AROUND

Indianapolis is a driving-oriented city. The city is easy to get around, based on a grid system. **Metro buses** (☎ **317/632-1900**) run on heavily traveled routes; fares are 75¢, $1 in rush hour. However, to get around the city you'll need a car. Call ahead if you want a taxi; taxis are radio-dispatched.

### WHAT TO SEE & DO

**ATTRACTIONS** The center of Indianapolis is **Monument Circle,** with the Soldiers' and Sailors' Monument at its center. The monument is 284 feet tall, crowned by a

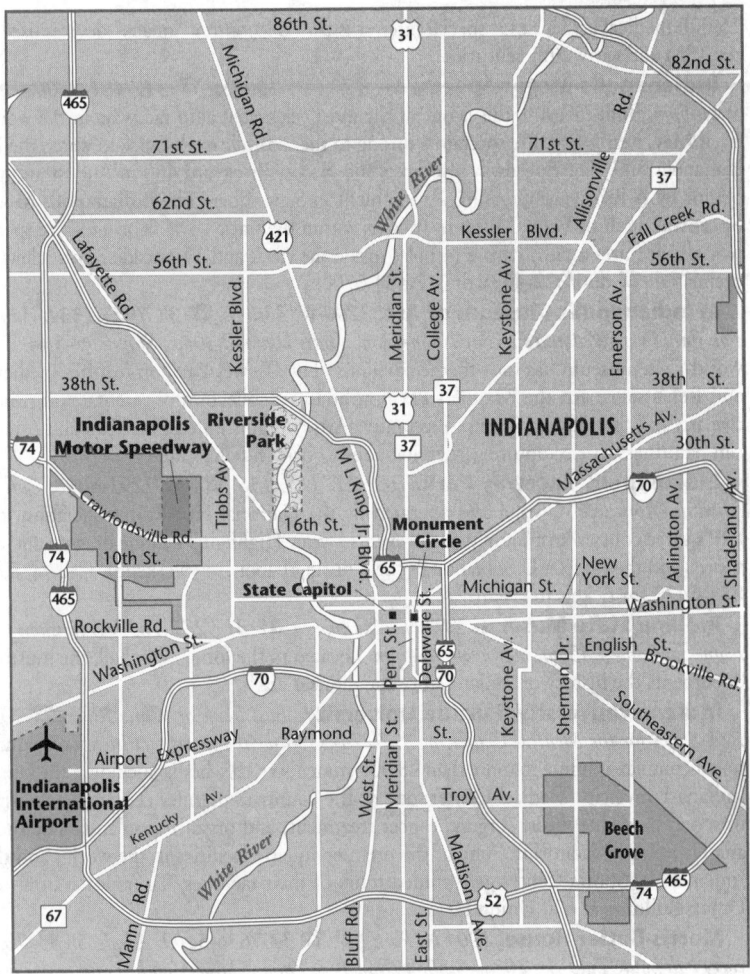

30-foot statute of Victory, known as *Miss Indiana*. An observation deck offers a panoramic view.

**Conner Prairie Pioneer Settlement.** *13400 Allisonville Rd., Noblesville.* ☎ *317/776-6000. Admission $9 adults, $8 seniors, $5 children. May–Oct, Tues–Sat 10am–5pm, Sun noon–5pm. Reduced hours off-season.* Located 30 miles northeast of downtown, this restored 19th-century village faithfully reproduces pioneer life between 1820 and 1840 with the help of 36 carefully restored buildings, craft demonstrations, and reenactments of events on the frontier.

**✪ Eiteljorg Museum of American Indian and Western Art.** *500 W. Washington St., White River State Park.* ☎ *317/636-9378. Admission $5 adults, $4 seniors, $2 students and children 5-17. June–Aug, Mon–Sat 10am–5pm, Sun noon–5pm. Reduced hours off-season.* This impressive $14-million building houses one of the country's most noted collections of Native American and Western art.

**Indiana Medical History Museum.** *3045 W. Vermont St.* ☎ *317/635-7329. Wed–Sat 10am–4pm.* Housed in the state's first medical center, this museum holds some

15,000 medical artifacts. Of special interest is the collection of "quack" devices used in the 19th and early 20th centuries.

**Indianapolis Motor Speedway.** *4790 W. 16th St.* ☎ *317/481-8500. Daily 9am–5pm.* Built in 1909, this is one of the most celebrated auto raceways in the world. Each May, nearly 400,000 spectators throng to the 2.5-mile oval course to watch the Indianapolis 500. The Speedway also hosts the Nascar Brickyard 400 in August and the Senior PGA Brickyard Crossing Tournament in September. The **Indianapolis Motor Speedway Hall of Fame Museum** (free) is within the track's oval. The 433-acre speedway also features a PGA course (4 holes inside the track and 14 outside). For tickets to events, call ☎ **800/822-4639** or 317/484-6700.

✪ **Indianapolis Museum of Art.** *1200 W. 38th St.* ☎ *317/923-1331. Admission free. Tues–Wed and Fri–Sat 10am–5pm, Thurs 10am–8:30pm, Sun noon–5pm.* This world-class museum has four theme pavilions: The Clowes Pavilion features medieval and Renaissance art; the Krannert Pavilion houses a collection of oriental and primitive art; and the Lilly Pavilion of Decorative Arts contains noted European and American paintings. The sculpture garden includes Robert Indiana's famed *LOVE.*

**Indianapolis Raceway Park.** *10267 E. U.S. 136.* ☎ *317/291-4090. Call for schedule. Apr–Sept.* Owned and operated by the National Hot Rod Association, the IRP's three courses host more than 60 events a year. Highlights include drag racing, car shows, and the NHRA U.S. Nationals (held during Labor Day weekend). Call ☎ **800/ 884-6472** for tickets to events.

**Indiana State Museum.** *202 N. Alabama St.* ☎ *317/232-1637. Admission free. Mon–Sat 9am–4:45pm, Sun noon–4:45pm.* Located in the former city hall, the museum documents the history of Indiana since the pioneer era.

**Indiana University/Purdue University.** *East bank of White River.* ☎ *317/ 274-5555 for the Medical Center, or 317/274-3518 for the sports facilities.* This educational complex is home to more than 28,000 students at 19 schools, including the famed Indiana University Medical Center, one of the country's premier centers for research in sports medicine, heart surgery, cancer treatment, and organ transplants. The Indiana University Natatorium, one of the premier aquatic facilities in the world, and the Indianapolis Sports Center give guided tours of their facilities. Tours leave from the Union Building at 620 Union Dr.

**Morris-Butler House.** *1204 N. Park Ave.* ☎ *317/636-5409. Admission $3. Tours every half hour, Tues–Sat 10am–3:30pm, Sun 1–3:30pm. Closed Mondays and major holidays.* Housed in a mid-Victorian mansion dating from 1862, this museum focuses on Victorian decorative arts such as fine silver, tapestries, and Belter & Meeks furniture.

**National Art Museum of Sport.** *111 Monument Circle.* ☎ *317/274-3627. Admission free. Mon–Fri 9am–5pm, Sat 10am–4pm.* This museum houses a collection of sports-related works of art through the ages. A Greek bronze from the 5th century B.C. depicts an Olympic athlete.

**RCA Dome.** *100 S. Capitol Ave.* ☎ *317/262-3410. Call for schedule. Guided daily 1-hour tours, $3 adults, $1 students and children 18 and under.* This 61,000-seat stadium with an air-supported dome is the home of the NFL's Indianapolis Colts, in addition to many conventions, concerts, and trade shows.

**PARKS & GARDENS** **Eagle Creek Park,** 7840 W. 56th St. (☎ 317/327-7110), is one of the largest municipal parks in the country, with 4,000 acres of wooded terrain for hiking, biking, and cross-country skiing, and a 1,300-acre reservoir. The main attraction of the 128-acre **Garfield Park Conservatory,** 2450 S. Shelby St. (☎ 317/327-7184), is a tropical greenhouse—complete with parrots and macaws, and waterfall-fed pools—planted with flora from around the world. There is also an amphitheater that presents live musical performances, a picnic area, swimming pool, and tennis and horseshoe courts. It's open Tues–Sun 10am–5pm.

The **Indianapolis Zoo,** 1200 W. Washington St. (☎ 317/630-2001), is the nation's first major totally new zoo in decades. This $64-million, 64-acre facility houses 2,000 animals roaming through simulated environments. The world's largest enclosed Whale and Dolphin Pavilion is among the highlights. The zoo is in the 250-acre **White River State Park,** 801 W. Washington St. (☎ 317/634-4567). Open from Memorial Day to Labor Day, daily 9am–7pm; reduced hours off-season.

**BEST BETS FOR KIDS**   All kids will enjoy the zoo, and older kids will be interested in the **Indiana State Museum,** the Native American artifacts at the **Eiteljorg Museum,** or a visit to the **Speedway.** The **Children's Museum of Indianapolis,** 3000 N. Meridian St. (☎ 317/924-5431), is one of the world's largest children's museums, with artifacts and interactive displays. The museum is open from Memorial Day to Labor Day, Mon–Sat 10am–5pm, Sun noon–5pm; reduced hours off-season.

**SHOPPING**   Downtown shopping was revitalized in 1995 with the opening of the **Circle Centre,** 49 W. Maryland St. (☎ 317/681-8000), with anchor stores Nordstrom and Parisian, 100 specialty shops, restaurants, nightclubs, and a cinema. The **Fashion Mall, Keystone at the Crossing,** 86th and Keystone Ave. (☎ 317/574-4000), is the city's other best mall, with anchor stores Jacobson's and Parisian, a number of national chain stores, and numerous specialty and designer boutiques. For something different, head to artsy Broad Ripple Village, a charming neighborhood 20 minutes north of downtown. For contemporary clothing and accessories for women, check out **Marigold** at 6323 Guilford Ave. and **Protocol** at 6317 Guilford Ave. **Artifacts,** 6327 Guilford Ave., features funky jewelry and gifts. The old **City Market,** 222 E. Market St. (☎ 317/634-9266), has diminished in recent years, but some food and produce stands are still here.

## ACCOMMODATIONS

While the more expensive hotels are downtown in Indianapolis, there are many moderate and budget hotels in the surrounding area. Most downtown hotels offer weekend or theme packages.

**Brickyard Resort & Inn.** *4400 W. 16th St. Indianapolis, IN 46222.* ☎ *800/926-8276 or 317/241-2500. Fax 317/241-2133. 108 rms. $58–$63 double. Extra person $8. Children under age 15 stay free in parents' room. AE, CB, DC, DISC, MC, V. Free outdoor parking.* Set on 600 acres, this conventional motel's location is unique—outside turn two on the Indianapolis Speedway—and it's quiet, except for race month in May. It offers standard rooms and a first-class 18-hole golf course. Rooms have refrigerators and some have terraces. The motel has a restaurant, bar, and pool.

✪ **Canterbury.** *123 S. Illinois St (south end of Circle Centre Mall), Indianapolis, IN 46225.* ☎ *800/538-8186 or 317/634-3000. Fax 317/685-2519. 99 rms and suites. $190–$220 double; $225–$1,100 suite. Extra person $25. Children under age 12 stay free in parents' room. AE, CB, DC, DISC, EC, JCB, MC, V. Indoor parking $5–$9 per day.* This charming European-style hotel offers "a bit of England." Rooms are large, with quality furniture, including four-posters, armoires, bathroom telephones, and refrigerators. Tea is served daily. A restaurant, bar, masseur, and health club are available to guests.

**Courtyard by Marriott.** *501 W. Washington St. Indianapolis, IN 46204.* ☎ *800/321-2211 or 317/635-4443. Fax 317/687-0029. 233 rms. $119 single or double. Extra person $10. Children under 18 stay free in parents' room. Free outdoor parking. AE, CB, DC, DISC, MC, V.* This downtown hotel is nicely situated on the edge of White River State Park and across the street from the Eiteljorg Museum. Unusually clean and well-maintained rooms are bright and cheerful, and some have terraces. Facilities include two restaurants, a bar, and a pool.

**Crowne Plaza at Union Station.** *123 W. Louisiana St. (between Illinois St. and Capitol Ave.), Indianapolis, IN 46206.* ☎ *800/2-CROWNE or 317/631-2221. Fax 317/ 236-7474. 275 rms and suites. $205–$230 double; $177–$207 suite. Extra person $15. Children under 18 stay free in parents' room. Indoor/outdoor parking $2.50–$8. AE, CB, DC, DISC, MC, V.* When Union Station became a marketplace, this hotel was built in railroad warehouses, with some rooms in Pullman cars, and a connecting corridor to the station. It's near the RCA Dome and Convention Center. On the premises are two restaurants, a bar, pool, fitness center, spa, whirlpool, games room, beauty salon, and playground.

**Embassy Suites Downtown.** *110 W. Washington St. Indianapolis IN 46204.* ☎ *800/362-2779 or 317/236-1800. Fax 317/236-1816. 360 suites. $159–$209 suite. Extra person $10. Children under 12 stay free in parents' room. AE, CB, DC, DISC, MC, V.* Connected by skybridge to Circle Centre Mall and other downtown sites, this plush hotel offers suites with two TVs, wet bars, refrigerators, and microwaves. Some suites have terraces or whirlpools, and you can enjoy complimentary beverages each evening. Also available are two restaurants (lunch and dinner only), a bar, pool, fitness center, whirlpool, and washer/dryer.

**Embassy Suites North.** *3912 Vincennes Rd. (south of I-465 on Michigan Rd.), Indianapolis, IN 46268.* ☎ *800/EMBASSY or 317/872-7700. 250 suites. $115–$179 suite. Children under 17 stay free in parents' room. AE, DC, DISC, MC, V. Free outdoor parking.* This beautiful hotel, resembling a Moorish castle, is a standout amid a busy area. An eight-story atrium greets you, and rooms are large, well furnished, and include refrigerators and two TVs. Facilities and services include one restaurant, two bars, a pool, fitness center, basketball court, sauna, whirlpool, games room, social director, and complimentary cocktails in the evening.

**Fairfield Inn College Park.** *9251 Wesleyan Rd. (exit 27 off I-465), Indianapolis IN 46268.* ☎ *800/228-2800 or 317/879-9100. Fax 317/879-9100. 131 rms. $45–$70 single or double. Children under 18 stay free in parents' room. AE, CB, DC, DISC, MC, V. Free outdoor parking.* This new facility, at College Park in the city's northwest corner, is within walking distance of dinner theater and restaurants. There's a pool, and guests get a complimentary pass to a nearby health club.

**Hampton Inn Downtown at Circle Centre.** *105 S. Meridian St., Indianapolis, IN 46255.* ☎ *800/426-7866 or 317/261-1200. Fax 317/261-1030. 163 rms, 17 suites. $89–$109 single or double; $149–$159 suite. Children under 18 stay free in parents' room. AE, DISC, MC, V.* Housed in a 1920s building on the National Register of Historic Places, this hotel is the newest downtown, and one of the few there moderately priced. It's convenient to all downtown attractions. There are two-room suites and king rooms with whirlpool tubs, an exercise room, complimentary newspaper, and free HBO.

**Omni Indianapolis North Hotel.** *8181 N. Shadeland Ave. (exit 1 off I-69), Indianpolis, IN 46250.* ☎ *800/THE-OMNI or 317/849-6668. Fax 317/849-4936. 215 rms and suites. $99–$149 single or double; $169–$250 suite. Children under 18 stay free in parents' room. AE, CB, DC, DISC, MC, V. Free outdoor parking.* This high-rise hotel and conference center with English ambience is the only full-service facility in the city's northeast corner, close to shopping and restaurants, Deer Creek Music Center, and Conner Prairie Pioneer Settlement. The hotel has two restaurants, a bar, pool, fitness center, sauna, social director, games room, children's program, and washer/dryer.

**✪ Omni Severin Hotel.** *40 W. Jackson Place, Indianapolis, IN 46225.* ☎ *800/ THE-OMNI or 317/634-6664. Fax 317/767-0003. 423 rms and suites. $119–$209* *single or double; $225–$280 suite. Extra person $20. Children under 18 stay free in parents' room. AE, CB, DC, DISC, MC, V.* This classy, beautifully restored hotel is directly across from Union Station. All rooms were recently redone, and some have terraces. Facilities include two restaurants, a bar, pool, and fitness center.

**✪ Radisson Plaza and Suite Hotel.** *8787 Keystone Crossing, Indianapolis, IN 46240.* ☎ *800/333-3333 or 317/846-2700. Fax 317/846-2700. 552 rms and suites. $104–$159 single or double; $149–$179 suite. Extra person $10. Children under 12 stay free in parents' room. Free indoor/outdoor parking. AE, CB, DC, DISC, ER, JCB, MC, V.* The largest major hotel outside the downtown area, the Radisson is located in the middle of an upscale fashion mall and office building complex. The large rooms offer beautiful furnishings and decor, and all have refrigerators. Some include terraces or whirlpools. On the premises are two restaurants, a bar, pool, fitness center, spa, sauna, steam room, whirlpool, games room, and washer/dryer.

**Renaissance Tower Historic Inn.** *230 E. 9th St (exit 113 off I-65), Indianapolis, IN 46204.* ☎ *800/676-7786 or 317/261-1652. Fax 317/262-8648. 81 suites. $75–$105 suite. Children under 18 stay free in parents' room. Lower rates off-season. AE, MC, V. Free outdoor parking.* Located in the historic St. Joseph District on the north side of downtown, this hotel is listed in the National Register of Historic Places. Suites have fully equipped kitchens.

**University Place Conference Center and Hotel.** *850 W. Michigan St., Indianapolis, IN 46202.* ☎ *800/626-2700 or 317/269-9000. Fax 317/231-5168. 276 rms and suites. $89–$169 single or double; $150–$500 suite. Extra person $15. Children under 18 stay free in parents' room. Indoor parking $4.75. AE, DISC, MC, V.* Located on the campus of Indiana and Purdue universities, this hotel offers well-furnished and functional rooms with refrigerators. Guests can use campus facilities, including a world-class natatorium, fitness center, and track-and-field stadium. Facilities include two restaurants, a food court, bar, basketball court, beauty salon, and day-care center.

**Westin Hotel Indianapolis.** *50 S. Capitol Ave, Indianpolis, IN 46204.* ☎ *800/228-3000 or 317/262-8100. Fax 317/231-3928. 573 rms and suites. $224 double; $195–$1,000 suite. Extra person $30. Children under 18 stay free in parents' room. AE, CB, DC, DISC, JCB, MC, V. Indoor parking $6.50–$13.* This luxury hotel with a sky-bridge to Circle Centre Mall and Convention Center/RCA Dome is within walking distance to Union Station and downtown attractions, restaurants, and shops. Guests can enjoy two restaurants, a bar, pool, fitness center, whirlpool, and children's program.

**OTHER ACCOMMODATIONS**   The **Days Inn,** 5860 Fortune Circle W. (Indianapolis International Airport), Indianapolis, IN 46241 (☎ **800/DAYS-INN** or 317/248-0621; fax 317/247-6737), is your standard budget motel near the airport. Facilities include a restaurant, bar, and pool. A special park-and-fly program is available. **Holiday Inn,** 2501 S. High School Rd., Indianapolis, IN 46241 (☎ **800/465-4329** or 317/244-6861; fax 317/243-1059), is a Holiday Inn Select facility on the grounds of Indianapolis International Airport and is 10 minutes from downtown. The noted Chanteclair restaurant is here, and some units have terraces or whirlpools.

## DINING

In addition to the places listed below, you'll find many new dining options in the Circle Centre Mall. Best bets include **Bertolini's Authentic Trattoria, California Cafe Bar & Grill, Johnny Rockets, Palomino Euro Bistro,** and the **Alcatraz Brewing Co.** If you are heading to Broad Ripple Village for shopping or nightlife, you can't go wrong at long-time favorites **Bazbeaux Pizza,** 929 E. Westfield Blvd. (☎ **317/255-5711**), for gourmet pizza, or **Renee's French Restaurant,** 839 E. Westfield Blvd. (☎ **317/**

**251-4142**), for casual French fare in an intimate, country atmosphere.

**Aristocrat Pub & Restaurant.** *5212 N. College Ave. (Broad Ripple).* ☎ *317/ 283-7388. Reservations not accepted. Main courses $8–$15. AE, DC, DISC, MC, V. Mon–Thurs 11am–11pm, Fri–Sat 11am–midnight, Sun 10am–11pm. AMERICAN.* You can enjoy a warm and comfortable ambience here, and fun and inventive dishes, including shrimp Vesuvius (with mushrooms, tomatoes, and an array of spices that includes jalapeños, served over fettuccine noodles).

**Battery Park Saloon.** *In the Capital Center Office Building, 201 N. Illinois (2 blocks east of the state capitol).* ☎ *317/237-3388. Reservations recommended. Main courses $7–$12. AE, DC, MC, V. Mon–Fri 11am–7:30pm. AMERICAN/PUB.* This trendy restaurant is popular with office workers from this twin-tower structure and nearby government facilities. The menu offers a few entrees, an unusually large number of appetizers, and sandwiches, salads, and pasta.

**✪ Benvenuti.** *36 S. Pennsylvania Ave.* ☎ *317/633-4915. Reservations recommended. Main dishes $21–$34. Dinner only Mon–Sat 5pm–9pm. Closed holidays. ITALIAN.* This elegant, European-decor restaurant is popular with business clientele at lunch. The restaurant specializes in northern Italian cuisine, featuring such dishes as cream of roasted bell pepper soup, lobster ravioli, and an array of fine desserts. The restaurant also has a deli/cafe that's open Mon–Sat 7am–6pm.

**✪ Chanteclair.** *In the Holiday Inn, 2501 S. High School Rd. (Indianapolis International Airport).* ☎ *317/244-6861. Reservations recommended. Main courses $25–$50. AE, CB, DC, DISC, MC, V. Mon–Sat 6–10pm. FRENCH.* This gourmet French restaurant occupies the top floor of the hotel, located across the street from the main airport entrance. Chanteclair has the city's largest wine cellar and offers expertly prepared cuisine in an exquisite setting, enhanced by a strolling violinist.

**Hollyhock Hill.** *8110 N. College Ave. (6 blocks east of Meridian St.; 5 blocks south of 86th St.).* ☎ *317/251-2294. Reservations recommended. Main courses $13–$18. AE, MC, V. Tues–Sat 5–8pm, Sun noon–7:30pm. REGIONAL AMERICAN.* This unique eatery is known for its country setting and family-style dining. The fried chicken dinner—with the chicken "hand-fried like mother used to do"—is the popular dish here.

**Iron Skillet.** *2489 W. 30th St. and Cold Spring Rd. (Riverside, 6 mi northwest of downtown).* ☎ *317/923-6353. Reservations recommended. Main courses $12–$16. AE, DC, MC, V. Wed–Sat 5–8:30pm, Sun noon–7:30pm. AMERICAN.* Since 1953, this city landmark has been serving family-style meals in a hilltop 1870s mansion above the city's busiest public golf courses. Hostesses in colonial costumes serve your choice of chicken, shrimp, fish, or steak.

**Jazz Cooker.** *In Broad Ripple Village, 925 E. Westfield Blvd.* ☎ *317/253-2883. Reservations recommended. Main courses $9–$16. AE, DC, DISC, MC, V. Daily 5–10pm. REGIONAL AMERICAN/CAJUN.* Fair-weather diners enjoy the jazz music and large, shady terrace of this trendy restaurant in the heart of young, artsy Broad Ripple Village. Jambalaya is a favorite Cajun dish.

**Keystone Grill.** *8650 Keystone at the Crossing.* ☎ *317/848-5202. Reservations recommended. Main courses $15–$60; fixed price dinner $17. AE, CB, DC, DISC, MC, V. Mon–Sat 11am–3pm; Mon–Thurs 5–11pm, Fri–Sat 5pm–midnight, Sun 3–10pm; Sun brunch 10am–1:30pm. SEAFOOD/STEAK.* This upscale but comfy restaurant is brass and glass, and jazz music. The chef here uses an Aztec wood grill to bring out the full flavor of meat. There's an extensive wine list, and fresh seafood is the Grill's trademark.

**Malibu Grill.** *4503 E. 82nd St. (1 mi west of Allisonville Rd. and I-465).* ☎ *317/ 845-4334. Reservations not accepted. Main courses $9–$19. AE, CB, DC, DISC, MC, V. Mon–Thurs 11:30am–2pm and 5:30–10pm; Fri–Sat 11:30am–11pm; Sun noon–9pm.*

*New American.* At this popular, award-winning eatery, diners can enjoy the casual and contemporary atmosphere while watching orders prepared in the glass-enclosed kitchen. Try the wood-grilled steaks.

**Marker.** *In Adam's Mark Hotel, 2544 Executive Dr. (2 blocks east of Indianapolis International Airport, just off Airport Expwy.).* ☎ *317/381-6146. Reservations recommended. Main courses $16–$24. AE, CB, DC, DISC, MC, V. Mon–Fri 11am–2pm; Mon–Sat 5:30–10pm, Sun 5:30–9pm; Sun brunch 10:30am–2pm. ECLECTIC.* Splendid cuisine is expertly served here, in an attractive French country setting. Dishes from the Americas include grilled swordfish with tortilla sauce.

**St. Elmo Steak House.** *127 S. Illinois (at the south edge of Circle Centre Mall).* ☎ *317/637-1811. Reservations recommended. Main courses $23–$33. AE, CB, DC, DISC, MC, V. Mon–Fri 4–10pm, Sun 5–9:30pm. AMERICAN/STEAK.* For more than 90 years at the same location, this has been the city's premier steak house—it's even on the National Register of Historic Places. The original bar and back bar are still in operation, and waiters wear tuxedos. With the capitol just blocks away, the eatery is popular with legislators and lobbyists.

**Teller's Cage.** *In the National Bank of Detroit Tower, 1 Indiana Square.* ☎ *317/ 266-5211. Reservations accepted. Main courses $9–$14. AE, CB, DC, DISC, MC, V. Mon–Fri 11am–2pm and 5–8:30pm. AMERICAN.* One of the best views of the city can be enjoyed from this eatery on the 35th floor. The food matches the view for enjoyment, with a diversified menu ranging from Jamaican chicken salad to chimichangas.

## INDIANAPOLIS AFTER DARK

**THE PERFORMING ARTS**   The **Indianapolis Symphony Orchestra** (☎ 317/ 262-1110) has its home in the **Circle Theater,** a vintage 1916 film palace on Monument Circle. **Clowes Memorial Hall,** 4600 Sunset Ave. (☎ 800/732-0804, 317/ 940-6444, or 317/940-9696), a performing arts center on the campus of Butler University, is home to the **Indianapolis Opera, Indianapolis Ballet Theater,** and **Indiana Chamber Orchestra.** The city's professional repertory company is the **Indiana Repertory Theatre,** 140 W. Washington St. (☎ 317/635-5277), with a Sept–May season. **Madame Walker Urban Life Center,** 617 Indiana Ave. (☎ 317/236-2099 for information and tickets), is an ornate, 1927 art deco theater offering jazz, gospel, drama, and dance performances. Every Friday, from 6 to 10pm, "Jazz on the Avenue" showcases local, regional, and national talent.

**CLUBS & BARS**   Indianapolis's nightlife action is primarily centered in downtown and in Broad Ripple Village, an artsy enclave of boutiques, bistros, and bungalows 15 minutes north of downtown.

For live jazz, downtowners head to the cozy **Chatterbox Tavern** at 435 Massachusetts Ave. (☎ 317/636-0584). Big-name acts playing in town sometimes stop by. Another downtown top spot for live music is the **Slippery Noodle Inn,** 372 S. Meridian St. (☎ 317/631-6974), Indiana's oldest standing bar (established 1850) and *the* place in the city for blues. If you're not sure what you're in the mood for, check out **World Mardi Gras** on the top level of the Circle Centre Mall (☎ 317/630-5483), with four connected clubs, including a New Orleans–style bar with live music, a 1970s-ish dance club, and the obligatory sports pub. Expect a younger crowd. Also on the top level of Circle Centre is **Ybor's Martini Bar** (☎ 317/951-1621), Indy's nod to the cigar bar craze. Settle into one of the overstuffed chairs, order a cognac, and light up. A more unusual offering is **Hollywood Bar & Filmworks,** 247 S. Meridian St. (☎ 317/ 231-9255), a state-of-the-art cinema with cabaret-style seating where you enjoy a movie while munching on pizza and sandwiches and sipping suds.

Broad Ripple Village, an easy drive north of downtown straight up Meridian Street, is where the local yuppies go for weekend fun. Mature audiences head to the **Jazz Cooker,** 925 E. Westfield Blvd. (☎ **317/253-2883**), for live contemporary jazz. But everybody goes to **The Vogue,** 6259 N. College Ave. (☎ **317/259-7029**), an Indianapolis institution where local bands and big names perform in a renovated movie theater. You can also check out live rock or blues at friendly **C. T. Peppers** at 6283 N. College Ave. (☎ **317/257-6277**). Other good bets in Broad Ripple are the casual **Broad Ripple Brew Pub,** 840 E. 65th St. (☎ **317/253-2739**), and the cigar/martini bar on the second floor of the **Broad Ripple Steak House** at 929 E. Westfield Blvd. (☎ **317/253-8101**).

## 3  Cleveland

The second largest city in Ohio sprawls for 50 miles along Lake Erie. A microcosm of American industrial evolution—steel mills, oil refineries, automobile plants, plus electronics and machine tool factories—has left behind gray, polluted suburbs cheek-by-jowl with upscale residential areas.

Today, however, things are changing in Cleveland—the lake and river are cleaned up, and The Flats, a former industrial area along the Cuyahoga River, has become a trendy area of restaurants and clubs. A new Science Museum has opened and the 52-story Terminal Tower, the second tallest building in Ohio, is the nucleus of a refurbished downtown complex for dining, retail, and entertainment. Cleveland is home to the prestigious Case Western Reserve University, and its Cleveland Clinic is known internationally for cardiac surgery. And last, but definitely not least, it's home to the Rock and Roll Hall of Fame.

### ARRIVING & DEPARTING

**BY PLANE**   Major airlines fly into **Cleveland Hopkins International Airport,** 10 miles south of downtown. From the airport, it's 20 minutes to downtown on the **RTA rail system;** fare is $1.50. A **taxi** takes about 45 minutes and costs $20.

**BY TRAIN & BUS**   Amtrak (☎ **800/872-7245**) trains arrive at **200 Memorial Shoreway Northeast.** The **Greyhound Lines** (☎ **800/231-2222**) arrive at East 15th Street and Chester Avenue.

### ESSENTIALS

**VISITOR INFORMATION**   The **Visitor Information Center** of the Cleveland Convention and Visitor Bureau is at 3100 Terminal Towers, 50 Public Square (☎ **800/ 321-1001** or 216/621-4110). Pick up a copy of "Walks," a brochure on Cleveland walking tours.

**EMERGENCIES & SAFETY**   In cases of serious emergency, call ☎ **911.** Avoid deserted downtown areas at night, and as in all unfamiliar cities, stay alert.

### GETTING AROUND

**BY PUBLIC TRANSPORTATION**   The **Rapid Transit Authority (RTA)** rail system is not extensive; it travels east to west with Terminal Tower as the hub. From Public Square, **RTA buses** cover five downtown loop routes. Call ☎ **216/621-9500** for information.

### WHAT TO SEE & DO

**ESCORTED TOURS**   Trolley Tours of Cleveland (☎ **216/771-4484**) offers narrated tours of the metropolitan area aboard a fleet of replica trolley cars. Tours are daily May–Oct, weekends only Nov–Apr.

**CRUISES**   Goodtime Cruises (☎ **216/861-5110**) offers boat trips on Lake Erie and the Cuyahoga River from June until Labor Day. The cost is $10 for adults, $9.50 for

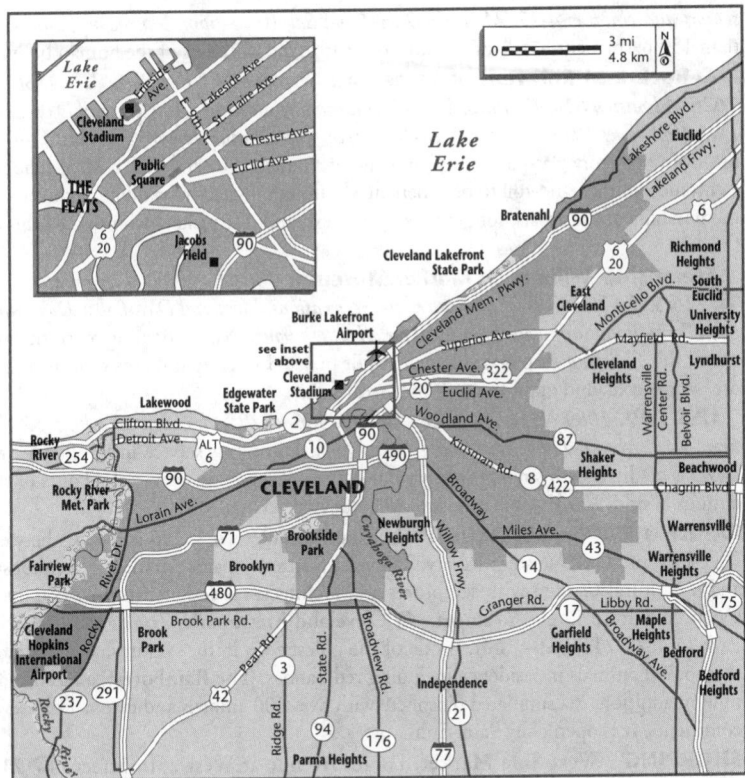

seniors, and $6 for children.

**ATTRACTIONS** Take a look at **Terminal Tower,** the city's central landmark, and **Public Square.** The **Old Arcade,** a short block east of Public Square between Superior and Euclid avenues, was built in 1890.

✪ **Cleveland Museum of Art.** *11150 East Blvd. (University Circle).* ☎ **216/ 421-7340.** *Admission free. Tues–Fri 10am–5:45pm, Sat 9am–4:45pm, Sun 1–5:45pm. Located in a marble Greek Revival building.* From *The Treasure of the Guelphs* to Rauschenberg, this exemplary regional collection boasts a rich panorama of Oriental, European, and American art.

**Cleveland Museum of Natural History.** *1 Wade Oval Dr. (University Circle).* ☎ **216/231-4600.** *Admission $6 adults, $4 seniors, students, and children 5-17; free on Tues and Thurs. Mon–Sat 10am–5pm, Sun 1–5:30pm; extended hours Wed and Fri (call for schedule).* Here you'll find a planetarium, Native American artifacts, and a fascinating array of fossils, dinosaurs, mammals, birds, and geological specimens, with a special emphasis on the geology of prehistoric Ohio.

✪ **Great Lakes Science Center.** *601 Erieside.* ☎ **216/694-2000.** *Museum, $6.75 adults, $4.50 children. Combination ticket, $9.95 adults, $7 children. Daily 9:30am–5:30pm. Omnimax Theater, Mon–Fri 10am–4pm, Sat–Sun 11am–5pm; shows every hour on the hour.* This museum focuses on the environment, particularly in relation to the Great Lakes.

**Health Museum.** *8911 Euclid Ave.* ☎ **216/231-5010.** *Admission $4.50 adults, $3* *seniors and children 4-17. Mon–Fri 9am–5pm, Sat 10am–5pm, Sun noon–5pm.* More than 150 permanent hands-on exhibits dramatize the workings of the human body.

○ **Rock and Roll Hall of Fame and Museum.** *1 Key Plaza.* ☎ *216/781-7625. Admission $14.95 adults, $11.50 seniors and children 4-11. Memorial Day–Labor Day, Mon–Tues 10am–5:30pm, Wed–Sun 10am–9pm. Reduced hours off-season.* This impressive seven-story glass-and-porcelain structure, designed by architect I. M. Pei, houses a chronicle of rock-and-roll to be experienced through interactive exhibits, archives, and memorabilia of the artists, songwriters, producers, and disc jockeys who created this art form.

**Steamship *William G. Mather* Museum.** *1001 E. 9th St. Pier (Waterfront).* ☎ *216/574-6262. Call for tour prices and reservations. Memorial Day–Labor Day, Mon–Sat 10am–5pm, Sun noon–5pm. Call for off-season hours.* Now a floating maritime museum, this 618-foot ship was originally built in 1925 to carry millions of tons of iron ore, stone, coal, and grain through the Great Lakes.

**USS COD.** *1089 N. Marginal Dr.* ☎ *216/566-8770. Admission $4 adults, $2 children 4-18. May 1–Labor Day, daily 10am–5pm.* During its service in the Pacific, the *COD* is credited with sinking nearly 30,000 tons of Japanese sea vessels. Tours of this famous World War II submarine are led by navy veterans.

**PARKS & ZOOS    Rockefeller Park,** Liberty Boulevard, a 296-acre oasis between Lake Erie and Case Western Reserve University, offers Japanese gardens, greenhouses, and a Cultural Garden with sculptures and architectural designs from 24 countries. Open daily from sunrise to sunset. ○ **Cleveland Metroparks Zoo,** 3900 Brookside Park Dr. (☎ 216/661-6500), is one of the oldest zoos in the country, and has more than 3,300 animals in residence including red pandas. **The RainForest,** a recent $30-million addition, is a simulated biosphere with over 600 animals and insects from seven continents. It is open daily 9am–5pm.

**SHOPPING    West Side Market,** Lorain Avenue at West 25th Street (☎ 216/664-3386), is a picturesque, Old European–style covered market with more than 100 food stalls where you can find regional cheese, fresh-baked bread, and fresh fruits and vegetables. It's open Mon, Wed, Fri, and Sat. Two downtown malls are the **Galleria,** 1301 E. 9th St. (☎ 216/861-4343), and the **Avenue,** Tower City Center (☎ 216/241-8550).

**BEST BETS FOR KIDS    For** "older" kids, you can't beat the **Rock and Roll Hall of Fame,** and youngsters of any age enjoy the zoo or a cruise on the steamship *Willy* (see above). At the Cleveland **Museum of Natural History,** there is plenty for kids to explore. The **Great Lakes Science Center's** Discover program offers kids over 350 hands-on exhibits, including the Polymer Funhouse and the Electric Show. Kids will also be thrilled by the center's six-story Omnimax Theater.

**SPECTATOR SPORTS    Jacob's Field,** 2401 Ontario St. (☎ 216/420-4200), is home to the 1995 American League champion Cleveland Indians. This gorgeous 42,000-seat stadium hosts concerts as well.

## ACCOMMODATIONS

Cleveland's former shortage of hotels is beginning to improve as new hotels open. Downtown hotels often offer weekend packages, while hotels away from the city center tend to offer lower rates on weekdays.

**Budgetel Inn.** *4222 W. 150th St., Cleveland, OH 44135.* ☎ *800/428-3438 or 216/251-8500. Fax 216/251-4117. 122 rms and efficiencies. $55–$58 double; $54–$61 efficiency. Extra person $7. Children under 21 stay free in parents' room. AE, DC, DISC, MC, V. Free outdoor parking.* Built in 1992, the Budgetel Inn is amid an industrial/

commercial area off a freeway near the airport, but it is immaculate and welcoming. Rooms include a refrigerator, and laundry facilities are available.

**Cleveland Marriott Society Center.** *127 Public Square, Cleveland, OH 44114.* ☎ *800/MARRIOT or 216/696-9200. Fax 216/696-8615. 400 rms and suites. $169 double; $380 suite. Weekend rates. Extra person $10. Children under 12 stay free in parents' room. Lower rates off-season. AE, CB, DC, DISC, EC, ER, JCB, MC, V. Indoor parking $12 per day.* This newer hotel off Public Square in downtown Cleveland is near The Flats, nightclubs, restaurants, and shopping. All rooms, decorated in light, warm colors, have minibars. Facilities include a restaurant, bar, fitness center, sauna, whirlpool, and washer/dryer.

**Embassy Suites Hotel.** *1701 E. 12th St., Cleveland, OH 44114.* ☎ *800/ EMBASSY or 216/523-8000. Fax 216/523-1698. 268 suites. $159 suite. Extra person $15. Children under 18 stay free in parents' room. Special weekend rates. AE, CB, DC, DISC, JCB, MC, V. Indoor/outdoor parking $3.50–$12.* Formerly the Radisson Plaza, this relatively new downtown hotel within a corporate apartment complex offers sophisticated decor and is close to shopping and major attractions. All rooms have minibars and some have terraces, and the indoor pool offers a view of the lake. Guests have access to a restaurant, bar, fitness center, basketball court, sauna, beauty salon, and washer/dryer.

**Glidden House.** *1901 Ford Dr. (University Circle), Cleveland, OH 44106.* ☎ *216/ 231-8900. Fax 216/231-2130. 62 rms and suites. $105–$129 double; $150–$165 suite. Extra person $10. Children under 18 stay free in parents' room. AE, DC, DISC, MC, V. Free outdoor parking.* This elegant 1910 mansion (listed on the National Register of Historic Places) has period furnishings and offers beautiful grounds and views. Nearby is the Cleveland Garden Center. There's a bar on the premises.

**Holiday Inn Lakeside.** *111 Lakeside Ave., Cleveland, OH 44114.* ☎ *800/ HOLIDAY or 216/241-5100. Fax 216/241-7437. 370 rms and suites. $109 single or double; $250 suite. Extra person $10. Children under 18 stay free in parents' room. AE, CB, DC, DISC, MC, V. Free indoor/outdoor parking.* This downtown, no-frills hotel is close to shopping, the waterfront, Rock and Roll Hall of Fame, stadium, city hall, and convention center. Some units offer minibars or whirlpools. The hotel has a restaurant, bar, pool, and sauna.

**Omni International Hotel.** *2065 E. 96th St. Cleveland, OH 44106.* ☎ *800/ THE-OMNI or 216/791-1900. Fax 216/231-3329. 274 rms and suites. $155 double; $225–$1,300 suite. Weekend rates. Extra person $10. Children under 18 stay free in parents' room. AE, DC, DISC, MC, V. Indoor/outdoor parking $8.* At the Cleveland Clinic, this elegant hotel is close to the Cleveland Playhouse, Case Western Reserve University, and museums. The elegant Classics restaurant is here (see "Dining," below). Live jazz is played in the atrium lobby. The recently renovated rooms include minibars, and some offer fireplaces or terraces. Conveniences include three restaurants, a bar, health club privileges, and business services.

**Renaissance Cleveland Hotel.** *24 Public Square. Cleveland, OH 44113.* ☎ *800/468-3571 or 216/696-5600. Fax 216/696-0432. 491 rms and suites. $109–$169 double; $225–$450 suite. Children under 18 stay free in parents' room. Lower rates off-season. AE, CB, DC, DISC, JCB, MC, V. Indoor parking $12.* A member of Historic Hotels of America, this elegant downtown hotel is connected to the Avenue at Tower City Center. The noted Sans Souci restaurant is here (see "Dining," below). All rooms have minibars, refrigerators, and bathroom TVs; some offer terraces or whirlpools. On the premises are two restaurants, a bar, fitness center, sauna, and beauty salon.

**Ritz-Carlton Cleveland.** *1515 W. 3rd St., Tower City Center, Cleveland, OH 44113.* ☎ *800/241-3333 or 216/623-1300. Fax 216/623-1492. 208 rms and suites.*

*$139 single or double; $300–$450 suite. AE, CB, DC, DISC, MC, V. Indoor parking $14.* Part of the restored Terminal Tower Rail Station, this hotel is connected to the Avenue at Tower City, Gund Arena, Jacobs Field, and the rapid transit terminal. It offers traditional Ritz-Carlton elegance with expansive windows overlooking the waterfront. All rooms have minibars. Facilities and amenities include two restaurants, two bars, a pool, fitness center, spa, sauna, masseur, and afternoon tea.

**Sheraton City Center.** *777 St. Clair Ave., Cleveland, OH 44114.* ☎ *800/ 321-1090 or 216/771-7600. Fax 216/771-5129. 470 rms and suites. $160 double; $300–$850 suite. Extra person $10. Children under 17 stay free in parents' room. Lower rates off-season. AE, DC, DISC, MC, V. Indoor parking $9.* This hotel is an ideal location for visitors to Cleveland's major attractions, and it affords a great view from upper stories. The hotel contains one restaurant, two bars, a fitness center, games room, and beauty salon.

**OTHER ACCOMMODATIONS**   A number of hotels are adjacent to or near the Cleveland Hopkins International Airport. The **Holiday Inn Airport,** 4181 W. 150th St. (☎ **800/HOLIDAY** or 216/252-7700; fax 216/252-3850), is a family-style hotel, with full facilities, including a pool, restaurant, and access to a health spa. The **Sheraton Hopkins Airport,** 5300 Riverside Dr. (☎ **800/362-2244** or 216/267-1500; fax 216/ 265-3177), is located at the airport entrance and caters to the business traveler, with full facilities, including a fitness center. The **Marriott Cleveland Airport,** 4277 W. 150th St. (☎ **800/MARRIOT** or 216/252-5333; fax 216/251-1508), is off the freeway near the airport and offers full facilities to the business traveler.

## DINING

Cleveland's restaurants reflect its ethnic mix. In addition to the restaurants listed below, there are restaurant rows in The Flats, around Gund Arena and Jacobs Field, and in Cleveland Heights on Coventry Road.

**Balaton.** *12523 Buckeye Rd. (between 116th and 130th sts.).* ☎ *216/921-9691. Reservations accepted. Main courses $7–$12. No credit cards. Tues–Wed 11:30am–8pm, Thurs–Sat 11:30am–9pm. HUNGARIAN.* Family owned and operated in an older neighborhood, this restaurant has an old-world atmosphere and a menu of familiar favorites, with Wiener schnitzel a specialty.

**Baricelli Inn.** *2203 Cornell Rd. (University Circle).* ☎ *216/791-6500. Reservations recommended. Main courses $20–$30. AE, MC, V. Mon–Thurs 5:30–10pm, Fri–Sat 5:30–11pm. Valet parking. ITALIAN.* This restaurant offers fine dining in a landmark turn-of-the-century brownstone mansion. The menu features pastas and breads made in-house.

**Classics.** *In the Omni International Hotel, 2065 E. 96th St. (University Circle).* ☎ *216/791-1300. Reservations recommended. Main courses $18–$25. AE, DC, DISC, MC, V. Daily 11:30am–2:30pm; Mon–Thurs 5:30–9:30pm, Fri 5:30–10pm, Sat 5–10pm. Valet parking. CONTINENTAL.* Elegant hotel dining with excellent service is found here, including tableside preparation of steak Diane or rack of lamb.

**Great Lakes Brewing Company.** *2516 Market St. (Ohio City, 3 miles west of downtown).* ☎ *216/771-4404. Reservations recommended. Main courses $9–$15. AE, CB, DC, MC, V. Mon–Thurs 11:30am–10:30pm, Fri–Sat 11:30am–11:30pm, Sun 3–8pm. ECLECTIC.* Many original fixtures are still used at this oldest working bar in Cleveland (dating from 1870). The menu is filled with simple, satisfying foods that go along with beer, such as Market Street ribs.

**Hyde Park Grille.** *1823 Coventry Rd. (between Cedar and Mayfield).* ☎ *216/ 321-6444. Reservations recommended. Main courses $15–$48. AE, CB, DC, DISC, MC, V. Mon–Thurs 5:30–10pm, Fri–Sat 5–11pm. STEAK.* This popular chophouse is known for its sophisticated decor, award-winning wine list, and hefty portions of steak, seafood, and chicken.

**Sammy's.** *1400 W. 10th St. (The Flats).* ☎ ***216/523-5560.*** *Reservations recommended. Main courses $22–$29. AE, CB, DC, DISC, MC, V. Mon–Thurs 5:30–10pm, Fri–Sat 5:30pm–midnight. Complimentary valet parking. NEW AMERICAN.* Popular with a young, business-type clientele, who come here for the contemporary decor and spectacular views of the Cuyahoga River, Sammy's is also romantic. There's an award-winning wine list. The menu leans toward seafood, and chocolate swans are a dessert favorite.

**Sans Souci Mediterranean Cuisine.** *In the Renaissance Cleveland Hotel, 24 Public Square.* ☎ ***216/696-5600.*** *Reservations recommended. Main courses $9–$18. AE, CB, DC, DISC, MC, V. Mon–Fri 11:30am–2:30pm; Sun–Thurs 5:30–10pm, Fri–Sat 5:30–11pm. MEDITERRANEAN.* The French-countryside ambience is enhanced by wall murals by French artists. Roman pillars and beautiful views from every table complement the dining, with sautéed snapper a highlight.

**Sfuzzi, An Italian Bistro.** *In the Avenue at Tower City, 230 Huron Rd. NW.* ☎ ***216/861-4141.*** *Reservations recommended. Main courses $9–$18. AE, DC, MC, V. Mon–Sat 11am–4pm; Mon–Thurs 4–9pm, Fri–Sat 4–10pm, Sun 4–8pm; Sun brunch 10:30am–3pm. Complimentary valet parking. ITALIAN.* Brick and stucco walls make an attractive background for the black bistro tables and secluded booths, and there's a view of the open kitchen. Favorite dishes—all of them made with the freshest ingredients—include oven-baked focaccia.

**Sterle's Slovenian Country House.** *1401 E. 55th St. (off I-90).* ☎ ***216/881-4181.*** *Reservations recommended. Main courses $6–$11. MC, V. Daily 11:30am–3pm; Tues–Sat 3:30–9pm, Sun 3:30–8pm. GERMAN.* An authentic central European beer hall, with a large, open dining room with hand-hewn beams, and the occasional live polka band. Try the pierogi.

**Swingos on the Lake.** *In Carlyle Towers, 12900 Lake Ave., Lakewood.* ☎ ***216/221-6188.*** *Reservations recommended. Main courses $15–$25. AE, DC, DISC, MC, V. Mon–Wed 11:30am–10pm, Thurs–Sat 11:30am–midnight, Sun 1–8pm. Complimentary valet parking. CONTINENTAL.* The atmosphere at this classy rooftop dining room is romantic, with windows overlooking Lake Erie, a dance area at the piano bar, and candlelight dining. The emphasis is on classic preparation of seafood, steak, and pasta, and there's an extensive wine list.

## CLEVELAND AFTER DARK

Tickets for many events are sold through **Ticketmaster** (☎ 216/241-5555) and **Advantix** (☎ 216/241-6000).

**THE PERFORMING ARTS** Severance Hall, 1100 Euclid Ave. (☎ 216/231-1111), is home to the world-renowned ✪ **Cleveland Orchestra,** led by music director Christoph Von Dohnànyi. In summer the orchestra performs in **Blossom Music Center,** an outdoor venue. The **Playhouse Square Center,** 1519 Euclid Ave. (☎ 216/241-6000 for the schedule), is a symbol of Cleveland's cultural renaissance, an urban-renewal project that endowed the city with one of the largest performance and concert hall complexes in the country. Three theaters (the Ohio, the State, and the Palace) and an elegantly restored cabaret present theatrical and musical performances of all kinds. **Square Center,** 1501 Euclid Ave. (☎ 216/771-8403), is home to the **Cleveland Ballet,** the **Cleveland Opera,** and the **Great Lakes Theater Festival.**

**BARS & CLUBS** Nightlife is concentrated in **The Flats,** Old River Road between Front Avenue and Center Street, a formerly industrial section near the mouth of the Cuyahoga River. The area draws a young crowd. For a look at the old-time Flats, drop in at the **Harbor Inn,** 1219 Main Ave. (☎ 216/241-3232). The **Improv Comedy Club** (☎ 215/696-4677) performs in the Powerhouse, a restored former power station at the south end of the Flats. In the Warehouse district, at **Liquid Café and Bar,** 1212 West 6th St. (☎ 216/479-7717), pub patrons can hang out in comfortable chairs and play board games.

## 4 Cincinnati

The poet Longfellow called Cincinnati the "Queen City of the West," and today it remains one of the most attractive and dynamic cities in the Midwest. Located in Ohio's southwestern corner on the Ohio River, Cincinnati has a more Southern flavor than the rest of the state. It originated as a river crossroads used by local Indian tribes, and the first settlers from the East arrived in 1788. In the 19th century it became an important rail and river hub, and entertained many interesting visitors, among them Charles Dickens, John Audubon, and, of course, Henry Wadsworth Longfellow.

Cincinnati blends its past with its progress. The original character of the downtown district has been largely preserved. Its older buildings are joined to its skyscrapers by a pedestrian walkway network. It is a dynamic city, connected to Kentucky by the Roebling Suspension Bridge, and to the world of the arts with a respected symphony and ballet company. It is home to the University of Cincinnati, Hebrew University, and Xavier University, and its zoo and botanical garden are among the best in the country.

### ARRIVING & DEPARTING

**BY PLANE**　Major airlines fly into the **Cincinnati/Northern Kentucky International Airport. ComAir** (☎ 800/354-9822) also flies into the airport. **Jetport Express** (☎ 606/767-3702) has regular service to downtown hotels; cost is $10 one way, $15 round-trip. Cab fare is about $20.

**BY TRAIN & BUS**　Amtrak trains arrive at **Union Terminal,** 1301 Western Ave. The **Greyhound bus station** is at 1005 Gilbert Ave.

### ESSENTIALS

**VISITOR INFORMATION**　The **Greater Cincinnati Convention & Visitor Bureau** is at 300 W. 6th St., Cincinnati, OH 45202 (☎ 513/621-2142).

**EMERGENCIES & SAFETY**　In a serious emergency, call ☎ **911.** Cincinnati has a good safety record, but in any strange city, always keep alert. It's never a good idea to walk down dark streets alone at night, and major tourist areas always attract pickpockets; keep your purse or wallet in a safe place.

### GETTING AROUND

Downtown Cincinnati is a very walkable area, and the Skywalk System connects hotels, stores, and buildings above street level.

**BY PUBLIC TRANSPORTATION**　The **Queen City Metro** provides bus service (☎ 513/621-4455). Fare is 80¢ during peak hours, and 65¢ off peak, 50¢ weekends; seniors pay 40¢ at all times. Exact change, token, or Metro Monthly Card (available at Queen City Metro sales office, 122 W. 5th St.) is required.

### WHAT TO SEE & DO

**SPECIAL EVENTS**　In mid-May, the **Appalachian Festival** is a celebration of the best of mountain music, handicrafts, and folkways. Call ☎ 800/282-5393 for information. **Tall Stacks,** a riverboat festival, is held every other year; it will be held in November 1997.

# Cincinnati

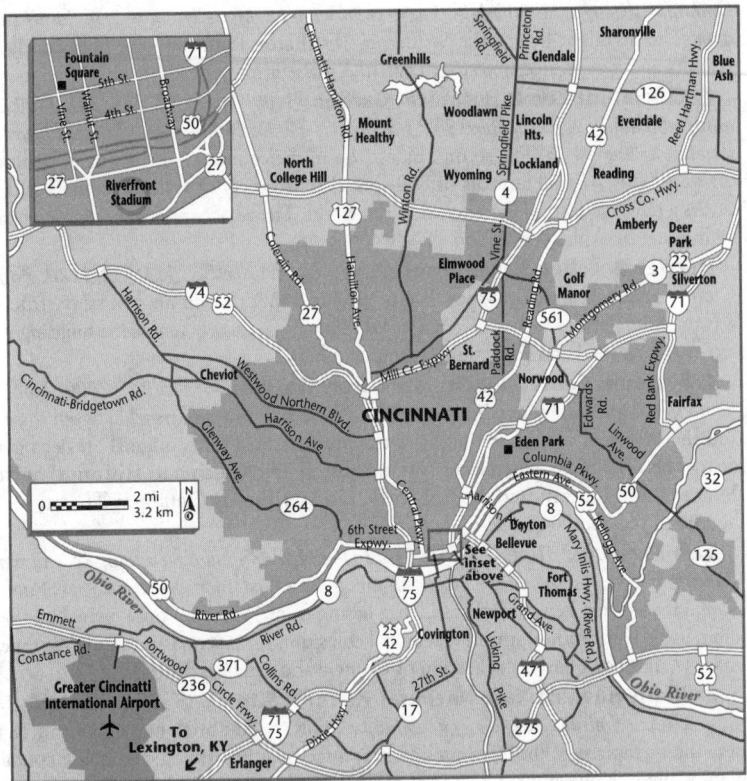

**ESCORTED TOURS**   The Museum Center offers a number of **Cincinnati Heritage Tours** by bus. Call ☎ **513/287-7000** for information about schedules and itineraries.

**CRUISES**   River cruises are offered by **BB Riverboats** near Covington Landing (☎ **606/261-8500**). The *Delta Queen* and the *Mississippi Queen,* historic paddle-steamers, dock at Cincinnati and offer cruises lasting from 3 to 10 days to St. Louis, Pittsburgh, and farther afield. Call ☎ **800/543-1949** for information.

**ATTRACTIONS**   The center of downtown Cincinnati is **Fountain Square,** a green oasis with gardens and a monumental fountain. East of downtown is the picturesque **Mt. Adams** section, with its old houses and narrow cobbled streets. The **Roebling Suspension Bridge** was built by John A. Roebling, later the builder of the Brooklyn Bridge; on the other side of the river, **Covington Landing** is a floating entertainment complex. For a great view of the city, visit the **Carew Tower Observatory,** 5th and Vine streets. The **Skywalk System** also offers views of the skyline.

   ✪ **Cincinnati Art Museum (CAM).** *Eden Park, off I-71.* ☎ **513/721-5204.** *Admission $5 adults, $4 for seniors and students, free for children under 18 and on Sat. Tues–Sat 10am–5pm, Sun noon–6pm.* The CAM houses a rich collection of European paintings, with emphasis on Impressionists and abstract painters. The permanent collection also includes sculptures, prints, photographs, costumes, tribal artifacts, and musical instruments.

   **Cincinnati Museum of Natural History.** *1301 Western Ave., in Union Station.* ☎ *513/287-7020. Admission $5.50 adults, $4.50 seniors, $3.50 for children 3-12.*

*Omnimax theater is $6.50 adults, $4.50 children 3-12. Mon–Sat 9am–5pm, Sun 11am–6pm.* The highlight here is the Wilderness Trail area, featuring local flora and fauna exhibits and a re-created limestone cavern. A planetarium offers shows.

✪ **Cincinnati Zoo & Botanical Garden.** *3400 Vine St.* ☎ *513/281-4700. Admission $8 adults, $5.75 seniors, $4.75 children 2-12. Daily 9am–5pm. Reduced hours off-season. Parking $4.75.* The second-oldest zoo in the country and still one of its finest, the park houses 6,000 animals of 800 species in a variety of realistic habitats and includes a feline collection unmatched in the world. The adjacent botanical garden boasts an international plant collection.

**Harriet Beecher Stowe House.** *2950 Gilbert Ave.* ☎ *513/632-5120. Admission free. Tues–Thurs 10am–4pm.* From 1832 to 1836, this simple two-story structure was the home of the author of *Uncle Tom's Cabin.* The newly renovated building now serves as a cultural and educational resource center.

✪ **Museum Center–Cincinnati Union Station.** ☎ *513/287-7000. Mon–Sat 9am–5pm, Sun 11am–6pm.* Built in 1931 to serve as a center of travel between the East and the Midwest, Union Station has since been restored to its original art deco grandeur. The Cincinnati Museum of Natural History, the **Cincinnati Historical Society Museum and Library,** and the **Robert D. Lindner Family Omnimax Theater** are all housed in the 50,000-square-foot complex.

**Taft Museum.** *316 Pike St.* ☎ *513/241-0343. Admission $4 adults, $2 seniors and students, free for children under 18. Admission free on Wed. Mon–Sat 10am–5pm, Sun 1–5pm.* Housed in a Federal-style residence dating from 1820 (and once owned by President Taft's half-brother), this fine regional collection focuses on paintings by European masters, and has a famous collection of Chinese and Limoges porcelain.

**William Howard Taft National Historic Site.** *2038 Auburn Ave.* ☎ *513/684-3262. Admission free. Daily 10am–4pm.* This modest brick home, built in 1840, was the birthplace of the 27th president. Now elegantly restored, the house contains family memorabilia and mementos from Taft's political and legal career.

**PARKS & GARDENS**   The 180-acre **Eden Park** on Mount Adams is the site of the **Krohn Conservatory** (☎ 513/421-4086) with more than 5,000 species of plants. **Bicentennial Commons** is an outdoor center at Sawyer Point on the Ohio River that tells the story of Cincinnati's river town origins.

**BEST BETS FOR KIDS**   The **zoo** and **parks** are favorites for kids, along with the **Omnimax theater** at the Museum Center in Union Station. Also at the Museum Center, the **Cincinnati Museum of Natural History** includes the Children's Discovery Center. Older kids may be interested in the **Harriet Beecher Stowe House** and the enduring impact of the author's *Uncle Tom's Cabin.* Kids will enjoy the **cruises** on the Ohio River (see above). In Kings Mills, 24 miles north of the city off I-71 at exit 24, is Paramount's **Kings Island Theme Park** (☎ 800/288-0808), which has a water park and the world's longest wooden roller coaster.

**SPORTS**   **Cinergy Field,** 201 E. Pete Rose Way (☎ 513/421-4510), located on the river, is the home of the **Cincinnati Reds** and the NFL's **Cincinnati Bengals.**

**SHOPPING**   There are many shops in the downtown area around 4th and 5th streets. Tower Place is an upscale mall at 4th and Race streets. It's connected by skywalks to Saks Fifth Avenue and McAlpin's.

## ACCOMMODATIONS

Many Cincinnati hotels offer weekend packages, including Cincinnati Reds games packages, or discount tickets to sights.

**Best Western Mariemont Inn.** *6880 Wooster Pike (exit 9 off I-71), Cincinnati, OH 45227.* ☎ *800/528-1234 or 513/271-2100. Fax 513/271-1057. 60 rms and suites.*

$60–$68 double; $75–$85 suite. Extra person $5. Children under 12 stay free in parents' room. AE, CB, DC, DISC, JCB, MC, V. Free outdoor parking. This landmark hotel in Cincinnati, in English Tudor style, dates back to 1926. Each room is different in size, shape, and style, and features antique wooden headboards.

○ **Cincinnatian Hotel Downtown.** *601 Vine St. (at 6th St.), Cincinnati, OH 45202.* ☎ *800/942-9000 or 513/381-3000, 800/332-2020 in Ohio. Fax 513/651-0256. 148 rms and suites. $175–$230 double; $200–$255 suite. Extra person $25. Children under 18 stay free in parents' room. Lower rates off-season. AE, CB, DC, DISC, ER, JCB, MC, V. Indoor parking $12.* This 1882 building, expensively renovated in 1987, offers elegance, from lobby to room furnishings. All units have minibars, and some offer terraces. The noted Palace restaurant here is highly recommended. There is a fitness center and sauna.

**Hampshire House Hotel & Conference Center.** *30 Tri-County Pkwy. (Springdale; 1 mile south off I-275), Cincinnati, OH 45246.* ☎ *800/543-4211 or 513/ 772-5440. Fax 513/772-1611. 150 rms and suites. $75 single or double; $125–$150 suite. Extra person $6. Children under 18 stay free in parents' room. Lower rates off-season. AE, DC, DISC, MC, V. Free outdoor parking.* This is a friendly, comfortable hotel in a quiet area near the Tri County Shopping Center, and it's a busy conference center. The sitting lobby is pleasant and the rooms are adequate. The restaurant serves breakfast and lunch only. There's a fitness center.

**Harley Hotel.** *8020 Montgomery Rd. (Kenwood; exit 12 off I-71), Cincinnati, OH 45236.* ☎ *800/321-2323 or 513/793-4300. Fax 513/793-1413. 152 rms and suites. $89–$99 double; $99–$110 suite. Extra person $10. Children under 18 stay free in parents' room. AE, CB, DISC, MC, V. Free outdoor parking.* Watch for the sign for the easily missed driveway here. All rooms have terraces and are well maintained and comfortable, with lounge chairs. There's a restaurant, two pools, and a fitness center.

**Imperial House Quality Inn West.** *5510 Rybolt Rd. (Western Hills; exit 11 off I-74 east and west), Cincinnati, OH 45248.* ☎ *800/543-3018 or 513/574-6000. Fax 513/574-6565. 197 rms, efficiencies, and suites. $48–$72 single or double; $72 efficiency; $110–$140 suite. Extra person $5. Children under 16 stay free in parents' room. During some weekends, rates increase. AE, CB, DC, DISC, MC, V. Free outdoor parking.* This hotel consists of two motel-style buildings and one four-story hotel-style building. Some rooms have terraces. There are laundry facilities and complimentary passes to a nearby fitness center.

○ **Omni Netherland Plaza.** *35 W. 5th St. (1 block west of Fountain Square), Cincinnati, OH 45202.* ☎ *800/843-6664 or 513/421-9100. Fax 513/421-4291. 621 rms, suites, and efficiencies. $165–$205 double; $350–$1,250 suite; $450 efficiency. Extra person $20. Children under 18 stay free in parents' room. AE, DC, DISC, MC, V.* The hotel is a National Historic Landmark, located downtown in the Carew Tower with shopping galore. It's popular with business travelers. The art deco style is carried out in room furnishings. Some units offer minibars, terraces, or whirlpools.

**Quality Inn Evendale.** *1717 Glendale Milford Rd. (exit 14 off I-75, 14 miles north of Cincinnati Center), Cincinnati, OH 45215.* ☎ *800/221-2222 or 513/771-5252. Fax 513/771-6569. 114 rms. $62–$68 double. Extra person $6. Children under 18 stay free in parents' room. Lower rates off-season. AE, DC, DISC, MC, V. Free outdoor parking.* Recently remodeled in a Southwestern decor, this hotel offers rooms with terraces, and has two pools, a sauna, and a steam room.

○ **Regal Cincinnati Hotel.** *150 W. 5th St. (1½ blocks west of Fountain Square), Cincinnati, OH 45202.* ☎ *800/876-2100 or 513/352-2100. Fax 513/352-2148. 887 rms and suites. $128–$138 single or double; $250–$350 suite. Extra person $10. Children under 17 stay free in parents' room. Lower rates off-season. AE, CB, DC, DISC, MC, V.*

A recent renovation gives this hotel a sparkling look. It is in the heart of downtown, across the street from the Cincinnati Convention Center. The beautiful Seafood 32 restaurant is highly recommended. The hotel offers basketball, racquetball, squash, and free passes to a fitness center.

**Signature Inn North.** *11385 Chester Rd. (exit 15 off I-75, next to Sharonville Convention Center), Cincinnati, OH 45246.* ☎ *800/822-5252 or 513/772-7877. Fax 513/ 772-7877. 130 rms. $63–$70 double. Extra person $7. Children under 17 stay free in parents' room. Rates increase during Jazz Festival in July. AE, DC, DISC, MC, V. Free outdoor parking.* This is an attractive property, with well-coordinated room decor, a pool, and a nearby fitness center.

**Travelodge.** *3244 Central Pkwy. (Clifton; exit 3 off I-75, two lefts to Central Pkwy.), Cincinnati, OH 45225.* ☎ *800/578-7878 or 513/559-1800. Fax 513/ 559-1807. 71 rms. $58–$68 double. Extra person $5. Children under 17 stay free in parents' room. Lower rates off-season. AE, CB, DC, DISC, MC, V. Free outdoor parking.* In the University of Cincinnati vicinity, this two-story hotel is built against a hill, affording no-stairs access to the second floor.

**♦ Vernon Manor.** *400 Oak St., Cincinnati, OH 45219 (Corryville; Taft Rd. exit off I-71).* ☎ *800/543-3999 or 513/281-3300. Fax 513/281-8933. 173 rms, suites, and efficiencies. $125–$145 double; $110–$425 suite; $125–$145 efficiency. Extra person $10. Children under 16 stay free in parents' room. Lower rates off-season. AE, CB, DC, DISC, MC, V. Free outdoor parking.* This 70-year-old Cincinnati landmark, noted for service and spaciousness, has hosted U.S. presidents and the Beatles. Near the University of Cincinnati, it offers suites or studio apartments. It has two restaurants and offers passes and transportation to a health club.

**Westin Hotel Cincinnati.** *21 E 5th St. (downtown), Cincinnati, OH 45202.* ☎ *800/228-3000 or 513/621-7700. Fax 513/852-5690. 448 rms and suites. $130–$195 single or double; $375–$1,200 suite. Extra person $25. Children under 18 stay free in parents' room. AE, CB, DC, DISC, ER, JCB, MC, V. Indoor self-parking $11; valet parking $14.* In the the center of Fountain Square, the centerpoint of downtown Cincinnati, this hotel is popular with businesspeople. Its location on the Skywalk connects it to many downtown locations, with shopping nearby. All units have minibars.

## DINING

Cincinnati offers visitors a range of outstanding restaurants. In addition to those listed below, check for recommended restaurants in the hotel descriptions above.

**Barresi's.** *4111 Webster Ave. (Deer Park).* ☎ *513/793-2540. Reservations recommended. Main courses $11–$24. AE, DC, DISC, MC, V. Mon–Sat 5–10:30pm. ITALIAN.* Patrons may feel they've arrived in Italy at this elegant restaurant, with a magnificent cappuccino and espresso machine, and a menu featuring both northern and southern Italian cuisine.

**Cherrington's.** *950 Pavilion St. (Mount Adams);* ☎ *513/579-0131. Reservations recommended. Main courses $10–$23. AE, MC, V. Tues–Fri 7–10am, Sat 8–11am; Tues– Fri 11am–3pm; Tues–Thurs 5–10pm, Fri–Sat 5–11pm, Sun 4–9pm; Sun brunch 11am– 3pm. Closed Aug 7–14. AMERICAN.* It looks like a tearoom, but this restaurant serves three meals a day. Order your ribeye roast beef with sautéed mushrooms from the large white menu board.

**El Coyote.** *7404 State Rd. (exit 69 off I-275 east).* ☎ *513/232-5757. Reservations not accepted. Main courses $7–$20. AE, DC, DISC, MC, V. Mon–Thurs 4–10pm, Fri 4– 11pm, Sat 1–11pm, Sun 1–10pm. TEX-MEX.* Patrons return again and again to this friendly Tex-Mex grill on a hill, with a fireplace and large portions of satisfying food served in two spacious dining rooms.

✪ **La Normandie.** *118 E. 6th St. (between Walnut and Main).* ☎ *513/721-2761. Reservations recommended. Main courses $14–$28. AE, CB, DC, DISC, MC, V. Mon– Fri 5–10pm, Sat 5–11pm. Valet parking. STEAK.* Popular in Cincinnati for 60 years, La Normandie is casual, with most seating in large booths or banquettes and peanut shells dotting the floor. The menu leans to steak, but other entrees are available.

✪ **Maisonette.** *114 E. 6th St. (between Walnut and Main).* ☎ *513/721-2260. Reservations recommended. Main courses $20–$75. AE, CB, DC, DISC, MC, V. Tues–Fri 11:30am–2pm; Mon–Fri 6–10:30pm, Sat 5:30–11pm. Free valet parking. FRENCH.* Unquestionably one of America's premier restaurants, founded in 1949, the Maisonette decor includes a large collection of paintings by Cincinnati artists offsetting the magnificent table settings. The menu is classic French cuisine, but includes dishes like red deer chop with pepper sauce.

**Morton's of Chicago.** *28 W. 4th St. (downtown, at Race St.).* ☎ *513/241-4104. Reservations recommended. Main courses $18–$30. AE, CB, DC, MC, V. Mon–Sat 5:30– 11pm, Sun 5–11pm. Valet parking. STEAK.* Dark wood and brick walls create a warm, comfortable ambience at this branch of a national chain noted for consistently top-quality steaks, with entrees cooked before your very eyes.

**Mullane's Parkside Cafe.** *723 Race St. (between 7th St. and Garfield Place).* ☎ *513/381-1331. Reservations not accepted. Main courses $6–$13. No credit cards. Mon– Thurs 11:30am–10pm, Fri 11:30am–11pm; Sat 5–11pm. ECLECTIC/HEALTH.* This smallish restaurant offers an art display, guitar music, and card readings for entertainment. Its most popular dish currently is spinach sautéed with zucchini, yellow squash, tomato, onion, black olives, basil, and feta cheese over rice and pasta.

**Orchids at Palm Court.** *35 W. 5th St. (1 block west of Fountain Square).* ☎ *513/564-6465. Reservations recommended. Main courses $16–$32. AE, DC, DISC, MC, V. Mon–Sat 11:30am–2pm; daily 6–10pm; Sun brunch 10am–2pm. Valet parking. REGIONAL AMERICAN/CONTINENTAL.* This famed restaurant is the essence of gourmet dining and diners enjoy the art deco stylings and jazz. Dine on grilled veal chop served on a giant marinated portobello mushroom.

**The Phoenix.** *812 Race St. (at 9th St.).* ☎ *513/721-8901. Reservations recommended. Main courses $11–$18. AE, CB, DC, DISC, MC, V. Tues–Fri 5–9pm, Sat 5:30– 10pm. Valet parking. AMERICAN.* Located in a century-old landmark building, with original architecture and features, The Phoenix offers a reasonably priced menu, including fettuccine with grilled chorizo sausage, roasted vegetables, garlic, and Parmesan.

**The Precinct.** *311 Delta Ave. (at Columbia Pkwy.).* ☎ *513/321-5454. Reservations recommended. Main courses $16–$29. AE, CB, DC, DISC, MC, V. Sun–Thurs 5– 9:45pm, Fri–Sat 5–10:45pm. Valet parking. STEAK.* This hot spot in a former police station is the place to go for high-energy atmosphere and top-flight steaks. You might rub shoulders with a celebrity.

**Skyline Chili.** *643 Vine St. (at 7th St.).* (☎ *513/241-2020. Reservations not accepted. Main courses $1–$5. No credit cards. Mon–Fri 10:30am–7pm, Sat 11am–3pm. CHILI.* Known across the country, Skyline Chili is a Cincinnati tradition. There are several ways to enjoy the uniquely flavored chili, including the "three-way" (spaghetti, chili, cheddar cheese), with diced onions and red beans. There are 80 Skyline Chili restaurants in the greater Cincinnati area, with 5 downtown. Additional locations include 580 Walnut (☎ 513/684-9600); 4th and Sycamore (☎ 513/241-4848).

## CINCINNATI AFTER DARK

To find out what's on, pick up two free newspapers, *City Beat* and *Everybody's News,* available in the downtown area, that provide detailed listings of concerts, performances, and clubs.

**THE PERFORMING ARTS** The **Music Hall,** 1241 Elm St. (☎ 513/721-8222), is the home of the ✪ **Cincinnati Symphony Orchestra.** The **Cincinnati Opera** and the **Cincinnati Pops Orchestra** also perform here.

Once dozens of river towns depended on traveling showboats for their entertainment. *Showboat Majestic,* 435 E. Mehring Way (☎ 513/241-6550), first launched in 1923, continues the tradition, presenting revues, comedies, dramas, and Broadway musicals. **Aronoff Center,** 6th and Walnut (☎ 513/621-2787), features Broadway shows, musical events, and plays, and is the home of the **Cincinnati Ballet** (☎ 513/621-5219), under artistic director Victoria Morgan.

**BARS & GRILLS** **Arnold's Bar and Grill,** 210 E. 8th St. (downtown between Main and Sycamore), (☎ 513/421-6234), is one of Cincinnati's oldest taverns and offers entertainment weekly, including Celtic, bluegrass, jazz, and swing. **Main Street** beyond Central Parkway has many bars, cafes, and microbreweries, many of which feature bands or other entertainment. **Upstairs at Carol's** at Carol's Corner Cafe, 825 Main St. (☎ 513/651-2667), is a piano bar and cabaret. There are many bars in Mount Adams with excellent city views that present nightly bands and other entertainment. **Incline,** the bar at the Celestial Restaurant, 1071 Celestial St. on Mount Adams (☎ 513/241-4455), features vocalists, cabaret, and jazz. **Rock Bottom Brewery,** 10 Fountain Square downtown (☎ 513/621-1588), often has bands on weekends.

## A DAY TRIP TO LEXINGTON, KENTUCKY

Historic Lexington, Kentucky, 72 miles south of Cincinnati, is the center of horse country. You can visit a training site and take a horse farm tour that includes the world-famous Calumet farm, birthplace of eight Kentucky Derby winners.

Take exit 20 off I-75 to reach the **Kentucky Horse Park,** 4089 Iron Works Pike (☎ 606/233-4303). This facility, complete with museums, offers horse-drawn carriage tours. A visit to the **Kentucky Horse Center,** an important training facility, will give you a behind-the-scenes look at thoroughbred racing. **Three Chimneys Farm,** where Triple Crown winner Seattle Slew was bred, is the place to tour for a view of breeding champions. Two- to 3-hour passenger van tours are offered by Margaret Woods's **Historic Horse Farm Tours,** 3429 Montavesta Rd. (☎ 606/268-2906). Tours include Keeneland Racecourse, Calumet and other farms, and vans pick up at all major hotels and motels.

Another interesting site in Lexington to visit is ✪ **Ashland,** the **Henry Clay Estate,** 120 Sycamore Rd. (☎ 606/266-8581). One of the most influential leaders in the pre–Civil War period, Clay's house contains personal furnishings from five generations of his family. The **Mary Todd Lincoln House,** 578 Main St. (☎ 606/233-9999), contains many Todd family pieces as well as her personal possessions.

Places to stay in Lexington include the **Campbell House Inn, Suites & Golf Club,** 1375 Harrodsburg Rd. (☎ 800/354-9235 outside Kentucky or 606/255-4281; fax 606/254-4368), a gracious hotel serving up Southern hospitality. The **Gratz Park Inn,** 120 W. 2nd St. (☎ 800/227-4362 or 606/231-1777; fax 606/233-1777), is a luxurious hotel in a historical district of downtown. The **Best Western Regency–Lexington Inn,** 2241 Elkhorn Rd. (☎ 800/528-1234 or 606/293-2202; fax 606/293-1821), is a good choice for families, offering extra-large rooms. **La Quinta Motor Inn,** 1919 Stanton Way (☎ 800/531-5900 or 606/231-7551; fax 606/281-6002), is conveniently located near the Kentucky Horse Park.

## 5 St. Louis

St. Louis began as a French trading post in 1764, and in pioneer days, it was the gateway to the west. Today its shining steel Gateway Arch, designed by Eero Saarinen in

# St. Louis

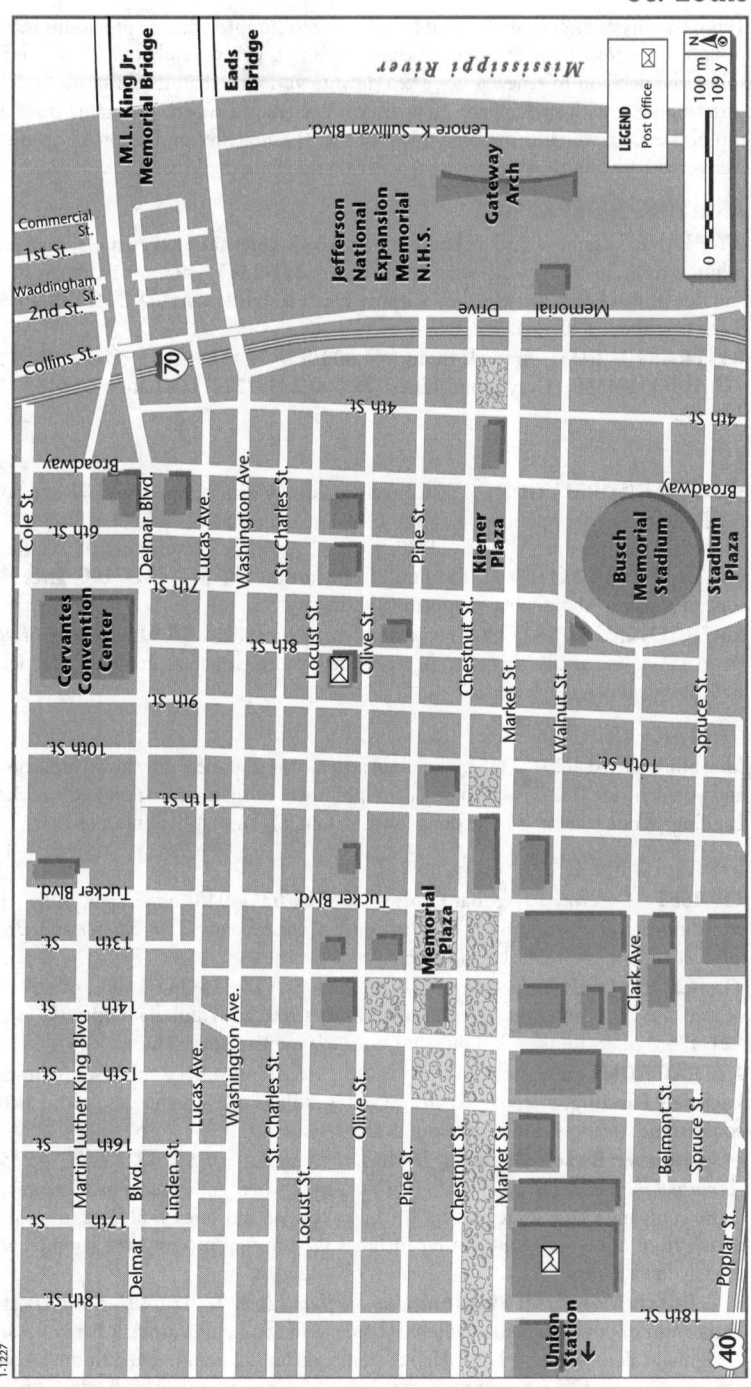

1966, commemorates western-bound pioneers who stopped here for provisions before pushing on across the great plains. The arch is also St. Louis's symbol of renewal: It inspired the decision to renew a neglected downtown rather than diminish the arch by surrounding it with skyscrapers. Now visitors can enjoy a superb panorama from the top of the arch, which is the centerpiece of the 91-acre Jefferson National Expansion Memorial Park and the picturesque renovated area along the Mississippi.

## ARRIVING & DEPARTING

**BY PLANE**    Flights arrive at **Lambert–St. Louis International Airport,** about 20 minutes from downtown. **Bi-State** bus (☎ **314/231-2345**) goes to downtown stops, and downtown hotels are served by **Airport Express** shuttle vans (☎ **314/429-4950**). Taxis cost about $20.

**BY TRAIN & BUS**    Amtrak trains (☎ **800/872-7245**) arrive at 550 S. 16th St. (☎ **314/331-3300**). **Greyhound Lines** (☎ **800/231-2222**) bus station is at 1450 N. 13th St.

## ESSENTIALS

**VISITOR INFORMATION**    The **Convention and Visitor Commission,** Metropolitan Building, 1 Metropolitan Sq., Suite 1100, St. Louis 63102 (☎ **800/888-3861** or 314/421-1023), is open weekdays 8:30am–5pm. A **visitor center** is at 308 Washington Ave. (☎ **314/241-1764**). The **Fun Phone hotline** (☎ **314/421-2100**) gives visitors information about what's happening in the city.

**EMERGENCIES & SAFETY**    For serious emergencies, call ☎ **911.** Whenever you are in an unfamiliar city, stay alert. In general, avoid deserted areas after dark, and don't walk alone on deserted streets.

## GETTING AROUND

**Metrolink** (☎ **314/231-2345**), a light-rail system, has stops near downtown attractions, and you can ride free on weekdays 10am–3pm between Union Station and Laclede's Landing. While you can explore downtown on foot, St. Louis is basically a driving city.

## WHAT TO SEE & DO

**CRUISES**    **Gateway Riverboat Cruises** (☎ **314/621-4040**) offers sightseeing trips and dinner cruises on replicas of 19th-century steamboats, *Tom Sawyer* and *Becky Thatcher,* leaving from St. Louis Levee.

**TOURS**    **St. Louis Tram Tours,** 1100 S. Sixth St. (☎ **314/241-1400**), offers tours of the city; in summer, in a replica of an open streetcar. **Vandalia Tours** (☎ **314/421-4753**) offers tours of St. Louis and tours to Grant's Farm by bus.

**ATTRACTIONS**    On the renewed Mississippi riverfront, you'll want to stroll through **Laclede's Landing,** a renovated area of old buildings and warehouses, with narrow cobblestone streets, and many boutiques and restaurants.

   **Anheuser-Busch Brewery Tours.** *13th and Lynch sts.* ☎ *314/577-2153. Admission free. Mon–Sat 9am–5pm.* This brewery is where Anheuser–Busch began and is the company's largest facility. Its 100 acres contain old brick buildings, the oldest dating from 1868. The guided tour includes the brewing process, free samples, and the Clydesdale horses.

   ✪ **Busch Memorial Stadium.** *100 Stadium Plaza.* ☎ *314/421-3060.* Located in the heart of downtown, the stadium is home to the St. Louis Cardinals baseball team. A highlight here is the St. Louis Hall of Fame, including items related to the legendary Stan Musial. On game evenings, the museum is open only to ticket holders. Tickets for tours of the stadium, including the press box and dugout, are available from the gift shop next to the Hall of Fame (☎ 314/421-3263).

✪ **Gateway Arch.** *Jefferson National Expansion Memorial, 11 N. 4th St.* ☎ *314/425-4465. Admission free. Memorial Day–Labor Day, daily 8am–10pm. Reduced hours off-season.* America's tallest monument commemorates westward expansion in the 1800s. Tram rides to the top can involve lengthy waits in summer and on weekends. Beneath the arch is the **Museum of Westward Expansion.**

**Missouri History Museum.** *Jefferson Memorial Building, Forest Park.* ☎ *314/746-4599. Admission free. Tues–Sun 9:30am–5pm.* This museum presents important events in the history of the city, the state of Missouri, and the American West. It also houses memorabilia from the people who played major roles in St. Louis's development, including Charles Lindbergh, Daniel Boone, and Lewis and Clark. Attached to the museum is the Missouri History Museum Library and Research Center (☎ 314/746-4500).

**Museum of Transportation.** *3015 Barrett Station Rd.* ☎ *314/965-7998. Admission $4 adults, $1.50 seniors and children 5-12. Daily 9am–5pm.* Exhibits cover 150 years of transportation history, including the Stanley Steamer and Model T.

✪ **St. Louis Art Museum.** *Forest Park.* ☎ *314/721-0067. Admission free. Tues 1:30–8:30pm, Wed–Sun 10am–5pm.* Housed in an American Renaissance–style building constructed for the 1904 World's Fair, this museum's pre-Colombian and German Expressionist collections are considered among the best in the world. Other galleries feature Islamic and ancient art, an Asian collection, an Egyptian collection, and art from Africa, Oceania, and the Americas. There are also displays of Chinese, European, and American decorative arts.

**St. Louis Cathedral.** *4431 Lindell Blvd.* ☎ *314/533-2824. Admission free. Daily 6am–6pm.* Something of a curiosity, this cathedral, begun in 1907, contains the largest collection of mosaics in the world, some 145 million pieces of stone and glass covering 83,000 square feet of ceilings, domes, arches, and wall panels.

**St. Louis Science Center.** *5050 Oakland Ave.* ☎ *800/456-7572 or 314/289-4444. Admission free. Sun–Thurs 9:30am–5pm, Fri–Sat 9:30am–9pm.* Interactive learning exhibits include dinosaurs, a laser show, and an earthquake center. There is also a live stage show featuring an "alien xenologist."

**St. Louis Union Station.** *1820 Market St.* ☎ *314/421-6655. Admission free. Mon–Thurs 10am–9pm, Fri–Sat 10am–10pm, Sun 11am–7pm.* At one time the busiest passenger-rail terminal in the United States, this restored 100-year-old terminal now contains a hotel, 80 specialty shops, restaurants, a 10-screen theater, and even a small lake.

**HISTORIC HOMES**   St. Louis has a number of unusually interesting 19th-century historic houses.

The **Campbell House Museum,** 1508 Locust St. (☎ 314/421-0325), is an elegant 1851 Victorian home with most of the original furnishings present. The Romanesque Revival–style 1889 **Cupples House,** 3673 W. Pine Blvd. (☎ 314/977-3025), is located on the campus of St. Louis University and contains 42 rooms and the McNamee Gallery, featuring modern paintings. The **Chatillon–De Menil Mansion,** 3352 De Menil Place (☎ 314/771-5828), was a four-room farmhouse in 1845, later expanded to 14 rooms in the Greek Revival style. It contains period furnishings and two oil paintings by Missouri artist George Caleb Bingham.

The oldest standing residence in downtown St. Louis, built in 1845, was the home of children's poet Eugene Field, who wrote "Little Boy Blue." The **Eugene Field House and Toy Museum,** 634 S. Broadway (☎ 314/421-4689), contains an antique toy and doll collection that spans more than 300 years.

The Greek Revival–style **Old Courthouse,** 11 N. 4th St. (☎ 314/425-4468), was the site of the 1857 Dred Scott trial and houses a museum and observation area in the rotunda.

The **Scott Joplin House,** 2658A Delmar Blvd. (☎ 314/533-1003), was the modest four-family antebellum home from 1900 to 1903 of the musician and composer known as the "King of Ragtime." Now a National Historic Landmark, guided tours are offered that include Joplin's second-floor apartment and conclude with a player-piano rendition of Joplin's best-known tunes.

**OTHER ATTRACTIONS**   Call for reservations and visit **Bob Kramer Marionettes,** 4143 Laclede Ave. (☎ 314/531-3313), to learn the history and craft of marionette making. At the **Dog Museum,** 1721 S. Mason Rd. (☎ 314/821-3647), you'll find a research library, lectures, art, artifacts, and literature dedicated to man's best friend. On Sunday, pedigree dogs are on display with their owners. The **National Bowling Hall of Fame,** 8th and Walnut streets (☎ 314/231-6340), presents the history of bowling from medieval Europe to the present. Housed here is a bowling alley as well as the American Bowling Congress and Women's International Hall of Fame.

**PARKS & ZOOS**   **Grant's Farm,** 10501 Gravois Rd. (☎ 314/843-1700), includes a log cabin built by Ulysses S. Grant in 1856, several years before he became the 18th president. Now a part of the 281-acre Busch estate (of Anheuser–Busch fame), the farm is open to the public, along with a game preserve, beer garden, antique carriage collection, and small zoo. The **Laumeier Sculpture Park,** 12580 Rott Rd., Sunset Hills (12 miles southwest of downtown) (☎ 314/821-1209), offers a 96-acre exhibition of freestanding contemporary sculpture in a rolling, partly wooded setting. Centered in the park, the **Laumeier Museum** mounts exhibits by contemporary artists. There are workshops for children, hiking trails, picnic sites, and live drama, music, and dance performances on summer evenings. Open daily 8am–sunset.

The **Missouri Botanical Garden,** 4344 Shaw (☎ 314/577-5100), opened in 1859, is the oldest botanical garden in the country. This 79-acre site is home to two rose gardens with 6,000 roses, as well as a Japanese garden and the world's first geodesic-dome greenhouse. Open daily 9am–8pm. The **St. Louis Zoological Park** (☎ 314/781-0900) spans 83 acres in Forest Park and is home to 2,800 animals. The Bird Cage dates from the 1904 World's Fair. Open daily 9am–5pm.

**BEST BETS FOR KIDS**   Children will enjoy many of the city's attractions, including the **Science Center** with its hands-on exhibits and the Discovery Room (for ages 4 to 10); the antique toys in the **Eugene Field House; Bob Kramer's Marionettes;** and the **zoo** (see above). **Magic House,** 516 S. Kirkwood Rd., Kirkwood (☎ 314/822-8900), 1 mile north of St. Louis, has a collection of interactive exhibits that encourage kids to challenge themselves and use all of their senses. **Six Flags Over Mid-America,** Allenton Road, Eureka (☎ 314/938-5300), is a huge amusement park about 30 miles southwest of St. Louis, off I-44. Among its attractions is a dolphin show.

## ACCOMMODATIONS

Many of St. Louis's big hotels are downtown or in the suburb of Clayton. For bed-and-breakfast options, contact **River Country Bed and Breakfasts,** 1900 Wyoming St., St. Louis 63118 (☎ 314-771-1993).

**✪ Adam's Mark Hotel.** *4th and Chestnut sts. (Memorial Dr. exit off I-70), St. Louis, MO 63102. ☎ 800/444-ADAM or 314/241-7400. Fax 314/241-6618. 910 rms and suites. $99–$209 double; $275–$1,200 suite. Children under 12 stay free in parents' room. AE, CB, DC, DISC, MC, V. Indoor parking $10.* An elegant hotel, Adam's Mark offers first-class rooms, some facing the Gateway Arch or the Mississippi River. The luxurious recommended **Faust's** restaurant is here. Facilities include two restaurants, two bars, two pools, a fitness center, racquetball court, spa, sauna, steam room, and whirlpool.

**Clarion Regal Riverfront Hotel.** *200 S. 4th St. (near Memorial Dr. exit off I-70), St. Louis, MO 63102. ☎ 800/325-7353 or 314/241-9500. Fax 314/241-6171.*

*780 rms and suites. $132–$152 double; $250–$1,000 suite. Extra person $10. Children under 18 stay free in parents' room. AE, CB, DC, DISC, MC, V. Indoor parking $9.* This popular, often busy convention hotel features two towers of rooms, some with terraces, and a revolving restaurant offering spectacular views. The hotel contains three restaurants, two bars, two pools, a fitness center, games room, and laundry facilities.

**Courtyard by Marriott.** *2340 Market St., St. Louis, MO 63101.* ☎ *800/ 321-2211 or 314/241-9111. Fax 314/241-8113. 151 rms and suites. $144 double; $400– $450 suite. Children under 18 stay free in parents' room. Lower rates on weekends. AE, CB, DC, DISC, MC, V. Free outdoor parking.* This hotel features rooms around an inner courtyard containing an expanse of green and a terrace. Some rooms offer views of downtown and the arch; most have king-size beds and sofas. Guests have access to one restaurant (breakfast only), a bar, fitness center, whirlpool, and laundry facilities. Another Courtyard by Marriott is at 11888 Westline Industrial Dr. (☎ 314/997-1200; fax 314/997-4215).

**✪ DoubleTree Mayfair Suites.** *806 St. Charles St., St. Louis, MO 63101.* ☎ *800/222-TREE or 314/421-2500. Fax 314/421-6254. 184 rms and suites. $155 double; $125–$175 junior suite. Extra person $10. Children under 19 stay free in parents' room. Lower rates off-season. AE, DC, DISC, JCB, MC, V. Outdoor parking $9.* Built in 1925, this luxury hotel was renovated in 1990 and is listed on the National Register of Historic Places. All of the spacious and modern rooms offer minibars, many have French doors separating the bedroom and parlor, and some have fireplaces or whirlpools. A restaurant, bar, and fitness center are on the premises.

**Drury Inn Gateway Arch.** *711 N. Broadway (near Convention Center St. exit off I-70), St. Louis, MO 63101.* ☎ *800/325-8300 or 314/231-8100. Fax 314/231-8100. 178 rms and suites. $99–$119 double or suite. Extra person $10. Children under 18 stay free in parents' room. Lower rates off-season. AE, CB, DC, DISC, MC, V. Free indoor parking.* Located in a building that once served as the city market, this newer hotel offers an array of services and fair rates and is well suited for business travelers and families. The soundproof rooms face either the inner atrium or outside. Guests appreciate the restaurant, bar, pool, and whirlpool.

**Embassy Suites.** *901 N. 1st St. (near Convention Center St. exit off I-70), St. Louis, MO 63102.* ☎ *800/362-2779 or 314/241-4200. Fax 314/241-6513. $125–$145 suite. Extra person $15. Children under 13 stay free in parents' room. Lower rates off-season. AE, CB, DC, DISC, JCB, MC, V. Outdoor parking $6.* This hotel features a skylight atrium with a courtyard, and extra nice touches and services. Rooms have refrigerators, and some rooms offer balconies or a view facing the arch. Facilities include a restaurant (lunch and dinner only), two bars, a pool, fitness center, sauna, steam room, whirlpool, games room, and washer/dryer.

**Hampton Inn.** *2211 Market St. (off U.S. 40), St. Louis, MO 63101.* ☎ *800/ HAMPTON or 314/241-3200. Fax 314/241-3200. 239 rms and suites. $105 double; $130 suite. Extra person $10. Children under 18 stay free in parents' room. Rates include continental breakfast. AE, DC, DISC, MC, V. Free indoor/outdoor parking.* This simple hotel, though tall, offers no view of downtown but is suitable for all travelers. The hotel has one restaurant (lunch and dinner only), a bar, pool, fitness center, whirlpool, and laundry facilities.

**Marriott Pavilion Downtown.** *1 Broadway (Memorial Dr. exit off I-70), St. Louis, MO 63102.* ☎ *800/228-9290 or 314/421-1776. Fax 314/331-9029. 672 rms and suites. $169–$185 double; $400–$550 suite. Extra person $10. Children under 12 stay free in parents' room. Lower rates off-season. AE, DC, DISC, JCB, MC, V. Indoor parking $11.* This plush, two-tower hotel is right beside Busch Stadium, home of the Cardinals. Some rooms provide views, minibars, or whirlpools. Extras include two restaurants, a bar, pool, fitness center, spa, sauna, steam room, whirlpool, games room, and laundry facilities.

**Oak Grove Inn.** *6602 S. Lindbergh Blvd. (at junction I-55), Mehlville, MO 63123.* ☎ *800/894-9449 or 314/894-9449. Fax 314/894-6859. 97 rms and suites. $47 double; $80 suite. Children under 13 stay free in parents' room. Lower rates off-season. AE, DC, DISC, MC, V. Free outdoor parking.* This is a comfortable, economy motel, and some units have whirlpools. Complimentary lobby coffee and juice, whirlpool, and laundry facilities are available.

**OTHER ACCOMMODATIONS** St. Louis's airport is on I-70 near many hotels and reliable budget motels. The **Holiday Inn Airport Oakland Park,** 4505 Woodson Rd., Woodson Terrace (exit 246 off I-70), St. Louis, MO 63134 (☎ 800/426-4700 or 314/427-4700; fax 314/427-6086), offers European character and homelike coziness. The **Radisson Hotel St. Louis Airport,** 11228 Lone Eagle Dr. (junction of I-70 and Lindberg), Brigeton, St. Louis, MO 66304 (☎ **800/333-3333** or 314/291-6700; fax 314/770-1205), greets guests with a large atrium lobby with a waterfall and fountain. The **St. Louis Airport Hilton,** 10330 Natural Bridge Rd., Woodson Terrace, St. Louis, MO 63134 (☎ **800/345-5500** or 314/426-5500), is directly across from the airport and offers a gracious, relaxing atmosphere.

## DINING

In addition to the choices below, many other restaurants are found in Laclede's Landing, in the Central West End, and in St. Louis Union Station. Also check hotel listings above for featured restaurants.

**Al's Steak House.** *1200 N. 1st St. (6th St. exit off I-70).* ☎ *314/421-6399. Reservations accepted. Main courses $20–$45. AE, MC, V. Mon–Sat 5–11pm. Free valet parking. SEAFOOD/STEAK.* A St. Louis favorite, Al's has been popular for business lunches and special occasions since 1926. No printed menu is offered at this old-time Italian restaurant; instead, the waiter displays a platter of steak, veal, rack of lamb, and seafood and carefully explains the preparations for each dish.

**Balban's.** *405 N. Euclid Ave. (Central West End).* ☎ *314/361-8085. Reservations recommended. Main courses $15–$20. AE, CB, DC, DISC, MC, V. Mon–Fri 11am–3pm, Sat–Sun 10am–3pm; Mon–Thurs 6–10:30pm, Fri–Sat 5:30–11:30pm, Sun 5–10:30pm. NEW AMERICAN.* One of the places to be seen in town, this hip, fun, cheerfully decorated West End standout offers some of the best New American food around. Chef David Timney works his magic with mesquite-grilled swordfish with wilted spinach and balsamic vinegar.

**Cafe de France.** *410 Olive St.* ☎ *314/231-2204. Reservations recommended. Main courses $17–$21; fixed-price meal $25–$28. AE, CB, DC, DISC, MC, V. Mon–Fri 11:30am–2pm; Mon–Thurs 5–10pm, Fri–Sat 5–11:30pm. FRENCH.* Crystal chandeliers and oil paintings set the scene for elegant, formal dining. Classic French cooking, marked by modern touches, is evident in the exquisite preparation and presentation. Poached salmon in red-wine sauce is a favorite specialty.

**Dierdorf & Hart's.** *In Union Station, 18th and Market sts.* ☎ *314/421-1772. Reservations recommended. Main courses $13–$37. AE, CB, DC, DISC, MC, V. Sun–Thurs 11am–10pm, Fri–Sat 11am–11pm. STEAK.* Relax in plush leather booths at this restaurant started by former local pro football stars Dan Dierdorf and Jim Hart. Enjoy excellent New York strip steak. Fresh fish, lobster, and sandwiches are also on the menu. An additional location is 734 Westport Plaza, Suite 262 (☎ **314/878-1808**).

✪ **Dominic's.** *5101 Wilson (The Hill).* ☎ *314/771-1632. Reservations recommended. Main courses $17–$23. AE, CB, DC, DISC, MC, V. Mon–Thurs 5–11pm,*

*Fri–Sat 5pm–midnight. ITALIAN.* Amid chandeliers and statuary, this formal temple of gourmet Italian dining provides seamless and classy service, a comprehensive wine list, and fantastic food. Veal saltimbocca is a reason to splurge.

**Gian-Peppe's.** *2126 Marconi.* ☎ *314/772-3303. Reservations recommended. Main courses $12–$24. AE, CB, DC, MC, V. Lunch Tues–Fri 11am–1:30pm; dinner Tues–Sat 5pm–10pm. Closed Mon. Free valet parking. ITALIAN.* Not the most famous Italian restaurant in St. Louis, but it does offer delicately prepared meals, and friendly and efficient service in a simple setting. You'll enjoy the veal, seafood, or pasta dishes offered here.

**Giovanni's.** *5201 Shaw.* ☎ *314/772-5958. Reservations recommended. Main courses $15–$39. AE, DC, DISC, MC, V. Mon–Sat 5–11pm. Valet parking. ITALIAN.* Elegant and romantic, this top trattoria offers some of the best pasta in town, served in a Renaissance-style room marked by large crystal chandeliers, paintings, and marble statues. Entrees include seafood, veal, lamb, chicken, and beef dishes. There is an additional location at 14560 Manchester Rd. (☎ *314/227-7230*).

✪ **Kemoll's.** *In Metropolitan Square, 211 N. Broadway (two blocks north of Busch Stadium).* ☎ *314/421-0555. Reservations recommended. Main courses $15–$30. AE, DC, DISC, MC, V. Mon–Fri 11am–2pm; Mon–Sat 5–10pm. Valet parking. Italian.* This attractive restaurant, decorated with paintings, elaborately framed mirrors, and luxurious drapes, offers a wonderful menu, including a noted selection of gourmet appetizers and salads. An excellent entree is the sautéed shrimp with sliced artichokes in a mustard cream sauce.

**Key West.** *In Union Station, 18th and Market sts.* ☎ *314/241-2566. Reservations not accepted. Main courses $6–$9. AE, CB, DC, DISC, MC, V. Mon–Sat 11am–2am, Sun 11am–midnight. Valet parking. SEAFOOD.* The emphasis here is on the sea, both in the decor and the cuisine. Fish nets and nautical photographs adorn the walls of this combination bar/restaurant. Great Key West specialties include conch fritters and shark. There is also a variety of burgers, sandwiches, and hot dogs.

**La Sala.** *513 Olive (between Broadway and 6th St.).* ☎ *314/231-5620. Reservations not accepted. Main courses $4–$8. AE, CB, DC, DISC, MC, V. Mon–Sat 11am–10pm. MEXICAN.* This local favorite for weekday happy hour offers fajitas, fajitas, and more fajitas. The menu at this dark and cozy place is also strong on burritos, enchiladas, and chimichangas.

**Patty Long's 9th St. Abby.** *1808 S. 9th St. (two blocks south of Soulard Market).* ☎ *314/621-9598. Reservations recommended. Lunch only. Main courses $7–$12. AE, DC, DISC, MC, V. Tues–Fri 11am–2pm, Sun 10am–2pm. Valet parking. ECLECTIC.* A renovated church, complete with high ceilings and stained-glass windows, Patty's menu includes a don't-miss turkey harvest pie: breast of turkey in a rich, white-wine cream sauce with fresh vegetables, topped with a flaky pastry.

✪ **Tony's.** *410 Market St. (Pine St. exit off I-70).* ☎ *314/231-7007. Reservations recommended. Main courses $19–$29. DC, DISC, MC, V. Mon–Thurs 5–11pm, Fri–Sat 5–11:30pm. Free valet parking. ITALIAN.* Agreement is near unanimous that Tony's is the finest restaurant in St. Louis. Great attention to detail—in the elegant setting, with its marble pillars, statues, and oil paintings, in the exquisite cuisine, and in the top-flight service—is the reason. Seafood is flown in daily. Try the thick veal chops.

## ST. LOUIS AFTER DARK

To find out what's on, consult the **St. Louis Post-Dispatch's** Thursday calendar or the free weekly *Riverfront Times*. For tickets to major events, call **Dialtix** (☎ **314/969-1800**) or Metro-Tix (☎ **314/534-1111**).

**THE PERFORMING ARTS**   **Powell Symphony Hall,** 718 N. Grand Blvd. (☎ 314/
533-2500), is the home of the ✪ **St. Louis Symphony Orchestra.** Shows, ballet, and
concerts are staged at the **Fabulous Fox Theatre,** 527 N. Grand Blvd. (☎ 314/
533-2500). The **Riverport Amphitheatre,** 14141 Riverport Dr. (☎ 314/298-9944),
presents big-name concerts by the likes of Jimmy Buffett, Tina Turner, and Santana.
The **Repertory Theater of St. Louis** (☎ 314/968-4925) presents a season of traditional and Broadway plays.

**CLUBS & CASINOS**   St. Louis's nightlife is concentrated around **Laclede's Landing** and in **Soulard,** on the south edge of downtown. You can gamble at the **President
Riverboat Casino,** 800 N. 1st St. (☎ 314/622-3000), the **Casino St. Charles,** South
5th Street (☎ 314/949-7777), or a dozen others.

## 6 Kansas City

Although it's Missouri's second-largest city, Kansas City, straddling the Missouri–Kansas
line, has managed to retain something of a small-town atmosphere, with tree-lined
streets and a large number of parks spread out over gently rolling hills. It has an interesting history as a frontier fur-trading post, a last stop for wagon trains heading over the
Santa Fe and Oregon trails. In one of the country's richest agricultural areas, it has been
home to the second-largest stockyard, and the largest slaughterhouse. Between the two
World Wars, along Vine and 18th streets in an area known as "Little New York" and
now a historic district, it produced musicians "Fats" Waller, Count Basie, and Charlie
Parker and his Kansas City bebop.

### ARRIVING & DEPARTING

**BY PLANE**   **Kansas City International Airport** is about 30 minutes north of downtown, served by major domestic airlines. **KCI Shuttle buses** (☎ 816/243-5950) goes
to downtown hotels; fare is $11. **Taxi** fares are zoned; the maximum fare to downtown
is $26.

**BY TRAIN & BUS**   **Amtrak trains** arrive at 2200 Main St. (☎ 816/421-3622). The
**Greyhound Bus** station is at 11th Street and Troost Avenue.

### GETTING AROUND

Kansas City is a driving city; while the downtown is compact, attractions are located
throughout the city. **Kansas City Trolley** (☎ 816/221-3399) runs a circuit through
downtown, Crown Center, Westport, and Country Club Plaza in replica trolleys.

### WHAT TO SEE & DO

**SPECIAL EVENTS**   The **Kansas City Blues and Jazz Festival** takes place the third
weekend in June. The first Friday and Saturday in October the **American Royal Barbecue contest** takes place in the American Royal Complex with teams competing from
all over the country.

**ATTRACTIONS**   Downtown Kansas City is a combination of old and new. The sky-
line is a blend of art deco buildings and modern skyscrapers, dominated by the "Sky
Stations/Pylon Caps," a set of four steel sculptures atop the city's convention center.
They look best when lighted at night.

   ***Arabia* Steamboat Museum.** *400 Grand Ave.* ☎ *816/471-4030. Admission
$6.50 adults, $6 seniors, $3.75 children 4-12. Mon–Sat 10am–6pm, Sun noon–5pm.* This
steamboat sank in 1856 and was preserved with its cargo in the cold mud of the Missouri River until it was unearthed in 1988. The many items on display range from china
to tools and hardware, from leather boots and shoes to jewelry, from glass bottles of
ketchup to perfume. A short film is also shown.

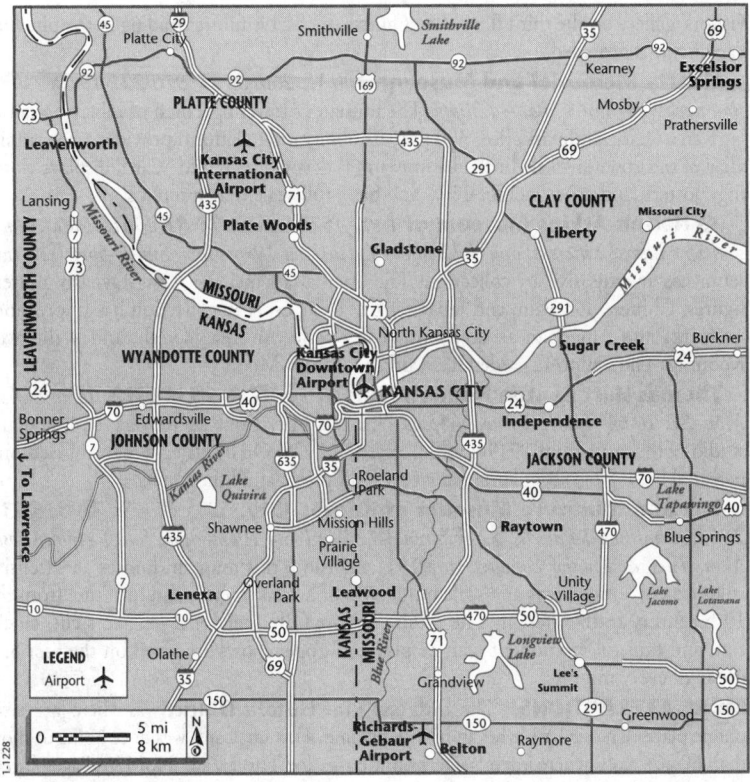

**Country Club Plaza.** *47th and Main sts.* ☎ *816/753-0100. Mon–Wed and Fri–Sat 10am–7pm, Thurs 10am–9pm, Sun noon–5pm.* The country's first suburban shopping center features Spanish courtyards and stucco buildings with red-tile roofs. Visitors can browse through shops and restaurants set among sculptures and fountains, and can take a ride in a horse-drawn carriage.

**Crown Center.** *2450 Grand Ave.* ☎ *816/274-8444. Mon–Wed and Sat 10am–6pm, Thurs–Fri 10am–9pm, Sun noon–5pm.* This 85-acre living-and-working environment, owned by the Hallmark Company, contains shops, restaurants, an outdoor ice-skating rink, a theater, a children's theater, and Kaleidoscope, a free creative art workshop for children. There's also the Hallmark Visitor Center with displays on Hallmark entertainment, products, and a film about craftspeople at work.

**John Wornall House Museum.** *146 W. 61st Terrace (Brookside).* ☎ *816/ 444-1858. Admission $3 adults, $2.50 seniors, $2 children 12 and under. Feb–Dec, Tues– Sat 10am–4pm, Sun 1–4pm. Closed Jan.* This Greek Revival farmhouse was built in 1858. Located near the dividing lines of the Civil War, it was the site of hospitals for both the Confederate and Union armies. Today tours re-create the daily life of a typical prosperous farm family in the years just before the Civil War. Tours include the gardens and open-hearth cooking demonstrations.

**Kansas City Board of Trade.** *4800 Main St., 3rd floor.* ☎ *816/753-7500. Mon–Fri 8:30am–3:15pm.* This is the world's predominant marketplace for wheat and grain sorghum, and a trading place for soybeans, corn, and oats, founded in 1856. A visitors' gallery on the third floor allows guests to observe futures trading in the pit, with explanations provided.

**Liberty Memorial and Museum.** *100 W. 26th St.* ☎ *816/221-1918. Admission free. Wed–Sun 9:30am–4:30pm.* The museum's towering Torch of Liberty, a familiar Kansas City landmark, rises 300 feet. Its observation platform provides a panoramic view of the downtown skyline. The museum is devoted to World War I, displays clothing, posters, and other memorabilia, and has a full-scale trench replica.

✪ **Nelson-Atkins Museum of Art.** *4525 Oak St.* ☎ *816/561-4000. Admission $5 adults, $2 students and children 6-18. Tues–Sat 10am–5pm, Sun 1–5pm.* The museum has an extensive art collection. The oriental art includes Tang Dynasty pottery figures, Chinese porcelain, and Japanese art. The European collection has Impressionist works and American artists Georgia O'Keeffe, Andrew Wyeth, and Willem de Kooning. The sculpture garden has works by Henry Moore.

**Thomas Hart Benton Home.** *3636 Belleview.* ☎ *816/931-5722. Admission $2. Mon–Sat 10am–4pm, Sun noon–5pm.* This 2½-story stone house was the home and studio of the artist from 1939 until his death in 1975. On display are many of Benton's personal belongings, some original works, and prints and lithographs.

**Toy and Minature Museum of Kansas City.** *5235 Oak St.* ☎ *816/333-2055. Admission $4 adults, $2 children 3-12. Wed–Sat 10am–4pm, Sun 1–4pm. Closed Mon, Tues, and major holidays.* In a 1911 mansion, this museum houses an extensive collection of antique toys and scale miniatures of houses, rooms, and furniture from the 19th century to the present. The miniatures are fully functional—scissors cut, clocks run, and musical instruments can be played. Puppet shows are given on the first Saturday of every month.

**MORE ATTRACTIONS** The **18th and Vine Historic District** was where jazz saxophone player Charlie Parker began his rise to fame. This small area was once home to more than 60 jazz clubs where legends like Count Basie, Joe Turner, and Hot Lips Page played. In the area is the **Negro Leagues Baseball Museum,** 160l E. 18th St. (☎ **816/221-1920**); baseball's Negro National League was founded in Kansas City in 1920. On the western edge of the city, **Westport** is a lively area of restored 19th-century streets and historic buildings, with festivals, shops, art galleries, restaurants, and live-music clubs.

**BEST BETS FOR KIDS** Children enjoy the *Arabia* Steamoat Museum and the Toy and Minatures Museum. **Worlds of Fun** and **Oceans of Fun,** 4545 Worlds of Fun Ave. (☎ **816/454-4545**), feature rides, water rides, pools, shows, and attractions. Worlds of Fun is open Sun–Fri 10:30am–sunset, Sat 10am–sunset; reduced hours off-season and closed Nov–Mar. Oceans of Fun is open the same hours from Memorial Day to Labor Day.

**SPECTATOR SPORTS** The **Kansas City Royals** play at Royals Stadium, and the **Kansas City Chiefs** football team plays at Arrowhead Stadium, both in the Harry S. Truman Sports Complex, on I-70 (☎ **816/921-8000** for the Royals, or **816/924-9400** for the Chiefs).

## ACCOMMODATIONS

If you'd prefer to stay in a B&B, contact **Bed and Breakfast Kansas City** (☎ **913/888-3636**), for bed-and-breakfast options.

✪ **Crowne Plaza.** *4445 Main St., Kansas City, MO 64111.* ☎ *800/2-CROWNE or 816/531-3000. Fax 816/531-3007. 296 rms and suites. $119–$149 double; $175–$350 suite. Extra person $10. Children under 18 stay free in parents' room. Lower rates off-season. Free parking. AE, CB, DC, DISC, MC, V.* Convenient and luxurious, for an exceptional vacation in the city, this hotel is worth the money. Floral drapes, potted trees, flowers, and plants accent the lobby. A honeymoon package is available. Facilities include a restaurant, bar, spa, and whirlpool.

**Historic Suites.** *612 Central Ave., Kansas City, MO 64105.* ☎ *800/733-0612 or 816/824-6544. Fax 816/842-0656. 100 suites. $79–$180 suite. AE, DC, DISC, MC, V. Free parking.* This tastefully decorated hotel in the garment district has hallways that overlook an atrium. Rooms have plants, sofas, refrigerators, and ceiling fans. VCRs are available on request. The hotel offers a spa, sauna, whirlpool, laundry facilities, free access to Gold's Gym, and complimentary shuttle to restaurants and shopping areas.

✪ **Hotel Savoy.** *219 W. 9th St., Kansas City, MO 64105.* ☎ *800/728-6922 or 816/842-3575. Fax 816/842-3575. 14 suites. $80–$120 suite. Extra person $20. Rates include breakfast. AE, CB, DC, DISC, MC, V. Free outdoor parking.* Kansas City's oldest hotel, in the old garment district, is slowly transforming itself into a European-style bed-and-breakfast. A gorgeous stained-glass dome lights the lobby, which is hung with paintings; an art gallery is adjacent. Furniture in the rooms is old but attractive. The hotel has a restaurant, bar, and laundry facilities.

**Park Place Hotel.** *1601 N. Universal Ave., Kansas City, MO 64120.* ☎ *800/ 821-8532 or 816/483-9900. Fax 816/231-1418. 328 rms. $59–$125 single or double. Packages available. AE, CB, DC, DISC, MC, V. Free outdoor parking.* This clean and bright hotel has friendly service and spacious public areas, and has easy access to I-435. Some units have terraces; some rooms have data ports. Extras include a restaurant, bar with entertainment, sauna, and steam room. Worlds of Fun and Oceans of Fun packages are available.

**Plaza Inn.** *1 E. 45th St., Kansas City, MO 64111.* ☎ *800/525-6321 or 816/ 753-7400. Fax 816/753-0359. 229 rms and suites. $69–$99 single or double; $109–$175 suite. Children under 17 stay free in parents' room. AE, CB, DC, DISC, JCB, MC, V. Free indoor/outdoor parking.* On Country Club Plaza, the Plaza Inn is near restaurants, shops, and entertainment spots. Some units have terraces; all have data ports and voice mail. Facilities include a restaurant, bar, and games room. Casino, shopping, and other packages are available.

✪ **The Raphael.** *325 Ward Pkwy., Kansas City, MO 64112.* ☎ *800/821-5343. 123 rms and suites. $95–$115 double; $120–$150 suite. Extra person $20. Children under 18 stay free in parents' room. AE, CB, DC, DISC, EC, JCB, MC, V. Free indoor/outdoor parking.* On Country Club Plaza, within walking distance of shops and restaurants, this hotel is wonderfully decorated with plants and marble tile. Rooms have refrigerators and minibars, data ports, and voice mail. The hotel has a restaurant (no breakfast), laundry facilities, and guests have access to a nearby fitness center and pool.

**Ritz-Carlton.** *401 Ward Pkwy., Kansas City, MO 64112.* ☎ *800/241-3333 or 816/756-1500. Fax 816/531-1483. 373 rms and suites. $149–$159 single or double; $159–$229 suite. AE, CB, DC, DISC, MC, V. Free indoor parking.* If you're looking for something extra, this is the place to stay. An elegant hotel with marble tiles and wooden pillars in the lobby, it's on Country Club Plaza near restaurants and shopping. Rooms are spacious, and have marble counters and crystal fixtures; all units have minibars and terraces, safes, and data ports. Baby-sitting is available. **The Grill** restaurant is highly recommended. There are two bars with entertainment, a spa, sauna, and steam room.

**Sheraton Suites Country Club Place.** *770 W. 47th St., Kansas City, MO 64112.* ☎ *800/227-2416 or 816/934-4400. Fax 816/561-7330. 259 suites. $159–$229 suite. Extra person $20. Children under 18 stay free in parents' room. AE, CB, DC, DISC, EC, ER, JCB, MC, V. Free indoor parking.* This better-than-average hotel is within walking distance of more than 180 shops, restaurants, and entertainment spots. It's a great place for weekend visits. Some units have terraces; all have refrigerators and data ports.

Baby-sitting and Nintendo games are available. The hotel has a restaurant, bar with entertainment, whirlpool, and laundry facilities.

**Southmoreland on the Plaza.** *116 E. 46th St., Kansas City, MO 64112. 12 rms.* ☎ *815/531-7979. Fax 816/531-2407. $100–$145 double. AE, MC, V. Free outdoor parking.* This bed-and-breakfast is in a peaceful setting with great views on a shaded, landscaped lot. Rooms are decorated with Shaker- and Chippendale-style furniture. Some units have terraces or fireplaces, and some have whirlpools. Service by a friendly staff is great. There's a guest lounge and free access to a nearby fitness center with a pool and tennis courts. Meals are served on a screened porch or solarium. It's not suitable for children under 15.

**Travelodge.** *1051 N. Cambridge Ave., Kansas City, MO 64120.* ☎ *800/500-7878 or 816/483-7900. Fax 815/483-8887. 134 rooms and suites. $50–$55 single or double; $75 suite. Extra person $5. Children under 19 stay free in parents' room. CB, DC, DISC, EC, ER, JCB, MC, V. Free outdoor parking.* Easy access to I-435 makes this small and comfortable property a convenient choice for an overnight or weekend stay. The hotel has a basketball court, whirlpool, and laundry facilities.

## DINING

Kansas City is known for steak and barbecue. Country Club Plaza and Westport have many eating places, from elegant restaurants to neighborhood cafes.

✪ **American Restaurant.** *In the Crown Center, 200 E. 25th St.* ☎ *816/426-1133. Reservations recommended. Main courses $18–$26. AE, CB, DC, MC, V. NEW AMERICAN.* One of the top places in the city for fine dining, this formal place has oak and satin-wood furniture and high ceilings. The extensive menu features Missouri farm-raised ostrich, and such dishes as coriander-encrusted rack of lamb with squash linguine and oven-roasted bell peppers, or seared sea scallops with lemongrass-shitake broth and jasmine rice.

**Arthur Bryant's.** *1727 Brooklyn.* ☎ *816/231-1123. Main courses $6–$14. AE, MC, V. Mon–Sat 5:30–10pm; Sun 10am–2pm and 5–9pm. BARBECUE.* Once you try the barbecue here, you might want to take a jar of the sauce home with you. The decor is clean and simple, fitting this barbecue sandwich joint.

**Cafe Allegro.** *1815 W. 39th St.* ☎ *816/561-3663. Reservations recommended. Main courses $16–$22. Mon–Fri 11:30am–2pm; Mon–Sat 6–10pm. NEW AMERICAN.* Casually elegant and cheerful, this restaurant draws a well-to-do older crowd. A favorite is the thick swordfish steak grilled over pecan wood atop a zesty couscous with a relish of roast tomato and niçoise olive. Some 40 wines are available by the glass.

**Fedora Cafe and Bar.** *210 W. 47th St.* ☎ *816/561-6565. Reservations recommended. Main courses $12–$24. AE, CB, DC, DISC, ER, MC, V. Mon–Sat 7–10:30am and 11:30am–4:30pm; Sun brunch 9am–4:30pm; Sun–Thurs 4:30–11pm, Fri–Sat 4:30pm–midnight. ECLECTIC.* On Country Club Plaza, this is a place for special occasions, handsomely decorated with stained-glass fixtures and dark wood dividers. The menu changes weekly and seasonally in order to take advantage of fresh vegetables and game available in the market. It's also known for its wide selection of handcrafted beers and single-malt scotches.

**Figlio.** *209 W. 46th St.* ☎ *816/561-0505. Reservations recommended. Main courses $8–$15. AE, DC, DISC, MC, V. Mon–Thurs 11am–10pm, Fri–Sat 11am–11pm, Sun 10:30am–10pm. ITALIAN.* On Country Club Plaza, this place is a fine choice for wood-fired pizza and homemade pasta. The simple dining area has old photographs from Italy on the walls. A favorite dish is Gorgonzola-stuffed veal scallopini, pan-seared and finished with port-wine glaze and shiitake mushrooms.

**Gates & Sons B-B-Q.** *47th and Paseo sts.* ☎ *816/921-0409. Reservations not accepted. Main courses $4–$11. Mon–Sat 10am–2am, Sun 10am–midnight. BARBECUE.* This joint ranks as one of the city's best, and it's been around since 1945. An ingratiating staff serves up tasty ribs with spicy sauce, sandwiches, sausages, and chicken.

**Hereford House.** *20th and Main sts.* ☎ *816/842-1080. Reservations recommended. Main courses $11–$24. AE, CB, DC, DISC, MC, V. Mon–Fri 11am–10pm, Sat 4–10:30pm, Sun 4–9pm. STEAK.* Here since 1957, this place serves prime beef; a favorite is steak Dijon, a filet topped with Dijon mustard and melted brown sugar. Lots of seating is in comfortable upholstered booths. The menu also has lobster, shrimp, and fish; burgers are on the lunch menu.

**✪ Jasper's.** *405 W. 75th St.* ☎ *816/363-3003. Reservations recommended. Main courses $16–$27. AE, CB, DC, DISC, MC, V. Mon–Thurs 6am–10pm, Fri–Sat 6am–11pm. CONTINENTAL/ITALIAN.* A Kansas City gem, offering fine dining and highly professional service. The formal, elegant setting includes Italian crystal and mirrors. A varied menu is offered; outstanding is conchiglia alla Sorrento (fresh scallops in a buttery sherry cream sauce over angel-hair pasta) and other pastas.

**Margarita's.** *2829 Southwest Blvd.* ☎ *816/931-4849. Reservations not accepted. Main courses $7–$8. AE, DISC, MC, V. Sun–Thurs 11am–10pm, Fri–Sat 11am–11:30pm. MEXICAN.* This lively, popular eatery offering Mexican fare and burgers is often crowded. Margarita's special is a flour tortilla stuffed with pork, beef, beans, cheese, and onions, topped with chili con queso.

**Metropolis.** *303 Westport Rd.* ☎ *816/753-1550. Reservations recommended. Main courses $8–$17. AE, CB, DC, DISC, ER, MC, V. Mon–Thurs 11:30am–10pm, Fri 11:30am–11pm; Sat 5–11pm, Sun 4–9pm. NEW AMERICAN/ECLECTIC.* This sophisticated spot is a hit with those looking for inspired grill fare. The decor is chic and very contemporary, and the menu shows a mix of American, Greek, Italian, and Vietnamese influences.

**✪ Plaza III—The Steakhouse.** *4749 Pennsylvania Ave.* ☎ *816/753-0000. Reservations recommended. Main courses $16–$29. AE, DC, MC, V. Mon–Sat 11:30am–2:30pm; Mon–Sun 5:30–10pm. STEAK.* This handsome restaurant in the Country Club Plaza is known throughout the country. It serves superb steaks, prime rib, and seafood, including its famous steak soup.

## KANSAS CITY AFTER DARK

For information check the Friday and Sunday editions of the *Kansas City Star*. For tickets to main events, call **TicketMaster** (☎ 816/931-3330). Much of the city's nightlife can be found in the Westport and the Country Club Plaza areas. For information about what's going on in Kansas City's jazz and blues clubs, call the **Jazz hotline** (☎ 816/763-1052).

**THE PERFORMING ARTS**   The **Lyric Theater,** 11th and Central streets (☎ 816/471-7344), is the venue for the **Kansas City Symphony** and the **Lyric Opera of Kansas City.** The city is home to the **State Ballet of Missouri** (☎ 816/931-2232), which performs at various venues. Concerts and events are presented at the **Midland Center for the Performing Arts,** 1228 Main St. (☎ 816/471-8600), and the **Folly Theater,** 12th and Central streets (☎ 816/842-5500).

**CLUBS & BARS**   Many bars and clubs are located in the Westport historic area and in the 18th and Vine Historic District. **Club 427,** 427 Main St. (☎ 816/421-2582), has live jazz nightly and offers a fine New American cuisine. **Jardine's Restaurant,** 5436 Main St. (☎ 816/561-6480), has live jazz nightly. **John's Food and Drink,** 928 Wyandotte (☎ 816/474-5668), is a three-story bar with live blues and jazz and a dance club. Live blues and jazz is also featured at the **Mardi Gras Club,** 1600 E. 19th St. (☎ **816/842-8463**). The **Mutual Musicians Foundation,** 1823 Highland Ave. (☎ **816/421-9297**), opens after midnight for jam sessions. The **Phoenix Club,** 302 W. Eighth St. (☎ **816/472-0001**), specializes in Kansas City–style jazz. **Blayney's,** 415 Westport Rd. (☎ **816/561-3747**), offers blues, jazz, R&B, and rock in a pub setting. For blues, try the **Grand Emporium,** 3832 Main St. (☎ **816/531-1504**).

**RIVERBOAT GAMBLING**   **Riverboat gambling** takes place on noncruising boats along the banks of the Missouri River. Some of those in the area are the *Argosy,* Mo. 9 and I-635, Riverside (☎ **816/741-7568**); *Harrah's Casino,* Armour Road, North Kansas City (☎ **816/471-3364**); and *Sam's Town,* East 18th Street, North Kansas City (☎ **816/764-4757**).

## 7 Branson & the Ozarks

The Ozark region of southern Missouri is a beautiful region of wooded hills, lakes, and clear, running streams, and it has become a popular playground area. Both indoor and outdoor recreation opportunities abound thanks to Branson—the self-proclaimed "Live Entertainment Capital of America"—along with Table Rock Lake and man-made Lake Taneycomo. Branson is second only to Nashville as a country music center—though it appeals to a more conservative audience. It is a popular family destination and boasts more than 30 music theaters.

## ARRIVING & DEPARTING

The nearest airport to the Branson area is **Springfield,** 40 miles to the north. The area is essentially a driving destination.

## ESSENTIALS

**VISITOR INFORMATION**   Call or write to the **Branson/Lakes Area Chamber of Commerce,** P.O. Box 1897, Branson, MO 65615 (☎ **417/334-4136**). For information on **Table Rock State Park,** contact **Table Rock Lake/Kimberling City Area Chamber of Commerce,** Box 495, Kimberling City, MO 65686 (☎ **417/739-2564**).

## GETTING AROUND

A car is a necessity in the area. Be warned, however, that traffic on "The Strip," or "Country Music Boulevard" (West Highway 26) is notorious, although a number of relief roads help access problems.

## WHAT TO SEE & DO

**THE SHOWS**   What started it all back in the mid-50s was the **Baldknobbers Hillbilly Jamboree Show** (☎ **417/334-4528**), and it's still going strong, along with dozens of others. Most theaters offer an afternoon and an evening show.

　　**Bobby Vinton Blue Velvet Theatre.** *2701 Mo. 76 west.* ☎ *800/US-BOBBY* or *417/334-2500. Admission $23 adults, $12 children 9 and under. Apr–Dec, Tues–Sun. Call for schedule.* At this 1,600-seat European-style theater, with a blue velvet curtain, Bobby Vinton performs hits from his long career, with backing from the Glenn Miller Orchestra.

　　**Grand Palace.** *2700 Mo. 76 west.* ☎ *800/5-PALACE or 417/33-GRAND. Admission $20–$40 depending on performer. Mar to mid-Dec, Sat–Tues 3 and 8pm, Wed–Fri 8pm.* This elaborate theater is the largest in town and hosts some of the biggest-name performers to come to Branson, such as Kenny Rogers (who is part owner).

　　**Mel Tillis Theater.** *2527 Mo. 248.* ☎ *417/335-6635. Admission $28.93 adult, $5.56 children under 12. Mid-March to Dec, daily.* At this 2,700-seat facility, country

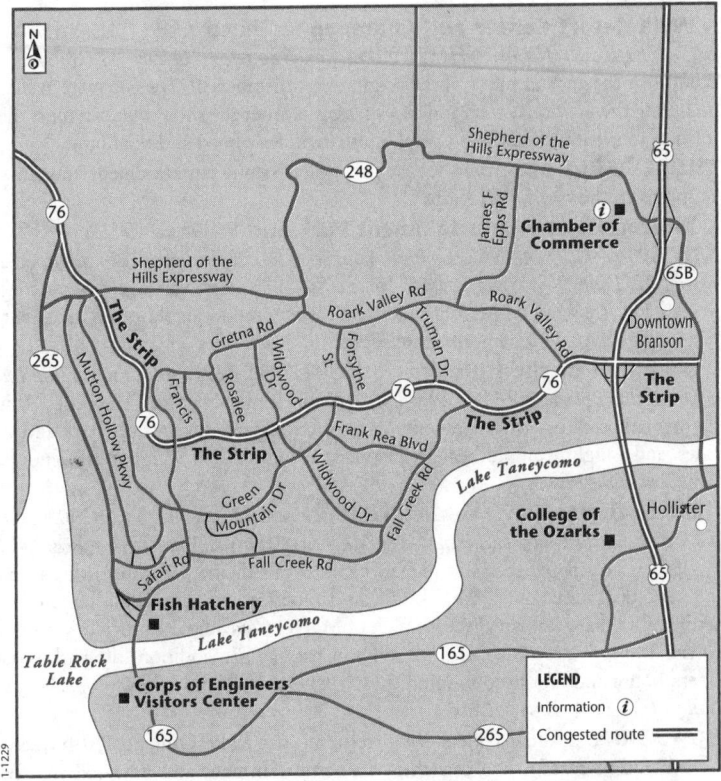

**Branson**

singer Tillis—who succeeded despite his stutter—is joined by a 20-piece band (the Stutterettes), and is often accompanied by his two daughters.

**Mickey Gilley Theatre.** *3455 Mo. 76 west.* ☎ *800/334-1936 or 417/334-3210. Admission $20 adult, $5 children 12 and under. Mar–Dec, daily.* Gilley performs his roadhouse hits with the Urban Cowboy Band. In a morning show, Jim Owen performs the songs of Hank Williams Sr.

**Pump Boys and Dinettes Dinner Theatre.** *625 Mo. 165 south.* ☎ *800/ 743-2386 or 417/336-4319. Dinner and show $29.25 adult, $9 children 14 and under.* At Branson's only Broadway musical dinner theater, waitresses and gas-station jockeys sing, dance, and joke while diners enjoy lunch or supper. A morning show features Buck Trent and other fiddlers and performers, as well as a breakfast buffet. Children under 14 eat free.

**76 Music Hall.** *76 Country Music Blvd.* ☎ *417/335-2484. Admission $16.50 adult, free for children under 12. Open daily.* Several shows are offered daily, including a music-and-dance show by the Memory Makers spanning the decades from the 1950s to the present. The adjoining 76 Mall Complex features a miniature-golf course, 3-D movies, shops, and a video arcade.

**Shoji Tabuchi.** *3260 Shepherd of the Hills Expwy.* ☎ *417/334-7469. Admission $29 adults, $28 seniors, and $20 children 12 and under. Mon–Fri 3 and 8pm.* This art deco, 2,000-seat theater offers one of the most popular shows in Branson, featuring elaborate production numbers, laser-light effects, an 18-piece orchestra, and the violin/ fiddling talent of Tabuchi.

**Welk Resort Center and Champagne Theatre.** *1984 Mo. 165.* ☎ *800/ 505-WELK or 417/337-SHOW. Admission $24. Apr 10–Dec 31.* Shows at this 2,300-seat theater star many of the original cast members of *The Lawrence Welk Show,* including the Lennon Sisters and Jo Ann Castle. After the show, you can meet the performers in the lobby, and the complex also includes a hotel and restaurant.

**THEME PARKS**  Branson's theme parks offer family entertainment and rides plus shopping in the many craft shops.

**Mutton Hollow Entertainment Park and Village.** *Mo. 76 west.* ☎ *800/ 531-7893 or 417/334-4947. Combination ticket for all attractions $25 adult, $14 children 4-12. Daily 9am–5pm. Reduced hours off-season. Closed Nov to mid-Apr.* Attractions here include shows of gospel, bluegrass, and country music; an old-time county fair with rides; craft shops with demonstrations; and horseback rides on Ozark trails.

**Shepherd of the Hills.** *Mo. 76.* ☎ *417/334-4191. Admission $20.28 adults, $9.60 children under 12. Apr–Dec, daily.* Located 2 miles west of "The Strip," this part theme park and part entertainment venue offers a scenic tower, horseback and wagon rides, and a nightly amphitheater enactment of Harold Bell Wright's 1907 novel, *The Shepherd of the Hills.*

**Silver Dollar City.** *Mo. 265.* ☎ *800/952-6626 or 417/338-8100. Admission $27.85 adult, $17.15 children 4-11. May–Aug, daily 9:30am–7pm. Reduced hours off-season.* This is the first and biggest of the area's theme parks, featuring rides, live entertainment, restaurants, shops, and craft demonstrations in an 1880s mountain-town setting. Originally known as the location of **Marvel Cave,** the site provides visitors access to the 200-foot-deep cave with 32 miles of passages. In addition, the park boasts an opera house and an outdoor amphitheater where the nightly show *Top 100 Country Songs of All Times* is performed.

**BOAT TRIPS**  Aboard the sternwheel riverboat **Lake Queen,** 280 N. Lake Dr. (☎ **417/334-3015**), you can enjoy live entertainment and narrated sightseeing, breakfast, and supper cruises on Lake Taneycomo. **Polynesian Princess,** Gage's Long Creek Marina, Mo. 86 (☎ **417/334-4191**), offers narrated tours of Table Rock Lake. Visitors can choose among breakfast, dinner, sightseeing, or sunset cruises, with dinner cruises featuring live Polynesian entertainment. **Ride the Ducks,** Mo. 76 west (☎ **417/334-3825**), takes passengers on clunky amphibious trucks on a 70-minute land-and-water sightseeing tour of Branson, including Table Rock Dam and Lake, the fish hatchery, and mountain scenery. On the **Showboat Branson Belle,** Mo. 265 (☎ **800/417-7770** or 417/336-7400), tourists can dine, view Ozark scenery, and watch a music-and-comedy revue aboard this multilevel, climate-controlled floating theater.

**OUTDOOR ACTIVITIES**  The cold waters of Lake Taneycomo serve up rainbow and brown trout and other game fish. For information on area fishing, contact the **Missouri Department of Conservation** (☎ **573/751-4115**). **Table Rock State Park** (☎ **417/ 334-4704**) offers hiking, camping, and is a favorite with scuba divers. **Snow Bluff Ski and Fun Area,** 5659 Mo. 13, Brighton (☎ **417/376-2201**), has nine ski trails, with special areas set aside for tubing and snowboarding. During the warm-weather months, visitors are offered a wide selection of outdoor and sports activities including swimming and bumper boats. **White Water Park,** on Highway 76 (☎ **417/334-7487** or 417/ 336-7100), has 12 acres of water rides, slides, a wave pool, and a rapids ride. It's open daily 9am–8pm, with reduced hours off-season.

## ACCOMMODATIONS

In addition to the listings below, there are a number of resorts around Indian Point on nearby Table Rock Lake. To find out about B&Bs in the Branson area, contact **Ozark**

**Mountain Country Bed and Breakfast** reservations service, Box 295, Branson, MO 65616 (☎ 800/695-1546 or 417/334-4720).

**Big Cedar Lodge.** *612 Devil's Pool Rd. (10 miles south of Branson at Table Rock Lake), Ridgedale, MO 65739.* ☎ *417/335-2777. Fax 417/335-2340. 208 rms, suites, and efficiencies; 61 cottages/villas. $125–$189 double; $229–$849 suite or efficiency; $139–$529 cottage/villa. Extra person $15. Children under 12 stay free in parents' room. Minimum stay on weekends. Lower rates off-season. Special packages available. AE, DISC, MC, V. Free outdoor parking.* This rustic and majestic Northwest-style lodge offers beautiful accommodations. Units have hand-carved furniture, and feature terraces, fireplaces, or whirlpools. A range of activities is offered, from boating and basketball to horseback riding and jogging. Conveniences include three restaurants, a bar, pool, fitness center, sauna, steam room, whirlpool, children's program, and laundry facilities.

**Bradford Inn.** *U.S. 265 (2 miles south of U.S. 76), Branson, MO 65616.* ☎ *800/3571-INN or 417/338-5555. 30 rms and suites. $49–$69 double; $79–$89 suite. Extra person $5. Children under 12 stay free in parents' room. Lower rates off-season. DISC, MC, V. Free outdoor parking.* This country setting offers views of the Ozarks. Each room is beautifully decorated and some feature antiques and reproductions, such as four-poster beds. All units have terraces and refrigerators, and some offer fireplaces or whirlpools. The inn has a guest lounge with TV.

**Crowne Plaza.** *120 S. Wildwood Dr., Branson, MO 65616.* ☎ *800/428-3386 or 417/335-5767. Fax 417/335-7979. 500 rms and suites. $65–$95 single or double; $150–$300 suite. Extra person $10. Children under 20 stay free in parents' room. Lower rates off-season. Special packages available. AE, CB, DC, DISC, EC, JCB, MC, V. Free outdoor parking.* This new nine-story hotel features contemporary rooms. Some units offer minibars, terraces, or whirlpools. A restaurant, bar, pool, fitness center, games room, sauna, and whirlpool are on the premises.

**Gazebo Inn.** *2424 Mo. 76 west, Branson, MO 65616.* ☎ *800/873-7990 or 417/335-3826. Fax 417/335-3889. 73 rms, suites, and efficiencies. No smoking. Children under 18 stay free in parents' room. $63 single or double; $83–$103 suite; $133 efficiency. Lower rates off-season. AE, DISC, MC, V. Free outdoor parking.* This Victorian hotel is near many music theaters. Some units have terraces and some offer whirlpools. The inn has a pool.

**Good Shepherd Inn.** *1023 W. Main St. (two blocks from junction U.S. 65 and Mo. 76), Branson, MO 65616.* ☎ *800/324-3457 or 417/334-1695. Fax 417/335-4295. 63 rms. $40 double. Extra person $5. Children under 15 stay free in parents' room. Lower rates off-season. AE, DC, DISC, MC, V. Free outdoor parking.* This basic economy motel is conveniently located and has a pool. Some rooms have VCRs.

**Lighthouse Inn.** *2375 Green Mountain Dr. (one block south of Mo. 76), Branson, MO 65616.* ☎ *800/237-5444 or 417/336-6161. Fax 417/336-2449. 91 rms. $67–$77 single or double. Extra person $2. Children under 18 stay free in parents' room. Lower rates off-season. Free outdoor parking. AE, DC, DISC, MC, V. Closed Jan–Feb.* There is a patio off the lobby and the inn has a pool. Some units have whirlpools.

**Rosebud Inn.** *2400 Roark Valley Rd., Branson, MO 65616.* ☎ *800/767-3522 or 417/336-4000. Fax 417/336-4919. 64 rms. $40–$59 single or double. Extra person $5. Children under 12 stay free in parents' room. Lower rates off-season. AE, DISC, MC, V. Free outdoor parking.* This attractive new hotel offers pleasant amenities and facilities including a pool and basketball court.

**Settle Inn.** *3050 Green Mountain Dr., Branson, MO 65616.* ☎ *800/677-6906 or 417/335-4700. Fax 417/335-3906. 300 rms and suites. $35–$69 single or double; $49–$129 suite. Children under 12 stay free in parents' room. Lower rates off-season. AE, DISC,*

*MC, V. Free outdoor parking.* This lovely motel is surrounded by trees and small pools. It offers theme suites, such as medieval-style rooms. Some units have terraces and some offer whirlpools. The inn includes a restaurant (lunch and dinner only), bar, two pools, games room, whirlpool, laundry facilities, and "Murder Mystery" dinner theater.

**Stonewall West Motor Inn.** *1030 W. Main St. (Mo. 76 west), Branson, MO 65616.* ☎ *417/334-5173. 26 rms. $22–$42 single or double. Extra person $4. Children under 12 stay free in parents' room. Lower rates off-season. AE, CB, DISC, MC, V. Closed Dec–Feb. Free outdoor parking.* This hotel supplies acceptable, affordable accommodations near all the popular attractions. It has a pool and is suitable for a brief stay.

## DINING

Most of Branson's restaurants offer regional or down-home cooking, featuring steak and country-fried chicken, but a few branch out and serve a lighter cuisine.

**Branson Cafe.** *120 W. Main St.* ☎ *417/334-3021. Reservations accepted. Main courses $5–$9. AE, CB, DC, DISC, MC, V. Mon–Sat 5:30am–8pm. REGIONAL AMERICAN/DINER.* This casual diner—a real regulars' hangout—is the place to go for down-home cooking. Sample one of the famous pies.

**BT Bones.** *Shepherd of the Hills Expwy. at Gretna Rd.* ☎ *417/335-2002. Reservations not accepted. Main courses $10–$18. AE, CB, DC, DISC, MC, V. Mon–Sat 11am–1am, Sun 11am–midnight. Closed Jan. AMERICAN/STEAK.* This dimly lit country bar offers country music/dancing and specializes in steaks, though chicken and fish dishes are available. Luckenbach Chicken, grilled with mushrooms, onions, cheese, bacon, and honey mustard, is recommended.

**Candlestick Inn.** *On Hwy. 76 east.* ☎ *417/334-3633. Main courses $13–$28. Dinner only. AE, DC, MC, V. SEAFOOD/STEAK.* On a bluff above Lake Taneycomo, the elegant dining rooms in this upscale restaurant offer a fine view. Aged beef is the specialty, along with fresh local trout and other seafood.

**Lone Star Steakhouse.** *201 Wildwood Dr.* ☎ *417/336-5030. Reservations not accepted. Main courses $8–$18. AE, DISC, MC, V. Sun–Thurs 11am–11pm, Fri–Sat 11am–midnight. STEAK.* In keeping with the country-western decor, this restaurant offers good solid steaks, but you can also enjoy the chili, burgers, and chicken kebab.

**Paradise Grill.** *3250 Shepherd of the Hills Expwy.* ☎ *417/337-7444. Reservations accepted. Main courses $10–$12. AE, DC, DISC, MC, V. July–Dec, Mon–Thurs 11am–9pm, Fri–Sat 11am–midnight, Sun 10:30am–9pm. AMERICAN.* This brightly decorated eatery, with neon and skylights, offers a variety of menu choices. Ozark Mountain Chicken, stuffed with ham and cheese, is a popular dish.

## A SIDE TRIP TO EUREKA SPRINGS

Just over the Missouri border in Arkansas, 50 miles southwest of Branson, Eureka Springs is a charming Victorian city that thrives as an antique and crafts center. Settled as a spa in the 1890s, it has country music performances, art galleries, and appealing public and botanical gardens.

Among the restored historic houses with period furnishings are the 1833 Queen Anne and Gothic-style **Rosalie House** at 282 Spring St.; and **Queen Anne Mansion,** U.S. 62 west, featuring hand-carved woodwork and stained-glass windows. The **Thorncrown Chapel,** U.S. 62 west, is a striking, mainly glass design (☎ 501/253-7401 for music performance times). The **Eureka Springs and North Arkansas Railway,** 299 N. Main St. (☎ 501/253-9623), is a restored 1906 steam railway that takes a scenic route through the Ozark Hills. It's open from May to November.

At the **Pine Mountain Jamboree,** U.S. 62 east (☎ 501/253-9156), visitors can enjoy bluegrass, country gospel, pop and rock, big band, and Cajun performers.

The **Great Passion Play,** U.S. 62 (☎ 800/882-7529), is a religious extravaganza on the life of Jesus. It takes place in an outdoor theater with a cast of 250 people and live animals, watched over by the seven-story **Christ of the Ozarks** statue.

About 10 miles southeast is the historic pioneer town of **Berryville,** also filled with crafts shops and museums.

There are plenty of places to stay in Eureka Springs. The **Crescent Hotel,** 75 Prospect St., Eureka Springs, AK 72632 (☎ 501/253-9766), sits on the mountain above town and is a National Historic Landmark. **East Mountain Lodge,** U.S. 62 (P.O. Box 87), Eureka Springs, AK 72632 (☎ 800/533-9521 or 502/253-9521), is a quaint lodge-style property near historic downtown. The **Best Western Inn of the Ozarks,** U.S. 62 (P.O. Box 431), Eureka Springs, AK 72632 (☎ 800/528-1234 or 501/253-9768), near the historic district, is a good place for extended stays.

**Essentials:** For more information, contact the Eureka Springs Chamber of Commerce, 81 Kings Highway (☎ 501/253-8737) or write to them at P.O. Box 551, Eureka Springs 72632.

## 8 Minneapolis

Minnesota's twin cities—Minneapolis and St. Paul—lie on either side of the Mississippi River, and both cities have riverboat traffic all the way up from New Orleans. When the first explorers ventured up the Mighty Mississippi, they found the river roaring over an 18-foot precipice here. Today the Falls of St. Anthony is tamed and bypassed by lock and dam.

Minneapolis was first settled by emigrants from New England in 1847, who were soon joined by waves of Scandinavians and Germans. Today it has the University of Minnesota, the famous Guthrie Theater, and miles and miles of a climate-controlled skyway system downtown that enables residents and visitors to do everything from parking and shopping to working and dining without stepping outdoors.

### ARRIVING & DEPARTING

**BY PLANE**   **Minneapolis/St. Paul International Airport,** located between the cities, is 8 to 10 miles south of downtown for both. The **Metropolitan Transit Commission** runs buses to both cities (☎ 612/349-7000) for a cost of $1 off-peak and $1.50 during rush hour. **Airport Express** (☎ 612/726-6400) runs vans to many hotels for about $10.50 one way. A taxi to downtown Minneapolis will cost $15 to $20.

**BY TRAIN & BUS**   Trains come into St. Paul. The **Greyhound Lines** station is at 29 N. 9th St. (☎ 612/371-3323).

**BY CAR**   The Twin Cities are circled by a beltway: I-494 goes through the southern suburbs, and I-694 through the northern suburbs.

### ESSENTIALS

**VISITOR INFORMATION**   The **Minneapolis Convention and Visitor Bureau** is at 4000 Multifoods Tower, 33 S. 6th St., Minneapolis, MN 55402 (☎ 612/661-4700). A general information line for parks, events, and attractions is **The Connection** (☎ 612/922-9000).

**EMERGENCIES & SAFETY**   Call ☎ 911 for emergencies. Minneapolis is one of the safest large cities in the country and has one of the lowest crime rates.

### GETTING AROUND

**BY PUBLIC TRANSPORTATION**   The **Metropolitan Transit Commission** (☎ 612/349-3333) operates buses between the Twin Cities. Rush-hour fare is $1.50; off-peak fare is $1, and 25¢ extra to some suburbs.

# Minneapolis/St. Paul Area

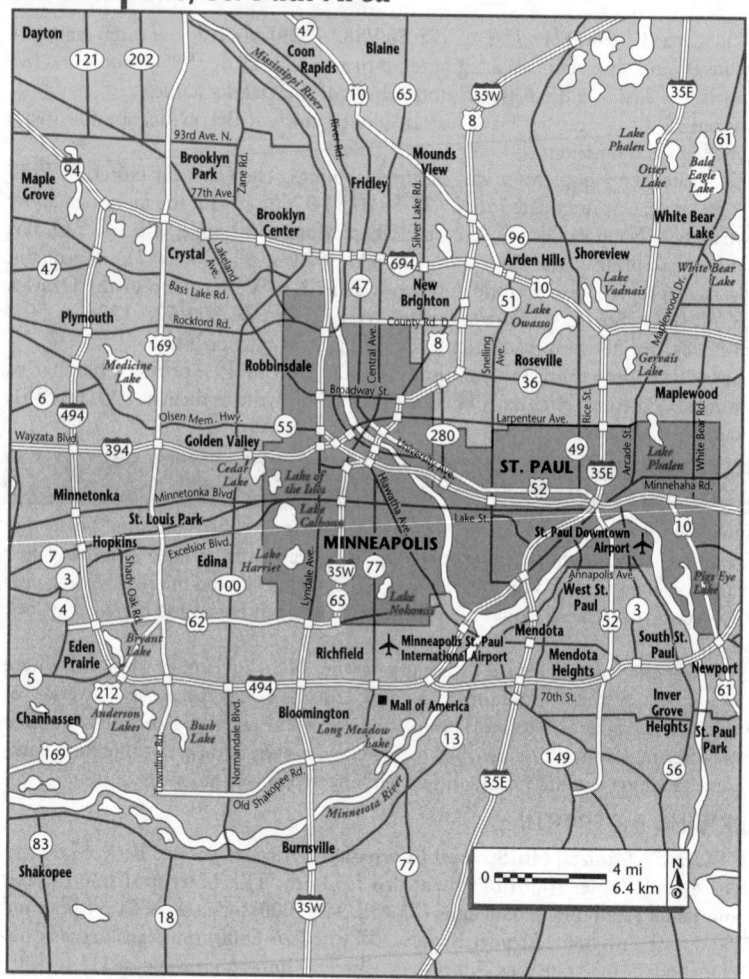

**BY CAR & ON FOOT**   The city is laid out on a grid system, but many downtown streets that parallel the Mississippi River run on a diagonal. The skyway system makes it easy to explore downtown on foot. You will need a car to reach many attractions outside the downtown area.

## WHAT TO SEE & DO

**ESCORTED TOURS**   **Gray Line Tours,** 835 Decatur Ave. N. (☎ 612/591-9099), offers tours of both cities and their surroundings.

**MUSEUMS**   As Minnesota's cultural center, Minneapolis offers many museums and galleries.

   **American Swedish Institute.** *2600 Park Ave.* ☎ *612/871-4907. Admission $3 adults, $2 seniors and children 6–18.* The institute offers rotating exhibits and a permanent collection tracing the history of Swedish immigration to Minnesota.

   **Flanders Contemporary Art Gallery.** *400 1st Ave. N.* ☎ *612/344-1700. Admission free. Tues–Sat 11am–4pm.* The works owned by this art gallery span all media: paintings, sculpture, drawings, photographs, and prints. Works are drawn from the

18th, 19th, and 20th centuries, with special emphases on French and American Impressionism. Masters from the 19th century are presented alongside modern masters.

**Frederick R. Weisman Art Museum.** *333 E. River Rd.* ☎ *612/625-9464. Admission free. Tues–Wed 10am–5pm, Thurs 10am–8pm, Fri 10am–5pm, Sat–Sun 11am–5pm.* High on a bluff overlooking the Mississippi River and the downtown Minneapolis landscape, this uniquely designed building, on the University of Minnesota campus, houses what one major art critic calls "five of the most gorgeous galleries on earth." The museum has more than 13,000 objects, with an emphasis on American art. It offers an extensive collection of Asian, American, European, and Native American ceramics. Group tours are available.

**Kramer Gallery.** *1012 Nicollet Mall.* ☎ *612/338-2911. Admission free. Mon–Fri 10am–6pm, Sat 10am–4pm.* This distinguished gallery specializes in local, national, and European artworks of the 19th and early 20th centuries; also featured is an extensive collection of Native American art and artifacts.

**Minneapolis Institute of Arts (MIA).** *2400 3rd Ave.* ☎ *612/870-3000. Admission free. Tues–Sat 10am–5pm, Thurs 10am–9pm, Sun noon–5pm.* The MIA's permanent collection of over 80,000 objects of fine and decorative art represents more than 25,000 years of history. Highlights include a 2,000-year-old mummy and a Paul Revere silver tea service. There are re-created period rooms; African, Oceanic, and New World galleries; collections of photographs, textiles, and prints; and paintings by European masters.

**Minnesota Air Guard Museum.** *Minnesota Air National Guard Base (located at the Minneapolis/St Paul International Airport).* ☎ *612/713-2523. Mid-Apr to mid-Sept, Sat–Sun 11am–4pm.* Vintage and current aircraft, artifacts, memorabilia, and photographs tell the story of the Minnesota Air Guard from 1921 to the present.

**Walker Art Center/Minneapolis Sculpture Garden.** *Vineland Place. Admission $4 adults, $3 seniors and students, free for children under 18.* ☎ *612/375-7622. Museum admission free Thurs and first Sat of every month. Museum: Tues–Sat 10am–8pm, Sun 11am–5pm. Sculpture garden: daily 6am–midnight.* The Walker Art Center is famous for its permanent collection of contemporary art, ranging from painting and sculpture to drawings, photographs, and multimedia installations. It is also known for the popular presentations it offers through its Departments of Film and Video, Performing Arts, and Education. Across Vineland Place is the Minneapolis Sculpture Garden, the most extensive garden of its kind in the United States, with a wide variety of 20th-century sculpture on display.

**OTHER ATTRACTIONS** New or notable architecture in the downtown area includes the 57-story **Norwest Center,** 77 S. 7th St.; the flat-topped multifaceted **IDS Tower,** 80 S. 8th St.; and Minneapolis's oldest skyscraper, **Foshay Tower,** 821 Marquette Ave., with an observation deck with a great view of the city. The **Hubert H. Humphrey Metrodome,** an indoor stadium, is one of the most recognized downtown structures.

**Fort Snelling.** *Minn. 55 (1 mile east of Minneapolis/St. Paul Airport).* ☎ *612/725-2413. Admission $4 adults, $3 seniors, $2 children 6–15. May–Oct, daily Mon–Sat 10am–5pm, Sun noon–5pm. Reduced hours off-season. Closed Dec–Mar.* This is a living history museum, commemorating the establishment of a fort here in the wilderness in 1819 by Col. Josiah Snelling and his troops, which opened the area for homesteaders. Costumed guides re-create the activities of everyday army life during the 1820s.

**Minneapolis City Hall.** *5th St. and 3rd Ave.* ☎ *612/673-2491. Admission free. Mon–Fri 9am–5pm.* The imposing 1891 City Hall, with its Big Ben–style clock tower, is a surprising contrast to its next-door neighbor, the ultramodern Hennepin County Government Center. Here you will find the *Father of Waters,* billed as the largest statue ever carved from a single block of Carrara marble.

**Minneapolis Planetarium.** *300 Nicollet Mall.* ☎ *612/372-6644. Call for schedule.* Located in the downtown branch of the Minneapolis Public Library, the Planetarium offers more than a dozen programs, including the immensely popular Skywatch (a "guided tour" of the night sky). Ticket prices vary from $2.50–$4.

**University of Minnesota.** *Located between Mississippi and University aves. and 10th Ave. and Oak St. SE.* ☎ *800/752-1000 or 612/625-5000. Admission free.* One of the Midwest's oldest (1851) and most important universities, with 41,000 students, the campus offers three significant museums—James Ford Bell Museum of Natural History, the University Art Gallery, and the Frederick R. Weisman Art Museum (see above). The 4,800-seat Northrop Auditorium has been a home for distinguished performances since 1929; the University Theatre has four separate stages. Guided tours leave from the admissions office, 240 Williamson Hall, Mon–Fri 10am and 1pm.

**PARKS** The **Eloise Butler Wildflower Garden and Bird Sanctuary,** Theodore Wirth Parkway (☎ 612/348-5702), is a 20-acre natural wildflower habitat offering bogs and swamp areas, with hiking and bicycle trails winding through. Guided tours are available. It's open Apr–Oct, daily from 7:30am until sunset. **Minnehaha Park,** Minnehaha Parkway (☎ 612/370-4939), on the Mississippi, is the site of the famed Minnehaha Falls, the "laughing water" Longfellow celebrated in his poem *Song of Hiawatha.* Other attractions include 15 miles of jogging and biking trails and a historic frame house that was the first built west of the Mississippi. It's open daily from sunrise to sunset.

**BEST BETS FOR KIDS** Kids enjoy the **Museum of Natural History** and **Planetarium** shows, and most kids love the **Baseball Museum.** A visit to **Fort Snelling** can be a high point of the visit (see "Other Attractions," above). The **Minnesota Zoo** in the suburb of Apple Valley houses more than 1,700 animals in natural settings. There's a monorail, a Zoo Lab, and a seasonal children's zoo. **UnderWater World** (☎ 612/888-3483) is an aquarium that simulates an underwater diving experience. The **Children's Theater Company,** 2400 3rd Ave. S. (☎ 612/874-0400), presents a season of plays for all age groups. At the Mall of America (see below) is **Camp Snoopy,** one of the country's largest enclosed amusement parks.

**SPORTS** The **Minnesota Twins** play baseball at Hubert H. Humphrey Metrodome, 501 Chicago Ave. S. (☎ 612/375-1116), April–October. The **Minnesota Timberwolves** play at their home base, **Target Center,** 801 1st Ave. N. (☎ 612/337-3865), November–April. Target Center (☎ 612/673-1300) is also a popular venue for rock bands. The **Minnesota Vikings** play football at the Metrodome (☎ 612/335-3370) August–December.

**SHOPPING** **Nicollet Mall** downtown has Dayton, Minneapolis's largest department store, and the upscale **Gaviidae Common** with a variety of shops. **City Center,** 7th Street and Hennepin Avenue, has about 60 shops and many restaurants. Hip galleries and antique stores abound in the restored **Warehouse District. Uptown** is *the* trendy place to shop—just 10 minutes south of downtown Minneapolis, it is full of specialty shops and botiques.

For shopping at the **Mall of America,** see "A Side Trip to the Mall of America," below.

## ACCOMMODATIONS

In addition to the hotels listed below, many accommodations are attached to shopping malls and along I-494 in the suburbs.

**Crowne Plaza Northstar Hotel.** *618 2nd Ave. S. (2 blocks south of Nicollet Ave.), Minneapolis, MN 55402.* ☎ *800/556-STAR or 612/338-2288. Fax 612/338-2288. 226 rms and suites. $97–$160 double; $175–$500 suite. Extra person $15. Children under 16*

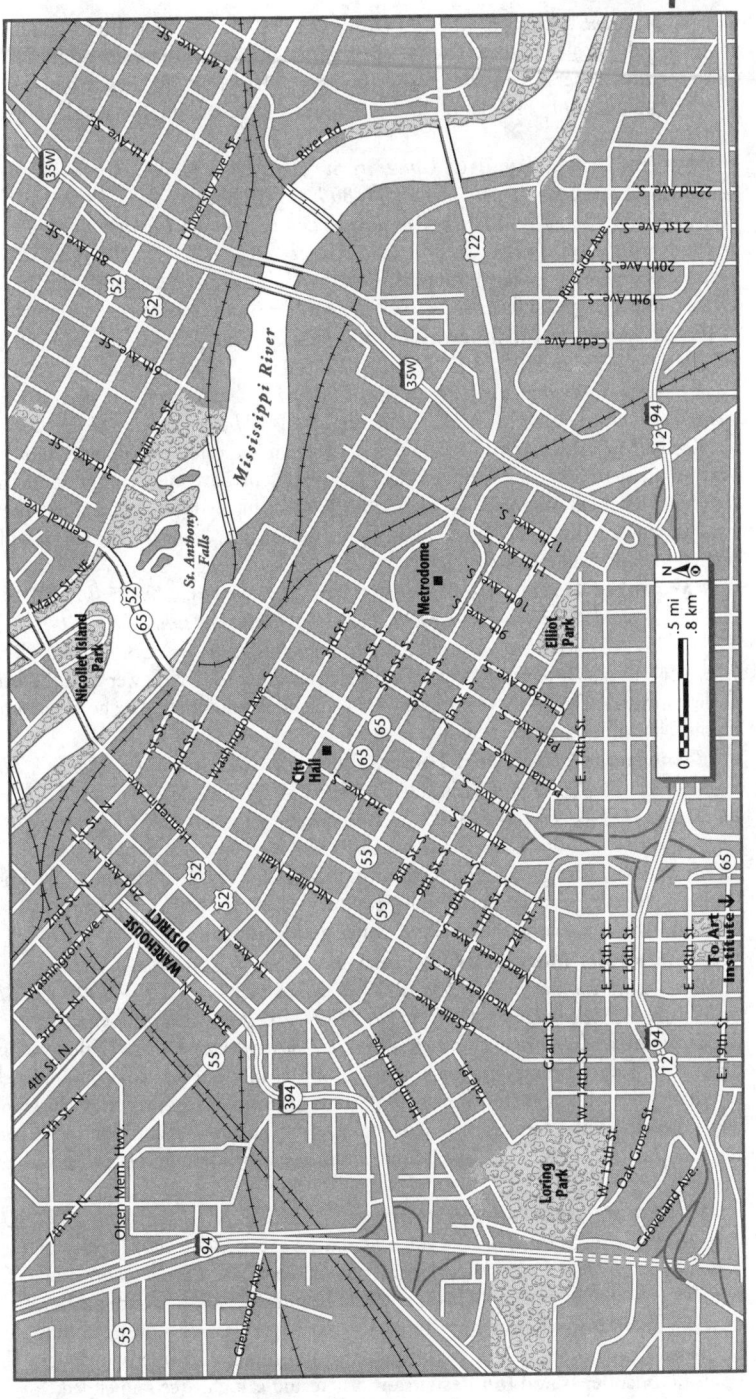

*stay free in parents' room. AE, CB, DC, DISC, EC, MC, V.* A bellhop directs you to the lobby past the small entrance. The average-size rooms, some with minibars, offer views of other skyscrapers. The hotel is on the route of Airport Express, which leaves every 15 minutes until midnight. On the premises are a restaurant, bar, and laundry facilities.

**Days Inn University.** *2407 University Ave. SE (I-94 to 35 west, then north to University Ave.), Minneapolis, MN 55414.* ☎ *800/375-3990 or 612/623-3999. Fax 612/331-2152. 131 rms. $59–$89 single or double. Extra person $6. Children under 17 stay free in parents' room. Lower rates off-season. AE, CB, DC, DISC, EC, ER, JCB, MC, V. Free outdoor parking.* Located 3 blocks from the University of Minnesota, this facility caters to business and university people. There is free shuttle service to the university.

**Hyatt Regency Minneapolis.** *1300 Nicollet Mall, Minneapolis, MN 55403.* ☎ *800/233-1234 or 612/370-1234. Fax 612/370-1333. 533 rms and suites. $210–$235 double; $290–$800 suite. Extra person $25. Children under 18 stay free in parents' room. Lower rates off-season. AE, CB, DC, DISC, EC, MC, V. Indoor parking $9.75.* Located at Nicollet Mall, this elegant hotel is close to uptown and caters to corporate and convention travelers. Some of the beautifully furnished rooms have minibars and some have terraces. The noted **Manny's** (☎ *612/339-9900*) is a highly recommended restaurant. Facilities include five restaurants, a bar, fitness center, spa, sauna, steam room, whirlpool, and basketball/racquetball courts.

**Marquette Hotel.** *710 Marquette Ave., Minneapolis, MN 55402.* ☎ *800/32-VISTA or 612/333-4545. Fax 612/376-7419. 278 rms and suites. $79–$200 double; $175–$349 suite. Children under 18 stay free in parents' room. AE, CB, DC, DISC, EC, JCB, MC, V. Indoor parking $6–$12.* This elegant hotel in IDS Tower is in the heart of downtown. All rooms have minibars and some offer whirlpools. The hotel has a restaurant, bar, fitness center, and sauna.

**Minneapolis Hilton and Towers.** *1001 Marquette Ave. S. (at 10th St.), Minneapolis, MN 55403.* ☎ *800/HILTONS or 612/376-1000. Fax 612/397-4875. 814 rms and suites. $175–$195 double; $700–$1,200 suite. Extra person $20. Children under 17 stay free in parents' room. Lower rates off-season. Indoor parking $9.50. AE, CB, DC, DISC, EC, JCB, MC, V.* In the heart of downtown, this hotel is connected to the Convention Center, Orchestra Hall, and many other facilities via the skyway. Guests enjoy two restaurants, two bars, a fitness center, spa, sauna, and whirlpool.

**Minneapolis Marriott City Center.** *30 S. 7th St. (between Hennepin and Nicollet aves.), Minneapolis, MN 55402.* ☎ *800/228-9290 or 612/349-4000. Fax 612/332-7165. 583 rms and suites. $189 double; $189–$269 suite. Children under 18 stay free in parents' room. Lower rates off-season. AE, CB. Indoor parking $3–11.* Within walking distance of Target Center and much nightlife, this facility caters to conventioneers. Its layout and furnishings are functional. Some units have minibars; some offer whirlpools. The noted Gustino's restaurant is here (see "Dining," below), in addition to a second restaurant, bar, fitness center, spa, sauna, steam room, whirlpool, social director, and masseur.

✪ **Nicollet Island Inn.** *95 Merriam St., Minneapolis, MN 55401.* ☎ *612/331-1800. Fax 612/331-6528. 24 rms and suites. $115–$130 double; $150 suite. Extra person $15. Children under 10 stay free in parents' room. AE, CB, DC, DISC, EC, JCB, MC, V. Free outdoor parking.* This lovely inn, begun in 1988, was once an 1893 window shade and blind company. It is close to Riverplace shopping, dining, and businesses. Each room is furnished differently and some units offer whirlpools. The beautiful **Nicollet Island Inn Restaurant** is here and is highly recommended.

**Normandy Inn.** *405 S. 8th St., Minneapolis, MN 55404.* ☎ *800/372-3131 or 612/370-1400. Fax 612/370-0351. 159 rms and suites. Apr–Nov, $85 single or double;*

*$95 suite. Extra person $10. Children under 12 stay free in parents' room. Lower rates off-season. AE, CB, DC, DISC, EC, MC, V. Free outside parking.* The exterior resembles a European chalet and inside the standard rooms are nicely furnished, some with terraces. The inn has a restaurant, bar, pool, fitness center, sauna, and whirlpool.

**Radisson Plaza Hotel Minneapolis.** *35 S. 7th St. (just off Hennepin Ave.), Minneapolis, MN 55402.* ☎ *800/333-3333 or 612/339-4900. Fax 612/337-9798. 357 rms and suites. $143 double; $255–$450 suite. Extra person $15. Children under 16 stay free in parents' room. Lower weekend rates. AE, CB, DC, DISC, EC, ER, JCB, MC, V. Indoor parking $10.* This gracious hotel across from City Center is a welcome respite from the downtown scene, with a 17-story atrium and comfortable rooms offering elegance and homeliness. Some units have terraces, whirlpools, or minibars. There are two restaurants, two bars, a fitness center, spa, sauna, whirlpool, masseur, and beauty salon.

**Radisson University Hotel.** *615 Washington Ave. SE (on University of Minnesota campus), Minneapolis, MN 55414.* ☎ *800/822-MPLS or 612/379-8888. Fax 612/379-8682. 304 rms and suites. $115 double; $135–$350 suite. Extra person $10. Children under 18 stay free in parents' room. AE, CB, DC, DISC, ER, JCB, MC, V. Outdoor parking $6.80.* The hotel's architecture blends in so well with the university's that it can be hard to locate. Most guests are here for university-related conferences. For $5, guests can use the University Health Club, a $30-million complex. On the premises are two restaurants, two bars, a fitness center, games room, beauty salon, and washer/dryer.

**Regal Minneapolis Hotel.** *1313 Nicollet Ave. (between 13th and Grant sts.), Minneapolis, MN 55403.* ☎ *800/222-8888 or 612/332-0371. Fax 612/359-2160. 330 rms and suites. $130–$169 double; $200–$250 suite. Extra person $10. Children under 17 stay free in parents' room. Lower rates off-season. AE, CB, DC, DISC, EC, MC, V. Indoor parking $8.* Built in 1962 and updated through the years, this comfortable, reliable hotel stands at one end of the Nicollet Mall. The older rooms feature exposed brick; new rooms have impressive furnishings. Conveniences include a restaurant, bar, pool, fitness center, sauna, whirlpool, and washer/dryer.

**Sheraton Minneapolis Metrodome.** *1330 Industrial Blvd. NE, Minneapolis, MN 55413.* ☎ *800/777-3277 or 612/331-1900. Fax 612/331-6827. 252 rms and suites. Aug–Nov, $79–$129 single; $89–$139 double; $150 suite. Extra person $10. Children under 18 stay free in parents' room. Lower rates off-season. AE, CB, DC, DISC, EC, MC, V. Free outdoor parking.* North of downtown and away from some congestion, this hotel sometimes attracts celebrities as guests, and offers an attractive courtyard area. A shuttle service within a 5-mile radius includes the aiport, Mall of America, and downtown. On the premises are a restaurant, bar, pool, fitness center, spa, sauna, whirlpool, games room, social director, and masseur.

**Sheraton Park Place.** *1500 Park Place Blvd., Minneapolis, MN 55416.* ☎ *800/542-5566 or 612/542-8600. Fax 612/542-8068. 297 rms and suites. $99–$109 single or double; $119 suite. Extra person $15. Children under 18 stay free in parents' room. Lower rates off-season. AE, CB, DC, DISC, EC, ER, JCB, MC, V. Free outdoor parking.* Located 3½ miles west of downtown, this hotel is close to business and commercial facilities and offers a spacious pool atrium area. Some rooms offer terraces; some have whirlpools. Extras include a restaurant, bar, pool, fitness center, sauna, whirlpool, games room, laundry facilities, and complimentary van shuttle within a 3-mile radius.

**Whitney Hotel.** *150 Portland Ave., Minneapolis, MN 55401.* ☎ *800/248-1879 or 612/339-9300. Fax 612/339-1333. 97 rms and suites. $160–$205 king-bedded room; $195–$205 suite. Extra person $10. Children under 18 stay free in parents' room. AE, CB, DC, DISC, EC, MC, V. Outdoor parking $6.* This 18th-century European-style hotel on the Mississippi River was once a 19th-century flour mill; it has been a hotel since 1987. The comfortable rooms are all shaped differently and feature minibars. Many have high ceilings. South-facing rooms offer views of the river and outdoor patio and fountain. The hotel has a restaurant and bar.

**OTHER ACCOMMODATIONS**   There are a number of hotels at or near the airport. The **Minneapolis/St. Paul Airport Hilton,** 3200 E. 80th St. (☎ **800/637-7453** or 612/854-2100; fax 612/854-8002), offers extensive facilities and services, including free shuttle service to the Mall of America and other locations, and is within walking distance of the Minnesota Valley National Wildlife Refuge. Also near the airport are the **Hotel Sofitel** (☎ **612/835-1900**), the **Marriott Minneapolis Bloomington** (☎ **612/ 854-7441**), and the **Embassy Suites Airport** (☎ **612/854-1000**).

## DINING

Minneapolis restaurants reflect Minnesota's heritage of German and Scandinavian cooking, and generally prefer a classic rather than exotic version of these cuisines. Also see recommended restaurants in hotel listings, above.

    **Black Forest Inn.** *1 E. 26th St.* ☎ *612/872-0812. Reservations not accepted. Main courses $7–$14. AE, DC, DISC, MC, V. Mon–Sat 11am–1am, Sun noon–midnight. German.* The building's exterior resembles an old German house, while the interior is distinguished by dark wood, stained-glass windows, and a rustic bar area. Authentic sauerbraten, Wiener schnitzel, bratwurst, and other German specialties await.

    **Buca.** *1204 Harmon Place (at 12th St.).* ☎ *612/638-2225. Reservations not accepted. Main courses $7–$20. AE, CB, DC, MC, V. Mon–Thurs 5–10pm, Fri 5–11pm, Sat 4:30– 11pm, Sun 4:30–10pm. Italian.* Located on the garden level of a downtown building, this popular, casual restaurant prepares Italian family-style meals. Garlic mashed potatoes and chicken marsala are recommended. You'll find an additional location at 2728 Gannon Rd., St. Paul (☎ *612/772-4388*).

    ✪ **Café Brenda.** *300 1st Ave.* ☎ *612/342-9230. Main courses $6–$12. AE, DC, MC, V. Mon–Fri 11:30am–2pm; Mon–Thurs 5:30–9pm, Fri–Sat 5:30–10pm. SEA-FOOD/VEGETARIAN.* This gourmet restaurant in the trendy Warehouse District has a simple but elegant atmosphere, and the emphasis is on the freshest possible ingredients.

    **D'Amico Cucina.** *In Butler Square, 100 N. 6th St.* ☎ *612/338-2401. Reservations recommended. Main courses $20–$26. AE, CB, DC, MC, V. Mon–Thurs 5:30–10pm, Fri–Sat 5:30–11pm, Sun 5–9pm. Valet parking. ITALIAN.* This beautifully decorated restaurant with a distinctive atmosphere, enhanced by whitewashed wood beams and French doors, offers creative Italian dishes and over 150 Italian wines. Try the pollo in tegame con gnocchi e taleggio (chicken with a potato dumpling and parsley sauce).

    **Edwardo's Natural Pizza Restaurant.** *1125 Marquette Ave. (at S. 12th St.).* ☎ *612/339-9700. Reservations accepted. Main courses $6–$15. AE, MC, V. Mon–Thurs 11am–10pm, Fri–Sat 11am–11pm. Pizza.* Part of a chain known for its stuffed pizza, this is a good choice for family dining. You'll find an additional location at 2633 Southtown Dr., Bloomington (☎ *612/884-8400*).

    **The Egg and I Restaurant.** *2828 Lyndale Ave. (at 28th St.).* ☎ *612/872-7282. Reservations accepted. Main courses $4–$6. No credit cards. Mon–Fri 6am–3pm, Sat–Sun 8am–3pm. AMERICAN.* This local favorite for 18 years serves home-cooked, breakfast-type meals at a good price in a comfortable atmosphere. Every month a different local artist's work is displayed for purchase. There's an additional location at 2550 University Ave., St. Paul (☎ *612/647-1292*).

    ✪ **Famous Dave's BBQ & Blues Club.** *Calhoun Square (at Lake St. and Hennepin Ave.).* ☎ *612/822-9900. Main courses $9–$17. AE, DC, DISC, MC, V. Daily 11am–1am. BARBECUE.* This funky place, with a 1930s Chicago alley decor, has some of the best barbecue in town. Live blues bands are featured Wednesday to Sunday.

**Figlio's.** *3001 Hennepin Ave.* ☎ *612/822-1688. Main courses $8–$19. Daily 11:30am–1am. AE, DISC, MC, V. UPSCALE ITALIAN.* This place is a trendy upscale bar/restaurant in the Uptown area with outdoor seating during the summer.

✪ **Giorgio's.** *2451 Hennepin Ave. S.* ☎ *612/374-5131. Main courses $10–$14. MC, V. Mon–Fri 11:30am–2:30pm; Mon–Sat 6–10pm. NORTHERN ITALIAN.* Located in Uptown, this upscale restaurant has an intimate, candlelight atmosphere. There are a variety of pastas and a selection of changing entrees. The garlicky Caesar salad is fabulous.

**Goodfellow's.** *In the City Center, 40 S. 7th St.* ☎ *612/332-4800. Reservations recommended. Main courses $19–$30. AE, CB, DC, DISC, MC, V. Mon–Fri 11:30am–2pm; Mon–Thurs 5:30–9pm, Fri–Sat 5:30–10pm. REGIONAL AMERICAN.* This comfortably elegant restaurant serves an American menu amid polished ambience with impressive table settings. The menu changes seasonally. All pastas, breads, stocks, and pastries are made from scratch and the extensive wine list highlights American vintages.

**Gustino's.** *In the Minneapolis Marriott City Center, 30 S. 7th St. (between Nicollet and Hennepin aves.).* ☎ *612/349-4075. Reservations recommended. Main courses $12–$24; fixed-price dinner $25. AE, CB, DC, DISC, MC, V. Mon–Thurs 6–10pm, Fri–Sat 6–11pm. Valet parking. ITALIAN.* Specializing in northern Italian food, this relaxed yet sophisticated restaurant offers a sixth-floor view of Minneapolis. A wait staff of professional singers entertains you. Popular choices include shrimp sautéed in olive oil, garlic, lemon, and white wine.

**Jax Cafe.** *1928 University Ave. NE (at 20th St.).* ☎ *612/789-7297. Reservations recommended. Main courses $15–$28. AE, CB, DC, DISC, MC, V. Mon–Sat 11am–3pm and 4–11pm; Sun 3:30–10pm; Sun brunch 10am–3pm. AMERICAN.* This elegant spot, which has been around since 1933, offers standard American fare in its five private dining rooms, each decorated differently. Outdoor dining provides a view of flower gardens, a waterfall, and mill wheel. Pick your own rainbow trout from the pond.

**Kikugawa.** *45 Main St. SE (Riverplace).* ☎ *612/378-3006. Reservations recommended. Main courses $8–$18; fixed-price dinner $25. AE, DISC, MC, V. Daily 11:30am–2pm and 5–10pm. Valet parking. JAPANESE.* Featuring views of Nicollet Island Park and the Mississippi River, this may be the city's best Japanese restaurant. The dining area offers both Japanese- and Western-style seating. There are unique dishes combining the cooking styles of Japan and Minnesota, like walleye kasuzuke, marinated in rice wine and then broiled.

✪ **Locanda Di Giorgio.** *4924 France Ave. S. (near 50th St.).* ☎ *612/928-0323. Main courses $8–$14. DC, DISC, MC, V. Tues–Sun 11:30am–2pm; Mon–Thurs 5–10pm, Fri–Sat 5–11pm. ITALIAN BISTRO.* This is a quiet, cozy restaurant in Uptown with a friendly staff. A flank steak with marsala and portobello mushrooms with a hint of Gorgonzola and rosemary is perfectly rendered; shrimp and lobster ravioli and stuffed spinach pasta in saffron cream sauce are also delicious.

**Loon Cafe.** *500 1st Ave. N. (at 5th St.).* ☎ *612/332-8342. Reservations accepted. Main courses $6–$11. AE, CB, DC, DISC, MC, V. Mon–Sat 11am–1am, Sun 11:30am–1am. AMERICAN.* This casual restaurant, close to the Target Center, is popular with a young professional crowd. The primarily American menu includes some Mexican dishes. An atmosphere of fun is reflected in whimsically named menu offerings like the tasty Loon Addict, a lightly breaded chicken breast sandwich.

**Lucia's Restaurant & Wine Bar.** *1432 W. 31st St.* ☎ *612/825-1572. Main courses $10–$19. MC, V. Daily 5:30–9:30pm. CONTINENTAL.* This restaurant/wine bar, located in Uptown, caters to a hip crowd. The menu changes weekly.

**Malt Shop.** *809 W. 50th St. (at Bryant).* ☎ *612/824-1352. Reservations not accepted. Main courses $4–$7. AE, CB, DC, DISC, MC, V. Daily 11am–10:30pm.*

*AMERICAN.* This old-style malt shop, with a jukebox and wooden booths, is just a few blocks from Lake Harriet. The menu ranges from vegetarian (ratatouille, pita stuffed with vegetables sautéed in peanut sauce) to gourmet burgers.

**Monte Carlo Bar & Grill.** *219 3rd Ave. N. (Warehouse District).* ☎ *612/333-5900. Reservations recommended. Main courses $7–$17. AE, CB, DC, DISC, MC, V. Daily 11am–1am. Valet parking. AMERICAN.* This favorite old-timer has been around since 1906. Textured ceilings, low lighting, and booths provide a comfortable ambience and a touch of elegance. Offerings include a variety of specialty sandwiches (crab salad sandwich, turkey Reuben) and classic pasta dishes.

**Morton's of Chicago.** *555 Nicollet Mall.* ☎ *612/673-9700. Reservations recommended. Main courses $17–$30. AE, CB, DC, MC, V. Mon–Fri 11:30am–2:30pm; Mon–Sat 5:30–11pm, Sun 5–10pm. Free valet parking. STEAK.* Located off the Nicollet Mall, this well-known steak house with dark wood furniture and booths offers a comfortable setting for elegant, intimate dining. Specialties include double filet mignon in béarnaise sauce.

**Mud Pie Vegetarian Restaurant.** *2549 Lyndale Ave. S. (at 26th St.).* ☎ *612/872-9435. Reservations accepted. Main courses $9–$13. AE, CB, DC, DISC, MC, V. Mon–Thurs 11am–10pm, Fri 11am–11pm, Sat 8am–11pm, Sun 8am–10pm. VEGETARIAN.* This very casual, highly regarded eatery offers veggie burgers, a Reuben made with a tempeh burger instead of corned beef, and Mexican dishes.

**Murray's.** *26 S. 6th St.* ☎ *612/339-0909. Reservations recommended. Main courses $10–$34. AE, CB, DC, DISC, MC, V. Mon–Thurs 11am–10:30pm, Fri 11am–11pm; Sat 4–11pm, Sun 4–10pm. AMERICAN.* Located in the heart of downtown, this family-owned establishment recently celebrated its 50th anniversary in Minneapolis. Enjoy piano and violin music as you dine on a special like Silver Butter Knife steaks and garlic toast. The award-winning wine list features over 500 wines.

**New French Cafe.** *128 N. 4th St. (betwen 1st and 2nd aves. N.)* ☎ *612/338-3790. Reservations accepted. Main courses $17–$21; fixed-price dinner $18. AE, DC, MC, V. Mon–Fri 7–11am and 12:30–2:30pm; Mon–Thurs 5:30–10pm, Fri–Sat 5:30–11pm; Sat–Sun brunch 8am–2pm. FRENCH.* Located in the Warehouse District, this restaurant offers a comfortable setting for French country cuisine, with the quaint bar and kitchen visible from the dining area. Satisfying entrees include Black Angus beef filet with a ragout of Roma tomatoes, mushrooms, and thyme.

**Nora's.** *3118 W. Lake St. (at Excelsior).* ☎ *612/927-5781. Reservations accepted. Main courses $6–$13. DISC, MC, V. Mon–Fri 11am–10pm, Sat–Sun 7am–10pm. AMERICAN.* This family-style restaurant, located just a few blocks from Lake Calhoun, features a casual dining room with flowered wallpaper and old photos for a distinctly homey quality. There is a soup and salad bar, breakfast buffet, and basics, like macaroni and cheese.

**Pickled Parrot.** *26 N. 5th St.* ☎ *612/332-0673. Main courses $9–$16. AE, DC, MC, V. Mon–Thurs 11am–10:30pm, Fri–Sat 11am–11:30pm; Sun 4:30–10pm. CARIBBEAN/SOUTHWESTERN.* In this Warehouse District restaurant, both the food and decor are eclectic. The outstanding award-winning ribs share the menu with salsa-flavored dishes and seafood.

**Sidney's.** *2120 Hennepin Ave. (at 22nd St.).* ☎ *612/870-7000. Reservations not accepted. Main courses $6–$10. AE, CB, DC, DISC, MC, V. Mon–Thurs 7am–11pm, Fri 7am–midnight, Sat 10am–midnight, Sun 10am–11pm. CALIFORNIAN.* This Uptown locale serves exceptional California cuisine, with excellent individual gourmet pizzas. Inside the comfortable, cedar interior with a gas-burning stone fireplace you can enjoy many specialties, including marinated rotisserie chicken Provençal (lemon, garlic, herbs) served with roasted potatoes and vegetables. There's an additional location in the Galleria Shopping Center, Edina (☎ 612/925-2002).

## MINNEAPOLIS AFTER DARK

To check on what's happening in Minneapolis, the free newsweekly *City Pages* lists all events. Other good sources are the *Star Tribune* and the monthly *Twin Cities Directory.*

**THE PERFORMING ARTS**   Minneapolis has a lively theater scene that includes two major companies as well as many smaller, cutting-edge theaters. The famous ✪ **Guthrie Theater,** 725 Vineland Place (☎ 612/377-2224), born in 1964, is the nation's premier classical repertory company. **Theater de la Jeune Lune,** 105 1st St. N. (☎ 612/333-6200), in the Warehouse District, is a strong and innovative acting company with a varied performance repertoire.

For more than 20 years, **Orchestra Hall,** 1111 Nicollet Mall (☎ 612/371-5656), has been home to the internationally acclaimed ✪ **Minnesota Orchestra.** Since 1980, the annual Viennese Sommerfest has drawn large audiences for programs including everything from light classics to orchestral masterworks. Antol Dorati is music director.

**THE CLUB & MUSIC SCENE**   The Warehouse District is the heart of Minneapolis nightlife. **First Avenue,** 701 1st Ave. N. (☎ 612/338-8388), is where Prince got his start. Connected to it is **7th Street Entry,** a small, loud venue for local music. **Blues Alley,** 15 N. Glenwood Ave. (☎ 612/333-1327), has live music Friday and Saturday and an open jam on Sunday. **South Beach,** 188 N. 4th St. (☎ 612/204-0790), is an upscale dance club targeting a slightly older nightclub crowd than 1st Avenue. **Fine Line Music Cafe,** 318 1st Ave. N. (☎ 612/338-8100), is an intimate music venue that caters to the 30-something crowd; musical groups vary from jazz trios to Alanis Morisette.

The **Loon Cafe,** 500 N. 1st Ave. (☎ 612/332 8352), was one of the first bars to set up shop in the Warehouse District; it has a crowded, casual atmosphere and is popular with the late 20s and early 30s downtown business crowd. **The Lounge,** 411 N. 2nd Ave. (☎ 612/333-8800), is a funky, relaxed bar set up with couches and comfortable chairs in various rooms—a good place to hang out and people-watch. **Rock Bottom Brewery,** 9th Street and Hennepin Avenue, in the Lasalle Plaza Building (☎ 612/332-2739), is a restaurant and brewery with pool tables. **City Billiards & Cafe,** 25 N. 4th St.(☎ 612/338-2255), is an upscale billiard hall and a staple of Warehouse District nightlife.

The **Gay 90's Theater Cafe & Bar,** 408 Hennepin Ave. (☎ 612/333-7755), caters to (but not exclusively) a gay clientele and features six bars and a show lounge presenting the finest female impersonators in the Midwest. **The Saloon,** 830 Hennepin Ave. (☎ 612/332-0835), is a gay nightclub downtown and has a younger crowd.

In Uptown, **Famous Dave's BBQ & Blues Club** (see above under "Dining") has live blues bands Wednesday through Friday. The **Uptown Bar & Cafe** is a popular grunge bar offering live music; it's a place to meet the locals. The **Smiling House,** 3018 Hennepin Ave. S. (☎ 612/822-5933), is a casual restaurant/bar.

## A SIDE TRIP TO THE MALL OF AMERICA

America's largest mall has everything—restaurants, major department stores like Bloomingdale's and Nordstrom, specialty stores, boutiques, movie theaters, night clubs, and even a golf course. On site is **Camp Snoopy,** America's largest enclosed theme park.

The mall is located in Bloomington, about a 20-minute drive from the city center during non-rush hours. Follow I-35W south to Minn. 62 East, go about 1 mile and exit onto Minn. 77 South (Cedar Avenue). Follow the signs to the mall. To get there by public transportation, take bus no. 80, which stops on Nicollet Mall near South 7th Street at the rounded glass booth. The trip takes about 30 minutes and costs $1.50

non-peak hours, $2 peak hours. Mall hours are Mon–Sat 10am-9:30pm, Sun 11am–7pm. Restaurants, nightclubs, and movies may have extended hours.

## 9 St. Paul

While St. Paul has its share of glass skyscrapers and 5 miles of skyways, it has preserved much of its Victorian architecture, and its downtown is a blend of the two styles. Somewhat smaller than Minneapolis, quieter and more conservative, it is also a cultural center with museums, universities, and theaters.

### ARRIVING & DEPARTING

**BY PLANE**   See "By Plane" in the Minneapolis section above. The airport is 8 miles south of downtown. A taxi to downtown will cost about $13 to $17.

**BY TRAIN & BUS**   The **Amtrak station** is at 730 Transfer Rd. (☎ 612/644-1127) and serves both cities. **Greyhound Lines** has a station at 25 W. 7th St. (☎ 612/222-0509).

### ESSENTIALS

**VISITOR INFORMATION**   The **St. Paul Convention and Visitor Bureau** is at 55 E. 5th St., Suite 102, St. Paul, MN 55101 (☎ 800/627-6101 or 612/297-6985).

**EMERGENCIES & SAFETY**   Call ☎ 911 in emergencies. Like its twin city of Minneapolis, St. Paul is one of the safest cities in the nation.

### GETTING AROUND

St. Paul has an extensive skyway system, which makes it easy to get around in all weather. St. Paul's downtown is easy to explore on foot, but a car will be needed to go into the suburbs. The **Metropolitan Transit Commission** (☎ 612/373-3333) runs buses between the two cities. Fares are $1 off-peak and $1.50 during rush hours.

### WHAT TO SEE & DO

A major cultural center, St. Paul has its share of museums, historic buildings, and other sights.

   **Alexander Ramsey House.** *265 S. Exchange St.* ☎ *612/296-8760. Admission $4 adults, $3 seniors, $2 children. May–Dec, Tues–Sat 11am–2pm.* The restored 1872 Victorian home of Minnesota's first territorial governor has been renovated and outfitted with period furnishings, black walnut woodwork, marble fireplaces, china and silver collections, and crystal chandeliers. Tours begin on the hour.

   **Cathedral of St. Paul.** *239 Selby Ave.* ☎ *612/228-1766. Admission free. Daily 8am–6pm.* Built in 1915 on the highest point in the city, this replica of St. Peter's in Rome boasts a 175-foot-high dome, a west-facing rose window, and massive granite-and-travertine construction.

   **James J. Hill House.** *240 Summit Ave.* ☎ *612/297-2555. Admission $4 adults, $3 seniors, $2 children. Wed–Sat 10am–3:30pm. Tours every 3 hours; call for reservations.* Situated on historic Summit Avenue, this was the house of the Great Northern Railway builder James J. Hill. Completed in 1891, the 36,000-square-foot red-sandstone residence has five floors, including 13 bathrooms, 16 crystal chandeliers, and a two-story skylit art gallery. Special events are held regularly and guided tours are offered Wednesday to Saturday.

   **Landmark Center.** *75 W. 5th St.* ☎ *612/292-3225. Admission free. Mon–Fri 8am–5pm, Sat 10am–5pm, Sun 1–5pm.* A fine 1902 example of the Roman Revival style, this restored Federal Court Building is capped by a tall belfry reminiscent of Trinity Church in Boston. You can still visit the courtrooms where notorious gangsters came

# St. Paul

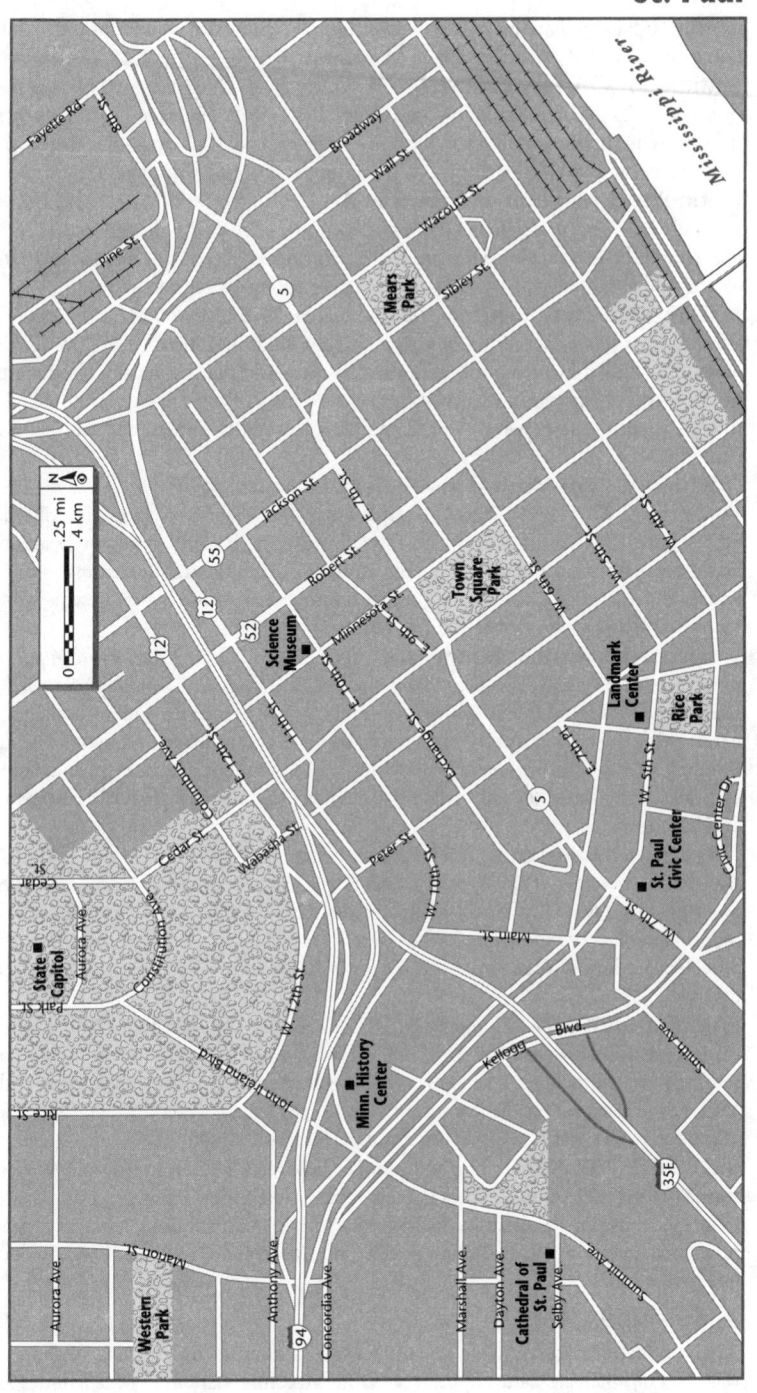

to trial. Today, the Landmark is an active cultural center with an auditorium, exhibition galleries, and the Schubert Piano Museum.

**Minnesota History Center.** *345 W. Kellogg Blvd.* ☎ *612/296-9131. Admission free. Tues–Wed and Fri–Sat 10am–5pm, Thurs 10am–9pm, Sun noon–5pm.* This three-story museum houses an impressive array of artifacts, books, photographs, maps, writings, videos, and interactive displays celebrating the history of Minnesota.

**Minnesota Museum of American Art.** *75 W. 5th St.* ☎ *612/292-4380. Admission free. Tues–Fri 10:30am–4:30pm, Sat–Sun 1–4:30pm.* Founded in 1927, this museum in the Landmark Center presents a permanent collection of more than 10,000 objects and a full range of art classes designed for young people and adults.

**Minnesota State Capitol.** *700 Wabasha St.* ☎ *612/296-2881. Admission free. Mon–Fri 9am–4pm, Sat 10am–3pm, Sun 1–3pm.* Built in 1905 on a hill overlooking downtown St. Paul, the capitol is crowned by the world's largest unsupported marble dome (modeled after the one Michelangelo created for St. Peter's Basilica in Rome). The interior is equally impressive, with its marble stairways, chambers, and halls, and oil paintings.

**Schubert Club Musical Instrument Museum.** *75 W. 5th St. (in the Land-mark Center).* ☎ *612/292-3267. Admission free. Mon–Fri 11am–3pm.* The collection here features 100 historical keyboard instruments spanning 450 years; a vast array of instruments from around the world; and a rotating exhibition of musical manuscripts, letters, and autographs. The distinguished International Artists Series presents world-renowned artists at the Ordway Music Theatre.

**Science Museum of Minnesota.** *30 E. 10th St.* ☎ *612/221-9444. Admission to exhibits, $5 adults, $4 children; Omnimax theater, $6 adults, $5 children; $2 extra for special exhibits. Mon–Sat 9:30am–9pm, Sun 10am–9pm.* Hands-on exhibits dealing with natural history, science, and technology are the focus at this massive museum. The East Building houses "Our Minnesota," featuring a 12-by-14-foot map that permits visitors to "walk" across the state. The Hall of Paleontology features a dinosaur lab. There's also an Omnitheater.

**Trains at Bandana.** *1021 Bandana Blvd. E. (Bandana Square).* ☎ *612/647-9628. Mon–Fri 10am–8pm, Sat 10am–6pm, Sun noon–5pm. Donation requested.* Sponsored by Twin City Model Railroad Club. Club members are assembling a scale-model panorama of railroading in the United States from the 1930s to the 1950s. The 3,000-square-foot O-scale layout features Twin Cities railroad landmarks, artifacts, and displays.

**PARKS & GARDENS    Como Park,** 1325 Aida Place (☎ **612/489-1740**), is one of the busiest and most beautiful parks in the Twin Cities, best known for its flower conservatory, which includes a Japanese garden, golf course, ski trails, and walking paths. Visitors will also find paddleboats, canoes, bikes, and in-line skates for rent. Open daily 10am–6pm peak season (Apr–Sept). Reduced hours off-season.

**BEST BETS FOR KIDS**    The **Minnesota Children's Museum,** 7th and Wabasha streets (☎ **612/225-6000**), offers popular features like a high-action maze and historic train. The museum also offers weekend programming, summer camps, and special group programs. Open daily 9am–5pm in peak season (Memorial Day–Labor Day). Reduced hours off-season.

## ACCOMMODATIONS

Accommodations are available downtown, and a number are attached to shopping centers. For hotels near the airport, see "Other Accommodations" in the Minneapolis section, above.

**Best Western Kelly Inn.** *161 St. Anthony Ave., St. Paul, MN 55103.* ☎ *800/ 528-1234 or 612/227-8711. 126 rms and suites. $79–$89 double; $125–$195 suite. Extra person $8. Children under 16 stay free in parents' room. Lower rates off-season. AE, CB, DC, DISC, MC, V. Free outdoor parking.* This older, plain facility still offers serviceable accommodations for the traveler on the go, and it is located minutes from downtown with views from some rooms. Some units have whirlpools. On the premises are a restaurant, bar, games room, sauna, and whirlpool.

**Days Inn Civic Center.** *175 7th St. W., St. Paul, MN 55102.* ☎ *800/DAYS-INN or 612/292-8929. Fax 612/292-1149. 203 rms and efficiencies. $63 double; $100–$139 efficiency. Extra person $8. Children under 12 stay free in parents' room. Lower rates off-season. AE, DC, DISC, MC, V. Free outdoor parking.* This unassuming tall building in the heart of downtown St. Paul is across the street from the Civic Center, and a skyway to it is being built. Some rooms offer views of downtown or the cathedral. It's well suited for people in town for special events and for groups. Facilities include a restaurant and bar.

**Radisson Hotel St. Paul.** *11 E. Kellogg Blvd. St. Paul, MN 55101.* ☎ *800/ 333-3333 or 612/292-1900. Fax 612/224-8999. 475 rms and suites. $89–$150 single or double; $150–$350 suite. Extra person $10. Children under 12 stay free in parents' room. Lower rates off-season. AE, CB, DC, DISC, MC, V. Indoor parking $9.* Located downtown, overlooking the Mississippi River, the Radisson's second-floor patio offers a nice river view, and the majority of rooms have views as well. The only revolving restaurant in the Twin Cities is here, as well as a bar, games room, pool, fitness center, and whirlpool.

**Ramada Hotel.** *1870 Old Hudson Rd. (White Bear exit off I-94), St. Paul, MN 55119.* ☎ *800/RAMADA or 612/735-2330. Fax 612/735-1953. 201 rms and suites. $94 double; $107–$125 suite. Extra person $10. Children under 18 stay free in parents' room, and under 12 eat free. AE, DC, DISC, JCB, MC, V. Free outdoor parking.* Two buildings connected by a corridor form this hotel. It is located in a busy commercial area dotted with fast-food restaurants and is 10 minutes from downtown. Some units offer terraces. The hotel has a restaurant, bar, games room, pool, sauna, whirlpool, social director, and washer/dryer.

**Saint Paul Hotel.** *350 Market St. (at 5th St.), St. Paul, MN 55102.* ☎ *800/ 292-9292 or 612/292-9292. Fax 612/228-9506. 254 rms and suites. $205 double; $230–$675 suite. Extra person $15. Children under 17 stay free in parents' room. AE, CB, DC, DISC, ER, JCB, MC, V. Indoor parking $10.* This beautiful, sophisticated hotel housed in a 1910 building is well suited to business travelers, with exquisite rooms decorated in European style, and offering fine views. The noted St. Paul Grill is here (see "Dining," below), in addition to another restaurant, a bar; and exercise equipment is provided upon request.

## DINING

As in Minneapolis, exotic cuisines are not favored, although there are a number of ethnic restaurants. Dress tends to be urban but casual.

**Bread & Chocolate.** *867 Grand Ave. (at Victoria).* ☎ *612/228-1017. Reservations not accepted. Main courses $3–$6. No credit cards. Mon–Fri 6:30am–5pm, Sat–Sun 7am–5pm. SANDWICHES/BAKERY.* A wonderful sandwich shop in Victoria Crossing West where you can get rolls, cookies, pies, and cakes, as well as a good selection of sandwiches with interesting spreads, like vegetable and crab and artichoke.

**Caravan Serai.** *2175 Ford Pkwy.* ☎ *612/690-1935. Reservations recommended. Main courses $9–$16. AE, DC, MC, V. Tues–Fri 11am–2pm; Mon–Thurs 5–9:30pm, Fri–Sat 5–10:30pm, Sun 4:30–9:30pm. AFGHANI.* This Afghani restaurant claims to be the first of its kind in the United States, with pillowed ceilings and Afghan treasures. Seating is American or Afghani style (low tables and pillows on the floor). Most dishes are cooked in a special clay pot, such as the half chicken marinated in 16 spices.

**Cognac McCarthy's Grill.** *162 N. Dale St. (a half mile west of the cathedral).* ☎ **612/224-4617.** *Reservations not accepted. Main courses $8–$10. AE, DC, MC, V. Mon–Sat 11am–1am, Sun 9am–9pm. AMERICAN.* Awnings and plants surround an inviting brick exterior, and the interior features large windows and lots of wood. Home-style cooking is the specialty, with one of the favorite items being the garlicky French–Cuban rotisserie chicken.

**Cossetta's Italian Market & Pizzeria.** *211 W. 7th St. (1 block west of the Civic Center, between Kellogg Blvd. and Chestnut).* ☎ **612/222-3476.** *Reservations not accepted. Main courses $5–$10. No credit cards. Mon–Sat 11am–10pm, Sun 11am–8pm. ITALIAN.* This enterprise began in 1911 as an Italian market; it was not until later that it was expanded to include this simple, fun, and charming restaurant. The menu features prize-winning pizzas and fine mostaccioli.

**Dakota Bar and Grill.** *1021 E. Bandana Blvd. (between Lexington and Snelling).* ☎ **612/642-1442.** *Reservations recommended. Main courses $12–$21; fixed-price dinner $20. AE, DC, DISC, MC, V. Mon–Thurs 5–10:30pm, Fri–Sat 5–11:30pm, Sun 5–9pm; Sun brunch 10am–2pm. REGIONAL AMERICAN.* All of the tables are decorated with flowers and offer a good view of the stage where live entertainment is regularly scheduled. The menu has a midwestern theme, with pork chops with cinnamon rhubarb sauce a standout.

**Dixie's.** *695 Grand Ave. (Summit Hill).* ☎ **612/222-7345.** *Reservations accepted. Main courses $6–$16. AE, DC, DISC, MC, V. Mon–Sat noon–1am, Sun 10am–11pm. CAJUN.* The menu offers burgers, sandwiches, and other items, all with a Cajun/Southern flair. Favorite items are fried salad, ribs, chili, and red beans and rice.

**Fabulous Ferns.** *400 Selby Ave. (at Western, 3 blocks west of the cathedral).* ☎ **612/225-9414.** *Reservations accepted. Main courses $9–$12. AE, DC, DISC, MC, V. Mon–Sat 11am–1am, Sun 10am–10pm. AMERICAN.* Well lighted with a fun upbeat ambience, this restaurant offers tasty modern American fare, such as chicken and dried-cranberry salad.

**Forepaugh's Restaurant.** *276 Exchange St. (3 blocks west of Civic Center).* ☎ **612/224-5606.** *Reservations recommended. Main courses $4–$18. AE, DC, MC, V. Mon–Fri 11:30am–2pm; Mon–Sat 5:30–9:30pm, Sun 5:30–8:30pm; Sun brunch 10:30am–1:30pm. Valet parking. FRENCH.* At this historic mansion, built in 1870 and adjacent to Irvine Park, the grace and grandeur of the architecture is matched only by the gracious French cuisine prepared by chef/owner Eric Schlenker. The formal, Victorian setting encompasses three floors and nine separate dining areas.

**Grandview Grill.** *1818 Grand Ave.* ☎ **612/698-2346.** *Reservations not accepted. Main courses $5–$8. No credit cards. Mon–Sat 6am–3pm, Sun 8am–3pm. AMERICAN.* This restaurant offers excellent food in a diner-style setting. The sister restaurant to Louisiana Cafe, you can expect the same great breakfasts—such as the elaborate Tex-Mex plates—with a touch less spice, and well-executed traditional American dishes for lunch.

**Green Mill.** *57 S. Hamlen Ave. (at Grand Ave.).* ☎ **612/690-0539.** *Reservations accepted. Main courses $8–$13. AE, DC, DISC, MC, V. Mon–Thurs 11am–11pm, Fri–Sat 11am–1am, Sun 10am–11pm. PIZZA.* Rich, dark woodwork, hanging plants, comfortable seating, and great, simple food make this an inviting place. You can order extra ingredients like spicy chicken or sun-dried tomatoes on any pizza. A brewery attached to the restaurant produces its own distinctive beer.

**Khyber Pass Cafe.** *1399 St. Clair Ave. (at Albert).* ☎ **612/698-5403.** *Reservations accepted. Main courses $6–$12. No credit cards. Tues–Sat 11am–1pm and 5–9pm.*

*AFGHANI.* This small, quaint neighborhood cafe offers authentic Afghani food. Family run, it attracts the locals with simple, hearty dishes like stewed chicken over rice.

**La Cucaracha.** *36 South Dale St.* ☎ *612/221-9682. Reservations accepted. Main courses $6–$10. AE, DC, MC, V. Mon–Thurs 11am–11pm, Fri–Sat 11am–midnight. MEXICAN.* Tucked away in a well-hidden spot on the block since 1961, this family-owned restaurant is worth the search. The menu offers authentic Mexican fare, with black-bean burritos and fajitas as favorites.

**Louisiana Cafe.** *518 Selby Ave. (at Dale).* ☎ *612/221-9140. Reservations not accepted. Main courses $3–$7. No credit cards. Mon–Sat 7am–2pm, Sun 8am–2pm. AMERICAN.* Housed in a brick building with attractive awnings and flowers, this bright, clean cafe is best known for its bountiful breakfast plates, including the popular Cajun breakfast.

**Old City Cafe.** *1571 Grand Ave. (near Macalester College).* ☎ *612/699-5347. Reservations not accepted. Main courses $4–$7. No credit cards. Mon–Thurs 11am–9pm, Fri 11am–2pm, Sun 11am–9pm. JEWISH/KOSHER.* This Kosher deli restaurant, located in an old building with huge windows, serves vegetarian, except for some tuna fish items. Falafel Parmesa (baked with vegetables and melted cheese) and Yemenite rice (with vegetables and spicy tomato sauce) are popular items.

**Ristorante Luci.** *470 Cleveland Ave. S.* ☎ *612/699-8258. Reservations recommended. Main courses $6–$20; fixed-price dinner $20. MC, V. Mon–Thurs 5–9:30pm, Fri–Sat 5–10:30pm, Sun 4:30–9pm. ITALIAN.* Small and intimate, this family-run restaurant offers homemade pastas and breads along with dishes representing different regions in Italy. The saltimbocca is highly recommended: medaillons of veal tenderloin layered with prosciutto and fontina cheese, topped with tomato and fresh sage.

**St. Paul Grill.** *In the Saint Paul Hotel, 350 Market St.* ☎ *612/224-7455. Reservations recommended. Main courses $10–$25. AE, CB, DC, DISC, ER, MC, V. Mon–Sat 11:30am–midnight, Sun 11am–midnight. Valet parking. AMERICAN GRILL.* Grilled meats and fish and excellent pastas are prepared here under the supervision of the hotel's executive chef, Robert Bach. The interior is enhanced by immaculate table settings and features views of the lovely English garden as well as Rice Park.

**Saji-ya.** *695 Grand Ave. (Summit Hill).* ☎ *612/292-0444. Reservations recommended. Main courses $11–$16. AE, DC, DISC, MC, V. Mon–Fri 11am–2pm; Sun–Thurs 5–10pm, Fri–Sat 5–11pm. JAPANESE.* A traditional Japanese restaurant where patrons enter across a bridge to be greeted by the Japanese staff. The dining area offers a view of the kitchen and there is a separate teppanyaki room.

**Table of Contents.** *1648 Grand Ave. (1 block west of Snelling Ave.).* ☎ *612/699-6595. Reservations recommended. Main courses $5–$20. DC, DISC, MC, V. Mon–Thurs 11:30am–9:30pm, Fri–Sat 11:30am–11:30pm, Sun 10am–9pm. NEW AMERICAN.* Located in the Macalester College area, this relaxed restaurant is connected to the Hungry Mind bookstore. A sure approach to New American cuisine, with creative use of herbs, produces tasty dishes like beef tenderloin with garlic mashed potatoes and olive tapenade. You'll find an additional location at 1310 Hen in Minneapolis (☎ *612/339-1133*).

**Tulips.** *452 Selby Ave. (just west of the cathedral, between Dale St. and Western Ave.).* ☎ *612/221-1061. Reservations accepted. Main courses $9–$18; fixed-price dinner $24–$29. AE, MC, V. Mon–Fri 11:30am–2pm; daily 5–9pm. FRENCH COUNTRY.* This small, comfortable establishment, in an otherwise unoccupied old brick building, presents the French country cooking of part owners David Wernz and Andy Klevn. Fine linens and tableware enhance menu offerings such as sautéed scallops with béarnaise sauce.

**W. A. Frost and Company.** *374 Selby Ave. (at Western).* ☎ *612/224-5715. Reservations recommended. Main courses $6–$20. AE, DC, DISC, MC, V. Daily*

*11am–midnight. AMERICAN.* This Victorian setting, in a historic red-stone building, offers a formal, dimly lit ambience and dark, solid furnishings and popular dishes like broiled lemon chicken with red peppers, served with pasta salad.

**White Lily.** *758 Grand Ave. (between Dale and Avon).* ☎ *612/293-9124. Reservations accepted. Main courses $5–$7. MC, V. Sun–Thurs 11am–9:30pm, Fri–Sat 11am–10:30pm. VIETNAMESE.* High wooden ceilings, windows the length of one wall, a red-tile floor, and many plants create an international flavor. The very popular Vietnamese salad has a base of chilled bean sprouts, rice noodles, and lettuce and is topped with hot, wok-cooked chicken and onions, sprinkled with carrots and peanuts.

## ST. PAUL AFTER DARK

To find out what's going on in St. Paul, check the calendar in the monthly *Minneapolis–St. Paul* magazine, the *St. Paul Pioneer Press,* and the free *City Pages* and *Twin Cities Directory.*

**THE PERFORMING ARTS** The **Schubert Club,** 301 Landmark Center (☎ 612/292-3267), was founded in 1882 and is now one of the oldest musical organizations in the United States. The Schubert brings celebrated artists to perform, and commissions works. The well-known ✪ **St. Paul Chamber Orchestra**'s home is the **Ordway Music Theater,** 345 Washington St. (☎ 612/224-4222). Opera, recitals, pop and classical concerts, and dance performances are also presented here.

**World Theater,** 10 E. Exchange St. (☎ 612/290-1221), is the home base of Garrison Keillor's famous radio show *Prairie Home Companion.* Touring companies also perform at this beautifully restored historic building. The **Great American History Theatre,** 30 E. 10th St. (☎ 612/292-4323), presents plays with themes relating to Minnesota history.

**THE CLUB & MUSIC SCENE** St. Paul has a big Irish neighborhood, and many Irish bars and clubs. **Chang O'Hara's Bistro,** 498 Selby Ave. (☎ 612/290-2338), is a bar/restaurant featuring fondue cooking at your table. There's local music almost every night and Dixieland jazz on Sunday. **O'Hara's Garage,** 164 N. Snelling Ave. (☎ 612/644-3333), is a dance club with live music, popular with the college crowd. **Sweeney's,** 96 N. Dale St. (☎ 612/221-9157), is a pub with a good beer selection where you can meet the locals.

For jazz, go to the **Artist's Quarter,** 366 Jackson St. (☎ 612/292-1359), which showcases national and local performers; or the **Dakota Bar and Grill,** 1021 E. Bandana Blvd. (☎ 612/642-1442), one of the Midwest's best jazz bars.

# 10 The Badlands & the Black Hills

When the Lakota tribe first encountered the mysterious buttes and spires of the Badlands they aptly named them *mako sica* ("bad land"). Depending on your frame of mind, the Badlands are a stark moonscape or a land of sun-kissed beauty. The Black Hills, with their wooded mountains, waterfalls, and rushing streams, present a startling contrast to the barren, rugged landscape of the Badlands.

## ESSENTIALS

**ARRIVING & DEPARTING** The **Rapid City Regional Airport,** on S.D. 44, is the area airport, and is served by Northwest Airlines, Skywest (Delta), and United Express. **Gray Line of the Black Hills,** Box 1106, Rapid City, SD 57709 (☎ 605/342-4461; fax 605/341-4614), offers bus tours of the Black Hills region. **Jack Rabbit Lines,** 301 N. Dakota, Sioux Falls, S.D. 57102 (☎ 800/454-6287), serves the towns of Wall and Rapid City.

A **car** is essential for exploring the area. Make rental reservations early; Rapid City car-rental agencies are often fully booked by business travelers.

**VISITOR INFORMATION**   For information about the area, contact **Black Hills, Badlands, and Lakes Association,** 900 Jackson Blvd., Rapid City, SD 57702 (☎ **605/ 341-1462;** fax 605/341-4614).

# BADLANDS NATIONAL PARK

A combination of volcanic ash, a sharp decrease in rainfall, and extreme temperatures have created the steep canyons and eerie-looking rock formations of the Dakota Badlands. Today the area is recognized as a geologic and ecological wonder worthy of preservation. Prairie dogs, badgers, coyotes, and a hardy band of surviving bison make the Badlands their home; yucca, cottonwood trees, and wild roses dot the landscape, and hundreds of wildflowers bloom.

**VISITOR CENTER**   For information about bird-watching, self-guided nature trails, and wildlife-watching, stop at the **Ben Reifel Visitor Center** (☎ 605/433-5361) at Cedar Pass, 9 miles south of I-90 on S.D. 240; it's open daily 8am–4:30pm, with extended hours in summer. The **White River Visitor Center,** operated in cooperation with the Pine Ridge Indian Reservation and open in summer only, has special cultural exhibits.

**ADMISSION COST & REGULATIONS**   Fees for entering the park are $10 per car, or $5 per person on foot. Bicycles and motorbikes are not allowed on trails or off the roads.

**INTERPRETIVE PROGRAMS**   Ranger-naturalists offer guided nature walks as well as evening programs and activities. Children can join a Junior Rangers program to learn about the geologic and other aspects of the park.

**WHEN TO GO**   The best times of year are fall and spring. In summer the temperature can be well above 100°F, and in winter winds are frigid and storms are common.

## EXPLORING THE PARK

From the northwestern Pinnacles entrance to the park, the 32-mile **Badlands Loop** along S.D. 240 gives a good overview of the park's rugged rock formations and changing vistas. The road has about a dozen scenic overlooks as well as a fossil exhibit trail. The topography of the Badlands has made it a natural site for filming: *Thunderheart* and *Dances with Wolves* were partially shot here and on the Pine Ridge Indian Reservation. The loop road passes through part of the **Buffalo Gap National Grasslands,** one of the last intact natural prairie landscapes.

On the 10-mile unsurfaced **Sage Creek Rim Road** the park's surviving herd of bison can be observed. Also on this road is a prairie-dog habitat, the **Robert Prairie Dog Town.**

Located 30 miles south of the park off S.D. 27 is **Wounded Knee National Historic Site,** commemorating the battle that was a turning point in U.S. government and American Indian relationships. The massacre there of unarmed Lakota by a U.S. cavalry contingent has never been forgotten and in 1973 it was the site of an Oglala Lakota protest.

**HIKING**   Six developed hiking trails are open to hikers, and the entire park, trails or not, is open to hikers.

**CAMPING**   There are two campgrounds in the park. The **Cedar Pass Campground** charges $8 per night and has some amenities. The **Sage Creek Wilderness Campground** is a primitive campground. Reservations are not accepted at either place. For information on nearby state campgrounds, contact the **Department of Game, Fish, and Parks** (☎ **605/773-3485**).

# The Badlands

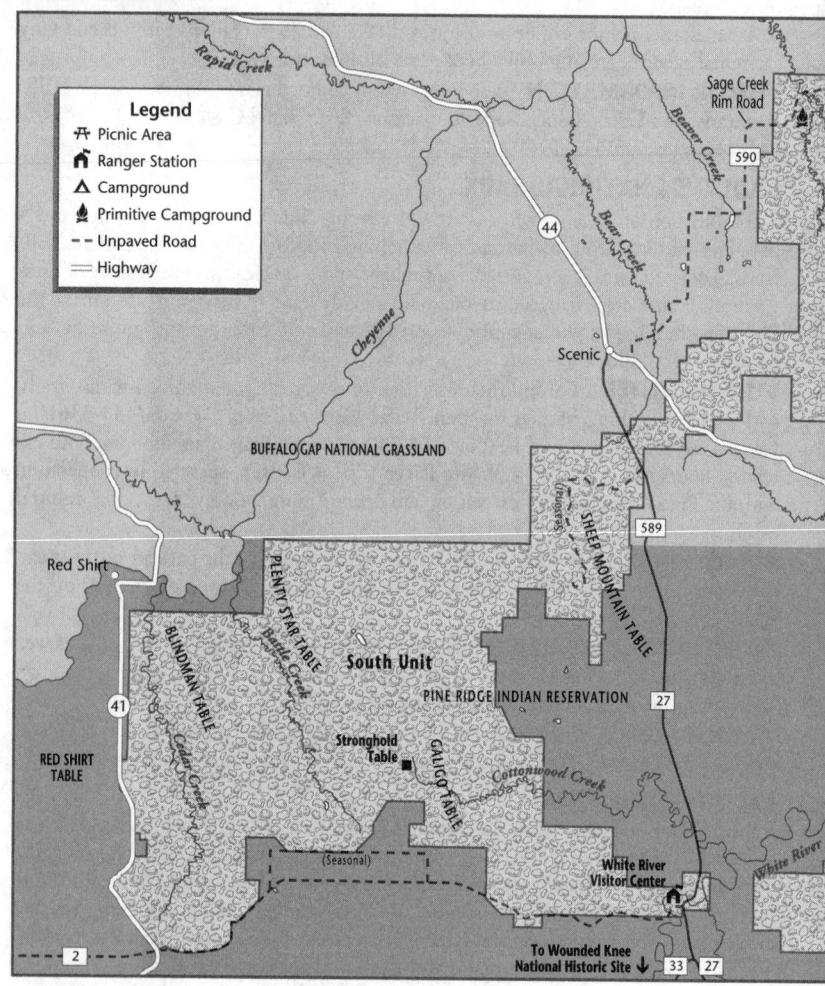

**Legend**
- 🏕 Picnic Area
- 🏠 Ranger Station
- △ Campground
- 🔥 Primitive Campground
- – – Unpaved Road
- ═══ Highway

## ACCOMMODATIONS

The only lodging in the park is the rustic **Cedar Pass Lodge,** Badlands National Park, Interior (☎ 605/433-5460). Accommodations are in one- or two-bedroom wood-frame cabins with a private bath; the cost is $47.25 per night plus $4 per person. The restaurant offers a meat-and-potatoes fare. It's closed mid-November to March.

## THE BLACK HILLS

The monumental faces of Mount Rushmore, South Dakota's most popular attraction, were carved into the granite of the Black Hills mountains. This is a magical area, with deep pine forests that look black from a distance, waterfalls, lakes, and caves. The gateway to the Black Hills National Forest is Rapid City, a town with a colorful mix of cowboy chic and Native American heritage, the cultural center of the western part of the state.

### EXPLORING THE BLACK HILLS

**IN RAPID CITY**   The **Dahl Fine Arts Center,** 7th and Quincy sts. (☎ 605/ 394-4101), features the work of local and regional painters and craftspeople and

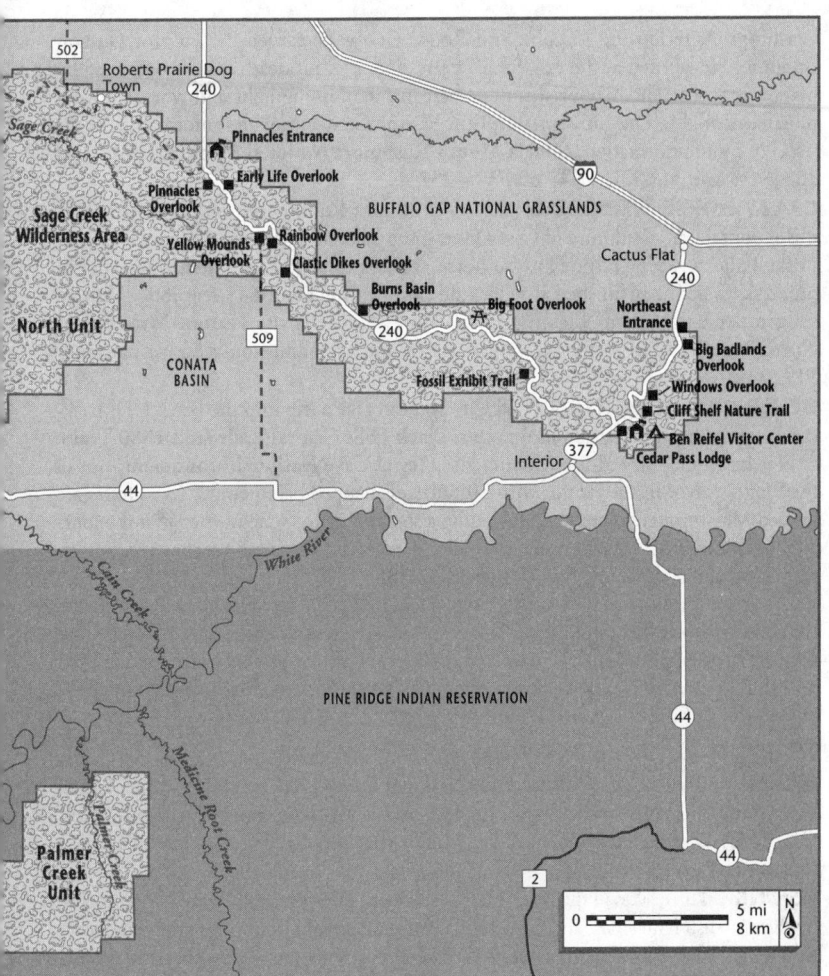

Native American artwork. The **South Dakota Air and Space Museum,** 2890 Davis Dr., Box Elder (☎ 605/385-5189), is at the entrance of Ellsworth Air Force Base and houses 23 vintage aircraft, including Gen. Eisenhower's personal B-25 bomber from World War II. Tours of the base leave the museum daily from mid-May to mid-September. The **Sioux Indian Museum,** 515 West Blvd. (☎ 605/348-0557), has an extensive display of ceremonial costumes, horse gear, weaponry, household articles, musical instruments, and more. Two exhibition galleries feature contemporary arts and crafts.

**BLACK HILLS NATIONAL FOREST**   This vast area covers more than 1 million acres. The area is a delight for the geologist—a domed mountain region composed of an ancient crystalline core with deep valleys, surrounded by ridges of sedimentary strata. The forest offers 28 campgrounds, picnic areas, lakes, and endless opportunities for the outdoor enthusiast (see "Sports & Outdoor Activities, "below). Its most famous sight, of course, is Mount Rushmore (see below). For information and camp reservations, contact the **Black Hills National Forest Superintendent's Office** (☎ 605/673-2251).

**MOUNT RUSHMORE NATIONAL MEMORIAL**   Some 24 miles southwest of Rapid City on U.S. 16 is the granite cliff where the faces of four presidents—

Washington, Jefferson, Lincoln, and Roosevelt—were carved by sculptor Gutzon Borglum. He labored at the task for 14 years, and after his death it was completed by his son Lincoln. The memorial is at its best in the morning light and when it is illuminated at night. The **Lincoln Borglum Visitor Center** provides information at the site. For more information, contact **Mount Rushmore National Memorial,** P.O. Box 268, Keystone, SD 57751 (☎ **605/574-2523**).

**CRAZY HORSE MEMORIAL**   A rival to Mount Rushmore in monumental scale, this mountain-size sculpture of Crazy Horse, the Lakota leader who defeated Custer at Little Bighorn, sitting astride his war horse, was begun in 1945 and remains a work in progress. When it is finished it will stand 563 feet high and 641 feet long. Visitors should expect frequent blasting at the site. On site is the **Indian Museum of North America.** The memorial is open year-round and admission is $6 per person or $15 per car.

**OTHER ATTRACTIONS**   In Hill City you can take a trip into the Black Hills backcountry on the antique steam locomotive, **Black Hills Central Railroad's 1880 Train.**

Not far from Crazy Horse Monument is **Jewel Cave National Monument,** one of the longest caves in the world, with 80 miles of mapped passageways. Cave tours are offered May through September, including a spelunking tour. Be warned that the tours are quite strenuous. The monument's visitor center has exhibits about the cave. For information about the tours, call ☎ **605/673-2288.**

To the southeast, south of Custer State Park, is **Wind Cave National Park,** one of the country's most beautiful natural caverns. In Lakota tradition it was from Wind Cave that the first Lakota people were tricked by Iktomi ("spider person") into leaving their ancestral home. An 8-mile walkway runs through the cavern. For information about guided tours of the cave, call ☎ **605/745-4600.**

## SPORTS & OUTDOOR ACTIVITIES

**BIKING**   Almost all of the **Black Hills National Forest** is open to bikers, while **Custer State Park** offers lots of back trails. Rapid City has a **9-mile trail** along Rapid Creek. U.S. 16A's 17-mile length, connecting Mount Rushmore and Custer State Park, is a fine stretch for views and sights.

**FISHING**   Three lakes in the Black Hills—Sheridan, Deerfield, and Pactola—are stocked by the state fish hatcheries, and numerous streams offer good trout fishing. If you like ice fishing, try Blue Dog, Enemy Swim, or Pickerel Lakes between December and March. Custer State Park has trout fishing in several lakes. Contact the **South Dakota Department of Game, Fish, and Parks** (☎ **605/773-3485**) for license information.

**HIKING**   The **Centennial Trail** runs 111 miles through the Black Hills National Forest, from Bear Butte, a site sacred to the Plains Indians, to Wind Cave National Park, passing through grasslands and high-country hills. Contact the state **Department of Tourism** (☎ **800/SDAKOTA**) for information. Trails in the **Black Elk Wilderness** and the **Norbeck Wildlife Preserve** include a climb to the top of 7,242-foot Harney Peak for a panoramic 60-mile view. Trail maps are available from **Black Hills National Forest** (☎ **605/673-2251**).

**HORSEBACK RIDING**   Horse trails cut through stunning buttes and rocky cliffs. An interesting trip is to Stronghold Table, site of the Sioux Ghost Dances. Call **Black Hills National Forest** (☎ **605/673-2251**) for information.

**SNOWMOBILING & SKIING**   The Black Hills is one of the country's premier spots for snowmobiling. More than 275 miles of groomed trails dip into canyons and deep pine forest. Cross-country skiing is available on 600 miles of abandoned logging roads, railroad beds, and fire trails. Call ☎ **800/445-3574** for maps of trails and information on snow quality.

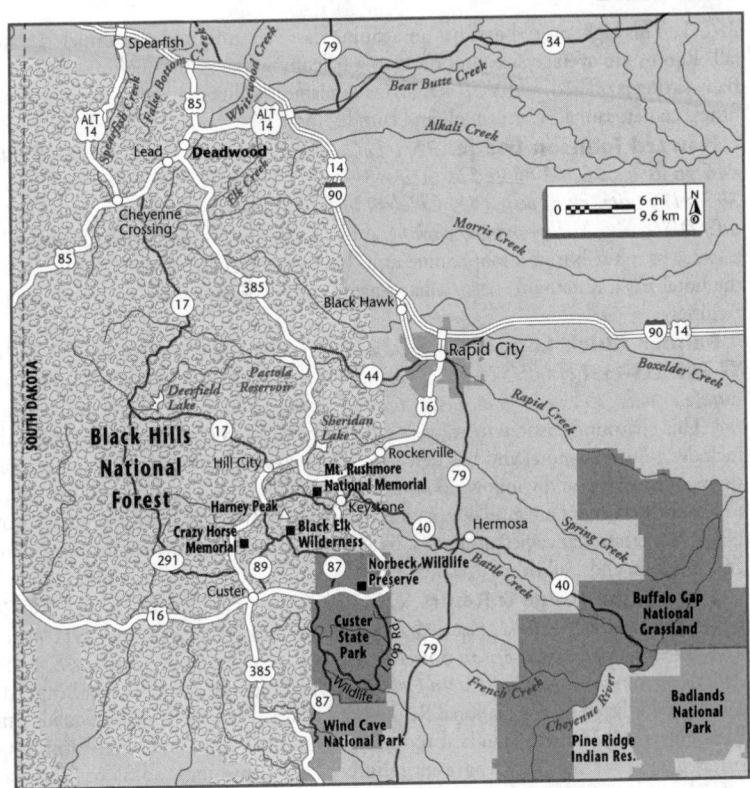

**WILDLIFE-WATCHING** **Custer State Park,** one of the largest state parks in the country, is the place to go. The park has a herd of 1,500 buffalo as well as elk, mule deer, mountain goats, and bighorn sheep. Visitors can take safari jeep rides to scout the animals. For information, contact the **Peter Norbeck Visitor Center** on S.D. 16A, or the **Wildlife Station Visitor Center** on the wildlife loop in the park, or call the director's headquarters at ☎ **605/255-4515.**

**CAMPING** For information about campgrounds, contact the **Department of Game, Fish, and Parks,** 523 E. Capitol Ave., Pierre, SD 57501 (☎ **800/710-2267** or 605/ 773-3485).

## ACCOMMODATIONS

There are accommodations in Rapid City, Hill City, Keystone, Hot Springs, and other towns in the vicinity, and Custer State Park has a number of resorts.

**Alex Johnson Hotel.** *523 Sixth St., Rapid City, SD 57701.* ☎ ***800/888-2539*** *or 605/342-1210. 109 rooms, 35 suites. $110–$120 double; $110–$250 suite. AE, DC, MC, V.* Listed on the National Register of Historic Places, this grand six-story hotel was featured in Hitchcock's *North by Northwest.* The lobby has a soaring beamed ceiling and a torch chandelier made of Lakota war lances. Rooms are furnished with replicas of the original furniture when the hotel opened in 1929. The hotel has a restaurant (see "Dining," below) and pub.

**Holiday Inn Rushmore Plaza & Convention Center.** *505 N. 5th St., Rapid City, SD 57701.* ☎ ***605/348-4000.*** *Fax 605/348-9777. 205 rms, 46 suites. AE, DC,*

*MC, V.* This eight-story hotel has an atrium, glass elevators, and a multitiered waterfall. Rooms are average size, and open to a balcony walkway overlooking the atrium. Baby-sitting is offered, and VCR rentals are available. Facilities include a restaurant, new fitness center, sauna, steam room, and laundry room.

**Howard Johnson Lodge.** *2211 LaCrosse St., Rapid City, SD 57701.* ☎ *800/446-4656 or 605/343-8550. Fax 605/343-9107. 272 rms and suites. $65–$90 double; $95–$175 suite. Extra person $8. Children under 18 stay free in parents' room. AE, CB, DC, DISC, MC, V. Free outdoor parking.* A block east of Rushmore Mall, this place has easy access to the business loop. Some units have terraces. Baby-sitting is available, and the hotel has a restaurant, bar, sauna, playground, pool with patio area, and laundry facilities.

**Palmer Gulch Lodge.** *On S.D. 244 (P.O. Box 295), Hill City, SD 57745.* ☎ *800/233-4331 or 605/574-2525. Fax 605/574-2574. 30 cottages and villas. $66–$50 cottage or villa. $5 extra person. Lower rates off-season. DISC, MC, V. Free outdoor parking.* This charming rustic retreat, with old and new cabins among the pine trees, also includes a 60-unit motel and has tent sites. The two-room cabins have wood-burning stoves or fireplaces and windows looking out to the hills. Baby-sitting and a free shuttle to Mount Rushmore are available. Extras include a restaurant, bar with entertainment, Native American dance performances, basketball, volleyball, games room, playground, golf facilities, and trail rides.

**State Game Lodge & Resort.** *U.S. 16A, Custer State Park, SD 57730.* ☎ *800/658-3530 or 605/255-4541. Fax 605/255-4706. 47 rms, 27 cottages. $80–$100 double; $65–$250 cottage. Extra person $5; cribs $5. Pets $5 extra (cabins only). AE, DISC, MC, V. Free outdoor parking. Closed Oct–Apr.* Set in a spectacular rustic landscape, this 1922 hotel is listed on the National Register of Historic Places. Presidents Coolidge and Eisenhower stayed here. Standard rooms have minimal decor and older furnishings; suites named for presidents have more interesting furnishings. Some cottages have housekeeping facilities. Baby-sitting is available. There's a restaurant, and jeep rides are offered.

## DINING

Most fare in the area is of the meat-and-potatoes and burgers variety with some seafood or Mexican dishes.

**Alpine Inn.** *225 Main St., Hill City.* ☎ *605/574-2749. Reservations not accepted. Main courses $6–$8. No credit cards. Mon–Sat 11am–2:30pm and 5–9:30pm. AMERICAN/GERMAN.* Once a hotel known as the "show place of Hill City," it now serves a German-inspired menu geared toward beef lovers.

✪ **Firehouse Brewing Company.** *610 Main St., Rapid City.* ☎ *605/348-1915. Reservations not accepted. Main courses $7–$14. AE, CB, DC, DISC, MC, V. Mon–Sat 11am–4pm; Mon–Sun 4–9pm. BREW PUB/ECLECTIC.* This brew pub is in a remodeled 1915 firehouse. An electic menu includes English pot pies, pasta, steak, seafood, burgers, burritos, and salads. A tasting sampler of the current house brews is offered for $5.

✪ **Landmark Restaurant.** *In the Alex Johnson Hotel, 523 6th St., Rapid City.* ☎ *605/342-1210. Reservations recommended. Main courses $6.95–$16.95. Mon–Sat 6am–2pm; daily 5–10pm; Sun brunch 10am–2pm. REGIONAL AMERICAN.* The restaurant has brick walls adorned with Native American artifacts and carvings. The menu offers traditional choices of chicken and beef and some specialties of freshwater fish and game.

✪ **Mediterranean Islands Restaurant.** *523 Main St., Rapid City.* ☎ *605/394-7727. Reservations recommended. Main courses $7.95–$15. AE, MC, V. Mon–Fri*

*11am–2pm and 5–9pm, Sun 11am–10pm. MEDITERRANEAN.* This small, bright restaurant has a pleasant scent of herbs and spices in the air. Menu choices include salads, pasta, chicken, and lamb, all prepared with Mediterranean influences.

✪ **Oriana's Bookcafe.** *349 Main St., Hill City.* ☎ *605/574-4878. Reservations not accepted. Main courses $4–$9. AE, DISC, MC, V. Daily 9am–9pm. TEX/MEX.* This three-level cafe/bookstore serves Mexican breakfast burritos or croissants to go with your coffee or espresso. Other specialties include enchiladas and black-bean tacos. It's a fine place to read or just browse.

**Uptown Grill.** *615 Main St., Rapid City.* ☎ *605/343-1942. Reservations not accepted. Main courses $6–$17; fixed-price menu $5–$6. DC, DISC, MC, V. Mon–Wed 11am–midnight, Thurs–Sat 11am–2am. AMERICAN.* Housed in a recently renovated historic building, the restaurant serves hamburgers, soups, and salads. Weekend jazz/blues performances make this place popular with locals.

## SIDE TRIPS

**A DAY IN DEADWOOD**  No trip to the area would be complete without a visit to Deadwood, the spot where Calamity Jane hung out and Wild Bill Hickok was shot dead during a poker game. This once rambunctious gold-mining boomtown rejuvenated itself after gambling was legalized in 1989. Gambling halls and casinos line the downtown and refurbished old hotels have their own gambling rooms. The **Adams Museum,** 54 Sherman St. (☎ 605/578-1714), is a treasure trove of Black Hills history and memorabilia, with photographs, minerals, guns, and Native American artifacts. The **Broken Boot Gold Mine** on U.S. 14A (☎ 605/578-1876) has guided tours of the mine and offers gold-panning. Wild Bill Hickok, Calamity Jane, and other notorious residents are buried in **Mt. Moriah Cemetery.** Today's list of movers and shakers include Kevin Costner, who owns the Midnight Star casino.

If you want to stay in Deadwood, try the **Bullock Hotel,** 633 Main St. (☎ 800/336-1876 or 605/578-1745), rumored to be haunted by its builder, the area's first sheriff. The **Historic Franklin Hotel and Gambling Hall,** 700 Main St. (☎ 800/688-1876 or 605/578-2241; fax 605/578-3452), retains a turn-of-the-century feel.

For more information, contact the **Deadwood/Lead Area Chamber of Commerce,** 735 Main St., Deadwood, SD 57732 (☎ 605/578-1876).

**DEVILS TOWER**  North and west of the Black Hills, over the border in Wyoming, you'll find this well-known image, featured in Steven Spielberg's *Close Encounters of the Third Kind.* It's about a 2 hour drive from Rapid City; follow I-90 to Sundance and turn north on Wy. 14. For information, call Devils Tower National Monument (☎ 307/467-5283). Also see "More Northwest Highlights" in part 8.

# 11 More Central State Highlights

## THE INDIANA DUNES NATIONAL LAKESHORE

"The Dunes," Carl Sandburg wrote, "are to the Midwest what the Grand Canyon is to Arizona. . . . They constitute a signature of time and eternity." The dunes rise 180 feet and more above Lake Michigan's southern shore, with uncrowded beaches, prairie, bird-filled marshes, and oak and maple forests. The area offers hiking, swimming, fishing, boating, and cross-country skiing in winter. The lakeshore's highest sand dune, the 192-foot Mount Tom, is in the 2,182-acre **Indiana Dunes State Park** (☎ 219/926-1952 for information). The **Dunes State Nature Preserve** boasts more species of trees than any other similar-size area in the Midwest. **Cowles Bog,** immediately south of Dune Acres, and **Pinhook Bog,** 6 miles south of Michigan City, are of special interest. This habitat includes the northern range of many birds and plants as well as plants representative of cooler climates. The **Paul H. Douglas Center for Environmental Education** (☎ 219/938-8221) is located in Miller Woods, a combination of open beach, dunes, and oak forest.

**Essentials:** For information about the Dunes National Lakeshore, contact the Superintendent, **Indiana Dunes National Lakeshore,** 1100 N. Mineral Springs Rd., Portage, IN 46304 (☎ 219/926-7561). Rangers lead birding walks, dune hikes, wildlife walks, and offer many other programs.

## SPRING GREEN & TALIESIN

Just north of the Wisconsin River in south-central Wisconsin is the Frank Lloyd Wright home and studio, **Taliesin.** The Welsh, with their lyrical speech and strong work ethic, settled in the rural countryside around Spring Green, and among them was Lloyd Jones, grandfather of architect Frank Lloyd Wright. Wright's house and school is built on the brow of a hill facing the Wisconsin River; its name, Taliesin, is Welsh for "shining brow." Visitors can observe architects and apprentices at work in the drafting studio, which Wright likened to "an abstract forest with light pouring in from the ceiling." They may also see Wright-designed furniture and take a 90-minute 2-mile country walk past gardens, ponds, and other buildings on the estate.

South of town, the **House on the Rock** defies description. Built as a retreat atop a 60-foot rock chimney, the house is an architectural curiosity, with massive fireplaces, pools of running water, and spectacular views of the surrounding landscape. Its museum collections of scrimshaw, miniature circuses, doll houses, and theater organs is equally curious. Outside the house is the world's largest carousel with 269 handcrafted animals—not one of them a horse.

You can stay at the **Silver Star,** on Limmex Hill Road (☎ 608/935-7297), a huge log building on 350 acres of woods and farmland with a very good restaurant. The area also offers over two dozen farm vacations where kids can milk a cow, pick raspberries, dine on homegrown vegetables, take a hay ride, paddle a canoe, or go fishing and stay in century-old farmhouses or rustic cabins.

**Essentials:** For information, contact the **Spring Green Area Chamber of Commerce,** P.O. Box 3, Spring Green, WI 53588 (☎ 608/588-2042). For information about farm vacations, call the **Wisconsin Department of Tourism** (☎ 800/432-TRIP).

## THE WISCONSIN DELLS

Although some decry the heavily touristed Wisconsin Dells, the bustling resort has a lot going for it. Its towering sandstone cliffs and cool fern-filled gullies remain relatively unspoiled. The Wisconsin River flowed through soft limestone for thousands of years to carve out the Dells. In summer, you can view the river and its spectacular rock formations by cruising with **Dells Boat Tours** (☎ 608/254-8555), or aboard World War II amphibious "ducks" at **Dells Ducks** (☎ 608/254-6080) or **Original Wisconsin Ducks** (☎ 608/254-8751).

Perennial family attractions in the Dells include **Tommy Bartlett's Ski, Sky, and Stage Show,** 560 Wisconsin Dells Pkwy. (☎ 608/254-2525), a well-produced variety of entertainment that includes a waterskiing show, stunt boats, and a laser/water spectacle after dark. **Noah's Ark Waterpark,** 1410 Wisconsin Dells Pkwy. (☎ 608/254-6351), and **Family Land,** Wisconsin Dells Parkway (☎ 608/253-7766), offer typical water-park attractions, including water slides, inner-tube rides, restaurants, shops, and picnic areas.

At nearby Baraboo, **Circus World Museum,** 426 Water St. (☎ 608/356-0800), pays homage to the birthplace of some of the greatest shows on earth. Once headquarters of

Ringling Brothers, the museum is a storehouse of gilded wagons, calliopes, costumes, and other circus memorabilia. Daily events include performances in the big top and a high-wire act across the Baraboo River. The lakeshore of **Mirror Lake State Park,** entry off Fern Dell Road (☎ **608/254-7951**), is formed by sandstone cliffs up to 50 feet high, and pine and oak woods surround the lake. Picknicking, boating, and camping are available.

There are many overnight options in the area: The **Quality Inn,** P.O. Box 84, Baraboo, WI 53913 (☎ **800/355-6422** or 608/356-6422), is a handy place for families, with many amenities and a bar/restaurant that serves all meals; **Holiday Inn,** 655 Frontage Rd. (P.O. Box 236), Wisconsin Dells, WI 53965 (☎ **800/543-3557** or 608/254-8306), is another family-oriented place; **Black Hawk,** 720 Race (P.O. Box 15), Wisconsin Dells, WI 53965 (☎ **608/254-7770**), is the oldest family-owned motel in Wisconsin, and has large rooms with terraces.

**Essentials:** For information, contact the **Wisconsin Dells Visitor and Convention Bureau,** 701 Superior St. (P.O. Box 390), Wisconsin Dells, WI 53965 (☎ **608/254-8088**).

# The Southwest, Texas & Colorado

A land of wide open spaces between big cities, the American Southwest begins in the humid flatlands of east Texas and sweeps across the continent to the majestic Rocky Mountains and on to the barren deserts of Arizona. This was America's last frontier, a place where rugged individualism flourished, and where fortunes were made overnight from oil.

Today Houston is known more for its jumble of freeways and former President George Bush than the oil that made it rich. Dallas has its football Cowboys and the lingering reputation of J.R. Ewing from the popular TV series. The population of San Antonio, where the Texas freedom fighters died at the Alamo fighting for independence from Mexico, is now nearly 60% Mexican-American, giving it a rich cultural life. Residents of high-tech, education-minded Austin let their hair down to listen to some of America's best country-and-western music.

Up in Colorado, the showcase city of Denver sits at the foot of the great Rocky Mountains, which have their own national park. Across the mountains, beside a great inland sea, you may still have trouble finding libation in Salt Lake City, home to the teetotaling Mormon Church. But in southern Utah, you can whet your eyesight on the geologic wonders of Bryce Canyon and Zion national parks. In the Rockies' southern foothills stand trendy Santa Fe and Taos, both filled with Native American culture, artists and writers, and rich expatriots from Los Angeles.

Follow the Colorado River southwest and you will come to its immense Grand Canyon, one of the great wonders of the world. Southeast of the canyon you will see a desert so colorful it actually is named Painted. And down in Arizona you'll visit the irrigated oases of Phoenix, Scottsdale, and Tucson, where Americans love to golf during pleasant winters.

Indeed, the Southwest today is as varied and as beautiful as ever.

## DRIVING TOUR
## Colorado's Western Slope

**Start:** Grand Junction
**Finish:** Durango
**Distance:** 213 miles
**Time:** 1–3 days
**Highlights:** Spectacular mountain scenery, dinosaurs, historic Old West towns, a steam train

This tour covers some of Colorado's most spectacular scenery, particularly at Colorado National Monument at the beginning of the trip and along the drive from Ouray to Durango near the end. Although the route from Grand Junction to Durango is considered all-weather and is maintained year-round, it includes several mountain passes that are often closed during winter snowstorms. If you have severe fear of heights, you can avoid the steep and somewhat scary drive over Red Mountain by turning back at Ouray.

Begin the tour at the junction of I-70 and U.S. 50 at:

1. **Grand Junction,** founded in 1882 where the spike was driven to connect Denver and Salt Lake City by rail. It quickly became the main trade center between the two state capitals. Its mild climate, together with fertile soil and irrigation from the Gunnison and Colorado rivers, helped it grow into an important agricultural area.

The primary attraction here is **Colorado National Monument** (☎ 970/858-3617). Although the east entrance is only 5 miles west of Grand Junction off Monument Road, the best way to explore the monument is to begin at the west entrance, following signs off I-70 from the small community of Fruita, 15 miles west of Grand Junction. It's here that the 23-mile **Rim Rock Drive** begins, snaking up dramatic Fruita Canyon and offering panoramic views across the Colorado River valley to the Grand Mesa and Book cliffs. Carved by millions of years of wind and water erosion, the park's spectacular landscape boasts red-rock canyons and sandstone monoliths—some towering more than 1,000 feet high—plus a variety of fanciful and sometimes bizarre rock formations. Bighorn sheep, mountain lions, and golden eagles are among the wildlife inhabiting the semidesert plateau. At the visitor center you'll find exhibits on the park's geology and history.

While in Fruita you might want to stop at **Devil's Canyon Science & Learning Center,** 550 Crossroads Court. Just south of I-70 off exit 19, the center is especially popular with kids, who can journey back to the Jurassic period to watch a mother stegosaurus defending her young or visit the last ice age alongside a mighty mammoth. Interactive exhibits will let you experience an earthquake, create a sandstorm, and feel the icy wall of a glacier. Nearby, **Rimrock Adventures,** on Colo. 340 about a half-mile south of I-70 off exit 19, is home to exotic deer from around the world; you can also see goats, sheep, and elk, and visit a wildlife museum.

Back in downtown Grand Junction, stop at the **Museum of Western Colorado,** 248 S. 4th St. Inside is a pioneer room and kitchen. The museum also houses an extensive firearms collection, Native American artifacts, natural history exhibits, and Western art. Operated by the museum, **Cross Orchards Historic Site,** 3079 F Road, is a re-creation of an early 20th-century farm, with a blacksmith shop, barn, workers' bunkhouse, and farm manager's home. Living history demonstrations are offered daily in summer, and various events are held throughout the year.

**Dinosaur Valley,** 362 Main St., contains animated replicas, complete with sound effects. Visitors can study regional paleontological history, examine a model of a dinosaur dig, and view plaster casts of dinosaur footprints. At **Doo Zoo Children's Museum,** 635 Main St., children 12 and younger get hands-on experience in a variety of activities, from art to science to the most real world of adult work. The museum's toy store specializes in educational items.

Before leaving Grand Junction, be sure to drive or walk by **Art on the Corner,** located along Main Street between 1st and 7th streets. This changing outdoor sculpture exhibit is part of a shopping park with wide tree-lined pedestrian walkways that also includes art galleries, antique shops, restaurants, and a variety of retail stores. The **Western Colorado Center for the Arts,** 1803 N. 7th St., contains works of art, many with western themes, plus more than 50 Navajo weavings

# Driving Tour: Colorado's Western Slope

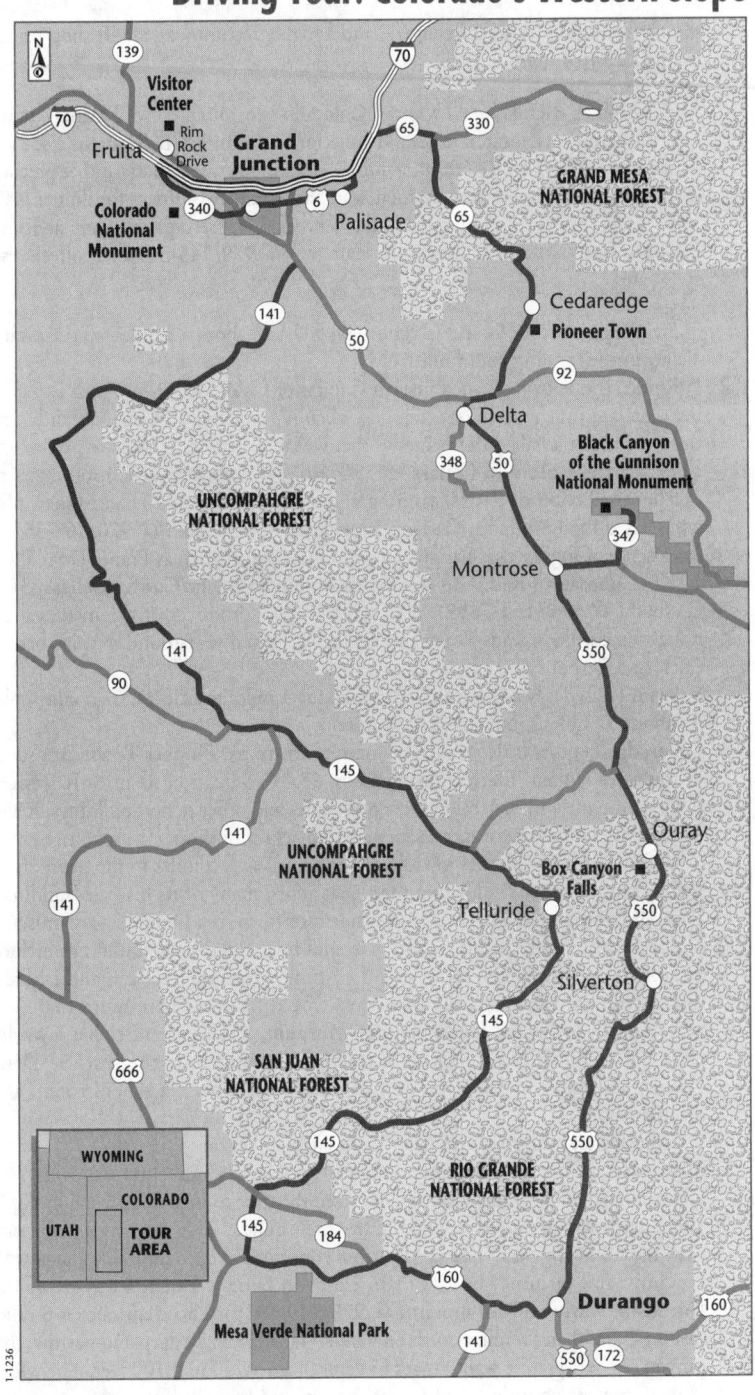

dating from the turn of the century, and a highly recommended gift shop featuring handcrafted items.

☕ **TAKE A BREAK** As western Colorado's major center of business, you'll find numerous restaurants in Grand Junction, including **GB Gladstone's,** 2531 N. 12th St. (☎ 970/241-6000), a quietly elegant, upscale restaurant that prepares interesting variations of beef, seafood, and pasta standards. Prices for dinner main courses are $5 to $18. For a quick sandwich, salad, or fresh pastry, shop at **Jitters Espresso Bar Cafe and Bakery,** 504 Main St. (☎ 970/245-5194), a coffeehouse-style cafe.

Heading east from Grand Junction, take U.S. 6 about 12 miles up the Grand Valley to the farming community of:

2. **Palisade,** the self-proclaimed "Peach Capital of Colorado." Most fruit is picked between late June and mid-September, when it's available at roadside stands, and there are about a half-dozen wineries that welcome visitors. The state's oldest existing winery, **Colorado Cellars,** 3553 E Rd. (☎ 800/848-2812), produces an excellent selection of award-winning chardonnay wines and champagnes, plus wine-based food products. **Carlson Vineyards,** 461 35 Rd. (☎ 970/464-5554), has a sense of humor that has given its products names such as Prairie Dog White and Tyrannosaurus Red. And **Rocky Mountain Meadery/Confre Cellars,** 3701 G Road (☎ 970/464-7899), is Colorado's only producer of the medieval-era honey wine called mead. Tours and tastings are given year-round, but it's best to call ahead for hours.

From Palisade, head east on I-70 for about 4 miles to exit 47, then take Colo. 65 about 52 miles southeast for a stop in:

3. **Cedaredge,** a quiet little residential community, to see **Pioneer Town,** just south of the town's main intersection on Colo. 65. A re-creation of an early western town, complete with jail, saloon, country store, and other period buildings, it also contains a Native American museum and a blacksmith shop.

Continue south 10 miles to Colo. 92 and head west 5 miles to the town of:

4. **Delta,** known for the colorful murals that adorn many of its historic buildings. **Fort Uncompahgre,** off U.S. 50 just north of town, is a living history museum in a reconstructed 1826 fur-trading post and fort. Hand-hewn buildings include a trade room and living quarters, and costumed traders, trappers, and laborers discuss the hard but exciting lives they would have led here more than 150 years ago. In town, the **Delta County Museum,** 251 Meeker St., has a world-class butterfly collection. Other attractions here include the historic Delta County Jail, built in 1886, pioneer tools and machinery, a school room, and dinosaur bones.

From Delta, head south on U.S. 50 about 21 miles to:

5. **Montrose,** in the Uncompahgre Valley where Ute chief Ouray and his wife Chipeta ranched until the government forced the tribe to migrate to Utah in 1881. White settlers then moved in, and the area grew quickly with the arrival of the railroad the following year. Today Montrose continues its agricultural heritage with ranching and farming, but its main claim to fame is **Black Canyon of the Gunnison National Monument** (☎ 970/249-1915), whose entrance is 8 miles east on U.S. 50 and 6 miles north on Colo. 347. Amazingly deep and narrow, this canyon of sheer granite walls ranges in depth from 1,730 to 2,700 feet. The width at its narrowest point is 1,100 feet at the rim and only 40 feet at the Gunnison River.

Although a summer-only access road winds to the bottom of the canyon at the East Portal Dam in the adjoining Curecanti National Recreation Area, access to the canyon floor in the national monument itself is limited to hiking trails that wind down steep side canyons. You can view the canyon from above, along the South Rim, site of a visitor center, or along the lesser-used North Rim. Short paths off both roads lead to viewpoints with signs explaining the canyon's unique geology. The visitor center is open daily in summer but has intermittent hours in spring and fall; it is closed in winter. The road to the South Rim is open 24 hours a day year-round, and the North Rim is open around the clock except when closed by snow, usually between December and March.

Nearby, **Fort Eagle Trail,** 72291 U.S. 50 east (5 miles east of Montrose), is a family-oriented living history museum that depicts the West from 1790 to 1860, with soldiers and other fort residents in period dress. Visitors can try their hand at tomahawk throwing and other activities.

Once you're back in downtown Montrose, stop at the **Montrose County Historical Museum,** West Main Street and Rio Grande Avenue, in the historic Denver and Rio Grande Railroad Depot. The museum includes an 1890s homesteader's cabin, railroad memorabilia, antique toys, a country store, and Native American artifacts. **Ute Indian Museum,** 17253 Chipeta Dr., is on the site of the final home of Chief Ouray and wife Chipeta. Situated 2 miles south of downtown off U.S. 550, it offers an extensive collection of Ute artifacts, including ceremonial items. Also on the grounds are Chipeta's grave and tiny, bubbling Ouray Springs.

You'll have several good choices of accommodations in Montrose, including the **Best Western Red Arrow,** 1702 E. Main St. (☎ **800/528-1234** or 970/249-9641), a handsome, moderately priced modern motel with particularly attractive rooms, and the independent **Red Barn Motel,** 1417 E. Main St. (☎ **970/249-4507**), with clean, comfortable rooms in the budget price range.

☕ **TAKE A BREAK**   Fresh baked goods and Southwestern dishes prepared over a mesquite grill are the specialties of **Camp Robber Cafe,** 228 E. Main St. (☎ **970/240-1590**). Prices for dinner are in the $6–$17 range. The **Whole Enchilada,** 44 S. Grand Ave. (☎ **970/249-1881**), offers Mexican dishes and burgers in a cheerful family-style atmosphere. Prices run $3–$12.

From Montrose, continue south on U.S. 550 for 37 miles to:

**6. Ouray,** named for the great chief of the southern Utes, who lived in this area. Ouray got its start in 1876 as a gold- and silver-mining camp. Within 10 years it had 1,200 residents, a school, several churches, a hospital, and dozens of saloons and brothels. Many of its original buildings still stand, and beautiful mountain scenery surrounds the town. Begin your visit at the **Ouray County Museum,** 420 Sixth Ave., in the town's first hospital, built by the Sisters of Mercy in 1887. Exhibits include memorabilia of Chief Ouray and the Utes, turn-of-the-century hospital equipment (including some truly frightening medical devices), and other historical items. Get a copy here of a **walking tour** guide to Ouray's historic buildings. To really get a taste of the community's early days, take the **Bachelor–Syracuse Mine Tour,** 2 miles north of Ouray via County Road 14. A train transports visitors deep inside an old mine, where over $100 million in gold, silver, and other minerals were mined after the first silver strike in 1884. Guides describe the mining process and tell stories of the mine.

Next head to **Box Canyon Falls,** off Oak Street above Third Avenue. Among the most impressive falls in the Rockies, they are created as the Uncompahgre River tumbles almost 300 feet through an opening in a cliff. For a soothing soak, stop at the large **Ouray Hot Springs Pool,** along U.S. 550 at the north end of town, where the odorless mineral water is cooled from its ground temperature of 150°F to 80°F.

The 23 miles on U.S. 550 south from Ouray over 11,000-foot Red Mountain Pass to Silverton are part of a spectacular drive. The road shimmies up the sheer sides of the Uncompahgre Gorge, through tunnels and past cascading waterfalls, then follows the route of a 19th-century toll road. Abandoned mining equipment and log cabins can be seen on the slopes of the steel-gray mountains, many of them over 14,000 feet. Soon you'll arrive in:

**7. Silverton,** perched at an altitude of 9,300 feet at the northern end of the Durango and Silverton Narrow Gauge Railroad. Now a National Historic Landmark District, the town was a silver mining camp in 1871, notorious for its saloons and brothels—so much so that famed lawman Bat Masterson, fresh from taming Dodge City, was called in to make Silverton suitable for decent folks. Today the original false-fronted buildings (sometimes used as movie sets) remain, but they now house restaurants and galleries.

The **San Juan County Historical Society Museum,** in the turn-of-the-century jail at Greene and 15th streets, displays memorabilia from Silverton's boom days. Other interesting buildings include the **San Juan County Courthouse** (next to the museum), with its gold-domed clock tower; and the recently restored **Town Hall** at 14th and Greene streets.

From Silverton continue 49 miles south on U.S. 550 as it climbs over the 11,000-foot Molas Divide and follows the tracks of the Durango and Silverton Narrow Gauge Railroad into:

**8. Durango,** born as a railroad town more than a century ago and still one—at least in summer, when thousands of visitors take a journey back in time aboard the Durango and Silverton Narrow Gauge Railroad (the **depot** is at 479 Main Ave.). In continuous operation since 1881, this coal-fired steam train, with its string of Victorian coaches, puffs its way 45 miles up scenic Animas Canyon, past relics of 19th-century mining and railroad days, to Silverton, before heading back to Durango. A center for outdoor recreation, Durango is a good base for whitewater rafting on the Animas River.

Good lodging possibilities here include the stately **Victorian Strater Hotel,** 699 Main Ave. (☎ **800/247-4431** or 970/247-4431), with moderate-to-expensive rates, and the inexpensive **Redwood Lodge,** 763 Animas View Dr. (☎ **970/247-3895**), a clean and comfortable independent motel.

☕ **TAKE A BREAK**   Durango has a number of good choices for a meal, including **Carver's Bakery/Cafe/Brewery,** 1022 Main Ave. (☎ **970/259-2545**), a friendly neighborhood restaurant that offers good Southwestern cooking. Dinner main courses range from $5 to $8.

To return to Grand Junction, you can either retrace your route or create a loop tour through more mountain scenery. Just follow U.S. 160 west, past Mesa Verde National Park, to Colo. 145, which you can take north through the San Juan National Forest to the ski resort of Telluride. Then follow Colo. 145 and Colo. 141 north back to Grand Junction. This return route is 271 miles long.

# DRIVING TOUR
## Phoenix, Prescott & Sedona

**Start:** Phoenix
**Finish:** Pioneer Arizona Living History Museum
**Distance:** 362 miles
**Time:** 3–5 days
**Highlights:** Rock formations, Victorian buildings, old mining towns, Native American ruins

From Phoenix's fine art museums to Sedona's red rocks, this tour of central Arizona's top attractions wanders through historic mining towns and modern communities as well as some of America's most spectacular scenery. Mileages listed are from stop to stop only and do not include travel within a stop or side trips, which may easily add another 100 miles. Some mountain driving is included, and although most roads are paved and well maintained, allow extra time. The section of Ariz. 89A north of Sedona, through spectacular Oak Creek Canyon, is not recommended for large trailers.

Start in America's eighth largest city:

**1. Phoenix,** which is what people mean when they talk about the "New West." Phoenix and its surrounding cities—known collectively as the Valley of the Sun—attract both visitors and transplants with over 300 days of sunshine a year, mild temperatures, a robust economy, and an easygoing outdoor lifestyle. See section 8 of this chapter, below, for details.

After you've visited Phoenix, head northwest out of the city on U.S. 60 (Grand Avenue), and follow the railroad for 58 miles to:

**2. Wickenburg,** founded in 1863 by Prussian immigrant Henry Wickenburg, who discovered what would become Arizona's richest gold and silver mine. Wickenburg is a good place to relive the Old West. As you enter on U.S. 60, turn right (north) onto Tegner Street, then left (west) on Yavapai Street, which takes you to Frontier Street and the **Chamber of Commerce,** in the Old Santa Fe Depot, where you can pick up a historic walking tour map. On Frontier Street, you'll see false-front buildings dating to the turn of the century. **Desert Caballeros Western Museum,** 21 N. Frontier St. (☎ 520/684-2272), displays a 1900 street scene, rooms from a Victorian home, minerals, and Native American artifacts. Don't miss the Jail Tree, near the corner of Wickenburg Way and Tegner Street, where outlaws were once chained because no one wanted to take time out from mining to build a real jail.

About 12 miles south of town on Vulture Mine Road, you'll find Wickenburg's original reason for existence, **Vulture Mine,** where you can take a self-guided, aboveground tour and explore some of the remaining 1884 buildings of Vulture City. About 3 miles south of Wickenburg on U.S. 60 is the **Hassayampa River Preserve** (☎ 520/684-2772), with self-guided nature walks along the Hassayampa River, Palm Lake, and through cottonwood-willow forests.

From Wickenburg, continue northwest on U.S. 93 for 6 miles to Ariz. 89, which branches off to the north along the railroad tracks for 10 miles to Congress, and continue north about 2 miles on Ariz. 89 to a rough dirt road heading east onto the plain. Follow that about 7 miles to:

**3. Stanton,** established in 1863 after gold nuggets reportedly the size of potatoes were discovered. Originally called Antelope Station, Stanton had 3,500 residents by 1868, but both its population and gold prospects had dwindled by the early

1900s. Today the town is owned by the **Lost Dutchman Mining Association** (☎ 520/427-9908), which hosts "recreational" miners. Drop-in visitors are also welcome, and they can visit the 1879 Stanton Hotel, opera house, saloon, and other original buildings.

From Stanton, drive back to Ariz. 89 and turn north. You'll soon climb Yarnell Hill, with a breathtaking valley view to the south. Follow Ariz. 89 north from the Stanton turnoff for 43 miles to:

**4. Prescott,** Another Arizona town (at 5,347 feet elevation) born during the 1860s gold rush. Prescott was twice the capital of the Arizona Territory—from 1864 to 1867 and from 1877 to 1889. Today this pleasant small city is notable for its historic sites, museums, and arts and crafts. Upon your arrival, stop at the **Chamber of Commerce,** 117 W. Goodwin St. (☎ 520/445-2000) for the Historic Downtown Walking Tour Guide, which describes close to three dozen historic buildings. Near the Chamber of Commerce, you can see the 1864 **Governor's Mansion,** built of logs, and a number of other historic edifices and exhibits at **Sharlot Hall Museum,** 415 W. Gurley St. (☎ 520/445-3122). The **Smoki Museum,** 147 N. Arizona St. (☎ 520/445-1230), contains baskets, rugs, pottery, and other artifacts from a variety of Indian tribes, as well as a collection of western art.

Prescott makes a good overnight stop. Among the local lodging choices are the historic 1927 **Hassayampa Inn,** 122 E. Gurley St. (☎ 800/322-1927 or 520/778-9434); the homey **Prescott Pines Inn,** 901 White Spar Rd. (☎ 800/541-5374 or 520/445-7270); and the economical **Super 8 Motel** (☎ 520/776-1282).

☕ **TAKE A BREAK**   For a trip back to the 1950s, head for **Kendall's Famous Burgers and Ice Cream,** 113 S. Cortez St. (☎ 520/778-3658), or for a more formal dinner in an 1892 building, try the beef, ribs, or pasta at **Murphy's,** 201 N. Cortez (☎ 520/445-4044).

Leaving Prescott, take Ariz. 89 north for 5 miles, passing through the beautiful, wild-looking red, pink, and gray rock formations of Granite Dells. Then branch off to the northeast on Ariz. 89A for 25 miles to:

**5. Jerome,** which once upon a time had 15,000 residents and was labeled "the wickedest town in the West" by a New York newspaper. But when the copper mines closed in 1950 after operating for more than 70 years, the town was practically deserted until it was rediscovered in the 1960s by artists attracted by the Verde Valley's magnificent scenery. Much of the old town has been restored, and in addition to exploring its art galleries and crafts shops, you can delve into its past. **Gold King Mine, Museum and Ghost Town,** 1 mile west of Main Street on Perkinsville Road (☎ 520/634-0053), has exhibits on Jerome's early mining days. **Jerome State Historic Park,** off Ariz. 89A (☎ 520/634-5381), features a 1916 mansion built for mine owner James "Rawhide Jimmy" Douglas that reveals how rich miners lived during that time. The park has a spectacular view of the town and Verde Valley.

From Jerome, continue north on Ariz. 89A about 4 miles, then leave Ariz. 89A and follow 11th Street into:

**6. Clarkdale,** where copper mined at Jerome was smelted. When the mines closed, Clarkdale almost shut down, but was revived by the establishment of a cement company in the 1950s. **Tuzigoot National Monument** (☎ 520/634-5564), about 2 miles east of Clarkdale (turn east on Main Street and follow the signs), contains remnants of a Sinaguan Indian village built of mud and rock between

# Driving Tour: Phoenix, Prescott & Sedona

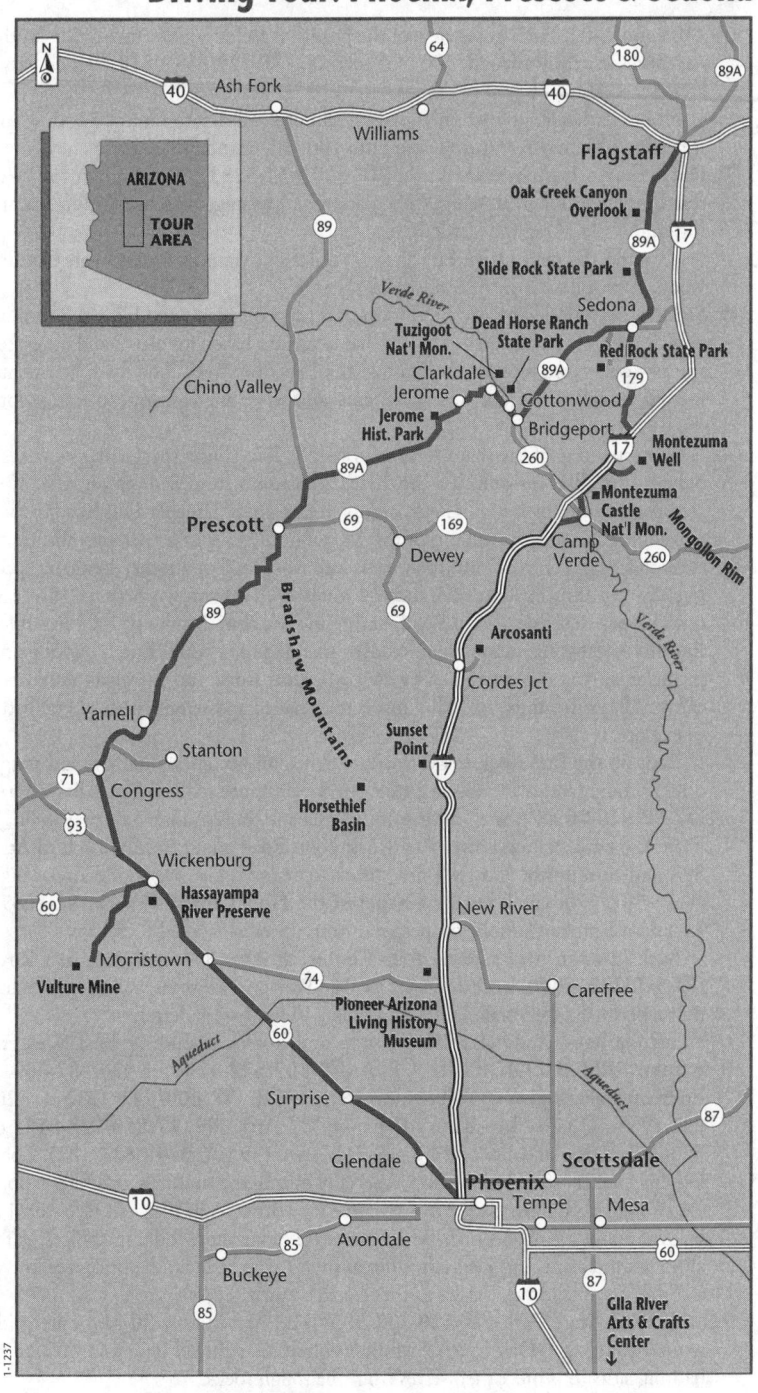

1125 and 1400. For a good view of the beautiful Verde Valley, take a ride on the **Arizona Central Railroad,** 300 N. Broadway (☎ **520/639-0010**), which passes areas inaccessible by car.

From Clarkdale, go east on Broadway about 2 miles into Cottonwood, where it becomes Main Street; turn north onto 10th Street and follow it to:

**7. Dead Horse Ranch State Park** (☎ **520/634-5283**), best known for bird-watching, it also has canoeing, stream and pond fishing, horseback riding, camping, and walks along the Verde River.

Leaving the park, drive east about 2 miles on Main Street through Cottonwood, then follow Ariz. 89A north 20 miles to:

**8. Sedona,** surrounded by huge red rocks and rugged terrain, and blessed by a mild climate. Sedona (elevation 4,400 feet) has become a haven for artists and other free spirits—and more recently, increasing numbers of retirees. The town boasts numerous art galleries, shops, and restaurants, and serves as a base for exploration into the backcountry.

Scenery is one of the main reasons to visit Sedona. For a spectacular view, visit **Schnebly Hill Overlook.** To get there, head south from Sedona on Ariz. 179, crossing a bridge over Oak Creek, and turn east onto Schnebly Hill Road, which you follow 12 miles to the top of the Mogollon Rim. It takes 40–60 minutes to drive this latter dirt road, but the view is well worth it. For another scenic perspective, drive south on Ariz. 89A about 4 miles from downtown Sedona, turn east onto Upper Red Rock Loop Road, and follow it about 2 miles to the turnoff for Red Rock Crossing. About 1 mile down this dirt road you'll find a parking and picnic area, from where you can view **Cathedral Rock** and the gigantic red box canyon that surrounds you. This area is tree-shaded and serene, with several paths to explore.

Back on the Red Rock Loop Road, which soon becomes a narrow and rough dirt thoroughfare, drive about 2 miles to the entrance to **Red Rock State Park** (☎ **520/282-6907**), with hiking and horseback trails available during the day. From the park, follow Lower Red Rock Loop Road about 3 miles back to Ariz. 89A and turn north, and go 5 miles back to Sedona. Just south of Sedona, high above Ariz. 179, you'll see the **Chapel of the Holy Cross** (☎ **520/282-4069**), a modern Roman Catholic chapel built from the canyon's red rock.

Back in town, the **Sedona Arts Center,** at Ariz. 89A and Art Barn Road (☎ **520/282-3809**), has exhibits of local and regional artists as well as theater and music performances. Sedona has more than 40 local art galleries.

Sedona has a number of fine resorts and hotels, including **Best Western Arroyo Roble Hotel,** 400 U.S. 89A (☎ **800/528-1234** or 520/282-4001); **Enchantment Resort,** 525 Boynton Canyon Rd. (☎ **800/522-2282** or 520/282-2900); **Quality Inn King's Ransom,** 771 Ariz. 179 (☎ **800/228-5151** or 520/282-7151); and **Sedona Motel,** 218 Ariz. 179 (☎ **520/282-7187**). Local lodging is likely to fill up quickly, especially during the summer, and reservations are strongly recommended. An alternative is to drive on to Flagstaff (see stop 11, below), about 28 miles north, where there are many more lodging choices. Also, although the scenery in Flagstaff is not as pretty as in Sedona, the prices are lower.

From Sedona, drive 7 miles farther north on Ariz. 89A to:

**9. Slide Rock State Park** (☎ **520/282-3034**). It's named for a 30-foot water slide worn into rocks in Oak Creek. Swimmers often wear cut-off blue jeans instead of bathing suits to protect themselves from the rough rocks.

After cooling off at the park, continue north on Ariz. 89A for another 8 miles to:

**10. Oak Creek Canyon Overlook,** where the stretch of highway through the inspirational red rocks and pine forests of Oak Creek Canyon is considered one of the most scenic in America. The overlook provides an awesome view down the valley.

Now, continue north on Ariz. 89A for another 13 miles to:

**11. Flagstaff,** at the junction of two interstate highways and within easy reach of Grand Canyon National Park. From here, you can head south down I-17 for 47 miles to exit 293 and then north 4 miles to Montezuma Well (see directions to stop 12, below), or drive back to Sedona, 28 miles south on Ariz. 89A, for a different perspective on beautiful Oak Creek Canyon. Along the way you'll pass U.S. Forest Service camp and picnic grounds, parking for hiking trails, and Slide Rock State Park, before finding yourself back in Sedona.

From Sedona, go south past more magnificent red rock formations on Ariz. 179 for 15 miles to I-17 (exit 298), and then head south on the interstate for 5 miles to exit 293, and then 4 miles north on an unmarked road, following signs to:

**12. Montezuma Well,** actually a limestone sink formed by the collapse of an ancient underground cavern. It was home to first the Hohokam and then the Sinagua, who built irrigation ditches for growing corn, beans, squash, and cotton. You can see remnants of the ditches, an A.D. 1100 Hohokam pit house, and a variety of structures used by the Sinaguan between 1125 and 1400. Montezuma Well is managed as part of Montezuma Castle National Monument (see below).

Now go back to I-17 and drive 4 miles south to exit 289 for:

**13. Montezuma Castle National Monument (☎ 520/567-3322),** where you'll find a five-story, 20-room cliff dwelling believed to have been constructed by the Sinagua some 800 years ago, plus the ruins of a larger, six-story pueblo built against the base of a cliff.

From here, head south 5 miles on Montezuma Castle Hwy., following signs into:

**14. Camp Verde,** east of I-17 off exit 287, established as a cavalry outpost in 1865 to protect settlers along the Verde River from raids by the Apache and Yavapai. **Fort Verde State Historic Park,** in the center of Camp Verde (☎ 520/567-3275), includes five of the fort's original buildings, with exhibits depicting life in a late 19th-century fort.

Now, go west through town to I-17, head south about 23 miles to Corde Junction (exit 262A), and go northeast about 3 miles on a dirt road, following signs to:

**15. Arcosanti (☎ 520/632-7135),** a city of the future designed by Paolo Soleri, still under construction by Soleri's students. When it is eventually completed, it will be an ecologically friendly, 25-story-tall city of some 5,000 residents, with solar energy for both heating and cooling. At present, Arcosanti has a visitor center, guest rooms, a bakery, and guided tours.

Leaving Arcosanti, return to I-17 and continue south about 10 miles to:

**16. Sunset Point,** an interstate rest stop between exits 256 and 248 on a promontory with a stunning view, taking in a ghost town site, an old stagecoach trail, Horsethief Basin, and the Bradshaw Mountains. It has photo displays and maps, as well as the usual rest stop facilities.

Now go south on I-17 about 26 more miles to Pioneer Road (exit 225) and:

**17. Pioneer Arizona Living History Museum (☎ 602/465-1052;** closed in summer), where costumed pioneers demonstrate life in Arizona's early days, with close to two dozen original and reconstructed buildings, including a stagecoach station, a Victorian mansion, a miners' cabin, a church, several farmhouses, and carpenters', blacksmiths', and wagon makers' shops. Melodramas and other performances are presented in the opera house, and each fall there is a reenactment of Civil War events.

From the museum it's about 12 miles south on I-17 back to Phoenix.

## 1 Denver

In the summer of 1858, a few flecks of gold were discovered where Cherry Creek empties into the shallow South Platte River in what was then the Kansas Territory. A tent camp quickly sprang up, and in 1859 militia Gen. William H. Larimer claim-jumped the land on the east side of the Platte and laid out a city that he named after James Denver, governor of the Kansas Territory. Denver is one of the few cities founded without the presence of an ocean, lake, navigable river, or railroad to give it a reason to exist.

Although the gold found in Denver was only a teaser for much larger strikes in the nearby mountains, the community grew as a shipping and trading center for the mining towns up in the hills. Leadville silver and Cripple Creek gold made Denver a showcase city in the late 19th and early 20th centuries.

In the years following World War II, Denver became the largest city between the Great Plains and the Pacific coast. Today it's noted for its dozens of tree-lined boulevards, its more than 20,000 acres of city parks, and its architecture, from Victorian to sleek contemporary.

## ARRIVING & DEPARTING

**BY PLANE**   The new **Denver International Airport,** 23 miles northeast of downtown, is served by all major American airlines, regional airlines, and by Martinair Holland and Mexicana. A city bus ride from the airport to downtown costs $6. Shuttle service is available from the **Airporter** (☎ **303/333-5833**), with door-to-door pickup and drop-off ($20–$40 one-way). Travelers should check on the availability and cost of hotel shuttle service when making reservations. The **Denver Airport Shuttle** (☎ **800/525-3177** or 303/342-5454) provides transportation to and from many hotels. Fares vary and may be paid partly or completely by the hotel. **Taxi fares** are generally in the $30–$50 range for one passenger.

**BY TRAIN & BUS**   Amtrak's **Union Station** is at 17th and Wynkoop streets (☎ **800/USA-RAIL** or 303/825-2583), in the lower downtown historic district. The **Greyhound bus station** is at 1055 19th St. (☎ **800/231-2222** or 303/293-6555).

## ESSENTIALS

**VISITOR INFORMATION**   Stop at the **Denver Metro Convention and Visitor Bureau,** 225 W. Colfax Ave., Denver, CO 80202 (☎ **800/645-3446** or 303/892-1112), for a copy of the "Official Visitors Guide." There's also an **Information Center** at the airport.

**EMERGENCIES & SAFETY**   Dial ☎ **911** in an emergency. Among Denver-area hospitals is **St. Joseph's,** 1835 Franklin St. (☎ **303/837-7111**), just east of downtown. Although Denver is generally a safe city, it is not crime-free. The 16th Street Mall is seldom a problem, but even streetwise Denverites avoid late-night walks along certain sections of East Colfax Avenue, just several blocks away.

## GETTING AROUND

Denver's good transportation system means that you don't really need a car in the downtown area.

**BY BUS & TRAIN**  The **Regional Transportation District (RTD)** (☎ **800/
366-7433** or 303/299-6000) calls itself "The Ride" for its bus routes and light-rail system, with transfer tickets available free. It serves Denver, its suburbs and outlying communities, including Boulder, and offers free car parking at 50 Park-n-Ride locations
throughout the Denver–Boulder metropolitan area. Local fare is $1 during peak hours;
50¢ other times, but **free buses** run up and down the 16th Street Mall between the
Civic Center and Market Street. Popular among visitors is the **Cultural Connection
Trolley** (☎ **303/299-6000**), which runs daily in summer, with stops at Denver's most
popular tourist attractions. A full-day pass costs $3.

**BY TAXI**  The main services are **Yellow Cab** (☎ 303/777-7777), **Zone Cab**
(☎ 303/444-8888), and **Metro Taxi** (☎ 303/333-3333). Rates are about $1.40 pickup
and $1.40 per mile.

## WHAT TO SEE & DO

**SPECIAL EVENTS**  The **National Western Stock Show and Rodeo** (☎ **303/
295-1660**), one of the world's richest rodeos, is held the second and third weeks of
January at the Denver Coliseum.

**ESCORTED TOURS**  Half- and full-day bus tours of Denver and the nearby Rockies
are offered by **Gray Line,** P.O. Box 17527, Denver, CO 80217-0527 (☎ **303/
289-2841**). A 3¹/₂-hour tour, leaving the Denver Bus Center at 19th and Curtis streets
at 2pm, takes in Denver, Red Rocks Park, and Buffalo Bill's Grave. For half- and full-
day bike tours of the Denver metropolitan area, contact **Two Wheel Tours** (☎ **800/
343-8940** or 303/798-4601).

**ATTRACTIONS**  Many of the attractions here are related to the city's history, particularly its glorious Victorian era, but Denver also has a large amount of green space.

 **Black American West Museum and Heritage Center.** *3091 California St.,
at 31st St.* ☎ *303/292-2566. Admission $3 adults, $2 seniors, $1 ages 12–17, 50¢ chil-
dren under 12, free for children under 3. Wed–Fri 10am–2pm, Sat noon–5pm, Sun
2–5pm.* Nearly a third of the cowboys in the Old West were black, and this museum
chronicles their history, along with that of black doctors, teachers, miners, farmers,
newspaper reporters, and state legislators. The 35,000-item collection is lodged in the
Victorian home of Dr. Justina Ford, the first black woman licensed to practice medicine in Denver.

 **Colorado History Museum.** *1300 Broadway.* ☎ *303/866-3682. Admission $3
adults, $2.50 seniors and students with an ID, $1.50 ages 6–16, free for children under 6.
Mon–Sat 10am–4:30pm, Sun noon–4:30pm.* Permanent exhibits include "The Colorado
Chronicle," an 1800 to 1949 timeline incorporating biographical plaques and a remarkable collection of photographs, news clippings, and paraphernalia from Colorado's past.
Dioramas portray episodes in state history, including an intricate re-creation of 19th-
century Denver.

 **Colorado State Capitol.** *Broadway and E. Colfax Ave.* ☎ *303/866-2604.
Admission free. Self-guided or guided 30-minute tours. Mon–Fri 9:30am–2:45pm (dome
is locked at 3:30pm).* Built to last 1,000 years, the capitol was constructed in 1886 of
Colorado granite. The dome was first sheathed in copper, but after a public outcry—
copper was not a Colorado product—it was replaced with 200 ounces of gold. Note
the murals that adorn the walls of the first-floor rotunda, which offers a view of the
underside of the dome. The House, Senate, and old Supreme Court chambers occupy
the second floor, with visitor galleries on the third.

 **Denver Art Museum.** *100 W. 14th Ave. Pkwy., at Civic Center Park.* ☎ *303/
640-4433. Admission $3 adults, $1.50 students and seniors, free for children under 6; free
for everyone Sat. Tues–Sat 10am–5pm, Sun noon–5pm.* Founded in 1893, this seven-story

# Denver

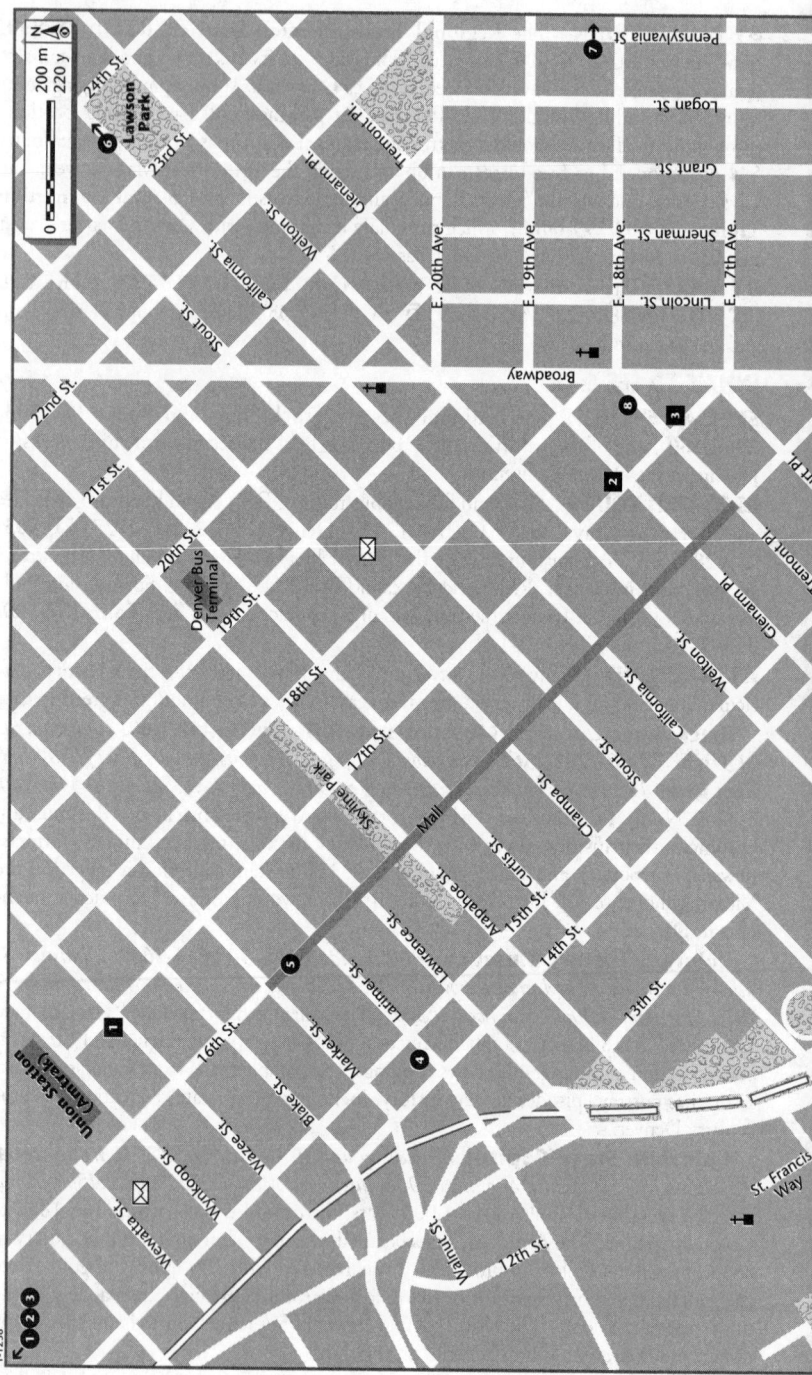

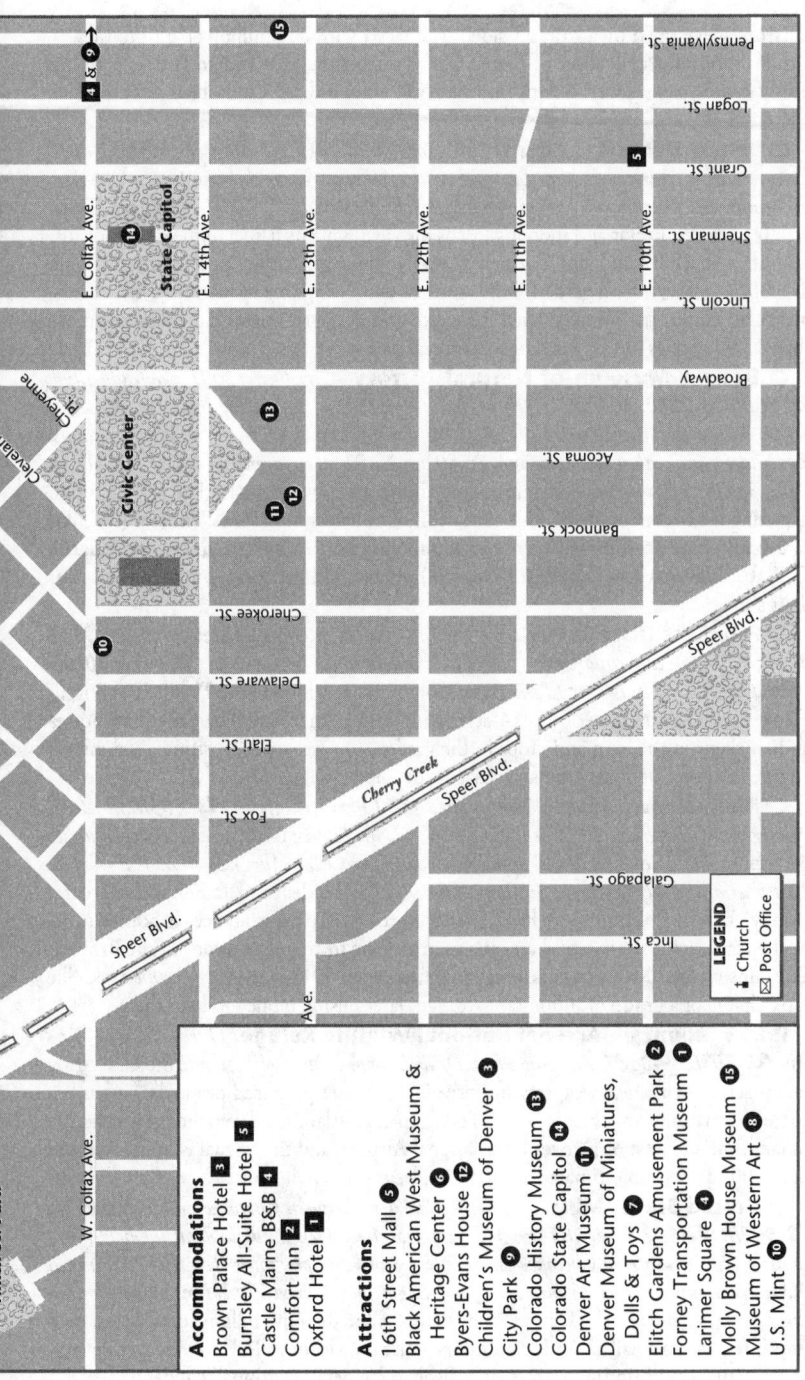

**Accommodations**
Brown Palace Hotel **3**
Burnsley All-Suite Hotel **5**
Castle Marne B&B **4**
Comfort Inn **2**
Oxford Hotel **1**

**Attractions**
16th Street Mall **5**
Black American West Museum & Heritage Center **6**
Byers-Evans House **12**
Children's Museum of Denver **3**
City Park **9**
Colorado History Museum **13**
Colorado State Capitol **14**
Denver Art Museum **11**
Denver Museum of Miniatures, Dolls & Toys **7**
Elitch Gardens Amusement Park **2**
Forney Transportation Museum **1**
Larimer Square **4**
Molly Brown House Museum **15**
Museum of Western Art **8**
U.S. Mint **10**

**LEGEND**
✝ Church
⊠ Post Office

525

museum is wrapped by a thin 28-sided wall faced with one million sparkling tiles. It has an important collection of pieces from North American Indian tribes spanning nearly 2,000 years, as well as African, Asian, Oceanic, and pre-Columbian artifacts, plus contemporary art.

✪ **Denver Botanic Gardens.** *1005 York St.* ☎ *303/331-4000, or 303/331-4010 for a recording. Admission May–Sept, $4 adults, $2 seniors and children 6–15; Oct–Apr, $3 adults, $1.50 seniors, $1 children; free for children under 6. Daily 9am–5pm.* There are 20 acres of outdoor and indoor gardens displaying plants native to the desert, plains, mountain foothills, and alpine zones; plus a Japanese garden, scripture garden (plants in biblical history), herb garden, water garden, and "wingsong" garden to attract songbirds. In winter, the dome-shaped, concrete-and-Plexiglas conservatory houses more than 1,000 species of tropical and subtropical plants.

✪ **Denver Museum of Natural History.** *City Park, 2001 Colorado Blvd.* ☎ *800/925-2250, 303/322-7009, or 303/370-8257 for the hearing impaired. Museum, $4.50 adults, $2.50 children 4–12, $2.50 seniors 65 and older. IMAX tickets, $5 adults, $4 children and seniors. Planetarium, $3.50 adults, $2.50 children and seniors. Sat–Thurs 9am–5pm, Fri 9am–9pm.* This three-story museum contains more than 90 dioramas, depicting the history of life on four continents. The museum's **IMAX Theater** (☎ **303/ 370-6300**) presents films with sense-surround sound on a huge screen; and the **Charles C. Gates Planetarium** (☎ **303/370-6487**) offers multimedia star programs and laser light shows.

✪ **Four Mile Historic Park.** *715 S. Forest St.* ☎ *303/399-1859. Admission $3.50 adults, $2 seniors and children 6–15, free for children under 5. Apr–Sept, Wed–Sun 10am– 4pm; Oct–Mar, Thurs–Sat 11am–3pm.* The oldest log home (1859) still standing in Denver is the centerpiece of this 14-acre living-history museum. There are draft horses and chickens in the barn and crops in the garden. On weekends, costumed volunteers engage in chores or crafts, and stagecoach rides are available.

✪ **Molly Brown House Museum.** *1340 Pennsylvania St.* ☎ *303/832-4092. Admission $5.00 adults, $3.50 seniors over 65, $1.50 children 6–12, free for children under 6. Year-round, Tues–Sat 10am–4pm, Sun noon–4pm; June–Aug, also Mon 10am–4pm. Last tour of the day begins at 3:30pm.* This was the residence of James and Margaret (Molly) Brown from 1894 to 1932. Restored to its 1910 appearance, it houses turn-of-the-century furnishings and art objects, many the former possessions of the Browns. The "unsinkable" Molly became a national heroine in 1912 when the *Titanic* sank: She took charge of a group of immigrant women, later raising money to help them.

**Rocky Mountain Arsenal National Wildlife Refuge.** *Quebec St. and 72nd Ave.* ☎ *303/289-0467. Admission free. Daylight hours.* Once a site where the U.S. Army manufactured chemical weapons and private businesses produced pesticides, it has become an environmental success story. Today open grasslands and wetlands cover the 27-square-mile site west of Denver International Airport, and the arsenal is home to more than 200 species. An estimated 100 bald eagles roost here in winter.

✪ **United States Mint.** *320 W. Colfax Ave., between Cherokee and Delaware sts.* ☎ *303/844-3582 or 303/844-3331. Admission free. Tickets available at the booth next to the visitor entrance on Cherokee St. Mon–Fri 8am–2:45pm; tours every 10–20 minutes. No reservations, so expect 45-min wait June–Labor Day. Closed 2 weeks in summer for audit; call for exact dates.* The Denver Mint stamps more than five billion coins a year, each imprinted with a small *D*. Video monitors along the visitor gallery provide a close view of the actual coin minting process, and displays are being continually added.

**Wings Over the Rockies Air and Space Museum.** *1750 E. Irvington Place in Lowry Air Force Base (entrances at Sixth Ave. and Dayton St., Quebec St. and 1st Ave.,* *and Alameda Ave. between Havana and Monaco sts.).* ☎ *303/360-5360. Admission $4 adults, $2 ages 6–17 and seniors, free for children under 6. Mon–Sat 10am–4pm, Sun noon–4pm.* When Lowry Air Force Base closed in 1995, the museum moved in. More than a dozen planes are housed in cavernous Hangar No. 1, including antique biplanes, a search and rescue helicopter, a massive B-1A bomber, and most of the F1 fighter series. Also on display is the dining room used by the Eisenhowers when Lowry was nick-named the "Summer White House."

**PARKS & ZOOS   City Park,** East 17th to East 26th Avenue, between York Street and Colorado Boulevard, is Denver's largest urban park, covering 314 acres on the east side of Uptown. Established in 1881, and still retaining Victorian touches, it includes two lakes, athletic fields, jogging and walking trails, playgrounds, tennis courts, picnic areas, and an 18-hole municipal golf course. In summer there are band concerts. Admission is free for the park, although the museum, golf course, and other sites charge independently. It's open daily 24 hours.

**Denver Zoo.** *City Park, 23rd Ave. and Steele St.* ☎ *303/331-4110. Admission $6 adults, $4 seniors, $3 children 4–12 (accompanied by an adult). Summer, daily 9am–6pm. Winter, daily 10am–5pm.* This spacious zoological park is home to 600 species. The 1918 Bear Mountain exhibit was the first in the United States to be constructed of simulated concrete rock-work. Northern Shores allows underwater viewing of polar bears and sea lions, and Tropical Discovery re-creates an entire tropical ecosystem. The Primate Panorama is a world-class primate exhibit. The zoo also has the nation's only natural gas-powered zoo train, touring all zoo paths, spring through fall.

**BEST BETS FOR KIDS**   Kids enjoy the zoo, the space museum, and the natural history museum. The **Children's Museum of Denver,** 2121 Children's Museum Dr. (☎ 303/433-7444), is Denver's best hands-on experience for kids, with a computer lab where they can log onto the Internet; lab areas to explore light, sound, electronics, and biology; a woodworking shop, a TV weather forecasting studio, plus an exhibit where participants learn what it feels like to have various disabilities. The **Elitch Gardens Amusement Park,** Speer Boulevard at I-25 exit 212 (☎ 800/ELITCHS or 303/595-4FUN), established in 1889, has close to two dozen rides including Twister II, a wooden roller coaster; Disaster Canyon, a raging river-rapids ride; the 300-foot Total Tower; and the newly renovated 1925 carousel with 67 hand-carved horses.

**SPORTS**   Baseball fever hits Denver when the **Colorado Rockies** (☎ 800/388-7625 or 303/762-5437) play at Coors Field. For basketball, head to McNichols Sports Arena for a **Denver Nuggets** (☎ 303/893-3865) game; and the **Denver Broncos** (☎ 303/433-7466) football team plays at Mile High Stadium. Denver's hockey team, the **Colorado Avalanche** (☎ 303/893-6700), plays at McNichols Sports Arena.

**SHOPPING**   Most visitors, especially those on foot, concentrate their shopping along the delightful **16th Street Mall**—with a slew of wonderful shops—and adjacent areas, including Larimer Square. The **Cherry Creek Shopping Center,** south of downtown (☎ 303/424-6360), is home to about 140 shops, and adjacent is the very upscale Cherry Creek North. Among Denver's special stores are **Caboose Hobbies,** 500 S. Broadway (☎ 303/777-6766), a gigantic mecca for model train buffs; and the **Tattered Cover Bookstore,** 2955 E. First Ave. (☎ 800/833-9327 or 303/322-7727), a wonderful four-story bookstore so huge it provides maps to help you find your way around.

## ACCOMMODATIONS

Although most hotels and motels in the Denver area do not change their rates on a seasonal basis, hotels that cater to business travelers frequently offer substantial discounts on weekends. **Mile High Adventure Club** (☎ 800/489-4888) offers discounted rates at more than 30 hotels, plus discounts on a wide variety of activities.

✪ **Brown Palace Hotel.** *321 17th St., Denver, CO 80202.* ☎ *800/321-2599 in North America, 800/228-2917 in Colorado, or 303/297-3111. Fax 303/293-9204. 205 rms, 25 suites. $185–$205 double; $245–$725 suite. Weekend rates start at $120. AE, CB, DC, DISC, ER, JCB, MC, V. Parking $14.* The elegant 1892 Brown Palace has a beautiful stained-glass ceiling soaring high above its lobby. Rooms are individually and meticulously decorated in either Victorian or art deco style, each having a desk and TV in an armoire. Extras include restaurants, bar, in-room massage, fitness center, business center, VCR rentals, boutiques, and beauty salon.

**Burnsley All Suite Hotel.** *1000 Grant St. (at E. 10th Ave.), Denver, CO 80203.* ☎ *800/231-3915 or 303/830-1000. 82 suites. $99–$145 suite. Weekend rates available. AE, CB, DC, MC, V. Free covered parking.* This small, elegant hotel offers suites with private balconies, and separate living, bedroom, dining, and fully stocked kitchen areas. Units are handsomely furnished, although slightly dated. The hotel has a pool, business center, and privileges at a nearby health club.

**Cameron Motel.** *4500 E. Evans Ave. (I-25, exit 203), Denver, CO 80222.* ☎ *303/757-2100. Fax 303/757-0974. 33 rooms, 2 suites. $43 double; $65 suite. AE, DISC, ER, MC, V.* This small mom-and-pop motel, about 10 minutes from downtown, was built in the 1940s. The renovated rooms have glazed-brick interiors, three have kitchenettes, and 14 have showers only.

**Castle Marne Bed & Breakfast.** *1572 Race St., Denver, CO 80206.* ☎ *800/92-MARNE for reservations, or 303/331-0621. Fax 303/331-0623. 7 rms, 2 suites. $85–$155 double; $180 suite. Rates include breakfast. AE, CB, DC, MC, V.* One of Denver's grandest historic mansions, Castle Marne is furnished with antiques and reproductions. Three rooms have private balconies and hot tubs for two, three have claw-foot tubs and pedestal sinks, and suites have Jacuzzi tubs for two. Facilities include a game room, library, and gift shop. No television, no smoking, unsuitable for children under 10.

**Cherry Creek Inn.** *600 S. Colorado Blvd., Denver, CO 80222.* ☎ *303/757-3341. Fax 303/756-6670. 323 rms. $90 double. AE, DC, DISC, MC, V.* This modern property is conveniently located just 10 minutes from downtown and about 45 minutes from Denver International Airport. The spacious rooms have minirefrigerators and coffeemakers. Guests enjoy the pool, access to a nearby health club, self-serve Laundromat, and beauty salon.

**Loews Giorgio Hotel.** *4150 E. Mississippi Ave., Denver, CO 80222.* ☎ *800/345-9172 or 303/782-9300. Fax 303/758-6542. 165 rms, 17 suites. $195–$215 double; $250 suite. Children under 18 stay free in parents' room. AE, CB, DC, DISC, JCB, MC, V. Free valet and self-parking.* The modern exterior belies the Romanesque decor inside—a wide use of floral patterns, Italian silk wall coverings, and marble-top furnishings. West-facing rooms have superb views of the mountains. Conveniences include a restaurant, fitness center, business center, and rooms for business travelers with two phone lines, modem hookups, and in-room fax.

**Oxford Hotel.** *1600 17th St. (at Wazee St.), Denver, CO 80202.* ☎ *800/228-5838 or 303/628-5400. Fax 303/628-5413. 79 rms, 2 suites. $135–$160 double; $180 suite. Children under 18 stay free in parents' room. AE, CB, DC, DISC, MC, V. Valet parking $12.* A fine example of Denver's 19th-century hotels, furnished with English and French antiques. No two rooms are alike, but each has a stocked minibar, dressing table, and large closet. Facilities include a restaurant, bar, fitness center, health spa, and beauty salon.

**OTHER ACCOMMODATIONS**  Many of the major chains provide reasonably priced lodging in Denver. Moderate and lower-priced options downtown include the

**Comfort Inn,** 401 17th St. (☎ **800/237-7431** or 303/296-0400), with 229 rooms in a convenient location; and **Ramada Inn–Mile High Stadium,** 1975 Bryant St., at I-25 exit 210B (☎ **800/272-6232** or 303/433-8331), with 167 rooms.

Outside downtown, chain lodgings include the **Hampton Inn,** 4685 Quebec St. (☎ **800/HAMPTON** or 303/388-8100), with 138 rooms; and **Quality Inn Denver South,** 6300 E. Hampden Ave. (☎ **800/647-1986** or 303/758-2211), with 182 rooms.

## DINING

Like most of America, Denver is plagued with an invasion of chain and franchise eateries, but you can still find that special place to dine.

**City Spirit Cafe.** *1434 Blake St.* ☎ *303/575-0022. Reservations not accepted. Main courses $5–$7. AE, CB, DC, DISC, MC, V. Mon–Thurs 11am–midnight, Fri–Sat 11am–2am. ECLECTIC/VEGETARIAN.* This casual, friendly restaurant offers an unusual blend of Mexican, Mediterranean, Far Eastern, and American sandwiches, salads, main dishes, and pizza. Menu items include a lamb sandwich, turkey and Swiss cheese sandwich, vegetarian green chili, and pasta dishes, plus several coffees and pastries.

✪ **Cliff Young's.** *700 E. 17th Ave.* ☎ *303/831-8900. Reservations recommended. Main courses $8–$16 at lunch, $20–$33 at dinner. AE, CB, DC, DISC, MC, V. Mon–Fri 11:30am–2pm; daily 6–9:30pm. NEW AMERICAN.* Cliff Young's is sophisticated but not pretentious, the ultimate upscale bistro. The dining room is spacious, elegant, and dimly lit, with a classical pianist playing nightly, joined by a violinist from Wednesday to Sunday. The menu changes seasonally, and includes seafood, game, and regional specialties.

✪ **Duffy's Shamrock.** *1635 Court Place.* ☎ *303/534-4935. Breakfast $1.75–$4.50; lunch $4–$7; dinner $5–$12. AE, CB, DC, MC, V. Daily 7am–1:30am. AMERICAN.* This traditional Irish pub has been going strong since the late 1950s. Specializing in Irish coffees and beers, sandwiches on practically every kind of bread include corned beef, Reuben, braunschweiger, and even a Dagwood. Daily specials might be prime rib, barbecued beef, fried prawns, or liver and onions.

✪ **The Fort.** *19192 Colo. 8, off W. Hampden Ave. (U.S. 285), Morrison.* ☎ *303/697-4771. Reservations recommended. Main courses $13.95–$34.95. AE, CB, DC, DISC, MC, V. Mon–Fri 5–10pm, Sat 5–11pm, Sun 5–8pm. ROCKY MOUNTAIN.* This is a full-scale reproduction of a historic fort, with the staff dressed as 19th-century Cheyenne. The Fort built its reputation on high-quality, low-cholesterol buffalo—steak, tongue, even broiled marrow bones. Other house specialties include a spicy-hot chicken stew, and elk medaillons with wild huckleberry sauce. Diehards can get beefsteak.

**Imperial Chinese Restaurant.** *431 S. Broadway.* ☎ *303/698-2800. Reservations recommended. Individual dishes $8–$28. Complete multicourse dinners $15–$25. AE, CB, DC, MC, V. Mon–Thurs 11am–10pm, Fri 11am–10:30pm, Sat noon–10:30pm, Sun 4–10pm. CHINESE.* Many locals consider this the best Chinese restaurant in Denver, offering classic and innovative Szechuan, Hunan, Mandarin, and Cantonese dishes. A laughing Buddha graces the entrance, with two rather large tropical fish tanks. Specialties include Nanking pork loin, seafood bird's nest, and sesame chicken.

✪ **La Bonne Soupe.** *1512 Larimer St., Writer Square.* ☎ *303/595-9169. Reservations accepted. Main courses $5.95–$9.95 at lunch, $7.95–$18.95 at dinner. AE, DC, MC, V. Mon–Thurs 11am–10pm, Fri–Sat 11am–11pm, Sun 11:30am–9:30pm. FRENCH.* A faithful replica of a French sidewalk bistro, this casual restaurant combines a patio cafe atmosphere with indoor seating overlooking Writer Square mall. The specialty soups here are meals in themselves, but you can also get sandwiches, fresh fish, pasta, and fondue.

**Marlowe's.** *511 16th St. (at Glenarm St.)* ☎ *303/595-3700. Reservations recommended. Main courses $6.95–$10.95 at lunch, $8.95–$24.95 at dinner. AE, DC, MC, V. Mon–Thurs 11am–11pm, Fri 11am–midnight, Sat 5pm–midnight. STEAK/ SEAFOOD.* This popular eatery and saloon occupies a corner of an 1891 building and boasts an antique cherry-wood bar, granite pillars, and brass rails. House specialties include a 20-ounce porterhouse steak, chicken marsala, and live Maine lobster. There are also "heart healthy" choices.

**T-Wa Inn.** *555 S. Federal Blvd., near W. Virginia Ave.* ☎ *303/922-4584. Lunch $4.50–$7.50; dinner $5–$14. AE, CB, DC, DISC, MC, V. Daily 11am–10pm. VIET- NAMESE.* Denver's first Vietnamese restaurant is still its best. The decor is simple but pleasant, with Viet folk songs providing atmospheric background. Try the eggrolls, with shrimp and crabmeat wrapped in rice paper, hearty meat-and-noodle soups, chicken salad, or soft-shell crab.

**Watson's.** *900 Lincoln St.* ☎ *303/837-1366. $2.25–$4.95 per item. AE, DISC, MC, V. Mon–Thurs 8am–10pm, Fri 8am–11pm, Sat 10am–11pm. AMERICAN.* A soda fountain and pharmacy since 1951, Watson's sports framed *Life* magazine covers and old-fashioned Coca-Cola advertising. The hand-dipped shakes and malts still come with the "leftovers" on the side. The menu includes meat loaf, a chili-cheese foot-long, a variety of sandwiches, plus daily lunch specials.

## DENVER AFTER DARK

Current entertainment listings can be found in special Friday-morning sections of the two daily newspapers, the *Denver Post* and *Rocky Mountain News. Westword,* a weekly newspaper distributed free throughout the city every Wednesday, has perhaps the best listings of all. The *Denver Post* provides information on movie show times and theaters at ☎ 303/777-FILM. Tickets for nearly all major entertainment and sporting events can be obtained from **Ticketmaster** (☎ 303/830-TIXS).

**THE PERFORMING ARTS**    Denver's performing arts are anchored by the huge **Denver Performing Arts Complex** downtown, with various theaters plus concert and symphony halls. It's home to the **Colorado Symphony Orchestra,** 1031 13th St. (☎ 303/98-MUSIC), offering classical concerts interspersed with pop concerts featuring top touring musicians; **Colorado Ballet,** 1278 Lincoln St. (☎ 303/837-TUTU); **Opera Colorado,** 695 S. Colorado Blvd., Suite 20 (☎ 303/778-1500); and the **Denver Center for the Performing Arts,** 1245 Champa St. (☎ 303/893-4000, or 303/ 893-DCPA for recorded information), an umbrella organization for resident and touring theater programs.

The **Cleo Parker Robinson Dance Ensemble,** 119 Park Ave. W. (☎ 303/ 295-1759), is a highly acclaimed multicultural modern dance ensemble and school, performing a varied selection of programs.

**THE CLUB & BAR SCENE**    On any given night you can hear live country, rock, jazz, or reggae somewhere in the city and surrounding area. The **Cactus Moon,** 1001 Grant St., Thornton Town Center, Thornton (☎ 303/451-5200), advertises that it provides "the most fun you can have with your boots on," with a 6,000-square-foot dance floor. At the **Grizzly Rose,** 5450 N. Valley Hwy. (☎ 303/295-1330), you might catch national acts like Garth Brooks, Willie Nelson, and Tanya Tucker.

For live rock, check out **Herman's Hideaway,** 1578 S. Broadway (☎ 303/ 777-5840), where bands on their way up perform original music. **Jimmy's Grille,** 320 S. Birch St., Glendale (☎ 303/322-5334), offers live reggae, blues, or jazz. Drop in at **El Chapultepec,** 1962 Market St. (☎ 303/295-9126), for live jazz.

Popular bars include **Broadway Brewery & Pub,** 2441 Broadway (☎ 303/ 292-2555), featuring the best dozen or so microbrews the state has to offer. The **Bull**

**& Bush Pub and Brewery,** 4700 Cherry Creek Dr. S., Glendale (☎ 303/759-0333), is a re-creation of a famous London pub offering good imported beer. One of the city's best watering holes is **Wynkoop Brewing Co.,** 1634 18th St., at Wynkoop Street (☎ 303/297-2700), Denver's first microbrewery, with a billiards hall and comedy club.

## A DAY TRIP TO GOLDEN

Best known for Coors beer, historic downtown Golden focuses on the 1861 Territorial Capitol, which housed the first state legislature from 1862 to 1867, when the capital was moved to Denver.

Sites of special interest here include the **Colorado Railroad Museum** (☎ 800/365-6263 or 303/279-4591), which occupies a replica of an 1880 railroad depot. On display are more than four dozen narrow- and standard-gauge locomotives and cars, plus other historic equipment and artifacts, historic photos and documents, and model trains. You can climb into many of the old locomotives and wander through the parlor cars. The **Colorado School of Mines Geology Museum** (☎ 303/273-3815) has a gold mine replica, fine mineral and gem collections from around the world, displays of geology, earth history, paleontology, and exhibits depicting Colorado's rich mining history.

Those who like to bend an elbow can taste the wares at the **Coors Brewing Company** (☎ 800/443-8242 or 303/277-BEER), the world's largest single-site brewery, which produces 1.5 million gallons of beer each day and conducts free public 40-minute tours followed by free samples. Children are welcome, and arrangements can be made for disabled or foreign-speaking visitors. Beer isn't the only intoxicant brewed here. **Hakushika Sake USA** (☎ 303/279-7253), founded in 1662 and today one of Japan's foremost sake makers, opened this brewery in Golden to produce sake for distribution throughout the United States and Europe. Free guided tours are by reservation only; children are welcome.

Nearby, the **Mother Cabrini Shrine** (☎ 303/526-0758) is dedicated to America's first citizen saint, St. Frances Xavier Cabrini, who founded the Order of the Missionary Sisters of the Sacred Heart. The **National Earthquake Information Center** (☎ 303/273-8500) is operated by the U.S. Geological Survey to collect rapid earthquake information and transmit warnings via the Earthquake Early Alerting Service. Tours of 30 to 45 minutes can be arranged.

**Essentials:** From Denver, head 15 miles west on U.S. 6 or Colo. 58 off I-70. For information, contact the **Greater Golden Area Chamber of Commerce,** 507 14th St. (P.O. Box 1035), Golden, CO 80402-1035 (☎ 303/279-3113).

## 2 Rocky Mountain National Park

Snow-covered peaks stand over lush valleys and shimmering alpine lakes. Certainly, this sort of beauty is not unusual in the Colorado Rockies, but the range in elevation and ecology is. In relatively low areas, about 7,500 to 9,000 feet, ponderosa pine and juniper cloak the sunny southern slopes, with Douglas fir on the cooler northern slopes. The thirstier blue spruce and lodgepole pine cling to streamsides, with occasional groves of aspen. Elk and mule deer thrive. On higher slopes, forests of Engelmann spruce and subalpine fir dominate, interspersed with wide meadows alive with wildflowers in spring and summer, and home to the bighorn sheep that have become a symbol of the park. Above 11,500 feet the trees gradually disappear altogether and alpine tundra takes over. Fully one-third of the park is in this bleak, rocky world, many of its plants identical to those found in the Arctic. Within the 415-square-mile park are 17 mountains above 13,000 feet. Longs Peak, at 14,255 feet, is the highest.

# ESSENTIALS

**ARRIVING & DEPARTING**   The closest airport is Denver International, about 80 miles southeast, where you can rent a car or hop a shuttle to the park. Entry is either from the east through Estes Park or west through Grand Lake. A road runs through the park, connecting the entrances in summer, but is closed by snow in winter. The Beaver Meadows entrance, leading to the main visitor center, is from Estes Park via U.S. 36. To the north but also from Estes Park is the Fall River entrance, via U.S. 34. South of Estes Park via Colo. 7 are two access roads to trailheads and camping in the park's southeast corner. The Grand Lake entrance is on the west side via U.S. 34.

**VISITOR INFORMATION**   For information, contact **Rocky Mountain National Park,** Estes Park, CO 80517-8397 (☎ **970/586-1206**). The **Rocky Mountain Nature Association** (☎ **800/816-7662** or 970/586-1258), sells maps, books, and videos.

**VISITOR CENTERS**   Entering the park from Estes Park, stop at the main visitor center at Park Headquarters, which has a good interpretive exhibit, a relief map of the park, and additional information. Those entering from the west can get information at the Kawuneeche Visitor Center, located at the Grand Lake end of Trail Ridge Road. There are several smaller summer-only visitor centers inside the park.

**ADMISSION COSTS & REGULATIONS**   Entrance permits for 7 consecutive days cost $10 per week per vehicle, $5 for bicyclists, motorcyclists, and pedestrians. Permits ($10 in summer, free in winter) are required for all backcountry camping. Bicycles and dogs are not permitted on any trails.

**INTERPRETIVE PROGRAMS**   Campfire talks and other programs are offered at visitor centers year-round, and rangers lead a variety of walks and hikes, including snowshoe hikes in winter. A variety of seminars and workshops are offered by **Rocky Mountain Nature Association** (☎ **970/586-1258**), with subjects such as songbirds, flowers, edible and medicinal herbs, painting, wildlife photography, tracking park animals, and edible mushrooms.

**WHEN TO GO**   Because much of the park's high country and its scenic Trail Ridge Road are closed by snow during winter—often from late October through May—most people visit during the remaining months. The very busiest time, though, is mid-June to mid-August, so just before or just after that period is best. For those who don't mind chilly evenings, late September and early October are less crowded and can be beautiful, although there's always the chance of an early winter storm.

# WHAT TO SEE & DO

Although Rocky Mountain National Park is generally considered the domain of hikers and climbers, ideal for those who want to head into the backcountry, it's surprisingly easy to enjoy this park without working up a sweat. For that we thank **Trail Ridge Road,** built in 1932 and undoubtedly one of America's most scenic highways, providing expansive and sometimes dizzying views in all directions. Traveling some 48 miles through the park, rising to over 12,000 feet in elevation, it offers spectacular vistas of snowcapped peaks, deep forests, and meadows of wildflowers where bighorn sheep, elk, and deer browse. Allow at least 3 hours for the drive, and consider a short walk or hike from one of the many vista points.

**CLIMBING & MOUNTAINEERING**   The most popular climb is **Longs Peak,** the highest mountain in the park. For the complete mountain experience, contact **Colorado Mountain School** (☎ **970/586-5758**), a year-round guide service and technical climbing school.

**FISHING**   Four species of trout are fished in park streams and lakes: brown, rainbow, brook, and cutthroat. A state fishing license is required, and only artificial lures or flies are permitted.

# Rocky Mountain National Park

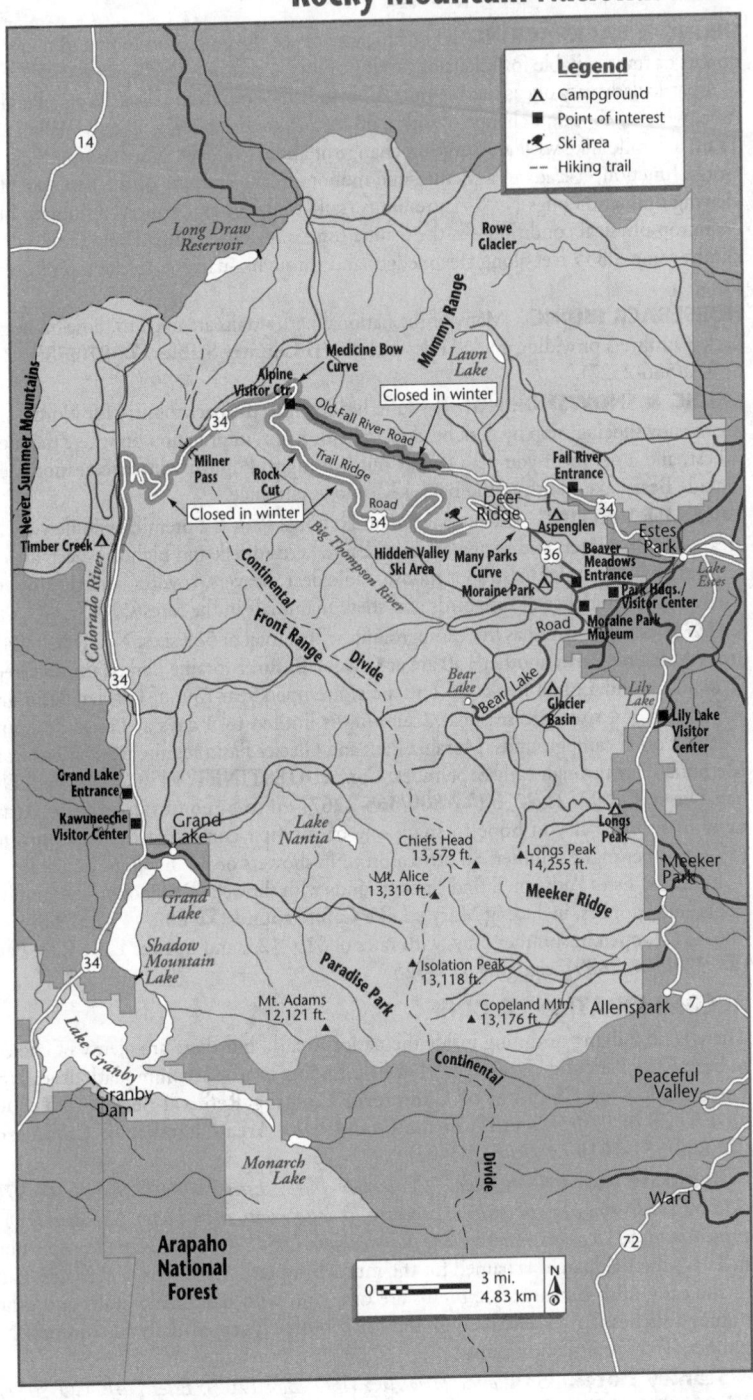

**Legend**
- △ Campground
- ■ Point of interest
- ⛷ Ski area
- --- Hiking trail

14

Long Draw Reservoir

Rowe Glacier

Mummy Range

Medicine Bow Curve

Alpine Visitor Ctr.

Lawn Lake

Closed in winter

Old Fall River Road

34

Milner Pass

Trail Ridge

Rock Cut

Closed in winter

Road

34

Fall River Entrance

34

Deer Ridge

Aspenglen

36

Estes Park

Lake Estes

Never Summer Mountains

Timber Creek △

Continental

Big Thompson River

Hidden Valley Ski Area

Many Parks Curve

Moraine Park △

Beaver Meadows Entrance

Park Hqds./ Visitor Center

Moraine Park Museum

Colorado River

Front Range

Divide

Road

7

34

Bear Lake

Bear Lake

Glacier Basin △

Lily Lake

Lily Lake Visitor Center

Grand Lake Entrance

Kawuneeche Visitor Center

Grand Lake

Lake Nantia

Chiefs Head 13,579 ft. ▲

Mt. Alice 13,310 ft. ▲

Longs Peak 14,255 ft. ▲

Longs Peak △

Meeker Park

34

Grand Lake

Shadow Mountain Lake

Meeker Ridge

Paradise Park

Isolation Peak 13,118 ft ▲

Copeland Mtn. 13,176 ft. ▲

Allenspark

7

Mt. Adams 12,121 ft. ▲

Continental

Peaceful Valley

Lake Granby

Granby Dam

Monarch Lake

Divide

Ward

Arapaho National Forest

72

0     3 mi.
      4.83 km

N

**HIKING & BACKPACKING**   The best way to see the park is on foot, and there are dozens of trails suitable for hikers of varying ability and fitness levels.

A particularly easy one is the 1.2-mile **Alberta Falls Trail** from Glacier Gorge Parking Area, with an elevation change of only 160 feet. A good moderate hike is **Mills Lake Trail,** a 5-mile hike with an elevation change of about 700 feet. Starting from Glacier Gorge Junction, it leads to a picturesque mountain lake and one of the best spots for viewing dramatic Longs Peak. A strenuous trail—only for experienced mountain hikers in top physical condition—is the 8-mile (one way) **East Longs Peak Trail,** which climbs some 4,855 feet along steep ledges and through a narrows to the top of Longs Peak.

**HORSEBACK RIDING**   Many of the national park's trails are open to those on horseback. Outfitters providing guided rides include **Hi Country Stables** (☎ 970/586-3244 or 970/586-2327).

**SKIING & SNOWSHOEING**   If you're headed into the backcountry for Nordic skiing or snowshoeing, stop by park headquarters for maps, information on where the snow is best, and a permit if you plan to stay out overnight. Popular winter recreation areas include Bear Lake, south of the Beaver Meadows entrance.

**WILDLIFE VIEWING**   Rocky Mountain National Park is a premier wildlife viewing area, and fall, winter, and spring are best. Large herds of elk and bighorn sheep are often seen, and you might also spot moose, mule deer, beavers, coyotes, and river otters. There is an abundance of songbirds and small mammals in the forests.

**CAMPING**   The park has five campgrounds with a total of 589 sites. Nearly half (247) are at **Moraine Park;** another 150 are at **Glacier Basin.** Moraine Park, **Timber Creek** (100 sites), and **Longs Peak** (26 tent sites) are open year-round; Glacier Basin and **Aspenglen** (54 sites) are seasonal. Camping is limited to 3 days at Longs Peak and 7 days at other campgrounds. Moraine Park and Glacier Basin require reservations from Memorial Day through early September. Contact **DESTINET,** 9450 Carroll Park Dr., San Diego, CA 92121-2256 (☎ 800/365-2267) up to 5 months in advance. Arrive early in summer if you hope to snare one of the first-come/first-served campsites ($10–$12 per night summer; $6 off-season). No showers or RV hookups available.

In nearby Estes Park you'll find campgrounds with showers, RV hookups, swimming pools, and supplies, including **Mary's Lake Campground** (☎ 800/445-6279 or 970/586-4411), open in summer only, with rates of $19–$23; and **Spruce Lake R.V. Park** (☎ 970/586-2889), charging $15–$25.

## ACCOMMODATIONS & DINING

There is no lodging or dining inside the national park, but there are plenty of choices in both Estes Park and Grand Lake. For help finding nearby accommodations, call the **Estes Park Area Chamber of Commerce Lodging Referral Service** (☎ 800/44-ESTES or 970/586-4431) or the **Grand Lake Area Chamber of Commerce** (☎ 800/531-1019 or 970/627-3402).

**Baldpate Inn.** *4900 S. Colo. 7 (P.O. Box 4445), Estes Park, CO 80517.* ☎ *970/586-6151. 13 rms (4 with bath), 3 cabins. $70 double with shared bath, $85 double with private bath; $125 cabin. Rates include full breakfast. DISC, MC, V. Closed Oct–Apr.* Built in 1917, the Baldpate was named for the murder mystery *Seven Keys to Baldpate.* Each of the early 20th-century style rooms are different, with handmade quilts and other homey touches. An excellent soup and salad buffet is served daily in summer. No phones, TVs, or air-conditioning.

**Stanley Hotel.** *333 Wonderview Ave. (P.O. Box 1767), Estes Park, CO 80517.* ☎ *800/976-1377 or 970/586-3371. Fax 970/586-3673. 129 units. $99–$169 double;*

*$159–$199 suite. AE, DISC, JCB, MC, V.* Built by the inventor of the Stanley Steamer in 1909, this elegant, historic hotel offers turn-of-the-century ambience and good mountain views. There are two restaurants. The hotel does not have air-conditioning.

## 3 Salt Lake City

Utah's capital, Salt Lake City attracts visitors from around the world, many to see Temple Square, international headquarters of the Church of Jesus Christ of Latter Day Saints. But while Mormonism may spring first to mind, it certainly isn't all the city offers. Here you can look up your family history, visit museums, attend the ballet or symphony, or drop in at a Utah Jazz basketball game. And within an hour's drive are lush forests, rugged mountains, and some of the country's best ski resorts.

Lying in a valley in north–central Utah, between the Wasatch Mountains and Great Salt Lake, Salt Lake City is both old and modern, small as cities go, with a population of 160,000, but with plenty of cultural attractions, restaurants, lodging, and easy access to an abundance of magnificent scenery and exhilarating outdoor recreation possibilities.

### ARRIVING & DEPARTING

**BY PLANE**  **Salt Lake City International Airport** is just north of I-80 off exit 115 on the west side of the city. A variety of ground transportation options are available, with information from the airport's central information number (☎ **801/575-2400**). The cost to downtown is generally about $12 for the first person, with lower rates for additional passengers.

**BY CAR, TRAIN & BUS**  I-80 cuts through the city east–west, and I-15 runs north–south. The **Amtrak** station is downtown at 320 S. Rio Grande Ave. (☎ **800/872-7245** or 801/364-8562), just west of Temple Square. **Greyhound** has a bus station downtown at 160 W. South Temple (☎ **800/231-2222** or 801/355-9581), a block west of Temple Square.

### ESSENTIALS

**VISITOR INFORMATION**  A downtown **Visitor Center** is operated by the **Salt Lake Convention and Visitor Bureau,** 180 S. West Temple, Salt Lake City, UT 84101 (☎ **800/541-4955** or 801/521-2868). Another **information center** is at **Salt Lake City International Airport Terminal II** (☎ **801/575-2800** or 801/575-2660).

**RESOURCES FOR TRAVELERS WITH SPECIAL NEEDS**  The information and referral line for **travelers with disabilities** is ☎ **800/333-8824.** The **Gay Help Line** (☎ **801/533-0927**) provides referral and counseling services, and can also suggest nightspots and accommodations.

**EMERGENCIES**  Dial ☎ **911** for police, fire, or ambulance. Hospitals include **LDS Hospital,** the closest to downtown, at 8th Avenue and C Street (☎ **801/321-1100**).

**LIQUOR LAWS**  Buying liquor, beer, or wine by the drink is somewhat more complicated in Utah than in most other states. Most of the better restaurants can serve alcoholic beverages with meals, starting at noon. Some establishments are licensed as taverns, and can sell 3.2% beer only. There are also establishments called private clubs, which are essentially bars, and may or may not be attached to restaurants. You have to be a member or a guest of a member to enter, but inexpensive, 2-week memberships (usually $5) are generally available. Private clubs can serve beginning at 10am from Monday to Saturday and at noon on Sunday. Liquor by the drink cannot be sold after 1am from Monday to Saturday or after midnight on Sunday.

## GETTING AROUND

Salt Lake City is laid out on a simple grid system centered on Temple Square. The road numbers increase by 100s in the four cardinal directions, with West Temple taking the place of 100 West, North Temple of 100 North, and State Street of 100 East. The "Salt Lake City Visitor's Guide," available free at the visitor center, has maps showing the approximate location of many restaurants, motels, and attractions.

**BY BUS**   The **Utah Transit Authority** (☎ **801/287-4636** or TDD 801/287-4657) provides bus service around the city, with a "free fare zone" in the downtown area. Outside the "free fare zone" the charge is 85¢, exact change required. Regular route schedules and maps are available at malls, libraries, and the visitor centers. The Centennial Discovery Trolley operates during the summer, offering transportation to historic sites and other attractions around the city. Tickets ($3) are available aboard the trolley or at the Visitor Center.

**BY TAXI**   For 24-hour taxi service, call **City Cab Co.** (☎ **801/363-5550**). Base fare is $1.25 plus $1.50 per mile.

## WHAT TO SEE & DO

The major attractions here are all related to the Church of Jesus Christ of Latter-Day Saints, also known as the Mormons, but there are also a number of other things to see and do.

**ATTRACTIONS**   For the best possible introduction to the state of Utah and its people, 70% of whom are Mormons, make your first stop at ✪ **Temple Square,** bounded by Main Street on the east, and North, South, and West Temple streets (☎ **801/240-2534**). The Mecca of the Church of Jesus Christ of Latter-Day Saints, this 4-block-square is enclosed by 15-foot walls, with a gate in the center of each. Inside are the Temple (closed to the public), Tabernacle, Assembly Hall, and North and South Visitor Centers. Short guided tours are offered every 10–15 minutes. The oval Tabernacle boasts one of the West's largest unsupported domed roofs, has incredible acoustics, and seats 6,500 people. The Mormon Tabernacle Choir can be heard here for free when not on tour; inquire at a visitor center. Admission is free, and it's open daily from 6:30am to 10:30pm, tours 8am to 9pm; shorter hours on Christmas Day.

All things in Salt Lake City start at Temple Square, and the bulk of what you want to see will be within walking distance.

   ✪ **Beehive House.** *67 E. South Temple.* ☎ *801/240-2672. Admission free. Mon–Sat 9:30am–4:30pm; Sun 10am–1pm. Closes at 1pm on all holidays.* Brigham Young built this house in 1854 as his family home, but he also had an office and entertained church and government leaders here. The house gives visitors a glimpse into the lifestyle of this famous Mormon. His bedroom is just to the left of the entrance, handy for when late callers arrived to confer with him. The sewing room was a gathering place for children. The house has been restored and furnished with period furniture, including many original pieces.

   **Capitol Building.** *Capitol Hill, at north end of State St.* ☎ *801/538-3000. Admission free. Memorial Day–Labor Day, Mon–Sat 6am–8pm. Labor Day–Memorial Day, Mon–Sat 6am–6pm. Closed major holidays.* Built of unpolished Utah granite and Georgia marble, the capitol rests on a beautifully landscaped hill in a 40-acre park. Guided tours are available (☎ 801/538-1030) or you may walk through on your own. The Rotunda stretches upward 165 feet, and is decorated with murals. The third floor houses the state supreme court and legislature.

   **Genealogy Research Center.** *35 N. West Temple.* ☎ *801/240-2331. Admission free. Mon 7:30am–6pm, Tues–Fri 7:30am–10pm, Sat 7:30am–5pm. Closed major holidays and July 24.* This incredible facility has a huge collection of genealogical records

# Salt Lake City

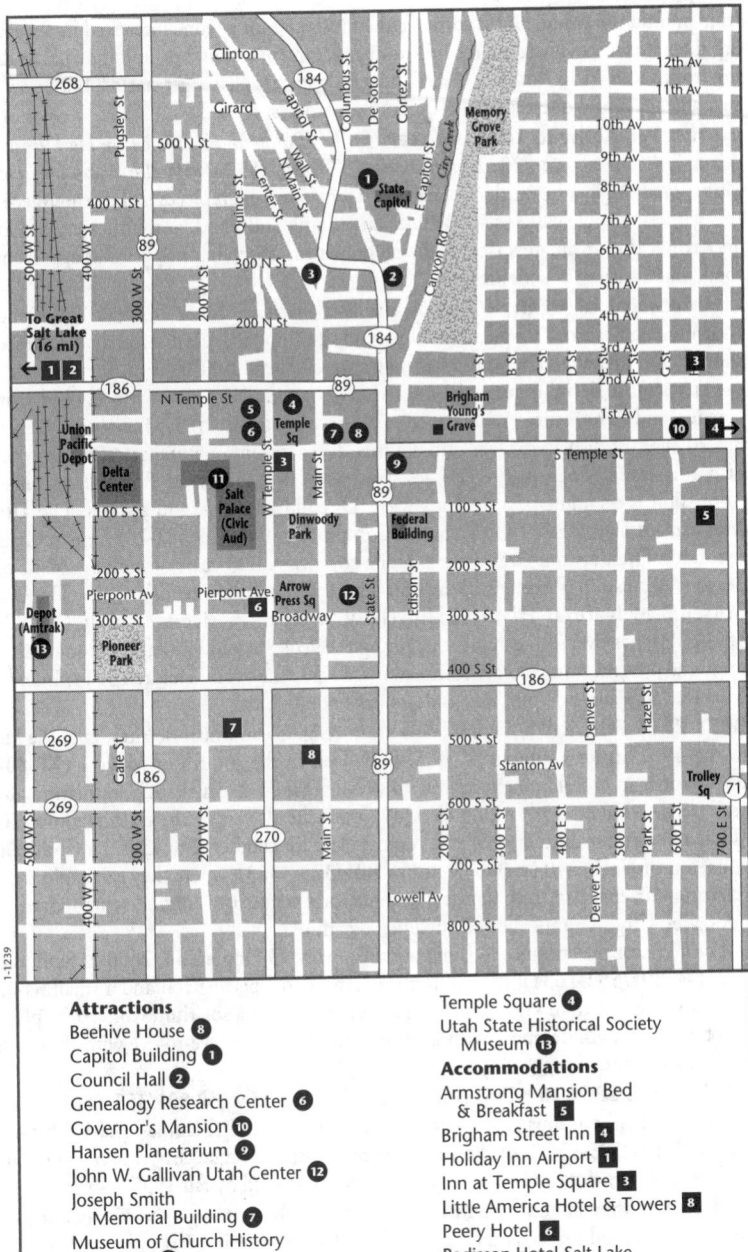

## Attractions

Beehive House **8**
Capitol Building **1**
Council Hall **2**
Genealogy Research Center **6**
Governor's Mansion **10**
Hansen Planetarium **9**
John W. Gallivan Utah Center **12**
Joseph Smith
  Memorial Building **7**
Museum of Church History
  and Art **5**
Pioneer Memorial Museum **3**
Salt Lake Art Center **11**
Temple Square **4**
Utah State Historical Society
  Museum **13**

## Accommodations

Armstrong Mansion Bed
  & Breakfast **5**
Brigham Street Inn **4**
Holiday Inn Airport **1**
Inn at Temple Square **3**
Little America Hotel & Towers **8**
Peery Hotel **6**
Radisson Hotel Salt Lake
  City Airport **2**
Salt Lake Hilton **7**

from around the world, and is considered a must-stop for anyone interested in researching their ancestors. There are records from governments, churches, and individuals dating from about 1550 to about 1920. The staff helps neophytes get started, but be aware that a genealogical quest is a time-consuming process.

**John W. Gallivan Utah Center.** *36 E. 200 South St. (the entire block between Main and State sts., and 200 and 300 South).* ☎ *801/532-0459. Admission free. Daily 7am–10pm.* A gigantic outdoor chess board with waist-high pieces is the centerpiece of this gathering spot, which also includes an ice rink and pond, amphitheater, and aviary. You'll find intimate spaces, vantage points for observing performing arts events, food, and a variety of activities.

**University of Utah.** *University and 200 South sts.* ☎ *801/581-6773.* Pioneer Mormons had a great respect for education, and opened the University of Deseret shortly after arriving. The university now sprawls over 1,500 acres on the east side of the city almost at the mouth of Emigration Canyon. The university's ✪ **Red Butte Garden and Arboretum** (☎ 801/581-4747 recording, 801/585-5322 Visitor Center) has 20 acres of display gardens and another 200 acres in a natural state, with 4 miles of nature trails. Open Apr–Oct Tues–Sun, and Nov–Mar Wed–Sun, 10am–sunset. Admission is $3 adults, $2 students with ID, children 4–15, and seniors. The **Utah Museum of Fine Arts,** 1530 E. South Campus Dr. (☎ 801/581-7332), is probably the state's finest art museum, with exhibits covering 4,000 years of human artistic endeavors. Admission is free; it's open Mon–Fri 10am–5pm, weekends 2–5pm. The **Utah Museum of Natural History,** University Street at President's Circle (☎ 801/ 581-4303), has over 200 exhibits describing the geologic and natural creation of Utah, up to the present. Admission is $3 for adults, $1.50 seniors and children 3–14. It's open Mon–Sat 9:30am–5:30pm, Sun and holidays noon–5pm.

**BEST BETS FOR KIDS**   For a break from religious and historic sites, take the kids to the **49th Street Galleria,** 4998 S. 360 West in the suburb of Murray (☎ **801/ 265-3866**), an entertainment mall with bowling alleys, roller skating, miniature golf, and arcades. Take I-15 exit 303 to 5300 South, head west to the traffic light at 700 West, and turn north to the Galleria. A great place for children 2 to 12 is the **Children's Museum of Utah,** 840 N. 300 West (☎ **801/328-3383**), where they can explore face painting and makeup, folk dancing and art, or operate a telephone switchboard, or pilot a jet. Children must be accompanied by adults.

Located near the entrance to Emigration Canyon, ✪ **Hogle Zoo,** 2600 E. Sunnyside Ave. (☎ **801/582-1631**), is small but modern, with a petting zoo and a small replica of an 1869 steam train kids can ride in summer. There's a solarium with exotic plants and birds and a giraffe house with a balcony so you can see eye-to-eye with those tall-necked creatures.

**SPECTATOR SPORTS**   Pro teams include the **Utah Jazz** (☎ **801/355-3865**), which plays basketball, not music, at Delta Center, 301 W. South Temple. The **Utah Grizzlies** (☎ **801/325-7328**) of the International Hockey League currently play in Delta Center, although a new arena is expected to be completed by fall 1997.

**SKIING**   Within an hour of downtown Salt Lake City are four super ski areas. If **driving,** take exit 7 off I-215, and follow Utah 210 south, turning east onto Utah 190 for Big Cottonwood Canyon's Solitude and Brighton ski areas; continue on Utah 210 south and east into Little Cottonwood Canyon's Snowbird and Alta ski areas. Driving time from the airport is approximately 1 hour to any of them. The **Utah Transit Authority** (☎ **801/287-4636** or TDD 801/287-4657) provides bus service from downtown hotels and various park-and-ride lots into Big and Little Cottonwood canyons during ski season. **Lewis Bros. Stages** (☎ **800/366-0288** or 801/359-8677) offers shuttles from the airport, downtown Salt Lake City, and among the ski resorts.

✪ **Alta Ski Area,** P.O. Box 8007, Alta, UT 84092-8007 (☎ **801/742-3333;** snow report 801/572-3939; ski school 801/742-2600; lodging 801/942-0404), at the top of Little Cottonwood Canyon, is an excellent choice for serious skiers of all levels. While the lifts and other facilities here are not state-of-the-art (some hiking is required), the emphasis is on quality skiing, and skiers are turned away if the ski gods determine there are already enough people on the mountain. The highly regarded ski school is recognized for its part in the development of professional ski instruction.

**Brighton Ski Resort,** Star Route, Brighton, UT 84121 (☎ **801/532-4731,** 800/ 873-5512, or 801/943-8309 for ski report), located at the top of Big Cottonwood Canyon, has been hosting skiers since 1936. There's a full range of terrain, a highly regarded ski school (including night ski lessons Thursday evenings), and a large day lodge. In addition, Brighton is considered one of the best snowboarding destinations in the state.

**Snowbird Ski and Summer Resort,** P.O. Box 929000, Snowbird, UT 84092-9000 (☎ **800/453-3000** for reservations; 801/742-2222, ext. 4285 for snow conditions; 801/ 521-6040 in Salt Lake City), consistently rated among America's top 10 ski resorts, is a full-service resort offering spectacular powder skiing and a wide range of upper-end amenities. The ski and snowboarding school, with about 200 instructors, provides private or group lessons; helicopter skiing is available mid-December to mid-May. Snowbird's Disabled Skier Program is among the best in the country.

**Solitude Ski Resort,** P.O. Box 21350, Salt Lake City, UT 84121-0350 (☎ **800/ 748-4754** or 801/534-1400), is a friendly, family-oriented ski area with virtually no lift lines. The mountain is well designed, with runs laid out so beginners won't suddenly find themselves in more difficult terrain. Solitude is the state's only downhill ski area with a world-class Nordic center out its back door.

## ACCOMMODATIONS

You'll have no trouble finding conveniently located lodging in Salt Lake City, wherever you want to be, at relatively reasonable rates.

**Brigham Street Inn.** *1135 E. South Temple, Salt Lake City, UT 84102.* ☎ *800/ 417-4461 or 801/364-4461. Fax 801/521-3201. 8 rms, 1 suite. $115–$135 double; $175–$195 suite. Rates include continental breakfast. AE, CB, DISC, MC, V.* Located in a handsome three-story historic mansion, the Brigham Street Inn is elegant yet relaxed. Most rooms have queen beds, and over half have fireplaces. The continental breakfast is a scrumptious offering that includes homemade pastries or croissants and fresh fruit.

✪ **Inn at Temple Square.** *71 W. South Temple, Salt Lake City, UT 84101.* ☎ *800/843-4668 or 801/531-1000. Fax 801/536-7272. 95 units including 10 suites. $113–$132 double; $155–$220 suite. Rates include breakfast. AE, DC, DISC, MC, V.* Built in 1930, this gracious hotel radiates 18th-century European elegance. Rooms are spacious, with at least one upholstered chair. Conveniences include a restaurant, library, free pass to nearby health club, valet parking, and airport shuttle.

✪ **Little America Hotel and Towers.** *500 S. Main St., Salt Lake City, UT 84101.* ☎ *800/453-9450 or 801/596-5785. Fax 801/322-1610. 850 units, including 17 suites. $73–$124 double; $114–$124 suite. AE, DC, DISC, MC, V.* Among the city's finest hotels, the Little America offers large, handsomely appointed rooms, all with 31-inch color televisions, and most with beautiful views of the city and mountains beyond. Facilities include restaurants, bar, health club, sundeck with indoor/outdoor pool, beauty salon, and shops.

**Peery Hotel.** *110 W. 300 South (Broadway), Salt Lake City, UT 84101.* ☎ *800/ 331-0073 or 801/521-4300. Fax 801/575-5014. 77 rms. $89–$109 double. Rates include continental breakfast. AE, DC, DISC, MC, V.* One of the few truly historic hotels left in Salt Lake City, the Peery, built in 1910, has been restored to its former understated elegance, offering comfortable, tastefully decorated rooms. Extras include a whirlpool and exercise room, restaurant, and airport shuttle.

**Radisson Hotel Salt Lake City Airport.** *2177 W. North Temple, Salt Lake City, UT 84116.* ☎ *800/333-3333 or 801/364-5800. Fax 801/364-5823. 127 units, including 29 suites. $129–$139 double; $139 suite. AE, CB, DC, DISC, ER, JCB, MC, V.* This rugged gray-stone building, reminiscent of a mountain hunting lodge, features attractive and spacious rooms with country French decor and gas fireplaces; top-floor rooms have cathedral ceilings, and there are loft suites. Guests appreciate the whirlpool, large outdoor pool, executive exercise room, and airport transportation.

**Salt Lake Hilton.** *150 W. 500 South, Salt Lake City, UT 84101.* ☎ *800/ 421-7602 or 801/532-3344. Fax 801/531-0705. 351 rms, including 33 suites. $130– $175 double; $135–$350 suite. AE, CB, DC, DISC, ER, MC, V.* Many rooms offer incredible views, some suites have large sunken baths, and courtyard king rooms overlook a lawn and trees. The hotel has restaurants, a bar, fitness center, hot tub, outdoor pool, sundeck, video game room, business center, laptop computer rental, airport shuttle, and secretarial service.

**OTHER ACCOMMODATIONS**   Additional lodging choices include **Armstrong Mansion Bed and Breakfast,** 667 E. 100 South, Salt Lake City, UT (☎ **800/ 708-1333** or 801/531-1333; fax 801/531-0282), with 14 charming, tastefully decorated rooms (most with whirlpool) in a historic building; and **Holiday Inn Airport,** 1659 W. North Temple, Salt Lake City, UT 84116 (☎ **800/HOLIDAY** or 801/533-9000; fax 801/364-0614), with 191 units, each furnished with a king or two queen beds, a comfortable easy chair, and a desk.

## DINING

Salt Lake City restaurants are more casual than in most major American cities, but the service is generally excellent. You will have to request alcoholic drinks except in what are called "private clubs." See "Liquor Laws" above. Also, the Utah Indoor Clean Air Act prohibits smoking in restaurants, although not in private clubs, lounges, or taverns.

**Café Trang.** *818 S. Main St.* ☎ *801/539-1638. Reservations recommended in winter. Main courses $5–$10. AE, MC, V. Sun–Thurs 11:30am–9:30pm, Fri–Sat 11:30am– 10pm. VIETNAMESE/CHINESE.* Known for the best Vietnamese food in the state, this restaurant has added Chinese dishes, mostly Cantonese. The 200 or so menu items are listed by number, with brief English descriptions of each, little hearts indicating dishes that are completely vegetarian, and stars to indicate spiciness.

**Crown Burgers.** *3190 S. Highland Dr.* ☎ *801/467-6633. Reservations not accepted. Main courses $3–$7. DISC, MC, V. Mon–Sat 10am–10pm. FAST FOOD.* The wall sconces, chandeliers, and stone fireplace almost seem out of place, since you still order at the counter and otherwise serve yourself. Known for the best fast-food burger around—a cheeseburger covered with pastrami—there's lots more, and the food is good, hot, and fast.

✪ **Lamb's Restaurant.** *169 S. Main St.* ☎ *801/364-7166. Main courses $3–$10 at breakfast, $13–$18 at lunch and dinner. AE, DC, DISC, MC, V. Mon–Sat 7am–9pm. AMERICAN/CONTINENTAL.* Lamb's consistently serves good food at reasonable prices, with friendly, efficient service. In front is a counter and booths, with more formal dining rooms in back. There are sandwiches and salads, Greek dishes, plus several lamb choices, such as broiled French-style lamb chops and barbecued lamb shanks.

**Marianne's Delicatessen.** *149 W. 200 South.* ☎ *801/364-0513. Main courses $4–$8. AE, MC, V. Daily 11am–3pm. GERMAN.* This cafe-style combination delicatessen and restaurant offers sandwiches, a variety of sausage platters, and soups. Portions are generous, and all the sausage is homemade.

**Market Street Grill.** *50 W. Market St.* ☎ *801/322-4668. Reservations not accepted. Breakfast $3–$7; lunch $5–$13; dinner $12–$24; Sun brunch $6. AE, DISC, MC, V. Mon–Thurs 6:30am–3pm and 5–10:30pm, Sat 7am–3pm and 5–11:30pm, Sun 9:30am–3pm and 4–9:30pm. SEAFOOD/STEAK.* Quite possibly Utah's best seafood restaurant, with fresh fish flown in daily from around the world, the grill is popular, so expect to wait before being led into the noisy, somewhat cramped dining room. There's Pacific red snapper, seafood stew, and more, plus beef, pastas, and salads.

✪ **New Yorker.** *60 W. Market St.* ☎ *801/363-0166. Reservations recommended. Lunch $7–$16, dinner $13–$50. AE, DISC, MC, V. Mon–Fri 11:30am–2:30pm; Mon–Thurs 5:30–10pm, Fri–Sat 5:30–11pm. (Private club, membership required—$5 for 2 weeks.) AMERICAN.* Salt Lake City's finest restaurant, with understated elegance, excellent food, and impeccable service. Dinner choices include sautéed sweetbreads, Dungeness crab cakes, and rack of lamb. Lunches offer sautéed chicken breast, tenderloin of beef, sandwiches, and salads. The less formal cafe offers similar but somewhat lighter selections at slightly lower prices.

**OTHER DINING**    A few other especially good restaurants are **Baci Trattoria,** 134 W. Pierpont Ave. (☎ **801/328-1500**), offering good northern Italian dishes in a distinctively outdoor Italian cafe atmosphere; **Diamond Lil's,** 1528 W. North Temple (☎ **801/533-0547**), with a good steak and seafood menu and Old West decor; and **Pierpont Cantina,** 122 W. Pierpont Ave. (☎ **801/364-1222**), serving tasty but not-too-spicy Mexican dishes.

## SALT LAKE CITY AFTER DARK

Pick up the Friday morning edition of the *Salt Lake Tribune* or Friday evening's *Deseret News* for listings of upcoming events.

**THE PERFORMING ARTS**    The historic **Capitol Theatre,** 50 W. 200 South (☎ 801/355-2787 for box office), is home to several performing arts companies. The nationally acclaimed **Ballet West** (☎ 801/363-9318) generally offers four productions at the Capitol Theatre between September and March. Modern dance lovers should check out the **Repertory Dance Theatre** (☎ 801/534-6345) and the **Ririe–Woodbury Dance Company** (☎ 801/328-1062). Also appearing at the Capitol is the **Utah Opera Company** (☎ 801/534-0842), which features international artists.

The widely acclaimed **Utah Symphony,** 123 W. South Temple (☎ 801/533-6683), performs year-round in **Symphony Hall,** and the summer series in July and August usually kicks off with a gala music and food event. The **Utah Music Festival** offers fine chamber music during July and most of August at the Utah Museum of Fine Arts and at Temple Square. Contact the festival at P.O. Box 3381, Logan, UT 84323-3381 (☎ 800/816-UTAH).

**THE CLUB & BAR SCENE**    Salt Lake City is not known for its wild nightlife, but there are at least a few popular clubs and bars. The **Club Baci,** 140 W. Pierpont Ave. (☎ 801/328-1333), has big-screen TVs that are terrific for sports events. For live music, try the well-established **D.B. Coopers,** 19 E. 200 South (☎ 801/532-2948), which features folk and rhythm and blues, including occasional big-name entertainers. At the **Dead Goat Saloon,** 156 S. West Temple, Arrow Press Square (☎ 801/328-4628), you'll find live country music nightly, plus satellite TV, darts, pool, grill food, and beer. And nearby, **Sandy's Station,** 8925 S. 255 West, Sandy (☎ 801/255-2078), is a popular swing bar, with country-western music.

## 4  Bryce Canyon National Park

One of America's most colorful national parks, Bryce Canyon offers spectacular beauty among thousands of intricately shaped sculptures called *hoodoos*. Geologists say these oddly shaped pinnacles of rock were created by millions of years of water and wind erosion, but a Paiute Indian legend says a people who once lived in this valley were turned to stone because of their evil ways. Whatever the cause, Bryce is unique, with its delicate and often whimsical formations, changing colors with the changing light of day.

## ESSENTIALS

**ARRIVING & DEPARTING**  The nearest commercial airports are **Cedar City Airport,** 78 miles to the west of the park, and **St. George Airport,** 125 miles southwest. Bryce Canyon Airport, several miles from the park entrance, has very limited service. The park is crossed by east–west Utah 12, with an access road to the south providing the main entrance.

**VISITOR INFORMATION**  For advance information, contact **Bryce Canyon National Park,** Bryce Canyon, UT 84717 (☎ 435/834-5322). You can order books, maps, and videos from Bryce Canyon Natural History Association, Bryce Canyon, UT 84717 (☎ 435/834-5322).

**VISITOR CENTER**  The visitor center, at the north end as you enter the park, has exhibits on the geology and history of the area and presents a short slide show.

**ADMISSION COSTS & REGULATIONS**  Entry into the park (for up to 7 days) costs $10 per private vehicle or $5 per motorcycle or bicycle. Free permits, available at the visitor center, are required for all overnight trips into the backcountry. Backcountry hikers are prohibited from building fires and must carry their own water. Both bicycles and dogs are prohibited in the backcountry and on all trails.

**SAFETY**  Sprained, twisted, and broken ankles are fairly common here, due to the nature of the trails, but can usually be prevented by wearing sturdy hiking boots. Another concern is bubonic plague, which, contrary to popular belief, is treatable with antibiotics if caught early. The plague bacteria has been found on fleas on prairie dogs in the park, so you should avoid contact with wild animals, especially prairie dogs, chipmunks, and ground squirrels.

**INTERPRETIVE PROGRAMS**  Ranger talks take place most summer evenings at campground amphitheaters. Topics vary, but could include the animals of the park, geology, and humans' role in the park's history. Rangers also give half-hour talks on similar subjects several times daily at various locations, and lead hikes and walks, including a moonlight hike and a wheelchair-accessible 1-hour canyon rim walk. During the summer, children 12 and younger can join the Junior Rangers, participate in a variety of programs, and earn certificates and patches.

**WHEN TO GO**  The park is particularly busy from mid-June to mid-September, when the campgrounds are often full by 2pm. A better time to visit is spring or fall. If you don't mind a bit of cold and snow, the park is practically deserted in winter, and bright red hoodoos capped with white snow are beautiful.

## WHAT TO SEE & DO

Your first stop should be the **visitor center** to see the short slide show on the park's geology—the why of Bryce. Then either drive the park road, stopping at viewpoints to gaze down into the canyon, or hop on the Bryce Tours van for a 1 1/2-hour **guided tour.** Whichever you choose, be sure to spend at least a moment at Inspiration Point, which offers splendid (and yes, inspirational) views into Bryce Amphitheater and its hundreds of statuesque pink, red, orange, and brown stone sculptures.

# Bryce Canyon National Park

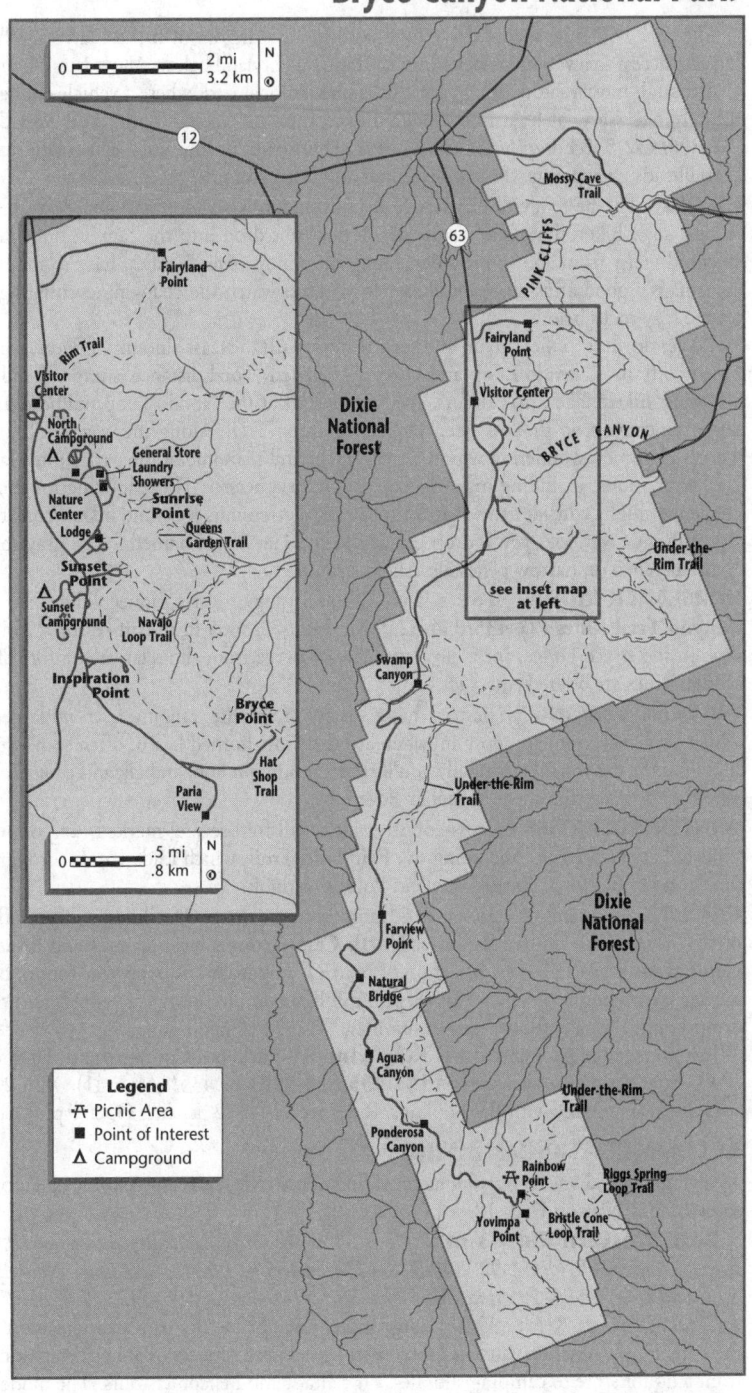

0 —— 2 mi
—— 3.2 km
N

⑫

㉖

Mossy Cave
Trail

PINK CLIFFS

Fairyland
Point

Fairyland
Point

Visitor
Center

Visitor Center

Rim Trail

North
Campground

General Store
Laundry
Showers

BRYCE CANYON

Nature
Center

Sunrise
Point

Lodge

Queens
Garden Trail

Under-the-
Rim Trail

Sunset
Point

see inset map
at left

Sunset
Campground

Navajo
Loop Trail

Dixie
National
Forest

Inspiration
Point

Bryce
Point

Swamp
Canyon

Hat
Shop
Trail

Under-the-Rim
Trail

Paria
View

0 —— .5 mi
—— .8 km
N

Dixie
National
Forest

Farview
Point

Natural
Bridge

Agua
Canyon

Under-the-Rim
Trail

## Legend
⊼ Picnic Area
■ Point of Interest
△ Campground

Ponderosa
Canyon

Rainbow
Point

Riggs Spring
Loop Trail

Yovimpa
Point

Bristle Cone
Loop Trail

The park's 17-mile **scenic drive** (one way) follows the rim of Bryce Canyon, offering easy access to a variety of views into the fanciful fairyland below. Allow 1 to 2 hours.

Although most visitors bring cars, this is one national park where a vehicle isn't absolutely necessary, at least in summer. **Bryce Canyon Scenic Tours and Shuttles** (☎ 800/432-5383 or 435/834-5200) runs a shuttle bus in July and August with stops at trailheads, viewpoints, the visitor center, and campgrounds.

**HIKING**  The best way to experience Bryce Canyon is on foot, and you don't have to be a superhiker. The **Rim Trail,** which does not drop into the canyon but offers splendid views from above, meanders along the rim for over 5 miles. Easy to moderate, this is a good after-dinner walk, when you can watch the changing evening light on the rosy rocks below.

To get down into the canyon and see the most with the least amount of sweat, combine two trails—**Navajo Loop** and **Queen's Garden.** Total distance is under 3 miles, and most hikers take 2 to 3 hours. It's best to start at the Navajo Loop trailhead and leave the canyon on the less-steep Queen's Garden Trail. Along the way you'll pass Thor's Hammer, wondering why it hasn't fallen; and see some of the park's most fanciful formations, including majestic Queen Victoria herself. Those looking for more challenge might consider the **Hat Shop Trail,** a strenuous 3.8-mile hike. From the Bryce Point Overlook, you'll drop quickly to the Hat Shop, named for its gray rock "hats" perched on narrow pedestals. Allow 4 hours.

**HORSEBACK RIDING**  To see Bryce Canyon the way early pioneers did, contact **Canyon Trail Rides** (☎ 435/834-5219, or 435/679-8665 in the off-season), with a desk inside Bryce Lodge, for a close-up view of Bryce from the relative comfort of a saddle. Rides are offered Apr–Oct.

**WILDLIFE VIEWING**  The park has a variety of wildlife, ranging from mule deer, which you're likely to see most anywhere, to the short-horned lizard, often seen while hiking in the canyon. Occasionally you'll spot a mountain lion, and elk and pronghorn antelope are sometimes seen at higher elevations.

**WINTER ACTIVITIES**  Cross-country skiers will find several marked, ungroomed trails (all above the rim), including the **Fairyland Trail,** which leads 1 mile through a pine and juniper forest to the Fairyland Point Overlook.

**CAMPING**  Typical of national park campgrounds, the two facilities at Bryce offer plenty of trees but limited facilities. **North Campground** has 105 sites and **Sunset Campground** has 111 sites. A section of North Campground is open year-round, but Sunset Campground is open May–Sept only. Reservations are not accepted, and the campgrounds usually fill by 2pm in summer. Cost is $10 per night.

Just outside the park entrance is **Ruby's Inn RV Park and Campground,** Utah 63 (P.O. Box 22), Bryce, UT 84764 (☎ 435/834-5301 or 435/834-5341), with 227 sites, including many with RV hookups. Rates are $14–$22 per site. Open Apr–Oct.

## ACCOMMODATIONS & DINING

More lodging and several restaurants providing home-style meals are available in Tropic, several miles away on Utah 12.

**Best Western Ruby's Inn.**  *Utah 63 at the entrance to Bryce Canyon (P.O. Box 1), Bryce, UT 84764.* ☎ *800/528-1234 or 435/834-5341. 369 units. Nov–Apr, $45–$80 double; $80–$95 suite. May–Oct, $80–$100 double; $95–$125 suite. AE, CB, DC, DISC, EC, JCB, MC, V.* This large motel just outside the park provides most of the beds for park visitors, and its lobby offers goods and services of almost every kind, from a liquor store to camping supplies, car rentals, and helicopter tours. The modern motel rooms have wood furnishings and art depicting scenes of the area. Some have whirlpool tubs.

**Bryce Canyon Lodge.** *Bryce Canyon National Park, UT.* ☎ *435/834-5361. For information and reservations: Amfac Parks & Resorts, 14001 E. Iliff Ave., Suite 600, Aurora, CO 80014.* ☎ *303/29PARKS; fax 303/ 338-2045. 114 units in motel rooms and cabins; 3 suites and 1 studio in lodge. $75–$80 motel; $87–$95 cabin; $112–115 lodge. AE, DISC, MC, V. Closed Nov to mid-Apr.* This is the only lodging located inside Bryce Canyon National Park. The handsome sandstone and pine lodge, which opened in 1924, contains luxurious suites. The adjacent motel rooms are just that—pleasant, modern motel rooms; and the small cabins offer rustic charm, with gas-burning stone fireplaces, pine walls, and log beams. Make reservations 4 to 6 months in advance. No air-conditioning.

# 5 Zion National Park

Named Zion by Mormon pioneers because it made them think of heaven, Zion National Park casts a spell over you, as you gaze upon its sheer multicolored walls of sandstone, explore its narrow canyons, hunt for hanging gardens of wildflowers, or just ponder the complexities of life while listening to the roar of the churning, tumbling Virgin River. A collage of images, Zion offers a smorgasbord of experiences, sights, and even smells, from its stone sculptures and gnarled trees to its lush forests and rushing rivers.

## ESSENTIALS

**ARRIVING & DEPARTING** The nearest airports are **St. George Airport,** 42 miles west of the park; and **Cedar City Airport,** 56 miles north. Both offer car rentals.

From the east, take Utah 9, reached from either the north or south via U.S. 89, to the park's main **Zion Canyon entrance.** From I-15 on the park's western side, the drive into Zion Canyon follows Utah 9, or Utah 17 and Utah 9. The **Kolob Canyons entrance,** in the park's northwest corner, is reached by an access road off I-15.

**VISITOR INFORMATION** For advance information, contact **Zion National Park,** Springdale, UT 84767-1099 (☎ **435/772-3256**). You can order books, maps, and videos from **Zion Natural History Association,** Zion National Park, Springdale, UT 84767 (☎ **800/635-3959** or 435/772-3264).

**VISITOR CENTERS** The park has two visitor centers. The more comprehensive **Zion Canyon Visitor Center** (☎ **435/772-3256**) has a museum with a slide show and exhibits on the geology and history of the area. The smaller **Kolob Canyon Visitor Center** (☎ **435/586-9548**) provides permits, books, and maps.

**ADMISSION COSTS & REGULATIONS** Entry into the park (for up to 7 days) costs $10 per private vehicle or $4 per motorcycle or bicycle. Oversized vehicles, such as motorhomes, are charged $10 extra (round-trip) to access the park from the east through Zion–Mt. Carmel Tunnel. Permits (fee), available at either visitor center, are required for overnight trips into the backcountry. Backcountry hikers should practice minimum impact techniques, are prohibited from building fires, and cannot travel in groups of 12 or more. Bicycles are prohibited in the Zion–Mt. Carmel Tunnel, the backcountry, and on most trails. Dogs must be leashed at all times and are prohibited on trails and in the backcountry.

**INTERPRETIVE PROGRAMS** Amphitheater programs take place most summer evenings at park campgrounds. Topics vary, but could include the animals or plants of the park, geology, or some unique aspect such as Zion's slot canyons. Rangers also give short talks on similar subjects several times daily at various locations, and lead hikes and walks. Kids from 6 to 12 years old can join the Junior Rangers, participate in a variety of programs, and earn certificates, badges, and patches.

# Zion National Park

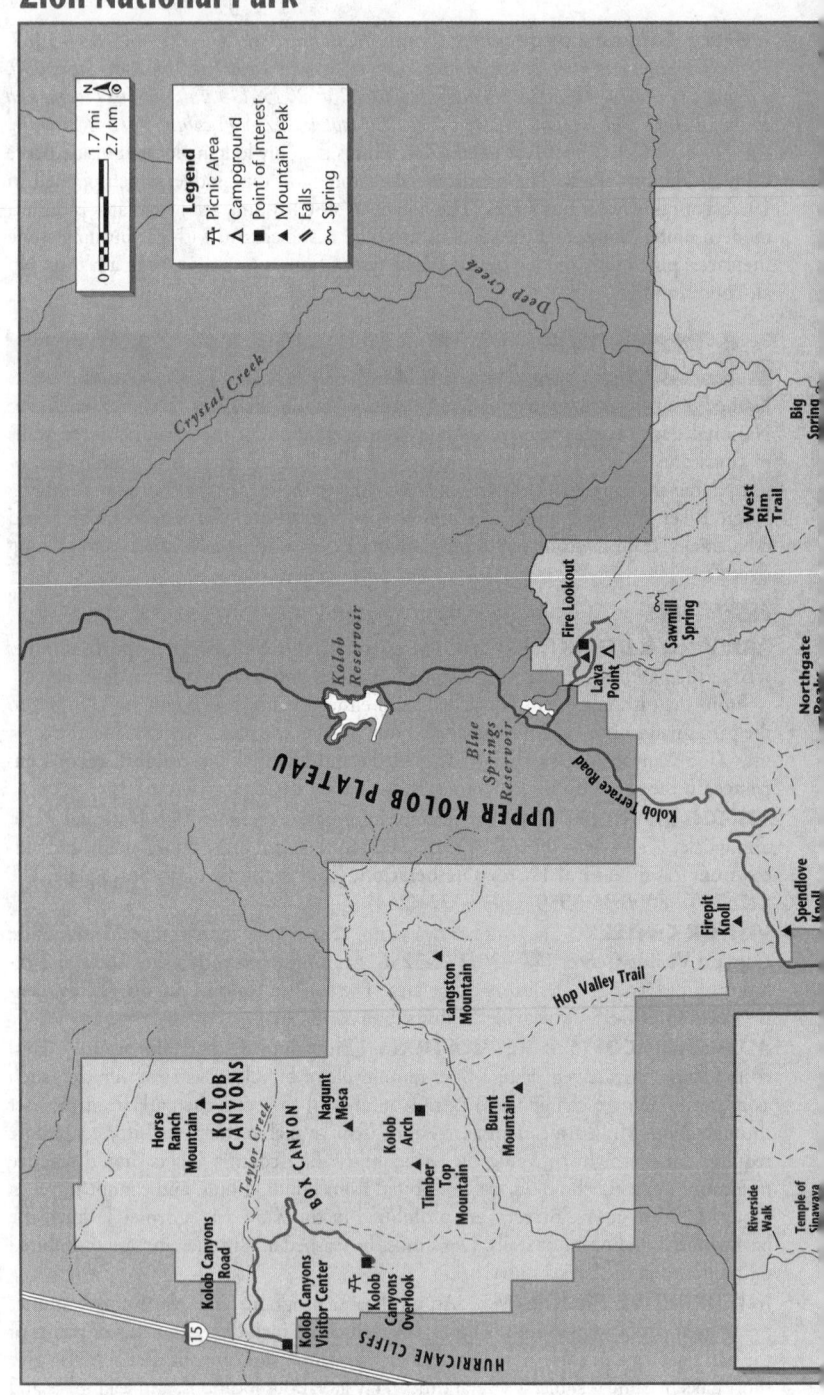

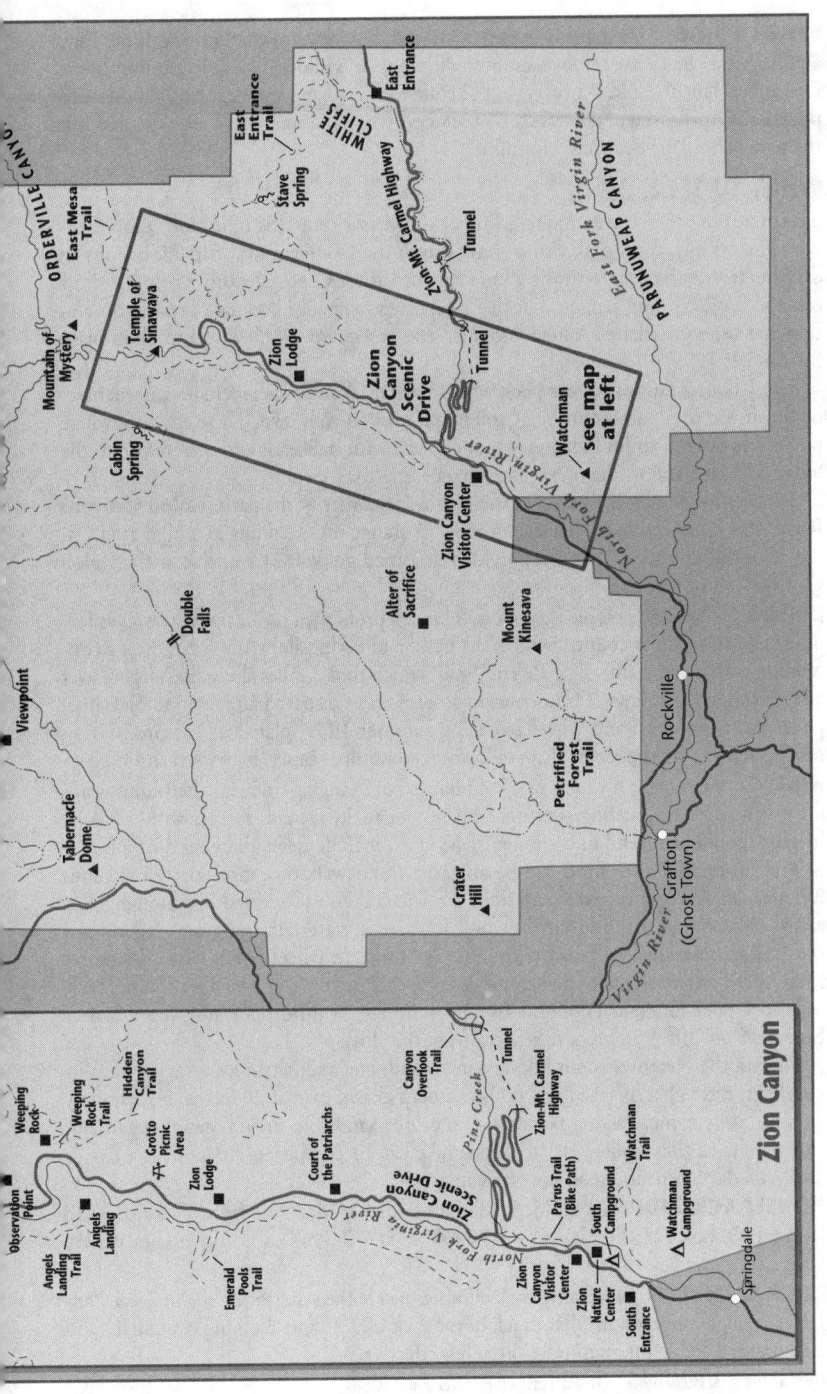

ORDERVILLE CANYON

East Mesa Trail

East Entrance Trail

WHITE CLIFFS

East Entrance

Mountain of Mystery ▲

Temple of Sinawava ▲

Stave Spring

Zion Lodge

Zion-Mt. Carmel Highway

Tunnel

Zion Canyon Scenic Drive

Tunnel

Watchman ▲

see map at left

Cabin Spring

Zion Canyon Visitor Center

North Fork Virgin River

PARUNUWEAP CANYON

East Fork Virgin River

Viewpoint ▼

Double Falls

Alter of Sacrifice ■

Mount Kinesava ▲

Tabernacle Dome ▲

Petrified Forest Trail

Rockville ◉

Crater Hill ▲

Virgin River Grafton
(Ghost Town) ◉

## Zion Canyon

Weeping Rock ■

Observation Point ◄

Hidden Canyon Trail

Weeping Rock Trail

Angels Landing ◄

Grotto Picnic Area

Angels Landing Trail

Zion Lodge ■

Court of the Patriarchs ■

Canyon Overlook Trail

Tunnel

Zion-Mt. Carmel Highway

Emerald Pools Trail

Zion Canyon Scenic Drive

Pine Creek

Pa'rus Trail (Bike Path)

North Fork Virgin River

South Campground △

Watchman Trail

Zion Canyon Visitor Center

Nature Center

Watchman Campground △

South Entrance

Springdale ◉

547

**WHEN TO GO**   The park is open year-round, but very crowded during June, July, and August, when Zion receives almost half its annual visitors. The quietest months are December, January, and February, but of course it's cold and snowy then. A good compromise is April, May, September, or October, when the weather is usually good but the park is less crowded than in summer.

## WHAT TO SEE & DO

The first thing to do, after a quick stop at the visitor center, is to explore Zion Canyon. Historically, most park visitors have driven the 14-mile round-trip **Zion Canyon Scenic Drive,** which starts at the Zion Canyon Visitor Center. At this writing, visitors can still drive into the canyon, but that's expected to change because of traffic congestion and other problems. A mandatory shuttle bus service is scheduled to be in place by summer 1999.

The 1-hour **Zion tram tour** (fee), which starts at Zion Lodge, includes commentary by the driver, who points out things you might miss on your own. There are stops where passengers can get off for better views, or connect with trailheads and then return to the lodge on a later tram. The tram generally operates May–Sept.

A less-crowded scenic drive is in the northwest corner of the park. **Kolob Canyons Road** runs 5 miles among spectacular red and orange rocks, ending at a high vista. Allow about 45 minutes. Detail is provided in a road guide ($1) available at the Kolob Canyon Visitor Center.

**BIKING**   With one notable exception, bikes are prohibited on all trails, as well as forbidden to travel cross-country within the park, and biking along the roads means contending with heavy traffic. The **Pa'rus Trail,** which runs 2 miles along the Virgin River and provides good views of numerous rock formations, is paved and open to bicyclists, pedestrians, strollers, and wheelchairs. By summer 1999, plans call for prohibiting private vehicles on the scenic drive, allowing only shuttle buses, bicyclists, and hikers.

**HIKING**   Zion offers a wide variety of hiking trails, ranging from easy half-hour walks on paved paths to grueling overnight hikes over rocky terrain. Hikers with a fear of heights should be careful in choosing trails; many include steep, dizzying drop-offs.

The **Emerald Pools Trail** can be an easy 1-hour walk or a moderately strenuous 2-hour hike. A 0.6-mile paved path from the Emerald Pools Parking Area through a forest of oak, maple, fir, and cottonwood leads to a waterfall, hanging garden, and the Lower Emerald Pool, and is suitable for those in wheelchairs, with assistance. From there, a steeper, rocky trail continues past cactus, yucca, and juniper another half-mile to Upper Emerald Pool and another waterfall. A third pool, just above Lower Emerald Pool, offers impressive reflections of the cliffs.

**Hiking the Narrows** is not hiking a trail at all, but walking and wading in the Virgin River, through a spectacular 1,000-foot-deep chasm that, at 20 feet wide, definitely lives up to its name. Passing fancifully sculptured sandstone arches, hanging gardens, and waterfalls, this moderately strenuous hike can be completed in less than a day or in several days, depending on how far you go.

**HORSEBACK RIDING**   Guided rides are available Mar–Oct from **Canyon Trail Rides,** P.O. Box 128, Tropic, UT 84776 (☎ **435/772-3967**), with ticket sales at Zion Lodge.

**ROCK CLIMBING**   Technical rock climbers tackle the sandstone cliffs in Zion Canyon, although rangers warn that much of the rock is loose and climbing equipment and techniques suitable for granite are often less effective.

**WILDLIFE VIEWING**   It's a rare visitor to Zion that does not see some form of wildlife, from mule deer to the numerous varieties of lizards. The ringtail cat prowls Zion Canyon at night, and the rare peregrine falcon, among the world's fastest birds, is sometimes seen. Also in the park are golden eagles, hummingbirds, ravens, piñon jays, and an occasional roadrunner.

**CAMPING**   The best camping is at one of the **national park campgrounds,** if you can find a site. Reservations are not accepted, and the campgrounds often fill by noon in summer. Both of Zion's main campgrounds, just inside the park's south entrance, have lots of trees but no showers. The charge is $10 per night. South Campground has 141 sites, and is usually open mid-Mar–mid-Oct; Watchman Campground has 228 sites and is open year-round. Lava Point, with six primitive sites, is located in Kolob Canyons. Use is free and it is usually open May–Oct.

The closest commercial campground, with hot showers and RV hookups, is **Zion Canyon Campground,** on Zion Park Boulevard a half mile south of the west park entrance (P.O. Box 99), Springdale, UT 84767 (☎ **435/772-3237**). It has 180 sites, many shaded, and is open year-round. Although crowded in summer, the campground is clean and well maintained. Rates are $14–$20.

## ACCOMMODATIONS & DINING

There is only one lodging and dining option actually in Zion National Park. For other lodging and dining head to Springdale, a village of some 350 at the park's south entrance, where there are a number of attractive motels, including a Best Western, plus about a half-dozen restaurants.

**Zion Lodge.** *Zion National Park.* ☎ *435/586-7686. For information and reservations: Amfac Parks & Resorts, 14001 E. Iliff Ave. Suite 600, Aurora, Co 80014. ☎ 303/ 29PARKS; fax 303/338-2045. 120 units. $75–$80 double; $113–$120 suite; $79–$85 cabin. AE, DISC, MC, V.* The charming cabins have private porches, gas-burning stone fireplaces, pineboard walls, and log beams. The comfortable motel units are basically that—motel units—with all the usual amenities except TVs. Motel suites have separate sitting rooms and refrigerators. No accommodations have air-conditioning. The lodge's restaurant offers fine food and spectacular views of the park.

# 6  The Grand Canyon

A mile deep, 277 miles long, and 18 miles wide in places, the Grand Canyon is truly one of the great wonders of the world. Banded layers of sandstone, limestone, shale, and schist give the canyon its color, and the interplay of shadows and light from dawn to dusk creates an ever-changing palette of hues and textures. Formed by the cutting action of the Colorado River as it flows through the Kaibab Plateau, the Grand Canyon is an open book exposing the secrets of the geologic history of this region. Twenty-one sedimentary layers, the oldest of which is more than a billion years old, can be seen in the canyon. And beneath these layers, at the very bottom, is a stratum of rock known as Vishnu schist, dating back 2 billion years.

Today the Grand Canyon is the last major undammed section of the Colorado River, and the river flows cold and clear from the bottom of the upriver Glen Canyon Dam. By raft, by mule, on foot, in helicopters and small planes, five million people come to the canyon each year seeking one of nature's meccas.

## ESSENTIALS

**ARRIVING & DEPARTING**   Air Nevada Airlines (☎ 800/634-6377) serves Grand Canyon Airport, 6 miles south of Grand Canyon Village in Tusayan (Grand Canyon).

The **Grand Canyon Railway** (☎ 800/843-8724) operates vintage steam and diesel locomotives and 1920s coaches between Williams and Grand Canyon Village. This is primarily a day-excursion train, but it's possible to ride up one day and return on another. **Amtrak** (☎ 800/USA-RAIL) provides service to Flagstaff, from where a bus connects directly to Grand Canyon Village. Another option is to take a Greyhound bus to Williams and then the steam train to Grand Canyon Village.

Bus service between Phoenix, Flagstaff, Williams, and Grand Canyon Village is provided by **Nava–Hopi Tours** (☎ 800/892-8687 or 520/774-5003). **Greyhound Lines** has service to Flagstaff and Williams (☎ 800/231-2222).

If you do drive, fill your gas tank before setting out for the canyon, since there are few service stations in this remote region. The South Rim of the Grand Canyon is 60 miles north of Williams and I-40 on Ariz. 64 and U.S. 180. Flagstaff, the nearest city of any size, is 78 miles south. From Flagstaff, it's possible to take U.S. 180 directly to the South Rim or U.S. 89 to Ariz. 64 and the east entrance to the park. The Grand Canyon is 230 miles north of Phoenix and 340 miles north of Tucson.

**VISITOR INFORMATION** For free information on the park, contact the **Grand Canyon National Park,** P.O. Box 129, Grand Canyon, AZ 86023-0129 (☎ 520/638-7888).

**VISITOR CENTERS** The **Grand Canyon National Park Visitor Center** is located on Village Loop Drive 6 miles north of the south entrance. *The Guide,* a small newspaper crammed with information about the park and its visitor programs, is available at all entrances.

**ADMISSION COSTS** Admission is $20 per car or $10 per person if you come in by bus, taxi, or on foot.

**SAFETY** Footing can be unstable near the edge of the canyon and the ground may give way. Keep your distance from wild animals, no matter how friendly they may appear. Don't hike alone. Wear proper footgear and carry adequate water. Don't leave valuables in your car or tent.

**INTERPRETIVE PROGRAMS** Park rangers lead nature hikes, walks, and lectures that explore various aspects of the canyon. Consult *The Guide* for times and meeting points.

**WHEN TO GO** In spring and fall there are smaller crowds and the weather can be quite comfortable, especially for hiking down into the canyon. Summertime temperatures can be unbearable. The North Rim is closed in winter.

## GETTING AROUND

Since the Grand Canyon Village area can be extremely congested, especially in summer, consider using a bus or taxi to avoid parking problems. The **Tusayan–Grand Canyon Shuttle** (☎ 520/638-0871 or 520/638-0821) runs between the Grand Canyon Airport in Tusayan and Grand Canyon Village, with stops in between. **Trans Canyon** (☎ 520/638-2820) offers shuttle-bus service between the South Rim and the North Rim. For **taxi service** to and from the airport, trailheads, and other destinations, call ☎ 520/638-2822.

## WHAT TO SEE & DO

**GRAND CANYON VILLAGE & VICINITY** Most visitors first glimpse the canyon at **Mather Point,** the first canyon overlook you encounter when entering the park through the south entrance. Continuing west toward Grand Canyon Village, you next come to **Yavapai Point,** a favorite spot for sunrise and sunset photos and the site of the Yavapai Observation Station (☎ 520/638-7890).

In the village, stop at the visitor center. From there, you can walk the 1½ miles to the historic section of the village on a paved trail that runs along the rim. There, you will see numerous canyon viewpoints and the El Tovar Hotel and Bright Angel Lodge, both worth brief visits (see "Accommodations," below). Adjacent to the El Tovar are

# The Grand Canyon & Northern Arizona

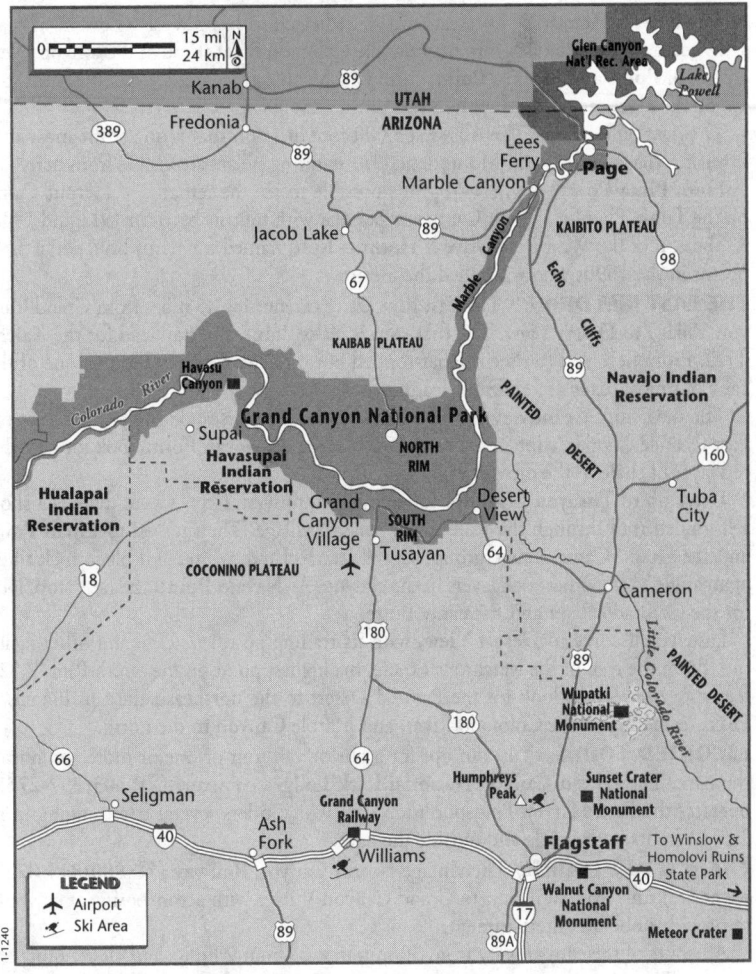

two historic souvenir and curio shops, **Hopi House Gift Store and Art Gallery** (☎ 520/638-2631, ext. 6383) and **Verkamps Curios** (☎ 520/638-2242). To the west of Bright Angel Lodge are the Lookout and Kolb studios. **Lookout Studio** (☎ 520/ 638-2631, ext. 6087) houses a souvenir store and two lookout points. **Kolb Studio** serves as a bookstore and features special exhibits. All four buildings are open daily; hours vary seasonally.

**THE WEST RIM DRIVE** The West Rim Drive is an 8-mile-long road leading west from Grand Canyon Village to Hermits Rest. During the summer, a free shuttle operates frequently and stops at all the scenic overlooks. The rest of the year you can drive this scenic road in your own car.

The first stops are **Trailview Overlook** and **Paiute Point.** From either of these points you have a view of Grand Canyon Village to the east. Next is **Maricopa Point,** where you can see the remains of the Orphan Mine, which began operation in 1893. And if you look carefully at the bottom of the canyon you can see some of the 2-billion-year-old black Vishnu schist.

The **Powell Memorial,** the next stop, is dedicated to John Wesley Powell, who, in 1869, became the first person to navigate the Colorado River through the canyon. Next are **Hopi Point** and **Mojave Point,** from which you can see (and sometimes hear) the Colorado River racing through rapids.

The next pull-off is at **The Abyss,** a 3,000-foot drop-off that is one of the most awe-inspiring views in the park. Monumental freestanding pillars are visible from here.

From **Pima Point,** the next stop, it's possible to see the remains of Hermit Camp on the Tonto Plateau. Hermit Camp was popular with tourists between 1911 and 1930. At the end of the West Rim Drive is **Hermits Rest,** named for Louis Boucher, a prospector in the 1890s who was called the Hermit.

**THE EAST RIM DRIVE**    The East Rim Drive extends for 25 miles from Grand Canyon Village to Desert View. The first stop is **Yaki Point,** the trailhead for the Kaibab Trail. From here you can see the flat-topped butte called Wotan's Throne, one of the canyon's most easily recognizable features.

The next stop, **Grandview Point,** affords a view of Horseshoe Mesa, the site of the Last Chance Copper Mine in the early 1890s. Next, at **Moran Point,** look for a bright-red layer of shale in the canyon walls.

Drive on to **Tusayan Museum** (open daily; admission free), where there is a short self-guided trail through the ruins of an Anasazi village. Then it's on to **Lipan Point** and the Grand Canyon supergroup: several strata of red, white, and black rock tilted at an angle to the other rock layers in the canyon. At **Navajo Point,** the next stop, look for the Colorado River and Escalante Butte.

Last, you'll come to **Desert View,** with its trading post, cafeteria, and other facilities. From the roof of the watchtower there, the highest point on the South Rim (7,522 feet above sea level), look for the Painted Desert to the northeast, the San Francisco Peaks to the south, the Colorado River, and Marble Canyon to the north.

**ESCORTED TOURS**    You can opt for a bus or van tour of one or more sections of the park. The **Grand Canyon National Park Lodges** company (☎ **303/297-2757**) operates the Fred Harvey Transportation Co., which offers several trips ranging from 2 to 11 hours both inside and outside the park.

**TRAIN & AIR TOURS**    The vintage **Grand Canyon Railway** (☎ **800/843-8724;** see above) runs from Williams to Grand Canyon Village with actors posing as cowboys to provide onboard entertainment.

Air tours of the canyon vary from 30 minutes to about 2 hours and all are quite expensive. There have been a few crashes over the years, but if you're still interested, contact **Air Grand Canyon** (☎ 800/AIR-GRAND or 520/638-2686); **Airstar Airlines** (☎ 800/962-3869 or 520/638-2622); **Grand Canyon Airlines** (☎ 800/528-2413 or 520/638-2407); and **Windrock Aviation** (☎ 800/247-6259 or 520/638-9591). For helicopter tours, call **Airstar Airlines** (☎ 800/962-3869 or 520/638-2622); **Kenai Helicopters** (☎ 800/541-4537 or 520/638-2412); and **Papillon Grand Canyon Helicopters** (☎ 800/528-2418 or 520/638-2419).

**MULE RIDES**    Mule rides into the canyon are extremely popular. The 1-day trip descends to Plateau Point, from which you can view the Colorado River 1,320 feet below. This is a grueling trip requiring 6 hours in the saddle. If you want to spend a night down in the canyon, choose an overnight trip to Phantom Ranch (see "Accommodations," below). From mid-November to mid-March there's also a 3-day/2-night trip to Phantom Ranch. Reserve a trail ride as soon as your itinerary is set; contact the **Grand Canyon National Park Lodges** (☎ 303/297-2757).

**HORSEBACK RIDING**    For trail rides of various lengths, or wagon rides, contact **Apache Stables** (☎ 520/638-2891 or 520/638-2424), located at the south entrance to the park.

**RAFTING**  Spend as few as 3 days or as many as 16 navigating the river in a huge motorized rubber raft, a paddled- or oar-powered raft, a kayak, or a wooden dory. Most trips start from Lees Ferry near Page and Lake Powell. You can also start or finish a trip at Phantom Ranch, hiking in or out from either the North or South Rim. The main rafting season is from April to October, but some companies operate year-round. A few to contact are **Arizona Raft Adventures** (☎ 800/786-RAFT or 520/526-8200); **Arizona River Runners** (☎ 800/477-7238 or 602/867-4866); **Colorado River and Trail Expeditions** (☎ 800/253-7328 or 801/261-1789); **Grand Canyon Expeditions Company** (☎ 800/544-2691 or 801/644-2691); **Hatch River Expeditions** (☎ 800/433-8966 or 801/789-3813); **Moki Mac River Expeditions** (☎ 800/284-7280 or 801/268-6667); **Outdoors Unlimited** (☎ 800/637-7238 or 520/526-4546); and **Western River Expeditions** (☎ 800/453-7450 or 801/942-6669).

For those not addicted to adrenaline, there are two Colorado River whitewater rafting alternatives. **Wilderness River Adventures** (☎ 800/528-6154 or 520/645-3279), which operates half-day smooth-water raft trips between the Glen Canyon Dam and Lees Ferry; and **Fred Harvey Transportation Co.** (☎ 520/638-2631), which will transport you between Grand Canyon Village and Page. West of Grand Canyon Village, on the Hualapai Indian Reservation, **Hualapai River Runners** (☎ 800/622-4409 or 520/769-2210), operates 1- and 2-day river trips that include a day of white water and a day of smooth water.

**HIKING**  The Grand Canyon offers some of the most rugged hiking anywhere in the United States, but be warned and be prepared: Each year several people are injured or killed because they set out without sturdy footgear or without food or adequate supplies of water. Just a short 30-minute hike in the summer can dehydrate you, and a long hike into or out of the canyon in the heat can necessitate drinking more than a gallon of water. Remember while hiking that mules have the right of way; always stay to the inside of the trail when being passed by a mule train. Don't attempt to hike from the rim to the Colorado River and back in 1 day.

Among the easiest day hikes is the 1 1/2-mile paved trail leading from the Yavapai Museum to the Powell Memorial. From there the trail becomes dirt and continues another 8 miles to Hermits Rest, from which, in summer, you can take a free shuttle back to Grand Canyon Village. For the more adventurous, four trails lead down into the canyon. If you plan to hike for more than 30 minutes, carry at least 2 quarts of water per person.

The **Bright Angel Trail** is the main route down to Phantom Ranch and is the most popular trail into the canyon. Day hikes on this trail include trips to Indian Gardens or Plateau Point. Both trips are long and strenuous. There are rest houses at 1 1/2 and 3 miles (during the summer they have water), which make good turnaround points for a 3-mile or 6-mile round-trip hike.

The **South Kaibab Trail** begins near Yaki Point and is the alternative route to Phantom Ranch. It also offers the best views of any of the day hikes. From the trailhead it's a 3-mile round-trip to Cedar Ridge. The hike is very strenuous and there's no water available along the trail.

The **Grandview Trail** is a steep, unmaintained trail that should be attempted only by experienced desert hikers. It's a 6-mile round-trip to Horseshoe Mesa, and there's no water available along the trail. Allow at least 7 hours for this rugged hike.

The **Hermit Trail** begins near Hermits Rest and is also steep and unmaintained. Don't attempt this trail unless you are an experienced desert hiker. It's a 5-mile round-trip to Santa Maria Springs and a 6-mile round-trip to Dripping Springs. Water from the springs must be treated before it is safe to drink.

**BACKPACKING**   There are many miles of trails deep in the canyon and several established campgrounds for backpackers. The best times of year are spring and autumn. During the summer, temperatures at the bottom of the canyon are regularly over 100°F, while in the winter, ice and snow at higher elevations make footing on trails precarious. Be sure to carry at least 2 quarts of water (preferably 1 gallon).

A **Backcountry Use Permit,** which costs $10, is required of all hikers planning to overnight in the canyon, unless you have reservations at Phantom Ranch. Because a limited number of hikers are allowed into the canyon on any given day, reserve by mail as soon as your itinerary is set. Contact the **Backcountry Reservations Office** (☎ 520/638-7875) for information. The office begins accepting reservations on the first of every month for the following 5 months. There are **campgrounds** at Indian Gardens, Bright Angel Campground (near Phantom Ranch), and Cottonwood, but hikers are limited to 2 nights per trip at each of these campgrounds (4 nights are allowed from Nov 15–Feb 28). Other nights can be spent camping at undesignated sites in certain regions of the park. The *Backcountry Trip Planner,* available through the Backcountry Office, has information to help you plan your itinerary.

**CAMPING**   On the South Rim, **Mather Campground,** in Grand Canyon Village, has 350 campsites. For reservations, contact DESTINET (☎ 800/365-2267), which takes reservations 5 months in advance  Dec 1–Mar 1. Other times of the year, no reservations are accepted. Campsites are $12 per night. **Desert View Campground,** with 50 sites, is 26 miles east of Grand Canyon Village, open mid-May–mid-Oct. No reservations are accepted. Campsites are $10 per night. For the **Trailer Village RV Park** in Grand Canyon Village, make reservations through the Grand Canyon National Park Lodges (☎ 303/297-2757; fax 303/297-3175). There are 192 full hookup sites here; they cost $18 per night for two people.

## ACCOMMODATIONS

Hotel rooms within the park are in high demand, so make reservations as far in advance as possible. Hotels outside the park are popular with tour groups, which keep many full during the busy summer months. The mailing address for all park lodges is 14001 E. Iliff Ave., Aurora, CO 80014.

**Bright Angel Lodge & Cabins.** ☎ *303/297-2757. Fax 303/297-3175. 34 rms, 55 cabins. $35 double with sink only, $44 double with sink and toilet, $53 double with bath; $61–$221 cabin. AE, DC, DISC, MC, V.* This is the most economical lodge in the park and offers a variety of accommodations. In addition to rooms with shared bathrooms, there are also roomier cabins, including four rim cabins with fireplaces. The **Bright Angel Coffee Shop** (☎ 520/638-2631) is a casual dining room specializing in Southwestern favorites and foods comforting to hungry hikers. Other facilities include a soda fountain, a tour desk, and a museum.

**El Tovar Hotel.** ☎ *303/297-2757. Fax 303/297-3175. 65 rms, 10 suites. $111 $166 double; $186–$271 suite. AE, DC, DISC, MC, V.* The El Tovar is a rustic yet luxurious mountain lodge perched on the edge of the canyon. Standard rooms are small; de luxe rooms provide more legroom. Suites, with private terraces and stunning views, are spacious. Services include concierge, room service, and tour desk. The El Tovar Dining Room (see "Dining," below) serves excellent continental and Southwestern cuisine. There is also a cocktail lounge.

**Phantom Ranch.** ☎ *303/29-PARKS. Fax 303/297-3175. Reconfirmations* ☎ *520/638-3283 or 520/638-2631, ext 6015. 11 cabins, 40 dorm beds. $58 double in the cabins; $21 dormitory bed. Packages available for mule riders. AE, MC, V.* This popular lodge, located at the bottom of the Grand Canyon, has a classic ranch atmosphere.

Rustic cabins and dormitories are cooled by evaporative coolers in the summer. Reserve up to a year in advance and be sure to reconfirm. Family-style meals in the dining hall must also be reserved in advance. The dining hall serves as a canteen and an after-dinner beer hall. Services include mule-back baggage transfer between Grand Canyon Village and Phantom Ranch.

**OTHER ACCOMMODATIONS**   Set back a bit from the rim, **Maswik Lodge** (☎ 303/297-2757; fax 303/297-3175) offers spacious rooms and rustic cabins. If you crave modern appointments, opt for one of the Maswik North rooms. More rugged types will prefer the economically priced old cabins. **Thunderbird & Kachina Lodges** (☎ 303/297-2757; fax 303/297-3175) are the two newest lodges on the canyon rim, and though they are both two-story motel-style buildings, their construction of native sandstone helps them blend in a bit with the adjacent historic lodges. **Yavapai Lodge** (☎ 303/297-2757; fax 303/297-3175), at the east end of Grand Canyon Village, is the largest in the park but there are no canyon views; it's less expensive than the other lodges, and is a mile hike from the main section of the village.

**OUTSIDE THE PARK**   Located a few miles outside the park, the **Best Western Grand Canyon Squire Inn** (☎ 800/622-6966 or 520/638-2681) offers large, comfortable rooms and a long list of amenities. The dining room is the best restaurant in the area. There's a pool, tennis courts, a whirlpool, sauna, bowling alley, pool room, video arcade, and tour desk.

Some of the 66 units at ♦ **Cameron Trading Post Motel,** P.O. Box 339, Cameron, AZ 86020 (☎ 800/338-7385 or 520/679-2231; fax 520/679-2350), 54 miles north of Flagstaff adjacent to the historic Cameron Trading Post, have views of the Little Colorado River canyon. There are two restaurants and one of the best trading posts in the state.

## DINING

For a quick, inexpensive meal, Grand Canyon Village choices include **cafeterias** at the Yavapai and Maswik lodges and a delicatessen at **Babbitt's General Store** (across from the visitor center). **Hermits Rest Fountain** on the West Rim Drive is a snack bar. At Desert View (on the West Rim Drive) is the **Desert View Trading Post Cafeteria.** All of these places are open daily for all three meals, and all serve meals for about $7 and under.

**Arizona Steak House.** *In the Bright Angel Lodge.* ☎ *520/638-2631. Reservations not accepted. Dinner $12–$20. AE, DC, DISC, MC, V. Daily 5–10pm. STEAK.* If you have a craving for a thick, juicy steak or a crisp, cool salad, visit this dining room. Since it's open only for dinner (only group tours do lunch here), you should arrive as early as possible to enjoy the sunset view of the canyon and avoid a long wait for a table.

**El Tovar Dining Room.** *In the El Tovar Hotel.* ☎ *520/638-2631, ext 6432. Reservations required at dinner. Main courses $14–$28. AE, DC, DISC, MC, V. Daily 6:30–11am, 11:30am–2pm, and 5–10pm. CONTINENTAL/SOUTHWESTERN.* El Tovar's dining room matches its world-class view with world-class continental cuisine accented by Southwestern touches. Most ingredients are flown in daily to ensure freshness and quality. On a recent visit the dinner menu featured medaillons of veal with apricots and red peppercorns in orange-muscat sauce. Reserve early to get the dinner time you prefer.

## THE NORTH RIM

Though the North Rim is only 10 miles as the raven flies from the South Rim, it's a 200-mile drive. It's open only from mid-May to late October or early November because, at 8,000 feet, it receives considerably more snow in the winter.

There are far fewer activities on the North Rim than on the South Rim, and not surprisingly there are fewer people. The three best spots for viewing the canyon are Bright Angel Point, Point Imperial, and Cape Royal, the real star.

Along the 23-mile road to Cape Royal are several scenic overlooks. Across the road from the **Walhalla Overlook** are the ruins of an Anasazi structure. And just before reaching Cape Royal, you'll come to the **Angel's Window Overlook,** which gives you a breathtaking view of the natural bridge that forms Angel's Window. Once at Cape Royal, you can follow a trail across this natural bridge to a towering promontory overlooking the valley.

If you want to go down into the canyon, there are day hikes of varying lengths here. The shortest is the half-mile paved trail to Bright Angel Point; the longest is the North Kaibab Trail to Roaring Springs and back, which takes 6 to 8 hours. You can also arrange mule rides that vary in length from 1 hour to a full day. Reserve through **Grand Canyon Trail Rides** (☎ 520/638-9875 in summer or 801/679-8665 in winter).

The only campground on the North Rim is the **North Rim Campground,** with 82 sites but no hookups for RVs. To reserve, call DESTINET (☎ 800/365-2267). Sites are $10 per night. Outside the park, in the Kaibab National Forest, is the **DeMotte Park Campground.** It's the closest to the park entrance, but has only 25 sites. **Jacob Lake Campground,** 30 miles north of the park entrance, has 50 sites. Both charge $10 per night. You can also camp anywhere in the Kaibab National Forest. The **Kaibab Lodge Camper Village** (☎ 520/643-7804) is a privately owned campground 30 miles north of the park entrance. It has 80 RV sites and 50 tent sites. Rates are $10 to $22 per night.

If you're looking for a hotel, the **Grand Canyon Lodge,** perched on the canyon rim, offers guest rooms and cabins. A large dining hall serves straightforward American food and is open daily for all three meals. There's also a snack bar, a saloon, and a tour desk. For information and reservations, contact Amfac Parks and Resorts (☎ 303/29-PARKS). Closed Nov–mid-May. On the edge of a large meadow, 5 miles north of the North Rim entrance is the **Kaibab Lodge.** Although the highway from Jacob Lake is closed by the first big snow, the lodge stays open for much of the winter, shuttling cross-country skiers in by snowcoach. Services include a dining room, a tour desk, hiking equipment and mountain-bike rentals, ski lessons, and ski tours. For information and reservations, call ☎ 800/525-0924, 520/638-2389, or 520/526-0924.

**Essentials:** The North Rim is at the end of Ariz. 67 (the North Rim Parkway), which is reached from U.S. 89A. It's 216 miles north of Grand Canyon Village (South Rim), 354 miles north of Phoenix, and 125 miles west of Page/Lake Powell. **Trans Canyon** (☎ 520/538-2820) operates a shuttle between the North Rim and South Rim. The park admission fee is $10 per car and is good for 1 week.

For information before leaving home, contact **Grand Canyon National Park,** P.O. Box 129, Grand Canyon, AZ 86023-0129 (☎ 520/638-7888). There's an information desk in the lobby of the Grand Canyon Lodge, open daily from 8am to 5pm, but no visitor center or museum. At the entrance gate, you'll receive a copy of *The Guide,* which will fill you in on North Rim park activities.

## 7  The Navajo & Hopi Reservations & Canyon de Chelly

The Navajo and Hopi reservation land in Arizona's Four Corners section is a spectacular countryside, with majestic mesas, rainbow-hued deserts, gravity-defying buttes, cliffs, and canyons. The 1,000-foot buttes of Monument Valley for years have been evocative symbols of the Wild West and John Wayne movies.

The Navajo and Hopi peoples, who dwelled in this arid land for hundreds of years, adapted different means of surviving. The Navajo are herders, and their homes,

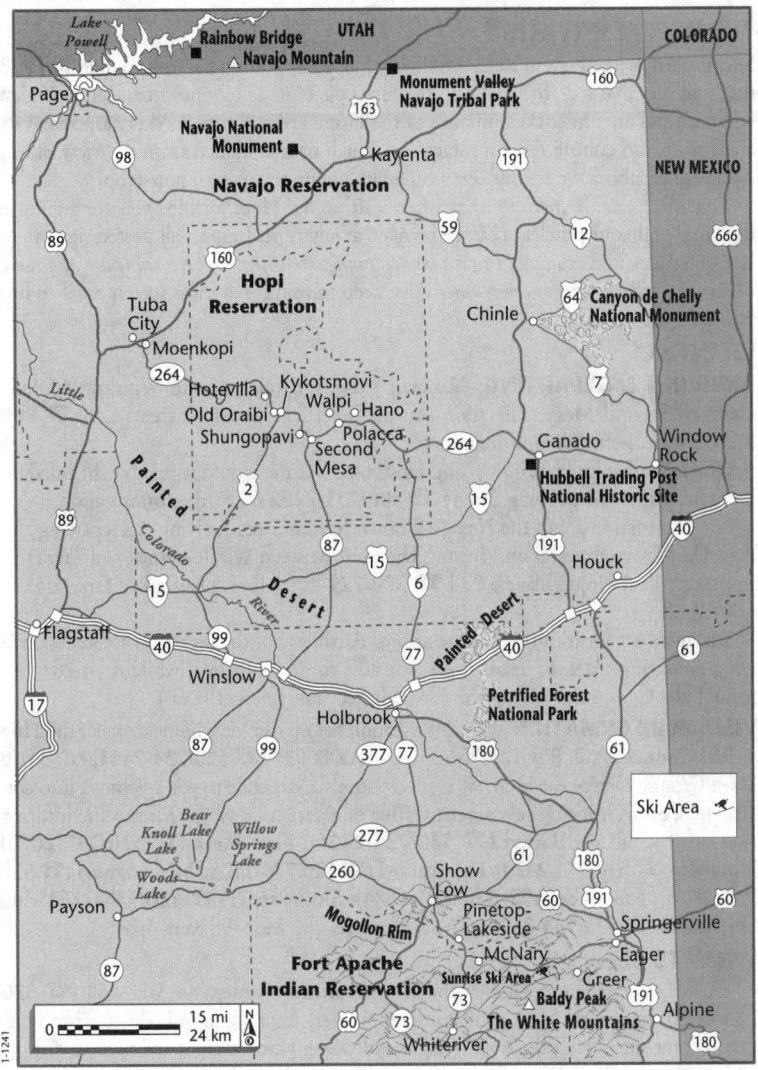

including traditional log-walled hogans, are scattered across the countryside. The Hopi congregated in villages atop mesas and built houses of stone. They farm the floors of narrow valleys at the feet of their mesas today in much the same way as they have done for centuries.

The ancient Anasazi also left their mark. Throughout the canyons of the region you can see cliff dwellings dating back 700 years and more; the most impressive are at Canyon de Chelly National Monument and Navajo National Monument. These cliff dwellings were mysteriously abandoned in the 13th century.

The 2,000-foot-high Mogollon Rim (pronounced "*Mug*-gee-un" by the locals) divides the arid lowlands from the cool mountain forests, and the climatic and vegetative change is dramatic. Western author Zane Grey lived near the Rim and many of his novels capture its scenic beauty.

# THE HOPI RESERVATION

Surrounded by the Navajo Reservation, the Hopi Reservation has at its center the handful of villages that together make up the Hopi pueblos. These ancient and independent communities are under the guidance of the Hopi Tribal Council. Many aspects of the ancient Pueblo culture remain intact, but much of it is hidden from the view of outsiders. The elaborate religious ceremonies are no longer open to non-Hopi.

*Important note:* Remember that when visiting the Hopi pueblos you are a guest of the Hopi and your privileges can be revoked at any time. Respect all posted signs at village entrances, and remember that *photographing, sketching, and recording are all prohibited in the villages and at ceremonies.* Also keep in mind that kivas (ceremonial rooms) and ruins are off-limits.

## ESSENTIALS

**ARRIVING & DEPARTING**    **Amtrak** passenger trains stop in Winslow, 67 miles south of Second Mesa. The train station is on East Second Street. Call ☎ 800/872-7245 for schedule information.

**Greyhound** stops in Winslow and Holbrook, but there is no regularly scheduled bus service north to the pueblos. Phone ☎ 800/231-2222 for further information.

For information about the **Navajo Transit System,** see "Arriving & Departing" under "The Navajo Reservation," below. The route between Window Rock and Tuba City stops at several Hopi villages. Call ☎ 520/729-4002 for schedule and fare information.

Distances are great in this remote area of Arizona, but the highways are generally in good condition. Ariz. 87 leads from Winslow to Second Mesa, while Ariz. 264 runs from Tuba City in the west to the New Mexico state line in the east.

**VISITOR INFORMATION**    For information before you leave home, contact the **Hopi Tribal Council,** P.O. Box 123, Kykotsmovi, AZ 86039 (☎ 520/734-2441, ext. 341 or 360). Because each of the Hopi villages is relatively independent, you might want to contact the **Community Development Office** of a particular village for specific information on that village: **Bacavi** (☎ 520/734-2404), **First Mesa** (☎ 520/737-2670), **Hotevilla** (☎ 520/734-2420), **Kykotsmovi** (☎ 520/734-2474), **Mishongnovi** (☎ 520/737-2520), **Moenkopi** (☎ 520/283-6684), **Shungopavi** (☎ 520/734-2262), and **Shipaulovi** (☎ 520/734-2570). These offices are open Mon–Fri 8am–5pm.

## WHAT TO SEE & DO

The place to start your visit is at the **Hopi Cultural Center,** on Ariz. 264 (☎ 520/734-6650) in Second Mesa. This museum, motel, and restaurant is the tourism headquarters for the area. Take note of signs indicating when villages are open to visitors. The museum is open Mon–Fri 8am–5pm, Sat–Sun 9am–3pm (closed Sunday in winter). Admission is $3 for adults and $1 for children.

**VILLAGES**    Most of the Hopi villages are built on three mesas, known simply as First, Second, and Third Mesa, which are numbered from east to west. The Hopi claim that Oraibi, on Third Mesa, is the oldest continuously inhabited town in the United States. Though it's possible to get permission to visit most villages, the easiest to visit is **Walpi,** on First Mesa (see below). Guided tours, led by young Hopi, are offered daily from about 9am to 5pm, and admission is by donation. To sign up for a tour, drive to the top of First Mesa (in Palacca, take the road that says to First Mesa villages) and continue through the village to the **information office** (☎ 520/737-2260).

**First Mesa** includes **Polacca,** a village at the base of the mesa founded in the late 1800s. At the mesa's top is **Walpi,** with small stone houses jutting from rocks and a view that extends for hundreds of miles. **Sichomovi,** lower down on the mesa, was founded in 1750 as a colony of Walpi. **Hano** was founded by Tewa peoples.

**Second Mesa** is the center of tourism in Hopiland (as the Hopi country is called) and here you'll find the Hopi Cultural Center. Villages on Second Mesa include **Shipaulovi, Shungopavi, Gray Spring,** where the Snake Dance is performed in even-numbered years, and **Mishongnovi,** named for a clan leader who came here from the San Francisco Peaks around A.D. 1200; the Snake Dance is held here in odd-numbered years.

**Third Mesa (Oraibi)** dates from 1150, and the ruins of a 1629 Spanish mission are still visible. In 1906, a schism among villagers occurred and some left to form **Hotevilla,** considered the most conservative of the villages. **Kykotsmovi** was founded in 1890 and **Bacavi** in 1907.

One last Hopi village, **Moenkopi,** is located 40 miles to the west, a few miles from Tuba City off U.S. 160. Founded in 1870 by people from Oraibi, it is located in the center of a wide, green valley where plentiful water makes farming more reliable.

**DANCES & CEREMONIES**   The Hopi have developed the most complex religious ceremonies of any of the Southwest tribes. For information about attending dances or ceremonies, call the **Hopi Tribal Council** (☎ 520/734-2441). Many are closed to non-Hopi, but it is worth checking.

The masked **kachina dances,** for which the Hopi are most famous, are held from January to July. Kachinas, whether as dolls or as masked dancers, represent the spirits of everything from plants and animals to ancestors and sacred places. The kachina ceremonies bring rain for the corn crop, and also ensure health, happiness, long life, and harmony. It is the **snake dance** that has captured the attention of the outside world; it involves the handling of both poisonous and nonpoisonous snakes.

**SHOPPING**   Native American crafts abound throughout both reservations, in trading posts to roadside stands and homes. **Hopi kachinas** are elaborately carved and decorated wooden dolls representing the spirits of plants, animals, ancestors, and sacred places. Older kachinas are simple, carved from a single piece of cottonwood. Prices today are in the hundreds of dollars for even a simple kachina. The **Hopi overlay silverwork**—with bola ties, belt buckles, earrings, and bracelets—is characteristic Hopi silverwork; two sheets of silver are used, one with a design cut in it. Though not noted for basketry, the **Hopi baskets** are beautiful, some made from rabbit brush and sumac (Third Mesa) and others from dyed yucca fibers (Second Mesa). Most **Hopi pottery** is produced on First Mesa, and there are a variety of styles, tending toward geometric patterns. A popular style is yellow-orange ware decorated with black-and-white designs.

On the Hopi reservation, perhaps the best place to shop is **Hopi Arts & Crafts—Silvercraft,** 100 yards from the Hopi Cultural Center on Second Mesa. This arts-and-crafts cooperative has more than 300 members. Other reliable sources are **McGee's Indian Art,** at Keams Canyon east of First Mesa (☎ 520/738-2295), and the **Honani Crafts Gallery** (☎ 520/737-2238), at the intersection of Ariz. 264 and Second Mesa.

## ACCOMMODATIONS & DINING

In **Second Mesa,** you'll find the **Hopi Cultural Center Restaurant and Motel,** P.O. Box 67, Second Mesa, AZ 86043 (☎ 520/734-2401), with 33 rooms costing $55–$60 for a double. This is the only lodging for miles around, so have a reservation before heading up for an overnight visit. The architecture is modern pueblo and the rooms are comfortable and warm. The restaurant serves American and traditional Hopi meals, including piki bread. There's also a museum here.

In **Winslow**—70 miles south of Second Mesa and the next-closest place to stay if you're planning to tour the pueblos—you'll find budget chain motels: **Best Western Adobe Inn** (☎ 520/289-4638); **Comfort Inn** (☎ 520/289-9581); **Econo Lodge** (☎ 520/289-4687); and **Super 8 Motel** (☎ 520/289-4606).

# THE NAVAJO RESERVATION

Roughly the size of West Virginia, the Navajo Reservation covers 25,000 square miles of northeastern Arizona, as well as parts of New Mexico, Colorado, and Utah. It's the largest Native American reservation in the United States and home to nearly 200,000 Navajo. Though there are now modern towns with supermarkets, shopping malls, and hotels on the reservation, many Navajo still follow a pastoral lifestyle and you'll encounter flocks of sheep or herds of cattle on the road. Animals have free range and often graze beside the highways, so drive carefully, especially at night.

As you travel in the reservation you'll see the traditional homes of the Navajo— **hogans,** small hexagonal buildings, usually made of wood and earth, with doorways facing east to greet the new day. Most Navajo now live in modest homes but keep a hogan for religious ceremonies. At Canyon de Chelly and Navajo National Monument visitor centers you can look inside hogans. If you take a tour at Canyon de Chelly or Monument Valley, you may be able to visit a hogan that is still someone's home. Monument Valley is operated as a tribal park, and there is also a Navajo-owned marina on Lake Powell in Utah.

The Navajo Reservation observes daylight saving time, unlike the rest of Arizona, so set your watch forward an hour if you're visiting in the summer. Also keep in mind that *alcohol is not allowed on the reservation.* Before taking a photograph of a Navajo, always ask permission. If permission is granted, a tip of $1 or more is expected.

## ESSENTIALS

**ARRIVING & DEPARTING**　　There is **Amtrak** passenger service to Winslow, south of the reservation. Call ☎ **800/872-7245** for schedules and fares.

The **Navajo Transit System** operates bus service Monday through Friday throughout the Navajo nation with service between the cities of Farmington, Gallup, and Crown Point (all in New Mexico), and Window Rock, Kayenta, Chinle, and Tuba City. Call ☎ **520/729-4002** for schedule information. **Greyhound** stops in Winslow, Holbrook, and Houck. Phone ☎ **800/231-2222** for schedules and fares.

The Navajo Indian Reservation is a vast area and is laced with a network of excellent paved roads as well as many unpaved roads that are not always passable to cars without four-wheel-drive. From Flagstaff, **Navajo National Monument** can be reached by taking U.S. 89 north to U.S. 160; **Monument Valley Navajo Tribal Park** is a bit farther on U.S. 163. The most direct route to **Canyon de Chelly National Monument** from Flagstaff is by way of I-40 to U.S. 191 North. **Window Rock** is east of the north end of U.S. 191 on Ariz. 264.

**VISITOR INFORMATION**　　For information before visiting, contact the **Navajoland Tourism Department,** P.O. Box 663, Window Rock, AZ 86515 (☎ **520/871-6436** or 520/871-7371).

## WHAT TO SEE & DO

**SPECIAL EVENTS**　　Unlike the village ceremonies of the Hopi, Navajo religious ceremonies tend to be held in the privacy of family hogans. However, there are numerous public events. The biggest is the **Navajo Nation Fair,** including a rodeo and powwow. It's held September in Window Rock. Other important fairs include the **Central Navajo Fair** at Chinle, Arizona, in August; the **Northern Navajo Fair** at Shiprock, New Mexico, in October; and the **Western Navajo Fair** at Tuba City, Arizona, in October.

**MONUMENT VALLEY NAVAJO TRIBAL PARK**　　Nature, in its role as sculptor, has created a garden of monoliths and spires in the north–central part of the Navajo Reservation at Monument Valley, and you may have seen this otherworldly landscape as a backdrop in many movies, television shows, and commercials. Located 30 miles north of Kayenta just across the Utah state line, Monument Valley is a vast flat plain punctuated by natural cathedrals of sandstone, with descriptive names like Elephant Butte and the Thumb. A 17-mile unpaved loop road winds among these awe-inspiring buttes and mesas. Within the park are more than 100 ancient Anasazi archeological sites, ruins, and petroglyphs dating to before A.D. 1300.

At the **valley overlook** parking area you'll find a small museum, gift shop, snack bar, and campground ($10 per night per site). You'll find numerous local **Navajo guides** here who offer tours of Monument Valley. Before leaving the area, you might also want to visit **Goulding's Museum and Trading Post** at Goulding's Lodge, a few miles from the park entrance, open daily 7:30am–9pm. **Goulding's Tours** (☎ 801/727-3231) offers half-day tours for $30 for adults and $18 for children 11 and under; full-day tours are $60 for adults and $45 for children 11 and under. For horseback exploration, contact **Ed Black's Stables** (☎ 800/551-4039 or 801/739-4285), located near the visitor center. Charges are $25 for a 1¹/₂-hour ride and $60 for an all-day ride. **Bigman's Horseback Riding** (☎ 520/677-3219) is located on the road to the monument entrance and charges $20 for a 1-hour ride and $55 for an all-day ride.

The park is open May–Sept, daily 8am–7pm; Oct–Apr, daily 8am–5pm. Admission is $2.50 for adults, $1 for seniors, and free for children 6 and under. For more information, contact **Monument Valley Navajo Tribal Park,** P.O. Box 360289, Monument Valley, UT 84536 (☎ 801/727-3287 or 801/727-3353).

**NAVAJO NATIONAL MONUMENT**    Located 30 miles west of Kayenta and 60 miles northeast of Tuba City, Navajo National Monument encompasses three of the best-preserved Anasazi cliff dwellings in the region—Betatakin, Keet Seel, and Inscription House. Fragile Inscription House is closed to the public.

**Betatakin,** which means "ledge house" in Navajo, can be easily viewed. Built in a huge amphitheater-like alcove in the canyon wall, Betatakin was occupied only from 1250 to 1300, and at its height may have housed only 125 people. A 1-mile round-trip paved trail from the visitor center leads to the Betatakin overlook. The strenuous 5-mile round-trip hike to Betatakin itself is ranger-led, takes about 6 hours, and involves descending more than 700 feet to the floor of Tsegi Canyon and later returning to the rim. In summer, there are two hikes a day, and one a day in spring and fall.

**Keet Seel,** which means "broken pieces of pottery" in Navajo, was occupied as early as A.D. 950 until 1300. The 17-mile round-trip hike or horseback ride to Keet Seel is strenuous. Hikers may stay overnight at a primitive campground near the ruins. Only 20 people a day are given permits to visit Keet Seel, and the trail is only open from Memorial Day to Labor Day.

The **visitor center** is open daily from 8am to 5pm (until 6pm in summer when daylight saving time is observed) and offers informative displays, including numerous artifacts from Tsegi Canyon. There's no lodge at the national monument, but there is a campground open year-round. About 30 campsites are here, with an overflow area containing about a dozen more. For more information, contact **Navajo National Monument,** HC 71, Box 3, Tonales, AZ 86044-9704 (☎ 520/672-2366).

Located just outside Ganado in the southeastern part of the reservation, **Hubbell Trading Post National Historic Site** (☎ 520/755-3475) is the oldest continuously operating trading post on the Navajo Reservation, established in 1876. It includes a small museum where you can watch Navajo weavers creating rugs. It's open Apr–Oct, daily 8am–6pm; Oct–Apr, daily 8am–5pm.

While in Ganado, you can get good, inexpensive cafeteria-style food at **Cafe Sage** (☎ 520/755-3411, ext. 294) on the grounds of Ganado's health clinic, which is across Ariz. 264 and half a mile east of the trading post.

**WINDOW ROCK**    Less than a mile from the New Mexico state line, Window Rock is the capital of the Navajo nation and is named for a huge natural opening in a sandstone cliff just outside town. At one time there was a spring at the base of the rock, with its water used by medicine men. Today Window Rock is preserved as the **Window Rock Tribal Park,** located 2 miles off Ariz. 264.

**OTHER ATTRACTIONS**    The **Four Corners Monument Navajo Tribal Park,** north of Teec Nos Pos in the very northeast corner of the state, is open daily. This is the only place in the U.S. where the corners of four states come together—Arizona, Colorado, Utah, and New Mexico. There's a visitor center, picnic ground, and crafts vendors. West of Tuba City and just off U.S. 160, you can see **dinosaur footprints** preserved in the stone surface of the desert. There may be people there to guide you to them, and a tip is expected.

The **Navajo Tribal Museum,** located in the Navajo Arts and Crafts Enterprise, West Ariz. 264, Window Rock (☎ 520/871-6673), is a small museum containing Navajo artifacts, old photos, and contemporary crafts. It's open in summer, Mon–Sat 8am–6pm; winter, Mon–Fri 8am–5pm. The **Navajo Nation Zoo and Botanical Park,** Ariz. 264, Window Rock (☎ 520/871-6573), features animals and plants significant in Navajo history and culture in its small collection. The setting, which includes "haystack" rocks, is striking. You'll find the park east of the Navajo Nation Inn. Admission free. Open daily 8am–5pm. Closed Christmas and New Year's Day.

**St. Michael's Historical Museum,** 3 miles south of Ariz. 264. (☎ 520/871-4171), chronicles the lives and effects of Franciscan friars who started a mission in this area in the 1670s. Admission is free. Open Memorial Day–Labor Day, daily 9am–5pm.

**SHOPPING**    File-and-chisel and sand-casting creates the distinctive **Navajo silverwork,** which highlights the silver itself. Wide bracelets and concha belts and the squash-blossom necklace are well-known styles in silver and turquoise jewelry. **Navajo rugs,** which take hundreds of hours to make, have become almost prohibitively expensive. The best are those made with homespun yarn and natural vegetal dyes, but commercial manufacturing is keeping costs down. Navajo weaving is recognized as the finest in the Southwest, and there are 15 regional styles, with much overlapping. The bigger, bolder patterns are likely to cost much less than the complex and detailed patterns. Navajo rug auctions are held at Window Rock and Crown Point.

You'll find roadside stalls throughout the Navajo Reservation, and you might find quality merchandise and bargain prices, but you'd do better to shop at trading posts, museum and park gift shops, and established shops in order to guarantee the quality of the pieces.

The **Hubbell Trading Post** (see above) in Ganado has a well-deserved reputation for having an excellent selection of rugs and jewelry. Prices are not low, but neither is the quality. Though it's possible to buy a small 12-by-18-inch rug for around $100, most cost in the thousands. There are also baskets, kachinas, and jewelry by Navajo, Hopi, and Zuñi. The **Cameron Trading Post** (☎ 800/338-7385 or 520/679-2231), at the crossroads of Cameron where Ariz. 64 branches off U.S. 89 to Grand Canyon Village, is another historic trading post that houses a gallery of old and antique Native American artifacts, clothing, and jewelry. This gallery may be the finest in the state and offers museum-quality pieces.

In Window Rock, visit the **Navajo Arts and Crafts Enterprise** (☎ 520/871-4090), which is adjacent to the Navajo Nation Inn and has been operating since 1941. Here you'll find high-quality silver-and-turquoise jewelry, Navajo rugs, sandpaintings, baskets, pottery, and clothing.

On the west side of the reservation, in Tuba City, you'll find the **Tuba Trading Post** (☎ 520/283-5441) on the corner of Main Street and Moenave Street. This trading post serves both as a small market and as a store selling Native American crafts. On the western outskirts of Tuba City, on U.S. 160, is **Van's Trading Co.** (☎ **520/283-5343**), which has a dead-pawn auction on the 15th of each month at 3pm. This auction provides opportunities to buy older pieces of Navajo silver-and-turquoise jewelry.

## ACCOMMODATIONS & DINING

Since lodging options in the reservation are limited, it's a good idea to reserve in advance.

**Anasazi Inn at Tsegi Canyon.** *U.S. 160 (P.O. Box 1543), Kayenta, AZ 86033.* ☎ *520/697-3793. Fax 520/697-8249. 56 rms. $80 double. Lower rates available Oct–Apr. AE, CB, DC, DISC, MC, V.* Take U.S. 160 west of Kayenta. Located about halfway between Kayenta and Navajo National Monument, the Anasazi Inn at Tsegi Canyon is a simple, somewhat maintained motel surrounded by wilderness, but it's the closest lodging to Navajo National Monument. The inn has a dining room.

✪ **Cameron Trading Post Motel.** *P.O. Box 339, Cameron, AZ 86020.* ☎ *800/ 338-7385 or 520/679-2231. Fax 520/679-2350. 62 rms, 4 suites. $69–$79 double; $175–$250 suite. AE, MC, V.* Located 54 miles north of Flagstaff, this motel offers some of the most attractive rooms anywhere in the Grand Canyon vicinity. It is adjacent to Cameron Trading Post and built around its terraced gardens. Some rooms offer balconies and/or views of the canyon or Little Colorado River. There are two restaurants.

✪ **Goulding's Lodge.** *P.O. Box 360001, Monument Valley, UT 84536-0001.* ☎ *801/727-3231. Fax 801/727-3344. 62 rms. Mar–Oct, $88–$108 double. Oct–Mar, $68–$78 double. AE, DC, MC, V.* This is the only lodge actually located in Monument Valley, and it offers superb views from the private balconies of the guest rooms, which are furnished with Southwestern decor. A restaurant serves Navajo and American dishes, and the view makes any meal an event. The lodge has an indoor pool, museum, gift shop, coin laundry, and gas station.

**Holiday Inn—Kayenta.** *At the junction of U.S. 160 and U.S. 163 (P.O. Box 307), Kayenta, AZ 86033.* ☎ *800/HOLIDAY or 520/697-3221. Fax 520/697-3349. 160 rms. May–Nov, $99–$119 double. Dec–Apr, $79 double. Nov–Apr, $89 double. AE, CB, DC, DISC, MC, V.* Located just 23 miles south of Monument Valley and 29 miles east of Navajo National Monument, this hotel is often crowded. The grounds are dusty, but the rooms are spacious and clean, and some are poolside. The restaurant offers both American and Navajo meals. Extras include an outdoor pool, tour desk, and room service.

**Navajo Nation Inn.** *48 W. Hwy. 264 (P.O. Box 2340), Window Rock, AZ 86515.* ☎ *800/662-6189 or 520/871-4108. Fax 520/871-5466. 54 rms, 2 suites. $62–$72 double; $72 suite. AE, DC, MC, V.* Located in the center of Window Rock, the Navajo Nation Inn is a modern motel with rustic pine furniture in the guest rooms. The restaurant and coffee shop, open daily from 6am to 9pm, serve American and traditional Navajo dishes. The inn has a tour desk.

**Tuba Trading Post Motel, Restaurant & RV Park.** *At the junction of U.S. 160 and Ariz. 264 (P.O. Box 247), Tuba City, AZ 86045.* ☎ *800/644-8383 or 520/283-5441. 80 rms, 2 suites. June–Oct, $80–$90 double; $125 suite. Nov–May, $65–$75 double; $105 suite. AE, DISC, JCB, MC, V.* Motels are scarce on the Navajo Reservation, so if you plan to be anywhere near the west side of the reservation, this is a good choice. Located adjacent to the historic Tuba City Trading Post, the motel offers comfortable, modern rooms. The restaurant serves Mexican and American meals.

**Wetherill Inn Motel.** *P.O. Box 175, Kayenta, AZ 86033-0175.* ☎ *520/ 697-3231. 54 rms. Apr–Oct, $78 double. Oct–Apr, $49.50 double. AE, CB, DC, DISC, MC, V.* Located 1 mile north of the junction of U.S. 160 and U.S. 163 and 20 miles south of Monument Valley, the Wetherill Inn Motel offers modern guest rooms with coffeemakers. There is a tour desk.

**CAMPGROUNDS** If you're headed to Monument Valley Navajo Tribal Park, you can camp in the park at the **Mitten View Campground** (☎ 801/727-3353) or just outside the park at **Goulding's Monument Valley Campground** (☎ 801/727-3231). North of Window Rock, there are **Wheatfields Lake Campground** and **Tsaile Lake Campground,** both of which are close to Canyon de Chelly. There's also a campground at **Navajo National Monument** (☎ 520/672-2366), west of Kayenta. At the **Tuba City Motel** (☎ 520/283-5441), you'll find an RV park.

## CANYON DE CHELLY

It's hard to imagine narrow canyons less than 1,000 feet deep being more spectacular than the Grand Canyon, but in some ways the canyons of Canyon de Chelly National Monument are just that. For more than 2,000 years people have called these canyons home. Today there are more than 100 prehistoric dwelling sites in the area.

   **Canyon de Chelly National Monument** consists of two major canyons—Canyon de Chelly (pronounced "Canyon de Shay," and derived from the Navajo word *tségi,* meaning "rock canyon") and Canyon del Muerto (Spanish for Canyon of the Dead)—and several smaller canyons. The canyons extend for more than 100 miles through the rugged slick-rock landscape of northeastern Arizona.

### ESSENTIALS

**ARRIVING & DEPARTING** There is **Amtrak** passenger service to Winslow, south of the Navajo Reservation. The train station is on East Second Street. Call ☎ 800/872-7245 for schedule and fare information.

   Chinle, 3 miles from the entrance to Canyon de Chelly National Monument, is served by the **Navajo Transit System.** Call ☎ 520/729-4002 for schedules and fares. Winslow, Holbrook, and Houck are all served by **Greyhound** (☎ 800/231-222).

   From Flagstaff, take I-40 to U.S. 191 to Ganado. At Ganado, drive west on Ariz. 264/U.S. 191 and head north on U.S. 191 to Chinle. If you're coming down from Monument Valley or Navajo National Monument, Indian Route 59, which connects U.S. 160 and U.S. 191, is an excellent, scenic road.

**VISITOR INFORMATION** Before leaving home you can contact **Canyon de Chelly National Monument,** P.O. Box 588, Chinle, AZ 86503 (☎ 520/674-5500).

### WHAT TO SEE & DO

The **visitor center,** open in summer, daily 8am–6pm (on daylight saving time), and in winter, daily 8am–5pm, should be your first stop. Out front is a traditional hogan structure and inside a small museum. If you want to drive your own four-wheeler into the canyon, this is where you need to get your permit, and you must hire a guide as well (see below). From May to the beginning of September, there are daily programs, including ranger-led canyon hikes, campfire programs, and natural history programs.

**ESCORTED TOURS** Access to the canyons is restricted, and in order to descend into the canyon you must be accompanied by either a park ranger or an authorized guide (see below for an exception, the White House Ruins trail). To hire a **Navajo guide** to lead you into the canyon on foot or in your own four-wheel-drive vehicle costs $10 per hour, with a 3-hour minimum. Another way to see the Canyons is to take one of the **four-** or **six-wheel-drive** trucks that operate out of Thunderbird Lodge (☎ 520/674-5841). Tours cost $31 per person for a half day ($23 for children 11 and under); all-day tours are $50. Half-day tours leave at 9am and 2pm in summer, at 9am and 1pm in winter; full-day trips leave at 9am and return at 5:30pm.

There are also two stables offering horseback tours into the canyon. **Justin Tso Horse Rental** (☎ 520/674-5678) and **Twin Trails Tours** (☎ 520/674-8425) both charge around $8 per hour for a horse and $8 per hour for a guide.

**THE RIM DRIVES**    A very different view of the canyons is provided by the North and South Rim drives. The North Rim Drive overlooks Canyon del Muerto, while the South Rim Drive overlooks Canyon de Chelly. Each of the rim drives is around 20 miles in each direction, and with stops it can easily take 3 hours to visit each rim.

On the **North Rim Drive,** the first stop is **Ledge Ruin Overlook.** The Ledge Ruin was occupied by the Anasazi between A.D. 1050 and 1275. Nearby, at the **Dekaa Kiva Viewpoint,** you can see a lone kiva (circular ceremonial building). The second stop is at the **Antelope House Overlook.** This ruin takes its name from the paintings of antelopes on a nearby cliff wall. Across the wash from Antelope House is the Tomb of the Weaver, discovered in the 1920s by archeologists. Also visible from this overlook is Navajo Fortress, a red sandstone butte. The third stop is at **Mummy Cave Overlook,** named for two mummies that were found in burial urns below the ruins. Archeological evidence indicates that this giant amphitheater consisting of two caves was occupied for 1,000 years from A.D. 300 to 1300. On the shelf between them there are 80 rooms, including three kivas. The fourth and last stop on the North Rim is at the **Massacre Cave Overlook.** The cave received its name after an 1805 Spanish military expedition killed more than 115 Navajo at this site. Also visible from this overlook is Yucca Cave, which was occupied about 1,000 years ago.

If you continue another 10 miles or so from the end of the North Rim Drive to the community of Tsaile, you can visit the **Hatathli Gallery** at Navajo Community College (☎ 520/724-3311). This modern art gallery has a small but interesting collection of Navajo art, crafts, and artifacts, old photos, and a collection of Plains Indian regalia and clothing. The gallery is open Mon–Fri 9am–4pm, and admission is free.

The **South Rim Drive** follows the south rim of Canyon de Chelly and climbs slowly but steadily. At each stop you're a little bit higher above the canyon floor. At the **Tségi Overlook** you'll see a rock canyon that feeds into Chinle Wash. The second stop is at the **Junction Overlook,** so named because it overlooks the junction of Canyon del Muerto and Canyon de Chelly. Visible here is the Junction Ruin, with its 10 rooms and one kiva. Also visible is First Ruin, perched precariously on a long, narrow ledge, with 22 rooms and two kivas.

The third stop, at **White House Overlook,** provides the only opportunity for descending 600 feet into Canyon de Chelly without a guide or ranger. The White House Ruins Trail leads to the White House Ruins, inhabited between 1040 and 1275, one of the largest ruins in the canyon, with 80 rooms. You're not allowed to wander off this trail and are asked to respect the privacy of those Navajo living here. The 2$^1$/2-mile round-trip hike takes about 2 hours.

The fourth stop is at **Sliding House Overlook,** built on a narrow shelf and inhabited from about 900 until 1200. This overlook is already more than 700 feet above the canyon floor, with sheer walls giving the narrow canyon a very foreboding appearance.

The next two stops, **Wild Cherry Overlook** and **Face Rock Overlook,** provide views 1,000 feet to the bottom of the canyon. The last stop on the South Rim is **Spider Rock Overlook,** one of the most spectacular, with a view of the junction of Canyon de Chelly and Monument Canyon, and the monolithic twin pinnacles called Spider Rock, a geologic wonder that rises 800 feet from the canyon floor. Across the canyon stands the striking Speaking Rock.

## ACCOMMODATIONS & DINING

Chinle has a few options for staying overnight.

**Best Western Canyon de Chelly Inn.** *P.O. Box 295, Chinle, AZ 86503.* ☎ *800/327-0354 or 520/674-5875. Fax 520/674-3715. 102 rms. $60–$104 double.*

*AE, DC, MC, V.* Located in the center of Chinle, this modern motel has medium- to large-size rooms that have beamed ceilings and coffeemakers. The restaurant features moderately priced American and Navajo meals. There's an indoor pool.

**Holiday Inn—Canyon de Chelly.** *Indian Route 7 (P.O. Box 1889), Chinle, AZ 86503.* ☎ *800/23-HOTEL or 520/674-5000. Fax 520/674-8264. 108 rms. Summer, $79–$95 double. Winter, $49–$69 double. AE, CB, DC, DISC, JCB, MC, V.* The newest hotel in Chinle, it incorporates an old trading post into the restaurant and gift shop building. The guest rooms all have patios or balconies, and most face the cottonwood-shaded pool courtyard. The restaurant serves American and Navajo meals. The hotel has a tour desk, room service, and Native American dance performances on Monday through Friday.

✪ **Thunderbird Lodge.** *P.O. Box 548, Chinle, AZ 86503.* ☎ *800/679-BIRD or 520/674-5841. Fax 602/674-5844. 72 rms, 1 suite. $79–$84 double; $145 suite. Lower rates Nov–Mar. AE, DC, DISC, MC, V.* The Thunderbird Lodge is the most appealing of the Chinle hotels, with pink adobe construction reminiscent of the pueblos, and guest rooms featuring rustic furniture and Navajo sandpaintings. An original trading post building now serves as the lodge cafeteria, where American and Navajo meals are served. The lodge has a tour desk, gift shop, and rug room.

**CAMPGROUNDS** There's a year-round free campground near Thunderbird Lodge that doesn't take reservations. In the summer the campground has water and rest-rooms, but in the winter you must bring your own water and only portable toilets are available.

## 8  Phoenix & Scottsdale

Tourists flock to Phoenix for its weather. Summers are hot, but the mountains—and cooler air—are only 2 hours away. However, it's in the winter that Phoenix truly shines. When most of the country is frozen solid, The Valley of the Sun is sunny and warm. Its great winter climate has helped make Phoenix and neighboring Scottsdale one of the resort capitals of the United States, meccas for golf, tennis, and lounging by the pool. With the cooler winter weather comes the cultural season, and between Phoenix and Scottsdale, there's an impressive array of music, dance, and theater to be enjoyed. Scottsdale is also well known as a center of the visual arts, ranking only behind New York and Santa Fe in the number of art galleries.

Over the years, Phoenix has enjoyed the benefits and suffered the problems of rapid urban growth. Today this sprawling cosmopolitan metropolis is a quintessential 20th-century American city. Shopping malls are raised to an art form in Phoenix. Luxurious resorts create fantasy worlds of waterfalls and swimming pools. Wide boulevards stretch for miles across land that was once desert but has been made green through irrigation. Perhaps it's this willingness to create a new world atop an old one that attracts people to Phoenix. Then again, maybe it's all that sunshine.

### ARRIVING & DEPARTING

**BY PLANE** **Sky Harbor Airport,** 3 miles from downtown Phoenix, is served by Aéro Mexico, Alaska, America West, Northwest, Southwest, and all major airlines. The **SuperShuttle** (☎ 800/258-3826 or 602/244-9000) and **Courier Transportation** (☎ 602/232-2222) offer 24-hour van service between the airport and hotels and homes throughout the valley. Fares average $7 to $12 to the downtown and Tempe areas, $16 to $35 to Scottsdale and points north.

**BY TRAIN & BUS** The Phoenix **Amtrak terminal** is at 401 W. Harrison St. (☎ 800/USA-RAIL). The **Greyhound terminal** is at 525 E. Washington St., near Fifth Street (☎ 800/231-2222).

## ESSENTIALS

**VISITOR INFORMATION**    The **Phoenix and Valley of the Sun Convention and Visitor Bureau,** One Arizona Center, 400 E. Van Buren St., Suite 600, Phoenix, AZ 85004-2290 (**☎ 602/254-6500**), operates an information desk at the airport and a visitor bureau at the northwest corner of Adams Street and Second Street. The **Information Hotline** (**☎ 602/252-5588**) lists current events in Phoenix.

**RESOURCES FOR TRAVELERS WITH SPECIAL NEEDS**    *Arizona Senior World Newspaper* (**☎ 602/438-1566**), sold in supermarkets and convenience stores, has information relevant to seniors. Contact the **Gay and Lesbian Community Center,** 3136 N. Third Ave. (**☎ 602/265-7283**) for information and publications about the local scene.

**EMERGENCIES & SAFETY**    Dial ☎ 911 for police, ambulance, or fire emergencies. The **Good Samaritan Regional Medical Center,** 1111 E. McDowell Rd. (**☎ 602/239-2000**), near downtown Phoenix, has an emergency room. After dark, take extra precautions in the south–central Phoenix area and downtown. Angry freeway drivers in Phoenix have been known to pull guns, so give aggressive drivers plenty of room.

## GETTING AROUND

The heat, bright sun, and great distances make a car, bus, or taxi essential for seeing the area.

**BY BUS & TROLLEY**    The **Downtown Area Shuttle (DASH)** provides bus service for 25¢ a ride within downtown Phoenix. These purple buses with orange stripes operate Mon–Fri 6:30am–6pm. In Scottsdale, **Ollie the Trolley** (**☎ 602/970-8130**) buses run between many area resorts and shopping areas. An all-day pass is $3.

**BY TAXI**    Yellow Cab (**☎ 602/252-5252**) and **Scottsdale Cab** (**☎ 602/994-1616**) provide service throughout the valley. Fares start at $2.70 for the first mile, then increase by $1.40 for each additional mile.

## WHAT TO SEE & DO

**ESCORTED TOURS**    Gray Line of Phoenix (**☎ 800/732-0327** or 602/495-9100) offers a tour of such local landmarks as the state capitol, downtown Phoenix, Barry Goldwater's home, the Wrigley Mansion, and Camelback Mountain.

Far more fun are desert Jeep tours, most of which offer a bit of six-gun target practice during the day's adventure. Ask the concierge at your hotel, or contact **Arizona Awareness Desert Jeep Tours** (**☎** 602/947-7852); **Carefree Jeep Adventures** (**☎** 800/294-JEEP or 602/488-0023); **Desert Mountain Jeep Tours** (**☎** 602/860-1777); **Desert Storm Hummer Tours** (**☎** 602/922-0020); or **Wild West Jeep Tours** (**☎** 602/941-8355). Some Jeep tour companies also offer the chance to do some gold panning. Contact **Arizona Awareness Desert Jeep Tours** (**☎** 602/947-7852), which also does ghost-town excursions, or **Arrowhead Desert Tours** (**☎** 602/942-3361).

The *Desert Princess* (**☎** 602/230-7600) offers sightseeing, breakfast, lunch, and dinner cruises on Lake Pleasant, a reservoir 45 minutes northwest of Phoenix.

**ATTRACTIONS**    Few would argue that sunshine, warm winter days, and the outdoor activities they allow are the valley's top attractions. But there are also a number of exceptional museums and historic sites to tempt you away from the pool or the greens.

**Arizona Historical Society Museum.** *1300 N. College Ave., Tempe.* ☎ *602/929-0292. Admission free. Mon–Sat 10am–4pm, Sun noon–4pm.* By focusing on the people who helped shape the region, this museum presents the history of 20th-century central Arizona. Exhibits feature life-size statues of everyday people; quotes relate their individual stories and props reveal what items they might have carried during their days in the desert. Characters include a Mexican miner and a Chinese laborer.

# Phoenix

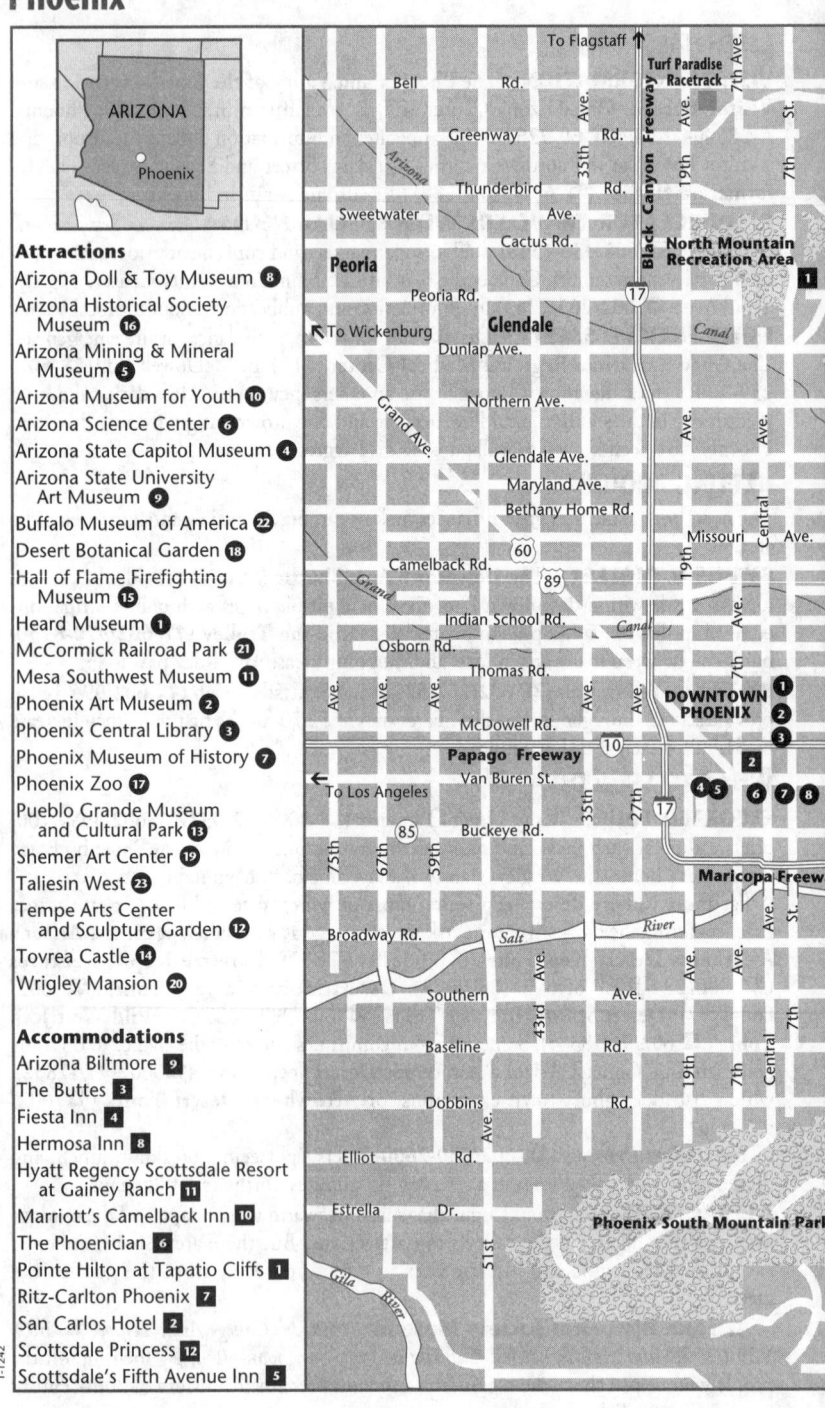

1-1242

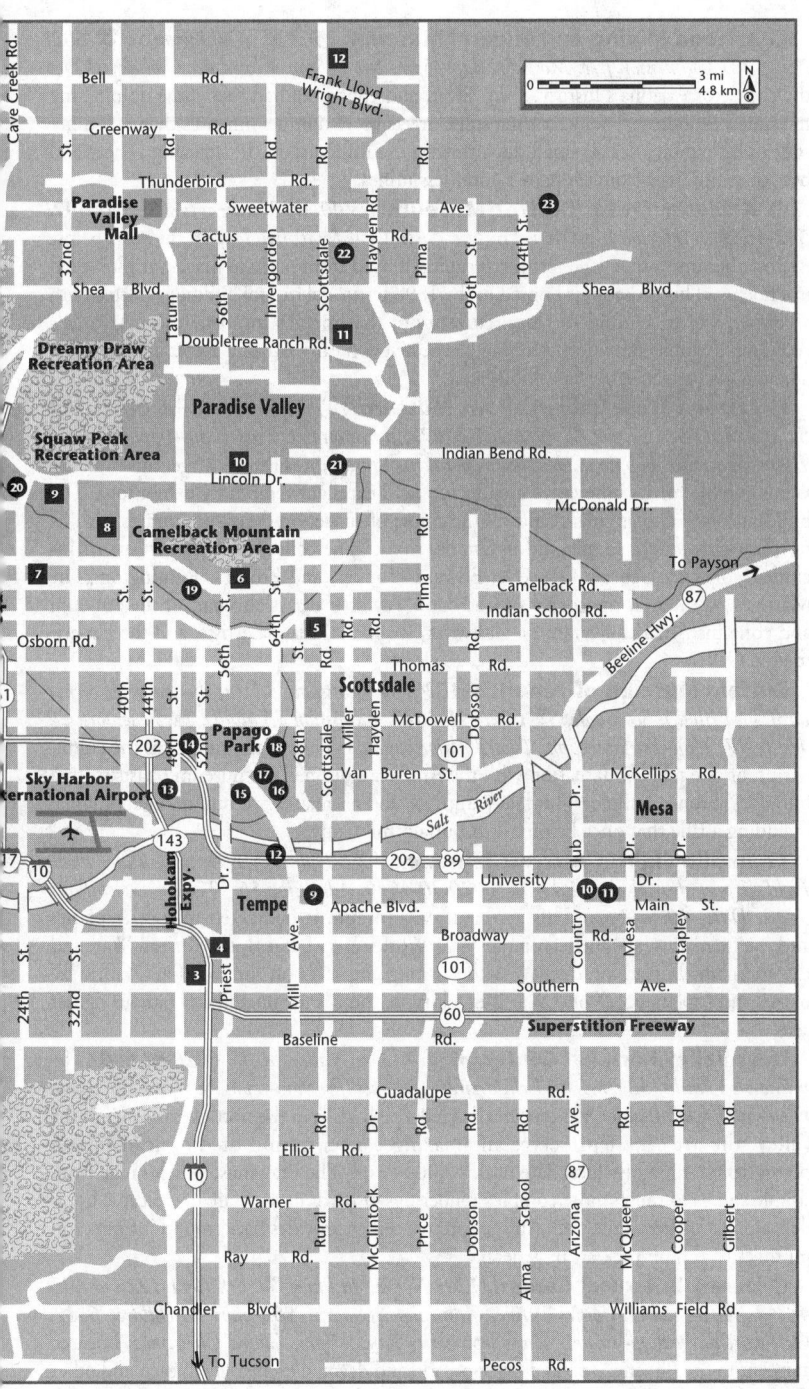

✪ **Arizona Mining and Mineral Museum.** *1502 W. Washington St.* ☎ *602/ 255-3791. Admission free. Mon–Fri 8am–5pm, Sat 1–5pm. Closed state holidays.* Over the course of Arizona's history, gold, silver, and copper all had their time dominating the state's economy. Today Arizona still extracts more nonfuel minerals than any other state. The exhibits in this small downtown museum focus on the amazing variety and beauty of minerals from the state's countless mines.

✪ **Arizona State Capitol Museum.** *1700 W. Washington St.* ☎ *602/ 542-4581. Admission free. Mon–Fri 8am–5pm. Closed state holidays.* In the years before Arizona became a state, the territorial capital moved from place to place until it settled in Phoenix. This museum is housed in the 1898 territorial capitol building, erected with a copper roof to remind the local citizenry of that metal's importance to Arizona's economy. Exhibits provide interesting perspectives on early Arizona events and lifestyles. There is also a USS *Arizona* exhibit here.

✪ **Arizona State University Art Museum.** *In the Nelson Fine Arts Center, 10th St. and Mill Ave., Tempe.* ☎ *602/965-2787. Admission free. Tues 10am–9pm, Wed–Sat 10am–5pm, Sun 1–5pm. Closed major holidays.* Though it isn't very large, this museum is memorable for its innovative architecture and excellent temporary exhibitions. The building, stark and angular, captures the colors of sunset on desert mountains with its purplish gray stucco facade and pyramidal shape. The collection of American art includes works by Georgia O'Keeffe, Edward Hopper, and Frederic Remington. The Matthews Center, at the corner of Cady and Taylor malls, is also part of the museum and contains American ceramics, glasswork, works by Arizona artists, and the Experimental Gallery.

**Buffalo Museum of America.** *10261 N. Scottsdale Rd. (at the southeast corner with Shea Blvd.), Scottsdale.* ☎ *602/951-1022. Admission $3 adults, $2.50 seniors, $2 ages 6–17. Mon–Fri 9am–5pm. Closed major holidays.* This small museum is the culmination of one man's infatuation with the American bison. The museum boasts stuffed buffaloes, bronze buffaloes, buffalo paintings, and all manner of buffalo memorabilia, including a rifle that once belonged to Buffalo Bill Cody.

**Champlin Fighter Aircraft Museum.** *4636 Fighter Aces Dr., Mesa (at Falcon Field Airport off McKellips Rd.).* ☎ *602/830-4540. Admission $6.50 adults, $3 children 5–12. Daily 10am–5pm.* This aeronautical museum is dedicated to fighter planes and the men who flew them. Aircraft from World Wars I and II, the Korean War, and the Vietnam War are on display, with a strong emphasis on the wood-and-fabric biplanes and triplanes of World War I. In addition, there is memorabilia of famous fighter aces.

**Deer Valley Rock Art Center.** *3711 W. Deer Valley Rd.* ☎ *602/582-8007. Admission $3 adults, $2 seniors, $1 children 6–12. Tues–Fri 9am–2pm, Sat 9am–5pm, Sun noon–5pm. Closed major holidays.* In the Hedgepeth Hills in the northwest corner of the valley, the art center preserves an amazing concentration of American Indian petroglyphs, some of which date back 10,000 years. The drawings, which range from simple spirals to much more complex renderings of herds of deer, are on volcanic boulders along a quarter-mile trail. An interpretive center provides background information on this site and on rock art in general.

✪ **Desert Botanical Garden.** *1201 N. Galvin Pkwy.* ☎ *602/941-1225 or 602/ 481-8134 (24-hour activities hotline). Admission $6 adults, $5 seniors, $1 children 5–12. Oct–Apr, daily 8am–sunset. May–Sept, daily 7am–10pm. Closed Christmas.* Located adjacent to the Phoenix Zoo and Papago Park, and devoted exclusively to cacti and other desert plants, the Desert Botanical Garden displays desert plants from all over the world. You can also practice grinding corn and pounding mesquite beans, or make a yucca-fiber brush.

**Hall of Flame Firefighting Museum.** *6101 E. Van Buren St.* ☎ *602/275-3473. Admission $5 adults, $4 seniors, $3 ages 6–17. Mon–Fri 9am–5pm, Sat 9am–4pm, Sun noon–4pm. Closed Thanksgiving, Christmas, and New Year's Day.* The world's largest firefighting museum contains a fascinating collection of vintage fire trucks, including a 1725 hand-pumper from England as well as classic fire engines from this century.

✪ **Heard Museum.** *22 E. Monte Vista Rd.* ☎ *602/252-8840. Admission $5 adults, $4 seniors and students, $3 ages 13–18, $2 children 4–12; free on Wed 5–9pm. Mon–Tues and Thurs–Sat 9:30am–5pm, Wed 9:30am–8pm, Sun noon–5pm. Closed some holidays.* The Heard is considered one of the nation's finest Native American museums. Extensive exhibits, some interactive, examine the culture of each of the region's major tribes. On weekends singers and dancers perform, and throughout the week artists demonstrate their work. The biggest event of the year is the Guild Indian Fair and Market, held the first weekend in March. The museum operates a satellite gallery in El Pedregal Festival Marketplace, 34505 N. Scottsdale Rd. (☎ 602/488-9817), adjacent to The Boulders resort and the town of Carefree.

**Heritage Square.** *115 N. Sixth St., at Monroe.* ☎ *602/262-5029 or 602/262-5071. Rosson House tours, $3 adults, $2 seniors, $1 children 6–12, free for children 5 and under. Wed–Sat 10am–3:30pm, Sun noon–3:30pm (shorter hours in summer); other hours vary. Arizona Doll and Toy Museum closed Aug.* Heritage Square is a collection of some of the few remaining houses that date to the last century and the original Phoenix town site. Among the buildings are the ornate Eastlake Victorian Rosson House; the Silva House, a neoclassical Revival–style home; an 1899 bungalow (now a tearoom); the Stevens–Haustgen House, devoted to Native American crafts and history; and the Arizona Doll and Toy Museum, housed in a 1912 schoolhouse.

**Phoenix Art Museum.** *1625 N. Central Ave. (at the northeast corner with McDowell Rd.).* ☎ *602/257-1222. Admission free; special exhibitions $5 adults, $4 seniors, $2 students and children 6–12, free for children 5 and under; free on Wed. Tues and Thurs–Sat 10am–5pm, Wed 10am–9pm, Sun noon–5pm. Closed major holidays.* This is the largest art museum in the Southwest, and houses a collection that spans major artistic movements from the Renaissance to the present. The holdings of modern and contemporary art are particularly good. The Thorne Miniature Collection of tiny, exquisitely detailed rooms is one of the most popular exhibits. Others include Spanish colonial furnishings and religious art, and of course, works by the Cowboy Artists of America.

**Phoenix Museum of History.** *105 N. Fifth St.* ☎ *602/253-2734. Admission $5 adults, $3.50 seniors, $2.50 children 6–11. Mon–Sat 10am–5pm, Sun noon–5pm. Closed major holidays.* Located adjacent to Heritage Square in downtown Phoenix, this museum presents an interesting, interactive look at unusual aspects of the city's history. Aroma barrels offer a sniff of how Phoenix once smelled. A beer-bottle sidewalk shows how one saloon-keeper solved the problem of muddy streets. Yet another exhibit shows how "lungers" (tuberculosis sufferers) inadvertently helped originate the tourism industry in Arizona.

**Pueblo Grande Museum and Cultural Park.** *4619 E. Washington St. (between 44th and 48th sts.).* ☎ *602/495-0901. Admission $2 adults, $1.50 seniors, $1 children; free on Sun. Mon–Sat 9am–4:45pm, Sun 1–4:45pm. Closed major holidays.* Located near downtown Phoenix, this museum contains the ruins of an ancient Hohokam village, one of several that were located along the Salt River between A.D. 300 and 1400. Before touring the grounds to view the partially excavated ruins, view the many artifacts from the site on display. Changing exhibits focus on different aspects of ancient and contemporary Native American cultures. The museum also sponsors demonstrations and workshops; past programs have included pottery, bow-and-arrow, and basketry classes.

**ARCHITECTURAL HIGHLIGHTS** The **Arizona Biltmore,** 24th Street and Missouri Avenue (☎ 602/955-6600), though not designed by Frank Lloyd Wright, shows the famed architect's influence in its distinctive cast-cement blocks, and displays objects designed by Wright. The architect loved the Arizona desert and in 1937 opened a winter camp here that served as his office and school. Today **Taliesin West,** 114th Street and Frank Lloyd Wright Boulevard, Scottsdale (☎ 602/860-8810 or 602/860-2700 for reservations), is the headquarters of the Frank Lloyd Wright Foundation and School of Architecture. Tours take you around campus buildings and introduce Wright's architectural theories, including his innovative methods for dealing with the extremes of a desert climate.

The **Phoenix Central Library,** 1221 N. Central Ave. (☎ 602/262-4636), is the most daring piece of public architecture in the city. The five-story cube, partially clad in ribbed copper sheeting, not only makes use of the desert's plentiful sunshine to provide light for reading but also incorporates computer-controlled louvers and shade sails to reduce heat and glare. The fifth-floor reading room, covering more than an acre, is topped by a "floating" ceiling suspended from cables.

**Tovrea Castle,** 5041 E. Van Buren St. (☎ 602/262-6412), has been likened to a giant wedding cake and is currently under renovation until some time in 1998. **Cosanti,** 6433 Doubletree Ranch Rd. (1 mile west of Scottsdale Road), in Scottsdale (☎ 602/948-6145), is a complex of cast-concrete structures that served as a prototype and learning project for architect Paolo Soleri's much grander Arcosanti project, currently under construction north of Phoenix. It's here at Cosanti that Soleri's famous bells are cast.

**PARKS & OUTDOOR AREAS** Among the city's most popular parks are its natural areas and preserves. These include South Mountain Park, Papago Park, Phoenix Mountains Preserve (site of Squaw Peak), North Mountain Preserve and North Mountain Recreation Area, and Camelback Mountain–Echo Canyon Recreation Area.

**BEST BETS FOR KIDS** The **Phoenix Zoo,** in Papago Park in central Phoenix (☎ 602/273-1341), is known for its mixed-species, 4-acre African veldt exhibit and its baboon colony. Kids will love the 11-acre children's zoo, where they can see baby animals and pet some of the more friendly residents. For the unusual of the animal kingdom, head for **Wildlife World Zoo,** 16523 W. Northern, Litchfield Park (☎ 602/935-9453). At this private zoo you'll see tiny mammals, mammals that fly, kangaroos and wallabies, white tigers and black panthers, and plenty of snakes and lizards. Several exhibits let visitors get close to the animals.

The **Arizona Science Center,** 600 E. Washington St. (☎ 602/716-2000), is a hands-on museum with a planetarium and large-screen theater. Dolls and toys have universal appeal. The **Arizona Doll and Toy Museum,** 602 E. Adams St. (☎ 602/253-9337), in the Stevens House on Heritage Square in downtown Phoenix, includes a 1912 schoolroom display in which the children are all antique dolls.

For a break from sightseeing, take the kids to **McCormick Railroad Park,** 7301 E. Indian Bend Rd., Scottsdale (☎ 602/994-2312), which boasts a five-twelfths-scale model railroad that visitors can ride as well as restored cars and engines and a 1929 carousel. In the spring and summer months there are concerts in the park.

**SPORTS** Starting in 1998, with the completion of the new Bank-One Ballpark, Phoenix will have its very own major league team—the **Arizona Diamondbacks.** Get a schedule from the convention and visitor bureau, or check the *Arizona Republic* newspaper. The NBA's **Phoenix Suns** play at America West Arena, 201 E. Jefferson St. (☎ 602/379-7867 or 602/379-7800). Tickets are available at the arena and at Dillard's Box Office locations. The **Arizona Cardinals** (☎ 602/379-0102) play NFL football at Arizona State University's Sun Devil Stadium, which also hosts the Fiesta Bowl Football Classic at New Year's.

**GOLF** Among the many PGA events held here, the **Phoenix Open Golf Tournament** (☎ 602/870-0163) in January is the largest. Other major tournaments include the LPGA's **Standard Register Turquoise Classic** (☎ 602/495-4653), played in March, and **The Tradition** (☎ 602/443-1597), a Senior PGA Tour event held in April.

With more than 100 courses in the valley, golf is the most popular sport in Phoenix. For information on area golf courses, call the **Phoenix and Valley of the Sun Convention and Visitor Bureau** (☎ 602/254-6500) or pick up the *Phoenix and Valley of the Sun Golf Guide,* available at the Visitor Bureau and at many hotels and resorts. It's smart to make reservations in advance, and many companies will book tee times for you. Some of these include **Golf Express** (☎ 800/878-8580 or 602/404-GOLF) or **Par-Tee Time** (☎ 800/827-2223 or 602/230-7223), or, for last-minute bookings, try **Stand-By Golf** (☎ 602/905-2665) or **Next Day Golf** (☎ 800/838-4637 or 602/994-4653).

**SHOPPING** **Scottsdale** and the **Biltmore District** of Phoenix are the valley's main upscale shopping areas. **Old Scottsdale** (one of the few outdoor shopping areas and the most popular) has a western atmosphere, with hundreds of boutiques, galleries, jewelry stores, and Native American crafts stores. It is also the heart of the valley's art market. For an extensive listing of galleries and exhibitions in the area, pick up a copy of *The Official Valley of the Sun Gallery Guide,* available at art galleries.

**Glendale** is the antiques center for the valley, with the highest concentration of shops in downtown Glendale and on Glendale Avenue in the 5000 and 6000 blocks.

## ACCOMMODATIONS

Phoenix's popularity as a winter refuge from cold and snow, has given it the greatest concentration of resorts in the continental United States, and in its winter season, some of the highest room rates in the country. Even moderately priced motels jack up their prices in winter. Luckily, no matter where you stay, even in a budget motel, you're likely to find a pool and whirlpool on the premises. When you reserve, keep in mind that most resorts offer a variety of weekend, golf, and tennis packages, as well as special discounts in the off-season.

✪ **Arizona Biltmore.** *24th St. and Missouri Ave., Phoenix, AZ 85016.* ☎ *800/950-0086 or 602/955-6600. Fax 602/954-2571. 600 rms including 50 suites. Early Sept–early June, $280–$360 double; from $420 suite. Early June–early Sept, $115–$155 double; from $300 suite. AE, CB, DC, DISC, EURO, JCB, MC, V.* Frank Lloyd Wright had a hand in designing the historic Biltmore, the premier Phoenix address. Rooms in the resort section are larger than those in the main building, and have balconies or patios, some offering views of Squaw Peak. Amenities include afternoon tea, two restaurants, bar, two golf courses, 18-hole putting course, five swimming pools, two whirlpools, eight lighted tennis courts, fitness center, sauna, steam room, jogging paths, children's activities center, bicycle rentals, shops, and business center.

✪ **The Buttes.** *2000 Westcourt Way, Tempe, AZ 85282.* ☎ *800/843-1986 or 602/225-9000. Fax 602/438-8622. 343 rms, 9 suites. Jan–late May, $215–$240 double; $375–$950 suite. Late May–early Sept, $110–$130 double; $275–$950 suite. Early Sept–Dec 31, $185–$205 double; $375–$950 suite. AE, CB, DC, DISC, JCB, MC, V.* Just 3 miles from Sky Harbor Airport, this spectacular resort makes the utmost of its craggy hilltop location. The Top of the Rock restaurant snags the best view around (see "Dining," below). Many guest rooms have good valley views. Forget long soaks: most bathrooms have only three-quarter-size tubs. Facilities include two restaurants, three bars/lounges, two pools with waterfalls and a connecting swim-through canal, four whirlpools (one's the most romantic in the valley), four tennis courts, and a fitness center.

**Doubletree Paradise Valley Resort.** *5401 N. Scottsdale Rd., Scottsdale, AZ 85250.* ☎ *800/222-TREE or 602/947-5400. Fax 602/946-1524. 387 rms, 17 suites. Jan–May, $155–$285 double; $425–$2,000 suite. June–Aug, $75–$125 double; $225–$500 suite. Sept–Dec, $145–$230 double; $425–$2,000 suite. AE, CB, DC, DISC, MC, V.* Built around several courtyards containing pools, fountains, palm trees, and desert gardens, this resort gives a nod to the pioneering architectural style of Frank Lloyd Wright. The guest rooms are large and comfortable. The resort has a restaurant, pool bar, two outdoor pools, two lighted tennis courts, fitness center, two racquetball courts, saunas, steam room, whirlpools, beauty salon, business center, and car rental.

**Fiesta Inn.** *2100 S. Priest Dr., Tempe, AZ 85282.* ☎ *800/528-6481 or 602/967-1441. Fax 602/967-0224. 270 rms, 4 suites. Jan 1–May 31, $119–$153 double; $225–$275 suite. June 1–Sept 30, $51–$79 double; $100–$135 suite. Oct 1–Dec 31, $95–$125 double; $150–$200 suite. AE, CB, DC, DISC, MC, V.* Reasonable rates, extensive recreational facilities, and a convenient location make this older, casual resort hotel one of the best deals in the valley. The grounds are lush and shaded, and the guest rooms are large, with refrigerators, coffeemakers, and hair dryers. Facilities include a restaurant, lounge, three tennis courts, putting green, driving range, pool, health club, and jogging trails.

**✪ Hermosa Inn.** *5532 N. Palo Cristi Rd., Paradise Valley, AZ 85253.* ☎ *800/241-1210 or 602/955-8614. Fax 602/955-8299. 17 rms, 18 suites. Late Nov–late Apr, $200–$225 double; $250–$500 suite. Late Apr–early June, $145–$150 double; $195–$325 suite. Early June to mid-Sept, $89–$99 double; $120–$250 suite. Mid-Sept to late Nov, $150–$175 double; $200–$350 suite. AE, CB, DC, DISC, MC, V.* Originally the 1930s home of western artist Lon Megargee, this renovated guest ranch is set on over 6 acres of neatly landscaped gardens. Accommodations vary from cozy rooms to spacious suites; the decor is one of tasteful contemporary western and Southwestern elegance. Lon's, the dining room in the original adobe home, serves excellent new American and Southwestern cuisine. The inn has a concierge, pool, whirlpool spas, and three tennis courts.

**✪ Hyatt Regency Scottsdale Resort at Gainey Ranch.** *7500 E. Doubletree Ranch Rd., Scottsdale, AZ 85258.* ☎ *800/233-1234 or 602/991-3388. Fax 602/483-5550. 493 rms, 7 casitas, 25 suites. Jan–May, $295–$415 double; $1,175–$2,070 casita; $385–$2,300 suite. May–Sept, $145–$270 double; $775–$1,800 casita; $215–$1,050 suite. Sept–Dec, $305–$350 double; $875–$1,075 casita; $375–$1,100 suite. AE, DC, DISC, MC, V.* Located north of Scottsdale's resort row, this resort has a 2 1/2-acre water playground as its focal point, and there are gorgeous views of the McDowell Mountains. The guest rooms have every amenity. Extras include three restaurants, three bars, and a grill near the pool. Guests also enjoy gondola rides, a 27-hole golf course, 10 pools, whirlpools, eight lighted tennis courts, a croquet court, jogging and bicycling trails, and a full-service health spa.

**Marriott's Camelback Inn.** *5402 E. Lincoln Dr., Scottsdale, AZ 85253.* ☎ *800/24-CAMEL or 602/948-1700. Fax 602/951-8469. 424 rms, 28 suites. Jan 1–early June, $309–$380 double; $500–$1,700 suite. Early June–early Sept, $109–$175 double; $200–$750 suite. Early Sept–Dec 31, $235–$280 double; $350–$1025 suite. AE, CB, DC, DISC, JCB, MC, V.* Opened in 1936, this was the first Marriott resort, in a tranquil setting only 5 minutes from downtown Scottsdale. The spa is among the finest in the state. Guest rooms all have balconies or patios, and some have their own sundecks. The excellent Chaparral serves continental fare. There are four other restaurants, three bars, two 18-hole golf courses, eight tennis courts, three pools, three whirlpools, a full-service health spa, beauty salon, lap pool, aerobics room, saunas, steam rooms, whirlpool, and fitness room.

✪ **The Phoenician.** *6000 E. Camelback Rd., Scottsdale, AZ 85251.* ☎ *800/ 888-8234 or 602/941-8200. Fax 602/947-4311. 555 rms, 92 suites. Jan–June, $350– $485 double; $1,000–$1,650 suite. June–Sept, $175–$305 double; $475–$1,095 suite. Sept–Dec, $355–$405 double; $1,075–$1,725 suite. AE, CB, DC, DISC, EURO, JCB, MC, V. Valet parking $8.* The Phoenician is the most ostentatious resort with the best service in town, the finest pool complex in the state, the Center for Well-Being spa offering all the pampering anyone could ever need, and 27 challenging holes of golf. Even the standard guest rooms include sunken bathtubs for two. Mary Elaine's and Windows on the Green are two of the area's finest restaurants (see "Dining," below). Conveniences include afternoon tea, bar/lounge, two cafes, seven pools, 12 tennis courts (11 lighted), whirlpool, lawn games, volleyball court, rental bikes, jogging trails, shopping arcade, full fitness center and spa, car-rental desk, and business center.

**Pointe Hilton at Tapatio Cliffs.** *11111 N. Seventh St., Phoenix, AZ 85020.* ☎ *800/876-4683 or 602/866-7500. Fax 602/993-0276. 584 suites. Jan–Apr, $199– $255 suite for two. May–Sept, $79–$215 suite for two. Sept–Dec, $165–$215 suite for two. AE, CB, DC, DISC, EURO, JCB, MC, V.* With two lagoon pools, complete with waterfall, water slide, and many other fun features, Tapatio Cliffs has family appeal. Situated on the shoulder of North Mountain, it also backs up to a nature preserve where guests can hike in the desert. The views are spectacular from both the lounge and dining room. All guest quarters are spacious suites. Guests can enjoy the complimentary afternoon cocktails, massages, car-rental desk, horseback riding, 18-hole golf course, 15 lighted tennis courts, seven swimming pools, full-service health spa, games room, rental bikes, gift shop, tennis shop, golf shop, and business center.

✪ **Ritz-Carlton Phoenix.** *2401 E. Camelback Rd., Phoenix, AZ 85016.* ☎ *800/ 241-3333 or 602/468-0700. Fax 602/468-9883. 281 rms, 14 suites. Sept–May, $190– $275 double; $250–$1,500 suite. May–Sept, $105–$165 double; $195–$1,500 suite. AE, CB, DC, DISC, EC, JCB, MC, V. Valet parking $9.50.* The Ritz-Carlton is the city's finest nonresort hotel and provides the usual impeccable Ritz service in elegant surroundings. The hotel has two restaurants, a lobby lounge/bar, afternoon tea, car-rental desk, massages, complimentary golf shuttle, small outdoor pool, tennis court, fitness center, and saunas.

**San Carlos Hotel.** *202 N. Central Ave., Phoenix, AZ 85004.* ☎ *800/528-5446 or 602/253-4121. Fax 602/253-6668. 115 rms, 11 suites. $79–$99 double; $129–$199 suite. AE, CB, DC, DISC, MC, V.* Built in 1928, the San Carlos is a small European-style hotel that provides that touch of elegance and charm missing from most high-rise hotels downtown. You're close to shopping, the Phoenix Convention Center, sightseeing, and theaters, which makes this a good choice for both tourists and conventioneers. The rooms are comfortable though small. Facilities include a restaurant, pub, bar, cafe, rooftop pool, and exercise room.

**Scottsdale's Fifth Avenue Inn.** *6935 Fifth Ave., Scottsdale, AZ 85251.* ☎ *800/ 528-7396 outside Arizona, or 602/994-9461. Fax 602/947-1695. 92 rms. Mid-Jan to Apr, $87–$92 double. May–Sept, $45–$50 double. Oct to mid-Jan, $57–$62 double. Rates include continental breakfast. AE, CB, DC, DISC, MC, V.* This motel is at the west end of Scottsdale's Fifth Avenue Shops, the city's best shopping and dining venue. The guest rooms are large. The three-story building is arranged around a central courtyard with a pool and whirlpool.

✪ **Scottsdale Princess.** *7575 E. Princess Dr., Scottsdale, AZ 85255.* ☎ *800/ 344-4758 or 602/585-4848. Fax 602/585-0086. 450 rms, 125 casitas suites, 75 villa suites. Jan 1–May 31, $320–$440 double; $480–$2,500 suite. June 1–Sept 3, $145–$185 double; $215–$1,250 suite. Sept 4–Dec 31, $260–$330 double; $380–$2,000 suite. AE, CB, DC, DISC, MC, V.* As host to the Phoenix Open golf tournament and a professional tennis tournament, this resort boasts top golf and tennis facilities, in addition to a full-service spa and fitness center. Yet the exotic atmosphere also makes it perfect for romantic getaways. The fully appointed guest rooms all have distinct living and work areas, with wet bars, refrigerators, and private balconies. The Marquesa (see "Dining," below) is a highly acclaimed—and high-priced—Spanish restaurant; equally praised is **La Hacienda.** There are three other restaurants, two lounge/bars, two 18-hole golf courses, seven tennis courts (six lighted), three pools, whirlpools, sports courts, a complete spa and fitness center, boutiques, pro shops, and a business center.

**NEARBY ACCOMMODATIONS**   Set amid a jumble of giant rocks 45 minutes north of Scottsdale, ✪ **The Boulders** (☎ **800/553-1717** or 602/488-9009) epitomizes the Southwest aesthetic and is the state's premier resort. Adobe buildings blend unobtrusively into the desert, as do the two golf courses, which feature the most breathtaking tee boxes in Arizona. There are two pools, tennis, and a full-service spa.

Located 20 minutes west of downtown Phoenix, **The Wigwam** (☎ **800/327-0396** or 602/935-3811) opened its doors to the public in 1929 and remains one of the nation's premier golf resorts. Three challenging golf courses are the main reason most people come here. Though elegant, the resort is set amid flatlands that lack the stunning desert scenery of the Scottsdale area.

## DINING

Scottsdale and the Biltmore District are home to most—but not all—of the excellent restaurants in the valley. If you can afford only one expensive meal while you're here, be sure to make it at one of the resort restaurants that offers a view of the city lights. Other meals not to be missed are the cowboy dinners served amid Wild West decor at such places as **Rawhide Western Town & Steakhouse.** Mexican food and Southwestern cuisine are Phoenix specialties.

**The Bistro.** *In the Biltmore Financial Center, 2398 E. Camelback Rd.* ☎ *602/ 957-3214. Reservations recommended. Main courses $6–$15 at lunch, $18–$23 at dinner. AE, CB, DC, MC, V. Mon–Fri 11am–10pm, Sat–Sun 5–10pm. FRENCH/ INTERNATIONAL.* From the same kitchen as the pricey Christopher's (see below), the main courses here are usually straightforward and paired with sauces that enhance the flavor of the dish, such as grilled prime beef with pepper sauce or grilled halibut with smoked tomato sauce.

**Café Terra Cotta.** *At the Borgata, 6166 N. Scottsdale Rd., Suite 100.* ☎ *602/ 948-8100. Reservations recommended for dinner. Main courses $11–$19. AE, CB, DC, MC, V. Sun–Thurs 11am–9:30pm, Fri–Sat 11am–10pm. SOUTHWESTERN/INTER-NATIONAL.* This casually sophisticated and low-key restaurant features wood-oven pizzas, sandwiches, and smaller meals as well as full-size main courses. Imaginative combinations are the rule here, as evidenced by the grilled chicken breast with achiote-sherry glaze on mole verde with garlic-chipotle whipped potatoes.

**Christopher's.** *In the Biltmore Financial Center, 2398 E. Camelback Rd.* ☎ *602/957-3214. Reservations highly recommended. Main courses $29; menu prestige $75 ($115 with wines). AE, CB, DC, DISC, MC, V. Tues–Sat 5–10pm. FRENCH/NOUVELLE AMERICAN.* This elegant dining room is small and attracts a well-heeled clientele. Chef Christopher Gross creates contemporary French cuisine, and his versions of traditional dishes (such as venison with shiitake mushrooms in a cognac and red-wine sauce) are truly memorable. The restaurant also has what may be the best wine collection in Phoenix.

**✪ Eddie's Grill.** *4747 N. Seventh St.* ☎ *602/241-1188. Reservations recommended. Main courses $7–$13 at lunch, $12–$20 at dinner. AE, DC, MC, V. Mon–Thurs 11:30am–2:30pm and 5–11pm, Fri 11:30am–2:30pm and 5pm–midnight, Sat 5pm–midnight, Sun 4–9pm. NEW AMERICAN.* Chef Eddie Matney is passionate about his grilled turkey meat loaf, which comes with herbed red-potato celery bread stuffing and cranberry au jus. His combination plate is filled with spicy, piquant, tongue-tingling crusted sea scallops with Cajun dill wasabi sauce and seared portobello mushrooms in a black-bean dressing with red-pepper coulis.

**El Guapo's Taco Shop & Salsa Bar.** *3015 N. Scottsdale Rd.* ☎ *602/423-8385. Main courses $2–$6. No credit cards. Mon–Sat 10:30am–8pm. MEXICAN.* This little taco shop offers up grilled mahimahi, carne asada, and marinated pork tacos, among others, which you can then douse with salsa and vegetable toppings from the salsa cart. Other good bets are the homemade-style cheese crisps, burritos, and nachos, and armadillo eggs—jalapeño peppers stuffed with cheese and deep fried.

**✪ Franco's Trattoria.** *8120 N. Hayden Rd., Scottsdale.* ☎ *602/948-6655. Reservations recommended. Main courses $13.75–$24.25. AE, MC, V. Mon–Thurs 5–10pm, Fri–Sat 5–10:30pm. Closed Mon in summer. TUSCAN ITALIAN.* The food here fairly bursts with flavor. Try the *insalata capricciosa,* a salad of fennel, goat cheese, sun-dried tomatoes, beans, arugula, radicchio, and red onion, or the *risotto coi carciof* (risotto with fresh baby artichokes and pancetta). Even the simple dishes, such as *bistecca fiorentina* (porterhouse steak with tomato and onion) are usually well prepared.

**✪ Lon's.** *5532 N. Palo Cristi Rd. (at the Hermosa Inn).* ☎ *602/955-7878. Reservations recommended for late in the week. Main courses $9–$12 at lunch, $17–$25 at dinner. AE, MC, V. Sun–Fri 11:30am–2pm and 5:30–10pm. SOUTHWESTERN.* At this most "Arizonan" restaurant—a Mexican-style hacienda with tile roof and gardens all around—you'll see both retirees and the power-lunching set eating rosemary-infused sourdough rolls, platters of fried sweet potatoes and onion rings, and juicy grilled pineapple chicken on focaccia bread. Dinner entrees include the likes of New York steak with horseradish mashed potatoes and a beer demiglace, and lamb with a shallot-basil couscous.

**✪ Marquesa.** *At the Scottsdale Princess Resort, 7575 E. Princess Dr. (about 12 miles north of downtown Scottsdale).* ☎ *602/585-4848. Reservations recommended. Main courses $23–$31; champagne brunch $29.95. AE, DC, DISC, MC, V. Mon–Sat 5–10pm, Sun 10:30am–2:30pm (brunch) and 5–10pm. SPANISH/CATALONIAN.* Paella with lobster, chicken, pork, shellfish, chistora, and saffron rice is the signature dish here. Some others are low in fat and sodium, but not the desserts—crème fraîche flan with a black-walnut crust is just one such temptation. There's a separate tapas bar. Sunday brunch is served on the patio.

**Mary Elaine's.** *At the Phoenician, 6000 E. Camelback Rd., Scottsdale.* ☎ *602/ 423-2530. Reservations required. Jacket required for men. Main courses $29–$34; 5-course tasting menu $76 ($111 with wine). AE, CB, DC, DISC, EURO, JCB, MC, V. Sun–Thurs 6–10pm, Fri–Sat 6–11pm. MODERN FRENCH.* Mary Elaine's is not only one of the finest hotel restaurants in the valley, it boasts one of the city's best views as well. Recent menu offerings have included roasted Arizona quail with Java pepper, figs, and Parma ham accompanied by a warm salad of butternut squash, red cabbage, and chanterelles. Some dishes are low in sodium, fat, and cholesterol.

**Oregano's Pizza Bistro.** *3622 N. Scottsdale Rd. (south of Indian School Rd.).* ☎ *602/970-1860. Reservations not accepted. Main courses $6–$17. AE, DISC, MC, V.*

*Mon–Thurs 11am–10pm, Fri–Sat 11am–11pm, Sun noon–10pm. PIZZA/PASTA.* The prices at Oregano's are very reasonable, and both the thin-crust pizzas—spread with the likes of pesto and Cajun chicken—and the Chicago stuffed pizza are all the good things pizza should be. You can also order artichoke lasagna with both a cream and a marinara sauce, barbecued wings, a variety of Caesar salads, and more.

**Rancho Pinot Grill.** *6208 N. Scottsdale Rd., Scottsdale.* ☎ *602/468-9463. Reservations recommended. Main courses $17–$22. MC, V. Tues–Sat 5:30–10pm. Closed first 2 weeks in Sept. NEW AMERICAN.* Rancho Pinot combines fun and kitschy 1950s cowboy memorabilia with an airy setting at the back of a shopping mall. The menu is short and changes regularly; on a recent visit, it featured a salad of shaved fennel, red onion, orange, and parsley with lemon and Parmesan.

**Rawhide Western Town & Steakhouse.** *23023 N. Scottsdale Rd. (4 miles north of Bell Rd.), Scottsdale.* ☎ *602/502-5600. Reservations accepted only for large parties. Main courses $10–$28. AE, DC, DISC, MC, V. June–Sept, daily 5–10pm. Oct–May, Mon–Thurs 5–10pm, Fri–Sun 11am–10pm. STEAK.* The real attraction here is the entertainment, including shootouts, stagecoach rides, and a petting zoo. Kids love dancing to the country music and pretending they're in a real Old-Western town, which isn't difficult, since Rawhide, with its wide street, looks pretty authentic. As for food, you'll find mesquite-broiled steaks, a few barbecued items, and fruit pie à la mode.

**Sam's Cafe.** *In the Arizona Center, 455 N. Third St.* ☎ *602/252-3545. Reservations recommended. Main courses $8–$19. AE, DC, DISC, MC, V. Sun–Thurs 11am–10pm, Fri–Sat 11am–midnight. SOUTHWESTERN.* Sam's Cafe offers imaginative Southwestern cuisine at affordable prices. Breadsticks served with picante-flavored cream cheese, grilled tuna tacos, and penne pasta in a spicy peanut sauce with black beans and goat cheese all have a nice balance of flavors and just the right amount of spice. Salads and dipping sauces are complex and interesting. There's another Sam's in the Biltmore Fashion Park at 2566 E. Camelback Rd. (☎ *602/954-7100).*

**✪ Such Is Life.** *3602 N. 24th St.* ☎ *602/955-7822. Reservations recommended. Main courses $13–$25. AE, DC, DISC, MC, V. Mon–Fri 11:30am–2pm and 5:30–9pm, Sat 5:30–9pm. MEXICAN.* This is simply the best Mexican food in Phoenix—the three salsas alone are enough to justify a visit. There are daily specials, but the restaurant is known for its *guisados,* or Mexican casseroles. The *mole poblano* is excellent, and fresh juices and creamy flan cheesecake also excel. There is a second location at 7000 E. Shea Blvd., Scottsdale (☎ *602/948-1753).*

**Texaz Grill.** *6003 N. 16th St.* ☎ *602/248-STAR. Reservations taken for six or more. Main courses $4–$6 at lunch, $7–$15 at dinner. AE, MC, V. Mon–Thurs 11am–10pm, Fri 11am–11pm, Sat noon–11pm, Sun 4–10pm. STEAK.* Outside the heat is blazing; inside, there's a twangy Texas favorite playing on the jukebox, and it's cool and dim, with a well-mannered chaos of stuffed armadillos, license plates, and other Texan memorabilia adorning every surface. The folks here are friendly and will be pleased to dish you up the house special—chicken-fried steak with mashed potatoes and gravy.

**✪ Top of the Rock.** *At the Buttes, 2000 Westcourt Way, Tempe.* ☎ *602/225-9000. Reservations recommended. Main courses $16–$26 at dinner, $25 Sun brunch. AE, CB, DC, DISC, MC, V. Mon–Thurs 5–10pm, Fri–Sat 5–11pm, Sun 10am–2pm (brunch) and 5–10pm. NEW AMERICAN/SOUTHWESTERN.* In addition to the stunning view (sunsets are packed), this resort restaurant serves up some standout creative cuisine such as blue crab cakes with smoked chile cream. Sauces on the entree menu offer a good range of mellow as well as bold flavors, so even those who aren't chile fanatics can enjoy dining here.

**✪ Vincent Guerithault on Camelback.** *3930 E. Camelback Rd.* ☎ *602/224-0225. Reservations highly recommended. Main courses $6–$10 at lunch, $15–$22 at* *dinner. AE, DC, MC, V. Mon–Fri 11:30am–2:30pm and 6–10:30pm, Sat 6–10:30pm, Sun 6–10pm. Closed Sun from after Mother's Day to the end of Oct. SOUTHWESTERN.* Local restaurant celebrity Vincent Guerithault serves Southwestern cuisine in an intimate, unpretentious French country atmosphere. Grilled meats and seafoods are his specialty and might come accompanied by an ancho-chili and honey glaze or by habañero pasta. The lunch menu is basically the same as at dinner, with nearly all items under $10.

**Vintage Market.** *24th St. and Camelback Rd. (Biltmore Fashion Park).* ☎ *602/ 955-4444. Reservations not necessary. Salads/sandwiches $4–$6. AE, DC, MC, V. Mon–Wed 10am–8pm, Thurs–Sat 10am–10pm, Sun 11am–6pm. UPSCALE DELI.* It's not likely that you could get the equivalent of a grilled vegetable tart with red-pepper coulis or a Southwest grilled chicken sandwich anywhere else in this neighborhood for such a reasonable price. In the wine bar, you can choose from a couple of dozen vintages, some of them local, by the glass.

✪ **Windows on the Green.** *At The Phoenician, 6000 E. Camelback Rd., Scottsdale.* ☎ *602/423-2530. Reservations recommended. Main courses $18–$25; lunch/ brunch $7–$15. AE, CB, DC, DISC, EC, JCB, MC, V. Tues–Fri 11am–3pm and 6–10pm, Sat–Sun 10am–3pm (brunch) and 6–10pm. SOUTHWESTERN.* This restaurant is slightly more casual than its sister, Mary Elaine's (see above), but no less elegant. Using ingredients native to the region, such as jicama, nopales (cactus), and cilantro, the kitchen produces such pleasures as lump crabmeat and black truffle tamale, tenderloin of beef with wild huckleberry sauce, and pan-roasted dorado with smoked tomato-roasted chile vinaigrette.

## PHOENIX AFTER DARK

For comprehensive nightlife listings, call the **Visitor Information Hotline** (☎ 602/ 252-5588), or scan the weekly *Phoenix New Times,* or the Friday Weekend section and the Sunday Arts Plus section of the *Arizona Republic.* Tickets to many concerts, theater performances, and sporting events are available through **Ticketmaster** (☎ 602/ 784-4444) and at all **Dillard's** department store box offices (☎ 800/638-4253 or 602/ 678-2222).

**THE PERFORMING ARTS** The **Herberger Theater Center,** 222 E. Monroe St. (☎ 602/252-8497), has two Broadway-style theaters that host productions by the **Actors Theatre of Phoenix (ATP)** (☎ 602/253-6701 or 602/252-8497), featuring lesser-known works, and the **Arizona Theatre Company (ATC)** (☎ 602/256-6899 or 602/ 252-8497), tending toward big productions. The **Valley Broadway Series** (☎ 602/ 965-3434 or 602/678-2222), held at the Gammage Auditorium in Tempe, focuses mostly on Broadway comedies and musicals.

The **Phoenix Symphony** (☎ 800/776-9080 or 602/264-6363), the Southwest's leading symphony orchestra, performs at the Phoenix Symphony Hall, while the **Scottsdale Symphony Orchestra** (☎ 602/945-8071) performs at the Scottsdale Center for the Arts. Opera buffs should check out the **Arizona Opera Company** (☎ 602/266-7464). **Ballet Arizona** (☎ 602/381-1096) performs at the Phoenix Symphony Hall and the Herberger Theater Center. The contemporary **Center Dance Ensemble** (☎ 602/482-6410) performs at the Herberger Theater and Scottsdale Center for the Arts. The **Scottsdale Center for the Arts,** 7380 E. Second St. (☎ 602/ 994-2787), hosts a wide variety of performances ranging from alternative dance to classical music.

For everything from barbershop quartets to touring Broadway plays, check the 3,000-seat Frank Lloyd Wright–designed **Grady Gammage Memorial Auditorium,** at Mill Avenue and Apache Boulevard on the Arizona State University campus in Tempe (☎ 602/965-3434). The city's top outdoor venue is the **Blockbuster Desert Sky**

**Pavilion** (☎ 602/254-7200), located half a mile north of I-10 between 79th Avenue and 83rd Avenue, open year-round.

**Westworld of Scottsdale,** 16601 N. Pima Rd., Scottsdale (☎ 800/488-4887 or 602/483-8800), provides such events as rodeos, polo matches, and Arabian horse shows. But when big-name music stars come to town, they often perform at the **America West Arena,** 201 E. Jefferson St. (☎ 602/379-7800), known locally as the Purple Palace.

**THE CLUB & BAR SCENE**     Most of the area's bars and clubs are spread out across the valley. **Phoenix Live!,** downtown at Arizona Center, 455 N. Third Ave. (☎ 602/252-2112), has four different clubs side-by-side in a modern shopping mall. Another area to wander until you hear your favorite type of music is **Mill Avenue** in Tempe. For an upscale crowd in more sophisticated surroundings, head for **Scottsdale's Resort Row** and **Old Scottsdale.**

One Scottsdale favorite is **Handlebar-J,** 7116 E. Becher Lane, Scottsdale (☎ 602/948-0110), where you'll hear live git-down two-steppin' music and can even get free dance lessons Wednesday and Thursday. The **Rockin' Horse,** 7000 E. Indian School Rd., Scottsdale (☎ 602/949-0992), mixes its country with blues, jazz, swing, and world music, but country still rules at **Toolie's Country Saloon and Dance Hall,** 4231 W. Thomas Rd., at SE 43rd Avenue (☎ 602/272-3100). At **Gecko's,** 7316 E. Stetson Dr., Scottsdale (☎ 602/947-1000), there is a large dance floor and state-of-the-art lighting and staging to accommodate concerts by national acts; otherwise the emphasis is on jazz and reggae.

For an elegant evening of dining and live jazz, **Timothy's,** 6335 N. 16th St. (☎ 602/277-7634), is hard to beat. If it's a Hard Rock Cafe imitation you're looking for, try **Studebakers,** 10345 N. Scottsdale Rd. (at Shea Blvd.), Scottsdale (☎ 602/443-3222 or 602/443-0303). This spot attracts singles and couples 25–50 years old; disc jockeys play music from 1950s to contemporary, and there's a free happy-hour buffet on weekdays from 5 to 8pm. **The Works,** 7223 E. Second St., Scottsdale (☎ 602/946-4141), in a cavernous neo-industrial building, is one of the most popular dance clubs in the valley, throbbing with the latest techno-industrial and alternative vibes. But if you're a beer drinker, your club is **Hops! Bistro & Brewery,** 7000 E. Camelback Rd., Scottsdale (☎ 602/945-4677), an upscale brew pub that includes a patio with live acoustic music, a bar, a separate sports-bar area, and a dining room serving creative contemporary American cuisine. There are other Hops! at the Biltmore Fashion Park, at 2584 E. Camelback Rd. (☎ 602/468-0500), and 8668 E. Shea Blvd., Scottsdale (☎ 602/998-7777).

## A DAY TRIP ON THE APACHE TRAIL

In addition to the driving tour of Phoenix, Prescott, and Sedona described earlier in this chapter, you'll find quite a bit of desert history an hour's drive east of Phoenix along the often winding, gravel roads of the Apache Trail.

Head east on U.S. 60 to the town of Apache Junction and then north on Ariz. 88 to **Goldfield ghost town,** 4650 N. Mammoth Mine Rd. (☎ 602/983-0333), a reconstructed 1890s gold-mining town. Though it's a bit of a tourist trap, it's also home to the **Superstition Mountain/Lost Dutchman Museum** (☎ 602/983-4888) with interesting exhibits about the history of the area.

Not far from Goldfield is **Lost Dutchman State Park** (☎ 602/982-4485), where you can hike into the rugged Superstition Mountains and see what the region's gold-seekers were up against. Park admission is $3 per vehicle. If you're game to see the Superstitions from horseback, contact **Superstition Riding Stables,** 2151 N. Warner Rd., Apache Junction (☎ 800/984-5488 or 602/982-6353). They offer rides, riding lessons, overnight pack trips, picnics, and hayrides. You can also try **OK Corral Horse Rentals** (☎ 602/982-4040), which is close to Goldfield ghost town.

Continuing northeast, you'll next come to **Canyon Lake,** the first of three reservoirs on the Salt River. You can go for a swim or take a cruise on the *Dolly* steamboat (☎ 602/827-9144), a reproduction paddlewheeler. You can also rent powerboats at the Canyon Lake Marina. If you're hungry, grab a bite at the Lakeside Restaurant, which overlooks the marina. However, for a taste of the Old West, hold out for **Tortilla Flat** (☎ 602/984-1776), an old stagecoach stop that has a restaurant, saloon, and general store. The prickly pear ice cream served here is worth a try (guaranteed no spines).

A few miles past Tortilla Flat, the pavement ends and the truly spectacular desert scenery—rocky ridges, arroyos, canyons, and cacti—begins. Next you'll come to **Apache Lake,** which is in a deep canyon flanked by colorful cliffs and rugged rock formations. This lake also has a marina, as well as a campground, motel, restaurant, and general store.

Shortly before reaching pavement again you'll come to the **Theodore Roosevelt Dam,** the largest masonry dam in the world. From there, continuing on Ariz. 88, you'll next come to **Tonto National Monument** (☎ 520/467-2241), which preserves the southernmost cliff dwellings in Arizona. These pueblos were built between 1100 and 1400 by the Salado people, and are some of their few remaining traces. The upper ruins are only open Nov–Apr, Sat–Sun, by reservation. The park is open daily from 8am to 5pm.

Continuing on Ariz. 88 will bring you to the copper-mining town of **Globe.** The mines here are open pits, and though you can't see the mines themselves, the tailings can be seen piled high all around the town. In Globe, be sure to visit **Besh-Ba-Gowah Archaeological Park** (☎ 520/425-0320), on the eastern outskirts of town (open daily 9am–5pm; admission $2). At the Salado Indian pueblo site here, you'll see some of the most fascinating ruins in the state. To reach Besh-Ba-Gowah, head out of Globe on South Broad Street to Jesse Hayes Road.

From Globe, head east on U.S. 60. On the west side of Superior, you'll come to **Boyce Thompson Southwestern Arboretum** (☎ 520/689-2811), dedicated to researching and propagating desert plants. At **Don Donnelly Stables,** 6010 S. Kings Ranch Rd. (☎ 602/982-7822), in the community of Gold Canyon, you can go horseback riding or arrange overnight rides, cookouts, and hayrides.

If after a long day on the road you're looking for a good place to eat, stop in at **Gold Canyon Ranch** (☎ 602/982-9090), which has a good, though expensive, dining room serving creative Southwestern cuisine. There's also a bar and grill serving basic burgers and sandwiches.

You can also finish this trip with an evening at the **Barleen Family Country Music Dinner Theatre,** 2275 Old West Hwy., Apache Junction (☎ 602/982-7991), which serves up Branson-style country music and comedy for the whole family.

If you'd rather leave the driving to someone else, you can take a tour of this area with **Apache Trail Tours** (☎ 602/982-7661), which offers a variety of four-wheel-drive tours as well as overnight hiking trips into the Superstition Mountains.

# 9 Tucson

Melding Hispanic, Anglo, and Native American roots, Tucson has become a city confident in its style. Although the city is undergoing the same sort of sprawl as Phoenix, advocates for controlled growth are fighting hard to preserve both Tucson's special charcter and its surrounding desert environment. It's the city's natural surroundings that make it unique. Four mountain ranges ring the city, and in those mountains and their

# Tucson

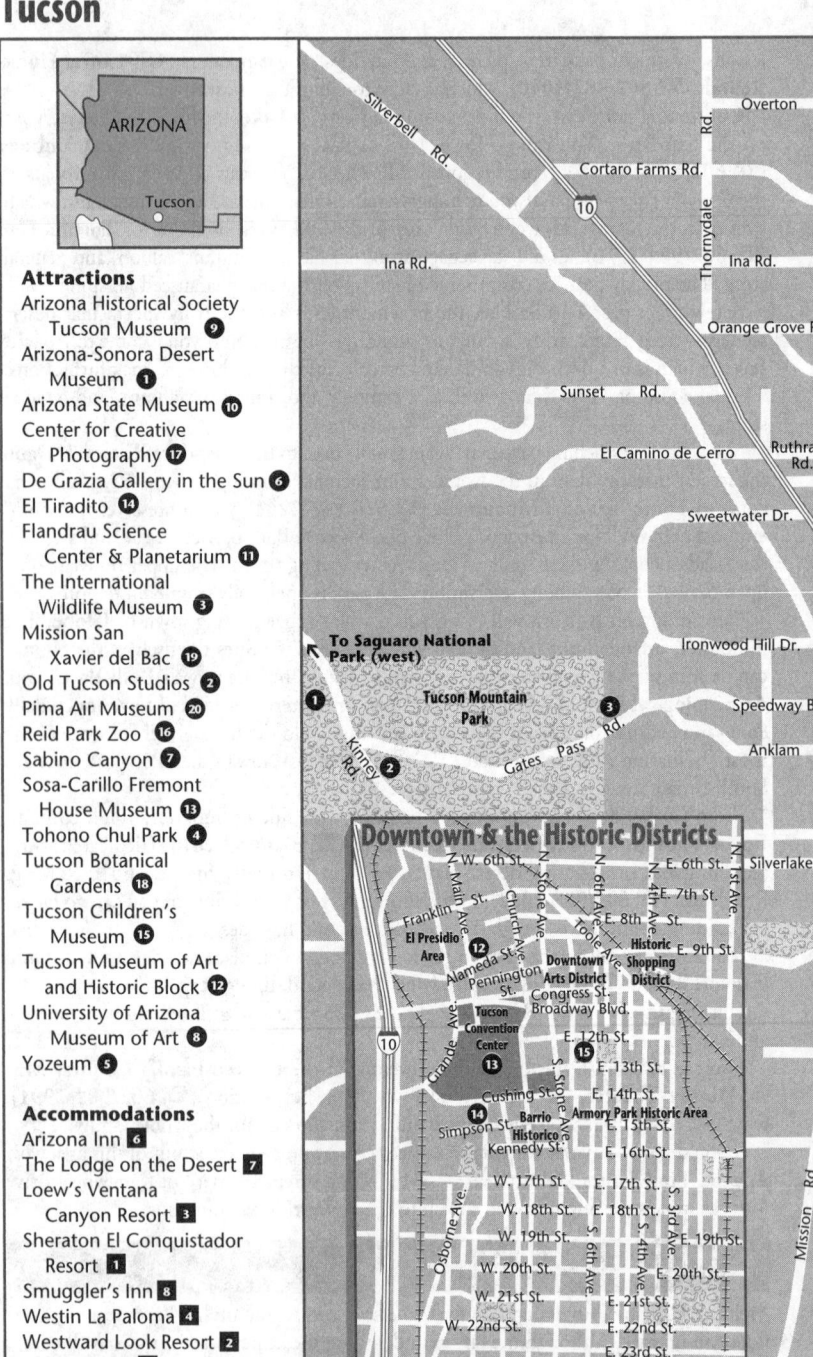

**Attractions**
Arizona Historical Society Tucson Museum **9**
Arizona-Sonora Desert Museum **1**
Arizona State Museum **10**
Center for Creative Photography **17**
De Grazia Gallery in the Sun **6**
El Tiradito **14**
Flandrau Science Center & Planetarium **11**
The International Wildlife Museum **3**
Mission San Xavier del Bac **19**
Old Tucson Studios **2**
Pima Air Museum **20**
Reid Park Zoo **16**
Sabino Canyon **7**
Sosa-Carillo Fremont House Museum **13**
Tohono Chul Park **4**
Tucson Botanical Gardens **18**
Tucson Children's Museum **15**
Tucson Museum of Art and Historic Block **12**
University of Arizona Museum of Art **8**
Yozeum **5**

**Accommodations**
Arizona Inn **6**
The Lodge on the Desert **7**
Loew's Ventana Canyon Resort **3**
Sheraton El Conquistador Resort **1**
Smuggler's Inn **8**
Westin La Paloma **4**
Westward Look Resort **2**
Windmill Inn **5**

1-1243

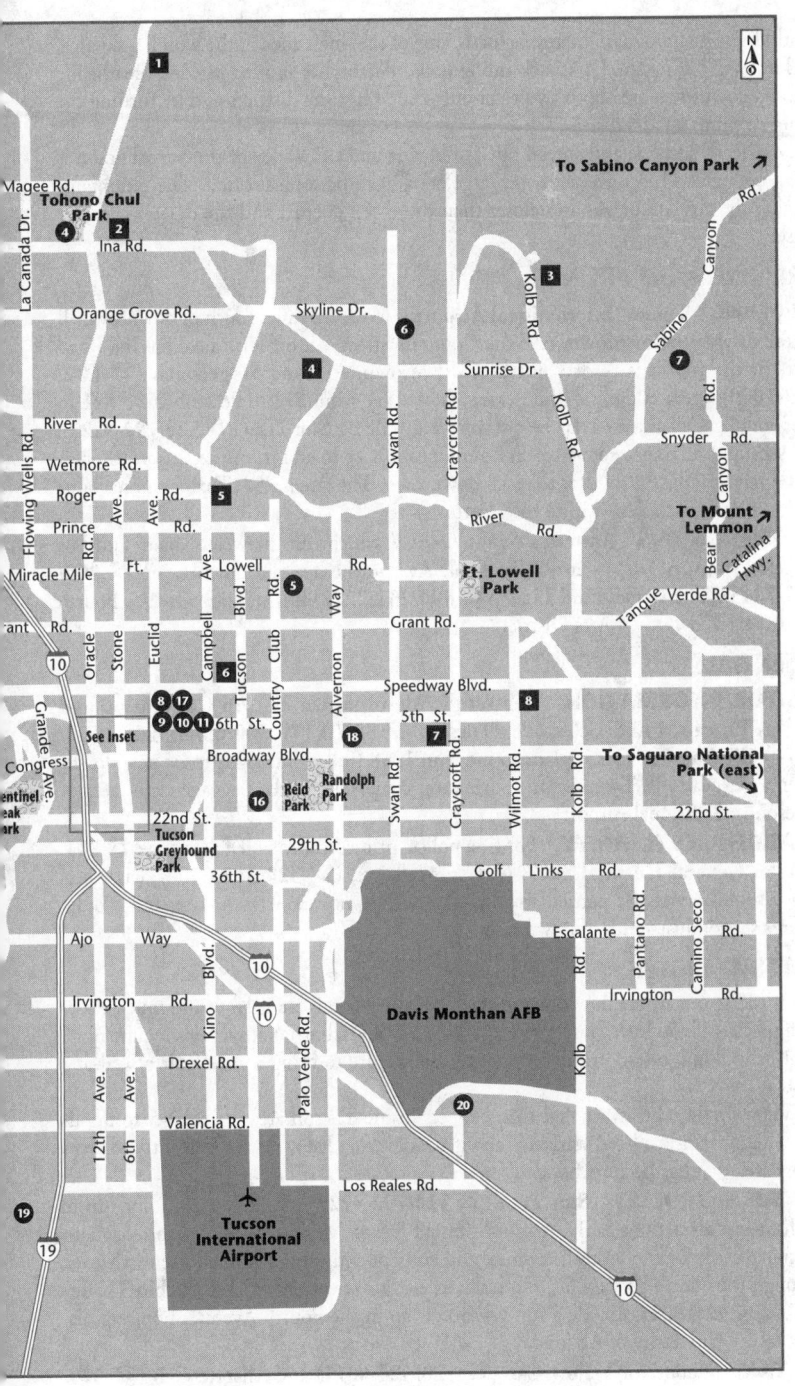

foothills are giant saguaro cactus, an oasis, one of the finest zoos in the world, a ski area, and miles of hiking and horseback-riding trails. Tucson has also managed to breathe life into its downtown area both by preserving several historic districts and by turning the inner city into an arts district.

Not nearly as large and spread out as Phoenix and the Valley of the Sun, Tucson is small enough to be convenient, yet large enough to be sophisticated. The mountains ringing the city are bigger and closer than those of Phoenix, and the desert is equally close.

## ARRIVING & DEPARTING

**BY PLANE**　**Tucson International Airport** is located 6 miles south of downtown. If you're driving to downtown, take the Congress Street exit off I-10; take the Ina Road exit for the foothills resorts north of downtown. **Arizona Stagecoach** (☎ 602/889-1000) operates daily 24-hour vans; fares range from $12 to downtown to $21 to the foothills. Call at least a day before your return flight. **Sun Tran** (☎ 520/792-9222), the local public transit, operates an hourly bus service to and from the airport, though you'll have to make a transfer to reach downtown. The fare is 75¢. Taxi fares are about $15 to downtown, $28–$38 to the resorts.

**BY TRAIN & BUS**　Amtrak's *Sunset Limited,* which runs between Miami and Los Angeles, stops in Tucson at 400 E. Toole Ave. in the heart of downtown (☎ 800/872-7245). The **Greyhound Lines** (☎ 800/231-2222) bus station is at 2 S. Fourth Ave. in the Downtown Arts District.

## ESSENTIALS

**VISITOR INFORMATION**　Contact the **Metropolitan Tucson Convention and Visitor Bureau,** 130 S. Scott Ave., Tucson, AZ 85701 (☎ 800/638-8350 or 520/624-1817), but note that it plans to move in 1998 (follow the signs to its new downtown area location). Two visitor information centers are in the baggage-claim area of Tucson International Airport.

**EMERGENCIES & SAFETY**　For fire, police, or medical emergency, phone ☎ 911. **Tucson General Hospital,** 3838 N. Campbell Ave. (☎ 520/318-6300), has emergency room service. Be particularly alert in the Downtown Arts District, and avoid a poorer section just south of downtown.

## GETTING AROUND

Many old streets in the downtown historic neighborhoods are narrow and much easier to appreciate if you leave your car in a parking lot. Several major attractions require quite a bit of walking, often on uneven footing, so be sure to bring a good pair of walking shoes.

When driving, be aware that many streets in the Tucson area are subject to flooding when it rains, so heed warnings about possible flooded areas and don't try to cross a low area that has become flooded.

**BY BUS & TROLLEY**　**Sun Tran** (☎ 520/792-9222) public buses do not run to such tourist attractions as the Arizona–Sonora Desert Museum, Old Tucson, Saguaro National Park, or the foothills resorts, and consequently are of limited use to visitors. Though they don't go very far, the restored electric streetcars of **Old Pueblo Trolley** (☎ 520/792-1802) provide a fun way to get from the Fourth Avenue shopping district to the University of Arizona.

**BY TAXI**　Phone for **Yellow Cab** (☎ 520/624-6611) and **Allstate Cab** (☎ 520/798-1111). Fares start at $2 and increase by $1.35 per mile.

## WHAT TO SEE & DO

**ESCORTED TOURS**   To get a thorough overview of Tucson, you can take a 6½-hour tour with **Old Pueblo Tours** (☎ 520/795-7448). The tour includes visits to a mountain, the downtown historic districts, and Mission San Xavier del Bac. To learn more about the history of Tucson, see if you can attach yourself to a group on one of Ken Scoville's **Old Pueblo Walking Tours** of the downtown area from November to May (☎ 520/323-9290). He has a wealth of knowledge about the city and can make the historic districts come alive. The **Center for Desert Archaeology** (☎ 520/881-2244), a nonprofit educational and research organization, can take you to view petroglyphs near Tucson and ruins of the Hohokam people in Catalina State Park. **High Desert Convoys** (☎ 800/93-TOURS or 520/323-3386) will take you into the wilds for a taste of pioneer history. They offer trips to Buenos Aires National Wildlife Refuge, to a ghost town, to some remote petroglyphs, and on a hike to a cave.

**✪ SAGUARO NATIONAL PARK**   Since 1933 the two sections of Saguaro National Park have protected the saguaro cactus, quintessential symbol of the American desert, as well as coyotes, foxes, squirrels, javelinas, and all the other inhabitants of this section of the Sonoran Desert. The west section is the more popular because of its proximity to both the Arizona–Sonora Desert Museum and Old Tucson Studios (see below). In the area near the Red Hills Information Center is a water hole that attracts wild animals, which you're most likely to see at dawn, dusk, or at night. The east section of the park contains an older area of forest at the foot of the Rincon Mountains. This section is popular with hikers because most of it has no roads. There's also a visitor center here. Both sections have loop roads, nature trails, hiking trails, and picnic grounds.

For more information, contact the east section (☎ 520/733-5100) or the west section (☎ 520/733-5153). Admission to the east section is $4 per car (free to west section). Park open daily 7am–sunset; visitor centers, daily 8:30am–5pm. To reach the west section, take Speedway Boulevard west from downtown Tucson (it becomes Gates Pass Boulevard); to reach the east section, take Speedway Boulevard east, then head south on Freeman Road to Old Spanish Trail.

**OTHER ATTRACTIONS**   In addition to the museums and historical buildings listed below, downtown Tucson has a couple of historic neighborhoods. Among the more interesting buildings are the restored homes maintained by the **Tucson Museum of Art,** 140 N. Main Ave. (☎ 520/624-2333), on the block surrounding the museum. These houses date from between 1850 and 1907 and are all built on the former site of the Tucson presidio. **La Casa Cordova,** the oldest and one of the city's earliest, serves as a Mexican Heritage Museum. The **Leonardo Romero House** is now part of the museum's art school; the **Stevens House** is home to Janos, one of the best restaurants in Tucson; and the **Fish House** contains the museum's western art collection. A map and descriptive brochures about the houses are available at the art museum's front desk.

**Arizona Historical Society Tucson Museum.** *949 E. Second St.* ☎ *520/628-5774. Admission free or by donation. Mon–Sat 10am–4pm, Sun noon–4pm. Closed major holidays.* This is a repository of all things Arizonan: a full-scale reproduction of an underground mine tunnel, a miner's tent, a blacksmith's shop, silver-studded saddles of Spanish ranchers, steam locomotives that opened Arizona to the world, "horseless carriages" that revolutionized life in the Southwest, and much more. The museum has a research library and a good gift shop.

**✪ Arizona–Sonora Desert Museum.** *2021 N. Kinney Rd.* ☎ *520/883-2702 or 502/883-1380. Admission $8.95 adults, $1.75 children 6–12, free for children 5 and under. Oct–Feb, daily 8:30am–5pm. Mar–Sept, daily 7:30am–6pm. From downtown*

*Tucson, go west on Speedway Blvd., which becomes Gates Pass Rd., and follow the signs.* Don't be fooled by the name, for this is one of the best zoos in the country. The full spectrum of Sonoran Desert life—from plants to insects to fish to reptiles to mammals—is on display here in natural settings: black bears, mountain lions, beavers, otters, frogs, fish, tarantulas, scorpions, prairie dogs, and javelinas (peccaries). There's also a simulated cave with exhibits on prehistoric desert life and aviaries holding hummingbirds and many other species. Guides explain everything from the life cycle of the saguaro cactus to the feeding habits of the tarantula. A restaurant serves excellent food and is well worth a stop.

**Center for Creative Photography.** *East of the corner of Park Ave. and Speedway Blvd.* ☎ *520/621-7968. Admission free. Mon–Fri 11am–5pm, Sun noon–5pm.* You can request to see an original Ansel Adams print and an Edward Weston or a Richard Avedon at this center, conceived by Adams. Negatives, study prints, and master prints by the greatest photographers make it one of the best and largest collections in the world. It's also a research facility that preserves complete photographic archives, including that of Adams. You're limited to two photographers per visit, so make an appointment and decide beforehand whose works you'd like to see.

**Flandrau Science Center and Planetarium.** *University of Arizona campus, Cherry Ave. and University Blvd.* ☎ *520/621-STAR or 520/621-4515. Admission to exhibits, $2 adults, $1 children; free on Wed. Telescope viewing free. Theater, $3–$8. Mon–Fri 9am–5pm, Sat–Sun 1–5pm; Wed–Thurs 7–9pm, Fri–Sat 7pm–midnight. Closed major holidays.* The planetarium offers programs on the stars as well as very popular laser shows set to music. Exhibit halls contain a mineral collection and hands-on science exhibits for people of all ages. On clear nights, you can gaze through the 16-inch telescope.

**✪ Mission San Xavier del Bac.** *1950 W. San Xavier Rd.* ☎ *520/294-2624. Admission free. Daily 9am–6pm. Take I-19 south about 9 miles to the Valencia Rd. exit (exit 92) and follow the signs.* Called the "White Dove of the Desert" and considered the finest example of mission architecture in the country, the church was built between 1783 and 1797 of adobe brick. It incorporates Moorish, Byzantine, and Mexican Renaissance styles. Faded murals cover the walls, and a statue of St. Francis Xavier is to the left of the ornate main altar. On a small hill just east of the church is a replica of the famous grotto in Lourdes, France.

**Old Tucson Studios.** *201 S. Kinney Rd.* ☎ *520/883-0100. Admission $14.95 adults, $9.45 children 4–11, free for children 3 and under. Daily 9am–9pm. Closed Thanksgiving and Christmas. Take Speedway Blvd. west, continuing in the same direction when it becomes Gates Pass Blvd., and turn left on South Kinney Rd.* This western town was built as the set for the 1939 movie *Arizona* and has been used in innumerable films. It's more than just a movie set; it's a Wild West theme park with diverse family-oriented activities and staged entertainment. There are also train rides, stagecoach rides, a storyteller's theater, restaurants, and circus acts.

**✪ Pima Air Museum.** *6000 E. Valencia Rd.* ☎ *520/574-9658 or 520/574-0646. Admission $6 adults, $5 seniors and military, $3 ages 10–17, free for children under 10. Daily 9am–5pm. Closed Christmas. Take the Valencia Rd. exit from I-10 and then drive east 2 miles to the museum entrance.* Located just south of Davis Monthan Air Force Base, the museum has one of the largest collections of historic aircraft in the world, covering the evolution of American aviation from replicas of the Wright brothers' 1903 Wright Flyer to the X-15.

**Sabino Canyon.** *5900 N. Sabino Canyon Rd.* ☎ *520/749-2861. Admission free. Sabino Canyon tram ride, $5 adults, $2 children 3–12, free for children 2 and under. Bear Canyon tram ride, $3 adults, $1.25 children 3–12, free for children 2 and under. Park: daily, dawn–dusk. Sabino Canyon tram rides: daily 9am–4:30pm; Bear Canyon tram rides:*

*daily 9am–4pm (both trams more limited in summer). Take Grant Rd. east to Tanque Verde Rd., continuing east; at Sabino Canyon Rd., turn north and watch for the sign.* In the Santa Catalina Mountains of Coronado National Forest, Sabino Canyon is a desert oasis that has attracted people and animals for thousands of years. These days it offers a chance to splash and swim in waterfalls and pools. There's also a narrated tram ride through the lower canyon. Hikers head to the picturesque Seven Falls at the end of a 2.2-mile hiking trail. Bring water.

✪ **Tucson Botanical Gardens.** *2150 N. Alvernon Way.* ☎ *520/326-9686. Admission $3 adults, $2 seniors, free for children under 12. Daily 8:30am–4:30pm. Closed July 4, Thanksgiving, Dec 24–25, Jan 1.* On the 5¹/₂-acre grounds are several small gardens, including a cactus garden, that have both educational and visual appeal. If you live in the desert, you'll benefit from learning how to harvest rainfall for the desert garden and how to design a water-conserving landscape. There's a cafe that serves lunch.

**Tucson Museum of Art and Historic Block.** *140 N. Main Ave.* ☎ *520/624-2333. Admission $2 adults, $1 students and seniors, free for children 12 and under; free on Tues. Mon–Sat 10am–4pm, Sun noon–4pm. Closed Mon in June, July, and Aug and all national holidays.* The museum is in a large modern building surrounded by historic adobes open to the public. A spacious plaza is frequently used to display sculptures. There is an excellent collection of pre-Colombian art and a large collection of western art.

**University of Arizona Museum of Art.** *Park Ave. and Speedway Blvd.* ☎ *520/621-7567. Admission free. Late Aug to mid-May, Mon–Fri 9am–5pm, Sun noon–4pm. Mid-May to late Aug, Mon–Fri 10am–3:30pm, Sun noon–4pm. Closed major holidays.* The collection here is more extensive and diverse than the Tucson Museum of Art and includes European and American works from the Renaissance to the 20th century. Notable are the *Retable of Ciudad Rodrigo,* paintings from 15th-century Spain, and more than 60 clay and plaster models and sketches by Jacques Lipchitz.

**BEST BETS FOR KIDS**   Located in the old Carnegie Library in downtown, the **Tucson Children's Museum,** 200 S. Sixth Ave. (☎ 520/792-9985), is filled with hands-on activities and exhibits that are fun and educational. Although small and overshadowed by its neighbor, the Arizona–Sonora Desert Museum, **Reid Park Zoo,** Lake Shore Lane and 22nd St., between Country Club Road and Alvernon Way (☎ 520/791-4022), is an important breeding center for several endangered species including giant anteaters, white rhinoceroses, tigers, ruffed lemurs, and zebras.

**SPORTS**   The **Colorado Rockies** (☎ 520/327-9467) pitch spring baseball training camp Feb–Mar at Hi Corbett Field, 900 S. Randolph Way, in Reid Park, which is also home to the **Tucson Toros** (☎ 520/325-2621), the Houston Astros AAA team in the Pacific Coast League. The Toros's season runs Apr–Aug.

In mid-March, women golfers compete for big prizes at the **Ping/Welch's LPGA Championship** (☎ 520/791-5742), at the Randolph North Golf Course. The **Tucson Chrysler Classic** (☎ 800/882-7660), Tucson's main PGA tournament, is held in mid-February at the Omni Tucson National Golf Resort and Spa.

The **CIGNA Beau Bridges Celebrity Tennis Classic** (☎ 520/623-6165) takes place at the Randolph Tennis Center at Randolph Park in late April, when more than 40 celebrity tennis players take on local tennis players.

**SHOPPING**   In downtown Tucson, the **North Fourth Avenue historic shopping district,** on Fourth Avenue between Congress Street and Speedway Boulevard, has more than 100 shops, galleries, and restaurants. Through the underpass at the south end of Fourth Avenue is Congress Street, the heart of the **Downtown Arts District,** where you'll find numerous galleries specializing in contemporary art, avant-garde boutiques, and a few trendy eating establishments.

The **El Presidio Historic District** around the Tucson Museum of Art is the city's center for crafts shops. Here are Old Town Artisans and the Tucson Museum of Art museum shop. The **"Lost Barrio"** on the corner of Southwest Park Avenue and 12th Street is a good place to look for Mexican imports and Southwest-style home furnishings at good prices.

You'll find concentrations of antiques shops along **Speedway Boulevard** between Swan and Craycroft roads and along **Grand Road** between Tucson Boulevard and Alvernon Way.

## ACCOMMODATIONS

Tucson is rapidly becoming known as a resort destination, with resorts that boast more spectacular settings than those in Phoenix and Scottsdale. Business and budget travelers are well served with downtown all-suite and conference hotels, and budget chain motels along I-10 and near the airport.

Room rates May–October are roughly half what they are in winter at the more expensive hotels and resorts; May and September are good times to visit. Ask about special packages, weekend rates, various discounts, and free accommodations for children.

✪ **Arizona Inn.** *2200 E. Elm St., Tucson, AZ 85719.* ☎ *800/933-1093 or 520/325-1541. Fax 520/881-5830. 66 rms, 15 suites, 2 houses. Mid-Jan–late May, $165–$195 double; from $210 suite. Late May–mid-Sept, $82–$100 double; from $110 suite. Mid-Sept–mid-Dec, $115–$156 double; from $178 suite. Mid-Dec–mid-Jan $134–$175 double; from $196 suite. AE, MC, V.* Opened in 1930, this is Tucson's most classically elegant lodging. Although the bathrooms are small and have their original fixtures, the guest rooms are often very spacious, and many have furniture made by disabled World War I veterans. Some also have fireplaces. Facilities include a casually elegant dining room, outdoor pool, two tennis courts, and a croquet court.

✪ **Lodge on the Desert.** *306 N. Alvernon Way (P.O. Box 42500), Tucson, AZ 85733.* ☎ *800/456-5634 or 520/325-3366. Fax 520/327-5834. 37 rms. Nov–May, $94–$180 double. June–Oct, $58–$137 double. Rates include continental breakfast. AE, CB, DC, DISC, MC, V.* This older, family-owned lodge's greatest draw is its old-world charm and hacienda styling, where manicured lawns and flower gardens offer a relaxing retreat. Several guest rooms are housed in buildings made of adobe blocks, and some have beamed ceilings or fireplaces. The lodge has a dining room, pool with mountain view, shuffleboard court, table tennis, croquet court, and library.

✪ **Loews Ventana Canyon Resort.** *7000 N. Resort Dr., Tucson, AZ 85715.* ☎ *800/234-5117 or 520/299-2020. Fax 520/299-6832. 372 rms, 26 suites. Jan 1–May 25, $295–$375 double; $700–$2,000 suite. May 26–Sept 8, $85–$135 double; $200–$1,100 suite. Sept 9–Dec 31, $225–$305 double; $550–$1,000 suite. AE, CB, DC, DISC, ER, JCB, MC, V.* The Santa Catalina Mountains provide a spectacular setting for the genteel comforts, golf courses, tennis courts, and other facilities of this haven of luxury. The guest rooms are designed to impress. The Ventana Room is one of Tucson's finest restaurants (see "Dining," below). There are also two more eateries, bars, a free shopping shuttle, bike rentals, two pools with mountain views, whirlpools, a health spa, and a beauty salon.

**Omni Tucson National Golf Resort and Spa.** *2727 W. Club Dr. (off Magee Rd.), Tucson, AZ 85742.* ☎ *800/528-4856 or 520/297-2271. Fax 520/297-7544. 167 rms. Jan–May, $275–$350 double. May–Sept, $150–$225 double. Sept–Jan, $165–$240 double. AE, CB, DC, MC, V.* Golf and a full-service health spa make for some serious stress reduction here. Guest rooms are the best and most luxurious in Tucson. A clublike gourmet dining room is among the dining choices. Facilities include a 27-hole golf course, four lighted tennis courts, two pools, basketball and volleyball courts, a pro shop, and a full-service health spa.

**Sheraton El Conquistador Resort and Country Club.** *10000 N. Oracle Rd., Tucson, AZ 85737.* ☎ *800/325-7832 or 520/544-5000. Fax 520/544-1228. 428 rms, 100 suites. Jan 10–Apr 30, $230–$315 double; $265–$1,200 suite. May 1–May 31, $125–$155 double; $160–$1,200 suite. June 1–Sept 10, $85–$105 double; $120–$600 suite. Sept 11–Jan 9, $160–$200 double; $195–$1,200 suite. AE, CB, DC, DISC, ER, JCB, MC, V.* A Santa Catalina Mountains backdrop gives this golf resort a spectacular setting. The majority of the Southwestern-influenced guest rooms fringe a central court-yard with a large pool, but those in the separate casitas are quieter and have their own pool. Three golf courses are the big draw, plus 31 tennis courts, racquetball courts, and two health clubs. Restaurants serve Southwestern and Mexican cuisine.

**Smuggler's Inn.** *6350 E. Speedway Blvd. (at Wilmot), Tucson, AZ 85710.* ☎ *800/ 525-8852 or 520/296-3292. Fax 520/722-3713. 121 rms, 28 suites. Jan–May, $109– $119 double; $125–$135 suite. May–Sept, $56–$63 double; $96 suite. Sept–Dec, $66– $73 double; $96 suite. AE, CB, DC, DISC, MC, V.* The Smuggler's Inn is a very com-fortable and economically priced hotel built around an attractive garden and pond. The guest rooms are spacious and all have modern furnishings and a balcony or patio. The inn has a restaurant, pool, whirlpool, and putting green.

**Westin La Paloma.** *3800 E. Sunrise Dr., Tucson, AZ 85718.* ☎ *800/876-3683 or 520/742-6000. Fax 520/577-5878. 487 rms, 41 suites. Early Jan–late May, $280– $360 double; from $475 suite. Late May–early Sept, $89–$200 double; from $300 suite. Early Sept–early Jan, $220–$300 double; $425 suite. AE, CB, DC, DISC, ER, JCB, MC, V.* Both this mission Revival resort and its surrounding golf course offer great views of the city and the Santa Catalinas. The associated country club keeps active guests busy with tennis and exercise facilities. Guest rooms in 27 low-rise buildings sport desert hues and western art. Facilities include restaurants, a pool with slide and swim-up bar, children's lounge, shopping arcade, beauty salon offering spa services, and health club.

**Westward Look Resort.** *245 E. Ina Rd., Tucson, AZ 85704.* ☎ *800/722-2500 or 520/297-1151. Fax 520/297-9023. 244 rms, 8 suites. Mid-Jan to mid-Apr, $179–$269 double; $508 suite. Mid-Apr to early June, $109–$189 double; $328 suite. Early June to early Sept, $89–$139 double; $188 suite. Early Sept to mid-Jan, $119–$189 double; $348 suite. AE, CB, DC, DISC, ER, JCB, MC, V.* Opened in 1929 as a dude ranch, this is now one of Tucson's most reasonably priced foothill resorts. There's no golf course, but guests enjoy tennis, a fitness center, jogging trails, three pools, and a health spa. Many of the large guest rooms have exposed-beam ceilings and great views of the city. A res-taurant and bar are on the premises.

**Windmill Inn at St. Philip's Plaza.** *4250 N. Campbell Ave., Tucson, AZ 85718.* ☎ *800/547-4747 or 520/577-0007. Fax 520/577-0045. 122 suites. Jan 1–Apr 20, $110–$145 suite for two. Apr 21–May 31 and Sept 15–Oct 31, $89–$109 suite for two, Nov–Dec $110–$145. June 1–Sept 15, $69 suite for two. Rates include continental break-fast. AE, DC, DISC, MC, V.* Conveniently located in St. Philip's Plaza, which has a couple of great restaurants and an array of upscale shops, this hotel offers spacious suites with couches, work desks, two TVs, three telephones (one in the bathroom; local calls are free), wet bars, small refrigerators, and microwaves. The inn has a pool and whirl-pool.

**GUEST RANCHES**   Homesteaded in 1933 and converted to a dude ranch in 1936, the **Lazy K Bar Ranch,** 8401 N. Scenic Dr., Tucson, AZ 85743 (☎ **800/321-7018** or 520/744-3050; fax 520/744-7628), covers 160 acres adjacent to Saguaro National Park about 20 minutes from downtown. Activities include horseback riding, hayrides, lunch rides, cookouts, and square dances. There are also nature walks and talks and weekly excursions to the Arizona–Sonora Desert Museum.

Far and away the most luxurious guest ranch in Tucson, the **Tanque Verde Ranch,** 14301 E. Speedway Blvd., Tucson, AZ 85748 (☎ **800/234-DUDE** or 520/296-6275; fax 520/721-9426), was founded in 1860 and still has some of its original buildings. It also borders both Saguaro National Park and the Coronado National Forest. The guest rooms are spacious and comfortable, but don't expect a TV here—ranch policy encourages guests to participate, not watch CNN.

## DINING

A few years back Tucson's mayor declared the city the Mexican restaurant capital of the universe. But there are dozens of other restaurants serving everything from the finest French cuisine to Southwestern. In summer, be on the lookout for early-bird dinners and summer sampler plates.

✪ **Arizona Inn Dining Room.** *In the Arizona Inn, 2200 E. Elm St.* ☎ *520/ 325-1541. Reservations recommended. Main courses $5–$13 at lunch; $16–$23 at dinner. AE, MC, V. Mon–Sat 7–10am, 11:30am–2pm, and 6–10pm; Sun 7–10am, 11am– 2pm (brunch), and 6–10pm. SOUTHWESTERN.* The dining room of one of the state's first resorts is a consistently excellent restaurant with reasonable prices. It's a treat to dine on the terrace overlooking the garden and croquet lawn. The menu is not extensive, but every dish, such as mesquite-smoked quail with candied pecan and apple dressing, is perfectly prepared. A guitarist entertains on Friday and Saturday.

**Boccata.** *In River Center, 5605 E. River Rd.* ☎ *520/577-9309. Reservations recommended. Main courses $11–$26. AE, MC, V. Sun–Thurs 5:30–9pm, Fri–Sat 5–10pm. MEDITERRANEAN/NEW AMERICAN.* Large windows frame the panoramic view of Tucson from this casually elegant restaurant at the back of the River Center complex in the foothills. Marble floors, rich colors, and works of contemporary art add the finishing touches. You might find such temptations as crayfish cakes made with just a hint of Creole fire on Chef Steven Michael Braun's seasonally changing menus.

✪ **Café Poca Cosa.** *88 E. Broadway Blvd.* ☎ *520/622-6400. Reservations highly recommended. Main courses $7–$15. MC, V. Mon–Thurs 11am–9pm, Fri–Sat 11am– 10pm. MEXICAN.* Owner-chef Suzana Davila creates imaginative and unique Mexican fare. You never know what her offerings will be, but there is always something great to try. The courteous service staff will recite the menu for you in both Spanish and English. There's another (smaller) Café Poca Cosa downtown at 20 S. Scott St., open for breakfast and lunch Mon–Fri 7:30am–2:30pm.

**Daniel's Restaurant and Trattoria.** *In St. Philip's Plaza, 4340 N. Campbell Ave.* ☎ *520/742-3200. Reservations recommended. Main courses $18–$27. AE, DC, MC, V. Daily 5–10pm. NORTHERN ITALIAN.* The elegant, art deco–tinged atmosphere here translates as a good place for business meetings or a romantic setting for an evening out—but what's most outstanding is the contemporary northern Italian cuisine. The pastry chef has a creative flair with fruits and chocolates, so save room for dessert.

✪ **El Charro Café.** *311 N. Court Ave.* ☎ *520/622-1922. Reservations recommended for dinner. Main courses $4–$16. AE, DISC, MC, V. Sun–Thurs 11:30am–10pm, Fri–Sat 11:30am–11pm. MEXICAN.* Sun-dried beef is the main ingredient in carne seca, El Charro's well-known specialty, which you will rarely find on a Mexican menu outside Tucson. The cafe can be packed at lunch, so arrive early or late. Other El Charro branches are in the Tucson International Airport and at 6310 E. Broadway (☎ *520/ 745-1922).* The family also runs the adjacent ¡Toma!, a colorful bar/cantina.

**El Corral Restaurant.** *2201 E. River Rd.* ☎ *520/299-6092. Reservations not accepted. Complete dinner $7–$11. AE, DC, DISC, MC, V. Mon–Fri 5–10pm, Sat–Sun 4:30–10pm. STEAK.* The inexpensive El Corral is very popular with retirees and families (expect long lines at the door). Flagstone floors and wood paneling make this hacienda dark and cozy. Prime rib is the house specialty, but there are also steaks, pork ribs, chicken, and burgers for the kids.

✪ **Janos.** *150 N. Main St.* ☎ *520/884-9426. Reservations highly recommended. Main courses $21–$32; five-course tasting menu $55 ($85 with wines); summer sampler $12.95. AE, DC, MC, V. Mon–Thurs 5:30–8:30pm, Fri–Sat 5:30–9:30pm. Closed Sun and Mon in summer. SOUTHWESTERN/REGIONAL.* Across the courtyard from the Tucson Museum of Art in a beautifully restored old adobe home, Chef Janos's stellar cuisine includes such creations as grilled ostrich with slow-roasted red-onion barbecue sauce and a blue-corn tamale pie. A low-priced summertime sampler menu is one of Tucson's best values. *Note:* Janos will move to a new location in 1998, so call ahead.

**Keaton's.** *6464 E. Tanque Verde Rd.* ☎ *520/721-1299. Reservations recommended on weekends. Main courses $11–$18. AE, DISC, MC, V. Mon–Thurs 11am–10pm, Fri–Sat 11am–10:30pm, Sun 10:30am–10pm. Nouvelle American.* Both the crunchy sourdough and zucchini breads here are excellent, but save room for the likes of seared and poached salmon with a pistachio crust at this roomy and sophisticated spot. An earlybird menu, served Mon–Thurs 3–6pm, is a very good deal. Another Keaton's is at 7401 N. La Cholla Blvd. (☎ **520/297-1999**).

**Le Rendez-Vous.** *3844 E. Fort Lowell Rd. (at Alvernon Way).* ☎ *520/323-7373. Reservations highly recommended. Main courses $14–$26. AE, DC, DISC, MC, V. Tues–Thurs 11:30am–2pm and 6–9:30pm, Fri 11:30am–2pm and 6–10pm, Sat 6–10pm, Sun 6–9:30pm. FRENCH.* Most patrons here are locals returning for the duck, mussels cooked in white wine, and the ultimate spinach salad. You might expect such rich and savory fare to be served amid rarefied elegance, but Le Rendez-Vous is housed in an unpretentious little stucco cottage. Despite waiters dressed in black tie, the atmosphere is strictly bistro.

✪ **Tack Room.** *2800 N. Sabino Canyon Rd.* ☎ *520/722-2800. Reservations recommended. Main courses $25–$34. AE, CB, DC, DISC, JCB, MC, V. May to mid-Jan, Tues–Sun 6–11pm; late Jan to Apr, daily 6–11pm. SOUTHWESTERN/AMERICAN.* The Tack Room is the city's most prestigious restaurant, housed in an older hacienda with an atmosphere of casual elegance in which a bevy of waiters in tuxedos make you feel pleasingly pampered. Plump guaymas shrimp subtly seasoned with orange zest and garlic are among the outstanding offerings.

✪ **Ventana Room.** *In Loews Ventana Canyon Resort, 7000 N. Resort Dr.* ☎ *520/ 299-2020. Reservations highly recommended. Main courses $20–$30. Chef's five-course tasting menu $45 without wine. AE, CB, DC, MC, V. Sun–Thurs 6–9pm, Fri–Sat 6–10pm. NOUVELLE AMERICAN.* With the spectacular setting and waterfall at the head of Ventana Canyon, it would be worth eating here even if the food weren't so good. Ethereal strains of a harp set the mood for memorable meals of venison, lamb, veal, and quail, which often appear on the changing menu.

**OTHER DINING** Located in the Trail Dust Town, a Wild West–themed shopping and dining center, the **Pinnacle Peak Steakhouse,** 6541 E. Tanque Verde Rd. (☎ 520/296-0911), specializes in family dining in a fun cowboy atmosphere. Stroll the wooden sidewalks past the opera house and saloon to these grand old dining rooms, which could be in Old Tombstone or Dodge City. Be prepared for crowds—this place is very popular with tour buses.

## TUCSON AFTER DARK

The **Downtown Arts District** is the center of all Tucson's nightlife action. The **University of Arizona campus,** only a mile away, is another hot spot for entertainment. Look for entertainment listings in the *Tucson Weekly,* available in convenience stores.

Tickets to many concerts and theater performances are available at **Dillard's** department store box offices or by calling the Dillard's telephone reservation line (☎ 800/638-4253). **Ticketmaster** (☎ 520/321-1000) also sells tickets to some Tucson performances.

**THE PERFORMING ARTS**    Three of Tucson's major performance companies—the Arizona Opera Company, Ballet Arizona, and the Arizona Theatre Company—spend half their time in Phoenix. This means that whatever gets staged in Phoenix also gets staged in Tucson. This city does, however, have its own symphony, and sustains a diversified theater scene as well—more experimental theater is staged here.

The **Tucson Symphony Orchestra** (☎ 520/792-9155 for information, 520/882-8585 for tickets) performs at the Tucson Convention Center Music Hall, 260 S. Church Ave., and is the oldest symphony in the Southwest. Opera fans can catch the **Arizona Opera Company** (☎ 520/293-4336), at the Tucson Convention Center Music Hall, 260 S. Church Ave. Tucson's dance scene is dominated by **Ballet Arizona** (☎ 520/882-5022), at different venues around town.

The **Temple of Music and Art,** 330 S. Scott Ave., a restored historic theater dating back to 1927, is the centerpiece of the Tucson theater scene and home to the **Arizona Theatre Company (ATC)** (☎ 520/622-2823), the state's top professional theater company. Each season sees a mix of comedy, drama, and Broadway-style musical shows. If you enjoy new works by unknown playwrights, check the schedule of the **A.K.A. Theatre,** 125 E. Congress St. (☎ 520/623-7852). **Centennial Hall,** on the campus of the University of Arizona, at University Boulevard and Park Avenue (☎ 520/621-3341), is one of Tucson's main venues for touring musical acts and Broadway shows.

The **Tucson Jazz Society** (☎ 520/743-3399), which manages to book a few well-known jazz musicians each year, sponsors different outdoor music series at various locations around the city including St. Philip's Plaza shopping center.

**THE CLUB & MUSIC SCENE**    A young to middle-aged crowd frequents the **Cactus Moon Café,** 5470 E. Broadway Blvd., on the east side of town at the corner of Craycroft Road (☎ 520/748-0049), a large and glitzy nightclub for country music. Another spot for country, **A Little Bit of Texas,** 4385 W. Ina Rd. (☎ 520/744-7744), has the biggest and best dance floor in Tucson. The crowd is mixed, and dance lessons are available. Just off the lobby of the restored Hotel Congress (now a youth hostel), **Club Congress,** 311 E. Congress St. (☎ 520/622-8848), is one of Tucson's main alternative-music venues, with a couple of nights of live music each week. **La Fuente,** 1749 N. Miracle Mile (☎ 520/623-8659), the largest Mexican restaurant in Tucson, serves up good food, but what really draws the crowds is the live mariachi music 7 nights a week; the music starts after 6pm, and if you don't want dinner, you can hang out in the lounge and listen to the music.

**THE BAR SCENE**    If you're looking for a quiet and comfortable bar, piano music in the Audubon Lounge of the **Arizona Inn,** 2200 E. Elm St. (☎ 520/325-1541), is sure to soothe your soul. In the El Presidio Historic District **¡Toma!,** 311 N. Court Ave. (☎ 520/622-1922), has a humorous and festive atmosphere. Happy hour is Friday 5–8pm, and Latino and salsa music happens weekend nights. **Gentle Ben's Brewing Co.,** 865 E. University Blvd. (☎ 520/624-4177), is Tucson's favorite microbrewery, with daily food and drink specials. The crowd is young and active. If you want your cocktails with a view, try the **Flying V Bar and Grill** in Loew's Ventana Canyon Resort, 7000 N. Resort Dr. (☎ 520/299-2020); the lounge at **Anthony's in the Catalinas,** 6440 N. Campbell Ave. (☎ 520/299-1771); or the **Lookout Lounge** in the Westward Look Resort, 245 E. Ina Rd. (☎ 520/297-1151).

## DAY TRIPS FROM TUCSON

By the time you arrive, **Kartchner Caverns State Park** (☎ 520/586-7257), 10 miles south of Benson, should be open to the public. These caverns, discovered in 1974 and kept secret for 14 years to protect them, are among the largest and most beautiful in the country. The park will include an exhibit hall and multimedia presentation as well as a campground.

**BIOSPHERE 2 VISITOR CENTER**    For 2 years, beginning in September 1991, four men and four women were locked inside this airtight, 3-acre greenhouse in the desert 35 miles north of Tucson near the town of Oracle. During their tenure in Biosphere 2 (earth is considered Biosphere 1) they conducted experiments on how the earth, basically a giant greenhouse, manages to support all the planet's life forms. Today this huge science project is a major attraction. Daily tours take you inside Biosphere 2 and through the Biome Ecology Laboratories. An interactive display area provides entertainment for children. Also on the grounds are a hotel, restaurant, cafe, bookstore, and gift shop.

   **Essentials:** Take Oracle Road north out of Tucson and continue north on U.S. 89 and Ariz. 77 until you see the Biosphere sign. Call ☎ **520/896-6200** for information.

**KITT PEAK NATIONAL OBSERVATORY**    Southern Arizona has come to be known as the "Astronomy Capital of the World." The largest of the astronomical observatories here is the famous Kitt Peak National Observatory. The observatory sits atop 6,882-foot Kitt Peak in the Quinlan Mountains. The darkness of the surrounding desert makes the night sky here as brilliant as anywhere on earth.

   There are five major telescopes operating at Kitt Peak, including the McMath telescope, the world's largest solar telescope. This telescope's system of mirrors channels an image of the sun deep into the mountain before reflecting it back up to the observatory where scientists study the resulting 30-inch-diameter image. The 158-inch Mayall telescope features a 30,000-pound quartz mirror and is used for studying distant regions of the universe.

   Guided tours are given daily at 10:30am and 1:30pm. There's also a visitor center and museum. There's no restaurant at the observatory, but there is a picnic area.

   **Essentials:** Take Ariz. 86 southwest from Tucson; in about 40 miles you'll see the turnoff for Kitt Peak; the observatory is about 16 miles from the turnoff. Call ☎ **520/322-3350** or 520/322-3426 for information.

**ORGAN PIPE CACTUS NATIONAL MONUMENT**    The Monument, 145 miles west of Tucson, is a preserve for the rare organ pipe cactus. This massive cactus resembles the saguaro in many ways, but instead of forming a single main trunk, it forms many trunks, some 20 feet tall, resembling organ pipes. This is a rugged region with few towns or services. Be sure to gas up your car before leaving Ajo. Inside the park there's only one campground, and the only roads other than Ariz. 85 are gravel. In the western section of the national monument, 15 miles down a gravel road, is Quitobaquito Spring, which was relied on by Native Americans and pioneers as the only reliable source of water for miles around.

   **Essentials:** Take Ariz. 86 west to Ariz. 85 south. Call ☎ **520/387-6849** for information.

**COLOSSAL CAVE MOUNTAIN PARK**    Colossal Cave may once have served as a bandit hangout. Today, tours through the cave combine a bit of history with a bit of geology. This is a dry cave, where the stalactites, stalagmites, and other formations are no longer actively growing. The 45-minute tours of the cave cover about half a mile, and the temperature is a comfortable 70° to 72°F.

   **Essentials:** The caves are located 22 miles east of Tucson off I-10. Call ☎ **520/647-7275** for information.

**SAN PEDRO & SOUTHWESTERN RAILROAD**   Railroad buffs and anyone else who wants to see the San Pedro River valley from a different perspective should check out this train excursion, which runs between Benson and the ghost town of Charleston. Along the route, the train passes ghost towns, the ruins of a Spanish outpost, stamp mill ruins, and abandoned ranches. Much of the trip is within the San Pedro Riparian National Conservation Area. In addition to desert scenery, the historical narration provides fascinating background, including stories from Tombstone's glory days.

**Essentials:** To reach the train depot, take I-10 east to exit 303 in Benson, drive through town, and take U.S. 80 south 1 mile, and then turn left on Country Club Drive. Call ☎ 520/586-2266 for the current schedule and prices.

**MADERA CANYON**   In the Coronado National Forest about 40 miles south of Tucson, Madera Canyon National Forest Recreation Area (☎ 520/281-2296) is one of southern Arizona's prime bird-watching spots. Avid birders flock to this canyon from around the country in hopes of spotting more than a dozen species of hummingbirds, an equal number of flycatchers, warblers, tanagers, buntings, grosbeaks, and many rare birds that are not found in any other state.

Before birding became a hot activity, this canyon was popular with families looking for an escape from the heat. The shady picnic areas and trails still get a lot of general use. If you're heading out here for the day, arrive early—parking is very limited.

**Essentials:** To reach Madera Canyon, take exit 39 from I-19; from the exit, it's another 12 miles southeast. Admission is a $2 donation and the canyon is open daily from dawn to dusk.

## 10  Santa Fe

Founded in 1610 as the seat of Spanish government in the upper Rio Grande Valley—a decade before the pilgrims set foot on Plymouth Rock—Santa Fe is caught in a time warp between the 17th and 21st centuries—between traditional American Indian and Hispanic cultures and a current-day onslaught of newcomers and high tech.

Today's visitor can explore New Mexico's best museums, visit numerous historic buildings, browse through dozens of art galleries, and dine at some of the West's most innovative restaurants.

### ARRIVING & DEPARTING

**BY PLANE**   The **Santa Fe Municipal Airport,** just southwest of the city, has only limited commercial service, and most air travelers fly to **Albuquerque International Airport** on America West, American, Continental, Delta, Southwest, TWA, and United, and either rent a car or take the **Shuttlejack** shuttle service (☎ 505/982-4311 or 505/243-3244), which charges $20 per person.

**BY TRAIN & BUS**   The **Amtrak** station is at Lamy, just east of Santa Fe (☎ 800/USA-RAIL or 505/842-9650). The bus station for the **Texas, New Mexico,** and **Oklahoma** line is at 858 St. Michael's Dr. (☎ 505/242-4998).

### ESSENTIALS

**VISITOR INFORMATION**   The **Santa Fe Convention and Visitor Bureau** is at 201 W. Marcy St., in Sweeney Center at the corner of Grant Street downtown (P.O. Box 909, Santa Fe, NM 87501-0909; ☎ 800/777-CITY or 505/984-6760).

**EMERGENCIES**   In an emergency, dial **911. St. Vincent Hospital** is located at 455 St. Michael's Drive (☎ 505/983-3361).

### GETTING AROUND

Street **parking** is difficult to find during summer months. The Convention and Visitor Bureau has a free wallet-size guide to Santa Fe parking areas, showing both street and lot parking.

# Santa Fe

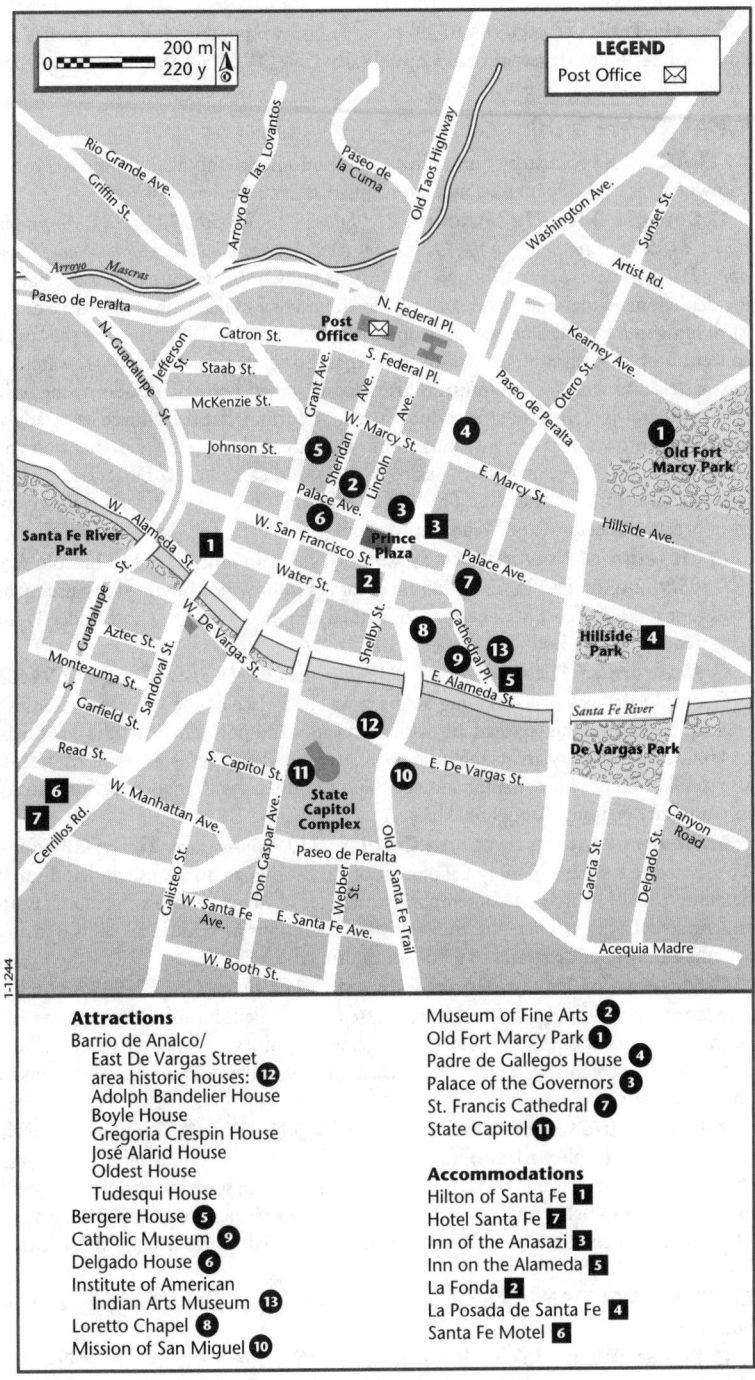

**Attractions**

Barrio de Analco/
  East De Vargas Street
  area historic houses: **12**
  Adolph Bandelier House
  Boyle House
  Gregoria Crespin House
  José Alarid House
  Oldest House
  Tudesqui House
Bergere House **5**
Catholic Museum **9**
Delgado House **6**
Institute of American
  Indian Arts Museum **13**
Loretto Chapel **8**
Mission of San Miguel **10**

Museum of Fine Arts **2**
Old Fort Marcy Park **1**
Padre de Gallegos House **4**
Palace of the Governors **3**
St. Francis Cathedral **7**
State Capitol **11**

**Accommodations**

Hilton of Santa Fe **1**
Hotel Santa Fe **7**
Inn of the Anasazi **3**
Inn on the Alameda **5**
La Fonda **2**
La Posada de Santa Fe **4**
Santa Fe Motel **6**

1-1244

**Santa Fe Trails** (☎ 505/984-6730) provides in-town bus service. Call for routes and fares. For 24-hour taxi service, call **Capital City Cab** (☎ 505/438-0000), with a base fair of $1.85 plus $1.50 per mile.

## WHAT TO SEE & DO

**ATTRACTIONS**    History and culture predominate in Santa Fe, home to world-renowned Santa Fe Opera plus numerous music festivals and art galleries.

✪ **Georgia O'Keeffe Museum.** *217 Johnson St.* ☎ *505/995-0785. Admission: $5 (4-day 5-museum passes to the Museum of New Mexico available). Tues–Sun 10am–5pm, Fridays 10am–8pm.* Although this artist is known the world over for her haunting depictions of the shapes and colors of northern New Mexico, until now little of her work hung in the state. The new museum, inaugurated in July 1997, contains the largest collection of O'Keeffes in the world, more than 80 oil paintings, drawings, watercolors, pastels and works in sculpture. This rich and varied body of art adorns the walls of a cathedral-like 10,000-square-foot space—a former Baptist church with adobe walls—downtown. It is the only museum in the U.S. dedicated solely to one woman's work. O'Keeffe first visited New Mexico in 1917 and came here for extended periods from the '20s through the '40s. The idea of bringing O'Keeffe's works together came from private collector Anne Windfohr Marion.

✪ **Museum of New Mexico System**    The main office is at 113 Lincoln Ave. (☎ 505/982-6366 or 505/827-6463 for recorded information). Four-day passes good at all four museums cost $8; one-time individual entrance costs $5. Those under 17 are admitted free. Open hours are Tues–Sun 10am–5pm.

✪ **Museum of Fine Arts.** *107 W. Palace (at Lincoln Ave.)* ☎ *505/827-4468.* This Pueblo Revival–style building across from the Palace of the Governors houses a collection emphasizing regional art, with landscapes and portraits by all the Taos masters plus contemporary artists including R. C. Gorman and Georgia O'Keeffe. There's also a collection of photographs and two sculpture gardens, with modern artists featured in temporary exhibits throughout the year.

**Museum of Indian Arts and Culture.** *710 Camino Lejo.* ☎ *505/827-6344.* The showcase for the adjoining Laboratory of Anthropology, this museum has displays detailing tribal history and contemporary lifestyles of New Mexico's Pueblo, Navajo, and Apache Indians. There are frequent demonstrations of traditional skills by tribal artisans and regular programs in a 70-seat multimedia theater.

✪ **Museum of International Folk Art.** *706 Camino Lejo.* ☎ *505/827-6350.* The largest of its kind in the world, this museum has a collection from more than 100 countries. The museum's Hispanic Heritage Wing houses the country's finest collection of Spanish colonial and Hispanic folk art, often with demonstrations, performances, and workshops.

**Palace of the Governors.** *North Plaza.* ☎ *505/827-6476.* Built in 1610 as the Spanish capitol of New Mexico, the palace has been in continuous public use longer than any other structure in the United States. It's now the state history museum, with exhibits that chronicle four centuries of New Mexico's Hispanic and American history. Outside, under the long portal, members of local Indian tribes display and sell their crafts.

**MORE ATTRACTIONS**    One of Santa Fe's major attractions is a living museum just outside of town.

✪ **El Rancho de las Golondrinas.** *334 Los Pinos Rd.* ☎ *505/471-2261. Admission $3.50 adults, $2.50 seniors and teens, $1.50 children 5–12; free for children under 5. Festival weekends, $5 adults, $3.50 seniors and teens, $2.50 children 5–12. June–Sept, Wed–Sun 10am–4pm. Apr–May and Oct, open by advance arrangement. Closed*

*Nov–Mar.* This 200-acre ranch, about 15 miles south of the Santa Fe Plaza (I-25 exit 276), was once a major stop on the 1,000-mile El Camino Real from Mexico City. Today it's a living 18th and 19th-century Spanish village, comprising a hacienda, village store, schoolhouse, chapels, kitchens, a working molasses mill, wheelwright and blacksmith shops, shearing and weaving rooms, threshing ground, vineyard and winery, and four water mills, plus dozens of farm animals.

**Loretto Chapel.** *207 Old Santa Fe Trail (between Alameda and Water sts).* ☎ *505/ 984-7971. Admission $1 adults, free for children 6 and under. Daily 9am–5pm.* Though no longer consecrated for worship, the chapel is noted for its spiral staircase, which makes two complete 360° turns. Patterned after the famous Sainte-Chapelle Church in Paris, it was constructed in 1873 for the Sisters of Loretto, who established a school for young ladies in Santa Fe in 1852.

**St. Francis Cathedral.** *Cathedral Place at San Francisco St.* ☎ *505/982-5619. Donations appreciated. Open daily. Visitors may attend mass Mon–Sat at 5:15pm, Sun at 6, 8, and 10am, noon, and 7pm.* Santa Fe's grandest religious structure is just a block east of the plaza. In the style of the great cathedrals of Europe, it was built over and around Our Lady of the Assumption Church, founded along with Santa Fe in 1610. The small adobe chapel on the northeast side of the cathedral is the only portion that remains of the original church.

**BEST BETS FOR KIDS** Designed for families to experience together, the **Santa Fe Children's Museum,** 1050 Old Pecos Trail (☎ 505/989-8359), offers interactive exhibits and hands-on activities in the arts, humanities, science, and technology. Special performances and hands-on sessions with artists and scientists are regularly scheduled.

**SKIING** **Ski Santa Fe,** 1210 Luisa St., Suite 5, Santa Fe, NM 87505 (☎ 505/ 982-4429), is about 16 miles northeast of Santa Fe via Hyde Park (Ski Basin) Road. There's something for every ability level, plus snowboarding (rentals available), sledding, and inner tubing. Ski packages available through **Santa Fe Central Reservations** (☎ 800/776-7669 outside New Mexico or 505/983-8200 within New Mexico).

**SHOPPING** For traditional Native American crafts as well as Hispanic folk art and abstract contemporary works, Santa Fe is the place to shop. Jewelry, pottery, and other American Indian crafts are sold beneath the portal of the Palace of the Governors. The main shopping area is the plaza and nearby streets, and Canyon Road is lined with fine art galleries. **Nedra Matteucci's Fenn Galleries,** 1075 Paseo de Peralta (☎ 505/ 982-4631), specializes in 19th- and 20th-century American art, offering early Taos and Santa Fe painters, classic American impressionism, historical western modernism, plus contemporary Southwestern landscapes and sculpture. **Owings–Dewey Fine Art,** 76 E. San Francisco St., upstairs (☎ 505/982-6244), offers 19th- and 20th-century American painting and sculpture. Works are by Georgia O'Keeffe, Robert Henri, Maynard Dixon, Fremont Ellis, and Andrew Dasburg. **Shidoni Foundry and Gallery,** Bishop's Lodge Road, Tesuque (☎ 505/988-8001), is one of the region's most exciting spots for sculpture enthusiasts. There's a 5,000-square-foot contemporary gallery, bronze gallery, and sculpture garden; visitors may tour the facilities to watch the casting processes.

## ACCOMMODATIONS

Be aware of the highly seasonal nature of the tourist industry in Santa Fe: accommodations are often booked solid through the summer months, and most establishments raise their prices accordingly. Rates go up even higher during Indian Market, the third weekend of August. During these periods, it's essential to make reservations well in advance. Contact **Santa Fe Central Reservations,** 320 Artist Rd., Suite 10 (☎ 800/ 776-7669 or 505/983-8200; fax 505/984-8682), for lodging reservations, plus reservations for a number of cultural events and recreational activities. **Emergency**

**Lodging Assistance**—especially helpful around fiesta time in September—is available free after 4pm daily (☎ **505/986-0043**).

✪ **El Rey Inn.** *1862 Cerrillos Rd. (P.O. Box 4759), Santa Fe, NM 87502.* ☎ *800/ 521-1349 or 505/982-1931. Fax 505/989-9249. 85 rms, 8 suites. $56–$115 single or double; $98–$207 suite. Rates include continental breakfast. Children under 18 stay free in parents' room. AE, CB, DC, DISC, MC, V.* Carefully tended shaded grounds surround well-maintained rooms. Some units have kitchenettes; others, refrigerators and/or fireplaces. Eight poolside units feature private patios. Ten deluxe units surround a courtyard. The inn has a sitting room with library and games tables, pool, hot tub, sauna, picnic area, and guest laundry.

**Hilton of Santa Fe.** *100 Sandoval St. (P.O. Box 25104), Santa Fe, NM 87504- 2387.* ☎ *800/HILTONS, 800/336-3676, or 505/988-2811. Fax 505/986-6435. 155 rms, 6 suites. May–Oct and Christmas, $170–$270 double. Nov–Apr, $90–$240 double. Year-round, $300–$700 suite. Additional person $20 extra. Children under 18 stay free in parents' room. AE, CB, DC, DISC, MC, V.* The Hilton, occupying a full city block, has spacious guest rooms with king, queen, or double beds and deck or balcony. Larger executive rooms have a couch or easy chairs. An adjacent building houses three exclusive suites. Conveniences include restaurants, a bar, pool, Jacuzzi, gift shop, car-rental and travel agencies, courtesy car, and valet laundry.

**Hotel Santa Fe.** *1501 Paseo de Peralta, Santa Fe, NM 87501.* ☎ *800/825-9876 or 505/982-1200. Fax 505/984-2211. 131 rms, 91 suites. Jan–Apr, $89–$119 double; from $129 suite. May–Oct, $139–$159 double; from $169 suite. Nov–Dec, $159–$179 double; from $199 suite. Additional person $20 extra. Children under 18 stay free in parents' room. AE, CB, DC, DISC, MC, V.* Most rooms in this three-story pueblo-style building feature California king beds, and all have attractive Southwest-style furnishings. Suites have a safe-deposit box and microwave oven. Facilities include a restaurant, bar, valet laundry, courtesy shuttle, massage room, guest laundry, gift shop, pool, and whirlpool.

**Hotel St. Francis.** *210 Don Gaspar Ave., Santa Fe, NM 87501.* ☎ *800/529-5700 or 505/983-5700. Fax 505/989-7690. 83 rms, 2 suites. May–Oct and Christmas holidays, $118–$188 double; $228–$353 suite. Nov–Apr, $88–$153 double; $178–$278 suite. Additional person $15 extra. Children under 12 stay free in parents' room. AE, CB, DC, DISC, MC, V.* This politicians' gathering spot (1930s–1940s) offers rooms with high ceilings and casement windows. Thirty have barely enough room for a double bed, table, and two chairs, but all have a refrigerator and closet safe. Most have brass or iron beds, antique cherry tables, and Mexican marble baths. A restaurant, bar, and valet laundry are on the premises.

✪ **Inn of the Anasazi.** *113 Washington Ave., Santa Fe, NM 87501.* ☎ *800/ 688-8100 or 505/988-3030. Fax 505/988-3277. 59 rms. Nov–Mar, $200–$350 double. Apr–Oct, $240–$400 double. Additional person $20 extra. Children under 12 stay free in parents' room. AE, CB, DC, DISC, MC, V. Valet parking $10.* This luxury hotel is named for the "enduring and creative spirit" of the Anasazi. The elegant, beautifully appointed rooms have VCRs, minibars, safes, coffeemakers, and walk-in closets. There's a living room with gas fireplace and a library. Extras include a restaurant, tours of galleries and museums, and massage and aromatherapy treatments.

**Inn on the Alameda.** *303 E. Alameda St., Santa Fe, NM 87501.* ☎ *800/ 289-2122 or 505/984-2121. Fax 505/986-8325. 66 rms and suites. Nov–Feb, $150– $200 single or double; $210–$320 suite. Mar–June, $165–$220 single or double; $235– $345 suite. July–Oct, $170–$225 single or double; $260–$350 suite. Rates include breakfast. AE, CB, DC, DISC, MC, V.* This attractive and intimate inn offers rooms furnished in Southwestern style, with a table and chairs and desk with three-drawer credenza. Some feature outdoor patios or private balconies, refrigerators, and fireplaces. Suites provide enclosed courtyards and portals, two TVs, and separate parking. Facilities include a bar, two Jacuzzis, a fitness facility, and massage room.

✪ **La Fonda.** *100 E. San Francisco St. (P.O. Box 1209), Santa Fe, NM 87501.* ☎ ***800/523-5002*** *or 505/982-5511. Fax 505/988-2952. 153 rms, 21 suites. $170–$190 double; $250–$500 suite. Additional person $15 extra. Children under 12 stay free in parents' room. AE, CB, DC, DISC, MC, V. Parking $4 per day in three-story garage.* La Fonda occupies a full block just east of Santa Fe Plaza. Rooms are distinct, with hand-carved Spanish-style furniture. Deluxe rooms have minirefrigerators and tiled baths. Suites feature fireplaces and balconies; some offer kitchenettes. La Fonda has a restaurant, bar, pool, two indoor Jacuzzis, massage room, and shopping arcade.

✪ **La Posada de Santa Fe.** *330 E. Palace Ave., Santa Fe, NM 87501.* ☎ ***800/ 727-5276*** *or 505/986-0000. Fax 505/982-6850. 119 rms, 40 suites. May–Oct and Christmas holidays, $119–$300 double; $189–$397 suite. Nov–Apr (except holidays), $119–$285 double; $149–$285 suite. Additional person $10 extra. Children under 12 stay free in parents' room. AE, DC, DISC, MC, V.* The hotel's 119 adobe-style buildings are spread across 6 beautifully landscaped acres. The comfortable units vary in size, shape, layout, and detail. Many have fireplaces or woodstoves; some have refrigerators, walk-in closets, and dressing tables. Facilities include a restaurant, bar, pool, boutique, and beauty salon.

**Santa Fe Motel.** *510 Cerrillos Rd., Santa Fe, NM 87501.* ☎ ***800/999-1039*** *or 505/982-1039. Fax 505/986-1275. 22 rms, 1 house. May–Oct, $85–$95 double; $180 Thomas House. Nov–Apr, $70–$80 double; $150 Thomas House. Rates include continental breakfast May–Sept. AE, MC, V.* This adobe-style motel south of the Santa Fe River consists of a modern, basic motel plus several historic buildings. Rooms have fully furnished kitchenettes and Southwestern motifs. One has a fireplace, another skylights, and several have private patios.

## DINING

Creative Southwestern cuisine—combining traditional Southwestern foods with nonindigenous ingredients—is especially good here.

**Bobcat Bite.** *Old Las Vegas Hwy.* ☎ ***505/983-5319.*** *Reservations not accepted. Menu items $4–$12. No credit cards. Wed–Sat 11am–7:50pm. STEAKS/BURGERS.* This local classic (in business for more than 40 years), located about 5 miles southeast of Santa Fe, is famed for its high-quality steaks—such as the 13-ounce ribeye—and huge hamburgers. The ranch-style atmosphere appeals to families.

✪ **Cafe Escalera.** *130 Lincoln Ave., 2nd floor* ☎ ***505/989-8188.*** *Reservations recommended. Main courses $8.50–$14.50 at lunch, $16.50–$24.50 at dinner. AE, MC, V. Mon–Fri 11:30–2pm; Mon–Wed 5:30–9pm, Thurs–Sat 5:30–9:30pm. CONTINENTAL/ MEDITERRANEAN.* Cafe Escalera's spacious, open, warehouse-like space is bright, airy, and filled with energy. The decor is understated modern; the focus here is on the food. A good lunch starter is Mediterranean olives and roasted almonds, or roasted peppers and goat cheese. Lunch and dinner appetizers are usually the same, but main courses differ. The risotto timbale with summer squash, spinach, and basil pesto is a good choice, as is the grilled king salmon with a tomato-basil vinaigrette. Those with heartier appetites might like the Niman-Schell Ranch fillet steak with garlic mashed potatoes. The menu changes daily. For dessert you can't go wrong with Blanco y Negro, the Creme Brolles, or pots de cremes. The waitstaff here is among Santa Fe's best.

**The Compound.** *653 Canyon Rd.* ☎ ***505/982-4353.*** *Reservations required. Main courses $18–$28. AE. Tues–Sat 6pm–close. Closed Jan. CONTINENTAL.* The

Compound, in an old adobe home set amid tall firs and pines, offers exceedingly attentive service in an elegant atmosphere. There's a wide choice of seafood, chicken, and meat dishes. A favorite house special is roast rack of lamb with mint sauce.

**Cowgirl Hall of Fame.** *319 S. Guadalupe St.* ☎ *505/982-2565. Reservations recommended. Main courses $3–$8 at lunch, $7–$14 at dinner. AE, DISC, MC, V. Mon–Thurs 11am–10:30pm, Fri–Sat 11am–11:30pm, Sun 10am–10pm. The bar is open until 2am (Sun until midnight). REGIONAL AMERICAN/BARBECUE.* This restaurant is *fun*—from cowgirl paraphernalia to the menu, which sports "chicken wing dings" (in a citrus-Tabasco marinade with a special dressing). Happy hour is 4–6pm, there's a children's play area, and live music or comedy performances take place almost every night.

**El Farol.** *808 Canyon Rd.* ☎ *505/988-9912. Reservations recommended. Main courses $11–$24. DC, DISC, MC, V. Daily 11am–10pm. SPANISH.* Housed in a charming old building with old-fashioned local ambiance, El Farol boasts one of the largest and most unusual assortments of tapas (bar snacks and appetizers). Thirty-five varieties are offered, including octopus, grilled cactus, rabbit, and Moroccan eggplant.

**Maria's New Mexican Kitchen.** *555 W. Cordova Rd.* ☎ *505/983-7929. Reservations recommended. Main courses $5–$9 at lunch, $8–$16 at dinner. AE, DC, DC, DISC, MC, V. Mon–Fri 11am–10pm, Sat–Sun noon–10pm. NEW MEXICAN.* Maria's, with Mexican tile floors and other authentic Mexican touches, centers on an open tortilla grill, where cooks make flour tortillas by hand. Tortillas are served with every dish, from beef, chicken, and vegetarian fajitas to blue-corn enchiladas and even the huge steaks. Strolling mariachi troubadours perform nightly.

**Old Mexico Grill.** *2434 Cerrillos Rd., College Plaza South.* ☎ *505/473-0338. Reservations recommended for large parties. Main courses $6–$10 at lunch, $8–$18 at dinner. DISC, MC, V. Mon–Fri 11:30am–2:30pm; Sun–Thurs 5:30–9pm, Fri–Sat 5:30–9:30pm. MEXICAN.* The Grill looks like a cafe in Mexico City, and the authentic Mexican cuisine won't let you down. The focal point is an open mesquite grill and French rotisserie where fajitas, tacos, and other specialties are prepared. Popular dishes include hickory-smoked baby-back ribs.

**Palace Restaurant.** *142 W. Palace Ave.* ☎ *505/982-9891. Reservations recommended. Main courses $6–$11 at lunch; $10–$24 at dinner. AE, CB, DC, DISC, MC, V. Mon–Sat 11:30am–3pm; daily 5:45–10pm. NORTHERN ITALIAN/CONTINENTAL.* Located in a historic building and oozing Santa Fe charm, the Palace is known for its Caesar salad. Specialties include crab-stuffed shrimp and New Mexican lamb. Pastas are made fresh daily on the premises, the wine list is long, and the bar has nightly entertainment.

**Pink Adobe.** *406 Old Santa Fe Trail.* ☎ *505/983-7712. Reservations recommended. Main courses $5–$9 at lunch, $11–$23 at dinner. AE, CB, DC, DISC, MC, V. Mon–Fri 11:30am–2:30pm; daily 5:30–9:30pm. CONTINENTAL/SOUTHWESTERN.* A Santa Fe institution since 1946, this cozy restaurant occupies an adobe home believed to be at least 350 years old. A wide variety of innovative dishes is offered, many with a Southwest flair. A house specialty is steak Dunnigan—charred sirloin with fresh mushrooms and green chile.

**Pranzo Italian Grill.** *540 Montezuma St., Sanbusco Center.* ☎ *505/984-2645. Reservations recommended. Main courses $6–10 at lunch, $9–$19 at dinner. AE, CB, DC, DISC, MC, V. Mon–Sat 11:30am–3pm; Sun–Thurs 5–10pm, Fri–Sat 5–11pm. REGIONAL ITALIAN.* Housed in a warehouse redecorated in warm Tuscan colors, the centerpiece of this restaurant is an open grill. Homemade soups, salads, creative pizzas, and fresh pastas are among the less expensive menu items. Steak, chicken, veal, and fresh seafood grills—heavy on the garlic—dominate the dinner menu.

✪ **Santacafé.** *231 Washington Ave.* ☎ *505/984-1788. Reservations recommended. Main courses $9–$12 at lunch, $18–$25 at dinner. AE, MC, V. Mon–Fri 11:30am–2pm; daily 6–10pm. NEW AMERICAN.* A favorite since 1983, Santacafé's service and presentation are impeccable. Its unique modern American cooking has a hint of Southwestern and Asian influences, and menus change seasonally. Breads and desserts are homemade.

**The Shed.** *113½ E. Palace Ave. in Sena Plaza.* ☎ *505/982-9030. Reservations accepted at dinner. Main courses $5–$7 at lunch, $7–$14 at dinner. DISC, MC, V. Mon– Sat 11am–2:30pm; Thurs–Sat 5:30–9pm. NEW MEXICAN.* The Shed occupies several rooms and the patio of a rambling 1692 hacienda. The food is basic but delicious, featuring enchiladas, tacos, and burritos, all served on blue corn tortillas. Green chile soup is a local favorite, and the menu includes vegetarian and low-fat Mexican dishes.

**Tiny's Restaurant & Lounge.** *In the Penn Rd. Shopping Center, 1015 Penn Rd.* ☎ *505/983-9817. Reservations recommended. Lunch $5.25–$8; dinner $6–$15. AE, CB, DC, DISC, MC, V. Mon–Fri 11:30am–2pm; Mon–Sat 6–10pm. Bar, Mon–Sat 10pm– 2am. STEAKS/NEW MEXICAN.* A local favorite, Tiny's sports 1950s decor. Steaks and shrimp complement a menu featuring fajitas and northern New Mexico dishes. The house specialty is baked chicken flautas. There's live entertainment on weekends from 9pm.

## SANTA FE AFTER DARK

Santa Fe is a city committed to the arts. Its night scene is dominated by high-brow cultural events, with the club and music scene running a distant second. Complete information on all major cultural events can be obtained from the **Santa Fe Convention and Visitor Bureau** (☎ **800/777-CITY** or 505/984-6760) or from the **City of Santa Fe Arts Commission** (☎ **505/984-6707**). Current listings are published each Friday in the *New Mexican,* a daily newspaper.

The **Galisteo News and Ticket Center,** 201 Galisteo St. (☎ **505/984-1316**), is the primary outlet for tickets to the opera and other major entertainment events. You can order by phone from **Ticketmaster** (☎ **505/842-5387** for information, 505/884-0999 to order).

**THE PERFORMING ARTS**  Current listings of what's happening are published each Friday in the "Pasatiempo" section of *The New Mexican,* the city's daily newspaper, and in the *Santa Fe Reporter,* published every Wednesday.

The city's premier performing arts experience is the ✪ **Santa Fe Opera** (☎ **505/ 986-5959**), one of the country's most highly regarded opera companies, which presents both classic and cutting-edge modern operas in a semiopen theater each summer. The **Santa Fe Symphony and Chorus** (☎ **505/983-1414**) presents a variety of works at Sweeney Center downtown, often with preconcert lectures. ✪ **Desert Chorale** (☎ **800/ 244-4011** or 505/988-7505) is nationally recognized for its blend of Renaissance melodies and modern avant-garde compositions. The **Serenata of Santa Fe** (☎ **505/ 989-7988**) specializes in lesser-known works of the masters. The 6-week season of the **Santa Fe Chamber Music Festival,** P.O. Box 853, Santa Fe, NM 87504 (☎ **505/ 983-2075** or 505/982-1890), brings an extraordinary group of international artists to Santa Fe from mid-July through mid-August. Chamber music, new music by a composer-in-residence, and jazz are featured.

Those looking for the excitement of true flamenco should try to catch a performance by **Maria Benitez Teatro Flamenco** (☎ **800/905-3315** for tickets, or 505/982-1237), which presents its "Estampa Flamenca" series each summer.

**THE CLUB & BAR SCENE**  No matter the impression given by the ritzy set at Santa Fe gallery openings and opera galas, this is still the Old West, and to get into the spirit you might want to stop in at **Rodeo Nites,** 2911 Cerrillos Rd. (☎ 505/473-4138), with live country dance music nightly. For a mix of jazz, folk, and ethnic music, try **El Farol,** 808 Canyon Rd. (☎ 505/983-9912); **Vanessie of Santa Fe,** 434 W. San Francisco St. (☎ 505/982-9966), is unquestionably Santa Fe's most popular piano bar, with a repertoire ranging from Bach to Billy Joel, Gershwin to Barry Manilow.

Good watering holes with large-screen TVs always tuned to sports include the **Green Onion Pub,** 1851 St. Michael's Dr. (☎ 505/983-5198); and **Season Tickets,** 2907 Cerrillos Rd., in the Ramada Inn (☎ 505/471-3000). **Dana's After Dark,** 222 W. Guadalupe (☎ 505/982-5225), is a cool after-hours lesbian and gay bar.

## 11 Taos

Known for its thriving art colony, historic American Indian pueblo, and highly regarded nearby ski resort, Taos remains in many ways a quiet little rural community of dirt roads and pickup trucks. The Spanish first visited this area in 1540, and during the 18th and 19th centuries Taos was an important trade center, and even put itself on the map for its whisky distillery, which produced the potent and widely consumed Taos Lightning. But when the railroad bypassed Taos in favor of Santa Fe, the population dwindled. Then, in 1898, two East Coast artists fell in love with the dramatic lighting, captured it on canvas, and began Taos's new life as one of America's foremost art colonies.

### ARRIVING & DEPARTING

**BY PLANE**  **Albuquerque International Airport,** 130 miles south of Taos, is served by America West, American, Continental, Delta, Southwest, TWA, and United. Car rentals are available at the airport, and **Pride of Taos** (☎ 505/758-8340) and **Faust Transportation, Inc.** (☎ 800/535-1106 or 505/758-3410) provide shuttle-bus service from the airport at $25–$30 one-way.

**BY CAR & BUS**  East-west U.S. 64 and north-south N.M. 68 and 522 intersect in the middle of town. The **Taos Bus Center,** Paseo del Pueblo Sur at the Chevron station (☎ 505/758-1144), has daily service from **Greyhound/Trailways** and **TNM&O Coaches.**

### ESSENTIALS

**VISITOR INFORMATION**  The **Taos Visitor Center** (☎ 505/758-3873) is at the junction of N.M. 68 and Paseo del Cañon on the south side of town. **Carson National Forest** has an information center in the same building. Tourist information is also available from the **Taos County Chamber of Commerce,** P.O. Drawer I, Taos, NM 87571 (☎ 800/732-TAOS or 505/758-3873).

**EMERGENCIES**  In an emergency, dial **911. Holy Cross Hospital,** 1397 Weimer Rd., off Paseo del Cañon (☎ 505/758-8883), has 24-hour emergency service.

### GETTING AROUND

Local bus service is provided by **Taos Chile Line** (☎ 505/751-7786). Fare is 50¢ for one ride or $1 for an all-day pass. **Pride of Taos** (☎ 505/758-8340) operates a summer historical sites trolley tour, which takes about 2¹/₂ hours and costs $15. **Faust Transportation** (☎ 505/758-3410) offers town taxi service, with fares to most parts of town in the $7–$8 range.

### WHAT TO SEE & DO

Taos, although best known for its art, pueblo, and ski area, also has several fine museums and historic sites.

**KIT CARSON MUSEUMS**  The **Kit Carson Historic Museums** (☎ 505/758-0505) operates three historic homes as museums. They're all different and well

# Taos Area

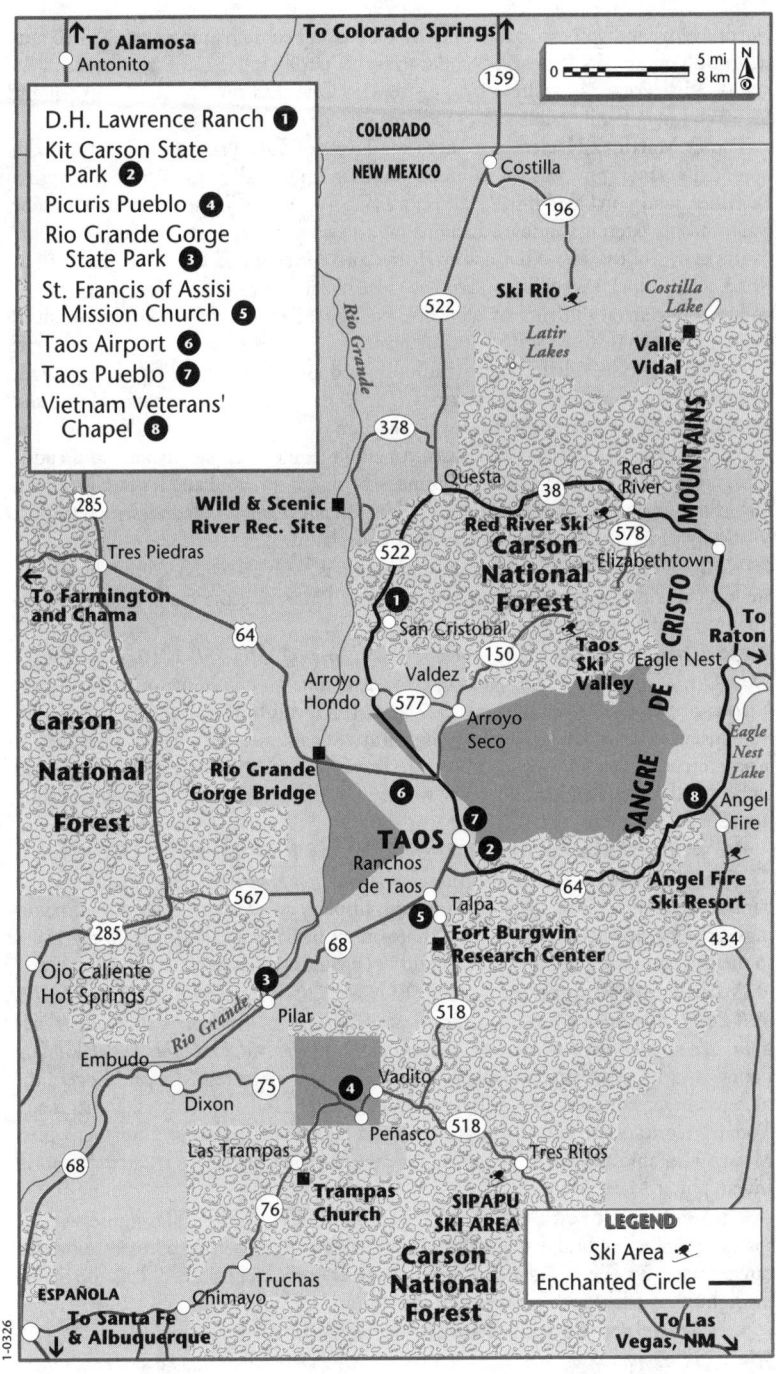

**LEGEND:**
- D.H. Lawrence Ranch ❶
- Kit Carson State Park ❷
- Picuris Pueblo ❹
- Rio Grande Gorge State Park ❸
- St. Francis of Assisi Mission Church ❺
- Taos Airport ❻
- Taos Pueblo ❼
- Vietnam Veterans' Chapel ❽

To Alamosa
Antonito

To Colorado Springs

(159)

COLORADO
NEW MEXICO

Costilla

(196)

Ski Rio

Costilla Lake

(522)

Latir Lakes

Valle Vidal

Rio Grande

(378)

Questa

(38)

Red River

(285)

Wild & Scenic River Rec. Site

Tres Piedras

(522)

Red River Ski

(578)

Carson National Forest

Elizabethtown

To Farmington and Chama

(64)

❶

San Cristobal

(150)

SANGRE DE CRISTO MOUNTAINS

Taos Ski Valley

To Raton

Eagle Nest

Arroyo Hondo

Valdez

(577)

Arroyo Seco

Eagle Nest Lake

Carson

National

Forest

Rio Grande Gorge Bridge

❻

TAOS

❼

❷

❽

Angel Fire

(567)

Ranchos de Taos

❺

Talpa

(64)

Angel Fire Ski Resort

(285)

(68)

Fort Burgwin Research Center

(434)

Ojo Caliente Hot Springs

❸

Pilar

(518)

Embudo

(75)

Vadito

Dixon

❹

(518)

(68)

Peñasco

Tres Ritos

Las Trampas

SIPAPU SKI AREA

(76)

Trampas Church

Carson

National

Forest

ESPAÑOLA

Truchas

Chimayo

To Santa Fe & Albuquerque

To Las Vegas, NM

**LEGEND**
Ski Area
Enchanted Circle

0   5 mi
    8 km
N

1-0326

worth seeing, and you can save money by purchasing combination tickets. Three museums, $8 adults, $6 seniors, $5 children 6–16; family rate $15. Two museums, $6 adults, $5 seniors, $4 children; family rate $13. One museum, $4 adults, $3 seniors, $2.50 children; family rate $6. All museums free for children under 5.

The ✪ **Martinez Hacienda,** 2 miles southwest of Taos Plaza on Ranchitos Road, open daily 9am–5pm, was the home of merchant and trader Don Antonio Severino Martinez, who purchased it in 1804. Built like a fortress, the hacienda has thick adobe walls and no exterior windows. Exhibits tell the story of the Martinez family and life in the early 1800s. The **Kit Carson Home and Museum of the West,** Kit Carson Road, a half-block east of Taos Plaza, open daily 8am–6pm in summer, 9am–5pm in winter, is a general museum of Taos history. The 12-room adobe home was built in 1825 and purchased in 1843 by Indian agent and scout Kit Carson as a wedding gift for his young bride. A living room, bedroom, and kitchen are furnished as they might have been when occupied by the Carsons. The ✪ **Ernest L. Blumenschein Home and Museum,** 222 Ledoux St., open daily 9am–5pm, re-creates the lifestyle of one of the founders of the Taos Society of Artists. An adobe home with garden walls and courtyard, it was the home and studio of Blumenschein (1874–1960) and his family. Period furnishings include European antiques and handmade Spanish colonial–style furniture. Works by early 20th-century Taos artists are displayed.

**OTHER ATTRACTIONS**   Most major attractions, with a few noteworthy exceptions, are located within easy walking distance of **Taos Plaza,** also the starting point for visiting some 50 art galleries.

✪ **Fechin Institute.** *227 Paseo del Pueblo Norte.* ☎ *505/758-1710. Admission $3. May–Oct, Wed–Sun 1–5pm. Nov–Apr, by appointment.* The home of Russian artist Nicolai Fechin (1881–1955) from 1927 until 1933, this historic building commemorates his life and art. Considered a 20th-century Renaissance man, he was acclaimed as a painter, sculptor, and woodworker. In Taos, he built this huge adobe home and embellished it with hand-carved doors, windows, and other features of a Russian country home.

**Harwood Museum of the University of New Mexico.** *238 Ledoux St.* ☎ *505/758-9826. Admission $4. Mon–Fri 10am–5pm, Sat 10am–4pm.* A cultural and community center since 1923, this museum displays an excellent collection of paintings, drawings, prints, sculpture, and photographs by Taos-area artists from the 1800s to the present, plus 19th- and 20th-century Hispanic arts and crafts.

✪ **Millicent Rogers Museum.** *Off N.M. 522, 4 miles north of Taos.* ☎ *505/ 758-2462. Admission $4 adults, $3 seniors and students, $2 children 6–16. Daily 10am– 5pm. Closed Mon in Nov–Mar, San Geronimo Day (Sept 30), and other major holidays.* Founded in 1953 by family members after the death of oil heiress Millicent Rogers, the museum began with Rogers's collection of Southwestern Indian jewelry and other items. Today it contains an acclaimed collection of American Indian and northern New Mexico Hispanic arts and crafts, including an extensive collection of pottery by famed Indian potter Maria Martinez.

**Rio Grande Gorge Bridge.** *U.S. 64, 10 miles west of Taos.* This impressive and sometimes dizzying bridge spans the Southwest's greatest river. At 650 feet above the canyon floor, it's one of America's highest bridges. At different times of day, the changing light plays tricks with the colors of the cliff walls.

**San Francisco de Asis Church.** *Just off N.M. 68, Ranchos de Taos.* ☎ *505/ 758-2754. Donations appreciated. Mon–Sat 9am–4pm. Closed daily noon–1pm. Visitors may attend mass Sat at 5:30pm and Sun at 7am (Spanish), 9am, and 11:30am.* From the back, your first view, this historic church appears as a massive adobe sculpture with no doors or windows. It has often been photographed (by Ansel Adams, among others) and painted (by Georgia O'Keeffe, for one) from this angle, although the front is equally attractive. A video presentation tells the history of the church.

✪ **Taos Pueblo.** *Access road north of downtown Taos, off N.M. 522.* ☎ *505/758-9593. Admission $5 per private vehicle, still camera $5; video camera $10; sketching $15; painting $35. Photography prohibited on feast days. Generally open daily 8am–5:30pm. Taos Pueblo closes to visitors for a month or more each year in late winter or early spring (call for exact dates).* No other site in Taos is as important or as famous. The community of 1,500—about 2¹/₂ miles north of the plaza—is the northernmost of New Mexico's 19 pueblos, and unquestionably the most stunning. The pueblo is comprised of two massive, centuries-old multistoried adobe apartment houses. The flowing lines of hand-shaped mud are typical of pueblo architecture throughout the Southwest. Remember, these are people's homes, so don't just walk in uninvited. You're expected to ask permission before taking anyone's photo; some will ask for payment.

**SPORTS**  Considered among the best ski resorts in the Rockies, **Taos Ski Valley,** NM 87525 (☎ **505/776-2291** or 505/776-2916), is internationally renowned for its light, dry powder, superb ski school, and intimate ambiance. It offers runs for intermediate skiers, but its greatest challenge is for experts.

Half- or full-day **whitewater rafting** trips down the Rio Grande originate in Taos, led by several professional outfitters. The wild Taos Box, a picturesque steep-sided canyon, is especially popular, but it's not a place to learn this exciting sport. May and June, when snowmelt is highest, are the best times. Contact **Rio Grande Rapid Transit,** P.O. Box A, Pilar, NM 87571 (☎ **800/222-RAFT** or 505/758-9700); or **Native Sons Adventures,** 715 Paseo del Pueblo Sur (☎ **800/753-7559** or 505/758-9342).

**SHOPPING**  Numerous shops and 60-odd art galleries offer hand-made jewelry, Southwest clothing, and American Indian and Hispanic crafts. Most are within walking distance of Taos Plaza, and a couple of dozen more are a short drive from downtown.

The best-known artist in modern Taos is Navajo R. C. Gorman, internationally acclaimed for his bright, somewhat surrealistic depictions of Navajo women. His **Navajo Gallery,** at 210 Ledoux St. (☎ **505/758-3250**), is a showcase for his work. Among other top galleries are **Gallery A,** 105–107 Kit Carson Rd. (☎ **505/758-2343**), offering contemporary and traditional paintings, sculpture, and graphics; **Creative Expressions,** 103 Kit Carson Rd. (☎ **505/758-7795**), with jewelry, pottery, and art in a wide variety of media; and **Alexandra Stevens Gallery of Fine Art,** 115 Bent St. (☎ **505/758-1399**), showing traditional and modern western art.

## ACCOMMODATIONS

For help with reservations, contact **Taos Central Reservations,** P.O. Box 1713, Taos, NM 87571 (☎ **800/821-2437** or 505/758-9767), or **Taos Valley Resort Association,** P.O. Box 85, Taos Ski Valley, NM 87525 (☎ **800/776-1111** or 505/776-2233; fax 505/776-8842).

**Best Western Kachina Lodge de Taos.** *413 Paseo del Pueblo Norte (P.O. Box NN), Taos, NM 87571.* ☎ *800/522-4462 or 505/758-2275. Fax 505/758-9207. 118 rms, 4 suites. $85–$125 double. Additional person $8 extra. Children under 12 stay free in parents' room. AE, DC, DISC, MC, V.* This long-established pueblo-style motel offers attractive guest rooms appointed with custom-made Southwest-style furniture. Two restaurants, a bar, summer guest services desk, pool, indoor hot tub, coin-op laundry, and ski shop are on the premises.

**El Monte Lodge.** *317 Kit Carson Rd. (P.O. Box 22), Taos, NM 87571.* ☎ *800/808-8267 or 505/758-3171. Fax 505/758-1536. 13 rms. $75–$125 double. Kitchenette units $10 extra. AE, DISC, MC, V.* Four blocks east of the plaza, El Monte is old-fashioned, homey, and well-maintained. The rooms, many with fireplaces, occupy eight small buildings. Four have fully stocked kitchenettes; there's a free guest laundry and a parklike picnic area, complete with barbecue grills and children's playground. No air-conditioning.

**El Pueblo Lodge.** *412 Paseo del Pueblo Norte (P.O. Box 92), Taos, NM 87571.* ☎ *800/433-9612 or 505/758-8700. Fax 505/758-7321. 60 units. $55–65 double; $58–$215 suite. Additional person $5–$10 extra. Rates include continental breakfast. AE, DISC, MC, V.* The setting is special: cottonwood and towering fir trees, gardens, barbecue pits, and lawn furniture on 3¹/₂ acres. All the brightly colored rooms feature Southwestern decor and refrigerators. Some have kitchenettes and fireplaces. There is free use of laundry facilities, pool, and hot tub. No air-conditioning.

**Fechin Inn.** *227 Paseo del Pueblo Norte (P.O. Box O), Taos, NM 87571.* ☎ *800/811-2933 or 505/751-1000. Fax 505/751-7338. 85 rms and suites. May to mid-Oct and Feb–Mar, $149–$210 double; $259–$350 suite. Apr and mid-Oct to Jan, $119–$180 double; $209–$325 suite. Additional person $15 extra. Rates include continental breakfast. AE, CB, DC, DISC, MC, V.* Named for famed Russian artist Nicolai Fechin, the hotel boasts handsome hand-carved doors, staircase, and reception desk. Rooms are beautifully appointed in Southwestern style, and many have kiva fireplaces, and balcony or private patio. The inn has a bar, fitness room, masseuse, and whirlpool.

**۞ Historic Taos Inn.** *125 Paseo del Pueblo Norte (P.O. Drawer N), Taos, NM 87571.* ☎ *800/TAOS-INN or 505/758-2233. Fax 505/758-5776. 37 rms and suites. $85–$225 double. AE, DC, MC, V.* Taos history lives within the walls of this inn, comprised of several mid-1800s adobe houses clustered around the original town well. Today, interior balconies in the lobby overlook the old well, now a fountain. All rooms have fireplaces and regional furnishings. The inn's restaurant, **Doc Martin's** (☎ *505/758-1977*) sewes an acclaimed contemporary southwestern cuisine. Amenities include a bar, room service, pool, and Jacuzzi.

**۞ Sagebrush Inn.** *Paseo del Pueblo Sur (P.O. Box 557), Taos, NM 87571.* ☎ *800/428-3626 or 505/758-2254. Fax 505/758-5077. 68 rms, 32 suites. $70–$95 standard double; $90–$110 deluxe double; $95–$115 minisuite; $105–$140 executive suite. Rates include breakfast. Additional person $10 extra. Children under 12 stay free in parents' room. AE, CB, DC, DISC, MC, V.* About 3 miles south of Taos Plaza, the Sagebrush, built in 1929, has long been a landmark and local gathering spot. Room sizes vary, but all have Southwestern decor. Suites have kiva fireplaces, king and Murphy beds, and two full baths. Extras include a restaurant, bar, courtesy van, swimming pool, hot tub, and tennis courts.

## DINING

Many restaurants offer interesting combinations of Southwestern flavors and the gamut from European to Oriental to South Seas.

**۞ Apple Tree.** *123 Bent St.* ☎ *505/758-1900. Reservations recommended. Main courses $5–$10 at lunch, $11–$19 at dinner. CB, DC, DISC, MC, V. Mon–Sat 11:30am–3pm; light meals and snacks daily 3–5pm; daily 5:30–9pm; Sun brunch 10am–3pm. SOUTHWESTERN.* Original Taos art overlooks the candlelit service in the elegant adobe rooms of this fine restaurant; outside are wooden tables sheltered by a spreading apple tree. Choices include innovative variations on Southwestern cuisine, such as mango chicken enchiladas.

**Casa Cordova.** *Arroyo Seco, 8 miles north of town on N.M. 150.* ☎ *505/776-2500. Reservations recommended. Main courses $15–$25. AE, DISC, MC, V. Mon–Sat 4–10pm. CONTINENTAL.* This elegant yet cozy restaurant has fireplaces, rough-hewn ceilings, and whitewashed adobe walls. Most of the seafood is farm-raised, and only free-range chickens, chemical-free beef, organic greens, and naturally fed veal are served.

**El Taoseño Restaurant.** *819 Paseo del Pueblo Sur.* ☎ *505/758-4142. Main courses $6–$12. AE, MC, V. Mon–Sat 6am–9pm, Sun 6:30am–3pm. NEW MEXICAN/ AMERICAN.* A long-established locals' favorite, El Taoseño features daily specials like barbecued chicken and Mexican plates. Standard fare includes huevos rancheros and enchiladas as well as burgers and sandwiches. The breakfast burrito is tops.

✪ **Lambert's of Taos.** *309 Paseo del Pueblo Sur.* ☎ *505/758-1009. Reservations recommended. Main courses $6–$12 at lunch, $8–$19 at dinner. AE, DC, MC, V. Mon– Fri 11:30am–2pm; daily 6–9pm. CONTEMPORARY AMERICAN.* The wooden floors and stucco walls of this historic home are an understated backdrop for the elegant and innovative dinners, such as pepper-crusted lamb with red-wine demiglace and garlic pasta. Many dishes have Southwestern or Oriental flavorings.

**Michael's Kitchen.** *304C Paseo del Pueblo Norte.* ☎ *505/758-4178. No reservations. Breakfast $2–$8; lunch $3–$10; dinner $6–$12. AE, DISC, MC, V. Daily 6am– 8:30pm. NEW MEXICAN/AMERICAN.* Michael's is a throwback to the 60s, with knickknacks everywhere. Breakfast dishes (including pancakes and eggs) and luncheon sandwiches (including Philly cheesesteak and a veggie) are served all day. Dinners range from veal cordon bleu to enchiladas rancheros to fish and chips.

## TAOS AFTER DARK

For a small town, Taos has more than its share of top entertainment, with annual music, dance, theater, and literary arts events. Many events are at the **Taos Community Auditorium,** 145 Paseo del Pueblo Norte (☎ **505/758-2052**). The weekly *Taos News* (Thursday), includes a current events section.

Fans of classical music visiting during the summer will not want to miss performances and seminars by the Taos School of Music's (☎ **505/776-2388**) **American String Quartet,** or pianist Robert McDonald. There is also an international group of student artists.

The bar action is at the hotels. The **Adobe Bar,** in the Historic Taos Inn, 125 Paseo del Pueblo Norte (☎ **505/758-2233**), is a favorite gathering place for locals as well as visitors. There's live music most evenings—jazz, folk, Hispanic, or acoustic—and it's a favorite for people-watching. Another lively spot is **Sagebrush Inn,** Paseo del Pueblo Sur (☎ **505/758-2254**), with regional country or rock performers nightly. The **Thunderbird Lodge,** in Taos Ski Valley (☎ **505/776-2280**), offers live entertainment and two-step dance lessons most of the year. Throughout January, the Thunderbird Jazz Festival hosts top-name jazz musicians.

## 12 Dallas

From its humble beginnings as an 1840 trading post along the Trinity River, Dallas has blossomed into a cosmopolitan and cultured city. Today this status-conscious city is a banking and insurance center, and the third-largest fashion center and film production area in the nation. And with space for architectural experimentation, its glittering skyline, creatively lighted at night, is one of the nation's most spectacular.

J. R. Ewing of TV's *Dallas* may have been too bad to be true, but the program put the city on the map all over the world. Tragic history was made here when President John F. Kennedy was fatally shot from the Texas School Book Depository on November 22, 1963.

"Big D" continues to look to the future, its hospitality still solid amid its Texas-size growth.

## ARRIVING & DEPARTING

**BY PLANE**   Domestic and international carriers fly into the **Dallas–Fort Worth International Airport (DFW),** and 24-hour van service is offered by the **Supershuttle** (☎ **800/258-3826**) to downtown Dallas for a charge of $11. The **Airporter Bus Service** (☎ **817/334-0092**) goes to a downtown terminal and some hotels, and costs $8. A taxi into Dallas will run you around $30. **Southwest Airlines** has its hub at **Love Field,** Cedar Springs (☎ **800/435-9792**), a $15 taxi ride to downtown Dallas.

**BY TRAIN & BUS**   Three **Amtrak** trains from Chicago per week pull into **Union Station,** 400 Houston St. (☎ **800/872-7245** or 214/653-1101). Amtrak also has trains to San Antonio and to points in east Texas. The **Greyhound Lines** (☎ **800/231-2222**) bus station is at 205 S. Lamar St.(☎ **214/655-7965**).

**BY CAR**   Dallas is circled by the I-635 ring road, also known as the LBJ Freeway. I-35 and Highway 75 (also known as Central Expressway) and the North Dallas Tollway run north-south. I-30 runs east-west.

## ESSENTIALS

**VISITOR INFORMATION**   The **Dallas Convention and Visitor Bureau** is located at 1201 Elm St., No. 2000, Dallas, TX 75270 (☎ **214/746-6677**).

**EMERGENCIES & SAFETY**   For emergencies, call ☎ **911.** In any strange city, you should always keep alert. It's never a good idea to walk down dark streets alone at night, and major tourist areas always attract pickpockets; keep your purse or wallet in a safe place.

## GETTING AROUND

**BY PUBLIC TRANSPORTATION**   The **Dallas Area Rapid Transit (DART)** operates citywide bus service, with stops indicated by yellow signs. Fare is $1, express fare $2, and seniors and persons with disabilities ride for 50¢; exact change is required. For information, call ☎ **214/979-1111.** A new **light-rail system** (☎ **214/979-1111**) connects Oak Cliff (Westmoreland) in the south and Park Lane in the north, with stops at the Dallas Zoo, Union Station, the West End, and the Convention Center; fare is $1. Buses connect with light-rail stops. A restored **trolley** (☎ **214/855-0006**) runs from McKinney Avenue, home of the Hard Rock, and the arts district.

## WHAT TO SEE & DO

**SPECIAL EVENTS**   The **Texas State Fair** (☎ **214/263-8374**), the largest state fair in the nation, takes place from late September to mid-October in Fair Park, which also has one of the nation's largest collections of art deco buildings. The **Cotton Bowl Football Game and Parade** (☎ **214/634-7525** or 214/638-2695) is an important event on January 1.

**ATTRACTIONS**   While the ranch you visit may be "pretend," the skyscrapers are real; however, Dallas has not totally demolished its past while building for the future. The revitalized **West End Historic District,** once a district of warehouses built between 1900 and 1930, is a big draw for visitors. Full of shops and restaurants, it is a good place for people-watching. The **Old Red Courthouse,** Main and Houston streets, is one of the city's oldest structures, and the nearby **John Neely Bryan Cabin** is a reconstruction of the trading post that was the city's first structure in 1841. Nearby is the Kennedy Memorial, designed by Philip Johnson.

Deep Ellum was once the city's blues and jazz center. It fell into squalor, but has gone through a SoHo-esque renaissance and now is a hip area with shops, galleries,

# Dallas

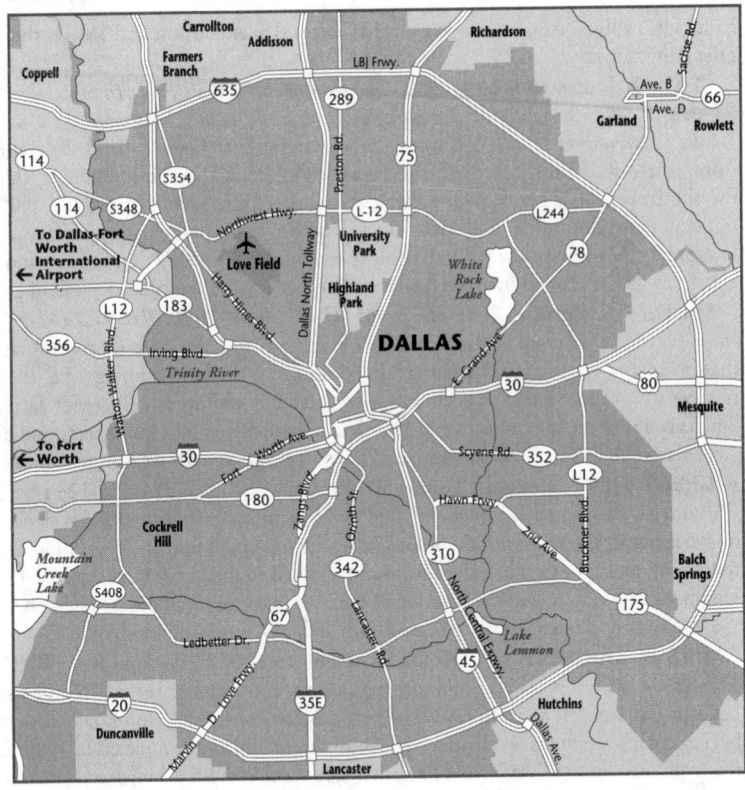

restaurants, and nightclubs. For information, call the Deep Ellum Association at ☎ 214/748-4332.

**Dallas Museum of Art.** *1717 N Harwood St.* ☎ *214/922-1200. Admission free. Tues, Wed, and Fri 11am–4pm, Thurs 11am–9pm, Sat–Sun 11am–5pm.* This most recent (1984) of the large Texas museums houses pre-Colombian art, works by Impressionist masters, modern American paintings (notably Jackson Pollock), and rich collections of African art. A giant sculpture by Claes Oldenburg, *Stake Hitch,* is also here. The building, designed by Edward Larrabee Barnes, features lovely gardens with waterfalls, shaded groves, and an unspoiled view of the Dallas skyline.

**Dallas Museum of Natural History.** *3535 Grand Ave.* ☎ *214/421-3466. Admission $4 adults, $2.50 children 3 and older. Daily 10am–5pm.* A neoclassical building houses this museum of Southwest and Texas natural history, offering more than 50 replicas of natural habitats plus rich zoological and botanical collections, including a 90-million-year-old fossil fish.

**Dallas World Aquarium.** *1801 N Griffin St.* ☎ *214/720-1801. Admission $5 adults, $3 seniors and children 3–11. Daily 10am–5pm.* One of the most modern and complete aquariums in the Southwest, with 350 species of fish, reptiles, and amphibians. The aquarium is home to indigenous species as well as tropical and exotic ones.

**Science Place.** *1318 2nd Ave.* ☎ *214/428-5555. Admission to exhibits $6 adults, $3 seniors and children 3–12; IMAX theater admission $6 adults, $5 children 3–12. Sun–Thurs 9:30am–5:30pm, Fri–Sat 9:30am–9pm.* Permanent and changing state-of-the-art, hands-on exhibits explore the world of science. A planetarium and IMAX theater offer daily shows.

✪ **Sixth Floor Museum.** *Elm and Houston sts. (West End Historic District).* ☎ *214/653-6659. Admission (including audio tour) $7 adults, $6 seniors, $5 ages 12–18, $4 children 6–11. Daily 9am–6pm.* Located on the sixth floor of the Dallas County Administration Building, formerly the Texas School Book Depository Building, this is the site from which Lee Harvey Oswald assassinated President Kennedy. A 9,000-square-foot exhibit, titled "The Sixth Floor," features films, photographs, artifacts, and interpretive displays on the cultural context of John F. Kennedy's death. The window area from which Oswald fired the fatal shots has been re-created behind a wall of glass.

**Southfork Ranch.** *3700 Hogge Rd.* ☎ *972/442-7800. Fax 972/442-5259. Admission $6.50 adults, $5.50 seniors, $4.50 children. Daily 9am–5pm.* The Texas ranch that became internationally famous as the location for the long-running CBS TV series *Dallas* operates today as both a tourist attraction and event/conference facility. Guests can tour the infamous Ewing Mansion and ranchland on a guide tram tour and view memorabilia in the *Dallas* museum. There is also a western-wear store and cafe.

**A GREAT VIEW**    **Reunion Tower,** 300 Reunion Blvd. (☎ **214/651-1234**), a 50-story tower, capped with a geodesic dome where computer-operated lights dance at night, is one of the new symbols of Dallas. At the top you'll find an observation deck, restaurant, and revolving lounge. The tower is linked to the Hyatt Regency Hotel, the Union railway station, and the Reunion Arena. Admission is $2 adults, $1 children, and the observatory is open Mon–Fri 9am–10pm and Sat–Sun 10am–midnight.

**PARKS & GARDENS**    The ✪ **Dallas Arboretum,** 8525 Garland Rd. (☎ **214/327-8263**), is 66 acres of beautiful gardens located on the eastern shore of White Rock Lake, just minutes from downtown. The headquarters are in the Camp Estate, designed by Texas's most famous residential architect, John Staub, and completed in 1938. On the grounds is historic DeGolyer House, a magnificent Spanish colonial–style mansion. More than 2,000 variations of azaleas are on display and 30 species of ferns. Enjoy the wildflower trail and 11-mile path around the lake. Tours are available. It's open daily 10am to 6pm; reduced hours off-season.

**BEST BET FOR KIDS**    Children enjoy the **Aquarium** (see above) and also the **Dallas Zoo,** 621 E. Clarendon St. (☎ **214/670-5656**); a highlight is the "Wilds of Africa" exhibit. Older children enjoy the Sixth Floor Museum as well as the Science Place with its many hands-on exhibits (see above).

**SPORTS**    The **Dallas Cowboys** play at **Texas Stadium,** 2401 E. Airport Freeway (☎ **214/579-5000**), from August through December. The **Dallas Mavericks** play in the **Reunion Arena** (☎ **214/748-1808**). The **Texas Rangers** play in the new **Ballpark at Arlington,** 1000 Ballpark Way, off I-30 (☎ **817/273-5100**).

**SHOPPING**    Shopping is sometimes called Dallas's number one indoor sport. **Highland Park Village** (☎ **214/559-2740**) was the first Dallas shopping center, opened in 1931. **Northpark Center** (☎ **214/363-7441**) is notable because developer Raymond Nasher displays pieces from his world-renown modern art collection throughout. The **Westend Market Place,** 603 Munger Ave. (☎ **214/748-4801**), once a candy factory, is now a five-story shopping center. Located in the southeast corner of Dallas, the **Farmers Produce Market,** 1010 S. Pearl (☎ **214/939-2808**), is open daily 7am–6pm. Special events, cooking classes, and educational classes on food-related, agricultural, and gardening topics are held year-round.

**The Galleria,** LBJ Freeway and Dallas North Tollway (☎ **214/702-7100**), is one of Dallas's largest upscale malls, with more than 200 shops, food court, and ice-skating rink. The **Shops at the Crescent** include the super-upscale department store,

Stanley Korshak (☎ **214/871-3600**), and the downtown Neiman Marcus (☎ **214/741-6911**) is a longtime institution. The **Quadrangle** (☎ **214/871-0878**) has great galleries, boutiques, and quirky shops such as Legacy Trading Co. (☎ 214/953-2222); Afterimage is a fine-art photo gallery (☎ 214/871-9140). For boutique shopping, people head to **Lower Greenville Avenue,** and **Deep Ellum** has kicky boutiques and hip clothing.

## ACCOMMODATIONS

Dallas's hotels tend to cater to the business traveler, and many of the hotels below have lower rates on the weekend.

✪ **Adam's Mark Resort & Hotel.** *400 N. Olive St. (between Live Oak and Pear sts.), Dallas, TX 75201.* ☎ **800/922-9222** *or 214/922-8000. Fax 214/922-0308. 502 rms and suites. $135–$155 single or double; $195–$225 suite. Additional person $10 extra. Children under 18 stay free in parents' room. Special weekend rates. AE, CB, DC, DISC, EC, JCB, MC, V. Indoor parking $8–$10.* This beautiful hotel, formerly the Harvey Hotel, is connected to many downtown buildings through an underground pedestrian system and skywalks. It is undergoing a renovation and expansion and adding a convention center that will more than triple the number of rooms by 1998.

✪ **Adolphus.** *1321 Commerce St., Dallas, TX 75202 (Financial District).* ☎ **800/221-9083** *or 214/742-8200. Fax 214/651-3561. 435 rms and suites. From $195 single or double; from $400 suite. Additional person $20 extra. Children under 12 stay free in parents' room. Rates vary by floor and size, with best values being the "superiors." AE, CB, DC, DISC, MC, V. Indoor parking $20.* Near the Arts Center, this modern 19-story hotel is attached to a smaller 1912 grand hotel. Large 10-foot ceiling rooms offer sitting area, minibar, and Queen Anne and Chippendale furnishings. The French Room serves outstanding cuisine. There is a courtesy town car to downtown, afternoon tea, and a day-care center.

**Courtyard by Marriott—LBJ at Josey.** *2930 Forest Lane (near I-35 and I-635), Dallas, TX 75229.* ☎ **800/321-2211** *or 972/620-8000. Fax 972/620-9267. 146 rms and suites. $75–$85 single or double; $89–$99 suite. Additional person $10 extra. Special weekend rates. Children under 16 stay free in parents' room. AE, CB, DC, DISC, MC, V. Free outdoor parking.* This cozy, friendly hotel in a quiet, shaded area is nicely secluded and safe. All rooms have terraces. Laundry facilities are available. The restaurant serves a buffet breakfast only.

**Dallas Grand Hotel.** *1914 Commerce St. (near Harwood).* ☎ **800/421-0011** *or 214/747-7000. Fax 214/742-1337. 710 rms and suites. $69–$129 single or double; $200–$500 suite. Additional person $10 extra. Special weekend rates. Children under 18 stay free in parents' room. AE, CB, DC, DISC, MC, V. Indoor parking $3–$9.50.* A large, arc-shaped budget hotel east of downtown, the Grand is spacious and uncrowded. It has two restaurants and laundry facilities.

**Embassy Suites Dallas Market Center.** *2727 Stemmons Freeway, Dallas, TX 75207.* ☎ **800/EMBASSY** *or 214/630-5332. 244 suites. $109–$169 suite. Additional person $10 extra. Children under 12 stay free in parents' room. Rates include breakfast and happy-hour cocktails. AE, CB, DC, DISC, JCB, MC, V. Free outdoor parking.* This all-suite hotel is friendly and convenient to downtown; it features a nine-story atrium. Executive, two-bedroom, king, and double units are available, some with sofa beds. All rooms have terraces and microwaves. The hotel has a restaurant (lunch and dinner only), sauna, steam room, and whirlpool, and offers transportation within a 3-mile radius of the hotel.

**Fairmont.** *1717 N. Akard St. (south of Woodall Rogers Freeway), Dallas, TX 75201.* ☎ **800/527-4727** *or 214/720-2020. Fax 214/720-5269. 600 rms and suites. $189–$219* *single or double; $249–$349 suite. Additional person $25 extra. Children under 18 stay free in parents' room. AE, CB, DC, DISC, ER, JCB, MC, V. Indoor parking $12.* An upscale, modern complex, the Fairmont affords easy access to downtown and specializes in conventions. Some rooms have minibars. The highly rated **Pyramid Room** is the elegant restaurant.

**Hawthorn Suites Hotel.** *7900 Brookriver Dr. (south of Mockingbird Lane, near I-35), Dallas, TX 75247.* ☎ *800/527-1133 or 214/688-1010. Fax 214/638-5215. 100 suites. $130–$168 suite. Special weekend rates. Children under 18 stay free in parents' room. AE, CB, DC, DISC, MC, V. Free outdoor parking.* Hawthorn is a growing and increasingly favored chain of suite hotels, great for extended stays. This hotel is located in a quiet and secluded section of town within minutes of I-35. Comfortable rooms offer terraces, refrigerators, and fireplaces. Conveniences include a pool, basketball, fitness club arrangement, and washer/dryer.

**Holiday Inn Aristocrat.** *1933 Main St. (between Harwood and Ervay), Dallas, TX 75201.* ☎ *800/231-4235 or 214/741-7700. Fax 214/939-3639. 172 rms and suites. $159–$169 double; $149–$189 suite. Additional person $10 extra. Children under 18 stay free in parents' room. AE, CB, DC, DISC, ER, JCB, MC, V. Indoor parking $3.* Built in 1925 by Conrad Hilton, this was the first property to bear the Hilton name. It became a Holiday Inn in 1992. A registered historic landmark, its original elegance and architectural features have been preserved. The hotel is connected to a downtown pedestrian system. Each room is individually decorated with antique furniture and has a minibar and refrigerator. The hotel has a restaurant, bar, complimentary coffee in the club room, and free access to a health and fitness center.

✪ **Hotel St. Germain.** *2516 Maple Ave. (near Cedar Springs Rd., across from the Crescent), Dallas, TX 75201.* ☎ *800/683-2516 or 214/871-2516. Fax 214/871-0740. 7 suites. $245–$600 suite. Unsuitable for children under 18. AE, MC, V.* This gem of an inn, located in an old house near downtown, offers 19th-century French motif rooms, with feather beds and lavish canopies. Some units have terraces or whirlpools, and all feature fireplaces. The attentive staff includes a full-time butler. The hotel has a restaurant (breakfast and dinner only), bar, and guest lounge.

**Hyatt Regency Dallas at Reunion.** *300 Reunion Blvd., Dallas TX 75207 (Downtown/West End).* ☎ *800/233-1234 or 214/651-1234. Fax 214/742-8126. 945 rms, 50 suites. $220–$250 double; $750–$2,300 suite. Children under 12 stay free in parents' room. Business rates available. AE, CB, DC, DISC, EC, JCB, MC, V. Indoor/outdoor parking $6–$12.* Featured in the opening sequence of *Dallas*, this hotel is near Reunions Arena, Dallas Convention Center, and connected by tunnel to Union Station. Rooms have minibars and all amenities, and there are special, well-equipped rooms for those with disabilities. The Antares restaurant is here (see "Dining," below). The hotel has three restaurants, two bars, a pool, spa, sauna, steam room, whirlpool, washer/dryer, and playground.

**Lexington Hotel Suites.** *4150 Independence Dr. (off Camp Wisdom Rd.), Dallas, TX 75237.* ☎ *800/53-SUITE or 972/298-7014. Fax 972/709-1680. 108 suites. $59–$169 suite. Children under 12 stay free in parents' room. AE, CB, DC, DISC, JCB, MC, V. Free outdoor parking.* Near I-20 and Redbird Mall, this attractive hotel is convenient and cozy for leisure travelers looking for something extra. Extras include a pool, whirlpool, washer/dryer, video games, refrigerators, Wednesday night cookouts in summer, transportation, and free pass to health club.

✪ **Mansion on Turtle Creek.** *2821 Turtle Creek Blvd. (Oaklawn/Turtle Creek), Dallas, TX 75219.* ☎ *800/527-5432 or 214/559-2100. Fax 214/528-4187. 141 rms and suites. $290–$350 double; $625–$1,500 suite. Additional person $40 extra. Children* *under 18 stay free in parents' room. AE, CB, DC, DISC, ER, JCB, MC, V. Indoor/ outdoor parking $10.* Near the Financial and Arts District, this flagship of the classy Rosewood Hotel group—cherished by an elite clientele for pampering—has large, refined rooms and suites, some with French windows and balconies. The **dining room** is one of the finest restaurants in Dallas and is highly recommended. There's a pool, sauna, steam room, business center, and a courtesy car for travel within a 5-mile radius.

**Radisson Hotel and Suites.** *2330 W. Northwest Hwy. (east of I-35), Dallas, TX 75220.* ☎ *800/333-3333 or 214/351-4477. Fax 214/351-4499. 198 rms and suites. $139 double; $149 suite. Additional person $10 extra. Children under 18 stay free in parents' room. AE, CB, DC, DISC, MC, V. Free outdoor parking.* This conveniently located hotel features poolside suites and is near Love Field, Texas Stadium, downtown, and "restaurant row." The hotel has a restaurant, two bars, two pools, whirlpool, and washer/ dryer.

**Stoneleigh Hotel.** *2927 Maple Ave., Dallas, TX 75201 (near Cedar Springs).* ☎ *800/255-9299 or 214/871-7111. 132 rms and suites. $125–$175 single or double; $215–$225 suite. Additional person $10 extra. Children under 18 stay free in parents' room. AE, CB, DC, DISC, MC, V. Free indoor/outdoor parking.* This historic 1924 hotel offers romantic ambiance in a posh Dallas area and is a home away from home to show business celebs. What it lacks in facilities it makes up for in coziness and elegance. Large rooms provide a view of downtown. The hotel has a restaurant, bar, masseur, complimentary newspapers, and nearby health/sporting facilities.

**Westin Hotel Galleria Dallas.** *13340 Dallas Pkwy. (I-635 and Dallas N. Tollway), Dallas, TX 75240.* ☎ *800/228-3000 or 972/934-9494. Fax 972/450-2979. 431 rms and suites. $144–$192 single or double; $525–$1,275 suite. Additional person $20 extra. Children under 18 stay free in parents' room. AE, CB, DC, DISC, ER, JCB, MC, V. Free indoor/outdoor parking.* Located in one of the most prestigious areas of Dallas, near the Galleria Mall. All units have minibars and some offer terraces. Conveniences include three restaurants, three bars, a pool, health/fitness facilities access, and a children's program.

**OTHER ACCOMMODATIONS**  A number of hotels are convenient to the DFW Airport. The **Hyatt Regency DFW Airport,** International Pkwy. (P.O. Box 619014), Dallas, TX 75261 (☎ **800/233-1234** or 972/453-1234; fax 972/456-8668), claims to be the world's largest airport hotel, with 1,400 rooms and suites, 1,500 free parking places, and an array of restaurants, bars, sports and health facilities, and shops. The bright pinkish **Doubletree Guest Suites,** 4650 W. Airport Freeway, Irving, TX 75062 (☎ **972/790-0093**), is located near the south entrance to DFW Airport and features a beautiful tropical atrium. The **Holiday Inn DFW Airport South,** 4440 W. Airport Freeway, Irving, TX 75062 (☎ **972/399-1010**), is located halfway between Dallas and Fort Worth. The **Harvey Hotel DFW Airport,** 4545 W. John Carpenter Freeway, Irving, TX 75063 (☎ **800/922-9222** or **972/929-4500;** fax 972/929-0733), is one of the largest hotels near the airport, suitable for all kinds of travelers.

## DINING

In addition to the listings below, check out the restaurants mentioned by name in the hotel section.

**Antares.** *In the Hyatt Regency Dallas at Reunion, 300 Reunion Blvd. (at Jct. I-35).* ☎ *214/651-1234. Reservations recommended. Main courses $15–$30. AE, CB, DC, DISC, MC, V. Valet parking. NEW AMERICAN.* The Hyatt's fine dining restaurant, located at the top of Reunion Tower, revolves every hour to provide some great views of Dallas. Patrons dine in a romantic setting, enjoying interesting New American preparations of beef, chicken, and seafood.

**Aw Shucks.** *3601 Greenville Ave. (south of Mockingbird).* ☎ *214/821-9449. Reservations not accepted. Main courses $5–$8. AE, DC, DISC, MC, V. Peak season (Feb–Oct), Mon–Thurs 11am–11pm, Fri–Sat 11am–11:45pm, Sun 11:30am–10pm. SEAFOOD.* Popular with locals and SMU students, this noisy and fast-paced eatery has outdoor tables on an active section of Greenville Avenue, making it a prime people-watching spot. Shrimp cocktail is a specialty of the house.

**Cerveceria—The Big Mex Cafe.** *1800 N. Market St. (near junction of Ross and Market sts., West End Historical District).* ☎ *214/969-0310. Reservations accepted. Main courses $3–$25. AE, CB, DC, DISC, MC, V. Sun–Thurs 11am–10pm, Fri–Sat 11am–midnight. TEX-MEX.* Located in the heart of the West End, this fun, colorful, multi-level Tex-Mex restaurant with Southwestern decor and lively service offers good food along with country music/jazz/reggae/rock. There's a children's menu.

**Dakota's.** *600 N. Akard St. (downtown, at San Jacinto).* ☎ *214/740-4001. Reservations recommended. Main courses $10–$20. AE, CB, DC, DISC, MC, V. Mon–Fri 11am–2:30pm; Mon–Thurs 5–10pm, Fri–Sat 5–10:30pm, Sun 5:30–9pm. Valet parking. NEW AMERICAN.* A unique, award-winning restaurant located below ground—the above-ground entrance is simply a canopied elevator. The elegant interior is marked by Italian marble, and the Sun Room features a cascading waterfall. Outdoor seating offers views of downtown. Mesquite-grilled items are popular and specialties include blackened red snapper.

**Deep Ellum Cafe.** *2706 Elm St. (in Deep Ellum).* ☎ *214/741-9012. Sandwiches $7, main courses $12–$14. AE, MC, V. Sun–Thurs 11am–10pm, Fri–Sat 11am–11pm. AMERICAN.* This chic, locally popular cafe is the place to go for sandwiches, pastry, and more substantial pasta dishes and meat dishes.

**Fog City Diner.** *2401 McKinney (near Pearl Expwy. and the Crescent).* ☎ *214/220-2401. Reservations recommended. Main courses $10–$16. AE, CB, DC, DISC, MC, V. Sun–Wed 11:30am–11pm, Thurs–Sat 11:30am–midnight. NEW AMERICAN.* Popular and trendy, this eatery (partially owned by Cowboys quarterback Troy Aikman) offers superb diner atmosphere. The classic look includes a reflective metal exterior and counter and booth seating inside.

✪ **Gloria's.** *600 W. Davis St. (west of Zangs Blvd. near I-35, Oak Cliff).* ☎ *214/948-3672. Reservations not accepted. Main courses $4–$11. AE, CB, DC, DISC, MC, V. Mon–Fri 11am–10pm, Sat–Sun 10am–10pm. LATIN AMERICAN.* This little storefront eatery has developed a strong reputation in Dallas for its excellent Latin American cuisine. Dishes like Salvadoran fried yucca or tamales wrapped in banana leaves make for deliciously different lunch or dinner fare. Additional location: 4140 Lemmon Ave. (☎ 214/521-7576).

✪ **Javier's.** *4912 Cole Ave.* ☎ *214/521-4211. Main courses $14–$20. Sun–Thurs 5:30–10:30pm, Fri–Sat 5:30–11pm. MEXICAN/CONTINENTAL.* This upscale restaurant is locally popular for its sophisticated Mexican cuisine in an antique Spanish setting.

**L'Ancestral.** *In Travis Walk, 4514 Travis (Knox exit off U.S. 75), Knox–Henderson).* ☎ *214/528-1081. Reservations recommended. Main courses $13–$20; fixed-price dinner $23. AE, CB, DC, DISC, MC, V. Mon–Sat 11:30am–2pm; Mon–Thurs 6–10pm, Fri–Sat 6–11pm. FRENCH.* Located in an upscale section of Dallas, this elegant French bistro has a decor highlighted by exquisite oil paintings. It offers excellent classic French fare, with steak tartare a standout.

**NorthSouth.** *In the Quadrangle.* ☎ *214/849-0000. Main courses $15–$26. Mon–Sat 11:30am–3pm; Tues–Thurs 5:30–10pm, Fri–Sat 5pm–midnight. AE, MC, V. ECLECTIC.* Local fitness guru Larry North recently opened this restaurant. If you order from the menu North, everything is fat-free; everything on the South menu has all fat intact. A pleasant, upscale spot with a varied menu.

**Old Warsaw.** *2610 Maple (between Cedar Springs and McKinney aves., Oak Lawn).* ☎ *214/528-0032. Reservations recommended. Main courses $21–$48. AE, CB, DC, DISC, MC, V. Daily 5:30–10:30pm. Valet parking. FRENCH.* Established in 1948, this elegant restaurant offers sophisticated dining amid music and candlelight, chandeliers, model ships, and oriental accents to create a unique ambiance. The wine room connects to a posh bar. Included on the menu are chicken, duck, veal, and lots of rich desserts.

**Pierre's by the Lake.** *3430 Shorecrest Dr. (between Lemmon Ave. and Denton Dr.).* ☎ *214/358-2379. Reservations recommended. Main courses $9–$12. AE, CB, DC, DISC, MC, V. Mon–Thurs 10am–10pm, Fri 10am–11pm, Sat 5–11pm. Valet parking. SEAFOOD/STEAK.* Overlooking Bachman Lake on the north side of Love Field, this elegant restaurant sits in the middle of Dallas but offers a peaceful setting. Dine on continental classics amid plush red carpeting and French Impressionist prints, and enjoy the fireplace and piano. Try the chateaubriand.

✪ **Pomodoro.** *2520 Cedar Springs Rd. (near Maple Ave.).* ☎ *214/871-1924. Reservations recommended. Main courses $6–$13. AE, DC, MC, V. Mon–Fri 11:30am–2pm; Mon–Thurs 6–10pm, Fri–Sat 6–11pm. Valet parking. ITALIAN.* Located in posh Turtle Creek, this popular upscale restaurant attracts a diverse clientele that includes celebrities. While it can be noisy, northern Italian cuisine is worth the trip. Try the swordfish carpaccio.

**Riviera.** *7709 Inwood Rd.* ☎ *214/351-0094. Reservations recommended. Main courses $26–$30. Mon–Thurs 6:30–10:30pm, Fri–Sat 6–11:30pm. AE, CB, DC, MC, V. MEDITERRANEAN.* A highly regarded upscale restaurant and a local favorite, featuring exceptional service and fine food by chefs David Holben and Michael Winsein. Beautiful decorations and gorgeous floral arrangements set the scene for such dishes as fettuccine with smoked chicken and wild mushrooms.

**S&D Oyster Company.** *2701 McKinney Ave. at Boll St.* ☎ *214/880-0111. Reservations not accepted. Main courses $3–$13. MC, V. Mon–Thurs 11am–10pm, Fri–Sat 11am–11pm. SEAFOOD.* The 1891 building and featured jazz bands lend New Orleans ambiance to this classy restaurant. Great oysters, shrimp, and other gulf seafood are presented smartly by the formally attired wait staff.

✪ **Seventeen-Seventeen.** *In the Dallas Museum of Art.* ☎ *214/880-0158. Main courses $18–$28. Tues–Sun 11am–2pm; Tues–Thurs 6–10pm, Fri–Sun 6–11pm. SOUTHWESTERN/NEW AMERICAN.* This upscale and sophisticated restaurant is a fine addition to downtown Dallas. The menu reflects the ever-inventive talents of executive chef Kent Rathbun.

**Sonny Bryan's.** *2202 Inwood Rd. (near Harry Hines, off I-35).* ☎ *214/357-7120. Reservations not accepted. Main courses $4–$10. No credit cards. Mon–Fri 10am–4pm, Sat 10am–3pm, Sun 11am–2pm. BARBECUE.* The nonchalant atmosphere and great barbecue bring many repeat customers. Eat outside in the large open parking lot or get your food to go; there's no seating available. Additional locations: 302 N. Market (☎ *214/ 744-1610*); 4701 Frankford (☎ *214/447-0102*).

**Star Canyon.** *In the Centrum, 3102 Oak Lawn (between Cedar Springs and Lennon, Oak Lawn).* ☎ *214/520-7827. Main courses $15–$29. AE, CB, DC, DISC, MC, V. Mon–Fri 11:30am–2pm; Mon–Thurs 6–10:30pm, Fri–Sat 6–11pm, Sun 6–10pm. Valet parking. NEW TEXAS.* This friendly and fashionable upscale restaurant features what innovative chef Stephan Pyles terms New Texas cuisine, incorporating Southwestern, Southern, Texas, and Latin influences. The popular barbecued shrimp enchilada is a fine way to sample his talents.

**Thai Soon.** *2018 Greenville Ave.* ☎ *214/821-7666. Reservations accepted. Main courses $7–$14. AE, DC, DISC, MC, V. Mon–Fri 11am–3pm; Mon–Thurs 5–10pm, Fri 5pm–midnight; Sat 11am–midnight, Sun noon–10pm. THAI.* Located on a busy stretch of Greenville Avenue, this small, modestly decorated restaurant serves authentic Thai cuisine to a devoted clientele. Fresh seafood and vegetarian dishes are specialties.

**Tolbert's Texas Chili Parlor.** *In One Dallas Center, 350 N. St. Paul, at Bryan St.* ☎ *214/953-1353. Reservations accepted. Main courses $6–$8. AE, CB, DC, DISC, MC, V. Mon–Fri 11am–7pm. TEX-MEX.* One of the state's most celebrated chili parlors, this Tex-Mex has been around for years. A fun, casual atmosphere and affordable prices make it easy for families to enjoy "donkey tails" (hot-dog tortillas).

## DALLAS AFTER DARK

**THE PERFORMING ARTS**   Home to the **Dallas Symphony,** the impressive **Morton H. Meyerson Symphony Center,** 2301 Flora St. (☎ 214/670-3600), is the only concert hall designed by I. M. Pei. The **Dallas Theater Center,** 3636 Turtle Creek Blvd. (☎ 214/526-8857), is also impressively designed, by Frank Lloyd Wright, and presents a 7-month season of productions ranging from Shakespeare to contemporary works.

**THE CLUB & BAR SCENE**   Hotlines for tickets are **Central Tickets** (☎ 214/335-9000) and the **Dallas Blues Society** (☎ 214/521-BLUE).

In Deep Ellum, **Club Dada,** 2720 Elm (☎ 214/744-3232), offering live music, was a pioneer in the neighborhood during the area's 1980s renaissance. **Club Clearview,** 2806 Elm (tel] 214/939-0077), is loud and attracts very young people with tattoos and earrings. Its spinoff clubs include the **Art Bar & Cafe** (☎ 214/939-0077) for recorded music and art, **Blind Lemon** (☎ 214/939-0202) for dancing, and **Red** (☎ 214/939-0077), the newest of the bunch. **Sambuca,** 15207 Addison (☎ 214/744-0820), is a Mediterranean restaurant that has live jazz on weekends.

For Blues, **Schooners,** 1212 Stillman (☎ 214/821-1934), is a neighborhood hangout; as is **Muddy Waters,** 1518 Greenville (☎ 214/823-1518). **Blue Cat Blues,** 2617 Commerce (☎ 214/744-CATS), is Deep Ellum's blues spot.

**Trees,** 2709 Elm (☎ 214/748-5009), is a cavernous club that gets the larger alternative rock touring acts. **Velvet Elvis,** 1906 McKinney (☎ 214/969-5586), has live blues, funk, and gospel, and recently won a lawsuit with the Presley estate to keep the name. The **Rehab Lounge,** 2614 Main (☎ 214/741-1311), is a multilevel club with everything from comedy to acid jazz.

For country, an all-time favorite spot is **Sons of Hermann Hall,** 3414 Elm (☎ 214/747-4422), a dance hall (and real fraternal organization) that has live music on weekends—often Texas pickers—and attracts everyone from Grandpa to the kids, from straight-ahead country types to alternative club dabblers. **Poor David's Pub,** 1924 Greenville (☎ 214/821-9891), just celebrated its 20th anniversary. It's a dive, but it brings in good live folk/country and other interesting acts such as Guy Clarke and the Roches.

**Starck** (☎ 214/922-9677) is the too-hip-to-breathe disco. **Red Jacket,** 3606 Lower Greenville (☎ 214/373-8000), is a disco that rides all the latest trends, with a Martini Night, lounge music, and cigar bar. **Mirage** (☎ 214/739-8063) is an all-out disco, reportedly popular with Dallas Cowboys. **Club Babalu,** 3878 Oak Lawn (☎ 214/521-3695), is an upscale Latin disco. **Village Station** (☎ 214/526-7171) is the popular gay disco in the Oak Lawn area, and the hub of the city's large gay community.

Hang out with well-dressed artsy types at the **Inwood Lounge** (☎ 214/350-7834) adjoining the Inwood art-house movie theater. **Lava Lounge,** 2604 Main (☎ 214/698-3020), has a cocktail menu and live music. **Java Jones** is a coffeehouse with live acoustic music on weekends in two locations, Oak Lawn (☎ **214/528-2099**) and Mockingbird (☎ **214/823-3345**).

## 13  Fort Worth

Established in 1849 as a frontier military post, Fort Worth was later nicknamed "Cowtown" because it was a major railhead for shipping cattle. Today Fort Worth is as sophisticated as its neighbor, Dallas. Its once rowdy cattle trading center and meatpackers' mecca is now the Stockyard Historic District where modern western-wear outlets sit cheek-by-jowl with turn-of-the-century wooden sidewalks and shopfronts, and three of the state's finest art museums are found in the city.

### ARRIVING & DEPARTING

**BY PLANE**   Flights to Fort Worth arrive at the **Dallas–Fort Worth International Airport (DFW);** see section 12 for details.

**BY TRAIN & BUS**   Trains arrive at the old **Santa Fe Depot,** 1501 Jones St. (☎ **817/332-2931**). The **Greyhound Bus Station** is at 901 Commerce St. (☎ **817/429-3089**).

### ESSENTIALS

**VISITOR INFORMATION**   The **Fort Worth Convention and Visitor Bureau** is at 415 Throckmorton St., Fort Worth, TX 76102 (☎ **800/433-5747** or 817/336-8791). The **Visitor Center/Uptown,** 130 E. Exchange Ave. (☎ **817/624-4741**), also has information on the area.

**EMERGENCIES & SAFETY**   Call ☎ **911** for emergencies. After dark, never walk alone in deserted areas.

### GETTING AROUND

**BY PUBLIC TRANSPORTATION**   The Fort Worth Transportation Authority (FWTA) operates 33 main bus routes citywide (the bus is also known as "the T." Standard fare is 80¢; children ages 6 to 18, seniors, and persons with disabilities pay half fare. Exact change is required. Call ☎ **817/871-6200** for information.

### WHAT TO SEE & DO

**SPECIAL EVENTS**   The **Southwestern Exposition Stock Show and Rodeo** takes place 2 weeks in early January or late February. Call ☎ **817/877-2400** for information. The third weekend in June brings the **Chisholm Trail Roundup,** with a cowboy parade, barbecue, and square dancing.

**TOURS**   The **Tarantula Excursion Train,** 2318 8th Ave. (☎ **817/625-7245**), offers tours from downtown to the Stockyards.

**THE TOP ATTRACTIONS**   The **Fort Worth Stockyard Historic District** recalls the time when Fort Worth was a major meatpacking center. Today the former cattle and sheep pens house shops and restaurants. Information is available at the **Stockyards Visitor Center,** 130 E. Exchange Ave. (☎ **817/624-4741**). The **Cultural District** is home to three of Texas's finest museums.

✪ **Amon Carter Museum.** *3501 Camp Bowie Blvd.* ☎ *817/738-1933. Admission free. Sept to mid-June, Tues–Sat 10am–5pm, Sun noon–5pm.* The collection, housed in a Philip Johnson–designed, international-style building, features outstanding works of 19th- and early 20th-century American art (paintings, sculpture, and prints), as well as an impressive collection of American photographs. The research library holds over 30,000 volumes and an extensive microfilm collection of 19th-century American newspapers, periodicals, and important rare publications. Special programs such as film series, gallery talks, and children's workshops are offered. The museum has a bookstore, and guided museum tours are available.

**Botanic Gardens.** *3200 Botanic Garden Dr.* ☎ *817/871-7686. Japanese Garden, $2 adults, $1 children. Conservatory, $1 adults, 50¢ children. Daily sunrise–sundown. Japanese garden, Nov–Mar, daily 10am–5pm. Conservatory, Mon–Fri 10am–9pm, Sat 10am–6pm, Sun 1–6pm.* The gardens showcase 150,000 plants representing 2,500 species, displayed in both formal and natural settings. A 10,000-square-foot glass conservatory is planted with more than 2,500 tropical plants native to Central and South America.

**Fort Worth Museum of Science and History.** *1501 Montgomery St.* ☎ *817/732-1631. Mon 9am–5pm, Tues–Thurs 9am–8pm, Fri–Sat 9am–9pm, Sun noon–8pm.* Nine galleries present hands-on exhibits dealing with the human body, rocks and fossils, medicine, dinosaurs, and computers. The Noble Planetarium offers astronomy programs, and the 80-foot domed Omni Theater presents films on science and nature. More than 600 classes and workshops are offered year-round.

✪ **Kimbell Art Museum.** *3333 Camp Bowie Blvd.* ☎ *817/332-8451. Admission free. Tues–Thurs 10am–5pm, Fri noon–8pm, Sat 10am–5pm, Sun noon–5pm.* Housed in an acclaimed modern building designed by renowned architect Louis I. Kahn, the collection ranges in period from antiquity to the 20th century. Included are masterworks from Fra Angelico, El Greco, and Matisse, to name a few, and a collection of Asian art, as well as a group of meso-American and African pieces and Mediterranean antiquities. Lectures, symposia, and workshops, as well as a Sunday family hour and a summer family film festival, are offered.

✪ **Modern Art Museum of Fort Worth.** *1309 Montgomery St.* ☎ *817/738-9215. Admission free. Tues–Fri 10am–5pm, Sat 11am–5pm, Sun noon–5pm.* Established in 1892, this is among the oldest art museums in Texas. The permanent collection contains works by modern and contemporary masters, such as Picasso and Rothko. Program offerings include lectures, gallery talks, children's workshops, intermuseum loans, educational programs, and guided tours. The **Modern at Sundance Square** (☎ 817/335-9215) is the museum annex, located on the ground floor of the historic Sanger Building downtown. It hosts selections from the Modern's permanent collection and small-scale traveling exhibitions.

**Sid Richardson Collection of Western Art.** *309 Main St.* ☎ *817/332-6554. Admission free. Tues–Wed 10am–5pm, Thurs–Fri 10am–8pm, Sat 11am–8pm, Sun 1–5pm.* This one-room gallery holds a collection of Western art assembled by the late oil tycoon Sid Richardson. Frederic Remington and Charles M. Russell are represented by some 50 paintings.

**Will Rogers Memorial Center.** *3400 W Lancaster St.* ☎ *817/871-8150. Admission free. Grounds, 8am–5pm. Call for events schedule.* Dedicated to the famous cinema cowboy and humorist, this vast exhibition center includes the Memorial Coliseum and the Will Rogers Auditorium, where concerts, rodeos, and other Fort Worth events take place.

**MORE ATTRACTIONS** **Thistle Hill,** 1509 Pennsylvania Ave. (☎ 817/336-1212), built in 1903, is one of the few remaining examples of Georgian Revival architecture in the Southwest, and is listed on the National Register of Historic Places. It's open Mon–Fri 10am–3pm, Sun 1–4pm. **Log Cabin Village,** 2100 Log Cabin Village Lane (☎ 817/926-5881), is a living history museum comprised of seven authentic log homes from the late 1800s, furnished with period antiques and implements. Historical interpreters demonstrate pioneer crafts and there is also a working grist mill. Admission is $1.50 adults, $1.25 seniors and children; it's open Tues–Fri 9am–5pm, Sat 10am–5pm, Sun 1–5pm.

**BEST BETS FOR KIDS** Kids enjoy the **Log Cabin Village** as well as the **Amon Carter Museum** with its Old West paintings. In Sundance Square, they will like the

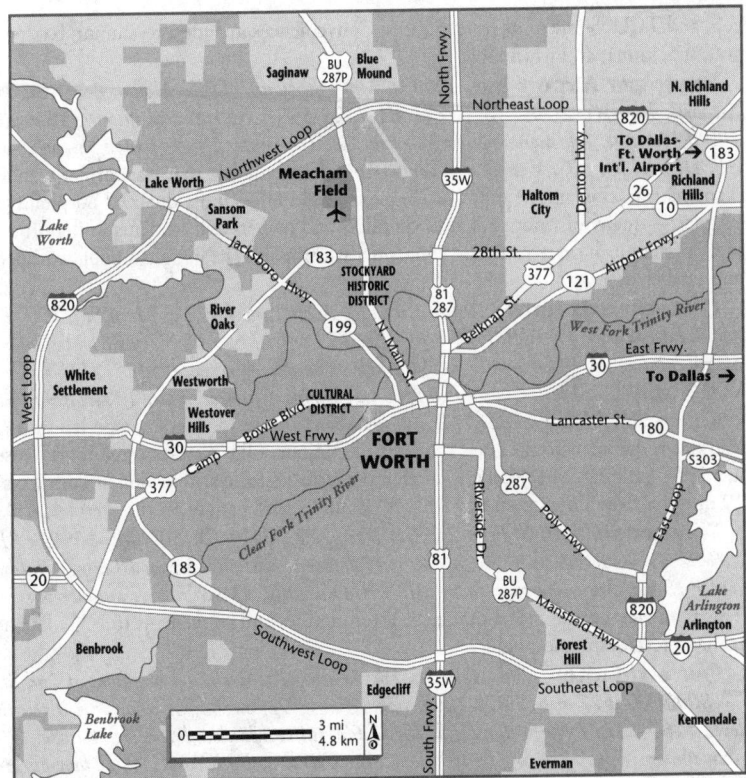

Fire Station Museum, 215 Commerce St., and the Fort Worth Museum of Science and History is fun. The Stockyards and the Stockyards Museum are a good bet (☎ 817/624-7117).

**SHOPPING**  Western wear is the thing to buy here, and many outlet stores in the Stockyards Historic District carry it. For western boots, try M. L. Leddy's Boot and Saddlery, 2455 Main St. (☎ 817/624-3149). There are also shops in Sundance Square.

## ACCOMMODATIONS

In addition to the hotels listed below, see "Other Accommodations" for hotels near the airport in the Dallas section.

**Courtyard by Marriott.** *3150 Riverfront Dr. (near University Dr. and I-30), Fort Worth, TX 76107.* ☎ *800/321-2211 or 817/335-1300. Fax 817/336-6926. $105 double; $122 suite. Additional person $10 extra. Children under 18 stay free in parents' room. AE, CB, DC, DISC, MC, V. Free outdoor parking.* Located in a wooded area across from the Trinity River, this better-than-average chain property is near Texas Christian University (TCU) and convenient to downtown but not amid its hustle and bustle. The hotel has a restaurant (breakfast only), pool, and washer/dryer.

**Green Oaks Inn and Conference Center.** *6901 West Freeway (at junction of Tex. 183 and I-30), Fort Worth, TX 76116.* ☎ *800/433-2174 or 817/738-7311, 800/772-2341 in Texas. Peak season (Oct), $94 double; $114 suite. Additional person $10 extra. Lower rates off-season. Children under 12 stay free in parents' room. Rates include breakfast. AE, CB, DC, DISC, JCB, MC, V. Free outdoor parking.* With its resort atmosphere, this facility draws vacationers and conventioneers. Close to Carswell AFB, the zoo, and TCU. Some units have terraces. Conveniences include a restaurant, bar, pool, golf, spa, sauna, and whirlpool.

**Sandpiper Airport Inn.** *4000 N. Main St. (south of Blue Mound near Meacham Airport), Fort Worth, TX 76106.* ☎ *817/625-5531. 81 rms and suites. $55 double; $80–$300 suite. Additional person $5 extra. Children under 18 stay free in parents' room. AE, DC, DISC, MC, V. Free outdoor parking.* In a building that was formerly an airplane hangar, this unique motel at Meacham Field offers individualized hospitality to its guests—many of whom are airplane pilots and owners and students in flight training. Some units have terraces and some offer whirlpools. The inn has a pool, whirlpool, and washer/dryer.

✪ **Stockyards Hotel.** *109 E. Exchange Ave. (1 block east of Main St.), P.O. Box 4558, Fort Worth, TX 76106.* ☎ *800/423-8471 or 817/625-6427. Fax 817/624-2571. 52 rms and suites. Weekdays, $85–$90 single or double. Weekends, $125–$135 single or double. $130–$350 suite. Additional person $10 extra. Children under 18 stay free in parents' room. AE, CB, DC, DISC, MC, V. Outdoor parking $5.* A grand wooden staircase leads from the lobby to the guest rooms at this unique, Old West–inspired hotel housed in a 1907 building. The hotel is located in the historic stockyards section of Fort Worth, 10 minutes from downtown and I-35. A restaurant and bar are on the premises.

**Travelodge.** *4201 S. Freeway, Fort Worth, TX 76115.* ☎ *800/446-4656 or 817/ 923-8281. Fax 817/926-8756. 98 rms. $45 double. Additional person $8 extra. Children under 18 stay free in parents' room. AE, CB, DC, DISC, MC, V. Free outdoor parking.* This is an economical motel that is great for families and convenient to I-35. The hotel has a restaurant and pool.

✪ **Worthington.** *200 Main St., Fort Worth, TX 76102 (downtown, at 2nd St.).* ☎ *800/433-5677 or 817/870-1000. Fax 817/338-9176. 504 rms and suites. Executive level, $165–$375 single or double; $275–$1,000 suite. Additional person $20 extra. Children under 18 stay free in parents' room. AE, CB, DC, DISC, MC, V. Indoor parking $6–$9.* Across from Sundance Square, this is one of the most luxurious hotels in Fort Worth. All units have minibars and some offer terraces. Conveniences include three restaurants, a bar, pool, spa, sauna, whirlpool, and masseur.

## DINING

Steak is the thing here, along with barbecue, but you can also choose from a variety of other cuisines.

**Angelo's Barbecue.** *2533 White Settlement Rd. (between Henderden and University, near downtown).* ☎ *817/332-0357. Reservations not accepted. Main courses $7–$12. No credit cards. Mon–Sat 11am–10pm. BARBECUE.* It's a western theme at this downhome barbecue joint, serving up spicy authentic Texas-style barbecue, and the numerous awards displayed on the wall attest to its quality.

**Bella Italia West.** *5139 Camp Bowie (west of University).* ☎ *817/738-1700. Reservations recommended. Main courses $8–$21. AE, CB, DC, DISC, MC, V. Mon–Fri 11:30am–2pm; Mon–Sat 6pm–close. ITALIAN.* This elegant restaurant, great for family dining, offers an extensive menu with something to please everyone, and a professional wait staff to do the serving.

✪ **Cattlemen's Steak House.** *2458 N. Main (near Exchange at Stockyards).* ☎ *817/624-3945. Reservations accepted. Main courses $10–$26. AE, DC, DISC, MC, V. Mon–Thurs 11am–10:30pm, Fri–Sat 11am–11pm; Sun 4–10pm. STEAK.* Suave, posh, and romantic, this authentic steak house in the old stockyards is well known in the Dallas–Fort Worth area—it's been around since 1947 and may well have perfected the steak.

**Edelweiss.** *3801A Southwest Blvd. (at junction of U.S. 377, Tex. 183, and Tex. 580).* ☎ *817/738-5934. Reservations accepted. Main courses $9–$16. AE, CB, DC, DISC,*

MC, V. *Tues–Thurs 5–10:30pm, Fri–Sat 5–11pm. GERMAN.* A noisy establishment with a gregarious clientele and staff, this is a great place for fun, where sing-alongs are held regularly. Weekday happy hours draw crowds, and the traditional German fare is tasty and filling.

**۞ Joe T. Garcia's.** *2201 N. Commerce St. (near Main St. and Stockyards).* **☎ 817/ 626-4356.** *Reservations accepted. Main courses $3–$10. No credit cards. Mon–Thurs 11am–2:30pm and 5–10pm, Fri–Sat 11am–11pm, Sun 11am–10pm. MEXICAN.* Behind the small entrance is a patio that seats 300 people amid fountains, a swimming pool, and a miniature park. Seating is also available indoors. The friendly and casual service remains unaffected by celebrity patrons. The two dinner entrees are beef or chicken fajitas, or a family-style enchilada dinner.

**Juanita's.** *In Sundance Square, 115 W. 2nd St.* **☎ 817/335-1777.** *Reservations accepted. Main courses $2–$12. AE, CB, DC, DISC, MC, V. Mon–Thurs 11am–midnight, Fri 11am–1am, Sat noon–1am, Sun noon–midnight. TEX-MEX.* A popular, festive Tex-Mex restaurant situated amid the downtown nightlife spots. Fajitas and other favorites, plus specialties like quail braised in tequila.

**۞ Kincaid's.** *4901 Camp Bowie Blvd. (at Eldridge, near Hulen Blvd.).* **☎ 817/ 732-2881.** *Reservations not accepted. Main courses $2–$5. No credit cards. Mon–Sat 11am–6pm. BURGERS.* Recognized for serving some the best burgers in Fort Worth, this well-known family-owned and -operated restaurant/grocery store has been serving quality food since 1946. Picnic seating in front of the restaurant is nice for lunch or early dinner. The grocery shelves serve as tables for the large lunch crowd.

**Michael's.** *3413 W. 7th St. (west of University).* **☎ 817/877-3413.** *Reservations accepted. Main courses $12–$25. AE, DC, DISC, MC, V. Mon–Fri 11am–2:30pm; Mon–Wed 5:30–10pm, Thurs–Sat 5:30–11pm. REGIONAL AMERICAN.* Unique floral arrangements and modern art decorate this contemporary restaurant where a professional staff serves up such specialties as pistachio-encrusted salmon.

**Ristorante La Piazza.** *3431 W. 7th St. (west of University).* **☎ 817/334-0000.** *Reservations recommended. Main courses $14–$26. AE, CB, DC, DISC, MC, V. Mon–Fri 11:30am–2:30pm; Mon–Thurs 5:30–10pm, Fri–Sat 5:30–11pm. ITALIAN.* This trendy, elegant trattoria may tend toward stuffiness, but the fine service and food compensate. A good bet is the veal parmigiana.

**Saint Emilion.** *3617 W. 7th St. (west of University).* **☎ 817/737-2781.** *Reservations accepted. Main courses $7–$20. AE, CB, DC, DISC, MC, V. Mon–Sat 6–10pm. FRENCH.* This charming restaurant, resembling a French country home, has a simple menu of good cuisine, like Australian rack of lamb.

**Star Cafe.** *111 W. Exchange (west of Main St.).* **☎ 817/624-8701.** *Reservations accepted. Main courses $5–$20. Mon–Fri 11am–9:30pm, Sat 11am–10:30pm. AE, MC, V. STEAK.* One of the few places in the Dallas–Fort Worth area serving prime steak, this tourist favorite located in the stockyards has two separate dining areas and an old-fashioned bar downstairs reserved for parties.

## FORT WORTH AFTER DARK

Texas's most famous theater-in-the-round is **Casa Mañana,** 3101 Lancaster (**☎ 817/ 332-2272**), housed in a geodesic dome. Broadway hits, concerts, and modern theater works are presented here.

There are many clubs and bars along Exchange Avenue in the Stockyard district, including **Billy Bob's Texas,** 2520 Rodeo Plaza (**☎ 817/624-7117**), which bills itself as "the world's largest honky-tonk." **Cowtown Coliseum,** 121 E. Exchange Ave. (**☎ 817/625-1025**), has rodeos on Saturday night.

# 14  Austin

Many Texans who live in faster-paced places like Dallas or Houston dream of someday escaping to Austin, a laid-back city set in lake-laced hills. This leafy home of the University of Texas, lying well outside the realm of Lone Star stereotypes, has been compared to Berkeley and Seattle, but it is at once its own place and entirely of Texas.

Born on the frontier out of the grandiose dreams of a man whose middle name was Buonaparte, Austin spent its formative years fighting to maintain its status as capital. Texan hubris and feistiness remain key to the city's character—from state legislators who descend, squabbling, on the town every other year, to the locals fighting to save the golden-cheeked warbler from the developer's bulldozer.

Despite an economic boom that has made it a high-tech center, Austin has taken full advantage of its natural endowments, establishing myriad bicycle trails and hiking paths. Bird-watchers find bliss here, and sailboard concessionaires do a brisk business. When they're not exercising—and often even when they are—Austinites are listening to music. The city's annual South by Southwest Conference is the music industry's influential gathering, and there are more than 50 live music venues in town.

Indeed, Austin indulges the good life with pure Texas excess. It has the largest travel store in the state, gigantic health food emporiums, supermarket-size bookstores—not to mention the most movie screens and restaurants per capita in the U.S.

## ARRIVING & DEPARTING

**BY PLANE**   **Robert Mueller Municipal Airport,** 3600 Manor Rd. (☎ 512/495-7550), about 2 miles north of downtown near I-35, is slated to be replaced by a larger facility at the former Bergstrom Air Force Base on the south side in May 1999. Airlines flying here are America West, American, Continental, Delta, Northwest, Southwest, TWA, United, and US Airways. Conquest is Austin's short-hop commuter airline. There is no direct international service to the city.

The 15-minute taxi ride between the airport and downtown generally costs $8 to $10. Capital Metro Transit's bus no. 20 takes about 20 minutes and costs 50¢ (☎ 512/474-1200; TDD 512/385-5872).

**BY TRAIN & BUS**   **Amtrak** (☎ 800/872-7245) has three trains a week between Austin and Chicago. You'll have to go to San Antonio for east–west connections. The Amtrak station is in the southwest corner of downtown, at Lamar and West First Street near the Seton Medical Center. The **Greyhound** bus station is at 916 E. Koenig Lane near Highland Mall, about 10 minutes north of downtown and just south of the I-35 motel zone (☎ 800/231-2222).

## ESSENTIALS

**VISITOR INFORMATION**   The **Austin Convention and Visitor Bureau,** 201 E. Second St., Austin, TX 78701 (☎ 800/926-2282 or 512/474-5171), is across the street from the Convention Center in the southeast section of downtown. A booth at the airport is often unattended. You can pick up tourist information pamphlets downtown at the **Old Bakery and Emporium,** 1006 Congress Ave. (☎ 512/477-5961). The **Capitol Complex Visitor Center,** 112 E. 11th St. (☎ 512/305-8400), dispenses information on the entire state of Texas.

**RESOURCES FOR TRAVELERS WITH SPECIAL NEEDS**   The **Old Bakery and Emporium,** 1006 Congress Ave. (☎ 512/477-5961), which sells crafts and baked goods made by senior citizens, is a good place to find out about any senior activities in town.

**Book Woman,** 918 W. 12th St., at Lamar (☎ 512/472-2785), and **Lobo,** 3204A Guadalupe St. (☎ 512/454-5406), are the best places to find gay and lesbian books and magazines. The *Austin Gay-Friendly Resource Directory,* published by Austin Media Visions, has gone online and can be accessed at **http://www.gayfriendly.com**; it's also available in a free hard-copy edition at Book Woman and Lobo. **Hippie Hollow,** near Lake Travis, is a popular daytime gathering spot for gays.

**EMERGENCIES & SAFETY**   Call ☎ **911** if you need the police, fire department, or an ambulance. Austin has the third-lowest crime rate of America's major cities, but that doesn't mean you should throw common sense to the wind. It's never a good idea to walk down dark streets alone at night, and major tourist areas always attract pickpockets; keep your purse or wallet in a safe place.

**Brackenridge,** 601 E. 15th St. (☎ 512/476-6461), and **St. David's,** 919 E. 32nd St. at I-35 (☎ 512/397-4240), have good and convenient emergency-care facilities.

## GETTING AROUND

It would be hard to find a city more accommodating to two-wheelers than Austin. Many city streets have separate bicycle lanes.

Austin's excellent **Capital Metropolitan Transportation Authority** has more than 50 bus lines. The regular adult one-way fare on Metro routes is 50¢; express service from various Park and Ride lots costs $1; three 'Dillo routes—Congress Street, Lavaca, and Old Pecan Street—are free. Call ☎ **800/474-1201** or 512/474-1200 from local pay phones (TDD ☎ **512/385-5872**) for routing information.

Cab companies are **Austin Cab** (☎ 512/478-2222), **Roy's Taxi** (☎ 512/482-0000), and **Yellow-Checker American Cab** (☎ 512/472-1111). Regulated rates are $1.50 for the first fifth of a mile, $1.50 for each additional mile.

## WHAT TO SEE & DO

**ESCORTED TOURS**   Whatever price you pay, you won't find better guided walks than the informative, entertaining, and free ones offered from March to November by the **Austin Convention and Visitor Bureau (ACVB),** 201 E. Second St., Austin, TX 78701 (☎ **800/926-2282** or 512/478-0098). The ACVB also publishes four excellent self-guided tour booklets.

**Capital Cruises** (☎ 512/480-9264) has sightseeing and other cruises on Town Lake from March to October, departing from the Hyatt Regency Town Lake dock. **Lone Star River Boat** (☎ 512/327-1388) goes upstream past Barton Creek, Zilker Park, 100-feet-high cliffs, and million-dollar estates. **Vanishing Texas River Cruise** (☎ 512/756-6986) plies Lake Buchanan, about 1½ hours from Austin.

**Hill Country Flyer Steam Train Excursion** (☎ 512/477-8468) takes five historic coaches and a 1916 locomotive on leisurely 33-mile excursions from Cedar Park, northwest of Austin, to scenic Hill Country vistas, especially pretty in spring and fall. An Old West gunfight is staged at Burnet, near Lake Buchanan.

**SPECIAL EVENTS**   The **Zilker Hillside Theater** in Zilker Park hosts free summer events. Starting in late April or early May, the city sponsors **free concerts** on Sunday afternoon. Call ☎ **512/442-2263** for current schedules and information about the free **Zilker Park Jazz Festival** in September. There are free performances by the **Austin Contemporary Ballet** (☎ 512/892-1298) the first weekend in June. Mid-July to late August, the theater hosts a **summer musical series** (☎ 512/397-1463). The summer **Austin Shakespeare Festival** is often held at the theater, too; call ☎ **512/454-BARD** for locations and dates.

**ATTRACTIONS**   Stroll up Congress Avenue and you'll see much the same sight as visitors to Austin did more than 100 years ago: a broad thoroughfare gently rising to

# Austin

## Attractions

Austin Children's Museum ⑪

Austin Museum of Art
  at Laguna Gloria ③

Austin Nature
  & Science Center ⑫

Barton Springs Pool ⑭

Elisabet Ney Museum ④

French Legation ⑧

George Washington
  Carver Museum ⑥

Governor's Mansion ⑩

Jourdan Bachman
  Pioneer Farm ①

LBJ Library and Museum ⑤

Mt. Bonnell ②

National Wildflower
  Research Center ⑯

O. Henry Museum ⑨

State Cemetery ⑦

Umlauf Sculpture Garden
  and Museum ⑮

Zilker Botanical Garden ⑬

## Accommodations

Austin Motel ⑩

Austin North Hilton
  and Towers ③

Barton Creek Resort ①

The Brook House ④

Driskill Hotel ⑥

Four Seasons Austin ⑧

Hyatt Regency Austin ⑨

The Inn at Pearl Street ⑤

Radisson Hotel
  on Town Lake ⑦

Renaissance Austin Hotel ②

0 ▭▬▭▬▭ 1 mile
              1.6 km

N

Bull Creek Rd.

City Park Rd.

Emma Long
Metropolitan
Park

Capital of Texas Hwy.

**Westlake Hills**

Westlake Dr.

Toro Canyon Dr.

L360

Wild Basin
Wilderness Park

Red Bud Trail

Bee Creek
Preserve

Bee Caves Rd.

**Rollingwoo**

Barton Creek

Mo-Pac Blvd.

L1

Gus Fruh
Dist. Park

Ben White Blvd.

290

Fredericksburg Rd.

⑯

1-1247

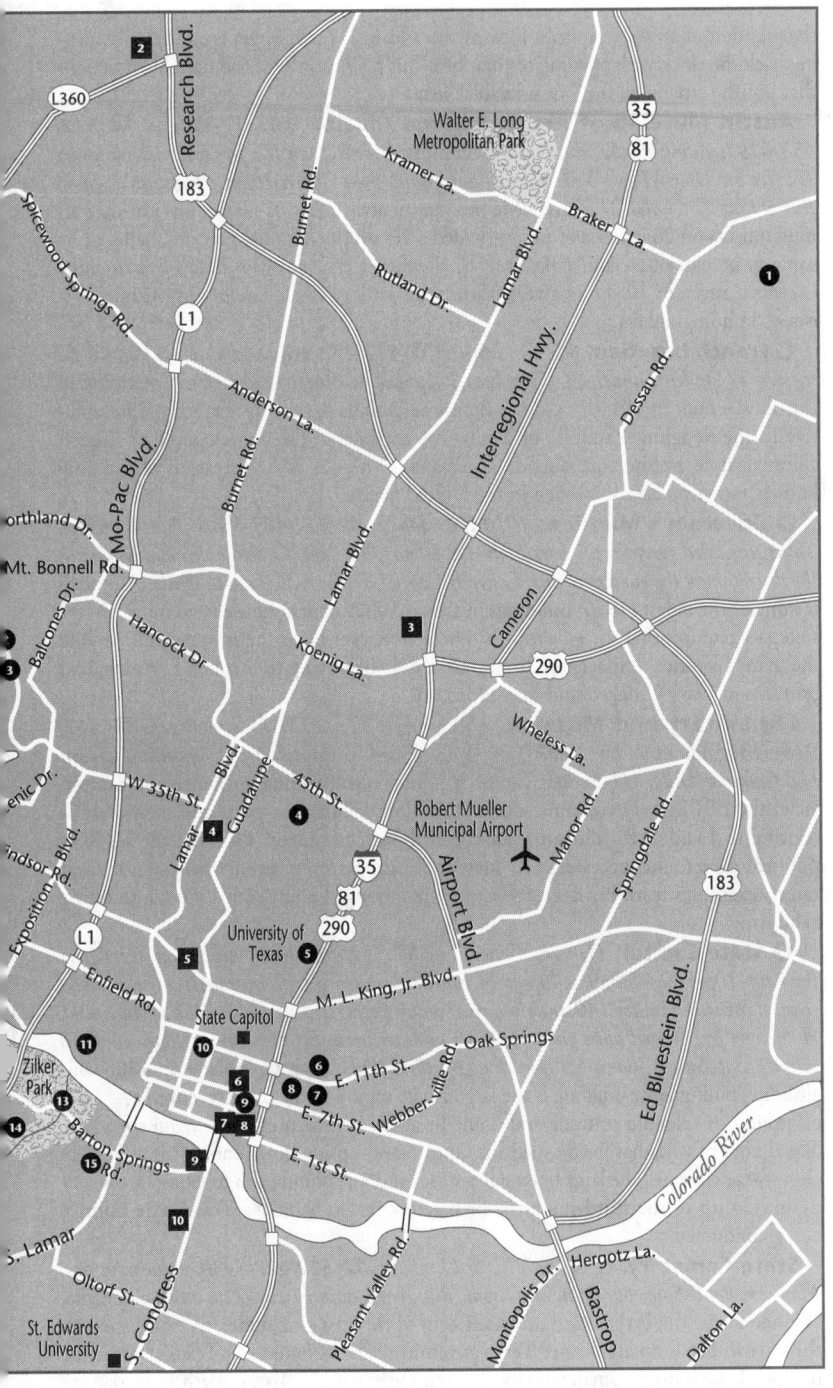

the grandest of all state capitols. Downtown's historic Sixth Street is continually turning back the clock with ongoing restorations. But it's Austin's myriad natural attractions that put the city on all the "most livable" lists.

**Austin Museum of Art at Laguna Gloria.** *3809 W. 35th St.* ☎ *512/ 458-8191. Admission $2 adults, $1 seniors and students with ID, free for children under 16; free on Thurs. Tues–Wed and Fri–Sat 10am–5pm, Thurs 10am–9pm, Sun 1–5pm. Bus: 9 (Sat–Sun only).* The lovely Mediterranean-style villa that houses this intimate art museum sits on 28 palm- and pecan-shaded acres overlooking Lake Austin, believed by some to be part of a claim staked out by Stephen F. Austin, who didn't live to enjoy the view. Seven to 10 shows a year feature the work of local, Texas, and Mexican artists and photographers.

✪ **French Legation.** *802 San Marcos.* ☎ *512/472-8180. Admission $3 adults, $2 seniors, $1 students under 18. Tues–Sun 1–5pm.* The oldest residence still standing in Austin was built in 1841 for Comte Alphonse Dubois de Saligny, France's representative to the fledgling Republic of Texas. It's considered the best example of French colonial–style architecture outside Louisiana. Out back is a re-creation of the only known authentic Creole kitchen in the United States.

✪ **Governor's Mansion.** *1010 Colorado St.* ☎ *512/463-5518. Admission free. Tours scheduled every 20 minutes Mon–Fri 10am–11:40am. Closed some holidays and at the discretion of the governor. Bus: Congress/Capitol 'Dillo, ACC/Lavaca 'Dillo.* Although it's one of the oldest (1856) buildings in the city, this opulent house is no museum, for state law requires that the governor live here whenever he or she is in Austin. Among the many historical artifacts on display are a desk belonging to Stephen F. Austin and portraits of Davy Crockett and Sam Houston.

**LBJ Library and Museum.** *University of Texas, 2313 Red River.* ☎ *512/ 916-5136. Admission free. Daily 9am–5pm. Closed Christmas. Bus: Convention Center/ UT Campus 'Dillo, UT Shuttle.* Set on a hilltop commanding an impressive campus view, the LBJ Library contains some 40 million documents, gifts, and memorabilia relating to Lyndon B. Johnson, our colorful 36th president. Photos trace his long political career and successes. LBJ loved political cartoons, even when he was their target; examples from his large collection are among the museum's most interesting exhibits.

✪ **State Capitol.** *11th and Congress sts.* ☎ *512/463-0063. Admission free. Mon–Fri 7am–10pm, Sat–Sun 9am–5pm; 24 hours a day during legislative sessions (held in odd years, starting in Jan, for 140 straight days; 30-day special sessions are also called sometimes). Hour-long free guided tours given every 15 minutes Mon–Fri 8:30am–4:30pm, every 30 minutes Sat–Sun 9:30am–4:30pm. Bus: All three 'Dillo lines.* Completed in 1888, this gleaming pink-granite building is the largest state capitol in the country, covering 3 acres of ground. A splendid rotunda and dome lie at the intersection of the main corridors. The design of what has been called the "inside-out, upside-down capitol" is extremely clever—for example, the large brass star on the outdoor rotunda also functions as a water drain. Go up to the third-floor visitor balcony if you want see Texas-style politics being conducted.

**State Cemetery.** *E. Seventh St. at Comal St.* ☎ *512/478-8930. Admission free. Mon–Fri 8am–5pm, Sat–Sun 9am–6pm. Bus: 4–18 stops nearby.* The city's namesake, Stephen F. Austin, is the best-known resident of this east-side cemetery, established by the state in 1851. So are former Texas governors, various fighters in Texas's battles for independence, and a woman who lived to tell the tale of the Alamo. Barbara Jordan recently became the first African-American to be interred here. An excellent self-guided tour pamphlet, available from the Austin Convention and Visitor Bureau, details headstone highlights.

**University of Texas at Austin.** *Main Campus, Guadalupe and I-35, Martin Luther King, Jr. Blvd., and 26th St.* ☎ *512/471-3434.* Nearly 50,000 students occupy 120 buildings on UT's main campus. Two visitor centers, one at Sid Richardson Hall, next to the LBJ Library, and the other in the Arno Nowotny Building, at I-35 and Martin Luther King, Jr. Boulevard, offer maps and other campus information; they're open weekdays 8am–4:30pm (☎ 512/471-6498). In addition to the LBJ Library and Museum (see above), the campus is home to the **Archer M. Huntington Art Gallery,** Harry Ransom Center, 21st and Guadalupe streets (☎ 512/471-7324), ranked among the top 10 university art museums in the United States. Among the permanent exhibits are the Mari and James Michener collection of 20th-century American masters and the largest gathering of Latin American art in the U.S. The special collections of the **Harry Ransom Research Center** (☎ 512/471-8944) contain approximately one million rare books, 36 million manuscripts, five million photographs, and more than 100,000 works of art. Permanent and rotating exhibits of HRC holdings are held in two buildings: the Harry Ransom Center and the Leeds Gallery of the Flawn Academic Center. A Gutenberg Bible—one of only five complete copies in the United States—is always on display on the first floor of the former. The **Texas Memorial Museum,** 2400 Trinity St. (☎ 512/471-1604), features displays detailing the geology, anthropology, and natural history of Texas. An intriguing exhibit on the history of firearms, the original zinc Goddess of Liberty that once sat on top of the capitol, and a good gift shop make it worth a visit.

**LITERARY LANDMARKS**   William Sidney Porter, better known as O. Henry, lived in Austin from 1884 to 1898 and published a popular satirical newspaper called the *Rolling Stone.* He also worked as a teller at the First National Bank of Austin, which accused him of embezzling funds. It was while he was serving time that he wrote the 13 short stories that established his reputation. The modest Victorian cottage in which he lived with his wife and daughter from 1893 to 1895 is now the free **O. Henry Museum,** 409 E. Fifth St. (☎ 512/472-1903).

**PARKS & GARDENS**   Comprising 347 acres, the first 40 donated to the city by the wealthy German immigrant for whom it's named, **Zilker Park,** 2201 Barton Springs Rd. (☎ 512/476-9044), is Austin's favorite public playground. Its centerpiece is amazingly clear ✪ **Barton Springs** (☎ 512/476-9044), a swimming pool with constant 68°F water—bracing in summer and warming in winter, when many hearty souls go for a dip. Visitors and locals alike flock to the soothing **Zilker Botanical Garden** (☎ 512/477-8672), with its Isamu Taniguchi–designed Oriental Garden particularly peaceful; the **Austin Nature Preserves;** and the **Umlauf Sculpture Garden and Museum** (☎ 512/445-5582), named for UT art instructor Charles Umlauf, whose pieces also reside in such places as the Smithsonian Institution and New York's Metropolitan Museum (you'll probably recognize the portrait of Umlauf's most famous UT student, actress Farrah Fawcett).

Researchers at the lovely, colorful **National Wildflower Research Center,** 4801 La Crosse Ave. (☎ 512/292-4100), have 42 acres of wildflowers for their personal laboratory. The main attractions are the display gardens and meadow, but the native stone architecture of the visitor center and observation tower is attention-grabbing too. Included among the interesting indoor displays is one of Lady Bird Johnson's wide-brimmed gardening hats and a talking lawn mower with a British accent.

**BEST BETS FOR KIDS**   Offering everything from tools for tots to a soundstage for teens, the **Austin Children's Museum,** 1501 W. Fifth St. (☎ 512/472-2499), appeals to a wide range of ages and interests with interactive exhibits. A working beehive and ant farm are among the displays in the hands-on Discovery Lab at the **Austin Nature and Science Center,** in Zilker Park (☎ 512/327-8181), where orphaned and injured wildlife are brought to mend and recuperate. Traveling back in time to the rural 1880s at the **Jourdan Bachman Pioneer Farm,** 11418 Sprinkle Cut Off Rd. (☎ 512/837-1215), might make kids appreciate today's conveniences.

**SPORTS**    There are no professional teams in Austin, but the University of Texas Longhorns are very, very big in most collegiate athletics. For information about schedules, call the **UT ticket office** (☎ 512/471-3333); to order tickets, contact **UTTM Charge-A-Ticket** (☎ 512/477-6060).

Fans turn out in droves each summer to watch the **Dallas Cowboys** in summer training camp at St. Edwards University, 3001 S. Congress. Dates and local contact numbers change each year, so call the Cowboys' office in Dallas (☎ 214/556-9327).

Pick your ponies at **Manor Downs,** 8 miles east of I-35 on U.S. 290 east (☎ 512/272-5581). Racing season is from March to June.

**SHOPPING**    Much of Austin's shopping has moved out to the suburban malls, and bargain hunters go even farther afield to the huge collections of factory outlet stores in San Marcos and New Braunfels. Little enclaves offering more intimate retail experiences can be found on **Sixth Street west of Lamar** and, nearby, north of 12th Street and West Lynn. In the vicinity of **Central Market,** between West 35th and 40th streets and Lamar and Mo-Pac, such small shopping centers as 26 Doors and Jefferson Square are similarly charming settings. **South Congress Avenue,** from Riverside south to Annie Street, has long been a fun place to seek vintage clothing and antiques, and it's lately been revitalized, as lots of hip restaurants and cafes are opening in the area.

Austin's commitment to music makes **Wild About Music,** 710 W. Sixth St. (☎ 512/708-1700), a perfect location for this new gallery and shop, strictly devoted to art with a musical theme. Some of the pieces are expensive, but nearly all of them are fun. The gift shop at the **Capitol Complex Visitor Center,** 112 E. 11th St. (☎ 512/305-8400), sells brass bookends made from the original molds used for the intricately designed door hinges of the capitol.

It's only been here since 1994, but the **Central Market,** 40th and Lamar (☎ 512/206-1000), is already an integral part of town, a gourmet megamarket with every imaginable food item and a restaurant section. The **Travis County Farmers' Market,** 6701 Burnet Rd. (☎ 512/454-1002), not only offers great fresh fruit and vegetables but also hosts monthly festivals honoring particular crops and seasons.

## ACCOMMODATIONS

Endless chain motels along I-35 north of the airport notwithstanding, Austin has a room shortage. When planning your trip, keep in mind that rooms are scarce during the state legislature's sessions and during University of Texas football games, graduations, and other big events. You'll get a feel for what makes Austin special if you stay in the verdant Town Lake area; hotels there are close to the major sights and near a hike-and-bike trail.

**Austin Motel.** *1220 S. Congress St., Austin TX 78704.* ☎ *512/441-1157. Fax 512/444-2610. 41 rooms, including 4 suites (1 with kitchenette). $46–$73 double; $99 suite. AE, DC, MC, V.* Nostalgia and a convenient (though not quiet) location just south of downtown draw repeat guests to this Austin institution, established in 1938. The renovated pool rooms are more expensive but also much more cheerful. The hotel has El Sol y Luna restaurant, a pool, and free local phone calls.

**Barton Creek Resort.** *8212 Barton Club Dr., Austin, TX 78735.* ☎ *800/336-6158 or 512/329-4000. Fax 512/329-4597. 147 rms, 4 suites. $210 double;*

*$350–$715 suite. Spa and golf packages available. AE, CB, DC, MC, V.* This gorgeous, chateaulike conference resort on 4,000 rolling acres has three 18-hole championship golf courses, 12 outdoor tennis courts, and a state-of-the-art spa and fitness center. Accommodations are large and high-toned, with that rarity in Texas—minibars. Some have balconies and superb views of the Texas Hill Country. Facilities include restaurants, bars, an indoor-outdoor pool, and a jogging course.

**Driskill Hotel.** *604 Brazos St., Austin TX 78701.* ☎ *800/252-9367 or 512/474-5911. Fax 512/474-2214. 160 rms, 15 suites. $105–$220 double; from $200 suite. Corporate and weekend rates and various packages available. AE, CB, DC, DISC, MC, V. Self-parking $4; valet parking $9.* An ongoing renovation is restoring the magnificent halls of Austin's only historic hotel to their former luxury. Many rooms have handmade wooden desks and other original 19th-century furnishings; other rooms have excellent reproductions. All offer modern amenities. The Driskill Grill looks like a ladies' tearoom but serves mainly Southwestern fare.

✪ **Four Seasons Austin.** *98 San Jacinto Blvd., Austin, TX 78701.* ☎ *800/332-3442 or 512/478-4500. Fax 512/478-3117. 251 rms, 28 suites. $170–$240 double; $245–$1,200 suite. Packages available. AE, CB, DC, MC, V. Self-parking $7; valet parking $12.* Elegant public and private rooms at this poshest of the Town Lake hotels have Southwestern touches. Enjoy the European-style pampering (there's even a room-service menu for pets). The city views are fine, but the ones of the lake are prime, especially from the dining venues. Extras include a pool, excellent health club and spa, 24-hour room and concierge service.

✪ **Hyatt Regency Austin on Town Lake.** *208 Barton Springs Rd., Austin, TX 78704.* ☎ *800/233-1234 or 512/477-1234. Fax 512/480-2069. 429 rms, 17 suites. $175–$185 double; $250–$650 suite. Weekend specials, corporate, and state government rates available. AE, CB, DC, DISC, MC, V. Free self-parking; valet parking $8.* A Hill Country tableau of limestone-banked flowing stream, waterfalls, and oak trees anchor the Hyatt signature atrium lobby here, but outdoor activities are the main draw: Bat tours depart from a private dock, which also rents paddleboats and canoes and lends mountain bikes to ride on the hike-and-bike trail, right outside the door.

✪ **Lake Austin Spa Resort.** *1705 Quinlan Park Rd., Austin, TX 78732.* ☎ *800/847-5637 in U.S., or 512/266-4362. Fax 512/266-1572. 40 rooms. $553.50 per person for 2 nights, double occupancy (2-night minimum). Rates include all meals, classes, and activities. Three-, 4-, and 7-night packages available. AE, MC, V. Free parking.* This luxury spa on Lake Austin takes advantage of its proximity to the lovely Texas Hill Country by offering such activities as combination canoe/hiking trips or excursions to view wildflowers. In lake-view cottages, rooms are country-French cheerful. Facilities include a dining room, indoor and outdoor pools, a sauna, steam room, Jacuzzi, and weight and cardio rooms.

**Radisson Hotel on Town Lake.** *11 E. First St., Austin, TX 78701.* ☎ *800/333-3333 or 512/478-9611. Fax 512/473-8399. 260 rms, 20 suites. $110–120 double; $135 suite. Corporate, family, and weekend rates available. AE, CB, DC, DISC, MC, V. Self-parking $4; valet parking $7.* A lower-priced alternative to the downtown luxury high-rises, the Radisson offers a prime Town Lake location along with many of the same perks. From the airy, open lobby to pleasant rooms in shades of turquoise or peach, the ambiance is light and cheery. Conveniences include a TGI Friday's chain restaurant, pool, and exercise room.

**Renaissance Austin Hotel.** *9721 Arboretum Blvd., Austin, TX 78759.* ☎ *800/HOTELS-1 or 512/343-2626. Fax 512/346-7945. 478 rms, including 43 suites. $175–$185 double; $230–$270 suite. Weekend packages available. AE, CB, DC, DISC, MC, V. Free self-parking; valet parking $8.* Anchoring the upscale Arboretum Mall on

Austin's northwest side, the luxurious Renaissance caters to executives visiting the nearby computer firms. But weekend rates allow even underlings to enjoy the silk wallpaper, lacquer chests, and Japanese-design draperies that add an oriental flavor to the oversized guest rooms. There are indoor and outdoor pools and an exercise room.

**OTHER ACCOMMODATIONS** The **Brook House,** 609 W. 33rd St., Austin, TX 78705 (☎ 512/459-0534), an immaculate but homey bed-and-breakfast in a 1922 colonial Revival–style home near the university, offers sunny, appealing quarters at reasonable rates. Rooms are in the main house, a carriage house, and a romantic private cottage. An 1896 Greek Revival–style house on a rise above one of Austin's busier streets, the **Inn at Pearl Street,** 809 W. Martin Luther King, Jr. Blvd., P.O. Box 201494, Austin, TX 78720-1494 (☎ 800/494-2261 or 512/477-2233; fax 512/477-4571), is unassuming on the outside, but inside is an interior decorator's dream. On nice days, you can enjoy breakfast on a tree-shaded deck.

Near the airport, **Austin North Hilton and Towers,** 6000 Middle Fiskville Rd., Austin, TX 78752 (☎ 800/347-0330 or 512/451-5757; fax 512/467-7644), adjoins Highland Mall, and is within walking distance of the tonier Lincoln Village. Doubles run $146–$166, suites $275–$350, with weekend and seasonal specials available.

## DINING

You might expect to eat well in a town where lawmakers schmooze power brokers. Downtown's West End/Warehouse district near 4th and Colorado streets is the hot new area to eat, with hip new restaurants opening up at a rapid rate. The other rapidly expanding restaurant area is the northwest, near the Arboretum Mall, where many popular downtown restaurants are installing branches. Wherever you eat, think casual.

**✪ Bitter End Bistro & Brewery.** *311 Colorado St.* ☎ *512/478-2337. Reservations accepted for five or more only. Pizzas $5.50–$6.50; main courses $9.50–$18.50. AE, DC, DISC, MC, V. Mon–Thurs 11:30am–1am, Fri 11:30am–2am, Sat 2pm–2am, Sun 5pm–midnight. REGIONAL AMERICAN.* The food is as good as the beer at this brew pub—and the beer is very good indeed, especially the smooth, light E-Z Wheat and the toasty Uptown Brown. One of the earliest of the downtown warehouses to have been renovated, the Bitter End is all tall windows, brick walls, and galvanized metal light fixtures.

**Fonda San Miguel.** *2330 W. North Loop.* ☎ *512/459-4121. Reservations advised. Main courses $10–$18. AE, CB, DC, DISC, MC, V. Sun–Thurs 5:30–9:30pm, Fri–Sat 5:30–10:30pm; Sun brunch 11:30am–2pm. MEXICAN REGIONAL.* Mexico City chefs' back-to-the-roots movement, which might involve ancient Aztec ingredients in their dishes, are carefully tracked and artfully translated by chef Ricardo Muñoz, making this the best place in town for Mexican regional cuisine. The huge dining room, with its carved wooden doors, colorful paintings, and live ficus tree, provides a gorgeous backdrop.

**Green Pastures.** *811 W. Live Oak Rd.* ☎ *512/444-4747. Reservations advised for lunch and dinner Thurs–Sat. Main courses $12–$25. AE, DC, DISC, MC, V. Daily 11am–2pm and 6–10pm. CONTINENTAL.* Peacocks strut their stuff among the 225 live oaks surrounding this 1894 mansion whose current owner's mother turned into a restaurant in 1945. You'll find Southern comfort in the gracious setting and polite service, as well as in a continental menu that nods only gently toward current culinary trends.

**✪ Güero's.** *1412 S. Congress.* ☎ *512/447-7688. Reservations not accepted. Main courses $6–$10. AE, DC, DISC, MC, V. Mon–Fri 7am–10pm, Sat–Sun 8am–10pm. MEXICAN.* This sprawling converted feed store has become the center of the newly hip South Austin scene, but it's fine for families, too. Although the menu listings are stylishly tongue-in-cheek, the food is seriously good. You can enjoy health-conscious versions of Tex-Mex standards as well as some dishes from the interior of Mexico. There's live music on Sunday afternoon.

**Hudson's on the Bend.** *3509 RR 620 North.* ☎ *512/266-1369. Reservations recommended, required on weekends. Main courses $20–$35. AE, DC, MC, V. Sun–Thurs 6–9pm, Fri–Sat 5:30–10pm (closing times may be earlier in winter; call ahead). SOUTH-WESTERN.* If you're game for things that once roamed the wild, served in a very civilized setting, come to Hudson's. Soft candlelight, fresh flowers, fine china, and attentive service combine with out-of-the-ordinary cuisine like rattlesnake cakes and javelina stuffed with boar and pecans. Hudson's can be very noisy on weekends; opt for the terrace in nice weather.

**Hula Hut.** *3826 Lake Austin Blvd.* ☎ *512/476-4852. Reservations not accepted. Main courses $7–$17. AE, DC, DISC, MC, V. Sun–Thurs 11am–11pm, Fri–Sat 11am–midnight. MEXICAN/POLYNESIAN/HAWAIIAN.* The Hula Hut has perfected the technique of cross-Polynesation: It's mixed Mexican with what usually masquerades as Pacific Island cooking, added decks reaching out over Lake Austin, and arrived at the formula for fun. This place is especially cheerful if you come with a group ready to experiment with different platters.

✪ **Jeffrey's.** *1204 W. Lynn.* ☎ *512/477-5584. Reservations advised. Main courses $19.75–$27.75; bistro menu $16–$19. AE, CB, DC, DISC, MC, V. Mon–Thurs 6–10pm, Fri–Sat 6–10:30pm. SOUTHWESTERN.* While chef David Garrido's innovative Texas fare is dazzling, the setting for his performance is low-key; people walk into this three-room former storefront, in the artsy Clarksville neighborhood, wearing anything from a T-shirt to a tux. You can depend on flavors and textures to dance wildly together without falling down.

✪ **Mars.** *1610 San Antonio, St.* ☎ *512/472-3901. Reservations advisable on weekends. Main courses $9.50–$17; bistro menu (noodle and rice dishes) $8–$10. AE, DISC, MC, V. Mon–Thurs 5:30–10:30pm, Fri–Sat 5:30–11pm, Sun 5:30–10pm. MEDITER-RANEAN/ASIAN.* Mars shines increasingly bright in Austin's growing constellation of interesting restaurants. Chef James Fischer picked up some interesting culinary influences when he lived in Cairo (tandoori lamb loin medaillons with pomegranate sauce). The dining room is a bit dark, but the food more than compensates for any trouble you might have seeing the menu.

**Mexico Tipico.** *1707 E. Sixth St.* ☎ *512/472-3222. Reservations accepted. Main courses $6–$14. AE, CB, DC, MC, V. Mon–Thurs 8am–3pm, Fri–Sun 8am–10pm ($6 all-you-can-eat buffet Mon–Fri 11am–3pm). MEXICAN.* Diners from both sides of Austin's Anglo-Hispanic divide pile into the red leather booths of this large, cheerful room for authentic versions of such specialties as *rajas con queso*, a dip of poblano peppers, ham, onions, and cheese served with hot corn tortillas. The cabrito (kid) is out of this world. There's live Latin-beat entertainment on weekends.

**Mezzaluna.** *310 Colorado St.* ☎ *512/472-6770. No reservations. Pasta $9–$14.50; main courses $13–$18.50. AE, DC, DISC, MC, V. Mon–Fri 11:30am–midnight; Sat 5pm–midnight, Sun 6–10pm. ITALIAN.* One of the first restaurants to open in the now-chic warehouse district, Mezzaluna was ahead of the pack with its contemporary Italian menu (the house lasagna is layered with smoked chicken and bell peppers along with the more conventional spinach, ricotta, and mozzarella).

**Threadgill's.** *6416 N. Lamar Blvd.* ☎ *512/451-5440. Reservations not accepted. Sandwiches and specials $4–$5.50; main courses $5–$17. MC, V. Daily 11am–10pm. AMERICAN/SOUTHERN.* Performers like Janis Joplin turned up regularly at his legendary Wednesday night hootenannies here in the 1960s. The down-home casual and good Southern-style diner added in 1980 is now legendary for its $4.95 blue-plate specials, huge chicken-fried steaks, and vegetables like jalapeño jambalaya, squash casserole, garlic cheese grits, and Cajun Italian eggplant.

✪ **Zoot.** *509 Hearn.* ☎ *512/477-6535. Reservations advised, especially on weekends. Main courses $13–$22. AE, CB, DC, DISC, MC, V. Sun–Thurs 5:30–10:30pm, Fri–Sat 5:30–11pm; Sun brunch 11am–2pm. AMERICAN REGIONAL.* Zoot is a prime example of a propitious Texas trend toward a cuisine that's delicious, fresh, and affordable. This cozy Enfield restaurant, set in a 1920s cottage, uses only organic vegetables and designs its dishes around ingredients grown in the area. Presentations are gorgeous and soft jazz plays in the background.

**Z'Tejas Grill.** *9400 Arboretum Blvd.* ☎ *512/346-3506. Reservations recommended. Main courses $8–$16. AE, DC, DISC, MC, V. Mon–Fri 11am–11pm, Sat 10am–midnight, Sun 10am–10pm. SOUTHWESTERN.* Like its popular downtown parent, this northwest branch has a terrifically zippy Southwest menu, here served amid Santa Fe–style decor and a fireplace under a soaring ceiling. The Navajo Taco with a variety of exotic but tasty ingredients heaped atop Indian herb bread is well worth a try.

**BARBECUE JOINTS**    Though C. B. Stubblefield, the Lubbock-based patron saint of Texas barbecue, has gone on to that big smoker in the sky, his vision lives on at ✪ **Stubb's Bar-B-Q,** 801 Red River (☎ 512/480-8341). Stubbs was a strong supporter of Texas musicians, so it is fitting that this has become one of the best live-music venues in town. The food is "big and simple" as Stubbs once put it, not to mention delicious.

It's 11¹⁄₂ miles from the junction of 290 West and F.M. 1826 to the **Salt Lick,** in Driftwood (☎ 512/858-4959), but you'll start smelling the smoke during the last five. Moist chicken, beef, and pork, as well as terrific homemade pickles, more than justify the drive. Some critics deride the **County Line** chain for its "suburban" barbecue, but Austinites love the two branches at 6500 W. Bee Cave Rd. (☎ 512/327-1742), with a deck and Hill Country views, and at 5204 F.M. 2222 (☎ 512/346-3664), near Lake Austin.

## AUSTIN AFTER DARK

The best sources for what's on around town are the *Austin Chronicle* and *XLent,* the entertainment supplement of the *Austin-American Statesman;* both are free and available in hundreds of outlets every Thursday. Two music hotlines offer quick takes on the local club action: **KLBJ** at ☎ 512/832-4094 and **KGSR** at ☎ 512/478-2842. The **Austin Circle of Theaters Hotline** (☎ 512/320-7168) can tell you what's on the boards each week. If you want to know who's kicking around, phone **Danceline** (☎ 512/474-1766). **Ticketmaster** handles most University of Texas and Paramount Theater events (☎ 512/477-6060). **Box Office** (☎ 512/499-TIXS) provides phone charges for many of the smaller theaters in Austin. **AusTix** (☎ 512/397-1450) is the city's half-price theater and performing arts outlet; call for what's available, then buy tickets at **Book People,** 603 N. Lamar Blvd Rd., or at the **Austin Visitor Center,** 201 E. Second St.

PBS's longest-running show, *Austin City Limits* is taped live from August to December at the KLRU-TV studio. Free tickets are distributed; phone the show's hotline at ☎ 512/475-9077 for details. Also see "Special Events," above.

**THE PERFORMING ARTS**    Much of the action, local and imported, goes on at the University of Texas's Performing Arts Center. The **Austin Symphony** performs at Bass Concert Hall (☎ 888-4-MAESTRO or 512/476-6064), as does the **Austin Lyric Opera** (☎ 512/472-5927).

**Live Oak Theatre,** State Theatre, 719 Congress St. (☎ 512/472-5143 or 512/472-7134), the city's most professional theater, puts on a wide variety of work, including original plays by the winners of the annual Texas Young Playwrights competition. The **Zachary Scott Theatre Center** (☎ 512/476-0594 or 512/476-0541), Austin's oldest, features Broadway and off-Broadway fare.

**Ballet Austin** (☎ 512/476-9051 or 512/476-2163) performs classic and modern works. The high-tech **Sharir Dance Company** (☎ 512/458-8158) first stretched the boundaries of dance toward virtual reality in 1994 when they included video projections and computer-generated images in the choreography.

**THE CLUB, MUSIC & BAR SCENE**   Willie Nelson, Waylon Jennings, and Jerry Jeff Walker gave Austin its reputation for alternative country in the early 1970s. One of the most appealing things about the local scene today is that you can find a wide range of good sounds at lots of unexpected places—barbecue joints, Mexican restaurants, converted gas stations—and hear legends like Bob Dylan and Joan Baez perform at intimate spots like The Backyard. The atmosphere almost everywhere is assiduously laid-back, and most cover charges are low.

Willie Nelson celebrated his 60th birthday at the cavernous **Antone's,** 2915 Guadalupe St. (☎ 512/474-5314), where country-and-western crossover bands like the Austin Lounge Lizards turn up all the time but where blues guitars are most likely to be heard. Although it also showcases rock, rockabilly, and new-wave sounds, the small, smoky **Continental Club,** 1315 S. Congress Ave. (☎ 512/441-2444), holds onto its roots in traditional country. A terrific sound system and a casual country atmosphere have helped make **The Backyard,** Hwy. 71 west at RR 620 in Bees Cave (☎ 512/236-4146), one of the hottest new venues in town. The **Broken Spoke,** 3201 S. Lamar Blvd. (☎ 512/442-6189), is the genuine item, a western honky-tonk with a wood-plank floor and a cowboy-hatted, two-steppin' crowd. The **Cactus Café,** in Texas Union on the University of Texas campus (☎ 512/475-6515), is singer/songwriter heaven, a place where dramatic stage antics take a backseat to engaged showmanship.

Film stars on location mingle with T-shirted students and well-dressed older jazz aficionados at the **Elephant Room,** 315 Congress Ave. (☎ 512/473-2279), an intimate downtown venue.

Good rock cover bands, a great selection of beers, and plenty of space set **Maggie Mae's,** 512 Trinity St. (☎ 512/478-8541), apart from the collegiate-crowded clubs lining Sixth Street. You might miss a couple of the punchlines if you're not in on the latest twists and turns of local politics, but the no-holds-barred **Esther's Follies,** 525 E. Sixth St. (☎ 512/320-0553), is very satirical, very irreverent, very Austin.

The **Waterloo Brewing Company,** 401 Guadalupe St. (☎ 512/477-1836), was the first brew pub in Texas. The pale ale is excellent and the full-bodied O. Henry's Porter is practically a meal in itself. Texas's oldest beer garden, **Scholz Garten,** 1607 San Jacinto Blvd. (☎ 512/474-1958), is a great place to drink in some Austin history. The martini and cigar crowd hang out at **Cedar Street,** 208 W. Fourth St. (☎ 512/708-8811), and actor Denzel Washington and music legend Bob Dylan have been seen here.

# 15  San Antonio

The Alamo City or the Fiesta City—either nickname reveals a truth about San Antonio. In America's ninth-largest city you can't help but remember the Alamo, where Texas's freedom fighters took their doomed, heroic stand. But even before Texas won its independence from Mexico, San Antonio was home to diverse groups with distinct goals: Spanish missionaries and militia men, Southern plantation owners and German merchants, western cattle ranchers and eastern architects. All left their mark, not only on the city's culture and cuisine, but more tangibly on its winding downtown streets.

# San Antonio

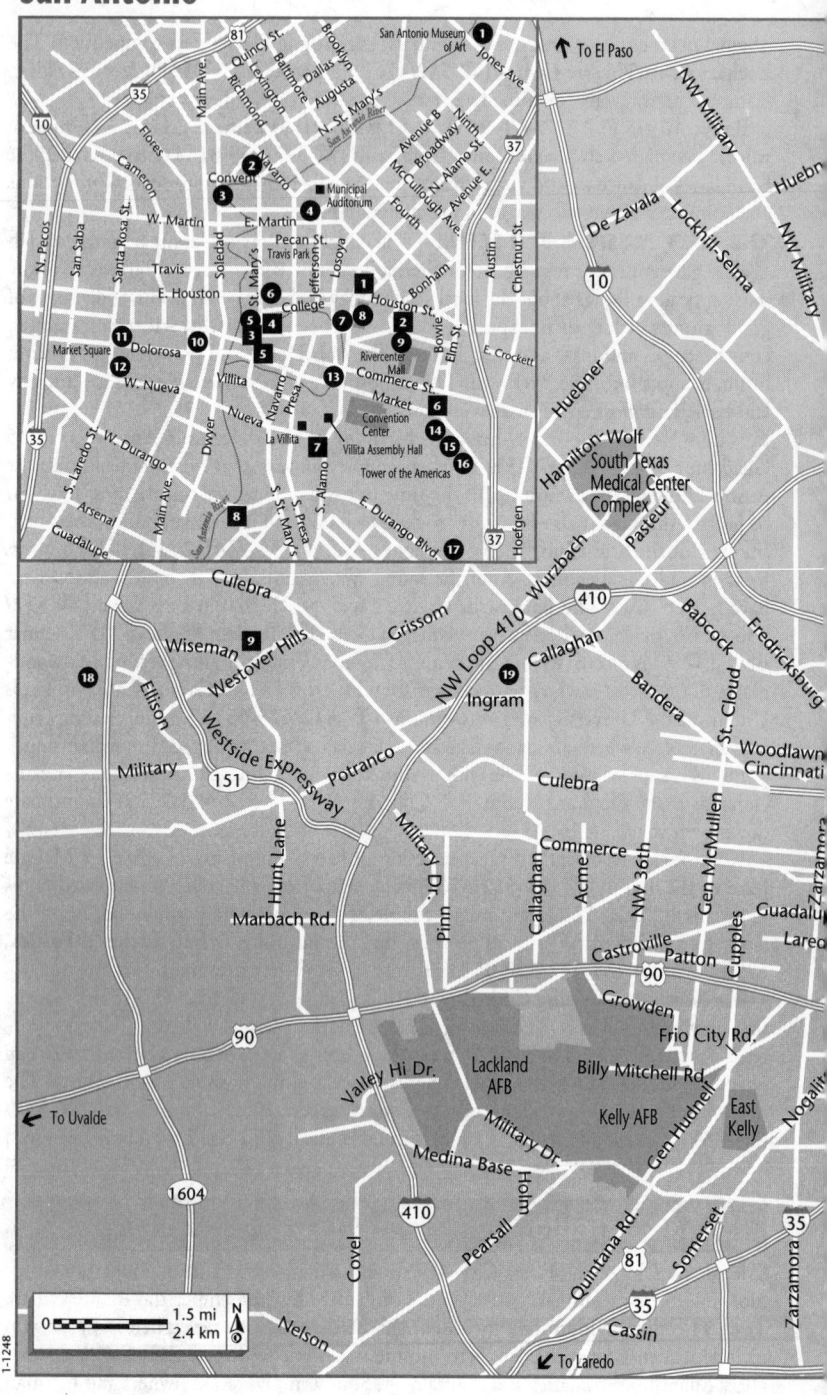

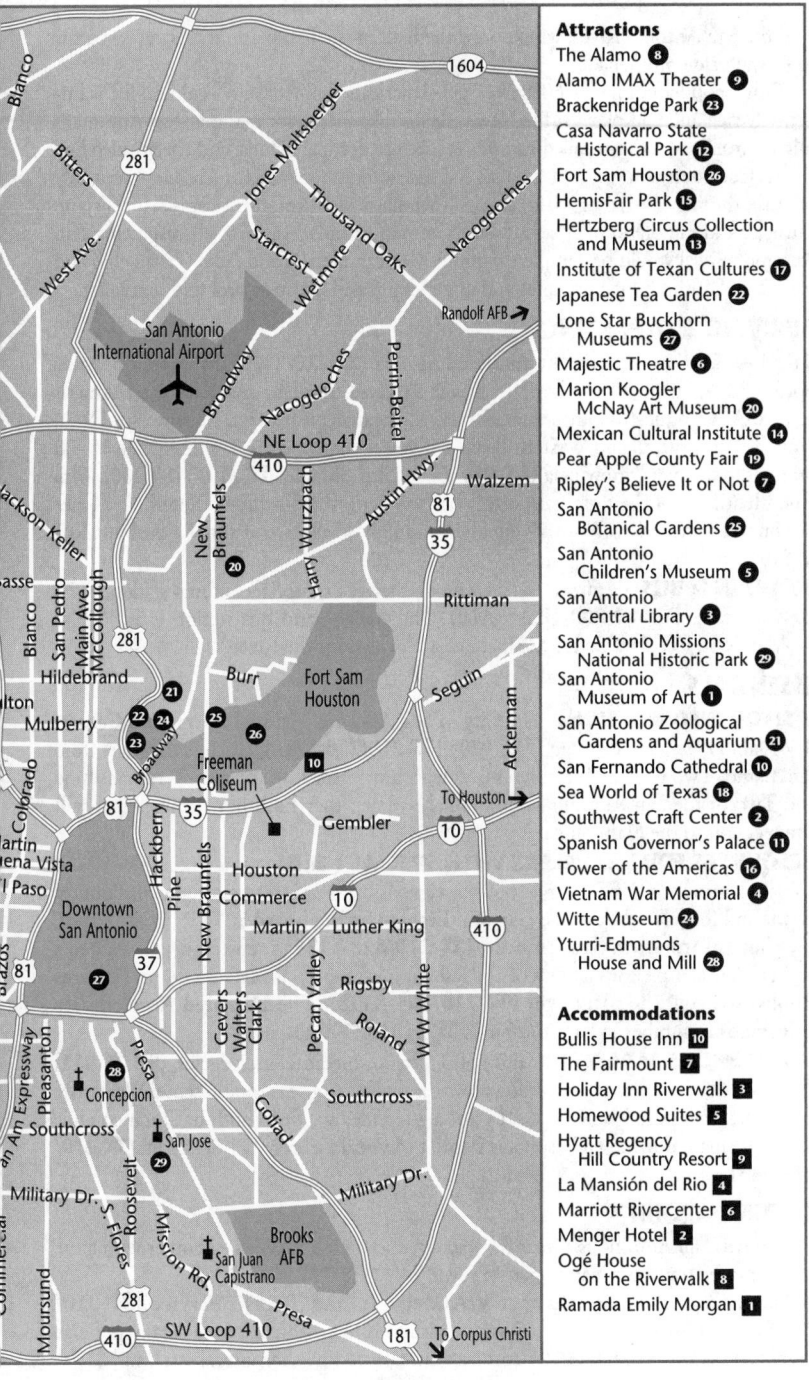

**Attractions**

The Alamo **8**
Alamo IMAX Theater **9**
Brackenridge Park **23**
Casa Navarro State Historical Park **12**
Fort Sam Houston **26**
HemisFair Park **15**
Hertzberg Circus Collection and Museum **13**
Institute of Texan Cultures **17**
Japanese Tea Garden **22**
Lone Star Buckhorn Museums **27**
Majestic Theatre **6**
Marion Koogler McNay Art Museum **20**
Mexican Cultural Institute **14**
Pear Apple County Fair **19**
Ripley's Believe It or Not **7**
San Antonio Botanical Gardens **25**
San Antonio Children's Museum **5**
San Antonio Central Library **3**
San Antonio Missions National Historic Park **29**
San Antonio Museum of Art **1**
San Antonio Zoological Gardens and Aquarium **21**
San Fernando Cathedral **10**
Sea World of Texas **18**
Southwest Craft Center **2**
Spanish Governor's Palace **11**
Tower of the Americas **16**
Vietnam War Memorial **4**
Witte Museum **24**
Yturri-Edmunds House and Mill **28**

**Accommodations**

Bullis House Inn **10**
The Fairmount **7**
Holiday Inn Riverwalk **3**
Homewood Suites **5**
Hyatt Regency Hill Country Resort **9**
La Mansión del Rio **4**
Marriott Rivercenter **6**
Menger Hotel **2**
Ogé House on the Riverwalk **8**
Ramada Emily Morgan **1**

And the San Antonio River, which drew them all in the first place, still attracts visitors to its waterside promenade.

With a population nearly 60% Mexican-American, San Antonio's cultural life is immensely rich and complex. At the New Orleans–like Fiesta, for example, San Antonians might break confetti eggs called *cascarones,* listen to oompah bands, and cheer rodeo bull riders. Countless country-and-western ballads twang on about San Antone—probably because the name rhymes with "alone"—which is also America's capital for Tejano music, a unique blend of Mexican and German sounds. And no self-respecting San Antonio festival would be complete without Mexican tamales and tacos, Texan chili and barbecue, Southern hush puppies and glazed ham, and German beer and bratwurst.

## ARRIVING & DEPARTING

**BY PLANE** San Antonio International Airport (☎ 210/207-3411), about 13 miles north of downtown, is served by Aerolitoral, Aeromar, Air Tran, America West, American, ASA, Conquest, Continental, Delta, Mexicana, Northwest, Southwest, TWA, United, US Airways, and Western Pacific. If you're renting a car, it should take 15–20 minutes to drive downtown via U.S. 281 south. Star Shuttle (☎ 210/341-6000), with a booth at each of the terminals, offers van service to the downtown hotels for $6 per person. Call ahead if you're arriving after midnight. Taxi fare into town is about $13 to $15.

**BY TRAIN & BUS** Amtrak has several trains a week to its San Antonio station, 1174 E. Commerce St. (☎ 800/USA-RAIL). The Greyhound bus station is at 500 N. St. Mary's St. (☎ 800/231-2222), about 2 blocks from the River Walk.

## ESSENTIALS

**VISITOR INFORMATION** The City of San Antonio Visitor Information Center, 317 Alamo Plaza, San Antonio, TX 78205 (☎ 210/270-8748), is across the street from the Alamo. Two unstaffed satellite offices with brochures are located in Terminals One and Two of the San Antonio International Airport; they both have phones that will connect you to the main office.

**RESOURCES FOR TRAVELERS WITH SPECIAL NEEDS** San Antonio's gay and lesbian community is fairly large, but not very visible. For information on community events and for referrals, call the Gay and Lesbian Switchboard at ☎ 210/733-7300. Lesbian Information San Antonio (☎ 210/828-LISA) focuses on gay women's events. You can pick up a copy of the lesbian newspaper, *Woman Space,* at Textures Bookstore, 5309 McCullough (☎ 210/805-8398). The Disabled Accessibility Information number in San Antonio is ☎ 210/207-7243.

**EMERGENCIES & SAFETY** For police, fire, or medical emergencies, dial ☎ 911. There are frequent police patrols downtown at night, but use common sense: Walk only in well-lit, well-populated streets. It's not a good idea to stroll south of Durango after dark. The main downtown hospital is Baptist Medical Center, 111 Dallas St. (☎ 210/222-8431).

## GETTING AROUND

Downtown San Antonio is a treat for walkers, and there's no need to bother with a car in this public transport–happy part of town.

Among regular bus routes that VIA Metropolitan Transit Service (☎ 210/227-2020) runs is 7/40, the Via Vistas Cultural Route, which stops at many popular tourist attractions. Fare is 75¢ for regular routes (including the cultural one), and $1.50 for express buses. In addition to its bus lines, VIA offers four convenient downtown streetcar routes that cover all the most popular tourist stops. The streetcars look like trolleys and cost 50¢.

Cabs are available outside the airport, near the Greyhound and Amtrak terminals, and at most major downtown hotels, but they're next to impossible to hail on the street. The best taxi company is **Checker Cab** (☎ 210/222-2151). **Yellow Cab** (☎ 210/226-4242) is a reasonable alternative. Most cabbies impose a minimum of $6 for trips from the airport, $3 for rides downtown.

## WHAT TO SEE & DO

**ESCORTED TOURS**   **Gray Line** (☎ 800/472-9546 or 210/226-1706) serves up a large menu of guided bus tours: Spanish missions, military bases, and museums to forays south of the border or to the Hill Country. Not to be confused with the city-run trolleys, **Lone Star Trolley** (☎ 210/224-9299) has hour-long narrated tours touching on all the downtown highlights, King William Historic District, Market Square, and more. **Yanaguana Cruises** (☎ 210/244-5700) offers an amusing, informative river tour lasting 35–40 minutes.

**ATTRACTIONS**   Just a few steps below the streets of downtown San Antonio lies another world, the ✪ **Paseo del Rio/River Walk.** The quieter areas of the 2¹/₂ paved miles of winding riverbank, shaded by cypresses, oaks, and willows, exude a tropical, exotic aura. The Big Bend section, filled with sidewalk cafes, tony restaurants, bustling bars, high-rise hotels, and even a huge shopping mall, has a festive, sometimes frenetic feel. Tour boats, water taxis, and floating picnic barges regularly ply the river, and local parades and festivals fill its banks with revelers.

✪ **The Alamo.** *300 Alamo Plaza.* ☎ *210/225-1391. Admission free (donations welcome). Mon–Sat 9am–5:30pm, Sun 10am–5:30pm, until 6:30pm Memorial Day–Labor Day. Closed Christmas Eve and Christmas. Streetcar: All streetcar lines.* Sitting smack in the heart of downtown, this graceful mission church was where 188 Texas volunteers defied the much larger army of Mexican dictator Santa Anna for 13 days in March 1836. The deaths of Davy Crockett, Jim Bowie, and all the others rallied Sam Houston's army to eventual victory. Only the Long Barrack and the mission church still stand. The former houses a history museum; the latter includes artifacts of the Alamo fighters, an information desk, and a small gift shop. A larger museum and gift shop are at the back of the complex. There's also a peaceful garden and an excellent research library (closed Sunday).

**Hertzberg Circus Collection and Museum.** *210 W. Market St.* ☎ *210/207-7810. Admission $2.50 adults, $2 seniors, $1 children 3–12. Mon–Sat 10am–5pm, Sun and holidays 1–5pm (June–Aug only). Streetcar: Near all four streetcar lines.* Displays chosen from the massive collection of "circusana" that Harry Hertzberg bequeathed to the San Antonio Public Library include Tom Thumb's carriage, a flea circus, and photographs of Buffalo Bill's Wild West show. Jugglers, mimes, face-painting workshops, and the like entertain kids on weekends.

**Institute of Texan Cultures.** *801 S. Bowie St., in HemisFair Park.* ☎ *210/558-2300. Admission $4 adults, $2 seniors and children 3–12. Tues–Sun 9am–5pm. Multimedia Dome shows at 10:15am, noon, 2 and 3:30pm. Closed Thanksgiving, Christmas. Streetcar: HemisFair Park/La Villita/Cattleman Square.* As many as 28 different cultures that have contributed to Texas history are represented in imaginative, hands-on displays at this educational center, part of the University of Texas at San Antonio.

**Lone Star Buckhorn Museums.** *600 Lone Star Blvd.* ☎ *210/270-9469. Admission $5 adults, $4 senior citizens, $1.75 children 6–11, free for children under 6. Daily 9:30am–5pm. Bus: 40.* With its huge stuffed animals, mounted fish, and Lone Star memorabilia, this complex on the grounds of an active brewery fulfills every out-of-stater's stereotype of what a Texas museum might be like: Hall of Horns, Hall of Feathers, Hall of Fins, and the Texas History Wax Museum. A free beer or soft drink is included in the price of admission.

○ **Marion Koogler McNay Art Museum.** *6000 N. New Braunfels Ave.* ☎ *210/824-5368. Admission free. Fee for special exhibits. Tues–Sat 10am–5pm, Sun noon–5pm. Docent tours Sun at 2pm (Oct–May). Closed Fourth of July, Thanksgiving, Christmas, New Year's Day. Bus: 7.* Set on a hill north of Brackenridge Park with a striking view of downtown, the sprawling Spanish Mediterranean–style mansion of oil-heiress and artist Marion Koogler McNay has been an art museum since 1954. Its main strength is French post-Impressionist and early 20th-century European painting, but there's also a fine collection of theater arts, some excellent special exhibits, and a well-stocked gift shop adjoining a shaded central patio.

○ **San Antonio Missions National Historic Park.** *2202 Roosevelt Ave.* ☎ *210/229-5701. Admission free (donations accepted). Daily 9am–5pm. Closed Christmas, New Year's Day. Call ahead to inquire about National Park Ranger tours. Bus: 40.* The Alamo was originally the first of five Franciscan missions along the San Antonio River. The four now under the aegis of the National Park Service are still active parishes. Built in 1731, **Concepción,** 807 Mission Rd. at Felisa (☎ 210/229-5732), looks much as it did 200 years ago. Established in 1720, **San José,** 6539 San José Dr. at Mission Road (☎ 210/229-4770 or 210/229-4771), was the largest, best-known, and most beautiful of the Texas missions. Reconstructed, it gives a complete picture of mission life. **San Juan Capistrano,** 9102 Graf at Ashley (☎ 210/229-5734), doesn't have the grandeur of the others, but the original simple chapel and the wilder setting give it a peaceful, spiritual aura. The southernmost mission, **San Francisco de la Espada,** 10040 Espada Rd. (☎ 210/627-2021), also has an ancient, isolated feel. Be sure to visit the **Espada Aqueduct,** part of the mission's original *acequia* (irrigation ditch) system and one of the oldest Spanish aqueducts in the United States. A handsome visitor center just outside Mission San José offers an excellent introduction to the park. There's also a good bookstore.

**San Antonio Museum of Art.** *200 W. Jones Ave.* ☎ *210/978-8100. Admission $4 adults, $2 senior citizens and students with ID, $1.75 children 4–11, free for children 3 and under; free on Tues 3–9pm. Mon and Wed–Sat 10am–5pm, Tues 10am–9pm, Sun noon–5pm. Bus: 7.* A number of the castlelike buildings of the 1904 Lone Star Brewery house this visually exciting exhibition space. The Latin American folk art collection is outstanding. The other collections range from early Egyptian, Greek, and Asian to 19th- and 20th-century American. A multiwindowed crosswalk between the two buildings affords fine views of downtown.

**Southwest Craft Center.** *300 Augusta.* ☎ *210/224-1848. Admission free. Galleries, Mon–Sat 10am–5pm. Streetcar: Romana Plaza/King William.* A stroll along the River Walk to the northern corner of downtown will bring you to this rare French-designed cloister, established by the Ursuline order in the mid-19th century, where contemporary crafts are now being created. Two exhibition galleries and artist studios-cum-classrooms occupy the garden-filled grounds of the first girls' school in San Antonio. The Ursuline Gallery's gift shop carries unique craft items, and you can enjoy lunch in the **Copper Kitchen Restaurant** (open Mon–Fri 11:30am–2pm).

**Spanish Governor's Palace.** *105 Plaza de Armas.* ☎ *210/224-0601. Admission $1 adults, 50¢ children 7–13, free for children 6 and under. Mon–Sat 9am–5pm, Sun 10am–5pm. Closed Christmas, New Year's Day, and Fiesta week. Streetcar: Romana Plaza/King William.* Never actually a palace, this 1749 adobe structure formerly served as the residence and headquarters for the captain of the Spanish presidio. It served as the capitol of the Spanish province of Texas in 1772. The building, with high ceilings crossed by protruding *viga* beams, is beautiful in its simplicity, and the 10 rooms crowded with period furnishings paint a vivid portrait of upper-class life in a rough-hewn society.

✪ **Witte Museum.** *3810 Broadway, at the edge of Brackenridge Park.* ☎ *210/ 820-2111. Admission $4 adults, $2 senior citizens and students with ID, $1.75 children 4–11, free for children 3 and under; free Tues 3–9pm. Mon and Wed–Sat 10am–5pm (until 6pm June–Aug), Tues 10am–9pm, Sun noon–5pm (until 6pm June–Aug). Closed Thanksgiving, Christmas. Bus: 7.* A family museum, the Witte focuses on Texas history, natural science, and anthropology. You might hear animal cries as you crouch through south Texas thorn brush, or feel rough-hewn stone carved with American Indian pictographs under your feet. An EcoLab is home to live Texas critters ranging from tarantulas to tortoises. There's a butterfly and hummingbird garden, three restored historic homes, and the H-E-B Science Treehouse, a four-level, 15,000-square-foot science center with hands-on activities for all ages.

**HISTORIC AREAS**   On the east bank of the river just south of downtown, the **King William Historic District** was settled in the late 19th century by prosperous German merchants who displayed their wealth through extravagant homes. They named the 25-block area after Kaiser Wilhelm of Prussia. Stop at the headquarters of the San Antonio Conservation Society, 107 King William St. (☎ **210/224-6163**), and pick up a self-guided walking tour booklet outside the gate. The neighborhood is within walking distance of the Convention Center and is on the VIA Romana/King William streetcar route.

**PARKS & GARDENS**   With its rustic stone bridges and winding walkways, **Brackenridge Park,** 2800 block of North Broadway (☎ **210/207-8480**), opened in 1899 and still has a charming, old-fashioned quality. It also serves as a popular center for recreational activities including golf, polo, biking, picnicking, horseback riding, and paddleboating. A cable-car sky ride offers a panoramic view of the San Antonio skyline, a miniature railway replicating an 1863 steam locomotive runs $3^1/2$ miles through the park, and a carousel features 60 antique horses. Also here are the **San Antonio Zoo,** 3903 N. St. Mary's St. (☎ **210/734-7183**), home to one of the largest animal collections in the U.S. (it produced the first white rhino born in the U.S.), and the **Japanese Tea Garden,** 3800 N. St. Mary's St., next to the zoo (☎ **210/821-3120**), also called the Japanese Sunken Garden, built by prison labor to beautify an abandoned quarry in the 1880s and 1890s.

An urban oasis, **HemisFair Park,** 200 S. Alamo (☎ **210/207-8572**), was built for the 1968 HemisFair, an exposition celebrating the 250th anniversary of the founding of San Antonio. It boasts water gardens and a wood-and-sand playground constructed by children. The Institute of Texan Cultures (see "Attractions," above) and the Tower of the Americas (see "The Club & Bar Scene," below) are here. Be sure to see the striking mosaic mural by Mexican artist Juan O'Gorman at the Henry B. Gonzales Convention Center.

Take a horticultural tour of Texas at **San Antonio Botanical Gardens,** 555 Funston (☎ **210/821-5115**), whose gracious 38 acres encompass everything from south Texas scrub to Hill Country wildflowers and east Texas formal rose gardens. Fountains, pools, paved paths, and examples of Texas architecture provide visual contrast. There's also a garden for the blind, an herb garden, a children's garden, and the $6.5-million Lucille Halsell Conservatory complex, a bermed, below-ground greenhouse replicating a variety of tropical and desert environments.

**BEST BETS FOR KIDS**   If you're traveling with children, don't miss the ✪ **San Antonio Children's Museum,** 305 E. Houston St. (☎ **210/21-CHILD**), for a wonderful introduction to the city. Local history, population, and geography are all explored through such features as a miniature riverwalk, a multicultural grocery store, and a bird-watching platform.

Leave it to Texas to provide Shamu, the performing killer whale, with his most spacious digs at the largest marine theme park in the world, **Sea World of Texas,** 16 miles northwest of downtown San Antonio at Ellison Drive and Westover Hills Boulevard (☎ 210/523-3611). Kids can get wet in the huge wave pool of the Lost Lagoon, the Texas Splashdown flume ride, and the Rio Loco river rapids. Younger kids can cavort in Shamu's Happy Harbor. **Six Flags Fiesta Texas,** at the corner of I-10 West and Loop 1604 (☎ 210/697-5050), has a vast variety of food booths to share the 200-acre amusement arena with rides, games, and craft demonstrations. Dramatic 100-foot cliffs surround the park, which is set in an abandoned limestone quarry on the north end of town.

**Alamo IMAX Theater,** 849 E. Commerce St., in the Rivercenter Mall (☎ 210/225-4629), presents *Alamo: Price of Freedom* on a six-story-high screen with a stereo sound system. Adults may get a bigger charge out of the waxy stars at **Ripley's Believe It or Not and Plaza Theater of Wax,** 301 Alamo Plaza (☎ 210/224-9299).

**SPORTS**   Spur madness hits San Antonio every year from mid-October through May, when the city's only major-league franchise, the **San Antonio Spurs,** shoot hoops at the huge Alamodome. Tickets are available at the Spurs Ticket Office (south end of the Alamodome) or by phoning Rainbow Ticketmaster (☎ 210/224-9600).

**Retama Park,** some 15 minutes north of San Antonio in Selma (☎ 210/651-7000), is the hottest place to play the ponies; take exit 174A from I-35, or the Lookout Road exit from Loop 1604.

**SHOPPING**   Most out-of-town shoppers will find all they need downtown at the large **Rivercenter Mall,** 849 E. Commerce between Alamo Plaza, and Bowie, Crockett, and Commerce; the boutiques and crafts shops of **La Villita;** the **Southwest Craft Center** (see "Attractions," above); and assorted retailers and galleries on and around Alamo Plaza. In the Southtown section near King William, the **Blue Star Arts Complex,** 1400 S. Alamo (☎ 210/227-6960), is the up-and-coming place to buy art.

San Antonians tend to shop the **Loop 410 malls,** especially North Star, Loop 410 at McCullough; and Central Park, Loop 410 and Blanco, near the airport. Among the upscale **strip centers along Broadway** in Alamo Heights, the posh Collection and Lincoln Heights are particularly noteworthy. Weekends might see locals poking around a number of terrific **flea markets.** For serious bargains on brand labels, they head out to the three large **factory outlet malls** at New Braunfels and San Marcos, about 45 minutes northeast on I-35.

With some buildings dating to the late 1800s, **Market Square,** between Dolorosa and Commerce streets, will transport you south of the border. Stalls sell everything from onyx chess sets and cheap serapes to beautifully made crafts from the interior of Mexico. Across the street, the Farmer's Market has carts with more modern goods. Most of the city's Hispanic festivals are held here, and mariachis usually stroll the square.

## ACCOMMODATIONS

San Antonio has the highest concentration of historic hotels in Texas; most are in the downtown area, within walking distance of many of the city's attractions. In recent years, a number of the old mansions in the King William and Monte Vista Historic Districts have been converted into bed-and-breakfasts. For information or reservations, contact **Bed & Breakfast Hosts of San Antonio,** P.O. Box 831203, San Antonio, TX 78283 (☎ 800/356-1605 for reservations, or 210/824-8036; fax 210/824-9926), or the **San Antonio Bed & Breakfast Association,** P.O. Box 830101, San Antonio TX 78283 (☎ 800/210-8422 or 210/212-8422). Book as far in advance as possible, and 6 months or more during Fiesta the third week in April. Rates here are highest from November to April. Room tax is 15%.

✪ **Fairmount.** *401 S. Alamo St., San Antonio, TX 78205.* ☎ *800/642-3363 or 210/224-8800. Fax 210/224-2767. 20 rms, 17 suites. $165–$200 double; $225–$475* *suite. Corporate rates and packages available. AE, DC, MC, V. Valet parking $8.* This lovely boutique establishment was built in an ornate Italianate-Victorian railway hotel in 1906, but today's clientele is more likely to fly in via private jet. Battle of the Alamo artifacts are showcased in the lobby. Even the so-called standard rooms here are outstanding. The romantic Polo's serves fine fare.

**Holiday Inn Riverwalk.** *217 N. St. Mary's St., San Antonio, TX 78205.* ☎ *800/ 465-4329 or 210/224-2500. Fax 210/226-0154. 303 rms, 10 suites. $125–$139 double; $175–$275 suite. AE, CB, DC, DISC, MC, V. Self-parking $5; valet parking $7.* This hotel offers a River Walk location at lower prices than usual. Guest rooms are done in attractive contemporary style, and almost all of them have balconies; you pay slightly more for a river view, although the urban vistas can be stunning at night. The hotel has a restaurant with river view, lounge, outdoor heated pool, whirlpool, exercise room, and gift shop.

**Homewood Suites.** *432 Market St., San Antonio, TX 78205.* ☎ *800/ CALL-HOME or 210/222-1515. Fax 210/222-1575. 146 suites. $119–$159 suite on weekends, lower on weekdays. Rates include continental breakfast. AE, CB, DC, DISC, MC, V. Valet parking $10.* Located on a quiet stretch of the river, this all-suites hotel is convenient to west side attractions such as Market Square and is only a few extra blocks from the Alamo. Microwave ovens, refrigerators with icemakers, dishwashers, and coffeemakers appeal to business travelers and families alike. Facilities include a heated rooftop pool and whirlpool, exercise room, guest laundry, and business center.

✪ **Hyatt Regency Hill Country Resort.** *9800 Hyatt Resort Dr., San Antonio, TX 78251.* ☎ *800/233-1234 or 210/647-1234. Fax 210/681-9681. 443 rms, 57 suites, 1 guest house. $240–$320 double; $435–$1,560 suite. AE, CB, DC, DISC, MC, V. Free self-parking; valet parking $8.* You might never want to leave this cushy resort on the far west side of town. On-site activities range from golf to tubing on a man-made river, and Sea World of Texas sits at your doorstep. The restaurants are excellent, the rooms are beautifully appointed, and there are even free laundry facilities and a country store for supplies.

**La Mansión del Rio.** *112 College St., San Antonio, TX 78205.* ☎ *800/292-7300 (U.S., Canada, or Mexico) or 210/225-2581. Fax 210/226-0389. 327 rms, 10 suites. $190–$260 single or double; $430–$1,500 suite. AE, CB, DC, DISC, MC, V. Valet parking $12.* Moorish arches, Mexican tile, a central patio, wrought-iron balconies, and antique pieces combine to create a low-glitz, high-tone Mediterranean atmosphere at this lushly landscaped Spanish hacienda–style hotel, converted from a 19th-century seminary. Guest rooms all have rough-hewn beamed ceilings, brick walls, and soothing earth-tone furnishings. Las Canarias dining room serves up a terrific river view. Facilities include an outdoor pool and gift shop.

**Marriott Rivercenter.** *101 Bowie St., San Antonio, TX 78205.* ☎ *800/228-9290 or 210/223-1000. Fax 210/223-4092. 1,000 rms, 86 suites. $205 double; $229–$900 suite. AE, DC, DISC, MC, V. Self-parking $9; valet parking $12.* This hotel has it all— transportation desks, a good range of dining and drinking areas, a large indoor/outdoor pool, and an extremely well-equipped exercise center, free washers and dryers, and a mall with 100 Rivercenter emporiums. Many of the well-appointed, contemporary but elegant guest rooms afford spectacular River Walk or city views.

✪ **Menger Hotel.** *204 Alamo Plaza, San Antonio, TX 78205.* ☎ *800/345-9285 or 210/223-4361. Fax 210/228-0022. 320 rms, 25 suites. $132 double; $182–$546 suite. Honeymoon packages available. AE, CB, DC, DISC, MC, V. Self-parking $6.95; valet parking $11.* Established in 1859, the Menger has gorgeous public areas, charming guest rooms, reasonable rates, and a great location. The Menger Bar is a great historic tavern (see "San Antonio After Dark," below). The hotel has a heated outdoor pool, hot tub, exercise room, spa, shopping arcade, tourist information center, game room, and gift shop.

○ **Ramada Emily Morgan.** *705 E. Houston St., San Antonio, TX 78205.* ☎ *800/ 824-6674 or 210/225-8486. Fax 210/225-7227. 154 rms, 11 Executive rms, 12 Plaza rms. $99 double on weekdays, $115 double on weekends. AE, CB, DC, DISC, MC, V. Self-parking $7.* One of the city's best bargains, the Ramada Emily Morgan is centrally located directly across Alamo Plaza in a beautiful 1926 Gothic Revival building, the first documented skyscraper built west of the Mississippi. Guest rooms are modern, bright, and immaculate. Conveniences include a restaurant, outdoor pool and whirlpool, exercise room, his-and-her saunas, and gift shop.

**OTHER ACCOMMODATIONS** One of the most glorious of the mansions that grace the King William Historic District, the Greek Revival–style ○ **Ogé House on the River Walk,** 209 Washington St., San Antonio, TX 78204 (☎ 800/242-2770 or 210/223-2353; fax 210/226-5812), is more boutique inn than folksy bed-and-breakfast. The five rooms and four suites range from $135 to $195, including breakfast.

For those who don't mind sharing a bath, the gracefully, neoclassical **Bullis House Inn,** 621 Pierce St., San Antonio, TX 78208 (☎ 210/223-9426), is the best bed-and-breakfast bargain in town. Just down the street from the Fort Sam Houston quadrangle, it was built between 1906 and 1909 for General John Lapham Bullis, a frontier Indian fighter who played a key role in capturing Geronimo. Rates are $49–$69 double, including continental breakfast.

## DINING

You can get great Tex-Mex food here, but you'll find less familiar, often sophisticated dishes from the interior of Mexico as well as Southwestern fare. Although dining on the River Walk is a not-to-be-missed experience, many riverside restaurants are overpriced and overcrowded. Most locals eat in the area around Broadway, where many good restaurants are concentrated.

○ **Boudro's.** *421 E. Commerce St./River Walk.* ☎ *210/224-8484. Reservations strongly recommended. Main courses $13–$25. AE, DC, DISC, MC, V. Sun–Thurs 11am–11pm, Fri–Sat 11am–midnight. SOUTHWESTERN.* Locals tend to look down their noses on River Walk restaurants, but not Boudro's. The kitchen uses fresh local ingredients—Gulf Coast seafood, Texas beef, Hill Country produce—and the preparations and presentations do them justice. The setting is also out of the ordinary: a turn-of-the-century limestone building with hardwood floors and handmade mesquite bar.

**Cappy's.** *5011 Broadway (behind Twig Bookstore).* ☎ *210/828-9669. Reservations recommended. Main courses $8.50–$17. AE, MC, V. Mon–Thurs 11am–10pm, Fri–Sat 11am–11pm, Sun 10:30am–10pm. REGIONAL AMERICAN.* In the burgeoning Alamo Heights neighborhood, Cappy's is set in an unusual broken-brick structure dating back to the late 1930s, but there's nothing outdated about this cheerful, light-filled place with colorful work by local artists. The enticing smell of the wood-burning grill gives a hint of some of the house specialties. **Cappyccino's,** just next door, is ideal for quick lunches, light dinners, or after-theater drinks.

**Chez Ardid.** *1919 San Pedro Ave.* ☎ *210/732-3203. Reservations recommended. Main courses $12.50–$25. AE, CB, DC, MC, V. Mon–Fri 11:30am–2pm; Mon–Sat 6–10pm. FRENCH.* Wedding classic French cuisine with regional ingredients, Chef Miguel Ardid presides over this restored 1902 home, one of the most enduring favorites here. The deboned pheasant stuffed with wild-boar sausage is an excellent entree selection, as is the tenderloin medaillon in green peppercorn sauce.

✪ **Koi Kawa.** *4051 Broadway.* ☎ *210/521-7421. Reservations recommended on the weekends. AE, DC, DISC, MC, V. Main courses $10–$22. Mon–Thurs 11:30am–2pm and 5:30–10pm, Fri–Sat 5:30–11pm. JAPANESE.* Devoted fans sit around Koi Kawa's sushi bar and watch David Mukai perform his magic. There are plenty of other options such as crispy tempuras and various udon (wheat noodle) and soba (cold buckwheat noodle) soups, meals in themselves. The unassuming Koi Kawa has a view of the tree-shaded riverbanks.

**Little Rhein Steak House.** *231 S. Alamo.* ☎ *210/225-2111. Reservations recommended. Main courses $14–$30. AE, DC, DISC, MC, V. Sun–Thurs 5–10pm, Fri–Sat 5–11pm. AMERICAN.* Built in 1847, the oldest two-story structure in San Antonio now houses this elegant steak house. Antique memorabilia and a miniature train deck the dining room. Leafy branches overhang the River Walk patio with little sparkling lights. Choice steaks come with salad, baked potato, and Texas caviar (deliciously seasoned black-eyed peas).

✪ **Mesteña.** *7959 Broadway.* ☎ *210/822-7733. Reservations recommended on weekends. Main courses $14–$24. AE, MC, V. Mon–Thurs 11:30am–2:30pm and 5:30–10pm; Fri–Sat 11:30am–2:30pm and 5:30–10:30pm; Sun 11am–3pm (brunch) and 5–9:30pm. SOUTHWESTERN.* Formerly of Washington, D.C.'s famed Red Sage Restaurant, chef Chris Swinyard brings creative dishes like seared rabbit loin entree in round cuts with cheddar cheese grits to the local scene. The wild horses for which the restaurant is named apply more to the exciting menu than to the stark, high-ceiling room. Presentations are gorgeous.

**Mi Tierra.** *218 Produce Row, Market Square.* ☎ *210/225-1262. Reservations accepted for large groups only. Main courses $7–$15. AE, MC, V. Open 24 hours. MEXICAN.* Open since 1946 but much expanded and gussied up since then, Mi Tierra still draws a faithful clientele of Latino families and businesspeople along with busloads of tourists. You can order anything from chorizo and eggs to an 8-ounce charbroiled ribeye—while being serenaded by mariachis—at all hours. Mi Tierra is justly renowned for its *panadería* (bakery).

**Paesanos Riverwalk.** *111 Crockett, Suite 101.* ☎ *210/22-PASTA. Reservations accepted for lunch only. Pasta $8–$14; main courses $16–$22. AE, DC, MC, V. Sun–Thurs 11am–11pm, Fri–Sat 11am–midnight. ITALIAN.* No Italian Chianti bottle–kitsch decor here, but a soaring ceiling and lots of inscrutable contemporary art. If you want to save money, order the crispy shrimp Paesanos as an appetizer: Portions are huge.

✪ **Restaurant Biga.** *206 E. Locust St.* ☎ *210/225-0722. Reservations accepted for five or more only. Main courses $14–$26. AE, CB, DC, DISC, MC, V. Mon–Thurs 5:30–10:30pm, Fri–Sat 5:30–11pm. NEW AMERICAN.* Giving the lie to the maxim "Never trust a thin chef," lanky Bruce Auden turns out some of the city's finest food in this 100-year-old house. Although his menu changes regularly, you can depend on seeing oak-roasted Nilgai antelope and quail or pheasant; the Texas-bred African game is remarkably tender.

✪ **Rosario's.** *1014 S. Alamo.* ☎ *210/223-1806. Reservations not accepted. Main courses $6–$13. Mon–Sat 10:45am–3pm; Tues–Thurs 3–10pm, Fri–Sat 3pm–12:30am. AE, DC, DISC, MC, V. MEXICAN.* This hip Mexican hangout is housed in a dimly lit, green-brick building with a pink neon sign and is hung with folk art and paintings by local artists. Large helpings come with rice, refried beans, and tortillas. The place sizzles when a tropical band plays on weekend nights, and weekday lunch specials draw a sizable local crowd.

**Schilo's.** *424 E. Commerce St.* ☎ *210/223-6692. Reservations not accepted. Sandwiches $2.50–$5; hot or cold plates $4–$5; main dishes (served after 5pm) $7–$9. AE, CB,*

*DC, DISC, MC, V. Mon–Sat 7am–8:30pm. GERMAN DELI.* You can't leave town without stopping into this San Antonio institution, if only for a hearty bowl of split-pea soup or a piece of the signature cherry cheesecake. The large, open room with its worn wooden booths gives a glimpse into the city's German past (an oompah band plays Saturday from 5 to 8pm).

**Zuni Grill.** *511 River Walk/223 Losoya St.* ☎ *210/227-0864. Reservations accepted only for parties of six or more. Main courses $11–$19. AE, DC, DISC, MC, V. Sun–Thurs 8am–11pm, Fri–Sat 8am–midnight. SOUTHWESTERN.* With its stylized cacti, metallic hump-backed flute players, and chic Southwestern menu, this popular River Walk cafe is a little bit of Santa Fe–on–the–San Antonio. The grilled chicken salad with goat cheese and spicy roasted pecans makes a nice, light meal. For something more substantial, try the honey coriander pork loin with adobo sauce.

**BARBECUE JOINTS** Emotions rise in San Antonio when the talk runs to barbecue, with many locals insisting that the place they go to is the best and most authentic. Favorites include **Rudy's,** 24152 I-10 West at Leon Springs/Boerne Stage Road exit (☎ 210/698-0418); the **County Line,** 111 W. Crockett St., Suite 104 (☎ 210/229-1941), River Walk, or 607 W. Afton Oaks, off F.M. 1604 (☎ 210/496-0011); **Bob's Smokehouse,** at 5145 Fredericksburg Rd. (☎ 210/344-8401), or 3306 Roland Ave. (☎ 210/333-9338), or 1219 S. St. Mary's St. (☎ 210/224-4717); **Texas Pride,** 2980 E. Loop 1604 S. at LaVernia Road (☎ 210/649-3730); and **Tommy Wilson's** (U.S. Hwy. 281 between Loop 1604 and Tex. 46 (☎ 210/980-3052).

## SAN ANTONIO AFTER DARK

A Latin flavor lends spice to some of the best local nightlife: San Antonio is America's capital for Tejano music, a unique blend of German polka and northern Mexico ranchero sounds, with a touch of pop for good measure. For the most complete listings of what's on, pick up a free copy of the weekly alternative newspaper, the *Current,* or the Friday "Weekender" section of the *San Antonio–Express.* You can also call the new San Antonio Arts Hotline at ☎ 800/894-3819 or 210/207-2166. There is no central office in town for tickets, discounted or otherwise; reserve seats directly through the theaters or clubs, or, in the case of large events, through Ticketmaster (☎ 210/224-9600).

**THE PERFORMING ARTS** The **San Antonio Symphony,** 222 E. Houston St. (☎ 210/554-1010), performs in the stunning **Majestic Theatre,** 230 E. Houston (☎ 210/226-3333), which also hosts major Broadway productions and big-name solo performers. With its shifting, night-sky ceiling, the Majestic also is a show unto itself. Built by the Works Project Administration in 1939 as part of architect Robert Hugman's design for the River Walk, the ✪ **Arneson River Theatre,** La Villita (☎ 210/927-3389), stages summertime shows on one side of the river while the audience watches from an amphitheater on the other.

There's always something happening at the **Guadalupe Cultural Arts Center,** 1300 Guadalupe (☎ 210/271-3151), the main locus for Latino cultural activity in San Antonio. Visiting or local directors put on six or seven plays a year, and the resident Guadalupe Dance Company might collaborate with the city's symphony or invite modern masters up from Mexico City.

**THE CLUB & BAR SCENE** The closest San Antonio comes to having a club district is the stretch of North St. Mary's between Josephine and Magnolia just north of downtown and south of Brackenridge Park. Known as **The Strip,** it draws locals on the weekends. Most visitors tend to stay around the River Walk.

Preppie and gallery types don't often mingle, but the popularity of the **Blue Star Brewing Company Restaurant & Bar,** in the Blue Star Arts Complex, 1414 S. Alamo (☎ 210/212-5506), demonstrates the transcendent power of good beer. Toss your peanut shells on the floor and sing along with the piano player at **Durty Nellie's Irish Pub,** Hilton Palacio del Rio Hotel, 715 River Walk (☎ **210/222-1400**), a wonderfully corny version of an Irish watering hole. In the 700-foot-high **Tower of the Americas,** 600 HemisFair Park (☎ **210/223-3101**), the bar affords dazzling views of the city.

In the hotels, cornetist Jim Cullum's popular national public radio program is broadcast live from ✪ **The Landing,** Hyatt Regency on River Walk (☎ **210/ 223-7266**), one of the best traditional jazz clubs in the country. Teddy Roosevelt recruited men for his Rough Riders unit at the dark, wooded **Menger Bar,** Menger Hotel, 204 Alamo Plaza (☎ **210/223-4361**). For piano music in a high-tone atmosphere from Tuesday to Saturday, come to **Polo's,** in the Fairmount Hotel, 40 S. Alamo St. (☎ **210/224-8800**). An older crowd sinks down into the plush green leather couches or perches on a stool at the marble bar.

Two miles north of Loop 1604, the ✪ **Floore Country Store,** 14664 Bandera Rd./ Hwy. 16, Helotes (☎ **210/695-8827**), has a half-acre-size dance floor—the largest in south Texas. Willie Nelson, Hank Williams, Sr., Conway Twitty, Ernest Tubb, and other country greats have played here—Willie still performs now and then, as does his friend Jerry Jeff Walker.

## 16 Houston

The largest city in Texas, Houston was founded as a real estate venture in 1836. It was hard hit by the oil crash of the early 1980s, and visitors may be struck by the contrast between downtown's glittering skyscrapers and the many boarded-up buildings in depressed areas nearby. However, Houston's economy has begun to turn itself around. A 50-mile long ship channel links this inland city with the Gulf of Mexico, making it the third-largest seaport in the United States.

Houston is a cosmopolitan cultural center, with internationally known universities, a symphony, and a world-class ballet and opera company. It's also home to a major branch of America's space program—the everywhere-present Disney teamed up with the National Aeronautics and Space Administration to create the dazzling Space Center Houston. Downtown Houston has the oldest and one of the largest indoor pedestrian tunnel systems in the nation—workers and visitors can avoid the city's heavy traffic and hot and humid climate in an underground landscape dotted with restaurants and shops.

### ARRIVING & DEPARTING

**BY PLANE** The **George Bush–Houston Intercontinental Airport (IAH)** is about an hour's ride north of downtown, with taxi fare around $30. The **W. P. Hobby Airport,** more convenient to downtown, is 45 minutes away; taxi fare is about $20. City **express bus service** (☎ **713/635-4000**) to downtown costs $1.20. **Shuttles** (☎ **713/ 523-8888**) to several locations serve both Hobby ($11) and IAH ($16).

**BY BUS & TRAIN** Amtrak (☎ **800/872-7245**) trains arrive at the old **Southern Pacific Station,** 902 Washington Ave. (☎ **713/224-1577**). The **Greyhound Lines** (☎ **800/231-2222**) bus station is at 2121 Main St.

**BY CAR** Houston is ringed by the I-610 beltway. A tighter loop, made up of several expressways, circles downtown, incidentally providing striking views of the city. Traffic can be extremely heavy during rush hours.

### ESSENTIALS

**VISITOR INFORMATION** The **Greater Houston Convention and Visitor Bureau's Houston Welcome Center** is at 801 Congress Ave., Houston, TX 77002

(☎ 800/4-HOUSTON or 713/227-3100; http://houston-guide.com), open Mon–Fri 8:30am–5pm.

**EMERGENCIES & SAFETY**   In a serious emergency, call ☎ **911.** For medical emergencies, the **Prime Care Emergency Ambulance Service, Inc.** can be reached at ☎ **713/521-1426.** The assistance center of the **Texas Medical Center** is at 1155 Holcombe (☎ **713/790-1136**). In general, avoid deserted areas at night, and be careful when parking your car on a deserted street.

## GETTING AROUND

**BY BUS**   The **Metropolitan Transportation Authority (MTA)** operates citywide bus service with stops indicated by red, white, or blue signs. Standard fare is $1; express fare is $1.50. Seniors and riders with disabilities pay 40¢; children under 4 ride free. The **Texas Special Red, White, and Blue** is a route servicing downtown only for a 25¢ fare. Call ☎ **713/739-4000** for information.

## WHAT TO SEE & DO

**SPECIAL EVENTS**   The **Houston Livestock Show and Rodeo** (☎ **713/791-9000**), in mid-February, is the largest event of its kind in the world. On the weekend nearest June 19, the **Juneteenth Festival** (☎ **713/227-3100** or 713/667-8000) celebrates the day slavery was abolished in Texas with blues, gospel, and other musicfests.

**MUSEUMS**   Houston has a number of important museums, housing treasures ranging from Etruscan sculpture to Picasso paintings.

   **Bayou Bend.** *1 Westcott St.* ☎ *713/639-7750. $10 adults, $8.50 seniors, $5 those 10–18. Tues–Fri 10am–2:45pm, Sat 10am–5pm, Sun 1–5pm.* A beautiful collection of 17th–19th-century furniture is housed here in 28 rooms of the vast Renaissance-style home of Ima Hogg, daughter of a former governor of Texas. Under the auspices of the Museum of Fine Arts; the collection can be viewed Tues–Sat by appointment; children under 10 not admitted except at certain times, so call for schedule.

   **Contemporary Arts Museum.** *5216 Montrose Blvd.* ☎ *713/284-8250. Admission free. Tues–Sat 10am–5pm, Sun noon–5pm; Thurs until 9pm. Closed Mon.* This unique, silvered-aluminum parallelogram presents temporary exhibitions of modern art and industrial design as well as films. It focuses on post-1945 American art. During 1996–97 the museum underwent massive renovation.

   ✪ **Houston Museum of Natural Science.** *1 Hermann Circle Dr.* ☎ *713/ 639-IMAX. Admission $3 adults, $2 children 3–11; IMAX tickets $5.50 adults, $3.50 children 3–11. Mon–Sat 9am–6pm, Sun 11am–6pm.* From the diplodocus to the space rocket, and from oil wells to artificial earthquakes, this is one of the biggest and most impressive natural science museums in the country. Special highlights include the Hall of Medical Science with giant models of the human body, and the Burke Baker Planetarium, where visitors follow the paths of comets and planetary motions.

   **Menil Collection.** *1515 Sul Ross.* ☎ *713/525-9400. Admission free. Wed–Sun 11am–7pm.* The personal collection of Dominique de Menil, which drew large crowds a few years ago at the Petit Palais in Paris, is now housed here. This is among the world's most highly regarded private museums, comprising more than 15,000 works of art spanning over 5,000 years of history, including Etruscan and Anatolian sculpture, medieval paintings, works from native cultures around the world, and the works of avant-garde painters such as Picasso and Pollock.

   ✪ **Museum of Fine Arts, Houston.** *1001 Bissonnet.* ☎ *713/639-7300. $3 adults, $1.50 seniors and children 6–18. Tues–Sat 10am–5pm, Thurs 10am–9pm, Sun 12:15–6pm.* This museum houses an impressive collection of European art from throughout the ages, as well as works by renowned American painters (particularly Frederic Remington),

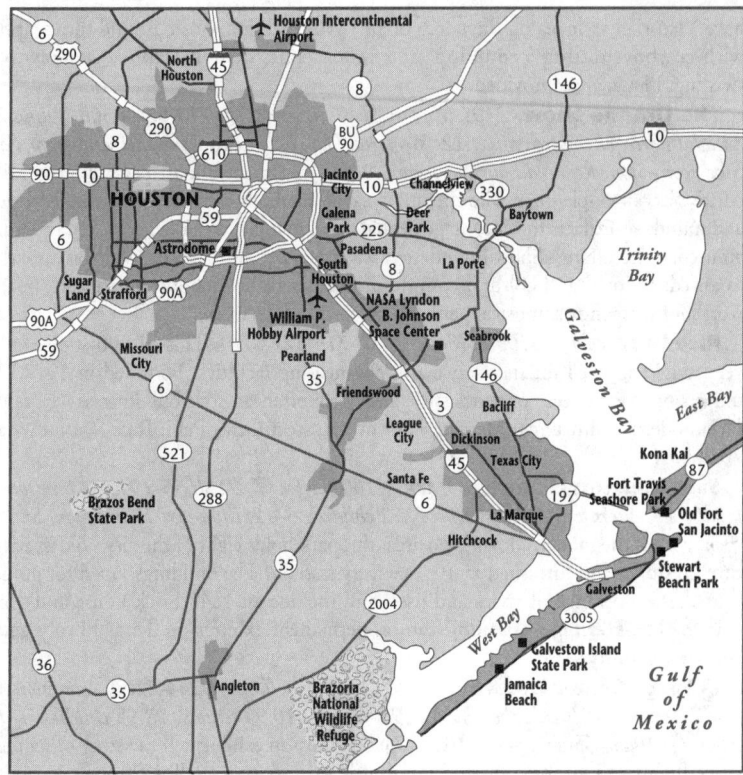

Native American pottery, and pre-Colombian art. The sculpture garden, created by distinguished sculptor Isamu Noguchi, provides a setting for major 19th- and 20th-century sculpture. The Glassell School of Art, established in 1927, is nationally known for its training in the fine arts, and it also offers a wide variety of programs and classes for adults and children. A reference library and guided tours are available.

⭐ **Rothko Chapel.** *3900 Yupon St.* ☎ *713/524-9839. Admission free. Daily 10am–6pm.* This octagonal chapel in an out-of-the-way district was designed by Philip Johnson and houses brooding paintings by Mark Rothko in 1965 and 1966. Barnett Newman's *Broken Obelisk*, a sculpture dedicated to Martin Luther King, Jr., sits in a reflection pool in front of the chapel.

**MORE ATTRACTIONS**  Houston's sprawling geography is matched by the range of its attractions. You might want to enjoy a cowboy campfire, or land a space shuttle.

⭐ **Astrodome USA.** *8400 Kirby Dr.* ☎ *713/799-9544. Tours $4 adults, $3 seniors and children 4–11. Tues–Sat 11am, 1pm, and 3pm.* One of the most visited structures in Texas, the Astrodome seats 76,000 people, and its 18-story dome is one of the highest in the world. It is home to the Astros baseball team, and is also used for concerts and exhibitions.

**George Ranch Historical Park.** *10215 F.M. 762, Richmond.* ☎ *281/545-9212. Admission Mon–Fri, $3 adults, $2 children 3–13; Sat–Sun $6 adults, $3 children 3–13. Apr–Dec, Sat–Sun 10am–6pm.* This 470-acre "working ranch" features a number of restored historic buildings (which can be toured) as well as demonstrations and historical reconstructions provided by costumed guides and craftsmen. Visitors can have Victorian-style tea on the porch of an 1890s mansion, or sit around the campfire with cowboys during a roundup, and watch crafts demonstrations such as rope twisting. Picnic areas provided.

**The Orange Show.** *2401 Munger St. (East End).* ☎ *713/926-6368. Admission $1 adults, free for children under 12. Memorial Day–Labor Day, Wed–Fri 9am–1pm, Sat–Sun noon–5pm. Reduced hours off-season.* A unique urban folk-art park built by Hjeff Mckissack, an ex-postman who spent 25 years assembling a collection of found objects and mundane artifacts to "encourage people to eat oranges, drink oranges, and be highly amused." The Orange Show Foundation has preserved the complex, which is also used as an educational and cultural community center to host children's theater, poetry workshops, art shows, musical performances, and art lectures.

**Rice University.** *6100 S. Main St.* ☎ *713/527-8101.* This 31,000-student university is renowned for its science and engineering faculties. Founded in 1912, the university boasts dozens of neoclassical and Mediterranean-style buildings as well as the ultramodern and original Herring Hall by architect Cesar Pelli. Rice Stadium seats 70,000.

**Sam Houston Historical Park.** *1100 Bagby.* ☎ *713/655-1912. Admission $6 adults, $4 seniors and children 13–17, $2 children 6–12. Mon–Sat 10am–4pm, Sun 1–5pm.* Part of the modern downtown area, this park holds eight of the city's oldest structures, restored and furnished in 19th-century fashion. The buildings, open for guided tours, reflect a range of styles and uses, and include an 1847 brick house and 1891 church. The **Heritage Museum** features permanent exhibits on Texas history and a complete country store.

✪ **Space Center Houston.** *1601 NASA Rd. 1.* ☎ *281/244-2100. Admission (including tours and IMAX theater) $11.95 adults, $10.95 seniors, $8.95 children 4–11. Mon–Fri 10am–5pm, Sat–Sun 10am–7pm.* Hands-on exhibits tell the story of manned space flight, and visitors can land the shuttle or retrieve a satellite through computer simulations, touch a moon rock, or try on space helmets. There are behind-the-scenes tram tours of NASA's Johnson Space Center (JSC), which includes a visit to Mission Control. Actual Mercury, Gemini, and Apollo spacecraft can be viewed, and information on space flight and training activities is provided. JSC scientists, engineers, and astronauts visit the facility daily to share their experiences and answer questions.

**PARKS & ZOOS**   The city's playground is **Hermann Park,** a 545-acre park a short way from downtown. It has an 18-hole golf course, picnic areas, the Garden Center, the Miller Outdoor Theater, and many other recreational facilities. It is also home to the **Houston Zoological Gardens,** 1513 N. MacGregor (☎ 713/523-5888); open daily 10am–6pm. This 50-acre zoo features a gorilla habitat, rare albino reptiles, cat facility, huge aquarium, and vampire bats that eat lunch every day at 2:30pm. The tropical bird house is home to more than 200 exotic birds in a rain-forest environment. The Brown Education Center, open daily from 10am–6pm, allows visitors to interact with the animals.

**BEST BETS FOR KIDS**   The youngsters will enjoy the **Museum of Science,** the **Space Center,** and the **Sam Houston Historical Park,** and, of course, the **Houston Zoological Gardens** (see above). The **Children's Museum of Houston,** 1500 Binz (☎ 713/522-1138), was designed by award-winning architect Robert Venturi and features an auditorium, resource center for parents and educators, and hands-on exhibits geared to children age 14 and under on science, history, culture, and the arts.

Houston is also home to two large amusement parks. **Six Flags AstroWorld,** 9001 Kirby Dr. (☎ 713/799-1234), is a 75-acre amusement park with more than 100 attractions, including the giant "Texas Cyclone" roller coaster. Shows and concerts are also presented. **Six Flags WaterWorld,** 9001 Kirby Dr. (☎ 713/799-1234), is an aquatic amusement park adjoining AstroWorld.

**SPORTS**  The **Houston Astros** play at the Astrodome (see above) Apr–Oct. The **Houston Rockets** play at **The Summit,** 10 Greenway Plaza (☎ 713/627-3865), Nov–Apr. Galveston has 32 miles of **beaches** and other recreational facilities. See "A Day Trip to Galveston" at the end of this section.

**SHOPPING**  The main shopping area in Houston is the upscale **Galleria,** Post Oak Boulevard and Westheimer Road. Even more expensive is the **River Oaks Shopping Center,** Shepherd Drive and Gray Street. The **Parks Shops** in Houston Center, 1200 McKinney St., is a more recently built downtown mall.

## ACCOMMODATIONS

Houston can roughly be divided into three major areas: downtown, west of downtown, and the area south of downtown near Rice University and the renowned Texas Medical Center.

**Adam's Mark.** *2900 Briarpark Dr. at Westheimer (near Beltway 8), Houston, TX 77042.* ☎ *800/444-ADAM or 713/978-7400. Fax 713/735-2727. 604 rms and suites. $165–$199 single or double; $185–$350 suite. Children under 18 stay free in parents' room. AE, CB, DC, DISC, MC, V. Free indoor/outdoor parking.* Located in a largely residential area, this extravagant hotel's main feature is the 10-story atrium, with shops and restaurants on its ground level. Some rooms offer minibars and some have terraces. Language interpreters and a day-care center are available.

**Allen Park Inn.** *2121 Allen Pkwy. (Taft between I-45 and Mantrose), Houston, TX 77019.* ☎ *800/231-6310 or 713/521-9321. Fax 713/521-9321. 242 rms and suites. $88–$110 single or double; $135–$250 suite. Additional person $8 extra. Children under 10 stay free in parents' room. AE, CB, DC, DISC, MC, V. Free outdoor parking.* It is hard to imagine you are in downtown Houston at this pleasant motel with beautiful landscaping and a pool area surrounded by palm trees, all within the lovely, secluded Bayou Park area. Some rooms offer terraces.

**Drury Inn Houston Galleria.** *1615 W. Loop South (east side of I-610, south of I-10), Houston, TX 77027.* ☎ *800/325-8300 or 713/963-0700. 134 rms. $77–$110 single or double. Additional person $10 extra. Children under 18 stay free in parents' room. AE, CB, DC, DISC, MC, V. Free outdoor parking.* An elegant atrium entrance sets the tone for this hotel, located near Galleria Mall. There's a pool, whirlpool, and complimentary evening cocktails from Monday to Thursday.

✪ **Four Seasons Hotel Houston Center.** *1300 Lamar St. (downtown, near the Convention Center), Houston, TX 77010.* ☎ *800/332-3442 or 713/650-1300. Fax 713/650-8169. 399 rms and suites. $245–$310 double; $275–$700 suite. Additional person $25 extra. Weekend city cultural packages. Children under 18 stay free in parents' room. AE, CB, DC, ER, JCB, MC, V. Indoor parking $14 per day.* This luxurious hotel offers a walkway to Houston Center shopping, and rooms with desks and armchairs. Some rooms are poolside, offering whirlpools or parlors, and all have minibars. The hotel has a complimentary town car for downtown, a fitness center, sauna, athletic club privileges, and a children's program. In the hotel is the highly rated **DeVille** restaurant, offering an American-Italian cuisine.

**Grant Motor Inn.** *8200 S. Main (near Kirby), Houston, TX 77025.* ☎ *800/255-8904 or 713/668-8000. 64 rms. June–Aug, $31–$48 single or double. Additional person $4 extra. Lower rates off-season. AE, CB, DC, DISC, MC, V. Free outdoor parking.* This independent motel with conscientious management and an attentive staff boasts a nicely landscaped courtyard and pool surrounded by palm trees. All rooms come with terraces. There's a pool, laundry facilities, and a playground.

**Holiday Inn Astrodome.** *8111 Kirby Dr., Houston, TX 77054.* ☎ *800/ HOLIDAY or 713/790-1900. 235 rms and suites. June–Aug, $79–$109 single or double; $225–$295 suite. Additional person $10 extra. Lower rates off-season. Children under 19 stay free in parents' room. AE, CB, DC, DISC, JCB, MC, V. Free outdoor parking.* Located near Old Spanish Trail on the north side of the Astrodome, this Holiday Inn has major changes planned to increase services.

**Houston Plaza Hilton.** *6633 Travis St., Houston, TX 77030.* ☎ *800/HILTONS or 713/313-4000. Fax 713/529-6806. 185 rms. $115–$165 double. Additional person $15 extra. Children under 17 stay free in parents' room. AE, CB, DC, DISC, JCB, MC, V. Indoor parking $7.* Located in the middle of the Texas Medical Center and near Rice University, this comfortable hotel faces a residential district. Rooms include a minibar. Aerobics classes and swimming lessons are available. The roof provides a pool, sundeck, and jogging path.

**Houstonian Hotel.** *111 N. Post Oak Lane (north of Woodway near I-610 West), Houston, TX 77024.* ☎ *800/231-2759 or 713/680-3805. Fax 713/686-3701. 291 rms and suites. $189 single or double; $305 suite. Children under 18 stay free in parents' room. AE, CB, DC, DISC, JCB, MC, V. Free indoor parking.* This comfortable hotel on 18 wooded acres has a country lodge look and feel. All rooms have minibars, and a social director, masseur, and children's program are available. The fitness facility is outstanding.

**Hyatt Regency Houston.** *1200 Louisiana St. (downtown, between Dallas and Polk sts.), Houston, TX 77002.* ☎ *800/233-1234 or 713/654-1234. Fax 713/951-0934. 959 rms and suites. $169–$204 single or double; $350–$650 suite. Children under 18 stay free in parents' room. AE, CB, DC, DISC, JCB, MC, V. Indoor parking $8.50–$16.* A dramatic, 30-story atrium is the central feature of this contemporary hotel, which is connected to the underground pedestrian system. All rooms have minibars. The hotel is a favorite with business travelers.

**JW Marriott Hotel Houston.** *5150 Westheimer Rd. (across from the Galleria, just west of I-610 W. Loop Fwy.), Houston, TX 77056.* (☎ *800/228-9290 or 713/ 961-1500. Fax 713/961-5045. 503 rms and suites. $149–$159 single or double, $175– $600 suite. Lower rates June-Aug. Extra person $10. Children under 18 stay free. AE, CB, DC, DISC, JCB, MC, V. Parking indoor/outdoor $6.* The attractive brick building stands among trees on a grassy lot. Soft lighting, wood paneling, and fresh flowers make an inviting lobby area. Rooms have satellite TV with movies, and voice mail. No-smoking rooms are available. The **Brasserie Restaurant** serves a buffet breakfast and lunch and dinner. Facilities include a restaurant, bar, basketball and raquetball courts, steam room, whirlpool, and games room. Room services and baby-sitting are offered.

**✪ Lancaster Hotel.** *701 Texas Ave. (at Louisiana in the Theater District), Houston, TX 77002.* ☎ *800/231-0336 or 713/228-9500. Fax 713/223-4528. 93 rms and suites. 120–$220 single or double; $300–$850 suite. Children under 18 stay free in parents' room. AE, CB, DC, DISC, MC, V. Indoor parking $12.* Dwarfed by nearby skyscrapers, this charming little hotel with personality is housed in a historic building. Friendly service and attention to detail distinguish this hotel from others. Antiques, original paintings, and fresh flowers add grace and beauty.

**Omni Richardson Hotel.** *701 E. Campbell Rd. (on U.S. 75 at Campbell), Richardson, TX 75081.* ☎ *800/THE-OMNI or 972/231-9600. Fax 972/907-2578. 342 rms and suites. $159–$199 single; $169–$209 double; $249–$809 suite. Children under 18 stay free in parents' room. AE, CB, DC, DISC, JCB, MC, V. Free outdoor parking.* Catering to business travelers, this attractive hotel, located near Southfork Ranch (featured in TV's *Dallas*), offers an elegant lobby with soft, contemporary colors.

**Renaissance Houston Hotel.** *6 Greenway Plaza E. (Buffalo Speedway/Edloe St. exit off U.S. 59), Houston, TX 77046.* ☎ *800/HOTELS-1 or 713/629-1200. Fax 713/629-4706. 389 rms and suites. $129–$169 single or double; $300–$750 suite. Children under 18 stay free in parents' room. AE, CB, DC, DISC, EC, JCB, MC, V. Complimentary valet parking.* Located in Greenway Plaza, this large hotel is convenient to downtown, shopping, and the Astrodome. Some rooms offer whirlpools. A courtesy shuttle within a 5-mile radius is available. The hotel is connected to a minimall with a food court and movie theaters.

✪ **Sara's Bed and Breakfast Inn.** *941 Heights Blvd. (between 9th and 10th sts. near I-10), Houston, TX 77008.* ☎ *800/593-1130 or 713/868-1130. Fax 713/868-1160. 14 rms, all with shared bath. $55–$95 single. Additional person $10 extra. AE, CB, DC, DISC, JCB, MC, V. Free outdoor parking.* A traditional B&B in a spotlessly maintained Victorian home. Located in a pretty, quaint neighborhood, the inn is perfect for that romantic getaway. Unsuitable for children under 12.

**Sheraton Astrodome Hotel.** *8686 Kirby Dr. (at junction I-610), Houston, TX 77054.* ☎ *800/627-6461 or 713/748-3221. Fax 713/795-8420. 669 rms and suites. $90–$150 single; $105–$165 double; $270–$370 suite. Additional person $15 extra. Children under 17 stay free in parents' room. AE, CB, DC, DISC, ER, JCB, MC, V. Free outdoor parking.* A large hotel in a great location near the Astrodome, AstroWorld, Rice University, and the Texas Medical Center. It caters to families as well as businesspeople. Some rooms have terraces.

**Westchase Hilton.** *9999 Westheimer (near Gessner), Houston, TX 77042.* ☎ *800/445-8667 or 713/974-1000. Fax 713/974-6866. 300 rooms and suites. $129–$184 single or double; $149–$189 suite. Additional person $15 extra. Children under 17 stay free in parents' room. AE, CB, DC, DISC, JCB, MC, V. Free outdoor parking.* This professional and businesslike hotel, with a multilingual staff, offers an inviting sunlit lobby and lounge areas. All rooms have minibars. Towers and concierge levels provide interesting amenities such as video phones, electric massage chairs, and cocktail bars.

**Westin Oaks.** *5011 Westheimer Rd. (at Post Oaks), Houston, TX 77056.* ☎ *800/228-3000 or 713/960-8100. Fax 713/960-6553. 406 rms and suites. $165–$210 single or double; $210–$1,200 suite. Additional person $15 extra. Lower rates off-season. Children under 18 stay free in parents' room. AE, CB, DC, DISC, JCB, MC, V. Free indoor parking; valet parking $15.* Linked with the Westin Galleria and the Galleria Mall, this property caters primarily to families and tourists. Services and facilities at both hotels are available to guests. All units offer minibars and terraces, and some have whirlpools. There's a fitness center, jogging, a children's program, and an AT&T language translation line is available.

✪ **Wyndham Warwick.** *5701 S. Main St. (near Hermann St.), Houston, TX 77251.* ☎ *800/822-4200 in the U.S., 800/631-4200 in Canada, or 713/526-1991. Fax 713/639-4545. 308 rms and suites. $115–$155 single or double; $165–$195 suite. Additional person $10 extra. Children under 12 stay free in parents' room. AE, CB, DC, DISC, EC, ER, JCB, MC, V. Indoor self-parking $6.50; valet parking $12.* Originally built in 1926, this elegant European-style hotel located in the museum district features authentic 18th-century antique furnishings and tapestries—some from the estate of Napoleón Bonaparte's sister. All units have terraces.

**OTHER ACCOMMODATIONS**    A number of good hotels are located at or near the airport, including the **Houston Airport Marriott,** 18700 John F. Kennedy Blvd., Houston, TX 77032 (tel] **800/228-9290** or 281/443-2310), located between terminals B and C and offering an executive level and shops and restaurants. The **Quality Inn Intercontinental Airport,** 6115 Will Clayton Pkwy., Houston, TX 77205 (☎ **800/221-2222** or 281/446-9131), is quiet and convenient, located among the trees in a forest that surrounds the airport. The **Days Inn Hobby Airport,** 1505 College Ave., Houston, TX 77587 (☎ 800/424-4777 or 713/946-5900), offers great access to the airport, the Astrodome, universities, and the medical center.

# DINING

Houston's large and varied population ensures that the city has many ethnic and some fine regional restaurants.

○ **Américas.** *1800 Post Oak Blvd. (Galleria, near San Felipe).* ☎ *713/961-1492. Reservations recommended. Main courses $12–$24. AE, CB, DC, DISC, MC, V. Mon–Thurs 11:30am–10pm, Fri 11:30am–11pm; Sat 5–11pm. SEAFOOD/SOUTH AMERICAN.* Named Restaurant of the Year for 1993 by *Esquire* magazine, Américas is fun and imaginative in both cuisine and decor. The setting is a version of a South American rain forest. Grilled poultry and seafood in a variety of tasty sauces are the most popular menu items.

**Anthony's.** *4007 Westheimer (between Wesleyan and I-610 West).* ☎ *713/ 961-0552. Reservations recommended. Main courses $14–$28. AE, CB, DC, DISC, MC, V. Mon–Fri 11:30am–2pm; Mon 5:30–10pm, Tues–Thurs 5:30–11pm, Sat 5:30–11:30pm. CONTINENTAL/FRENCH.* Stained-glass fixtures and reproductions of Greek and Roman sculptures characterize the beautiful interior of this elegant and trendy restaurant. Enjoy watching the cooks through a large window while seated in either the wine storage room or main dining area. Fine European-accented American cuisine is presented by a highly professional staff.

**Ashland House Tea Room & Restaurant.** *7611 Westview Rd., between Work and Antoine.* ☎ *713/682-7611. Reservations recommended. Main courses $6–$7. AE, DISC, MC, V. Mon–Sat 11am–3pm. ECLECTIC.* The menu at this elegant restaurant changes daily, but the Victorian building that houses it, listed on the National Register of Historic Places, hasn't changed in years. Lace curtains and ceiling fans create a casual, homey atmosphere. Great home-style meals and an alcohol-free environment are pluses for families with children.

**Brennan's.** *3300 Smith St. (at Stuart near Spur 527 terminus).* ☎ *713/522-9711. Reservations recommended. Main courses $24–$31. AE, CB, DC, DISC, MC, V. Mon–Fri 11:30am–1:30pm; Sun–Thurs 5:45–9pm; brunch Sat 11am–1:30pm, Sun 10am–2pm. Valet parking. CREOLE.* This spacious, elegant restaurant may have one of the loveliest patios in Houston, and jazz, but it is the delicious Creole cuisine that you are likely to remember. This is true New Orleans–style dining, with specialties such as shrimp rémoulade.

**Cafe Annie.** *1728 Post Oak Blvd. (Galleria, near San Felipe).* ☎ *713/840-1111. Reservations recommended. Main courses $19–$35. AE, CB, DC, DISC, ER, MC, V. Mon–Fri 11:30am–2pm; Mon–Thurs 6:30–10pm; Fri 6:30–10:30pm; Sat 6–10:30pm. Valet parking. SOUTHWESTERN.* Cutting-edge cuisine is the draw at this upscale, elegant restaurant—a favorite among those in the know. The contemporary design features beautiful tile floors and a lovely mural. Always interesting Southwestern creations include such items as grilled sea scallops with roasted tomato sauce and garlic cream.

**Cafe Express.** *1800 Post Oak Blvd. (Galleria, near San Felipe).* ☎ *713/963-9222. Reservations not accepted. Main courses $5–$8. AE, CB, DC, DISC, MC, V. Sun–Thurs 11am–11pm, Fri–Sat 11am–midnight. ECLECTIC.* A self-serve restaurant with a trendy decor of bright colors with tropical accents such as a fountain and lush plants. An eclectic menu includes fruits and vegetables, grilled items, and sandwiches. There are additional locations at 3200 Kirby (☎ 713/522-3994), and 1422 W. Gray (☎ 713/ 522-3100).

**Churrascos.** *2055 Westheimer at Shepherd.* ☎ ***713/527-8300.*** *Reservations suggested. Main courses $12–$22. AE, CB, DC, DISC, MC, V. Mon–Thurs 11am–10pm, Fri 11am–11pm; Sat 5–11pm. SOUTH AMERICAN.* This lively, informal place has great South American fare. The dish that is the restaurant's namesake consists of butterflied beef tenderloin in a garlicky sauce.

**County Line Barbecue.** *13850 Cutten Rd. (1 mile north of F.M. 1960).* ☎ ***281/537-2454.*** *Reservations recommended. Main courses $4–$13. AE, CB, DC, MC, V. Wed–Fri 11:30am–2pm; Sat noon–10pm; Sun 11:30am–3:30pm; Tues–Thurs 5:30–9pm; Fri 5–10pm; Sun 3:30–9pm. BARBECUE.* This lodge-type restaurant, secluded on a wooded estate in far north Houston, offers a western-theme decor with cowhide-covered chairs and cacti light fixtures. There is an all-you-can-eat buffet, and smoked prime rib is a popular menu choice.

**Damian's Cucina Italiana.** *3011 Smith St. (near downtown and junction Elgin).* ☎ ***713/522-0439.*** *Reservations recommended. Main courses $15–$25. AE, CB, DC, MC, V. Mon–Fri 11am–2pm; Mon–Thurs 5:30–10pm, Fri 5:30–11:30pm, Sat 5–11:30pm. Valet parking. ITALIAN.* A light and refreshing atmosphere, along with formal and polished service, make this a pleasant setting for fine Italian dining. Enjoy the large antipasti selection.

**Goode Company Texas Barbecue.** *5109 Kirby Dr. (south of U.S. 59 SW Fwy.).* ☎ ***713/522-2530.*** *Reservations not accepted. Main courses $6–$8. AE, CB, DC, DISC, MC, V. Daily 11am–10pm. BARBECUE.* Buffalo trophies, snake skins, and stuffed armadillos adorn this very popular cowboy barbecue pit—a prime destination for those who love great, authentic barbecue. An additional location is at 8911 Katy Fwy. (☎ **713/464-1901**).

**Kim Son.** *2001 Jefferson (downtown, at Chartres, near U.S. 59).* ☎ ***713/222-2461.*** *Reservations accepted. Main courses $4–$11. AE, CB, DC, DISC, MC, V. Daily 10:30am–11pm. VIETNAMESE.* With some 100 menu options, this highly regarded Vietnamese restaurant demonstrates that more can be better. Enjoy finely prepared delicacies as well as expected fare, like terrific spring rolls, in a lovely contemporary setting. Look for the exotic fish pool at the entrance. An additional location is at 8200 Wilcrest (☎ **281/498-7841**).

**✪ La Mora Cucina Toscana.** *912 Lovett (at Montrose near Westheimer).* ☎ ***713/522-7412.*** *Reservations recommended. Main courses $10–$21. AE, CB, DC, DISC, MC, V. Tues–Fri 11am–2pm; Mon–Thurs 5:30–10pm, Fri–Sat 5:30–11pm. Valet parking. ITALIAN.* Situated atop a beautiful wooded lot, this restaurant serves up wonderful Tuscan cuisine in a lovely atrium dining room with fireplace, or in the garden area. Try the quail with polenta, and enjoy selecting from an excellent Italian wine list.

**✪ La Réserve.** *Four Riverway (Galleria, in the Omni Houston hotel near Woodway).* ☎ ***713/871-8177.*** *Reservations recommended. Main courses $19–$37; fixed-price dinner $50–$70. AE, CB, DC, DISC, ER, MC, V. Mon–Thurs 6:30–10pm, Fri–Sat 6–10:30pm. Valet parking. FRENCH.* One of Houston's best restaurants serves wonderful haute cuisine in a dining room decorated with tasteful yet unique furnishings, elaborate floral arrangements, and myriad plants and trees. Caviar pie is a luxurious specialty. Ask about the grand menu, which offers the best specialties and includes wine.

**Nino's.** *2817 W. Dallas (between Yale and Montrose).* ☎ ***713/522-5120.*** *Reservations recommended. Main courses $9–$26. AE, CB, DC, MC, V. Mon–Fri 11am–2:30pm; Mon–Thurs 5:30–10pm, Fri–Sat 5:30–11pm. ITALIAN.* A great place for a fun evening with friends or family, this upbeat, semicasual two-story restaurant offers an excellent, large antipasti bar and a fine veal chop.

**Pappas Seafood House.** *6894 Southwest Fwy. (on U.S. 59 near Savoy and Regency Sq.).* ☎ *713/784-4729. Reservations not accepted. Main courses $10–$20. AE, MC, V. Sun–Thurs 11am–10pm, Fri–Sat 11am–11pm. SEAFOOD.* This busy, casual seafood restaurant lets you choose your fish or shellfish blackened, broiled, or fried. Healthy menu items are available and gumbo and Greek salad are house favorites. Additional locations are at 12010 I-10 East (☎ **713/453-3265**) and 3001 S. Shepherd (☎ **713/ 522-4595**).

✪ **Rotisserie for Beef and Bird.** *2200 Wilcrest Dr. (3 blocks north of Westheimer, near Beltway 8).* ☎ *713/977-9524. Reservations recommended. Main courses $18–$29. AE, CB, DC, DISC, MC, V. Mon–Fri 11:30am–2pm; Mon–Sat 6–10pm. Valet parking. CONTINENTAL.* Owned by well-known Houston chef Joe Mannke, this serene restaurant located in a residential area is predictably elegant and upscale, yet unpretentious. A rotisserie and an open hearth face one of the dining areas. Enjoy food cooked to perfection, like roast duckling.

**Sammy's Lebanese Restaurant.** *5825 Richmond (near Fountainview; accessible from U.S. 59).* ☎ *713/780-0065. Main courses $9–$15. AE, CB, DC, DISC, MC, V. Mon–Fri 11am–10:30pm, Sat 11am–11pm, Sun noon–10pm. LEBANESE.* This very casual and friendly restaurant serves up great inexpensive Middle Eastern food. It is popular for its appetizer platters, and offers a range of menu items, including a large seafood selection and vegetarian dishes.

## HOUSTON AFTER DARK

**THE PERFORMING ARTS**   Houston has an important performing arts scene with world-class companies. Call ☎ 713/227-5134 for ticket information for all venues.

**Jesse H. Jones Hall for the Performing Arts,** 615 Louisiana St. (☎ **713/ 227-3974**), is the home of the **Houston Symphony Orchestra.** The **Wortham Theater Center,** 500 Texas Corner (☎ **713/237-1439**), opened in 1987 and is home to the innovative ✪ **Houston Grand Opera,** whose season runs from September to March. The world-famous ✪ **Houston Ballet** also performs here. The **Society for the Performing Arts (SPA),** 615 Louisiana St. (☎ **800/346-4462** or 713/227-1111), is the largest nonprofit organization of its kind in the Southwest. SPA sponsors distinguished artists and productions from all areas of the performing arts. Educational programs, master classes, and lectures are also included in its regular season schedule.

The **Nina Vance Alley Theatre,** 615 Texas Ave. (☎ **713/228-8421**), presents productions ranging from Shakespeare to contemporary plays in one of Houston's most innovative and futuristic structures, designed by Ulrich Fransen.

**THE CLUB & MUSIC SCENE**   There are many bars and clubs along Richmond Avenue. **Billy Blues Bar and Club,** at 6025 Richmond (☎ **713/266-9294**), features blues performers like Clarence "Gatemouth" Brown and Bo Didley. For country-and-western and all kinds of music, try **City Streets,** 5078 Richmond (☎ **713/840-8555**). **Fitzgerald's,** 2706 White Oaks Dr. (☎ **713/862-7580**), is a top venue for pop performers.

Popular brew pubs are **The Ale House,** 2425 W. Alabama (☎ **713/521-2333**); **McGonigel's Mucky Duck,** 2425 Norfolk (☎ **713/528-5999**); and **Rock Bottom Brewery,** 6111 Richmond Ave. (☎ **713/974-2739**). In the city's oldest commercial building, **La Carafe,** 813 Congress Ave. (☎ **713/229-9399**), is one of the city's more interesting bars. Cigar smokers can head for **Downing Street Ltd.,** 2549 Kirby, (☎ **713/523-2291**).

## A DAY TRIP TO GALVESTON

Galveston was Texas's largest city until a hurricane swept it away in 1900. Today this barrier island city, 50 miles south of Houston, is undergoing a renaissance. Restored buildings and landmarks have recaptured a historic feel and recall its 19th-century glory days. Among the interesting historic buildings is the **Grand 1894 Opera House,** 2020 Post Office St. (☎ **409/765-1894**), where Sarah Bernhardt and Anna Pavlova once performed.

Galveston is connected to the mainland by a causeway and a bridge. The island has more than 32 miles of **beaches** offering recreational opportunities, although some of the many developments are of the Coney Island type.

If you want to stay in Galveston, the **Flagship Hotel Over the Water** (☎ **409/762-9000**) offers great views. The grand **Tremont House** (☎ **800/874-2300** or 409/763-0300) is an elegant Victorian hotel in the heart of the historic district. You can reach Galveston from Houston by taking **Texas Bus Lines** (☎ **409/765-7731**), which arrive at 714 25th St. in Galveston. For more information, contact the **Galveston Island Convention and Visitor Bureau,** 2106 Seawall Blvd., Galveston, TX 77550 (☎ **409/763-4311**).

# 17  More Southwest, Texas & Colorado Highlights

## LAKE HAVASU & THE LONDON BRIDGE

In the mid-1960s the British government decided to sell the London Bridge, which was indeed falling down—or, more correctly, sinking into the Thames River because of too much heavy car and truck traffic. Robert McCulloch, founder of the tourist-starved Lake Havasu City resort in western Arizona, and his partner paid $2.4 million for the famous bridge and had it shipped 10,000 miles to Long Beach, California, then trucked to Lake Havasu City. Reconstruction of the bridge was begun in 1968 and the grand reopening was held in 1971. At first the 900-foot-long bridge connected only desert to more desert, but eventually a 1-mile-long channel was dredged, thus creating an island offshore from Lake Havasu City.

Today the London Bridge sits like a mirage on the banks of Lake Havasu in this dusty desert town where summer temperatures are often over 110°F. An unlikely place for a bit of British heritage, it's true, but Lake Havasu City and the London Bridge have become the second-most-popular tourist destination in Arizona. Only the Grand Canyon gets more visitors.

At the base of the bridge you'll find **English Village,** done up in proper English style with shops, restaurants, and a waterfront promenade. Here you'll find several cruise boats and small-boat rental docks. After the London Bridge, water sports on 45-mile-long Lake Havasu are the most popular local attraction. And Lake Havasu City has four golf courses, all open to the public.

Merrie Olde England was once the theme at **London Bridge Resort** (☎ **800/624-7939** or 520/855-0888), built after the bridge came here, with Tudor half-timbers jumbled up with turrets, towers, ramparts, and crenellations. Though the bridge is just out the hotel's back door, and inside the lobby is a replica of Britain's gold State Coach, guests are more interested in the three pools, the tropical-theme outdoor nightclub, and the Mexican cantina. Even the English dining room now serves Southwestern food.

You can also stay at the clean and inexpensive **Bridgeview Motel** (☎ **520/855-5559**), with a view of the bridge, or the **Island Inn Resort** (☎ **800/243-9955** or 520/680-0606), across the bridge from downtown. One of the most popular ways to enjoy Lake Havasu is on a rented houseboat from **Havasu Springs Resorts** (☎ **520/667-3361**).

**Essentials:** Lake Havasu City is on the Colorado River 21 miles south of I-40 via Ariz. 95. Regional airlines serve **Lake Havasu City Airport.** For more information, contact the **Lake Havasu City Visitor and Convention Bureau,** 314 London Bridge Rd., Lake Havasu City, AZ 86403 (☎ **800/242-8278** or 520/453-3444).

# METEOR CRATER

In the middle of the Arizona desert lies Meteor Crater, a gaping round hole nearly a mile across and 570 feet deep. Standing on a platform on the crater rim, it's difficult to imagine the instant devastation that occurred 49,000 years ago when a meteorite estimated to be about 100 feet in diameter slammed into the ground here at 45,000 mph.

Billed as "this planet's most penetrating natural attraction," this is the best-preserved crater in the world. Its resemblance to the surface of the moon prompted NASA to train Apollo program astronauts here in the 1960s. There's a small museum, part of which is dedicated to the exploration of space, with an Apollo space capsule on display. The rest of the museum is devoted to astrogeology and includes a meteorite weighing nearly three quarters of a ton. Guided tours along the rim leave on the hour from 9am to 2pm (closed-toe shoes required).

**Essentials:** You'll need a car to reach Meteor Crater, which is south of I-40 between Winslow and Flagstaff, Arizona. Admission is $8 adults, $7 seniors, $2 ages 6–17, free for children under 6. It's open mid-May–mid-Sept, daily 6am–6pm; the rest of the year, daily 8am–5pm. For information, call ☎ 520/289-2362.

# THE PETRIFIED FOREST & THE PAINTED DESERT

Though petrified wood can be found in almost every state, the "forests" of downed logs in the Painted Desert of northeastern Arizona are by far the most spectacular. It's hard to believe when you drive across this arid landscape, but 225 million years ago, when dinosaurs and huge amphibians ruled the earth, this area was a vast humid swamp surrounded by giant, now-extinct trees. Fallen trees were eventually covered over with silt, mud, and volcanic ash. Preserved from decay, the logs lay as they were when they fell until water bearing dissolved silica seeped into the logs. The dissolved silica filled the cells of the wood and eventually recrystallized into stone to form petrified wood.

Eventually wind and water eroded the landscape to create the many colorful and spectacular features of northern Arizona, including the Painted Desert, and the petrified logs were once again exposed on the surface of the land. Throughout the region you'll see petrified wood in all sizes and colors, natural and polished, being sold in gift stores. This petrified wood comes from private land. No matter how small, no petrified wood may be removed from Petrified Forest National Park.

The petrified logs are concentrated in the southern part of the monument, while the northern section overlooks the Painted Desert. At the north end, the **Painted Desert Oasis Visitor Center** shows a 17-minute film explaining the fossilizing process. Also here, the **Painted Desert Oasis** provides a full-service cafeteria. At the south end, exhibits at **Rainbow Forest Museum** chronicle the area's geologic and human history, including letters from people who had taken pieces of petrified wood and who later felt guilty and returned the stones. There's a snack bar near the museum.

A 27-mile scenic road with more than 20 overlooks connects the two visitor centers. Erosion has played a major role in the formation of the Painted Desert, and to the north of Blue Mesa you'll see **The Teepees.** It's quite evident how these conical hills of sandstone and clay got their name. The Painted Desert itself is named for the vivid colors of the soil and stone here, a Technicolor dreamscape of pastels washed across a barren expanse of eroded hills.

Human habitation of the area dates back more than 2,000 years, and at **Newspaper Rock** you can see petroglyphs left by generations of Native Americans. At **Puerco Indian Ruins** you can see the homes of the people who made the carvings prior to the area's abandonment around 1400.

There's a picnic area at Chinde Point overlook, and at Kachina Point, where you'll find the **Painted Desert Inn Museum.** From here, there's access to the park's other wilderness area.

You may also want to stop at the **Navajo County Museum** in downtown Holbrook. This old and dusty museum has exhibits on local history, but is most interesting for having the town's old jail cells on display. The museum sponsors Native American dancers June–Aug, Mon–Fri 7–9pm on its lawn. There are also several rock shops in Holbrook where you can buy petrified wood and other fascinating stones. Also here in town is **McGee's Beyond Native Tradition Gallery,** 2114 E. Navajo Blvd. (☎ 520/524-1977), a Native American crafts gallery with a wide selection of typical crafts at reasonable prices.

Also in Holbrook you'll find branches of Comfort Inn, Days Inn, Motel 6, and Super 8 motels, but its most unique accommodations are the small, wigwam-shaped buildings of the **Wigwam Motel** (☎ 520/524-3048), built in the 1940s when unusual architecture was springing up all along famous Route 66. It's been renovated, but you'll still find the original rustic furniture and colorful bedspreads.

**Essentials:** The north entrance to Petrified Forest National Park is 25 miles east of Holbrook on I-40. The south entrance is 20 miles east of Holbrook on U.S. 180. Amtrak passenger trains stop at Winslow, 33 miles west of Holbrook (☎ 800/USA-RAIL). Holbrook is served by Greyhound/Trailways buses (☎ 800/231-2222). The park is open daily from 8am to 5pm, with longer hours in summer. Admission is $10 per car or $5 per individual. National Park Service passports are accepted. For further information, contact the **Petrified Forest National Park,** P.O. Box 2217, Petrified Forest National Park, AZ 86028 (☎ 520/524-6228). For information on Holbrook and the surrounding region, contact the **Holbrook Chamber of Commerce,** 100 E. Arizona St., Holbrook, AZ 86025 (☎ 800/524-2459 or 520/524-6558).

## WHITE SANDS NATIONAL MONUMENT

Arguably the most memorable natural area in southeastern New Mexico, White Sands National Monument preserves the best part of the world's largest gypsum dune field. An area of 275 square miles of pure white gypsum sand reaches out over the floor of the Tularosa Basin in wavelike dunes. Plants and animals have evolved in special ways here, some with bleached coloration to match the brilliant whiteness all around them. The dunes are in fact all moving slowly to the northeast, pushed by prevailing southwest winds, some at the rate of as much as 20 feet per year.

A 16-mile Dunes Drive loops through the "heart of sands" from the visitor center, where you can pick up information about what you will see. Occasionally the road is rerouted by drifting dunes or closed for a few hours during missile tests at nearby White Sands Missile Range. Most of the time, however, you can get out of your car at designated parking areas and explore—perhaps climb a dune for a better view of this endless sea of sand. Park rangers lead nature walks and interpretive programs during the summer; ask about the full-moon presentations, which are worth the drive out here. A picnic area among the dunes has shelters and rest rooms but no drinking water.

This region plays a leading role in America's space research and military technology industries, especially nearby **Alamogordo,** where you can visit the **Space Center** (☎ 505/545-4021), recalling the accomplishments of the first astronauts and cosmonauts with a spacecraft, a lunar module, and other exhibits. Ham, the world's first chimp to fly in space, is buried in the front lawn of the center's **International Space Hall of Fame,** which inducts its new members the first Saturday in October. Other attractions include the **Toy Train Depot** (☎ 505/437-2855), housed in a genuine 1898 train depot and a favorite of model train buffs. The **Tularosa Basin Historical Museum** (☎ 505/437-6120), beside the chamber of commerce, displays artifacts and photographs recalling local history. Next door, the **Alameda Park Zoo** (☎ 505/439-4290) has hundreds of mammals and birds from around the world.

The world's first atomic bomb was exploded on July 16, 1945, at **Trinity Site,** 60 air miles northwest of Alamogordo. A small lava monument commemorates the explosion, which left a quarter-mile, 8-foot-deep crater and transformed the desert sand into a jade-green glaze called "Trinitite" that remains today. The site is strictly off-limits to civilians except in early April and early October. Call the public affairs office at **White Sands Missile Range** (☎ 505/678-1134) for information.

**Essentials:** White Sands National Monument is 15 miles southwest of Alamogordo on U.S. 70. Admission is $4 per vehicle. National Park Service passports are accepted. For information, contact the site at P.O. Box 458, Alamogordo, NM 88310 (☎ 505/479-6124). You can stay in Alamogordo, which has a Days Inn and a Holiday Inn. For information about the city, contact the **Alamogordo Chamber of Commerce,** 1301 N. White Sands Blvd. (P.O. Box 518), Alamogordo, NM 88311 (☎ 800/545-4021 or 505/437-6120).

## CARLSBAD CAVERNS NATIONAL PARK

Among the largest and most spectacular cave systems in the world, Carlsbad Caverns comprise some 80 known caves that snake through a porous limestone reef in southeastern New Mexico. Fantastic and grotesque formations fascinate visitors, who find every shape imaginable naturally sculpted in the underground—from frozen waterfalls to strands of pearls and miniature castles.

Known to American Indians for centuries, the caverns were not discovered by whites until the 1880s, when settlers noticed sunset flights of bats. Mining of bat guano led to tourism, and the caverns became a national park in 1930. Development has been confined to the largest of the caverns, where the famous Big Room has a ceiling 60 stories high and a floor large enough to hold 14 football fields.

It's easy to visit the main cavern, with elevators, a paved walkway, and a nursery. The fairly strenuous guided tour of undeveloped Slaughter Canyon Cave lasts about 2½ hours and requires a flashlight, stout hiking shoes, and drinking water. Several other specialized cave tours are also offered. There is a 10-mile one-way scenic loop drive, and several hiking trails.

The visitor center has displays depicting the history of the caverns and information about the different tours available. A ranger program on bats is offered about 7pm each evening in summer at the natural entrance to the cavern, where the bat flight usually begins about sunset. There are also guided nature walks.

The temperature in the caverns is 56°F year-round, regardless of the weather on top, where winters are mild and summers hot. Crowds are thickest in summer, so visiting from Labor Day to Memorial Day is best.

There are no accommodations or campgrounds inside the park, but there is a restaurant at the visitor center. The closest lodging and camping is in White's City, about 7 miles from the visitor center, where you'll find **Best Western Cavern Inn** (☎ 800/CAVERNS or 505/785-2291). It and two adjacent properties have 132 rooms, two swimming pools, two hot tubs, a sports court, and two casual restaurants. A campground and RV park is under the same management and has the same phone number. There are additional campgrounds, motels, and restaurants in the city of Carlsbad. Contact the **Carlsbad Convention and Visitor Bureau,** P.O. Box 910, Carlsbad, NM 88220 (☎ 800/221-1221 or 505/887-6516).

**Essentials:** The closest airport is in the city of Carlsbad, about 27 miles to the northeast. There is no shuttle service to the park, but rental cars are available. The park **entrance** is reached via U.S. 62/180 and N.M. 7. General admission fees are $5 adults, $3 children 6–12, free for children under 5. A variety of tours cost extra. Strollers are not permitted in the caves. Pets are also forbidden in the caves and on the trails, but a kennel is available. Spelunkers need special permission to explore the park's

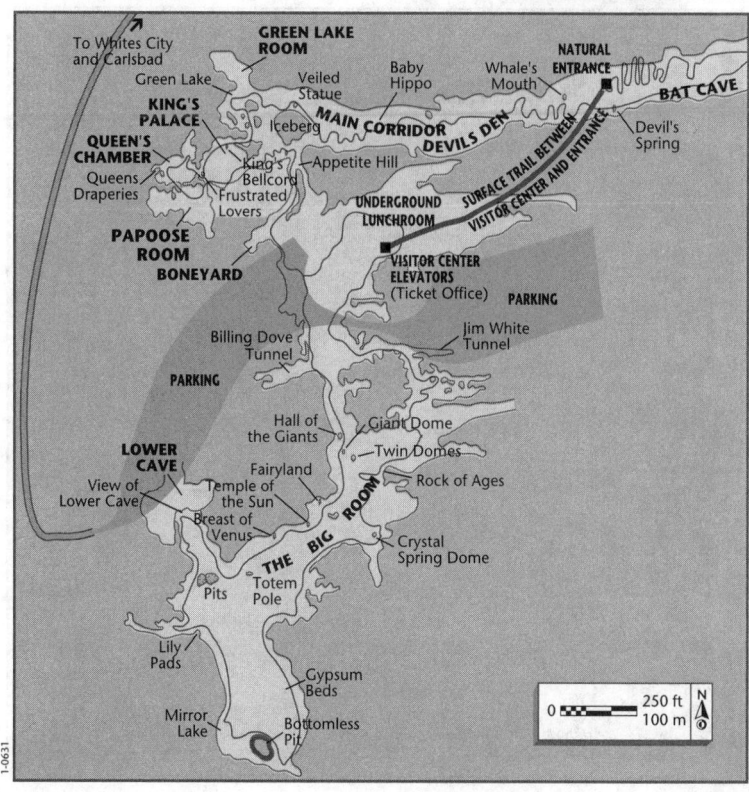

Map labels: To Whites City and Carlsbad · GREEN LAKE ROOM · Green Lake · Veiled Statue · Baby Hippo · Whale's Mouth · NATURAL ENTRANCE · BAT CAVE · KING'S PALACE · MAIN CORRIDOR · DEVILS DEN · Iceberg · Devil's Spring · QUEEN'S CHAMBER · Appetite Hill · SURFACE TRAIL BETWEEN VISITOR CENTER AND ENTRANCE · Queens Draperies · King's Bellcord · Frustrated Lovers · UNDERGROUND LUNCHROOM · PAPOOSE ROOM · BONEYARD · VISITOR CENTER ELEVATORS (Ticket Office) · PARKING · Billing Dove Tunnel · Jim White Tunnel · PARKING · Hall of the Giants · Giant Dome · LOWER CAVE · Twin Domes · Fairyland · Rock of Ages · View of Lower Cave · Temple of the Sun · Breast of Venus · THE BIG ROOM · Crystal Spring Dome · Pits · Totem Pole · Lily Pads · Gypsum Beds · Mirror Lake · Bottomless Pit · 0 250 ft / 100 m · N

1-0631

undeveloped caves. For information, contact **Carlsbad Caverns National Park,** 3225 National Parks Hwy., Carlsbad, NM 88220 (☎ **505/785-2232**).

## THE TEXAS HILL COUNTRY

Anchored on the northeast by Austin and on the southwest by San Antonio, the Hill Country is one of Texas's prettiest regions, especially in early spring when wildflowers daub it with every pigment in nature's palette. Dotted with old dance halls, country stores, and quaint Teutonic towns—more than 30,000 Germans emigrated to Texas during the great land-grant years of the Republic—and birthplace to one of the U.S.'s more colorful recent presidents, the region also presents a riveting tableau of the state's history.

The town of **Boerne** (rhymes with "journey") was settled in the 1850s by freedom-seeking German intellectuals. A number of the town's 19th-century limestone buildings house small historical museums, boutiques, and restaurants, but Boerne's biggest draw for many is its antique shops—more than 20 line the "Hauptstrasse," or main street.

On a scenic bend of the Medina River, **Castroville** was founded by émigrés from the Rhine Valley and especially from the French province of Alsace (you can still hear Alsatian spoken by some older residents). Almost 100 of the original settlers' unevenly slope-roofed houses remain. The oldest standing structure, the First St. Louis Catholic Church, went up in 1846, and many of the European-style headstones in the cemetery at the western edge of town date back to the 1840s.

# The Texas Hill Country

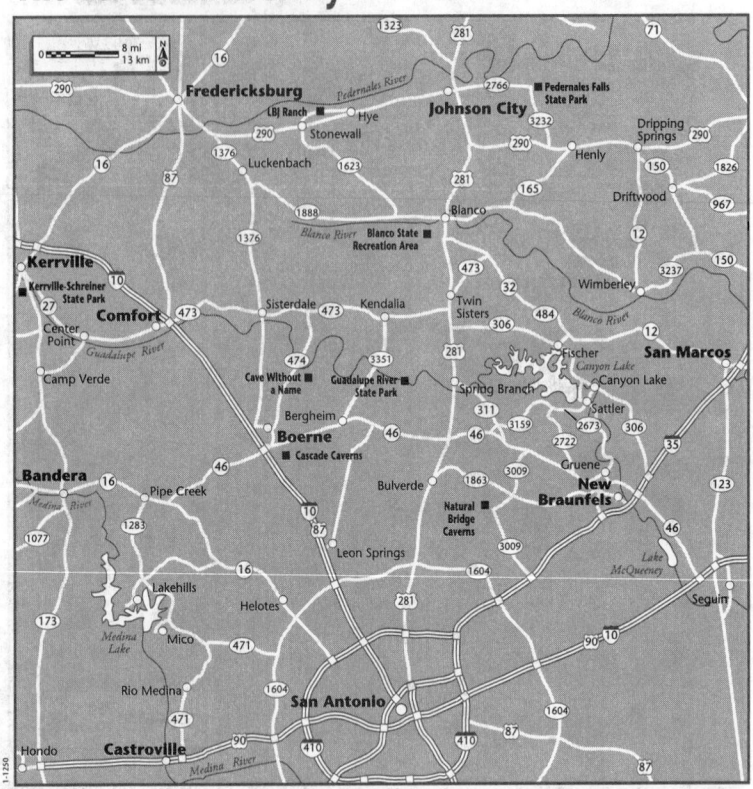

**Bandera** is a slice of life out of the Old West. Established as a lumber camp in 1853, this popular guest-ranch center still has the feel of the frontier. Many of its historic buildings are intact, including St. Stanislaus (1855), the second-oldest Polish church in the country. You can watch craftspeople create traditional cowboy gear and pop into **Arkey Blue's Silver Dollar Saloon** (☎ 210/796-8826), a genuine spit-and-sawdust cowboy honky-tonk, along Main Street.

San Antonians and Austinites flock to **Fredericksburg** on the weekends for fine shopping, interesting historic attractions, and some of the most unusual accommodations around—all in a lovely rural setting. Movie star spottings are increasingly common there these days, but Fredericksburg also remains devoted to its European past. The 1852 Steamboat Hotel, originally owned by the grandfather of World War II naval hero Chester A. Nimitz, is now home to the **Admiral Nimitz Museum State Historical Park,** 340 E. Main St. (☎ 210/997-4379).

From Fredericksburg, U.S. 290 leads east 16 miles to the entrance of the **Lyndon B. Johnson State and National Historical Parks at LBJ Ranch** (☎ 210/868-7128 or 210/644-2252), co-run by the Texas Parks and Wildlife Department and the National Park Service. Crossing over the swift-flowing Pedernales River to fields filled with phlox, Indian blanket, and other wildflowers, one can easily see why LBJ used the ranch as a second, more comfortable White House, and why he chose to be buried here.

It's 14 miles farther east along U.S. 290 to **Johnson City,** a pleasant agricultural town named for founder James Polk Johnson, LBJ's second cousin. The **Lyndon B. Johnson National Historical Park** (☎ 210/868-7128) contains LBJ's Boyhood Home and the

Johnson Settlement, where you can visit the rustic dogtrot cabin from which his grandfather and great uncle ran a successful cattle speculation in the 1860s. The park's visitor center has a number of excellent displays and a moving film about Johnson's presidency.

**San Marcos,** the temporary site of two Spanish missions in the late 1700s, was settled by Anglos in the middle of the 19th century and is now home to Southwest State University, the alma mater of both LBJ and singer George Strait. Most visitors come here to the clear, cool springs that well up from the Balcones Fault to form Spring Lake. On its shores sits **Aquarena Springs Resort,** 1 Aquarena Springs Dr. (☎ **800/ 999-9767** or 512/396-8900), renowned for glass-bottomed boats from which you can view some of the rare flora and fauna that the springs support, as well as for Ralph the Swimming Pig, who performs at a submarine theater. Also, the **Tanger Factory Outlet Center** (☎ **800-4TANGER** or 512/396-7444) and the larger and tonier **San Marcos Factory Shops** (☎ **800/628-9465** or 512/396-7183) are Texas's largest shop fest.

At the junction of the Comal and Guadalupe rivers, **New Braunfels** was founded by Germans in 1845 and by the 1850s was the fourth-largest city in Texas. These days it's home to the **Mill Store Plaza,** 651 Business Loop I-35 North (☎ **210/620-6806**), another popular factory outlet mall. You can still get a glimpse of the past in tiny **Gruene** (pronounced "Green"), a former ghost town crowded with day-trippers browsing its specialty shops in wonderfully restored structures. Big names have played at **Gruene Hall** (☎ **210/606-1281**), the oldest country-and-western dance hall in Texas and still one of the most mellow places to listen to music.

**Essentials:** The nearest airports are in Austin and San Antonio. For general information about the region, contact the **Hill Country Tourism Association,** 1700 Sidney Baker, Suite 200, Kerrville, TX 78028 (☎ **210/895-5505**). Ask for a schedule of the many food-and-music fests celebrated here throughout the year.

# California & Nevada

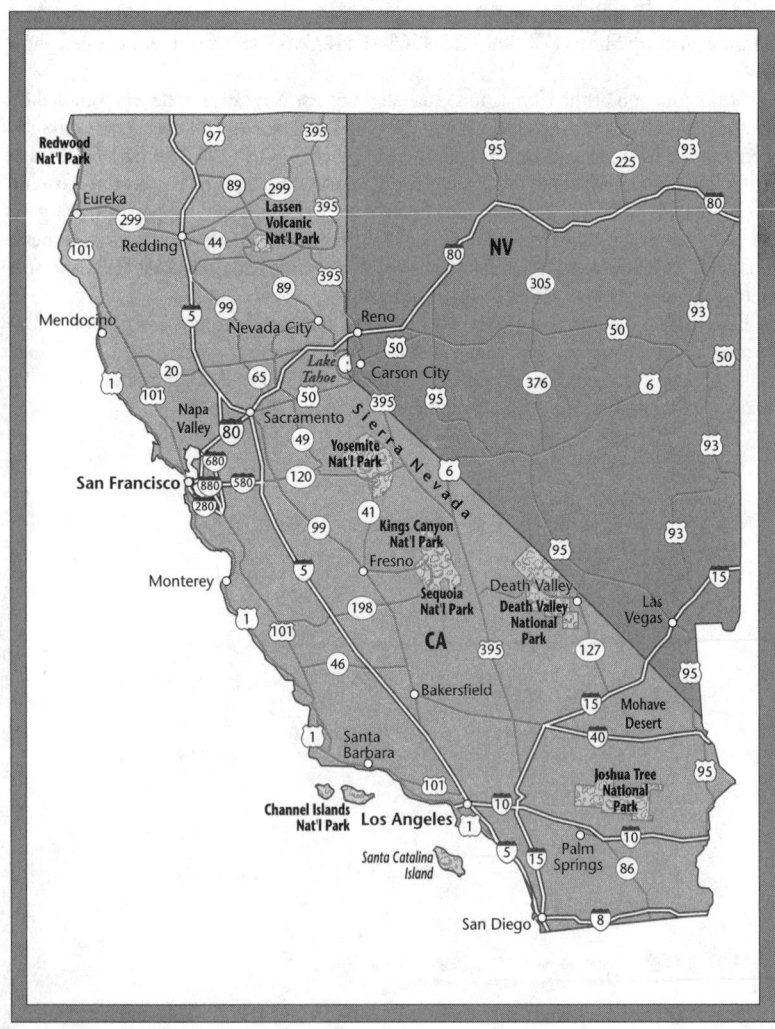

With its terrain rising from sea-battered coast to soaring Sierras, with a climate ranging from redwood rain forests to bone-dry deserts, with its cities spanning the gamut from sprawling Los Angeles to sophisticated San Francisco, with every ethnic group imaginable represented in its 30 million–plus population, and with an economy that would make it the world's tenth-largest nation, California has something for everyone.

Here you can spy for movie stars on the "Tinsel Town" streets of Hollywood, rub shoulders with the filthy rich in Beverly Hills and Palm Springs, spend a day frolicking with Mickey Mouse at Disneyland, explore the scorched depths of Death Valley, hang off the sheer face of El Capitan in Yosemite National Park, taste the Wine Country's fine vintages, and dine Beijing style in San Francisco's Chinatown. And that's only the tip of California's attractions iceberg.

Head east across the Mojave Desert into Nevada, and you come to neon-lit Las Vegas, a town that never sleeps, a place devoted to the jackpot. Fortunes are won and lost—okay, usually lost—in Vegas's glittering casinos, but the city has diversified of late, offering mega-attractions for kids and a constant parade of entertainment superstars for grown-ups. And if you don't lose your wad, it's a surprisingly affordable destination.

## DRIVING TOUR
## The Big Sur Coast

**Start:** Monterey
**Finish:** Santa Barbara
**Distance:** Approximately 275 miles
**Time:** 2–3 days
**Highlights:** Phenomenal scenery, seaside towns, redwood forests, Spanish missions, factory outlets, America's most outrageous castle

This tour follows Calif. 1, one of the world's most scenic highways. It starts on the Monterey peninsula, which forks the southernmost nub of Monterey Bay and encompasses four distinct communities: Monterey, Pacific Grove, Pebble Beach, and Carmel-by-the-Sea. Calif. 1 then heads south through the Big Sur, America's most dramatically scenic coastline, at times hugging the cliffs high above the surf crashing on rocks below. Later you will pass San Simeon, the garish castle built by controversial publisher William Randolph Hearst. You will end up in Santa Barbara, a pleasant seaside city that has more than its share of artists, writers, photographers, and a few movie stars.

To reach Monterey from San Francisco, take I-280 south to San Jose, then U.S. 102 south. At Prunedale, take Calif. 156 west, which merges into Calif. 1, and proceed south to:

**1.** **Monterey,** which owes its prominence to its immense bay, measuring almost 60 miles long and 13 miles wide. First settled in 1770, Monterey served as the capital of Alta (Upper) California originally for the Spanish and later for the Mexicans. Step back into the past along Monterey's "Path of History," a self-guided walking tour past about a dozen well-preserved 18th- and 19th-century adobe structures, including the Spanish colonial–style **Larkin House,** 510 Calle Principal, and **Colton Hall,** 522 Pacific St. between Madison and Jefferson streets, where California's first constitution was written in 1849. You can obtain a free walking-tour map from **Monterey State Historic Park,** Cooper–Molera Adobe, Polk and Alvarado streets (☎ **408/649-7118**).

Next head for the waterfront and **Fisherman's Wharf.** Although the pier is lined with T-shirt and souvenir shops, it still retains a seafaring spirit, amplified by the gulls' squawks and briny aromas from the boiling crab pots. Pick up a "walkaway" shrimp or crab cocktail from a food stall, or enjoy a seafood dinner at **Abalonetti** or **Domenico's.**

From the 1920s to the 1940s, Monterey was the sardine-packing capital of the world. John Steinbeck vividly captured this raucous era of factory workers, fishermen, and hustlers in his novel *Cannery Row.* Today, Cannery Row, on Monterey Bay between David and Drake avenues, has been reborn, with souvenir shops and restaurants occupying former bards and bordellos. The biggest attraction here is the **Monterey Bay Aquarium,** 886 Cannery Row (☎ **408/648-4888**), located in the former Hovden sardine cannery. The star exhibit is the three-story kelp forest aquarium, where leopard sharks and schools of silver sardines cruise. Visitors can also watch the captivating sea otters, aquatic clowns who float on their backs and whack open clams with small stones.

From Cannery Row, drive southwest (inland) on David Avenue, then turn right on Lighthouse Avenue. Proceed through the town of **Pacific Grove,** which was founded at the turn of the century as a strict Methodist summer community; several of the ornate Victorian houses have been converted into bed-and-breakfast inns. Turn left onto:

**2.** **17 Mile Drive,** a scenic excursion among homes of the rich and famous. Pay the $6.50 toll and set your odometer to "zero," since mileages given in this section are calculated from the entrance gate. The route runs through privately owned, 5,000-acre **Del Monte Forest** and **Pebble Beach,** twining its way past wave-lashed seacoast and through pine groves shrouded in mist. Much of the vegetation you see is unique to this region, and some plant species are endangered. The **Coastal Bluff Walking Trail** (mile 2.2) offers a good opportunity to stretch your legs and observe the scenery. At mile 3.4, you'll come to **Bird and Seal Rocks,** offshore outcrops where sea lions and harbor seals ("downstairs") and thousands of cormorants and seagulls ("upstairs") share their rocky roost in cacophonous harmony. You can gaze at this scene through fuzzy-quality telescopes for 25¢. The symbol of the Monterey peninsula, the famous **Lone Cypress,** stands grandly on a nearly barren rock facing the sea (mile 6). Experts estimate the tree is between 200 and 300 years old.

The next section of roadway is flanked by some spectacular homes—minicastles, really, in styles ranging from Mediterranean to Norman to Cape Cod. Indeed, Pebble Beach's 93953 zip code vanquishes Beverly Hills in terms of exclusivity. At mile 8, you'll pass the elegant Lodge at Pebble Beach, known for its top-ranked **Pebble Beach Golf Links.** Since 1919, this beautiful course designed by Jack Neville and Douglas Grant has been home to some of golf's most prestigious

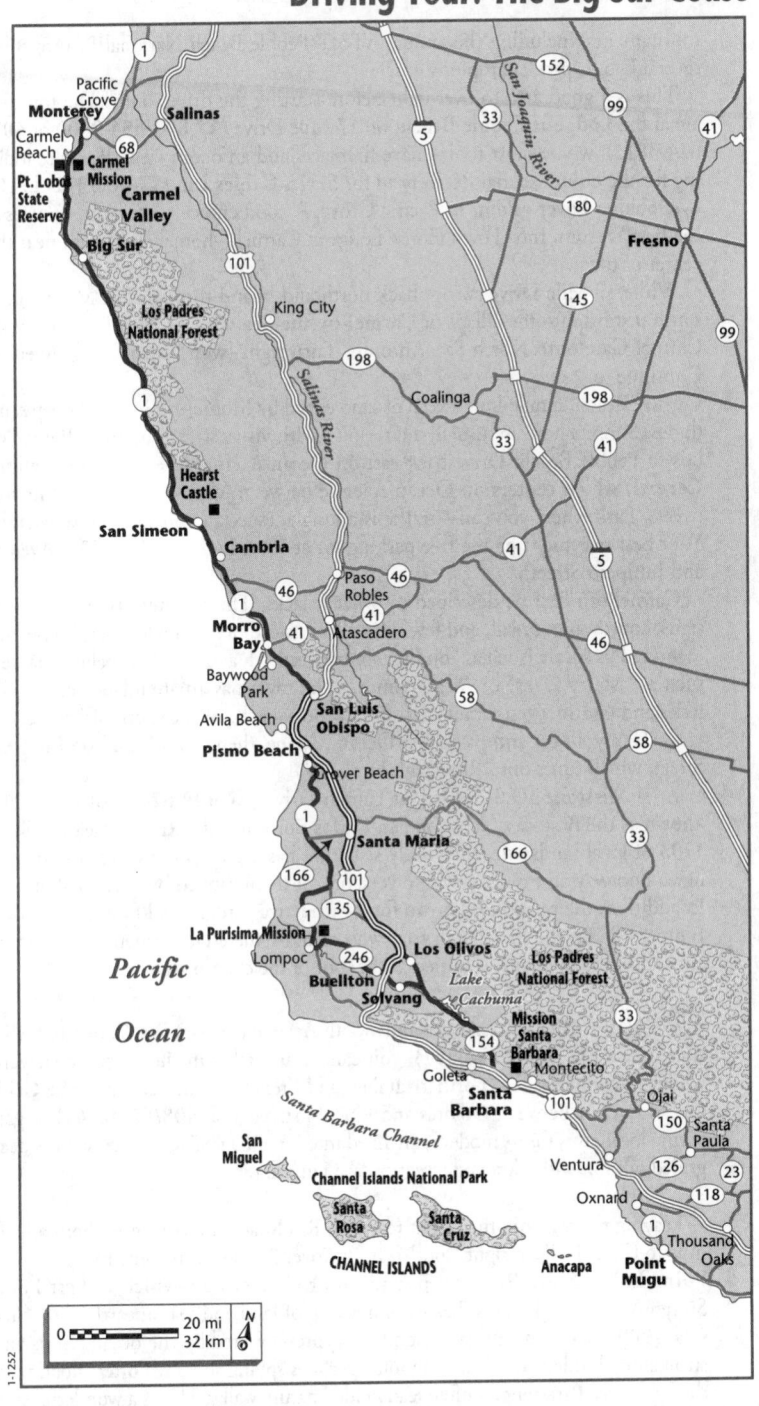

# Driving Tour: The Big Sur Coast

Monterey
Pacific Grove
Salinas
Carmel Beach
Carmel Mission
Pt. Lobos State Reserve
Carmel Valley
Big Sur
Los Padres National Forest
King City
Salinas River
Hearst Castle
San Simeon
Cambria
Paso Robles
Atascadero
Morro Bay
Baywood Park
Avila Beach
San Luis Obispo
Pismo Beach
Grover Beach
Santa Maria
La Purisima Mission
Lompoc
Los Olivos
Los Padres National Forest
Buellton
Solvang
Lake Cachuma
Mission Santa Barbara
Montecito
Goleta
Santa Barbara
Ojai
Santa Paula
Ventura
Oxnard
Thousand Oaks
Point Mugu

San Joaquin River
Fresno
Coalinga

Pacific Ocean

Santa Barbara Channel
San Miguel
Channel Islands National Park
Santa Rosa
Santa Cruz
Anacapa
CHANNEL ISLANDS

0    20 mi
     32 km

N

tournaments, including the annual AT&T Pebble Beach National ProAm, plus several U.S. Open Championships.

This is a good area to overnight before starting the drive south. The top digs are at the **Lodge at Pebble Beach,** on 17 Mile Drive (☎ **800/654-9300** or 408/624-3811), where most rooms have fireplaces and an ocean view. If you're looking for the quintessential B&B, head for **Seven Gables Inn** (☎ **408/372-4341**), overlooking Lover's Point in Pacific Grove. A good choice for bargain hunters is the Best Western Inn–Town House Lodge in Carmel—homely, but right near the center of town.

While 17 Mile Drive swings back north and inland through Del Monte, bear south instead into the village of **Carmel-by-the-Sea.** Exit 17 Mile Drive through Carmel Gate onto North San Antonio. Turn right (west) onto Ocean Avenue. Continue to:

3. **Carmel Beach,** a mile-long sweep of sand edged by Monterey pines and steep sand dunes. Sunsets here are usually marvelous, with vistas stretching from Point Lobos to Pebble Beach. Drive back east on Ocean Avenue to explore the town of **Carmel,** which centers on Ocean Avenue between Monte Verde and Mission streets. Park where you can—traffic is a jungle, especially on summer weekends. Your best bet might be the free parking lot at Vista Lobos Park (on 3rd Avenue and Junipero Street).

   Carmel can best be described by what it lacks. The community has no neon signs, courthouse, or jail, and few sidewalks. Instead of street addresses, houses are identified by locale (such as "on Lincoln between 7th and 8th") or melodic names, such as "Merry Oaks" or "Sea Nymph." The town has an abundance of art galleries and gourmet restaurants that give it the panache of the south of France.

   Reclaim your car and go east on Ocean Avenue, then south (right) on Junipero Street, which turns onto Rio Road. Drive to:

4. **Carmel Mission,** 3080 Rio Rd. at Lausen Drive (☎ **408/624-3600**), officially known as the Basilica of Mission San Carlos Borromeo del Rio Carmelo. Built in 1793 of local sandstone, this lovely structure has a star window over the rough-hewn doorway and two uneven towers, one of them capped by a Moorish dome. In addition, the mission is known for its attractive gardens and fountains. Father Junípero Serra, the Franciscan friar who oversaw the establishment of 21 different California missions, is buried at the foot of the church altar.

   ☕ **TAKE A BREAK**  At **Casanova,** 5th Avenue between San Carlos and Mission streets (☎ **408/625-0501**), you can sit at a table in the garden courtyard while enjoying excellent northern Italian and French country cuisine. **The Grill,** Ocean Avenue between Dolores and Lincoln streets (☎ **408/624-2569**), is garnering local raves for its modern, art-filled interior and creative cuisine, such as oak-grilled salmon with okra and sweet-potato tempura.

   Leaving the mission, turn right (east) on Rio Road, and continue about a half-mile to Calif. 1. Turn right (south). In just over 2 miles, you come to:

5. **Point Lobos State Reserve,** just south of Carmel Bay, which Robert Louis Stevenson called "the most beautiful meeting of land and sea on earth" (☎ **408/624-4909**). You can hike past stands of cypress twisted by the ocean winds and stroll along hidden covers and lagoons, perhaps spying some sea otters floating in the kelp beds. Park rangers often lead guided nature walks. This is a wonderful spot for a picnic.

Retrace your route back to Calif. 1 and turn south. The roadway sidewinds the cliffs, with nothing between you and the blue Pacific but a sheer 1,000-foot drop. There are plenty of scenic overlooks, so you can pull over to photograph the views. About 11 miles after Point Lobos, you'll come to a Calif. 1 landmark:

6. **Bixby Creek Bridge,** which looks as if it were spun by a drunken spider. Measuring 260 feet high and 700 feet long, it was the highest single-arch bridge in the world when constructed in 1932.

Roughly 9 miles after the bridge, your next stop is:

7. **Point Sur Lighthouse,** a State Historic Park and the only intact 19th-century lighthouse open to the public in California (☎ **408/625-4419**). The beacon stands 361 feet above the surf at what was once a notorious ships' graveyard. Three-hour tours of the area are offered Wednesday and weekends, weather permitting.

The landscape changes dramatically in about 9 miles, heading inland from sun-bleached coastal grasslands to cool green redwoods and oaks. You are now entering famous:

8. **Big Sur,** one of the last American frontiers, a place where the highway first came through in the 1930s, and phone service began in the 1950s. Residents still have to drive 30 miles to Carmel to pick up their dry cleaning or a new oil filter for the pickup. The name comes from the Spanish, who referred to the entire unexplored region south of the settlement in Monterey as El Sur Grande. Vistas offer contrasts: jagged cliffs and smooth white beaches, towering redwoods and scruffy chaparral. For years, the region has been a haven for avant-garde writers such as Henry Miller and Jack Kerouac. You can hike through the forests at Pfeiffer Big Sur State Park (☎ **408/667-2315**), where the **Waterfall Trail** climbs through a redwood canyon to 40-foot falls. **Andrew Molera State Park** (☎ **408/667-2315**) covers 9,000 acres and has a variety of hiking trails along the river, cliffs, and beach.

☕ **TAKE A BREAK** Time your drive so you can ogle the views from one of Big Sur's clifftop restaurants, all 2 to 3 miles south of Molera State Park. Major gourmet American food is happening at **Ventana** (☎ **408/667-2331**), where you can dine on a deck beneath trees, under white umbrellas, or in a ridgetop pergola woven with vines. Perched at the very brink of the cliffs, **Sierra Mar** at **Post Ranch Inn** (☎ **408/667-2200**) offers views heretofore known only by seagulls, and excellent contemporary Californian cuisine. Or slip into a 1960s hippie time warp at **Nepenthe** (☎ **408/667-2345**), serving basic burgers, sandwiches, chicken, and fish in a casual atmosphere.

Once again, head south on Calif. 1, which continues its scenic crescendos with the unusual boulder formations at **Pacific Valley** (23 miles south of Nepenthe) and the vista point at **Willow Creek** in Los Padres National Forest (34 miles south of Nepenthe), commanding spectacular views of sentinel-like rocks and pounding surf. About 60 miles south of Nepenthe, the road suddenly levels off into undulating green cow country. About 70 years ago, everything you can see around you—about 50 miles of prime coastline—belonged to publisher William Randolph Hearst. Your next stop is:

9. **Hearst Castle (San Simeon),** his most outrageous and most lasting achievement. Some 130 rooms; art treasures ranging from tapestries by Rubens to a wine bucket made from 30 pounds of pure silver; a dining room lined with a 13th-century Italian choir stall. This is the larger-than-life world of what Hearst called his La Cuesta Encantada—the Enchanted Hill. In 1935, Hearst was worth $220 million—the equivalent of $2 billion today. Working with architect Julia Morgan, he spent

$3 million and almost 30 years crafting this extravagant Mediterranean Revival mansion, which in fact was never completed. Hearst heirs donated the castle to the state in 1958, and the California Park Service now runs several different tours of the grounds.

On the tour, you experience the castle as guests would have, sauntering past the magnificent white Carrera marble Neptune pool, walking through a guest "cottage" with its plaster ceiling leafed in 22-karat gold, and entering the castle itself, known as La Casa Grande. In its heyday, guests included luminaries from the world of politics (Winston Churchill, Calvin Coolidge); royalty (the Duke and Duchess of Windsor); and Hollywood (Cary Grant, Vivien Leigh, Rudolph Valentino).

Because of the tremendous popularity of Hearst Castle, it is absolutely essential to purchase your tickets in advance. To make reservations, call ☎ **800/444-4445.**

Leaving Hearst Castle, turn left (south) on Calif. 1. From here to Santa Barbara, you'll be driving along both good roads and highways, with none of the vertiginous curves found between Carmel and Hearst Castle. Continue another 5 miles to:

10. **Morro Strand State Park,** a 2-mile-long beach where you might see surfers shredding the waves against the backdrop of Morro Rock, a 576-food outcrop attached to the mainland by a skinny sand isthmus. Unfortunately, the vistas are marred by a trio of smoke stacks from Pacific Gas & Electric Company. Swimming is usually safe at Morro Strand, although no lifeguards are on duty.

Continue south on Calif. 1. On the outskirts of San Luis Obispo, Calif. 1 joins up with U.S. 101, a main north–south route through California. You can continue south on U.S. 101 or straight on Calif. 1, which becomes Santa Rosa Street in town. Go right on Monterey Street, which dead-ends at:

11. **Mission San Luis Obispo de Tolosa,** with its shady plaza and thick walls (☎ **805/543-6850**). Founded in 1772, it has three bells hanging from an opening above the entrance and was one of the first buildings in California to have a red clay–tile roof—now a fixture of West Coast architecture. In addition to early photos, artifacts on view include a re-creation of a friar's bedroom.

Retrace your route and pick up U.S. 101 south. In a little over 8 miles, you'll reach Pismo Beach, where you should continue south on U.S. 101 to Buellton; then take Calif. 246 west 15 miles to Purisima Road. After 2 miles, you'll arrive at:

12. **La Purisima Mission State Historic Park,** dating to 1787 and the most completely restored of California's 21 missions (☎ **805/733-3713**). It's one of the best places to get a sense of early mission life, with re-created workshops including a soap factory and tannery, and real cattle, sheep, and horses grazing the corrals.

Leaving the mission, turn east (left) on Calif. 246. Continue approximately 18 miles to:

13. **Solvang,** founded in 1911 by Danish-American educators. Most of the town features Old World architecture. The result is Scandinavia as it might have been rendered by Walt Disney, with half-timbered and thatched storefronts, cobblestone walks, and a few windmills. There is a good selection of shops selling such Danish treats as *ableskivers,* a rounded pancake drizzled with jam and powdered sugar, and *medisterpole,* a locally made sausage. But the main draw here is the factory outlets for brands like Izod, Dansk, and Oneida.

A slice of old-time California lies just up the road in the rolling hills of **Santa Ynez Valley.** Resume your route east on Calif. 246. At the last light leaving

Solvang, turn left on Alamo Pintado Road. Continue about 5 miles, then turn right at the only road stop sign for miles, onto an unmarked road. A hundred yards later, turn left at the next stop sign onto Grand Avenue. Drive about a half-mile and you're in:

**14. Los Olivos,** formerly a stagecoach stop at a narrow-gauge railroad. This quintessential small town—all 2 blocks of it—has one- and two-story wood-frame buildings, and a flagpole plunked in the middle of the main street, Grand Avenue. Men ride fine Arabian horses through the center of town, and kids wander barefoot into the grocery store. There are also some fine shops for browsing.

From Los Olivos, retrace your route back on Grand Avenue and Alamo Pintado Road. Turn left (east) on Calif. 246. If you've got wine-tasting on your mind, stop at:

**15. Gainey Vineyard,** 3950 E. Calif. 246, Santa Ynez (☎ 805/688-0558), part of 1,800-acre Gainey Ranch in the Santa Ynez Valley. This Spanish-style winery opened in 1984 and soon achieved a reputation for its premium varieties, including cabernet sauvignon, pinot noir, and chardonnay. In addition to winery tours and tastings, there's a vineyard garden with picnic tables.

Leaving Gainey, turn right (east) on Calif. 246. Proceed a half-mile to Calif. 154 and turn right (south). Designated a California Scenic Highway, Calif. 154 lives up to its appellation as you leave Santa Ynez, curving through a lovely valley backed by the crumpled green face of the Santa Ynez Mountains. Shortly, on the left, you'll pass **Lake Cachuma,** a shimmering blue mirror washing into the receding lines of ridges. Watch for the Vista Point on your left.

☕ **TAKE A BREAK**   About 8 miles after you merge onto Calif. 154 from Calif. 246, look for the Stagecoach Road exit on your right. Turn right and head for a drink at **Cold Spring Tavern,** 5995 Stagecoach Rd. (☎ 805/967-0066), a 126-year-old former stagecoach stop. There's great live music Wednesday to Sunday nights, featuring anything from country-and-western to jazz.

About 30 miles from Los Olivos, Calif. 154 shimmies its way down through narrow mountain passes to Santa Barbara. Turn left on State Street, then left on Contstand and left on Los Olivos to:

**16. Mission Santa Barbara,** 2201 Laguna St. (☎ 805/682-4713), which was established in 1786 and called the "Queen of the Missions." It commands a beautiful view of the Pacific, with twin bell towers set against a backdrop of eucalyptus-clad foothills. Its unusual design blends classical and colonial styles: The padres adapted a design from a Roman temple. Today, the former living quarters house an excellent museum tracing mission history.

After leaving the mission, turn right on Los Olivos, then left on State Street to downtown **Santa Barbara.** Snuggled between the Santa Ynez Mountains and the Pacific about 90 miles north of Los Angeles, the city's setting equals that of any village along the Côte d'Azur. Santa Barbara has always appealed to major power brokers from business (the Armours and Freestones), movies and television (Michael Douglas, Jonathan Winters, Jane Seymour), and politics (Ronald Reagan had his "White House West" here).

Santa Barbara's finest accommodations match the scenic setting. Queen of the city is the **Four Seasons Biltmore** (☎ 800/332-3442 or 805/969-2261), built Spanish style with tranquil courtyards and located right across from the beach. Located in the Santa Ynez foothills, the individual cottages at **San Ysidro Ranch** (☎ 800/868-6788 or 805/969-5046) offer hideaway seclusion on 540 acres.

**Harbor View Inn** (☎ 800/755-0222 or 805/963-0780) is located directly across from Stearns Wharf and the Pacific Ocean.

With the improvement of U.S. 101 so that it no longer slices downtown Santa Barbara in half, State Street is booming with recently opened shops and restaurants. State Street ends at the oceanfront and:

17. **Stearns Wharf,** which extends a half-mile over the Pacific. The wharf, which was owned by actor Jimmy Cagney and his brother in the 1940s, offers a picture-postcard California view—sailboats heeling with the wind, sunbathers strolling along the shore, and a chorus line of swaying palm trees along the esplanade.

# DRIVING TOUR
## California's Gold Country

**Start:** Nevada City
**Finish:** Jamestown
**Distance:** 230 miles, including side trips
**Time:** 3–4 days
**Highlights:** Columbia State Historical Park, Railtown 1897, Gold Rush–era towns, natural caverns, whitewater rafting

This tour follows Calif. 49—the Golden Chain Highway—which slices a nearly 300-mile route through Gold Country, linking the main towns and villages created in the Sierra foothills by the Gold Rush of 1848–59. The region, about 150 miles east of San Francisco, is awash in history, and following this former stagecoach and supply route is tantamount to a historic adventure.

Beginning in the spring of 1848, the cry of "Gold!" brought tens of thousands of settlers to the western foothills of the Sierras. The peak mining years lasted a decade, during which over $600 million in gold was plucked from the hills. The flood of wannabe millionaires ended with the last of the gold, and disappeared as quickly as the miners, who migrated to San Francisco and other cities. Today, many communities in the region pride themselves on their well-preserved Gold Rush–era buildings, with main streets straight out of the old western movies. The rustic mining towns have antiques shops, pioneer cemeteries, and general stores, while ubiquitous museums tell the history of Gold Country. Peaceful back roads lead to boutique wineries in sheltered valleys.

The gently sloping terrain is cut through by fast-flowing rivers—the American, Stanislaus, Mokelumne, and Tuolumne—that offer whitewater thrills for kayakers, canoers, and rafters. You can also take advantage of rock climbing, caving, and hiking. The region is full of natural splendors: rolling whalebacked foothills and dramatic canyons; woodlands of blue oak, incense cedar, and ponderosa pine dominating the hills; poplar, alder, and willow lining the riverbanks; and groves of giant sequoia sequestered in cooler hollows. With luck, you may sight black bears, raccoons, skunks, and deer, which are abundant throughout the foothills. Be wary, however, of poison oak, which is also common.

Calif. 49 can be reached from San Francisco or Sacramento by traveling east on I-80 to exit 14, at Auburn. Alternately, take I-580 to I-205 to I-5 to Manteca to Calif. 120, which meets Calif. 49 at Chinese Camp, near Jamestown. A longer but prettier route follows Calif. 24 from Oakland to I-680 to Calif. 4, a two-lane road that snakes through farmland to Calif. 49 at Angels Camp. From the Lake Tahoe area, head north on Calif. 89 to I-80 and west to Calif. 20 to Nevada City. Located at the junction of Calif. 49 and Calif. 20 is the heart of:

1. **Nevada City,** a pretty town where at one point during the Gold Rush 10,000 miners worked every foot of ground within a radius of 3 miles. Later, Nevada City

became the inland retreat of wealthy San Francisco families, whose carefully preserved Victorian houses still hug the hillsides. The town is a happy blend of Old West and art deco, exemplified by the **Nevada County Courthouse.** Take a carriage ride through the narrow, historic streets, or opt for a self-guided walking tour. The **Chamber of Commerce** (☎ 916/265-2692), in the old assay office at 132 Main St., has free guides and maps. The slender 1861 **Firehouse Number 1,** 214 Main St., is festooned with gingerbread trim and houses the Nevada County **Historical Society Museum** (☎ 916/265-5468), with its collection of Gold Rush relics. Dominating the gaslit town center is the handsome, three-story, green-and-white 1856 **National Hotel,** 211 Broad St. (☎ 916/265-4551). The **Miners Foundry and Cultural Center,** in the old foundry building at 325 Spring St. (☎ 916/265-5804), is a showplace of Victorian arts and crafts. Linger overnight to take in a performance of the **Nevada Theater,** 401 Broad St. (☎ 916/265-8587); built in 1865, it hosted Mark Twain's first-ever lecture. Afternoon tours are offered Friday and Saturday at the **Nevada City Brewing Company,** 75 Bost Ave. (☎ 916/265-2446). The **Nevada City Winery,** 321 Spring St. (☎ 916/265-9463), also offers tastings and tours.

At the junction of Broad and Union streets is the ramp onto Calif. 49. Go south 3.3 miles to East Main Street and turn left into:

2. **Grass Valley,** the former hard-rock capital of the Northern Mines that yielded $14 million in the year of the Gold Rush. Today it lures tourists with its balconies, Victorian-era buildings, and gaslight along Main and Mill streets; its Cornish heritage (many Cornish hard-rock miners once settled here); and the colorful saga of Irish-born Lola Montez, paramour of European royals and notables, who scandalized Europe with her racy "spicer dance" before making her way across America to settle in Grass Valley in 1852. Lola passed her skills on to a young local lass, Lotta Crabtree, who captivated the minerals and the rest of America and eventually amassed a fortune. The **Lola Montez Home,** a replica of the original, at 248 Mill St. (☎ 916/273-4667), is now the local **tourist information office.** The **Grass Valley Museum,** corner of Church and Chapel streets (☎ 916/273-5509), boasts historical displays and a collection of 10,000 antiquarian books in the town's former (1865) schoolhouse.

**☕ TAKE A BREAK**  Follow the locals to **Moore's Cafe,** 216 Broad St. (☎ 916/265-9440), a hole-in-the-wall diner serving down-to-earth breakfast. Omelets run the gamut from plain to bacon and avocado, and zesty green chile and cheese. Filling meals at '50s prices.

While here, you also can tour the:

3. **Empire Mine State Historic Park,** 10791 E. Empire St., site of the deepest, richest, and largest hard-rock gold mine in California (☎ 916/273-8522). Its owner, William Bourne, became one of the wealthiest men in California. A shaft leads more than a mile down to 367 miles of underground mines. A model of the tunnel complex can be viewed near the park entrance. Some 10 miles of hiking trails lead past mining relics, old shafts, and forest. Bourne's baronial cottage, replete with original furnishings, overlooks the site amid imposing formal gardens.

Return via East Empire Street to Calif. 49 and continue south. The route narrows down to a single lane, but passing lanes are spaced at regular intervals. After 2 miles, a sign advises you to "Turn on headlights for the next 14 miles." Proceed south to Lincoln Way. Turn right and enter historic:

**4. Auburn,** whose 5-square-block, perfectly preserved "old town" is steeped in Gold Rush flavor. A walk along Lincoln Way, and Commercial, Court, and Sacramento streets takes you back into the past; the **Chamber of Commerce,** 601 Lincoln Way (☎ 916/885-5616), has a walking tour brochure. Begin at the base of Washington Street and the massive **statue of Claude Chana** making his historic find of gold in Auburn Creek in 1848. Nearby is the 1893 **Hook and Ladder Company Firehouse,** still home to California's first motorized fire engine. The **post office** at the corner of Lincoln and Sacramento streets opened in 1851 and is the oldest continuously used post office in California. The stately, neoclassical structure clinging to the hill above Old Town is the 1894 **Placer County Courthouse,** featuring an impressive dome. Downtown Auburn, centered on Lincoln Way, is a piece of homey 1950s Americana. At 1273 High St., a log-and-stone building (a 1940s WPA project) houses the **Placer County Museum** (☎ 916/888-6891), home to a walk-through mining tunnel and historical items telling the tale of Placer County.

Exit Auburn along Lincoln Way, which merges with Calif. 49 (High Street). Continue south as Calif. 49 scales the flanks of the American River ravine. After 16 miles enter Coloma and the:

**5. Marshall Gold Discovery Site,** 310 Back St. (☎ 916/622-3470), which changed the history of the West. The 240-acre historic park contains a functioning full-size replica of **John Sutter's sawmill** where, in 1848, overseer James Marshall found flecks of gold on the banks of the American River. Within a year, 10,000 miners poured in. Sutter lost most of his land with the invasion and died impoverished in 1880. Marshall was tricked out of his claim and died in poverty in 1879. He lies buried on the hillside, where his massive effigy (reached via One Way Road) overlooks the site of his momentous find. A nature trail begins here and is particularly pleasing in fall when the leaves turn gold. Demonstrations of panning for gold are given at Sutter's Mill each afternoon. Most of Columa lies within the Historic Park, and includes a working smithy, Chinese stores, a theater, and a pioneer cemetery. In summer, Columa is also a mecca for white-water enthusiasts who push off here to run the American River's south fork.

🍵 **TAKE A BREAK**   For a taste of the Gold Country's Chinese connection, try **Shanghai Restaurant,** 289 Washington St. (☎ 916/823-2613), which dishes out standard but flavorful Cantonese fare at budget prices.

Continue 7 miles south through pine and oak forest to the junction with U.S. 50. Cross, staying on Calif. 49, and enter:

**6. Placerville,** where you can take a sidewalk stroll that brings you back to the '50s— of both this century and last. Placerville was formerly known as Hangtown, named for the "necktie party" by which three desperadoes met their demise in 1849. A dummy strung up outside the **Hangman's Tree Bar,** 905 Main St. (☎ 707/622-3878), reminds us to behave. Many of California's richest men made their fortunes in Placerville catering to the mining stampede. Mark Hopkins, who rose to become a railroad magnate, began his steam-powered ascent selling groceries on Main Street, where Leland Standford (later founder of Stanford University) also had a store; and John Studebaker launched his success with wheeled vehicles by building wheelbarrows. You can see one of his barrows at the **El Dorado County Historical Museum,** 104 Placerville Dr. (☎ 916/621-5865), 2 miles west of town, which also displays Native American baskets and arts, mining equipment, plus an old stagecoach and steam locomotive. Northwest of town is the **Gold Bug Mine,** Bedford Avenue (☎ 916/642-5232), America's only city-owned gold

# Driving Tour: California's Gold Country

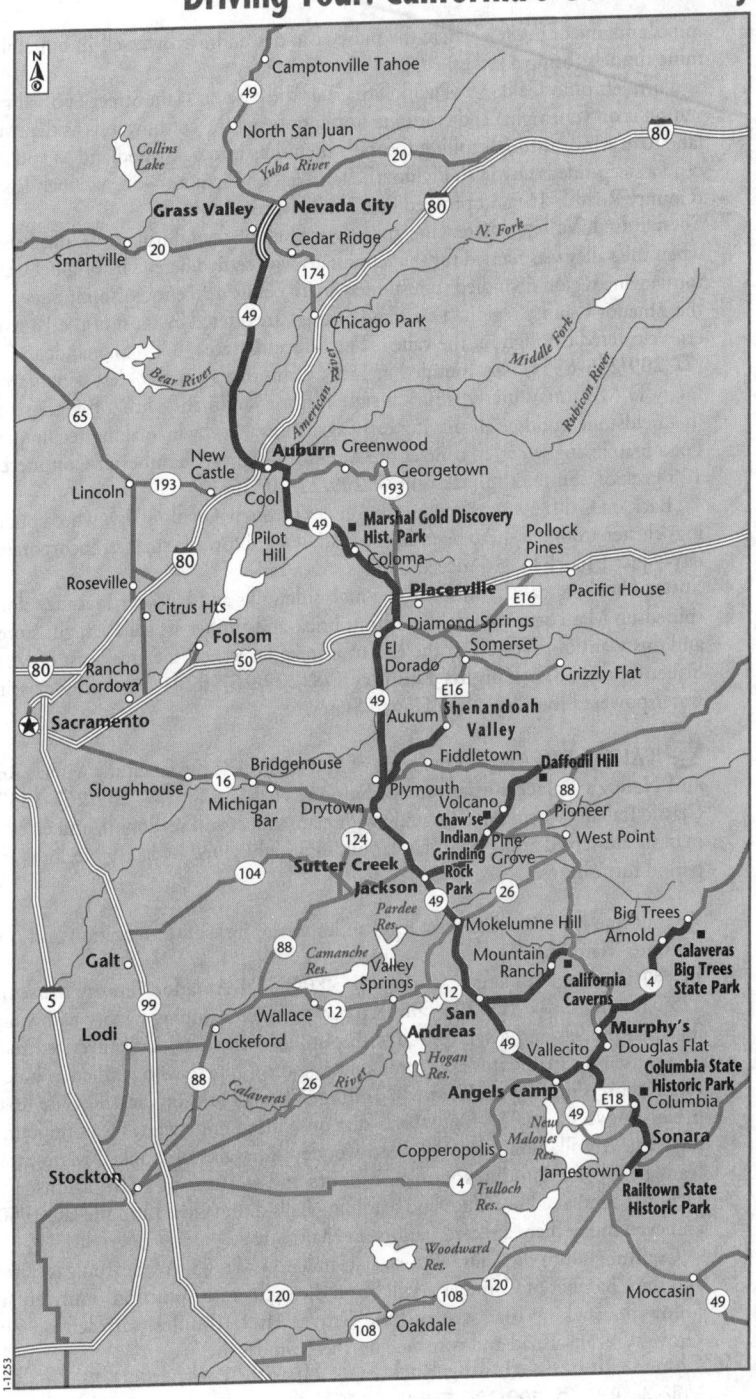

mine, and one of the few where the public can descend narrow, well-lit but chilly mine tunnels (bring a jacket).

Turn left onto Calif. 49 (Pacific Street) at the base of Main Street (a Shell gas station is on your right) and continue south, noticing the cottonwoods as the two-lane road winds through rolling foothills then dips into oak woodland as you ascend a steep-sided canyon to Plymouth. Turn left on Plymouth–Shenandoah Road (County Road E-16) and proceed east 7 miles through the:

7. **Shenandoah Valley,** where wine grapes were first planted during the Gold Rush, when the valley was named for the Virginians who settled here. The original California wine region dwindled to just one winery before a recent blossoming revived the Amador County region. Tours and tastings are offered by most of the 18 wineries clustered throughout the valley. The **Sobon Estate,** 14430 Shenandoah Rd. (☎ 209/245-6554), was founded in 1856. California's fourth oldest winery (formerly D'Agostini Winery) is now a state historic landmark, with a free museum in a fieldstone building displaying early agricultural and winemaking techniques. For a map listing wineries, contact the **Amador County Chamber of Commerce,** 125 Peek St., Suite B, in Jackson (☎ 209/223-0350).

Back on Calif. 49, continue south 6 miles through Amador City, whose buildings cluster around a sharp bend in the road; it's California's smallest incorporated city—just 1 block long. Proceed 2 miles south to:

8. **Sutter Creek,** a real charmer with its high sidewalks and balconied facades along spiffed-up Main Street, full of false-front brick-and-timber art galleries, gift stores, and dusty antiques stores. At the end of Eureka Street, on the creek east of Main Street, is the 1873 **Knights Foundry** (☎ 209/267-0201), the only existing water-powered foundry in the United States.

☕ **TAKE A BREAK** In the heart of Sutter Creek is the fancifully named **Ron and Nancy's Palace Restaurant & Saloon,** 76 Main St. (☎ 209/267-1355). Classic Italian favorites like linguine with clam sauce, veal scallopini, and chicken marsala are served amid historic surroundings highlighted by lace tablecloths and period furnishings.

Continue south on Calif. 49 for 4 miles to the Jackson Fire Station and turn left onto Main Street in:

9. **Jackson,** the region's largest town (pop. 3,800). The **Amador County Museum,** 225 Church St. (☎ 209/223-6386), parlays Jackson's mining history with working scale models and a stamp mill with pistonlike crushers that pulverized rock. The museum's mementos also commemorate the Chinese who worked as indentured laborers in the area. **Kennedy Tailing Wheels Park,** on Jackson Gate Road, preserves two soaring 58-foot wheels that once lifted mine waste to an impounding dam. A walk along the well-worn wooden sidewalks of crooked Main Street leads past brick buildings with iron doors and shutters to guard against fire. Jackson's renowned bordellos and gambling halls didn't close until the late 1950s, and even today there are card parlors on Main Street.

Continue south on Calif. 49 for a half-mile to Calif. 88. A Chevron gas station and the Chamber of Commerce will be on the right, at the junction. Turn left and follow the snaking road east to Pine Grove. After 10 miles, turn left on Pine Grove–Volcano Road and continue north 1½ miles to:

10. **Chaw'se Indian Grinding Rock State Historic Park,** 14881 Pine Grove–Volcano Rd. (☎ 209/296-7488), a 136-acre preserve of grassy meadows, black oaks, and pine that was once home to the Miwok tribe. Gold miners brutally

chased out and decimated the largely peaceable Native American populations who inhabited the Sierra foothills. The **Chaw'se Regional Indian Museum** profiles their vibrant culture and features a reconstructed, native village replete with bark teepees, a granary, a roundhouse (or *hun'ge*), and a Miwok ball field.

Continue north on Pine Grove–Volcano Road to the Y-junction with Pioneer–Volcano Road (be wary of merging traffic). Proceed into:

11. **Volcano,** a remote hamlet nestled in a deep, craterlike setting. Little remains to remind visitors that Volcano was once sinfully sybaritic, or that in its Gold Rush heyday it boasted the state's first observatory, lending library, literary and debating societies, and community theater. Performances by Volcano Pioneers Community Theater Group at the **Cobblestone Theater** (☎ 209/296-4696), a former assay office on Main Street, are a far cry from Volcano's once bawdy nightlife.

☕ **TAKE A BREAK**   The place to eat hereabouts is the **St. George Hotel,** 16104 Pine Grove–Volcano Rd. (☎ 209/296-4458), an 1864 structure on the National Register of Historic Places, with maple vines clambering up the outside walls. Inexpensive American fare, including a special Sunday chicken brunch, are served in the genteel dining room.

In Volcano, Pioneer–Volcano Road swings right and becomes Ram's Horn Grade. In springtime, follow Ram's Horn north 3 miles to the junction of Shake Ridge Road and:

12. **Daffodil Hill,** where the McLaughlin family has been planting daffodils—over 300,000 at current count—for over 140 years. Mid-March to mid-April, the forested hillside explodes in a stunning floral display.

Return via Volcano and Pine Grove to Jackson. Turn left on Calif. 49 and proceed south on the meandering road for 16 miles to:

13. **Mokelumne Hill,** another once-bawdy town where gold claims were limited to 16 square feet because the local hills were so rich. Fires ravaged Mokelumne in 1864 and 1874, but the now-sleepy village still has several venerable Victorian structures.

Back on Calif. 49, the road straightens out for most of the 7 miles south to the T-junction with Calif. 12. Turn left and continue on Calif. 49 for 1 mile to:

14. **San Andreas,** named for the mission church that served the Mexicans who founded the town in 1848. The charming classical Revival buildings date from 1858, after a fire destroyed the town; the Queen Anne homes sprang up during the 1893–1905 boom, when San Andreas thrived as a copper-producing town. The handsome brick **County Courthouse,** 30 N. Main St., has been immaculately restored and now houses the **Calaveras County Museum** (☎ 209/754-6513), which provides a pamphlet that describes a self-guided historic walking tour of the town. The museum pays deference to the Miwok Indians. It also features recreations of a miner's cabin and general store. The gentleman bandit Black Bart (alias Charles Bolton) was tried and sentenced here in 1883; he robbed gold from 28 Wells Fargo stagecoaches between 1875 and 1883.

Continue south on Calif. 49 and turn left after 1 mile onto Mountain Ranch Road (opposite the law offices of Airola & Airola). After 8 miles, turn right onto Michel Road to Cave City Road. Turn left and continue as the road descends to:

15. **California Caverns** (☎ 209/736-2708), within whose bowels noted 19th-century naturalist John Muir recorded "chamber after chamber more and more magnificent, all a-glitter like a glacier cave with icicle-like stalactites and stalagmites combining in forms of indescribable beauty." The caverns opened to the public in 1850, and a small resort town, Cave City, grew around the small inconspicuous entrance,

which gives no hint of the grandeur of the many crystal chambers within. The 1-hour "Trail of Lights" tour gives no indication, either, of the size of the caverns, which have not yet been fully explored. Adventurous souls can take a Wild Expedition tour to reach underground lakes.

Return to Calif. 49 and continue south 11 miles to:

**16. Angels Camp,** whose name is derived from commercial, not spiritual, reasons—Henry Angel was the first storekeeper. The town began life in 1849 as a Gold Rush boomtown and later became a hard-rock gold-mining capital. Mark Twain worked the diggings briefly from 1864 to 1865 and heard the tale that inspired his first successful short story, "The Celebrated Jumping Frog of Calaveras County." The annual **Jumping Frog Jubilee**—in which frogs compete over three measured hops for a $1,500 prize for the winner's owner—is held the third weekend in May in the Frogtown Fairgrounds south of town. A short hop west of town is the **Angels Camp Museum,** 753 S. Main St. (☎ 209/736-2963), displaying Gold Rush artifacts and horse-drawn wagons.

Turn left onto Calif. 4 (Vallecito Road) at the south end of town, head east 10 miles, and take the "Business District" turnoff to the left into historic:

**17. Murphys,** an attractive one-street former Gold Rush town shaded by cottonwoods, sycamores, and elms, and known to locals as "Queen of the Sierras." Murphys is named for two Irish brothers who founded the town in 1848. The **Black Bart Playhouse** (☎ 209/728-8842) has weekend performances in April and November. Black Bart, Ulysses S. Grant, Mark Twain, and William Randolph Hearst were among the famous lodgers at the 1856 **Murphys Hotel.** The hostelry once had a reputation for Wild West violence. Its atmosphere bar has many tales to tell—the bullet holes in the doors are real—and it's the place to enjoy a cool beer from the **Murphys Creek Brewing Company.**

☕ **TAKE A BREAK** The historic **Murphys Hotel Restaurant,** Main Street (☎ 209/728-3444), serves liver and onions and other steadfast meat-based American fare, alongside pastas, cioppino, pork dijonnaise, and seafood fettuccine.

Opposite the Murphys Hotel is the narrow entrance to Sheep Ranch Road. Turn right and follow the bumpy road uphill 1 mile to:

**18. Mercer Caverns,** 1665 Sheep Ranch Rd. (☎ 209/728-2101), exhibiting an enormous variety of bizarre and exotic limestone formations within its 10 subterranean caverns. Miwok Indians used to bury their dead inside the chilly caves, which Mother Nature maintains at a steady 55°F.

Back in Murphys, return to Calif. 4 and continue east, following the snaking road uphill for 14 miles through stately pine to:

**19. Calaveras Big Tree State Park,** at an elevation of between 4,000 and 5,000 feet, and well worth the detour (☎ 209/795-2334). The park protects two magnificent **groves of giant sequoias,** which grow only on the western slopes of the Sierra Nevada. The North Grove offers an easy mile-long loop trail; the larger South Grove, 9 miles south, is easily seen on the Big Trees Creek self-guided loop. A longer Lava Bluffs Trail leads to ancient lava formations. There are also deep canyons for exploring, riverside beaches for picnicking, guided hikes, fishing, and winter snowshoeing and cross-country skiing.

Return via Murphys on Calif. 4 to Parrotts Ferry Rd (County Rd. E-18). Turn left and proceed south 1½ miles to:

**20. Moaning Caverns,** 5350 Moaning Cave Rd. (☎ 209/736-2708), where a 100-foot spiral staircase leads down to the floor of a natural limestone cavern, the deepest in the state and large enough to hold the Statue of Liberty. Native Americans held the caves in awe because of the moans that emanated from the entrance. Alas, the staircase altered the acoustics, and the caves no longer moan. The oldest human remains ever found in America were discovered here, preserved in the mineral deposits (they date back more than 13,000 years).

Continue on Parrotts Ferry Road as it winds south through the ravine of the Stanislau River to:

**21. Columbia State Historic Park,** where you recall a time when the "Gem of the Southern Mines" was the state's second-largest city (☎ 209/532-4301). Gone are the bordellos and 159 gambling halls where dirty, bearded miners rubbed shoulders with bankers and ladies of the night. But the whole 12-square-block "downtown" has been restored as an outdoor living-history museum where shop clerks wear period costumes, a blacksmith forges tools, and a saloon with swing doors still serves sarsaparilla. You can also take a bumpy, 15-minute ride in an authentic stagecoach.

"Talking buttons" on building exteriors provide information for a **self-guided tour.** Highlights include California's oldest barbershop (dating back to 1865), an early dentist's office, and the **Livery Stable,** at Fulton Street and Broadway, with displays of old-time wagons. **Engine Co. No. 1 firehouse,** on State Street, houses the restored, fancifully decorated Papeete fire pumper acquired in 1859. The **Columbia Gazette and Printing Museum,** housed in a replica of the original 1855 building, has exhibits on printing and newspaper life in early California. "Mellerdramers" by the Columbia Actors' Repertory are still offered at the **Fallon House Theatre** (☎ 209/532-4644) in the restored Fallon Hotel on Washington Street. Finally, don't leave town before visiting the **Nelson Candy Kitchen,** on Main Street, to purchase hand-dipped chocolates made using Gold Rush–era recipes. The kitchen is open daily from 9am to 5pm.

☕ **TAKE A BREAK**   Crisp linens, high-back chairs, and period decor add to the pleasure of eating at the **City Hotel Dining Room,** Main Street (☎ 209/532-1479). The moderately priced French cuisine is delicious—typical treats include angel-hair pasta, roast leg of lamb, and duck breast with black fig and apple-raisin sauce.

Continue south on Parrott's Ferry Road until reaching the T-junction with Calif. 49. Turn left and proceed 2 miles to:

**22. Sonora,** founded by Mexican miners who were soon driven out by greedy gringo miners. Sonora's Big Bonanza was the richest pocket mine in the Mother Lode, and the town was known as "Queen of the Southern Mines." The town continues to prosper thanks to its impressive, well-preserved Victorian homes and a tranquillity that attracts tourists and retirees, young and old. Washington Street, the main drag, has 19th-century mansions as well as the 1859 **St. James Episcopal Church.** Old West paintings and local history exhibits are on display at the **Tuolumne County Museum and History Center,** 158 W. Bradford Ave. (☎ 209/532-1317), housed in the town's 1857 jail. The **Tuolumne County Courthouse,** on West Yankey Street, is an intriguing amalgam of marble, green sandstone, and yellow brick; it has a copper door and a Byzantine clock tower.

Turn right at the Bank of America in downtown Sonora to continue on Calif. 49, which after 2 miles merges with Calif. 108. Turn left at the T-junction and continue 1½ miles south to 5th Avenue. Turn left and after a quarter-mile enter:

23. **Railtown 1897 State Historic Park,** which preserves the locomotives and carriages of the Sierra Railway Company in the old Sierra Railway Depot (☎ 209/984-3953). Trains began operating from Jamestown in 1897, hauling passengers and freight throughout the Mother Lode. The 23-acre, open-air museum includes the West's only operating steam roundhouse. During summer weekends, board the 80-year-old steam-powered Mother Lode Cannon for excursions through the Sierra foothills.

Return along 5th Avenue to Willow Street. Turn left and follow Willow to Main Street, in the heart of downtown:

24. **Jamestown,** which, beloved by Hollywood, has starred in such films and TV shows as *High Noon, Lassie, The Lone Ranger, Butch Cassidy and the Sundance Kid,* and *Little House on the Prairie.* The half-mile-long **Main Street** features shops, galleries, and breakfast inns. Kids can pan for fake gold in the horse trough outside the **livery stable** at 18170 Main St.; adults can sign up with **Gold Prospecting Expeditions** (☎ 209/984-4653) and go panning for the real thing.

The end of Main Street merges with Calif. 49, announcing the end of your tour.

# 1 San Francisco

Consistently rated one of the top tourist destinations in the world, San Francisco is awash with multiple dimensions. Its famous, thrilling streets go up, and they go down; its multifarious citizens—and their adopted cultures, architectures, and cuisines—span from San Antonio to Singapore; and its politics range from hyperliberalism to an ever-encroaching wave of conservatism. Even something as mundane as fog takes on a new dimension as it creeps from the ocean and slowly envelops San Francisco in a resplendent blanket of mist.

The result is a bit of heaven for everyone. In a city so multifaceted, so enamored with itself, it's truly hard not to find what you're looking for. Feel the cool blast of salt air as you stroll across the Golden Gate. Stuff yourself on Chinatown dim sum. Browse the Haight for incense and crystals. Walk along the beach, pierce your nose, see a play, rent a Harley—the list is endless. Like an eternal World's Fair, it's all happening in San Francisco, and everyone's invited.

## ARRIVING & DEPARTING

**BY PLANE**    Two major airports serve the Bay Area. **San Francisco International Airport** (☎ 415/761-0800) is 14 miles south of downtown on U.S. 101. A cab to downtown will cost $25–$30 and takes about 40 minutes during rush hour; otherwise it's 20–25 minutes. The **SFO Airporter** bus (☎ 415/495-8404) picks up passengers in front of the baggage-claim area every 15–30 minutes daily from 6:20am to midnight and stops at most of the major downtown hotels. No reservations are needed. It costs $10 one-way, children under 2 ride free. Other private shuttle companies offer door-to-door airport service, in which you share a van with other passengers. SuperShuttle (☎ 415/558-8500) charges $10 to downtown; a second passenger pays only $8 each way. **Yellow Airport Shuttle** (☎ 415/282-7433) charges $10 per person. Each shuttle stops every 20 minutes or so. The San Mateo County Transit system, **SamTrans** (☎ 800/660-4287 within northern California, or ☎ 415/508-6200), runs two buses between the airport and the Transbay Terminal at First and Mission streets. The 7B bus costs $1 and takes about 55 minutes. The 7F bus costs $2 and takes only 35 minutes, but permits only one carry-on bag. Both buses run daily, every half hour from about 6am to 7pm, then hourly until about midnight.

**Oakland International Airport,** located about 5 miles south of downtown Oakland, at the Hegenberger Road exit of Calif. 17/U.S. 880 (☎ 510/577-4000), is used primarily by passengers with East Bay destinations. Taxis from here to the center of San Francisco cost about $45 plus tip; trip time is about an hour. The cheapest way downtown is via **Bay Area Rapid Transit (BART)** (☎ 415/992-2278), the high-speed rail system linking San Francisco with the East Bay. The **AirBART shuttle bus** (☎ 510/562-8428) runs about every 15 minutes, from Terminals 1 and 2, and will take you to BART for $2. The BART fare to downtown San Francisco costs $2.45 and takes 20 minutes once onboard. AirBART operates Mon–Sat 6am–midnight and Sun 8am–midnight.

**BY TRAIN & BUS** Amtrak (☎ 800/USA-RAIL) arrives at the Emeryville depot just north of the East Bay side of the Bay Bridge (☎ 800/872-7245). Free shuttles connect the depot with San Francisco's Ferry Building and CalTrain Station. None of the major car-rental agencies are at the train station; pick up your car from downtown Oakland or San Francisco.

**Greyhound/Trailways** (☎ 800/231-2222) buses arrive and depart from the Transbay Terminal at First and Mission streets in downtown San Francisco.

## ESSENTIALS

**VISITOR INFORMATION** The **San Francisco Visitor Information Center,** on the lower level of Hallidie Plaza, 900 Market St., at Powell Street (☎ 415/391-2000), provides information in several languages (open Mon–Fri 9am–5:30pm, Sat 9am–3pm, Sun 10am–2pm). Dial ☎ 415/391-2001 anytime for a recorded message about current cultural, theater, music, sports, and other special events.

**SAFETY** We don't recommend walking alone late at night in the Tenderloin, between Union Square and the Civic Center; the Mission District, around 16th and Mission streets; the Fillmore area, around lower Haight Street; and the SoMa area south of Market Street.

**EMERGENCIES** Dial ☎ 911 for police, ambulance, or the fire department. Emergency hotlines include the **Poison Control Center** (☎ 800/523-2222) and **Rape Crisis** (☎ 415/647-7273). **Saint Francis Memorial Hospital,** 900 Hyde St., between Bush and Pine streets on Nob Hill (☎ 415/353-6000), provides urgent-care service 24 hours.

## GETTING AROUND

You don't need a car to explore downtown San Francisco and central areas, for this is one of the West Coast's few great walking cities. It's compact enough so that you can roam from Downtown/Union Square, through Chinatown, into North Beach, and out to Fisherman's Wharf in an afternoon. Furthermore, the city's notorious parking regulations can make a car your worst nightmare.

**BY PUBLIC TRANSPORTATION** The **San Francisco Municipal Railway,** better known as **Muni** (☎ 415/673-6864), operates the city's cable cars, buses, and Metro streetcars. For detailed route information, phone Muni, check the map in the Yellow Pages, or purchase a route map ($2) at the San Francisco Visitor Information Center (see "Essentials," above) or another store. The fare on buses and Metro streetcars is $1 for adults (payable in exact change or bills) and 35¢ for kids under 17 and seniors over 65. Cable cars, packed primarily with tourists, cost $2 ($1 for seniors from 6 to 7am and 9pm to midnight). "Passports," allowing unlimited rides on any Muni vehicle, cost $6 for 1 day, $10 for 3 days, and $15 for a week. The passport also grants admission discounts at 24 city attractions, including the Museum of Modern Art, the Exploratorium, and the museums in Golden Gate Park. It is available at the Visitor Information Center (see "Essentials," above) and the TIX booth at Union Square.

# San Francisco

## Accommodations
Archbishop's Mansion **4**
Commodore International **11**
Cow Hollow Motor Inn & Suites **2**
Golden Gate Hotel **12**
Grant Plaza Hotel **14**
Holiday Lodge & Garden Hotel **17**
Hotel Bedford **9**
Hotel Bohème **18**
Hotel Diva **7**
Hotel Majestic **3**
Hotel Milano **5**
Hotel Monaco **8**
Hotel Triton **13**
Huntington Hotel **16**
Prescott Hotel **10**
Ritz-Carlton San Francisco **15**
San Francisco International Hostel **1**
Tuscan Inn **19**
Westin St. Francis **6**

## Attractions
Alcatraz Island **1**
Ansel Adams Center for Photography **8**
Cable Car Museum **15**
Coit Tower **16**
Exploratorium/Palace of Fine Arts **2**
Ghiradelli Square **18**
Grace Cathedral **14**
Jewish Museum **11**
Lombard Street **17**
Mexican Museum **3**
Mission Dolores **7**
Museum of the City of San Francisco
  (the Cannerly) **19**
Names Project Visitors Center **6**
Octagon House **4**
St. Mary's Cathedral **5**
San Francisco Maritime
  National Historic Park **20**
San Francisco Museum of Modern Art **10**
Transamerica Pyramid **12**
Wells Fargo History Museum **13**
Yerba Buena Gardens **9**

Municipal Pier    Pier 45    Pier 43 1/2

Pier 43

Pier 41

Aquatic
Park

Pier 39

Pier 35

San Francisco

Pier 33

Bay

Jefferson St.
Beach St.

Pier 31

North Point St.

Pier 27

Bay St.

Francisco St.

Chestnut St.

Pier 23

Lombard St.

Pier 19

Greenwich St.

Pier 17

Filbert St.

Pier 15

Union St.

Pier 9

Green St.

Pier 7

Vallejo St.

Pier 5

Broadway

Pier 3

Tunnel

Pacific Ave.

Pier 1

Chinatown

Jackson St.

Justin
Herman
Plaza

Ferry Building
(World Trade Center)

Union
Square

San Francisco–
Oakland
Bay Bridge

80

Geary St.

O'Farrell St.

ddy St.

Market St.

Moscone
Convention
Center

South Park

Mission St.

Howard St.

Folsom St.

Harrison St.

Bryant St.

Brannan St.

Townsend St.

King St.

Berry St.

Channel St.

China Basin

Division St.

Alameda St.

280

15th St.

**BART,** an acronym for Bay Area Rapid Transit (☎ **415/992-2278**), is a high-speed rail network connecting San Francisco with the East Bay—Oakland, Richmond, Concord, and Fremont—as well as southern Daly City. Four stations are located along Market Street. Fares range from 90¢ to $3.55, depending on how far you go. Tickets are dispensed from machines in the stations. Children 4 and under ride free. Trains run every 15–20 minutes, Mon–Fri 4am–midnight, Sat 6am–midnight, and Sun 8am–midnight. A line to the airport is scheduled to open in 1997.

**BY TAXI**   If you're downtown during rush hours or leaving from a major hotel, you can easily hail a cab. Otherwise, call one of the following companies: **Veteran's Cab** (☎ 415/552-1300), **Desoto Cab Co.** (☎ 415/673-1414), **Luxor Cabs** (☎ 415/282-4141), **Yellow Cab** (☎ 415/626-2345), **City** (☎ 415/468-7200), and **Pacific** (☎ 415/986-7220). Rates are approximately $2 for the first mile and $1.80 for each mile thereafter.

**BY FERRY**   The **Golden Gate Ferry Service** (☎ **415/923-2000**) operates between the San Francisco Ferry Building, at the foot of Market Street, and downtown Sausalito (30 minutes) and Larkspur (45 minutes). The frequent Sausalito service takes a half hour and costs $4.25 for adults, $3.20 for kids 6–12, and $2.10 for seniors and the disabled. The Larkspur ferry is primarily a weekday commuter service, with limited service on weekends. The 13-mile trip takes about 45 minutes and costs $2.50 for adults, $1.90 for kids 6–12, and $1.25 for seniors and the disabled; on weekends, prices rise to $4.25, $3.20, and $2.10 respectively. The **Blue and Gold Fleet** (☎ **415/705-5444** or 510/522-3300) operates daily from the Ferry Building and Pier 39 to Oakland, Alameda, and Vallejo. Fares to Oakland are $3.75 adult, $1.50 children, and $2.50 seniors; to Vallejo, $7.50, $4, and $6, respectively. The **Red & White Fleet,** Piers 41 and 43½ (☎ **800/229-2784** or 415/546-2700), operates from Pier 43½ to Sausalito, Tiburon, Angel Island, and Vallejo. *Note:* At press time, the Blue & Gold Fleet had just purchased the Red & White Fleet and schedule changes were yet to be determined. Call either number for updated schedules and fare changes.

## WHAT TO SEE & DO

Some of the city's best attractions are its diverse, lively neighborhoods. **Castro Street** around Market and 18th streets is the center of the city's gay community, replete with restaurants, bars, shops, and other institutions that cater to the city's large gay population. Among the landmarks are Harvey Milk Plaza, the Quilt Project, and the Castro Theater, a fabulous 1920s movie palace. California Street to Broadway and Kearny to Stockton streets are the boundaries of today's **Chinatown.** The gateway at Grant and Bush marks the entry to Chinatown; Stockton Street is the main shopping drag.

Unless you come really early in the morning, you won't catch many traces of the traditional waterfront life that once existed around **Fisherman's Wharf.** Most of the fishing going on around here is for tourist dollars, as T-shirt and trinket shops line the waterfront from Ghirardelli Square to **Pier 39** (☎ **415/981-8030**), the busiest mall of the group, with more than 100 stores and restaurants.

Once inhabited almost entirely by Irish immigrants, the **Mission District** is now the center of the city's Latino community, an oblong area from 14th to 30th streets between Dolores and Potrero. The heart of the community lies along 24th Street between Van Ness and Potrero, where dozens of excellent ethnic restaurants, bakeries, bars, and specialty stores attract people from all over the city.

When the cable car was invented in 1873, **Nob Hill** became the city's most exclusive residential area. The 1906 earthquake destroyed most of the big mansions, but the Flood mansion, which serves today as the Pacific Union Club, and the Fairmont (which was under construction when the earthquake struck) were spared. Today the area is home to some of the city's most upscale hotels.

In the late 1800s, an enormous influx of Italian immigrants into **North Beach** firmly established this area as San Francisco's "Little Italy." The aromas of pasta sauce and roasting coffee compete for olfactory attention along Columbus Avenue, drawing visitors into the dozens of eclectic little cafes, delis, bakeries, and coffee shops that give North Beach its Italian–Bohemian character.

**ESCORTED TOURS**   Cruisin' the Castro (☎ 415/550-8110) will give you a totally new insight into the gay community's contribution to San Francisco. Tours are personally conducted by Ms. Trevor Hailey, who was involved in the development of the Castro in the 1970s and knew Harvey Milk, the first openly gay politician elected to office in the United States.

Rachel Heller's **Haight–Ashbury Walking Tours** (☎ 415/221-8442) will take you to the city's hippie haunts, including the Grateful Dead's crash pad, Janis Joplin's house, and other monuments to the Summer of Love.

**Javawalk** (☎ 415/673-9255) is a 2-hour walking tour by self-described "coffeehouse lizard" Elaine Sosa. Aside from visiting North Beach's cafes, Javawalk also serves up a good share of the district's historical, architectural, and coffee-related trivia. Sosa keeps the tour interactive and fun.

Founded by author, TV personality, and restaurant critic Shirley Fong-Torres, **Wok Wiz Chinatown Walking Tours** (☎ 415/355-9657) takes you into nooks and crannies not usually seen by tourists. Her guides are intimately acquainted with all of Chinatown's backways and small businesses. Fong-Torres also operates a gastronomical tour.

The self-guided **49-Mile Scenic Drive** is one easy way to orient yourself and to grasp the beauty of San Francisco. It begins in the city, follows a rough circle around the bay, and passes virtually all the best-known sights. The route is marked with blue-and-white seagull signs, but free maps are available at the San Francisco Visitor Information Center, at Powell and Market streets. Try to avoid the downtown area during the weekday rush hours from 7 to 9am and 4 to 6pm.

**Gray Line** bus tours, Transbay Terminal, First and Mission streets (☎ 800/826-0202 or 415/558-9400), offers several daily itineraries with free transfers from centrally located hotels to departure points.

**CRUISES & BOAT TOURS**   One of the best ways to look at San Francisco is from a boat tour on the bay. There are two major companies: **Red and White Fleet,** at Pier 41, Fisherman's Wharf (☎ 800/229-2784 in California, or 415/546-2700), is the city's largest boat tour operator, offering more than half a dozen itineraries on the bay.

**Blue and Gold Fleet,** at Pier 39, Fisherman's Wharf (☎ 415/705-5444), tours the bay year-round in a sleek, 400-passenger sightseeing boat, complete with food and beverage facilities. The fully narrated, $1\frac{1}{4}$-hour cruise passes beneath the Golden Gate and Bay bridges, and comes within yards of Alcatraz Island.

**ATTRACTIONS**   It's not surprising that in "The City by the Bay" most of the top attractions are on, near, or over water. Fisherman's Wharf is the best-known tourist spot, and the jumping-off point for cruises around the bay, trips to Alcatraz, and walks along the waterfront. Golden Gate Park extends out to the water, Coit Tower provides the best views of it, and the Golden Gate Bridge spans across it.

The city's legendary hills are another source of entertainment, whether it's a **cable car** ride up to Nob Hill or a drive down the serpentine **Lombard Street.** All around and in between are some of the finest and most diverse shopping streets in the country.

✪ **Alcatraz Island.** *Pier 41, near Fisherman's Wharf.* ☎ *415/705-1045. Admission (including ferry trip and audio tour) $10 adults, $8.25 seniors, $4.75 children 5–11. Winter, daily 9:30am–2:45pm. Summer, daily 9:15am–4:15pm. Ferries depart at 15 and*

*45 minutes after the hour.* Surrounded by frigid waters with treacherous tides, Alcatraz ("The Rock") was believed to be an escape-proof federal prison. From 1934 to 1963, it was home to gangsters like Al Capone, Machine Gun Kelly, and Alvin Karpis. It cost a fortune to keep them imprisoned here because all supplies, including water, had to be shipped in. The government closed the prison in 1963, and in 1972 it became part of the Golden Gate National Recreation Area. Allow slightly more than 3 hours for the entire excursion.

**Asian Art Museum.** *In Golden Gate Park near 10th Ave. and Fulton St.* ☎ *415/668-8921. Admission (including the M. H. de Young Memorial Museum and California Palace of the Legion of Honor) $6 adults, $4 seniors, $3 ages 12–17, free for children under 12. Wed–Sun 10am–4:45pm. Bus: 44.* Adjacent to the M. H. de Young Museum and the Japanese Tea Garden, this museum can only display about 1,800 pieces from its vast collection of 12,000 at any given time. About half of the works exhibited are in the ground-floor Chinese and Korean galleries, including sculptures, paintings, bronzes, ceramics, jades, and decorative objects. There is also a wide range of exhibits from Pakistan, India, Tibet, Japan, and Southeast Asia, including the world's oldest-known dated Chinese Buddha.

**✪ The Cable Cars.** ☎ *415/673-6864. Fares $2; $1 seniors 6–7am and 9pm–midnight.* Designated official historic landmarks by the National Park Service in 1964, the city's beloved cable cars clank across the hills like mobile museum pieces. Each weighs about 6 tons and is hauled along by a steel cable, enclosed under the street in a center rail. They move at a constant $9^1/_2$ mph—never more, never less. This may strike you as slow, but it doesn't feel that way when you're cresting an almost perpendicular hill and look down at what seems like a bobsled dive straight into the ocean. But in spite of the thrills, they're perfectly safe.

**Cable Car Barn Museum.** *Washington and Mason sts.* ☎ *415/474-1887. Admission free. Apr–Oct, daily 10am–6pm. Nov–Mar, daily 10am–5pm. Cable Car: Powell St. lines stop at the museum.* If you've ever wondered how cable cars work, this nifty museum will explain (and demonstrate!) it all to you. This working museum is the living powerhouse, repair shop, and storage place of the cable-car system. The exposed machinery, which pulls the cables under San Francisco's streets, looks like a Rube Goldberg invention. Watch the massive groaning and vibrating winches as they thread the cable that hauls the cars through a huge figure '8' and back into the system via slack-absorbing tension wheels.

**California Academy of Sciences.** *On the Music Concourse of Golden Gate Park.* ☎ *415/221-5100 or 415/750-7145 for recorded information. Admission $7 adults, $4 seniors and students 12–17, $1.50 children 6–11, free for children under 6. Planetarium shows cost an additional $2.50 adults, $1.25 seniors and students under 18. Labor Day–July 3, daily 10am–5pm. July 4–Labor Day, daily 10am–7pm. Muni Metro: N line (Judah) to Golden Gate Park. Bus: 5 (Fulton), 71 (Haight–Noreiga), or 44 (O'Shaughnessy).* This is actually a group of three related museums: the Steinhart Aquarium, the Morrison Planetarium, and the Natural History Museum. The aquarium contains a California tide pool and a hands-on area where children can touch starfish and sea urchins. The living coral reef is the largest such display in the country. The Morrison Planetarium presents sky shows as well as laser-light shows. At the Natural History Museum, you can experience a simulation of two of San Francisco's biggest earthquakes in the Hohfeld Earth and Space Hall.

**✪ California Palace of the Legion of Honor.** *In Lincoln Park (at 4th Ave. and Clement St.).* ☎ *415/750-3600 or 415/863-3330 for recorded information. Admission (including the Asian Art Museum and M. H. de Young Memorial Museum) $6 adults,*

*$4 seniors, $3 ages 12–17, free for children under 12. Tues–Sun 10am–4:45pm. Bus: 18, 38.* Designed as a memorial to California's World War I casualties, the neoclassical structure is an exact replica of the Legion of Honor Palace in Paris, right down to the inscription *honneur et patrie* above the portal. Reopened after a 2-year, $29-million renovation and seismic upgrading project that was stalled by the discovery of almost 300 turn-of-the-century coffins, the museum's collection contains paintings, sculptures, and decorative arts from Europe, as well as international tapestries, prints, and drawings. The chronological display of more than 800 years of European art includes a fine Rodin sculpture collection.

✪ **Coit Tower.** *Atop Telegraph Hill.* ☎ *415/362-0808. Admission $3 adults, $2 seniors and students, $1 children 6–12. Daily 10am–6pm. Bus: 39 (Coit).* Just east of North Beach, this round, stone tower offers stunning 360° views of the city and the bay. Inside the base of the tower are the impressive WPA murals completed during the New Deal by more than 25 artists, many of whom had studied under master muralist Diego Rivera. On a clear day, walk up the Filbert Steps (thereby avoiding a traffic nightmare) and take in the panorama at the tower base. In fact, we recommend not paying the admission and going to the top; the view is just as good from the parking area and you can see the murals for free.

✪ **Golden Gate Bridge.** ☎ *415/921-5858. Bridge-bound Golden Gate Transit buses (☎ 415/332-6600) depart every half hour from the Transbay Terminal at Mission and First sts.* With its gracefully swung single span, spidery bracing cables, and sky-high towers, the bridge looks more like a work of art than one of the greatest engineering feats of the 20th century. Despite Cassandra-like predictions that it would collapse in an earthquake, the bridge revitalized the city during the Depression and opened areas north of San Francisco to development. Crossing by foot is the best way to experience the immense scale of the structure; millions of pedestrians walk across the mile-long steel link each year. Marin's Vista Point, at the bridge's northern end, boasts one of the most famous cityscape views in the world.

**Golden Gate Park.** *Entrance at Kezar Dr., an extension of Fell St. Bus: 16AX, BX, 6, 7, 66, 71. For information, head first to the McClaren Lodge and Park Headquarters (open Mon–Fri).* In addition to housing numerous tennis courts, baseball fields, and riding stables, this landmark park is home to some impressive gardens. The Conservatory of Flowers, a striking glass structure, was modeled on the famous glass house at Kew Gardens in London. The orchids are a highlight. The Japanese Tea Garden is a quiet haven of cherry trees, shrubs, and bonsai, crisscrossed by winding paths and highbacked bridges extending over pools of water. Strawberry Hill, a 430-foot-high artificial island, lies at the center of Stow Lake. The boathouse on the lake rents pedal and rowboats. Several museums are located within the park.

**Lombard Street.** Known as the "crookedest street in the world," the whimsically winding block of Lombard Street, between Hyde and Leavenworth streets, puts smiles on the faces of thousands of visitors each year. The elevation is so steep that the road has to snake back and forth to make a descent possible.

**M. H. de Young Memorial Museum.** *In Golden Gate Park (near 10th Ave. and Fulton St.). ☎ 415/750-3600, or 415/863-3330 for recorded information. Admission (including the Asian Art Museum and California Palace of the Legion of Honor) $6 adults, $4 seniors, $3 ages 12–17, free for children under 12. Wed–Sun 10am–4:45pm. Bus: 44.* Best known for its American art from colonial times to the 20th century, this museum displays paintings, sculptures, furniture, and decorative arts by such diverse talents as Paul Revere, Winslow Homer, John Singer Sargent, and Georgia O'Keeffe. Note in particular the American landscapes, as well as the trompe-l'oeil and still-life works from the turn of the century. There's also an important textile collection, with primary emphasis on rugs from Central Asia and the Near East. The museum's Café de Young is exceptional. In summer, visitors can dine in the garden, among bronze statuary. The cafe is open Wed–Sun 10am–4pm.

**Mission Dolores.** *16th St. (at Dolores St.).* ☎ *415/621-8203. Admission $2 adults, $1 children 5–12. May–Oct, daily 9am–4:30pm. Nov–Apr, daily 9am–4pm. Muni Metro: J line to the corner of Church and 16th sts. Bus: 22.* This is the oldest structure in the city, built on order of Franciscan Father Junípero Serra by Father Francisco Palou. It was constructed of 36,000 sun-baked bricks and dedicated in June 1776 at the northern terminus of El Camino Real, the Spanish road from Mexico to California. It's a moving place to observe the cool, serene buildings with their thick adobe walls, and most of all, the cemetery gardens where the early settlers are buried.

**Museum of Modern Art.** *151 Third St. (2 blocks south of Market St., across from Yerba Buena Gardens).* ☎ *415/357-4000. Admission $7 adults, $3.50 seniors and students 14–18, free for children under 14. Tues–Sun 11am–6pm (until 9pm Thurs). Muni Metro: J, K, L, M to Montgomery Station. Bus: 15, 30, 45.* Swiss architect Mario Botta designed this $62-million building, which doubled the museum's space when it opened south of Market Street in 1995. MOMA's collection consists of more than 15,000 works, including close to 5,000 paintings and sculptures by artists such as Henri Matisse, Jackson Pollock, and Willem de Kooning. MOMA's extensive photography collection includes over 9,000 photographs by such notables as Ansel Adams, Alfred Steiglitz, and Henri Cartier-Bresson.

**NAMES Project AIDS Memorial Quilt Visitor Center.** *2362A Market St. Admission free.* ☎ *415/863-1966. Wed noon–10pm, Thurs–Tues noon–5pm. Muni Metro: J, K, L, M line to Castro St. Station; F line to Church and Market sts.* The NAMES Project began in 1987 as a memorial to those who have died of AIDS. Sewing machines and fabric were acquired, and the public was invited to make coffin-sized panels for a giant memorial quilt. More than 28,000 individual panels—which would cover an area the size of 11 football fields if laid end-to-end—now commemorate the lives of those who have died. Each has been uniquely designed and sewn by the victims' friends, lovers, and family members. The quilt was first displayed on the Capitol Mall in Washington, D.C., during a 1987 national march on Washington for lesbian and gay rights.

**San Francisco Maritime National Historical Park and Museum.** *At the foot of Polk St. (near Fisherman's Wharf).* ☎ *415/556-3002. Admission to museum free; to ships $2 adults, $1 ages 11–17, free for seniors and children under 11. Museum: daily 10am–5pm. Ships: May 16–Sept 15, daily 10am–6pm; Sept 16–May 15, daily 9:30am–5pm. Cable Car: Hyde St. line to the last stop. Bus: 19, 30, 32, 42, 47.* Shaped like an art deco ship, the National Maritime Museum is filled with sailing, whaling, and fishing lore. Exhibits include intricate model craft, scrimshaw, and historic marine scenes. Two blocks east, at Aquatic Park's Hyde Street Pier, are several historic ships open to the public. The *Balclutha,* one of the last surviving square-riggers, carried grain from California around Cape Horn at a near-record speed of 300 miles a day. Visitors can spin the wheel and climb into the bunking quarters. Other ships of note include the 1890 paddlewheeled ferry *Eureka* and the three-masted lumber ship *C. A. Thayer.*

**Yerba Center of the Arts Galleries.** *701 Mission St.* ☎ *415/978-2700. Admission $4 adults, $2 seniors and students; free Thurs 11am–3pm. Tues–Sun 11am–6pm. Muni Metro: Powell or Montgomery. Bus: 30, 45, 9X.* Cutting-edge computer art and multimedia shows are on view in the high-tech galleries. The initial exhibition, "The Art of Star Wars," which featured the special effects created by George Lucas for the film, was a prime example.

**GREAT WALKS** The **Filbert Street Steps,** 377 of them running between Sansome Street and Telegraph Hill, scale the eastern face of Telegraph Hill, from Sansome and Filbert past charming 19th-century cottages and lush gardens. Napier Lane, a narrow wooden plank walkway, leads to Montgomery Street. Turn right, and follow the path to the end of the cul-de-sac where another stairway continues to Telegraph's panoramic summit. The **Lyon Street Steps,** between Green Street and Broadway, comprise another historic stairway street, containing four steep sets of stairs totaling 288 steps. Begin at Green Street and climb all the way up, past manicured hedges and flower gardens, to an iron gate that opens into the Presidio. A block east, on Baker Street, another set of 369 steps descends to Green Street.

**BEST BETS FOR KIDS** The 65-acre **San Francisco Zoo and Children's Zoo,** Sloat Boulevard and 45th Avenue (☎ 415/753-7080), in the southwest corner of the city, is among America's highest-rated animal parks. Most of the 1,000-plus inhabitants are contained in landscaped enclosures guarded by concealed moats. The innovative Primate Discovery Center is particularly noteworthy for its many rare and endangered species. The **Exploratorium,** 3601 Lyon St., in the Palace of Fine Arts at Marina Boulevard (☎ 415/563-7337), is a fun, hands-on science fair with exhibits that explore everything from color theory to Einstein's Theory of Relativity. Optics are demonstrated in booths where you can see a bust of a statue in three dimensions—but when you try to touch it, you discover it isn't there! Or you can whisper into a concave reflector and have a friend hear you 60 feet away.

**SPORTS** Formerly known as Candlestick Park, **3COM Park,** Giants Drive and Gilman Avenue (☎ 415/467-8000), is home to the **San Francisco Giants** baseball team and the **San Francisco 49ers** during football season. Baseball's **Oakland Athletics,** football's **Oakland Raiders,** and basketball's **Golden State Warriors** play their home games at **Oakland Coliseum Complex,** Hegenberger Road exit off I-880 (☎ 510/430-8020). Tickets to sporting events throughout the Bay Area are available by phone through BASS Ticketmaster (☎ 510/762-2277). Thoroughbred races are held at **Golden Gate Fields,** Gilman Street, off I-80 in Albany, 10 miles northeast of the city (☎ 510/559-7300), Jan–Mar and Apr–June.

**SHOPPING** San Francisco shopping is as diverse and sophisticated as its population. Every persuasion, style, era, and fetish is represented here, not in a big, tacky shopping mall, but rather in hundreds of quaint and dramatically different boutiques scattered throughout the city. The **Pacific Heights/Cow Hollow** and upper **Fillmore** offer strolling streets packed with handcrafts, hip fashions, and home accessories. **Haight Street's** 6 blocks between Central Avenue and Stanyan Street are still the best place to shop for inexpensive funky styles, antique and vintage clothing, Grateful Dead memorabilia, and kitsch. **Fisherman's Wharf** and environs, the nonstop strip of waterfront malls that runs along Jefferson Street, includes hundreds of shops filled with tourist trinkets. However, San Francisco's most congested and popular shopping mecca is **Union Square,** where most of the big department stores and high-end specialty shops mingle with major hotels and a handful of exceptional restaurants.

## ACCOMMODATIONS

San Francisco is an outstanding hotel town, especially considering its relatively small size. Most of the hotels listed below are within easy walking distance of Union Square, and accessible via cable car. Union Square is near the city's major shops, the Financial District, and all transportation. Prices listed below do not include state and city taxes, which total 12%. Other hidden extras include parking and hefty surcharges for telephone use.

**Andrews Hotel.** *624 Post St. (between Jones and Taylor sts.), San Francisco, CA 94109.* ☎ *800/926-3739 or 415/563-6877. Fax 415/928-6919. 43 rms, 5 suites.*

*$86–$109 double; $119 petite suite. AE, DC, MC, V. Parking $15. Cable car: Powell–Hyde and Powell–Mason lines (3 blocks east). Bus: 2, 3, 4, 30, 38, 45.* A European-style hotel with small but well-kept rooms. White lace curtains and fresh flowers add a light touch. Some rooms have shower only, and bathrooms in general tend to be tiny. A great value for the location. There's an adjoining restaurant.

○ **Archbishop's Mansion.** *1000 Fulton St. (at Steiner St.), San Francisco, CA 94117.* ☎ *800/543-5820 or 415/563-7872. 15 rms. $129–$385 double. AE, MC, V. Free parking. Bus: 19, 31, 38.* Drippingly romantic, the Archbishop's Mansion is one of the most opulent and fabulously adorned B&Bs you could possibly hope to find. The Don Giovanni suite—larger than most San Francisco houses—comes with a huge, angel-encrusted French four-poster bed, a palatial fireplace, and a seven-head shower that you won't want to leave. This B&B has laundry/valet service, a concierge, limousine service, and complimentary morning newspaper.

**Brady Acres.** *649 Jones St. (between Geary and Post sts.), San Francisco, CA 94102.* ☎ *800/627-2396 or 415/929-8033. Fax 415/441-8033. 25 rms. $60–$85 double. Weekly rentals only Oct–Apr. MC, V. Parking garage nearby. Bus: 2, 3, 4, 27, 38.* Here's a penny-pincher's dream come true. You'll find everything you need to keep home-away-from-home costs to a minimum. The small but very clean rooms have a microwave oven, small refrigerator, toaster, coffeemaker, hair dryer, direct-dial phone with free local calls, answering machine, and VCR. There are laundry facilities too.

**Commodore International.** *825 Sutter St. (at Jones St.), San Francisco, CA 94109.* ☎ *800/338-6848 or 415/923-6800. Fax 415/923-6804. 113 rms. $79–$89 double or twin. AE, DC, MC, V. Parking $12. Bus: 2, 3, 4, 27, 76.* The Commodore was pretty bad before hotelier Chip Conley let his hip-hop designers loose. Now it's one groovy hotel. Stealing the show is the Red Room, a Big Apple–style bar and lounge (you gotta see it). The first four floors feature no-frills—though clean and comfortable—rooms; the top two floors boast the neo-deco decor. There's an adjoining restaurant.

**Cow Hollow Motor Inn & Suites.** *2190 Lombard St. (between Steiner and Fillmore sts.), San Francisco, CA 94123.* ☎ *415/921-5800. Fax 415/922-8515. 117 rms, 12 suites. $80 double; from $175 suite. Additional person $10 extra. AE, DC, MC, V. Free parking. Bus: 28, 43, 76.* If you don't need to be downtown, check out this modest hotel in the beautiful bayfront marina district. There's no fancy theme here, but each room comes loaded with amenities like cable TV and in-room coffeemakers. All the rooms were renovated in 1996, so you'll sleep on a nice firm mattress.

**Golden Gate Hotel.** *775 Bush St. (between Powell and Mason sts.), San Francisco, CA 94108.* ☎ *800/835-1118 or 415/392-3702. Fax 415/392-6202. 23 rms (14 with bath). $65–$99 double without bath; $99–109 double with bath. AE, CB, DC, MC, V. Parking $12. Cable car: Powell–Hyde and Powell–Mason lines (1 block east). Bus: 2, 3, 4, 30, 38, 45.* This is a small, family-run hotel in a historic turn-of-the-century building, and it's a real gem. Innkeepers John and Renate Kenaston take obvious pleasure in making their guests comfortable. Each individually decorated room has handsome antique furnishings, quilted bedspreads, and fresh flowers. Most, but not all, rooms have phones.

**Grant Plaza Hotel.** *465 Grant Ave. (at the corner of Pine St.), San Francisco, CA 94108.* ☎ *800/472-6899 or 415/434-3883. Fax 415/434-3886. 72 rms. $49–$75 double. MC, V. Parking $11.50. Cable car: Powell–Hyde and Powell–Mason lines.* You won't find any free little bottles of shampoo here, just cheap accommodations and basic—and we mean basic—rooms right in the middle of Union Square/Chinatown. Many of the small rooms overlook Chinatown's main street. Corner rooms on higher floors are both larger and brighter. No visitors are permitted after 11pm.

**Holiday Lodge & Garden Hotel.** *1901 Van Ness Ave. (between Clay and Washington sts.), San Francisco, CA 94109.* ☎ *415/776-4469. Fax 415/474-7046. 75 rms (12 with kitchenettes), 2 suites. $99–$109 double; $119 double with kitchenette; $125–$135 suite. AE, DC, DISC, MC, V. Free parking. Cable car: Powell–Hyde line. Bus: 42, 47, 49.* Decorated in what could be called tropical contemporary style, this property centers on the outdoor heated pool and courtyard. The modern rooms were recarpeted in 1996 and contain a TV with HBO. Kids are welcomed with coloring books, crayons, board games, and rubber ducks for the tub. The hotel has a concierge, laundry/valet, and masseuse.

**Hotel Bedford.** *761 Post St. (between Leavenworth and Jones sts.), San Francisco, CA 94109.* ☎ *800/227-5642 or 415/673-6040. Fax 415/563-6739. 137 rms, 7 suites. $109–$129 double; from $175 suite. AE, CB, DC, JCB, MC, V. Parking $18. Cable car: Powell–Hyde and Powell–Mason lines (4 blocks east). Bus: 2, 3, 4, 27.* For the price and location (3 blocks from Union Square), the Bedford offers a great deal. You won't be paying for lavish furniture, but you will find clean, large, sunny rooms (many with terrific views), each furnished with a VCR, desk, and armchair. The staff is incredibly enthusiastic. Conveniences include a bar, restaurant, video library, and free morning limousine to financial district.

✪ **Hotel Bohème.** *444 Columbus St. (between Vallejo and Green sts.), San Francisco, CA 94133.* ☎ *415/433-9111. Fax 415/362-6292. 15 rms. $130 double. AE, DC, DISC, MC, V. Parking $20 at nearby public garage. Cable car: Powell–Mason line. Bus: 12, 15, 30, 41, 45, 83.* Although located on the busiest strip in North Beach, this recently renovated hotel feels more like a prestigious Nob Hill home. The rooms are small but hopelessly romantic, with gauze-draped canopies. It's a few steps to some of the greatest cafes and shops in the city; Union Square is within walking distance.

**Hotel Diva.** *440 Geary St. (between Mason and Taylor sts.), San Francisco, CA 94102.* ☎ *800/553-1900 or 415/885-0200. Fax 415/346-6613. 98 rms, 12 suites. $135 double; $155 junior suite; $300 villa suite. AE, DC, DISC, JCB, MC, V. Parking $17. Bus: 38, 38L.* Appropriately named, the Diva is the prima donna of San Francisco's modern hotels and one of our favorites. A stunning profusion of curvaceous glass, marble, and steel mark the Euro-tech lobby, while the rooms—each spotless and neat—are softened with utterly fashionable "Italian Modern" furnishings. Reserve a room ending in '09—they have extra-large bathrooms. VCRs, Nintendo, and complimentary breakfast in your room. Valet parking, fitness and business centers are available.

✪ **Hotel Majestic.** *1500 Sutter St. (between Octavia and Gough sts.), San Francisco, CA 94109.* ☎ *800/869-8966 or 415/441-1100. Fax 415/673-7331. 51 rms, 9 suites. $135–$170 double; from $260 suite. AE, DC, MC, V. Parking $14. Bus: 2, 3, 4.* Built in 1902, the Majestic meets every professional need while retaining the ambiance of a luxurious Old World hotel. Rooms are furnished with French and English antiques, including a large four-poster canopy bed, custom-made mirrored armoires, and antique reproductions. Conveniences include a full-size, well-lit desk. Some rooms also have fireplaces. Conveniences include a bar, restaurant, laundry/valet, concierge, complimentary newspaper, and afternoon sherry.

**Hotel Milano.** *55 Fifth St. (between Market and Mission sts.), San Francisco, CA 94103.* ☎ *800/398-7555 or 415/543-8555. Fax 415/543-5843. 108 rms. $129–$189 double. AE, DC, JCB, MC, V. Parking $19. Bus: All Market St. routes.* Contemporary Italian design, simple and elegantly streamlined rooms, and a central location make Hotel Milano a popular choice for tourists and businesspeople alike. Guest rooms feature everything a business executive could want—from fax/computer modem hookups to a Nintendo game system. Some have spa tub, bidet, double lavatories, and VCR. The hotel also has a restaurant, concierge, laundry/valet, fitness center and spa, and business center.

○ **Hotel Monaco.** *501 Geary St. (at Taylor St.), San Francisco, CA 94102.* ☎ *800/214-4220 or 415/292-0100. Fax 415/292-0111. 177 rooms, 24 suites. From $170 double; from $295 suite. AE, DC, DISC, JCB, MC, V. Parking $20. Bus: 2, 3, 4, 27, 38.* This remodeled 1910 beaux-arts building debuted in June 1995 and is the new diva of Union Square luxury hotels. Most rooms are too small, but the decor makes this our favorite luxury hotel in the city. The hotel's restaurant, the Grand Cafe, is the best hotel dining room downtown. Extras include computers, complimentary wine hour nightly, concierge, secretarial services, extensive health club and spa.

**Hotel Triton.** *342 Grant Ave. (at Bush St.), San Francisco, CA 94108.* ☎ *800/433-6611 or 415/394-0500. Fax 415/394-0555. 140 rms, 7 suites. $119–179 double; $199–279 suite. AE, DC, DISC, MC, V. Parking $20. Cable car: Powell–Hyde and Powell–Mason lines (2 blocks west).* Hotelier Bill Kimpton asked a cadre of local artists and designers to "do their thing"; the result was San Francisco's first three-star hotel to finally break the boring barrier. Described as vogue, chic, retro-futuristic, and even neo-Baroque, the Triton is stylish, though far from perfect; the service could be snappier. Facilities include a restaurant, laundry, business center, and exercise room.

**Huntington Hotel.** *1075 California St. (between Mason and Taylor sts.), San Francisco, CA 94108.* ☎ *800/227-4683, 800/652-1539 in California, or 415/474-5400. Fax 415/474-6227. 110 rms, 30 suites. $190–$240 double; $290–$790 suite. AE, CB, DC, MC, V. Parking $19.50. Cable car: California St. line (direct stop). Bus: 1.* One of the kings of Nob Hill, the stately, family-owned Huntington Hotel has long been a favorite retreat for Hollywood stars and political VIPs who desire privacy and security, not pomp and circumstance. The petite lobby belies large guest rooms decorated in French-style furnishings with views of the city. The hotel has a restaurant, lounge, concierge, complimentary limousine to the Financial District and Union Square, laundry, and access to an off-premises health club and spa.

○ **Prescott Hotel.** *545 Post St. (between Mason and Taylor sts.), San Francisco, CA 94102.* ☎ *800/283-7322 or 415/563-0303. Fax 415/563-6831. 167 rms, 35 suites. $175 double; from $265 suite. AE, CB, DC, MC, V. Parking $21. Cable car: Powell–Hyde and Powell–Mason lines. Bus: 2, 3, 4, 30, 38, 45.* The Prescott has always been one of our favorite hotels in San Francisco. The staff treats you like royalty, the rooms are beautiful and immaculate, the location—1 block from Union Square—is perfect, and room service is provided by Postrio, one of the best restaurants in the city. Extras include a concierge, limousine service to Financial District, same-day valet/laundry service, and access to an off-premises health club. There is no restaurant, but the hotel provides preferred seating at Postrio Restaurant.

○ **Ritz-Carlton San Francisco.** *600 Stockton St. (between Pine and California sts.), San Francisco, CA 94108.* ☎ *800/241-3333 or 415/296-7465. Fax 415/296-0288. 292 rms, 44 suites. $275 double; $395 club-level double; from $575 suite. AE, CB, DC, DISC, MC, V. Parking $27. Cable car: Powell–Hyde and Powell–Mason lines.* The Ritz-Carlton has been ranked among the top hotels in the world since it opened in this Nob Hill landmark building in 1991. The rooms offer every possible service and amenity, including Italian marble bathrooms with double sinks. The more expensive rooms have great views of the city. The ○ **Ritz Carlton Dining Room** will treat you like royalty, and is known for its outstanding California/French cuisine. There's a concierge, child care, business center, and outstanding fitness center with pool.

**San Francisco International Hostel.** *Fort Mason, Building 240 Fort Mason, San Francisco, CA 94123.* ☎ *415/771-7277. Fax 415/771-1468. 155 beds. $13–$15* *bed. MC, V.* Unbelievable but true: bay views for a mere $13–$15 nightly. The hostel provides dorm-style accommodations for 155 guests (three or four to a room), and offers easy access to the marina's shops and restaurants. Communal space includes a fireplace, pool table, kitchen, dining room, laundry facilities, and free parking.

**Tuscan Inn.** *425 North Point St. (at Mason St.), San Francisco, CA 94133.* ☎ *800/ 648-4626 or 415/561-1100. Fax 415/561-1199. 209 rms, 12 suites. $165–$198 double; $218–$258 suite. AE, DC, DISC, MC, V. Parking $13. Cable car: Powell–Mason line. Bus: 42, 15, 32.* Like an island of respectability in a sea of touristy schlock, the Tuscan exudes a level of style and comfort far beyond its neighbors. Each room is equipped with desks, armchairs, and handsome bedspreads. The only drawback is the lack of scenic views; a small price for a good hotel in a great location. The inn has an adjoining restaurant, concierge, and laundry; the valet parking here is cheaper than any nearby garage.

**Westin St. Francis.** *335 Powell St. (between Geary and Post sts.), San Francisco, CA 94102.* ☎ *800/228-3000 or 415/397-7000. Fax 415/774-0124. 1,192 rms, 83 suites. Main building, $209–$290 double; from $295 suite. Tower, $300–$375 double; from $550 suite. AE, DC, DISC, JCB, MC, V. Parking $24. Cable car: Powell–Hyde and Powell–Mason lines (direct stop). Bus: 2, 3, 4, 30, 45, 76.* Emperor Hirohito, Queen Elizabeth II, and every U.S. president since Taft have stayed at this world-class hotel. The 32-story Tower was added in 1972, doubling the capacity and adding the requisite conference centers. Rooms in the main building have more charm; Tower rooms above the 18th floor have tremendous views. Facilities include four restaurants, laundry, Westin Kids Club, fitness center, business center, and barber/beauty salon.

**BED & BREAKFASTS**   One of the most delightful B&Bs in California, the **Union Street Inn,** 2229 Union St. (between Fillmore and Steiner streets), San Francisco, CA 94123 (☎ **415/346-0424;** fax 415/922-8046), is a two-story Edwardian fronting the perpetually busy Union Street, but it's as quiet as a church on the inside. All individually decorated rooms are comfortably furnished with canopied or brass beds with down comforters, fresh flowers, bay windows, and private baths (some with Jacuzzi tubs).

While it lacks the casual ambience of neighboring Union Street Inn, the ✪ **Bed & Breakfast Inn,** 4 Charlton Court (off Union Street, between Buchanan and Laguna streets), San Francisco, CA 94123 (☎ **415/921-9784**), is loaded with charm. This trio of Victorian houses, all gussied up in English country style, hides in a cul-de-sac off Union Street.

Reminiscent of a traditional English inn right down to the cucumber sandwiches served during afternoon tea, the comely **Washington Square Inn,** 1660 Stockton St. (between Filbert and Union streets), San Francisco, CA 94133 (☎ **800/388-0220** or 415/981-4220; fax 415/397-7242), is ideal for those who prefer a quiet refuge amid the bustle of North Beach. Not all rooms here have air-conditioning and TVs.

For more choices, **Bed and Breakfast International,** P.O. Box 282910, San Francisco, CA 94128 (☎ **800/872-4500** or 415/696-1690; fax 415/696-1699; World Wide Web: **http://www.bbintl.com**), offers a selection of B&Bs ranging from $60 to $150 per night, with a 2-night minimum. Accommodations range from simple rooms in private homes to luxurious, full-service carriage houses, houseboats, and Victorian homes.

## DINING

San Francisco diners spend more money eating out than those in any other city in the nation. And at last count they had more than 3,000 reasons to avoid cooking at home. The city is blessed with a cornucopia of cuisines. Afghan, Cajun, Burmese, Jewish, Moroccan, Persian, Cambodian, vegan—whatever you're in the mood for tonight, this town has it covered. Note that at the most popular and most expensive restaurants, you will need to make reservations several weeks in advance.

✪ **Alain Rondelli.** *126 Clement St. (between Second and Third aves.).* ☎ *415/ 387-0408. Reservations necessary Fri–Sat. Main courses $19–$23; tasting menu from $52. MC, V. Tues–Sun 5:30–10:30pm. Bus: 2, 38. FRENCH.* Chef Rondelli dishes up an innovative gastronomic experience you're likely to dream about for years to come. Choose from the 6-, 9-, 12-, or 20-course tasting menus (for the entire table only). To complete the experience, wine can be ordered by the half glass.

✪ **Aqua.** *252 California St. (between Battery and Front sts.).* ☎ *415/956-9662. Reservations recommended. Main courses $26–$32; six-course tasting menu $65; vegetarian tasting menu $45. AE, DC, MC, V. Mon–Fri 11:30am–2pm; Mon–Sat 5:30–10:30pm. Bus: all Market St. routes. SEAFOOD.* Without question, Aqua is San Francisco's finest seafood restaurant. The salmon, for example, is glazed in ginger, then spiced with sweet orange marmalade that contrasts perfectly with the sour reduction sauce of braised red cabbage. The chocolate tasting dessert plate is a feast for the eyes as well as the palate.

**Bix.** *56 Gold St. (between Sansome and Montgomery sts.).* ☎ *415/433-6300. Reservations recommended. Main courses $5–$12 at lunch, $11–$25 at dinner. AE, CB, DC, DISC, MC, V. Mon–Thurs 11:30am–11pm, Fri–Sat 11:30am–midnight, Sun 5–10pm. Bus: 15, 30, 41, 45. CALIFORNIA.* Bix is best known for its martinis, but its menu isn't bad either. Massive silver columns and deco-style lighting set the stage for dancing to live music, though most locals settle for chatting with the friendly bartenders. The lobster linguine with fresh prawns and mussels in a sun-dried tomato broth is the undisputed favorite.

**Bizou.** *598 Fourth St. (at Brannan St.).* ☎ *415/543-2222. Reservations recommended. Main courses $10.50–$17.50. AE, MC, V. Mon–Fri 11:30am–2:30pm; Mon–Thurs 5:30–10pm, Fri–Sat 5:30–10:30pm. Bus: 15, 30, 32, 42, 45. FRENCH/ITALIAN.* Bizou's friendly and professional waiters, fresh and creative fare, and sizable portions keep locals coming back. Starters include pizzas or grilled calamari with a citrus salsa; main courses include a sautéed sea bass with olive couscous. Our only complaint is that literally every dish is extremely rich, even the salads.

✪ **Boulevard.** *1 Mission St. (at Embarcadero and Stewart sts.).* ☎ *415/543-6084. Reservations recommended. Main courses $17.75–$22. AE, DC, MC, V. Mon–Fri 11:30am–2pm; daily 5:30–10:30pm. Bus: 15, 30, 32, 42, 45. AMERICAN.* Art nouveau interior-vaulted brick ceilings, floral-design banquettes, and fluid, tulip-shaped lamps set a dramatic scene for equally impressive dishes. Start with the delicate, soft egg ravioli with spinach, ricotta, and shaved white truffles, then embark on wood oven–roasted sea bass on a bed of sun-dried tomatoes and roasted garlic mashed potatoes.

**Cha Cha Cha.** *1801 Haight St. (at Schrader St.).* ☎ *415/386-5758. Reservations not accepted. Tapas $4–$7; main courses $9–$13. No credit cards. Mon–Sun 11:30am– 4pm; Sun–Thurs 5–11pm, Fri–Sat 5–11:30pm. Bus: 6, 7, 66, 71, 73. Muni Metro: N line. CARIBBEAN.* The hour-long wait for a table is just part of the party atmosphere at this festive, loud (and we mean loud) restaurant. Dine amid Santeria altars, banana trees, and plastic, tropical tablecloths while you sample fried calamari, fried new potatoes, or Cajun shrimp from the extensive family-style tapas menu.

✪ **Fleur de Lys.** *777 Sutter St. (at Jones St.).* ☎ *415/673-7779. Reservations required. Main courses $29–$35; five-course tasting menu $65; four-course vegetarian menu $55. AE, CB, DC, MC, V. Mon–Thurs 6–10pm, Fri–Sat 5:30–10:30pm. Bus 2, 3, 4, 27, 38. FRENCH.* Imagine a life-size *I Dream of Jeannie* bottle: dark, cozy, with 700 yards of floor-to-ceiling fabric enclosing the room. Throw in 20 tables and well-dressed diners—wear a dinner jacket—and voilà!: one of San Francisco's most renowned dining rooms. The food may even surpass the decor; desserts are sumptuous.

✪ **Fringale Restaurant.** *570 Fourth St. (between Brannan and Bryant sts.).* ☎ *415/543-0573. Reservations recommended at least a week in advance. Main courses*

$9–$18; lunch $4–$12. AE, MC, V. Mon–Fri 11:30am–2:30pm; Mon–Sat 5:30–10:30pm. Bus: 30, 45. FRENCH.* Fringale, French for "sudden urge to eat," has enjoyed a week-long waiting list since it opened. The dining room's serene atmosphere is all but shattered, though, when the 15-table room inevitably fills with fans of chef Gerald Hirigoyen's potato and goat cheese galette with black olives, or fillet of tuna basquaise.

**Greens Restaurant, Fort Mason.** *Building A, Fort Mason Center (enter Fort Mason opposite the Safeway at Buchanan and Marina sts.).* ☎ *415/771-6222. Reservations recommended 2 weeks in advance. Main courses $10–$13; fixed-priced dinner $38; brunch $7–$10. DISC, MC, V. Mon–Sat 8am–9pm, Sun 9am–2pm. Bakery, Tues–Sat 9:30am–4:30pm, Sun 10am–3pm. Bus: 28, 30. VEGETARIAN.* Executive chef Annie Somerville cooks with the seasons, using local organic produce, in this old warehouse with enormous windows overlooking the bay. A weeknight dinner might feature such appetizers as grilled asparagus with lemon, Parmesan cheese, and watercress. Main courses might include spring vegetable risotto with asparagus, peas, and shiitake and crimini mushrooms.

**Harris'.** *2100 Van Ness Ave. (at Pacific Ave.).* ☎ **415/673-1888.** *Reservations recommended. Main courses $18–$30. AE, CB, DC, DISC, JCB, MC, V. Mon–Fri 6–11pm, Sat–Sun 5–11pm. Bus: 38, 45. AMERICAN.* Proprietor Ann Lee Harris knows steaks; she grew up on a cattle ranch and married the owner of the largest feedlot in California. The restaurant's steaks, which hang in a glass-windowed aging room, are cut thick—either New York style or T-bone—and served with a baked potato and seasonal vegetables.

**Hawthorn Lane.** *22 Hawthorn Lane (at Howard St. between Second and Third sts.).* ☎ *415/777-9779. Reservations recommended. Main courses $9.50–$13 lunch, $19.50–$24 dinner. CB, DC, DISC, JCB, MC, V. Jacket appropriate but not required. Mon–Fri 11:30am–2pm, Sun–Thurs 5:30–10pm. BART: Montgomery Station. Muni Metro: F, J, K, L, M, N. Bus: 12, 30, 45, 76. CALIFORNIA.* Anne and David Gingrass's seasonal menus reflect the Asian and European influences that made them famous under Wolfgang Puck. The dining room is not too fancy or pretentious, but it's the food that people come for. The bread alone is worth writing home about. If it's available, don't miss the black cod appetizer served with a miso glaze and spinach rolls.

**Hayes Street Grill.** *320 Hayes St. (near Franklin St.).* ☎ *415/863-5545. Reservations recommended. Main courses $14–$18. AE, DC, MC, V. Mon–Fri 11:30am–2pm and 5–8:30pm, Sat 6–10:30pm, Sun 5–8:30pm. Bus: 19, 31, 38. SEAFOOD.* This small, no-nonsense seafood restaurant has built a solid reputation among San Francisco's picky epicureans for its impeccably fresh fish. Choices ranging from Hawaiian swordfish to Puget Sound salmon—cooked to perfection, naturally—are matched with your sauce of choice: Szechuan peanut, tomato salsa, herb shallot butter, etc.

**Hong Kong Flower Lounge.** *5322 Geary Blvd. (between 17th and 18th aves.).* ☎ *415/668-8998. Most main dishes $6–$11; dim sum dishes $1.20–$3.20. Mon–Fri 11am–2:30pm, Sat–Sun 10am–2:30pm; daily 5–9:30pm. Bus: 1, 2, 38. CHINESE/ DIM SUM.* You know you're at a good Chinese restaurant when most customers are Chinese. But expect to wait in line, because you're not the only one who's heard this is the best dim sum in town. Every little dish is so darn good. Don't pass up tarot cake, salt-fried shrimp, or shark-fin soup.

**House of Nanking.** *919 Kearny St. (at Columbus Ave.).* ☎ *415/421-1429. Reservations not accepted. Main courses $4.95–$7.95. No credit cards. Mon–Fri 11am–10pm, Sat noon–10pm, Sun 4–10pm. Bus: 9, 12, 15, 30. CHINESE.* This inconspicuous little shoebox of a diner is one of San Francisco's worst-kept secrets. Legions wait up to an hour for the best potstickers we've ever tasted, or for chef/owner Peter Fang's signature shrimp-and-green-onion pancake served with peanut sauce. The tight seating and lack-luster service are all part of the Nanking experience.

**Kabuto Sushi.** *5116 Geary Blvd. (at 15th Ave.).* ☎ *415/752-5652. Sushi $3–$8; main courses $12–$20. AE, MC, V. Tues–Sat 5:30–11pm. Bus: 2, 28, 38. JAPANESE.* Kabuto is one of the best (and most expensive) sushi houses in town. Chef Sachio Kojima, who presides over the small, ever-crowded sushi bar, constructs each dish with smooth, lightning-fast movements known only to master chefs. If you're big on wasabe, ask for the stronger stuff Kojima serves on request.

✪ **La Folie.** *2316 Polk St. (between Green and Union sts.).* ☎ *415/776-5577. Reservations recommended. Main courses $22–$28; five-course tasting menu $45. AE, DC, JCB, MC, V. Mon–Sat 5:30–10:30pm. Bus: 19, 41, 45, 47, 49, 76. FRENCH.* The minute you walk in, you'll know why this is many locals' favorite restaurant. The country French decor is tasteful but not too serious, the staff is friendly and knowledgeable, and the food is outstanding. Try the roti of quail and squab stuffed with wild mushrooms, wrapped in crispy potato strings.

**Lulu.** *816 Folsom St. (at Fourth St.).* ☎ *415/495-5775. Reservations recommended. Main courses $7–$13 at lunch, $9–$17 at dinner. AE, MC, V. Mon–Fri 7am–midnight, Sat 9am–midnight, Sun 9am–11pm. Bus: 15, 30, 32, 42, 45. CONTINENTAL.* The energy of this enormous, converted warehouse, the pizzas sliding in and out of the wood-fired oven, and the chefs communicating via headsets makes every meal an event. Everything is served family style and is meant to be shared. Don't pass up the roasted mussels, piled high on an iron skillet.

**Mario's Bohemian Cigar Store.** *566 Columbus Ave.* ☎ *415/362-0536. Sandwiches $5–$6. No credit cards. Daily 10am–11pm. Closed Dec 24–Jan 1. Bus: 15, 30, 41, 45. ITALIAN.* The small, well-worn, and perpetually busy century-old bar is best known for its focaccia sandwiches, including meatball or eggplant. Wash it all down with an excellent cappuccino or a house Campari as you watch the tourists stroll by. And no, they don't sell cigars.

✪ **Masa's.** *In the Hotel Vintage Court, 648 Bush St. (at Stockton St.).* ☎ *415/ 989-7154. Reservations required; accepted up to 21 days in advance. Main courses $30–$40; fixed-price dinner $70–$75. AE, CB, DC, DISC, MC, V. Tues–Sat 6–9:30pm. Closed first week in Jan and fourth week in July. Cable Car: Powell–Mason and Powell–Hyde lines. Bus: 2, 3, 4, 30, 45. FRENCH.* Dinner here is a memorable experience, matched by memorable prices, whether you order à la carte or from the fixed-price menu. The service is exemplary (even unpretentious), and the wine list is flawless, making this one of the best French restaurants in San Francisco, and perhaps the entire country.

✪ **Pane e Vino.** *3011 Steiner St. (at Union St.).* ☎ *415/346-2111. Reservations recommended. Main courses $10–$18. AE, MC, V. Mon–Sat 11:30am–2:30pm; daily 5–10pm. Bus: 41, 45. ITALIAN.* This is one of San Francisco's most authentic Italian restaurants. The food is consistently excellent, the prices reasonable, and the mostly Italian-accented staff always smooth and efficient. The two small dining rooms, separated by an open kitchen emanating heavenly aromas, offer only limited seating, so expect a wait even if you have reservations.

**PlumpJack Café.** *3127 Fillmore St. (between Filbert and Greenwich sts.).* ☎ *415/ 563-4755. Reservations recommended. Main courses $14–$20. AE, MC, V. Mon–Fri 11:30am–2pm and 5:30–10:30pm, Sat 5:30–10:30pm. Bus: 41, 45. CALIFORNIA/ MEDITERRANEAN.* Wildly popular among San Francisco's style-setters, this small Cow Hollow restaurant is the *in* place to dine. The food is just plain good and the whimsical decor is a veritable work of art. Though the menu changes weekly, you might find dishes like roasted portobello mushroom with vegetable stuffing and cippolini onions.

✪ **Postrio.** *545 Post St. (between Mason and Taylor sts.).* ☎ *415/776-7825. Reservations required. Main courses $6–$15 at breakfast, $14–$15 at lunch, $20–$26 at dinner. AE, CB, DC, DISC, MC, V. Mon–Fri 7–10am, 11:30am–2pm, and 5:30–10:30pm; Sat–Sun 9am–2pm. Bar, daily 11:30am–2am. Cable car: Powell–Mason and Powell–Hyde lines. Bus: 2, 3, 4, 38. INTERNATIONAL.* When chefs Anne and David Gingrass departed, rumors began that San Francisco's top restaurant was no longer what it once was. But you'd never guess by the nightly packed house that comes as much for the atmosphere as for the Italian/Asian/French/California cuisine. The perpetually happening bar fronts an antebellum staircase down to the cavernous dining room.

**Rumpus.** *One Tillman Place (off Grant Ave., between Sutter and Post sts.).* ☎ *415/421-2300. Reservations recommended. Main courses $12–$17. AE, DC, MC, V. Mon–Sat 11:30am–2:30pm; Sun–Thurs 5:30–10pm, Fri–Sat 5:30–11pm. CALIFORNIA.* Rumpus is a fantastic new restaurant serving well-prepared California fare at reasonable prices. It's architecturally playful, and usually buzzing with the conversations of friends dining together. The pan-roasted chicken has a delightfully crispy and flavorful crust. The pudding-like chocolate brioche cake is one of the best desserts we've ever had.

**Scala's Bistro.** *In Sir Francis Drake Hotel, 432 Powell St. (at Sutter St.).* ☎ *415/395-8555. Reservations recommended. Breakfast $6–$9; lunch and dinner main courses $8–$17. AE, CB, DC, DISC, MC, V. Mon–Sun 6:30am–midnight. Cable car: Powell–Hyde line. Bus: 2, 3, 4, 30, 45, 76. FRENCH/ITALIAN.* Giovanni (the host) and his wife Donna (the chef) Scala have created one of the best new restaurants in the city. The Parisian bistro/Old World atmosphere blends just the right balance of elegance and informality. And Donna's fantastic array of Italian and French dishes (don't miss the seared salmon) have surprisingly low prices.

**Swan Oyster Depot.** *1517 Polk St. (between California and Sacramento sts.).* ☎ *415/673-1101. Reservations not accepted. Seafood cocktails $5–$8, clams and oysters on the half shell $6–$7.50 per half dozen. No credit cards. Mon–Sat 8am–5:30pm. Bus: 27. SEAFOOD.* Almost 85 years old and looking even older, this hole-in-the-wall with the city's friendliest servers is little more than a fish market that decided to slap down some stools. Most patrons come for the oysters or a cup of chowder. The menu is limited to fresh crab, shrimp, oysters, clams, chowder, and Maine lobster.

**Tadich Grill.** *240 California St. (between Battery and Front sts.).* ☎ *415/391-1849. Reservations not accepted. Main courses $12–$19. MC, V. Mon–Fri 11am–9:30pm, Sat 11:30am–9:30pm. Muni Metro: all Market St. trams. Bus: all Market St. routes. SEAFOOD.* This venerated California institution arrived with the Gold Rush in 1849 and claims to be the first to broil seafood over mesquite charcoal, back in the early 1920s. The charcoal-broiled petrale sole with butter sauce is a local favorite. Almost everyone gets a side order of big, tasty french fries.

**Zinzino.** *2355 Chestnut St. (at Divisadero St.).* ☎ *415/346-6623. Reservations for six or more only. Main courses $4–$9 at brunch, $9–$17 at lunch and dinner. MC, V. Tues–Fri 5:30–10pm; Sat–Sun 10am–4pm and 5:30–10pm. Bus: 22, 30. ITALIAN.* The Italian movie posters, magazines, and furnishings at this cavernous restaurant evoke memories of past vacations, but we rarely recall the food in Italy being this good or this cheap. Start with roasted jumbo prawns wrapped in crisp pancetta, or proceed directly to the eggplant and Italian sausage pizza.

✪ **Zuni Café.** *1658 Market St. (at Franklin St.).* ☎ *415/552-2522. Reservations recommended. Main courses $16–$22.50. AE, MC, V. Tues–Sat 7:30am–midnight, Sun 7:30am–11pm. Bus: 6, 7, 71, 75. Muni Metro: all Market St. trams. MEDITERRANEAN.* Despite its snotty waiters, Zuni Café is still one of our favorite lunch spots. Its expanse of windows and prime Market Street location guarantee good people-watching. For the full effect, sit at the bustling bar and peruse the foot-long oyster menu. The ever-changing menu always includes meat and fish, grilled in the brick oven.

## SAN FRANCISCO AFTER DARK

For a city with fewer than a million inhabitants, San Francisco's overall artistic enterprise is nothing short of phenomenal. The city's opera is justifiably world renowned, the ballet is well respected, and the theaters are high in both quantity and quality. Dozens of piano bars and top-notch lounges are augmented by one of the best dance club cultures this side of New York. And skyscraper lounges offer some of the most dazzling city views in the world. To find out what's hot, check the *San Francisco Bay Guardian* and the *San Francisco Weekly,* available free at bars and restaurants, and from streetcorner boxes. Also check the Sunday edition of the *San Francisco Chronicle,* which contains a "Datebook" section.

**Tix Bay Area,** Stockton Street between Post and Geary (☎ 415/433-7827), sells half-price tickets to theater, dance, and music performances on the day of the show only starting at 11am. Tickets to most theater and dance events can also be obtained through **City Box Office,** 153 Kearny St., Suite 402 (☎ 415/392-4400), and **BASS Ticketmaster** (☎ 510/762-2277). You can also try **Wherehouse** stores throughout the city; the most convenient is at 30 Powell St.

**THE PERFORMING ARTS** Acclaimed by the *New York Times* as "the country's leading early-music orchestra," the **Philharmonia Baroque Orchestra** (☎ 415/391-5252) performs usually at Herbst Theatre from September to April. And the **San Francisco Contemporary Music Players** (☎ 415/978-ARTS) feature modern chamber works by international artists. Founded in 1911, the internationally respected ✪ **San Francisco Symphony**—now under the baton of Michael Tilson Thomas—performs at Louise M. Davies Hall, 201 Van Ness Ave. (☎ 415/864-6000). The season runs from September to May. Summer symphony activities include a Composer Festival and a Summer Pops series.

The ✪ **San Francisco Opera** (☎ 415/864-3330) was the first municipal opera in the United States and is one of the city's cultural icons. It features celebrated stars, along with promising newcomers, in traditional and avant-garde productions, all with English supertitles. The season starts in September and runs 14 weeks, with nightly performances (except on Monday) and matinees on Sunday.

The ✪ **American Conservatory Theater (ACT)** troupe, based in the Geary Theater, 415 Geary St. (☎ 415/749-2228), has been compared to the British National Theatre, the Berliner Ensemble, and the Comédie Française. The season runs from October through May and features both classical and experimental works. San Francisco's top African-American theater group performs at the 300-seat **Lorraine Hansberry Theatre** in the Sheehan Hotel, 620 Sutter St. (☎ 415/474-8800). Special adaptations from literature are performed along with contemporary dramas, classics, and world premieres. Check the daily or weekly papers to see current productions at the city's dozens of other theaters.

Winner of high international praise, the ✪ **San Francisco Ballet** (☎ 415/861-5600 or 415/865-2000) is the oldest permanent ballet company in the United States. Under the artistic direction of Helgi Tomasson, the company performs an eclectic repertoire of full-length neoclassical and contemporary ballets. The season opens with performances of *The Nutcracker* in December and continues through May.

**CLUBS** The hippest dance places are South of Market Street (SoMa), in former warehouses, but the most popular music and cafe culture is still centered in North Beach.

A San Francisco tradition, **Beach Blanket Babylon,** at Club Fugazi, 678 Green St. (☎ 415/421-4222), is a comedic musical send-up, best known for its outrageous costumes and oversize headdresses. It's been playing almost 22 years now and still sells out. **Bay Area Theatresports (BATS),** Bayfront Theater at the Fort Mason Center, Bldg. B, Third Floor (☎ 415/824-8220), is an improvisational tournament, in which four-actor teams compete against each other. Monday only. For more than 50 years, **Finnochio's,** 506 Broadway (☎ 415/982-9388), a family-run cabaret club, has showcased the best female impersonators in a funny, kitschy show, nightly Thurs–Sat.

New Orleans–style **Slim's,** 333 11th St. (☎ 415/522-0333), is co-owned by Boz Scaggs, who sometimes takes the stage under the name "Presidio Slim." This glitzy restaurant/bar seats 300, serves California cuisine, and specializes in homegrown rock, jazz, blues, and alternative music. At **Cesar's Latin Palace,** 3140 Mission St. (☎ 415/648-6611), live Latin bands perform to a very mixed crowd. **Jazz at Pearl's,** 256 Columbus Ave. (☎ 415/291-8255), is one of the best venues for jazz in the city.

The dance club scene is always changing. Most of the venues below are promoted as different clubs on various nights of the week, each with its own look, sound, and style. **Club DV8,** 540 Howard St. (☎ 415/777-1419 or 415/957-1730), attracts the black-garb crowd where two deejays spin music on separate dance floors. Dance floors on three levels have made **Club Ten 15,** 1015 Folsom St. (☎ 415/431-1200), a stylish stop along the nightclub circuit. The labyrinthine **Paradise Lounge,** 1501 Folsom St. (☎ 415/861-6906), features three dance floors simultaneously vibrating to different beats, with smaller spaces devoted to pool tables and to poetry readings. **Blues,** 2125 Lombard St. (at Fillmore St.) (☎ 415/771-BLUE), has mostly a local crowd. The bands are pretty good and easy to dance to. Cover is $5–$6. **181 Eddy,** 181 Eddy St. at Taylor (☎ 415/673-8181), a dark retro club crammed with twenty-somethings looking to gyrate the night, has a combination of great ambience, decent food, and throw-down funk and acid jazz. Early evening there's live entertainment and later a DJ spinning slamming old-school. Cover is $5–$10.

**BARS** The city's best bars include some of the following: **Edinburgh Castle,** 950 Geary St. (☎ 415/885-4074), a legendary Scottish pub known for unusual British ales on tap; **Gordon–Biersch Brewery,** on the Embarcadero, 2 Harrison St. (☎ 415/243-8246), a large brew-restaurant serving a tasty brew to a lively yuppie crowd; **Harry Denton's,** 161 Steuart St. (☎ 415/882-1333), filled with working "suits" and secretaries on the prowl early in the evening, who give way to a glitzier crowd after dinner. The front lounge features R&B or jazz performers while there's disco and pop dancing in the back room. **Johnny Love's,** 1500 Broadway (☎ 415/931-6053), is the city's quintessential singles bar. The magnificent **Redwood Room,** in the Clift Hotel, 495 Geary St. (☎ 415/775-4700), completely paneled by the wood of a single redwood tree, features a fabulous martini menu and a pianist who specializes in tunes from the 1930s and 1940s. **The Saloon,** 1232 Grant Ave. (at Vallejo St.) (☎ 415/989-7666), is an authentic Gold Rush survivor, the oldest extant bar in the city. It's popular with both bikers and daytime pinstripers; there's live blues nighly. Cover is $3–$5 Fri–Sat. The huge, upscale **20 Tank Brewery,** 316 11th St. (☎ 415/255-9455), is known for good ale, plus live jazz 2 nights a week.

**CAFES** At most North Beach cafes, patrons are encouraged to linger. **Caffè Greco,** 423 Columbus Ave. (☎ 415/397-6261), opened in the late 1980s and has quickly become one of the best such places. Opera is always on the jukebox at **Caffè Trieste,** 601 Vallejo St. (☎ 415/392-6739), a classic Italian coffeehouse, where on Saturday afternoon the family performs arias to the assembled crowd. **Vesuvio,** 255 Columbus Ave. (☎ 415/362-3370), is one of North Beach's best beatnik-style hangouts, popular with neighborhood writers, artists, and songsters, as well as longshoremen, cab drivers, and businesspeople. At **Savoy Tivoli,** 1434 Grant Ave. (☎ 415/362-7023), Euro-trash wannabes crowd the few pool tables and indoor and patio seating to smoke cigarettes and look cool. **Spec's,** 12 Saroyan Place (☎ 415/421-4112), is one of the liveliest and most likable pubs in North Beach.

**COCKTAILS & VIEWS**   Many of the top hotels offer cocktails high above the city, with magnificent views. The Fairmont Hotel's **Crown Room,** 950 Mason St., 24th Floor (☎ 415/772-5131), is definitely the plushest, reached by a trip via a glass elevator. The **Carnelian Room,** Bank of America Building, 555 California St. (☎ 415/433-7500), requires jackets and ties for men to partake of the view from the 52nd floor. **Harry Denton's Starlight Room,** Sir Francis Drake Hotel, 450 Powell St., 21st Floor (☎ 415/395-8595), features live swing and big-band tunes after dark in this classic 1930s San Francisco room. During World War II, countless Pacific-bound servicemen toasted their good-bye to the States at **Top of the Mark,** Mark Hopkins Hotel, California and Mason streets (☎ 415/392-3434). The glass-walled room with the unparalleled view was renovated in 1996.

**GAY & LESBIAN CLUBS**   San Francisco's gay life is centered in the Castro, with establishments also in SoMa, along Polk Street, and in the Mission. Check the *Bay Area Reporter* or the *San Francisco Bay Guardian* for more information about what's currently hot. The major lesbian community is in Oakland, though there are a few hangouts in San Francisco. **Alta Plaza,** 2301 Fillmore St. (☎ 415/922-1444), is where Pacific Heights's wealthy gays flock. **Badlands,** 4121 18th St. (☎ 415/626-9320), is a cruise bar popular with patrons clad in tight Levi's. A well-known gay hangout, **Castro Station,** 456 Castro St. (☎ 415/626-7220), is popular with the leather and Levi's crowd, and trendy boys from around the country show up here looking for action. **Detour,** 2348 Market St. (☎ 415/861-6053), attracts a young crowd of boys, with its low lighting and throbbing house music. **Metro,** 3600 16th St. (☎ 415/703-9750), seems to attract people of all ages who enjoy the friendly bartenders, the highly charged, cruisy atmosphere, and the best view of the Castro district from its large balcony. **The Mint,** 1942 Market St. (☎ 415/626-4726), is a gay and lesbian karaoke bar where show tunes reign. **The Stud,** 399 Ninth St. (☎ 415/863-6623), has been around for 30 years, is one of the most successful gay establishments in town, and is mellow enough for straights as well as gays.

## DAY TRIPS FROM SAN FRANCISCO

The Bay City is, without question, captivating, but don't let it ensnare you to the point of ignoring its environs. They contain a multitude of natural spectacles like Mount Tamalpais and Muir Woods; scenic communities like Tiburon and Sausalito; and cities like gritty Oakland and its youth-oriented next-door neighbor, Berkeley. A little farther north stretch the valleys of Napa, Sonoma, and Alexander, the finest wine region in the nation. From San Francisco you can reach any of these points in a few hours or less by car or public transport.

**ANGEL ISLAND & TIBURON**   A federal and state wildlife refuge, **Angel Island** is the largest islet in San Francisco Bay. The island has been, at various times, a prison, a quarantine station for immigrants, a missile base, and even a favorite site for duels. Nowadays, though, most of the people who visit here are content with picnicking on the large green lawn that fronts the docking area. Hiking, mountain biking, and guided tram tours are also popular options. Among the 12 miles of Angel Island's hiking and mountain-bike trails is the **Perimeter Road,** a partly paved path that circles the island and winds its way past disused troop barracks and other military buildings; several turn-offs lead up to the top of Mount Livermore, 776 feet above the bay. **Sea Trek** (☎ 415/488-1000) offers guided sea kayak tours around the island. The daylong trips include a catered lunch and combine the thrill of paddling with an informative, naturalist-led tour. All equipment is provided, kids are welcome, and no experience is necessary.

**Tiburon,** situated on a peninsula of the same name, looks like a cross between a fishing village and a Hollywood western set. This seacoast town rambles over a series of green hills and ends up at a spindly, multicolored pier on the waterfront, like a miniature Fisherman's Wharf. But in reality it's an extremely plush patch of yacht-club suburbia. **Main Street** is lined with ramshackle, color-splashed old frame houses that shelter chic boutiques, souvenir stores, antiques shops, and art galleries. Other roads are narrow, winding, and hilly, and lead up to dramatically situated homes with stunning (and stunningly expensive) views of San Francisco's skyline. For a taste of the Wine Country, stop in at **Windsor Vineyards,** 72 Main St. (☎ **800/214-9463** or 415/435-3113). Their Victorian tasting room, where 35 choices are available for free tasting, dates from 1888.

**Essentials:** Ferries of the **Blue and Gold Fleet** (☎ **800/229-2784,** or 415/546-2700 in California) leave from Fisherman's Wharf for both Angel Island and Tiburon on seasonal schedules. By car from San Francisco, take U.S. 101 to the Tiburon/Highway 131 exit, then follow Tiburon Boulevard all the way into town. The trip takes about 40 minutes. Catch the ferry (☎ **415/435-2131** or 415/388-6770) to Angel Island from the dock located at Tiburon Boulevard and Main Street.

**SAUSALITO**    Just off the northern end of the Golden Gate Bridge is the eclectic little town of Sausalito, a slightly Bohemian, nonchalant, and studiedly quaint adjunct to San Francisco. With approximately 7,500 residents, Sausalito feels rather like St-Tropez on the French Riviera—minus the starlets and the social rat race. It has its quota of paper millionaires, but they rub their permanently suntanned shoulders with a good number of hard-up artists, struggling authors, shipyard workers, and fishers. Next to the swank restaurants, plush bars, and antiques shops and galleries, you'll see hamburger joints, beer parlors, and secondhand bookstores. Sausalito's main touring strip is **Bridgeway,** which runs along the water, but those in the know make a quick detour to **Caledonia Street,** 1 block inland; not only is it less congested, there's a far better selection of cafes and shops. Above all, Sausalito has scenery and sunshine, for once you cross the Golden Gate Bridge you're out of the San Francisco fog patch and under blue California sky (we hope). Almost all the tourist action, which is almost singularly limited to window-shopping and eating, takes place at sea level on Bridgeway. For picnic fixin's, try one of these establishments: **Café Soleil,** 37 Caledonia St. (☎ **415/331-9355**), for soups, salads, and sandwiches, not to mention killer smoothies; **Caledonia Kitchen,** 400 Caledonia St. (☎ **415/331-0220**), a beautiful little cafe, serves a huge assortment of fresh salads, soups, chili, sandwiches, and inexpensive entrees; **Hamburgers,** 737 Bridgeway (☎ **415/332-9471**), which serves what you would imagine; **Stuffed Croissant, Etc.,** 43 Caledonia St. (☎ **415/332-7103**), where you can get anything from a snack to a meal; and **Venice Gourmet Delicatessen,** 625 Bridgeway (☎ **415/332-3544**), a classic old deli with all the makings for a superb picnic—wines, cheese, fruits, stuffed vine leaves, mushroom and artichoke salad, quiche, olives, and fresh-baked pastries.

**Essentials:** Ferries of the **Blue and Gold Fleet** (☎ **800/229-2784,** or 415/546-2700 in California) leave from Fisherman's Wharf on a seasonal schedule. By car from San Francisco, take U.S. 101 north, then the first right after the Golden Gate Bridge (Alexander exit). Alexander becomes Bridgeway in Sausalito.

**MUIR WOODS & MOUNT TAMALPAIS**    While the rest of Marin County's redwood forests were being devoured to feed the building spree in San Francisco around the turn of the century, the trees of **Muir Woods,** in a remote ravine on the flanks of **Mount Tamalpais,** escaped destruction in favor of easier pickings. The coast redwood, or *Sequoia sempervirens,* is the tallest tree in the immediate region, and the largest-known specimen towers 367.8 feet. Soaring toward the sky like a wooden cathedral, Muir Woods is unlike any other forest in the world. You can drive the 2,600 feet to the top of Mount Tam, as the locals call it, or hike along one of two clearly marked trails (one gentle, the other fairly rough) to the summit.

**Essentials:** Drive across the Golden Gate Bridge and take the exit for Calif. 1/Mount Tamalpais. Follow the Shoreline Highway about 2½ miles and turn onto the Panoramic Highway. After about 5½ miles, turn onto Pantoll Road and continue for about a mile to Ridgecrest Boulevard. Ridgecrest winds to a parking lot below East Peak. From there, it's a 15-minute hike up to the top. To get to Muir Woods, follow the Mount Tamalpais directions to the Panoramic Highway. After about a mile, take the signed turnoff and follow successive signs.

**POINT REYES NATIONAL SEASHORE**   The national seashore system was created to protect rural and undeveloped stretches of the coast from the pressures brought on by soaring real estate values and increasing population. Nowhere is the success of the system more evident than at Point Reyes. Comprised primarily of sand beach and scrubland, it's home to birds, sea lions, and a variety of tide-pool creatures. In November 1995, the Bay Area suffered a great loss when 12,000 acres of Point Reyes burned in an uncontrollable brush fire. However, there's still plenty of pristine property in this 65,000-acre park and even the areas that suffered the worst damage are quickly replenishing themselves. The park encompasses several surf-pounded beaches, bird estuaries, open swaths of land with roaming elk, and the **Point Reyes Lighthouse** (☎ 415/669-1534), a favorite among visitors who are awestruck by the spectacular views of the coast, wildflowers, and **gray whales** on their seasonal journey between Alaska and Baja. The 10,000 mile round-trip passes through here in December and January (southbound) and March (northbound). Come early, dress warmly, and bring bino-culars.

North and South **Point Reyes Beaches** face the Pacific and withstand the full brunt of ocean tides and winds, making the water much too rough for even wading. It's no longer illegal to enter the bone-chilling waters (thanks to a lawsuit by some persistent surfers), but it's still stupid. Along the south coast, **Drake's Beach's** waters can be as tranquil and serene as Point Reyes's are turbulent. Locals come here to sun and picnic and occasionally a hearty soul ventures into the cold waters of Drake's Bay. But a powerful weather front can turn wispy waves into torrential tides.

Park rangers conduct many different tours at Point Reyes, including a hike to the promontory overlooking **Chimney Rock** to see the sea lions, harbor seals, and seabirds; the **Limantour** wetlands, home to some of North America's most beautiful ducks; and a guided walk along the **San Andreas fault** to observe the site of the epicenter of the 1906 earthquake. Call the **Ranger Station** (☎ 415/663-1092) or request a copy of *Park Paper,* which includes a schedule of activities and other useful information.

**Essentials:** Cross the Golden Gate Bridge and stay on U.S. 101 North. Shortly before Corte Madera, turn left onto Sir Francis Drake Boulevard and drive 20 miles to Bear Valley Road. The information center is a half-mile down Bear Valley Road. To get to the infamous Point Reyes Lighthouse, return to Sir Francis Drake Boulevard and continue to its end at a parking lot. The lighthouse is a half-mile walk down a paved road.

## 2 The Wine Country

California's adjacent Napa and Sonoma valleys comprise one of the world's most famous wine-growing regions. Hundreds of wineries nestle among the vines of this beautiful countryside, and most welcome visitors to explore the winemaking process and sample their produce. Even if you can spend only a day, Napa and Sonoma are well worth the 90-minute drive up from San Francisco.

Unlike most tourist destinations, the Wine Country is still remarkably rural and has little in the way of public transportation. In order to truly explore the vicinity, you'll need a car. Most of the wineries, hotels, shops, and restaurants are located along two roads: Calif. 29, which starts at the mouth of the Napa River near the north end of San Francisco Bay and continues north through the Napa Valley; and Calif. 12, which runs through the Sonoma Valley.

## ESSENTIALS

**ARRIVING & DEPARTING**   There's no commercial airport in Napa, but United Express has flights to **Sonoma County Airport,** 6 miles north of Santa Rosa. Alternatively, you can fly to **San Francisco International Airport** and catch an **Evans Airport Service shuttle** (☎ 707/255-1559) to Napa or **Sonoma Airport Shuttle** (☎ 707/938-4246) to Sonoma.

Greyhound (☎ 800/231-2222) has bus service to Napa and Sonoma, but you'll still need a car to see the vineyards and other attractions.

**VISITOR INFORMATION**   In San Francisco, you can pick up free maps and brochures from the **Wine Institute,** 425 Market St., Suite 1000, San Francisco, CA 94105 (☎ 415/512-0151). Once you're here, stop at the **Napa Valley Conference and Visitor Bureau,** 1310 Town Center Mall, off First Street, Napa, CA 94559 (☎ 707/226-7455), or the **Sonoma Valley Visitor Bureau,** 453 First St. E., Sonoma, CA 95476 (☎ 707/996-1090; fax 707/996-9212). The **Sonoma County Convention and Visitor Bureau,** 5000 Roberts Lake Rd., Suite A, Rohnert Park, CA 94928 (☎ 800/326-7666 or 707/586-8100; fax 707/586-8111), offers a free 48-page visitor guide with information about the whole county.

If you need help organizing your vacation, **Wine Country Referrals,** P.O. Box 543, Calistoga, CA 94515 (☎ 707/942-2186; fax 707/942-4681), offers extensive information on inns, hotels, motels, resorts, and vacation homes, as well as wineries, limousine tours, restaurants, spas, ballooning, gliders, and train rides.

**GETTING AROUND**   Valley Cab (☎ 707/257-6444) and **Yellow Cab** (☎ 707/226-3731) offer metered taxi service.

## NAPA VALLEY

Napa Valley is home to more than 250 wineries, as well as to an exceptional selection of fine restaurants and hostelries for every taste and budget. The valley is just 35 miles long, so any of its towns—Napa, Yountville, Rutherford, Oakville, St. Helena, Calistoga—make a convenient base for wining, dining, shopping, and sightseeing.

The most popular pastime here is wine tasting, of course, but you don't have to worry about drinking and driving if you take the **Napa Valley Wine Train,** a rolling restaurant that makes a 3-hour, 36-mile journey through the Napa vineyards (sit on the west side for the best views). The vintage-style cars evoke the opulent sophistication of the 1920s and 1930s. Three- or four-course gourmet meals are served by an attentive staff, complete with all the luxurious details. Tours depart from the McKinstry Street Depot, 1275 McKinstry St., near First Street and Soscol Avenue in Napa (☎ 800/427-4124 or 707/253-2111).

**TOURING THE WINERIES**   Along with on-site samplings, most wineries offer tours daily from 10am to 5pm, usually charting the process of winemaking. They vary in length, detail, and formality, depending on the winery. Most are free.

Be sure to get a wine map to give you a complete listing of vintners. When choosing which to visit, keep in mind that the big, commercially oriented wineries offering tours are not to be missed, for sure, but don't pass up the other, more personal side of the Wine Country experience either.

**Trefethen Vineyards,** 1160 Oak Knoll Ave., Napa (☎ 707/255-7700), has tours by appointment only, but they are well worth arranging. The main structure, built in 1886, with bucolic brick courtyard surrounded with oak and cork trees, is listed on the National Register of Historic Places. Tastings take place in their inviting wood-beamed, jazz-filled tasting room.

✪ **Domaine Chandon,** California Drive at Calif. 29, Yountville (☎ 707/944-2280), annually produces about 500,000 cases of Chandon Brut Cuvée, Carneros Blanc de Noirs, Chandon Réserve, and Etoile *méthode champenoise* sparkling wines. Also on the property is the Domaine Chandon restaurant, one of the best in the valley (see "Dining," below).

**Stag's Leap Wine Cellars,** 5766 Silverado Trail, Napa (☎ 707/944-2020), guided by noted vintner Warren Winiarski, produces the renowned Cabernet Sauvignon Cask 23 as well as good, lower-priced wines under the Hawk Crest label.

**Robert Mondavi Winery,** 7801 St. Helena Hwy. (Hwy. 29), Oakville (☎ 800/MONDAVI), is the ultimate high-tech Napa Valley winery, with computers controlling almost every variable in their winemaking process. The Vineyard Room usually features an art show, and you'll find some exceptional antiques in the reception hall. During the summer, the winery hosts outdoor jazz concerts. Make tour reservations at least a week in advance, especially in summer.

**Beaulieu Vineyard,** 1960 St. Helena Hwy. (Hwy. 29), Rutherford (☎ 707/963-2411), produces world-class wines that have been served by every American president since Franklin D. Roosevelt. They offer a complimentary glass of chardonnay the minute you walk through the door.

✪ **Flora Springs Wine Co.,** 1978 W. Zinfandel Lane (just off Hwy. 29), St. Helena (☎ 707/963-5711), is well known for its barrel-fermented chardonnay, a cabernet sauvignon, and "Trilogy," a Bordeaux-style blend. An excellent 1-hour "familiarization seminar" can be tailored to suit all levels of wine enthusiasts.

**Beringer Vineyards,** 2000 Main St. (just north of St. Helena's business district, on Hwy. 29), St. Helena (☎ 707/963-7115), with its hand-dug tunnels carved out of the mountainside, is the oldest continuously operating Napa winery (it made "sacramental" wines during Prohibition).

**Sterling Vineyards,** 1111 Dunaweal Lane (a half-mile east of Hwy. 29), Calistoga (☎ 800/726-6136 or 707/942-3344), is more startling in appearance than any of its neighbors: Perched atop an island of rock and looking like a Greek or Italian monastery, it's reached by an aerial gondola with panoramic views of the valley. The very informative tour is self-directed.

**BALLOONING & GLIDING**   Alcoholic grape juice isn't the only thing the Wine Country has to offer. Believe it or not, the Napa Valley is the world's most popular hot-air balloon "flight corridor." Most flights go early in the morning, last about an hour, and end with a traditional champagne celebration and breakfast. Reservations are required and should be made as far in advance as possible. Contact **Bonaventura Balloon Company** (☎ 800/FLY-NAPA or 707/944-2882) or **Adventures Aloft** (☎ 800/944-4408 or 707/944-4408).

Over in Sonoma, the town of Calistoga offers a unique way of seeing the vineyard-filled valleys—from a **glider.** These quiet birds leave from the **Calistoga Gliderport** (☎ 707/942-5000).

**GOLF**   Another way to spend a less alcoholic afternoon is at the **Chardonnay Club,** Hwy. 12 south of downtown Napa, 1¹/₃ miles east of Hwy. 29 (☎ 707/257-8950), a challenging 36-hole land-links golf complex with first-class service. The course ambles through and around 325 acres of vineyards, hills, creeks, canyons, and rock ridges.

**GEYSERS, SPAS & MUD BATHS**   Old Faithful Geyser of California, at 1299

# The Wine Country

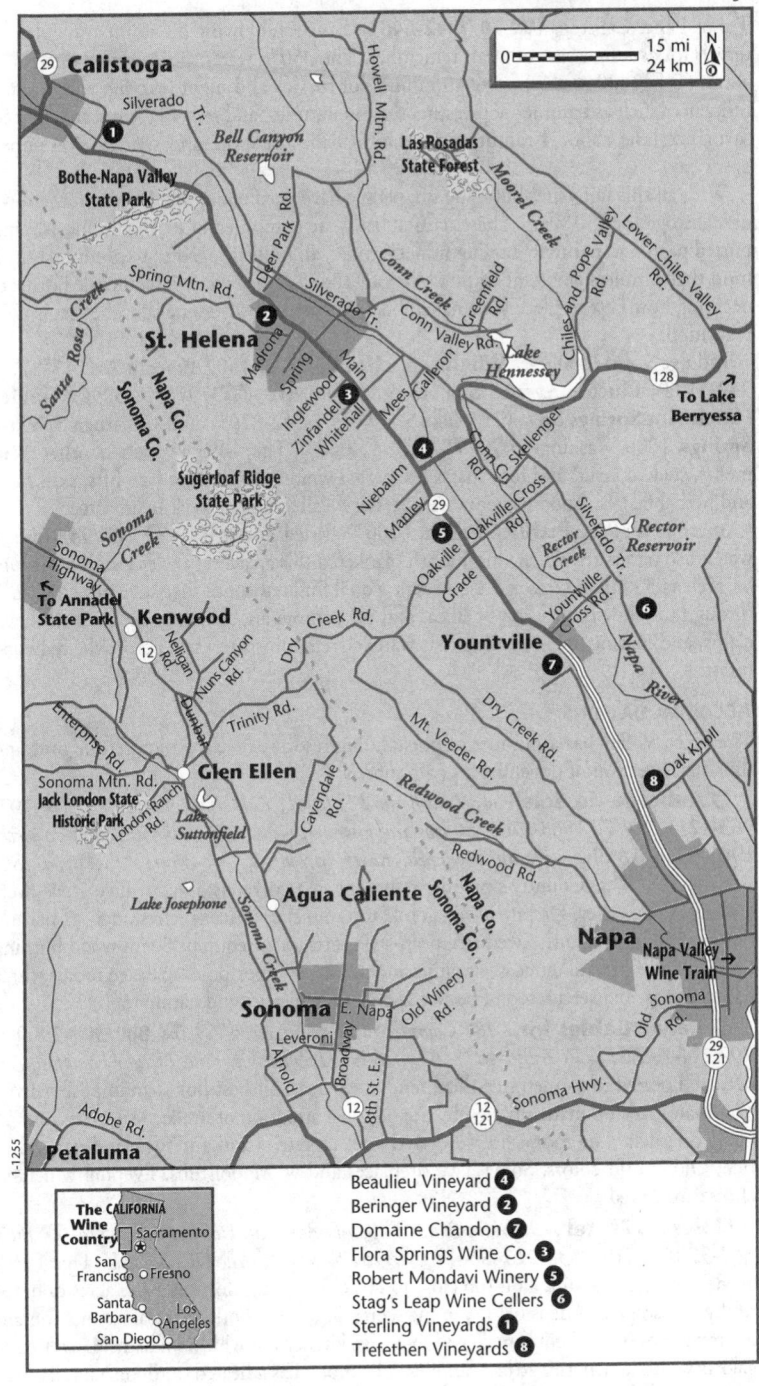

**Calistoga** 29

Silverado Tr. 1

Bell Canyon Reservoir

Bothe-Napa Valley State Park

Deer Park Rd.

Howell Mtn. Rd.

Las Posadas State Forest

Moorel Creek

Lower Chiles Valley Rd.

Chiles and Pope Valley Rd.

Spring Mtn. Rd.

**St. Helena** 2

Silverado Tr.

Conn Creek

Greenfield Rd.

Conn Valley Rd.

Lake Hennessey

128

↗ To Lake Berryessa

Madrona

Spring

Main

Inglewood

Zinfandel

Whitehall

Mees

Galleron

3

Santa Rosa Creek

Napa Co.

Sonoma Co.

Sugarloaf Ridge State Park

Sonoma Creek

Niebaum

Manley

29

4

Conn Cr. Stellenger Rd.

Oakville Cross Rd.

Silverado Tr.

Rector Creek

Rector Reservoir

5

Oakville Grade

Yountville Cross Rd.

6

Sonoma Highway

← To Annadel State Park

**Kenwood**

Nelligan Rd.

Nuns Canyon Rd.

Dunbar

Dry Creek Rd.

**Yountville** 7

Napa River

Trinity Rd.

12

**Glen Ellen**

Mt. Veeder Rd.

Dry Creek Rd.

Oak Knoll 8

Enterprise Rd.

Sonoma Mtn. Rd.

Jack London State Historic Park

London Ranch Rd.

Lake Suttonfield

Cavendale Rd.

Redwood Creek

Napa Co.

Sonoma Co.

Redwood Rd.

Lake Josephone

**Agua Caliente**

Sonoma Creek

**Napa**

Napa Valley Wine Train →

**Sonoma**

E. Napa

Old Winery Rd.

Old Sonoma Rd.

29 121

Leveroni

Broadway

8th St. E.

Arnold

12 121

Sonoma Hwy.

Adobe Rd.

**Petaluma**

1-1255

0  15 mi
   24 km
N

## The CALIFORNIA Wine Country

Sacramento ★

San Francisco

Fresno

Santa Barbara

Los Angeles

San Diego

Beaulieu Vineyard 4
Beringer Vineyard 2
Domaine Chandon 7
Flora Springs Wine Co. 3
Robert Mondavi Winery 5
Stag's Leap Wine Cellers 6
Sterling Vineyards 1
Trefethen Vineyards 8

703

Tubbs Lane, Calistoga (☎ **707/942-6463**), has been blowing off steam at regular intervals for as long as anyone can remember. The 350°F water spews out to a height of about 60 feet (20 meters) every 40 minutes or so, day and night (varying with natural influences such as barometric pressure, the moon, tides, and tectonic stresses). The performance lasts about 3 minutes. An exhibit hall, gift shop, and snack bar are open every day.

With all this hot water bubbling up, people have been taking mud baths in the town of Calistoga for 150 years. These natural baths are composed of local volcanic ash, imported peat, and naturally boiling mineral water, all mulled together to produce a thick mud that simmers at a temperature of about 104°F. Once you overcome the hurdle of deciding how best to place your naked body into the mushy stone tub, the rest is pure relaxation.

Indulge yourself at **Dr. Wilkinson's Hot Springs,** 1507 Lincoln Ave. (☎ 707/942-4102); **Lincoln Avenue Spa,** 1339 Lincoln Ave. (☎ 707/942-5296); **Golden Haven Hot Springs Spa,** 1713 Lake St. (☎ 707/942-6793); and **Calistoga Spa Hot Springs,** 1006 Washington St. (☎ 707/942-6269). They offer a variety of other treatments, such as hand and foot massages, herbal wraps, acupressure face-lifts, skin rubs, and herbal facials. Appointments are necessary; call at least a week in advance.

Specimens at the **Petrified Forest,** 4100 Petrified Forest Rd. (☎ **707/942-6667**), weren't so pampered when volcanic ash blanketed this area after the eruption of Mount St. Helena 3 million years ago. As a result, you'll find redwoods that have turned to rock through the slow infiltration of silicas and other minerals, as well as petrified seashells, clams, and marine life indicating that water covered this area even before the redwood forest.

## ACCOMMODATIONS

The Napa Valley has a number of outstanding resorts as well as picturesque inns and the usual selection of dependable chain motels.

✪ **Auberge du Soleil.** *180 Rutherford Hill Rd., Rutherford, CA 94573.* ☎ **707/963-1211.** *Fax 707/963-8764. 50 rms and suites. Apr–Nov, $175–$750 double on weekdays; $250–$850 double on weekends. Rates discounted Dec–Mar. AE, DC, DISC, MC, V.* The Wine Country's premier resort sits in a gorgeous 33-acre olive grove overlooking Napa Valley. Despite its high rank, the ambience remains refreshingly casual and unpretentious. Romantic, Mediterranean-style cottages are equipped with wood-burning fireplaces and private terraces. Facilities include an outdoor pool, massage rooms, three tennis courts, an exercise room, beauty salon, and sculpture and nature trail.

✪ **Cedar Gables Inn.** *486 Coombs St., Napa, CA 94559.* ☎ **800/309-7969** *or 707/224-7969. Fax 707/224-4838. 6 rms. $99–$169 double. Rates include breakfast. AE, MC, V.* Located in a quiet, tree-filled residential area, this best-buy is an imposing 1892 Victorian mansion made inviting by the personal attention of innkeepers Margaret and Craig Snasdell. The rooms are decorated with tapestries and antiques, and painted in rich, Old World colors. Some have fireplaces and whirlpool tubs. Evening wine and cheese are served.

**El Bonita Motel.** *195 Main St. (at El Bonita Ave.), St. Helena, CA 94574.* ☎ **800/541-3284** *or 707/963-3216. 26 rms. $79–$120 double. AE, DC, MC, V.* This 1930s art deco motel was built a bit too close to Hwy. 29 for comfort, but 2¹/₂ acres of beautifully landscaped gardens help even the score. Small but spotlessly clean rooms contain microwave ovens and coffeemakers; some have kitchens or whirlpool baths. Larger bungalows with kitchenettes attract families. The motel has a heated outdoor pool, Jacuzzi, sauna, and massage facility.

**Harvest Inn.** *1 Main St., St. Helena, CA 94574.* ☎ **800/950-8466** *or 707/*

*963-9463. 54 rms. $185–$220 double. AE, DC, DISC, MC, V.* Ornate brick walkways constructed of bricks harvested from turn-of-the-century San Francisco homes cross the beautifully landscaped grounds to this Tudor-style inn. Each of the immaculate rooms is furnished with oak beds and dressers, black leather chairs, and antique furnishings; most have brick fireplaces, wet bars, and refrigerators. The inn has a wine bar, heated swimming pools, and outdoor spas.

✪ **Meadowood Resort.** *900 Meadowood Lane, St. Helena, CA 94574.* ☎ *707/ 458-8080. Fax 707/963-3532. 85 rms. $320–$465 double; $540–$1,520 suite. Ask about promotional offers and off-season rates. Two-night minimum stay. AE, DC, DISC, MC, V.* This summer camp for grown-ups is tucked away on 250 acres of pristine mountainside. Suites are decorated with American country classics and equipped with beamed ceilings, private patios, stone fireplaces, and wilderness views. The resort has a nine-hole golf course, tennis courts, croquet lawns, two outdoor swimming pools, and health spa.

✪ **Mount View Hotel.** *1457 Lincoln Ave., Calistoga, CA 94515.* ☎ *707/ 942-6877. Fax 707/942-6904. 22 rms, 8 suites, 3 cottages. $110–$140 double; $155– $200 suite; $200 cottage. Two-night minimum during high-season weekends. Packages available. AE, MC, V.* Listed on the National Register of Historic Places, this hotel offers 1920s- and 1930s-style "European eclectic" rooms, self-contained cottages, and suites named for movie idols. The cottages have wet bars, private decks, and hot tubs. Catahoula's restaurant is here (see "Dining," below). No smoking is permitted in rooms. Guests enjoy the heated swimming pool, European spa, and Jacuzzi.

**Napa Valley Budget Inn.** *3380 Solano Ave., Napa, CA 94558.* ☎ *707/ 257-6111. 58 rms. $56–$79 double. AE, DC, DISC, MC, V.* The best thing going for this no-frills inn is its excellent location—close to Hwy. 29 and just across the street from convenient shopping. Rooms are simple, clean, and comfortable. There's a small heated pool on the premises.

✪ **Silverado Country Club & Resort.** *1600 Atlas Peak Rd., Napa, CA 94558.* ☎ *800/532-0500 or 707/257-0200. Fax 707/257-2867. 281 rms, 28 suites. $195 studio; $255 one-bedroom suite; $365–$470 two- or three-bedroom suite. Golf and promotional packages available. AE, CB, DC, MC, V.* If you long for the opulence of an East Coast country club, bring your racket and golf clubs to this 1,200-acre resort. The accommodations range from very large studios to one-, two-, or three-bedroom cottage suites, each with a wood-burning fireplace. The resort keeps guests busy with two restaurants, a bar, two golf courses, tennis courts, and several swimming pools.

**Vintage Inn.** *6541 Washington St., Yountville, CA 94599.* ☎ *800/351-1133 or 707/944-1112. Fax 707/944-1617. 72 rms, 8 minisuites. $150–$275 double; $240–$325 minisuite or villa. Additional person $25 extra. Rates include continental breakfast. AE, CB, DC, MC, V.* This sprawling, contemporary hideaway resides on an old 23-acre winery estate in the center of Yountville. Rooms are well equipped, with fireplaces, ceiling fans, oversize beds, coffeemakers, refrigerators, plush bathrobes, tubs with Jacuzzi jets, and a complimentary bottle of wine. A limousine to the wineries is provided, as well as a heated pool, whirlpool, and tennis courts.

## DINING

For a picnic, try the **Oakville Grocery Co.,** 7856 St. Helena Hwy., in Oakville (☎ 707/944-8802), one of the finest gourmet food stores in California.

**All Seasons Café.** *1400 Lincoln Ave. (at Washington St.), Calistoga.* ☎ *707/ 942-9111. Reservations recommended on weekends. Main courses $13–$19 at dinner. MC, V. Thurs–Tues 11am–3pm and 5:30–10pm; brunch Sat–Sun 9am–noon. Wine shop, Thurs–Tues 11am–8pm. CALIFORNIAN.* Wine Country devotees come here because Chef John Coss matches wines to his dishes. Buy a bottle from the cafe's wine shop, then pay a corkage fee of $7.50 instead of triple the price if they deliver it. Anything with the house-smoked salmon or spiced sausages is a safe bet.

✪ **Auberge du Soleil.** *180 Rutherford Hill Rd., Rutherford.* ☎ **707/963-1211.** *Reservations recommended. Main courses $25–$30; fixed-price dinner $60. AE, DISC, MC, V. Daily 7–11am, 11:30am–2:30pm, and 6–9:30pm. WINE COUNTRY CUISINE.* Auberge du Soleil may be better known as an inn, but it was the restaurant that started all the fuss about this world-class resort. Chef Andrew Sutton's "Wine Country cuisine" reflects the region's produce and international influences. Be sure to arrive before sunset and beg for terrace seating.

✪ **Brava Terrace.** *3010 St. Helena Hwy., St. Helena.* ☎ **707/963-9300.** *Reservations recommended. Main courses $8–$15. AE, DC, DISC, MC, V. Thurs–Tues noon–9pm. CALIFORNIA/MEDITERRANEAN.* Fred Halpert, who earned acclaim as the head chef at the Portman Hotel in San Francisco, works his magic here on both good and reasonably priced fare. The main dining room has an open kitchen and handsome stone fireplace; there's also a glass-enclosed dining area and a large terrace with umbrella-covered tables.

✪ **Catahoula.** *1457 Lincoln Ave., Calistoga.* ☎ **707/942-2275.** *Reservations recommended. Main courses $11–$20. MC, V. Mon and Wed–Fri noon–2:30pm, Sat–Sun noon–3:30pm; Mon, Wed–Thurs, and Sun 5:30–10pm, Fri–Sat 5:30–10:30pm. AMERICAN/SOUTHERN.* The domain of chef Jan Birnbaum, this restaurant is Calistoga's current favorite, and with good reason: Here you can get a decent rooster gumbo, and you'd have to travel all over Louisiana to find another pan-fried jalapeño-pecan catfish like the one they serve here. Catahoula is funky and fun.

✪ **Domaine Chandon.** *One California Dr., Yountville.* ☎ **707/944-2892.** *Reservations required. Main courses $13–$17 at lunch, $24–$28 at dinner. AE, DC, MC, V. Summer, daily 11:30am–2:30pm; Wed–Sun 6–9:30pm. Winter, Wed–Sun 11:30am–2:30pm and 6–9:30pm. Closed first 3 weeks of Jan. CALIFORNIA/FRENCH.* Hidden in an idyllic locale beside a tree-shaded creek, one of California's most celebrated restaurants has large picture windows to take full advantage of the vineyard views. At night, candles romantically illumine the fir-paneled room. The full-flavored cuisine is carefully orchestrated to go with the Napa Valley wines offered. Alfresco dining on nice days.

✪ **French Laundry.** *6640 Washington St. (at Creek St.), Yountville.* ☎ **707/944-2380.** *Reservations required. Fixed-price menu $49–$57. AE, MC, V. Tues–Thurs 5:30–9:30pm, Fri–Sun noon–1:30pm and 5:30–9:30pm. AMERICAN/FRENCH.* Dinner at renown chef/owner Thomas Keller's restaurant, housed in a converted fieldstone cottage that was once a French steam laundry, is an all-night affair; when it's finally over, you're ready to sit down and do it all over again. On warm summer nights, request a table in the flower-filled garden.

✪ **Mustards Grill.** *7399 St. Helena Hwy. (1 mile north of Yountville on Hwy. 29).* ☎ **707/944-2424.** *Reservations required. Main courses $11–$17. CB, DC, MC, V. Apr–Oct, daily 11:30am–10pm. Nov–Mar, daily 11:30am–9pm. CALIFORNIAN.* Food critics call this often boisterous and noisy place "the quintessential Napa Valley wine restaurant." A bronze of a bowler-hatted gentleman greets you at the door of the barnlike building. Inside, you'll find a bilevel, black-and-white–tiled dining room with cathedral ceilings, a small bar, a glass-enclosed outer dining area, and blue-jeaned, white-shirted servers.

✪ **Restaurant at Meadowood.** *At Meadowood Resort, 900 Meadowood Lane, St. Helena.* ☎ **707/963-3646.** *Reservations recommended. Fixed-price dinner $45; vegetarian dinner $39. AE, DC, DISC, MC, V. Daily 6–10pm. AMERICAN/FRENCH.* One of Napa's more ambitious four-course dinners is served at Meadowood, a top-rated resort whose gazebo-style clubhouse dining room overlooks the golf course. Every Southern French–influenced course is well balanced and delicious. Take a little stroll around the tranquil grounds afterward.

✪ **Terra.** *1345 Railroad Ave. (between Adams and Hunt sts.), St. Helena.* ☎ *707/963-8931. Reservations recommended. Main courses $14–$23. DC, MC, V. Sun–Thurs 6–9pm, Fri–Sat 6–10pm. CONTEMPORARY AMERICAN.* St. Helena's restaurant of choice, Terra is the creation of Lissa Doumani and her husband, Hiro Sone, a master chef who hails from Japan. Coaxing every nuance of flavor from his fine local ingredients, his main dishes successfully fuse different cooking styles: grilled salmon with Thai red-curry sauce; sake-marinated sea bass with shrimp dumplings in shiso broth.

✪ **Tra Vigne Restaurant and Cantinetta.** *1050 Charter Oak Ave. (at Hwy. 29), St. Helena.* ☎ *707/963-4444, or 707/963-8888 for the cantinetta. Reservations recommended. Main courses $13–$16; cantinetta $4–$8. CB, DC, DISC, MC, V. Restaurant, daily 11:30am–9:30pm. Cantinetta, daily 11:30am–6pm. ITALIAN.* They may be fancier, but no other local restaurant measures up to the combined qualities of atmosphere, food, and prices found here. Whether seated next to the immense curved windows opening onto a large veranda, or on the heated veranda itself, diners usually are thrilled. The adjoining cafe, **Cantinetta,** offers a small selection of sandwiches, pizzas, and lighter meals, and packs picnics.

**Wappo Bar & Bistro.** *1226B Washington St. (off Lincoln Ave.), Calistoga.* ☎ *707/942-4712. Main courses $8.50–$14.50. AE, DC, MC, V. Wed–Mon 11:30am–2:30pm; Thurs–Mon 6–9:30pm. INTERNATIONAL.* One of the best alfresco dining experiences in the Wine Country is under Wappo's honeysuckle and vine-covered arbor, but you'll also be comfortable at one of the well-spaced, well-polished tables inside this small bistro. The menu offers a wide range of choices, from roast vegetables with polenta to rabbit pie with wild mushrooms and puff pastry.

## SONOMA VALLEY

Often thought of as the "other" Wine Country, the Sonoma Valley has far fewer wineries—and far, far fewer tourists—but its wines have actually won more awards than Napa's. Sonoma County, which stretches west to the coast, also is more rural and less traveled. Small family-owned wineries are its mainstay. Unlike the corporate-run tours at many Napa wineries, tastings on the west side of the Mayacamas Mountains are usually free, low-key, and come with plenty of friendly banter between the winemakers and their guests.

**TOURING THE WINERIES**   Sonoma is home to about 35 wineries, most still family owned and more spread out than those in Napa, yet they're still easy to find. California's first winery, Buena Vista, was founded here in 1857, and it's still in operation (see below). Today, Sonoma is most noted for chardonnay.

**Ravenswood Winery,** 18701 Gehricke Rd., Sonoma (☎ 707/938-1960), built right into the hillside, is best known for its big, bold zinfandels, but it also produces a merlot, a cabernet sauvignon, and some whites. A "Barbecue in the Vineyards" is held weekends from Memorial Day through September.

**Sebastiani Vineyards Winery,** 389 Fourth St. E., Sonoma (☎ 800/888-5532 or 707/938-5532), doesn't occupy the most scenic setting or structures in Sonoma Valley, but its place in the history and development of the region is unique, and its 25-minute tour through aging stone cellars containing more than 300 carved casks is well worth the time.

**Buena Vista,** 18000 Old Winery Rd., Sonoma (☎ 707/938-1266), the patriarch of California wineries, was founded in 1857 by Count Agoston Haraszthy, the Hungarian émigré who is called the father of the California wine industry. Although the winemaking now takes place in an ultramodern facility outside Sonoma, the winery still maintains a complimentary tasting room here, inside the restored 1862 Press House.

**Château St. Jean,** 8555 Sonoma Hwy. (Hwy. 12), Kenwood (☎ 707/833-4134), formerly a 250-acre country retreat built in 1920, is notable for its exceptionally beautiful buildings, well-landscaped grounds, and elegant tasting room. A well-manicured lawn is now a picnic area, complete with a fountain and benches.

## ACCOMMODATIONS

In the more laid-back Sonoma Valley, you can relax in a spa or stay in a friendly farmhouse hotel.

✪ **Beltane Ranch.** *11775 Sonoma Hwy., Glen Ellen, CA 95442.* ☎ *707/ 996-6501. 4 rms. $120–$160 double. No credit cards; checks accepted.* Surrounded by pastures on the slopes of the Mayacamas, the Beltane Ranch is an honest-to-Betsy 1892 double-porched farmhouse. A terrace around the house looks out over flower-filled gardens and fields beyond. Rooms are comfortably furnished in a homey style and with the occasional family antique. There are hiking trails and a tennis court.

**El Dorado Hotel.** *405 First St. W. (at W. Spain St.), Sonoma, CA 95476.* ☎ *800/ 289-3031 or 707/996-3030. Fax 707/996-3148. 27 rms. Winter, $85–$110 double. Summer, $105–$145 double. Rates include continental breakfast and split of wine. AE, MC, V.* The El Dorado Hotel may look like a 19th-century Wild West relic from the outside, but you won't be sleeping on a rickety antique bed and bathing in a cramped clawfoot tub here—inside it's all 20th-century deluxe. Each guest room has a canopy bed. The popular Piatti restaurant is here.

**El Pueblo Inn.** *896 W. Napa St., Sonoma, CA 94576.* ☎ *800/900-8844 or 707/ 996-3651. 38 rms. May–Oct, $70–$80 double. Mar–Apr and Nov, $60–$70 double. Dec–Feb, $59 double, except during holidays when rates are higher. AE, DISC, JCB, MC,V.* It ain't the Ritz, but the Pueblo offers some of the best-priced accommodations around here. The rooms are pleasant enough, with post-and-beam construction, exposed brick walls, light wood furniture, and geometric prints. Reserve at least a month in advance for spring and summer. There's an outdoor heated pool.

✪ **Kenwood Inn & Spa.** *10400 Sonoma Hwy., Kenwood, CA 95452.* ☎ *800/ 353-6966 or 707/833-1293. 12 rms. April 1–Oct 31, $195–$315 (2-night minimum stay on weekends). Nov 1–Mar 31, $165–$275. Rates include breakfast and bottle of wine. AE, MC, V.* This Tuscan-inspired inn and full spa will make any northern Italian homesick. Equipped with fireplaces, balconies, feather beds, and down comforters, the sumptuous rooms have been exquisitely decorated with imported tapestries and furnishings. A celebrated three-course breakfast is served poolside or in the Mediterranean-style kitchen. A minor caveat: road noise.

✪ **Sonoma Chalet.** *18935 Fifth St. W. (at the northwest end of town), Sonoma CA 95476.* ☎ *707/938-3129. 3 rms, 3 cottages, 1 suite. Apr–Oct, $95–$140 double. Nov–Mar, $80–$130 double. Rates include continental breakfast. AE, MC, V.* One of the valley's few secluded accommodations, this chalet is in a peaceful country setting overlooking a 200-acre ranch (gaggles of ducks, chickens, and ornery geese wander the grounds). Accommodations are in a Swiss-style farmhouse and several cottages, but they're by no means rustic. Breakfast is served either in the country kitchen or in your room.

**Sonoma Mission Inn & Spa.** *18140 Hwy. 12, Boyes Hot Springs, CA 94576.* ☎ *800/862-4945 or 707/938-9000. Fax 707/938-4250. 170 rms, 3 suites. Nov–Mar, $115–$350 double. Apr–Oct, $140–$365 double. Year-round, suites from $325. AE, DC, MC, V.* Clara Bow or Mary Pickford would have felt at home at this sprawling 1920s-era resort housed in a three-story pink mission-style structure set on 8 landscaped

1920s-era resort housed in a three-story pink mission-style structure set on 8 landscaped acres. Though comfortable and well-equipped, rooms are short on style. The Grille is known for its low-calorie, low-sodium, and low-cholesterol cuisine. There are full spa facilities, a health club, tennis courts, and golf club privileges.

## DINING

On a sunny day, the Wine Country is made for a picnic. Stop in Sonoma at **Angelo's Wine Country Deli,** 23400 Arnold Dr. (☎ 707/938-3688), or at the **Sonoma Cheese Factory,** on the Plaza at 2 Spain St. (☎ 707/996-1000), to pick up your picnic.

✪ **John Ash & Co.** *4330 Barnes Rd., Santa Rosa.* ☎ **707/527-7687.** *Reservations recommended. Main courses $15–$23. AE, MC, V. Tues–Sat 11:30am–2pm, Sun 10:30am–2pm; Sun–Thurs 5–9pm, Fri–Sat 5–10pm. Cafe menu, Tues–Sun 11:30am– close. Hours change seasonally. From Hwy. 101, exit west at River Rd. CALIFORNIAN.* The bounty of California is celebrated at this Southwestern-inspired restaurant, whose dining rooms are light and airy with high vaulted ceilings, terra-cotta tile floors, and large local landscapes on the walls. Whenever possible, the chef uses Sonoma-grown foods: luscious lamb, other meats, vegetables, and fruits. There's alfresco dining on a heated terrace with pleasant vineyard views.

✪ **Kenwood Restaurant & Bar.** *9900 Sonoma Hwy., Kenwood.* ☎ **707/ 833-6326.** *Reservations recommended. Main courses $12.50–$23.50. MC, V. Tues–Sun 11:30am–9pm. CALIFORNIAN/CONTINENTAL.* This Sonoma-style roadhouse is what Wine Country dining should be but often is not. In good weather you can dine on the terrace; on nippy days, retreat inside to cushioned rattan chairs set at white cloth– covered tables. Perfectly balanced between tradition and innovation, the first-rate cuisine is complemented by a reasonably priced wine list.

# 3 Redwood National & State Parks

It's impossible to explain the feeling you get in the old-growth forests of Redwood National and State Parks, in California's northwest corner, without resorting to Alice-in-Wonderland comparisons. Like a tropical rain forest, these are multistoried affairs, the tall trees being only the top layer. Everything is big, misty, and primeval; flowering bushes cover the ground, 10-foot-tall ferns line the creeks, and the smells are rich and musty. It's so Jurassic Park–like that you can't help but half expect to turn the corner and see a dinosaur.

When Archibald Menzies first noted the botanical existence of the coast redwood in 1794, more than 2 million acres of redwood forest carpeted the north coast. Heavy logging had reduced that to 300,000 acres by the 1960s, and in 1968 the federal government created Redwood National Park to complement several state parks established around individual groves in the 1920s.

## ESSENTIALS

U.S. 101 barrels north–south right through the Redwoods. At the south end of Redwood National Park near the town of Orick on Highway 101 is the sleek **Redwood National Park Information Center,** P.O. Box 7, Orick, CA 95555 (☎ 707/ 464-6101). Stop here first to pick up a free map and see the displays of fauna and wildlife. Free guides and information are also available at the **Redwood National Park Headquarters and Information Center** at 1111 2nd St. at K Street in Crescent City (☎ 707/464-6101).

**Admission** to the national park is free, but there's a $20 per person interpretive fee. The three state parks (which contain the best redwood groves) charge a $6-per-person day-use fee, good at all three. Pets are prohibited on all of the parks' trails.

Beach, and Redwood information centers during summer months, year-round at the park headquarters in Crescent City (☎ 707/464-6101). State rangers lead campfire programs and numerous other activities throughout the year. Call the Parks Information Service for both the national and state parks (☎ 707/464-6101) to get current schedules and events.

## WHAT TO SEE & DO

A number of scenic drives cut through the park off U.S. 101. Steep, windy **Bald Hills Road** will take you back into the Redwood Creek watershed and up to the shoulder of 3,097-foot Schoolhouse Peak. Don't even think of pulling a trailer or driving a motor home up here.

The partially paved 8-mile **Coastal Drive** wanders among redwood groves and along the banks of the Klamath River. The southern section is okay for RVs, but don't go past Alder Camp Road going north or Flint Ridge heading south. Watch for the old World War II radar tracking station disguised as a barn and farmhouse to fool the Japanese.

**BEACHES & BOATING**    The park's beaches vary from long white-sand strands to cobblestone pocket coves. The water temperature is in the high 40s to low 50s year-round and it's often rough out there, so swimmers and surfers should be prepared for chilly, often adverse conditions. **Crescent Beach** is a long sandy beach just 2 miles south of Crescent City that's popular with beachcombers, surf fishermen, and surfers. Just south of Crescent Beach is **Endert's Beach,** a protected spot with a hike-in campground and tide pools at the southern end of the beach.

**Klamath River Jet Boat Tours,** Klamath (☎ 800/887-JETS or 707/482-7775), has jet-boat tours upriver from the Klamath River estuary to view bear, deer, elk, osprey, hawks, otters, and more along the riverbanks.

**CAMPING**    Five small campgrounds are located in the national park proper. Four are walk-in camps and are free, but you must get a permit from the visitor center in advance. A car-camping strip along the freeway at Freshwater Lagoon requests an $8 donation.

Most car campsites are in the **Prairie Creek** and **Jebediah Smith State Parks,** which lie entirely inside the national park. Sites there are $14 per night and can be reserved by calling the Destinet reservation system (☎ 800/444-7275), which requires an additional $6.75 reservation fee.

An interesting option is the **boat-in campground** at Stone Lagoon in Humboldt Lagoons State Park. Reachable only by canoe, kayak, or rowboat, it is on the bank of the lagoon and a short walk to the ocean beach.

Farther from the park attractions but also farther from the crowds are four **National Forest Campgrounds** in the mountains above the park. Sites are $8 per night and can be reserved by calling ☎ 800/280-2267—where an actual person can help you make decisions.

**FISHING**    The area streams are some of the best steelhead trout and salmon breeding habitat in California. Park beaches are good for surf casting, but be prepared for heavy wave action. A California fishing license is required and you should check with rangers about any special closures before wetting a line.

**HIKING**    The park map and guide, available at any of the information centers, provides a good map of hiking trails. Backpackers can tackle the **Coastal Trail,** which runs the entire length of the park, as near the ocean as possible. There are several backcountry camps on the route, making for a great 3- or 4-day trip. More manageable segments of the Coastal Trail can be hiked in a day. One of the nicest runs is from Crescent Beach south into the Del Norte Coast Redwoods State Park.

The 8-mile **Redwood Creek Trail** will take you to the Tall Trees Grove, where the

# Redwood National & State Parks

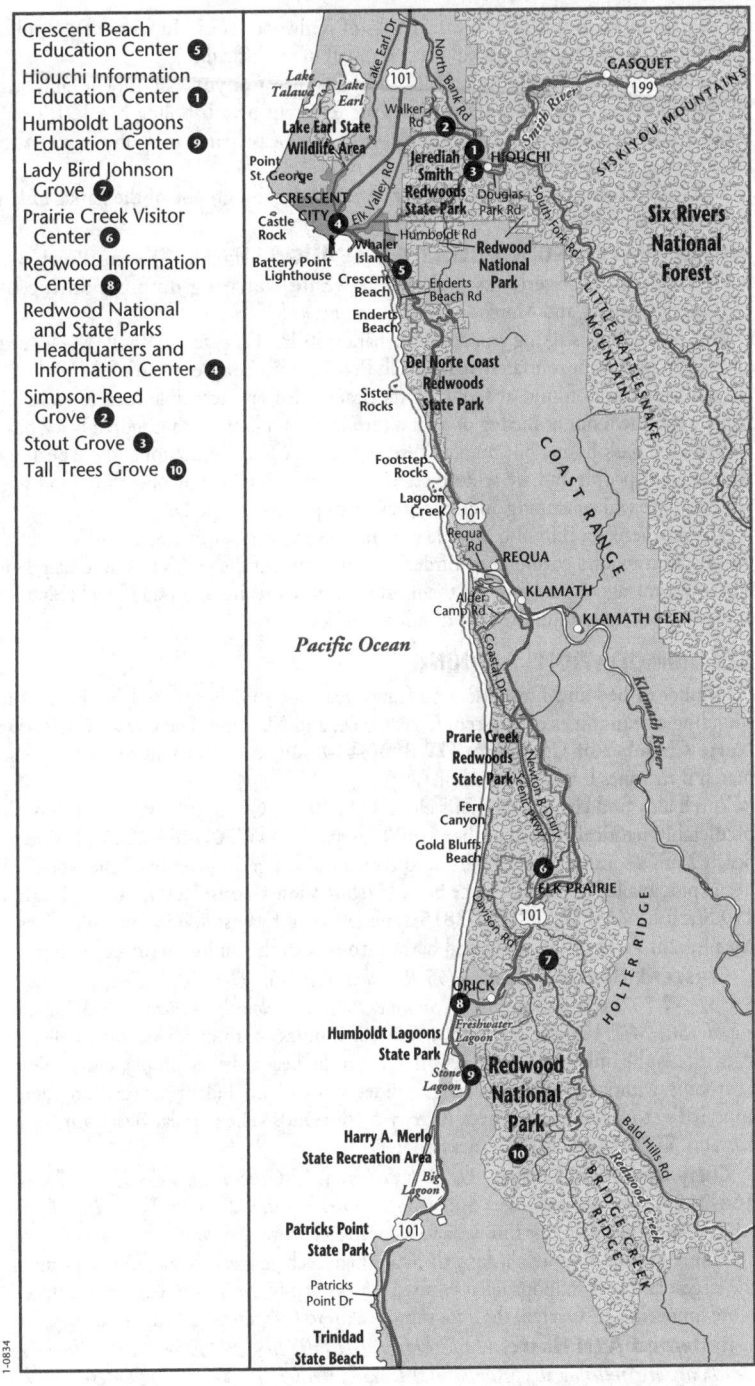

Crescent Beach
Education Center **5**

Hiouchi Information
Education Center **1**

Humboldt Lagoons
Education Center **9**

Lady Bird Johnson
Grove **7**

Prairie Creek Visitor
Center **6**

Redwood Information
Center **8**

Redwood National
and State Parks
Headquarters and
Information Center **4**

Simpson-Reed
Grove **2**

Stout Grove **3**

Tall Trees Grove **10**

711

tallest trees in the world grow on the banks of Redwood Creek. In winter two bridges are removed from the trail, making access much more difficult.

Smaller day hikes include the walk through **Fern Canyon,** an unbelievably lush grotto of sword, five-finger, and maidenhair ferns cut by a babbling brook. It's only about a 1¹/₂-mile walk from Gold Bluffs beach, but be prepared to scramble across the creek several times on your way.

**Lady Bird Johnson Grove Loop** is a short stroll through one of the park's lushest groves of redwoods.

**WHALE-WATCHING & WILDLIFE VIEWING**　　Klamath, Crescent Beach, and other high coastal overlooks make great **whale-watching** outposts during the December–January and March–April migrations.

One of the most striking aspects of the park is its herd of gigantic Roosevelt elk, usually found in the appropriately named Elk Prairie in the southern end of the park. Elk are also sometimes found at Gold Bluffs Beach—it's an incredible rush to suddenly come upon them out of the fog or after a turn in the trail. Nearly a hundred black bears also call the park home, but unlike those at Yosemite and Yellowstone, these bears are still afraid of people and are seldom seen. Keep them that way by observing food storage etiquette while camping and by disposing of garbage properly.

The northern sea cliffs also provide valuable nesting sites for marine birds like auklets, puffins, murres, and cormorants. Birders will also thrill at the park's freshwater lagoons. These coastal lagoons are some of the most pristine shorebird and waterfowl habitat left and are chock-full of hundreds of different species.

## ACCOMMODATIONS & DINING

A number of bed-and-breakfasts and funky roadside motels are available in the surrounding communities of Crescent City, Orick, and Klamath. The **Crescent City/Del Norte Chamber of Commerce** (☎ **800/343-8300**) can steer you toward a proper match if the ones listed here are full.

You'll also find chain restaurants along U.S. 101 in Crescent City. In addition, the predictably nautical **Beachcomber,** 1400 Hwy. 101 (☎ **707/464-2205**), beside the beach 2 miles south of town, offers inexpensive seafood grilled over madrone-wood barbecue pits. Hailed as the best place here, **Harbor View Grotto Restaurant & Lounge,** 150 Starfish Way (☎ **707/464-3815**), specializes in fresh seafood at market prices. It has pleasant views of the ocean and harbor from both the dining room and lounge.

**Crescent Beach Motel.** *1455 Redwood Hwy. S. (U.S. 101), Crescent City, CA 95531.* ☎ **707/464-5436.** *28 rms. Summer, $63–$68 double. Winter, $49–$52 double. AE, DISC, MC, V.* Near the highway, about 2 miles south of town, this single-story structure is the only local motel set directly on the beach. It has simple, old-fashioned bedrooms, without phone or cooking facilities, but with an undeniably rustic, outdoorsy appeal. Try to get one with a deck directly on the sands. The popular Beachcomber restaurant (☎ **707/464-2205**) is next door.

**Curly Redwood Lodge.** *701 Redwood Hwy. S., Crescent City, CA 95531.* ☎ **707/ 464-2137.** *36 rms. Summer, $59–$64 double. Winter, $37–$39 double. AE, DC, MC, V.* Built in 1959, this throw-back is completely trimmed with lumber from a single ancient redwood. Although lacking the latest high-tech gadgets, the bedrooms are among the largest and best-soundproofed in town, and certainly the most evocative of a bygone, more innocent age. Overall, the aura is more akin to Oregon than California.

**Redwood AYH Hostel.** *14480 Hwy. 101 (off Hwy. 101 across from Wilson Creek Beach, about 7 miles north of Klamath), Klamath, CA 95548.* ☎ **707/482-8265.** *30 beds. $9–$11 per person. MC, V.* In a turn-of-the-century logger's mansion, this hostel is the only lodging actually within the park, a mere 100 yards from the beach and surrounded by hiking trails. Family rooms are available with advance notice, and credit-card reservations are strongly recommended in summer. The staff leads nature walks and is well versed in local history.

# 4 Lake Tahoe

Nestled in the mountains on the California–Nevada border, Lake Tahoe has long been this region's most popular recreational playground. Its list of outdoor activities is almost endless, from boating and water sports in summer to ice skating and skiing in winter (it's one of America's premier ski areas). Year-round activities include tennis, fishing, and gambling and big-name entertainment in the casinos just across the Nevada line.

All this is set in a stunning location, for the lake is one of the most beautiful in the world. Its water is so pure that a white dinner plate is clearly visible at a depth of 75 feet, and it's so immense that it holds up to 40 trillion gallons, enough to cover the entire state of California with $14^1/_2$ inches of water. Its average depth is 989 feet, although it reaches 1,645 feet in places, making it the second deepest lake in the U.S. (after Crater Lake, Oregon) and the eighth deepest in the world.

## ESSENTIALS

**ARRIVING & DEPARTING**   **Reno/Tahoe International Airport,** 40 miles northeast of Lake Tahoe (about a 50-minute drive), is served by American, Delta, and United airlines. Trans World Express flies into **South Lake Tahoe Airport** (☎ 916/542-6180), just south of town. **Amtrak** (☎ 800/USA-RAIL) services Truckee, 10 miles north of the lake, with shuttle service to North Lake Tahoe.

**VISITOR INFORMATION**   Call the **Tahoe North Visitor and Convention Bureau,** 1156 Ski Run Blvd., South Lake Tahoe, CA 96150 (☎ 800/824-6348 or 916/583-3495), or stop by the **North Lake Tahoe Chamber of Commerce,** 245 North Lake Blvd., Tahoe City (☎ 916/581-6900). In South Lake Tahoe, there's the **South Lake Tahoe Visitor Authority,** 1156 Ski Run Blvd. (☎ 800/288-2463 or 916/544-5050), and the **South Lake Tahoe Chamber of Commerce,** 3066 Lake Tahoe Blvd. (☎ 916/541-5255), which is open Monday to Friday from 8:30am to 5pm and Saturday from 9am to 4pm (it's closed on major holidays).

## WHAT TO SEE & DO

While you can gamble the night—and your fortune—away here, outdoor activities are equally as important. In summer you can enjoy boating and water sports, plus in-line skating, bungee jumping, camping, ballooning, horseback riding, bicycling, parasailing, and much more. In winter Lake Tahoe boasts 13 downhill resorts and 15 cross-country skiing centers. There's also sleigh riding, ice skating, snowmobiling, and snowshoeing.

You'll have no trouble finding the activities once you arrive—in fact, the operators will find *you.*

**DOWNHILL SKIING**   The ski season usually lasts from November to May, but frequently extends into summer. Lift tickets cost about $42 per day, $30 per half day, and $6 for children under 13. Alpine Meadows, Heavenly Resort, Kirkwood, Northstar-at-Tahoe, and Squaw Valley (see below) offer an interchangeable Ski Lake Tahoe lift ticket. Most hotels and resorts offer money-saving ski packages.

Site of the 1960 Olympic Winter Games, ✪ **Squaw Valley USA** (☎ 800/545-4350 or 916/583-6985) offers the most challenging array of runs. Another Tahoe legend, **Heavenly Resort** (☎ 702/586-7000) is one of the area's largest ski resorts, with trails and slopes for all skill levels. Sitting at 8,637 feet, the season at **Alpine Meadows** (☎ 800/441-4423 or 916/583-4232) lasts through May, but it's best for intermediate and advanced skiers. More than 50% of snow-making coverage and a full-time kids program make **Northstar-at-Tahoe** (☎ 800/466-6784 or 916/562-1010) a top choice for families. Facilities include on-site lodging and restaurants, and it's only 45 minutes from the Reno–Tahoe airport. The smaller, less crowded, and less expensive **Diamond Peak** (☎ 702/832-1177 or 702/831-3249) plugs itself as the "premier family ski resort." It's primarily a mountain for intermediate skiers, but kids love its snowboard park. A homey little resort with lean lift lines and gorgeous views of the lake, **Ski Homewood** (☎ 916/525-2992) also is a good family resort, with child care for 2- to 5-year-olds and a special ski and play program for kids 6 to 12. Known for its deep snowpack and great powder skiing, the mid-sized **Sugar Bowl** (☎ 916/426-3651) was ranked by *Ski* magazine in 1994 as one of the top 30 resorts in the nation. It's 30 miles from South Lake Tahoe. **Kirkwood,** P.O. Box 1, Kirkwood, CA 95646, off Hwy. 88 (☎ 209/258-6000), is one of the top areas, with one of the highest average snowfalls and excellent spring skiing often running into June.

**CROSS-COUNTRY SKIING**   **Lakeview Cross Country** (☎ 916/583-9353) has 37 miles of groomed trails, a full-service day lodge, and three warming huts. It's only 2 miles from Tahoe City off Calif. 28, making it very accessible. The **Royal Gorge Cross-Country Ski Resort** (☎ 800/500-3871 or 916/426-3871) is one of the largest cross-country facilities anywhere, with 88 trails (203 miles), including 28 novice trails and four ski lifts. **Sugar Pine Point State Park** (☎ 916/525-7982) also has cross-country skiing on well-maintained trails. The **Squaw Creek Cross-Country Ski Center,** at the Resort at Squaw Creek (☎ 916/583-6300), has 400 acres for touring and 28 miles of groomed trails.

**GOLF**   The area has two Robert Trent Jones, Jr. championship courses: **Incline Village Championship Course,** 955 Fairway Blvd. (☎ 702/832-1144), and **Squaw Creek Golf Course,** at the Resort at Squaw Creek (☎ 916/583-6300), which is the most expensive course at Tahoe. Other challenging courses include the **Northstar Golf Course** (☎ 916/562-2490), which has water hazards on 14 holes, and South Lake's **Edgewood Tahoe,** site of the Isuzu Celebrity Gold Championship (☎ 702/588-3566).

**OTHER OUTDOOR ACTIVITIES**   Miles of excellent paved bike paths around the lake beckon bicyclists and in-line skaters. You can rent bikes and skates in Tahoe City, Incline, and South Lake Tahoe. You can take your mountain bike up the cable cars and cycle back down the trails at both Northstar-at-Tahoe and Squaw Valley ski resorts (see above).

Fishing in the crystal-clear waters of the lake presents a special challenge to anglers, with kokanee salmon catchable from May to June, rainbow trout in fall and winter, and Mackinaw trout year-round. Dozens of charter companies offer daily excursions on Lake Tahoe year-round.

The mountains surrounding Lake Tahoe are crisscrossed with hiking trails graded for all levels of experience. Contact the local visitor bureau for a map and more in-depth information on particular trails (see "Essentials," above).

Stables with horseback riding include **Camp Richardson Corral,** South Lake Tahoe (☎ 916/541-3113); **Northstar Stables,** at the Northstar-at-Tahoe resort (☎ 916/562-1230); **Squaw Valley Stables,** on Squaw Valley Road (☎ 916/583-7433); and **Sunset Ranch,** on Hwy. 50, South Lake Tahoe (☎ 916/541-9001), the only stable to allow unescorted riding.

One of the world's most unusual ice rinks is 8,200 feet above sea level at **Squaw Valley's High Camp** (☎ 916/583-6985). The ice is accessible only by cable car—a scenic ride that's included with rink admission. The rink is open year-round, but call first, since it closes a few days in the spring and fall for repairs.

The Truckee River—Lake Tahoe's only outlet—dumps plenty of water for a swift,

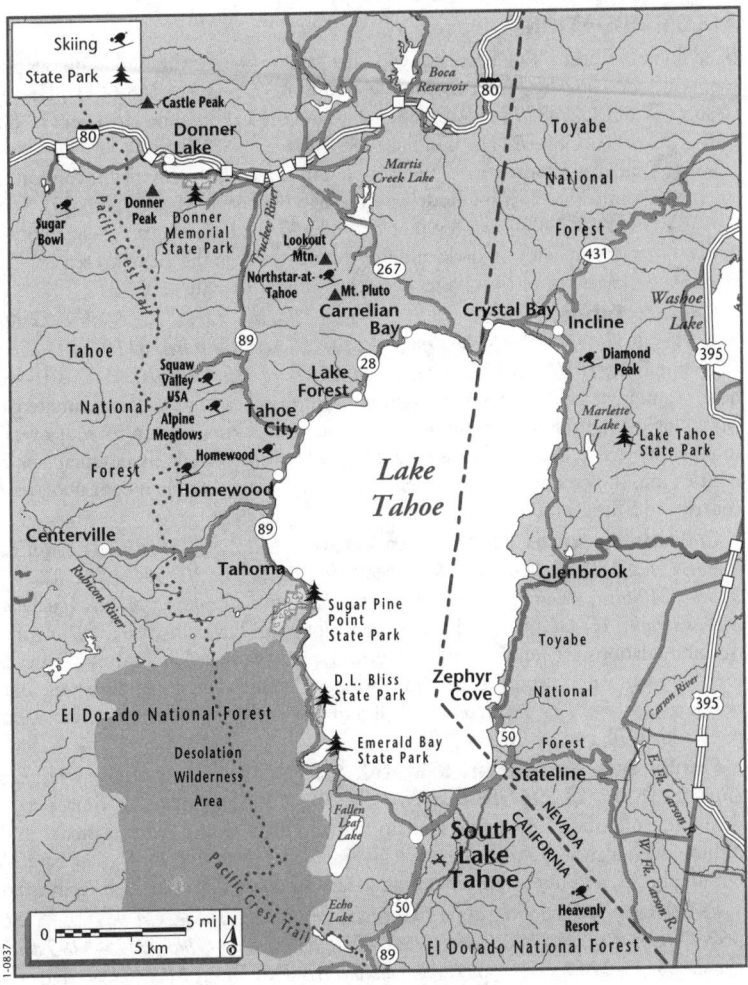

but gentle, whitewater ride. Rafting outfits include **Truckee River Raft Rental** (☎ 916/583-0123), **Fanny Bridge Rafts** (☎ 916/581-0123), and **Truckee River Rafting/Mountain Air Sports** (☎ 916/583-7238).

**LAKE CRUISES**   The best way to experience the lake is to get out on it aboard *M.S. Dixie II* (☎ 702/588-3508), a 570-passenger vessel with bars, a dance floor, and a full dining room; or the *Tahoe Queen* (☎ 800/238-2463 or 916/541-3364), a 500-passenger sternwheeler offering daily Emerald Bay cruises, sunset dinner-dance cruises, and shuttle service between the lake's north and south shores during the ski season. On the North Shore, the *Tahoe Gal* (☎ 800/218-2464 or 916/583-0141), a Mississippi River paddlewheeler, departs from the Lighthouse Marina in Tahoe City (behind Safeway). *Woodwind* **Sailing Cruises,** in the Zephyr Cove Resort, on U.S. 50, Zephyr Cove (☎ 702/588-3000), offers daily sailing trips aboard a 41-foot trihull craft that takes up to 30 passengers. The boat's glass bottom allows for good underwater viewing. Reservations are recommended.

## ACCOMMODATIONS

In addition to Caesars Tahoe (see below), other gaming houses with multitudinous guest rooms include **Harrah's Hotel Casino** (☎ 800/648-3773 or 916/588-6611), **Harvey's Resort** (☎ 800/427-8397 or 916/588-2411), and the **Lake Tahoe Horizon** (☎ 800/648-3322 or 916/588-6211), all in Stateline, Nevada.

Among the chain motels here, two people can share a perfectly plain, comfortable room for about $35 each at the **Rodeway Inn,** 645 N. Lake Blvd. (P.O. Box 29), Tahoe City, CA 96145 (☎ 800/624-8590 or 916/583-3711), including access to a hot tub, heated outdoor pool with sundeck, and free shuttle service to the major ski resorts. Generous ski packages are an even better deal from Sunday to Thursday.

**Caesars Tahoe.** *P.O. Box 5800, 55 Hwy. 50, Lake Tahoe, NV 89449.* ☎ *800/648-3353 or 702/588-3515. 410 rms, 31 suites, 7 executive suites. $110–$195 double; $375 minisuite; $650 suite. Additional person $10 extra. AE, DC, MC, V.* This 16-story hotel is a more intimate version of its glittery, glitzy, and campy Las Vegas counterpart. Mythological figures even cavort across the elevators taking you up to your oversize room with views of the lake across the highway. Facilities include six restaurants, a 24-hour casino, showrooms with major entertainment, a lagoon-style indoor pool, tennis courts, and a fitness room.

**✪ Embassy Suites Resort Lake Tahoe.** *4130 Lake Tahoe Blvd., South Lake Tahoe, CA 96150.* ☎ *800/988-9850 or 916/544-5400. Fax 916/544-4900. 400 suites. $150–$240 suite. Additional person $20 extra. Rates include continental breakfast. Packages available. AE, DC, MC, V.* Family skiers fill up this Bavarian-style hotel in winter. Accommodations are nothing unusual for those who've stayed at Embassy Suites before: dark hardwood furniture, tasteful fabrics, well-chosen carpets, and such useful extras as microwaves. On the premises you'll find a 24-hour restaurant, sports bar, indoor pool, whirlpool, and small gym.

**Family Tree Restaurant & Motel.** *551 N. Lake Blvd., P.O. Box 551, Tahoe City, CA 96145.* ☎ *916/583-0287. 10 rms. $43–$60 double. MC, V.* Smack dab in the middle of Tahoe City, this restaurant first and hotel second (you register with the cashier) offers a great deal. Though ordinary, rooms are clean and comfy; they have TVs but no phones, and not all are air-conditioned. This place fills up fast, so reserve early.

**✪ Fantasy Inn.** *3696 Lake Tahoe Blvd., South Lake Tahoe, CA 96150.* ☎ *800/367-7736 or 916/541-6666. Fax 916/541-6798. 53 rms. Sun–Thurs, $115–$195 double. Fri–Sat, $155–$240 double. Packages available. AE, DC, DISC, MC, V.* Catering exclusively to adults, this place sports sexually provocative art, porno flicks, lots of wall and ceiling mirrors, surround-sound stereo systems, and twin showerheads. Some suites have round beds or "waveless" water beds (the Graceland model has a heart-shaped bed and mucho Elvis memorabilia). You're on your own: no restaurant or casino here.

**Lakeland Village Beach & Ski Resort.** *3535 Lake Tahoe Blvd. (between Ski Run Blvd. and Fairway Ave.), P.O. Box 1356, South Lake Tahoe, CA 96150.* ☎ *800/822-5969 or 916/544-1685. Fax 916/541-3539. 212 units. $75–$345 double. AE, MC, V.* This condo complex on 19 lightly forested acres is a hybrid mix of residential apartments and holiday resort. Ranging from studios to four-bedroom lakeside apartments, units are streamlined California architecture, many with upstairs sleeping lofts. The resort has two outdoor pools, three saunas, tennis and volleyball courts, bicycle rentals, a health club, and a large private beach.

**Lamplighter Motel.** *4143 Cedar Ave. South Lake Tahoe, CA 96159.* ☎ *916/544-2936. Fax 916/544-5249. 28 rms. $36–$55 double. Ski packages available. AE, DISC, JCB, MC, V.* This family-run motel is clean, cozy, and loaded with perks like cable TV, in-room coffee brewer, ceiling fans, open-air spa and sundeck. It's in a great spot, only

3 blocks from the beach and 50 yards from the casinos. Not all units are air-conditioned, so ask for one in summer.

✪ **Resort at Squaw Creek.** *400 Squaw Creek Rd., P.O. Box 3333, Olympic Valley, CA 96146.* ☎ *800/327-3353 or 916/583-6300. Fax 916/581-6632. 196 rms, 201 suites. $180–$250 double; $280–$395 suite. AE, CB, DC, DISC, MC, V. Free self-parking; valet parking $10.* A Squaw Valley chairlift lands at the door of this luxurious lodge, and lots more sports facilities keep active travelers happy. Accommodations are well equipped if not particularly spacious. There are restaurants, bars, an 18-hole golf course, three heated swimming pools, three outdoor whirlpools, eight tennis courts, a fitness center, a shopping arcade, 18¹/₂ miles of groomed cross-country skiing trails (marked for hiking and biking in the summer), an ice-skating rink (winter only), and an equestrian center.

**Richardson's Resort.** *Hwy. 89 at Jamison Beach, South Lake Tahoe, CA 96158.* ☎ *800/544-1801 or 916/541-1801. Fax 916/541-2791. 29 rooms, 39 cabins. $64–$74 double per night; $495–$1,095 cabin per week. AE, MC, V.* This armada of condominiums, homey little log cabins, classic lodge rooms, and tent/RV sites spread out over several acres of wooded grounds adjacent to a gold-sand beach is one of the most enjoyable places to stay in Lake Tahoe. There are plenty of sports activities on-site and nearby.

✪ **Shore House.** *7170 N. Lake Blvd., Tahoe Vista, CA 96148.* ☎ *800/207-5160 or 916/546-7270. 9 rms. $125–$165 double. Rates include breakfast. MC, V.* Hosts Marty and Barb have made pampering an art form at this cozy, romantic bed-and-breakfast right on Lake Tahoe's shoreline. Their individually decorated rooms have their own entrances, fabulous rough-hewn log furniture, private bathrooms, minifridges, and blissfully comfortable featherbeds. You won't soon forget a romantic weekend here.

**Sunnyside Lodge.** *1850 W. Lake Blvd. (off Calif. 89), P.O. Box 5969, Tahoe City, CA 96145.* ☎ *800/822-2754 or 916/583-7200. 23 rms. Apr 7–May 23 and Oct 7–Dec 12, $110–$125 double. May 24–Oct 6, $145–$160 double. Dec 13–Apr 6, $130–$145 double. Rates include continental breakfast. AE, MC, V.* Built as a private home in 1908, this cabinlike wooden structure is one of the grand old lodges still left on the lake. Individually decorated bedrooms have homey bark-covered timber tables and chairs, and all but four have nice views. The popular Sunnyside Restaurant takes up the first floor (see "Dining," below).

**Tamarack Lodge.** *2311 N. Lake Tahoe Blvd., P.O. Box 859, North Lake Tahoe, CA 96145.* ☎ *916/583-3350. 21 rms, 4 cabins. $35–$65 room; $45–$110 cabin. DISC, MC, V.* A favorite haunt of Clark Gable and Gary Cooper, this old lodge now is one of the best bets for cost-conscious travelers. A few old cabins, five hokey old "poker rooms," and a modern, far less nostalgic motel unit are hidden among a cadre of pines just east of Tahoe City.

## DINING

**Bridgetender Tavern and Grill.** *30 W. Lake Blvd. (at Fanny Bridge), Tahoe City.* ☎ *916/583-3342. Items $5–$7. No credit cards. Daily 11am–2am. PUB FOOD.* Though it's in Fanny Bridge, one the most popular tourist areas in North Lake, locals as well as visitors come here for cheap pub grub and a huge selection of draft beers. The tavern is built around a trio of ponderosa pines that meld in with the decor. Dine outside among the pines in summer.

**Cantina Los Tres Hombres.** *765 Emerald Bay Rd.* ☎ *916/544-1233. Main courses $7–$13. AE, MC, V. Daily 11:30am–10:30pm. MEXICAN.* While this busy restaurant's cavernous tiki bar is South Seas, the food is unmistakably south of the border—albeit tried-and-true tacos, burritos, and enchiladas. The chilies rellenos and

crabmeat- and mushroom-stuffed enchiladas get thumbs-up. The portions are mountainous, and service is brisk but not unfriendly. Some patrons may have had more than
their share of tequila.

**✪ Fire Sign Café.** *1785 W. Lake Blvd., Tahoe City.* ☎ *916/583-0871. Items
$4–$9. MC, V. Daily 7:30am–2pm. AMERICAN.* This has been the local's favorite
breakfast joint since the 1970s. Just about everything is made from scratch: soft buttermilk biscuits, coffee cake, and blackberry-buckwheat pancakes. The salmon for the
legendary salmon omelet is even smoked in-house. Lunch also is quite popular, particularly when the outdoor patio is open.

**Nepheles.** *1169 Ski Run Blvd.* ☎ *916/544-8130. Main courses $12–$18. AE,
MC, V. Daily 5–10pm. CALIFORNIAN.* This old home complete with stained-glass
windows stops the traffic en route to Heavenly Ski Resort. The basically Californian
cuisine uses market-fresh ingredients, including venison, elk, wild boar, or whatever
other game's in season. If you demand ketchup here, it's likely to be a bottle from
Indonesia.

**Scusa!** *1142 Ski Run Blvd.* ☎ *916/542-0100. Main courses $9–$15. MC, V. Daily
5–10pm. ITALIAN.* Also on the trail to the Heavenly Ski Resort, this cozy, civilized,
basic but clean Italian eatery may have a decor that errs a little garishly on the neon side,
but the food more than compensates. Standard dishes are interspersed with enough surprises to keep the locals happy.

**Sunnyside Restaurant.** *In Sunnyside Lodge, 1850 W. Lake Blvd., Tahoe City.*
☎ *916/583-7200. Main courses $13–$19. AE, MC, V. Oct–June, daily 5:30–9:30pm.
July–Sept, daily 10am–10pm. Sun brunch 9:30am–2pm. SEAFOOD/AMERICAN.*
There's no more highly coveted table in Tahoe than one on the Sunnyside Lodge's
lakeside veranda in summer, but you can dine any season in the traditional dining room
with its 1930s aura. Lunch is nothing special, but dinners feature the likes of Australian lobster tail and oven-roasted shiitake pork tenderloin.

**✪ Wolfdale's.** *640 N. Lake Blvd., Tahoe City.* ☎ *916/583-5700. Reservations recommended. Main courses $15–$20. MC, V. July–Aug, daily 6–10pm. Sept–June, Wed–
Mon 6–10pm. CALIFORNIAN/JAPANESE.* Situated in an idyllic lakeside setting, the
visually modest Wolfdale's is one of Tahoe's top restaurants. A rather unassuming wood-
shingle exterior fronts a simple, clean interior combining country-style American furnishings with Japanese-style blond woods and screens. The chefs dare to be innovative
and aren't afraid of blending flavors and textures of the East and the West.

**Za's.** *395 N. Lake Blvd. (across from the fire station), Tahoe City.* ☎ *916/583-1812.
Main courses $6–$10. MC, V. Daily 4:30–9:30pm. ITALIAN.* This little gem serves great
Italian food at bargain prices: a hefty plate of smoked chicken fettuccini in a garlic cream
sauce with roasted bell peppers, fresh artichoke hearts, and mushrooms sells for under
$10. Za's is a bit hard to find (look behind Pete-n-Peter's Saloon), but *mama-mia,* it's
worth the search.

## TAHOE AFTER DARK

There's always something going on in the showrooms of the major casino hotels in
Stateline, Nevada. Call **Harrah's** (☎ 916/588-6611), **Harvey's** (☎ 916/588-2411),
**Caesars Tahoe** (☎ 916/588-3515), and the **Lake Tahoe Horizon** (☎ 916/588-6211)
for current show schedules and prices. Headliners are likely to include the likes of Jay
Leno or perhaps Johnny Mathis.

Otherwise, there's usually live music nightly in **Bullwhackers Pub,** at the Resort at
Squaw Creek (☎ 916/583-6300), 5 miles west of Tahoe City. The **Pierce Street Annex,** 850 N. Lake Blvd. (☎ 916/583-5800), behind the Safeway in Tahoe City, has

pool tables, shuffleboard, and deejay dancing every night. It's one of the livelier places around.

## 5  Yosemite National Park

What most sets the dramatic Yosemite National Park apart is its incredible geology. At least three glaciers flowed through the Yosemite Valley during the last Ice Age, sheering vertical faces of stone and hauling away the rubble. They left an incredible number of waterfalls pouring into the valley from hanging side canyons. Combined with the shadows and lighting of the deep valley, the effect of all this falling water is mesmerizing. On a clear spring morning you'll see more rainbows than you can count, and a bass note of roaring water echoes through the entire valley.

The 7-square-mile valley is really a huge bathtub drain for the combined runoff of hundreds of square miles of snow-covered peaks. The 8,000-foot tops of El Capitan, Half Dome, and Glacier Point look like the top of the world, but they're small in comparison to the highest peaks in the park, some of which reach almost 14,000 feet. All that vertical stone gets put to use by hundreds who flock to the park for some of the finest climbing anywhere.

Deer and coyote frequent the valley, often causing vehicular mayhem as one heavy-footed tourist after another slams on brakes to whip out the camera. The name "Yosemite" derives from the Native American word *Yohamite*, "killer among us." Grizzly bears are gone from the park now, but black bears make their presence known through late-night plundering of ice chests and food in the campgrounds.

While it's easy to let the tremendous beauty of the valley monopolize your attention, remember that 95% of Yosemite is wilderness. Of the 4 million visitors who come to the park each year, very few ever get more than a mile from their car. That leaves most of Yosemite's 750,000 acres open for anyone adventurous enough to hike a few miles. In the park's southwest corner, the Mariposa Grove is a striking forest of rare sequoias, the world's largest trees, as well as several meadows and the rushing south fork of the Merced River.

Unfortunately, popularity isn't always the greatest thing for wild places. Over the last 20 years, tourist-magnet Yosemite Valley has set records for the worst crowding, noise, crime, and traffic in any California national park. More than 4.1 million visitors came in 1995.

### ESSENTIALS

**ARRIVING & DEPARTING**   The nearest airport is in Merced. From there, it's 65 miles to Yosemite Village via Calif. 140. You will need a car.

There are four main **entrances** to the park. Most valley visitors enter through the **Arch Rock Entrance Station** on Calif. 140. The best entrance for Mariposa Grove and Wawona is the **South entrance** on Calif. 41 from Mariposa. If you're going to the high country you'll save a lot of time by coming in through the **Big Oak Flat entrance,** which puts you straight onto Tioga Road without forcing you to deal with the congested valley. The **Tioga Pass entrance** is only open in summer and is relevant only if you're coming from the east side of the Sierra (in which case it's your only choice). A fifth, little-used entrance is the **Hetch Hetchy entrance** in the euphonious Poopenaut Valley, on a dead-end road.

**VISITOR INFORMATION**   There is a central, 24-hour recorded information line for the park (☎ 209/372-0200). All visitor-related service lines including hotels and information can be accessed by touch-tone phone at ☎ 209/372-1000.

**VISITOR CENTERS**    Right in the middle of the valley's thickest urban cluster is the **Valley Visitor Center** (☎ 209/372-0299), with exhibits that will teach you about glacial geology, history, and the park's flora and fauna. Check out the **Indian Cultural Museum** next door for insight into what life in the park was once like. The **Wawona Ranger Station** (☎ 209/372-0564) and **Big Oak Flat Information Center** (☎ 209/372-0615) give general park information. For interesting biological and geological displays about the high sierra, as well as trail advice, the **Tuolumne Meadows Visitor Center** (☎ 209/372-0263) is great. All three can provide you with maps plus more newspapers, books, and photocopied leaflets than you'll ever read.

**ADMISSION COSTS & REGULATIONS**    Entrance fees are $10 per car or $5 per person, good for 7 days. Annual Yosemite Passes cost $40. Park entrance is free for holders of the National Park Service's Golden Eagle ($50), Golden Access (free to disabled U.S. citizens), and Golden Age ($10 for U.S. citizens 62 or older) passports.

Wilderness permits are required for all overnight backpacking trips. They are free, but reserving them requires a $3 fee. Fishing licenses are required. Utilize proper food storage methods in bear country. Don't collect firewood around campgrounds. No off-road bicycle riding. Dogs are allowed in the park but must be leashed and are forbidden on the trails. Don't feed the animals.

**WHEN TO GO**    Yosemite Valley becomes a total zoo between Memorial Day and Labor Day. If you must go in summer, park your car, and bike, hike, or ride the shuttle buses that go everywhere in the valley. Curry Village and Yosemite Lodge also rent bikes in the summer (☎ 209/372-8367). It may take longer to get from point A to point B, but you're in one of the most gorgeous places on earth—so why hurry?

Winter is one of the nicest times to visit the valley—it isn't crowded, and a dusting of snow provides a stark contrast to all that granite. To see the waterfalls at their best, come in spring when snowmelt is at its peak. Fall can be cool, but it's beautiful and much less crowded than summer.

The high country is under about 20 feet of snow from November to May, so unless you are snow camping, summer is pretty much the only season. Even in summer, thundershowers are an almost daily occurrence and snow is not uncommon. Mosquitoes can be a plague during the peak of summer but get better after the first freeze.

**INTERPRETIVE PROGRAMS**    Even though they are overworked just trying to keep the peace, Yosemite's wonderful rangers also take time to lead a number of educational and interpretive programs ranging from backcountry hikes to fireside talks to snow-country survival clinics. Call the main park information number with specific requests for the season and park area you'll be visiting. Also a great service are the free painting, drawing, and photography classes offered from spring through fall and holiday weekends in winter at the Art Activity Center next to the Museum Gallery.

## WHAT TO SEE & DO

Before setting out, buy the excellent "Map and Guide to Yosemite Valley" at a visitor center; it describes many excellent hikes and short nature walks. Walking and biking are the best ways to get around. To cover longer distances, shuttles run frequently to all major parts of the park.

**SEEING THE VALLEY**    The first two things you'll see in the valley are the delicate and beautiful **Bridal Veil Falls** and the immense face of **El Capitan,** a beautiful and anything but delicate 3,593-foot-tall solid granite rock. A short trail leads to the base of Bridal Veil, which at 620 feet tall is only a medium-size fall by park standards, but one of the prettiest.

The best single view in the valley is from **Sentinel Bridge** over the Merced River. At sunset, Half Dome's face functions as a projection screen for all the sinking sun's hues

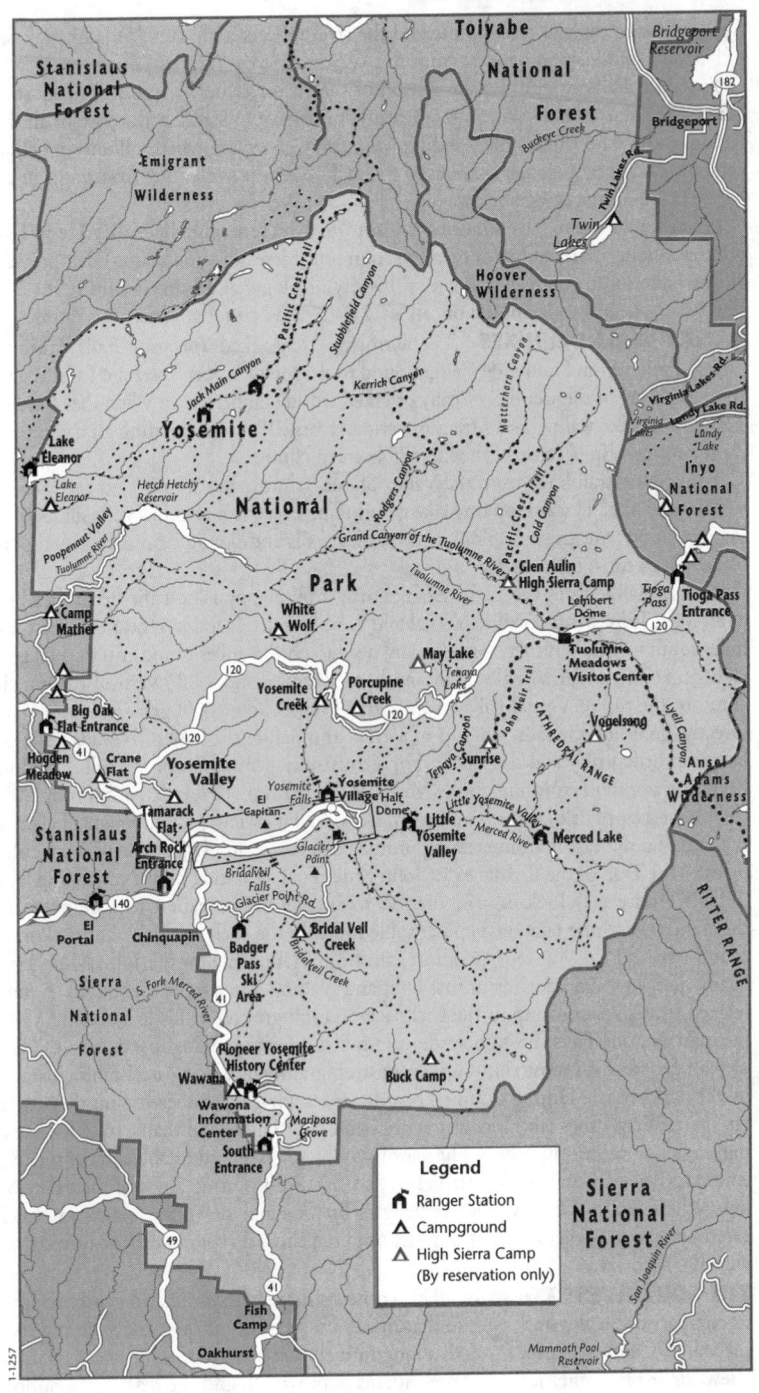

# Yosemite National Park

Toiyabe

National

Forest

Bridgeport Reservoir

182

Bridgeport

Stanislaus National Forest

Emigrant Wilderness

Buckeye Creek

Hoover Wilderness

Pacific Crest Trail

Stubblefield Canyon

Jack Main Canyon

Kerrich Canyon

Matterhorn Canyon

Twin Lakes

Virginia Lakes Rd.

Lundy Lake Rd.

Virginia Lakes

Lundy Lake

Lake Eleanor

Lake Eleanor

Yosemite

Rodgers Canyon

Cold Canyon

Pacific Crest Trail

I'nyo

National

Forest

Hetch Hetchy Reservoir

Grand Canyon of the Tuolumne River

Poopenaut Valley

Tuolumne River

National

Glen Aulin High Sierra Camp

Tuolumne River

Lembert Dome

Tioga Pass

Tioga Pass Entrance

120

Camp Mather

Park

White Wolf

May Lake

Tenaya Lake

Tuolumne Meadows Visitor Center

120

Big Oak Flat Entrance

Hogden Meadow

Crane Flat

120

Yosemite Creek

Porcupine Creek

120

Vogelsong

Lyell Canyon

Ansel Adams Wilderness

Tenaya Canyon

John Muir Trail

CATHEDRAL RANGE

Yosemite Valley

Yosemite Falls

El Capitan

Yosemite Village

Half Dome

Sunrise

Tamarack Flat

Arch Rock Entrance

Glacier Point

Little Yosemite Valley

Little Yosemite Valley

Merced River

Merced Lake

RITTER RANGE

El Portal

140

Bridalveil Falls

Glacier Point Rd.

Chinquapin

Badger Pass Ski Area

Bridal Veil Creek

Bridalveil Creek

Stanislaus National Forest

Sierra

National

Forest

S. Fork Merced River

41

Pioneer Yosemite History Center

Wawona

Buck Camp

Wawona Information Center

South Entrance

Mariposa Grove

Sierra

National

Forest

49

## Legend

🏠 Ranger Station

△ Campground

△ High Sierra Camp
(By reservation only)

San Joaquin River

41

Fish Camp

Oakhurst

Mammoth Pool Reservoir

1-1257

from yellow to pink to dark purple and the river reflects it all. Ansel Adams took one of his most famous photographs from this very spot.

**Yosemite Falls** is within a short stroll of the visitor center. You can actually see it better elsewhere in the valley, but it's really impressive to stand at the base of all that falling water. The wind, noise, and blowing spray generated when millions of gallons catapult 2,425 feet through space onto the rocks below is sometimes so strong you can barely stand on the bridge below.

If you would like to have someone explain what you're seeing, the **Valley Floor Tour** offers a 2-hour, narrated bus or open-air tram tour (depending on season) that provides an introduction to the valley's natural history, geology, and human culture for $15. Purchase tickets at valley hotels or call ☎ **209/372-1240** for advance reservations.

**VALLEY WALKS & HIKES**    The narrow, switchbacked **Yosemite Falls Trail** zig-zags 3¹/₂ miles from Sunnyside Campground to the top of Upper Yosemite Falls. It gives you an inkling of the weird, vertically oriented world climbers enter when they head up Yosemite's sheer walls. It's a little unnerving at first. Plan on spending all day on this 7-mile round-trip because of the incredibly steep climb.

A mile-long trail leads from the Valley Stables (shuttle bus stop 17; no car parking) to **Mirror Lake.** The already tiny lake is shrinking every year as it fills with silt, becoming a meadow, but the reflections of the valley walls and sky on its surface remain one of the park's most introspective sights.

Also accessible from the Valley Stables or nearby Happy Isles is the best valley hike of all—the **John Muir Trail** to Vernal and Nevada Falls. It follows the Sierra crest 200 miles south to Mt. Whitney, but you only need to go 1¹/₂ miles round-trip to get a great view of 317-foot Vernal Falls. Add another 1¹/₂ miles and 1,000 vertical feet for the climb to the top of Vernal Falls on the **Mist Trail,** where you'll get wet as you climb directly alongside the falls. On top of Vernal and before the base of Nevada Falls is a beautiful little valley and deep pool. For a truly outrageous view of the valley and one heck of a workout, continue up the Mist Trail to the top of Nevada Falls. From 2,000 feet above Happy Isles where you began, it's a dizzying view straight down the face of the falls. To the east is an interesting profile perspective on Half Dome. Return either by the Mist Trail or the slightly easier John Muir Trail for a total 7-mile round-trip hike.

**Half Dome** may look insurmountable to anyone but an expert rock climber, but thousands every year take the popular cable route up the back side. It's almost 17 miles round-trip and a 4,900-foot elevation gain from Happy Isle on the John Muir Trail. Many do it in 1 day, starting at first light and rushing home to beat nightfall. A more relaxed strategy is to camp in the backpacking campground in Little Yosemite Valley just past Nevada Falls. From here the summit is an easy striking distance to the base of Half Dome. You must climb up a very steep granite face using steel cables installed by the park service. During summer, boards are installed as crossbeams, but they're still far apart. Wear shoes with lots of traction, and your hands will thank your for bringing leather gloves for the cables. The view from the top is an unbeatable vista of the high country, Tenaya Canyon, Glacier Point, and the awe-inspiring abyss of the valley below. When you shuffle up to the overhanging lip for a look down the face, be extremely careful not to kick rocks or anything else onto the climbers below who are earning this view the hard way.

**THE SOUTHWEST CORNER**    This corner is densely forested and gently sculpted in comparison to the stark granite that makes up so much of the park. Coming from the valley, Calif. 41 passes through a long tunnel. Just prior to the entrance is **Tunnel View,** sight of another famous Ansel Adams photograph, and the best scenic outlook of the valley accessible by automobile. Virtually the whole valley is laid out below:

Half Dome and Yosemite Falls straight ahead in the distance, Bridal Veil to the right, and El Capitan to the left.

A few miles past the tunnel, Glacier Point Road turns off to the east. Closed in winter, this winding road leads to a picnic area at **Glacier Point,** site of another fabulous view of the valley, this time 3,000 feet below. Schedule at least an hour to drive here from the valley and an hour or two to absorb the view. This is a good place to study the glacial scouring of the valley below.

On Calif. 41, 30 miles south of the valley, is the **Wawona Hotel** and the **Pioneer Yosemite History Center.** In 1879 the Wawona was the first lodge built in the state reserve that would later become the national park. Its Victorian architecture evokes a time when travelers spent several days in horse-drawn wagons to get to the park. What a welcome stop it must have been. The Pioneer center is a collection of early homesteading log buildings across the river from the Wawona.

One of the primary reasons Yosemite was first set aside as a park was the **Mariposa Grove** of sequoias. Many good trails lead through the grove. These huge trees have personalities that match their gargantuan size. Single limbs on the biggest tree in the grove, the Grizzly Giant, are 10 feet thick. The tree itself is 209 feet tall, 32 feet in diameter, and more than 2,700 years old. Totally out of proportion with the size of the trees are the tiny cones of the sequoia. Smaller than a baseball and tightly closed, the cones will not release their cargo of seeds until opened by fire.

**THE HIGH COUNTRY**   Yosemite's high country has the most grandiose landscape in the entire Sierra Nevada. Dome after dome of beautifully crystalline granite reflects the sunlight above deep green meadows and icy-cold rivers.

**Tioga Pass** is the gateway to the high country. At times it clings to the side of steep rock faces; in other places it weaves through canyon bottoms. Several good campgrounds make it a pleasing overnight alternative to fighting summertime crowds in the valley, though use is increasing here, too. Unlike the valley, a car is vital to getting around as the only public transportation is the once-a-day bus to Tuolumne Meadows. Leaving the valley at 8am, the bus will let you off anywhere along the way. The driver waits 2 hours at Tuolumne Meadows, which isn't much time to see anything, then heads back down to the valley, returning around 4pm. One-way fare is $12, or slightly less to intermediate destinations.

**Tenaya Lake** is a popular windsurfing, fishing, canoeing, sailing, and swimming spot. The water is very chilly. Many good hikes lead into the high country from here and the granite domes surrounding the lake are popular with climbers. Fishing varies greatly from year to year.

Near the top of Tioga Pass is stunning **Tuolumne Meadows.** This enormous meadow covering several square miles is bordered by the Tuolumne River on one side and spectacular granite peaks on the other. The meadow is cut by many stream channels full of trout, and herds of mule deer are almost always present. The **Tuolumne Meadows Lodge** and store is a welcome counterpoint to the overdeveloped valley. In winter the canvas roofs are removed and the buildings fill with snow. You can buy last-minute backpacking supplies here, and there is a basic burgers-and-fries cafe.

**TUOLUMNE MEADOWS HIKES & WALKS**   So many hikes lead from here into the backcountry that it's impossible to do them justice. A good day hike is the 5-mile climb to **Cathedral Lake.** This steep but shady trail passes an icy-cold spring and traverses several meadows.

On the far bank of the Tuolumne from the meadow a trail leads downriver, eventually passing through the grand canyon of the Tuolumne and exiting at Hetch Hetchy. Shorter hikes will take you downriver past rapids and cascades.

An interesting geological quirk is the **Soda Spring** on the far side of Tuolumne Meadow from the road. This bubbling spring gushes carbonated water from a hole in the ground. A small log cabin marks its site.

For a great selection of Yosemite high country hikes and backpacking trips, consult some of the specialized guidebooks to the area. *Tuolumne Meadows,* a hiking guide by Jeffrey B. Shaffer and Thomas Winnett, and *Yosemite National Park* by Thomas Winnett and Jason Winnett, both published by Wilderness Press, are two of the best.

**OTHER OUTDOOR ACTIVITIES** Biking is the perfect way to see the valley, with 8 miles of bike paths in addition to the roads. You can rent one-speeds at the Yosemite Lodge or Curry Village (see "Accommodations & Dining," below). If you want a fancier bike, you'll have to bring it from home. All trails in the park are closed to mountain bikes.

Fishing in the Merced River in the valley is catch and release only, and barbless hooks are required. High country lakes and streams are literally leaping with trout. A California license is required and available in the park at the Yosemite Village Sportshop.

Four stables offer scenic day rides and multiday pack excursions in the park. **Yosemite Valley Stables** (☎ 209/372-8348) is open spring through fall. The other three, **Wawona** (☎ 209/375-6502), **White Wolf** (☎ 209/372-1323), and **Tuolumne Meadows** (☎ 209/372-8427), only operate during summer. The park wranglers can be hired to make resupply drops at any of the backcountry High Sierra camps if you want to arrange for a food drop while on an extended trip.

Much of the most important technical advancement in rock climbing came out of the highly competitive Yosemite Valley climbing scene of the 1970s and 1980s. Though other places have taken some of the limelight, Yosemite is still one of the most desirable climbing destinations in the world. **Yosemite Mountaineering School** runs classes for beginners through advanced climbers (☎ 209/372-8444 in the Valley; 209/372-8435 at Tuolumne Meadows). Considered one of the best climbing schools in the world, it offers classes from early spring to early October in the valley, less often in Tuolumne Meadows.

Opened in 1935, **Badger Pass** (☎ 209/372-8430) is the oldest operating ski area in California. Four chairs and two T-bars cover a compact mountain of beginner and intermediate runs. It's not great, but it's a fine place to learn how to ski or snowboard. Yosemite is a better destination for cross-country skiers and snowshoers. Both the Badger Pass ski school and the mountaineering school run trips and lessons for all abilities, ranging from basic technique to trans-Sierra crossings. If you're on your own, Crane Flat is a good place to go, as is the groomed track up to Glacier Point, a 20-mile round-trip.

In winter the **Curry Village Ice Rink** is a lot of fun. It's outdoors and melts quickly when the weather warms up.

**CAMPING** Campgrounds in Yosemite can be reserved up to 4 months in advance through **DESTINET** (☎ 800/436-7275). During the busy season all valley campsites sell out within hours of becoming available on the service.

The five car-campgrounds in the valley are along the Merced River and cost $15 per night. All have drinking water, flush toilets, pay phones, fire pits, and a heavy ranger presence. Showers are available for a cost at Curry Village. Three campgrounds—**North Pines, Upper Pines,** and **Lower River**—allow RVs less than 35 feet long. Upper River is for tents only.

**Sunnyside Campground** is the only walk-in campground in the valley and fills up with climbers since it is only $3 per night. Hard-core climbers used to live here for months at a time, but the Park Service has cracked down on that. It's still a much more Bohemian atmosphere than any of the other campgrounds.

Two campgrounds near the south entrance of the park, **Wawona** and **Bridal Veil Creek,** offer a total of 210 sites with all the amenities. Wawona is open year-round on a first-come first-served basis. Because it sits well above snowline at more than 7,000 feet, Bridal Veil is open summer only. Both cost $10 per night.

Crane Flat, Hodgdon Meadow, and Tamarack Flat are all in the western corner of the park near the Big Oak Flat entrance. **Crane Flat** is the nearest to the valley, about a half-hour drive, with 166 sites, water, flush toilets, and fire pits. Its rates are $12 per night, and it's open May through October. **Hodgdon Meadow** is directly adjacent to the Big Oak Flat entrance at 4,800 feet elevation. It's open year-round and charges $12 per night. Facilities include flush toilets, running water, ranger station, and pay phone. It's one of the least crowded low-elevation car campgrounds, but there's not a lot to do here.

**Tamarack Flat** is a waterless, 52-site campground with pit toilets, open June through October. It's a bargain at $6 per night.

In the high country, **Tuolumne Meadows** is the largest campground in the park, with more than 300 spaces, but it absorbs the crowd well and has all the amenities, including campfire programs and slide shows in the outdoor amphitheater. Half the sites are reserved in advance, the rest are first-come, first-served. Rates are $12 per night. **White Wolf,** west of Tuolumne Meadows, is the other full-service campground in the high country, with 87 sites available for $10 per night. It offers a drier climate than the meadow and doesn't fill up as quickly. Two primitive camps, **Porcupine Flat** and **Yosemite Creek,** are the last to fill up in the park. Both have pit toilets and no running water, and charge $6 per night. High country campgrounds are open summer only.

## ACCOMMODATIONS & DINING
### IN THE PARK

To reserve at any accommodation in the park, call ☎ 209/252-4848 as far in advance as possible.

The grand **Ahwahnee Hotel,** in the valley, about three-quarters of a mile from the visitor center, is one of the most romantic and beautiful hotels in California. This native granite-and-timber lodge was built in 1927 and reflects an era when grand hotels were, well, grand. Fireplaces bigger than most Manhattan studio apartments warm the immense common rooms. Parlors and halls are filled with antique Native American rugs. With its ballroom, pool, tennis, gourmet dining, outstanding views, and high-digit price tag, it's a special-occasion sort of affair. Rooms are booked a year in advance. Rooms and cottages both cost $229.50 double. The cottages are more spacious than rooms in the main hotel.

The next best thing is the **Wawona Hotel** near the south entrance. Now a National Historical Landmark, the Wawona is a romantic throwback to another century. That has its ups and downs. Private bathrooms were not a big hit in the 19th century and rooms were small to hold in heat. Still, the Wawona is a great place to play make-believe. It offers a restaurant, pool, stables, and a lounge. Rooms cost $71 without bath, $97.50 with bath.

**Yosemite Lodge** is the next step down. It's actually a huge complex, not a lodge, with an array of accommodations ranging from luxurious suites with outdoor balconies and striking views of Yosemite Falls to one-room cabins with shared baths in a separate building. There is a pool. Two restaurants and a cafeteria serve mediocre meals. Rates are $101 double.

**Curry Village** is the valley's low-rent district. This compound of almost 200 cabins and 400 tent cabins varies widely in quality. Some have private baths. Others share campground-style bathrooms. Ironically, the oldest cabins are the nicest. Shoddy construction gives the others a slapped-together appearance, not to mention making them cold and drafty in winter. The tent cabins have wood floors and canvas walls; without real walls to stop noise, they lack any sort of privacy, but they're fun in that summer camp way. You'll have to sustain yourself with fast food from the Curry Village shopping center, as no cooking is allowed in the rooms. Rates range from $40 for tent cabins to $87 for rooms.

An intriguing option is Yosemite's five backcountry **High Sierra Camps.** These wilderness lodges are simple tent cabins and cafeteria tents located in some of the most beautiful, remote parts of the park. The five camps—Glen Aulin, May Lake, Sunrise, Merced Lake, and Vogelsang—make for good individual destinations. Or you can link several together, since they're arranged in a loose loop about a 10-mile hike from each other—a nice wilderness circuit. Overnight rates include a tent cabin, breakfast, dinner, bathrooms, and showers. Only one problem: They are assigned through a lottery system almost a year in advance of each summer season; call in May for an application for the following year.

### OUTSIDE THE PARK

Some luxurious lodgings are available not far from the park.

✪ **Estate by the Elderberries.** *48688 Victoria Lane, P.O. Box 577, Oakhurst, CA 93644.* ☎ *209/683-6860 (Château du Sureau); 209/683-6800 (Erna's Elderberry House restaurant). Fax 209/683-0800. 9 rms. $310–$410 double. Additional person $65 extra. Rates include full breakfast. AE, MC, V.* A perfect marriage of luxurious lodging and decadent dining, the Château Sureau and Erna's Elderberry House in Oakhurst, a 20-minute drive from the southern entrance to Yosemite via Calif. 41, gives even Wine Country retreats a run for their money. The interior is exquisitely furnished with fine antiques, rugs, and fabrics. Each room is decorated differently, but all have king-size beds with the finest Italian linens, goose-down comforters, wood-burning fireplaces, wrought-iron balconies, and CD sound systems with a selection of discs. The restaurant has been hailed as one of California's best places to dine. There's an outdoor pool and sundeck.

✪ **Tenaya Lodge.** *1122 Hwy. 41, Fish Camp, CA 93623.* ☎ *800/635-5807 or 209/683-6555. Fax 209/683-8684. 224 rms, 20 suites. Winter, $129–$159 double. Summer, $159–$239 double. Add $20–$80 for suites. Children stay free in parents' room. AE, DC, MC, V.* This three- and four-story resort sits on a 35-acre tract of forested land loaded with hiking trails. It's the centerpiece of Fish Camp, a village whose only other attraction is a gas station and a general store. The inside decor combines Adirondack hunting lodge and Southwestern pueblo. A massive river-rock fireplace rising three stories dominates the lobby. Rooms are ultramodern, with three phones and other amenities including in-room safes. The three restaurants draw huge crowds. The lodge has indoor and outdoor swimming pools, on-site massage specialists, a health club, games room, sleigh and hay rides.

## 6 Sequoia & Kings Canyon National Parks

While the National Park Service has taken every opportunity to modernize, accessorize, and urbanize Yosemite, it has treated the wilderness beauty of Sequoia and Kings Canyon national parks with respect and care. Only one road loops through the parks, the Generals Highway, and no road traverses the Sierra here. The park service doesn't recommend vehicles over 22 feet long for the steep and windy stretch between Potwisha Campground and the Giant Forest in Sequoia National Park. As a result, the park is much less accessible by car than most, but spectacular for those willing to head out on foot.

Saving the giant sequoias was the reason Sequoia National Park was created in 1890 at the request of San Joaquin Valley residents, making it America's second-oldest national park. Unlike the coast redwoods, which reproduce either by sprouting or by seeds, giant sequoias only reproduce by seed. The tiny cones require fire to open, so decades can pass between generations. Adult sequoias don't die of old age and are protected from fire by thick bark. The huge trees have surprisingly shallow roots, and most die when they topple in high winds or heavy snows. These groves, like the ones in Yosemite, were first explored by conservationist and nature writer John Muir.

**Mt. Whitney,** the highest point in the Lower 48 at 14,495 feet, is just one of many high peaks in Sequoia and Kings Canyon. The Pacific Crest Trail reaches its highest point here too, crossing north to south through both parks. Besides the rocky, snow-covered peaks, Sequoia and Kings Canyon are also home to the largest groves of giant sequoias in the Sierra Nevada, as well as the headwaters of the Kern, Kaweah, and Kings rivers. A few small, high-country lakes are home to some of the only remaining pure-strain golden trout. Bear, deer, and numerous smaller animals and birds depend on the park's miles of wild habitat for summer breeding and feeding grounds.

Technically two separate parks, Sequoia and Kings Canyon are contiguous and managed jointly from the park headquarters near Ash Mountain off Calif. 198 east of Visalia.

## ESSENTIALS

**ARRIVING & DEPARTING**   The nearest airport is in Fresno, 46 miles west of the parks. You'll need a car to reach the parks. The **entrances** to Sequoia are at Grant Grove (on Calif. 180) and at Ash Mountain (on Calif. 198). These two highways join in the park, making a loop that most visitors follow between the two entrances. Kings Canyon is entered via Calif. 180.

To escape the crowds and see less-used areas of the park, enter on one of the dead-end roads to Mineral King, South Fork, or Cedar Grove. The lack of through traffic makes these parts of the park incredibly peaceful even at full capacity and they are gateways to the parks' best hiking.

**VISITOR INFORMATION**   For information, contact **Sequoia and Kings Canyon National Parks,** Three Rivers, CA 93271 (☎ 209/565-3708).

**VISITOR CENTERS**   Lodgepole and **Grant Grove** visitor centers are the largest, with a full selection of park information and displays about the history, biology, and geology of this incredible place. Some time spent here will pay off by letting you decide which parts of the widely dispersed park you most want to concentrate on.

**ADMISSION FEES & REGULATIONS**   A $10 per car or $5 per individual fee is good for 1 week's worth of entry at any park entrance. An annual pass is $20. Entrance is free for holders of the National Park Service's Golden Eagle ($50), Golden Access (free to disabled U.S. citizens), and Golden Age ($10 for U.S. citizens 62 or older) passports. Backcountry permits are required for all backpacking trips ($10 per person). You can reserve permits in advance by writing the park headquarters. Mountain bikes are forbidden on all park trails. Dogs are only permitted in developed areas and must be leashed. The park service allows firewood gathering at campgrounds, but removing wood from living or standing trees is forbidden.

You can reserve permits for Mt. Whitney and Inyo National Forest by phone, fax, or mail through **Wilderness Reservations,** P.O. Box 430, Big Pine, CA 93513 (☎ **888-374-3773** or 619/938-1136; fax 619/938-1137).

**SAFETY**   Winter driving in the Sierra Nevada range can be dangerous. While the most hazardous roads are often closed, others are negotiable by four-wheel-drive or with chained tires. Check road conditions before setting out by calling ☎ **800/427-7623.**

**WHEN TO GO**   In the middle to high altitudes, where most Sequoia and Kings Canyon visitors are headed, summers are short and winters are cold. Spring can come as early as April and as late as June. Snow is not unheard of in July and August. Afternoon showers are common. Only the main roads through the parks are usually open during winter months when the climate can range from bitter cold to pleasant and changes minute by minute. Be ready for anything if you head into the backcountry on skis. Mosquitoes, poison oak, and rattlesnakes are common in lower elevations during summer.

**RANGER PROGRAMS**   Park rangers lead hikes, campfire talks, and slide shows at several campgrounds and visitor centers during the summer.

## WHAT TO SEE & DO

There are some 75 groves of giant sequoias in the park, but the easiest places to see them are **Grant Grove,** in Kings Canyon near the park entrance on Calif. 180 from Fresno, or **Giant Forest,** a huge grove of trees containing 40 miles of footpaths 16 miles from the entrance to Sequoia National Park on Calif. 198.

The 2-mile **Congress Trail** loop in the Giant Forest starts at the base of the **General Sherman tree,** the largest living thing in the world. Single branches of this monster are more than 7 feet thick. Each year it grows enough wood to make a 60-foot-tall tree of normal dimensions. Other trees in the grove are nearly as large, and many of the peaceful-looking trees have also been saddled with strangely militaristic and political monikers like General Lee and Lincoln. Longer trails lead to remote reaches of the grove and nearby meadows.

Besides the sequoia groves, Sequoia and Kings Canyon is home to the most pristine wilderness in the Sierra Nevada. At **Roads End** on the Kings Canyon Highway (open May–Nov) you can stand by the banks of the Kings River and stare up at 5,000-foot-tall granite walls rising above the river, the deepest canyon in the United States.

Near Giant Forest Village, **Moro Rock** is a 6,725-foot-tall granite dome formed by exfoliation of layers of the rock. A quarter-mile trail scales the dome for a spectacular view of the adjacent Kaweah Canyon. The trail gains 300 feet in 400 yards, so be ready for a climb.

**Boyden Cavern** on Calif. 180, in neighboring Sequoia National Forest, is a large cave where you can take a 45-minute tour to see stalactites and stalagmites. A fee is charged; call ☎ 209/736-2708 for details.

**Crystal Cave** is located 15 miles from the Calif. 198 park entrance and an additional 7 miles to cave parking. Here you can take a 50-minute tour of Crystal's beautiful marble interior. The tour costs $4 for adults and children 12 and older, $2 for children 6–11 and senior citizens, free for kids under 6. Tickets are not sold at the cave and must be purchased at Lodgepole or Foothills visitor centers at least 1 1/2 hours in advance. Be sure to wear sturdy shoes and bring a jacket.

**HIKING**   Hiking and backpacking are what this park is really all about, with 700 miles of trails connecting canyons, lakes, and high alpine meadows and snowfields.

Some of the park's most impressive hikes start in the **Mineral King** section in the southern end of Sequoia. Beginning at 7,800 feet, trails lead onward and upward to destinations like Sawtooth Pass, Crystal Lake, and the old White Chief Trail to the now-defunct White Chief Mine.

The **John Muir Trail,** which begins in Yosemite National Park (see section 5, above), ends here just below Mount Whitney. For many miles it coincides with the **Pacific Crest Trail** as it skirts the highest peaks in the park. This is the most difficult part of the Pacific Crest, remaining above 10,000 feet most of the time and crossing 12,000-foot-high passes.

# Sequoia & Kings Canyon National Parks

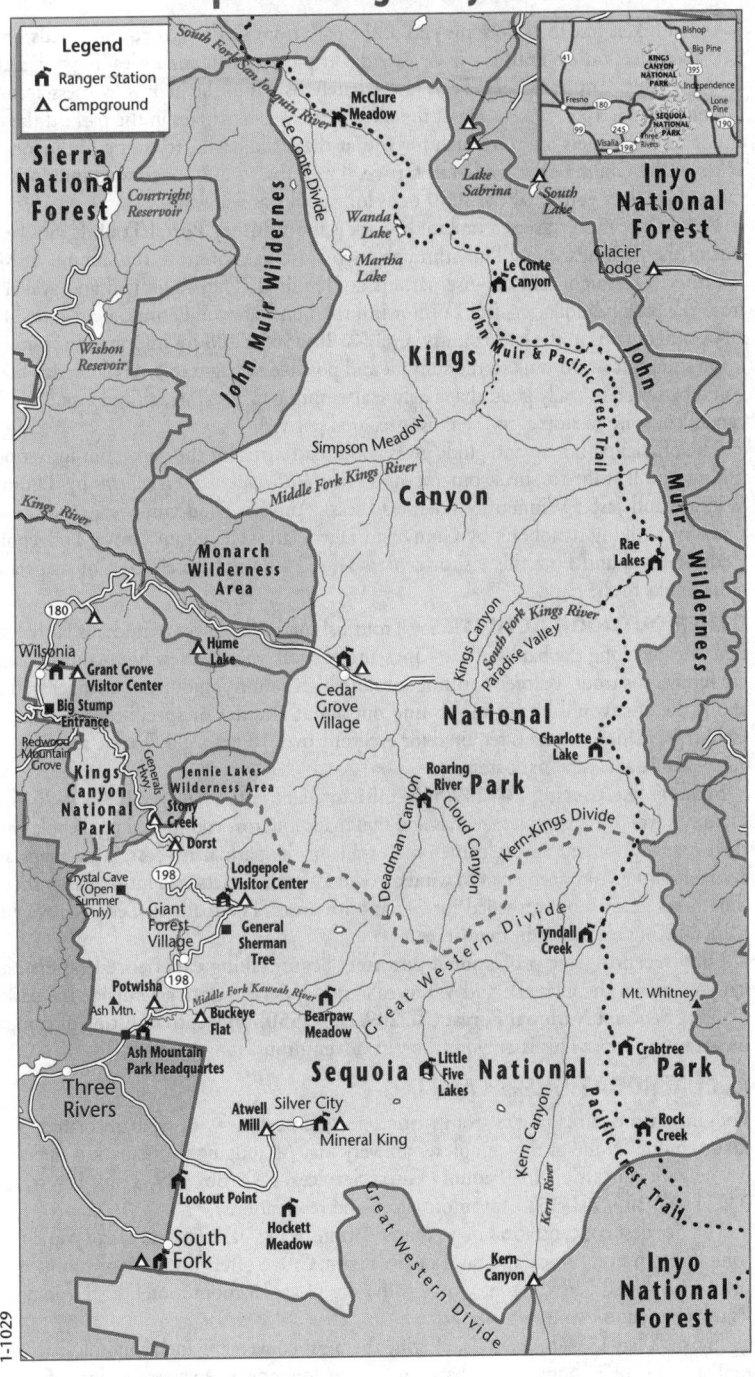

**Legend**

🏠 Ranger Station
△ Campground

Sierra National Forest

Inyo National Forest

Courtright Reservoir

McClure Meadow

Lake Sabrina

South Lake

Glacier Lodge

Le Conte Canyon

Wanda Lake

Martha Lake

Wishon Reservoir

John Muir Wilderness

Le Conte Divide

Kings

John Muir & Pacific Crest Trail

Simpson Meadow

Middle Fork Kings River

Canyon

Kings River

Monarch Wilderness Area

Rae Lakes

John Muir Wilderness

Wilsonia

Grant Grove Visitor Center

Hume Lake

Cedar Grove Village

Kings Canyon

South Fork Kings River

Paradise Valley

National

Charlotte Lake

Big Stump Entrance

Redwood Mountain Grove

Kings Canyon National Park

Generals Hwy.

Jennie Lakes Wilderness Area

Stony Creek

Roaring River

Park

Kern-Kings Divide

Crystal Cave (Open Summer Only)

Dorst

Lodgepole Visitor Center

Giant Forest Village

General Sherman Tree

Deadman Canyon

Cloud Canyon

Great Western Divide

Tyndall Creek

Mt. Whitney

Potwisha

Ash Mtn.

Middle Fork Kaweah River

Buckeye Flat

Bearpaw Meadow

Little Five Lakes

Crabtree

Ash Mountain Park Headquartes

Sequoia

National

Park

Rock Creek

Three Rivers

Atwell Mill

Silver City

Mineral King

Kern Canyon

Lookout Point

Hockett Meadow

Great Western Divide

Kern River

South Fork

Kern Canyon

Inyo National Forest

Bishop

Big Pine

KINGS CANYON NATIONAL PARK

Independence

Fresno

Lone Pine

SEQUOIA NATIONAL PARK

Visalia

Three Rivers

1-1029

729

Other hikers like to explore the end of the park from **Cedar Grove** and **Roads End.** The **Paradise Valley Trail** is a fairly easy day trip by park standards leading to beautiful Mist Falls. **Copper Creek Trail** immediately rises into the high wilderness around Granite Pass at 10,673 feet, one of the most strenuous day hikes in the park. If the altitude and steepness are too much for you at these trailheads, try some of the longer hikes in the **Giant Forest** or **Grant Grove.** These forests are woven with interlocking loops that allow you to take as short or as long a hike as you want.

Perhaps the most traversed trail to the park is the **Whitney Portal Trail.** It runs from east of the park near Lone Pine, through Inyo National Forest, to the summit of Mt. Whitney. Overnight and day-use permits are required. They're limited and available from the park headquarters (see "Visitor Information," above). Permits are required for all overnight trips to the backcountry. Call ☎ **209/565-3708** for information. Though it is a straightforward walk to the summit and possible to bag it in a very long day hike, you'd better be in really good shape before attempting it. Weather, altitude, and fatigue can all conspire to stop even the most prepared party.

The official park map and guide gives good road maps for the parks, but for serious hiking you'll want to check out *Sierra South: 100 Back-Country Trips* by Thomas Winnett and Jason Winnett (Wilderness Press). Another good guide is *Kings Canyon Country,* a hiking handbook by Ginny and Lew Clark. The Grant Grove, Lodgepole, Cedar Grove, and Foothills visitor centers all sell a complete selection of maps and guidebooks to the park.

**OTHER OUTDOOR ACTIVITIES**    Trout fishing in the lower altitudes is fairly limited, mostly along the banks of the Kings and Kaweah rivers. A few high-country lakes are refuges for trout. Before venturing into the high country, inquire at a ranger station about the area you'll be visiting to find out about closures or specific regulations. A California fishing license is required for everyone over 16 years old. Tackle and licenses are available at several park stores.

**Sequoia Ski Touring** (☎ **209/565-3381** in Giant Forest Village, 209/335-2314 in Grant Grove) offers complete rentals and trail maps for cross-country skiing. People with their own equipment are welcome on all trails in the park at no cost. Trail maps are available at the visitor centers. On winter weekends park rangers lead introductory snowshoe hikes (snowshoes provided for $1) at both areas. The roads to Cedar Grove and Mineral King are closed in the winter.

Only recently have professional outfitters begun taking experienced rafters and kayakers down the Class IV and V Kaweah and Upper Kings rivers outside the parks. Contact **Sequoia National Forest** (☎ **209/784-1550**) for a current listing of companies running trips. This is only for the very adventurous.

## ACCOMMODATIONS & CAMPING

Lodging in the parks ranges from rustic one-room cabins with no bath or heat to a luxury motel. None of the complexes are very big. All lodging in the park is operated by the park concessionaire, **Sequoia Guest Services,** P.O. Box 789, Three Rivers, CA 93271 (☎ **209/561-3314** for information and reservations).

The heaviest concentration of accommodations is in Giant Forest, where you'll find something in every price and taste range. Grant Grove offers a variety of cabins with private or shared baths. Cedar Grove is the site of an 18-room motel. Each room has its own bath and two queen-size beds.

The park has 13 campgrounds, offering the most convenient and economical accommodations here, although none have hookups. Only one accepts reservations: **Lodgepole Campground** on the Kaweah River in Sequoia. Others are first-come, first-served and often fill up on weekends. Three campgrounds—Azalea, Lodgepole, and

Potwisha—are year-round. The rest are open from snowmelt through September. Even in summer, campers should prepare for rain and cold temperatures. Bring a good tent and warm sleeping bags.

Two large campgrounds in Sequoia are **Dorst** and Lodgepole. Both are close to the Giant Forest. Lodgepole is within a short stroll of a restaurant, gas station, and visitor center. With more than 200 sites each, they tend to be the noisiest campgrounds in Sequoia. Lodgepole is the most expensive in the park at $14 per site. Dorst is $12.

Smaller and more peaceful are **South Fork, Potwisha, Buckeye Flats, Atwell Mill,** and **Cold Springs.** South Fork, Atwell Mill, and Cold Springs have pit toilets and are $6 per night. The others, with flush toilets, running water, and public phones, charge $12.

Campers in the remote Cedar Grove area of Kings Canyon National Park near the Kings River gorge can choose from **Moraine, Sentinel, Sheep Creek,** and **Canyon View,** a group camp. All four have flush toilets and are convenient to some of the park's best hiking. The small **Cedar Grove Village** offers a restaurant, store, showers, and gas. Sites are $12.

Three campgrounds in the Grant Grove area will put you near the sequoias without the noise and crowds of Giant Forest Village. All three—**Sunset, Azalea,** and **Crystal Springs**—have flush toilets and phones. Azalea has an RV disposal site and ranger station. Showers are nearby. The cost is $12 per site.

## 7  Los Angeles & Disneyland

Los Angeles is not a humble city. Like a celebrity who chooses a front table at Spago, L.A. is a star that just loves to be noticed. And noticed it is. The movies, TV, and music made here are seen, heard, and felt throughout the world. The city is America's—and often the world's—pop tastemaker. When it comes to what's hot and what's not, Angelenos can confidently say that they heard—or started—the buzz first.

L.A. is a cosmopolitan city in the true sense of the word, a cornucopia of lifestyles and cultures and a sometimes uneasy mix of races that's at once both thrilling and uncomfortable. It's not an easy place to master. The sprawling city has no cultural center, and its layout is difficult to grasp. Despite all appearances, however, L.A. is a very welcoming place. Often criticized for having few historical or cultural attributes, Los Angeles is anxious to prove its critics wrong, and any resident will gladly tell of the hidden corners and secret treasures that make living here a nonstop adventure.

The best way to approach this colossal, Technicolor city is with a critical conscience and tongue firmly in cheek. Recognize its influence and humor its self-importance. Keep in mind your media-made preconceptions, then discover L.A. for what it is: glitzy, grimy, glittery, powerful—the world capital of pop culture—and a city resplendent in the sunny climate and Mediterranean topography that have drawn admirers here for centuries. Put on your shades, take the top down, and get ready to roll—this is Hollywood.

### ARRIVING & DEPARTING

Los Angeles is infamous for its freeways and monumental traffic jams. Whichever way you approach the area by car, study a good map—and avoid morning and evening rush hours if you can.

**BY PLANE**    The huge **Los Angeles International Airport,** better known as LAX, is one of the major gateways to the United States, with most domestic airlines and Pacific Rim international carriers landing here. Many domestic airlines also serve smaller **Burbank–Glendale–Pasadena Airport** (☎ 626/840-8840) in the San Fernando Valley, a convenient option if you're staying in Hollywood or the valleys.

You'll probably need a car, and the major car-rental firms provide shuttles from the terminals to their off-site branches, where they'll give you a complimentary map and outline the route to your hotel. Many city hotels provide free shuttles for their guests; ask about transportation when you make reservations. **Super Shuttle** (☎ 800/ BLUE-VAN or 310/782-6600) operates shared minivans from LAX and Burbank airports to anywhere in the city. Fares range from $10 to $50 depending on your destination, and you can call from the airport (expect a short wait during peak times if you don't reserve). Metered **taxis** line up outside each terminal; expect to pay about $30 from LAX to Hollywood and downtown, $25 to Beverly Hills, and $20 to Santa Monica. The cab fare from Burbank Airport to Universal City is about $18, and $30 to Hollywood. The city's MTA **buses** also go between LAX and many parts of the city; phone **MTA Airport Information** (☎ 800/252-7433 or 213/626-4455) for schedules and fares. They'll also provide information on the new **MetroRail** line from LAX to either downtown or Long Beach.

**BY TRAIN & BUS**  Amtrak (☎ 800/USA-RAIL) passengers disembark at Union Station, on downtown's northern edge. Many taxis line up outside. The main Los Angeles **Greyhound/Trailways** bus station is downtown at 1716 E. 7th St., east of Alameda (☎ 800/231-2222).

## ESSENTIALS

**VISITOR INFORMATION**  The **Los Angeles Convention and Visitor Bureau,** 633 W. 5th St., Suite 6000, Los Angeles, CA 90071 (☎ 213/624-7300), is the city's main source for information. The bureau staffs a **Visitor Information Center** at 685 S. Figueroa St., between Wilshire Boulevard and 7th Street; it's open Mon–Fri 8am– 5:30pm and Sat 8:30am–5pm. Several city-oriented newspapers and magazines offer up-to-date information on current happenings, including the *L.A. Weekly,* a free weekly newspaper packed with information on current events around town. It's available from sidewalk news racks and in many stores and restaurants around the city. The monthly magazines *Los Angeles* and *Buzz* are also good sources of information.

**RESOURCES FOR TRAVELERS WITH SPECIAL NEEDS**  The **Los Angeles County Commission on Disabilities,** 383 Hall of Administration, 500 W. Temple St., Los Angeles, CA 90012 (☎ 213/974-1053 or TDD 213/974-1707), publishes a free brochure listing services and facilities offered by various city agencies, and the **Junior League of Los Angeles,** Farmers Market, 3rd and Fairfax streets, Gate 12, Los Angeles, CA 90036 (☎ 213/937-5566), distributes *Round the Town with Ease* free to visitors with disabilities.

Senior discounts abound in Los Angeles—at hotels, movie theaters, museums, restaurants, and attractions—always inquire before you pay the regular rate.

The highest concentration of gay- and lesbian-oriented businesses and services is in West Hollywood, including **A Different Light** bookstore, 8853 Santa Monica Blvd. (☎ 310/854-6601), which has a large selection of gay-oriented books, magazines, and newspapers, including biweekly *Frontiers* and weekly *Nightlife,* both excellent sources of information and up-to-date listings.

**EMERGENCIES & SAFETY**  In case of life-threatening emergencies, including fires, call ☎ 911. Many area hospitals have 24-hour emergency rooms, including world-famous **Cedars–Sinai Medical Center** (☎ 310/855-5000), located at 8700 Beverly Blvd., near the Beverly Center shopping mall.

Los Angeles is a lot safer than many big American cities, but don't make yourself a target of common crimes. When walking after dark, or in a doubtful neighborhood (some parts of Hollywood, for example), walk briskly and with purpose. If you feel you are being followed, proceed to a well-lighted and/or populated area.

## GETTING AROUND

**BY CAR**   Driving is the most common way to get around L.A., a fact of life both necessitated and frustrated by the fact that this is not a single compact city, but a sprawling suburbia comprising dozens of disparate communities on the flatlands of a huge basin between mountains and ocean. A good map of the area is essential. Foldout maps are available at gas stations, hotels, bookshops, and tourist-oriented shops around the city. If you're a member of the AAA auto club, stop by your local office for excellent free maps of the entire L.A. area, including a special freeway guide.

**BY TAXI**   Cabs can be an efficient if slightly expensive way to get around. They do not cruise L.A. streets looking for fares, so you can't count on hailing one on the street anywhere except central downtown or the theater districts. They do, however, queue up at airports and large hotels, or call **Checker Cab** (☎ 213/221-2355), **L.A. Taxi** (☎ 213/627-7000), or **United Independent Taxi** (☎ 213/483-7604).

## WHAT TO SEE & DO

**ESCORTED TOURS**   Oskar J's Tours (☎ 818/501-2217) operates regularly scheduled panoramic motorcoach tours of the city. Buses (or plush minivans) pick up passengers from major hotels for morning or afternoon tours of Sunset Strip, the movie studios, Farmer's Market, Hollywood, homes of the stars, and other attractions. Tours vary in length and cost, so call for details and reservations.

Grave Line Tours (☎ 213/469-4149) is a terrific journey in a renovated hearse to the sites of famous scandals and murders, including a stop at star-filled cemeteries. Reservations are required.

The **L.A. Conservancy** (☎ 213/623-2489) hosts guided walking tours of historic downtown Los Angeles. They're usually held on Saturday mornings. Call Mon–Fri 9am–5pm for an exact schedule and information.

**FESTIVALS & SPECIAL EVENTS**   All the world watches the annual **Tournament of Roses Parade** each New Year's Day; call ☎ 626/449-4100 for details. The first Sunday in March, local athletes take to the streets alongside world-champion runners in the 26-mile **Los Angeles Marathon.** Call ☎ 310/444-5544 for spectator information. The city of West Hollywood hosts the **Gay & Lesbian Pride Celebration** the last weekend in June; the festivities culminate in a flamboyant parade. Call ☎ **213/860-0701.**

**STUDIO TOURS & TV SHOW TAPINGS**   Get a behind-the-scenes look at movie making during tours offered by **Paramount Pictures,** 5555 Melrose Ave., Hollywood (☎ 213/956-1777); **NBC Studios,** 3000 W. Alameda Ave., Burbank (☎ 626/840-3537); and **Warner Brothers Studios,** Olive Avenue at Hollywood Way, Burbank (☎ 626/972-TOUR). For TV fans, **Audiences Unlimited** (☎ 818/506-0043, or 818/506-0067 for ticket information hotline) distributes free tickets for the top sitcoms, and **Television Tickets** (☎ 213/467-4697) can get you into popular talk- and game-show audiences. The tickets, and their services, are free.

**ATTRACTIONS**   The granddaddy of major theme parks, **Disneyland** is in Anaheim, 27 miles southeast of Los Angeles. Since a visit to this West Coast version of the Magic Kingdom will take at least a day, we have provided full coverage in "A Day Trip to Disneyland," at the end of this section.

✪ **Autry Museum of Western Heritage.** *4700 Western Heritage Way, in Griffith Park.* ☎ *213/667-2000. Admission $7 adults, $5 seniors 60 and over and students 13–18, $3 children 2–12, free for children under 2. Tues–Sun 10am–5pm.* Gene Autry, the Texas-born "Singing Cowboy" who starred in 82 western movies, opened this museum in 1988 to house an enormous, remarkably comprehensive, and well-displayed collection of art and artifacts of the European conquest of the West. Evocative

# Los Angeles

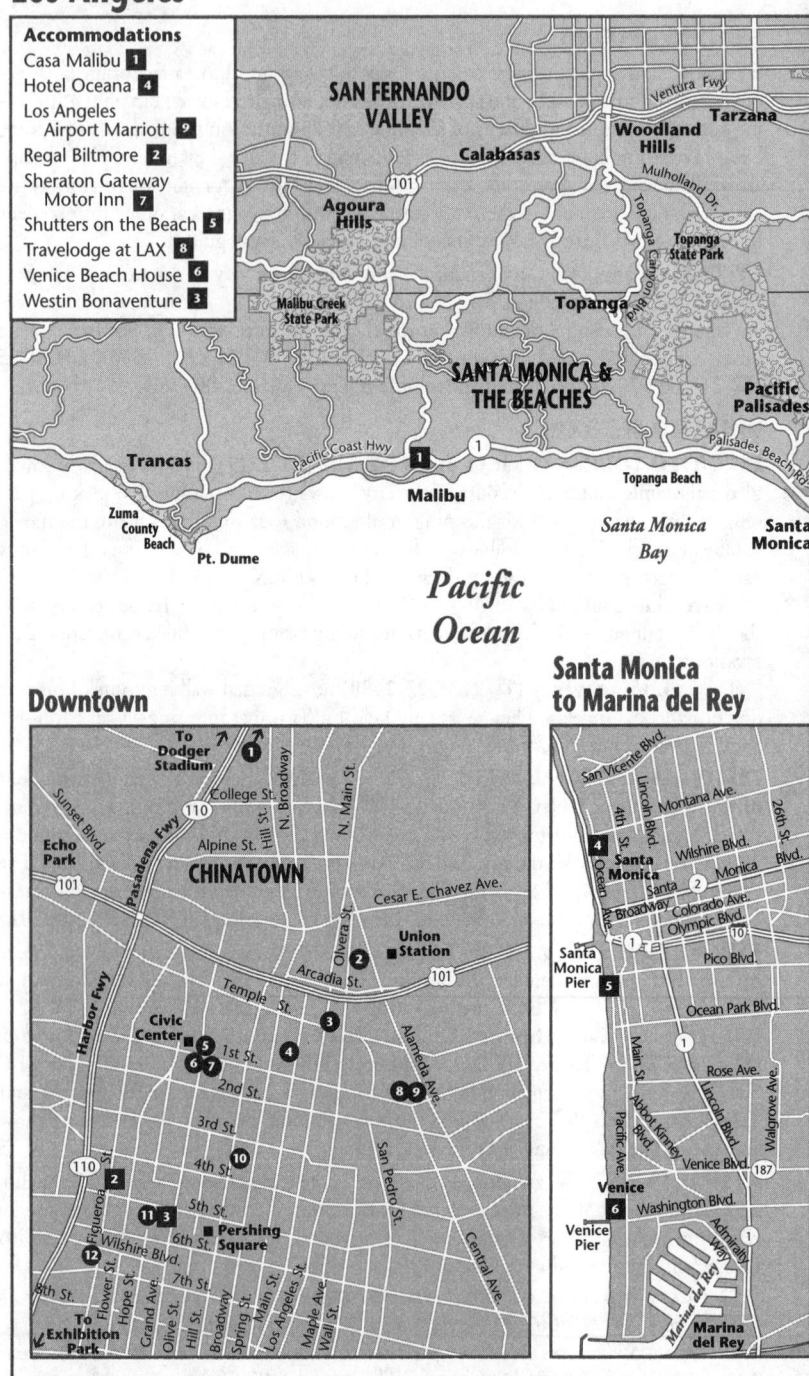

**Accommodations**

Casa Malibu **1**
Hotel Oceana **4**
Los Angeles
 Airport Marriott **9**
Regal Biltmore **2**
Sheraton Gateway
 Motor Inn **7**
Shutters on the Beach **5**
Travelodge at LAX **8**
Venice Beach House **6**
Westin Bonaventure **3**

SAN FERNANDO
VALLEY

Ventura Fwy

Woodland
Hills

Tarzana

Calabasas

Mulholland Dr.

101

Agoura
Hills

Topanga
State Park

Malibu Creek
State Park

Topanga

SANTA MONICA &
THE BEACHES

Pacific
Palisades

Trancas

Pacific Coast Hwy

1

Palisades Beach Rd.

Topanga Beach

Malibu

Zuma
County
Beach

Pt. Dume

*Santa Monica
Bay*

Santa
Monica

*Pacific
Ocean*

## Downtown

To
Dodger
Stadium

College St.

Sunset Blvd

110

Hill St.

N. Broadway

N. Main St.

Pasadena Fwy

Alpine St.

Echo
Park

101

**CHINATOWN**

Cesar E. Chavez Ave.

Olvera St.

Union
Station

Harbor Fwy

Arcadia St.

101

Temple St.

Civic
Center

1st St.

2nd St.

3rd St.

4th St.

110

San Pedro St.

Alameda Ave.

Central Ave.

5th St.

6th St.

Pershing
Square

Figueroa St.

Wilshire Blvd.

7th St.

8th St.

To
Exhibition
Park

Flower St.

Hope St.

Grand Ave.

Olive St.

Hill St.

Broadway

Spring St.

Main St.

Los Angeles St.

Maple Ave.

Wall St.

## Santa Monica
## to Marina del Rey

San Vicente Blvd.

Lincoln Blvd.

Montana Ave.

4th St.

26th St.

Wilshire Blvd.

Ocean Ave.

Santa
Monica

2

Santa

Monica

Blvd.

Broadway

Colorado Ave.

Olympic Blvd.

10

1

Santa
Monica
Pier

Pico Blvd.

Ocean Park Blvd.

1

Main St.

Rose Ave.

Abbot Kinney Blvd.

Pacific Ave.

Lincoln Blvd.

Walgrove Ave.

Venice Blvd.

187

**Venice**

Washington Blvd.

Venice
Pier

Admiralty Way

1

Via Marina

**Marina
del Rey**

734

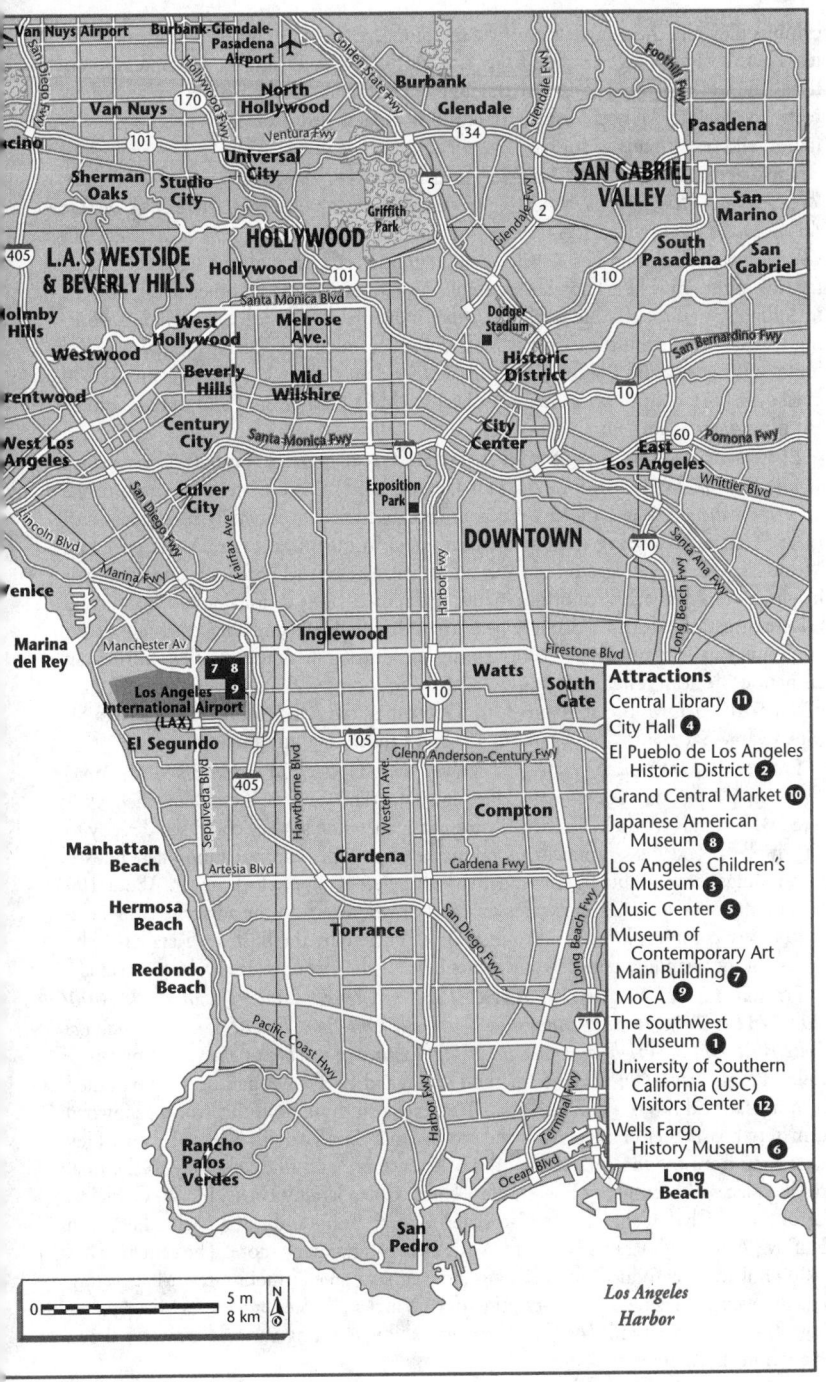

**Attractions**

Central Library ⓫

City Hall ➍

El Pueblo de Los Angeles
    Historic District ➋

Grand Central Market ➓

Japanese American
    Museum ➑

Los Angeles Children's
    Museum ➌

Music Center ➎

Museum of
    Contemporary Art
Main Building ➐

MoCA ➒

The Southwest
    Museum ➊

University of Southern
    California (USC)
    Visitors Center ⓬

Wells Fargo
    History Museum ➏

exhibits illustrate the everyday lives of early pioneers, including many hands-on exhibits. There's film footage ranging from *Buffalo Bill's Wild West Show* to contemporary films, the works of Wild West artists, and plenty of memorabilia from Autry's own career. The Hall of Merchandising displays Roy Rogers bedspreads, Hopalong Cassidy radios, and other items to stir baby boomers' collective instincts.

**California Museum of Science and Industry.** *700 State Dr., Exposition Park.* ☎ *213/744-7400, or 213/744-2014 for the IMAX theater. Museum: free. IMAX theater: $6 adults, $4.75 ages 18–21, $4 seniors and children. Multishow discounts available. Daily 10am–5pm.* Celebrating Los Angeles's longstanding romance with the aerospace industry, this museum is best known for its collection of airplanes and other flying objects, including several rockets and satellites. Other industrial science exhibits include a working winery and a behind-the-scenes look at a functioning McDonald's restaurant. Exhibits on robotics and fiber optics thrill kids, as does the hatchery, where almost 200 chicks are born daily. The museum's spherical IMAX theater shows up to three different films daily 10am–9pm.

**El Pueblo de Los Angeles Historic District.** *Enter on Alameda St. across from Union Station.* ☎ *213/628-1274.* This Los Angeles Historic District was built in the 1930s, on the site where the city was founded, and has proven wildly successful, with L.A.'s Latinos adopting it as an important cultural monument. At its core is a Mexican-style marketplace on old Olvera Street. The carnival of sights and sounds is heightened by mariachis, colorful piñatas, and more than occasional folkloric dancing. Olvera Street, the district's primary pedestrian thoroughfare, and adjacent Main Street are home to about two dozen 19th-century buildings; one houses La Golondrina, an authentic Mexican restaurant. Stop in at the visitor center, 622 N. Main St. (☎ 213/628-1274); open Mon–Sat 10am–3pm. Don't miss the Avila Adobe, E-10 Olvera St. (open Mon–Sat 10am–5pm); built in 1818, it's the oldest building in the city.

**Farmer's Market.** *6333 W. 3rd St. (near Fairfax Ave.).* ☎ *213/933-9211. Mon–Sat 9am–6:30pm, Sun 10am–5pm.* The original market was little more than a field clustered with stands set up by farmers during the Depression so they could sell directly to city dwellers. Today it's a sprawling food marketplace with a carnival atmosphere housed in buildings recognizable by the trademark shingled 10-story clock tower. About 100 restaurants, shops, and grocers cater to a mix of workers from the adjacent CBS Television City complex, locals, and tourists brought here by the busload. Retailers sell a variety of merchandise, but everyone comes here for the vast offerings of the food stands.

**Forest Lawn Memorial Park.** *1712 S. Glendale Ave., Glendale.* ☎ *800/ 204-3131 or 213/254-3131. Admission free. Daily 8am–5pm. From I-5, exit east onto Los Feliz Blvd. and turn right on Glendale Ave.; the entrance is 2 blocks ahead.* Lenny Bruce called Forest Lawn "Disneyland for the Dead," and Evelyn Waugh brutally parodied it in his satirical novel *The Loved One.* Whatever you think of it, this world-renowned cemetery boasts even more stars in the ground than Hollywood's Walk of Fame. Pick up a map from the information booth at the entrance and find your way to the final resting places of Humphrey Bogart, Nat "King" Cole, Sammy Davis, Jr., W. C. Fields, Errol Flynn, Clark Gable, Karen Carpenter, George Burns and wife Gracie Allen, Jean Harlow, Alan Ladd, Carole Lombard, Walt Disney, and many more. The cemetery has 1,000 full-scale reproductions of Renaissance statuary, an enormous Great Mausoleum, and an oversized stained-glass re-creation of da Vinci's *The Last Supper.* Its prized paintings *The Resurrection* and *The Crucifixion* are exhibited during narrated cemetery shows every hour from 10am to 4pm.

**✪ Griffith Observatory.** *2800 E. Observatory Rd. (in Griffith Park, at the end of Vermont Ave.).* ☎ *213/664-1191, or 213/663-8171 for the Sky Report, a recorded* *message on current planet positions and celestial events. Admission free. Planetarium show tickets, $4 adults, $3 seniors, $2 children. June–Aug, daily 12:30–10pm. Sept–May, Tues–Fri 2–10pm, Sat–Sun 12:30–10pm.* These bronze domes on the south slope of Mt. Hollywood have been Hollywood Hills landmarks since 1935 and offer unparalleled city views (this is one of the most romantic places in L.A. on warm nights). The main dome houses a planetarium, where narrated projection shows reveal the stars and planets that are hidden from the naked eye by the city's lights and smog. The adjacent Hall of Science holds exhibits on galaxies, meteorites, and other cosmic objects, including a telescope trained on the Sun. On clear nights you can gaze at the heavens through the powerful 12-inch telescope.

**Hollywood Sign.** *At the top of Beachwood Dr., Hollywood.* These 50-foot-high white sheet-metal letters have come to symbolize both the movie industry and the city itself. Erected in 1923 as an advertisement for a fledgling real-estate development, the full text originally read "Hollywoodland." The recent installation of motion detectors around the sign made it even more of a graffiti tagger's target. A thorny hiking trail leads to it from near Beachwood Drive, but the best view is from down below, at the corner of Sunset Boulevard and Bronson Avenue.

**Hollywood Walk of Fame.** *Hollywood Blvd., between Gower St. and La Brea Ave; and Vine St., between Yucca St. and Sunset Blvd.* ☎ *213/469-8311.* More than 2,500 celebrities are honored along the world's most famous sidewalk. Each bronze medallion, set into the center of a granite star, pays homage to names like James Dean (1719 Vine St.), John Lennon (1750 Vine St.), Marlon Brando (1765 Vine St.), Rudolph Valentino (6164 Hollywood Blvd.), Greta Garbo (6901 Hollywood Blvd.), Louis Armstrong (7000 Hollywood Blvd.), and Barbra Streisand (6925 Hollywood Blvd.). Contact the Hollywood Chamber of Commerce, 6255 Sunset Blvd., Suite 911, Hollywood, CA 90028 (☎ **213/469-8311**), to find out who'll be honored when you're in town; it's a good way to star-gaze.

**Los Angeles Children's Museum.** *310 N. Main St. (at Los Angeles St.).* ☎ *2 13/ 687-8800. Admission $5; free for children under 2. Summer, Tues–Fri 11:30am–5pm, Sat–Sun 10am–5pm. Fall–spring, Sat–Sun 10am–5pm.* This thoroughly enchanting museum is a place where children learn by doing—they even can become "stars" in the museum's own TV studio. Everyday experiences are demystified by interesting interactive exhibits displayed in a playlike atmosphere. In the Art Studio, kids are encouraged to make finger puppets from a variety of media, and shiny rockets out of Mylar. In the City Street, kids can sit on a policeman's motorcycle or pretend to drive a bus or a fire truck. Kids (and adults) can see their shadows freeze in the Shadow Box, and play with giant foam-filled, Velcro-edged building blocks in Sticky City.

✪ **Los Angeles County Museum of Art.** *5905 Wilshire Blvd.* ☎ *213/857-6111, or 213/857-6000 for a recording. Admission $6 adults, $4 students and seniors 62 and over, $1 ages 6–17, free for children 5 and under; regular exhibitions free for everyone the second Wed of every month. Tues–Thurs 10am–5pm, Fri 10am–9pm, Sat–Sun 11am–6pm.* One of the finest art museums in the United States, this huge complex was designed by three very different architects over a span of 30 years. The architectural fusion can be migraine-inducing, but this city landmark is well worth delving into. If you fear getting lost forever, head straight for the Japanese Pavilion, a highly aesthetic building housing a collection of Japanese Edo paintings that's rivaled only by the holdings of the emperor of Japan. The collection also includes an entire building of 20th-century painting and sculpture by artists like Matisse, Magritte, and representative Dada works; plus everything from 2,000-year-old pre-Columbian Mexican ceramics to a unique glass collection spanning the centuries to 19th-century portraiture, one of the nation's largest holdings of costumes and textiles, and an important Indian and Southeast Asian art collection. Major special exhibitions are always taking place and the museum offers free guided tours of the collection's highlights.

**Mann's Chinese Theatre.** *6925 Hollywood Blvd. (3 blocks west of Highland Ave.).* ☎ *213/464-8111 or 213/461-3331. Movie tickets $7.50. Call for show times.* Outrageously conceived, with both authentic and simulated Chinese embellishments, this gaudy theater is one of the world's great movie palaces, and one of Hollywood's finest landmarks. It was opened in 1927 by entertainment impresario Sid Grauman, a brilliant promoter who originated paparazzi-packed movie "premières." Original Chinese heaven doves top the facade, and two of the theater's exterior columns once propped up a Ming Dynasty temple. In the world-famous entry court, stars like Elizabeth Taylor, Paul Newman, Ginger Rogers, Humphrey Bogart, Frank Sinatra, Marilyn Monroe, and about 160 others set their signatures and hand- and footprints in concrete. It's not always hands and feet, though: Betty Grable made an impression with her shapely leg, Gene Autry with his horse Champion's hoofprints, and Jimmy Durante and Bob Hope used their trademark noses.

**Museum of Contemporary Art.** *250 S. Grand Ave. and 152 N. Central Ave.* ☎ *213/621-2766. Admission $6 adults, $4 seniors and students, free for children 11 and under. Tues–Wed and Fri–Sun 11am–5pm, Thurs 11am–8pm.* These two buildings, which are not within walking distance of each other, house Los Angeles's only institution exclusively devoted to art from 1940 to the present. Displaying works in a variety of media, the museum is particularly strong in works by Cy Twombly, Jasper Johns, and Mark Rothko. It's not world class, but its shows are often superb. The Grand Avenue main building is a contemporary red sandstone structure by renowned Japanese architect Arata Isozaki. The second venue on Central Avenue in Little Tokyo houses a superior permanent collection in a warehouse-type space. Unless there's a visiting exhibit of great interest at the main museum, start at the Little Tokyo building where parking is easier.

**Museum of Television and Radio.** *465 N. Beverly Dr. (at Santa Monica Blvd.), Beverly Hills.* ☎ *310/786-1000. Admission $6 adults, $4 students and seniors, $3 children 12 and under. Wed and Fri–Sun noon–5pm, Thurs noon–9pm. Closed July 4, Thanksgiving, Christmas, New Year's Day.* Want to see the Beatles on *The Ed Sullivan Show* (1964) or watch Arnold Palmer win the 1958 Masters Tournament, listen to radio excerpts like FDR's first "Fireside Chat" (1933) or Orson Welles's famous *War of the Worlds* UFO hoax (1938)? All these, plus a gazillion episodes of *The Twilight Zone, I Love Lucy,* and other beloved series, can be viewed within the starkly white walls of architect Richard Meier's neutral, contemporary museum building. It becomes quickly apparent that "library" would be a more fitting name for this West Coast branch of the 20-year-old New York facility, since the main attractions are requested via sophisticated computer "catalogs" and viewed in private consoles.

**Museum of Tolerance.** *9786 W. Pico Blvd. (at Roxbury Dr.).* ☎ *310/553-8403. Admission $8 adults, $6 seniors, $5 students, $3 children 3–12, free for children 2 and under. Advance purchase recommended. Mon–Thurs 10am–5pm, Fri 10am–3pm (Nov–Mar until 1pm), Sun 11am–5pm. Closed many Jewish and secular holidays; call for schedule.* Located in the Simon Wiesenthal Center, an institute founded by the legendary Nazi-hunter, this museum is designed to expose prejudices and teach racial and cultural tolerance. While the Holocaust figures prominently here, this is not just a Jewish museum—it's an academy that broadly campaigns for a live-and-let-live world. Tolerance is an abstract idea that's hard to display, so most of this $50-million museum's exhibits are high tech and conceptual in nature. Fast-paced interactive displays are designed

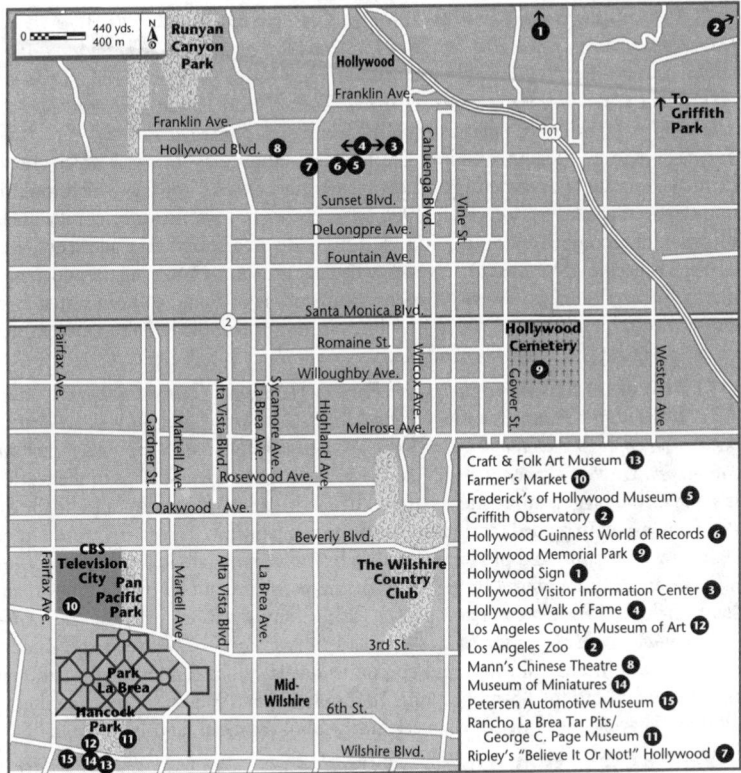

0 ╾ 440 yds. / 400 m

N

Runyan Canyon Park

Hollywood

Franklin Ave.

Franklin Ave.

To Griffith Park

101

Franklin Ave.

Hollywood Blvd. **8**

←**4**→**3**

**7** **6** **5**

Sunset Blvd.

DeLongpre Ave.

Fountain Ave.

Cahuenga Blvd.

Vine St.

Santa Monica Blvd.

Romaine St.

Willoughby Ave.

Melrose Ave.

Hollywood Cemetery **9**

Wilcox Ave.

Gower St.

Western Ave.

Fairfax Ave.

Alta Vista Blvd.

La Brea Ave.

Sycamore Ave.

Martell Ave.

Gardner St.

Highland Ave.

Rosewood Ave.

Oakwood Ave.

Beverly Blvd.

CBS Television City

Pan Pacific Park **10**

Fairfax Ave.

Martell Ave.

Alta Vista Blvd.

La Brea Ave.

The Wilshire Country Club

3rd St.

Park La Brea

Hancock Park

Mid-Wilshire

6th St.

**15** **12** **11**

**15** **14** **13**

Wilshire Blvd.

Craft & Folk Art Museum **13**
Farmer's Market **10**
Frederick's of Hollywood Museum **5**
Griffith Observatory **2**
Hollywood Guinness World of Records **6**
Hollywood Memorial Park **9**
Hollywood Sign **1**
Hollywood Visitor Information Center **3**
Hollywood Walk of Fame **4**
Los Angeles County Museum of Art **12**
Los Angeles Zoo **2**
Mann's Chinese Theatre **8**
Museum of Miniatures **14**
Petersen Automotive Museum **15**
Rancho La Brea Tar Pits/
  George C. Page Museum **11**
Ripley's "Believe It Or Not!" Hollywood **7**

to touch the heart as well as the mind, and engage both serious investigators and the MTV crowd.

**Natural History Museum of Los Angeles County.** *900 Exposition Blvd., Exposition Park.* ☎ *213/744-3466. Admission $6 adults; $3.50 ages 12–17, seniors, and students with ID; $2 children 5–12; free for children 4 and under; free for everyone the first Tues of every month. Tues–Sun 10am–5pm. Free docent-led tours offered daily at 1pm. Closed Thanksgiving, Christmas, New Year's Day.* The "Fighting Dinosaurs"—*Tyrannosaurus rex* and *triceratops* skeletons poised in a stance so realistic that every kid feels inspired to imitate their *Jurassic Park* bellows—are the trademark symbol of this massive museum. Opened in 1913 in a beautiful columned and domed Spanish Renaissance building, the museum is a 35-hall warehouse with a mind-numbing number of exhibits chronicling the planet and its inhabitants from 600 million years ago to the present day. The best permanent displays include the world's rarest shark, a walk-through vault of priceless gems, and an Insect Zoo.

✪ **Petersen Automotive Museum.** *6060 Wilshire Blvd. (at Fairfax Ave.).* ☎ *213/930-2277. Admission $7 adults, $5 seniors and students, $3 children 5–12, free for children 4 and under. Tues–Sun 10am–6pm.* Named for Robert Petersen, the publisher responsible for *Hot Rod* and *Motor Trend* magazines, the four-story museum displays over 200 cars and motorcycles, from the historic to the futuristic. Cars on the first floor are depicted chronologically, in period settings. Other floors are devoted to frequently changing shows of race cars, early motorcycles, and famous movie vehicles.

✪ **Rancho La Brea Tar Pits/George C. Page Museum.** *5801 Wilshire Blvd. (east of Fairfax Ave.), Los Angeles.* ☎ *213/936-2230 or 213/857-6311. Admission $6 adults, $3.50 seniors 62 and older and students with ID, $2 children 5–12, free for children 4 and under, free for everyone the second Tues. of every month. Museum, Tues–Sun 10am–5pm. Paleontology Laboratory, Wed–Sun 10am–5pm. Tar Pits, Sat–Sun 10am–5pm.* Thousands of mammals, birds, amphibians, and insects—many of which are now extinct—mistakenly crawled into these glistening pools of hot tar, which look like murky water, and stayed forever. In 1906 scientists began a systematic removal and classification of entombed specimens. The best finds are on display in the adjacent George C. Page Museum of La Brea Discoveries, where an excellent 15-minute film documenting the recoveries is also shown. Archeological work is ongoing; you can watch as scientists clean, identify, and catalog new finds in the Paleontology Laboratory. Guided tar pit tours are given Saturday and Sunday at 1pm.

✪ **Universal Studios.** *Hollywood Freeway (Universal Center Dr. exit), Universal City.* ☎ *818/508-9600. Admission $34 adults, $28 seniors 65 and older and children 3–11, free for children 2 and under. Parking $5. Summer, daily 7am–11pm. Fall–spring, daily 9am–7pm.* Universal is more than just one of the largest movie studios in the world—it's one of the biggest amusement parks. The main attraction continues to be the Studio Tour, a 1-hour guided tram ride around the company's 420 acres. En route you pass stars' dressing rooms and production offices before visiting famous backlot sets. Other attractions are more typical of high-tech theme-park fare, but all have a film-oriented slant, including *Back to the Future—The Ride,* a fiery *Backdraft* ride, the *E.T. Adventure,* a *Waterworld* live-action stunt show, and *Jurassic Park—The Ride,* a special-effects showcase of dinosaur illusions and computer magic. Lines can be long—sometimes more than an hour for a 5-minute ride. In summer the stifling valley heat can dog you all day. To avoid the crowds, skip weekends, school vacations, and Japanese holidays.

**Venice Ocean Front Walk.** *On the beach, between Venice Blvd. and Rose Ave.* It's no exaggeration to say that no visit to L.A. would be complete without a stroll along Venice's famous beach path, an almost surreal assemblage of every L.A. stereotype—and then some. Among stalls and stands selling cheap sunglasses, Mexican blankets, and "herbal ecstasy" pills swirls a carnival of humanity that includes bikini-clad roller skaters, tattooed bikers, muscle-bound pretty boys, panhandling vets, beautiful wannabes, and plenty of tourists and gawkers. On any given day you're bound to come across all kinds of performers: white-faced mimes, breakdancers, buskers, chainsaw jugglers, talking parrots, or an occasional apocalyptic evangelist.

**PARKS**    Mining tycoon Griffith J. Griffith donated the 4,000 acres of ✪ **Griffith Park,** with three entrances along Los Feliz Boulevard between Western Avenue and Riverside Drive (☎ 213/665-5188), one of the largest city parks in America. There's a lot to do here, including hiking, horseback riding, golfing, swimming, biking, and picnicking. For a general overview, drive the mountainous loop road that winds from the top of Western Avenue, past Griffith Observatory, and down to Vermont Avenue. For a more extensive foray, turn north at the loop road's midsection, onto Mt. Hollywood Drive. The park is also home to the Los Angeles Zoo, Autry Museum, and Travel Town Museum.

Between Santa Monica and Malibu, the 168-acre **Will Rogers State Historic Park,** 1501 Will Rogers State Park Rd., Pacific Palisades (☎ 310/454-8212), was once the cowboy/humorist's private ranch and grounds. You can explore the grounds, the former stables, and the 31-room house filled with the original furnishings, including a porch swing in the living room and many Native American rugs and baskets. There are picnic tables, but no food is sold. Admission is $5 per vehicle.

**BEACHES**   Shoulder-to-shoulder during the summer, and never empty even in winter, the southern California beach is a place to swim, surf, sunbathe, picnic, people-watch, play volleyball, and much more. Los Angeles has 72 miles of beaches, the largest of which is **Zuma Beach,** off the Pacific Coast Highway (Calif. 1) a mile north of Kanan Dume Road. It's not the loveliest beach in the Southland, but Zuma has the most comprehensive facilities: plenty of rest rooms, lifeguards, playgrounds, volleyball courts, and snack bars. The southern stretch, toward Point Dume, is Westward Beach, separated from the noisy highway by sandstone cliffs. A trail leads over the point's headlands to Pirate's Cove, once a popular nude beach.

**Malibu Lagoon State Beach** isn't just a pretty white-sand beach, but an estuary and wetlands area as well, plus Malibu Lagoon is the historic home of the Chumash Indians. The entrance is on the Pacific Coast Highway (Calif. 1) south of Cross Creek Road, and there's a small admission charge. Marine life and shorebirds teem where the creek empties into the sea, and the waves are always mild. The historic Adamson House is here, a showplace of Malibu tile now operating as a museum.

Without a doubt, L.A.'s best waves roll ashore at **Surfrider Beach,** a popular surfing spot located between the Malibu Pier and the lagoon. In surf lingo, few "locals only" wave wars are ever fought here—surfing is not as territorial here as it can be in other areas, where out-of-towners can be made to feel unwelcome. Surrounded by all of Malibu's hustle and bustle, don't come to Surfrider for peace and quiet.

Three miles along the Pacific Coast Highway (Calif. 1) between Sunset Boulevard and the Santa Monica border is **Will Rogers State Beach,** named for the American humorist whose ranch–turned–state historic park (see "Parks," above) is nestled above the palisades that provide the striking backdrop for this popular beach. A pay parking lot extends the entire length of Will Rogers, and facilities include rest rooms, lifeguards, and a snack hut in season. While the surfing is only so-so, the waves are friendly for swimmers of all ages.

**Santa Monica State Beach,** on either side of the Santa Monica Pier, is popular for its white sands and easy accessibility. There are big parking lots, eateries, and lots of well-maintained rest rooms. A paved beach path runs along here, allowing you to walk, bike, or skate to Venice and points south. Colorado Boulevard leads to the pier; turn north on the Pacific Coast Highway (Calif. 1) below the coastline's striking bluffs, or south along Ocean Avenue; you'll find parking lots in both directions.

**Venice Beach** reaches an apex at Washington Boulevard and the Venice fishing pier. Although there are people who swim and sunbathe, Venice Beach's character is defined by the sea of humanity that gathers here, plus the bevy of boardwalk vendors and old-fashioned "walk-streets" a block away (see above). Park on the side streets or in the plentiful lots west of Pacific Avenue.

The Beach Boys used to hang out (and surf, of course) at **Manhattan State Beach,** whose wide, friendly sands are backed by beautiful ocean-view homes. Plenty of parking on 36 blocks of side streets (between Rosecrans Avenue and the Hermosa Beach border) draws weekend crowds from the L.A. area. Manhattan has some of the best surfing around, along with rest rooms, lifeguards, and volleyball courts.

**Hermosa City Beach** is a very, very wide white-sand beach with tons to recommend it, extending to either side of the pier and including "The Strand," a pedestrian lane that runs its entire length. Main access is at the foot of Pier Avenue, which itself is lined with interesting shops. There's plenty of street parking, rest rooms, lifeguards, volleyball courts, a fishing pier, playgrounds, and good surfing.

County beaches are operated by the **Department of Beaches and Harbors,** 13837 Fiji Way, Marina del Rey (☎ **310/305-9503**). County-run beaches usually charge for parking ($4–$8), and alcohol, bonfires, and pets are prohibited. For recorded surf conditions (and coastal weather forecast), call ☎ **310/457-9701.**

**BEST BETS FOR KIDS**   Much of larger-than-life L.A. is as appealing to kids as it is to adults. The number-one kid-pleaser obviously is **Disneyland** out in Anaheim (see "A Day Trip to Disneyland," below). Many of the city's best attractions, like Venice's **Ocean Front Walk,** Hollywood's **Farmer's Market, Universal Studios,** and downtown's **Olvera Street** in the El Pueblo de Los Angeles Historic District have a kid-friendly carnival-like atmosphere. The novelty of sights such as the **Walk of Fame** and **Mann's Chinese Theatre** appeals to kids from 6 to 60 and beyond; curious kids of all ages will enjoy the **Rancho La Brea Tar Pits** and **Griffith Observatory.** Older kids, in particular, also love to go on **studio tours** and attend **TV tapings,** both of which take them behind the scenes of their favorite shows. The **Los Angeles Children's Museum** is a thoroughly enchanting place where kids learn by doing. The **Los Angeles Zoo,** 5333 Zoo Dr., in Griffith Park (☎ 213/666-4090), is an easy place to tote the kids around. The best features are the zoo's walk-in aviary and Adventure Island, an excellent children's zoo that re-creates mountain, meadow, desert, and shoreline habitats.

Universal Studios, Universal CityWalk, the **carousel at the Santa Monica Pier** (☎ 310/458-8900), and the **Travel Town Transportation Museum,** 5200 Zoo Dr. in Griffith Park (☎ 213/662-5874), also are popular with kids. And if all this doesn't keep the children happy, you can always take them to the beaches.

**SPORTS**   During baseball season, the **Los Angeles Dodgers** (☎ 213/224-1500) play at Dodger Stadium, near downtown. Basketball fans can see the **L.A. Lakers** (☎ 310/419-3100) play at the Great Western Forum in Inglewood, near the airport. The **L.A. Clippers** (☎ 213/745-0400) shoot hoops in the Los Angeles Sports Arena, near downtown. The Forum is also home to the NHL's **L.A. Kings** (☎ 310/673-6003). You can play the ponies at **Hollywood Park Racetrack** (☎ 310/419-1500) near the airport, where thoroughbreds run from April to July and November to December, and at **Santa Anita Racetrack** (☎ 626/574-7223) in Arcadia, northeast of downtown. Santa Anita's season runs from October to early April.

**SHOPPING**   Whether you take home souvenirs with traditional southern California images or fine goods available only here, you'll enjoy the diversity of the city's shopping scene as much as the residents do. The **sales tax** in Los Angeles is 8.25%, but savvy shoppers know to have larger items shipped directly home and save the tax.

Packed with chain stores and boutiques as well as dozens of restaurants and a large, multiscreen movie theater, **Santa Monica's 3rd Street Promenade** from Broadway to Wilshire Boulevard is one of the most popular shopping areas in the city. The pedestrian-only Promenade bustles on into the evening with a seemingly endless assortment of street performers and an endless parade of souls. Stores stay open late (often until 1 or 2am on the weekends) for the moviegoing crowds. There's plenty of metered parking in structures on the adjacent streets, so bring lots of quarters. Another good place for strolling in Santa Monica is **Main Street** between Pico Boulevard and Rose Avenue, which boasts a healthy combination of mall standards like The Gap, as well as upscale, left-of-center individual boutiques. You'll also find plenty of casually hip cafes and restaurants. This primary strip connecting Santa Monica and Venice has a relaxed, beach-community vibe that sets it apart from similar strips. The stores here straddle the fashion fence between upscale trendy and beach-bum edgy.

Once a station for the Red Car trolley line, the industrial space of **Bergamot Station,** at the terminus of Michigan Avenue west of Cloverfield Boulevard in Santa Monica (☎ 310/829-5854), is now home to about two dozen art galleries, a cafe, a bookstore, and offices. Most of the galleries are closed on Monday. Exhibits change often and vary widely, ranging from a Julius Shulman black-and-white photo retrospective of L.A.'s Case Study Houses, to a provocative exhibit of Vietnam War propaganda posters from the U.S. and Vietnam, to whimsical furniture constructed entirely of corrugated cardboard.

You can shop till you drop on **West 3rd Street** (between Fairfax Avenue and Robertson Boulevard), a newly trendy street in the shadow of the behemoth Beverly Center and anchored on the east end by the Farmer's Market. Many of Melrose Avenue's shops have relocated here, alongside some terrific up-and-comers, several cafes, and the much-lauded restaurant Locanda Veneta. "Fun" is more the catchword here than "funky," and the shops (including the vintage clothing stores) tend a bit more to the refined than do those along Melrose; you'd never find upscale bookshops dedicated to travel tomes and cookbooks in that neck of the woods—but you will here.

The monster-size billboards advertising the latest rock god make it clear that the **Sunset Strip** between La Cienega Boulevard and Doheny Drive in West Hollywood is rock 'n' roll territory. The "Strip" is lined with trendy restaurants, music industry–oriented hotels, and dozens of shops offering outrageous fashions and chunky stage accessories. One anomaly is Sunset Plaza, an upscale cluster of Georgian-style shops resembling Beverly Hills at its snootiest.

**La Brea Avenue** north of Wilshire Boulevard is L.A.'s artsiest shopping strip. Anchored by the giant American Rag, Cie. alterna-complex, La Brea is home to lots of great urban antiques stores dealing in deco, arts and crafts, 1950s modern, and the like (there's even a great antiques-hardware store). You'll also find vintage clothiers, furniture galleries, and other warehouse-size stores, as well as some of the city's hippest restaurants, such as Campanile.

Everyone knows about **Rodeo Drive,** the city's most famous shopping street. Couture shops from high fashion's Old Guard are located along its 3 hallowed blocks, along with plenty of newer high-end labels. The 16-square-block area surrounding Rodeo Drive is known as the **Golden Triangle.** Shops off Rodeo are generally not as name conscious as those on the strip (you might actually be able to buy something!), but they're nevertheless plenty upscale. Little Santa Monica Boulevard has a particularly colorful line of specialty stores, and Brighton Way is as young and hip as relatively staid Beverly Hills gets.

It's showing some wear—some stretches have become downright ugly—but **Melrose Avenue** between Fairfax and La Brea avenues is still one of the most exciting shopping streets in the country for cutting-edge fashions—and some eye-popping people-watching to boot. There are scores of shops selling the latest in clothes, gifts, jewelry, and accessories. Melrose is a playful stroll, dotted with plenty of hip restaurants and funky shops that are sure to shock. Where else could you find green patent-leather cowboy boots, a working 19th-century pocket watch, an inflatable girlfriend, and glow-in-the-dark condoms in the same shopping spree?

**Hollywood Boulevard** between Gower Street and La Brea Avenue is one of Los Angeles's most famous streets and, for the most part, a sleazy strip. But along the Walk of Fame, between the T-shirt shops and greasy pizza parlors, you'll find some excellent poster shops, souvenir stores, and Hollywood memorabilia dealers.

A pedestrian promenade next door to Universal Studios, **Universal CityWalk,** Universal Center Dr., Universal City (☎ 818/622-4455), is utterly unique. It's dominated by brightly colored, outrageously surreal oversize storefronts. The heavily touristed faux street is home to an inordinate number of restaurants, including B. B. King's Blues Club, the newest Hard Rock Cafe, and a branch of the Hollywood Athletic Club featuring a restaurant and pool hall.

# ACCOMMODATIONS

Choosing the right neighborhood as a base can make or break your vacation in this sprawling megalopolis. In general, downtown hotels are business oriented. A better bet is the city's Westside, a short drive from the beach and close to the most colorful sights. The city's most elegant—and expensive—accommodations are in Beverly Hills and Bel Air; a few of the hotels in this neighborhood have become attractions themselves. West Hollywood is an action-packed neighborhood with many hotel bargains. In Hollywood itself the action is a little grittier, but rates are friendly and you'll be centrally located to most of L.A. The smog-free coastal areas are extremely popular, especially in summertime; book hotels early in the beach towns of Santa Monica, Venice, and Malibu. The San Fernando Valley is popular with families who want to be near Universal Studios.

✪ **The Argyle.** *8358 Sunset Blvd., West Hollywood, CA 90069.* ☎ *800/225-2637 or 213/654-7100. Fax 213/654-9287. 19 rms, 48 suites. $225 double; from $325 suite. AE, CB, DC, EC, MC, V.* Completed in 1929, this landmark 15-story hotel is one of the most pristine art deco buildings in the city; it's also terrifically located, at the base of the Hollywood Hills between Beverly Hills and Hollywood. Once home to Golden Age movie stars, the hotel has small, lovely rooms with deco reproductions and specially commissioned handcrafted Italian furnishings, such as unique gondola-like beds. Modern conveniences haven't been overlooked—all rooms come equipped with VCRs, CD players, fax machines, and space-age phones. Facilities include a heated outdoor pool, exercise room, sundeck, and car-rental desk.

**Beverly Garland Holiday Inn.** *4222 Vineland Ave., North Hollywood, CA 91602.* ☎ *800/BEVERLY or 818/980-8000. Fax 818/766-5230. 258 rms, 12 suites. $139–$149 double; from $189 suite. AE, DC, DISC, MC, V. Free parking.* This hotel is named for its owner, the actress Beverly Garland (of *My Three Sons* fame). Grassy areas and greenery abound. Southwestern-themed fabrics complement the natural-pine furnishings in the guest rooms, whose painted cinderblock walls give off something of a college dorm feel. The hotel has a restaurant, pool, sauna, two tennis courts, and complimentary shuttle to Universal Studios.

✪ **Beverly Hills Hotel & Bungalows.** *9641 Sunset Blvd. (at Rodeo Dr.), Beverly Hills, CA 90210.* ☎ *800/283-8885 or 310/276-2251. Fax 310/281-2905. 194 rms, 21 bungalows and garden suites. $300–$350 double; from $300 bungalow; from $595 suite. AE, DC, EC, MC, V. Parking $15.* This legendary "Pink Palace" was center stage for deal—and star—making in Hollywood's golden days. It has been reconfigured to compete in today's luxury market, but the best original touches have been retained as well, like a butler on call at the touch of a button. Restaurants include the iconic Polo Lounge, nouvelle Polo Grill, and casual Fountain Coffee Shop. The hotel has a large outdoor heated pool, fitness room, Jacuzzi, sundeck, car-rental desk, beauty salon, and boutiques.

**Beverly Hills Inn.** *125 S. Spalding Dr., Beverly Hills, CA 90212.* ☎ *800/463-4466 or 310/278-0303. Fax 310/278-1728. 45 rms, 4 suites. $125–$175 double; from $175 suite. Rates include breakfast. AE, DC, EC, MC, V. Free parking.* This newly renovated inn is within walking distance of both Rodeo Drive and Century City. Thoughtfully designed rooms have a slightly Asian style. The least expensive tend to be smallish. The best overlook the pool and courtyard instead of the parking lot. Every room has a refrigerator. Guests enjoy the restaurant, bar, exercise room, and sauna.

✪ **Casa Malibu.** *22752 Pacific Coast Hwy. (about a quarter-mile south of Malibu Pier), Malibu, CA 90265.* ☎ *800/831-0858 or 310/456-2219. Fax 310/456-5418. 19 rms, 2 suites. $99–$135 double with garden view; $150 double with ocean view; $169 beachfront double; from $169 suite. Room with kitchen $10 extra. AE, EC, MC, V. Free* *parking.* This modest two-story motel wraps around a palm-studded inner courtyard just yards away from the blue Pacific and a large swath of private Malibu beach for the exclusive use of hotel guests. Rooms are surprisingly contemporary and cheerful, with top-quality mattresses, bathrobes, coffeemaker, and refrigerator; some rooms come with a fireplace and/or air-conditioning.

○ **Chateau Marmont.** *8221 Sunset Blvd. (between La Cienega and Crescent Heights blvds.), West Hollywood, CA 90046.* ☎ *800/242-8328 or 213/656-1010. Fax 213/655-5311. 63 rms, 53 suites, 4 bungalows. $190 double; from $240 suite; from $550 bungalow. AE, CB, DC, EC, MC, V. Valet parking $12.50.* This Norman-style 1920s landmark is close to the Hollywood action yet a luxurious world away at the same time. You expect to find John Barrymore or Errol Flynn holding inebriated court in the baronial living room here. Standard rooms have city views; some have kitchenettes. Their faux English and Formica furnishings are kitsch but not rustic. The poolside Cape Cod bungalows—large, secluded, cozy, with full kitchens—are some of the most coveted in town. A large outdoor heated pool, small fitness room, and sundeck are on the premises.

○ **Hollywood Roosevelt.** *7000 Hollywood Blvd., Hollywood, CA 90028.* ☎ *800/ 252-7466 or 213/466-7000. 311 rms, 19 suites. $109–$129 double; from $200 suite. AE, CB, DC, DISC, EC, MC, V. Valet parking $9.50.* This 12-story movie-city landmark is located on a slightly seedy, very touristy part of Hollywood Boulevard, across from Mann's Chinese Theatre and just down the street from the Walk of Fame. The Roosevelt was one of the city's grandest hotels when it opened its doors in 1927, and was home to the first Academy Awards ceremony. The rooms, however, are typical of chain hotels, far less appealing—in both size and decor—than the public areas; but a few are charmed with their original 1920s-style bathrooms, and high floors have unbeatable skyline views. The Cinegrill supper club draws locals with a zany cabaret show and guest chanteuses from Eartha Kitt to Cybill Shepherd.

○ **Hotel del Capri.** *10587 Wilshire Blvd. (at Westholme Ave.), Los Angeles, CA 90024.* ☎ *800/444-6835 or 310/474-3511. Fax 310/470-9999. 36 rms, 45 suites. $85– $105 double; from $110 suite. Rates include continental breakfast. AE, CB, DC, EC, MC, V. Free parking.* The Capri is one of the best values in trendy Westwood, popular with casual visitors, business travelers, and parents visiting their UCLA offspring. Though showing wear and tear, rooms are of good quality and have electrically adjustable beds—a decidedly novel touch. Larger models have whirlpool baths, and suites have kitchenettes. There's a free shuttle to nearby shopping and attractions in Westwood, Beverly Hills, and Century City.

**Hotel Oceana.** *849 Ocean Ave., Santa Monica, CA 90403.* ☎ *800/777-0758 or 310/393-0486. 63 suites. $170–$325 suite. AE, DC, DISC, MC, V. Rates include breakfast. Parking $10.* Excellently located in a residential neighborhood, this all-suite hotel is great for families. The beachy lobby is light and airy, and the newly renovated suites are filled with bright Matisse-inspired colors and cushy IKEA-ish furniture. Some suites have ocean views; VIP suites feature air-conditioning and two-person Jacuzzi tubs. In-room lunch and dinner service is provided by Wolfgang Puck's Cafe, but all suites come with fully equipped kitchens.

○ **Le Montrose Suite Hotel.** *900 Hammond St., West Hollywood, CA 90069.* ☎ *800/776-0666 or 310/855-1115. Fax 310/657-9192. 125 suites. $160–$475 suite. AE, CB, DC, EC, MC, V. Parking $13.* Nestled on a quiet residential street just 2 blocks from the bustling Strip, this hotel features large, condolike one-bedroom apartments. Each has a sizable sunken living room complete with gas fireplace, fax machine, and Nintendo games. There's a rooftop pool and lighted tennis court. For location, quality, and price, this is one of L.A.'s best values. A small exercise room, Jacuzzi, sauna, sundeck, and complimentary bicycles add to the appeal.

**Mansion Inn.** *327 Washington Blvd., Marina del Rey, CA 90291.* ☎ *800/ 828-0688 or 310/821-2557. Fax 310/827-0289. 38 rooms, 5 suites. $79–$89 double; $125 suite. Additional person $10 extra. Children under 12 stay free in parents' room. Rates include breakfast. AE, CB, DC, DISC, EC, JCB, MC, V. Free parking.* This charming, friendly, affordable inn is just 3 blocks from the ocean. Rooms all have balconies and refrigerators. There's an endless parade out front of people exploring Marina del Rey, the beach, or Venice canals on foot, bike, or in-line skates . . . rentals are 2 blocks away. Suites are the best deal here: a high-ceiling living room and spacious sleeping loft with queen bed.

**Regal Biltmore.** *506 S. Grand Ave. (between 5th and 6th sts.), Los Angeles, CA 90071.* ☎ *800/245-8673 or 213/624-1011. Fax 213/612-1545. 640 rms, 43 suites. $225–$235 double; from $350 suite. AE, CB, DC, DISC, EC, MC, V. Parking $20.* Built in 1923, the historic—and opulent—Biltmore is considered the grand dame of L.A. hotels. During the 1930s and 1940s the Academy Awards were held in the spectacular Crystal Ballroom (which appeared upside-down in *The Poseidon Adventure*), and the hotel was the top choice for presidents and the elite. Today, although the hotel's over-all elegance has been slightly compromised, a sense of refinement and graciousness still endures. Though small, rooms are attentively decorated and have marble baths. Some units are enchanting Old World suites. There are two restaurants, a swimming pool, health club, and business center.

**✪ Regent Beverly Wilshire.** *9500 Wilshire Blvd. (east of Santa Monica Blvd.), Beverly Hills, CA 90210.* ☎ *800/421-4354 or 310/275-5200. Fax 310/274-2851. 300 rms, 144 suites. $255–$405 double; from $425 suite. AE, CB, DC, DISC, EC, MC, V. Parking $15.* You might recognize this sophisticated hotel from its role in the film *Pretty Woman.* It's close to Rodeo Drive shops and an easy cruise down Wilshire to just about anywhere else. The rooms are refined, with a mix of period furniture, three phones, three TVs, an extra-deep soaking tub, and a glass-enclosed shower large enough for at least two. There's steward service on every floor and butlers can be called from a bedside bell. The hotel also has a small outdoor heated pool, large health club, hot tubs, sundeck, masseuse, and shops.

**✪ Shutters on the Beach.** *1 Pico Blvd. (at the beach), Santa Monica, CA 90405.* ☎ *800/334-9000 or 310/458-0030. Fax 310/458-4589. 186 rms, 12 suites. $290–$475 double; from $675 suite. AE, DC, DISC, EC, MC, V. Parking $16.* Light and luxurious Shutters is the only Santa Monica hotel directly on the beach. Cottagelike beachfront rooms are the most desirable, but all rooms enjoy the views and sounds of the ocean; some have fireplaces and Jacuzzis. Many celebrities stay here for the relaxed and elegant atmosphere sort of like an opulent Cape Cod estate. Luxuries include in-room massage, outdoor heated pool, exercise room, Jacuzzi, sauna, sundeck, beach equipment, and bicycle rental.

**Universal City Hilton & Towers.** *555 Universal Terrace Pkwy., Universal City, CA 91608.* ☎ *800/HILTONS or 818/506-2500. Fax 818/509-2031. 446 rms, 26 suites. $125–$165 double; from $175 suite. AE, DC, DISC, EC, MC, V. Valet parking $13.* Though this 24-story hotel sits right outside the Universal Studios theme park, there's more of a conservative, business-traveler feel than the raucous family-with-young-children ambience you might expect. The rooms are tastefully decorated in light earth tones with English-style furniture. The Cafe Sierra serves California cuisine. Guests appreciate the heated pool, Jacuzzi, and health club.

**Venice Beach House Historic Inn.** *15 30th Ave. (off Pacific Ave.), Venice, CA 90291.* ☎ *310/823-1966. Fax 310/823-1842. 4 rms, none with private bath; 5 suites. $85–$95 double; $130–$165 suite. Rates include continental breakfast. AE, EC, MC, V.*

*Free parking.* Built in 1922, this former family home is now a fine bed-and-breakfast on one of Venice's unique sidewalk streets. With hardwood floors, bay windows, a lattice porch, and large oriental rugs, it will make you forget the hustle and bustle of the beach just steps away. In addition to breakfast, afternoon tea or cool lemonade is served with fresh-baked cookies daily.

**Westin Bonaventure.** *404 S. Figueroa St. (between 4th and 5th sts.), Los Angeles, CA 90071.* ☎ *800/228-3000 or 213/624-1000. Fax 213/612-4800. 1,368 rms, 155 suites. $175–$215 double; from $190 suite. AE, CB, DC, EC, MC, V. Parking $18.50.* The 35-story Bonaventure is one of downtown's most distinctive landmarks, an enormous convention hotel designed on the scale of a minicity. The six-story skylit lobby houses splashing fountains, gardens, trees, even a large lake. One of the towers is an all-suite facility. The rooftop Top of Five restaurant and Bona Vista cocktail lounge have spectacular views. The hotel includes a large outdoor pool, sundeck, and five levels of shops and boutiques.

**OTHER ACCOMMODATIONS**  While it's slightly dingy, the **Beverly Laurel Motor Hotel,** 8018 Beverly Blvd., west of Fairfax (☎ 800/962-3824 or 213/651-2441; fax 213/651-5225), is ultra-cheap by L.A. standards and ideally located for exploring most of the area. Attached is the enormously popular Swingers coffee shop (see "Dining," below). The **Los Angeles West Travelodge,** 10740 Santa Monica Blvd., at Overland Ave. (☎ 310/474-4576; fax 310/470-3117), is a clean and friendly motel offering good value in a high-priced area, close to all Westside destinations. The **Best Western Hollywood Motor Hotel,** 6141 Franklin Ave., between Vine and Gower streets (☎ 800/287-1700 in California, or 213/464-5181; fax 213/962-0536), is within walking distance of the famed Hollywood and Vine intersection. Like the Beverly Laurel, the coffee shop is also a favorite among local hipsters.

Near LAX airport, the **Sheraton Gateway Hotel—Los Angeles Airport,** 6101 W. Century Blvd., near Sepulveda Boulevard (☎ 800/325-3535 or 310/642-1111), is a comfortable, California-style hotel that literally overlooks the runway. The **Los Angeles Airport Marriott,** Century and Airport boulevards (☎ 800/228-9290 or 310/641-5700), is a reliable choice. The inexpensive **Travelodge at LAX,** 5547 W. Century Blvd. (☎ 800/421-3939 or 310/649-4000), has a surprisingly beautiful tropical garden surrounding the pool area.

## DINING

When it comes to culinary innovation and architectural design, L.A.'s restaurants are tops, plus recent economic and social trends have led to a whole new crop of places serving bone-china cuisine at blue-plate prices. Reservations are recommended almost everywhere, particularly on weekends and during peak lunch and dinner times on weekdays.

**Alice's.** *23000 Pacific Coast Hwy. (at the Malibu Pier), Malibu.* ☎ *310/456-6646. Reservations recommended. Main courses $9–$18; lunch $7–$15. MC, V. Mon–Fri 11:30am–10pm, Sat–Sun 11am–11pm. CALIFORNIA.* Alice's has a long history as a Malibu fixture, situated on the Pacific Coast Highway on the pier above the beach. It's dining room is glassed in and faces the ocean; everyone has a million-dollar view. It's a light and airy place, with a casual menu to match. Seared yellowtail tuna is served simply, on a bed of spinach, with lemon and tarragon butter. Grilled chicken breast is marinated in garlic and soy and served with tomato-cilantro relish. Pastas and pizzas are also available, and there's a full bar.

**Apple Pan.** *10801 Pico Blvd. (east of Westwood Blvd.).* ☎ *310/475-3585. Main courses $6–$7. No credit cards. Tues–Thurs and Sun 11am–midnight, Fri–Sat 11am–1am. SANDWICHES/AMERICAN.* There are no tables, just a U-shaped counter, at this classic (circa 1947) American burger shack and L.A. landmark. It's famous for juicy burgers, bullet-fast service, and an authentic frills-free atmosphere. The hickory burger is best, though the tuna salad sandwich also has its huge share of fans. If your waistline can take it, order fries and home-baked apple pie.

**Authentic Cafe.** *7605 Beverly Blvd. (at Curson Ave.).* ☎ *213/939-4626. Reservations not accepted. Main courses $8–$13. AE, MC, V. Mon–Thurs 11:30am–10pm, Fri 11:30am–11pm, Sat 10am–11pm, Sun 10am–10pm. SOUTHWESTERN.* True to its name, this excellent restaurant serves authentic Southwestern food in a casual atmosphere known for hip people-watching, large portions, and good food. You'll sometimes find an Asian flair to chef Roger Hayot's Southwestern-style meals; look for brie, papaya, and chili quesadillas; other worthwhile dishes are the chicken casserole with a cornbread crust, fresh corn and red peppers in chile-cream sauce, and meat loaf with caramelized onions.

**Bombay Cafe.** *12113 Santa Monica Blvd. (at Bundy Dr.).* ☎ *310/820-2070. Reservations not accepted. Main courses $9–$15. MC, V. Tues–Thurs 11:30am–10pm, Fri–Sat 11:30am–11pm, Sun 11:30am–4pm. INDIAN.* Indian is the cuisine of the moment in L.A., and nowhere is it done better than at the Bombay Cafe. The unlikely and plain mini-mall location belies excellent curries and kurmas that are typical of South Indian street food. Once seated, immediately order *sev puri* for the table—crispy little chips topped with chopped potatoes, onions, cilantro, and chutneys. Also recommended are the burrito-like "frankies," juicy little bread rolls stuffed with lamb, chicken, or cauliflower. The best dishes come from the 800°F tandoor, and include yogurt-marinated swordfish, lamb, and chicken, all served spicy.

**Camelions.** *246 26th St. (south of San Vicente Blvd.), Santa Monica.* ☎ *310/395-0746. Reservations required. Main courses $10–$13 at lunch, $14–$22 at dinner. AE, CB, DC, MC, V. Tues–Sun 11:30am–2:30pm and 6–9:30pm. CALIFORNIA/FRENCH.* Served in a romantic Provençal setting (either indoors or out), Camelions's tasty French-inspired cuisine is plenty California trendy. Red-lentil crepes arrive garnished with smoked salmon and arugula salad, and roasted duck breast is sliced thin and fanned out over a plate of walnut-merlot sauce, accompanied by a risotto-and-berry timbale. A large selection of sandwiches and salads (like spinach with warm new potatoes, bacon, and mustard vinaigrette) are available at lunch.

**Campanile.** *624 S. La Brea Ave. (north of Wilshire Blvd.).* ☎ *213/938-1447. Reservations required. Main courses $18–$28. AE, MC, V. Mon–Thurs 7:30am–2:30pm and 6–10pm, Fri 7:30am–2:30pm and 5:30–11pm, Sat 8am–1:30pm and 5:30–11pm, Sun 8am–1:30pm. CALIFORNIA/MEDITERRANEAN.* Built as Charlie Chaplin's private offices in 1928, this lovely building has a skylight through which diners can see the *campanile* (bell tower). The kitchen, headed by Spago alumnus chef/owner Mark Peel, gets a giant leg up from baker (and wife) Nancy Silverton, who runs the now-legendary La Brea Bakery next door, and whose chewy breads and heavenly desserts round out a menu of grilled and roasted meat, fish, and poultry.

**✪ El Cholo.** *1121 S. Western Ave. (south of Olympic Blvd.).* ☎ *213/734-2773. Reservations recommended. Main courses $7–$13. AE, DC, MC, V. Mon–Thurs 11am–10pm, Fri–Sat 11am–11pm, Sun 11am–9pm. MEXICAN.* There's *authentic* Mexican and then there's *traditional* Mexican—El Cholo is comfort food of the latter variety, south-of-the-border cuisine traditionally craved by Angelenos. They've been serving it up in this pink adobe hacienda since 1927; El Cholo's expertly blended margaritas, invitingly messy nachos, and classic combination dinners don't break new culinary ground, but the kitchen has perfected these standards over 70 years. The atmosphere is festive, as people from all parts of town dine happily in the many rambling rooms that comprise the restaurant. There's valet parking as well as a free self-park lot directly across the street.

**Il Pastaio.** *400 N. Canon Dr. (at Brighton Way), Beverly Hills.* ☎ *310/205-5444. Reservations not accepted. Main courses $7–$12 at lunch, $12–$23 at dinner. AE, MC, V. Mon–Sat 11am–11pm. ITALIAN.* Sicilian-born chef Drago has been helming the kitchens of high-profile L.A. restaurants for years, but this value-priced restaurant is a simple place with white walls, a long bar, and a pasta-making area. It's as narrow as a bowling alley and almost as loud. Only starters, pastas, and desserts are served, but the selections are vast and great for grazing. *Be warned:* Il Pastaio is small, and there is often a wait.

**Kate Mantilini.** *9101 Wilshire Blvd. (at Doheny Dr.), Beverly Hills.* ☎ *310/ 278-3699. Reservations suggested. Main courses $7–$16. AE, MC, V. Mon–Thurs 7:30am–1am, Fri 7:30am–3am, Sat noon–3am, Sun 10am–midnight. AMERICAN.* It's rare to find a restaurant that feels comfortably familiar yet trendy and cutting edge and is also one of L.A.'s few late-night eateries. Kate Mantilini fits the bill perfectly. One of the first to bring meat loaf back into fashion, Kate's offers a huge menu of upscale truck-stop favorites. At 2am nothing quite beats a steaming bowl of lentil-vegetable soup and some garlic-cheese toast—unless your taste runs to fresh oysters and a dry martini. Kate has it all.

**Kay 'n Dave's Cantina.** *262 26th St. (south of San Vicente Blvd.), Santa Monica.* ☎ *310/260-1355. Reservations not taken. Main courses $5–$12. AE, MC, V. Mon–Thurs 7:30am–9:30pm, Fri 7:30am–10pm, Sat 8am–10pm, Sun 8am–9:30pm. HEALTHY MEXICAN.* A beach community favorite for "really big portions of really good food at really low prices," Kay 'n Dave's cooks with no lard and has a vegetarian-friendly menu with plenty of meat items, too. Come early (and be prepared to wait) for breakfast, as local devotees line up for five kinds of fluffy pancakes, zesty omelets, or bulging breakfast burritos. Grilled tuna Veracruz, spinach and chicken enchiladas in tomatillo salsa, vegetable-filled corn tamales, and other Mexican specialties really are served in huge portions; bring the family—there's a kids' menu and crayons on every table. Kay 'n Dave's also has cantinas in Malibu at 18763 Pacific Coast Hwy. (☎ **310/456-8800**) and in Pacific Palisades at 15246 Sunset Blvd. (☎ **310/459-8118**). The Malibu location opens later in the mornings.

✪ **Locanda Veneta.** *8638 W. 3rd St. (between San Vicente and Robertson blvds.).* ☎ *310/274-1893. Reservations required. Main courses $10–$22. AE, DC, DISC, MC, V. Mon–Thurs 11:30am–2:30pm and 5:30–10:30pm, Fri 11:30am–2:30pm and 5:30–11pm, Sat 5:30–11pm. ITALIAN/VENETIAN.* Locanda Veneta's citywide renown belies its tiny size and unpretentious setting. L.A.'s "foodies" flock here to sample the latest creations of chef Massimo Ormani, whose signature dishes include pasta-and-bean soup, veal chops, lobster ravioli, shrimp risotto, and perfectly grilled vegetables—plus a thick vanilla custard with chocolate and caramel sauces.

✪ **Matsuhisa.** *129 N. La Cienega Blvd. (north of Wilshire Blvd.), Beverly Hills.* ☎ *310/659-9639. Reservations required. Main courses $14–$22; sushi $20–$30. AE, DC, MC, V. Mon–Fri 11:45am–2:45pm and 5:45–10:15pm, Sat–Sun 5:45–10:15pm. JAPANESE/PERUVIAN.* Japanese chef/owner Nobuyuki Matsuhisa arrived in Los Angeles via Peru and creates fantastic, unusual dishes by combining Japanese flavors with South American spices and salsas. Broiled sea bass with black truffles, sautéed squid with garlic and soy, and Dungeness crab tossed with chiles and cream are good examples. Both tight and bright, the restaurant's small, crowded main dining room fills up quickly—make your reservation in advance. Celebrities are commonplace, and Matsuhisa is fantastically popular with hard-core foodies, who continually return for the savory surprises that come with every bite.

**✪ Michael's.** *1147 3rd St. (west of Wilshire Blvd.), Santa Monica.* ☎ *310/ 451-0843. Reservations required. Main courses $15–$25. AE, CB, DC, DISC, MC, V. Tues–Fri noon–3pm and 6–10:30pm, Sat 6–10:30pm. CALIFORNIA.* If Wolfgang Puck is the father of contemporary California cuisine, then Michael McCarty is the grandfather. Born in New York and schooled in France, McCarty opened this self-consciously modern American restaurant in 1979, when he was only 25 years old, and this fetching Santa Monica eatery remains one of the city's best. A recent price rollback has made dishes like Michael's simple grilled pork tenderloin with cream sauce and apples, and duck with Grand Marnier and oranges, even more appetizing. Spaghetti tossed in a creamy chardonnay sauce with large sea scallops, roasted sweet peppers, baby asparagus, and American golden caviar is just one example of the delicious, complex pastas here.

**Musso & Frank Grill.** *6667 Hollywood Blvd. (at Cahuenga Blvd.).* ☎ *213/ 467-7788. Reservations recommended. Main courses $13–$22. AE, CB, DC, DISC, MC, V. Tues–Sat 11am–11pm. AMERICAN/CONTINENTAL.* As L.A.'s oldest eatery (since 1919), Musso & Frank is the paragon of Old Hollywood grill rooms, where Faulkner and Hemingway drank during their screenwriting days, where Orson Welles used to hold court. The restaurant is still known for its bone-dry martinis and perfectly seasoned Bloody Marys. Regulars flock in for Thursday-only chicken pot pie, and Musso's trademark "flannel cakes," crepe-thin pancakes flipped to order.

**✪ Patina.** *5955 Melrose Ave. (west of Cahuenga Blvd.).* ☎ *213/467-1108. Reservations required. Main courses $18–$26. AE, DC, DISC, MC, V. Sun–Mon 6–9:30pm, Tues–Thurs 11:30am–2pm and 6–9:30pm, Fri 11:30am–2pm and 6–10:30pm, Sat 6–10:30pm. CALIFORNIA/FRENCH.* Superstar chef Joachim Splichal's Patina routinely wins the highest praise from demanding gourmands, who are happy to empty their bank accounts for unbeatable meals that almost never miss their intended mark. The dining room is professional, without the slightest hint of stuffiness, and the seasonal menu features partridge, pheasant, venison, and other game in winter and spotlights exotic local vegetables in warmer months.

**✪ Spago.** *1114 Horn Ave. (at Sunset Blvd.), West Hollywood.* ☎ *310/652-4025. Reservations required. Main courses $18–$28. DC, DISC, MC, V. Daily 6–11:30pm. CALIFORNIA.* German-born Wolfgang Puck is a masterful businessman and publicist who has made Spago one of the best-known restaurants in America; he's also a great chef, and Spago remains one of L.A.'s top-rated eateries. The menu stars imaginative "gourmet" pizzas topped with goodies like duck sausage, shiitake mushrooms, leeks, and artichokes, and other combinations once considered to be on the culinary edge. Of the other items on the bistro-inspired menu, roast Sonoma lamb with braised shallots, and grilled chicken with garlic and parsley are two perennial favorites. The celebrated (and far from secret) off-menu meal is Jewish pizza, a crispy pie topped with smoked salmon, crème fraîche, dill, red onion, and dollops of caviar.

**Swingers.** *8020 Beverly Blvd. (west of Fairfax).* ☎ *213/653-5858. Reservations not accepted. Most items under $8. AE, MC, V. Sun–Thurs 6am–2am, Fri–Sat 9am–4am. DINER/AMERICAN.* Swingers was transformed by a couple of L.A. hipster nightclub owners from a dismal motel coffee shop into a '90s shrine to comfy Americana. Guests at the attached Beverly Laurel Motor Hotel chow down alongside body-pierced Industry hounds from nearby Maverick Records (Madonna's company), while outside orthodox Jews stroll to and from Fairfax Avenue. Swingers serves high-quality diner favorites spiked with trendy crowd-pleasers like steel-cut Irish oatmeal, *challah* French toast, grilled Jamaican jerk chicken, and a nice selection of tofu-enhanced vegetarian dishes.

**OTHER DINING**   For a true L.A. dining experience, be sure to try at least one of chef Wolfgang Puck's restaurants. In addition to Spago (see above), there's **Chinois on**

**Main,** 2709 Main St., Santa Monica (☎ **310/392-9025**), which serves terrifically quirky East–meets–West Franco–Chinese cuisine. At **Granita,** in the Malibu Colony Mall, 23725 W. Malibu Rd., Malibu (☎ **310/456-0488**), Puck applies his signature California style to seafood. His latest venture is the affordable Pan-Asian bistro and satay bar **ObaChine,** 242 N. Beverly Dr., Beverly Hills (☎ **310/274-4440**).

## LOS ANGELES AFTER DARK

The *L.A. Weekly,* a free weekly paper available at sidewalk stands, shops, and restaurants, is the best place to find out what's going on about town, especially for club happenings. The "Calendar" section of the Sunday *Los Angeles Times* is also a good place to find out what's going on after dark. For weekly updates on music, art, dance, theater, special events, and festivals, call the **Cultural Affairs Hotline** (☎ **213/688-ARTS**), a 24-hour directory listing a wide variety of events, most of which are free. **Ticketmaster** (☎ 213/480-3232) and **Telecharge** (☎ 800/447-7400) are the major charge-by-phone ticket agencies in the city, selling tickets to concerts, sporting events, plays, and special events.

**THE PERFORMING ARTS** The ✪ **Los Angeles Philharmonic** (☎ **213/850-2000**) isn't just the city's top symphony; it's the only major classical music company in Los Angeles. Finnish-born music director Esa-Pekka Salonen concentrates on contemporary compositions; despite complaints from traditionalists, he does an excellent job attracting younger audiences. In addition to regular performances at the **Music Center's Dorothy Chandler Pavilion,** 135 N. Grand Ave., downtown, the Philharmonic also plays a popular summer season at the Hollywood Bowl (☎ **213/850-2000**), an outdoor amphitheater cradled in the hills and recognized by its distinctive, Frank Lloyd Wright–designed band shell. Summer season also includes jazz performances and pop vocalists; attendees usually make a night of it by picnicking on the grounds before the performance.

Slowly but surely, the **L.A. Opera** (☎ **213/972-8001**) is gaining both respect and popularity with inventive stagings of classic operas, usually with guest divas. The opera also calls the Music Center home.

The 120-voice **Los Angeles Master Chorale** (☎ **213/626-0624**) sings a varied repertoire that includes classical and pop compositions. Concerts are usually held at the Music Center from October to June.

Major theatrical productions are held at the two theaters of the **Music Center,** 135 N. Grand Ave., downtown. The **Ahmanson Theater** (☎ **213/972-7401**) reopened in 1995, after a $71-million renovation that improved acoustics and seating. In-house shows are usually revivals of major Broadway plays, starring famous film and TV actors; a few years ago, we saw *Dangerous Liaisons* with Lynn Redgrave and Frank Langella, and *The Little Shop Around the Corner* with Pam Dawber and Christopher Reeve. Traveling shows are usually West Coast premieres of plays such as Neil Simon's *Broadway Bound* or Andrew Lloyd Webber's *Phantom of the Opera;* the renovated theater debuted with *Miss Saigon.*

The **Mark Taper Forum** (☎ **213/972-0700**) is a more intimate, circular theater staging contemporary works by international and local playwrights. Kenneth Branagh's Renaissance Theatre Company staged its only American productions of *King Lear* and *A Midsummer Night's Dream* at the Mark Taper, to give you an idea of the quality of the shows here. Productions are usually excellent, run with plenty of spirit and no shortage of controversy. Ticket prices vary depending on the performance. Discounted tickets are usually available on the day of the performance for students and seniors.

Big-time traveling troupes and Broadway-bound musicals that don't go to the Ahmanson head instead for the **Shubert Theater,** in the ABC Entertainment Center,

2020 Avenue of the Stars, Century City (☎ 800/233-3123). This plush playhouse presents major Broadway musicals. Top-quality Broadway-caliber productions are also staged at the **UCLA James A. Doolittle Theater,** 1615 N. Vine St., Hollywood (☎ 213/462-6666 or 213/972-0700).

For the current schedule at any of the above theaters, check the listings in *Los Angeles* magazine or the "Calendar" section of the Sunday *Los Angeles Times,* or call the box offices directly at the numbers listed above.

**SMALLER PLAYHOUSES**  Like New York's off-Broadway or London's fringe, Los Angeles's small-scale theaters often outdo the slick, high-budget shows. Because this is Tinseltown, movie and TV stars sometimes headline, but more often than not the talent is up-and-coming. See them at the **Colony Studio Theater,** 1944 Riverside Dr., Silver Lake (☎ 213/665-3011); the **Actors Circle Theater,** 7313 Santa Monica Blvd., West Hollywood (☎ 213/882-8043); or the restored former movie palace **Los Angeles Theater,** 615 S. Broadway (☎ 213/629-2939). In addition to those listed above, there are about 100 other stages of varying quality throughout the city. Tickets for most plays usually cost $10 to $30. Check newspaper listings for current offerings.

**THE CLUB & MUSIC SCENE**  This is a town where only the strongest—and the most resourceful—survive, and too many folks are angling to get into the hot clubs and see the hot shows. You can still make a fabulous night of it by doing a little advance research and copping some L.A. attitude of your very own.

Like the popular "House of Blues" franchise, **B. B. King's Blues Club,** CityWalk, Universal City (☎ 818/622-5464), is designed to make you feel like you just stepped into a murky bayou, but feels a bit more "real" than its Hollywood cousin. The music stays closer to authentic blues, and it also offers a fine, though overpriced, Sunday gospel brunch.

With a gala opening in August 1996 that closed down the Sunset Strip for the first time in history, the three-tier, $5¹/₂-million **Billboard Live,** 9039 Sunset Blvd., West Hollywood (☎ 310/786-1712), promised to breathe some life into the legendary Strip. Among its state-of-the-art distinctions: two gigantic exterior "Jumbotrons," whose screens reveal the onstage performances to passersby and, during the day, feature continuous music programming. Numerous monthly performances are selected from *Billboard*'s "Heatseekers" charts, so you can be the first to see the Next Big Thing.

Over in the east Hollywood neighborhood of Los Feliz Village, **The Derby,** 4500 Los Feliz Blvd., Los Feliz (☎ 213/663-8979), is a luscious club at a former Brown Derby site with a heavy 1940s edge. Despite its Disneyland-ish decor and co-ownership by such strange bedfellows as Jim Belushi, Dan Ackroyd, Aerosmith, and Harvard University, the **House of Blues,** 8430 Sunset Blvd., West Hollywood (☎ 213/650-0247), is permeated with industry types more interested in being seen than hearing the music. Even so, there's enough top-notch music here to keep many who routinely bad-mouth the place coming back. The Sunday gospel brunch, though a bit overpriced, is a rousing diversion.

During the summer, crowds flock to the outdoor **John Anson Ford Theatre,** 2580 Cahuenga Blvd. W., Los Angeles (☎ 213/464-2826), where rock shows were once banned after the punk sounds of a Ramones's late-'80s concert carried across U.S. 101 and into the ears of people who were trying to hear the L.A. Symphony play Beethoven at the Hollywood Bowl. But lately it's been back, and a night with a rising star under the stars can be wonderful. Arrive early for the best parking, or face a hike uphill from your car.

Proprietor Jean-Pierre Boccarra has turned **LunaPark,** 665 N. Robertson Blvd., West Hollywood (☎ 310/652-0611), into one of the most unpredictable yet reliable venues in the area—not just for music but for performance art, cabaret, and comedy. The

Date Street 6

Cedar Street
Beech Street
Ash Street

India St.
Columbia St.

4th Ave.
5th Ave.
6th Ave.
7th Ave.

8th Ave.
9th Ave.
10th Ave.
11th Ave.

Drive

Highway

A Street
B Street

7

C Street
Broadway

1 8

Harbor

Pacific

Kettner Blvd.

State Street
Union Street
Front Street

E Street
F Street
G Street

2

Market Street

1st Ave.
2nd Ave.
3rd Ave.

4

5

Harbor Dr.

6

Island Avenue
J Street

K Street

9

Gaslamp
Quarter

3

**Downtown**

**Hillcrest/
Uptown**

Pacific Hwy.

5

1st Ave.

5th Ave.

163
**Balboa
Park**

14

Park Blvd.

805

Ash Street
Broadway

**SAN DIEGO**

15

94

13

15

Euclid Ave.

3rd St.
4th St.

Orange Ave.

San Diego–Coronado
Bay Bridge (Toll)

National
Ave.

Logan Ave.

11

12

16

Silver

75

Division St.

**National
City**

8th St.

805

8

7

8

10

Vista Rd.

Linda

Friars Rd.

River

**Visitor Information Center,** 2688 E. Mission Bay Dr., San Diego, CA 92109 (☎ 619/276-8200). The **North County Convention and Visitor Bureau,** 720 N. Broadway, Escondido (☎ 800/848-3336 or 619/745-4741), can provide information on La Jolla and excursion areas in San Diego County, including Escondido, Julian, and Anza-Borrego Desert State Park.

**RESOURCES FOR TRAVELERS WITH SPECIAL NEEDS** The special senior citizens referral and information line is ☎ 619/560-2500. The Travelers with Disabilities hotline (☎ 619/279-0704) helps disabled visitors link up with hotels, tours, attractions, and transportation accessible to them. Or send a $5 donation for a 25-page access guide that includes a listing of local social service agencies to P.O. Box 124526, San Diego, CA 92112-4526. The San Diego Convention and Visitor Bureau's dining and accommodations guide carries the wheelchair symbol indicating handicapped accessibility. Bus stops served by accessible buses are marked with a wheelchair symbol.

The free *San Diego Gay & Lesbian Times,* published every Thursday, is often available at Quel Fromage coffeehouse and the Blue Door Bookstore, both in Hillcrest near Balboa Park. The active **Lesbian and Gay Men's Community Center** is at 3916 Normal St. (☎ 619/692-2077). **AIDS Foundation San Diego,** 4080 Centre St. (☎ 619/686-5000), provides information and educational programs on AIDS and social services for people with AIDS.

**EMERGENCIES & SAFETY** For police, fire, highway patrol, or life-threatening medical emergencies, dial ☎ 911 from any phone. **UCSD Medical Center,** 200 W. Arbor Dr. in Hillcrest (☎ 619/543-6400), has the best-located, almost-downtown emergency room. As cities go, San Diego is relatively safe, but do use caution on the beaches after dark. Stay on designated walkways and away from secluded areas in Balboa Park—night or day. In the Gaslamp Quarter, don't wander east of 5th Avenue.

## GETTING AROUND

**BY BUS** The **Metropolitan Transit System (MTS)** includes 101 routes and provides a **Transit Store,** 102 Broadway, at First Avenue (☎ 619/233-3004), where you can get information, passes, timetables, maps, and ID cards for seniors and disabled travelers. It's open 8:30am to 5:30pm on weekdays, and until 4pm on weekends. Call ☎ 619/233-3004 or TTY/TDD 619/234-5005 for specifics on reaching a particular destination, or ☎ 619/685-4900 for schedule information. Local fare is $1.50 one way, exact change required ($1 bills are accepted); express buses cost $1.75. A **Day Tripper Pass,** which allows unlimited rides on any bus or trolley route for 1 day, costs $5 (4 days for $15), and the pass is also good on the San Diego–Coronado ferry.

**BY TROLLEY** The bright-red **San Diego Trolley** is a fun and efficient way to get around. Trolleys generally operate daily from 5am to 12:30am (the San Ysidro line runs 24 hours on Saturday). Machine purchase your ticket before boarding, and it is good for 2 hours in one direction, except in the "Center Zone," where it is good in any direction. (Fare inspectors randomly board trains and check proof of payment.) Trolley travel within the downtown area costs $1; the fare to the U.S.–Mexican border is $1.75. For recorded trolley information, call ☎ 619/231-8549; to get a real person on the line, call ☎ 619/233-3004 or TTY/TDD 619/234-5005 from 5:30am to 8:30pm daily.

**BY FERRY & WATER TAXI** Ferries between San Diego and Coronado (☎ 619/234-4111) leave from the Broadway Pier on the hour Sun–Thurs 9am–9pm, Fri–Sat until 10pm. The fare is $2 one way, or free if you have an MTS Day Tripper Pass. Purchase tickets in advance for the 15-minute ride at the Harbor Excursion kiosk on the pier in San Diego or at the Old Ferry Landing in Coronado. **Water taxis** (☎ 619/235-TAXI) will take you anywhere you want to go on San Diego Bay for $5.

**BY TAXI**   Cab companies don't have standardized rates, except from the airport into town, which costs $1.80 per mile. Taxis are not easily hailed on the street, so phone for a guaranteed pickup. Companies include **Orange Cab** (☎ 619/291-3333), **San Diego Cab** (☎ 619/226-TAXI), **Yellow Cab** (☎ 619/234-6161), and **La Jolla Cab** (☎ 619/453-4222). The **Coronado Cab Company** (☎ 619/435-6211) serves Coronado.

## WHAT TO SEE & DO

San Diego is more a chain of separate neighborhoods than a single cohesive city. Each area is well defined and relatively compact, and each offers a wonderful variety of experience for visitors. **Downtown** includes **Horton Plaza,** a 6-block shopping mall; the **Gaslamp Quarter,** the heart of San Diego's dining and entertainment in a Victorian-style National Historic District; the **Embarcadero,** the waterfront; **Seaport Village,** a themed shopping/dining area; and the **Convention Center. Old Town,** northwest of downtown, is a state historic park with museums and restaurants. **Hillcrest/Uptown,** adjoining neighborhoods near Balboa Park, offers a slightly funky dining and nightlife scene, with Hillcrest the center of San Diego's gay community. **Mission Bay/Pacific Beach** is the water playground area and is known for its nightlife.

   **Coronado** is actually a lovely, upscale city in its own right. Enjoy a boat ride over (see "Getting Around," above) or cross the **Coronado Bay Bridge** (free for two or more people in car) and enjoy a self-guided tour of the famous **Hotel Del Coronado's** grounds and photo gallery. You can enjoy a walk on the beach and continue on to the **Coronado Beach Historical Museum.**

**ESCORTED TOURS**   The **Old Town Trolley** (☎ 619/298-8687) is a privately operated open-air tour bus that travels in a continuous loop around the city, providing access to sightseeing highlights. It stops at more than a dozen places and you can hop on and off as often as you please. Old Town Trolley is the only company allowed on military bases in San Diego. The tours operate daily 9am–5pm in summer; until 4pm the rest of the year. The cost is $17 for adults and $8 for children 6 to 12 (under 5 ride free). For information on base tours, call ☎ 800/NARY-TOUR. There's usually a discount coupon in the Visitor Value Pack (see "Visitor Information," above). **Walkabout International** (☎ 619/231-7463) sponsors 150 free walking tours every month, led by volunteers.

**BALBOA PARK**   This urban enclave comprises more than 1,400 acres northeast of downtown and contains the San Diego Zoo and numerous museums. The park is the city's cultural center and a recreational paradise. It ranks as one of the nation's largest, loveliest, and most important municipal greenbelts, with gardens, historical buildings, restaurants, and a pavilion. Entry to the park is free, but most of its museums have admission charges, though one free day a month is offered (call for information), and open hours vary. A free tram will transport you around the park. A **Balboa Park Pass** is good for 10 museums and can be purchased for $18 at the Visitor Center. The museums include: ✪ **Aerospace Museum and International Aerospace Hall of Fame** (☎ 619/234-8291); **Museum of Art** (☎ 619/232-7931); ✪ **Museum of Photographic Arts** (☎ 619/239-5262); **Natural History Museum** (☎ 619/232-3821); **Museum of Man** (☎ 619/239-2001); **San Diego Automotive Museum** (☎ 619/231-2886); **Botanical Museum** (☎ 619/235-1100); **Hall of Champions** (☎ 619/234-2544); **Marston House Museum** (☎ 619/232-6203); **Model Railroad Museum** (☎ 619/696-0199); **Museum of San Diego History** (☎ 619/232-6203); **Timken Museum of Art** (☎ 619/239-5548); and the **Reuben H. Fleet Space Theater and Science Center** (☎ 619/238-1233, or 619/232-6866 for advance ticket sales), the busiest museum, so you may want to call to charge tickets in advance to save a long wait in line. At the **Sprekels Organ Pavilion** (☎ 619/226-0819), free concerts are given on Sunday at 2pm and in summer on Monday at 8pm.

✪ **San Diego Zoo.** ☎ *619/234-3153 or 619/231-1515. Admission $15 adults, $6 children 3–11, free for children 2 and under. Free to everyone on the first Mon in Oct and free to children ages 11 and under all through Oct. July–Labor Day, daily 9am–9pm. Rest of year, daily 9am–4pm. Bus: 7, 7A, 7B.* More than 3,500 animals call this world-famous zoo home and the zoo is noted for its rare and exotic species. It is also a botanical garden, representing over 6,500 species of flora from many climate zones, all installed to help simulate native environments for the animals. The zoo offers two types of bus tours—both provide a narrated overview and you see 75% of the park. You can get an aerial perspective via the Skyfari.

**OLD TOWN & BEYOND**  The birthplace of San Diego—indeed, of California—Old Town is Mexican California, which existed here until the mid-1800s. You can get here on the trolley. Free walking tours leave daily at 2pm from the **Old Town State Historic Park's** visitor center (☎ **619/220-5422**), located at the head of the pedestrian walkway that is the continuation of San Diego Avenue. Admission to the center is free. Open daily 10am–5pm. There are a number of highlights to enjoy. **Heritage Park,** 2455 Heritage Park Row (☎ **619/694-3049**), is filled with seven original 19th-century houses, now home to shops and inns. Admission is free. Open daily 9:30am–3pm. The **Junípero Serra Museum,** 2727 Presidio Dr., Presidio Park (☎ **619/297-3258**), is the site of a 1769 mission and the first nonnative West Coast settlement. **Mission Basilica San Diego de Alcala,** 10818 San Diego Mission Rd., Mission Valley (☎ **619/281-8449**), was the first link, in 1769, in a chain of 21 missions founded by Spanish missionary Junípero Serra. Admission is $2 adults, $1 seniors and students, 50¢ children 12 and under. **Whaley House,** 2482 San Diego Ave. (☎ **619/298-2482**), was built in 1856 and is one of two authenticated haunted houses in the state, and the home of treasures such as the spinet piano used in the movie *Gone with the Wind.* Admission is $4 adults, $3 seniors 65 and over, $2 ages 5–16.

**MORE ATTRACTIONS**

✪ **Cabrillo National Monument.** *1800 Cabrillo Memorial Dr., Point Loma.* ☎ *619/557-5450. Admission $4 per vehicle, $2 for walk-ins; free for seniors 62 and over (with a National Park Service Golden Age Passport) and free for those 16 and younger. Daily 9am–5:15pm. Follow I-5 or I-8 to Rosecrans St. (Calif. 209), which leads to Point Loma and the monument via Catalina Blvd.* Enjoy stunning views while you're learning about California history at this monument commemorating Juan Rodríguez Cabrillo, the European discoverer of America's west coast. From mid-Dec–Feb, the Old Point Loma lighthouse is a good vantage point for watching the migration of the Pacific gray whales.

**Maritime Museum.** *1306 N. Harbor Dr.* ☎ *619/234-9153. Admission (to all three ships) $5 adults, $4 seniors and ages 13–17, $2 children 6–12. Daily 9am–8pm.* This nautical museum consists of three restored historic vessels docked downtown at the Embarcadero: the *Berkeley,* a propeller-driven ferry launched in 1898; the *Meadea,* a 1904 steam yacht; and the 1863 *Star of India,* the oldest square-rigged merchant vessel still afloat.

**Mission Bay/Pacific Beach Giant Dipper Roller Coaster.** *3146 Mission Blvd.* ☎ *619/488-1549. Summer, Sun–Mon and Thurs 11am–8pm, Tues–Wed 11am–9pm, Fri–Sat 11am–10pm. Closes earlier rest of the year. Admission to the park is free; a ride on Giant Dipper is $2.50. Take I-5 to the Sea World exit, and follow W. Mission Bay Dr. to Belmont Park.* A local landmark for 70 years, the Giant Dipper is one of two surviving fixtures from the original Belmont Amusement Park (the other is the Plunge indoor swimming pool). This vintage wooden roller coast features over 2,600 feet of track and 13 hills, and other rides are available. At the Plunge (☎ **619/488-3110**), you can watch "dive-in movies" while floating on rafts.

**Museum of Contemporary Art.** *Downtown (MCA). 1001 Kettner Blvd. (at Broadway).* ☎ *619/234-1001. Admission $4 adults, 50¢ children 5–12; free on first Tues of month. Tues–Sun 10:30am–5:30pm, Fri 10:30am–8pm.* Four galleries present changing exhibitions of distinguished contemporary artists. Lectures and tours for adults and children are offered.

**Villa Montezuma.** *1925 K St. (at 20th Ave.).* ☎ *619/239-2211. Admission $3 adults, $5 in combination with Marston House, free for children 12 and under. Jan–Nov, Sat–Sun noon–4:30pm. Dec, Thurs–Sun noon–4:30pm.* Just east of downtown, this stunning mansion, on the National Register of Historic Places, was built in 1887 for then internationally acclaimed musician and author Jesse Shepard. Lush with quirky Victoriana, it features stained-glass windows depicting notables such as Mozart and Reubens.

✪ **Wild Animal Park.** *15500 San Pasqual Valley Rd., Escondido (30 miles north of San Diego).* ☎ *619/747-8702. Admission $18.95 adults, $11.95 children 3–11, free for children 2 and under. Daily 9am–4pm; extended summer hours. Take I-15 to Via Rancho Pkwy. and follow signs. Public transportation takes 3¹/₂ hours; Gray Line (☎ 619/ 491-0011) offers a 7-hour tour for $40 for adults and $24 for children, including admission.* Over 3,000 animals, many of them endangered species, roam freely on more than 2,200 acres, while the humans are enclosed. The best way to see the animals is by riding the 5-mile monorail (included in admission). Photo tours run May through September on Wednesday, Thursday, Saturday, and Sunday. They cost $60 or $85 depending on the tour.

**LA JOLLA** About 12 miles north of downtown San Diego and home to the University of California San Diego, La Jolla is one of the prettiest parcels of San Diego County. For over half a century, the wealthy and successful have chosen to live in lovely homes here amid lush landscaping, beautiful beaches, and good restaurants. Some folks just enjoy driving around La Jolla, taking in the sea views and the 360° vista from the top of **Mount Soledad.** Hiking trails with ocean views are found in the **Torrey Pines State Reserve** (☎ 619/755-2063). Enjoy the **free outdoor concerts** at Scripps Park from mid-June to mid-September, on Sunday from 2 to 4pm (☎ 619/525-3160). As you walk along the ocean in La Jolla you'll see the **harbor seal colony** at the **Children's Pool** near the intersection of Coast Boulevard and Jenner.

The **Museum of Contemporary Art,** 700 Prospect St.(☎ 619/454-3541), offers ocean views and works produced primarily since 1950. Admission is $4 adults, free for children under 12; free to all the first Tuesday of each month. The **Stephen Birch Aquarium-Museum** at the Scripps Institution of Oceanography, 2300 Expedition Way (☎ 619/534-3474 for a recording), is a branch of the University of California San Diego (UCSD), with an aquarium-museum offering close-up views of the Pacific Ocean in 33 marine-life tanks, and a giant kelp forest. Admission is $6.50 adults, $3.50 children 3–12. The **Stuart Collection** (☎ 619/534-2117), at the UCSD campus, is a still-growing collection of site-related sculptures by leading contemporary artists placed throughout the 1,200-acre campus. Pick up a brochure and map at the information booth at the Northview Drive or Gilman Drive entrance to the campus. Admission is free.

**BEACHES** San Diego County is blessed with 70 miles of sandy coastline and more than 30 beaches that attract surfers, snorkelers, swimmers, and sunbathers. As is true throughout California, beaches here are public to the mean high-tide line.

**Ocean Beach,** near the pier off I-8 and Sunset Cliffs Boulevard, is a surfers' and sunset lovers' heaven. Not far away are **Dog Beach,** where four-legged beach lovers roam unleashed, and **Garbage Beach,** another surfing spot (it doesn't live up to its name).

**Mission Bay Park** is a 4,600-acre aquatic playground with 27 miles of bayfront, 17 miles of oceanfront beaches, picnic areas, children's playgrounds, and paths for biking, roller skating, and jogging. The bay lends itself to windsurfing, sailing, jet skiing, waterskiing, and fishing. There are dozens of access points; one of the most popular is off I-5 at Clairemont Drive, where there's a visitor information center.

**Pacific Beach** is popular for its boardwalk, eateries, jogging, biking, and in-line skating. It runs along Ocean Boulevard (just west of Mission Boulevard), north of Pacific Beach Drive. At **Mission Beach,** surfing is popular year-round. The long beach and boardwalk extend from Pacific Beach Drive south to Belmont Park and beyond to the jetty. Facing Mission Bay in South Mission Beach, **Bonita Cove/Mariner's Point** and **Mission Point** are perfect for families, with calm waters, grassy areas for picnicking, and playground equipment.

**Windansea** is one of California's finest surfing beaches, and this area, along Neptune Street in La Jolla, achieved cult status in 1968, when the surfers who rode its waves were the subject of Tom Wolfe's book *The Pumphouse Gang.* ✪ **La Jolla Cove** offers calm waters, praised as the clearest on the state's coast, and there's a small sandy beach on the cliffs above. The Cove's "look but don't touch" policy protects the colorful Garibaldi, California's state fish, plus other marine life. The unique Underwater Park stretches from here to the northern end of Torrey Pines State Reserve. **La Jolla Shores Beach** is a mile-long flat stretch of beach, popular for jogging, swimming, and body and board surfing for beginners. Families often come here, where lifeguards are on duty year-round. **Black's Beach,** set out of the way below steep cliffs between La Jolla Shores Beach and Torrey Pines State Beach, is the area's unofficial nude beach. (*Note:* Though the water at this beach is pleasant for wading, this area is known for its rip currents.)

**OUTDOOR ACTIVITIES**   **Ballooning** provides a bird's-eye view of the area at sunrise or sunset, followed by champagne and hors d'oeuvres. Contact **A Skysurfer Balloon Company** (☎ 619/481-6800), **Pacific Horizon Balloon Tours** (☎ 800/244-1790), or **California Dreamin** (☎ 800/748-5959).

**Seaforth Boat Rental,** 1641 Quivira Rd., Mission Bay (☎ 619/223-1681), offers all kinds of boats for rent, from fishing boats for bay and ocean, powerboats, and sailboats, to canoes and pedal boats. **Downtown Boat Rental** (at the Marriott), 333 W. Harbor Dr. (☎ 619/437-1514), has similar rentals. **Club Nautico,** a concession at the San Diego Marriott Marina, 333 W. Harbor Dr. (☎ 619/233-9311), provides guests and nonguests with an exhilarating way to see the bay by the hour, half day, or full day in offshore powerboats. You can rent Wave Runners and boats to be taken into the ocean. The club also provides diving, waterskiing, and fishing packages. **Coronado Boat Rental,** 1715 Strand Way, in Coronado (☎ 619/437-1514), has a full range of boats for half- and full-day rates. **Sail USA** (☎ 619/298-6822) offers custom-tailored skippered cruises on a 34-foot Catalina sloop. Full-day and overnight trips are also available, as are trips up the coast and to Catalina.

**Fishing** piers are at Shelter Island, Ocean Beach, and Imperial Beach. Fishing charters depart from Harbor and Shelter islands, Point Loma, the Imperial Beach pier, and Quivira Basin in Mission Bay (near the Hyatt Islandia Hotel). Participants over the age of 16 need a California fishing license. For sportfishing, the summer and fall are excellent times for excursions. The following outfitters offer short or extended outings with daily departures: **H&M Landing** (☎ 619/222-1144), **Islandia Sportfishing** (☎ 619/222-1164), **Lee Palm Sportfishers** (☎ 619/224-3857), **Point Loma Sportfishing** (☎ 619/223-1627), and **Seaforth Boat Rentals** (☎ 619/223-1681).

**Golf** is popular here, with nearly 80 courses, 50 of them open to the public. Courses are diverse, some with vistas of the Pacific, others with views of country hillsides or of desert. **Par-Tee Golf** (☎ 800/PAR-TEE-1) and **M&M Tee Times**

(☎ 619/456-8366) can arrange tee times for you at most golf courses. **Greenlink** (☎ 619/I-LOVE-GOLF) is a source for information about golf courses, schools, and equipment. Practice your golf swing right in town at the **Harborside Golf Center,** on Broadway at Pacific Highway (☎ 619/239-GOLF). ✪ **Torrey Pines Golf Course,** 11480 Torrey Pines Rd., La Jolla (☎ 619/552-1784 for information; 619/570-1234 to book a tee time; 619/452-3226 for the pro shop), offers two gorgeous 18-hole championship courses located on the coast between La Jolla and Del Mar, only 15 minutes from downtown San Diego. **Coronado Municipal Golf Course,** 2000 Visalia Row, Coronado (☎ 619/435-3121), is an 18-hole, par-72 course overlooking Glorietta Bay.

The Bayside Trail near **Cabrillo National Monument** is popular because hikers can stop and look in the tide pools. ✪ **Mission Trails Regional Park,** 8 miles northeast of downtown between Highway 52 and I-8 (access via Mission Gorge Road), offers a glimpse of what San Diego looked like before development, with rugged hills and valleys. A visitor and interpretive center (☎ 619/668-3275) is open daily from 9am to 5pm. **Torrey Pines State Park** in La Jolla is another great spot for hiking.

Mission Bay and Coronado are fun for biking and in-line skating. Boardwalks in Pacific Beach and Mission Beach can get crowded. Most major thoroughfares offer a bike lane (a helmet is the law). For gliding around in Mission Bay, rent a pair of regular or in-line skates from **Skates Plus,** 3830 Mission Blvd. (☎ 619/488-PLUS); or **Hamel's Action Sports Center,** 704 Ventura Place, off Mission Boulevard at the roller coaster (☎ 619/488-5050); and in Pacific Beach, at **Pacific Beach Sun & Sea,** 4539 Ocean Blvd. (☎ 619/483-6613). In Coronado, go to **Mike's Bikes,** 1343 Orange Ave. (☎ 619/435-7744); or **Bikes & Beyond,** 1201 First St. and at the Ferry Landing (☎ 619/435-7180).

For **mountain biking,** try the **Palomar Plunge,** the 16-mile 5,000-foot drop from Palomar Mountain, or the **Desert Descent,** a 12-mile, 3,700-foot descent down the Montezuma Valley Grade to the desert floor, followed by a visitor center tour and lunch. **Gravity Activated Sports** (☎ 800/985-4427 or 619/742-2294) supplies all you need, including a souvenir photo. **Adventure Bike Tours,** based at the Hyatt (☎ 619/234-1500, ext. 6514), offers a "Bay to Breakers" bike ride that starts downtown and includes Coronado. **Backroads Bicycle Touring** (☎ 800/BIKE-TRIP or 415/527-1555) offers cycling packages to San Diego.

Public **tennis** courts are located throughout the city, including the **La Jolla Recreation Center** (☎ 619/295-9278) and **Morley Field** (☎ 619/459-9950) in Balboa Park.

**BEST BETS FOR KIDS**   At the San Diego Zoo (See "Balboa Park," above), kids enjoy the nursery with baby animals and a petting area with sheep, goats, and the like. The **Children's Museum of San Diego,** 200 W. Island Ave. (☎ 619/233-8792), encourages hands-on participation and provides supervised activities. A big draw is the indoor and outdoor art studio. **Sea World,** 1720 S. Shores Rd., Mission Bay (☎ 619/226-3901), is a 150-acre aquatic playground and showplace for marine mammals, from otters to walruses. It is a family entertainment center with shows presented continuously throughout the day. A Dolphin Interaction Program ($125 per person) is available to eight people a day, so advance reservations are required. Admission is $30.95 adults, $25.45 seniors, $21.95 children 3–11, and it's open mid-June–Aug, daily 9am–11pm, Sept–mid-June, daily 10am–5pm. Exit I-5 west onto Sea World Drive.

**SPORTS**   Baseball's **San Diego Padres** play from April to September at San Diego Jack Murphy Stadium, 9449 Friars Rd., in Mission Valley (☎ 619/283-4494 for schedules and information; 619/29-PADRES for tickets). San Diego's professional football team, the **San Diego Chargers,** also plays their home games at San Diego Jack Murphy Stadium (☎ 619/280-2121), Aug–Dec.

San Diego hosts some of the country's most important golf tournaments, including the **Mercedes Championships,** held at La Costa Resort in Carlsbad in early January (☎ 800/918-4653 for tickets and information). The **Buick Invitational of California,** in February, is played at Torrey Pines Golf Course in La Jolla (☎ 800/888-BUICK or 619/281-4653). The **HGH Pro-Am Golf Classic** is held at Carlton Oaks Country Club every September (☎ 619/448-8500).

Live thoroughbred horse racing takes place at the famous **Del Mar Racetrack** (☎ 619/755-1141 for info; 619/792-4242 for the ticket office) from late July to mid-September. You can watch polo matches on Sunday from June to October at the **Rancho Santa Fe Polo Club,** 14555 El Camino Real, Rancho Santa Fe (☎ 619/481-9217). Major tennis tournaments are hosted by San Diego, including the **Toshiba Tennis Classic** (☎ 619/438-LOVE), held at the La Costa Resort and Spa in Carlsbad.

**SHOPPING**    Shops in San Diego tend to stay open late, and you'll find plenty of variety. **Horton Plaza** (☎ 619/238-1596) is in the heart of the revitalized city center downtown. This Disneyland of shopping malls, eclectic and colorful, covers $6^1/_2$ city blocks and offers 140 specialty shops, including art galleries, fun shops for kids, seven-screen cinema, three major department stores, and a variety of restaurants and eateries. Other malls you might check out include **Fashion Valley,** 352 Fashion Valley Rd. (☎ 619/297-3381); **Mission Valley,** 1640 Camino del Rio N. (☎ 619/296-6375); and **University Towne Center,** 4545 La Jolla Village Dr., San Diego (☎ 619/546-8858). It is fun to shop in **Tijuana,** Mexico, just across the border, and you can also shop on the north side of the international border at the **San Diego Factory Outlet Center.** In addition, bargain hunters will want to attend **Kobey's Swap Meet** at the San Diego Sports Arena from Thursday to Sunday.

At **Bazaar del Mundo,** 2754 Calhoun St., Old Town State Historic Park (☎ 619/296-3161), the central courtyard vibrates with mariachi music, and, while the shops are pricey, one-of-a-kind folk art is featured as well as textiles from Mexico and South America.

The **Ferry Landing Market Place,** 1201 1st St., at B Avenue, Coronado (☎ 619/435-8895), is a stroll up the pier to the turreted red rooftop entrance to shops filled with gifts, imported and designer fashions, jewelry, and crafts.

**Seaport Village,** 849 W. Harbor Dr., at Kettner Boulevard. (☎ 619/235-4014, or 619/235-4013 for events information), is a 14-acre ersatz village alongside San Diego Bay built to resemble a Cape Cod community, but the 75 shops are the southern California variety, such as the Seasick Giraffe for resort wear and the Upstart Crow bookshop/coffeehouse with the Crow's Nest children's bookstore inside.

The old village in **La Jolla,** at Prospect Street and Girard Avenue, has become sort of a cross between Rodeo Drive and a shopping mall. A few of the old-time stores remain, such as Warwick's (books and stationery) and Burns Drugs, but these are outnumbered by glossy newcomers like Armani Exchange, Banana Republic, and Polo Ralph Lauren. Bargain hunters can browse in one of the many resale shops, like Encore, 7850 Herschel St.

## ACCOMMODATIONS

San Diego offers the cost-conscious traveler a good selection of lodgings. Remember to factor in the city's 10.5% hotel tax and to keep in mind that rates are often higher in summer (especially true of beach hotels).

You might want to compare the price you're quoted with those available through **San Diego Hotel Reservations** (☎ 800/SAVE-CASH or 619/627-9300). For information on 30 bed-and-breakfasts in the San Diego area, send $3.95 for a 20-page directory to **B&B Resources,** P.O. Box 3292, San Diego, CA 92163 (☎ 800/619-ROOM or

619/297-3130). You can also get information from the **Bed & Breakfast Guild** of San Diego (☎ **619/523-1300**).

**۞ Beach Cottages.** *4255 Ocean Blvd. (a block south of Grand Ave.), San Diego (Pacific Beach), CA 92109. ☎ 619/483-7440. 78 units including 28 motel rms, 12 studios, 18 apts, 17 cottages, and 3 suites. Winter (Oct–mid-May), $60–$70 double motel room; $80 studio for up to 4; $95–$120 apt for up to 6; $90–$130 cottage for up to 6; $180–$200 two-bedroom, two-bath suite for up to 6. Weekly rates available except in summer. AE, CB, DC, DISC, MC, V. Free parking.* Directly on the beach, all accommodations come with country-flavor decor, and all, except motel rooms, with full kitchens. Cottages have patios, and the third-floor balcony/walkway affords a great ocean view. Within walking distance of shops and restaurants, the Beach Cottages have barbecue grills, shuffleboard courts, table tennis, and a laundry.

**Clarion Hotel Bay View San Diego.** *660 K St. (at Sixth) San Diego, CA 92101. ☎ 800/766-0234 or 619/696-0234. 312 rms and suites. $109–$139 double; $149–$169 suite. Children under 18 stay free in parents' room. AE, CB, DC, DISC, MC, V. Parking $8.* Close to the Convention Center and the Gaslamp Quarter, the Clarion offers spacious, bright, and modern rooms, many with a harbor view and all with sliding-glass doors and in-room safes. The carpeted rooftop sundeck offers a great view as well as a Jacuzzi, sauna, workout room, and video arcade. The hotel has a cafe, bar, and coin-operated laundry.

**۞ Crystal Pier Hotel.** *4500 Ocean Blvd., San Diego (Pacific Beach), CA 92109. ☎ 800/748-5894 or 619/483-6983. 26 cottages. Mid-June to mid-Sept, $145–$225 cottage for up to 4 people. Mid-Sept to mid-June, $95–$190. Three-day minimum in summer. Weekly and monthly rates available. DISC, MC, V. Free parking.* This historic 1927 property, with some cottages added later and others renovated, is on a private pier jutting into the ocean. Quarters have a living room, bedroom, kitchenette, and private deck. Quietest units are furthest out on the pier, away from the boardwalk. Fishing poles, beach chairs, and umbrellas are available.

**۞ El Cordova Hotel.** *1351 Orange Ave.(at Adella St.), Coronado, CA 92118. ☎ 800/229-2032 or 619/435-4131. 14 rms, 26 suites. $75–$95 double; $85–$105 studio with kitchen; $110–$140 one-bedroom suite; $135–$170 two-bedroom suite. Weekly and monthly rates available off-season. Children under 12 stay free in parents' room. AE, DC, DISC, MC, V.* This Spanish-style hotel has a south-of-the-border flavor, with colorful little shops and hacienda-style furnishings in the comfortable rooms and suites, some with kitchenettes. About half the rooms are air-conditioned. The hotel is popular with families because of the restaurant, heated pool, barbecue area, and coin-op laundry.

**Glorietta Bay Inn.** *1630 Glorietta Blvd. (near Orange Ave.), Coronado, CA 92118. ☎ 800/283-9383 or 619/435-3101. 81 rms, 17 suites. Mansion: $145–$155 double; $165–$179 suite; $279–$299 penthouse. Annex: $79–$89 economy double; $109–$139 contemporary double; $139–$179 family suite with kitchen. AE, DC, DISC, MC, V. Free parking.* Once the 1908 mansion of 19th-century multimillionaire John Spreckels, former owner of the Hotel del Coronado, this beautifully restored house offers well-appointed rooms amid lush gardens. Mansion rooms have Victorian styling, while others are contemporary, with windows overlooking Glorietta Bay. One block from the beach. A pool, laundry, and morning coffee are provided.

**Hacienda Hotel.** *4041 Harney St. (just east of San Diego Ave.), San Diego, CA 92110. ☎ 800/888-1991 or 619/298-4707. 150 suites. $109–$119 double. Children under 16 stay free in parents' room. AE, CB, DC, DISC, ER, MC, V. Free underground parking.* Perched above Old Town, this Best Western all-suite hotel affords excellent views of Old Town from its outdoor pool and patio. Comfortable suites, with Southwest furnishings, have high ceilings, ceiling fans, refrigerators, microwaves, and VCRs. Conveniences include a restaurant, complimentary airport/train transportation, pool, Jacuzzi, spa with fitness center, and coin-operated laundry.

**Holiday Inn on the Bay.** *1355 N. Harbor Dr. (at Ash St.), San Diego, CA 92101-3385.* ☎ *800/HOLIDAY or 619/232-3861. 563 rms, 17 suites. $135–$155 single or double; from $400 suite. Children under 18 stay free in parents' room. AE, DC, MC, V.* Renovated in 1992, this hotel is ideally located on the harbor. The rooms are California contemporary, offering harbor views. The king rooms are a good choice for families. The hotel has two restaurants, a bar, lobby lounge with entertainment, babysitting, outdoor pool, self-service laundry, and some rooms with voice mail or minibars.

**La Jolla Cove Travelodge.** *1141 Silverado St. (corner of Herschel St.), La Jolla, CA 92037.* ☎ *800/578-7878 or 619/454-0791. 30 rms. $49–$89 double. Additional person $5 extra. Children 17 and under stay free in parents' room. AE, DC, DISC, MC, V. Free parking.* No deferred maintenance here, despite the price range, and all rooms—queen, king, or two double beds—were refurbished in 1996. Convenient to La Jolla shopping, dining, and nightlife, the hotel supplies coffeemakers, free HBO, and a modest sundeck on the third floor.

✪ **La Pensione.** *1700 India St. (at Date St.), San Diego, CA 92101.* ☎ *619/236-8000. 80 rms. $44–$70 double. AE, CB, DC, MC, V. Free daily parking, or $10 per week.* This modern, clean place, within walking distance of the business district, is a good value. Built around a courtyard, the rooms are small but comfy, all with microwave and refrigerator. There are two restaurants, one with jazz on weekends, and laundry facilities. Another La Pensione, 1654 Columbia St. between Cedar and Date streets (☎ 619/232-3400), rents by the week or month only; no parking. Both properties are within walking distance of eateries and nightspots.

**Ocean Park Inn.** *710 Grand Ave., San Diego (Pacific Beach), CA 92109.* ☎ *800/231-7735 or 619/483-5858. 73 rms, 4 suites. Summer, $99–$149 double; from $159 suite. Lower rates rest of the year. Rates include continental breakfast. AE, DC, DISC, MC, V. Free indoor parking.* On Pacific Beach's boardwalk, this Spanish-Mediterranean facility is appealing, with comfortable, contemporary rooms. All units have terraces and refrigerators. The most expensive rooms have oceanfront balconies but can be noisy. King suites offer Roman tubs; some have kitchenettes. The inn has a sundeck, heated pool, outdoor Jacuzzi, vending machines, and coin laundry.

✪ **Prospect Park Inn.** *1110 Prospect St. (at Coast Blvd.), La Jolla, CA 92037.* ☎ *800/433-1609 or 619/454-0133. 23 rms and suites. $95–$140 double. AE, DC, DISC, MC, V. Rates include continental breakfast. Free off-site indoor parking.* This spotless, 1947 three-story hotel, once a boardinghouse, offers European charm, with afternoon snacks in the library and breakfast on the ocean-view sundeck. Rooms are charming, some with balconies or terraces and an ocean view. This nonsmoking hotel is close to the beach, shops, and restaurants. Beach towels and chairs are provided free.

✪ **Sommerset Suites Hotel.** *606 Washington St. (at Fifth Ave.), San Diego, CA 92103.* ☎ *800/356-1787 in California, 800/962-9665 elsewhere, or 619/692-5200. 80 suites. $90 studio suite; $160 one-bedroom suite; $180 executive suite. Children under 12 stay free in parents' room. Rates include large continental breakfast. AE, CB, DC, DISC, MC, V. Free covered parking.* Located in the Hillcrest/Uptown area, this friendly hotel serves complimentary snacks in the guest lounge and encourages barbecues (gas grills provided) on the poolside patio. All quarters are spacious, tastefully furnished, with kitchens and balconies. The hotel has a concierge, baby-sitting, courtesy airport/attractions van, outdoor pool, Jacuzzi, snack room, and coin-operated laundry.

**OTHER ACCOMMODATIONS**    Hostelling International—San Diego (☎ 619/ 525-1531) was moving at press time, but it should offer dorm beds and couples rooms for $12–$14 for members, $15–$17 for nonmembers. Call for the new location. The serenely situated **De Anza Bay Resort RV Park,** 2727 De Anza Rd., San Diego (Mission Bay), CA 92109 (☎ **800/924-PLAY** in California, or 619/273-3211), has 250 hookup sites for RV vacationers, offering everything from a private beach and floating dock to potluck dinners and dancing. Small pets are welcome. It's adjacent to an executive 18-hole golf course.

## DINING

San Diego offers a good selection of inexpensive and interesting dining. You can find standard fare, or go a little daring.

   **✪ The Atoll.** *In the Catamaran Resort Hotel, 3999 Mission Blvd.* ☎ **619/539-8635.** *Reservations recommended for Sunday brunch. Main courses $8–$20. AE, CB, DC, DISC, MC, V. Sun–Thurs 6:30am–10pm, Fri–Sat 6:30am–11pm. Free self-parking with validation; valet parking $7. CALIFORNIAN.* You can dine at a wrought-iron table on the waterfront patio here and take in the view of Mission Bay, or inside, where the interior is made elegant by rattan chairs, and Villeroy and Boch china. The spicy crab cakes with lime and ginger-butter sauce are recommended.

   **Bay Beach Cafe.** *1201 1st St. (in the Ferry Landing Marketplace).* ☎ **619/ 435-4900.** *Main courses $8.95–$16.95. AE, DISC, MC, V. Daily 7am–10:30pm. Free parking. AMERICAN/SEAFOOD.* You can't beat the views at the Bay Beach Cafe. Dine indoors or alfresco, and choose from items such as daily fresh fish specials, vegetarian pasta, and roasted free-range chicken with wild-mushroom sauce. There's also a bar menu featuring sandwiches and burgers.

   **Brockton Villa.** *1235 Coast Blvd. (across from the La Jolla Cove), La Jolla, CA 92037.* ☎ **619/454-7393.** *Reservations: call by Thurs for Sun brunch. Breakfast $3.95– $7.25. Dinner main courses $7.95–$13.95. AE, DISC, MC, V. Mon–Wed 8am–5pm, Thurs–Sun 8am–9pm (later in summer). Validated parking in Coast Walk Shopping Center. CALIFORNIAN.* Located in an 1894 beach cottage, Brockton Villa offers good food, a view of the La Jolla Cove, and charming historic surroundings. Dine inside or outside on the patio or porch. A favorite here is the basil ravioli with saffron shrimp sauce.

   **Cafe Pacifica.** *2414 San Diego Ave.* ☎ **619/291-6666.** *Reservations recommended. Main courses $11–$18. AE, CB, DC, DISC, MC, V. Tues–Fri 11:30am–2pm; daily 5:30– 10pm. Valet parking free at lunch, $4 at dinner. CALIFORNIAN.* Excellent fresh fish, grilled over mesquite, keeps visitors happy and locals returning. The setting is charming, with tiny twinkling lights overhead and candles adorning the tables, and slightly formal. Try the Hawaiian ahi with shiitake mushrooms and ginger butter.

   **✪ Corvette Diner.** *3946 Fifth Ave. (between Washington and University).* ☎ **619/ 542-1001.** *Reservations not accepted. Main courses $4.50–$9.95. AE, DC, DISC, MC, V. Sun–Thurs 11am–11pm, Fri–Sat 11am–midnight. Bus: 1, 3. AMERICAN.* The centerpiece in this art deco diner is a corvette. A deejay plays your requests at night and a magician performs on Tuesday and Wednesday. Enjoy the soda fountain, or the full bar. The menu features burgers and other diner fare. The diner is popular with the young crowd.

   **✪ The Cottage.** *7702 Fay Ave. (at Kline), La Jolla, CA 92037.* ☎ **619/454-8409.** *Reservations accepted for dinner only. Breakfast and lunch $4.95–$6.95; dinner main courses $6.95–$11.95. MC, V. Daily 7:30am–3pm. June–Sept, daily 4–9pm. LIGHT FARE.* This turn-of-the-century cottage in downtown La Jolla is airy inside, with booths and tables under a skylight; outside there's a large brick patio. Start the day with a vegetable frittata. The dinner menu (summer only) features California bistro cuisine. The Cottage bakery makes its own *wonderful* desserts, pastries, and bread.

**✪ Croce's Restaurant and Jazz Bar.** *802 Fifth Ave. (at F St.).* ☎ *619/233-4355. Fax 619/232-9836. Reservations recommended. Main courses $13.50–$17.95. AE, DC, DISC, MC, V. Daily 7:30am–3pm and 4pm–midnight. Valet parking $5 with validation. AMERICAN.* Try the salmon baked in puff pastry, served with wild spinach hollandaise. Besides the main restaurant, there's Ingrid's Cantina & Sidewalk Cafe next door for Southwestern cuisine, and Upstairs at Croce's for cocktails, coffee, and desserts. Two adjacent nightspots, the Jazz Bar and the Top Hat, serve up jazz and R&B.

**✪ D'Lish.** *7514 Girard Ave. (at Pearl St.), La Jolla, CA 92037.* ☎ *619/459-8118. Main courses $5.95–$8.99. AE, DC, DISC, MC, V. Sun–Thurs 11:30am–10pm, Fri–Sat 11:30am–11pm. Free off-street parking. CONTEMPORARY ITALIAN.* This is the place for one of those trendy wood-fired pizzas with designer toppings you wouldn't have imagined a decade ago. A favorite is the Greek grilled chicken.

**Firehouse Beach Cafe.** *722 Grand Ave.* ☎ *619/272-1999. Reservations recommended on weekends. Main courses $8–$12. AE, CB, DC, DISC, MC, V. Sun–Thurs 7am–9pm, Fri–Sat 7am–10pm. Free parking. AMERICAN.* This casual place is always packed (though not oppressively so), and if you're lucky, you can get an umbrella table on the upstairs deck with an ocean view. The locals love eating breakfast here—the omelets are especially popular. The kitchen turns out one of the best burgers in San Diego.

**✪ George's Ocean Terrace and Café/Bar.** *1250 Prospect St., La Jolla, CA 92037.* ☎ *619/454-4244. Reservations not accepted. Main courses $7.50–$10.75 at lunch, $9.50–$14.95 at dinner. AE, DC, DISC, MC, V. Sun–Thurs 11am–10pm, Fri–Sat 11am–11pm. Valet parking available. CALIFORNIAN.* The main dining room at George's is legendary and has won numerous awards for its haute cuisine. However, the Ocean Terrace and Café/Bar serve some of the same dishes. These two areas offer indoor and outdoor seating overlooking La Jolla Cove. For dinner you could choose something out of the ordinary like George's meat loaf served with mushroom and corn mashed potatoes.

**Green Flash.** *701 Thomas Ave. (at Mission Blvd.).* ☎ *619/270-7715. Main courses $10–$25. AE, DC, DISC, MC, V. Mon–Thurs 8am–9:30pm, Fri 8am–10pm, Sat 7:30am–10pm, Sun 7:30am–9:30pm. SEAFOOD/INTERNATIONAL.* You can eat a lot or a little in this lively oceanfront place, which has a menu to match a variety of budgets and hankerings. It's known for its fresh fish. Salads and sandwiches are available at lunch. The outdoor tables here are prime real estate at sunset.

**✪ Kung Food.** *2949 Fifth Ave. (between Palm and Quince).* ☎ *619/298-7302 (deli/takeout* ☎ *619/298-9232). Reservations not accepted. Main courses $6.50–$9.55. DISC, MC, V. Mon–Thurs 11:30am–9pm, Fri 11:30am–10pm, Sat 8:30am–10pm, Sun 8:30am–9pm. VEGETARIAN.* San Diego's best-known vegetarian eatery offers an extensive menu created from natural ingredients. The menu includes Greek spinach pie. There is indoor and outdoor seating, and soothing music sets the scene. Beer and wine are served. No smoking.

**✪ Mandarin House.** *2604 Fifth Ave. (at Maple).* ☎ *619/232-1101. Most main courses $6.50–$9.95. AE, DC, MC, V. Mon–Thurs 11am–10pm, Fri 11am–11pm, Sat noon–11pm, Sun 2–10pm. CHINESE.* This award-winning restaurant is the most popular Chinese restaurant in San Diego and offers a pleasant and surprising sea-foam-and-peach color scheme. Try the kung pao chicken, hot and spicy Szechuan style. Mandarin House also has locations in La Jolla and Pacific Beach.

**Old Spaghetti Factory.** *Fifth Ave. and K St.* ☎ *619/233-4323. Main courses $4.25–$8.10. DISC, MC, V. Mon–Thurs 11:30am–10pm, Fri 11:30am–10pm, Sat–Sun noon–10pm. ITALIAN.* Located in the Gaslamp Quarter area, this popular Victorian-atmosphere restaurant offers dining in a trolley car. Main courses—mostly old stand-bys such as lasagna and spaghetti—come with lots of extras, such as salad, sourdough bread, and ice cream. There's a small play area for kids.

✪ **Old Town Mexican Cafe.** *2489 San Diego Ave.* ☎ *619/297-4330. Reservations accepted for parties of 10 or more. Most main courses under $10. AE, DISC, MC, V. Daily 7am–11pm. MEXICAN.* A fun margarita bar and homemade tortillas are the primary draws of this boisterous Mexican restaurant that's popular with both families and couples (expect a wait). All the south-of-the-border standards are available. Check out the Mexican-style rotisserie pork ribs.

✪ **Primavera.** *932 Orange Ave.* ☎ *619/435-0454. Reservations recommended. Main courses $10.95–$19.95. AE, DC, DISC, MC, V. Mon–Fri 11am–2:30pm; daily 5–10:30pm. Free parking. NORTHERN ITALIAN.* The lovely dining room at Primavera is the setting for delicious, creatively prepared Italian dishes. One of the most popular appetizers is bagna caoda primavera (grilled eggplant, roasted red peppers, sun-dried tomatoes, Montrachet, and Parmesan, with bagna caoda sauce). This has been called the best restaurant in Coronado.

**OTHER DINING**   Southern Californians have a reputation for eating in their cars. One local favorite is **Rubios,** home of the fish taco, mahimahi burrito, and other Cali–Mex specialties. You'll find these emporia scattered around the city. Some of the most convenient locations are at 901 Fourth Ave., at E Street (☎ 619/231-7731); in Pacific Beach at 910 Grand Ave. (☎ 619/270-4800); and at 3555 Rosecrans St., near Midway Drive (☎ 619/223-2631). Another chain, **In-N-Out Burgers,** offers thin meat patties doused in secret sauce. There is an **In-N-Out** just off I-5 in Pacific Beach at 2910 Damon Ave., near East Mission Bay Drive (no phone).

Because the benign climate lends itself to alfresco dining, portable meals often take the form of picnics. A favorite spot to pick up sandwiches is the **Cheese Shop,** 401 G St., downtown (☎ 619/232-2303), or in La Shores at 2165 Avenida de La Playa (☎ 619/459-3921). Another spot that's very popular with San Diegans is **Point Loma Seafoods,** 2805 Emerson, near Scott Street south of Rosecrans and west of Harbor Drive (☎ 619/223-1109), which is on the water's edge in front of the Municipal Sportfishing Pier (a fish market here sells seafood sandwiches and salads to go).

## SAN DIEGO AFTER DARK

It's no "wild 'n' crazy" place, but San Diego offers pockets of lively entertainment, and both the Old Globe and La Jolla Playhouse have won Tonys for "best regional theater." For a rundown of the latest performances, gallery openings, and other events in the city, check the listings in *Night and Day,* the Thursday entertainment section of the *San Diego Union–Tribune,* or *The Reader,* San Diego's free alternative newspaper, published weekly on Thursday. For what's happening at the gay clubs, get the weekly *San Diego Gay & Lesbian Times.*

Half-price tickets to theater, music, and dance events are available at the **Times Arts Tix** booth, in Horton Plaza Park, at Broadway and Third Avenue. The kiosk, which doubles as a Ticketmaster outlet, is open Tues–Sat 10am–7pm. Half-price tickets for Sunday performances are sold on Saturday. Only cash payments are accepted. For a daily listing of half-price offerings, call ☎ 619/497-5000.

**THE PERFORMING ARTS**   The **San Diego Repertory Theatre** offers professional, culturally diverse productions of contemporary and classic dramas, comedies, and musicals at the Lyceum Theatre, 79 Horton Plaza (☎ 619/235-8025 or 619/231-3586).

In Coronado, **Lamb's Players Theatre,** 1142 Orange Ave. (☎ 619/437-0600), is a professional repertory company whose season runs from February to December in Coronado's historic Spreckels building, where no seat is more than seven rows from the stage.

The award-winning ✪ **Old Globe Theatre,** in Balboa Park (☎ 619/239-2255, or 619/23-GLOBE for 24-hour hotline), is fashioned after Shakespeare's own. It's part of the **Simon Edison Centre for the Performing Arts,** which also includes the 245-seat Cassius Carter Centre Stage and the 620-seat open-air Lowell Davies Festival Theatre, and mounts a dozen plays a year on the three stages from January to October. Tours are offered Saturday and Sunday at 11am. The box office is open Tues–Sun noon–8:30pm.

The **La Jolla Playhouse,** La Jolla Village Drive and Torrey Pines Road (☎ 619/550-1010), also award-winning, stages six productions from May to November each year in its 500-seat Mandell Weiss Theater and 400-seat Mandell Weiss Forum on the UCSD campus. The box office is open Mon noon–6pm and Tues–Sun noon–8pm. Each show designates one Saturday matinee as a "pay-what-you-can performance." Reduced-price "Public Rush" tickets are available 10 minutes before curtain, subject to availability.

The **San Diego Opera** performs at the Civic Theater, 202 C St. (☎ 619/232-7636), and often showcases international stars. The box office, open Mon–Fri 9am–5pm, is across the plaza from the theater. Standing-room tickets are available an hour before the performance.

The **San Diego Symphony,** whose future is up in the financial air at press time, performs at Copley Symphony Hall, 750 B St. (☎ 619/699-4205), and gives outdoor pops concerts at Embarcadero Marina Park in summer.

**THE CLUB & MUSIC SCENE**   Clubs do come and go, so your best bet for finding the latest, hottest spot is to stroll through the Gaslamp Quarter. The current favorites are **Johnny Loves,** 664 Fifth Ave. (☎ 619/595-0123), which endears itself to an over-30 crowd; **Club 66,** at 901 Fifth Ave. (☎ 619/234-4166), catering to those ages 25 to 45; **E Street Alley,** on the north side of E Street between Fourth and Fifth avenues (☎ 619/231-9200), which is a dressier club; **Ole Madrid,** 751 Fifth Ave. (☎ 619/557-0146), the destination of choice for Europhiles; **Dick's Last Resort,** 345 Fourth Ave., with entrances on both Fourth and Fifth avenues (☎ 619/231-9100), popular with the college crowd; and **Buffalo Joe's Saloon,** 600 Fifth Ave. (☎ 619/236-1616), a country-and-western nightclub.

Fans of alternative music might enjoy the **Casbah,** 2501 Kettner Blvd. (☎ 619/232-4355), where break-through bands are the norm, or **Bodies,** 528 F St. (☎ 619/236-8988), where live original music is played nightly. If you're under 21, **SOMA Live,** 5305 Metro St., Mission Bay (☎ 619/239-SOMA), is the place for you, with concerts by folks such as Courtney Love and Social Distortion.

From May to October a series of contemporary concerts takes place outdoors at **Humphrey's,** 2241 Shelter Island Dr., San Diego (☎ 619/523-1010). Videos and live bands (sometimes local, sometimes nationally known) take center stage in the **Cannibal Bar,** 3999 Mission Blvd. (in the Catamaran Hotel; ☎ 619/539-8650).

Top L.A. comics regularly visit the **Comedy Store,** 916 Pearl St., La Jolla (☎ 619/454-9176). Monday and Tuesday are amateur nights.

For jazz and blues, visit **Croce's,** 802 Fifth Ave. at F Street (☎ 619/233-4355). There is no cover to either Croce's Jazz Bar (traditional jazz) or Croce's Top Hat (rhythm and blues) if you have dinner at Croce's Restaurant or Ingrid's Cantina. Jim Croce's son sometimes performs in this popular spot, owned by the late singer's wife.

Gay and lesbian nightspots include **The Flame,** 3780 Park Blvd.(☎ **619/295-4163**), with a large dance floor and two bars; **Kickers/Hamburger Mary's,** 308 University Ave.(☎ **619/491-0400**) is adjacent to an outdoor restaurant and is a foot-stomping informal place for country-and-western dancing and line dancing (lesson early each evening); and **Rich's,** 1051 University Ave. (☎ **619/295-2195,** or 619/497-4588 for upcoming events), a popular club/dance space, welcomes primarily gay men 21 and older.

## A DAY TRIP TO JULIAN

A trip to the old gold mining town of Julian, 60 miles northeast of San Diego, is a trip back in time. Now known for its apples, it offers shops, eateries, a pioneer museum, cider mill, and antiques. (Remember when it's sunny in San Diego, it may be snowing in Julian, perched 4,235 feet above sea level). **Country Carriages** (☎ **619/765-1471**) will show you the sights in a horse-drawn wagon; or try **Llama Trek** (☎ **800/ LAMAPAK** or 619/765-1890), with trips that include a historic gold mine and the local winery.

If you come via Calif. 78, you'll pass the mission church of **Santa Ysabel** (1812), with a tiny museum and a large Native American cemetery, on your right, as well as **Dudley's Bakery,** noted for its breads, off to the left at the junction with Calif. 79 and just 7 miles from Julian.

The **Eagle and High Peak Mines** in Julian (☎ **619/765-0036**) operate daily from 9am to 4pm but only for educational reasons, since the gold is long gone.

You can mix culture with barbecue at the **Pine Hills Dinner Theater** on weekend nights at Pine Hills Lodge, a few miles from Julian off Pine Hills Road (☎ **619/ 765-1100**). To hear some music on Saturday night—folk music or piano or maybe the strains of a hammered dulcimer—head out to the **Wynola Coffee Company** (☎ **619/ 765-2023**), in a big red barn just over 3 miles south of town on Calif. 78. People of all ages come to this local hangout.

Exploring the countryside is easy from Julian. You'll pass rolling hills, country stores, fruit stands, and small towns. Just outside of town, 2 miles out Farmer's Road, is the **Menghini Winery** (☎ **619/765-2072**), where you can enjoy a bottle of wine right away in the picnic area in the apple orchard.

If you don't make it to the desert this trip, take a moment to gaze at it and the Salton Sea from **Inspiration Point,** just 1$^{1}$/2 miles south of Julian on Calif. 79, opposite Pinecroft Park. **Lake Cuyamaca** (pronounced *kwee*-yah-*mack*-ah), 10 miles south on Calif. 79, offers boating, fishing, and RV camping on a first-come, first-served basis. Its facilities are open from sunrise to sunset daily (☎ **619/765-0515** or 619/447-8123). **Essentials:** Take Calif. 78, winding through scenic Rancho Cuyamaca State Park, or I-8 to Calif. 79, which traverses open country and farmland. Town maps and flyers are at **Town Hall** on Main Street at Washington Street. The town has a 24-hour hotline (☎ **619/765-0707**) for information on lodging, dining, shopping, activities, upcoming events, weather, and driving conditions. For a brochure on what to see and do, contact the **Julian Chamber of Commerce** (☎ **619/765-1857**). The **Julian Arts Guild** (☎ **619/765-0560**) can answer questions about the Fine Arts Show.

# 9  Las Vegas

Las Vegas is an anything-goes kind of place where you're encouraged to eat too much (at lavish low-priced buffets), drink too much (liquor is gratis at gaming tables), and sleep too little (this city is always awake). But the real attraction in this desert city is gambling.

Even if you don't hit the tables or play slots, the plush hotels offer numerous resort facilities at about half of what you'd pay in other cities. Food is cheap, and many great attractions are within easy driving distance—especially Hoover Dam and the recreational pleasures of Lake Mead.

If you can endure the summer heat, avoid the crowds, and keep a tight rein on your wallet, a brief sojourn to this city of bright lights is a uniquely American experience.

## ARRIVING & DEPARTING

**BY PLANE**    Most major domestic airlines fly into **McCarran International Airport,** just a few minutes' drive from the southern end of the "Strip." **Bell Trans** (☎ 702/ 739-7990) runs minibuses daily between the airport and all major Las Vegas hotels and motels almost around the clock. The cost is less than $5 per person.

## ESSENTIALS

**VISITOR INFORMATION**    For advance information, contact the **Las Vegas Convention and Visitor Authority** (☎ 702/892-0711), the **Las Vegas Chamber of Commerce** (☎ 702/735-1616), or the **Nevada Commission on Tourism** (☎ 800/ 638-2328).

**RESOURCES FOR TRAVELERS WITH SPECIAL NEEDS**    The **Independent Living Program** (☎ 702/870-7050) can recommend hotels and restaurants accessible to the handicapped, and address any other concerns. The **Nevada Commission on Tourism** (☎ 800/638-2328) offers a free accommodations guide to Las Vegas hotels that includes access information.

The *Las Vegas Bugle* (☎ 702/369-6260), a monthly magazine, provides information about the gay community.

**EMERGENCIES & SAFETY**    Dial ☎ 911 for police, ambulance, or fire emergencies. **University Medical Center,** 1800 W. Charleston Blvd., at Shadow Lane (☎ 702/ 383-2661), has 24-hour emergency service.. Money is always on display in Las Vegas, and pickpockets and thieves hang around at casinos, restaurants, and outdoor shows. Know where your wallet or handbag is at all times.

## GETTING AROUND

Las Vegas is easy to navigate. The hotels are the major attractions, and they're clustered in two areas—on and around the Strip/Convention Center area, and Downtown. If the heat isn't too overbearing, many people walk.

**BY BUS & TROLLEY**    The no. 301 bus operated by **Citizens Area Transit** (☎ 702/ CAT-RIDE) runs round the clock between the Downtown Transportation Center (at Casino Center Boulevard and Stewart Avenue) and a few miles beyond the southern end of the Strip. The fare is $1.50 for adults, 50¢ for seniors (62 and older) and ages 5–17, and free for those under 5. CATs are wheelchair accessible.

**Las Vegas Strip Trolley** (☎ 702/382-1404) operates a classic streetcar replica that runs northward from Hacienda Avenue, stopping at all major hotels en route to the Sahara, and then looping back via the Las Vegas Hilton. They do not, however, go to the Stratosphere Tower or downtown. Trolleys run about every 15 minutes daily from 9:30am to 2am. The fare is $1.30 (free for children under 5), and exact change is required.

**BY TAXI**    Taxis are metered and line up at all hours in front of the major hotels. Up to five people can ride for the same fare. Reputable companies are **Desert Cab Company** (☎ 702/376-2688), **Whittlesea Blue Cab** (☎ 702/384-6111), and **Yellow/ Checker Cab/Star Company** (☎ 702/873-2000).

# Las Vegas

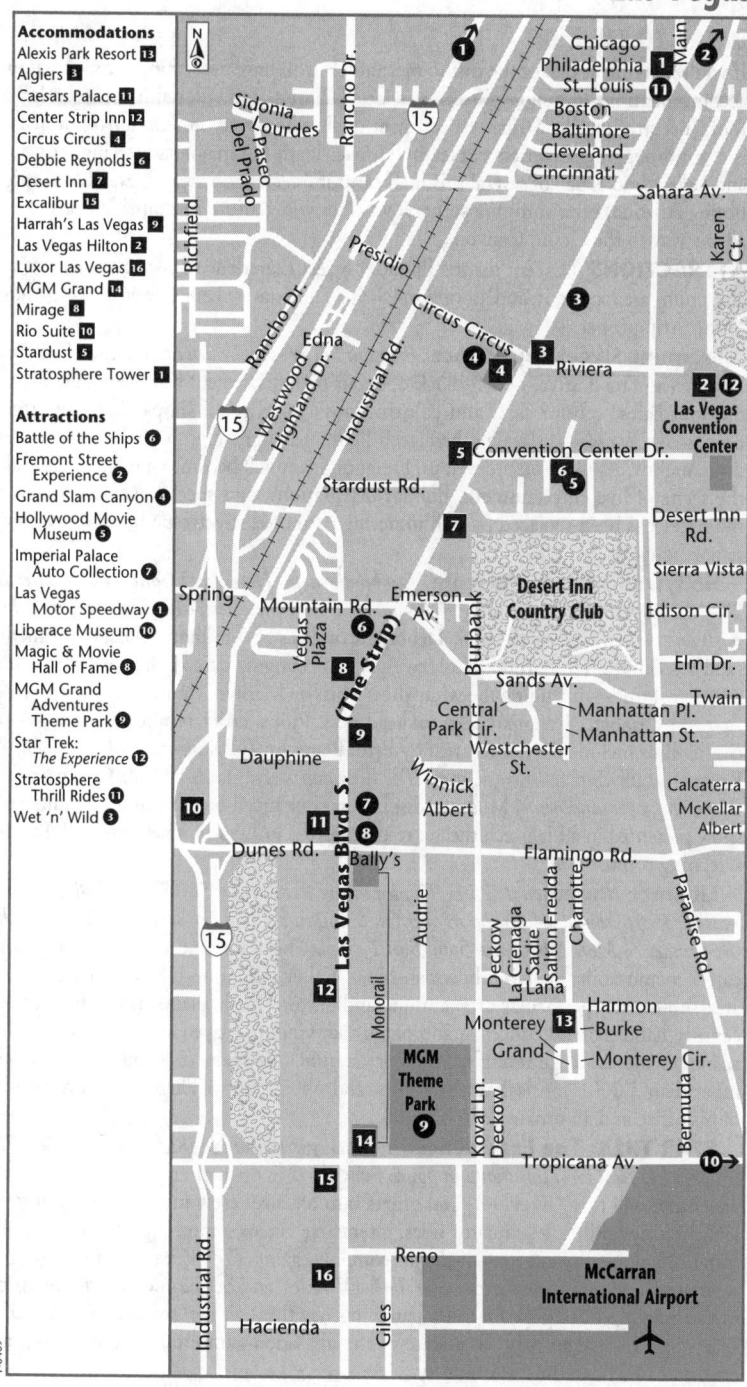

**Accommodations**
Alexis Park Resort 13
Algiers 3
Caesars Palace 11
Center Strip Inn 12
Circus Circus 4
Debbie Reynolds 6
Desert Inn 7
Excalibur 15
Harrah's Las Vegas 9
Las Vegas Hilton 2
Luxor Las Vegas 16
MGM Grand 14
Mirage 8
Rio Suite 10
Stardust 5
Stratosphere Tower 1

**Attractions**
Battle of the Ships 6
Fremont Street Experience 2
Grand Slam Canyon 4
Hollywood Movie Museum 5
Imperial Palace Auto Collection 7
Las Vegas Motor Speedway 1
Liberace Museum 10
Magic & Movie Hall of Fame 8
MGM Grand Adventures Theme Park 9
Star Trek: The Experience 12
Stratosphere Thrill Rides 11
Wet 'n' Wild 3

1-0409

## WHAT TO SEE & DO

If you're staying at one of the casino megahotels, you have everything—casino gaming, accommodations, dining, sightseeing, sports facilities, and entertainment—under one roof. Just strolling the Strip—especially at night when every hotel is ablaze in neon—is a mind-boggling experience. Nearby Hoover Dam is a major sightseeing attraction, and Lake Mead is one of several pristinely beautiful recreation areas. Nevada, and neighboring Arizona, offer stunning scenery, whether you venture just outside Las Vegas or all the way to the Grand Canyon.

**ATTRACTIONS**   Except for the Fremont Street Experience downtown, most major attractions are located in and around the Strip. The Stratosphere Tower is slightly north of the Strip proper.

**Fremont Street Experience.** *Fremont St., between Main St. and Las Vegas Blvd., downtown.* This festive, new 5-block open-air pedestrian mall will eventually include outdoor cafes, vendor carts and colorful kiosks, and retail shops. The centerpiece now is *Sky Parade*—a dazzling high-tech light and laser show that takes place several times nightly. As the project develops, Fremont Street will become an ongoing festival—the scene of live entertainment, holiday celebrations, and special events. Asphalt on the street has been replaced by a shimmering patterned streetscape lit by runway-type strobe lights.

**Hollywood Movie Museum.** *Debbie Reynolds Hotel, 305 Convention Center Dr.* ☎ *702/7-DEBBIE. Admission $7.95 adults, $5.95 children 3–12. Daily 11am–10pm, with tours every hour on the hour.* Debbie Reynolds's $30-million collection of memorabilia celebrates Hollywood's Golden Age, and changing exhibits here showcase some 3,000 costumes—including the white dress worn by Marilyn Monroe in *The Seven Year Itch* and Elizabeth Taylor's *Cleopatra* headdress. Props, artifacts, and furnishings from classic films include the dagger used by Errol Flynn in *The Adventures of Don Juan;* Yul Brynner's bullwhip and throne from *The King and I;* and the Ark of the Covenant from *The Ten Commandments.* Museum displays are enhanced by a 35-minute multimedia show presented in a high-tech theater re-creating the intimate ambience of a Hollywood screening room.

**Liberace Museum.** *1775 E. Tropicana Ave., at Spencer St.* ☎ *702/798-5595. Admission $6.50 adults, $4.50 seniors over 60, $3.50 students, $2 children 6–12, free for children under 6. Mon–Sat 10am–5pm, Sun 1–5pm.* This entire museum is devoted to the career memorabilia of "Mr. Showmanship," Walter Valentino Liberace. Three exhibit areas house his spectacular cars, antique and custom-made pianos (including a 19th-century hand-painted concert grand piano that Chopin played at Versailles), dazzling costumes and capes, glittering stage jewelry, a miniature piano collection (fans gave him more than 3,000), musical arrangements, and photographs. There's also a re-creation of his office and an ornate bedroom suite.

**STAR TREK: The Experience.** *In Las Vegas Hilton, 3000 Paradise Rd.* ☎ *702/732-5111. Call for admission and hours.* Scheduled to open after we went to press, this adventure will turn "Trekkies" and others into Starfleet crew members on an intergalactic journey utilizing simulator rides, interactive videos, morphing and virtual-reality stations, holograms, and state-of-the-art computer games. You'll see authentic costumes, weaponry, and props used in the *Star Trek* TV series, and be "beamed up" to the Bridge of the Starship Enterprise for a simulated journey through the universe. You "land" at Deep Space Nine to play (in a state-of-the-art video-game room), dine, shop, and encounter aliens in the 24th century.

**Stratosphere Thrill Rides.** *Stratosphere, 2000 Las Vegas Blvd. S.* ☎ *702/380-7777. Admission for either ride is $5, plus $5 to ascend the tower (no tower charge if you dine in the buffet room or Top of the World). Sun–Thurs 10am–midnight, Fri–Sat*

*10am–2am. Minimum height requirement for both rides is 48 inches.* Atop the 1,149-foot Stratosphere Tower are two marvelous thrill rides. The **Let It Ride High Roller,** the world's highest roller coaster, zooms around a hilly track that is seemingly suspended in midair. The **Big Shot,** a breathtaking free-fall ride, thrusts you 160 feet in the air along a 228-foot spire at the top of the tower, then plummets back down again. Sitting in an open car, you seem to be dangling in space over Las Vegas.

**BEST BETS FOR KIDS**   Las Vegas used to be an adults-only kind of town, but now it's actively pursuing families by offering dozens of child-oriented activities. Just be aware that if you bring your children, most of the attractions for them are expensive. And despite the pitch to families, the town's atmosphere is not terribly wholesome.

Many key kids' attractions are at the hotels; see "Accommodations," below, for particulars.

**Circus Circus Hotel/Casino** has ongoing circus acts throughout the day, a vast video game and pinball arcade, and dozens of carnival games on its mezzanine level. Behind the hotel is **Grand Slam Canyon Theme Park** (☎ 702/734-3939), an indoor amusement park with games and rides. **Excalibur** offers video and carnival games, plus thrill cinemas and free shows with jugglers, puppets, and more. At **Caesars Palace,** both the Magical Empire (for kids 12 and older only) and an IMAX theater are a thrill. The ship battle in front of **Treasure Island at the Mirage** is sure to please, as will the erupting volcano and the dolphin habitat; while you're here, see the tigers and the sharks. Appropriate shows for kids include *King Arthur's Tournament* at Excalibur, *Siegfried & Roy* at the Mirage, *Lance Burton* at the Monte Carlo, *Starlight Express* at the Hilton, *EFX* at the MGM Grand, and Cirque du Soleil's *Mystère* at Treasure Island.

**MGM Grand Adventures,** behind the MGM Grand Hotel (☎ 702/891-7777), is an amusement park featuring games, shows, and thrill rides. **Wet 'n' Wild,** 2601 Las Vegas Blvd. S., just south of Sahara Avenue (☎ 702/878-7811), is a great outdoor water park. But try to find a discount admission coupon as the entry fee is too high.

**GAMBLING**   Both **Caesars Palace** and the **Desert Inn** are two of the more upscale casinos on the Strip; downtown, it's the casino at the **Golden Nugget.** The casino at the **Hard Rock Hotel** is a favorite with the under-35 crowd, and they may also be interested in the new Spacequest Casino at the **Las Vegas Hilton.** Another good choice is the casino at the **Luxor Las Vegas.** The **MGM Grand's** casino is supposedly the world's largest, but you'll find slots for days at the sprawling casino in the **Stardust.**

**GOLF**   There are dozens of local golf courses, but two of the best are attached to hotels. The course at the **Desert Inn Golf Club** (☎ 702/733-4290) is the most famous and demanding course in Las Vegas. It's an 18-hole, par-72 resort course with driving range, putting green, pro shop, and restaurant. You can reserve 90 days in advance for Sunday to Thursday; 2 days in advance for Friday and Saturday. The **Las Vegas Hilton Country Club** (☎ 702/796-0016) course is an 18-hole, par-72 public affair with pro shop, golf school, driving range, restaurant, and cocktail lounge. Hilton guests enjoy preferred tee times and rates.

**SHOPPING**   No one comes here to shop, but several malls can amply supply the basics. **Boulevard Mall,** 3528 S. Maryland Pkwy., between Twain Avenue and Desert Inn Road (☎ 702/732-8949), has more than 144 stores. The well-located **Fashion Show Mall,** 3200 Las Vegas Blvd. S., at the corner of Spring Mountain Road (☎ 702/369-8382), has more than 130 stores and some decent restaurants. The fastest-growing shopping mecca is at **Caesars Palace.**

## ACCOMMODATIONS

You'll probably want to stay on the Strip if it's your first visit to Las Vegas, but with a lot of construction recently, Downtown is on a roll. All hotels here have free self- and valet parking.

**Alexis Park Resort.** *375 E. Harmon Ave., between Koval Lane and Paradise Rd., Las Vegas, NV 89109.* ☎ *800/453-8000 or 702/796-3300. Fax 702/796-4334. 600 suites. $105–$250 double one-bedroom suite; $175–$400 double one-bedroom loft suite; $350–$1,500 larger suite. Additional person $15 extra. Children 18 and under stay free in parents' room. AE, CB, DC, DISC, JCB, MC. V.* Because of its low-key atmosphere, luxurious digs, and superb service, many celebrities choose this hotel. Spacious suites are decorated in light colors with taupe lacquer furnishings. All are equipped with refrigerators, wet bars, two-line phones with computer jacks, and TVs. Many have working fireplaces and/or Jacuzzi tubs. There are restaurants, bars/lounges, three pools, two lighted tennis courts, a fitness center, and a nine-hole putting green. Note that there is no casino.

**Caesars Palace.** *3570 Las Vegas Blvd. S., just north of Flamingo Rd., Las Vegas, NV 89109* ☎ *800/634-6661. 1,305 rms, 190 suites. $115–$190 double; $450–$7,500 suite. Additional person $20 extra. Children under 12 stay free in parents' room. AE, CB, DC, DISC, MC, V.* In this world-class resort, guests are greeted by gladiators and centurions, and its several entrances are graced by Roman fountains, temples, and heroic arches. Guest rooms have a lavish bath with an oversized marble tub. Many have four-poster beds with mirrored ceilings, and all are equipped with three phones, cable TV, and private safes. The palace has a casino, restaurants, buffet, bars/lounges, IMAX theater, shops, pool, fitness center and spa, and four tennis courts.

**Circus Circus Hotel/Casino.** *2880 Las Vegas Blvd. S., between Circus Circus Dr. and Convention Center Dr., Las Vegas, NV 89109.* ☎ *800/444-CIRC, 800/634-3450, or 702/734-0410. Fax 702/734-2268. 2,674 rms, 126 suites. Sun–Thurs, $36–$40 for up to four people; Fri–Sat $50–$55; holidays $65. Sun–Thurs, $46 suite; Fri–Sat, $65 suite; holidays and convention times, $85–$100 suite; $129 two-bedroom parlor suite. AE, CB, DC, DISC, MC, V.* A 123-foot clown named Lucky and a festive pink-and-white circus tent beckon visitors to Circus Circus, which holds the record as the world's largest permanent circus. Kids love it. Choose from tower rooms decorated in contemporary style or rooms in three-story buildings. All rooms have safes. There are three casinos, restaurants, a buffet, bars/lounges, a wedding chapel, tour and show desk, car-rental desk, three pools, two video arcades, shops, and an amusement park.

**Debbie Reynolds Hotel.** *305 Convention Center Dr., between Las Vegas Blvd. S. and Paradise Rd., Las Vegas, NV 89109.* ☎ *800/633-1777 or 702/734-0711. Fax 702/ 734-2954. 197 rms, 7 suites. Sun–Thurs, $49–$69 double. Fri–Sat $59–$79 double. Rates can go as high as $175 during conventions and peak seasons. Additional person $10 extra. AE, DC, DISC, MC, V.* Actress Debbie Reynolds has turned this hotel into a minimuseum of Hollywood memorabilia. And not only does she perform, but Strip entertainers often unwind and take the stage in her after-hours lounge as well. Large rooms offer great views of the Strip, and large black-and-white photographs of movie legends adorn the walls. On the top three floors are luxurious time-share units. The hotel has a casino, restaurants, bars/lounges, sightseeing/show/tour desk, shops, pool, and nearby fitness center.

✪ **Desert Inn Country Club Resort & Casino.** *3145 Las Vegas Blvd. S., between Desert Inn Rd. and Sands Ave., Las Vegas, NV 89109.* ☎ *800/634-6906 or 702/ 733-4444. Fax 702/733-4744. 566 rms, 136 suites/minisuites. $175–$185 double; $215– $225 minisuite; $350–$555 suite. Golf Digest* calls the 18-hole course here one of America's top resort courses, and the spa offers all the facilities and treatments one would expect in a world-class establishment. Many of the rooms and suites have spacious marble baths with Jacuzzi tubs. Some suites have private pools. Facilities include a casino, restaurants, bars/lounges, tour and show desks, car-rental desk, shops, golf, fitness center and spa, pool, five lighted tennis courts, and two shuffleboard courts.

**Four Queens.** *202 Fremont St., at Casino Center Blvd., Las Vegas, NV 89101.* ☎ *800/634-6045 or 702/385-4011. Fax 702/387-5133. 700 rms, 38 minisuites. Sun–Thurs, $54–$79 double; Fri–Sat, $65–$79 double; $99–$125 minisuite. Additional person $10 extra. Children under 2 stay free in parents' room. AE, CB, DC, DISC, MC, V.* The Four Queens is a major Downtown property occupying an entire city block. Notably nice rooms are located in 19-story twin towers; many offer views of the Fremont Street Experience. Minisuites, decorated in traditional styles, have living rooms and dining areas; some rooms are equipped with small refrigerators and coffeemakers. The hotel has a casino, restaurant, bars/lounges, car-rental desk, show desk, video arcade, and gift shop.

**✪ Golden Nugget.** *129 E. Fremont St., at Casino Center Blvd., Las Vegas, NV 89101.* ☎ *800/634-3454 or 702/385-7111. Fax 702/386-8362. 1,805 rms, 102 suites. Sun–Thurs, $59–$159 double; Fri–Sat, $99–$259 double; $275–$475 suite. Additional person $20 extra. AE, CB, DC, DISC, MC, V.* Gleaming white and gold in the Las Vegas sun, the Golden Nugget is a magnificent European-style resort with a stunning chandeliered white-marble lobby. Resort-style rooms are light and airy, with valanced beds, Indian batik-look bedspreads and draperies, and prints of 19th-century Rangoon and botanicals adorning the walls. The Golden Nugget has a casino, restaurants, buffet, bars/lounges, car-rental desk, shops, fitness center and spa, pool, and whirlpool.

**Hard Rock Hotel and Casino.** *4455 Paradise Rd., at Harmon Ave., Las Vegas, NV 89109.* ☎ *800/473-ROCK or 702/693-5000. Fax 702/693-5010. 316 rms, 24 suites. Sun–Thurs, $85–$250 double; Fri–Sat, $135–$300 double; $250–$350 suite. Additional person $25 extra. Children 12 and under stay free in parents' room. AE, DC, DISC, MC, V. Free valet and self-parking.* As you might guess, everything here is rock music–themed. Even the casino features piano-shaped roulette tables and guitar-neck-handle slot machines. The large, attractive rooms have French windows that actually open to fresh air and 27-inch TVs—both a rarity in Las Vegas hotels. Facilities include a casino, restaurants, bar/lounges, fitness center, video arcade, retail store, show desk, and pool.

**Harrah's Las Vegas.** *3475 Las Vegas Blvd. S., between Flamingo and Spring Mountain rds., Las Vegas, NV 89109.* ☎ *800/634-6785, 800/HARRAHS, or 702/369-5000. Fax 702/369-5008. 1,675 rms, 36 suites. $50–$250 double. Additional person $15 extra. Children 12 and under stay free in parents' room. AE, CB, DC, DISC, MC, V.* Harrah's has abandoned its landmark Mississippi riverboat facade for a new Mardi Gras/Carnival theme. Included in the renovation are additional rooms, restaurants, and casino space. Rooms are tastefully decorated, and spacious minisuites are especially desirable. The hotel has a casino, restaurants, fitness center, car-rental desk, video arcade, shops, and wedding chapel.

**Las Vegas Hilton.** *3000 Paradise Rd., at Riviera Blvd., Las Vegas, NV 89109.* ☎ *800/732-7117 or 702/732-5111. Fax 702/732-5805. 2,900 rms, 274 suites. $89–$269 double; $310–$1,520 suite. Additional person $25 extra. Children of any age stay free in parents' room. Off-season rates may be lower, subject to availability. Inquire about attractively priced golf and other packages. AE, CB, DC, DISC, JCB, MC, V.* The Hilton is simply magnificent—from its lobby and casino glittering with Austrian crystal chandeliers to its comprehensive resort facilities. A 40,000-square-foot Star Trek attraction is also expected to draw crowds. Rooms are southwestern in motif; most contain safes. Facilities include a casino, restaurant, buffet, bar/lounges, showroom, car-rental desk, tour desk, travel agency, shops, jogging trail, 18-hole golf course, video arcade, pool, six lighted tennis courts, fitness center, and convention center.

**Luxor Las Vegas.** *3900 Las Vegas Blvd. S., between Reno and Hacienda aves., Las Vegas, NV 81119.* ☎ *800/288-1000. 3,986 rms, 488 suites. Sun–Thurs, $49–$259 double; Fri–Sat, $99–$299 double. Concierge level $179–$279 double; $99–$329 Jacuzzi suite; $500–$800 other suites. Additional person $10 extra. Children under 12 stay free in* *parents' room. AE, CB, DC, DISC, MC, V.* This Egyptian-themed resort is a 30-story bronze pyramid fronted by a 191-foot obelisk and guarded by a 10-story sphinx. At night, a 315,000-watt light beam searches the heavens from the pyramid's apex. The rooms are among the most appealing in town; note, however, that most baths have showers only—no tubs. Extras include a casino, restaurants, buffet, bars/lounges, showroom, pool, fitness center and spa, arcade, wedding chapel, foreign currency exchange, car-rental desk, and tour/show/sightseeing desks.

✪ **MGM Grand Hotel/Casino.** *3799 Las Vegas Blvd. S., at Tropicana Ave., Las Vegas, NV 89109.* ☎ *800/929-1111 or 702/891-7777. Fax 702/891-1112. 4,254 rms, 751 suites. $69–$119 double; concierge floor $79–$129 double with breakfast; $99–$2,500 suite. Additional person $10 extra. Children under 12 stay free in parents' room. AE, DC, DISC, MC, V.* This 112-acre megaresort—an immense emerald-green monolith fronted by a towering MGM lion—is the world's largest. The casino is the size of four football fields, and the hotel's "backyard" is a 33-acre theme park. Guest rooms carry Hollywood, Wizard of Oz, Casablanca, and Old South motifs; all offer gorgeous marble baths. The hotel has a casino, restaurants, buffet, theme-park pool, four lighted tennis courts, fitness center and spa, business center, show/sporting events ticket desk, tour desk, America West airline desk, two wedding chapels, video arcade, and carnival midway.

✪ **Mirage.** *3400 Las Vegas Blvd. S., between Flamingo Rd. and Sands Ave., Las Vegas, NV 89109.* ☎ *800/627-6667 or 702/791-7111. Fax 702/791-7446. 3,044 rms, 279 suites. Sun–Thurs, $79–$399 double; Fri–Sat and holidays, $159–$399 double; $250–$3,000 suite. Additional person $30 extra. AE, CB, DC, DISC, MC, V.* The Mirage is fronted by waterfalls and tropical foliage centering on a "volcano" that erupts every 15 minutes after dark. Inside, you're in a verdant rain forest, which includes habitats for the rare white tigers belonging to Siegfried & Roy and for seven Atlantic bottlenose dolphins. The tasteful guest rooms have every amenity; superdeluxe rooms have whirlpool tubs. Facilities include a casino, restaurants, buffet, cafes, bars, golf, pool, fitness center and spa, shops, and car-rental desk.

**Rio Suite Hotel & Casino.** *3700 W. Flamingo Rd., at I-15, Las Vegas, NV 89103.* ☎ *800/752-9746 or 702/252-7777. Fax 702/252-0080. 1,555 suites. Sun–Thurs, $85 double; Fri–Sat and holidays, $103–$150 double. Additional person $15 extra. Children under 12 stay free in parents' room. Inquire about golf packages. AE, CB, DC, MC, V. Free valet and self-parking.* The Rio's palm-fringed facade heralds a luxurious tropical resort done in a carnival theme. The suites are spacious and, with the tropical decor, most appealing. Each has a stunning bath and picture windows provide panoramic views of the Strip. You'll also find a safe, refrigerator, and coffeemaker. Some suites have two phones. The hotel has a casino, restaurants, buffet, bar/lounges, car-rental desk, tour and show desks, foreign currency exchange, shops, two pools, three whirlpools, and two volleyball courts.

**Showboat.** *2800 Fremont St., between Charleston Blvd. and Mojave Rd., Las Vegas, NV 89104.* ☎ *800/826-2800 or 702/385-9123. Fax 702/383-9283. 451 rms, 4 suites. Sun–Thurs, $30–$65 double; Fri–Sat, $30–$85 double; holidays, $85 double; $130–$195 suite. Additional person $10 extra. Children under 12 stay free in parents' room. AE, CB, DC, DISC, MC, V.* Despite its slightly out-of-the-way location, this New Orleans–themed hotel is popular for its extensive facilities, friendliness, and delightful interior. Its gorgeous 24-hour bingo parlor is famous, both for its flower garden murals and for the highest payouts in town. And the bowling alley hosts major PBA tournaments. The rooms are spacious and cheerfully decorated, with an extra phone in the bath. A casino, restaurants, buffet, bars/lounges, bowling center, video arcade, pool, and child-care center are on the premises.

**Stardust Resort & Casino.** *3000 Las Vegas Blvd. S., at Convention Center Dr., Las Vegas, NV 89109.* ☎ *800/634-6757. 2,271 rms, 160 suites. Tower room: Sun–Thurs, $75–$150 double; Fri–Sat, $75–$300 double. Villa room: Sun–Thurs $40–$70 double; Fri–Sat $60–$100 double. Motor Inn room: Sun–Thurs $24–$36 double; Fri–Sat $45–$65 double; $150–$500 suite. Additional person $10 extra. Children 12 and under stay free in parents' room. AE, CB, DC, MC, V.* The sign in front of the venerable Stardust is one of America's most recognized landmarks. In the 32-story tower, you can rent an adjoining parlor with a sofa bed, Jacuzzi tub, refrigerator, and wet bar—a good choice for families. The two-story Villa buildings surround a large pool and have private shaded patios. The Stardust's Motor Inn is a block from the casino, but a good value. All rooms have safes. Facilities include a casino, restaurants, buffet, bar/lounge, car-rental desk, tour and show desks, shops, two pools, three whirlpools, fitness center, and video arcade.

**Stratosphere Las Vegas.** *2000 Las Vegas Blvd. S., between St. Louis St. and Baltimore Ave., Las Vegas, NV 89104.* ☎ *800/99-TOWER or 702/380-7777. Fax 702/383-5334. 1,278 rms, 222 suites. Sun–Thurs, $39–$93 double; Fri–Sat, $59–$129 double; $69–$400 suite. Additional person $15 extra. Children 18 and under stay free in parents' room. Rates may be higher during special events. AE, CB, DC, DISC, JCB, MC, V.* At 1,149 feet, the Stratosphere is the tallest building west of the Mississippi. It offers panoramic vistas from a revolving rooftop restaurant, and the world's highest roller coaster—108 stories aboveground. Notably good restaurants and shows are also pluses here, as are rooms furnished in handsome Biedermeier-style cherrywood pieces with black lacquer accents. Guests enjoy the pool, beauty salon, and shops.

✪ **Treasure Island at the Mirage.** *3300 Las Vegas Blvd. S., at Spring Mountain Rd., Las Vegas, NV 89109.* ☎ *800/944-7444 or 702/894-7111. Fax 702/894-7446. 2,688 rms, 212 suites. Sun–Thurs, $69–$149 double; Fri–Sat $129–$269 double; $109–$500 suite. Additional person $30 extra. Inquire about packages. AE, CB, DC, DISC, JCB, MC, V.* The Strip in front of this hotel has been transformed into a long wooden dock overlooking "Buccaneer Bay," where live sea battles between two full-scale ships take place at regular intervals. The 36-story hotel towers above the bay and a ramshackle pirate village. Within, public areas all maintain the pirate theme. Rooms are done in soft hues and nautical themes. Extras include a casino, restaurants, buffet, cafes, bars, pool, video arcade and carnival midway, two wedding chapels, fitness center and spa, shops, limo rental, foreign currency exchange, car-rental desk, and travel agency.

**OTHER ACCOMMODATIONS**   The **Excalibur,** 3850 Las Vegas Blvd. S., at Tropicana Avenue (☎ 800/937-7777), is a moderately priced option if you like the Medieval theme.

Vegas is also awash in nonthemed hotels and motels, most moderate to inexpensive in price. In addition to the **Days Inn Downtown,** 707 E. Fremont St., at 7th Street (☎ 800/325-2344), which has a casino, there are two independent Las Vegas stalwarts that don't: the **Algiers Hotel,** 2845 Las Vegas Blvd. S., between Riviera Boulevard and Sahara Avenue (☎ 800/732-3361), and the **Center Strip Inn,** 3688 Las Vegas Blvd. S., at Harmon Avenue (☎ 800/777-7737).

Chains in town include Marriott, which operates a Fairfield Inn, a Residence Inn, and a Courtyard by Marriott; Motel 6, which has two big complexes; La Quinta, which operates a Motor Inn and a more upscale La Quinta Inn; and Super 8.

## DINING

From the vantage point of value for your money, Las Vegas is a great restaurant town. After all, profits here are made at the gaming—not dining—tables.

**Alpine Village Inn.** *3003 Paradise Rd., between Riviera Blvd. and Convention Center Dr.* ☎ *702/734-6888. Reservations recommended. Fixed-price dinners $10–$19.50; children's portions (under 12 only) about half price. AE, CB, DC, DISC, MC, V. Sun–Thurs 5–10pm, Fri–Sat 5–11pm. SWISS/GERMAN.* Amid murals of snowy Alpine scenery and twinkling Christmas lights, diners in this popular family restaurant can expect a multicourse feast served by waiters in Tyrolean costume. Entrees such as roast duckling with sausage stuffing or roast chicken with chestnut stuffing are accompanied by an array of side dishes and topped off by warm strudel for dessert.

**Big Sky.** *In Stratosphere Las Vegas Hotel, 2000 Las Vegas Blvd. S., between St. Louis St. and Baltimore Ave.* ☎ *702/780-7777. All-you-can-eat dinner $12.99, free for children under 6. AE, CB, DC, DISC, JCB, MC, V. Sun–Thurs 5–11pm, Fri–Sat 5pm–midnight. PRIME RIB/BARBECUE.* The food here is one of the best bargains in town. There are all-you-can-eat feasts of prime rib with creamed horseradish sauce or a barbecue combination (beef brisket, St. Louis ribs, Carolina pulled pork, and fried chicken), with sides of salad, corn muffins, corn on the cob, fries, cole slaw, baked beans—and, of course, dessert. Country music sets the tone, and service is down-home and friendly.

**Center Stage.** *In Jackie Gaughan's Plaza Hotel Casino, 1 Main St., at Fremont St.* ☎ *702/386-2110. Reservations essential. Main courses $6–$16 (many under $10). AE, DISC, MC, V. Daily 5–11pm. STEAK AND SEAFOOD.* This is the best place in town for viewing the Fremont Street Experience (see "Attractions," above). The food can be lackluster, however, so stick to basic items. Order the prime rib au jus, served with onion soup or salad (take the salad), warm sourdough bread, a vegetable, and baked potato, rice, or fettuccine Alfredo (take the potato). It's just $7.95, and you get to see the show. Be sure to make reservations and arrive early for a good seat.

**Country Star.** *3724 Las Vegas Blvd. S., at Harmon Ave.* ☎ *702/740-8400. Reservations for large parties only. Main courses $5.95–$21.95 (most under $14). AE, CB, DC, DISC, MC. V. Mon–Thurs 11am–midnight, Fri–Sun 11am–1am. AMERICAN COWBOY COOKING.* This is a vast establishment filled with country music memorabilia and equipped with a dance floor, stage, and sound system for the frequent live entertainment. Specialties include barbecued beef or pork ribs (consider a platter of both, with hickory-smoked chicken, salad, barbecued beans, fries, and cornbread), homemade sausage platter, and pulled pork sandwich. For dessert, there's peanut butter pie.

**✪ Coyote Cafe.** *In the MGM Grand, 3799 Las Vegas Blvd. S.* ☎ *702/891-7349. Reservations recommended for the Grill Room, not accepted for the Cafe. Grill Room main courses $15–$32. Cafe main courses $7.50–$17.50 (many under $10). AE, CB, DC, DISC, JCB, MC, V. Grill Room, daily 5:30–10pm. Cafe, daily 9am–11pm. MODERN SOUTHWESTERN.* Coyote Cafe combines traditional Mexican, Native American, Creole, and Cajun cookery with cutting-edge culinary trends. The Grill Room menu, which changes monthly, recently featured salmon fillet crusted with ground pumpkin seeds and corn tortillas topped with roasted chile/pumpkin-seed sauce. The Cafe menu offers similar but somewhat lighter fare. Southwestern breakfasts ($6 to $9.50) range from *huevos rancheros* to blue-corn pancakes with toasted pine nuts and honey butter.

**Dive!** *In the Fashion Show Mall, 3200 Las Vegas Blvd. S.* ☎ *702/369-DIVE. Reservations not accepted. Main courses $7–$14. AE, CB, DC, DISC, MC. V. Sun–Thurs 11:30am–10pm, Fri–Sat 11:30am–11pm. AMERICAN.* DIVE!'s exterior is designed as a whimsical yellow submarine crashing through a 30-foot wall of water that cascades into an oversized pool erupting with depth-charge blasts. The submarine theme continues inside, where you can get good "sub" sandwiches (such as grilled shrimp with smoked peppered bacon), as well as delicious pasta dishes, pizzas, burgers on brioche onion rolls, and wood oven–roasted herbed chicken.

**Fiore.** *In Rio Suite Hotel, 3700 W. Flamingo Rd., at I-15.* ☎ *702/252-7702. Reservations recommended. Main courses $21–$36. AE, CB, DC, DISC, MC, V. Daily 5–11pm. NORTHERN ITALIAN/PROVENÇAL.* Recent offerings in this spacious, mahogany-ceilinged dining room included sautéed herb-crusted prawns in a buttery mustard/anise sauce, and barbecued Atlantic salmon in honeyed hickory sauce, served with grilled polenta, portobello mushrooms, roasted Roman tomatoes, and grilled asparagus. For dessert, try the warm chocolate torte on crème anglaise embellished with raspberry stars and chocolate hearts.

**Monte Carlo Pub & Brewery.** *In Monte Carlo Resort, 3770 Las Vegas Blvd. S., between Flamingo Rd. and Tropicana Ave.* ☎ *702/730-7777. Main courses $6–$8. AE, CB, DC, DISC, MC, V. Sun–Thurs 11am–1am, Fri–Sat 11am–3am. PUB FARE AND BREWS.* The Pub is a cigar-friendly place with a touch of elegance—somewhat mitigated by rock videos blaring from TV screens all around the room. The fare is somewhat sophisticated, and portions are enormous. Choices include pizza with lamb, eggplant, and goat cheese; penne pasta with wild mushrooms in garlic cream sauce; and sausages with warm potato salad. Only pizza is served after 9pm, and dueling pianos provide entertainment.

**Ricardo's.** *2380 Tropicana Ave., at Eastern Ave. (northwest corner).* ☎ *702/ 798-4515. Reservations recommended. Main courses $7.50–$13; lunch buffet $7; children's plates $3–$3.50, including milk or soft drink with complimentary refills. AE, CB, DC, DISC, MC, V. Mon–Thurs 11am–10pm, Fri–Sat 11am–11pm, Sun 11am–10pm. MEXICAN.* This hacienda-style restaurant is another local favorite. Start off with deep-fried battered chicken wings served with melted cheddar, or nachos smothered with cheese and guacamole. For an entree, you can't go wrong with the fajitas or any of the usual taco/enchilada/tamale combinations. The margaritas are great, and the fried ice cream is a delicious end to the meal. Arrive early to snag a good seat.

✪ **Tillerman.** *2245 E. Flamingo Rd., at Channel 10 Dr. (just west of Eastern Ave.).* ☎ *702/731-4036. Reservations not accepted. Main courses $16–$37. AE, CB, DC, DISC, MC, V. Daily 5–11pm; bar/lounge until midnight. STEAK/SEAFOOD.* Popular with local residents, Tillerman offers seating amid a grove of ficus trees, under a lofty cathedral ceiling. Portions are immense, but such appetizers as blackened medaillons of yellowfin tuna in spicy mustard sauce are hard to resist. Meat entrees include prime center-cut New York strip steak and a center-cut veal chop. And there are at least a dozen fresh seafood specials and a list of homemade desserts each night.

**OTHER DINING**   You can enjoy veritable food orgies at low-priced buffets, many of them consisting of incredible arrays of good, fresh food, creatively prepared and attractively displayed. Some of the better buffets include those at **Bally's,** 3645 Las Vegas Blvd. S. (☎ 702/739-4111); **Caesars Palace,** 3570 Las Vegas Blvd. S. (☎ 702/ 731-7110); **Excalibur,** 3850 Las Vegas Blvd. S. (☎ 702/597-7777); **Rio,** 3700 W. Flamingo Rd. (☎ 702/252-7777); and **Sam Boyd's Fremont** (☎ 702/385-3232).

And off-hours specials can be tremendous. Be sure to check out the coffee shop at **Binion's Horseshoe** downtown, or the 24-hour coffee shop of virtually any hotel.

Steak eaters will enjoy **Morton's of Chicago,** 3200 Las Vegas Blvd. S., in the Fashion Show Mall (☎ 702/893-0703), which has everything you've come to expect in this sophisticated chain. A Las Vegas version of Wolfgang Puck's **Spago** can be found at the Forum Shops at Caesars Palace, 3500 Las Vegas Blvd. S. (☎ 702/369-6300). Memorabilia-lovers and kids will enjoy the local edition of **Planet Hollywood,** also located in the Forum Shops at Caesars Palace, 3500 Las Vegas Blvd. S. (☎ 702/ 791-STAR), and the **Hard Rock Cafe,** 4475 Paradise Rd., at Harmon Avenue (☎ 702/733-8400), with its attached hotel and casino.

## LAS VEGAS AFTER DARK

No city in the world offers more excitement after dark than Las Vegas, and you can't leave without enjoying a show. Admission ranges from about $20 for a show at a lesser hotel to $80 and more for top headliners or *Siegfried & Roy*. Prices usually include two drinks or, in rare instances, dinner. For a performance schedule, call the **Las Vegas Convention and Visitor Authority** (☎ **702/892-0711**).

**THE SHOWS**   **Boylesque,** at the Debbie Reynolds Hotel (☎ **800/633-1777** or 702/ 7-DEBBIE), is a slick female-impersonator revue. **Cirque de Soleil's Mystère,** in Treasure Island, 3300 Las Vegas Blvd. S. (☎ **800/392-1999** or 702/894-7723), has sophisticated circus acts by a French–Canadian troupe. **Country Fever,** in the Golden Nugget, 129 E. Fremont St. (☎ **800/777-4658** or 702/386-8100), is a foot-stompin', hand-clappin' country music show of singers and dancers.

In the 1,700-seat Grand Theatre at the MGM Grand, 3799 Las Vegas Blvd. S. (☎ **800/929-1111** or 702/891-7777), you'll find **EFX,** a multimedia musical extravaganza starring David Cassidy (of *Partridge Family* fame). **Lance Burton: Master Magician** appears at the Monte Carlo, 3770 Las Vegas Blvd. S. (☎ **800/311-8999** or 702/ 730-7000), while **Siegfried & Roy,** illusionists par excellence, pack the house at The Mirage, 3400 Las Vegas Blvd. S. (☎ **800/627-6667** or 702/792-7777).

**THE CLUB & BAR SCENE**   You can dance the night away at several local establishments, including **The Beach,** 365 S. Convention Center Dr., at Paradise Road (☎ **702/ 731-9298**), an immense two-story affair with singing staff. **Bobby McGee's,** 1030 E. Flamingo Rd., at Cambridge Street (☎ **702/733-0388**), is the kind of hang-loose club where dance contests, trivia games, putting contests, and the like are frequent events. **Club Rio,** Rio Suite Hotel, 3700 W. Flamingo Rd. (☎ **800/634-6787** or 702/597-5970), is one of the hottest spots in town for young sophisticates ages 25–40. **Drink,** 200 E. Harmon Ave., at Koval Lane (☎ **702/796-5519**), is decidedly more sophisticated than the ultra-casual Beach, but not quite as serious as Club Rio. And there's **Cleopatra's Barge Nightclub,** in Caesars Palace, 3570 Las Vegas Blvd. S. (☎ **702/731-7110**).

The 24-hour **Angles,** 4633 Paradise Rd. at Naples Street (☎ **702/791-0100**), though upscale, is a casual neighborhood hangout compared to gay bars in other cities.

Comedy Clubs here featuring national talent include **Catch a Rising Star,** in the MGM Grand, 3799 Las Vegas Blvd. S. (☎ **800/929-1111** or 702/891-7777), and **The Improv,** in Harrah's, 3475 Las Vegas Blvd. S. (☎ **800/392-9002** or 702/369-5111).

## A DAY TRIP TO HOOVER DAM

Until Hoover Dam harnessed the Colorado River, much of the southwestern United States was plagued by parched, sandy terrain for most of the year, and extensive flooding in spring and summer. Of course, left unchecked for billions of years beforehand, the river's rushing, turbulent waters had carved the mighty Grand Canyon.

Completed in 1936, the dam stopped the annual floods and conserved water for irrigation, industrial, and domestic uses. Equally important, it became one of the world's major hydroelectric plants. The dam is a massive curved wall, 660 feet thick at the bottom and tapering to 45 feet thick at the top, where a road crosses. It towers 726 feet above bedrock (about the height of a 60-story skyscraper) and acts as a plug between the canyon walls to hold back up to 9.2 trillion gallons in Lake Mead, America's largest man-made reservoir. All the architecture is on a grand scale, with beautiful art deco elements unusual in an engineering project. Note the monumental 30-foot bronze sculpture, *Winged Figures of the Republic,* flanking a 142-foot flagpole at the Nevada entrance.

The dam is a major sightseeing attraction, and Lake Mead is a major Nevada recreation area.

**Essentials:** Take U.S. 93 south from Las Vegas (it's a continuation of Fremont Street). As you near the dam, you'll see a five-story parking structure tucked into the canyon wall on your left. Park here and head to the **Hoover Dam Visitor Center.** The Visitor Center is open daily from 8:30am to 6:30pm except Christmas Day. Thirty-minute tours of the dam depart from the lobby every few minutes daily except Christmas. Admission is $5 for adults, $2.50 for senior citizens and ages 10–16, free for children under 10. There are more extensive—and expensive—hard-hat tours, offered every half hour from 9:30am to 4pm. They can be arranged by calling in advance (☎ **702/294-3522**).

When you're through touring, you can enjoy the nearby Lake Mead National Recreation Area (☎ **702/293-8990**).

## 10 More California & Nevada Highlights

### LASSEN VOLCANIC NATIONAL PARK

Up in rugged northeastern California, Lassen Volcanic National Park is a remarkable reminder that North America is still forming, and that the ground below is alive with the forces of creation and, sometimes, destruction. Lassen Peak, the southernmost of a chain of volcanoes (including Mount Saint Helens), stretching all the way from British Columbia, is dormant but still very much alive. It last awakened in May 1914, beginning a cycle of eruptions that spit lava, steam, and ash until 1921. The eruption climaxed in 1915 when Lassen blew its top, sending a mushroom cloud of ash 7 miles high that was seen from hundreds of miles away. The area still boils with a ferocious intensity: Hot springs, fumaroles, and mud pots are all indicators that Lassen hasn't had its last word. Monitoring of geothermal features in the park shows that they are getting hotter, not cooler, and some scientists take this as a sign that the next big eruption in the Cascades is likely to happen here.

Until then, the park offers an interesting chance to watch a landscape recover from the massive destruction brought on by an eruption. To the northeast of Lassen Peak is the aptly named **Devastated Area,** a huge swath of volcanic destruction steadily repopulating with conifer forests. Botanists have revised their earlier theories that forests must be preceded by herbacious growth after watching the Devastated Area immediately revegetate with a diverse mix of different conifer species.

The 106,000-acre park is a place of great beauty. The flora and fauna here are an interesting mix of species from the Cascade Range, which stretches north from Lassen, and species from the Sierra Nevada, which stretches south. The resulting blend accounts for an enormous diversity of plants—715 distinct species have been identified here. Though it's snowbound in winter, Lassen is an important summer feeding ground for transient herds of mule deer and numerous black bears.

In addition to the volcano and all its geothermal features, Lassen Volcanic National Park includes miles of hiking trails, huge alpine lakes, large meadows, cinder cones, lush forests, cross-country skiing, and great camping. Only one major road, Calif. 89 (the Park Road), crosses the park in a 39-mile half circle with entrances and visitor centers at either end. Three-quarters of the park is designated wilderness.

Backcountry camping is allowed almost everywhere, and traffic is light. Ask about closed areas when you get your wilderness permit. Car campers have their choice of seven park campgrounds, but so few people camp here that there is no reservation system except for the **Lost Creek Group Campground,** and stays are granted a generous 14-day limit. Sites do fill up on weekends, so your best bet is to get to the park early on Friday to secure a place. If the park is packed, there are 43 campgrounds in surrounding Lassen National Forest, so you'll find a site somewhere.

Only one lodge operates within the park: **Drakesbad Guest Ranch,** famous for its rustic cabins, lodge, and steaming hot spring pool. Drakesbad is deluxe as only a place with no electricity or phones can be, with handmade quilts on every bed and kerosene lamps to read by. Full meal service is available and is very good. The lodge is extremely popular and is only open from June to September. Reservations are booked as far as a year in advance; contact **California Parks Co.,** 2150 N. Main St. #5, Red Bluff, CA 96080 (☎ **916/529-3376,** or 916/529-1512 in the off-season).

**Essentials:** Calif. 89 passes north–south through the park. Most visitors enter at the southwest entrance station, drive through the park, and leave through the northwest entrance, or vice versa. Two other entrances lead to remote portions of the park. Ranger stations are near each entrance and provide the full spectrum of interpretive displays, ranger-led walks, informational leaflets, and emergency help. The largest visitor center is located just outside the northwest entrance station before Manzanita Lake. The best time to visit is in summer, and even then, you should plan for possible rain and snow. For information and wilderness permits, contact **Lassen Volcanic National Park,** P.O. Box 100, Mineral, CA 96063-0100 (☎ **916/595-4444**).

# MENDOCINO

It's easy to see why artists are attracted to idyllic Mendocino, a cluster of New England–style sea captains' homes and stores set on headlands overlooking the Pacific. It's so scenic that it's been used for dozens of movies and the TV series *Murder, She Wrote.*

Mendocino was an important port during the logging boom, when it had three hotels, 17 saloons, and more than a dozen bordellos. Today it has about 1,000 residents, although it swarms with people, especially on weekends. The brothels are gone, but Mendocino still retains its charm. In fact, the entire town has been declared a national historic monument.

You can easily spend a day browsing through dozens of galleries and shops and walking out on the surrounding headlands, now constituting **Mendocino Headlands State Park** (the visitor center is in Ford House on Main Street). Three miles of trails wind through the park, providing panoramic views of sea arches and hidden grottoes. The headlands are home to many unique species of birds, including the black oystercatcher. A trail behind the Presbyterian church on Main Street goes down to a small but picturesque beach where driftwood formations wash ashore. South of town off Calif. 1, **Big River Beach** is good for picnicking, walking, and sunbathing.

The **Mendocino Art Center,** 45200 Little Lake Rd. (☎ **707/937-5818**), is the town's unofficial cultural headquarters, known for its gardens, galleries, and shops displaying local fine arts and crafts. For a special treat, go to **Sweetwater Gardens,** 955 Ukiah St. ☎ **707/937-4140**), which offers group and private saunas and hot-tub soaks, plus massages.

You can explore the Big River by renting a canoe, sea cycle, kayak, or outrigger from **Catch a Canoe & Bicycles Too** (☎ **707/937-0273**). Horseback riding on the beach is offered by **Lari Shea's Ricochet Ridge Ranch,** north of Mendocino in Fort Bragg (☎ **707/964-7669**).

Accommodations are available at the rustic but elegant **Standord Inn by the Sea,** just south of town (☎ **800/331-8884** or 707/937-5615; fax 707/937-0305); the **Joshua Grindle Inn** (☎ **707/937-4143**), a Victorian built in 1879; the **MacCallum House** (☎ **707/937-0289**), an 1882 Victorian gingerbread mansion; and the inexpensive **Mendocino Village Inn** (☎ **800/882-7029** or 707/937-0246), across the street from the sea.

**Essentials:** Mendocino is about a 4-hour drive north of San Francisco via U.S. 101 to Cloverdale, then Calif. 128 west to Calif. 1, then north along the coast. For information, contact the **Fort Bragg/Mendocino Coast Chamber of Commerce,**

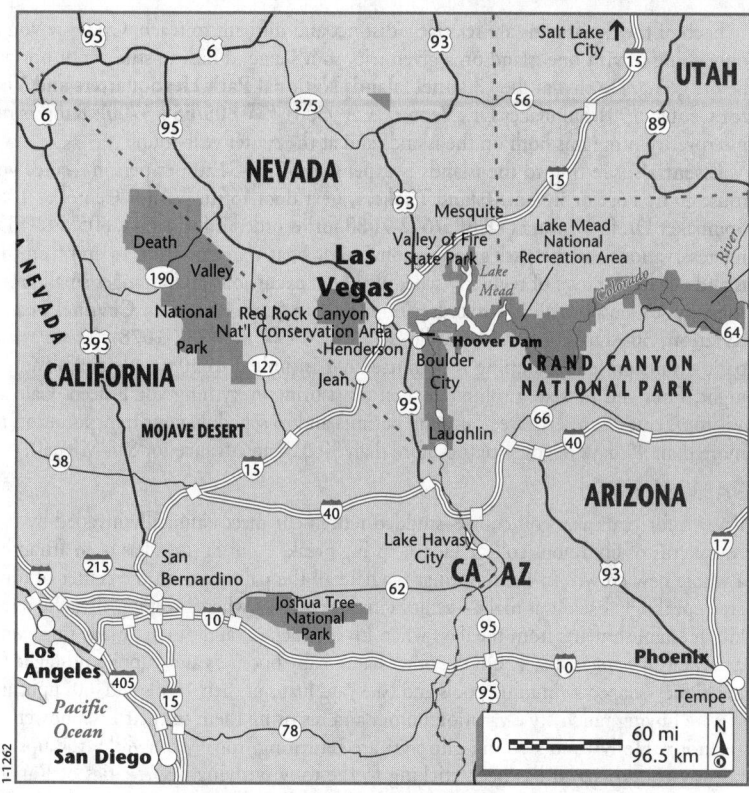

## The California Desert


95, 6, 375, 93, Salt Lake City, 15, UTAH, 6, 95, 56, 89, NEVADA, 93, Mesquite, Lake Mead National Recreation Area, Death, 190, Valley, **Las Vegas**, Valley of Fire State Park, *Lake Mead*, Colorado River, 64, National Park, Red Rock Canyon Nat'l Conservation Area, Henderson, **Hoover Dam**, Boulder City, GRAND CANYON NATIONAL PARK, 395, CALIFORNIA, 127, Jean, 95, MOJAVE DESERT, Laughlin, 66, ARIZONA, 58, 15, 40, 40, San Bernardino, 215, Lake Havasy City, 62, CA AZ, 93, 17, 5, Joshua Tree National Park, 10, 95, **Phoenix**, **Los Angeles**, 405, 10, Tempe, 15, 78, *Pacific Ocean*, **San Diego**, 0   60 mi / 96.5 km, N

1-1262

332 N. Main St. (P.O. Box 1141), Fort Bragg, CA 95437 (☎ **800/726-2780** or 707/961-6300).

## CHANNEL ISLANDS NATIONAL PARK

There's nothing like a visit to the Channel Islands for discovering the sense of awe the explorers must have felt nearly 400 years ago. It's miraculous what 25 miles of ocean can do, for compared to the mainland, this is a wild and empty land. Whether you approach the islands by sea or air, you'll be bowled over by how untrammeled they remain, despite being next-door neighbors with southern California's teeming masses.

Channel Islands National Park encompasses the five northernmost islands of the eight-island chain: Santa Barbara, Anacapa, Santa Cruz, Santa Rosa, and San Miguel. Tiny Santa Barbara Island sits very much by itself, about 46 miles off Santa Barbara. The other four are clustered in a 40-mile-long chain that begins with tiny Anacapa; it continues with Santa Cruz, then Santa Rosa, and ends with wild and windy San Miguel. The park also protects the ocean 1 mile offshore from each island, thereby prohibiting oil drilling, shipping, and other industrial uses.

The islands are the meeting point of two distinct marine ecosystems: The cold waters of northern California and the warmer currents of southern California swirl together here, creating an awesome array of marine life. On land, the relative isolation from mainland influences has allowed distinct species, like the island fox and the night lizard, to develop and survive here. The islands are also the most important seabird nesting area in California, and home to the biggest seal and sea lion breeding colony in the United States.

Each of the five islands are relatively distinct and difficult to reach. Odds are you're only going to visit one island on a given trip, so it's a good idea to study your options before going. Do that at the **Channel Islands National Park Headquarters and Visitor Center,** 1901 Spinnaker Dr., Ventura, CA 93001 (☎ 805/658-5700). Rangers run interpretive programs both on the islands and at the center year-round.

**Essentials:** Getting to the islands is expensive—$25–$120 per person—since you must go by boat or fly out. **Island Packers,** next door to the Visitor Center at 1867 Spinnaker Dr. in Ventura (☎ **805/642-7688** for recorded information, 805/642-1393 for reservations), is the park's concessionaire for boat transportation to and from the islands. It has a range of regularly scheduled boat excursions and arranges small group tours by sea kayak to all five islands. You can fly to Santa Rosa with **Channel Islands Aviation,** 305 Durley Ave, Camarillo, CA 93010 (☎ **805/987-1678**). There are no park admission fees. Camping is permitted but is limited to 30 people per island per night. Fires and pets are prohibited. You must bring everything you'll need. Call the Visitor Center to reserve free camping permits and to schedule your transportation no more than 90 days in advance (no more than 30 days in advance for San Miguel).

## PALM SPRINGS

Known for years as a golf course–studded retirement mecca annually invaded by raucous herds of libidinous college kids at spring break, Palm Springs has been attracting a whole new crowd. In Palm Springs—where all the palm trees in the center of town are appealingly backlit at night—senior citizens are everywhere, keeping alive the retro-kitsch establishments from the days when Elvis, Liberace, and Sinatra made this balmy desert city a *swingin'* place. On the other hand, baby boomers and yuppies nostalgic for the kidney-shaped swimming pools and backyard luaus of their 1950s and '60s upbringing are buying ranch-style vacation homes and restoring them to their Eisenhower-era splendor. Hollywood's young glitterati are returning, too. Meanwhile, the upscale fairway-condo crowd has been sticking to the tony outlying resort cities of Rancho Mirage, Palm Desert, Indian Wells, and La Quinta.

An important presence in Palm Springs has little to do with socialites and Americana, for the *Agua Caliente* band of *Cahuilla* Indians settled in this area 1,000 years before the first golf ball was ever teed up. Recognizing the beauty and spirituality of this wide-open space, they lived a simple life around the natural mineral springs on the desert floor, and would migrate into the cool canyons during the hot summer months. Under a treaty with the railroad companies and the U.S. government, the tribe owns half the land on which Palm Springs is built and actively works to preserve Native American heritage. It's easy to learn about the American Indians during your visit, and it will definitely add to your appreciation of this part of California.

This area is a world-famous mecca for golfers, with 85 public, semiprivate, and private courses. If you're an avid duffer, you're best off staying at one of the valley's many golf resorts, such as **Marriott's Desert Springs Resort** in Palm Desert (☎ 619/341-2211), **Marriott's Rancho Las Palmas** in Rancho Mirage (☎ **619/568-2727**), **Hyatt Grand Champions** in Indian Wells (☎ **619/341-1000**), **La Quinta Resort & Club** in La Quinta (☎ **619/346-2904**), and the **Estrella Inn** (☎ **800/237-3687** or 619/320-4417). There you can enjoy the proximity of your hotel facilities as well as economically smart package deals that give a taste of country club membership.

On the other hand, there are courses at all levels open to the general public, mostly in Palm Springs, and all the principal clubs have resident pros to sharpen your game. There are several schools and clinics including **Indian Wells Golf School** at Indian Wells Resort (☎ **800/241-5782** or 619/346-4653), the **Golf Center at Palm Desert** (☎ **619/779-1877**), and **Leadbetter Golf Academy** at PGA West in La Quinta (☎ **800/424-3542** or 619/564-0777).

Nonguests cannot book tee times at many courses more than a few days in advance, but several companies can make arrangements several months earlier, and even construct a custom package for you with accommodations, golf, meals, and other extras. Among them are **Golf a la Carte** (☎ **619/324-5012;** fax 619/321-1242) and **Palm Springs Golf and Tours** (☎ **800/PS-GOLF-1** or 619/346-3331; fax 619/346-4473).

This also is a great area to watch the pros in action. February brings the PGA Tour **Bob Hope Chrysler Classic** and the **Frank Sinatra Celebrity Invitational.** In March, catch the LPGA Tour **Nabisco Dinah Shore,** then in April the Senior PGA **Liberty Mutual Legends of Golf.** November brings two of the desert's longest-running charity events: the **Frostig Center/Chris Korman Celebrity Tournament** and the **Billy Barty/7Up Celebrity Golf Classic.** Also in November, check out the wacky **Palm Desert Golf Cart Parade.**

Of course, there are many other outdoor activities here, including ballooning, biking, horseback riding, hiking, and skydiving. It's also a good place to shop, with many art galleries and antiques stores. And with older residents passing on, consignment and estate sale companies are better stocked than ever before.

**Essentials:** Several airlines serve **Palm Springs Regional Airport.** If you're driving from Los Angeles, take I-10 to the Calif. 111 turnoff to Palm Springs. You'll breeze into town on North Palm Canyon Drive, the main thoroughfare. The trip from downtown L.A. takes about 2 hours. If you're driving from San Diego, take I-15 north to I-10 east; it's 135 miles. For information, contact the **Palm Springs Desert Resorts Convention and Visitor Bureau,** in the Atrium Design Centre, 69–930 Calif. 111, Suite 201, Rancho Mirage, CA 92270 (☎ **800/417-3529** or 619/770-9000). In town, the **Palm Springs Visitor Information Center,** 2781 N. Palm Canyon Dr. (☎ **800/34-SPRINGS**), offers maps, brochures, advice, souvenirs, and a free hotel reservation service.

## JOSHUA TREE NATIONAL PARK

Sometimes known as the "in-between" desert because of its location between the Mojave and the Colorado deserts, Joshua Tree National Park shares characteristics of each. The mountainous, Joshua tree-studded Mojave Desert is relatively cooler, wetter, and higher; it forms the northern and western parts of the park. Hotter, drier, lower, and characterized by a wide variety of desert flora including ironwood, smoketree, and native California fan palms, the Colorado Desert comprises the southern and eastern sections of the park. Cacti, especially cholla and ocotillo, thrive in the more southerly Colorado Desert (a part of the larger Sonoran Desert).

The Joshua tree is said to have been given its name by early Mormon settlers traveling west. Its upraised limbs and bearded appearance reminded them of the prophet Joshua leading them to the promised land. Other observers were not so kind. Nature writer Charles Francis Saunders opined: "The trees themselves were as grotesque as the creations of a bad dream; the shaggy trunks and limbs were twisted and seemed writhing as though in pain, and dagger-pointed leaves were clenched in bristling fists of inhospitality."

The trees grow at the foot of mountain slopes and capture the surface and groundwater draining from higher elevations. Pale yellow, lilylike flowers festoon their limbs in March, April, or May, depending on rainfall.

An excellent first stop is the main **Oasis Visitor Center,** south of the town of Twentynine Palms on Calif. 62. For many generations, the native Serrano lived at this "place of little springs and much grass." Get maps, books, and the latest in road, trail, and weather conditions before beginning your tour.

You'll want to explore **Jumbo Rocks,** which captures the complete essence of the park with a vast array of rock formations, a Joshua tree forest, and wide-open yucca-dotted desert. Many rocks in the area appear to resemble humans, dinosaurs, monsters, cathedrals, and castles. A 1½-mile-long nature trail provides an introduction to the park's flora, wildlife, and geology.

Beginning in Queen Valley, just west of Jumbo Rocks, a rough track known as **Geology Tour Road** (four-wheel-drive recommended) extends 18 miles into the heart of the park. Farther west, **Indian Cave** is typical of the kind of shelter sought by the nomadic Cahuilla and Serrano Indian clans that traveled this desert land. A 4-mile round-trip trail climbs through a lunar landscape of rocks and Joshua trees to the top of 5,470-foot Ryan Mountain. Your reward for making this climb is one of the park's best panoramic views.

At Cap Rock Junction, the paved park road swings north toward the **Wonderland of Rocks,** a curious, 12-square-mile maze of massive jumbled granite. From Cap Rock Junction, dirt Keys View Road dead-ends at mile-high **Keys View,** at the crest of the Little San Bernardino Mountains, with grand views encompassing both the highest (Mt. San Gorgonio) and lowest (Salton Sea) points in southern California.

Pinto Basin Road tours the forbidding Colorado Desert side of the park, a barren lowland surrounded by austere mountains and punctuated by trackless sand dunes. **Cholla Cactus Garden** preserves an unusually thick concentration of cholla, often called teddy-bear cactus because of the soft, fluffy appearance of its spines. Don't be deceived: they pierce the skin with only the lightest touch.

The park is one of the world's premier **rock-climbing** destinations, with some 3,000 routes ranging from the easiest of bouldering to some of the sport's most difficult technical climbs. Superstars of the sport can be seen surmounting flared chimneys and difficult jam cracks from November to May. There's good hiking and mountain biking here, too.

Nine campgrounds scattered throughout the park offer pleasant though often spartan accommodations. Only two—**Black Rock Canyon** and **Cottonwood**—have water.

If you're staying in the Palm Springs area, it's entirely possible to make a day trip here. For a complete listing of Yucca Valley Lodging, contact the **Yucca Valley Chamber of Commerce,** 56300 Twentynine Palms Hwy., Yucca Valley, CA 92284 (☎ 619/365-6323). Yucca Valley has lots of restaurants and every fast-food franchise imaginable.

**Essentials:** From Los Angeles, the usual route to the Oasis Visitor Center is via I-10 to its intersection with Calif. 62 (some 45 miles east of San Bernardino). Calif. 62 leads north and east for about 43 miles to the town of Twentynine Palms. From town, follow the park signs a short distance to the visitor center. In addition to the main Oasis Visitor Center at the Twentynine Palms entrance, there is Cottonwood at the south entrance, and Black Rock Canyon, located at the campground southeast of Yucca Valley. For more information, contact **Joshua Tree National Park,** 74485 National Park Dr., Twentynine Palms, CA 92277 (☎ 619/367-7511).

## MOJAVE NATIONAL PRESERVE

To many motorists, the East Mojave Desert is a vast, bleak, interminable stretch of wasteland to be crossed as quickly as possible on I-15 between Los Angeles and Las Vegas. Few realize that the freeway is the northern boundary of what desert rats have long considered the crown jewel of the California desert—the Mojave National Preserve.

With few campgrounds and even fewer motels—without even a visitor center—this land is a hard one to get to know. But it's an easy one to get to like. Its 1.4 million acres include the world's largest Joshua tree forest, wild burros and grazing cattle, spectacular canyons and volcanic formations, nationally honored scenic back roads and footpaths to historic mining sites, tabletop mesas, and a dozen mountain ranges.

One of the preserve's spectacular sights is the **Kelso Dunes,** the most extensive dune field in the West. The 45-square-mile formation of magnificently sculpted sand is famous for its "booming": visitors' footsteps cause miniavalanches and the dunes to go "sha-boom-sha-boom-sha-boom." Sometimes the low rumbling sound resembles a Tibetan gong; other times it sounds like a 1950s doo-wop musical group. From atop the dunes is a stunning view of the Kelso Mountains to the north, the Bristol Mountains to the southwest, the Granite Mountains to the south, and the Providence Mountains to the east.

A 10-mile drive from the Kelso Dunes is the Spanish Revival–style **Kelso Depot,** built by Union Pacific railroad in 1924. Train passengers and visitors ate meals in a restaurant nicknamed "The Beanery." The National Park Service is considering refurbishing the building for use as the preserve's visitor center.

Another preserve highlight is **Cima Dome,** a 75-square-mile chunk of uplifted volcanic rock. A geological rarity, Cima has been called the most symmetrical natural dome in the U.S. Another distinctive feature is its handsome rock outcroppings—the same type found in Joshua Tree National Park to the south, and a lure for rock climbers and hikers. On and around Cima Dome grows the world's largest and densest **Joshua tree forest,** some more than 25 feet high and several hundred years old.

Hole-in-the-Wall and Mid Hills are the centerpieces of the preserve. Linking them is the preserve's best drive, **Wildhorse Canyon Road,** which loops from Mid Hills Campground to Hole-in-the-Wall Campground, crossing wide-open country dotted with cholla and, in season, delicate purple, yellow, and red wildflowers. Mile-high **Mid Hills** recalls the Great Basin Desert topography of Nevada and Utah. Mid Hills Campground offers a grand observation point from which to gaze out at the coffee-with-cream-colored Pinto Mountains to the north and the rolling Kelso Dunes shining on the western horizon. **Hole-in-the-Wall** is the kind of place Butch Cassidy and the Sundance Kid would have chosen as a hideout. This twisted maze of rocks called rhyolite is a form of crystallized red lava rock. A series of iron rings aids descent into Hole-in-the-Wall; they're not particularly difficult for those who are reasonably agile and take their time.

**Mid Hills Campground** is located in a pinyon pine–juniper woodland and offers outstanding views. This mile-high camp is the coolest in the East Mojave. Nearby **Hole-in-the-Wall Campground** is perched above two dramatic canyons. **Afton Canyon Campground,** 33 miles east of Barstow, can be easily reached via the Afton exit off I-15 and a well-graded 3-mile dirt road. Barstow has a great many restaurants and motels. Call the **Barstow Chamber of Commerce** (☎ 619/256-8617) for suggestions. Accommodations and food also are available in Baker.

**Essentials:** I-15 extends along the northern boundary of the preserve. I-40 is the southern access route to the East Mojave. Spring is a splendid time (autumn is another) to visit this desert. From March to May, temperatures are mild, the Joshua trees are in bloom, and the lower Kelso Dunes are bedecked with yellow and white desert primrose and pink sand verbena. The **California Desert Information Center,** 831 Barstow Rd. in Barstow (☎ 619/255-8760), has maps, brochures, a selection of guidebooks, and information about camping, lodging, and desert attractions, and National Park Service and U.S. Bureau of Land Management staff are on hand to help.

## DEATH VALLEY NATIONAL PARK

The Forty-niner prospectors, whose suffering gave this valley its name, would have howled at the notion of a Death Valley National Park. To them, this was the closest place to hell on earth. It's been called the land God made in anger. Mountains stand naked, unadorned. The bitter waters of saline lakes evaporate into bizarre, razor-sharp crystal formations. Jagged canyons jab deep into the earth. Ovenlike heat, frigid cold, and the driest air imaginable combine to make this one of the most inhospitable locations in the world.

**Badwater,** the lowest point in the western hemisphere at 282 feet below sea level, is also one of the hottest places in the world, with regularly recorded summer temperatures of 120°F. At **Racetrack Playa,** a dry lake bed, you will puzzle over rocks that weigh as much as one-quarter ton and move mysteriously across the mud floor, leaving trails as a record of their movement. Research suggests that a combination of powerful winds and rain may skid the rocks over slick clay.

A good first stop after checking in at the main park visitor center in Furnace Creek is the **Harmony Borax Works**—a rock-salt landscape as tortured as you'll ever find. From 1883 to 1888, famous 20-mule teams pulled more than 20 million pounds of borax to a railhead 165 miles away. A short trail with interpretive signs leads past the ruins of the old borax refinery. To learn more about this colorful era, visit the **Borax Museum** at Furnace Creek Ranch.

**Salt Creek** is the home of the **Salt Creek pupfish,** found nowhere else on earth. The little fish, which has made some amazing adaptations to survive in this arid land, can be glimpsed from a wooden boardwalk nature trail. In spring, a million pupfish might be wriggling the creek; by summer's end, only a few thousand remain.

Before sunrise, photographers point their cameras from **Zabriskie Point** down at the pale mudstone hills of Golden Canyon and the great valley beyond. Another grand vista is seen at **Dante's View,** a 5,475-foot viewpoint in the Black Mountains.

A 14-square-mile field of dunes and bizarre geology are some of the attractions at the **Stove Pipe Wells** area. Those surreal corn stalks you see across Calif. 190 from the dunes are actually clumps of arrowweed. The **Devil's Cornstalks** are perched on wind- and water-eroded pedestals. **Mosaic Canyon,** located near Stovepipe Wells, displays mosaics of water-polished white, gray, and black rock. The long, narrow, white marble walls of the canyon seem like an art gallery.

**Scotty's Castle,** a Mediterranean-to-the-max mega-hacienda in the northern part of the park, is unabashedly Death Valley's premier tourist attraction. This villa was built in 1924 as a winter retreat for eccentric Chicago millionaire Albert Johnson, whose unlikely friendship with prospector/cowboy/spinner-of-tall-tales Walter Scott put the structure on the map. "Scotty" greeted visitors and told them fanciful stories from the early hard-rock mining days of Death Valley. Near Scotty's Castle is half-mile-wide **Ubehebe Crater,** from which hot magma blasted. To the south is Little Hebe Crater and a cluster of smaller holes.

If you can stand the heat, the park has a number of good hiking trails. Bicycling is not allowed on hiking trails. The park's nine **campgrounds** are located at elevations ranging from below sea level to 8,000 feet. In Furnace Creek, Sunset offers 1,000 spaces with water and flush toilets. Furnace Creek has 200 similarly appointed spaces. Stovepipe Wells has 200 spaces with water and flush toilets. **Furnace Creek Ranch** (☎ 619/786-2345) has 225 no-frills cottage units with air-conditioning and showers. The swimming pool is a popular hangout for tired lodgers. Nearby are a coffee shop, cafeteria, steak house, Mexican restaurant, and general store. The **Furnace Creek Inn** (☎ 619/786-2345), an elegant resort, boasts 67 deluxe rooms with a formal dining room, heated pool, golf, and tennis courts. **Stove Pipe Wells Village** (☎ 619/786-2387) has 74 modest rooms with air-conditioning and showers. The town of **Lone Pine,** on the west side of the park, and **Baker,** on the south, also have accommodations.

**Essentials:** Perhaps the most scenic entry to the park is via Calif. 190, east from Calif. 395 through Towne Pass. Another scenic drive to the park is by way of Calif. 127 and Calif. 190 from Baker. The **Death Valley Visitor Center** at Furnace Creek, 15 miles inside the eastern park boundary on Calif. 190 (☎ 619/786-3244), offers well-done interpretive exhibits and an hourly slide program. Ask at the information desk for ranger-led nature walks and evening naturalist programs. Admission to the park is $10 per vehicle or $5 for an individual. Annual entrance permits cost $20. For information, contact **Death Valley National Park,** Death Valley, CA 92328 (☎ 619/786-2331).

# Part 8

# The Northwest

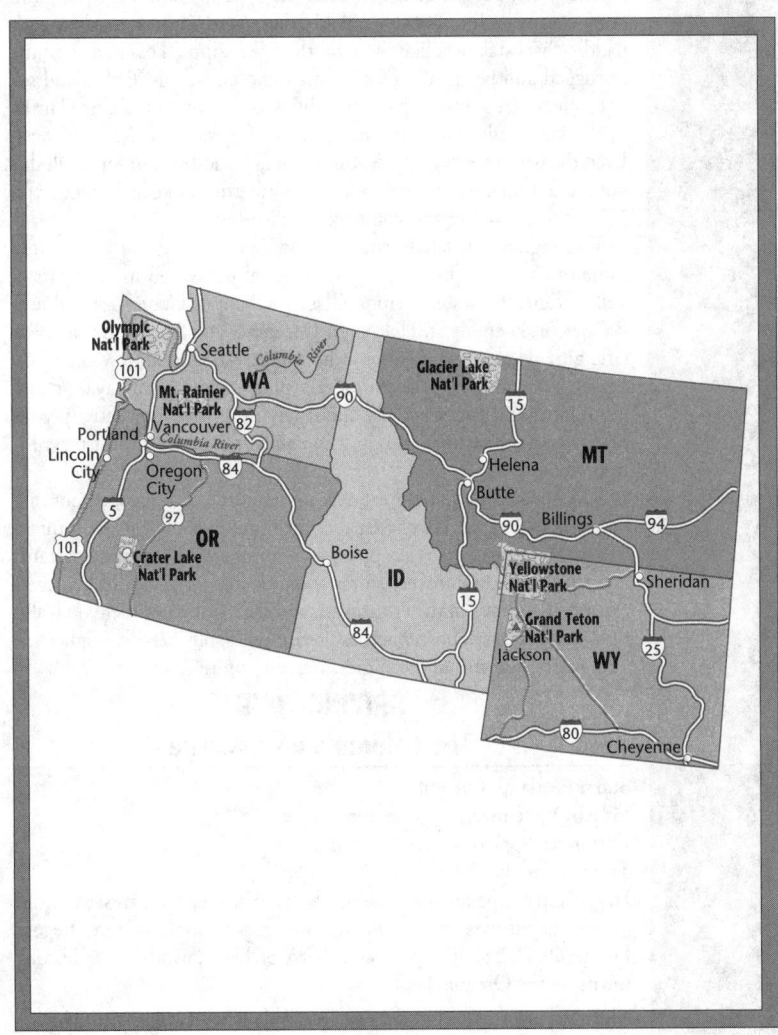

The upper left-hand corner of the nation offers an amalgam of American life and landscapes. Take a bit of New England's rural beauty with covered bridges, steepled churches, and familiar place names like Portland and Springfield. Bring in low rolling mountains like the Appalachians, some rugged glaciated peaks like the Colorado Rockies, and even volcanoes like Hawaii's. Add a large and important river with paddlewheel steamers like those on the Mississippi. Toss in a coastline as rugged and beautiful as California's and an island-filled inland sea that offers as many sailing opportunities as the coast of Maine. Throw in the sagebrush, cowboys, and Indians of Texas and the Southwest. Even the wheat fields of the Midwest could be added. On top of all this put a beautiful city, one with hills and a waterfront like San Francisco's. Mix all this together and you have the Northwest.

This region will satiate your outdoor spirit. Here you can explore some of America's most stunning national parks and monuments— Yellowstone, the Grand Tetons, Glacier, Olympia, Crater Lake, Mount Rainier, and Mount St. Helens. In December and April you watch Pacific gray whales migrate along the rugged Oregon and Washington coasts. You can backpack, mountain bike, canoe, hike, kayak, climb mountains and rocks, or just about any other outdoor activity your mind can conjure up—and do it in some of America's most magnificent scenery.

You'll be in for some great eats up here, too. Smoked salmon has been a staple of the Northwest diet for thousands of years, and thick-legged Dungeness crabs are prepared a number of ways by restaurants and sold cooked in grocery stores at reasonable prices. Wild blackberries are ubiquitous in the Northwest, and during the summer you'll also find marionberries, boysenberries, loganberries, ollieberries, raspberries, and others at farm stands, in groceries, and on restaurant menus.

## DRIVING TOUR
## The Columbia River Gorge

**Start:** Portland, Oregon
**Finish:** Vancouver, Washington
**Distance:** Approximately 165 miles
**Time:** 1 1/2 days
**Highlights:** Spectacular waterfalls; volcanic cliffs; forested trails; second-largest river in the United States; highest mountain in Oregon; Bonneville Dam; apple, pear, and cherry orchards; windsurfing; historic towns on the Oregon Trail; gorge artifacts

This tour goes up and down the Columbia River Gorge, justifiably an official National Scenic Area. Beautiful trails wind through the shady forests, and waterfalls cascade in profusion as the creeks and streams

# Driving Tour: The Columbia River Gorge

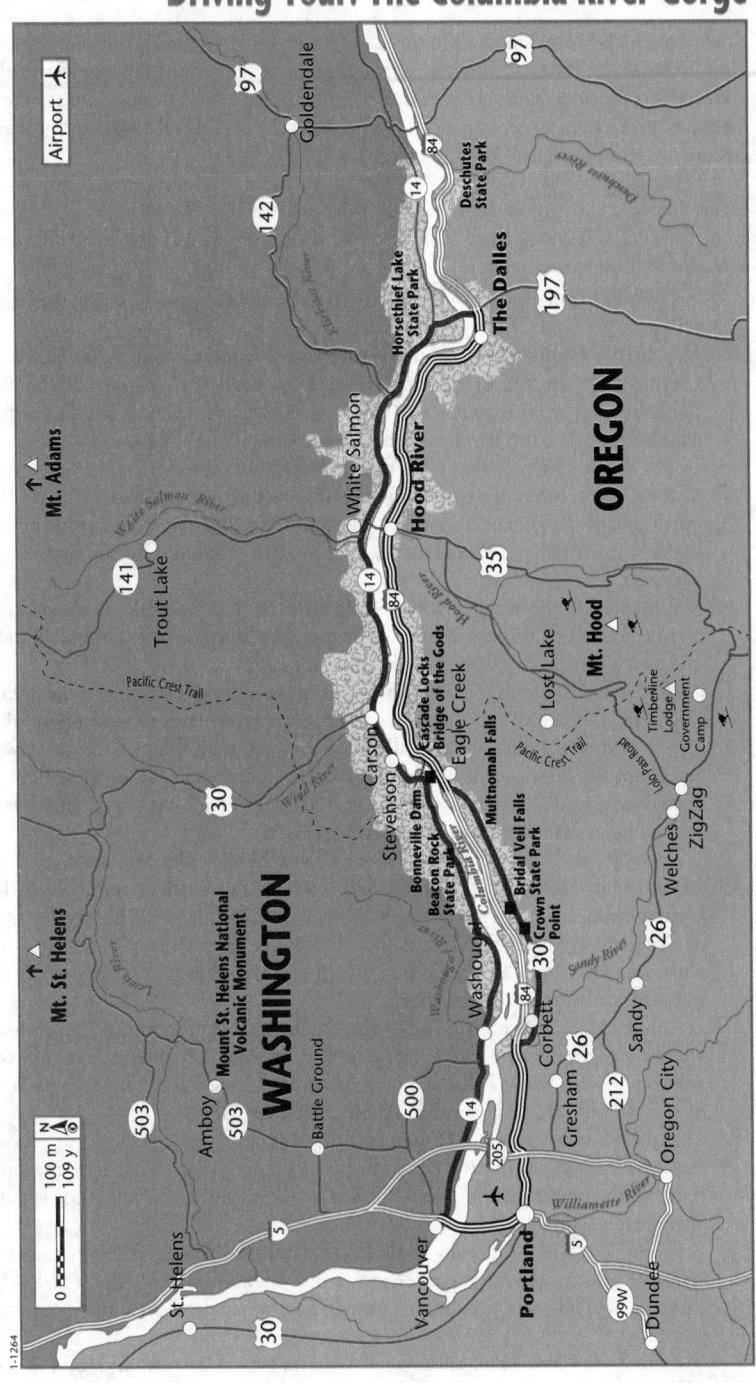

flow from Larch Mountain and Mount Hood (at 11,235 feet, the highest point in Oregon) toward the broad Columbia. The Columbia is the second-largest river in the country and the only sea-level break in a mountain range that extends from northern California to Canada. Sheer basalt cliffs rising above the river reveal a dramatic geologic history of volcanic eruptions and immense floods.

I-84 runs beside the river on the Oregon side; Wash. 14 follows the Washington shore. Historic U.S. Scenic Highway 30, which parallels I-84 for 22 miles, is the best route for a more leisurely trip and close-up views of the falls and greenery. This tour includes all three roads.

From Portland, drive I-84 east about 20 miles to Corbett and exit 22, then turn off on:

**1. U.S. Scenic Highway 30,** a winding road edged by mossy stone walls, The road, cut into the steep cliffs of the gorge between 1913 and 1915, is listed on the National Register of Historic Places. Taking exit 22 will place you on a hill road that travels to a fork. Turn left; this road becomes U.S. 30, heading east.

The Scenic Highway rises from river level up 720 feet to:

**2. Crown Point,** offering a panoramic overview of the river and forest and, on the north side of the gorge, Mount St. Helens and Mount Adams. The stone building on Crown Point is **Vista House,** built in 1918 to honor Oregon pioneers. It has maps, brochures, and a gift shop.

Continue on the Scenic Highway for a little less than 2¹/₂ miles to the parking area for **Latourell Falls.** A 2-mile scenic trail curves up the hill through tall trees and past ferns and wildflowers to the 100-foot falls.

More accessible from the road is **Sheppers's Dell,** east of Latourell on the Scenic Highway. A paved path, beside a low, moss-covered wall, leads to these pretty falls.

The next stop is **Bridal Veil Falls State Park,** on a bluff high above the river. In the spring, meadows of blue camas flowers bloom; the roots of these flowers were once a staple of the Native American diet. The park has picnic tables, rest rooms, and a paved trail with wheelchair access.

You will pass Wahkeena Falls on your way to the showpiece of the gorge:

**3. Multnomah Falls,** with a drop of 620 feet, the fourth-tallest waterfall in the United States. Interpretive signs at the base of the falls explain the history, botany, and geology of the region. A partially paved trail leads to the top of the falls and a dizzying view from an observation platform. Take a break here for snacks and meals in **Multnomah Falls Lodge.**

A mile east of Multnomah Falls is the **Oneonta Gorge Botanical Area,** where wildflowers grow on the banks of a narrow ravine. After Oneonta on U.S. 30 you will come to **Horsetail Falls,** and then **Ainsworth State Park,** where the portion of U.S. 30 officially designated as a Scenic Highway ends.

Join I-84 at this point and drive east for 5 miles to:

**4. Bonneville Dam,** the oldest dam on the river (operating since 1938) and providing much of the power for the region. There's a visitor center, and self-guided tours are available daily.

One mile east of Bonneville, **Eagle Creek Trail** rises beside a rippling brook toward the heart of the inner gorge. It's a 2-mile walk through the forest to lovely **Punchbowl Falls,** and 6 miles to **Tunnel Falls,** which drops in a misty veil over a cavern.

From Eagle Creek Trail, drive 23 miles east on I-84 to the town of **Hood River.** Along the way you'll pass **Cascade Locks,** which has a historical museum and marine park. Next to the Locks is the **Bridge of the Gods,** which Native

American legend says is on the site of an ancient stone bridge used by the gods. The present structure was built in 1926. The town of Cascade Locks was named for the shipping locks that were constructed here in 1896, allowing boats to navigate the river's rapids. The town is now headquarters of the sternwheeler **Columbia Gorge,** which offers narrated river cruises in the summer.

From I-84, take exit 64 at:

5. **Hood River,** a small town with a big reputation. Long known for its apple and pear orchards, in recent years it has gained renown as the windsurfing capital of the world. Thanks to the constant winds of the Columbia Gorge, windsurfers skim the river's waves like hundreds of colorful birds. Port Marina Park is the most popular site. Hood River is also becoming famous for its microbreweries and wineries. Follow the signs to **Port Marina Park,** where the **Hood River Visitor Center** offers maps and brochures. Next to the center is the **Hood River County Historical Museum,** which offers an interesting look at life on the river, from early Native American settlements to pioneer days.

The fruit orchards outside of town draw hordes of visitors in spring, when some 15,000 acres of trees explode with pink and white blooms. With snow-capped Mount Hood rising behind them, they're a photographer's dream. Festivals take place in spring and fall to celebrate the area's abundant crops. The old-fashioned **Mount Hood Railroad** offers orchard tours in vintage train cars. The refurbished depot is listed on the National Register of Historic Places.

East of Hood River you're on the dry side of the Cascade Range. The lush green forests are behind you; wheat fields and sagebrush lie ahead. From Hood River, drive 24 miles east on I-84 and take exit 84 to:

6. **The Dalles,** which was the end of the overland Oregon Trail. Here pioneers were faced with two options, both of them dangerous: Load their covered wagon onto a raft and float it down the Columbia, or take the southern land route around Mount Hood's steep shoulders. Stop in the **Dalles Convention and Visitor Bureau,** 404 W. 2nd St. (☎ **503/296-2231**), and pick up a walking-tour map and brochures. Adjacent to the visitor center is the original **Wasco County Courthouse,** now a museum. The restored building looks as it did in 1858, when Wasco was the largest county in the United States, covering 130,000 square miles from Oregon to Wyoming.

Three blocks away, at West 3rd and Lincoln streets, stands the historic **St. Peter's Landmark.** The steeple on this red-brick Gothic Revival church rises 176 feet and is topped by a cross and a rooster weather vane that can be seen from all over town.

In 1850, an army post later named **Fort Dalles** was established here. The remains of the post can be seen at 15th and Garrison streets. The original Surgeon's Quarters, today the **Fort Dalles Museum,** contains memorabilia from those early frontier days.

Cherry orchards thrive near the Dalles, and a cherry festival is held here every spring. The area is also noted for its wildflower displays, especially west of town at **Rowena Crest.** The Nature Conservancy maintains the **Tom McCall Preserve** on this grassy plateau; there are guided walks when the flowers are in bloom and the hillsides blaze with color. The plateau, high above the river, provides a broad view of the gorge and mountains.

Leaving the Dalles, head north across the bridge that spans the Columbia to Washington State. If you have time for an interesting side trip, turn east on Wash. 14 and travel 20 miles to **Maryhill Museum,** perched on a windswept cliff above the river, which maintains an excellent collection of sculptures by Auguste Rodin. A nearby **replica of England's Stonehenge,** built as a World War I memorial, is another point of interest.

If you don't take this side trip, turn west on Wash. 14 and drive about 44 miles to Stevenson. One mile west of town, turn right at the sign to Skamania Lodge and stop at the:

**7.** **Columbia Gorge Interpretive Center,** which overlooks the river and forest, for a glimpse of the history of the gorge. On display are an immense fishing wheel and sawmill, a room full of Japanese immigrants' artifacts, petroglyph replicas, a fascinating collection of Asian art and furniture, the world's largest rosary collection, and more.

If you're looking for an overnight stop, you might try the **Skamania Lodge,** P.O. Box 189, Stevenson, WA 98648 (☎ **800/221-7117** or 509/427-7700). Its comfortable and moderately priced rooms have river and forest views, and the luxurious lodge/conference center is full of amenities.

☕ **TAKE A BREAK**  The restaurant at **Skamania Lodge** (☎ **509/427-7700**), on the hillside above the Interpretive Center, overlooks a field of wildflowers and the Columbia River, with the cliffs of Oregon rising beyond. Excellent Northwest cuisine, focusing on fresh local ingredients and prepared in an open kitchen, is featured. Dinner entrees range from $12 to $20.

From Stevenson, head west on Wash. 14, driving about 45 miles past Beacon Rock, where a trail winds up to the summit of this 800-foot-high volcanic remnant; you'll be rewarded with stunning views up and down the river. **Beacon Rock State Park** has a picnic area and playground.

Keep going on Wash. 14 to:

**8.** **Vancouver,** on the Washington side of the river opposite Portland. Turn right on Grand Boulevard, go about 1 mile to 5th Street, and turn left. Continue on 5th Street to **Fort Vancouver National Historic Site,** 1501 E. Evergreen Blvd. This was the headquarters for the Hudson's Bay Company trading post in the mid-1800s. You can visit the partially reconstructed fort and watch volunteers demonstrate frontier skills. A visitor center and museum stand on the hill above the fort.

Across the road is **Officers' Row,** the oldest residential neighborhood in the Northwest. This group of 21 gracious Queen Anne–style homes once housed the likes of Ulysses S. Grant; now most of them have been turned into condos or office buildings. Top-quality craft items are sold in the **Folk Art Center** in the Grant House.

Other points of interest in Vancouver are the **Pearson Air Museum,** 1105 E. 5th St.; **Covington House,** 4208 Main St. (one of the oldest remaining log cabins in the area); **Esther Short Park,** 8th and Esther streets (Washington's first public square); and **Columbia Arts Center,** 400 W. Evergreen Blvd. The Arts Center houses most of the city's visual and performing arts organizations and has a continuing schedule of art exhibits, plays, and concerts.

To return to the starting point of the tour, it's a direct route across the Columbia River on I-5 from Vancouver to Portland.

☕ **TAKE A BREAK**  **Sheldon's Cafe,** 1101 Officers' Row (☎ **360/ 699-1213**), offers light but filling lunch fare from Tuesday to Friday. Specialties include unusual sandwiches such as fried eggplant and grilled chicken-apple sausage. Several tables on the veranda and garden patio are available in warm weather. Lunch entrees are $4 to $7.

## DRIVING TOUR
# The Oregon Coast

**Start:** Lincoln City
**Finish:** Coos Bay
**Distance:** 170 miles
**Time:** 2–3 days
**Highlights:** Spectacular stretch of the Pacific Coast; wide, sandy beaches; short hikes; Oregon Coast Aquarium; wildlife sanctuaries and sea lion viewing; fresh seafood restaurants; historic lighthouses; scenic fishing villages; microbreweries

Hugging the rustic Oregon coastline, scenic U.S. 101 covers some of the most diverse and memorable terrain along the West Coast. The Coast Range Mountains to the east separate small, oceanside fishing towns from the interior of Oregon, creating an out-of-the-way but friendly atmosphere. State parks offer access to wide, sandy beaches and unlimited strolling aside the crashing surf, while rocky beaches expose some of the best tide pools found anywhere. Almost all accommodations, restaurants, and scenic attractions are on, or adjacent to, U.S. 101, and all streets and roads lead back to the highway, creating little chance for getting lost and ample opportunities for relaxed wandering.

Lincoln City is approximately 90 miles from Portland. From the center of Portland, take I-5 or Ore. 99W (follow the signs to Tigard). Ore. 99W becomes Ore. 18, which will take you all the way to U.S. 101 and:

**1.** **Lincoln City,** one of the larger towns on the Oregon Coast and the area's hub for dining, recreation, overnight accommodations, and shoreline activities. During July and August, motels and hotels can fill up and eateries can be crowded. The town's **visitor center,** U.S. 101 and SW 8th Street (☎ **541/994-8378**), is a good stop on your way out of town to pick up information about places to see and events to attend, particularly during the summer months. Seven miles south of Lincoln City is **Siletz Bay** (suh-LETS), a beautiful and protected estuary that offers the tour's first wildlife views.

☕ **TAKE A BREAK** Perhaps the best restaurant on the coast, the **Bay House,** just south of Lincoln City at 5911 SW U.S. 101 (☎ **541/996-3222**), is sophisticated and casual at the same time. Carefully prepared seafood and pastas provide a wonderful introduction to Northwest cuisine. Picture windows provide views of the wildlife in Siletz Bay, and the wine list is excellent. Entrees range from $13 to $25.

Continuing approximately 14 miles south on U.S. 101 you will find the small town of:

**2.** **Depoe Bay,** where a tiny but beautiful harbor protects a small fleet of boats and the road winds along bluffs that drop to the Pacific below. Two miles south of town is a short but worthwhile side trip, called the **Otter Crest Loop** (look for the highway signs). An Oregon State Park lookout at **Cape Foulweather** offers stunning coastal vistas and the chance to see blue whales during their migration. The **Lookout Gift Shop** sells knickknacks and dispenses tourist information at 500 feet above the crashing surf; coin-operated binoculars are available.

Another natural attraction that shouldn't be missed is at the southern end of the Otter Crest Loop where it rejoins U.S. 101. **Devils Punchbowl State Park** has a marine garden ocean-shore preserve that can be reached by taking the short path from the parking lot. The preserve allows you to walk among the intertidal zone and see (depending on the tide) purple shore crabs, common sea stars, red sea cucumbers, and gooseneck barnacles, as well as peregrine falcons, western gulls, and black oyster catchers. The main attraction at the park is Devils Punchbowl, a large hole formed in the seaside rock that fills with churning, foaming water at high tide.

About 20 miles south of Depoe Bay on U.S. 101, you will discover a clearly marked turnoff to the **Yaquina Head Outstanding Natural Area** and its post–Civil War lighthouse. The lighthouse has been carefully restored and maintained, and tours are available. The area, a breeding ground for seabirds, offers excellent bird-watching (especially during the spring and summer months) and outstanding views. The turnoff is just north of:

3. **Newport,** whose historic waterfront district along Bay Boulevard, off U.S. 101, is lined with shops and restaurants, side-by-side with canneries and working fishing boats. Many of the attractions on Bay Boulevard can be somewhat touristy, but worth noting is the **Wood Gallery,** 818 SW Bay Blvd. (☎ **541/265-6843**), which displays sculpture, furniture, musical instruments, and jewelry—all made from wood—as well as paintings and metal sculptures. Many local artists are represented in the store's collection. Just south of the impressive bridge that takes U.S. 101 across Yaquina Bay you will find the **Mark O. Hatfield Marine Science Center,** operated by Oregon State University, offering an excellent introduction to the sea's geology, ecology, and wildlife; there's even a tank where kids can touch a sampling of the slithering, swimming, and sticky marine life of the region.

Following a quarter-mile drive back toward U.S. 101, you will find the more high-tech (and more crowded, particularly in the summer) **Oregon Coast Aquarium** (☎ **541/867-3474**). This well-designed facility includes a small theater showing a film on whale migration, a display on the ecology of wetlands, a sandy beach with a wave machine, and a touch tank for kids. On the way back to U.S. 101, you will also pass the **Rogue Ale Brewery Tasting Room,** which dispenses a different kind of introduction to the area. The brewery has become an institution along Oregon's central coast, with its line of imaginatively named microbrews. The tasting room gives visitors a chance to sample standard brews and seasonal specialties.

Continue south on the coast highway until you reach:

4. **Waldport,** where a small, unassuming building at the foot of the Alsea Bay Bridge, just as you enter town, is the **Alsea Bay Bridge Interpretive Center.** This delightful center offers a history of the area from its settlement by Native Americans to the arrival of white settlers and the establishment of sawmills, canneries, fishing fleets, rail lines, and bridges. Here, you can get an idea of the effort that went into creating the roadway that has carried you on your travels.

Southbound again, you will enter:

5. **Yachats** (pronounced YAH-hots), a town that calls itself the Gem of the Oregon Coast. Yachats is indeed a fine place to behold—small but sophisticated, with a great little cove and adjoining beaches. Park your car anywhere; you can walk the length of town in a matter of minutes. Plan to stop in at **Clark's Market,** in the center of the 3-block business district on U.S. 101, to pick up picnic supplies and other necessities. While you are there, you can drop in at the **tourist information center** next door, where a helpful staffer is on hand to answer questions or dispense information.

One of the best spots to enjoy a picnic lunch is **Yachats State Park,** 2 blocks toward the sea on Ocean View. You can picnic on the wide lawn overlooking the inlet, or take the stairs to the rocky shoreline and its impressive collection of

# Driving Tour: The Oregon Coast

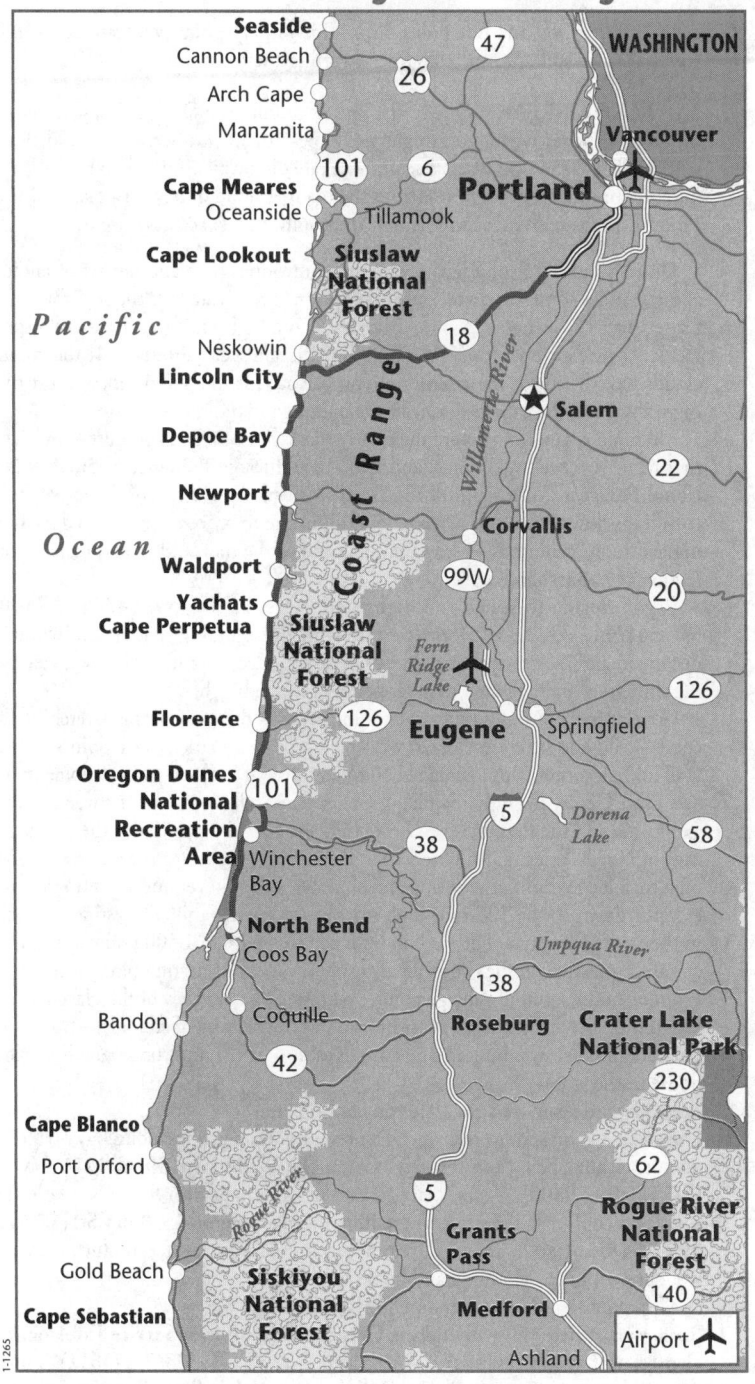

beached driftwood and tide pools. From this vantage point, you can see the hills above Yachats spill into the coastline, dwarfing the town.

☕ **TAKE A BREAK** One of the joys of driving the Oregon Coast is finding pleasant surprises where you might not expect them. **La Serre,** 2nd and Beach streets (☎ **541/547-3420**), is one of those rare discoveries. A modern but welcoming interior offers a pleasant rest from the road. Seafood dishes are a mainstay, but carefully prepared meats complement the menu. Entrees cost $11 to $21.

Driving south out of Yachats, you are confronted with another set of choices about 2 miles south of town. Your first option is to turn left at the sign for:

6. **Cape Perpetua,** where a 1-mile drive leads to a high bluff overlook and a spectacular, hawk's-eye view of the mountain, sea, and coastal terrain. If the coastal clouds have lifted for the afternoon, you can see for miles and miles. Short hiking trails along the cape begin from the parking lot and the overlook.

Alternately, you can explore the clearly marked 19-mile, 45-minute **loop drive** that takes you back to Yachats and U.S. 101, through the heart of **Suislaw National Forest,** or turn right off the Devil's Churn. At one end of the lot, a paved path leads down the bluff, where a long slit in the rocky coast has created a whirling, frothing "cauldron" of seawater. The end of the trail lands you on a table-flat section of rocky shoreline.

If you decide to spend the night here, **Oregon House,** 94288 U.S. 101 (☎ **541/547-3329**), is a former estate with five buildings and 10 individually decorated and moderately priced units. The secluded grounds offer great views of the shoreline, and a lighted path leads down to the beach.

Continuing south, you will encounter perhaps the most scenic stretch of the coast—wild and little-developed, with plenty of well-marked vista points to take it all in. In a turnout approximately 10 miles south of Yachats, you will come upon:

7. **Sea Lion Caves,** the only mainland rookery for Steller's sea cow between central California and the Bering Sea (☎ **541/547-3111**). Signs claim it's the largest sea cave in North America. An observation deck allows you to see the animals outside on a rock ledge during the spring and summer, but it's even more fun to take the elevator down to the 125-foot-high sea cave to see the animals nesting on rocks in the cavernous room. The sea lion bulls can weigh up to 1,500 pounds, and they cut an impressive profile. You can also spot a variety of nesting birds in the cave. From one underground vantage point, you can get a clear view of the Haceta Head Lighthouse perched on a sea-coast promontory. The Spanish colonial–style Coast Guard lighthouse was built in 1894 and is said to be the most photographed lighthouse in the world.

Southward again on U.S. 101, you continue to:

8. **Florence,** a good spot to recharge. The restaurants and shops along Bay Street are quaint without being too touristy. **Catch the Wind Kite Shop,** 1251 Bay St. (☎ **541/997-9500**), a good place to find just the right flyer for a sea breeze and a wide beach. Down the street, **Incredible Edible Oregon,** 1350 Bay St. (☎ **541/997-7018**), offers made-in-Oregon products and produce including wine, woodcrafted items, clothing, and books.

Keep going south 21 miles on U.S. 101 to:

9. **Reedsport,** where you will find the **Oregon Dunes Forest Service Information Center,** at the intersection of U.S. 101 and Ore. 38 (☎ **503/271-3611**). This is the gateway to the **Oregon Dunes National Recreation Area.** The center features interpretive exhibits and dispenses information about dune-buggy rides, camping,

beachcombing, fishing, and hikes in the area as well as interpretive programs offered by the Forest Service.

In addition, there are great opportunities for bird-watching a few miles east on Ore. 38, which follows the Umpqua River, and just off U.S. 101 you find yourself in a beautiful river valley, with sheer cliffs rising on the other side of the Umpqua. Great blue herons, egrets, ospreys, and stately elk make their home in this area. (Clearly marked wildlife viewing areas with information boards dispense wildlife facts and figures.) Fishermen will find shad, smallmouth bass, steelhead, and coho and chinook salmon in the Umpqua River.

A wonderful place to stay is the **Salbasgeon Inn,** situated 7 miles east on Ore. 38 (☎ **541/271-4831**). The moderately priced motel is on the banks of the river and is a relaxing spot for bird-watching, fishing, or just watching the river flow outside your window.

As you continue south from Reedsport, U.S. 101 leaves the coast to swing around the Oregon Dunes National Recreation Area, so the drive is less scenic along the stretch. About 27 miles south of Reedsport is the town of:

**10. North Bend,** where there's a **visitor center** at 1380 Sherman Ave. (☎ **541/756-4613**). Stop there for directions to the nearby **Coos County Historical Museum** or to find out where the best antique stores are in the business district, which has retained its small-town character.

Look for the clearly marked signs on Virginia Street and U.S. 101 in North Bend and follow the Cape Arago Hwy. to Charleston Harbor. Six miles past Charleston Harbor, along a winding country road, you'll reach **Cape Arago State Park,** which has a protected beach for swimming (a rarity on the rugged coastline), views of the Cape Arago Lighthouse, a beautiful botanical garden, scenic picnic areas, and short hiking paths. On the horseshoe-shaped reef just offshore, you can see a sea lion breeding and resting ground. The constant barking of the sea lions adds a natural "soundtrack" to the park.

From the park follow the Cape Arago Hwy. back to U.S. 101 and then south a few miles into:

**11. Coos Bay,** a decades-old working timber and wood town. Drop in the **Bay Area Visitor Center,** Commercial Street and U.S. 101 (☎ **541/269-0215**), and pick up a walking-tour map with numbered sites including the Elk's Temple, the Methodist Hospital, several Victorian homes, and the Tioga and Chandler hotels. The boardwalk in front of the center also has interpretive exhibits.

☕ **TAKE A BREAK**    A Coos Bay culinary favorite, **Kum Yon's,** 835 S. Broadway (☎ **541/269-2662**), is always bustling. The eclectic marriage of Chinese, Japanese, and American cuisine is pulled off admirably and offers a nice change from the standard seafood served at many restaurants along the coast. Entree prices range from $7 to $14.

## DRIVING TOUR
## Montana's Glacier Country

**Start:** Missoula
**Finish:** Glacier National Park
**Distance:** Approximately 280 miles
**Time:** 2–3 days
**Highlights:** Wildlife viewing opportunities—from waterfowl and raptors to big game animals; glacial lake valley and majestic mountains; Native American and early pioneer

heritage sites and museums; lakeside communities and recreation; historic railroad hotels

Montana's name is derived from a Spanish word meaning "mountainous region"—a very appropriate moniker considering the numerous mountain ranges within view of this driving tour around the northwestern part of the state. The route will lead you through the pastoral landscapes of Mission and Flathead Lake Valleys and into the snowcapped mountains forming the Continental Divide, with the showcase being the Warton/Glacier International Peace Park. A large part of the valley lands and mountains are home to the Confederated Salish and Kootenai tribes and the Blackfeet Nation. A multitude of recreational opportunities is available on the tribal lands (tribal recreation permits are required) and in the bordering state and national forests. Nearby Flathead Lake, the largest body of fresh water west of the Mississippi River, offers all forms of water sports and recreation.

The tour follows one of the routes of the Trail of the Great Bear, a scenic corridor linking America's first national park (Yellowstone) to the world's first international peace park (Waterton/Glacier) and to Canada's first national park (Banff). The region's mountainous terrain is still home to the grizzly bear, the trail's symbol. It is the spirit of this great bear that prevails in the wild lands along the corridor.

You may not spot a grizzly, but you are likely to see hundreds of other wildlife species. The large stick nests of bald eagles and osprey are commonly sighted on the tops of utility poles and ponderosa pine trees, while the nests of great blue heron can be spotted in cottonwood trees. Raptors perch on fence posts, mountain bluebird boxes form "bluebird trails" along fence rows, and the melodious song of the state bird—the distinctively marked western meadowlark—is heard throughout the region. (Bird and flower identification field guides will enhance your viewing and photographing pleasure.) Soft evening breezes often carry the coyote's tune and the gray wolf's howl.

I-90 gives easy access to the first stop:

1. **Missoula,** the largest city in western Montana and the educational, recreational, and entertainment hub of the region. The city is home to the University of Montana, which offers a wide range of sporting events and theatrical performances.

   Missoula has Holiday Inn, Best Western, Days Inn, Econo Lodge, and Roadway Inn chain motels, so you can easily overnight here before launching on the tour.

   From Missoula, take exit 96 off I-90 and follow U.S. 93 north. You will travel through a canyon and over a low-elevation pass, forested on both sides with thick stands of evergreens. This area is the last remaining natural wildlife corridor for grizzlies, wolves, and other wildlife species. The animals use the corridor to travel between the high-elevation mountain habitats located on the west and east sides of U.S. 93.

   As you drive north through the small town of Ravalli, you'll see a large tree-covered hill directly in front of you; this is your next stop. Drive 6 miles west of Ravalli on Mont. 200 to its junction with Mont. 212. Then follow Mont. 212 north for 5 miles to the entrance of:

2. **The National Bison Range,** a wildlife refuge for a free-roaming herd of 300–500 American bison. Numerous other big game animals (such as deer and elk) and large populations of songbirds and raptors also inhabit the refuge, which was established in 1908 when the bison was nearly extinct. The refuge has a **visitor center** (☎ 406/644-2211) with exhibits and displays, two scenic drives, a nature trail and picnic area (both accessible for guests with disabilities), and a bison paddock for close-up viewing and photos. The most scenic and interesting option is the

# Driving Tour: Montana's Glacier Country

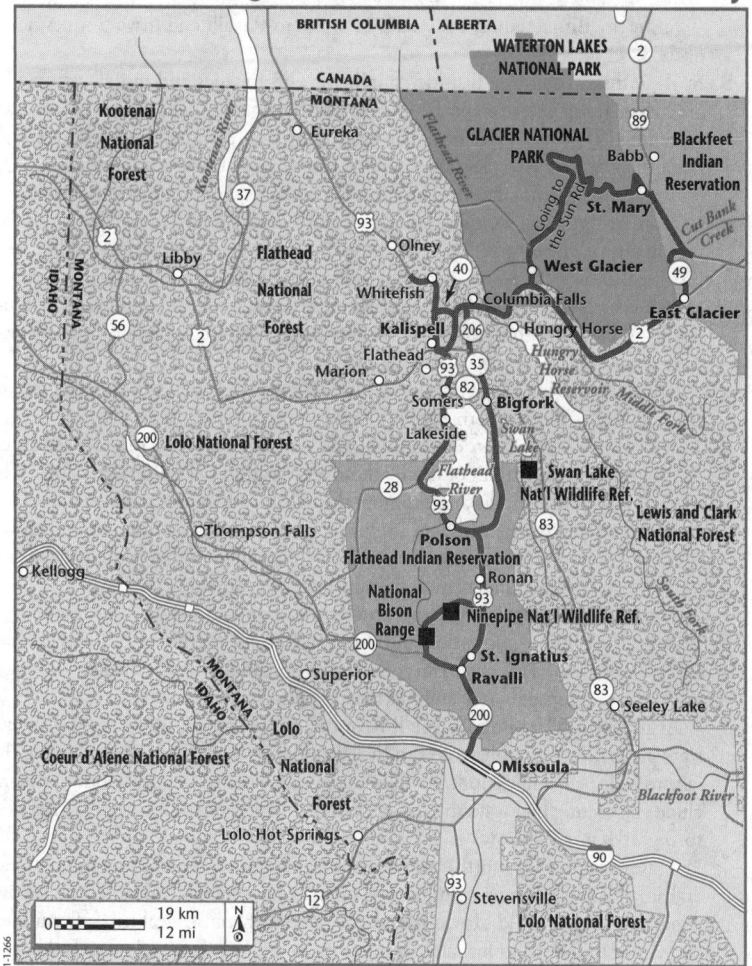

19-mile, self-guided **Red Sleep Mountain Drive.** It climbs 2,000 feet through four types of habitat (grassland, riparian, wetland, and mountain forest) on a winding, narrow gravel road with tight turns, no guard rails, and a long, steep downgrade. (Trailers and towed units are not allowed on the mountain drive; bicycles and motorcycles are prohibited on the driving loops.)

The best time to visit the refuge is early morning and late evening, when the animals are most likely to be moving around and feeding. Bring binoculars and a telephoto lens for your camera. The entry fee is $4 per car (during the dry summer months when the Red Sleep Mountain Drive is open). The visitor center is open 8am–4:30pm daily. The refuge itself is open dawn to dusk.

☕ **TAKE A BREAK**   You can sample a low-fat, low-cholesterol buffalo burger at the **Burger "B"** (☎ 406/644-2385) in Moises, on Mont. 212 near the entrance to the Bison Range. It offers walk-up window service only and has a couple of picnic tables. Most travelers prefer to take their burgers and beverages to the refuge's shaded picnic area. Lunch items cost $2–$5. Open daily 11:30am–7:30pm.

From the Bison Range, backtrack 11 miles to Ravalli and drive 5 miles north on U.S. 93 to:

3. **St. Ignatius Mission,** a historic church with 58 frescoes and murals painted by an Italian Jesuit priest/cook, Brother Joseph Carignano, who had no formal art schooling (☎ 406/745-2768). The beautifully colored murals tell various stories from the Old and New Testaments. The mission and town was founded in 1854 by Jesuit missionaries. Parking for large RV units; wheelchair access available.

From St. Ignatius, continue your drive north on U.S. 93. The majestic mission mountains will be on your right (to the east). There are several scenic, wildlife, and historical interpretive sites along the side of the highway. The route also passes through the **Ninepipe Wildlife Management Area,** a collection of glacial pothole lakes and ponds surrounded by native grassland. The refuge is home to a large variety of wildlife, waterfowl, and songbirds.

Continue driving north on U.S. 93 for 19 miles to Pablo. On the west side of the highway at the northern edge of Pablo is:

4. **The People's Center,** an educational and cultural center of the Confederated Salish and Kootenai tribes of the Flathead Reservation (☎ 406/675-2700). The center's goal is to preserve and promote the Salish and Kootenai cultures. Guided tours are offered daily from 9am to 9pm during the peak tourist season. Admission is $2 for adults, $1 for seniors, and $5 for families. Pablo is the tribal headquarters, so tribal land recreation permits may be acquired here.

From the People's Center, drive 7 miles north on U.S. 93 to:

5. **Polson,** the outdoor recreation and vacation hub for the south end of **Flathead Lake.** Water sports are the main focus at the 23-mile-long by 15-mile-wide lake, but the area offers golf and summer theater performances as well.

At milepost 59 at Polson, you'll have two route choices. Both pass by several state parks offering public access to the lake. U.S. 93 follows the west shore of the lake to Kalispell, while Mont. 35 follows the east shore to Bigfork. Both routes include connecting highways to Glacier National Park. For the east shore drive, skip to Bigfork (stop 7, below).

Travelers going up (north) the west side of Flathead Lake will pass through several small lakeside towns with marinas offering boat rentals. According to Native American legend, **Wild Horse Island** got its name because local tribes swam their horses out to the island for safekeeping from raiding parties. Today, several horses are allowed to roam the island as a reminder of its heritage. The island, now managed by the state as a day-use park, is a popular picnicking, hiking, and wildlife-viewing location. A large population of deer and bighorn sheep—popular photo subjects—make their home here.

For overnight accommodations, **KwaTaqNuk Resort** (☎ 800/882-6363 or 406/883-3636) is operated by the local Salish and Kootenai tribes. Also on the lake, **Marina Kay Resort** (☎ 800/433-6516 or 406/837-5861) caters to families. Less expensive are the **Port Polson Inn** (☎ 800/654-0682 or 406/883-5385), with lake and mountain views, and the budget-priced **Timbers Motel** (☎ 800/821-4546 or 406/837-6200).

Continue driving north on U.S. 93. In Dayton, watch for the **Mission Mountain Winery** (☎ 406/849-5524) on the east side of the highway. Montana's only winery, Mission Mountain offers complimentary tastings of its award-winning varietals. Tastings and tours are available May–Oct, daily 10am–5pm.

From the winery, drive 27 miles north on U.S. 93 to:

6. **Kalispell,** the northern gateway to Flathead Valley and the surrounding mountains. A popular shopping, dining, and lodging stop, Kalispell makes a good

overnight stop. The modern, full-service **Cavanaugh's at Kalispell Center,** 20 N. Main St. (☎ **800/843-4667** or 406/752-6660), and the historic **Kalispell Grand Hotel,** 8 First St. W. (☎ **800/858-7422** or 406/755-8100), are good choices for downtown lodging close to specialty stores and restaurants. You can also make a 20-mile trip to **Big Mountain Ski and Summer Resort** (☎ **800/858-5439** or 406/862-2918), north of Whitefish. It is noted for its views of Glacier National Park, summer festivals, alpine nature trails, guided trail rides and dinners, and mountain biking (rentals available). Lodging options on the mountain range from family budget accommodations (Alpinglow Inn) to more luxurious accommodations (Kandahar Lodge) offering a quiet romantic ambience.

If you are heading directly to Glacier National Park, follow U.S. 2 from Kalispell for 32 miles to West Glacier (stop 8).

**7.** **Bigfork** is the summer playground for the north end of Flathead Lake. The drive along the eastern shoreline from Polson to Bigfork on Mont. 35 passes through fruit orchards and small lakeside communities. Roadside stands with seasonal fresh fruit, berries, and farm produce dot the scenic route. Bigfork has the renowned Bigfork Summer Playhouse. You can stay here at **Eagle Bend Golf and Yacht Community** (☎ **800/255-5641** or 406/837-7333), a full-service golf and boating resort beside the Flathead River. You can engage in horse and ranching activities at **Flathead Lake Lodge** (☎ **406/837-4391**), a dude ranch on the north end of the lake. The town offers easy access to mountain getaways.

From Bigfork, follow the combination of Mont. 35 and Mont. 206 north for 22 miles to Columbia Falls, and then follow U.S. 2 north for 15 miles to:

**8.** **West Glacier,** the west entrance to **Glacier National Park** (see section 4, below). The West Glacier area is a good place to make some outdoor adventure plans. Llama trekking into national forest lands and fishing float trips and whitewater rafting adventures on designated branches of the Flathead River are very popular. Several companies, situated along both sides of U.S. 2, offer helicopter sightseeing flights over Glacier National Park; the views are breathtaking. For information on these and other activities, call **Glacier Country** (☎ **800/338-5072**) and ask for a free Glacier country guide.

The national park entrance kiosk is about 1 mile north off U.S. 2, where you can pick up the designated 141-mile Glacier Park driving loop. The first building complex you come to is:

**9.** **Apgar Village,** about 1 mile from the kiosk, where a visitor center provides information on narrated lake cruises, driving tours aboard historic red jammer buses, guided trail rides, and educational field trips.

From Apgar Village, follow the **Going-to-the-Sun Road,** a 50-mile-long highway that bisects the park. Completed in 1932 and listed on the National Register of Historic Places, this narrow and winding road is considered a great feat of engineering because of the steep and rocky terrain. Some portions have vehicle size limitations and bicycling restrictions. (The road is closed by snow Oct–June.)

☕ **TAKE A BREAK** The **Cedar Dining Room** (☎ **406/888-5431**) is located in the historic Lake McDonald Lodge on the northeastern shore of Lake McDonald. Even if you aren't hungry, stop and marvel at the interior cedar-log architecture of the lobby. Lunch specials cost under $7, while dinner entrees are $11 to $18.

Follow the serpentine road through the western side of the park up to the **Logan Pass Visitor Center,** taking time to stop at the scenic overlooks. The road crosses the Continental Divide at Logan Pass (at an elevation of 6,648 feet). Continuing down the east side, stop to view the roadside waterfalls, flora and fauna, and regal mountains. (You'll know when wildlife is on or near the road because of the traffic jams.) The road will take you to:

**10. St. Mary,** a small tourist town located just outside the park's main east entrance. It is a popular stop for food, fuel, and shopping before heading into the remote east-side locations of the park.

From St. Mary, you can drive 33 miles north on U.S. 89, Mont. 17, and Canada 6 to reach the Waterton entrance of the international peace park. The U.S.–Canada border is located 17 miles north of St. Mary. Be sure to carry proof of citizenship (passport, birth certificate, voter's registration card). A state driver's license is not proof of U.S. citizenship.

To complete the Glacier National Park loop, leave St. Mary and drive 31 miles south on U.S. 89 and Mont. 49 to:

**11. East Glacier Park,** a small town located outside the park's boundary. As an Amtrak stop, the town continues to serve rail travelers arriving to see the park.

From East Glacier Park, follow U.S. 2 for a 56-mile drive back to West Glacier via the 5,216-foot Marias Pass at the Continental Divide. U.S. 2 loops around the southern boundary of the park. There are several roadside turnoffs for wildlife viewing; the most popular is **Goat Lick** (near milepost 189), a natural mineral salt lick along the Middle Fork of the Flathead River that attracts mountain goats.

☕ **TAKE A BREAK**   The **Steak & Rib House** in the grand, historic Glacier Park Lodge (☎ 406/226-9311) is a place to stop for lunch or dinner. Sixty immense ponderosa logs support the structure of the huge lobby, which is worthy of a photo stop and tour even if you are not hungry.

Continue west on U.S. 2 for about 2 miles to the Essex turnoff (near milepost 180) to reach the:

**12. Izaak Walton Inn,** on U.S. 2 (☎ 406/888-5700), a historic railroad hotel currently served by Amtrak. The inn is about a half-mile south of the highway. Built in 1939 by the Great Northern Railroad and filled with railroad memorabilia, the Izaak Walton is a popular vacation destination for rail fans. Besides the hotel rooms, guests can stay in refurbished cabooses. In the winter, the inn is a highly rated cross-country ski destination; summer guests can go mountain biking, horseback riding, hiking, and wildlife-watching. The appropriately decorated Dining Car restaurant offers breakfast, lunch, and dinner.

From Izaak Walton Inn, drive 27 miles west on U.S. 2 to West Glacier to complete the Glacier Park loop.

# 1  Seattle

When Seattle was voted "America's most livable city" a few years ago, Californians by the drove picked up stakes and relocated here. Another influx of refugees arrived when the rock-music industry decided that Seattle's guitar-driven grunge rock would be the next sound to hit it big, and America's guitar-toting youth headed for the city by the sound (Puget Sound, that is) with dreams of Nirvana dancing in their heads.

Although it has brought fine restaurants, a new art museum, rock-music fame, and national recognition of the city's arts scene, Seattle's popularity and rapid growth has had its price. The streets and highways are unable to handle the increased traffic

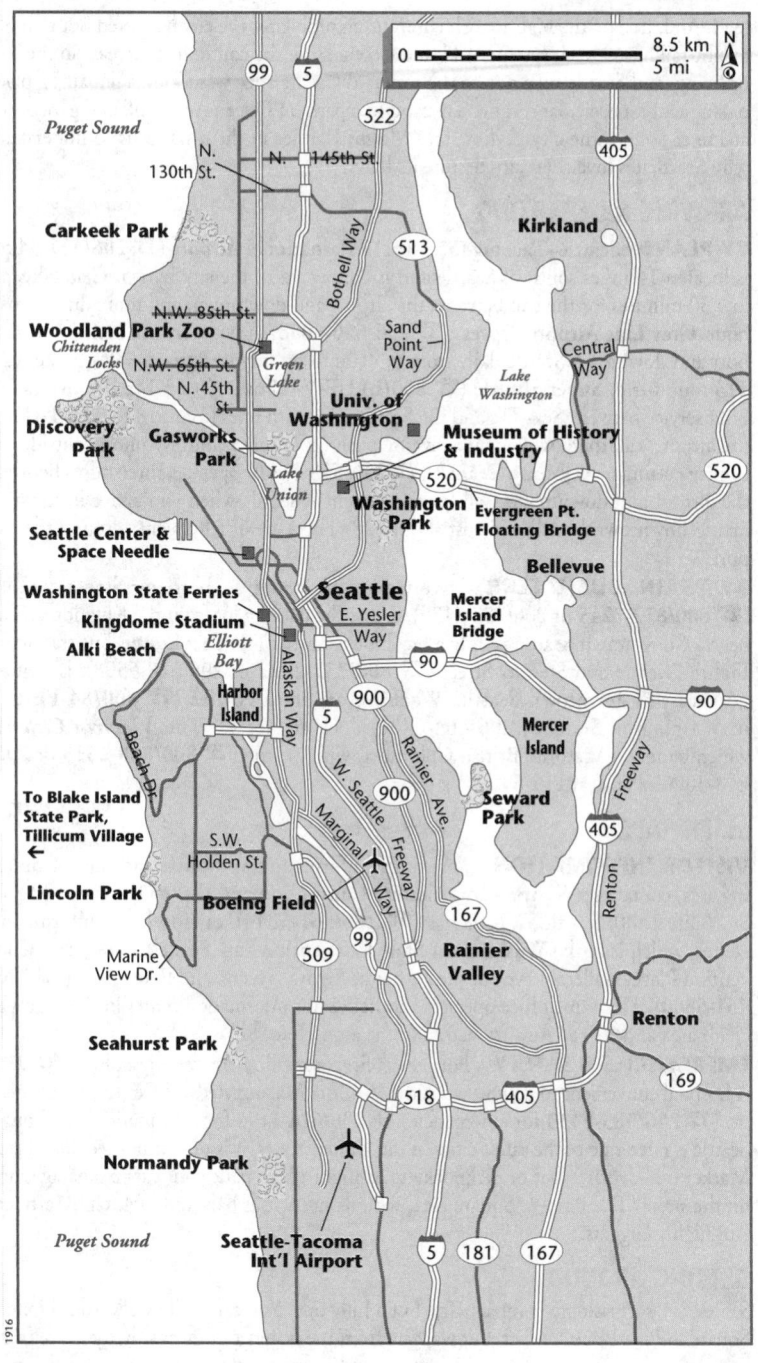

# Greater Seattle

0   8.5 km
    5 mi

N

*Puget Sound*

99  5

522

405

N. 130th St.   N. 145th St.

**Carkeek Park**

Bothell Way

513

**Kirkland**

N.W. 85th St.

Sand Point Way

Central Way

**Woodland Park Zoo**

*Chittenden Locks*

N.W. 65th St.   *Green Lake*

N. 45th St.

**Univ. of Washington**

*Lake Washington*

**Discovery Park**

**Gasworks Park**

**Museum of History & Industry**

*Lake Union*

520

520

**Washington Park**

Evergreen Pt. Floating Bridge

**Seattle Center & Space Needle**

**Bellevue**

**Washington State Ferries**

**Seattle**

E. Yesler Way

**Mercer Island Bridge**

**Kingdome Stadium**

*Elliott Bay*

90

**Alki Beach**

Alaskan Way

Harbor Island

5

900

90

**To Blake Island State Park, Tillicum Village**
←

*Beach Dr.*

W. Seattle Freeway

900

Rainier Ave

**Mercer Island**

405

Renton Freeway

S.W. Holden St.

W. Marginal Way

**Seward Park**

**Lincoln Park**

*Marine View Dr.*

**Boeing Field**

167

509

99

**Rainier Valley**

**Renton**

169

**Seahurst Park**

518   405

**Normandy Park**

*Puget Sound*

**Seattle-Tacoma Int'l Airport**

5   181   167

807

load. And, despite the nightmarish commuting problems, the city has voted not to build a light-rail mass transit system. Add to the congestion the continuing increase in the cost of living, and Seattle may not be the Emerald City it once was. Still, it remains a place of singularly spectacular setting. To stand in a park on Queen Anne Hill and gaze down at Puget Sound, the city skyline, and Mount Rainier in the distance is to understand why Seattleites love their city despite its flaws.

## ARRIVING & DEPARTING

**BY PLANE**    Seattle–Tacoma (Sea–Tac) International Airport (☎ 206/431-4444) is located 14 miles south of Seattle and is connected to the city by I-5. Generally, allow 30 minutes for the trip between the airport and downtown, and more during rush hour. **Gray Line Airport Express** (☎ 206/626-6088) provides service between the airport and downtown Seattle daily from 5:30am to midnight. Rates are $7.50 one-way, $13 round-trip. **Super Shuttle** (☎ 800/BLUE-VAN or 206/622-1424) provides 24-hour service between Sea–Tac and the Seattle area, with rates from $18 to $23. To leave the airport, call them when you arrive by pushing **48** on a courtesy phone outside the baggage claim areas. **Metro Transit** (☎ 206/553-3000) operates three buses between the airport and downtown. Call for the current schedule when you arrive in town. A taxi to downtown Seattle will cost about $28. There are usually plenty around the airport.

**BY TRAIN, BUS & FERRY**    Amtrak trains arrive at the **King Street Station** (☎ 800/872-7245 or 206/382-4125), across the parking lot from the Kingdome. The heart of downtown Seattle is only a few blocks north. The **Greyhound** bus station, at Eighth Avenue and Stewart Street (☎ 800/231-2222 or 206/628-5508), is slightly northeast of downtown Seattle. **Washington State Ferries** (☎ 800/84-FERRY in Washington State, or 206/464-6400) dock at Pier 52. The *Victoria Clipper,* which connects Victoria, British Columbia, with Seattle (☎ 800/888-2535 or 206/448-5000), docks at Pier 69.

## ESSENTIALS

**VISITOR INFORMATION**    For tourist information on Seattle and the surrounding area, contact the **Seattle–King County Convention and Visitor Bureau,** 520 Pike St., Suite 1300, Seattle, WA 98101 (☎ 206/461-5840), or stop by its information center, which is at the **Washington State Convention and Trade Center,** 800 Convention Place, Galleria Level, at the corner of Eighth Avenue and Pike Street (☎ 206/461-5840). This same office operates another visitor information center in the baggage-claim area at Sea–Tac Airport, across from carousel no. 8.

**EMERGENCIES & SAFETY**    For police, fire, or medical emergencies, phone ☎ 911. A hospital convenient to downtown is the **Virginia Mason Medical Center,** 925 Seneca St. (☎ 206/583-6433 for emergencies, or 206/624-1144 for information). Although Seattle is rated one of the safest cities in the United States, it is not crime-free. Pike Place Market is a favorite spot of pickpockets. At night try to park your car in a garage, not on the street. The Pioneer Square area, with its numerous bars and nightclubs, attracts late-night muggers.

## GETTING AROUND

Seattle is a surprisingly compact city, but a hilly one. You can easily walk from Pioneer Square to Pike Place Market, but walking from the waterfront means that you are tackling a steep hill. Traffic congestion is severe and streets are almost all one-way. On-street parking is extremely limited and very expensive. Downtown parking decks (either above or below ground) charge from $8 to $16 per day. You'll save money by parking up toward the Space Needle, where parking lots charge around $7 per day, and taking the monorail into downtown.

**BY BUS, MONORAIL & STREETCAR**   The **Metro bus** (☎ 206/553-3000 for information) is free between 6am and 7pm in the **Ride Free Area** between Alaskan Way in the west, Sixth Avenue in the east, Battery Street in the north, and South Jackson Street in the south. Within this area are many of Seattle's most popular attractions. Outside the Ride Free Area, fares range from 85¢ to $1.60, depending on the distance and time of day. Exact change is required.

Seattle's monorail, leaving every 15 minutes daily, connects Westlake Center, Fifth Avenue, and Pine Street with Seattle Center and it covers the 1.2 miles in 90 seconds. The one-way fare is $1 for adults, 75¢ for children 5–12, and 50¢ for seniors and the disabled.

Old-fashioned streetcars run along the waterfront from Pier 70 to the corner of Fifth Avenue South and South Jackson Street on the edge of the International District. The trolley operates Monday to Friday from around 7am to around 6:30pm, departing every 20–30 minutes; weekends and holidays from just after 10am to almost 7pm, departing about every 20 minutes. One-way fare is 85¢ during off-peak hours and $1.10 during peak hours. Metrobus transfers are available, and streetcars are wheelchair accessible.

**BY TAXI**   Taxis can be difficult to hail on the street in Seattle, so it's best to call or wait at the taxi stands at the major hotels. **Yellow Cab** (☎ 206/622-6500) and **Farwest Taxi** (☎ 206/622-1717) charge $1.80 for flag drop and $1.80 per mile after that. **Graytop Cab** (☎ 206/282-8222) charges $1.20 for the flag drop and $1.40 per mile.

**BY FERRY**   The Washington State Ferries system (☎ 800/84-FERRY in Washington, or 206/464-6400) connects Seattle with Bainbridge Island, Vashon Island, Bremerton, and Southworth. At press time, fares from Seattle to Bremerton or Bainbridge Island were $5.90 one-way for a car and driver, $3.50 for passengers, $1.75 for children and seniors. Fares for passengers are collected on westbound journeys only, though cars and drivers must pay in both directions.

## WHAT TO SEE & DO

Seattle's downtown area and main business district is characterized by high-rise office buildings and steep streets, and also offers the city's greatest diversity of retail shops. The International District is home to the city's Asian population. Bordering it is the Pioneer Square Historic District, noted for its restored old buildings full of shops, galleries, restaurants, and bars. Capitol Hill, Seattle's cutting-edge shopping district and gay community, is centered along Broadway near Volunteer Park. The "U" District, or University District, surrounds the University of Washington in the northeast section of the city and provides all the amenities of a college neighborhood.

**ESCORTED TOURS**   Seattle's most popular guided walking excursion is the **Underground Tour,** 610 First Ave. (☎ 206/682-4646), offering a seamier side of city history and humor, below the Pioneer Square area where vestiges of businesses built before the great 1889 fire remain. **Tillicum Village Tours** at Pier 56 (☎ 206/443-1244) takes you to an island, across Puget Sound from Seattle at Lake Island Marine State Park, where the culture of the Northwest tribes comes alive, from tribal masked dances to a meal of alder-smoked salmon. Daily tours run May to October (other months vary).

**Gray Line of Seattle** (☎ 800/426-7532 or 206/626-5208) has half-day bus tours of Seattle's main tourist attractions and trips outside the city.

**BOAT TOURS**   Seattle is surrounded by water, and in addition to the boat tours mentioned here, take your own low-budget cruise by hopping one of the ferries operated by Washington State Ferries. Try the Bainbridge Island or Bremmerton ferries out of Seattle for a 2-hour round-trip. *Argosy,* at Pier 55 (☎ 206/623-4252) offers cruises. There's a Seattle harbor cruise (departs from Pier 55), a cruise through the Hiram Crittenden Locks to Lake Union (departs from Pier 57), and a cruise around Lake Washington (departs from downtown Kirkland and Chandler's Cove on Lake Union).

**ATTRACTIONS**   The waterfront is the city's main draw for visitors to Seattle, who stroll along Alaskan Way visiting the many tourist-oriented shops and restaurants. Pike Place Market, with its rabbit warren of shops and dozens of restaurants, is also one of Seattle's most popular attractions.

   **Burke Museum.** *17th Ave. NE and NE 45th St.* ☎ *206/543-5590. Donation, $3 adults, $2 students and seniors, $1.50 ages 6–18. Daily 10am–5pm. Closed July 4, Thanksgiving, Christmas, New Year's Day.* Located on the University of Washington campus, the Burke Museum features exhibits on the natural and cultural heritage of the Pacific Rim. It is noteworthy primarily for its Northwest Native American art collection. Try to visit on a Saturday afternoon or a Sunday when parking is cheaper.

   **Freeway Park.** *Sixth Ave. and Seneca St. Admission free. Daily dawn to dusk.* What do you do when an interstate runs through the middle of your city and you don't have enough parks for all the suntanners and Frisbee throwers? Put a roof on the highway and build a park over the rushing cars and trucks. Terraced gardens, waterfalls, grassy lawns—they're all here.

   **Hiram M. Chittenden Locks.** *3015 NW 54th St.* ☎ *206/783-7059. Admission free. Park and locks, daily 7am–9pm. Visitor center, June–Sept, daily 10am–7pm; Oct–May, Thurs–Mon 11am–5pm. Closed Thanksgiving, Christmas, New Year's Day.* These locks connect Lake Washington and Lake Union to Puget Sound and allow boats to travel from the lakes onto open water. The locks are a popular spot to watch salmon jumping up the fish ladder cascades. The best time of year to see salmon is July and August.

   **Japanese Gardens.** *Washington Park Arboretum, Lake Washington Blvd. E., north of E. Madison St.* ☎ *206/684-4725. Admission $2.50 adults, $1.50 seniors, the disabled, and ages 6–18. Mar 1–Apr 30, daily 10am–6pm; May 1–May 31, daily 10am–7pm; June 1–Aug 31, daily 10am–8pm; Sept 1–Oct 30, daily 10am–6pm; Nov 1–Nov 30, daily 10am–4pm. Closed Dec–Feb.* Situated on $3^{1}/_{2}$ acres of land, the Japanese Gardens are a world unto themselves, with brooks, cherry orchard, and an iris-rimmed lake with colorful koi (Japanese carp). Unfortunately, noise from a nearby road can be distracting at times.

   ✪ **Museum of Flight.** *9404 E. Marginal Way S.* ☎ *206/764-5720. $8 adults, $7 seniors, $4 ages 6–15; free first Thurs 5–9pm. Daily 10am–5pm (until 9pm Thurs). Closed Thanksgiving, Christmas. Take exit 158 off I-5. Next door to Boeing Field, 10 miles south of Seattle.* One of the world's best aviation museums, a six-story glass-and-steel building holds most of the collection, which ranges from a replica of the Wright brothers' first glider to an Apollo command module. See "Day Trips from Seattle," below, for information on a tour of the Boeing plant.

   **Museum of History and Industry.** *2700 24th Ave. E.* ☎ *206/324-1126. Admission $5.50 adults, $3 seniors and children 6–12, $1 children 2–5. Daily 10am–5pm. Closed Thanksgiving, Christmas, New Year's Day.* You can learn about the history of Seattle and the Northwest in this museum at the north end of Washington Park Arboretum. There is a Boeing mail plane from the 1920s and an exhibit on the 1889 fire that leveled Seattle. Re-created storefronts provide glimpses of 19th-century living.

   **Omnidome Film Experience.** *Pier 59, Waterfront Park.* ☎ *206/622-1868 or 206/622-1869. Admission $6.95 adults, $5.95 seniors and ages 6–18, $4.95 children 3–5. Sun–Thurs 10am–9pm, Fri–Sat 10am–11pm.* The Omnidome, for those who have never experienced it, is a movie theater with a 180-degree screen that fills your

# Seattle

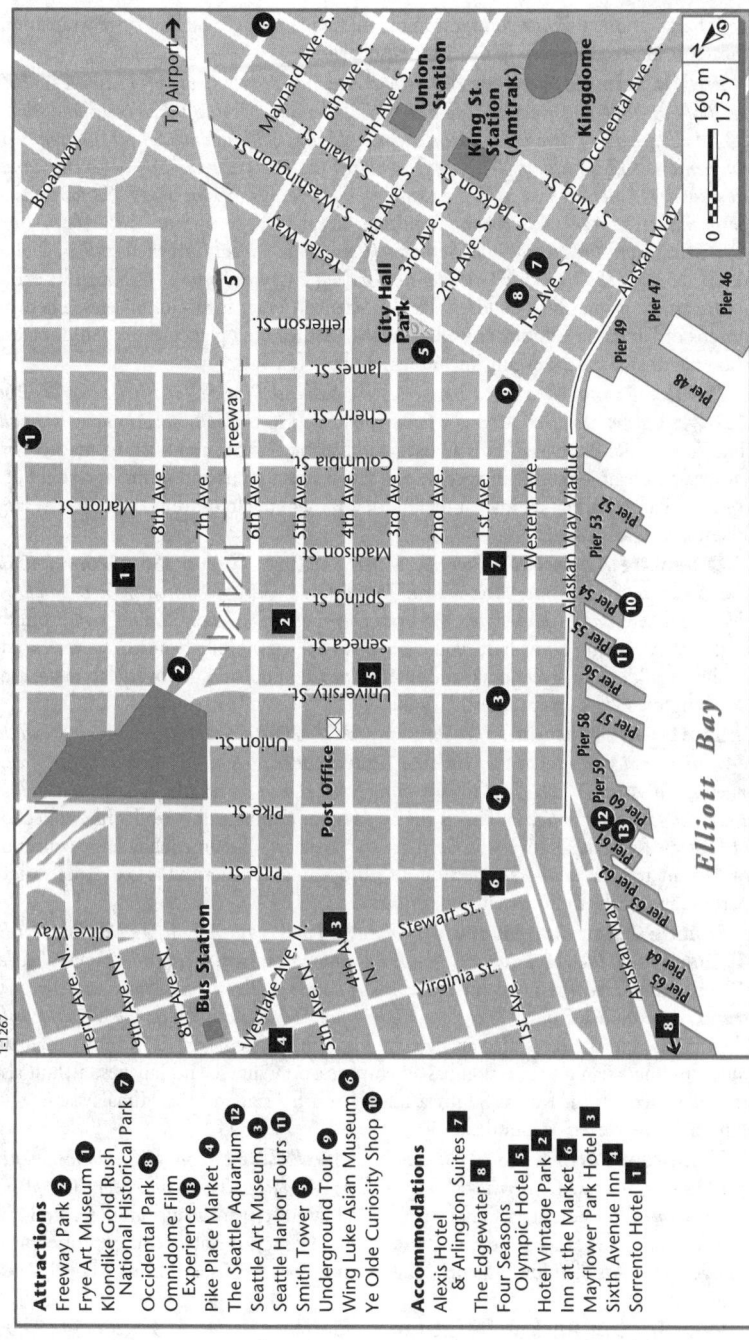

**Attractions**
Freeway Park ❷
Frye Art Museum ❶
Klondike Gold Rush
National Historical Park ❼
Occidental Park ❽
Omnidome Film
Experience ⑬
Pike Place Market ❹
The Seattle Aquarium ⑫
Seattle Art Museum ❸
Seattle Harbor Tours ⑪
Smith Tower ❺
Underground Tour ❾
Wing Luke Asian Museum ❻
Ye Olde Curiosity Shop ❿

**Accommodations**
Alexis Hotel
& Arlington Suites ▣7
The Edgewater ▣8
Four Seasons
Olympic Hotel ▣5
Hotel Vintage Park ▣2
Inn at the Market ▣6
Mayflower Park Hotel ▣3
Sixth Avenue Inn ▣4
Sorrento Hotel ▣1

1-1267

811

peripheral vision and puts you right in the middle of the action. This huge wraparound theater is located adjacent to the Seattle Aquarium.

**Pacific Science Center.** *200 Second Ave. N., Seattle Center.* ☎ *206/443-2001 or 206/443-2880 (information). Admission $7.50 adults, $5.50 children 6–13 and seniors, $3.50 children 2–5, free for children under 2. IMAX, $5.50 adult, $4.50 children 6–13 and seniors, $3.50 children 2–5, free for children under 2 ($2 as add-on to general admission ticket). Laser show, $6.75 for evening performances ($3 on Tues), $2 for matinee performances as add-on to general admission ticket only. June–Sept, daily 10am–6pm; Oct–May, Mon–Fri 10am–5pm, Sat–Sun 10am–6pm. Closed Christmas. Bus: 1, 2, 3, 4, 6, 13, 15, 16, 18, 19, 24, 33. Monorail: To Seattle Center Station.* Although its exhibits are aimed primarily at children, Pacific Science Center is fun for all ages. There are dozens of hands-on exhibits as well as an IMAX theater, a planetarium that does laser shows, and also special events, including a bubble festival.

✪ **Pike Place Market.** *Between Pike St. and Pine St. at First Ave.* ☎ *206/ 682-7453. Admission free. Mon–Sat 9am–6pm, Sun 11am–5pm. Bus: Any downtown bus.* The 7-acre Pike Place Market is a National Historic District and bustling market with farmers and fishmongers, craftspeople and artists, restaurants and shops, and street performers. Pick up a market map at the information booth almost directly below the large Pike Place Market sign.

✪ **Seattle Aquarium.** *Pier 59, Waterfront Park.* ☎ *206/386-4320. Admission $7.15 adults, $5.70 senior citizens, $4.70 ages 6–18, $2.45 children 3–5. Labor Day– Memorial Day, daily 10am–5pm; Memorial Day–Labor Day, daily 10am–7pm.* From the underwater viewing dome here, you'll get a fish-eye view of life beneath the waves, and a salmon ladder, coral-reef tank, and interactive tide-pool and discovery lab re-creating Washington's wave-swept intertidal zone.

**Seattle Art Museum.** *100 University St.* ☎ *206/654-3100. Admission $6 adults, $4 seniors and students, free for children 12 and under. Free to all on first Thurs of each month. Tues–Sun 10am–5pm (Thurs until 9pm). Open on certain holidays that fall on Mon. Closed major holidays.* This is the city's premier museum, with its fine collection of Northwest Coast Native American art and artifacts, and an equally large collection of African art. It also offers collections of European and American art covering various periods and 18th- to 20th-century exhibitions.

**Seattle Asian Art Museum.** *Volunteer Park, 14th Ave. E. and E. Prospect St.* ☎ *206/654-3100. Admission $6 adults, $4 students and senior citizens, free for children 12 and under. Free first Thurs of each month. Admission ticket also valid at Seattle Art Museum if used within 2 days. Tues–Sun 10am–5pm (Thurs until 9pm). Closed major holidays.* Housed in the renovated art deco building that once served as the city's main art museum, the Asian art collection has an emphasis on Chinese and Japanese art but also includes pieces from Korea, Southeast Asia, South Asia, and the Himalayas. Special exhibits change every 6 months.

**Volunteer Park.** *E. Prospect St. and 14th Ave. E.* ☎ *206/684-4743. Admission free. Daily dawn to dusk. Conservatory, May 1–Sept 15, daily 10am–7pm; Sept 16–Apr 30, daily 10am–4pm.* Volunteer Park is surrounded by the elegant mansions of Capitol Hill and is a popular spot for suntanning and playing Frisbee. A stately conservatory houses a large collection of tropical plants. The Seattle Asian Art Museum (see above) is also here.

**Washington Park Arboretum.** *2300 Arboretum Dr. E.* ☎ *206/543-8800. Admission free. Daily dawn to dusk. Visitor Center, Mon–Fri 10am–4pm, Sat–Sun noon–4pm.* This 200-acre arboretum, stretching from Capitol Hill to the Montlake Cut, offers quiet trails (most beautiful in spring) and over 5,000 plant varieties. The marshland is home to ducks and herons, and popular with kayakers and canoeists (see below for information on renting a canoe or kayak).

**Wing Luke Asian Museum.** *407 Seventh Ave. S.* ☎ *206/623-5124. Admission $2.50 adults, $1.50 students and seniors, 75¢ children 5–12. Free to all on Thurs. Tues–Fri 11am–4:30pm, Sat–Sun noon–4pm. Closed Easter, July 4, Veteran's Day, Thanksgiving, Christmas, New Year's Day.* In the heart of the International District, the museum features Asian American culture, art, and history. The emphasis is on the life of Asian immigrants in the Northwest, and special exhibits are intended to help explain foreign customs to non-Asians.

✪ **Woodland Park Zoo.** *5500 Phinney Ave. N.* ☎ *206/684-4800. Admission $7.50 adults, $5.75 seniors and students, $5 ages 6–17 and disabled, $2.75 children 3–5. Parking $3.50. Mar 15–Oct 14, daily 9:30am–6pm; Oct 15–Mar 14, daily 9:30am–4pm.* This sprawling zoo in north Seattle has outstanding new exhibits focusing on such bioclimatic zones as Alaska, tropical Asia, the African savanna, and the tropical rain forest. The tropical nocturnal house offers a view of seldom-seen night animals in action. For the little ones, there is a farm animal area.

**Ye Olde Curiosity Shop.** *Pier 54, Alaskan Way.* ☎ *206/682-5844. Admission free. Mon–Thurs 9:30am–6pm, Fri–Sat 9am–9pm, Sun 9am–7pm.* It's a museum. It's a souvenir shop. It's weird! It's tacky! If you have a fascination with the bizarre, shoulder your way in to see treasures such as Siamese-twin calves, a natural mummy, and the Lord's prayer on a grain of rice.

**NEIGHBORHOODS** Seattle's **International District,** Fifth Avenue South to Eighth Avenue South between South Main and South Lane streets, has been the Asian neighborhood for 100 years or more, and you can learn about the history of the neighborhood at the Wing Luke Museum (see above). There are, of course, lots of restaurants and import and food stores, including the huge Uwajimaya.

The funky **Fremont District,** north end of Fremont Bridge around the intersection of Fremont Avenue North and North 36th Street, goes by the name of Republic of Fremont, with a motto that translates to, "free to be peculiar." Enjoy outdoor art, the Sunday Market, vintage clothing and furniture stores, a brew pub, and other unusual shops, galleries, and cafes.

**TOTEM POLES** Totem poles are the quintessential symbol of the Northwest, and although this Native American art form actually comes from farther north, there are quite a few around Seattle. The largest concentration is at the Burke Museum (see above), and in the triangular park of Pioneer Place is the most famous one. Those in Occidental Park at Occidental Avenue South and South Washington Street were carved by local artist Duane Pasco. Near Pike Place Market, in Victor Steinbrueck Park, at the intersection of Pike Place, Virginia Street, and Western Avenue, are two 50-foot-tall totem poles.

**GREAT VIEWS** If you want to take home a drop-dead photo of the Seattle skyline at sunset, head up to Highland Park on Queen Anne Hill. To reach the park, head north from Seattle Center on Queen Anne Avenue North and turn left on West Highland Drive. The **Space Needle,** 219 Fourth Ave. N., Seattle Center (☎ 206/443-2100), was erected for the 1962 World's Fair, and the 605-foot tower is the most popular tourist site in town. There is an observation deck, lounge, and two expensive restaurants. The lines are long and it's pricey, but an elevator ride here can quickly orient you to the city. **Smith Tower,** 508 Second Ave. (☎ 206/682-9393), sits like a tall white needle on the edge of the Pioneer Square District. There is an observation platform near the top of the 42 stories, but call ahead to ensure it isn't closed for a special function.

**BEST BETS FOR KIDS**   In addition to the Seattle Aquarium, the Pacific Science Center, and Woodland Park Zoo (see "Attractions," above), the **Seattle Center,** 305 Harrison St. (☎ 206/684-7200 or 206/728-1586), is a 74-acre amusement park and cultural center on the north end of downtown, built for the 1964 World's Fair. It offers rides and arcade games, and is the city's main site for festivals, especially during summer months. The **Children's Museum,** Center House, Seattle Center (☎ 206/441-1768), includes plenty of hands-on cultural exhibits, workshops, a mountain wilderness area, and other exhibits to keeps kids busy.

**SPORTS**   The American League's **Seattle Mariners** (☎ 206/628-3555) play in the Kingdome Apr–Oct. The NBA's **Seattle SuperSonics** (☎ 206/281-5800) play basketball in the Key Arena Nov–May. The **Seattle Seahawks** NFL football team plays in the Kingdome Sept–Dec. Tickets are difficult to get, but call ☎ 206/827-9777 for information. Parking in the Kingdome area is nearly impossible during games, so take the bus. Tickets for major sporting events can be purchased through **Ticketmaster** (☎ 206/628-0888) or **Pacific Northwest Ticket Service** (☎ 206/232-0150).

**SHOPPING**   The heart of Seattle's shopping district is at the corner of Pine Street and Westlake Avenue. Within 1 block of this intersection are two major department stores— Nordstrom and the Bon Marché—and a shopping mall. If you're young at heart and possess a very personal idea of style, head over to Broadway on Capitol Hill to do your shopping. Pioneer Square, Seattle's historic district, is filled with art galleries, antique shops, and other unusual stores. Seattle's most famous shopping area is **Pike Place Market,** a produce market, but also much more (see "Markets," below).

For an absolutely astonishing selection of antiques, head north of Seattle to the town of **Snohomish** (near Everett), where you'll find more than 150 antique shops.

**MARKETS**   **Pike Place Market,** between Pike and Pine streets at First Avenue (☎ 206/682-7453), is one of Seattle's major attractions (see above). The second favorite is **Fremont Sunday Market,** Fremont Avenue North and North 35th Street (☎ 206/282-5706), with crafts, imports, antiques, collectibles, fresh produce, and live music. The underground **Pioneer Square Mall,** 602 First Ave., in the heart of Pioneer Square (☎ 206/624-1164), contains about 80 shops selling all manner of antiques and collectibles. **Uwajimaya,** 519 Sixth Ave. S., in the heart of the International District (☎ 206/624-6248), is like your local supermarket with nothing *but* Asian foods, housewares, produce, and toys.

## ACCOMMODATIONS

Seattle's largest concentrations of hotels are in downtown and near the airport, with a few good hotels in the University District and over in the Bellevue/Kirkland area. If you don't mind the high prices, the downtown hotels are the most convenient for most visitors. However, if your budget won't allow for a first-class business hotel, you'll have to stay near the airport or elsewhere on the outskirts of the city. Among the better and more convenient chain motel choices at Sea–Tac Airport, 30 minutes south of downtown Seattle, are Motel 6, Super 8 Motel, and Travelodge Seattle Airport.

✪ **Alexis Hotel and Arlington Suites.** *1007 First Ave. (at Madison St.), Seattle, WA 98104.* ☎ *800/426-7033 or 206/624-4844. Fax 206/621-9009. 109 rms, 44 suites. $190–$210 double; $235–$360 suite. Rates include continental breakfast. AE, CB, DC, MC, V. Parking $16.* This elegant little hotel halfway between Pike Place Market and Pioneer Square offers fireplace suites with whirlpool baths and wet bars. Alexis's larger Arlington Suites with kitchens are adjacent. Extras include a Painted Tables restaurant, bar, complimentary newspaper, evening sherry, shoe-shine service, fitness room, steam room, and privileges at two sports clubs.

**The Edgewater.** *Pier 67, 2411 Alaskan Way, Seattle, WA 98121.* ☎ *800/624-0670 or 206/728-7000. Fax 206/441-4119. 240 rms, 3 suites. $129–$220 double; $325 suite. AE, CB, DC, DISC, MC, V. Parking $8–$10.* Seattle's only waterfront hotel has the feel of a deluxe mountain lodge with rustically furnished rooms, some small but most with minibars and balconies overlooking Elliott Bay. The hotel has a dining room, piano-bar lounge, courtesy shuttle downtown, and privileges at nearby health clubs.

✪ **Four Seasons Olympic Hotel.** *411 University St., Seattle, WA 98101.* ☎ *800/332-3442 or 206/621-1700, or 800/821-8106 in Washington, or 800/268-6282 in Canada. Fax 206/623-2681. 450 rms, 200 suites. $250–$320 double; $600–$1,425 suite. AE, CB, DC, ER, JCB, MC, V. Parking $11–$15.* Old-fashioned grandeur is found at this ornate Italian Renaissance palace with spacious and tasteful rooms. The elegant **Georgian Room** is here as well as an English pub and the Garden Court restaurant. Guests enjoy the indoor pool, whirlpool spa, sauna, health club, shopping arcade, 24-hour room service, complimentary shoe shine, and masseuse.

**Hotel Vintage Park.** *1100 Fifth Ave., Seattle, WA 98101.* ☎ *800/624-4433 or 206/624-8000. Fax 206/623-0568. 126 rms, 1 suite. $190–$210 double; $375 suite. AE, CB, DC, DISC, JCB, MC, V. Valet parking $17.* Classically elegant, with stunning Italianate and contemporary decor, the Vintage offers small, comfortable rooms and deluxe rooms with rare luxury for the price. For a splurge, try the Chateau Ste. Michele suite. The hotel offers evening wine tastings, a restaurant, bar, health club access, complimentary morning newspaper and coffee, and use of in-room exercise equipment.

✪ **Inn at the Market.** *86 Pine St., Seattle, WA 98101.* ☎ *800/446-4484 or 206/443-3600. 65 rms, 6 suites. $130–$190 double; $225–$325 suite. AE, CB, DC, DISC, MC, V. Parking $15.* French country decor is found in this small, elegant hotel in the Pike Place Market. Bay windows open to Puget Sound. Refrigerators and bathroom telephones are among the amenities. There is a bistro, cafe, and the Campagne dining room (see "Dining," below). The hotel also has a hair salon, athletic club privileges, and complimentary van service.

**Mayflower Park Hotel.** *405 Olive Way, Seattle, WA 98101.* ☎ *800/426-5100 or 206/623-8700. Fax 206/382-6996. 172 rms, 20 suites. $135–$165 double; $175–$355 suite. AE, CB, DC, DISC, MC, V. Parking $9.* This 1927 hotel offers subdued elegance and shopping convenience. All rooms have been remodeled and most are furnished with a blend of contemporary Italian and traditional European with Chinese accents. Some bathrooms are old-fashioned and small but have large tubs. The Mayflower has a restaurant, lounge, 24-hour room service, and athletic club privileges.

**Meany Tower Hotel.** *4507 Brooklyn Ave. NE, Seattle, WA 98105.* ☎ *800/899-0251 or 206/634-2000. 155 rms. $91–$98 double. AE, DC, MC, V. Free parking.* If you need to be near the university and want superb views of downtown Seattle and environs, book a room in this moderately priced high-rise hotel. Every room is a corner room, with a large television. Facilities include a fitness room and restaurant, and complimentary newspapers are provided.

✪ **Seattle Marriott Hotel Sea-Tac.** *3201 S. 176th St., Seattle, WA 98188.* ☎ *800/228-9290 or 206/241-2000. 459 rms, 5 suites. $129–$149 double; $195–$550 suite. AE, CB, DC, DISC, MC, V. Free parking.* You can't pick a better place to stay in the airport area. This Marriott offers a soaring atrium, waterfalls and totem poles, and large rooms attractively decorated. The concierge-level rooms are particularly appealing and extras include a restaurant, free airport shuttle, car-rental desk, indoor pool, whirlpools, health club, sauna, and game room.

**Sixth Avenue Inn.** *2000 Sixth Ave., Seattle, WA 98121.* ☎ *800/648-6440 or 206/441-8300. Fax 206/441-9903. 166 rms. $90–$130 double (lower rates are for off-season).*

*Children under 17 stay free in parents' room. AE, CB, MC, V. Free parking*. This is not your standard moderately priced hotel, with brass beds, and old hardcover books and photos of Seattle in every room. Wicker furniture and potted plants provide a tropical greenhouse feeling. Facilities include a restaurant and lounge.

✪ **Sorrento Hotel.** *900 Madison St., Seattle, WA 98104-9742.* ☎ *800/426-1265 or 206/622-6400. Fax 206/343-6155. 76 rms, 42 suites. $180–$200 double; $220–$1,200 suite. AE, DC, DISC, MC, V. Parking $15.* From the wrought-iron gates of the courtyard entrance to rooms with armoires, refrigerators, and plush robes, the Sorrento offers the finest decor and service. The intimate **Hunt Club** restaurant is here. Extras include a bar, afternoon tea, complimentary car service in downtown Seattle, morning paper, fitness center, and florist.

✪ **University Inn.** *4140 Roosevelt Way NE, Seattle, WA 98105.* ☎ *800/733-3855 or 206/632-5055. Fax 206/547-4937. 102 rms, 12 junior suites. $100 double; $120 junior suite. All rates include continental breakfast. AE, DC, DISC, MC, V. Free parking*. Within easy walking distance of the university, this hotel offers very attractive rooms, many with a view of Lake Union. The standard rooms have only bathroom showers, but compensate with small balconies. Deluxe rooms are spacious, and junior suites are available with microwaves and refrigerators. Facilities include a heated outdoor pool and whirlpool.

**ACCOMMODATIONS IN BELLEVUE & KIRKLAND**  On the east side of Lake Washington and at the heart of the region's high-tech industrial growth, Bellevue and Kirkland are two of Washington's fastest-growing cities. From here it's only 15 minutes to downtown Seattle if it isn't rush hour.

**Hyatt Regency Bellevue.** *900 Bellevue Way NE, Bellevue, WA 98004.* ☎ *800/ 233-1234 or 206/462-1234. Fax 206/646-7567. 382 rms, 21 suites. $119–$185 double; $250–$800 suite. Self-parking $7; valet parking $11.* Located across from the Northwest's largest shopping mall and connected to an exclusive shopping center, this high-rise hotel offers some rooms with a Lake Washington and skyline view. Rooms include marbletop desks and rattan chairs. Regency Club floors offer extra amenities and access to a concierge lounge. Facilities include a restaurant, bar, and adjacent health club.

✪ **Woodmark Hotel at Carillon Point.** *1200 Carrillon Point, Kirkland, WA 98033.* ☎ *800/822-3700 or 206/822-3700. Fax 206/822-3699. 100 rms, 25 suites. $180–$230 double; $250–$1,250 suite. AE, CB, DC, ER, JCB, MC, V. Self-parking $9; valet parking $11.* The most luxurious waterfront hotel in the Seattle area, the Woodmark offers impressive guest rooms with many amenities, such as robes and VCR, and most rooms view Lake Washington. Conveniences include a restaurant, lounge, exercise room, business center, courtesy local shopping van, complimentary newspaper and late-night snacks, and video library.

## DINING

With its cosmopolitan population, Seattle's restaurants serve a wide range of cuisines. However, it should come as no surprise that seafood is emphasized. Views of the water, whether it be Puget Sound, Lake Union, or Lake Washington, are an added bonus at many restaurants.

✪ **Café Campagne.** *1600 Post Alley.* ☎ *206/728-CAFE. Reservations accepted for dinner. Main courses $8–$15; lunches $6–$10. AE, MC, V. Mon–Fri 8am–10pm, Sat 8am–11:30pm, Sun brunch 8am–3pm. FRENCH.* This cozy cafe in the Pike Place Market neighborhood, an offshoot of the Campagne Inn, offers a restful Parisian atmosphere, with glass cases displaying roast chickens, tarts, and other delicacies. The menu is seasonal and might include a lamb burger with aïoli. The cafe doubles as a wine bar.

**Café Flora.** *2901 E. Madison St.* ☎ *206/325-9100. Reservations taken for 8 or more. Main courses $9–$14. MC, V. Tues–Fri 11:30am–10pm, Sat 5:30–10pm; brunch*

*Sat–Sun 9am–2pm. VEGETARIAN.* Big and bright and airy, this cafe offers meatless gourmet cooking that is delicious. The menu changes weekly and might include a sauté of seasoned shiitake mushrooms, onion, peppers, carrots, and celery served with basmati rice and fruit chutney. Patio dining is available in the summer.

**Campagne.** *86 Pine St.* ☎ *206/728-2800. Reservations highly recommended. Main courses $19–$28. AE, CB, DC, MC, V. Daily 5:30–10pm (cafe dining until midnight). FRENCH.* Cheerful and unpretentious, Campagne is one of the most enjoyable French restaurants in Seattle. The cuisine is excellent and Provence is the specialty of the house. There are daily fish-soup specialties and entrees like lamb loin encrusted with truffles. Lighter pasta dishes are available, and the desserts are equal to the entrees.

**Canlis.** *2576 Aurora Ave. N.* ☎ *206/283-3313. Reservations highly recommended. Jacket required for men. Main courses $20–$30. AE, DC, MC, V. Mon–Thurs 5:30–9:30pm, Fri–Sat 5:30–10pm. AMERICAN/CONTINENTAL.* Canlis has enjoyed unflagging popularity for 40 years. The reason could be perfectly prepared steaks and seafoods, or excellent service by kimono-clad waitresses, or a hilltop view across Lake Union. A stone fireplace and columns add to the ambience. The baked potato is legendary, and Grand Marnier soufflé is excellent.

✪ **Chez Shea.** *94 Pike St., Suite 34, Pike Place Market.* ☎ *206/467-9990. Reservations highly recommended. Main courses $23; fixed-price 4-course dinner $38. AE, MC, V. Tues–Sun 5:30–10pm. NORTHWEST.* Dark and intimate, this is one of Seattle's finest. Candlelit tables and views across Puget Sound to the Olympic Mountains add to the food, prepared with the freshest ingredients from the market. Weeknight à la carte dinners are available. The menu changes seasonally and might feature a fillet of salmon with savory cabbage. Shea's Lounge serves lighter meals.

✪ **Dahlia Lounge.** *1904 Fourth Ave.* ☎ *206/682-4142. Reservations highly recommended. Main courses $12–$20. AE, DC, DISC, MC, V. Mon–Fri 11:30am–2:30pm; Mon–Thurs 5:30–10pm, Fri–Sat 5:30–11pm, Sun 5–9pm. NORTHWEST.* The neon chef holding a flapping fish may suggest a roadside diner, but a glimpse inside at the stylish decor of Dahlia Lounge says otherwise. Mouthwatering and succulent Dungeness crab cakes are the house specialty. The lunch menu offers slightly lower prices.

**Emmett Watson's Oyster Bar.** *1916 Pike Place No. 16.* ☎ *206/448-7721. Reservations not accepted. Main courses $4–$6. No credit cards. Mon–Thurs 11:30am–9pm, Fri–Sat 11:30am–10pm, Sun 11:30am–6pm; in winter, closes 2 hours earlier except for Sun. SEAFOOD.* Tucked away across from Pike Place Market, Emmett Watson's looks like a fast-food place but its service is infamously slow. Booths are tiny, but there is a courtyard. Oysters on the half shell are its raison d'être but the fish dishes are often memorable.

✪ **Fuller's.** *Seattle Sheraton Hotel, 1400 Sixth Ave.* ☎ *206/447-5544. Reservations highly recommended. Main courses $18–$25; 5- or 6-course tasting menu $50; lunches $8–$16. AE, CB, DC, DISC, JCB, MC, V. Mon–Fri 11:30am–1:45pm; Mon–Sat 5:30–10pm. NORTHWEST.* Fuller's, named for the Seattle Art Museum founder, is dedicated to Northwest culinary and visual arts, with dishes artfully designed and superbly prepared, and an elegant dining room with works by the Northwest's best artists. A specialty is roast venison with pear-armagnac sauce. Lunch, with its lower-price menu, is popular.

**Gravity Bar.** *113 Virginia St.* ☎ *206/448-8826. Also at 415 E. Broadway.* ☎ *206/325-7186. Meals $4–$7; juices $2.50–$4. MC, V. Downtown, Mon–Thurs 11am–9pm, Fri 11am–10pm, Sat 10am–10pm, Sun 10am–8pm. Broadway, Sun–Thurs 10am–10pm, Fri–Sat 10am–11pm. NATURAL.* If you're young at heart or hip to healthy, the Gravity is your place. Postmodern neoindustrial decor (lots of sheet metal) is the antithesis of the wholesome juices and meals they serve here. The juice list includes unusual combinations, all with catchy names like Martian Martini or 7 Year Spinach.

**Ivar's Salmon House.** *401 NE Northlake Way.* ☎ *206/632-0767. Reservations recommended. Main courses $10–$23; fish bar $4–$7. AE, MC, V. Main restaurant, Mon–Fri 11:30am–2:30pm; Mon–Thurs 4:30–10pm, Fri 4:30–11pm; Sat noon–3:30 and 4–11pm, Sun 10am–2pm (brunch) and 4–10pm. Fish bar, Sun–Thurs 11am–10pm, Fri–Sat 11am–11pm. SEAFOOD.* The Salmon House, with a Northwest theme, offers a view of the skyline from Lake Union and floating docks out back. It's famous for alder-smoked salmon. The building received an award from the Seattle Historical Society for its replica of a tribal longhouse. Kids and adults love this place.

**McCormick & Schmick's.** *1103 First Ave.* ☎ *206/623-5500. Reservations recommended. Main courses $10–$20. AE, DC, DISC, MC, V. Mon–Fri 11am–11pm, Sat–Sun 4pm–12:30am. SEAFOOD.* Get past the crowds of business suits at the bar and you'll find a classic fish house. From the polished brass to dark-wood paneling, everything here shines. A recent menu included blackened Canadian lingcod with tomato-ginger chutney. From 3 to 6pm and 10 to closing, bar appetizers are only $1.95.

**Pink Door.** *1919 Post Alley.* ☎ *206/443-3241. Reservations recommended. Pastas $8–$14; main dishes $13–$17. AE, MC, V. Tues–Sat 11:30am–2:30pm and 5:30–10pm. ITALIAN.* There's no sign, so watch for the pink door between Stewart and Virginia streets. Inside you'll find hanging Chianti bottles, a fountain, a tarot card reader, cabaret singers, and a weekend accordion player. A deck offers harbor and downtown views in summer. Cioppino, a flavorful seafood stew, is recommended.

✪ **Pirosmani.** *2220 Queen Anne Ave. N.* ☎ *206/285-3360. Reservations recommended. Main courses $16–$23. AE, DC, MC, V. Tues–Sat 5:30–10pm. GEORGIAN/ MEDITERRANEAN.* Named after the Georgian Republic's most famous artist, Pirosmani is a small, informal restaurant in a Victorian home in the Queen Anne district. The chef draws from both Georgia and the Mediterranean and each dish is distinctively different. Try the tuna wrapped in grape leaves in pomegranate-mix sauce.

✪ **Ponti Seafood Grill.** *3014 Third Ave. N.* ☎ *206/284-3000. Reservations recommended. Main courses $14–$24; early dinners $13.95. AE, MC, V. Mon–Thurs 11:30am–2:30pm and 5–10pm; Fri 11:30am–2:30pm and 5–11pm; Sat 5–11pm; Sun 10am–2:30pm (brunch) and 5–10pm. SEAFOOD.* Overlooking the Lake Washington Ship Canal at Fremont Bridge's south end, Ponti's is one of Seattle's most elegant restaurants, offering an international menu and northwestern creations. One tantalizing appetizer is smoked salmon served with a corn pancake, vodka crème fraîche, chives, and caviar. Early dinners are served between 5 and 6pm.

✪ **Queen City Grill.** *2201 First Ave.* ☎ *206/443-0975. Reservations recommended. Dinner main courses $9–$20; lunch main courses $10–$14. AE, DC, DISC, MC, V. Mon– Thurs 11:30am–11pm, Fri 11:30pm–midnight, Sat 5pm–midnight, Sun 5–11pm. INTERNATIONAL.* Battered wooden floors and high-backed booths provide a weathered look, and the spare decor and sophisticated lighting underscore an exciting menu. Seafood is the specialty and some people come just for the crab cakes. The wine list has over 500 labels from the Northwest and around the world.

**Ray's Boathouse and Café.** *6049 Seaview Ave. NW.* ☎ *206/789-3770. Reservations recommended on weekends; not necessary for upstairs cafe. Main courses $12–$28; cafe prices slightly less. AE, CB, DC, MC, V. Cafe, Mon–Fri 11:30am–2pm and 5–10pm; Sat 4:30–10pm, Sun 4:30–9pm. Restaurant, Mon–Sat 5–10pm, Sun 5–9pm. SEAFOOD.* At Ray's, considered one of Seattle's best restaurants, you'll find the upstairs lounge pretty rowdy with suntanned boaters, but the price is reduced here. Downstairs is quiet and cozy. Entrees include manila clam fettuccine with peppered bacon and fresh herbs in garlic lemon cream.

⊗ **Rover's.** *2808 E. Madison St.* ☎ *206/325-7442. Reservations required. Main courses $22–$29; 5-course menu degustation $60, 8 courses $90. AE, DC, MC, V. Tues–Sat 5:30–9:30pm. NORTHWEST.* Tucked away in a quaint clapboard house behind a chic little shopping center is one of Seattle's most talked about restaurants. Chef Thierry Rautureau received classic French training before falling in love with the Northwest and the wonderful ingredients available here. Main dishes include salmon or halibut, with pomme mousseline.

**Serafina.** *2043 Eastlake Ave. E.* ☎ *206/323-0807. Reservations recommended. Main courses $10–$17; pastas $9–$14. MC, V. Mon–Fri 11:30am–2pm; Sun–Thurs 5–10pm, Fri–Sat 5–11pm. ITALIAN/EUROPEAN.* Serafina's rustic atmosphere underscores its earthy Italian country dishes. The casual ambience is enhanced by jazz and Latin-influenced live music most evenings. For a main dish, try Italian sausages sautéed with grapes and onions and served with soft polenta.

**Siam on Broadway.** *616 Broadway E.* ☎ *206/324-0892. Reservations recommended on weekends. Main courses $7–$9. AE, MC, V. Mon–Thurs 11:30am–10pm, Fri 11:30am–11pm, Sat 5–11pm, Sun 5–10pm. THAI.* At the north end of the Broadway shopping district in trendy Capitol Hill is one of Seattle's best inexpensive Thai restaurants. Small and casual, its tom yum soups, with either shrimp or chicken, are the creamiest anywhere. Superhot is indeed that, so tell your waiter if you prefer milder dishes. Another Siam restaurant, on Lake Union at 1880 Fairview Ave. E. (☎ **206/323-8101**), is larger and has the same good food but less personality.

**OTHER DINING**  Fremont is Seattle's most eclectic neighborhood, and **Still Life in Fremont Coffeehouse,** 709 N. 35th St. (☎ **206/547-9850**), reflects this eclecticism. It's big, crowded, and serves good vegetarian meals. The Belltown burger at the **Belltown Pub,** 2322 First Ave. (☎ **206/728-4311**), might be the best burger in town. This neighborhood pub is a few blocks north of Pike Place Market.

## SEATTLE AFTER DARK

Seattle has been making a splash on the national performance scene for several years now with its world-class opera company and its prolific theater scene. Seattle Center and Pioneer Square are the city's focal points for evening entertainment, with the former area housing several theaters and the latter being home to numerous rock and jazz clubs.

**Ticketmaster Northwest** (☎ 206/628-0888) handles most theaters, large concert halls, and sporting events tickets. For half-price, day-of-show tickets, contact **Ticket/Ticket** (☎ 206/324-2744) at Pike Place Market, First Avenue and Pike Street (open Tues–Sun noon–6pm), or at the Broadway Market, 401 Broadway E. (open Tues–Sun 10am–7pm).

To find out what's going on when you are in town, pick up a copy of *Seattle Weekly,* which is Seattle's weekly arts-and-entertainment newspaper. In the Friday *Seattle Times's* "Tempo" section, you'll also find a guide to the week's arts-and-entertainment offerings.

**THE PERFORMING ARTS**  At Seattle Center, in the shadow of the Space Needle, you'll find the **Seattle Opera House** (☎ 206/389-7676), **Bagley Wright Theater** (☎ 206/443-2222), **Intiman Playhouse** (☎ 206/269-1900), **Seattle Children's Theatre** (☎ 206/441-3322), and **The Group** theater (☎ 206/441-1299), as well as the Seattle Center Coliseum, and Memorial Stadium.

The ⊗ **Seattle Opera Association,** Seattle Opera House, Third Avenue North and Mercer Street (☎ 206/389-7699), is the contact for the Seattle Opera, considered one of the finest opera companies in the country, and is *the* Wagnerian opera company. The season also includes a contemporary musical. The ⊗ **Seattle Symphony Orchestra,** Seattle Opera House, Fourth Avenue and Mercer Street (☎ 206/443-4747), under the baton of Gerard Schwarz, offers an amazingly diverse musical season that runs from September to May and includes children's concerts and guest artists. In addition to these two major companies, the **Northwest Chamber Orchestra** (☎ 206/343-0445), which performs primarily in Kane Hall on the University of Washington campus, is worthy of note. This company is a showcase for Northwest performers.

The **Intiman Theatre Company** (☎ 206/269-1900), which performs at the Intiman Playhouse, Seattle Center, 201 Mercer St., is over 30 years old and is a favorite of Seattle theatergoers, with a season that starts in May and ends in December. The **Seattle Repertory Theater** (☎ 206/443-2222) performs at the Bagley Wright Theater, Seattle Center, 155 Mercer St. The season (Oct–May) fills in where the Intiman leaves off, giving Seattle excellent year-round professional theater. Productions range from classics to world premiers to Broadway musicals.

Among the city's smaller theater companies, **A Contemporary Theater (ACT),** 700 Union St. (☎ 206/292-7676), is known for staging adventurous productions. The **Paramount Theater,** Pine Street and Ninth Avenue (☎ 206/682-1414), is a popular venue for touring rock bands and stage companies. The **5th Avenue Theatre,** 1308 Fifth Ave. (☎ 206/625-1418), the city's most beautiful theater, is a loose re-creation of the imperial throne room in Beijing's Forbidden City. It has its own resident musical theater company, and also stages productions by major touring companies.

The **Pacific Northwest Ballet** (☎ 206/292-2787) performs at the Seattle Opera House, Third Avenue North and Mercer Street, and presents classics, new works, and Ballanchine ballets. For modern dance enthusiasts, **On the Boards** (☎ 206/325-7901), performs at Washington Hall Performance Gallery, 153 14th Ave., and provides innovative contemporary dance performances.

**THE CLUB & MUSIC SCENE**   An eclectic assortment of musical styles are featured on the bandstand of the **Ballard Firehouse,** 5429 Russell St. (☎ 206/784-3516). **The Crocodile,** 2200 Second Ave. (☎ 206/441-5611), is a combination nightclub, bar, and restaurant amid rambunctious decor. Grunge dominates, but folk and jazz sometimes show up. In the heart of the Pioneer Square area, **Fenix/Fenix Underground,** 315 and 323 Second Ave. (☎ 206/467-1111), book an eclectic blend of rock, reggae, and world-beat music by primarily regional acts. **Doc Maynard's,** 610 First Ave. (☎ 206/682-4649), by day is the starting point of the Underground Tour, but by night is one of Seattle's most popular clubs for live rock 'n' roll. This place attracts all types of rock music lovers. For a friendly Irish pub, **Kells,** 1916 Post Alley, Pike Place Market (☎ 206/728-1916), offers good Guinness stout and live traditional Irish music. On the jazz and blues scene is ✪ **Dimitriou's Jazz Alley,** 2033 Sixth Ave. (☎ 206/441-9729). Cool and sophisticated, it is reminiscent of New York jazz clubs and books only the very best performers.

**THE BAR SCENE**   **Pacific NW Brewing Co.,** 322 Occidental Ave. S. (☎ 206/621-7002), usually has six of its own brews on tap, plus plenty of other popular local micros. The **Pub at the Hart Brewery,** 1201 First Ave. S. (☎ 206/682-8322), south of the Kingdome, serves Thomas Kemper lagers and Pyramid ales and offers brewery tours, good pub food, and other special events.

**Fx Mcrory's Steak, Chop, and Oyster House,** 419 Occidental Ave. S. (☎ 206/623-4800), is an upscale sports bar where you're likely to see members of the Seahawks or the Supersonics, as well as find Seattle's largest selection of bourbons and microbrew beers and ales. **McCormick & Schmick's,** 1103 First Ave. (☎ 206/623-5500), is very busy during happy hour as brokers wind down. If you long to rub shoulders with the movers and shakers of Seattle, this is the place for you. **Wildrose,** 1021 E. Pike St. (☎ 206/324-9210), is a friendly restaurant/bar that is a long-time favorite with the Capitol Hill women's and lesbian community.

# DAY TRIPS FROM SEATTLE

**ACROSS PUGET SOUND**   Pick and choose what you like, for there's more than one day's worth of adventures here. You start on one ferry and end on another and along the way can visit sites ranging from a Native American museum to the picturesque bedroom community of Bainbridge Island, noted for miles of waterfront and gorgeous views.

Start with the Bainbridge Island ferry, Pier 52, which affords views that include Mount Rainier and the Olympic Mountains. For a current sailing schedule, contact **Washington State Ferries** (☎ 800/84-FERRY in Washington State, or 206/464-6400). Up the hill from the ferry terminal is the island's main shopping district. Drop in at the **Bainbridge Island Winery** (☎ 206/842-WINE), or visit **Fort Ward State Park** at the island's south end. The **Bainbridge Island Historical Museum** (☎ 206/842-2773), located at Strawberry Hill Park 1¹/₂ miles west of Wash. 305 on High School Road, houses a restored 1908 schoolhouse. Garden enthusiasts will want to visit the **Bloedel Reserve,** 7571 NE Dolphin Dr. (☎ 206/842-7631), which is 6 miles north of the ferry terminal off Wash. 305 (turn right on Agate Point Road). Nearby you'll find **Fay Bainbridge State Park,** which offers camping and great views across the sound.

After crossing the Agate Passage Bridge to the mainland of the Kitsap Peninsula, take your first right for the town of Suquamish and the grave of **Chief Sealth,** for whom Seattle was named. To visit the site of the **Old Man House,** which was a large Native American longhouse, return to Wash. 305, continue west, turn left at the Suquamish Hardware building, and watch for the sign. The Old Man House itself is long gone, but you'll find a small park with picnic tables. Continuing on Wash. 305, you'll find the **Suquamish Museum,** 15838 Sandy Hook Rd. (☎ 360/598-3311), on the Port Madison Indian Reservation. Continuing north on Wash. 305, you reach Poulsbo, a Scandinavian-inspired town that overlooks Liberty Bay and offers interesting shops. Between downtown and the waterfront, you'll find **Liberty Bay Park,** and at the south end of Front Street, you'll find the **Marine Science Center,** 18743 Front St. (☎ 360/779-5549), which houses interpretive displays on Puget Sound. If you have a sweet tooth, don't miss **Sluys Poulsbo Bakery,** 18924 Front St. NE (☎ 360/697-BAKE). For microbrewery ales, head north of Poulsbo 2 miles to the **Thomas Kemper Brewery,** 22381 Foss Rd. NE (☎ 360/697-1446), which is also a good spot for lunch. If you have time, continue north from Poulsbo on Wash. 3 to reach the 1853 historic town of Port Gamble, with Victorian homes and the **Port Gamble Country Store** (☎ 360/297-2623), which now houses the Port Gamble Historical Museum as well as the Of Sea and Shore Museum. From Port Gamble, head south on Wash. 3 toward Bremmerton to begin an exploration of the area's naval history. Between Poulsbo and Silverdale, you will pass just east of the **Bangor Navy Base,** home port on Hood Canal for a fleet of Trident nuclear submarines. Near the town of Keyport, you can visit the **Naval Undersea Museum** (☎ 360/396-4148), which is located 3 miles east of Wash. 3 on Wash. 308.

Continuing south, you come to Bremmerton, which is home to the **Puget Sound Naval Shipyard,** where the mothballed destroyer USS *Turner Joy* (docked some 150 yards east of the Ferries terminal) is now operated by the **Bremmerton Historic Ships Association** (☎ 360/792-2457) and is open to the public. It was involved in the Tonkin Gulf incident, which led to large-scale U.S. intervention in Vietnam in 1964. Nearby is the **Bremmerton Naval Museum,** 130 Washington Ave. (☎ 360/479-7447). You can park your car and board one of the last remaining private mosquito fleet ferries (small ferries) to cross the bay to the waterfront town of Port Orchard, offering several antique malls. To return to Seattle, take the foot ferry back to Bremmerton, pick up your car, and drive onto the car ferry to Seattle.

For an alternative excursion with less driving and more time on the water, take the Bremmerton ferry from Seattle. In Bremmerton, you can then take the **Kitsap Harbor Tours** (☎ 360/377-8924) fast ferry that offers various tours of the area. When you return to Bremmerton, you can visit Port Orchard.

**NORTH OF THE CITY** This driving excursion takes in the world's largest building, a town full of antique stores, wineries, and a picturesque lakeshore community.

Roughly 30 miles north of Seattle on I-5 on the shore of Puget Sound is the city of Everett, a bedroom community for Seattle and home to the region's single largest employer—**Boeing.** Its main assembly plant is the single largest building, by volume, in the world. For information on guided tours, contact the Boeing Tour Center, Wash. 526, Everett (☎ 206/342-4801).

A few miles east of Everett, off U.S. 2, is the historic town of **Snohomish,** established in 1859 on the banks of the Snohomish River, and home today to more than 300 antique dealers in turn-of-the-century buildings as well as restored Victorian homes, a Pioneer village, and Victorian home museum. You can pick up a copy of a guide to the stores and homes by stopping by or contacting the **Snohomish Chamber of Commerce,** corner of Avenue A and Second Street (P.O. Box 135), Snohomish, WA 98291 (☎ 360/568-2526).

Heading south from Snohomish to Woodinville brings you into the Puget Sound's small winery region. Largest and most famous of the wineries in the area is **Chateau Ste. Michelle,** One Stimson Lane, Woodinville (☎ 206/488-4633), which is located in a grand chateau on a 1912 historic estate. An amphitheater on the grounds stages music performances in summer. To reach the winery, head south from Woodinville on Wash. 202 and watch for signs.

Finish your day with a walk around downtown **Kirkland,** along the Moss Bay waterfront. Here you'll find interesting shops and more than a dozen art galleries. There are also several decent restaurants in the area, including the **Cafe Juanita,** 9702 NE 120th Place (☎ 206/823-1505), an excellent Italian restaurant. To get back to Seattle, take I-405 south to I-90.

**EAST OF THE CITY** This tour offers mountain scenery and the most spectacular waterfall in the Seattle area. You may also recognize some scenery from old television shows like *Twin Peaks* and *Northern Exposure.*

**Snoqualmie Falls,** located 35 to 45 minutes east of downtown Seattle on I-90, plummet 270 feet into a pool of deep blue water. The falls are surrounded by a park with two overlooks near the lip of the falls and a half-mile-long trail leading down to the base of the falls. Nearby, off exit 22 from I-90, you'll find one of the Northwest's best-loved farms—**The Herbfarm,** 32804 Issaquah–Fall City Rd. (☎ 206/784-2222), with a country store, school, theme gardens, mail-order business, and the region's most famous restaurant. Anyone interested in seeing other *Twin Peaks* filming sites should stop by the **Salish Lodge** before heading into the town of North Bend to the **Mar-T Cafe** (☎ 206/888-1221), where you can still get "damn good pie."

One of the best ways to see this area is from a rail car on the **Puget Sound and Snoqualmie Railroad** (☎ 206/746-4025), which has historic depots in Snoqualmie and North Bend.

Continuing east on I-90 another 50 miles or so will bring you to the remote town of **Roslyn,** once a decaying old coal-mining town and now a major tourist attraction since it became "Cicely, Alaska," for *Northern Exposure.* Besides dining at the **Roslyn Cafe,** Pennsylvania and Second streets (☎ 509/649-2763), you can pay a visit to the

**Roslyn Museum** next door, or wander through the town's 25 **cemeteries,** each containing the graves of different nationalities of miners who lived and died in Roslyn.

On your way back to Seattle, you may want to stop in **Issaquah,** at Gilman Village, an interesting collection of old homes that have been restored and turned into shops and restaurants. Take exit 17.

## 2  Olympic National Park & the Olympic Peninsula

Olympic National Park is unique in the contiguous United States for its temperate rain forests, which are found in the valleys of the Hoh, Queets, Bogachiel, Clearwater, and Quinault rivers. In these valleys, rainfall can exceed 140 inches per year, trees grow more than 200 feet tall, and mosses hang from every limb. Trails lead from these valleys (and other points around the peninsula) into the interior of the park, providing access to hundreds of miles of hiking trails. In fact, trails are the only access to most of the park, which has fewer than a dozen roads, none of which lead more than a few miles into the park.

Though much of the Olympic Peninsula was designated a national forest preserve in 1897, and in 1909 became a national monument, it was not until 1938 that the heart of the peninsula—the jagged, snowcapped Olympic Mountains—became a national park.

Within a few short miles of the park's rain forests, the Olympic Mountains rise up to the 7,965-foot peak of Mount Olympus and produce an alpine zone where no trees can grow. Together, elevation and heavy rainfall combine to form 60 glaciers within the park. It is these glaciers that have carved the Olympic Mountains into the jagged peaks that mesmerize visitors and beckon to hikers and climbers. Rugged and spectacular sections of the coast have also been preserved as part of the national park, and offshore waters are designated as the Olympic Coast National Marine Sanctuary.

### ESSENTIALS

**ARRIVING & DEPARTING**   **Fairchild International Airport** in Port Angeles is served by Horizon Airlines. There is bus service from **Sea–Tac Airport** to Port Angeles on **Olympic Bus Lines** (☎ **800/550-3858** or 360/452-3858). There is service to Lake Quinault from Olympia and Aberdeen on **Grays Harbor Transit** (☎ **800/ 562-9730** or 360/532-2770). Two ferries, one for pedestrians only and the other for both vehicles and pedestrians, connect Port Angeles and Victoria, British Columbia. The ferry terminal for both ferries is at the corner of Laurel and Railroad streets. **Victoria Express** (☎ **800/633-1589** in Washington, 360/452-8088 or 250/361-9144 in Victoria) is the faster of the two ferries and carries foot passengers only. This ferry operates only between May and October. The crossing takes 1 hour. The **Black Ball Transport ferry** (☎ **360/457-4491,** or 250/386-2202 in Victoria) operates year-round, except for 2 weeks in late January and early February, and carries both vehicles and walk-on passengers. The crossing takes slightly more than an hour and a half.

U.S. 101 circles Olympic National Park with **main park entrances** south of Port Angeles, at Lake Crescent, and at the Hoh River. The Port Angeles park entrance is 48 miles west of Port Townsend and 55 miles east of Forks.

**VISITOR INFORMATION**   For information, contact **Olympic National Park,** 3002 Mt. Angeles Rd., Port Angeles, WA 98362 (☎ **360/452-0330**). For the Port Angeles area, contact the **Port Angeles Visitor Center,** 121 E. Railroad Ave., Port Angeles, WA 98362 (☎ **360/452-2363**). For the rest of the north Olympic Peninsula, contact the **North Olympic Peninsula Visitor and Convention Bureau,** P.O. Box 670, Port Angeles, WA 98362 (☎ **800/942-4042** or 360/452-8552).

**VISITOR CENTERS** The **Olympic National Park Visitor Center** is at 3002 Mt. Angeles Rd., on the south edge of Port Angeles on the road leading to Hurricane Ridge (☎ 360/452-0330). Open summer, daily 8:30am–6pm; winter, daily 9am–4pm. The center offers maps, park books, and exhibits.

Roughly 8 miles south of Forks is the turnoff for the Hoh River valley. Travel 17 miles to the **Hoh Visitor Center** (☎ 360/374-6925), campground, and trailheads. This valley receives an average of 140 inches of rain per year, making it the wettest region in the continental United States. At the visitor center, open 9am–4pm daily with longer hours in summer, you can learn about the natural forces that cause this tremendous rainfall.

**ADMISSION COSTS** Park admission is $10 per vehicle and $5 per pedestrian or cyclist. Here you can also buy a **Golden Eagle Passport,** an annual pass good at all national parks and recreation areas, for $50. If you are over 62, you can get a Golden Age Passport for $10, and if you have a disability, you can get a free Golden Access Passport.

**INTERPRETIVE PROGRAMS** In summer, there are evening campfire programs, ranger-led talks, walks in the forest, and intertidal beach walks. Consult a copy of the park newspaper for the current schedule.

**WHEN TO GO** June to September are much less wet than the other months. In winter, the road to Hurricane Ridge can be "iffy"; it is plowed only Saturday to Monday.

## WHAT TO SEE & DO

**OUTDOOR ACTIVITIES & TOURS** With its rugged beaches, rain-forest valleys, alpine meadows, and mountaintop glaciers, the park offers a variety of hiking opportunities. Among the most popular hikes are those along the coast between La Push and Oil City and from Rialto Beach north to Lake Ozette and onward to Shi Shi Beach. Day hikes, overnight trips, and longer backpacking trips are all possible, though you'll need a special advance-reservation permit to overnight along the Ozette Loop Trail (☎ 360/452-0300 for reservations). For most other overnight hikes, pick up a permit at the trailhead, though there are a few exceptions in the high country. If in doubt, check with a park ranger. Other noteworthy hikes include the trails in the Hoh and Quinault River rain-forest valleys. For alpine hikes, head up to Hurricane Ridge or Deer Park. There are also many trails outside the boundaries of the park. For information, contact the **Olympic National Forest,** 1835 Black Lake Blvd. SW, Olympia, WA 98512-5623 (☎ 360/956-2300).

If you'd like to have a llama carry your gear, contact **Wooley Packer Llama Co.,** 5763 Upper Hoh Rd., Forks, WA 98331 (☎ 360/374-9288). If you want to do a one-way backpacking trip, you can arrange a shuttle through **Olympic Van Tours** (☎ 800/550-3858 or 360/452-3858).

The Elwha and Hoh rivers afford great whitewater rafting. Contact **Olympic Raft and Guide Service,** U.S. 101 W., Port Angeles, WA 98363 (☎ 360/452-1443). Rates start at $35. For sea kayak tours on Lake Crescent and Lake Aldwell, and in salt water near Port Angeles, the rate is $36–$55.

The town of Sekiu, on Clallam Bay, is a popular spot for both sport fishing and scuba diving. For salmon or deep-sea fishing, contact **Herb's Charters** (☎ 360/963-2346) or **Olson's Charters** (☎ 360/963-2311). Divers will want to stop in at the **Sekiu Dive Shop** (☎ 360/963-2281), which is on the main road through town.

In Lakes Crescent and Ozette, you can fish for such elusive species as Beardslee and Crescenti trout. **Four Seasons Guide Service** (☎ 360/327-3380) will take you fishing for $180 per day for one person, $225 for two people.

The **Olympic Park Institute,** 111 Barnes Point Rd., Port Angeles, WA 98363 (☎ **360/928-3720**), located in the Rosemary Inn on Lake Crescent, offers summer field seminars ranging from landscape painting to multiday backpacking. **Olympic Van Tours** (☎ **360/452-3858**) offers guided tours to Hurricane Ridge, the Hoh River rain forest, and ocean beaches ($13–$50).

**TOURING THE PENINSULA**  From the Olympic Park Visitor Center, continue 17 miles up to **Hurricane Ridge,** which offers breathtaking views of the park. Several hiking trails lead into the park, and in winter, Hurricane Ridge is a popular cross-country skiing area. The **Hurricane Ridge Visitor Center** has exhibits on alpine plants and wildlife.

West of **Port Angeles** on U.S. 101 lies **Lake Crescent,** a glacier-carved lake and one of the state's most beautiful. Between late May and early October, you can cruise the lake on the paddlewheeler *Storm King* (☎ **360/452-4520**), which has its ticket office at the Shadow Mountain General Store, milepost 233 on U.S. 101 (tickets $15 adults, $14 seniors, $10 ages 6–17). Near the east end of the lake, you'll find an information center and the 1-mile trail to 90-foot-tall Marymere Falls. At the west end, you'll find **Fairholm General Store** (☎ **360/928-3020**), which has rowboats, canoes, and motorboats for rent.

Continuing west from Lake Crescent, watch for the turn off to **Sol Duc Hot Springs** (☎ **360/327-3583**); open May–Sept, daily; Oct–Apr, Sat–Sun (admission $6 adults, $5 seniors). For 14 miles the road follows the Soleduck River passing the Salmon Cascades along the way. Sol Duc Hot Springs were for centuries considered healing waters, and today, in addition to the hot swimming pools and soaking tubs, you'll find cabins, a campground, a restaurant, and a snack bar. A 6-mile loop trail leads to **Sol Duc Falls.**

Continuing west on U.S. 101 from the junction with the road to Sol Duc Hot Springs, you will come to the crossroads of Sappho. Heading north at Sappho will bring you to Wash. 112, an alternate route from Port Angeles. About 40 miles west, Wash. 112 brings you to the community of **Neah Bay** on the Makah Indian Reservation. The reservation land includes Cape Flattery, which is the northwesternmost point of land in the contiguous United States. Just off the cape lies **Tatoosh Island,** site of one of the oldest lighthouses in Washington. Neah Bay is a busy commercial and sport-fishing port, and is also home to the impressive **Makah Museum** (☎ **360/645-2711;** open June 1–Sept 15, daily 10am–5pm; Sept 16–May 31, Wed–Sun 10am–5pm; admission $4 adults, $3 students and seniors). Here is the most perfectly preserved collection of Native American artifacts in the Northwest. Each year in late August, Makah Days are celebrated with canoe races, Indian dancing, a salmon bake, and other events.

A turnoff 16 miles east of Neah Bay leads south to **Ozette Lake,** where there are boat ramps, a campground and, stretching north and south, miles of beaches that are only accessible on foot. A 3.3-mile trail on a raised boardwalk leads from the Ozette Lake trailhead to Cape Alava, which, along with Cape Blanco in Oregon, claims to be the westernmost point in the contiguous United States.

Returning to U.S. 101, you soon reach the lumber town of **Forks.** At the heart of the controversy over protecting the northern spotted owl, Forks has long suffered high unemployment. The **Forks Timber Museum,** south of town on U.S. 101 (☎ **360/ 374-9663**), chronicles the history of logging in this region, and has displays on Native American culture and pioneer days (open mid-April to October, daily 10am–4pm; admission by donation).

Just west of Forks is the first place you can drive to the Pacific Ocean. At the end of a spur road you come to the **Quileute Indian Reservation** and the community of

**La Push.** In town is a beach at the mouth of the Quileute River; however, before you reach La Push, you'll see signs for **Third Beach** and **Second Beach,** two of the prettiest beaches on the peninsula. Third Beach is a 1.6-mile walk and Second Beach is just over a half-mile from the trailhead. **Rialto Beach** is just north of La Push and may be reached from a turnoff east of La Push.

This region's most notable feature is its rain, which has produced forests with some of the largest trees on earth. The rainiest spots are in westward-facing Bogachiel, Hoh, Queets, and Quinault river valleys. However, only the Hoh and Bogachiel valleys are easily accessible. Accessible short trails along the coast lead through groves of old-growth trees. Among these are trails in the Hoh Valley (see below), the **Ancient Groves Trail** at Soleduck and a **short trail** near the Lake Quinault Lodge.

Roughly 8 miles south of Forks is the turnoff for the Hoh River valley. It's 17 miles up to the **Hoh Visitor Center** (☎ 360/374-6925), campground, and trailheads. Walk the three-quarter-mile **Hall of Mosses Trail** where the trees tower for 200 feet above thick carpets of moss. For a longer walk, try the **Spruce Nature Trail.** If you've come with a backpack, there's no better way to see the park than by hiking the **Hoh River Trail,** which is 17 miles long and leads past Blue Glacier to Glacier Meadows on the flanks of Mount Olympus.

Continuing south on U.S. 101, but before crossing the Hoh River, you'll come to a secondary road heading west from the Hoh Oxbow campground. From the end of the road it's a hike of less than a mile to a rocky beach at the mouth of the Hoh River. Sea lions and harbor seals feed just off shore here, and to the north are several haystack rocks that are nesting sites for numerous seabirds. Primitive camping is permitted on this beach, and from here, hikers can continue hiking for 17 miles north along a pristine wilderness of rugged headlands and secluded beaches.

U.S. 101 finally reaches the coast at **Ruby Beach,** noted for its pink sand. For another 17 miles, the highway parallels the wave-swept coastline. Along this stretch of highway there are pulloffs and short trails down to six numbered beaches. Near the south end of this stretch of road, you'll find Kalaloch Lodge, which has a gas station, and the **Kalaloch Information Station,** which is only open during the summer.

Shortly beyond Kalaloch, the highway turns inland again, passing through the community of Queets on the river of the same name. If you'd like to do some rainy valley hiking away from the crowds, head up the gravel road to the **Queets campground** to find the trail leading up the valley. A little more than 2 miles up is one of the world's largest Douglas firs.

A long stretch of clear-cuts and tree farms, mostly on the Quinault Indian Reservation, will bring you to **Quinault Lake.** Surrounded by forested mountains, this deep lake offers boating and freshwater fishing as well as more rain forests to explore. This is also a good area in which to spot Roosevelt elk.

The **Arthur D. Feiro Marine Lab,** Port Angeles City Pier (☎ 360/452-3940), offers a close-up look at some of the peninsula's aquatic inhabitants (open Tues–Sat 10am–5pm in summer, Sat–Sun noon–4pm in winter; admission $1 adults, 50¢ seniors and children 6–12).

## ACCOMMODATIONS

Beyond Port Angeles, accommodations are scarce, and places worth recommending tend to be popular, so it is wise to have reservations before heading west from Port Angeles. As the peninsula's biggest town and a base of operations for families exploring the national park, Port Angeles abounds in budget hotels. You'll find dozens along the section of U.S. 101 east of downtown.

✪ **Domaine Madeleine.** *146 Wildflower Lane, Port Angeles, WA 98362.* ☎ *360/457-4174. Fax 360/457-3037. 5 rms. $125–$165 double. Rates include full breakfast.*

*MC, V.* Located 7 miles east of Port Angeles, this secluded B&B with a waterfront setting offers guest rooms in several different buildings surrounded by colorful gardens, and with views of the Strait of Juan de Fuca and the mountains. Four rooms have whirlpools. Rooms have fireplaces and VCRs.

✪ **Lake Crescent Lodge.** *416 Lake Crescent Rd., Port Angeles, WA 98363-8672.* ☎ *360/928-3211. 52 rms and cabins (48 with bath). $70–$120 double with shared bath, double with private bath, or cottage. AE, CB, DC, MC, V. Open Apr–Oct.* This historic lodge, 20 miles west of Port Angeles on picturesque Lake Crescent, offers rustic wood paneling and stone floors. Except in the Lodge, rooms afford a lake or mountain view. Motel-style rooms and cottages are available, some with fireplaces. A dining room, lobby lounge, and rowboat rentals are on the premises.

**Red Lion Bayshore Inn.** *221 N. Lincoln St., Port Angeles, WA 98362.* ☎ *800/ 733-5466 or 360/452-9215. Fax 206/452-4734. 187 rms, 3 suites. $130–$150 double; $160 suite. Lower rates in off-season. AE, CB, DC, DISC, MC, V.* Located on the waterfront, the Red Lion is only steps from the ferry terminal, making it convenient when traveling to or from Victoria. Most rooms have balconies and large bathrooms, and the more expensive rooms overlook the Strait of Juan de Fuca. Extras include an adjacent seafood restaurant, outdoor pool, and hot tub.

**Sol Duc Hot Springs Resort.** *P.O. Box 2169, Sol Duc Rd., Hwy. 101, Port Angeles, WA 98362.* ☎ *360/327-3583. 32 cabins. $80–$95 double. AE, DISC, MC, V. Open mid-May to Sept.* The Springs, long a popular family vacation spot, attract campers, day-trippers, and resort guests to three hot spring–fed swimming pools. The resort grounds are grassy and open, but the forest is nearby. The modern cabins are comfortable if not spacious. The resort has a restaurant, poolside deli, and grocery store. Massages are available.

**Tudor Inn.** *1108 S. Oak St., Port Angeles, WA 98362.* ☎ *360/452-3138. 5 rms. Summer, $85–$120 double. Other months, $75–$110 double. Rates include full breakfast. MC, V.* In a residential neighborhood 13 blocks from the waterfront, this 1910 Tudor home is surrounded by a large yard and lovely gardens. Furnished with European antiques, the inn offers a lounge and library, both with fireplaces. Some rooms have a view of the Olympic Mountains.

**ON THE WEST SIDE OF THE PARK**  The town of Forks has several inexpensive motels and is a good place to look if you happen to be out this way without a reservation.

✪ **Kalaloch Lodge.** *157151 Hwy. 101, Forks, WA 98331.* ☎ *360/962-2271. Fax 360/962-3391. 18 rms, 40 cabins. $100–$116 double; $116–$176 double in cabins. Lower weekday rates in off-season. AE, MC, V.* Perched on a bluff above the thundering Pacific Ocean, the Kalaloch Lodge provides a breathtaking setting, making it very popular (book 4 months ahead). Ocean-view bluff cabins are most in demand. The Sea Crest House motel-style rooms are great for comfort. Facilities include a coffee shop, dining room, general store, and gas station.

✪ **Lake Quinault Lodge.** *P.O. Box 7, Quinault, WA 98575.* ☎ *800/562-6672 in Washington and Oregon, or 360/288-2900. 92 rms. June–Oct, $100–$135 double; $195 suite. Oct–June, $65–$110 double; $175 suite. AE, MC, V.* Situated on Lake Quinault, this peninsula grand dame possesses ageless tranquillity, with towering firs and cedars shading the rustic lodge and deck. Some rooms have balconies or fireplaces, but none have TVs or telephones. Guests enjoy the dining room, indoor pool, sauna, lawn games, canoe and paddleboat rentals, and massages.

**CAMPGROUNDS**  For information on the 16 campgrounds within the national park, contact the Olympic National Park or Olympic National Forest (see above for addresses and phone numbers). Campground fees are $10 per night. The **Deer Park campground,** in the high country south of Port Angeles, is one of the most spectacular, and **Sol Duc Hot Springs campground** is one of the most popular. If you want to say you've camped in the wettest campground in the contiguous U.S., head for the Hoh River valley. At the west end of Lake Crescent, you'll find the **Fairholm Campground.** On the banks of the Bogachiel River, **Bogachiel State Park** is another area option, as well as national park and private campgrounds along the shores of Lake Quinault.

North of the park, on the Strait of Juan de Fuca shore, are two county parks with campgrounds. **Salt Creek County Park** is 13 miles west of Port Angeles on Wash. 112 and **Pillar Point County Park** is another 22 miles further west.

The beaches offer some of the best camping but do not have established campgrounds. Several beaches are within 3 miles or so of the nearest road, while others require several days of walking.

## DINING

Outside of Port Angeles, the restaurant choices become exceedingly slim. The dining rooms at the lodges listed above are your best choices.

**C'est Si Bon.** *23 Cedar Park Rd., Port Angeles.* ☎ *360/452-8888. Reservations recommended. Main courses $19–$21. AE, CB, MC, V. Tues–Sun 5–11pm. FRENCH.* Four miles south of town off U.S. 101, C'est Si Bon offers classic decor, including European artworks. The limited menu assures each dish's quality, and the service is very French. Among the flavorful dishes, there are surprising sauces. The beef tenderloin comes in a red-currant sauce.

**Coffee House Restaurant.** *118 E. First St., Port Angeles.* ☎ *360/452-1459. Main courses $9–$13. MC, V. Mon–Sat 8am–8pm, Sun 9am–1pm. INTERNATIONAL.* This casual cafe draws on the cuisines of the world, with an emphasis on Mediterranean and Middle Eastern. There is an impressive pastry case and a modest selection of wines and, of course, espresso.

**Downriggers.** *115 E. Railroad Ave., Port Angeles.* ☎ *360/452-2700. Reservations recommended. Main courses $10–$19. DISC, MC, V. Mon–Sat 11:30am–11pm, Sun 11:30am–10pm. Closed later in summer. SEAFOOD.* This casual restaurant on the second level of the Landing Mall provides a glass-walled view of the ferries (so you don't miss yours) and great sunsets. A long menu offers a wide selection, including interesting dishes like salmon Wellington.

# 3 Portland

To appreciate this city at the confluence of the Columbia and Willamette rivers, one must cultivate an appreciation for Portland's subtle charms. A stroll through the Japanese Gardens on a misty May morning; a latte on the bricks at Pioneer Courthouse Square as the Weather Machine sculpture goes through its motions; an evening spent perusing the acres of books at Powell's City of Books; shopping for crafts at the Saturday Market; a summer festival on the banks of the Willamette River; a quick trip to the beach or Mount Hood—these are the quintessential Portland experiences. The city has museums, with the noteworthy Oregon Museum of Science and Industry leading the list. And there are theaters for live stage shows.

Portland seems to be a city on the verge. Restaurants and nightclubs are proliferating as never before, the city is extending its modern light-rail system into the western suburbs, and companies such as Nike and Intel are feeding the local economy. Attracted by the quality of life, more and more people are moving to Portland from across the country.

While Portland is growing quickly, so far it has done so deliberately without compromising its values and uniqueness. It's both cosmopolitan and accessible, with a subtle appeal and a laid-back attitude that is refreshing in this high-speed, high-stress age.

## ARRIVING & DEPARTING

**BY PLANE**   **Portland International Airport** is 10 miles northeast of downtown. By car or taxi, the trip into downtown takes about 20 minutes. Taxi fare is around $23. Many Portland hotels provide courtesy shuttle service to and from the airport, so check when you make your hotel reservation. The **Raz Transportation Downtown Shuttle** (☎ **503/246-3301**), located outside the baggage-claim area, will take you directly to your hotel for $8.50. They operate every 30 minutes daily from 5am to midnight. **Tri-Met public bus no. 12 (Sandy Boulevard)** leaves the airport for downtown approximately every 15 minutes from about 5:30am to 11:43pm. The trip takes about 40 minutes and costs $1.05.

**BY TRAIN & BUS**   **Amtrak** trains use the historic Union Station at 800 NW Sixth Ave., in northwest Portland near downtown (☎ **800/872-7245**). The **Greyhound** bus station is at 550 NW Sixth Ave., also in northwest Portland near downtown (☎ **800/ 231-2222**).

## ESSENTIALS

**VISITOR INFORMATION**   The walk-in office for the **Portland Oregon Visitor Association Information Center** is at Two World Trade Center, 25 SW Salmon St., in downtown Portland (☎ **800/345-3214** or 503/222-2223). The mailing address is Three World Trade Center, 26 SW Salmon St., Portland, OR 97204-3299. There is also an information booth by the baggage-claim area at Portland International Airport.

**EMERGENCIES & SAFETY**   For emergencies, phone ☎ **911.** The **Legacy Good Samaritan,** 1015 NW 22nd Ave. (☎ **503/229-7711**), in the heart of the northwest neighborhood, has an emergency room. Due to its small size and emphasis on a vibrant downtown, Portland remains a relatively safe city, but take extra precautions if venturing at night into the entertainment district along West Burnside Street or Chinatown. Parts of northeast Portland are controlled by street gangs, so get detailed directions before visiting this area. Don't leave anything valuable in your car anywhere.

## GETTING AROUND

City blocks in Portland are about half the average length, and since the entire downtown area is only some 13 by 26 blocks, it's easy to explore the city on foot.

**BY LIGHT RAIL & BUS**   The **Metropolitan Area Express (MAX)** is Portland's aboveground light-rail system connecting downtown Portland with the suburb of Gresham, 15 miles to the east. The ticket-vending machines at all MAX stops give change and the fare schedule for destinations. Light-rail trolleys are free within an area known as the **Fareless Square** between I-405 on the south and west, Hoyt Street on the north, and the Willamette River on the east. Otherwise, fares on Tri-Met buses are $1.05 or $1.35, depending on how far you travel. A $3.25 day ticket is good for all zones and valid on both buses and MAX. The **Tri-Met** information office (☎ **503/ 238-7433**) is open Mon–Fri 9am–5pm.

**BY TAXI**   Since nearly everything in Portland is close by, taxi travel can be economical. Taxis line up at major hotels, but otherwise you'll have to call **Broadway Cab** (☎ **503/227-1234**) or **Radio Cab** (☎ **503/227-1212**).

## WHAT TO SEE & DO

You can see Portland's attractions in a day or two. Portlanders prefer gardening to museum visits, so you'll find few museums—but can enjoy world-class public gardens here.

# Portland

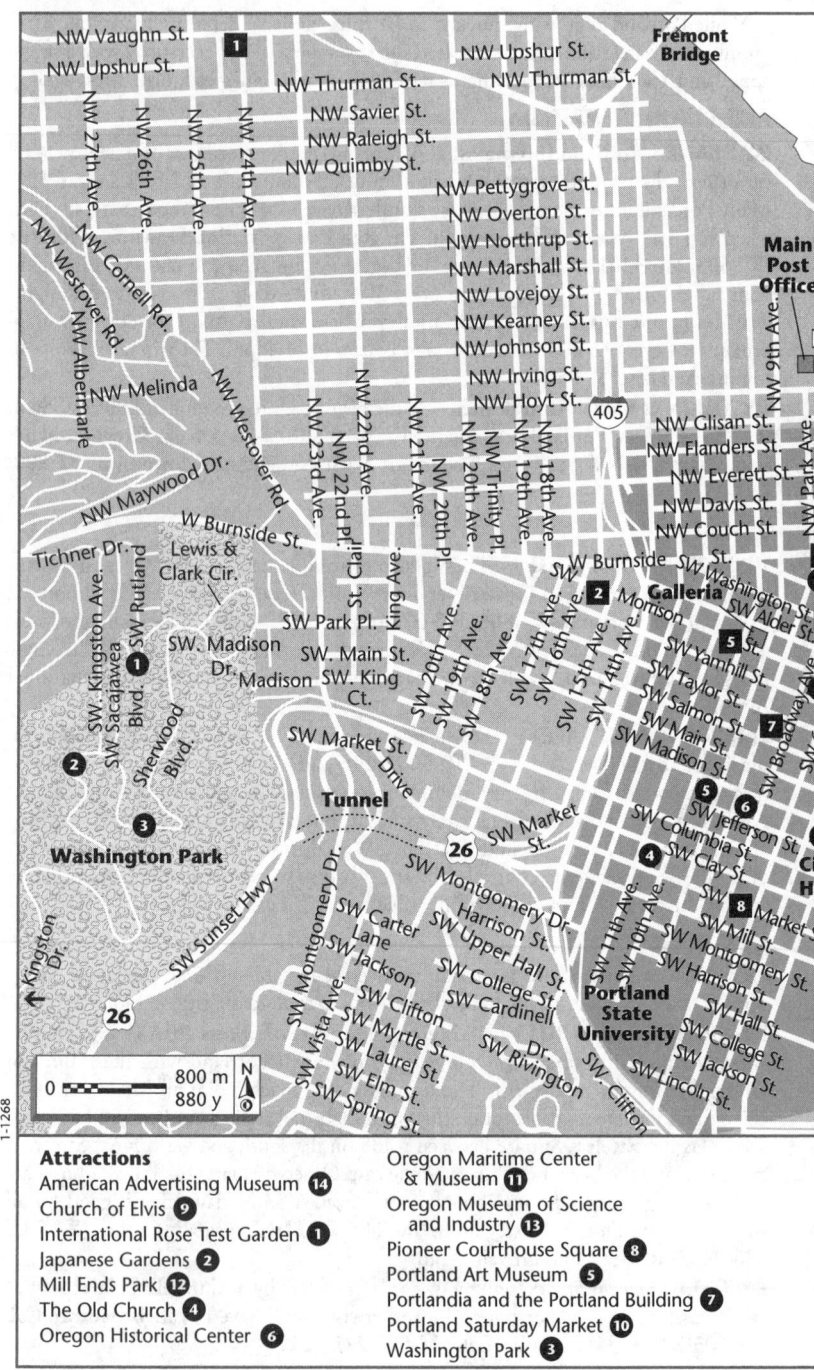

NW Vaughn St.
NW Upshur St.
NW Upshur St.
NW Thurman St.
NW Thurman St.
**Fremont Bridge**
NW 27th Ave.
NW 26th Ave.
NW 25th Ave.
NW 24th Ave.
NW Savier St.
NW Raleigh St.
NW Quimby St.
NW Pettygrove St.
NW Overton St.
NW Northrup St.
NW Marshall St.
NW Lovejoy St.
NW Kearney St.
NW Johnson St.
NW Irving St.
NW Hoyt St.
**Main Post Office**
NW Cornell Rd.
NW Westover Rd.
NW Albermarle
NW Melinda
NW Maywood Dr.
NW 23rd Ave.
NW 22nd Ave.
NW 22nd Pl.
NW 21st Ave.
NW 20th Ave.
NW Trinity Pl.
NW 19th Ave.
NW 18th Ave.
405
NW Glisan St.
NW Flanders St.
NW Everett St.
NW Davis St
NW Couch St.
NW 9th Ave.
NW Park Ave.
Tichner Dr.
W Burnside St.
Lewis & Clark Cir.
SW Kingston Ave.
SW Rutland
SW Sacajawea Blvd.
SW. Madison Dr.
Madison
SW. Madison Dr.
SW. Main St.
SW. King Ct.
Clair St.
King Ay Pky
SW Park Pl.
W Burnside
SW Washington St.
SW Morrison
**Galleria**
SW Alder St.
SW Yamhill St.
SW Taylor St.
SW Salmon St.
SW Main St.
SW Madison St.
SW Broadway Ave.
SW 6th
Sherwood Blvd.
SW Market St.
SW 20th Ave.
SW 19th Ave.
SW 18th Ave.
SW 17th Ave.
SW 16th Ave.
SW 15th Ave.
SW 14th Ave.
SW Jefferson St.
SW Columbia St.
SW Clay St.
SW Market St.
**Washington Park**
**Tunnel**
26
SW Market St.
SW Montgomery Dr.
Harrison St.
SW Upper Hall St.
SW Mill St.
SW Montgomery St.
SW Harrison St.
**Cit Ha**
SW Sunset Hwy.
Kingston Dr.
26
SW Montgomery Dr.
SW Carter Lane
SW Jackson
SW College St.
SW Cardinell
Dr.
SW Rivington
SW. Clifton
SW 11th Ave.
SW 10th Ave.
SW Hall St.
SW College St.
SW Jackson St.
SW Lincoln St.
**Portland State University**
SW Vista Ave.
SW Clifton
SW Myrtle St.
SW Laurel St.
SW Elm St.
SW Spring St.

0  800 m / 880 y
N

1-1268

## Attractions

American Advertising Museum ⑭
Church of Elvis ⑨
International Rose Test Garden ①
Japanese Gardens ②
Mill Ends Park ⑫
The Old Church ④
Oregon Historical Center ⑥

Oregon Maritime Center & Museum ⑪
Oregon Museum of Science and Industry ⑬
Pioneer Courthouse Square ⑧
Portland Art Museum ⑤
Portlandia and the Portland Building ⑦
Portland Saturday Market ⑩
Washington Park ③

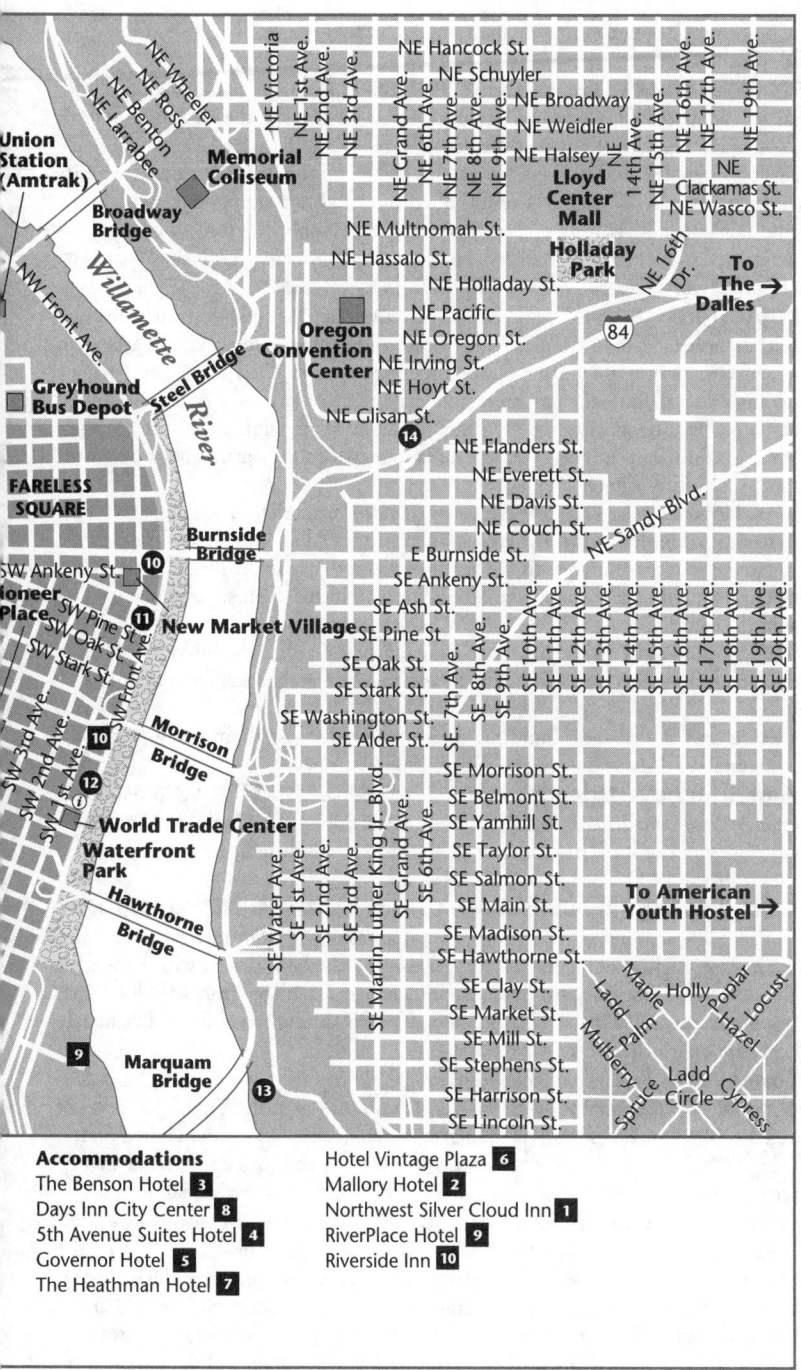

**Accommodations**

The Benson Hotel **3**
Days Inn City Center **8**
5th Avenue Suites Hotel **4**
Governor Hotel **5**
The Heathman Hotel **7**

Hotel Vintage Plaza **6**
Mallory Hotel **2**
Northwest Silver Cloud Inn **1**
RiverPlace Hotel **9**
Riverside Inn **10**

The beautiful Oregon countryside itself is a key attraction (see "Day Trips from Portland," below).

**ESCORTED TOURS** Gray Line (☎ 503/285-9834) offers half-day and full-day tours, including one for the International Rose Test Garden and the grounds of Pittock Mansion, and one for the Japanese Gardens and the World Forestry Center. A seasonal excursion offered is to Columbia Gorge and includes a sternwheeler ride. **Rose City Riverboat Cruises** (☎ 503/234-6665) offers modern catamaran power yacht cruises on the Willamette River from mid-April to October. Moonlight, Portland Harbor, and historical river tours are also available. For an in-depth winery tour of the Willamette Valley, call **Grape Escape** (☎ 503/282-4262).

**ATTRACTIONS** Bounded by Broadway, Sixth Avenue, Yamhill Street, and Morrison Street, Pioneer Courthouse Square is the heart of downtown Portland and acts as an outdoor stage for everything from flower displays to protest rallies. The square, with its tumbling waterfall fountain and freestanding columns, is Portland's favorite gathering spot, especially at noon when the "Weather Machine," a mechanical sculpture, predicts the weather for the upcoming 24 hours. Keep your eyes on the square's brick pavement for some surprising names.

A few blocks away, at 1120 SW Fifth Ave., stands **Portlandia,** the symbol of the city. This hammered bronze statue, reminiscent of a Greek goddess, is the second largest such statue in the country (the largest is the Statue of Liberty). Classically designed, the statue rests above the entrance to the Portland Building, considered the first postmodern structure in the country.

Three of Portland's major attractions—the Japanese Garden, the International Rose Test Garden, and the Metro Washington Park Zoo—are at the International Rose Test Garden.

Leisure time is well spent amid the cafes, restaurants, and shops along Portland's Northwest 23rd Avenue, starting at West Burnside Street.

**American Advertising Museum.** *50 SW Second Ave.* ☎ *503/226-0000. Admission $3 adults and seniors; $1.50 children under 12. Wed–Sat 11am–5pm, Sun noon–5pm.* Here you can learn or reminisce about historic advertisements, celebrities, and jingles from the 1700s until now.

**Crystal Springs Rhododendron Garden.** *SE 28th Ave.* ☎ *503/777-1734. Admission $2 from Mar 1 to Labor Day, Thurs–Mon 10am–6pm; free all other times. Daily dawn to dusk.* Eight months out of the year this is a tranquil garden, with a waterfall and ducks to feed. But when the rhododendrons and azaleas bloom from March to June, it becomes a spectacular mass of blazing color. The Rhododendron Show and Plant Sale is held here on Mother's Day weekend.

**Forest Park.** *Bounded by W. Burnside St., Newberry Rd., St. Helens Rd., and Skyline Rd.* ☎ *503/823-4492. Admission free. Daily dawn to dusk.* With 4,800 acres of forested wilderness, Forest Park is the largest forested city park in the United States, offering 50 miles of trails and old fire roads for hiking and jogging. More than 100 species of birds call these forests home, making this a bird-watchers' paradise.

✪ **International Rose Test Garden.** *400 SW Kingston Ave., Washington Park.* ☎ *503/823-3636. Admission free. Daily dawn to dusk.* Established in 1917 by the American Rose Society, these are the largest and oldest rose test gardens in the U.S., covering 4¹/₂ acres of hillsides above downtown Portland, which is known as the City of Roses. You'll find familiar roses, new hybrids, a separate garden of miniature roses, and a Shakespearean garden. The Rose Festival is the biggest celebration of the year in Portland.

✪ **Japanese Garden Society of Oregon.** *Off Kingston Ave. in Washington Park.* ☎ *503/223-1321. Admission $5 adults, $2.50 students and seniors, and children 6 and* *over. Apr 1–May 31 and Sept 1–Sept 30, daily 10am–6pm; June 1–Aug 31, daily 9am–8pm; Oct 1–Mar 31, daily 10am–4pm. Closed Thanksgiving, Christmas, and New Year's Day.* This tranquil garden is special not only for its design and plantings but the view afforded on a clear day of Portland and spectacular Mt. Hood beyond.

○ **Metro Washington Park Zoo.** *4001 SW Canyon Rd., Washington Park.* ☎ *503/226-1561. Admission $5.50 adults, $4 seniors, $3.50 children ages 3–11; free second Tues of each month from 3pm to closing. Memorial Day–Labor Day, daily 9:30am–6pm; Labor Day–Memorial Day, daily 9:30am–4pm.* This zoo has the largest breeding herd of elephants in captivity and an African exhibit with an impressive simulated rain forest, as well as a convincing Alaskan tundra exhibit. The Washington Park and Zoo Railway travels between the zoo and the International Rose Test Garden and Japanese Gardens. In the summer there are concerts on Wednesday and Thursday from 7 to 9pm.

**Oregon Historical Center.** *1200 SW Park Ave.* ☎ *503/222-1741. Admission $6 adults and seniors, $3 students, $1.50 children 6–12, free for seniors on Thurs. Tues–Sat 10am–5pm, Sun noon–5pm. Bus: Any downtown bus.* The Oregon Territory was a land of promise and plenty. Thousands of hardy individuals set out along the Oregon Trail to cross a vast and rugged country to reach the fertile valleys of Oregon's rivers. Oregon history from before the first white men arrived to well into this century is chronicled in educational and fascinating exhibits.

**Oregon Maritime Center and Museum.** *113 SW Front Ave.* ☎ *503/224-7724. Admission $4 adults, $3 seniors, $2 students, free for children under 8. Summer, Wed–Sun 11am–4pm. Winter, Fri–Sun 11am–4pm.* On display here are models of ships that once plied the Columbia and Willamette rivers, early navigation instruments, and maritime memorabilia. The historic sternwheeler *Portland,* moored across Waterfront Park, is also open to the public.

○ **Oregon Museum of Science and Industry (OMSI).** *1945 SE Water Ave.* ☎ *800/955-6674 or 503/797-4000. Admission $6 adults, $4.50 seniors and children 4–13. IMAX and light shows cost extra, although discounted combination tickets are available. Thurs 3pm until closing all tickets are 2-for-1. Tues–Sat 9:30am–5:30pm (until 7pm in summer), Thurs 9:30am–8pm. Closed Christmas.* The impressive OMSI building on the east bank of the Willamette River has six huge halls, and kids and adults enjoy the exhibits, including two that allow visitors to touch a tornado or ride an earthquake. This is a hands-on museum and everyone is urged to get involved with displays. Entertainment is offered at an IMAX theater and the Murdock Sky Theater, which features laser-light shows and astronomy presentations. The USS *Blueback* submarine is docked here, with daily tours offered. Also, a small train makes runs to the Oaks Park amusement park.

**Pittock Mansion.** *3229 NW Pittock Dr.* ☎ *503/823-3624. Admission $4.25 adults, $3.75 seniors, $2 ages 6–18. Daily noon–4pm. Closed 3 days in late Nov, most major holidays, and the first 3 weeks of Jan.* Once slated for demolition, this 1914 French Renaissance–style chateau has been restored and furnished with 18th- and 19th-century antiques. Lunch and afternoon tea are available in the **Gate Lodge** (☎ *503/823-3627*), where reservations are recommended.

**Portland Art Museum.** *1219 SW Park Ave.* ☎ *503/226-2811. Admission $6 adults, $4.50 seniors and students, $2.50 children 6–15, seniors half price on Thurs. Half price 4–9pm on the first Thurs of each month. Tues–Sun 10am–5pm; first Thurs of each month 10am–9pm.* Although this small museum has a respectable collection of European, Asian, and American art, it is the Northwest Coast Native American exhibit that requires a special visit. Particularly fascinating are the transformation masks, worn during ritual dances, and the totem pole and woodcarvings of the Northwest tribes. There are also exhibits of regional contemporary art, Asian antiquities, primitive African art from Cameroon, and a large hall for temporary exhibits. On Wednesday night (except in summer), the Museum After Hours program presents live music.

**World Forestry Center.** *4033 SW Canyon Rd.* ☎ *503/228-1367. $3 adults, $2 seniors and children 6–18. Daily 9am–5pm (10am–5pm in winter). Closed Christmas.* This center serves to educate visitors about forest resources and offers exhibits on forests of the world and old-growth trees. A vintage carousel is on the grounds in summer.

**BEST BETS FOR KIDS** Children will get a kick at the **Oregon Museum of Science and Industry (OMSI),** the **World Forestry Center,** and the **Metro Washington Park Zoo** (see above). In addition, the **Portland Children's Museum,** 3037 SW Second Ave. (☎ 503/823-2227), offers a variety of participatory activities, from a kid-size medical center to a clay shop. **Oaks Park,** at the east end of the Sellwood Bridge (☎ 503/ 233-5777), is the complete amusement park, from wild rides to waterfront picnic sites. The largest roller-skating rink in the Northwest is here.

**SPORTS** The **Portland Trail Blazers,** one of the hottest NBA teams in recent years, pound the boards Oct–Apr at the Rose Garden, at the Broadway exit off I-5 (☎ 503/ 231-8000).

**SHOPPING** Over the past few years Portland has preserved and restored much of its historic architecture, and some late 19th-century and early 20th-century buildings now serve as unusual and attractive shopping centers. **New Market Village** (50 SW Second Ave.), **Morgan's Alley** (515 SW Broadway), and **Skidmore Fountain Square** (28 SW First Ave.) are fine examples.

Portland's most "happening" areas for shopping, along with downtown Portland, are in the northwest neighborhood along Northwest 23rd Avenue beginning at West Burnside Street; Northeast Broadway around Northeast 15th Avenue; and Southeast Hawthorne Street around Southeast 32nd Avenue. Here you'll find antique stores, boutiques, card shops, design studios, ethnic restaurants, florists, galleries, home furnishings stores, interior decorators, pubs, and the other necessities of Bohemian neighborhoods gone upscale.

With its old Victorian homes and turn-of-the-century architecture, Sellwood is Portland's main antique district, with 13 blocks of antique dealers and restaurants at the east end of Sellwood Bridge on SE 13th Street.

Worth a visit are **Powell's "City of Books,"** 1005 W. Burnside St. (☎ 800/ 878-7323 or 503/228-4651), one of the largest bookstores on the West Coast; and the **Real Mother Goose,** 901 SW Yamhill St. (☎ 503/223-9510), showcasing only the very finest contemporary American crafts, and also located at the Portland Airport, Main Terminal (☎ 503/284-9929).

Oregon charges no sales tax, which adds to any bargains you will find here.

**MARKETS** The **Portland Saturday Market,** beneath the Burnside Bridge between SW First Avenue and SW Ankeny Street (☎ 503/222-6072), is a Sunday market as well. Open March–Christmas Eve, this is arguably Portland's single best-loved event, with some 300 artists and craftspeople selling crafts and creations, and flowers, fresh produce, ethnic and unusual foods, with free entertainment available.

## ACCOMMODATIONS

If you are planning to visit Portland during the busy summer months, make your reservations as far in advance as possible and be sure to ask if there are any special rates available. Almost all large hotels offer weekend discounts of as much as 50%. In fact, you might even be able to get a discount simply by asking for one. Chain motels are plentiful in the Tigard–Tualitin I-5 corridor about 10 miles south of Portland.

**Benson Hotel.** *309 SW Broadway, Portland, OR 97205.* ☎ *800/426-0670 or 503/228-2000. Fax 503/226-4603. 287 rms, 46 junior suites, 9 suites. $190 double; $210–$600 suite. AE, CB, DC, DISC, ER, JCB, MC, V. Valet parking $12.* The vintage 1912 Benson, with a French baroque lobby, exudes Old World charm. The guest rooms, in two towers above the lobby, offer classic French Second Empire furnishings. The noted London Grill restaurant is here, and two lounges. Extras include in-room modems, 24-hour room service, a gift shop, and a weight room.

**Days Inn City Center.** *1414 SW Sixth Ave., Portland, OR 97201.* ☎ *800/899-0248 or 503/221-1611. 175 rms. $100–$111 double. AE, CB, DC, MC, V. Free parking.* In the heart of downtown Portland, this hotel is an excellent choice for budget-minded business travelers and family vacationers. Each room offers a small library, brass beds, and picture window. With its brass rails and wood trim, the restaurant is popular with the business set for lunch. Room service and complimentary newspapers are available.

**5th Avenue Suites Hotel.** *506 SW Washington St., Portland, OR 97204.* ☎ *800/711-2971 or 503/222-0001. Fax 503/222-0004. 221 rooms, 139 suites. $160 double; $170–$225 suite. AE, DC, DISC, JCB, MC, V. Valet parking $13.* Conveniently located a block from Pioneer Square, this hotel is a converted department store. Turn-of-the-century country rooms offer plush chairs and brocade headboards. The popular Red Star Tavern and Roast House is here. The hotel provides complimentary wine, morning coffee and newspaper, turndown service, 24-hour room service, a fitness center, spa, and business center.

**Governor Hotel.** *SW 10th Ave. and Alder St., Portland, OR 97205.* ☎ *800/554-3456 or 503/224-3400. Fax 503/241-2122. 100 rms, 27 suites. $180–$185 double; $195–$235 suite. AE, CB, DC, JCB, MC, V. Valet parking $13.* Rooms here feature Asian influence, including porcelain lamps and lacquered tables. Some rooms are small but nevertheless comfortable. Suites are spacious, some with patios overlooking the city. The fully equipped athletic club includes a lap pool, indoor running track, and whirlpool spa. The hotel has a restaurant, 24-hour room service, complimentary morning newspaper and coffee, and business center.

✪ **Heathman Hotel.** *SW Broadway at Salmon St., Portland, OR 97205.* ☎ *800/551-0011 or 503/241-4100. Fax 503/790-7110. 150 rms, 30 suites. $160–$205 double; $225–$575 suite. AE, CB, DC, MC, V. Parking $12.* Portland's finest hotel, the Heathman features original art in each room. There are two restaurants, including the Heathman Restaurant, one of Portland's best (see "Dining," below), and a Mezzanine Bar offering daily tea and jazz some evenings. Guests appreciate the 24-hour room service, complimentary newspaper, business services, athletic club, and on-site fitness suite.

✪ **Hotel Vintage Plaza.** *422 SW Broadway, Portland, OR 97205.* ☎ *800/243-0555 or 503/228-1212. Fax 503/228-3598. 107 rms, 21 suites. $175–185 double; $205–$225 suite. All rates include continental breakfast. AE, CB, DC, DISC, MC, V. Valet parking $13.* An interesting Italianate and wine decor prevails, with Roman shades and pink-granite bathroom counters in the rooms. Starlight rooms with ceiling windows and two-level suites, some with soaking tubs, are stunning. There is an Italian restaurant (see "Dining," below). Complimentary evening wine, morning newspaper and coffee, an executive gym, and a business center are conveniences at this hotel.

**Mallory Hotel.** *729 SW 15th Ave., Portland, OR 97205-1994.* ☎ *800/228-8657 or 503/223-6311. Fax 503/223-0522. 136 rms, 26 suites. $70–$110 double; $110 suite. AE, CB, DC, MC, V.* The Mallory, a long-time favorite of Portland visitors seeking inexpensive downtown lodging, is a faded grandeur old hotel but with clean and comfortable rooms and huge suites with refrigerators and sofa beds. The dining room continues the grand design of the lobby. Local calls are free.

**Northwest Silver Cloud Inn.** *2426 NW Vaughn St., Portland, OR 97210-2540.* ☎ *800/551-7207 or 503/242-2400. Fax 503/242-1770. 81 rms. $78 double; $95 minisuite. Rates include continental breakfast. AE, DC, DISC, MC, V.* This attractive and comfortable newer hotel north of Portland's trendy northwest neighborhood is near the best restaurants, although it edges an industrial area (get a room away from Vaughn Street). Rooms have refrigerators; minisuites have wet bars and microwaves; and king rooms offer whirlpools. Local calls are free and a fitness room and whirlpool are on the premises.

**Park Lane Inn and Suites.** *809 SW King St., Portland, OR 97205.* ☎ *800/532-9543 or 503/226-6288. Fax 503/274-0038. 82 rms. $59–$89 double. Rates include continental breakfast. AE, DC, DISC, MC, V.* This motel sits a little up into the hills west of downtown and offers views of the city. A plus here is that you are within walking distance of both the northwest shopping and restaurant district and Washington Park, home of the Japanese Garden and the Rose Test Gardens.

✪ **Riverplace Hotel.** *1510 SW Harbor Way, Portland, OR 97201.* ☎ *800/227-1333 outside Oregon, or 503/228-3233. Fax 503/295-6161. 84 rms, 47 suites. $185–$225 double; $210–$375 suite. Rates include continental breakfast. AE, CB, DC, JCB, MC, V. Valet parking $14.* With European resort charm and spacious rooms and suites, some with fireplaces and whirlpools, the Riverplace sits beside the Willamette River and Waterfront Park. The **Esplanade** restaurant offers a river view. Extras include 24-hour room service, in-room computers, whirlpools, saunas, and privileges at an athletic club.

**Riverside Inn.** *50 SW Morrison Ave., Portland, OR 97204.* ☎ *800/899-0247 or 503/221-0711. Fax 503/274-0312. 140 rms. $170 double. AE, CB, DC, DISC, MC, V.* Overlooking Waterfront Park and located on the MAX light-rail line, the Riverside is steps from the Willamette River, restaurants, and shopping. The rooms, many with river views, offer modern furnishings and a small library of books. The restaurant affords a lovely water view. A complimentary newspaper and use of a fitness club are offered.

## DINING

The Portland restaurant scene is hopping. Good new restaurants seem to open weekly, many of them in the northwest neighborhood, and especially along NW 21st Avenue.

**Bima.** *1338 NW Hoyt St.* ☎ *503/241-3465. Reservations recommended. Main courses $12–$16. AE, MC, V. Mon–Thurs 11:30am–10pm, Fri–Sat 11:30am–11pm. GULF COAST.* This warehouse restaurant has softened the cavernous space with lighting and oversized booths. The food combines Southern and Caribbean styles, much of it fiery, and affords a contrast to other Portland restaurants. Try an appetizer of kumomoto oysters, thick cornbread, or the catfish fillets covered in crushed pecans.

**B. Moloch/Heathman Bakery and Pub.** *901 SW Salmon St.* ☎ *503/227-5700. Reservations not accepted. Main courses $8–$13. AE, DC, DISC, MC, V. Mon–Thurs 7am–10pm, Fri 7am–11:30pm, Sat 8am–11:30pm, Sun 8am–10:30pm. NORTHWEST.* Corporate climbers and bicycle messengers rub shoulders here, quaffing microbrews and enjoying wood-oven pizzas. The bright, noisy atmosphere amid industrial decor is softened by colorful images of salmon. Gourmet pizzas are the mainstay, and there are sandwiches, pasta dishes, and great salads. Beyond a glass wall is a microbrewery.

✪ **Caprial's Bistro and Wines.** *7015 SE Milwaukee Ave.* ☎ *503/236-6457. Reservations highly recommended. Main courses $14–$19. MC, V. Tues–Fri 11am–3:30pm, Sat noon–3:30pm; Wed–Thurs 5–8:30pm, Fri–Sat 5–9pm. NORTHWEST.* Chef Caprial Pence helped put the Northwest on the national restaurant map, and Caprial's, while small and casual, is a contender for best restaurant in Portland. Wines and wine bar dominate, and four or five main dishes are offered. Entrees include roast pork loin or lightly breaded oysters.

**Esparzaõs Tex–Mex Café.** *2725 SE Ankeny St.* ☎ *503/234-7909. Reservations not accepted. Main courses $5–$11. MC, V. Tues–Sat 11:30am–10pm (in summer, Fri– Sat until 10:30pm). TEX–MEX.* The Tex-clectic decor includes cow skulls and stuffed armadillos. The equally eclectic menu offers standards like tamales, but stuffed with buffalo. Rest assured you can get regular chicken and beef. Main courses come with some of the best rice and beans ever. The *nopalitos* (fried cactus) are worth a try.

**Fernando's Hideaway.** *824 SW First Ave.* ☎ *503/248-4709. Reservations recommended. Main courses $13–$20. AE, DC, MC, V. Mon–Thurs 5–10pm, Fri–Sat 5–11pm, Sun noon–9pm. SPANISH.* Fernando's is enormously popular for good tapas, such as spicy oysters, but the Spanish entree is also a delight. Roasted chicken with an apricot and nut sauce is artfully arranged with potato wedges and spinach dollops. The service is professional without a trendy attitude.

**✪ Heathman Restaurant and Bar.** *In the Heathman Hotel, SW Broadway at Salmon St.* ☎ *503/241-4100. Reservations highly recommended. Main courses $10–$25. AE, CB, DC, MC, V. Daily 6:30am–2pm and 5–11pm. NORTHWEST/FRENCH.* The menu in this elegant hotel dining room changes seasonally, but the ingredients remain the freshest Northwest seafoods, meats, wild game, and produce. Both the adventurous diner and the traditionalist will find dishes here, like red snapper with a potato and parsley crust, or venison wrapped in applewood-smoked bacon.

**Higgins.** *1239 SW Broadway.* ☎ *503/222-9070. Reservations highly recommended. Main courses $13–$19. AE, DC, MC, V. Mon–Fri 11:30am–2pm; daily 5–10:30pm; bistro menu served Mon–Fri 2pm–midnight. NORTHWEST/MEDITERRANEAN.* Wood paneling and hanging copper pots provide classic ambience for chef Greg Higgins's creations. His menu is contemporary with offerings such as duck liver flan with green peppercorns and walnut crackers. Entrees include such dishes as grilled sausage made from chicken.

**✪ Il Piatto.** *2348 SE Ankeny St.* ☎ *503/236-4997. Reservations highly recommended Thurs–Sat. Dinner main courses $7–$13; lunch main courses $6–$9. MC, V. Tues–Fri 11:30am–2:30pm; Sun–Thurs 5:30–10pm, Fri–Sat 5:30–11pm. NORTHERN ITALIAN.* Il Piatto is a small neighborhood restaurant with a relaxed atmosphere, including a comfy lounge area for coffee sipping. The marinated rabbit gets rave reviews. Italian desserts are all made by the pastry chef. Il Piatto is open throughout the day for coffee and pastry.

**Jake's Famous Crawfish.** *401 SW 12th St.* ☎ *503/226-1419. Reservations recommended. Main courses $11–$27. AE, DC, DISC, MC, V. Mon–Thurs 11:30am–11pm, Fri 11:30am–midnight, Sat 5pm–midnight, Sun 5–10pm (until 11pm in summer). SEAFOOD.* Jake's has been serving up crayfish since 1909, and the decor is well worn. The noise level can be loud and the wait long without reservations, but it is one of Portland's most popular restaurants, offering 15 to 20 daily specials and, of course, crayfish prepared several different ways.

**L'Etoile.** *4627 NE Fremont St.* ☎ *503/281-4869. Reservations recommended. Main courses $17–$24. MC, V. Tues–Sat 5–9pm. FRENCH.* With its *fin de siècle* decor, intimate Parisian bar, and Edith Piaf on the stereo, L'Etoile is quintessentially French. Rich classic French cuisine prevails, from crusty French bread to escargots. Main courses might include venison with a chestnut, fennel, walnut, and onion compote or duck breast with tangerines and cranberries.

**McCormick & Schmick's.** *235 SW First Ave.* ☎ *503/224-7522. Reservations highly recommended. Main courses $9–$20; bar meals $1.95; lunches $6–$12. AE, DC,*

*MC, V. Mon–Thurs 11:30am–10:30pm, Fri 11:30am–11pm; Sat 4:30–11pm, Sun 4:30–10pm. SEAFOOD.* The oysters go by first names, like Olympia, and the daily fresh menu might list 25 seafoods, including grilled rainbow trout with apple-smoked bacon and currant chutney. Oregon wines are featured on the extensive wine list. There is an $8.25 dinner menu daily from 5 to 6:15pm and 9:30pm until closing.

✪ **Pazzo Ristorante.** *627 SW Washington St. (at Broadway).* ☎ *503/228-1515. Reservations highly recommended. Main courses $8–$17; lunch $8–$14. AE, CB, DC, DISC, MC, V. Mon–Fri 7–10:30am, Sat 8–10:30am, Sun 8–11am; Mon–Sat 11:30am–2:30pm; Mon–Thurs 5–10pm, Fri–Sat 5–11pm, Sun noon–10pm. NORTHERN ITAL-IAN.* The atmosphere here is not as rarefied as in the adjacent hotel lobby, and you may duck hanging hams and sausages at the bar. Rustic decor speaks of an Italian country ristorante. Garlicky dishes abound, but departures include grilled duck with braised red cabbage or ravioli stuffed with smoked salmon.

✪ **Ron Paul Charcuterie.** *1441 NE Broadway.* ☎ *503/284-5347. Also at 6141 SW Macadam Ave.* ☎ *503/977-0313. Reservations not accepted. Sandwiches $5–$8; main courses $6–$15. AE, MC, V. Mon–Thurs 8am–10:30pm, Fri 8am–midnight, Sat 9am–midnight, Sun 9am–4pm. MEDITERRANEAN/DELI.* A casual deli-style place in an upwardly mobile neighborhood offering long cases of tempting fare like pasta-and-vegetable salads and decadent desserts. After 5pm, there are specials such as lamb in filo with goat cheese. Both locations serve Saturday and Sunday brunch and have extensive selections of Northwest wines.

✪ **Wildwood.** *1221 NW 21st Ave.* ☎ *503/248-WOOD. Reservations highly recommended. Main courses $14–$22. AE, MC, V. Mon–Sat 11:30am–2:30pm; Mon–Thurs 5:30–10pm, Fri–Sat 5:30–10:30pm, Sun 5–8:30pm; Sun brunch 10am–2pm. MEDITERRANEAN.* A hit with urban sophisticates, Wildwood offers booths, a meal counter, bar area, and patio. The short menu, changed daily, relies primarily on the subtle flavors of the Mediterranean. Entrees include roast lamb with a white-bean puree.

✪ **Zefiro Restaurant and Bar.** *500 NW 21st Ave.* ☎ *503/226-3394. Reservations highly recommended. Main courses $14–$18. AE, DC, MC, V. Mon–Fri 11:30am–2:30pm; Mon–Thurs 5:30–10pm, Fri–Sat 5:30–10:30pm. MEDITERRANEAN.* Chef Christopher Israel's creativity stands out amid minimalist decor at this popular restaurant. The Mediterranean menu is dominated by old-style Italian and French cuisine, but includes influences ranging from Moroccan to Asian. Roasted mahimahi with an herb salsa verde made from seven spices captures a Mediterranean herb garden in one dish.

## PORTLAND AFTER DARK

To find out what's going on during your visit, pick up the arts-and-entertainment newspaper, *Willamette Week.* You can also check the Friday *A & E* section and Sunday edition of the *Oregonian,* the city's daily newspaper. Many theaters and performance halls offer student and senior discounts, and buying your ticket on the day of a performance or within a half hour of curtain time can often save you some money. Tickets for many of the venues listed below can be purchased through **GI Joe's/Ticketmaster** (☎ **503/224-4400**) or **Fastixx** at Fred Meyer (☎ **503/224-TIXX**).

**THE PERFORMING ARTS**    The **Portland Center for the Performing Arts,** 1111 SW Broadway, is comprised of four theaters in three buildings, including the **Arlene Schnitzer Concert Hall,** Southwest Broadway and Southwest Main Street, an immaculately restored movie palace; the Intermediate and Winningstad theaters in the New Theatre Building, across the street from Schnitzer Hall; and the **Portland Civic Auditorium,** Southwest Third Avenue and Southwest Clay Street. The center plays host to the Oregon Symphony (☎ **800/228-7343** or 503/228-1353), the Oregon Ballet

Theatre (☎ 503/222-5538), the Portland Opera (☎ 503/241-1802), the Portland Center Stage (☎ 503/274-6588), and touring companies.

The **Portland Repertory Theater,** World Trade Center, 25 SW Salmon St. (☎ 503/224-4491), is the city's oldest Equity theater and offers excellent productions. The **Tygres Heart Shakespeare Co.,** 309 SW Sixth Ave., Suite 102 (☎ 503/222-9220), performs only Shakespearean works.

**THE CLUB & MUSIC SCENE**    The **Aladdin Theater,** 3017 SE Milwaukee Ave. (☎ 503/233-1994), once a movie theater, now serves as one of Portland's main venues for touring performers from a diverse musical spectrum. The **Brasserie Montmartre,** 626 SW Park Ave. (☎ 503/224-5552), offers live jazz nightly. Both food and music are popular with a largely middle-aged clientele who like to dress up when out of town. ✪ **La Luna,** 215 SE Ninth Ave. (☎ 503/241-5862), with its stage in a cavernous room, offers a wide range of lesser-known national acts for a reasonable price. ✪ **Rock n' Rodeo,** 220 SE Spokane St. (☎ 503/235-2417), is the place for fans of western dancing, with lessons offered. As the evening progresses, it is a swirl of cowboy boots, skirts, and jeans. ✪ **Atwaters,** 111 SW Fifth Ave. (☎ 503/275-3600), is located on the 30th floor of the U.S. BanCorp building, and affords the best view in Portland. Thursday through Saturday evenings there is live jazz.

There are a number of popular "brew pubs." **Bridgeport Brewery & Brew Pub,** 1313 NW Marshall St. (☎ 503/241-7179), is Portland's oldest microbrewery, founded in 1984, and is housed in the city's oldest industrial building. Windows behind the bar allow a view of the brewers. It has four to seven of its brews on tap, and great pizza. ✪ **Hillsdale Brewery & Public House,** 1505 SW Sunset Blvd. (☎ 503/246-3938), was the cornerstone of the McMenamin brothers' microbrewery empire that now includes more than 20 pubs in the greater metropolitan area. These pubs craft flavorful and unusual ales. Other McMenamin pubs include the **Blue Moon Tavern,** 432 NW 21st St. (☎ 503/223-3184), on a fashionable street in northwest Portland; and the **Ram's Head,** 2282 NW Hoyt St. (☎ 503/221-0098), between 21st and 22nd avenues.

## DAY TRIPS FROM PORTLAND

**VANCOUVER, WASHINGTON**    This often overlooked city offers several historic sites and other attractions that make it a good day-long excursion from Portland. The first three attractions listed here are all in the 1-square-mile Central Park, just east of I-5 (take the East Mill Plain Boulevard exit just after you cross the bridge into Washington).

It was in the U.S. Vancouver (as opposed to the Canadian city) that much of the Northwest's important early pioneer history unfolded at the Hudson's Bay Company's Fort Vancouver. Fur trappers, mountain men, missionaries, explorers, and settlers all made Fort Vancouver their first stop in this area. Today the **Fort Vancouver National Historic Site,** 1501 E. Evergreen Blvd. (☎ 360/696-7655), houses several reconstructed buildings with mid-19th-century furnishings (open daily 9am–5pm, until 4pm in the winter; free admission in winter, $2 in summer).

When Fort Vancouver became a U.S. military post, stately officers' homes were built and these have been preserved as the **Officers' Row National Historic District.** Stop in at the **Grant House Folk Art Center** (☎ 360/694-5252), named for President Ulysses S. Grant, who was stationed here as quartermaster in the 1850s (open Tues–Sun 10am–5pm). A cafe here serves good lunches. Further along Officers' Row, you'll find the **George C. Marshall House** (☎ 360/693-3103), a Victorian-style building that replaced the Grant House as the commanding officer's quarters (open Mon–Fri 9am–5pm).

The nearby **Pearson Air Museum,** 1115 E. Fifth St. (☎ 360/694-7026), offers dozens of vintage aircraft, including several World War I biplanes. This airfield was established in 1905 and is the oldest operating airfield in the U.S. (open Wed–Sun noon–5pm; admission $4 adults, $3 seniors, $1.50 students).

In the town of **Washougal,** 16 miles east of Vancouver on Wash. 14, you can visit the **Pendleton Woolen Mills and Outlet Shop,** 2 17th St., Washougal (☎ 360/835-2131), and see how the famous wool blankets and classic wool fashions are made (open Mon–Fri 8am–5pm, Sat 9am–5pm; free mill tours Mon–Fri at 9, 10, and 11am, and 1:30pm).

Ten miles north at the town of Battle Ground, you can ride a diesel-powered **Lewis River Excursion Train,** which has its depot at 1000 E. Main St. in Battle Ground (☎ 360/687-2626). The 2-hour excursions run from Battle Ground to Moulton Falls County Park. Call for a schedule; tickets for regular excursions are $10 adults, $5 children.

In the town of **Woodland,** 23 miles north of Vancouver, are the **Hulda Klager Lilac Gardens,** 115 S. Pekin Rd., Woodland (☎ 360/225-8996). Between late April and Mother's Day, these gardens burst into color (open daily dawn–dusk; admission $1).

Ten miles east of Woodland off NE Cedar Creek Road, the **Cedar Creek Grist Mill,** Grist Mill Road (☎ 360/225-9552), is the only remaining 19th-century grist mill in Washington (open Sat 1–4pm, Sun 2–4pm; admission by donation).

**OREGON CITY & THE END OF THE OREGON TRAIL**   When the first settlers began crossing the Oregon Trail in the early 1840s, their destination was Oregon City and the fertile Willamette Valley. At the time Portland had yet to be founded, and Oregon City, set beside powerful Willamette Falls, was the largest town in Oregon. However, with the development of Portland and the shifting of the capital to Salem, Oregon City began to lose its importance. Today this is primarily an industrial town, though one steeped in Oregon history and well worth a visit.

To get to Oregon City from Portland, you can take I-5 south to I-205 east or you can head south from downtown Portland on SW Riverside Drive and drive through the wealthy suburbs of Lake Oswego and West Linn. Once in Oregon City, your first stop should be just south of town at the **Willamette Falls Overlook** on Ore. 99E. Though the falls have been much changed by industry over the years, they are still an impressive sight.

Oregon City is divided into upper and lower sections by a steep bluff. A 100-foot free municipal elevator, at the corner of Seventh Street and Railroad Avenue, connects the two halves of the city and affords a great view from its observation area at the top of the bluff. In the upper section of town are many historic homes.

Oregon City's most famous citizen was retired Hudson's Bay Company chief factor John McLoughlin, who helped found Oregon City in 1829. By the 1840s, immigrants were pouring into Oregon, and McLoughlin provided food, seeds, and tools to many. Upon retirement in 1846, McLoughlin moved to Oregon City where he built what was at that time the most luxurious home in Oregon. Today the **McLoughlin House,** 713 Center St. (☎ 503/656-5146), is a National Historic Site and is open to the public (open Tues–Sat 10am–4pm, Sun 1–4pm; admission $3 adults, $2.50 seniors, $1 children).

Several other Oregon City historical homes are also open to the public. The **Clackamas County Historical Museum,** 211 Tumwater Dr. (☎ 503/655-5574), houses collections of historic memorabilia and old photos from this area (open Mon–Fri 10am–4pm, Sat–Sun 1–5pm; admission $3.50 adults, $2.50 seniors, $1.50 children 6–12). The **Stevens–Crawford House,** 603 Sixth St. (☎ 503/655-2866), is a foursquare-style home furnished with late-19th-century antiques (open Tues–Sun 10am–4pm; in summer, Mon 1–4pm also; admission $3 adults, $2 seniors, $1.50 children 6–12).

The story of the settlers who traveled the Oregon Trail is told at the **End of the Oregon Trail Interpretive Center,** 1726 Washington St. (☎ **503/657-9336**), which is designed to resemble three giant covered wagons (open Mon–Sat 9am–5pm, Sun 10am–5pm; admission $4.50 adults, $2.50 seniors and children 5–12).

Another interesting chapter in Oregon pioneer history is preserved 13 miles south of Oregon City in the town of **Aurora,** which was founded in 1855 as a Christian communal society that lasted some 20 years. Today Aurora is a National Historic District and the large old homes of the community's founders have been restored. Many of the old commercial buildings house antique stores, which are the main reason most people visit Aurora. At the **Old Aurora Colony Museum** (☎ **503/678-5754**) you can learn about the history of Aurora (open Tues–Sat 10am–4pm, Sun noon–4pm; admission $3.50 adults, $3 seniors, $1.50 for those under 18).

On your way back to Portland, consider taking the **Canby ferry,** one of the last remaining ferries on the Willamette River. To take the ferry, head 4 miles north on Ore. 99E to Canby and watch for ferry signs.

# 4 Glacier National Park

Glacier National Park is so named because 48 slow-moving glaciers continue to carve valleys throughout its incredible expanse of nearly a million majestic, wild acres. From the incredible wildflowers that coat the springtime meadows to the astonishing peaks that remain snowcapped even in summer, Glacier is a postcard come to life. Moose and elk still roam the land and can be found virtually anywhere. But the unofficial mascot in these parts is the grizzly bear, a refugee from the High Plains who now inhabits the Montana mountains.

Along with adjoining Waterton Lakes National Park in Canada, Glacier makes up the world's first international park—officially known as Glacier–Waterton International Peace Park—a gesture of goodwill and friendship between the two countries.

## ESSENTIALS

**ARRIVING & DEPARTING**　**Glacier Park International Airport,** north of Kalispell on U.S. 2, is served by Skywest, Delta, and Horizon (a commuter carrier for Northwest). **Great Falls International Airport** has daily service on Delta, Northwest, Horizon, and Frontier. Rental cars are available in Kalispell, Great Falls, Whitefish, East Glacier, and West Glacier. By car, you can reach the park from U.S. 2 and U.S. 89. **Amtrak's** Chicago–Seattle *Empire Builder* (☎ **800/872-7245**) stops at East Glacier and West Glacier from mid-May to October, and at Essex, near the southern tip of the park, year-round.

Access is primarily at West Glacier on the southwest side and St. Mary on the east, at either end of Going-to-the-Sun Road, which cuts across the park. There are four other entrances: Camas Road, Many Glacier, Two Medicine, and Polebridge.

**VISITOR INFORMATION**　For advance information, contact **Glacier National Park,** West Glacier, MT 59936 (☎ **406/888-5441**). The park's "Nature with a Naturalist" publication contains current program information, including suggestions for visitors with disabilities.

**VISITOR CENTERS**　For up-to-date information on park activities, check with the visitor centers located at **Apgar** (open daily May–Oct, weekends Nov–Apr), **Logan Pass** (open mid-June to Sept), and **St. Mary** (open mid-May to Sept). You can also get information from the Many Glacier Ranger Station.

**ADMISSION COSTS & REGULATIONS**　Entrance fees are $10 per vehicle or $5 for an individual on foot or bike. An annual pass costs $20. Admission is free for holders of the National Park Service's Golden Eagle Passport ($50), Golden Access (free to disabled U.S. citizens), and Golden Age (U.S. citizens 62 or older) passports. A separate entrance fee is charged for visitors to Waterton Lakes National Park in Canada.

Backcountry permits must be obtained in person from the visitor centers at Apgar and St. Mary, or the ranger station at Many Glacier. They cost $2 per person per night and may be obtained no earlier than 24 hours before your trip during summer, 7 days ahead during winter. Backcountry camping trips are limited to 6 nights, with no more than 3 nights allowed at each campground. Groups of five have to reserve two campsites, which can be tricky during the crowded summer months. Check with the rangers before setting out for seasonal regulations.

Vehicles over 20 feet long are prohibited on the 24-mile stretch of Going-to-the-Sun Road between Avalanche Campground and Sun Point on St. Mary Lake. No wheeled vehicles are allowed on park trails, and that includes bicycles. Bikes are restricted to bike routes, parking areas, and established roads (restrictions apply on Going-to-the-Sun Road during peak summer periods).

All pets must be on a leash no longer than 6 feet, and under physical restraint or caged while in the park. While boating is permitted on some lakes, motor size is restricted to 10hp on most.

**SAFETY** Park officials are serious when they say don't mess with the bears who live in the park. Don't try to get a bear to pose for photographs, don't pet it, don't look it in the eyes, don't approach it, and don't leave food at ground level in your campground.

**INTERPRETIVE PROGRAMS** "Nature for Kids" activities, evening campfire and slide-show programs, and guided hikes are all offered daily throughout the park. The park's "Nature with a Naturalist" publication—free upon entering the park and also available at visitor centers—is a thorough source for days, times, and locations of various educational programs. Most programs are free, although those including boat trips may include a minimal charge.

**Guided trail rides** have traditionally been offered at Apgar, Lake McDonald, and Many Glacier; inquire at the closest ranger station as to the nearest corral before planning a trail ride.

**WHEN TO GO** By far the most popular time to visit is during the summer, when Going-to-the-Sun Road is fully open. Spring and fall are equally magnificent, with budding wildflowers and variegated leaves and trees, but these sights can only be viewed from the park's outer boundaries and a limited stretch of the scenic highway. In winter, snow shuts Glacier off from the motorized world. Even snowmobiles are forbidden here. All unplowed roads become trails for snowshoers and cross-country skiers.

Most visitors don't stray too far from Going-to-the-Sun Road. Therefore, if you want to avoid most of the crowds, visit just after the road is opened in early summer or just before it's closed in the fall.

## WHAT TO SEE & DO

Two of the park's most popular destinations, Granite Park and Sperry Chalets—National Historic Landmarks built by the Great Northern Railway between 1912 and 1914—have been closed for extensive restoration. Call to see if they have reopened.

**Going-to-the Sun Shuttle Bus Service** (☎ 406/862-2539) runs midsize historic motorcoaches from virtually every major picnic area and campground to other points in the park. Costs for the shuttle service range from $2 for a short distance to $14 for a one-way long-distance excursion. If you plan to use the shuttle extensively, a 1-day unlimited pass costs $28. Unlimited 2-day passes are $35. Children under 12 ride for half price and babies ride free. The maximum price for a family traveling one-way is $50. Reservations are recommended.

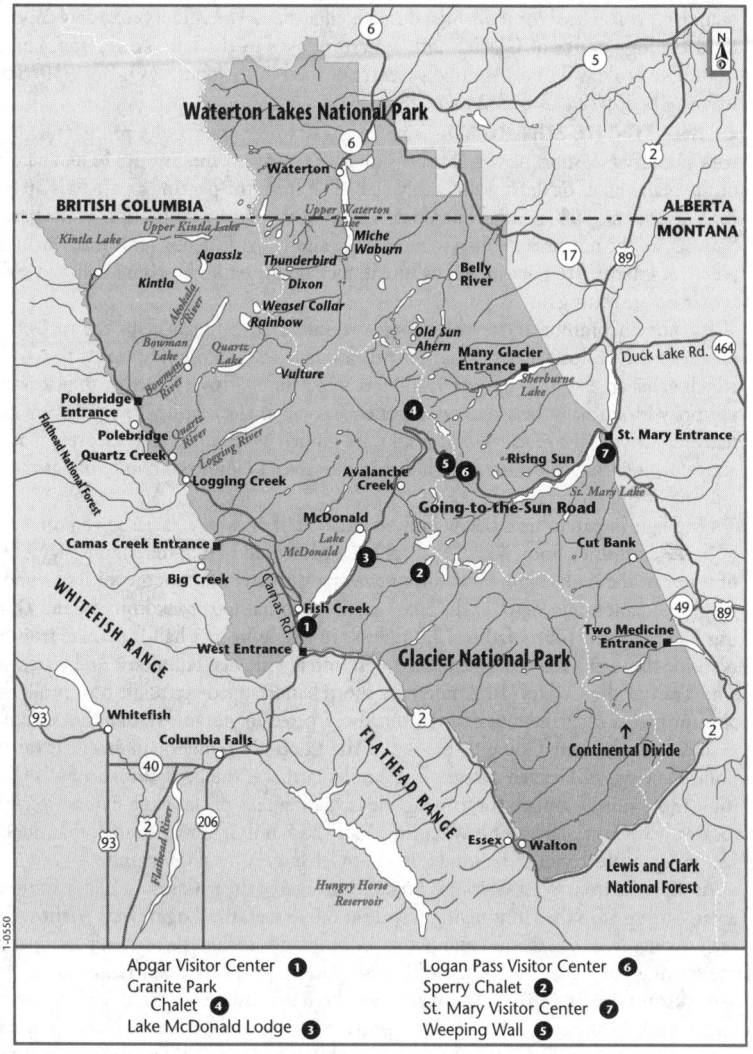

Apgar Visitor Center ❶
Granite Park
Chalet ❹
Lake McDonald Lodge ❸

Logan Pass Visitor Center ❻
Sperry Chalet ❷
St. Mary Visitor Center ❼
Weeping Wall ❺

**ESCORTED TOURS** Glacier Park, Inc. has unique **coach tours** aboard a scarlet 1936 "Jammer" coach—so named because of its standard transmission—along Going-to-the-Sun Road. Drivers give insightful commentary about the park and its history. For schedules, call ☎ 602/207-6000.

Glacier Park Boat Co. (☎ 406/752-5488) offers **narrated boat tours** from Lake McDonald, St. Mary, Two Medicine, and Many Glacier from mid-June to mid-September. **Scenic helicopter tours** are offered by Eagle Aviation (☎ 406/387-4160), Glacier Heli Tours (☎ 800/879-9310), and Kruger Helicopters (☎ 406/387-4565). All are within 2 miles of West Glacier off U.S. 2.

The Glacier Institute (☎ 406/756-3911) conducts **field classes** each summer that examine Glacier's cultural and natural resources. The institute's Big Creek Outdoor Education Center, on the North Fork of the Flathead River near the park's western boundary, is also used for residential outdoor education. The Audubon Society conducts **field ecology tours** of Glacier and Waterton lakes in the fall. To register, contact Audubon Ecology Tours, Audubon Center of the Northwoods, P.O. Box 530, Sandstone, MN 55072 (☎ 612/245-2648).

**GOING-TO-THE-SUN ROAD**  The best way to experience the full gamut of the park's beauty in a short period of time is to drive **Going-to-the-Sun Road** and take one of the many hikes or short walks easily accessible from the parking areas. This 50-mile road bisects the park, going from West Glacier in the southwest portion of the park to St. Mary in the northeast. Points of interest are clearly marked along this road, including plenty of interpretive signage, but be sure to pick up the park's brochure-map at a visitor center before setting out.

It's not uncommon to see the curious wildlife that can wander to the roadside in search of the prohibited food that tourists attempt to dispense. However, the road—which gains an elevation of over 1,400 feet in 32 miles—is very narrow in places, and visitors with a fear of heights may experience some anxiety while driving it. An alternative to driving the road yourself is taking a guided coach tour (see "Escorted Tours," above). (Note that this route is included in the Glacier Country driving tour at the beginning of this chapter.)

Numbers in parentheses below indicate mileage from West Glacier as you drive east.

Just a short drive from West Glacier is **Lake McDonald** (10.8 miles), the largest body of water in the park. Numerous turnouts along the way offer opportunities to photograph the panoramic views of the lake with its mountainous backdrop. **Sacred Dancing Cascade** and **Johns Lake** (12.8 miles) are visible from a half-mile hike from the roadside through a red cedar/hemlock forest, often with views of moose and waterfowl. The **Trail of the Cedars** (16.2 miles) is a short, handicapped-accessible boardwalk trail, also through a cedar/hemlock forest, thickly carpeted in vibrant, verdant hues. Almost exactly halfway along Going-to-the-Sun is the **Loop** (24.6 miles), an excellent vantage point for views of **Heaven's Peak.** Just 2 miles farther is the **Bird Woman Falls Overlook** (26.8 miles), a place for viewing the cascading falls of the same name, which are located across the valley. The **Weeping Wall** (28.7 miles), a wall of rock that does, in fact, weep profusely in the summer, is a popular subject for photographers.

At 32 miles from West Glacier is **Logan Pass,** one of the park's most highly trafficked areas. Sitting atop the Continental Divide at 6,646 feet, the **Logan Pass Visitor Center** provides free information and naturalist programs, includes a souvenir shop, and is the starting point for one of the park's most popular hikes, **Hidden Lake.**

**Jackson Glacier** (36.1 miles) is perhaps the most easily recognizable glacier in the entire park; turnouts at the overlook provide you with excellent vantage points for picture-taking. **Sunrift Gorge** (39.4 miles) and **Sun Point** (40 miles) are two short trails with spectacular views and opportunities for wildlife viewing. **St. Mary** (50.1 miles) is the terminus for this road, with extensive visitor services, including restaurants, places to stay, gas stations, and gift shops.

**OTHER ROADS**  About 4 miles north of Babb is the junction with **Chief Mountain International Highway** (Mont. 17), a 30-mile road cutting across the park's northeastern boundary and across the U.S.–Canada border. At this point, you enter Canada's Waterton Lakes National Park.

To see Glacier's western boundary, take the **North Fork Road** (Mont. 486) from Columbia Falls. Though largely gravel and rife with potholes, it follows the North Fork of the Flathead River, with outstanding views into the park. The road continues on to the U.S./Canadian border 22 miles north of Polebridge, one of the park's most popular areas in which to hike, camp, fish, or cross-country ski. Hugely popular in spite of its outhouses and lack of electricity, the area around Polebridge is perfect for experiencing what Montana and its natural beauty have to offer without modern-day distractions like telephones and TVs.

**Camas Road,** just inside the park's West Glacier entrance, runs northwest from its junction with Going-to-the-Sun Road to the North Fork Road. It's a popular stretch of highway on which to catch a glimpse of a black bear or moose and provides an alternate route to the park's northwestern entrance at Polebridge.

**FISHING**   The crystal-clear mountain streams and lakes of Glacier are home to many native species of fish. Anglers looking to hook a big one should try the North Fork of the Flathead for cutthroat and bull trout and Bowman Lake, St. Mary Lake, and Lake McDonald for rainbow and brook trout, and whitefish. Generally, the park's fishing season is late May–Nov. A fishing license isn't required inside the park boundaries. **Glacier Fishing Charters** in Columbia Falls (☎ **800/735-9244** or 406/892-2377) provides full- or half-day charters with lunch and fishing equipment.

**HIKING**   Hiking is the best way to truly explore the park in depth. Trail maps are available at outdoor stores in Whitefish and Kalispell as well as at the major ranger stations at each entry point. Before striking off into the wilderness, however, check with the nearest ranger station to determine the accessibility of your destination, trail conditions, and recent bear sightings.

Notable of the park's 700 miles of trails is **Kintla Lake to Upper Kintla Lake,** 12 miles skirting the north shore of Kintla Lake. This stretch of the Boulder Pass hike is a breeze, but you may want to stop once you hit Kintla Creek. Once it breaks into the clear, the trail offers views of several peaks, including Kinnerly Peak to the south of Upper Kintla Lake. The 14-miles **Bowman Lake Trail** passes the lake on the north. The growth along the trail once you've passed the head of the lake is thick, especially after a really wet season, but an occasional glimpse of Hole-in-the-Wall Falls makes it worthwhile. Jumping 2,000 feet in less than 3 miles, the trail joins the Kintla Trail at Brown Pass.

Cross the bridge over Bowman Creek and you're on your way to **Quartz Lake,** a 12-mile loop over a ridge and down to the south end of Lower Quartz Lake. From there it's a level 3-mile hike to the west end of Quartz Lake, then 6 miles back over the ridge to Bowman Lake. You'll probably be able to see evidence of the Red Bench Fire of 1988, which took a chunk out of the North Fork area. The **Lake McDonald–Trout Creek Loop** is like reliving an Evel Knievel motorcycle experience in slow motion: straight up and straight down. The trail to the foot of Trout Lake and back is roughly 8 miles and begins from the north end of Lake McDonald. The relatively easy **Highline Trail,** which gains a mere 200 feet in elevation over 7.6 miles, begins at the Logan Pass Visitor Center and skirts the Garden Wall at heights of over 6,000 feet to Granite Park Chalet. It is extremely popular in midsummer, when the wildflowers are in full bloom, though acrophobics may not want to attempt its high, often narrow, snow-covered path. The **Dawson and Pitamakan Pass Loop** is a doozy—3 easy miles in, then you climb 3,000 feet in 4 miles. The strain leads to an awesome view of Oldman Lake and its 9,225-foot Flinsch Peak backdrop. It's a 16.9-mile loop that begins at the Two Medicine campground trailhead.

**KAYAKING**   Most kayakers in the park are crossing lakes. Flat-water kayakers make their way across Bowman Lake with regularity. For whitewater voyagers, the North Fork of the Flathead River (Class 2–3) and the Middle Fork (Class 3) are the best bets. Inquire at any ranger station for details and conditions.

**MOUNTAIN CLIMBING**   Glacier has some incredibly difficult climbs, and you must inquire at the ranger station before setting out. The rangers do not screen climbers for ability, and they make it clear that you will pay for search and rescue should anything happen. Climbers should complete the Voluntary Climbers Registration form available at any ranger station and at the Apgar Visitor Center.

**RAFTING**   Though the waters in the park don't lend themselves to whitewater rafting, the boundary forks of the Flathead River are some of the best in the northwest corner of Montana. For just taking it easy and floating on your back in the summer sun, the North Fork of the Flathead River stretching from Polebridge to Columbia Falls and into Flathead Lake is ideal. Portaging in Polebridge can be difficult if there's not a good sport waiting for you downstream, however. This goes for the Middle Fork of the Flathead, which forms the southern border of the park, as well. The Middle Fork is a little more severe and isn't the sort of river you enjoy with an umbrella drink in your hand. The names of certain stretches of the Middle Fork are terror-inspiring in themselves (the Narrows, Jaws, Bonecrusher).

To assuage that terror, several outfitters offer expert and sanctioned guides to make sure you're not floating downstream facedown. **Montana Raft Company** (☎ **800/521-7238** or 406/888-5466) offers Middle Fork expertise and can even arrange for a side trip into the mountains of Glacier. **Glacier Raft Company** (☎ **800/ 332-9995**) has been taking trips since 1976. **Great Northern Whitewater and Chalet** (☎ **800/735-9244** or 406/387-5340) offers summer trips and year-round accommodations if for some reason you decide to hold on through the winter. **Wild River Adventures** (☎ **800/826-2724** or 406/387-9453) also takes river rats on the Middle Fork.

**SNOWSHOEING & CROSS-COUNTRY SKIING**   Glacier offers several cross-country trails, the most popular of which is the **Upper Lake McDonald Trail** to the Avalanche picnic area. This 8-mile trail offers a relatively flat route up Going-to-the-Sun Road with views of McDonald Creek and the surrounding mountains looming above the McDonald Valley. For advanced skiers, this area offers a more intense 1 1/2-mile trip in a roundabout fashion to the Apgar Lookout; it offers great views but may be too tough for beginners.

On the east side, the **Autumn Creek Trail** near Marias Pass is the most popular. Though getting into the park this way doesn't have traditional drive-up window accessibility, the views of the mountains heading west are spectacular. However, avalanche paths cross this area, so, as always, inquire as to current weather conditions before heading into the wild. Another popular spot is in **Essex** along the southern boundary of the park at the Izaak Walton Inn (see "Nearby Accommodations," below).

**CAMPING**   Camping is permitted only at designated locations and is strictly prohibited on the roadside. See "Essentials," above, for information about backcountry permits.

The park has seven campgrounds accessible by paved road: **Apgar,** near the West Glacier entrance; **Avalanche Creek,** just up from the head of Lake McDonald; **Fish Creek,** on the west side of Lake McDonald; **Many Glacier,** in the northeast part of the park; **Rising Sun,** on the north side of St. Mary Lake; **St. Mary,** on the east side of the park; and **Two Medicine,** at the southeast part of the park near East Glacier. Though they don't have utility connections, they are equipped with fireplaces, picnic tables, washrooms, and cold running water. The nightly fee is $10, and reservations are not accepted.

For a more rustic camping experience with fewer people and minimal amenities, try the sites located off gravel roads in **Cut Bank** (on the east side, off U.S. 89), Bowman and Kintla lakes (north of Polebridge), and Quartz Creek (south of Polebridge). Stop at any ranger station for information on closures, prices, and availability.

Glacier has 63 backcountry campgrounds. Some are at high elevations requiring difficult hikes, but many are on lower-elevation trails of moderate difficulty. Inquire at the ranger station for an accurate depiction of your itinerary's difficulty and advice on what may be needed. Also helpful are the topographical section maps of the park, available at each ranger station.

## ACCOMMODATIONS

With the exception of Apgar Village Lodge, all lodging in the park is operated by **Glacier Park, Inc. (GPI),** Dial Tower, Station 0928, Phoenix, AZ 85077 (☎ **602/ 207-6000** for reservations). Reservations are highly recommended, usually a year in advance.

When making your choice, consider that Apgar Village is convenient to the Apgar corral, the Lake McDonald docks, and the ubiquitous hiking trails. It bustles with activity during the summer and is a great choice for families or anyone who likes to people-watch.

**Apgar Village Lodge.** *Apgar Village, Box 398, West Glacier, MT 59936.* ☎ *406/ 888-5484. 28 cabins, 20 motel rms. $57–$86 double; $69–$210 cabin. DISC, MC, V. Closed mid-Oct to Apr.* In Apgar Village on the south end of Lake McDonald, this is a less expensive alternative to the park's GPI-owned properties. The log and frame cabins have a rustic charm but lack in-room amenities.

✪ **Glacier Park Lodge.** *Glacier National Park, MT 59936.* ☎ *406/226-9311. 154 rms. $105–$142 lodge; $151–$187 suite. AE, DISC, MC, V.* Conveniently located just inside the southeast entrance at East Glacier, this is the park's flagship inn, an imposing timbered structure built by the Great Northern Railroad to lure tourists to Glacier. The interior features massive Douglas-fir pillars, some 40 inches in diameter and 40 feet tall. Each of the rooms has a private bath and telephone and is located either in the main lodge around the balconies or in an annexed building. The lodge has a dining room, coffee shop, evening entertainment, outdoor heated pool, and nine-hole golf course.

✪ **Lake McDonald Lodge.** *Glacier National Park, MT 59936.* ☎ *602/ 207-6000. 62 rms in lodge and motel, 38 cottage rms (some without private bath). $106 lodge room; $75 motel unit; $61–$106 cottage. AE, DISC, MC, V.* On the shore of the park's largest lake, this rustic hunting lodge is a hive of activity in the summer, with scenic lake cruises and canoe rentals. It's also a marvelous base for exploring the western part of the park. It features an enormous lobby with imposing wood beams. The rooms are old but comfortable; be sure to request a private bath, as some don't have them. One of the larger complexes in the park, it includes a dining room, coffee shop and post office.

✪ **Many Glacier Hotel.** *Glacier National Park, MT 59936.* ☎ *602/207-6000. 208 rms. $87–$106 lodge room; $146–$156 suite. AE, DISC, MC, V.* This alpine-style hotel on the banks of Swiftcurrent Lake is probably the most-photographed building in the park. Built in 1915 by the Great Northern Railway, it's the largest lodge in the park and, though not close to Going-to-the-Sun Road, it is among the most popular. Rooms are either in the main lodge around the balconies overlooking the lobby or in the adjoining annex. The walls are extremely thin, so try for a room well away from the exit doors. The hotel has a dining room, coffee shop, and nightly cabaret performances midsummer.

**Rising Sun Motor Inn.** *Glacier National Park, MT 59936.* ☎ *602/207-6000. 63 rms. $72–$75 motor inn unit; $61 cottage unit. AE, DISC, MC, V.* Located 6½ miles from St. Mary, just off Going-to-the-Sun Road, this complex has a restaurant, motor inn, cottages, camp store, gift shop, and service station. While the rooms are comfortable enough, and you'll be ideally located to explore the eastern side of the park, Rising Sun is a lot of asphalt and plain brown buildings. Nine of the 28 motel rooms are located in the same building as the camp store; others are in duplex cottages. The lake is across the road.

**Swiftcurrent Motor Inn.** *Glacier National Park, MT 59936.* ☎ *602/207-6000. 88 rms and cabins (most cabins without private bath). $66–$75 motor inn unit; $26–$45 cabin. AE, DISC, MC, V.* Though modest in decor as well as price, this is a less expensive alternative to Many Glacier Hotel if you plan to explore this part of the park. It's beautifully set against a mountain backdrop and is generally considered a hiker's paradise. There's a mix of motor inn rooms, motel rooms, and cabins. Cabins are outfitted with kitchenettes, one or two bedrooms, but not all have private baths. There's a coffee shop/ restaurant on the premises.

**Village Inn.** *Glacier National Park, MT 59936.* ☎ *602/207-6000. 36 rms. $80– $100 double; $100–$111 suite. AE, DISC, MC, V.* Located in Apgar Village, this inn is convenient to the general store, cafes, and boat docks. It's comfortably outfitted with modest furnishings, making it a cozy and convenient place to hang your hat. All 36 rooms are on two floors of the inn. There are kitchenettes in 12 rooms, but none of the rooms have air-conditioning, phones, or TVs. The restaurants of Lake McDonald and Apgar are nearby.

## NEARBY ACCOMMODATIONS

The following are in so-called "Gateway" communities close to the park. Farther away, you'll find a range of accommodations in Whitefish, Kalispell, and Columbia Falls.

In Essex, the Tudor-style ✪ **Izaak Walton Inn,** P.O. Box 653, Essex, MT 59916 (☎ **406/888-5700**), was built in 1939 by the Great Northern Railway. Located just off U.S. 2 on the southern boundary of the park, it's now extremely popular with tourists and locals alike, many of whom choose to travel there via Amtrak trains, which arrive a mere 50 feet from the front door.

Situated at the St. Mary end of Going-to-the-Sun Road, the **St. Mary Lodge,** U.S. 89 and Going-to-the-Sun Road, St. Mary, MT 59417 (☎ **800/452-7275** or 406/ 732-4431), is one of only a handful of conveniently located accommodations that aren't owned by GPI. Once you see it, you'll understand why it is often mistaken as a sister property to those in the park. The main lodge and attendant rooms are standard Montana fare, with the ubiquitous yet tasteful western lodgepole furniture and furnishings. The Snow Goose Grille serves up breakfast, lunch, and dinner with specialties that include fresh whitefish and sourdough scones.

In East Glacier, the dorm-style **Backpacker's Inn,** P.O. Box 94, East Glacier, MT 59434 (☎ **406/226-9392**), has three cabins—one for men, one for women, and one coed—each sleeping up to six people, at $8 per person. It may be spartan, but adjacent Serrano's is one of the most popular restaurants hereabouts. Closed mid-October to April. Reservations are recommended at **Brownies Grocery and AYH Hostel,** P.O. Box 229, East Glacier, MT 59434 (☎ **406/226-4426** or 406/226-4456), a popular grocery store/hostel combination. Closed October to early May, depending on the weather.

Motel rooms or remodeled forest service cabins are your options at **East Glacier Motel,** P.O. Box 93, East Glacier, MT 59434 (☎ **406/226-5593**). Located in a nicely wooded area, the 12 quaint cottages at **Jacobson's Cottages,** P.O. Box 216, East Glacier, MT 59434 (☎ **406/226-4422**), are small but comfortable. They don't have TVs or kitchens (with one exception), but entertainment and good food are short walks away.

Near Polebridge, the **North Fork Hostel and Cabins,** P.O. Box 1, Polebridge, MT 59928 (☎ **800/775-2938** or 406/888-5241), was moved in the late 1960s from within the park to its present location a stone's throw from the North Fork of the Flathead River. The lodge features complete kitchen facilities. If you can make the trek up the gravelly North Fork Road, then the four bare-bones cabins and one teepee at **Polebridge**

**Mercantile and Cabins,** P.O. Box 2, Polebridge, MT 59928 (☎ 406/888-9926), are a steal at $35 a night, especially if you brought the kids.

In West Glacier, **Glacier Highland Resort,** U.S. 2, West Glacier, MT 59936 (☎ 406/888-5427), is a good place to stay in summer, and with its close proximity to a snowmobile rental facility, it's even better in winter. A 40-acre ranch bordered by the Flathead River 7 miles north of the West Glacier entrance, **Glacier River Ranch Bed & Breakfast,** P.O. Box 176, Coram, MT 59913 (☎ 406/387-4151), offers a framed lodge with five bedrooms, a TV room (with cable, no less), a hot tub, and a main room. They'll even put up your horse overnight. Rates are affordable for the area (for people, anyway).

Surrounded by Forest Service lands, the lodges at the year-round **Glacier Wilderness Resort,** P.O. Box 295, West Glacier, MT 59936 (☎ 406/888-5664), are as private as you can get. Each has a stereo, VCR, and a hot tub on the front porch. Families will find the two-bedroom lodges to their liking, and kids can play outdoors during the day on 23 undeveloped acres and at the Recreation Center at night. Make summer reservations before March. Five-night minimum stay required.

Tucked away on the other side of the Flathead River near the south side of the park is the cozy ✪ **Mountain Timbers,** P.O. Box 84, West Glacier, MT 59936 (☎ 800/841-3835 or 406/387-5830). Situated on 260 acres, this beautiful 5,000-square-foot lodge offers everything from easy access to the park to more than 10 miles of gorgeous hiking and biking trails of its own.

Perched atop a hill at the park's west entrance, the **Vista Motel,** P.O. Box 98, West Glacier, MT 59936 (☎ 406/888-5311), boasts the best views of the mountains from anywhere around. There's only one catch—you'll have to visit between March and October to see them. The motel is nothing special to look at, but the rooms are clean and comfortable, and there's an outdoor heated pool. Golf, raft trips, riding stables, and restaurants are all nearby.

## DINING

Food options along Going-to-the-Sun Road are limited to dining rooms operated by GPI and, regrettably, are overpriced and unimaginative more often than not. You will probably enjoy your surroundings more than you'll enjoy your meal. The dining rooms are convenient, however, and you're almost always assured of friendly service from a staff of twentysomething college students from around the country.

**Glacier Park Lodge** has the Goatlick Steak & Rib House and the Teepee Room; **Lake McDonald Lodge** has the Cedar Dining Room and the Coffee Shop; **Many Glacier Hotel** has the Ptarmigan Dining Room and Heidi's; the **Rising Sun Motor Inn** has the Coffee Shop; and the **Swiftcurrent Motor Inn** has the Coffee Shop. There is no restaurant associated with the Village Inn at Apgar. However, Lake McDonald Lodge and restaurants at Apgar Village are convenient to the hotel.

The dining rooms open with the park and close sometime in September, depending on the facility. At each, breakfast is served 6:30–9:30am; lunch 11:30am–2pm; and dinner 5:30–9:30pm. Coffee and snack shops open either at 7am or 8am and close at 9pm. They accept traveler's checks and Discover, MasterCard, and Visa credit cards.

For light snacks or a cold drink, stock up in West Glacier or at Lake McDonald; the next place to grab something quick is Rising Sun, at the other end of Going-to-the-Sun Road. You'll find ample restaurants in all the nearby towns.

## 5  Yellowstone National Park

At the mention of Yellowstone, visions spring to mind of magnificent geysers, steaming hot springs, thundering waterfalls, pristine forests, great herds of bison and elk, and giant silvertip grizzly bears. As the world's first, most famous, and most treasured national park, Yellowstone stands alone. The birthplace of conservation and natural preservation, Yellowstone has served as an example for parks around the world for well over a century.

Whether it's your first or 21st visit, you don't have to look far to find extremes and drama in this ever-evolving park. Most famous are its signature geological wonders, which tell the story of a tumultuous volcanic past. Approximately 600,000 years ago eruptions created the 28-by-47-mile volcanic crater, or caldera, which is central to Yellowstone's present geography, and still accounts for the thermal activity that powers Old Faithful and the park's other famous spouting geysers, boiling springs, steaming fumaroles, and bubbling mud pots.

The only year-round inhabitants here in early times were a small band of Shoshones (they were removed to the Shoshone Wind River Reservation in 1871). Stories began to circulate in the 1800s about a land of boiling cauldrons of mud and spewing steam holes, stories that were dismissed at first as wild tales. However, in 1870 Montana's surveyor general, Nathaniel P. Langford, actually visited this strange land, and convinced the director of the U.S. Geological Survey, Dr. Ferdinand Hayden, to mount an official exploration. Hayden took along landscape artist Thomas Moran and photographer William Henry Jackson, and the findings of the expedition convinced Congress to set up some 2.2 million acres as Yellowstone National Park on March 1, 1872.

## ESSENTIALS

**ARRIVING & DEPARTING**   The nearest airport is the **West Yellowstone Airport** on U.S. 191 a mile north of West Yellowstone, which provides commercial air service from June to September only on Delta's commuter service, **Skywest** (☎ 800/453-9417 or 406/646-7351). West Yellowstone is just outside the park's western entrance. The nearest airports served by domestic carriers are **Jackson Airport** at Grand Teton National Park, **Fanning Field** at Idaho Falls, Idaho, and **Gallatin Field** at Bozeman, Montana. From Jackson, head north 45 miles on U.S. 89/191. From Idaho Falls, take I-15 south from the airport to exit 119 and head east on U.S. 20, roughly a 107-mile drive. From Bozeman you can take U.S. 191 south for 91 miles to its junction with U.S. 287 and south into West Yellowstone, or you can proceed east toward Livingston on I-90, turning south on U.S. 89 to Gardiner, the northern gateway to the park, about an 80-mile drive.

Throughout the summer, Yellowstone is accessible through five major **entrances.** Gateway towns are West Yellowstone, the biggest and most commercial, and Gardiner and Cooke City. The north entrance is at Mammoth Hot Springs, just south of Gardiner, Montana. In winter, this is the only access into Yellowstone by car. The west entrance is just outside the town of West Yellowstone, Montana, and is open to wheeled vehicles Apr–Nov, and to snowmobiles Dec–Mar. The south entrance is from Grand Teton National Park, open to wheeled vehicles May–Nov, and to snowmobile traffic Dec–Mar. The east entrance is 52 miles west of Cody, Wyoming, and is open to wheeled traffic May–Sept and to snowmobiles Dec–Mar. The northeast entrance, at Cooke City, Montana, is open throughout the year to wheeled vehicles, but in the late fall, when the Beartooth Pass is closed, the only route to Cooke City is through Mammoth Hot Springs.

Check road conditions before entering the park by calling the visitor center at ☎ 307/344-7381. As winter approaches, early snows can close roads temporarily. Note that a massive road project in progress may cause delays.

**VISITOR INFORMATION**   If you wish to have maps and information mailed to you before you leave home, contact **Yellowstone National Park,** WY 82190

# Yellowstone National Park

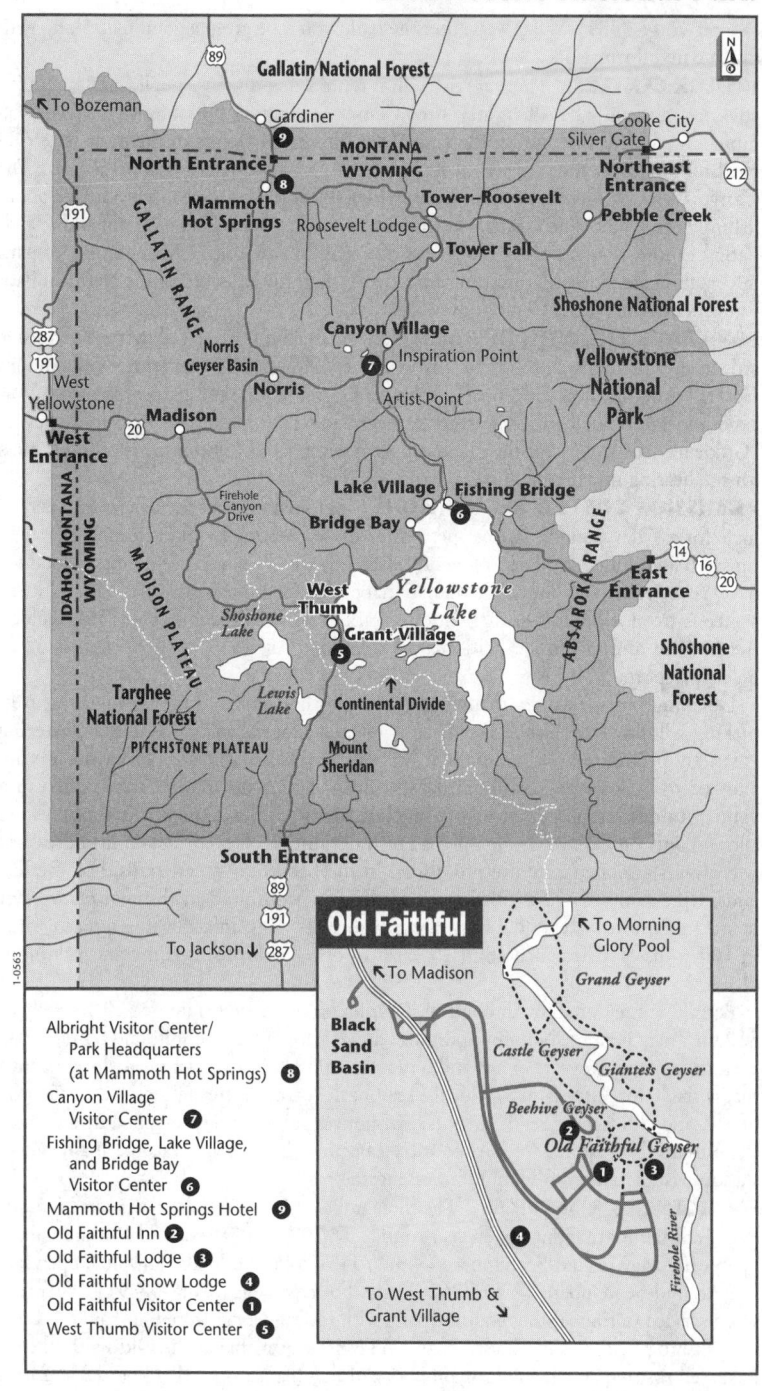

(☎ 307/344-7381). When you enter the park, you'll be given a good map along with up-to-date information.

**VISITOR CENTERS**   There are five visitor centers that dispense publications, permits, advice, and maps. The **Albright Visitor Center** at Mammoth Hot Springs also has exhibits on park history and on the recently reintroduced wolves in the park. The **Old Faithful Visitor Center** offers a movie on geysers and up-to-date geyser predictions. The **Canyon Visitor Center** and **Fishing Bridge Visitor Center** can give advice about fishing in the park. The **Grant Village Visitor Center** has a slide program and a fascinating exhibit that examines the effects of fire in Yellowstone. Other sources of park information are at the Madison Information Station, the Museum of the National Park Ranger, and the Norris Geyser Basin Museum.

**FOR TRAVELERS WITH DISABILITIES**   A large number of Yellowstone's roadside attractions, including the Grand Canyon of the Yellowstone's south rim, West Thumb Geyser Basin, much of the Norris and Upper Geyser basins, and parts of the Mud Volcano and Fountain Paint Pot areas are negotiable by wheelchair. Pick up a copy of "Guide to Accessibility for the Handicapped Visitor" at any visitor center. TDD access for the hearing impaired is at ☎ **307/344-2386.**

**ADMISSION COSTS & REGULATIONS**   The cost to enter the park is $20 per vehicle for a 7-day period, $10 per person for those entering by other means; however, those 16 and under or 62 and older are admitted free. The entrance permit is good for both Yellowstone and Grand Teton national parks. An annual pass costs $40. Park entrance is free for holders of the National Park Service's Golden Eagle ($50), Golden Access (free to disabled U.S. citizens), and Golden Age ($10 for U.S. citizens 62 or older) passports.

Defacing park features, throwing coins or other objects into thermal features, picking wildflowers, or collecting natural or archeological objects is illegal. **Littering** is strictly prohibited—if you pack it in, you have to pack it out. **Firearms** are not allowed in Yellowstone National Park; unloaded firearms may be transported in a vehicle under strict regulations. **Bicycles, motorcycles,** and **motorscooters** are allowed only on park roads; no off-road or trail riding is allowed. **Pets** must be leashed and always attended, and are prohibited in the backcountry, on trails, boardwalks, and in thermal areas. **Swimming** or **wading** is prohibited in thermal features or in streams whose waters flow from thermal features. It is unlawful to approach within 100 yards of a **bear** or within 25 yards of other **wildlife.** Feeding any wildlife is illegal.

Permits are required for all **boating.** Permits for motorized craft are $20 annually or $10 for 7-day permits. Nonmotorized fees are $10 for annual permits and $5 for 7-day permits. Anglers 16 years of age and older must purchase a special-use **fishing permit** that costs $5 for 7 days and $10 for the season; the permit is free to those 12 to 15 years of age, and children under 12 may fish without a permit if accompanied by an adult. Permits are also required for **backcountry camping.** Permits are available at any ranger station, visitor center, or Hamilton Store in the park.

**EMERGENCIES & SERVICES**   The three **medical facilities** in Yellowstone National Park are Mammoth Clinic, open year-round (☎ 307/344-7965); Old Faithful Clinic, open early May to mid-September (☎ 307/545-7325); and Lake Hospital, open late May to mid-September (☎ 307/242-7241). For emergencies, dial ☎ **911.** There are seven **service stations** throughout the park, with towing service from Old Faithful, Canyon, Fishing Bridge, and Grant Village. **ATMs** are available at the Old Faithful Inn, Lake Yellowstone Hotel, and Canyon Lodge during regular operating hours. **Hamilton Stores, Inc.** offer a wide array of items and outdoor gear.

**INTERPRETIVE PROGRAMS**   Park ranger programs and activities include demonstrations and talks at visitor centers, guided walks and hikes, and evening programs at the park's many amphitheaters (many of these activities are accessible to the disabled). Be on the lookout for "roving" ranger/naturalists at major park features—they are there to help you appreciate your park. Kids 7–12 are encouraged to become Junior Rangers, a program that introduces them to the wonders of Yellowstone and teaches the importance of its preservation. The **Yellowstone Institute** (☎ **307/344-2294**) offers educational seminars and classes that cover such topics as birding, wolf tracking, canoeing, and fly-fishing. Headquarters are at the historic Buffalo Ranch in Yellowstone's Lamar Valley, but courses are conducted throughout the park. Call for a detailed course listing.

**WHEN TO GO**   Yellowstone National Park is open all year long, but access is limited in winter months. Summer finds the park populated with millions of visitors, so if you want to miss the crowds, avoid the busy summer season, especially July and August. Few of Yellowstone's visitors venture far past the roadside attractions, so plan a backcountry camping trip and experience the essence of Yellowstone's wilderness. In winter, Yellowstone is transformed into a surreal wonderland of snow and ice, and trees in the geyser basins become "snow ghosts" of frozen thermal vapors. Cross-country skiing is a great way to see the winter face of Yellowstone. Spring can be a roll of the dice—roads may or may not be open and heavy spring storms can arise. But there are no crowds in spring, and during a good year most roads open by Memorial Day. The Old Faithful area is usually cleared by the middle of April.

## WHAT TO SEE & DO

**ORGANIZED TOURS**   Guided all-day **motorcoach tours** are available from all of Yellowstone's villages. The Upper Loop, Lower Loop, and Grand Loop tours stop at all major points of interest, and short guided walks are conducted. Fares are $23 for adults, $12 for ages 12 to 16, and free for children under 12. At Bridge Bay Marina, 1-hour **scenicruiser tours** explore the northern part of Yellowstone Lake. Fares are $7 for adults, $4 for children, free for children under 2 (held on lap). Reservations can be made through **TW Recreational Services, Inc.** (☎ **307/344-7311**).

Guided **horseback trail rides** of 1 or 2 hours are available at Mammoth Hot Springs, Roosevelt Lodge, and Canyon Village corrals. Tour prices are $15 for a 1-hour ride and $24 for a 2-hour ride. Children must be 8 years old and at least 48 inches tall. Check any activity desk for times and dates and to make reservations. **Stagecoach rides** leave from Roosevelt Lodge throughout the day; fares are $6 for adults and $5 for children 2 to 11. The Lodge's **Old West cookouts** combine a trail ride and dinner with old-fashioned entertainment.

**Yellowstone Guidelines** (☎ **800/314-4506**), based in Bozeman, Montana, provides private customized itineraries, with prices starting at $125 per person per day, that include excursions to lesser-known attractions. Although camping is encouraged (and all equipment is supplied), hotel and cabin accommodations can be arranged at additional expense. Their season runs from June to September; advance reservations are required. Call for more information.

For a memorable wildlife expedition, check out biologist Ken Sinay's **Northern Rockies Natural History Tours,** P.O. Box 42, Bozeman, MT (☎ **406/586-1155**). Tours cost $65 per person for a half day and $125 per person for a full day.

### TOURING YELLOWSTONE BY CAR

**Self-guided car audio tours** are a great way to get the most out of a drive through the park. The system plugs into your car's cigarette lighter, costs $25 for a full day or $16 for a half day, and is available through activity desks.

The main roads in Yellowstone form a "figure 8," commonly divided into the Upper Loop and Lower Loop. The Grand Loop Tour combines the major elements of both of these.

In summer, traffic can proceed at a slow crawl, and to make matters worse, Yellowstone is currently in the throes of an 8-year construction project begun in 1994 and designed to improve driving conditions throughout the park. In the meantime, expect delays and nightly sectional road closings. Some of the roads being repaired are barely passable. Check with the visitor information center ( ☎ 307/344-7381) before entering the park to determine the best times and routes.

Plan carefully if you have limited time in Yellowstone. The park's north entrance, 5 miles south of Gardiner, Montana, is the best entrance for first-time visitors because of its history as park headquarters and traditional entry point. In the two driving tours outlined below, the highlights that you should not miss are starred.

**THE UPPER LOOP**    This tour is 70 miles long and begins at Mammoth Hot Springs, where you should take the one-way **Upper Terrace Loop** drive. ✪ **Mammoth Hot Springs Terraces** is one of Yellowstone's unique and beautiful attractions. Mineral-rich hot waters flow to the surface at an unusually constant rate, bringing new deposits to the remarkable succession of ever-changing limestone terraces. Enjoy a ranger-guided tour or pick up a self-guiding trail map. Those interested in the history of Yellowstone should take time to explore the **Albright Visitor Center** and its exhibits.

Heading east from Mammoth, drive 6 miles to the **Children's Fire Trail,** a relatively flat and easy walk, built after the fires of 1988 to show the effects of forest fires. A few miles farther, **Blacktail Plateau Drive** is an alternative to the main road, a one-way dirt road that exits to the south and offers great wildlife-viewing. Shortly after you get back to the main road, a short spur road leads to one of northern Yellowstone's many ancient **petrified trees.** Stop at **Roosevelt Lodge** for a taste of the Old West if a 1-hour guided horseback tour or stagecoach ride appeals to your sense of adventure.

Head south toward Canyon Village, and stop at **Tower Falls,** a 132-foot waterfall surrounded by volcanic pinnacles. Continuing south, the road climbs Mount Washburn to **Dunraven Pass** (elevation 8,859 feet), where keen eyes might be rewarded with a glimpse of a grizzly bear in an open meadow—this is one of their prime habitats. South of the pass an **overlook** provides views as far as the Teton Mountain range to the southeast on a clear day.

Head toward Canyon Village and the ✪ **Grand Canyon of the Yellowstone River.** The intense thermal forces here have colored the canyon walls with many hues of reds, oranges, yellows, tans, and browns. The canyon, 24 miles long and up to 1,200 feet deep, begins at a dramatic waterfall more than twice as tall as Niagara Falls. The **Lower Falls** plunges 308 feet; the **Upper Falls,** just upstream, 109 feet. There are trails and roads along both rims of the canyon. **Inspiration Point** and **Artist Point** (handicapped accessible) are especially noteworthy. For the more adventurous, a hike 500 feet down **Uncle Tom's Trail** provides a vantage point for viewing the Lower Falls. Be sure to watch for osprey fishing the river or nesting along the canyon walls.

On the 12-mile drive west from Canyon Village to Norris Geyser Basin, the alternate road, **Virginia Cascades Drive,** is well worth the extra few miles. Plan to spend some time walking and exploring the ✪ **Norris Geyser Basin** area, which has the park's most dynamic concentration of thermal features. Three faults in the earth's crust intersect here, and any movement in these faults can change the face of the geyser basin. A walk of less than 2 miles will take you past both the northern **Porcelain Basin** and the southern **Back Basin.** At the right time of day you can hear the haunting music of Porcelain Basin. These basins contain a great variety of geysers, and if you're lucky, you may witness a rare eruption of **Steamboat Geyser,** which has been known to shoot up to 400 feet. The nearby **Norris Geyser Basin Museum** explains geothermal features.

Drive back north toward Mammoth Hot Springs. You will first pass **Obsidian Cliff,** a source once tapped by ancient peoples of North America. Obsidian is a black volcanic glass used for weapons and tools; through trade, it traveled great distances across the continent (please remember that it's unlawful to remove any natural features from a national park). Farther ahead is a picnic area at the turnoff at **Sheepeater Cliff.** Continuing north, watch for moose at **Swan Lake Flats** on your left. The final few miles into Mammoth take you through a small canyon and along the unusual formations of limestone boulders called "hoodoos" on your left.

**THE LOWER LOOP**  This tour is 96 miles long and can easily take up most of your day. Old Faithful is the starting point. Stop first at the visitor center at Old Faithful and pick up the Yellowstone Association's guides for the surrounding geyser basins.

✪ **Old Faithful** is undoubtedly the world's most famous geyser. It's aptly named: Over the last 120 years, its eruptions have been remarkably consistent—21 to 23 times daily at about 74-minute intervals, with a column averaging about 134 feet and a duration of about 40 seconds. Visit the visitor center for predictions of nearby geyser eruptions or stop in at the National Historic Landmark **Old Faithful Inn** (see "Accommodations," below). The log structure, finished in 1904, is an impressive attraction in itself. Accessible by walkways from Old Faithful Village is the **Upper Geyser Basin.** Among the attractions here are Beehive Geyser, Grand Geyser, Castle Geyser, Riverside Geyser, and the beautiful Morning Glory Pool.

Leaving Old Faithful Village and driving toward Madison Junction, stop at **Black Sand Basin** to view **Emerald Pool.** A little farther up the road is **Biscuit Basin,** named for biscuit-shaped formations that were later destroyed by natural causes. A short stop here will allow you to see Jewel Pool, Sapphire Pool, and Mystic Falls on the **Little Firehole River.** The ✪ **Midway Geyser Basin's** major attractions are the **Grand Prismatic Spring,** Yellowstone's largest hot spring, and the **Excelsior Geyser,** once the park's most powerful geyser.

On your way to the Lower Geyser Basin, take the one-way **Firehole Lake Drive** to Firehole Lake, **Great Fountain Geyser,** and **Three Senses Trail.** At the Lower Geyser Basin view the **Fountain Paint Pots** and **White Dome Geyser.** The small detour to **Firehole Canyon Drive** is worth the time—there are great views of the canyon and the **Firehole Falls.** Before turning north at Madison Junction, a 9-mile detour to the west to **Two Ribbons Trail,** which winds its way through the burned forest along the Madison River, provides a fascinating look at fire ecology. North from Madison to Norris, follow the Gibbon River, which runs along the volcanic caldera's rim. About halfway to Norris is **Gibbon Falls,** where the river tumbles over the caldera wall. In the Norris area is ✪ **Norris Geyser Basin, Norris Geyser Basin Museum,** and the **Museum of the National Park Ranger.**

Heading east toward Canyon Village, take the **Virginia Cascades Drive** alternate road, a one-way west-to-south road, along the Gibbon for some lovely views. Near Canyon Village is the magnificent ✪ **Grand Canyon of the Yellowstone** (see details in the Upper Loop tour section, above).

To the south the road follows the Yellowstone River from the Upper Falls to Yellowstone Lake. **Hayden Valley** is a wide sprawling former extension of Yellowstone Lake, where a 6-mile section of the river has been closed to fishing, leaving the natural state of the valley relatively undisturbed. Herds of bison roam the area and can be seen occasionally fording the river. Watch the marshy areas for trumpeter swans, white pelicans, and Canadian geese. Moose also frequent the area, as well as river otters and the occasional grizzly bear. Ten miles south of Canyon Village is the **Mud Volcano** area. Follow the two-thirds-mile trail to see Mud Geyser, Black Dragon's Cauldron, Dragon's Mouth Spring, and Sulfur Caldron. Major features here are all handicapped accessible.

A little more than 2 miles farther is **Le Hardy Rapids.** Here you can enjoy a shaded stroll in the trees and perhaps a glimpse of **spawning cutthroat trout** in the early summer. Because of the spawn, Fishing Bridge is a prime grizzly bear habitat. The **museum** here features exhibits of Yellowstone's birds and animals, which can help you to put names to the wildlife you will spot in the park. ✪ **Yellowstone Lake** is North America's largest high-altitude lake at 7,733 feet. The lake reaches depths of 320 feet, has more than 100 miles of shoreline, and is roughly 20 miles long by 14 miles wide. Wildlife abounds in and around the lake area—osprey, bald eagles, white pelicans, cormorants, moose, and grizzly bears. The lake has the largest population of native cutthroat trout in North America and makes an ideal fishing spot in summer. On the south shore of the lake, **Grant Village** is the newest of Yellowstone's villages and the Grant Visitor Center offers an exhibit exploring the history of fires in Yellowstone. At **Bridge Bay Marina** you can take a 1-hour **scenicruiser tour** of the northern part of the lake or a guided fishing trip; small boat rentals, dock rentals, and a tackle shop are available. The majestic 100-year-old **Lake Yellowstone Hotel** on the north shore has been beautifully restored, and a stop in its sunroom makes a relaxing break.

From the Lake Village area, the road follows the lake's western shore to the **West Thumb Geyser Basin.** The bay of West Thumb is a caldera, or volcanic crater. West Thumb was an early center of park activity and the log structure that functioned as the original West Thumb Ranger Station still stands here. A **self-guided walking tour** takes you through a wonderfully concentrated collection of thermal features, geysers, hot pools, and mud pots on the lake's shore.

The final leg of this tour leads east over the **Continental Divide** at Craig Pass and back to Old Faithful. At **Shoshone Lake Overlook** there are views of the lake and valley below, and of the distant Tetons.

## OUTDOOR ACTIVITIES

Yellowstone offers year-round outdoor activities. For additional information, contact **TW Recreational Services, Inc.** (☎ 307/344-7311). See also "Admission Costs & Regulations," above. In addition to park services, there are many activities, outfitters, and rental shops in the park's gateway towns.

**BIKING**    Biking in Yellowstone is permitted on established public roads, campgrounds, parking areas, and designated routes only. Inquire at a visitor center for information on bike trails. The park roads themselves are usually narrow and winding and can be quite dangerous because of heavy traffic. There are no bike lanes. Bicycles are not allowed on backcountry trails and boardwalks. Gateway communities usually rent bicycles and can recommend rides. Try Bill Blackford's **Cooke City Bike Shop** (☎ 406/838-2412), located in Cooke City, near the northeast entrance of the park.

**BOATING**    The best place is on Yellowstone Lake, which has easy access and beautiful, panoramic views. The lake is also one of the few areas where powerboats are allowed; rowboats and outboard motorboats can be rented at **Bridge Bay Marina** (☎ 307/344-7381). For a fully guided 3- or 4-day paddling/camping experience, call **Far and Away Adventures** (☎ 800/232-8588). Permits are required for all types of boating. Inquire at a ranger station for more detailed boating restrictions and permit information.

**CROSS-COUNTRY SKIING**    Yellowstone's light, powdery snow is a skier's dream. There are backcountry and skied-in trails suitable for every level of expertise. Equipment rentals (about $12 per day), ski instruction, ski shuttles to various locations, and guided ski tours are all available at the park's two winter lodging options: the Old Faithful Snow Lodge and the Mammoth Hot Springs Hotel. Discounts are available for multiday rentals. Ski instruction costs $17 per person for a 2-hour group lesson. A half-day guided excursion (two-person minimum) is around $32 per person; a full day is $69 per person. If your group has three or more people, the cost is $21 per person for a half day,

$48 per person for a full day. **Yellowstone Nordic Guides,** 511 Gibbon Ave., in West Yellowstone (☎ **406/646-9333**), offers cross-country tours and maintains a yurt in the park.

**FISHING**   The fishing season in Yellowstone begins as early as late May and continues into early November. Permits are available at any ranger station, visitor center, or Hamilton store in the park. The large population of native cutthroat trout in the park's lakes, rivers, and streams provides a challenging and exciting angling experience. You can rent fishing equipment and/or a small boat at the Bridge Bay Marina or arrange a guided fishing trip on one of the available cabin cruisers (tackle is included). Fishing tackle is available at any Hamilton store. Contact **Yellowstone Visitor Services** (☎ **307/344-2107**) for information on fishing guides.

**HIKING**   The vast backcountry area of Yellowstone is accessible only by leaving your car behind and hitting the trail. There are more than 1,200 miles of walking and hiking trails. Even on a short hike just out of sight of the road the park takes on an entire new identity. Trails vary greatly in length and level of difficulty; check with the nearest ranger station if you are in doubt, and ask for details of bear activity, damaged bridges, or weather that affect accessibility. For hikes and campsites in the backcountry, you must have a permit (free), which can be issued by any ranger. The **Bechler River Trail** to Old Faithful from the Bechler Ranger Station goes through country that was not scarred by the 1988 fire, and offers cascades, waterfalls, and thermal areas along the 30-mile route. The **Thorofare Trail** is a hike that covers over 70 miles through isolated and pristine wilderness. The **Sportsman Lake Trail,** which begins near Mammoth Hot Springs, will take you to Electric Peak, named for its uncanny ability to attract lightning in a storm, in the park's scenic northwestern corner. *Yellowstone Trails: A Hiking Guide,* by Mark C. Marschall (Yellowstone National Park, WY: Yellowstone Association, 1990), covers more than 1,000 miles of trails. If you want the services of a backcountry guide, call **Yellowstone Visitor Services** (☎ **307/344-2107**) for leads on local experts.

**HORSEBACK RIDING**   Throughout the summer season, Canyon Village, Roosevelt Lodge, and Mammoth Hot Springs offer 1- and 2-hour guided trail rides daily. Roosevelt Lodge also offers evening rides from June into September. For a more extensive riding experience, sign on with **Yellowstone Mountain Guides** (☎ **406/ 388-0148**) for a backcountry adventure.

**SNOWMOBILING**   Roads specifically groomed for snowmobile travel are found throughout the park. A driver's license is required for rental ($130 per day for two riders at Mammoth Hot Springs Hotel or Old Faithful Snow Lodge) and a quick lesson will put even a first-timer at ease. A snowmobiler's clothing package is also available. At Mammoth, Indian Creek, Canyon, Madison, West Thumb, and Fishing Bridge are warming huts, which offer food and beverages. Half- and full-day guided snowmobile tours are available. Snowmobile rentals are also available in the gateway communities of Gardiner and West Yellowstone.

**SNOWCOACH TOURS**   This distinctively Yellowstone mode of transportation isn't merely a fancy name for a tour bus—imagine an Econoline van with tank treads for tires and water skis extending from its front, and you won't be surprised when you see this unusual-looking vehicle. Interiors are toasty warm, with seating for a large group. They are also available for rent if you want to drive yourself.

**CAMPING**   Camping is allowed only in designated areas and is limited to 14 days between June 15 and Labor Day, and to 30 days the rest of the year. Checkout time for all campgrounds is 10am. Quiet hours are strictly enforced between 8pm and 8am. Of the 12 campgrounds in Yellowstone, 7 are operated by the National Park Service, available on a first-come, first-served basis. Mammoth and Norris offer showers and disposal stations; Indian Creek, Lewis Lake, Pebble Creek, Slough Creek, and Tower Fall are primitive campsites. If you arrive before noon, you run the best chance of getting a campsite for the evening.

**TW Recreational Services, Inc.** (☎ **307/344-7311**) accepts reservations for campgrounds at Canyon, Grant Village, Madison, and Fishing Bridge that have all amenities. The **Fishing Bridge RV Park** is the only campground offering water, sewer, and electrical hookups and accepts hard-sided vehicles only (no tents or tent trailers). Reservations for **Bridge Bay Campground** may be made no more than 8 weeks in advance by calling MISTIX reservations at ☎ **800/365-2267.**

## ACCOMMODATIONS

Lodgings inside Yellowstone are booked through **TW Recreational Services, Inc.,** P.O. Box 165, Yellowstone National Park, WY 82190 (☎ **307/344-7311**), the company that operates all accommodations, restaurants, and snack bars in the park. Yellowstone's accommodations are open from early summer to late September; snowmobilers and cross-country skiers can stay at Mammoth Hot Springs from mid-December to early March or at Old Faithful Snow Lodge and Cabins, which opens early December and stays open all winter. Summer reservations should be made well in advance. Many alternatives exist outside the park in the gateway communities. Most accommodations in the park are rustic, many lack private baths, and there's no television. Most are priced in the moderate range, though there are also expensive options.

Located in unsightly and overdeveloped Canyon Village, the **Canyon Lodge and Cabins** offers comfortable rooms in the three-story lodge building and slightly less expensive cabins scattered throughout the village. **Grant Village** on the West Thumb of Yellowstone Lake is the southernmost place to stay in the park, and one of the newest. It's also one of the few places where you're going to find a private bath with a shower. Other guest services include a dining room, lounge, marina steak house, and laundry facility. **Lake Lodge Cabins** on Lake Yellowstone are located just down from the Lake Yellowstone Hotel and Cabins. Lake Lodge, with its cafeteria dining room facing the lake, serves as home base for the cabins. Both Western and Frontier cabins offer at least one bath (unlike some other cabins in Yellowstone). **Lake Yellowstone Hotel and Cabins** are on the north side of the lake. This recently restored historic 1920s hotel also has comfortable, rustic cabins. The main lodge has a beautiful sunroom and bar. The hotel annex offers some of the most expensive rooms in the park (a parlor and bedroom suite goes for $342 per night).

**Mammoth Hot Springs Hotel and Cabins** is the only place to stay year-round in the north part of the park, and the Mammoth Ranger Station is the only station open throughout the year. Mammoth Hot Springs is one of the older park settlements, dating back to the late 19th century when Fort Yellowstone was still around. The actual lodge was built in 1937. Rooms are hotel style and the cabins are cottage style (a few units have private hot tubs).

✪ **Old Faithful Inn** was designated a National Historic Landmark in 1987. Built of local logs and stone in 1904, it's a remarkable gabled mansion with a central lobby that towers six stories high (you can visit the roof) and has intricate logwork from nearby trees. Views of the geyser are best from the third floor of the recently remodeled East Wing. The rustic **Old Faithful Lodge and Cabins** will suit the tightest of budgets. The Frontier cabin units are the most expensive units and come with a full bath. The Economy cabin units have a sink and toilet, and the Budget units with no conveniences don't cost much more than a tent site; showers and rest rooms are located nearby. **Old Faithful Snow Lodge and Cabins** offers a remarkably inexpensive way to stay inside the park in winter near many cross-country skiing trails. And don't worry—the giant geyser continues its famous eruptions throughout winter with an even more dramatic effect. The cabins, tastefully furnished in western motifs, seem more cozy than cramped.

**Roosevelt Lodge Cabins** are named for Theodore Roosevelt, who camped here and loved this area. The Roughriders are bare-bone cabins of frame construction with showers and facilities nearby. Rustic Shelters are even more basic because they're smaller. However, the location just north of the Grand Canyon of the Yellowstone and Tower Falls makes this an ideal spot for exploring the northeast part of Yellowstone.

## DINING

Eating in the park can be a nightmare if you're trying to save money—lines in the affordable cafeterias can be extraordinarily long at normal mealtimes. On the other hand, if you dine in one of the nicer restaurants, you may find that you're paying *a lot* for not standing in line. On the whole the food is well prepared, and some of it is very good, but what you ate on Tuesday at Grant Village you can enjoy again on Wednesday in another part of the park.

What is different at the ✪ **Old Faithful Inn** is the atmosphere. The dining room is always filled with interesting people, and the wait in line can offer a chance to meet fellow travelers or to marvel silently at the surroundings. **Grant Village** occasionally offers some more enterprising items, such as pan-fried trout covered with toasted pecans and lemon butter, and has good steaks and seafood. At **Mammoth Hot Springs Hotel** you can watch the resident herd of elk that frequents the lawn while you dine. At **Lake Yellowstone Hotel,** the view over the lake in the mornings as you watch the sun come up can be exceptional, and a late sunset dinner is just as spectacular.

Cafeterias and fast food are convenient, if less appetizing, alternatives to the more formal dining rooms. There are cafeterias in Mammoth Hot Springs, Canyon Village, Grant Village, Old Faithful, and West Thumb.

## 6  Grand Teton National Park & Jackson Hole

While Yellowstone is the premier attraction of the northwestern section of Wyoming, the rugged, gray-granite Tetons are also remarkable, not only for their visual power but as an enduring wildlife habitat. From rodeo to rock climbing to backcountry hiking, or just sightseeing, this area has Wyoming's widest selection of outdoor activities. Jackson Hole, close to the edge of Grand Teton National Park and within an easy drive of Yellowstone, is one of the nation's premier ski resorts and has all kinds of other outdoor recreation.

### GRAND TETON NATIONAL PARK

The Tetons themselves seem to shoot straight out of the earth at odd angles, stretching toward the sky—six of the peaks tower more than 12,000 feet. Formed by massive earthquakes, the Tetons rose from the depths of the earth at a typically geologic pace—they began their upward path some 9 million years ago.

In the winter of 1807, wilderness man extraordinaire John Colter was the first to make his way into this spectacular area. The French-Canadian fur trappers who followed him are responsible for naming these rugged granite peaks the Grand Tetons—"Big Tits." The area achieved park status only in 1929, when it became the refuge for wildlife that we see today.

#### ESSENTIALS

**ARRIVING & DEPARTING**   American, Continental, and United flights arrive at **Jackson Airport at Grand Teton National Park,** just south of the park. There are three ways to enter the park by road: the **Yellowstone South** entrance through the John D.

Rockefeller Jr. Memorial Parkway; the **Moran entrance station** on the east side of the park; and the **Moose entrance station,** 15 miles north of Jackson. There are park rangers at each of the entrance stations to answer any questions you may have.

**VISITOR INFORMATION**   For advance information, contact **Grand Tetons National Park,** P.O. Drawer 170, Moose, WY 83012 (☎ **307/739-3399**). See "Essentials" in the Jackson Hole section, below, for sources outside the park.

**VISITOR CENTERS**   The **Moose Visitor Center** (☎ **307/739-3399**), 8 miles north of the park's southern boundary, is a half-mile west of Moose Junction on the Teton Park Road. It's open May 15–early June, daily 8am–6pm; June 5–Labor Day, 8am–7pm. Winter hours (8am–5pm) begin after Labor Day and continue through mid-May. The **Colter Bay Visitor Center** (☎ **307/739-3594**) is a half-mile west of Colter Bay Junction on U.S. 191. Open mid-May–early June, daily 8am–7pm; early June–Labor Day 8am–8pm. The **Jenny Lake Visitor Center** is open early June–Labor Day, daily 8am–7pm; closed the remainder of the year.

**FOR TRAVELERS WITH DISABILITIES**   Although the visitor centers are wheelchair accessible, the Grand Tetons are not an easily navigable environment for those with physical disabilities. The park's telecommunication device (TDD) for the deaf can be reached at ☎ **307/739-3400.**

**ADMISSION COSTS & REGULATIONS**   A $10 fee per vehicle or $4 for pedestrians or bicyclists is required to enter at Moose or Moran and is good for 7 days. If you enter from the north, the park assumes you've paid in Yellowstone. National Park Service passports are accepted and sold at Moose and Moran entries.

A Wyoming **fishing license** is required for fishing anywhere in the park or at the Rockefeller Parkway, and may be purchased at the Moose Village store, Signal Mountain Lodge, Colter Bay Marina, or Flagg Ranch Village. Fishing in Yellowstone requires a separate permit. A **backcountry permit** is required for all hikers planning to spend the night and may be obtained at any visitor center. **Boat permits** are required ($10 motorized, $5 nonmotorized) and may be obtained at Moose or Colter Bay visitor centers. You do not have to register to **climb** in the park unless it'll be an overnight trek.

**Bikes** are allowed on major roads throughout the park but not on trails or in the backcountry. **Pets** must be attended and on a leash at all times, and are not allowed on trails, in the backcountry, in boats on the lakes (except Jackson) or the Snake River, in visitor centers, or on ranger-led activities. Kennels are available in Jackson. **Swimming** is allowed in all lakes, although there are no lifeguards on duty.

**INTERPRETIVE PROGRAMS**   Ranger-led activities in the park run from early June to early September. The park newspaper, *Teewinot,* has a complete activities guide. Most activities are hour-long programs scheduled from 9am to 9pm and are free, though some programs charge a nominal fee. The **Teton Science School,** P.O. Box 68, Kelly, WY 83011 (☎ **307/733-4765**), in the southwest part of the park, offers programs on the ecology of the park and the surrounding area. The school also houses the Murie Collection of birds, skulls, and animal tracks.

**WHEN TO GO**   July and August are the crowded months, when days are warm and nights cool; by August the divides between mountain canyons are usually free of snow. Early June or mid-September are ideal times to visit: Rates at most of the lodges surrounding the park have dropped, roads are less traveled, and days are still mild. Before June you may encounter occasional rain or snow, but the snow-encrusted Tetons make a striking contrast to the deep-blue skies and the blooming wildflowers along the southern part of the park. Trails are not always clear of snow in higher elevations in the spring, so check with one of the ranger stations for trail conditions. By mid-September, fall colors are beginning.

# Grand Teton National Park & Jackson Hole

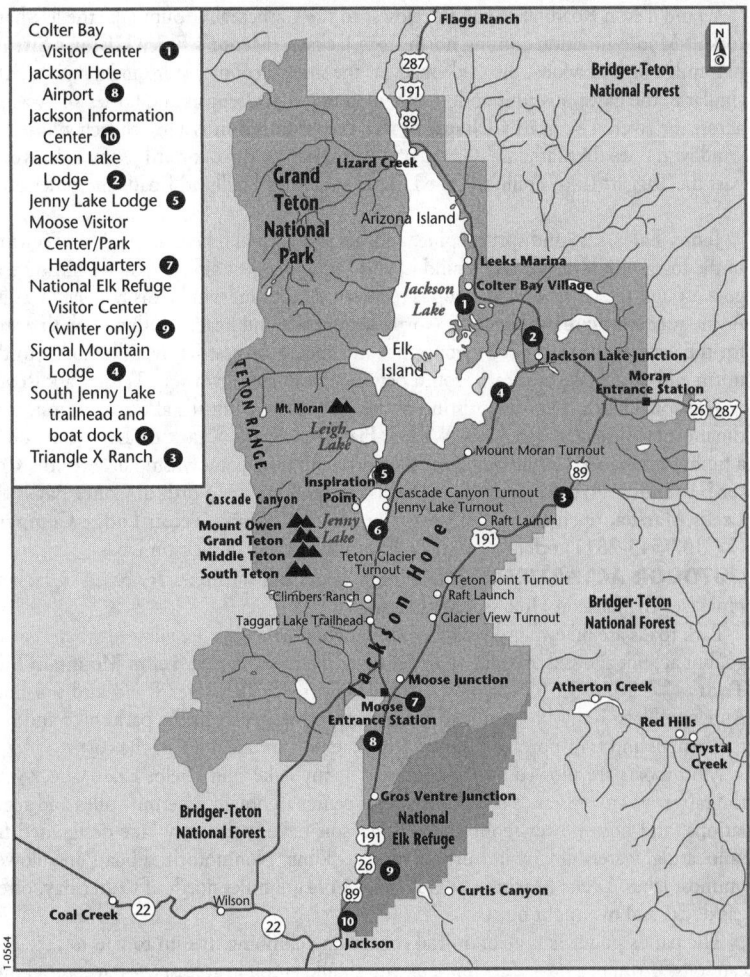

Colter Bay
 Visitor Center **1**
Jackson Hole
 Airport **8**
Jackson Information
 Center **10**
Jackson Lake
 Lodge **2**
Jenny Lake Lodge **5**
Moose Visitor
 Center/Park
 Headquarters **7**
National Elk Refuge
 Visitor Center
 (winter only) **9**
Signal Mountain
 Lodge **4**
South Jenny Lake
 trailhead and
 boat dock **6**
Triangle X Ranch **3**

## WHAT TO SEE & DO

**ORGANIZED TOURS**   The Colter Bay Village Corral offers sightseeing **wagon rides** in the summer. The Jackson Lake Lodge Corral offers similar adventures. The Grand Teton Lodge Company (☎ 307/543-2811) offers **bus tours** and charters to and from Jackson as well as through Yellowstone and Grand Teton national parks.

**TOURING THE PARK**   The most spectacular group of mountains in the Teton Range is the **Cathedral Group:** the **Grand Teton,** 13,766 feet, and a major challenge for technical climbers; the **Middle Teton;** the **South Teton;** and **Mt. Owen,** which is named for the second man who actually climbed it. **Teewinot** is the third highest Teton peak. **Signal Mountain,** east of Jackson Lake, is not so impressive, but is the most accessible lookout point; a narrow, winding road leads to the summit, where you'll have a fabulous view over Jackson Lake and the range (note that the road is too narrow for most RVs). To the north is the fourth tallest Teton, **Mt. Moran,** the 12,605-foot peak you'll see first when driving south from Yellowstone.

Grand Teton Road takes you the closest to the Cathedral Group; take the left-hand fork at Moose Junction coming north from Jackson. **Menor's Ferry Historic Site** is a half-mile north of Moose on a side road. At the site is a country store and a replica ferry, similar to the ingenious contraption once used to ferry passengers and horses and wagons across the river. The nearby **Chapel of the Transfiguration** is a log church whose rear window frames the Cathedral Group of Tetons. As you drive toward Jenny Lake, you'll pass the Taggart Lake Trailhead, the Lupine Meadows Trailhead Road, and other turnouts.

**Jenny Lake,** set amid spruce, pine, and fur, is a natural reflecting pool for Teewinot in the foreground, the Grand behind it, and Mt. Owen just off the right. A **hiking trail** goes around the lakeshore; the loop is relatively simple and can be easily done in a day. A one-way **scenic drive** begins at North Jenny Lake and heads southwest, with a stop for the view at the Cathedral Group turnout, then goes past Jenny Lake Lodge to the north end of the lake and turns south before rejoining the two-way Teton Park Road.

**Jackson Lake** is the least pristine of the Teton lakes, but it's also the biggest, with the most facilities for recreation. **Willow Flats,** just north of Jackson Lake Junction, is a freshwater marsh. **Colter Bay,** near the north entrance, is a township of sorts; the **Colter Bay Indian Arts Museum** is in the visitor center there. North of Colter Bay is the **Leeks Marina,** open throughout the summer. The **Grand Teton Lodge Company** (☎ 307/543-2811) offers three daily 90-minute cruises of Jackson Lake.

**OUTDOOR ACTIVITIES**    Many guides, tours, and outfitters are based in Jackson Hole (see the Jackson Hole section, below).

Park roads are bike-friendly, with wide shoulders. Bicycles are allowed wherever cars go, but are not allowed on trails or anywhere in the backcountry. **Teton Mountain Bike Tours** (☎ 307/733-0712) offers trips along the Snake River Road and a 4-hour Antelope Flats–Kelly Loop tour through the southwest part of the park; bike and helmet rentals and transportation to and from Jackson are included in the cost.

Motorboats are allowed on Jackson Lake, Jenny Lake, and Phelps Lake. Check with the ranger at any entrance station or visitor center to obtain a permit, rules and regulations, and horsepower requirements. Jackson Lake is the only lake designated for sailboating, waterskiing, windsurfing, and jet-skiing. Nonmotorized boats are allowed on most lakes. **Leeks Marina** (☎ 307/543-2494), 2 miles north of Colter Bay, offers gas docks and overnight buoys.

The park's policy is noncommittal concerning climbing. It's up to you to take precautions. If you're a novice at climbing, you should enroll in at least a 1-day basic climbing course at one of the local climbing schools. Sign in for your climb at **Jenny Lake Ranger Station** where climbing rangers are stationed from June until mid-September. A backcountry permit is required if the climb is an overnight trek. It's also a good idea to sign out. The park does not check on climbers who have not signed out, and a search-and-rescue attempt is begun only after the park is certain you are missing. Solo climbing is not advised. **Jackson Hole Mountain Guides and Climbing School** (☎ 307/733-4979) offers 1-day courses as well as guided climbs. The school is an accredited member of the American Mountain Guides Association. **Exum Mountain Guides** in Moose (☎ 307/733-2297) offers guided climbs to the summit of the Grand Teton for those with the requisite skills; they have a base camp at 11,600 feet.

In winter the roads in the park become trails for cross-country skiers. Snowmobiling is allowed, but is discouraged; most snowmobilers find Yellowstone more accommodating.

Self-guided hiking trail information is available at each visitor center. North of Menor's Ferry are trailheads leading to **Taggart Lake** and **Bradley Lake,** and there are good trails for day hikes around **Jenny Lake.** The trail leading to **Emma Matilda** and

**Two Ocean Lakes** near Jackson Lake is a 14-mile route with excellent wildlife spotting. **Lupine Meadows** is an arduous climb to Amphitheater Lake, and takes you to the edge of the cliffs for spectacular views of the Jackson Hole valley. **Teton Crest** is the main trail in a system that starts from the south near the Teton Pass and runs to the center of the park near Cascade Canyon. **Cascade Canyon Loop,** the most popular of the backcountry hikes, forms a 20-mile loop that begins and ends at the String Creek Trailhead north of Jenny Lake. See "Essentials," above, for permit requirements.

Most river rafting inside the park is scenic; the calmer waters of the Snake River flow through the park. For rafting on the river, register at the Moose Visitor Center, or the Colter Bay Visitor Center; a nonmotorized boat fee is required. **Solitude Float Trips** in Moose (☎ 307/733-2871) offers 5- and 10-mile scenic trips as well as guided fishing trips throughout the summer. Other trips are run by **Flagg Ranch,** in the north part of the park (☎ 800/443-2311 or 307/543-2861); and **Signal Mountain Lodge,** in the park (☎ 307/543-2831). A number of operators based in Jackson Hole offer whitewater or scenic trips; see "Outdoor Activities" in the Jackson Hole section, below.

**CAMPING**   Five campgrounds—Colter Bay, Gros Ventre, Jenny Lake, Lizard Creek, and Signal Mountain—are operated on a first-come, first-served basis, so the earlier you set out to find a spot, especially in midsummer, the better. All campgrounds except Lizard Creek have amenities such as flush toilets. Jenny Lake fills up faster than the others; the maximum stay is 7 days. All others have 14-day maximums. Colter Bay Campground, with group sites accommodating 10–75 people, accepts reservations Jan–mid-May; write to the **Permits Office** at Grand Teton National Park, P.O. Drawer 170, Moose, WY 83012. Colter Bay and Flagg Ranch (see below) have RV sites with hookups; reservations are advised.

### ACCOMMODATIONS & DINING

The **Grand Teton Lodge Company** (☎ 800/628-9988 for reservations) runs three properties in the park. **Colter Bay Cabins,** Grand Teton National Park, WY 83012 (☎ 307/543-2811), is a moderately priced place to stay, open mid-May to September. Near Jackson Lake, the cabins are quaint and the views spectacular, but walls are so thin that you can hear your neighbors at night. Colter Bay offers a full-service marina. **Jackson Lake Lodge,** Grand Teton National Park, WY 83012 (☎ 307/543-2811), is more expensive, and is not actually on the lake, though it has great views. It's open late May to mid-October. A better bet on the expensive side is **Jenny Lake Lodge,** in an ideal setting of pine trees and meadows. Breakfast, dinner, bicycles, and horseback riding come with the package.

**Flagg Ranch and Riverside Motel,** Grand Teton National Park, WY 83012 (☎ 800/443-2311), north of the park on the John D. Rockefeller Jr. Memorial Parkway, is 5 minutes away and 2 minutes from Yellowstone, on the Snake River. There are 100 spots for RVs complete with electricity, sewer, and water. It's open mid-May to mid-October and mid-December to mid-March. One of the best places to stay is **Signal Mountain Lodge,** Grand Teton National Park, WY 83012 (☎ 307/543-2831). The lakefront cabins, with kitchenettes, offer the best value at moderate rates. The lodge is decorated in a comfortable western style with a large fireplace for those less than balmy nights. It's open mid-May to mid-October. **Spur Ranch Cabins at Dornan's,** P.O. Box 39, Moose, WY 83012 (☎ 307/733-2522), is on the Snake River with wonderful Teton views. The cabins are some of the newer units in the park and have full kitchens.

## JACKSON HOLE

When wilderness man John Colter traversed these parts in the winter of 1807, Jackson was a pristine mountain valley, teeming with wildlife, called Teewinot by the Shoshone. Jackson Hole grew into a quaint, quiet little western town on the fringe of Grand Teton

National Park. But 20 years ago it began to change, and today it has more than 2 million annual visitors, three major ski resorts, and a real estate boom.

## ESSENTIALS

**ARRIVING & DEPARTING**    American, Continental, and United serve **Jackson Airport at Grand Teton National Park,** north of town and just south of the park. Many hotels and car-rental agencies in the Jackson area offer free shuttle service to and from the airport. Taxi service is available from **A-1 Taxi** (☎ 307/733-5089), **All Star Taxi** (☎ 800/378-2944 or 307/733-2888), **Buckboard Cab** (☎ 307/733-1112), **Jackson Hole Transportation** (☎ 307/733-3135), and **Tumbleweed Taxi** (☎ 307/733-0808).

**VISITOR INFORMATION**    The **Jackson Hole Visitor Council and Chamber of Commerce,** P.O. Box E, Jackson, WY 83001 (☎ **800/443-6931** or 307/733-3316), is at the Wyoming Information Center at 532 N. Cache. Here you can pick up brochures on activities in and outside the park as well as up-to-date weather and road condition information. You can also contact the Wyoming road and travel hotline for the Jackson area (☎ **307/733-9966**).

**GETTING AROUND**    **Southern Teton Area Rapid Transit (START)** offers bus transport from Teton Village to Jackson daily (every other hour 7am–10pm) on the Green Line for $2. The Blue Line runs daily (on the same schedule) from Jackson to Hoback throughout the summer for $1 each way. A season pass may be purchased for $35. Senior citizens and children 8 and under ride free. Winter service runs as frequently as summer, but during the off-season months in spring and fall, START slows down with the rest of the town. For specific schedule information, contact START at ☎ **307/733-4521.**

## WHAT TO SEE & DO

**OUTDOOR ACTIVITIES**    Jackson is full of outfitters. **Adventure Sports,** at Dornan's in Moose (☎ **307/733-3307**), has mountain-bike, kayak, and canoe rentals. Across from the old post office is a snowboard shop, the **Boardroom,** 245 Pearl (☎ **307/733-8327**). The **Jack Dennis Outdoor Shop** on the south side of Town Square (☎ **307/733-3270**) has fishing supplies, skis, and outdoor clothing. In Teton Village the Jack Dennis branch (☎ **307/733-6838**), along with **Pepi Steigler Sports** (☎ **307/733-4505**), accommodates winter and summer outdoor enthusiasts with guides, instruction, and the best equipment. **Hoback Sports,** 40 S. Millward (☎ **307/733-5335**), has three locations around town; others are Snow King (☎ 307/733-5200) and the Aspens (☎ 307/733-4664). **Skinny Skis,** at 65 W. Deloney off Town Square (☎ **307/733-6094**), is a year-round specialty sports shop, the best place in town for free recreational literature.

For bicycle rentals, maps, and reliable information about trails and equipment, drop by **Teton Cyclery** at 175 N. Glenwood (☎ **307/733-4386**) and **Wilson Backcountry Sports,** 5 miles west of Jackson in Wilson, at the Fish Creek Center (☎ **307/733-5228**). Closer to the park, **Adventure Sports** at Dornan's in Moose (☎ **307/733-3307**) offers hourly, daily, weekly, and even monthly rentals. For rentals and tour information, both guided and unguided, contact **Fat Tire Tours** at Hoback Sports, 40 S. Millward (☎ **307/733-5335**), or **Teton Mountain Bike Tours** at 430 S. Cache (☎ **307/733-0712**).

**Jackson Hole Iditarod,** P.O. Box 1940, Jackson, WY 83001 (☎ **800/554-7388**), offers both half- and full-day trips in five-person dog sleds (four passengers; the fifth is your guide). You can also take a full-day excursion out to Granite Hot Springs, a 22-mile trip.

**High Country Flies,** 165 N. Center St. (☎ **307/733-7210**), has all the goods and offers guided fishing trips and schools. Fishing experts assemble at the **Jack Dennis**

**Outdoor Shop,** downtown on the Town Square at 50 E. Broadway (☎ **307/ 733-3270**). A branch is in Teton Village (☎ 307/733-6838). **Westbank Anglers,** 3670 N. Moose–Wilson Rd. (☎ **307/733-6483**), is a full-service fly shop offering guides and fishing trips in Jackson Hole.

The **Jackson Hole Golf and Tennis Club** (☎ 307/733-3111), north of Jackson off U.S. 89, has an 18-hole golf course that's one of the best in the country. The **Teton Pines Resort,** 3450 N. Clubhouse Dr. (☎ **800/238-2223** or 307/733-1005), has a course that was designed by Arnold Palmer (it becomes a cross-country ski center in winter). Both courses are open to the public.

Less-traveled alternatives than the park's hiking trails (see above) are those in the **Bridger–Teton National Forest** just east of Jackson. A **visitor center** is located in the log cabin at 340 N. Cache in downtown Jackson (☎ 307/739-5500) and has hiking and access information for the national forest, Gros Ventre, and Teton Wilderness areas. The **Wind River Range** is southeast of Jackson in the Bridger–Teton National Forest. Information on the peaks and trails can be obtained by contacting the U.S. Forest Service at the Bridger–Teton office in Jackson mentioned above.

A few of the places ready to put you in the saddle are **Bridger–Teton Outfitters** (☎ 307/739-4314 or 307/733-7745), **Green River Outfitters** in Pinedale (☎ 307/ 733-1044 or 307/367-2416), **Jackson Hole Trail Rides** (☎ 307/733-6992), **Snow King Stables** (☎ 307/733-5781), and the **Mill Iron Ranch** (☎ 307/733-6390).

Kayaking is popular on the Snake River, but it's not for beginners, who should stick to the relatively calm waters of the lakes in Yellowstone National Park. Schools and guide services include Greg Winston's **Wilderness Exposure Expeditions** (☎ 307/ 733-1026), offering specialized custom trips into the Yellowstone backcountry on Lewis and Shoshone lakes; **Greater Yellowstone Sea Kayaking** (☎ 800/733-2471), with similar trips; the **Snake River Kayak and Canoe School** (☎ 307/733-3127), which has 1-day classes for canoes and inflatable kayaks, as well as an indoor kayak school in their 45,000-gallon teaching facility.

Contact the **National Park Service** (☎ 307/739-3300) for information on rafting in the park. Outside the park, you're in the jurisdiction of the **National Forest Service;** the Bridger–Teton supervisor's office is in Jackson at 340 N. Cache (☎ 307/739-5500). Outfits offering whitewater rafting and/or scenic tours along the Snake include **Barker–Ewing** (☎ 307/733-1800); **Charlie Sands Wildwater** (☎ 800/358-8184 or 307/ 733-4410); **Dave Hansen Whitewater** (☎ 307/733-6295); **Fort Jackson River Trips** (☎ 800/735-8430 or 307/733-2583); **Grand Teton Lodge Company** (☎ 307/543-2811); **Jackson Hole Whitewater** (☎ 800/648-2602 or 307/733-1007); **Lewis and Clark Expeditions,** at Snow King Ski Resort (☎ 800/824-5375 or 307/ 733-4022); **O.A.R.S.** (☎ 307/733-3379); **Triangle X Ranch with Osprey,** in Moose (☎ 307/733-5500); and **Mad River Boat Trips** (☎ 800/458-7238 or 307/733-6203).

**WINTER SPORTS** Jackson is a premier destination for **downhill skiing. ✪ Jackson Hole Ski Resort,** 7658 Teewinot, Teton Village, WY 83025 (☎ **800/443-6931** for central reservations; 307/733-2292 or 307/733-4005; 307/733-2291 for snow conditions), is the number-one ski area in this part of the country. Aprés Mountain, at 8,481 feet, is a network of beginner and intermediate slopes; the 10,450-foot Rendezvous Mountain has black diamond and double black diamond runs that head straight for the bottom. There are 2,500 acres of skiable terrain, 62 named runs, 9 lifts, and an aerial tram to the top of Rendezvous. ✪ **Grand Targhee Resort,** Hill Road, Alta, WY 83422 (☎ **800/827-4433** or 307/353-2300), is 40 miles from Jackson, and is a good area for beginning and intermediate skiers. Targhee is a powder mountain with a beginner's powder area and wide-open powder slopes for intermediates. The resort has a program for kids and an in-room baby-sitting service. **Snow King Resort,**

100 E. Snow King, Jackson, WY 83001 (☎ 800/533-5464, or 800/522-7669 within Wyoming, or 307/733-5200; 307/734-2020 for snow conditions), is mainly for experts, with steep grades and mostly black diamond runs. Wind and cold can be a problem on "Town Hill."

Contact the **National Forest Service** in downtown Jackson at 340 N. Cache (☎ 307/739-5500) for information on cross-country skiing. **Teton Pines Cross Country Skiing Center** (☎ 307/733-1005) has 13km of groomed trails that wind over the resort's golf course. **Spring Creek Resort** (☎ 307/733-1004) has an excellent facility with 14km of groomed trails. **Grand Targhee** (see above) has 12 km of groomed trails. **Teton Parks and Recreation** (☎ 307/733-5056) has instructional programs for those who bring their own equipment. Keep in mind that many of the trails used by cross-country skiers are also used by snowmobiles.

**High Country Snowmobile Tours** (☎ 800/524-0130 or 307/733-5017) has a touring service for Jackson Hole, Yellowstone, and the Gros Ventre Mountains. **Rocky Mountain Snowmobile Tours** (☎ 800/647-2561 or 307/733-2237) offers 1-day trips in Yellowstone and multiday trips along the Continental Divide.

**WILDLIFE-WATCHING** The **National Elk Refuge,** U.S. 26, P.O. Box C, Jackson, WY 83001 (☎ 307/733-9212), is winter home to the largest gathering of elk in North America. Thinly timbered stretches along the Gros Ventre River that roll into grassy meadows and sagebrush form an ideal habitat for elk, moose, bighorn sheep, and more than 175 species of birds. Winter is the best time to view the migrating elk herd, which moves down from higher elevations to the valley floor during the first snows of late autumn. The Fish and Wildlife Service offers **horse-drawn sleigh rides** that provide up-close glimpses of the 8,000 elk. Tickets can be purchased at the National Museum of Wildlife Art across from the refuge. Headquarter hours for the refuge are Mon–Fri 8am–4:30pm.

**OTHER ATTRACTIONS** A ride to the top of Rendezvous Mountain between late May and September on the **aerial tram** at Jackson Hole Ski Resort (see above) will give you a view of the Tetons from an elevation of 10,000 feet. The **National Museum of Wildlife Art,** 2820 Rungius Rd., 3 miles north on U.S. 89 (☎ 307/733-5771), is one of the largest museums devoted to wildlife in the country. It houses a collection of paintings by wildlife artist Carl Rungius and is a repository for wildlife films. A quirky downtown museum is the **Jackson Hole Museum,** 105 N. Glenwood (☎ 307/733-2414), with a collection of early photographs, artifacts, and other items of local historical significance. The **Teton County Historical Center,** 105 N. Mercill St. (☎ 307/733-9605), open by appointment only, takes a more scholarly look at local history.

**Old West cookouts** with entertainment are offered by the **A/OK Corral,** 10 minutes south of town at 9600 U.S. 191 S. (☎ 307/733-6556); the **Bar-J Ranch** (☎ 307/733-3370) has a meal with a real western show. To get there, head for Wilson and turn right toward Teton Village; watch for the ranch about a mile down the road on your left. **Bar-T-5,** 790 E. Cache Creek, Jackson (☎ 800/772-5386 or 307/733-5386), has a covered wagon ride, a cookout, and after-dinner songs.

**SHOPPING** Among the more than 20 art galleries in downtown Jackson, the **American Legends Gallery,** at 365 N. Cache, has an array of bronze sculptures and features the works of several local artists. **Images of Nature Gallery,** 170 N. Cache, exhibits Tom Mangelson's excellent wildlife photography; a number are signed and numbered. The **Center Street Gallery,** 172 Center St., shows abstract western art. The **Moynihan Gallery,** at 120 E. Broadway, displays some of Russell Chatham's landscapes (Chatham's own gallery is in Livingston, Montana). A mile north of town is the **Wilcox Gallery,** 1975 U.S. 89, which showcases more than 20 painters and sculptors.

## ACCOMMODATIONS

There are few moderate or inexpensive accommodations in the area. It's advisable to make reservations as far ahead as possible, especially in summer. **Business and Vacation Planning** (☎ 800/733-6431) can make reservations and other arrangements for visitors. In addition to the listings below, property management companies offer lodging options for skiers in Teton Village. **Jackson Hole Property Management** (☎ 800/443-8613 or 307/733-7945) has 85 condominium units, and **Teton Village Property Management** (☎ 307/733-4610) runs the Village Center Inn and the Crystal Springs Inn. The **Jackson Hole Racquet Club** (☎ 800/443-8616 or 307/733-3990) has a resort with 120 condominium units.

✪ **Days Inn of Jackson Hole.** *1280 W. Broadway (just off the junction of Hwy. 22 and U.S. Hwy. 191), Jackson, WY 83001.* ☎ *800/329-7466 or 307/733-0033. 91 rms, 13 suites. $149 double; $159–209 suite. Off-season rates considerably lower. Rates include continental breakfast. AE, DC, DISC, MC, V.* An above-average Days Inn, this one has an extremely helpful staff and beautiful and spacious suites with fireplaces and hot tubs.

✪ **Flying A Ranch.** *Rte. 1 (P.O. Box 7), Pinedale, WY 82941.* ☎ *307/367-2385. 6 cabins. $1,500–$1,575 per person per week. Rates include all meals and ranch activities. No credit cards.* This guest ranch in a high mountain valley 50 miles southeast of Jackson is surrounded by the Gros Ventre and Wind River ranges. The resort provides a low-key ranch experience for adults, with gourmet meals and unparalleled opportunities for fly-fishing and exploring the outdoors.

**Gros Ventre River Ranch.** *P.O. Box 151, Moose, WY 83012.* ☎ *307/733-4138. 8 cabins. $945–$1,854 per person per week. No credit cards. Call for directions.* This year-round guest ranch, about 18 miles north of Jackson, keeps the Old West alive, but with all the comforts of home. Horseback rides and fly-fishing dominate the program of events. Four log cabins and four log lodges are spread out on this property, which looks straight out to the Teton Range. There's a full array of summer sports, and in winter, cross-country skiing and snowmobiling.

✪ **Heart 6 Ranch.** *P.O. Box 70, Moran, WY 83013.* ☎ *307/543-2477. 15 cabins. $1,072–$1,265 per person per week. MC, V.* A little more than an hour north of Jackson, 5 miles outside Grand Teton National Park, this guest ranch is not fancy, but not short on activities either—fishing, horseback riding, and hiking lead the long list. A naturalist from the park service is often on hand. There are extensive children's programs; baby-sitting is available for infants and children up to 4.

✪ **Red Rock Ranch.** *P.O. Box 38, Kelly, WY 83011.* ☎ *307/733-6288. 9 cabins. $1,085 per week. Minimum 7-day stay (Sun to Sun). Closed Oct–May. No credit cards.* With excellent fly-fishing on the ranch's private stretch of Crystal Creek, horseback riding in the mountains, and activities that include overnighters for the kids and trips to the rodeo in Jackson, this is a great family place, northeast of Jackson. A late 19th-century homestead surrounded by the mountains, it's also a working cattle ranch. All nine log cabins have small refrigerators and charming wood stoves (electric heat is also available). Amenities include a recreation room for the kids and a heated pool.

**Rusty Parrot Lodge.** *175 N. Jackson, Jackson, WY 83001.* ☎ *800/458-2004 or 307/733-2000. 31 rms, 1 suite. $98–$215 double; $300 suite. Rates include full breakfast. AE, DISC, MC, V.* If it weren't right in the middle of town, you'd think this was a country lodge. It's decorated in the new western style of peeled log, pine furniture, and river rock fireplaces; rooms are gigantic and several have private balconies.

✪ **Spring Creek Resort.** *P.O. Box 3154, Jackson, WY 83001.* ☎ *800/443-6139 or 307/733-8833. 116 units. $200–$950 per unit per night. AE, MC, V.* Spring Creek sits atop Gros Ventre Butte, but it's only a 4-mile drive from Jackson's Town Square. The freestanding units can sleep eight people and come equipped with all the amenities and plenty of living space. Condominiums accommodate fewer people and cost less. Nearly every room has a view of the Teton range. There is shuttle service to the Jackson Hole Ski Resort, a swimming pool, and tennis courts. The Granary offers great food and views.

**Teton Pines Resort.** *3450 N. Clubhouse Dr., Jackson, WY 83001.* ☎ *800/ 238-2223 or 307/733-1005. 16 suites. Summer, $250–$360 suite; rest of year, $125– $195 suite. Closed Nov.* This luxury resort has a country club conveniently attached, along with an 18-hole golf course designed by Arnold Palmer and Ed Seay, and 8 miles of groomed Nordic trails. The Grille at the Pines, in the clubhouse, has an impressive menu and is one of the better places to eat in Jackson.

**Trapper Inn.** *235 N. Cache, Jackson, WY 83001.* ☎ *800/341-8000 or 307/ 733-2648. 54 rms, 1 suite. $85–$105 double; $195 suite. AE, DC, DISC, MC, V.* The staff here know all the best deals in town, and they're not afraid to share. Though the decor of the rooms is average, the newest building, erected in 1991, has units that are larger than normal; many come with miniature refrigerators. Laundry facilities and an indoor/outdoor hot tub are also on hand.

**Village Center Inn.** *3275 W. McCollister, Teton Village, WY 83025.* ☎ *307/ 733-3155. 16 rms. Winter, $102–$132 double. AE, MC, V.* At the base of the hill next to the Jackson Hole tram, the units here resemble efficiency apartments, with cable television, small kitchens, and a living area. In summer, rates are reduced.

**Virginian Lodge.** *750 W. Broadway, Jackson, WY 83001.* ☎ *800/262-4999 or 307/733-2792. 135 rms, 12 minisuites, 11 suites. $95–$105 double; $110 minisuite; $115–$155 suite. AE, DC, DISC, MC, V.* With its overhaul in 1995, the Virginian is one of the best affordable hotels in Jackson. The hotel's Old West flavor is delightful. The Virginian has an outdoor heated pool, an average family-style restaurant, an arcade for the youngsters, and laundry facilities.

**CAMPING**   Most campgrounds are open from late spring to early fall. **Astoria Mineral Springs,** also known as Astoria Hot Springs, at 12500 S. U.S. 89 (☎ 307/733-2659), has 110 tent and RV sites; it's about 17 miles south of town toward Pinedale. The **Snake River Park KOA Campground** is also on U.S. 89, 10 miles south of town (☎ 307/733-7078). In town, the **Wagon Wheel Campground** is at the Wagon Wheel Motel. The **Teton Village KOA** (☎ 307/733-5354) is 12 miles northwest of Jackson.

## DINING

Jackson has some pleasant dining surprises, but like everything else here, restaurant prices are high.

✪ **Acadian House.** *170 N. Millward.* ☎ *307/739-1269. Reservations recommended. Lunch $3–$7; main courses $9–$17. AE, DC, MC, V. Tues–Fri 11:30am–2pm; daily 5:30–10pm. CAJUN.* Traditional dishes like boudin—a sausage-and-rice bratwurst look-alike—next to red beans and rice, and shrimp étouffée, make an appearance along with continental-style creations such as crawfish fettuccine. The blackened-to-perfection catfish in white wine is topped with almonds and pecans.

✪ **Blue Lion.** *160 N. Millward.* ☎ *307/733-3912. Reservations recommended. Main courses $15–$26. AE, DC, MC, V. Daily 6–9:30pm. Closed Tues off-season. CONTINENTAL.* The menu at this quaint restaurant off the Town Square is filled with a delicious array of creative entrees. Rack of lamb, beef tenderloin medaillons, and wild game, including elk loin grilled and served in a peppercorn sauce, are specialties of the Blue Lion. Vegetarian entrees are also prepared with zest.

**The Bunnery.** *130 N. Cache St.* ☎ *307/733-5474. Breakfast $3–$6; lunch $5–$6. MC, V. Year-round, daily 7am–3pm. Summer, daily 7am–3pm and 5:30–9:30pm. SANDWICHES/SOUPS/SALADS.* A Jackson mainstay, this bakery and restaurant is a great place to have one of the famous Bunnery breakfasts outside on a cool morning, or to drop by for a sunny-day lunch.

**Cadillac Grille.** *55 N. Cache.* ☎ *307/733-3279. Reservations recommended. Lunch $5–$8; main courses $15–$25. AE, MC, V. Daily 11am–3pm and 5:30–9:30pm. CONTINENTAL.* This trendy California-influenced restaurant with its nationally acclaimed cuisine is Jackson's premier see-and-be-seen restaurant. The menu changes seasonally, but has included such creative items as stuffed Dakota pheasant, bleu cheese tournedos, and steamed Alaskan halibut.

**Jedidiah's House of Sourdough.** *135 E. Broadway.* ☎ *307/733-5671. Reservations not accepted. Breakfast $4–$8; lunch $3–$7. AE, DC, MC, V. Daily 7am–2pm. AMERICAN.* Jedidiah's is known throughout the valley for its breakfast and its log-cabin atmosphere. Sourjacks are a stack of sourdough pancakes, served with blueberries, and the omelet is a big three-egg concoction stuffed with bacon, onions, and cheddar cheese.

✪ **Nani's Genuine Pasta House.** *240 N. Glenwood (2 blocks north of Broadway at the El Rancho Motel).* ☎ *307/733-3888. Reservations recommended. Main courses $8–$14. MC, V. Tues–Sat 5:30–9:30pm. ITALIAN.* Each month Nani's explores a new regional cuisine. The residents call it one of the best restaurants in town for the fresh handmade ravioli alone.

**Nora's Fish Creek Inn.** *5600 W. Wyo. 22, Wilson.* ☎ *307/733-8288. Reservations not accepted. Breakfast $3–$7; lunch $4–$6; main courses $8–$14. DISC, MC, V. Daily 6am–9:30pm. AMERICAN.* This little place outside Wilson is a great spot for a weekend breakfast because it's all-you-can-eat pancakes. One of Jackson Hole's institutions, and food isn't gourmet, but prices are inexpensive compared to other restaurants in town.

**Stiegler's.** *Teton Village Rd., Teton Village.* ☎ *307/733-1071. Reservations recommended. Main courses $14–$24. AE, MC, V. Tues–Sun 5:30–10pm. AUSTRIAN/CONTINENTAL.* Peter Stiegler, the chef, invites you to "find a little *genutlichkeit*," and enjoy such dishes as venison filet mignon morel and other Austrian dishes. The restaurant is in the Jackson Hole Racquet Club.

✪ **Vista Grande.** *Teton Village Rd., Teton Village.* ☎ *307/733-6964. Reservations not accepted. Main courses $9–$17. AE, MC, V. Daily 5–10pm. MEXICAN.* The food is great south-of-the-border cuisine, and the portions are plentiful. Along with the usual fajitas and burritos, you'll find chicken asados (grilled chicken on a bed of rice with pico de gallo), blackened tuna, and a vegetarian plate.

### JACKSON AFTER DARK

Throughout the summer, the **Grand Teton Music Festival,** 4015 N. Lake Creek (☎ 307/733-3050), brings in world-class musicians for classical concerts. The **Jackson Hole Playhouse,** 145 W. Deloney (☎ 307/733-6994), and the **Lighthouse Theatre,** 49 W. Broadway (☎ 307/733-3670), always have something in production during the summer months. For family fun in an Old West atmosphere, head to **Dirty Jack's Wild West Musical Theatre,** 140 N. Cache (☎ 307/733-4775). The jokes are run-of-the-mill, but the cast loves telling them.

At the **Silver Dollar Bar,** 50 N. Glenwood in the Wort Hotel, you can have a drink with real or imagined cowpokes at the bar. The very famous **Million Dollar Cowboy Bar** down the street packs in the western crowd for cocktails. The **Mangy Moose,** 3285 W. McCollister in Teton Village, is where up-and-coming bands play when they stop in Jackson Hole. For Sunday night drink and merriment, try the **Stagecoach** on Wyo. 22 in Wilson.

# 7  More Northwest Highlights

## CRATER LAKE NATIONAL PARK

At 1,932 feet deep, Crater Lake is the deepest lake in the United States and the seventh deepest in the world. But depth alone is not what makes this one of the most visited spots in the Northwest—it's the startling sapphire-blue waters. They've mesmerized visitors ever since a prospector searching for gold stumbled on the high mountain lake in 1853. The lake and its surroundings are the only national park in Oregon.

The caldera (crater) that today holds the serene lake was born in an explosive volcanic eruption 7,700 years ago. When the volcano now known as Mount Mazama erupted, its summit—thought to have been around 12,000 feet high—collapsed, leaving a crater 4,000 feet deep. Thousands of years of rain and melting snow have created the cold, clear lake surrounded by crater walls nearly 2,000 feet high.

The drive into the park winds through forests that hold not a hint of the spectacular sight that lies hidden among these mountains. With no warning except the signs leading to Rim Village, you suddenly find yourself gazing down into this vast bowl full of blue water. Toward one end of the lake rises the cone of Wizard Island, the tip of a volcano that has been slowly building since the last eruption of Mount Mazama.

After your first breathtaking view of the lake, you may want to stop by one of the park's two visitor centers—**Steel Information Center** and the **Rim Village Visitor Center.** Though the park is open year-round, in winter deep snows blanket the region and only the road to Rim Village is kept clear. During the summer (roughly beginning in late June), the **Rim Drive** provides many stunning viewpoints as it makes a 39-mile-long circuit of the lake.

There are many activities available in the park, but the most popular are 2-hour **boat trips** around the lake beginning at Cleetwood Cove, at the bottom of a very steep 1-mile trail descending 700 feet from the rim to the lakeshore. Be sure you're in good enough physical condition to make the steep climb back up to the rim. Also bring warm clothes, as it can be quite a bit cooler on the lake than on the rim. A naturalist on each boat provides a narrative on the ecology and history of the lake, and all tours include a stop on Wizard Island. Tours are offered late June–mid-Sept.

Other park activities include children's programs, campfire ranger talks, history talks, and guided walks.

Many miles of **hiking trails** can be found within the park, but the Cleetwood Trail down to the boat dock is the only one from the rim to the lake. Although it's a rigorous 2¹/₂-mile climb, the trail to the top of Mount Scott is the park's most rewarding hike. Shorter trails with good views include the 0.8-mile trail to the top of the Watchman, which overlooks Wizard Island, and the 1.7-mile trail up Garfield Peak. The short Castle Crest Wildflower Trail is best hiked in late July and early August. Backpackers can hike the length of the park on the Pacific Crest Trail, which is being rerouted to travel along the rim.

In winter, **cross-country skiing** is popular on the park's snow-covered roads and in the backcountry. The **Diamond Lake Resort Cross-Country Ski Center** (☎ 800/733-7593) in Diamond Lake offers Sno-Cat ski tours on the north side of the park.

You'll have two lodging options in the park (☎ 541/594-2511 or fax 541/594-2622 to reserve at either). Overlooking the lake from the rim, ✪ **Crater Lake Lodge** has the look and feel of a historic mountain lodge yet has modern conveniences. Stone fireplace and ponderosa pine–bark walls grace the Great Hall. About half the guest rooms overlook the lake, and the dining room provides a view of both the lake and the Klamath

River basin. Although it isn't on the rim of the crater, **Mazama Village Motor Inn** is just a short drive away. Its 10 steep-roofed buildings look much like traditional mountain cabins. A laundry, gas station, and general store make Mazama Village a busy spot in the summer. Both facilities are closed mid-Oct–May.

On the shores of Diamond Lake near the north entrance, **Diamond Lake Resort** (☎ 800/733-7593 or 541/793-3333) enjoys one of the most picturesque settings in the Oregon Cascades. The variety of accommodations includes lakefront cabins with great mountain and lake views. Cabins and studios have kitchenettes, and the lodge offers several dining options. Boat and mountain-bike rentals are available, and there's a small sandy beach.

Lodging options in the tiny hamlet of Prospect, 30 miles from Rim Village, include **Prospect Historical Hotel and Motel** (☎ 800/944-6490 or 541/560-3664), a combination of an 1889 vintage hotel and a modern motel, and **Union Creek Resort** (☎ 541/560-3339 or 541/560-3565), across the road from the Rogue River Gorge.

Tent camping and RV spaces are available on the south side of the park at the **Mazama Village Campground,** where there are 198 sites. There are also 16 tent sites available at **Lost Creek Campground** on the park's east side. They are open June–Oct, and reservations are not accepted. Backpackers can camp in the park's backcountry. Four miles north of the park's north entrance, Diamond Lake has three **U.S. Forest Service campgrounds**—Diamond Lake, Broken Arrow, and Thielsen View—with a total of 450 campsites. The private **Diamond Lake RV Park** (☎ 541/793-3318) is 4 miles north of the park's north entrance.

**Essentials:** Crater Lake is 57 miles north of Klamath Falls via U.S. 97 and Ore. 62, and 71 miles northeast of I-5 at Medford via Ore. 62. Entrance fees are $10 per vehicle or $5 per individual. National Park Service passports are accepted. For information, contact **Crater Lake National Park,** P.O. Box 7, Crater Lake, OR 97604 (☎ 541/594-2211). For more information on activities just outside the park, contact the **Diamond Lake Ranger District,** HC 60, Box 101, Idleyld Park, OR 97447 (☎ 541/498-2531); the **Umpqua National Forest,** 2900 NW Stewart Pkwy. (P.O. Box 1008), Roseburg, OR 97470 (☎ 541/672-6601); or the **Diamond Lake Visitor Center,** Chemult, OR 97731 (☎ 541/793-3310).

## MOUNT RAINIER NATIONAL PARK

At 14,410 feet high, Mount Rainier is the highest point in Washington, and to the sun-starved residents of Seattle the dormant volcano is a giant weather gauge. When the skies clear over Puget Sound, "The Mountain is out" is a phrase often heard around the city. And when the Mountain is out, all eyes turn to admire its broad slopes, which remain snow-covered throughout the year. The region's infamous moisture-laden air has made Mount Rainier one of the snowiest spots in the country, and in 1972, the mountain set a record when 93$^1$/$_2$ feet of snow fell in 1 year. Such record snowfalls have created numerous glaciers on the mountain's flanks, and one of these, the Carbon Glacier, is the lowest-elevation glacier in the continental United States.

Snow and glaciers notwithstanding, Rainier has a heart of fire. Steam vents at the mountain's summit are evidence that, though this volcanic peak has been dormant for more than 150 years, it could erupt again at any time. However, scientists believe that Rainier's volcanic activity occurs in 3,000-year cycles—and luckily we have another 500 years to go before there's another big eruption.

Known to Native Americans as Tahoma, Mount Rainier received its current name in 1792 when British explorer Capt. George Vancouver named the mountain for a friend who never visited the region. The first ascent to the mountain's summit was made in 1870 by Gen. Hazard Stevens and Philemon Van Trump, and it was 14 years later that James Longmire built the first hotel on the flanks of Mount Rainier. In 1889 Mount Rainier became the fifth national park. Today the park covers 235,612 acres and is visited by more than two million people a year.

The park's **main entrance** is Nisqually, at its southwest corner. Just past there, you'll come to **Longmire,** site of the National Park Inn, the **Longmire Museum** (with exhibits on the park's natural and human history), a hiker information center that issues backcountry permits, and a ski-touring center where you can rent cross-country skis in winter.

The road then continues climbing to **Paradise** (elevation 5,400 feet), the aptly named mountainside aerie from which you get a breathtakingly close-up view of the mountain. Paradise is the park's most popular destination, so expect crowds. During July and August the meadows here are ablaze with wildflowers. The circular **Henry M. Jackson Memorial Visitor Center** (☎ 360/569-2211, ext. 2328) provides 360° panoramic views, and includes exhibits on the flora, fauna, and geology of the park, as well as a display on mountain climbing. The visitor center is open daily early May–mid-Oct and on weekends and holidays mid-Oct–early May. A 1.2-mile walk from the visitor center will bring you to a spot from which you can look down on the **Nisqually Glacier.** It's not unusual to find plenty of snow at Paradise as late as July.

In the summer months you can continue beyond Paradise to the **Ohanapecosh Visitor Center** (☎ 360/569-2211, ext. 2352), which is open weekends late May–mid-June and daily mid-June–early Oct. Nearby, you can walk through the **Grove of the Patriarchs,** a forest of old-growth trees, some of which are more than 1,000 years old.

Continuing around the mountain, you'll come to the turnoff for **Sunrise,** at 6,400 feet the highest spot accessible by car. A beautiful old log lodge serves as the **Sunrise Visitor Center** (☎ 360/569-2211, ext. 2357). From here you get a superb view of Mount Rainier and **Emmons Glacier,** which is the largest glacier in the 48 contiguous states.

If you want to avoid the crowds and see a bit of dense old-growth forest, or do a bit of uncrowded hiking, head for the park's **Carbon River entrance** in the northwest corner. This is the least visited region of the park because it only offers views to those willing to hike several miles uphill. Carbon River has another distinction as well. It's formed by meltwater from the Carbon Glacier, which descends lower than any other glacier in the continental United States.

Hikers have more than 240 miles of trails to explore within the park. Although Paradise sees a lot of visitors, it also offers many excellent day hikes. The 5-mile **Skyline Trail** is the highest trail at Paradise and climbs above the tree line. Along the way there are views of Mount Adams, Mount St. Helens, and the Nisqually Glacier. The **Lakes Trail,** of similar length, heads downhill to the Reflection Lakes. The 95-mile-long **Wonderland Trail,** which circles the mountain, is the quintessential Mount Rainier backpacking trip. This trail takes 10 days to 2 weeks to complete. For the less adventurous, there are naturalist-led programs and walks throughout the spring, summer, and fall. Check the park newspaper for schedules.

Mount Rainier is a training ground for making mountain-climbing attempts on higher peaks, such as Mount Everest. **Rainier Mountaineering, Inc.,** 535 Dock St., Tacoma, WA 98402 (☎ 360/569-2227 in summer, or 206/627-6242 in winter), teaches classes.

In winter, miles of trails are open to **cross-country skiing,** but there is limited access because of road closures. At Longmire, you'll find a ski touring and a rental shop (☎ 360/569-2411). There are also **guided snowshoe walks** at Paradise.

Lodging is available at the **National Park Inn,** in Longmire in the southwest corner of the park, a rustic lodge opened in 1920 and fully renovated in 1990. With only

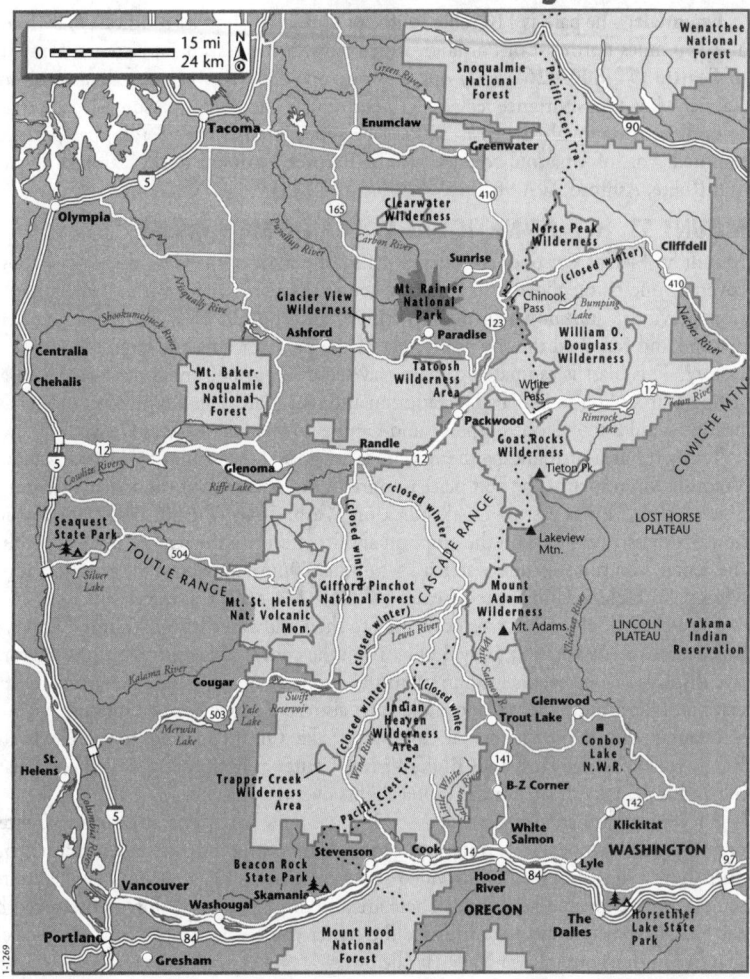

25 rooms and open all year, it makes a great little getaway or base for exploring the mountain. The front veranda has a view of Mount Rainier, and inside there's a guest lounge with a river-rock fireplace that's perfect for winter-night relaxing. Up at Paradise, the rustic **Paradise Inn** offers breathtaking views of the mountain and the nearby Nisqually Glacier. Miles of trails and meadows make this the perfect spot for some relatively easy alpine exploring. Cedar-shake siding, huge exposed beams, cathedral ceilings, and a gigantic stone fireplace all add up to a quintessential mountain retreat. Both inns have dining rooms. For information or reservations, contact either at P.O. Box 108, Ashford, WA 98304 (☎ **360/569-2275**).

Nearby lodging is available in the towns of Greenwater, Ashford, Elbe, and Packwood.

There are five campgrounds within the park, all available on a first-come, first-served basis. They stay full throughout the summer, so arrive early. No electrical or water hookups are available. Only the **Sunshine Point Campground** (☎ **360/569-2211,** ext. 3314) is open year-round. There are also numerous National Forest Service campgrounds along Wash. 410 east of the park.

**Essentials:** The park is 110 miles southeast of Seattle, 70 miles southeast of Tacoma, and 150 miles northeast of Portland, which have the nearest major airports. **Grayline of Seattle** (☎ 800/426-7532) operates one bus daily between Seattle and Mount Rainier May–Oct. Entrance fees are $10 per vehicle and $5 per person for pedestrians or cyclists. An annual pass costs $20 per person. National Park Service passports are honored. For information, contact **Mount Rainier National Park,** Tahoma Woods, Star Route, Ashford, WA 98304 (☎ 206/569-2211).

## MOUNT ST. HELENS NATIONAL VOLCANIC MONUMENT

Mount St. Helens was once considered the most perfect of the Cascade peaks, a snow-covered cone rising above lush forests. Then on May 18, 1980, with a violent explosion previously unknown in modern times, an eruption blew out the side of the volcano and removed the top 1,300 feet of the peak, causing the largest landslide in history. This blast is estimated to have traveled at up to 650 miles per hour, with air temperatures of up to 800°F. The eruption also sent more than 540 million tons of ash nearly 16 miles into the atmosphere and raining down as far away as Denver.

Today the area surrounding the volcano is designated the Mount St. Helens National Volcanic Monument. The best place to start an exploration is at the **Visitor Center** at Silver Lake, 5 miles east of Castle Rock on Wash. 504 (☎ 360/274-2100), which houses extensive exhibits on the eruption and its effects on the region. Before reaching the center, you can stop and watch a 25-minute, 70mm film about the eruption at the **Mount St. Helens Cinedome Theater** (☎ 360/274-8000), at exit 49 off I-5.

For a closer look at the crater, continue to the **Coldwater Ridge Visitor Center,** at milepost 47 on Wash. 504, only 8 miles from the crater. This center features interpretive displays on the events leading up to the eruption and the subsequent slow regeneration of life around the volcano. Coldwater also has a picnic area, an interpretive trail, a restaurant, and a boat launch at Coldwater Lake. On the road up to the Coldwater Ridge, you'll pass the **Hoffstadt Bluffs Visitor Center** at milepost 27, which has a snack bar and is the takeoff site for helicopter flights over the volcano.

A few miles farther, just past milepost 33, you'll come to the **Forest Learning Center,** open May to October. It's primarily a promotional center for the timber industry but does show a short but fascinating video about the eruption in a theater designed to resemble an ash-covered landscape. There are also displays on how forests destroyed by the blast have been replanted. Outside the center you can look down on a herd of elk that live in the Toutle River Valley far below.

You must drive around to the monument's east side for a close-up view of the forest blown down by the eruption. For the best views, take U.S. 12 east from exit 68 off I-5. In Randle, head south on Forest Road 25 and then take Wash. 26. The **Woods Creek Information Center,** on Wash. 25 just before the junction with Wash. 26, has information on this part of the monument. Wash. 26 travels through mile after mile of blown-down trees felled by the single blast. Life is slowly returning to this devastated forest.

At Meta Lake, Wash. 26 joins Wash. 99, which continues to the **Windy Ridge Viewpoint,** where you can get your closest look at the volcano. Below Windy Ridge lies **Spirit Lake,** which was once one of the most popular summer vacation spots in the Washington Cascades. Today the lake is desolate and lifeless.

Experienced hikers in good physical condition can climb to the top of what's left of the peak. It's an 8- to 10-hour, 10-mile hike and can require an ice axe. The trailhead is on the south side of the monument. Permits are required May 15–Oct 31, available at **Jack's Restaurant and Store** on Wash. 503, 5 miles west of Cougar (☎ 360/750-3920). On the south side of the monument you can hike to the **Ape Cave,** a

2-mile-long lava tube that was formed 1,900 years ago when lava poured from the volcano. Other hiking trails are in blast zones and some are in forests that were left undamaged by the eruption. Ask at any visitor center for trail information.

Mountain-bike tours just outside the monument are offered by **Volcano View Mountain Bike Tours** (☎ 360/274-4341). **Mount St. Helens Adventure Tours** (☎ 360/274-6542) offers a variety of personalized tours including van tours, cross-country ski tours, mountain-bike tours, horse tours, and others, including a tent-and-breakfast tour that includes a night in the blast zone.

You'll find 11 campgrounds near the monument. **Sequest State Park,** on Wash. 504, is the closest to Coldwater Ridge, and **Iron Creek Campground** is the closest to Windy Ridge.

**Timberland Inn and Suites** in Castle Rock (☎ 360/274-6002; fax 360/274-6335), is the closest motel, right off I-5 at exit 49 adjacent to the Cinedome Theatre.

**Essentials:** The Coldwater Ridge Visitor Center is 90 miles north of Portland via I-5 and Wash. 504. It's 168 miles south of Seattle. For more information, contact **Mount St. Helens National Volcanic Monument,** 42218 NE Yale Bridge Rd., Amboy, WA 98601 (☎ 360/750-3900).

## DEVILS TOWER

This spectacular, 865-foot monument rises out of the prairie, a landmark visible for miles away. A natural rock formation, known to the Indians as Mateo Tipi, the huge isolated crag was declared the country's first national monument in 1906. It formed some 60 million years ago when hot magma thrust itself up to the rock surface, where it cooled into a highly resistant and tightly packed cluster of columns. It was used as a landmark by westward bound pioneers.

A unique American symbol, it has been particularly popular since it was featured in the movie, *Close Encounters of the Third Kind.* Annually more than 5,000 climbers come here to scale the rock.

The monument's visitor center has displays on the tower's history and geology, and in summer guided walks, campfire programs, and climbing demonstrations are offered. There are five nature trails and a campground. On the southeast side of the tower is a colony of prairie dogs.

**Essentials:** Devils Tower is 27 miles northeast of Sundance, Wyoming on Wy. 110. For information, contact the Superintendent, Devil's Tower National Monument, P.O. Box 8, Devils Tower, WY 82714 (☎ 307/467-5283). Note that visitors who want to climb the tower must register with a ranger.

# Alaska

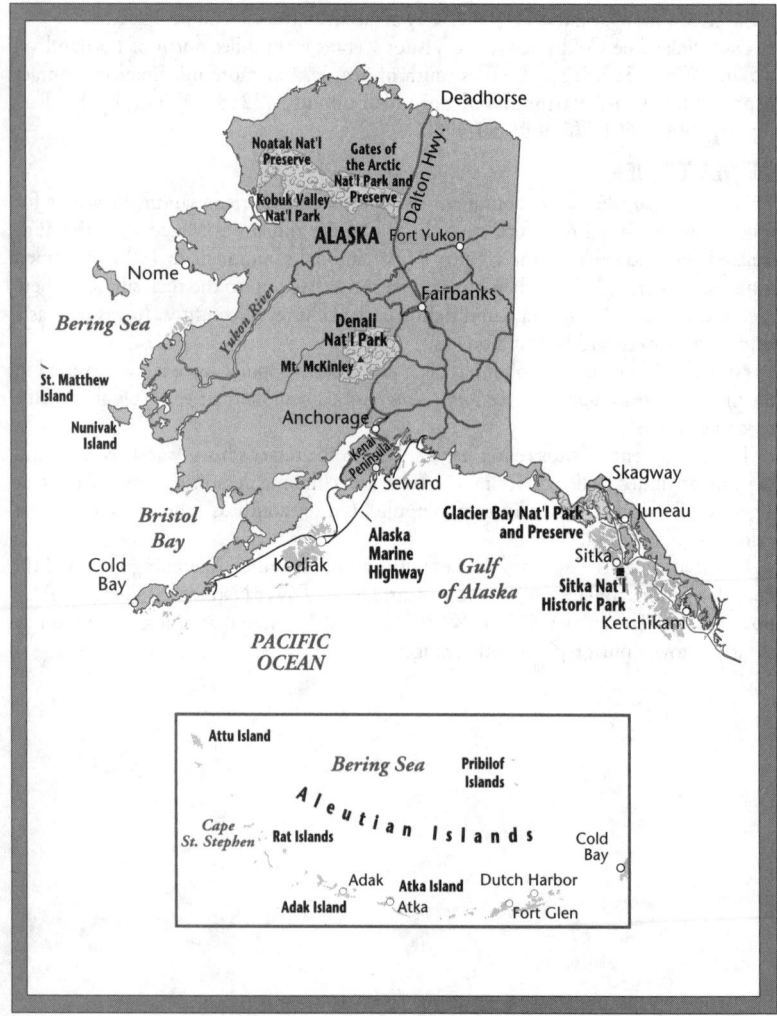

Deadhorse

Noatak Nat'l Preserve

Gates of the Arctic Nat'l Park and Preserve

Kobuk Valley Nat'l Park

**ALASKA** Fort Yukon

Dalton Hwy.

Nome

*Bering Sea*

*Yukon River*

Fairbanks

**Denali Nat'l Park**

Mt. McKinley

St. Matthew Island

Nunivak Island

Anchorage

Kenai Peninsula

Skagway

Juneau

Seward

**Glacier Bay Nat'l Park and Preserve**

Sitka

*Bristol Bay*

**Alaska Marine Highway**

*Gulf of Alaska*

**Sitka Nat'l Historic Park**

Cold Bay

Kodiak

Ketchikam

*PACIFIC OCEAN*

Attu Island

*Bering Sea*

Pribilof Islands

A l e u t i a n   I s l a n d s

Cape St. Stephen

Rat Islands

Cold Bay

Adak

Atka Island

Dutch Harbor

Adak Island

Atka

Fort Glen

To many of us, the lower 48 states are a fairly homogeneous land of freeways and fast food, a well-mapped network of established places. Alaska, on the other hand, isn't even completely explored. Natural forces of vast scale and subtlety are still shaping the land, inscribing a different story on each of an infinite number of unexpected places. Unlike those places where human endeavor holds sway, Alaska feels vast, unconquered, and exquisitely real. In any attempt to capture the state's grandeur in mere words, adjectives like spectacular, majestic, vast, or magnificent are quickly exhausted.

This chapter does not crystallize the entire state, but it does give you an idea of the best places to make your own discoveries, and to help take care of the details on the way. When you get home, if your trip has been especially successful, you may find that you, too, are at a loss for words for what you've seen and experienced.

# 1 Southeast Alaska

Within Alaska, the Southeast stands apart, and not only because most of it can't be reached by road. No other part of the state shares the mysterious spirit-ridden quality of the coastal rain forest. No other area gets so much rain (precious few places anywhere on earth do, for that matter). If Alaska sometimes feels like a different country from the rest of the United States, its southeast certainly feels like a different state from the rest of Alaska. Unlike most of the state, the southeast has a well-diversified economic base—fishing, timber, tourism, and government—and the region is generally more stable and prosperous than other areas. The weather, while wet, is mild, more akin to the Pacific Northwest than to the heart of Alaska. The Natives' heritage is richer: the Tlingit, Haida, and Tsimshian exploited the wealth that nature gave them and amplified it by trading successfully with tribes to the south and over the mountains in today's British Columbia and Yukon Territory. In their early contact, the Tlingits even defeated the Russian invaders in the Battle of Sitka, and after white dominance was established, they saved many of their cultural artifacts and stories.

Along with its other riches and complexity, Southeast Alaska also has many small towns and villages—too many to include in this brief chapter. They await your discovery.

## ARRIVING & DEPARTING

**BY PLANE**    Air travel is the primary link between the Southeast's towns and the rest of the world. The major towns all have jet service, provided by Alaska Airlines. Juneau also receives less frequent flights from Delta. Juneau is Southeast Alaska's travel hub, but Ketchikan and

Sitka also have a number of daily flights from Seattle and Anchorage. Some of the larger commuter operators are **L.A.B. Flying Service** (☎ 907/983-2471), **Wings of Alaska** (☎ 907/983-2442), and **Skagway Air Service** (☎ 907/983-2218).

**BY FERRY**   Thanks to steep island terrain and icy mountains, no roads connect the communities of Southeast Alaska. But the islands of the region form a protected waterway called the Inside Passage, along which almost all of the towns are arrayed. The state-run **Alaska Marine Highway Ferry System,** P.O. Box 25535, Juneau, AK 99802-5535 (☎ 800/642-0066), is a subsidized fleet of oceangoing ferries that connects the roadless coastal towns. It's cheap, convenient, and safe, though it gets crowded and backed up in the busy July season, when there is almost always a shortage of cabins.

The main line runs from Prince Rupert, British Columbia, north to Skagway, a voyage of about 38 hours if you never get off to visit any of the worthwhile towns in between. The foot passenger fare is $118 for adults and half that for children under 12. If you're bringing a car or definitely need a cabin during the June-through-August high season, you *must* reserve well in advance. Prices depend on how far you take your car.

The superb **B.C. Ferries** system, 1112 Fort St., Victoria, B.C., Canada V8V 4V2 (☎ 604/386-3431; fax 604/381-5452), docks right next to the Alaska ferry in Prince Rupert, so you can easily connect to wonderful places like Vancouver Island. Smaller commuter ferries throughout Southeast Alaska connect the main stops to smaller towns and villages. If you have the time, take one; they are the definition of off the beaten track.

## ESSENTIALS

**VISITOR INFORMATION**   The **Southeast Alaska Visitor Information Center,** 50 Main St., Ketchikan, AK 99901 (☎ 907/228-6214), dispenses information about the entire region. It's open May–Sept, daily 8:30am–4:30pm; in winter, Mon–Fri 8:30am–4:30pm.

## KETCHIKAN

There was a time when Ketchikan would have provided the perfect backdrop to a Humphrey Bogart movie. Pelting rains, suspicious figures darting through saloon doors and into the lobbies of concrete-faced hotels, a forest of workboat masts fading into the midsummer twilight amid the floating docks, and legal prostitutes along the main street gave the town its gritty character.

Today, though, the saloons have been replaced by T-shirt shops, the hotels have given way to bright streetfront stores selling plastic gewgaws, and the workboats have been shoved out by an ever-increasing flow of cruise ships. Up to five ships at a time are in port during the summer, dumping tourists by the hundreds into the town at certain hours, and making Ketchikan feel like a big carnival. But after the cruise ships pack up and slide off to their next port, a sense of the old, misty, mysterious Ketchikan starts to return.

Whatever the feel of the place, there's plenty to see. The state's fourth-largest city is a transportation hub, making it a great starting-off point for some spectacular outdoor experiences. Seaplanes based on docks along the waterfront are the taxis of the region, and a massive interagency visitor center can get you started. Ketchikan also is one of the wettest spots on earth, with rain measured in the hundreds of inches, so any activity requires serious rain gear.

It's also a center of Tlingit and Haida culture. There are two replica clan houses and totem pole parks, as well as the only museum dedicated to preserving the old, original poles from the days when the Tlingit and Haida cultural traditions were more intact.

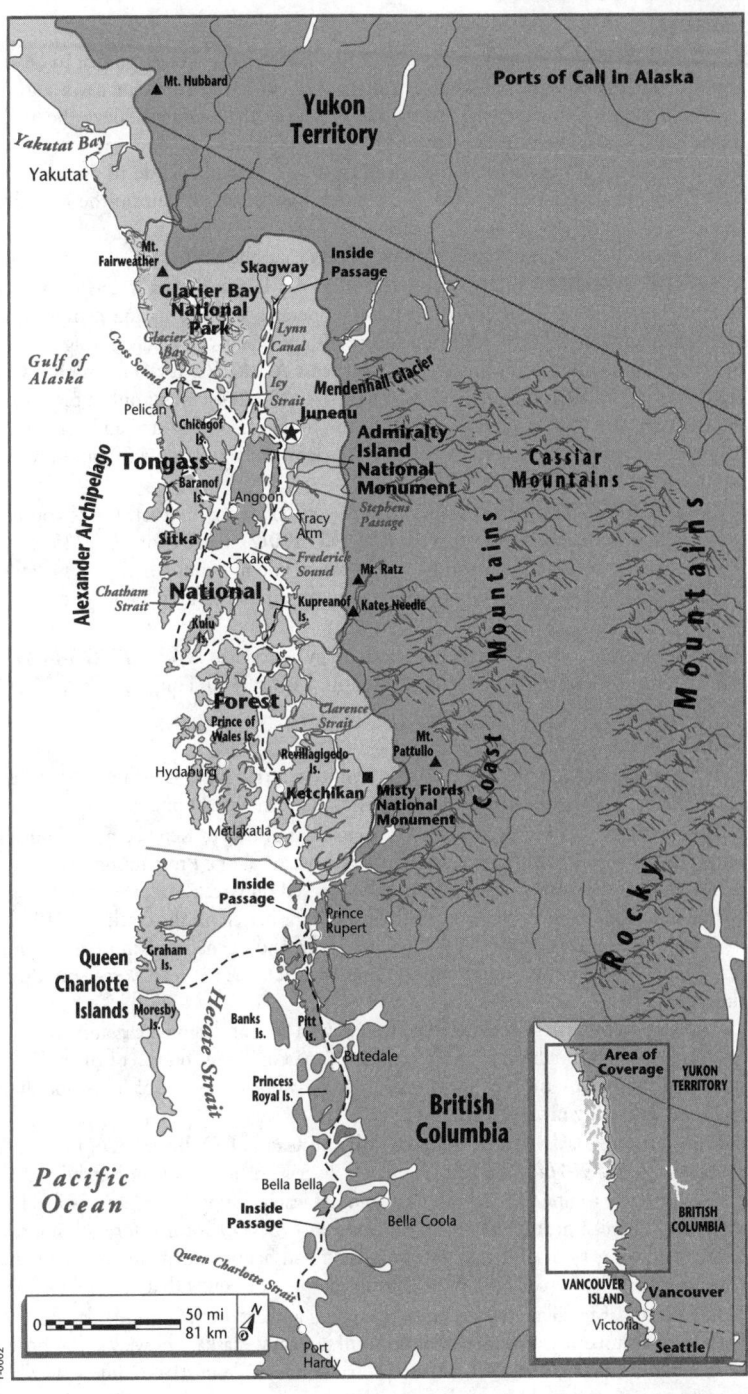

# Southeast Alaska

**Ports of Call in Alaska**

Mt. Hubbard

**Yukon Territory**

*Yakutat Bay*

Yakutat

Mt. Fairweather

Skagway

**Inside Passage**

**Glacier Bay National Park**

*Glacier Bay*

*Cross Sound*

*Lynn Canal*

*Gulf of Alaska*

*Icy Strait*

Mendenhall Glacier

Pelican

Chichagof Is.

**Juneau**

**Admiralty Island National Monument**

**Cassiar Mountains**

**Tongass**

Baranof Is.

Angoon

*Stephens Passage*

**Sitka**

*Tracy Arm*

*Chatham Strait*

Kake

*Frederick Sound*

Mt. Ratz

**National**

Kupreanof Is.

Kates Needle

Kuiu Is.

*Clarence Strait*

**Forest**

Prince of Wales Is.

Revillagigedo Is.

Mt. Pattullo

**Coast Mountains**

**Rocky Mountains**

Hydaburg

**Ketchikan**

**Misty Fiords National Monument**

Metlakatla

*Alexander Archipelago*

**Inside Passage**

Prince Rupert

**Queen Charlotte Islands**

Graham Is.

Moresby Is.

Banks Is.

Pitt Is.

Butedale

*Hecate Strait*

Princess Royal Is.

**British Columbia**

*Pacific Ocean*

Bella Bella

**Inside Passage**

Bella Coola

*Queen Charlotte Strait*

Port Hardy

0    50 mi
0    81 km

N

**Area of Coverage**

YUKON TERRITORY

BRITISH COLUMBIA

VANCOUVER ISLAND

Vancouver

Victoria

**Seattle**

1-0002

## ESSENTIALS

**GETTING THERE** **Alaska Airlines** provides Ketchikan with jet service to Seattle, Juneau, and Anchorage. The airport is on a different island from the town and can be reached only by a ferry that runs each way every half hour. Believe the airline when it tells you when to catch the ferry for your plane. The one-way ferry fare is $2.50 for adults and well worth it: a cab from the Ketchikan side to downtown is $10; from the airport side it's $70. Most hotels have courtesy vans on the Ketchikan side.

The **ferry** dock is out of town, although closer than the airport.

**VISITOR INFORMATION** The **Ketchikan Visitor Bureau,** 131 Front St., Ketchikan, AK 99901 (☎ **907/225-6166**), operates an information center on the cruise-ship dock, at Front and Mission streets; it's open 8am–5pm daily during the summer, weekdays only in the winter. The **Southeast Alaska Visitor Information Center,** 50 Main St., Ketchikan, AK 99901 (☎ **907/228-6214**), is not only a place to get guidance on your visit, it's also the best museum of the region's natural and cultural history and contemporary society. It's open May–Sept, daily 8:30am–4:30pm; in winter, Mon–Fri 8:30am–4:30pm.

**GETTING AROUND** You can do most of your exploring by foot, but if you need a car, call **Practical/All Star Car Rental** (☎ **800/770-8778** or 907/225-8774). They'll deliver the car to you and pick it up when you're done. For a cab, try **Yellow Taxi** (☎ **907/225-5555**). A city bus runs from the airport parking lot and ferry downtown.

**EMERGENCIES** Dial ☎ 911. The **police** can be reached at ☎ **907/225-6631** for nonemergencies. **Ketchikan General Hospital** is at 3100 Tongass Ave. (☎ **907/225-5171**).

## WHAT TO SEE & DO

Ketchikan highlights include the usual downtown attractions, as well as unparalleled fishing, Native Alaskan totem pole parks, and, increasingly, shopping.

**DOWNTOWN** ✪ **Creek Street** was the red-light district of Ketchikan until not that long ago; now it's a tourist attraction thronged with visitors. Prostitution was legal in Alaska until 1952; some of the women who worked on Creek Street are still living in Ketchikan. Dolly Arthur, who started in business for herself on the creek in 1919, died in 1975; her house was kept as it had always been and opened as a museum soon after. Dolly's House is well worth the $3 admission; it's open at least 9am–4pm during the summer.

The **Cape Fox Hill–Creek Street Funicular,** a sort of diagonal elevator, runs 211 feet from the boardwalk up to the Westmark Cape Fox Lodge on top of the hill. Take it up and then enjoy the walk down through the woods; the fare of $1 is not always collected, especially in the evening.

**FISHING** The **Alaska Department of Fish and Game,** P.O. Box 25526, Juneau, AK 99802-5526 (☎ **907/465-4112**), produces a 24-page fishing guide to Ketchikan, with details on where to find fish in both fresh and salt water, listing 17 spots accessible from the roads. You can pick up a copy at the Southeast Alaska Visitor Information Center or by mail. To get out on the water for salmon and halibut, there are plenty of charters available. The Ketchikan Visitor Bureau can provide you with a list.

**SHOPPING** Ketchikan has become a shopping and art destination thanks to the explosion of visitors. If you want something authentically Alaskan, however, you have to be careful. Generally, items for sale are probably not made in Alaska unless they have one of two marks: a made-in-Alaska polar bear sticker or a silver hand sticker that marks authentic Native art. ✪ **Coho Soho,** 5 Creek St., open daily in summer 9am–5:30pm, is worth a visit even if you aren't shopping. Owner Ray Troll is Alaska's leading fish-obsessed artist. His gallery shows his work and other Ketchikan artists from the same school of surreal rain-forest humor. Troll's popular T-shirts are both works of art and a comment on the commercialism of the region. "Curios Kill the Cat" shows a cat falling under a rain of plastic totem poles, igloos, and polar bear paper weights.

**TLINGIT, HAIDA & TSIMSHIAN CULTURAL HERITAGE**    The Ketchikan area has two totem pole parks and a totem pole museum, as well as a wealth of contemporary Native art displayed all over town.

The city-owned **Totem Heritage Center,** 601 Deermount St. (☎ 907/225-5900), near City Park, contains the largest collection of original 19th-century totem poles in the United States. The poles are displayed indoors, unpainted, many with the grass and moss still attached where it was when they were rescued from villages where they had been mounted up to 160 years ago. Totem poles were never meant to be maintained or repainted, instead disintegrating after about 70 years and replaced, but these were preserved to help keep the culture alive. Guides are on hand from May to September to explain what you're looking at, and there are occasional demonstrations of Native arts. Admission is $3 in summer, open daily 8am–5pm; it's free in winter, open Tues–Fri 1–5pm.

The ✪ **Totem Bight State Historical Park** was a New Deal–era work project to save disappearing Tlingit cultural artifacts by replicating them in an authentic setting. The park, now run by the State of Alaska Division of Parks (☎ 907/762-2600), is unique among the clan houses and outdoor totem pole collections in the southeast for having excellent interpretive signs and a printed guide that explains what you're looking at. It sits at a peaceful spot on the edge of Tongass Narrows, at the end of a short walk through the woods, 10 miles out of town on North Tongass Highway. Guided bus tours are available.

The **Saxman Totem Pole Park** stands on a lawn above the Tlingit town of Saxman, 2$^1/_2$ miles south of Ketchikan on the South Tongass Highway. Its artifacts are similar to those at Totem Bight Park, but here's an added resource: master carvers are still at work here, and sometimes you can get a glimpse of them carving in a workshop at the park.

## ACCOMMODATIONS

In addition to the prices quoted below, Ketchikan charges an 11.5% bed tax.

✪ **Captain's Quarters Bed & Breakfast.** *325 Lund St., Ketchikan, AK 99901.* ☎ *907/225-4912. 3 rms. High season, $75 double. Low season, $65 double. MC, V.* These huge, quiet, immaculate rooms, with a sweeping view of the city and ocean, private telephone lines, and a self-service breakfast room, rival the best in Ketchikan, but cost half as much. Marv Wendeborn built the place with his own hands, carrying the nautical theme through fine oak woodwork. Children are not allowed.

✪ **New York Hotel.** *207 Stedman St., Ketchikan, AK 99901.* ☎ *907/225-0246. 8 rms. High season, $79 double. Low season, $55 double. Additional person $10 extra. AE, MC, V.* It took 6 years to restore this 1924 building, but the loving work was worth the trouble. It's a special place to stay: very clean, with a balance of authentic atmosphere and modern comforts. The location is the best in town, right on the boat harbor. It's quickly developing a following, so reserve ahead.

✪ **Westmark Cape Fox Lodge.** *800 Venetia Way, Ketchikan, AK 99901.* ☎ *800/544-0970 or 907/225-8001. Fax 907/225-8286. 70 rms, 2 suites. High season, $155 double weekday, $99 weekend. Low season, $129 double weekday, $79 weekend. Year-round, $175 suite. Additional person $15 extra. AE, DC, DISC, MC, V.* Sitting atop the hill that dominates Ketchikan, this is the most beautiful hotel in Southeast Alaska. The hotel is interwoven with red cedar and masterpieces of Tlingit art. Even if you can't afford to stay, the elegance and view are worth a visit.

## DINING

In addition to the establishments listed below, the **Heen Kahadi,** in the Westmark Cape Fox Lodge (see above), is one of Ketchikan's best restaurants.

**Annabelle's Famous Keg and Chowder House.** *326 Front St.* ☎ *907/ 225-9423. Lunch $7.50–$16; dinner $12–$35. AE, CB, DC, DISC, MC, V. High season, daily 7am–11pm. Low season, Sun–Thurs 11am–9:30pm, Fri–Sat 11am–10:30pm. STEAK/SEAFOOD.* The prices are high, but the turn-of-the-century decor, attentive service, and extensive seafood and steak menu make Annabelle's the chief competitor with the Westmark Cape Fox Lodge for the title of the best restaurant in Ketchikan.

✪ **Five Star Cafe.** *5 Creek St.* ☎ *907/247-STAR. Lunch/dinner $1.25–$8.25. No credit cards. High season, daily 7am–6pm. Low season, 7:30am–5:30pm. SANDWICHES/ VEGETARIAN.* Like a place you'd find in a college town, the Five Star has good, reasonably priced sandwiches, soups, and vegetarian dishes, served up in an atmosphere conducive to journal writing among the young patrons. The black-bean burrito is delicious and healthy. Ketchikan Creek flows under and outside the windows.

## SITKA

Sitka sits on the west side of Baranof Island, a detour from the Inside Passage, and many ferries on the Alaska Marine Highway System bypass the stop. However, the ride through narrow Peril Straits is definitely worth the trip.

The town is a living monument to the cultural conflict between Alaska Natives and their white invaders. Here, 18th-century Russian conquerors who had successfully enslaved the Aleuts to the west met their match in battle against the rich, powerful, and sophisticated Tlingit. Sitka remains an oasis of Russian Orthodox religious influence to this day.

Besides its historic significance, Sitka is fun to visit. Somehow it has retained a friendly, authentic feel, despite the crush of thousands of visitors. Perhaps because cruise-ship travelers must ride smaller boats to shore, or because Sitka is a slightly inconvenient, out-of-the-way stop on the Alaska Marine Highway's main-line ferry routes, the city's streets haven't been choked by solid rows of seasonal gift shops. It remains picturesque; historic photographs bear a surprising resemblance to today's city.

### ESSENTIALS

**GETTING THERE**　**Alaska Airlines** (☎ 800/426-0333 or 907/966-2422) flies jets daily to Seattle and Anchorage. The little "local" ferries stop at all the villages on the way to Sitka. The fare to either Juneau or Petersburg is $26.

**VISITOR INFORMATION**　The **Harrigan Centennial Hall,** next to the Crescent Boat Harbor at 330 Harbor Dr., houses the summer visitor center. The main offices of the **Sitka Convention and Visitor Bureau** are at 303 Lincoln St., Suite 4, and can be reached at P.O. Box 1226, Sitka, AK 99835 (☎ 907/747-5940; fax 907/747-3739).

**GETTING AROUND**　Sitka is a walker's paradise. Competing shuttles charge $3 to get to town from the ferry dock or airport. **Sitka Cab** is available at **907/747-5001.** Rental cars are available at the airport. **Sitka Tours** (☎ 907/747-8443) takes cruise-ship passengers and anybody else on historical bus tours of the city for $24.

**EMERGENCIES**　Dial ☎ 911. For nonemergencies, call the **police** at ☎ 907/ 747-3245. The **Sitka Community Hospital** (☎ 907/747-3241) is at 209 Moller Dr.

### WHAT TO SEE & DO

Sitka has a long Russian and Tlingit heritage, dating back to 1799, when the Russian America Company established Redoubt St. Michael (now the Old Sitka State Historic Site, 7$^1$/$_2$ miles north of town) to control the lucrative fur trade. The Tlingit attacked and destroyed the Redoubt in 1802, killing most of the Russians, but vacated after a

Russian counterattack in 1804. The Russians fortified the town, which they called New Archangel, but the Tlingit name is the one that stuck: Shee Atika, or Sitka.

**✪ Russian Bishop's House.** *Lincoln and Monastery sts. No phone; call Historical Park Visitor Center. Admission free; $2 for upstairs tour. Summer, daily 9:30am–noon and 1–3pm. Winter, by appointment.* Father Ivan Veniaminov (later Bishop Innocent) translated the Bible into Tlingit and trained deacons to carry Russian Orthodoxy back to Native villagers. In 1842, the Russian America Company erected this extraordinary house for him. Despite years of neglect, the incredibly well-built house remains to this day. So does the bishop's legacy: few Russians stayed after the U.S. bought Alaska in 1867, but the Russian Orthodox faith that Veniaminov planted remains strong. There are 89 parishes, primarily in tiny Native villages.

**✪ Sheldon Jackson Museum.** *104 College Dr.* ☎ *907/747-8981. Admission $3 adults, free for students and age 18 and under. Mid-May to mid-Sept, daily 8am–5pm; mid-Sept to mid-May, Tues–Sat 10am–4pm.* The best collections of Alaska Native artifacts on display anywhere are kept here in a restored building, now run by the state museum, on the campus of Sheldon Jackson College. Jackson, a Presbyterian missionary and beloved figure in Alaska history, started the collection in 1888.

**✪ Sitka National Historical Park.** *106 Metlakatla St.* ☎ *907/747-6281. Admission free. Visitor center open daily 8am–5pm. Closed on weekends in winter.* President Benjamin Harrison recognized the importance of this battle site in 1890 and preserved it as a national historical park. In 1905, a collection of totem poles was brought here (the originals are in storage; replicas are on display). The totems stand tall and forbidding along a pathway through massive spruce and hemlock, where misty rain wanders down from an unseen sky. The historic park emphasizes the Native perspective. In the visitor center, Tlingit craftsmen labor in workshops making traditional carvings, jewelry, drums, and costumes. You can watch them work.

**✪ EXPLORING SITKA SOUND** The little islands and rocks that dot Sitka Sound are an invitation to the sea otter in all of us; you must get out on the water. In fact, otters are so numerous in the area that **Allen Marine Tours** (☎ 907/747-8100) guarantees a 50% refund if you don't see wildlife on its 3¹/₂-hour cruise. It costs $85 ($40 under age 12) and leaves Sun–Tues and Fri at 2pm from the boat harbor downtown during summer. You're likely to see sea otters, seals, sea lions, eagles and, in season, whales.

Local boosters claim that Sitka has the best **sea kayaking** in the world, and I won't dispute it: these protected waters and little-used shorelines are inviting. **Baidarka Boats** (☎ 907/747-8996) offers customized day trips, and also rents kayaks and provides instruction. The guided trips are around $50 for a half day, $100 for a full day.

## ACCOMMODATIONS

Sitka is a popular bed-and-breakfast town. The Sitka **Convention and Visitor Bureau** (☎ 907/747-5940; fax 907/747-3739) produces a chart listing B&Bs, with rates and facilities. The bed tax in Sitka is an additional 9%.

**✪ Alaska Ocean View Bed and Breakfast.** *1101 Edgecumbe Dr., Sitka, AK 99835.* ☎ *and fax 907/747-8310. 3 rms. High season, $79 double; $129 suite. Low season, $69 double; $99 suite. AE, MC, V.* Bill and Carol Denkinger have made their bed-and-breakfast one you'll recommend for years. They've thought of everything: a covered outdoor spa where you can watch eagles, games for the kids, VCRs in the rooms, even wildflower seeds to take home. It's a bit far from the sights, unless you have a car.

**Potlatch Motel.** *713 Katlian St., Sitka, AK 99835.* ☎ *800/354-6017 or 907/747-8611. Fax 907/747-5810. 32 rms. High season, $83 double. Low season, $59 double. Additional person $8 extra. AE, DC, MC, V.* A clean, comfortable motel-style building located in the business district, a 10-minute walk to the sights. The rooms are reasonably priced and there's a coin-op laundry and a fish cleaning and freezing facility in the motel. We found the service kid-friendly. Courtesy van service is provided to the ferry, airport, and downtown.

**Westmark Shee Atika.** *330 Seward St., Sitka, AK 99835-7523.* ☎ *800/ 544-0970 or 907/747-6241. Fax 907/747-5486. 100 rms. High season, $139 double. Low season, $109 double. AE, DC, DISC, MC, V.* This large, upscale chain hotel stands in a central location in the heart of the historic district. Most rooms have good views, as do the restaurant and lounge. You can book tours and activities in the lobby. The service in the Raven Dining Room restaurant is friendly and efficient.

## DINING

For burgers and sandwiches, try **Lulu's Diner,** a streetfront cafe at 116 Lincoln St.

**El Dorado Restaurant.** *714 Katlian St.* ☎ *907/747-5070. Lunch $5–$8; dinner $9–$14. DISC, MC, V. High season, daily 10:30am–11pm. Low season, Tues– Sat 11am–10pm, Sun–Mon 11:30am–9:30pm. MEXICAN.* The menu has separate lists of American/Mexican and authentic Mexican dishes. The portions are large, the prices low, and the service jolly and efficient. Our Mexican dinners were excellent— subtly flavored, despite the casual, small-town, family-restaurant atmosphere. Pizza is also available.

✪ **VanWinkle and Daigler.** *228 Harper Dr.* ☎ *907/747-3396. Reservations recommended. Lunch $5–$9; dinner $16–$19. AE, MC, V. High season, Mon–Sat 11:30am– 10pm, Sun 5–10pm. Low season, Tues–Sat 11:30am–2pm, Wed–Sun 5–9pm. STEAK/ SEAFOOD.* A nice balance of the casual and fine, the dining room has shelves of old books, but also tablecloths. The Pacific Northwest–style cuisine concentrates on local seafood. Portions are huge and service quick, but the cooking is still subtle and expert. The wine list and entrees are well priced.

# JUNEAU

Juneau (JUNE-oh) hustles and bustles like no other city in Alaska. The steep downtown streets echo with the mad shopping sprees of cruise-ship passengers in the summer tourist season and the whispered intrigues of the politicians during the winter legislative session. Miners, loggers, and ecotourism operators come to lobby for their share of the southeast's forest. Even bears and eagles don't seem able to leave the place alone. Bears have always been a problem, wandering into town to dig through garbage and terrorize neighbors. And every couple of years an eagle makes off with a tourist's chihuahua.

Juneau is Alaska's third-largest city, with a population of almost 30,000, but it feels like a small town that's just been stuffed with people. It's splattered on the sides of Mt. Juneau and Mt. Roberts along Gastineau Channel, where there really isn't room for much of a town. Gold-mine tailings dumped into the Gastineau created the flat land near the water where much of the downtown area now stands. Further development up the mountains is hemmed in by avalanche danger; beyond is the 1,500-square-mile Juneau Icefield, an impenetrable barrier. There's no road to the outside world; jets and boats are the only way in and out.

The relatively sophisticated population of government workers supports good restaurants and amenities not found elsewhere in the southeast. Also, Juneau is a starting point for outdoor travel in the area, and in all of Southeast Alaska. The crush of visitors can be overwhelming when many cruise ships are in port at once, and the streets around the docks have been entirely taken over by shops and other touristy businesses. But despite the onslaught, it's still just a short walk from the rackety downtown streets to the land of bear and salmon, fiddlehead ferns and massive rain-forest spruces.

## ESSENTIALS

**GETTING THERE**   Alaska Airlines (☎ 800/426-0333) has numerous daily flights from Seattle and Anchorage and to the smaller Southeast Alaska towns. The mountainside airport is a hair-raising place to land, frequently forcing flights to alight elsewhere. The airline will put you on the next flight back to Juneau, but won't pay for hotel rooms or give you a refund, meaning that any Juneau itinerary is at best a work in progress. Most of the commuter and air-taxi operators in the southeast also maintain a desk at the airport. All main-line **Alaska Marine Highway ferries** stop at the dock in Auke Bay, a 15-minute drive from town.

**VISITOR INFORMATION**   The **Davis Log Cabin Visitor Center,** 134 Third Ave. (at Seward, downtown), Juneau, AK 99801 (☎ 907/586-2201; fax 907/586-6304), is a replica of Juneau's first school, a log cabin with a little log belfry. The center is open daily 9am–5pm, year-round.

The **U.S. Forest Service headquarters** for the 17-million-acre Tongass National Forest—encompassing the vast majority of Southeast Alaska—is at Ninth Street and Glacier Avenue. The **Forest Service Visitor Information Center** is located in the Centennial Hall Convention Center, 101 Egan Dr., Juneau, AK 99801 (☎ 907/586-8751; fax 907/586-7894).

**GETTING AROUND**   A cab in from the airport costs about $20, but the **Capital Transit city bus** (☎ 907/789-6901) runs every hour at 11 minutes past the hour and costs $1.25; your luggage must fit under your seat. A cab to the ferry dock costs even more than to the airport, but **Mendenhall Glacier Transport (MGT)** (☎ 907/789-5460) meets the boats with a blue school bus and goes to town for $5. Most of the major car-rental companies are based at the airport, but you'll only need a car if you're going to see the Mendenhall Glacier or any of the attractions on the road. MGT arranges 2-hour tours of downtown Juneau and the Mendenhall Glacier for $12.50.

**EMERGENCIES**   Dial ☎ 911. For nonemergency calls to the **police,** dial ☎ 907/586-2780. The **hospital** (☎ 907/586-2611) is 3 miles out the Glacier Highway.

## WHAT TO SEE & DO

**IN TOWN**   The **Alaska State Capitol** on Main Street may be the least impressive state capitol in the most beautiful setting in the nation. Juneau has considered replacing it as an incentive to keep the rest of the state from voting to move it to another town. Free tours start every half hour, 9am–4:30pm during the summer; the legislature is in session from January to May.

The **Mt. Roberts Tramway** (☎ 907/463-3412) leaves every 15 minutes from downtown Juneau to the top of Mt. Roberts, high above the city and the Gastineau Channel. It costs $17.75 for adults, $10.45 for children 7–12, free for children under 7. A restaurant, theater, and shops are at the top and are still in the planning stages.

✪ **Alaska State Museum.** *395 Whittier St.* ☎ *907/465-2901. Admission $3 adults, free for students and children. Summer, Mon–Fri 9am–6pm, Sat–Sun 10am–6pm. Winter, Tues–Sat 10am–4pm.* A visit to this small museum will help put the rest of what you see in Alaska in context. It contains a huge collection of Alaskan art and Alaska Native and historical artifacts, but it is the presentation, not the volume, that edifies. A clan house in the Alaska Native Gallery, for example, teaches more than the outdoor houses you see in Wrangell or Ketchikan because it contains the authentic art that you'd really find there in its functional place.

**Juneau–Douglas City Museum.** *At the corner of Fourth and Main sts.* ☎ *907/586-3572. Admission $1, free for children. Summer, Mon–Fri 9am–6pm, Sat–Sun 10am–6pm. Winter, Fri–Sat noon–4pm or by appointment.* This museum concentrates on the city's history, especially gold mining. There's a large relief map of the town, historic artifacts and displays, a video, and a hands-on display for children. Pick up a historic walking tour map and maps of the Evergreen Cemetery and the old Treadwell Mine.

✪ **St. Nicholas Orthodox Church.** *Fifth and Gold sts.* This tiny, octagonal chapel was built in 1893 by local Tlingits. Under pressure from the government to convert to Christianity, they chose the only faith that allowed them to keep their language (Father Ivan Veniaminov had translated the Bible into Tlingit 50 years earlier when the Russians were still in nearby Sitka). The church still has an active Tlingit parish. Services in English, Tlingit, and Slavonic are on Sat at 6pm and on Sun at 10am.

**SHOPPING**  Juneau, like Ketchikan and Skagway, has developed a shopping district catering primarily to the cruise ships. To buy authentic Alaskan items you have to be careful—look for the MADE IN ALASKA polar bear sticker or the silver hand sticker, which authenticates Alaska Native art.

**WILDLIFE-WATCHING**  The drive out the four-lane Egan Expressway to the Mendenhall Valley crosses tidal flats that are a place to see birds, especially **bald eagles.** The tidal marsh near the airport also is good bird-watching territory.

**DIPAC Gastineau Salmon Hatchery.** *2697 Channel Dr.* ☎ *907/463-4810. Admission $2.75 adults, $1 children under 12. Mon–Fri 10am–6pm, Sat–Sun noon–5pm. Closed Oct 15–May 15.* Its saltwater aquariums contain indigenous marine life and there's a fish ladder with an underwater window through which salmon can be seen swimming upstream beginning in July. In May and June the tour includes the incubation process.

**GLACIERS**  **Mendenhall Glacier** is the easiest glacier in Alaska to get to. The **Forest Service** maintains a **visitor center** (☎ **907/586-8800**) that's open in summer, daily 8:30am–5pm; Oct–May, Sat–Sun 9am–5pm. The glacier is on the opposite side of a lake from the visitor center and parking lot; a wheelchair-accessible trail leads down to the lake. In late summer you can watch salmon spawning in Steep Creek. There are several **trails** at the glacier, ranging from a half-mile nature trail loop to two fairly steep, 3¹/₂-mile hikes. The ✪ **East Glacier Loop Trail** is a beautiful day hike leading to a waterfall near the glacier's face. The trail has steep parts, but is okay for school-age children.

The glaciers around Juneau are rivers of ice flowing off a frozen ocean behind the mountains, the **Juneau Icefield.** You can fly over it in a plane, or land on it in a helicopter, a humbling experience that will teach you how small you really are. **Era Helicopters** (☎ **800/843-1947** or 907/586-2030), a company with an excellent reputation, offers a 40-minute flight and 20-minute glacier landing for $162.

**KAYAKING & CANOEING**  Alaska Rainforest Tours (☎ **907/463-3466;** fax 907/463-4453) specializes in environmentally conscious trips. The most established operator is ✪ **Alaska Discovery,** 5449 Shaune Dr., Suite 4, Juneau, AK 99801 (☎ **800/586-1911** or 907/780-6226; fax 907/780-4220), with dozens of trips in the southeast and in the Arctic National Wildlife Refuge. An 8-hour wildlife-watching sea kayak paddle from Juneau is $95 per person. Trips to Admiralty Island include a $349 day trip to the Pack Creek Bear Observatory, one of the best places to see brown bear in Alaska.

**FISHING & WHALE-WATCHING**  Juneau is well protected behind layers of islands, so the calm waters here offer an  opportunity to see whales without the seasickness that usually accompanies such an adventure. More than two dozen charter companies will take you fishing from Juneau and Auke Bay; you can fish or watch whales or do both. The Juneau Convention and Visitor Bureau maintains a list of outfitters, but **Juneau Sportfishing and Sightseeing,** on Merchants Wharf (P.O. Box 20438), Juneau, AK 99802 (☎ **907/586-1887;** fax 907/586-9769), is one of the largest operators; they charge $185 per person for a full day of fishing or sightseeing.

## ACCOMMODATIONS

Hotel rooms are tight in the summer, so book ahead; the convention and visitor bureau can give you a complete list. The **Alaska Bed and Breakfast Association,** 369 S. Franklin St., Suite 200, Juneau, AK 99801 (☎ **907/463-3466;** fax 907/463-4453), books many of the B&Bs in Juneau. Juneau's bed tax is an additional 11%.

**Blueberry Lodge.** *9436 N. Douglas Hwy., Juneau, AK 99801.* ☎ *and fax 907/463-5886. 5 rms, none with bath. High season, $85 double. Low season, $75 double. Rates include full breakfast. MC, V.* A beautiful log building in the woods near the Eaglecrest Ski Area, 6 miles out of town, overlooks an eagle's nest and the Mendenhall Wetlands Refuge. You can borrow binoculars or rubber boots. The breakfast is deluxe, the rooms homey and very clean, and the atmosphere social. You'll need a car.

**Driftwood Lodge.** *435 Willoughby Ave., Juneau, AK 99801.* ☎ *800/544-2239 or 907/586-2280. Fax 907/586-1034. 30 rms, 32 suites. High season, $78 double; $85–$95 suite. Low season, $62 double; $72–$89 suite. AE, DC, DISC, MC, V.* This three-story motel right downtown is popular with families and houses legislators and aides in the winter in its apartment-like kitchenette suites. The rooms, although clean, are threadbare and the walls are of cinder block, but the managers are hospitable. The lodge has a courtesy car to the airport and coin-op laundry.

**Prospector Hotel.** *375 Whittier St., Juneau, AK 99801.* ☎ *800/331-2711 or 907/ 586-3737, or 800/478-5866 in Alaska. Fax 907/586-1204. 58 rms. High season, $100 double; $125–$135 kitchenette. Low season, $75 double; $85–$95 kitchenette. AE, DC, MC, V.* A comfortable hotel right on the waterfront, the Prospector has the best rates for a good, chain-style room downtown. The lower level is a half basement and somewhat dark; the rooms facing the channel have great views, but also traffic noise. Kitchenette rooms with water views cost $10 more.

## DINING

In addition to the places listed below, you might try **T.K. Maguire's,** in the Prospector Hotel (see above), where fresh fish and prime rib are a specialty.

**Armadillo Tex–Mex Cafe.** *431 S. Franklin St.* ☎ *907/586-1880. Lunch/dinner $6–$16. MC, V. Daily 11am–10pm. MEXICAN.* Popular with locals and visitors alike for its convenient location, reasonable prices, unpretentious atmosphere, and good ranch-style Mexican food, this restaurant is known merely as "Tex–Mex." Chicken is the specialty, and the homemade salsa, served free with chips, is famous.

✪ **Second Course.** *213 Front St.* ☎ *907/463-5533. Dinner $10–$20; buffet-style lunch $10. MC, V. Tues–Fri noon–2pm and 5–9pm, Sat–Sun 5–9pm. Closed for dinner in winter, except by arrangement. CHINESE/THAI.* Heidi Grimes does "New Asian cuisine" that draws on Cantonese, Thai, Vietnamese, and other Far Eastern styles to create something completely new and different with fresh local seafood. The menu changes with constant experimentation. The storefront dining room, with white tablecloths and plastic garden furniture, is a bit odd, but perfectly comfortable.

## JUNEAU AFTER DARK

Juneau's **Perseverance Theatre,** 914 Third St., Douglas, AK 99824 (☎ **907/ 364-2421**), is Alaska's largest professional theater. Starting in September and ending in May, the troupe produces five serious offerings for Juneau audiences and multicultural shows such as Yup'ik Antigone, which toured internationally.

The new Sealaska Cultural Arts Center presents the ✪ **Naa Kahidi Theater** (☎ **907/ 463-4844**) in a mock clan house next to the cruise-ship dock. The professionally produced story-telling and dance performances are entertaining for a wide age range and present Tlingit, Haida, and Tsimshian artifacts as they were meant to be seen. The hour-long shows are presented frequently during the May–Sept season; tickets are $16 for adults, $10 for children.

The **Red Dog Saloon,** at 278 S. Franklin St., is the town's most famous bar, with a sawdust-strewn floor and slightly contrived historic atmosphere. It's a fun place with lots of Alaskana on the walls, and the live music doesn't entail a cover charge. The **Alaskan Bar,** a block away at 167 S. Franklin St., has brass and wood decor, and blues, jazz, and folk music.

## GLACIER BAY NATIONAL PARK

Glacier Bay is a work in progress. The bay John Muir discovered in a canoe in 1879 didn't exist a hundred years earlier; 18th-century explorers had found instead a wall of ice a mile thick where the entrance to the branching, 65-mile-long fjord now opens to the sea. Receding faster than any other glacier on earth, the ice melted into the ocean and opened a spectacular and still-unfinished land. As your vessel retraces Muir's path, the story of this new world unravels in reverse. The trees on the shore get smaller, then disappear, then all vegetation disappears, and finally, at the head of the bay, the ice stands at the water's edge surrounded by barren rock, rounded and scored by the passage of the ice.

It's often windy and cold at the head of the bay, near the glaciers. Precipitation and cold add up to glaciers, so be prepared for bad weather. It rains a lot in Glacier Bay, and fog clings to the water and the ice. The mist and rain contribute their own beauty— at times the smooth, silver water, barren rock, white clouds, and ice create an ethereal study in white.

There really is no cheap way to visit Glacier Bay—any trip entails a boat or a plane ride—but many visitors feel compelled to go. It is a grand and fascinating place, but you can see Alaska without seeing Glacier Bay. The uniqueness of the glaciers of Glacier Bay lies in their size and geological activity, in their number, and in the opportunity to see them fairly close up in a remote setting.

### ESSENTIALS

**GETTING THERE**   Commuter flights by various operators land at the runway in Gustavus, where vans are available for the 10-mile drive to the park headquarters. Or take the **Auk Nu passenger ferry** (☎ 800/820-2628) from Juneau, for an $85 round-trip.

The ✪ *Spirit of Adventure,* operated by park concessionaire **Glacier Bay Tours and Cruises,** is the main way for independent travelers to see the park. The fast, quiet tour boat carries up to 250 passengers. Bring binoculars and heavy rain gear, as the windows can fog up and you'll want to spend as much time as possible outside. The 9-hour cruise leaves Bartlett Cove at 7am and costs $150.

**VISITOR INFORMATION**   The park service's address is **Glacier Bay National Park and Preserve,** Gustavus, AK 99826 (☎ 907/687-2230). But the concessionaire, **Glacier Bay Tours,** operates most of the activities in the park. During the summer you can reach them at P.O. Box 199, Gustavus, AK 99826 (☎ 907/697-2226; fax 907/697-2408); or year-round at 520 Pike St., Suite 1400, Seattle, WA 98101 (☎ 800/451-5952 or 206/623-7110; fax 206/623-7809). The park service interprets the park mainly by placing well-prepared rangers on board all cruise and tour vessels entering the bay. The park also maintains a modest visitor center at Bartlett Cove.

### WHAT TO SEE & DO

There are two short **hiking trails,** right at the Bartlett Cove compound, for an afternoon walk. A ranger leads a daily nature walk, and there are displays upstairs in the lodge.

A popular way to see Glacier Bay is ✪ **sea kayaking,** and there are several remote yet protected places to paddle. I can only imagine what it's like to see humpback whales from a kayak. Make sure you calibrate the length of your trip to your outdoors experience—this is remote territory. For guided kayak trips, **Alaska Discovery,** 5449 Shaune Dr., Suite 4, Juneau, AK 99801 (☎ **907/780-6226;** fax 907/780-4220), offers trips ranging from 6 hours (for $119) to 8 days (for $1,890).

## ACCOMMODATIONS & DINING

There's only one place to stay in the park, although Gustavus, 10 miles down the road, has some of the most attractive accommodations in Alaska, some for the same price or less.

**Glacier Bay Lodge.** *Bartlett Cove (P.O. Box 199), Gustavus, AK 99826.* ☎ *800/451-5952 or 907/697-2226. Fax 206/623-7809 or 907/697-2408. 56 rms. $156 double. Hostel bunks $28 per person (six to a room). AE, DC, DISC, MC, V. Closed Sept 21–May 5.* The lodge rooms are comfortable but, for the price, nothing special; they're in buildings accessed from the main lodge by boardwalks. Laundry is available. The restaurant has great views of Bartlett Cove. There are inexpensive main courses on the dinner menu, but mainly it's a fine-dining establishment with dishes in the $20 range. Breakfast is available as early as 5:45am and dinner as late as 10pm. Meals are buffet style in May and September. Alcohol is available with meals, but there is no bar at the lodge. The lodge also provides showers for the free park service campground.

# SKAGWAY

Skagway is probably the best-preserved gold-rush town in the United States. What happened here in a 2-year period 100 years ago was certainly extraordinary, even if the phenomenon the town celebrates is one of mass insanity based on greed, inhumanity, thuggery, prostitution, waste, and, for most, abject failure. In 1897 a group of prospectors showed up on the dock in Seattle with steamer trunks full of gold, and all of a sudden the rush was on. Even the mayor of Seattle joined the stampede. Skagway instantly grew from a single homestead to a population of 15,000 to 25,000—no one knows exactly how many, in part because the people were flowing through so fast. Soapy Smith, a con artist turned organized crime boss, ruled the lawless city; the governor offered to put him officially in charge as a territorial marshall and rode with him in the 1898 Independence Day parade.

By 1899, the rush was over, but 10 years later, local businessmen were already recreating the history in an attempt to attract tourism. Picturesque gold-rush buildings were moved to Broadway, the main street, to create a more unified image when visitors arrived on the steamers, gardens were planted, and tourists began contributing a large portion of the local economy.

Today's Skagway is a town of 800 residents, but 400,000 visitors. Most of the people you'll meet are fellow visitors, usually from the abundant cruise ships that pack the wharves. But there are plenty of highway and ferry travelers too, and outdoor enthusiasts here to do the Chilkoot Trail, just as the stampeders did. There's a new gold rush going on, a new stampede 10 times larger than the original one they're coming to see—and probably richer for the town, too. With the approaching centennial of the '98 gold rush coming up, this new gold rush shows no signs of fading.

## ESSENTIALS

**GETTING THERE**    Skagway is one of the few Southeast towns accessible by car. Since 1978 ✪ **Klondike Highway 2** has traced the route of the Stampeders through the White Pass, a parallel route to the Chilkoot Trail, into Canada. The road runs 99 miles, then meets the Alaska Highway a dozen miles southeast of Whitehorse. The border is at the top of the pass, 14 miles from Skagway. This is one of the most spectacular drives anywhere in Alaska. Make sure you do it in clear weather. Car rentals are available from Avis (☎ **800/331-1212** or 907/983-2247), at the Westmark Inn Skagway.

Two bus lines have daily summer service to Whitehorse, where you can make connections to Anchorage or Fairbanks 3 days a week. **Gray Line's Alaska-Yukon Express** (☎ 800/544-2206) stops at the Westmark Inn Skagway.

The **Alaska Marine Highway Ferry System** connects Skagway with Haines and Juneau; the fare is $14 to Haines, $26 to Juneau. Haines is 15 miles away by boat but more than 350 by road.

**VISITOR INFORMATION** The ✪ **National Park Service Visitor Center,** in the restored railroad depot at Second Avenue and Broadway (P.O. Box 517), Skagway, AK 99840 (☎ 907/983-2921), is the focal point for activities in Skagway. It's open June–Aug 8am–7pm, closing an hour earlier in late May and September; it's closed in winter except when ferries are in town. The **Skagway Convention and Visitor Bureau** (P.O. Box 415), Skagway, AK 99840 (☎ 907/983-2854), maintains a visitor center on Fifth Avenue just north of Broadway, with listings of local hotels and restaurants. It's open in summer, daily 8am–5pm; closed weekends in the off-season.

**GETTING AROUND** Skagway's main sights can all be reached on foot. Don't miss the exceptionally good **Skagway Walking Tour Map,** provided free by the Skagway Convention and Visitor Bureau. Various companies offer car, van, or bus tours of Skagway, but none goes to greater lengths for an authentic experience than Steve Hites, whose **Skagway Street Car Company,** at 270 Second Ave. (☎ 907/983-2908), uses antique touring vehicles and costumed guides. The 2¹/₂-hour streetcar tour and slide show is $34 for adults, $17 for children. Book well in advance.

**EMERGENCIES** Dial ☎ **911.** For nonemergencies, call the **police** at ☎ 907/ 983-2232. The **Dahl Memorial Health Center** in Skagway (☎ 907/983-2255) is on 11th Avenue between Broadway and State streets.

## WHAT TO SEE & DO

**ATTRACTIONS** An amazing collection of miscellaneous memorabilia and an immense display of animal mounts reside in the **Alaska Wildlife Adventure and Museum** at Fourth and Spring streets. Open in summer, daily 8am–6pm. Admission $7 adults, $4 children.

The **Gold Rush Cemetery** is 1¹/₂ miles from town, up State Street. Used until 1908, it's small and overgrown with spruce trees, but some of the charm and mystery of the place are largely lost because of the number of visitors and the shiny new paint and maintenance of the wooden markers. The graves of Soapy Smith and Frank Reid are the big attractions, but don't miss the short walk up to Reid Falls.

The city-owned ✪ **Trail of '98 Historical Museum and Archives,** currently housed in a single room in the Arctic Brotherhood Hall, on Broadway, contains Skagway's best collection of gold-rush artifacts. The museum is open in summer, daily 9am–5pm; in winter by appointment. Admission $2 adults, $1 students and children.

The ✪ **White Pass and Yukon Route Railway,** P.O. Box 435, Dept. B, Skagway, AK 99840 (☎ 800/343-7373 or 907/983-2217), a narrow-gauge line that originally ran to Whitehorse, was completed after only 2 years in 1900. It's an engineering marvel and a fun way to see spectacular, historic scenery. Tickets are expensive ($75 for adults, $37.50 for kids), however, and I wouldn't recommend going in bad weather, when all you'll see out the window are clouds. The 3-hour excursion climbs steeply up tracks chipped out of the side of the mountains, gaining 2,865 feet in elevation over 20 miles.

**SHOPPING** With almost 100 years of experience, Skagway knows how to do gift shops—and now has more than 50. ✪ **Kirmse's Jewelry and Curios,** at Fifth Avenue and Broadway, has been in business since 1897. Besides the jewelry and gifts, there are huge gold nuggets and Soapy Smith's gun on display. Across the street is **Curringtons,** a large gift store with an entire free museum attached. **Lynch and Kennedy,** at Fourth Avenue and Broadway, is in a building owned and restored by the National Park Service; it carries fine art, jewelry, and high-quality gifts.

**SPECIAL PLACES**    The famous 33-mile long **Chilkoot Pass Trail** was traversed by gold rushers from Dyea—9 miles from Skagway—to Lake Bennett, where they could launch boats for Dawson City. It's now managed by the National Park Service and Canadian Park Service and attracts about 3,600 hikers a year. It's a challenging 3- to 5-day hike; people tend to underestimate it, which is odd, since the reason for going is to see and experience the difficulties faced by gold rushers. Most of the 3,600-foot elevation gain comes in a 3-mile stretch, with some passes reaching 45° angles! Contact the National Park Service to plan your climb and pickup at Lake Bennett, and check in at the visitor center for current trail conditions.

**FLIGHT-SEEING**    Skagway is a good place for a flight-seeing trip. Glacier Bay National Park is just to the west; a small plane is a great way to see it, and less expensive, all things considered, than journeying to the bay and seeing it by boat. **L.A.B. Flying Service** (☎ **907/983-2471**), **Wings of Alaska** (☎ **907/983-2442**), and **Glacier Bay Airways** (☎ **907/697-2249**) have flights.

### ACCOMMODATIONS

The bed tax in Skagway is an additional 8%.

   ✪ **Skagway Inn Bed and Breakfast.** *Seventh Ave. and Broadway (P.O. Box 500), Skagway, AK 99840.* ☎ *907/983-2289. Fax 907/983-2713. 12 rms, none with bath. High season, $72–$86 double. Low season, $65–$79 double. DISC, MC, V. Closed Oct–Apr.* Built in 1897, this perfect little Victorian inn has rooms named after the prostitutes who worked in them when it was a brothel (the owners researched old police records). There are six bathrooms for the 12 guest rooms, and they're kept immaculate. Some of the rooms are quite small. Extras include a courtesy van and restaurant (see Lorna's, below).

   **Wind Valley Lodge.** *22nd Ave. and State St. (P.O. Box 354), Skagway, AK 99840.* ☎ *907/983-2236. Fax 907/983-2957. 29 rms. High season, $75–$85 double. Low season, $55 double. AE, DISC, MC, V. Closed Oct 15–Mar 15.* These are good rooms for a reasonable price. The main building contains a pleasant lobby with a fireplace, gift shop, and 12 smaller double rooms. The larger rooms in the new building are $10 more. The only drawback is the location—quiet, but a mile from the sights on Broadway. The lodge has a courtesy van, coin-op laundry, and free coffee.

### DINING

You also can enjoy a vegetarian lunch at **Mabel G. Smith's** (☎ **907/983-2609**), a new-age bakery just off Broadway.

   ✪ **Lorna's at the Skagway Inn.** *Seventh Ave. and Broadway.* ☎ *907/ 983-2289. Reservations recommended. Main courses $17–$26. MC, V. May–Sept, daily 5–9pm. FRENCH.* Lorna's recent diplomas from Le Cordon Bleu are posted by the dining room entrance, tantalizing diners on their way in. The intimate dining room is lovely, decorated with antiques, and seats only 27 people. The menu changes every night, but it always emphasizes Alaska seafood and French country cuisine.

   **Siding 21 Restaurant.** *21st Ave. and State St.* ☎ *907/983-3328. Lunch $5–$9.50; dinner $12–$15. DISC, MC, V. Daily 6am–10pm. AMERICAN.* Built to look like an old-fashioned railway depot inside and out, this is a wonderful family restaurant. There's a complete children's menu and the regular menu is reasonably priced. The service is friendly and quick. It's a mile out of town, next to the Wind Valley Lodge.

## SKAGWAY AFTER DARK

Incredibly, the **Days of '98 Show** has been playing since 1927 in the **Fraternal Order of Eagles Hall No. 25,** Sixth Avenue and Broadway (☎ **907/983-2545**). Jim Richards carries on the tradition each summer with professional actors from all over the United States. The evening shows begin at 7:30pm with mock gambling at a casino run by the actors. The performance, at 8:30pm, includes singing, can-can dancing, and the story of the shooting of Soapy Smith. The play money you win in the gambling hall can be used to bid for a garter from one of the can-can dancers in the show. Matinees are $12 and evening shows are $14.

The **Red Onion Saloon,** Second Avenue and Broadway, is an authentic-feeling old bar with live music some nights. It was a brothel originally; look in the upstairs windows.

## 2  South-Central Alaska: Anchorage & the Kenai Peninsula

Dominated by Anchorage, the state's largest city, with 40% of Alaska's population, South-Central doesn't have an identity of its own. Anchorage is accused of being just like a city in the Lower 48, not really part of Alaska at all, although it sits in the lap of the wild Chugach Mountains. The Kenai Peninsula is famous for the crowding on its salmon streams, not the secret and grand places it contains. The Copper River country and Prince William Sound have their own definitions, made up of the huge and spectacular land and the few little towns they host. As a region, South-Central is more of an area on a map than an interconnected way of life.

For the visitor, that's an advantage, because South-Central Alaska's diversity contains almost everything that people come to the state to see. The glaciers are most numerous and largest here. The mountains are the most massive, if not quite the tallest. The waters of Prince William Sound and the Kenai Peninsula have the same allure as Southeast Alaska, but are more accessible by road. The towns have art to see, if not much history. And in some of them, there's a new sophistication that has removed some of the crude edges that accompanies much Alaska travel.

The disadvantage, of course, is that there are more people in the way. The closer you get to Anchorage, the more human development will remind you of the outskirts of any town in the United States, with fast-food franchises, occasional traffic jams, and even crime-ridden neighborhoods. But if that starts to bother you, do what Anchorage residents do—head up to the Chugach Mountains, down to the Kenai Peninsula, or out on Prince William Sound.

### ARRIVING & DEPARTING

Most trips to South-Central begin with a flight into Anchorage, which has daily jet service from Seattle and other smaller cities. It has by far the most flights linking Alaska to the rest of the world. You can also make the long drive up the Alaska Highway, or, if you're on a cruise ship, you'll likely come in on a tour bus from Seward.

### ANCHORAGE

Anchorage started as a tent camp for workers mobilized to build the Alaska Railroad in 1915, but for 40 years afterward, it was never more than a remote, sleepy railroad town. But oil was discovered here in 1957, bringing prospectors as fast as they had come to other parts of the state 60 years earlier looking for gold. Fortunes came fast, development was haphazard, and a lot was built that we'd all soon regret. Coming home from college to the town where I grew up, I had the bizarre experience of getting completely lost in a large area of the city that had been nothing but moose browse the last time I'd seen it.

In the city's adolescence, visitors found a city full of life, but empty of charm. But in the last 10 years that has started to change. Anchorage is still young, prosperous, vibrant—exhausting, at times, when the summer sun refuses to set. But now it also has some excellent restaurants, a good museum, a nice little zoo, and things to do in the evening. Some people complain that Anchorage isn't really Alaska. In Fairbanks, they call it "Los Anchorage." (In Anchorage, Fairbanks is known as "Squarebanks.") Yet the wilderness remains close by, right at the edge of town, and often intertwined with it. With around a quarter-million people, Anchorage still has problems in the winter with pesky moose. And a system of greenbelts and bike trails, the city's best feature, brings the woods into almost every neighborhood. Good downhill skiing is available, as is some of the best Nordic skiing in the United States.

There's a downtown area of about 6 by 20 blocks, near Ship Creek where it all started, but the rest of the city spreads some 5 miles east and 15 miles south along broad commercial strips and freeway frontages. Like many cities in the western United States built in the era of the car, the layout is not particularly conducive to any other form of transportation. But the city's boundaries go far beyond the reach of cars, taking in the Chugach, Turnagain Arm all the way to Portage, and even reaching over to Prince William Sound. Most of that land is there only to be explored, a land containing unnamed and many rarely climbed mountain peaks.

## ESSENTIALS

**GETTING THERE**   The Anchorage International Airport is a major hub. Flights from the Lower 48 to Russia and Asia often stop over here; there are also frequent flights from Seattle. In addition, flights between small towns within Alaska often route through Anchorage. **Alaska Airlines** (☎ 800/426-0333) is the dominant carrier. A ride downtown from the airport runs about $12; try **Alaska Cab** (☎ 907/563-5353).

There are two roads out of town. The southbound **Seward Highway** is a dead end, leading only to the Kenai Peninsula. The **Glenn Highway** is a four-lane freeway heading north to the intersection with the Parks Highway, which leads to Denali National Park and Fairbanks. All major car-rental companies operate in Anchorage, at the airport or at other locations in town.

**Gray Line's Alaskon Express** (☎ 800/544-2206 or 907/277-5581) links Anchorage to Seward, Valdez, and points on the Alaska Highway.

The **Alaska Railroad** (☎ 800/544-0552 or 907/265-2494) connects Anchorage to Seward, Fairbanks, and Denali National Park. The run to Seward, which operates only in the summer, is incredibly spectacular; the fare is $50 one way, $80 round-trip. The fare to Fairbanks is $149 year-round.

**VISITOR INFORMATION**   The **Anchorage Convention and Visitor Bureau** (☎ 907/276-4118; fax 907/278-5559), 524 W. Fourth Ave., Anchorage, AK 99501, operates five visitor information centers, distributing brochures and providing guidance for the whole state. The main location is the **Log Cabin Visitor Information Center**, downtown at Fourth Avenue and F Street (☎ 907/274-3531; fax 907/272-9564). It's open daily: June–Aug 7:30am–7pm; May and Sept 8am–6pm; Oct–Apr 9am–4pm.

The ✪ **Alaska Public Lands Information Center,** 605 W. Fourth Ave., Suite 105, Anchorage, AK 99501 (☎ 907/271-2737), in the old concrete federal building across the intersection from the log cabin at Fourth and F, has guidance for anyone planning to spend time in the outdoors.

**GETTING AROUND**   You can do downtown Anchorage on foot or by taking the **People Mover** city bus system (☎ 907/343-6543), which operates a free zone in the downtown core area. The fare for service all over town is $1. Buses generally come every half hour, but are much less frequent on weekends. **Taxis** are quite expensive in Anchorage because of the spread-out urban design. Call **Alaska Cab** (☎ 907/563-5353).

To visit some of the best of Anchorage, or to get into the outdoors, you'll need to get beyond the downtown area. All the major rental agencies have offices in Anchorage.

There isn't that much to see on a bus tour of Anchorage unless it's going specifically to one of the attractions I've listed below and you can get off. **Princess Tours** (☎ 907/276-7711) offers a 5¹/₂-hour Best of Anchorage tour that includes several stops for $40.

**EMERGENCIES** Call ☎ **911.** To reach the **Anchorage Police Department** for nonemergency problems, call ☎ **907/786-8500.** For police business outside the city, call the Alaska State Troopers (☎ **907/269-5511**). There are two hospitals serving the general public in Anchorage: the **Alaska Regional Hospital,** at 2801 DeBarr Rd. (☎ **907/276-1131**), and **Providence Hospital,** at 3200 Providence Dr. (☎ **907/562-2211**).

## WHAT TO SEE & DO

✪ **Alaska Zoo.** *4731 O'Malley Rd.* ☎ *907/346-3242. Admission $6 adults, $5 seniors, $4 ages 13–17, $3 children 3–12. Opens at 10am; closing time depends on sunset. Closed Tues in winter. Drive out the New Seward Hwy. to O'Malley Rd., then turn left and go 2 miles; it's at least 15 minutes from downtown, without traffic.* If you're expecting a big-city zoo, you'll be disappointed, but the Alaska Zoo has a charm all its own. Anchorage residents have developed personal relationships with the animals. Gravel paths wander through the woods past bears, seals and otters, musk oxen, mountain goats, moose, caribou, waterfowl—all the animals you were supposed to see in Alaska but may have missed.

✪ **Anchorage Museum of History and Art.** *121 W. Seventh Ave.* ☎ *907/343-4326. Admission $4 adults, $3.50 seniors 65 and older, free for children. High season, daily 9am–6pm. Low season, Tues–Sat 10am–6pm, Sun 1–5pm.* This is the state's largest museum, and it serves as a regional center of contemporary culture. Here you can learn about the history and anthropology of the state, or you can see what's happening in art in Alaska today. It also gets the best touring shows. In the summer, Native dancers perform in the atrium daily at 12:15, 1:15, and 2:15pm.

**Imaginarium.** *737 W. Fifth Ave., Suite 140.* ☎ *907/276-3179. Admission $5 adults, $4 seniors 65 and older and children 2–12. Mon–Sat 10am–6pm, Sun noon–5pm.* This is a science museum geared to children, where grown-ups can learn, too. While they're running around having a great time, kids may accidentally learn something; at least, the displays will excite a sense of wonder.

**Oscar Anderson House.** *420 M St.* ☎ *907/274-2336. Admission $3 adults. Summer, Tues–Sat noon–4pm. Call for winter schedule.* This house museum shows how an early Swedish butcher lived. Although far from grand, the house is quaint, surrounded by a lovely little garden, and the tour provides a good explanation of Anchorage's short history. If you come the first 2 weekends in December, don't miss the Swedish Christmas tours.

**WALKING TOURS** **Anchorage Historic Properties,** 645 W. Third Ave. (☎ 907/274-3600), a city-funded historical preservation group, offers a ✪ **Guided Walking Tour of Historic Downtown Anchorage,** June–Aug, Mon–Fri at 1pm. The volunteer guides are fun and knowledgeable. The 1-hour tour covers 2 miles and costs $5 for adults, $4 for seniors over age 65, and $1 for children. Highlights include Fourth Avenue, where the Iditarod Trail Sled Dog Race starts each year in March (at Fourth

Avenue and D Street, a bronze of a dog commemorates the race, and a mural depicts a relief map of the state with the Iditarod Trail marked); ✪ **Alaska Center for the Performing Arts,** Anchorage's most controversial building (the lobby is usually open for a look inside that is sure to spark a discussion); **Alaska Experience Center** (Sixth Avenue and G Street), a 40-minute IMAX movie about Alaska that's so spectacular that some people get motion sickness; and the restored ✪ **Fourth Avenue Theater** (between F and G streets), Anchorage's most attractive historic building. Don't miss going in and looking at the bas-relief murals and the blinking big dipper on the ceiling.

**BIKING, WALKING, & SKIING TRAILS**   My favorite thing about Anchorage is a ride or walk on a sunny summer afternoon on the ✪ **Tony Knowles Coastal Trail.** You can join the wide, paved trail at various points; Elderberry Park, at the western end of Fifth Avenue, is the most popular. There's a **bike-rental pavilion** right in the park. I've ridden my bike parallel with beluga whales swimming along the trail at high tide; toward the Kincaid Park end of the trail, I've often had moose stop me.

At Westchester Lagoon, 10 blocks south of Elderberry Park, the coastal trail meets the **Lanie Fleischer Chester Creek Trail,** which runs about 4 miles through the center of town to Goose Lake, where you can swim in a cool, wooded lake at the end of a hot ride. The trail follows a greenbelt the whole way, so you rarely see a building, and road and railroad crossings on all the trails have bridges or tunnels, so you're never in traffic.

✪ **Kincaid Park** itself is one of the best cross-country skiing areas in the country, and in the summer it's a great place for mountain biking, running, or day hiking, and it has an archery range. Little Campbell Lake is a picturesque swimming hole. The whole place is crawling with moose. There are about 30 miles of groomed ski trails ranging from easy to killer. Seven miles are lighted and open until 11pm nightly. An **outdoor center** (☎ 907/248-4346) is open Mon–Fri 1–9pm and Sat–Sun 10am–9pm.

**BIRD-WATCHING**   Potter Marsh, at the south end of the Anchorage bowl, is terrific for bird-watching. Boardwalks and interpretive signs help, but you can also pull out anywhere along the Seward Highway to set up a tripod for a camera or spotting scope.

**CHUGACH MOUNTAINS**   The mountains behind Anchorage are wonderfully accessible, and as beautiful as areas much further away. There's plenty of alpine terrain to wander in, and it's possible to get off by yourself on multiday trips where you'll see few other people but still be in cellular-phone range of Anchorage. You don't need a permit to camp, but you should get out of sight of trails. The best trail guide to the entire region, a really essential purchase, is Helen Neinhueser and John Wolfe, Jr.'s *55 Ways to the Wilderness,* published by The Mountaineers, 1011 SW Klickitat Way, Seattle, WA 98134; it's available in any bookstore in the area.

✪ **Flattop Mountain,** right behind Anchorage, is a great family climb. It's an easy afternoon hike for fit adults, and younger children can go partway and still get to see memorable views above the tree line. From New Seward Highway, drive east on O'Malley Road, turn right on Hillside Drive and left on Upper Huffman Road, then right on the twisting, gravel Toilsome Hill Drive. The parking area at Glen Alps, above tree line, is a starting point for lots of winter and summer trips.

North of Anchorage, on the Glenn Highway, there are trails at the head of Eagle River Road, around the park visitor center, and, from the Thunderbird Falls exit, 25 miles from Anchorage, an easy mile-long hike leads to a crashing cataract of water.

**EKLUTNA**   About 25 miles out the Glenn Highway (take the Eklutna exit, then go left over the overpass), the Native village of Eklutna has a fascinating old cemetery in which each grave is enclosed by a highly decorated spirit house, the size of a large dollhouse. The spirit houses excite the imagination in a way no ordinary marker would. The **Eklutna Tribe** (☎ 907/688-6026 or 907/696-2828) leads a 30-minute tour of the cemetery for $3.50. If you don't take the tour, you have to stay outside the cemetery fence. The park is open in summer only, 10am–6pm.

**FISHING** Serious fishermen use Anchorage as a base for a ✪ **fly-in fishing trip** on a remote lake or river. Several companies offer fly-in trips; two of the largest and best established are **Ketchum Air Service** (☎ 800/433-9114 or 907/243-5525) and **Rust's Flying Service** (☎ 800/544-2299 or 907/243-1595). They can take you out guided or on your own. There's nothing like the silence that falls as the float plane that dropped you off disappears over the horizon. Prices start around $200 per person for an unguided day trip.

**FLIGHT-SEEING** There are more than two dozen operators anxious to take you on a flight-seeing tour—check the visitor center for names—but the most comfortable and memorable is probably the restored DC-3 operated by ✪ **Era Aviation** (☎ 800/866-8394 or 907/248-4422). The plane re-creates the classic days of air travel—you can pretend to be Ingrid Bergman or Spencer Tracy while gazing out the oversize windows at a glacier. The daily summer flights from the **South Airpark,** off Raspberry Road, go to Mt. McKinley for 2 hours for $185 or to Prince William Sound for 1 hour and 15 minutes for $130; the route is tailored to the weather and viewing opportunities.

**SPECTATOR SPORTS** The **University of Alaska–Anchorage** fields an NCAA Division I hockey team, the Seawolves, which plays at the Sullivan Arena. The men's basketball team hosts a major Division I preseason tournament over Thanksgiving weekend, the **Great Alaska Shoot-Out,** and plays the regular season at the Sullivan Arena and at the University Sports Center, on campus on Providence Drive. Tickets are available from **Carrs Tix** (☎ 800/478-7328 or 907/263-2787).

## ACCOMMODATIONS

Rooms can be hard to find in Anchorage in the summer. I've provided full listings for my top recommendations in each price category below, but Anchorage also has almost all the chain motels and they all have the standard rooms you'd find anywhere in the country. There are several booking agencies that can put you together with the right bed-and-breakfast. **Alaska Private Lodgings,** P.O. Box 200047, Anchorage, AK 99520-0047 (☎ 907/258-1717; fax 907/258-6613), is the most established of the agencies. It has a downtown office at 704 W. Second Ave. The bed tax in Anchorage is an additional 8%.

**Bonanza Lodge.** *4455 Juneau St., Anchorage, AK 99503.* ☎ *800/478-3590 or 907/563-3590. Fax 907/563-5560. 48 suites. High season, $100 suite for two. Low season, $55–$70 suite for two. AE, DISC, MC, V.* This comfortable, family hotel is located in midtown, somewhat convenient to the airport but not the sights. All rooms are suites with full kitchens and large balconies. The industrial neighborhood is completely screened off by trees and nicely landscaped. The staff is friendly and competent. Pets are allowed in some rooms. The lodge has coin-op laundry and free coffee in the lobby.

✪ **Hotel Captain Cook.** *Fourth Ave. and K St. (P.O. Box 102280), Anchorage, AK 99510-2280.* ☎ *800/843-1950 or 907/276-6000. Fax 907/278-5366. 566 rms, 77 suites. High season, $205–$240 double; $250–$1,500 suite. Low season, $80–$140 double; $150–$1,500 suite. AE, DC, DISC, JCB, MC, V.* This is Alaska's great, grand hotel. Former Gov. Wally Hickel built it to demonstrate his commitment to the state's future after the 1964 earthquake. Today its three red towers help define the skyline. The rooms are large and sumptuous, with great views from all sides; you don't pay more to be higher. There's a concierge, and facilities include tour desks, a barbershop and beauty

# Anchorage

**Accommodations**

Hostelling International, Anchorage **3**
Hotel Captain Cook **1**
Oscar Gill House B&B **5**
Snowshoe Inn **4**
Voyager Hotel **2**

**Attractions**

Alaska Center for the Performing Arts **8**

Alaska Experience Theater **7**
Anchorage Museum of History and Art **10**
Coastal Trail Trailhead **5**
Fifth Avenue Mall **9**
The Imaginarium **6**
Log Cabin Visitor Information Center **3**
Oscar Anderson House **4**
Public Lands Information Center **2**
Saturday Market **1**

salon, business center, full-service health club, pool, racquetball court, three restaurants, and three lounges.

✪ **Oscar Gill House Bed and Breakfast.** *1344 W. 10th Ave. (P.O. Box 200047), Anchorage, AK 99520-0047.* ☎ *907/258-1717. Fax 907/258-6613. 3 rms, 1 with bath. High season, $85 double. Low season, $65 double. The room with bath costs $10 more. Rates include full breakfast. AE, DISC, MC, V (5% surcharge).* Oscar Gill was an early civic leader. His house was built in 1913, in Knik, before Anchorage was founded, and later moved here on a barge. Innkeepers Mark and Susan Lutz authentically restored it in 1994 as a cozy, friendly bed-and-breakfast. The house is full of appropriate antiques. Free laundry machines and bicycles are available.

✪ **Snowshoe Inn.** *826 K St., Anchorage, AK 99501.* ☎ *907/258-7669. Fax 907/258-7463. 14 rms, 6 with bath. High season, $89 double. Low season, $44 double. Rooms with bath cost $10 more. AE, MC, V.* This family-operated hotel on a quiet downtown street is so clean it feels like you're the first one ever to stay there. The rooms are comfortable, light, and attractively decorated in bright fabrics. There are only two rooms for each shared bathroom and they couldn't be closer or more secure.

✪ **Voyager Hotel.** *501 K St., Anchorage, AK 99501.* ☎ *800/247-9070 or 907/277-9501. Fax 907/274-0333. 38 rms. High season, $149 double. Low season, $79–$99 double. AE, DC, DISC, JCB, MC, V.* Everything about the Voyager is just right: the small size; the central location; the large, light rooms, all with kitchens; the exceptional housekeeping; and the warm yet highly professional hospitality. There's nothing ostentatious or outwardly remarkable about the hotel, yet the most experienced travelers rave about it the loudest.

## DINING

Anchorage is full of take-out and fast-food restaurants: The **Lucky Wishbone,** 1033 E. Fifth Ave., has the best fried chicken in town, and **Benny's Food Wagon** has been parked at Benson Boulevard and Seward Highway for more than 20 years. In addition, there are coffeehouses all over the city that offer poetry readings and conversation. Try the **Java Joint** at Northern Lights and Spenard or **Cafe del Mundo** at Northern Lights and Denali.

✪ **CampoBello.** *601 W. 36th St., Suite 10.* ☎ *907/563-2040. Main courses $9–$16; lunch $7–$10. MC, V. Mon–Sat 11am–9pm. NORTHERN ITALIAN.* This small midtown trattoria, improbably located in a shopping center, has sophisticated Northern Italian cuisine in a low-key setting, with wonderfully hospitable service and low prices. It stands with the best of Alaska's restaurants, but charges half of what you might pay in a comparable establishment.

**Crows Nest.** *Fourth Ave. and K St.* ☎ *907/276-6000. Main courses $25–35. Mon–Sat 6–10pm; Sun brunch 10am–2pm. AE, MC, V. AMERICAN.* An old-fashioned formal-style dining room at the top of the highest tower in the Hotel Captain Cook is the city's finest restaurant. The dining room is well divided to lend intimacy to the many booths and has stupendous views in all directions.

**Dianne's Restaurant.** *550 W. Seventh Ave., Suite 110.* ☎ *907/279-7243. All items $4–$8. MC, V. Mon–Fri 7am–4pm. SOUP AND SANDWICHES.* Dianne's has developed such a reputation for great baking, soups, sandwiches, and specials that at lunch hour it's clogged with people in suits and dresses. The line at the cafeteria moves fast, however, and the bright, casual atmosphere is full of energy. My first choice for a healthy lunch downtown.

✪ **Marx Brothers Cafe.** *627 W. Third Ave.* ☎ *907/278-2133. Reservations recommended. Main courses $17.50–$28.50. AE, DC, MC, V. Summer, daily 6–9:30pm. Winter, Mon–Sat 6–9:30pm. REGIONAL AMERICAN.* A restaurant that began as a hobby 20 years ago among friends is still a labor of love. Dinner takes all night—you'll want an appetizer while you watch the chef picking herbs and vegetables for your meal from the garden—but is worth the wait. The cuisine is varied and creative, ranging from Asian to Italian.

✪ **Sacks Cafe.** *625 W. Fifth Ave.* ☎ *907/274-4022. Reservations not accepted. Main courses $12–$19.50; lunch $4.50–$9. AE, MC, V. Sun–Thurs 11am–9:30pm, Fri–Sat 11am–11pm. NEW AMERICAN.* We like to come here for a special meal because the food is creative and occasionally inspired, the atmosphere is light, and the prices are reasonable. At times the place takes itself a bit too seriously, but the (seasonal) mussels in white wine will make you forgive anything.

✪ **Simon and Seafort's Saloon and Grill.** *420 L St.* ☎ *907/274-3502. Reservations essential. Lunch/dinner $16–$35. AE, MC, V. Daily 11:15am–2:30pm and 4:30–10:30pm. STEAK AND SEAFOOD.* Simon's is a jolly grill where hearty voices boom off the high ceilings and brass turn-of-the-century saloon decor. On sunny summer evenings, the rooms fill with light off Cook Inlet; the views are magnificent. I've never been disappointed by the salmon or prime rib; the service is always efficient and highly professional.

## ANCHORAGE AFTER DARK

Alaska's largest city has more varied nightlife than anywhere else in the state. Pick up a copy of the Friday edition of the *Anchorage Daily News* for current event listings in the "8" section; it's also for sale separately in boxes around town all week.

The **Anchorage Symphony** performs regularly during the concert season. There's also an opera company and the **Anchorage Concert Association,** which promotes a schedule of international-caliber music and other performing arts. The **Anchorage Festival of Music** presents a summer program of visiting classical musicians. The **Anchorage Center for the Performing Arts,** at 621 W. Sixth Ave., on town square, has three beautiful theaters ranging in size from 350 to 2,000 seats. A ticket office in the lobby is operated by **Carrs Tix** (☎ 800/478-7328 or 907/263-2787), the main ticket agency in town, which is associated with Carrs grocery stores and has outlets at each store. Popular music and other large-venue performances take place at the 8,500-seat **Sullivan Arena,** at 16th Avenue and Gambell Street (New Seward Highway); call ☎ 907/279-2596 for a recorded listing of events.

For a funny night out, nothing in town compares to ✪ **Mr. Whitekeys' Fly By Night Club,** Spenard Road south of Northern Lights Boulevard (☎ 907/279-SPAM). This drinking establishment seems to be an excuse for the goateed proprietor, a consummate vulgarian, to ridicule Anchorage in his crude, political, local-humor musical comedy shows. The summer show is Tues–Sat at 8pm; tickets are $12–$17, and reservations are necessary well in advance.

The largest bar in town is **Chilkoot Charlie's,** Spenard Road and Fireweed Lane (☎ 907/272-1010), yet on the weekend the place is packed and there are lines for the 657-person standing-room capacity. There are three stages with live rock music, generally of the Top-40 variety.

## A ROAD TRIP TO TURNAGAIN ARM & PORTAGE GLACIER

One of the world's great drives starts in Anchorage and leads roughly 50 miles south on the Seward Highway to Portage Glacier. It's the trip, not the destination, that makes it worthwhile. The two-lane highway along Turnagain Arm, chipped from the foot of the rocky Chugach Mountains, provides a platform to see a magnificent, ever-changing, mostly untouched landscape full of wildlife. There are trails into Chugach State Park all along the drive. It will take at least half a day, and there's plenty to do for an all-day excursion. There are lots of bus tours that follow the route and visit Portage Glacier. **Gray Line** (☎ 907/277-5581) offers a 7-hour trip that includes a stop in Girdwood and the boat ride on Portage Lake for $59, twice daily in summer. Here are some highlights:

**BELUGA POINT**   When the state highway department put up scenic overlook signs on this pullout, they weren't kidding. The terrain is simply awesome, as the highway traces the edge of Turnagain Arm, below the towering cliffs of the Chugach Mountains. If the tide and salmon runs are right, you may see beluga whales accidentally beaching themselves in their search for fish.

**WINDY POINT**   Be on the lookout in this section, 4 miles south of Beluga Point, on the mountain side of the road, where Dall sheep are frequently seen picking their way along the cliffs. It's a unusual spot, for they get much closer to people here than is usual in the wild; apparently, they know they're safe. Although Windy Point is the prime spot, you have a decent chance of seeing sheep virtually anywhere along this stretch of road. If cars are stopped, that's probably why.

**THE FLATS**   Nine miles beyond Bird Creek, the highway descends from the mountainside to the flats. At high tide, water comes right up to the highway. At low tide, all of Turnagain Arm (so named by Capt. James Cook, who had to keep turning around in its confines) narrows to a winding channel through the mud. Since the 1964 Good Friday earthquake, the arm has not been navigable.

**OLD PORTAGE**   All along the flats at the head of Turnagain Arm are large marshes full of birds and what looks like standing driftwood. These are trees killed by salt water that flowed in when the 1964 quake lowered the land as much as 10 feet. On the right, 9 miles beyond the Girdwood turnoff, a few ruins of the abandoned town of Portage are still visible, more than 30 years after the great earthquake. *Warning:* There is good bird-watching from the turn-outs, but don't think of venturing out on Turnagain Arm's tidal mud flats. They suck people up and drown them in the incoming tide. A woman died a few years ago in the arms of rescuers, who were not strong enough to pull her out of the quicksand-like mud as the water covered her.

**PORTAGE GLACIER**   When the National Forest Service spent $8 million on a new visitor center in 1985, Portage Glacier was predicted to keep depositing icebergs into its 800-foot-deep lake until the year 2020. But within 10 years, the glacier had receded completely out of sight of the visitor center. So nowadays, a cruise boat operated by **Gray Line of Alaska** (☎ 907/783-2983), under license with the Forest Service, traverses the lake hourly to get right up to Portage Glacier, ice conditions permitting. This isn't the best glacier in Alaska (Columbia, Exit, and Mendenhall glaciers, and Glacier Bay National Park are all better), but it's a good choice if it's your lone opportunity.

## GIRDWOOD & MT. ALYESKA

The Girdwood area—actually still part of the Municipality of Anchorage—is a small town on the threshold of turning into a major resort. Originally a mining community, it still has a sleepy, offbeat character. Retired hippies, ski bums, and a few old-timers live in the houses and cabins among the big spruce trees in the valley below the Mt. Alyeska ski resort. They've all got their eye on the development bonanza expected to come with the discovery of uncrowded skiing here—but so far the town is still an authentically funky community.

The primary summer attractions are the hiking trails, the tram to the top of Mt. Alyeska, and the Crow Creek Mine. In winter, it's skiing. Mt. Alyeska doesn't have the size or the fame of resorts in the Rockies, but it's certainly large and challenging enough—Olympian Tommy Moe trained here. Skiers used to more crowded slopes rave about the skiing here, with views of the Chugach Mountains and, between their parted, snowy, rocky peaks, Turnagain Arm.

**VISITOR INFORMATION**   For Girdwood-specific arrangements, the **Alyeska Booking Company,** on Linblad Street (P.O. Box 330), Girdwood, AK 99587 (☎ 907/783-4FUN), takes care of accommodations, rafting trips, rentals, and so on.

### WHAT TO SEE & DO

**ALYESKA RESORT**   Owned by the Japanese Seibu company, Alyeska is trying to transform itself from a local ski area to an international resort. The work is going well, but it's not there yet—and that's good for skiers who enjoy a varied, challenging mountain with a long season, low lift-ticket prices, and no crowds.

**SKIING**   **Mt. Alyeska,** at 3,939 feet, has 786 acres of skiing, beginning from a base elevation of only 250 feet and rising 2,500 feet. The normal season is early November to April. The average snowfall is 556 inches, but because it's near the water, the weather is temperate. Light is more of an issue, as the days are short in winter. There are 75 acres of lighted skiing on 19 trails. Lift tickets are $38 for adults, $24 for students, and $17 for seniors and kids under 14. There are excellent cross-country trails as well.

A new **center for people with disabilities** was opened in the fall of 1995 by Challenge Alaska, 720 W. 58th Ave., Anchorage, AK 99518 (☎ 907/783-2925 or 907/563-2635), allowing disabled skiers to use the mountain without assistance.

**THE TRAM**   At $16 per person for a 6-minute summertime ride up the mountain, the tram leaving from the Alyeska Prince Hotel isn't cheap, but I think it's worth it for people who can't make the climb on foot. The view looks up and down the valley and below at the treetops and, perhaps, the back of a grazing moose or bear. This is an opportunity for everyone, no matter how young, old, or infirm, to experience the pure light, limitless surroundings, and crystalline quiet of an Alaskan mountaintop. Dress very warmly.

## ACCOMMODATIONS & DINING

If you don't want to pay the rates charged by the Alyeska Prince Hotel, there are other nice places to stay in Girdwood. Contact the **Alyeska Booking Company,** on Linblad Street (P.O. Box 330), Girdwood, AK 99587 (☎ **907/783-4FUN**), to find a bed-and-breakfast, with rates starting at $80 a night.

✪ **Alyeska Prince Hotel.** *1000 Arlberg Ave. (P.O. Box 249), Girdwood, AK 99587.* ☎ *800/880-3880 or 907/754-1111. Fax 907/754-2200. 303 rms, 4 suites. Summer, $230–$450 double; $700–$1,500 suite. Winter, $150–$400 double; $500–$1,000 suite. AE, DC, DISC, JCB, MC, V.* Completed in 1994, the Alyeska is unusual in Alaska, a large, first-class hotel in a nearly pristine mountain valley. The accommodations and service are close to perfect—so perfect, in fact, as to seem inappropriately solemn at times. The standard rooms are not large, but have extraordinary views. The hotel has a concierge, fitness center, and out-of-this-world swimming pool.

Two of the hotel's four restaurants are on Mt. Alyeska, reached only by tram. Check which restaurants are open when you come; some close in certain seasons. The Japanese cuisine (the property is Japanese owned) in particular has developed a reputation. Whether you're dining or sleeping here, you'll need a car. The hotel is convenient to nothing except its own spectacular surroundings.

# SEWARD

The main reason to go to Seward is Resurrection Bay and the access the port provides to the great mass of Alaska. Most visitors are on their way to the excellent ocean fishing, especially for silver salmon, or to Kenai Fjords National Park, which is described below. But the path left by generations of earlier travelers and settlers makes Seward an unusual and attractive town in its own right. It's also a good starting point for hiking on publicly owned wild lands. Until the age of jet travel, most people coming to Alaska arrived by steamer in Seward and then traveled north by rail. The train ride to Anchorage, daily during the summer, is supremely beautiful.

## ESSENTIALS

**GETTING THERE**  The Seward Highway leads 127 miles from Anchorage. All major car-rental agencies are represented in Anchorage. **Hertz** has an office in Seward during the summer (☎ **800/654-3131** or 907/224-6097).

The **Seward Bus Line** (☎ **907/224-3608;** fax 907/224-7237) makes one trip daily, year-round, starting in Seward and going to Anchorage and back; the fare is $30 one-way.

Everyone should take the run between Anchorage and Seward on the ✪ **Alaska Railroad,** 411 W. First Ave., Anchorage, AK 99501 (☎ **800/544-0552** or 907/265-2494), which runs daily in summer. It's even more spectacular than the highway route, passing close by glaciers and following a ledge halfway up the narrow, vertical Placer River gorge, where it ducks into tunnels and pops out at bends in the river. The terrain around the tracks is completely undeveloped and looks just as it did when the first person beheld it. The fare for the summer-only run is $80 round-trip or $50 one-way.

**VISITOR INFORMATION**  The **Kenai Fjords National Park Visitor Center,** at the boat harbor (P.O. Box 1727), Seward, AK 99664 (☎ **907/224-3175;** fax 907/224-2144), open in summer, daily 8am–5pm, closed on weekends in winter, is worth a stop for park information and other outdoor opportunities (see the section on the national park, below, for more specifics on the visitor center). The **Seward Chamber of Commerce,** P.O. Box 749, Seward, AK 99664 (☎ **907/224-8051**), has four visitor centers: one on the Seward Highway as you enter town, open year-round, and summer locations at a kiosk at the boat harbor, in an old Alaska Railroad car at the corner of Third Avenue and Jefferson Street, downtown, and at the cruise-ship dock, when ships are in town.

**GETTING AROUND**   You can easily cover downtown Seward on foot, although a little help is handy to get back and forth from the boat harbor. The **Chamber of Commerce Trolley** runs every half hour from 10am to 7pm, daily in summer, with stops at the railroad depot, the cruise-ship dock, and the harbor visitor center. **Independent Taxi** (☎ **907/224-5000**) is one of the cab companies.

**EMERGENCIES**   Dial ☎ **911.** For nonemergency situations, call the **Seward Police Department** (☎ **907/224-3338**) or, outside the city limits, the **Alaska State Troopers** (☎ **907/224-3346**). **Providence Seward Medical Center** is at 417 First Ave. (☎ **907/224-5205**).

## WHAT TO SEE & DO

The main thing to do in Seward is visit the Kenai Fjords National Park, which includes the fjords and Exit Glacier. See the separate section below.

**FISHING**   Seward is renowned for its saltwater silver salmon fishing, and there's a harbor full of large and small charter boats waiting to take you. There's also good halibut fishing. The going rate for a charter is $130 per person for salmon, or $150 for halibut. The **Fish House,** P.O. Box 1209, Seward, AK 99664 (☎ **800/257-7760** or 907/224-3674; fax 907/224-7108), is the old, established booking agency, and has a big store for supplies at the boat harbor. You can fish from shore for silvers when they're running in the late summer, although your chances aren't as good as if you use a boat. The beach below the downtown area is a popular spot.

**HIKING**   There are several excellent hiking trails near Seward. You can get a complete list at the Kenai Fjords National Park Visitor Center (see "Visitor Information," above). The **Mt. Marathon Trail** is a vigorous hike to the top of a 3,000-foot mountain. The route of the famous Mt. Marathon foot race is the more strenuous choice, basically going straight up from the end of Jefferson Street; the hikers' route starts at the corner of First Avenue and Monroe Street. Either trail rises steeply to the top of the rocky pinnacle and the incredible views there.

## ACCOMMODATIONS

The tax on rooms in Seward is an additional 9%.

   ✪ **Best Western Hotel Seward.** *217 Fifth Ave., Seward, AK 99664.* ☎ *800/ 478-4050 or 907/224-2378. Fax 907/224-3112. 38 rms. High season, $178–$198 double. Low season, $79 double. AE, MC, V.* Brad Snowden, who also owns the neighboring New Seward Hotel, has created a hotel that's in a league of its own. The rooms are large, fresh, and nicely decorated; many have big bay windows. The view rooms in front go for a premium; avoid the south-facing rooms, which look out on the back of another hotel.

   The **New Seward Hotel** operates out of a connected lobby with the Best Western. The rooms are smaller and less expensive, ranging from $58 to $96 for a double during the summer season. It has been called the "New Seward" since 1945, but some rooms have been recently remodeled with pleasant country decor.

## DINING

**The Depot,** at the north end of the harbor, is a good fast-food place, with burgers and fish sandwiches.

# The Kenai Peninsula & Prince William Sound

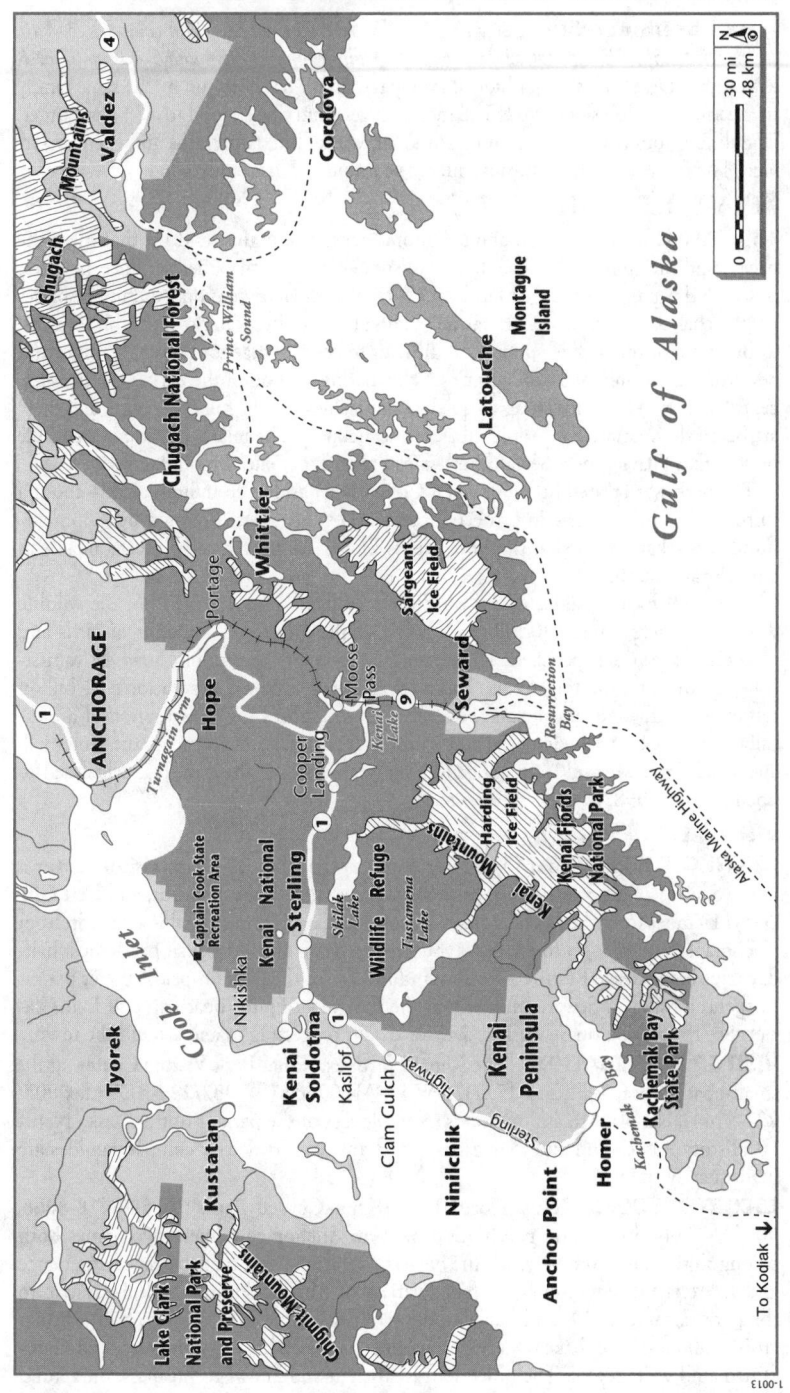

**Harbor Dinner Club.** *220 Fifth Ave.* ☎ *907/224-3012. Main courses $13–$40; lunch $5–$8.50. AE, CB, DC, DISC, MC, V. Daily 11am–2:30pm and 5–11pm. STEAK AND SEAFOOD.* This old-fashioned family restaurant has been run by the same family in the same location since 1962. The menu ranges from fine seafood to a $3 hamburger. The dining room is attractive and traditional, with white tablecloths and friendly service. The food is not adventurous, but we've found it consistently good.

## KENAI FJORDS NATIONAL PARK

This 580,000-acre park is all about remote rocks, mountains, and ice that meet the ocean, and the animals that live there. For some it's a natural cathedral: the experience of seeing the grand and rugged terrain takes on a spiritual dimension. And in few places are the chances better of seeing marine mammals or adding waterfowl to a birder's list.

But most of the park is remote and difficult to get to. Large tour boats, leaving from Seward, are the only practical way to see the marine portion of the park—the truly exceptional part. That's not cheap or quick if you really want the full experience, and there are better destinations for people subject to seasickness. The inland portion is accessible only at Exit Glacier, near Seward, unless you're an experienced mountaineer.

The park was created in 1980, when Congress set aside 106 million acres—about a third of the entire state—in protected parks and wilderness. Although development-minded Alaskans howled at the time, Kenai Fjords has proven to be most valuable as a tourist attraction.

The 1989 Exxon Valdez oil spill in Prince William Sound caused horrific wildlife destruction here, some 140 miles southwest of the disaster. Thousands of birds and hundreds of sea otters perished. That damage is no longer perceptible, however, to first-time visitors, and the tragedy has had a silver lining. Exxon Corporation's $1 billion settlement with state and federal governments will afford the construction of a $50-million sea-life center in downtown Seward. Both an aquarium and a lab, the center will allow visitors to see and learn about the marine biology of the area. It is scheduled to open in May 1998.

### ESSENTIALS

**GETTING THERE**    **Seward** is the threshold to the park. The park **visitor center** is at the Seward small-boat harbor, **tour boats** leave from Seward harbor, and **Exit Glacier** is 13 miles from the town by road. I recommend against making this a day trip from Anchorage. To really get to the park, you need to be on an all-day boat trip—most half-day trips barely leave Resurrection Bay and hardly see the park proper. A better plan is to spend a night in Seward and take in the full Kenai Fjords boat trip and Exit Glacier. See the section on Seward, above, for details on getting to and around the town.

**VISITOR INFORMATION**    The **Kenai Fjords National Park Visitor Center,** at the small-boat harbor (P.O. Box 1727), Seward, AK 99664 (☎ **907/224-3175;** fax 907/224-2144), is a place to ask questions of employees of the park or of the Alaska Natural History Association and to get the correct answer (many tour company guides are inadequately trained).

**ESCORTED TOURS**    Kenai Fjords Tours/Kenai Coastal Tours (☎ **800/478-8068,** 907/224-8068 in Seward, or 907/276-6249 in Anchorage). These two names both belong to the same company. It's the biggest operation, with many years of experience and an excellent reputation. It offers a variety of trips, including the full-day trip to the park (around $130) and half-day Resurrection Bay tours (closer to $60), dinner cruises, and a salmon bake on a remote island. Its vessels are large and fast, well maintained, and well crewed. The office staff is efficient and knows its business; the refund policy is generous. The only drawback: seating here is airline style, rather than around tables.

**WHAT TO SEE & DO**

Kenai Fjords is essentially a marine park. On a boat tour, you'll see its mountains, glaciers, and wildlife. On any of the tours, you're likely to see sea otters and sea lions and you have a good chance of seeing humpback whales, orcas, mountain goats, and black bears. Bird-watchers will see bald eagles, puffins, cormorants, murres, and various sea ducks.

Depending on the time and money you have to spend, you can choose to take a half-day trip (which stays primarily in Resurrection Bay) or a full-day trip that travels to Aialik Bay or Harris Bay, in the heart of the park. Find out exactly where your boat is going—some tour companies call their trips Kenai Fjords tours, but are really just Resurrection Bay tours. Resurrection Bay contains plenty of impressive scenery—its cliffs are as if chiseled from the mountains—but the fjords within the park itself are even grander. The glaciers in the park are also more impressive than those in Resurrection Bay.

How much wildlife you see also depends on the trip you take. The half-day cruises have less of a chance of seeing whales and will see puffins and other birds in lesser numbers. But on a full-day trip, if you're lucky with the weather, you may make it to the exposed Chiswell Islands, which have among the greatest bird rookeries in Alaska, supporting more than 50,000 seabirds of 18 species.

If you get seasick easily, stick to the half-day cruise. The water in the Kenai Fjords is calm. But the passage from Resurrection Bay to the fjords is through the unprotected waters of the North Pacific, where large, rolling waves are inevitable. On a rough day, most boats will turn back for the comfort of the passengers and change the full-day trip into a Resurrection Bay cruise, refunding the difference in fare. Ask about your company's refund policy, but more importantly, plan a boat trip on the first day of your stay, so if the weather is bad, you can wait and go the next day.

**EXIT GLACIER**   Although relatively small, Exit Glacier really is unusual, and I enjoyed a visit even as a jaded lifelong Alaskan. It's possible to walk quite close to Exit Glacier, see its brittle texture, and feel the cold, dense spires of ice looming over you (don't go beyond the warning signs, though; ice can fall off and crush you). The pattern of vegetation reclaiming the land that the glacier has uncovered is well explained by interpretive signs and a nature trail. At the same time, however, the area remains refreshingly primitive. Often, a spotting scope is set up to see mountain goats up in the rocky cliffs. (To get to the glacier, turn off the Seward Highway 3.7 miles north of town and follow the signs down the 9-mile gravel road.) If you don't have a car, **Kenai Fjords Tours** (☎ 907/224-8068) takes daily trips to Exit Glacier, combined with a Seward town tour. It starts at 2pm, takes 2¹/₂ hours, and costs $19.

## 3  Denali National Park

Denali (den-AL-ee) National Park contains Mt. McKinley, at 20,320 feet the tallest mountain in North America; but you don't need to go to the park to see the mountain, and you probably won't see it even if you do. Denali encompasses a broad expanse of alpine tundra and taiga populated by bears, wolves, Dall sheep, caribou, moose, eagles, fox, beavers, and small mammals; but that's typical of much of interior and Arctic Alaska. And in and around the park, opportunities exist for river rafting, flight-seeing, hiking, and tourist activities; but again, you don't have to go to the park for that.

What makes Denali special is the fact that anyone can get into a relatively pristine natural environment and see wildlife in its natural state. A single National Park Service decision makes that possible: the only road through the park is closed to cars. To get into the park, you must ride a crowded bus over a dusty gravel road hour after hour.

The upside of this inconvenience, though, is that the animals aren't scared away by the cars or the half-million visitors who come to the park every summer. From the window of the bus, you're likely to see grizzly bears doing what they would be doing even if you weren't there.

More important and more valuable, you can get off the bus pretty much whenever you want to, walk away from the road, and be alone in a primeval wilderness utterly undisturbed by human development. Unless you're up for a rugged trek into the wilderness, this kind of perfect moment would cost you thousands of dollars to experience elsewhere. But at Denali, it costs $20, plus the cost of your accommodations. And when you're ready to go back to civilization, you just walk to the road and catch the next bus—they come every half hour.

Most visitors to the park are on an 18-hour-long package tour, which is about the worst way to see the park. Such tours allow you to say you went to the park, but they don't actually give you much chance to see anything. There's a dinner-theater show the night before, and then a ride in a tour bus that has time to go only partway into the park. In the past few years, the bus turned around short of where the bears were most often seen. The scenery on the drive is spectacular, many package-tour visitors doubtless saw bears, and some even saw the mountain. But it's just about impossible to schedule a perfect moment into an 18-hour day, especially with dozens of other tourists around you.

## ESSENTIALS

**ARRIVING & DEPARTING**   The most popular way to get to Denali is by train. The **Alaska Railroad,** P.O. Box 107500, Anchorage, AK 99510-7500 (☎ **800/544-0552** or 907/265-2494), has daily service in the summer from Anchorage and Fairbanks. Trains leave both cities at 8:15am, arriving at the park from Fairbanks at noon and from Anchorage at 3:45pm, then continue to the opposite city for arrival at 8:15pm. The one-way fare from Anchorage to Denali is $99. Fares are slightly lower in May and September, though service is less frequent; in winter, a single car makes the trip once a week. The Alaska Railroad locomotives also pull two sets of luxury cars owned by **Princess Cruises** (☎ **800/835-8907**) and **Holland America Westours/Gray Line of Alaska** (☎ **800/628-2449** or 907/277-5581). Most of these passengers are on the company's cruises, but they do sell train tickets separately (they cost more than the Alaska Railroad cars).

The drive from Anchorage to Denali takes about $4^1/2$ hours ($2^1/2$ hours from Fairbanks) on a good two-lane highway. Many of the views along the George Parks Highway are equal to the views on the train, but large stretches, especially in the Matanuska and Susitna valleys, have been spoiled by the worst kind of roadside development, which you don't see on the train. Car-rental agencies are located in downtown Anchorage and at the airport.

The **Alaska Backpacker Shuttle** (☎ **800/266-8625** or 907/344-8775) carries passengers from Anchorage in a van that leaves from the youth hostel at 700 H St., downtown, or picks up elsewhere by arrangement. The fare is $35 one-way.

**GETTING AROUND**   You don't need a car at Denali; in fact, you can't bring your car into the park. Virtually all accommodations have arrangements to get you around. If your hotel doesn't have a courtesy van of its own, you can always take a scheduled shuttle.

**VISITOR INFORMATION**   The park service has placed most of its dealings with the public in the hands of a concessionaire, **ARA's Denali Park Resorts,** P.O. Box 87, Denali Park, AK 99755, or 241 W. Ship Creek Ave., Anchorage, AK 99501 (☎ **800/ 622-7275** or 907/272-7275; fax 907/264-4684). ARA also operates the buses and

# Denali National Park

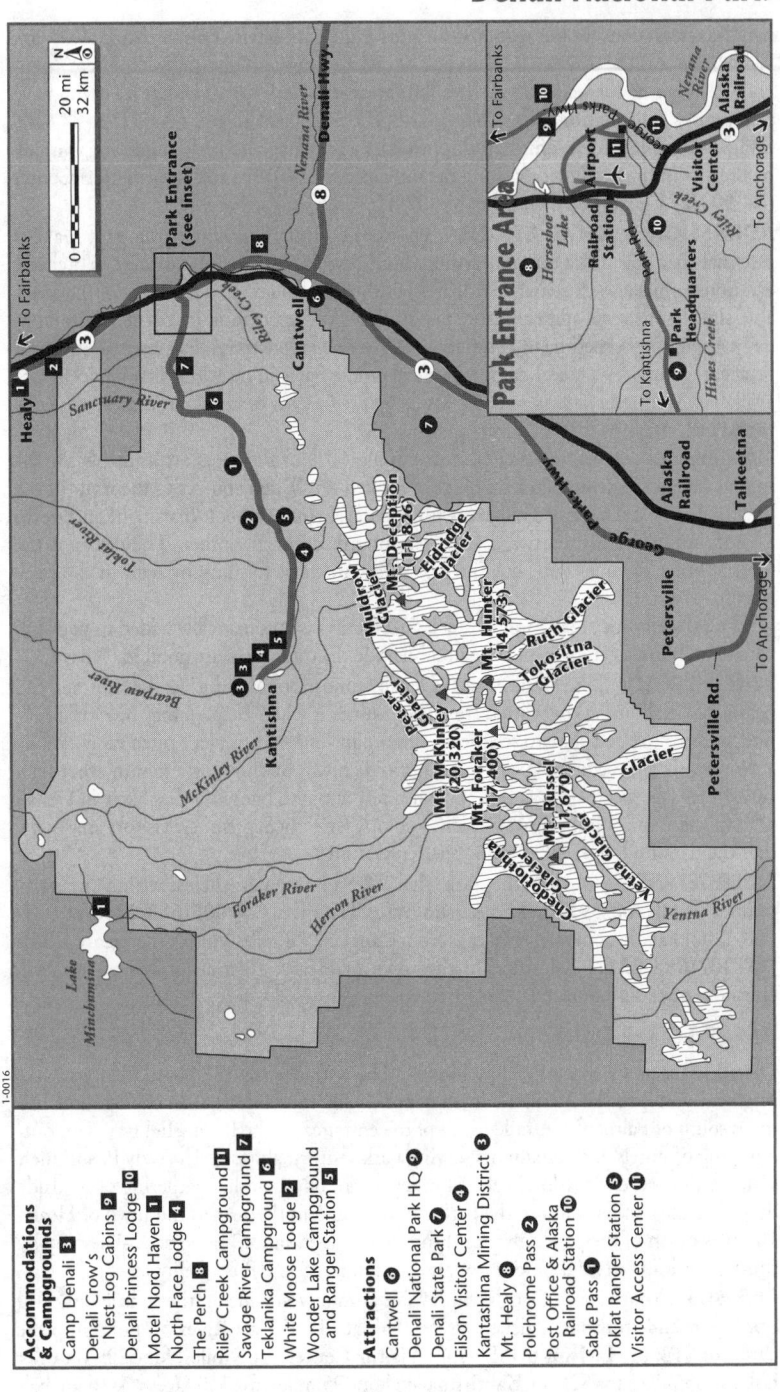

**Park Entrance Area**

## Accommodations & Campgrounds

Camp Denali **3**
Denali Crow's Nest Log Cabins **9**
Denali Princess Lodge **10**
Motel Nord Haven **1**
North Face Lodge **4**
The Perch **8**
Riley Creek Campground **11**
Savage River Campground **7**
Teklanika Campground **6**
White Moose Lodge **2**
Wonder Lake Campground and Ranger Station **5**

## Attractions

Cantwell **6**
Denali National Park HQ **9**
Denali State Park **7**
Eilson Visitor Center **4**
Kantishna Mining District **3**
Mt. Healy **8**
Polchrome Pass **2**
Post Office & Alaska Railroad Station **10**
Sable Pass **1**
Toklat Ranger Station **5**
Visitor Access Center **11**

1-0016

handles reservations for bus seats and for sites at the park service campgrounds. The park visitor center is the place to pick up bus tickets and campground permits. There's generally a long line for walk-in purchase, but a will-call desk speeds things up if you have reservations. The **National Park Service,** P.O. Box 9, Denali Park, AK 99755 (☎ **907/ 683-9640** for recorded information), provides a free map and park guide; you can talk to a real person by calling or visiting the interagency **Public Lands Information Center** (☎ **907/271-2737** in Anchorage, or 907/456-0527 in Fairbanks).

**ADMISSION & REGULATIONS**   The traffic limitations within the park make it essential that you make bus and campground reservations well in advance. Hotel reservations, while also extremely tight, are slightly easier to get. Forty percent of the available shuttle-bus seats and campsites are available for reservation by phone, 7am–5pm daily, beginning sometime in February until the day before travel. Fax reservations must be accompanied by a credit card; include alternate dates in case your first choice is unavailable. Mail reservations must be made by credit card or check at least 30 days before travel.

Beginning 2 days in advance, the remaining 60% of the spots are available in person, at the visitor center, and are quickly booked up. When you get to the front of the line, if there's still a night available within 2 days, you can book that night and up to 14 continuous nights afterward at that campground or any other. The doors of the visitor center open at 7am, but the line to get in starts forming by 6am in the peak season.

The park entrance fee ($5 individual, $10 family) is automatically added to your bill when you book a campground site or a bus ride. Entrance fees are good for 7 days.

**WHEN TO GO**   Like all of Alaska, Denali is most popular during the summer and nearly deserted during the winter. Ironically, winter is when the park may be most beautiful, and it's the best time to see the mountain; in June and July, it's often rainy. While a winter visit may be impractical, you can avoid crowds by choosing a month other than July. In fall, the weather starts getting a bit nippy at night, but rain is less likely in Denali and the trees and tundra turn wonderful colors. By early September, visitors are so few that the park no longer takes telephone reservations.

**EMERGENCIES**   Outside the park, dial ☎ **911** in emergencies; within the park, phone ☎ **907/683-9100.** The **Alaska State Troopers** (☎ **907/683-2232** or 907/ 768-2202) handle nonemergency calls from Cantwell, 28 miles south. The **Healy Clinic** (☎ **907/683-2211**) is located in the town of Healy, 10 miles north of the park entrance, open 24 hours a day for emergencies.

## WHAT TO SEE & DO

Denali is about the size of Massachusetts. The entrance, on the paved George Parks Highway and near the Alaska Railroad depot, is 230 miles north of Anchorage and 120 miles south of Fairbanks. A mile north of the entrance on the Parks Highway is an outcropping of hotels and restaurants serving park visitors, almost exclusively in summer. Other services are at Carlo Creek, 14 miles south, or at another gathering of roadside development 7 miles south of the park entrance, and in the year-round town of Healy, 10 miles north of the park entrance. From the park entrance, a road accessible only by shuttle bus leads west 90 miles through the park (see "The Bus," below).

**THE BUS**   Your visit to Denali will revolve around your ride on the shuttle bus. You can buy round-trip shuttle tickets to the **Toklat** (TOE-klat) **River** 53 miles into the park, for $12; the **Eielson** (AISLE-son) **Visitor Center** at 66 miles, for $20; **Wonder Lake** at 85 miles, for $26; or **Kantishna** at about 95 miles, for $30 (ages 13–16 are half price, free for children 12 and under). Of course, you have to go both ways unless you have a campground reservation, a backcountry permit, or accommodations in

Kantishna's wilderness lodge, which means that you're in for a long drive. If you don't get off the bus along the way, the round-trip takes 6½ hours to Toklat, 8 hours to Eielson, 11 hours to Wonder Lake, and 12 hours to Kantishna. The farther you go, the better your chances of seeing wildlife, but the less time you'll have for day hikes. I think Eielson is the best destination for most people, offering the chance to see the mountain and some wildlife while leaving some time to get out and walk. But going the extra miles to Wonder Lake allows you to see the classic image of Mt. McKinley across the wooded lake.

Reserve your ticket for as early as you can stand to get up in the morning. You're more likely to see wildlife early in the morning (especially on hot days), and you'll have more time for day hikes. Bring food and plenty of water with you. Wear good walking shoes, dress in layers, and bring rain gear. Binoculars and insect repellent are a must. Shuttle-bus etiquette is to yell out when you see wildlife. The driver will stop and everyone will rush to your side of the bus.

**CAMPING**    All sites must be reserved, except the Marino Backpacker campground, which has a self-registration system. However, the Sanctuary and Igloo campgrounds can be reserved only in person—which means you'll most likely have to reserve your spot, then wait 2 nights until a site is open. There's a one-time reservation fee of $4 per campground in addition to the campground permit fees. See the section on campgrounds below for detailed information about specific campgrounds. The permit system for staying overnight in the undeveloped backcountry is onerous enough to weed out those who aren't serious about a wilderness experience. Backcountry permits are free, but can be obtained only 24 hours in advance and only in person at the backcountry desk in the visitor center.

**HIKING**    The park service is making a concerted effort to discourage the making of trails in the tundra or taiga of the park proper, but there are six easy, well-maintained trails around the park entrance area, the longest of which is the Mt. Healy Overlook, a 5-mile round-trip. The others are strolls of 2 miles or less.

The park service offers three **guided hikes** out in the park, beyond the 14-mile checkpoint. The daily **Discovery Hike** lasts 4 hours and goes somewhere different every day. You need to wear hiking boots and bring food, water, and rain gear. A special bus carrying the hikers leaves the visitor center at 8am, starting in mid-June. Reserve a place in advance. The **Toklat Trek** is an irregularly scheduled ranger-led walk in the Toklat River streambed; the **Tundra Walk,** at 1:30pm daily starting in late June, is a short guided stroll from the Eielson Visitor Center, at milepost 66 on the park road. Check in at the visitor center for late word on all the hikes before heading out on a long bus trip.

**BACKCOUNTRY HIKING**    Trekking the backcountry on a multiday backpacking journey is challenging and rugged, but also the most authentic way to see the park. Only people with strong outdoor skills who are in good physical condition should attempt a strenuous backcountry overnight, however, as there are no trails or other people to guide you. You must be flexible about where you're going and be prepared for any kind of terrain, because you can't choose your backcountry unit until you arrive at the visitor center and find out what's available.

Buy the $7 **Denali National Park and Preserve topographical map** published by Trails Illustrated, P.O. Box 3610, Evergreen, CO 80439-3425 (☎ **800/962-1643**), sold at the visitor center, which includes the boundaries of the 43 backcountry units. Also, you'll want to consult *Backcountry Companion*, by Jon Nierenberg, a book that describes each of the units. Published by the Alaska Natural History Association (605 W. Fourth Ave., Anchorage, AK 99501), it's for sale at the visitor center. The alpine backcountry units are most popular. That's where you get broad views and can cross heathery valleys walking in any direction. But to go far, you'll also have to be ready to climb over some rugged, rocky terrain. The best routes for making time are along the braided river valleys; you need to be ready for a lot of stream crossings.

**RANGER PROGRAMS & ACTIVITIES**  You may be anxious to get deep into the park as soon as you arrive, but the park service does offer lectures, guided hikes, and a ✪ **Sled-Dog Demonstration** at the park entrance to keep you entertained and interpret the park while you wait for a bus or permit.

In the winter, rangers patrol the park by sled dog, as they have for decades. In the summer, to keep the dogs active and amuse the tourists, they pull a sled on wheels around the kennel and a ranger gives a talk two to three times a day. A free bus leaves the visitor center for each show, at the kennels near the headquarters at milepost 3.4 on the park road. Or you can take a guided walk to the kennels, along the 2-mile-long Rock Creek Trail.

**FLIGHT-SEEING**  Getting a good, close look at Mt. McKinley is best accomplished by air. Frequently, when you can't see McKinley from the ground, you can see it from above the clouds. It's an impressive mountain, standing huge and white far above most of the surrounding terrain. The best flights take at least 90 minutes and circle McKinley. **Denali Air** (☎ **907/683-2261**) has an office at the airstrip in the park and several single- and two-engine planes. An hour-long flight going within a mile of the mountain costs around $150.

✪ **RAFTING & BOATING**  Floating the swift, glacial water of the Nenana River Canyon as it passes the park entrance has become a major activity at the park, because it's convenient and fun. The entire trip is outside the park. Several companies compete for your business, most offering a choice of slow Class II water, or a whitewater trip with numerous Class III and IV rapids. Each trip takes 2 to 2¹/₂ hours and costs $40–$47. Be prepared to get soaked. You'll want a shower afterward, as the glacial silt sticks to your hair and skin. The **Denali Outdoor Center** (☎ **907/683-1925**), a cooperative of five guides, is across from the McKinley Chalet Hotel on the Parks Highway.

## ACCOMMODATIONS

The furious pace of development around Denali has led to a hodgepodge of roadside hotels, cabins, lodges, and campgrounds in pockets arrayed along more than 20 miles of the Parks Highway. The most expensive rooms, and the first booked, are in the immediate area of the park entrance. Next are the hotels south of the park. Both these areas are entirely seasonal. The best deals are in Healy, 10 miles north of the park, where you can find a room for $50 less than what you'd pay near the park entrance. The other choice is to stay at a remote wilderness lodge: accommodations within the park borders for a hefty price. If you can afford them, though, there's no better way to be in the wilderness without giving up creature comforts. The local bed tax is 7%.

**Camp Denali/North Face Lodge.** *Kantishna Mining District (P.O. Box 67), Denali National Park, AK 99755.* ☎ *907/683-2290. Fax 907/683-1568. 17 cabins (Camp Denali); 15 rms, none with bath (North Face Lodge). $855 cabin per person double occupancy, for minimum 3-day stay at Camp Denali; $570 per person double, for minimum 2-day stay at North Face Lodge. Rates include all meals, transportation from park entrance, and guided activities. No credit cards. Closed early Sept–early June.* These pioneering ecotourism establishments under the same ownership are deep in the park, close to Mt. McKinley, away from roads used by tour buses. And they make good use of the opportunity, offering guests the chance to explore the wilderness on guided natural history hikes, bike rides, and lake canoe trips. Camp Denali cabins each have their own outhouse and share a central bathhouse.

**Denali Crow's Nest Cabins.** *Milepost 238.5, Parks Hwy. (P.O. Box 70), Denali National Park, AK 99755.* ☎ *907/683-2723. Fax 907/683-2323. 39 cabins. $134 cabin for two. MC, V.* Near the park entrance, on the mountainside above Nenana Canyon, looking down on Horseshoe Lake, these simple cabins are large, homey, and distinctly Alaskan. You'll spend a lot of time climbing stairs, however, and despite the great views, the cabins aren't as luxurious as you might expect for the price. Extras include the Overlook Bar and Grill (see "Dining," below), courtesy van, and outdoor Jacuzzis.

**Denali Princess Lodge.** *Milepost 238.5, Parks Hwy. (P.O. Box 110), Denali National Park, AK 99755.* ☎ *800/426-0500. Fax 907/683-2545; fax for reservations 206/443-1979. 280 rms, 7 suites. High season, $169 double; $250–$275 suite. Low season, $99 double; $180–$205 suite. AE, DC, MC, V. Closed late Sept to mid-May.* This is the best of the big hotels right at Denali, with a resort-hotel feel. The comfortable and attractively furnished rooms are nothing special for the high price. The hotel is used primarily for the cruise line's tours, and is booked mostly with their elderly passengers. There is a restaurant here.

✪ **Motel Nord Haven.** *Milepost 249.5, Parks Hwy. (P.O. Box 458), Healy, AK 99743.* ☎ *800/683-4501 in Alaska, or 907/683-4500. 24 rms. High season, $103 double. Low season, $65 double. AE, MC, V.* This new, family-run motel is a gem. Large, immaculate rooms branch off a hallway with a central sitting room. They're equal to the best in the Denali Park area, and a lot less expensive. The motel is open year-round. Extras include free coffee and Anchorage newspapers.

**The Perch.** *Milepost 224, Parks Hwy. (HC2, Box 1525), Healy, AK 99743.* ☎ *and fax 907/683-2523. 11 cabins, 4 with bath. $75–$105 cabin for 2. Rates include breakfast. Additional person in cabin $10 extra. AE, MC, V. Closed Sept 15–May 16.* Located south of the park, these are attractive, well-kept cabins in the woods. The adorable A-frames share a bathhouse; large, modern rooms in duplex buildings have private baths. The restaurant and bar on the top of a knoblike hill is a friendly place with good fish and beef at reasonable prices.

**White Moose Lodge.** *Milepost 248, Parks Hwy. (P.O. Box 68), Healy, AK 99743.* ☎ *800/481-1232 or 907/683-1233. 9 rms. $85 double. Rates include coffee, tea, and pastry breakfast. AE, DC, DISC, MC, V. Closed Oct to mid-May.* This old, low-slung building among stunted black spruce contains an unlikely find—fresh, new rooms inside, and a hospitable host: a former professional wildlife photographer. These are excellent basic rooms for a reasonable price.

**CAMPGROUNDS**  The park has eight campgrounds. Recreational vehicles can find a place, as can tent campers who want to be away from people out in the wilderness. The campgrounds range from 7 to 100 sites each. Here are the best and most popular.

**Riley Creek** is open all year (no water in winter). Camping fees are $12 per night. This is the traditional family campground, right at the park entrance. It's far from wilderness, but it's easy to get a permit here. It has 100 sites, paved roads, flush toilets, and a sewage dump station. For more ambitious campers, it's still a good stop for your first night in the park, when you need time to get your bearings before heading to a more remote area.

**Savage River** costs $12 per night. Just a mile short of the park road checkpoint beyond which vehicles cannot go, Savage River is both easily accessible and relatively remote, 13 miles from the park entrance. It's the best choice for car or RV campers who want to get away from the park entrance but don't have 3 days to spend camping at Teklanika. There are 33 sites. The rest rooms have flush toilets.

**Teklanika River** charges $12 per night. At milepost 29 on the park road, this is the only campground for car or RV camping beyond the checkpoint. You can drive in if you agree not to move your vehicle for at least 3 days. With 53 sites, it's a large campground, but the sites are adequately separated by trees. It has chemical toilets.

**Wonder Lake** costs $12 per night. The 28 tent-camping sites at this campground near the end of the park road are in high demand, in the woods next to a placid mountain lake below spectacular views of Mt. McKinley. Despite the remote location, it has flush toilets and a ranger station is only 2 miles away. It doesn't open until mid-June, or whenever winter finally ends.

## DINING

Most of the good restaurants are located at hotels, including **The Perch** (see Accommodations, above) and the **Chalet Center Cafe** at the McKinley Resorts Chalets, which I recommend.

**Lynx Creek Pizza.** *Milepost 238.6, Parks Hwy.* ☎ *907/683-2547. All items $6–$8.25. AE, DISC, MC, V. Daily 11am–11:30pm. Closed early Sept to late May. PIZZA.* This ARA-owned pizza restaurant is a center of activity for the less–well-heeled visitors to Denali, more for being the only place to get a slice and a cheap beer than for the quality of the food, which wouldn't be so popular if there were any competition.

✪ **Overlook Bar and Grill.** *Milepost 238.5, Parks Hwy., up the hill above the Denali Canyon area.* ☎ *907/683-2723. Lunch main courses $9–$17; dinner $8.50–$28. MC, V. Daily 11am–11pm. Closed mid-Sept to mid-May. STEAK AND SEAFOOD.* This is a fun, noisy place with lodge decor and a terrific view. The salmon and filet mignon are well seasoned and done to a turn, and the service is friendly, although the main course was slow to arrive. An extraordinary variety of microbrews is available.

# 4  Fairbanks

Discovered by accident and later fortified by gold-rushers, Fairbanks is now Alaska's second-largest city, with a population of about 38,000, but it has never learned to put on airs. It sprawls, broad and flat, along big highways and the Chena River. It's a friendly, easygoing town, but one where people still take gold and their independence seriously. There's another gold rush going on, north of the city, and plenty of prospectors are still searching the hills. And Fairbanks is the hotbed of the Alaskan Independence Party, whose platform advocates the state's secession from the Union and recognition as an independent nation. Former Gov. Wally Hickel was elected under its banner in 1990, although he didn't adopt all its positions. Fairbanks is an adamant, loopy, affable place; it doesn't seem to mind being a little bizarre or residing far from the center of things. And that makes it an intensely Alaskan city, for those are the qualities Alaskans most cherish in their myth of themselves.

Anchorage and Fairbanks maintain a great rivalry. In Fairbanks, they say Anchorage is as close as you can get to Alaska without actually being there. In Anchorage, Fairbanks is known as "Squarebanks." It's 40° below zero in winter, but in summer, under seemingly endless blue 85° skies, Fairbanksans wonder how anyone could live anywhere else. There's plenty to do in Fairbanks, much of it at least a little corny. It's a terrific destination for families; there are good opportunities for hiking and mountain biking, and great opportunities for canoeing and slow river float trips.

## ARRIVING & DEPARTING

**BY PLANE**    **Fairbanks International Airport** has direct jet service on **Alaska Airlines** (☎ 800/426-0333 or 907/474-9175) from Anchorage, and has flights with various carriers to many of Alaska's Interior and Arctic communities.

**BY CAR**   Fairbanks is a transportation hub. Exploring the region on your own requires a car. **Avis** and **Hertz** are at the airport; **Affordable** is at 3101 S. Cushman St. (☎ **907/ 452-7341**).

**BY BUS**   Gray Line's **Alaskon Express** (☎ **907/456-7741**) offers service 3 days a week from the Westmark Fairbanks down the Alaska Highway to Haines and Skagway.

**BY RAIL**   The **Alaska Railroad** (☎ **800/544-0552** or **907/456-4155**) links Fairbanks to Denali National Park and Anchorage to the south, with connections to Seward in the summer. The fare is $53 to Denali and $149 to Anchorage.

## ESSENTIALS

**VISITOR INFORMATION**   The **Fairbanks Convention and Visitor Bureau** maintains a comprehensive visitor center in a large log building on the Chena River by Golden Heart Plaza, at 550 First Ave. (at Cushman Street), Fairbanks, AK 99701 (☎ **800/327-5774** or **907/456-5774**), open in summer, daily 8am–8pm; in winter, Mon–Fri 8am–5pm. Get maps, including a road map and the good downtown walking-tour map.

The ✪ **Alaska Public Lands Information Center,** at 250 Cushman St. (at Third Avenue), Suite 1A, Fairbanks, AK 99701 (☎ **907/456-0527**), open in summer, daily 9am–6pm, and in winter, Tue–Sat 10am–6pm, is an indispensable stop for anyone planning to spend time in the outdoors. Besides providing detailed information on all of Alaska's public lands and answering questions and giving advice on outings, the center has a small museum about the state's regions and the gear needed to explore them.

**GETTING AROUND**   It's possible to see much of Fairbanks without a car, staying in the downtown area and making excursions by bus, but the city is designed around the car and that's the easiest way to see the best sights. **Fairbanks Taxi** (☎ **907/ 456-3333**) is liable to be an expensive choice because everything is so far apart.

To see the widely scattered attractions without a car, try the **G.O. Shuttle Service** (☎ **800/478-3847** or **907/474-3847**), a special bus, van, and car system geared to independent travelers. The company offers a regular route of the tourist areas throughout the day (an all-day pass costs $25), as well as on-call shuttle service to the airport, train depot, and major attractions.

**EMERGENCIES**   Dial ☎ **911.** For nonemergencies, call the **Alaska State Troopers** (☎ **907/452-2114**) or the **Fairbanks Police Department** (☎ **907/459-6500**). **Fairbanks Memorial Hospital** is at 1650 Cowles St. (☎ **907/452-8181**).

## ATTRACTIONS

To explore downtown Fairbanks, pick up the walking-tour map available at the visitor center. Don't miss the **Fairbanks Ice Museum** to see what Alaska is like most of the year.

✪ **Alaskaland.** *Airport Way and Peger Rd. Admission free. Memorial Day–Labor Day, daily 11am–9pm.* Alaskaland is called a theme park, but it's more like a city park with a theme. Most of Fairbanks's history has been moved here. A village of log cabins contains shops and restaurants, each marked with its original location. But the SS *Nenana* is the park's centerpiece. This huge sternwheeler plied the Yukon and Tanana rivers until 1957. It had nearly collapsed from rot by 1982 before a major community restoration effort saved it from the scrap heap. Tour groups generally come for the $18.95 all-you-can-eat **Alaska Salmon Bake** (☎ **907/452-7274**), and the nightly **Golden Heart Revue** at the Palace Theater (☎ **907/456-5960**), which covers the founding of Fairbanks with comedy and song.

✪ **Creamers's Field.** *Off College Rd. For information, call the Alaska Department of Fish and Game (☎ 907/459-7200) Summer, Tues–Fri 10am–5pm, Sat 10am–3pm.*

This migratory waterfowl refuge is an old dairy homestead right in Fairbanks. The pastures are a prime stopover point for Canada geese, pintails, and golden plovers in the spring and fall. Sandhill cranes, shovelers, and mallards show up all summer. I especially enjoyed the well-interpreted boreal forest nature walk.

✪ **Riverboat _Discovery_.** ☎ *907/479-6673. Admission $36.95 adults, $25.95 children.* There's nothing intimate or spontaneous about this 3¹/₂-hour ride with 700 passengers down the Chena and Tanana rivers. But the Binkley family, who have been in the riverboat business since the Klondike gold rush and still run the boat today, still provide a fun, educational experience for a bargain price. Onshore demonstrations include a bush plane taking off and landing, fish cutting at a Native fish camp, and the backyard of five-time Iditarod champion Susan Butcher, who often shows off the dogs herself. The boat leaves from a landing off Dale Road near the airport.

✪ **University of Alaska Museum.** *At the University of Alaska–Fairbanks, University Ave. Admission $5. June–Aug, daily 9am–7pm; May, 9am–5pm; winter, Sat–Sun noon–7pm.* This is the state's largest research museum, containing nine labs and huge cultural and scientific collections. In fact, its only weakness is that it tries to do so much in too small a space: a display on emission spectrums is side-by-side with a stuffed lynx, a woven root basket, and a broad-view aurora camera. Don't miss the daily shows: There's a presentation of Native games and dance at 11am and 2pm daily, and an aurora presentation at 10am and 3pm daily, during the summer. They cost extra.

## ACCOMMODATIONS

The **Bed and Breakfast Reservation Service,** P.O. Box 71131, Fairbanks, AK 99707 (☎ **800/770-8165** or 907/479-8165; fax 907/474-8448), represents more than 50 B&Bs, including the All Seasons, listed below. You can also get detailed information at the visitor center. The local bed tax is 8%.

✪ **All Seasons Bed and Breakfast.** *763 Seventh Ave., Fairbanks, AK 99701.* ☎ *888/457-6649 or 907/451-6649. Fax 907/474-8448. 8 rms. High season, $100 double. Low season, $65 double. Rates include full breakfast. Additional person $20 extra. AE, CB, DC, DISC, MC, V.* More of an inn than a bed-and-breakfast, this attractive house close to downtown was recently renovated, and the result is inspired. The rooms are elegant and have VCRs; there's a common room downstairs if you want to socialize, and a glassed-in sunporch. It's quite a value in overpriced Fairbanks. Newspapers are free.

**Fairbanks Hotel.** *517 Third Ave., Fairbanks, AK 99701.* ☎ *888/329-4685 or 907/456-6411. Fax 907/456-1792. 35 rms, 11 with bath. High season, $65–$89 double. Low season, $55–$70 double. AE, MC, V.* Four women took over a notorious flop house in 1996 and transformed it into a charming art deco historic hotel, in the core of downtown. Although small, the rooms are light and attractively decorated, including brass beds and other period touches. And, still undiscovered, they're quite a bargain.

**Golden North Motel.** *4888 Old Airport Way, Fairbanks, AK 99701.* ☎ *800/447-1910 in the U.S., 800/478-1910 in Canada, or 907/479-6201. 41 rms, 21 suites. High season, $69 double; $99 suite. Low season, $50 double; $75 suite. AE, DISC, MC, V.* The Baer family, owners since 1971, keep the rooms in this motel clean and up-to-date, making it a good bargain favored by Alaskans in town from the Bush to shop or just visiting Fairbanks by car. The rooms are small, but the reasonably priced suites are a good choice for families. A courtesy van and free coffee and pastry in the lobby is available.

✪ **Wedgewood Resort.** *212 Wedgewood Dr., Fairbanks, AK 99701.* ☎ *800/528-4916 or 907/452-1442. Fax 907/451-8184. 150 rms, 300 apts. High season, $180 double; $150–$160 apt for 2. Low season, $70–$80 apt for 2. AE, DC, DISC, MC, V.*

Off College Road, this huge property has both upscale standard hotel rooms and a large complex of guest apartments. The decor in the apartments is dark, but there's no better place for a family or business traveler to stay. The new rooms, open in the summer only, are among the best in Fairbanks. The resort provides a courtesy van, free newspapers, and a coin-op laundry. There are two restaurants and a lounge (summer only).

## DINING

For a family pizza, try **Pizza Bella** on Airport Way; for burgers go to the **Food Factory** on South Cushman Street.

**The Bakery.** *69 College Rd.* ☎ *907/456-8600. Lunch $6–$7; dinner $7–$14. No credit cards. Mon–Sat 6am–9pm, Sun 7am–4pm. DINER.* There are an infinite number of old-fashioned coffeehouses in Fairbanks—where a gold miner can find a hearty meal, a motherly waitress, and a bottomless cup of coffee. This is the best of the lot— quite a statement. The sourdough pancakes are mind-expanding, the service friendly, and the prices low.

✪ **Gambardella'a Pasta Belle.** *706 Second Ave.* ☎ *907/456-3417. Main courses $12–$15; lunch $4.25–$10.50. 15% gratuity added for parties of 5 or more, or for split checks. AE, MC, V. Mon–Sat 11am–10pm, Sun 5–10pm. ITALIAN.* The quality of the southern Italian cuisine—the lasagna particularly—is a cut above everything else in Fairbanks, the prices are low, and the service efficient. You can eat in an attractive dining room on white tablecloths, but on a sunny day nothing could be more pleasant than dining on the patio among the hanging flowers.

**Plate and Palette Gallery Cafe.** *310 First St.* ☎ *907/451-9294. Lunch $6– $8. No credit cards. Daily 7am–10am and 11am–3pm. SANDWICHES AND SALADS.* There's no more delightful place for a healthy sandwich, quiche, salad, or other light fare. The dining room is a serious gallery of art and crafts, the various little chambers each containing a table or two and the diverse output of this college town's visual artists. Children are exceptionally well treated.

## FAIRBANKS AFTER DARK

Fairbanks has a lot of tourist-oriented evening activities, as well as entertainment also attended by locals. Call the 24-hour event recording of what's playing currently, or check the *Fairbanks Daily News–Miner.* The best of the performing-arts scene is at the ✪ **Fairbanks Summer Arts Festival** (☎ 907/474-8869) and **Fairbanks Shakespeare** (☎ 907/457-POET), both special summer festivals. The **Ester Gold Camp,** P.O. Box 109, Ester, AK 99725 (☎ **907/479-2500;** fax 907/474-1780), is an 11-building historic site—an old mining town that's been turned into an evening tourist attraction. The main event is a gold-rush theme show at the **Malamute Saloon,** with singing and Robert Service poetry, nightly at 9pm; admission is $12.

# Hawaii

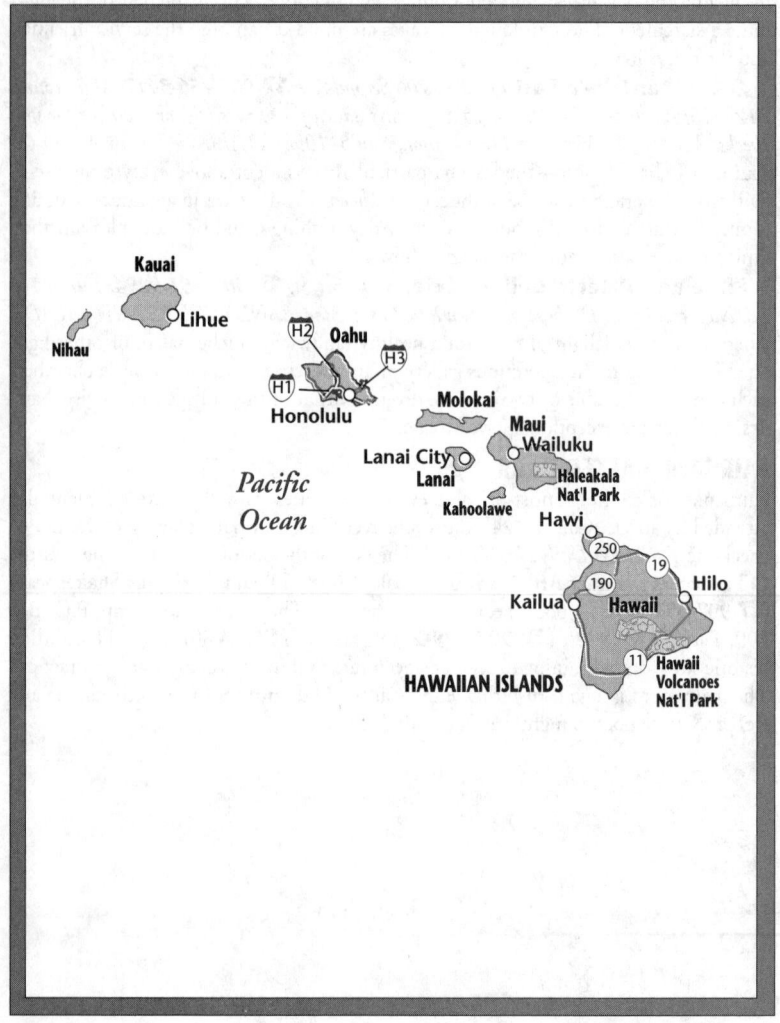

There's no place quite like this handful of sun-drenched mid-Pacific islands, so remote from any continent yet visited by nearly seven million guests a year. They come from the far corners of the globe seeking relaxation under the Hawaiian sun, and leave feeling good inside and out.

Yes, the mythical Hawaii of South Seas literature and Hollywood films really does exist, and the possibilities for adventure are endless. Each of the six main islands is separate and distinct, larger than life and infinitely complex, as anyone who ventures here soon discovers. You'll find palm-fringed blue lagoons, verdant rain forests, singing waterfalls, rugged canyons, and a bubbling volcano soaring 2 miles into the sky. And the beaches: With gold, red, black, and even green sands caressed by an endless surf, they're just as you imagined they would be. Come and see.

# 1 Honolulu & Oahu

It's astounding to spend hours flying across the barren blue of the Pacific and then to suddenly see below you the whites and pastels of Honolulu, the most remote big city on earth. Most visitors here end up along the canyonlike streets of Waikiki, Honolulu's famous hotel district and its most densely populated neighborhood. Some days it seems like the entire world is sunning itself on Waikiki's famous beach.

Out in the country, the island of Oahu can be as down-home as a slack-key guitar. That's where you'll find a big blue sky, perfect waves, empty beaches, rainbows and waterfalls, sweet tropical flowers, and fiery Pacific sunsets.

## ARRIVING & DEPARTING

**Honolulu International Airport** is the major gateway to all the islands. All major American and many international carriers fly here from the mainland U.S., and most major Pacific Rim international carriers land here as well.

The 30-minute taxi ride to downtown Honolulu costs about $18; about $25 to Waikiki. **Trans-Hawaiian Services** (☎ **808/566-7000**) provides van service every 20–30 minutes; it's $7 one-way to Waikiki, $12 round-trip. Book ahead for hotel pickup for a departing flight. **TheBUS** nos. 10 and 20 (Waikiki Beach and Hotels) take about an hour to get from the airport to downtown Honolulu and Waikiki; the one-way fare is $1, and students pay 50¢, exact change only. You can bring a carry-on or small suitcase on TheBUS as long as it fits under the seat.

# ESSENTIALS

**VISITOR INFORMATION** The **Hawaii Visitor and Convention Bureau,** has an office at 2270 Kalakaua Ave., 7th floor, Honolulu, HI 96815 (☎ 808/923-1811). **Waikiki Oahu Visitor Association** is at 1001 Bishop St., Pauahi Tower, Suite 47, Honolulu, HI 96813 (☎ 800/OAHU-678 or 808/524-0722).

**RESOURCES FOR TRAVELERS WITH SPECIAL NEEDS** The **Commission on Persons with Disabilities,** 919 Ala Moana Blvd., Honolulu, HI 96814 (☎ 808/586-8121), and the **Hawaii Center for Independent Living,** 677 Ala Moana Blvd., Suite 118, Honolulu, HI 96813 (☎ 808/537-1941), can provide information and send you a copy of the *Aloha Guide to Accessibility* ($3). **HandiCabs of the Pacific** (☎ 808/524-3866) provides wheelchair taxi service and a variety of wheelchair-accommodated activities.

**EMERGENCIES** Call ☎ 911 for police, fire, and ambulance. Hospitals offering 24-hour emergency care in Honolulu include **Queens Medical Center,** 1301 Punchbowl St. (☎ 808/538-9011), and **Kaiser Permanente Medical Center,** Honolulu Clinic, 1010 Pensacola St. (☎ 808/593-2950).

# GETTING AROUND

Having a car is the best way to see the countryside, but traffic can be heavy on the mostly two-lane roads beyond the city. You can avoid the gridlock by driving between 9am and 3pm or after 6pm. All of the major car-rental firms have agencies on Oahu.

**BY BUS** One of the best deals anywhere, **TheBUS** (☎ 808/848-4444, or 808/296-1818 for recorded information) goes around the whole island for $1. You can buy a Visitor Pass for $10 at any ABC convenience store in Waikiki; it's good for unlimited rides anywhere on Oahu for 4 days. The most popular route is no. 8, which shuttles between Waikiki and Ala Moana Center every 10 minutes or so (the ride takes 15–20 minutes). To see the island, take Circle Island–North Shore no. 52 (Wahaiwa/Circle Island); it leaves from Ala Moana Shopping Center every half hour and takes about 4½ hours to circle the island. The Circle Island–South Shore route is no. 55 (Kaneohe/Circle Island) and also leaves Ala Moana every half hour and takes about 3 hours to circle the island.

**BY TROLLEY** The 34-seat, open-air, motorized **Waikiki Trolley** (☎ 800/824-8804 or 808/596-2199) loops around Waikiki and downtown Honolulu, stopping every 40 minutes at 12 key places. A 1-day pass at $17 for adults, $5 for children under 12, allows you to jump on and off all day long.

**BY TAXI** Try **Aloha State Cab** (☎ 808/847-3566); **Charley's Taxi & Tours** (☎ 808/531-1333); **City Taxi** (☎ 808/524-2121); **Royal Taxi & Tour** (☎ 808/944-5513); **Sida Taxi & Tours** (☎ 808/836-0011); **Star Taxi** (☎ 808/942-7827); or **TheCab** (☎ 808/422-2222). **Coast Taxi** (☎ 808/261-3755) serves Windward Oahu; **Hawaii Kai Hui/Koko Head Taxi** (☎ 808/396-6633) serves East Honolulu/Southeast Oahu.

# WHAT TO SEE & DO

**BEACHES** No beach anywhere is so widely known or so universally sought after than **Waikiki Beach,** a 1½-mile-long crescent of sand at the foot of a string of high-rise hotels that's home to the world's longest-running beach party. Waikiki is fabulous for swimming, surfing, diving, sailing, and snorkeling. But Oahu's most popular snorkel spot is **Hanauma Bay,** a marine life conservation district where the fish are so friendly they'll eat right out of your hand. Go early—it gets crowded. If you're looking for a postcard-perfect Hawaiian beach, head to the Windward Coast's **Lanikai Beach.**

Because golden Lanikai is in a residential neighborhood, it's the perfect place to enjoy a quiet day at the beach. If you're looking for the perfect spot to watch world-class surfers ride the legendary North Shore winter waves, head to **Sunset Beach, Waimea Bay,** or—you've seen it on TV in the opening shot of *Hawaii Five-O*—the **Banzai Pipeline,** where daredevils shoot perfect wave tubes. They'll keep you spellbound for hours.

**ATTRACTIONS**    For just about as long as anyone can remember, the Eastman Kodak Company has been hosting the **Kodak Hula Show** at the Waikiki Band Shell at Kapiolani Park on Tuesday, Wednesday, and Thursday 10–11:15am. Admission is free. For more information, call ☎ **808/627-3300.**

**Bishop Museum.** *1525 Bernice St.* ☎ *808/847-3511 or 808/848-4129. Admission $8 adults, $7 ages 6–17 and seniors. Daily 9am–5pm.* The world's greatest collection of natural and cultural artifacts from Hawaii and the Pacific are found here. The Bishop is jam-packed with more than 20 million acquisitions—there are 12 million insect specimens alone—from ceremonial spears to calabashes to old photos of topless hula dancers.

**Iolani Palace.** *King and Richards sts.* ☎ *808/522-0832. Admission $6 adults, $1 children 5–13. Guided tours conducted Wed–Sat 9am–2:15pm. Call ahead to reserve. You must be booked on a guided tour to enter the palace; children under 5 not permitted.* This royal palace was built by King David Kalakaua, who spared no expense. The 10-room palace attracts 100,000 visitors a year in groups of 20, who must don denim booties to scoot across the royal floors. The 45-minute tour is well worth your time.

**National Cemetery of the Pacific.** *Punchbowl Crater, 2177 Puowaina Dr.* ☎ *808/541-1434. Admission free. Daily 8am–5:30pm (until 6pm Mar–Sept).* The old Punchbowl crater is a burial ground for 35,000 victims of World War II and the Korean and Vietnam wars. Among the graves you'll find many unmarked ones of servicemen killed during the Japanese attack on Pearl Harbor on December 7, 1941. Some forever will be unknown; others are famous, like war correspondent Ernie Pyle, killed by a Japanese sniper in April 1945 on Okinawa.

**Polynesian Cultural Center.** *55–370 Kamehameha Hwy., Laie.* ☎ *808/ 293-3333. Waikiki office, 2255 Kuhio Ave., Suite 1601.* ☎ *808/923-2911. Admission $44 adults, $27 children 5–11. Luau, $57 adults, $37 children. Ambassador VIP (deluxe) tour, $92 adults, $61 children. Mon–Sat 12:30–9:30pm.* This 42-acre lagoon park makes it easy to experience the authentic songs, dance, costumes, and architecture of seven Pacific islands by re-creating villages of Hawaii, Tonga, Fiji, Samoa, the Marquesas, New Zealand, and Easter Island. You "travel" through this kind of "living" museum by canoe on a man-made freshwater lagoon. Each village is "inhabited" by native students from Polynesia, who attend Hawaii's Bright Young University. Operated by the Mormon Church, the park also features a variety of stage shows, which celebrate the music, dance, history, and culture of Polynesia. There's a luau every evening. Since a visit can take up to 8 hours, it's a good idea to arrive in the morning.

**USS *Arizona* Memorial at Pearl Harbor.** *Pearl Harbor.* ☎ *808/422-0561. Daily 7:30am–5pm (shuttles run 8am–3pm). Admission free. Children under 12 must be accompanied by adults.* During the December 7, 1941, Japanese attack, the 608-foot battleship USS *Arizona* sank in 9 minutes without firing a shot, taking 1,177 sailors and marines to a fiery death. The memorial is a stark-white 184-foot rectangle that spans the sunken hull of the ship. Try to arrive early at the visitor center to avoid the huge crowds; 1- to 3-hour waits are common. No reservations are taken. Allow at least 4 hours to visit the memorial.

**Waikiki Aquarium.** *2777 Kalakaua Ave.* ☎ *808/923-9741. Admission $6 adults, $4 seniors and students, $3 ages 13–17. Daily 9am–5pm.* This is a small but first-class

# Honolulu

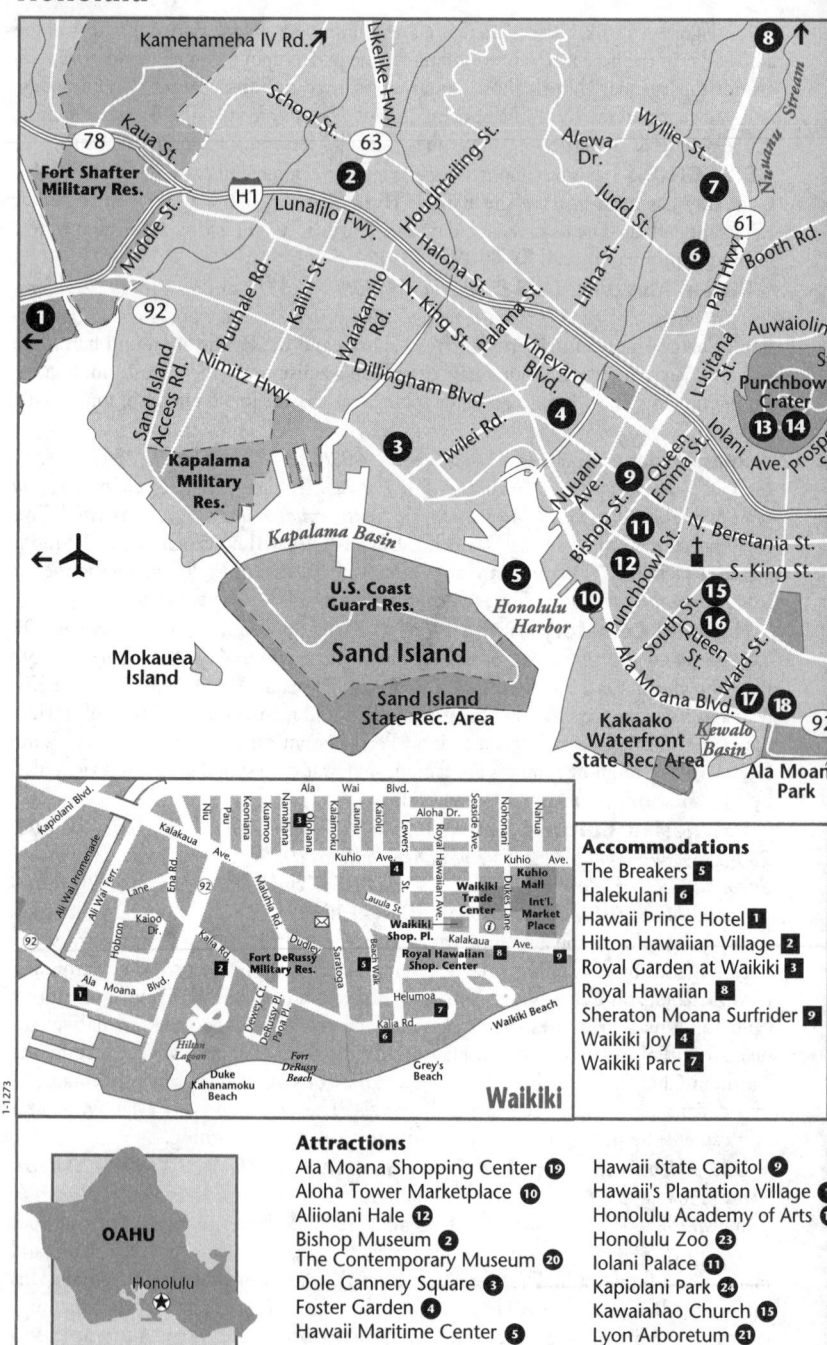

**Accommodations**
The Breakers **5**
Halekulani **6**
Hawaii Prince Hotel **1**
Hilton Hawaiian Village **2**
Royal Garden at Waikiki **3**
Royal Hawaiian **8**
Sheraton Moana Surfrider **9**
Waikiki Joy **4**
Waikiki Parc **7**

**Attractions**
Ala Moana Shopping Center **19**
Aloha Tower Marketplace **10**
Aliiolani Hale **12**
Bishop Museum **2**
The Contemporary Museum **20**
Dole Cannery Square **3**
Foster Garden **4**
Hawaii Maritime Center **5**

Hawaii State Capitol **9**
Hawaii's Plantation Village **6**
Honolulu Academy of Arts **1**
Honolulu Zoo **23**
Iolani Palace **11**
Kapiolani Park **24**
Kawaiahao Church **15**
Lyon Arboretum **21**

1-1273

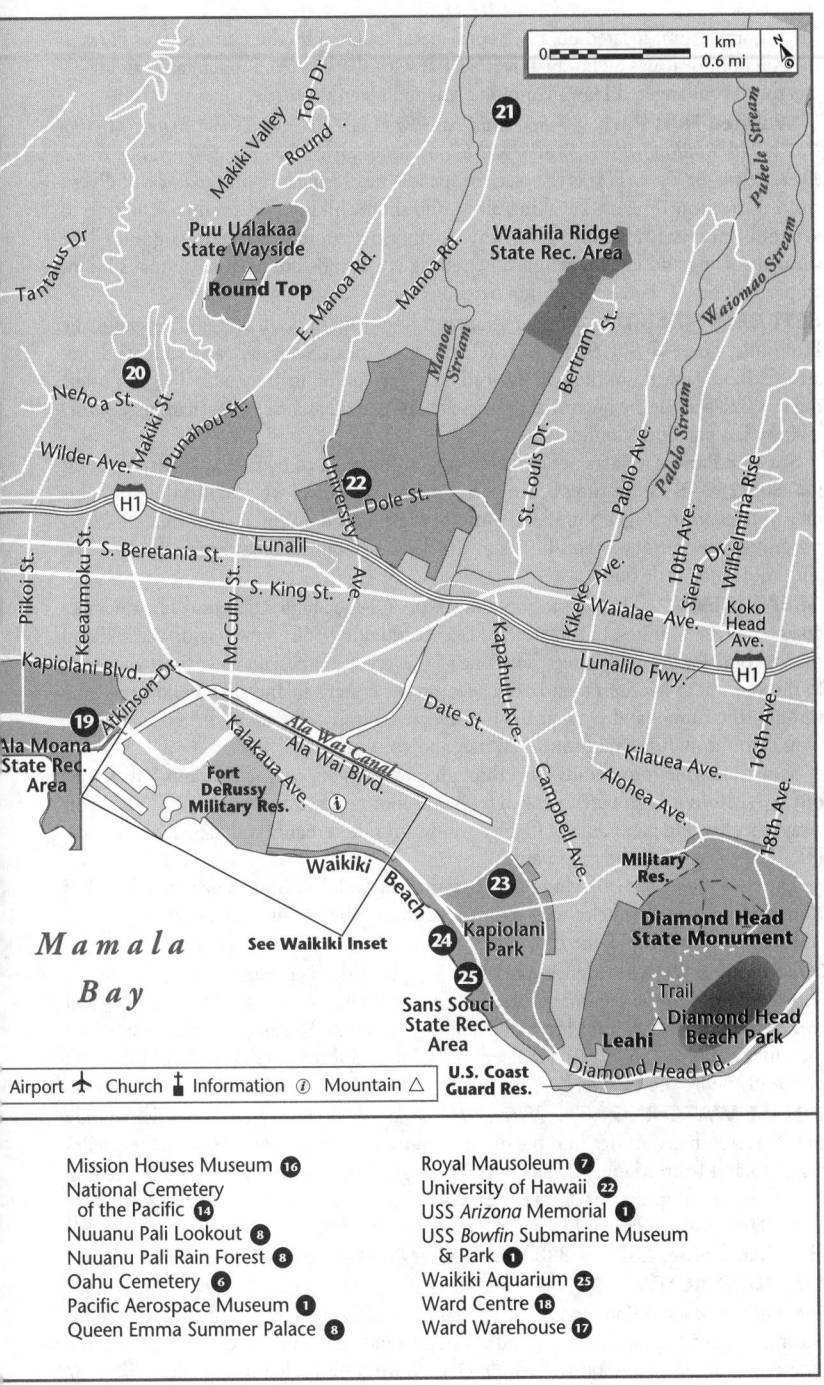

Airport ✈ Church ⌖ Information ⓘ Mountain △ U.S. Coast Guard Res.

| | |
|---|---|
| Mission Houses Museum ⑯ | Royal Mausoleum ⑦ |
| National Cemetery of the Pacific ⑭ | University of Hawaii ㉒ |
| | USS *Arizona* Memorial ① |
| Nuuanu Pali Lookout ⑧ | USS *Bowfin* Submarine Museum |
| Nuuanu Pali Rain Forest ⑧ | & Park ① |
| Oahu Cemetery ⑥ | Waikiki Aquarium ㉕ |
| Pacific Aerospace Museum ① | Ward Centre ⑱ |
| Queen Emma Summer Palace ⑧ | Ward Warehouse ⑰ |

tropical aquarium, located on a live coral reef. Operated by the University of Hawaii, the aquarium features a Hawaiian reef habitat with sharks, eels, a touch tank, and habitats for the endangered Hawaiian monk seal and green sea turtle.

**Waimea Falls Park.** *59–864 Kamehameha Hwy., Haleiwa (North Shore).* ☎ *800/ 767-8046, 808/638-8511, or 808/942-5700. Admission $20 adults, $10 children 6–12. Daily 10am–5:30pm.* This is the place to spend a day seeing ancient hula or cliff divers, sniffing tropical flowers, kayaking along the shore, hiking and mountain biking to archeological sites and a waterfall, or playing ancient Hawaiian games like spear-throwing and lawn bowling. The setting is a 1,800-acre river valley that's full of tropical blooms. There's something here for everyone.

**BEST BETS FOR KIDS**   At the entrance to Kapiolani Park on Kapahula Avenue, the **Honolulu Zoo** (☎ 808/971-7171) features the African Savannah, a 10-acre wild preserve exhibit with more than 40 African critters roaming in the open. The zoo offers night walks—when the nocturnal beasties are out—and has a rare Hawaiian nene goose, a Hawaiian pig, and Mouflon sheep.

**Sea Life Park,** a 62-acre ocean theme park on Kalanianaole Hwy. at Makapuu Point (☎ 808/259-7933), features a "wolphin," a cross between a whale and a dolphin, plus orca whales from Puget Sound, Atlantic bottle-nosed dolphins, California sea lions, penguins going through their hoops to the delight of children, and more to entertain and inform the little ones.

**GREAT VIEWS**   The hike to the summit of 760-foot-high **Diamond Head Crater** takes about 45 minutes, but the reward is a breathtaking 360° view—with Waikiki and the vast blue Pacific at your feet. This one's for everyone, especially kids. Start your hike to the summit at Monserrat and 18th aves. on the crater's inland side. Follow the road through the tunnel and park in the lot; the paved trail starts there. Bring a flashlight (you'll go through several tunnels), water, and your camera.

Sometimes gale-force winds howl through the mountain pass at **Nuuanu Pali Lookout,** a 1,186-foot-high perch flanked by 3,000-foot peaks. If the winds don't blow you away, the dizzying panorama of Oahu's windward side certainly will. The lookout is on Hi. 61 at the crest of the mountain.

The best sunset view of Honolulu is from **Puu Ualakaa State Park,** at the end of Round Hill Drive. On a clear day you can see almost the length of Oahu. At night, several scenic overlooks provide romantic spots for lovers.

**SUBMARINE DIVES**   Here's your chance to play Jules Verne and experience the underwater world in the comfort of a submarine. It'll take you on a 2-hour ride 60–100 feet below the surface. Subs leave from Hilton Hawaiian Village Pier. The cost is $85 for adults, $39 for kids 12 and younger; call **Atlantis Submarines** at ☎ 800/548-6262 or 808/973-9811 to reserve.

**WHALE-WATCHING**   The *Navatek II,* the so-called "no seasick" boat, is the only tourist vessel that ventures into the often choppy waters off Koko Head, where whales cruise to and from Maui. In whale season (roughly January to April), whale-watching cruises depart from Pier 6, on the Diamond Head side of Aloha Tower Marketplace, at 8:30am, and return at 11am. The cost is $39 adults, $24 children 2–11. Call **Hawaiian Cruises Ltd.** (☎ 800/852-4183 or 808/848-6360) to reserve.

**OUTDOOR ACTIVITIES**   Oahu is a wonderful place to scuba dive, from the famous wreck of the *Mahi* to Kahuna Canyon, a massive underwater Grand Canyon, with crabs, octopi, slippers, spiny lobsters, and an occasional shark in the distance. Hawaii's oldest and largest dive shop is **Aaron's Dive Shop,** 602 Kailua Rd., Kailua (☎ 808/ 262-2333).

For snorkeling, there's no place like **Hanauma Bay:** clear, warm water and an abundance of fish that are so friendly they'll eat out of your hand. The best thing about this underwater park is that anyone can join the fun: Just wade in and look down. It can get crowded, so go early. Braver snorkelers may want to head to **Shark's Cove,** on the North Shore just off Kamehameha Highway, between Haleiwa and Pupukea. This big, lava-edged pool is one of Oahu's best snorkel spots in summer.

A wonderful adventure is to rent a kayak, arrive at **Lanikai Beach** just as the sun is appearing, and paddle across the emerald lagoon to the pyramid-shaped islands off the beach called Mokulua—it's an experience you won't forget. First-timers should go to **Waimea Falls Park** (☎ 808/638-8511), on the North Shore, for lessons and equipment.

When they come to Hawaii, otherwise rational people who have never set foot on a boat in their life suddenly want to go out to sea. If you can afford it, go with **Hawaiian Cruises Ltd.** (☎ 800/852-4183 or 808/848-6360), which charges $155 adults, $115 children for sunset dinner cruises, $45 for lunch voyages.

Summer is surf season in Waikiki, the best place to learn how to ride the boards on Oahu. Go early to **Aloha Beach Service,** next to the Sheraton Moana Surfrider (☎ 808/922-3111), where beach boys offer surfing lessons. You must know how to swim.

The island's 33 major **hiking trails** take you across razor-thin ridge backs, or deep into waterfall valleys. Check out Stuart Ball's *The Hikers Guide to Oahu* (Honolulu: University of Hawaii Press, 1993) before you go. For a free Oahu Recreation Map, listing all 33 trails, contact the **Department of Land and Natural Resources,** 1151 Punchbowl St., Room 130, Honolulu, HI 96813 (☎ 808/587-0300). They'll also send you free trail maps upon request and issue camping permits.

Oahu has 35 golf courses. Among them, *Golf Digest* named 6,867-yard, par-72 **Ko Olina Golf Course** (☎ 808/676-5300) one of America's top 75 resort courses in 1992 and rated **Turtle Bay Hilton Golf & Tennis Club** (☎ 808/293-8574) the fourth best new resort course in 1994. **Hawaii Kai Golf Course** (☎ 808/395-2358), on east Oahu, is a moderately challenging option.

**SHOPPING**   Real Tahitians fly in to do their Christmas shopping at **Ala Moana Center,** at Ala Moana Boulevard and Atkinson Drive (☎ 808/946-2811), a teeming megalopolis of mainland chain stores anchored by Sears and JC Penney. There's a good food court here. Both dining and shopping diversions abound at **Aloha Tower Marketplace,** on the Honolulu waterfront between piers 8 and 11 (☎ 808/528-5700). Various Honolulu trolleys stop at the Marketplace, but if you want a direct ride from Waikiki, take the $2 Aloha Tower Marketplace Express, which continues on to **Hilo Hattie's,** Hawaii's most famous name in aloha wear, in Iwilei.

## ACCOMMODATIONS

**AN ACCOMMODATIONS BOOKING AGENCY**   Barbara Campbell can help you find your dream accommodation through her booking agency, **Hawaii's Best Bed & Breakfast** (☎ 800/262-9912 or 808/885-4550; fax 808/885-0559; e-mail: bestbnb.@aloha.net). Barbara books only the best bed-and-breakfasts in Hawaii; she also happens to run her own fantastic B&B in Waimea: **Waimea Garden Cottages** (☎ 800/262-9912 or 808/885-4550).

○ **The Breakers.** *250 Beach Walk, Honolulu, HI 96815.* ☎ *800/426-0494 or 808/923-3181. Fax 808/923-7174. 70 rms. $91–$97 double; $120–$146 suite. AE, DC, MC, V.* A little gem in the midst of high-rise Waikiki, The Breakers is full of old-fashioned Hawaiian aloha, and it's only a few steps to the beach. It's set in six buildings around a tropical garden and pool, and it captures the tropical ambience with wooden jalousies and shoji doors. Slightly oversize rooms have a lanai and kitchen.

○ **Halekulani.** *2199 Kalia Rd., Honolulu, HI 96815.* ☎ *800/367-2343 or 808/ 923-2311. Fax 808/926-8004. 500 rms. $275–$440 double; from $595 suite. Packages available. AE, DC, JCB, MC, V. Valet parking $10.* This graceful example of old-style Hawaii architecture first rose in 1907 as bungalows by the sea but is today a world-class resort. It has only a thin sliver of beach, but the biggest and best appointed rooms in Waikiki all have memorable views of Diamond Head. Facilities include a restaurant, pool, seven upscale shops, hair salon, conference facilities, and fitness room.

**Hawaii Prince Hotel & Golf Club.** *100 Holomoana St., Honolulu, HI 96815.* ☎ *800/321-6248 or 808/956-1111. Fax 808/946-0811. 578 rms. $220–$350 double; from $450 suite. Packages available. AE, DC, DISC, JCB, MC, V. Self-parking $8, valet parking $12.* Overlooking Ala Wai Yacht Harbor, Waikiki's newest is a world-class city hotel that happens to be near the beach. It may not have its own beach, but every room has an ocean view. The 27-hole championship course designed by Arnold Palmer is in west Oahu (free shuttle). There's a pool on the premises.

**Hilton Hawaiian Village.** *2005 Kalia Rd., Honolulu, HI 96815.* ☎ *800/ HILTONS or 808/949-4321. Fax 808/947-7898. 2,907 rms. $165–$335 double; from $305 suite. Packages available. AE, DC, DISC, JCB, MC, V. Self-parking $9; valet parking $12.* Hawaii's largest resort is a fanciful modern re-creation of a Hawaiian village including a man-made lagoon near the beach and Waikiki's largest swimming pool. Big, beautiful rooms and suites are dazzling by Waikiki standards. Dinner theater stars Charo. The resort includes a shopping village, fitness center, 36-hole minigolf course, and wedding chapel.

**Manoa Valley Inn.** *2001 Vancouver Dr., Honolulu, HI 96822.* ☎ *800/535-0085 or 808/947-6019. Fax 808/946-6168. 8 rms, 1 suite, 1 cottage. $99–$190 double. Rates include continental breakfast and evening wine and cheese. AE, DC, JCB, MC, V. Free parking.* Off the tourist trail and far from the beach and Waikiki, this historic 1915 eclectic Carpenter Gothic home on a quiet residential street near the University of Hawaii campus offers guests a taste of lifestyles of the rich in early Honolulu. Rooms have old-fashioned decor, and a genteel manner pervades the place.

**Outrigger Coral Seas.** *250 Lewers St., Honolulu, HI 96815.* ☎ *800/688-7444 or 808/923-3881. 932 rms. $60–$75 double; $125 suite. Packages available. AE, CB, DC, DISC, JCB, MC, V. Parking $7.* At the heart of Waikiki on busy little Lewers Street, this small, clean hotel is one of the great bargains here. The rooms don't have ocean views and aren't grand, but this is the top choice in Waikiki for budget travelers.

○ **Royal Garden at Waikiki.** *440 Olohana St., Honolulu, HI 96815.* ☎ *800/ 367-5666 or 808/943-0202. Fax 808/946-8777. 249 rms. $120–$500 double; $295–$500 suite. Rates include continental breakfast. AE, DC, DISC, JCB, MC, V. Valet parking $7.* Tucked in a quiet side street in Waikiki, all this little gem lacks is the beach, which is a bit of a hike away. The rooms have VCRs, minikitchens, robes and slippers, and marble baths. A Euro-Asian restaurant opens to a pool with waterfall, and there's a great Japanese sushi bar. Laundry machines and a free shopper shuttle are available.

○ **Royal Hawaiian Hotel.** *2259 Kalakaua Ave., Honolulu, HI 96815.* ☎ *800/ 325-3535 or 808/923-7311. Fax 808/924-7098. 585 rms. $275–$475 double; from $425 suite. Packages available. AE, DC, JCB, MC, V. Self-parking $9; valet parking $13.* Built in 1927 with Moorish fantasy turrets and curlicues, this hotel resembles a Valentino movie set come to life in radiant flamingo pink. The old glamour is expressed in octagonal suite drawing rooms, custom-made floral wool carpets, koa wood doors carved with the Hawaiian royal seal, and other flourishes. There's a freshwater pool.

**Sheraton Moana Surfrider Hotel.** *2365 Kalakaua Ave., Honolulu, HI 96815.* ☎ *800/325-3535 or 808/922-3111. Fax 808/923-0308. 835 rms. $210–$350 double;*

*from $650 suite. Packages available. AE, CB, DC, ER, JCB, MC, V. Self-parking $9; valet parking $15.* A registered national landmark, this striking Victorian "First Lady of Waikiki" launched tourism here a century ago. Banyan Wing rooms aren't large by today's standards, but they have an inimitable Victorian charm. Others are in an adjoining concrete high-rise tower. The hotel has a pool and shops. Guests can use the fitness center at Sheraton Waikiki.

**Waikiki Joy.** *320 Lewers St., Honolulu, HI 96815.* ☎ *800/922-7866 or 808/ 923-2300. Fax 808/924-4010. 94 rms. $115–$165 double; $175–$190 club suite; $240– $260 executive suite. Additional person $15 extra. Rates include continental breakfast. Call about special deals. AE, CB, DC, MC, V. Valet parking $10.* This is a hidden jewel, an oasis right in the heart of busy Waikiki, offering not only outstanding personal service but also a Bose entertainment system and Jacuzzi in every room. The tropical veranda with swimming pool, sauna, and furnished deck sets the scene for the beautifully decorated guests rooms.

**Waikiki Parc.** *2233 Helumoa Rd., Honolulu, HI 96815.* ☎ *800/422-0450 or 808/ 921-7272. Fax 808/923-1336. 298 rms. $170–$255 double. Additional person $30 extra. Packages available. AE, CB, DC, JCB, MC, V. Valet parking $9.* Just 100 yards from the beach at Waikiki, this 22-story luxury property has been dubbed the "Halekulani, Jr.," since it's similar to its parent hotel in its elegant simplicity, personalized service, and sophisticated style. Rooms here are beautifully done with ceramic tile floors and inlaid carpeting, conversation areas, armoires, and custom rattan furniture. There's a freshwater pool.

**WINDWARD OAHU ACCOMMODATIONS**   Pat O'Malley of **Pat's Kailua Beach Properties,** 204 S. Kalaheo Ave., Kailua, HI 96734 (☎ **808/261-1653** or 808/ 262-4128; fax 808/262-8275 or 808/261-0893), offers more than 25 houses and cottages near Kailua Beach, from a million-dollar estate right on the water to cottages on or close to the beach. Each unit is different, but all are fully furnished and include cooking and dining utensils, bedding and towels, telephone and TV. Rates range from $60 to $325.

On Oahu's most scenic gold-sand beach, the gracious and nostalgic 1924 **John Walker's Beach House,** 826 Mokulua Dr., Lanikai Beach, HI 96734 (☎ **800/ 258-7895** or 808/261-7895; fax 808/262-2181), is a fully equipped, restored hideaway with modern amenities. The lanai is exactly three giant steps to the beach.

**NORTH SHORE ACCOMMODATIONS**   **Ke Iki Hale,** 59–579 Ke Iki Rd., Haleiwa, HI 96712 (☎ **800/377-4030** or 808/638-8229), is a collection of rustic one- and two-bedroom duplex cottages snuggled on a stretch of beach between two legendary surf spots, Waimea Bay and the Banzai Pipeline. Kitchens, barbecues, hammocks, and laundries provide some of the comforts of home.

**BED & BREAKFASTS**   Windward Oahu is the B&B capital of Hawaii. Prices start at $55 a night for accommodations that can range from a room with bath in a private home to a $1,000-a-night Lanikai beachfront estate. **Hawaii Islands Bed-and-Breakfast & Vacation Rentals,** 572 Kailua Rd., Suite 201, Kailua, HI 96734 (☎ **800/ 258-7895** or 808/261-7895), has more than 400 B&Bs and vacation rentals available on all the islands; it also offers plane/car-rental packages at deep discounts. **Honolulu Bed-and-Breakfast (Statewide),** 3242 Kaohinani Dr., Honolulu, HI 96817 (☎ **800/ 288-4666** or 808/595-7533), also offers low-cost alternatives to hotels.

## DINING

Dining out is a popular pastime in Honolulu, and Hawaii regional cuisine has recently been gaining recognition for its blending of influences and its use of native Hawaiian foodstuffs.

**A Pacific Cafe Oahu.** *At Ward Centre, 1200 Ala Moana Blvd., Honolulu.* ☎ *808/593-0035. Reservations recommended. Main courses $19–$26. AE, DC, DISC, MC, V. Mon–Fri 11:30am–2pm; daily 5:30–10pm; appetizer bar, Fri–Sat 5:30–11pm. PACIFIC RIM/FRENCH/MEDITERRANEAN.* Noted Chef Jean Josselin sealed his fate as the brightest star in Hawaii's culinary galaxy. An informal, elegant, and inviting ambience sets the tone for an unforgettable celebration of epicurean joy. Try the warm tiger-eye ahi sushi tempura, pan-seared salmon, or any of the fresh fish dishes seared and cradled in sumptuous seasonings.

✪ **Akasaka.** *1646B Kona St., Honolulu.* ☎ *808/942-4466. Reservations recommended. Main courses $10–$19. AE, DC, DISC, MC, V. Mon–Sat 11am–2:30pm and 5pm–2am. JAPANESE.* Cozy, busy, casual, and occasionally smoky, with a tiny tatami room for small groups, Akasaka wins top scores for sushi, sizzling tofu and scallops, miso-clam soup, and overall quality and integrity of its Japanese cuisine.

✪ **Alan Wong's Restaurant.** *1857 S. King St., 5th Fl.* ☎ *808/949-2526. Reservations recommended. Main courses $15–$20. AE, MC, V. Daily 5–10pm. HAWAII REGIONAL.* Vertical cuisine is the trend at Chef Alan Wong's busy restaurant, a 90-seat room with a glassed-in terrace and open kitchen. Many dishes on his daily menus come in high-rise towers of multiple layers and colors, such as his famous ahi cake with layers of grilled eggplant, Maui onion, seared ahi, and Big Island goat cheese with lemongrass sauce.

**Broke the Mouth.** *Puck's Alley, 1023 University Ave., Moiliili.* ☎ *808/955-5599. Plate lunches $4–$6. Mon 9am–8pm, Tues–Sat 9am–9pm. It's open Mon–Fri 7am–5:30pm, Sat 10am–2pm. HEALTH FOOD/PLATE LUNCHES.* Big Island farmer Tip Davis successfully cloned his Hilo plate-lunch stand to rave reviews by busy diners who continue to embrace his taro/sweet-potato salad and tofu manapua. Everything is healthy, vegetarian, and inexpensive. Best bets: Mamo plate lunch, with greens, pesto pasta, for $5. There's another Broke the Mouth at 1148 Bishop St. in Honolulu (☎ *808/524-0355*).

**Cha Cha Cha.** *342 Seaside Ave., Waikiki.* ☎ *808/395-7797. Complete dinners $7–$9. MC, V. Daily 7:30am–midnight. MEXICAN/CARIBBEAN.* Nothing wimpy about the flavors here; the lime, coconut, and Caribbean spices make Cha Cha Cha more than plain ole Mex, adding zing to the fresh fish and shrimp ceviche, the jerk-chicken breast, and the shrimp and fish stew in lime broth.

**Chan's Chinese Restaurant.** *2600 S. King St., Honolulu.* ☎ *808/949-1188. Reservations recommended for large groups. Main courses $6–$14. AE, MC, V. Sun–Thurs 10:30am–midnight. CANTONESE/NORTHERN CHINESE.* Chan's is the quintessential, modest neighborhood eatery that opens early and closes late, doesn't oversalt its food, and serves noodles, seafood, and dim sum that would hold its own in Hong Kong. Ignore the decor; no one comes here for style.

**Diem.** *2633 S. King St., Honolulu.* ☎ *808/941-8657. Reservations recommended for dinner. Main courses $6–$10. AE, DISC, JCB, MC, V. Daily 10am–10pm. VIETNAMESE.* The tiny eatery in the university area has earned its following by word of mouth and spreads the taste treats with a thriving catering business. Best bets: Royal Seafood Noodle Soup, the best pho in town, and roll-up appetizers (fish, shrimp, beef, seafood).

**Hanaki.** *Sam Sung Plaza 101, 655 Keeaumoku St., Honolulu.* ☎ *808/955-1347. Reservations recommended for groups. Main courses $5–$14; Kaiseki $18–$20. AE, JCB, MC, V. Daily 11am–2pm and 5–10pm. JAPANESE.* Nabeyaki and noodles are Hanaki's specialties. Small and newly renovated, with a pleasantly quirky mix of Japanese noodles and oddities, Hanaki crosses many barriers in delivering simple, good food that is anything but boring.

✪ **Hawaii Seafood Paradise.** *1830 Ala Moana Blvd., Waikiki.* ☎ *808/ 946-4514. Reservations recommended. Main courses $7–$32. AE, DC, JCB, MC, V. Daily 6:30am–3am. CHINESE/SEAFOOD.* You can dine as simply or as lavishly as you choose in this quirky, unpretentious restaurant that serves the best Chinese food on Oahu. A few of the best items on the menu are written in Chinese with no English translation, so don't be afraid to ask questions.

I ♥ **Country Cafe.** *In Ala Moana Plaza, 451 Piikoi St., Honolulu.* ☎ *808/ 596-8108. Main courses $5–$9. MC, V. Mon–Sat 10:30am–9pm, Sun 10:30am–8pm. INTERNATIONAL.* Give yourself time to peruse the lengthy list of specials posted on the menu board, as well as the prodigious printed menu. This place is a beehive, with a mind-boggling selection that includes everything from shredded, moist roast turkey that may be better than grandma's to vegetarian tofu.

**Kahala Moon Cafe.** *4614 Kilauea Ave.* ☎ *808/732-7777. Reservations recommended. Main courses $15–$24. AE, MC, V. Tues–Fri 11am–2pm and 5:30–9:30pm; Fri–Sat 5:30–10pm; Sun 5:30–9:30pm. HAWAII REGIONAL.* With designer flowers in behemoth pots accenting a windowless room, Kahala Moon is a top choice for lunch and one of the top values for a special-occasion dinner. It isn't cheap, but many other restaurants of this ilk charge far more for far less culinary enjoyment. Don't miss the sake-steamed clams and lemon-herb–crusted crab cakes.

✪ **La Mer.** *In the Halekulani, 2199 Kalia Rd., Waikiki.* ☎ *808/923-2311. Reservations recommended. Main courses $34–$41; fixed-price dinner $85–$105. AE, CB, DC, JCB, MC, V. Daily 6–10pm. Jackets required for men. NEOCLASSIC FRENCH.* Honolulu's most elegant, sumptuous, and expensive dining takes place in this second-floor, open-sided, oceanside room with views of Diamond Head and the sunset between palm fronds. Southern French influences meld seamlessly with the fresh island ingredients that La Mer has always celebrated.

**Legend Seafood Restaurant.** *In Chinese Cultural Plaza, 100 N. Beretania St., Honolulu.* ☎ *808/532-1868. Reservations recommended. Most items under $15. AE, DC, MC, V. Mon–Fri 10:30am–2pm, Sat–Sun 8am–2pm; daily 5:30–10pm. DIM SUM/ SEAFOOD.* It's like dining in Hong Kong here, with a Chinese-speaking clientele poring over Chinese newspapers, and the clatter of chopsticks punctuating conversations. Excellent dim sum comes in bamboo steamers that parade by in carts. Dim sum is only served at lunch, but at dinner the seafood shines.

✪ **Parc Cafe.** *In the Waikiki Parc Hotel, 2233 Helumoa Rd., Waikiki.* ☎ *808/ 921-7272. Reservations recommended. Buffets $12–$23. Mon–Sat 7–10am and 11:30am– 2pm, Sun 7–9:30am and 11am–2pm; daily 5:30–9:30pm. BUFFETS/BRUNCH.* The Halekulani's sister hotel may not be on the beach, but it's made a name for itself as Honolulu's top spot for buffets, with food and prices so good it has won over even the most dedicated buffet bashers. Regulars flock to the dining room for the Wednesday and Friday Hawaiian buffet, the finest such spread around at $16.

**Roy's Restaurant.** *6600 Kalanianaole Hwy., Hawaii Kai.* ☎ *808/396-7697. Reservations recommended. Main courses $9–$25. AE, JCB, MC, V. Daily 5:30–9:15pm. EUROPEAN/ASIAN.* This was the first of Roy Yamaguchi's chain of 10 throughout Hawaii and the Pacific. The formula—open kitchen, fresh ingredients, ethnic touches, and a good dose of nostalgia mingling with European techniques and traditions— is smashingly successful. The menu changes nightly, but you can generally count on individual pizzas, a small pasta selection, and several types of fresh catch prepared at least five different ways.

**Sam Choy's Diamond Head Restaurant.** *449 Kapahulu Ave., Honolulu.* ☎ *808/732-8645. Reservations required. Main courses $19–$30. AE, MC, V.*

*Mon–Thurs 5:30–9:30pm, Fri–Sun 5–9:30pm. HAWAII REGIONAL.* It's noisy, informal, and full of hearty diners sitting in front of embarrassingly gargantuan-sized servings. The master of poke, Choy serves several of the best versions ever invented. The entrees are served with salad and soup, which doubles the generosity and makes each meal more than most single diners can consume.

**Wahoo Kitchen.** *3046A Monserrat Ave.* ☎ *808/732-5594. Main courses $7–$11. No credit cards. Mon–Sat 11am–2pm and 5:30–9pm. JAPANESE/LOCAL.* A shedlike atmosphere here sets the tone for a charmingly oddball and affordable dining experience. The food, especially the seafood at these prices, is a bargain. A menu board announces the constantly changing specials: a parade of fresh fish and chicken dishes cooked in Japanese or island style. No booze served, so bring your own.

**OTHER DINING**   It's hard to spend more than $5 at the **Ba-le Sandwich Shops,** whose French and Vietnamese specialties such as *pho* (the noodle soup that's a national ritual in Vietnam), croissants as good as the espresso, and wonderful taro/tapioca desserts have won an islandwide following. Branches are in Ala Moana Center (☎ **808/ 944-4752**); at 333 Ward Ave. (☎ **808/591-0935**); in Kahala Mall, 4211 Waialae Ave. (☎ **808/735-6889**); in Manoa Marketplace, 2855 E. Manoa Rd. (☎ **808/988-1407**); and in Chinatown at 150 N. King St. (☎ **808/521-3973**).

With branches in Waikiki, Kaimuki, Kailua, Wahiawa, and Kaneohe, the high-profile **Boston's North End Pizza Bakery** chain has an enthusiastic following among pizza lovers, and not just because it boasts "Hawaii's largest slice." The Waikiki branch is at 2145 Kuhio Ave. (☎ **808/922-7992**).

The largest food court for a cheap meal on the run is the Makai Court in **Ala Moana Shopping Center,** at Ala Moana Blvd. and Atkinson Dr. (☎ **808/946-2811**). There are 17 different types of cookery in this busy, noisy complex on the ground floor of the rambling mall.

## OAHU AFTER DARK

For what's going on, check the multitudinous tourist give-away publications and the daily editions of the *Honolulu Advertiser* and the *Honolulu Star–Bulletin.*

**CATCHING THE SUNSET**   Waikiki's beachfront bars offer many possibilities, from the Royal Hawaiian Hotel's **Mai Tai Bar,** a few feet from the sand, to the ever-enchanting **House Without a Key** at the Halekulani, where the breathtaking **Kanoelehua Miller** dances hula to the riffs of Hawaiian steel-pedal guitar under a century-old kiawe tree. With the sunset and ocean glowing behind her and Diamond Head visible in the distance, the scene is straight out of Somerset Maugham—romantic, evocative, nostalgic.

At **Duke's Canoe Club** at the Outrigger Waikiki Hotel, it's always three deep at the beachside bar when the sun is setting and the fabulous **Moe Keale** is playing with his trio, 4 to 6pm on weekends, but call ☎ **808/923-0711** to see if there's anything cooking later in the evening.

**THE PERFORMING ARTS**   Aloha-shirt-to-Armani is what locals call the night scene in Honolulu—mostly casual but with ample opportunity to dress up if you dare to part with your flip-flops. The **Hawaii Theatre,** 1130 Bethel St., downtown (☎ **808/ 528-0506**), is a neoclassical beaux-arts landmark featuring a 1922 dome, 1,400 plush seats, a hydraulically elevated organ, Corinthian columns, and gilt galore, which offers a range of productions including the **Honolulu Symphony Orchestra.** Meanwhile, the highly successful **Hawaii Opera Theatre** still draws fans to the **Neal Blaisdell Concert Hall,** as do many of the performances of Hawaii's four ballet companies: **Hawaii Ballet Theatre, Ballet Hawaii, Hawaii State Ballet,** and **Honolulu Dance Theatre.**

Showroom acts are still led by the tireless, ageless **Don Ho,** who still sings "Tiny Bubbles" in his **Waikiki Beachcomber Hana Hou** nightly except Monday.

**THE CLUB & MUSIC SCENE**   Jazz Hawaii (☎ **808/737-6554**) has an updated list of who's playing where. Big names and regular venues include **Duc's Bistro,** 1188 Maunakea St., Chinatown (☎ **808/531-6325**), where the silky smooth chords of **Azure McCall** deliver everything from "Paradise Cafe" to "Stormy Weather," from 8 to 10pm on Thursday and until midnight on Friday and Saturday; and **Alana Waikiki Hotel's Cafe Picasso,** 1956 Ala Moana Blvd. (☎ **808/941-7275**), where **Jimmy Borges** and **Betty Loo Taylor** cling to the classics.

The **Jungle,** 311 Lewers St., Waikiki (☎ **808/922-7808**), open 10pm to 4am, is the hot scene for alternative music these days. You can be as cheesy as you want here and no one will notice. The **Wave Waikiki,** 1877 Kalakaua Ave., Waikiki (☎ **808/941-0421**), is rough around the edges but still popular, serving up alternative music to the heavily body-pierced crowd on the same stage that Grace Jones once spat from.

**LOUNGES**   Waikiki is peppered with casual, lively nightspots into which you can saunter spontaneously for some consummate entertainment, which often includes impromptu hula and spirited music from the family and friends of the performers. Foremost among these venues is the Hilton Hawaiian Village's **Paradise Lounge,** which (despite its pillars) serves as a large living room for the full-bodied music of **Olomana** on Friday and Saturday from 8pm to midnight. Nearby, the Sheraton Moana Surfrider offers a regular program of Hawaiian music in the **Banyan Veranda,** on a spot where Robert Louis Stevenson loved to linger. *Hint:* Drinks, though not as elegantly presented, cost much less from the ground-level bar than from the elegant veranda with the high-backed chairs, and you still get to enjoy the music.

## A DAY TRIP TO THE NORTH SHORE

Rent a bright shiny convertible—the perfect car for Oahu since you can tan as you go—and head for the North Shore and Hawaii's surf city: **Haleiwa,** a quaint turn-of-the-century sugar plantation town designated a historic site. A collection of faded clapboard stores with a picturesque harbor, it has evolved into a surfer outpost and major roadside attraction with an eclectic collection of galleries, restaurants, and shops.

Stop by the **Haleiwa Surf Museum,** North Shore Marketplace, 66–250 Kamehameha Hwy. (☎ **808/637-3406**), which celebrates the sport of Hawaiian kings, before heading just down the road to some of the fabled shrines of surfing—**Waimea Bay, Banzai Pipeline, Sunset Beach**—where the world's largest waves, reaching 20 feet and more, rise up between November and March, drawing professional surfers, reckless daredevils, and hoards of onlookers when "surf's up." Don't forget your binoculars.

Getting to the North Shore is half the fun. From Waikiki you have a choice: Cruise up the H-2 through Oahu's broad and fertile central valley, past **Pearl Harbor** and **Schofield Barracks** of *From Here to Eternity* fame and through the pineapple and sugarcane fields until the sea reappears on the horizon. We recommend the Windward Coast route, which will take you around **Koko Head,** an arid moonscape with prickly cacti on shore and, in winter, whales cavorting in the water. The beaches here—especially **Sandy's, Makapuu,** and **Waimanalo**—are long, wide, and popular with daredevil bodysurfers and boogie boarders. This scenic coast is the best place on Oahu to birdwatch, and the night sky is ideal for amateur astronomers to watch meteors, comets, and stars.

Farther along the Windward Coast is a profusion of fluted green mountains and strange peaks, edged by golden beaches and the blue Pacific. The 3,000-foot-high Koolau range plunges almost straight down, presenting an irresistible jumping-off spot for hang-glider pilots, who catch the thermals on hours-long rides.

Eventually you'll wander into **Kailua,** Hawaii's biggest beach town, with more than 50,000 residents and two special beaches, **Kailua** and **Lanikai,** begging for visitors. Next is incredibly scenic **Kaneohe Bay,** which has a barrier reef and four tiny islets, one of which is known as **Coconut Island.** Don't be surprised if it looks familiar—it appeared in *Gilligan's Island.* At **Heeia State Park** (☎ 808/247-3156) is **Heeia Fishpond,** which ancient Hawaiians built by enclosing natural bays with rocks to trap fish on the incoming tide.

Everyone calls it Chinaman's Hat, but the tiny island off the eastern shore of **Kualoa Regional Park** is really Mokolii. At low tide, you can swim out to the island, but keep watch on the changing tide. The islet has a small sandy beach and is a bird preserve, so don't spook the red-footed boobies.

Farther along, on the east side of Kahana Bay by Kamehameha Highway is **Huilua Fishpond.** This National Historic Landmark is one of Oahu's most beautiful fishponds and the easiest to see.

From here, continue along Kamehameha Hwy. (Hi. 83) to the North Shore.

# 2 Maui

On a map, Maui doesn't look like much, but this 727-square-mile island has three peaks more than a mile high, thousands of waterfalls and pools, 120 miles of shoreline, more than 80 golden-sand beaches (including two more than a mile long), some great seaside hotels, and endless sunshine.

Maui was formed by the marriage of two shield volcanoes, 10,023-foot-high Haleakala and 5,788-foot-high Puu Kukui, creating a valley between them. Thanks to this unusual makeup, Maui has a variety of tropical delights, from cloud-wreathed peaks to coral reefs. Its microclimates offer distinct variations on the theme: The island is as lush as an equatorial rain forest in Hana; dry as the Arizona desert in Makena; hot as Mexico in Lahaina; and cool and misty, like Oregon, up in Kula.

Anytime's the right time to be in Lahaina, the historic port town, where a Friday-night party mood prevails any day of the week. Go gallery hopping, pub crawling, dine on a fabulous meal as the sun sets over the harbor, and end a perfect Maui day by watching the moonbeams dance on the crashing surf.

## ARRIVING & DEPARTING

Delta, Hawaiian, and United airlines fly from the U.S. mainland to **Kahului Airport,** on the island's north shore about a 40-minute drive to West Maui's resort area. Hawaiian, Aloha, and Mahalo airlines have service to Kahului from Honolulu and the other islands. You can avoid Kahului altogether by taking Aloha to **Kapalua–West Maui Airport,** which is only a 10- or 15-minute ride to the Kapalua resorts and 20 to 25 minutes to Kaanapali.

**SpeediShuttle** (☎ 808/875-8070) runs between Kahului Airport and all the major resorts daily from 5am to 9pm. Rates vary, but figure on $22 for two to Makena, and $40 for two to Kapalua. Be sure to call before your return flight to arrange pickup.

## ESSENTIALS

**VISITOR INFORMATION**   The **Maui Visitor Bureau** is located at 1727 Wili Pa Loop, Wailuku, Maui, HI 96793 (☎ 800/525-MAUI or 808/244-3530; fax 808/244-1337).

**EMERGENCIES**   Call ☎ 911 for police, fire, and ambulance. The hospitals are **Maui Memorial Hospital,** 221 Mahalani, Wailuku (☎ 808/244-9056); **Hana Medical Center,** on Hana Highway (☎ 808/248-8924); and **Kula Hospital,** 204 Kula Hwy., Kula (☎ 808/878-1221).

# Maui

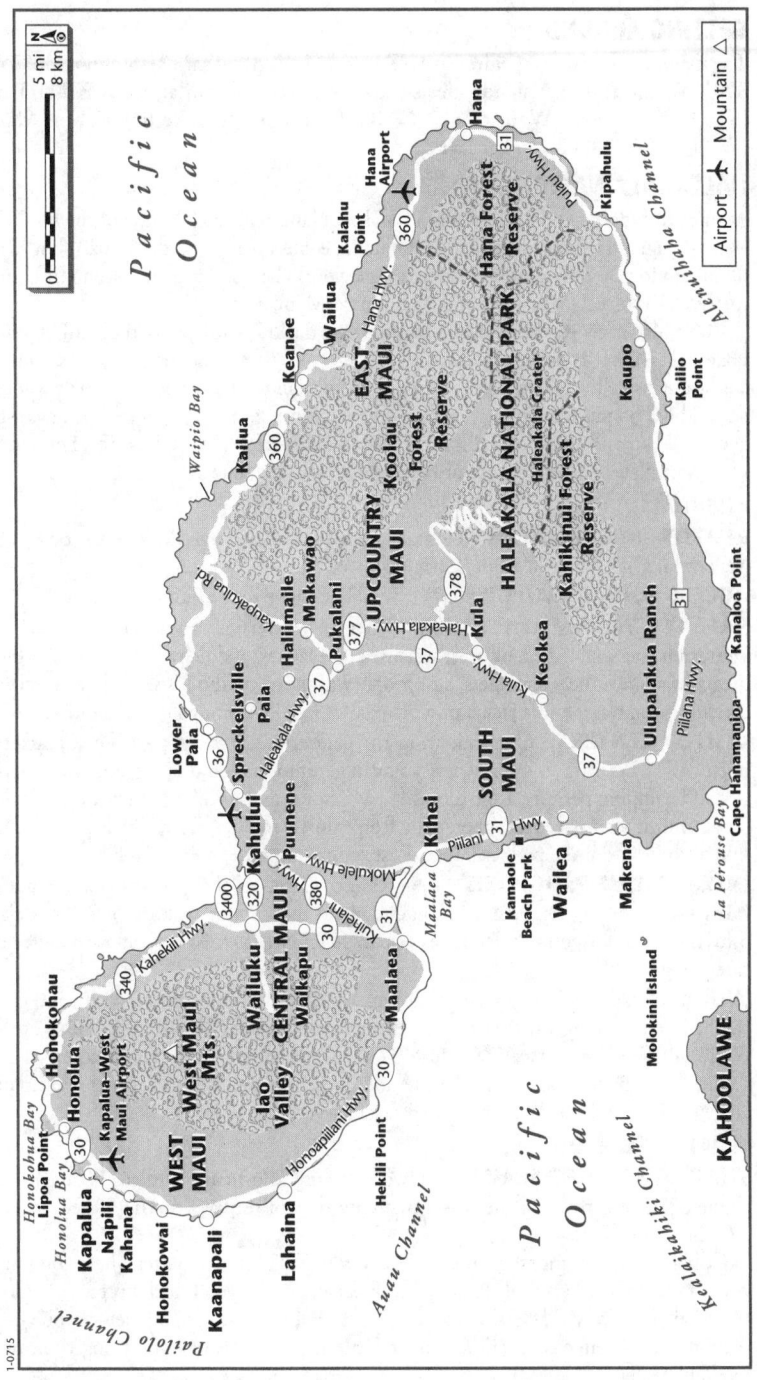

## GETTING AROUND

The major car-rental companies have offices on Maui. **Alii Taxi** (☎ 808/661-3688 or 808/667-2605) offers islandwide, 24-hour service. You can also call **Kihei Taxi** (☎ 808/879-3000), **Wailea Taxi** (☎ 808/874-5000), and **Yellow Cab of Maui** (☎ 808/877-7000) if you need a ride.

## HALEAKALA NATIONAL PARK

At once forbidding and compelling, Haleakala National Park ("House of the Sun") is Maui's main attraction. More than 1.3 million people a year go up the 10,023-foot-high mountain to peer down into the crater of the world's largest dormant volcano (it hasn't spewed lava since 1790). That hole would hold Manhattan.

Many drive up to the summit in predawn darkness to watch the sunrise over Haleakala (sunset is no less spectacular); others take a trail ride inside the bleak lunar landscape inside the crater. Hardy adventurers hike and camp inside the crater's wilderness. Those bound for the interior bring their survival gear, for the terrain is raw, rugged, and punishing—not unlike the moon. However you choose to experience Haleakala National Park, it will prove memorable—guaranteed.

### ESSENTIALS

**VISITOR INFORMATION**   Contact **Haleakala National Park,** P.O. Box 369, Makawao, HI 96768 (☎ **808/572-9306**).

**ACCESS POINTS & ADMISSION**   See "The Drive to the Summit," below.

**SAFETY**   You're entering a high-altitude wilderness area. You may suffer lightheadedness, shortness of breath, nausea, headaches, and dehydration. Asthmatics, pregnant women, heavy smokers, and people with heart conditions should be especially careful. Bring water and a jacket or a blanket, especially if you go up for sunrise.

**VISITOR CENTERS**   One mile from the park entrance is the **park headquarters,** open daily from 7am to 4pm, where you can get information on programs and activities and camping permits. Rest rooms, a pay phone, and drinking water are available. The **summit visitor center,** open daily from sunrise to 3pm, is near Haleakala's summit, 11 miles from the park entrance. Rest rooms and water are available.

**INTERPRETIVE PROGRAMS**   Rangers also offer excellent, informative, free **naturalist talks** at 9:30, 10:30, and 11:30am daily in the summit visitor center. They also offer free 2- and 3-hour guided hikes usually four times a week; call for a schedule before you go.

**WHEN TO GO**   Weather changes fast at the summit. Temperatures with wind chill can be below freezing any time of year. Always call the park (☎ **808/572-9306**) or the **National Weather Service** (☎ **808/871-5054**) for current conditions before you go.

The best time for photos is in the afternoon, when the sun lights the crater and clouds are few. Go on full-moon nights for spectacular viewing.

### WHAT TO SEE & DO

**THE DRIVE TO THE SUMMIT**   Hwy. 378, also known as Haleakala Crater Road, is one of the few roads in the world that climbs from sea level to 10,000 feet in just 37 miles.

Going to the summit takes about 2 hours from Kahului. No matter where you start, you'll follow Hi. 37 (Haleakala Hwy.) to Pukalani, where you'll pick up Hi. 377 (also Haleakala Hwy.), which you'll take to Hi. 378. Fill up your gas tank before you go— the only gas available is 27 miles below the summit at Pukalani—and bring your own food and water.

At the **park entrance,** you'll pay an entrance fee of $4 per car (or $2 for a bicycle). About a mile from the entrance is **Park Headquarters,** where an endangered **nene,** or

Hawaiian goose, may greet you with its unique call ("nay-nay"). With a black face, buff cheeks, and partially webbed feet, the gray-brown bird looks like a small Canadian goose with zebra stripes.

Beyond headquarters are two scenic overlooks on the way to the summit. Stop at **Leleiwi Overlook,** just beyond mile post 17, on the way up, if only to get out, stretch, and get accustomed to the heights. Take a deep breath, a good look around, and pop your ears. If you feel dizzy, drowsy, or get a sudden headache, consider turning around and going back down.

Two miles along is **Kalahaku Overlook.** You can only turn into it when you're descending from the top. This is the best place to see a rare silversword, its silvery bayonets displaying tiny purple bouquets—like a spacey artichoke with an attitude.

Continue on, and you'll quickly reach **Haleakala Visitor Center,** which offers a panoramic view of the volcanic landscape and exhibits that explain what you see. But don't turn around here; the actual summit is a little farther on, at **Puu Ulaula Overlook** (also known as Red Hill), where you'll find a mysterious cluster of buildings officially called Haleakala Observatories, but known as **Science City.** If you do go up for sunrise, the building at Puu Ulaula Overlook is the best viewing spot.

Put your car in low gear for the ride down.

**HIKING HALEAKALA**   Hiking into the volcano is really the way to see it. The crater has 36 miles of hiking trails, two campsites, and three cabins. The best route takes you into the crater along **Sliding Sands Trail,** which begins on the rim and descends to the floor, and back out along **Halemauu Trail.** For hiking and camping information and maps before you go, contact **Haleakala National Park,** P.O. Box 369, Makawao, HI 96768 (☎ **808/572-9306**).

Or, hire a guide. Naturalist Ken Schmidt at **Hike Maui** (☎ **808/879-5270**) is an excellent guide, who knows Maui's backcountry well. He'll take you on the trip of a lifetime into Haleakala.

**HALEAKALA ON HORSEBACK**   **Pony Express Tours** (☎ **808/667-2200** or 808/878-6698; fax 808/878-3581) can also take you into the crater. They offer half- and full-day rides to the crater floor and back, as well as gentler 1- and 2-hour rides at Haleakala Ranch, on the volcano's beautiful lower slopes.

## MORE TO SEE & DO ON MAUI

**BEACHES**   Hitting the beach is at the top of everyone's list of things to do on Maui. The most famous is **Kaanapali Beach,** a 4-mile-long stretch in front of the resorts along the west coast. From here you have great views down the channel between Molokai and Lanai (on a clear day you can even see Oahu on the horizon). In a cove fronting the Kapalua Bay Hotel and Villas, **Kapalua Beach** is the stuff of dreams: a golden crescent bordered by two palm-studded points, a sandy bottom sloping gently to deep water. It's great for snorkelers and swimmers of all ages and abilities. On the southern end of Maui's resort coast, development falls off dramatically, leaving a wild, dry countryside of green kiawe trees backing **Maluaka (Makena) Beach,** a short, wide, palm-fringed crescent of golden, grainy sand set between two lava points and bounded by big sand dunes. The drive to Hana is worth it just to see **Hamoa Beach,** a half-moon–shaped, gray-sand beach set below black lava cliffs (the Hotel Hana–Maui maintains the beach and tries to act like it's theirs, but it's not).

**WHALE-WATCHING**   The Pacific humpback whale is one of the largest creatures on earth, averaging 40 to 50 feet in length and weighing up to 90,000 pounds. These majestic mammals commute from Alaska to Maui each winter, where they're protected and celebrated as the star attraction of the annual whale-watch season. For a closer look, take a whale-watching cruise. The **Pacific Whale Foundation** (☎ **808/879-8811**) is a nonprofit foundation in Kihei that helps whales instead of just gawking at them. The organization supports its whale research by offering cruises and snorkel tours, some to Molokini and Lanai. They operate a 3-hour whale-watch cruise from December to May.

**DRIVING THE HEAVENLY ROAD TO HANA** Driving the incredibly winding, in places one-way, coastal road to Hana is all about the journey, not the destination. Go slow, top down, early in the morning—dawn isn't too early. Take your time and go with the flow. Stop at Puohokamoa Falls and take a splash, buy a pandanus hat from a Samoan weaver, nibble on some fresh apple bananas, and smell the wild ginger. Spend the day at Waianapanapa Beach, or take a dip in the **Seven Sacred Pools.** None of them is sacred, but they're all beautiful, spilling seaward at Oheo Gulch. (Check with the Kipahulu Ranger Station, ☎ 808/248-7375, before swimming in the pools, and always keep one eye on the water in the streams; the sky can be sunny near the coast, but flood waters travel 6 miles down from Kipahulu Valley and can rise 4 feet in less than 10 minutes.) Don't hurry back to civilization from Hana; stay in a romantic B&B and drive back tomorrow—or the next day.

**OUTDOOR ACTIVITIES** Maui's best snorkeling beaches include **Kapalua; Black Rock,** at Kaanapali; along the Kihei coastline, especially at **Kamaole III;** and along the Wailea coastline, particularly at **Ulua Beach. Maui Classic Charters** (☎ 808/879-8188) will take you out on a boat.

Everyone dives at Molokini, an underwater marine-life park in a sunken crater off the Wailea coast. Its calm, clear, protected waters harbor an abundance of marine life, from manta rays to clouds of yellow butterfly fish. For personalized diving, **Ed Robinson's Diving Adventures** (☎ 808/879-3584) is the best on Maui. In Lahaina, call **Lahaina Divers** (☎ 808/667-7496).

Marlin, tuna, ono, and mahimahi abound in Maui's coastal and channel waters, making for great deep-sea fishing. No license is required; just book a sportfishing vessel through your hotel activities desk or at the **Maalaea Activities** desk at Lahaina harbor (☎ 808/242-6982).

The trade winds ripping through Maui's isthmus make for exciting sailing. Many boats, from a three-masted schooner to spacious trimarans, offer day cruises. You can experience the thrill of competition sailing with **Alihilani Yacht Charters** (☎ 808/667-7733), whose two boats meet off west Maui's coast for a daily duel in the wind.

Maui has Hawaii's best windsurfing beaches. **Hookipa,** known all over the globe for its brisk winds and excellent waves, is the site of several world championship contests. When conditions are right, **Kanaha** is also packed with colorful sails. Equipment rental and lessons are available from **Hawaiian Island Windsurfing** (☎ 808/871-4981), **Hawaiian Sailboarding Techniques** (☎ 808/871-5423), **Maui Windsurf Co.** (☎ 808/877-4696), and **Second Wind Windsurfing** (☎ 808/877-7467), all in Kahului.

Maui's challenging and beautiful golf courses offer a range of opportunities. The views from **Kapalua Resort's** three championship courses—the Bay, Village, and Plantations—are worth the greens fees, which can run up to $110 (☎ 808/669-8044). **Wailea** has three courses to choose from: the Blue, Orange, and Gold (☎ 808/879-2966 or 808/875-5111).

**SHOPPING** On the west coast, you can blow a wad at Kaanapali's beachfront **Whalers Village** (☎ 808/661-4567), with the likes of Tiffany, Chanel, Gucci, Louis Vuitton, Coach, and Sharper Image, among its 70 shops and restaurants. In Lahaina, shopping means the half-dozen blocks along **Front Street,** which has everything from sunglasses to T-shirts to expensive art.

The main mall here is **Kaahumanu Center,** on Kaahumanu Avenue, 5 minutes from the Kahului Airport. It covers all the bases, from the finest arts and crafts to a supermarket. Dining and upscale shopping have sprouted up overnight in **Dairy Center,** a commercial center on the way to the Kahului Airport that harbors chic boutiques and Maui's ultimate bathing-suit shop.

**BEST BETS FOR KIDS**   Kids will love a trip on **Atlantis Submarines** (☎ 800/548-6262 or 808/667-2224), a real sub that takes you and them down into the shallow coastal waters off Lahaina to see plenty of fish, who come around to be fed by chumming divers—a shark or two may join them. On dry land, a steam engine pulls the **Sugar Cane Train** (☎ 808/661-0089) on a 30-minute, 12-mile round-trip through sugar-cane fields between Lahaina and Kaanapali. The conductor sings and calls out the landmarks. Along the way, you can see Molokai, Lanai, and the backside of Kaanapali.

In the Hyatt Regency Maui's lobby, **Incredible Journeys!** (☎ 808/661-0092) is a virtual reality flight trainer that replicates a seven-passenger helicopter that "lifts off" with vibrations and sounds, then shows off Maui on a wraparound dome-shaped theater screen before "touching down" in the Hyatt's lobby. For the real thing, go to Kahului Heliport.

Adults as well as kids can explore the tropical night skies through **Star Search,** the world's first recreational computer-driven telescope, on the rooftop of the Hyatt Regency Maui (☎ 808/661-1234).

## ACCOMMODATIONS
### WEST MAUI

The region around Kapalua is one of Hawaii's most desirable vacation areas. About 30 miles away, Lahaina is an old whaling town on Maui's exquisite west coast.

**Lahaina Inn.** *127 Lahainaluna Rd., Lahaina, HI 96761-1502.* ☎ *800/669-3444 or 808/661-0577. Fax 808/667-9480. 12 rms. $89–$129 double. Rates include continental breakfast. AE, DISC, JCB, MC, V. Next-door parking $5.* If you like old hotels with a genuine historic feel, you'll love this charming place in the heart of Lahaina. The Victorian-style, antique-stuffed rooms all have private baths and lanais. David Paul's Lahaina Grill (see "Dining," below) is here. No TV and no kids under 15.

**Maui Islander.** *660 Wainee St. (between Dickenson and Prison sts.), Lahaina, HI 96761.* ☎ *800/367-5226 or 808/667-9766. Fax 808/661-3733. 372 rms. High season, $92 double; $105–$114 studio; $125 one-bedroom; $182 two-bedroom ($10 off in low season). AE, DC, DISC, JCB, MC, V.* With kitchenettes in all units, this wooden complex on a quiet street within walking distance of restaurants, shops, attractions, and the beach is one of Lahaina's great buys. Tennis courts, pool, sundeck, barbecue and picnic area, and an aloha-friendly staff are here. Sizable units have tropical decor.

**Mauian on Napili Bay.** *5441 Lower Honoapiilani Rd. (Napili), Lahaina, HI 96761.* ☎ *800/367-5034 or 808/669-6205. Fax 808/669-0129. 44 units. Low season, $100–$125. High season, $115–$140. Additional person $9 extra. Three-night minimum. AE, DISC, MC, V.* Run by a Hawaiian family, this low-rise hotel on a beautiful, half-mile-long beach is the place to get away from it all (no phones or TVs in rooms). The renovated rooms feature hardwood floors, island-style furniture, and big lanais with great views. Great restaurants and Kapalua Resort are nearby.

**Napili Bay.** *33 Hui Dr. (off Lower Honoapiilani Hwy., Napili), Lahaina, HI 96761.* ☎ *808/661-3500 or 888/661-7200. Fax 808/661-5210. 33 units. $58–$75 double. Five-night minimum. MC, V.* A bargain on Maui, this small, two-story complex sits right on Napili Beach's gorgeous, half-mile white-sand beach. The compact studio apartments have kitchens and roomy lanais for enjoying the sunsets. Louvred windows and ceiling fans keep the units cool. Restaurants and shopping are nearby.

**Noelani Condominium Resort.** *4095 Lower Honoapiilani Rd. (Kahana), Lahaina, HI 96761.* ☎ *800/367-6030 or 808/669-8374. Fax 808/669-7904. 50 units.*

*$87–$107 studio double; $110–$120 one-bedroom; $167 two-bedroom; $197 three-bedroom. Rates include first morning continental orientation breakfast. Three-night mini-mum. AE, MC, V.* Studios and three-bedroom units at this first-class property are a good value. Units feature complete kitchens, stereo entertainment centers, and spectacular views. Fine snorkeling and whale-watching are next door. Two pools (one heated) and a Jacuzzi are on the premises.

**Papakea.** *3600 Lower Honoapiilani Rd. (Honokowai), Maui Resort Management, Lahaina, HI 96761.* ☎ *800/367-5037 or 808/669-1902. Fax 808/669-8790. 28 units. $80–$119 studio double; $120–$165 one-bedroom; $120–$210 two-bedroom. Seven-night minimum. AE, DISC, MC, V.* Just a mile down the beach from Kaanapali, these low-rise buildings have landscaped grounds and ocean views galore. A putting green wraps around the resort's two kidney-shaped pools, each with its own private cabana with sauna, Jacuzzi, and barbecue grills. The units have big lanais, dishwashers, and washer/dryers. Definitely a value property.

**Puamana.** *P.O. Box 11108, Lahaina, HI 96760.* ☎ *800/669-6284 or 808/667-2712. Fax 808/661-5875. E-mail: robyn@maui.com. 40 condo units. $100–$175 one-bedroom double; $140–$250 two-bedroom; $300–$350 three-bedroom. Three-night minimum. AE, MC, V.* This peaceful town-house complex is on the water in a quiet section of Lahaina. Each unit is a freestanding, privately owned home (most are exquisitely decorated) with full kitchen, TV, at least two baths, lanai, and barbecue. Conveniences include three pools (one for adults only), tennis, table tennis, and clubhouse with oceanfront lanai, library, card room, and sauna.

○ **Ritz-Carlton, Kapalua.** *1 Ritz-Carlton Dr., Kapalua, HI 96761.* ☎ *800/262-8440 or 808/669-6200. Fax 808/669-1566. 550 rms, 48 suites. $285–$2,800 double. Wedding/honeymoon and other packages available. AE, DC, DISC, MC, V. Free self-parking; valet parking $10.* The Ritz rises spectacularly on a knoll overlooking the sea at the northern end of West Maui. The style is fancy plantation, elegant but not imposing. Rooms are up to the usual Ritz standard and have private lanais. The hotel provides exemplary service, three top-rated golf courses, a nine-hole putting green, tennis complex, three pools, croquet lawn, fitness center, and salon.

## SOUTH MAUI

The south coast is blessed with the best weather on Maui, a windswept stretch of sea and sand with miles of unspoiled beaches.

**Aston Maui Lu Resort.** *575 S. Kihei Rd., Kihei, HI 96753.* ☎ *800/92-ASTON or 808/879-5881. Fax 808/879-4627. 120 rms. Winter, $119–205. Low season, $99–$185. AE, DC, DISC, JCB, MC, V.* This resort on the quiet northern end of Kihei of-fers a nostalgic Old Hawaii atmosphere. Ask for a beach unit if you like to be right on the sand; the others are up on a rise, around a pool. The big, airy rooms have ceiling fans, coffeemakers, and minifridges. Tennis, laundry, and a surprisingly good restaurant are on the premises.

○ **Four Seasons Resort Wailea.** *3900 Wailea Alanui Dr., Wailea, HI 96753.* ☎ *800/334-MAUI or 808/874-8000. Fax 808/874-6449. 380 rooms, 73 suites. $295–$610 double; from $515 suite. Packages available. Second room $250 for families. AE, DC, JCB, MC, V.* It's hard to beat this four-time Five Diamond Award winner, a modern Hawaiian palace by the sea. The open courtyard of pools and gardens creates its own world so you don't feel like you're in resort row. Each large, recently renovated room has a grand marble bath and a furnished lanai, nearly all with ocean views. The resort has restaurants, a fitness center, game room, salon, putting green, shops, beach pavil-ion, tennis, and nearby golf.

**Kea Lani Hotel Suites & Villas.** *4100 Wailea Alanui Dr., Wailea, HI 96753.* ☎ *800/882-4100 or 808/875-4100. Fax 808/875-1200. 413 units. $265–$450 suite (sleeps up to 4); $795–$1,195 one- to three-bedroom villas. Packages available. AE, DC, DISC, JCB, MC, V.* This is Hawaii's only all-suite luxury resort. Each 840-square-foot creamy white suite has a microwave kitchenette, living room with a high-tech media center and pullout sofa, wet bar, an oversized marble bathroom with a shower big enough for a party, and a private lanai with ocean views. Conveniences include restaurants, three pools, a fitness center, shops, salon, tennis and golf nearby.

**Maui Coast Hotel.** *2259 S. Kihei Rd., Kihei, HI 96753.* ☎ *800/895-6284 or 808/ 874-6284. Fax 808/875-4731. 257 rms, 113 one- and two-bedroom suites. $119–$139 double; $179–$300 suite. Room/car packages available. AE, DC, DISC, JCB, MC, V.* This off-beach midrise is one of Hawaii's best-priced new hotels—and it's just a block from a great beach and within walking distance of restaurants and shopping. The comfortable, clean rooms have lots of extras: sitting areas, coffeemakers, hair dryers, whirlpools, minifridges, ceiling fans, and furnished lanais. The hotel has two restaurants, room service, an activities desk, laundry facilities, two pools, two Jacuzzis, tennis, and a gift shop.

## UP COUNTRY

**ACCOMMODATIONS**   A quiet retreat at 4,000 feet, surrounded by Haleakala Ranch, towering eucalyptus groves, and a protea farm, **Olinda Country Cottage & Inn,** 536 Olinda Rd., Makawao, HI 96768 (☎ **808/572-1453**), will definitely give you a different take on Maui. The beautiful Tudor-style home has two two-room suites with private baths and a huge living area to share; there's also a suite with its own living room, kitchenette, and cozy bedroom, as well as a romantic, antique-filled cottage with kitchen, fireplace, washer/dryer, VCR, and views. Breakfast is included, there's a 2-night minimum, and no credit cards are accepted.

## EAST MAUI

**ON THE HANA ROAD**   On a spectacular, remote sea cliff near a waterfall stream, **Huelo Point Flower Farm,** P.O. Box 1195, Paia, HI 96779 (☎ **808/572-1850**), is a little Eden by the sea, a 2-acre estate overlooking Waipio Bay, with two guest cottages and a main house to rent. The Carriage House apartment has glass walls facing mountain and sea, while the two-bedroom main house has an exercise room, fireplace, cathedral ceilings, and other extras. There's a natural pool with a waterfall and an oceanfront hot tub.

**ACCOMMODATIONS IN HANA**   **Hana Plantation Houses,** c/o 2957 Kalakaua Ave., Honolulu, HI 96815 (☎ **800/228-HANA** or 808/923-0772), has rentals throughout the Hana area. These lovely folks will set you up with an accommodation that's right for you, whether you're looking for a romantic cottage or a house for the family. Their fully equipped rentals all come with kitchens; some are waterfront and others have ocean views or tropical garden settings. Rates run $100 to $160; minimum stay is 2 nights.

**Ekena,** P.O. Box 728, Hana, HI 96713 (☎ **808/248-7047**), lies on a piece of rural paradise with 360° views. You can rent an ultra-private two-bedroom apartment in this spacious, elegantly furnished open Hawaiian-style home, with floor-to-ceiling sliding glass doors that bring the outside in. There's a 3-night minimum and no credit cards are accepted.

## DINING
### WEST MAUI
Lahaina is Maui's most enjoyable dining area, with everything from bistros to barbecue as well as oceanside watering spots.

✪ **Avalon.** *844 Front St., Lahaina.* ☎ *808/667-5559. Reservations recommended. Main courses $15–$37. AE, CB, DC, JCB, MC, V. Daily 11:30am–10pm. HAWAII REGIONAL.* One of the originators of Hawaii regional cuisine, Mark Ellman has remained one of Hawaii's avant-garde chefs, and casual Avalon is his proving ground. His clean, crisp flavors suggest California, Indonesia, Thailand, China, Japan, and Vietnam. Personal favorites: Maui onions with a zesty tamarind ketchup, Asian pasta with seafood in a tomato-ginger sauce, and Szechuan sugar-snap peas.

**Cheeseburger in Paradise.** *811 Front St., Lahaina.* ☎ *808/661-4855. Main courses $6–$10. AE, MC, V. Daily 11am–11pm. AMERICAN.* Always crowded, highly visible, and very noisy (with live music in the evenings), Cheeseburger is a shrine to the American classic. This is burger country, tropical style, with everything from tofu and garden burgers to the biggest, juiciest beef and chicken burgers, served on buns baked fresh daily. Good value, good grinds, and a great ocean view.

**David Paul's Lahaina Grill.** *127 Lahainaluna Rd., Lahaina.* ☎ *808/667-5117. Reservations required. Main courses $19–$38. Fixed-price dinner $45. AE, DC, DISC, MC, V. Daily 5:30–10pm, bar until midnight. NEW AMERICAN.* Chef David Paul is a creative genius. His menu is determined by the availability of the best fresh ingredients, but expect one culinary marvel after another: tequila shrimp with firecracker rice, kalua duck in reduced plum wine sauce, maybe even the pricey-but-worth-it lobster risotto with wild mushrooms and Gorgonzola cheese.

**Lahaina Coolers.** *180 Dickensen St., Lahaina.* ☎ *808/661-7082. Most items under $14. AE, MC, V. Daily 7am–2am (kitchen open until midnight). AMERICAN.* This indoor/outdoor restaurant serves up good, reasonably priced food in a cheerful atmosphere. The Surfer Special (a gourmet bean burrito) or fruit pancakes go great with their famous mango daiquiri. A new pasta machine promises great things—shrimp pesto linguine, smoked salmon fettuccine in dill-caper cream sauce—and the nightly steak and fish specials are terrific deals.

**Maui Tacos.** *Napili Plaza, 5095 Napili Hau St., Napili.* ☎ *808/665-0222. Most items under $7. No credit cards. Mon–Sat 11am–9pm, Sun 11am–8pm. MEXICAN.* As if he had anything more to prove, Mark Ellman of Avalon fame put gourmet Mexican on paper plates and on Maui's culinary map. The food is top quality: excellent fresh fish tacos, chimichangas, searing salsas, and other mouth-breaking compositions—the green spinach burrito is a knockout. Also in Kahului, Lahaina, and Kihei.

✪ **Roy's Kahana Bar & Grill.** *Kahana Gateway, 4405 Honoapiilani Hwy., Kahana.* ☎ *808/669-6999. Reservations strongly suggested. Main courses $12–$25. AE, DC, DISC, MC, V. Daily 5:30–10pm. EUROASIAN.* It's big, noisy, and important, bustling with young, hip servers impeccably trained to deliver the blackened ahi or perfectly seared lemongrass *shutome* (broadbill swordfish) hot to your table. The room sizzles with cross-cultural tastings. Roy's is known for its rack of lamb, fresh seafood, and a large, open kitchen that turns out everything from pizza to sake-grilled New York steak.

## SOUTH MAUI

In south Maui, you have a choice, from inexpensive restaurants in the Kihei area to top-of-the-line places in Wailea-Makena.

**A Pacific Cafe Maui.** *Azeka's Place II, 1279 S. Kihei Rd., Kihei.* ☎ *808/879-0069. Reservations recommended. Main courses $21–$24. AE, DC, CB, MC, V. Daily 5:30–10pm. HAWAII REGIONAL.* Jean-Marie Josselin brought his singular talents from Kauai to a Kihei strip mall and made it a cornerstone of exemplary cuisine. From the open kitchen comes a stream of unforgettables: tiger-eye ahi sushi tempura, steamed mussels in lemongrass ginger broth, garlic-sesame mahimahi in lime-ginger sauce. You'll be so busy enjoying the food, you won't notice the parking lot.

**Alexander's Fish & Chicken & Chips.** *1913 S. Kihei Rd., Kihei.* ☎ *808/ 874-0788. Fish-and-chips $6–$11. MC, V. Daily 11am–9pm. FISH-AND-CHIPS/ SEAFOOD.* A friendly neighborhood take-out stand with patio seating and a very busy kitchen producing fresh ono, mahimahi, and ahi, broiled or fried, with baskets of fries or rice. Equally popular are the family-sized 13-piece shrimp, chicken, oyster, calamari, rib, or fish baskets.

**Coffee Store.** *Azeka's Place II, 1279 Kihei Rd., Kihei.* ☎ *808/875-4244. Most items under $9. AE, CB, DC, DISC, MC, V. Sun–Thurs 6am–10pm, Fri–Sat 6am–11pm. COFFEEHOUSE.* This simple, classic coffeehouse serves two dozen different types of coffee drinks, from mochas, lattés, and frappés to cappuccino, espresso, and toddies. Breakfast items include lox and bagels, quiches, granola, and an egg-and-mushroom breakfast quesadilla. Pizza, salads, vegetarian lasagna, and sandwiches also move briskly from the take-out counter.

**Joe's Bar & Grill.** *Above the Wailea Tennis Club, 131 Wailea Ike Place, Wailea.* ☎ *808/875-7767. Reservations recommended. Main courses $14–$28. AE, DC, MC, V. Daily 11am–2pm and 5:30–10pm. AMERICAN REGIONAL.* Bev and Joe Gannon of up-country Maui's acclaimed Haliimaile General Store don't disappoint with their new restaurant. The 360° view spans golf course, ocean, and Haleakala; after dark, the rich interior and theatrical lighting take over. Succulent grilled quail, smoked salmon quesadilla, lobster pot pie, grilled lamb chops in mint balsamic glaze . . . the menu is brilliant in its simplicity.

**✪ Seasons.** *Four Seasons Resort Wailea.* ☎ *808/874-8000. Reservations recommended. Main courses $29–$42; fixed-price dinner $62–$95. AE, CB, DC, DISC, JCB, MC, V. Daily 6:30–9:30pm. HAWAII REGIONAL/PROVENÇAL.* George Mavrothalassitis, formerly the wunderkind behind La Mer and Orchids in Honolulu, is renowned for his use of local ingredients and the most vaunted traditions of his native Provence—his bouillabaisse still reigns supreme. Other favorites: Hawaiian salt-crusted red snapper in *ogo* (seaweed) sauce, and papillote of kumu (parchment-baked goat fish with shiitake mushrooms, ogo, and Maui onion).

**Shaka Sandwich & Pizza.** *1295 S. Kihei Rd., Kihei.* ☎ *808/874-0331. Pizzas up to $26. Daily 10am–9pm (delivery hours 10:30am–9pm). PIZZA.* Award-winning pizzas share the limelight with New York–style hoagies and Philly cheesesteaks, and they're all terrific. You can have your pie delivered, take it out, or dine in Shaka's modest new dining room.

## EAST MAUI

**ON THE ROAD TO HANA: PAIA**   There are a number of simple and satisfying places to eat in Paia.

**Charley's Restaurant.** *142 Hana Hwy., Paia.* ☎ *808/579-9453. Reservations accepted. Main courses $10–$19. AE, DISC, MC, V. Daily 7am–2:30pm and 5–10pm. Pupu bar, daily 2:30–5pm. AMERICAN/PIZZA.* This little tavern has a big and skillful kitchen. Any day starts splendidly with Cajun-style eggs Benedict made with fresh ono (wahoo), or plate-sized whole wheat, blueberry, or macadamia nut pancakes. At lunch, the quarter-pound hamburgers are served on home-baked Kaiser buns; at dinner, the pizzas, pastas, kiawe-smoked ribs, and fresh steamers steal the show.

**Pic-nics.** *30 Baldwin Ave., Paia.* ☎ *808/579-8021. Most items under $7. No credit cards. Daily 7am–7pm. SANDWICHES/PICNIC LUNCHES.* If there were a nut burger Hall of Fame, Pic-nics would be a lifetime member. The spinach nut burger, an ingenious vegetarian blend topped with vegetables and cheddar, is the signature item on a varied menu of elegant and no-fuss picnic fare for the drive to Hana or up-country Maui.

**Pauwela Cafe.** *375 W. Kuiaha Rd., Haiku.* ☎ *808/575-9242. Most items under $6. No credit cards. Mon–Sat 7am–3pm, Sun 8am–2pm. INTERNATIONAL.* This tiny cafe in an industrial center is a long drive from anywhere, but the kalua turkey sandwich—warm, moist, smoky shredded turkey served with cheese on home-baked French bread and covered with a green chili and cilantro sauce—is reason enough for the journey. We never dreamed we could dine so well on Styrofoam plates.

**HANA DINING** Your best options after a long day's drive to Heavenly Hana are the **Cafe at Hana Gardenland,** Hana Hwy. at Kalo Rd. (☎ 808/248-8975), where the light, healthy fare and atmosphere are pure, garden-style Hana; and the **Hana Ranch Restaurant,** Hana Hwy. (☎ 808/248-8255), a good casual restaurant with prices that seem exploitative given the paucity of restaurants in Hana—but the adjoining take-out stand offers reasonable plate lunches and saimin.

## Up Country

**DINING** This area has a not-to-be missed restaurant, ✪ **Haliimaile General Store,** Haliimaile Rd., Haliimaile (☎ 808/572-2666). What was once an old plantation store in the middle of the cane fields is now one of Maui's most appealing restaurants. The food, a blend of eclectic American with ethnic touches, avoids the same-old, same-old, I'm-bored-with-seared-ahi Hawaii regional syndrome with such dishes as spicy rack of lamb Hunan style, Brie and grape quesadilla, and Chinese roasted duck taco. Main courses cost $16–$24, and there's a sushi bar. It's open daily 11am–2:30pm and 5:30–9:30pm. Sun brunch starts at 10am. Reservations are recommended.

# MAUI AFTER DARK

The best way to find out what's going on when you're on Maui is to check the *Maui News.*

**PERFORMING ARTS** The island's most prestigious entertainment venue is the $28-million **Maui Arts and Cultural Center** in Kahului (☎ 808/242-7469), a long-awaited, first-class visual and performing arts center with an art gallery, an outdoor amphitheater, a 300-seat theater for experimental performances, and a 1,200-seat main theater. Since its 1994 opening, the state-of-the-art facilities have attracted first-rate performers and sold-out shows, from Tony Bennett to Hawaii's premier cultural event of the decade, the Halau o Kekuhi's riveting five-act saga of Pele's migration, "Holo Mai Pele."

**LIVE MUSIC & DANCING** With a few exceptions (Makawao's **Casanova,** ☎ 808/572-0220; and **Wunderbar,** ☎ 808/579-8808, in Paia), your other options for live entertainment are pretty much limited to the resort areas, where the major hotels generally have lobby lounges offering regular Hawaiian music, soft jazz, or hula. In west Maui, the only real after-dark action is at **Blue Tropix Nightclub** (☎ 808/667-5309), located upstairs and past the pool hall at the Lahaina Center (900 Front St.). The Grand Wailea Resort's **Tsunami** (☎ 808/875-1234), Maui's most high-tech club, happens to be south Maui's only nightspot for dancing.

To find out what's happening in blues or jazz, look in at **La Pastaria** (☎ 808/879-9001) in Kihei. It's the nightlife nexus for this genre, with quality music and overflow crowds that linger into the wee hours.

**LUAU!** Maui's—maybe Hawaii's—best luau is the nightly **Old Lahaina Luau,** on the beach side of 505 Front St. in Lahaina (☎ 808/667-1998). This is the consummate luau, with a healthy balance of good food, showmanship, educational value, and sheer romantic beauty. It begins at sunset, on a grassy lawn with a view of Kahoolawe,

Molokai, and Lanai, and features Tahitian and Hawaiian entertainment, including ancient hula, which is riveting even for jaded locals. The food is authentic: imu-roasted kalua pig, lomi salmon, poi, dried fish, poke, breadfruit, sweet potato, and, for the more cautious, teriyaki steak, barbecued chicken, and mahimahi. They're often booked a week in advance, so call ahead (at press time, there are plans to move the luau a few blocks north, so check the location when you reserve).

## A DAY TRIP TO LANAI

If you have only 1 day to spare but you still want to experience the essence of the island of Lanai, there are several ways to see it (see "More Hawaii Attractions," at the end of this chapter, for coverage of Lanai).

**Trilogy Excursions** (☎ 800/874-2666 or 808/661-4743) will take you to Lanai for a day of snorkeling, swimming, and whale-watching on a 50-foot catamaran. This is the only outfitter with access to Hulopoe Bay and offering a ground tour of Lanai. **Club Lanai** (☎ 808/871-1144) will take you on a trimaran from Lahaina to Lanai's eastern shore, where you spend the day snorkeling, kayaking, and biking at an 8-acre beachfront estate.

Catch an inflatable black rubber Zodiac (the boats Jacques Cousteau made famous) to Lanai for a day of snorkeling with **Ocean Riders** (☎ 808/661-3586). On the way, they'll take you on a wet and often wild cruise exploring reefs, shipwrecks, and coves.

If that's not your style, consider the **Navatek II** (☎ 800/852-4183 or 808/661-8787). The unusual 82-foot vessel is designed to operate in heavy seas without spilling your Mai Tai. The ship's superstructure (the part you ride on) rests on twin torpedo-like hulls that create a remarkably smooth ride—you couldn't get sick if you tried.

# 3  Hawaii: The Big Island

The Big Island of Hawaii—the island that lends its good name to the entire 1,500-mile-long Hawaiian archipelago—is like no other place on earth. Simply put, it's spectacular.

This is where Mother Nature pulled out all stops. The island looks like the inside of a barbecue pit on one side and a legendary Green Mansion jungle on the other. The Big Island has it all: fiery volcanoes and sparkling waterfalls, black lava deserts and snowcapped mountain peaks, tropical rain forests and alpine meadows, a glacial lake and miles of beaches—with a rainbow of black, green, and golden sands. A 50-mile drive will take you from snowy winter to sultry summer, passing through spring or fall along the way. Five volcanoes—one still erupting—have created a continental island that's as big as Connecticut, and it's growing bigger daily.

## ARRIVING & DEPARTING

The Big Island has two major airports: **Keahole International Airport** ("the Kona Airport"), on the island's west coast, is the island's main port of entry; you can also fly into **Hilo International Airport** on the other side of the island. United flies directly from Los Angeles and San Francisco to the Kona Airport. Otherwise, you'll have to pick up an interisland flight in Honolulu on Aloha, Hawaiian, or Mahalo airlines.

## ESSENTIALS

**VISITOR INFORMATION**   The **Hawaii Visitor and Convention Bureau** has offices at 250 Keawe St., Hilo, HI 96720 (☎ 808/961-5797; fax 808/961-2126); and at 75–5719 W. Alii Dr., Kailua–Kona, HI 96740 (☎ 808/329-7787; fax 808/326-7563). The **Kohala Coast Resort Association** is at 69–275 Waikoloa Beach Dr., Kamuela, HI 96743 (☎ 808/885-4915; fax 808/885-1044).

**EMERGENCIES**    For ambulance, fire, and rescue, call ☎ **808/961-6022,** or dial
☎ **911. Hilo Hospital,** 1190 Waianuenue Ave. (☎ **808/969-4111**), and **Kona Hospital** in Kealakekua (☎ **808/322-9311**), both have 24-hour urgent-care facilities.

## GETTING AROUND

All the major car-rental agencies are represented at both major airports and at Kohala
coast resort hotels.

**TAXIS**    Taxis are readily available at both Keahole and Hilo airports. In Hilo, call
**A-1 Bob's Taxi.** In Kona, call **Kona Airport Taxi** (☎ **808/329-7779**).

**BUSES**    This is the cheapest way to see the Big Island, but you've got to be flexible.
The **Hele-On Bus** is a commuter bus service based in Hilo that goes almost everywhere
7 days a week, including Waimea, Kailua–Kona, South Kohala, and Volcano, with regular stops along the way. Eighteen Greyhound-sized buses run between 3:45am and 7pm
daily. You can board with backpacks, and there's storage for bicycles and other gear. The
most popular route, from Hilo to Volcano, is $1.50—the best transit deal on the island.
The 140-mile route from Hilo to Captain Cook, on the Kona coast, is $6. Call ☎ **808/
961-8744** for routes and schedules.

## HAWAII VOLCANOES NATIONAL PARK

Hawaii Volcanoes National Park, Hawaii's premier natural attraction, is a work in
progress thanks to Kilauea volcano, which pours red-hot lava into the sea and adds land
to the already big Big Island every day. Since the explosive fountaining stopped in 1986,
Kilauea has been bubbling and oozing in a mild-mannered way that lets you walk right
up to the creeping lava flow for an up-close-and-personal encounter.

You can see the highlights by car (the park has 45 miles of good roads, some of them
often covered by lava flows) if you only have a day to spare. If you can, allow 3 days
to explore the park fully; it has hiking trails, rain forests, and campgrounds in addition
to some of the world's weirdest landscape.

### ESSENTIALS

**VISITOR INFORMATION**    Contact **Hawaii Volcanoes National Park,** P.O. Box
52, Volcano, HI 96718 (☎ **808/967-7184**). **Kilauea Visitor Center** is at the park's
entrance, just off Hi. 11 (open daily 7:45am–5pm). For the latest **eruption update** in
the park, call ☎ **808/967-7977.** Daily updates on volcanic activity are also posted on
the visitor center's bulletin board.

**ACCESS POINTS**    The park is 29 miles from Hilo on Hawaii Belt Road (Hi. 11).
From Kailua–Kona, it's 100 miles, or a 2¹⁄₂-hour drive. For information where to stay
in nearby Volcano Village, see "Accommodations," below.

**ADMISSION**    Entry fees to the park (good for 1 week) are $10 per vehicle, $5 for
walk-ins and bicyclists.

**WHEN TO GO**    The best time to go is when Kilauea is really pumping. Go after dark
for the best look at the flowing lava.

**VOLCANO VOCABULARY**    The lava that looks like swirls of chocolate frosting is
called *pahoehoe,* which results from a fast-moving flow. The big, blocky lava that looks
like a chopped-up parking lot is *aa.* It's caused by lava that moves slowly, pulling apart
as it overruns itself. *Vog* is smog made of volcanic gases and smoke from forests set on
fire by aa and pahoehoe. *Laze* results when sulfuric acid hits the water and mixes with
chlorine to become hydrochloric acid. Both vog and laze sting your eyes and can cause
respiratory illness; don't subject yourself to either for too long. Anyone with breathing
or heart problems should take heed to avoid both vog and laze.

# The Big Island

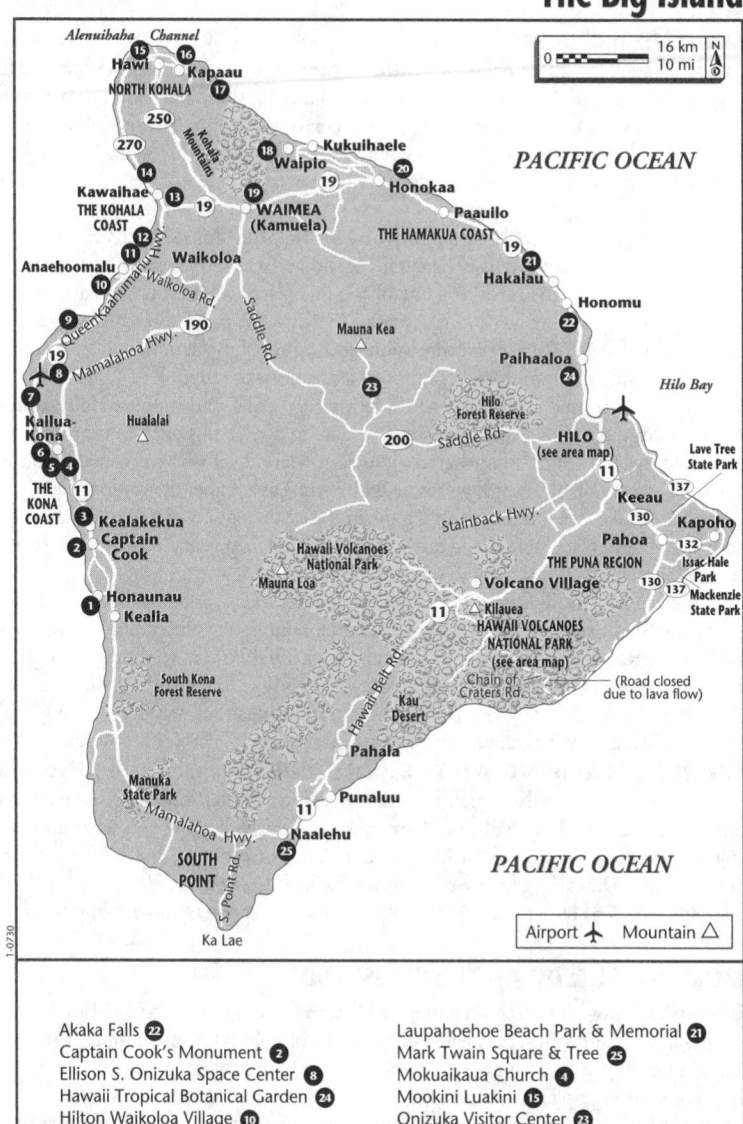

## SEEING THE HIGHLIGHTS

Your first stop should be **Kilauea Visitor Center,** just inside the park entrance. Here you can get up-to-the-minute reports on the volcano's activity and learn how volcanoes work. Then walk across the street to **Volcano House;** go through the lobby and out the other side, where you can have a good look at **Kilauea Caldera,** a $2^{1}/_{2}$-mile-wide, 500-foot-deep pit, once known as one of "the greatest wonders of the globe." You can still see wisps of steam.

Now, get out on the highway and drive by the **Sulphur Banks,** which smell like rotten eggs, and the **Steam Vents,** where trails of smoke, once molten lava, rise from within the inner reaches of the earth. It's one of the few places where you can have the sensory experience that the volcano is actually alive. Stop at the **Thomas A. Jaggar Museum** (open daily 8:30am–5pm; admission free), which shows eruption videos, explains the Pele legend, and monitors earthquakes (a precursor of eruptions).

Next, drive around the caldera to the other side, park, and walk to **Halemaumau Crater's edge** to stand at the overlook and stare in awe at this once-fuming and bubbling old fire pit, which still generates ferocious heat out of vestigial vents. If you feel the need to cool off afterward, go to the **Thurston Lava Tube,** the coolest place in the park. You'll hike down into a natural bowl in the earth, a forest preserve the lava didn't touch, and see a black hole in the earth; step in. It's all drippy and cool, with bare roots hanging down.

If the volcano is still erupting, be sure to see it after dark as it snakes down the side of the mountain and pours into the sea. About an hour before sunset, head down **Chain of Craters Road.** Get ready to see the red—it's a vivid display you'll never forget. At the barricades, park rangers will direct you where to hike to the current site of the lava flow. Remember that new lava can be unstable and break off without warning. Take water, a flashlight, your camera, and wear sturdy shoes.

**HIKING & CAMPING AT THE VOLCANO** The moderate **Kilauea Iki** and **Halemaumau trails,** which start at the Visitor Center, both take you into the still-fuming crater. Easy half-mile **Devastation Trail** will show you what an erupting volcano did to a once-flourishing ohia forest. For camping and hiking information, contact **Hawaii Volcanoes National Park,** P.O. Box 52, Volcano, HI 96718 (☎ **808/967-7311**). Trail maps are sold at park headquarters and are highly recommended.

## MORE TO SEE & DO ON THE BIG ISLAND

**BEACHES** Just off Queen Kaahumanu Highway, south of the Hapuna Beach Prince Hotel, lies **Hapuna Beach,** a half-mile crescent of gold sand. In summer, this is the island's best beach for swimming, snorkeling, and bodysurfing; in winter, its thundering waves, strong rip currents, and lack of lifeguards can be dangerous. Hawaii has lots of extraordinary snorkel and dive sites, but none are so easily accessible or have as much to offer as mile-wide **Kealakekua Bay,** an uncrowded marine preserve on the south Kona coast (take Napoopoo Road off Hi. 11). You can swim with dolphins, sea turtles, octopi, and every species of tropical fish that calls Hawaii's waters home—simply dazzling. **Kahaluu Beach Park,** the best all-around beach on Kailua–Kona's Alii Drive, is a great place for beginning snorkelers and children to get their fins wet—the water is so shallow you can literally stand up if you feel uncomfortable. Its unusual emerald sands attract thousands each year to Hawaii's famous **Green Sand (Papakolea) Beach,** at the island's South Point. Follow a well-worn four-wheel-drive–only road for $2^{1}/_{2}$ miles to the top of a cliff, which you have to climb down to reach the beach (the south end offers the safest path).

**SAMPAN TOURS OF HILO** Here's an ideal way to sightsee: Catch a sampan (an open-air sedan) and ride around Hilo like everyone did back in the 1930s. The sampans run hourly from the pier, but you can pick them up anywhere along the route; call for the location nearest you (☎ 808/959-7864). The driver delivers an animated running commentary on Hilo's history. If you buy a $7 all-day pass, you can jump on and off whenever the fancy strikes you.

**WAIPIO VALLEY**    Pack a picnic and head for this gorgeously lush valley that time forgot. Delve deep into the jungle on foot, comb the black-sand beach, or just laze the day away by a babbling stream, the tail end of a 1,000-foot waterfall. No matter how you see Waipio Valley, it's an unforgettable experience.

To get to Waipio Valley, take Hi. 19 from Hilo to Honokaa, then Hi. 240 to **Waipio Valley Lookout,** a grassy park on the edge of Waipio Valley's sheer cliffs with splendid views of the wild oasis below. From the lookout, you can hike down into the valley, or take the **Waipio Valley Shuttle** (☎ 808/775-7121) on a 90-minute guided tour. The shuttle runs Mon–Sat 9am–4pm; it's $35 for adults, $14 for kids under 11. Get your tickets at Waipio Valley Art Works on Hi. 240, 2 miles from the lookout.

**STARGAZING FROM MAUNA KEA**    Mauna Kea's summit is the best place on earth for astronomical observations because its mid-Pacific site is near the equator and enjoys clear, pollution-free skies and pitch-black nights with no urban light to interfere with the "seeing." The stargazing from here is fantastic even with the naked eye; all you need are binoculars to see the Milky Way.

On Friday, Saturday, and Sunday from 6:30 to 10pm, you can do some serious stargazing from the **Onizuka Visitor Center** (☎ 808/961-2180). There's a free lecture at 7pm, and you'll have a chance to peer through an 11-inch telescope.

You need four-wheel-drive to make the drive to the peak, Observatory Hill; always check the weather and Mauna Kea Road conditions before you head out (☎ 808/969-3218). If you'd rather not go it alone, you can caravan up as part of a **free summit tour;** the tours are offered Saturday and Sunday at 2pm from the visitor center; you must be at least 16 years old and have a four-wheel-drive vehicle. Call ☎ 808/935-3371 if you'd like to participate.

**BEST BETS FOR KIDS**    Hawaii Volcanoes National Park's Thurston Lava Tube is scary, spooky, and perfect for any kid. You hike downhill through a rain forest to enter this huge, silent black hole full of drips, cobwebs, and tree roots that stretches underground for almost a half mile. And any kid who doesn't get a kick out of seeing a **live volcano** set the night on fire has been watching too much TV. Take hot dogs, bottled water, and go to it.

**Atlantis Submarine** (☎ 800/548-6262 or 808/329-6626) offers real submarine tours of the underwater world hourly from Kailua Pier 7 days a week. Your kids are gonna love it—but a mask, snorkel, and some fins do the trick just as well.

When your kid **catches a fish** bigger than you, that's something to write home about. It can happen any day of the year on the Kona coast, marlin capital of the world. See "Outdoor Activities," below.

**WHALE-WATCHING**    Hawaii's most impressive visitors—45-foot humpback whales—return to the waters off Kona every winter, roughly December to April. To see the whales up close and personal, book a 3¹/₂-hour cruise with **Captain Dan McSweeney's Year-Round Whale-Watching** (☎ 808/322-0028).

**OUTDOOR ACTIVITIES**    Deep-sea fishing doesn't get any better than Kona. When anglers here catch marlin that weigh 1,000 pounds or more, they call them "granders." Many now tag and release so the marlin can live to fight again. You can arrange a charter through **Kona Charter Skippers Association** (☎ 808/329-3600), which serves as a booking desk for local boats.

The leeward coast offers some of the best diving and snorkeling in the world, thanks to year-round calm, warm, clear waters that are home to spectacular marine life. For day or night scuba dives, contact **Jack's Diving Locker** in Kona (☎ 808/329-7585), **Kona Coast Divers** (☎ 808/329-8802), or **Red Sail Sports,** on the Kohala coast (☎ 808/ 885-2876 or 808/885-2000). Some of the best snorkeling areas include **Hookena, White Sands, Kahaluu, Kona Coast,** and **Spencer beach parks.** Or take a snorkeling cruise to an underwater park on a 60-foot catamaran with **Fair Wind Snorkeling and Diving Adventures** (☎ 800/677-9461 or 808/322-2788).

For guided day hikes ranging from shoreline hikes to ancient petroglyphs to hikes up Mauna Kea to one of the world's highest glacial lakes, contact Dr. Hugh Montgomery of **Hawaiian Walkways,** P.O. Box 2193, Kamuela, HI 96743 (☎ 800/457-7759).

Most of the Big Island's golf courses are carved out of lava beds. Among the island's best are **Mauna Kea Beach Golf Course,** a Robert Trent Jones, Jr. course that's consistently rated one of the top courses in the U.S. (☎ 808/882-7222 or 808/882-5888); **Hapuna Golf Course,** which the U.S. Golf Association named "The Course of the Future" (☎ 808/882-1111); and **Mauna Lani Frances I'i Brown Championship Courses,** two courses with breathtaking vistas (☎ 808/885-6655).

**SHOPPING**    Kailua–Kona's shopping prospects pour out into the streets in a festival of T-shirts, trinkets, and dime-a-dozen souvenirs, with Alii Drive at the center of the activity. The **Kona Inn Shopping Village** on Alii Drive includes shops galore for vacationers' needs. In Kohala, the **King's Shops** has a variety of shops specializing in children's and women's fashion and hip aloha shirts. Shopping in Waimea centers around **Parker Square** and **Waimea Center,** at Hi. 19 and Hi. 190, with everything from one-of-a-kind Hawaiian artifacts to sun hats. Shopping in Hilo is centered around the **Bayfront** area downtown, where the hippest new businesses have taken up residence in the historic buildings lining Kamehameha Avenue.

## ACCOMMODATIONS
### THE KONA COAST
The Kona coast is a collection of tiny communities along the sun-baked leeward side of the island.

✪ **Four Seasons Resort Hualalai at Historic Kaupulehu.** *P.O. Box 1119, Kailua–Kona, HI 96745.* ☎ *800/332-3443 or 808/325-8000. Fax 808/325-8100. 243 rms, 31 suites. From $450 double. AE, DC, JCB. MC, V.* These brand-new clusters of oceanfront villas are nestled between the sea and a new, private Jack Nicklaus–designed golf course. The rooms are furnished in Pacific tropical style, and the bathrooms have private gardens, so you can shower naked under the sun. Facilities include restaurants, a sports club, spa, three swimming pools, tennis courts, Hawaiian culture center, and conference facilities.

**Kanaloa at Kona.** *78–261 Manukai St., Kailua–Kona, HI 96740.* ☎ *800/ 688-7444 or 808/322-9625. Fax 808/322-3618. 166 units. $175–$210 one-bedroom apt; $205–$245 two-bedroom apt; $245–$265 three-bedroom apt. AE, CB, DC, DISC, JCB, MC, V.* These well-managed, spacious condos border the rocky coast beside Keauhou Bay, 6 miles south of Kailua–Kona. The units have all the comforts of home (and then some), such as the huge bathrooms with spas, dressing rooms, and bidets. Spacious lanais, tropical decor, and lots of appliances make for free and easy living. Ideal for families.

**Keauhou Beach Hotel.** *78–6740 Alii Dr., Kailua–Kona, HI 96740 (6 miles south of Kailua in Keauhou).* ☎ *800/367-6025 or 808/322-3441. Fax 808/322-6586. 317 units. $98–$170 double; $240–$415 suite. $99 room/car/breakfast package for 2. AE, DC, JCB, MC, V.* The best package in town is available year-round at this older hotel, set on lush, well-maintained, historic royal grounds and adjacent to Kona's best swimming and snorkeling beach. Some of the rooms are slipping—torn bedspreads, stained carpets—so insist on a renovated room, preferably on the south side for the best views. There's a restaurant on the premises.

**Kona Magic Sands.** *77–6452 Alii Dr., Kailua–Kona, HI 96740.* ☎ *and fax 808/ 326-5622. E-mail: lacertee@aol.com. 37 studio apts with showers only. Low season, $65 apt. High season, $75 apt. No credit cards.* Every unit in this older condo has a lanai that steps out over the ocean and sunset views you'll dream about long afterward. The small, cozy units (two people max) are one long, narrow room with a kitchenette at one end and lanai at the other, with living/dining/bedroom combo in between. There's a restaurant on the premises.

**Kona Riviera Villas.** *c/o Knudson & Associates, 75–6082 Alii Dr., Kailua–Kona, HI 96740.* ☎ *800/800-6202 or 808/329-6311. Fax 808/326-2178. E-mail: knutson@aloha.net. 12 one-bedroom units. Low season, $65–$90. High season, $75–$100. Three-night minimum. No credit cards.* This older condominium is set back from the ocean, but still has the view, plus a freshwater pool and patio with barbecue right on the water. Swimming is too rough here, but you can watch the surfers ride the waves. All units are one bedroom; most have ocean-view lanais, and some have sofa beds. Book early.

**Kona Tiki Hotel.** *75–5968 Alii Dr. Kailua–Kona, HI 96740.* ☎ *808/329-1425. Fax 808/327-9402. 15 rms. $56 double; $62 double with kitchenette. Rates include breakfast. Three-night minimum. No credit cards.* This motel on the ocean is one of the hottest budget deals in Hawaii. All of the tastefully decorated rooms feature oceanfront lanais, ceiling fans, and a minifridge (no TV or phones). This family-run operation is like a large B&B, with lots of aloha and a morning continental breakfast buffet at the pool. Book *way* in advance.

**Kona Village Resort.** *P.O. Box 1299, Kailua–Kona, HI 96745.* ☎ *800/ 367-5290 or 808/325-5555. Fax 808/325-5124. 125 bungalows. Full American Plan (all meals, tennis, water sports, walking tours, airport transfers, welcome lei, and Friday luau), $395–$680 double. Packages available. AE, DC, JCB, MC, V.* This is the place to get away from it all—a Polynesian paradise where no money is exchanged (everything is all-inclusive, except liquor). The tastefully decorated thatch-roof bungalows all have separate bedroom, lanai, and such extras as grind-and-perk coffeemakers, but no phones or TVs; some have outdoor hot tubs. Conveniences include the beach, water sports, tennis, two pools, and outdoor cocktail lounges.

## UP COUNTRY KONA

**BED & BREAKFASTS** Holualoa Inn, P.O. Box 222, Holualoa, HI 96725 (☎ 800/ 392-1812 or 808/324-1121; fax 808/322-2472), a fabulous contemporary Hawaiian home on 40 pastoral acres in artsy Holualoa village, has six suites with stunning panoramic views of Kailua–Kona and the entire Kona coast.

Everything about **Merryman's Bed & Breakfast,** P.O. Box 474, Kealakekua, HI 96750 (☎ 800/545-4390 or 808/323-2276; fax 808/323-3749), above the Captain Cook–Kealakekua area, is impeccable, from the fresh flowers throughout to the memorable breakfast. You can watch the sun set from the lanai, or gaze at the star-studded sky as you soak in the hot tub.

## THE KOHALA COAST

Along this black lava coast are world-class beachfront hotels, golden beaches, golf courses, and historic sites.

**Hilton Waikoloa Village.** *69–425 Waikoloa Beach Dr., Kamuela, HI 96743.* ☎ *800/445-8667 or 808/885-1234. Fax 808/885-2900. 1,294 units. Winter, $210–$1,455 double or suite. Lower prices in off-season. AE, CB, DC, DISC, JCB, MC, V.* If you love Las Vegas and Disneyland, this is where you belong—especially if you're bringing the kids. It's a tropical fantasy world all its own, featuring waterfalls, wildlife, a water slide, lagoons (one with dolphins), and more. Everything is luxurious. Conveniences include restaurants, bars, boutique shops, a spa, three pools, tennis courts, two championship golf courses, American Express and Avis desks.

**Royal Waikoloan.** *69–275 Waikoloa Beach Rd., Kamuela, HI 96743.* ☎ *800/688-7444 or 808/885-6789. Fax 808/885-7852. 555 units. Winter, $135–$750 double. Low-season, $120–$750 double. Rates are all-inclusive. AE, DC, DISC, JCB, MC, V.* Here's the bargain of the Kohala coast: a resort with food and drink included in the rate! Older and more basic than its neighbors, the comfortable Waikoloan has a breathtaking beach, a historic fishpond, and petroglyphs. Smoke lingers in some of the smallish rooms, but you can always get fresh air out on the lanai. The resort has a bar, golf, tennis, and health club.

**WAIPIO VALLEY**   Jackie Horne's 1930s plantation home, **Waipio Wayside B&B Inn,** P.O. Box 840, Honokaa, HI 96727 (☎ **800/833-8849** or 808/775-0275), has five rooms (some with shared bath), done in old Hawaii style. The place abounds with thoughtful touches, such as a help-yourself tea and cookies bar. A sunny lanai with hammocks overlooks a yard that blooms with trees and orchids. Jackie's friendly hospitality and excellent breakfasts really round out the experience. Rates, including breakfast, are $65–$110 for a double.

## HILO

Hawaii's second largest city is a quaint, misty flower-filled city of Victorian houses overlooking a half-moon bay.

**✪ Dolphin Bay Hotel.** *333 Iliahi St., Hilo, HI 96720.* ☎ *808/935-1466. Fax 808/935-1523. 18 studio, one-, and two-bedroom apts. $55–$89 double. MC, V.* This clean, family-run motel offers good value in a quiet, Edenlike garden setting: Ripe starfruit hang from the trees, flowers abound, and there's a jungly trail by a stream. The tidy, brightly decorated concrete-block apartments are small and often breezeless, but they're equipped with ceiling fans and jalousies (but no phones).

**Hawaii Naniloa Hotel.** *93 Banyan Dr., Hilo, HI 96720.* ☎ *800/367-5360 or 808/969-3333. Fax 808/969-6622. 336 units. $100–$240 double or suite. Rates include airport shuttle. AE, JCB, MC, V.* This 9-story hotel on Hilo Bay is a generally characterless place to stay, but, in terms of comfort and amenities, one of the best that Hilo has to offer, with nice rooms with lanais and a quiet, leafy setting across from the ocean. Facilities include restaurants, lounges, pools, spa, and shops.

**A HILO BED-&-BREAKFAST**   A stately, completely restored, century-old Victorian, **Shipman House Bed and Breakfast,** 131 Kaiulani St., Hilo, HI 96720 (☎ **800/MAP-THIS** or 808/934-8002; fax 808/935-1032), is the island's grande dame of historic B&Bs, outfitted with such details as antique koa beds and a 1903 Steinway along with modern amenities like full baths, ceiling fans, and minifridges in each room.

## VOLCANO

The village sits in a rain forest on the edge of America's most exciting national park.

**Chalet Kilauea: The Inn at Volcano.** *P.O. Box 998, Volcano, HI 96785.* ☎ *800/937-7786 or 808/967-7786. Fax 800/577-1849 or 808/967-8660. E-mail: bchawaii@aol.com. 6 units. $125–$395 double. Rates include full breakfast. AE, DISC, MC, V.* This AAA triple Diamond Award winner, nestled in the forest just a mile from Hawaii Volcanoes National Park, features two rooms, three suites, and a separate elegant cottage. From the personal service at check-in to the art-filled rooms to the afternoon tea to the excellent gourmet breakfast, this place is worth every penny.

The same owners also run **Volcano Bed & Breakfast** (☎ **800/736-7140** or 808/967-7779; same fax as above), a restored 1912 home with six rooms (all with shared baths). It's not as luxurious as Chalet Kilauea, but it's comfortable, quiet, and a bargain: $45–$65 double, including continental breakfast.

**OTHER VOLCANO-AREA BED & BREAKFASTS**  Comfortable **Carson's Volcano Cottage,** Mauna Loa Estates, 501 Sixth St., Volcano, HI 96785 (☎ **800/845-5282** or 808/967-7683), has three rooms, three cottages, and five vacation rental homes just around the corner from the national park, as well as other well-appointed accommodations nearby. **Kilauea Lodge,** P.O. Box 116, Volcano, HI 96785 (☎ **808/967-7366;** fax 808/967-7367), is a pleasant and popular roadside lodge on 10 acres of wooded, landscaped grounds.

## DINING

### THE KONA COAST

This is where the Kona coffee mania began. Coffeehouses are a burgeoning aspect of Big Island dining, some of them very touristy. The north and south Kona districts, where coffee is a viable industry is *the* place for coffee lovers to buy their brew.

    **Aloha Cafe.** *Hi. 11, Kainaliu.* ☎ *808/322-3383. Reservations recommended for large parties. Most items under $7. MC, V. Mon–Sat 8am–9pm, Sun 9am–2pm. AMERICAN/VEGETARIAN.* This roadside oasis dispenses healthy food with many special touches. Expect heroic burgers and omelets, a "broke-your-mouth" breakfast burrito, fresh-squeezed orange juice, fresh fruit smoothies, and carrot cake of the gods.

    **Manago Hotel Restaurant.** *Manago Hotel, Hi. 11, Captain Cook.* ☎ *808/ 323-2642. Reservations recommended for dinner. Main courses $7–$11. DISC, MC, V. Daily 7–9am and 11am–2pm; Tues–Thurs 5–7:30pm, Fri–Sun 5–7pm. AMERICAN.* This place is a local legend, greatly loved for its unpretentious, tasty food at family prices. You can dine handsomely on local favorites: a 12-ounce T-bone, fried ahi, or the house specialty, pork chops, for $11 or less. It's nothing fancy, and there's a lot of frying going on, but there would be riots if anything changed after 80 years.

    ✪ **Palm Cafe.** *75–5819 Alii Dr.* ☎ *808/329-7765. Reservations recommended. Main courses $19–$26. AE, DC, DISC, JCB, MC, V. Daily 5:30–10pm. PACIFIC RIM.* The casual, elegant ambience of this open-air restaurant matches the fresh and brilliantly prepared island cuisine, which is sophisticated without being pretentious. Signature dishes include Hunan-style lamb chops with Puna goat cheese and roasted sweet peppers; and marinated mahimahi served on a rich concoction of lobster sauce and coconut cream on noodle crisps.

    **Sam Choy's Restaurant.** *Kaloko Light Industrial Park, 73–5576 Kauhola St.* ☎ *808/326-1545. Reservations recommended for dinner. Main courses $18–$30. No credit cards. Mon–Sat 6am–2pm, Wed–Sat 5–9pm. HAWAII REGIONAL.* Jovial chef-owner Sam Choy hit upon a smashing formula: informal environs, humongous servings, and high-volume local food with a gourmet twist. Sam's legendary dinners include top-of-the-line fresh opakapaka, oriental lamb chops with shiitake-vegetable pasta, and seafood laulau, his signature dish of fresh fish with julienned vegetables and seaweed, wrapped and steamed in ti leaves.

### THE KOHALA COAST

    ✪ **Cafe Pesto.** *Kawaihae Shopping Center.* ☎ *808/882-1071. Main courses $7–$17. AE, DC, DISC, MC, V. Mon–Fri 11am–9pm, Fri–Sat 11am–10pm. PIZZA/ ITALIAN.* The first rave we ever heard about Cafe Pesto was years ago, from a visiting New York food editor who stumbled upon its organic greens, sizzling sauces, and world-class dressings. Adoring devotees still drive many miles for its gourmet pizza, calzones, and salads.

    **CanoeHouse.** *Mauna Lani Bay Hotel and Bungalows.* ☎ *808/885-6622. Reservations recommended. Main courses $25–$37. AE, CB, DC, DISC, JCB, MC, V. Daily*

*5:30–9pm. HAWAII REGIONAL.* Chef David Abella's penchant for Asian cooking, strengthened during his tenure in Hong Kong, is becoming apparent: seared fresh ahi (a CanoeHouse signature), marinated rack of lamb, nori-wrapped ahi, and other standouts are presented with a balance of European sophistication and assertive Asian flavors, either under the stars or in the open-air dining room.

## WAIMEA (KAMUELA)

This is an old up-country cow town set in a countryside of rolling green pastures and wide-open spaces.

**Ann Sutherland's Mean Cuisine.** *Opelo Plaza, Hi. 19.* ☎ *808/885-6325. Main courses $4–$13. MC, V. Mon–Sat 6am–8pm, Sun 8am–2pm. AMERICAN ECLECTIC.* Ann Sutherland has proven that busy people can eat well, too. Streaming out of this busy kitchen/bakery are breads, pastries, cakes, and pies baked fresh daily, and a host of meals to eat in or take home—sandwiches, soups, salads, and daily specials ranging from lamb stew to spinach crepes—that are as good as mom's home cooking.

✪ **Maha's Cafe.** *Spencer House, Hi. 19.* ☎ *808/885-0693. Main courses $6–$11. DC, DISC, MC, V. Mon–Sat 9am–6pm, Sun 10am–5pm. COFFEEHOUSE/ SANDWICHES.* The island's best sandwiches are served in a tiny room of Waimea's first frame house (1852). What a find! Harriet-Ann Namahaokalani Schutte, who first made her culinary mark at Mauna Lani Resort, dispenses hotcakes and granola for breakfast, delectable sandwiches at lunch, finger sandwiches and homemade scones (with lilikoi butter!) at teatime, and cookies all day long.

**Merriman's.** *Opelu Plaza, Hi. 19.* ☎ *808/885-6822. Reservations recommended. Main courses $12–$24 (market price for ranch lamb or ahi). AE, MC, V. Mon–Fri 11:30am–1:30pm; daily 5:30–9pm. HAWAII REGIONAL.* Foodies the world over know Merriman's as one of Hawaii's top palate-pleasers. The brilliant, unassuming Peter Merriman has won accolades for pioneering the use of fresh local products long before it became fashionable—organic greens, vine-ripened Lokelani tomatoes, lamb from the Kohala mountains, corn from Pahoa, fish straight off the hook—but it's his imaginative and respectful preparations that make them sizzle.

## HILO

With many reasonably priced restaurants, Hilo is a bargain for budget travelers.

**Broke the Mouth.** *55 Mamo St.* ☎ *808/934-7670. Plate lunches $3.50–$5.50. MC, V. Tues–Sat 7am–2pm. ORGANIC/VEGETARIAN.* The healthful Hawaiian pleasures here include *manapua* (sweet buns) filled with sweet-potato basil or taro and cheese, and fresh baked goods like ginger buns sweetened with banana and ohelo berries. The house-special sauce uses macadamia nuts instead of peanuts, and starchy taro is seasoned and whipped into a mayonnaise that could give Best Foods a run for its money.

✪ **Cafe Pesto Hilo Bay.** *S. Hata Building, 308 Kam Ave.* ☎ *808/969-6640. Pizzas $6.95–$16.95. AE, CB, DC, DISC, JCB, MC, V. Sun–Thurs 11am–9pm, Fri–Sat 11am–10pm. PIZZA/PACIFIC RIM.* The island's only wood-fired brick oven turns out toothsome pizzas topped with fresh organic herbs and island-grown produce. Favorites include the Four Seasons (dripping with prosciutto, bell peppers, and mushrooms), smoked salmon pizza with Gorgonzola, and flash-seared poke salad on organic greens with tamarind dressing—gourmet all the way.

**Fiascos.** *Waiakea Sq., 200 Kanoelehua Ave.* ☎ *808/935-7666. Reservations recommended for more than 4. Main courses $6.95–$15.95. AE, DC, DISC, MC, V. Sun–Thurs 11am–10pm, Fri–Sat 11am–11pm. AMERICAN/MEXICAN/ECLECTIC.* All the makings of fantastic fajitas arrive on sizzling platters so you build your own at the table.

Fiascos also offers a huge soup-and-salad bar (with four different soups daily), fresh fish sandwiches, bountiful salads, pastas, burgers, steaks, fried chicken, smoked chicken breast with sesame dressing—something for everyone, even fried ice cream for dessert.

**Nihon Restaurant & Cultural Center.** *Liliuokalani Gardens, 123 Lihiwai St.* ☎ *808/969-1133. Reservations recommended. Main courses $8.95–$19.95. AE, DC, DISC, MC, V. Mon–Sat 11am–1:30pm and 5–8pm. JAPANESE.* The room faces beautiful Hilo Bay on one side and soothing Liliuokalani Gardens on the other. The menu features steak-and-seafood combos and selections from the sushi bar, including innovative poke and lomi salmon hand rolls. This isn't inexpensive dining, but the return on your dollar is high, with a presentation that matches the setting.

## VOLCANO

For a quick bite, you can go to the **Steam Vent Cafe,** Haunani Road (between markers 26 and 27 on Hi 11; ☎ 808/985-8744), is *the* place to stop for gourmet coffee, sandwiches, salads, and pastries—it's all fabulous. Even more important, the only ATM in a 60-mile stretch is here.

**Kilauea Lodge.** *Hi. 11 (Volcano Village exit).* ☎ *808/967-7366. Reservations recommended. Main courses $14.75–$28.50. MC, V. Daily 5:30–9pm. CONTINENTAL.* Some of us would cross the tundra to dine at Kilauea Lodge, a fine culinary act on the volcano. But my last visit was disappointing: The quality had noticeably declined. Let's hope that the duck a l'orange regains the excellence we remember. Other offerings: pastas, rack of lamb, fresh fish, and a winning potato-leek soup.

## THE BIG ISLAND AFTER DARK

Jokes abound about the neighbor islands and nightlife being oxymorons, but there are a few pockets of entertainment, most of it in the Kona and Kohala coast resorts. Your best bet is to check the local newspapers—*Honolulu Advertiser, West Hawaii Today*—for special shows. Other than that, regular entertainment in the local clubs usually consists of mellow Hawaiian music at sunset, small hula groups, or jazz trios.

Some of the island's best events are usually held at **Kahilu Theatre** in Waimea (☎ 808/885-6017), so be on the lookout for any mention of it during your stay. Hula, the top Hawaiian music groups from all over Hawaii, drama, and all aspects of the performing arts use Kahilu as a favored venue.

**King Kamehameha's Kona Beach Hotel** (☎ 808/329-2911) holds a luau and Polynesian revue on the beach on Tuesday, Wednesday, Thursday, and Sunday. Elsewhere in Kailua–Kona, the **Jolly Roger,** on Waterfront Row (☎ 808/329-1344), is the spot for live entertainment on Friday and Saturday—Top 40s, Hawaiian music, and dancing.

Hilo's most notable event is the **Merrie Monarch Hula Festival,** which continues for a week after Easter Sunday with hula competition from all over the world, demonstrations and craft fairs, and a colorful spirit of pageantry that takes over the entire town. Tickets are always hard to come by; call ☎ 808/935-9168 well ahead of time. Special concerts are also held at the **Hawaii Naniloa Hotel's Crown Room** (☎ 808/969-3333), the Hilo venue for name performers. If you're a blues lover, see what's playing at **Lehua's Bay City Bar and Grill** (☎ 808/935-8055). Live blues pours out onto the streets twice a month, on Friday and Saturday nights.

**LUAU!** **Kona Village Luau,** Kona Village Resort (☎ 808/325-5555), held Friday at 6pm (reservations required), is the longest continuously running luau on the island—and it's still the best, a combination of an authentically Polynesian venue with a menu that works, impressive entertainment, and the spirit of Old Hawaii. The bounty and generosity of the Polynesian buffet are striking, and the Polynesian revue manages, miraculously, to avoid being corny.

# 4 Kauai

Aloof and beautiful, Kauai is the realization of the dream—a tropical island paradise come to life. All the elements are here: moody rain forests, majestic cliffs, jagged peaks, emerald valleys, palm trees swaying in the breeze, daily rainbows, and some of the most spectacular golden beaches you'll find anywhere.

Kauai's beauty has won a best supporting role in more than 40 Hollywood films, from *South Pacific* and *Blue Hawaii* to *Jurassic Park*. But it's not just another pretty face: The island's raw wilderness is daunting, its seas challenging, its canyons forbidding; two-thirds of this island is impenetrable. This great green place remains a sanctuary for native birds and plants and fish and, in a larger sense, even humans.

## ARRIVING & DEPARTING

No carriers fly direct from the mainland to Kauai; you'll have to pick up a 20-minute interisland flight in Honolulu to **Lihue Airport,** on Kauai's eastern shore; Aloha, Hawaiian, and Mahalo airlines will get you there.

## ESSENTIALS

**VISITOR INFORMATION**    The Kauai chapter of the **Hawaii Visitor and Convention Bureau** is on the second floor of Lihue Plaza at 3016 Umi St., Lihue (☎ **800/ 262-1400** or 808/245-3971). For a free *Kauai Vacation Planner,* call ☎ **800/ AH-KAUAI.**

**EMERGENCIES**    Dial ☎ **911** for emergencies. **Wilcox Memorial Hospital,** 3420 Kuhio Hwy., Lihue (☎ **808/245-1100**), has emergency services available around the clock.

## GETTING AROUND

All major car-rental agencies have cars available on Kauai.

**BY BUS**    Kauai Bus (☎ **808/241-6410**) is good for day trips if you know your way around, but you can't take anything larger than a shopping bag aboard and it doesn't stop at any of the resorts. Buses run more or less hourly from 5:30am to 6pm. The fare is $1 (50¢ for seniors, students, and disabled passengers).

**BY TAXIS & AIRPORT SHUTTLE SERVICE**    Call **Al's VIP Limo Taxicab** (☎ **808/742-1390**) or **Kauai Cab Service** (☎ **808/246-9554**).

## WHAT TO SEE & DO

**BEACHES**    Kauai is renowned for its beaches; three of the most beautiful are Tunnels, Haena, and Ke'e on the North Shore. Postcard-perfect, gold-sand **Tunnels Beach** is one of Hawaii's most beautiful, excellent for swimming nearly year-round, and safe for snorkeling since it's protected by a fringing coral reef (the waters can get rough in winter, though). Around the corner is **Haena Beach Park,** with grainy, golden sand, excellent swimming in summer, and great snorkeling in crystal-clear waters amid clouds of tropical fish. **Ke'e Beach State Park,** where the road ends on the north shore, is a little reddish-gold sand beach almost too beautiful to be real. Don't be surprised if it looks familiar; it was featured in *The Thornbirds.* Swimming and snorkeling are safe inside the reef, but dangerous outside. On the sunny South Shore, big, wide **Poipu Beach Park** has excellent swimming, small tide pools for exploring, great reefs for snorkeling and diving, nice waves for surfers, and a steady wind for windsurfers.

**WAIMEA CANYON & KOKEE STATE PARK**    **Waimea Canyon** is quite a sight; no other island has anything else like it. To get there, turn up Waimea Canyon Dr. (Hi. 550) or Kokee Road (Hi. 55) from Hi. 50. This valley, known for its reddish lava beds, reminds everyone who sees it of the Grand Canyon. Kauai's version is bursting

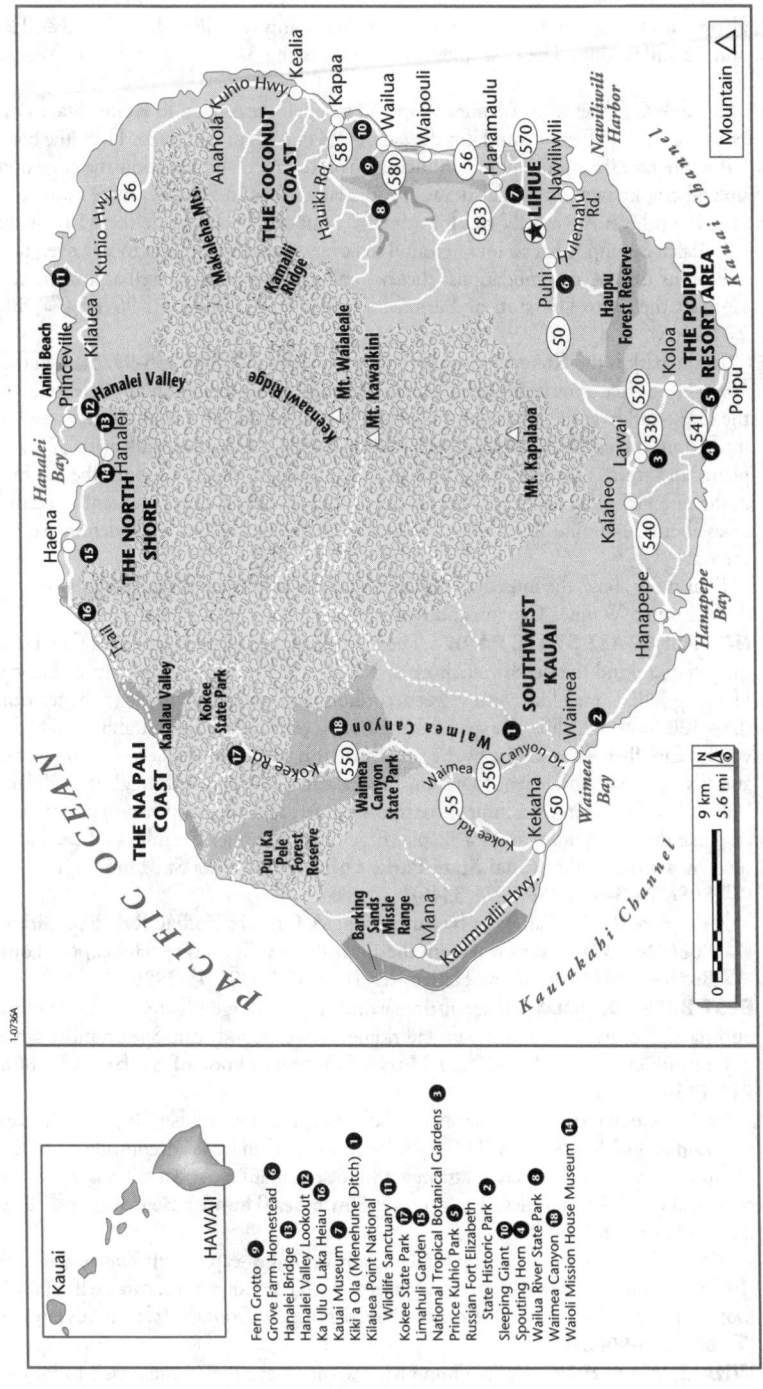

# Kauai

Mountain △

**THE NA PALI COAST**

**THE NORTH SHORE**

**THE COCONUT COAST**

**SOUTHWEST KAUAI**

**THE POIPU RESORT AREA**

PACIFIC OCEAN

Hanalei Bay

Anini Beach
Princeville
Kilauea
Kuhio Hwy

Haena
Trail
Kalalau Valley
Kokee State Park
Puu Ka Pele Forest Reserve

Barking Sands Missle Range
Mana
Kaumualii Hwy.
Kekaha
Waimea Bay
Waimea
Canyon Dr.

Makaleha Mts.
Kamalii Ridge
Keenawai Ridge

Mt. Waialeale △
Mt. Kawaikini △
Mt. Kapalaoa △

Anahola
Kealia
Kapaa
Wailua
Waipouli
Hanamaulu
LIHUE ★
Nawiliwili
Puhi
Haupu Forest Reserve
Koloa
Lawai
Kalaheo
Hanapepe
Poipu

Kauai Channel
Nawiliwili Harbor
Hanapepe Bay
Kaulakahi Channel

Kuhio Hwy
56
581
580
570
583
50
520
530
540
541
550
55

Waimea Canyon State Park
Waimea Canyon
Kokee Rd.

**HAWAII**

Kauai

Fern Grotto ⑨
Grove Farm Homestead ⑥
Hanalei Bridge ⑬
Hanalei Valley Lookout ⑫
Ka Ulu O Laka Heiau ⑯
Kauai Museum ⑦
Kiki a Ola (Menehune Ditch) ①
Kilauea Point National Wildlife Sanctuary ⑪
Kokee State Park ⑰
Limahuli Garden ⑮
National Tropical Botanical Gardens ③
Prince Kuhio Park ⑤
Russian Fort Elizabeth State Historic Park ②
Sleeping Giant ⑩
Spouting Horn ⑧
Wailua River State Park ⑩
Waimea Canyon ⑱
Waioli Mission House Museum ⑭

9 km
5.6 mi
0

1-0736A

also with ever-changing color, but it's smaller—only a mile wide, 3,567 feet deep, and 12 miles long. The best hike for families is the 3-hour round-trip to Waipoo Falls.

It's only 20 miles from Waimea town and through the canyon to **Kokee State Park,** but it's a whole different world, for the park is 4,345 acres of rain forest. Here, the breeze has a bite and trees look quite continental. You're in a cloud forest on the edge of an upland bog known as the Alakai Swamp, the largest bog in Hawaii. There's lots to see and do up here: Anglers fly-fish for rainbow trout and hikers tackle the 45 trails that lace Alakai Swamp. That's a lot of ground to cover, so you might want to stay over; there are cabins (see "Accommodations," below) and campgrounds, as well as a rustic cafe. Contact the **State Division of Parks,** P.O. Box 1671, Lihue, HI 96766 (☎ **808/ 274-3446**).

In the park is the **Kokee Natural History Museum** (☎ **808/335-9975;** open daily 10am–4pm; free admission). This small, vital museum is the best place to learn about the forest and swamp before you set off hiking in the wild. The shop has great trail information, including the official park trail map (50¢). A **nature walk** with 35 native plants and trees is the best mini-intro to this rain forest; it starts behind the museum at the rare Hawaiian koa tree. This easy, self-guided walk of about one-tenth of a mile takes about 20 minutes if you stop and look at all the plants; they're all identified along the way.

Four miles above the museum is ✪ **Kalalau Lookout,** the spectacular climax of your drive through Waimea Canyon and Kokee.

**NA PALI COAST STATE PARK**   The Na Pali coast, a 22-mile stretch of fluted cliffs that wrap around the northwest shore of Kauai, is the most beautiful part of Hawaii. Hanging valleys open like green velvet accordions and waterfalls tumble to the sea from the 4,120-foot-high cliffs; the spatial experience is exhilarating and humbling. Whether you hike in, fly over, or cruise by, be sure to see this park. It's only accessible on foot— and it's not easy. An ancient footpath, the Kalalau Trail, winds through it to Kalalau Valley. It's only open on a limited basis in summer, and you must have a permit (you can hike the first 2 miles, to Hanakapiai Beach, without one). Permits are free, and issued in person, at the **Kauai State Parks Office,** 3060 Eiwa St., Lihue, HI 96766 (☎ **808/274-3445** or 808/274-3346).

To explore the Na Pali coast by water, contact **Captain Zodiac Raft Expeditions** (☎ **808/826-9371**). To view it from the air, contact **Will Squyres Helicopter Tours** (☎ **808/245-7541**) or **Ohana Helicopter Tours** (☎ **808/245-3996**).

**BEST BETS FOR KIDS**   If seven-time world champ Margo Oberg, a member of the Surfing Hall of Fame, can't get your kid riding a wave, nobody can. She promises same-day results even for a klutz. Call **Margo Oberg's School of Surfing** (☎ **808/ 742-1750**).

Go flying down the spectacular Na Pali coast on a 23-foot rubber life raft with **Captain Zodiac** (☎ **808/826-9371**). This is Jacques Cousteau–style adventuring at its best. Or you can race along the coast fast in a 38-foot Fountain race boat. This is no wimpy eco-kayak—it's Thunder Road at sea. Call **South Sea Thunder Boat Ride** (☎ **808/ 245-2222** or 808/241-3444).

Indiana Jones ran for his life up the Huleia River to his seaplane in *Raiders of the Lost Ark.* Now, you and the kids can venture down the picturesque Huleia yourself, in a 12-foot-long, virtually unsinkable canoe-shaped pirogue. Contact **Island Adventures** (☎ **808/245-9662**).

**WHALE-WATCHING**   When humpback whales make their annual visit to Hawaii from December to March, they swim right by Kauai. **Liko Kauai Cruises** (☎ **808/ 338-0333**) offers a 4¹/₂-hour Na Pali coast tour/deep-sea fishing/historical lecture/

whale-watching extravaganza on their 37-foot cabin cruiser. **Captain Zodiac** (☎ 808/826-9371) will also take you whale-watching in season.

**OUTDOOR ACTIVITIES**   Kauai's kaleidoscopic marine world makes it a must for divers. Since the best dives are offshore, we suggest you book a two-tank dive off a dive boat with **Bubbles Below Scuba Charters** (☎ 808/822-3483). In summer, they offer all-day trips to dive the waters off the "forbidden" island of Niihau.

Kauai has lots of inshore reefs to make snorkelers happy. You can rent gear at **Snorkel Bob's Kauai, Inc.,** 4480 Ahukini Rd., Lihue (☎ 808/245-9433), or in Poipu (☎ 808/742-8322). For great offshore snorkeling, try **Ke'e Beach, Haena State Park, Anini Beach, Poipu Beach Park,** and **Salt Pond Beach Park.** For sail-snorkel cruises, check out **Captain Andy's Sailing Adventures** (☎ 808/822-7833), **Captain Sundown's Catamaran Sailing** (☎ 808/245-6117), or **Bluewater Sailing** (☎ 808/828-1142).

Kauai provides some of Hawaii's last sanctuaries for endangered native birds and oceanic birds, such as the albatross. Great places to spot native birds are **Kokee State Park** in southwest Kauai, and **Kilauea Point National Wildlife Refuge,** a mile north of Kilauea on the North Shore (☎ 808/828-1413).

From high handicapper to pro, Kauai's courses will challenge every golfer. Two of Kauai's finest are **Poipu Bay Resort Golf Course** (☎ 808/742-8711; call early for tee times), a 6,959-yard, par-72 course with a links-style layout designed by Robert Trent Jones, Jr.; and **Princeville Golf Club, Prince Course** (☎ 808/826-5000), another Trent Jones, Jr.–designed devil of a course—it's the island's most challenging; everyone wants a crack at this course, so call now.

**SHOPPING**   Expect mostly touristy shops in Poipu, the island's resort mecca. A quick stroll through the characterless **Poipu Shopping Village** (2360 Kiahuna Plantation Dr.), as well as the dependably overpriced resort shops, will give you an idea of what's available.

The only hope is the North Shore. Chic galleries and shops like **Kong Lung** in Kilauea, off Hi. 56 on Kilauea Road; **Ola's,** by the Hanalei River on Hi. 560 (after the bridge); and **Yellowfish Trading Company** in Hanalei Center have launched these former hippie villages as must-stop shopping spots.

## ACCOMMODATIONS
### THE POIPU RESORT AREA

Poipu Beach, on the sun-soaked South Shore, is a pleasant resort destination of low-rise hotels.

✪ **Hyatt Regency Kauai Resort & Spa.** *1571 Poipu Rd., Koloa, HI 96756.* ☎ *800/233-1234 or 808/742-1234. Fax 808/742-1557. 641 units. $275–$485 double; from $425 suite. Packages available. AE, CB, DC, DISC, EC, JCB, MC, V.* This is one of Hawaii's best luxury hotels, more environmentally attuned and with more Hawaiian influences than most. The most distant quarters are a good 5-minute hike from the lobby, but you'll find oversized rooms elegantly outfitted in rattan, marble baths, and spacious lanais; most have ocean views. Facilities include restaurants, lounges, a spa, tennis, fantasy pool and slide, and golf.

**Kiahuna Plantation Resort.** *2253 Poipu Rd., Koloa, HI 96756.* ☎ *800/688-7444 or 808/742-6411. Fax 808/742-7233. 333 one- and two-bedroom apts. $155–$390 one-bedroom apt; $290–$450 two-bedroom apt. AE, CB, DC, DISC, JCB, MC, V.* This cluster of condos sits on a gold-sand beach at the heart of Poipu. The gracious two-story plantation-style buildings, loaded with Hawaii style and spirit, are sprinkled throughout a garden. All units have full kitchens, daily maid service, and lanais; there's also a big pool and a sundeck with lounges.

**Poipu Kapili Resort.** *2221 Kapili Rd., Koloa, HI 96756.* ☎ *800/443-7714 or 808/742-6449. Fax 808/742-9162. 60 one- and two-bedroom apts; 2 two-bedroom pent-houses. $150–$244 one-bedroom apt; $200–$375 two-bedroom apt. Three-night mini-mum. Discounts for longer stays; packages available. MC, V.* This quiet, upscale ocean-front cluster of condos is outstanding in every area but one: The beach is a block away. There are video and book-lending libraries, barbecues, tennis courts, a pool, even an herb garden you're welcome to take samples from. All units have full kitchens, ceiling fans, lanais, and free continental breakfast on Friday.

## SOUTHWEST KAUAI

This region is more remote, but is near the spectacular Waimea Canyon and the Kokee State Park.

**Kokee Lodge Cabins.** *P.O. Box 819, Waimea, HI 96796.* ☎ *808/335-6061. 12 cabins. $35 dormitory-style one-room cabins; $45 two-bedroom cabins. Five-night limit. No credit cards; send personal check for full amount.* These are an excellent choice for those who plan on hiking Waimea Canyon and Kokee State Park. The older cabins are dorm style; the new ones have two bedrooms. Both sleep six and come with utensils, bedding, and linens. The lodge sells firewood and has a restaurant open for breakfast and lunch.

✪ **Waimea Plantation Cottages.** *P.O. Box 367, Waimea, HI 96796.* ☎ *800/ 9-WAIMEA or 808/338-1625. Fax 808/338-1619. 48 one- to five-bedroom cottages. Win-ter, $135–$480 cottage. Off-season, $115–$450 cottage. AE, DC, DISC, JCB, MC, V.* This beachfront retreat is like no other: Among groves of coco palms are restored plan-tation cottages from the 1880s to the 1930s transformed into cozy guest units with pe-riod rattan, wicker, and fabrics; each has a furnished lanai and modern kitchen and bath. The black-sand beach is lovely but not for swimming. A restaurant and pool are on the premises.

## NORTH SHORE

Kauai's north shore is one of the most beautiful places in Hawaii, the land of double rainbows, waterfalls, and lush valleys.

✪ **Hanalei Bay Resort & Suites.** *P.O. Box 220, Hanalei, HI 96714.* ☎ *800/ 477-2329 or 808/826-6522. Fax 808/826-6680. 256 units. $140–$230 double; $155– $240 studio; $260–$500 one-bedroom suite; $360–$750 two-bedroom suite; from $650 three-bedroom suite. AE, DC, DISC, MC, V.* This 22-acre resort is next door to the ritzy Princeville Hotel, overlooking the same fabled Bali Hai cliffs and Hanalei Bay; it has the same majestic view, but for as little as half the price. The island-style rooms have lanais overlooking the bay, the lush grounds, and the distant mountains.

**Hanalei Colony Resort.** *P.O. Box 206, Hanalei, HI 96714-9985.* ☎ *800/ 628-3004 or 808/826-6235. Fax 808/826-9893. 52 two-bedroom apts. $100–$210 apt. Seventh night free; condo/car packages from $123. Five-night minimum at Christmas. AE, MC, V.* If you love the wild beauty of the North Shore, you'll love this condo complex, on the sand at Haena. It's quiet, comfortable, unpretentious, and scrupulously tended. The two-bedroom units have full kitchens, but since this little gem prides itself on be-ing a peaceful getaway, there are no phones or TVs.

**Princeville Hotel.** *P.O. Box 3069, 5520 Kahaku Rd., Princeville, HI 96722-3069.* ☎ *800/826-4400 or 808/826-9644. Fax 808/826-1166. 304 rms. $290–$525 double; from $925 suite. Packages available. AE, DC, DISC, JCB, MC, V.* Princeville enjoys one of the world's finest settings, between Hanalei Bay and Kauai's Bali Hai mountains. The gilt and butler service may be a bit too much for this down-to-earth island, but each opulent room is filled with extras. There are no lanais, but oversized windows let in the awesome view. The hotel has two restaurants, two championship golf courses, tennis, a pool, three spas, shops, a business center, and riding stables.

## DINING
### THE POIPU RESORT AREA
Between this area and the Coconut Coast, you may want to stop in Lihue at **Hamura's Saimin Stand,** 2956 Kress St. (☎ 808/245-3271), for their world-renowned saimin and teriyaki barbecue sticks. It's literally just a few U-shaped counters, but it attracts an all-day, late-night, pre- and post-movie crowd. It's open Mon–Thurs 10am–midnight, Fri–Sat 10am–1am, Sun 10am–10pm.

✪ **Beach House.** *5022 Lawai Rd., Poipu.* ☎ *808/742-1424. Reservations recommended. Main courses $20–$24. AE, DC, DISC, MC, V. Daily 5:30–9:30pm. HAWAII REGIONAL/MEDITERRANEAN.* With or without the sunset, this is one of Kauai's top culinary experiences. Menus are printed daily, but look forüber-chef Jean-Marie Josselin's signature touches: wok-charred mahimahi, tiger-eye ahi sushi tempura, tenderloin, and a host of premium poultry and fresh-fish fantasies. Potatoes in any form catapult the spud to new levels of respect.

✪ **Roy's Poipu Bar & Grill.** *Poipu Shopping Village, 2360 Kiahuna Plantation Dr.* ☎ *808/742-5000. Reservations recommended. Main courses $15–$26. AE, CB, DC, DISC, JCB, MC, V. Daily 5:30–9:30pm. EUROASIAN.* Roy Yamaguchi's (of Roy's on Oahu and Maui) signature touches are present in abundance: an excellent and affordable wine list and fresh local ingredients prepared with a nod to Europe, Asia, and the Pacific. The menu is achingly seductive: blackened sea scallops with sweet chile butter, garlic mustard short ribs, kiawe-grilled hibachi-style salmon, and legendary Chinese-style roasted duck.

### THE COCONUT COAST
Along this condo coast, you can find just about anything you might need. Kapaa, a restored plantation town by the sea has a funky charm.

**A Pacific Cafe Kauai.** *Kauai Shopping Village, 4–831 Kuhio Hwy., Kapaa.* ☎ *808/822-0013. Reservations recommended. Main courses $20–$24. AE, DC, DISC, MC, V. Daily 5:30–9:30pm. HAWAII REGIONAL/MEDITERRANEAN.* Jean-Marie Josselin's wizardry with island ingredients and cross-cultural preparations has kept A Pacific Cafe on the A-list of national food critics. Signature dishes—herb-crusted opakapaka with black rice, Chinese roast duck, blackened ono with papaya basil sauce, and clams in any form—are the mainstays of a menu that changes daily and is relentlessly creative without being cloying.

**Bubba's Burgers.** *1384 Kuhio Hwy., Kapaa.* ☎ *808/823-0069. Most items under $6. MC, V. Mon–Sat 10:30am–8pm. AMERICAN.* They dish out irreverence, great T-shirts, and authentic, old-fashioned hamburgers—as well as chicken and veggie burgers, fish-and-chips, and Bubba's famous Budweiser chili—at this tiny stand. The freshly ground Kauai beef is 88% fat-free and served on a toasted bun with the appropriate condiments and diced onions, of course.

### THE NORTH SHORE
Picture-postcard Hanalei is the center of North Shore life, and Kilauea is home to Kauai's oldest general store, Kong Lung Company, founded in 1892.

✪ **Casa di Amici.** *2484 Keneke St., Kilauea.* ☎ *808/828-1555. Reservations recommended. Main courses $12–$24. MC, V. Daily 11:30am–2:30pm and 6–9pm. ITALIAN/MEDITERRANEAN.* Randall Yates's brawny Italian cuisine is served in a cordial, comfortable atmosphere. Expect perfectly cooked risotto awash in mushrooms, tarragon, and cracked pepper; a tower of polenta with Gorgonzola, Molokai sweet potato, and a drizzle of tomato sauce; and the best linguine Alfredo in the state—light, garlicky, and perfectly balanced in flavor and texture.

**Kilauea Bakery & Pau Hana Pizza.** *Kong Lung Center (on the way to Kilauea Lighthouse).* ☎ *808/828-2020. Pizzas $11–$26. No credit cards. Mon–Sat 6:30am–9pm. PIZZA/BAKERY.* It's amazing what pours out of here: basil-pesto Provençale; classic scampi with tiger prawns; and other pizzas, all made with organically grown olive oil, whole-milk mozzarella, whole-wheat or traditional crust, and long-simmering sauces. The Billie Holiday—with Swiss chard, roasted onions, Gorgonzola-rosemary sauce, and mozzarella cheese—is guaranteed to obliterate the blues.

**Postcards.** *In the old Hanalei Museum, Kuhio Hwy., Hanalei.* ☎ *808/826-1191. Reservations recommended for dinner. Main courses $7–$14. AE, DC, MC, V. Daily 6:30am–2:30pm and 5:30–9:30pm. GOURMET VEGETARIAN/SEAFOOD.* Excellent gourmet vegetarian fare (plus fresh fish) is prepared fresh with locally grown organic herbs and produce and other low-fat, no-cholesterol, high-protein ingredients, and presented in an impressive menu that roams the planet. Main dishes include shredded lobster tacos; vegetable curry in phyllo pastry; and a light, comforting medley of soup, salad, and warm corn bread.

## KAUAI AFTER DARK

Suffice it to say that one does not come to Kauai to trip the night fantastic. This is the island for winding down. There are two dance clubs on the island: **Gilligan's Disco** at the Outrigger Kauai Beach Hotel, 4331 Kauai Beach Dr., Lihue (☎ **808/245-1955**); and **Kuhio's** at Poipu's Hyatt Regency Kauai Resort (☎ **808/742-1234**). In the Outrigger's **Mele Lounge,** Pua Kaholokula and her husband, gifted musician Robbie Kaholokula, blend their talents in Hawaiian music and dance on Monday, Thursday, Friday, and Saturday from 7:30 to 10pm. The Outrigger's **Jasmine Ballroom** is the scene for an all-Hawaiian buffet dinner show produced by the Kaholokulas.

# 5 More Hawaii Highlights

## MOLOKAI

The cradle of Hawaiian dance, aquaculture, and sacred rites, Molokai lives on its reputation as the most Hawaiian place chiefly through its lineage; there are more people here of Hawaiian blood than on any other island. The simple life of the people and the absence of contemporary landmarks is what attracts those in search of the "real" Hawaii. But what makes them stand in awe is this little island's diverse natural wonders: Hawaii's highest waterfall and greatest collection of fishponds, the world's tallest sea cliffs, sand dunes, coral reefs, rain forests, hidden coves—and empty, gloriously empty beaches.

Even if you have only a day to spend on Molokai, spend it on a mule ride to Kalaupapa. You can sit back and let the mule do the walking on the precipitous path—down 26 switchbacks and past cliffs taller than 300-story skyscrapers—to Molokai's wide remote shore, home to the island's historic leper colony. Contact **Molokai Mule Ride** (☎ **800/567-7550** or 808/567-6088); advance reservations required. You can also visit Kalaupapa on a helicopter flight with **Damien Tours** (☎ **808/567-6171**).

The **Molokai Ranch Wildlife Park,** Maunaloa (☎ **808/552-2681**), is probably the best of its kind anywhere. Exotic wild animals freely roam 350 acres of west Molokai, which look like Africa's savanna. You ride slowly through the game preserve in a guided van, which stops periodically so you can peer and photograph antelope, oryx, Indian black buck, Greater Kudu, Barbary sheep, and giraffes.

In a wagon drawn by two horses, bump along a dirt trail through an incredible mango grove, bound for an ancient temple of human sacrifice right out of *Indiana Jones.* After a visit to the awesome temple, the horse-drawn wagon takes you back to the mango grove for a beachside lunch and an old-fashioned backyard ukulele songfest. Contact **Molokai Wagon Rides** (☎ **808/558-8380**).

**Fun Hogs,** Kaluakoi Hotel & Golf Club Beach Activities Center, Maunaloa (☎ 808/552-2555), is the place to go if you want to enjoy the great outdoors. Mike Holmes shares his adventures, dispenses good local advice on where to go, and rents everything you need, including boogie boards, kayaks, mountain bikes, and snorkel gear.

Shoppers shouldn't expect much. Downtown Kaunakakai has mainly grocery stores and a few variety stores. On the west end is inveterate Bali-philes Jonathan and Daphne Socher's **Big Wind Kite Factory & the Plantation Gallery,** Maunaloa (☎ 808/552-2634). Maunaloa's naturally windy conditions make it ideal for kite-flying classes, offered free when conditions are right.

Of all the islands, Molokai is the most affordable island to stay on, although accommodations are more Motel 6 than Ritz-Carlton. **Molokai Shores Suites,** P.O. Box 1037, Kaunakakai, HI 96748 (☎ 800/535-0085 or 808/553-5954; fax 800/633-5085), offers bright, clean, basic units with kitchens and large lanais facing a small gold-sand beach and the ocean beyond. Old and funky **Pau Hana Inn,** P.O. Box 860, Kaunakakai, HI 96748 (☎ 800/423-6656 or 808/553-5342; fax 808/553-5047), is a no-frills cottage-style complex, but the grounds are tropically lush, and the pool's always crystal clear. Airy, homey **Paniolo Hale,** Kaluakoi Resort (P.O. Box 190), Maunaloa, HI 96770 (☎ 800/367-2984 or 808/552-2731; fax 808/552-2288), is far and away Molokai's most charming lodging, and probably its best value. The one- and two-bedrooms come with two baths, so they accommodate three or four easily. **Dunbar's Beachfront Cottages,** c/o Sunscapes, 3538 207th SE, Issaquah, WA 98029 (☎ 800/225-7978 or 206/391-8932; fax 206/391-9121), has two wonderful plantation-style cottages, each on its own secluded stretch of swimmable beach; you'll feel like you're on your own island.

Dining on Molokai is casual and affordable. Options include **Kanemitsu's Bakery & Restaurant,** 79 Ala Malama St., Kaunakakai (☎ 808/553-5855), a third-generation bakery that has expanded its repertoire to include such fare as mahi burgers, egg-salad sandwiches, and honey-dipped fried chicken. Excellent pizzas and sandwiches have made **Molokai Pizza Cafe,** Kahua Center, on the old Wharf Road (☎ 808/553-3288), a Kaunakakai staple. The freshest and healthiest food on the island is served at **Outpost Natural Foods,** 70 Makaena, Kaunakakai (☎ 808/553-3377); the closet-sized lunch counter pumps out salads, burritos, tofu-spinach lasagna, and other guilt-free fare. **Pau Hana Inn,** Oceanfront, Kaunakakai (☎ 808/553-5342), affectionately regarded more for its character and value than for its culinary excellence, features local food: teriyaki short ribs, prime rib, roast pork, and saimin. Local food, or American food with a local twist, is also the dominant genre at **Kualapuu Cook House,** on the way to the north coast (☎ 808/567-6185). Gourmet burgers, chili, and a rich steak-and-shrimp plate keep the cooks in nonstop action.

**Essentials:** Hawaiian, Aloha, and Mahalo airlines and **Molokai Air Shuttle** (☎ 808/545-4988) fly from Honolulu into Molokai. Rental cars can be hard to find on Molokai, so book with Budget or Dollar before you go. **Molokai Off-Road Tours & Taxi** (☎ 808/553-3369) and **Kukui Tours & Limousines** (☎ 808/553-5133) offer taxi and tour service. For more information, contact the **Molokai Visitor Association,** P.O. Box 960, Kaunakakai, HI 96748 (☎ 800/800-6367 or 808/553-3876; interisland ☎ 800/553-0404); or the **Hawaii Visitor and Convention Bureau,** 2270 Kalakaua Ave., Suite 801, Honolulu, HI (☎ 808/923-1811).

## LANAI

Hawaii's sixth largest island and the nation's biggest defunct pineapple patch, Lanai now claims to be one of the world's top tropical destinations. What you have here is something quite rare: an almost virgin island, unspoiled by what passes for progress, except for a little hard-scrabble plantation town—and its fancy new neighbors, two first-class luxury hotels where a decent room starts at $300 a night.

Palm-fringed, gold-sand **Hulopoe Beach,** at the foot of the Manele Bay Hotel, is a protected marine preserve, and the schools of colorful fish know it. Spinner dolphins come here to play, and humpback whales cruise by in winter. In summer, Hulopoe is perfect for swimming, snorkeling, or just lolling about; swells can kick up in winter. Other beaches (accessible by four-wheel-drive only) are **Shipwreck** and **Polihua.**

On a clear day, you can see all the main islands in the Hawaiian chain, except Kauai, from the top of Mt. Lanaihale, the 3,370-foot summit of Lanai. The hearty will hike the strenuous 11-mile, 7-hour (round-trip) uphill climb along the **Munro Trail** through the groves of Norfolk pines; the rest of us four-wheel-it to the top. The trail begins at Lanai Cemetery along Keomoku Road (Hi. 44); go in the morning for the best visibility.

**Garden of the Gods** is the ultimate rock garden: a barren, mysterious, beautiful place full of rocks strewn by volcanic forces and shaped by the elements into an infinite variety of shapes and colors—brilliant reds, oranges, ochres, and yellows.

On the outskirts of Lanai City, on a hillside site known as **Luahiwa Petroglyph Field,** are ancient characters incised on boulders, including a running man, a deer, a turtle, a bird, a goat, and even a rare, curly-tailed Polynesian dog.

For golfers, the **Experience at Koele** is indeed quite an experience. An 18-hole, par-72 championship course at 2,500 feet, designed by Greg Norman with Ted Robinson as the architect, is often shrouded in fog and mist. Call ☎ **808/565-GOLF** for tee times.

It'll be difficult to keep your credit card warm on Lanai. Exceptions are the gift shops at the **Lodge at Koele** and the **Manele Bay Hotel,** where you can find luxury items and sunwear. The stores in Lanai City are basically purveyors of necessities.

Lanai's two fabulous sister resorts are the up-country **Lodge at Koele** and the ocean-front **Manele Bay Hotel** (☎ **800/321-4666,** or 808/565-7700 for both). The Lodge stands in a cool, often misty 21-acre grove of Norfolk pines; it looks like an English hunting lodge, with giant stone fireplaces, stuffed furniture, and lavishly chintzed rooms. If you want to stay at the beach, head to the Manele Bay, an open, airy, luxury resort on a sunwashed bluff overlooking one of Hawaii's best stretches of sand. For something a little more affordable, try the **Hotel Lanai** (☎ **800/321-4666** or 808/565-7211), a recently redecorated plantation-era relic that has retained its quaint character.

The big resorts have wonderful restaurants, including the Lodge's **Formal Dining Room** (☎ **808/565-4580**), where Chef Edwin Goto's American menu soars in a grand atmosphere; and the Manele Bay Hotel's top-quality trio of restaurants: **Hulopoe Court** (☎ **808/565-7700**), which is casual compared to the hotel's fine dining room, **Ihilani** (☎ **808/565-2290**), but formal compared to the **Pool Grille** (☎ **808/565-7700**), the outdoor lunchtime oasis. If you'd like something a little less fancy—and a little less expensive—head to **Blue Ginger Cafe,** 409 Seventh St., Lanai City (☎ **808/565-7016**), a very local, very casual restaurant offering solid, no-nonsense everyday fare; or **S.T. Properties,** 419 Seventh St., Lanai City (☎ **808/565-6537**), whose homemade hamburgers and bento lunches (a plantation legacy) have fed two generations of Lanai residents.

**Essentials:** Lanai is a 25-minute flight from Honolulu on Hawaiian, Aloha, and Mahalo airlines. A free airport shuttle runs between the island's three hotels every 30 minutes from 7am to 11pm. You'll need four-wheel-drive if you plan on exploring; contact **Lanai City Service** (☎ **808/244-9538** or 808/565-7227). For more information, contact **Destination Lanai** (☎ **808/565-7600;** fax 808/565-9316), the **Hawaii Visitor and Convention Bureau** (☎ **808/923-1811**), or the **Island of Lanai** (☎ **800/ 321-4666**).

# Appendix

## Toll-Free Telephone Numbers

**HOTEL CHAINS**

**Best Western International, Inc.**
800/528-1234 North America
800/528-2222 TDD

**Budgetel Inns**
800/4-BUDGET Continental USA and Canada

**Budget Host**
800/BUD-HOST Continental USA

**Clarion Hotels**
800/CLARION Continental USA and Canada
800/228-3323 TDD
http://www.hotelchoice.com/cgi-bin/res/webres?clarion.html

**Comfort Inns**
800/228-5150 Continental USA and Canada
800/228-3323 TDD
http://www.hotelchoice.com/cgi-bin/res/webres?comfort.html

**Courtyard by Marriott**
800/321-2211 Continental USA and Canada
800/228-7014 TDD
http://www.marriott.com/lodging/courtyar.htm

**Days Inn**
800/325-2525 Continental USA and Canada
800/325-3297 TDD
http://www.daysinn.com/daysinn.html

**Doubletree Hotels**
800/222-TREE Continental USA and Canada
800/528-9898 TDD

**Drury Inn**
800/325-8300 Continental USA and Canada
800/325-0583 TDD

**Econo Lodges**
800/55-ECONO Continental USA and Canada
800/228-3323 TDD
http://www.hotelchoice.com/cgi-bin/res/webres?econo.html

**Embassy Suites**
800/362-2779 Continental USA and
Canada
800/458-4708 TDD
http://www.embassy-suites.com/

**Exel Inns of America**
800/356-8013 Continental USA and
Canada

**Fairfield Inn by Marriott**
800/228-2800 Continental USA and
Canada
800/228-7014 TDD
http://www.marriott.com/lodging/
fairf.htm

**Fairmont Hotels**
800/527-4727 Continental USA

**Forte Hotels**
800/225-5843 Continental USA and
Canada

**Four Seasons Hotels**
800/332-3442 Continental USA
800/268-6282 Canada

**Friendship Inns**
800/453-4511 Continental USA
800/228-3323 TDD
http://www.hotelchoice.com/cgi-bin/res/
webres?friendship.html

**Guest Quarters Suites**
800/424-2900 Continental USA

**Hampton Inn**
800/HAMPTON Continental USA and
Canada
800/451-HTDD TDD
http://www.hampton-inn.com/

**Hilton Hotels Corporation**
800/HILTONS Continental USA and
Canada
800/368-1133 TDD
http://www.hilton.com

**Holiday Inn**
800/HOLIDAY Continental USA and
Canada
800/238-5544 TDD
http://www.holiday-inn.com/

**Howard Johnson**
800/654-2000 Continental USA and
Canada
800/654-8442 TDD
http://www.hojo.com/hojo.html

**Hyatt Hotels and Resorts**
800/228-9000 Continental USA and
Canada
800/228-9548 TDD
http://www.hyatt.com

**Inns of America**
800/826-0778 Continental USA and
Canada

**Intercontinental Hotels**
800/327-0200 Continental USA and
Canada

**ITT Sheraton**
800/325-3535 Continental USA and
Canada
800/325-1717 TDD

**La Quinta Motor Inns, Inc.**
800/531-5900 Continental USA and
Canada
800/426-3101 TDD

**Loews Hotels**
800/223-0888 Continental USA and
Canada
http://www.loewshotels.com

**Marriott Hotels**
800/228-9290 Continental USA and
Canada
800/228-7014 TDD
http://www.marriott.com/
MainPage.html

**Master Hosts Inns**
800/251-1962 Continental USA and
Canada

**Meridien**
800/543-4300 Continental USA and
  Canada

**Motel 6**
800/4motel6

**Omni Hotels**
800/843-6664 Continental USA and
  Canada

**Park Inns International**
800/437-PARK Continental USA and
  Canada
http://www.p-inns.com/parkinn.html

**Quality Inns**
800/228-5151 Continental USA and
  Canada
800/228-3323 TDD
http://www.hotelchoice.com/cgi-bin/res/
  webres?quality.html

**Radisson Hotels International**
800/333-3333 Continental USA and
  Canada

**Ramada**
800/2-RAMADA Continental USA and
  Canada
http://www.ramada.com/ramada.html

**Red Carpet Inns**
800/251-1962 Continental USA and
  Canada

**Red Lion Hotels and Inns**
800/547-8010 Continental USA and
  Canada

**Red Roof Inns**
800/843-7663 Continental USA and
  Canada
800/843-9999 TDD
http://www.redroof.com

**Renaissance Hotels International**
800/HOTELS-1 Continental USA and
  Canada
800/833-4747 TDD

**Residence Inn by Marriott**
800/331-3131 Continental USA and
  Canada
800/228-7014 TDD
http://www.marriott.com/lodging/
  resinn.htm

**Ritz-Carlton**
800/241-3333 Continental USA and
  Canada

**Rodeway Inns**
800/228-2000 Continental USA and
  Canada
800/228-3323 TDD
http://www.hotelchoice.com/cgi-bin/res/
  webres?rodeway.html

**Scottish Inns**
800/251-1962 Continental USA and
  Canada

**Shilo Inns**
800/222-2244 Continental USA and
  Canada

**Signature Inns**
800/822-5252 Continental USA and
  Canada

**Super 8 Motels**
800/800-8000 Continental USA and
  Canada
800/533-6634 TDD
http://www.super8motels.com/
  super8.html

**Susse Chalet Motor Lodges & Inns**
800/258-1980 Continental USA and
  Canada

**Travelodge**
800/255-3050 Continental USA and
  Canada

**Vagabond Hotels Inc.**
800/255-3050 Continental USA and
  Canada

**Westin Hotels and Resorts**
800/228-3000 Continental USA and
  Canada
800/254-5440 TDD
http://www.westin.com/

**Wyndham Hotels and Resorts**
800/822-4200 Continental USA and
  Canada

## CAR-RENTAL AGENCIES

**Alamo Rent A Car**
800/327-9633 Continental USA and
  Canada
http://www.goalamo.com/

**Avis**
800/331-1212 Continental USA
800/TRY-AVIS Canada
800/331-2323 TDD
http://www.avis/com/

**Budget Rent A Car**
800/527-0700 Continental USA and
  Canada
800/826-5510 TDD

**Dollar Rent A Car**
800/800-4000 Continental USA and
  Canada

**Enterprise Rent-A-Car**
800/325-8007 Continental USA and
  Canada

**Hertz**
800/654-3131 Continental USA and
  Canada
800/654-2280 TDD

**National Car Rental**
800/CAR-RENT Continental USA and
  Canada
800/328-6323 TDD
http://www.nationalcar.com/index.html

**Rent-A-Wreck**
800/535-1391 Continental USA

**Sears Rent A Car**
800/527-0770 Continental USA and
  Canada

**Thrifty Rent-A-Car**
800/367-2277 Continental USA and
  Canada
800/358-5856 TDD

**Value Rent-A-Car**
800/327-2501 Continental USA and
  Canada
http://www.go-value.com/

## AIRLINES

**American Airlines**
800/433-7300 Continental USA and
  Western Canada
800/543-1586 TDD
http://www.americanair.com/aa_home/
  aa_home.htm

**Continental Airlines**
800/231-0856 Continental USA
800/343-9195 TDD
http://www.flycontinental.com:80/
  index.html

**Delta Air Lines**
800/241-4141 Continental USA
800/831-4488 TDD
http://www.delta-air.com/index.html

**Northwest Airlines**
800/225-2525 Continental USA and
  Canada
http://www.nwa.com/

**Southwest Airlines**
800/435-9792 Continental USA and
  Canada
http://www.iflyswa.com

**Trans World Airlines**
800/221-2000 Continental USA
http://www2.twa.com/TWA/Airlines/
  home/home.htm

**United Airlines**
800/241-6522 Continental USA and
  Canada
http://www.ual.com/

**US Airways**
800/428-4322 Continental USA and
  Canada
http://www.usair.com/

## State Tourism Offices

**Alabama Bureau of Tourism & Travel**
Box 4927
Montgomery, AL 361036-4927
800/ALABAMA
334/242-4169

**Alaska Division of Tourism**
Box 110801 TIA
Juneau, AK 99811-0801
907/465-2010

**Arizona Office of Tourism**
1100 W. Washington
Phoenix, AZ 85007
602/230-7733
800/888-520-3434

**Arkansas Department of Parks &
Tourism**
1 Capitol Mall, Dept. 7701
Little Rock, AR 72201
800/NATURAL
501/682-7777

**California Division of Tourism**
Box 1499
Sacramento, CA 95812-1499
800/TO-CALIF
916/322-2881

**Colorado Tourism Board**
340 Highway 340
Fruita, CO
303/296-3384
800/COLORADO

**Connecticut Dept. of Economic
Development**
Tourism Division
505 Hudson St.
Hartford, CT 06106
800/282-6863
860/270-8080

**Delaware Tourism Office**
99 King's Highway
Box 1401, Dept. TIA
Dover, DE 19903
800/441-8846
302/739-4271

**Florida Tourism Industry Marketing
Group**
661 E. Jefferson St.
Tallahassee, FL 32301
904/488-5607
888/7-FLA-USA

**Georgia Dept. of Industry, Trade
& Tourism**
Box 1776, Dept. TIA
Atlanta, GA 30301
800/VISIT-GA
404/656-3590

**Hawaii Dept. of Business, Economic
Development, and Tourism**
Box 2359
Honolulu, HI 96804
808/586-2550
Hawaii Visitors Bureau:
  800/GO-HAWAII

**Illinois Bureau of Tourism**
100 W. Randolph, Suite 3-400
Chicago, IL 60601
800/2-CONNECT
312/814-4732

**Indiana Dept. of Commerce/Tourism**
1 North Capitol, Suite 700
Indianapolis, IN 46204
800/289-6646
317/232-8860

**Iowa Division of Tourism**
200 E. Grand
Des Moines, IA 50309
Vacation kit: 800/345-IOWA

**Kansas Travel & Tourism Division**
700 SW Harrison St., Suite 1300
Topeka, KS 66603-3712
800/2-KANSAS
913/296-2009

**Kentucky Dept. of Travel
Development**
500 Mero St., 22nd Floor, Dept. DA
Frankfort, KY 40601
800/225-TRIP
502/564-4930

**Louisiana Office of Tourism**
Box 94291
Baton Rouge, LA 70804
800/334-8626
504/342-8119

**Maine Office of Tourism**
189 State St.
Augusta, ME 04333
800/533-9595
207/287-5711

**Maryland Office of Tourism
Development**
217 E. Redwood St., 9th Floor
Baltimore, MD 21202
410/767-3400
Vacation kit: 800/543-1036

**Massachusetts Office of Travel
& Tourism**
100 Cambridge St., 13th Floor
Boston, MA 02202
617/727-3201
Vacation kit: 800/447-MASS

**Michigan Travel Bureau**
Box 3393
Livonia, MI 48151-3393
800/5432-YES

**Minnesota Office of Tourism**
121 Seventh Place East
St. Paul, MN 55101
800/657-3700
612/296-5029

**Mississippi Division of Tourism
Development**
Box 1705
Ocean Springs, MS 39566
800/927-6378
601/359-3297

**Missouri Division of Tourism**
Box 1055, Dept. TIA
Jefferson City, MO 65102
800/877-1234
573/751-4133

**Travel Montana**
Room TIA
Deer Lodge, MT 59722
800/VISIT-MT
406/444-2854

**Nebraska Division of Travel
& Tourism**
Box 94666
Lincoln, NE 68509
800/228-4307
402/471-3796

**Nevada Commission of Tourism**
Capitol Complex
Dept. TIA
Carson City, NV 89710
800/NEVADA-8
702/687-4322

**New Hampshire Office of Travel
& Tourism**
Box 1856
Concord, NH 09302
800/386-4664
603/271-2343

**New Jersey Division of Travel
& Tourism**
20 West State Street, CN 820
Trenton, NJ 08625
800/JERSEY-7
609/292-2470

**New Mexico Dept. of Tourism**
491 Old Santa Fe Trail
Santa Fe, NM 87503
800/545-2070
505/827-7400

**New York State Travel Information Center**
1 Commerce Plaza
Albany, NY 12245
800/CALL-NYS
518/474-4116

**North Carolina Division of Travel & Tourism**
430 N. Salisbury St.
Raleigh, NC 27603
800/VISIT-NC
919/733-4171

**North Dakota Dept.**
Liberty Memorial Building
604 East Boulevard
Bismarck, ND 58505
800/HELLO-ND
701/328-2525

**Ohio Division of Travel & Tourism**
Box 1001
Columbus, OH 43216-1001
800/BUCKEYE
614/466-8844

**Oklahoma Tourism & Recreation Department**
2401 Lincoln Blvd., Room 505-DA595
Oklahoma City, OK 73105-4492
800/654-8240
405/521-3981

**Oregon Tourism Division**
775 Summer St., NE
Salem, OR 97310
800/547-7842
503/986-0000

**Pennsylvania Office of Travel Marketing**
Forum Building
Room 453
Harrisburg, PA 17120
800/VISIT-PA
717/787-5453

**Rhode Island Tourism Division**
7 Jackson Walkway, Dept. TIA
Providence, RI 02903
800/556-2484
401/277-2601

**South Carolina Division of Tourism**
Box 71
Columbia, SC 29202
803/734-0122
800/346-3634

**South Dakota Department of Tourism**
711 E. Wells Ave.
Pierre, SD 57501-3369
800/SDAKOTA
605/773-3301

**Tennessee Dept. of Tourism Development**
Box 23107 TNDA
Nashville, TN 37202
800/836-6200
615/741-2158

**Texas Dept. of Commerce, Tourist Division**
Box 12728
Austin, TX 78711-2728
800/888-8TEX
512/462-9191

**Utah Travel Council**
Council Hall, Capitol Hill
Salt Lake City, UT 84114
800/200-1160
801/538-1030

**Vermont Dept. of Tourism**
Box 1471
Montpelier, VT 05601-1471
800/VERMONT
802/828-3237

**Virginia Division of Tourism**
901 E. Byrd Street
Richmond, VA 23219
800/VISIT-VA
804/786-4484

**West Virginia Division of Tourism**
2101 Washington St. East
Charleston, WV 25305
800/225-5982
304/558-2766

**Wisconsin Division of Tourism**
Box 7606
Madison, WI 53707
In-state: 800/372-2737
Out-of-state: 800/432-TRIP
608/266-2161

**Wyoming Division of Tourism**
I-25 at College Drive, Dept. WY
Cheyenne, WY 82002
800/225-5996
307/777-7777

# Index

# WHEREVER YOU TRAVEL, *H*ELP IS NEVER FAR AWAY.

From planning your trip to

providing travel assistance along

the way, American Express®

Travel Service Offices are

always there to help

you do more.

For the office nearest you, call
1-800-AXP-3429

**do more** AMERICAN EXPRESS

**Travel**

http://www.americanexpress.com/travel

# GMAT® Foundations of Math

## Strategy Guide Supplement

This supplemental guide provides in-depth and
easy-to-follow explanations of the fundamental math skills
necessary for a strong performance on the GMAT.

GMAT® Foundations of Math, Sixth Edition

10-digit International Standard Book Number: 1-5062-0764-2
13-digit International Standard Book Number: 978-1-5062-0764-3
eISBN: 978-1-5062-1245-6

Layout Design: Derek Frankhouser
Cover Design: Andrew Au and Frank Callaghan
Cover Photography: Alli Ugosoli

# GMAT® STRATEGY GUIDES

0. GMAT Roadmap
1. Fractions, Decimals, & Percents
2. Algebra
3. Word Problems
4. Geometry

5. Number Properties
6. Critical Reasoning
7. Reading Comprehension
8. Sentence Correction
9. Integrated Reasoning & Essay

# STRATEGY GUIDE SUPPLEMENTS

**Math**

GMAT Foundations of Math

GMAT Advanced Quant

**Verbal**

GMAT Foundations of Verbal

October 4, 2016

Dear Student,

Thank you for picking up a copy of *GMAT Foundations of Math*. I hope this book provides the guidance you need to get the most out of your studies.

At Manhattan Prep, we continually aspire to provide the best instructors and study resources possible. We hope that you will find our commitment manifest in this book. If you have any questions or comments, please email us at gmat@manhattanprep.com. Our Student Services and curriculum teams are very interested to hear what you have to say.

Many people were involved in the creation of this book. First and foremost is Zeke Vanderhoek, the founder of Manhattan Prep. Zeke was a lone tutor in New York when he started the company in 2000. Now, more than a decade and a half later, the company serves the needs of thousands of students each year.

Our books are based on the continuing experiences of our instructors and students. Stacey Koprince led the rewriting of *GMAT Foundations of Math*, resulting in this new edition. Numerous other instructors have made contributions to this title over the years. For this edition, I'd like to send particular thanks to Whitney Garner, Andrea Pawliczek, Emily Meredith Sledge, and Ryan Starr.

Our colleagues at Kaplan Publishing managed the production process and made sure all the moving pieces came together at just the right time.

At Manhattan Prep, we are proud of this book and of the people who have worked hard to bring it to you.

Thanks again for trusting us to help you prepare for the GMAT. Best of luck!

Sincerely,

Chris Ryan
Vice President of Academics
Manhattan Prep

# HOW TO ACCESS YOUR ONLINE RESOURCES

## IF YOU ARE A REGISTERED MANHATTAN PREP STUDENT

and have received this book as part of your course materials, you have *automatic* access to *all* of our online resources. This includes all practice exams, Question Banks, and online updates to this book. To access these resources, follow the instructions in the Welcome Guide provided to you at the start of your program.

## IF YOU PURCHASED THIS BOOK FROM MANHATTANPREP.COM
## OR AT ONE OF OUR CENTERS

1. Go to: **www.manhattanprep.com/gmat/studentcenter**
2. Log in with the username and password you chose when setting up your account.

## IF YOU PURCHASED THIS BOOK AT A RETAIL LOCATION

1. Create an account with Manhattan Prep at this website:

**www.manhattanprep.com/gmat/register**

2. Follow the instructions on the screen.

Your one year of online access begins on the day that you register your book at the above URL.

You only need to register your product *once* at the above URL. To use your online resources any time *after* you have completed the registration process, log in at the following URL:

**www.manhattanprep.com/gmat/studentcenter**

Please note that online access is nontransferable. This means that only *new* and *unregistered* copies of the book will grant you online access. Previously used books will not provide any online resources.

## IF YOU PURCHASED AN EBOOK VERSION OF THIS BOOK

1. Create an account with Manhattan Prep at this website:

**www.manhattanprep.com/gmat/register**

2. Email a copy of your purchase receipt to **gmat@manhattanprep.com** to activate

your resources. Please be sure to use the same email address to create an account that you used to purchase the eBook.

Email **gmat@manhattanprep.com** or call **800-576-4628** with any questions.

Please refer to the following page for a description of the online resources that come with this book.

# YOUR ONLINE RESOURCES

## YOUR PURCHASE INCLUDES ONLINE ACCESS TO THE FOLLOWING:

## GMAT FOUNDATIONS OF MATH QUESTION BANK

This bank consists of extra practice questions (with detailed explanations) that test the variety of foundational math concepts and skills covered in this book. These questions provide you with extra practice beyond the problem sets contained in this book. You may use our online timer to practice your pacing by setting time limits for each question in the bank.

## GMAT MATH READINESS ASSESSMENTS

Know when you're ready to move on to GMAT Math. These four online assessments – designed to be taken during and at the end of your fundamental math prep – test your readiness for higher-level GMAT Math.

## 5 FREE INTERACT™ LESSONS

Interact™ is a comprehensive self-study program that is fun, intuitive, and directed by you. Each interactive video lesson is taught by an expert Manhattan Prep instructor and includes dozens of individual branching points. The choices you make determine the content you see. This book comes with access to the *first five lessons* of GMAT Interact. Lessons are available on your computer or iPad so you can prep where you are, when you want. For more information on the full version of this program, visit **www.manhattanprep.com/gmat/interact**.

## ONLINE UPDATES TO THE CONTENT IN THIS BOOK

The content presented in this book is updated periodically to ensure that it reflects the GMAT's most current trends. You may view all updates, including any known errors or changes, upon registering for online access.

**The above resources can be found in your Student Center at manhattanprep.com/gmat/studentcenter.**

# TABLE OF CONTENTS

# Arithmetic

# In this chapter...

- Quick-Start Definitions
  - Basic Numbers
  - Greater Than and Less Than
  - Adding and Subtracting Positives and Negatives
  - Multiplying and Dividing
  - Distributing and Factoring
  - Multiplying Positives and Negatives
  - Fractions and Decimals
  - Divisibility and Even and Odd Integers
  - Exponents and Roots (and Pi)
  - Variable Expressions and Equations
- PEMDAS
  - PEMDAS Overview
  - Combining Like Terms
  - Distribution
  - Pulling Out a Common Factor
  - Long Addition and Subtraction
  - Long Multiplication
  - Long Division

Chapter 1

# Arithmetic

Your goal in this book is twofold: to review fundamental math skills and to practice applying these skills. To this end, there are a number of "Check Your Skills" questions throughout each chapter. After learning a topic, try these problems (one at a time, if more than one), checking your answers at the back of the chapter as you go.

*If you find these questions challenging, reread the section you just finished.* Then try the questions again. Whenever needed, use the solution to help you work through the math step-by-step. When you get stuck, don't read the entire solution immediately. Read as much as you need to get yourself unstuck, then continue to try to do the work on your own.

## In This Chapter, You Will Learn To:

- Recognize math vocabulary and calculate accordingly
- Apply PEMDAS
- Combine like terms and pull out common factors

## Quick-Start Definitions

Whether you work with numbers every day or avoid them diligently, give a good read to this first section, which provides definitions for certain core concepts in order to give your studies a quick start. We'll come back to many of these concepts throughout the book. Moreover, **bolded** terms in this section can be found in the glossary at the back of the book.

## Basic Numbers

All the **numbers** that we care about on the GMAT can be shown as a point somewhere on the **number line**:

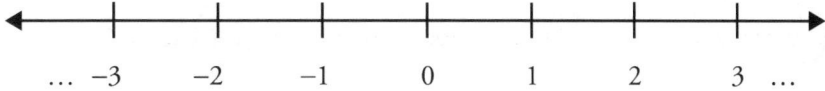

Another word for number is **value**.

**1**

**Counting numbers** are 1, 2, 3, and so on. These are the first numbers that you ever learned—the numbers that you use to count individual items.

**Digits** are 10 symbols (0, 1, 2, 3, 4, 5, 6, 7, 8, and 9) used to represent numbers. If the GMAT asks you specifically for a digit, it wants one of these 10 symbols.

Counting numbers above 9 are represented by two or more digits. The number *four hundred twelve* is represented by three digits in this order: 412.

**Place value** tells you how much a digit in a specific position is worth. The 4 in 412 is worth 4 hundreds (400), so 4 is the *hundreds digit* of 412. Meanwhile, 1 is the *tens digit* and is worth 1 ten (10). Finally, 2 is the *units digit* and is worth 2 units, or just plain old 2.

| 412 | = | 400 | + | 10 | + | 2 |
|---|---|---|---|---|---|---|
| Four hundred twelve | equals | four hundreds | plus | one ten | plus | two units (or two) |

The GMAT always separates the thousands digit from the hundreds digit by a comma. For readability, big numbers are broken up by commas placed three digits apart.

1,298,023 equals one million two hundred ninety-eight thousand twenty-three.

**Addition** (+, or *plus*) is the most basic operation in arithmetic. If you add one counting number to another, you get a third counting number farther to the right on the number line.

| 7 | + | 5 | = | 12 |
|---|---|---|---|---|
| Seven | plus | five | equals | twelve |

$$+5$$
$$0 \qquad 7 \longrightarrow 12$$

Therefore, 12 is the **sum** of 7 and 5.

You can always add in either order and get the same result.

| 5 | + | 7 | = | 12 |
|---|---|---|---|---|
| Five | plus | seven | equals | twelve |

$$+7$$
$$0 \qquad 5 \longrightarrow 12$$

**Subtraction** (−, or *minus*) is the opposite of addition. Subtraction undoes addition.

| 7 | + | 5 | − | 5 | = | 7 |
|---|---|---|---|---|---|---|
| Seven | plus | five | minus | five | equals | seven |

**MANHATTAN PREP**

1

Order matters in subtraction: $6 - 2 = 4$, but $2 - 6 =$ something else (more on this in a minute). By the way, since $6 - 2 = 4$, the **difference** between 6 and 2 is 4.

Any number minus itself equals **zero** (0).

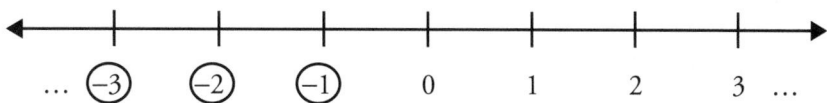

| 7 | – | 7 | = | 0 |
|---|---|---|---|---|
| Seven | minus | seven | equals | zero |

Any number plus zero equals that starting number. The same is true if you subtract zero. In either case, you're moving *zero* units away from the original number on the number line.

$$8 + 0 = 8 \qquad\qquad 9 - 0 = 9$$

**Negative counting numbers** are $-1, -2, -3$, and so on. These numbers, which are written with a **minus sign** or **negative sign**, show up to the left of zero on a number line.

You need negative numbers when you subtract a bigger number from a smaller number. Say you subtract 6 from 2.

| 2 | – | 6 | = | –4 |
|---|---|---|---|---|
| Two | minus | six | equals | negative four |

Negative numbers can be used to represent deficits. If you have $2 but you owe $6, your net worth is –$4.

If you're having trouble computing *small minus big,* figure out *big minus small,* then make the result negative.

$35 - 57 = ?$
$$\begin{array}{r} 57 \\ -35 \\ \hline 22 \end{array}$$
So $35 - 57 = -22$

**Positive** numbers are to the right of zero on a number line. **Negative** numbers are to the left of zero. Zero itself is neither positive nor negative—it's the only number right in the middle.

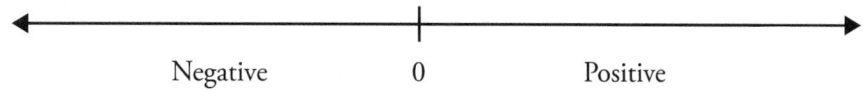

The **sign** of a number indicates whether the number is positive or negative.

**1**

**Integers** include all the numbers discussed so far:

- Counting numbers (1, 2, 3, …), also known as **positive integers**
- Negative counting numbers (−1, −2, −3, …), also known as **negative integers**
- Zero (0)

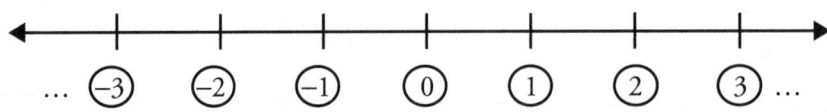

## Check Your Skills

Perform addition and subtraction.

1. 37 + 141 =
2. 23 − 136 =

*Answers can be found on page 37.*

# Greater Than and Less Than

*Greater than* (>) means *to the right of* on a number line. You can also say *bigger* or *larger*, but there is one drawback to using this terminology. Take a look at this example.

| 7 | > | 3 |
|---|---|---|
| Seven | is | greater (bigger) (larger) | than | three |

0      3⟶⑦

Careful! This definition of *greater than* means that, for negative numbers, bigger numbers are *closer* to zero. This may be counterintuitive at first. For example:

| −3 | > | −7 |
|---|---|---|
| Negative three | is | greater (bigger) (larger) | than | negative seven |

−7⟶⊖3      0

Don't think in terms of "size," even though *bigger* and *larger* seem to refer to size. Bigger numbers are *to the right of* smaller numbers on the number line.

The left-to-right order of the number line is negatives, then zero, then positives. So any positive number is greater than any negative number. For example:

| 2 | > | −3 |
|---|---|---|
| Two | is | greater | than | negative three |

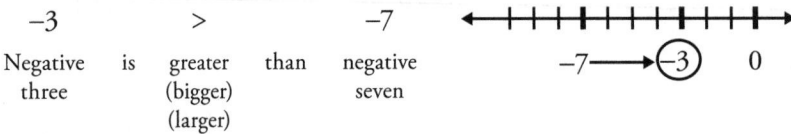

**MANHATTAN** PREP

Likewise, zero is greater than every negative number.

| | | |
|---|---|---|
| 0 | > | −3 |
| Zero is greater than | | negative three |

$$-3 \rightarrow \boxed{0}$$

*Less than* (<) means *to the left of* on a number line. You can always re-express a *greater than* relationship as a *less than* relationship—just flip it around.

| | | |
|---|---|---|
| 7 | > | 3 |
| Seven is greater than | | three |

$$0 \qquad 3 \rightarrow \boxed{7}$$

| | | |
|---|---|---|
| 3 | < | 7 |
| Three is less than | | seven |

$$0 \qquad \boxed{3} \leftarrow \boxed{7}$$

If 7 is greater than 3, then 3 is less than 7.

If you think you are more likely to make mistakes with negatives, test out the following true statements on a number line.

| | |
|---|---|
| −7 is less than −3 | −7 < −3 |
| −3 is less than 2 | −3 < 2 |
| −3 is less than 0 | −3 < 0 |

**Inequalities** are statements that involve greater than (>) or less than (<) relationships.

## Check Your Skills

3. What is the sum of the greatest negative integer and the smallest positive integer?

For questions 4 and 5, plug in > and < symbols, and say the resulting statement aloud.

4. 5 __ 16
5. −5 __ −16

*Answers can be found on page 37.*

## Adding and Subtracting Positives and Negatives

**Positive** *plus* **positive** gives you a third positive. For example:

| | | | | |
|---|---|---|---|---|
| 7 | + | 5 | = | 12 |
| Seven | plus | five | equals | twelve |

$$+5$$
$$0 \qquad 7 \rightarrow \boxed{12}$$

Remember that, when adding, you move even farther to the right of zero, so the result is always bigger than either starting number.

**Positive** *minus* **positive** could give you either a positive or a negative.

*big positive – small positive = positive*

|     |     |     |     |     |
| :-: | :-: | :-: | :-: | :-: |
|  8  |  –  |  3  |  =  |  5  |
| Eight | minus | three | equals | five |

*small positive – big positive = negative*

|     |     |     |     |     |
| :-: | :-: | :-: | :-: | :-: |
|  3  |  –  |  8  |  =  |  –5  |
| Three | minus | eight | equals | negative five |

Either way, the result is less than where you started, because you move left.

*Adding a* negative is the same as subtracting a positive—you move left.

|     |     |     |     |     |
| :-: | :-: | :-: | :-: | :-: |
|  8  |  +  |  –3  |  =  |  5  |
| Eight | plus | negative three | equals | five |

**Negative** *plus* **negative** always gives you a negative, because you move even farther to the left of zero.

|     |     |     |     |     |
| :-: | :-: | :-: | :-: | :-: |
|  –3  |  +  |  –5  |  =  |  –8  |
| Negative three | plus | negative five | equals | negative eight |

*Subtracting a* **negative** is the same as adding a positive—you move right. Think "two wrongs (*subtracting* and *negative*) make a right." Add in parentheses so you keep the two minus signs straight.

|     |     |     |     |     |     |
| :-: | :-: | :-: | :-: | :-: | :-: |
|  7  |  –  |  (–5)  |  =  |  7  +  5  |
| Seven | minus | negative five | equals | seven plus five, |

|     |     |
| :-: | :-: |
|  =  |  12  |
| and this equals | twelve |

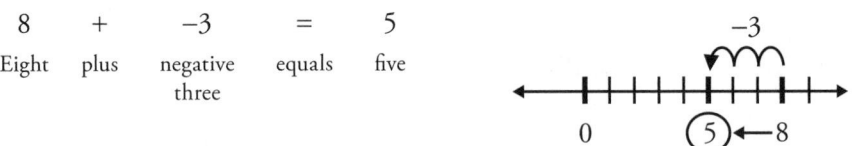

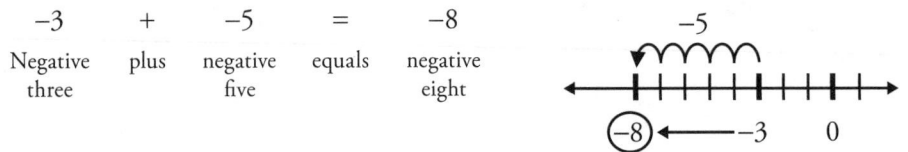

**MANHATTAN** PREP

In general, any subtraction can be rewritten as an addition. If you're subtracting a positive, that's the same as adding a negative. If you're subtracting a negative, that's the same as adding a positive.

## Check Your Skills

6. Which is greater, a positive minus a negative or a negative minus a positive?

*Answer can be found on page 37.*

## Multiplying and Dividing

**Multiplication** (×, or *times*) is repeated addition.

| 4 | × | 3 | = | 3 + 3 + 3 + 3 | = | 12 |
|---|---|---|---|---|---|---|
| Four | times | three | equals | four threes added up, | and this equals | twelve |

Therefore, 12 is the **product** of 4 and 3, which are **factors** of 12.

**Parentheses** can be used to indicate multiplication. Parentheses are usually written with ( ), but brackets [ ] can also be used, especially if you have parentheses within parentheses.

If a set of parentheses bumps up right against something else, multiply that something by whatever is in the parentheses.

$$4(3) = (4)3 = (4)(3) = 4 \times 3 = 12$$

When writing a multiplication sign, you can use a big dot. Just make the dot big and high so it doesn't look like a decimal point.

$$4 \bullet 3 = 4 \times 3 = 12$$

You can always multiply in either order; you will get the same result.

| 4 | × | 3 | = | 3 + 3 + 3 + 3 | = | 12 |
|---|---|---|---|---|---|---|
| Four | times | three | equals | four threes added up, | and this equals | twelve |

| 3 | × | 4 | = | 4 + 4 + 4 | = | 12 |
|---|---|---|---|---|---|---|
| Three | times | four | equals | three fours added up, | and this equals | twelve |

**Division** (÷, or *divided by*) is the opposite of multiplication. Division undoes multiplication.

| 2 | × | 3 | ÷ | 3 | = | 2 |
|---|---|---|---|---|---|---|
| Two | times | three | divided by | three | equals | two |

Order matters in division. $12 \div 3 = 4$, but $3 \div 12 =$ something else (more on this soon).

Multiplying any number by 1 leaves the number the same. One times anything *is* that thing.

| 1 | × | 5 | = | 5 | = | 5 |
|---|---|---|---|---|---|---|
| One | times | five | equals | one five by itself, | and this equals | five |

| 5 | × | 1 | = | 1 + 1 + 1 + 1 + 1 | = | 5 |
|---|---|---|---|---|---|---|
| Five | times | one | equals | five ones added up, | and this equals | five |

Multiplying any number by zero (0) gives you zero. Anything times zero is zero.

| 5 | × | 0 | = | 0 + 0 + 0 + 0 + 0 | = | 0 |
|---|---|---|---|---|---|---|
| Five | times | zero | equals | five zeros added up, | and this equals | zero |

Since order doesn't matter in multiplication, this means that zero times anything is zero, too.

| 0 | × | 5 | = | 5 × 0 | = | 0 |
|---|---|---|---|---|---|---|
| Zero | times | five | equals | five times zero, | and this equals | zero |

Multiplying a number by zero destroys it permanently, in a sense. So you're not allowed to undo that destruction by dividing by zero:

*Never divide by zero*: 13 ÷ 0 = undefined. Stop right there—don't do this!

You *are* allowed to divide zero by any nonzero number. The answer is—surprise!—zero.

| 0 | ÷ | 13 | = | 0 |
|---|---|---|---|---|
| Zero | divided by | thirteen | equals | zero |

## Check Your Skills

Complete the operations.

7. $7 \times 6 =$
8. $52 \div 13 =$

*Answers can be found on page 37.*

## Distributing and Factoring

What is $4 \times (3 + 2)$? Here's one way to solve it.

| 4 | × | (3 + 2) | = | 4 × 5 | = | 20 |
|---|---|---|---|---|---|---|
| Four | times | the quantity three plus two | equals | four times five, | and this equals | twenty |

Turn (3 + 2) into 5, then multiply 4 by that 5.

The other way to solve this problem is to **distribute** the 4 to both the 3 and the 2.

| 4 | × | (3 + 2) | = | 4 × 3 | + | 4 × 2 |
|---|---|---------|---|-------|---|-------|
| Four | times | the quantity three plus two | equals | four times three | plus | four times two, |

| | | | = | 12 | + | 8 |
|---|---|---|---|----|---|---|
| | | | and this equals | twelve | plus | eight, |

| | | | = | 20 | |
|---|---|---|---|----|---|
| | | | and that equals | twenty | |

Notice that you multiply the 4 into *both* the 3 and the 2.

Distributing is extra work in this case, but the technique will come in handy down the road.

Another way to see how distributing works is to put the sum in front.

| | 20 | | = | | 20 | |
|---|----|---|---|---|----|---|
| (3 + 2) | × | 4 | = | 3 × 4 | + | 2 × 4 |
| 5 | | | | | | |
| Five | times | four | equals | three times four | plus | two times four |

| Five fours added together | | | equals | three fours added together | plus | two fours added together |
|---|---|---|---|---|---|---|
| Twenty | | | equals | twenty | | |

In a sense, you're splitting up the sum 3 + 2. Just be sure to multiply both the 3 and the 2 by 4.

You distribute when the terms inside the parentheses are connected by addition or subtraction signs. Do *not* distribute if the terms inside the parentheses are connected by multiplication or division; in that case, just drop the parentheses and multiply or divide straight across. For example:

| DO distribute: | $3(4 + y) = (3)(4) + (3)(y) = 12 + 3y$ |
|---|---|
| DO NOT distribute: | $3(4 × y) = 3 × 4 × y = 12y$ |

**1**

Distributing works similarly for subtraction. Just keep track of the minus sign.

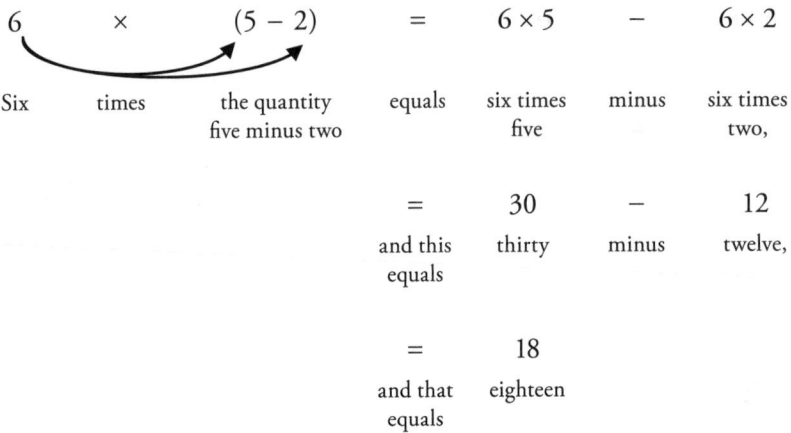

| 6 | × | (5 − 2) | = | 6 × 5 | − | 6 × 2 |
| Six | times | the quantity five minus two | equals | six times five | minus | six times two, |

| | | | = | 30 | − | 12 |
| | | | and this equals | thirty | minus | twelve, |

| | | | = | 18 | | |
| | | | and that equals | eighteen | | |

You can also go in reverse. You can **factor** the sum of two products if the products contain the same factor:

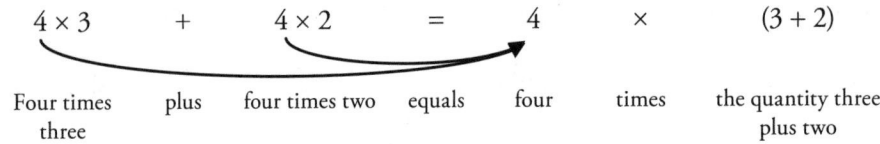

| 4 × 3 | + | 4 × 2 | = | 4 | × | (3 + 2) |
| Four times three | plus | four times two | equals | four | times | the quantity three plus two |

Pull out the **common factor** of 4 from each of the products 4 × 3 and 4 × 2. Next, put the sum of 3 and 2 into parentheses. By the way, *common* here doesn't mean *frequent* or *typical*. Rather, it means *belonging to both products*. A common factor is a factor in common (like a friend in common).

You can also put the common factor at the back of each product, if you like:

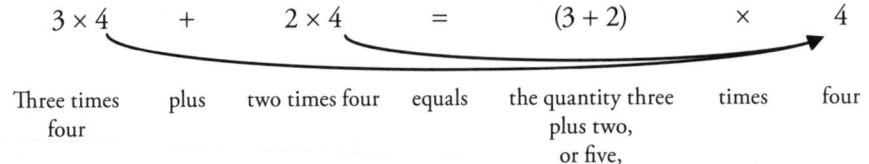

| 3 × 4 | + | 2 × 4 | = | (3 + 2) | × | 4 |
| Three times four | plus | two times four | equals | the quantity three plus two, or five, | times | four |

As mentioned before, you can distribute when the math in the parentheses is added or subtracted. Don't distribute if the math in the parentheses is multiplied or divided. For example:

| Example | Can I distribute? | |
|---------|-------------------|--|
| 3(4 + 5) | Yes! The math in the parentheses is added. | $3(4 + 5) =$ <br> $(3)(4) + (3)(5) = 27$ |
| 3(4 × 5) | No. When the math in the parentheses is also multiplied (or divided), do the math straight out. | $3(4 × 5) =$ <br> $3 × 4 × 5 = 60$ |

You will use both distributing and factoring in more advanced ways later. Using simple numbers to understand the concepts now will help you to apply these same concepts to more complex problems in future.

## Check Your Skills

9.  Use distribution to solve: $5 \times (3 + 4) =$
10. Factor a 6 out of the following expression: $36 - 12$

*Answers can be found on page 37.*

## Multiplying Positives and Negatives

**Positive** $\times$ **positive** is always **positive**:

| 3 | $\times$ | 4 | $=$ | $4 + 4 + 4$ | $=$ | 12 |
|---|---|---|---|---|---|---|
| Three | times | four | equals | three fours added up, | and this equals | twelve |

**Positive** $\times$ **negative** is always **negative**:

| 3 | $\times$ | $-4$ | $=$ | $-4 + (-4) + (-4)$ | $=$ | $-12$ |
|---|---|---|---|---|---|---|
| Three | times | negative four | equals | three negative fours, all added up, | and this equals | negative twelve |

Since order doesn't matter in multiplication, the same outcome happens when you have *negative times positive*. You again get a **negative**:

| $-4$ | $\times$ | 3 | $=$ | $3 \times (-4)$ | $=$ | $-12$ |
|---|---|---|---|---|---|---|
| Negative four | times | three | equals | three times negative four, | and this equals | negative twelve |

What is **negative** $\times$ **negative**? **Positive**. This fact may seem weird, but it's consistent with the rules developed so far. In the same way that something minus a negative turns into something plus a positive ($7 - (-3) = 7 + 3$), a negative times a negative also turns positive. In either case, two negatives make a positive.

All the same rules hold true for division:

| **Positive Result** | **Negative Result** |
|---|---|
| Positive $\div$ Positive = Positive | Positive $\div$ Negative = Negative |
| Negative $\div$ Negative = Positive | Negative $\div$ Positive = Negative |
| Positive $\times$ Positive = Positive | Positive $\times$ Negative = Negative |
| Negative $\times$ Negative = Positive | Negative $\times$ Positive = Negative |

## Check Your Skills

11. $(3)(-4) =$
12. Use distribution to solve: $-6 \times (-3 + (-5))$

*Answers can be found on page 37.*

# Fractions and Decimals

Adding, subtracting, or multiplying integers always results in an integer, whether positive or negative.

$$\text{Int} \quad + \quad \text{Int} \quad = \quad \text{Int}$$
$$\text{Int} \quad - \quad \text{Int} \quad = \quad \text{Int}$$
$$\text{Int} \quad \times \quad \text{Int} \quad = \quad \text{Int}$$

(*Int* is a handy abbreviation for a random integer, by the way, although the GMAT won't demand that you use it.)

However, dividing an integer by another integer does not always give you an integer.

$$\text{Int} \quad \div \quad \text{Int} \quad = \quad \text{sometimes an integer,}$$
$$\text{sometimes not!}$$

When you don't get an integer, you get a **fraction** or a **decimal**—a number between the integers on the number line.

$$7 \div 2 \quad = \quad \frac{7}{2} \quad = \quad 3.5$$

| Seven divided by two | equals | seven halves, | and this equals | three point five |
|---|---|---|---|---|

Fraction          Decimal

A horizontal **fraction line,** or bar, expresses the division of the **numerator** (above the fraction line) by the **denominator** (below the fraction line).

$$\text{Numerator} \searrow$$
$$\text{Fraction line} \longrightarrow \frac{7}{2} \quad = \quad 7 \div 2$$
$$\text{Denominator} \nearrow$$

In fact, the division symbol ÷ is just a miniature fraction. People often say things such as "seven *over* two" rather than "seven halves" to express a fraction.

You can express division in three ways: with a fraction line, with the division symbol ÷, or with a slash (/).

$$\frac{7}{2} \quad = \quad 7 \div 2 \quad = \quad 7/2$$

A **decimal point** is used to extend place value to the right for decimals. Each place to the right of the decimal point is worth a tenth $\left(\dfrac{1}{10}\right)$, a hundredth $\left(\dfrac{1}{100}\right)$, and so on.

$$3.5 \quad = \quad 3 \quad + \quad \frac{5}{10}$$

| Three point five | equals | three | plus | five-tenths |
|---|---|---|---|---|

$$1.25 \quad = \quad 1 \quad + \quad \frac{2}{10} \quad + \quad \frac{5}{100}$$

| One point two five | equals | one | plus | two-tenths | plus | five-hundredths |

A decimal such as 3.5 has an **integer part** (3) and a **fractional part** or **decimal part** (0.5). In fact, an integer is just a number with no fractional or decimal part.

Every fraction can be written as a decimal, although you might need an unending string of digits in the decimal to properly express the fraction.

$$4 \div 3 \quad = \quad \frac{4}{3} \quad = \quad 1.333\ldots \quad = \quad 1.\overline{3}$$

| Four divided by three | equals | four-thirds (or four over three), | and this equals | one point three three three dot dot dot, forever and ever, | and that equals | one point three repeating |

Fractions and decimals obey all the rules you've seen so far about how to add, subtract, multiply, and divide. Everything you've learned for integers applies to fractions and decimals as well: how positives and negatives work, how to distribute, etc.

## Check Your Skills

13.  Which arithmetic operation involving integers does NOT always result in an integer?

14.  $2 \div 7 = 2 \times \underline{\quad}$?

*Answers can be found on page 37.*

## Divisibility and Even and Odd Integers

Sometimes you do get an integer out of integer division.

$$15 \div 3 \quad = \quad \frac{15}{3} \quad = \quad 5 \quad = \quad \text{int}$$

| Fifteen divided by three | equals | fifteen-thirds (or fifteen over three), | and this equals | five, | which is | an integer |

In this case, 15 and 3 have a special relationship. You can express this relationship in several equivalent ways.

1

15 is **divisible** by 3.

    15 divided by 3 equals an integer: $15 \div 3 = \text{int}$

15 is a **multiple** of 3.

    15 equals 3 times an integer: $15 = 3 \times \text{int}$

3 is a **factor** of 15.

3 **goes into** 15 evenly.

3 **divides** 15 evenly.

**Even integers** are divisible by 2.

    14 is even because $14 \div 2 = 7 =$ an integer.

All even integers have 0, 2, 4, 6, or 8 as their units digit (the digit just to the left of the decimal point).

**Odd integers** are not divisible by 2.

    15 is odd because $15 \div 2 = 7.5 =$ not an integer.

All odd integers have 1, 3, 5, 7, or 9 as their units digit.

Even and odd integers alternate on the number line.

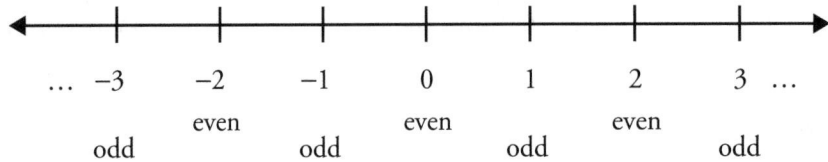

Zero is even because it is divisible by 2.

    $0 \div 2 = 0$, which is an integer

Only integers can be said to be even or odd. Fractions or decimals are not considered even or odd.

## Check Your Skills

15. Fill in the blank. If 7 is a factor of 21, then 21 is a _____ of 7.
16. Is 2,284,623 divisible by 2?

*Answers can be found on page 37.*

## Exponents and Roots (and Pi)

**Exponents** represent repeated multiplication. (Remember, multiplication was repeated addition, so this is just the next step up the food chain.)

In $5^2$, the **exponent** is 2, and the **base** is 5. The exponent tells you how many bases you multiply together in the product. When the exponent is 2, you usually say *squared*.

| $5^2$ | = | $5 \times 5$ | = | 25 |
|-------|---|--------------|---|-----|
| Five squared | equals | two fives multiplied together, or five times itself, | and this equals | twenty-five |

When the exponent is 3, you usually say *cubed*.

| $4^3$ | = | $4 \times 4 \times 4$ | = | 64 |
|-------|---|------------------------|---|-----|
| Four cubed | equals | three fours multiplied together, or four times four times four, | and this equals | sixty-four |

For other exponents, you say *to the ____ power* or *raised to the ____ power*. You could also say *to the power of ____*. For example:

| $2^5$ | = | $2 \times 2 \times 2 \times 2 \times 2$ | = | 32 |
|-------|---|------------------------------------------|---|-----|
| Two to the fifth power | equals | five twos multiplied together, | and this equals | thirty-two |

When you write exponents on your own paper, be sure to make them much tinier than regular numbers, and put them *clearly* up to the right. You don't want to mistake $5^2$ for 52, or vice versa.

By the way, a number raised to the first power equals the original number.

| $7^1$ | = | 7 | = | 7 |
|-------|---|---|---|---|
| Seven to the first power | equals | just one seven in the product, | and this equals | seven |

A **perfect square** is the square of an integer.

  25 is a perfect square because $25 = 5^2 = \text{int}^2$.

A **perfect cube** is the cube of an integer.

  64 is a perfect cube because $64 = 4^3 = \text{int}^3$.

**Roots** undo exponents. The simplest and most common root is the **square root**, which undoes squaring. The square root is written with the **radical sign** ($\sqrt{\phantom{x}}$); if a problem refers to the **radical**, it's talking about that symbol.

| $5^2$ | = | $5 \times 5$ | = | 25, | so | $\sqrt{25}$ | = | 5 |
|-------|---|--------------|---|-----|-----|-------------|---|---|
| Five squared | equals | five times five, | and this equals | twenty-five, | so | the square root of twenty-five | equals | five |

As a shortcut, *the square root of twenty-five* can just be called *root twenty-five*.

Asking for the square root of 49 is the same as asking what number, times itself, gives you 49.

$$\sqrt{49} \qquad = \qquad 7 \qquad \text{because} \qquad 7 \times 7 \qquad = \qquad 7^2 \qquad = \qquad 49$$

| Root forty-nine | equals | seven, | because | seven times seven | equals | seven squared, | and this equals | forty-nine |

The square root of a perfect square is an integer, because a perfect square is an integer squared.

$$\sqrt{36} \qquad = \qquad \text{int} \qquad \text{because} \qquad 36 \qquad = \qquad \text{int}^2$$

| The square root of thirty-six | is | an integer, | because | thirty-six | equals | an integer squared |

The square root of any *non*-perfect square is an unending decimal that never even repeats, as it turns out.

$$\sqrt{2} \qquad \approx \qquad 1.414213562\ldots \qquad \text{because} \qquad (1.414213562\ldots)^2 \qquad \approx \qquad 2$$

| Root two | is about | one point four one four two blah blah, | because | that thing squared | is about | two |

The square root of 2 can't be expressed as a simple fraction, either. So you can leave it as is ( $\sqrt{2}$ ), or you can approximate it ( $\sqrt{2} \approx 1.4$ ).

You'll encounter one other number with an ugly decimal in geometry: **pi** ($\pi$).

Pi is the ratio of a circle's circumference to its diameter. It's about 3.14159265… without ever repeating.

Since pi can't be expressed as a simple fraction, it is typically represented by the Greek letter for *p* ($\pi$), or you can approximate it ($\pi \approx 3.14$, or a little more than 3).

**Cube roots** undo cubing. The cube root has a little 3 tucked into its notch ( $\sqrt[3]{\phantom{x}}$ ):

$$\sqrt[3]{8} \qquad = \qquad 2 \qquad \text{because} \qquad 2^3 \qquad = \qquad 8$$

| The cube root of eight | equals | two, | because | two cubed | equals | eight |

Other roots occasionally show up. For example, the **fourth root** undoes the process of taking a base to the fourth power.

$$\sqrt[4]{81} \qquad = \qquad 3 \qquad \text{because} \qquad 3^4 \qquad = \qquad 81$$

| The fourth root of eighty-one | equals | three, | because | three to the fourth power | equals | eighty-one |

## Check Your Skills

17. $2^6 =$
18. $\sqrt[3]{27} =$

*Answers can be found on page 38.*

# Variable Expressions and Equations

Up to now, every number you've dealt with has been an actual, known number. **Algebra** is the art of dealing with *unknown* numbers.

A **variable** is an unknown number, also called an **unknown**. You represent a variable with a single letter, such as $x$ or $y$.

When you see $y$, imagine that it represents a number that you don't happen to know. At the start of a problem, the value of $y$ is hidden from you. It could be anywhere on the number line, in theory, unless you're told something about $y$.

The letter $x$ is the stereotypical letter used for an unknown. Since $x$ looks so much like the multiplication symbol ×, you generally stop using × when writing out algebra to prevent confusion. To represent multiplication, you do other things.

To multiply variables, just put them next to each other.

| *What you see* | *What you say* | *What it means* |
|---|---|---|
| $xy$ | "x y" | $x$ times $y$ |
| $abc$ | "a b c" | The product of $a$, $b$, and $c$ |

To multiply a known number by a variable, write the known number in front of the variable.

| *What you see* | *What you say* | *What it means* |
|---|---|---|
| $3x$ | "three x" | 3 times $x$ |

Here, 3 is called the **coefficient** of $x$. If you want to multiply $x$ by 3, write $3x$, not $x3$, which could look too much like $x^3$ ("*x cubed*").

All the operations besides multiplication look the same for variables as they do for known numbers.

| *What you see* | *What you say* | *What it means* |
|---|---|---|
| $x + y$ | "x plus y" | $x$ plus $y$, or the sum of $x$ and $y$ |
| $x - y$ | "x minus y" | $x$ minus $y$ |
| $\dfrac{x}{y}$ | "x over y" or "x divided by y" | $x$ divided by $y$ |
| $x^2$ | "x squared" | $x$ squared, which is just $x$ times $x$ |
| $\sqrt{x}$ | "the square root of x" | the square root of $x$ |

**1**

By the way, be careful when you have variables in exponents.

| What you see | What you say | What it means |
|:---:|:---:|:---:|
| $3x$ | "three x" | 3 times $x$ |
| $3^x$ | "three to the x" | 3 raised to the $x$th power, or 3 multiplied by itself $x$ times |

Never call $3^x$ "three x." It's called "three *to the* x." If you don't call $3^x$ by its correct name, then you'll never keep it straight.

An **expression** is something that ultimately represents a number; for example, $x + 3$ is an expression. You might not know that number, but you *express* it using variables, numbers you know, and operations such as adding, subtracting, etc.

An expression is like a recipe. If you follow the recipe, you will get the right number, as shown in the examples below:

| Expression | What you say | The number represented by the expression |
|:---:|:---:|:---:|
| $x + y$ | "x plus y" | The sum of $x$ and $y$. In other words, the recipe is "add $x$ and $y$." The result is the number. |
| $3xz - y^2$ | "3 x z minus y squared" | First, multiply 3, $x$, and $z$, then subtract the square of $y$. The result is the number. |
| $\dfrac{\sqrt{2w}}{3}$ | "The square root of 2 w, all over 3" | First, multiply 2 and $w$ together. Next, take the square root. Finally, divide by 3. The result is the number. |

Within an expression, you have one or more **terms**. A single term involves no addition or subtraction (typically). Often, a term is just a product of variables and known numbers.

It's useful to notice terms so that you can **simplify** expressions, or reduce the number of terms in those expressions. Here are the terms in the previous expressions.

| Expression | Terms | Number of terms |
|:---:|:---:|:---:|
| $x + y$ | $x, y$ | Two |
| $3xz - y^2$ | $3xz, y^2$ | Two |
| $\dfrac{\sqrt{2w}}{3}$ | $\dfrac{\sqrt{2w}}{3}$ | One |

If the last step in the expression recipe is adding or subtracting, then you can split up the expression into more than one term. Many expressions contain just one term, though (just as that last one did).

An **equation** sets one expression equal to another using the **equals sign** (=), which you've seen plenty of times in your life—and in this book already.

MANHATTAN PREP

What you might not have thought about, though, is that the equals sign is a *verb*. In other words, an equation is a complete, grammatical sentence or statement:

Something    *equals*    something else.

Some expression    *equals*    some other expression.

Here's an example:

$$3 + 2x \qquad = \qquad 11$$

Three plus two $x$   equals   eleven

Each equation has a *left side* (the subject of the sentence) and a *right side* (the object of the verb *equals*). You can say *is equal to* instead of *equals* if you want:

$$3 + 2x \qquad = \qquad 11$$

Three plus two $x$   is equal to   eleven

Solving an equation is solving this mystery:

What is $x$?

Or, more precisely:

What is the value or values of $x$ that make the equation *true*?

Since an equation is a sentence, it can be true or false, at least in theory. You always want to focus on how to make the equation *true*, or keep it so, by finding the right values of any variables in that equation.

The process of solving an equation usually involves rearranging the equation and performing identical operations on each side until the equation tells you what the variable equals.

| $3 + 2x$ | $=$ | $11$ | Three plus two $x$ | equals | eleven |
|---|---|---|---|---|---|
| $-3$ | | $-3$ | Subtract 3 | | Subtract 3 |
| $2x$ | $=$ | $8$ | Two $x$ | equals | eight |
| $\div 2$ | | $\div 2$ | Divide by 2 | | Divide by 2 |
| $x$ | $=$ | $4$ | $x$ | equals | four |

The solution to the original equation is $x = 4$. If you replace $x$ with 4 in the equation $3 + 2x = 11$, then you get $11 = 11$, which is always true. Any other value of $x$ would make the equation false.

If the GMAT gives you the equation $3 + 2x = 11$, it's telling you something very specific about $x$. For this particular equation, in fact, just one value of $x$ makes the equation work (namely, 4).

## Check Your Skills

19.  What is the value of the expression $2x - 3y$ if $x = 4$ and $y = -1$?

*Answer can be found on page 38.*

# 1 PEMDAS

Consider the expression $3 + 2 \times 4$.

Should you add 3 and 2 first, then multiply by 4? If so, you get 20.

Or should you multiply 2 and 4 first, then add 3? If so, you get 11.

There's no ambiguity—mathematicians have decided on the second option. **PEMDAS** is an acronym to help you remember the proper **order of operations**.

## PEMDAS Overview

When you simplify an expression, don't automatically perform operations from left to right, even though that's how you read English. Instead, follow PEMDAS:

| | |
|---|---|
| **P**arentheses | Do P first |
| **E**xponents | Then E |
| **M**ultiplication | Then either M or D |
| **D**ivision | |
| **A**ddition | Then either A or S |
| **S**ubtraction | |

For $3 + 2 \times 4$, you do the M first (multiply 2 and 4), then the A (add 3 to the result).

$$3 + 2 \times 4 \qquad = 3 + 8 \qquad = 11$$

If you want to force the addition to go first, add parentheses. P always goes first:

$$(3 + 2) \times 4 \qquad = 5 \times 4 \qquad = 20$$

Multiplication and division are at the same level of importance in PEMDAS, because any multiplication can be expressed as division, and vice versa. For example:

$$7 \div 2 = 7 \times \frac{1}{2}$$

In a sense, multiplication and division are two sides of the same coin.

Likewise, addition and subtraction are at the same level of importance. Any addition can be expressed as subtraction, and vice versa.

$$3 - 4 = 3 + (-4)$$

So you can think of PEMDAS this way:

$$PE^M/_D{}^A/_S$$
$$\longrightarrow$$

If you have two operations of equal importance, do them *left to right*.

$$3 - 2 + 3 \qquad = 1 + 3 \qquad = 4$$

However, *override this order* if you have parentheses:

$$3 - (2 + 3) \qquad = 3 - 5 \qquad = -2$$

Consider a more complicated expression:

$$3 + 4(5 - 1) - 3^2 \times 2 = ?$$

Here is the correct order of steps to simplify:

$$3 + 4(5 - 1) - 3^2 \times 2$$

**P**arentheses              $3 + 4(4) - 3^2 \times 2$

**E**xponents                $3 + 4(4) - 9 \times 2$

**M**ultiplication or **D**ivision     $3 + 16 - 18$

**A**ddition or **S**ubtraction       $3 + 16 - 18 = 19 - 18 = 1$

Try this problem on your own:

$$5 - 3 \times 2^3 \div (7 - 1)$$

**P**

**E**

**M/D**

**A/S**

Here's the solution:

$$5 - 3 \times 2^3 \div \left( 7 - 1 \right)$$
$$5 - 3 \times 2^3 \div 6$$
$$5 - 3 \times 8 \div 6$$
$$5 - 24 \div 6$$
$$5 - 4$$
$$1$$

The answer is 1.

Try one more:

$$32 \div 2^4 \times (5 - 3^2)$$

**P**

**E**

**M/D**

**A/S**

Here's the solution:

$$32 \div 2^4 \times (5 - 3^2)$$

$$32 \div 2^4 \times (5 - 9)$$

$$32 \div 2^4 \times (-4)$$

$$32 \div 16 \times (-4)$$

$$2 \times (-4)$$

$$-8$$

## Check Your Skills

Evaluate the following expressions.

20. $-4 + \dfrac{12}{3}$

21. $(5 - 8) \times 10 - 7 =$

22. $-3 \times 12 \div 4 \times 8 + (4 - 6) =$

23. $\dfrac{2^4 \times (8 \div 2 - 1)}{(9 - 3)} =$

*Answers can be found on page 38.*

## Combining Like Terms

How can you simplify this expression?

$$3x^2 + 7x + 2x^2 - x$$

Remember, an expression is a recipe. Here's the recipe in words:

> Square $x$, then multiply that by 3, then separately multiply $x$ by 7 and add that product in, then square $x$ again, multiply that by 2, and add that product into the whole thing, and then finally subtract $x$.

That recipe is pretty annoying. Is there a way to simplify it?

There is! First, focus on **like terms**, which contain very similar elements.

Again, a term is an expression that doesn't contain addition or subtraction. Quite often, a term is just a bunch of things multiplied together.

Like terms are very similar to each other. They only differ by a numerical coefficient (the number in front of the variable). Everything else in them is the same.

The expression above contains four terms, separated by + and − operations:

$$3x^2 \qquad + \qquad 7x \qquad + \qquad 2x^2 \qquad - \qquad x$$

Three $x$ squared — plus — seven $x$ — plus — two $x$ squared — minus — $x$

There are two pairs of like terms:

Pair one: $\qquad 3x^2 \qquad$ and $\qquad 2x^2$

Pair two: $\qquad 7x \qquad$ and $\qquad -x$

Make sure that the variables are identical, including exponents. Otherwise, the terms aren't *like*.

What can you do with two or more like terms? Combine them into one term by adding or subtracting the coefficients. Keep track of + and − signs. For example:

$$3x^2 \qquad + \qquad 2x^2 \qquad = \qquad 5x^2$$

Three $x$ squared — plus — two $x$ squared — equals — five $x$ squared

$$7x \qquad - \qquad x \qquad = \qquad 6x$$

Seven $x$ — minus — $x$ — equals — six $x$

Whenever a variable does not have a number in front, the coefficient is 1. In the example above, $x$ can be rewritten as $1x$.

$$7x \qquad - \qquad 1x \qquad = \qquad 6x$$

Seven $x$ — minus — one $x$ — equals — six $x$

Or you could say that you're adding $-1x$.

$$7x \qquad + \qquad -1x \qquad = \qquad 6x$$

Seven $x$ — plus — negative one $x$ — equals — six $x$

1

Either way is fine. A negative sign in front of a term on its own is really a $-1$ coefficient. For instance, $-xy^2$ has a coefficient of $-1$.

Combining like terms works because, for like terms, everything *but* the coefficient is a **common factor**. So you can *pull out* that common factor and group the coefficients into a sum (or difference). This is when factoring starts to become really useful.

For a review of factoring, see pages 10–12.

In the first case, the common factor is $x^2$.

$$3x^2 \qquad + \qquad 2x^2 \qquad = \qquad (3+2)x^2$$

Three $x$ squared    plus    two $x$ squared    equals    the quantity three plus two, times
$x$ squared

The right side then reduces by PEMDAS to $5x^2$. Of course, once you can go straight from $3x^2 + 2x^2$ to $5x^2$, you'll save a step.

By the way, when you *pronounce* $(3+2)x^2$, you should technically say "the quantity three plus two…" The word *quantity* indicates parentheses. If you just say "three plus two $x$ squared," someone could (and should) interpret what you said as $3 + 2x^2$, with no parentheses.

In the case of $7x - x$, the common factor is $x$. Remember that $x$ should be thought of as $1x$.

$$7x \qquad - \qquad 1x \qquad = \qquad (7-1)x$$

Seven $x$    minus    one $x$    equals    the quantity seven minus one,
times $x$

Again, the right side reduces by PEMDAS to $6x$.

So, if you combine like terms, you can simplify the original expression this way:

$$3x^2 + 7x + 2x^2 - x$$

$$(3x^2 + 2x^2) + (7x - x)$$

$$5x^2 + 6x$$

The common factor in like terms does not have to be a simple variable expression such as $x^2$ or $x$. It could involve more than one variable:

$$-xy^2 + 4xy^2 = (-1 + 4)xy^2 = 3xy^2 \qquad\qquad \text{Common factor: } xy^2$$

Remember that the coefficient on the first term should be treated as $-1$.

Be careful when you see multiple variables in a single term. For two terms to be like, the exponents have to match for every variable.

In $-xy^2 + 4xy^2$, each term contains a plain $x$ (which is technically $x$ raised to the first power) and $y^2$ (which is $y$ raised to the second power, or $y$ squared). All of the exponents match. So the two terms are like, and you can combine them to $3xy^2$.

Now suppose you had the following series of terms:

| $2xy$ | $+$ | $xy^2$ | $-$ | $4x^2y$ | $+$ | $x^2y^2$ |
|---|---|---|---|---|---|---|
| Two $x\,y$ | plus | $x\,y$ squared | minus | four $x$ squared $y$ | plus | $x$ squared $y$ squared |

*None* of the terms above can combine to a single term. They all have different combinations of variables and exponents. For now, you're stuck. (In the next section, you'll see that there's *something* you can do with that expression, but you can't combine terms.)

The two terms in the following expression *are* like:

| $xy^2$ | $+$ | $3y^2x$ |
|---|---|---|
| $x\,y$ squared | plus | three $y$ squared $x$ |

The order of the variables does not matter, since you can multiply in any order. All that matters is that the variables and exponents all match. You can flip around $3y^2x$ to $3xy^2$ to get:

| $xy^2$ | $+$ | $3y^2x$ | $=$ | $4xy^2$ | $=$ | $4y^2x$ |
|---|---|---|---|---|---|---|
| $x\,y$ squared | plus | three $y$ squared $x$ | equals | four $x\,y$ squared, | and that equals | four $y$ squared $x$ |

In general, be ready to flip around products as you deal with numbers times variables. The order of multiplication does not matter. For example

| $x(-3)$ | $=$ | $-x(3)$ | $=$ | $-3x$ |
|---|---|---|---|---|
| $x$ times negative three | equals | negative $x$ times three | equals | negative three $x$ |

The last form, $-3x$, is the standard form. You can encounter the others as you rearrange terms.

A common factor in like terms could be the square root of a number:

$$\sqrt{2} + 3\sqrt{2} = 1\sqrt{2} + 3\sqrt{2} = \left(1 + 3\right)\sqrt{2} = 4\sqrt{2} \quad \text{Common factor: } \sqrt{2}$$

Or the common factor could include pi ($\pi$):

$$2\pi r + 9\pi r = (2 + 9)\pi r = 11\pi r \qquad \text{Common factor: } \pi r$$

When terms are *not* like, tread carefully. Don't automatically combine everything; see what you can combine and what you cannot.

As you practice simplifying expressions, keep in mind that your main goal is to reduce the overall number of terms by combining like terms.

**1**

PEMDAS becomes more complicated when an expression contains terms that are not like and so cannot be combined. Be especially careful when you see terms buried within part of an expression, as in the following cases that you'll come back to later:

*Terms inside parentheses*

$$-3(x - 2) \qquad x \text{ and } 2 \text{ are not like}$$

*Terms in the numerator or denominator of a fraction*

$$\frac{1}{1 - x} = 2 \qquad x \text{ and } 1 \text{ are not like}$$

*Terms involving exponents*

$$\frac{x^{-3} + \left(x^2\right)^4}{x^5} \qquad x^{-3} \text{ and } (x^2)^4 \text{ are not like}$$

*Terms under a root sign*

$$\sqrt{x^2 + y^2} \qquad x^2 \text{ and } y^2 \text{ are not like}$$

*Terms in parentheses, with the parentheses raised to an exponent*

$$(x + y)^2 \qquad x \text{ and } y \text{ are not like}$$

## Check Your Skills

Combine as many like terms as possible in each of the following expressions.

24. $-3 + 4\sqrt{2} + 6$
25. $4\pi r^2 - 3\pi r + 2\pi r$
26. $8ba + ab^2 - 5ab + ab^2 - 2ba^2$

*Answers can be found on page 38.*

## Distribution

Things become more complicated when multiple terms are found within a set of parentheses.

For a quick review of distribution, go back to pages 10 and 11.

Start by distributing the example from the previous section: $-3(x - 2)$. Remember that you're multiplying $-3$ by $(x - 2)$. To keep track of minus signs as you distribute, you can think of $(x - 2)$ as $(x + (-2))$. The following example shows the multiplication sign ($\times$) to make it clear that you're multiplying.

**MANHATTAN** PREP

$$-3 \quad \times \quad (x-2) \quad = \quad -3 \times x \quad + \quad -3 \times -2 \quad = \quad -3x + 6$$

| Negative three | times | the quantity $x$ minus two | equals | negative three times $x$ | plus | negative three times negative two, | and that equals | negative three $x$ plus six |

Remember that the negative sign (on $-3$) distributes across both terms in the parentheses.

When you do all this on your paper, don't use $\times x$ to show multiplication, because you could confuse it with the variable $x$. Use a big dot or put each term to be multiplied in its own set of parentheses, such as $(-3)(-2)$. You might also put parentheses around the second product to help keep track of sign.

$$-3 \quad \times \quad (x-2) \quad = \quad -3x \quad + \quad (-3 \bullet -2) \quad = \quad -3x + 6$$

| Negative three | times | the quantity $x$ minus two | equals | negative three times $x$ | plus | negative three times negative two, | and that equals | negative three $x$ plus six |

How can you simplify this expression?

$$4y^2 - y(5 - 2y)$$

First, distribute negative $y$, $(-y)$, to both terms in the parentheses:

$$4y^2 - y(5 - 2y) = 4y^2 - 5y + 2y^2$$

Notice that $-y$ times $-2y$ becomes $+2y^2$.

Next, combine $4y^2$ and $2y^2$ because they are like terms:

$$4y^2 - y(5 - 2y) = 4y^2 - 5y + 2y^2 = 6y^2 - 5y$$

Sometimes the term being distributed involves a root or pi. Consider this tougher example:

$$\sqrt{2}\,(1 - x\sqrt{2}\,)$$

The principle is the same. Distribute the first $\sqrt{2}$ to both terms in the parentheses.

$$\sqrt{2} \quad \times \quad (1 - x\sqrt{2}\,) \quad = \quad \sqrt{2} \times 1 \quad + \quad \sqrt{2} \times -x\sqrt{2} \quad = \quad \sqrt{2} - 2x$$

| Root two | times | the quantity one minus $x$ root two | equals | root two times one | plus | root two times negative $x$ root two, | and that equals | root two minus two $x$ |

It turns out that $\sqrt{2}$ times $\sqrt{2}$ is 2.

$$\sqrt{2} \times \sqrt{2} = 2$$

For a more in-depth look at multiplying roots, go to page 111 (or just wait until you get there).

Here's an example with pi:

$$\pi(1 + r)$$

Distribute the pi:

$$\pi \quad \times \quad (1 + r) \quad = \quad \pi \times 1 \quad + \quad \pi \times r \quad = \quad \pi + \pi r$$

| pi | times | the quantity one plus $r$ | equals | pi times one | plus | pi times $r$, | and that equals | pi plus pi $r$ |

## Check Your Skills

27. $x(3 + x)$
28. $4 + \sqrt{2}(1 - \sqrt{2})$

*Answers can be found on page 39.*

# Pulling Out a Common Factor

Earlier, you saw the long expression below:

$$3x^2 + 7x + 2x^2 - x$$

This expression has four terms. By combining two pairs of like terms, you can simplify this expression to $5x^2 + 6x$, which has only two terms.

This expression can't go below two terms. The two remaining terms ($5x^2$ and $6x$) aren't *like*, because the variable parts aren't identical. However, these two terms do still have a common factor—namely, $x$. Each term is $x$ times something, and you can use this fact to rewrite $5x^2 + 6x$.

$x$ is a factor of $6x$, because $6x = 6$ times $x$.

$x$ is also a factor of $5x^2$, because $x^2 = x$ times $x$, so $5x^2 = 5x$ times $x$.

Since $x$ is a factor of both $5x^2$ and $6x$, you can factor it out and group what's left as a sum within parentheses.

$$5x^2 \quad + \quad 6x \quad = \quad x(5x + 6)$$

| Five $x$ squared | plus | six $x$ | equals | $x$ times the quantity five $x$ plus six |

If in doubt, distribute the $x$ back through to verify that you're back where you started.

$$x(5x + 6) \quad = \quad 5x^2 \quad + \quad 6x$$

| The quantity five $x$ plus six, times $x$ | equals | five $x$ squared | plus | six $x$ |

In addition, $x(5x + 6)$ can also be written as $(5x + 6)x$. Either way, it may or may not be truly "simpler" than $5x^2 + 6x$. However, pulling out a common factor can be the key move when you solve a GMAT problem.

MANHATTAN PREP

Sometimes, the common factor is hidden among more complicated variable expressions. In the example below, the common factor is *xy*.

$$x^2y \qquad - \qquad xy^2 \qquad = \qquad xy(x-y)$$

x squared y        minus        x y squared        equals        x y times the quantity x minus y

Sometimes, the common factor involves a root or pi.

$$\sqrt{2} \qquad + \qquad \sqrt{2}\,\pi \qquad = \qquad \sqrt{2}\,(1+\pi)$$

Root two        plus        root two times pi        equals        root two times the quantity one plus pi

Here, the common factor is $\sqrt{2}$. Notice that the first term ($\sqrt{2}$) is the same as the common factor. Whenever the factor you are pulling out is the same as the term, leave a 1 in its place (in the parentheses). For example:

$$\pi r^2 \qquad - \qquad \pi \qquad = \qquad \pi(r^2-1)$$

pi r squared        minus        pi        equals        pi times the quantity r squared minus one

In the example above, the common factor is $\pi$. Again, when you pull $\pi$ out of the second term (which is $\pi$), leave a 1 behind in its place. You can check that this works by distributing $\pi$ back through.

You might only factor out an integer, or even a negative sign.

$$2 \qquad + \qquad 4x \qquad = \qquad 2(1+2x)$$

Two        plus        four x        equals        two times the quantity one plus two x

$$3 \qquad - \qquad x \qquad = \qquad -(x-3)$$

Three        minus        x        equals        the negative of quantity x minus three

Remember this monster from a couple of sections ago?

$$2xy \qquad + \qquad xy^2 \qquad - \qquad 4x^2y \qquad + \qquad x^2y^2$$

Two x y        plus        x y squared        minus        four x squared y        plus        x squared y squared

What is the common factor that you can pull out?

Answer: *xy*

$$2xy + xy^2 - 4x^2y + x^2y^2 = xy(2 + y - 4x + xy)$$

## Check Your Skills

29. Factor a negative *x*, (–*x*), out of the expression $-2x^3 + 5x^2 + 3x$.
30. Factor the following expression: $4x^2 + 3xy - yx + 6x$

*Answers can be found on page 39.*

# 1 | Long Addition and Subtraction

Sometimes you'll need to add or subtract larger numbers. It has probably been quite some time since you last had to do this on paper, so here's a refresher.

Try this problem.

$$\begin{array}{r} 283 \\ +\ 654 \\ \hline \end{array}$$

Here are the steps to find the sum of two larger numbers such as these.

$$\begin{array}{r} 283 \\ +\ 654 \\ \hline \end{array}$$

Begin with the right-most column of numbers and work your way to the left. The right-most column contains the units digits 3 and 4.

$$\begin{array}{r} 283 \\ +\ 654 \\ \hline 7 \end{array}$$

Sum the units digits: 3 + 4 = 7.

$$\begin{array}{r} {}^{1}283 \\ +\ \ 654 \\ \hline 37 \end{array}$$

Move to the next column, the tens digits 8 and 5, where 8 + 5 = 13. Place the 3 below and *carry* the 1 (from 13) above the top number in the next column, the hundreds digits.

$$\begin{array}{r} {}^{1}283 \\ +\ \ 654 \\ \hline 937 \end{array}$$

Move to the next column, the hundreds digit. Now, there are three numbers: the carried 1, as well as the 2 and 6. Add all of these together to get 9.

When conducting long addition, add the columns of numbers: units digit + units digit, tens digit + tens digit, and so on. If one of those sums is a number greater than 9, you'll need to carry over part of the number to the next column. For example, if the sum is 15, then place the units digit of the sum (the 5) below, but carry the extra part (the tens digit, 1) over to the next column and add it there instead.

Subtraction works similarly, although there is one special circumstance to note.

Try this example:

$$\begin{array}{r} 653 \\ -\ 472 \\ \hline \end{array}$$

**MANHATTAN** PREP

Here's how you subtract when the top number in a column is smaller than the bottom number.

$$
\begin{array}{r}
653 \\
-\ 472 \\
\hline
\end{array}
$$

Begin with the right-most column of numbers and work your way to the left. The right-most column contains the units digits 3 and 2.

$$
\begin{array}{r}
653 \\
-\ 472 \\
\hline
1
\end{array}
$$

Subtract: $3 - 2 = 1$.

$$
\begin{array}{r}
{}^{5}\!\!\not{6}\,{}^{1}53 \\
-\ \ 472 \\
\hline
81
\end{array}
$$

$5 - 7 = -2$, but you aren't allowed to put $-2$ down below. Instead, *borrow* a 10 from the next column. The tens column becomes $15 - 7 = 8$. The 6 in the hundreds column turns into a 5.

$$
\begin{array}{r}
{}^{5}\!\!\not{6}\,{}^{1}53 \\
-\ \ 472 \\
\hline
181
\end{array}
$$

Finally, subtract the hundreds column: $5 - 4 = 1$.

As long as the top number is greater than the bottom one, you can subtract normally. If the top number is smaller, though, then borrow a 10 from the next number to the left. Once you've done that, proceed normally.

## Long Multiplication

In this section, you'll review the basics of long multiplication. It is useful to know this skill for the GMAT, but long multiplication takes time, so think carefully before you use it. Can you simplify the math in any way before you have to multiply? Don't forget to look ahead to the next step or two in the problem: The next step might be to divide. If you do that first, then the multiplication might be easier.

When multiplying two numbers, always put the smaller number in the bottom row. For example, here's how to write $8 \times 57$:

$$
\begin{array}{r}
57 \\
\times\ \ 8 \\
\hline
\end{array}
$$

Multiply the two numbers in the right-most column: $7 \times 8 = 56$. Put the 6 underneath, then carry the 5.

$$
\begin{array}{r}
{}^{5}57 \\
\times\ \ 8 \\
\hline
6
\end{array}
$$

Multiply the next number over in the top row by the number in the bottom row: $5 \times 8 = 40$, + the 5 you carried = 45.

$$
\begin{array}{r}
57 \\
\times\ \ 8 \\
\hline
456
\end{array}
$$

Because you're at the end, put the whole 45 underneath.

**1**

You may also need to multiply two two-digit numbers, such as 12 × 85.

$^{1}$85

× 12

0

Start with the 2 in the bottom row: 5 × 2 = 10.

Put the 0 underneath, then carry the 1.

$^{1}$85

× 12

170

8 × 2 = 16, + the 1 you carried = 17. Because you are done multiplying by 2, place the 17 underneath.

$\cancel{1}$85

× 12

170

0

Now deal with the 1 in the second row. Remember that the 1 actually represents 10.

Place a 0 underneath the right-most column. Don't forget to cross out the 1 you carried last time!

$\cancel{1}$85

× 12

170

50

5 × 1 = 5. Place the 5 underneath.

$\cancel{1}$85

× 12

170

850

8 × 1 = 8. Place the 8 underneath.

$^{1}$170

+ 850

1020

Now add the rows underneath, starting from the right: 0 + 0 = 0; 7 + 5 = 12, so place the 2 underneath and carry the 1; 1 + 8 + the carried 1 = 10. Because you are done with the addition, place the 10 underneath.

12 × 85 = 1,020

Don't let multiplication slow you down on the GMAT. Do multiplication drills to become quick and accurate; 5 minutes a day will make a big difference after a few weeks!

**MANHATTAN** PREP

# Long Division

As with long multiplication, think carefully before you dive into long division. For instance, what would you do with this problem?

What is 468 divided by 26?

(A)  12

(B)  18

(C)  22

You could do long division…but you don't need to! You can estimate.

$26 \times 10 = 260$

$26 \times ?? = 486$

$26 \times 20 = 520$

Answer (C) is definitely too large. Answer (A) is between 260 and 520, but since 486 is closer to 520 than 260, the answer should be closer to 20 than 10; answer (A) is too small. Therefore, the answer must be (B), 18. Done without having to resort to long division!

On other problems, you may be able to simplify before you do long division. For example:

What is the result when 440 is divided by 11 and then divided by 2?

Don't be fooled by the language! When multiplying or dividing, you can do the work in any order; that's why M and D go together in the PEMDAS order of operations. You don't have to do the work in the order presented. In this case, it's easier to divide by 2 first:

$440 \div 2 = 220$

Now, if you can't simplify any further or estimate your way to an answer, you can try long division.

$$11\overline{)220}$$

11 goes into 22 two times.

$$\begin{array}{r} 2 \\ 11\overline{)220} \\ -22 \\ \hline 0 \end{array}$$

Place a 2 on top of the unit's digit of the portion of the number you used. In this case, place the 2 above the second 2 in 22.

$$\begin{array}{r} 20 \\ 11\overline{)220} \\ -22 \\ \hline 00 \end{array}$$

Bring down the next digit in 220 (in this case 0). 11 goes into 0 zero times, so add a 0 to the top row and you're done. The answer is 20.

**1**  In the previous example, the answer was an integer ($220 \div 11 = 20$). However, the answer will not always be an integer.

Try dividing 123 by 6.

$$6\overline{)123}$$

6 doesn't go into 1, but it does go into 12 two times.

$$\begin{array}{r} 2 \\ 6\overline{)123} \\ -12 \\ \hline 03 \end{array}$$

Place a 2 on top of the digit farthest to the right in 12.

$2 \times 6 = 12$, so subtract 12 from 12, then bring down the next digit (3).

$$\begin{array}{r} 20 \\ 6\overline{)123.0} \\ -12 \\ \hline 030 \end{array}$$

6 doesn't go into 3, so place a 0 on top of the 3.

You're not done! 123 is equal to 123.0. Add the decimal point and a 0 in the tenths column. Bring down the 0.

$$\begin{array}{r} 20.5 \\ 6\overline{)123.0} \\ -12 \\ \hline 030 \\ -30 \\ \hline 0 \end{array}$$

6 goes into 30 five times. Place a 5 on top of the 0. Don't forget to put a decimal between the 0 and the 5.

Also, check your answers. Only carry the calculation as far as you need to in order to find the answer.

## Check Your Skills Answer Key

1. **178:**

$$
\begin{array}{r}
141 \\
+37 \\
\hline
178
\end{array}
$$

2. **−113:** Do the subtraction in reverse to find the positive difference, then add a negative sign (so the answer is −113, not +113).

$$
\begin{array}{r}
136 \\
-23 \\
\hline
113
\end{array}
$$

3. **0:** The greatest negative integer is −1 and the smallest positive integer is 1: −1 + 1 = 0.

4. **5 < 16:** 5 is less than 16.

5. **−5 > −16:** Negative 5 is greater than negative 16.

6. **A positive minus a negative:** (+) − (−) will always be positive, whereas (−) − (+) will always be negative. Any positive number is greater than any negative number.

7. **42:** $7 \times 6 = 42$

8. **4:** $52 \div 13 = 4$

9. **35:** $5 \times (3 + 4) = (5 \times 3) + (5 \times 4) = 15 + 20 = 35$

10. **6(6 − 2):** $36 − 12 = (6 \times 6) − (6 \times 2) = 6(6 − 2)$

11. **−12:** $(3)(−4) = −12$

12. **48:** $−6 \times (−3 + (−5)) = (−6 \times −3) + (−6 \times −5) = 18 + 30 = 48$

13. **Division:** Sometimes an integer divided by an integer equals an integer (e.g., 6 ÷ 2 = 3), and sometimes it does not (e.g., 8 ÷ 5 = 1.6).

14. $2 \times \dfrac{1}{7}$ **:** $2 \div 7 = 2 \times$ the reciprocal of 7, or $\dfrac{1}{7}$.

15. **Multiple:** If 7 is a factor of 21, then 21 is a multiple of 7.

16. **No:** 2,284,623 ends in 3, which means that it is an odd number. It is not divisible by 2.

**1**

17. **64:** $2^6 = (2 \times 2) \times (2 \times 2) \times (2 \times 2) = 4 \times 4 \times 4 = 64$

18. **3:** $\sqrt[3]{27} = 3$ because $3^3 = 27$.

19. **11:** Plug the values of the variables back into the expression to find the value of the expression.
$2x - 3y = 2(4) - 3(-1) = 8 + 3 = 11$

20. **0:**

$$-4 + \frac{12}{3} =$$         Divide first.

$$-4 + 4 = 0$$         Next, add the two numbers.

21. **−37:**

$$(5 - 8) \times 10 - 7 =$$

$$(-3) \times 10 - 7 =$$      First, combine what is inside the parentheses.

$$-30 - 7 =$$      Next, multiply −3 and 10.

$$-30 - 7 = -37$$      Subtract the two numbers.

22. **−74:**

$$-3 \times 12 \div 4 \times 8 + (4 - 6) =$$

$$-3 \times 12 \div 4 \times 8 + (-2) =$$      First, combine what is inside the parentheses.

$$-36 \div 4 \times 8 + (-2) =$$      Multiply −3 and 12.

$$-9 \times 8 + (-2) =$$      Divide −36 by 4.

$$-72 + (-2) = -74$$      Multiply −9 by 8 and subtract 2.

23. **8:**

$$\frac{2^4 \times (8 \div 2 - 1)}{(9 - 3)} =$$      $8 \div 2 = 4$ and $9 - 3 = 6$.

$$\frac{2^4 \times (4 - 1)}{(6)} =$$      $4 - 1 = 3$ and $2^4 = 16$.

$$\frac{16 \times (3)}{6} =$$

$$\frac{16 \times \cancel{3}^{1}}{\cancel{6}_{2}} =$$      When you have larger numbers, simplify (divide) before you multiply.

$$\frac{^{8}\cancel{16} \times 1}{\cancel{2}_{1}} =$$

$$= 8$$

24. $\mathbf{3 + 4\sqrt{2}}$ **:** $(-3 + 6) + 4\sqrt{2} = 3 + 4\sqrt{2}$

25. $\mathbf{4\pi r^2 - \pi r}$ **:** $4\pi r^2 + (-3\pi r + 2\pi r) = 4\pi r^2 - \pi r$

26. $\mathbf{3ab + 2ab^2 - 2a^2b}$ **:** $(8ab - 5ab) + (ab^2 + ab^2) + (-2a^2b) = 3ab + 2ab^2 - 2a^2b$

27. **$3x + x^2$:** $x(3 + x) = (3)(x) + (x)(x) = 3x + x^2$

28. **$2 + \sqrt{2}$:** $4 + \sqrt{2}\left(1 - \sqrt{2}\right) = 4 + \left(\sqrt{2} \times 1\right) + \left(\sqrt{2} \times -\sqrt{2}\right) = 4 + \sqrt{2} - 2 = 2 + \sqrt{2}$

29. **$-x(2x^2 - 5x - 3)$:** Pull an $x$ out of each term. Switch the sign on each term in the parentheses in order to pull out a negative sign.

30. **$2x(2x + y + 3)$:** First, combine the two middle terms, which are like terms: $3xy - yx = 2xy$. In the expression $4x^2 + 2xy + 6x$, the terms all contain $2x$. Pull $2x$ out of each term.

# Chapter Review: Drill Sets

## Drill 1

Evaluate the following expressions.

1.  $39 - (25 - 17)$
2.  $3(4 - 2) \div 2$
3.  $15 \times 3 \div 9$
4.  $(7 - 5) - (3 - 6)$
5.  $14 - 3(4 - 6)$
6.  $-5 \times 1 \div 5$
7.  $(5)(-3)(-4)(2)$
8.  $5 - (4 - (3 - (2 - 1)))$
9.  $-4(5) - \dfrac{12}{2 + 4}$
10.  $17(6) + 3(6)$

## Drill 2

Evaluate the following expressions.

11.  $-12 \times -2 + 5$
12.  $\dfrac{24}{2 + 6 \div 3}$
13.  $-10 - (-3)^2$
14.  $-5^2$
15.  $\dfrac{-2^3}{2}$
16.  $5^3 - 5^2$
17.  $5^{(2+1)} + 25$
18.  $(-2)^3 - 5^2 + (-4)^3$
19.  $7(4) + 7(3) + 7(2) + 7(1)$
20.  $3 \times 99 - 2 \times 99 - 1 \times 99$

## Drill 3

Combine as many like terms as possible.

21.  $\pi r^2 - (2\pi r + \pi r^2)$
22.  $5\sqrt{3} + 5\sqrt{2} - 2\sqrt{3}$
23.  $12xy^2 - 6x^2y^2 + (2)^2x^2y^2$
24.  $3\pi + x\pi - 2\pi$

25.  $\sqrt{2} + x\sqrt{2} - 2\sqrt{2}$
26.  $12xy - (6x + 2y)$
27.  $5x - (4x + 2 - (5x - 3))$
28.  $\pi^2r^2 - \pi r + 2\pi r^2 + \pi r^2 + \pi^2r^2 + 2\pi r$
29.  $2x^2 - (2x)^2 - 2^2 - x^2$
30.  $4x^2 + 2x - (2\sqrt{x})^2$

## Drill 4

Distribute the following expressions. Simplify as necessary.

31.  $3(5 - y)$
32.  $-(a - b)$
33.  $(m + 2n)4m$
34.  $2b(3a + b)$
35.  $52r(2t - 10s)$
36.  $(-37x + 63)10^2$
37.  $6kl(k - 2l)$
38.  $-\sqrt{2}(18 - 8x)$
39.  $d(d^2 - 2d + 1)$
40.  $xy^2z(x^2z + yz^2 - xy^2)$

# Drill Sets Solutions

## Drill 1

1. **31:**

$$39 - (25 - 17) =$$
$$39 - 8 = 31$$

Tip: You could also distribute the minus sign if you prefer: $(39 - 25 + 17) = 14 + 17 = 31$.

2. **3:**

$$3 \times (4 - 2) \div 2 =$$
$$3 \times (2) \div 2 =$$
$$6 \div 2 = 3$$

3. **5:**

$$15 \times 3 \div 9 =$$
$$45 \div 9 = 5$$

4. **5:**

$$(7 - 5) - (3 - 6) =$$
$$(2) - (-3) =$$
$$2 + 3 = 5$$

5. **20:**

$$14 - 3\,(4 - 6) =$$
$$14 - 3(-2) =$$
$$14 + 6 = 20$$

6. **−1:**

$$-5 \times 1 \div 5 =$$
$$-5 \div 5 = -1$$

7. **120:**

$$(5)(-3)(-4)(2) =$$

$$(10)(12) = 120$$

Tip #1: When multiplying several numbers together, look for 5s and 2s in the product. Combine these first to create 10; it is easier to multiply 10 into other numbers.

**1**

Tip #2: To determine whether a product will be positive or negative, count the number of negative terms you are multiplying. An even number of negative terms will give you a positive product; an odd number of negative terms will give you a negative product.

8. **3:**
$$5 - (4 - (3 - (2 - 1))) =$$
$$5 - (4 - (3 - 1)) =$$
$$5 - (4 - 2) =$$
$$5 - (2) = 3$$

Tip: Start with the innermost parentheses. Write everything down, and don't try to do multiple steps at once; you'll just open yourself up to careless mistakes.

9. **−22:**
$$-4(5) - \frac{12}{2+4} =$$
$$-20 - \frac{12}{6} =$$
$$-20 - 2 = -22$$

Tip: In order to avoid making a careless mistake with negatives, you may want to write the last line as $-20 + (-2) = -22$.

10. **120:** Most people would think of this path first:

$$17(6) + 3(6) =$$
$$102 + 18 = 120$$

However, if you find that math annoying (most people would), then don't just start doing it. Take a moment: Is there an easier way to do this math? Yes! Factor a 6 out of both terms:

$$17(6) + 3(6) =$$
$$6(17 + 3) =$$
$$6(20) = 120$$

# Drill 2

11. **29:** Do the multiplication first, then the addition.

$$(-12 \times -2) + 5 =$$
$$24 + 5 = 29$$

12. **6:**

$$\frac{24}{2 + (6 \div 3)} =$$

$$\frac{24}{2 + 2} =$$

$$\frac{24}{4} = 6$$

13. **−19:**

$$-10 - (-3)^2 =$$
$$-10 - (-3)(-3) =$$
$$-10 - (9) = -19$$

You could also write the last line as $-10 + (-9) = -19$.

14. **−25:**

$$-5^2 =$$
$$-(5^2) = -25$$

15. **−4:**

$$\frac{-2^3}{2} =$$

$$\frac{-8}{2} = -4$$

16. **100:**

$$5^3 - 5^2 =$$
$$125 - 25 = 100$$

17. **150:**

$$5^{(2+1)} + 25 =$$
$$5^3 + 25 =$$
$$125 + 25 = 150$$

18. **−97:**

$$(-2)^3 - 5^2 + (-4)^3 =$$
$$(-2)(-2)(-2) - (5^2) + (-4)(-4)(-4) =$$
$$(-8) - 25 + (-64) =$$
$$-33 - 64 = -97$$

19. **70:** To make the math faster, factor a 7 out of each term:

$$7(4) + 7(3) + 7(2) + 7(1) =$$
$$7(4 + 3 + 2 + 1) =$$
$$7(10) = 70$$

You can also multiply out each term and then add, as shown below, but that will generally take longer when the numbers are at all large or annoying:

$$7(4) + 7(3) + 7(2) + 7(1) =$$
$$28 + 21 + 14 + 7 = 70$$

20. **0:** Think a moment before you work. Because the number 99 is large, the math is made easier if you factor 99 out of each term:

$$3 \times 99 - 2 \times 99 - 1 \times 99 =$$
$$99(3 - 2 - 1) =$$
$$99(0) = 0$$

Here is the longer way to do the math:

$$3 \times 99 - 2 \times 99 - 1 \times 99 =$$
$$297 - 198 - 99 =$$
$$99 - 99 = 0$$

# Drill 3

21. **$-2\pi r$**: The two terms in the parentheses cannot be combined, so start by distributing the negative sign before combining like terms:

$$\pi r^2 - (2\pi r + \pi r^2) =$$
$$\pi r^2 - 2\pi r - \pi r^2 =$$
$$(1\pi r^2 - 1\pi r^2) - 2\pi r =$$
$$0 - 2\pi r = -2\pi r$$

Tip: You don't have to write out a coefficient of 1, but consider doing so if this helps you to minimize careless mistakes.

22. **$3\sqrt{3} + 5\sqrt{2}$** : Group and combine like terms.

$$5\sqrt{3} + 5\sqrt{2} - 2\sqrt{3}$$
$$\left(5\sqrt{3} - 2\sqrt{3}\right) + 5\sqrt{2}$$
$$3\sqrt{3} + 5\sqrt{2}$$

23. **$12xy^2 - 2x^2y^2$**: Simplify before grouping and combining like terms.

$$12xy^2 - 6x^2y^2 + (2)^2x^2y^2 =$$
$$12xy^2 - 6x^2y^2 + 4x^2y^2 =$$
$$12xy^2 + (-6 + 4)x^2y^2 =$$
$$12xy^2 + (-2)x^2y^2 =$$
$$12xy^2 - 2x^2y^2$$

24. **$(x + 1)\pi$:** Group like terms and then combine.

$$3\pi + x\pi - 2\pi =$$
$$3\pi - 2\pi + x\pi =$$
$$(3 - 2)\pi + x\pi =$$
$$1\pi + x\pi =$$
$$(1 + x)\pi = (x + 1)\pi$$

25. **$(x - 1)\sqrt{2}$:**

$$\sqrt{2} + x\sqrt{2} - 2\sqrt{2} =$$
$$1\sqrt{2} + x\sqrt{2} - 2\sqrt{2} =$$
$$(1 + x - 2)\sqrt{2} =$$
$$(-1 + x)\sqrt{2} = (x - 1)\sqrt{2}$$

26. **$12xy - 6x - 2y$:** The terms in the parentheses are not like terms, so distribute the negative sign before grouping and combining like terms.
$$12xy - (6x + 2y) =$$
$$12xy - 6x - 2y$$

Note that you cannot actually combine any of the terms in this problem; none are like terms!

27. **$6x - 5$:** Work from the innermost parentheses out.

$$5x - (4x + 2 - (5x - 3)) =$$
$$5x - (4x + 2 - 5x + 3) =$$
$$5x - (4x - 5x + 2 + 3) =$$
$$5x - (-x + 5) =$$
$$5x + x - 5 = 6x - 5$$

28. **$2\pi^2 r^2 + \pi r + 3\pi r^2$:**
$$\pi^2 r^2 - \pi r + 2\pi r^2 + \pi r^2 + \pi^2 r^2 + 2\pi r =$$
$$(1\pi^2 r^2 + 1\pi^2 r^2) + (-1\pi r + 2\pi r) + (2\pi r^2 + 1\pi r^2) =$$
$$2\pi^2 r^2 + 1\pi r + 3\pi r^2$$

29. **$-3x^2 - 4$:**
$$2x^2 - (2x)^2 - 2^2 - x^2 =$$
$$2x^2 - 2^2 x^2 - 4 - 1x^2 =$$
$$2x^2 - 4x^2 - 1x^2 - 4 =$$
$$(2 - 4 - 1)x^2 - 4 =$$
$$(-3)x^2 - 4 =$$
$$-3x^2 - 4$$

**1**

30. $4x^2 - 2x$:

$$4x^2 + 2x - (2\sqrt{x})^2 =$$
$$4x^2 + 2x - 2^2(\sqrt{x})^2 =$$
$$4x^2 + 2x - 4x =$$
$$4x^2 + (2 - 4)x =$$
$$4x^2 + (-2)x =$$
$$4x^2 - 2x$$

# Drill 4

31. $15 - 3y$:

$$3(5 - y) =$$
$$3 \times 5 + 3 \times (-y) =$$
$$15 - 3y$$

32. $-a + b$ **OR** $b - a$: The minus sign in front of the left parenthesis should be interpreted as: $-1$ times the expression $(a - b)$. Because $(-1) \times a = -a$ and $(-1) \times (-b) = b$, the solution is: $-(a - b) = (-1) \times (a - b) = -a + b$.

33. $4m^2 + 8mn$: Ordinarily, you see the Distributive Property in this form:

$$a(b + c) = ab + ac$$

If you place $a$ to the right of the parentheses, you can still distribute in the same way.

$$(b + c)a = ba + ca$$

This works because the order in which numbers are multiplied does not matter. The GMAT sometimes disguises a possible distribution by presenting it in this alternative form:

$$(m + 2n)4m = 4m^2 + 8mn$$

34. $6ab + 2b^2$:

$$2b(3a + b) = (2b)(3a) + (2b)(b) = 6ab + 2b^2$$

35. $104rt - 520rs$: When distributing more complicated expressions, remember to multiply out numbers and combine any copies of the same variable.

$$52r(2t - 10s) =$$
$$(52r)(2t) - (52r)(10s) =$$
$$104rt - 520rs$$

36. $-3,700x + 6,300$:

$$(-37x + 63)10^2 =$$
$$(-37x)(100) + (63)(100) =$$
$$-3,700x + 6,300$$

**MANHATTAN** PREP

37. $6k^2l - 12kl^2$: First, distribute normally. Next, combine like terms. (Note: This solution shows what it looks like to use a big dot to mean multiplication. You can also use parentheses, as other explanations do.)

$$6kl(k - 2l) =$$
$$6kl \cdot k - 6kl \cdot 2l =$$
$$6k^2l - 12kl^2$$

38. $-18\sqrt{2} + 8x\sqrt{2}$ : Distribute carefully to keep track of those negative signs!

$$-\sqrt{2}\left(18 - 8x\right) =$$
$$\left(-\sqrt{2}\right)(18) + \left(-\sqrt{2}\right)(-8x) =$$
$$-18\sqrt{2} + 8x\sqrt{2}$$

39. $d^3 - 2d^2 + d$: Even though there are three terms inside the parentheses, distribution works exactly the same. Multiply $d$ by every term in the parentheses.

$$d(d^2 - 2d + 1) =$$
$$(d \times d^2) - (d \times 2d) + (d \times 1) =$$
$$d^3 - 2d^2 + d$$

40. $x^3y^2z^2 + xy^3z^3 - x^2y^4z$: The term $xy^2z$ on the outside of the parentheses must be multiplied by each of the three terms inside the parentheses. You can then simplify the expression as much as possible.

$$xy^2z(x^2z + yz^2 - xy^2) =$$
$$(xy^2z)(x^2z) + (xy^2z)(yz^2) - (xy^2z)(xy^2) =$$
$$x^3y^2z^2 + xy^3z^3 - x^2y^4z$$

# Divisibility

# In this chapter...

- Divisibility
  - Memorize Divisibility Rules for Small Integers
  - Factors Are Divisors
  - Prime Number: Only Divisible by 1 and Itself
  - Prime Factorization: All the Primes on the Tree
  - Every Number Is Divisible by the Factors of Its Factors
  - Factors: Built Out of Primes
  - Factor Tree of a Variable: Contains Unknowns
  - Factors of $x$ with No Common Primes: Combine
  - Factors of $x$ with Primes in Common: Combine to LCM

# Chapter 2
# Divisibility

## In This Chapter, You Will Learn To:

- Apply divisibility rules
- Find the factors of a number
- Answer GMAT questions related to divisibility

## Divisibility

**Divisibility** has to do with **integers**. Recall that integers are the counting numbers (1, 2, 3, etc.), their opposites (−1, −2, −3, etc.), and 0. Integers have no decimals or fractions attached.

Also recall that most integer arithmetic is boring:

| | |
|---|---|
| integer + integer = always an integer | $4 + 11 = 15$ |
| integer − integer = always an integer | $-5 - 32 = -37$ |
| integer × integer = always an integer | $14 \times 3 = 42$ |

However, when you divide an integer by another integer, sometimes you get an integer ($18 \div 3 = 6$), and sometimes you don't ($12 \div 8 = 1.5$).

If you get an integer out of the division, then the first number is **divisible by** the second. For example, 18 is divisible by 3 because $18 \div 3 =$ an integer. On the other hand, 12 is *not* divisible by 8 because $12 \div 8$ is not an integer.

## Memorize Divisibility Rules for Small Integers

These rules come in very handy. An integer is divisible by:

**2 if the integer is even.**

> Even numbers, such as the number 12, are integers that end in 0, 2, 4, 6, or 8. The number 12 is divisible by 2 because $12 \div 2 = 6$, an integer. Any even number is always divisible by 2.

**3 if the sum of the integer's digits is a multiple of 3.**

> Take the number 147. Its digits are 1, 4, and 7. Add those digits to get the sum: $1 + 4 + 7 = 12$. The sum, 12, is a multiple of 3, so 147 is divisible by 3.

**5 if the integer ends in 0 or 5.**

> The numbers 75 and 80 are divisible by 5, but 77 and 84 are not. Any integer that ends in 0 or 5 is divisible by 5. Any integer that ends in something other than 0 or 5 is *not* divisible by 5.

**9 if the sum of the integer's digits is a multiple of 9.**

> This rule is very similar to the divisibility rule for 3. Take the number 288. Add the digits: $2 + 8 + 8 = 18$. The sum, 18, is a multiple of 9, so 288 is divisible by 9.

**10 if the integer ends in 0.**

> The number 8,730 is divisible by 10, but 8,753 is not. Any integer that ends in 0 is divisible by 10. Any integer that ends in something other than 0 is *not* divisible by 10.

### Check Your Skills

1. Is 123,456,789 divisible by 2?
2. Is 732 divisible by 3?
3. Is 989 divisible by 9?

*Answers can be found on page 73.*

## Factors Are Divisors

The integer 6 is divisible by what positive integers?

Test the positive integers less than or equal to 6: 1, 2, 3, 4, 5, and 6.

$6 \div 1 = 6$       Any number divided by 1 equals itself, so an integer divided by 1 will always be an integer.

$6 \div 2 = 3$
$6 \div 3 = 2$       6 is divisible by 2, and 6 is divisible by 3. Note that these form a pair: $3 \times 2 = 6$.

  **MANHATTAN** PREP

$6 \div 4 = 1.5$
$6 \div 5 = 1.2$ — Not integers, so 6 is *not* divisible by 4 or by 5.

$6 \div 6 = 1$ — Any number divided by itself equals 1, so an integer is always divisible by itself.

Therefore, 6 is divisible by 1, 2, 3, and 6. That means that 1, 2, 3, and 6 are **factors** of 6. Learn all the ways you might see this relationship expressed on the GMAT.

| | |
|---|---|
| 2 is a factor of 6 | 6 is a multiple of 2 |
| 2 is a divisor of 6 | 6 is divisible by 2 |
| 2 divides 6 | 2 goes into 6 (evenly, without a remainder) |

To find all the factors of a small number, use **factor pairs**. A factor pair of 60 is a pair of integers that multiplies together to 60. For instance, 15 and 4 are a factor pair of 60 because $15 \times 4 = 60$.

Here's an organized way to make a table of factor pairs of 60:

1.  Label two columns Small and Large.

2.  Start with 1 in the small column and 60 in the large column. (The first set of factor pairs will always be 1 and the number itself.)

3.  After 1, try the next smallest integer: 2. Since 2 is a factor of 60, write 2 underneath the 1 in your table. Divide 60 by 2 to find 2's "sibling" in the pair: $60 \div 2 = 30$. Write 30 in the large column.

4.  Repeat this process until the numbers in the small and the large columns run into each other. In this case, 6 and 10 are a factor pair, but 7, 8, and 9 are not factors of 60. The next number after 9 is 10, which appears in the large column, so you can stop.

| If you... | Then you... | Like this: | |
|---|---|---|---|
| | | Small | Large |
| | | 1 | 60 |
| | Make a table of factor pairs, starting with 1 and 60 | 2 | 30 |
| Want all the factors of 60 | | 3 | 20 |
| | | 4 | 15 |
| | | 5 | 12 |
| | | 6 | 10 |

## Check Your Skills

4. Find all the factors of 90.
5. Find all the factors of 72.
6. Find all the factors of 105.
7. Find all the factors of 120.

*Answers can be found on pages 73–74.*

## Prime Number: Only Divisible by 1 and Itself

The integer 7 is divisible by what positive integers?

Test out the positive integers less than or equal to 7: 1, 2, 3, 4, 5, 6, and 7.

$7 \div 1 = 7$    Every number is divisible by 1—no surprise there!

$7 \div 2 = 3.5$

$7 \div 3 = 2.33...$

$7 \div 4 = 1.75$    7 is not divisible by *any* integer besides 1 and itself. (You don't need to do these calculations. It's enough to know that the answer is not an integer.)

$7 \div 5 = 1.4$

$7 \div 6 = 1.16...$

$7 \div 7 = 1$    Every number is divisible by itself—boring!

So 7 has only two factors—1 and itself. Numbers that have exactly two factors are called **prime numbers**. Primes are extremely important in any question about divisibility.

There are a few key details to note. First, the concept of prime applies only to positive integers. Second, note that 1 is *not* prime; it has exactly one factor (itself!). Finally, 2 is the only even prime number. Every even number greater than 2 has at least one more factor besides 1 and itself, namely the number 2.

Every positive integer can be placed into one of two categories—prime or not prime. Memorize the smaller primes: 2, 3, 5, 7, 11, 13, 17, and 19.

## Check Your Skills

8.  List all the prime numbers between 20 and 50.

*Answer can be found on page 74.*

## Prime Factorization: All the Primes on the Tree

Take another look at the factor pairs of 60. It had 12 factors and 6 factor pairs.

$60 = 1 \times 60$    Always the first factor pair—boring!

*and* $2 \times 30$

*and* $3 \times 20$

*and* $4 \times 15$    5 other factor pairs—interesting!
Let's look at these in a little more detail.

*and* $5 \times 12$

*and* $6 \times 10$

Consider $4 \times 15$. One way to think about this pair is that 60 breaks down into 4 and 15. Use a **factor tree** to show this relationship.

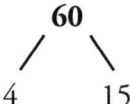

Keep going. Neither 4 nor 15 is prime, so they both have factor pairs that you might find interesting: 4 breaks down into 2 × 2, and 15 breaks down into 3 × 5.

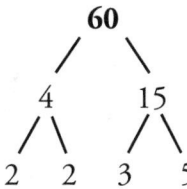

Can you break it down any further? Not with interesting factor pairs. For instance, 2 = 2 × 1, but that's nothing new. The numbers you have reached (2, 2, 3, and 5) are all primes.

When you find a prime factor, that branch on the factor tree has reached the end. Circle prime numbers as you go, as if they were fruit on the tree. The factor tree for 60 looks like this:

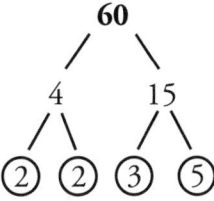

After you break down 60 into 4 and 15, and then break 4 and 15 down further, you end up with 60 = 2 × 2 × 3 × 5.

What if you start with a different factor pair of 60? Create a factor tree for 60 in which the first breakdown you make is 6 × 10.

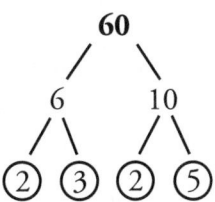

According to this factor tree 60 = 2 × 3 × 2 × 5. These are the same primes as before (though in a different order). Any way you break down 60, you end up with the same prime factors: two 2's, one 3, and one 5. The **prime factorization** of 60 is 2 × 2 × 3 × 5.

Note: The factor tree doesn't list *all* factors of 60; for that, make a table of factor pairs. The factor tree represents the *prime* factors of 60.

Prime factors are like the DNA or the fingerprint of a number. Every number has a unique prime factorization. Sixty is the only number that can be written as 2 × 2 × 3 × 5.

Your first instinct on divisibility problems should be to *break numbers down to their prime factors*. A factor tree is the best way to find a prime factorization.

Find the prime factorization of 630.

One way to start is by finding the smallest prime factor of 630. Check 2 first: 630 is even, so it is divisible by 2. On your factor tree, break down 630 into 2 and 315.

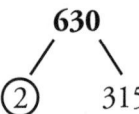

Now you still need to factor 315. It's not even, so it's not divisible by 2. Check 3 by adding up the digits of 315. That's $3 + 1 + 5 = 9$, which is a multiple of 3, so 315 is divisible by 3. Add this next level of information, $315 = 3 \times 105$, to your factor tree.

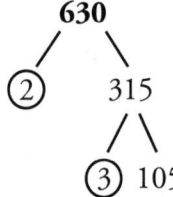

The number 105 might still be divisible by another integer. Check it out: $1 + 0 + 5 = 6$, so 105 is divisible by 3. Since $105 \div 3 = 35$, the tree now looks like this:

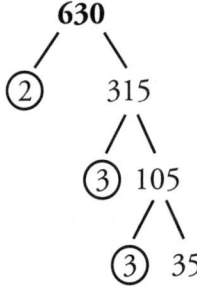

The number 35 is not divisible by 3 ($3 + 5 = 8$, which is not a multiple of 3), so the next number to try is 5. The number 35 ends in a 5, so it is divisible by 5. Since $35 \div 5 = 7$, the tree now looks like this:

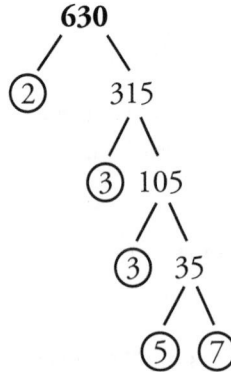

Every number on the tree has now been broken down as far as it can go. The prime factorization of 630 is $2 \times 3 \times 3 \times 5 \times 7$.

Alternatively, you could have split 630 into 63 and 10, since it's easy to see that 630 is divisible by 10. Then you would proceed from there, breaking 10 into 2 and 5 and breaking 63 into 7 and 9 (which then breaks down into 3 and 3). As you practice, you'll spot shortcuts.

Either way will get you to the same set of prime factors.

| If you… | Then you… | Like this: |
|---|---|---|
| Want the prime factorization of 96 | Break 96 down to primes using a tree | 96<br>2   48<br>12   4<br>3  4  2  2<br>2  2 |

## Check Your Skills

9.  Find the prime factorization of 90.
10. Find the prime factorization of 72.
11. Find the prime factorization of 105.
12. Find the prime factorization of 120.

*Answers can be found on page 74.*

# Every Number Is Divisible by the Factors of Its Factors

If *a* is divisible by *b*, and *b* is divisible by *c*, then *a* is divisible by *c* as well. For instance, 12 is divisible by 6, and 6 is divisible by 3. Therefore, 12 is divisible by 3 as well.

This **factor foundation rule** also works in reverse to a certain extent. If *d* is divisible by two different *primes*, *e* and *f*, then *d* is also divisible by *e* × *f*. In other words, if 20 is divisible by 2 and 5, then 20 is also divisible by 2 × 5 (or 10).

Divisibility travels up and down the factor tree. Consider the factor tree of 150:

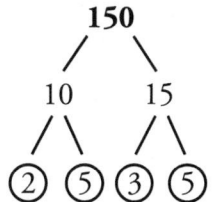

**Prime factors** are *building blocks*. In the case of 150, you have one 2, one 3, and two 5's at your disposal to build other factors of 150. In the example above, you're moving down the tree—from 150 down to 10 and 15, and then down again to 2, 5, 3, and 5. But you can also build upward, starting with the four building blocks. For instance, $2 \times 3 = 6$, and $5 \times 5 = 25$, so your tree could also look like this:

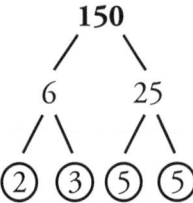

(Even though 5 and 5 are not different primes, 5 appears twice on 150's tree. So you are allowed to multiply those two 5's together to produce another factor of 150, namely 25.)

The tree above isn't even the only other possibility. Here are more:

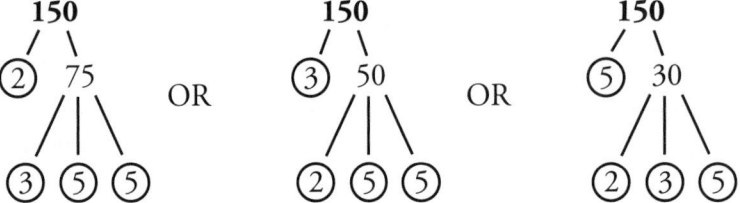

Beginning with four prime factors of 150 (2, 3, 5, and 5), you build different factors by multiplying any two, any three, or even all four of those primes together in different combinations. All of the factors of a number (except for 1) can be built with different combinations of that number's prime factors.

## Factors: Built Out of Primes

Take one more look at the number 60 and its factors. Consider the prime factorization of each factor.

| Building blocks | Small | Large | Building blocks |
|:---:|:---:|:---:|:---:|
| 1 | 1 | 60 | $2 \times 2 \times 3 \times 5$ |
| 2 | 2 | 30 | $2 \times 3 \times 5$ |
| 3 | 3 | 20 | $2 \times 2 \times 5$ |
| $2 \times 2$ | 4 | 15 | $3 \times 5$ |
| 5 | 5 | 12 | $2 \times 2 \times 3$ |
| $2 \times 3$ | 6 | 10 | $2 \times 5$ |

*All* of the factors of 60 (except 1) are different combinations of some or all of the four prime factors of 60. To say this another way, every factor of a number (again, except 1) can be expressed as the product of a subset of its prime factors. This relationship between factors and prime factors is true of every number.

To recap what you've learned so far:

1. If *a* is divisible by *b*, and *b* is divisible by *c*, then *a* is divisible by *c* as well. For instance, 100 is divisible by 20, and 20 is divisible by 4, so 100 is divisible by 4 as well.

2. If *d* has *e* and *f* as prime factors, *d* is also divisible by *e* × *f*. For instance, 90 is divisible by 5 and by 3, so 90 is also divisible by 5 × 3 = 15. You can let *e* and *f* be the same prime, as long as there are at least two copies of that prime in *d*'s factor tree.

3. Every factor of a number (except 1) is the product of a different combination of that number's prime factors. For example, 30 = 2 × 3 × 5. The factors of 30 are 1, 2, 3, 5, 6 (2 × 3), 10 (2 × 5), 15 (3 × 5), and 30 (2 × 3 × 5).

4. To find all of the factors of a number in a methodical way, set up a factor pairs table. For example, 30 has the factor pairs (1, 30), (2, 15), (3, 10), and (5, 6).

5. To find all of the *prime* factors of a number, use a factor tree.

## Check Your Skills

13. The prime factorization of a number is 3 × 5. What is the number and what are all of its factors?
14. The prime factorization of a number is 2 × 5 × 7. What is the number, and what are all of its factors?
15. The prime factorization of a number is 2 × 3 × 13. What is the number and what are all of its factors?

*Answers can be found on page 75.*

## Factor Tree of a Variable: Contains Unknowns

Say that you are told that some unknown positive number *x* is divisible by 6. You can represent this fact on paper in several different ways. For instance, you could write "*x* = multiple of 6" or "*x* = 6 × integer." You could also write the information as the result of division: $\frac{x}{6}$ = integer.

You could also represent the information with a factor tree. Since the top of the tree is a variable, add in a branch to represent what you *don't* know about the variable. Label this branch with a question mark (?), three dots (...), or something to remind yourself that you have *incomplete* information about *x*:

What *else* do we know about *x*? What can you definitely say about *x* right now?

Take a look at these three statements. For each statement, decide whether it *must* be true, whether it *could* be true, or whether it *cannot* be true.

>   I.      *x* is divisible by 3.
>   II.     *x* is even.
>   III.    *x* is divisible by 12.

Begin with statement I: *x* is divisible by 3. Think about the multiples of 6. If *x* is divisible by 6, then *x* is a multiple of 6. List out the first several multiples of 6 to see whether they're divisible by 3.

$$x \text{ is a number on this list.} \left\{ \begin{array}{ll} 6 & 6 \div 3 = 2 \\ 12 & 12 \div 3 = 4 \\ 18 & 18 \div 3 = 6 \\ 24 & 24 \div 3 = 8 \\ \ldots & \ldots \end{array} \right\} \text{All of these numbers are also divisible by 3.}$$

At this point, you can be fairly certain that *x* is divisible by 3. In divisibility problems (and elsewhere), listing out possible values of a variable can help you wrap your head around a question or a pattern.

But you can also *prove* that *x* is divisible by 3. Just make one modification to the tree.

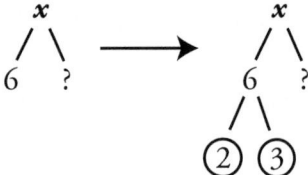

The purpose of the tree is to break integers down into primes, which are the building blocks of greater integers. Now that the factor tree is broken down as far as it will go, apply the factor foundation rule. Since *x* is divisible by 6, and 6 is divisible by 3, you can definitively say that *x* is divisible by 3. Statement I *must* be true.

Statement II says *x* is even. Must that be true? Return to your factor tree.

Again, make use of the factor foundation rule: 6 is divisible by 2, so you know that *x* is divisible by 2 as well. Since *x* is divisible by 2, *x* is even. Statement II *must* be true.

Statement III says *x* is divisible by 12. Compare the factor tree of *x* with the factor tree of 12.

**MANHATTAN** PREP

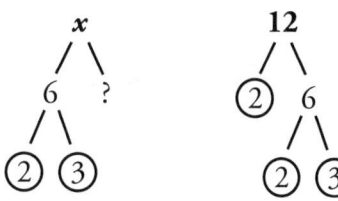

What would you have to know about *x* to guarantee that it is divisible by 12?

The number 12 is 2 × 2 × 3, so 12's building blocks are two 2's and a 3. To guarantee that *x* is divisible by 12, you need to know for sure that *x* has two 2's and one 3 among its prime factors. That is, *x* would have to be divisible by everything that 12 is divisible by.

Look at the factor tree for *x*. There is a 3 but only *one* 2. So you can't claim that *x* *must be* divisible by 12. But *could x* be divisible by 12?

Consider the question mark on *x*'s factor tree. That question mark is there to remind you that you *don't* know everything about *x*. After all, *x could* have other prime factors. If one of those unknown factors were another 2, your tree would look like this:

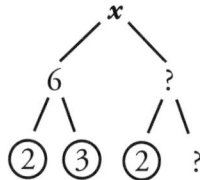

If an unknown factor were a 2, then *x* would indeed be divisible by 12. So *x could* be divisible by 12.

To confirm this thinking, list out a few multiples of 6 and check whether they are divisible by 12.

Some of the possible values of *x* are divisible by 12, and some aren't. *x could* be divisible by 12. Statement III *could* be true but doesn't have to be true.

$$
x \text{ is a number on this list.}
\begin{cases}
6 & 6 \div 12 = 0.5 \\
12 & 12 \div 12 = 1 \\
18 & 18 \div 12 = 1.5 \\
24 & 24 \div 12 = 2 \\
\dots & \dots
\end{cases}
\quad
\begin{array}{l}
\text{Some, but not all, of these} \\
\text{numbers are also divisible} \\
\text{by 12.}
\end{array}
$$

| If you… | Then you… | Like this: |
|---|---|---|
| Use a factor tree with a variable on top | Put in a question mark (or something similar) to remind yourself what you *don't* know | $x$ ∕ \ 6 ? |

## Check Your Skills

For each question, the following is true: $x$ is divisible by 24. Determine whether each statement below *must* be true, *could* be true, or *cannot* be true.

16. $x$ is divisible by 6.
17. $x$ is divisible by 9.
18. $x$ is divisible by 8.

*Answers can be found on pages 75–76.*

# Factors of $x$ With No Common Primes: Combine

Try this problem.

> $x$ is divisible by 3 and by 10. Decide whether each statement below *must* be true, *could* be true, or *cannot* be
> true.
>
>     I.    $x$ is divisible by 2.
>     II.   $x$ is divisible by 15.
>    III.  $x$ is divisible by 45.

First, create two factor trees to represent the given information.

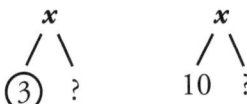

Why not write them together at once? "$x$ is divisible by 3" is a different fact from "$x$ is divisible by 10." *Initially, always write two given facts about a variable separately.* That way, you can think carefully about how to combine those facts.

Continue to break down the factors until you have only primes:

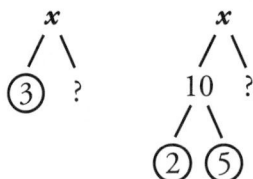

Now you can examine statement I. $x$ is divisible by 10, and 10 is divisible by 2, so $x$ is definitely divisible by 2. Statement I *must* be true.

Statement II is more difficult. Study the trees. Neither one provides complete information about $x$, but you know for certain that $x$ is divisible by 3 and that $x$ is divisible by 2 and by 5. These primes are all different. *When the primes from two trees are all different, you can put all the primes on one tree.*

**MANHATTAN** PREP

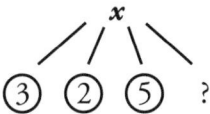

Return to the statement: *x* is divisible by 15. Can you guarantee this? If *x* definitely has all the prime factors that 15 has, then you can guarantee that *x* is divisible by 15.

The prime factors of 15 are 3 and 5. Being divisible by 15 is the same as being divisible by 3 and by 5.

Look at the combined factor tree. *x* has both a 3 and a 5, so *x* is definitely divisible by 15. Statement II *must* be true.

In order to understand better how prime factors work, you may want to sketch out some other possible factor trees for this information. If you know that *x* is divisible by 3, 2, and 5, you can combine these primes to form other definite factors of *x*.

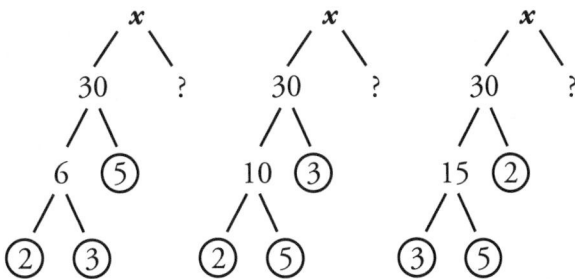

You get 15 on the third tree (don't write all this out on the test, of course). Notice what all three trees have in common. No matter how you combine the prime factors, each tree ultimately leads to 30, which is 2 × 3 × 5.

Therefore, you know that *x* is divisible by 2 × 3 × 5 = 30. And if *x* is divisible by 30, it is also divisible by everything 30 is divisible by. Since 15 is a factor of 30, *x* must be divisible by 15. Statement II *must* be true.

Statement III says that *x* is divisible by 45. What do you need to know in order to claim that *x* is divisible by 45? Build a factor tree of 45:

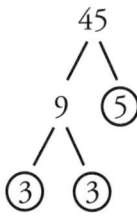

Your tree shows that 45 is divisible by 3, 3, and 5. For *x* to be divisible by 45, you need to know that *x* has all the same prime factors. Does it?

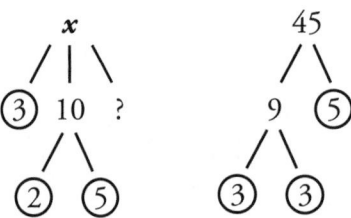

*x* has a 5, but only *one* 3 for sure. Since you don't know whether *x* has the second 3 that the 45 needs, you can't say for certain whether *x* is divisible by 45. *x could* be divisible by 45, but you don't know what the question mark contains. If it contains a 3, then *x* is divisible by 45. If not, then *x* is not divisible by 45. Statement III *could* be true but does not have to be.

| If you… | Then you… | Like this: |
|---|---|---|
| Know two factors of *x* that have no primes in common | Combine the two trees into one | *x* (3, ?) and *x* (10, ?) becomes *x* (3, 2, 5, ?) |

## Check Your Skills

For each question, the following is true: *x* is divisible by 28 and by 15. Determine whether each statement below *must* be true, *could* be true, or *cannot* be true.

19. *x* is divisible by 14.
20. *x* is divisible by 20.
21. *x* is divisible by 24.

*Answers can be found on pages 76–77.*

# Factors of *x* with Primes in Common: Combine to LCM

In the last section, you were told that *x* was divisible by 3 and by 10, and you figured out the consequences. For instance, you could conclude that *x* was divisible by 30, the product of 3 and 10.

Now consider a slightly different situation. Let's say that *x* is divisible by 6 and by 9. Is *x* divisible by 54, the product of 6 and 9?

MANHATTAN PREP

Here is the question in tree form:

Given:                                              Question: Do we necessarily get this tree?

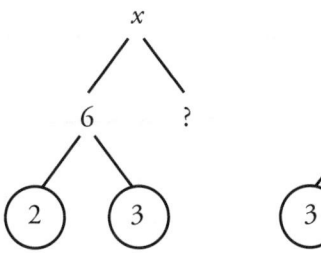  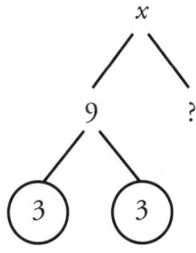                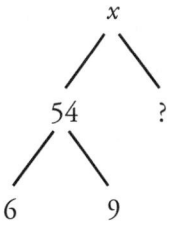

The earlier situation, in which *x* was divisible by 3 and by 10, was simpler, because 3 and 10 do not share any prime factors. You were able to keep all of the prime factors because no factors were shared. If you multiply those factors together, you'll find find the **least common multiple**, or **LCM**. The least common multiple of two numbers, say *A* and *B*, is the smallest number that is a multiple of both *A* and *B*. For the 3 and 10 example, the LCM is $3 \times 10 = 30$.

In the new question, though, 6 and 9 do share a prime factor, namely a 3.

Try listing out the multiples of each number, 6 and 9, to find the first number that appears on both lists:

| Multiples of 6 | Multiples of 9 |
|---|---|
| 6 | 9 |
| 12 | **18** |
| **18** | 27 |
| 24 | |

The LCM of 6 and 9 is 18. This is *not* the same number as $6 \times 9$, which equals 54. You can't just multiply the two numbers together this time. Why is that?

Take a look at how this works when you are using factor trees:

Given:                                              Conclusion:

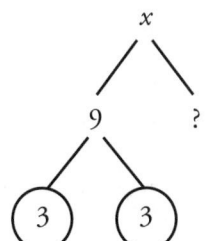                                 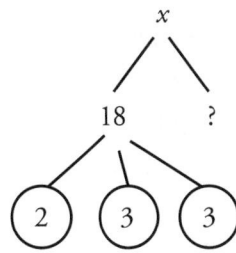

The conclusion contains only two of the three 3's that were part of the given information. The third 3 was dropped.

Imagine this scenario. On a table in front of you sits a box. Sally looks in that box and tells you, "I see an apple and an orange in the box." Linus looks in the box and tells you, "I see two oranges in the box." (Assume Sally and Linus are both telling the truth; they just may not be telling you *everything* they see in the box.)

2

Does that mean that the box contains three oranges?

No, it doesn't. Linus did see two oranges. But Sally's orange could have been one of those same two that Linus saw. Therefore, at a *minimum*, the box contains two oranges and one apple. You have to strip out one orange, because it represents overlap between the two pieces of information. (Note: The box *could* contain more oranges or apples; it could even contain bananas! You just don't know for sure that it does.)

In the same way, you need to strip out the 3 from the factor tree of 6, because that 3 could just be an overlap with the two 3's from the factor tree of 9. At a minimum, you have a 2 and two 3's. The LCM of 6 and 9 is $2 \times 3 \times 3 = 18$, so $x$ must be divisible by 18, but it does not have to be divisible by 54.

Here's why the LCM is important: *If $x$ is divisible by A and by B, then $x$ is divisible by the LCM of A and B, no matter what.*

For instance, if you are told that $x$ is divisible by 3 and by 10, then you can conclude that $x$ is definitely divisible by the LCM of 3 and 10, which equals 30 (since 3 and 10 don't overlap at all).

The same principle holds true for 6 and 9, though you have to *strip out any common factors*. If $x$ is divisible by 6 and 9, then $x$ is definitely divisible by 18, the LCM of 6 and 9.

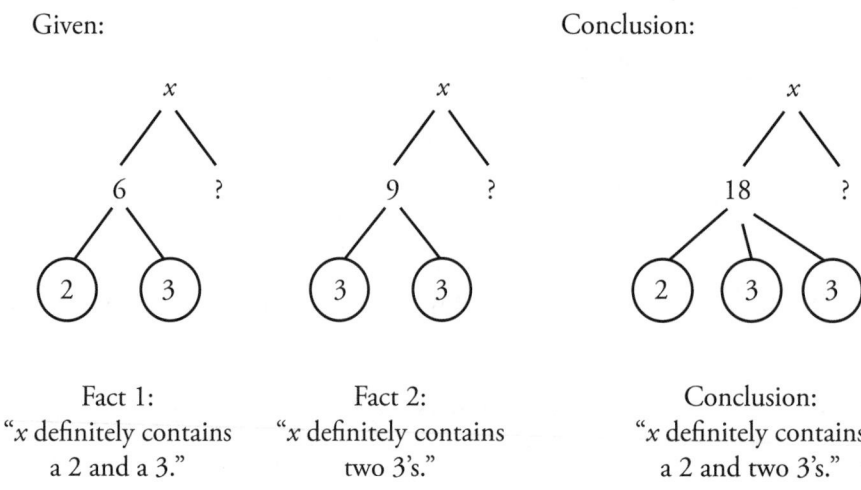

Given:                                            Conclusion:

Fact 1:                    Fact 2:                    Conclusion:
"$x$ definitely contains      "$x$ definitely contains      "$x$ definitely contains
a 2 and a 3."               two 3's."                  a 2 and two 3's."

The two given facts are like statements given by two witnesses. The witnesses aren't lying, but they could have seen the same things. *Don't double-count the evidence.* All you can prove about $x$ is that it contains a 2 and *two* 3's. The two witnesses could have seen the *same* 3, as Sally and Linus could have seen the same orange.

When two numbers don't share prime factors, their LCM is their product. For example:

3 and 10 don't share any prime factors, so their LCM = $3 \times 10 = 30$.

However, when two numbers share prime factors, their LCM will be *smaller* than their product, because you have to strip out overlap.

6 and 9 share prime factors, so their LCM is not 6 × 9 = 54. In fact, their LCM (18) is smaller than 54.

Listing the two sets of multiples to find the smallest number on both lists works well for small numbers, but it can be messy when the numbers are greater. In that case, break the numbers into their primes and then take only the *greater number of instances of* any particular prime.

For instance:

6 = 2 × 3 and 9 = 3 × 3
How many 2's should you take? The number 6 has one 2 and 9 has no 2's, so take one 2.
How many 3's should you take? The number 6 has one 3 and 9 has two 3's, so take two 3's.

The LCM = 2 × 3 × 3 = 18. That's a lot of steps to find the LCM when the numbers are small, but for more complicated situations, it's definitely faster.

Try another question.

If *x* is divisible by 8, 12, and 45, what is the greatest number that *x* must be divisible by?

The "greatest number that *x* must be divisible by" is code for: *What is the LCM of 8, 12, and 45?*

First, draw three separate trees for the given information:

Given:

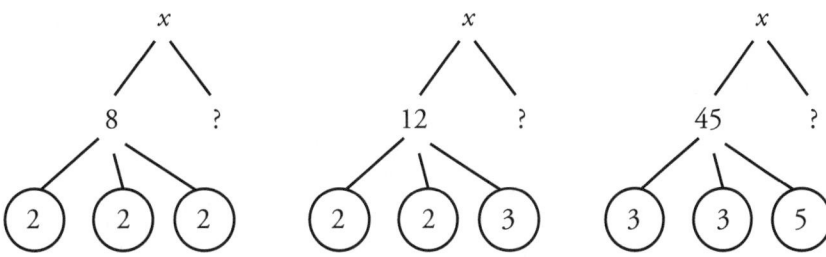

You could find this number by listing all the multiples of 8, 12, and 45 and looking for the first number on all three lists. That would be annoying. Instead, find the LCM by counting up prime factors that you *know* are in *x*, while stripping out the overlap.

Start with 2. How many 2's are guaranteed to be in *x*? There are three 2's in 8, two 2's in 12, and none in 45. To cover all the bases, there must be at least *three* 2's in *x*.

Take 3 next. Since 45 has two 3's, the most in any tree above, *x* must contain at least *two* 3's. Finally, *x* must have at least *one* 5 because of the 45. So here's the picture:

**2**

Given:                                                          Conclusion:

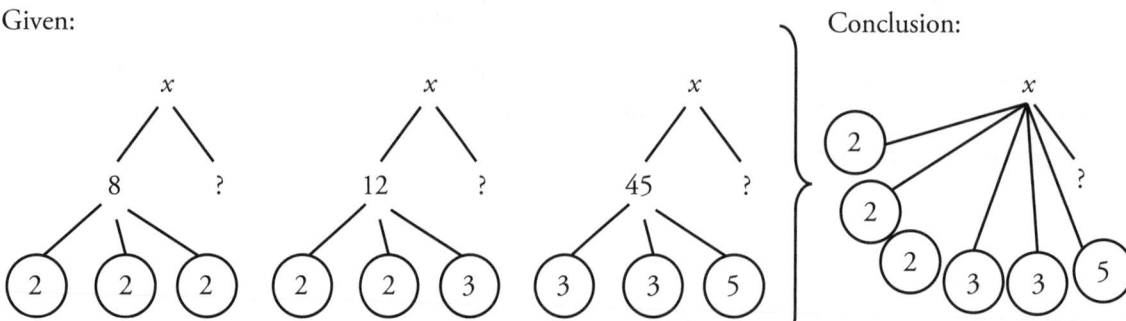

Now calculate the LCM:

$$2 \times 2 \times 2 \times 3 \times 3 \times 5 = (2 \times 2) \times (3 \times 3) \times (2 \times 5) = 4 \times 9 \times 10 = 360$$

Tip: Whenever you have to multiply a lot of numbers, try to pair 2's and 5's to create 10's, because 10 is an easy number to multiply into the greater number.

The LCM of 8, 12, and 45 is 360. It is the greatest number that *x must* be divisible by.

One final note: If the facts are about different variables (e.g., *x* and *y*), then the facts don't overlap when multiplying *x* and *y*.

Given:                                                          Conclusion:

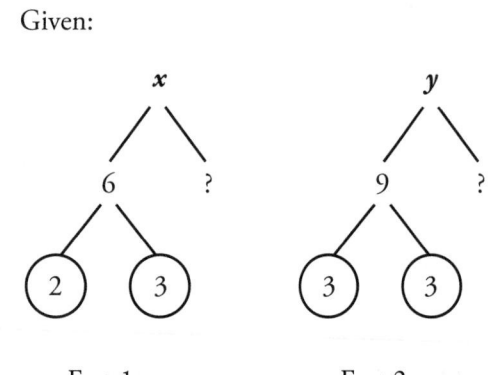
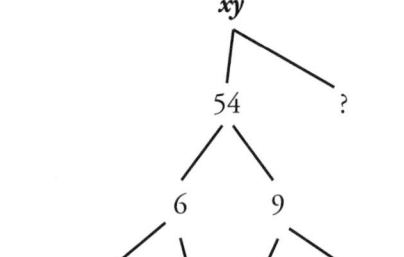

Fact 1:
"*x* definitely contains
a 2 and a 3."

Fact 2:
"*y* definitely contains
two 3's."

Conclusion:
"*xy* definitely contains
a 2 and ***three*** 3's."

The two witnesses are looking at different crime scenes ($x$ and $y$), so the product counts up everything you see across all the trees. Therefore:

| If you... | Then you... | Like this: |
|---|---|---|
| Know two factors of $x$ that have primes in common | Combine the two trees into one, eliminating the overlap $=$ Know that $x$ is divisible by the LCM of the factors | $x$ is divisible by 6 $x$ is divisible by 9 becomes $x$ is divisible by 18, the LCM of 6 and 9 |

## Check Your Skills

For each question, the following is true: $x$ is divisible by 6 and by 14. Determine whether each statement below *must* be true, *could* be true, or *cannot* be true.

22. $x$ is divisible by 42.
23. $x$ is divisible by 84.

*Answers can be found on page 77.*

# Check Your Skills Answer Key

1. **No:** 123,456,789 is an odd number, because it ends in 9. Therefore, 123,456,789 is *not* divisible by 2.

2. **Yes:** The digits of 732 sum to a multiple of 3 (7 + 3 + 2 = 12), so 732 is divisible by 3.

3. **No:** The digits of 989 do not sum to a multiple of 9 (9 + 8 + 9 = 26), so 989 is *not* divisible by 9.

4. The factors of 90 are:

| Small | Large |
|-------|-------|
| 1 | 90 |
| 2 | 45 |
| 3 | 30 |
| 5 | 18 |
| 6 | 15 |
| 9 | 10 |

5. The factors of 72 are:

| Small | Large |
|-------|-------|
| 1 | 72 |
| 2 | 36 |
| 3 | 24 |
| 4 | 18 |
| 6 | 12 |
| 8 | 9 |

6. The factors of 105 are:

| Small | Large |
|-------|-------|
| 1 | 105 |
| 3 | 35 |
| 5 | 21 |
| 7 | 15 |

**2**

7. The factors of 120 are:

| Small | Large |
|-------|-------|
| 1 | 120 |
| 2 | 60 |
| 3 | 40 |
| 4 | 30 |
| 5 | 24 |
| 6 | 20 |
| 8 | 15 |
| 10 | 12 |

8. **23, 29, 31, 37, 41, 43, and 47** are the prime numbers between 20 and 50.

9.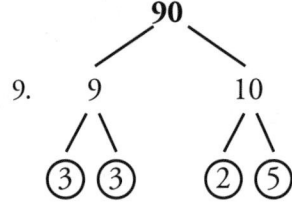

10.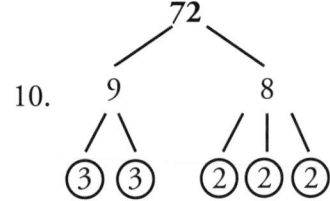

11.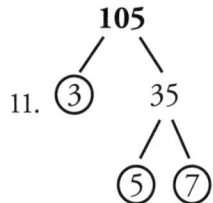

12.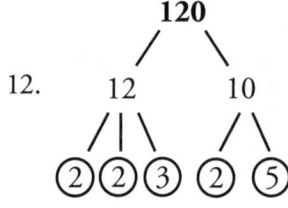

MANHATTAN PREP

13. **15**:

    $3 \times 5 = 15$

| Small | Large |
|-------|-------|
| 1     | 15    |
| 3     | 5     |

14. **70**:

    $2 \times 5 \times 7 = 70$

| Building blocks | Small | Large | Building blocks |
|-----------------|-------|-------|-----------------|
| 1               | 1     | 70    | $2 \times 5 \times 7$ |
| 2               | 2     | 35    | $5 \times 7$    |
| 5               | 5     | 14    | $2 \times 7$    |
| 7               | 7     | 10    | $2 \times 5$    |

15. **78**:

    $2 \times 3 \times 13 = 78$

| Building blocks | Small | Large | Building blocks |
|-----------------|-------|-------|-----------------|
| 1               | 1     | 78    | $2 \times 3 \times 13$ |
| 2               | 2     | 39    | $3 \times 13$   |
| 3               | 3     | 26    | $2 \times 13$   |
| $2 \times 3$    | 6     | 13    | 13              |

**For questions 16–18, $x$ is divisible by 24.**

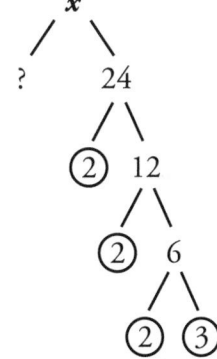

16.

**Must be true:** For $x$ to be divisible by 6, it must contain the same prime factors as 6, which contains a 2 and a 3. $x$ also contains a 2 and a 3, so $x$ must be divisible by 6.

17.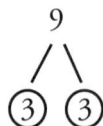

> **Could be true:** For $x$ to be divisible by 9, it must contain the same prime factors as 9, which contains two 3's. $x$ only contains one known 3. But the question mark means $x$ may have other prime factors and may contain another 3. For this reason, $x$ could be divisible by 9 but does not have to be.

18.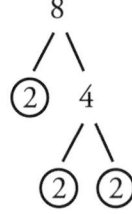

> **Must be true:** For $x$ to be divisible by 8, it must contain the same prime factors as 8, which contains three 2's. $x$ also contains three 2's, so $x$ must be divisible by 8.

**For questions 19–21, $x$ is divisible by 28 and by 15.**

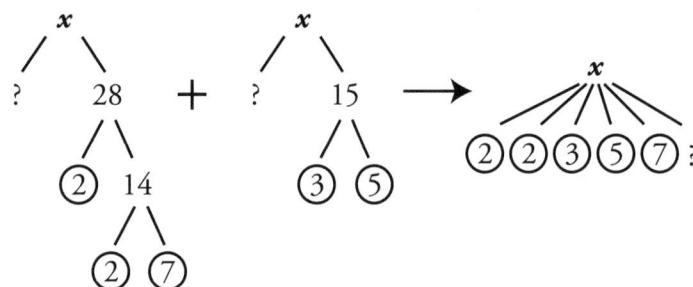

19.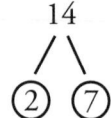

> **Must be true:** For $x$ to be divisible by 14, it must contain the same prime factors as 14, which contains a 2 and a 7. $x$ also contains a 2 and a 7, so $x$ must be divisible by 14.

20.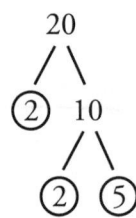

> **Must be true:** For $x$ to be divisible by 20, it must contain the same prime factors as 20, which contains two 2's and a 5. $x$ also contains two 2's and a 5, so $x$ must be divisible by 20.

21.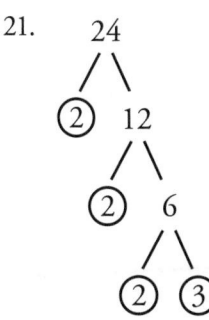

**Could be true:** For *x* to be divisible by 24, it must contain the same prime factors as 24, which contains three 2's and a 3. *x* contains a 3, but only two 2's for sure. But the question mark indicates that *x* may have other prime factors, so it may contain another 2. For this reason, *x* could be divisible by 24 but does not have to be.

**For questions 22–23, *x* is divisible by 6 and by 14.**

22.  $6 = 2 \times 3$ and $14 = 2 \times 7$. Therefore, the LCM of 6 and 14 is $2 \times 3 \times 7 = 42$. (Remember to strip out the overlapping 2.)

**Must be true:** Since the LCM of 6 and 14 is 42, *x* must be divisible by 42.

23.  **Could be true:** The LCM is 42. *x* could be divisible by 84, but it does not have to be.

# Chapter Review: Drill Sets

## Drill 1

1. Is 4,005 divisible by 5?
2. Does 51 have any factors besides 1 and itself?
3. $x = 20$
The prime factors of $x$ are:
The factors of $x$ are:
4. If 33 is a factor of 594, is 11 a factor of 594?
5. Is 6,750 divisible by 18?

## Drill 2

6. Is 123 divisible by 3?
7. Does 23 have any factors other than 1 and itself?
8. $x = 100$
The prime factors of $x$ are:
The factors of $x$ are:
9. If 2,499 is divisible by 147, is 2,499 divisible by 49?
10. What are all of the positive multiples of 18 that are less than 60?

## Drill 3

11. Is 285,284,901 divisible by 10?
12. Is 539,105 prime?
13. If $x = 36$, what are all of the factors of $x$?
    (A) 2, 2, 3, 3
    (B) 2, 3, 4, 6, 9, 12, 18
    (C) 1, 2, 3, 4, 6, 9, 12, 18, 36
14. Find at least four even divisors of 84.
15. What are the prime factors of $30 \times 49$?

## Drill 4

16. Is 9,108 divisible by 9 and/or by 2?
17. Is 937,184 prime?
18. $x = 39$
The prime factors of $x$ are:
The factors of $x$ are:
19. How many more prime factors does the product of $42 \times 120$ have than the product of $21 \times 24$?

## Drill 5

20. Is 43,360 divisible by 5 and/or by 3?
21. Is 513,501 prime?
22. $x = 37$
The prime factors of $x$ are:
The factors of $x$ are:
23. What are the two greatest odd factors of 90?

## Drill 6

24. Determine which of the following numbers are prime numbers. A prime number has exactly two factors: 1 and itself.

| 2 | 3 | 5 | 6 |
|---|---|---|---|
| 7 | 9 | 10 | 15 |
| 17 | 21 | 27 | 29 |
| 31 | 33 | 258 | 303 |
| 655 | 786 | 1,023 | 1,325 |

**2**

## Drill 7

25. If $x$ is divisible by 33, what other numbers is $x$ divisible by?

26. The prime factorization of a number is $3 \times 3 \times 7$. What is the number, and what are all of its factors?

27. If 6 and 14 are factors of $y$, must $y$ be divisible by 21?

28. If $7y$ is a multiple of 210, must $y$ be a multiple of 12?

29. If integer $a$ is *not* a multiple of 30, but $ab$ is, what is the smallest possible value of integer $b$?

## Drill 8

30. If 40 is a factor of $x$, what other numbers must be factors of $x$?

31. The only prime factors of a number are 5 and 17. What is the number, and what are all of its factors?

32. 5 and 6 are factors of $x$. Is $x$ divisible by 15?

33. If $q$ is divisible by 2, 6, 9, 12, 15, and 30, is $q$ divisible by 8?

34. If $p$ is a prime number, and $q$ is a non-prime integer, what are the minimum and maximum numbers of factors $p$ and $q$ can have in common?

## Drill 9

35. If 64 divides evenly into $n$, what are all of the known divisors of $n$?

36. The prime factorization of a number is $2 \times 3 \times 11$. What is the number, and what are all of its factors?

37. 14 and 3 divide evenly into $n$. Is 12 a factor of $n$?

38. The sum of the positive integers $x$ and $y$ is 17. If $x$ has only two factors and $y$ is a multiple of 5, which of the following is a possible value of $x$?

    (A) 3
    (B) 7
    (C) 12

39. If $n$ is the product of 2, 3, and a two-digit prime number, how many of its factors are greater than 6?

## Drill 10

40. If $n$ is a multiple of both 35 and 44, is 14 a divisor of $n$?

41. 4, 21, and 55 are factors of $n$. Is $n$ divisible by 154?

42. If $n$ is divisible by both 196 and 15, is 270 a factor of $n$?

# Drill Sets Solutions

## Drill 1

1. **Yes:** 4,005 ends in 5, so it is divisible by 5.

2. **Yes:** The digits of 51 sum to a multiple of 3 (5 + 1 = 6), so 3 is a factor of 51. (In fact, both 3 and 17 are factors of 51, since 3 × 17 = 51.)

3. **Prime factors: 2, 2, 5**
   **Factors: 1, 2, 4, 5, 10, 20**
   The prime factors of *x* are:

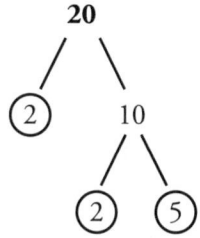

The factors of *x* are:

| Small | Large |
|-------|-------|
| 1 | 20 |
| 2 | 10 |
| 4 | 5 |

4. **Yes:** You could divide 594 by 11 to determine divisibility, but it is faster to use the Factor Foundation rule. If 594 is divisible by 33, 594 is also divisible by all of the factors of 33. The number 11 is a factor of 33 (33 = 11 × 3). Therefore, 594 is also divisible by 11.

5. **Yes:** In order to be divisible by 18, a number must be divisible by both 2 and 9, factors that make up 18. Because 6,750 ends in a 0, it is even, so it is divisible by 2. The digits of 6,750 sum to 18 (6 + 7 + 5 = 18), and 18 is divisible by 9, so 6,750 is also divisible by 9. Because 6,750 is divisible by both 2 and 9, it is also divisible by 18.

## Drill 2

6. **Yes:** The digits of 123 sum to a multiple of 3 (1 + 2 + 3 = 6), so 123 is divisible by 3.

7. **No:** 23 is a prime number. It has no factors other than 1 and itself.

**2**

8. **Prime factors: 2, 2, 5, 5**
   **Factors: 1, 2, 4, 5, 10, 20, 25, 50, 100**
   The prime factors of *x* are:

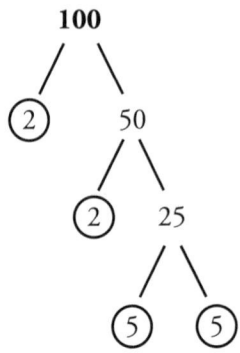

The factors of *x* are:

| Small | Large |
|-------|-------|
| 1     | 100   |
| 2     | 50    |
| 4     | 25    |
| 5     | 20    |
| 10    | 10    |

9. **Yes:** The Factor Foundation rule is helpful in this question. The problem states that 2,499 is divisible by 147. The Factor Foundation rule states that if 2,499 is divisible by 147, then 2,499 is also divisible by all of the factors of 147. And 147 is divisible by 49 (147 ÷ 49 = 3). Since 2,499 is divisible by 147, it is also divisible by 49.

10. **18, 36, and 54:** In order to generate multiples of 18 that are less than 50, multiply 18 by small integers.

    18 × 1 = 18
    18 × 2 = 36
    18 × 3 = 54

    All other positive multiples of 18 are greater than 60.

# Drill 3

11. **No:** 285,284,901 ends in a 1, not a 0. It is not divisible by 10.

12. **No:** 539,105 ends in a 5, so 5 is a factor of 539,105. So are 1 and 539,105. There are other factors, such as 107,821, since 539,105 = 5 × 107,821. Prime numbers have only two factors, so 539,105 is not prime.

13. **(C):** The question asks for *all* of the factors of *x*, not just the prime factors. Use a table to find the factor pairs of 36. (Note: 1 and the number itself are always your first factor pair; don't forget them! Also, trap answer (A) represents only the prime factors, not all factors.)

| Small | Large |
|-------|-------|
| 1 | 36 |
| 2 | 18 |
| 3 | 12 |
| 4 | 9 |
| 6 | 6 |

14. **2, 4, 6, 12, 14, 28, 42, and 84:** Make a factor pair table to see which factors are even:

| Small | Large |
|-------|-------|
| 1 | **84** |
| **2** | **42** |
| 3 | **28** |
| **4** | 21 |
| **6** | **14** |
| 7 | **12** |

15. **2, 3, 5, 7, and 7:** While you could multiply the numbers together to find the prime factors (annoying because the numbers are large!), there is a faster way. The prime factors of the product of 30 and 49 will consist of the prime factors of 30 and the prime factors of 49. The prime factors of 30 are 2, 3, and 5. The prime factors of 49 are 7 and 7. Therefore, the prime factors of 30 × 49 are 2, 3, 5, 7, and 7.

# Drill 4

16. **9,108 is divisible by 9 AND by 2:** The digits of 9,108 sum to a multiple of 9 (9 + 1 + 0 + 8 = 18), so it is a multiple of 9. Because 9,108 ends in 8, it is even, which means it is divisible by 2.

17. **No:** 937,184 ends in 4, which means it's even. Therefore, it's divisible by 2. It's also divisible by 1 and itself. Prime numbers have only two factors, so 937,184 is not prime.

18. **Prime factors: 3, 13**
    **Factors: 1, 3, 13, 39** The prime factors of *x* are:

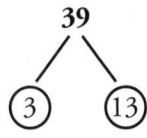

The factors of *x* are:

| Small | Large |
|-------|-------|
| 1     | 39    |
| 3     | 13    |

19. **Two:** You could multiply these products out or identify all of the prime factors of each number, but there is a more efficient way. Because the question asks you to make a comparison, focus only on the *differences* between the two products.

$$42 \times 120$$
$$21 \times 24$$

Compare 42 and 21: 42 = 21 × 2. That is, 42 contains 21 (and all of its factors), but 42 also has one additional factor of 2.

Compare 120 and 24: 120 = 24 × 5. That is, 120 contains 24 (and all of its factors), but 120 also has one additional factor of 5.

Therefore, the only *additional* prime factors in 42 × 120 are the 2 in 42 and the 5 in 120. The product of 42 × 120 has two more prime factors than the product of 21 × 24.

# Drill 5

20. **43,360 is divisible by 5 but is NOT divisible by 3:** 43,360 ends in 0, so it is divisible by 5. The digits of 43,360 do not sum to a multiple of 3 (4 + 3 + 3 + 6 + 0 = 16), so it is not divisible by 3.

21. **No:** The sum of the digits is 5 + 1 + 3 + 5 + 0 + 1 = 15. The number 15 is divisible by 3, so the number 513,501 is also divisible by 3. Prime numbers have only themselves and 1 as factors, so 513,501 is not prime.

22. **Prime factors: 37**
    **Factors: 1, 37**

| Small | Large |
|-------|-------|
| 1     | 37    |

23. **15, 45:** Break 90 down into its factor pairs.

| Small | Large |
|-------|-------|
| 1     | 90    |
| 2     | **45** |
| 3     | 30    |
| 5     | 18    |
| 6     | **15** |
| 9     | 10    |

The two greatest odd factors of 90 are 45 and 15.

# Drill 6

24. **Prime numbers: 2, 3, 5, 7, 17, 29, 31:** The numbers in bold below are prime numbers.

| | | | |
|---|---|---|---|
| **2** | **3** | **5** | 6 |
| 7 | 9 | 10 | 15 |
| **17** | 21 | 27 | **29** |
| **31** | 33 | 258 | 303 |
| 655 | 786 | 1,023 | 1,325 |

All of the even numbers other than 2 (6, 10, 258, 786) are not prime, since they are divisible by 2.

All of the multiples of 5 other than 5 itself (10, 15, 655, 1,325) are not prime, because they are divisible by 5.

Next, check whether any remaining numbers have digits that sum to a multiple of 3: 9, 21 (digits sum to 3), 27 (digits sum to 9), 33 (digits sum to 6), 303 (digits sum to 6), and 1,023 (digits sum to 6). All of these numbers are divisible by 3.

For the remaining numbers, you may already know that certain ones are prime. For the rest, check to see whether they are divisible by any prime numbers smaller than the number you are checking. For instance, to check 17, determine that it is not divisible by 2 (it's not even), by 3 (the digits don't sum to a multiple of 3), by 5 (it does not end in 0 or 5), or by 7 (actually check the division here: you don't get an integer).

# Drill 7

25. **1, 3, 11:** If $x$ is divisible by 33, then $x$ is also divisible by everything 33 is divisible by. The factors of 33 are:

| Small | Large |
|---|---|
| 1 | 33 |
| 3 | 11 |

26. **The number is 63, and the factors are 1, 3, 7, 9, 21, and 63:**

$3 \times 3 \times 7 = 63$.

| Small | Large |
|---|---|
| 1 | 63 |
| 3 | 21 |
| 7 | 9 |

27. **Yes:**

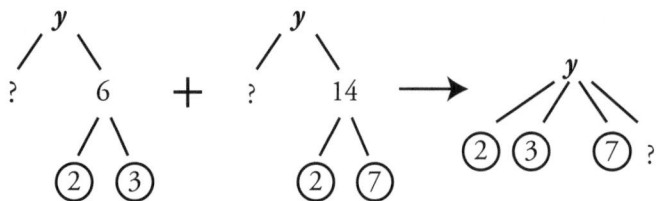

The factors of 6 are 2 and 3. The factors of 14 are 2 and 7. The 2's do overlap, so strip out one instance of that double-counted factor. The combined factors are 2, 3, and 7. The 3 and 7 can be used to create 21 (3 × 7 = 21), so $y$ must be a multiple of 21.

28. **No:** For $y$ to be a multiple of 12, it would need to contain all of the prime factors of 12: 2, 2, and 3. $7y$ is a multiple of 210, so $7y$ contains the prime factors 2, 3, 5, and 7 (because 2 × 3 × 5 × $y$ = 210). However, the question asks about $y$, not $7y$, so divide out the 7. Therefore, $y$ must contain the remaining primes: 2, 3, and 5. Compare this to the prime factorization of 12: $y$ does have a 2 and a 3, but it does not necessarily have *two* 2's. Therefore, $y$ could be a multiple of 12, but it doesn't have to be.

Alternatively, you could start by dividing out the 7. If $7y$ is divisible by 210, $y$ is divisible by 30. Therefore, $y$ contains the prime factors 2, 3, and 5, and you can follow the remaining reasoning from above. Alternatively, since $y$ is divisible by 30, $y$ could be 30, which is *not* divisible by 12, or $y$ could be 60, which *is* divisible by 12.

29. **2:** For integer $a$ to be a multiple of 30, it would need to contain all of the prime factors of 30: 2, 3, and 5. Since $a$ is not a multiple of 30, it must be missing at least one of these prime factors. So if $ab$ is a multiple of 30, $b$ must supply any missing prime factors. The smallest possible missing prime is 2. If $b = 2$ and $a = 15$ (or any odd multiple of 15), then the initial constraints will be met: $ab$ will be a multiple of 30, but $a$ by itself will not be.

## Drill 8

30. **1, 2, 4, 5, 8, 10, and 20:** If 40 is a factor of $x$, then any factor of 40 is also a factor of $x$. List out the factors of 40.

| Small | Large |
|-------|-------|
| 1 | 40 |
| 2 | 20 |
| 4 | 10 |
| 5 | 8 |

31. **The number is 85, and the factors are 1, 5, 17, and 85:** If 5 and 17 are the only prime factors of the number, then the number equals 5 × 17, which means the number is 85.

| Small | Large |
|-------|-------|
| 1 | 85 |
| 5 | 17 |

MANHATTAN PREP

2

32. **Yes:**

None of the factors overlap, so you can combine them all: *x* is divisible by 2 × 3 × 5. For *x* to be divisible by 15, it must contain all of the prime factors of 15 (3 × 5). Since *x* does contain a 3 and a 5, *x* is divisible by 15.

33. **Maybe:** To be divisible by 8, *q* needs three 2's in its prime factorization. Don't find the full list of (non-overlapping) factors. Concentrate only on the 2's, since that's all you need to answer the question.

Because there might be some overlapping factors of 2, you cannot simply count all of the numbers that contain 2. For instance, 6 is a multiple of 2 and 3, so the fact that *q* is divisible by both 2 and 6 indicates only that there is at least one 2 (and at least one 3); there aren't necessarily two factors of 2 just because *q* has the factors 2 and 6.

Instead, look for the greatest number of 2's *in one factor*. The number 12 contains two known 2's, so *q* must be a multiple of 4, but it's unclear whether *q* contains three 2's. It might or it might not.

If you ever do need to check all of the factors, not just the 2's, then do this:

2: *q* must be divisible by 2.

6: The 3 is new. Ignore the overlapping 2 and add a 3 to your list of factors: *q* must be divisible by 2 and 3.

9: The second 3 is new. Add it to your list: *q* must be divisible by 2, 3, and 3.

12: The second 2 is new. Add it to your list: *q* must be divisible by 2, 2, 3, and 3.

15: The 5 is new. Add it to your list: *q* must be divisible by 2, 2, 3, 3, and 5.

30: Nothing new. *q* must be divisible by 2, 2, 3, 3, and 5.

There are only two 2's for certain. Therefore, *q* must be a multiple of 180 (i.e., 2 × 2 × 3 × 3 × 5), but it does not necessarily have to be a multiple of 8.

34. **Minimum = one; maximum = two:** Start with the more constrained variable: *p*. Because it is prime, it has exactly two factors—itself and 1. Therefore, the maximum number of "factors in common" cannot be more than two. Can *p* and *q* have exactly two factors in common? Certainly; *q* can be a multiple of *p*. (For instance, if *p* = 3 and *q* = 12, the common factors are 1 and 3.)

What about the minimum? Can $p$ and $q$ have absolutely no factors in common? Try some numbers. If $p = 3$ and $q = 10$, then the two numbers don't have any prime factors in common, but notice that they are both divisible by 1. Any integer has 1 as a factor. Therefore, the minimum possible number of shared factors is one (the number 1 itself), and the maximum is two (the two factors of prime number $p$).

# Drill 9

35. **1, 2, 4, 8, 16, 32, 64:** If 64 divides evenly into $n$, then any divisors of 64 will also be divisors of $n$.

| Small | Large |
|-------|-------|
| 1 | 64 |
| 2 | 32 |
| 4 | 16 |
| 8 | 8 |

36. **The number is 66, and the factors are 1, 2, 3, 6, 11, 22, 33, and 66:** $2 \times 3 \times 11 = 66$.

| Small | Large |
|-------|-------|
| 1 | 66 |
| 2 | 33 |
| 3 | 22 |
| 6 | 11 |

37. **Maybe:**

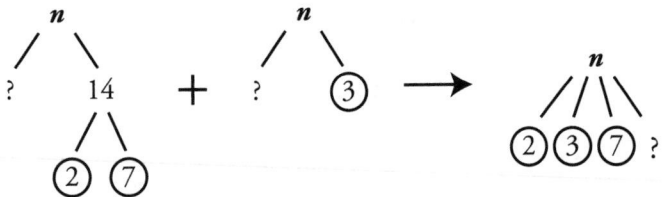

The two sets of factors don't overlap, so you can keep them all. For 12 to be a factor of $n$, $n$ must contain all of the prime factors of 12 ($2 \times 2 \times 3$). $n$ contains a 3, but only contains one 2 for sure, so 12 *could* be a factor of $n$ but does not have to be.

38. **(B):** Since $x$ has only two factors, it must be a prime number (with factors itself and 1). Since $y$ is a positive multiple of 5, it must be 5, 10, or 15. List out the possible scenarios; start with $y$ since you know there are only three possible values.

> $y + x = 17$
> $5 + 12 = 17$ No good: 12 isn't a prime number.
> $10 + 7 = 17$ Bingo! 10 is a multiple of 5, and 7 is a prime number.

You could write out the third scenario, but wait! Check the answers whenever you have a possible solution. There is a 7 in the answers, so you're done. (It turns out that 15 + 2 = 17 also fits the criteria given in the problem, but 2 is not among the answer choices.)

39. **Four:** Because you have been asked for a concrete answer, you can infer that the answer will be the same regardless of which two-digit prime you pick. So, to make your job easier, pick the smallest one: 11.

If *n* is the product of 2, 3, and 11, then *n* = 66, and its factors are:

| Small | Large |
|-------|-------|
| 1     | **66** |
| 2     | **33** |
| 3     | **22** |
| 6     | **11** |

There are four factors greater than 6: 11, 22, 33, and 66.

Why is the answer always four factors, even if you try a different two-digit prime number? Notice that because the other given prime factors of *n* (2 and 3) multiply to get exactly 6, you have to multiply by the third factor, the two-digit prime number, in order to get a number greater than 6. The right-hand column represents that third factor multiplied by all of the other factors: 11 × 6, 11 × 3, 11 × 2, and 11 × 1. If you replace 11 with another two-digit prime, you will get the same result. (If you're not sure, test it out! That's a great way to prove a principle to yourself.)

# Drill 10

40. **Yes:**

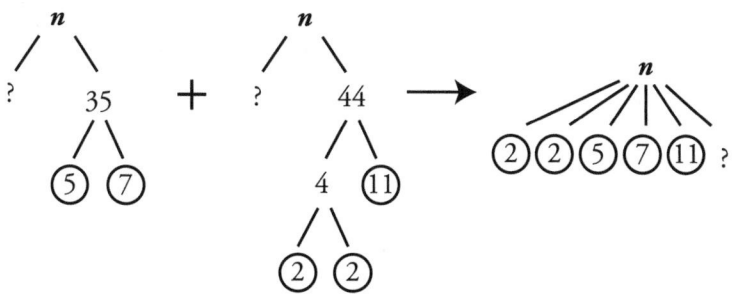

There is no overlap among the factors, so you can keep them all. In order for 14 to be a divisor of *n*, *n* has to contain all of the prime factors of 14 (2 × 7). Since *n* does contain 2 and 7, 14 is a divisor of *n*.

**2**

41. **Yes:**

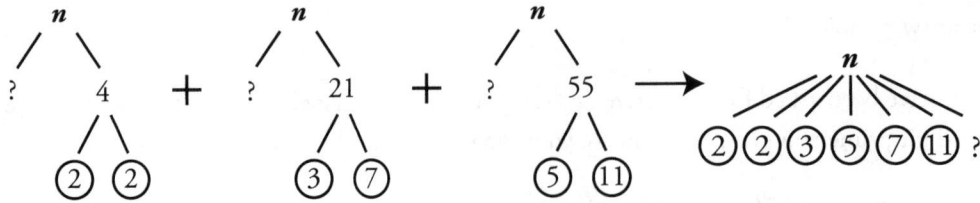

None of the factors overlap, so you can keep all of them. For 154 to divide evenly into *n*, *n* has to contain all the same prime factors as 154 (2 × 7 × 11). *n* also contains 2, 7, and 11, so *n* is divisible by 154.

42. **Maybe:**

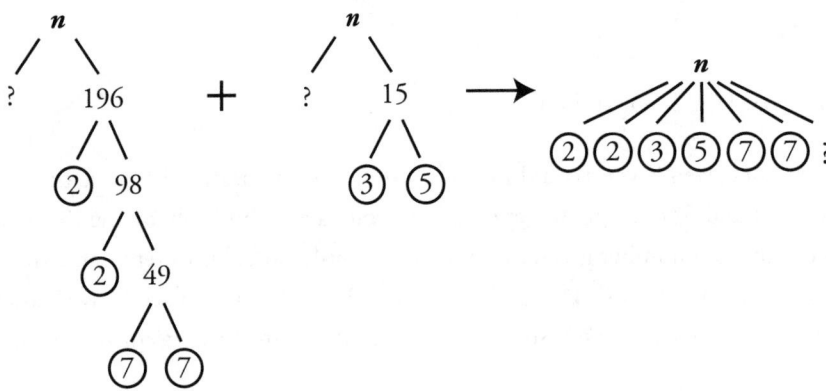

None of the factors overlap, so you can keep all of them. For 270 to be a factor of *n*, *n* must contain all the same prime factors as 270 (2 × 3 × 3 × 3 × 5). *n* contains a 2 and a 5, but only one known 3. Therefore, 270 *could* be a factor of *n*, but it does not have to be.

# Exponents & Roots

# In this chapter...

- Basics of Exponents
- Multiply Terms with Same Base: Add the Exponents
- Divide Terms with Same Base: Subtract the Exponents
- Pretty Much Anything to the Power of Zero: One
- Negative Power: One Over a Positive Power
- Apply Two Exponents: Multiply the Exponents
- Apply an Exponent to a Product: Apply the Exponent to Each Factor
- Add or Subtract Terms with the Same Base: Pull Out a Common Factor
- Roots: Opposite of Exponents
- Square Root: Power of One-Half
- Cube Roots Undo Cubing
- Multiply Square Roots: Put Everything Under the Root
- Simplify Square Roots: Factor Out Squares
- Add or Subtract Under the Root: Pull Out Common Square Factors

# Chapter 3
# **Exponents & Roots**

## In This Chapter, You Will Learn To:

- Apply exponent rules to solve problems
- Manipulate square and cube roots

## Basics of Exponents

Exponents represent repeated multiplication. The **exponent**, or power, tells you how many **bases** to multiply together. In the example below, 5 is the base and 3 is the exponent.

$$5^3 \qquad = \qquad 5 \times 5 \times 5 \qquad = \qquad 125$$

Five cubed    equals    three fives multiplied together, or five times five times five,    which equals    one hundred twenty-five

An **exponential expression** or term is one that contains an exponent. Exponential expressions can contain variables as well. The variable can be the base, the exponent, or even both. For example:

$$a^4 \qquad = \qquad a \times a \times a \times a$$

*a* to the fourth    equals    four *a*'s multiplied together, or *a* times *a* times *a* times *a*

$$3^x \qquad = \qquad 3 \times 3 \times \ldots \times 3$$

Three to the *x*    equals    three times three times ... times three (there are *x* three's in the product, whatever *x* is)

Any base to the first power equals that base.

$$7^1 \qquad = \qquad 7$$

Seven to the first    equals    seven

**3**

Memorize the following powers of positive integers. Create flash cards for any that you don't already know.

| _Squares_ | _More Squares_ | _Cubes_ |
|---|---|---|
| $1^2 = 1$ | $10^2 = 100$ | $1^3 = 1$ |
| $2^2 = 4$ | $11^2 = 121$ | $2^3 = 8$ |
| $3^2 = 9$ | $12^2 = 144$ | $3^3 = 27$ |
| $4^2 = 16$ | $13^2 = 169$ | $4^3 = 64$ |
| $5^2 = 25$ | $14^2 = 196$ | $5^3 = 125$ |
| $6^2 = 36$ | $15^2 = 225$ | $10^3 = 1,000$ |
| $7^2 = 49$ | $20^2 = 400$ | |
| $8^2 = 64$ | $30^2 = 900$ | |
| $9^2 = 81$ | | |

| _Powers of 2_ | _Powers of 3_ | _Powers of 5_ |
|---|---|---|
| $2^1 = 2$ | $3^1 = 3$ | $5^1 = 5$ |
| $2^2 = 4$ | $3^2 = 9$ | $5^2 = 25$ |
| $2^3 = 8$ | $3^3 = 27$ | $5^3 = 125$ |
| $2^4 = 16$ | $3^4 = 81$ | |
| $2^5 = 32$ | | |
| $2^6 = 64$ | _Powers of 4_ | _Powers of 10_ |
| $2^7 = 128$ | $4^1 = 2^2 = 4$ | $10^1 = 10$ |
| $2^8 = 256$ | $4^2 = 2^4 = 16$ | $10^2 = 100$ |
| $2^9 = 512$ | $4^3 = 2^6 = 64$ | $10^3 = 1,000$ |
| $2^{10} = 1,024$ | $4^4 = 2^8 = 256$ | |
| | $4^5 = 2^{10} = 1,024$ | |

Remember PEMDAS? Exponents come before everything else, except parentheses. That includes negative signs. For example:

| $-3^2$ | = | $-(3^2)$ | = | $-9$ |
|---|---|---|---|---|
| The negative of three squared | equals | the negative of the quantity three squared, | and this equals | negative nine |

To calculate $-3^2$, square the 3 _before_ you multiply by negative one ($-1$). If you want to square the negative sign, throw parentheses around $-3$.

| $(-3)^2$ | = | 9 |
|---|---|---|
| The square of negative three | equals | nine |

In $(-3)^2$, the negative sign and the 3 are both inside the parentheses, so they both get squared. If you say _negative three squared_, you probably mean $(-3)^2$, but someone listening might write down $-3^2$, so say _the square of negative three_ instead.

Negative numbers raised to an even power are always positive. Negative numbers raised to an odd number are always negative.

$$(\text{Negative})^{\text{even}} = \text{Positive} \qquad (\text{Negative})^{\text{odd}} = \text{Negative}$$

The powers of −1 alternate between 1 and −1. Even powers of −1 are always 1 (e.g., $(-1)^2 = 1$), while odd powers of −1 are always −1 (e.g., $(-1)^3 = -1$).

A positive base raised to any power is always positive, because positive times positive is positive—no matter how many times you multiply. For example $2^{45}$ is positive because it represents 2 multiplied by itself 45 times.

Since an even exponent always gives a positive result, *an even exponent can hide the sign of the base.* Consider this equation:

$$x^2 = 16$$

In Chapter 6, Equations, you will cover in greater depth how to solve an equation such as this one. For now, notice that *two* different numbers for $x$ would make the equation true:

$$4^2 = 16 \qquad\qquad (-4)^2 = 16$$

The value of $x$ could be either 4 or −4. *Always be careful when dealing with even exponents in equations.* Look for more than one possible solution.

## Check Your Skills

1.  Which is greater, $-5^8$ or $(-5)^8$?

*Answer can be found on page 117.*

## Multiply Terms with Same Base: Add the Exponents

Imagine that you multiply together a string of five $a$'s. Now multiply a second string of three $a$'s together. Finally, because you love multiplication, go ahead and multiply the two strings together. How many $a$'s do you end up with?

Write it all out longhand:

$$(a \times a \times a \times a \times a) \times (a \times a \times a) = a \times a \times a \times a \times a \times a \times a \times a$$

Now use exponential notation:

$$a^5 \qquad \times \qquad a^3 \qquad = \qquad a^8$$

$a$ to the *fifth*    times    $a$ to the *third*    equals    $a$ to the *eighth*

What happens to the exponents 5 and 3? They add up: $5 + 3 = 8$. This works because there are only $a$'s in the equation. The two terms on the left ($a^5$ and $a^3$) have the same base ($a$), so there are eight $a$'s on each side of the equation.

*When you multiply exponential terms that have the same base, add the exponents.*

Treat any term without an exponent as if it had an exponent of 1.

$$y(y^6) = y \times y^6 = y^1 \times y^6 = y^{(1 + 6)} = y^7$$

Adding exponents works with numbers in the base, even weird numbers such as $\pi$. You just have to make sure that the bases are the same.

$$5^3 \times 5^6 = 5^9 \qquad \pi \times \pi^2 = \pi^3$$

The rule also works with variables in the exponent.

$$2^3 \times 2^z = 2^{(3+z)} \qquad 6(6^x) = 6^1 \times 6^x = 6^{1+x} \text{ or } 6^{x+1}$$

You can choose whether to use parentheses around the exponent, as in the first example—this can help to minimize careless mistakes. If you don't think you're likely to make a careless mistake here, then feel free to skip the parentheses, as in the second example.

## Check Your Skills

Simplify the following expressions.

2. $b^5 \times b^7$
3. $(x^3)(x^4)$

*Answers can be found on page 117.*

# Divide Terms with Same Base: Subtract the Exponents

Now divide a string of five $a$'s by a string of three $a$'s. Again, these are strings of *multiplied a*'s. What is the result?

$$\frac{a \times a \times a \times a \times a}{a \times a \times a} = \frac{a \times \cancel{a} \times \cancel{a} \times \cancel{a} \times a}{\cancel{a} \times \cancel{a} \times \cancel{a}} = a \times a$$

In exponential notation, you have this: $\dfrac{a^5}{a^3} = a^2$

What happens to the exponents? You subtract the bottom exponent from the top exponent: $5 - 3 = 2$.

*When you divide exponential terms that have the same base, subtract the exponents.*

This rule works the same for numbers as for variables.

$$\frac{2^{16}}{2^{13}} = 2^{16-13} = 2^3 = 8 \qquad\qquad \frac{x^y}{x^2} = x^{y-2}$$

As before, treat any term without an exponent as if it had an exponent of 1.

$$\frac{f^9}{f} = \frac{f^9}{f^1} = f^8$$

Just make sure that the bases are the same. If the bases are not the same, then you can't combine the two terms into one.

MANHATTAN PREP

Here's the rule book so far.

| If you... | Then you... | Like this: |
|---|---|---|
| Multiply exponential terms that have the same base | Add the exponents | $a^2 \times a^3 = a^5$ |
| Divide exponential terms that have the same base | Subtract the exponents | $\dfrac{a^5}{a^3} = a^2$ |

## Check Your Skills

Simplify the following expressions.

4. $\dfrac{y^5}{y^2}$

5. $\dfrac{d^8}{d^7}$

*Answers can be found on page 117.*

# Pretty Much Anything to the Power of Zero: One

Divide a string of five *a*'s by a string of five *a*'s. As before, each string is internally multiplied. What do you get?

Using longhand, you get 1.

$$\frac{a \times a \times a \times a \times a}{a \times a \times a \times a \times a} = \frac{\not{a} \times \not{a} \times \not{a} \times \not{a} \times \not{a}}{\not{a} \times \not{a} \times \not{a} \times \not{a} \times \not{a}} = 1$$

Using the exponent subtraction rule, you get $a^0$.

$$\frac{a^5}{a^5} = a^{5-5} = a^0$$

So $a^0$ must equal 1. That's true for practically any value of *a*. For example:

$$1^0 = 1 \qquad 6.2^0 = 1 \qquad (-4)^0 = 1 \qquad \left(\frac{3}{4}\right)^0 = 1 \qquad \left(\sqrt{2}\right)^0 = 1$$

The *only* base value for which this doesn't work is 0 itself. The expression $0^0$ is called *undefined*. Notice that the exponent subtraction rule above required you to divide by *a*. Since you can't divide by 0, you can't raise 0 to the 0 power either. The GMAT will never ask you to do so.

For any nonzero value of *a*, $a^0 = 1$.

Now you can extend the powers of 2 to include $2^0$.

<u>Powers of 2</u>

$2^0 = 1$

$2^1 = 2$

$2^2 = 4$

$2^3 = 8$

$2^4 = 16$

Notice the pattern: Each power of 2 is 2 times the previous power of 2.

# Negative Power: One Over a Positive Power

What happens if you divide a string of three $a$'s by a string of five $a$'s?

Using longhand, you get a leftover $a^2$ in the denominator of the fraction.

$$\frac{a \times a \times a}{a \times a \times a \times a \times a} = \frac{\cancel{a} \times \cancel{a} \times \cancel{a}}{a \times a \times \cancel{a} \times \cancel{a} \times \cancel{a}} = \frac{1}{a \times a} = \frac{1}{a^2}$$

Using the exponent subtraction rule, you get $a^{-2}$.

$$\frac{a^3}{a^5} = a^{3-5} = a^{-2}$$

So those two results must be equal. *Something with a negative exponent is "1 over" that same thing with a positive exponent.*

$$a^{-2} \qquad\qquad = \qquad\qquad \frac{1}{a^2}$$

$a$ to the negative two          equals          one over $a$ squared

In other words, $a^{-2}$ is equal to the **reciprocal** of $a^2$. The reciprocal of 5 is 1 *over* 5, or $\frac{1}{5}$. You can also think of reciprocals this way: Something times its reciprocal always equals 1. For example:

$$5 \times \frac{1}{5} = 1 \qquad\qquad a^2 \times \frac{1}{a^2} = 1 \qquad\qquad a^2 \times a^{-2} = a^{2-2} = a^0 = 1$$

Now you can extend the powers of 2 to include negative exponents.

<u>Powers of 2</u>

$$2^{-3} = \frac{1}{2^3} = \frac{1}{8} = 0.125$$

$$2^{-2} = \frac{1}{2^2} = \frac{1}{4} = 0.25$$

$$2^{-1} = \frac{1}{2} = 0.5$$

$$2^0 = 1$$
$$2^1 = 2$$
$$2^2 = 4$$
$$2^3 = 8$$
$$2^4 = 16$$

The pattern still holds! Each power of 2 is 2 times the previous power of 2.

The rules you've seen so far work the same for negative exponents.

$$5^{-3} \times 5^{-6} = 5^{-3 + (-6)} = 5^{-9}$$

$$\frac{x^3}{x^{-5}} = x^{3-(-5)} = x^8$$

Negative exponents are tricky, so it can be useful to *rewrite negative exponents using positive exponents*. A negative exponent in a term on top of a fraction becomes positive when you move the term to the bottom.

$$\frac{5x^{-2}}{y^3} = \frac{5}{x^2 y^3}$$

Here, $x^{-2}$ moved from the numerator to the denominator and the sign of the exponent switched from $-2$ to 2. Everything else stayed the same.

Likewise, a negative exponent in the bottom of a fraction becomes positive when the term moves to the top.

$$\frac{3}{z^{-4} w^2} = \frac{3z^4}{w^2}$$

Here, $z^{-4}$ moved from the denominator to the numerator and the sign of the exponent switched from $-4$ to 4.

If you move the entire denominator, leave a 1 behind.

$$\frac{1}{z^{-4}} = \frac{1 \times z^4}{1} = z^4$$

The same is true for a numerator.

$$\frac{w^{-5}}{2} = \frac{1}{2w^5}$$

*Don't confuse the sign of the base with the sign of the exponent.* The sign of the base does not change.

A positive base raised to a negative exponent stays positive. For example:

$$3^{-3} = \frac{1}{3^3} = \frac{1}{27}$$

A negative base stays negative. Odd powers of a negative base still produce negative numbers.

$$(-4)^{-3} = \frac{1}{(-4)^3} = \frac{1}{-64} = -\frac{1}{64}$$

Even powers of a negative base still produce positive numbers.

$$\frac{1}{(-6)^{-2}} = (-6)^2 = 36$$

Here are additional rules for the rule book.

| If you… | Then you… | Like this: |
|---------|-----------|------------|
| Raise anything to the power of zero (besides zero itself) | Get 1 | $a^0 = 1$ |
| Raise anything to a negative power | Get 1 over that same thing to the corresponding positive power | $a^{-2} = \dfrac{1}{a^2}$ |
| Move a term from top to bottom of a fraction (or vice versa) | Switch the sign of the exponent | $\dfrac{2a^{-2}}{3} = \dfrac{2}{3a^2}$ |

## Check Your Skills

Simplify the following expressions.

6. $2^{-3}$

7. $\dfrac{1}{3^{-3}}$

*Answers can be found on page 117.*

# Apply Two Exponents: Multiply the Exponents

How do you simplify this expression?

$(a^2)^4$

Use the definition of exponents. First you square $a$. Next, you multiply four separate $a^2$ terms together. In longhand:

$(a^2)^4 = a^2 \times a^2 \times a^2 \times a^2 = a^{2+2+2+2} = a^8$

What happens to the exponents 2 and 4? You multiply them: $2 \times 4 = 8$. On each side, you have eight $a$'s multiplied together.

*When you raise something that already has an exponent to another power, multiply the two exponents together.*

Always keep these two cases straight:

If you multiply the bases, *add* the exponents.          $a^2 \times a^4 = a^{2+4} = a^6$

If you raise a power to a power, *multiply* the exponents.          $(a^2)^4 = a^{2 \times 4} = a^8$

If you see see *two* bases multiplied together, as in $a^2 \times a^4$, then you'll add the exponents. If you see just *one* base with two exponents, as in $(a^2)^4$, then you'll multiply the exponents.

The "apply two exponents" rule works perfectly with negative exponents as well.

$$(x^{-3})^5 = x^{-3 \times 5} = x^{-15}$$

$$(4^{-2})^{-3} = 4^{-2 \times -3} = 4^6$$

| If you... | Then you... | Like this: |
|-----------|-------------|------------|
| Raise something to two successive powers | Multiply the powers | $(a^2)^4 = a^8$ |

Put it all together. Now you can handle this expression:

$$\frac{x^{-3}\left(x^2\right)^4}{x^5}$$

First, simplify the parentheses $(x^2)^4$.

$$(x^2)^4 = x^{2 \times 4} = x^8$$

The fraction now reads:

$$\frac{x^{-3}x^8}{x^5}$$

Now follow the rules for multiplying and dividing terms that have the same base. That is, add and subtract the exponents.

$$\frac{x^{-3}x^8}{x^5} = x^{-3+8-5} = x^0 = 1$$

If you have *different* bases that are numbers, try breaking the bases down to prime factors. You might discover that you can express everything in terms of one base. For example:

$$2^2 \times 4^3 \times 16 =$$

(A) $2^6$

(B) $2^{12}$

(C) $2^{18}$

The bases are all different, but they have something in common: Both 4 and 16 are powers of 2. Try rewriting those terms with 2 as the base.

$$4 = 2^2 \text{ and } 16 = 2^4$$

Everything can now be expressed with 2 as the base.

$$
\begin{aligned}
2^2 \times 4^3 \times 16 \quad &= 2^2 \times (2^2)^3 \times 2^4 \\
&= 2^2 \times 2^6 \times 2^4 \\
&= 2^{2+6+4} \\
&= 2^{12}
\end{aligned}
$$

The correct answer is (B).

## Check Your Skills

Simplify the following expressions.

8. $\left(x^3\right)^4$

9. $\dfrac{a^{15}}{a^0\left(a^3\right)^3}$

*Answers can be found on page 117.*

# Apply an Exponent to a Product: Apply the Exponent to Each Factor

Consider this expression:

$(xy)^3$

How can you rewrite this? Use the definition of exponents. You multiply three $xy$ terms together.

$(xy)^3 = xy \times xy \times xy$

So you have three $x$'s multiplied together and three $y$'s multiplied together. You can group these separately, because everything's multiplied.

$(xy)^3 = xy \times xy \times xy = (x \times x \times x)(y \times y \times y) = x^3 y^3$

*When you apply an exponent to a product, apply the exponent to each factor in the product.*

This rule works with every kind of base and exponent you've seen so far. For example:

$(3x)^4 = 3^4 x^4 = 81x^4$

$(wz^3)^x = w^x z^{3x}$

$\left(2^{-2} y^2\right)^{-3} = 2^{-2\times-3} y^{2\times-3} = 2^6 y^{-6} = 64y^{-6} = \dfrac{64}{y^6}$

Do the same thing with division. In particular, if you raise an entire fraction to a power, separately apply the exponent to the numerator and to the denominator.

$\left(\dfrac{3}{4}\right)^{-2} = \dfrac{3^{-2}}{4^{-2}} = \dfrac{4^2}{3^2} = \dfrac{16}{9}$

In this example, the top and the bottom of the fraction each have a negative exponent. In this case, you can flip the whole fraction and get rid of the negative exponents in both pieces.

Notice that the following case is different.

$\dfrac{3^{-2}}{4} = \dfrac{1}{4\times3^2} = \dfrac{1}{36}$

**MANHATTAN** PREP

In $\dfrac{3^{-2}}{4}$, the exponent applies only to the numerator (3). Respect PEMDAS, as always. Here's more for the rule book.

| If you... | Then you... | Like this: |
|---|---|---|
| Apply an exponent to a product | Apply the exponent to each factor in the product | $(ab)^3 = a^3 b^3$ |
| Apply an exponent to an entire fraction | Apply the exponent separately to the top and bottom | $\left(\dfrac{a}{b}\right)^4 = \dfrac{a^4}{b^4}$ |

You can use this principle to write the prime factorization of big numbers without computing those numbers directly. For example:

What is the prime factorization of $18^3$?

Don't multiply out $18 \times 18 \times 18$. Instead, figure out the prime factorization of 18 itself, then apply the rule above.

$18 = 2 \times 9 = 2 \times 3^2$

$18^3 = (2 \times 3^2)^3 = 2^3 \times 3^6 = 2^3 3^6$

The prime factorization of $18^3$ is 2, 2, 2, 3, 3, 3, 3, 3, 3.

Simplify this harder example.

$$\dfrac{12^2 \times 8}{18} =$$

First, break each base into its prime factors.

$12 = 2^2 \times 3 \qquad\qquad 8 = 2^3 \qquad\qquad 18 = 2 \times 3^2$

$$\dfrac{12^2 \times 8}{18} = \dfrac{\left(2^2 \times 3\right)^2 \times 2^3}{2 \times 3^2}$$

Next, apply the exponent to the parentheses.

$$\dfrac{\left(2^2 \times 3\right)^2 \times 2^3}{2 \times 3^2} = \dfrac{2^4 \times 3^2 \times 2^3}{2 \times 3^2}$$

Finally, combine the terms with 2 as their base. Remember that a 2 without a written exponent really has an exponent of 1. Separately, combine the terms with 3 as their base.

$$\dfrac{2^4 \times 3^2 \times 2^3}{2 \times 3^2} = 2^{4+3-1} \times 3^{2-2} = 2^6 \times 3^0 = 2^6 \times 1 = 2^6 = 64$$

Occasionally, it's faster *not* to break down all the way to primes. If you spot a greater common base, feel free to use it. Try this example:

$$\dfrac{36^3}{6^4} =$$

You can simplify this expression by breaking 36 and 6 down to primes. But if you recognize that $36 = 6^2$, then you can go much faster.

$$\frac{36^3}{6^4} = \frac{\left(6^2\right)^3}{6^4} = \frac{6^6}{6^4} = 6^2 = 36$$

One last point: Be ready to rewrite $a^3b^3$ as $(ab)^3$.

Consider $2^4 \times 3^4$. Here's a way to see that $2^4 \times 3^4$ equals $(2 \times 3)^4$, or $6^4$:

$$2^4 \times 3^4 = (2 \times 2 \times 2 \times 2) \times (3 \times 3 \times 3 \times 3)$$

$$= (2 \times 3) \times (2 \times 3) \times (2 \times 3) \times (2 \times 3) \qquad \text{by regrouping}$$

$$= (2 \times 3)^4 = 6^4$$

More often you'll need to change $(ab)^3$ into $a^3b^3$, but occasionally it's handy to go in reverse.

| If you... | Then you... | Like this: |
|---|---|---|
| See two factors with the same exponent | Might regroup the factors as a product | $a^3b^3 = (ab)^3$ |

## Check Your Skills

Simplify the following expressions.

10. $\left(\dfrac{x^2y}{z^{-3}}\right)^2$

11. $\dfrac{75^3 \times 45^3}{15^8}$

*Answers can be found on pages 117–118.*

# Add or Subtract Terms with the Same Base: Pull Out a Common Factor

Every case so far in this chapter has involved *only* multiplication and division. What if you are adding or subtracting exponential terms?

Consider this example:

$$13^5 + 13^3 =$$

*Do **not** add the exponents* to get $13^8$. That is the answer to a similar but different question (namely, $13^5 \times 13^3$), so it can't also be the correct answer when the multiplication symbol has changed to an addition symbol.

Instead, *look for a common factor and pull it out*. Both $13^5$ and $13^3$ are divisible by $13^3$, so that's the common factor. If necessary, rewrite $13^5$ as $13^3 13^2$ first.

$$13^5 + 13^3 = 13^3 13^2 + 13^3 = 13^3(13^2 + 1)$$

  **MANHATTAN** PREP

You could go farther and rewrite $13^2$ as 169. The right answer choice would possibly look like this: $13^3(170)$.

Remember that whenever you pull a term out of itself (e.g., pull $13^3$ out of $13^3$), you'll always be left with 1.

If you were given $x$'s instead of 13's as bases, the factoring would work the same way.

$$x^5 + x^3 = x^3x^2 + x^3 = x^3(x^2 + 1)$$

Now try this example:

$3^8 - 3^7 - 3^6$

(A)  $3^6(5)$
(B)  $3^6$
(C)  $3^{-5}$

All three terms ($3^8$, $3^7$, and $3^6$) are divisible by $3^6$, so pull $3^6$ out of the expression.

$$3^8 - 3^7 - 3^6 = 3^6(3^2 - 3^1 - 1) = 3^6(9 - 3 - 1) = 3^6(5)$$

The correct answer is (A).

This time, note that when you're pulling from a term whose exponent is just one number higher, you're always left with that term to the first power: Pulling $3^6$ from $3^7$ returns $3^1$, which is the same as 3. Once you get used to that, feel free to skip the step of writing out $3^1$ and just write 3 (or whatever number is in the base) directly.

Now try to simplify this fraction:

$$\frac{3^4 + 3^5 + 3^6}{13}$$

Ignore the 13 on the bottom of the fraction for the moment. On the top, each term is divisible by $3^4$.

$$\frac{3^4 + 3^5 + 3^6}{13} = \frac{3^4\left(1 + 3^1 + 3^2\right)}{13}$$

Continue to simplify the small powers of 3 in the parentheses.

$$\frac{3^4 + 3^5 + 3^6}{13} = \frac{3^4\left(1 + 3^1 + 3^2\right)}{13} = \frac{3^4(1 + 3 + 9)}{13} = \frac{3^4(13)}{13}$$

The 13's on the top and bottom of the fraction can cancel.

$$\frac{3^4 + 3^5 + 3^6}{13} = \frac{3^4\left(1 + 3^1 + 3^2\right)}{13} = \frac{3^4(1 + 3 + 9)}{13} = \frac{3^4(\cancel{13})}{\cancel{13}} = 3^4$$

If you *don't* have the same bases in what you're adding or subtracting, you can't immediately factor. If the bases are numbers, break them down to smaller factors to see whether you now have anything in common. Try this example:

$4^6 + 20^6 =$

Again, don't answer the wrong question. $4^6 \times 20^6 = (4 \times 20)^6 = 80^6$, but that doesn't answer this question. This problem asks you to *add* $4^6$ and $20^6$, *not* multiply them.

Since 4 is a factor of 20, rewrite 20 as $4 \times 5$ and apply the exponent to that product.

$$4^6 + 20^6 = 4^6 + (4 \times 5)^6 = 4^6 + (4^6 \times 5^6)$$

Now pull out the common factor of $4^6$.

$$4^6 + 20^6 = 4^6 + (4 \times 5)^6 = 4^6 + (4^6 5^6) = 4^6(1 + 5^6)$$

That's as far as you'd reasonably go, given the size of $4^6$ and $5^6$. Finally, try simplifying this one:

$$4^5 + 20^3 =$$

Start it the same way as before. Rewrite 20 as $4 \times 5$ and apply the exponent.

$$4^5 + 20^3 = 4^5 + (4 \times 5)^3 = 4^5 + (4^3 \times 5^3)$$

Now the common factor is $4^3$, so pull it out:

$$4^5 + 20^3 = 4^5 + (4 \times 5)^3 = 4^5 + (4^3 \times 5^3) = (4^3 4^2) + (4^3 5^3) = 4^3(4^2 + 5^3)$$

The result isn't especially pretty, but it's legitimate. Here's more to add to the rule book:

| If you… | Then you… | Like this: |
|---|---|---|
| Add or subtract terms with the same base | Pull out the common factor | $2^3 + 2^5$ $= 2^3(1 + 2^2)$ |
| Add or subtract terms with different bases | Break down the bases and pull out the common factor | $2^3 + 6^3$ $= 2^3 + (2^3 3^3)$ $= 2^3(1 + 3^3)$ |

## Check Your Skills

Simplify the following expression by factoring out a common term.

12. $5^5 + 5^4 - 5^3$

*Answer can be found on page 118.*

## Roots: Opposite of Exponents

Squaring a number means raising it to the second power (or multiplying it by itself). Square-rooting a number undoes that process. For example:

| $3^2$ | $=$ | 9 | and | $\sqrt{9}$ | $=$ | 3 |
|---|---|---|---|---|---|---|
| Three squared | is | nine, | and | the square root of nine | is | three |

If you square-root first, then square, you get back to the original number.

$$\left(\sqrt{16}\right)^2 \qquad = \qquad \sqrt{16} \times \sqrt{16} \qquad = \qquad 16$$

| The square of the square root of sixteen | equals | the square root of sixteen times the square root of sixteen, | and that equals | sixteen |

If you square first, then square-root, you get back to the original number if the original number is positive.

$$\sqrt{5^2} \qquad = \qquad \sqrt{5 \times 5} \qquad = \qquad 5$$

| The square root of five squared | equals | the square root of five times five, | and that equals | five |

If the original number is negative, you just flip the sign, so you end up with a positive.

$$\sqrt{(-5)^2} \qquad = \qquad \sqrt{25} \qquad = \qquad 5$$

| The square root of the square of negative five | equals | the square root of twenty-five, | and that equals | five |

| If you... | Then you... | Like this: |
|-----------|-------------|------------|
| Square a square root | Get the original number | $\left(\sqrt{10}\right)^2 = 10$ |
| Square-root a square | Get the positive value of the original number | $\sqrt{10^2} = 10$ <br> $\sqrt{(-10)^2} = 10$ |

Because 9 is the square of an integer ($9 = 3^2$), 9 is called a **perfect square**: its square root is an integer. In contrast, 2 is not the square of an integer, so its square root is an ugly decimal, as you saw in Chapter 1.

Memorize the perfect squares on page 94 so you can take their square roots easily. Also memorize these approximations:

$$\sqrt{2} \approx 1.4 \qquad\qquad \sqrt{3} \approx 1.7$$

Here's a neat way to remember them: February 14th, or the date 2/14, is Valentine's Day, and March 17th, or the date 3/17, is St. Patrick's Day.

You can approximate the square root of a non-perfect square by looking at nearby perfect squares. Try this example:

$\sqrt{70}$ is between which two consecutive integers?

Two nearby perfect squares are 64 and 81. $\sqrt{64} = 8$ and $\sqrt{81} = 9$, so $\sqrt{70}$ must be between 8 and 9. It's almost halfway in between, so you could say that $\sqrt{70} \approx 8.5$.

When you take the square root of any number greater than 1, your answer will be smaller than the original number.

$$\sqrt{2} < 2 \qquad \sqrt{21} < 21 \qquad \sqrt{1.3} < 1.3$$

However, the square root of a number between 0 and 1 is *greater* than the original number.

$$\sqrt{0.5} > 0.5 \qquad\qquad \sqrt{\frac{2}{3}} > \frac{2}{3}$$

$$\sqrt{0.5} \approx 0.7 \qquad\qquad \left( \sqrt{\frac{2}{3}} \approx 0.8 \right)$$

Whether a number is greater than 1 or between 0 and 1, the square root of the number is **always closer to 1** than is the original number.

The square root of 1 is 1, since $1^2 = 1$. Likewise, the square root of 0 is 0, since $0^2 = 0$.

$$\sqrt{1} = 1 \qquad \sqrt{0} = 0$$

You cannot take the square root of a negative number in GMAT world. What is inside the radical sign must never be negative.

Likewise, the square root symbol never gives a negative result. This may seem strange. After all, both $5^2$ and $(-5)^2$ equal 25, so shouldn't the square root of 25 be either 5 or −5? No. Mathematicians like to have symbols mean one thing.

$$\sqrt{25} = 5, \text{ and that's that.}$$

When you see the square root symbol on the GMAT, *only consider the positive root.*

In contrast, when *you* take the square root of both sides of an equation, you have to consider both positive and negative roots.

$$x = \sqrt{25} \qquad \text{Solution: } x = 5$$
$$x^2 = 25 \qquad \text{Solutions: } x = 5 \text{ OR } x = -5$$

Be careful with square roots of variable expressions. The expression must not be negative, or the square root is illegal.

| If you... | Then you... | Like this: |
|---|---|---|
| Take the square root of a number greater than 1 | Get a smaller number (a number that is closer to 1) | $\sqrt{25} = 5$ |
| Take the square root of a number between 0 and 1 | Get a greater number (a number that is closer to 1) | $\sqrt{0.5} \approx 0.7$ |
| Take the square root of 1 or 0 | Get the number you started with | $\sqrt{1} = 1$ <br> $\sqrt{0} = 0$ |

## Check Your Skills

13. $\sqrt{27} \times \sqrt{27} =$

*Answer can be found on page 118.*

**3**

# Square Root: Power of One-Half

Consider this equation:

$$\left(9^x\right)^2 = 9$$

Rewrite the expression using the tools you already have.

$$\left(9^x\right)^2 = 9$$
$$9^{2x} = 9^1$$

Since the bases are equal, the exponents must also be equal. Therefore, $2x = 1$, or $x = \dfrac{1}{2}$.

Consider this equation:

$$\left(9^{\frac{1}{2}}\right)^2 = 9$$

The equation above is true because the exponents are multiplied together: $\left(\dfrac{1}{2}\right)(2) = 1$. You also learned earlier that $\left(\sqrt{9}\right)^2 = 9$.

Put these two equations together:

$$\text{If } \left(9^{\frac{1}{2}}\right)^2 = 9 \text{ and } \left(\sqrt{9}\right)^2 = 9,$$

$$\text{then } 9^{\frac{1}{2}} = \sqrt{9}.$$

For expressions with positive bases, *a square root is equivalent to an exponent of* $\dfrac{1}{2}$.

Try to simplify this example:

$$\sqrt{7^{22}} =$$

You can approach the problem in either of two ways.

1. Rewrite the square root as an exponent of $\dfrac{1}{2}$, then apply the two-exponent rule (multiply exponents).

$$\sqrt{7^{22}} = \left(7^{22}\right)^{\frac{1}{2}} = 7^{\frac{22}{2}} = 7^{11}$$

2. Rewrite what's inside the square root as a product of two identical numbers. The square root is therefore one of those numbers.

$$7^{22} = 7^{11} \times 7^{11}$$

$$\sqrt{7^{22}} = \sqrt{7^{11} \times 7^{11}} = 7^{11}$$

Notice that you get an exponent that is an integer. This tells you that the number $7^{22}$ is a perfect square, or the square of another integer: $7^{22} = \left(7^{11}\right)^2$. An integer raised to a positive, even power is always a perfect square.

Here's the rule book:

| If you... | Then you... | Like this: |
|---|---|---|
| Take a square root of a positive number raised to a power | Rewrite the square root as an exponent of $\frac{1}{2}$, then multiply exponents | $\sqrt{5^{12}} = \left(5^{12}\right)^{\frac{1}{2}}$ $= 5^6$ |
| | *OR* Rewrite what's inside the root as a product of two identical numbers | $\sqrt{5^{12}} = \sqrt{5^6 \times 5^6}$ $= 5^6$ |

Avoid changing the square root to an exponent of $\frac{1}{2}$ when you have variable expressions underneath the square root (or radical) sign, since the output depends on the sign of the variables.

## Check Your Skills

14. If $x$ is positive, $\sqrt{x^6} =$

*Answer can be found on page 118.*

# Cube Roots Undo Cubing

Cubing a number means raising it to the third power. Cube-rooting a number undoes that process. For example:

| $4^3$ | $=$ | $64$ | and | $\sqrt[3]{64}$ | $=$ | $4$ |
|---|---|---|---|---|---|---|
| Four cubed | is | sixty-four, | and | the cube root of sixty-four | is | four |

Many of the properties of square roots carry over to cube roots. You can approximate cube roots the same way.

$\sqrt[3]{66}$ is a little more than 4, but less than 5, because $\sqrt[3]{64} = 4$ and $\sqrt[3]{125} = 5$

Like square-rooting, cube-rooting a positive number pushes it toward 1.

$\sqrt[3]{17} < 17$      but      $\sqrt[3]{0.17} > 0.17$

The main difference in behavior between square roots and cube roots is that you *can* take the cube root of a negative number. You wind up with a negative number.

$\sqrt[3]{-64} = -4$      because $(-4)^3 = -64$

As a fractional exponent, cube roots are equivalent to exponents of $\frac{1}{3}$, just as square roots are equivalent to exponents of $\frac{1}{2}$. Going further, fourth roots are equivalent to exponents of $\frac{1}{4}$, and so on.

Now you can deal with **fractional exponents**. Consider this example:

$$8^{\frac{2}{3}} =$$

Rewrite $\frac{2}{3}$ as $2 \times \frac{1}{3}$, making two successive exponents. This is the same as squaring first, then cube-rooting.

$$8^{\frac{2}{3}} = 8^{2 \times \frac{1}{3}} = \left(8^2\right)^{\frac{1}{3}} = \sqrt[3]{8^2} = \sqrt[3]{64} = 4$$

You could also rewrite $\frac{2}{3}$ as $\frac{1}{3} \times 2$ instead, allowing you to take the cube root first and then square the result. Look at the numbers; which way is easier for this math?

$$8^{\frac{2}{3}} = 8^{\frac{1}{3} \times 2} = \left(8^{\frac{1}{3}}\right)^2 = \left(\sqrt[3]{8}\right)^2 = 2^2 = 4$$

Whichever path you choose, you don't have to write out every step of the math above. Talk yourself through the steps:

$\sqrt[3]{8^2}$ — First, I square the 8 to get 64, and then I take the cube root of the 64 to get 4.

$\left(\sqrt[3]{8}\right)^2$ — First, I take the cube root of 8 to get 2, and then I square the 2 to get 4.

| If you… | Then you… | Like this: |
|---|---|---|
| Raise a number to a fractional power | Apply two exponents—the numerator as a power and the denominator as a fractional root, in whatever order seems easiest to you | $125^{\frac{2}{3}} = \left(\sqrt[3]{125}\right)^2$ $= 5^2 = 25$ |

## Check Your Skills

15. $64^{2/3} =$

*Answer can be found on page 118.*

## Multiply Square Roots: Put Everything Under the Root

Consider this example:

$$\sqrt{8} \times \sqrt{2} =$$

Earlier, you learned that $8^a 2^a = (8 \times 2)^a$. This principle holds true for fractional exponents as well.

$$\sqrt{8} \times \sqrt{2} = 8^{\frac{1}{2}} \times 2^{\frac{1}{2}} = (8 \times 2)^{\frac{1}{2}} = \sqrt{8 \times 2}$$

In practice, you can usually skip the fractional exponents. *When you multiply separate square roots, you can put everything under the same radical sign.*

$$\sqrt{8} \times \sqrt{2} = \sqrt{8 \times 2} = \sqrt{16} = 4$$

This shortcut works for division, too. *When you divide square roots, you can put everything under the same radical sign.*

$$\frac{\sqrt{27}}{\sqrt{3}} = \sqrt{\frac{27}{3}} = \sqrt{9} = 3$$

As long as you're only multiplying and dividing, you can deal with more complicated expressions.

$$\frac{\sqrt{15} \times \sqrt{12}}{\sqrt{5}} = \sqrt{\frac{\cancel{15}^{3} \times 12}{\cancel{5}_{1}}} = \sqrt{36} = 6$$

Don't forget to simplify before you multiply!

| If you... | Then you... | Like this: |
|-----------|-------------|------------|
| Multiply or divide square roots | Combine everything under one radical sign, then simplify | $\sqrt{a} \times \sqrt{b} = \sqrt{ab}$  $\frac{\sqrt{a}}{\sqrt{b}} = \sqrt{\frac{a}{b}}$ |

## Check Your Skills

Simplify the following expressions.

16. $\sqrt{20} \times \sqrt{5}$

17. $\dfrac{\sqrt{216}}{\sqrt{2} \times \sqrt{3}}$

*Answers can be found on page 118.*

## Simplify Square Roots: Factor Out Squares

What does this product equal?

$$\sqrt{6} \times \sqrt{2} =$$

First, put everything under one radical.

$$\sqrt{6} \times \sqrt{2} = \sqrt{12}$$

You might think that you're done—after all, 12 is not a perfect square, so you won't get an integer out of $\sqrt{12}$. But what if you glance at the answers and $\sqrt{12}$ isn't there? It turns out that $\sqrt{12}$ is mathematically correct, but it can be simplified further.

Here's how: $12 = 4 \times 3$ and 4 is a perfect square, so it can be pulled out from under a square root sign.

$$\sqrt{12} = \sqrt{4 \times 3} = \sqrt{4} \times \sqrt{3}$$

Nicely, $\sqrt{4} = 2$, so finish up:

$$\sqrt{12} = \sqrt{4 \times 3} = \sqrt{4} \times \sqrt{3} = 2\sqrt{3}$$

If the answer you get isn't a perfect square itself but does have a perfect square as a factor, then the GMAT will typically expect you to simplify that answer as far as it can go. Glance at the answers before you actually do that simplification, just to make sure—but expect that you will probably have to do so.

*To simplify square roots, factor out squares.*

| If you… | Then you… | Like this: |
|---|---|---|
| Have the square root of a large number (or a root that doesn't match any answer choices) | Pull perfect-square factors out of the number under the radical sign | $\sqrt{50} = \sqrt{25 \times 2}$ $= \sqrt{25} \times \sqrt{2}$ $= 5\sqrt{2}$ |

Sometimes you can spot the square factor, if you know your perfect squares. Consider this example:

$$\sqrt{360} =$$

If you have your perfect squares memorized, then 360 will likely make you think of the perfect square 36.

$$\sqrt{360} = \sqrt{36 \times 10} = \sqrt{36} \times \sqrt{10} = 6\sqrt{10}$$

What if you don't spot a perfect square? You can always **break the number down to primes**. This method will take longer, but it will work when you need it.

Consider $\sqrt{12}$ again. The prime factorization of 12 is $2 \times 2 \times 3$, or $2^2 \times 3$. Therefore, you can break it down:

$$\sqrt{12} = \sqrt{2^2 \times 3} = \sqrt{2^2} \times \sqrt{3} = 2\sqrt{3}$$

Each pair of prime factors under the radical ($2 \times 2$, or $2^2$) turns into a single copy as it emerges (becoming the 2 in $2\sqrt{3}$). In this exercise, it can be useful to write out the prime factorization without exponents so that you can spot the prime pairs quickly.

Take $\sqrt{360}$ again. Say you don't spot the perfect square factor (36). Write out the prime factorization of 360.

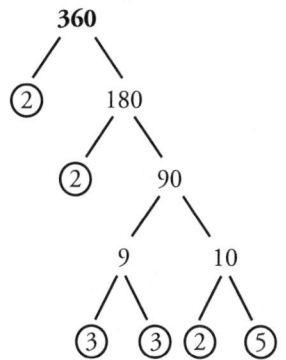

$$360 = 2 \times 2 \times 2 \times 3 \times 3 \times 5$$

Now pair off two 2's and two 3's, leaving an extra 2 and 5. Any pair of primes under a radical sign becomes a single copy of that prime outside the radical.

$$\sqrt{360} = \sqrt{2 \times 2} \times \sqrt{3 \times 3} \times \sqrt{2 \times 5} = 2 \times 3 \times \sqrt{2 \times 5} = 6\sqrt{10}$$

## Check Your Skills

Simplify the following roots.

18. $\sqrt{96}$

19. $\sqrt{225}$

*Answers can be found on page 118.*

# Add or Subtract Under the Root: Pull Out Common Square Factors

Consider this example:

$$\sqrt{3^2 + 4^2} =$$

Don't fall into the trap. You *cannot* break this root into $\sqrt{3^2} + \sqrt{4^2}$. You can only break up *products*, not sums, under the square root. For instance, this is correct:

$$\sqrt{3^2 \times 4^2} = \sqrt{3^2} \times \sqrt{4^2} = 3 \times 4 = 12$$

But you can't do that when you're adding under the root. To evaluate $\sqrt{3^2 + 4^2}$, follow PEMDAS under the radical, *then* take the square root.

$$\sqrt{3^2 + 4^2} = \sqrt{9 + 16} = \sqrt{25} = 5$$

The same goes for subtraction.

$$\sqrt{13^2 - 5^2} = \sqrt{169 - 25} = \sqrt{144} = 12$$

Often, you have to crunch the numbers if they're small. However, when the numbers get large, the GMAT will give you a necessary shortcut: factoring out squares.

You'll need to find a square factor that is common to both terms under the radical. Consider this example:

$$\sqrt{3^{10} + 3^{11}} =$$

First, consider $3^{10} + 3^{11}$ by itself. What is the greatest factor that the two terms in the sum have in common? $3^{10}$. Note that $3^{11} = 3^{10} \times 3$. Therefore, you can put that in the equation:

$$3^{10} + 3^{11} = 3^{10}(1 + 3) = 3^{10}(4)$$

Now plug that back into the square root.

$$\sqrt{3^{10} + 3^{11}} = \sqrt{3^{10}(1+3)} = \sqrt{3^{10}(4)} = \sqrt{3^{10}} \times \sqrt{4}$$

Since $3^{10} = \left(3^5\right)^2$, $\sqrt{3^{10}} = 3^5$.

Alternatively, apply the square root as an exponent of $\dfrac{1}{2}$.

$$\sqrt{3^{10}} = \left(3^{10}\right)^{\frac{1}{2}} = 3^{\frac{10}{2}} = 3^5$$

And, of course, $\sqrt{4} = 2$. Plug everything back in.

$$\sqrt{3^{10} + 3^{11}} = \sqrt{3^{10}(1+3)} = \sqrt{3^{10}(4)} = \sqrt{3^{10}} \times \sqrt{4} = 3^5 \times 2$$

The answer also might be in the form $3^5(2)$.

| If you… | Then you… | Like this: |
|---|---|---|
| Add or subtract underneath the square root symbol | Factor out a square factor from the sum or difference  OR  Go ahead and crunch the numbers as written, *if they're small* | $\sqrt{4^{14} + 4^{16}} = \sqrt{4^{14}\left(1+4^2\right)}$ $= \sqrt{4^{14}} \times \sqrt{1+16}$ $= 4^7\sqrt{17}$ $\sqrt{6^2 + 8^2} = \sqrt{36+64}$ $= \sqrt{100} = 10$ |

## Check Your Skills

20. $\sqrt{10^5 - 10^4} =$

*Answer can be found on page 118.*

# Check Your Skills Answer Key

1. **$(-5)^8$:** $-5^8 = -1 \times 5^8$, and is thus negative. $(-5)^8$ will be positive, since the exponent is even. A positive is always greater than a negative.

2. **$b^{12}$:** The bases are the same, so add the exponents.
   $$b^5 \times b^7 = b^{5+7} = b^{12}$$

3. **$x^7$:** The bases are the same, so add the exponents.
   $$x^3 \times x^4 = x^{3+4} = x^7$$

4. **$y^3$:** The bases are the same, so subtract the bottom exponent from the top exponent.
   $$\frac{y^5}{y^2} = y^{5-2} = y^3$$

5. **$d$ or $d^1$:** The bases are the same, so subtract the bottom exponent from the top exponent. $d^1$ is more commonly written $d$.
   $$\frac{d^8}{d^7} = d^{8-7} = d^1 = d$$

6. **$\dfrac{1}{8}$:**
   $$2^{-3} = \frac{1}{2^3} = \frac{1}{8}$$

7. **27:**
   $$\frac{1}{3^{-3}} = 3^3 = 27$$

8. **$x^{12}$:**
   $$(x^3)^4 = x^{3 \times 4} = x^{12}$$

9. **$a^6$:**
   $$\frac{a^{15}}{a^0 \left(a^3\right)^3} = \frac{a^{15}}{a^0 a^9} = a^{15-0-9} = a^6$$

10. **$x^4 y^2 z^6$:**
   $$\left(\frac{x^2 y}{z^{-3}}\right)^2 = \frac{x^{2 \times 2} y^{1 \times 2}}{z^{-3 \times 2}} = \frac{x^4 y^2}{z^{-6}} = x^4 y^2 z^6$$

11. **15:**

$$\frac{75^3 \times 45^3}{15^8} = \frac{\left(3 \times 5^2\right)^3 \times \left(3^2 \times 5\right)^3}{\left(3 \times 5\right)^8} = \frac{3^3 \times 5^6 \times 3^6 \times 5^3}{3^8 \times 5^8} = \frac{3^9 5^9}{3^8 5^8} = 3^1 5^1 = 15$$

12. **$5^3(5^2 + 5 - 1)$ or $5^3(29)$:**

$$5^5 + 5^4 - 5^3 = 5^3(5^2 + 5^1 - 1) = 5^3(25 + 5 - 1) = 5^3(29)$$

13. **27:** Any square root times itself equals the number underneath the square root symbol.

14. **$x^3$:** Since $x$ is positive, $x^3$ is positive, too.

$$\sqrt{x^6} = \sqrt{x^3 \times x^3} = x^3$$

15. **16:**

$$64^{\frac{2}{3}} = \left(\sqrt[3]{64}\right)^2 = 4^2 = 16$$

You could also square the 64 first, but that would be very annoying math to do without a calculator.

16. **10:**

$$\sqrt{20} \times \sqrt{5} = \sqrt{20 \times 5} = \sqrt{100} = 10$$

17. **6:**

$$\frac{\sqrt{216}}{\sqrt{2} \times \sqrt{3}} = \sqrt{\frac{\overset{108}{\cancel{216}}}{\cancel{2} \times 3}} = \sqrt{\frac{108}{3}} = \sqrt{36} = 6$$

Simplify before you multiply!

18. **$4\sqrt{6}$ :**

$$\sqrt{96} = \sqrt{3 \times (2 \times 2) \times (2 \times 2) \times 2} = (2 \times 2)\sqrt{3 \times 2} = 4\sqrt{6}$$

19. **15:** Did you recognize this root? This is one of the common ones; if you have it memorized, you don't have to do any work at all! The square root of 225 is 15. Here's the math:

$$\sqrt{225} = \sqrt{(3 \times 3) \times (5 \times 5)} = 3 \times 5 = 15$$

20. **300:**

$$\sqrt{10^5 - 10^4} = \sqrt{10^4(10 - 1)} = \sqrt{10^4 9} = 10^2 \times 3 = 300$$

# Chapter Review: Drill Sets

## Drill 1

Simplify the following expressions by combining like terms. If the base is a number, leave the answer in exponential form (e.g., use $2^3$, not 8).

1. $x^5 \times x^3$
2. $7^6 \times 7^9$
3. $\dfrac{5^5}{5^3}$
4. $(a^3)^2$
5. $7^{-4} \times 7^3$
6. $\dfrac{(-3)^a}{(-3)^2}$
7. $(3^2)^{-3}$
8. $\dfrac{11^4}{11^x}$
9. $x^2 \times x^3 \times x^5$
10. $(5^2)^x$

## Drill 2

Simplify the following expressions by combining like terms. If the base is a number, leave the answer in exponential form (e.g., use $2^3$, not 8).

11. $3^4 \times 3^2 \times 3$
12. $\dfrac{x^5 \times x^6}{x^2}$
13. $\dfrac{5^6 \times 5^{4x}}{5^4}$
14. $y^7 \times y^8 \times y^{-6}$
15. $\dfrac{x^4}{x^{-3}}$
16. $\dfrac{z^5 \times z^{-3}}{z^{-8}}$
17. $\dfrac{3^{2x} \times 3^{6x}}{3^{-3y}}$
18. $(x^2)^6 \times x^3$
19. $(m^y)^5 \times m^{y+5}$
20. $\dfrac{\left(2^x\right)^{-2} \times 2^3}{2^{2x}}$

## Drill 3

Follow the directions for each question.

21. Compute the sum of $27^{\frac{1}{3}} + 9^{\frac{1}{2}} + \dfrac{3}{9^0}$.

22. Which of the following has the greatest value?
    (A) $-5^6$
    (B) $6^{-5}$
    (C) $(-6)^5$
    (D) $(-5)^6$
    (E) $5^{-6}$

23. Compute the sum of $6^{-3} - \left(\dfrac{1}{6}\right)^3 + 8^{\frac{2}{3}}$.

24. Which of the following is equal to $\left(\dfrac{4}{7}\right)^{-4}$?
    (A) $-\left(\dfrac{4}{7}\right)^4$
    (B) $\left(\dfrac{7}{4}\right)^4$
    (C) $\left(\dfrac{4}{7}\right)^{\frac{1}{4}}$
    (D) $\left(-\dfrac{4}{7}\right)^{\frac{1}{4}}$
    (E) $-\left(\dfrac{7}{4}\right)^4$

25. Which of the following has a value less than 1? (Select all that apply.)
    (A) $\dfrac{2^{-2}}{3^0}$
    (B) $\dfrac{3^{-2}}{4^{-2}}$
    (C) $\dfrac{(-3)^3}{(-5)^2}$
    (D) $\left(\dfrac{2}{3}\right)^{-2}$
    (E) $(-4)^3$

## Drill 4

Simplify the following expressions by finding common bases. If the base is a number, leave the answer in exponential form (e.g., use $2^3$, not 8).

26. $8^3 \times 2^6$

27. $\dfrac{36^3}{6^4}$

28. $25^4 \times 125^3$

29. $9^{-2} \times 27^2$

30. $2^{-7} \times 8^2$

## Drill 5

Simplify the following expressions by pulling out as many common factors as possible.

31. $6^3 + 3^3$
    (A) $3^5$
    (B) $3^9$
    (C) $2(3^3)$

32. $81^3 + 27^4$
    (A) $3^7(2)$
    (B) $3^{12}(2)$
    (C) $3^{14}$

33. $15^2 - 5^2$
    (A) $5^2(2)$
    (B) $5^2 2^3$
    (C) $5^2 3^2$

34. $4^3 + 4^3 + 4^3 + 4^3 + 3^2 + 3^2 + 3^2$
    (A) $4^4 + 3^3$
    (B) $4^{12} + 3^6$
    (C) $4^3(3^2)$

35. $\dfrac{3^{12} - 9^4}{27^2 + 9^4}$
    (A) $3^2(8)$
    (B) $\dfrac{5}{3^3}$
    (C) $3^3(20)$

## Drill 6

Simplify the following expressions. All final answers should be integers.

36. $\sqrt{3} \times \sqrt{27}$

37. $\sqrt{2} \times \sqrt{18}$

38. $\dfrac{\sqrt{48}}{\sqrt{3}}$

39. $\sqrt{5} \times \sqrt{45}$

40. $\dfrac{\sqrt{5,000}}{\sqrt{50}}$

41. $\sqrt{36} \times \sqrt{4}$

42. $\dfrac{\sqrt{128}}{\sqrt{2}}$

43. $\dfrac{\sqrt{54} \times \sqrt{3}}{\sqrt{2}}$

44. $\dfrac{\sqrt{640}}{\sqrt{2} \times \sqrt{5}}$

45. $\dfrac{\sqrt{48} \times \sqrt{7}}{\sqrt{21}}$

## Drill 7

Simplify the following roots. Not every answer will be an integer.

46. $\sqrt{32}$

47. $\sqrt{24}$

48. $\sqrt{180}$

49. $\sqrt{490}$

50. $\sqrt{216}$

51. $\sqrt{135}$

52. $\sqrt{224}$

53. $\sqrt{343}$

54. $\sqrt{208}$

55. $\sqrt{432}$

# Drill 8

Simplify the following roots. You will be able to eliminate the root completely in every question. Express answers as integers.

56. $\sqrt{36^2 + 15^2}$

57. $\sqrt{35^2 - 21^2}$

58. $\sqrt{10(11^5 - 11^4)}$

59. $\sqrt{8^4 + 8^5}$

60. $\sqrt{2^9 + 2^7 - 2^6}$

61. $\sqrt{50^3 - 50^2}$

62. $\sqrt{\dfrac{10\left(13^4 + 13^2\right)}{17}}$

63. $\sqrt{5^7 - 5^5 + 5^4}$

# Drill Sets Solutions

## Drill 1

1. $x^8$:

   $$x^5 \times x^3 = x^{(5+3)} = x^8$$

2. $7^{15}$:

   $$7^6 \times 7^9 = 7^{(6+9)} = 7^{15}$$

3. $5^2$:

   $$\frac{5^5}{5^3} = 5^{(5-3)} = 5^2$$

4. $a^6$:

   $$(a^3)^2 = a^{(3 \times 2)} = a^6$$

5. $7^{-1}$ or $\dfrac{1}{7}$:

   $$7^{-4} \times 7^3 = 7^{(-4+3)} = 7^{-1} = \frac{1}{7}$$

6. $(-3)^{a-2}$:

   $$\frac{(-3)^a}{(-3)^2} = (-3)^{(a-2)}$$

7. $3^{-6}$:

   $$(3^2)^{-3} = 3^{(2 \times -3)} = 3^{-6}$$

8. $11^{4-x}$:

   $$\frac{11^4}{11^x} = 11^{(4-x)}$$

9. $x^{10}$:

   $$x^2 \times x^3 \times x^5 = x^{(2+3+5)} = x^{10}$$

10. $5^{2x}$:

    $$(5^2)^x = 5^{(2 \times x)} = 5^{2x}$$

## Drill 2

11. $3^7$:

$$3^4 \times 3^2 \times 3 = 3^{(4+2+1)} = 3^7$$

12. $x^9$:

$$\frac{x^5 \times x^6}{x^2} = x^{(5+6-2)} = x^9$$

13. $5^{4x+2}$:

$$\frac{5^6 \times 5^{4x}}{5^4} = 5^{(6+4x-4)} = 5^{4x+2}$$

14. $y^9$:

$$y^7 \times y^8 \times y^{-6} = y^{(7+8+(-6))} = y^9$$

15. $x^7$:

$$\frac{x^4}{x^{-3}} = x^{(4-(-3))} = x^7$$

16. $z^{10}$:

$$= \frac{z^5 \times z^{-3}}{z^{-8}} = z^{(5+(-3)-(-8))} = z^{10}$$

17. $3^{8x+3y}$:

$$\frac{3^{2x} \times 3^{6x}}{3^{-3y}} = 3^{(2x+6x-(-3y))} = 3^{8x+3y}$$

18. $x^{15}$:

$$(x^2)^6 \times x^3 = x^{(2 \times 6 + 3)} = x^{(12+3)} = x^{15}$$

19. $m^{6y+5}$:

$$(m^y)^5 \times m^{y+5} = m^{(5 \times y + y + 5)} = m^{(5y+y+5)} = m^{6y+5}$$

20. $2^{-4x+3}$:

$$\frac{\left(2^x\right)^{-2} \times 2^3}{2^{2x}} = 2^{-2 \times x + 3 - 2x} = 2^{(-2x+3-2x)} = 2^{-4x+3}$$

## Drill 3

21. **9**: If you are comfortable handling fractional exponents, you do not need to rewrite those forms using radical signs, as shown below.

$$27^{\frac{1}{3}} + 9^{\frac{1}{2}} + \frac{3}{9^0} = \sqrt[3]{27} + \sqrt{9} + \frac{3}{1} = 3 + 3 + 3 = 9$$

**MANHATTAN** PREP

22. **(D):** The question asks for the answer with the greatest value. How can you compare efficiently? In general, don't calculate actual values unless you have to; without a calculator, this math would be messy.

(A) $-5^6$: Since there are no parentheses around $-5$, apply the exponent first, then apply the negative. This value will be negative, so if any answer is positive, that answer will automatically be greater than this answer.

(B) $6^{-5}$. A positive value raised to a negative power always stays positive. Cross off answer (A). To get rid of the negative exponent, take the reciprocal: $\dfrac{1}{6^5}$.

(C) $(-6)^5$. A negative number raised to an odd exponent will stay negative. Answer (B) is positive, so eliminate this choice.

(D) $(-5)^6$. A negative number raised to an even exponent will turn positive. This value is equivalent to $5^6$, which is greater than answer (B). Eliminate (B).

(E) $5^{-6}$. This choice is similar to choice (B): to get rid of the negative, take the reciprocal: $\dfrac{1}{5^6}$. This is also smaller than answer (D), so eliminate (E).

23. **4:**

$$6^{-3} - \left(\frac{1}{6}\right)^3 + 8^{\frac{2}{3}} = \frac{1}{6^3} - \frac{1^3}{6^3} + \left(\sqrt[3]{8}\right)^2 = \frac{1}{6^3} - \frac{1}{6^3} + 2^2 = 4$$

The first two terms in the expression are in fact the same. Because these terms are equal, when the second is subtracted from the first, they cancel out leaving only the third term.

24. **(B):** Make the answer choices work for you. Glance at them before you start manipulating the given statement. Two of them flip the fraction and the question prompt has a negative exponent, which involves taking a reciprocal or flipping a fraction. Try that:

$$\left(\frac{4}{7}\right)^{-4} = \left(\frac{7}{4}\right)^4$$

25. **(A), (C), and (E):** The problem asks for values less than 1, so any expressions with negative values, zero itself, or values between 0 and 1 will work:

(A) $\dfrac{2^{-2}}{3^0} = \dfrac{1}{3^0 \times 2^2} = \dfrac{1}{1 \times 4} = \dfrac{1}{4}$

Answer (A) is less than 1. Note: Dividing a smaller positive number by a greater positive number will result in a number less than 1. If you know this, you can stop at the second step.

(B) $\dfrac{3^{-2}}{4^{-2}} = \dfrac{4^2}{3^2} = \dfrac{16}{9}$

Answer (B) is greater than 1. Note: Dividing a greater positive number by a smaller positive number will result in a number greater than 1. If you know this, you can stop at the second step.

$$(C) \quad \frac{(-3)^3}{(-5)^2} = \frac{-27}{25} = \text{negative}$$

Answer (C) is negative; therefore, it is less than 1. As soon as you realize this one is negative, you can stop.

$$(D) \quad \left(\frac{2}{3}\right)^{-2} = \left(\frac{3}{2}\right)^2 = \frac{3^2}{2^2} = \frac{9}{4}$$

Answer (D) is greater than 1. As with (B), dividing a greater positive number by a smaller positive number will result in a number greater than 1.

$$(E) \quad (-4)^3 = \text{negative}$$

Answer (E) is negative; therefore, it is less than 1.

# Drill 4

26. $2^{15}$:
$$8^3 \times 2^6 = (2^3)^3 \times 2^6 = 2^9 \times 2^6 = 2^{9+6} = 2^{15}$$

27. $6^2$:
$$\frac{36^3}{6^4} = \frac{(6^2)^3}{6^4} = \frac{6^6}{6^4} = 6^{6-4} = 6^2$$

28. $5^{17}$:
$$25^4 \times 125^3 = (5^2)^4 \times (5^3)^3 = 5^8 \times 5^9 = 5^{17}$$

29. $3^2$:
$$9^{-2} \times 27^2 = (3^2)^{-2} \times (3^3)^2 = 3^{-4} \times 3^6 = 3^2$$

30. $2^{-1}$:
$$2^{-7} \times 8^2 = 2^{-7} \times (2^3)^2 = 2^{-7} \times 2^6 = 2^{-1}$$

# Drill 5

31. **(A):** Begin by breaking 6 down into its prime factors:
$$6^3 + 3^3 =$$
$$(2 \times 3)^3 + 3^3 =$$
$$(2^3)(3^3) + 3^3$$

Now each term contains $3^3$. Factor it out.

$$(2^3)(3^3) + 3^3 =$$
$$3^3(2^3 + 1) =$$
$$3^3(9) =$$
$$3^3(3^2) = 3^5$$

32. **(B):** Both bases are powers of 3. Rewrite the bases and combine.

$$81^3 + 27^4 =$$
$$(3^4)^3 + (3^3)^4 =$$
$$3^{12} + 3^{12} =$$
$$3^{12}(1 + 1) =$$
$$3^{12}(2)$$

33. **(B):** Begin by breaking 15 down into its prime factors.

$$15^2 - 5^2 =$$
$$(3 \times 5)^2 - 5^2 =$$
$$(3^2)(5^2) - 5^2$$

Now both terms contain $5^2$. Factor it out.

$$(3^2)(5^2) - 5^2 =$$
$$5^2(3^2 - 1) =$$
$$5^2(9 - 1) =$$
$$5^2(8)$$

Compare that to the answers. What else can you manipulate?

$$5^2(8) =$$
$$5^2(2^3)$$

34. **(A):** Factor $4^3$ out of the first four terms and factor $3^2$ out of the last three terms.

$$4^3 + 4^3 + 4^3 + 4^3 + 3^2 + 3^2 + 3^2 =$$
$$4^3(1 + 1 + 1 + 1) + 3^2(1 + 1 + 1) =$$
$$4^3(4) + 3^2(3) =$$
$$4^{3+1} + 3^{2+1} =$$
$$4^4 + 3^3$$

35. **(A):** Every base in the fraction is a power of 3. Begin by rewriting every base.

$$\frac{3^{12} - 9^4}{27^2 + 9^4} = \frac{3^{12} - (3^2)^4}{(3^3)^2 + (3^2)^4} = \frac{3^{12} - 3^8}{3^6 + 3^8}$$

The terms in the numerator both contain $3^8$, and the terms in the denominator both contain $3^6$. Factor the numerator and denominator.

$$\frac{3^{12}-3^8}{3^6+3^8} = \frac{3^8\left(3^4-1\right)}{3^6\left(1+3^2\right)} = \frac{3^8(80)}{3^6(10)}$$

Simplify the numerator and denominator.

$$\frac{3^8(80)}{3^6(10)} = 3^{8-6}(8) = 3^2(8)$$

# Drill 6

36. **9**: Before you multiply larger numbers together, think about whether you can make the math easier by breaking down into primes and pairing integers to pull out of the square root.

$$\sqrt{3}\times\sqrt{27} = \sqrt{3\times27} = \sqrt{3\times3\times3\times3} = 3\times3 = 9$$

In this case, you can break 27 down into three 3's. Then, each pair of 3's can be pulled out of the square root to give one 3.

37. **6**:
$$\sqrt{2}\times\sqrt{18} = \sqrt{2\times18} = \sqrt{36} = 6$$

38. **4**:
$$\frac{\sqrt{48}}{\sqrt{3}} = \sqrt{\frac{48}{3}} = \sqrt{16} = 4$$

39. **15**: You can break 45 down to get a second 5 to match the first one.

$$\sqrt{5}\times\sqrt{45} = \sqrt{5\times5\times9} = 5\times3 = 15$$

Alternatively, you can multiply first and then simplify, as shown below. Which way is easier for you?

$$\sqrt{5}\times\sqrt{45} = \sqrt{5\times45} = \sqrt{225} = 15$$

40. **10**:
$$\frac{\sqrt{5,000}}{\sqrt{50}} = \sqrt{\frac{5,000}{50}} = \sqrt{100} = 10$$

41. **12**: Careful! You might get so used to combining automatically that you fail to notice that these two are already perfect squares. They can be simplified first and then multiplied.

$$\sqrt{36}\times\sqrt{4} = 6\times2 = 12$$

3

42. **8**:

$$\frac{\sqrt{128}}{\sqrt{2}} = \sqrt{\frac{128}{2}} = \sqrt{64} = 8$$

43. **9**: Simplify the numerator and denominator before you multiply, then break 27 down into 3's.

$$\frac{\sqrt{54} \times \sqrt{3}}{\sqrt{2}} = \sqrt{\frac{\overset{27}{\cancel{54}} \times 3}{\cancel{2}_1}} = \sqrt{3 \times 3 \times 3 \times 3} = 3 \times 3 = 9$$

44. **8**:

$$\frac{\sqrt{640}}{\sqrt{2} \times \sqrt{5}} = \sqrt{\frac{640}{2 \times 5}} = \sqrt{\frac{640}{10}} = \sqrt{64} = 8$$

45. **4**: Simplify before you multiply.

$$\frac{\sqrt{48} \times \sqrt{7}}{\sqrt{21}} = \sqrt{\frac{48 \times \overset{1}{\cancel{7}}}{\cancel{21}_3}} = \sqrt{\frac{\overset{16}{\cancel{48}} \times 1}{\cancel{3}_1}} = \sqrt{16} = 4$$

# Drill 7

46. $4\sqrt{2}$ : Keep track of all those 2's carefully!

$$\sqrt{32} = \sqrt{2 \times 2 \times 2 \times 2 \times 2} = \sqrt{2 \times 2} \times \sqrt{2 \times 2} \times \sqrt{2} = 2 \times 2 \times \sqrt{2} = 4\sqrt{2}$$

47. $2\sqrt{6}$ :

$$\sqrt{24} = \sqrt{2 \times 2 \times 2 \times 3} = \sqrt{2 \times 2} \times \sqrt{2 \times 3} = 2\sqrt{6}$$

48. $6\sqrt{5}$ : If needed, use a factor tree to break down large numbers.

$$\sqrt{180} = \sqrt{2 \times 2 \times 3 \times 3 \times 5} = \sqrt{2 \times 2} \times \sqrt{3 \times 3} \times \sqrt{5} = 2 \times 3 \times \sqrt{5} = 6\sqrt{5}$$

49. $7\sqrt{10}$ :

$$\sqrt{490} = \sqrt{2 \times 5 \times 7 \times 7} = \sqrt{7 \times 7} \times \sqrt{2 \times 5} = 7\sqrt{10}$$

50. $6\sqrt{6}$ : Break 216 down into its primes.

$$\sqrt{216} = \sqrt{2 \times 2 \times 2 \times 3 \times 3 \times 3} = \sqrt{2 \times 2} \times \sqrt{3 \times 3} \times \sqrt{2 \times 3} = 2 \times 3 \times \sqrt{2 \times 3} = 6\sqrt{6}$$

51. $3\sqrt{15}$ :

$$\sqrt{135} = \sqrt{3 \times 3 \times 3 \times 5} = \sqrt{3 \times 3} \times \sqrt{3 \times 5} = 3\sqrt{15}$$

**3**

52. $4\sqrt{14}$ : Count out those 2's carefully.

$$\sqrt{224} = \sqrt{2\times2\times2\times2\times2\times7} = \sqrt{2\times2}\times\sqrt{2\times2}\times\sqrt{2\times7} = 2\times2\times\sqrt{14} = 4\sqrt{14}$$

53. $7\sqrt{7}$ :

$$\sqrt{343} = \sqrt{7\times7\times7} = \sqrt{7\times7}\times\sqrt{7} = 7\sqrt{7}$$

54. $4\sqrt{13}$ :

$$\sqrt{208} = \sqrt{2\times2\times2\times2\times13} = \sqrt{2\times2}\times\sqrt{2\times2}\times\sqrt{13} = 2\times2\times\sqrt{13} = 4\sqrt{13}$$

55. $12\sqrt{3}$ :

$$\sqrt{432} = \sqrt{2\times2\times2\times2\times3\times3\times3} = \sqrt{2\times2}\times\sqrt{2\times2}\times\sqrt{3\times3}\times\sqrt{3} = 2\times2\times3\times\sqrt{3} = 12\sqrt{3}$$

# Drill 8

56. **39:** It is tempting to use the square root to eliminate the exponents on 36 and 15 immediately, but you cannot break up a root over addition. You could multiply out both terms and add them, but you should always try to simplify before doing large calculations. Pull out the greatest common factor of $36^2$ and $15^2$, namely $3^2$. (Tip: Find the greatest number that 36 and 15 have in common. Then square that number. $15 = 3 \times 5$. 36 contains a 3 but not a 5.)

$$\sqrt{3^2\left(12^2+5^2\right)} = \sqrt{3^2\left(144+25\right)} = \sqrt{3^2\left(169\right)}$$

Both $3^2$ and 169 are perfect squares ($169 = 13^2$). Therefore:

$$\sqrt{3^2\left(169\right)} = \sqrt{3^2\left(13^2\right)} = 3\times13 = 39$$

57. **28:** Pull out the greatest common factor of $35^2$ and $21^2$, namely $7^2$.

$$\sqrt{7^2\left(5^2-3^2\right)} = \sqrt{7^2\left(25-9\right)} = \sqrt{7^2\left(16\right)}$$

Both $7^2$ and 16 are perfect squares ($16 = 4^2$). Therefore:

$$\sqrt{7^2\left(16\right)} = \sqrt{7^2\left(4^2\right)} = 7\times4 = 28$$

58. **1,210:** Pull out the greatest common factor of $11^4$ and $11^5$, namely $11^4$.

$$\sqrt{10(11^5-11^4)} = \sqrt{10\left(11^4\left(11-1\right)\right)} = \sqrt{10\left(11^4\left(10\right)\right)}$$

$(10)(10)$ is the same as $10^2$. The other term, $11^4$, is also a perfect square ($11^4 = 11^2 \times 11^2$). Pull the squares out of the square root.

$$\sqrt{10\left(11^4\left(10\right)\right)} = (10)\left(11^2\right) = (10)(121) = 1,210$$

59. **192**: Pull out the greatest common factor of $8^4$ and $8^5$, namely $8^4$.

$$\sqrt{8^4(1+8)} = \sqrt{8^4(9)} = \sqrt{8^4(3^2)}$$

Both $8^4$ and $3^2$ are perfect squares ($8^4 = 8^2 \times 8^2$). Therefore:

$$\sqrt{8^4(3^2)} = 8^2 \times 3 = 64 \times 3 = 192$$

60. **24**: Pull out the greatest common factor of $2^9$, $2^7$, and $2^6$, namely $2^6$.

$$\sqrt{2^6(2^3 + 2 - 1)} = \sqrt{2^6(8 + 2 - 1)} = \sqrt{2^6(9)} = \sqrt{2^6(3^2)}$$

Both $2^6$ and $3^2$ are perfect squares ($2^6 = 2^3 \times 2^3$). Therefore:

$$\sqrt{2^6(3^2)} = 2^3 \times 3 = 8 \times 3 = 24$$

61. **350**: Pull out the greatest common factor of $50^3$ and $50^2$, namely $50^2$.

$$\sqrt{50^2(50-1)} = \sqrt{50^2(49)} = \sqrt{50^2(7^2)} = 50 \times 7 = 350$$

62. **130**: First focus on the numerator of the fraction under the radical. Pull out the greatest common factor of $13^4$ and $13^2$, namely $13^2$.

$$\sqrt{\frac{10(13^2(13^2+1))}{17}} = \sqrt{\frac{10(13^2(169+1))}{17}} = \sqrt{\frac{10(13^2(170))}{17}}$$

The denominator (17) divides evenly into 170, and the remaining terms are perfect squares:

$$\sqrt{\frac{10(13^2(170))}{17}} = \sqrt{10(13^2(10))} = \sqrt{(10^2)(13^2)} = (10)(13) = 130$$

63. **275**: Pull out the greatest common factor of $5^7$, $5^5$, and $5^4$, namely $5^4$.

$$\sqrt{5^4(5^3 - 5 + 1)} = \sqrt{5^4(125 - 5 + 1)} = \sqrt{5^4(121)} = \sqrt{5^4(11^2)}$$

Both $5^4$ and $11^2$ are perfect squares ($5^4 = 5^2 \times 5^2$). Therefore:

$$\sqrt{5^4(11^2)} = 5^2 \times 11 = 25 \times 11 = 275$$

# Fractions

# In this chapter...

- Basics of Fractions
- Add Fractions with the Same Denominator: Add the Numerators
- Add Fractions with Different Denominators: Find a Common Denominator
- Compare Fractions: Use the Double-Cross
- Change an Improper Fraction to a Mixed Number: Divide
- Change a Mixed Number to an Improper Fraction: Add
- Simplify a Fraction: Cancel Common Factors on the Top and Bottom
- Multiply Fractions: Simplify First, Then Multiply
- Square a Proper Fraction: It Gets Smaller
- Take a Reciprocal: Flip the Fraction
- Divide by a Fraction: Multiply by the Reciprocal
- Addition in the Numerator: Pull Out a Common Factor
- Addition in the Numerator: Split into Two Fractions (Maybe)
- Addition in the Denominator: Pull Out a Common Factor, but Never Split
- Add, Subtract, Multiply, Divide Nasty Fractions: Add Parentheses
- Fractions within Fractions: Work Your Way Out

Chapter 4

# Fractions

## In This Chapter, You Will Learn To:

- Add, subtract, multiply, and divide fractions
- Manipulate fractions in complex scenarios

## Basics of Fractions

A fraction expresses division.

The **numerator** on top is divided by the **denominator** on bottom.

Numerator ⟶

Fraction line ⟶ $\dfrac{3}{4}$ = 3 ÷ 4

Denominator ⟶

Three-fourths is three divided by four.

The result of the division is a number. If you punch "3 ÷ 4 =" into a calculator, you get the decimal 0.75. But you can also think of 0.75 as $\dfrac{3}{4}$, because $\dfrac{3}{4}$ and 0.75 are two different ways to write the same number. (You'll learn about decimals in the next chapter.)

Fractions express a part-to-whole relationship.

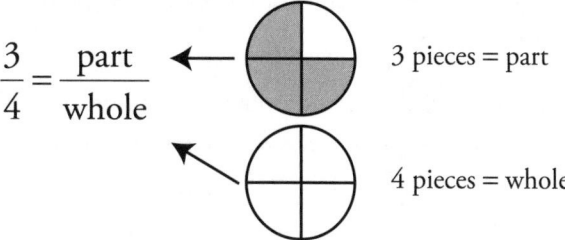

$$\frac{3}{4} = \frac{\text{part}}{\text{whole}}$$

3 pieces = part

4 pieces = whole

In the above figure, a circle represents a whole unit—a full pizza. The pizza has been divided into four equal parts, or fourths, because the denominator of the fraction is 4. In any fraction, the denominator tells you how many equal slices something has been broken into, in this case a pizza. In other words, the denominator indicates the size of a slice: Each slice is one-quarter of the pizza.

The numerator of the fraction is 3. This means that the fraction is talking about three slices of the pizza.
In any fraction, the numerator tells you how many of the slices you are talking about. Together, you are talking about three slices out of four total, or three parts to the total four. You can also say that you are talking about three-quarters of the pizza.

Since fractions express division, all the arithmetic rules of division apply. For instance, a negative divided by a positive gives you a negative, and so on.

$$\frac{-3}{4} = -3 \div 4 = -0.75 \qquad\qquad \frac{3}{-4} = 3 \div (-4) = -0.75$$

So $\frac{-3}{4}$ and $\frac{3}{-4}$ represent the same number. You can also write that number as $-\frac{3}{4}$. Just don't mix up the negative sign with the fraction bar.

PEMDAS also applies. The fraction bar means that you always *divide the entire numerator by the entire denominator.*

$$\frac{3x^2 + y}{2y^2 - z} = \left(3x^2 + y\right) \div \left(2y^2 - z\right)$$

The entire quantity $3x^2 + y$ is being divided by the entire quantity $2y^2 - z$.

If you rewrite a fraction, be ready to put parentheses around the numerator or denominator to preserve the correct order of operations.

Finally, remember that you can't divide by zero. So *a denominator can never equal zero.* If you have a variable expression in the denominator, that expression cannot equal zero. If a problem contains the fraction $\frac{x}{y}$, then $y$ cannot equal zero. The problem will tell you that $y \neq 0$ (that's a "does not equal" sign).

If the problem tells you that $\frac{3x^2 + y}{2y^2 - z}$, then what cannot equal zero?

The entire denominator cannot equal zero. In other words:

$$2y^2 - z \neq 0 \qquad \text{or} \qquad 2y^2 \neq z$$

If the GMAT tells you that something does *not* equal something else (using the $\neq$ sign), the purpose is often to rule out dividing by zero somewhere in the problem.

To compare positive fractions with the same *denominator*, compare the numerators. The numerator tells you how many pieces you have. *The greater the numerator, the greater the fraction* (assuming positive numbers and the same denominators). You have more same-sized slices of pie.

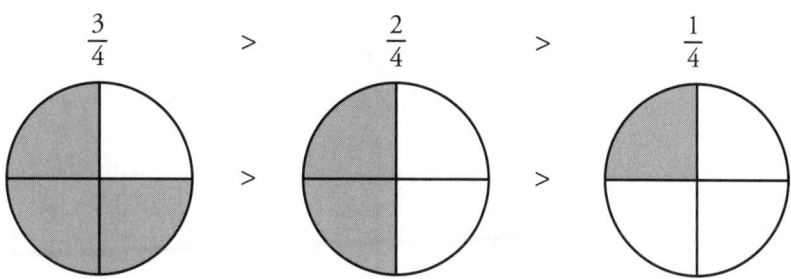

To compare positive fractions with the same *numerator*, compare the denominators. *The greater the denominator, the smaller the fraction.* Each slice of pie is smaller. So the same number of smaller slices represents a smaller amount of the pie.

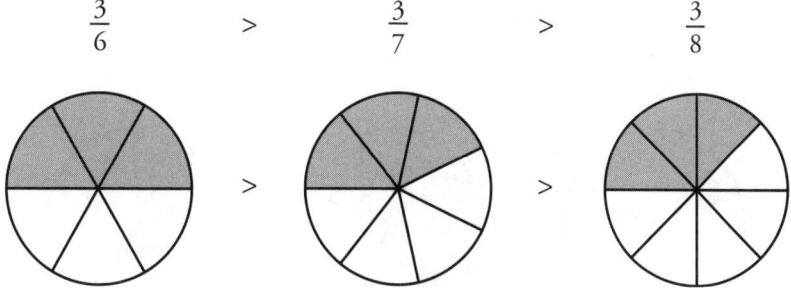

If the numerator and denominator are the same, then the fraction equals 1.

$$\frac{4}{4} \qquad = \qquad 4 \div 4 \qquad = \qquad 1$$

Four-fourths      equals      four divided by    and that equals    one
                          four,

If the numerator is greater than the denominator (again, assume positive numbers), then you have more than one pizza.

$$\frac{5}{4} \qquad = \qquad 5 \div 4 \qquad = \qquad 1 \qquad + \qquad \frac{1}{4}$$

Five-fourths   equals   five divided   and that   one   plus   one-fourth
                  by four,   equals

Another way to write $1 + \frac{1}{4}$ is $1\frac{1}{4}$ (read *one and one-fourth*). This is the only time in GMAT math when you put two things next to each other (1 and $\frac{1}{4}$) in order to *add* them. In all other circumstances, two things right next to each other means *multiplication*.

A **mixed number** such as $1\frac{1}{4}$ contains both an integer part, 1, and a fractional part, $\frac{1}{4}$. You can always rewrite a mixed number as a sum of the integer part and the fractional part: just split the integer and the fraction.

$$3\frac{3}{8} = 3 + \frac{3}{8}$$

In an **improper fraction** such as $\dfrac{5}{4}$, the numerator is greater than the denominator. Improper fractions and mixed numbers are two different ways to express the same thing. Later, you'll learn how to convert between them.

A **proper fraction** such as $\dfrac{3}{4}$ has a value between 0 and 1. In a proper fraction, the numerator is smaller than the denominator.

## Add Fractions with the Same Denominator: Add the Numerators

The numerator of a fraction tells you how many slices of the pizza you have. So when you add fractions, you add the numerators. You just have to make sure that the slices are the same size—in other words, that the denominators are equal.

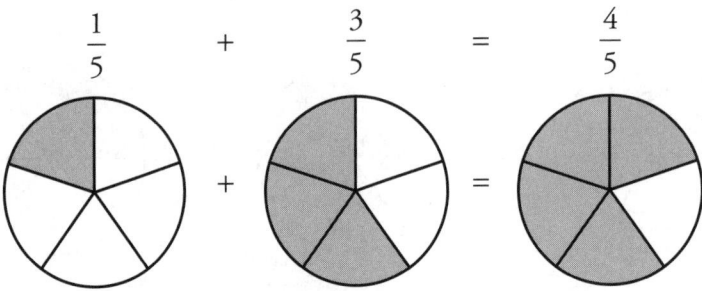

In words, one-fifth plus three-fifths equals four-fifths. The *fifth* is the size of the slice, so the denominator (5) doesn't change.

Since 4 = 1 + 3, you can write the fraction with 1 + 3 in the numerator.

$$\frac{1}{5}+\frac{3}{5}=\frac{1+3}{5}=\frac{4}{5}$$

The same process applies with subtraction. Subtract the numerators and leave the denominator the same.

$$\frac{9}{14}-\frac{4}{14}=\frac{9-4}{14}=\frac{5}{14}$$

If variables are involved, add or subtract the same way. Just make sure that the denominators in the original fractions are equal. It doesn't matter how complicated they are.

$$\frac{3a}{b}+\frac{4a}{b}=\frac{3a+4a}{b}=\frac{7a}{b}\qquad\frac{5x^2}{z+w}-\frac{2x^2}{z+w}=\frac{5x^2-2x^2}{z+w}=\frac{3x^2}{z+w}$$

If you can't simplify the numerator, leave it as a sum or a difference. Remember that the denominator stays the same, because it just tells you the *size* of the slices you're adding or subtracting.

$$\frac{x}{y}+\frac{z}{y}=\frac{x+z}{y}\qquad\frac{3n}{2w^3}-\frac{5m}{2w^3}=\frac{3n-5m}{2w^3}$$

**MANHATTAN** PREP

Here's another rule for your book:

| If you… | Then you… | Like this: |
|---|---|---|
| Add or subtract fractions that have the same denominator | Add or subtract the numerators, leaving the denominator alone | $\frac{2}{7}+\frac{3}{7}=\frac{2+3}{7}$ $=\frac{5}{7}$ |

## Check Your Skills

1. $\dfrac{3x}{yz^2}+\dfrac{7x}{yz^2}=$

*Answer can be found on page 163.*

# Add Fractions with Different Denominators: Find a Common Denominator

Consider this example:

$$\frac{1}{4}+\frac{3}{8}=$$

The denominators (the sizes of the slices) aren't the same, so you can't just add the numerators this time.

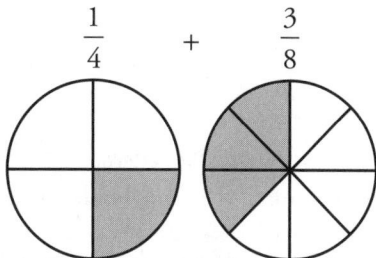

To add these fractions correctly, you will need to manipulate the fractions so that the slices are the same size. In other words, the fractions need to have a **common denominator**—that is, the *same* denominator. Once they have the same denominator, you can add the numerators.

Since a fourth of a pizza is twice as big as an eighth, take the fourth in the first circle and cut it in two.

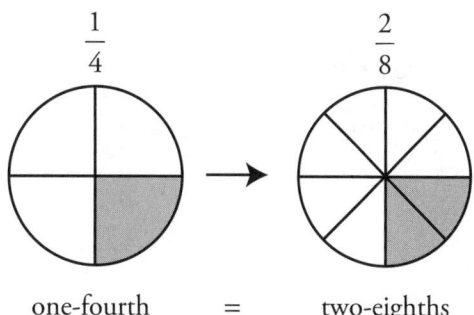

one-fourth     =     two-eighths

You have the same amount of pizza—the shaded area hasn't changed in size. So one-fourth $\left(\dfrac{1}{4}\right)$ equals two-eighths $\left(\dfrac{2}{8}\right)$.

When you cut the fourth in two, you end up with twice as many slices. So the numerator is doubled. But you're breaking the whole circle into twice as many pieces, so the denominator is doubled as well. If you double both the numerator and the denominator, the fraction's value stays exactly the same (this is why you are allowed to make this move!).

$$\frac{1}{4} = \frac{1 \times 2}{4 \times 2} = \frac{2}{8}$$

Without changing the value of $\dfrac{1}{4}$, you have renamed it $\dfrac{2}{8}$. Now you can add it to $\dfrac{3}{8}$.

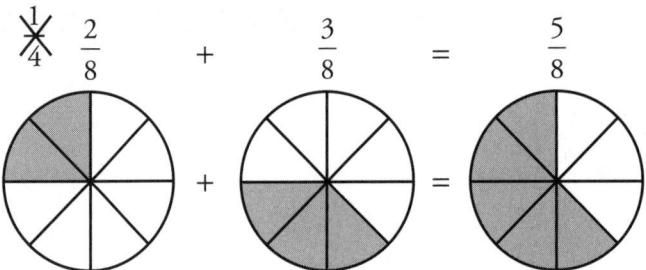

All in one line:

$$\frac{1}{4} + \frac{3}{8} = \frac{1 \times 2}{4 \times 2} + \frac{3}{8} = \frac{2}{8} + \frac{3}{8} = \frac{5}{8}$$

*To add fractions with different denominators, find a common denominator.* That is, rename the fractions so that they have the same denominator. Then add the new numerators. The same holds true for subtraction.

How do you rename a fraction without changing its value? Multiply the top and bottom by the same number. For example:

$$\frac{1}{4} = \frac{1 \times 2}{4 \times 2} = \frac{2}{8} \qquad \frac{3}{4} = \frac{3 \times 25}{4 \times 25} = \frac{75}{100} \qquad \frac{5}{9} = \frac{5 \times 7}{9 \times 7} = \frac{35}{63}$$

Here's why this works. Doubling the top and doubling the bottom of a fraction is the same as multiplying the fraction by $\dfrac{2}{2}$. (More on fraction multiplication later.)

Notice that $\dfrac{2}{2}$ is equal to 1. And multiplying a number by 1 doesn't change the number. So when you multiply by $\dfrac{2}{2}$, you aren't really changing the number, you're just changing its appearance.

$$\frac{1}{4} = \frac{1}{4} \times \frac{2}{2} = \frac{1 \times 2}{4 \times 2} = \frac{2}{8}$$

**MANHATTAN** PREP

You can rename fractions that have variables in them, too. You can even multiply the top and bottom by the same variable.

$$\frac{x}{y} = \frac{x}{y} \times \frac{2}{2} = \frac{x \times 2}{y \times 2} = \frac{2x}{2y} \qquad\qquad \frac{a}{2} = \frac{a}{2} \times \frac{b}{b} = \frac{a \times b}{2 \times b} = \frac{ab}{2b}$$

Just make sure the expression on the bottom can never equal zero, of course. Here's another rule for your book:

| If you… | Then you… | Like this: |
|---|---|---|
| Want to give a fraction a different denominator but keep the value the same | Multiply the top and bottom of the fraction by the same number | $\frac{1}{4} = \frac{1 \times 2}{4 \times 2} = \frac{2}{8}$ |

Say you have this problem:

$$\frac{1}{4} + \frac{1}{3} =$$

What should the common denominator of these fractions be? It needs to be both a multiple of 4 *and* a multiple of 3. That is, it should be a multiple that 3 and 4 have in common. The easiest multiple to pick is usually the **least common multiple** (LCM) of 3 and 4. If you need a refresher on that concept, return to Chapter 2.

The least common multiple of 4 and 3 is 12. Rename the two fractions so that they each have a denominator of 12.

$$\frac{1}{4} = \frac{1 \times 3}{4 \times 3} = \frac{3}{12} \qquad\qquad \frac{1}{3} = \frac{1 \times 4}{3 \times 4} = \frac{4}{12}$$

Once you have a common denominator, add the numerators.

$$\frac{1}{4} + \frac{1}{3} = \frac{1 \times 3}{4 \times 3} + \frac{1 \times 4}{3 \times 4} = \frac{3}{12} + \frac{4}{12} = \frac{7}{12}$$

The process works the same if you subtract fractions or even have more than two fractions. Try this example:

$$\frac{5}{6} + \frac{2}{9} - \frac{3}{4} =$$

First, find the common denominator by finding the least common multiple. All three denominators (6, 9, and 4) are composed of 2's and 3's.

$$6 = 2 \times 3 \qquad\qquad 9 = 3 \times 3 \qquad\qquad 4 = 2 \times 2$$

The LCM will contain two 2's (because there are two 2's in 4) and two 3's (because there are two 3's in 9).

$$2 \times 2 \times 3 \times 3 = 36$$

To make each of the denominators equal 36, multiply the fractions by $\frac{6}{6}$, $\frac{4}{4}$, and $\frac{9}{9}$, respectively.

$$\frac{5}{6} = \frac{5 \times 6}{6 \times 6} = \frac{30}{36} \qquad\qquad \frac{2}{9} = \frac{2 \times 4}{9 \times 4} = \frac{8}{36} \qquad\qquad \frac{3}{4} = \frac{3 \times 9}{4 \times 9} = \frac{27}{36}$$

Now that the denominators are all the same, add and subtract normally.

$$\frac{5}{6}+\frac{2}{9}-\frac{3}{4}=\frac{30}{36}+\frac{8}{36}-\frac{27}{36}=\frac{30+8-27}{36}=\frac{11}{36}$$

The process works even if you have variables. Try adding these two fractions:

$$\frac{2}{x}+\frac{3}{2x}=$$

First, find the common denominator by finding the least common multiple of $x$ and $2x$. The LCM is $2x$. So give the first fraction a denominator of $2x$, then add:

$$\frac{2}{x}+\frac{3}{2x}=\frac{2\times2}{x\times2}+\frac{3}{2x}=\frac{4}{2x}+\frac{3}{2x}=\frac{4+3}{2x}=\frac{7}{2x}$$

Now that you know how to do the math in the traditional way, it's time to learn a useful shortcut: the double-cross. (In general, you'll be better able to remember how to implement a shortcut when you first understand the textbook approach.)

Here's an example that you solved earlier.

$$\frac{1}{4}+\frac{1}{3}=\frac{1\times3}{4\times3}+\frac{1\times4}{3\times4}=\frac{3}{12}+\frac{4}{12}=\frac{7}{12}$$

This time, you're going to take some different steps. First, draw three arrows on the problem and rewrite the addition sign just above the top arrows.

The arrows mean multiplication. Multiply along each arrow, and place the product where the arrow points.

The new denominator, 12, is the result of multiplying along the bottom, as shown above.

To get the new numerator, add the two new numbers on top.

The result is the same whether you use the shortcut or do the math in the traditional way; the shortcut just compresses several steps.

The double-cross will always work, and it is usually faster, but there is one circumstance in which the traditional approach is faster.

Take a look at this example:

$$\frac{1}{3} + \frac{1}{6}$$

In this case, 3 and 6 share a common denominator of 6, so you only need to change one fraction: $\frac{1}{3}$. Since this is the case, it's faster to find common denominators.

$$\frac{1}{3} + \frac{1}{6} = \frac{2}{6} + \frac{1}{6} = \frac{3}{6} = \frac{1}{2}$$

Try one more.

$$\frac{5}{6} + \frac{3}{8}$$

| Traditional | The Double-Cross |
|---|---|
| Find a common denominator. The smallest one is 24: $$\frac{5 \times 4}{6 \times 4} + \frac{3 \times 3}{3 \times 3}$$ Add the two fractions: $$\frac{20}{24} + \frac{9}{24} = \frac{29}{24}$$ | Draw your arrows and multiply. Add the numerators. Note that 58 and 48 are both divisible by 2, so simplify as a last step: $$\frac{58}{48} = \frac{29 \times \cancel{2}}{24 \times \cancel{2}} = \frac{29}{24}$$ |

As usual, the traditional method has more work up front (finding a common denominator), but this time the shortcut had an extra step at the end: You have to simplify. Why?

This will happen when the two denominators share factors, as 6 and 8 do. The smallest common denominator, 24, is smaller than multiplying those two numbers together: 6 × 8 = 48. If you choose the double-cross in this circumstance, be aware that you will need to simplify at the end (you'll learn various methods for doing this later in this chapter). If the numbers are large enough to be annoying, then you may want to use the traditional method, even though you do have to find common denominators.

| If you... | Then you... | Like this: |
|---|---|---|
| Add or subtract fractions with different denominators | Put the fractions in terms of a common denominator, then add or subtract  OR  Use the double-cross shortcut | $$\frac{1}{3} - \frac{1}{6} = \frac{1 \times 2}{3 \times 2} - \frac{1}{6}$$ $$= \frac{2}{6} - \frac{1}{6} = \frac{1}{6}$$  OR  |

## Check Your Skills

2. $\dfrac{1}{2} + \dfrac{3}{4} =$

4

3. $\dfrac{2}{3} - \dfrac{3}{8} =$

*Answers can be found on page 163.*

# Compare Fractions: Use the Double-Cross

The double-cross is very versatile; it can also be used to compare two fractions.

Which is greater, $\dfrac{3}{5}$ or $\dfrac{4}{7}$?

Use a modified version of the double-cross. Multiply along the top two crossed arrows, but ignore the denominator:

1. Set the two fractions up near each other.

$$\dfrac{3}{5} \qquad \dfrac{4}{7}$$

2. Multiply "up" the arrows. Be sure to put the resulting number at the top of each respective arrow.

$$21 \nwarrow \dfrac{3}{5} \diagdown \dfrac{4}{7} \nearrow 20$$

3. Compare the numbers. The side with the bigger number is the bigger fraction. 21 > 20, so $\dfrac{3}{5}$ is greater than $\dfrac{4}{7}$.

This process generates the same numerators as before (21 and 20), and the numerators are all you need to compare. The common denominator is the same for both terms, so it doesn't matter.

| If you… | Then you… | Like this: |
|---|---|---|
| Want to compare fractions | Do the two top calculations of the double-cross | 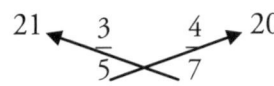 |

## Check Your Skills

For each of the following pairs of fractions, decide which fraction is greater.

4. $\dfrac{5}{7}, \dfrac{3}{7}$

5. $\dfrac{3}{10}, \dfrac{3}{13}$

*Answers can be found on page 163.*

**MANHATTAN** PREP

# Change an Improper Fraction to a Mixed Number: Divide

What is $\frac{13}{4}$ as a mixed number? Note that $\frac{13}{4}$ is an improper fraction, because 13 > 4.

Since the fraction bar represents division, go ahead and divide 13 by 4. Try doing this by long division:

$$\begin{array}{r} 3 \\ 4\overline{)13} \\ \underline{12} \\ 1 \end{array}$$

The number 4 goes into 13 three times, with 1 left over. Since it goes in three times, the number 3 is called the **quotient**. It represents how many whole times the denominator (4) goes into the numerator (13). The number one is called the **remainder**. It represents what is left over.

So $\frac{13}{4}$ equals 3 plus a remainder of 1. This remainder of 1 is literally "left over" the 4, so write it out this way:

$$\frac{13}{4} = 3 + \frac{1}{4}$$

As a mixed number, $\frac{13}{4}$ equals $3\frac{1}{4}$.

*To convert an improper fraction to a mixed number, divide the numerator by the denominator.* The quotient is the integer part of the mixed number. The remainder over the denominator equals the leftover fractional part of the mixed number.

To do the division, look for the greatest multiple of the denominator that is less than or equal to the numerator. In the case of $\frac{13}{4}$, 12 is the greatest multiple of 4 that is still less than 13, and since 12 = 4 × 3, the number 3 is the quotient. 13 − 12 = 1, so 1 is the remainder.

Here's another way to understand this process. Fraction addition can be done both forward and in reverse.

Forward: $\frac{2}{7} + \frac{4}{7} = \frac{2+4}{7} = \frac{6}{7}$          Reverse: $\frac{6}{7} = \frac{2+4}{7} = \frac{2}{7} + \frac{4}{7}$

In other words, you can *rewrite a numerator as a sum, then split the fraction.* Try this with $\frac{13}{4}$.

Rewrite 13 as 12 + 1, then split the fraction:

$$\frac{13}{4} = \frac{12+1}{4} = \frac{12}{4} + \frac{1}{4}$$

Since $\frac{12}{4} = 12 \div 4 = 3$, the expression becomes $\frac{13}{4} = \frac{12}{4} + \frac{1}{4} = 3 + \frac{1}{4} = 3\frac{1}{4}$.

| If you... | Then you... | Like this: |
|---|---|---|
| Want to convert an improper fraction to a mixed number | Divide the numerator by the denominator OR Rewrite the numerator as a sum, then split the fraction | $\dfrac{13}{4} = 13 \div 4$ $= 3 \text{ remainder } 1$ $= 3\dfrac{1}{4}$ $\dfrac{13}{4} = \dfrac{12+1}{4}$ $= \dfrac{12}{4} + \dfrac{1}{4}$ $= 3\dfrac{1}{4}$ |

## Check Your Skills

Change the following improper fractions to mixed numbers.

6. $\dfrac{11}{6}$

7. $\dfrac{100}{11}$

*Answers can be found on pages 163–164.*

# Change a Mixed Number to an Improper Fraction: Add

What is $5\dfrac{2}{3}$ as an improper fraction?

First, rewrite the mixed number as a sum: $5\dfrac{2}{3} = 5 + \dfrac{2}{3}$.

Now add these two numbers together by rewriting 5 as a fraction. You can always write any integer as a fraction by putting it over 1

$$5 = \dfrac{5}{1} \qquad \text{This is true because } 5 \div 1 = 5.$$

So $5\dfrac{2}{3} = 5 + \dfrac{2}{3} = \dfrac{5}{1} + \dfrac{2}{3}$. At this point, you're adding fractions with different denominators, so find a common denominator.

The least common multiple of 1 and 3 is 3, so convert $\dfrac{5}{1}$ to a fraction with a 3 in its denominator.

$$\dfrac{5}{1} = \dfrac{5 \times 3}{1 \times 3} = \dfrac{15}{3}$$

**MANHATTAN** PREP

Finally, complete the addition. Here are the steps from start to finish:

$$5\frac{2}{3} = 5 + \frac{2}{3} = \frac{5}{1} + \frac{2}{3} = \frac{15}{3} + \frac{2}{3} = \frac{15+2}{3} = \frac{17}{3}$$

If you'd like, learn this shortcut: the new numerator is $3 \times 5 + 2 = 17$. That is: (denominator)(integer part of the mixed number) + numerator = the new numerator. The denominator, 3, stays the same, so the complete fraction is $\frac{17}{3}$.

If you understand how this shortcut is equivalent to the addition process above, you'll be better able to remember the shortcut.

| If you... | Then you... | Like this: |
|---|---|---|
| Want to convert a mixed number to an improper fraction | Convert the integer to a fraction over 1, then add it to the fractional part  OR  Use the shortcut:  $\dfrac{(\text{denom})(\text{integer})+\text{num}}{\text{denom}}$ | $7\dfrac{3}{8} = \dfrac{7}{1} + \dfrac{3}{8}$ $= \dfrac{56}{8} + \dfrac{3}{8}$ $= \dfrac{59}{8}$  $\dfrac{8 \times 7 + 3}{8} = \dfrac{56+3}{8} = \dfrac{59}{8}$ |

## Check Your Skills

Change the following mixed numbers to improper fractions.

8. $3\dfrac{3}{4}$

9. $6\dfrac{3}{4}$

*Answers can be found on page 164.*

## Simplify a Fraction: Cancel Common Factors on the Top and Bottom

Consider this problem:

$$\frac{5}{9} + \frac{1}{9} =$$

(A) $\dfrac{4}{9}$

(B) $\dfrac{6}{18}$

(C) $\dfrac{2}{3}$

You know how to add fractions with the same denominator: $\dfrac{5}{9} + \dfrac{1}{9} = \dfrac{5+1}{9} = \dfrac{6}{9}$. This is mathematically correct so far.

But $\dfrac{6}{9}$ is not among the answer choices. Try **simplifying** or **reducing** the fraction to its lowest terms.

*To simplify a fraction, cancel out common factors from the numerator and denominator.*

$$\frac{6}{9} = \frac{2 \times 3}{3 \times 3}$$

Since 3 is a common factor on the top and bottom, cancel it.

$$\frac{6}{9} = \frac{2 \times \cancel{3}}{3 \times \cancel{3}} = \frac{2}{3}$$

Earlier, you learned that you can multiply the top and bottom of a fraction by the same number without changing the value of the fraction. The fraction stays the same because you are multiplying the whole fraction by the equivalent of 1. For example:

$$\frac{2}{3} = \frac{2 \times 3}{3 \times 3} = \frac{6}{9}$$

Now you're just dividing the fraction by the equivalent of 1; this also leaves the value unchanged. As you divide away the $\frac{3}{3}$ (which equals 1), the look of the fraction changes from $\frac{6}{9}$ to $\frac{2}{3}$, but the value of the fraction is the same.

This process works with both numbers and variables. Try reducing the following fraction:

$$\frac{18x^2}{60x} =$$

Start canceling common factors on the top and bottom. You can do so in any order. If you want, you can even break all the way down to primes, then cancel. (The math below uses the × symbol to be very explicit about all the multiplication.)

$$\frac{18x^2}{60x} = \frac{2 \times 3 \times 3 \times x \times x}{2 \times 2 \times 3 \times 5 \times x}$$

The top and the bottom each contain a 2, a 3, and an $x$. These are the common factors to cancel. Here's one way to do so:

$$\frac{18x^2}{60x} = \frac{\cancel{2} \times 3 \times \cancel{3} \times x \times \cancel{x}}{\cancel{2} \times 2 \times \cancel{3} \times 5 \times \cancel{x}} = \frac{3x}{10}$$

Here's another way to do so:

$$\frac{18x^{\cancel{2}}}{60\cancel{x}} = \frac{18x}{60} = \frac{\cancel{2} \times 9x}{\cancel{2} \times 30} = \frac{9x}{30} = \frac{\cancel{3} \times 3x}{\cancel{3} \times 10} = \frac{3x}{10}$$

If you feel comfortable canceling all at once, feel free to do so—but if this opens you up to careless mistakes, write the math out more fully. Here's a more compressed version:

$$\frac{\overset{3}{\cancel{18}}x^{\cancel{2}}}{\underset{10}{\cancel{60}}\,x} = \frac{3x}{10}$$

| If you... | Then you... | Like this: |
|:---:|:---:|:---:|
| Want to simplify a fraction | Cancel out common factors from the top and bottom | $\dfrac{14}{35} = \dfrac{2 \times \cancel{7}}{5 \times \cancel{7}} = \dfrac{2}{5}$ |

**4**

## Check Your Skills

Simplify the following fractions.

10. $\dfrac{25}{40}$

11. $\dfrac{16}{24}$

*Answers can be found on page 164.*

# Multiply Fractions: Simplify First, then Multiply

What is $\dfrac{1}{2}$ of 6?

One-half of 6 is 3. When you take $\dfrac{1}{2}$ of 6, you divide 6 into two equal parts (since the denominator of $\dfrac{1}{2}$ is 2).

Then you keep one part (since the numerator of $\dfrac{1}{2}$ is 1). If your starting point is 6, then that one part equals 3.

One-half *of* 6 is the same thing as one-half *times* 6. It's also the same thing as 6 divided by 2. Either way, you get 3.

$$\frac{1}{2} \times 6 = 3 \qquad\qquad \frac{6}{2} = 6 \div 2 = 3$$

Now consider this problem:

What is $\dfrac{1}{2}$ of $\dfrac{3}{4}$?

In other words, what is $\dfrac{1}{2} \times \dfrac{3}{4}$?

*To multiply two fractions, multiply the tops together and multiply the bottoms together.*

$$\frac{1}{2} \times \frac{3}{4} = \frac{1 \times 3}{2 \times 4} = \frac{3}{8}$$

The rule works for integers, too. Just put the integer over 1.

$$\frac{3}{4} \times \frac{5}{7} = \frac{3 \times 5}{4 \times 7} = \frac{15}{28} \qquad\qquad \frac{1}{2} \times 6 = \frac{1}{2} \times \frac{6}{1} = \frac{6}{2} = 3$$

But wait! Don't multiply immediately. Whenever possible, *cancel factors before you multiply out*, or simplify before you multiply. Take a look at these numbers; can you simplify first?

$$\frac{33}{7} \times \frac{14}{3} =$$

The terribly long way to do this multiplication is to multiply the tops, then multiply the bottoms, then reduce the numerator and denominator. You'd first have to multiply $33 \times 14$ (ugh) and then take whatever that big number is and divide it by $7 \times 3 = 21$ (double ugh).

But you *can* cancel factors before multiplying! Break the numerators into smaller factors.

$$\frac{33}{7} \times \frac{14}{3} = \frac{11 \times 3}{7} \times \frac{7 \times 2}{3} = \frac{11 \times \cancel{3}^{1}}{\cancel{7}_{1}} \times \frac{\cancel{7}^{1} \times 2}{\cancel{3}_{1}} = \frac{11 \times 2}{1 \times 1} = 22$$

You are allowed to cancel across the multiplication sign ($\times$). In other words, a factor on top of fraction #1 can cancel with a factor on the bottom of fraction #2.

If you prefer, you can also write out the work in this way:

$$\frac{33}{7} \times \frac{14}{3} = {}^{11}\frac{\cancel{33}}{7} \times \frac{14}{\cancel{3}} = {}^{11}\frac{\cancel{33}}{\cancel{7}} \times {}^{2}\frac{\cancel{14}}{\cancel{3}} = 11 \times 2 = 22$$

When a factor in the denominator cancels to 1, you don't need to write it down. If *all* of the factors in the denominator cancel to 1, the answer will not be a fraction. Technically, the bottom of the calculation shown above is $1 \times 1 = 1$, but the answer $\frac{22}{1}$ simplifies to 22.

Negative signs can make fraction multiplication trickier. Again, a negative sign can appear anywhere in a fraction:

$$-\frac{2}{3} = \frac{-2}{3} = \frac{2}{-3}$$

When you multiply a fraction by $-1$, you put a negative sign in the fraction. Where you put it is up to you, though the most common place to put the negative sign is out in front of the fraction. For example:

$$-1 \times \frac{3}{5} = -\frac{3}{5} = \frac{-3}{5} = \frac{3}{-5}$$

In general, think of it as multiplying *either* the numerator *or* the denominator by $-1$.

$$-1 \times \frac{8}{7} = -\frac{8}{7} \text{ OR } \frac{-8}{7} \text{ OR } \frac{8}{-7}$$

If the fraction already contains a negative sign, then cancel out both negatives, because $-1 \times -1 = 1$.

$$-1 \times -\frac{8}{7} = -1 \times -1 \times \frac{8}{7} = \frac{8}{7}$$

$$-1 \times \frac{-8}{7} = \frac{-1 \times (-8)}{7} = \frac{8}{7}$$

| If you... | Then you... | Like this: |
|---|---|---|
| Multiply two fractions | Multiply tops and multiply bottoms, canceling common factors first | $\frac{20}{9} \times \frac{6}{5} = \frac{\overset{4}{\cancel{20}}}{\underset{3}{\cancel{9}}} \times \frac{\overset{2}{\cancel{6}}}{\cancel{5}}$ $= \frac{4 \times 2}{3} = \frac{8}{3}$ |

## Check Your Skills

Evaluate the following expressions. Simplify all fractions.

12. $\dfrac{3}{7} \times \dfrac{6}{10} =$

13. $\dfrac{5}{14} \times \dfrac{7}{20} =$

*Answers can be found on page 164.*

## Square a Proper Fraction: It Gets Smaller

What is $\left(\dfrac{1}{2}\right)^2$ ?

Now that you can multiply fractions, you can apply exponents.

$$\left(\frac{1}{2}\right)^2 = \frac{1}{2} \times \frac{1}{2} = \frac{1}{4}$$

Notice that $\dfrac{1}{4}$ is *less* than $\dfrac{1}{2}$. When you square a number greater than 1, it gets bigger. When you square a negative number, it also gets bigger. But when you square a proper fraction (between 0 and 1), it gets *smaller*.

The same is true for greater powers (cubes, etc.). *If you square, cube, or apply any greater power to a proper fraction (between 0 and 1), the number will get smaller.*

In general, if you multiply *any* positive number by a proper fraction, the result is smaller than the original number. You are taking a *fraction* of that number. For instance, if you take $\dfrac{1}{2}$ of 3, you will get $\dfrac{1}{2} \times 3 = \dfrac{3}{2}$. The answer is smaller than the starting number, 3.

By the way, what happens if you square 0 or 1?

You get the same number! $0^2 = 0$ and $1^2 = 1$. Here are some more rules for your book:

| If you... | Then you... | Like this: |
|---|---|---|
| Square a proper fraction (between 0 and 1) | Get a smaller number | $\left(\dfrac{1}{3}\right)^2 = \dfrac{1}{9}$  $\dfrac{1}{9} < \dfrac{1}{3}$ |
| Square a number greater than 1 or square a negative number | Get a greater number | $2^2 = 4$  $(-3)^2 = 9$ |
| Square 0 or 1 | Get the same number | $0^2 = 0$  $1^2 = 1$ |

# Take a Reciprocal: Flip the Fraction

The **reciprocal** of an integer is "1 over" that number. For example, the reciprocal of 5 is 1 over 5, or $\dfrac{1}{5}$.

Any number times its reciprocal equals 1:

$$5 \times \frac{1}{5} = \frac{5}{1} \times \frac{1}{5} = \frac{5}{5} = 1$$     (You could also cancel all the factors as you multiply.)

Consider this example:

What is the reciprocal of $\dfrac{2}{3}$?

To find the reciprocal of a fraction, *flip the fraction*. The reciprocal of $\dfrac{2}{3}$ is $\dfrac{3}{2}$, since the product of $\dfrac{2}{3}$ and $\dfrac{3}{2}$ is 1.

$$\frac{2}{3} \times \frac{3}{2} = \frac{6}{6} = 1$$

If you write an integer as a fraction over 1, then the flipping rule works for integers as well. The integer 9 is $\dfrac{9}{1}$, and the reciprocal of 9 is $\dfrac{1}{9}$.

Keep track of negative signs. The reciprocal of a negative fraction will also be negative.

$$\frac{-5}{6} \times \frac{6}{-5} = \frac{-30}{-30} = 1$$

The reciprocal of $\dfrac{-5}{6}$ is $\dfrac{6}{-5}$, more commonly written as $-\dfrac{6}{5}$.

| If you... | Then you... | Like this: |
|---|---|---|
|  |  | Fraction       Reciprocal |
| Want the reciprocal of a fraction | Flip the fraction | $\dfrac{4}{7} \rightarrow \dfrac{7}{4}$  $\dfrac{4}{7} \times \dfrac{7}{4} = 1$ |

**MANHATTAN PREP**

# Divide by a Fraction: Multiply by the Reciprocal

What is $6 \div 2$?

Interestingly, $6 \div 2$ gives the same result as $6 \times \dfrac{1}{2}$:

$$6 \div 2 = 6 \times \frac{1}{2} = 3$$

The numbers 2 and $\dfrac{1}{2}$ are reciprocals of each other. This pattern generalizes: *Dividing by a number is the same as multiplying by its reciprocal.* Try this example:

$$\frac{5}{6} \div \frac{4}{7} =$$

First, find the reciprocal of the second fraction (the one you're dividing *by*). Then multiply the first fraction by that reciprocal.

$$\frac{5}{6} \div \frac{4}{7} = \frac{5}{6} \times \frac{7}{4} = \frac{35}{24}$$

Sometimes you see a double-decker fraction. It's just one fraction divided by another. The longer fraction bar is the primary division.

$$\frac{\dfrac{5}{6}}{\dfrac{4}{7}} = \frac{5}{6} \div \frac{4}{7} = \frac{5}{6} \times \frac{7}{4} = \frac{35}{24}$$

This works with variables as well. Flip the bottom fraction and multiply.

$$\frac{\dfrac{3}{x}}{\dfrac{5}{x}} = \frac{3}{x} \times \frac{x}{5} = \frac{3}{\cancel{x}} \times \frac{\cancel{x}}{5} = \frac{3}{5}$$

As always, dividing by 0 is forbidden, so $x$ cannot equal 0 in this case.

| If you… | Then you… | Like this: |
|---------|-----------|------------|
| Divide something by a fraction | Multiply by that fraction's reciprocal | $\dfrac{3}{2} \div \dfrac{7}{11} = \dfrac{3}{2} \times \dfrac{11}{7}$ |

## Check Your Skills

Evaluate and simplify the following expressions.

14. $\dfrac{1}{6} \div \dfrac{1}{11}$

15. $\dfrac{8}{5} \div \dfrac{4}{15}$

*Answers can be found on pages 164–165.*

# Addition in the Numerator: Pull Out a Common Factor

If a fraction contains addition or subtraction in the numerator or denominator, tread carefully.

The fraction bar always tells you to *divide the entire numerator by the entire denominator*. To respect PEMDAS, think of the fraction bar as a grouping symbol, like parentheses. For example:

$$\frac{3x^2 + y}{2y^2 - z} = (3x^2 + y) \div (2y^2 - z)$$

Consider a cleaner example, one with simple terms and one subtraction in the numerator:

$$\frac{9x - 6}{3x}$$

The entire quantity $9x - 6$ is divided by $3x$. In other words, you have $(9x - 6) \div 3x$.

To simplify $\dfrac{9x - 6}{3x}$, you need to *find a common factor of the entire numerator and the entire denominator*. That is, you need to find a common factor that you can pull out of both the $9x$ *and* the 6, as well as the $3x$ in the denominator.

What factor does $3x$ have in common with the quantity $9x - 6$? Notice that $x$ is not a common factor, because you can't pull it out of the *entire* numerator; the 6 does not contain an $x$. But you can pull a 3 out because both 9 and 6 have 3 as a factor.

In the numerator, $9x - 6 = 3 \times (3x - 2)$, or $3(3x - 2)$.

$$\frac{9x - 6}{3x} = \frac{3(3x - 2)}{3x}$$

Now cancel out the common factor on the top and bottom.

$$\frac{9x - 6}{3x} = \frac{\cancel{3}(3x - 2)}{\cancel{3}x} = \frac{3x - 2}{x}$$

The common factor could include a variable.

$$\frac{9y^2 - 6y}{12y} = \frac{\cancel{3y}(3y - 2)}{\cancel{3y}(4)} = \frac{3y - 2}{4}$$

If you feel comfortable simplifying without explicitly pulling out the common factor first, you can do so. Remember that you have to cancel from each separate term, $9y^2$, $6y$, and $12y$:

$$\frac{9y^2-6y}{12y} = \frac{^3\cancel{9}y^2 - {}^2\cancel{6}\cancel{y}}{_4\cancel{12}\cancel{y}} = \frac{3y-2}{4}$$

If you find yourself making too many careless mistakes that way, though, then pull out the common factor before you cancel.

| If you… | Then you… | Like this: |
|---|---|---|
| Have addition or subtraction in the numerator | Pull out a factor from the entire numerator and cancel that factor with the same one in the denominator | $\dfrac{5x+10y}{25y} = \dfrac{\cancel{5}(x+2y)}{\cancel{5}(5y)}$ $= \dfrac{x+2y}{5y}$ |

## Check Your Skills

Simplify the following expression.

16. $\dfrac{4x^2+20xy}{12x}$

Answer can be found on page 165.

# Addition in the Numerator: Split into Two Fractions (Maybe)

After you've canceled common factors, you still might not see your answer among the answer choices. In that case, you can try one more thing. Remember this?

$$\frac{13}{4} = \frac{12+1}{4} = \frac{12}{4} + \frac{1}{4}$$

*If you have a sum in the numerator, you can rewrite the fraction as the sum of two fractions.* The same is true if you have a difference (subtraction).

Consider this example again.

$$\frac{9x-6}{3x} =$$

The first step is to cancel common factors from the numerator and denominator.

$$\frac{9x-6}{3x} = \frac{\cancel{3}(3x-2)}{\cancel{3}x} = \frac{3x-2}{x}$$

It's often fine to stop there. But since you have a difference on top, you can go farther by splitting the fraction into two fractions:

$$\frac{3x-2}{x} = \frac{3x}{x} - \frac{2}{x}$$

Now you can simplify the first fraction further by canceling the common factor of $x$ on the top and bottom. Here's the full math:

$$\frac{9x-6}{3x} = \frac{\cancel{3}(3x-2)}{\cancel{3}x} = \frac{3x-2}{x} = \frac{3\cancel{x}}{\cancel{x}} - \frac{2}{x} = 3 - \frac{2}{x}$$

That's as far as you can possibly go. Is $3 - \dfrac{2}{x}$ simpler than $\dfrac{3x-2}{x}$? In a technical sense, no. But you still might have to split the fraction, depending on the available answer choices. In fact, one of the main reasons you simplify is to make an expression or equation look like one of the answer choices.

Consider this problem involving square roots:

$$\frac{10\sqrt{2} + \sqrt{6}}{2\sqrt{2}} =$$

(A) $\dfrac{5 + \sqrt{6}}{2}$

(B) $5 + \dfrac{\sqrt{6}}{2}$

(C) $5 + \dfrac{\sqrt{3}}{2}$

It's hard to spot a common factor in the numerator that will cancel with one in the denominator. So, if you're stuck, try splitting the fraction in two.

$$\frac{10\sqrt{2} + \sqrt{6}}{2\sqrt{2}} = \frac{10\sqrt{2}}{2\sqrt{2}} + \frac{\sqrt{6}}{2\sqrt{2}}$$

Now deal with the two fractions separately. Cancel a $\sqrt{2}$ out of the top and bottom of the first fraction.

$$\frac{10\cancel{\sqrt{2}}}{2\cancel{\sqrt{2}}} = \frac{10}{2} = 5$$

The second fraction is trickier. A rule from the Exponents & Roots chapter is that when you divide roots, you can combine the numbers under one square root sign: $\dfrac{\sqrt{6}}{\sqrt{2}} = \sqrt{\dfrac{6}{2}} = \sqrt{3}$ . That's not exactly the second fraction, but it's close. Just keep the extra 2 on the bottom, separated out. Introduce a factor of 1 on top as a temporary placeholder.

$$\frac{\sqrt{6}}{2\sqrt{2}} = \frac{1 \times \sqrt{6}}{2 \times \sqrt{2}} = \frac{1}{2} \times \sqrt{\frac{6}{2}} = \frac{1}{2} \times \sqrt{3} = \frac{\sqrt{3}}{2}$$

Putting it all together, you have $5+\dfrac{\sqrt{3}}{2}$. The answer is (C).

| If you... | Then you... | Like this: |
|:---:|:---:|:---:|
| Have addition or subtraction in the numerator | Might split the fraction into two fractions | $\dfrac{a+b}{c}=\dfrac{a}{c}+\dfrac{b}{c}$ |

## Check Your Skills

17. $\dfrac{x+y}{xy}$ is equivalent to which of the following for all nonzero values of $x$ and $y$?

(A) $\dfrac{1}{x}+\dfrac{1}{y}$

(B) $\dfrac{1+y}{y}$

(C) $\dfrac{x+1}{x}$

*Answer can be found on page 165.*

# Addition in the Denominator: Pull Out a Common Factor, but Never Split

To simplify a fraction with addition (or subtraction) in the *denominator*, you can do one of the same things as before. You can *pull out a common factor from the denominator, and cancel with a factor in the numerator.*

Consider this example:

$$\frac{4x}{8x-12}=$$

You can factor a 4 out of $8x - 12$ and cancel it with the 4 in the numerator.

$$\frac{4x}{8x-12}=\frac{4x}{4(2x-3)}=\frac{\cancel{4}x}{\cancel{4}(2x-3)}=\frac{x}{2x-3}$$

That's all legal so far. But you *cannot* go any farther. *Never split a fraction in two because of addition or subtraction in the denominator.* Consider this example:

Is $\dfrac{1}{3+4}$ equal to $\dfrac{1}{3}+\dfrac{1}{4}$?

No, because $\dfrac{1}{3+4}=\dfrac{1}{7}$, while $\dfrac{1}{3}+\dfrac{1}{4}=\dfrac{7}{12}$.

Do not be tempted to split $\dfrac{x}{2x-3}$ into anything else. That's as far as you can go.

| If you... | Then you... | Like this: |
|-----------|-------------|------------|
| Have addition or subtraction in the denominator | Pull out a factor from the entire denominator and cancel that factor with one in the numerator...but *never* split the fraction in two! | $\dfrac{3y}{y^2+xy} = \dfrac{3\cancel{y}}{\cancel{y}(y+x)}$ $= \dfrac{3}{y+x}$ |

## Check Your Skills

18. $\dfrac{5a^3}{15ab^2 - 5a^3}$ is equivalent to which of the following?

(A) $\dfrac{a^2}{3b^2} - 1$    (B) $\dfrac{a^2}{3b^2 - a^2}$    (C) $\dfrac{1}{15ab^2}$

*Answer can be found on page 165.*

# Add, Subtract, Multiply, Divide Nasty Fractions: Add Parentheses

Complicated fractions, such as $\dfrac{4x}{8x-12}$, can be a headache, but they follow the same rules of addition, subtraction, multiplication, and division as do all other fractions.

> **Addition:** Use the double-cross, or find a common denominator, then add numerators.
> **Subtraction:** Use the double-cross, or find a common denominator, then subtract numerators.
> **Multiplication:** Cancel common factors, then multiply tops and multiply bottoms.
> **Division:** Flip, then multiply.

With complicated fractions, the most important point to remember is this: *Treat the numerators and denominators as if they have parentheses around them.* This preserves the order of operations (PEMDAS).

Consider this sum:

$$\frac{1}{y+1} + \frac{2}{y} =$$

The same principle of addition holds. Do these fractions have the same denominator?

No. So use the double-cross to add. $\dfrac{1}{y+1} + \dfrac{2}{y} = \dfrac{y + (2y+2)}{y(y+1)} = \dfrac{3y+2}{y(y+1)}$

You could also write the answer as $\dfrac{3y+2}{y^2+y}$.

Consider this product:

$$\left(\frac{2w+4}{z^3+z}\right)\left(\frac{z}{2}\right) =$$

**MANHATTAN** PREP

You could just multiply the tops and multiply the bottoms, but don't forget to cancel common factors as best as you can *before* you multiply. Start by pulling out factors from the ugly fraction on the left.

$$\frac{2w+4}{z^3+z} = \frac{2(w+2)}{z(z^2+1)}$$

Now plug that back into the product, and cancel common factors.

$$\left(\frac{2w+4}{z^3+z}\right)\left(\frac{z}{2}\right) = \left(\frac{2(w+2)}{z(z^2+1)}\right)\left(\frac{z}{2}\right) = \left(\frac{\cancel{2}(w+2)}{\cancel{z}(z^2+1)}\right)\left(\frac{\cancel{z}}{\cancel{2}}\right) = \frac{w+2}{z^2+1}$$

| If you... | Then you... | Like this: |
|-----------|-------------|------------|
| Add, subtract, multiply, or divide fractions with complicated numerators and/or denominators | Throw parentheses around those numerators and/or denominators, then proceed normally—find common denominators, cancel common factors, etc. | $\frac{3}{m+2} - \frac{2}{m} = \frac{(3)(m)}{m+2} \overset{-}{\underset{m}{\searrow\nearrow}} \frac{(2)(m+2)}{m}$ $= \frac{3m-(2m+4)}{m(m+2)}$ $= \frac{m-4}{m(m+2)}$ |

## Check Your Skills

19. $\dfrac{x+1}{x-1} - \dfrac{3}{4} =$

*Answer can be found on page 165.*

## Fractions within Fractions: Work Your Way Out

Remember double-decker fractions in fraction division?

$$\frac{\dfrac{5}{6}}{\dfrac{4}{7}} = \frac{5}{6} \div \frac{4}{7} = \frac{5}{6} \times \frac{7}{4} = \frac{35}{24}$$

When you see a fraction within a fraction, *work your way out from the deepest level inside.* Try this example:

$$\frac{1}{1+\dfrac{1}{3}} =$$

Forget about the entire expression for a moment. Just focus on the deepest level: $1+\dfrac{1}{3}$.

Find a common denominator.

$$1 + \frac{1}{3} = \frac{3}{3} + \frac{1}{3} = \frac{4}{3}$$

Now move up a level in the original expression.

$$\frac{1}{1 + \frac{1}{3}} = \frac{1}{\frac{4}{3}}$$

The number 1 divided by a fraction is the same as taking the reciprocal of that fraction in the denominator. Here's how that works:

$$\frac{1}{1 + \frac{1}{3}} = \frac{1}{\frac{4}{3}} = \frac{1}{1} \div \frac{4}{3} = \frac{1}{1} \times \frac{3}{4} = \frac{3}{4}$$

That's the answer. Try another one, this time a three-level problem:

$$\frac{1}{2 + \frac{1}{3 + \frac{1}{4}}} =$$

Again, start at the deepest level: $3 + \frac{1}{4}$. Turn this into a mixed fraction: $3 + \frac{1}{4} = \frac{12}{4} + \frac{1}{4} = \frac{13}{4}$. Now move up a level:

$$\frac{1}{2 + \frac{1}{3 + \frac{1}{4}}} = \frac{1}{2 + \frac{1}{\frac{13}{4}}}$$

Remember that 1 divided by a fraction is the same thing as taking the reciprocal of the fraction in the denominator:

$$\frac{1}{2 + \frac{1}{3 + \frac{1}{4}}} = \frac{1}{2 + \frac{1}{\frac{13}{4}}} = \frac{1}{2 + \frac{4}{13}}$$

Now add the two terms in the bottom part:

$$2 + \frac{4}{13} = \frac{26}{13} + \frac{4}{13} = \frac{30}{13}$$

Now replace that in the original fraction. You've almost reached the surface:

$$\cfrac{1}{2+\cfrac{1}{3+\cfrac{1}{4}}} = \cfrac{1}{2+\cfrac{1}{\frac{13}{4}}} = \cfrac{1}{2+\cfrac{4}{13}} = \cfrac{1}{\frac{30}{13}}$$

Finally, you have another 1 divided by a fraction. Take the reciprocal:

$$\cfrac{1}{2+\cfrac{1}{3+\cfrac{1}{4}}} = \cfrac{1}{2+\cfrac{1}{\frac{13}{4}}} = \cfrac{1}{2+\cfrac{4}{13}} = \cfrac{1}{\frac{30}{13}} = \frac{13}{30}$$

That was a lot of steps! If you can do that problem, then you can tackle any fraction within a fraction that you might see on the real test.

| If you… | Then you… | Like this: |
|---|---|---|
| Encounter a fraction within a fraction | Work your way out from the deepest level inside | $$\cfrac{1}{y+\cfrac{1}{2-\cfrac{3}{y}}}$$ Focus here |

## Check Your Skills

20. $\dfrac{1+\dfrac{3}{4}}{2} =$

*Answer can be found on page 165.*

# Check Your Skills Answer Key

1. $\dfrac{10x}{yz^2}$ : The denominator stays the same. Add the numerators.

$$\frac{3x}{yz^2}+\frac{7x}{yz^2}=\frac{3x+7x}{yz^2}=\frac{10x}{yz^2}$$

2. $\dfrac{5}{4}$ **or** $1\dfrac{1}{4}$ : The denominator 4 is already a multiple of the denominator 2. Because only one of the fractions needs to change, use the traditional method to solve this one.

$$\frac{1}{2}+\frac{3}{4}=\frac{1\times2}{2\times2}+\frac{3}{4}=\frac{2}{4}+\frac{3}{4}=\frac{2+3}{4}=\frac{5}{4}$$

3. $\dfrac{7}{24}$ : This time, the 3 and the 8 don't share any factors, so the double-cross is the best way to proceed.

$$\frac{2}{3}\overset{16}{\underset{\diagup}{-}}\overset{9}{\underset{8}{3}}=\frac{7}{24}$$

Here is the traditional approach:

$$\frac{2}{3}-\frac{3}{8}=\frac{2\times8}{3\times8}-\frac{3\times3}{8\times3}=\frac{16}{24}-\frac{9}{24}=\frac{16-9}{24}=\frac{7}{24}$$

4. $\dfrac{5}{7}$ : The denominators of the two fractions are the same, but the numerator 5 is greater, so $\dfrac{5}{7}>\dfrac{3}{7}$.

5. $\dfrac{3}{10}$ : The numerators of the two fractions are the same, but the denominator of $\dfrac{3}{10}$ is smaller, so $\dfrac{3}{10}>\dfrac{3}{13}$.
Alternatively, you could double-cross.

$$\overset{39}{\underset{10}{3}}\overset{30}{\underset{13}{\diagdown}}\overset{30}{3}$$

39 is greater than 30, so $\dfrac{3}{10}$ is the greater fraction.

6. $1\dfrac{5}{6}$ : The denominator 6 goes into 11 just once, so the quotient is 1 and the remainder is $11-6=5$. Alternatively, split the numerator into two parts.

$$\frac{11}{6}=\frac{6+5}{6}=\frac{6}{6}+\frac{5}{6}=1+\frac{5}{6}=1\frac{5}{6}$$

7. $9\dfrac{1}{11}$ : Think of multiples of 11. How close can you get to 100 without going over? $11 \times 9 = 99$, with 1 left over.

$$\frac{100}{11} = \frac{99+1}{11} = \frac{99}{11} + \frac{1}{11} = 9 + \frac{1}{11} = 9\frac{1}{11}$$

8. $\dfrac{15}{4}$ : The shortcut is $\dfrac{4 \times 3 + 3}{4} = \dfrac{12+3}{4} = \dfrac{15}{4}$. Here's the full path:

$$3\frac{3}{4} = 3 + \frac{3}{4} = \frac{3}{1} \times \frac{4}{4} + \frac{3}{4} = \frac{12}{4} + \frac{3}{4} = \frac{15}{4}$$

9. $\dfrac{27}{4}$ : The shortcut is $\dfrac{6 \times 4 + 3}{4} = \dfrac{24+3}{4} = \dfrac{27}{4}$. The full path is:

$$6\frac{3}{4} = 6 + \frac{3}{4} = \frac{6}{1} \times \frac{4}{4} + \frac{3}{4} = \frac{24}{4} + \frac{3}{4} = \frac{27}{4}$$

10. $\dfrac{5}{8}$ :

$$\frac{25}{40} = \frac{5 \times 5}{8 \times 5} = \frac{5 \times \cancel{5}}{8 \times \cancel{5}} = \frac{5}{8}$$

11. $\dfrac{2}{3}$ :

$$\frac{16}{24} = \frac{2 \times 8}{3 \times 8} = \frac{2 \times \cancel{8}}{3 \times \cancel{8}} = \frac{2}{3}$$

12. $\dfrac{9}{35}$ :

$$\frac{3}{7} \times \frac{6}{10} = \frac{3}{7} \times \frac{\overset{3}{\cancel{6}}}{\underset{5}{\cancel{10}}} = \frac{9}{35}$$

13. $\dfrac{1}{8}$ : When a factor in the numerator cancels to 1, do still write it down; in this problem, the numerator simplifies to 1. It's safe to ignore a 1 only when a factor in the *denominator* cancels to 1.

$$\frac{5}{14} \times \frac{7}{20} = \frac{\overset{1}{\cancel{5}}}{\underset{2}{\cancel{14}}} \times \frac{\overset{1}{\cancel{7}}}{\underset{4}{\cancel{20}}} = \frac{1}{2} \times \frac{1}{4} = \frac{1}{8}$$

14. $\dfrac{11}{6}$ :

$$\frac{1}{6} \div \frac{1}{11} = \frac{1}{6} \times \frac{11}{1} = \frac{11}{6}$$

15. **6:**

$$\frac{8}{5} \div \frac{4}{15} = \frac{8}{5} \times \frac{15}{4} = \frac{{}^2\cancel{8}}{\cancel{5}} \times \frac{{}^3\cancel{15}}{\cancel{4}} = 6$$

16. $\dfrac{x+5y}{3}$:

$$\frac{4x^2 + 20xy}{12x} = \frac{\cancel{4x}\,(x+5y)}{\cancel{4x}\,(3)} = \frac{x+5y}{3}$$

17. **(A):** Split the fraction into two.

$$\frac{x+y}{xy} = \frac{\cancel{x}}{\cancel{x}\,y} + \frac{\cancel{y}}{x\,\cancel{y}} = \frac{1}{y} + \frac{1}{x}$$

18. **(B):** Don't split the denominator!

$$\frac{5a^3}{15ab^2 - 5a^3} = \frac{\cancel{5}\,a^{\cancel{3}\,2}}{\cancel{5}\,\cancel{a}\,(3b^2 - a^2)} = \frac{a^2}{3b^2 - a^2}$$

19. $\dfrac{x+7}{4x-4}$:

$$\frac{x+1}{x-1} - \frac{3}{4} = \overset{(4)(x+1)}{\underset{x-1}{\cancel{\frac{x+1}{\phantom{x}}}}} - \overset{(3)(x-1)}{\underset{4}{\cancel{\frac{3}{\phantom{x}}}}} = \frac{(4x+4)-(3x-3)}{4(x-1)} = \frac{x+7}{4x-4}$$

20. $\dfrac{7}{8}$:

$$\frac{1+\dfrac{3}{4}}{2} = \frac{\dfrac{4}{4}+\dfrac{3}{4}}{2} = \frac{\dfrac{7}{4}}{2} = \frac{7}{4} \times \frac{1}{2} = \frac{7}{8}$$

# Chapter Review: Drill Sets

## Drill 1

For each of the following pairs of fractions, decide which fraction is greater.

1. $\dfrac{1}{4}, \dfrac{3}{4}$

2. $\dfrac{1}{5}, \dfrac{1}{6}$

3. $\dfrac{53}{52}, \dfrac{85}{86}$

4. $\dfrac{7}{9}, \dfrac{6}{10}$

5. $\dfrac{700}{360}, \dfrac{590}{290}$

## Drill 2

Add or subtract the following fractions. Answers should be in their most simplified form. For any problems with variables in the denominator, assume that the denominator does not equal zero.

6. $\dfrac{7}{9} - \dfrac{2}{9}$

7. $\dfrac{2}{3} + \dfrac{5}{9}$

8. $\dfrac{4}{9} + \dfrac{8}{11}$

9. $\dfrac{20}{12} - \dfrac{5}{3}$

10. $\dfrac{52}{11x} + \dfrac{25}{11x}$

11. $\dfrac{a}{12} - \dfrac{b}{6} - \dfrac{b}{4}$

12. $\dfrac{u}{w} + 1$

13. $\sqrt{\dfrac{7}{5}} - \sqrt{\dfrac{5}{7}}$

   (A) $\dfrac{2}{\sqrt{35}}$

   (B) $\sqrt{35}$

   (C) $\dfrac{\sqrt{2}}{\sqrt{35}}$

14. $\dfrac{x^2 z}{yz} - \dfrac{x^2 z}{xy} + \dfrac{3xz}{y}$

   (A) $\dfrac{x^2 - 4xz}{y}$

   (B) $\dfrac{x(x+2z)}{y}$

   (C) $\dfrac{2x^2 z + 3xz}{xyz}$

15. $\dfrac{24}{3\sqrt{2}} - \dfrac{4}{\sqrt{2}}$

   (A) $2\sqrt{2}$

   (B) $4$

   (C) $8\sqrt{2}$

## Drill 3

Convert the following improper fractions to mixed numbers.

16. $\dfrac{9}{4}$

17. $\dfrac{31}{7}$

18. $\dfrac{47}{15}$

19. $\dfrac{70}{20}$

20. $\dfrac{72}{12}$

## Drill 4

Convert the following mixed numbers to improper fractions.

21. $3\dfrac{2}{3}$

22. $2\dfrac{1}{6}$

23. $6\dfrac{3}{7}$

24. $4\dfrac{5}{9}$

25. $12\dfrac{5}{12}$

## Drill 5

Simplify the following expressions. For any problems with variables in the denominator, assume that the denominator does not equal zero.

26. $\dfrac{5}{8} - \dfrac{4}{8}$

27. $\dfrac{7}{9} - \dfrac{2}{9}$

28. $\dfrac{1}{3} + \dfrac{7}{5}$

29. $\dfrac{3}{4} - \dfrac{10}{4}$

30. $\dfrac{2\sqrt{18}}{15}$

31. $\dfrac{17^2 \times 22}{11 \times 34}$

32. $\dfrac{48yz^3}{12z}$

33. $\dfrac{2r\sqrt{54}}{r^2 s\sqrt{12}}$

34. $\dfrac{6x^8 yz^5}{46x^6 y^2 z^3}$

35. If $a > 0$, $\dfrac{3ab^2\sqrt{50}}{\sqrt{18a^2}}$

## Drill 6

Multiply or divide the following fractions. Resulting fractions should be put in their most simplified form. For any problems with variables in the denominator, assume that the denominator does not equal zero.

36. $\dfrac{14}{20} \times \dfrac{15}{21}$

37. $\dfrac{6}{25} \div \dfrac{9}{10}$

38. $\dfrac{3}{11} \div \dfrac{3}{11}$

39. $\dfrac{x^4}{wyz} \times \dfrac{w^2 z}{x^2 y}$

40. $\dfrac{3^2}{4^2} \times \dfrac{2^2}{5^2} \times \dfrac{10}{3}$

41. $\dfrac{\sqrt{25}}{\sqrt{10}} \times \dfrac{\sqrt{8}}{\sqrt{15}}$

42. $\dfrac{\sqrt{12}}{5} \times \dfrac{\sqrt{60}}{2^4} \times \dfrac{\sqrt{45}}{3^2}$

43. $\dfrac{\sqrt{18}}{\sqrt{4}} \div \dfrac{\sqrt{9}}{\sqrt{18}}$

44. $\dfrac{xy^3 z^4}{x^3 y^4 z^2} \div \dfrac{x^6 y^3 z}{x^3 y^5 z^2}$

45. $\dfrac{12^2}{9^2} \div \dfrac{6^3}{3^5}$

# Drill 7

Simplify the following fractions. For any problems with variables in the denominator, assume that the denominator does not equal zero.

46. $\dfrac{6x+8}{2x}$

47. $\dfrac{9a+4b}{3ab}$

   (A) $\dfrac{13}{3}$

   (B) $\dfrac{3a+4b}{ab}$

   (C) $\dfrac{3}{b}+\dfrac{4}{3a}$

48. $\dfrac{6a}{33a+21ab}$

49. $\dfrac{2y\sqrt{5}}{5y\sqrt{20}-2y\sqrt{45}}$

50. $\dfrac{8x^2+40x}{32x-24x^2}$

# Drill 8

Simplify the following expressions. Final answers should be in their most simplified forms, but it is not necessary to convert improper fractions into mixed fractions. For any problems with variables in the denominator, assume that the denominator does not equal zero.

51. $\dfrac{3+4}{1+2}-\dfrac{1+2}{3+4}$

52. $\dfrac{3}{x+2}\times\dfrac{1}{5}$

53. $\dfrac{7}{n+3}\times\dfrac{n+1}{2}$

54. $\dfrac{x+2}{4}+\dfrac{x+3}{4}$

55. $\dfrac{-t+1}{t-2}\times\dfrac{-t}{2}$

56. $\dfrac{b+6}{6}-\dfrac{3+b}{6}$

57. $\dfrac{x(3+\sqrt{3})}{9}-\dfrac{x}{3}$

58. $\dfrac{3x^2+3y}{40}+\dfrac{x^2+y}{8}$

# Drill 9

Match the following expressions to their simplified forms. For any problems with variables in the denominator, assume that the denominator does not equal zero.

59. $\dfrac{4t}{6}\times\dfrac{-3}{t-3}$

   (A) $\dfrac{-2t}{t-3}$

   (B) $\dfrac{4t-3}{6t-18}$

   (C) $\dfrac{2}{3}$

60. $\dfrac{x+3}{15}\times\dfrac{10}{x+3}$

   (A) $\dfrac{2}{3}$

   (B) $2x+6$

   (C) $\dfrac{2(x+3)}{3}$

61. $\dfrac{m^3}{m-2}\times\dfrac{m+3}{m^2}$

   (A) $m+1$

   (B) $\dfrac{m^2+3m}{m-2}$

   (C) $\dfrac{m^3+3m^2}{2m}$

62. $\dfrac{(n+2n)}{n^4} \times \dfrac{(2n)^2}{(15n-5n)}$

    (A) $\dfrac{2n^2+4n^3}{15n^4-5n^5}$

    (B) $\dfrac{6}{5n^2}$

    (C) $\dfrac{n^7}{n^{16}}$

## Drill 10

Simplify the following complex fractions. For any problems with variables in the denominator, assume that the denominator does not equal zero.

63. $\dfrac{3}{3+\dfrac{3}{4}}$

64. $\dfrac{8}{2-\dfrac{2}{3}}$

65. $\dfrac{\dfrac{1}{2}+\dfrac{1}{3}}{\dfrac{7}{6}-\dfrac{3}{4}}$

66. $1-\dfrac{\dfrac{1}{2}}{y+1}$

    (A) $\dfrac{y+3}{y+1}$

    (B) $\dfrac{y}{y-1}$

    (C) $\dfrac{y+1}{y-1}$

**MANHATTAN** PREP

# Drill Sets Solutions

## Drill 1

1. $\frac{3}{4}$: When denominators are the same, the *greater* numerator is the *greater* fraction. The numerator of $\frac{3}{4}$ is greater, so $\frac{3}{4} > \frac{1}{4}$.

2. $\frac{1}{5}$: When numerators are the same, the *smaller* denominator is the *greater* fraction. The denominator of $\frac{1}{5}$ is smaller, so $\frac{1}{5} > \frac{1}{6}$.

3. $\frac{53}{52}$: Finding a common denominator or using the double-cross would both involve ugly multiplication. Instead, consider estimating using some things you know about fractions. In the first fraction, $\frac{53}{52}$, the numerator is greater than the denominator, so the fraction is greater than 1. In the second fraction, $\frac{85}{86}$, the denominator is greater than the numerator, so the fraction is less than 1. Therefore, $\frac{53}{52} > \frac{85}{86}$.

4. $\frac{7}{9}$: Consider using what you know about fractions to compare the relative size of these. The first fraction $\frac{7}{9}$ has both a greater numerator and a smaller denominator than the second fraction. Therefore, $\frac{7}{9} > \frac{6}{10}$. Alternatively, use the double-cross: 70 > 54.

5. $\frac{590}{290}$: Comparing these using the double-cross is going to involve some very ugly math! Try simplifying and estimating. First, simplify each fraction by dropping the extra zeros! Now compare $\frac{70}{36}$ and $\frac{59}{29}$. The first fraction is greater than 1 but less than 2, because 70 is less than twice 36 ($2 \times 36 = 72$). The second fraction is greater than 2, because 59 is more than twice 29 ($2 \times 29 = 58$). So $\frac{590}{290} > \frac{700}{360}$.

## Drill 2

6. $\dfrac{5}{9}$ : The denominators are already the same, so subtract the numerators.

$$\frac{7}{9} - \frac{2}{9} = \frac{7-2}{9} = \frac{5}{9}$$

7. $\dfrac{11}{9}$ : Only the first fraction needs to change, so the traditional method may be faster than the double-cross.

$$\frac{2}{3} + \frac{5}{9} = \frac{2}{3} \times \frac{3}{3} + \frac{5}{9} = \frac{6}{9} + \frac{5}{9} = \frac{6+5}{9} = \frac{11}{9}$$

8. $\dfrac{116}{99}$ : The denominators don't share any factors, so use the double-cross.

$$\frac{4}{9} + \frac{8}{11} = \overset{44}{\underset{9}{4}} \overset{+}{\times} \overset{8}{\underset{11}{72}} = \frac{116}{99}$$

9. **0:** Only the second fraction needs to change, so the traditional method may be faster than the double-cross.

$$\frac{20}{12} - \frac{5}{3} = \frac{20}{12} - \frac{5}{3} \times \frac{4}{4} = \frac{20}{12} - \frac{20}{12} = 0$$

10. $\dfrac{7}{x}$ : The denominators are already the same. Add the numerators and reduce.

$$\frac{52}{11x} + \frac{25}{11x} = \frac{77}{11x} = \frac{7}{x}$$

11. $\dfrac{a-5b}{12}$ : Find a common denominator and subtract. Because both 6 and 4 are factors of 12, 12 is the lowest common denominator.

$$\frac{a}{12} - \frac{b}{6} - \frac{b}{4} = \frac{a}{12} - \frac{2b}{12} - \frac{3b}{12} = \frac{a-2b-3b}{12} = \frac{a-5b}{12}$$

12. $\dfrac{u+w}{w}$ : The common denominator of $\dfrac{u}{w}$ and 1 is $w$.

$$\frac{u}{w} + 1 = \frac{u}{w} + \frac{w}{w} = \frac{u+w}{w}$$

13. **(A):** First, break out the square root signs.

$$\sqrt{\frac{7}{5}} - \sqrt{\frac{5}{7}} = \frac{\sqrt{7}}{\sqrt{5}} - \frac{\sqrt{5}}{\sqrt{7}}$$

Then use the double-cross.

$$\sqrt{(7)(7)} \quad \frac{\sqrt{7}}{\sqrt{5}} - \frac{\sqrt{5}}{\sqrt{7}} \quad \sqrt{(5)(5)}$$
$$\longrightarrow \sqrt{(5)(7)}$$

Now, you can simplify. $\sqrt{(7)(7)}$ reduces to 7 and $\sqrt{(5)(5)}$ reduces to 5.

$$\frac{7-5}{\sqrt{35}} = \frac{2}{\sqrt{35}}$$

14. **(B):** Start by simplifying the individual fractions.

$$\frac{x^2 z}{yz} - \frac{x^2 z}{xy} + \frac{3xz}{y} = \frac{x^2 \not{z}}{y \not{z}} - \frac{x^{\not{2}} z}{\not{x} y} + \frac{3xz}{y} = \frac{x^2}{y} - \frac{xz}{y} + \frac{3xz}{y}$$

Now you have common denominators, so you can add and subtract.

$$\frac{x^2}{y} - \frac{xz}{y} + \frac{3xz}{y} = \frac{x^2 - xz + 3xz}{y} = \frac{x^2 + 2xz}{y}$$

Glance at the answers. No match yet, but can you see a way to manipulate what you have to match one of the answers?

$$\frac{x^2 + 2xz}{y} = \frac{x(x + 2z)}{y}$$

15. **(A):** Glance at the answers. They aren't fractions, so there must be some way to eliminate the denominators. Keep that in mind. First, find a common denominator to combine the two terms. Multiply the second term by $\frac{3}{3}$.

$$\frac{24}{3\sqrt{2}} - \frac{4}{\sqrt{2}} = \frac{24}{3\sqrt{2}} - \frac{12}{3\sqrt{2}} = \frac{24 - 12}{3\sqrt{2}} = \frac{12}{3\sqrt{2}} = \frac{4}{\sqrt{2}}$$

When you see a root on the bottom of a fraction, get rid of it by multiplying by that root over itself. In this case, the root is $\sqrt{2}$, so multiply the fraction by $\frac{\sqrt{2}}{\sqrt{2}}$.

$$\frac{4}{\sqrt{2}} \times \frac{\sqrt{2}}{\sqrt{2}} = \frac{4\sqrt{2}}{2} = 2\sqrt{2}$$

## Drill 3

16. $2\dfrac{1}{4}$:

$$\frac{9}{4} = \frac{8+1}{4} = \frac{8}{4} + \frac{1}{4} = 2 + \frac{1}{4} = 2\frac{1}{4}$$

17. $4\dfrac{3}{7}$:

$$\frac{31}{7} = \frac{28+3}{7} = \frac{28}{7} + \frac{3}{7} = 4 + \frac{3}{7} = 4\frac{3}{7}$$

18. $3\dfrac{2}{15}$:

$$\frac{47}{15} = \frac{45+2}{15} = \frac{45}{15} + \frac{2}{15} = 3 + \frac{2}{15} = 3\frac{2}{15}$$

19. $3\dfrac{1}{2}$:

$$\frac{70}{20} = \frac{60+10}{20} = \frac{60}{20} + \frac{10}{20} = 3 + \frac{10}{20} = 3 + \frac{1}{2} = 3\frac{1}{2}$$

20. **6:** This one simplifies to an integer.

$$\frac{72}{12} = 6$$

## Drill 4

21. $\dfrac{11}{3}$: Via the shortcut, the numerator is (3)(3) + 2 = 11, and the denominator remains 3. Here's the full calculation:

$$3\frac{2}{3} = 3 + \frac{2}{3} = \frac{3 \times 3}{1 \times 3} + \frac{2}{3} = \frac{9}{3} + \frac{2}{3} = \frac{11}{3}$$

22. $\dfrac{13}{6}$: Via the shortcut, the numerator is (6)(2) + 1 = 13, and the denominator remains 6. Here's the full calculation:

$$2\frac{1}{6} = 2 + \frac{1}{6} = \frac{2 \times 6}{1 \times 6} + \frac{1}{6} = \frac{12}{6} + \frac{1}{6} = \frac{13}{6}$$

23. $\dfrac{45}{7}$ : Via the shortcut, the numerator is $(7)(6) + 3 = 45$, and the denominator remains 7. Here's the full calculation:

$$6\frac{3}{7} = 6 + \frac{3}{7} = \frac{6 \times 7}{1 \times 7} + \frac{3}{7} = \frac{42}{7} + \frac{3}{7} = \frac{45}{7}$$

24. $\dfrac{41}{9}$ : Via the shortcut, the numerator is $(9)(4) + 5 = 41$, and the denominator remains 9. Here's the full calculation:

$$4\frac{5}{9} = 4 + \frac{5}{9} = \frac{4 \times 9}{1 \times 9} + \frac{5}{9} = \frac{36}{9} + \frac{5}{9} = \frac{41}{9}$$

25. $\dfrac{149}{12}$ : Via the shortcut, the numerator is $(12)(12) + 5 = 149$, and the denominator remains 12. Here's the full calculation:

$$12\frac{5}{12} = 12 + \frac{5}{12} = \frac{12 \times 12}{1 \times 12} + \frac{5}{12} = \frac{144}{12} + \frac{5}{12} = \frac{149}{12}$$

# Drill 5

26. $\dfrac{1}{8}$ :

$$\frac{5}{8} - \frac{4}{8} = \frac{5-4}{8} = \frac{1}{8}$$

27. $\dfrac{5}{9}$ :

$$\frac{7}{9} - \frac{2}{9} = \frac{7-2}{9} = \frac{5}{9}$$

28. $\dfrac{26}{15}$ **OR** $1\dfrac{11}{15}$ :

$$\frac{1}{3} \overset{+}{\underset{}{\times}} \frac{7}{5} = \frac{26}{15} \text{ or } 1\frac{11}{15}$$

29. $-\dfrac{7}{4}$ **OR** $-1\dfrac{3}{4}$ :

$$\frac{3}{4} - \frac{10}{4} = \frac{3-10}{4} = \frac{-7}{4} \text{ OR } -1\frac{3}{4}$$

30. $\dfrac{2\sqrt{2}}{5}$ : Begin by simplifying the square root in the numerator. When simplifying a square root, always look for factors that are perfect squares; in this example, $18 = 2 \times 9 = 2 \times 3^2$. The $3^2$ can be removed from the square root to become 3.

$$\frac{2\sqrt{18}}{15} = \frac{2\sqrt{2 \times 3 \times 3}}{15} = \frac{2 \times \cancel{3} \times \sqrt{2}}{\cancel{3} \times 5} = \frac{2\sqrt{2}}{5}$$

31. **17** :

$$\frac{17^2 \times 22}{11 \times 34} = \frac{17 \times \cancel{17} \times \cancel{2} \times \cancel{11}}{\cancel{11} \times \cancel{2} \times \cancel{17}} = 17$$

32. $4yz^2$ : Cancel a 12 from both 48 and 12. Use your exponent rules to simplify $z$.

$$\frac{48\,yz^3}{12z} = \frac{\overset{4}{\cancel{48}}\,yz^{3-1}}{\cancel{12}} = 4\,yz^2$$

33. $\dfrac{3\sqrt{2}}{rs}$ : To begin, simplify the square roots in the numerator and denominator by looking for factors that have pairs.

$$\begin{aligned}
\sqrt{54} &= \sqrt{2 \times 3 \times 3 \times 3} = 3\sqrt{2 \times 3} \\
\sqrt{12} &= \sqrt{2 \times 2 \times 3} = 2\sqrt{3}
\end{aligned}$$

Because the numbers remaining inside the square roots have a factor of 3 in common, it's useful to leave the numerator broken into the root of 2 and 3.

$$3\sqrt{2 \times 3} = 3\sqrt{2}\sqrt{3}$$

Therefore:

$$\frac{2r\sqrt{54}}{r^2 s\sqrt{12}} = \frac{2r\left(3\sqrt{2}\sqrt{3}\right)}{r^2 s\left(2\sqrt{3}\right)} = \frac{\cancel{2}\,r\left(3\sqrt{2}\,\cancel{\sqrt{3}}\right)}{r^{\cancel{2}}s\left(\cancel{2}\,\cancel{\sqrt{3}}\right)} = \frac{3\sqrt{2}}{rs}$$

34. $\dfrac{3x^2 z^2}{23y}$ : There are two good ways to simplify a fraction with variables raised to powers. One approach is to use exponent rules to rewrite the expression so that the cancellations are more clear.

$$\frac{6x^8 yz^5}{46x^6 y^2 z^3} = \frac{\overset{3}{\cancel{6}} \times \cancel{x^6} \times x^2 \times \cancel{y} \times \cancel{z^3} \times z^2}{\underset{23}{\cancel{46}} \times \cancel{x^6} \times \cancel{y} \times y \times \cancel{z^3}} = \frac{3x^2 z^2}{23y}$$

Alternatively, if you are comfortable with the exponent rules, use the rules to simplify directly.

$$\frac{6}{46} \times \frac{x^8}{x^6} \times \frac{y}{y^2} \times \frac{z^5}{z^3} = \frac{3}{23} x^2 y^{-1} z^2$$

To combine these into one fraction, leave $x^2$ and $z^2$ in the numerator but place $y$ in the denominator because $y^{-1} = \frac{1}{y}$.

$$\frac{3}{23} x^2 y^{-1} z^2 = \frac{3x^2 z^2}{23y}$$

35. **$5b^2$** : Begin by simplifying the square roots then pull any squares out.

$$\sqrt{50} = \sqrt{2 \times 25} = 5\sqrt{2}$$
$$\sqrt{18a^2} = \sqrt{2 \times 9 \times a^2} = 3a\sqrt{2}$$

Cancel common terms on the top and bottom.

$$\frac{3ab^2 \sqrt{50}}{\sqrt{18a^2}} = \frac{\cancel{3}\,\cancel{a}b^2 \times 5\sqrt{\cancel{2}}}{\cancel{3}\,\cancel{a}\,\cancel{\sqrt{2}}} = 5b^2$$

# Drill 6

36. $\dfrac{1}{2}$ : Remember, you *can* cancel across the multiplication sign.

$$\frac{14}{20} \times \frac{15}{21} = \frac{^2\cancel{14}}{20} \times \frac{15}{\cancel{21}_3} = \frac{^2\cancel{14}}{_4\cancel{20}} \times \frac{\cancel{15}^3}{\cancel{21}_3} = \frac{^1\cancel{2}}{\cancel{4}_2} \times \frac{\cancel{3}^1}{\cancel{3}_1} = \frac{1}{2}$$

37. $\dfrac{4}{15}$ : This is starting further left than those prior flip the second fraction to multiply.

$$\frac{6}{25} \div \frac{9}{10} = \frac{6}{25} \times \frac{10}{9} = \frac{^2\cancel{6}}{_5\cancel{25}} \times \frac{\cancel{10}^2}{\cancel{9}_3} = \frac{4}{15}$$

38. **1:**

$$\frac{3}{11} \div \frac{3}{11} = \frac{3}{11} \times \frac{11}{3} = \frac{\cancel{3} \times \cancel{11}}{\cancel{11} \times \cancel{3}} = 1$$

**4**

39. $\dfrac{x^2 w}{y^2}$ :

$$\dfrac{x^4}{wyz} \times \dfrac{w^2 z}{x^2 y} = \dfrac{x^4}{wy\cancel{z}} \times \dfrac{w^2 \cancel{z}}{x^2 y} = \dfrac{x^{4-2} w^{2-1}}{y^2} = \dfrac{x^2 w}{y^2}$$

40. $\dfrac{3}{10}$ : Simplify the bases to their prime components, then cancel. $4^2$ is the same as $\left(2^2\right)^2$, which equals $(2^2)(2^2)$.

$$\dfrac{3^2}{4^2} \times \dfrac{2^2}{5^2} \times \dfrac{10}{3} = \dfrac{3^{\cancel{2}}}{\left(2^{\cancel{2}}\right)\left(2^{\cancel{2}}\right)} \times \dfrac{2^{\cancel{2}}}{5^{\cancel{2}}} \times \dfrac{\cancel{2} \times \cancel{5}}{\cancel{3}} = \dfrac{3}{10}$$

41. $\dfrac{2}{\sqrt{3}}$ : Combine everything under one square root sign (you're allowed to do this because everything is multiplication or division), and simplify.

$$\dfrac{\sqrt{25}}{\sqrt{10}} \times \dfrac{\sqrt{8}}{\sqrt{15}} = \sqrt{\dfrac{25 \times 8}{10 \times 15}} = \sqrt{\dfrac{^5\cancel{25} \times \cancel{8}^4}{_5\cancel{10} \times \cancel{15}_3}} = \sqrt{\dfrac{^{\cancel{5}}\cancel{25} \times \cancel{8}^4}{_{\cancel{5}}\cancel{10} \times \cancel{15}_3}} = \sqrt{\dfrac{4}{3}} = \dfrac{2}{\sqrt{3}}$$

42. $\dfrac{1}{4}$ : Begin by factoring the roots, keeping an eye on what they have in common with each other and with the terms on the bottom. Then combine everything into one big fraction.

$$\dfrac{\sqrt{12}}{5} \times \dfrac{\sqrt{60}}{2^4} \times \dfrac{\sqrt{45}}{3^2} = \dfrac{\sqrt{4}\sqrt{3} \times \sqrt{4}\sqrt{15} \times \sqrt{3}\sqrt{15}}{5 \times \left(2^2 \times 2^2\right) \times 3^2}$$

Note that you can combine each pair of roots in the numerator to get integers that will cancel with the denominator.

$$\dfrac{\sqrt{3}\sqrt{3}\sqrt{4}\sqrt{4}\sqrt{15}\sqrt{15}}{5 \times 4 \times 4 \times 3 \times 3} = \dfrac{\cancel{3} \times \cancel{4} \times \cancel{15}}{\cancel{5} \times \cancel{4} \times 4 \times \cancel{3} \times \cancel{3}} = \dfrac{1}{4}$$

43. **3:** To divide by a fraction, multiply by its reciprocal.

$$\dfrac{\sqrt{18}}{\sqrt{4}} \div \dfrac{\sqrt{9}}{\sqrt{18}} = \dfrac{\sqrt{18}}{\sqrt{4}} \times \dfrac{\sqrt{18}}{\sqrt{9}}$$

Feel free to simplify the perfect squares as soon as you spot them.

$$\dfrac{\sqrt{18}}{\sqrt{4}} \times \dfrac{\sqrt{18}}{\sqrt{9}} = \dfrac{18}{2 \times 3} = \dfrac{18}{6} = 3$$

44. $\dfrac{yz^3}{x^5}$ : To divide, multiply by the reciprocal.

$$\frac{xy^3z^4}{x^3y^4z^2} \div \frac{x^6y^3z}{x^3y^5z^2} = \frac{xy^3z^4}{x^3y^4z^2} \times \frac{x^3y^5z^2}{x^6y^3z}$$

If you'd like, first rearrange to place the like terms together (to minimize careless mistakes). Cancel any terms that match exactly.

$$\frac{(x)\cancel{(x^3)}}{\cancel{(x^3)}(x^6)} \times \frac{\cancel{(y^3)}(y^5)}{(y^4)\cancel{(y^3)}} \times \frac{(z^4)\cancel{(z^2)}}{\cancel{(z^2)}(z)} = \frac{x}{x^6} \times \frac{y^5}{y^4} \times \frac{z^4}{z}$$

For the remaining terms, use exponent rules to simplify the like variables.

$$\frac{x}{x^6} \times \frac{y^5}{y^4} \times \frac{z^4}{z} = x^{(1-6)}y^{(5-4)}z^{(4-1)} = x^{-5}y^1z^3 = \frac{yz^3}{x^5}$$

45. **2:** Begin by multiplying by the reciprocal.

$$\frac{12^2}{9^2} \div \frac{6^3}{3^5} = \frac{12^2}{9^2} \times \frac{3^5}{6^3}$$

Break the larger numbers down into numbers with similar bases, then use exponent rules to simplify.

$$\frac{12^2}{9^2} \times \frac{3^5}{6^3} = \frac{(2\times6)^2}{(3\times3)^2} \times \frac{3^5}{6^3} = \frac{2^2\times6^2}{3^2\times3^2} \times \frac{3^5}{6^3} = \frac{2^2}{1} \times \frac{3^5}{3^4} \times \frac{6^2}{6^3} = \frac{2^23^1}{6^1} = \frac{12}{6} = 2$$

# Drill 7

46. $3+\dfrac{4}{x}$ **OR** $\dfrac{3x+4}{x}$ : When the numerator of a fraction consists of two or more terms added together, but the denominator is a single term, you can split the fraction into two fractions, and then simplify further.

$$\frac{6x+8}{2x} = \frac{6x}{2x} + \frac{8}{2x}$$

Now simplify both fractions. (Don't cancel across the two fractions; that isn't allowed when adding or subtracting.)

$$\frac{6x}{2x} + \frac{8}{2x} = \frac{\overset{3}{\cancel{6}}\cancel{x}}{\cancel{2}\cancel{x}} + \frac{\overset{4}{\cancel{8}}}{\cancel{2}x} = 3 + \frac{4}{x}$$

Alternatively, you can leave this in the starting form and cancel out the common term of 2.

$$\frac{6x+8}{2x} = \frac{\cancel{2}(3x+4)}{\cancel{2}x} = \frac{3x+4}{x}$$

47. **(C):** Split this fraction into two fractions with a common denominator of $3ab$, and then simplify further.

$$\frac{9a+4b}{3ab} = \frac{9a}{3ab} + \frac{4b}{3ab} = \frac{\overset{3}{\cancel{9}}\,\cancel{a}}{\cancel{3}\,\cancel{a}b} + \frac{4\cancel{b}}{3a\cancel{b}} = \frac{3}{b} + \frac{4}{3a}$$

48. $\dfrac{2}{11+7b}$ : Be careful when dealing with addition or subtraction in the denominator; you can't split these into two separate fractions. Instead, look for a common term that you can cancel.

$$\frac{6a}{33a+21ab} = \frac{3a \times 2}{(3a \times 11)+(3a \times 7b)} = \frac{\cancel{3a} \times 2}{\cancel{3a}\,(11+7b)} = \frac{2}{11+7b}$$

49. $\dfrac{1}{2}$ : Begin by simplifying the square roots in the denominator.

$$\frac{2y\sqrt{5}}{5y\sqrt{20}-2y\sqrt{45}} = \frac{2y\sqrt{5}}{5y\sqrt{4}\sqrt{5}-2y\sqrt{9}\sqrt{5}} = \frac{2y\sqrt{5}}{5y\left(2\sqrt{5}\right)-2y\left(3\sqrt{5}\right)}$$

All three terms have a common factor of $2y\sqrt{5}$. Pull this factor out of each term.

$$\frac{2y\sqrt{5}}{5y\left(2\sqrt{5}\right)-2y\left(3\sqrt{5}\right)} = \frac{\cancel{2y\sqrt{5}}}{\cancel{2y\sqrt{5}}\,(5)-\cancel{2y\sqrt{5}}\,(3)} = \frac{1}{5-3} = \frac{1}{2}$$

If you feel comfortable canceling from all three terms without pulling out the common factor first, feel free to do so. Make sure to cancel a 2, a $y$, and a $\sqrt{5}$ from each of the three terms, the one on the top and the two on the bottom.

$$\frac{2y\sqrt{5}}{5y\left(2\sqrt{5}\right)-2y\left(3\sqrt{5}\right)} = \frac{\cancel{2}\,\cancel{y}\,\cancel{\sqrt{5}}}{5\cancel{y}\left(\cancel{2}\,\cancel{\sqrt{5}}\right)-\cancel{2}\,\cancel{y}\left(3\cancel{\sqrt{5}}\right)} = \frac{1}{5-3} = \frac{1}{2}$$

50. $\dfrac{x+5}{4-3x}$ : Notice that every term has the common factor of $8x$. Pull this out and cancel.

$$\frac{8x^2+40x}{32x-24x^2} = \frac{\cancel{8x}\,(x+5)}{\cancel{8x}\,(4-3x)} = \frac{x+5}{4-3x}$$

# Drill 8

51. $\dfrac{40}{21}$ : Begin by simplifying each fraction.

$$\frac{3+4}{1+2} - \frac{1+2}{3+4} = \frac{7}{3} - \frac{3}{7}$$

**MANHATTAN** PREP

Use the double-cross method to subtract.

$$\overset{49}{7} \overset{-}{\nearrow} \overset{9}{3} = \frac{40}{21}$$
$$\underset{3}{\phantom{x}} \underset{\phantom{x}}{\times} \underset{7}{\phantom{x}}$$

4

52. $\dfrac{3}{5x+10}$ :

$$\frac{3}{x+2} \times \frac{1}{5} = \frac{3 \times 1}{(x+2) \times 5} = \frac{3}{5x+10}$$

53. $\dfrac{7n+7}{2n+6}$ :

$$\frac{7}{n+3} \times \frac{n+1}{2} = \frac{7 \times (n+1)}{(n+3) \times 2} = \frac{7n+7}{2n+6}$$

54. $\dfrac{2x+5}{4}$ :

$$\frac{x+2}{4} + \frac{x+3}{4} = \frac{(x+2)+(x+3)}{4} = \frac{2x+5}{4}$$

55. $\dfrac{t^2-t}{2t-4}$ :

$$\frac{-t+1}{t-2} \times \frac{-t}{2} = \frac{(-t+1) \times (-t)}{(t-2) \times 2} = \frac{t^2-t}{2t-4}$$

56. $\dfrac{1}{2}$ : When subtracting fractions with more than one term in the numerator, put the subtracted term in parentheses to remind yourself to distribute the negative sign.

$$\frac{b+6}{6} - \frac{3+b}{6} = \frac{b+6-(3+b)}{6} = \frac{b+6-3-b}{6} = \frac{3}{6} = \frac{1}{2}$$

57. $\dfrac{x\sqrt{3}}{9}$ :

$$\frac{x(3+\sqrt{3})}{9} - \frac{x}{3} = \frac{3x+x\sqrt{3}}{9} - \frac{3x}{9} = \frac{(3x+x\sqrt{3})-(3x)}{9} = \frac{x\sqrt{3}}{9}$$

58. $\dfrac{x^2+y}{5}$ :

$$\frac{3x^2+3y}{40}+\frac{x^2+y}{8}=\frac{3x^2+3y}{40}+\frac{5x^2+5y}{40}=\frac{\left(3x^2+3y\right)+\left(5x^2+5y\right)}{40}=\frac{8x^2+8y}{40}$$

Don't stop yet! All three terms are divisible by 8.

$$\frac{8x^2+8y}{40}=\frac{\cancel{8}x^2+\cancel{8}y}{\cancel{40}\,_5}=\frac{x^2+y}{5}$$

# Drill 9

59. **(A):** Simplify before you multiply. Take a 2 out of the 4 and 6, then take a 3 out of the 3 and −3.

$$\frac{4t}{6}\times\frac{-3}{t-3}=\frac{^2\cancel{4}t}{\cancel{6}\,_{\cancel{3}}}\times\frac{\cancel{-3}^{\,-1}}{t-3}=\frac{2\times t\times-1}{t-3}=\frac{-2t}{t-3}$$

60. **(A):** Simplify before you multiply.

$$\frac{x+3}{15}\times\frac{10}{x+3}=\frac{\cancel{(x+3)}}{\cancel{15}\,_3}\times\frac{^2\cancel{10}}{\cancel{(x+3)}}=\frac{2}{3}$$

61. **(B):** Simplify before you multiply. $m^3$ divided by $m^2$ equals $m^1$, which is just $m$.

$$\frac{m^3}{m-2}\times\frac{m+3}{m^2}=\frac{m^{\cancel{3}}}{m-2}\times\frac{m+3}{\cancel{m}^{\cancel{2}}}=\frac{m(m+3)}{m-2}=\frac{m^2+3m}{m-2}$$

62. **(B):** First, combine the like terms in the numerator of the first fraction and the denominator of the second fraction.

$$\frac{(n+2n)}{n^4}\times\frac{(2n)^2}{(15n-5n)}=\frac{3n}{n^4}\times\frac{4n^2}{10n}$$

If you like, rearrange to place the numbers and variables near each other (to minimize careless mistakes), then simplify.

$$\frac{(3)(4)}{(10)}\times\frac{(n)(n^2)}{(n^4)(n)}=\frac{(3)(^2\cancel{4})}{(\cancel{10}\,_5)}\times\frac{(n^{1+2})}{(n^{4+1})}=\frac{6}{5}\times n^{3-5}=\frac{6}{5}\times n^{-2}=\frac{6}{5n^2}$$

If you feel comfortable with exponents, you can do the exponent simplification in one long step (but, if you do, use parentheses to make sure you keep the signs straight!).

$$\frac{(n)\left(n^2\right)}{\left(n^4\right)(n)} = n^{(1+2)-(4+1)} = n^{3-5} = n^{-2}$$

# Drill 10

63. $\dfrac{4}{5}$ : Begin by simplifying the denominator.

$$\frac{3}{3+\dfrac{3}{4}} = \frac{3}{\dfrac{12}{4}+\dfrac{3}{4}} = \frac{3}{\dfrac{15}{4}}$$

Dividing by $\dfrac{15}{4}$ is the same as multiplying by $\dfrac{4}{15}$.

$$\frac{3}{\dfrac{15}{4}} = 3\times\frac{4}{15} = \cancel{3}\times\frac{4}{\cancel{15}_5} = \frac{4}{5}$$

64. **6:** Begin by simplifying the denominator:

$$\frac{8}{2-\dfrac{2}{3}} = \frac{8}{\dfrac{6}{3}-\dfrac{2}{3}} = \frac{8}{\dfrac{4}{3}}$$

Dividing by $\dfrac{4}{3}$ is the same as multiplying by $\dfrac{3}{4}$.

$$\frac{8}{\dfrac{4}{3}} = 8\times\frac{3}{4} = \cancel{8}^2\times\frac{3}{\cancel{4}} = 6$$

65. **2:** To begin, simplify the numerator and the denominator.

$$\frac{\dfrac{1}{2}+\dfrac{1}{3}}{\dfrac{7}{6}-\dfrac{3}{4}} = \frac{\dfrac{3}{6}+\dfrac{2}{6}}{\dfrac{14}{12}-\dfrac{9}{12}} = \frac{\dfrac{5}{6}}{\dfrac{5}{12}}$$

Now divide.

$$\frac{\dfrac{5}{6}}{\dfrac{5}{12}} = \frac{5}{6} \times \frac{12}{5}$$

Simplify before you multiply.

$$\frac{5}{6} \times \frac{12}{5} = \frac{\cancel{5}}{\cancel{6}} \times \frac{^2\cancel{12}}{\cancel{5}} = 2$$

66. **(C):** Work from the inside out. First, combine the terms in the denominator.

$$\frac{1}{1 - \dfrac{2}{y+1}} = \frac{1}{\dfrac{y+1}{y+1} - \dfrac{2}{y+1}} = \frac{1}{\dfrac{(y+1)-(2)}{y+1}} = \frac{1}{\dfrac{y-1}{y+1}}$$

A numerator of 1 divided by a fraction is just the reciprocal of that fraction (no matter how ugly that fraction is).

$$\frac{1}{\dfrac{y-1}{y+1}} = \frac{y+1}{y-1}$$

# Fractions, Decimals, Percents, & Ratios

# In this chapter...

- Four Ways to Express Parts of a Whole

- Convert 0.25 to 25%: Move the Decimal Point Two Places Right

- Convert 0.25 or 25% to $\frac{1}{4}$: Put 25 over 100 and Simplify

- Convert $\frac{1}{4}$ to 0.25 or 25%: Long-Divide 1 by 4

- Multiply a Decimal by a Power of Ten: Shift the Decimal Point

- Add or Subtract Decimals: Line Up the Decimal Points

- Multiply Two Decimals: Ignore Decimal Points at First

- Multiply a Decimal and a Big Number: Trade Decimal Places

- Divide Two Decimals: Move Points in the Same Direction to Kill Decimals

- 20% of $55 = 0.2 × $55

- Percent Change: Divide Change in Value by Original Value

- Percent of a Percent of: Multiply Twice

- Ratio: Part-to-Part and Part-to-Whole

- Ratios and Percents: Convert Fractions to Percents

# Fractions, Decimals, Percents, & Ratios

## In This Chapter, You Will Learn To:

- Understand relationships among fractions, decimals, percents, and ratios
- Convert from one form to another

## Four Ways to Express Parts of a Whole

Say you have the shaded part of this orange. You can express how much you have in four ways.

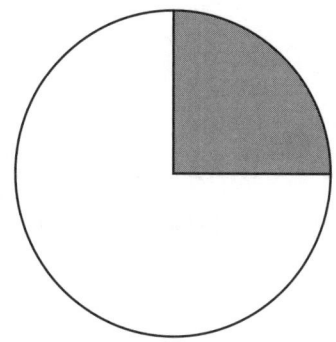

1. You have $\frac{1}{4}$ of the orange.  **Fraction**

2. You have 0.25 of the orange.  **Decimal**

3. You have 25% of the orange.  **Percent**

4. The ratio of your piece to the whole orange is 1 part to 4 parts, or 1 : 4.  **Ratio**

Any of these four forms can express a *part-to-whole relationship*. The main difference between the forms is how you think about the whole:

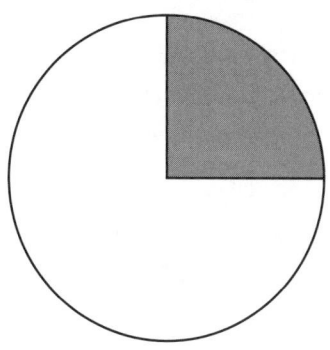

$\frac{1}{4}$ = 1 out of 4 pieces of the whole

0.25 = 0.25 of the whole

25% = 25 out of 100 pieces of the whole

1 : 4 = ("1 to 4") 1 out of 4 pieces of the whole

In other words, what is each form "out of"? What is the whole that you are dividing by?

Fractions are *out of* the denominator (4 in this case).

Decimals are *out of* 1 (the whole). You've already done the division.

Percents are *out of* 100. *Percent* literally means "per hundred," or divided by 100.

Part-to-whole ratios are *out of* the second term in the ratio (4 in this case). Ratios can also be part-to-part; you'll learn more about this later. A ratio can be written with a colon between the two numbers (3 : 7) or as a fraction ($\frac{3}{7}$).

Which form is most useful depends on the problem at hand. You might say any of the following:

The container is $\frac{1}{2}$ full.

The container is filled to 0.5 of its capacity.

The container is 50% full.

The ratio of the contents of the container to its total capacity is 1 to 2.

By the way, the part can be greater than the whole.

I ate $\frac{5}{4}$ boxes of cereal. (I ate more than one box.)

I ate 1.25 boxes of cereal.

I ate 125% of one box of cereal.

The ratio of what I ate to a whole box of cereal was 5 to 4.

# Convert 0.25 to 25%: Move the Decimal Point Two Places Right

Decimals are out of 1. Percents are out of 100. So, to convert a decimal to a percent, move the decimal point to the *right two places*. Add zeros if necessary:

0.53 = 53%      0.4 = 0.40 = 40%      0.03 = 3%      1.7 = 1.70 = 170%

A percent might still contain a visible decimal point when you're done.

0.4057 = 40.57%      0.002 = 0.2%      0.0005 = 0.05%

Note that, when converting from a decimal to a percent, the new number seems greater than the original. In reality, the two are equal; they represent the exact same number. But the way you write the number makes it *look* greater in percent form and smaller in decimal form. This can help you to remember to move the decimal point to the *right* when converting to the percent form.

To convert a percent to a decimal, *go in reverse*. That is, move the decimal point two places to the *left*. If the decimal point isn't visible, it's actually just before the percent sign. Add zeros if necessary as you move left.

$$39\% = 39.\% = 0.39 \qquad 60\% = 0.60 = 0.6 \qquad 8\% = 0.08 \qquad 225\% = 2.25$$

$$13.4\% = 0.134 \qquad 0.7\% = 0.007 \qquad 0.001\% = 0.00001$$

Remember: The decimal form of the number *looks* smaller than the percent form. That can help you to remember to move the decimal point to the *left* when converting to decimal form. Here are a couple more rules for your book:

| If you… | Then you… | Like this: |
|---|---|---|
| Want to convert a decimal to a percent | Move the decimal point two places to the right to make the number seem greater (though it isn't really) | $0.036 = 3.6\%$ |
| Want to convert a percent to a decimal | Move the decimal point two places to the left to make the number seem smaller (though it isn't really) | $41.2\% = 0.412$ |

## Check Your Skills

1. Convert 0.035 to a percent.

*Answer can be found on page 217.*

# Convert 0.25 or 25% to $\frac{1}{4}$: Put 25 over 100 and Simplify

The decimal 0.25 is twenty-five one-hundredths. Rewrite that as 25 over 100.

$$0.25 = \frac{25}{100}$$

Now simplify by canceling common factors from the top and bottom.

$$0.25 = \frac{25}{100} = \frac{\overset{1}{\cancel{25}}}{\underset{4}{\cancel{100}}} = \frac{1}{4}$$

When you convert a decimal to a fraction, put a power of 10 (10, 100, 1,000, etc.) in the denominator of the fraction. Which power of 10? It depends on how far the decimal goes to the right.

Put as many zeros in your power of 10 as you have digits to the right of the decimal point.

| | | |
|---|---|---|
| 0.3 | = | $\frac{3}{10}$ |
| Zero point three | is | three-tenths, or three over ten |
| 0.23 | = | $\frac{23}{100}$ |
| Zero point two three | is | twenty-three one-hundredths |
| 0.007 | = | $\frac{7}{1,000}$ |
| Zero point zero zero seven | is | seven one-thousandths |

As with any fractions, cancel common terms to simplify.

$$0.4 = \frac{4}{10} = \frac{\overset{2}{\cancel{4}}}{\underset{5}{\cancel{10}}} = \frac{2}{5} \qquad 0.75 = \frac{75}{100} = \frac{\overset{3}{\cancel{75}}}{\underset{4}{\cancel{100}}} = \frac{3}{4}$$

In the second case, you cancel 25 from the top and bottom, leaving 3 and 4.

In the numerator, keep any zeros in the middle of two numbers, such as the 0 between the 1 and the 2 in 0.0102 in the problem shown below. Otherwise, drop any zeros (such as the 0's to the left of the 1). However, base the number of zeros in the denominator on the total number of starting decimal places (before you dropped any zeros). In the example below, there are four decimal places in 0.0102, so there are four zeros in the power of 10 in the denominator.

$$0.0102 = \frac{102}{10,000} = \frac{\overset{51}{\cancel{102}}}{\underset{5,000}{\cancel{10,000}}} = \frac{51}{5,000}$$

To convert a percent to a fraction, write the number over 100. Remember that *percent* literally means "per hundred." For example:

$$45\% = \frac{45}{100} = \frac{\overset{9}{\cancel{45}}}{\underset{20}{\cancel{100}}} = \frac{9}{20} \qquad 8\% = \frac{8}{100} = \frac{\overset{2}{\cancel{8}}}{\underset{25}{\cancel{100}}} = \frac{2}{25}$$

Alternatively, you can first convert the percent to a decimal by moving the decimal place. Then follow the process given earlier.

$$2.5\% = 0.025 = \frac{25}{1,000} = \frac{\overset{1}{\cancel{25}}}{\underset{40}{\cancel{1,000}}} = \frac{1}{40}$$

If you don't convert to a decimal first, be sure to write the fraction over 100.

$$2.5\% = \frac{2.5}{100}$$

You'll learn how to divide decimals a little farther on.

| If you… | Then you… | Like this: |
|---|---|---|
| Want to convert a decimal to a fraction | Put the digits to the right of the decimal point over the appropriate power of 10, then simplify | $0.036 = \frac{36}{1,000}$ $= \frac{9}{250}$ |
| Want to convert a percent to a fraction | Write the percent over 100, then simplify  *OR*  Convert first to a decimal, then follow the process for converting decimals to fractions | $4\% = \frac{4}{100}$ $= \frac{1}{25}$ $3.6\% = 0.036$ $0.036 = \frac{36}{1,000}$ $= \frac{9}{250}$ |

## Check Your Skills

2. Convert 0.375 to a fraction.
3. Convert 24% to a fraction and simplify fully.

*Answers can be found on page 217.*

# Convert $\frac{1}{4}$ to 0.25 or 25%: Long-Divide 1 by 4

A fraction represents division. The decimal equivalent is the result of that division.

*To convert a fraction to a decimal*, long-divide the numerator by the denominator. As you're doing the math, keep track of the decimal point on top (in the solution), but don't worry about keeping the decimals down below.

$$\frac{1}{4} = ?$$    Divide 1 by 4.

$$\begin{array}{r} 0.25 \\ 4\overline{)1.00} \\ \underline{-8} \\ 20 \\ \underline{-20} \\ 0 \end{array}$$

$$\frac{1}{4} = 0.25$$

$$\frac{5}{8} = ?$$    Divide 5 by 8.

$$\begin{array}{r} 0.625 \\ 8\overline{)5.000} \\ \underline{-48} \\ 20 \\ \underline{-16} \\ 40 \\ \underline{-40} \\ 0 \end{array}$$

$$\frac{5}{8} = 0.625$$

On the GMAT, most cases in which you might need to do this math will involve common fractions that you can memorize. For instance, $\frac{1}{4}$ is a common fraction. Memorize the fact that $\frac{1}{4} = 0.25 = 25\%$. At the end of this section, you'll find more common fractions to memorize.

In some cases, the decimal never ends because the long division never ends. You get a repeating decimal.

$$\frac{1}{3} = 0.333... = 0.\overline{3}$$

$$\begin{array}{r} 0.33... \\ 3\overline{)1.000} \\ \underline{-\ 9} \\ 10 \\ \underline{-\ 9} \\ 10 \\ ... \end{array}$$

If the denominator contains only 2's and/or 5's as factors, the decimal will end (this is called a *terminating decimal* because it terminates, or ends). In this case, you can find the decimal equivalent using the earlier method: Multiply the numerator and denominator by the same number—whatever number turns the denominator into a power of 10. For example:

$$\frac{1}{4} = \frac{1 \times 25}{4 \times 25} = \frac{25}{100} = 0.25 \qquad\qquad \frac{1}{20} = \frac{1 \times 5}{20 \times 5} = \frac{5}{100} = 0.05$$

However, if the denominator contains factors other than 2's and 5's, you must use long division to convert to a percent (this is because powers of 10 are only multiples of 2 and 5).

*To convert a fraction to a percent*, first convert it to a decimal, then convert the decimal to a percent.

$$\frac{1}{2} = \frac{1 \times 5}{2 \times 5} = \frac{5}{10} = 0.5 = 50\%$$

| If you... | Then you... | Like this: |
|---|---|---|
| Want to convert a fraction to a decimal | Do long division<br><br>*OR*<br><br>Multiply the top and bottom by the same number such that the denominator becomes a power of 10, but only if the denominator contains only 2's and 5's as factors | $\dfrac{7}{8} \rightarrow 8\overline{)7.000}\,^{0.875}$<br><br>$\dfrac{1}{50} = \dfrac{1 \times 2}{50 \times 2}$<br>$= \dfrac{2}{100}$<br>$= 0.02$ |

Memorize the following conversions. Flash cards are a great tool to help; grab some index cards and start writing.

*Tenths and Fifths*

| Fraction | Decimal | Percent |
|---|---|---|
| $\dfrac{1}{10}$ | 0.1 | 10% |
| $\dfrac{2}{10} = \dfrac{1}{5}$ | 0.2 | 20% |
| $\dfrac{3}{10}$ | 0.3 | 30% |
| $\dfrac{4}{10} = \dfrac{2}{5}$ | 0.4 | 40% |
| $\dfrac{5}{10} = \dfrac{1}{2}$ | 0.5 | 50% |
| $\dfrac{6}{10} = \dfrac{3}{5}$ | 0.6 | 60% |
| $\dfrac{7}{10}$ | 0.7 | 70% |

| Fraction | Decimal | Percent |
|---|---|---|
| $\dfrac{8}{10} = \dfrac{4}{5}$ | 0.8 | 80% |
| $\dfrac{9}{10}$ | 0.9 | 90% |
| $\dfrac{10}{10} = \dfrac{5}{5} = 1$ | 1.0 | 100% |
| $\dfrac{11}{10}$ | 1.1 | 110% |
| $\dfrac{12}{10} = \dfrac{6}{5}$ | 1.2 | 120% |

*Eighths and Fourths*

| Fraction | Decimal | Percent |
|---|---|---|
| $\dfrac{1}{8}$ | 0.125 | 12.5% |
| $\dfrac{2}{8} = \dfrac{1}{4}$ | 0.25 | 25% |
| $\dfrac{3}{8}$ | 0.375 | 37.5% |
| $\dfrac{4}{8} = \dfrac{2}{4} = \dfrac{1}{2}$ | 0.5 | 50% |
| $\dfrac{5}{8}$ | 0.625 | 62.5% |
| $\dfrac{6}{8} = \dfrac{3}{4}$ | 0.75 | 75% |
| $\dfrac{7}{8}$ | 0.875 | 87.5% |
| $\dfrac{8}{8} = \dfrac{4}{4} = 1$ | 1 | 100% |
| $\dfrac{10}{8} = \dfrac{5}{4}$ | 1.25 | 125% |
| $\dfrac{12}{8} = \dfrac{6}{4} = \dfrac{3}{2}$ | 1.5 | 150% |

For the set above, note that $\frac{1}{8}$ is half of $\frac{2}{8}$. You may already know that $\frac{2}{8} = \frac{1}{4} = 25\%$. Use this to help memorize the fact that $\frac{1}{8}$ is half that, or 12.5%. Every eighth fraction then increases by another 12.5%.

*Thirds*

| Fraction | Decimal | Percent |
|---|---|---|
| $\frac{1}{3}$ | 0.3333… | 33.33…% |
| $\frac{2}{3}$ | 0.6666… | 66.66…% |
| $\frac{3}{3} = 1$ | 1 | 100% |

*You're almost done!*

| Fraction | Decimal | Percent |
|---|---|---|
| $\frac{1}{100}$ | 0.01 | 1% |
| $\frac{1}{20}$ | 0.05 | 5% |

## Check Your Skills

4   Change $\frac{3}{5}$ to a decimal.

5.  Convert $\frac{3}{8}$ to a percent.

*Answers can be found on page 217.*

# Multiply a Decimal by a Power of 10: Shift the Decimal Point

Decimals are tenths, hundredths, thousandths, and so on. One-tenth is a power of 10, namely $10^{-1}$. One-hundredth is also a power of 10, namely $10^{-2}$.

You can write any decimal as a fraction with a power of 10 in the denominator, or as a product involving a power of 10. For example, $0.03 = \frac{3}{100} = \frac{3}{10^2}$. The power of 10 determines where the decimal point is. In this example, the power of 10 is 2. In the decimal form, the decimal point is two places to the left of 3.

So if you multiply or divide a decimal by a power of 10, you move the decimal point to the right or to the left.

If you multiply by 10 itself, you shift the decimal point one place to the right.

$$0.004 \times 10 = 0.04$$

The 10 cancels with one power of 10 in the denominator.

$$\frac{4}{1,000} \times 10 = \frac{4}{1,00\cancel{0}} \times \cancel{10} = \frac{4}{100}$$

You can also see it in terms of exponents. The additional 10 increases the overall exponent from $-3$ to $-2$.

$$4 \times 10^{-3} \times 10 = 4 \times 10^{-2}$$

If you multiply by 100, or $10^2$, you shift the decimal point two places to the right.

$$0.004 \times 100 = 0.4 \qquad \text{That is, } \frac{4}{1,000} \times 100 = \frac{4}{10} \qquad 4 \times 10^{-3} \times 10^2 = 4 \times 10^{-1}$$

When you multiply by a power of 10, the exponent of that power is the number of places you move the decimal. If the power of 10 is positive, move the decimal to the *right* to make the number *greater*.

$$43.8723 \times 10^3 = 43,872.3 \quad \text{Move the decimal 3 places to the right.}$$

If you divide by a power of 10, move to the *left* to make the number *smaller*.

$$782.95 \div 10 = 78.295 \quad \text{Move the decimal 1 place to the left.}$$

$$57,234 \div 10^4 = 5.7234 \quad \text{Move the decimal 4 places to the left.}$$

If you're asked to multiply by a negative power of 10, flip the power to positive and divide instead. Move the decimal to the left to make the number smaller, since you're dividing.

$$4 \times 10^{-3} = 4 \div 10^3 = 0.004 \quad \text{Move 3 places to the left.}$$

Likewise, if you're asked to divide by a negative power of 10, change the power to positive and multiply instead. Move the decimal to the right to make the number greater, since you're multiplying.

$$62 \div 10^{-2} = 62 \times 10^2 = 6,200 \quad \text{Move 2 places to the right.}$$

All of these procedures work the same for repeating decimals.

$$\frac{1}{3} \times 10 = 0.333... \times 10 = 3.33... \quad \text{Move 1 place to the right.}$$

| If you... | Then you... | Like this: |
|---|---|---|
| Multiply a decimal by a positive power of 10 | Move the decimal point right a number of places, corresponding to the exponent of the 10 | $0.007 \times 10^2 = 0.7$ <br><br> $7 \div 10^{-2} = 7 \times 10^2 = 700$ |
| Divide a decimal by a positive power of 10 | Move the decimal point left a number of places, corresponding to the exponent of the 10 | $6 \div 10^3 = 0.006$ <br><br> $6 \times 10^{-2} = 6 \div 10^2 = 0.06$ |

## Check Your Skills

Multiply. Give each answer as a single value.

6. $32.753 \times 10^2$
7. $43,681 \times 10^{-4}$

*Answers can be found on pages 217-218.*

# Add or Subtract Decimals: Line Up the Decimal Points

When you add or subtract decimals, write the decimals vertically, with the decimal points lined up.

$$0.3 + 0.65 = \qquad\qquad 0.65 - 0.5 =$$

$$
\begin{array}{r}
0.3 \\
+\ 0.65 \\
\hline
0.95
\end{array}
\qquad\qquad
\begin{array}{r}
0.65 \\
-\ 0.50 \\
\hline
0.15
\end{array}
$$

You can add zeros on the right to help you line up. For instance, turn 0.5 into 0.50 before you subtract it from 0.65.

| If you... | Then you... | Like this: |
|---|---|---|
| Add or subtract decimals | Line up the decimal points vertically | $\begin{array}{r} 4.035 \\ +0.120 \\ \hline 4.155 \end{array}$ |

## Check Your Skills

Add or subtract. Give each answer as a single value.

8. $3.128 + 0.045$
9. $1.8746 - 0.313$

*Answers can be found on page 218.*

**MANHATTAN** PREP

# Multiply Two Decimals: Ignore Decimal Points at First

Consider this example:

$$0.25 \times 0.5 =$$

First, multiply the numbers together as if they were integers. In other words, ignore the decimal points.

$$25 \times 5 = 125$$

Now count all the digits to the right of the original decimal points.

0.25 has 2 digits to the right.     0.5 has 1 digit to the right.

There were a total of three digits originally to the right, so move the decimal point of the answer three places to the *left*, in order to compensate. In other words, since there were three digits to the right of the decimal originally, the result should also have three digits to the right of the decimal.

125 becomes 0.125.     Therefore, $0.25 \times 0.5 = 0.125$.

Here's why this process works:

$$0.25 = 25 \times 10^{-2} \qquad\qquad 0.5 = 5 \times 10^{-1}$$
$$0.25 \times 0.5 = (25 \times 10^{-2}) \times (5 \times 10^{-1}) = 125 \times 10^{-3} = 0.125$$

The powers of 10 tell you where to put the decimal point. Here is another example:

| | |
|---|---|
| $3.5 \times 20 =$ | There is one digit to the right of the decimal point. |
| $35 \times 20 = 700$ | Ignore the decimals and multiply. |
| $3.5 \times 20 = 70.0$ | Account for the one decimal place in 3.5 by moving the final decimal point one |
| $= 70$ | place to the left. |

Count the zeros to the right of the decimal point as well.

| | |
|---|---|
| $0.01 \times 0.05 =$ | There are four digits (including zeros) to the right of the decimal points. |
| $1 \times 5 = 5$ | Ignore the decimals and multiply. |
| $0.01 \times 0.05 = 0.0005$ | Account for the original four decimal places by moving the decimal point four places to the left. |

| If you... | Then you... | Like this: |
|:---:|:---:|:---:|
| Multiply two decimals | Ignore the decimal points, multiply integers, then place the decimal point by counting the original number of decimals | $0.2 \times 0.5 = ?$<br>$2 \times 5 = 10$<br>$10 \rightarrow 0.10$<br>$0.2 \times 0.5 = 0.1$ |

## Check Your Skills

Multiply. Give each answer as a single value.

10. $0.6 \times 1.1$
11. $0.004 \times 0.032$

*Answers can be found on page 218.*

# Multiply a Decimal and a Big Number: Trade Decimal Places

Now consider this example:

$$4{,}000{,}000 \times 0.0003 =$$

When one number is very big and the other one is very small, you can trade powers of 10 from the big one (4,000,000) to the small one (0.0003). In other words, move one decimal point *left* and the other one *right*. Just make sure that you move the same number of places.

This multiplication would be easier if you had no decimals at all. To make this happen, move the decimal in 0.0003 to the right four places to get 3. To compensate, move the decimal in 4,000,000 to the left four places. That makes that number more manageable, too.

$$4{,}000{,}000 \times 0.0003 = 4{,}000{,}000 \times 0.0003 = 400 \times 3 = 1{,}200$$

You can justify these maneuvers with powers of 10.

$$4{,}000{,}000 \times 0.0003 = (4 \times 10^{6}) \times (3 \times 10^{-4}) = 12 \times 10^{6-4} = 12 \times 10^{2} = 1{,}200$$

| If you… | Then you… | Like this: |
|---------|-----------|------------|
| Multiply a small decimal and a big number | Trade decimal places from the big number to the decimal | $50{,}000 \times 0.007 =$ <br> $50 \times 7 = 350$ |

## Check Your Skills

Multiply. Give the answer as a single value.

12. $520{,}000 \times 0.0004$

*Answer can be found on page 218.*

# Divide Two Decimals: Move Points in the Same Direction To Kill Decimals

When you divide decimals, first write the division as a fraction if it isn't in that form already.

$$\frac{300}{0.05} =$$

Now move the decimals in the *same* direction on the top and bottom. This is the same as multiplying the top and bottom by the same power of 10. Do this to eliminate decimals.

In this case, turn 0.05 into 5 by moving its decimal two places to the right. Then do the same thing on top. Add zeros as necessary.

$$\frac{300}{0.05} = \frac{300_{\rightarrow\rightarrow}}{0.0\underset{\rightarrow}{5}} = \frac{30,000}{5} = 6,000$$

This is equivalent to multiplying the top and bottom by 100.

$$\frac{300}{0.05} = \frac{300 \times 100}{0.05 \times 100} = \frac{30,000}{5} = 6,000$$

One decimal may need more moves than the other. Try this example:

$$\frac{12.39}{0.003} =$$

The 12.39 only needs two moves to get rid of the decimal, while 0.003 needs three moves. Go with the greater number of moves. You can always add zeros to the other number.

$$\frac{12.39}{0.003} = \frac{12.39_{\rightarrow\rightarrow\rightarrow}}{0.00\underset{\rightarrow\rightarrow\rightarrow}{3}} = \frac{12,390}{3} = 4,130$$

| If you... | Then you... | Like this: |
|:---:|:---:|:---:|
| Divide two decimals | Move the decimal points in the same direction to eliminate decimals as far as you can | $\frac{0.002_{\rightarrow\rightarrow\rightarrow}}{0.000\underset{\rightarrow\rightarrow\rightarrow}{4}} = \frac{20}{4} = 5$ |

## Check Your Skills

13. Simplify $\dfrac{0.00084}{0.00007}$.

*Answer can be found on page 218.*

# 20% of \$55 = 0.2 × \$55

In everyday life, percents are the most common way of expressing part-to-whole relationships. You often see signs advertising "25% off," but you don't see as many signs advertising "$\frac{1}{4}$ off" or "0.75 of the original price." So your intuition about percents is probably pretty good, and that's useful on the GMAT.

However, percents are not necessarily the most useful form for actual *computation*. If you need to crunch numbers, think about what form would be easiest to use: *fractions, decimals, or percents*.

Consider this problem:

   30% of \$60 =

The word *of* means *times* in math terms. In other words, *of* indicates multiplication.

You could start by taking 10% of 60. This is the same as $(0.1)(60) = 6$. Since 30% is three times as much as 10%, multiply: $6 \times 3 = 18$.

Alternatively, you could convert 30% to a decimal, trade decimal places, and then multiply.

30% of $60 = 0.30 \times \$60 = 3 \times \$6 = \$18$

You even have a third option: use the fraction form of 30%.

$$30\% \text{ of } \$60 = \frac{30}{100} \times \$60 = \frac{3\cancel{0}}{10\cancel{0}} \times \$60 = \frac{3}{1\cancel{0}} \times \$6\cancel{0} = \$18$$

Which path did you find the easiest?

A problem could also be worded as a question.

What is 20% of $55?

In the Word Problems chapter, you'll learn more about translating words into math. For now, know these translations:

| **What** | can be translated as | *x* | (some variable) |
| **is** | can be translated as | = | (the equals sign) |

Translate the full question to math as follows:

| What | is | 20% | of | $55? |
| *x* | = | 0.20 | × | $55 |

Now crunch the numbers on the right. Note that when there are zeros at the end of a decimal, you don't count those zeros when counting decimals.

| $0.20 \times \$55 =$ | For purposes of counting the decimal point, do not include the 0 after the 2. |
| $0.2 \times \$55 =$ | Compute $2 \times \$55 = \$110$, then move the decimal point. |
| $0.2 \times \$55 = \$11$ | |

Alternatively, translate 20% to a fraction rather than to a decimal.

$$20\% = \frac{20}{100} = \frac{1}{5}$$

$$\frac{1}{5} \times \$55 = \frac{1}{\cancel{5}} \times {}^{11}\cancel{\$55} = \$11$$

Or, find 10% and then multiply by 2 to get 20%.

$(10\%)(55) = (0.1)(55) = 5.5$

$5.5 \times 2 = 11$

The translation gets a little tougher when you encounter the phrase "what percent." Consider this example:

What percent of 125 is 25?

Use a variable to represent the word *what*. Remember that the word percent by itself means "divided by 100," so it can be translated as $\dfrac{\phantom{x}}{100}$.

As a result, "what percent" can be translated as $\dfrac{x}{100}$.

Translate the question now.

| What percent | of | 125 | is | 25? |
|---|---|---|---|---|
| $\dfrac{x}{100}$ | $\times$ | 125 | $=$ | 25 |

You can now find the answer by solving for $x$. Solving equations for $x$ will be covered in depth in the Equations chapter later in this book. Here's how to solve this question:

$$\frac{x}{100} \times 125 = 25$$

$$\frac{x}{\cancel{100}^{4}} \times {}^{5}\cancel{125} = 25$$

$$\frac{x}{4} \times 5 = 25$$

$$\frac{x}{4} = 25$$

$$x = 20$$

In practice, use something other than $\times$ (multiplication sign) to indicate multiplication when you have an $x$ (variable) around, so that you don't mix up $\times$ and $x$ on your paper. You can use parentheses or a big dot.

$$\left(\frac{x}{100}\right)125 = 25 \qquad \frac{x}{100} \bullet 125 = 25$$

Here's a last example:

16 is 2% of what?

Translate word by word. Change 2% either to 0.02 or to $\dfrac{2}{100} = \dfrac{1}{50}$.

| 16 | is | 2% | of | what? |
|---|---|---|---|---|
| 16 | $=$ | 0.02 | $\times$ | $x$ |

Now solve for $x$.

$$16 = (0.02)x$$

$$\frac{16}{0.02} = x$$

$$\frac{16}{0.02} = x$$

$$\frac{1,600}{2} = x$$

$$800 = x$$

| If you... | Then you... | Like this: |
|---|---|---|
| See "30% of" | Convert 30% into a decimal or fraction, then multiply; alternatively, when appropriate, find 10%, then multiply by 3 to reach 30% | 30% of 200 = 0.30 × 200 = 60<br><br>10% of 200 = (0.1)(200) = 20<br>30% = 20 × 3 = 60 |
| See "what percent of" | Turn what percent into $\dfrac{x}{100}$, then multiply | What percent of 200 is 60?<br><br>$\left(\dfrac{x}{100}\right)200 = 60$ |

## Check Your Skills

Translate the following and solve.

14.  21 is 30% of what number?

*Answer can be found on page 219.*

## Percent Change: Divide Change in Value by Original Value

Consider this example.

> You have $200 in a bank account. You deposit an additional $30 in that account. By what percent did the value of the bank account increase?

Whenever some amount changes and you care about percents, set up this equation:

Original + Change = New

This equation holds true in two ways. First, it holds true for the actual amounts or values, which in this case are in dollars. This is unsurprising. Here is the first equation:

| Original value | + | Change in value | = | New value |
|---|---|---|---|---|
| $200 | + | $30 | = | $230 |

This equation *also* holds true for percents, as long as you mean percents *of the original value.* For example:

| Original percent | + | Change percent | = | New percent |
|---|---|---|---|---|
| (% of original) | | (% of original) | | (% of original) |
| 100% | + | ? | = | ? |

The original percent is always 100%, since the original value is always 100% of itself.

The change percent is better known as the **percent change**.

You had $200 in your bank account. You added $30. What percent of $200 is $30?

Turn *what percent* into $\dfrac{x}{100}$, translate the rest, and solve for *x*.

$$\left(\frac{x}{100}\right)200 = 30$$

$$\left(\frac{x}{100}\right)2\cancel{00} = 30$$

$$2x = 30$$

$$x = 15$$

The percent change is 15%.

Alternatively, if you feel pretty comfortable working with percentages, you can try a "back-of-the-envelope" approach. How can you get to the value of 30 using some combination of "easy" small percentages of the original number?

| | |
|---|---|
| 200 = 100% | The starting number is always 100% of itself. |
| 20 = 10% | 20 (or 10%) is close to 30, but not quite there… |
| 10 = 5% | …add 10 (or 5% more) to get to 30! |
| | 20 + 10 = 30, which represents 10% + 5% = 15%. |

Therefore, 15% is the percent change.

To do this kind of back-of-the-envelope calculation in the future, break the starting 100% figure down into more manageable pieces: 50%, 10%, 5%, or 1%. Then add up (or subtract) what you need in order to find the right percent.

So the original percent is 100%, and the percent change is 15%. What is the new percent? Add them up!

| Original percent | + | Change percent | = | New percent |
|---|---|---|---|---|
| (% of original) | | (% of original) | | (% of original) |
| 100% | + | 15% | = | 115% |

In the future, you can use a formula to calculate the percent change more directly. The percent change equals the change in value divided by the original value.

$$\text{Percent change (as \% of original)} = \frac{\text{Change in value}}{\text{Original value}}$$

$$\frac{\text{Change in value}}{\text{Original value}} = \frac{\$30}{\$200} = \frac{\overset{15}{\cancel{\$30}}}{\underset{100}{\cancel{\$200}}} = \frac{15}{100} = 15\%$$

The additional \$30 corresponds to a 15% change in the value of the account. Take note of the way that the math was simplified. You're looking for a percent, so you want the denominator to be 100 (since *per cent* means *of 100*). Don't simplify to $\frac{3}{20}$, since you'd just have to do more math to figure out what percent that is.

You can also directly calculate the *new percent*. Here's the formula:

$$\text{New percent (as \% of original)} = \frac{\text{New value}}{\text{Original value}}$$

$$\frac{\text{New value}}{\text{Original value}} = \frac{\$230}{\$200} = \frac{115}{100} = 115\%$$

As last time, make the denominator 100; divide by 2 and you're there.

If the value of the account *decreases*, the equations still hold true. You just have a negative change. In other words, subtract the change this time. Consider this example:

> You have \$200 in a bank account. You make a withdrawal that reduces the value of the account by 40%. How much money remains in the account?

Solve for the new percent first. A 40% decrease from the original is a negative 40% change.

| Original percent (% of original) | + | Change percent (% of original) | = | New percent (% of original) |
|---|---|---|---|---|
| 100% | + | −40% | = | 60% |

If you take out 40%, what's left is 60% of the original. Now find that new value.

$$\text{New percent (as \% of original)} = \frac{\text{New value}}{\text{Original value}}$$

$$60\% = \frac{\text{New value}}{\$200}$$

$$\left(\frac{60}{100}\right)200 = x$$

$$\left(\frac{60}{\cancel{100}}\right)2\cancel{00} = x$$

$$120 = x$$

Therefore, $120 remains in the account.

Alternatively, you could use the back-of-the-envelope approach. How can you get to 60% using values for some combination of 50%, 10%, 5%, and 1%?

60% = 50% + 10%

| 200 = 100% | The original value is always 100% of itself. |
| 100 = 50% | 50% is half of the original value. |
| 20 = 10% | To find 10%, move the decimal one place to the left. |

Therefore, 60% = 100 + 20 = 120, so $120 remains in the account.

| If you... | Then you... | Like this: |
|---|---|---|
| Need to find percent change of an original percent | Use the formula:<br><br>$\% \text{ Change} = \dfrac{\text{Change in value}}{\text{Original value}}$ | Original = $200; $30 added:<br><br>$\dfrac{\$30}{\$200} = 15\%$ |
| Need to find a new percent of an original percent | Use the formula:<br><br>$\text{New } \% = \dfrac{\text{New value}}{\text{Original value}}$ | Original = $200; $30 added:<br><br>$\dfrac{230}{200} = 115\%$ |

If you learn the following shortcuts, you'll make your job easier on the GMAT.

| A percent INCREASE of... | ...is the same as this NEW percent... | ...which is the same as multiplying the ORIGINAL VALUE by... |
|---|---|---|
| 10% | 110% | 1.1 |
| 20% | 120% | 1.2, or $\dfrac{6}{5}$ |
| 25% | 125% | 1.25, or $\dfrac{5}{4}$ |
| 50% | 150% | 1.5, or $\dfrac{3}{2}$ |
| 100% | 200% | 2 |

| A percent DECREASE of... | ...is the same as this NEW percent... | ...which is the same as multiplying the ORIGINAL VALUE by... |
|---|---|---|
| 10% | 90% | 0.9 |
| 20% | 80% | 0.8, or $\frac{4}{5}$ |
| 25% | 75% | 0.75, or $\frac{3}{4}$ |
| 50% | 50% | 0.5, or $\frac{1}{2}$ |
| 75% | 25% | 0.25, or $\frac{1}{4}$ |

*Percent more than* is just like *percent increase*. You do exactly the same math. Consider this example:

$230 is what percent more than $200?

Think of $230 as the new value and $200 as the original value. Again, 230 is 15% more than the starting point of $200.

Likewise, *percent less than* is just like *percent decrease*. Consider this example:

$120 is what percent less than $200?

Think of $120 as the new value and $200 as the original value. Again, you'll get a 40% decrease or difference.

Which number you call the original value matters. The original value is always after the word *than*. It's the value you're comparing the other value *to*.

$230 is what percent *more than* $200?

Therefore, $200 is the original value. You're comparing $230 to a starting point of $200, not the other way around.

Finally, watch out for the language *percent OF* versus *percent MORE THAN*. These two expressions don't mean the same thing. Consider these examples:

30 is what percent *of* 20?

30 is what percent *more than* 20?

For the first question (*of*), you are including the original 20 as part of the percent calculation. Since 20 is 100% of 20, you have to have at least 100% already. Then, you still have to get up to 30. What additional percentage do you need to add to get from 20 to 30?

$$20 = 100\%$$
$$10 = 50\%$$

$$20 + 10 = 30$$
$$100\% + 50\% = 150\%$$

In other words, 30 is 150 percent *of* 20. Translate the equation to check the math if you're not confident.

$$30 = \frac{150}{100} \times 20$$

$$30 = \frac{15\cancel{0}}{1\cancel{0}\,\cancel{0}} \times 2\cancel{0}$$

$$30 = 30$$

In contrast, the second question (*more than*) is asking you to find only the *increase* from 20 to 30. The baseline 100% that 20 represents is *not* included in this calculation. This time, only count the difference: 30 − 20 = 10.

What percent of the original number does 10 represent?

$$20 = 100\%$$

$$10 = 50\%$$

In other words, 30 is 50 percent *more than* 20. Again, check the math if you're not sure; use the percent change formula, since *more than* is a signal to use percent change.

$$\% \text{ change } = \frac{10}{20} = \frac{50}{100} = 50\%$$

The math above works the same way for *less than* problems, except you'll be subtracting the change rather than adding it.

By the way, did you happen to notice that the answer to the first one (150%) is exactly 100% more than the second one (50%)? This isn't a coincidence! It will always be the case that the *percent of* question will be 100% more than the *percent more than* question for the exact same original and resulting numbers.

Recall how the *percent of* question includes the original number in the calculation but the *percent more than* question does not? The original number is always 100% of itself, so the *percent of* calculation will always include this 100% and the *percent more than* question will not.

Keep *percent of* and *percent more than* or *percent less than* distinct; they mean different things!

| If you... | Then you... | Like this: |
|---|---|---|
| Need to find a *percent more than* or *percent less than* | Treat the problem like a percent increase or a percent decrease | $230 is what % more than $200? $$\frac{\$30}{\$200} = 15\%$$ |
| Need to find a *percent of* | Translate the equation and solve OR Use back-of-the-envelope approach; set the starting number to 100% | 50 is what % of 25? $$50 = \frac{x}{100}(25)$$ $$50 = \frac{x}{4}$$ $$200 = x$$ $$25 = 100\%$$ $$50 = 200\%$$ |

## Check Your Skills

15. What is the percent decrease from 90 to 72?

*Answer can be found on page 219.*

# Percent of a Percent of: Multiply Twice

Consider this example:

What is 120% of 150% of 30?

These are *percents of*, so turn the percents into decimal or fractional equivalents and multiply 30 by *both* of those equivalents. Don't forget to simplify before you multiply.

$$120\% = \frac{6}{5} \qquad 150\% = \frac{3}{2}$$

120% of 150% of 30 =

$$\frac{6}{5} \times \frac{3}{2} \times 30 = \frac{\overset{3}{\cancel{6}}}{5} \times \frac{3}{\cancel{2}} \times 30 = \frac{\overset{3}{\cancel{6}}}{\cancel{5}} \times \frac{3}{\cancel{2}} \times \overset{6}{\cancel{30}} = 9 \times 6 = 54$$

Percent changes often come one after the other. *When you have successive percent changes, multiply the original value by each new percent* (converted to a suitable fraction or decimal).

Consider another example.

> The price of a share, originally $50, goes up by 10% on Monday and then by 20% on Tuesday. What is the overall change in the price of a share, in dollars?

A percent increase of 10% is equivalent to a new percent of 110%, or multiplying the original value by 1.1 or $\frac{11}{10}$.

A percent increase of 20% is equivalent to a new percent of 120%, or multiplying the original value by 1.2 or $\frac{6}{5}$.

Compute the new value by multiplying the original value by each of these factors.

$$\$50 \times \frac{11}{10} \times \frac{6}{5} = \cancel{\$50} \times \frac{11}{\cancel{10}} \times \frac{6}{\cancel{5}} = 11 \times 6 = \$66$$

The change in value is $66 − $50 = $16.

Notice that that change is *not* 30% of $50 = $15. Never *add* successive percents (e.g., 10% and 20%). If you add the percents, the answer will be approximately right ($15 is *close* to $16), but it will not be the exact number.

| If you... | Then you... | Like this: |
|:---:|:---:|:---:|
| Have successive percent changes | Multiply the original value by the new percents for *each* percent change | $50 is increased by 10%, and the result is increased by 20% $$\$50\left(\frac{11}{10}\right)\left(\frac{6}{5}\right) = \$66$$ |

## Check Your Skills

16. What is 80% of 75% of 120?

*Answer can be found on page 219.*

## Ratio: Part-to-Part and Part-to-Whole

Ratios or proportions express a particular kind of relationship between two quantities. That relationship is division. Consider this example:

> For every 2 bananas in a certain basket of fruit there are 3 apples.

This relationship can be rewritten this way:

$$\frac{\text{Number of bananas}}{\text{Number of apples}} = \frac{2}{3}$$

In words, the number of bananas divided by the number of apples is $\frac{2}{3}$.

In the example above, the ratio is expressing a *part-to-part relationship*. There are 2 "parts" bananas to 3 "parts" apples (though you still have only whole pieces of fruit).

You could also write this same information as a *part-to-whole relationship*. There are 2 bananas for every 5 pieces of fruit (because $2 + 3 = 5$), and there are 3 apples for every 5 pieces of fruit.

$$\frac{\text{Number of bananas}}{\text{Number of apples}} = \frac{2}{3} \qquad \frac{\text{Number of apples}}{\text{Total pieces}} = \frac{3}{5}$$

The language and symbols of ratios are peculiar. Note the following equivalent expressions:

> For every 2 bananas, there are 3 apples.
> There are 2 bananas for every 3 apples.
> The ratio of bananas to apples is 2 to 3.
> The ratio of bananas to apples is 2 : 3.
> The ratio of bananas to apples is $\frac{2}{3}$.

Next, the ratio, by itself, does not actually indicate how many bananas and apples there really are. In other words, *a ratio tells you the relationship between two things, but not necessarily the actual numbers of those two things.*

In this case, there are at least 2 bananas and at least 3 apples in this basket—but there may be more. There could also be 4 bananas and 6 apples, or 6 bananas and 9 apples, or 20 bananas and 30 apples, and so on.

Notice what those pairs of numbers have in common? The number of bananas divided by the number of apples must equal $\frac{2}{3}$. There are many different possible combinations of actual numbers that will make this true.

By the way, use full words for the units *bananas* and *apples*. *Never* write 2*B* to mean 2 bananas or 3*A* to mean 3 apples because you may confuse those labels with variables. Single letters (such as *B* and *A*) should always represent variables, not units. The expression 2*B* would mean "2 times the number of bananas."

If you know that the ratio of bananas to apples is 2 to 3 and you are given one of the real numbers, then you can figure out the other real number. For instance, if there are 15 apples, then how many bananas are there?

|          | Part (bananas) | Part (apples) | Whole/Total   |
|----------|:--------------:|:-------------:|:-------------:|
| **Ratio**   | 2           | 3             | $2 + 3 = 5$   |
| **Actual**  |             | 15            |               |

If you know that the 15 apples represent 3 parts of the ratio, then you can calculate a new number: **the unknown multiplier**. The unknown multiplier is the number by which you multiply the *ratio* to get to the *actual* number. In this case, the unknown multiplier is 5, because $3 \times 5 = 15$.

*The unknown multiplier is always the same for all parts of a ratio.* Once you know what it is, apply it to everything in the ratio.

|  | Part (bananas) | Part (apples) | Whole/Total |
|---|---|---|---|
| **Ratio** | 2 | 3 | 5 |
| **× Unknown Multiplier** | × 5 | × 5 | × 5 |
| **= Actual** | 10 | 15 | 25 |

Now you also know the actual number of bananas (10) and the actual total number of pieces of fruit (25).

When you don't yet know what the unknown multiplier is, call it $x$, and write out an algebraic representation for the actual numbers.

|  | Part (bananas) | Part (apples) | Whole/Total |
|---|---|---|---|
| Ratio | 2 | 3 | 5 |
| × | $x$ | $x$ | $x$ |
| Actual | $2x$ | $3x$ | $5x$ |

If there are 12 bananas, how many apples are there?

Set up what you know: $12 = 2x =$ the actual number of bananas, so $x = 6$. The actual number of apples, therefore, is $3x = 3(6) = 18$.

Take a look at the table again. The actual number of bananas is always $2x$, and the actual number of apples is always $3x$. This formulation *guarantees* the ratio of 2 to 3.

$$\frac{\text{Number of bananas}}{\text{Number of apples}} = \frac{2x}{3x} = \frac{2\cancel{x}}{3\cancel{x}} = \frac{2}{3}$$

The unknown multiplier $x$ is a common factor that cancels out to leave $\dfrac{2}{3}$, every single time.

Since the actual values will always simplify down to the same ratio, you can always set up an algebraic representation to solve. Consider this new problem:

> The ratio of apples to bananas in a certain display is 4 to 7. If there are 63 bananas, how many apples are there?

The ratio of apples to bananas is 4 : 7. The actual number of apples is $4x$, and the actual number of bananas is $7x$, where $x$ represents the unknown multiplier. The problem states that there are 63 actual bananas, so set up an equation to solve:

$$7x = 63$$
$$x = 9$$

Now plug in the unknown multiplier to solve for the number of apples: $4x = 4(9) = 36$. There are 36 apples.

Alternatively, you can set up the table.

|   | Apples | Bananas | Total |
|---|--------|---------|-------|
| **R** | 4 | 7 | |
| × | × 9 | × 9 | |
| **A** | 36 | 63 | |

You don't need to fill out every cell in the table. Feel free to fill in only the parts you need to answer the question. Consider this example:

> The ratio of apples to bananas in a certain display is 4 to 7. If there are 28 apples, how many total pieces of fruit are there?

Again, you can set up an equation or use the table to solve—use what you find easier.

This time, you need the ratio total, which is equal to the sum of the individual parts of the ratio: $4 + 7 = 11$. The actual number of apples is $4x$ and the actual number of pieces of fruit is $11x$. Therefore:

$4x = 28$

$x = 7$

Total pieces of fruit = $11x = 11 \times 7 = 77$

Here's the table approach.

|   | A | B | Total |
|---|---|---|-------|
| **R** | 4 | 7 | 11 |
| × | × 7 | | × 7 |
| **A** | 28 | | 77 |

If there are 28 apples, then there are 77 total pieces of fruit.

| If you… | Then you… | Like this: | | | |
|---------|-----------|------------|---|---|---|
| Are told that "the ratio of sharks to dolphins is 3 to 13" | Write each quantity in terms of the unknown multiplier<br><br>OR<br><br>Create the table | Sharks = 3x<br><br>Dolphins = 13x | | | |
| | | | **S** | **D** | **Total** |
| | | **R** | 3 | 13 | |
| | | × | | | |
| | | **A** | 3x | 13x | |

## Check Your Skills

17. The ratio of blue marbles to white marbles in a bag is 3 : 5. If there are 15 white marbles in the bag, how many blue marbles are in the bag?

*Answer can be found on page 220.*

## Ratios and Percents: Convert Fractions to Percents

You can now write two-way ratios between any two components.

Cars : Trucks = 2 : 3
Cars : Total Vehicles = 2 : 5
Trucks : Total Vehicles = 3 : 5

You can use this information to determine percents of the whole. Because there is a 2 : 5 ratio of cars to vehicles, $\frac{2}{5}$, or 40%, of the vehicles are cars. Likewise, $\frac{3}{5}$, or 60%, of the vehicles are trucks.

Here are a few other common Part : Part ratios and the resulting percents of the whole.

| Cars : Trucks | Cars : Trucks : Total | Cars : Total | Trucks : Total |
|:---:|:---:|:---:|:---:|
| 1 : 1 | 1 : 1 : 2 | 1 : 2<br>50% | 1 : 2<br>50% |
| 1 : 2 | 1 : 2 : 3 | 1 : 3<br>33.33…% | 2 : 3<br>66.66…% |
| 1 : 3 | 1 : 3 : 4 | 1 : 4<br>25% | 3 : 4<br>75% |

Consider this problem:

A bouquet contains white roses and red roses. If the ratio of white to red roses is 5 : 3, what percent of all the roses are red?

(A) 37.5%    (B) 40%    (C) 60%    (D) 62.5%    (E) 80%

Set up a Part : Part : Whole ratio using just the top row of the standard ratio table:

|   | White | Red | Total |
|:---:|:---:|:---:|:---:|
| **R** | 5 | 3 | 8 |

The ratio of red to total is 3 to 8, or $\frac{3}{8}$. As a percent, $\frac{3}{8}$ = 37.5%. The correct answer is (A).

If you are given the percents of the two parts of the whole, you can set up a Part : Part : Whole ratio with the percents. Use 100 for the whole. Then reduce by removing common factors and you'll have the ratio. Here's an example.

If 20% of the animals in a certain zoo are skunks, what is the ratio of non-skunk animals to skunks in the zoo?

The Part + Part = Whole equation is Skunks + Non-skunks = Animals. If 20% of the animals are skunks, then 100% − 20% = 80% are non-skunks. Reduce those numbers as far as possible to get the ratio.

|     | S    | N-S  | Total |
| --- | ---- | ---- | ----- |
| %   | 20%  | 80%  | 100%  |
| R   | 1    | 4    | 5     |

The three numbers share a common factor of 20. Take out that common factor, and you have 1 : 4 : 5 as the ratio of skunks to non-skunks to total animals at the zoo.

Thus, the ratio of non-skunk animals to skunks is 4 to 1. When answering ratio questions, double-check the order in which you were asked to present the desired categories. A ratio of 1 to 4 would be incorrect for this question.

Try this problem:

> A car lot contains only sedans and trucks. There are 4 sedans for every 5 trucks on the lot. If there are 12 sedans on the lot, how many total vehicles are there?

Set up the table and solve.

|     | S    | T   | Total |
| --- | ---- | --- | ----- |
| R   | 4    | 5   | 9     |
| ×   | × 3  |     | × 3   |
| A   | 12   |     | 27    |

Alternatively, set up an equation.

> Number of sedans = $4x$ = 12 sedans
> $x = 3$

Now plug in this multiplier to find the total number of vehicles.

> Total number of vehicles = $(4 + 5)x = 9(3) = 27$ vehicles

Notice that when the quantities are counting real things, you have to stick to positive integers: 1, 2, 3, etc. In that case, the unknown multiplier itself is restricted to positive integers as well. In other words, the parts and the whole must be multiples of the numbers in the ratio.

Take the bananas and apples example again.

> Bananas : Apples : Pieces of fruit = 2 : 3 : 5

The number of bananas is $2x$, and $x$ must be an integer, so the number of bananas must be even (a multiple of 2).

Likewise, the number of apples ($3x$) must be a multiple of 3, and the total number of pieces of fruit ($5x$) must be a multiple of 5. If the GMAT asks you what *could* be the total number of pieces of fruit, then the right answer will be a multiple of 5, and the four wrong answers will not be.

In real life, you encounter ratios in recipes. You usually have more than two ingredients. But you can still use the unknown multiplier.

Take this recipe:

> 3 cups of olive oil
> + 1 cup of vinegar
> + ½ cup of lemon juice
> + ½ cup of mustard                    = 5 cups of salad dressing

What if you need 7.5 cups of salad dressing for a big party? Find the unknown multiplier.

> Cups of salad dressing: $5x = 7.5$
> Therefore: $x = 1.5$

The multiplier is 1.5. Every ingredient is multiplied by the same factor (1.5 in this case). Note that you can have a non-integer multiplier when you are working with something that can be split into fractional parts, such as the number of cups of salad dressing. You couldn't do this for a problem about people; you don't want to have half of a person!

> Cups of olive oil      $= 3x$      $= 3(1.5)$      $= 4.5$ cups
> Cups of vinegar       $= 1x$      $= 1(1.5)$      $= 1.5$ cups
> Cups of lemon juice  $= \dfrac{1}{2}x$      $= \dfrac{1}{2}(1.5)$      $= \dfrac{3}{4}$ cup
> Cups of mustard      $= \dfrac{1}{2}x$      $= \dfrac{1}{2}(1.5)$      $= \dfrac{3}{4}$ cup

| If you... | Then you... | Like this: |
|---|---|---|
| Have two parts that make a whole and that have a ratio of 3 to 4 | Write the Part : Part : Whole ratio as 3 : 4 : 7, and use the unknown multiplier as needed | Oranges = $3x$<br>Apples = $4x$<br>so<br>Pieces of fruit = $7x$ |

## Check Your Skills

18. A flowerbed contains only roses and tulips. If the ratio of tulips to the total number of flowers in the bed is 5 : 11, and there are 121 flowers in the bed, how many roses are there?

*Answer can be found on page 220.*

# Check Your Skills Answer Key

1. **3.5%:** Make the number seem greater; move the decimal to the right two places: $0.035 = 3.5\%$.

2. $\dfrac{3}{8}$: If you notice that 375 and 1,000 are both divisible by 125, then you can perform the simplification in one step. If not, simplify by smaller numbers until you can't go any further. The solution below shows dividing the top and bottom by 5 first and then dividing the top and bottom by 25.

$$0.375 = \frac{\overset{75}{\cancel{375}}}{\underset{200}{\cancel{1{,}000}}} = \frac{\overset{3}{\cancel{75}}}{\underset{8}{\cancel{200}}} = \frac{3}{8}$$

3. $\dfrac{6}{25}$:

$$24\% = \frac{\overset{6}{\cancel{24}}}{\underset{25}{\cancel{100}}} = \frac{6}{25}$$

4. **0.6:** This one is on the list to memorize. Because the denominator is 5, you can multiply the numerator and denominator by the same number to turn the denominator into a power of 10.

$$\frac{3}{5} \times \frac{2}{2} = \frac{6}{10} = 0.6$$

Alternatively, perform long division to convert a fraction to a decimal.

$$
\begin{array}{r}
0.6 \\
5\overline{)3.0} \\
-30 \\
\hline
0
\end{array}
$$

5. **37.5%:** This one is also on the list to memorize. Alternatively, perform long division.

$$
\begin{array}{r}
0.375 \\
8\overline{)3.000} \\
\underline{24\phantom{00}} \\
60\phantom{0} \\
\underline{56\phantom{0}} \\
40 \\
\underline{40} \\
0
\end{array}
$$

6. **3,275.3:**

$$32.753 \times 10^2 = 3{,}275.3$$

7. **4.3681:**

   $$43{,}681 \times 10^{-4} = 43{,}681 \div 10^4 = 4.3681$$

8. **3.173:** Make sure to carry over the 1 from the units digit column. Since $8 + 5 = 13$, then 3 becomes the units digit and the tens digit becomes $4 + 2 + 1 = 7$.

   $$
   \begin{array}{r}
   3.128 \\
   +\ \ 0.045 \\
   \hline
   3.173
   \end{array}
   $$

9. **1.5616:**

   $$
   \begin{array}{r}
   1.8746 \\
   -\ \ 0.3130 \\
   \hline
   1.5616
   \end{array}
   $$

10. **0.66:**

    $$0.6 \times 1.1 =$$
    $$6 \times 11 = 66$$
    $$0.6 \times 1.1 = 0.66$$

11. **0.000128:**

    $$0.004 \times 0.032$$
    $$4 \times 32 = 128$$
    $$0.004 \times 0.032 = 0.000128$$

12. **208:** Move the decimal in 520,000 to the left four places and move the decimal in 0.0004 to the right four places.
    $$520{,}000 \times 0.0004 = 52 \times 4 = 208$$

13. **12:** Move each decimal to the right five places.

    $$\frac{0.00084}{0.00007} = \frac{84}{7} = 12$$

14. **70:**

| 21 | = | $\dfrac{30}{100}$ | × | $x$ |
|----|----|----|----|----|
| 21 | is | 30 percent | of | what number? |

$$21 = \frac{30}{100}x$$

$$\frac{10\cancel{0}}{3\cancel{0}} \times 21 = x$$

$$\frac{10 \times \overset{7}{\cancel{21}}}{\underset{1}{\cancel{3}}} = x$$

$$70 = x$$

15. **20%:** To find the percent decrease, focus on the amount by which 90 was reduced. Since $90 - 72 = 18$, then:

$$\frac{18}{90} = \frac{\overset{2}{\cancel{18}}}{\underset{10}{\cancel{90}}} = \frac{2}{10} = 20\%$$

Alternatively, use the back-of-the-envelope approach. How do you go from 90 to 18?

90 = 100%
9 = 10%

Multiply 9 by 2 to get 18, so multiply 10% by 2 to get 20%.

16. **72:** Convert 80% and 75% to fractions: $80\% = \dfrac{4}{5}$ and $75\% = \dfrac{3}{4}$. Set up the equation and solve.

$$x = \frac{\cancel{4}}{5} \times \frac{3}{\cancel{4}} \times 120$$

$$x = \frac{\cancel{4}}{\cancel{5}} \times \frac{3}{\cancel{4}} \times \overset{24}{\cancel{120}}$$

$$x = 3 \times 24 = 72$$

17. **9:** The ratio of blue to white is 3 : 5. There are 15 white marbles, so set the 15 equal to $5x$, and solve for the unknown multiplier.

$5x = 15$

$x = 3$

Therefore, the number of blue marbles is $3x$, which is $3(3) = 9$.

Alternatively, use the table to solve.

|   | **B** | **W** | **Total** |
|---|---|---|---|
| **R** | 3 | 5 | |
| × | × 3 | × 3 | |
| **A** | 9 | 15 | |

18. **66:** If the ratio of tulips to all flowers is 5 : 11, then roses must represent $11 - 5 = 6$ in the ratio. The ratio of roses to tulips to all flowers is 6 : 5 : 11.

Use the total number of flowers, 121, to find the unknown multiplier.

$11x = 121$

$x = 11$

The total number of roses is $6x$, which is $6(11) = 66$.

# Chapter Review: Drill Sets

## Drill 1

1. Fill in the missing information in the chart below. See the third line for an example.

| Fraction | Decimal | Percent |
|----------|---------|---------|
|  |  | 1% |
| $\frac{1}{20}$ |  |  |
| $\frac{1}{10}$ | 0.1 | 10% |
| $\frac{1}{8}$ |  |  |
|  | 0.2 |  |
|  |  | 25% |
|  | 0.3 |  |
|  |  | 33.33…% |
| $\frac{3}{8}$ |  |  |
|  |  | 40% |
| $\frac{1}{2}$ |  |  |
|  | 0.6 |  |
|  |  | 66.66…% |
|  |  | 70% |
|  | 0.75 |  |
| $\frac{4}{5}$ |  |  |
|  | 0.875 |  |
| $\frac{9}{10}$ |  |  |
|  |  | 100% |
|  | 1.1 |  |
| $\frac{6}{5}$ |  |  |
|  |  | 125% |
|  | 1.5 |  |

## Drill 2

2. Convert 45% to a decimal.
3. Convert 0.20 to a percent.
4. Convert $\frac{4}{5}$ to a percent.
5. Convert 13.25% to a decimal.
6. Convert $\frac{6}{20}$ to a percent.
7. Convert 0.304 to a percent.
8. Convert 0.02% to a decimal.
9. Convert 0.375 to a fraction.
10. Convert $\frac{3}{2}$ to a percent.

## Drill 3

Simplify the following expressions. Answers in the explanations may appear in more than one form (e.g., fraction and decimal).

11. $\frac{1}{2} \times 50\%$
12. $25\% - 0.1$
13. $\frac{2}{3} + 0.3$
14. $\frac{16}{5} \div 0.8$
15. $\frac{3}{8} \div 10\%$
16. What is 30% of $3.50?
17. What is 0.3 times 110%?
18. Simplify $\frac{2}{5} + 20\% + 0.7$.
19. Simplify $1.5 \div \left( \frac{5}{8} - 50\% \right)$.
20. Simplify $190\% - \left( 1.2 \div \frac{4}{5} \right)$.

## Drill 4

Simplify the following expressions.

21. $6.75 \times 10^3$
22. $1 + 0.2 + 0.03 + 0.004$
23. $0.27 \times 2$
24. $72.12 \times 10^{-3}$
25. $0.6 \times 0.4$
26. $0.48 + 0.02$
27. $\frac{4}{0.2}$
28. $20 \times 0.35$
29. $\frac{54.197}{10^2}$
30. $\frac{12.6}{0.3}$

## Drill 5

Simplify the following expressions.

31. $2,346 \times 10^{-2}$
32. $1.21 + 0.38$
33. $\frac{6}{0.5}$
34. $2.1 \times 0.04$
35. $0.03 \times 0.05$
36. $0.370 + 0.042$
37. $\frac{3.2}{0.04}$
38. $0.6(50) + 0.25(120)$
39. $\frac{0.49}{0.07}$
40. $100 \times 0.01 \times 0.01$

# Drill 6

41. $4.672 \times 10^4$ equals which of the following?
    (A) 4,672
    (B) 46,720
    (C) 467,200

42. $337 \times 10^{-4}$ equals which of the following?
    (A) 3,370,000
    (B) 0.0337
    (C) 0.0000337

43. $8.25 \times 10^5$ equals which of the following?
    (A) $825 \times 10^7$
    (B) $825 \times 10^4$
    (C) $825 \times 10^3$

44. 0.003482 equals which of the following?
    (A) $34.82 \times 10^{-4}$
    (B) $34.82 \times 10^2$
    (C) $34.82 \times 10^4$

45. $12.12 \times 10^{-3}$ equals which of the following?

    (A) $-1.21 \times 10^3$
    (B) $0.00001212 \times 10^3$
    (C) $0.01212 \times 10^3$

# Drill 7

46. What is 15% of 40?
47. 12 is 5% of what number?
48. 4 is what percent of 32?
49. 7% of 9 is what percent of 7?
50. 25% of 30 is 75% of what number?
51. What percent of 6 is 37.5% of 160?
52. If 14 is added to 56, what is the percent increase?
53. What is the percent increase from 50 to 60?
54. What number is 40% more than 30?
55. What is 60% less than 60?

## Drill 8

56. If $m$ is reduced by 55%, the resulting number is 90. What is the value of $m$?
57. If 75 reduced by $x$ percent is 54, what is the value of $x$?
58. If $x$ is 15% more than 20, what is 30% of $x$?
59. What is 50% of 12% of 50?
60. What is 120% of 30% of 400?
61. If 45% of 80 is $x$ percent more than 24, what is the value of $x$?
62. 10% of 30% of what number is 200% of 6?
63. If $q \neq 0$, what percent of 25% of $q$ is $q$ percent of 20?
64. If $a \neq 0$, 200% of 4% of $a$ is what percent of $\dfrac{a}{2}$?

65. If positive integer $m$ is first increased by 20%, then decreased by 25%, and finally increased by 60%, the resulting number is what percent of $m$?

## Drill 9

66. If there are 20 birds and 6 dogs in a park, which of the following is the ratio of dogs to birds?
    (A) $3:13$
    (B) $3:10$
    (C) $10:3$

67. In a class of 24 students made up of only juniors and seniors, 12 are juniors. Which of the following is the ratio of juniors to seniors in the class?
    (A) $1:1$
    (B) $1:2$
    (C) $2:1$

68. If there are 45 red marbles and 35 green marbles in a bag, which of the following is the ratio of green to red marbles?
    (A) $9:16$
    (B) $7:9$
    (C) $9:7$

69. There are 21 trout and 24 catfish in a pond. There are no other fish in the pond. What is the ratio of catfish to the total number of fish in the pond?
    (A) $7:15$
    (B) $8:15$
    (C) $7:8$

## Drill 10

70. Fill in the missing information in the table below.

| 1 : 2 | = | 3 : __ | = | __ : 14 | = | __ : 22 |
|---|---|---|---|---|---|---|
| 1 : __ | = | 4 : 20 | = | __ : 25 | = | 15 : __ |
| 3 : __ | = | __ : 8 | = | __ : 36 | = | 33 : 44 |
| __ : 7 | = | 20 : __ | = | 40 : 56 | = | 60 : __ |
| 4 : 11 | = | __ : 22 | = | 36 : __ | = | __ : 132 |

## Drill 11

71. A recipe calls for 1 cup of cheese and $\frac{1}{2}$ cup of sauce in order to make 1 pizza. If Bob used 15 cups of sauce to make pizzas, how much cheese did he use?

72. On a safari, Sofia saw only giraffes and lions. If she saw 7 giraffes for every 3 lions, and she saw 60 animals in total, how many lions did she see?
    (A) 18
    (B) 21
    (C) 42

73. The ratio of oranges to peaches to strawberries in a fruit basket is 2 : 3 : 4. If there are 8 oranges, how many pieces of fruit are in the basket?

74. A certain automotive dealer sells only cars and trucks and currently has 51 trucks for sale. If the ratio of cars for sale to trucks for sale is 1 to 3, how many cars are for sale?

75. Mustafa has invented a new dance in which he moves 3 steps forward for every 4 steps he moves back. If the dance requires 49 steps in total, how many total steps forward has Mustafa taken at the completion of the dance?
    (A) 7
    (B) 21
    (C) 28

76. A steel manufacturer combines 98 ounces of iron with 2 ounces of carbon to make 1 sheet of steel. How much iron is used in $\frac{1}{2}$ of a sheet of steel?

77. To make a 64-ounce smoothie, Malin must use 4 bananas, 2 apples, 6 cups of yogurt, and 8 teaspoons of protein powder. How many cups of yogurt will she need to make a 16-ounce smoothie?

# Drill Sets Solutions

## Drill 1

1.

| Fraction | Decimal | Percent |
|----------|---------|---------|
| $\frac{1}{100}$ | 0.01 | 1% |
| $\frac{1}{20}$ | 0.05 | 5% |
| $\frac{1}{10}$ | 0.1 | 10% |
| $\frac{1}{8}$ | 0.125 | 12.5% |
| $\frac{1}{5}$ | 0.2 | 20% |
| $\frac{1}{4}$ | 0.25 | 25% |
| $\frac{3}{10}$ | 0.3 | 30% |
| $\frac{1}{3}$ | 0.3333… | 33.33…% |
| $\frac{3}{8}$ | 0.375 | 37.5% |
| $\frac{2}{5}$ | 0.40 | 40% |
| $\frac{1}{2}$ | 0.50 | 50% |
| $\frac{3}{5}$ | 0.6 | 60% |
| $\frac{2}{3}$ | 0.6666… | 66.66…% |
| $\frac{7}{10}$ | 0.7 | 70% |
| $\frac{3}{4}$ | 0.75 | 75% |

| Fraction | Decimal | Percent |
|:---:|:---:|:---:|
| $\dfrac{4}{5}$ | 0.8 | 80% |
| $\dfrac{7}{8}$ | 0.875 | 87.5% |
| $\dfrac{9}{10}$ | 0.9 | 90% |
| 1 | 1.0 | 100% |
| $\dfrac{11}{10}$ | 1.1 | 110% |
| $\dfrac{6}{5}$ | 1.2 | 120% |
| $\dfrac{5}{4}$ | 1.25 | 125% |
| $\dfrac{3}{2}$ | 1.5 | 150% |

# Drill 2

2. **0.45:** To convert from a percent to a decimal, move the decimal point two places to the left (to make it appear *smaller*), so 45% becomes 0.45.

3. **20%:** To convert from a decimal to a percent, move the decimal point two places to the right (to make it appear *greater*) and add a percent sign, so 0.20 becomes 20%.

4. **80%:** This one is on the conversion list to memorize. Alternatively, perform long division to find the decimal form, then convert to a percent.

> Step 1: $4 \div 5 = 0.8$          $5\overline{)4.0}^{\,0.8}$
> Step 2: 0.8 becomes 80%

An additional shortcut is to convert the denominator to 100 by multiplying both the numerator and denominator by 20.

$$\frac{4}{5} \times \frac{20}{20} = \frac{80}{100} = 80\%$$

5. **0.1325:** 13.25% becomes 0.1325.

6. **30%:** $\dfrac{6}{20}$ simplifies to $\dfrac{3}{10}$, which is on the list to memorize. Alternatively, perform long division to find the

   decimal form, then convert to a percent.

   Step 1: $6 \div 20 = 0.30$

   Step 2: 0.30 becomes 30%

   $$20\overline{)6.0} \quad \dfrac{0.3}{}$$

   An additional shortcut is to convert the denominator to 100 by multiplying both the numerator and denominator by 5.

   $$\dfrac{6}{20} \times \dfrac{5}{5} = \dfrac{30}{100} = 30\%$$

7. **30.4%:** 0.304 becomes 30.4%.

8. **0.0002:** Careful! To convert from a percent to a decimal, still move the decimal point two places to the *left*, even though this creates a really small number, as 0.02% becomes 0.0002.

9. $\dfrac{\mathbf{3}}{\mathbf{8}}$ **:** This one is on the list to memorize. Alternatively, 0.375 becomes $\dfrac{375}{1,000}$, which reduces to $\dfrac{3}{8}$.

10. **150%:** This one is on the list to memorize. Alternatively, perform long division to find the decimal form, then convert to a percent.

    Step 1: $3 \div 2 = 1.5$

    Step 2: 1.5 becomes 150%

    $$2\overline{)3.0} \quad \dfrac{1.5}{}$$

    An additional shortcut is to convert the denominator to 100 by multiplying both the numerator and denominator by 50.

    $$\dfrac{3}{2} \times \dfrac{50}{50} = \dfrac{150}{100} = 150\%$$

# Drill 3

11. $\dfrac{1}{4}$ **or 25%:**

| | |
|---|---|
| $\dfrac{1}{2} \times 50\% =$ | Convert percent to fraction because fractions are easier to multiply than percents. |
| $\dfrac{1}{2} \times \dfrac{50}{100} =$ | Simplify before you multiply. |
| $\dfrac{1}{2} \times \dfrac{1}{2} =$ | |
| $\dfrac{1}{4}$ | or 25% |

12. **15% or 0.15:**

| | |
|---|---|
| $25\% - 0.1 =$ | Convert decimal to percent because 1) it's easier to add or subtract integers, and 2) 0.1 is easy to convert to a percent (if you don't already have it memorized). |
| $25\% - 10\% =$ | |
| $15\%$ | |

13. $\dfrac{29}{30}$ **:**

| | |
|---|---|
| $\dfrac{2}{3} + 0.3 =$ | Convert decimal to fraction because $\dfrac{2}{3}$ is a repeating decimal (that is, it can't be converted to an easy decimal form). |
| $\dfrac{2}{3} + \dfrac{3}{10} =$ | |
| $\overset{20}{\underset{3}{2}} \overset{+}{\underset{10}{\times}} \overset{9}{\underset{}{3}} = \dfrac{29}{30}$ | Use the double-cross to add. |

14. **4:**

| | |
|---|---|
| $\dfrac{16}{5} \div 0.8 =$ | Convert decimal to fraction because 1) this decimal is a "have this memorized" decimal, and 2) you will then be able to simplify before multiplying. |
| $\dfrac{16}{5} \div \dfrac{4}{5} =$ | |
| $\dfrac{16}{5} \times \dfrac{5}{4} =$ | |
| $\dfrac{\overset{4}{16}}{\cancel{5}} \times \dfrac{\cancel{5}}{\cancel{4}} = 4$ | Simplify before you multiply. |

15. **3.75 or $\dfrac{15}{4}$ or $3\dfrac{3}{4}$ :**

   $\dfrac{3}{8} \div 10\% =$          Convert percent to fraction because fractions are easier to divide than percents.

   $\dfrac{3}{8} \div \dfrac{1}{10} =$

   $\dfrac{3}{8} \times \dfrac{10}{1} =$

   $\dfrac{3}{\underset{4}{\cancel{8}}} \times \dfrac{\cancel{10}^{5}}{1} =$          Simplify before you multiply.

   $\dfrac{15}{4}$

16. **$1.05:**

   30% of $3.50          How can you get to 30% using the "easy" percentages of 50%, 10%, 5%, or 1%?

   100%: $3.50
   10%: $0.35          Take 10% of $3.50.

   (0.35)(3) = $1.05          Multiply by 3 to get 30%.

17. **0.33 or $\dfrac{33}{100}$ or 33%:** If you feel comfortable taking percents, you can take 10% of 0.3 and add that to 100% of 0.3 to get 110% of 0.3.

   100% of 0.3 is 0.3
   10% of 0.3 is 0.03 (move the decimal one place to the left)
   0.3 + 0.03 = 0.33

   Alternatively, convert both values to fractions (because fractions are easier to simplify and multiply), and solve from there.

   $$0.3 \times 110\% = \dfrac{3}{10} \times \dfrac{11\cancel{0}}{10\cancel{0}} = \dfrac{33}{100} = 33\% = 0.33$$

18. **130% or $\dfrac{13}{10}$ or 1.3:** Note that all of the forms are part of your memorized lists. It's easier to add integers (in the form of percents) than decimals or fractions, so convert all three terms to percents.

$$\frac{2}{5} + 20\% + 0.7 =$$

$$40\% + 20\% + 70\% =$$

$$130\%$$

19. **12 or 1,200%:**

$$1.5 \div \left( \frac{5}{8} - 50\% \right) =$$  Convert percent to fraction because 50% is easier to convert than $\dfrac{5}{8}$.

$$1.5 \div \left( \frac{5}{8} - \frac{1}{2} \right) =$$

$$1.5 \div \left( \frac{5}{8} - \frac{4}{8} \right) =$$

$$= 1.5 \div \left( \frac{1}{8} \right) =$$

$$\frac{3}{2} \div \frac{1}{8} =$$  Convert decimal to fraction because 1) 1.5 is easier to convert than $\dfrac{1}{8}$,

$$\frac{3}{2} \times \frac{8}{1} =$$  and 2) it's easier to divide fractions as factors often cancel.

$$\frac{3}{\cancel{2}} \times \frac{\cancel{8}^{4}}{1} =$$

$$12$$

20. **40% or 0.4 or $\dfrac{2}{5}$:**

$$190\% - \left(1.2 \div \dfrac{4}{5}\right) =$$   Convert decimal to fraction because fractions are easier to divide than decimals.

$$190\% - \left(\dfrac{6}{5} \div \dfrac{4}{5}\right) =$$

$$190\% - \left(\dfrac{6}{5} \times \dfrac{5}{4}\right) =$$

$$190\% - \left(\dfrac{3}{2}\right) =$$

$$190\% - 150\% =$$   Convert fraction to percent because $\dfrac{3}{2}$ is easier to convert than 190%, and percents are easier to subtract.

40%

# Drill 4

21. **6,750:** Move the decimal to the right three places.

$$6.75 \times 10^3 = 6,750$$

22. **1.234:** Line up the decimals and add.

$$
\begin{array}{r}
1.000 \\
+\ 0.200 \\
+\ 0.030 \\
+\ 0.004 \\
\hline
1.234
\end{array}
$$

23. **0.54:** First, ignore the decimals and multiply the numbers. Then move the decimal two places to the left to account for the two decimals in the initial problem.

$$0.27 \times 2 =$$
$$27 \times 2 = 54$$
$$0.27 \times 2 = 0.54$$

24. **0.07212:** Move the decimal three places to the left.

$$72.12 \times 10^{-3} = 0.07212$$

25. **0.24:** First, ignore the decimals and multiply the numbers. Then move the decimal two places to the left to account for the two decimals in the initial problem.

$$0.6 \times 0.4 =$$
$$6 \times 4 = 24$$
$$0.6 \times 0.4 = 0.24$$

26. **0.50:** Line up the decimal points and add.

$$
\begin{array}{r}
0.48 \\
+\ 0.02 \\
\hline
0.50
\end{array}
$$

27. **20:** Multiply the top and bottom by 10 to get rid of the decimal.

$$\frac{4}{0.2} \times \frac{10}{10} = \frac{40}{2} = 20$$

28. **7:** Trade off a decimal place to make the math easier.

$$20 \times 0.35 =$$
$$2 \times 3.5 = \qquad \text{Take a decimal from 20 and give it to 0.35.}$$
$$2 \times 3.5 = 7$$

29. **0.54197:** Divide by 100, or move the decimal two places to the left.

$$\frac{54.197}{10^2} = \frac{54.197}{100} = 0.54197$$

30. **42:** Multiply the top and bottom by 10, or move each decimal one place to the right, in order to get integers.

$$\frac{12.6}{0.3} \times \frac{10}{10} = \frac{126}{3} = 42$$

# Drill 5

31. **23.46:** Move the decimal two places to the left.

$$2{,}346 \times 10^{-2} = 23.46$$

32. **1.59:** Line up the decimal points and add.

$$
\begin{array}{r}
1.21 \\
+\ 0.38 \\
\hline
1.59
\end{array}
$$

33. **12:** Multiply the top and bottom by 10 (or move the decimal one place to the right on both the top and bottom).

$$\frac{6}{0.5} \times \frac{10}{10} = \frac{60}{5} = 12$$

34. **0.084:** Ignore the decimals and multiply the numbers. Then move the decimal three places to the left.

$$
\begin{aligned}
2.1 \times 0.04 &= ? \\
21 \times 4 &= 84 \\
2.1 \times 0.04 &= 0.084
\end{aligned}
$$

35. **0.0015:** Ignore the decimals and multiply the numbers. Then move the decimal four places to the left.

$$
\begin{aligned}
0.03 \times 0.05 &= ? \\
3 \times 5 &= 15 \\
0.03 \times 0.05 &= 0.0015
\end{aligned}
$$

36. **0.412:** Line up the decimals, then add.

$$
\begin{array}{r}
\overset{1}{0.3}70 \\
+\ 0.042 \\
\hline
0.412
\end{array}
$$

37. **80:** Multiply the top and bottom by 100 (or move both decimal points to the right two places) to get rid of the decimals. Then simplify.

$$\frac{3.20}{0.04} \times \frac{100}{100} = \frac{320}{4} = 80$$

38. **60:** Convert the decimals to fractions because fractions are easier to multiply. Then simplify.

$$0.6(50) + 0.25(120) =$$

$$\left(\frac{3}{5} \times 50\right) + \left(\frac{1}{4} \times 120\right) =$$

$$\left(\frac{3}{\cancel{5}} \times \cancel{50}^{10}\right) + \left(\frac{1}{\cancel{4}} \times \cancel{120}^{30}\right) =$$

$$30 + 30 =$$

$$60$$

39. **7:** Multiply the top and bottom by 100 (or move the decimal point two places to the right on the top and bottom).

$$\frac{0.49}{0.07} \times \frac{100}{100} = \frac{49}{7} = 7$$

40. **0.01:** Ignore the decimals and multiply the numbers first, then insert the missing decimal by moving the decimal point four places to the left.

$$100 \times 0.01 \times 0.01 = ?$$
$$100 \times 1 \times 1 = 100$$
$$100 \times 0.01 \times 0.01 = 0.01$$

# Drill 6

41. **(B):** The answer choices don't use a power of 10, so you need to multiply that $10^4$ into the starting number. Since the exponent is a positive 4, move the decimal four places to the right.

$$4.6720$$

The number becomes 46,720.

42. **(B):** Multiplying by $10^{-4}$ will make the resultant number smaller. Because the exponent is $-4$, move the decimal four places to the left.

$$0337.$$

The number becomes 0.0337.

43. **(C):** Glance at the answers. All are 825 multiplied by a power of 10. What math occurs to turn 8.25 into 825?

$$8.25$$

In other words, 8.25 increases by two decimal places to 825. In order to balance out that increase, reduce the exponent by 2; $10^5$ becomes $10^3$. The new form of the number is $825 \times 10^3$.

44. **(A):** Glance at the answers. All start with the form 34.82, so first figure out how may decimal places you need to move in order to get to that number.

$$0.00\underset{\sim\sim\sim\sim}{3482}$$

The number 0.003482 increased by four decimal places. In order to balance out that increase, multiply by a power of $10^{-4}$, since the exponent is equivalent to the number of decimal places moved: $34.82 \times 10^{-4}$.

You can also write the original number this way: $0.003482 \times 10^0$ (note that $10^0 = 1$). Therefore, if you add four decimal points to the starting number, then subtract four from the exponent: $0.003482 \times 10^0 = 34.82 \times 10^{-4}$.

45. **(B):** Glance at the answers. Each one uses the form $10^3$. If you change the exponent from $-3$ to 3, how do you need to change the starting number?

To go from $-3$ to 3, add 6. If the exponent adds 6, then the starting number needs to lose six decimal places.

$$\underset{\sim\sim\sim\sim\sim}{00001}2.12$$

The number becomes $0.00001212 \times 10^3$.

# Drill 7

46. **6:**

| What | is | 15% | of | 40? |
|------|-----|-----|-----|-----|
| $x$ | $=$ | $\dfrac{15}{100}$ | $\times$ | 40 |

$$x = \frac{15}{100} \times 40$$

$$x = \frac{3}{20} \times 40$$

$$x = \frac{3}{\cancel{20}} \times {}^2 \cancel{40}$$

$$x = 6$$

47. **240:**

| 12 | is | 5% | of | what number? |
|----|-----|-----|-----|-----|
| 12 | $=$ | $\dfrac{5}{100}$ | $\times$ | $x$ |

$$12 = \frac{5}{100} \times x$$

$$12 = \frac{1}{20} \times x$$

$$20(12) = x$$

$$x = 240$$

48. **12.5%:**

| 4 | is | what percent | of | 32? |
|---|----|----|----|-----|
| 4 | = | $\dfrac{x}{100}$ | × | 32 |

$$4 = \frac{x}{100} \times 32$$

$$400 = x \times 32$$

$$\frac{400}{32} = x$$

$$\frac{100}{8} = x$$

$$12.5 = x$$

49. **9%:**

| 7% | of | 9 | is | what percent | of | 7 |
|----|----|---|----|----|----|---|
| $\dfrac{7}{100}$ | × | 9 | = | $\dfrac{x}{100}$ | × | 7 |

$$\frac{7}{100} \times 9 = \frac{x}{100} \times 7 \qquad \text{Multiply both sides by 100.}$$

$$7 \times 9 = x \times 7$$

$$9 = x$$

50. **10:** Use your memorized equivalents for 25% and 75%.

| 25% | of | 30 | is | 75% | of | what? |
|-----|----|----|----|-----|----|------|
| $\dfrac{1}{4}$ | × | 30 | = | $\dfrac{3}{4}$ | × | $x$ |

$$\frac{1}{4} \times 30 = \frac{3}{4} \times x \qquad \text{Multiply both sides by 4.}$$

$$30 = 3 \times x$$

$$10 = x$$

**MANHATTAN** PREP

51. **1,000%:** 37.5% is on the list of common equivalents to memorize.

| What percent | of | 6 | is | 37.5% | of | 160 |
|---|---|---|---|---|---|---|
| $\dfrac{x}{100}$ | $\times$ | 6 | $=$ | $\dfrac{3}{8}$ | $\times$ | 160 |

$\dfrac{x}{100} \times 6 = \dfrac{3}{8} \times 160$     Simplify before you multiply.

$\dfrac{x}{100} \times 6 = \dfrac{3}{\cancel{8}} \times \cancel{160}^{\,20}$

$\dfrac{x}{100} \times 6 = 60$

$\dfrac{x}{100} = 10$

$x = 1,000$

52. **25% increase:** In this percent change problem, the change is 14 and the original number is 56. Use the Percent Change formula.

$$\text{Percent change} = \frac{\text{Change}}{\text{Original}}$$

$$\frac{14}{56} = \frac{1}{4} = 25\%$$

53. **20% increase:** If the increase is 50 to 60, then the change is $60 - 50 = 10$, and 50 is the original number. Use the Percent Change formula:

$$\text{Percent change} = \frac{\text{Change}}{\text{Original}}$$

$$\frac{10}{50} = \frac{1}{5} = 20\%$$

54. **42:** There are two ways to represent "40% more than 30." The first is a literal translation—30 plus an additional 40% of 30.

$$x = 30 + \left( \frac{40}{100} \times 30 \right)$$

Find 40% of 30, then add to 30.

| | |
|---|---|
| 100% = 30 | Find 10% of 30. |
| 10% = 3 | |
| (10%)(4) = 40% | To find 40%, multiply 10% by 4. |
| (3)(4) = 12 | |
| 30 + 12 = 42 | Add 30 + 40% of 30. |

Alternatively, 40% more than a number is the same as 100% of that number plus an additional 40%, or 140%. In that case, "40% more than 30" can be represented this way:

$$x = \frac{140}{100} \times 30$$

$$x = \frac{14\cancel{0}}{1\cancel{0}\cancel{0}} \times 3\cancel{0}$$

$$x = 42$$

55. **24:** You can use fractions to set this up:

$$x = 60 - \left( \frac{60}{100} \times 60 \right)$$

60% of 60 is equivalent to 10% of 60 multiplied by 6. Do the math in two steps: 10% of 60 is 6, and $6 \times 6 = 36$. Therefore:

$$x = 60 - 36 = 24$$

Alternatively, "60% less than" 60 is equivalent to "40% of" 60.

$$x = \frac{40}{100} \times 60$$

40% of 60 is equivalent to 10% of 60 multiplied by 4. Do the math in two steps: 10% of 60 is 6, and $6 \times 4 = 24$.

# Drill 8

56. **200:** If m is *reduced* by 55%, then 45% of *m* remains. Use the 45% figure in the translation.

$$0.45m = 90$$ — Multiply both sides by 100 to get rid of the decimal.

$$45m = 9,000$$ — Simplify before you divide!

$$m = \frac{^2 \cancel{9,000}}{\cancel{45}}$$ — The 90 and 45 cancel. Don't forget about the two leftover zeros!

$$m = 200$$

Glance at the answer in the context of the question stem. Does it make sense? When 200 is reduced by 55%, the answer is 90. In other words, 200 is reduced by a little more than half, so what remains (90) is a little less than half; the answer does make sense.

When you have lots of zeros or are shifting decimals, you may want to double-check the solution in this way to make sure that it makes sense. If you had gotten an answer of 2, for example, you would have asked yourself: Does it make sense that 2 reduced by 55% equals 90? No! In this way, you might catch a careless mistake.

57. **28:** Translate the problem. As always, simplify before you multiply.

$$75 - \left(\frac{x}{100} \times 75\right) = 54$$

$$75 - 54 = \frac{75x}{100}$$

$$21 = \frac{3x}{4}$$

$$^7 \cancel{21}\left(\frac{4}{\cancel{3}}\right) = x$$

$$28 = x$$

You could also use the percent change formula. If 75 has been reduced to 54, then the change is 75 − 54 = 21. The original number is 75. Use the formula:

$$\text{Percent change} = \frac{\text{Change}}{\text{Original}}$$

$$\frac{21}{75} = \frac{7}{25}$$

Now what? Get the denominator to be 100 so that the number is expressed as a percent.

$$\frac{7}{25} = \frac{28}{100} = 28\%$$

58. **6.9 or $\dfrac{69}{10}$**: There are two equations—"$x$ is 15% more than 20" and "what is 30% of $x$?" Also, the question stem specifies a variable named $x$ already, so translate the word *what* as a different variable. Use $y$. Now set up your equations:

$$x = \frac{115}{100} \times 20$$

$$y = \frac{3}{10} \times x$$

Solve the first equation for $x$.

$$x = \frac{115}{100} \times 20$$

$$= \frac{115}{\cancel{100}\,_5} \times \cancel{20}$$

$$= \frac{115}{5}$$

$$= 23$$

Plug $x = 23$ into the second equation to find $y$.

$$y = \frac{3}{10} \times 23$$

$$y = \frac{69}{10}$$

$$y = 6.9$$

59. **3**: Use a fractional representation here because fractions are easier to multiply:

$$x = \frac{1}{2} \times \frac{12}{100} \times 50$$

$$x = \frac{1}{2} \times \frac{6}{\cancel{50}} \times \cancel{50}$$

$$x = 3$$

60. **144**: Translate and simplify. Note that there are three zeros on top and three on the bottom; cancel them all.

$$x = \frac{120}{100} \times \frac{3}{10} \times 400$$

$$x = \frac{12\cancel{0}}{1\cancel{00}} \times \frac{3}{1\cancel{0}} \times 4\cancel{00}$$

$$x = 12 \times 3 \times 4$$

$$x = 144$$

61. **50:** Translate and simplify. Because the translation is decently long, it might be helpful to figure out the parts separately.

For the left-hand side of the equation, you can make 45% by adding 10% + 10% + 10% + 10% + 5%, or 10% four times and 5% once. First, find the individual percentages: 10% of 80 is 8 and 5% of 80 is half of 8, or 4. Now solve:

$(8)(4) + 4 = 36$

Alternatively, you can make 45% by taking 50% − 5%. Again, find the individual percentages first: 50% of 80 is 40. To get 5% from 50%, move the decimal one place to the left: 40 becomes 4. Now subtract:

$40 − 4 = 36$

Either way, the equation in the question stem is now "36 is $x$ percent more than 24." This is a percent change problem! The original number is the "more than" number, 24. The change is the difference between the two numbers: $36 − 24 = 12$. Use the Percent Change formula to solve:

$$Percent\ change = \frac{12}{24} = \frac{1}{2} = 50\%$$

Note that the answer is 50, not 50%. The question stem refers to $x$ percent and asks for $x$ by itself. If you plug 50 for $x$ into the question stem, the equation will then say 50%.

62. **400:** Use your memorized percent equivalents. If you know that 200% = 2, you can skip the first line of math and go straight to the second.

$$\frac{1}{10} \times \frac{3}{10} \times x = \frac{200}{100} \times 6$$

$$\frac{1}{10} \times \frac{3}{10} \times x = 2 \times 6$$

$$x = \left(2 \times \cancel{6}^2\right)\left(\frac{100}{\cancel{3}}\right)$$

$$x = 400$$

63. **80%:** The question already contains a variable ($q$), so use another variable to represent the unknown "what" percent. Try $n$.

$$\frac{n}{100} \times \frac{1}{4} \times q = \frac{q}{100} \times 20$$

$$\frac{n}{\cancel{100}} \times \frac{1}{4} \times \cancel{q} = \frac{\cancel{q}}{\cancel{100}} \times 20$$

$$\frac{n}{4} = 20$$

$$n = 80$$

64. **16%:**

$$\frac{200}{100} \times \frac{4}{100} \times a = \frac{x}{100} \times \frac{a}{2}$$

$$2 \times \frac{4}{100} \times a = \frac{x}{100} \times \frac{a}{2} \qquad \text{Divide both sides by } a.$$

$$2 \times 4 = \frac{x}{2} \qquad\qquad \text{Multiply both sides by 100.}$$

$$2 \times 2 \times 4 = x$$

$$16 = x$$

65. **144%:** Assign a new variable for "what" percent. Try $x$. Notice that both sides of the equation below are multiplied by the variable $m$. Cancel it immediately (since it is not zero), and solve for $x$.

$$m \times \frac{120}{100} \times \frac{75}{100} \times \frac{160}{100} = \frac{x}{100} \times m$$

$$\frac{6}{5} \times \frac{3}{4} \times \frac{8}{5} = \frac{x}{100}$$

$$\frac{6}{5} \times \frac{3}{4} \times \frac{8^2}{5} = \frac{x}{100}$$

$$\frac{36}{25} = \frac{x}{100}$$

$$^4\,100 \times \frac{36}{25} = x$$

$$144 = x$$

# Drill 9

66. **(B):** The information was given in the order birds : dogs, but the question asks about dogs : birds. Make sure to put the info in the right order. If there are 6 dogs and 20 birds in the park, the ratio of dogs to birds is 6 : 20. Divide by 2 to simplify this ratio to its base form, 3 : 10.

67. **(A):** If 12 of 24 students in the class are juniors, then the remainder, 24 − 12 = 12, are seniors. Therefore, the ratio of juniors to seniors in the class is 12 : 12. Divide by 12 to simplify the ratio to its base form, 1 : 1.

68. **(B):** The question first presents the information in the order of red marbles to green, but the question asks about the ratio of green to red. There are 35 green to 45 red, or 35 : 45. Divide each number by 5 to simplify the ratio to its base form, 7 : 9.

69. **(B):** If there are 21 trout and 24 catfish, then there are 21 + 24 = 45 total fish in the pond. The ratio of catfish to the total is therefore 24 : 45. Simplify the ratio to its base form. The number 3 is a factor of both numbers, so divide by 3 to get 8 : 15.

# Drill 10

70. If the table does not give you the most basic form of the ratio, find that basic form first. Use it to find the other answers.

| 1 : 2 | = | 3 : **6** | = | **7** : 14 | = | **11** : 22 |
|---|---|---|---|---|---|---|
| 1 : **5** | = | 4 : 20 | = | **5** : 25 | = | 15 : **75** |
| 3 : **4** | = | **6** : 8 | = | **27** : 36 | = | 33 : 44 |
| **5** : 7 | = | 20 : **28** | = | 40 : 56 | = | 60 : **84** |
| 4 : 11 | = | **8** : 22 | = | 36 : **99** | = | **48** : 132 |

# Drill 11

71. **30 cups:** The ratio of cheese to sauce is $1 : \frac{1}{2}$, and Bob uses 15 cups of sauce. Use the table to find the unknown multiplier.

|   | Cheese | Sauce | Total |
|---|---|---|---|
| **R** | 1 | $\frac{1}{2}$ | |
| × | × 30 | × 30 | |
| **A** | **30** | 15 | |

72. **(A):** The ratio of giraffes to lions is 7 : 3, and Sofia saw 60 animals total. Set up a table to figure out how many lions she saw.

|   | G | L | Total |
|---|---|---|---|
| **R** | 7 | 3 | 10 |
| × | | × 6 | × 6 |
| **A** | | **18** | 60 |

73. **36 pieces of fruit:** The ratio of oranges to peaches to strawberries is 2 : 3 : 4, and there are 8 oranges total. Set up a table to solve for the number of pieces of fruit.

|   | **O** | **P** | **S** | **Total** |
|---|---|---|---|---|
| **R** | 2 | 3 | 4 | 9 |
| × | × 4 | | | × 4 |
| **A** | 8 | | | **36** |

74. **17 cars:** The ratio of cars to trucks is 1 : 3, and there are 51 trucks for sale. Set up a table to solve for the number of cars.

|   | **C** | **T** | **Total** |
|---|---|---|---|
| **R** | 1 | 3 | |
| × | × 17 | × 17 | |
| **A** | **17** | 51 | |

75. **(B):** The ratio of forward to back is 3 : 4, and the dance consists of 49 steps in total. Use a table to determine how many forward steps Mustafa takes.

|   | **F** | **B** | **Total** |
|---|---|---|---|
| **R** | 3 | 4 | 7 |
| × | × 7 | | × 7 |
| **A** | **21** | | 49 |

76. **49 ounces:** The ratio of iron to carbon to sheets of steel is 98 : 2 : 1. You can set up a table to find how much iron to use to make just $\frac{1}{2}$ of a sheet of steel. But reflect for a moment first.

You might notice that $\frac{1}{2}$ of a sheet of steel is exactly half of 1 full sheet of steal. As a result, you would need half

as much iron, or $\frac{98}{2} = 49$ ounces. No table needed!

77. **(C):** The ratio of bananas to apples to yogurt to protein powder is 4 : 2 : 6 : 8 for a 64-ounce smoothie. Set up a table to determine the number of cups of yogurt needed to make a 16-ounce smoothie. Note that, in this case, the total is the 64 ounces of smoothie, not the total number of various ingredients.

| | **B** | **A** | **Y** | **P** | **Total ounces in smoothie** |
|---|---|---|---|---|---|
| **R** | 4 | 2 | 6 | 8 | 64 |
| × | | | $\times \dfrac{1}{4}$ | | $\times \dfrac{1}{4}$ |
| **A** | | | $1\dfrac{1}{2}$ | | 16 |

Alternatively, you might notice that a 16-ounce smoothie is exactly one-quarter of a 64-ounce smoothie. As a result, Malin will need one-quarter as much yogurt, or $6 \times \dfrac{1}{4} = 1.5$, or $1\dfrac{1}{2}$ cups.

# Equations

# In this chapter...

- Expressions Don't Have Equals Signs
- An Equation Says "Expression A = Expression B"
- Golden Rule of Equations: Do the Same Thing to Both Sides
- Isolate a Variable: Work Your Way In by Doing PEMDAS in Reverse
- Clean Up an Equation: Combine Like Terms and Eliminate Denominators
- Variables in the Exponent: Make the Bases Equal
- Systems of Equations
- Kill an Equation and an Unknown: (A) Isolate, Then Substitute
- Kill an Equation and an Unknown: (B) Combine Equations
- Three or More Variables: Isolate the Expression You Want

Chapter 6

# Equations

## In This Chapter, You Will Learn To:

- Manipulate expressions and equations to solve for variables

Manipulating expressions and equations is at the core of algebra. The first step is to understand the distinction between expressions and equations.

## Expressions Don't Have Equals Signs

An **expression** such as $3y + 8z$ ultimately represents a number. It has a value, although you may not know that value. The expression $3y + 8z$ contains numbers that are known (3 and 8) and unknown ($y$ and $z$) and that are linked by arithmetic operations (in this case, $+$ and $\times$).

Here are more expressions:

$$12 \qquad x - y \qquad 2w^3 \qquad 4(n + 3)(n + 2) \qquad \frac{\sqrt{x}}{3b - 2}$$

These all have one thing in common: They do *not* have an equals sign. An expression never contains an equals sign.

When you **simplify** an expression, you reduce the number of separate terms. You might also pull out and cancel common factors. In other words, you make the expression simpler. However, *you never change the expression's value as you simplify*. Examples of simplifying equations are in the table:

| Unsimplified | | Simplified | How |
|:---:|:---:|:---:|:---:|
| $3x + 4x$ | $\rightarrow$ | $7x$ | Combine like terms |
| $\dfrac{2y^2}{3} + \dfrac{3y^2}{5}$ | $\rightarrow$ | $\dfrac{19y^2}{15}$ | Find a common denominator and then combine |
| $x + xy$ | $\rightarrow$ | $x(1 + y)$ | Pull out a common factor |
| $\dfrac{3x^2}{6x}$ | $\rightarrow$ | $\dfrac{x}{2}$ | Cancel common factors |

At times you might go in reverse. For instance, you might **distribute** a common factor.

$$x(1 + y) \quad \longrightarrow \quad x + xy$$

Or you might multiply the top and bottom of a fraction by the same number to change its look. The result may seem even *less* simplified, temporarily. But by finding a common denominator, you can add fractions and get a simpler final result. For example:

| Unsimplified | | Even less simple | | Simplified |
|:---:|:---:|:---:|:---:|:---:|
| $\dfrac{w}{2} + \dfrac{w}{4}$ | $\longrightarrow$ | $\dfrac{w \times 2}{2 \times 2} + \dfrac{w}{4}$ | $\longrightarrow$ | $\dfrac{3w}{4}$ |

As you simplify an expression (or even complicate one), the value of the expression must never change.

When you *evaluate* an expression, you figure out its value—the actual number represented by that expression.

To evaluate an expression, *substitute numbers in for any variables, then simplify*. In other words, *swap out the variables*, replacing them with numbers. Then do the arithmetic.

Some people say "plug and chug." You *plug* in the values of the variables, then you *chug* through the simplification. Some people also call this "subbing in."

Whatever you call this process, you have to know the values of the variables to evaluate the expression. Otherwise, you're stuck.

Finally, remember PEMDAS! Follow PEMDAS when you plug and chug. Consider this example:

Evaluate the expression $3\sqrt{2x}$ given that $x$ has the value of 8.

First, substitute in 8 for $x$.

$$3\sqrt{2x} \text{ becomes } 3\sqrt{2(8)}$$

Now simplify the expression.

$$3\sqrt{2(8)} = 3\sqrt{16} = 3 \times 4 = 12$$

You have now evaluated the expression $3\sqrt{2x}$ when $x = 8$. For that particular value of $x$, the value of the expression is 12.

Pay attention to negative signs, especially if the value you're subbing in is negative. Put in parentheses to obey PEMDAS. Consider this example:

If $y = -2$, what is the value of $3y^2 - 7y + 4$?

Substitute $-2$ for $y$. Put parentheses around the $-2$ to clarify that you're subbing in negative 2, not subtracting 2 somehow. Therefore:

$$3y^2 - 7y + 4 \text{ becomes } 3(-2)^2 - 7(-2) + 4$$

Now simplify.

$$3(-2)^2 - 7(-2) + 4 = 3(4) - (-14) + 4 = 12 + 14 + 4 = 30$$

Be sure to square the negative sign and to subtract $-14$ (in other words, add 14). The value of the expression is 30.

You might have to plug into expressions in answer choices. Here's another one:

If $y = 6$, then which of the following expressions has the value of 20?

(A) $y + 14$      (B) $y - 14$      (C) $20y$

When you substitute 6 in for $y$ in the answer choices, only $y + 14$ results in 20. The answer is (A).

Other expressions involving $y$ could also equal 20 when $y = 6$, such as $2y + 8$ or $y^2 - 16$. On the GMAT, you would not be forced to pick between these expressions, because they'd all be correct answers to this question.

| If you... | Then you... | Like this: |
|---|---|---|
| Simplify an expression | Combine like terms or perform other legal algebra moves | $3x + 4x$ becomes $7x$ |
| Evaluate an expression | Substitute numbers in for unknowns, then simplify | When $x = 2$, $7x$ becomes $7(2)$ or 14 |

## An Equation Says "Expression A = Expression B"

An equation is a complete sentence that has a subject, a verb, and an object. The sentence always takes this form:

Subject *equals* object.

One expression equals another expression.

| $2x$ | $-$ | $z$ | $=$ | $y$ | $+$ | $4$ |
|---|---|---|---|---|---|---|
| Two $x$ | minus | $z$ | equals | $y$ | plus | four |

An equation always sets one expression $(2x - z)$ equal to another expression $(y + 4)$.

Everything you know about simplifying or evaluating expressions applies in the world of equations, because equations are made up of expressions.

You can *simplify* an expression on just one side of an equation, because you are not changing the value of that expression. So the equation still holds true, even though you're ignoring the other side.

For instance, simplify the left side but leave the right side alone.

$3x + 5x = y$      becomes      $8x = y$

You can also *evaluate* an expression on just one side. For instance, say you have $\frac{8x}{15} = y$ and you know that $x = 5$. Then you can plug and chug just on the left side:

$$\frac{8x}{15} = y \qquad \text{becomes} \qquad \frac{8(5)}{15} = y \qquad \text{and finally} \qquad \frac{8}{3} = y$$

Throughout all these changes on the left side, the right side has remained *y*.

If all you could do to equations was to simplify or evaluate expressions, then your toolset would be limited. However, you can do much more.

You can truly *change* both sides. You can actually alter the values of the two expressions on either side of an equation.

You just have to follow the Golden Rule.

## Golden Rule of Equations: Do the Same Thing to Both Sides

You can change the value of the *left* side any way you want…

… as long as you change the *right* side in *exactly the same way*.

Take this example:

$$x + 5 = 8$$

If you subtract 5 from the left side, you must subtract 5 from the right side. You get a new equation with new expressions. If the first equation isn't lying, then the second equation is true, too.

$$\begin{array}{r} x + 5 = \phantom{-}8 \\ -5 \phantom{=} -5 \\ \hline x = \phantom{-}3 \end{array}$$

Here is a table of the major Golden Rule moves you can do to both sides of an equation.

| 1. **Add the same thing** to both sides. <br> • That "thing" can be a number or a variable expression. <br> • Show the addition underneath to be safe. (Later, if you feel comfortable with the steps, you can stop writing out the addition.) | $\begin{array}{r} y - 6 = 15 \\ +6 \phantom{=} +6 \\ \hline y = 21 \end{array}$ |
|---|---|
| 2. **Subtract the same thing** from both sides. | $\begin{array}{r} z + 4 = \phantom{-}k \\ -4 \phantom{=} -4 \\ \hline z \phantom{+4} = k - 4 \end{array}$ |

**MANHATTAN** PREP

| 3. **Multiply both sides by the same thing.** <br>• Put parentheses in so that you multiply *entire* sides. | $n+m=\dfrac{3w}{4}$ <br><br> $4\times(n+m)=\left(\dfrac{3w}{4}\right)\times 4$ <br><br> $4n+4m=3w$ |
|---|---|
| 4. **Divide both sides by the same thing** (except 0, of course). <br>• Extend the fraction bar all the way so that you divide *entire* sides. | $a+b=5d$ <br> $\dfrac{a+b}{5}=\dfrac{5d}{5}$ <br> $\dfrac{a+b}{5}=d$ |
| 5. **Square both sides**, cube both sides, etc. <br>• Put parentheses in so you square or cube *entire* sides. | $x+\sqrt{2}=\sqrt{7w}$ <br> $\left(x+\sqrt{2}\right)^2=\left(\sqrt{7w}\right)^2$ <br> $\left(x+\sqrt{2}\right)^2=7w$ |
| 6. **Take the square root of both sides**, the cube root of both sides, etc. <br>• Extend the radical so you square-root or cube-root *entire* sides. | $z^3=64$ <br> $\sqrt[3]{z^3}=\sqrt[3]{64}$ <br> $z=4$ |

One warning about square-rooting both sides of an equation: The equation usually splits into *two* separate equations. For example:

$$x^2=49$$
$$\sqrt{x^2}=\sqrt{49}$$
Square-root both sides

$$x=7 \quad \textbf{OR} \quad x=-7$$

There are two numbers that, when squared, equal 49. Remember that when negative numbers are squared, they become positive. So when you take a square root of a squared number, you'll need to find the negative solution as well. For example:

When you square $\quad y=6 \quad$ you always get $\quad y^2=36.$
But if you solve $\quad y^2=36 \quad$ you get $\quad y=6$ OR $y=-6.$

Essentially, the square hides the fact that the base could be positive or negative, leaving you with two possible solutions.

*Perform the same action to an entire side of an equation.* Pretend that the expression on each side of the equation is surrounded by parentheses—and actually write those parentheses in as necessary. Consider this equation:

$$x+4=\dfrac{x}{2}$$

To multiply both sides by 2, add in parentheses.

$$2(x+4) = \left(\frac{x}{2}\right)2$$

Now simplify. Distribute the 2 to both the $x$ and the 4 and cancel the 2's on the right.

$$2x + 8 = x$$

This is why multiplying to get rid of a denominator is sometimes called *cross-multiplication*. You can imagine that the 2 that *was* in the denominator on the right side moves to the left side, where it is multiplied by the $x + 4$. Cross-multiplication is even more useful when both sides have denominators to begin with.

Let's go back to the equation at hand. You can simplify further with more Golden Rule moves: subtracting $x$ from both sides, and then subtracting 8.

$$
\begin{array}{rcl}
2x + 8 &=& x \\
-x & & -x \\
\hline
x + 8 &=& 0 \\
-8 & & -8 \\
\hline
x & =& -8
\end{array}
$$

You now have $x$ by itself on one side, so the equation says that the value of $x$ is $-8$. What you did here was *isolate the variable* or *solve for the variable*.

To isolate $x$, get $x$ by itself on one side of the equation. The equation should wind up reading "$x = \ldots$"

The thing on the right side is often a number, as in the case above ($x = -8$).

In a more complicated equation, the right side could be an expression that contains other variables. Either way, the important thing when you isolate $x$ on the left is that the right side *cannot* have any terms containing $x$. Otherwise, you haven't truly *isolated* the $x$ on the left side.

You can isolate the $x$ on the *right* side if you want, of course. If you do that, make sure that the *left* side has no terms containing $x$.

When you get "$x = $ a number" or "a number $= x$," then you have *solved the equation*. The number you get is a *solution* to the equation.

When you plug a solution into an equation (i.e., into the *variable* in an equation), you make the equation true. For example:

"4 is a solution to the equation $2x + 7 = 15$."

This sentence means that if $x = 4$, that equation is true.

If you have more than one variable in an equation, you may still want to isolate one variable for some reason. Consider this example:

If $3x + 5y = 12$, what is $x$ in terms of $y$?

"What is $x$ in terms of $y$" means "get $x$ by itself and put $y$ and everything else on the opposite side of the equals sign."

**ⓜ MANHATTAN** PREP

For example, "*a* in terms of *b*" is the right side of this equation:

$$a = 3 + b^2$$

There cannot be any *a*'s on the right side. And there are only *a*'s on the left side.

To get *x* in terms of *y*, isolate *x* on one side by applying Golden Rule moves to the given equation.

$$3x + 5y = 12$$
$$\underline{\quad -5y \qquad -5y \quad}$$
$$3x \quad = 12 - 5y$$

$$x = \frac{12 - 5y}{3}$$

So *x* in terms of *y* is this expression: $\frac{12 - 5y}{3}$ . This contains no *x*'s. If you're looking for "*x* in terms of *y*," the answer will contain *y*'s, not *x*'s.

If you want *y* in terms of *x* instead, then isolate *y* on one side. You'll get this expression on the other side: $\frac{12 - 3x}{5}$ .

| If you... | Then you... | Like this: |
|---|---|---|
| Want to change an expression on one side of an equation | Apply the Golden Rule: Change both sides in exactly the same way | $y - 3 = 9$<br>$\underline{\quad +3 \quad +3 \quad}$<br>$y \quad = 12$ |
| Want to isolate the variable *x* in an equation | Perform Golden Rule moves and simplify until the equation reads "*x* = something else" | $7x + 4 = 18$<br>$\underline{\quad -4 \quad -4 \quad}$<br>$7x \quad = 14$<br>$\frac{7x}{7} = \frac{14}{7}$<br>$x = 2$ |
| Need *x* in terms of *y* | Perform Golden Rule moves and simplify until the equation reads "*x* = everything else" | $7x + 4 = y$<br>$\underline{\quad -4 \quad -4 \quad}$<br>$7x \quad = y - 4$<br>$\frac{7x}{7} = \frac{y - 4}{7}$<br>$x = \frac{y - 4}{7}$ |

## Check Your Skills

1. If $\sqrt{x + 2} = 4$, what is *x*?
2. If $\frac{y - 3}{x} = 2$, what is *y* in terms of *x*?

*Answers can be found on page 273.*

# Isolate a Variable: Work Your Way In by Doing PEMDAS in Reverse

If an expression is complicated, you might get confused about how to isolate the variable inside.

Consider the following equation:

$5(x - 1)^3 - 30 = 10$

The expression on the left side is a complicated recipe that builds from the inside out.

| 1. | Start with $x$. | $x$ |
| 2. | Subtract 1. | $x - 1$ |
| 3. | Cube the result. | $(x - 1)^3$ |
| 4. | Multiply by 5. | $5(x - 1)^3$ |
| 5. | Subtract 30. | $5(x - 1)^3 - 30$ |

The recipe follows PEMDAS, as you'd expect. The result of this recipe equals 10, because that's what the equation says:

$5(x - 1)^3 - 30 = 10$

To isolate $x$ on the left, you need to work your way through from the outside in. So you need to *undo* the PEMDAS steps by working in the *reverse order*.

The last step of the recipe was to subtract 30. To undo that step first, add 30 to both sides.

$$\begin{array}{rcl} 5(x-1)^3 - 30 & = & 10 \\ +30 & & +30 \\ \hline 5(x-1)^3 & = & 40 \end{array}$$

You have now gotten rid of 30 on the left side. You've "moved" it to the other side.

Now undo the previous step of the original recipe, which was to multiply by 5. Divide both sides by 5.

$$\frac{5(x-1)^3}{5} = \frac{40}{5}$$

$(x - 1)^3 = 8$

Next, undo the cubing. The opposite of exponents is roots, so take the cube root of both sides.

$$\sqrt[3]{(x-1)^3} = \sqrt[3]{8}$$

$(x - 1) = 2$

You don't need the parentheses anymore, so drop them.

$x - 1 = 2$

Finally, undo the subtraction by adding 1 to both sides, and you get $x = 3$.

In summary, you *added* 30, then *divided* by 5, then got rid of the *exponent*, then simplified what was inside the *parentheses*. You did PEMDAS backwards, from the outside in.

If you want to isolate a variable deep inside an expression, but you are unsure about the order of steps to perform, do PEMDAS in reverse. Try another example.

If $4\sqrt{x-6}+7=19$, what is the value of *x*?

**A/S**

**M/D**

**E**

**P**

Here's the solution path. First, *subtract* 7 from both sides.

$$\begin{array}{r}4\sqrt{x-6}+7=19\\ \underline{-7\quad-7}\\ 4\sqrt{x-6}\quad=12\end{array}$$

Next, *divide* both sides by 4.

$$\frac{\cancel{4}\sqrt{x-6}}{\cancel{4}}=\frac{12}{4}$$
$$\sqrt{x-6}=3$$

Now, undo the square root by *squaring* both sides.

$$\sqrt{x-6}=3$$
$$\left(\sqrt{x-6}\right)^2=(3)^2$$
$$x-6=9$$

Finally, *add* 6 to both sides, and you end up with *x* = 15.

The original equation did not contain explicit parentheses, but the square root symbol extended over two terms: $\sqrt{x-6}$. That's just like putting parentheses around *x* – 6 and raising that whole quantity to the $\frac{1}{2}$ power: $(x-6)^{\frac{1}{2}}$.

A square root sign acts like parentheses when it extends over more than one term. Likewise, a fraction bar acts like parentheses when it's stretched over multiple terms.

| If you... | Then you... | Like this: |
|---|---|---|
| Want to isolate a variable inside an expression | Follow PEMDAS in reverse as you undo the operations in the expression—in other words, work your way in from the outside | $2y^3 - 3 = 51$ <br> $\underline{\quad +3 \quad +3}$ <br> $2y^3 \quad\quad = 54$ <br> $\dfrac{2y^3}{2} = \dfrac{54}{2}$ <br> $y^3 = 27$ <br> $\sqrt[3]{y^3} = \sqrt[3]{27}$ <br> $y = 3$ |

## Check Your Skills

Solve for $x$.

3. $3(x+4)^3 - 5 = 19$

4. $\sqrt[3]{(x+5)} - 7 = -8$

*Answers can be found on page 273.*

# Clean Up an Equation: Combine Like Terms and Eliminate Denominators

What happens when $x$ shows up in multiple places in an equation? Consider this question:

If $\dfrac{5x - 3(4-x)}{2x} = 10$, what is $x$?

To isolate $x$, you have to get all the $x$'s together on one side. How? *Combine like terms.*

If there is a denominator, get rid of that right away, especially if the denominator contains $x$. *Always get variables out of denominators.*

This should be the first move in the case above. Undo the division by multiplying both sides by the entire denominator, which is $2x$.

$$2x\left(\dfrac{5x - 3(4-x)}{2x}\right) = (10)\,2x$$
$$5x - 3(4-x) = 20x$$

At this point, to combine like terms, get $x$ out of the parentheses. Distribute the $-3$ on the left side (be careful with the negative sign).

$$5x - 3(4-x) = 20x$$
$$5x - 12 + 3x = 20x$$

Now combine like terms. First add $5x$ and $3x$ on the left side.

$$5x - 12 + 3x = 20x$$
$$8x - 12 = 20x$$

Next, subtract $8x$ from both sides and immediately combine like terms on the right.

$$
\begin{array}{r}
8x - 12 = 20x \\
-8x \qquad -8x \\
\hline
-12 = 12x
\end{array}
$$

The right side could be written as $20x - 8x$, but you should combine into $12x$ as you perform the subtraction.

Why subtract $8x$ rather than $20x$? If you subtract $8x$, you get all the $x$ terms on one side and numbers on the other side. You also get a positive coefficient on the $x$ (i.e., positive 12). These results are both nice to have.

Finally, divide by 12 to isolate $x$ on the right.

$$\frac{-12}{12} = \frac{12x}{12}$$
$$-1 = x$$

You now have the answer to the question: $x = -1$.

| If you… | Then you… | Like this: |
|---------|-----------|-----------|
| Have a variable in multiple places in an equation | Combine like terms, which might be on different sides of the equation | $\begin{array}{r} 9y + 30 = 12y \\ -9y \qquad -9y \\ \hline 30 = 3y \end{array}$ |
| Have a variable in a denominator | Multiply to eliminate the denominator right away | $\dfrac{2z - 3}{z} = 4$ <br> $z\left(\dfrac{2z-3}{z}\right) = 4(z)$ <br> $2z - 3 = 4z$ |

## Check Your Skills

Solve for $x$.

5.  $\dfrac{2x + 6(9 - 2x)}{x - 4} = -3$

*Answer can be found on page 273.*

# Variables in the Exponent: Make the Bases Equal

If a variable is in the exponent, the typical PEMDAS moves aren't going to help much. Consider this example:

If $3^x = 27^4$, what is $x$?

The key is to rewrite the terms so they have the *same base*. Usually, the best way to do this is to *factor bases into primes*.

On the left side, 3 is already a prime, so leave it alone. On the right side, 27 is not prime. Since $27 = 3^3$, replace 27 with $3^3$. Put in parentheses to keep the exponents straight.

$$3^x = (3^3)^4$$

Simplify the right side by applying the "two exponent" rule: $(3^3)^4 = 3^{3 \times 4} = 3^{12}$. Therefore:

$$3^x = 3^{12}$$

In words, this equation says, "3 raised to the power of $x$ is equal to 3 raised to the power of 12."

This is only true if $x$ itself is equal to 12.

$$3^x = 3^{12} \quad \longrightarrow \quad x = 12$$

*Once the bases are the same, the exponents must be the same.*

This rule has exactly three exceptions: a base of 1, a base of 0, and a base of −1. The exceptions occur because more than one exponent of these particular bases results in the same number. For example:

$$1^2 = 1^3 = \ldots = 1 \qquad 0^2 = 0^3 = \ldots = 0 \qquad (-1)^2 = (-1)^4 = 1, \text{ while } (-1)^1 = (-1)^3 = -1$$

However, for every other base, the rule works. Try this example:

If $4^y = 8^{y+1}$, what is the value of $2^y$?

(A) −8

(B) $\dfrac{1}{8}$

(C) $\dfrac{1}{4}$

(D) 1

(E) 8

Look at the answer choices. Since none of them contain a $y$, that's your clue that the equation can be manipulated to find the value of $y$. You just need to figure out how!

Look at the given equation. The variable $y$ is in two exponents.

$$4^y = 8^{y+1}$$

To figure out what this tells you about $y$, make the bases the same. Rewrite both 4 and 8 as powers of 2.

$$4 = 2^2 \quad 8 = 2^3$$

$$4^y = 8^{y+1} \quad \longrightarrow \quad (2^2)^y = (2^3)^{y+1}$$

Next, apply the "two exponent" rule on both sides.

$$(2^2)^y = (2^3)^{y+1}$$

$$2^{2y} = 2^{3(y+1)}$$

Now that the bases are the same (and the common base is not 1, 0, or −1), you can set the exponents equal to each other. Write a brand-new equation that expresses this fact.

$$2y = 3(y + 1)$$

At this point, solve for $y$. To start, distribute the 3 on the right.

$$2y = 3y + 3$$

Next, subtract $2y$ from both sides to combine like terms.

$$0 = y + 3$$

Finally, subtract 3 from both sides.

$$-3 = y$$

Now that you've solved for $y$, find the value of $2^y$, which is what the question asked. To do this, replace $y$ with −3.

$$2^y = 2^{-3} = \frac{1}{8}$$

The correct answer is (B).

| If you... | Then you... | Like this: |
|---|---|---|
| Have a variable in an exponent or exponents | Make the bases equal, usually by breaking the given bases down to primes | $3^x = 27^4$ <br> $3^x = (3^3)^4$ <br> $3^x = 3^{12}$ <br> $x = 12$ |

## Check Your Skills

6. If $4^6 = 64^{2x}$, what is the value of $16^x$?

*Answer can be found on page 274.*

# Systems of Equations

Many GMAT problems will force you to deal with two variables. In most of those cases, you'll also have two equations. For example:

(a)   $2x - 3y = 16$                    (b)   $y - x = -7$

A group of more than one equation is often called a *system of equations*. Solving a system of two equations with two variables, for example, $x$ and $y$, means finding values for $x$ and $y$ that make both equations true *at the same time*.

The systems of equations discussed in this section only have one solution. That is, only one set of values of $x$ and $y$ makes the system work.

To solve a system of two equations and two unknowns, you can use either of two good strategies:

  1.  Isolate, then substitute          2.   Combine equations

These strategies are similar at a high level. In both, here's what you do:

  1. Kill off one equation and one unknown.
  2. Solve the remaining equation for the remaining unknown.
  3. Plug back into one of the original equations to solve for the other variable.

However, the two strategies take very different approaches to step #1: how to kill off one equation and one unknown. Let's examine these approaches in turn.

## Kill an Equation and an Unknown: (A) Isolate, Then Substitute

This strategy is also known as *substitution*. Consider this system again:

  (a)   $2x - 3y = 16$          (b)   $y - x = -7$

To follow the substitution strategy, first isolate one variable in one of the equations. Next, substitute into the other equation.

*Which variable should you isolate?* The one you *don't* ultimately want. If the problem asks for $x$, first isolate $y$.

Why $y$? Because the variable you first isolate is the one you will then kill off. You're left with one equation containing $x$—the variable you want. This way, you save work.

Conversely, if the problem asks for $y$, first isolate $x$, so you can kill it off early.

Let's say that the question asks for the value of $x$. Then you want to isolate $y$ in one of the given equations. In which equation should you isolate your variable? The one that's easier to deal with.

In the example above, it looks easier to isolate $y$ in equation (b). All you have to do is add $x$ to both sides. So go ahead and do so.

$$
\begin{array}{ll}
\text{(a)} \quad 2x - 3y = 16 & \text{(b)} \quad \begin{aligned} y - x &= -7 \\ \underline{+x \qquad +x} & \\ y \quad\; &= -7 + x \\ y \quad\; &= \; x - 7 \end{aligned}
\end{array}
$$

By the way, when you use this method, it's good practice to write the two equations in the system side by side. That way, you can do algebra down your page to isolate one variable without running into the other equation.

Now you have expressed $y$ in terms of $x$. Since $y = x - 7$, you can replace $y$ with $(x - 7)$ anywhere you see $y$. This will remove any references to $y$ in the first equation. In essence, you are killing off $y$. Now go ahead and replace the $y$ in the first equation:

(a)  $2x - 3y = 16$          (b)  $y - x = -7$

$$\frac{+x \qquad\qquad +x}{}$$

$$y \qquad = -7 + x$$

$$y \qquad = \ x - 7$$

$2x - 3(x - 7) = 16$

When you sub in an expression such as $x - 7$, place parentheses around the expression. This way, you avoid PEMDAS errors.

Now that you have killed off one variable ($y$) and one equation (the second one), you have just one variable left ($x$) in one equation. Solve for that variable:

$$2x - 3(x - 7) = 16$$

$2x - 3x + 21 = 16$ 　　　　　Distribute the $-3$.

$-x + 21 = 16$ 　　　　　Combine $2x$ and $-3x$ (like terms).

$-x = -5$ 　　　　　Subtract 21 from both sides.

$x = 5$ 　　　　　Multiply both sides by $-1$.

At this point, you're done if the question only asks for $x$. If the question asks for $x + y$ or some other expression involving both $x$ and $y$, then you need to solve for $y$. Do so by plugging your value of $x$ into either of the original equations.

Which equation should you plug back into? The one in which you isolated $y$. In fact, you should plug into the revised form of that equation—the one that looks like "$y =$ something." This is the easiest way to solve for $y$, so this is the equation you'll want to use:

$y = x - 7$

To start, swap out $x$ and replace it with 5, since you found that $x = 5$.

$y = (5) - 7$

$y = -2$

Now you have the complete solution: $x = 5$ and $y = -2$. These are the *solutions* of the system; in other words, these are the values that make *both* of the original equations true at the same time:

(a)  $2x - 3y = 16$          (b)  $y - x = -7$

$2(5) - 3(-2) = 16$          $(-2) - (5) = -7$

True                                    True

| If you… | Then you… | Like this: |
|---|---|---|
| Have two equations and two unknowns | Isolate one unknown, then substitute into the other equation | $2x - 3y = 16$ and $y - x = -7$<br>$y = -7 + x = x - 7$<br>$2x - 3(x - 7) = 16$<br>…<br>$x = 5$<br>$y = -2$ |

## Check Your Skills

Solve for $x$ and $y$.

7.  $6y + 15 = 3x$
    $x + y = 14$

*Answer can be found on page 274.*

# Kill an Equation and an Unknown: (B) Combine Equations

Substitution will always work. But some GMAT problems can be solved more easily with another method, known as *combination* or *elimination*.

Here's how combination works. You can always *add two equations together*. Just add the left sides up and put the result on the left, then add the right sides up and put that result on the right.

$$x = 4$$
$$+ \ y = 7$$
$$\overline{x + y = 4 + 7}$$

Why is this allowed? You are actually adding the same thing to both sides of an equation. Since $y$ equals 7, you can legally add $y$ on the left side of $x = 4$ and add 7 on the right side. You are making the same change on each side of the first equation.

In this example, the resulting equation ($x + y = 11$) is more complicated than the starting equations. However, adding equations can sometimes actually eliminate a variable—*and that's why you do it.*

Consider this system of equations:

$a + b = 11$ $\qquad$ $a - b = 5$

What happens when you add these equations together?

$$a + b = 11$$
$$+ \ \underline{a - b = 5}$$
$$2a \ = 16$$

**MANHATTAN** PREP

The $b$'s cancel out of the resulting equation completely. It's now easy to solve for $a$.

$$2a = 16 \quad \longrightarrow \quad a = 8$$

Finally, solve for $b$ by plugging back into one of the original equations.

$$a + b = 11 \quad \longrightarrow \quad (8) + b = 11 \quad \longrightarrow \quad b = 3$$

So the complete solution to the original system of equations is $a = 8$ and $b = 3$.

If you solve that system by substitution, you will need to take a few more steps. Every extra step takes time and presents an additional opportunity for error. If you learn to combine equations to eliminate, you can often kill off a variable easily and safely.

Combination isn't restricted to adding equations. You can also subtract equations. Say you are given these two equations:

$$5n + m = 17 \qquad\qquad 2n + m = 11$$

Since "$+ m$" shows up in both equations, we can kill $m$ by subtracting the second equation from the first.

$$\begin{array}{r} 5n + m = 17 \\ -\ \underline{2n + m = 11} \\ 3n \quad\ \ = 6 \end{array}$$

Realize that you are subtracting the whole left side, as well as the right side. If you are concerned that you might not follow PEMDAS, put in parentheses around the whole equation.

$$\begin{array}{r} 5n + m = 17 \\ -\ \underline{\left(2n + m = 11\right)} \\ 3n \quad\ \ = 6 \end{array}$$

Now you can solve for $n$, then plug back in to get $m$.

$$3n = 6 \quad \longrightarrow \quad n = 2$$

$$2n + m = 11 \quad \longrightarrow \quad 2(2) + m = 11 \quad \longrightarrow \quad m = 7$$

To set up a good elimination, you can even multiply a whole equation by a number. That's the same thing as multiplying the left side and the right side by the same number. This is a Golden Rule move.

Consider this system of equations from earlier:

$$\text{(a)} \qquad 2x - 3y = 16 \qquad\qquad \text{(b)} \qquad y - x = -7$$

To take the combination approach, first rewrite the equations vertically and line up the variables. Here, you *want* to write one equation below the other (not *next to* each other as you do with substitution). Space the terms to line up $x$ with $x$ and $y$ with $y$.

$$2x - 3y = 16$$
$$-x + y = -7$$

If you add the equations now, neither variable will die; you're left with $x - 2y = 9$. That's not helpful.

However, if you multiply the second equation by 2 on both sides, you'll be able to cancel when you add.

$$2x - 3y = 16 \quad \longrightarrow \quad 2x - 3y = 16$$
$$2(-x + y) = (-7)2 \quad \longrightarrow \quad -2x + 2y = -14$$

Now add. The $2x$ term will cancel with the $-2x$ term:

$$2x - 3y = 16$$
$$+ \quad -2x + 2y = -14$$
$$\overline{\hspace{2cm}}$$
$$-y = 2$$
$$y = -2$$

Finally, use this value of $y$ in one of the original equations to solve for $x$.

$$y - x = -7 \quad \longrightarrow \quad (-2) - x = -7 \quad \longrightarrow \quad -x = -5 \quad \longrightarrow \quad x = 5$$

This is the same solution as before. In this case, you only saved a little work by combining equations to eliminate rather than isolating and substituting. However, some problems are *much* easier to solve by combining equations. Take a look at this last example:

For this system of equations, what is the value of $x + y$?

$$\frac{1}{2}x + \frac{1}{3}y = 3$$
$$2x + y = 11$$

If you try direct substitution, you will need to make a lot of messy calculations involving fractions.

Instead, try combination. First, multiply the top equation through by 6 to eliminate all fractions.

$$6\left(\frac{1}{2}x + \frac{1}{3}y\right) = (3)6$$
$$3x + 2y = 18$$

Next line up the two given equations, which now look much better.

$$3x + 2y = 18$$
$$2x + y = 11$$

Before going further, consider: What does the question specifically ask for? It does not ask for $x$ or $y$ separately. Rather, it asks for $x + y$.

You can certainly solve for one of the variables, then find the other. But there's a shortcut.

If you look carefully, you might notice that you can solve for $x + y$ directly by *subtracting* the equations.

$$3x + 2y = 18$$
$$- (2x + y = 11)$$
$$x + y = 7$$

Ta-da! The answer to the question is 7.

Combination isn't always appropriate. Become very comfortable with substitution as a default method. But as you spot opportunities to eliminate a variable by adding or subtracting equations, seize those opportunities.

| If you… | Then you… | Like this: |
|---|---|---|
| Have two equations and two unknowns | Add or subtract equations to eliminate a variable | $2x - 3y = 16$ and $y - x = -7$<br><br>Multiply 2nd equation by 2:<br><br>$2(y - x) = (-7)2$<br><br>Add equations:<br><br>$-2x + 2y = -14$<br>$+2x - 3y = \phantom{-}16$<br>$- y = \phantom{-}2$<br>$y = -2$ |

## Check Your Skills

Solve for $x$ and $y$.

8.  $x + 4y = 10$
    $y - x = -5$

*Answer can be found on page 274.*

## Three or More Variables: Isolate the Expression You Want

A few problems involve even more than two variables. Fortunately, all the procedures you've learned so far still work.

Focus on exactly what the question asks for and isolate that on one side of the equation. Try this example:

If $\sqrt{\dfrac{a}{b}} = c$ and $abc \neq 0$, what is the value of $b$ in terms of $a$ and $c$?

Since the question asks for $b$, you should isolate $b$. The answer will contain $a$ and $c$, because the question asks for an expression "in terms of" $a$ and $c$.

Take the given equation and do Golden Rule moves to isolate $b$.

$$\sqrt{\frac{a}{b}} = c$$

$$\left(\sqrt{\frac{a}{b}}\right)^2 = c^2 \qquad \text{Square both sides.}$$

$$\frac{a}{b} = c^2$$

$$b\left(\frac{a}{b}\right) = \left(c^2\right)b \qquad \text{Multiply both sides by } b.$$

$$a = c^2 b$$

$$\frac{a}{c^2} = \frac{c^2 b}{c^2} \qquad \text{Divide both sides by } c^2.$$

$$\frac{a}{c^2} = b$$

The answer to the question is $\dfrac{a}{c^2}$.

By the way, the "non-equation" $abc \neq 0$ was only there to prevent division by zero. You rarely wind up using this sort of information in any other way.

Here is another tough question:

$$\frac{w}{x-y} = 3 \qquad\qquad y - x = 4$$

In the system of equations above, what is the value of $w$?

(A) $-12$

(B) $-\dfrac{3}{4}$

(C) $\dfrac{3}{4}$

(D) $\dfrac{4}{3}$

(E) $12$

You are asked for the value of $w$, so you want to manipulate the equations to get "$w = \ldots$"

Notice that the answer choices are all numbers. This means that the other variables $x$ and $y$ must disappear along the way.

One approach to this problem is to isolate $x$ or $y$ in the second equation, then substitute into the first equation. This way, you at least get rid of one variable. It's a start—let's see where it goes.

Isolate $y$ by adding $x$ to both sides of the second equation.

$$
\begin{array}{rl}
y - x = & 4 \\
\underline{+\ x \quad\ +x} & \\
y \quad\ \ = & x + 4
\end{array}
$$

Now substitute $x + 4$ into the first equation in place of $y$. Be sure to put parentheses around $x + 4$.

$$\frac{w}{x-y} = 3$$

$$\longrightarrow \quad \frac{w}{x-(x+4)} = 3$$

$$\longrightarrow \quad \frac{w}{x-x-4} = 3$$

$$\longrightarrow \quad \frac{w}{-4} = 3$$

Look what happened—the variable $x$ disappeared as well. This is a good sign. If $x$ didn't cancel out, then you'd be in trouble. You can solve for $w$ now.

$$\frac{w}{-4} = 3 \qquad \longrightarrow \qquad w = -12 \qquad \text{The answer is (A).}$$

Another approach to the problem is to recognize that $x - y$ is very similar to $y - x$. In fact, one is the negative version of the other.

$$x - y = -(y - x)$$

If you recognize this, then multiply the second equation by $-1$ so that it has $x - y$ on one side:

$$
\begin{array}{c}
y - x = 4 \\
(-1)(y - x) = (4)(-1) \\
x - y = -4
\end{array}
$$

Now you can *substitute for a whole expression*. That is, you can swap out $x - y$ in the first equation and replace that entire thing with $-4$.

$$\frac{w}{x-y} = 3 \qquad \longleftarrow \quad \boxed{x - y = -4}$$

$$\frac{w}{(-4)} = 3$$

This gets you to the same point as the first method, and you end up with $w = -12$.

However many variables and equations you have, pay close attention to what the question is asking for.

- If the question asks for the variable $x$, isolate $x$, so you have "$x = \ldots$"
- If the question asks for $x$ in terms of $y$, after you isolate $x$ on one side of the equation, the other side should contain $y$.
- If the question asks for $x + y$, isolate that expression, so you have "$x + y = \ldots$"
- If a variable does not appear in the answer choices, help it vanish. Isolate it and substitute for it in another equation.
- If an expression such as $x - y$ shows up in two different equations, feel free to substitute for it so that the whole thing disappears.

| If you... | Then you... | Like this: |
|---|---|---|
| Have three or more unknowns | Isolate whatever the question asks for, and use substitution to eliminate unwanted variables | If $a + b - c = 12$ and $c - b = 8$, what is the value of $a$? <br><br> Isolate $a$: <br> $a = 12 + c - b$ <br><br> Substitute for $c - b$: <br> $a = 12 + (8)$ <br> $a = 20$ |

## Check Your Skills

9.  If $\dfrac{a}{c} + \dfrac{b}{3c} = 1$, what is $c$ in terms of $a$ and $b$?

*Answer can be found on page 275.*

# Check Your Skills Answer Key

1. **14:** In order to find the value of $x$, isolate $x$ on one side of the equation.

$$\sqrt{x+2} = 4$$
$$\left(\sqrt{x+2}\right)^2 = 4^2$$
$$x+2 = 16$$
$$x = 14$$

2. **$2x + 3$:** In order to find $y$ in terms of $x$, isolate $y$ on one side of the equation.

$$\frac{y-3}{x} = 2$$
$$\cancel{x}\left(\frac{y-3}{\cancel{x}}\right) = (2)\,x$$
$$y - 3 = 2x$$
$$y = 2x + 3$$

3. **$x = -2$:**

$$3(x+4)^3 - 5 = 19$$

| | |
|---|---|
| $3(x+4)^3 = 24$ | Add 5 to both sides. |
| $(x+4)^3 = 8$ | Divide both sides by 3. |
| $(x+4) = 2$ | Take the cube root of both sides. |
| $x = -2$ | Remove the parentheses and subtract 4 from both sides. |

4. **$x = -6$:**

$$\sqrt[3]{(x+5)} - 7 = -8$$

| | |
|---|---|
| $\sqrt[3]{(x+5)} = -1$ | Add 7 to both sides. |
| $x + 5 = -1$ | Cube both sides and remove parentheses. |
| $x = -6$ | Subtract 5 from both sides. |

5. **$x = 6$:**

$$\frac{2x + 6(9 - 2x)}{x - 4} = -3$$

| | |
|---|---|
| $2x + 6(9 - 2x) = -3(x - 4)$ | Multiply by the denominator $(x - 4)$. |
| $2x + 54 - 12x = -3x + 12$ | Simplify grouped terms by distributing (be careful of the signs!). |
| $-10x + 54 = -3x + 12$ | Combine like terms ($2x$ and $-12x$). |
| $54 = 7x + 12$ | Add $10x$ to both sides. |
| $42 = 7x$ | Subtract 12 from both sides. |
| $6 = x$ | Divide both sides by 7. |

6. **16:** You could answer this question by breaking each base down to a power of 2, but you'll save some time if you notice that all three bases in the question (4, 64, and 16) are powers of 4. Solve for $x$ by rewriting 64 as $4^3$.

$$4^6 = 64^{2x}$$
$$4^6 = (4^3)^{2x}$$
$$4^6 = 4^{6x}$$
$$6 = 6x$$
$$1 = x$$

If $x = 1$, then $16^x = 16^1 = 16$.

7. **$x = 11, y = 3$:**

(a)  $6y + 15 = 3x$          (b)  $x + y = 14$

       $2y + 5 = x$

|  |  |
|---|---|
| | Divide the first equation by 3 to isolate $x$. |

$$(2y + 5) + y = 14$$
$$3y + 5 = 14$$
$$3y = 9$$
$$y = 3$$

Substitute $(2y + 5)$ for $x$ in the second equation and solve for $y$.

$$x + (3) = 14$$
$$x = 11$$

Substitute $y = 3$ in the second equation to solve for $x$.

8. **$x = 6, y = 1$:** Notice you have positive $x$ in the first equation and negative $x$ in the second equation. Rearrange the second equation and line it up under the first equation.

$$x + 4y = 10$$
$$\underline{-x + y = -5}$$
$$5y = 5$$
$$y = 1$$

Now that you know $y = 1$, plug it back into either equation to solve for $x$.

$$x + 4y = 10$$
$$x + 4(1) = 10$$
$$x = 6$$

9. $\dfrac{3a+b}{3}$ OR $a+\dfrac{b}{3}$: The wording "$c$ in terms of..." means that you have to isolate $c$ on one side of the equation. To do so, first combine the fractions on the left side of the equation to combine like terms.

$$\frac{a}{c}+\frac{b}{3c}=1$$

$$\frac{3a}{3c}+\frac{b}{3c}=1$$

$$\frac{3a+b}{3c}=1$$

$$\frac{3a+b}{3}=c$$

If you split the numerator, then you would get:

$$\frac{\cancel{3}a}{\cancel{3}}+\frac{b}{3}=c$$

$$a+\frac{b}{3}=c$$

# Chapter Review: Drill Sets

## Drill 1

1. If $x = 2$, what is the value of $x^2 - 4x + 3$?
2. If $x = 3$, what is the value of $x + \sqrt{48x}$?
3. If $x = -4$, what is the value of $\dfrac{5 - x}{3} - x^2$?
4. If $c = 100$ and $p = 30c^2 - c$, what is the value of $p$?
5. If $y - 3 = \dfrac{xy}{2}$ and $x = 3$, what is the value of $y$?

## Drill 2

Solve for the variable in the following equations.

6. $14 - 3x = 2$
7. $3(7 - x) = 4(1.5)$
8. $7x + 13 = 2x - 7$
9. $3t^3 - 7 = 74$
10. $\dfrac{z - 4}{3} = -12$
11. $1,200x + 6,000 = 13,200$
12. $\sqrt{x} = 3 \times 5 - 20 \div 4$
13. $-(y)^3 = -27$
14. $2 - \dfrac{\sqrt{2x + 2}}{2} = -1$
15. $5\sqrt{x} + 6 = 51$

## Drill 3

Solve for $x$ in the following equations.

16. $3x + 2(x + 2) = 2x + 16$
17. $\dfrac{3x + 7}{x} = 10$
18. $4(-3x - 8) = 8(-x + 9)$
19. $3x + 7 - 4x + 8 = 2(-2x - 6)$
20. $2x(4 - 6) = -2x + 12$
21. $\dfrac{3(6 - x)}{2x} = -6$

22. $\dfrac{13}{x + 13} = 1$
23. $\dfrac{10(-3x + 4)}{10 - 5x} = 2$
24. $\dfrac{15 - 3(5x - 3)}{3 - 2x} = 6$
25. $\dfrac{50(10 + 3x)}{50 + 7x} = 50$

## Drill 4

Solve for the values of both variables in each system of equations using substitution. The explanations will use substitution to solve.

26. $7x - 3y = 5$
    $y = 10$
27. $y = 4x + 10$
    $y = 7x - 5$
28. $2h - 4k = 0$
    $k = h - 3$
29. $5x - 3y = 17$
    $2x - y = 8$
30. $12b = 2g$
    $4g - 3b = 63$

## Drill 5

Solve for the values of both variables in each system of equations using elimination. The explanations will use elimination to solve.

31. $x - y = 4$
    $2x + y = 5$
32. $x + 2y = 5$
    $x - 4y = -7$
33. $a + b = 8$
    $2a + b = 13$
34. $7m - 2n = 1$
    $3m + n = 6$

35. $y - 2x - 1 = 0$
    $x - 3y - 1 = 0$

36. $\dfrac{1}{3}r - \dfrac{1}{6}s = 0$

    $2r + \dfrac{1}{2}s - 3 = 0$

## Drill 6

Solve for the values of both variables in each system of equations. Decide whether to use substitution or elimination. Explanation will use one of the two methods and explain why that is the better solution method.

37. $5x + 2y = 12$

    $y = \dfrac{1}{2}x + 3$

38. $y - 1 = x + 2$
    $2y = x + 1$

39. $8a - 2b - 5 = 0$
    $2b + 4a - 4 = 0$

40. $3x = 6 - y$
    $6x - y = 3$

41. $x = 2y - \dfrac{1}{2}$

    $y - x = -\dfrac{3}{2}$

## Drill 7

Solve for the indicated value in each system of equations.

42. $4x + y + 3z = 34$
    $4x + 3z = 21$

    What is $y$?

43. $\dfrac{x - 3}{y - 2} = 4z$

    What is the value of $x$ in terms of $y$ and $z$?

    (A) $4yz - 8z + 3$

    (B) $4yz - 5$

    (C) $y - 8z - 3$

44. $3x + 5y + 2z = 20$
    $6x + 4z = 10$

    What is $y$?

45. $\dfrac{a - b}{4} = c + 1$

    $c = b + 2$

    What is $b$ in terms of $a$?

## Drill 8

Solve for the indicated value in each system of equations.

46. $\dfrac{a + b}{c + d} = 10$

    $3d = 15 - 3c$

    What is $a + b$?

47. $x = \dfrac{y}{5}$

    $2z - 1 = \dfrac{x + y}{2}$

    What is $z$ in terms of $x$?

48. $2^{x+y} = \sqrt{z - 2}$

    $x = 2 - y$

    What is $z$?

49. $\dfrac{3x}{z + 4} = 4$

    $4z = 3y$

    What is $x - y$?

    (A) $4z + 3$

    (B) $\dfrac{16}{3}$

    (C) $\dfrac{4}{3}$

# Drill Sets Solutions

## Drill 1

1. **−1:** To evaluate the expression, replace $x$ with 2.

$$x^2 - 4x + 3 =$$
$$(2)^2 - 4(2) + 3 =$$
$$4 - 8 + 3 = -1$$

2. **15:** To evaluate the expression, replace $x$ with 3. Rather than multiply 48 by 3, pull a 3 out of 48 in order to create a perfect square that you can then remove from under the square-root symbol.

$$x + \sqrt{48x} =$$
$$3 + \sqrt{48(3)} =$$
$$3 + \sqrt{(16)(3)(3)} =$$
$$3 + (4)(3) =$$
$$3 + 12 = 15$$

3. **−13:** To evaluate the expression, replace $x$ with −4 everywhere in the equation. Be extra careful with the negative signs; use parentheses to help keep track.

$$\frac{5-x}{3} - x^2 =$$
$$\frac{5-(-4)}{3} - (-4)^2 =$$
$$\frac{5+4}{3} - (16) =$$
$$\frac{9}{3} - 16 =$$
$$3 - 16 = -13$$

4. **299,900:** To find the value of $p$, first replace $c$ with 100.

$$p = 30c^2 - c$$
$$p = 30(100)^2 - 100$$
$$p = 30(10,000) - 100$$
$$p = 300,000 - 100 = 299,900$$

5. **−6**: First, replace $x$ with 3 in the equation.

$$y - 3 = \frac{xy}{2}$$

$$y - 3 = \frac{(3)y}{2}$$

Now, to find the value of $y$, isolate $y$ on one side of the equation.

$$y - 3 = \frac{3y}{2}$$

$$2(y - 3) = 3y$$

$$2y - 6 = 3y$$

$$-6 = y$$

# Drill 2

6. **4**: Apply PEMDAS in reverse.

$$14 - 3x = 2$$
$$-3x = -12 \qquad \text{Subtract 14.}$$
$$x = 4 \qquad \text{Divide by −3.}$$

7. **5**: Apply PEMDAS in reverse.

$$3(7 - x) = 4(1.5)$$
$$21 - 3x = 6 \qquad \text{Distribute.}$$
$$-3x = -15 \qquad \text{Subtract 21.}$$
$$x = 5 \qquad \text{Divide by −3.}$$

8. **−4**: Apply PEMDAS in reverse.

$$7x + 13 = 2x - 7$$
$$5x + 13 = -7 \qquad \text{Subtract } 2x.$$
$$5x = -20 \qquad \text{Subtract 13.}$$
$$x = -4 \qquad \text{Divide by 5.}$$

9. **3**: Apply PEMDAS in reverse.

$$3t^3 - 7 = 74$$
$$3t^3 = 81 \qquad \text{Add 7.}$$
$$t^3 = 27 \qquad \text{Divide by 3.}$$
$$t = 3 \qquad \text{Take the cube root.}$$

10. **−32:** Apply PEMDAS in reverse.

$$\frac{z-4}{3} = -12$$

$$z - 4 = -36 \qquad \text{Multiply by 3.}$$
$$z = -32 \qquad \text{Add 4.}$$

11. **6:** Apply PEMDAS in reverse.

$$1{,}200x + 6{,}000 = 13{,}200$$
$$1{,}200x = 7{,}200 \qquad \text{Subtract 6,000.}$$
$$x = 6 \qquad \text{Divide by 1,200.}$$

12. **100:** Note that the right side contains no variables. First, simplify that side using standard PEMDAS rules.

$$\sqrt{x} = 3 \times 5 - 20 \div 4$$
$$\sqrt{x} = (3 \times 5) - (20 \div 4)$$
$$\sqrt{x} = 15 - 5$$
$$\sqrt{x} = 10$$
$$x = 100 \qquad \text{Square both sides.}$$

13. **3:** Be careful with the negatives!

$$-(y)^3 = -27$$
$$(y)^3 = 27 \qquad \text{Divide by −1.}$$
$$y = 3 \qquad \text{Take the cube root.}$$

14. **17:**

$$2 - \frac{\sqrt{2x+2}}{2} = -1$$

$$-\frac{\sqrt{2x+2}}{2} = -3 \qquad \text{Subtract 2 from both sides.}$$

$$\sqrt{2x+2} = 6 \qquad \text{Multiply by −2.}$$

$$2x + 2 = 36 \qquad \text{Square.}$$
$$2x = 34 \qquad \text{Subtract 2.}$$
$$x = 17 \qquad \text{Divide by 2.}$$

15. **81:**

$$5\sqrt{x} + 6 = 51$$
$$5\sqrt{x} = 45 \qquad \text{Subtract 6.}$$
$$\sqrt{x} = 9 \qquad \text{Divide by 5.}$$
$$x = 81 \qquad \text{Square}$$

# Drill 3

16. **4:**

$$3x + 2(x + 2) = 2x + 16$$
$$3x + 2x + 4 = 2x + 16$$
$$5x + 4 = 2x + 16$$
$$3x + 4 = 16$$
$$3x = 12$$
$$x = 4$$

17. **1:**

$$\frac{3x + 7}{x} = 10$$
$$3x + 7 = 10x$$
$$7 = 7x$$
$$1 = x$$

18. **−26:**

$$4(-3x - 8) = 8(-x + 9)$$
$$-12x - 32 = -8x + 72$$
$$-32 = 4x + 72$$
$$-104 = 4x$$
$$-26 = x$$

19. **−9:**

$$3x + 7 - 4x + 8 = 2(-2x - 6)$$
$$-x + 15 = -4x - 12$$
$$3x + 15 = -12$$
$$3x = -27$$
$$x = -9$$

20. **−6:**

$$2x(4 - 6) = -2x + 12$$
$$2x(-2) = -2x + 12$$
$$-4x = -2x + 12$$
$$-2x = 12$$
$$x = -6$$

21. **−2:**

$$\frac{3(6-x)}{2x} = -6$$

$$3(6-x) = -6(2x)$$

$$18 - 3x = -12x$$

$$18 = -9x$$

$$-2 = x$$

22. **0:**

$$\frac{13}{x+13} = 1$$

$$13 = 1(x + 13)$$

$$13 = x + 13$$

$$0 = x$$

23. **1:**

$$\frac{10(-3x+4)}{10-5x} = 2$$

$$10(-3x+4) = 2(10 - 5x)$$

$$-30x + 40 = 20 - 10x$$

$$40 = 20 + 20x$$

$$20 = 20x$$

$$1 = x$$

24. **2:**

$$\frac{15 - 3(5x - 3)}{3 - 2x} = 6$$

$$15 - 3(5x - 3) = 6(3 - 2x)$$

$$15 - 15x + 9 = 18 - 12x$$

$$24 - 15x = 18 - 12x$$

$$24 = 18 + 3x$$

$$6 = 3x$$

$$2 = x$$

25. **−10:**

$$\frac{\cancel{50}(10+3x)}{50+7x} = {}^{1}\cancel{50}$$

$$(10 + 3x) = (50 + 7x)$$

$$10 = 50 + 4x$$

$$-40 = 4x$$

$$-10 = x$$

## Drill 4

26. **$x = 5, y = 10$:** Equation 1 is $7x - 3y = 5$, and equation 2 is $y = 10$.

> Eq. (1):
> $7x - 3y = 5$
> $7x - 3(10) = 5$
> $7x - 30 = 5$
> $7x = 35$
> $x = 5$

> Eq. (2):
> $y = 10$
>
> Substitute 10 for $y$ in Eq. (1) and solve for $x$.

27. **$x = 5, y = 30$:**

> Eq. (1):
> $y = 4x + 10$
>
>
>
>
>
> $y = 4(5) + 10$
> $y = 30$

> Eq. (2):
> $y = 7x - 5$
> $(4x + 10) = 7x - 5$
> $10 = 3x - 5$
> $15 = 3x$
> $5 = x$
>
> Substitute $(4x + 10)$ for $y$ in Eq. (2), and solve for $x$.
>
> Substitute 5 for $x$ in Eq. (1), and solve for $y$.

28. **$h = 6, k = 3$:**

> Eq. (1):
> $2h - 4k = 0$
> $2h - 4(h - 3) = 0$
> $2h - 4h + 12 = 0$
> $-2h = -12$
> $h = 6$

> Eq. (2):
> $k = h - 3$
>
> Substitute $(h - 3)$ for $k$ in Eq. (1), and solve for $h$.
>
> $k = (6) - 3$
> $k = 3$
>
> Substitute 6 for $h$ in Eq. (2), and solve for $k$.

29. **$x = 7, y = 6$:**

> Eq. (1):
> $5x - 3y = 17$

> Eq. (2):
> $2x - y = 8$
> $-y = -2x + 8$
> $y = 2x - 8$
>
> Isolate $y$ in Eq. (2).

$$5x - 3(2x - 8) = 17$$
$$5x - 6x + 24 = 17$$
$$-x + 24 = 17$$
$$-x = -7$$
$$x = 7$$

Substitute $(2x - 8)$ for $y$ in Eq. (1), and solve for $x$.

$$y = 2(7) - 8$$
$$y = 14 - 8$$
$$y = 6$$

Substitute 7 for $x$ in the rephrased Eq. (2) to solve for $y$.

30. **$b = 3$, $g = 18$:**

Eq. (1):                        Eq. (2):
$$12b = 2g$$                    $$4g - 3b = 63$$

$$6b = g$$

Isolate $g$ in Eq. (1).

$$4(6b) - 3b = 63$$
$$24b - 3b = 63$$
$$21b = 63$$
$$b = 3$$

Substitute $(6b)$ for $g$ in Eq. (2), and solve for $b$.

$$6(3) = g$$
$$18 = g$$

Substitute 3 for $b$ in the rephrased Eq. (1) to solve for $g$.

# Drill 5

31. **$x = 3$, $y = -1$:** Notice that the first equation has the term $-y$ while the second equation has the term $+y$. If you add the equations together, these two terms will cancel.

$$x - y = 4$$
$$+(2x + y = 5)$$
$$\overline{\qquad 3x = 9 \qquad}$$

Therefore, $x = 3$. Plug this value into the first equation.

$$x - y = 4$$
$$(3) - y = 4$$
$$-y = 1$$
$$y = -1$$

32. **$x = 1$, $y = 2$:** Both equations have the term $+x$, so eliminate the variable $x$ by subtracting the second equation from the first.

$$\begin{array}{r} x + 2y = 5 \\ -(x - 4y = -7) \\ \hline 2y + 4y = 5 + 7 \end{array}$$

The new equation simplifies to $6y = 12$, or $y = 2$. Then plug this value for $y$ into the first equation and solve for $x$.

$$\begin{aligned} x + 2y &= 5 \\ x + 2(2) &= 5 \\ x + 4 &= 5 \\ x &= 1 \end{aligned}$$

Be very careful to change the sign of each term in the second equation when subtracting (e.g., $-4y$ becomes $-(-4y) = +4y$, and $-7$ becomes $-(-7) = +7$). Alternatively, you could have multiplied the entire second equation by $-1$ to get $-x + 4y = 7$ and then added this equation to the first.

$$\begin{array}{r} x + 2y = 5 \\ + (-x + 4y = 7) \\ \hline 6y = 12 \end{array}$$

This yields the same solution: $y = 2$ and $x = 1$.

33. **$a = 5$, $b = 3$:** Both equations have the term $+b$, so eliminate the variable $b$ by subtracting the second equation from the first.

$$\begin{array}{r} a + b = 8 \\ - (2a + b = 13) \\ \hline -a = -5 \end{array}$$

Hence, $a = 5$. Plug this value for $a$ into the first equation, and solve for $b$.

$$\begin{aligned} a + b &= 8 \\ (5) + b &= 8 \\ b &= 3 \end{aligned}$$

34. **$m = 1$, $n = 3$:** None of the variables have the same coefficient (the number in front of a variable), so no variables will cancel as the equations are currently written. Multiply one of the equations by a constant so that one of the variables will then cancel when you add or subtract the equations.

The second equation has an $n$, and the first equation has a $-2n$. Multiply the second equation by 2 to get $6m + 2n = 12$, then add the two equations.

**MANHATTAN** PREP

$$7m - 2n = 1$$
$$\underline{+(6m + 2n = 12)}$$
$$13m \qquad = 13$$

Therefore, $m = 1$. Plug this value into the second equation and solve for $n$.

$$3m + n = 6$$
$$3(1) + n = 6$$
$$n = 3$$

35. $x = -\dfrac{4}{5}, \; y = -\dfrac{3}{5}$ : First, manipulate the two equations so that the variables are nicely aligned on the left-hand side and the constant terms are all on the right.

$$-2x + y = 1$$
$$x - 3y = 1$$

Multiply one of the equations by a constant that will allow you to cancel one of the variables when you add or subtract. There are multiple correct ways to do this; one way is to multiply the second equation by 2, thereby replacing it with the equation $2x - 6y = 2$, then add the original first equation to the new second equation.

$$-2x + y = 1$$
$$\underline{+(2x - 6y = 2)}$$
$$-5y = 3$$

Therefore, $y = -\dfrac{3}{5}$. Glance at the two original equations. Which one is easiest to use to solve for $x$? In either case, you're still going to have to deal with the fractional value for $y$, but the second equation is a little easier because the $x$ variable has a coefficient of 1. In other words, you won't have to divide at the end in order to solve.

$$x - 3\left(-\frac{3}{5}\right) = 1$$
$$x + \frac{9}{5} = 1$$
$$x = \frac{5}{5} - \frac{9}{5}$$
$$x = -\frac{4}{5}$$

36. **$r = 1$, $s = 2$:** The coefficients in this problem are messy. Take a little time to think about the best way to proceed. It might be easiest to eliminate the fractions in both equations before proceeding.

Notice that if you multiply the first equation by 6, you will cancel out all denominators. Do the same for the second equation by multiplying everything by 2.

$$2r - s = 0$$
$$4r + s - 6 = 0$$

Notice that the coefficients on $s$ are both 1 but with different signs. This means that when you add the equations, they will cancel. Next, rearrange the second equation so that the constant terms are on the right side.

$$
\begin{array}{r}
2r - s = 0 \\
+\,(4r + s = 6) \\
\hline
6r \phantom{+s} = 6
\end{array}
$$

Then, plug $r = 1$ into the first equation to get:

$$2(1) - s = 0$$
$$2 = s$$

# Drill 6

37. **$x = 1$, $y = 3.5$:** When one of the two equations is already solved for one of the variables, substitution is usually the better method. In this particular problem, the second equation is solved for $y$, so take the right-hand side of the second equation and substitute it for $y$ in the first equation.

$$5x + 2\left(\frac{1}{2}x + 3\right) = 12$$
$$5x + x + 6 = 12$$
$$6x = 6$$
$$x = 1$$

Plug this value for $x$ into either of the original equations to solve for $y$; in this case, it will be easiest to use the equation that was used for the substitution (since it is already solved for $y$).

$$y = \frac{1}{2}x + 3$$
$$y = \frac{1}{2}(1) + 3$$
$$y = 3.5 \text{ or } 3\frac{1}{2}$$

38. **$x = -5, y = -2$:** For this system of equations, either method would be appropriate. Both equations would require some manipulation before you could stack-and-add, and neither equation is already solved for one of its variables. When neither method seems to have an advantage, pick whichever you like best.

    If you use substitution, it might be easier to solve the first equation for $y$: $y = x + 3$. Then substitute this into the second equation.

    $$2(x + 3) = x + 1$$
    $$2x + 6 = x + 1$$
    $$x = -5$$

    Plug this into the equation used for the substitution step.

    $$y = x + 3$$
    $$y = (-5) + 3$$
    $$y = -2$$

    If you use elimination, manipulate the first equation to combine the constant terms ($y = x + 3$). Now the two equations have the same order, and the coefficient on $x$ is the same, so if you subtract the second from the first, the variable $x$ will disappear.

    $$\begin{array}{r} y = x + 3 \\ -(2y = x + 1) \\ \hline -y = 2 \end{array}$$

    Therefore, $y = 2$; plug this value in for $y$ in either equation to solve for $x$: $x = -5$.

39. **$a = \dfrac{3}{4}, b = \dfrac{1}{2}$:** Even though some manipulations will be required to line up the variables nicely in this system, elimination is the optimal method because the $-2b$ in the first equation will cancel the $+2b$ in the second. Start by rearranging the two equations.

    $$8a - 2b = 5$$
    $$4a + 2b = 4$$

    Then add them together.

    $$\begin{array}{r} 8a - 2b = 5 \\ +(4a + 2b = 4) \\ \hline 12a = 9 \end{array}$$

Therefore, $a = \dfrac{9}{12} = \dfrac{3}{4}$. Plug this value into one of the two original equations, and solve for $b$. Note that the second equation has a $4a$ term, which will cancel nicely with the fraction $\dfrac{3}{4}$.

$$2b + 4\left(\frac{3}{4}\right) - 4 = 0$$
$$2b + 3 - 4 = 0$$
$$2b = 1$$
$$b = \frac{1}{2}$$

40. **$x = 1$, $y = 3$:** For this system of equations, either method would be appropriate. Both equations would require some manipulation before you could stack-and-add, and neither equation is already solved for one of its variables. When neither method seems to have an advantage, pick whichever you like best.

To solve via substitution, isolate $y$ in the first equation to get $y = 6 - 3x$, and then substitute this for $y$ in the second equation.

$$6x - (6 - 3x) = 3$$
$$6x - 6 + 3x = 3$$
$$9x = 9$$
$$x = 1$$

Next, plug $x = 1$ into the same equation used above for the substitution step.

$$y = 6 - 3x$$
$$y = 6 - 3(1)$$
$$y = 3$$

To solve using the elimination method, rearrange the first equation to get $3x + y = 6$, and then add the equations together to eliminate $y$.

$$3x + y = 6$$
$$+(6x - y = 3)$$
$$\overline{\phantom{+}9x \quad\;\; = 9}$$

Plug $x = 1$ into either of the equations to solve for $y$.

$$3x + y = 6$$
$$3(1) + y = 6$$
$$y = 3$$

41. **$x = 3.5$, $y = 2$:** The first equation is solved for $x$, which points to substitution. At the same time, the first equation has $+x$ on the left side while the second equation has $-x$. Either method will work; choose the one you like best.

To solve using the elimination method, rearrange the equations to line up all the variables. Next, add the two equations in order to eliminate the $x$ term.

$$x - 2y = -\frac{1}{2}$$
$$+\left( -x + y = -\frac{3}{2} \right)$$
$$\overline{\qquad\qquad -y = -2}$$

Therefore, $y = 2$. Plug this into the first equation, since that equation already isolates $x$ on one side.

$$x = 2y - \frac{1}{2}$$
$$x = 2(2) - \frac{1}{2}$$
$$x = 3.5$$

To solve by substitution, take the first equation, which is already solved for $x$, and substitute into the second equation.

$$y - \left( 2y - \frac{1}{2} \right) = -\frac{3}{2}$$
$$y - 2y + \frac{1}{2} = -\frac{3}{2}$$
$$-y = -\frac{3}{2} - \frac{1}{2}$$
$$-y = 2$$

Therefore, $y = -2$. As before, plug this value into the first equation to get $x = 3.5$.

# Drill 7

42. **13:** This question contains only two equations, but three variables. To isolate $y$, you need to get rid of both $x$ and $z$. Try to eliminate both variables at the same time. The coefficients of $x$ and $z$ are the same in both equations, so subtract the second equation from the first to eliminate both.

$$4x + y + 3z = 34$$
$$-\left( 4x \quad\ + 3z = 21 \right)$$
$$\overline{\qquad\qquad\quad y = 13}$$

43. **(A):** To find the value of $x$ in terms of the other variables, isolate $x$ on one side of the equation, and put everything else on the other side. Begin by getting rid of the fraction.

$$\frac{x-3}{y-2} = 4z$$

$$x - 3 = 4z(y-2)$$

$$x = 4z(y-2) + 3$$

The answers don't contain parentheses, so distribute to get rid of them.

$$x = 4yz - 8z + 3$$

44. **3:** In order to isolate $y$, you need to eliminate both $x$ and $z$. Find a way to eliminate both variables at the same time.

Notice that the coefficients for $x$ and $z$ in the second equation (6 and 4, respectively) are exactly double their coefficients in the first equation (3 and 2, respectively). If you divide the second equation by 2, the coefficients will be the same.

$$\longrightarrow\ 3x + 5y + 2z = 20$$
$$3x + 5y + 2z = 20 \longrightarrow 3x + 2z = 5$$
$$6x + 4z = 10$$

Now, subtract the second equation from the first.

$$3x + 5y + 2z = 20$$
$$-(3x \qquad + 2z = 5)$$
$$\overline{\phantom{xxxxxxx}5y = 15}$$
$$y = 3$$

45. $b = \dfrac{a-12}{5}$: To solve for $b$ in terms of $a$, isolate $b$ on one side of the equation, and put everything else on the other side. Furthermore, you will need to eliminate the variable $c$, because the question does not mention $c$.

The second equation is already solved for $c$, so start by substituting $b + 2$ for $c$ in the first equation.

$$\frac{a-b}{4} = c + 1$$

$$\frac{a-b}{4} = (b+2) + 1$$

Now isolate $b$ on one side of the equation.

$$\frac{a-b}{4} = b+3$$
$$a-b = 4(b+3)$$
$$a-b = 4b+12$$
$$a-12 = 5b$$
$$\frac{a-12}{5} = b$$

# Drill 8

46. **$a + b = 50$:** In order to find the value of $a + b$, you need to eliminate $c$ and $d$ from the first equation, but there are only two equations total. Is there a way to eliminate $c + d$ at once?

Try manipulating the second equation to give you $c + d$.

$$3d = 15 - 3c$$
$$3c + 3d = 15$$
$$c + d = 15$$

Next, substitute $c + d = 5$ into the first equation and isolate $a + b$.

$$\frac{a+b}{c+d} = 10$$
$$\frac{a+b}{(5)} = 10$$
$$a+b = 50$$

47. **$z = \dfrac{3x+1}{2}$:** In order to solve for $z$ in terms of $x$, you need to isolate $z$ on one side of an equation that contains only the variable $x$ and plain numbers on the other side of the equals sign. In other words, you have to get rid of the $y$ somehow. Therefore, kill off $y$ by isolating it in the first equation.

$$x = \frac{y}{5}$$
$$5x = y$$

Now substitute. In the second equation, replace $y$ with $5x$.

$$2z - 1 = \frac{x+y}{2}$$
$$2z - 1 = \frac{x+(5x)}{2}$$

Finally, isolate $z$.

$$2z - 1 = \frac{6x}{2}$$
$$2z - 1 = 3x$$
$$2z = 3x + 1$$
$$z = \frac{3x + 1}{2}$$

48. **18:** In order to isolate $z$, you have to eliminate $x$ and $y$. The combination $x + y$ is in the exponent of the first equation, so try to isolate that same combination (or combo) in the second equation.

$$x = 2 - y$$
$$x + y = 2$$

In the first equation, substitute 2 for the combo $x + y$, then solve for $z$.

$$2^{x+y} = \sqrt{z - 2}$$
$$2^{(2)} = \sqrt{z - 2}$$
$$4 = \sqrt{z - 2}$$
$$(4)^2 = (\sqrt{z - 2})^2$$
$$16 = z - 2$$
$$18 = z$$

49. **(B):** Both equations contain a $z$, but the question stem asks only for $x - y$. How can you get rid of that $z$?

First, get rid of the fraction in the first equation.

$$\frac{3x}{z + 4} = 4$$
$$3x = 4(z + 4)$$
$$3x = 4z + 16$$

You could solve the second equation for $z$ and then substitute. However, did you notice that both equations now have a $4z$ term? You can directly substitute $3y$ for $4z$ into the equation to get rid of the $z$ variable, then solve for $x - y$.

$$3x = 4z + 16$$
$$3x = (3y) + 16$$
$$3x - 3y = 16$$
$$x - y = \frac{16}{3}$$

# Quadratic Equations

# In this chapter...

- Mechanics of Quadratic Equations
    - Distribute $(a + b)(x + y) \rightarrow$ Use FOIL
    - Factor $x^2 + 5x + 6 \rightarrow$ Find the Original Numbers in $(x + ...)$ $(x + ...)$
    - Solve a Quadratic Equation: Set Quadratic Expression Equal to 0, Factor, Then Set Factors to 0
    - Solve a Quadratic Equation with No $x$ Term: Take Positive and Negative Square Roots
    - Solve a Quadratic Equation with Squared Parentheses: Take Positive and Negative Square Roots
    - Higher Powers: Solve Like a Normal Quadratic
- Other Instances of Quadratics
    - See a Quadratic Expression in a Fraction: Factor and Cancel
    - See a Special Product: Convert to the Other Form

# Quadratic Equations

## In This Chapter, You Will Learn To:

- Manipulate quadratic expressions and solve quadratic equations

## Mechanics of Quadratic Equations

In high school algebra, you learned a number of skills for dealing with quadratic equations. You will need those skills again on the GMAT.

Let's define terms first. A **quadratic expression** contains a squared variable, such as $x^2$, and no higher power. The word *quadratic* comes from the Latin word for *square*. Here are a few quadratic expressions:

$$z^2 \qquad\qquad y^2 + y - 6 \qquad\qquad x^2 + 8x + 16 \qquad\qquad w^2 - 9$$

A quadratic expression can also be disguised. You might not see the squared exponent on the variable explicitly. Here are some disguised quadratic expressions:

$$z \times z \qquad\qquad (y+3)(y-2) \qquad\qquad (x+4)^2 \qquad\qquad (w-3)(w+3)$$

If you multiply these expressions out—that is, if you distribute them—then you will have exponents on the variables. Note that each expression in the second list equals the corresponding expression in the first list (once you multiply out).

A **quadratic equation** contains a quadratic expression and an equals sign.

Quadratic expression = something else

*A quadratic equation usually has two solutions.* That is, in most cases, *two* different values of the variable each make the equation true. Solving a quadratic equation means finding those values.

Before you can solve quadratic equations, you have to be able to distribute and factor quadratic expressions.

# Distribute $(a + b)(x + y)$ → Use FOIL

Recall that distributing means applying multiplication across a sum. For example:

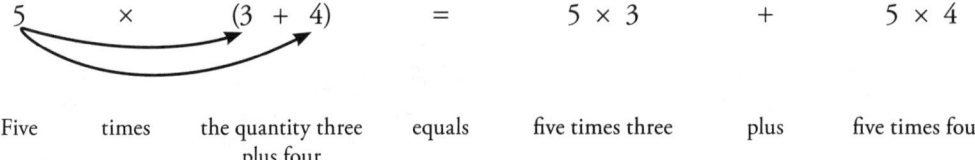

| Five | times | the quantity three plus four | equals | five times three | plus | five times four |

You can omit the multiplication sign next to parentheses. Also, the order of the product doesn't matter, and subtraction works the same way as addition. Here are more examples:

$$3(x + 2) = 3x + 6 \qquad (z - 12)y = zy - 12y \qquad w(a + b) = wa + wb$$

What if you have to distribute the product of two sums? Try this example:

$$(a + b)(x + y) =$$

*Multiply every term in the first sum by every term in the second sum, then add all the products up.* This is just distribution on steroids.

To make the products, use the acronym **FOIL: First, Outer, Inner, Last** (or **First, Outside, Inside, Last**). For example:

$(\boldsymbol{a} + b)(\boldsymbol{x} + y)$    F – multiply the First term in each of the parentheses:    $(a)(x) = ax$

$(\boldsymbol{a} + b)(x + \boldsymbol{y})$    O – multiply the Outer term in each:    $(a)(y) = ay$

$(a + \boldsymbol{b})(\boldsymbol{x} + y)$    I – multiply the Inner term in each:    $(b)(x) = bx$

$(a + \boldsymbol{b})(x + \boldsymbol{y})$    L – multiply the Last terms in each:    $(b)(y) = by$

Now add up the products.

$$(a + b)(x + y) = ax + ay + bx + by$$

By the way, you can even FOIL numbers. Try this example:

What is $102 \times 301$?

If you express 102 as $100 + 2$ and 301 as $300 + 1$, you can rewrite the question as a product of two sums:

What is $(100 + 2)(300 + 1)$?

Now FOIL it out.

$$(100 + 2)(300 + 1) = (100 \times 300) + (100 \times 1) + (2 \times 300) + (2 \times 1)$$
$$= 30,000 + 100 + 600 + 2$$
$$= 30,702$$

You get the same answer if you multiply these numbers in longhand. In fact, longhand multiplication is just distribution. You're essentially FOILing as you multiply the digits and add up the results.

$$102$$
$$\times\, 301$$
$$\overline{\phantom{0}102\phantom{0}}$$
$$30,600$$
$$\overline{30,702}$$

Now try to FOIL this disguised quadratic expression: $(x + 2)(x + 3)$.

$(\boldsymbol{x} + 2)(\boldsymbol{x} + 3)$     F – multiply the First term in each of the parentheses:   $(x)(x) = x^2$

$(\boldsymbol{x} + 2)(x + \boldsymbol{3})$     O – multiply the Outer term in each:   $(x)(3) = 3x$

$(x + \boldsymbol{2})(\boldsymbol{x} + 3)$     I – multiply the Inner term in each:   $(2)(x) = 2x$

$(x + \boldsymbol{2})(x + \boldsymbol{3})$     L – multiply the Last terms in each:   $(2)(3) = 6$

Add up the products.

$$(x + 2)(x + 3) = x^2 + 3x + 2x + 6$$

Notice that you can combine the like terms in the middle ($3x$ and $2x$).

$$(x + 2)(x + 3) = x^2 + \underbrace{3x + 2x}\ + 6 = x^2 + 5x + 6$$

Now compare the expression you started with and the expression you ended up with.

$$(x + 2)(x + 3) \qquad\qquad x^2 + 5x + 6$$

Study how the numbers on the left relate to the numbers on the right.

The 2 and the 3 *multiply* to give you the 6.
The 2 and the 3 *add* to give you the 5 in $5x$.

What if you have subtraction? Attach the minus signs to the second term in each pair of parentheses. Next, multiply according to the rules of arithmetic and add the products. Try this example:

$$(y - 5)(y - 2) =$$

First, FOIL. Keep track of minus signs. Put them in the products. For example:

$(\boldsymbol{y} - 5)(\boldsymbol{y} - 2)$     F – multiply First terms:         $(y)(y) = y^2$

$(\boldsymbol{y} - 5)(y - \boldsymbol{2})$     O – multiply Outer terms:       $(y)(-2) = -2y$

$(y - \boldsymbol{5})(\boldsymbol{y} - 2)$     I – multiply Inner terms:        $(-5)(y) = -5y$

$(y - \boldsymbol{5})(y - \boldsymbol{2})$     L – multiply Last terms:         $(-5)(-2) = 10$

Finally, add the products and combine like terms.

$$(y - 5)(\, y - 2) = y^2 - 2y - 5y + 10 = y^2 - 7y + 10$$

Again, study how the numbers on the left relate to the numbers on the right.

The −5 and the −2 *multiply* to give you the positive 10.
The −5 and the −2 *add* to give you the −7 in −7*y*.

Here's one last wrinkle. In the course of doing these problems, you might encounter a sum written as $4 + z$ rather than as $z + 4$. You can FOIL it as is, or you can flip the sum around so that the variable is first. Either way works fine.

| If you… | Then you… | Like this: |
|---|---|---|
| Want to distribute $(x + 5)(x − 4)$ | FOIL it out and combine like terms | $(x + 5)(x − 4)$ $= x^2 − 4x + 5x − 20$ $= x^2 + x − 20$ |

## Check Your Skills

FOIL the following expressions.

1. $(x + 4)(x + 9)$
2. $(y + 3)(y − 6)$

*Answers can be found on page 319.*

# Factor $x^2 + 5x + 6$ ➤ FIND the Original Numbers in $(x + …)(x + …)$

FOILing is a form of distribution. So going in reverse is a form of *factoring*. To factor a quadratic expression such as $x^2 + 5x + 6$ means to *rewrite the expression as a product of two sums*. For example:

$$x^2 + 5x + 6 = (x + …)(x + …)$$

The form on the right is called the **factored form**. (You can call $x^2 + 5x + 6$ the **distributed form**.)

You already know the answer, because earlier you turned $(x + 2)(x + 3)$ into $x^2 + 5x + 6$.

$$(x + \mathbf{2})(x + \mathbf{3}) = x^2 + 3x + 2x + 6 = x^2 + \mathbf{5}x + \mathbf{6}$$

Consider the relationship between the numbers one more time.

$2 + 3 = 5$, the coefficient of the $x$ term　　　$2 \times 3 = 6$, the constant term on the end

This is true in general. The two numbers in the factored form *add* to the $x$ coefficient, and they *multiply* to the constant.

Now think about how to work backwards.

$$x^2 + \mathbf{5}x + \mathbf{6} = (x + …)(x + …)$$

You need two numbers that multiply together to 6 and sum to 5.

*Look first for factor pairs of the constant*—in this case, two numbers that multiply to 6. Then check the sum.

> 2 and 3 are a factor pair of 6, because $2 \times 3 = 6$.
> 2 and 3 also sum to 5, so this is the correct pair.
>
> $x^2 + \mathbf{5}x + \mathbf{6} = (x + \mathbf{2})(x + \mathbf{3})$

Try this slightly different example:

> $y^2 + \mathbf{7}y + \mathbf{6} = (y + \ldots)(y + \ldots)$

The constant is the same: 6. So you need a factor pair of 6. But now the pair has to sum to 7.

Therefore, 2 and 3 no longer work. But 1 and 6 are also a factor pair of 6. So factor $y^2 + 7y + 6$ like this:

> $y^2 + 7y + 6 = (y + 1)(y + 6)$

Now try to factor this quadratic:

> $z^2 + 7z + 12 = (z + \ldots)(z + \ldots)$

Again, start with the constant. Look for a factor pair of 12 that sums to 7.

It might help to list the factor pairs of 12:

> $1 \times 12$
>
> $2 \times 6$
>
> $3 \times 4$

The only factor pair of 12 that sums to 7 is 3 and 4. Therefore:

> $3 \times 4 = 12 \qquad 3 + 4 = 7$
>
> $z^2 + \mathbf{7}z + \mathbf{12} = (z + \mathbf{3})(z + \mathbf{4})$

What if you have subtraction? The same principles hold. Just think of the minus signs as part of the numbers themselves. Try this example:

> $x^2 - \mathbf{9}x + \mathbf{18} = (x + \ldots)(x + \ldots)$

You need two numbers that multiply to 18, but now they have to add up to $-9$. Think about rules of negatives and positives. If the sum is negative, then at least one of the terms must be negative. And for the product to be positive, the terms must have the same sign.

> Both numbers must be negative.   Neg × Neg = Pos       Neg + Neg = Neg

Again, consider listing out the factor pairs of 18, and don't forget that both terms are negative.

$-1 \times -18$
$-2 \times -9$
$-3 \times -6$

The answer is $-3$ and $-6$.          $-3 \times -6 = 18$          $-3 + (-6) = -9$

Now, write the factored form of the quadratic expression.

$$x^2 - 9x + 18 = (x - 3)(x - 6)$$

If the constant (in the case above, 18) is positive, then the two numbers in the factored form must *both be positive* or *both be negative*, depending on the sign of the $x$ term.

If the sign of the constant (in the case below, 12) and the $x$ term ($7z$) are both positive, then the two numbers in factored form are positive.

$$z^2 + 7z + 12 = (z + 3)(z + 4)$$

If, on the other hand, the constant (18) is positive but the $x$ term ($9x$) is negative, then both numbers in factored form are negative.

$$x^2 - 9x + 18 = (x - 3)(x - 6)$$

What if the constant is negative? Again, *think of the minus sign as part of the number.* Try this example:

$$w^2 + 3w - 10 = (w + \ldots)(w + \ldots)$$

You need two numbers that multiply to negative 10 and that sum to 3.

For the product to be $-10$, one number must be positive and the other one must be negative. That's the only way to get a negative product of two numbers.

Pos × Neg = Neg

*If the constant is negative*, then in the factored form, *one number is positive and the other one is negative.*

This means that you are adding a positive and a negative to get 3:

Pos + Neg = 3

If you think about the negative as subtracting a positive, then you are looking for a difference of 3. Here's how to find the two numbers you want. First, pretend that the constant is positive. Think of the normal, positive factor pairs of 10. Which pair *differs* by 3?

$1 \times 10$
$2 \times 5$

The answer is 5 and 2.

$5 \times 2 = 10$

$5 - 2 = 3$

But now you must decide which is positive and which is negative. Because the sum is positive, it must be the case that the larger factor is the positive one.

The answer is 5 and –2.    $5 \times (-2) = -10$        $5 + (-2) = 3$

Notice that –5 and 2 would give you the correct product (–10) but the incorrect sum (–5 + 2 = –3).

Now you know where to place the signs in the factored form. Place the minus sign with the 2.

$w^2 + 3w - 10 = (w + 5)(w - 2)$

When the *constant is negative*, start by testing the positive factor pairs and asking which pair *differs* by the right amount.

Once you find a good factor pair for the constant (say 5 and 2), then determine which term is negative and which is positive by asking whether the sum is negative or positive. If the sum is positive, the larger term must be positive. If the sum is negative, the larger term must be negative. If you're ever not sure, try both possibilities!

Consider this example:

$y^2 - 4y - 21 = (y + \ldots)(y + \ldots)$

You need two numbers that multiply to *negative* 21 and that sum to *negative* 4.

Again, one number must be positive, while the other is negative.

Start by looking for the positive factor pairs of 21. Which pair *differs* by 4?

Only 7 and 3 work.    $7 \times 3 = 21$        $7 - 3 = 4$

Now you need to make one number negative, so that the product is now –21 and the *sum* is now –4. Which number should be negative?

The sum is negative, so make the larger term negative. Because 7 is larger than 3, 7 is the negative term.

$(-7) \times 3 = -21$    $(-7) + 3 = -4$

Write the factored form:

$y^2 - 4y - 21 = (y - 7)(y + 3)$

Finally, the GMAT can make factoring a quadratic expression harder in a couple of ways.

(1) Every term in the expression is multiplied through by a common numerical factor, including the $x^2$ term.

$3x^2 + 21x + 36 = \ldots$

In this case, *pull out the common factor first*. Put parentheses around what's left. Then factor the quadratic expression as usual.

$3x^2 + 21x + 36 = 3(x^2 + 7x + 12) = 3(x + 3)(x + 4)$

If the $x^2$ term is negative, factor out a common factor of −1 *first*. That will flip the sign on every term.

$$-x^2 + 9x - 18 = \ldots$$

Pull out the −1, which becomes a minus sign outside a set of parentheses. Don't forget to flip the sign of every term. Then factor the quadratic expression as usual.

$$-x^2 + 9x - 18 = -(x^2 - 9x + 18) = -(x - 3)(x - 6)$$

(2) Sometimes the $x^2$ term has a coefficient, but you can't divide it out without creating fractions for the other terms. *Avoid fractional coefficients at all costs.* If you cannot pull out a common factor from the $x^2$ term without turning coefficients into fractions, then keep a coefficient on one or even both $x$'s in your factored form. At this point, *experiment with factor pairs of the constant* until you get a match. Try this example:

$$2z^2 - z - 15 = \ldots$$

Don't factor a 2 out of all the terms. Rather, set up the parentheses on the right. Put a $2z$ in one set.

$$2z^2 - z - 15 = (2z + \ldots)(z + \ldots)$$

At least you've got the F of FOIL covered.

What you already know how to do is still useful. Since the constant is negative (−15), one of the numbers must be negative, while the other must be positive.

Pretend for a minute that the constant is positive 15. You still need a factor pair of 15. There are only two factor pairs of 15:

$$1 \times 15 = 15 \qquad 3 \times 5 = 15$$

But which pair do you want? Which number becomes negative? And where does that one go—with the $2z$ or the $z$?

The middle term is your guide. The coefficient on the $z$ term is only −1, so it's very unlikely that the "1 and 15" factor pair will work. The numbers must be 3 and 5, with a minus sign on exactly one of them. This covers the L of FOIL.

Finally, experiment. Try the numbers in different configurations. Examine only the OI of FOIL (Outer and Inner) to see whether you get the right middle term.

$$2z^2 - z - 15 = (2z + \ldots)(z + \ldots) = (2z + 3)(z - 5)? \quad \textbf{FOIL} \longrightarrow (2z)(-5) + 3z \text{ does not equal } -z$$

Learn after each attempt. Since −10$z$ and 3$z$ are too far apart, swap the numbers.

$$2z^2 - z - 15 = (2z + \ldots)(z + \ldots) = (2z - 5)(z + 3)? \quad \textbf{FOIL} \longrightarrow (2z)(3) - 5z \text{ equals } z, \text{ not } -z$$

The coefficient, 1, is correct this time, but not the sign. Switch the signs.

$$2z^2 - z - 15 = (2z + \ldots)(z + \ldots) = (2z + 5)(z - 3)? \quad \textbf{FOIL} \longrightarrow (2z)(-3) + 5z \text{ equals } -z \quad \text{YES}$$

So $2z^2 - z - 15$ factors into $(2z + 5)(z - 3)$. You can always check your work by FOILing the result.

$$(2z + 5)(z - 3) = 2z^2 - 6z + 5z - 15 = 2z^2 - z - 15$$

*If you're ever in doubt, FOIL it back out!* Luckily, you won't often see a FOIL this complex on the GMAT. (You might even decide that a problem this complex isn't worth your time.)

| If you… | Then you… | Like this: |
|---|---|---|
| Want to factor $x^2 + 11x + 18$ | Find a factor pair of 18 that sums to 11 | $x^2 + 11x + 18$ <br> $= (x + 9)(x + 2)$ <br><br> $9 + 2 = 11$ <br> $9 \times 2 = 18$ |
| Want to factor $x^2 - 8x + 12$ | Find a factor pair of 12 that sums to 8, then make both numbers negative | $x^2 - 8x + 12$ <br> $= (x - 6)(x - 2)$ <br><br> $(-6) + (-2) = -8$ <br> $(-6) \times (-2) = 12$ |
| Want to factor $x^2 + 6x - 16$ | Find a factor pair of 16 that *differs* by 6, then make the bigger number *positive* so that the sum is 6 and the product is −16 | $x^2 + 6x - 16$ <br> $= (x + 8)(x - 2)$ <br><br> $8 + (-2) = 6$ <br> $8 \times (-2) = -16$ |
| Want to factor $x^2 - 5x - 14$ | Find a factor pair of 14 that *differs* by 5, then make the bigger number *negative* so that the sum is −5 and the product is −14 | $x^2 - 5x - 14$ <br> $= (x - 7)(x + 2)$ <br><br> $(-7) + 2 = -5$ <br> $(-7) \times 2 = -14$ |
| Want to factor $-2x^2 + 16x - 24$ | Factor out −2 from all terms first, then factor the quadratic expression normally | $-2x^2 + 16x - 24$ <br> $= -2(x^2 - 8x + 12)$ <br> $= -2(x - 6)(x - 2)$ |

## Check Your Skills

Factor the following expressions.

3.  $x^2 + 14x + 33$
4.  $x^2 - 14x + 45$
5.  $x^2 + 3x - 18$
6.  $x^2 - 5x - 66$

*Answers can be found on page 319.*

# Solve a Quadratic Equation: Set Quadratic Expression Equal to 0, Factor, Then Set Factors to 0

So far, you've dealt with quadratic expressions—distributing them and factoring them.

Now how do you solve quadratic *equations*? Try this example:

If $x^2 + x = 6$, what are the possible values of $x$?

Notice that you are asked for *possible* values of $x$. Usually, two different values of $x$ will make a quadratic equation true. In other words, expect the equation to have two solutions.

The best way to solve most quadratic equations involves a particular property of the number 0. For example:

If $ab = 0$, then either $a = 0$ or $b = 0$ (or both, potentially).

In words, if the product of two numbers is 0, then you know that at least one of the numbers is 0. (This is known as the Zero Product rule.)

This is true no matter how complicated the factors. For example:

If $(a + 27)(b - 12) = 0$, then either $a + 27 = 0$ or $b - 12 = 0$ (or both).

In words, if the quantity $a + 27$ times the quantity $b - 12$ equals 0, then at least one of those quantities must be 0.

This gives you a pathway to solve quadratic equations.

1.  Rearrange the equation to make one side equal 0. The other side will contain a quadratic expression.
2.  Factor the quadratic expression. The equation will look like this:
    (Something)(Something else) = 0
3.  Set each factor equal to 0.
    Something = 0    or    Something else = 0

These two equations will be much easier to solve. Each one will give you a possible solution for the original equation.

Try this with the problem above. First, rearrange the equation to make one side equal to 0.

$$
\begin{array}{rcr}
x^2 + x & = & 6 \\
-6 & & -6 \\
\hline
x^2 + x - 6 & = & 0
\end{array}
$$

Next, factor the quadratic expression on the left side.

$$x^2 + x - 6 = 0$$
$$(x + 3)(x - 2) = 0$$

Finally, set each factor (the quantities in parentheses) equal to 0, and solve for $x$ in each case.

$$
\begin{array}{ccc}
x + 3 = 0 & & x - 2 = 0 \\
x = -3 & \text{or} & x = 2
\end{array}
$$

Now you have the two possible values of $x$, which are the two solutions to the original equation.

$$
\begin{array}{lll}
x^2 + x = 6 & x \text{ could be } -3 & (-3)^2 + (-3) = 6 \\
& \text{or } x \text{ could be } 2 & 2^2 + 2 = 6
\end{array}
$$

By the way, the two equations you get at the end can't both be true at the same time. What $x^2 + x = 6$ tells you is that $x$ must equal either −3 or 2. The value of $x$ is one or the other; it's not both simultaneously. The variable has multiple *possible* values.

The solutions of a quadratic equation are also called its **roots**.

If an additional condition is placed on the variable, you can often narrow down to one solution. Try this example:

> If $y < 0$ and $y^2 = y + 30$, what is the value of $y$?

First, solve the quadratic equation. Rearrange it so that one side equals 0.

$$
\begin{array}{rl}
y^2 & = \; y + 30 \\
\underline{-y - 30} & \underline{\; -y - 30} \\
y^2 - y - 30 & = \; 0
\end{array}
$$

Next, factor the quadratic expression.

$$y^2 - y - 30 = 0$$
$$(y - 6)(y + 5) = 0$$

Set each factor equal to 0.

$$
\begin{array}{ccc}
y - 6 = 0 & & y + 5 = 0 \\
y = 6 & \text{or} & y = -5
\end{array}
$$

At this point, you can definitively say that $y$ is either 6 or −5. Go back to the question, which gives the additional condition that $y < 0$. Since $y$ is negative, $y$ cannot be 6. Thus, the answer to the question is −5. The quadratic equation gave you two possibilities, but only one of them fits the constraint that $y < 0$.

Occasionally, a quadratic equation has only one solution on its own. Try this example:

> If $w^2 - 8w + 16 = 0$, what is the value of $w$?

The quadratic equation already has one side equal to 0, so go ahead and factor the quadratic expression:

$$w^2 - 8w + 16 = 0$$
$$(w - 4)(w - 4) = 0$$

The two factors in parentheses happen to be identical. In this special case, you don't get two separate equations and two separate roots.

$$w - 4 = 0 \qquad \text{so} \qquad w = 4$$

The only solution is 4.

Lastly, *never factor before you set one side equal to 0.* Try this example:

If $z$ is positive and $z^2 + z - 8 = 4$, what is the value of $z$?

You might be tempted to factor the left side right away. But the Zero Product rule only works when the product equals 0. Why? Imagine the easier example that $xy = 4$. Must it be true that $x = 4$ or $y = 4$? No! They could both equal 2, or you could have a combination of non-integer values. This means that you can really only solve these quadratics when you set them equal to 0.

Avoid the temptation to factor right away, and instead rearrange to make the right side 0 first.

$$
\begin{array}{rcr}
z^2 + z - 8 &=& 4 \\
-4 && -4 \\
\hline
z^2 + z - 12 &=& 0
\end{array}
$$

*Now* factor the left side.

$$z^2 + z - 12 = 0$$
$$(z + 4)(z - 3) = 0$$

Finally, set each factor equal to 0 and solve for $z$.

$$z + 4 = 0 \qquad \text{or} \qquad z - 3 = 0$$

Thus, $z$ equals either $-4$ or $3$. Since you are told that $z$ is positive, $z$ must be 3.

It's legal to factor a quadratic expression whenever you want to. But if you factor the expression *before* setting one side equal to zero, your factors don't tell you anything useful. You can't set them individually to 0.

When you solve a quadratic equation, always set one side equal to 0 *before* you factor.

| If you… | Then you… | Like this: |
|---|---|---|
| Want to solve $x^2 + 11x = -18$ | Rearrange to make one side 0, factor the quadratic side, then set the factors equal to 0 | $x^2 + 11x = -18$ <br> $x^2 + 11x + 18 = 0$ <br> $(x + 9)(x + 2) = 0$ <br> $(x + 9) = 0$ or $(x + 2) = 0$ <br> $x = -9$ or $x = -2$ |

## Check Your Skills

Solve the following quadratic equations.

7. $x^2 + 2x - 35 = 0$
8. $x^2 - 15x = -26$

*Answers can be found on page 320.*

**MANHATTAN** PREP

# Solve a Quadratic Equation with No *x* Term: Take Positive and Negative Square Roots

Occasionally, you encounter a quadratic equation with an $x^2$ term but no $x$ term. For example:

If $x$ is negative and $x^2 = 9$, what is $x$?

Here's the fast way to solve: *Take positive and negative square roots.*

$$x^2 = 9$$
$$\sqrt{x^2} = \sqrt{9}$$
$$x = 3 \text{ OR } -3$$

Since you are told that $x$ is negative, the answer to the question is $-3$.

You can also solve this problem using the method of the previous section. Although the method is longer in this case, it's worth seeing how it works.

1.  Rearrange the equation to make one side 0:

    $$x^2 = 9$$
    $$x^2 - 9 = 0$$

2.  Factor the quadratic expression. The strange thing is that there is no $x$ term, but you can imagine that it has a coefficient of 0.

    $$x^2 - 9 = 0$$
    $$x^2 + 0x - 9 = 0$$

    Because the constant $(-9)$ is negative, you need a factor pair of 9 that *differs* by 0. In other words, you need 3 and 3. Make one of these numbers negative to fit the equation as given.

    $$x^2 + 0x - 9 = 0$$
    $$(x + 3)(x - 3) = 0$$

    You can FOIL the result back out to see how the $x$ terms cancel in the middle.

    $$(x + 3)(x - 3) = x^2 - 3x + 3x - 9 = x^2 - 9$$

3.  Finally, set each of the factors in parentheses equal to 0, and solve for $x$.

    $$x + 3 = 0 \qquad \text{OR} \qquad x - 3 = 0$$

Thus, $x$ equals either $-3$ or 3. Again, the question tells you that $x$ is negative, so $-3$ is the answer.

Obviously, the second method is overkill in this case. It's important to understand, though, so that you know that $x^2 - 9$ factors to $(x + 3)(x - 3)$. You'll come back to that point later in this chapter.

| If you... | Then you... | Like this: |
|---|---|---|
| Want to solve $x^2 = 25$ | Take the positive and negative square roots of both sides | $x^2 = 25$<br>$\sqrt{x^2} = \sqrt{25}$<br>$(x + 5)(x - 5) = 0$<br>$x = -5$ or $x = 5$ |

## Check Your Skills

9. If $x^2 - 3 = 1$, what are all the possible values of $x$?

*Answer can be found on page 320.*

## Solve a Quadratic Equation with Squared Parentheses: Take Positive and Negative Square Roots

Try this example:

If $(y + 1)^2 = 16$, what are the possible values of $y$?

Notice that the variable $y$ only shows up once in your expression, not as both a $y$ and a $y^2$ term (the $y$ is isolated within the parentheses).

This means you can do this problem in either of two ways.

One way is to treat $y + 1$ as if it were a new variable, $z$. In other words, $z = y + 1$.

Solve $z^2 = 16$ by taking positive and negative square roots.

$(y + 1)^2 = 16 \longrightarrow z^2 = 16 \longrightarrow z = 4$ or $z = -4$

Go back to $y$.

$(y + 1)^2 = 16 \longrightarrow z^2 = 16 \longrightarrow z = 4$ or $z = -4 \longrightarrow y + 1 = 4$ or $y + 1 = -4$

In fact, you didn't need $z$. You could have just taken the positive and negative square roots right away:

$(y + 1)^2 = 16$
$y + 1 = 4$ or $y + 1 = -4$

Finally, solve the simpler equations for $y$: $y = 3$ or $y = -5$.

Alternatively, expand $(y + 1)^2$ into $(y + 1)(y + 1)$. Next, you can FOIL this product out.

$$(y + 1)(y + 1) = y^2 + y + y + 1 = y^2 + 2y + 1$$

Now solve the quadratic equation normally: set one side equal to 0, and factor.

$$y^2 + 2y + 1 = 16$$
$$y^2 + 2y - 15 = 0$$
$$(y + 5)(y - 3) = 0$$
$$y = -5 \text{ or } 3$$

Which way is faster depends on the numbers involved. With big numbers, the first way is easier.

| If you... | Then you... | Like this: |
|---|---|---|
| Want to solve $(z - 7)^2 = 225$ | Take the positive and negative square roots of both sides | $(z - 7)^2 = 225$ $\sqrt{(z - 7)^2} = \sqrt{225}$ $z - 7 = 15 \text{ or } z - 7 = -15$ $z = 22 \text{ or } z = -8$ |

## Check Your Skills

10. If $(z + 2)^2 = 144$, what are the possible values of $z$?

*Answer can be found on page 320.*

## Higher Powers: Solve Like a Normal Quadratic

If you have a higher power of $x$ in the equation, look for solutions as if the equation were a typical quadratic: Set one side equal to 0, factor as much as you can, and then set factors equal to 0:

$$x^3 = 3x^2 - 2x$$

What are all of the roots of the equation above?

(A)  –3, 1, 2
(B)  –2, 1, 3
(C)  0, 1, 2
(D)  0, 1
(E)  1, 2

Recall that a *root* of an equation is a solution—a value for the variable that makes the equation true.

First, set one side of the equation equal to 0:

$$x^3 = 3x^2 - 2x$$
$$\underline{-3x^2 + 2x - 3x^2 + 2x}$$
$$x^3 - 3x^2 + 2x = 0$$

You may notice that every term on the left contains an $x$. In other words, $x$ is a common factor. You might be tempted to divide both sides by $x$ to eliminate that factor.

Resist that temptation. *Never divide an equation by x unless you know for sure that x is not 0 (x ≠ 0).* You could be dividing by 0 without realizing it.

The problem doesn't tell you that $x \neq 0$. So, rather than divide away the $x$, pull it out to the left and keep it around.

$$x^3 - 3x^2 + 2x = 0$$
$$x\left(x^2 - 3x + 2\right) = 0$$

Now factor the quadratic expression in the parentheses normally, and rewrite the equation.

$$x\left(x^2 - 3x + 2\right) = 0$$
$$x\left(x - 2\right)\left(x - 1\right) = 0$$

There are *three* factors on the left side: $x$, $(x - 2)$, and $(x - 1)$. Set each one of them equal to 0 to get *three* solutions to the original equation.

$$x = 0 \qquad\qquad x - 2 = 0 \qquad\qquad x - 1 = 0$$
$$x = 2 \qquad\qquad\qquad x = 1$$

By the way, the presence of the $x^3$ term should alert you that there could be three solutions. The number of the largest exponent generally signals the number of solutions (unless two of the solutions turn out to be the same number, as in the example you saw earlier in this chapter).

If you had divided away the $x$ earlier, you would have missed the $x = 0$ solution. The question asks for all of the roots, so the answer is 0, 1, and 2, or (C).

| If you... | Then you... | Like this: |
|-----------|-------------|------------|
| Want to solve $x^3 = x$ | Solve like a normal quadratic: set the equation equal to 0, factor, and set factors equal to 0 | $x^3 = x$ <br> $x^3 - x = 0$ <br> $x\left(x^2 - 1\right) = 0$ <br> $x\left(x + 1\right)\left(x - 1\right) = 0$ <br> $x = 0$  or  $x + 1 = 0$  or  $x - 1 = 0$ <br> $x = 0, -1,$ or $1$ |

## Check Your Skills

11. What are all of the possible solutions to the equation $x^3 - 2x^2 = 3x$?

*Answer can be found on page 321.*

# Other Instances of Quadratics

You will come across quadratic expressions in various circumstances other than the ones already given. Fortunately, the skills of FOILing and factoring are still relevant as you try to simplify the problem.

## See a Quadratic Expression in a Fraction: Factor and Cancel

Take a look at this problem:

If $x \neq -1$, then $\dfrac{x^2 - 2x - 3}{x + 1}$ is equivalent to which of the following?

(A) $x + 1$
(B) $x + 3$
(C) $x - 3$

This question doesn't involve a typical quadratic expression. However, the numerator of the fraction is a quadratic. To simplify the fraction, *factor* the quadratic expression.

$$x^2 - 2x - 3 = (x - 3)(x + 1)$$

Now substitute the factored form back into the fraction.

$$\frac{x^2 - 2x - 3}{x + 1} = \frac{(x - 3)(x + 1)}{x + 1}$$

Finally, you can cancel a common factor from the top and bottom of the fraction. The common factor is the entire quantity $x + 1$. Since that is the denominator, you cancel the whole thing out, and the fraction is gone.

$$\frac{x^2 - 2x - 3}{x + 1} = \frac{(x - 3)(x + 1)}{(x + 1)} = \frac{(x - 3)\,\cancel{(x + 1)}}{\cancel{(x + 1)}} = x - 3$$

The correct answer is (C).

The constraint that $x \neq -1$ is mentioned only to prevent division by 0 in the fraction. You don't have to use this fact directly.

If you see a quadratic expression in a numerator or denominator, try factoring the expression. Then cancel common factors.

Common factors can be disguised, of course, even when you don't have quadratics. Take a look at this example:

If $x \neq y$, then $\dfrac{y-x}{x-y}$ is equivalent to which of the following?

(A)  $-1$

(B)  $x^2 - y^2$

(C)  $y^2 - x^2$

The numerator $y - x$ may look different from the denominator $x - y$. However, these two expressions are actually identical except for a sign change throughout.

$$y - x = -(x - y) \qquad\qquad \text{because} \qquad\qquad -(x - y) = -x + y = y - x$$

In other words, these expressions only differ by a factor of $-1$. The GMAT loves this little disguise. Expressions that differ only by a sign change are different by a factor of $-1$.

Rewrite the numerator: Pull a $-1$ out of the $(y - x)$ term.

$$\frac{y-x}{x-y} = \frac{-(x-y)}{x-y}$$

Now you can cancel $x - y$ from both the top and bottom. You are left with $-1$ on top. So the whole fraction is equal to $-1$.

$$\frac{y-x}{x-y} = \frac{-(x-y)}{x-y} = \frac{-\cancel{(x-y)}}{\cancel{(x-y)}} = -1$$

The correct answer is (A).

Try this last example:

If $y \neq -8$, then $\dfrac{(y+7)^2 + y + 7}{y+8}$ is equivalent to which of the following?

(A)  $y + 7$

(B)  $y + 8$

(C)  $2y + 14$

The long way to solve this is to expand $(y + 7)^2$, then add $y + 7$, then factor and cancel. This approach will work. Fortunately, there's a faster way.

Put parentheses around the last $y + 7$ on top of the fraction.

$$\frac{(y+7)^2 + y + 7}{y + 8} = \frac{(y+7)^2 + (y+7)}{y + 8}$$

This subtle change can help you see that you can factor the numerator. You can *pull out a common factor*—namely, $y + 7$—from both the $(y + 7)^2$ and from the $(y + 7)$.

When you pull out $(y + 7)$ from $(y + 7)^2$, you are left with $(y + 7)$. And when you pull out $(y + 7)$ from $(y + 7)$, you are left with 1.

$$\frac{(y + 7)^2 + (y + 7)}{y + 8} = \frac{(y + 7)\left[(y + 7) + 1\right]}{y + 8}$$

Since $y + 7 + 1 = y + 8$, you can simplify the second factor on top.

$$\frac{(y + 7)^2 + (y + 7)}{y + 8} = \frac{(y + 7)\left[(y + 7) + 1\right]}{y + 8} = \frac{(y + 7)(y + 8)}{y + 8}$$

Finally, cancel the $y + 8$ quantity from the top and bottom as a common factor of both.

$$\frac{(y + 7)^2 + (y + 7)}{y + 8} = \frac{(y + 7)\left[(y + 7) + 1\right]}{y + 8} = \frac{(y + 7)(y + 8)}{y + 8} = \frac{(y + 7)\cancel{(y + 8)}}{\cancel{(y + 8)}} = y + 7$$

The correct answer is (A).

The recurring principle is this: Look for ways to pull out common factors from complicated fractions and cancel them.

| If you... | Then you... | Like this: |
|:---:|:---:|:---:|
| See a quadratic expression in a fraction | Factor the quadratic and cancel common factors | $(z \neq -3)$ <br> $\dfrac{z^2 + 5z + 6}{z + 3} = \dfrac{(z + 2)(z + 3)}{(z + 3)}$ <br> $= z + 2$ |

## Check Your Skills

Simplify the following fraction by factoring the quadratic expression.

12. If $x \neq -3$, $\dfrac{x^2 + 7x + 12}{x + 3} =$

*Answer can be found on page 321.*

## See a Special Product: Convert to the Other Form

Three quadratic expressions are so important on the GMAT that we call them **special products**. Here they are:

| | | |
|:---:|:---:|:---:|
| $(x + y)^2 = x^2 + 2xy + y^2$ | $(x - y)^2 = x^2 - 2xy + y^2$ | $(x + y)(x - y) = x^2 - y^2$ |
| **Square of a sum** | **Square of a difference** | **Difference of squares** |

First, memorize these forms. Second, whenever you see one of these forms, *write down both forms*. Ask yourself which form is the better one to use for this particular problem; often, the better one is the one that the problem did *not* give you outright.

The GMAT often disguises these forms using different variables, numbers, roots, and so on. For example:

$$x^2 + 8x + 16 \qquad\qquad a^2 - 4ab + 4b^2 \qquad\qquad \left(1+\sqrt{2}\right)\left(1-\sqrt{2}\right)$$

Square of a sum              Square of a difference          Difference of squares

The first example can be factored normally.

$$x^2 + 8x + 16 = (x + 4)(x + 4) = (x + 4)^2$$

The test likes "square of a sum" and "square of a difference" because the two forms can be used to create quadratic equations that have only one solution. For instance:

$$x^2 + 8x + 16 = 0$$
$$(x+4)^2 = 0$$

There is only one solution: $x + 4 = 0$, or $x = -4$. The only number that makes $x^2 + 8x + 16 = 0$ true is $-4$.

The second example above, $a^2 - 4ab + 4b^2$, is tougher to factor. First, recognize that the first and last term are both perfect squares:

$$a^2 = \text{the square of } a \qquad\qquad 4b^2 = \text{the square of } 2b$$

This can provide a hint as to how to factor. Set up $(a - 2b)^2$, and FOIL it to check that it matches.

$$(a - 2b)^2 = (a - 2b)(a - 2b)$$
$$= a^2 - 2ab - 2ab + 4b^2$$
$$= a^2 - 4ab + 4b^2$$

It does, so $(a - 2b)^2$ is indeed the other form.

The third example above, $\left(1+\sqrt{2}\right)\left(1-\sqrt{2}\right)$, matches the factored form of the "difference of squares," the most important of the three special products.

In distributed or expanded form, the difference of squares has no middle term. In the process of FOILing, the Outer and the Inner terms cancel.

$$\left(1+\sqrt{2}\right)\left(1-\sqrt{2}\right) = 1^2 + \left(-\sqrt{2}\right) + \sqrt{2} + \sqrt{2}\left(-\sqrt{2}\right)$$
$$= 1^2 - \left(\sqrt{2}\right)^2$$
$$= 1 - 2$$
$$= -1$$

It's not a coincidence that the middle terms cancel. If you multiply $x + y$ by $x - y$, the middle terms, or *cross-terms*, will be $-xy$ and $+xy$, which sum to 0 and drop out every time.

As a result, don't FOIL every time you multiply a sum of two things by the difference of those same two things. You'll waste time.

Rather, match up to the "difference of squares" template. Square the first thing, and subtract the square of the second thing. Try this problem:

$$\left(3 + 2\sqrt{3}\right)\left(3 - 2\sqrt{3}\right) =$$

The two terms are 3 and $2\sqrt{3}$. Always make sure that the other expression in parentheses is the *difference* of the same exact terms. Since that's true, you can square the 3, square the $2\sqrt{3}$, and subtract the second from the first.

$$\left(3 + 2\sqrt{3}\right)\left(3 - 2\sqrt{3}\right) = 3^2 - \left(2\sqrt{3}\right)^2$$
$$= 9 - (4)(3)$$
$$= 9 - 12$$
$$= -3$$

Try this same type of special product, but going in the other direction:

$$16x^4 - 9y^2 =$$

To treat this as a difference of squares, figure out what each term is the square of.

$$16x^4 = (4x^2)^2 \qquad\qquad 9y^2 = (3y)^2$$

So the first term of the difference ($16x^4$) is the square of $4x^2$, and the second term ($9y^2$) is the square of $3y$.

Take those square roots ($4x^2$ and $3y$) and place them in two sets of parentheses.

$$16x^4 - 9y^2 = (4x^2 \quad 3y)(4x^2 \quad 3y)$$

Put a + sign in one place and a − sign in the other.

$$16x^4 - 9y^2 = (4x^2 + 3y)(4x^2 - 3y)$$

Now you have factored a difference of squares.

A couple of sections ago, you saw $x^2 - 9 = 0$. The left side is the difference of squares.

$$x^2 - 9 = (x + 3)(x - 3)$$

Now, you can factor difference-of-squares equations much more quickly; you don't have to do the full reverse FOIL process.

To match a special products template, you might have to rearrange an equation. Take a look at this example:

If $x^2 + y^2 = -2xy$, what is the sum of $x$ and $y$?

You need to find $x + y$. Look at the equation. It doesn't exactly match a special product, but it does have some squares. Try rearranging the equation.

$$\begin{array}{r} x^2 \qquad\quad + y^2 = -2xy \\ + 2xy \qquad\quad + 2xy \\ \hline x^2 + 2xy + y^2 = 0 \end{array}$$

The left side now matches the square of a sum.

$$x^2 + 2xy + y^2 = 0$$
$$\left(x + y\right)^2 = 0$$

The right side is also now equal to 0—a double benefit of the first move you made.

Since the square of $x + y$ equals 0, you know that $x + y$ itself must equal 0. That is the answer to the question.

| If you… | Then you… | Like this: |
|---|---|---|
| See a special product | Write down both forms, then decide which is better to use | $4w^2 - 25z^4$ $\left(2w\right)^2 - \left(5z^2\right)^2$ $\left(2w + 5z^2\right)\left(2w - 5z^2\right)$ |
| See something close to a special product | Rearrange the equation to try to fit the special product template | $m^2 + n^2 = 2mn$ $m^2 - 2mn + n^2 = 0$ $\left(m - n\right)\left(m - n\right) = 0$ $m - n = 0$ $m = n$ |

## Check Your Skills

Factor the following quadratic expressions.

13. $25a^4b^6 - 4c^2d^2$
14. $4x^2 + 8xy + 4y^2$

*Answers can be found on page 321.*

# Check Your Skills Answer Key

1. $x^2 + 13x + 36$:

   $(x + 4)(x + 9)$

   | | | |
   |---|---|---|
   | $(\boldsymbol{x} + 4)(\boldsymbol{x} + 9)$ | F — multiply First terms: | $(x)(x) = x^2$ |
   | $(\boldsymbol{x} + 4)(x + \boldsymbol{9})$ | O — multiply Outer terms: | $(x)(9) = 9x$ |
   | $(x + \boldsymbol{4})(\boldsymbol{x} + 9)$ | I — multiply Inner terms: | $(4)(x) = 4x$ |
   | $(x + \boldsymbol{4})(x + \boldsymbol{9})$ | L — multiply Last terms: | $(4)(9) = 36$ |

   $x^2 + 9x + 4x + 36 \longrightarrow x^2 + 13x + 36$

2. $y^2 - 3y - 18$:

   $(y + 3)(y - 6)$

   | | | |
   |---|---|---|
   | $(\boldsymbol{y} + 3)(\boldsymbol{y} - 6)$ | F — multiply First terms: | $(y)(y) = y^2$ |
   | $(\boldsymbol{y} + 3)(y - \boldsymbol{6})$ | O — multiply Outer terms: | $(y)(-6) = -6y$ |
   | $(y + \boldsymbol{3})(\boldsymbol{y} - 6)$ | I — multiply Inner terms: | $(3)(y) = 3y$ |
   | $(y + \boldsymbol{3})(y - \boldsymbol{6})$ | L — multiply Last terms: | $(3)(-6) = -18$ |

   $y^2 - 6y + 3y - 18 \longrightarrow y^2 - 3y - 18$

3. $(x + 3)(x + 11)$: Find a pair of numbers that multiplies to +33 and sums to +14. The factor pairs $1 \times 33$ and $3 \times 11$ multiply to +33, but only 3 and 11 also sum to +14.

4. $(x - 5)(x - 9)$: Ultimately, both numbers will need to be negative because the product (45) is positive, but ignore the signs for now. Find a pair that multiplies to +45 and sums to 14. The factor pairs of 45 are $1 \times 45$, $3 \times 15$, and $5 \times 9$. Only 5 and 9 sum to 14. Turn both negative: $-5 + -9 = -14$.

5. $(x + 6)(x - 3)$: The final term is negative, so you need one positive and one negative term. The middle term is positive, so the larger of the two numbers has to be the positive one. Finally, you need something that multiplies to $-18$ but whose *difference* is +3. The factor pairs $1 \times 18$, $2 \times 9$, and $3 \times 6$ multiply to 18. The difference of 3 and 6 is 3, so this is the correct pair. Make the 6 positive and the 3 negative.

6. $(x + 6)(x - 11)$: The final term is negative, so there will be one positive and one negative term. The middle term is also negative, so the larger of the two numbers has to be negative. You need something that multiplies to $-66$ and whose difference is $-5$. The pairs $1 \times 66$, $2 \times 33$, $3 \times 22$, and $6 \times 11$ multiply to 66. The difference of 6 and 11 is 5, so this is the correct pair. Make the 11 negative and the 6 positive.

7. **$x = 5$ or $-7$:** Find a factor pair that multiplies to 35 and has a difference of 2. The pair 5 times 7 multiplies to 35, and the difference between the factors is 2. The middle term is positive, so the larger of the two numbers (7) is positive.

$$x^2 + 2x - 35 = 0$$
$$(x - 5)(x + 7) = 0$$

$x - 5 = 0$        OR        $x + 7 = 0$
$x = 5$                         $x = -7$

8. **$x = 2$ or $13$:** Set the equation equal to 0, then solve.

$$x^2 - 15x = -26$$
$$x^2 - 15x + 26 = 0$$

The pair $2 \times 13$ multiply to 26 and sum to 15

$$x^2 - 15x + 26 = 0$$
$$(x - 2)(x - 13) = 0$$

$x - 2 = 0$        OR        $x - 13 = 0$
$x = 2$                        $x = 13$

9. **$x = 2$ or $-2$:** Since there is no $x$ term, you can isolate $x^2$ on one side of the equation. Next, take the square root of both sides.

$$x^2 - 3 = 1$$
$$x^2 = 4$$
$$\sqrt{x^2} = \sqrt{4}$$
$$x = \pm 2$$

10. **$z = 10$ or $-14$:** Begin by taking the square root of both sides. Remember to include the negative solution as well:

$$(z + 2)^2 = 144$$
$$\sqrt{(z + 2)^2} = \sqrt{144}$$

$z + 2 = 12$      OR      $z + 2 = -12$
$z = 10$                      $z = -14$

11. **$x = -1, 0,$ or $3$:** Begin by setting the equation equal to 0.

$$x^3 - 2x^2 = 3x$$
$$x^3 - 2x^2 - 3x = 0$$

Notice that all the terms contain $x$. Factor $x$ out of the left side of the equation. Then factor the quadratic and solve for $x$.

$$x^3 - 2x^2 - 3x = 0$$
$$x(x^2 - 2x - 3) = 0$$
$$x(x - 3)(x + 1) = 0$$

$x = 0$           $x - 3 = 0$           $x + 1 = 0$

                    $x = 3$                $x = -1$

The three values of $x$ that will make the equation true are 0, 3, and −1.

12. **$x + 4$:** Factor the numerator, then cancel.

$$\frac{x^2 + 7x + 12x}{x + 3} = \frac{(x + 3)(x + 4)}{(x + 3)} = x + 4$$

13. **$(5a^2b^3 + 2cd)(5a^2b^3 - 2cd)$:** Any expression that contains one term subtracted from another can be expressed as a difference of squares. Take the square root of each term. The square root of $25a^4b^6$ is $5a^2b^3$, and the square root of $4c^2d^2$ is $2cd$. In one set of parentheses, add the square roots; in the other, subtract: $(5a^2b^3 + 2cd)(5a^2b^3 - 2cd)$.

14. This is a more complicated version of the form $(x + y)^2 = x^2 + 2xy + y^2$. Take the square root of the first term to get $(2x)$ and the square root of the last term to get $(2y)$: $4x^2 + 8xy + 4y^2 = (2x + 2y)(2x + 2y)$.

# Chapter Review: Drill Sets

## Drill 1

Distribute the following expressions.

1. $(x + 2)(x - 3)$
2. $(2s + 1)(s + 5)$
3. $(5 + a)(3 + a)$
4. $(3 - z)(z + 4)$
5. $(3p + 2q)(p - 2q)$

## Drill 2

Solve the following equations. List all possible solutions.

6. $x^2 - 2x = 0$
7. $z^2 = -5z$
8. $y^2 + 4y + 3 = 0$
9. $r^2 - 10r = 24$
10. $y^2 + 3y = 0$
11. $y^2 + 12y + 36 = 0$
12. $a^2 - a - 12 = 0$
13. $x^2 + 9x - 90 = 0$
14. $2a^2 + 6a + 4 = 0$
15. $2b^3 + 6b^2 - 36b = 0$

## Drill 3

Simplify the following expressions.

16. If $a \neq b$, then $\dfrac{a^2 - b^2}{a - b}$ is equivalent to which of the following?
    (A) $a - b$
    (B) $a + b$
    (C) $a^2 + b^2$

17. If $|r| \neq |s|$, then $\dfrac{r^2 + 2rs + s^2}{r^2 - s^2}$ is equivalent to which of the following?
    (A) $\dfrac{r + s}{r - s}$
    (B) $\dfrac{r - s}{r + s}$
    (C) $2rs$

18. If $x \neq 1$, then $\dfrac{5x^3}{x - 1} - \dfrac{5x^2}{x - 1}$ is equivalent to which of the following?
    (A) $\dfrac{x}{x - 1}$
    (B) $5x^2$
    (C) $0$

19. If $y \neq -5$, then $\dfrac{y + 5 - (y + 5)^2}{y + 5}$ is equivalent to which of the following?
    (A) $y + 5$
    (B) $2y$
    (C) $-y - 4$

20. If $m \neq -7$, then $\dfrac{m^2 + 2m}{m + 7} + \dfrac{49 + 12m}{m + 7}$ is equivalent to which of the following?
    (A) $1$
    (B) $(m + 7)^2$
    (C) $m + 7$

## Drill 4

Simplify the following expressions.

21. If $z \neq -1$, then $\dfrac{4z^2 - 12z - 16}{2z + 2}$ is equivalent to

which of the following?

   (A) $z - 4$

   (B) $2z - 8$

   (C) $4z - 16$

22. If $c \neq -5$, then $\dfrac{5ab + abc}{abc^2 + 10abc + 25ab}$ is equivalent

to which of the following?

   (A) $\dfrac{1}{(c+5)^2}$

   (B) $c + 5$

   (C) $\dfrac{1}{c+5}$

23. If $x \neq 0$ or $1$, then $\dfrac{\left(x^5 - x^3\right)}{\left(x^3 - x^2\right)} \times \dfrac{x}{5}$ is equivalent to

which of the following?

   (A) $\dfrac{x^2}{5}$

   (B) $\dfrac{x^3 - x^2}{5}$

   (C) $\dfrac{x^3 + x^2}{5}$

24. If $x \neq 2$, then $\left(x^2 - 7x + 10\right) \times \dfrac{x + 5}{x - 2}$ is equivalent

to which of the following?

   (A) $x^2 - 25$

   (B) $x^2 + 10x + 25$

   (C) $x + 5$

25. If $x \neq 3$, then $\dfrac{x^2 - 6x + 9}{3 - x}$ is equivalent to which

of the following?

   (A) $x - 3$

   (B) $3 - x$

   (C) $(x - 3)^2$

# Chapter Review: Drill Sets

## Drill 1

1. $x^2 - x - 6$:

    $(x + 2)(x - 3)$

    $x^2 - 3x + 2x - 6$

    $x^2 - x - 6$

2. $2s^2 + 11s + 5$:

    $(2s + 1)(s + 5)$

    $2s^2 + 10s + s + 5$

    $2s^2 + 11s + 5$

3. $15 + 8a + a^2$:

    $(5 + a)(3 + a)$

    $15 + 5a + 3a + a^2$

    $15 + 8a + a^2$

4. $-z^2 - z + 12$:

    $(3 - z)(z + 4)$

    $3z + 12 - z^2 - 4z$

    $-z^2 - z + 12$

5. $3p^2 - 4pq - 4q^2$:

    $(3p + 2q)(p - 2q)$

    $3p^2 - 6pq + 2pq - 4q^2$

    $3p^2 - 4pq - 4q^2$

## Drill 2

6. $x = 0$ or $2$:

    $$x^2 - 2x = 0$$
    $$x(x - 2) = 0$$

    $x = 0$ $\qquad\qquad\qquad$ $(x - 2) = 0$

    $\qquad\qquad\qquad\qquad\qquad$ $x = 2$

7. $z = 0$ or $-5$:

    $$z^2 = -5z$$
    $$z^2 + 5z = 0$$
    $$z(z + 5) = 0$$

    $z = 0$ $\qquad\qquad\qquad$ $(z + 5) = 0$

    $\qquad\qquad\qquad\qquad\qquad$ $z = -5$

8. **$y = -1$ or $-3$:**

$$y^2 + 4y + 3 = 0$$
$$(y + 1)(y + 3) = 0$$

$(y + 1) = 0$                             $(y + 3) = 0$
$\quad y = -1$                             $\quad y = -3$

9. **$r = -2$ or $12$:**

$$r^2 - 10r = 24$$
$$r^2 - 10r - 24 = 0$$
$$(r + 2)(r - 12) = 0$$

$(r + 2) = 0$                             $(r - 12) = 0$
$\quad r = -2$                             $\quad r = 12$

10. **$y = 0$ or $-3$:**

$$y^2 + 3y = 0$$
$$y(y + 3) = 0$$

$y = 0$                             $(y + 3) = 0$
                                    $\quad y = -3$

11. **$y = -6$:** If you notice that the two factors are identical (both are $y + 6$), then you don't have to solve each one. The answer will be the same.

$$y^2 + 12y + 36 = 0$$
$$(y + 6)(y + 6) = 0$$

$(y + 6) = 0$                             $(y + 6) = 0$
$\quad y = -6$                             $\quad y = -6$

12. **$a = 4$ or $-3$:**

$$a^2 - a - 12 = 0$$
$$(a - 4)(a + 3) = 0$$

$(a - 4) = 0$                             $(a + 3) = 0$
$\quad a = 4$                             $\quad a = -3$

13. **$x = -15$ or $6$:**

$$x^2 + 9x - 90 = 0$$
$$(x + 15)(x - 6) = 0$$

$(x + 15) = 0$                             $(x - 6) = 0$
$\quad x = -15$                             $\quad x = 6$

14. **$a = -2$ or $-1$:** Ignore the 2 term that you pull out front because it doesn't contain a variable.

$$2a^2 + 6a + 4 = 0$$
$$2(a^2 + 3a + 2) = 0$$
$$2(a + 2)(a + 1) = 0$$

$(a + 2) = 0$                                                    $(a + 1) = 0$
    $a = -2$                                                         $a = -1$

15. **$b = 0, -6,$ or $3$:** The $2b$ term that you pull out front does have to be set equal to 0, because it contains a variable.

$$2b^3 + 6b^2 - 36b = 0$$
$$2b(b^2 + 3b - 18) = 0$$
$$2b(b + 6)(b - 3) = 0$$

$2b = 0$                          $(b + 6) = 0$                          $(b - 3) = 0$
$b = 0$                           $b = -6$                               $b = 3$

# Drill 3

16. **(B):** The key to simplifying this expression is to recognize the special product:

$a^2 - b^2 = (a + b)(a - b)$

After replacing the original numerator with $(a + b)(a - b)$, cancel the $(a - b)$ in the numerator with the $(a - b)$ in the denominator.

$$\frac{a^2 - b^2}{a - b} = \frac{(a + b)\,\cancel{(a - b)}}{\cancel{(a - b)}} = a + b$$

17. **(A):** Both the numerator and the denominator contain special products. Factor each one to find common terms to cancel.

$$\frac{r^2 + 2rs + s^2}{r^2 - s^2} = \frac{\cancel{(r + s)}\,(r + s)}{\cancel{(r + s)}\,(r - s)} = \frac{r + s}{r - s}$$

18. **(B):** First perform the subtraction to combine the two terms:

$$\frac{5x^3}{x - 1} - \frac{5x^2}{x - 1} = \frac{5x^3 - 5x^2}{x - 1}$$

Next, pull out the common term $(5x^2)$ in the numerator.

$$\frac{5x^3 - 5x^2}{x - 1} = \frac{5x^2\,\cancel{(x - 1)}}{\cancel{(x - 1)}} = 5x^2$$

19. **(C):** It is tempting to expand the quadratic term in the numerator, but notice all those $y$'s and 5's? Also, none of the answer choices are fractions, so the denominator must cancel out somehow.

Group the $y + 5$ terms.

$$\frac{(y + 5) - (y + 5)^2}{(y + 5)}$$

You can cancel a $(y + 5)$ from each term (remember that the numerator contains two separate terms, separated by the subtraction sign).

$$\frac{\cancel{(y + 5)} - (y + 5)^2}{\cancel{(y + 5)}} = \frac{1 - (y + 5)}{1} = -y - 4$$

If you think you might make a mistake doing it that way, you can first pull the common $y + 5$ term out of the numerator.

$$\frac{(y + 5) - (y + 5)^2}{(y + 5)} = \frac{\cancel{(y + 5)} \left[ 1 - (y + 5) \right]}{\cancel{(y + 5)}} = 1 - y - 5 = -y - 4$$

20. **(C):** The denominators are the same, so add the fractions:

$$\frac{m^2 + 2m}{m + 7} + \frac{49 + 12m}{m + 7} = \frac{m^2 + 14m + 49}{m + 7}$$

None of the answer choices are fractions, so find a way to eliminate the denominator. Start by factoring the numerator.

$$\frac{m^2 + 14m + 49}{m + 7} = \frac{\cancel{(m + 7)} (m + 7)}{\cancel{(m + 7)}} = m + 7$$

# Drill 4

21. **(B):** Simplify this problem by factoring a 4 out of the numerator and a 2 out of the denominator.

$$\frac{4z^2 - 12z - 16}{2z + 2} = \frac{\overset{2}{\cancel{4}} \left( z^2 - 3z - 4 \right)}{\cancel{2} (z + 1)} = \frac{2 \left( z^2 - 3z - 4 \right)}{(z + 1)}$$

The answers don't contain fractions, so the denominator must cancel somehow. Factor the numerator.

$$\frac{2 \left( z^2 - 3z - 4 \right)}{(z + 1)} = \frac{2 \cancel{(z + 1)} (z - 4)}{\cancel{(z + 1)}} = 2(z - 4) = 2z - 8$$

22. **(C):** This might seem nearly impossible to factor. Glance at the answers. Notice anything?

The variables *a* and *b* have disappeared. It must mean that these variables will cancel out as you solve! Notice that every term has an *ab* piece; factor it out and cancel.

$$\frac{5ab + abc}{abc^2 + 10abc + 25ab} = \frac{\cancel{ab}(5 + c)}{\cancel{ab}(c^2 + 10c + 25)} = \frac{5 + c}{c^2 + 10c + 25}$$

That's more manageable. None of the answers matches yet, so factor the denominator to see whether you can cancel any further.

$$\frac{5 + c}{c^2 + 10c + 25} = \frac{5 + c}{(c + 5)(c + 5)} = \frac{\cancel{(c + 5)}}{\cancel{(c + 5)}(c + 5)} = \frac{1}{c + 5}$$

23. **(C):** There's no obvious way to proceed through this question. The best bet is to try to simplify before multiplying. Notice that $x^3$ can be factored out of the numerator and $x^2$ can be factored out of the denominator.

$$\frac{\left(x^5 - x^3\right)}{\left(x^3 - x^2\right)} \times \frac{x}{5} = \frac{x^3\left(x^2 - 1\right)}{x^2\left(x - 1\right)} \times \frac{x}{5}$$

Cancel $x^2$ from the top and bottom. Also, the numerator now contains $(x^2 - 1)$. Factor this.

$$\frac{x^3\left(x^2 - 1\right)}{x^2\left(x - 1\right)} \times \frac{x}{5} =$$

$$\frac{x^{\cancel{3}^1}(x + 1)\cancel{(x - 1)}}{\cancel{x^2}\cancel{(x - 1)}} \times \frac{x}{5} =$$

$$\frac{x(x + 1) \times x}{5}$$

Glance at the answer choices. None of the numerators in the answer choices has parenthetical expressions, so multiply the numerator out.

$$\frac{x(x + 1)(x)}{5} = \frac{x^2(x + 1)}{5} = \frac{x^3 + x^2}{5}$$

24. **(A):** Simplify before you multiply. Are there any common factors to cancel?

$$\left(x^2 - 7x + 10\right) \times \frac{x+5}{x-2} =$$

$$\frac{(x-5)\,(x-2)}{1} \times \frac{x+5}{x-2} =$$

$$(x-5)(x+5) =$$

$$x^2 - 25$$

25. **(B):** Glance at the answers: no fractions. Factor the numerator to try to cancel the denominator.

$$\frac{x^2 - 6x + 9}{3 - x} = \frac{(x-3)(x-3)}{3-x}$$

Neither of the expressions in the numerator matches the denominator. However, $(x-3) = -(3-x)$. Factor out a $(-1)$ from the denominator, then cancel:

$$\frac{(x-3)(x-3)}{3-x} = \frac{(x-3)\,(x-3)}{-(x-3)} = \frac{x-3}{-1} = -x+3 \text{ or } 3-x$$

# Beyond Equations: Inequalities & Absolute Value

# In this chapter...

- An Inequality with a Variable: A Range on the Number Line

- Many Values "Solve" an Inequality

- Solve Inequalities: Isolate Variable by Transforming Each Side

- Multiply or Divide an Inequality by a Negative: Flip > to < or Vice Versa

- Absolute Value: The Distance from Zero

- Replace $|x|$ with $x$ in One Equation and with $-x$ in Another

- Inequalities + Absolute Values: Set Up Two Inequalities

# Beyond Equations: Inequalities & Absolute Value

## In This Chapter, You Will Learn To:

- Manipulate and solve inequalities
- Work with absolute values

## An Inequality with a Variable: A Range on the Number Line

Inequalities use $<$, $>$, $\leq$, or $\geq$ to describe the relationship between two expressions. For example:

$$5 > 4 \qquad y \leq 7 \qquad x < 5 \qquad 2x + 3 \geq 0$$

Like equations, *inequalities are full sentences.* Always read from left to right.

| | | |
|---|---|---|
| $x < y$ | $x$ is less than $y$. | |
| $x > y$ | $x$ is greater than $y$. | |
| $x \leq y$ | $x$ is less than or equal to $y$. | $x$ is at most $y$. |
| $x \geq y$ | $x$ is greater than or equal to $y$. | $x$ is at least $y$. |

You can also have two inequalities in one statement. Make a compound sentence.

| | |
|---|---|
| $9 < g < 200$ | 9 is less than $g$, and $g$ is less than 200. |
| $-3 < y \leq 5$ | $-3$ is less than $y$, and $y$ is less than or equal to 5. |
| $7 \geq x > 2$ | 7 is greater than or equal to $x$, and $x$ is greater than 2. |

To visualize an inequality that involves a variable, *draw the inequality on a number line.* Recall that "greater than" means "to the right of" on a number line. Likewise, "less than" means "to the left of."

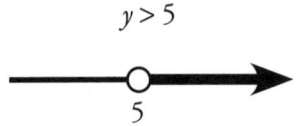

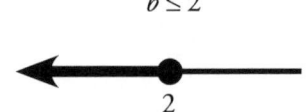

*y* is to the right of 5, which is *not* included in the line (as shown by the empty circle around 5), because 5 is not a part of the solution—*y* is greater than 5, but not equal to 5.

*b* is to the left of 2 (or on top of 2). Here, 2 is included in the solution, because *b* can equal 2. A solid black circle indicates that you include the point itself.

Any number covered by the black arrow (or a filled-in circle) will make the inequality true and so is a possible solution to the inequality. Any number not covered by the black arrow (or covered with an empty circle) is not a solution.

| If you... | Then you... | Like this: |
|---|---|---|
| Want to visualize an inequality | Put it all on a number line, where < means "to the left of" and > means "to the right of" |  |

## Check Your Skills

Draw the following equations or inequalities on the number line provided.

1. $x > 3$

2      3      4

2. $b \geq -2$

−3     −2     −1

3. $y = 4$

3      4      5

Translate the following into inequality statements.

4. *z* is greater than *v*.
5. The total amount is greater than $2,000.

*Answers can be found on page 343.*

## Many Values "Solve" an Inequality

*What does it mean to "solve an inequality"?*

It means the same thing as to solve an equation: Find the value or values of *x* that make the inequality true. When you plug a solution back into the original equation or inequality, you get a *true statement*.

Here's what's different. Equations have only one (or just a few) value as a solution. In contrast, *inequalities give a whole range of values as solutions*—often way too many to list individually. For example:

**Equation:** $x + 3 = 8$

The solution to $x + 3 = 8$ is $x = 5$, which is the *only* number that will make the equation true.

Plug back in to check: $5 + 3 = 8$. True.

**Inequality:** $x + 3 < 8$

The solution to $x + 3 < 8$ is $x < 5$. The number 5 itself is not a solution because $5 + 3 < 8$ is not a true statement. But 4 is a solution because $4 + 3 < 8$ is true. For that matter, 4.99, 3, 2, 2.87, −5, and −100 are also solutions. The list goes on.

For all of the correct answers: (any number less than 5) $+ 3 < 8$. True.

## Check Your Skills

6. If $x < 10$, what is a possible value of $x$?

   (A) −3
   (B) 2.5
   (C) −3/2
   (D) 9.999
   (E) All of the above

*Answer can be found on page 343.*

## Solve Inequalities: Isolate Variable by Transforming Each Side

As with equations, your objective is to isolate a variable on one side of the inequality. When the variable is by itself, you can see what the solution (or range of solutions) really is.

For example, $2x + 6 < 12$ and $x < 3$ provide the same information. But you understand the full range of solutions more easily when you see the second inequality, which literally says that "$x$ is less than 3."

Many manipulations are the same for inequalities as for equations. First of all, you are *always* allowed to simplify an expression on just one side of an inequality. Just don't change the expression's value.

    $2x + 3x < 45$      is the same as      $5x < 45$

The inequality sign isn't involved in this simplification.

Next, some Golden Rule moves work the same way for inequalities as for equations. For instance, you can *add* anything you want to both sides of an inequality. Just make sure you do the same thing to both sides. You can also *subtract* anything you want from both sides of an inequality.

$$a - 4 > 6$$
$$\underline{+4\quad +4}$$
$$a \qquad > 10$$

$$y + 7 < 3$$
$$\underline{-7\quad -7}$$
$$y \quad < -4$$

You can also add or subtract variables from both sides of an inequality. It doesn't matter what the signs of the variables might be.

| If you... | Then you... | Like this: |
|---|---|---|
| Want to add or subtract the same quantity on both sides of an inequality | Go ahead and do so | $x + y > -4$ $\underline{-y \quad -y}$ $x > -4 - y$ |

## Check Your Skills

Isolate the variable in the following inequalities.

7. $x - 6 < 13$
8. $y + 11 \geq -13$
9. $x + 7 > 7$

*Answers can be found on page 343.*

## Multiply or Divide an Inequality by a Negative: Flip > to < or Vice Versa

If you multiply both sides of an inequality by a positive number, leave the inequality sign alone. The same is true for division. For example:

$$\frac{x}{3} < 7$$
$$3\left(\frac{x}{3}\right) < (7)3$$
$$x < 21$$

$$4y > 12$$
$$\frac{4y}{4} > \frac{12}{4}$$
$$y > 3$$

However, *if you multiply or divide both sides of an inequality by a negative number, flip the inequality sign.* "Greater than" becomes "less than" and vice versa.

$$-2x > 10$$
$$\left(\frac{-2x}{-2}\right) < \left(\frac{10}{-2}\right)$$
$$x < -5$$

$$-b \geq 10$$
$$(-1)(-b) \leq (10)(-1)$$
$$b \leq -10$$

If you didn't switch the sign, then inequalities such as $5 < 7$ would become false when you multiply them by, say, $-1$. You must flip the sign.

$$5 < 7$$                    but                    $$-5 > -7$$

5 is less than 7                                   $-5$ is greater than $-7$

What about multiplying or dividing an inequality by a variable? If you aren't given the sign of the variable, then avoid taking this step! If you don't know the sign of the "hidden number" that the variable represents, then you don't know whether to switch the sign.

If the problem tells you the variable is positive, or if the variable has to be positive (e.g., it counts people or measures a length), then you can go ahead and multiply or divide. If you're told the variable is negative, flip the sign when you multiply or divide by that variable. If you're not told, don't multiply or divide by that variable.

| If you... | Then you... | Like this: |
|-----------|-------------|------------|
| Multiply or divide both sides of an inequality by a *negative* number | Flip the inequality sign | $45 \quad < \quad -5w$ $\left(\dfrac{45}{-5}\right) > \left(\dfrac{-5w}{-5}\right)$ $-9 \quad > \quad w$ |

## Check Your Skills

Isolate the variable in the following inequalities.

10. $x + 3 \geq -2$
11. $-2y < -8$
12. $a + 4 \geq 2a$

*Answers can be found on pages 343–344.*

## Absolute Value: The Distance from Zero

The **absolute value** of a number describes how far that number is away from 0. It is the distance between that number and 0 on a number line.

The symbol for absolute value is |number|. For instance, write the absolute value of $-5$ as $|-5|$.

The absolute value of 5 is 5. This is how it would look on a number line:

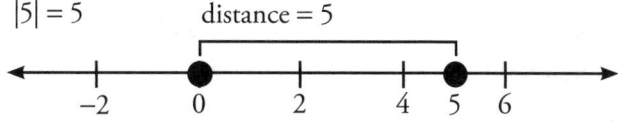

The absolute value of −5 is also 5:

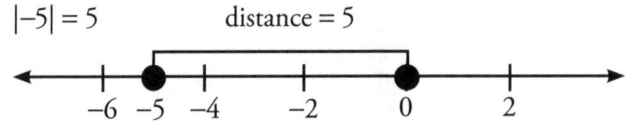

$$|-5| = 5 \qquad \text{distance} = 5$$

In either case, the number is 5 units away from 0 on the number line.

When you face an expression like $|4 - 7|$, treat the absolute value symbol like parentheses. Solve the arithmetic problem *inside* first, and then find the absolute value of the answer.

$$|4 - 7| = ?$$
$$4 - 7 = -3$$
$$|-3| = 3$$

Almost every absolute value is positive. There is one exception.

$$|0| = 0$$

Except for 0, every absolute value is positive.

## Check Your Skills

Mark the following expressions as TRUE or FALSE.

13. $|3| = 3$

14. $|-3| = -3$

15. $|3| = -3$

16. $|-3| = 3$

17. $|3 - 6| = 3$

18. $|6 - 3| = -3$

*Answers can be found on page 344.*

# Replace $|x|$ with $x$ in One Equation and with $-x$ in Another

You may see a variable inside the absolute value sign.

$$|y| = 3$$

This equation has *two solutions*. There are two numbers that are 3 units away from 0, namely 3 and −3. Both of these numbers could be the value of *y*, but not simultaneously, so *y* is *either* 3 *or* −3.

When you see a variable inside an absolute value, look for the variable to have two possible values. Here is a step-by-step process for finding both solutions:

| | |
|---|---|
| $\|y\| = 3$ | Step 1: Isolate the absolute value expression on one side of the equation. Here, the expression is already isolated. |
| $+(y) = 3$ or $-(y) = 3$ | Step 2: Drop the absolute value signs and *set up two equations*. The first equation has the positive value of what's inside the absolute value. The second equation has the negative value. |
| $y = 3$  or  $-y = 3$ | Step 3: Solve both equations. |
| $y = 3$  or  $y = -3$ | There are two possible values for $y$. |

For equations only (*not* inequalities), you can take a shortcut and go right to "$y$ equals plus or minus 3." This shortcut works as long as the absolute value expression is by itself on one side of the equation. As always, only use a shortcut if you know it well enough to avoid careless mistakes.

Here's a more difficult problem:

$$6 \times |2x + 4| = 30$$

To solve this problem, use the same approach.

| | |
|---|---|
| $6 \times \|2x + 4\| = 30$ <br> $\|2x + 4\| = 5$ | Step 1: Isolate the absolute value expression on one side of the equation or inequality. |
| $+(2x + 4) = 5$   or   $-(2x + 4) = 5$ <br> $-2x - 4 = 5$ | Step 2: Set up two equations—one positive and one negative. |
| $2x = 1$   or   $-2x = 9$ | Step 3: Solve both equations/inequalities. |
| $x = \dfrac{1}{2}$   or   $x = \dfrac{-9}{2}$ | There are two possible values for $x$. |

| If you... | Then you... | Like this: |
|:---:|:---:|:---:|
| Have a variable inside absolute value signs | Drop the absolute value and set up two equations, one positive and one negative | $\|z\| = 4$ <br><br> $+(z) = 4$ or $-(z) = 4$ <br><br> $z = 4$ or $z = -4$ |

## Check Your Skills

Solve the following equations with absolute values in them.

19. $|a| = 6$

20. $|x + 2| = 5$

21. $|3y - 4| = 17$

22. $4\left|x + \dfrac{1}{2}\right| = 18$

*Answers can be found on pages 344–345.*

# Inequalities and Absolute Values: Set Up Two Inequalities

Some tough problems include both inequalities and absolute values. To solve these problems, combine what you have learned about inequalities with what you have learned about absolute values. Try an example:

$$|x| \geq 4$$

The basic process for dealing with absolute values is the same for inequalities as it is for equations. The absolute value is already isolated on one side, so now drop the absolute value signs and *set up two inequalities*. The first inequality has the positive value of what was inside the absolute value signs, while the second inequality has the negative value.

$$+(x) \geq 4 \qquad \text{or} \qquad -(x) \geq 4$$

Next, isolate the variable in each inequality, as necessary.

$$+(x) \geq 4 \quad \text{or} \quad -(x) \geq 4$$
$$x \geq 4 \qquad\qquad -x \geq 4 \qquad \text{Divide by } -1 \text{ (in the negative example).}$$
$$x \leq -4 \qquad \text{Remember to flip the sign when dividing by a negative.}$$

The two solutions to the original equation are $x \geq 4$ or $x \leq -4$. Draw those two inequalities on a number line.

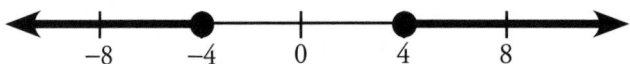

As before, any number that is covered by the black arrow will make the inequality true. Because of the absolute value, there are now two arrows instead of one, but nothing else has changed. $-4$ and any number to the left of $-4$ will make the inequality true, as will 4 and any number to the right of 4.

Looking back at the inequality $|x| \geq 4$, you can also interpret it in terms of distance. For example, $|x| \geq 4$ means "$x$ is at least 4 units away from 0, in either direction." The black arrows indicate all numbers for which that statement is true.

Here is a harder example, with a twist:

$$|y + 3| < 5$$

Once again, the absolute value is already isolated on one side, so set up the two inequalities.

$$+(y + 3) < 5 \quad \text{or} \quad -(y + 3) < 5$$

Next, isolate the variable.

$$y + 3 < 5 \qquad \text{or} \qquad -y - 3 < 5$$
$$y < 2 \qquad\qquad\qquad -y < 8$$
$$y > -8$$

The two inequalities are $y < 2$ and $y > -8$. If you plot those results, something curious happens.

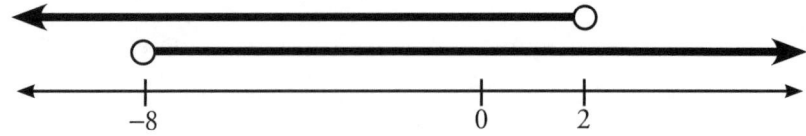

**MANHATTAN** PREP

It seems as if every number should be a solution to the equation. But try plugging $y = 5$ into $|y + 3| < 5$. What happens?

It doesn't work: $|5 + 3|$ is not less than 5. In fact, the only numbers that make the inequality true are those that are true for *both* inequalities. The number line should look like this:

In other words, $-8 < y < 2$.

When the two solutions overlap, as in this example, only the numbers that fall in the range of both arrows will be solutions to the inequality, so combine the solutions into one big inequality: $-8 < y < 2$.

If your two arrows do *not* overlap, as in the first example, any number that falls in the range of *either* arrow will be a solution to the inequality, so leave the solutions as two separate inequalities: $x \geq 4$ or $x \leq -4$.

You can also interpret $|y + 3| < 5$ in terms of distance: "$(y + 3)$ is less than 5 units away from from 0, in either direction." The shaded segment indicates all numbers $y$ for which this is true. As inequalities get more complicated, don't worry about interpreting their meaning—just solve them algebraically!

| If you... | Then you... | Like this: |
|---|---|---|
| Have an inequality with a variable inside absolute value signs | Drop the absolute value and set up two inequalities, one positive and one negative. If the two solutions don't overlap, write *or* between them and leave them as two inequalities. If the two solutions do overlap, combine them into one big inequality. | $|z| > 4$ $+(z) > 4 \quad -(z) > 4$ no overlap $z > 4$ or $z < -4$ $|a| < 4$ $+(a) < 4 \quad -(a) > 4$ $a < 4 \quad a > -4$ overlap! $-4 < a < 4$ |

## Check Your Skills

Solve the following inequalities with absolute values in them.

23.  $|x + 1| > 2$

24.  $|-x - 4| \geq 8$

25.  $|x - 7| < 9$

*Answers can be found on page 345.*

# Check Your Skills Answer Key

1. 

2. 

3. 

4. **$z > v$:** $z$ *is greater than* $v$ is translated as $z > v$.

5. **$a > \$2,000$:** Let $a$ = total amount. *The total amount is greater than $2,000* is translated as $a > 2,000$.

6. **(E):** All of the numbers in the answer choices are to the left of 10 on the number line, so all of them are possible values for $x$.

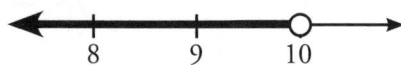

7. **$x < 19$:**

$$x - 6 < 13$$
$$\underline{+6\quad +6}$$
$$x < 19$$

8. **$y \geq -24$:**

$$y + 11 \geq -13$$
$$\underline{-11\qquad -11}$$
$$y \geq -24$$
$$y \geq -24$$

9. **$x > 0$:**

$$x + 7 > 7$$
$$\underline{-7\quad -7}$$
$$x > 0$$

10. **$x \geq -5$:**

$$x + 3 \geq -2$$
$$\underline{-3\quad -3}$$
$$x \geq -5$$

11. $y > 4$:

$$-2y < -8$$
$$\left(\frac{-2y}{-2}\right) > \left(\frac{-8}{-2}\right)$$
$$y > 4$$

12. $4 \geq a$:

$$a + 4 \geq 2a$$
$$\underline{\phantom{a+4}-a \quad -a}$$
$$4 \geq a$$

13. **True:** The absolute value of 3 is 3.

14. **False:** The absolute value of $-3$ is *not* $-3$; rather, the absolute value of $-3$ is 3. Note that an absolute value is *never* negative.

15. **False:** The absolute value of 3 is 3. An absolute value is never negative.

16. **True:** The absolute value of $-3$ is 3.

17. **True:** $|3 - 6| = |-3| = 3$

18. **False:** $|6 - 3| = |3| = 3$. An absolute value is never negative.

19. $a = 6$ **or** $-6$:

$$|a| = 6$$

$$+(a) = 6 \qquad \text{or} \qquad -(a) = 6$$
$$a = 6 \qquad\qquad\qquad a = -6$$

20. $x = 3$ **or** $-7$:

$$|x + 2| = 5$$

$$+(x + 2) = 5 \qquad \text{or} \qquad -(x + 2) = 5$$
$$x + 2 = 5 \qquad\qquad\qquad -x - 2 = 5$$
$$x = 3 \qquad\qquad\qquad -x = 7$$
$$x = -7$$

21. $y = 7$ **or** $-\dfrac{13}{3}$:

$$|3y - 4| = 17$$

$$+(3y - 4) = 17 \qquad \text{or} \qquad -(3y - 4) = 17$$
$$3y - 4 = 17 \qquad\qquad\qquad -3y + 4 = 17$$
$$3y = 21 \qquad\qquad\qquad -3y = 13$$
$$y = 7 \qquad\qquad\qquad y = -\frac{13}{3}$$

22. **$x = 4$ or $-5$:**

$$4\left|x+\frac{1}{2}\right| = 18$$

$$\left|x+\frac{1}{2}\right| = \frac{18}{4}$$

$$\left|x+\frac{1}{2}\right| = \frac{9}{2}$$

$$+\left(x+\frac{1}{2}\right) = \frac{9}{2} \qquad\qquad \text{or} \qquad\qquad -\left(x+\frac{1}{2}\right) = \frac{9}{2}$$

$$x+\frac{1}{2} = \frac{9}{2} \qquad\qquad\qquad\qquad -x-\frac{1}{2} = \frac{9}{2}$$

$$x = \frac{8}{2} = 4 \qquad\qquad\qquad\qquad -x = \frac{10}{2} = 5$$

$$\qquad\qquad\qquad\qquad\qquad\qquad\qquad x = -5$$

23. **$x < -3$ or $x > 1$:**

$$|x+1| > 2$$

$$+(x+1) > 2 \qquad\qquad\qquad -(x+1) > 2$$

$$x+1 > 2 \qquad\qquad\qquad\qquad -x-1 > 2$$

$$x > 1 \qquad\qquad\qquad\qquad\qquad -x > 3$$

$$\qquad\qquad\qquad\qquad\qquad\qquad x < -3$$

24. **$x \le -12$ or $x \ge 4$:**

$$|-x-4| \ge 8$$

$$+(-x-4) \ge 8 \qquad\qquad\qquad -(-x-4) \ge 8$$

$$-x-4 \ge 8 \qquad\qquad\qquad\qquad x+4 \ge 8$$

$$-x \ge 12 \qquad\qquad\qquad\qquad\qquad x \ge 4$$

$$x \le -12$$

25. **$-2 < x < 16$:**

$$|x-7| < 9$$

$$+(x-7) < 9 \qquad\qquad\qquad -(x-7) < 9$$

$$x-7 < 9 \qquad\qquad\qquad\qquad -x+7 < 9$$

$$x < 16 \qquad\qquad\qquad\qquad\qquad -x < 2$$

$$\qquad\qquad\qquad\qquad\qquad\qquad x > -2$$

# Chapter Review: Drill Sets

## Drill 1

Draw the following inequalities on the number line provided.

1. $x > 4$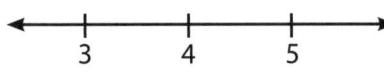

2. $a \geq 3$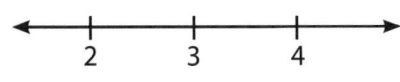

3. $y = 2$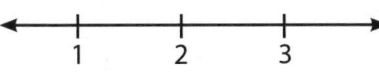

4. $x < 5$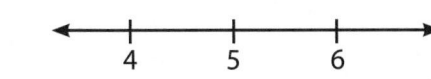

5. $6 < x$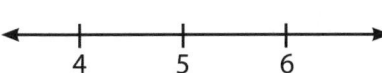

## Drill 2

Translate the following into inequality statements.

6. $a$ is less than $b$.

7. 5 times $x$ is greater than 10.

8. 6 is less than or equal to $4x$.

9. The price of an apple is greater than the price of an orange.

10. The total number of members is at least 19.

## Drill 3

Solve the following inequalities.

11. $x + 3 \leq -2$

12. $t - 4 \leq 13$

13. $3b \geq 12$

14. $-5x > 25$

15. $-8 < -4y$

## Drill 4

Solve the following inequalities.

16. $2z + 4 \geq -18$

17. $7x + 5 \geq 10x + 14$

18. $\dfrac{b}{5} \leq 4$

19. $d + \dfrac{3}{2} < 8$

20. $\dfrac{2a}{3} > 10 - a$

## Drill 5

Solve the following inequalities.

21. $3(x - 7) \geq 9$

22. $\dfrac{x}{3} + 8 < \dfrac{x}{2}$

23. $2x - 1.5 > 7$

24. $\dfrac{6(2x + 8)}{5} \leq 0$

25. $\dfrac{2(3 - x)}{5x} \leq 4$ and $x > 0$

## Drill 6

Solve the following inequalities.

26. $4\sqrt{3x - 2} > 20$

27. $\dfrac{2(8 - 3x)}{7} > 4$

28. $0.25x - 3 \leq 1$

29. $2(y + 2)^3 - 5 \geq 49$

30. $\dfrac{4\sqrt[3]{5x - 8}}{3} \geq 4$

8

## Drill 7

Solve the following absolute value equations.

31. $|x| = 5$
32. $|5a| = 15$
33. $|x + 6| = 3$
34. $|4y + 2| = 18$
35. $|1 - x| = 6$

## Drill 8

Solve the following absolute value equations.

36. $3|x - 4| = 18$
37. $2|x + 0.3| = 7$
38. $|3x - 4| = 2x + 6$
39. $|6z - 3| = 4z + 11$
40. $\left|\dfrac{x}{4} + 3\right| = 0.5$

## Drill 9

Solve each of the following inequalities. Then draw the solution on a number line.

41. $|x + 3| < 1$
42. $|3x| \geq 6$
43. $5 \geq |2y + 3|$
44. $6 \leq |5b - 9|$
45. $|-12a| < 15$

## Drill 10

Solve each of the following inequalities. Then draw the solution on a number line.

46. $|-x| \geq 6$
47. $\dfrac{|x + 4|}{2} > 5$
48. $|z^3| \leq 27$
49. $|0.1x - 3| \geq 1$
50. $\left|\dfrac{3x}{2} + 7\right| \leq 11$

## Drill 11

Solve each of the following inequalities. Then draw the solution on a number line.

51. $\left|\dfrac{-x}{5} + \dfrac{2}{3}\right| \leq \dfrac{7}{15}$
52. $|3x - 7| \geq 2x + 12$
53. $|3 + 3x| < -2x$
54. $|-9 - 5x| \leq -4x$
55. $2\left|\dfrac{7y}{4} - 7\right| < \dfrac{3y}{2} + 10$

# Drill Sets Solutions

## Drill 1

1. $x > 4$

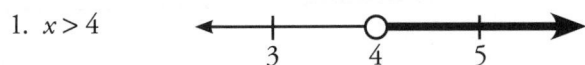

2. $a \geq 3$

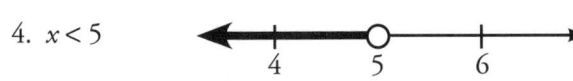

3. $y = 2$

4. $x < 5$

5. $6 < x$: You can flip inequalities around, moving the left side to the right and vice versa, as long as you flip the sign, too. In this case, $6 < x$ becomes $x > 6$:

## Drill 2

6. **$a < b$**: *a is less than b* translates as $a < b$.

7. **$5x > 10$**: *5 times x is greater than 10* is translated as $5x > 10$.

8. **$6 \leq 4x$**: *6 is less than or equal to 4x* is translated as $6 \leq 4x$.

9. **$a > o$**: Let *a* price of an apple and *o* equal to the price of an orange. *The price of an apple is greater than the price of an orange* is translated as $a > o$.

    Note: In this problem, the variables refer to prices—not the number of apples and oranges.

10. **$m \geq 19$**: Let *m* equal the number of members. *The total number of members is at least 19* is translated as $m \geq 19$.

## Drill 3

11. $x \leq -5$:

$$x + 3 \leq -2$$
$$x \leq -5$$

12. $t \leq 17$:

$$t - 4 \leq 13$$
$$t \leq 17$$

13. $b \geq 4$:

$$3b \geq 12$$
$$b \geq 4$$

14. $x < -5$:

$$-5x > 25$$
$$x < -5$$

15. $2 > y$:

$$-8 < -4y$$
$$2 > y$$

## Drill 4

16. $z \geq -11$:

$$2z + 4 \geq -18$$
$$2z \geq -22$$
$$z \geq -11$$

17. $x \leq -3$: The answer can also be written as $-3 \geq x$. It's more common to write the variable first.

$$7x + 5 \geq 10x + 14$$
$$5 \geq 3x + 14$$
$$-9 \geq 3x$$
$$-3 \geq x$$

18. $b \leq 20$:

$$\frac{b}{5} \leq 4$$
$$b \leq 20$$

**MANHATTAN** PREP

19. **$d < 6.5$ or $\dfrac{13}{2}$:** You can choose to convert to decimals or fractions, as you prefer.

$$d + \frac{3}{2} < 8$$
$$d < 8 - \frac{3}{2}$$
$$d < 8 - 1.5$$
$$d < 6.5$$

20. **$a > 6$:**

$$\frac{2a}{3} > 10 - a$$
$$2a > 30 - 3a$$
$$5a > 30$$
$$a > 6$$

## Drill 5

21. **$x \geq 10$:**

$$3(x - 7) \geq 9$$
$$x - 7 \geq 3$$
$$x \geq 10$$

22. **$x > 48$:** The answer can also be written $48 < x$. It is more common to put the variable first.

$$\frac{x}{3} + 8 < \frac{x}{2}$$
$$6\left(\frac{x}{3} + 8\right) < 6\left(\frac{x}{2}\right)$$
$$2x + 48 < 3x$$
$$48 < x$$

Multiply by 6 to get rid of fractions.

23. **$x > 4.25$:**

$$2x - 1.5 > 7$$
$$2x > 8.5$$
$$x > 4.25$$

24. $x \le -4$: You are allowed to multiply or divide by a constant (a number) even when one side of the equation is 0. That side of the equation just remains 0.

$$\frac{6(2x + 8)}{5} \le 0$$
$$6(2x+8) \le 0$$
$$2x+8 \le 0$$
$$2x \le -8$$
$$x \le -4$$

25. $x \ge \dfrac{3}{11}$ : The answer can also be written $\dfrac{3}{11} \le x$ .

$$\frac{2(3-x)}{5x} \le 4 \qquad \text{Since } x > 0, \text{ you can multiply both sides by } 5x$$
$$2(3-x) \le 20x \qquad \text{and keep the inequality sign as it is.}$$
$$3-x \le 10x$$
$$3 \le 11x$$
$$\frac{3}{11} \le x$$

# Drill 6

26. $x > 9$: Both sides of an inequality can be squared as long as both sides are positive. In this case, the square-root side of the equation must be positive because it is greater than the positive number 5.

$$4\sqrt{3x-2} > 20$$
$$\sqrt{3x-2} > 5$$
$$3x-2 > 25$$
$$3x > 27$$
$$x > 9$$

27. $x < -2$:

$$\frac{2(8-3x)}{7} > 4$$
$$2(8-3x) > 28$$
$$8-3x > 14$$
$$-3x > 6$$
$$x < -2$$

28. **$x \leq 16$:** If you are more comfortable working with fractions, you can convert 0.25 to $\dfrac{1}{4}$, before you solve:

$$0.25x - 3 \leq 1$$
$$0.25x \leq 4$$
$$x \leq 16$$

29. **$y \geq 1$:** When you take a cube root, there is only one solution: the cube has the same sign as the cube root. In this case, the cube root of positive 27 is positive 3:

$$2(y + 2)^3 - 5 \geq 49$$
$$2(y + 2)^3 \geq 54$$
$$(y + 2)^3 \geq 27$$
$$y + 2 \geq 3$$
$$y \geq 1$$

30. **$x \geq 7$:**

$$\frac{4\sqrt[3]{5x - 8}}{3} \geq 4$$
$$4\sqrt[3]{5x - 8} \geq 12$$
$$\sqrt[3]{5x - 8} \geq 3$$
$$\left(\sqrt[3]{5x - 8}\right)^3 \geq (3)^3$$
$$5x - 8 \geq 27$$
$$5x \geq 35$$
$$x \geq 7$$

# Drill 7

31. **$x = 5$ or $-5$:**

$$|x| = 5$$
$$+(x) = 5 \qquad \text{or} \qquad -x = 5$$
$$x = 5 \qquad\qquad\qquad x = -5$$

32. **$a = 3$ or $-3$:**

$$|5a| = 15$$
$$+(5a) = 15 \qquad \text{or} \qquad -(5a) = 15$$
$$5a = 15 \qquad\qquad\qquad -5a = 15$$
$$a = 3 \qquad\qquad\qquad\quad a = -3$$

33. **$x = -3$ or $-9$:**

$$|x + 6| = 3$$

$+(x + 6) = 3$         $-(x + 6) = 3$

$x + 6 = 3$      or      $-x - 6 = 3$

$x = -3$               $-x = 9$

$x = -9$

34. **$y = 4$ or $-5$:**

$$|4y + 2| = 18$$

$+(4y + 2) = 18$       $-(4y + 2) = 18$

$4y + 2 = 18$      or      $-4y - 2 = 18$

$4y = 16$           $-4y = 20$

$y = 4$             $y = -5$

35. **$x = -5$ or $7$:**

$$|1 - x| = 6$$

$+(1 - x) = 6$       $-(1 - x) = 6$

$1 - x = 6$      or      $-1 + x = 6$

$-x = 5$           $x = 7$

$x = -5$

# Drill 8

36. **$x = 10$ or $-2$:** Isolate the absolute value first. Next, split into two equations and solve:

$$3|x - 4| = 18$$
$$|x - 4| = 6$$

$+(x - 4) = 6$       $-(x - 4) = 6$

$x - 4 = 6$      or      $-x + 4 = 6$

$x = 10$           $-x = 2$

$x = -2$

37. **$x = 3.2$ or $-3.8$:** Isolate the absolute value first. Next, split into two equations and solve:

$$2|x + 0.3| = 7$$
$$|x + 0.3| = 3.5$$

$+(x + 0.3) = 3.5$       $-(x + 0.3) = 3.5$

$x + 0.3 = 3.5$      or      $-x - 0.3 = 3.5$

$x = 3.2$           $-x = 3.8$

$x = -3.8$

38. $x = 10$ or $-\dfrac{2}{5}$:

$$|3x - 4| = 2x + 6$$

$$+(3x - 4) = 2x + 6 \qquad \text{or} \qquad -(3x - 4) = 2x + 6$$

$$3x - 4 = 2x + 6 \qquad\qquad\qquad\qquad -3x + 4 = 2x + 6$$

$$x - 4 = 6 \qquad\qquad\qquad\qquad\qquad 4 = 5x + 6$$

$$x = 10 \qquad\qquad\qquad\qquad\qquad\qquad -2 = 5x$$

$$-\dfrac{2}{5} = x$$

39. $z = 7$ or $-\dfrac{4}{5}$:

$$|6z - 3| = 4z + 11$$

$$+(6z - 3) = 4z + 11 \qquad \text{or} \qquad -(6z - 3) = 4z + 11$$

$$6z - 3 = 4z + 11 \qquad\qquad\qquad\qquad -6z + 3 = 4z + 11$$

$$2z - 3 = 11 \qquad\qquad\qquad\qquad\qquad 3 = 10z + 11$$

$$2z = 14 \qquad\qquad\qquad\qquad\qquad\qquad -8 = 10z$$

$$z = 7 \qquad\qquad\qquad\qquad\qquad\qquad -\dfrac{8}{10} = z$$

$$-\dfrac{4}{5} = z$$

40. $x = -10$ or $-14$:

$$\left|\dfrac{x}{4} + 3\right| = 0.5$$

$$+\left(\dfrac{x}{4} + 3\right) = 0.5 \qquad \text{or} \qquad -\left(\dfrac{x}{4} + 3\right) = 0.5$$

$$\dfrac{x}{4} + 3 = 0.5 \qquad\qquad\qquad\qquad -\dfrac{x}{4} - 3 = 0.5$$

$$\dfrac{x}{4} = -2.5 \qquad\qquad\qquad\qquad\qquad -\dfrac{x}{4} = 3.5$$

$$x = -10 \qquad\qquad\qquad\qquad\qquad\qquad x = -14$$

# Drill 9

41. **$-4 < x < -2$:** Because the two solutions overlap, combine them into one inequality: $x$ is greater than $-4$ *and* less than $-2$.

$$|x + 3| < 1$$

| | |
|---|---|
| $+(x + 3) < 1$ | $-(x + 3) < 1$ |
| $x + 3 < 1$ | $-x - 3 < 1$ |
| $x < -2$ | $-x < 4$ |
| | $x < -4$ |

$$-4 < x < -2$$

42. **$x \le -2$ or $x \ge 2$:** The two solutions do not overlap, so leave them as two separate inequalities: $x$ is less than or equal to $-2$ *or* greater than or equal to 2.

$$|3x| \ge 6$$

| | |
|---|---|
| $+(3x) \ge 6$ | $-(3x) \ge 6$ |
| $3x \ge 6$ | $-3x \ge 6$ |
| $x \ge 2$ | $x \le -2$ |

$$x \le -2 \text{ or } x \ge 2$$

43. **$-4 \le y \le 1$:** If you prefer to have the variable on the left-hand side, you can rewrite, as shown in the last line below. If, when rewriting, you flip the two sides of the inequality, make sure to flip the inequality sign, too. (In this problem, it isn't necessary to flip the inequalities.)

$$5 \ge |2y + 3|$$

| | |
|---|---|
| $5 \ge +(2y + 3)$ | $5 \ge -(2y + 3)$ |
| $5 \ge 2y + 3$ | $5 \ge -2y - 3$ |
| $2 \ge 2y$ | $8 \ge -2y$ |
| $1 \ge y$ | $-4 \le y$ |
| $y \le 1$ | |

$$-4 \le y \le 1$$

**MANHATTAN** PREP

44. $b \geq 3$ or $b \leq \dfrac{3}{5}$:

$$6 \leq |5b - 9|$$

$6 \leq +(5b - 9)$                              $6 \leq -(5b - 9)$

$6 \leq 5b - 9$                                  $6 \leq -5b + 9$

$15 \leq 5b$                                     $-3 \leq -5b$

$3 \leq b$                                        $\dfrac{3}{5} \geq b$

$$b \geq 3 \text{ or } b \leq \dfrac{3}{5}$$

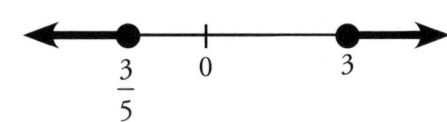

45. $-\dfrac{5}{4} < a < \dfrac{5}{4}$:

$$|-12a| < 15$$

$+(-12a) < 15$                                $-(-12a) < 15$

$-12a < 15$                                   $12a < 15$

$a > -\dfrac{15}{12}$                               $a < \dfrac{15}{12}$

$a > -\dfrac{5}{4}$                                 $a < \dfrac{5}{4}$

$$-\dfrac{5}{4} < a < \dfrac{5}{4}$$

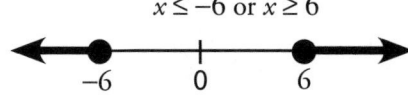

## Drill 10

46. $x \leq -6$ or $x \geq 6$:

$$|-x| \geq 6$$

$+(-x) \geq 6$                                $-(-x) \geq 6$

$-x \geq 6$                                   $x \geq 6$

$x \leq -6$

$$x \leq -6 \text{ or } x \geq 6$$

47. **$x < -14$ or $x > 6$:**

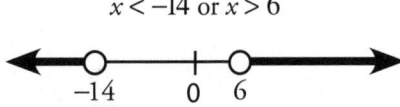

$$\frac{|x + 4|}{2} > 5$$

$$|x + 4| > 10$$

| | |
|---|---|
| $+(x + 4) > 10$ | $-(x + 4) > 10$ |
| $x + 4 > 10$ | $-x - 4 > 10$ |
| $x > 6$ | $-x > 14$ |
| | $x < -14$ |

$$x < -14 \text{ or } x > 6$$

48. **$-3 \leq z \leq 3$:**

$$|z^3| \leq 27$$

| | |
|---|---|
| $+(z^3) \leq 27$ | $-(z^3) \leq 27$ |
| $z^3 \leq 27$ | $z^3 \geq -27$ |
| $z \leq 3$ | $z \geq -3$ |

$$-3 \leq z \leq 3$$

49. **$x \leq 20$ or $x \geq 40$:**

$$|0.1x - 3| \geq 1$$

| | |
|---|---|
| $+(0.1x - 3) \geq 1$ | $-(0.1x - 3) \geq 1$ |
| $0.1x - 3 \geq 1$ | $-0.1x + 3 \geq 1$ |
| $0.1x \geq 4$ | $-0.1x \geq -2$ |
| $x \geq 40$ | $x \leq 20$ |

$$x \leq 20 \text{ or } x \geq 40$$

50. $-12 \leq x \leq \dfrac{8}{3}$:

$$\left|\dfrac{3x}{2}+7\right| \leq 11$$

$$+\left(\dfrac{3x}{2}+7\right) \leq 11 \qquad\qquad -\left(\dfrac{3x}{2}+7\right) \leq 11$$

$$\dfrac{3x}{2}+7 \leq 11 \qquad\qquad -\dfrac{3x}{2}-7 \leq 11$$

$$\dfrac{3x}{2} \leq 4 \qquad\qquad -\dfrac{3x}{2} \leq 18$$

$$3x \leq 8 \qquad\qquad -3x \leq 36$$

$$x \leq \dfrac{8}{3} \qquad\qquad x \geq -12$$

$$-12 \leq x \leq \dfrac{8}{3}$$

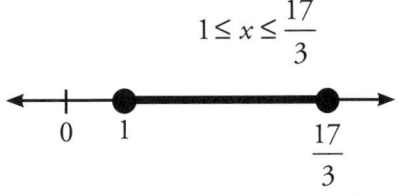

# Drill 11

51. $\mathbf{1 \leq x \leq \dfrac{17}{3}}$: The second number can also be written as a mixed fraction, $5\dfrac{2}{3}$.

$$\left|\dfrac{-x}{5}+\dfrac{2}{3}\right| \leq \dfrac{7}{15}$$

$$+\left(\dfrac{-x}{5}+\dfrac{2}{3}\right) \leq \dfrac{7}{15} \qquad\qquad -\left(\dfrac{-x}{5}+\dfrac{2}{3}\right) \leq \dfrac{7}{15}$$

$$-\dfrac{x}{5}+\dfrac{2}{3} \leq \dfrac{7}{15} \qquad\qquad \dfrac{x}{5}-\dfrac{2}{3} \leq \dfrac{7}{15}$$

$$15\left(-\dfrac{x}{5}+\dfrac{2}{3}\right) \leq \left(\dfrac{7}{15}\right)15 \qquad\qquad 15\left(\dfrac{x}{5}-\dfrac{2}{3}\right) \leq \left(\dfrac{7}{15}\right)15$$

$$-3x+10 \leq 7 \qquad\qquad 3x-10 \leq 7$$

$$-3x \leq -3 \qquad\qquad 3x \leq 17$$

$$x \geq 1 \qquad\qquad x \leq \dfrac{17}{3}$$

$$1 \leq x \leq \dfrac{17}{3}$$

**52. $x \leq -1$ or $x \geq 19$:**

$$|3x - 7| \geq 2x + 12$$

| | |
|---|---|
| $+(3x - 7) \geq 2x + 12$ | $-(3x - 7) \geq 2x + 12$ |
| $3x - 7 \geq 2x + 12$ | $-3x + 7 \geq 2x + 12$ |
| $x - 7 \geq 12$ | $7 \geq 5x + 12$ |
| $x \geq 19$ | $-5 \geq 5x$ |
| | $-1 \geq x$ |

$x \leq -1$ or $x \geq 19$

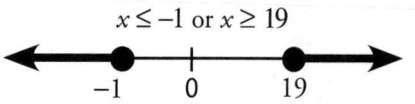

**53. $-3 < x < -\dfrac{3}{5}$:**

$$|3 + 3x| < -2x$$

| | |
|---|---|
| $+(3 + 3x) < -2x$ | $-(3 + 3x) < -2x$ |
| $3 + 3x < -2x$ | $-3 - 3x < -2x$ |
| $3 + 5x < 0$ | $-3 < x$ |
| $5x < -3$ | |
| $x < -\dfrac{3}{5}$ | |

$-3 < x < -\dfrac{3}{5}$

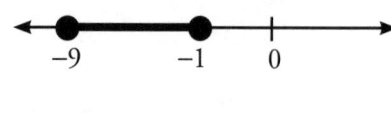

**54. $-9 \leq x \leq -1$:**

$$|-9 - 5x| \leq -4x$$

| | |
|---|---|
| $+(-9 - 5x) \leq -4x$ | $-(-9 - 5x) \leq -4x$ |
| $-9 - 5x \leq -4x$ | $9 + 5x \leq -4x$ |
| $-9 \leq x$ | $9 + 9x \leq 0$ |
| | $9x \leq -9$ |
| | $x \leq -1$ |

$-9 \leq x \leq -1$

55. $\dfrac{4}{5} < y < 12$: Isolate the absolute value, and then split into two equations.

$$2\left|\frac{7x}{4} - 7\right| < \frac{3y}{2} + 10$$

$$\left|\frac{7y}{4} - 7\right| < \frac{3y}{4} + 5$$

$$+\left(\frac{7y}{4} - 7\right) < \frac{3y}{4} + 5 \qquad\qquad -\left(\frac{7y}{4} - 7\right) < \frac{3y}{4} + 5$$

$$\frac{7y}{4} - 7 < \frac{3y}{4} + 5 \qquad\qquad -\frac{7y}{4} + 7 < \frac{3y}{4} + 5$$

$$7y - 28 < 3y + 20 \qquad\qquad -7y + 28 < 3y + 20$$

$$4y < 48 \qquad\qquad\qquad 8 < 10y$$

$$y < 12 \qquad\qquad\qquad \frac{8}{10} < y$$

$$\frac{4}{5} < y$$

$$\frac{4}{5} < y < 12$$

# Word Problems

# In this chapter...

- Solve Word Problems: Follow Four Steps to Turn Words into Math

- Common Word Problem Phrases

- Express Revenue as Price × Quantity

- Add Units: Add Apples to Apples

- Multiply and Divide Units: Treat Them Just Like Numbers or Variables

- Rate × Time: Distance, Follow the Units

- Rate × Time: Work, Define the Work Unit and Add Rates

- Fractions and Percents in Word Problems: *Of* Means *Times*

# Chapter 9

# Word Problems

## In This Chapter, You Will Learn To:

• Translate and solve word problems

## Solve Word Problems: Follow Four Steps to Turn Words into Math

Word problems are everywhere on the GMAT. They come in all sorts of shapes and sizes. The descriptions can be confusing and unfamiliar.

Fortunately, the process for tackling almost all word problems is fundamentally the same. You can solve word problems by asking yourself the following four questions:

1. **What do they want?**

   Identify what the problem is specifically asking for. Name that thing and write it down. This is the unknown that you care about the most.

2. **What do they give me?**

   The problem typically gives you some numbers. It also gives you relationships between things. Clearly identify all of this given information. You may have to name additional unknowns.

3. **How do I turn this information into equations?**

   An equation is a sentence: *The left side equals the right side.* You can express most relationships using the equals sign (=) or the inequalities signs. A few common relationships show up over and over again; you can learn to recognize them.

4. **How do I solve those equations for the desired value?**

   Use methods from the Equations chapter, the Quadratic Equations chapter, and so on, to manipulate the equations you've created. You'll eliminate any secondary unknowns until you find the value you want.

*It is crucial to write things down.* Do not wait for lightning to strike. Often, the entire process will not be completely clear from the beginning. That's fine—just start writing, and be methodical and patient.

The four questions above correspond to the four steps of a general process of solving word problems.

Consider this example:

> The annual profit for a mattress company is defined by the equation $p = 200m - 3{,}000$, where $p$ is the profit, in dollars, and $m$ is the number of mattresses sold. How much profit does the company make, in dollars, from the sale of 40 mattresses in a particular year?

Start with step #1: **What do they want?**

The question is asking for the *profit* in a particular year. This unknown has already been named for you. Profit is represented by $p$.

If you were not given a letter for the variable, you would make up your own.

Write "$p$ = profit = ?" on your paper. By writing an actual question mark, you flag the most important unknown.

You may even want to draw a circle or box around this text to help you remember that it is the question. This will help you to forestall one of the most common careless mistakes on word problems: solving for the wrong thing.

Next is step #2: **What do they give me?**

In this problem, you are given two specific pieces of information:

1.   The relationship between number of mattresses and profit
2.   A specific number of mattresses

Step #3: **How do I turn this information into equations?**

The first bit of information is already in equation form. Write "$p = 200m - 3{,}000$."

The same relationship could have been given in words: "The profit, in dollars, is $200 times the number of mattresses, minus a $3,000 fixed cost." You would translate those words to the same equation.

The second bit of given information is this: There are 40 mattresses. Write "$m = 40$" on your scrap paper. This is actually a second equation.

Don't just write "40." Put information down in the form of equations.

Finally, step #4: **How do I solve the equations for the desired value?**

$$p = 200m - 3{,}000 \qquad m = 40 \qquad p = \text{profit} = ?$$

To get $p$, you'll need to eliminate the variable $m$. Plug in 40 for $m$ in the first equation and simplify.

$p = 200(40) - 3,000$

$p = 8,000 - 3,000$

$p = 5,000$

Therefore, the answer to the problem is $5,000.

Even as the problems become more complicated, follow these same four steps. Let's try another problem:

> A steel rod 50 meters long is cut into two pieces. If one piece is 14 meters longer than the other, what is the length, in meters, of the shorter piece?

Again, start with step #1: **What do they want?**

The question asks specifically for the "length … of the shorter piece." This length is the number you want.

Since the problem did not give you a letter to represent this length, pick one. Don't just pick $x$. Choose a letter that will easily remind you of the quantity you are trying to find. For instance, you might choose $S$ for "shorter." Write this down:

$S$ = length short = ?

Note: "Length short" is shorthand for "the length of the shorter piece."

Step #2: **What do they give me?**

Reread the first sentence: "A steel rod 50 meters long is cut into two pieces."

It might not be obvious at first, but this sentence provides a relationship between a few lengths:

- The length of the whole rod, which is 50 meters
- The length of the shorter piece, which you've already called $S$
- The length of the longer piece (which must be longer, because the other piece is shorter)

Before trying to represent the relationship, name the length of the longer piece. Write this down:

$L$ = length long

Now you can express the relationship between all the lengths. This relationship is very common:

Part + Part = Whole

If you break something into two parts, you can add the parts back up to get the original thing. That's true of lengths, weights, and so on.

Go ahead and do step #3 right now: **How do I turn this information into an equation?** Write this relationship down using the numbers and letters for each quantity.

$$S + L = 50$$

As you identify each relationship, you will often want to go ahead and express it on paper in the form of an equation right away. You can go back and forth between steps #2 and #3.

The equation $S + L = 50$ is a good start, but it's not enough on its own to solve for $S$. Go back to step #2 and ask: **What ELSE do they give me?**

Keep reading: "If one piece is 14 meters longer than the other ..." Stop there. In a math problem, anything after an "if" is true. You are told that one piece is 14 meters longer than the other.

This relationship is also very common: *Different values are made equal.* You have two different values that are definitely not equal, but you are told exactly how the values differ, so you can set up an equivalence.

If the shorter piece were 14 meters longer, it would have the *same* length as the longer piece. *Same* always means *equal.* Therefore:

Shorter piece, if made 14 meters longer = Longer piece

Now do step #3 again: **How do I turn THIS information into an equation?**

To make something 14 meters longer, add 14 meters to its length. Write the equation using letters and numbers:

$$S + 14 = L$$

Be careful not to write this equation down backward. If you need to check, mentally test a number for $S$ and verify that the longer piece comes out longer. Alternatively, remind yourself that $S$ is the *shorter* piece, so logically it makes sense that you have to add something to it to match the longer piece.

At last you have two equations and two variables ($S$ and $L$), and you have no more information to process from the problem. Move on to step #4: **How do I solve the equations for the desired value?**

$$S + L = 50 \qquad S + 14 = L \qquad S = ?$$

Since you ultimately want $S$, eliminate $L$ by replacing it in the first equation with $S + 14$.

$$S + L = 50$$
$$S + (S + 14) = 50$$
$$2S + 14 = 50$$
$$2S = 36$$
$$S = 18$$

The answer to the question is 18.

Try a harder problem. Despite new challenges, the process remains the same. As needed, move back and forth among the first three steps: Identify what the question asks for, identify given quantities and relationships, and represent those quantities as variables and those relationships as equations.

Over a period of 5 days at a donut shop, the average (arithmetic mean) number of donuts sold per day was 80. In the 4 days after that period, the shop sold a total of 500 donuts. What was the average number of donuts sold per day over the entire 9-day period?

Start by identifying what they want: the average (arithmetic mean) number of donuts sold per day over 9 days. Use the letter $a$ to represent this value. (Note: *arithmetic mean* is a synonym for *average*. The test will often use both terms; all you need to find is the regular average.)

$a$ = average # donuts sold a day = ?

The problem also mentions the concept of an average. This is one of the formulas that you need to memorize for the GMAT: The average of a group of numbers is the sum of those numbers divided by the number of terms, which is the number of numbers you have.

$$\text{Average} = \frac{\text{Sum}}{\text{\# of terms}}$$

When you see that a problem mentions some concept for which you have memorized a formula, immediately write down the "generic" form of that formula, as shown above.

Include units as well. The average is in *donuts a day*, or donuts *per* day. *Per* means *divided by*, so this unit is donuts/day or $\frac{\text{donuts}}{\text{day}}$. The sum is the total number of donuts, and you divide by the number of days. Here is the average formula customized for this problem:

$$\text{Average donuts per day} = \frac{\text{Total donuts}}{\text{Total days}}$$

To find the average, you need both the total number of donuts and the total number of days.

Do you know either of these values? Yes. You are asked for the average *over the entire 9-day period*. So the total number of days is 9.

However, the total number of donuts is unknown. Make up a variable—say, $d$ for donuts.

Now rewrite the average formula.

$$a = \frac{d}{9}$$

You may not think that you've accomplished much yet, but now you know that to get $a$, you need $d$.

That's important. Now you should focus on $d$. What else can you find out about the total number of donuts sold over the 9 days?

Reread the problem. The first sentence indicates something about the donuts sold during the first 5 days. The next sentence indicates that a total of 500 donuts were sold in the last 4 days. And you are looking for $d$, the total donuts sold over all 9 days.

What is the relationship between the donuts sold during these periods?

- Donuts sold over the first 5 days
- Donuts sold over the last 4 days
- Donuts sold over all 9 days

This is Part + Part = Whole again.

$$\text{Donuts sold in the first 5 days} \quad + \quad \text{Donuts sold in the last 4 days} \quad = \quad \text{Total donuts sold over all 9 days}$$

As word problems get harder, they make relationships harder to see. You also have to perform more steps.

Now you have two more unknowns to worry about on the left side of the equation above. Do you know either unknown?

Yes. You do know how many donuts were sold in the last 4 days: 500 donuts. However, the number of donuts sold in the first 5 days is still unknown. Use an $n$ to represent that quantity and rewrite the Part + Part = Whole equation.

$$n + 500 = d$$

You're almost there. If you can find $n$, you can find $d$. Then you can find $a$, and that's the answer.

What do you know about $n$, the number of donuts sold over the first 5 days? You know something about that period from the first sentence: on average, 80 donuts per day were sold. Once again, you can use the average formula to create an equation. Notice that you're focusing on a different period now—just the first 5 days.

$$\text{Average donuts per day} = \frac{\text{Total donuts}}{\text{Total days}} \qquad 80 = \frac{n}{5}$$

At last, you can solve the problem. First, solve for $n$.

$$80 = \frac{n}{5} \quad \longrightarrow \quad 400 = n$$

Next, find $d$.

$$n + 500 = d \quad \longrightarrow \quad 400 + 500 = d \quad \longrightarrow \quad 900 = d$$

Finally, solve for $a$.

$$a = \frac{d}{9} \quad \longrightarrow \quad a = \frac{900}{9} \quad \longrightarrow \quad a = 100$$

The average number of donuts sold per day over the entire 9-day period is 100. That is, on average, 100 donuts were sold each day for 9 days.

As you solve word problems, sometimes you'll notice relationships first. At other times, you'll notice unknowns first. The order is not important. Just keep extracting information from the problem and representing that information on paper.

Turn unknowns into letters, and turn relationships into equations. Observe how the equations hook together. In the previous problem, you ultimately wanted $a$, but you needed $d$ first, and before that $n$.

The last value you solve for is the one you really want ($a$). When you identify other unknowns, realize that you will likely need to solve for them first.

| If you... | Then you... | Like this: |
|---|---|---|
| Want to solve a word problem:<br><br>Kelly is three times as old as Bill. In 5 years, Kelly will be twice as old as Bill will be. How old is Bill? | Follow the four steps:<br>1. Identify what they want<br>2. Identify what they give you<br>3. Represent relationships as equations<br>4. Solve the algebra | $B = ?$<br><br>$K = 3B$<br><br>$K+5 = 2(B+5)$<br>$(3B)+5 = 2(B+5)$<br>$3B+5 = 2B+10$<br>$B = 5$<br><br>Bill is 5 years old. |

To help you translate, here are several phrases commonly found in word problems to describe mathematical relationships. Study this list.

# Common Word Problem Phrases

## Addition

Add, Sum, Total (of parts), More Than: +

The sum of $x$ and $y$: $x + y$

The sum of the three funds combined: $a + b + c$

If Anuj were 50 years older: $a + 50$

Six pounds heavier than Dave: $d + 6$

A group of men and women: $m + w$

The cost is marked up: $c + m$

## Subtraction

Minus, Difference, Less Than: −

$x$ minus five: $x - 5$

The positive difference between Quentin's and Rachel's heights (if Quentin is taller): $q - r$

Four pounds less than expected: $e - 4$

The profit is the revenue minus the cost: $P = R - C$

## Multiplication

The product of $h$ and $k$: $h \times k$

The number of reds times the number of blues: $r \times b$

One-fifth of $y$: $\left(\dfrac{1}{5}\right) \times y$

$n$ persons have $x$ beads each: total number of beads $= nx$

## Ratios and Division

Quotient, Per, Ratio, Proportion: $\div$ or $/$

Five dollars every two weeks: $\left(\dfrac{5 \text{ dollars}}{2 \text{ weeks}}\right)$ ⟶ 2.5 dollars a week

The ratio of $x$ to $y$: $\dfrac{x}{y}$

The proportion of girls to boys: $\dfrac{g}{b}$

## Average or Mean (sum of terms divided by the total number of terms)

$$\text{Average} = \frac{\text{Sum}}{\text{\# of terms}}$$

The average of $a$ and $b$: $\dfrac{a+b}{2}$

The average salary of the three doctors: $\dfrac{x+y+z}{3}$

A student's average score on 5 tests was 87: $\dfrac{\text{sum}}{5} = 87$ or $\dfrac{a+b+c+d+e}{5} = 87$

# Check Your Skills

1.  The total weight of two jugs of milk is 2.2 kilograms. The lighter jug weighs 0.4 kilogram less than the heavier jug. What is the weight of the lighter jug?

2.  Jan makes a salary of $10,000 per month for 3 months. Then her salary drops to $6,000 per month. After 9 months at $6,000 per month, what will Jan's average (arithmetic mean) monthly pay be for the whole period?

*Answers can be found on page 387.*

ⓜ **MANHATTAN** PREP

# Express Revenue as Price × Quantity

The GMAT expects you to know certain basic money relationships. Try this example:

> At a certain store, 7 shirts cost $63. If each shirt costs the same amount, what is the cost of 3 shirts, in dollars?

Solve the problem methodically. First, what is the question specifically asking for? It's asking for the total cost to buy 3 shirts, in dollars (represented by $). This cost for the consumer can also be thought of as revenue for the company selling the shirts.

What are you given? You are given the cost of 7 shirts ($63); again, this cost to the buyer represents revenue for the seller. You are also told that every shirt has the same price, and you are given another quantity of shirts to care about (3).

When every unit of something has the same price, you can use this equation:

**Total revenue = Price × Quantity**

This can also be written: **Total cost to consumer = Price × Quantity**

Name the variables $R$ for revenue (in this case, you can also use $C$ for cost, since that's what the problem says), $P$ for price, and $Q$ for quantity.

$$C = P \times Q$$

What is the question asking for again? It asks for the total cost of 3 shirts. In other words, the question asks for the value of $C$ when $Q = 3$:

$$C = P \times 3 = ?$$

To find $C$, then, you need $P$—the price of each shirt. Price is always in dollars *per unit*. It is the cost of one unit of whatever is being sold or bought—in this case, shirts.

How can you find the price of each shirt? You know something else related to the price: "...7 shirts costs $63."

This is another instance of Total cost to consumer = Price × Quantity. You have a different quantity (7) and a different total cost ($63), but the problem says that the price per shirt is always the same. So $P$ is the same in both equations.

Set up a second equation:

$$\$63 = P \times 7$$

Next, solve for $P$, the price per shirt.

$$63 = P \times 7$$
$$\frac{63}{7} = P$$
$$9 = P$$

Therefore, $P = 9$, so each shirt costs $9.

Finally, solve the other equation for the total cost of 3 shirts by substituting 9 for $P$.

$$C = P \times 3$$
$$C = 9 \times 3$$
$$C = 27$$

The total cost of 3 shirts is $27.

Here's how the problem would look from the store's point of view.

> A certain store sold 7 shirts for $63. If every shirt has the same price, how much revenue, in dollars, would the store receive from selling 3 shirts?

The answer is the same: $27. Instead of Total cost, write Total revenue.

> Total revenue = Price × Quantity

Or, you can focus on the units. The total on the left is in dollars, while the price is in dollars per shirt.

$$\text{Total money (\$)} = \text{Price}\left(\frac{\$}{\text{shirt}}\right) \times \text{Quantity (shirts)}$$

Try a more complicated example.

> Five apples and four bananas cost $2.10, while three apples and two bananas cost $1.20. If the cost of each apple is the same, and if the cost of each banana is the same, what is the cost of two apples and one banana?

Take this one step at a time.

The cost of five apples and four bananas is $2.10. This $2.10 is a whole made up of two parts: the cost of five apples and the cost of four bananas. Each of *those* costs is a price times a quantity. Set up an equation:

| **Total Cost** | = | **Price × Quantity** | + | **Price × Quantity** |
|---|---|---|---|---|
| | | for apples | | for bananas |

What are you given? You are given the cost of five apples and four bananas ($2.10). You are also given the cost of three apples and two bananas ($1.20).

Furthermore, you are told that the cost (or price) of each apple is the same, and likewise for bananas. These last facts allow you to use the Total cost = Price × Quantity relationship.

What are you asked for? The total cost of two apples and a banana.

The simplest unknowns to name are the price (or cost) of one apple and the price of one banana. Call these $A$ for apple and $B$ for banana. You're going to write everything in terms of these unknowns.

For each total cost you are given, write a separate equation.

| | Total Cost | | Price × Quantity | | Price × Quantity | | |
|---|---|---|---|---|---|---|---|
| | $2.10 | = | $A \times 5$ | + | $B \times 4$ | = | $5A + 4B$ |
| | $1.20 | = | $A \times 3$ | + | $B \times 2$ | = | $3A + 2B$ |

You are looking for the cost of two apples and a banana: $A \times 2 + B \times 1 = 2A + B = ?$

Solve for $A$ and $B$. Try combining the equations. First, multiply the second equation by 2.

Equation 1:                            Equation 2:

$2.10 = 5A + 4B$                   $2(1.20) = (3A + 2B)2$

$2.40 = 6A + 4B$

Now subtract the first equation from the second.

$$
\begin{array}{rcl}
2.40 & = & 6A + 4B \\
-(2.10 & = & 5A + 4B) \\
\hline
0.30 & = & A
\end{array}
$$

Plug back into one of the original equations to solve for $B$.

$1.20 = 3A + 2B$          $\longrightarrow$

$$
\begin{array}{rcl}
1.20 & = & 3(0.30) + 2B \\
1.20 & = & 0.90 + 2B \\
0.30 & = & 2B \\
0.15 & = & B
\end{array}
$$

Finally, answer the question.

$2A + B = 2(0.30) + (0.15) = 0.60 + 0.15 = 0.75$

The cost of two apples and one banana is $0.75.

Sometimes the price is known and the quantity is not. The cost in dollars of $x$ books priced at $12 each is $12x$. Notice that $12x$ is also the cost of 12 pens, if each pen costs $x$. When you write the total cost as a product of price and quantity, keep track of which is which.

Occasionally, you encounter an up-front **fixed cost**. Cell phone minutes used to be priced this way: You had a fixed cost per call (including the first 2 or 3 minutes), and then you paid for additional minutes at a certain price per minute. The equation looks like this:

**Total cost**     =     **Fixed cost**     +     **Price** × *Additional* **quantity**

Consider this example:

> The charge to reserve a box seat at Colossus Stadium is $1,000, which includes attendance at two games, plus $300 for each additional game attended. If Sam wants to spend no more than $4,000 on his box seat at Colossus Stadium, what is the maximum number of games he can attend?

What is the question looking for? The maximum number of games that Sam can attend. Call that $n$.

What information are you given? You are told that the cost to reserve a box seat is $1,000 (which includes two games), plus $300 each additional game. You are also told that Sam wants to spend no more than $4,000 on his seat.

Sam attends $n$ games in all, but he had passes for two of them (included in the $1,000 up front).

So he attends $n - 2$ games at the $300 ticket price.

Finally, this is an inequality: Sam wants to spend less than or equal to $4,000. Set up an equation:

| **Fixed cost** | | **Price $\times$ _Additional_ quantity** | $\leq$ | **Total cost** |
|---|---|---|---|---|
| $1,000 | + | $300 $\times (n - 2)$ | $\leq$ | $4,000 |

Next, solve for $n$.

$$1,000 + 300(n - 2) \leq 4,000$$
$$300(n - 2) \leq 3,000$$
$$n - 2 \leq 10$$
$$n \leq 12$$

At most, Sam can attend 12 total games.

Last but not least, don't forget this classic relationship:

**Profit = Revenues − Costs**

This one shows up in business school quite a bit, of course! You also need it on the GMAT, sometimes in combination with the other relationships above.

| If you... | Then you... | Like this: |
|---|---|---|
| Encounter a money relationship: "The cost of 8 watches is $1,200..." | Write the equation: Total Cost = Price $\times$ Quantity, including more items or a fixed cost as necessary | $P$ = Price of one watch <br> $1,200 = P \times 8$ <br> $1,200 = 8P$ <br> $150 = P$ <br><br> One watch costs $150. |

## Check Your Skills

3. A candy shop sold 50 candy bars in January for $3 each. In February, the shop increased the price by $1, but its revenue from candy bar sales only increased by $10. By how many units did the number of candy bars sold decrease from January to February?

4. At a particular store, seven staplers and five coffee mugs cost $36, while two staplers and one coffee mug cost $10. If each stapler costs the same, and if each coffee mug costs the same, how much more does a stapler cost than a coffee mug?

*Answers can be found on pages 388.*

# Add Units: Add Apples to Apples

When you solve pure algebra problems, the numbers don't represent anything in particular. In contrast, word problems have a context. Every number has a meaning. That is, every number has a natural **unit** attached.

Up to this point, the units have worked out naturally. For instance, in the steel rod question (on page 367), all the lengths were already in meters, so you could ignore the units.

$$S + L = 50 \qquad S + 14 = L$$
$$\text{meters} \quad \text{meters} \quad \text{meters} \qquad \text{meters} \quad \text{meters} \quad \text{meters}$$

If some units were meters and others were feet, you couldn't add or subtract them. *When you add or subtract quantities, they must have exactly the same units.*

What is $2 plus 45 cents, if $1 = 100 cents? Choose a common unit. It doesn't matter which one you pick, but you must express both quantities in that same unit before you add.

$$2 + 0.45 = 2.45 \qquad 200 + 45 = 245$$
$$\text{dollars} \quad \text{dollars} \quad \text{dollars} \qquad \text{cents} \quad \text{cents} \quad \text{cents}$$

*The result has the same unit as the original quantities.* When you add or subtract units, the units do not change. For example:

$$\text{meters} + \text{meters} = \text{meters} \quad \text{dollars} - \text{dollars} = \text{dollars} \quad \text{puppies} + \text{puppies} = \text{puppies}$$

# Multiply and Divide Units: Treat Them Just Like Numbers or Variables

In contrast, when you multiply units, the result has a different unit. A good example is area.

If a room is 6 feet long and 9 feet wide, what is the area of the room?

Area is length times width, so multiply:

Area = 6 feet × 9 feet = 54...

What happens to the feet? "Feet" times "feet" equals "feet *squared*." Therefore:

$$\text{Area} = 6 \text{ feet} \times 9 \text{ feet} = 54 \text{ feet squared} = 54 \text{ feet}^2 = 54 \text{ square feet}$$

*If you multiply two quantities that each have units, multiply the units, too.*

Not every multiplication in a word problem changes the units. If Alex is twice as old as Brenda, in years, then you can represent that relationship like so:

$$\begin{array}{ccccc} \text{A} & = & 2 & \times & \text{B} \\ \text{years} & & & & \text{years} \end{array}$$

The word *twice* has no units (it just means *two times*, or $2 \times$).

Some units are naturally ratios of other units. Look for the words *per, a, for every,* and so on.

$$3 \text{ books a week} = 3\,\frac{\text{books}}{\text{week}} \qquad\qquad 17 \text{ miles per gallon} = 17\,\frac{\text{miles}}{\text{gallon}}$$

Prices and averages often have units that are ratios of other units.

$$9 \text{ dollars a shirt} \;=\; 9\,\frac{\text{dollars}}{\text{shirt}} \qquad\qquad 100 \text{ donuts per day} \;=\; 100\,\frac{\text{donuts}}{\text{day}}$$

The average formula actually shows the division of units.

$$\text{Average donuts per day} = \frac{\text{Total donuts}}{\text{Total days}}$$

Likewise, the Total cost relationship demonstrates that *units cancel in the same way as numbers and variables do.*

$$\text{Total cost} = \text{Price} \times \text{Quantity}$$

$$\text{dollars} = \frac{\text{dollars}}{\text{shirt}} \times \text{shirts}$$

The units match on both sides of the equation, because you can cancel the "shirt" unit just as you would with anything else in its place.

$$\text{dollars} = \frac{\text{dollars}}{\cancel{\text{shirt}}} \times \cancel{\text{shirts}}$$

This cancellation property allows you to convert from a larger to a smaller unit, or vice versa. Try another example:

How many minutes are in two days?

First, convert 2 days into hours: 1 day = 24 hours. You could convert 2 days to 48 hours in your head, but do it on paper with unit cancellation:

$$2 \text{ days} \times \frac{24 \text{ hours}}{1 \text{ day}} = 48 \text{ hours} \qquad \cancel{\text{days}} \times \frac{\text{hours}}{\cancel{\text{day}}} = \text{hours}$$

Notice that the "day" unit cancels, leaving you with "hours" on top. The fraction you use to multiply is called a *conversion factor*. It's a fancy form of the number 1, because the top (24 hours) equals the bottom (1 day). When you write conversion factors, put the units in place first so that they cancel correctly. Then place the corresponding numbers so that the top equals the bottom.

Keep going to minutes. Set up the conversion factor using 60 minutes = 1 hour.

$$48 \text{ hours} \times \frac{60 \text{ minutes}}{1 \text{ hour}} = 2{,}880 \text{ minutes} \qquad \cancel{\text{hrs}} \times \frac{\text{min}}{\cancel{\text{hr}}} = \text{min}$$

By the way, always write out at least a few letters for every unit. "Hours" can be "hr," and "minutes" can be "min," but never write "h" or "m." You might confuse a single letter for a variable.

You can do two or more conversions in one step:

$$2 \text{ days} \times \frac{24 \text{ hours}}{1 \text{ day}} \times \frac{60 \text{ minutes}}{1 \text{ hour}} = 2{,}880 \text{ minutes} \qquad \cancel{\text{days}} \times \frac{\cancel{\text{hrs}}}{\cancel{\text{day}}} \times \frac{\text{min}}{\cancel{\text{hr}}} = \text{min}$$

A common conversion is between miles and kilometers. You don't have to know that 1 mile is approximately 1.6 kilometers; the GMAT will give you this information. However, you will have to be able to use this information to convert between these units. For example:

A distance is 30 miles. What is the approximate distance in kilometers? (1 mile = 1.6 kilometers)

Multiply the given distance by the conversion factor, which you should set up to cancel units.

$$30 \text{ miles} \times \frac{1.6 \text{ kilometers}}{1 \text{ mile}} = 48 \text{ kilometers} \qquad \cancel{\text{miles}} \times \frac{\text{km}}{\cancel{\text{miles}}} = \text{km}$$

| If you... | Then you... | Like this: |
|---|---|---|
| Add or subtract quantities with units | Ensure that the units are the same, converting first if necessary | 30 minutes + 2 hours <br> = 30 min + 120 min <br> = 150 min <br> *or* <br> $= \frac{1}{2} \text{ hr} + 2 \text{ hr} = 2\frac{1}{2} \text{ hr}$ |
| Multiply quantities with units | Multiply the units, canceling as appropriate | $10 \frac{\text{bagels}}{\text{hr}} \times 3 \text{ hrs} = 30 \text{ bagels}$ |
| Want to convert from one unit to another | Multiply by a conversion factor and cancel | $20 \text{ min} \times \frac{60 \text{ sec}}{1 \text{ min}} = 1{,}200 \text{ sec}$ |

## Check Your Skills

5.  How many hours are there in two weeks? Do this problem with conversion factors.
6.  How long after midnight is 1:04am, in seconds?

*Answers can be found on pages 388–389.*

# Rate × Time: Distance, Follow the Units

A **rate**, or speed, can be expressed in "miles per hour" $\left(\dfrac{\text{miles}}{\text{hour}}\right)$ or in "feet per second" $\left(\dfrac{\text{feet}}{\text{sec}}\right)$. In other words, the

unit of this kind of rate is a *distance* unit (*miles*, *feet*) divided by a *time* unit (*hour*, *second*).

$$\text{Rate} = \frac{\text{Distance}}{\text{Time}} \qquad\qquad 60 \text{ miles per hour} = \frac{60 \text{ miles}}{1 \text{ hour}}$$

You also can rearrange this relationship to isolate distance on one side.

$$\text{Rate} \times \text{Time} = \text{Distance} \qquad\qquad 60 \, \frac{\text{miles}}{\text{hour}} \times 1 \text{ hour} = 60 \text{ miles}$$

This version is very similar to the Total cost equation:

$$\text{Price} \times \text{Quantity} = \text{Total cost/Revenue} \qquad\qquad 9 \, \frac{\text{dollars}}{\text{shirt}} \times 4 \text{ shirts} = 36 \text{ dollars}$$

A price is a kind of rate, too, because it's *per* something. In distance problems, most rates are *per* time, but occasionally, you see a rate *per* something else, such as miles per gallon.

Avoid expressing rates as time divided by distance. Instead, *always put time in the denominator*. It doesn't matter how the words are expressed. "It took Joe 4 hours to go 60 miles" means that Joe's rate was 60 miles ÷ 4 hours, or 15 miles per hour.

You can combine the Rate × Time = Distance relationship with other relationships already covered. For instance, you have worked with the average formula, as in the "donuts per day" problem:

$$\text{Average donuts per day} = \frac{\text{Total donuts}}{\text{Total days}}$$

The same formula works for rates as well.

$$\text{Average miles per hour} = \frac{\text{Total miles}}{\text{Total hours}}$$

To get the totals on the top and bottom, you often need another relationship you're familiar with:

Part + Part = Whole

Miles for first part of a trip + Miles for second part = Total miles

Hours for first part of a trip + Hours for second part = Total hours

Try this problem:

Nancy takes 2 hours to bike 12 kilometers from home to school. If she bikes back home by the same route at a rate of 4 kilometers per hour, what is her average speed, in kilometers per hour, for the entire trip?

Be careful. The average rate for a journey is the *total* distance divided by the *total* time. Do not simply take an average of the rates given.

You are asked for the average rate for the whole trip. Call this *a* and write an equation.

Average kilometers per hour = *a*                  $a = \dfrac{\text{Total kilometers}}{\text{Total hours}}$

Do you know either of the missing numbers on the right? Yes. You can figure out the total kilometers. The route from home to school is 12 kilometers, and Nancy comes home by the *same* route, so the total kilometers is equal to 12 + 12 = 24. This is Part + Part = Whole.

$$a = \frac{24}{\text{Total hours}}$$

Now, to find the total time in hours, use Part + Part = Whole again.

Total hours = Hours spent on the first part of the trip + Hours spent on the second part

Do you know either of *these* numbers? Yes—you have the first number directly from the problem.

Total hours = 2 hours + Hours spent on the second part

What do you know about the second part of the trip? You know that Nancy's rate was 4 kilometers per hour. You also know that this route was the *same* as for the first leg—so the distances are equal. It's easy to miss this information. Whenever the GMAT says "the same," pay attention! It always represents an equation.

Write Rate × Time = Distance again, this time just for the second leg of the journey.

Rate × Time = Distance                  $4 \dfrac{\text{kilometers}}{\text{hour}} \times \text{Time (hours)} = 12 \text{ kilometers}$

You now have enough to solve. Call this time *t*.

$$4t = 12$$
$$t = 3$$

9

Plug into the previous equation to find the total time spent on the trip.

Total hours = 2 hours + Hours spent on the second part

Total hours = 2 hours + 3 hours

Total hours = 5 hours

Finally, plug into the first equation you wrote.

$$a = \frac{24}{\text{Total hours}} = \frac{24}{5} = 4.8$$

Nancy's average rate for the whole trip is 4.8 kilometers per hour.

Rate problems can become tricky when you have to use the same relationship repeatedly (Rate × Time = Distance). To keep the various rates, times, and distances straight, you might use subscripts or even whole words.

$t_1 = 2$ hours          $t_2 = 3$ hours          Time #1 = 2 hrs          Time #2 = 3 hrs

If you have more than one time in the problem, then using $t$ everywhere for every time is likely to lead to mistakes. Tables or grids can help keep quantities straight.

| If you... | Then you... | Like this: |
|---|---|---|
| See a rate problem | Use Rate × Time = Distance, putting in units to keep the math correct | $7\ \dfrac{\text{miles}}{\text{hr}} \times 3\ \text{hrs} = 21\ \text{miles}$ |

## Check Your Skills

7. Amanda ran 24 miles at a rate of 3 miles per hour, then took 4 hours to run an additional 6 miles. What was her average speed for the entire run?

*Answer can be found on page 389.*

# Rate × Time: Work, Define the Work Unit and Add Rates

Work problems are very similar to Rate-Time-Distance problems. The main difference is that work takes the place of distance.

Rate × Time = Distance                    Rate × Time = Work

$20\ \dfrac{\text{miles}}{\text{hour}} \times 3\ \text{hours} = 60\ \text{miles}$          $20\ \dfrac{\text{chairs}}{\text{hour}} \times 3\ \text{hours} = 60\ \text{chairs}$

*Define work by the task done.* It could be building chairs, painting houses, manufacturing soda cans, etc. One unit of output (chairs, houses, cans) is one unit of work.

If the "job" is to paint a house or fill a warehouse, you can still call that one: filling the warehouse once is one unit of output. Occasionally, it can be helpful to invent small units of work ("widgets") so that you avoid dealing with fractions. If the problem references "half a warehouse per day," say that a warehouse contains 10 boxes. The rate then becomes 5 boxes per day.

Again, always put time in the denominator. "It takes Sally 3 minutes to build a chair" should be translated as 1 chair per 3 minutes. As a rate, this translates to $\frac{1}{3}$ of a chair per minute.

$$\text{Rate} = 1 \text{ chair per 3 minutes} \qquad\qquad \text{Rate} = \frac{1 \text{ chair}}{3 \text{ minutes}} = \frac{1}{3} \text{ chair per minute}$$

If two people or machines work at the same time side by side, you can *add* their rates. Try this example:

> Jay can build a chair in 3 hours. Kay can build a chair in 5 hours. How long will it take both of them, working together, to build 8 chairs?

First, focus on Jay. What is his rate of work? Put time in the denominator.

$$\text{Jay's rate} = \frac{1 \text{ chair}}{3 \text{ hours}} = \frac{1}{3} \text{ chair per hour}$$

In 1 hour, Jay can build $\frac{1}{3}$ of a chair.

Now, figure out Kay's rate of work.

$$\text{Kay's rate} = \frac{1 \text{ chair}}{5 \text{ hours}} = \frac{1}{5} \text{ chair per hour}$$

In 1 hour, Kay can build $\frac{1}{5}$ of a chair.

Together, then, Jay and Kay can build $\frac{1}{3} + \frac{1}{5}$ of a chair in an hour. This is the "adding rates" principle in action.

Simplify the sum of fractions.

$$\overset{5}{\underset{3}{\cancel{\frac{1}{3}}}} \overset{+}{\underset{+}{\times}} \overset{3}{\underset{5}{\cancel{\frac{1}{5}}}} = \frac{8}{15} \text{ chair per hour}$$

Together, Jay and Kay build $\frac{8}{15}$ of a chair in 1 hour.

Now use the full Rate × Time = Work equation. The Work is 8 chairs. The Time is unknown. Therefore:

$$\text{Rate} \times \text{Time} = \text{Work}$$

$$\frac{8}{15} \times T = 8 \text{ chairs}$$

$$T = 8\left(\frac{15}{8}\right)$$

$$T = 15$$

It takes Jay and Kay, working together, 15 hours to build 8 chairs.

As with Rate-Time-Distance problems, keep the various quantities separate. If you need to use the same equation more than once, distinguish the different cases clearly. For instance, there could be three cases in this problem: Jay working alone, Kay working alone, or the two of them working together.

| If you... | Then you... | Like this: |
|---|---|---|
| See a work problem | Use Rate × Time = Work, choosing work units and often adding rates | $7 \dfrac{\text{goblets}}{\text{hr}} \times 3 \text{ hrs} = 21 \text{ goblets}$ |

## Check Your Skills

8.  It takes Albert 6 hours to build a shelf. Betty can do the same work twice as fast. How many shelves can Albert and Betty, working together, build in a 24-hour period?

*Answer can be found on pages 389–390.*

# Fractions and Percents in Word Problems: *Of* Means *Times*

Many word problems involve fractional amounts or percents. Remember that word problems always have a real context. This means that fractional amounts are fractional amounts *of* something. Percents are percents *of* something. Neither fractions nor percents live in a vacuum.

As you already know, *of* means *times* in the context of fractions and percents. Try an example:

At a birthday party, children can choose one of the following 3 flavors of ice cream: chocolate, vanilla, or strawberry. If $\dfrac{1}{2}$ of the children choose chocolate, 20% of the children choose vanilla, and the remaining 15 children choose strawberry, how many children are at the party?

First, identify what the question wants. It asks for the total number of kids at the party. Label that number $n$.

The problem contains a Part + Part = Whole relationship—or rather, Part + Part + Part = Whole.

Kids who choose chocolate + Kids who choose vanilla + Kids who choose strawberry = Total kids

Replace all of these with variables for the moment.

$c + v + s = n$

The question gives you $s$ directly. It tells you 15 kids choose strawberry, so this can be put in your equation:

$c + v + 15 = n$

How many kids choose chocolate? You don't have an absolute number, but you know that $\frac{1}{2}$ of the kids choose this flavor. To emphasize the point, you can say that $\frac{1}{2}$ of *all* kids choose chocolate. Express this as an equation.

$\frac{1}{2}$ of all kids choose chocolate             $\frac{1}{2}n = c$

Note that the verb—in this case, *choose*—represents the equals sign.

Likewise, 20% of the kids (all kids) choose vanilla.

20% of all kids choose vanilla                $0.2n = v$

Rewrite $\frac{1}{2}n$ as $0.5n$. Replace $c$ and $v$ in the main Part + Part + Part equation.

$c + v + 15 = n$

$0.5n + 0.2n + 15 = n$

Now solve for $n$.

$$0.7n + 15 = n$$
$$15 = 0.3n$$
$$150 = 3n$$
$$50 = n$$

There are 50 kids at the party.

| If you… | Then you… | Like this: |
|---|---|---|
| See a fraction or a percent in a word problem | Figure out what the fraction or percent is *of*, and write *of* as *times*. The verb in the sentence represents the equals sign. | $\frac{1}{2}$ of kids choose chocolate $\frac{1}{2}n = c$ 20% of kids choose vanilla $0.2n = v$ |

## Check Your Skills

9. Every junior at Central High School studies exactly one language: 75 percent of the juniors study Gaelic, one-sixth of the juniors study Spanish, and the other 7 juniors study Tagalog. How many juniors are there at Central High School?

*Answer can be found on page 390.*

# Check Your Skills Answer Key

1. **0.9 kg:** First, translate the information in the question stem. Then, use algebra rules to solve for the weight of the lighter jug.

$$H = \text{weight heavy}$$
$$L = \text{weight light} = ?$$

| | |
|---|---|
| $H + L = 2.2$ | "The total weight...is 2.2 kilograms." |
| $L = H - 0.4$ | "The lighter jug weighs 0.4 kilogram less than the heavier jug." |
| $L + 0.4 = H$ | Rearrange. |
| $H + L = 2.2$ | Substitute. |
| $(L + 0.4) + L = 2.2$ | |
| $2L + 0.4 = 2.2$ | Simplify. |
| $2L = 1.8$ | |
| $L = 0.9$ | |

2. **$7,000 per month:** First, translate. When the problem mentions something for which you know a standard formula (in this case average), write down that standard formula. Also, when the problem has multiple time periods, organize the information carefully.

First 3 months:

$$\text{Average monthly pay} = \frac{\text{Total pay for 3 months}}{\text{Months}}$$

$$\$10,000 = \frac{\text{Total pay for 3 months}}{3}$$

The total pay for the first 3 months is $10,000 \times 3 = \$30,000$.

Last 9 months:

$$\text{Average monthly pay} = \frac{\text{Total pay for 9 months}}{\text{Months}}$$

$$\$6,000 = \frac{\text{Total pay for 9 months}}{9 \text{ months}}$$

The total pay for the last 9 months is $6,000 \times 9 = \$54,000$.

Next, set up the formula to find the average for the overall 12-month period and solve.

$$\text{Average monthly pay} = \frac{\text{Total pay for all months}}{\text{All months}}$$

$$\text{Average monthly pay} = \frac{30,000 + 54,000}{3 + 9}$$

$$\text{Average} = \frac{\overset{7}{\cancel{84}},000}{\cancel{12}} = 7,000$$

3.  **10:** The candy shop sold 50 candy bars in January, but only 40 in February, for a decrease of 10 candy bars. Here's how to do the math:

January: Total revenue = Price × Quantity = $3 per bar × 50 bars = $150

February: New price = Old price + $1 = $3 + $1 = $4 per bar

New total revenue = Old revenue + $10 = $150 + $10 = $160

| Total revenue | = | Price × Quantity |
|---|---|---|
| $160 | = | $4 per bar × $Q$ bars |
| 40 candy bars | = | $Q$ |

January Qty − February Qty = 50 bars − 40 bars = 10 bars

4.  **$4:** If the price of one stapler is $S$ and the price of one coffee mug is $C$, then $S - C$ represents the difference in price between the two items. In other words, the question is, "What is $S - C$?"

Translate the rest of the math in the question stem.

$$7S + 5C = \$36 \qquad 2S + C = \$10 \qquad S - C = ?$$

When you're asked for a combo, or combination of variables, examine the equations to see whether you can solve directly for the entire combo (in this case, $S - C$). That's faster than finding $S$ and $C$ individually.

Take a look at what happens when you multiply the second equation by 4.

$$2S + C = 10$$

$$8S + 4C = 40$$

Subtract the first equation from the new second equation.

$$
\begin{array}{rcl}
8S + 4C & = & 40 \\
-(7S + 5C & = & 36) \\
\hline
S - C & = & 4
\end{array}
$$

A stapler costs $4 more than a coffee mug. You might be thinking that you would never think to do this yourself. Now that you know it's possible, though, you can think about it. In the future, take a moment to examine the equations to see whether this shortcut exists. It often does! If not, you can solve for the variables individually, with substitution or elimination.

5.  **336 hours:**

1 week = 7 days

$$2 \text{ weeks} \times \frac{7 \text{ days}}{1 \text{ week}} = 14 \text{ days} \qquad\qquad \cancel{\text{weeks}} \times \frac{\text{days}}{\cancel{\text{week}}} = \text{days}$$

1 day = 24 hours

$$14 \text{ days} \times \frac{24 \text{ hours}}{1 \text{ day}} = 336 \text{ hours} \qquad \cancel{\text{days}} \times \frac{\text{hours}}{\cancel{\text{day}}} = \text{hours}$$

Or, in one line:

$$2 \text{ weeks} \times \frac{7 \text{ days}}{1 \text{ week}} \times \frac{24 \text{ hours}}{1 \text{ day}} = 336 \text{ hours}$$

6. **3,840 seconds:** Convert 1 hour to seconds and 4 minutes to seconds.

$$1 \text{ hours} \times \frac{60 \text{ minutes}}{1 \text{ hour}} \times \frac{60 \text{ seconds}}{1 \text{ minute}} = 3,600 \text{ seconds}$$

$$4 \text{ minutes} \times \frac{60 \text{ seconds}}{1 \text{ minute}} = 240 \text{ seconds}$$

3,600 seconds + 240 seconds = 3,840 seconds

7. **2.5 miles per hour:** To find Amanda's average speed, find the total distance and the total time.

Total distance = 24 miles + 6 miles = 30 miles
Total time = time for first part of trip + 4 hours

Now find the time Amanda took for the first part of the trip.

Rate × Time = Distance
3 miles per hour × $t$ = 24 miles
$t$ = 8 hours

The total time is 8 + 4 = 12 hours. Finally, calculate her average speed.

$$\text{Average} = \frac{\text{Total distance}}{\text{Total time}}$$

$$a = \frac{30 \text{ miles}}{12 \text{ hours}} = 2.5 \text{ miles per hour}$$

8. **12:** First, find Albert's rate, using the formula Rate × Time = Work.

$$r \times 6 \text{ hours} = 1 \text{ shelf}$$
$$r = \frac{1 \text{ shelf}}{6 \text{ hours}}$$

Albert's rate is $\frac{1}{6}$ shelf per hour.

Betty can work twice as fast, so her rate is $2 \times \frac{1}{6} = \frac{1}{3}$ shelf per hour.

Add the rates to find their combined rate:

$$\frac{1}{6} + \frac{1}{3} = \frac{1}{6} + \frac{2}{6} = \frac{3}{6} = \frac{1}{2}$$

Together, they can build $\frac{1}{2}$ of a shelf per hour. Finally, calculate how much work is completed in 24 hours at their combined rate:

$$\frac{1}{2} \text{ shelf per hour} \times 24 \text{ hours} = 12 \text{ shelves}$$

9. **84:** Define variables and translate the information.

> $G$ = the number of juniors studying Gaelic
> $S$ = the number of juniors studying Spanish
> $T$ = the number of juniors studying Tagalog
> $J$ = the total number of juniors

$J$ = total number of juniors = $G + S + T = ?$

75% of juniors study Gaelic: $\frac{3}{4}J = G$

One-sixth of juniors study Spanish: $\frac{1}{6}J = S$

The other 7 study Tagalog: $7 = T$

Now substitute these values into the equation $G + S + T = J$, and solve for $J$.

$$\frac{3}{4}J + \frac{1}{6}J + 7 = J$$

$$\frac{9}{12}J + \frac{2}{12}J + 7 = J$$

$$\frac{11}{12}J + 7 = J$$

$$7 = J - \frac{11}{12}J$$

$$7 = \frac{1}{12}J$$

$$(7)(12) = J$$

$$84 = J$$

# Chapter Review: Drill Sets

## Drill 1

Translate and solve the following problems.

1.  In an office, there are 5 more computers than there are employees. If there are 10 employees in the office, how many computers are there?

2.  If −5 is 7 more than $z$, what is $\dfrac{z}{4}$?

3.  Two conference rooms have a combined capacity of 75 people. Conference Room A can accommodate 15 fewer people than Conference Room B. How many people can Conference Room B accommodate?

4.  Norman is 12 years older than Michael. In 6 years, he will be twice as old as Michael. How old is Norman now?

5.  Three lawyers each earn an average (arithmetic mean) of $300 per hour. How much money have they earned in total after each has worked 4 hours?

6.  A clothing store bought a container of 100 shirts for $20. If the store sold all of the shirts at $0.50 per shirt, what is the store's gross profit on the box?

7.  There are 2 trees in the front yard of a school. The trees have a combined height of 60 feet, and the taller tree is three times the height of the shorter tree. What is the height, in feet, of the shorter tree?

8.  Louise is three times as old as Mary. In 5 years, Louise will be twice as old as Mary. How old is Mary now?

9.  The average of 2, 13, and $x$ is 10. What is $x$?

10.  Four children collect 33 candies that fall out of a piñata. If 3 of the children pick up the same number of candies and the fourth child picks up three fewer candies than each of the other children, how many candies does the fourth child collect?

## Drill 2

Translate and solve the following problems.

11.  To put on a concert, a band pays $10,000 to rent a venue and another $15,000 for security; the band has no other costs. Attendees at the concert pay an average price of $40 for a ticket to the concert. If everyone who attends the concert must purchase a ticket, how many tickets must the band sell to make a gross profit of $7,000 on the concert?

12.  Toshi is 7 years older than his brother Kosuke, who is twice as old as their younger sister Junko. If Junko is 8 years old, how old is Toshi?

13. A plane leaves Chicago in the morning and makes 3 flights before returning. The plane traveled twice as far on the first flight as on the second flight, and the plane traveled three times as far on the second flight as on the third flight. If the third flight was 45 miles, how many miles was the first flight?

14. It costs a certain bicycle factory $10,000 to operate for one month, plus $300 for each bicycle produced during the month. Each of the bicycles sells for a retail price of $700. The gross profit of the factory is measured by total income from sales minus the production costs of the bicycles and the factory operation cost. If 50 bicycles are produced and sold during the month, what is the factory's gross profit?

15. Arnaldo earns $11 for each ticket that he sells, plus a bonus of $2 per ticket for each ticket he sells over the first 100 tickets. If Arnaldo was paid $2,400, how many tickets did he sell?

16. If the average (arithmetic mean) of the five numbers $x - 3$, $x$, $x + 3$, $x + 4$, and $x + 11$ is 45, what is the value of $x$?

17. Ten years ago, Sana was half as old as Byron. If Byron is now 15 years older than Sana, how old will Sana be in 7 years?

18. John buys 5 books with an average (arithmetic mean) price of $9. If John then buys another book with a price of $15, what is the average price of the 6 books?

19. Alicia is producing a magazine that costs $3 per magazine to print. In addition, she has to pay $10,500 to her staff to design the issue. If Alicia sells each magazine for $10, how many magazines must she sell to break even?

20. Every week, Renee is paid $40 per hour for the first 40 hours she works and $80 per hour for each hour she works after the first 40 hours. If she earned $2,000 last week, how many hours did she work?

## Drill 3

Translate and solve the following unit conversion problems.

21. An American football field is 100 yards long. What is this length in feet? (1 yard = 3 feet)

22. How many gallons of water would it take to fill a tank with a capacity of 200 pints? (1 gallon = 8 pints)

23. A 40 kilogram suitcase weighs how many pounds? (1 kilogram = 2.2 pounds)

24. Boston received 2.5 feet of snow yesterday. How many inches of snow did Boston receive? (1 foot = 12 inches)

25. What is the temperature in Fahrenheit when it is 30 degrees Celsius? $\left( C = \dfrac{5}{9}(F - 32) \right)$

26. How many minutes are there in 10 days?

27. On her bicycle, Miriam travels 50 yards in 10 seconds. How many feet does she travel in 2 minutes?
(1 yard = 3 feet)

   (A) 500
   (B) 900
   (C) 1,800

28. A recipe calls for 1.6 cups of sugar and 2 quarts of flour. How many gallons is the resulting mixture of sugar and flour? (1 gallon = 4 quarts; 1 quart = 4 cups) Leave your answer in decimal form. (For you chefs: ignore the difference between dry measures and liquid measures.)

29. How many 1-inch-square tiles would it take to cover the floor of a closet that has dimensions 5 feet by 4 feet? (1 foot = 12 inches)

30. A pool has sprung a leak and is losing water at a rate of 5 milliliters per second. How many liters of water is this pool losing per hour? (1 liter = 1,000 milliliters)

# Drill 4

Translate and solve the following rate problems.

31. Jiang drove away from Marksville at a constant speed of 64 miles per hour. How far was she from Marksville after 2 hours and 15 minutes of driving?

32. Tyrone began the drive from Billington to Camville at 7:30. He drove at a constant speed of 40 miles per hour for the first hour and 50 miles per hour after that. If the distance from Billington to Camville is 160 miles, at what time did Tyrone arrive in Camville?

   (A) 10:30
   (B) 10:54
   (C) 11:00

33. If Roger took 2 hours to walk to a store that is 3 miles away, and then ran home along the same path in 1 hour, what was Roger's average speed, in miles per hour, for the round trip?

34. Sue and Rob began running a 10-mile path around a lake at the same time. Sue ran at a constant rate of 8 miles per hour. Rob ran at a constant rate of $6\frac{2}{3}$ miles per hour. Sue finished running the 10-mile path how much sooner than Rob did?

35. Svetlana ran the first 5 kilometers of a 10-kilometer race at a speed of 12 kilometers per hour. At what speed will she have to run the last 5 kilometers of the race if she wants to complete the 10-kilometer race in 55 minutes?

# Drill 5

Translate and solve the following work problems.

36.  A factory must complete production of 1,400 plastic bottles in 4 hours. How many bottles must be produced per hour (at a constant rate) to meet this deadline?

37.  A standard machine can fill 15 gallons of paint per hour. A deluxe machine fills gallons of paint at twice the rate of a standard machine. How long will it take a deluxe machine to fill 150 gallons of paint?

38.  Machine A produces 15 widgets per minute. Machine B produces 18 widgets per minute. How many widgets will the machines produce together in 20 minutes?

39.  At 2:00pm, a hose was placed into an empty pool and turned on. The pool, which holds 680 gallons of water, reached its capacity at 5:24pm. How many gallons of water per hour did the hose add to the pool?

40.  Machine X, working alone at a constant rate, can produce a certain number of chocolates in 5 hours. Machine Y, working alone at a constant rate, can produce the same number of chocolates in 2 hours. If Machine X produces 180 chocolates per hour, how many chocolates does Machine Y produce per hour?
    (A) 72
    (B) 450
    (C) 900

# Drill 6

Translate and solve the following word problems.

41.  If Ken's salary were 20% higher, it would be 20% less than Lorena's. If Lorena's salary is $60,000, what is Ken's salary?

42.  A $10 shirt is marked up by 30%, then by an additional 50%. What is the new price of the shirt?

43.  A share of Stock Q increased in value by 20%, then decreased in value by 10%. The new value of a share of Stock Q is what percent of its initial value?

44.  In a class of 200 students, 40 students earned A's on their test, while 64 of the students received B's, 18 received D's, and 6 received F's. If students can receive only A, B, C, D, or F as grades, what percent of the students received C's?

45.  Akira currently weighs 160 pounds. If he must lose 8 pounds in order to qualify for a certain sporting event, what percent of his body weight must he lose in order to qualify?
    (A) 0.05%
    (B) 0.5%
    (C) 5%

**MANHATTAN** PREP

## Drill 7

Translate and solve the following word problems.

46. Lily stayed up all last night to watch a meteor shower from her roof. Ten percent of the meteors visible from her roof were exceptionally bright, and of these, 80 percent inspired Lily to write a haiku. If Lily was inspired to write a haiku by 20 exceptionally bright meteors, how many meteors were visible from her roof last night?

47. Bingwa the African elephant can lift 6% of his body weight using his trunk alone. If Bingwa weighs 1,000 times as much as a white-handed gibbon, how many gibbons can Bingwa lift at once with his trunk?

48. Last year, Country X received $\frac{7}{4}$ as much precipitation as Country Y, which received $\frac{2}{3}$ as much precipitation as Country Z. If Country X received 280 centimeters of precipitation, how much precipitation, in centimeters, did Country Z receive?

   (A) 160
   (B) 240
   (C) 420

49. In Farrah's workday playlist, $\frac{1}{3}$ of the songs are jazz, $\frac{1}{4}$ are R & B, $\frac{1}{6}$ are rock, $\frac{1}{12}$ are country, and the remainder are world music. What fraction of the songs in Farrah's playlist are world music?

50. At a music convention, $\frac{2}{5}$ of the attendees play no musical instrument, $\frac{1}{4}$ play exactly one musical instrument, $\frac{3}{10}$ play exactly two musical instruments, and the remaining 8 attendees play three or more musical instruments. How many people are attending the convention?

## Drill 8

Translate and solve the following word problems.

51. Yemi wants to buy a blue umbrella for no more than $25. At a certain store, $\frac{3}{5}$ of the umbrellas cost more than $25, and of the remaining umbrellas, $\frac{7}{8}$ are not blue. If the store has 400 umbrellas, how many of the umbrellas meet Yemi's requirements?

   (A) 20
   (B) 140
   (C) 210

52. To make one serving of her signature punch, Mariko mixes $\frac{1}{2}$ cup of grape juice, $\frac{3}{4}$ cup of passion fruit juice, and $\frac{1}{8}$ cup of sparkling water. If Mariko makes 22 cups of punch, how many servings of punch will there be?

   (A) 16

   (B) 20

   (C) 30

53. Of the movies in Santosh's collection, $\frac{1}{3}$ are animated features, $\frac{1}{4}$ are live-action features, and the remainder are documentaries. If $\frac{2}{5}$ of the documentaries are depressing, what fraction of the films in Santosh's collection are depressing documentaries?

54. Of all the homes on Gotham Street, $\frac{1}{3}$ are termite-ridden, and $\frac{3}{5}$ of these are collapsing. What fraction of the homes are termite-ridden, but NOT collapsing?

55. A bag contains only red and green marbles. Of these, $\frac{3}{4}$ of the marbles in the bag are green. Of the green marbles, $\frac{1}{3}$ are cracked. If there are 6,000 red marbles in the bag, how many cracked green marbles are there?

# Drill Sets Solutions

## Drill 1

1. **15 computers:** Let $c$ = the number of computers and $e$ = the number of employees.

   The "more…than" translation is tricky. Which are there more of, computers or employees? There are more computers, so add 5 to the smaller group, employees: $c = e + 5$. The bigger number equals the smaller number plus 5.

   $$c = e + 5$$
   $$e = 10$$
   $$c = (10) + 5 = 15$$

2. **−3:**

   $$-5 = z + 7$$
   $$-12 = z$$

   $$\frac{z}{4} = \frac{-12}{4} = -3$$

3. **45 people:** Let $a$ = the capacity of Conference Room A, and let $b$ = the capacity of Conference Room B.

   $$\text{Eq 1: } a + b = 75$$
   $$\text{Eq 2: } a = b - 15$$

   The second translation is tricky. Which room can hold more people, A or B? Room B is bigger, so subtract 15 from room B to get the capacity in room A.

   The second equation already isolates $a$. Substitute into the first equation, and solve for $b$.

   $$(b - 15) + b = 75$$
   $$2b - 15 = 75$$
   $$2b = 90$$
   $$b = 45$$

4. **18 years old:** Make a table to keep track of the two people and the two points in time.

   |         | Now | In 6 years |
   |---------|-----|------------|
   | Norman  | $N$ | $N + 6$    |
   | Michael | $M$ | $M + 6$    |

$$N = M + 12$$     Translate the first sentence into an equation.

$$(N + 6) = 2\,(M + 6)$$     Translate the second sentence into an equation. Use the ages in 6 years, not the ages now.

$$N - 12 = M$$     You want to solve for $N$, so rewrite the first equation to isolate the variable you *don't* want: $M$.

$$N + 6 = 2(N - 12 + 6)$$     Insert $N - 12$ for $M$ in the second equation and simplify.
$$N + 6 = 2(N - 6)$$
$$N + 6 = 2N - 12$$
$$18 = N$$

5. **$3,600:** The lawyers each earn the same amount, so calculate what one lawyer earns, then multiply by 3:

One lawyer earns:          $4 \times \$300 = \$1,200$

The three lawyers together earn:    $\$1,200 \times 3 = \$3,600$

6. **$30 profit:** Let $p$ = profit, $r$ = revenue, and $c$ = cost.

While the question specifies the cost of the 100 shirts, it doesn't give you the revenue directly; use Revenue = Price (per shirt) × Quantity (of shirts). Therefore:

$$\text{Profit} = \text{Revenue} - \text{Cost}$$
$$p = (\$0.50 \times 100) - (\$20)$$
$$p = \$50 - \$20$$
$$p = \$30$$

7. **15 feet:** Let $s$ = the height of the shorter tree and $t$ = the height of the taller tree. Translate the equations.

$$s + t = 60$$
$$3s = t$$

The second equation is already isolated for $t$; substitute into the first equation and solve.

$$s + (3s) = 60$$
$$4s = 60$$
$$s = 15$$

8. **5 years old:**

|  | Now | In 5 years |
|---|---|---|
| Louise | $L$ | $L + 5$ |
| Mary | $M$ | $M + 5$ |

$$L = 3M$$     Translate the first sentence into an equation.

$$(L + 5) = 2(M + 5)$$     Translate the second sentence into an equation.

$$(3M + 5) = 2(M + 5)$$     Insert $3M$ for $L$ in the second equation and solve.

$$3M + 5 = 2M + 10$$
$$M = 5$$

9. **15:**

$$\text{Average} = \frac{\text{Sum}}{\text{\# of terms}}$$

$$10 = \frac{2 + 13 + x}{3}$$

$$30 = 2 + 13 + x$$

$$30 = 15 + x$$

$$15 = x$$

10. **6 candies:** Let $c$ stand for each of the three children who pick up the same number of candies. Let $f$ stand for the fourth child. Therefore:

　　　Eq 1: $c + c + c + f = 33$ or $3c + f = 33$
　　　Eq 2: $f = c - 3$

If you substitute the second equation into the first, note that you will be solving for $c$, not $f$. Make sure to solve for $f$ at the end.

$$3c + f = 33$$
$$3c + (c - 3) = 33$$
$$4c = 36$$
$$c = 9$$

Therefore, $f = c - 3 = 9 - 3 = 6$.

Alternatively, you can rearrange the second equation to isolate $c$. The second equation becomes $f + 3 = c$. When you plug into the first equation, you will be able to solve directly for $f$.

$$3c + f = 33$$
$$3(f + 3) + f = 33$$
$$3f + 9 + f = 33$$
$$4f = 24$$
$$f = 6$$

# Drill 2

11. **750 tickets:** Let $n =$ the number of tickets sold. Recall that Profit = Revenue − Cost. The problem indicates that the band wants a profit of $7,000. What are the revenues and the costs? Set up what you know:

　　　Revenue: $40n$
　　　Costs: $10,000 + 15,000 = 25,000$
　　　Profit = 7,000

$$\text{Profit} = \text{Revenue} - \text{Cost}$$
$$7{,}000 = 40n - 25{,}000$$

$$32{,}000 = 40n$$

$$\frac{32{,}000}{40} = n$$

$$\frac{3{,}200}{4} = n \qquad \text{Divide top and bottom of fraction by 10.}$$

$$800 = n \qquad \text{Divide top and bottom of fraction by 4.}$$

12. **23 years old:** Let $T =$ Toshi's age, $K =$ Kosuke's age, and $J =$ Junko's age.

$$T = K + 7$$
$$K = 2J$$
$$J = 8$$

Substitute and solve.

$$K = 2 \times J = 2 \times (8) = 16$$
$$T = K + 7 = (16) + 7 = 23$$

13. **270 miles:** Let $F =$ the distance of the first flight, $S =$ the distance of the second flight, and $T =$ the distance of the third flight. What is $F$?

$F = 2S$       The first flight traveled twice as far as the second flight.

$S = 3T$       The second flight traveled three times as far as the third flight.

$T = 45$

Substitute and solve.

$$S = 3 \times (45) = 135$$
$$F = 2 \times (135) = 270$$

14. **$10,000 profit:** Recall that Profit = Revenue − Cost. Set up equations to find the revenues and costs?

$$\text{Revenue} = 50 \times 700 = 35{,}000$$
$$\text{Cost} = 10{,}000 + (50 \times 300) = 10{,}000 + 15{,}000 = 25{,}000$$
$$\text{Profit} = \text{Revenue} - \text{Cost} = 35{,}000 - 25{,}000 = 10{,}000$$

15. **200 tickets:** Let $x$ equal the total number of tickets sold. Therefore, $(x - 100)$ is equal to the number of tickets Arnoldo sold beyond the first 100.

$$11x + 2(x - 100) = 2{,}400$$
$$11x + 2x - 200 = 2{,}400$$
$$13x = 2{,}600$$
$$x = 200$$

16. **42:** Multiplying 45 by 5 is a little annoying (because the number is large), so don't immediately multiply. Hold off to see whether you can simplify any part of the math first.

$$\frac{(x-3)+(x)+(x+3)+(x+4)+(x+11)}{5} = 45$$

$$\frac{5x+15}{5} = 45$$

$$x + 3 = 45$$

$$x = 42$$

17. **32 years old:** Let $S$ = Sana's age and $B$ = Byron's age. What is $S + 7$? Set up a table:

|        | 10 years ago | Now | 7 years from now |
|--------|--------------|-----|------------------|
| Sana   | $S - 10$     | $S$ | $S + 7$          |
| Byron  | $B - 10$     | $B$ | $B + 7$          |

$$S - 10 = \frac{B - 10}{2}$$

$$B = S + 15$$

Substitute the second equation into the first, and solve for $S$.

$$
\begin{aligned}
S - 10 &= \frac{(S+15)-10}{2} \\
2S - 20 &= S + 5 \\
S &= 25
\end{aligned}
$$

You're not quite done! The question asks for $S + 7$: $(25) + 7 = 32$.

18. **$10:** To find the average, you need to know the sum John spent on all 6 books. First, find the cost of the original 5 books.

$$\frac{\text{Sum}}{\text{\# of Terms}} = \text{Average}$$

Sum = (Average)(# of terms) = ($9)(5) = $45

Next, find the sum of the cost for all 6 books, and use that to find the new average.

Sum of the cost of all 6 books = $45 + $15 = $60
Number of books = 6

$$\text{New Average} = \frac{\$60}{6} = \$10$$

19. **1,500 magazines:** Let $m$ = the number of magazines sold.

$$\text{Total cost} = 3m + 10{,}500$$
$$\text{Total revenue} = 10m$$

Breaking even occurs when total revenue equals total cost. In other words, profit is $0. Therefore:

$$3m + 10{,}500 = 10m$$
$$10{,}500 = 7m$$
$$1{,}500 = m$$

20. **45 hours:** Let $h$ equal the number of hours Renee worked. She must have worked more than 40 hours, because she earned more than ($40/hour)(40 hours) = $1,600. Therefore, let $h - 40$ represent the number of hours she worked after the first 40 hours.

$$40(40) + (h - 40)(80) = 2{,}000$$
$$1{,}600 + 80h - 3{,}200 = 2{,}000$$
$$80h - 1{,}600 = 2{,}000$$
$$80h = 3{,}600$$
$$h = 45$$

# Drill 3

21. **300 feet:**

$$100 \ \text{yards} \times \frac{3 \text{ feet}}{1 \text{ yard}} = 300 \text{ feet}$$

22. **25 gallons:**

$$200 \ \text{pints} \times \frac{1 \text{ gallon}}{8 \text{ pints}} = \frac{200}{8} \text{ gallons} = 25 \text{ gallons}$$

23. **88 pounds:**

$$40 \ \text{kilograms} \times \frac{2.2 \text{ pounds}}{1 \text{ kilogram}} = 40 \times 2.2 \text{ pounds}$$

Swap a decimal place between the 40 and the 2.2: 40 loses one decimal place to become 4, and 2.2 gains one decimal place to become 22. Now multiply:

$$4 \times 22 = 88$$

24. **30 inches:**

$$2.5 \ \text{feet} \times \frac{12 \text{ inches}}{1 \text{ foot}} = 30 \text{ inches}$$

25. **86° Fahrenheit:** Use the conversion formula, replacing the variable $C$ with the temperature in Celsius.

$$C = \frac{5}{9}(F-32)$$

$$30 = \frac{5}{9}(F-32)$$

$$\overset{6}{\cancel{30}} \times \frac{9}{\cancel{5}} = F-32$$

$$54 = F-32$$

$$86 = F$$

26. **14,400 minutes:** One day has 24 hours. Each of those hours has 60 minutes. Set up conversion ratios to solve.

$$10 \ \cancel{\text{days}} \times \frac{24 \ \cancel{\text{hours}}}{1 \ \cancel{\text{day}}} \times \frac{60 \ \text{minutes}}{1 \ \cancel{\text{hour}}} = 14,400 \ \text{minutes}$$

To make the math a little easier, multiply 24 by 6, then add two zeros.

27. **(C):** Set up conversion ratios to solve.

$$\frac{50 \ \cancel{\text{yards}}}{1\cancel{0} \ \cancel{\text{seconds}}} \times \frac{3 \ \text{feet}}{1 \ \cancel{\text{yard}}} \times \frac{6\cancel{0} \ \cancel{\text{seconds}}}{1 \ \text{minute}} = 50 \times 3 \times 6 = 900 \ \frac{\text{feet}}{\text{min}}$$

Don't stop yet! The question asks how far Miriam can travel in 2 minutes, not just 1 minute. If she can travel 900 feet in 1 minute, then she can travel $900 \times 2 = 1,800$ feet in 2 minutes.

Alternatively, the answers are far enough apart to allow you to estimate. If Miriam can travel 50 yards in 10 seconds, then she can travel $50 \times 6 = 300$ yards in 60 seconds, or 1 minute. She can travel 600 yards, then, in 2 minutes. Since there are 3 feet for every yard, the answer has to be greater than 900. (Specifically, it is $600 \times 3 = 1,800$, but you can stop your calculations at any point that you realize only one answer would work.)

28. **0.6 gallons:** Convert both 1.6 cups and 2 quarts into gallons using conversion ratios.

$$1.6 \ \cancel{\text{cups}} \times \frac{1 \ \cancel{\text{quart}}}{4 \ \cancel{\text{cups}}} \times \frac{1 \ \text{gallon}}{4 \ \cancel{\text{quarts}}} = \frac{1.6}{16} \ \text{gallons} = 0.1 \ \text{gallons}$$

$$2 \ \cancel{\text{quarts}} \times \frac{1 \ \text{gallon}}{4 \ \cancel{\text{quarts}}} = \frac{2}{4} \ \text{gallons} = 0.5 \ \text{gallons}$$

0.1 gallons + 0.5 gallons = 0.6 gallons

29. **2,880 tiles:** There is a hidden trap in this question. The dimensions of this room are in square feet, not feet (because 5 feet × 4 feet = 20 square feet). To avoid this trap, convert the dimensions to inches first, then multiply.

$$5 \text{ feet} \times \frac{12 \text{ inches}}{1 \text{ foot}} = 60 \text{ inches}$$

$$4 \text{ feet} \times \frac{12 \text{ inches}}{1 \text{ foot}} = 48 \text{ inches}$$

The dimensions of the closet in inches are 60 inches by 48 inches, or 60 × 48 = 2,880 square inches. Each tile is 1 square inch, so it will take 2,880 tiles to cover the floor.

30. **18 liters per hour:** There is no mandatory order for processing the conversions. Start with 5 milliliters per second, and make the appropriate conversions.

$$\frac{5 \text{ milliliters}}{\text{second}} \times \frac{60 \text{ seconds}}{1 \text{ minute}} \times \frac{60 \text{ minutes}}{1 \text{ hour}} = \frac{5 \times 60 \times 60 \text{ milliliters}}{\text{hour}}$$

Don't multiply yet. Continue with the conversion to see whether you can simplify before you multiply.

$$\frac{5 \times 60 \times 60 \text{ milliliters}}{\text{hour}} \times \frac{1 \text{ liter}}{1,000 \text{ milliliters}} = \frac{5 \times 6 \times 6 \text{ liters}}{10 \text{ hours}} = \frac{18 \text{ liters}}{\text{hour}}$$

# Drill 4

31. **144 miles:** Use the $D = RT$ formula to solve for Jiang's distance. Note that the time must be converted so that it is expressed only in hours rather than hours and minutes.

$$15 \text{ min} \times \left( \frac{1 \text{ hr}}{60 \text{ min}} \right) = \frac{1}{4} \text{ hr} = 0.25 \text{ hr}$$

Therefore, 2 hours and 15 minutes is equivalent to 2.25 hours. Now set up a table and solve:

| D (mi) | = | R (mi/hr) | × | T (hr) |
|--------|---|-----------|---|--------|
| d | = | 64 | × | 2.25 |

$$\frac{64 \text{ miles}}{\text{hour}} \times 2.25 \text{ hours} = 64 \times \frac{9}{4} = 16 \times 9 = 144 \text{ miles}$$

32. **(B):** Process the math in steps. For the first hour only, Tyrone drove 40 miles per hour (mph), so he drove a total of 40 miles in that first hour. After that, he still had another 160 − 40 = 120 miles to go at a speed of 50 mph. Use the $D = RT$ formula to determine how long this took.

$$50t \ = \ 120$$
$$t \ = \ \frac{120}{50} = \frac{12}{5} = 2\frac{2}{5} = 2.4 \text{ hours}$$

Tyrone started at 7:30. As of 8:30, he had driven 40 miles. Then he took 2.4 hours to drive the remaining 120 miles. This took more than 2 hours, so the time is later than 10:30, but not as long as 2.5 hours, so the time is not yet 11:00. The only answer that works is answer (B).

If you want to calculate exactly, the math is shown below, but remember: On the GMAT, it's only necessary to find the right answer. It's not always necessary to do all of the official math!

$$\frac{2}{\cancel{5}} \text{ hours} \times \frac{\cancel{60}^{12} \text{ minutes}}{1 \text{ hour}} = 2 \times 12 = 24 \text{ minutes}$$

The additional time after 8:30 is 2 hours and 24 minutes, so Tyrone arrived in Camville at 10:54.

33. **2 miles per hour:** Find the average rate by dividing the total distance traveled by the total time spent traveling. In this case, Roger traveled 3 miles to the store and 3 miles back, covering a total of 6 miles in 3 hours.

$$R = \frac{(3+3) \text{ miles}}{(2+1) \text{ hours}} = \frac{6 \text{ miles}}{3 \text{ hours}} = 2 \frac{\text{miles}}{\text{hour}}$$

34. **15 minutes:** Use the $D = RT$ equation to calculate how long it took each individual to run the path. Sue ran the 10-mile path at a rate of 8 miles per hour. To get her time, set up a table and solve:

| D (mi) | = | R (mi/hr) | × | T (hr) |
|--------|---|-----------|---|--------|
| 10 | = | 8 | × | t |

$$10 = 8t$$
$$\frac{5}{4} = t$$

Therefore, Sue completed the path in 1 hour and 15 minutes.

Rob ran the 10-mile path at a rate of $6\frac{2}{3}$ mi/hr = $\frac{20}{3}$ mi/hr. To get his time, set up a table and solve:

| D (mi) | = | R (mi/hr) | × | T (hr) |
|--------|---|-----------|---|--------|
| 10 | = | $\frac{20}{3}$ | × | t |

$$10 = \frac{20}{3}t$$

$$\frac{3}{_2\cancel{20}} \times \cancel{10} = t$$

$$\frac{3}{2} = t$$

Therefore, Rob ran the path in 1 hour and 30 minutes.

Finally, subtract Sue's time from Rob's time to calculate how much sooner Sue finished.

$$1 \text{ hour } 30 \text{ min} - 1 \text{ hour } 15 \text{ min} = 15 \text{ min}$$

35. **10 kilometers per hour:** In order to calculate Svetlana's speed during the second half of the race, first calculate how long it took her to run the first half of the race. The first half of the race is 5 kilometers in length, and Svetlana ran at a speed of 12 kilometers per hour. Set up a table and solve:

| D (km) | = | R (km/hr) | × | T (hr) |
|--------|---|-----------|---|--------|
| 5      | = | 12        | × | t      |

$$5 = 12t$$

$$t = \frac{5}{12} \text{ hr}$$

To calculate the time Svetlana has available to run the second half of the race, subtract her time for the first half of the race from her goal time for the entire race. To do this calculation, first convert her goal time from minutes to hours.

$$55 \text{ min} \times \frac{1 \text{ hr}}{60 \text{ min}} = \frac{55}{60} \text{ hr} = \frac{11}{12} \text{ hr}$$

Then subtract Svetlana's time for the first half of the race from this value.

$$\frac{11}{12} \text{ hr} - \frac{5}{12} \text{ hr} = \frac{6}{12} \text{ hr} = \frac{1}{2} \text{ hr} = 0.5 \text{ hr}$$

Svetlana must complete the second 5 kilometers in 0.5 hours. Use the $D = RT$ equation to solve for Svetlana's required speed.

| D (km) | = | R (km/hr) | × | T (hr) |
|--------|---|-----------|---|--------|
| 5      | = | r         | × | 0.5    |

$$5 = 0.5r$$
$$10 = r$$

Svetlana must run the second half of the race at a speed of 10 kilometers per hour in order to finish the entire race in 55 minutes.

# Drill 5

36. **350 bottles per hour:** Use the $W = RT$ formula to solve for the number of bottles produced per hour.

| $W$ (bot) | = | $R$ (bot/hr) | × | $T$ (hr) |
|-----------|---|--------------|---|----------|
| 1,400     | = | $r$          | × | 4        |

$$1,400 = 4r$$
$$350 = r$$

37. **5 hours:** First, calculate the rate of the deluxe machine by multiplying the rate of the standard machine by 2. If the standard machine can fill 15 gallons per hour, then the deluxe machine can fill 30 gallons per hour.

Use the $W = RT$ formula to solve for the amount of time the machine takes to fill 150 gallons of paint.

| $W$ (gal) | = | $R$ (gal/hr) | × | $T$ (hr) |
|-----------|---|--------------|---|----------|
| 150       | = | 30           | × | $t$      |

$$150 = 30t$$
$$t = \frac{15\cancel{0}}{3\cancel{0}} = \frac{15}{3} = 5$$

38. **660 widgets:** Use two separate $W = RT$ equations, one for Machine A and one for Machine B, to calculate how many widgets each machine produces in 20 minutes.

|           | $W$ (wid) | = | $R$ (wid/min) | × | $T$ (min) |
|-----------|-----------|---|---------------|---|-----------|
| Machine A | $a$       | = | 15            | × | 20        |
| Machine A | $b$       | = | 18            | × | 20        |

Machine A: $a = 15 \times 20 = 300$ widgets
Machine B: $b = 18 \times 20 = 360$ widgets

To calculate the total number of widgets produced, add the values for the individual machines:

$$300 \text{ widgets} + 360 \text{ widgets} = 660 \text{ widgets}$$

39. **200 gallons per hour:** First, find the time it took to fill the pool.

$$5:24pm - 2:00pm = 3 \text{ hours } 24 \text{ minutes}$$

Next, convert the minutes portion of this time to hours.

$$24 \text{ min} \times \left(\frac{1 \text{ hr}}{60 \text{ min}}\right) = \frac{24}{60} \text{ hr} = \frac{2}{5} \text{ hr} = 0.4 \text{ hr}$$

It took 3.4 hours to fill the pool and the capacity of the pool is 680 gallons. Use the $W = RT$ equation to solve for the rate.

| $W$ (gal) | = | $R$ (gal/hr) | × | $T$ (hr) |
|-----------|---|--------------|---|----------|
| 680       | = | $r$          | × | 3.4      |

$$680 = 3.4r$$

$$r = \frac{680}{3.4} = \frac{6800}{34} = \frac{\overset{2}{\cancel{68}}00}{\cancel{34}} = 200 \frac{\text{gallons}}{\text{hour}}$$

40. **(B):** Machine X produces 180 chocolates per hour; use the $W = RT$ formula to determine how many chocolates it produces in 5 hours.

| $W$ (choc) | = | $R$ (choc/hr) | × | $T$ (hr) |
|------------|---|---------------|---|----------|
| $W$        | = | 180           | × | 5        |

$$W = 180 \times 5$$
$$W = 900$$

Machine Y is capable of producing the same number, 900 chocolates, but in just 2 hours. Use the $W = RT$ formula again to find the rate for Machine Y.

| $W$ (choc) | = | $R$ (choc/hr) | × | $T$ (hr) |
|------------|---|---------------|---|----------|
| 900        | = | $r$           | × | 2        |

$$900 = r \times 2$$
$$450 = r$$

# Drill 6

41. **$40,000:** Use decimal equivalents here, using 1 (or 100%) as a starting point and adding to 1 for an increase or subtracting from 1 for a decrease. For example, "If Ken's salary were 20% higher" can be translated as $1 + (20\%)(1) = 1 + 0.2 = 1.2$. Similarly, "20% less than" can be translated as $1 - (20\%)(1) = 1 - 0.2 = 0.8$. Therefore, 120% of Ken's salary is equal to 80% of Lorena's salary. Translate this into math and solve.

$$1.2K = 0.8(60,000)$$

$$K = \frac{0.8(60,000)}{1.2} \times \frac{10}{10}$$

$$K = \frac{8\left(\,^{5}\cancel{60},000\right)}{\cancel{12}}$$

$$K = 8(5,000)$$

$$K = 40,000$$

42. **$19.50:** When you are asked to multiply percents, it is usually best to use a fractional representation because you can then simplify before you multiply.

$$\$10 \times \frac{13\cancel{0}}{10\cancel{0}} \times \frac{15\cancel{0}}{10\cancel{0}}$$

$$= \$\cancel{10} \times \frac{13}{\cancel{10}} \times \frac{15}{10}$$

$$= \$13 \times \frac{3}{2}$$

$$= \$19.50$$

Multiplying by $\frac{3}{2}$, or 1.5, is the same as adding 50% of the starting number to the starting number:

$13 + \$6.50 = \$19.50$.

43. **108%:** If the stock increased 20%, then the resulting value is 120% of the original. If the stock then goes down 10%, the final value is 90% of that intermediate value.

| $\frac{120}{100}$ | $\times$ | $\frac{90}{100}$ | $\times$ | $Q$ | $=$ | $\frac{x}{100}$ | $\times$ | $Q$ |
|---|---|---|---|---|---|---|---|---|
| 120 percent | of | 90 percent | of | $Q$ | is | what percent | of | $Q$? |

$$\frac{120}{100} \times \frac{90}{100} \times Q = \frac{x}{100} \times Q \qquad \text{Divide both sides by Q and simplify.}$$

$$\frac{6}{5} \times \frac{9}{10} = \frac{x}{100}$$

$$\frac{54}{50} = \frac{x}{100}$$

$$\overset{2}{\cancel{100}} \times \frac{54}{\cancel{50}_1} = x$$

$$108 = x$$

Alternatively, pretend that the initial price was $100. If it increased in value by 20%, then the new value is $100 + $20 = $120. If that new value decreases by 10%, then the final value is $120 − $12 = $108. This final value is $\frac{108}{100} = 108\%$ of the starting value.

44. **36%:** Because all of the students sum to 200, write the following equation:

$$A + B + C + D + F = \text{Total}$$
$$40 + 64 + C + 18 + 6 = 200$$
$$128 + C = 200$$
$$C = 200 - 128$$
$$C = 72$$

Therefore, $\frac{72}{200}$ of the grades are C's. Percents are defined in terms of 100. Divide the top and bottom by 2 to find the percent directly.

$$\frac{72}{200} = \frac{36}{100}$$

Therefore, 36% of the students got a C.

45. **(C):** You can use the percent change formula or you can calculate directly.

Direct calculation:
160 = 100%            This is the starting fact.
16 = 10%              Move the decimal one to the left to get 10%.
8 = 5%               Divide by 2 to get 5%.

Percent change: $\% \text{ change} = \dfrac{\text{change}}{\text{original}}$

$$\% \text{ change} = \frac{\overset{1}{\cancel{8}}}{\underset{2}{\cancel{160}}} = \frac{1}{20}$$

This value is on the to-memorize list from the Fractions chapter: $\frac{1}{20} = 5\%$. If you forget the conversion, you can also find the percentage by making the fraction "of 100" or "per cent": $\frac{1}{20} = \frac{5}{100} = 5\%$.

# Drill 7

46. **250 meteors:** Let $m$ equal the number of meteors visible from Lily's roof. The 20 meteors that inspire Lily represent 10% of 80% of the visible meteors.

$$20 = \frac{10}{100}\left(\frac{80}{100}\right)m$$

$$20 = \frac{1}{10}\left(\frac{4}{5}\right)m$$

$$\left(\frac{50}{\cancel{4}}\right)\left(^5\cancel{20}\right) = m$$

$$250 = m$$

47. **60 gibbons:** Bingwa weighs the same as 1,000 gibbons. Therefore, he can lift 6% of this weight with his trunk.

$$\frac{6}{1\cancel{00}}\times 1,0\cancel{00}\text{ gibbons} = 6\times 10\text{ gibbons} = 60\text{ gibbons}$$

48. **(B):** Let $x$ equal the precipitation in Country X, $y$ equal the precipitation in Country Y, and $z$ equal the precipitation in Country Z. Translate the equations.

$$x = \frac{7}{4}y$$

$$y = \frac{2}{3}z$$

Since the question tells you the value of $x$ and you are solving for the value of $z$, substitute the second equation into the first to simplify to a single equation with $x$ and $z$.

$$x = \frac{7}{4}\left(\frac{2}{3}z\right)$$

$$x = \frac{7}{6}z$$

Now plug in for $x$ and solve for $z$:

$$280 = \frac{7}{6}z$$

$$\left(\frac{6}{7}\right)(280) = z$$

$$(6)(40) = z$$

$$240 = z$$

49. $\dfrac{1}{6}$ : In order to determine the fraction of the songs that are world music, first figure out what fraction of the songs are not world music. Add the fractions for the other types of music.

$$\begin{aligned}
\text{Not world} &= \frac{1}{3} + \frac{1}{4} + \frac{1}{6} + \frac{1}{12} \\
&= \frac{4}{12} + \frac{3}{12} + \frac{2}{12} + \frac{1}{12} \\
&= \frac{10}{12} \\
&= \frac{5}{6}
\end{aligned}$$

Of the songs in Farrah's playlist, $\dfrac{5}{6}$ are *not* world music, so the remaining $\dfrac{1}{6}$ of the songs are world music.

50. **160 people:** Let $p$ = the total number of people attending the convention. In order to find the total number, determine what fraction of the total the 8 people (who play three or more instruments) represent, and then use that to find the total.

You could add up the three fractions and subtract from 1—but wait! Adding fractions is annoying because you have to find a common denominator. Take a look at those fractions again: they are all on the to-memorize conversion list. Convert them to percentages.

$$\frac{2}{5} = 40\%$$

$$\frac{1}{4} = 25\%$$

$$\frac{3}{10} = 30\%$$

The sum is 40% + 25% + 30% = 95%. The 8 people who play three or more instruments must represent the remaining 5%. Use this fact to find 100%, or the total number of attendees.

| | |
|---|---|
| 5% = 8 | This is the starting fact. |
| 10% = 16 | Double the number to get 10%. |
| 100% = 160 | Add a 0 to get 100%. |

# Drill 8

51. **(A):** First, determine how many umbrellas fit Yemi's price range. There are 400 umbrellas total, but $\frac{3}{5}$ cost more than the \$25 that Yemi is willing to pay.

$$400\left(1-\frac{3}{5}\right) = \text{umbrellas under \$25}$$

$$\overset{8}{\cancel{400}}\left(\frac{2}{\cancel{5}}\right) = \text{umbrellas under \$25}$$

$$160 = \text{umbrellas under \$25}$$

There are 160 *remaining* umbrellas. According to the problem, $\frac{7}{8}$ of these are not blue, so $\frac{1}{8}$ are under \$25 and blue. Therefore:

$$\overset{2}{\cancel{160}}\left(\frac{1}{\cancel{8}}\right) = \text{blue umbrellas under \$25}$$

$$20 = \text{blue umbrellas under \$25}$$

52. **(A):** First, figure out how many cups of liquid are in one serving of Mariko's punch.

$$\frac{1}{2}+\frac{3}{4}+\frac{1}{8} = \frac{4}{8}+\frac{6}{8}+\frac{1}{8} = \frac{11}{8}$$

Each serving of punch consists of $\frac{11}{8}$ cups of liquid. (This is a weird number. Don't try to turn it into a mixed fraction yet. Glance at the answers: something must cancel out later to make a "nicer" number, so just keep going.)

Next, you know that $\frac{11}{8}$ times the number of servings equals 22 cups. Let *s* equal the number of servings and solve:

$$\frac{11}{8}s = 22$$

$$s = 22\left(\frac{8}{11}\right)$$

$$s = 2(8) = 16$$

53. $\dfrac{1}{6}$ : Begin by finding the fraction of the movies that are documentaries. Let $M$ equal the total number of movies and $d$ equal the number of documentaries. Notice that you can simplify the math by multiplying both sides by the common denominator, 12.

$$M = \frac{1}{3}M + \frac{1}{4}M + d$$

$$(12)(M) = \left(\frac{1}{3}M + \frac{1}{4}M + d\right)(12)$$

$$12M = 4M + 3M + 12d$$

$$5M = 12d$$

$$\frac{5}{12}M = d$$

Of the movies, $\dfrac{5}{12}$ are documentaries. Of these, $\dfrac{2}{5}$ are depressing. Therefore:

$$\frac{\cancel{5}}{12}M \times \frac{2}{\cancel{5}} = \frac{2}{12}M = \frac{1}{6}M$$

Of the movies in Santosh's collection, $\dfrac{1}{6}$ are depressing documentaries.

Alternatively, because the problem discusses only fractions (never any real numbers), you can work through the problem using a real number. Choose a number that is a multiple of all of the denominators of the fractions in the problem. In this case, choose $3 \times 4 \times 5 = 60$.

Assuming that there are 60 total movies, then $\dfrac{1}{3}$, or 20 movies, are animated, and $\dfrac{1}{4}$, or 15 movies, are live-action. The remainder, or $60 - 20 - 15 = 25$, are documentaries.

Of the documentaries, $\dfrac{2}{5}$, or $25\left(\dfrac{2}{5}\right) = 10$, documentaries are depressing. These 10 depressing documentaries represent $\dfrac{10,}{60}$ or $\dfrac{1}{6}$, of all of the movies.

54. $\dfrac{2}{15}$ : Let $h$ = the total number of homes. You know that $\dfrac{1}{3}$ of the homes are termite-ridden. If $\dfrac{3}{5}$ of the termite-ridden homes are collapsing, then $1 - \dfrac{3}{5} = \dfrac{2}{5}$ of the termite-ridden homes are NOT collapsing. Therefore:

$$\left( h \times \dfrac{1}{3} \right) \times \dfrac{2}{5} = \dfrac{2}{15} h$$

Alternatively, because the problem only mentions fractions (no real numbers), you can choose your own real number to solve. Choose a number that is a multiple of all of the denominators in the problem. In this case, choose $3 \times 5 = 15$.

Assuming that there are 15 homes total, then $\dfrac{1}{3}$, or 5 homes, are termite-ridden. Of these 5 homes, $\dfrac{3}{5}$, or 3 homes, are collapsing. That leaves 2 homes that are both termite-ridden and NOT collapsing; this represents $\dfrac{2}{15}$ of the total homes.

55. **6,000 cracked green marbles:** If $\dfrac{3}{4}$ of the marbles are green, then $\dfrac{1}{4}$ are red. If 6,000 represents $\dfrac{1}{4}$ (or 25%) of the total, then $\dfrac{3}{4}$ (or 75%) of the total is three times as much. There are $6{,}000 \times 3 = 18{,}000$ green marbles. Determine how many of these are cracked.

$$\overset{6}{\cancel{18}}{,}000 \times \dfrac{1}{\cancel{3}} = 6{,}000$$

It may seem odd that you're back at 6,000. It is sometimes the case that the answer is the same as another number in the problem!

# Geometry

# In this chapter...

- Circles
  - Know One Thing about a Circle: Know Everything Else
  - Sector: Slice of Pizza
- Triangles
  - Sum of Any Two Sides > Third Side
  - Sum of the Three Angles = 180°
  - Same Sides = Same Angles, and Vice Versa
  - Perimeter: Sum of Sides
  - Apply Area Formula: Any Side Can Be the Base
  - Know Two Sides of a Right Triangle: Find the Third Side
- Quadrilaterals
  - Parallelogram: Cut into Triangles OR Drop Height
  - Rectangles = Parallelogram + Four Right Angles
  - Squares = Rectangle + Four Equal Sides
- Geometry: "Word" Problems with Pictures
- Coordinate Plane—Position Is a Pair of Numbers
  - Know Just One Coordinate = Find a Line
  - Know a Range = Shade a Region
  - Read a Graph = Drop a Line to the Axes
  - Plot a Relationship: Given an $x$, Find a $y$
  - Lines in the Plane: Use Slope and y-Intercept to Plot

Chapter 10

# Geometry

## In This Chapter, You Will Learn To:

- Work with the basic shapes that the GMAT tests, including key facts, rules, and formulas
- Apply these rules and equations to solve GMAT geometry problems
- Solve coordinate plane problems

For many students, geometry brings to mind complicated shapes and the need to memorize lots of formulas. It's true that you will need to memorize some rules and formulas, but you can generally get away with limiting your studies to triangles, squares, rectangles, circles, and the coordinate plane.

On occasion, someone will be given a more complicated shape, such as a cylinder or a rhombus, but these shapes don't often appear on the GMAT. If you like, you can choose not to study the "weird" shapes and to make a guess if one happens to pop up on your test.

In this chapter, you'll learn the properties of the basic shapes most commonly tested on the GMAT. You'll also learn how the GMAT tests your knowledge of these shapes and how to work your way through Geometry questions.

## Circles

A circle is a set of points that are all the same distance from a central point. By definition, every circle has a center, usually labeled *O*, which is not itself a point on the circle. The **radius** of a circle is the distance between the center of the circle and a point on the circle. *Any* line segment connecting the center and *any* point on the circle is a radius (usually labeled *r*). All radii in the same circle have the same length. For example:

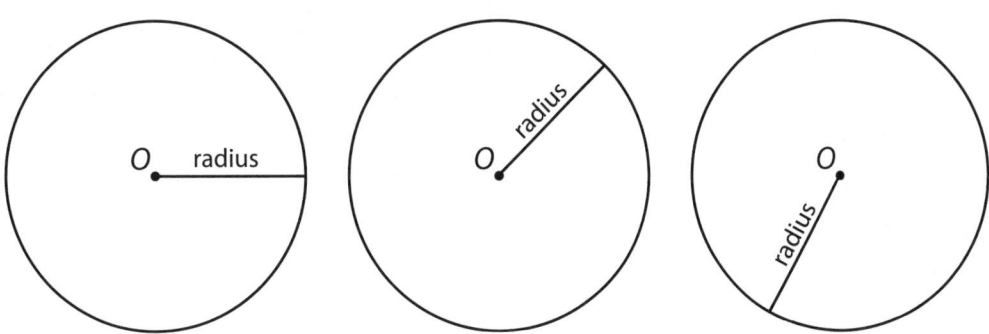

## Know One Thing about a Circle: Know Everything Else

Now imagine a circle of radius 7. What else can you figure out about that circle?

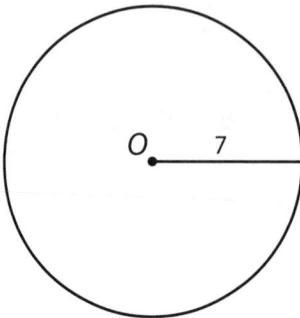

The next easiest thing to figure out is the **diameter** (usually labeled *d*), which passes through the center of a circle and connects two opposite points on the circle:

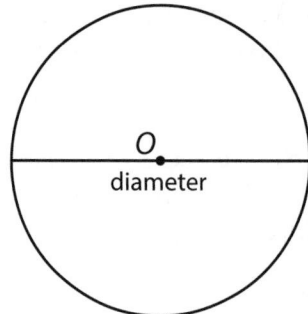

A diameter is two radii laid end to end, so it will always be exactly twice the length of the radius. This relationship can be expressed as $d = 2r$. A circle with radius 7 has a diameter of 14.

The **circumference** (usually referred to as *C*) is a measure of the distance around a circle. The circumference is essentially the perimeter of a circle:

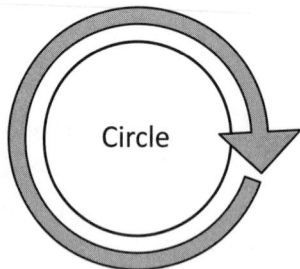

For any circle, the circumference and the diameter have a consistent relationship. If you divide the circumference by the diameter, you always get the same number: 3.14… This number has decimals that continue forever and it is indicated by the Greek letter $\pi$ (pi). To recap:

$$\frac{\text{Circumference}}{\text{Diameter}} = \pi \quad \text{or} \quad \pi d = C$$

In a circle with a diameter of 14, the circumference is $\pi(14)$, or $14\pi$. Most of the time, you will not approximate this as 43.96 (which is $14 \times 3.14$). Instead, keep it as $14\pi$.

You can relate the circumference directly to the radius, since the diameter is twice the radius. This relationship is commonly expressed as $C = 2\pi r$. Be comfortable with using either equation.

Finally, the **area** (usually labeled $A$) is the space inside the circle.

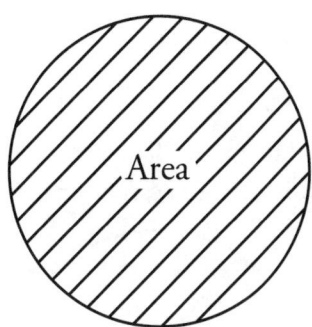

The area of a circle and its radius always have the same relationship. If you know the radius of the circle, then you can find the area using the formula $A = \pi r^2$. For a circle of radius 7, the area is $\pi(7)^2$, or $49\pi$. *Once you know the radius, you can find the diameter, the circumference, and the area.*

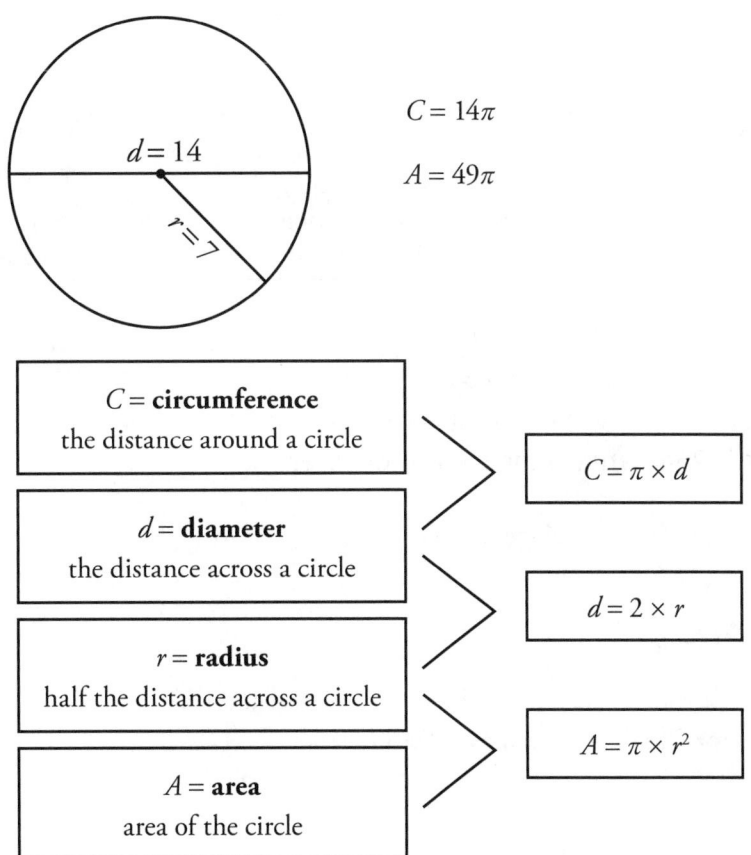

These relationships are true of any circle. What's more, *if you know any one of these values, you can determine the rest,* since they're all connected.

Say that the area of a circle is $36\pi$. How do you find the other measures? Start with the formula for the area, which involves the radius.

$$36\pi = \pi r^2$$

Solve for the radius by isolating $r$.

$36\pi = \pi r^2$        Divide by $\pi$.

$36 = r^2$        Take the square root of both sides.

$6 = r$

Now that you know the radius, multiply it by 2 to get the diameter, which is 12. Finally, to find the circumference, multiply the diameter by $\pi$. The circumference is $12\pi$. You can fill in the measurements on your circle:

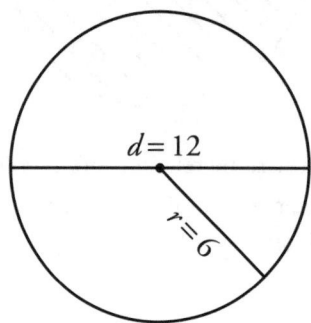

| If you... | Then you... | Like this: |
|---|---|---|
| Know one thing about a circle | Can find out everything else about the circle by using the standard formulas | If $r = 4$, then $d = 8$, $C = 8\pi$, and $A = 16\pi$ |

## Check Your Skills

1. The radius of a circle is 9. What is the area?
2. The circumference of a circle is $17\pi$. What is the diameter?
3. The area of a circle is $25\pi$. What is the circumference?

*Answers can be found on page 467.*

## Sector: Slice of Pizza

Imagine that you have a circle with an area of $36\pi$. Now cut it in half and make it a semicircle. Any fractional portion of a circle is known as a **sector**. Think of a sector as a slice of pizza.

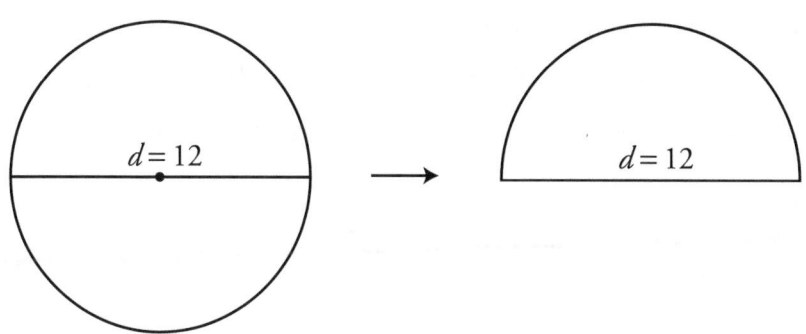

What effect does cutting the circle in half have on the basic elements of the circle? The diameter stays the same, as does the radius. But the area and the circumference are cut in half. The area of the semicircle is $18\pi$, and the curved part of the semicircle's perimeter is $6\pi$. When you deal with sectors, you call the remaining portion of the circumference the **arc length**. For this sector, the arc length is $6\pi$.

If, instead of cutting the circle in half, you cut it into quarters, each piece of the circle would have $\frac{1}{4}$ the area of the entire circle and $\frac{1}{4}$ the circumference.

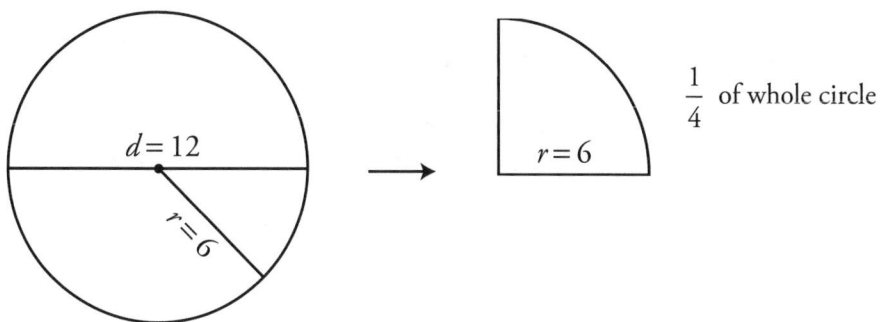

Now, on the GMAT, you're unlikely to be told that you have one-quarter of a circle. Rather, you would be told something about the **central angle**, which is the degree measure between two given radii. Take a look at the quarter circle. Normally, there are 360° in a full circle. What is the degree measure of the angle between the two radii? The same thing that happens to area and circumference happens to the central angle. It is now $\frac{1}{4}$ of 360°, which is 90° (you illustrate a 90° angle with a box at the angle).

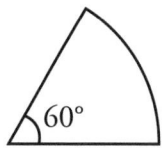

$$\frac{1}{4} = \frac{90°}{360°}$$

Let's see how you can use the central angle to determine sector area and arc length. Imagine that the original circle still has area $36\pi$, but now the sector, or slice of pie, has a central angle of 60°.

60°

What fractional amount of the circle remains if the central angle is 60°? The whole is 360°, and the part is 60°, so $\frac{60}{360}$ is the relevant fraction, which reduces to $\frac{1}{6}$. In other words, a sector with a central angle of 60° is $\frac{1}{6}$ of the entire circle. The sector area is $\frac{1}{6}$ × (Area of circle), and the arc length is $\frac{1}{6}$ × (Circumference of circle).

$$\text{Sector area} = \frac{1}{6} \times (36\pi) = 6\pi$$

$$\text{Arc length} = \frac{1}{6} \times (12\pi) = 2\pi$$

$$\frac{1}{6} = \frac{60°}{360°} = \frac{\text{Sector area}}{\text{Circle area}} = \frac{\text{Arc length}}{\text{Circumference}}$$

In the last example, the central angle indicated the fractional amount that the sector represented. But any of the three properties of a sector, namely central angle, arc length, and area, could be used to convey that same information, since all three measures are related.

Consider this example:

A sector has a radius of 9 and an area of $27\pi$. What is the central angle of the sector?

You still need to determine the fraction of the circle that the sector represents. This time, however, use the radius to figure out the area of the whole circle. From that, you can figure out what fractional amount the sector is.

$$\text{Area} = \pi r^2 = \pi(9)^2 = 81\pi$$

$$\frac{27\pi}{81\pi} = \frac{1}{3}$$

The sector is $\frac{1}{3}$ of the entire circle. The full circle has an angle of 360°, so multiply that by $\frac{1}{3}$ to find the angle of the sector.

$$\frac{1}{3} \times 360 = 120$$

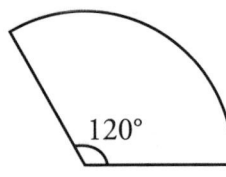

$$\frac{1}{3} = \frac{120°}{360°} = \frac{27\pi \ (\text{Sector area})}{81\pi \ (\text{Circle area})}$$

**MANHATTAN** PREP

Every question about sectors will provide you with enough information to calculate one of the following fractions, which represent the sector as a fraction of the circle.

$$\frac{\text{Central area}}{360} \qquad\qquad \frac{\text{Sector area}}{\text{Circle area}} \qquad\qquad \frac{\text{Arc length}}{\text{Circumference}}$$

All of these fractions have the same value for the same sector of a circle (in other words, each fraction is equal). Once you know this value, you can find any measure of the sector of the original circle.

| If you... | Then you... | Like this: |
|---|---|---|
| Encounter a sector | Figure out the fraction of the circle that the sector represents | If central angle = 45° and radius = 5, then $\text{fraction} = \dfrac{45}{360} = \dfrac{1}{8}$, and area = $\dfrac{1}{8}\pi r^2 = \dfrac{1}{8}\pi(5)^2 = \dfrac{25}{8}\pi$ |

## Check Your Skills

4. A sector has a central angle of 270° and a radius of 2. What is the area of the sector?
5. A sector has an arc length of $4\pi$ and a radius of 3. What is the central angle of the sector?
6. A sector has an area of $40\pi$ and a radius of 10. What is the arc length of the sector?

*Answers can be found on pages 467–468.*

# Triangles

Triangles are relatively common in GMAT geometry problems. You'll often find them hiding in problems that seem to be about rectangles or other shapes. Many properties of triangles are tested.

## Sum of Any Two Sides > Third Side

The sum of any two side lengths of a triangle will always be greater than the third side length.

Grab your pen and draw two dots (the endpoints), then connect them with a straight line. Now use that straight line as one side of a triangle, and draw two more lines to create the full triangle. The other two lines added together have to be longer than the straight line that you started from, since the straight line is the shortest possible distance between the two endpoints.

10

A related idea is that any side is greater than the *difference* of the other two side lengths. Otherwise, you can't even connect the dots and draw a complete triangle. The pictures below illustrate these points:

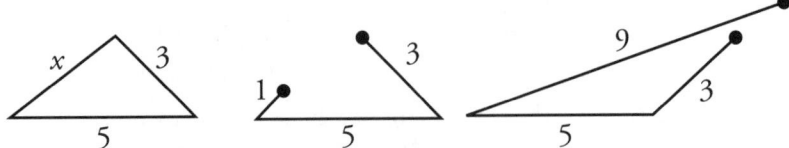

In the first triangle, what is the largest number *x* could be? What's the smallest? Could it be 9? 1?

    *x* must be less than $3 + 5 = 8$

    *x* must be greater than $5 - 3 = 2$

    $2 < x < 8$

| If you… | Then you… | Like this: |
|---------|-----------|------------|
| Want to know how long the third side of a triangle could be | Find the sum and the difference of the other two sides; the length of the third side must be less than the sum, but more than the difference | First side = 6<br>Second side = 4<br><br>Third side must be less than $6 + 4 = 10$ and greater than $6 - 4 = 2$ |

## Check Your Skills

7.  Two sides of a triangle have lengths 5 and 19. Can the third side have a length of 13?

8.  Two sides of a triangle have lengths 8 and 17. What is the range of possible values of the length of the third side?

*Answers can be found on page 468.*

# Sum of the Three Angles = 180°

The internal angles of a triangle must sum to 180°. As a result, if you know two angles in the triangle, you can find the third angle. Take a look at this triangle:

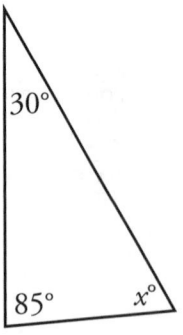

The three internal angles must sum to 180°, so $30 + 85 + x = 180$, so $x = 65$. The third angle is 65°.

MANHATTAN PREP

The GMAT can also test you in more complicated ways. Consider this triangle:

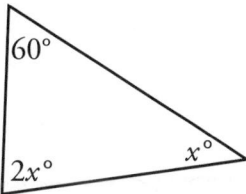

You only know one of the angles, but the other two are both given in terms of *x*. Again, the three angles must sum to 180°.

$$60 + x + 2x = 180$$
$$3x = 120$$
$$x = 40$$

The angle labeled *x* has a measure of 40°, and the angle labeled 2*x* has a measure of 80°.

By the way, a straight line also has a measure of 180°.

The GMAT does not always draw triangles to scale. On Problem Solving questions (one of the two types of GMAT Quant questions), figures will be drawn to scale unless there is a note saying that it is not drawn to scale. On Data Sufficiency questions (the other type of GMAT Quant question), the figures will not say whether they are drawn to scale, so assume they are not.

| If you… | Then you… | Like this: |
|---|---|---|
| Know two angles of a triangle or can represent all three in terms of a single variable | Can find all angles using the "sum to 180" principle | First angle = 3*x* <br> Second angle = 4*x* <br> Third angle = 40° <br> 3*x* + 4*x* + 40 = 180 <br> 7*x* = 140 or *x* = 20 |

## Check Your Skills

Find the missing angle(s).

9. 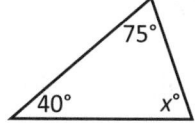     10. 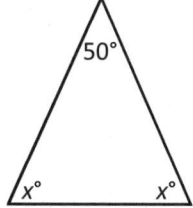     11.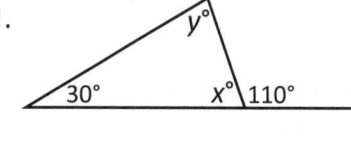

*Answers can be found on pages 468–469.*

## Same Sides = Same Angles, and Vice Versa

Internal angles of a triangle are important on the GMAT for another reason: *sides correspond to their opposite angles.* That is, the longest side is opposite the largest angle, and the smallest side is opposite the smallest angle. Think about an alligator opening its mouth. As the angle between its upper and lower jaws increases, the distance between its top and bottom teeth gets bigger.

For example:

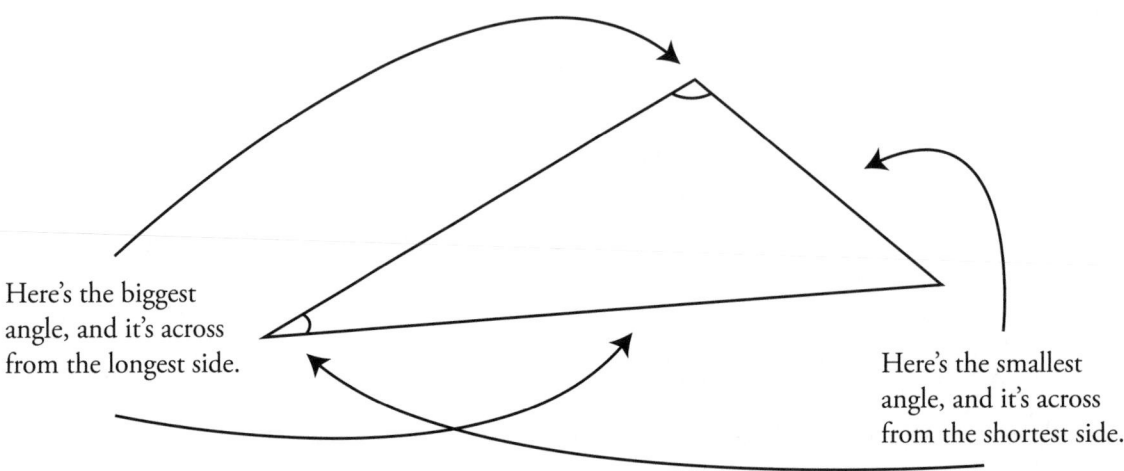

Here's the biggest angle, and it's across from the longest side.

Here's the smallest angle, and it's across from the shortest side.

This relationship works both ways. If you know the sides of the triangle, you can make inferences about the angles. If you know the angles, you can make inferences about the sides. (Note: In the diagram below, a two-letter designation, such as *AC*, refers to the line that lies between the points *A* and *C*. The three-letter designation. ∠*ABC*, refers to the angle traced by starting from the letter *A*, going through *B*, and ending on *C*.)

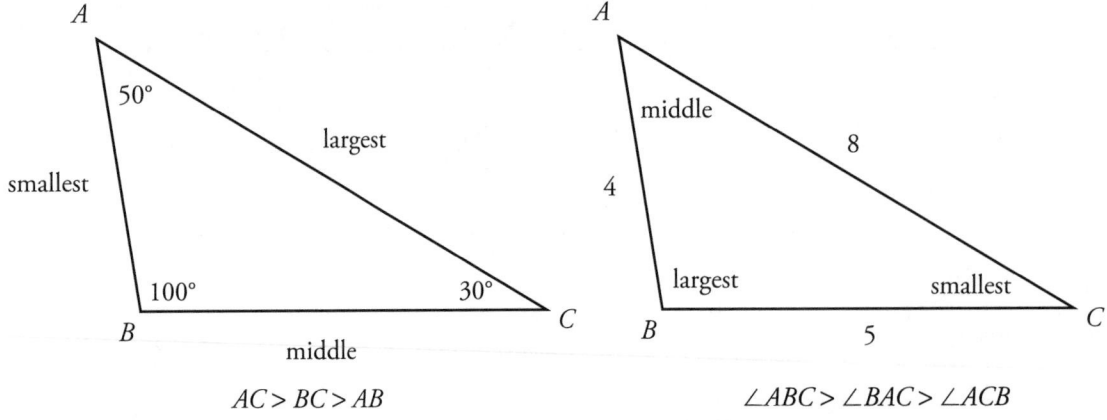

$$AC > BC > AB$$

$$\angle ABC > \angle BAC > \angle ACB$$

Lots of triangles have two or even three equal sides. These triangles also have two or three equal angles, respectively. You can classify triangles by the number of equal sides or angles that they have.

- A triangle that has two equal angles and two equal sides is an **isosceles** triangle.

- A triangle that has three equal angles (all 60°) and three equal sides is an **equilateral** triangle.

The relationship between equal angles and equal sides works in both directions. Take a look at these isosceles triangles, and think about what additional information you can infer from them:

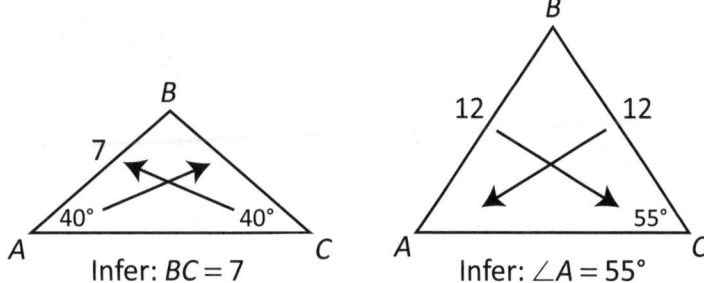

The GMAT loves isosceles triangles. Examine this challenging example:

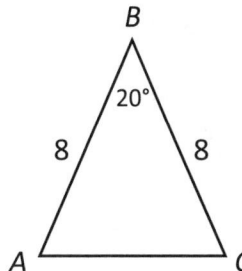

Take a look at the triangle to see what other information you can fill in. Specifically, do you know the degree measure of either angle *BAC* or angle *BCA*?

Because side *AB* is the same length as side *BC*, angle *BAC* must have the same degree measure as angle *BCA*. Label each of those angles $x°$:

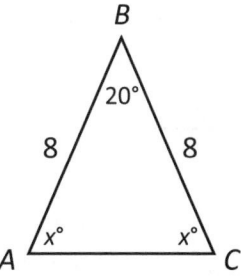

The three internal angles will sum to 180. So $20 + x + x = 180$, so $x = 80$. Therefore, the two angles, *BAC* and *BCA*, each equal 80°. You can't find the side length *AC* without more advanced math; the GMAT doesn't test that more advanced math.

| If you... | Then you... | Like this: |
|---|---|---|
| See two equal sides in a triangle | Set the angles opposite each side equal | Two sides both equal 8, so the angles opposite those sides are equal |
| See two equal angles in a triangle | Set the sides opposite each angle equal | Two angles equal 30°, so the sides opposite those angles are equal |

## Check Your Skills

Find the value of *x*.

12.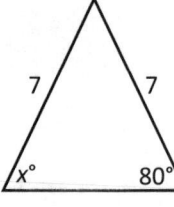

13.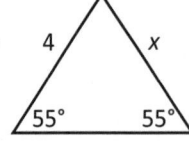

14.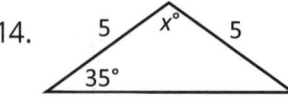

*Answers can be found on pages 469–470.*

# Perimeter: Sum of Sides

The **perimeter** of a triangle is the sum of the lengths of all three sides. Look at the triangle below:

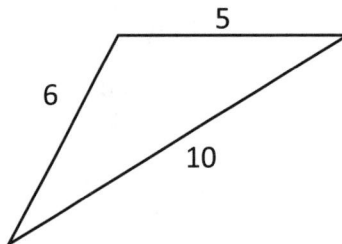

In this triangle, the perimeter is 5 + 6 + 10 = 21. This is a relatively simple property of a triangle, so often it will be used in combination with another property. Try this next problem. What is the perimeter of triangle *PQR*?

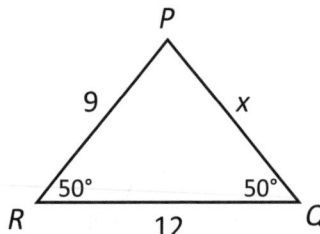

To solve for the perimeter, you need to determine the value of *x*. Because angles *PQR* and *PRQ* are both 50°, their opposite sides (*PR* and *PQ*) will have equal lengths. Therefore, side *PQ* also has a length of 9. The perimeter of triangle *PQR* is therefore 9 + 9 + 12 = 30.

## Check Your Skills

Find the perimeter of each triangle.

15.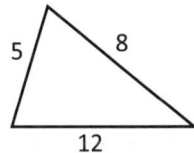

Note: Figure not drawn to scale.

16.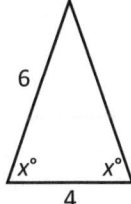

*Answer can be found on page 470.*

## Apply Area Formula: Any Side Can Be the Base

The area of a triangle equals $\frac{1}{2}$ × (base) × (height). In area formulas for any shape, be clear about the relationship between the base and the height. *The base and the height must be perpendicular to each other.*

In a triangle, one side of the triangle is the base. Any of the sides can be the base, but it is most common to make the bottom side the base.

The height is formed by dropping a line from the third point of the triangle straight down toward the base so that it forms a 90° angle with the base. The small square located where the height and base meet is used to denote a right angle (see the figure below). You can also say that the height is **perpendicular** to the base, or vice versa.

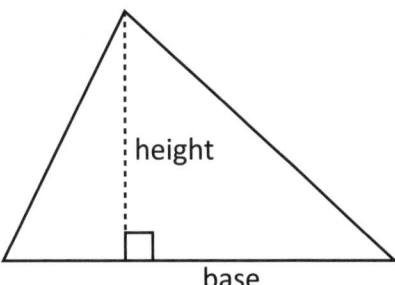

The GMAT often asks you about familiar shapes while presenting them in unfamiliar orientations. In particular, the triangle may be oriented in a way that makes it difficult to call the bottom side the base. The three triangles below are all the same triangle, but in each one a different side is the base. The diagrams also show the corresponding height.

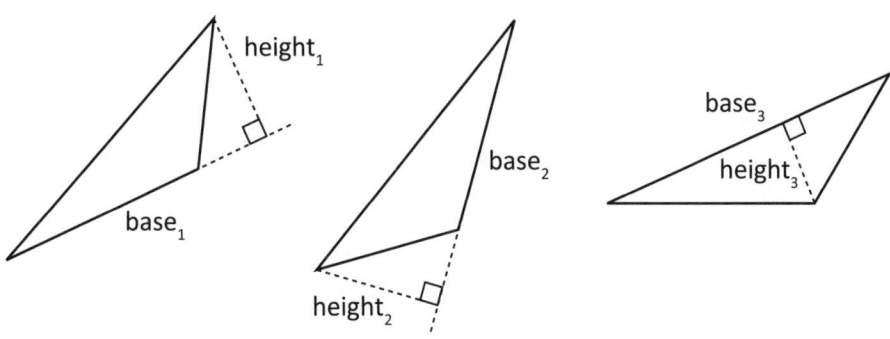

As in the first two examples, the height can be *outside* the triangle! You can extend the base farther in order to create the 90° angle. As long as there is a right angle between the base and the height, any orientation is permitted.

| If you… | Then you… | Like this: |
|---|---|---|
| Need the area of a triangle | Apply the area formula, using *any* convenient side as the base | $A = \frac{1}{2}$ (base) (height)<br>Use any side as the base; draw the right-angle height from the corner opposite the base |

## Check Your Skills

Find the area of each triangle.

17.

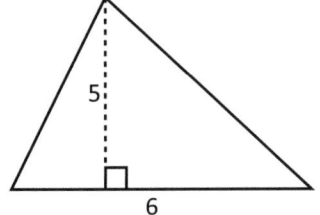

18.

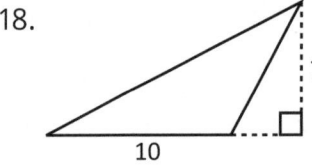

*Answers can be found on page 470.*

# Know Two Sides of a Right Triangle: Find the Third Side

**Right triangles** are very common on the GMAT. A right triangle is any triangle in which one of the angles is a right angle (90°). Consider this example:

What is the perimeter of triangle *ABC*?

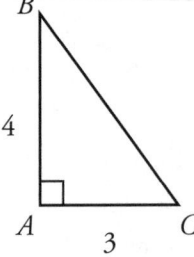

With only two sides of the triangle, how do you get the perimeter? Because this is a right triangle, you can use the Pythagorean theorem, which applies only to right triangles. According to the theorem, the lengths of the three sides of a right triangle are related by the equation $a^2 + b^2 = c^2$, where $a$ and $b$ are the lengths of the sides touching the right angle, also known as **legs**, and $c$ is the length of the side opposite the right angle, also known as the **hypotenuse**.

In the given triangle, sides $AB$ and $AC$ are $a$ and $b$ (it doesn't matter which is which), and side $BC$ is $c$. Therefore:

$$a^2 + b^2 = c^2$$
$$(3)^2 + (4)^2 = (BC)^2$$
$$9 + 16 = (BC)^2$$
$$25 = (BC)^2$$
$$5 = BC$$

The triangle looks like this:

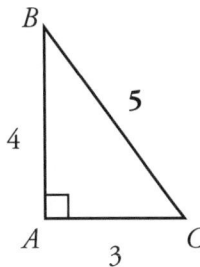

The perimeter is equal to $3 + 4 + 5 = 12$.

Often, you can take a shortcut around using the Pythagorean theorem. The GMAT favors a subset of right triangles, called *Pythagorean triples*. The triangle above is an example. The side lengths are 3, 4, and 5—all integers—and this triple is called a 3-4-5 triangle.

While there are quite a few of these triples, only a couple are useful to commit to memory for the GMAT; if you memorize them, you can save yourself from having to calculate them on the test. For each triple, the first two numbers are the lengths of the sides that touch the right angle, and the third (and greatest) number is the length of the hypotenuse.

3-4-5, or its "double" 6-8-10

5-12-13

Note that you can double, triple, or otherwise apply a common multiplier to these lengths; 3-4-5 is really a ratio of 3 : 4 : 5.

Consider this example:

What is the area of triangle *DEF*?

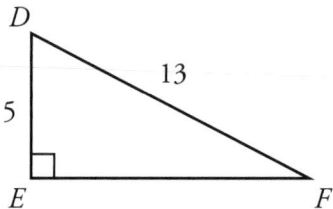

What do you need in order to find the area of triangle *DEF*? The area formula is $\frac{1}{2}$ × (base) × (height). This is a right triangle, so sides *DE* and *EF* are already perpendicular to each other. Treat one of them as the base and the other as the height.

How do you find the length of side *EF*? First, you can always use the Pythagorean theorem to find the length of the third side of a right triangle if you know the lengths of the other two sides. In this case, the formula would look like this: $(DE)^2 + (EF)^2 = (DF)^2$.

But don't follow through on that calculation! If you have memorized the Pythagorean triples, then when you see a right triangle in which one of the legs has a length of 5 and the hypotenuse has a length of 13, you will know that the length of the other leg must be 12.

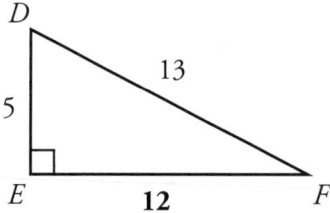

Now you have what you need to find the area of triangle *DEF*.

Area = $\frac{1}{2}$ × (12) × (5) = (6)(5) = 30

| If you... | Then you... | Like this: |
|---|---|---|
| Know two sides of a right triangle | Can find the third side, either by recognizing a triple or by using the full Pythagorean theorem | A leg of a right triangle has length 18, while the hypotenuse has length 30. How long is the third side? $18^2 + x^2 = 30^2$ and solve for $x$, or recognize that this is a multiple of the 3 : 4 : 5 triple (each side is multiplied by 6), $x = 24$ |

## Check Your Skills

Solve the following problems.

19.

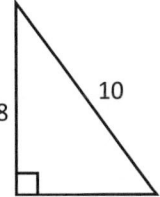

What is the length of the third side of the triangle in the figure above?

20.

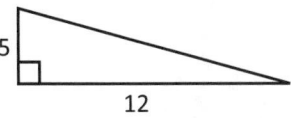

What is the length of the third side of the triangle in the figure above?

21.

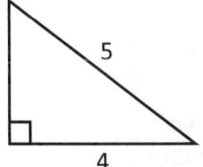

What is the area of the triangle in the figure above?

*Answers can be found on page 471.*

# Quadrilaterals

A quadrilateral is any figure with *four* sides. Quadrilaterals can always be cut up into two triangles by slicing across the middle to connect opposite corners. Therefore, what you know about triangles could apply in a problem involving quadrilaterals. In many cases, you won't want to cut up the quadrilateral that way, but it's good to know you could.

## Parallelogram: Cut into Triangles OR Drop Height

The GMAT frequently deals with **parallelograms**. A parallelogram is any four-sided figure in which the opposite sides are parallel and equal. Opposite angles are also equal, and adjacent angles (angles that are next to each other without another angle in between) add up to 180°.

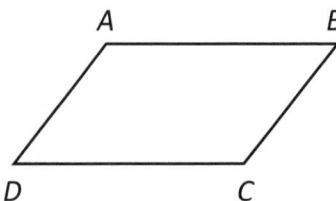

In the parallelogram above, sides *AB* and *CD* are parallel and have equal lengths. Sides *AD* and *BC* are parallel and have equal length. Angles *ADC* and *ABC* are equal. Angles *DAB* and *DCB* are equal. This is shown below:

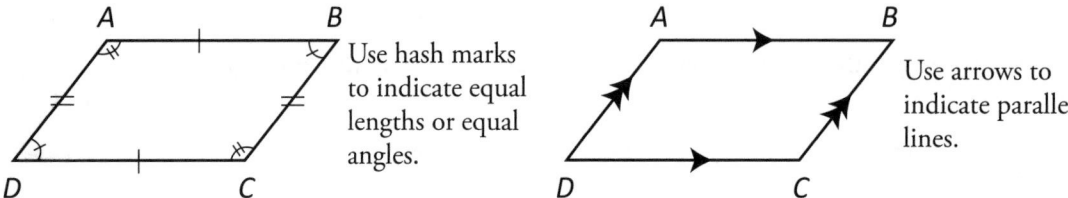

In any parallelogram, the diagonal will divide the parallelogram into two equal triangles.

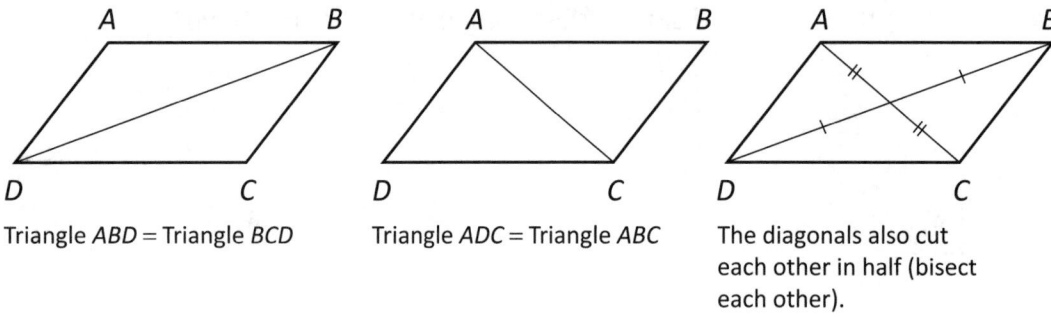

Triangle *ABD* = Triangle *BCD*     Triangle *ADC* = Triangle *ABC*     The diagonals also cut
each other in half (bisect
each other).

For any parallelogram, the perimeter is the sum of the lengths of all the sides and the area is equal to (base) × (height). With parallelograms, as with triangles, remember that the base and the height *must* be perpendicular to one another:

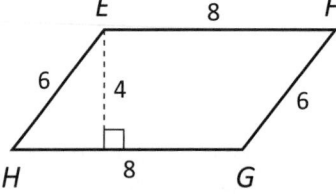

In the above parallelogram, what is the perimeter and what is the area? The perimeter is the sum of the sides: 6 + 8 + 6 + 8 = 28.

Alternatively, you can use one of the properties of parallelograms to calculate the perimeter in a different way. Parallelograms always have two sets of equal sides. In this parallelogram, two of the sides have a length of 6 and two of the sides have a length of 8. Therefore, the perimeter equals (2)(6) + (2)(8). You can factor out a 2 and say that the perimeter equals 2(6 + 8) = 28.

To calculate the area, you need a base and a height. It might be tempting to say that the area is 6 × 8 = 48. But the two sides of this parallelogram are not perpendicular to each other. The dotted line drawn into the figure, however, is perpendicular to side *HG*. You need to "drop a height," or draw a perpendicular line, to the base. The area of parallelogram *EFGH* is 8 × 4 = 32.

| If you... | Then you... | Like this: |
|---|---|---|
| Want the perimeter or area of a parallelogram | Find all sides (for the perimeter) or drop a height (for the area) | 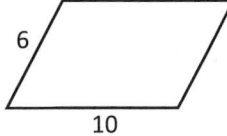 Perimeter = 2(6 + 8) = 28<br>Area = 8 × 4 = 32 |

## Check Your Skills

22. What is the perimeter of the parallelogram?

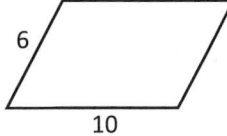

23. What is the area of the parallelogram?

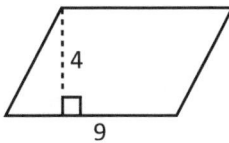

*Answers can be found on pages 471–472.*

## Rectangles = Parallelogram + Four Right Angles

Rectangles are a specific type of parallelogram. Rectangles have all the properties of parallelograms, plus one more: *all four internal angles of a rectangle are right angles*. With rectangles, you refer to one pair of sides as the length and one pair of sides as the width. It doesn't matter which is which, though traditionally the shorter side is the width and the longer side is the length.

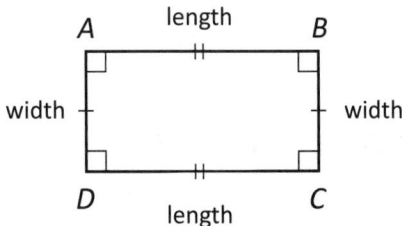

10

The formula for the perimeter of a rectangle is the same as for the perimeter of a parallelogram. You can sum the lengths of the four sides, or you can sum the length and the width and multiply by 2: $2(l + w)$.

The formula for the area of a rectangle is also the same as for the area of a parallelogram. But for any rectangle, the length and width are by definition perpendicular to each other, so you don't need to find a separate height. For this reason, the area of a rectangle is commonly expressed as (length) × (width), or $A = lw$.

For the following rectangle, find the perimeter and the area.

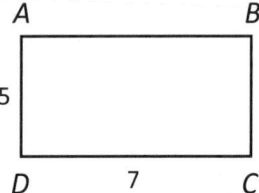

Start with the perimeter. The perimeter is $2(5 + 7) = 24$. Alternatively, $5 + 5 + 7 + 7 = 24$.

Now find the area. The formula for area is (length) × (width), or $(7)(5) = 35$.

Finally, the diagonal of a rectangle cuts the rectangle into two equal *right* triangles, with all the properties you expect of right triangles.

## Check Your Skills

Find the area and perimeter of each rectangle.

24.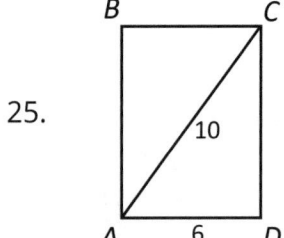

25.

*Answers can be found on page 472.*

## Squares = Rectangle + Four Equal Sides

The most special type of rectangle is a square. *A square is a rectangle in which all four sides are equal.* Knowing only one side of a square is enough to determine the perimeter and area of a square.

For instance, if the length of the side of a square is 3, then all four sides have a length of 3:

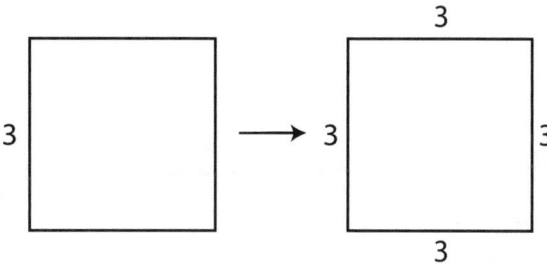

The perimeter of the square is 3 + 3 + 3 + 3, which equals 12. Alternatively, once you know the length of one side of a square, multiply that length by 4 to find the perimeter: $4s = (4)(3) = 12$.

To find the area, use the same formula as for a rectangle: Area = length × width.

But, because the shape is a square, the length and the width are equal. Therefore, the area of a square is Area = (side)², which is the side length squared.

In this case, the area is equal to $s^2$, or $(3)^2 = 9$.

Squares are like circles: if you know one measure, you can find everything. This is because they are both "regular" figures. All circles look like each other, and all squares look like each other. For circles, the most fundamental measure is the radius, and then you can calculate everything else. For squares, the most fundamental measure is the side length.

## Geometry: "Word" Problems with Pictures

Now that you know various properties of shapes, such as perimeter and area, how do you use these properties to answer GMAT geometry questions, especially ones with more than one figure? Consider this problem:

> Rectangles *ABCD* and *EFGH*, shown below, have equal areas. The length of side *AB* is 5. What is the length of diagonal *AC*?

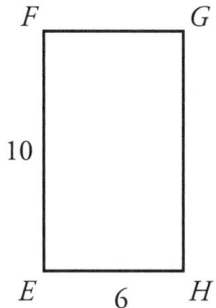 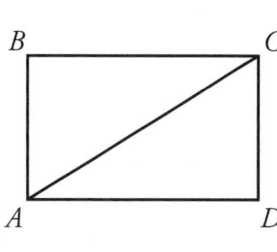

First, *draw your own copies of the shapes, and fill in everything you know.* For this problem, redraw both rectangles. Label side *AB* with a length of 5. Also, make note of what you're looking for—in this case, you want the length of diagonal *AC*. Label that diagonal with a question mark.

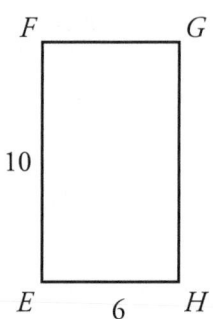

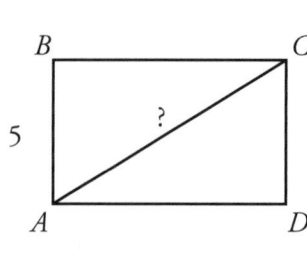

Now turn to the question. Many geometry questions are similar to the word problems discussed in Chapter 9. Both types of problems provide you with information that may be disguised. The information is related through common mathematical relationships, which also may be disguised or implied. In word problems, the information is given in words. In geometry, the information can be presented in words or visually.

So has the question above provided you with any information that can be expressed mathematically? Can you create equations?

Yes. The two rectangles have equal areas: $\text{Area}_{ABCD} = \text{Area}_{EFGH}$. You can do even better than that. The formula for area of a rectangle is Area = (length) × (width). The equation can be rewritten as $(\text{length}_{ABCD}) \times (\text{width}_{ABCD}) = (\text{length}_{EFGH}) \times (\text{width}_{EFGH})$.

The length and width of rectangle *EFGH* are 6 and 10, and the length of *AB* is 5.

$$(5) \times (\text{width}_{ABCD}) = (6) \times (10)$$
$$(5) \times (\text{width}_{ABCD}) = 60$$
$$\text{width}_{ABCD} = 12$$

Any time you learn a new piece of information, add that information to your picture.

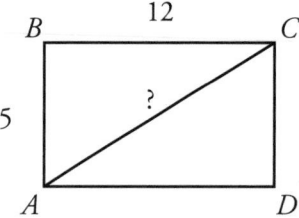

To recap, you've redrawn the shapes and filled in all the given information (such as side lengths, angles, etc.). You've made note of what the question wants. Just as you start a word problem by identifying unknowns, creating variables, and writing down givens, the first steps for geometry problems are to draw or redraw figures, add all of the given information, and confirm what you're being asked to find.

Next, you made use of additional information provided. The question stated that the two rectangles had equal areas. You created an equation to express this relationship, and then you plugged in the values you knew to solve for the width of rectangle *ABCD*. This process is identical to the process used to solve word problems—you identify relationships and create equations. After that, you solve the equations for the missing value (in this case, the width of *ABCD*).

MANHATTAN PREP

In some ways, all you have done so far is set up the problem. In fact, aside from noting that you need to find the length of diagonal *AC*, nothing you have done so far seems to have directly helped you actually solve for that value. So far, you have found that the width of rectangle *ABCD* is 12.

So why bother solving for the width of rectangle *ABCD* when you're not even sure why you'd need it? You are *likely* to need that missing value. On the vast majority of GMAT problems, two general principles hold:

> 1. Intermediate steps are required to solve for the value you want.
> 2. The GMAT almost never provides extraneous information.

As a result, something that you *can* solve for is likely to be a stepping stone on the way to the answer.

This doesn't mean that you should run hog-wild and calculate quantities at random. Rather, as you practice these problems, you'll gain a sense of the kinds of stepping stones that the GMAT prefers.

Now that you know the width of *ABCD*, what can you figure out that you couldn't before? Take another look at the value you're looking for: the length of *AC*.

You've already identified a relationship mentioned in the question—that both rectangles have equal areas. But for many geometry problems, there are additional relationships that aren't as obvious.

The key to this problem is to recognize that *AC* is not only the diagonal of rectangle *ABCD*, but also the hypotenuse of a right triangle, because all four interior angles of a rectangle are right angles.

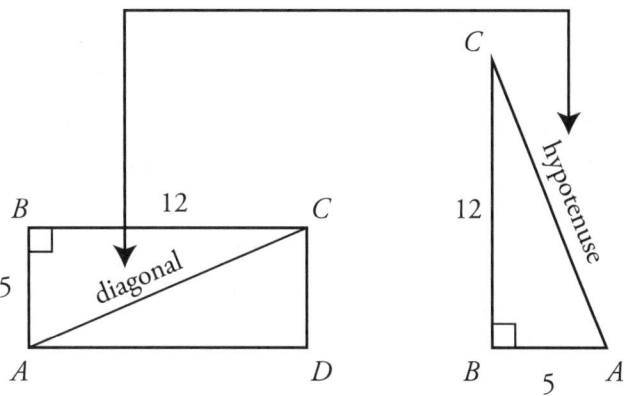

Now that you know *AC* is the hypotenuse of a right triangle, you can use two sides to find the third. One way to get the number is through the Pythagorean theorem.

This is a Pythagorean triple, though! The hypotenuse is *AC* = 13.

If you do want to use the Pythagorean theorem, sides *BC* and *AB* are the legs of the triangle, and *AC* is the hypotenuse. Therefore:

$$(BC)^2 + (AB)^2 = (AC)^2$$
$$(12)^2 + (5)^2 = (AC)^2$$
$$144 + 25 = (AC)^2$$
$$169 = (AC)^2$$
$$13 = AC$$

Let's recap what happened in the last portion of this question. You needed an insight that wasn't obvious: that the diagonal of rectangle *ABCD* is also the hypotenuse of right triangle *ABC*. Once you had that insight, you could apply "right triangle" thinking to get that unknown side. The last part of this problem required you to make inferences from the figures.

Sometimes you need to make a jump from one shape to another through a common element. For instance, you needed to see *AC* as both a diagonal of a rectangle and as a hypotenuse of a right triangle. Here, *AC* was common to both a rectangle and a right triangle, playing a different role in each.

These inferences can also make you think about what information you need to find another value.

Putting this all together, we recommend a 4-step process that you can apply to any Geometry problem.

Step 1:   *Draw or redraw figures, fill in all given information, and identify the target.*
          Fill in all known angles and lengths, and make note of any equal sides or angles.

Step 2:   *Identify relationships and create equations.*
          Start with relationships that are explicitly stated somewhere.

Step 3:   *Solve the equations for the missing value.*
          If you can solve for a value, you will almost always need that value to answer the question.

Step 4:   *Make inferences from the figures.*
          You often need to use relationships that are not explicitly stated.

Try this problem:

> Rectangle *PQRS* is inscribed in circle *O* pictured below. The center of circle *O* is also the center of rectangle *PQRS*. If the circumference of circle *O* is 5π, what is the area of rectangle *PQRS*?

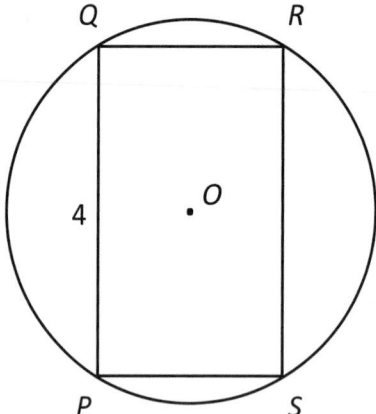

*Inscribed* means that the inside shape is just large enough to exactly touch the edges of the outside shape. The four corners of the rectangle just touch the circle.

First, redraw the figure on your paper and fill in all of the given information. The question didn't explicitly give you the value of any side lengths or angles, but it did say that *PQRS* is a rectangle. That means all four internal angles are right angles. This is how the GMAT tests what you know about the key properties of different shapes. Also identify what you're looking for: the rectangle's area. Here's what your picture should look like:

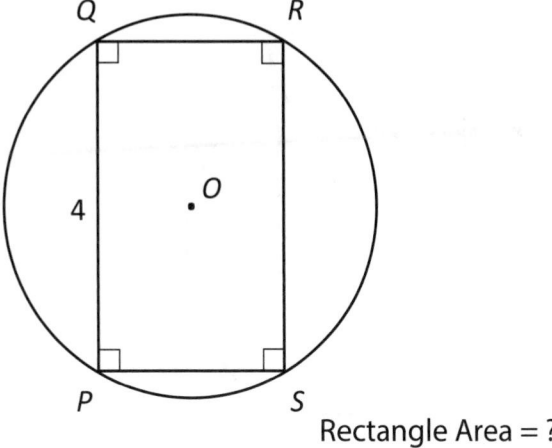

Rectangle Area = ?

Now identify relationships and create equations. The question stated that the circumference of circle $O$ is $5\pi$. Find the radius of the circle.

$$C = 2\pi r$$
$$5\pi = 2\pi r$$
$$5 = 2r$$
$$2.5 = r$$

If the radius is 2.5, then the diameter of circle $O$ is 5.

Why do you find the radius and diameter? *This is how you will make a connection between the circle and the rectangle.* Now is the time to make inferences from the figures.

Ultimately, this question is asking for the area of rectangle $PQRS$. What information do you need to find that value? You have the length of $QP$. If you can find the length of either $QR$ or $PS$, you can find the area of the rectangle.

What is the connection between the rectangle and the radius or diameter? Put in a diameter.

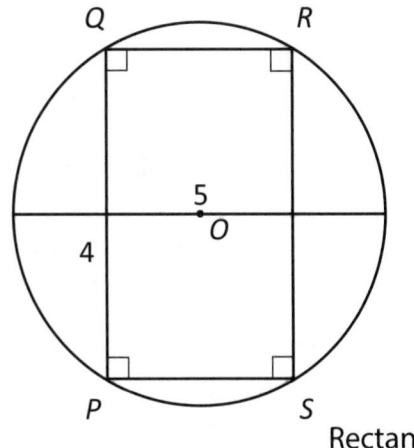

Rectangle Area = ?

That didn't help much. What if you drew the diameter so that it passed through the center but touched the circle at points *P* and *R*? The center of the circle is also the center of the rectangle, so the diameter of the circle is also the diagonal of the rectangle.

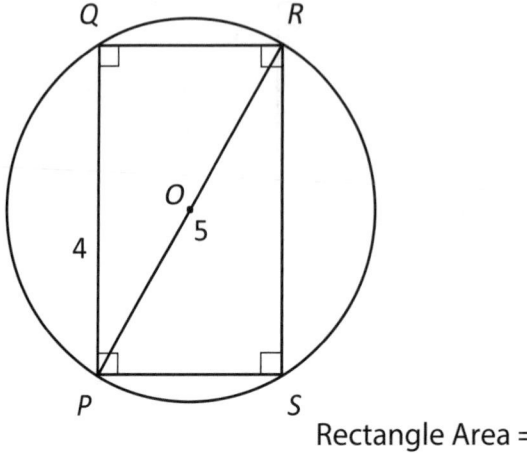

Rectangle Area = ?

Connection made! *PR* is the "bridge" between the two figures. (You could also draw the diagonal *QS*.)

Where do you go from here? You still need the length of either *QR* or *PS* (which are the same, because this is a rectangle). Can you get either one of those values? Yes. *PQR* is a right triangle. Maybe it's not oriented the way you are used to, but all the elements are there: it's a triangle and one of its internal angles is a right angle. You also know the lengths of two of the sides: *QP* and *PR*.

Triangle *PQR* is a 3-4-5 Pythagorean triple, so the length of *QR* is 3.

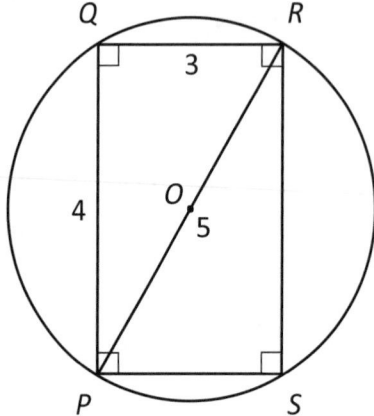

Rectangle Area = ?

At last, you have what you need to find the area of rectangle *PQRS*. Since the area is equal to (length) × (width), the area is (4) × (3) = 12.

The key insight in this problem was to realize that you could draw a diameter that would also act as the diagonal of the rectangle, linking the two figures together. You also had to recognize that *PQR* was a right triangle, even though it may have been hard to see. These kinds of insights will be crucial to success on the GMAT.

| If you... | Then you... | Like this: |
|---|---|---|
| Face a geometry problem with more than one figure | Follow the basic 4-step process to solve, finding intermediate unknowns and looking for bridges or links between the shapes | 1. Redraw, fill in, label target<br>2. Spot relationships & write equations<br>3. Solve for what you can<br>4. Make inferences |

## Check Your Skills

26. In rectangle *ABCD*, the distance from *A* to *C* is 10. What is the area of the circle tangent to sides *AD* and *BC* of the rectangle?

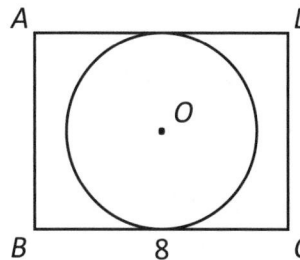

*Answer can be found on pages 472-473.*

# Coordinate Plane—Position Is a Pair of Numbers

A **coordinate plane** is a more advanced version of a number line.

| Position | Number | Number Line |
|---|---|---|
| "Two units right of 0" | 2 | |
| "One and a half units left of 0" | −1.5 | |

A **number line** is a ruler or measuring stick that goes as far as you want in both directions. With the number line, you can say where something is with a single number. In other words, you can link a position with a number.

You use either positive or negative numbers to indicate the position of a **point** either left or right of 0. When you are dealing with the number line, a point and a number mean the same thing.

If you're shown where the point is on the number line, you can tell the number.          → *The point is at −2.*

If you're told the number, you can show where the point is on the number line.          *The point is at 0.*  →

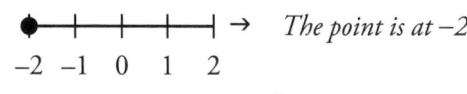

This works even if you have only partial information about the point. If you are told something about where the point is, you can tell *something* about the number, and vice versa.

For instance, if the number is positive, then the point lies somewhere to the right of 0 on the number line. Even though you don't know the exact location of the point, you do know a range of potential values.

*The number is positive.*
In other words, the number
is greater than (>) 0.

→

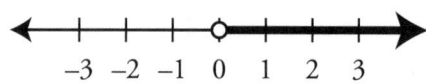

This also works in reverse. If you are given a range of potential positions on a number line, you can tell what that range is for the number:

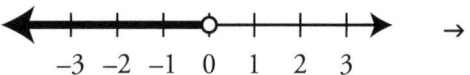

→        The number is less than (<) 0.

How does this get more complicated? What if you want to be able to locate a point that's not on a straight line, but on a page?

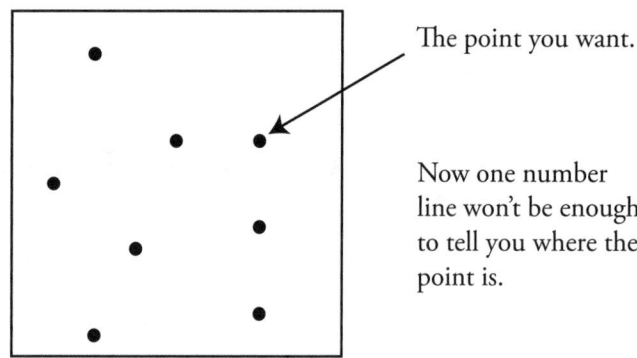

The point you want.

Now one number
line won't be enough
to tell you where the
point is.

Begin by inserting the number line into the picture. This will help you determine how far to the right or left of 0 the point is:

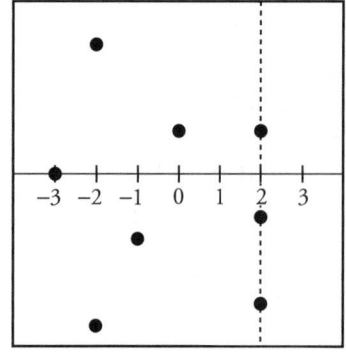

The point is two units to the right of 0.

But all three points that touch the dotted line are two units to the right of 0. You don't have enough information to determine the unique location of the point.

To locate the point, you also need to know how far up or down the dotted line the point is. For that, you'll need another number line. This number line, however, is going to be vertical. Using this vertical number line, you can measure how far above or below 0 a point is.

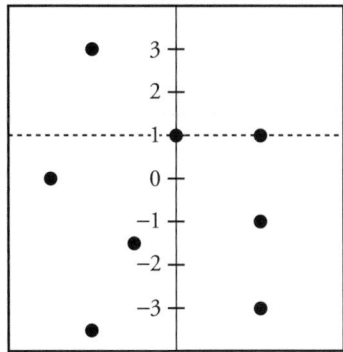

The point is one unit above 0.

Notice that this number line by itself also does not provide enough information to determine the unique location of the point.

If you combine the information from the two number lines, you can determine both how far left or right *and* how far up or down the point is.

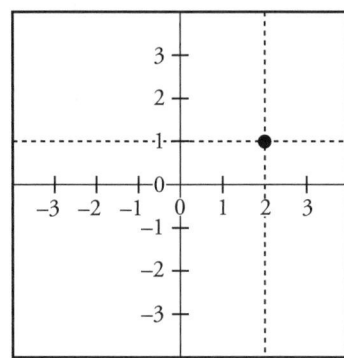

The point is 2 units to the right of 0.

AND

The point is 1 unit above 0.

Now you have a unique description of the point's position. Only one point on the page is *both* 2 units to the right of 0 *and* 1 unit above 0. On a page, you need two numbers to indicate position.

As with the number line, information can travel in either direction. If you're told the two numbers that indicate a point's location, you can place that point on the page.

The point is 3 units to the left of 0.

AND

The point is 2 units below 0.

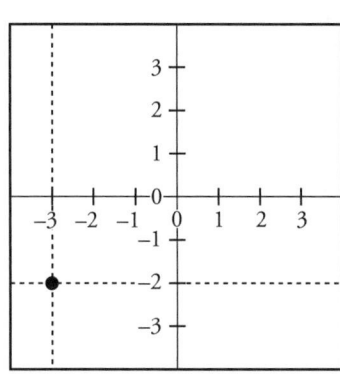

If, on the other hand, you see a point on the page, you can identify its location and extract the two numbers:

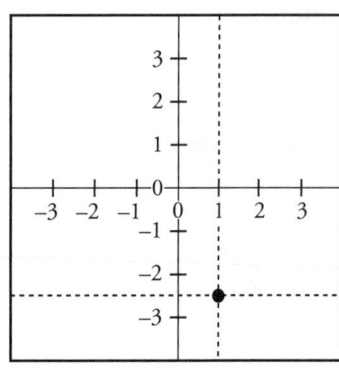

The point is 1 unit to the right of 0.

AND

The point is 2.5 units below 0.

Now that you have two pieces of information for each point, you need to keep straight which number is which. In other words, you need to know which number gives the left-right position and which number gives the up-down position:

The **x-coordinate** is the left-right number.

> Numbers to the right of 0 are positive.
> Numbers to the left of 0 are negative.

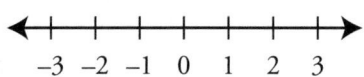

This number line is the **x-axis**.

The **y-coordinate** is the up-down number.

> Numbers above 0 are positive.
> Numbers below 0 are negative.

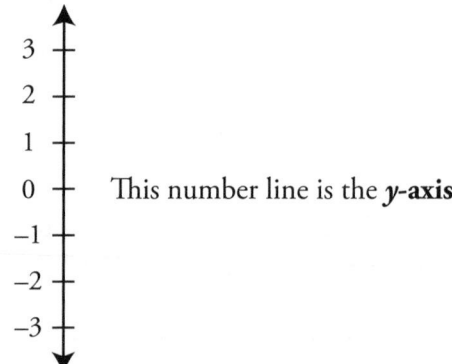

This number line is the **y-axis**.

The point where the x-axis and the y-axis cross is called the **origin**. This is always 0 on both axes.

Now when describing the location of a point, you can use the technical terms: x-coordinate and y-coordinate.

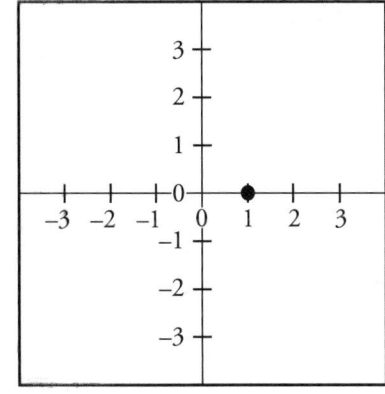

The *x*-coordinate of the point is 1 and the *y*-coordinate of the point is 0.

In short, you can say that, for this point, $x = 1$ and $y = 0$. In fact, you can go even farther. You can say that the point is at (1, 0). This shorthand always has the same basic layout. The first number in the parentheses is the *x*-coordinate and the second number is the *y*-coordinate: (*x*, *y*). One easy way to remember this is that *x* comes before *y* in the alphabet. The origin has coordinates (0, 0). For example:

The point is at (−3, −1).

OR

The point has an *x*-coordinate of −3 and a *y*-coordinate of −1.

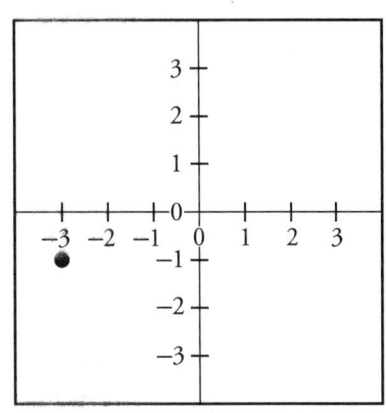

Now you have a fully functioning **coordinate plane**: an *x*-axis and a *y*-axis drawn on a page. The coordinate plane allows you to determine the unique position of any point on a **plane** (essentially, a big, flat sheet of paper).

And in case you were ever curious about what **one-dimensional** and **two-dimensional** mean, now you know. A line is one-dimensional, because you only need one number to identify a point's location. A plane is two-dimensional, because you need two numbers to identify a point's location.

| If you... | Then you... | Like this: |
|---|---|---|
| Want to plot a point on the coordinate plane | Use the *x*-coordinate for right-left of (0, 0), and use the *y*-coordinate for up-down from (0, 0) | (3, 2) is three units right of and two units up from the origin |

## Check Your Skills

27. Draw a coordinate plane and plot the given points.
    1. (3, 1)
    2. (−2, 3.5)
    3. (0, −4.5)
    4. (1, 0)

28. Match each coordinate with the appropriate point on the coordinate plane.
    1. (2, −1)
    2. (−1.5, −3)
    3. (−1, 2)
    4. (3, 2)

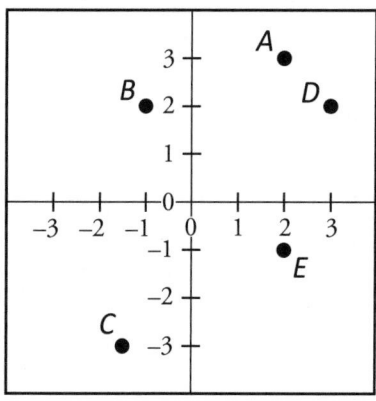

*Answers can be found on page 474.*

# Know Just One Coordinate = Find a Line

You need to know both the *x*-coordinate and the *y*-coordinate to plot a point exactly on the coordinate plane. If you only know one coordinate, you can't tell precisely where the point is, but you can narrow down the possibilities.

Let's say that all you know is that the point is 4 units to the right of 0.

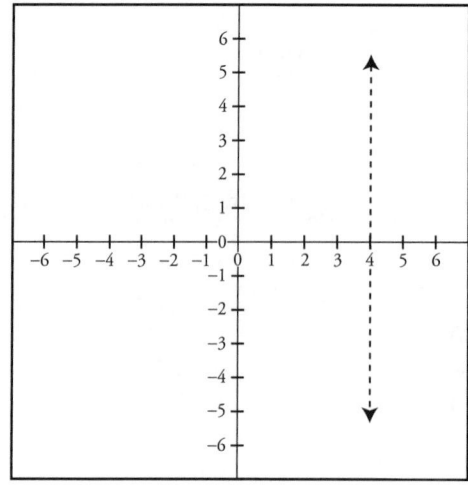

The *x*-coordinate still indicates left-right position. If you fix the left-right position but not the up-down position, then the point can only move up and down—forming a vertical line.

In this case, any point along the vertical dotted line is 4 units to the right of 0. In other words, every point on the dotted line has an *x*-coordinate of 4. You could shorten that and say $x = 4$. You don't know anything about the *y*-coordinate, which could be any number. All the points along the dotted line have different *y*-coordinates but the same *x*-coordinate, which equals 4.

So if you know that $x = 4$, then the point can be anywhere along a vertical line that crosses the *x*-axis at (4, 0). Let's try another example.

If you know that $x = -3$…

Then you know…

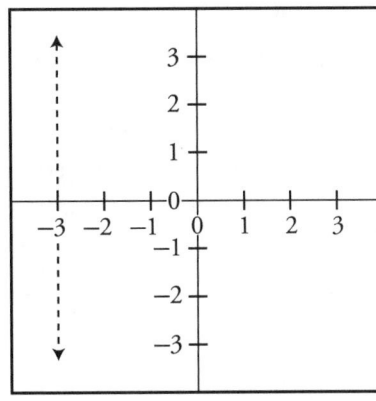

Every point on the dotted line has an *x*-coordinate of –3.

Points on the dotted line include (–3, 1), (–3, –7), (–3, 100), and so on. In general, if you know the *x*-coordinate of a point and not the *y*-coordinate, then all you can say about the point is that it lies on a vertical line.

Now imagine that all you know is the *y*-coordinate of a number. Say you know that $y = -2$. How could you represent this on the coordinate plane? In other words, what are all the points for which $y = -2$?

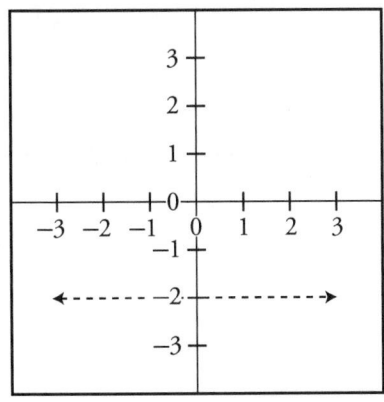

Every point 2 units below 0 fits this condition. These points form a horizontal line. You don't know anything about the *x*-coordinate, which could be any number. All the points along the horizontal dotted line have different *x*-coordinates but the same *y*-coordinate, which equals –2. For instance, (–3, –2), (–2, –2), and (50, –2) are all on the line.

Let's try another example. If you know that $y = 1$...

Then you know...

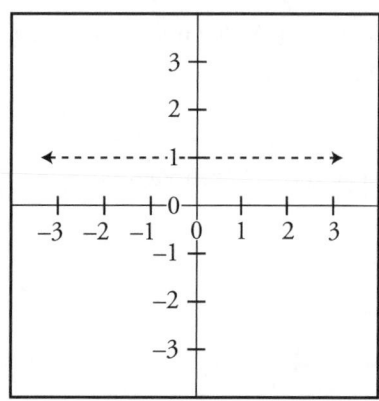

Every point on the dotted line has a $y$-coordinate of 1.

If you know the $y$-coordinate but not the $x$-coordinate, then you know the point lies somewhere on a horizontal line.

| If you... | Then you... | Like this: |
|---|---|---|
| Know just one coordinate | Have either a horizontal or a vertical line | If $x = 3$, then a vertical line runs through the number 3 on the $x$-axis. The $y$-coordinate could be anything. |

## Check Your Skills

Draw a coordinate plane and plot the following lines.

29. $x = 6$
30. $y = -3$
31. $x = 0$

*Answers can be found on pages 474–475.*

## Know a Range = Shade a Region

What do you do if all you know is that $x > 0$? To answer that, return to the number line for a moment. As you saw earlier, if $x > 0$, then the target is anywhere to the right of 0.

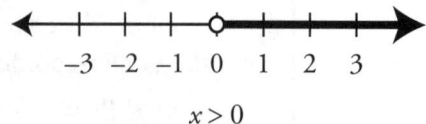

$x > 0$

Now look at the coordinate plane. All you know is that *x* is greater than 0. And you don't know *anything* about *y*, which could be any number.

How do you show all the possible points? You can shade in part of the coordinate plane: the part to the right of 0.

If you know that $x > 0$...

Then you know...

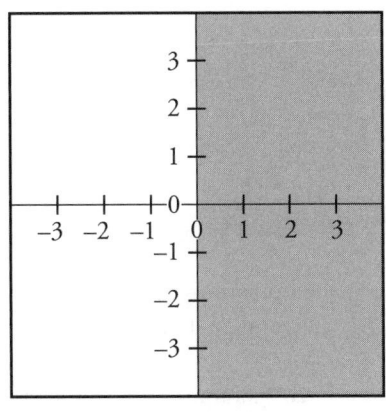

Every point in the shaded region has an *x*-coordinate greater than 0.

What if you know that $y < 0$? Then you can shade in the bottom half of the coordinate plane—where the *y*-coordinate is less than 0. The *x*-coordinate can be anything.

If you know that $y < 0$...

Then you know...

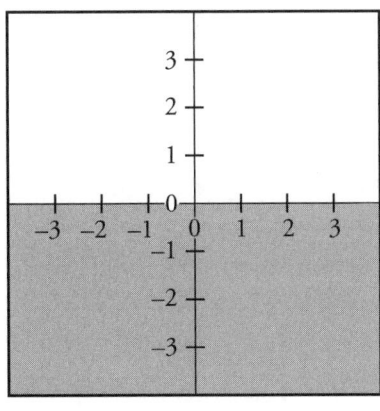

Every point in the shaded region has a *y*-coordinate less than 0.

Finally, if you know information about both *x* and *y*, then you can narrow down the shaded region.

If you know that $x > 0$ AND $y < 0$...

Then you know...

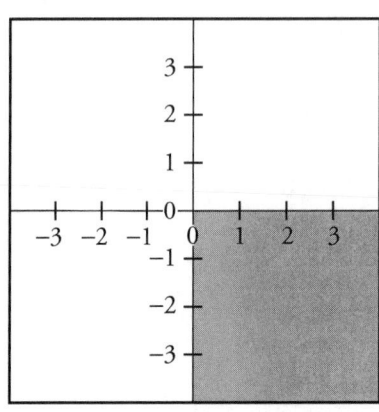

10

The only place where $x$ is greater than 0 AND $y$ is less than 0 is the bottom right quarter of the plane. So you know that the point lies somewhere in the bottom right quarter of the coordinate plane.

The four quarters of the coordinate plane are called **quadrants**. Each quadrant corresponds to a different combination of signs of $x$ and $y$. The quadrants are numbered I, II, III, or IV, as shown below, starting with the top right quadrant and moving counter-clockwise:

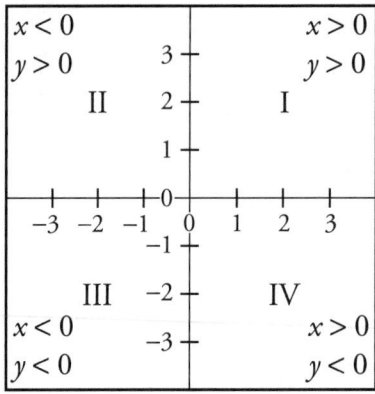

| In quadrant: | The $x$-coordinate is: | The $y$-coordinate is: |
|:---:|:---:|:---:|
| I | positive | positive |
| II | negative | positive |
| III | negative | negative |
| IV | positive | negative |

| If you... | Then you... | Like this: |
|:---:|:---:|:---:|
| Only know ranges for one or both coordinates | Can plot a shaded region corresponding to the proper range | If $x < 0$, then shade all of the points to the left of the $y$-axis |

## Check Your Skills

32. In which quadrant do the following points lie?

    1. (1, –2)

    2. (–4.6, 7)

    3. (–1, –2.5)

    4. (3, 3)

33. Which quadrant or quadrants are indicated by the following?

    1. $x < 0, y > 0$

    2. $x < 0, y < 0$

    3. $y > 0$

    4. $x < 0$

*Answers can be found on pages 475–476.*

# Read a Graph = Drop a Line to the Axes

If you see a point on a coordinate plane, how do you determine its coordinates? To find an *x*-coordinate, drop an imaginary line down to the *x*-axis (or up to it) and find the corresponding number.

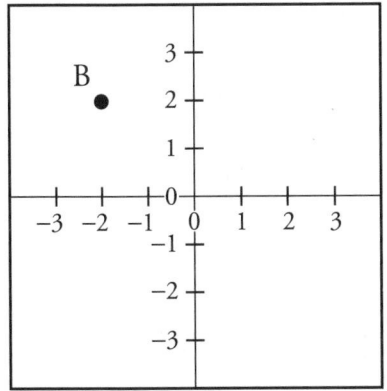 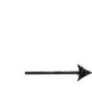 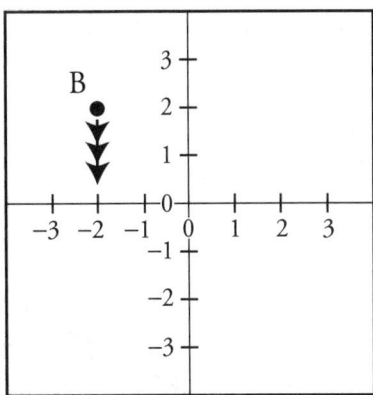

The line hits the *x*-axis at –2, so the *x*-coordinate of the point is –2. Now to find the *y*-coordinate, employ a similar technique. This time, draw a horizontal line instead of a vertical line.

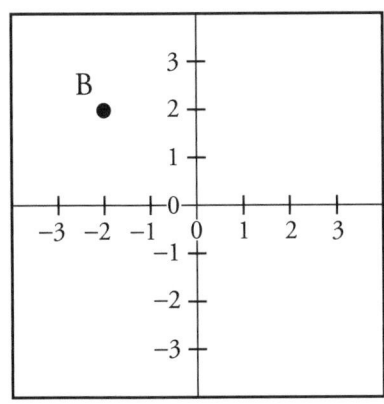  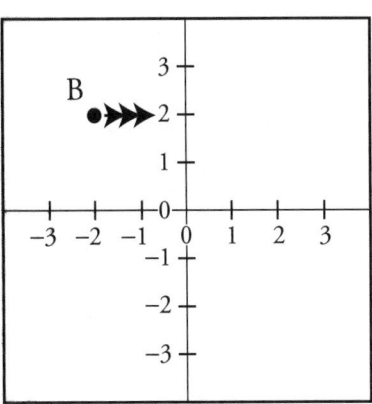

The line touches the *y*-axis at 2, which means the *y*-coordinate of the point is 2. Thus, the coordinates of point *B* are (−2, 2).

Now suppose that you know that the point is on a slanted line in the plane. Try this problem.

On the line shown, what is the *y*-coordinate of the point that has an *x*-coordinate of −4?

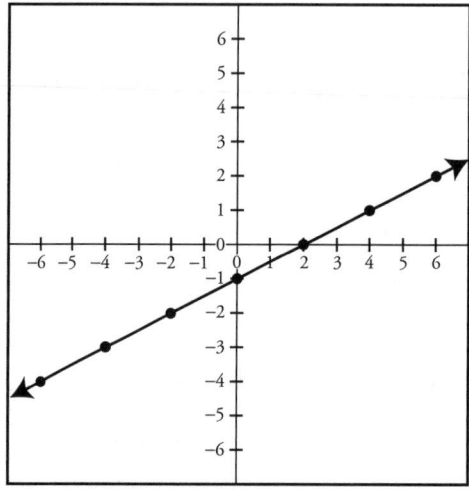

Go from the axis that you know (here, the *x*-axis) to the line that contains the point, and then to the *y*-axis (the axis you don't know).

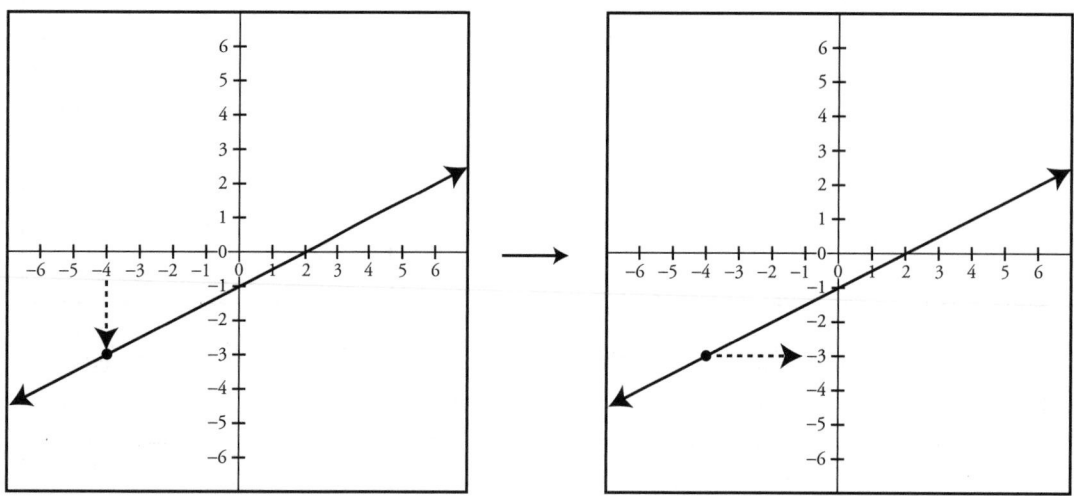

So the point on the line that has an *x*-coordinate of −4 has a *y*-coordinate of −3.

This method of locating points applies equally well to any shape or curve you may encounter on a coordinate plane. Try this next problem.

On the curve shown, what is the value of *y* when *x* = 2?

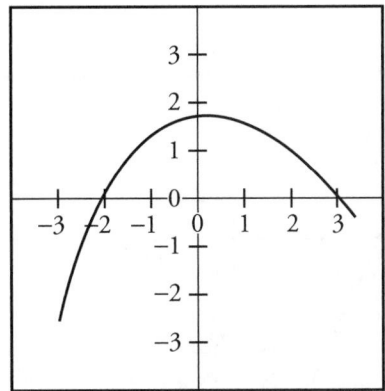

Once again, you know the *x*-coordinate, so draw a line from the *x*-axis (where you know the coordinate) to the curve, and then draw a line to the *y*-axis.

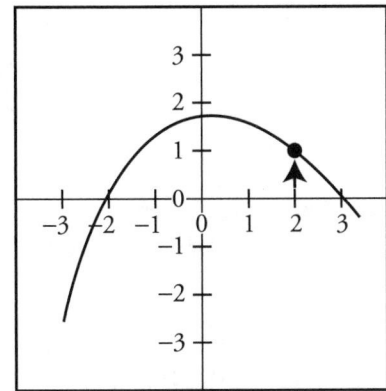     ⟶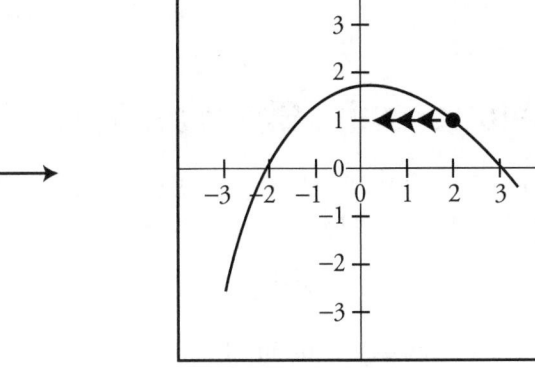

On the curve shown, the point that has an *x*-coordinate of 2 has a *y*-coordinate of 1.

Note that the GMAT will mathematically define each line or curve, so you will never be forced to guess visually where a point falls. This discussion is meant to convey how to use any graphical representation.

## Check Your Skills

34. On the following graph, what is the *y*-coordinate of the point on the line that has an *x*-coordinate of –3?

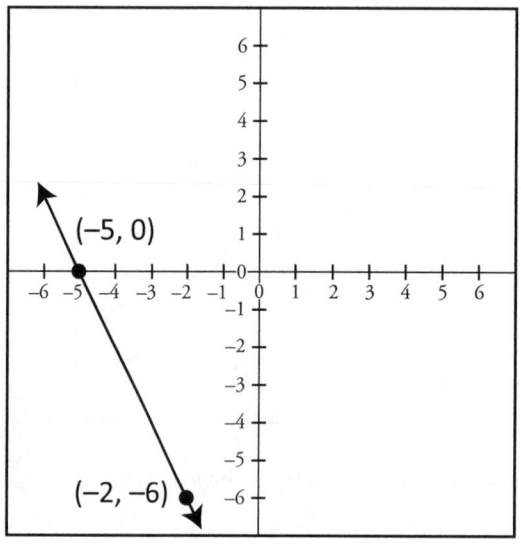

*Answer can be found on page 476.*

# Plot a Relationship: Given an *X*, Find a *Y*

The most frequent use of the coordinate plane is to display a relationship between *x* and *y*. Often, this relationship is expressed this way: If you tell me *x*, I can tell you *y*.

As an equation, this sort of relationship looks like this:

$y =$ some expression involving *x*

Another way of saying this is that you have *y* "in terms of" *x*.

Examples:     $y = 2x + 1$

$y = x^2 - 3x + 2$

$y = \dfrac{x}{x + 2}$

If you plug a number in for *x* in any of these equations, you can calculate a value for *y*.

Take $y = 2x + 1$. You can generate a set of *y*'s by plugging in various values of *x*. Start by making a table.

| *x* | $y = 2x + 1$ |
|---|---|
| –1 | $y = 2(-1) + 1 = -1$ |
| 0 | $y = 2(0) + 1 = 1$ |
| 1 | $y = 2(1) + 1 = 3$ |
| 2 | $y = 2(2) + 1 = 5$ |

Now that you have some values, see what you can do with them. You can say that when $x$ equals 0, $y$ equals 1. These two values form a pair. You express this connection by plotting the point (0, 1) on the coordinate plane. Similarly, you can plot all the other points that represent an $x$-$y$ pair from the table.

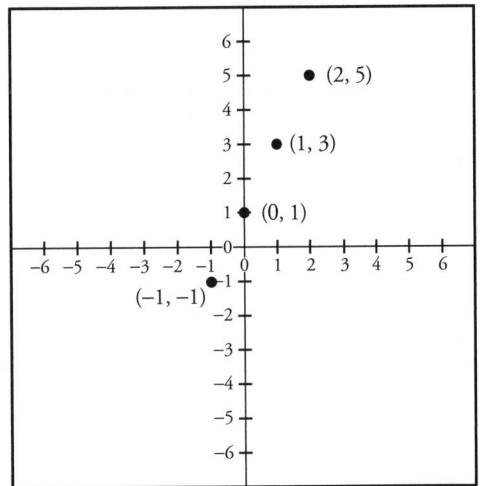

You might notice that these points seem to lie on a straight line. You're right—they do. In fact, any point that you can generate using the relationship $y = 2x + 1$ will also lie on the line.

This line is the graphical representation of $y = 2x + 1$:

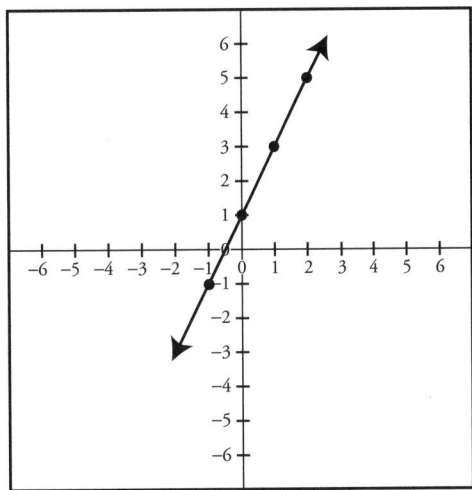

So now you can talk about equations in visual terms. In fact, that's what lines and curves on the coordinate plane are—they represent all the $x$-$y$ pairs that make an equation true. Take a look at the following example:

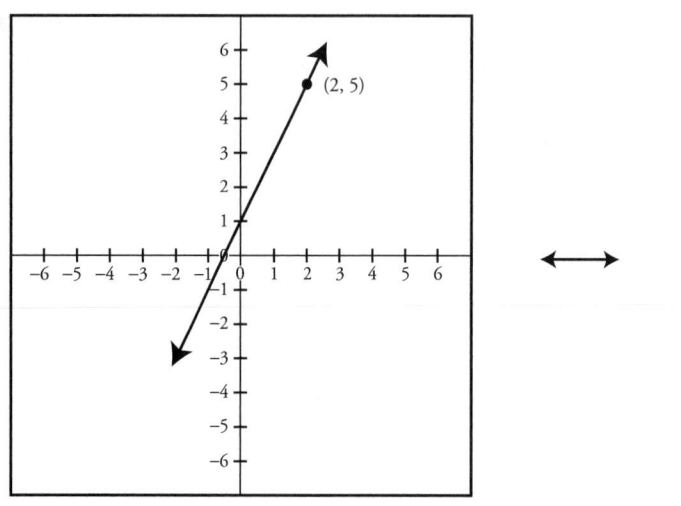

$$y = 2x + 1$$
$$5 = 2(2) + 1$$

The point (2, 5) lies on the line $y = 2x + 1$.   $\longleftrightarrow$   If you plug in 2 for $x$ in $y = 2x + 1$, you get 5 for $y$.

You can even speak more generally, using variables.

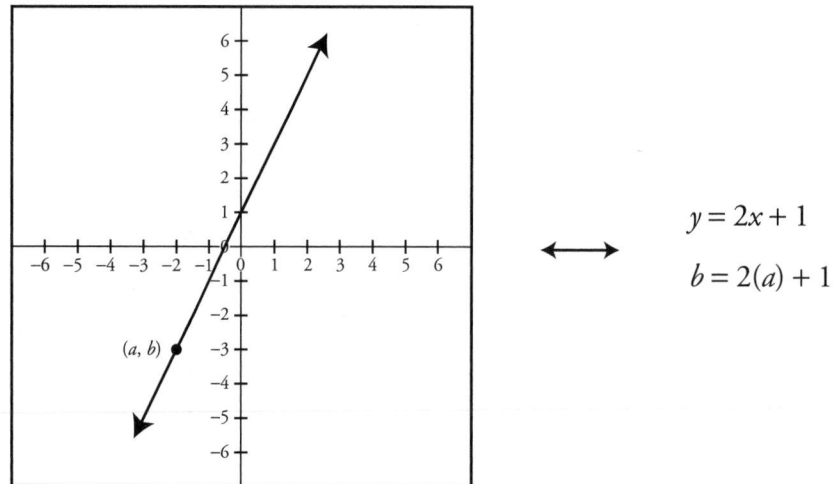

$$y = 2x + 1$$
$$b = 2(a) + 1$$

The point $(a, b)$ lies on the line $y = 2x + 1$.   $\longleftrightarrow$   If you plug in $a$ for $x$ in $y = 2x + 1$, you get $b$ for $y$.

| If you... | Then you... | Like this: |
|---|---|---|
| Want to plot a relationship in the $x$-$y$ plane | Input values of $x$ into the relationship, get values of $y$ back, then plot the $(x, y)$ pairs | Plot $y = 4 - x$<br>If $x = 0$, then $y = 4$, etc.<br>Then plot (0, 4), etc. |

## Check Your Skills

35. True or False? The point (9, 21) is on the line $y = 2x + 1$.
36. True or False? The point (4, 14) is on the curve $y = x^2 - 2$.

*Answers can be found on page 476.*

MANHATTAN PREP

# Lines in the Plane: Use Slope and *y*-Intercept to Plot

The relationship $y = 2x + 1$ formed a line in the coordinate plane. You can generalize this relationship. Any relationship of the following form represents a line:

$y = mx + b$                    *m* and *b* represent numbers (positive or negative).

For instance, in the equation $y = 2x + 1$, $m = 2$ and $b = 1$.

A **linear equation** is one that forms a straight line when it is plotted on a coordinate plane. A linear equation does not contain any exponents and, if you put *x* and *y* on the same side of the equation, the two variables are not multiplied together.

<u>Lines</u>                                              <u>Not Lines</u>

$y = 3x - 2$          $m = 3, b = -2$          $y = x^2$

$y = -x + 4$          $m = -1, b = 4$          $y = \dfrac{1}{x}$

$y = \dfrac{1}{2}x$          $m = \dfrac{1}{2}, b = 0$

These are called linear equations.          These equations are not linear.

The variables *m* and *b* have special meanings when you are dealing with linear equations. The variable *m* represents the **slope** of the line. The slope tells you how steep the line is and whether the line is rising or falling.

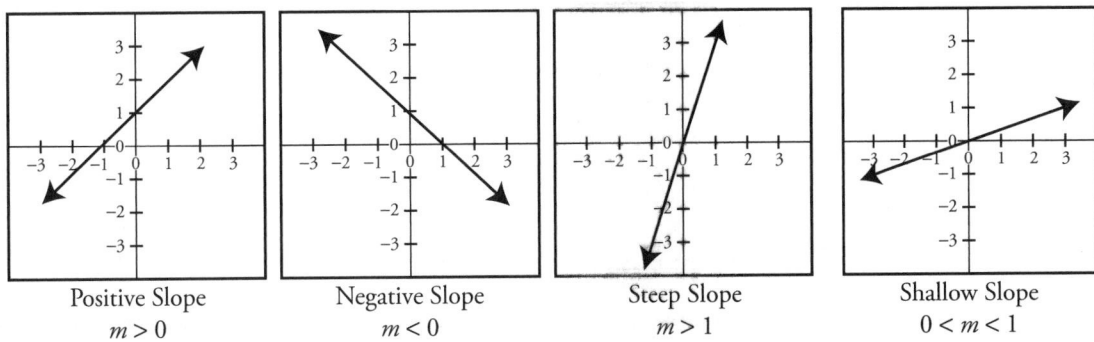

| Positive Slope | Negative Slope | Steep Slope | Shallow Slope |
| $m > 0$ | $m < 0$ | $m > 1$ | $0 < m < 1$ |

Imagine someone walking along the line from left to right. When the person is walking uphill, the slope is positive. If the person is walking downhill, the slope is negative. If the slope is very gradual, it is called a shallow slope. If it would be very hard to walk uphill, the slope is considered steep. (And if you'd be in danger of tumbling down while walking downhill, that's also very steep!)

The variable *b* represents the **y-intercept**. The *y*-intercept indicates where the line crosses the *y*-axis. Any line or curve always crosses the *y*-axis when $x = 0$. To find the *y*-intercept, plug in 0 for *x* in the equation and find *y*.

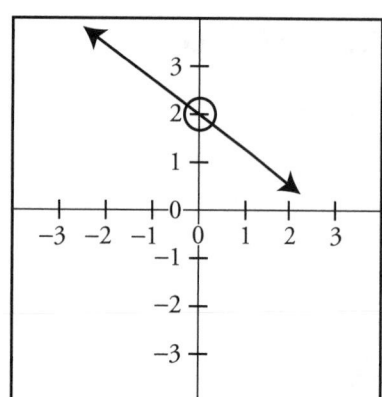   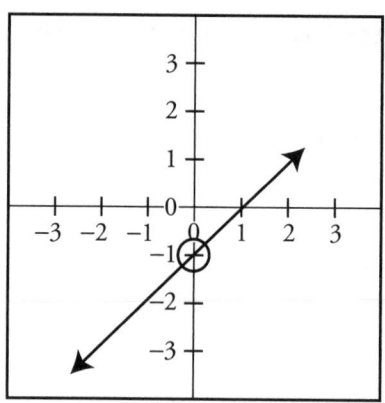

In the first image above, the *y*-intercept is 2, because the line crosses the *y*-axis at $y = 2$. In the second image, the *y*-intercept is −1.

As you saw earlier, you can graph an equation by solving the equation for various values of *x* to obtain a value of *y*, and then plot and connect those points. However, you can use *m* and *b* in a linear equation to plot a line more quickly than by plotting several points on the line. Here's how to plot the line $y = \dfrac{1}{2}x - 2$.

Begin with the *y*-intercept: $b = -2$, so the line crosses the *y*-axis at $y = -2$. Plot that point on the coordinate plane.

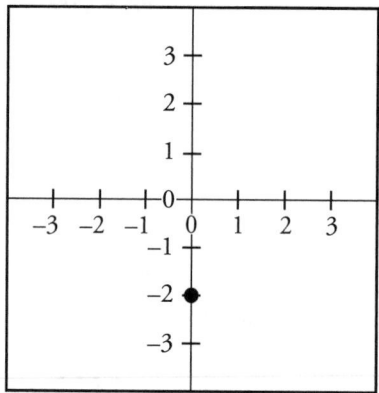

Now you're going to use the slope in order to finish drawing the line. Every slope, whether an integer or a fraction, can be thought of as a fraction. In this equation, $m = \dfrac{1}{2}$.

$$\dfrac{1}{2} \;\rightarrow\; \dfrac{\text{Numerator}}{\text{Denominator}} \;\rightarrow\; \dfrac{\text{Rise}}{\text{Run}} \;\rightarrow\; \dfrac{\text{Change in } y}{\text{Change in } x}$$

The numerator of the fraction indicates how many units you want to move in the *y* direction—in other words, how far up or down you want to move. The denominator indicates how many units you want to move in the *x* direction—in other words, how far left or right you want to move. For this particular equation, the slope is $\dfrac{1}{2}$, which means you want to move up 1 unit and right 2 units from the *y*-intercept.

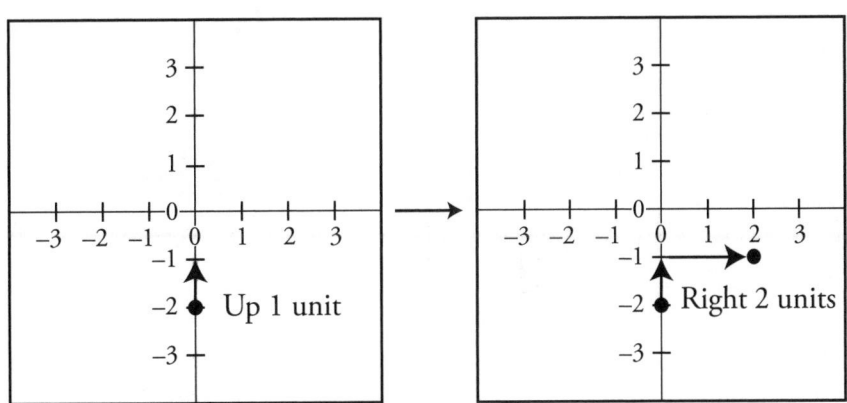

If you start from the point (0, −2) and go 1 unit up and 2 units to the right, you'll end up at the point (2, −1). The point (2, −1) is also a point on the line and a solution to the equation $y = \frac{1}{2}x - 2$. In fact, you can plug in the $x$ value and solve for $y$ to check that you did this correctly.

$$y = \frac{1}{2}x - 2$$
$$y = \frac{1}{2}(2) - 2$$
$$y = -1$$

If you go up another 1 unit and right another 2 units, you will end up with another point that appears on the line. Although you could keep doing this indefinitely, in reality, you need only two points to draw a line. Connect the dots and you're done! Here's what the equation will look like graphically:

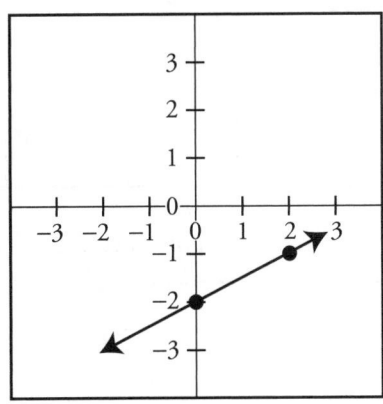

$$y = \frac{1}{2}x - 2$$

Try another one. Graph the equation $y = -\frac{3}{2}x + 4$.

Start by plotting the $y$-intercept. In this equation, $b = 4$, so the line crosses the $y$-axis at the point (0, 4).

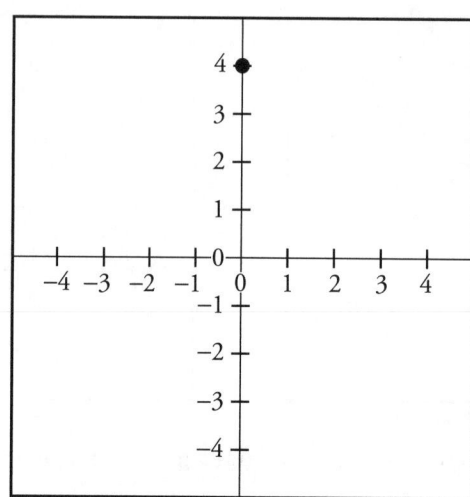

Now use the slope to find a second point. This time, the slope is $-\dfrac{3}{2}$, which is a negative slope. Associate the negative sign with the numerator: $-3$. To find the next point, go *down* 3 units and right 2 units.

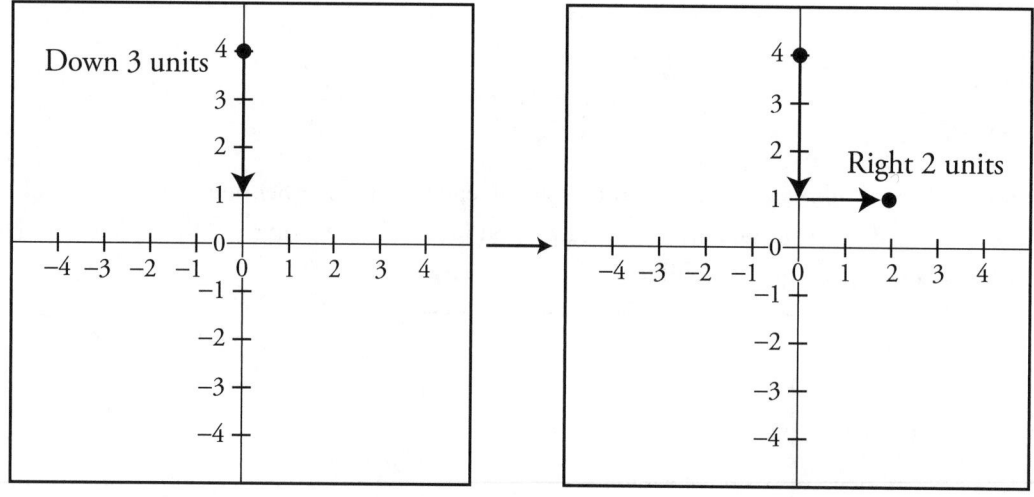

Therefore, $(2, 1)$ is another point on the line. Now that you have 2 points, you can draw the line.

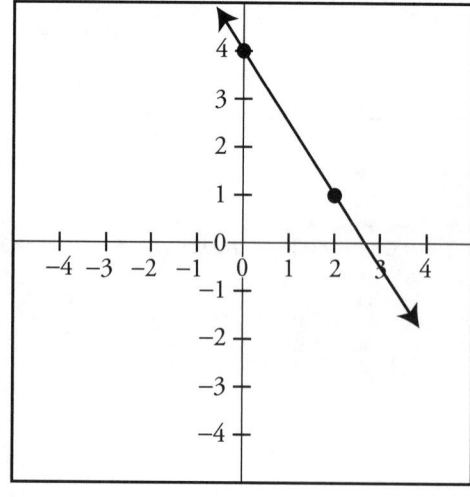

$$y = -\frac{3}{2}x + 4$$

| If you... | Then you... | Like this: |
|-----------|-------------|------------|
| Want to plot a linear equation in the *x-y* plane | Put the equation in the form of $y = mx + b$, then use $m$ and $b$ to draw the line | Plot $y = 4 - x$<br>Rearrange the equation:<br>$y = -1x + 4$<br>Slope is $-1$,<br>*y*-intercept is $(0, 4)$ |

## Check Your Skills

For questions 37 and 38, what are the slope and *y*-intercept of the given lines?

37. $y = 3x + 4$
38. $2y = 5x - 12$
39. Draw a coordinate plane and graph the line $y = 2x - 4$. Identify the slope and the *y*-intercept.

*Answers can be found on pages 476–477.*

10

# Check Your Skills Answer Key

1. **81$\pi$:** The formula for area is $A = \pi r^2$. The radius is 9, so the area is equal to $\pi(9)^2 = 81\pi$.

2. **17:** Circumference of a circle is either $C = 2\pi r$ or $C = \pi d$. The question asks for the diameter, so use the latter formula.

    $17\pi = \pi d$
    $17 = d$

3. **10$\pi$:** Both the area and circumference of a circle are defined in terms of the radius. Use the given area of $25\pi$ to find the radius.

    $A = \pi r^2$
    $25\pi = \pi r^2$
    $25 = r^2$
    $5 = r$

    Now use the radius of 5 to find the circumference.

    $C = 2\pi r$
    $C = 2\pi(5)$
    $C = 10\pi$

4. **3$\pi$:** If the central angle of the sector is 270°, then it is $\frac{3}{4}$ of the full circle, because $\frac{270°}{360°} = \frac{3}{4}$.

    Since the radius is 2, the area of the full circle is $\pi(2)^2 = 4\pi$. The area of the sector is $\frac{3}{4} \times 4\pi = 3\pi$.

5. **240°:** Because you are given the arc length, find the circumference of the full circle and use that to determine what fraction the sector represents.

    $C = 2\pi r = 2\pi(3) = 6\pi$

    Fraction of total $= \frac{4\pi}{6\pi} = \frac{2}{3}$

    The central angle is $\frac{2}{3} \times 360° = 240°$.

6. **$8\pi$:** Begin by finding the area of the whole circle; use that information to determine what fraction the sector represents.

$$\text{Area} = \pi(10)^2 = 100\pi$$
$$\text{Fraction of sector} = \frac{40\pi}{100\pi} = \frac{4}{10} = \frac{2}{5}$$

The circumference of the whole circle is $2\pi r = 20\pi$. Use this, coupled with the fraction of the sector, to determine the arc length.

$$\text{Arc length} = \frac{2}{5} \times 20\pi = 8\pi$$

7. **No:** The two known sides of the triangle are 5 and 19. The third side of the triangle must be greater than $19 - 5$ but less than $19 + 5$. In other words, the third side must be between 14 and 24. The number 13 is less than 14, so 13 cannot be the length of the third side.

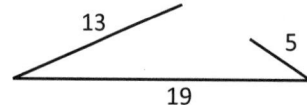

No possible triangle
with these lengths.

8. **$9 < \text{third side} < 25$:** If the two known sides of the triangle are 8 and 17, then find the range for the third side by taking the sum and the difference of the known sides.

Sum = $8 + 17 = 25$
Difference = $17 - 8 = 9$
The third side must be greater than 9 but less than 25.

9. **$x = 65°$:** The internal angles of a triangle sum to 180°.

$40 + 75 + x = 180$
$115 + x = 180$
$x = 65$

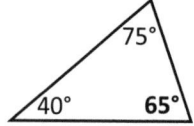

**MANHATTAN** PREP

10. **x = 65°:** The three angles of the triangle sum to 180°, so 50 + x + x = 180.

$$50 + x + x = 180$$
$$2x = 130$$
$$x = 65$$

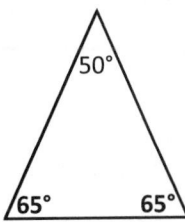

11. **x = 70° and y = 80°:** In order to determine the missing angles of the triangle, you'll need to do a little work with the picture. Start with x. Straight lines have a degree measure of 180°, so 110 + x = 180, and x = 70. Now find y.

$$30 + 70 + y = 180$$
$$y = 80$$

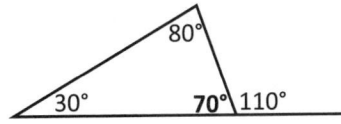

12. **x° = 80°:** In this triangle, two sides have the same length (so this triangle is isosceles). Therefore, the two angles opposite the two equal sides will also be equal: x must be 80°.

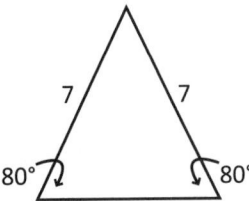

13. **x = 4:** In this triangle, two angles are equal (so this triangle is isosceles). The two sides opposite the equal angles must also be equal, so x must equal 4.

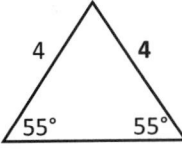

14. $x° = 110°$: Two sides have the same length, so the angles opposite the equal sides must also be equal. (This is an isosceles triangle.)

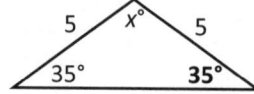

   Now solve for $x$.

   $35 + 35 + x = 180$
   $x = 110$

15. **25:**

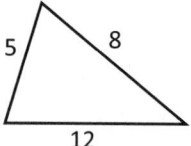

   The perimeter of a triangle equals the sum of the three sides, or $5 + 8 + 12 = 25$.

16. **16:** The two angles labeled $x$ are equal, so the sides opposite the equal angles must also be equal.

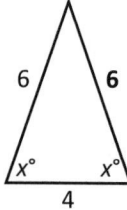

   The perimeter is $6 + 6 + 4 = 16$.

17. **15:** In the triangle shown, the base is 6 and the height is 5. Therefore, you can find the area:

   $$A = \frac{1}{2}bh$$
   $$A = \frac{1}{2}(6)(5)$$
   $$A = 15$$

18. **35:** In this triangle, the base is 10 and the height is 7. Remember that the height must be perpendicular to the base, but the height doesn't need to lie within the triangle. Now find the area:

   $$A = \frac{1}{2}bh$$
   $$A = \frac{1}{2}(10)(7)$$
   $$A = 35$$

   When you see a problem like this one on the GMAT, you will probably not be given the dotted lines; you'll likely have to realize yourself that the height can be drawn outside of the triangle.

19. **6:** This is a right triangle, so you can use the Pythagorean theorem to solve for the length of the third side. First, though, check to see whether this is one of the Pythagorean triples. It is a multiple of the 3-4-5 triangle; the sides here are 6-8-10. The third side must equal 6.

   If you don't recognize the triple, you need to use the Pythagorean theorem to solve.

   $a^2 + 8^2 = 10^2$
   $a^2 + 64 = 100$
   $a^2 = 36$
   $a = 6$

20. **13:** This triangle is one of the Pythagorean triples, a 5-12-13 triangle. The hypotenuse equals 13.

   Alternatively, use the Pythagorean theorem to solve.

   $5^2 + 12^2 = c^2$
   $25 + 144 = c^2$
   $169 = c^2$
   $13 = c$

21. **6:** This is a 3-4-5 triple, so the length of the third side is 3.

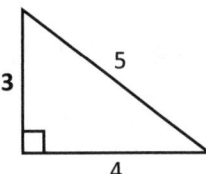

   The base of the triangle is 4 and the height is 3. Plug this into the area formula.

   $A = \dfrac{1}{2}bh$
   $A = \dfrac{1}{2}(4)(3)$
   $A = 6$

22. **32:** In parallelograms, opposite sides have equal lengths, so two of the sides of the parallelogram have a length of 6 and two sides have a length of 10.

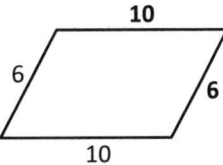

   The perimeter is 2(6 + 10) = 32.

23. **36:** The area of a parallelogram is $b \times h$. In this parallelogram, the base is 9 and the height is 4, so the area is $(9) \times (4) = 36$.

24. **$A = 21$ and $P = 20$:** In rectangles, opposite sides have equal lengths, so the rectangle looks like this:

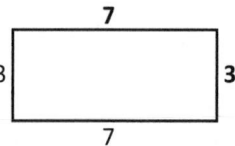

The perimeter is $2(l + w) = 2(3 + 7) = 20$. The area is $l \times w = (7)(3) = 21$.

25. **$A = 48$ and $P = 28$:** The diagonal of the rectangle creates a right triangle, so you can use the Pythagorean theorem to find the length of side $CD$. Alternatively, triangle $ACD$ is a 6-8-10 triangle, so the length of side $CD$ is 8.

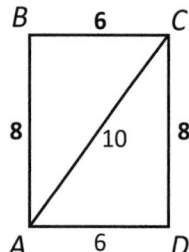

The perimeter of the rectangle is $2(l + w) = 2(8 + 6) = 28$. The area is $l \times w = (8)(6) = 48$.

26. **$9\pi$:** Redraw the diagram *without* the circle, so that you can focus on the rectangle. Add in the diagonal $AC$, as well as its length.

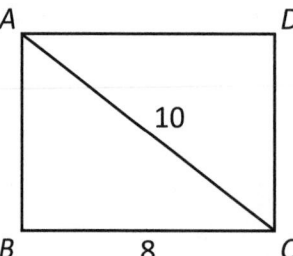

Look at right triangle *ABC*. *AC* functions not only as the diagonal of rectangle *ABCD* but also as the hypotenuse of right triangle *ABC*. Find the third side of triangle *ABC*, either using the Pythagorean theorem or by recognizing a Pythagorean triple (6-8-10).

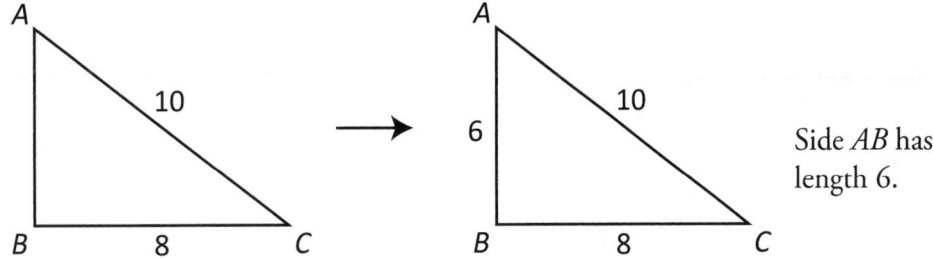

Side *AB* has length 6.

Now redraw the diagram *with* the circle but without the diagonal, since you've gotten what you need from that: the other side of the rectangle.

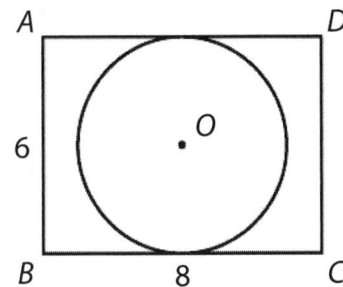

Since the circle touches both *AD* and *BC*, its diameter must be 6.

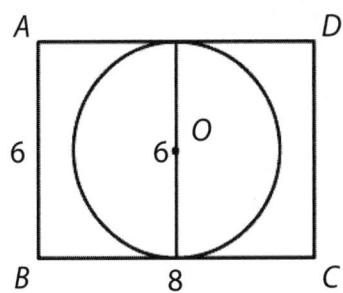

Finally, find the radius and compute the area:

$$d = 6 = 2r$$
$$3 = r$$

$$\text{Area} = \pi r^2$$
$$= \pi (3)^2$$
$$\text{Area} = 9\pi$$

27.

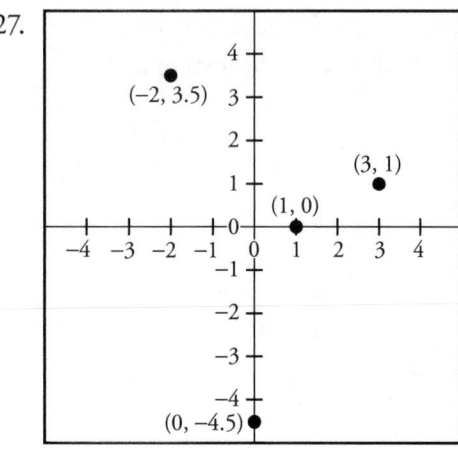

28. 1. (2, −1): **E**
    2. (−1.5, −3): **C**
    3. (−1, 2): **B**
    4. (3, 2): **D**

**10**

29.

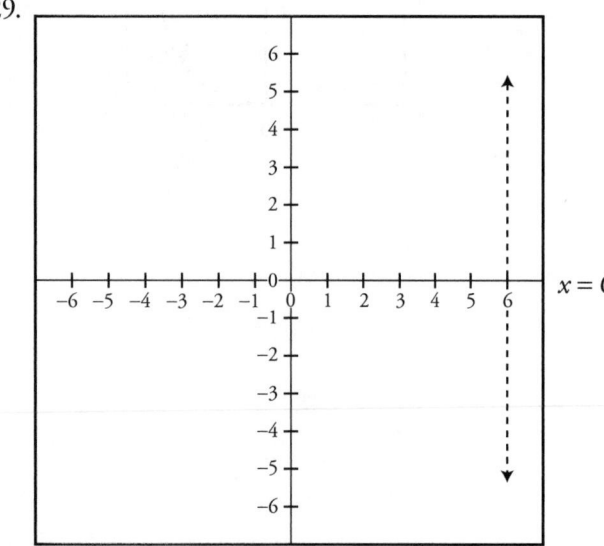

30.

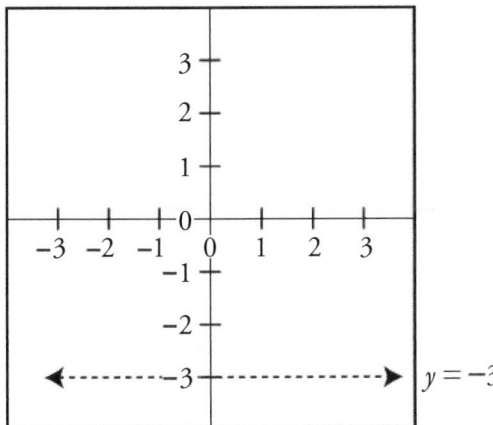

$y = -3$

31.

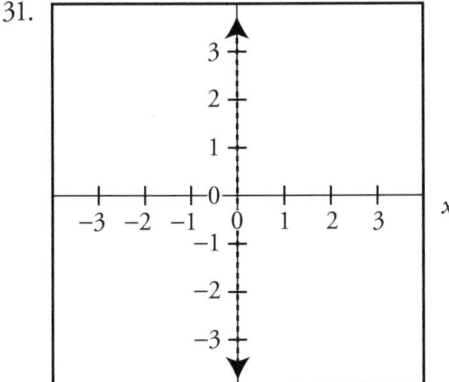

$x = 0$ is the $y$-axis.

32.  1.  $(1, -2)$ is in **Quadrant IV**
    2.  $(-4.6, 7)$ is in **Quadrant II**
    3.  $(-1, -2.5)$ is in **Quadrant III**
    4.  $(3, 3)$ is in **Quadrant I**

33.  1. $x < 0$, $y > 0$ indicates **Quadrant II**
     2. $x < 0$, $y < 0$ indicates **Quadrant III**
     3. $y > 0$ indicates **Quadrants I and II**
     4. $x < 0$ indicates **Quadrants II and III**

34. $y = -4$: The point on the line with $x = -3$ has a $y$-coordinate of $-4$.

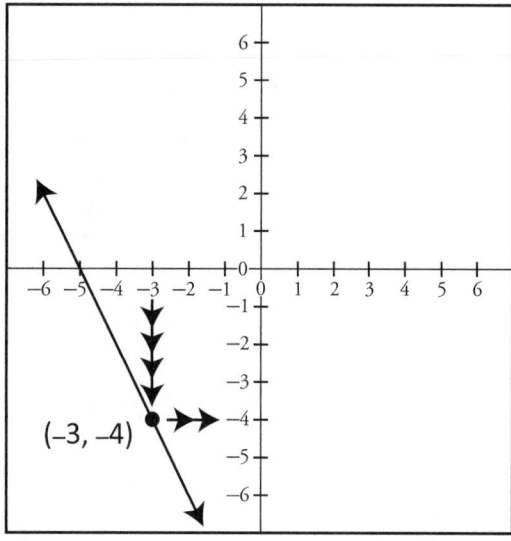

35. **False:** Test the point $(9, 21)$ in the equation $y = 2x + 1$. Plug in 9 for $x$ to see whether you get 21 for $y$.

    $y = 2(9) + 1 = 19$

    Because 19 does not equal 21, the point $(9, 21)$ does not lie on the line.

36. **True:** Test the point $(4, 14)$ in the equation $y = x^2 - 2$. Plug in 4 for $x$ to see whether you get 14 for $y$.

    $y = (4)^2 - 2 = 14$

    Because 14 is the desired number, the point $(4, 14)$ does lie on the curve defined by the equation $y = x^2 - 2$.

37. **slope = 3, $y$-intercept = 4:** The equation $y = 3x + 4$ is already in $y = mx + b$ form, so you can directly find the slope and $y$-intercept. The slope, $m$, is 3, and the $y$-intercept, $b$, is 4.

38. **slope = 2.5 (or $\frac{5}{2}$), $y$-intercept = −6:** To find the slope and $y$-intercept of a line, put the equation in $y = mx + b$ form. Next, divide the original equation by 2 to make that happen. Therefore, $2y = 5x - 12$ becomes $y = 2.5x - 6$. The slope, $m$, is 2.5 (or $\frac{5}{2}$) and the $y$-intercept, $b$, is $-6$.

39.

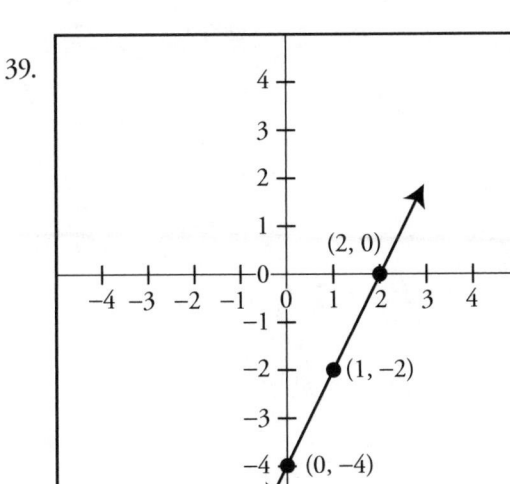

$y = 2x - 4$

slope = 2

$y$-intercept = $-4$

Think of the slope, 2, as a fraction: $\dfrac{2}{1}$. Go up 2 and to the right 1.

# Chapter Review: Drill Sets

## Drill 1

1. The radius of a circle is 4. What is its area?
2. The diameter of a circle is 7. What is its circumference?
3. The radius of a circle is 3. What is its circumference?
4. The area of a circle is $25\pi$. What is its diameter?
5. The circumference of a circle is $18\pi$. What is its area?

## Drill 2

6. The area of a circle is $100\pi$. What is its circumference?
7. The diameter of a circle is 16. Calculate its radius, circumference, and area.
8. Circle $A$ has a circumference of $6\pi$ and circle $B$ has an area of $8\pi$. Which circle has the greater area?
9. Circle $C$ has a diameter of 10 and circle $D$ has a circumference of $12\pi$. Which circle has the greater area?
10. Circle $A$ has an area of $64\pi$ and circle $B$ has an area of $16\pi$. The radius of circle $A$ is how many times the radius of circle $B$?

## Drill 3

11. A sector has a central angle of 90°. If the sector has a radius of 8, what is the area of the sector?
12. A sector has a central angle of 45° and a radius of 12. What is the arc length of the sector?
13. A sector has an arc length of $7\pi$ and a diameter of 14. What is the central angle of the sector?
14. A sector has a central angle of 270°. If the sector has a radius of 4, what is the area of the sector?
15. A sector has an area of $24\pi$ and a radius of 12. What is the central angle of the sector?

## Drill 4

16. The area of a sector is $\frac{1}{10}$ of the area of the full circle. What is the central angle of the sector?
17. What is the perimeter of a sector with a central angle of 60° and a radius of 18?
18. A sector has a radius of 8 and an area of $8\pi$. What is the arc length of the sector?
19. A sector has an arc length of $\frac{\pi}{2}$ and a central angle of 45°. What is the radius of the sector?
20. Sector $A$ has a radius of 4 and a central angle of 90°. Sector $B$ has a radius of 6 and a central angle of 45°. Which sector has the greater area?

## Drill 5

Note: Figures are not necessarily drawn to scale.

21. A triangle has two sides with lengths of 5 and 11, respectively. What is the range of values for the length of the third side?
22. The length of the hypotenuse of a right triangle is 10, and the length of one of the legs is 6. What is the length of the other leg?
23. What is the area of triangle $DEF$?

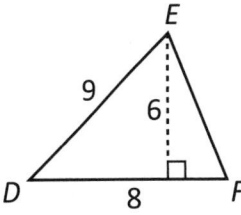

24. Which side of triangle $GHI$ has the longest length?

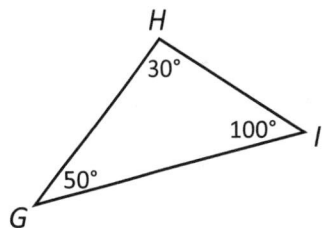

25. What is the value of *x*?

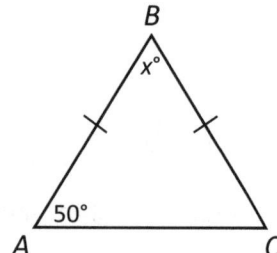

## Drill 6

Note: Figures are not necessarily drawn to scale.

26. Two sides of a triangle have lengths 4 and 8. Which of the following are possible side lengths of the third side? (More than one answer may apply.)

    (A) 2
    (B) 4
    (C) 6
    (D) 8

27. What is the value of *x*?

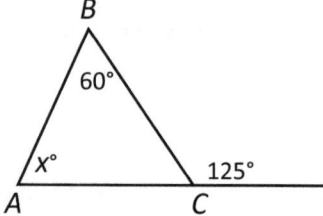

28. Isosceles triangle *ABC* has two sides with lengths 3 and 9. What is the length of the third side?

29. Which of the following could be the length of side *AB*, if *x* < *y* < *z*?

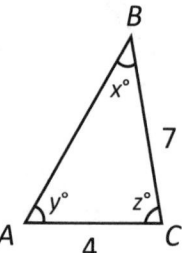

    (A) 6
    (B) 10
    (C) 14

30. What is the area of right triangle *ABC*?

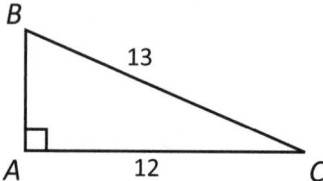

## Drill 7

Note: Figures are not necessarily drawn to scale.

31. What is the perimeter of triangle *ABC*?

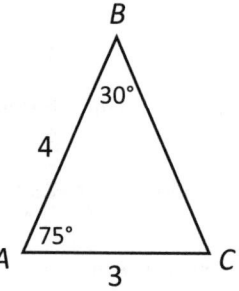

32. The area of right triangle *XYZ* is 12. What is the length of its hypotenuse?

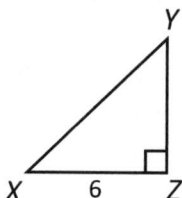

33. What is the length of side *HI*?

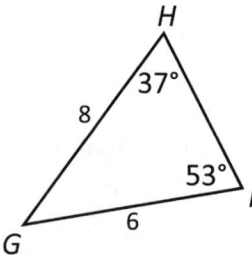

34. Which triangle has the greater perimeter?

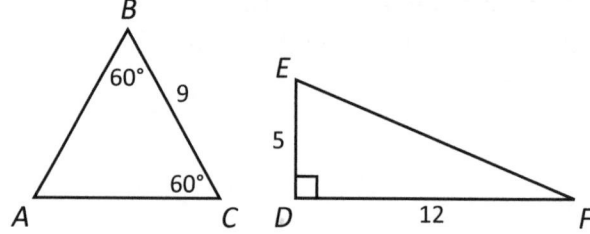

**MANHATTAN** PREP

35. *ZW* has a length of 3 and *XZ* has a length of 6. What is the area of triangle *XYZ*?

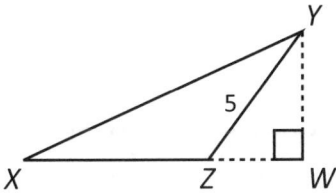

# Drill 8

Note: Figures are not necessarily drawn to scale.

36. What is the perimeter of parallelogram *ABCD*?

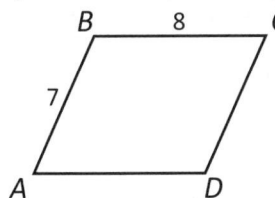

37. What is the area of parallelogram *EFGH*?

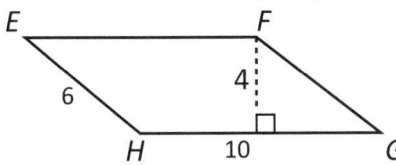

38. The rectangle and the parallelogram pictured below have the same perimeters. What is the length of side *EF*?

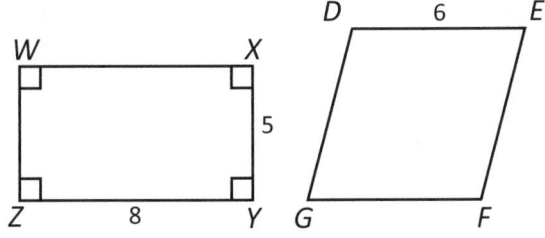

39. In parallelogram *ABCD*, triangle *ABC* has an area of 12. What is the area of triangle *ACD*?

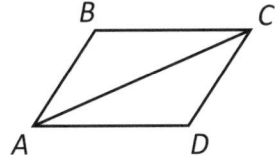

40. Rectangle *WXYZ* and rectangle *OPQR* have equal areas. What is the length of side *PQ*?

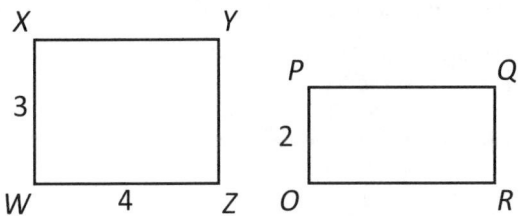

# Drill 9

Note: Figures are not necessarily drawn to scale.

41. What is the area of rectangle *ABCD*?

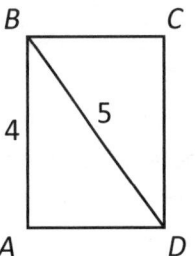

42. In rectangle *ABCD*, the area of triangle *ABC* is 30. What is the length of diagonal *AC*?

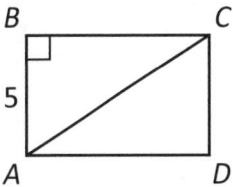

43. Rectangle *EFGH* has an area three times that of rectangle *ABCD*. What is the length of side *FG*?

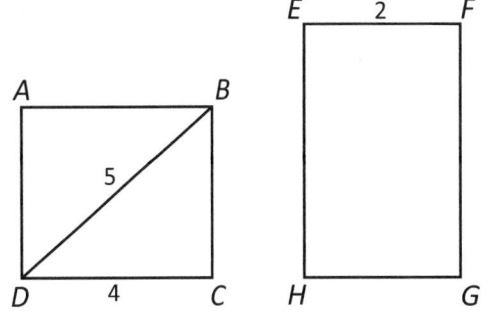

10

44. A rectangle has an area of 22 and a perimeter of 26. What are the length and width of the rectangle?

45. Right triangle *ABC* and rectangle *JKLM* have equal areas. What is the perimeter of rectangle *JKLM*?

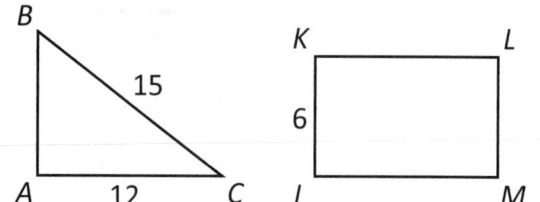

## Drill 10

Note: Figures are not necessarily drawn to scale.

46. What is the perimeter of a square with an area of 25?

47. A rectangle and a square have the same area. The square has a perimeter of 32, and the rectangle has a width of 4. What is the length of the rectangle?

48. A circle is inscribed in a square, as shown in the diagram. If the area of the circle is $16\pi$, what is the perimeter of the square?

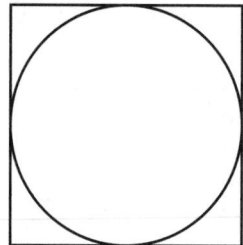

49. Square *WXYZ* has an area of 36. What is the length of diagonal *XZ*?

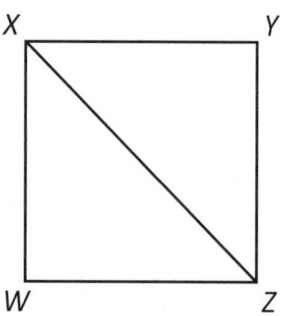

50. Right triangle *ABC* and rectangle *EFGH* have the same perimeter. What is the value of *x*?

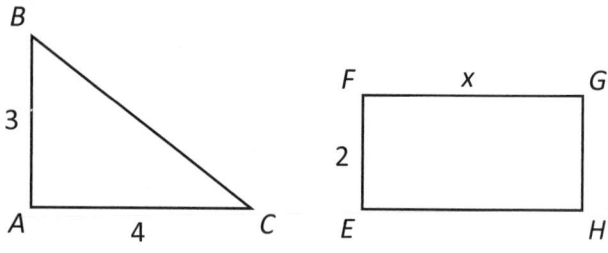

## Drill 11

51. Draw a coordinate plane and plot the following points.

    1. (2, 3)
    2. (−2, −1)
    3. (−5, −6)
    4. (4, −2.5)

52. What are the *x*- and *y*-coordinates of the following points?

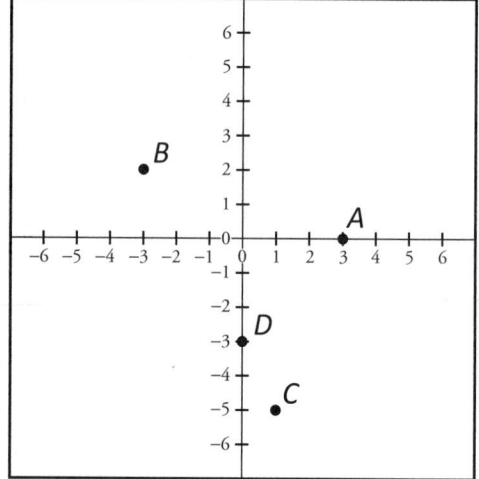

53. What is the *y*-coordinate of the point on the line that has an *x*-coordinate of 3?

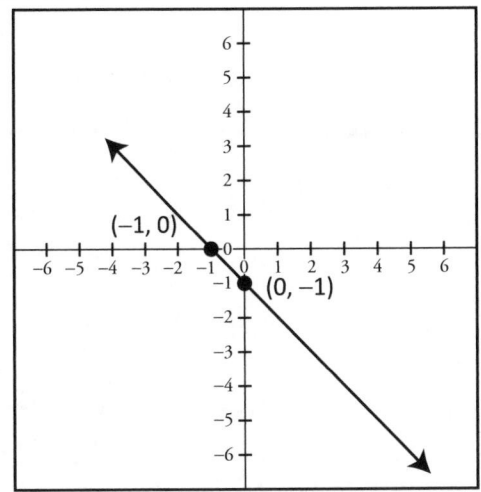

54. What is the *x*-coordinate of the point on the line that has a *y*-coordinate of −4?

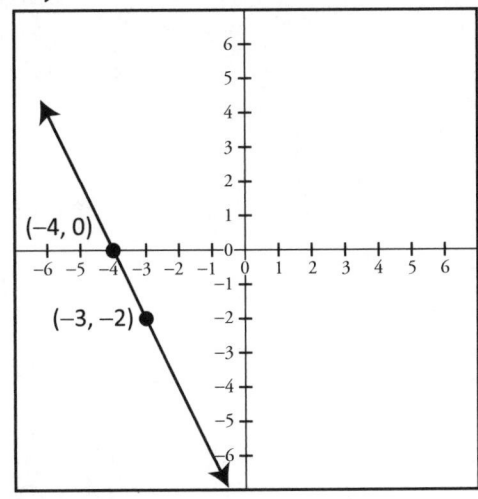

55. Does the point (−3, 5) lie on the line
$y = -2x - 1$?

## Drill 12

56. Does the point (−3, 0) lie on the curve
$y = x^2 - 3$?

57. For the line $y = 3x - 4$, what is the *y*-coordinate when $x = 2$?

58. What is the *y*-intercept of the line $y = -2x - 7$?

59. Graph the line $y = \dfrac{1}{2}x + 3$.

60. Graph the line $\dfrac{1}{2}y = -\dfrac{1}{2}x + 1$.

**10**

# Drill Sets Solutions

## Drill 1

1. **16$\pi$:**

   $$A = \pi r^2$$
   $$A = \pi(4)^2$$
   $$A = 16\pi$$

2. **7$\pi$:**

   $$C = \pi d$$
   $$C = \pi(7) = 7\pi$$

3. **6$\pi$:**

   $$C = 2\pi r$$
   $$C = 2\pi(3)$$
   $$C = 6\pi$$

4. **10:**

   $$A = \pi r^2$$
   $$25\pi = \pi r^2$$
   $$25 = r^2$$
   $$5 = r$$
   $$d = 2r = 2(5) = 10$$

5. **81$\pi$:** The connection between circumference and area is radius. Use the circumference to solve for the radius.

   $$C = 2\pi r$$
   $$18\pi = 2\pi r$$
   $$18 = 2r$$
   $$9 = r$$

   Use the radius to find the area.

   $$A = \pi r^2$$
   $$A = \pi(9)^2$$
   $$A = 81\pi$$

# Drill 2

6. **$20\pi$:**

$$A = \pi r^2$$
$$100\pi = \pi r^2$$
$$100 = r^2$$
$$10 = r$$

Use the radius to find the circumference.

$$C = 2\pi r$$
$$C = 2\pi(10)$$
$$C = 20\pi$$

7. **$r = 8$, $C = 16\pi$, and $A = 64\pi$:**

$$d = 2r$$
$$16 = 2r$$
$$8 = r$$

$$C = 2\pi r$$
$$C = 2\pi(8)$$
$$C = 16\pi$$

$$A = \pi r^2$$
$$A = \pi(8)^2$$
$$A = 64\pi$$

8. **Circle $A$:** Find the radius of circle $A$, and then calculate its area.

$$C_A = 2\pi r_A$$
$$6\pi = 2\pi r_A$$
$$3 = r_A$$

$$A_A = \pi r_A^{\,2}$$
$$A_A = \pi(3)^2$$
$$A_A = 9\pi$$

Because $9\pi$ is greater than $8\pi$, circle $A$ has the greater area.

9. **Circle $D$:** You could find the area of each circle and compare. Note, though, that it is sufficient to find the radii of both circles. The one with the greater radius will also have the greater area. Don't do more work than you're asked to do! You only need to tell which circle has the greater area; you don't need to be able to say what that area is.

$$d_C = 10$$
$$r_C = 5$$
$$C_D = 2\pi r_D$$
$$12\pi = 2\pi r_D$$
$$6 = r_D$$

Since circle $D$ has the greater radius, it will have the greater area.

10. **Two times:** The radius of circle $A$ is two times the radius of circle $B$.

Careful: Don't use the areas to determine the ratio of the two circles' radii. Find the radii.

$$A_A = \pi r_A^2 \qquad\qquad A_B = \pi r_B^2$$
$$64\pi = \pi r_A^2 \qquad\qquad 16\pi = \pi r_B^2$$
$$64 = r_A^2 \qquad\qquad 16 = r_B^2$$
$$8 = r_A \qquad\qquad 4 = r_B$$

Thus, 8 is 2 times 4.

# Drill 3

11. **$16\pi$:** If the sector has a central angle of 90°, then the sector is $\dfrac{90}{360} = \dfrac{1}{4}$ of the circle. Next, find the area of the entire circle

$$A = \pi r^2$$
$$A = \pi(8)^2$$
$$A = 64\pi$$

The area of the sector is $\dfrac{1}{4}$ of the total area: $64\pi \times \dfrac{1}{4} = 16\pi$.

12. **$3\pi$:** A central angle of 45° corresponds to $\dfrac{45}{360} = \dfrac{1}{8}$ of the circle. Next, find the circumference of the entire circle.

$$C = 2\pi r$$
$$C = 2\pi(12)$$
$$C = 24\pi$$

The arc length of the sector is $\dfrac{1}{8}$ of the total circumference: $24\pi \times \dfrac{1}{8} = 3\pi$.

13. **180°:** To find the central angle of the sector, you need to determine what fraction of the full circle the sector represents. Because you were given the arc length, find the circumference of the circle, and use those two numbers to determine the fraction.

$$C = \pi d$$
$$C = \pi(14) = 14\pi$$

$$\frac{7\pi}{14\pi} = \frac{1}{2}$$

The arc length represents $\frac{1}{2}$ of the circle. The central angle, therefore, also represents $\frac{1}{2}$ of the total 360°: $360° \times \frac{1}{2} = 180°$.

14. **12π:** The sector represents $\frac{270°}{360°} = \frac{3}{4}$ of the circle. Next, find the area of the whole circle:

$$A = \pi r^2$$
$$A = \pi (4)^2$$
$$A = 16\pi$$

The area of the sector is $\frac{3}{4}$ of the total area: $16\pi \times \frac{3}{4} = 12\pi$.

15. **60°:** First, find the area of the whole circle.

$$A = \pi r^2$$
$$A = \pi (12)^2$$
$$A = 144\pi$$

The sector represents $\frac{24\pi}{144\pi} = \frac{1}{6}$ of the circle. The central angle is also $\frac{1}{6}$ of the circle: $360° \times \frac{1}{6} = 60°$.

# Drill 4

16. **36°:** If the area of the sector is $\frac{1}{10}$ of the area of the full circle, then the central angle is also $\frac{1}{10}$ of the degree measure of the full circle.

$$360° \times \frac{1}{10} = 36°$$

17. **6π + 36:** The perimeter of a sector equals the arc length plus two radii.

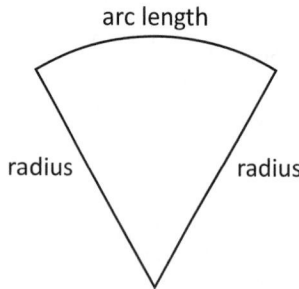

arc length

radius                radius

Begin by finding the circumference and the fraction of the total circle that the central angle represents.

$$C = 2\pi r$$
$$C = 2\pi(18) = 36\pi$$
$$\frac{\text{Central angle}}{\text{Total angle}} = \frac{60}{360} = \frac{1}{6}$$

The arc length is $\frac{1}{6}$ of the circumference: $36\pi \times \frac{1}{6} = 6\pi$.

The perimeter is $6\pi + 18 + 18 = 6\pi + 36$.

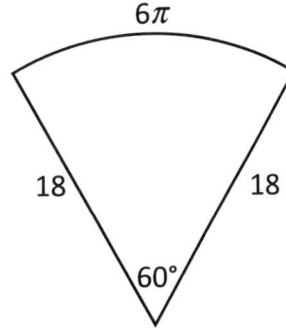

18. **$2\pi$:** First, determine what fraction of the circle the sector represents. Since you were given the area of the sector, find the area of the whole circle.

$$A = \pi r^2$$
$$A = \pi(8)^2$$
$$A = 64\pi$$
$$\frac{\text{Area of sector}}{\text{Area of circle}} = \frac{8\pi}{64\pi} = \frac{1}{8}$$

The sector represents $\frac{1}{8}$ of the circle. To find the arc length, find the circumference of the whole circle.

$$C = 2\pi r$$
$$C = 2\pi(8) = 16\pi$$
$$\text{Arc length} = 16\pi \times \frac{1}{8} = 2\pi$$

19. **2:** Begin by determining what portion of the circle the sector represents.

$$\frac{\text{Central angle}}{\text{Total angle}} = \frac{45}{360} = \frac{1}{8}$$

The sector represents $\frac{1}{8}$ of the circle. If the arc length of the sector is $\frac{\pi}{2}$, then the circumference of the whole circle is

$$\frac{\pi}{2} \times 8 = 4\pi.$$

$$C = 2\pi r$$
$$4\pi = 2\pi r$$
$$2 = r$$

20. **Sector B:** First, calculate what you can for sector $A$. Determine the fraction that the sector represents, the area of the entire circle, and finally the area of sector $A$.

$$\frac{\text{Central angle}}{\text{Total angle}} = \frac{90}{360} = \frac{1}{4}$$

$$A_A = \pi r_A^2$$
$$A_A = \pi(4)^2$$
$$A_A = 16\pi$$

Area of sector $A = \dfrac{1}{4} \times 16\pi = 4\pi$

Calculate the equivalent information for sector $B$.

$$\frac{\text{Central angle}}{\text{Total angle}} = \frac{45}{360} = \frac{1}{8}$$

$$A_B = \pi r_B^2$$
$$A_B = \pi(6)^2$$
$$A_B = 36\pi$$

Area of sector $B = \dfrac{1}{8} \times 36\pi = \dfrac{9}{2}\pi = 4.5\pi$

Because $4.5\pi > 4\pi$, the area of sector $B$ is greater than the area of sector $A$.

# Drill 5

21. **6 < third side < 16:** The sum of the lengths of any two sides of a triangle must be greater than the length of the third side. Therefore, the third side must be less than $5 + 11 = 16$. The third side must also be greater than the difference of the lengths of the other two sides: $11 - 5 = 6$. Therefore, the third side must be between 6 and 16.

22. **8:** This is a Pythagorean triple, a 6-8-10 triangle. When you think you may have a triple, do make sure that the longest measure corresponds to the hypotenuse. If you were told that the two *legs* were 6 and 10, then the hypotenuse could not be 8, since the hypotenuse is the longest side of the triangle.

Alternatively, use the Pythagorean theorem to solve.

$$a^2 + b^2 = c^2$$
$$6^2 + b^2 = 10^2$$
$$b^2 = 100 - 36$$
$$b^2 = 64$$
$$b = 8$$

23. **24:**

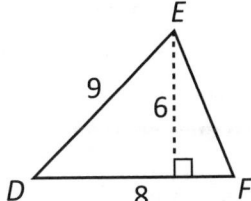

Side *DF* can act as the base, and the line dropping straight down from point *E* to touch side *DF* at a right angle can act as the height. The base is 8 and the height is 6, so you can find the area:

$$A = \frac{1}{2}bh$$

$$A = \frac{1}{2}(8)(6)$$

$$A = 24$$

24. **GH:**

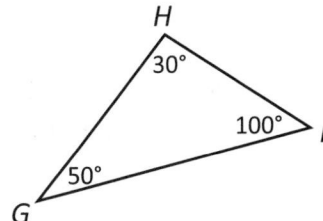

Although *GI* looks like the longest side, don't trust how the picture looks when the question states that the picture is not drawn to scale. In any triangle, the longest side is opposite the largest angle. Angle *GIH* is the largest angle in the triangle, so side *GH* is the longest side.

25. **80°:** In triangle *ABC*, sides *AB* and *BC* are equal, so their opposite angles are also equal. Therefore, angle *ACB* is also 50°.

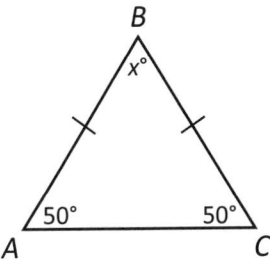

Now find angle *x*.

$$50 + 50 + x = 180$$
$$100 + x = 180$$
$$x = 80$$

# Drill 6

26. **(C) and (D):** The sum of the lengths of any two sides of a triangle must be greater than the length of the third side. Therefore, the third side must be less than $4 + 8 = 12$. In addition, the third side must be greater than the difference of the other two sides: $8 - 4 = 4$. Only values between 4 and 12 are possible values for the third side of the triangle. (Note that 4 itself is not a possible value. The third side must be greater than 4.)

27. $x = 65°$: First, solve for angle *BCA*. A straight line equals 180°, so angle *BCA* equals $180 - 125 = 55$.

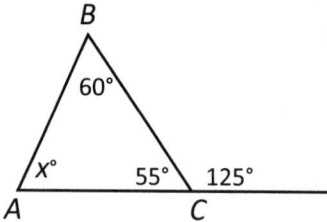

    Now solve for *x*.

    $$60 + 55 + x = 180$$
    $$x = 65$$

28. **9:** This is a tricky one. If the triangle is isosceles, then two sides have equal length, but is the unknown third side 3 or 9? If the third side were 3, then the lengths of two of the sides would not sum to greater than the length of the third side, because $3 + 3$ is not greater than 9.

    Use the rule about the third side of any triangle: The third side must be greater than the difference of the other two sides but smaller than the sum of the other two sides. The third side, then, has to be between $9 - 3 = 6$ and $9 + 3 = 12$.

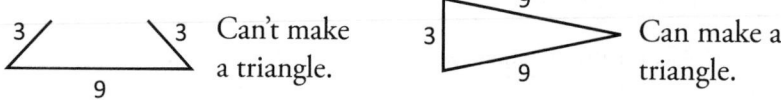

    Because 3 is not a valid possibility, the length of the third side must be 9.

29. **(B):** Start with the rule about the third side of any triangle. The third side must be between $7 - 4 = 3$ and $7 + 4 = 11$. That knocks out answer (C), 14.

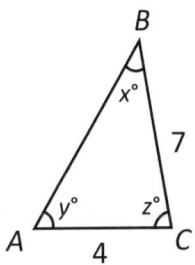

$$3 < \text{third side} < 11$$

Both 6 and 10 are still possibilities according to the rule about the third side of any triangle, though. Did the problem provide any other information that you haven't used yet?

Yes: angle $x$ < angle $y$ < angle $z$. If this is the case, then side $AC$ < side $BC$ < side $AB$, or $4 < 7 <$ side $AB$. Side $AB$ cannot be 6, but it could be 10.

30. **30:** Find the base and the height. Because this is a right triangle, the base can be 12 and the height can be the leg $AB$. The triangle is a Pythagorean triple, so side $AB = 5$.

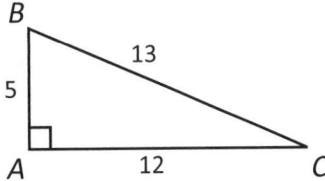

Now calculate the area.

$$A = \frac{1}{2}bh$$
$$A = \frac{1}{2}(12)(5)$$
$$A = 30$$

# Drill 7

31. **11:** The perimeter is the sum of the three sides of the triangle. This triangle is not a Pythagorean triple, nor is it a right triangle, so there must be some other way to figure out the unknown third side.

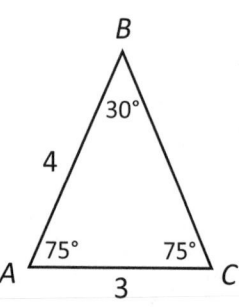

Let $x$ equal the unknown third angle:

$30 + 75 + x = 180$

$x = 75$

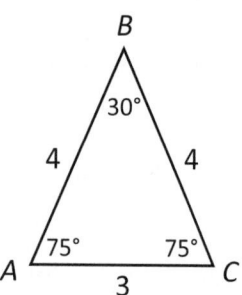

Angle $BAC$ and angle $BCA$ are both 75, so the triangle sides opposite those angles are also equal. Side $AB$ has a length of 4, so side $BC$ also has a length of 4.

The perimeter is $4 + 4 + 3 = 11$.

32. $\sqrt{52}$ *or* $2\sqrt{13}$ : The area of a right triangle can be calculated using the two legs as the base and height, so use the given area to find the length of the unknown leg.

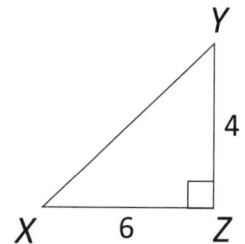

$$A = \frac{1}{2}bh$$

$$12 = \frac{1}{2}(6)h$$

$$12 = 3h$$

$$4 = h$$

Now use the Pythagorean theorem to find the length of the hypotenuse.

$$a^2 + b^2 = c^2$$
$$4^2 + 6^2 = c^2$$
$$16 + 36 = c^2$$
$$52 = c^2$$
$$\sqrt{52} = c$$

You can also write $\sqrt{52}$ as $\sqrt{52} = \sqrt{4 \times 13} = 2\sqrt{13}$ .

33. **10:** First, calculate the value of the unknown third angle.

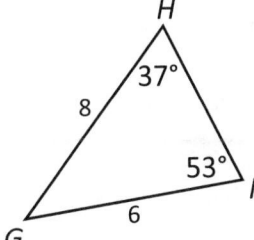

Let $x$ = the third angle.
$37 + 53 + x = 180$
$90 + x = 180$
$x = 90$

It turns out that the third angle is a right angle! Remember that the chapter directions indicated that figures are not necessarily drawn to scale (as is always the case on Data Sufficiency problems on the GMAT). It may help to redraw the triangle in a way that more closely approximates the real dimensions.

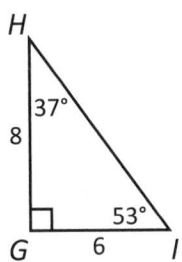

Now, you have a chance to recognize that this is a Pythagorean triple in disguise. It's a 6-8-10 triangle, so the hypotenuse equals 10:

34. **Triangle DEF:** Start with triangle *ABC*. Two of the angles equal 60°. The third angle must also be 60°, since $60 + 60 + 60 = 180$. Because the triangle is equilateral (all of the angles are the same), all of the sides are the same length, 9. The perimeter is $3(9) = 27$.

Triangle *DEF* is a right triangle and a Pythagorean triple. The hypotenuse equals 13, and the perimeter is $5 + 12 + 13 = 30$.

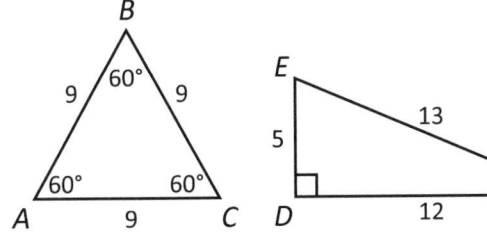

Because 30 > 27, triangle *DEF* has the greater perimeter.

35. **12:** Redraw the diagram, and fill in everything you know about triangle *XYZ*.

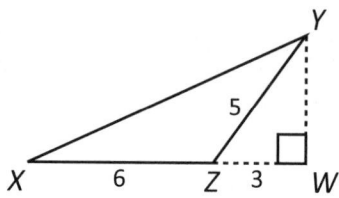

If *XZ* is the base, then *YW* can act as the height. Triangle *ZYW* is a right triangle and Pythagorean triple, a 3-4-5 triangle. Side *YW* = 4.

Now calculate the area of the triangle.

$$A = \frac{1}{2}bh$$

$$A = \frac{1}{2}(6)(4)$$

$$A = 12$$

## 10

# Drill 8

36. **30:** Opposite sides of a parallelogram are equal, so side *CD* has a length of 7 and side *AD* has a length of 8. The perimeter is 2(7 + 8) = 2(15) = 30.

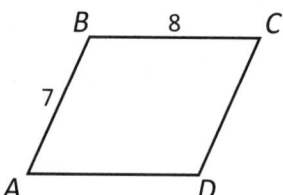

37. **40:** The area of a parallelogram is base × height. In this parallelogram, the base is 10 and the height is 4 (the base and height need to be perpendicular). The area is 10 × 4 = 40.

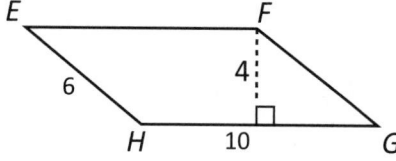

38. **7:** Start with the rectangle, since it provides enough information to calculate the perimeter.

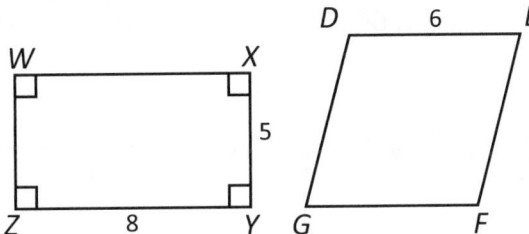

The opposite sides of a rectangle are the same length, so the perimeter of the rectangle is $2(5 + 8) = 2(13) = 26$.

The problem indicates that the perimeters of the two shapes are the same, so use this information to find the length of the unknown side of the parallelogram, *EF*.

$26 = 2(6 + EF)$
$26 = 12 + 2EF$
$14 = 2EF$
$7 = EF$

39. **12:** When you split any parallelogram by its diagonal, you create two identical triangles. In this case, since triangle *ABC* has an area of 12, triangle *ACD* must also have an area of 12.

40. **6:** Start by finding the area of rectangle *WXYZ*. The area of a rectangle $= lw = (3)(4) = 12$.

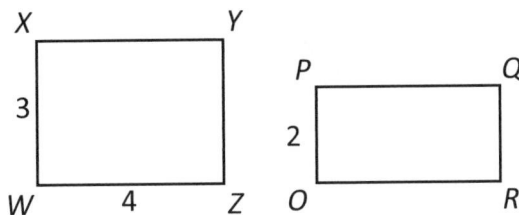

Since the two rectangles have equal areas, rectangle *OPQR* also has an area of 12. Use this information to find the length of side *PQ*. You know the length of side *OP*, so that is the width of rectangle *OPQR*. Side *PQ* is the length of rectangle *OPQR*. Therefore:

$A = lw$
$12 = l(2)$
$6 = l$

# Drill 9

41. **12:** The area of a rectangle equals the length times the width. The length, 4, is already given. Find the width, *AD* (or *BC*).

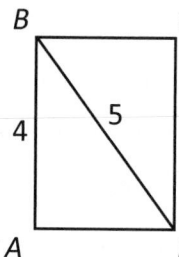

The triangle *ABD* is a Pythagorean triple—a 3-4-5 triangle. The length of side *AD* is therefore 3.

$A = lw$

$A = (4)(3)$

$A = 12$

42. **13:** First, use the area of the triangle to find the length of side *BC*.

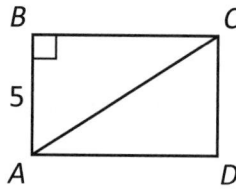

$$A = \frac{1}{2}bh$$

$$30 = \frac{1}{2}(5)h$$

$$\frac{2}{\cancel{5}}\left(\cancel{30}^{6}\right) = h$$

$$12 = h$$

The triangle is a 5-12-13 Pythagorean triple, so the length of the hypotenuse is 13. The hypotenuse, *AC*, is also the diagonal of the rectangle.

43. **18:** Use the information given for rectangle *ABCD* to find the area.

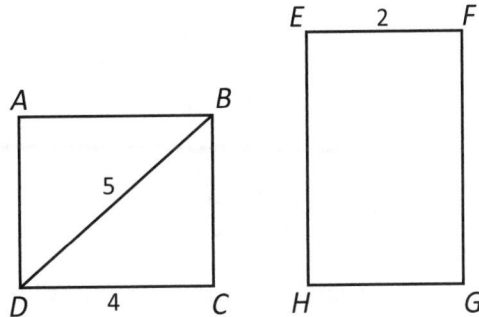

Triangle *BCD* is a 3-4-5 Pythagorean triple, so the side of length *BC* equals 3. The area of rectangle *ABCD* = $lw$ = (3)(4) = 12.

According to the question stem, the area of rectangle *EFGH* is three times the area of rectangle *ABCD*, so the area of rectangle *EFGH* equals (3)(12) = 36. Use this information to find the length of side *FG*. Let *l* equal the length of *FG*.

$$A = lw$$
$$36 = l(2)$$
$$18 = l$$

44. **11 and 2:** The question stem allows you to write two equations.

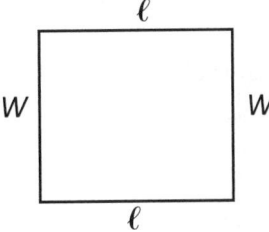

The area of the rectangle is 22, and the perimeter of the rectangle is 26.

$$A = lw = 22$$
$$P = 2(l + w) = 26$$

The second equation can be simplified to $l + w = 13$.

Substitute to solve for the values of the variables. In the second equation, isolate *w* (or *l*, your choice).

$$l = 13 - w$$

Substitute $(13 - w)$ for $l$ in the first equation.

$(13 - w)w = 22$

$13w - w^2 = 22$      This is a quadratic, so move everything
to one side to set it equal to 0.

$0 = w^2 - 13w + 22$

$0 = (w - 11)(w - 2)$      Factor the equation and solve.

$w = 11$ or $w = 2$

Which is it, 11 or 2? Plug the values into one of the original equations. What happens? It turns out that when $w = 11$, $l = 2$, and when $w = 2$, $l = 11$. Traditionally, the length is considered longer than the width, so the width is 2 and the length is 11.

45. **30:** Start with triangle $ABC$, since more information is provided for that shape.

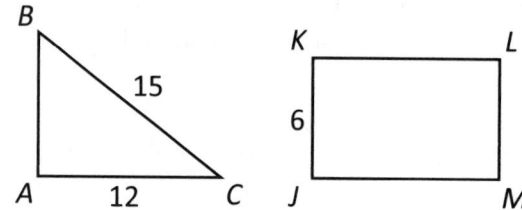

You can use the Pythagorean theorem to find side $AB$...but examine that triangle for a second. Does anything look familiar?

A 9-12-15 triangle is a 3-4-5 triangle in disguise; all of the measurements are tripled. Therefore, side $AB = 9$. Use that information to find the area of the triangle.

$A = \dfrac{1}{2}bh$

$A = \dfrac{1}{2}(12)(9)$

$A = 54$

Since the areas of the two shapes are the same, rectangle $JKLM$ also has an area of 54. Use this information to find the length of the rectangle.

$A = lw$

$54 = l(6)$

$9 = l$

Now calculate the perimeter: $2(l + w) = 2(9 + 6) = 2(15) = 30$.

# Drill 10

46. **20:** A square has four equal sides, so the area of a square is the length of one side squared.

$$A = s^2$$
$$25 = s^2$$
$$5 = s$$

The perimeter of a square is equal to four times the length of one side.

$$P = 4s$$
$$P = 4(5) = 20$$

47. **16:** Begin by drawing the shapes described in the problem.

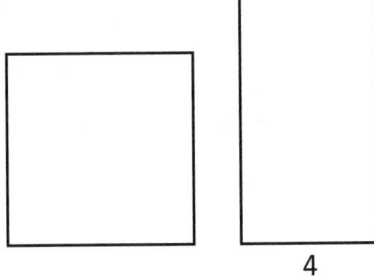

4

A square has four equal sides, so the perimeter is four times the length of one side. Let $s$ = length of a side of the square. Solve for $s$, then find the area of the square.

$$4s = 32$$
$$s = 8$$
$$A = s^2 = (8)^2 = 64$$

Since the two shapes have the same area, the area of the rectangle is also 64. The width of the rectangle is 4, so solve for the length.

$$A = lw$$
$$64 = l(4)$$
$$16 = l$$

48. **32:** Whenever you're given a diagram that combines shapes, find a common link between the two shapes. When a circle is inscribed in a square, the diameter of the circle is the same as the length of one side of the square.

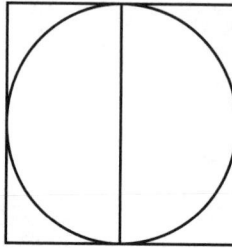

You can use the area of the circle to find the radius and then the diameter.

$$A = \pi r^2$$
$$16\pi = \pi r^2$$
$$16 = r^2$$
$$4 = r$$

If the radius is 4, then the diameter is 8. The diameter also equals one side of the square, so you can find the perimeter:

$$P = 4s$$
$$P = 4(8) = 32$$

49. $\sqrt{72}$ *or* $6\sqrt{2}$: Use the area of the square to find the length of one side.

$$A = s^2$$
$$36 = s^2$$
$$6 = s$$

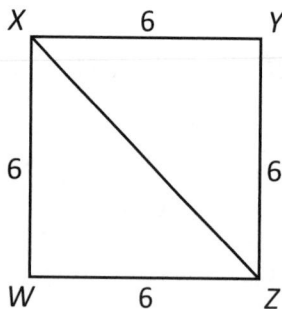

Now use the Pythagorean theorem to find the length of the diagonal *XZ*.

$$a^2 + b^2 = c^2$$
$$6^2 + 6^2 = c^2$$
$$36 + 36 = c^2$$
$$72 = c^2$$
$$\sqrt{72} = c$$

$\sqrt{72}$ can also be written as $\sqrt{72} = \sqrt{36 \times 2} = 6\sqrt{2}$.

50. **$x = 4$:** Start with the triangle. It's a 3-4-5 Pythagorean triple, so the hypotenuse is 5.

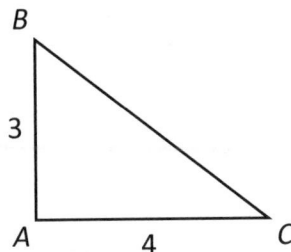 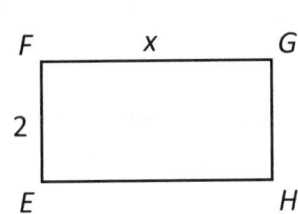

The perimeter of triangle *ABC* is 3 + 4 + 5 = 12.

Since the two shapes have the same perimeter, the perimeter of rectangle *EFGH* is also 12. Use this information to find the value of *x*.

$$P = 2(l + w)$$
$$12 = 2(2 + x)$$
$$12 = 4 + 2x$$
$$8 = 2x$$
$$4 = x$$

# Drill 11

51.

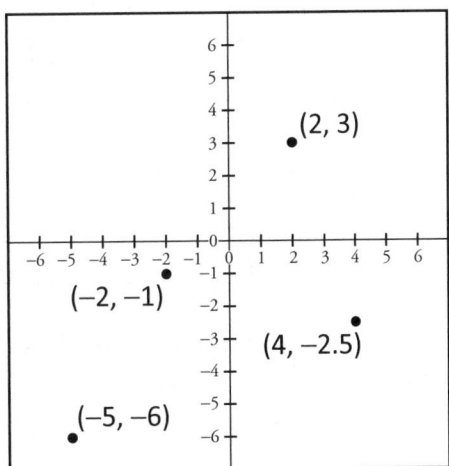

52.  A. (3, 0)
   B. (−3, 2)
   C. (1, −5)
   D. (0, −3)

53. **−4:** Find $x = 3$ on the $x$-axis, then go straight down to the line and draw a point. Next, move straight left to the $y$-axis to find the corresponding $y$-value. The point is $(3, −4)$.

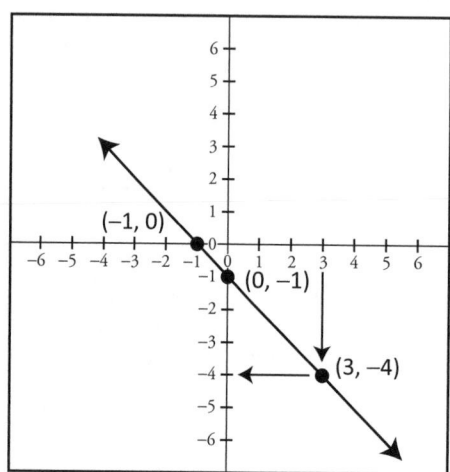

54. **−2:** Find $y = −4$ on the $y$-axis, then go straight left to the line and draw a point. Next, move straight up to the $x$-axis to find the corresponding $x$-value. The point is $(−2, −4)$.

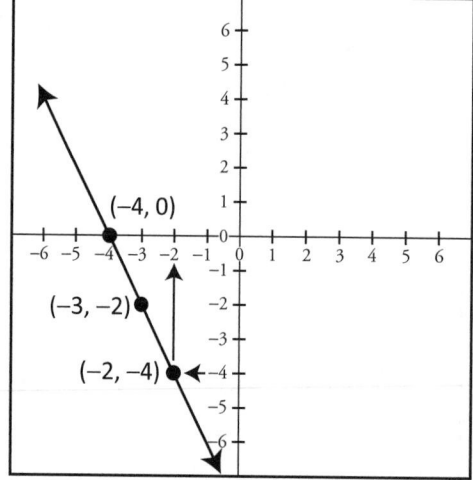

55. **Yes:** Plug the point $(−3, 5)$ into the equation $y = −2x − 1$. If the math works, then this point does lie on this line. If the math does not work, then this point does not lie on this line.

$$y = −2x − 1$$
$$(5) = −2(−3) − 1$$
$$5 = 6 − 1$$
$$5 = 5 \text{ True!}$$

The math is true, so this point does lie on this line.

# Drill 12

56. **No:** Plug the point $(-3, 0)$ into the equation $y = x^2 - 3$. If the math works, then this point does lie on this curve. If the math does not work, then this point does not lie on this curve.

$$y = x^2 - 3$$
$$0 = (-3)^2 - 3$$
$$0 = 9 - 3$$
$$0 = 6 \text{ False!}$$

The math is false, so this point does not lie on this curve.

57. **2:** To find the $y$-coordinate, plug in 2 for $x$ and solve for $y$.

$$y = 3(2) - 4$$
$$y = 6 - 4 = 2$$

The $y$-coordinate is 2. The point is $(2, 2)$.

58. **−7:** The equation of the line $y = -2x - 7$ is already in $y = mx + b$ form. In this form, $b$ stands for the $y$-intercept, so look at the equation to find the $y$-intercept. The $y$-intercept is $b = -7$. The point is $(0, -7)$. (For the $y$-intercept, the $x$ value is always 0.)

59. The equation is in $y = mx + b$ form. The $y$-intercept, $b$, is 3, so place a point at $(0, 3)$. The slope, $m$, is $\dfrac{1}{2}$. Count up 1 and to the right 2 to get to the point $(2, 4)$. Draw a line to connect the two points.

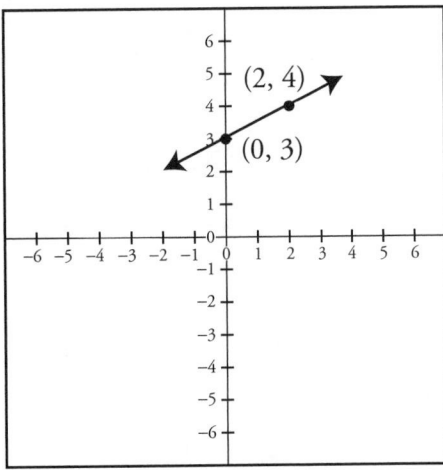

60. First, put the equation into $y = mx + b$ form. Multiply both sides by 2.

$y = -x + 2$

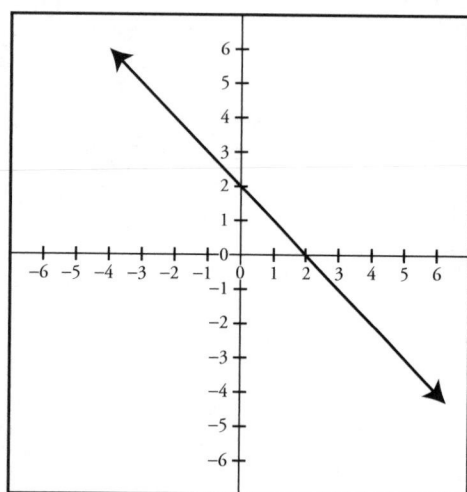

The $y$-intercept is 2, so place a point at $(0, 2)$.

The slope ($m$) is $-1$, so the line drops to the right. Count down 1, right 1 and place another dot.

Draw a line to connect the two dots.

**10**

# Glossary

**absolute value:** The distance from 0 on the number line for a particular term. E.g., the absolute value of −7 is 7, or $|-7| = 7$.

**arc length:** A section of a circle's circumference.

**area:** The space enclosed by a given closed shape on a plane; the formula depends on the specific shape. E.g., the area of a rectangle equals *length* × *width*.

**axis:** One of the two number lines ($x$-axis or $y$-axis) used to indicate position on a coordinate plane.

**base:** 1) In the expression $b^n$, the variable $b$ represents the base. The base is multiplied by itself $n$ times. E.g., $3^4 = 3 \times 3 \times 3 \times 3$. 2) Can refer to a side of a triangle when calculating the area of the triangle.

**center (circle):** The point from which any point on a circle's circumference is equidistant. The distance from the center to any point on the circumference is called the *radius*.

**central angle (circle):** The angle created by any two radii (lines drawn from the center of the circle to any point on the circumference).

**circle:** A set of points in a plane that are equidistant from a fixed center point.

**circumference:** The measure of the perimeter of a circle. The circumference of a circle can be found with the formula $C = 2\pi r$, where $C$ is the circumference, $r$ is the radius, and $\pi$ is a constant (which you can approximate as 3.14).

**coefficient:** A number that is multiplied by a variable. In the equation $y = 2x + 5$, the coefficient of the $x$ term is 2.

**common denominator:** When adding or subtracting fractions, first find a common denominator, generally the smallest common multiple of both numbers. (Note: You can also use the double-cross technique to add fractions.)

*Example:*

Given $\dfrac{3}{5} + \dfrac{1}{10}$, the two denominators are 5 and 10. The smallest multiple that works for both numbers is 10. The common denominator, therefore, is 10.

**constant:** In an equation or expression, a number that doesn't change. E.g., in the equation $y = 3x + 2$, the numbers 3 and 2 are constants. In the equation $y = mx + b$, $m$ and $b$ are also constants: once you know the value of $m$ or $b$ for a particular equation, it never changes. The $x$ and $y$, on the other hand, are *variables*; they can have many possible values.

**coordinate plane:** Consists of a horizontal axis (typically labeled "$x$") and a vertical axis (typically labeled "$y$"), crossing at the number 0 on both axes.

**decimal:** Most commonly refers to numbers that fall in between integers, such as 1.5. An integer can be expressed in decimal form, though, such as 2.00 or $3.4 \times 10^2$. A decimal can express a part-to-whole relationship, just as a percent or fraction can.

*Example:*

1.2 is a decimal. The integers 1 and 2 are not decimals. An integer written as 1.0, however, is considered a decimal. The decimal 0.2 is equivalent to 20% or to $\frac{2}{10} = \frac{1}{5}$.

**denominator:** The bottom of a fraction. In the fraction $\frac{7}{2}$, 2 is the denominator.

**diameter:** A line segment that passes through the center of a circle and whose endpoints lie on the circle's circumference.

**difference:** When one number is subtracted from another, the difference is what is left over. The difference of 7 and 5 is 2, because $7 - 5 = 2$.

**digit:** The ten numbers 0, 1, 2, 3, 4, 5, 6, 7, 8, and 9. Used in combination to represent other numbers (e.g., 12 or 0.38).

**distribute:** To multiply a term across other terms. For example, given the expression $3(x + 2)$, to distribute the 3, multiply each term in the parentheses by 3: $3(x + 2) = 3x + 6$. For the reverse math, see: *factor (verb)*.

**distributed form:** Presenting an expression as a sum or difference. In distributed form, terms are added or subtracted. $x^2 - 1$ is in distributed form, as is $x^2 + 2x + 1$. In contrast, $(x + 1)(x - 1)$ is not in distributed form; it is in factored form.

**divisible:** If an integer $x$ divided by another number $y$ yields an integer, then $x$ is said to be divisible by $y$.

*Example:*

Because 12 divided by 3 yields the integer 4, 12 is divisible by 3. On the other hand, 12 divided by 5 does not yield an integer. Therefore, 12 is not divisible by 5.

**divisor:** The part of a division operation that comes after the division sign. In the operation $22 \div 4$ (or $\frac{22}{4}$), 4 is the divisor. *Divisor* is also a synonym for *factor (noun)*.

**equation:** A combination of mathematical expressions and symbols that contains an equals sign. For example, $3 + 7 = 10$ is an equation, as is $x + y = 3$. An equation makes a statement: left side equals right side.

**equilateral triangle:** A triangle in which all three angles are equal (and all three are 60°); in addition, all three sides are of equal length.

**even:** An integer is even if it is divisible by 2. The integer 14 is even because $\frac{14}{2} = 7$, which is an integer.

**exponent:** In the expression $b^n$, the variable $n$ represents the exponent. The exponent indicates how many times to multiply the base, $b$, by itself. For example, $4^3 = 4 \times 4 \times 4$, or 4 multiplied by itself three times.

**expression:** A combination of numbers and mathematical symbols that does not contain an equals sign. For example, $xy$ is an expression, as is $x + 3$. An expression represents a quantity.

**factor (noun):** Integers that divide evenly into an integer. For instance, 6 is a factor of 12 because $12 \div 6 = 2$, an integer. On the GMAT, problems about factors are typically limited to positive integers; in this case, factors are equal to or smaller than the integer in question. The factors of 12 are 1, 2, 3, 4, 6, and 12. Note: For any given number, 1 and the number itself are always factors of that number.

**factor (verb):** To pull a common factor out of multiple terms. For example, given the expression $3x + 6$, factor out the common term of 3: $3x + 6 = 3(x + 2)$. For the reverse math, see: *distribute*.

**factored form:** Presenting an expression as a product. In factored form, expressions are multiplied together. The expression $(x + 1)(x - 1)$ is in factored form: $(x + 1)$ and $(x - 1)$ are the factors. In contrast, $x^2 - 1$ is not in factored form; it is in *distributed form*.

**factor foundation rule:** If $a$ is a factor of $b$, and $b$ is a factor of $c$, then $a$ is also a factor of $c$. For example, 2 is a factor of 10, and 10 is a factor of 60. Therefore, 2 is also a factor of 60.

**factor tree:** Use the "factor tree" to break any number down into its prime factors (see: *prime number*). For example:

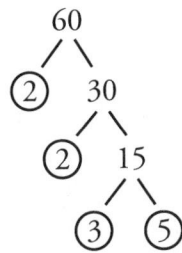

**FOIL:** First, Outside, Inside, Last; an acronym to remember the method for converting from factored to distributed form in a quadratic equation or expression. For example, $(x + 2)(x - 3)$ is a quadratic expression in factored form. Multiply the First, Outside, Inside, and Last terms to get the distributed form.

*Example:*

    Factored form: $(y + 2)(y - 3)$

    First: $y \times y = y^2$
    Outside: $y \times (-3) = -3y$
    Inside: $y \times 2 = 2y$
    Last: $2 \times (-3) = -6$

    Distributed form: $y^2 - 3y + 2y - 6 = y^2 - y - 6$

**fraction:** A way to express numbers that fall in between integers (though integers can also be expressed in fractional form). A fraction expresses a part-to-whole relationship in terms of a numerator (the part) and a denominator (the whole). For example, $\frac{3}{4}$ is a fraction, as is $\frac{6}{5}$. (The latter fraction has a special name. See: *improper fraction*.)

**hypotenuse:** The longest side of a right triangle. The hypotenuse is opposite the right angle.

**improper fraction:** Fractions that are greater than 1, such as $\frac{7}{2}$. Improper fractions can also be written as mixed numbers, such as, $\frac{7}{2} = 3\frac{1}{2}$.

**inequality:** A comparison of quantities that have different values. There are four ways to express inequalities: less than (<), less than or equal to (≤), greater than (>), or greater than or equal to (≥). Inequalities can be manipulated in the same way as equations with one exception: when multiplying or dividing by a negative number, the inequality sign must be flipped to the other direction.

**integers:** Numbers, such as −1, 0, 1, 2, and 3, that have no fractional part. Integers include the counting numbers (1, 2, 3, …), their negative counterparts (−1, −2, −3, …), and 0.

**interior angles:** The angles that appear in the interior of a closed shape. For example, a triangle has three interior angles.

**isosceles triangle:** A triangle in which two of the three angles are equal; in addition, the sides opposite the two equal angles are equal in length.

**line:** A set of points that extend infinitely in both directions without curving. On the GMAT, lines are by definition perfectly straight. They equal 180°.

**line segment:** A continuous, finite section of a line. The sides of a triangle or of a rectangle are line segments.

**linear equation:** An equation that does not contain exponents or multiple variables multiplied together. For example, $x + y = 3$ is a linear equation, but $xy = 3$ and $y = x^2$ are not. When plotted on a coordinate plane, linear equations create lines.

**mixed number:** An integer combined with a proper fraction. For example, $3\frac{1}{2}$ is a mixed number. Mixed numbers can also be written as improper fractions: $3\frac{1}{2} = \frac{7}{2}$.

**multiple:** Multiples are integers formed by multiplying some integer by any other integer. For example, 12 is a multiple of 12 ($12 \times 1$), as are 24 ($= 12 \times 2$), 36 ($= 12 \times 3$), 48 ($= 12 \times 4$), and 60 ($= 12 \times 5$). (Negative multiples are possible in mathematics, but you typically don't have to use them to get GMAT questions right. You can usually just stick with positive multiples.)

**negative:** Any number to the left of 0 on a number line; can be integer or non-integer.

**negative exponent:** Any exponent less than 0. To find a value for a term with a negative exponent, put the term containing the exponent in the denominator of a fraction and make the exponent positive, such as, $4^{-2} = \frac{1}{4^2}$. Alternatively, if the term with the negative exponent is already in the denominator of a fraction, flip the fraction and make the exponent positive: $\frac{1}{3^{-2}} = 3^2 = 9$.

**number line:** A straight line that represents all of the numbers from negative infinity to infinity.

**numerator:** The top of a fraction. In the fraction $\frac{7}{2}$, the numerator is 7.

**odd:** An odd integer is not divisible by 2 (i.e., division by 2 results in a non-integer value). The number 15 is odd because $\frac{15}{2} = 7.5$, which is not an integer.

**order of operations:** The order in which mathematical operations must be carried out in order to simplify an expression. See: *PEMDAS*.

**origin:** The coordinate pair (0, 0) represents the origin of a coordinate plane.

**parallelogram:** A four-sided closed shape composed of straight lines in which the opposite sides are equal and the opposite angles are equal.

**PEMDAS:** An acronym that stands for Parentheses, Exponents, Multiplication, Division, Addition, Subtraction; used to remember the order of operations.

**percent:** Literally, "per 100"; expresses a special part-to-whole relationship between a number (the part) and 100 (the whole). A special type of fraction or decimal that involves the number 100 (e.g., 50% = 50 out of 100).

**perimeter:** In a polygon, the sum of the lengths of the sides.

**perpendicular:** Lines that intersect at a 90° angle.

**plane:** A flat, two-dimensional surface that extends infinitely in every direction.

**point:** An object that exists in a single location on the coordinate plane. Each point has a unique *x*-coordinate and *y*-coordinate that together describe its location. For example, (1, −2) is a point.

**polygon:** A two-dimensional, closed shape made of line segments. For example, a triangle is a polygon, as is a rectangle. A circle is a closed shape, but it is not a polygon because it does not contain line segments.

**positive:** Any number to the right of 0 on a number line; can be an integer or a non-integer.

**prime factorization:** A number expressed as a product of its *prime numbers*. For example, the prime factorization of 60 is $2 \times 2 \times 3 \times 5$. Every number has a unique prime factorization; that is, no two numbers have the same prime factorization.

**prime number:** A positive integer with *exactly* two different factors: 1 and itself. The number 1 does not qualify as prime because it has only one factor, not two. The number 2 is the smallest prime number; it is also the only even prime number. The numbers 2, 3, 5, 7, 11, 13, and so on are prime.

**product:** The end result when two numbers are multiplied together. For example, the product of 4 and 5 is 20.

**Pythagorean theorem:** A formula used to calculate the sides of a right triangle: $a^2 + b^2 = c^2$, where $a$ and $b$ are the two sides (legs) that create the 90° angle, and $c$ is the length of the side (hypotenuse) across from the 90° angle.

**Pythagorean triple:** A set of three numbers that describes the lengths of the three sides of a right triangle in which all three sides have integer lengths. Common Pythagorean triples are 3-4-5, 6-8-10, and 5-12-13.

**quadrant:** One-quarter of the coordinate plane. Bounded on two sides by the *x*- and *y*-axes.

**quadratic expression:** An expression including a variable raised to the second power (and no higher powers). Commonly of the form $ax^2 + bx + c$, where *a*, *b*, and *c* are constants. (A **quadratic equation** contains both a quadratic expression and an equals sign.)

**quotient:** The result of dividing one number by another. The quotient of $10 \div 5$ is 2.

**radius:** A line segment that connects the center of a circle with any point on that circle's circumference. Plural: *radii*.

**reciprocal:** The product of a number and its reciprocal is always 1. To get the reciprocal of an integer, put that integer in the denominator of a fraction with numerator 1. The reciprocal of 3 is $\frac{1}{3}$. To get the reciprocal of a fraction, switch the numerator and the denominator. The reciprocal of $\frac{2}{3}$ is $\frac{3}{2}$.

**rectangle:** A four-sided closed shape in which all of the angles equal 90° and in which the opposite sides are equal. Rectangles are also parallelograms.

**right triangle:** A triangle that includes a 90°, or right, angle.

**root:** The opposite of an exponent (in a sense). The square root of 16 (written $\sqrt{16}$) is the number (or numbers) that, when multiplied by itself, will yield 16. In this case, both 4 and −4 equal 16 when squared. However, when the GMAT provides the root sign for an even root, such as a square root, the only accepted answer is the positive root. That is, $\sqrt{16} = 4$, *not* +4 or −4. In contrast, the equation $x^2 = 16$ has *two* solutions, +4 and −4.

**sector:** A "wedge" or "slice of pie" of a circle, bounded by two radii and the arc connecting those two radii.

**simplify (in general):** Change the form of given math to a simpler form. For example, add two numbers in parentheses, combine like terms, or divide every term in an equation by the same number.

**simplify (fractions):** Reducing numerators and denominators to their smallest form by taking out common factors. Dividing the numerator and denominator by the same number does not change the value of the fraction.

*Example:*

Simplify $\frac{21}{6}$. Divide both the numerator and the denominator by a common factor, in this case, 3: $\frac{21}{6} = \frac{7}{2}$.

**slope:** In a coordinate plane, "rise over run," or the distance the line runs vertically over the distance the line runs horizontally. The slope of any given line is constant over the length of that line.

**special products:** The set of three commonly used quadratic forms found on the GMAT:

**square of a sum:** $(x + y)^2 = x^2 + 2xy + y^2$

**square of a difference:** $(x - y)^2 = x^2 - 2xy + y^2$

**difference of squares:** $(x + y)(x - y) = x^2 - y^2$

**square:** A four-sided closed shape in which all of the angles equal 90° and all of the sides are equal. Squares are also rectangles and parallelograms.

**sum:** The result when two numbers are added together. The sum of 4 and 7 is 11.

**term:** Parts within an expression or equation that are separated by either a plus sign or a minus sign. For example, in the expression $x + 3$, "$x$" and "3" are each separate terms.

**triangle:** A three-sided closed shape composed of straight lines; the interior angles sum to 180°.

**two-dimensional:** A shape containing a length and a width.

**variable:** Letter used as a substitute for an unknown value, or number. Common letters for variables are $x$, $y$, $z$, and $t$. In contrast to a constant, a variable is a value that can change (hence the term *variable*). In the equation $y = 3x + 2$, both $y$ and $x$ are variables.

**$x$-axis:** A horizontal number line that indicates left-right position on a coordinate plane.

**$x$-coordinate:** The number that indicates where a point lies along the $x$-axis. The $x$-coordinate is always written first in the parentheses. The $x$-coordinate of $(2, -1)$ is 2.

**$x$-intercept:** The point where a line crosses the $x$-axis (that is, when $y = 0$).

**$y$-axis:** A vertical number line that indicates up-down position on a coordinate plane.

**$y$-coordinate:** The number that indicates where a point lies along the $y$-axis. The $y$-coordinate is always written second in the parentheses. The $y$-coordinate of $(2, -1)$ is $-1$.

**$y$-intercept:** The point where a line crosses the $y$-axis (that is, when $x = 0$). In the equation of a line $y = mx + b$, the $y$-intercept equals $b$. The coordinates of the $y$-intercept are $(0, b)$.

# Go beyond books.
# Try us for free.

## In Person

Find a GMAT course near you and attend the first session free, no strings attached.

**Find your city at manhattanprep.com/gmat/classes**

## Online

Enjoy the flexibility of prepping from home or the office with our online course.

**See the full schedule at manhattanprep.com/gmat/classes**

## On Demand

Prep where you are, when you want with GMAT Interact™— our on-demand course.

**Try 5 full lessons for free at manhattanprep.com/gmat/interact**

# Not sure which is right for you? Try all three! Or, give us a call, and we'll help you figure out which program fits you best.

**Toll-Free U.S. Number** 800.576.4628 | **International** 001 212.721.7400 | **Email** gmat@manhattanprep.com

# Prep made personal.

**Whether you want quick coaching in a particular GMAT subject area or a comprehensive study plan developed around your goals, we've got you covered. Our expert GMAT tutors can help you hit your top score.**

## CHECK OUT THESE REVIEWS FROM MANHATTAN PREP TUTORING STUDENTS.

 **VERIFIED REAL STUDENT** · reviews.beatthegmat.com

### Highly Recommend MPREP for a 700 Score
★★★★★ *June 1, 2014*

**Company**: Manhattan Prep *296 Reviews*
**Course**: Manhattan Prep Private Tutoring *24 Reviews*
**GMAT Scores — Before**: 680 **After**: 720

I bought the MPREP books and started studying on my own. Along with using the MPREP materials I also met with a Manhattan private tutor. He was fantastic. He really [listened] to my concerns and tried to understand what was holding me back. He's very down to earth and pragmatic. Not only did he help me understand the test material better, he helped me to have a better mental game while taking it. After meeting with him and studying with the MPREP materials I boosted my score to a 720.

 **VERIFIED REAL STUDENT** · reviews.beatthegmat.com

### A one-hour private tutoring session took me to the next level.
★★★★★

**Company**: Manhattan Prep *296 Reviews*
**Course**: Manhattan Prep Private Tutoring *24 Reviews*
**GMAT Scores — Before**: N/A **After**: 730

I purchased the MPREP materials second-hand and pursued a self-study strategy. I was stuck between 700 and 720 on all my practice exams, but was hoping to get into the mid-700s. I thought a private tutoring session would really help me go to the next level in my scoring. [My instructor] asked me beforehand (via email) what I was struggling with and what I thought I needed. Marc was able to quickly talk me through my struggles and give me concise, helpful tips that I used during the remainder of my study time and the actual exam.

 **VERIFIED REAL STUDENT** · reviews.beatthegmat.com

### Best Prep Out There!
★★★★★

**Company**: Manhattan Prep *296 Reviews*
**Course**: Manhattan Prep Private Tutoring *24 Reviews*
**GMAT Scores — Before**: 560 **After**: 750

I just took my GMAT and scored a 750 (Q49, V42). This was a pretty amazing feat for me considering I scored only 560 my first time taking the GMAT. Only by sitting down with the Manhattan Prep books and really learning the content contained in them was I able to get into the 700 range. Then, when I was consistently scoring in the 90+ percentile, Manhattan tutoring got me my 750 and into the 98th percentile. If you want a 700+ on the GMAT, use Manhattan Prep. PERIOD!!

 **VERIFIED REAL STUDENT** · reviews.beatthegmat.com

### Manhattan Prep is Best in Class!
★★★★★

**Company**: Manhattan Prep *296 Reviews*
**Course**: Manhattan Prep Private Tutoring *24 Reviews*
**GMAT Scores — Before**: N/A **After**: 750

I signed up for the self study so that I could review the materials on my own time. After completing the basic course content and taking a couple practice tests I signed up for private tutoring. Andrea helped me to develop a game plan to address my weaknesses. We discussed the logic behind the problem and practical strategies for eliminating certain answers if time is running short. Originally I had planned on taking the GMAT two times. But, MPREP and Andrea helped me to exceed my goal on the first attempt, allowing me to focus on the rest of my application.

**Contact us at 800.576.4628 or gmat@manhattanprep.com for information on rates and to get paired with your GMAT tutor.**